DECISIONS OF THE FEDERAL LABOR RELATIONS AUTHORITY

Volume 65

August 1, 2010 through July 31, 2011
(Cite as 65 FLRA_)

FEDERAL LABOR RELATIONS AUTHORITY
Washington, D.C. 20424

FLRA Doc. 1515

Issued February 2012

For sale by the Superintendent of Documents, U.S. Government Printing Office
Internet: bookstire.gpo.gov Phone: toll free (866) 512- 1800; DC area (202) 512 -1800
Fax: (202) 512 - 2104 Mail: Stop IDCC, Washington, DC 20402-0001

ISBN 978-0-16-089341-4

UNITED STATES OF AMERICA
FEDERAL LABOR RELATIONS AUTHORITY

MEMBERS

Honorable CAROL WALLER POPE, *Chairman*

Honorable THOMAS M. BECK Honorable ERNEST DUBESTER

GENERAL COUNSEL

Honorable JULIE AKINS CLARK

CONTENTS

Part I. TABLE

Office of Case Intake and Publication
Issuance Numbers and Volume 65 Page Numbers

No.	Page	No.	Page	No.	Page	No.	Page	No.	Page
1	1	45	185	89	430	133	624	177	843
2	1	46	191	90	433	134	630	178	849
3	2	47	194	91	437	135	632	179	853
4	5	48	201	92	442	136	635	180	857
5	9	49	208	93	447	137	638	181	860
6	13	50	219	94	451	138	642	182	870
7	21	51	224	95	452	139	647	183	877
8	23	52	239	96	456	140	651	184	887
9	27	53	242	97	460	141	657	185	892
10	30	54	252	98	465	142	666	186	895
11	35	55	256	99	471	143	668	187	897
12	40	56	259	100	472	144	672	188	898
13	45	57	264	101	473	145	677	189	901
14	50	58	267	102	474	146	687	190	905
15	54	59	272	103	477	147	699	191	908
16	60	60	281	104	483	148	704	192	911
17	61	61	286	105	487	149	713	193	921
18	69	62	290	106	491	150	720	194	924
19	74	63	302	107	495	151	723	195	928
20	75	64	310	108	502	152	726	196	931
21	76	65	312	109	509	153	730	197	933
22	79	66	320	110	523	154	734	198	939
23	88	67	325	111	529	155	738	199	946
24	91	68	330	112	539	156	746	200	950
25	97	69	334	113	544	157	752	201	957
26	98	70	339	114	547	158	756	202	960
27	102	71	344	115	552	159	781	203	969
28	113	72	348	116	557	160	786	204	975
29	121	73	356	117	561	161	787	205	978
30	125	74	364	118	564	162	792	206	988
31	130	75	369	119	565	163	797	207	996
32	131	76	373	120	568	164	799	208	1003
33	137	77	379	121	575	165	802	209	1004
34	141	78	383	122	580	166	806	210	1009
35	142	79	387	123	583	167	809	211	1012
36	148	80	390	124	588	168	817	212	1013
37	153	81	395	125	592	169	820	213	1015
38	157	82	402	126	596	170	823	214	1017
39	160	83	405	127	603	171	826	215	1022
40	167	84	411	128	607	172	830	216	1023
41	170	85	416	129	610	173	833	217	1040
42	171	86	417	130	615	174	834	218	1047
43	175	87	421	131	619	175	835	219	1049
44	179	88	422	132	623	176	836	220	1052

Part II. TEXT OF DECISIONS

65 FLRA No. 1

AMERICAN FEDERATION
OF GOVERNMENT EMPLOYEES
LOCAL 2437
(Union)

and

UNITED STATES
DEPARTMENT OF VETERANS AFFAIRS
NORTH TEXAS HEALTH CARE SYSTEM
MEDICAL CENTER
DALLAS, TEXAS
(Agency)

0-AR-4664

DECISION

August 20, 2010

Before the Authority: Carol Waller Pope, Chairman, and Thomas M. Beck and Ernest DuBester, Members

This matter is before the Authority on exceptions to an award of Arbitrator Barry E. Shapiro filed by the Union under § 7122(a) of the Federal Service Labor-Management Relations Statute (the Statute) and part 2425 of the Authority's Regulations. The Agency filed an opposition to the Union's exceptions.

Under § 7122(a) of the Statute, an award is deficient if it is contrary to any law, rule, or regulation, or it is deficient on other grounds similar to those applied by federal courts in private sector labor-management relations. Upon careful consideration of the entire record in this case and Authority precedent, the Authority concludes that the award is not deficient on the grounds raised in the exceptions and set forth in § 7122(a). *See AFGE, Local 2921,* 50 FLRA 184, 185-86 (1995) (arbitrator's determination of the procedural arbitrability of a grievance is subject to challenge only on grounds other than those that directly challenge the procedural arbitrability determination); *AFGE, Local 1840,* 45 FLRA 497, 499 (1992) (award not deficient as contrary to law where excepting party fails to specify law on which the party relies).

Accordingly, the Union's exceptions are denied.

65 FLRA No. 2

AMERICAN FEDERATION
OF GOVERNMENT EMPLOYEES
LOCAL 1906
(Union)

and

UNITED STATES
DEPARTMENT OF DEFENSE
DEFENSE CONTRACT
MANAGEMENT AGENCY
(Agency)

0-AR-4663

DECISION

August 20, 2010

Before the Authority: Carol Waller Pope, Chairman, and Thomas M. Beck and Ernest DuBester, Members

This matter is before the Authority on exceptions to an award of Arbitrator Susan R. Meredith filed by the Union under § 7122(a) of the Federal Service Labor-Management Relations Statute (the Statute) and part 2425 of the Authority's Regulations. The Agency filed an opposition to the Union's exceptions.

Under § 7122(a) of the Statute, an award is deficient if it is contrary to any law, rule, or regulation, or it is deficient on other grounds similar to those applied by federal courts in private sector labor-management relations. Upon careful consideration of the entire record in this case and Authority precedent, the Authority concludes that the award is not deficient on grounds raised in the exceptions and set forth in § 7122(a). *See U.S. Dep't of Transp., Fed. Aviation Admin., Portland, Me.*, 64 FLRA 772, 774 (2010) (arbitrator's determination of procedural arbitrability of a grievance is not deficient when excepting party fails to establish that the determination is contrary to procedural requirements established by statute that apply to the parties' negotiated grievance procedure or is deficient on grounds that do not directly challenge the procedural-arbitrability determination).

Accordingly, the Union's exceptions are denied.

65 FLRA No. 3

AMERICAN FEDERATION
OF GOVERNMENT EMPLOYEES
LOCAL 3438
(Union)

and

SOCIAL SECURITY ADMINISTRATION
(Agency)

0-AR-4639

DECISION

August 20, 2010

Before the Authority: Carol Waller Pope, Chairman, and Thomas M. Beck and Ernest DuBester, Members

I. Statement of the Case

This matter is before the Authority on exceptions to an award of Arbitrator Michael L. Allen filed by the Union under § 7122(a) of the Federal Service Labor-Management Relations Statute and part 2425 of the Authority's Regulations. The Agency filed an opposition to the Union's exceptions.[1]

The Arbitrator concluded that the Union failed timely to invoke arbitration and that, even if the Union had timely invoked arbitration, he would not grant the grievant's request for relief. Accordingly, he denied the grievance.

For the reasons that follow, we deny the exceptions.

II. Background and Arbitrator's Award

The Agency reimbursed the grievant for certain expenses. *See* Award at 2-3. Subsequently, the Agency notified the grievant that she had been overpaid and initiated debt collection for the amount of overpayment. *Id.* at 4. The grievant contested her liability and alternatively sought a waiver. *See id.* at 4-5. In accordance with the parties' Memorandum of Understanding (MOU),[2] they moved to expedited arbitration. *See id.* Without a stipulation of issues, the Arbitrator proceeded to determine: (1) whether the Union invoked arbitration within "the time limit permitted by the MOU[;]" and, if arbitration had been timely invoked, (2) whether "the debt . . . under review is justly due and owing by the [g]rievant[.]" *Id.* at 8.

The Arbitrator found that the Union did not invoke arbitration within the time frame permitted by the MOU, *id.* (quoting MOU, cl. 12), and that, "as a threshold matter, [this] fatal flaw" required him to deny the grievance. *Id.* at 7. He further explained that, "[e]ven assuming, *arguendo*, that the . . . challenge . . . could somehow be deemed . . . timely," he would deny the grievance on its merits. *Id.* at 8-9.

III. Preliminary Matter

In its amended, sworn statement of service (Statement), the Union avers that it served its exceptions on the Agency by certified mail on March 19, 2010.[3] *See* Union's Am. Statement of Serv. (June 17). After receiving the Statement, the Authority's Office of Case Intake and Publication issued an order to the Agency, explaining that, although the Agency in its opposition asserted that the Union's exceptions were postmarked on March 23, "the Agency did not provide any evidence or documentation of the . . . postmark." Order to Show Cause (June 23) (Order) at 2 (citing Opp'n at 2). The Order further explained that, if the Union served the exceptions on March 19, as indicated by the Statement, then "the Agency's opposition had to be postmarked . . . no later than April 26[] in order to be considered timely." Order at 1-2 (citing 5 C.F.R. §§ 2425.1(c), 2429.21(b), 2429.22). As the opposition was postmarked on April 27, the Agency was ordered to show cause why the Authority should consider the opposition. *Id.* at 2.

The Agency timely responded to the Order, but its response included only a copy of the Order and a copy of an envelope bearing a March 23 postmark. *See* Resp. to Order. Although the copied envelope is addressed to the prior Agency representative in this case and bears the return address of the Agency facility at which the Union is located, the Agency

1. We address the timeliness of the Agency's opposition below.

2. The MOU provides for expedited arbitration in cases where an employee disputes indebtedness or seeks a waiver of debt. *See* Award at 5; *see also* Exceptions, Attach. 1 at 8 (MOU, cl. 12).

3. All subsequent dates in this section refer to 2010.

provides no further explanation of its submission. In particular, the Agency does not contest the accuracy of the Union's sworn statement that the Union served its exceptions on March 19. The copied envelope submitted by the Agency, without more, does not establish that the exceptions were served on March 23; it merely establishes that an envelope with a preprinted return address was mailed to the prior Agency representative and that the envelope was postmarked on March 23. In particular, the submission establishes neither the contents of the depicted envelope nor the identity of its sender. As such, the Agency has not demonstrated that the Union's exceptions were served on March 23. Accordingly, we conclude that the Agency's opposition is untimely, and we do not consider it. *See* 5 C.F.R. § 2425.1(c).

IV. Union's Exceptions

The Union asserts that the Arbitrator "did not consider material evidence and facts presented[.]" Exceptions at 3. According to the Union, the Arbitrator "ignored" an email that the Union argues is evidence of its timely invocation of arbitration. *See id.* at 5. The Union asserts that the Arbitrator denied it a fair hearing and exhibited bias by "willful[ly] and deliberate[ly] exclu[ding]" this piece of evidence, which he does not reference in the award. *Id.* In addition, the Union contends that the Arbitrator exhibited bias by failing to address the Union's argument that the Agency waived its right to challenge the timeliness of the Union's invocation of arbitration. *Id.* (citing Art. 24, § 6 of the parties' agreement).[4] Moreover, the Union argues that the award is contrary to law, rule, or regulation because the Arbitrator "ignored [f]ederal [l]aw" when he determined that the Agency properly denied the grievant's request for a waiver of her liability. *Id.* at 6-7 (citing 4 C.F.R. pts. 91-92 (standards for evaluating waiver requests)).

V. Analysis and Conclusions

A. The Arbitrator did not deny a fair hearing or exhibit bias.

The Union challenges the Arbitrator's determination that it failed to timely invoke arbitration. An arbitrator's timeliness determination is a procedural-arbitrability ruling. *See AFGE, Local 1501*, 56 FLRA 632, 636 (2000). The Authority generally will not find an arbitrator's ruling on procedural arbitrability deficient on grounds that directly challenge the procedural-arbitrability ruling itself. *See AFGE, Local 3882*, 59 FLRA 469, 470 (2003). However, the Authority has stated that a procedural-arbitrability determination may be found deficient on grounds that do not directly challenge the determination itself, which, as relevant here, include claims that an arbitrator denied a party a fair hearing or was biased. *See AFGE, Council of Prison Locals, Local 3977*, 62 FLRA 41, 43-44 (2007); *see also U.S. Equal Emp't Opportunity Comm'n*, 60 FLRA 83, 86 (2004) (citing *AFGE, Local 2921*, 50 FLRA 184, 185-86 (1995)).

The Authority will find an award deficient on the ground that the arbitrator failed to provide a fair hearing when it determines that an arbitrator's refusal to hear or consider pertinent and material evidence, or other actions in conducting the proceeding, prejudiced a party and affected the fairness of the proceeding as a whole. *See AFGE, Local 1668*, 50 FLRA 124, 126 (1995). To establish that an arbitrator was biased, the moving party must demonstrate that the award was procured by improper means, that there was partiality or corruption on the part of the arbitrator, or that the arbitrator engaged in misconduct that prejudiced the rights of the party. *See U.S. Dep't of Veterans Affairs Med. Ctr., N. Chi., Ill.*, 52 FLRA 387, 398 (1996) (*VAMC, N. Chi., Ill.*). The fact that an arbitrator does not mention a particular evidentiary item in his or her award does not demonstrate that the arbitrator refused to consider it or failed to provide a fair hearing. *See, e.g., AFGE, Local 3615*, 57 FLRA 19, 22 (2001). Further, the Authority will not find an award deficient merely because it does not address every argument raised by the parties. *See, e.g., U.S. Dep't of Homeland Sec., Customs & Border Prot. Agency, N.Y., N.Y.*, 60 FLRA 813, 816 (2005) (*DHS*); *NFFE, Local 259*, 45 FLRA 773, 777 (1992) (citing *U.S. Dep't of Labor, Wash., D.C.*, 41 FLRA 472, 476-77 (1991) (an arbitrator's failure to set forth specific findings does not provide a basis for finding an award deficient)).

With regard to the fairness of the hearing, the Union does not establish that the Arbitrator "ignored" or "exclu[ded]" material evidence, as opposed to crediting other evidence, when determining that the Union failed timely to invoke arbitration. *See* Award at 8 (crediting Agency Ex. 18 and finding untimely invocation); *see also AFGE, Local 22*, 51 FLRA 1496, 1497 (1996); *cf. U.S. Dep't of the Air Force,*

4. Article 24, Section 6 of the parties' agreement provides, in relevant part, "The parties agree to raise any questions of grievability or arbitrability of a grievance prior to the limit for the written answer in the final step of this procedure." Exceptions at 5 (internal quotation omitted).

Okla. City Air Logistics Ctr., Tinker Air Force Base, Okla., 42 FLRA 680, 684 (1991) (declining to find procedural-arbitrability ruling deficient, despite allegation that arbitrator "ignore[d]" parties' agreement). In addition, as set forth above, the fact that the award does not mention the email referenced by the Union does not establish that the Arbitrator refused to consider it or failed to conduct a fair hearing. *See AFGE, Local 3615*, 57 FLRA at 22. Therefore, the Union has not established that the Arbitrator's conduct prejudiced it such that the fairness of the proceeding as a whole was affected, *see AFGE, Local 1668*, 50 FLRA at 126, and, consequently, has not established that the Arbitrator denied it a fair hearing.

With regard to the Union's allegation of bias, for the same reason that the Arbitrator's failure to mention an email does not establish that he denied the Union a fair hearing, it does not establish that the Arbitrator was biased. *See AFGE, Local 3615*, 57 FLRA at 22 (arbitrators need not mention every evidentiary submission in their awards). The only additional argument that the Union offers as an indication of bias is that the Arbitrator allegedly failed to address the Union's claim that, under the parties' agreement, the Agency waived any right to challenge the timeliness of the Union's invocation of arbitration. However, the Arbitrator was not required to address every argument raised by the parties. *See DHS*, 60 FLRA at 816. In addition, the Union does not allege that the award was procured by improper means, that the Arbitrator was corrupt, or that the Arbitrator engaged in misconduct that prejudiced the rights of the Union. *See VAMC, N. Chi., Ill.*, 52 FLRA at 398. Therefore, it has failed to establish that the Arbitrator was biased.

For the foregoing reasons, we deny the Union's fair-hearing and bias exceptions.

B. The Union's contrary-to-law exception does not provide a basis for setting aside the award.

The Union's contrary-to-law exception challenges the Arbitrator's determination that the Agency properly denied the grievant a waiver of the debt she owed. The Authority has recognized that when an arbitrator bases an award on separate and independent grounds, an appealing party must establish that all of the grounds are deficient in order to demonstrate that the award is deficient. *See, e.g., U.S. Dep't of the Treasury, Internal Revenue Serv., Oxon Hill, Md.*, 56 FLRA 292, 299 (2000) (*Oxon Hill*). In such circumstances, if the excepting party does not demonstrate that the award is deficient on one of the grounds relied on by the arbitrator, it is unnecessary to address exceptions to the other grounds. *See id.*

The Arbitrator determined that the Union's failure timely to invoke arbitration was a "fatal flaw" that required him to deny the grievance. *See* Award at 7. This timeliness determination constitutes a separate and independent basis for the award, and the Union has not established that this determination is deficient, *see supra* Part V.A. As such, it is unnecessary to address the Union's contention that the Arbitrator's alternative finding – that the Agency properly denied the grievant a waiver of debt – is contrary to law, rule, or regulation. *See Oxon Hill*, 56 FLRA at 299. Accordingly, we deny the exception.

VI. Decision

The Union's exceptions are denied.

65 FLRA No. 4

UNITED STATES
DEPARTMENT OF THE INTERIOR
BUREAU OF INDIAN AFFAIRS
WAPATO IRRIGATION PROJECT
(Agency)

and

INDIAN EDUCATORS FEDERATION
LOCAL 4526
AMERICAN FEDERATION OF TEACHERS
(Union)

0-AR-4406

DECISION

August 20, 2010

Before the Authority: Carol Waller Pope, Chairman, and Thomas M. Beck and Ernest DuBester, Members[1]

I. Statement of the Case

This matter is before the Authority on exceptions to an award of Arbitrator Vern E. Hauck filed by the Agency under § 7122(a) of the Federal Service Labor-Management Relations Statute (the Statute) and part 2425 of the Authority's Regulations. The Union filed an opposition to the Agency's exceptions.

For the reasons set forth below, we conclude that the Authority lacks jurisdiction over the Agency's exceptions.

II. Background and Arbitrator's Award

A. Background

The Union filed a grievance alleging that the Agency's removal of the grievant from his position as an Irrigation System Operator "was not for just cause." Opp'n at 2. The Union argued that an Agency policy that provided the basis for the grievant's removal violated the collective bargaining agreement (CBA) and Title VII of the Civil Rights Act. *Id.*

B. Arbitrator's Award

The claim advanced before the Arbitrator presented the issue of the grievant's removal. As the Arbitrator framed the issue, it stated:

> Was the grievant's removal in accordance with law, rule, regulation and/or the parties' negotiated labor agreement? If not, what is the remedy?

Award at 3.

The Arbitrator ruled that the grievant was improperly removed. The Arbitrator found that the grievant was removed because he was unable to perform the duties of his position. *Id.* at 8. The grievant occupied a position that required him to operate a motor vehicle. The Arbitrator found that the grievant was unable to perform the duties of his position because of an Agency policy requiring the termination of driving privileges for motor vehicle operators who have been "[a]rrested for . . . Driving Under the Influence [(DUI)]." *Id.* at 7; Opp'n, Attach., Volume 1, Agency Hearing Ex. 3, Notice of Proposal to Remove at 9. After the Agency learned that the grievant had been arrested for DUI, it terminated the grievant's driving privileges, and then removed him because he could no longer perform his position's driving duties.

The Arbitrator ordered the Agency to reinstate the grievant and to cease implementation of the policy on which the grievant's removal was based. Award at 21. The Arbitrator concluded that the Agency's policy has a disparate impact on Native American Agency employees. *Id.* at 18, 20. Consequently, the Arbitrator determined that both the Agency's policy and the grievant's removal violated the CBA. *Id.* at 14-15, 20. The Arbitrator therefore sustained the grievance.

1. Member Beck's dissent is set forth at the end of this decision.

III. Positions of the Parties[2]

A. Agency's Exceptions

The Agency seeks review of the Arbitrator's determination that the Agency's DUI policy violates the CBA and that, therefore, the Agency must cease implementing it. The Agency argues that the Authority has jurisdiction to review this portion of the award because it is not "inextricably intertwined" with the Arbitrator's decision to reverse the grievant's removal. Exceptions at 8. According to the Agency, "the second ruling" regarding the policy is separate from the ruling on the removal because the facts that formed the basis for the Arbitrator's decision to reinstate the grievant are unrelated to those that led to the decision concerning the DUI policy. *Id.* at 8-9.

In addition, the Agency claims that the Authority is the correct forum to review the portion of the award concerning the DUI policy because the Merit Systems Protection Board (MSPB) – which normally reviews appeals pertaining to removals – would not address the Arbitrator's ruling on the policy. *Id.* at 8.

B. Union's Opposition

The Union argues that the Authority does not have jurisdiction to review the award. In the Union's view, the Arbitrator did not make "two distinct rulings." Opp'n at 4 (quoting Exceptions at 1). To the contrary, the Union argues, the Arbitrator identified the DUI policy as playing a central role in the Agency's decision to remove the grievant. Opp'n at 4.

The Union also contends that the Agency erroneously claims that the MSPB would not review the Arbitrator's determination concerning the DUI policy. According to the Union, the MSPB has jurisdiction to resolve discrimination claims raised as affirmative defenses in cases involving removals. *Id.*

IV. Analysis and Conclusions

For the reasons set forth below, we find that the Authority lacks jurisdiction to review the Agency's exceptions.

Under § 7122(a) of the Statute, the Authority lacks jurisdiction to resolve exceptions to awards "relating to" a matter described in § 7121(f) of the Statute.[3] Matters described in § 7121(f) include adverse actions, such as removals, that are covered under 5 U.S.C. § 7512.[4] Such matters are appealable to the MSPB and reviewable by the United States Court of Appeals for the Federal Circuit. *See, e.g., U.S. Dep't of Commerce, Patent & Trademark Office, Arlington, Va.,* 61 FLRA 476, 477 (2006) (*PTO*).

The Authority will determine that an award relates to a matter described in § 7121(f) when it resolves, or is inextricably intertwined with, a § 7512 matter. *See AFGE, Local 1013*, 60 FLRA 712, 713 (2005). In making that determination, the Authority looks not to the outcome of the award, but to whether the claim advanced in arbitration is one reviewable by the MSPB, and, on appeal, by the United States Court of Appeals for the Federal Circuit. *See id.; Panama Canal Comm'n,* 49 FLRA 1398, 1402 (1994).

Applying this precedent, we conclude that the award relates to a matter described in § 7121(f) of the Statute. The sole claim advanced in arbitration was that the grievant was improperly removed from his position as an Irrigation System Operator. *See* Award at 2-3 (framing the issue before the Arbitrator). The Arbitrator's determination that the grievant was improperly removed resolved that claim. In these circumstances, we find that the award relates to the grievant's removal for purposes of § 7121(f). *See U.S. EPA, Narragansett, R.I.,* 59 FLRA 591, 592 (2004). Accordingly, we conclude that the Authority lacks jurisdiction to review the Agency's exceptions.

The dissent's position that we should exercise jurisdiction in this case is inconsistent with the plain language of the Statute. Section 7122(a) of the Statute specifically provides that the Authority lacks jurisdiction over "an award relating to a matter described in section 7121(f)[.]" It is clear, and

2. As we dismiss the exceptions for lack of jurisdiction, we do not address the parties' arguments on the merits.

3. Section 7122(a) provides, in pertinent part: "Either party to arbitration . . . may file with the Authority an exception to any arbitrator's award pursuant to the arbitration (other than an award relating to a matter described in § 7121(f) of this title)." Section 7121(f) provides, in pertinent part: "In matters covered under §§ 4303 and 7512 of this title which have been raised under the negotiated grievance procedure . . ., § 7703 of this title pertaining to judicial review shall apply to the award of an arbitrator . . . ."

4. Section 7512 covers removals, suspensions for more than fourteen days, reductions in grade or pay, and furloughs for thirty days or less.

undisputed by the dissent, that the award in this case relates to the grievant's removal, a matter described in § 7121(f). Indeed, as the dissent acknowledges, "[t]he issue to be addressed, as expressly framed by the Arbitrator, relates only to the grievant's removal[.]" Dissent at 6 (citing Award at 3).

The dissent's concerns with the breadth of the Arbitrator's remedy and the absence of a forum in which the Agency can challenge the award do not provide a legal foundation for Authority jurisdiction. In the dissent's view, the Arbitrator's determinations went beyond what was necessary to resolve the propriety of the grievant's removal. In addition, the dissent is concerned that unless the Authority exercises jurisdiction, the Agency may not have a forum in which to challenge the award.

With regard to the breadth of the remedy, Authority precedent explicitly directs that "the existence of Authority jurisdiction to review an award does not properly rest on the outcome of an award but, rather, depends on whether the claim advanced in arbitration is one that would be reviewed by the MSPB and, on appeal, by the Federal Circuit." *Panama Canal Comm'n,* 49 FLRA at 1402; *see also PTO,* 61 FLRA at 478-79 (noting, among other things, the Statute's legislative history "confirm[ing] that the statutory scheme of which § 7122(a) is a part was specifically designed to promote consistency and uniformity of process and to discourage forum shopping."). As discussed above, the claim advanced in arbitration went to the propriety of the grievant's removal. We therefore reject the dissent's reliance on the award's outcome as a basis for asserting jurisdiction.

In addition, the dissent's reluctance to risk leaving the Agency without a forum to challenge the award's outcome does not provide a foundation for overcoming the jurisdictional restrictions of § 7122(a). As the Authority has stated: "We recognize that our refusal to assert jurisdiction may leave the Agency without a forum to challenge the Arbitrator's award. . . . Nevertheless, we conclude that the advancement of the Congressional policies of uniformity, discouragement of forum shopping, and avoidance of multiple litigation, as well as the need for clarity and predictability on questions concerning jurisdiction, clearly override any potential for unreviewable awards." *U.S. Dep't of Veterans Affairs Med. Ctr., Newington, Conn.,* 53 FLRA 440, 443 (1997); *see also PTO,* 61 FLRA at 478 (noting that "[a]s a general matter, . . . under the statutory scheme enacted by Congress, there may be some awards that are not reviewable at all." (citation omitted)).

For these reasons, we reject the position taken by the dissent and conclude that we lack jurisdiction over the Agency's exceptions.

V. Decision

The Agency's exceptions are dismissed.

Member Beck, Dissenting:

I agree with the Majority that the Arbitrator enjoyed latitude to consider certain aspects of the Agency's Motor Vehicle Operation Policy (Part III.B.6.) (the Policy) on the way to resolving the specific issue that was before him: "was the grievant's removal in accordance with law, rule, regulation and/or the parties' [CBA]?" Award at 3.

I do not agree with my colleagues, however, that the Arbitrator's prospective invalidation of the Policy in its entirety "relates to" the grievant's removal such that we lack jurisdiction to consider the Agency's exceeds authority and contrary to law exceptions.

To the extent the Award purports to invalidate the Agency's policy, it neither "resolves" nor is "inextricably intertwined" with the grievant's removal. The issue to be addressed, as expressly framed by the Arbitrator, relates only to the grievant's removal. *Id.* at 3. Further, the Union requested relief only for the grievant – a clean record, reinstatement, and make-whole relief. *Id.* Consequently, the Arbitrator was not asked to, did not need to, and was not authorized to award a remedy directed at the Policy in general.

The validity of the policy is a question separate and distinct from the propriety of the grievant's removal and is a matter over which the Authority – and not the MSPB – has jurisdiction. Jurisdiction of the Board is limited strictly to those matters over which it has been given jurisdiction by law, rule, or regulation – i.e. 5 U.S.C. §§ 7701 (adverse actions), 7702 (certain actions involving discrimination). *Maddox v. MSPB*, 759 F.2d 9, 10 (Fed. Cir. 1985). The Board's jurisdiction does not extend, in general, to matters that involve an agency's policies* and conditions of employment. *NTEU v. OPM*, 110 M.S.P.R. 237, 239 (2008) (personal appearance standards); *Gore v. Dep't of Labor,* 101 M.S.P.R. 320, 322 (2006) (flexiplace); *Campbell v. Dep't of Veterans Affairs*, 93 M.S.P.R. 70, 72 (2002) (loss of locality pay).

The Arbitrator exceeded his authority when he went beyond the scope of the framed issue (and the relief requested by the Union) to invalidate the Policy itself and to direct the Agency to implement and negotiate an entirely new policy.

Stating my view of this case somewhat differently, one of these propositions must be true:

1. The Arbitrator's decision to direct a remedy at the Policy in general was inappropriate, in which case we have jurisdiction to consider the Agency's exception that the Arbitrator exceeded his authority; or
2. The Arbitrator's decision to direct a remedy at the Policy in general was appropriate, in which case we have jurisdiction to consider the Agency's exception that this portion of the Arbitrator's award is contrary to law.

In either event, we have jurisdiction to consider the Agency's exceptions. To conclude otherwise is to leave the Agency with no forum before which it can challenge the Arbitrator's invalidation of the Policy.

* The Board has original jurisdiction, nevertheless, to grant a petition to review a rule or regulation issued by the Office of Personnel Management (OPM) (see *Blanton v. OPM*, 105 M.S.P.R. 496, 498 (2007); 5 U.S.C. § 1204) to determine whether the regulation requires the agency to commit a prohibited personnel practice. *Prewitt v. MSPB*, 133 F.3d 885, 887 (Fed.Cir. 1998). Under these limited circumstances, the Board may declare such a regulation to be invalid. *Id.*

65 FLRA No. 5

AMERICAN FEDERATION
OF GOVERNMENT EMPLOYEES
LOCAL 933
(Union)

and

UNITED STATES
DEPARTMENT OF VETERANS AFFAIRS
MEDICAL CENTER
DETROIT, MICHIGAN
(Agency)

0-AR-4408

DECISION

August 25, 2010

Before the Authority: Carol Waller Pope, Chairman, and Thomas M. Beck and Ernest DuBester, Members

I. Statement of the Case

This matter is before the Authority on exceptions to an award of Arbitrator John S. Weisheit filed by the Union under § 7122(a) of the Federal Service Labor-Management Relations Statute (the Statute) and part 2425 of the Authority's Regulations. The Agency filed an opposition to the Union's exceptions.[1]

The Arbitrator found that the grievance was untimely filed in part, and that the Agency did not violate the parties' agreement by temporarily assigning the grievant additional duties without providing extra compensation or notifying the Union. For the following reasons, we dismiss the Union's exceptions in part and deny them in part.

II. Background and Arbitrator's Award

The grievant was employed as a licensed practical nurse. Award at 5. From 2001-2003 and again in 2006, the Agency assigned the grievant to an acting Clinical Coordinator position. *Id.* at 6.

The Union filed grievances alleging that the Agency violated the parties' agreement by: (1) temporarily promoting the grievant without proper compensation; (2) not filling the temporary promotion through competitive procedures; (3) bypassing the Union by not notifying it of the grievant's temporary promotion; and (4) preselecting the grievant for the Clinical Coordinator position. *Id.* at 1-2, 7-8.

The grievances were unresolved and submitted to arbitration, where the Arbitrator framed the issues as follows: (1) "[w]ere the grievances timely filed"; (2) "did the [Agency] violate the [parties' agreement] in bypassing the Union in its right to represent a bargaining unit member"; and (3) "did the [Agency] violate Article 12, Section 2 (A) or 2 (B) in not temporarily reassigning the [g]rievant to the position of temporary Clinic[al] Coordinator at the pay rate set forth [by] the [g]rievant and the Union?"[2] *Id.* at 11-12.

As an initial matter, the Arbitrator found that the grievance was untimely filed with respect to alleged contract violations between 2001 and 2003. *Id.* at 11. Specifically, the Arbitrator determined that the actions were not of a continuing nature and that the Union did not file the grievance "within 30 days of the date the employee or Union became aware [of] or should have become aware of the act or occurrence" as required by Article 42, Section 7 of the parties' agreement. *Id.*

Next, the Arbitrator found that the Agency did not violate the parties' agreement by assigning the grievant additional duties as acting Clinical Coordinator without notifying the Union. *Id.* at 12. The Arbitrator found that the Agency's obligations

---

1. As discussed further below, the Union also filed a supplemental submission in response to the Agency's opposition.

2. Article 12, Section 2 of the parties' agreement provides, in pertinent part:

> (A) Employees detailed to a higher grade position for a period of more than ten (10) consecutive work days must be temporarily promoted. The employee will be paid for the temporary promotion beginning the first day of the detail
>
> . . . .
>
> (B) Temporary promotions in excess of sixty (60) calendar days shall be filled through competitive procedures. Temporary promotions of less than sixty (60) days shall be made in accordance with Section 1 among qualified employees.

Award at 4.

and Union's rights had limitations, specifically, that Article 1, Section 3(B) requires the Agency to allow Union representation only during "formal discussions[,]" which does not include "routine work assignments." *Id.* (emphasis omitted).

With respect to whether the Agency violated Article 12, Section 2(A) or 2(B) of the parties' agreement, the Arbitrator found unpersuasive the Union's arguments regarding "'Details', 'Reassignments' and 'Temporary Promotions'" because "[t]he relevant [c]ontract terms clearly state that the [Agency] retains the right to determine if and when such assignments are to be implemented." *Id.* at 13.

III. Positions of the Parties

A. Union's Exceptions

The Union asserts that the Arbitrator erred in finding that the grievance was untimely filed in part. In this connection, the Union claims that the Agency's actions are "of a continuing nature[,]" and that the Union filed a grievance when it learned of the violations. Exceptions at 1-2. In addition, relying on § 7114(a)(2)(A) of the Statute and Articles 1 and 46 of the parties' agreement, the Union argues that the Agency was obligated to notify the Union before engaging in a formal discussion with the grievant concerning the assignment of additional duties because her service as acting Clinical Coordinator constituted a temporary promotion, as opposed to a routine work assignment.[3] *Id.* at 2. The Union further asserts that the Arbitrator took Article 1 "out of its context" by "assign[ing] new meaning to" the word "routine[.]" *Id.* The Union also argues that the Arbitrator's finding that the grievant was not entitled to additional compensation while serving as acting Clinical Coordinator is inconsistent with Article 12, Sections 1(C)(6) and 2(A).[4] *Id.* at 2-3. In this connection, the Union claims that the Agency did not refute the Union's claim to the contrary. *Id.* at 3.

B. Agency's Opposition

The Agency argues that the Union has failed to state a basis on which to set aside the award. Opp'n at 6. First, the Agency contends that the Union's timeliness argument directly challenges the Arbitrator's procedural-arbitrability finding and, therefore, does not provide a basis for finding the award deficient. *Id.* at 7-8. Second, the Agency asserts that the Union has presented "no argument or reasoning as to why [the award] is contrary to any law, rule, or regulation or asserted any other ground similar to those applied by Federal courts in private sector labor-management relations." *Id.* at 11.

IV. Preliminary Issues

A. The Authority will not consider the Union's supplemental submission.

After the thirty-day time period for filing exceptions had expired, the Union filed a supplemental submission in response to the Agency's opposition. However, the Union did not request permission to file this submission. Section 2429.26 of the Authority's Regulations requires a party filing a supplemental submission to request permission to file such a submission. 5 C.F.R. § 2429.26; *see also AFGE, Local 1061*, 63 FLRA 317, 317 n.1 (2009). Accordingly, we do not consider the Union's submission.

B. The Union's claims relating to § 7114(a)(2)(A) of the Statute and Article 12, Section 1(C)(6) of the parties' agreement are barred by § 2429.5 of the Authority's Regulations.

Under § 2429.5 of the Authority's Regulations, the Authority will not consider issues that could have been, but were not, presented in the proceedings before the arbitrator. *See, e.g., U.S. Dep't of the Air Force, Air Force Materiel Command, Robins Air Force Base, Ga.*, 59 FLRA 542, 544 (2003). In its

---

3. Section 7114(a)(2)(A) of the Statute states, in pertinent part:

> (2) An exclusive representative of an appropriate unit in an agency shall be given the opportunity to be represented at - -
>
> (A) any formal discussion between one or more representatives of the agency and one or more employees in the unit or their representatives concerning any grievance or any personnel policy or practices or other general condition of employment[.]

5 U.S.C. § 7114(a)(2)(A).

The Union does not cite to specific sections of Articles 1 and 46 in its exceptions. However, with regard to Article 1, it refers to wording contained in Article 1, Section 3(B), which is set forth *supra*. We construe the Union's exceptions as relying on that section.

4. Article 12, Section 1(C)(6) provides, in relevant part: "The Department will notify the Union of all details." Exceptions, Attach., Master Agreement at 32.

exceptions, the Union argues that § 7114(a)(2)(A) of the Statute and Article 12, Section 1(C)(6) of the parties' agreement required the Agency to notify the Union before assigning the grievant additional duties. Exceptions at 2. However, there is no evidence that the Union raised these issues before the Arbitrator, although it could have done so. We note that, although the Union cited other agreement provisions regarding details at arbitration, it did not raise a claim concerning Article 12, Section 1(C)(6). Accordingly, the Union is not permitted to raise such issues for the first time here, and we dismiss these exceptions.

V. Analysis and Conclusions

A. The Arbitrator's procedural-arbitrability determination is not deficient.

The Authority generally will not find an arbitrator's ruling on the procedural- arbitrability of a grievance deficient on grounds that directly challenge the procedural- arbitrability ruling itself. *See AFGE, Local 3882*, 59 FLRA 469, 470 (2003). However, the Authority has stated that a procedural-arbitrability determination may be found deficient on grounds that do not directly challenge the determination itself, which include claims that an arbitrator was biased or that the arbitrator exceeded his or her authority. *See id*; *see also U.S. Equal Emp't Opportunity Comm'n*, 60 FLRA 83, 86 (2004) (citing *AFGE, Local 2921*, 50 FLRA 184, 185-86 (1995)). An arbitrator's determination regarding the timeliness of a grievance constitutes a determination regarding the procedural-arbitrability of that grievance. *United Power Trades Org*., 63 FLRA 208, 209 (2009).

Here, the Arbitrator found that the Union's grievance was untimely filed with respect to alleged contract violations between 2001 and 2003. This finding constitutes a procedural-arbitrability determination. *See id.* As the Union's exception directly challenges this procedural-arbitrability determination, we deny the exception. *See AFGE, Local 3882*, 59 FLRA at 470.

B. The award draws its essence from the parties' agreement.

We construe the Union's argument that the award is inconsistent with Article 1, Section 3(B), Article 46, and Article 12, Section 2(A) of the agreement as a claim that the award fails to draw its essence from the parties' agreement. To demonstrate that an award fails to draw its essence from a collective bargaining agreement, a party must show that the award: (1) is so unfounded in reason and fact and so unconnected with the wording and purposes of the collective bargaining agreement as to manifest an infidelity to the obligation of the arbitrator; (2) does not represent a plausible interpretation of the agreement; (3) cannot in any rational way be derived from the agreement; or (4) evidences a manifest disregard of the agreement. *See U.S. Dep't of Labor (OSHA)*, 34 FLRA 573, 575 (1990) (*OSHA*). The Authority and the courts defer to arbitrators in this context "because it is the arbitrator's construction of the agreement for which the parties have bargained." *Id.* at 576.

With regard to Article 46 of the parties' agreement, the Union does not state what section of that Article it is relying on or provide any support for its claim that the award is inconsistent with that Article. Accordingly, we deny the Union's claim as a bare assertion. *See U.S. Dep't of Homeland Sec., U.S. Customs & Border Prot., Port of Seattle, Seattle, Wash.*, 60 FLRA 490, 492 n.7 (2004) (Chairman Cabaniss concurring).

With regard to Article 1, Section 3(B), the Arbitrator found that the Agency's obligations and Union's rights had limitations, specifically, that Article 1, Section 3(B) requires the Agency to allow Union representation only during "formal discussions[,]" which does not include "routine work assignments." Award at 12. (emphasis omitted). However, the Arbitrator made no finding that a formal discussion occurred, and the Union does not provide a basis for finding otherwise. Further, to the extent that the award can be construed as finding that the assignment to the Coordinator position was a "routine work assignment[,]" the Union's reliance on a dictionary definition of the word "routine" does not demonstrate that the Arbitrator's interpretation of "routine work assignments" in Article 1, Section 3(B) is implausible, unfounded, irrational, or in manifest disregard of the agreement. *OSHA*, 34 FLRA at 575. Accordingly, we find that the award does not fail to draw its essence from Article 1, Section 3(B), and we deny the exception.

Finally, with respect to Article 12, Section 2(A), the Arbitrator found that "the Union's arguments raised on this issue are found unpersuasive regarding detailed rights in attaining 'Details', 'Reassignments' and 'Temporary Promotions'" because "[t]he relevant [c]ontract terms clearly state that the [Agency] retains the right to determine if and when such assignments are to be implemented." Award at 13. The Union provides no basis for finding that the Arbitrator erred in finding that the Agency retained discretion to decide whether an assignment is a detail, reassignment or temporary promotion. Thus, the Union fails to show that the Arbitrator's finding that the Agency's assignment of the grievant to the acting Clinical Coordinator position did not violate this Article is implausible, unfounded, irrational, or in manifest disregard of the agreement. Accordingly, we find that the award does not fail to draw its essence from Article 12, Section 2(A), and we deny the exception.

VI. Decision

The Union's exceptions are dismissed in part and denied in part.

65 FLRA No. 6

UNITED STATES
DEPARTMENT OF COMMERCE
PATENT AND TRADEMARK OFFICE
(Agency)

and

NATIONAL TREASURY
EMPLOYEES UNION
CHAPTER 243
(Union)

0-AR-4045

DECISION

August 25, 2010

Before the Authority: Carol Waller Pope, Chairman, and Thomas M. Beck and Ernest DuBester, Members[1]

I. Statement of the Case

This matter is before the Authority on exceptions to an award of Arbitrator Earle William Hockenberry filed by the Agency under § 7122(a) of the Federal Service Labor-Management Relations Statute (the Statute) and part 2425 of the Authority's Regulations. The Union filed an opposition to the Agency's exceptions.

The Arbitrator concluded that the selecting official's determination that the grievant did not meet the qualifications of a position for which she had applied violated the parties' collective bargaining agreement and the Agency's merit assignment program (MAP). For the reasons that follow, we deny the Agency's exceptions.

II. Background and Arbitrator's Award

The grievant applied for promotion to a computer specialist position, but was informed by the office of human resources that she was not qualified because she failed to meet selective placement factors for the position. She filed a grievance that was submitted to arbitration where the parties stipulated that an issue for resolution was whether the selecting official's determination that the grievant did not meet the qualifications for the position was proper.[2]

Before the Arbitrator, the Union argued that the selecting official's determination violated the MAP and the agreement because the determination preceded the rating and ranking by the MAP panel and was not applied to all candidates. Award at 9. The Agency argued to the contrary that nothing prevented the human resources specialist from consulting the selecting official as a subject-matter expert for advice on whether the grievant met the selective qualification factors for the position. *Id.* at 10.

The Arbitrator found that the applications of only the grievant and three or four other applicants out of more than twenty-five applicants were sent by the human resources specialist to the selecting official prior to review by the MAP panel for evaluation of whether their applications met the selective placement factors for the position. He additionally found that it was the selecting official, and not the human resources specialist, who made the determination that the grievant was not qualified for the position. *Id.* at 15-16. The Arbitrator concluded that such conduct was inconsistent with the roles defined for the MAP panel and the selecting official in the MAP and the instructions to MAP panel members.[3] The Arbitrator also concluded that the conduct was not "supported or endorsed by" the MAP and the panel instructions. *Id.* at 15. Accordingly, he found that the selecting official's actions violated the MAP[4] and the agreement. *Id.*

In this regard, the Arbitrator explained that the MAP requires uniform and equitable consideration for promotion and establishes separate roles for the selecting official and the MAP panel to ensure that competing candidates are evaluated and ranked by the panel prior to consideration by the selecting official. He found that, in accordance with these roles, the panel rates the candidates as the end product of the

1. Member Beck's dissenting opinion is set forth at the end of the decision.

2. The Arbitrator also addressed whether: (1) the grievant was denied a promotion in retaliation for having filed grievances or a discrimination complaint; (2) the grievant was treated disparately in training or job assignments; and (3) the selecting official preselected the applicant selected for promotion. He found that the grievant had not proven any of these allegations. No exceptions have been filed to these findings, and they will not be addressed further.

3. The instructions reiterate the provisions of the MAP for members of MAP panels. *See* Award at 8-9.

4. The relevant provisions of the MAP are set forth in an appendix to this decision.

evaluation process and that any advice by the selecting official is normally provided before the panel considers actual applicants. The Arbitrator noted that there was no argument that the disputed promotion action occurred under other than normal circumstances. *Id.* at 15-16.

In the circumstances of this case, the Arbitrator concluded that the mandated roles and sequence requirements of the MAP were not followed. *Id.* He found that the selecting official's determination "blurs the roles of the appointed panel and the selecting official set out in the [MAP and] creates an additional step involving the selecting official that is not sanctioned in the [p]rogram[.]" *Id.* at 16 (footnote omitted). He also found that the selecting official's conduct was improper because it "occur[ed] prior to rating and ranking by the Panel of any candidates or an independent assessment of the [g]rievant's qualifications by the Office of Human Resources[.]" *Id.*

For all of these reasons, the Arbitrator found in resolution of the stipulated issue that the determination by the selecting official that the grievant did not meet the qualifications for the position was an improper interference with the promotion process. *Id.* at 18. In sum, he concluded that the determination violated the MAP, the MAP panel instructions, and the agreement. *Id.* at 16.

III. Positions of the Parties

A. Agency's Exceptions

The Agency contends that the award is contrary to management's rights to assign work under § 7106(a)(2)(B) and to make selections for appointments under § 7106(a)(2)(C). The Agency also contends that the award is contrary to the MAP and fails to draw its essence from the agreement.

As to management's right to assign work, the Agency maintains that the right includes the assignment of individuals to evaluate applicants for positions. The Agency claims that the award affects the right because the award precludes assigning the determination of whether an applicant meets the selective qualification factors to a selecting official or subject-matter expert. Exceptions at 13-14. The Agency maintains that, consequently, the award is deficient as it pertains to the MAP because the MAP does not constitute an applicable law within the meaning of § 7106(a)(2). *Id.* at 15. In this regard, the Agency maintains that there is no support for finding that the MAP has the force and effect of law under the standards applied by the Authority. *Id.* at n.3.

As to whether the Arbitrator enforced a contract provision, the Agency notes that the Arbitrator did not find a violation of a specific provision of the agreement. However, the Agency asserts that, to the extent that the Arbitrator found that the Agency violated either Article 38, Section 9(A), or Article 2, Section 2, the award is contrary to § 7106(a)(2)(B) because neither provision was negotiated pursuant to § 7106(b). *Id.* at 15-19.

As to management's right to select, the Agency maintains that the right includes the right to determine whether applicants are qualified for the position. The Agency claims that the award affects management's right to select because the award negated management's determination that the grievant was not qualified for the position. *Id.* at 20. In contending that the award is deficient, the Agency primarily argues that, "to the extent that the Arbitrator interprets the MAP to have required the grievant's application to be sent to the MAP panel for rating and ranking[,]" the award is contrary to § 7106(a)(2)(C) because the MAP is not an applicable law and was not incorporated into the agreement. *Id.* at 20. The Agency alternatively argues that, even if the MAP were incorporated into the agreement, the award is still contrary to § 7106(a)(2)(C) because the incorporated MAP provision was not negotiated pursuant to § 7106(b)(3). *Id.* at 21.

As to the MAP, the Agency maintains that, as found by the Arbitrator, the MAP constitutes an Agency regulation and that the Authority defers to an agency's interpretation of its own regulations when the interpretation is not clearly erroneous or inconsistent with the regulation. *Id.* at 9. In the Agency's view, nothing in the MAP precludes a human resources specialist from seeking advice from a subject-matter expert, including a selecting official, on whether an applicant meets selective qualification factors. *Id.* at 7. In addition, the Agency argues that the Arbitrator's interpretation of the MAP is without support because he prescribed an incorrect standard of proof and improperly placed the burden of proof on the Agency rather than the Union. *Id.* at 9. The Agency also argues that, to the extent the Arbitrator applied the MAP to have required the human resources specialist to refer the grievant to the MAP panel, the award is contrary to the MAP because only candidates determined to be qualified may be referred to the panel. *Id.* Consequently, the Agency asserts that the award is deficient because it is contrary to the MAP, as the Agency interprets the MAP, and such interpretation is not plainly erroneous or inconsistent with the MAP. *Id.*

As to essence, the Agency argues that, to the extent that the Arbitrator found a violation of either Article 38, Section 9(A), or Article 2, Section 2, the award is deficient because it does not represent a plausible interpretation of the agreement. *Id.* at 10-11.

B. Union's Opposition

As to management's rights, the Union disputes that the award affects the rights cited by the Agency. Opp'n at 18, 23. However, the Union argues that, to the extent the award does affect those rights, the award is not deficient. In this regard, the Union argues that the Arbitrator enforced provisions of Article 38 of the agreement and provisions of the MAP that were incorporated into the agreement by Article 2 and that these provisions were negotiated pursuant to § 7106(b)(2) or (b)(3) of the Statute. *Id.* at 19, 24. The Union also argues that the MAP has the force and effect of law and, thus, constitutes an applicable law within the meaning of § 7106(a)(2). *Id.* at 24.

As to the MAP, the Union additionally claims that, because the MAP was incorporated into the agreement, any alleged conflict between the award and the MAP is a question of contract interpretation and essence and not a question of whether the award is contrary to an Agency regulation. *Id.* at 9. In this regard, the Union contends that the Arbitrator's interpretation of the MAP draws its essence from its provisions.

Alternatively, the Union argues that, even if the MAP is not incorporated into the agreement, the award is not contrary to the MAP because the award is consistent with the MAP's plain meaning. *Id.* he Union maintains that the MAP makes clear that the human resources office is responsible for determining whether candidates are minimally qualified for positions and that a selecting official cannot evaluate qualifications until after the MAP panel has developed the best-qualified list. *Id.* at 29. The Union further maintains that, as the Arbitrator recognized, the MAP requires uniform and equitable consideration for promotions. Consequently, the Union asserts that the Arbitrator's finding that the selecting official reviewed some, but not all, of the applications supports the finding of a violation of the MAP because the selection process was neither uniform nor equitable. *Id.* at 14. Finally, the Union contends that the Authority should not defer to the Agency's interpretation of the MAP to find a conflict because the Agency's interpretation does not reflect the longstanding view of the Agency and is litigation inspired. *Id.* at 29-30.

As to Article 38 of the agreement, the Union contends that the award draws its essence from both Section 1(A) and Section 9(A). *Id.* at 15-16. As to Article 2, Section 2, the Union contends that the selecting official's determination violated the MAP and therefore Section 2, which incorporates the MAP. *Id.* at 14.

IV. Analysis and Conclusions

A. The award is not contrary to § 7106(a) of the Statute.

In resolving exceptions that contend that an award is contrary to a management right, the Authority first assesses whether the award affects the exercise of a right set forth in § 7106(a). The right to assign work under § 7106(a)(2)(B) includes the right to determine the particular duties to be assigned, when work assignments will occur, and to whom, or what positions, the duties will be assigned. *E.g., U.S. Dep't of the Treasury, U.S. Customs Serv., El Paso, Tex.*, 55 FLRA 553, 558 (1999). The right to select under § 7106(a)(2)(C) includes the right to determine the qualifications needed to perform the work of a position and to determine whether applicants possess such qualifications. *E.g., U.S. Dep't of the Navy, Supervisor of Shipbuilding, Conversion & Repair, Newport News, Va.*, 56 FLRA 339, 343 (2000). In this case, the Arbitrator concluded that the selecting official's determination that the grievant did not meet the qualifications for the position was improper. By precluding the selecting official from determining whether the grievant was qualified, the award affects management's rights to assign work and to select.

Both parties acknowledge that, if the MAP constitutes an applicable law within the meaning of § 7106(a)(2), then the award is not deficient. However, the parties dispute whether the MAP constitutes an applicable law.

A regulation constitutes an "applicable law" within the meaning of § 7106(a)(2) when it has "the force and effect of law." *NTEU*, 42 FLRA 377, 390-91 (1991), *enforcement denied on other grounds,* 996 F.2d 1246 (D.C. Cir. 1993). Regulations have the force and effect of law when they: (1) affect individual rights and obligations; (2) were promulgated pursuant to an explicit or implicit delegation of legislative authority by Congress; and (3) were promulgated in conformance with any procedural requirements imposed by Congress. *Id.* at 391-93.

The Authority has considered whether agency regulations constitute an applicable law under the *NTEU* requirements in three cases: *U.S. Dep't of the Air Force, Air Force Academy, Colo. Springs, Colo.*, 59 FLRA 888 (2004) (*Air Force*) (then-Member Pope dissenting as to another matter); *U.S. Dep't of the Army, Army Missile Command, Army Commc'ns Command Agency, Redstone Arsenal, Ala.*, 59 FLRA 154 (2003) (then-Member Pope dissenting) (*Army*); *U.S. Dep't of the Navy, Naval Undersea Warfare Ctr., Newport, R.I.*, 55 FLRA 687 (1999) (*Navy*). In *Air Force* and *Navy*, the Authority held that the regulations had the force and effect of law and constituted applicable laws. In *Army*, the Authority held that there was no basis on which to conclude that the agency regulation had the force and effect of law.

In *Navy*, the Authority held that the agency's Performance Appraisal Review System (PARS) regulation met all three *NTEU* requirements. 55 FLRA at 691. The Authority first concluded that PARS affected individual rights and obligations, noting that a regulation affects individual rights when it is mandatory and establishes obligations of agencies and rights of employees. The Authority found that PARS obligated the agency to conduct the performance appraisal process in a certain manner and affected the right of employees to obtain a particular rating. *Id.* at 690. The Authority further concluded that PARS was promulgated pursuant to an explicit delegation of legislative authority by Congress because, under 5 U.S.C. § 4302, each agency is required to establish certain performance appraisal systems and PARS stated that it was developed under this authority. *Id.* at 690-91. As to the third requirement, the Authority explained that, to meet this requirement, the regulation must be promulgated in accordance with applicable statutory procedures and be within the scope of delegated duties. The Authority acknowledged that, to be validly promulgated under the Administrative Procedures Act (APA), many regulations must be published through notice of the proposed rule in the Federal Register with an opportunity for interested parties to comment. However, the Authority noted the exception set forth in 5 U.S.C. § 553(a)(2) to the notice and comment requirements of the APA for agency rulemaking involving a matter related to agency management or personnel. The Authority found that PARS was excepted from the notice and comment requirements under § 553(a)(2) and was otherwise promulgated in conformance with the procedural requirements of law, regulation and OPM policy. Accordingly, the Authority concluded that PARS was promulgated in conformance with the procedural requirements imposed by Congress. *Id.* at 691.

In *Air Force*, the Authority held that Air Force Instruction (AFI) 38-203, which pertained to procurement and contracting out, met all three *NTEU* requirements. 59 FLRA at 893. The Authority first concluded that AFI-28-203 affected individual rights and obligations because it was mandatory for contracting-out studies and established the obligations of the agency and the right of employees as they pertained to such studies. *Id.* at 891. The Authority further concluded that AFI-38-203 was promulgated pursuant to a delegation of legislative authority by Congress. *Id.* at 892. Finally, the Authority concluded that AFI 38-203 was promulgated in conformance with the procedural requirements imposed by Congress. *Id.* at 892-93.

In *Army*, the arbitrator specifically cited MICOM 690-12.5 and 690-28.11, agency regulations pertaining to promotion. The Authority concluded that the citations did not constitute express findings that the agency violated the regulations. However, assuming that the arbitrator implicitly found that the agency violated the regulations, the Authority determined that "there [wa]s no evidence or assertion that either regulation constitute[d] an applicable law within the meaning of § 7106(a)(2) of the Statute." 59 FLRA at 156.

Applying the foregoing here, there is no dispute that the MAP is mandatory and that it establishes the obligations of the Agency and the rights of employees with respect to promotions and assignments within the Agency. Accordingly, the first requirement of *NTEU* is satisfied. As to the second requirement, Congress has expressly authorized OPM to prescribe rules governing the competitive service. 5 U.S.C. § 3302. Consistent with this authority, OPM has promulgated rules governing agency promotion and placement programs from which the MAP specifically states that it is derived. MAP Section I (Purpose); Section III (Authority). In this regard, the express purpose of the MAP is to assure that employees receive equitable consideration for promotion and placement solely on merit and fitness. MAP Section I. Accordingly, the second requirement is satisfied because the MAP is consistent with, and derived from, authorized OPM-imposed requirements. *See Navy*, 55 FLRA at 690-91. As to the third requirement, § 553(a)(2) excepts matters relating to agency management and personnel from the notice and comment requirements of the APA. *Id.* at 691. As a matter relating to agency management and personnel, the promulgation of the

MAP was excepted from the notice and comment requirements of the APA. *See id.* The Agency does not contend that the MAP was not promulgated in conformance with the procedural requirements of law and OPM rules and policy. Moreover, the Agency maintains that the MAP is a binding regulation that governs the disposition of this matter. Accordingly, the third requirement is satisfied. The Authority's decision in *Army* does not establish otherwise because, unlike that case, the Union specifically asserts, and the record supports, that, under Authority precedent, the MAP has the force and effect of law.

Accordingly, we conclude that the MAP constitutes an applicable law within the meaning of § 7106(a)(2). As the effect on management's rights is based on the Arbitrator's enforcement of such applicable law, the Agency fails to establish that the award is contrary to § 7106(a). Consequently, we deny this exception.

B. The award is not contrary to the MAP.

In the resolution of grievances under the Statute, arbitrators are empowered to interpret and apply agency rules and regulations. An arbitration award that conflicts with a governing agency regulation is deficient under § 7122(a)(1) of the Statute. *E.g., U.S. Dep't of Transp., Fed. Aviation Admin.*, 64 FLRA 513, 514 (2010). In reviewing arbitration awards for consistency with agency regulations, the Authority reviews the questions of law raised by the award and the exception *de novo*.[5] *Id.*

An agency's interpretation of its own regulations is controlling unless it is "plainly erroneous or inconsistent" with the language of the regulation. *Id.* (quoting *FLRA v. U.S. Dep't of the Treasury, Fin. Mgmt. Serv.*, 884 F.2d 1446, 1454 (D.C. Cir. 1989)) (*FLRA v. Treasury*). However, consistent with the approach of the courts, the Authority declines to defer to an agency's "litigative position[]." *Id.* (quoting *FLRA v. Treasury*, 884 F.2d at 1455)). In this regard, the Authority has explained that such positions may not reflect the views of the agency head and may have been developed "hastily, or under special pressure, or without an adequate opportunity for presentation of conflicting views." *Id.* Accordingly, for an agency's interpretation to be entitled to deference, the interpretation asserted in exceptions must have been publicly articulated prior to "litigation[.]" *Id.* (quoting *Nordell v. Heckler*, 749 F.2d 47, 48 (D.C. Cir. 1984)).

In the Agency's view, nothing in the MAP precludes a human resources specialist from seeking advice from a subject-matter expert, including a selecting official, on whether an applicant meets selective qualification factors. To the extent that this constitutes the Agency's interpretation of the MAP to which it alleges the Authority must defer, the Agency does not assert that this interpretation of the MAP reflects the views of the Agency head rather than the litigative position of the Agency before the Authority. *See id.* There is also no indication that this interpretation was developed in a manner that reflects deliberate consideration or that it was previously publicly articulated. *See id.* (citing *FLRA v. Treasury*, 884 F.2d at 1455). As such, the Agency has not established that its interpretation of the regulation is entitled to deference. *See id.*

In circumstances where an agency fails to establish that deference is due its alleged interpretation of an agency regulation, the Authority independently assesses whether the arbitrator's interpretation of the regulation is consistent with its provisions. *Id.* The Union argued to the Arbitrator that the selecting official's determination violated the MAP because it was not applied to all candidates. In assessing the selecting official's determination, the Arbitrator found that the MAP requires uniform and equitable treatment. In this regard, MAP, Section I (Purpose) specifically provides that employees will receive equitable treatment, and Section II (Policy) specifically provides that all vacancies will be treated uniformly. In finding a violation of the MAP, the Arbitrator found that the selecting official reviewed some, but not all, of the applications for the vacancy.[6] It is not disputed that these provisions must be strictly applied. Section XIII of the MAP expressly provides for the remedy awarded by the Arbitrator "[w]hen there is a failure to adhere strictly to the provisions of" the MAP. Award at 8. The Agency does not address these findings in its exception. Consequently, the

---

5. In this regard, the Union asserts that the MAP was incorporated into the agreement and that any alleged conflict between the award and the MAP is a question of contract interpretation that should be resolved under the deferential essence standard. Opp'n at 10. However, the Union concedes that the Arbitrator did not specifically interpret the agreement to incorporate the MAP. *Id.* at 10 n.13. Moreover, the Arbitrator treated the MAP and the agreement separately. *See* Award at 15-16. Consequently, we review *de novo* whether the award conflicts with the MAP.

6. The dissent argues that the requirement of uniformity applies to vacancies, not to candidates. *See* Dissent at 13. However, the dissent does not demonstrate that the vacancy was treated uniformly, particularly given the Arbitrator's finding that the selecting official reviewed some, but not all, of the applications for the vacancy.

Agency fails to demonstrate that, contrary to the conclusion of the Arbitrator, it strictly treated the grievant equitably and the vacancy uniformly, as required by the MAP.

Further, the Agency does not demonstrate how the selecting official's determination prior to evaluation by the MAP panel is strictly consistent with the mandated roles and sequence requirements of the placement process. The MAP assigns the office of human resources, the selecting official, and the rating and ranking panel distinct roles in the selection process. Pursuant to Section V of the MAP, the human resources office is responsible for screening applications and evaluating candidates for positions. Section IX of the MAP emphasizes that evaluations will be made by the human resources office and specifies only one exception: when the selecting official specifically requests the establishment of a panel. In such cases, the panel determines the qualifications, and the selecting official advises the panel on the interpretation of qualifications, but has no vote. The Arbitrator found that the selecting official, rather than the human resources specialist, determined that the grievant was not qualified prior to the establishment of the MAP panel, and there is no dispute that the selecting official did not request the establishment of a panel. This finding supports the Arbitrator's conclusion that the selecting official's determination violated the MAP.[7]

The Agency also contends that the Arbitrator's interpretation of the MAP is deficient because the Arbitrator prescribed an incorrect standard of proof and improperly placed the burden of proof on the Agency. If a standard of proof is set forth in applicable law or regulation or the parties' collective bargaining agreement, then the arbitrator must apply the prescribed standard. *E.g., U.S. Dep't of Commerce, Patent & Trademark Office, Arlington, Va.*, 60 FLRA 869, 881 (2005). When no standard is prescribed, arbitrators are empowered to prescribe whatever standard they consider appropriate, and their awards will not be found deficient on the basis that they applied an incorrect standard of proof. *Id.* Moreover, unless otherwise provided, prescribing the standard of proof encompasses specifying which party has the burden of proof. *Id.* In this case, the Agency does not claim that law, regulation, or the agreement prescribed the standard of proof or which party had the burden of proof, and its contentions provide no basis for finding the award deficient. *See id.*

For all of these reasons, we deny this exception.

C. The award does not fail to draw its essence from the agreement.

The Authority has consistently held that, when an arbitrator bases the award on two or more separate and independent grounds, the appealing party must establish that all of the grounds on which the arbitrator relied are deficient in order for the Authority to find that the award is deficient. *E.g., Broad. Bd. of Governors, Office of Cuba Broad.*, 64 FLRA 888, 892 (2010). As we have concluded that the Agency fails to establish that the award is contrary to the MAP, the Agency's essence exception provides no basis for finding the award deficient. *See id.* Accordingly, we deny this exception.

V. Decision

The Agency's exceptions are denied.

APPENDIX

The MAP provides, in pertinent part, as follows:

<u>Section I. Purpose</u>

> The Merit Assignment Program (MAP) . . . is hereby established to assure that all . . . employees . . . receive equitable consideration for promotion and placement based solely on merit and fitness. . . .

<u>Section II. Policy</u>

> All vacancies filled under the provisions of this Program will be treated uniformly and all candidates will be considered without regard to race, color, religion, national origin, marital status, age, sex, non-disqualifying physical handicap, political or labor organization affiliation, or any other non-merit factor. . . .

7. The Agency further claims that, to the extent that the Arbitrator concluded that the human resources specialist should have referred the grievant to the MAP panel, the award is inconsistent with the MAP. However, the Arbitrator made no such conclusion. Thus, we reject the claim.

In addition, we note that the dissent neither addresses the wording of the MAP requiring the Agency to "adhere strictly to the provisions of" the MAP – including the provisions designating which offices will engage in which aspects of the selection process – nor explains how the Agency adhered strictly to those provisions. Award at 8. Accordingly, the dissent does not demonstrate that the Arbitrator erred in concluding that the Agency violated the MAP.

. . . .

Section V. Responsibilities

A. Office of [Human Resources]. The Office of [Human Resources] is responsible for . . . [s]creening and evaluating qualifications against basic civil service requirements and standards.

. . . .

Section IX. Evaluation, Ranking, and Panels

A. All eligible candidates will be evaluated. . . . The evaluations will be made by the Personnel Office unless the selecting official specifically requests the establishment of a panel. . . .

B. Merit assignment panels will be constituted in the following manner:

1. A panel . . . will consist of at least three members . . . . When advice and guidance on the interpretation of qualifications is considered essential, the selecting official may advise the panel but has no vote. Such advice should normally be provided before the panel received the names and applications of the candidates.

Section XIII. Complaints and Corrective Actions

. . . . When there is a failure to adhere strictly to the provisions of the FPM, the DAO, or this [Program], corrective measures shall be applied [promptly] and in accordance with the corrective action guidance set forth in FPM Chapter 335.

Award at 5-8.

Member Beck, Dissenting:

I disagree with my colleagues that the Agency's contrary to regulation and essence exceptions should be denied.

The Arbitrator treated the Agency's Merit Assignment Program (MAP) as a binding Agency regulation. While it is not entirely evident to me that this is a correct characterization of the MAP, the Agency does not appear to take exception to such characterization.

Assuming that the provisions of the MAP were binding on the Agency, I believe the Arbitrator's interpretation and application of the MAP in this case is neither plausible nor rationally derived from the plain language of that document. *U.S. Dep't of Veterans Affairs, Medical & Reg'l Ctr., Togus, Maine*, 55 FLRA 1189, 1196 (1999) (citing *Carter v. Tisch*, 822 F.2d 465, 468-69 (4th Cir. 1987) (award that is inconsistent with regulation's plain language is unenforceable); *U.S. Dep't of the Treasury, Brooklyn Dist., Brooklyn, N.Y.*, 51 FLRA 1487, 1494 (1996) (award that is contrary to the plain language of regulation must be set aside)).

The Arbitrator's core concern about how the Agency handled the selection process was that the personnelist who initially assessed the threshold qualifications of applicants informally sought input from the selecting official who would later make the final selection decision. The Arbitrator concluded that such conduct ran afoul of the MAP because "such conduct is not supported or endorsed by the clear language of the Agency's Merit Assignment Program." Award at 15. But this is not the correct approach when determining whether an employer engaged in impermissible conduct. The proper question is not whether the applicable contract or regulation affirmatively endorses the conduct in question; rather, the question is whether the contract or regulation *prohibits* the conduct in question. That which is not prohibited is permitted. *Shroyer v. New Cingular Wireless Servs. Inc.*, 498 F.3d 976, 992 (9th Cir. 2007) (citing *Green Tree Financial Corp. v. Bazzle*, 539 U.S. 444, 454-55 (2003) (actions not prohibited by agreement are permitted); *Gold Line Refining, Ltd. v. United States*, 54 Fed. Cl. 285, 290 (Fed. Cl. 2002) (EPA clause that is not prohibited by the FAR is permitted)). The MAP does not prohibit the Agency conduct that is the subject of the grievance.

The crux of the Arbitrator's reasoning in finding a violation by the Agency is that "the MAP requires *uniform* and *equitable* consideration for Agency promotion actions . . . ." Award at 15 (emphasis in original). This is an over-generalization and a material misstatement of what the MAP actually requires.

To be sure, the MAP does use the phrase "equitable consideration" (MAP Section I), but it then goes on to explain precisely what is meant by this phrase, and thereby limits substantially the scope of what would otherwise be a vague phrase very much subject to interpretation. In the context of the MAP, "equitable consideration" is that which is "based solely on merit and fitness." MAP Section I. Thus, to establish agency conduct inconsistent with this requirement, a grieving party would need to prove that the Agency used selection criteria other than merit and fitness. No evidence was adduced to establish, and the Arbitrator did not find, that the grievant's non-selection was based on factors other than merit and fitness. Consequently, if the Arbitrator concluded that the grievant was not given "equitable consideration" within the meaning of the MAP, it is a conclusion that could only be reached by applying the pertinent MAP language in an overly expansive and implausible fashion.

Similarly, the Arbitrator misapplied the perceived requirement of uniformity. At Section II, the MAP states that:

> All vacancies . . . will be treated uniformly and all candidates will be considered without regard to race, color, religion, national origin, marital status, age, sex, non-disqualifying physical handicap, political or labor organization affiliation, or any other non-merit factor . . . .

Award at 5.

"Vacancies" and "candidates" are distinct terms that have different meanings. The requirement of uniformity applies to vacancies, not to candidates. To the extent the Arbitrator applied a uniformity requirement to the Agency's consideration of the grievant, he was misapplying language that self-evidently should not be applied to her as a candidate.*

As a "candidate" under the MAP, the grievant was entitled to be considered for promotion without regard to non-merit factors. Again, no evidence was adduced to establish, and the Arbitrator did not find, that the grievant's non-selection was based on any non-merit factor. Accordingly, to the extent the Arbitrator found a violation of the MAP, he did so by engaging in an implausible reading of the pertinent MAP language.

The Arbitrator's conclusions are inconsistent with the plain language of the MAP and do not represent a plausible interpretation of the parties' agreement.

---

* To the extent the Arbitrator may have obtained his perceived uniformity requirement from Article 38, Section 9 of the collective bargaining agreement, he misapplied contract language that should not have been applied to the grievant. This contractual uniformity requirement attaches only once a candidate reaches the "best qualified" stage of the selection process. Award at 4 (quoting Article 39, Section 9). The grievant never reached this stage.

65 FLRA No. 7

AMERICAN FEDERATION
OF GOVERNMENT EMPLOYEES
LOCAL 3937
(Union)

and

SOCIAL SECURITY ADMINISTRATION
REGION X
(Agency)

0-AR-4648
(64 FLRA 1113 (2010))

ORDER DENYING MOTION
FOR RECONSIDERATION

August 25, 2010

Before the Authority: Carol Waller Pope, Chairman, and Thomas M. Beck and Ernest DuBester, Members

I. Statement of the Case

This matter is before the Authority on the Union's motion for reconsideration of the Authority's decision in *AFGE, Local 3937*, 64 FLRA 1113 (2010) (*Local 3937*). The Agency filed an opposition to the Union's motion.

The Authority's Regulations permit a party to request reconsideration of an Authority decision where it can establish extraordinary circumstances. 5 C.F.R. § 2429.17. For the reasons that follow, we find that the Union has failed to establish that extraordinary circumstances exist warranting reconsideration of the Authority's decision. Therefore, we deny the Union's motion.[1]

II. Background

As discussed in greater detail in *Local 3937*, the Arbitrator found that, upon the effective date of the parties' national agreement (the 2005 MLA), twelve local memoranda of understanding (the 12 MOUs) "ceased to exist[,]" and the Agency was no longer "obligated to honor" the conditions of employment contained therein after that date. 64 FLRA at 1113 (quoting Award at 18). Accordingly, he found that the Agency did not violate the 2005 MLA when it denied the Union's request to bargain over its announcement that the 12 MOUs would no longer be followed. *Id.*

The Union filed exceptions alleging that the award was based on a nonfact (the Arbitrator's finding that the conditions of employment covered by the 12 MOUs were not in effect on the effective date of the 2005 MLA), failed to draw its essence from that MLA, and was contrary to §§ 7117, 7102(2), and 7114 of the Federal Service Labor-Management Relations Statute (the Statute). *Id.* at 1114. The Authority found that the parties disputed before the Arbitrator whether the conditions of employment covered by the 12 MOUs were in effect on the effective date of the 2005 MLA and, accordingly, denied the nonfact exception. *Id.* at 1115 (citing Award at 14 & 16). As the Union's essence exception and exceptions regarding §§ 7102(2) and 7114 were premised on the argument in the Union's nonfact exception, the Authority also denied those exceptions. *Id.* at 1115. In addition, the Authority dismissed the § 7117 exception because the Union had not raised § 7117 before the Arbitrator. *Id.* at 1114.

III. Positions of the Parties

A. Union's Motion for Reconsideration

The Union asserts that, in *Local 3937*, the Authority "missed the central and uncontested point" of its exceptions, specifically, that the Arbitrator erred in his "alleged finding 'that the conditions of employment set forth in the 12 MOUs were not in effect as of the effective date of the 2005 MLA[.]'" Union's Motion at 2. The Union asserts that the Authority's statement that the Agency disputed this fact before the Arbitrator "misunderstands" the award. *Id.* at 2 n.3. According to the Union, although the Arbitrator found that the Agency had argued that the "terms" embodied in the 12 MOUs ceased to exist upon the effective date of the 2005 MLA, he then stated that the Agency acknowledged that the "conditions of employment" embodied in the 12 MOUs did not change until the 2005 MLA was signed. *Id.* at 3 n.4. The Union asserts that "once it is understood that these conditions of employment" were being followed on the effective date of the 2005 MLA, it becomes "clear" that the award does not

1. The Union also asserts that "[o]ral [a]rgument is [r]equested." Union's Motion at 1. The Agency opposes that request. Agency's Opp'n at 2. As the record is sufficient to resolve the Union's motion, we deny the request. *See* 5 C.F.R. § 2429.6.

draw its essence from the parties' agreement. *Id.* at 4.

In addition, the Union asserts that an alleged violation of § 7116(a)(1) and (5) of the Statute was before the Arbitrator, that the Arbitrator addressed only a contractual issue, and that the Authority "failed to recognize" the § 7116(a)(1) and (5) issue. *Id.* at 6-7. In this regard, the Union concedes that it "did not separately list" § 7116(a)(1) and (5) in its exceptions, but claims that other references in its exceptions were "sufficient to put the [Authority] on notice that this case alleged and has always alleged a ULP or a [§] 7116(a)(1) and (5) violation in addition to a contract violation." *Id.* at 8.

B. Agency's Opposition

The Agency argues that the Authority should deny the Union's motion because: (1) the motion fails to state with particularity the extraordinary circumstances that warrant reconsideration, and fails to provide supporting citations, Opp'n at 2-5; (2) even assuming that the motion is not deficient in this regard, the Union fails to meet its "heavy burden" of proving extraordinary circumstances, *id.* at 5; (3) *Local 3937* does not require reconsideration because the Authority found no violation of the Statute, and the Authority is entitled to deference in this regard, *id.* at 6-7; and (4) the Arbitrator had discretion to frame the issue before him as purely contractual, given the parties' failure to stipulate the issues before him, *id.* at 7-9.

IV. Analysis and Conclusions

Section 2429.17 of the Authority's Regulations permits a party that can establish extraordinary circumstances to request reconsideration of an Authority decision. The Authority has repeatedly recognized that a party seeking reconsideration under § 2429.17 bears the heavy burden of establishing that extraordinary circumstances exist to justify this unusual action. *See Int'l Ass'n of Firefighters, Local F-25*, 64 FLRA 943, 943 (2010) (*IAF*). The Authority has identified a limited number of situations in which extraordinary circumstances have been found to exist. These include situations where: (1) an intervening court decision or change in the law affected dispositive issues; (2) evidence, information, or issues crucial to the decision had not been presented to the Authority; (3) the Authority erred in its remedial order, process, conclusion of law, or factual finding; and (4) the moving party has not been given an opportunity to address an issue raised sua sponte by the Authority in its decision. *See id.*

The Union's motion for reconsideration does not cite any of these situations. To the extent that the Union's first argument asserts that the Authority erred in a factual finding, the factual question of whether the conditions of employment set forth in the 12 MOUs continued to exist after the effective date of the 2005 MLA was clearly disputed by the parties at arbitration, *see* Award at 14 & 16, and, therefore, the Authority appropriately denied the Union's exception challenging that factual finding. *See IAF*, 64 FLRA at 943-44 (citation omitted). Thus, the Union's first argument does not demonstrate extraordinary circumstances warranting reconsideration of *Local 3937*.

To the extent that the Union's second argument asserts that the Authority misconstrued its exceptions, the Union acknowledges that it did not cite § 7116(a)(1) and (5) in its exceptions, and the Union's motion does not demonstrate that it sufficiently raised those specific statutory sections before the Authority. Thus, in effect, the Union raises new issues that were not raised in its exceptions. In resolving a request for reconsideration, the Authority will not consider issues that were not raised in its review of an award upon a party's exceptions. *See Bremerton Metal Trades Council*, 64 FLRA 543, 545 (2010) (Member DuBester concurring). Accordingly, the Union's second argument does not demonstrate extraordinary circumstances warranting reconsideration of *Local 3937*.

For the foregoing reasons, we deny the Union's motion for reconsideration.

V. Decision

The Union's motion for reconsideration is denied.

65 FLRA No. 8

UNITED STATES
DEPARTMENT OF THE TREASURY
INTERNAL REVENUE SERVICE
SMALL BUSINESS/SELF EMPLOYED
OPERATING DIVISION
(Agency)

and

NATIONAL TREASURY
EMPLOYEES UNION
CHAPTER 68
(Union)

0-AR-4480

DECISION

August 25, 2010

Before the Authority: Carol Waller Pope, Chairman, and Thomas M. Beck and Ernest DuBester, Members

I. Statement of the Case

This matter is before the Authority on exceptions to an award of Arbitrator Thomas N. Rinaldo filed by the Agency under § 7122(a) of the Federal Service Labor-Management Relations Statute (the Statute) and part 2425 of the Authority's Regulations. The Union filed an opposition to the Agency's exceptions.

The Union filed a grievance alleging that the Agency incorrectly set the grievant's rate of pay upon her permanent promotion. The Arbitrator sustained the grievance and directed the Agency to correct the grievant's pay rate and provide a make-whole remedy.

For the reasons that follow, we deny the Agency's exceptions.

II. Background and Arbitrator's Award

The grievant worked for the Agency in a permanent position at General Schedule (GS) grade-level five, step four (GS-05, Step 4). *See* Award at 10. The Agency subsequently granted her a temporary promotion at GS grade-level six, step four (GS-06, Step 4). *See id.* After holding her temporary promotion for more than a year, the grievant received a permanent promotion to a different position. The Agency concluded that the grievant's compensation after permanent promotion should be set at GS grade-level seven, step one (GS-07, Step 1), based on the grievant's previous rate of pay in her position of record, at GS-05, Step 4. *Id.* The Union filed a grievance contending that the Agency had erred in its compensation calculations and that the grievant's pay after permanent promotion should have been set at GS grade-level seven, step three (GS-07, Step 3), based on the grievant's previous rate of pay during her temporary promotion.[1] *Id.* at 2. The grievance went unresolved, and the parties proceeded to arbitration on the following stipulated issue:

> Whether [g]rievant's pay was appropriately set when she was promoted to the GS-07 . . . position . . ., and if not, what shall be the remedy?

Id.

The Agency argued that, in accordance with its standard practice, it had "returned" the grievant from her temporarily promoted position to her "position of record, which was GS-05, Step 4 . . . before promoting her to the GS-07 position." *Id.* at 7. Therefore, the Agency contended that it had: (1) properly identified GS-05, Step 4 as the grievant's existing rate of pay immediately prior to permanent promotion; and (2) correctly applied the "two step promotion rule," 5 U.S.C. § 5334(b), and Agency regulations to calculate the compensation rate for the grievant's permanent promotion.[2] *Id.* Using those calculations, the Agency

1. The table below shows the grievant's positions and their respective compensation ratings, side-by-side:

Grievant's Position	*GS Grade and Step*
pre-promotion	GS-05, Step 4
temporary promotion	GS-06, Step 4
permanent promotion (Agency's calculation)	GS-07, Step 1
permanent promotion (Union's calculation)	GS-07, Step 3

2. The Agency argued that it relied on 5 U.S.C. § 5334(b) and provisions of the Internal Revenue Manual (IRM) to set the grievant's compensation. *See, e.g.*, Exceptions, Attach. E, Agency's Post-Hearing Brief at 3 & n.1, 4-5. Referred to

set the grievant's rate of pay at GS-07, Step 1. *See* Award at 7.

The Union characterized the Agency's claim that it had returned the grievant to a GS-05, Step 4 position before permanently promoting her to the GS-07 position as "pure fiction." *Id.* at 5 (internal quotation marks omitted). According to the Union, the Agency should have identified the grievant's temporary-promotion compensation rate – *i.e.*, GS-06, Step 4 – as the grievant's existing rate of pay immediately prior to permanent promotion, which, after applying the "two step promotion rule," would have resulted in a permanent-promotion compensation rate of GS-07, Step 3. *Id.* at 4-5.

The Arbitrator determined that, "[al]though [the] [g]rievant's Personnel Action Report shows a change to the lower grade GS-05 position, in fact[, the g]rievant was never returned to that position[,] but went from the GS-06[,] Step 4 [temporary-promotion] position to the GS-07 [permanent-promotion] position." *Id.* at 10. Having found that the grievant was not returned to her position of record, the Arbitrator determined that the Agency should have calculated the grievant's permanent-promotion compensation rate using her temporary-promotion rate as her existing rate of pay. *Id.* at 15. Therefore, the Arbitrator sustained the grievance and ordered a make-whole remedy. *Id.* at 16.

III. Positions of the Parties

A. Agency's Exceptions

The Agency contends that the award is contrary to law because, according to the Agency, the Arbitrator's compensation calculations fail to account for the grievant's "return" to her position of record before her permanent promotion. Exceptions at 3. The Agency asserts that, after it "returned" the grievant to her position of record, it correctly calculated her permanent-promotion compensation rate in accordance with its regulations and applicable statutory authority, including the "two step promotion rule." *Id.* at 3-5, 8 (citing 5 U.S.C. § 5334(b); IRM §§ 6.500.1.4.4(4) & 6.500.1.4.7(1)). In particular, the Agency asserts that: (1) IRM, Section 6.500.1.4.4(4) "does not allow" the Agency to use the grievant's temporary-promotion compensation rate to determine her permanent-promotion rate, Exceptions at 5-6; and (2) IRM, Section 6.500.1.4.7(1)(B) required the Agency to set the grievant's permanent-promotion compensation based on her position of record, *see* Exceptions at 8.[3] Moreover, the Agency argues that its position is supported by decisions of the Comptroller General in similar cases, and that, consequently, the Arbitrator's interpretation of the IRM is "contrary to applicable Comptroller General case law." *Id.* at 8; *see also id.* at 5-6 (citing *Catherine L. Drake*, B-247553, 1992 WL 109481 (Comp. Gen. May 8, 1992); *Benjamin C. Smith*, B-202631, 1982 WL 27213 (Comp. Gen. Aug. 24, 1982)).

B. Union's Opposition

The Union opposes the Agency's exceptions because, according to the Union, they constitute "no[thing] more than disagreement with the Arbitrator's findings of fact and conclusions drawn from those facts." Opp'n at 4.

IV. Analysis and Conclusions

When an exception involves an award's consistency with law, rule, or regulation, the Authority reviews any question of law raised by the exception and the award *de novo*. *See NTEU, Chapter 24*, 50 FLRA 330, 332 (1995) (citing *U.S. Customs Serv. v. FLRA*, 43 F.3d 682, 686-87 (D.C. Cir. 1994)). In applying the standard of *de novo* review, the Authority assesses whether an arbitrator's legal conclusions are consistent with the applicable standard of law. *See U.S. Dep't of Def., Dep'ts of the Army & the Air Force, Ala. Nat'l Guard, Northport, Ala.*, 55 FLRA 37, 40 (1998) (*Ala. Nat'l Guard*). In making that assessment, the Authority defers to the arbitrator's underlying factual findings. *See id.*

---

as the "two step promotion rule," *e.g.*, Exceptions, Attach. F at 6 (quoting IRM § 6.500.1.4.7(4)(B)), 5 U.S.C. § 5334(b) provides, in pertinent part:

> (b) An employee who is promoted . . . to a position in a higher grade is entitled to basic pay at the lowest rate of the higher grade which exceeds his existing rate of basic pay by not less than two step-increases of the grade from which he is promoted[.]

5 U.S.C. § 5334(b).

The pertinent provisions of the IRM are set forth *infra* Part IV.B.

3. The IRM provisions, as well as the Agency's contentions regarding their application to the grievant's circumstances, are set forth *infra* Part IV.B.

A. The award is not contrary to 5 U.S.C. § 5334(b).

The Agency alleges that the "two step promotion rule," 5 U.S.C. § 5334(b), "does not prohibit the Agency from returning [g]rievant to her position of record on paper . . . prior to her permanent[] promot[ion.]" Exceptions at 8. However, the award does not hold to the contrary. Rather, the Arbitrator relied on 5 U.S.C. § 5334(b) to support his finding that "a promotion can occur . . . from 'a grade held under temporary promotion'" – a proposition that the Agency does not dispute. Award at 14. Thus, the Agency has not established that the award is contrary to 5 U.S.C. § 5334(b), and we deny the exception. *See Ala. Nat'l Guard*, 55 FLRA at 40.

B. The award is not contrary to the IRM.

The Agency contends that the Arbitrator misinterpreted the IRM when he determined that the "'mere chang[ing] of an employee's status on the Personnel Action Report[,]' as was done [in the grievant's case], cannot suffice for a 'return'" to the grievant's position of record, prior to her permanent promotion. *See* Exceptions at 8-9. The Agency asserts that a paper-record notation is sufficient to effect a "return," and the Arbitrator erred in finding that provisions of the IRM require anything more than a return "on paper only." *Id.* at 8. We construe the Agency's argument as a claim that the award is deficient because the Arbitrator did not defer to the Agency's interpretation of its own regulations.

In the resolution of grievances under the Statute, arbitrators are empowered to interpret and apply agency rules and regulations. *See U.S. Dep't of Justice, Immigration & Naturalization Serv., Wash., D.C.*, 48 FLRA 1269, 1275 (1993). In this regard, an agency's prior interpretation of its own regulation is controlling unless it is "plainly erroneous or inconsistent" with the language of the regulation. *U.S. Dep't of Justice, Fed. Bureau of Prisons, Med. Facility for Fed. Prisons*, 51 FLRA 1126, 1136 (1996) (*DOJ*) (quoting *FLRA v. U.S. Dep't of the Treasury, Fin. Mgmt. Serv.*, 884 F.2d 1446, 1454 (D.C. Cir. 1989) (*FLRA v. Treasury*)). However, the Authority declines to defer to an agency's "litigative positions." *Id.* (quoting *FLRA v. Treasury*, 884 F.2d at 1455)). Accordingly, for an agency's interpretation to be entitled to deference, the interpretation asserted in exceptions must have been publicly articulated prior to "litigation[.]" *Id.* (quoting *Nordell v. Heckler*, 749 F.2d 47, 48 (D.C. Cir. 1984)). In circumstances where an agency fails to establish that deference is due to its interpretation of its regulation, the Authority independently assesses whether the arbitrator's interpretation of the regulation is consistent with its provisions. *U.S. Dep't of Transp., Fed. Aviation Admin.*, 56 FLRA 627, 630 (2000) (*FAA*); *DOJ*, 51 FLRA at 1137.

First, the Agency asserts that IRM, Section 6.500.1.4.4 "does not allow" the Agency to use the grievant's temporary-promotion compensation rate to determine her permanent-promotion rate. Exceptions at 5-6. Section 6.500.1.4.4 provides, in pertinent part:

> **Maximum Payable Rate Rules**
>
> . . . .
>
> 4. The maximum payable rate rule, considering an employee's highest previous rate, will not be used to set the pay of an employee who is [returned] to lower grade as the result of the termination or expiration of a temporary promotion when the employee is likely to be promoted within 6 months of the date of the [return] to lower grade.

Id., Attach. F at 4-5 (quoting IRM § 6.500.1.4.4(4)).

According to the Agency, it had already selected the grievant for her permanent-promotion position when it "end[ed]" her temporary promotion "on paper[,]" Exceptions at 3, and, therefore, the Agency argues that it properly considered the grievant "likely to be promoted within 6 months" of her "return . . . on paper" to her position of record, *id.* at 5-6. Given those circumstances, the Agency asserts that: (1) it acted as required by Section 6.500.1.4.4(4), *supra*, in declining to apply the "maximum payable rate rule" to set the grievant's compensation when the Agency "returned" her to her position of record "on paper[;]" and (2) the Arbitrator's finding to the contrary is erroneous. *Id.* at 4.

Second, the Agency asserts that its actions in setting the grievant's compensation were consistent with IRM, Section 6.500.1.4.7(1), which states:

> **Promotions and Transfers**
>
> 1. As provided by 5 U.S.C. [§] 5334(b), upon promotion[,] the pay of a [GS] employee will be set at the lowest step of the higher grade that exceeds the employee's existing rate of basic pay by the value of two steps of the grade held immediately before the promotion.

> A. This includes a grade held under a temporary promotion if the promotion action is effected from the temporarily held grade.
>
> B. If the employee is returned to the lower permanent grade before the subsequent action is processed, the promotion action must be based on the lower grade.

Exceptions, Attach. F at 5 (quoting IRM § 6.500.1.4.7(1)).

In particular, the Agency contends that the grievant's situation is governed by § 6.500.1.4.7(1)(B), *supra*, because, according to the Agency, the grievant was returned "on paper" to her "lower permanent grade" before her subsequent permanent promotion was processed. *See* Exceptions at 8. The Agency maintains that the Arbitrator "ignored" the aforementioned IRM provisions – i.e., §§ 6.500.1.4.4(4) and 6.500.1.4.7(1) – when he interpreted the word "return" and found that the grievant had not been "returned" to her position of record prior to her permanent promotion. *See id.*

Although the Agency asserts that a notation in the grievant's Personnel Action Report constitutes a "return" to her position of record, the Agency does not cite, and the IRM provisions on which the Agency relies do not contain, a regulatory definition of "return." *Cf. DOJ*, 51 FLRA at 1137 (agency provided no basis for finding an award contrary to agency regulation when the regulation did not define the term in dispute). Moreover, the Agency provides no evidence that it formally promulgated or otherwise publicly announced its interpretation of the IRM's use of the word "return" prior to the instant dispute. Therefore, the Agency's interpretation of "return" is not entitled to deference. *See id.* at 1136 (citing *FLRA v. Treasury*, 884 F.2d at 1455); *cf. United States v. Paddack*, 825 F.2d 504 (D.C. Cir. 1987) (Foreign Service Grievance Board did not err in refusing to accord deference to agency's interpretation of regulation issued only after formal grievance litigation was commenced).

Thus, in accordance with Authority precedent on *de novo* regulatory interpretation, we independently assess whether the Arbitrator's interpretation of "return" is consistent with the text of the relevant IRM provisions. *See FAA*, 56 FLRA at 630. As mentioned above, the IRM does not define "return." In addition, the IRM expressly recognizes that the Agency may use an employee's temporary-promotion compensation rate to set the employee's pay upon promotion. *See supra* IRM § 6.500.1.4.7(1)(A). In these circumstances, we find no inconsistency between the text of the IRM and the Arbitrator's conclusion that a "return" requires more than a mere paper-record notation. Accordingly, we deny the Agency's exception.

C. The award is not inconsistent with Comptroller General decisions.

The Agency further asserts that the Arbitrator's interpretation of "return" is inconsistent with certain decisions of the Comptroller General – namely, *Catherine L. Drake* and *Benjamin C. Smith*. *See* Exceptions at 5-6. However, neither of those decisions dealt with interpretations of the IRM. *Cf. DOJ*, 51 FLRA at 1136 (responding to agency's assertion that its interpretation of regulation was consistent with certain court decisions, and noting that "[n]one of the cases cited by the Agency concerns an interpretation" of the regulation in dispute). Moreover, neither of those decisions held that, in every circumstance involving the "two step promotion rule," a purported change in an employee's position "on paper only" would establish, as a matter of law, that the affected employee had "returned" to the position indicated.[4] Thus, the Agency has failed to establish that the award is contrary to law due to inconsistency with *Catherine L. Drake* or *Benjamin C. Smith.*[5] Consequently, we deny the exception.

V. Decision

The Agency's exceptions are denied.

---

4. The word "return" does not even appear in *Catherine L. Drake*; in addition, the agency in that dispute had no written policy or regulation regarding the compensation matter at issue. *See id.*, B-247553, 1992 WL 109481, at *2. Similarly, in *Benjamin C. Smith*, the claimant-employee's agency had no written policy regarding the compensation matter in dispute. *See id.*, B-202631, 1982 WL 27213, at *2. As neither decision concerned a written policy or regulation, neither involved an interpretation of the word "return."

5. We note that, in any event, decisions of the Comptroller General are not binding on the Authority. "Although a Comptroller General opinion serves as an expert opinion that should be prudently considered, a prior assessment of the Comptroller General is not one to which deference must be given." *AFGE, Local 1458*, 63 FLRA 469, 471 (2009) (citations omitted).

65 FLRA No. 9

UNITED STATES
DEPARTMENT OF VETERANS AFFAIRS
G. V. (SONNY) MONTGOMERY
VA MEDICAL CENTER
JACKSON, MISSISSIPPI
(Agency)

and

AMERICAN FEDERATION
OF GOVERNMENT EMPLOYEES
LOCAL 589
(Union)

0-AR-4345

DECISION

August 26, 2010

Before the Authority: Carol Waller Pope, Chairman, and Thomas M. Beck and Ernest DuBester, Members

I. Statement of the Case

This matter is before the Authority on exceptions to an award and supplemental award of Arbitrator Patrick Hardin filed by the Agency under § 7122(a) of the Federal Service Labor-Management Relations Statute and part 2425 of the Authority's Regulations. The Union did not file an opposition to the Agency's exceptions.

The Union filed a grievance alleging that the grievants were not properly compensated when they were required to perform duties of a higher-graded position for twenty-three months. The Arbitrator determined that the employees at issue were entitled to backpay for performing the duties of the higher-graded position. For the reasons set forth below, we dismiss the Agency's exceptions.

II. Background and Arbitrator's Award

A. Background

The Union filed a grievance alleging that the Agency did not properly compensate the GS-6 Police Officer grievants when they were required to conduct training duties of higher-graded GS-7 Police Officer Instructors for twenty-three months.[1] Original Award at 3.

The Agency failed to timely respond to the grievance. Article 42, Section 9 of the Master Agreement provides that if the Agency fails to timely respond to a grievance, the dispute is to be resolved "in favor of the grievant" as long as the requested remedy is legal and reasonable. *Id.* at 4 (quoting Article 42, Section 9 of the Master Agreement).

The parties submitted the matter to arbitration. The Arbitrator framed the issue as whether the requested remedy was "'legal and reasonable under the circumstances of the grievance' within the meaning of Article 42, Section 9, of the parties' Master Agreement[?]" Original Award at 2. The issue further stated that if the Arbitrator determined that the remedy was not legal or reasonable, he was to decide what the remedy should be.

B. Arbitrator's Award

At the arbitration hearing, the Union requested three remedies. First, the Union asked that the grievants be temporarily promoted to the GS-7 Police Officer Instructor position for the twenty-three months during which they performed training duties. Second, the Union requested that the grievants be awarded a "16-hours time-off award[.]" *Id.* at 4. Third, the Union requested that the grievants receive a special contribution award totaling $9,568. *Id.*

Before the Arbitrator, the Agency argued that the Union's requested remedies were not legal or reasonable for several reasons. First, the Agency claimed that the grievants had not met the requirements of Article 12, Section 2.a of the Master Agreement to be compensated at the GS-7 pay rate. *Id.* at 6. Second, the Agency contended that the 16-hours time-off award requested by the Union was unreasonable. Third, the Agency argued that the monetary award requested by the Union was not legal because each of the grievants had already received a $2,500 special contribution award for the training that they conducted. Award at 5. The Agency claimed that it was illegal to grant a special contribution award in excess of $5,000 to any employee.

1. The original grievance concerned three GS-6 Police Officer grievants. The Agency's exceptions pertain to just two of the grievants.

The Arbitrator made several determinations with regard to the Union's request that the Agency temporarily promote the grievants. The Arbitrator rejected the Agency's argument that the grievants were not entitled to temporary promotions under Article 12, Section 2.a of the Master Agreement. In this regard, the Arbitrator concluded that the Agency could not argue on the merits that the grievants were not entitled to the temporary promotions because Article 42 of the Master Agreement required that the grievance be resolved in the grievants' favor. Moreover, the Arbitrator found that, in any event, Article 12, Section 2.a did not forbid the temporary promotions. *Id.* at 7. Accordingly, the Arbitrator found that the temporary promotions were both legal and reasonable. *Id.* at 7-8.

The Arbitrator directed the Agency to provide the grievants with backpay for sixteen hours per week, for the entire twenty-three month period during which they performed the training duties. The Arbitrator determined that the amount of backpay should be calculated based on the difference between the GS-6 rate of pay that the grievants received for the hours that they performed training duties and the GS-7 rate of pay that they should have received for performing the duties. *Id.* at 9.

Turning to the Union's two other requested remedies, the Arbitrator determined that the Union's request that each of the grievants receive sixteen hours of time off was not reasonable. *Id.* at 8. In addition, the Arbitrator concluded that the Union's request that each of the grievants receive a special contribution award totaling $9,568 was also not reasonable. *Id.*

C. Arbitrator's Supplemental Award

A dispute arose between the parties concerning the Agency's interpretation of, and compliance with, the Arbitrator's award. The Agency took the position that it did not need to provide the grievants with any backpay. Supplemental Award 2-3. In the Agency's view, the $2,500 special contribution award already provided to each of the grievants covered the total amount of backpay due to the grievants because it exceeded the amount each was due under the award. Consequently, the Agency did not provide any backpay to either grievant. *Id.* The Union disputed the offset and initiated supplemental proceedings before the Arbitrator to resolve the issue.

In his supplemental award, the Arbitrator determined that the offset was not authorized by his original award. *Id.* at 3. According to the Arbitrator, the Agency did not argue at the arbitration hearing that any backpay awarded to the grievants should be offset by the amount of the special contribution awards that the grievants had received. The Arbitrator also found that such an argument lacked merit. Accordingly, the Arbitrator ordered the Agency to award the grievants backpay as directed in his original award. *Id.* at 4.

III. Agency's Exceptions[2]

The Agency argues that the Arbitrator's awards are contrary to law for several reasons. The Agency claims that the award is contrary to the VA Handbook, which incorporates 5 C.F.R. § 335.103(c)(i), governing temporary promotions. Exceptions at 4. The Agency argues that both the handbook and the regulation provide that backpay for temporary promotions of more than 120 days cannot be awarded in the absence of competitive procedures. *Id.* at 4 (citing VA Handbook 5005/13, Part III, Chapter 3; VA Handbook 5005/2, Chapter 4, Section 15; 5 C.F.R. § 335.103(c)(i)).[3] Accordingly, the Agency asks that the award be vacated in its entirety or, alternatively, that the temporary promotions be limited to 120 days.

The Agency also contends that the award violates Article 22, Section 7 of the parties' Master Agreement. According to the Agency, this provision would only allow the grievants two sixty-day temporary promotions, with each in a separate twelve-month period. Exceptions at 5.

In addition, the Agency claims that the award violates VA Directive 5017, which the Agency argues prohibits the distribution of special

2. The Arbitrator issued his original award on October 19, 2007. The Agency's exceptions were filed with the Authority on February 8, 2008. *See* former 5 C.F.R. § 2429.21(b) (effective through November 8, 2009). The time limit for filing an exception to an arbitration award is thirty (30) days beginning on the date the award is served on the filing party. 5 C.F.R. § 2425.1(b). Therefore, to the extent that the exceptions pertain to the original award, they are untimely.

3. 5 C.F.R. § 335.103(c) states, in pertinent part:

> Covered personnel actions--(1) Competitive actions. Except as provided in paragraphs (c)(2) and (3) of this section, competitive procedures in agency promotion plans apply to all promotions under § 335.102 of this part and to the following actions: (i) Time-limited promotions under § 335.102(f) of this part for more than 120 days to higher-graded positions[.]

contribution awards for the same duties for which temporary promotions are given. *Id.* The Agency notes that special contribution awards in the amount of $2,500 were already given to each of the grievants for the training duties that they performed from April through October 2006. Exceptions, Ex. C at 1-4. Therefore, the Agency asks that the Authority limit the grievants' temporary promotions to the seventeen months to which the special contribution awards did not apply. The Agency notes that such a modification would still violate 5 C.F.R. § 335.103 to the extent that it would exceed 120 days. In the alternative, the Agency requests that the Authority set aside the award in its entirety.

IV. Analysis and Conclusions

For the following reasons, we dismiss the Agency's exceptions.

The Agency's arguments claiming that the award is contrary to law and the parties' agreement are not properly before the Authority. Exceptions are barred by 5 C.F.R. § 2429.5 of the Authority's Regulations when they pertain to an issue that could have been but was not presented to an arbitrator. *See U.S. Dep't of the Air Force, Air Force Materiel Command, Robins Air Force Base, Ga.*, 59 FLRA 542, 544 (2003); *see also U.S. Dep't of Energy, Oak Ridge Office, Oak Ridge, Tenn.*, 64 FLRA 535, 536 n.5 (2010) (pursuant to 5 C.F.R. § 2429.5, Authority declined to consider argument that regulation supported agency's claim that arbitration award required candidates to meet higher qualification standards than those promulgated by Office of Personnel Management where that argument was not presented to the arbitrator); *U.S. Dep't of Agric. Animal & Plant Health Inspection Serv., Plant Prot. & Quarantine*, 57 FLRA 4, 5 (2001) (consistent with 5 C.F.R. § 2429.5, Authority refused to consider agency's argument that award granting temporary promotions violated Back Pay Act because agency failed to make that argument before arbitrator).

The Agency had the opportunity to argue before the Arbitrator that the Union's requested remedies violated the Master Agreement, government-wide regulations governing temporary promotions, and Agency directives. However, there is no evidence in the record that the Agency did so.

The case law interpreting 5 C.F.R. § 2429.5 makes clear that the Authority will not consider a contention that could have been, but was not, presented to the Arbitrator. As there is no evidence in the record that the Agency raised any of the arguments before the Arbitrator that it is now raising in its exceptions, we conclude that the Agency's exceptions are not properly before the Authority.

Based on the foregoing, we dismiss the Agency's exceptions contending that the award is contrary to law and the parties' Master Agreement.

V. Decision

The Agency's exceptions are dismissed.

65 FLRA No. 10

AMERICAN FEDERATION
OF GOVERNMENT EMPLOYEES
LOCAL 3506
(Union)

and

SOCIAL SECURITY ADMINISTRATION
OFFICE OF DISABILITY
ADJUDICATION AND REVIEW
SHREVEPORT, LOUISIANA
(Agency)

0-AR-4306

DECISION

August 30, 2010

Before the Authority: Carol Waller Pope, Chairman, and Thomas M. Beck and Ernest DuBester, Members

I. Statement of the Case

The matter is before the Authority on exceptions to an award of Arbitrator John B. Barnard filed by the Union under § 7122(a) of the Federal Service Labor-Management Relations Statute (the Statute) and part 2425 of the Authority's Regulations. The Agency filed an opposition to the Union's exceptions.

The Arbitrator denied a grievance alleging that the grievant's non-selection for a Lead Case Technician (LCT), GS-9 position (position) violated the parties' agreement. For the reasons that follow, we deny the exceptions.

II. Background and Arbitrator's Award

The Agency's Office of Disability Adjudication and Review posted a vacancy announcement for the position in its Shreveport, Louisiana facility. Award at 4. The grievant, a GS-8 senior case technician, and Union member, applied for the position and was one of the five employees listed on the well-qualified list. *Id.* at 4 & 6; *see also* Exceptions, Attach., Jt. Ex. 14. The grievant ultimately was not selected for the position. Award at 4.

The grievant then filed a grievance claiming that his non-selection violated the parties' agreement. *Id.* The matter was unresolved and was submitted to arbitration. The Arbitrator did not frame an issue, but set forth the issue proposed by each party. *Id.* at 2. The Agency proposed: "Did the Agency violate the 2000 National Agreement, . . . [the parties' agreement] or any federal law or regulations, when it did not select the grievant for [the position] . . . . If so, what is the appropriate remedy?" *Id.* The Union proposed: "Whether or not the Agency violated the [parties' agreement], Articles 1, 2, 3, 18 or 26, when it non[-]selected the grievant for [the position] . . . . (If so, what is the proper remedy?) ."[1] *Id.*

Before the Arbitrator, the Union argued that the grievant was not selected for the position because of his "age, race, sex and Union membership." *Id.* at 10. The Union also contended that the parties' agreement provided the grievant "with more serious consideration than the other applicants" and noted that the grievant had "the most . . . experience of all the applicants and was stagnated in grade." *Id.* at 10, 8.

The Agency argued that the grievant had "presented no evidence" that the Agency's stated reasons for not selecting him were "pretextual." *Id.* at 13. The Agency also contended that Union had failed to present "any persuasive evidence" that anti-union animus played a role in the selection process and maintained that its reasons for hiring the selectee were "legitimate and non-discriminatory."[2] *Id.* at 13-14. According to the Agency, "after giving full and fair consideration," the Agency "properly exercised its right to select the candidate whose overall qualifications demonstrated the greatest potential for successful job performance." *Id* at 14.

As to the claim that the grievant was not selected because of his Union membership, the Arbitrator found that, although the testimony and evidence could give "the impression that anti[-]union sentiment" existed during the time of the grievant's non-selection, "nothing in [the grievant's] testimony" indicated "such described bias was . . . directed towards him." *Id.* at 16. The Arbitrator further determined that "no evidence or testimony" was

1. The relevant text of Articles 1, 2, 3, 18 and 26 is set forth in the appendix to this decision.

2. The Agency also claimed that the grievance was not arbitrable, but the Arbitrator rejected this contention. The Agency does not except to this finding; accordingly, we will not address it further.

presented regarding "alleged anti-[union] bias to the grievant, specifically as it relates to his non[-]selection." *Id.* The Arbitrator stated that he could not "conclude with any certainty that the grievant was not selected because of his Union membership." *Id.*

With respect to the claim that the grievant was not selected because of his race, sex, or age, the Arbitrator determined that the Agency had demonstrated legitimate business reasons for its selection of the selectee. Specifically, the Arbitrator found that the position includes some supervisory functions and that the evidence "demonstrate[d]" that the selectee has some experience in this regard. *Id.* at 17. The Arbitrator also found that the position requires "communicating with various levels of representatives" and that the selectee was rated as "possessing good communication skills[.]" *Id.*

Accordingly, the Arbitrator denied the grievance.

III. Positions of the Parties

A. Union's Exceptions

The Union asserts that the award is deficient because the Arbitrator failed to: (1) "follow the burdens in regard to reprisal for Union activity"; and (2) address the issue of grade stagnation in the award. Exceptions at 6.

As to the first assertion, the Union contends that the Arbitrator failed to follow appropriate law in finding that the grievant's non-selection was not based on his Union membership and sets forth a test which it contends the Authority applies in determining whether a "violation of the Statute" has occurred concerning a claim of reprisal for Union activity.[3] *Id.* at 3. The Union contends that the Agency "did not meet its burden . . . to justify its actions or to show that it would have taken the same action if the grievant had not been a Union member." *Id.* at 4. The Union asserts that it submitted "considerable unrebutted testimony and documentation that would lead a reasonable person to conclude that Union activity was a motivating factor in decision[]making" in the Shreveport office during the time of the disputed matter. *Id.* However, according to the Union, the Arbitrator "dismissed th[is] evidence[.]" *Id.*

As to the second assertion, the Union contends that the Arbitrator did not "consider the grievant's stagnation in grade." *Id.* The Union asserts that it "submitted" that Article 26, Section 11(C) of the parties' agreement "called for serious consideration of well-qualified candidates who were stagnated in grade[,]" and that the grievant, who has been in the same position for seven years, "should have received such consideration." *Id.* According to the Union, the award, therefore, is "legally deficient" because the Arbitrator failed to resolve all matters before him. *Id.* at 5.

B. Agency's Opposition

The Agency asserts that the parties, by stipulation, "submitted one issue" to the Arbitrator – whether the Agency violated the parties' agreement or any federal laws or regulations when it did not select the grievant for the position. Opp'n at 2. The Agency asserts that the Union presented no persuasive evidence that either of the selecting officials "violated [the parties' agreement] based on . . . anti-union animus or any illegal discrimination." *Id.* at 6. The Agency argues that it provided substantial testimony demonstrating that the selection was based on "legitimate business interests." *Id.* Furthermore, the Agency contends that a comparison of the grievant's qualifications with those of the selectee shows that no "illegal discriminatory factors [were] at work in the process." *Id.* at 8. The Agency also notes that the Arbitrator found that: (1) the grievant "did not testify that any anti-union bias was in any way directed toward him" and (2) there was no evidence or testimony of alleged bias toward the grievant regarding his non-selection. *Id.* at 10.

The Agency contends that the Union "has waived the issue of stagnation-in-grade." *Id.* at 9. The Agency asserts that "stagnation-in-grade" was not included in "any step of the grievance process" or discussed at the arbitration hearing, and that the matter was "only briefly alleged in the Union's [p]ost-[h]earing" brief without support. *Id.* at 6, 9. The Agency argues that, even if grade stagnation was properly raised, "that factor, in and of itself, would not entitle [the] [g]rievant to be selected for the position . . . when the Agency had a legitimate business reason" for the selection that it made. *Id.* at 9.

The Agency contends that the Union has not presented any evidence that demonstrates either that the Agency's stated reasons for its hiring decision were pretextual or that the real reason for the grievant's non-selection were his age, sex, race, or

3. Although the Union does not cite any case, the elements of the test that it sets forth are the same as those set forth in *Letterkenny Army Depot*, 35 FLRA 113, 118 (1990).

Union membership. *Id.* at 11. The Agency further contends that the requirement for "full and fair consideration" under Article 26 of the parties' agreement "was fulfilled" in the selection process and that the reasons for its hiring decision were "legitimate and non-discriminatory." *Id.* at 11 & 12.

IV. Analysis and Conclusions

A. The award is not contrary to law.

The Union asserts that the award is contrary to law because the Arbitrator "failed to follow the burdens in regard to reprisal for Union activity." Exceptions at 6. When an exception involves an award's consistency with law, the Authority reviews any question of law raised by the exception and the award *de novo*. *See NTEU, Chapter 24*, 50 FLRA 330, 332 (1995) (citing *U.S. Customs Serv. v. FLRA*, 43 F.3d 682, 686-87 (D.C. Cir. 1994)). In applying the standard of *de novo* review, the Authority assesses whether an arbitrator's legal conclusions are consistent with the applicable standard of law. *See U.S. Dep't of Def., Dep'ts of the Army & the Air Force, Ala. Nat'l Guard, Northport, Ala.*, 55 FLRA 37, 40 (1998). In making that assessment, the Authority defers to the arbitrator's underlying factual findings. *See id.*

The Union argues in its exception that the Agency committed a statutory unfair labor practice (ULP) when it allegedly based the grievant's non-selection on anti-union animus and that the Arbitrator erred by failing to so find. However, it is unclear from the issues proposed by the parties whether the Arbitrator was resolving statutory or contractual issues. *See* Award at 2. While the issue proposed by the Agency concerned both contractual and statutory issues, the issue proposed by the Union raised only contractual issues. Nevertheless, the Authority has applied statutory standards in assessing the application of contract provisions that mirror, or are intended to be interpreted in the same manner as, the Statute. *See, e.g., AFGE, Local 1164*, 64 FLRA 599, 600-01 (2010) (statutory principles applied in circumstance where exception was based on an alleged violation of the Statute and issue before the arbitrator was framed in contractual terms, which mirrored or were intended to be interpreted in the same manner as provision of the Statute); *NLRB*, 61 FLRA 197, 199 (2005) (*NLRB*) (same); *AFGE*, 59 FLRA 767, 769-70 (2004) (*AFGE*) (same). The issue proposed by the Union referenced certain contract articles, including Article 1, Section 1, which provides that the parties "shall be governed by existing or future laws . . . [,]" and Article 3, Section 1, which provides that "[e]ach employee shall have the right to join[] or assist the Union . . . without fear or penalty of reprisal . . . ." Award at 2. Therefore, assuming that the Arbitrator resolved statutory issues, we find, for the following reasons, that the Union has not established that the award is contrary to law.

Where statutory issues concerning Union discrimination are raised, the Authority reviews the award under the statutory principles applicable to § 7116(a)(2). *See, e.g., NLRB*, 61 FLRA at 199; *AFGE*, 59 FLRA at 769-70; *see also U.S. Dep't of Justice, Fed. Bureau of Prisons, Fed. Corr. Complex, Coleman, Fla.*, 63 FLRA 351, 354 (2009). Section 7116(a)(2) of the Statute provides that it is a ULP for an agency to encourage or discourage membership in a union by discrimination in connection with hiring, tenure, promotion, or other conditions of employment. When a grievance under § 7121 of the Statute involves an alleged ULP, the arbitrator must apply the same standards and burdens that would be applied by an administrative law judge in a ULP proceeding under § 7118. *See, e.g., AFGE, Local 3529*, 57 FLRA 464, 465 (2001). In a grievance alleging a ULP by an agency, the union bears the burden of proving the elements of the alleged ULP by a preponderance of the evidence. *See id.* As in other arbitration cases, the Authority defers to an arbitrator's findings of fact. *See id.*

Further, in cases alleging discrimination, the Authority applies the framework in *Letterkenny Army Depot*, 35 FLRA 113, 118 (1990) (*Letterkenny*). *See AFGE, Local 2145*, 64 FLRA 661, 664 (2010) (*AFGE, Local 2145*) (Member Beck dissenting, in part). Under that framework, the party making such an assertion establishes a *prima facie* case of discrimination by demonstrating that: (1) the employee against whom the alleged discriminatory action was taken was engaged in protected activity; and (2) such activity was a motivating factor in the agency's treatment of the employee. Once the *prima facie* showing is made, an agency may seek to establish the affirmative defense that: (1) there was a legitimate justification for the action; and (2) the same action would have been taken even in the absence of the protected activity.

In this case, although the Arbitrator did not expressly apply the *Letterkenny* framework, the record is sufficient for the Authority to do so. The Arbitrator found that the grievant was a Union member; however, the Arbitrator rejected the Union's claim that the grievant's non-selection for the position was motivated by his Union membership. Award at 16. The Arbitrator found that the evidence was insufficient to conclude that the "grievant was not selected because of his Union membership." *Id.*

A review of the record provides no basis for concluding that the Arbitrator's finding is deficient. In this regard, the record shows that the Arbitrator evaluated testimony and evidence offered by the Union and found that there was nothing in this evidence that showed the selection officials were biased towards the grievant in his non-selection. *Id.* at 15, 16. Although the Union asserts that it submitted "considerable unrebutted testimony and documentation that would lead a reasonable person to conclude that Union activity was a motivating factor in decision[]making[,]" Exceptions at 4, in the Shreveport office during the time of the disputed matter, the Union has not pointed to any evidence that demonstrates the grievant's non-selection was predicated on his Union membership.

Because the Union has not pointed to any evidence that demonstrates the grievant's non-selection was predicated on his Union membership and because the record does not establish that the selecting officials were biased towards the grievant in his non-selection, the Union has not satisfied the second part of its *prima facie* case under the *Letterkenny* framework. As a result, no *prima facie* case of discrimination based on protected activity has been established. *See, e.g., AFGE, Local 2145*, 64 FLRA at 664 (Member Beck dissenting on other grounds) (finding no *prima facie* case of discrimination where evidence did not show that agency's action in disciplining employee for being absent without leave was motivated by employee's protected activities).[4]

Accordingly, we find that the award is not contrary to law, and we deny this exception.

B. The Arbitrator did not exceed his authority.

We construe the Union's contention that the Arbitrator failed to address Article 26, Section 11(C) of the parties' agreement as it concerns grade stagnation as an exception that the Arbitrator exceeded his authority. Arbitrators exceed their authority when they fail to resolve an issue submitted to arbitration, resolve an issue not submitted to arbitration, disregard specific limitations on their authority, or award relief to those not encompassed within the grievance. *AFGE, Local 1617*, 51 FLRA 1645, 1647 (1996).

As noted previously, the Arbitrator did not frame the issue but set forth the issue proposed by each party. As relevant here, the Agency proposed: "Did the Agency violate the [parties' agreement] or any federal law or regulations, when it did not select the grievant for [the position . . . [,]" and the Union proposed: "Whether or not the Agency violated the [parties' agreement], Articles 1, 2, 3, 18 or 26 when it non[-]selected the grievant for the [LCT]. Award at 2. In resolving these issues, the Arbitrator specifically considered the parties' arguments, including both the Union's contention that the grievant was "stagnated in grade" and the Agency's contention that its non-selection of the grievant for the disputed position did not constitute a violation of the parties' agreement. *Id.* at 10, 12. After weighing such arguments and the record evidence, the Arbitrator determined that he "[could] not argue with [the selecting official's] rationale in her selection of [the selectee] over the grievant" and that the Agency had "met the burden of demonstrating that there were legitimate business reasons" for selecting the selectee instead of the grievant. *Id.* at 17, 18. The Arbitrator, thus, resolved the issues that were before him. Furthermore, that an award does not mention a specific provision of an agreement does not establish that such provision was not considered by the arbitrator and does not provide a basis for finding the award deficient. *See U.S. Dep't of the Army, Transp. Ctr., Fort Eustis, Va.*, 45 FLRA 480, 482 (1992); *Ill. Air Nat'l Guard, 182nd Tactical Air Support Group*, 34 FLRA 591, 593-94 (1990). Accordingly, we find that the Union has not demonstrated that the Arbitrator exceeded his authority, and we deny this exception.

V. Decision

The Union's exceptions are denied.

---

4. Even assuming the Union established a *prima facie* case, the Arbitrator's factual findings show that the Agency established a legitimate justification for its actions consistent with *Letterkenny*. Specifically, the Arbitrator found, among other things, that the disputed position includes some supervisory duties and the selectee had some experience in this regard while the grievant did not. Award at 17. Also, communication skills were important for the position and the selectee was rated as possessing good skills in this area. *Id.* In sum, after evaluating the evidence, the Arbitrator found that the Agency had "met the burden" of demonstrating that there was legitimate business reasons for the selection of the selectee over the grievant. *Id.* at 18. The Union has not established that the Arbitrator's evaluation of the evidence and his conclusions based thereon are improper. As the Authority defers to an arbitrator's factual findings, the Union has not demonstrated that the award is contrary to § 7116(a)(2) of the Statute.

APPENDIX

Article 1
Section 1

In the administration of all matters covered by this agreement, officials and employees shall be governed by existing or future laws and existing government wide rules and regulations as defined in U.S. [Chapter] 71, and by subsequently enacted government-wide rules and regulations implementing 5 U.S.C. [§] 2302.

Article 3
Section 1

Each employee shall have the right to join[] or assist the Union, or to refrain from such activity, freely and without fear of penalty or reprisal, and each employee shall be protected in the exercise of such right . . . .

Article 3
Section 5A

Except as specifically authorized by this agreement, the SF-7B Extension file is the only authorized file for personnel records, which may be maintained by a supervisor, other than the official personnel file.

Article 18
Section 1

The Administration and the Union affirm their commitment to the policy of providing equal employment opportunities to all employees and to prohibit discrimination because of race, color, religion, sex, national origin, disabling condition, or age . . . .

Article 18
Section 6B

An employee has the option of filing a complaint under the negotiated grievance procedure (Article 24) or under the Agency EEO complaint procedure, but not both . . . .

Article 24
Section 2

A grievance means any complaint,

A. by an employee(s) concerning any matter relating to the employment of the employee.

. . . .

Article 26
Section 1

It is the intent of the parties to redesign the merit promotion process as a corollary to the two[-]tier appraisal system created in Article 21 and to assure openness and objectivity in merit promotion selections.

The parties agree that the purpose and intent of the provisions contained herein are to ensure that merit promotion principles are applied in a consistent manner with equity all employees . . . .

Award at 2-3.

Article 26
Section 11C

If the vacancy is one for which an under-representation exists and is a targeted occupation as identified in the Affirmative Employment Plan, and there are well-qualified candidates who would reduce the under-representation, then the selecting official will give serious consideration to those individuals who would reduce the under-representation. If an under-representation is not present, then the selecting official will seriously consider providing upward mobility for those well-qualified candidates who have been stagnated in grade.

Exceptions, Attach., Union's Post-Hearing Brief at 6.

65 FLRA No. 11

UNITED STATES
DEPARTMENT OF JUSTICE
FEDERAL BUREAU OF PRISONS
FEDERAL CORRECTIONAL COMPLEX
OAKDALE, LOUISIANA
(Agency)

and

AMERICAN FEDERATION
OF GOVERNMENT EMPLOYEES
LOCAL 1007
COUNCIL OF PRISON LOCALS
(Union)

0-AR-4489

DECISION

August 31, 2010

Before the Authority: Carol Waller Pope, Chairman, and Thomas M. Beck and Ernest DuBester, Members

I. Statement of the Case

This matter is before the Authority on exceptions to an initial award and supplemental award of Arbitrator E. Gayle Sheridan filed by the Agency under § 7122(a) of the Federal Service Labor-Management Relations Statute (the Statute) and part 2425 of the Authority's Regulations. The Union filed an opposition to the Agency's exceptions.[1]

The Arbitrator concluded that the Agency violated a settlement agreement with the Union by requiring the grievants to perform higher-graded duties. As a remedy, the Arbitrator ordered the Agency to pay the grievants backpay plus interest and to reimburse the Union for attorney fees and related costs. For the reasons set forth below, the Agency's exceptions are dismissed in part and denied in part.

1. The Authority has consolidated AR-4489 (excepting to initial award) and AR-4489 (excepting to supplemental award). Accordingly, this decision addresses the Agency's exceptions to both the Arbitrator's initial award and his supplemental award.

II. Background and Arbitrator's Award

The Federal Detention Center (FDC) is a part of the Federal Correctional Complex, Oakdale, Louisiana. Initial Award at 8. The FDC primarily houses federal inmates who have completed their terms of incarceration and are awaiting deportation and undocumented immigrants who are awaiting deportation. *Id.* The grievants work as Correctional Counselors (Counselors) at the Alexandria and Ville Platte Units in the FDC. *Id.*

Counselors work as a "team" with Case Managers and Unit Managers. *Id.* Counselors address detainees' internal social needs and "top out" at the GS-9 pay level. *Id.* Case Managers address detainees' external needs and are paid at the GS-11 level. *Id.* Finally, Unit Managers have supervisory responsibility over the "team's" performance. *Id.* During the period at issue in this case, no Case Manager was assigned to the Alexandria and Virginia Platte units. *Id.*

In 2004, the Union filed a grievance over the assignment of certain higher-graded Case Manager duties to the Counselors. *Id.* at 9. Ultimately, the parties settled the grievance. *Id.* Under the terms of the settlement agreement, the parties agreed that the Unit Manager, rather than the Counselors, would perform the higher-graded Case Manager duties involved in detainee screening. *Id.*

In March 2007, the Agency hired a new Acting Unit Manager. *Id.* Shortly after this manager was hired, several Counselors brought the settlement agreement to her attention and told her that, as Unit Manager, she was obliged to perform the Case Manager duties involved in detainee screening. *Id.* The new Manager told the Counselors that, because of a nationwide initiative that the Bureau of Prisons (BOP) was instituting at the time, "those duties were no longer required of the Case or Unit Manager . . . ." *Id.* Based on her statements, the Counselors concluded that the settlement agreement was no longer in effect, and they began to perform the higher-graded Case Manager duties. *Id.*

During the fall of 2007, the FDC conducted a preliminary audit of Unit operations; the audit revealed that the nationwide BOP initiative did not in fact alter the settlement agreement. *Id.* In early November 2007, the Counselors discussed the results of the audit with the Union President, and, immediately thereafter, the Union President discussed the matter with the Assistant Warden. *Id.* The Assistant Warden admitted that the Agency had breached the settlement agreement but refused to compensate the Counselors "for their performance of the higher[-]graded duties because the breach was unintentional."[2] *Id.* Subsequently, a grievance was filed on December 17, 2007; the grievance alleged a violation of the 2004 settlement agreement and requested backpay. *Id.* at 4-5, 9.

The matter was unresolved and was submitted to arbitration. The Arbitrator framed the following relevant issues: "Did the Agency breach the parties' . . . [s]ettlement [a]greement when . . . the [g]rievants' supervisor assigned various GS-11 Case Manager's duties to the[m] . . . ?" and, if so, "[w]hat should be the remedy?" *Id.* at 17.

The Arbitrator determined that, based on the evidence, testimony, and arguments, the Union proved by "a preponderance of evidence" that the Agency had violated the Agreement "when the Acting Unit Manager assigned certain duties to the Counselors." *Id.* at 21. As a remedy, the Arbitrator ordered the Agency to pay the grievants backpay "plus interest . . . for the period . . . when they were assigned . . . certain Case Manager duties by [the] Acting Unit Manager" and to "reimburse the Union for attorney fees and related cost[s]." *Id.* at 22. The Arbitrator also retained jurisdiction for thirty days "to assist in the resolution of this remedy." *Id.*

On February 2, 2009, the Union's counsel requested that the Arbitrator provide a supplemental arbitration award clarifying the Agency's obligation to pay attorney fees and related costs. Supplemental Award, Attach. A at 1. On February 8, 2009, the Arbitrator sent the parties a letter, providing "the Agency [an] opportunity to submit its position regarding [the Union counsel's] request" and stating that he would issue a supplemental award by March 5, 2009. *Id.* The Agency, however, "elected to not submit [its] position at th[at] time, but instead requested [that] the Agency's position be deferred until after [it] filed its exceptions and obtained a ruling from the . . . Authority[;]" the Agency ultimately filed exceptions to the Arbitrator's initial award on February 23, 2009. *Id.*; Initial Exceptions at 10.

On March 5, 2009, the Arbitrator rejected this request, finding that the Agency's filing of exceptions and the Authority's ultimate decision on those exceptions had no impact on his ability to issue a supplemental arbitration award, and issued his supplemental award. Supplemental Award, Attach. A at 1. In that award, the Arbitrator specifically articulated why the award of attorney fees was appropriate under 5 U.S.C. § 7701(g) and ordered the Agency to pay the Union's counsel $25,676.06 in attorney fees and related expenses. Supplemental Award at 3-4. Noting that he had been advised that the Agency had failed to pay the grievants the backpay that he had ordered in his initial award, the Arbitrator further directed the Agency to make such payment within ten days. *Id.* at 4.

III. Positions of the Parties

A. Agency's Exceptions to Initial Award

The Agency alleges that the award is contrary to law because the Arbitrator failed to identify a government-wide regulation, Agency-wide policy, or provision of the parties' agreement that makes "temporary promotions mandatory for details to higher-graded positions, thereby establishing a nondiscretionary agency policy which would provide a basis for back pay." Initial Exceptions at 4-5. According to the Agency, under Authority precedent, the mere fact that a grievant has performed higher-graded duties is insufficient to entitle him or her to backpay; rather, the Agency asserts, a grievant is entitled to backpay only when a government-wide regulation, agency-wide policy, or provision of the parties' agreement mandates compensation for the temporary performance of the higher-graded duties. *Id.* The Agency contends that the 2004 settlement agreement does not satisfy this requirement. *Id.* at 5-6.

The Agency also alleges that the Arbitrator's initial award of attorney fees is premature and contrary to law. *Id.* at 7. The Agency claims that the award is premature because, although the Arbitrator retained jurisdiction to decide the issue of attorney fees, he ordered that the Agency pay the Union attorney fees and related costs in his initial award, without giving the parties the opportunity to make arguments and submit briefs on the issue. *Id.* at 7-8. The Agency also contends that the initial award of attorney fees is contrary to law because "the Arbitrator did not specifically articulate any of the reasons pursuant to 5 U.S.C. § 7701(g) that such an award was appropriate." *Id.* at 8. Finally, the Agency contends "that the award of attorney fees should be denied because . . . [the] award is not in the interest of justice [as] the Agency did not know, nor should it have known, that it would not be the

2. The Counselors' performance of higher-graded duties ceased shortly after the conversation between the Union President and the Assistant Warden took place. Initial Award at 9.

prevailing party in this case on the merits." *Id.* at 9. According to the Agency, it believed that it had "acted in good faith and that its actions comported with law, rule and regulation." *Id.*

B. Union's Opposition to Agency's Exceptions to Initial Award

The Union asserts that the Agency failed to argue before the Arbitrator that the 2004 settlement agreement "did not establish the kind of non-discretionary rule concerning the temporary promotion of Counselors . . . that could form the basis for a[n]" award of backpay; accordingly, the Union argues that the Agency's exception regarding this issue must be dismissed pursuant to 5 C.F.R. § 2429.5. Initial Opp'n at 2-4. The Union argues that it informed the Arbitrator of the "legal requirement that there must be . . . a non-discretionary [A]gency policy [in place] to justify a back pay [sic] award based on a temporary promotion." *Id.* at 6. The Union contends that the Arbitrator found that the 2004 settlement agreement satisfied this requirement. *Id.* at 7-8; *see also id.* at 6 (noting that Arbitrator found that Agency had "made a binding commitment in the 2004 settlement agreement to temporarily promote Counselors to Case Manager positions when they were required to perform those higher[-]graded duties").

Additionally, the Union contends that the Agency's second exception regarding the Arbitrator's initial award of attorney fees "was premature and is now moot." *Id.* at 8. The Union argues that the Arbitrator retained jurisdiction over the case and provided both parties an opportunity to present briefs on the issue of attorney fees; however, the Union asserts, the Agency never filed a response to the Union's fee request. *Id.* at 9. The Union notes that the Arbitrator issued a supplemental award in which he explained fully "how the Union's fee request comports with the legal requirements for a fee award under the Back Pay Act." *Id.* The Union contends that, given the issuance of the supplemental award, the Agency should have excepted to the merits of that award and that the Agency's exception to the initial award is now moot. *Id.*

C. Agency's Exception to Supplemental Award

The Agency filed a single exception to the Arbitrator's supplemental fee award. Supplemental Exception at 4. The Agency alleges that the Arbitrator's supplemental award is contrary to law because it requires the Agency to pay the backpay and attorney fees immediately, before the underlying award and the supplemental award are "final and binding." *Id.* at 4-6. The Agency contends that, because it filed timely exceptions to both awards, neither award is final and binding. *Id.* at 5-6. According to the Agency, such awards will not be final and binding until all exceptions are fully resolved by the Authority. *Id.* at 6.

D. Union's Opposition to Agency's Exception to Supplemental Award

The Union argues that, under Authority precedent, "an arbitrator is not required to refrain from granting a request for attorney fees until after the Authority resolves any exceptions that may have been filed to the underlying award." Supplemental Opp'n at 3 (quoting *U.S. GSA, Ne. & Caribbean Region*, 61 FLRA 68, 70 (2005)). The Union contends that the Agency's concern that it must pay attorney fees before the Authority resolves all of the exceptions is unwarranted and does not provide a basis for overturning the Arbitrator's supplemental fee award. *Id.* The Union argues that, because arbitration awards are not self-enforcing, the "Agency's concern about being forced to comply with an arbitration award that is not yet final and binding does not become timely until . . . [an unfair labor practice (ULP)] charge is filed." *Id.* According to the Union, it had not filed a ULP charge and did not contemplate filing one at that time. *Id.*

IV. Analysis and Conclusions

When an exception involves an award's consistency with law, the Authority reviews any question of law raised by the exception and the award *de novo*. *See NTEU, Chapter 24*, 50 FLRA 330, 332 (1995) (citing *U.S. Customs Serv. v. FLRA*, 43 F.3d 682, 686-87 (D.C. Cir. 1994)). In applying the standard of *de novo* review, the Authority assesses whether an arbitrator's legal conclusions are consistent with the applicable standard of law. *See U.S. Dep't of Def., Dep'ts of the Army & the Air Force, Ala. Nat'l Guard, Northport, Ala.*, 55 FLRA 37, 40 (1998). In making that assessment, the Authority defers to the arbitrator's underlying factual findings. *See id.*

A. The award of backpay is not contrary to law.

The Agency alleges that the award of backpay is contrary to law because the Arbitrator failed to identify a government-wide regulation, Agency-wide policy, or provision of the parties' agreement that makes "temporary promotions mandatory for details to higher graded positions, thereby establishing a nondiscretionary agency policy which would provide a basis for back pay." Initial Exceptions at 4-5.

Under § 2429.5 of the Authority's Regulations, the Authority will not consider issues that could have been, but were not, presented to the arbitrator. *See, e.g., U.S. DHS, U.S. Customs & Border Prot., JFK Airport, Queens, N.Y.*, 64 FLRA 841, 843 (2010) (*JFK Airport*). However, where an issue arises from the issuance of the award and could not have been presented to the arbitrator, it is not precluded by § 2429.5. *U.S. Dep't of Agric., Animal & Plant Health Inspection Serv., Plant Prot. & Quarantine*, 57 FLRA 4, 5 (2001) (citing *Prof'l Airways Sys. Specialists, Dist. No. 1, MEBA/NMU (AFL-CIO)*, 48 FLRA 764, 768 n.* (1993)).

The record establishes that the Agency was on notice that the Union raised the temporary promotion issue before the Arbitrator. The grievance clearly alleged a violation of the 2004 settlement agreement and requested backpay, thereby putting the Agency on notice that it should have made the argument that it now makes in its exceptions. *See* Initial Award at 4-5. Despite this notice, the record contains no indication that the Agency ever argued to the Arbitrator that the settlement agreement does not establish an Agency policy mandating compensation for the temporary performance of higher-graded duties; rather, the Agency claimed only that: (1) the requested remedy of temporary promotion would exceed 120 days, in violation of 5 C.F.R. § 335.103(c)(1)(i); (2) the work assigned to the Counselors was not, in fact, higher-graded; and (3) the extent of the extra duties performed by Counselors was *de minimis* in nature. Initial Award at 16, 20; *see also* Initial Opp'n at 2-3.

Because the Agency did not present to the Arbitrator its argument regarding the lack of a nondiscretionary Agency policy regarding compensation for the temporary performance of higher-graded duties, it may not do so now. *See JFK Airport*, 64 FLRA at 843 (finding § 2429.5 barred arguments that arbitrator's remedy was contrary to law because arguments could have been, but were not, presented to arbitrator). Accordingly, we find that the Agency's exception is barred by § 2429.5 of the Authority's Regulations and dismiss it.

B. The award of attorney fees is not contrary to law.

The Back Pay Act expressly provides that an employee affected by an unjustified or unwarranted personnel action is entitled, on correction of the personnel action, to receive "reasonable attorney fees related to the personnel action . . . ." 5 U.S.C. § 5596(b)(1)(A)(ii).

The Agency contends that the attorney fee award is contrary to law because it is premature. Initial Exceptions at 7-8. The Agency asserts that the award is premature because the Arbitrator awarded attorney fees at the same time he made a decision on the merits. *Id.* The Authority has determined that arbitrators may rule on requests for attorney fees simultaneous to rendering a decision on the merits of a grievance. *See Health Care Fin. Admin., Dep't of HHS*, 35 FLRA 274, 290 (1990) (citations omitted). Therefore, the Agency's assertion that the Arbitrator's initial award of attorney fees is premature because it was made at the same time the Arbitrator issued his decision on the merits of the case is without merit.

The Agency also contends that the award is premature because the Agency had no opportunity to respond to the Union's attorney fee request. Initial Exceptions at 7-8. However, after the Arbitrator issued his initial award, the Agency had at least two opportunities to respond to the Union's fee request. The Agency could have submitted its position after the Union submitted its fee request to the Arbitrator on February 2, 2009. Moreover, the Agency could have filed a response after the Arbitrator informed the Agency on February 8, 2009 that he was providing it an opportunity to respond to the Union's fee request. Instead of submitting its position before the Arbitrator issued his supplemental award on March 5, 2009, however, the Agency elected to file exceptions on February 23, 2009, and seek a ruling from the Authority. Ultimately, because the Arbitrator gave the Agency an opportunity to respond to the fee request and issued the second award only after giving the Agency that opportunity, the exception to the original award is moot. *See U.S. Dep't of the Army, Army Info. Sys. Command, Savanna Army Depot*, 38 FLRA 1464, 1468 (1991) (*Savanna Army Depot*) (finding that, because a deficiency in the initial award was later cured when the arbitrator issued a supplemental award, the union's exceptions to the initial award were moot).

The Agency further contends that the initial award of attorney fees is contrary to law because "the Arbitrator did not specifically articulate any of the reasons pursuant to 5 U.S.C. § 7701(g) that such an award was appropriate." Initial Exceptions at 8. Although the Arbitrator's initial award failed to explain the prerequisites for an award of attorney fees under § 7701(g)(1), his supplemental award specifically addressed these factors. Consequently, in view of the Arbitrator's supplemental award, this exception also is now moot. *See U.S. Dep't of the Army, Corpus Christi Army Depot, Corpus Christi, Tex.*, 56 FLRA 1057, 1074 n.17 (2001) (dismissing agency's exception that arbitrator failed to define employees entitled to environmental differential pay in his initial award as moot because arbitrator corrected this deficiency when he issued a supplemental award); *Savanna Army Depot*, 38 FLRA at 1468.

Finally, the Agency contends that the attorney fee award is contrary to law because it is not in the interest of justice; the Agency alleges that it "did not know, nor should it have known, that it would not be the prevailing party in this case on the merits." Initial Exceptions at 9. As stated above, under § 2429.5 of the Authority's Regulations, the Authority will not consider issues that could have been, but were not, presented to the arbitrator. *See, e.g., U.S. Dep't of Def. Educ. Activity*, 56 FLRA 985, 987 (2000). After the Union submitted its fee request, and the Arbitrator gave the Agency an opportunity to respond, the Agency could, and should, have submitted to the Arbitrator its position that an award of attorney fees is not in the interest of justice; however, the Agency failed to do so. Thus, because the Agency failed to raise this issue before the Arbitrator, the Agency is barred from doing so now.

Accordingly, we deny the Agency's exception that the award is contrary to law because the Arbitrator prematurely awarded attorney fees at the same time he made a decision on the merits; we dismiss as moot the exceptions pertaining to the Agency's inability to respond to the attorney fee request and the failure to address the prerequisites for an award of attorney fees under § 7701(g); and we find that the exception claiming the award is not in the interest of justice is barred from the Authority's consideration by § 2429.5 of the Authority's Regulations.

V. Decision

The Agency's exceptions are dismissed in part and denied in part.[3]

3. The Agency also alleges that the Arbitrator's supplemental award is contrary to law because it requires the Agency to pay the award of backpay and attorney fees immediately, before the underlying award and the supplemental award are "final and binding." Supplemental Exception at 4-6. We find it unnecessary to resolve this exception because, as we have fully resolved the Agency's exceptions in our decision, both awards are now final and binding. *See U.S. Dep't of Transp., FAA, Nw. Mountain Region, Renton, Wash.*, 55 FLRA 293, 296 (1999) (determining that an award becomes final and binding when timely filed exceptions are denied by the Authority).

65 FLRA No. 12

AMERICAN FEDERATION
OF GOVERNMENT EMPLOYEES
LOCAL 1102
(Union)

and

UNITED STATES
DEPARTMENT OF JUSTICE
FEDERAL BUREAU OF PRISONS
FEDERAL DETENTION CENTER
SEATAC, WASHINGTON
(Agency)

0-AR-4599

DECISION

August 31, 2010

Before the Authority: Carol Waller Pope, Chairman, and Thomas M. Beck and Ernest DuBester, Members

I. Statement of the Case

This matter is before the Authority on exceptions to an award of Arbitrator Vern E. Hauck filed by the Union under § 7122(a) of the Federal Service Labor-Management Relations Statute (the Statute) and part 2425 of the Authority's Regulations. The Agency filed an opposition to the Union's exceptions.

The Arbitrator concluded that: (1) the Agency was exempt from certain Bureau of Alcohol, Tobacco, Firearms, and Explosives (ATF) regulations; (2) the Agency's storage of explosive material at the Federal Detention Center SeaTac Armory (FDC SeaTac Armory) did not violate Article 27 of the Master Labor Agreement (Agreement); and (3) one grievant was entitled to a hazard pay differential. For the reasons set forth below, the Union's exceptions are dismissed in part and denied in part.

II. Background and Arbitrator's Award

The grievants work at the FDC SeaTac Armory located in Seattle, Washington. *See* Award at 4; *see also* Exceptions at 2. Two of the three grievants work as full-time Lock and Security Specialists; the other grievant works only part-time in that position when the full-time Lock and Security Specialists are unavailable or need assistance. Award at 4, 15. Lock and Security Specialists maintain "the armory where institution weapons and ammunition are stored" and are required to know how to use "emergency entry equipment, riot control equipment, chemical munitions, and all Special Operations Response Team (SORT) equipment . . . ."[1] *Id.* at 16. The position involves a high "level of risk for hazardous and stressful working conditions . . . ." *Id.*

The Union filed a grievance alleging, among other things, that employees working in the Armory should receive a 25% hazard pay differential for storing explosives. *See id.* at 3. After the Agency denied the Union's grievance, the Union invoked arbitration. *Id.* The Arbitrator framed the following relevant issues:

> 1. Were the grievants entitled to be paid a hazard pay differential for working with or in close proximity to explosive material in accordance with applicable law and the [Agreement]? If so, what shall be the remedy?
>
> 2. Has the Agency failed to follow Article 27 of the [Agreement] in the storage of explosive material at the FDC SeaTac Armory? If so, what shall be the remedy?

Id.

The Arbitrator determined that the Armory room, magazines, and bins were constructed in conformance with applicable law and regulations pursuant to Articles 6 and 27 of the Agreement.[2] *Id.* at 14. According to the Arbitrator, of the "few violations of construction codes and magazine storage capability that . . . exist at the Armory[,]" all were *de minimis* and "some of these possible violations [were] attributable to code and regulation changes post Armory room, magazine and bin construction and installation." *Id.* The Arbitrator also found that, based on 27 C.F.R. § 555.141, the

1. "Weapons include rifles, carbines, stun guns, less lethal munitions, pistols, riot shotguns, gas guns, ammunition for these weapons, chemical agents, riot equipment and protective gear." Award at 16.

2. The relevant provisions of the Agreement are set forth in the appendix to this decision.

Agency was exempt from ATF regulations relating to explosives.[3] *Id.* at 15.

The Arbitrator found that the grievants who were full-time Lock and Security Specialists were not entitled to a hazard pay differential. *Id.* at 16-17. The Arbitrator noted that "the Agency has properly included an adjustment for hazardous duty in the wage rate paid to [these individuals] pursuant to the Major Duties and Responsibilities, Factor 1 and Factor 9 of the grievant's [sic] position descriptions and GS-10 wage rate." *Id.* Moreover, the Arbitrator determined that these grievants had been trained to perform hazardous duties in the FDC SeaTac Armory. *Id.* at 17. However, the Arbitrator found that the grievant who was a part-time Lock and Security Specialist was entitled to a hazard pay differential because the position description and wage rate classification of his full-time position did not adequately compensate him for the hazardous duty work that he performed as an alternate Lock and Security Specialist. *Id.*

III. Positions of the Parties

A. Union's Exceptions

First, the Union alleges that the award is contrary to law because the Arbitrator determined that certain ATF regulations did not apply to the Armory. Exceptions at 5-7. The Union claims that, in finding that the Agency is exempt from the ATF regulations, "the arbitrator fail[ed] to recognize that [the] ATF regulations are specifically applicable to the Agency through application of the Occupational Safety and Health Act – as administered by the US Department of Labor (OSHA)." *Id.* at 7.

Second, the Union alleges that the award is contrary to the Agreement. *Id.* The Union claims that, by "improvising a '*de minim[i]s*' standard by which ATF regulations can be violated, [the award] has clearly run afoul of the [Agreement's] requirement [in Article 27, Section a] that the Agency 'lower . . . inherent hazards to the lowest possible level.'" *Id.* Moreover, the Union contends that, even if the ATF regulations do not apply, the Agency has violated this contractual duty "[b]y having no policies in place regarding the storage of firearms; providing no training on the storage and handling of explosive material; and by not even implementing minimum standards of safe storage as promulgated by ATF . . . ." *Id.* at 7-8.

Third, the Union alleges that the Arbitrator's failure to award a hazard pay differential is based on a nonfact because the Arbitrator incorrectly found that the disputed hazardous duties were taken into account in the classification of the grievants' position. *Id.* at 13-14. The Union contends that it introduced sufficient evidence and testimony at arbitration demonstrating that the disputed hazardous duties were not considered when the grievants' position was classified; according to the Union, the position description does not mention the performance of certain hazardous duties, and testimony demonstrates that the classifiers could not have considered the performance of certain hazardous duties in classifying the grievants' position. *Id.* (citing Tr. at 254, 260).

Finally, the Union argues that the award is contrary to law because, if the classification of the Lock and Security Specialist position does not account for the hazardous duties performed by the grievants, then all of the requirements entitling them to a hazard pay differential are met. *See id.* at 9-14.

B. Agency's Opposition

First, the Agency argues that the award is not contrary to law. Opp'n at 3-5. The Agency contends that the OSHA regulation cited by the Union does not cover the Agency because "part 1926 of 29 CFR applies to the Safety and Health Regulations for *Construction* [and] . . . 29 CFR 1926.904(a) falls under 1926 Subpart U-Blasting and the Use of Explosives." *Id.* at 4. Moreover, the Agency argues that, because the Union failed to raise, before the Arbitrator, its argument that the ATF regulations apply to the Agency through OSHA, it is barred from doing so now. *Id.* at 5.

Second, the Agency argues that the award is in accordance with the Agreement. *Id.* at 5-7. The Agency contends that "the Arbitrator found that the Armory room, magazines and bins [were] constructed in conformance with all relevant law and regulations pursuant to Article 6 and 27 of the labor agreement." *Id.* at 7. The Agency argues that the Arbitrator's finding that a few *de minimis* violations of construction codes and magazine storage capability exist at the FDC SeaTac Armory does not undermine the Arbitrator's conclusion that the Armory, magazines, and bins were constructed in accordance with the Agreement. *Id.* According to the Agency,

3. 27 C.F.R. § 555.141(a)(6) states that "[a]rsenals, navy yards, depots, or other establishments owned by, or operated by or on behalf of, the United States" are exempt from part 555.

"the Arbitrator has done nothing more than interpret the parties' agreement in a rational and reasonable way, which is exactly what the parties enlisted him to do." *Id.*

Third, the Agency argues that the award is not based on a nonfact. *Id.* at 7-9. The Agency contends that, while the Arbitrator may not have made any specific findings regarding whether "the Lock and Security Specialist's exposure to explosive munitions was considered when the position was classified[,]" the Arbitrator did find that "the Agency properly considered, took into account and adjusted the wage rate to reflect the hazards faced by the occupants of the job explained in the [Lock and Security Specialist] Position Description in the Armory." *Id.* at 8. The Agency argues that, for the Union to prove that the Arbitrator's award is based on a nonfact, it must specifically show a clearly erroneous mistake involving a central fact, rather than merely dispute the Arbitrator's findings. *Id.* at 8-9.

IV. Analysis and Conclusions

A. The Union's exception alleging that ATF regulations apply to the Agency through OSHA is dismissed.

Under § 2429.5 of the Authority's Regulations, the Authority will not consider issues that could have been, but were not, presented to the arbitrator. *See, e.g., U.S. DHS, U.S. Customs & Border Prot., JFK Airport, Queens, N.Y.*, 64 FLRA 841, 843 (2010) (finding § 2429.5 barred arguments that the arbitrator's remedy was contrary to law because arguments could have been, but were not, presented to the arbitrator). However, where an issue arises from the issuance of the award and could not have been presented to the arbitrator, it is not precluded by § 2429.5. *U.S. Dep't of Agric., Animal & Plant Health Inspection Serv., Plant Prot. & Quarantine*, 57 FLRA 4, 5 (2001).

The Union raises a new issue -- that the ATF regulations apply to the Agency through OSHA -- for the first time in its exceptions. There is no indication in the record that the Union ever mentioned OSHA, or any regulation promulgated pursuant to it, during arbitration, although the Union could have done so. Accordingly, we find that § 2429.5 bars the Union's exception, and we dismiss the exception.

B. The award does not fail to draw its essence from the Agreement.

In reviewing an arbitrator's interpretation of a collective bargaining agreement, the Authority applies the deferential standard of review that federal courts use in reviewing arbitration awards in the private sector. *See* 5 U.S.C. § 7122(a)(2); *AFGE, Council 220*, 54 FLRA 156, 159 (1998). Under this standard, the Authority will find that an arbitration award is deficient as failing to draw its essence from the collective bargaining agreement when the appealing party establishes that the award: (1) cannot in any rational way be derived from the agreement; (2) is so unfounded in reason and fact and so unconnected with the wording and purposes of the collective bargaining agreement as to manifest an infidelity to the obligation of the arbitrator; (3) does not represent a plausible interpretation of the agreement; or (4) evidences a manifest disregard of the agreement. *See U.S. Dep't of Labor (OSHA)*, 34 FLRA 573, 575 (1990). The Authority and the courts defer to arbitrators in this context "because it is the arbitrator's construction of the agreement for which the parties have bargained." *Id.* at 576.

The Union contends that the award fails to draw its essence from the Agreement because it conflicts with Article 27, Section a of the Agreement, which requires the Agency to lower certain inherent hazards to the lowest possible level. Exceptions at 7-8. The Union argues that "in improvising a '*de minim[i]s*' standard by which ATF regulations can be violated," the Arbitrator "has clearly run afoul" of this requirement. *Id.* at 7.

Contrary to the Union's argument, it is not implausible or irrational to interpret Article 27, section a as permitting *de minimis* violations of regulations that the Arbitrator found do not even apply to the Agency. Further, in making this argument, the Union ignores that, in this same provision of the Agreement, it agreed that the hazards at issue "can never be completely eliminated." *Id.* at 5. Thus, the provision itself, when read as a whole, clearly contemplates the existence of some inherent hazards. Therefore, the Union has not demonstrated that the Arbitrator's interpretation of the Agreement is irrational, implausible, unfounded, or in manifest disregard of the Agreement. *See U.S. Dep't of Transp., FAA*, 63 FLRA 15, 18 (2008).

Accordingly, we deny the Union's exception.

C. The award of a hazard pay differential is not based on a nonfact.

To establish that an award is based on a nonfact, the appealing party must show that a central fact underlying the award is clearly erroneous, but for which the arbitrator would have reached a different result. *See NFFE, Local 1984*, 56 FLRA 38, 41 (2000). However, the Authority will not find an award deficient on the basis of an arbitrator's determination of any factual matter that the parties disputed at arbitration. *See id.*; *see also U.S. Dep't of the Navy, Naval Explosive Ordinance Disposal Tech. Div., Indian Head, Md.*, 56 FLRA 280, 286 (2000) (citing *U.S. Dep't of the Air Force, Lowry Air Force Base, Denver, Colo.*, 48 FLRA 589, 594 (1993)). In addition, the Authority has long held that disagreement with an arbitrator's evaluation of evidence and testimony, including the determination of the weight to be accorded such evidence, provides no basis for finding the award deficient. *See U.S. Dep't of Veterans Affairs, Med. Ctr., Richmond, Va.*, 63 FLRA 553, 556 (2009); *AFGE, Local 3295*, 51 FLRA 27, 32 (1995).

The Hazardous Duty Act, codified at 5 U.S.C. § 5545, authorizes the payment of hazard pay differentials to employees who perform hazardous duties. *NTEU, Chapter 51*, 40 FLRA 614, 621 (1991). Before an Arbitrator may award hazardous duty pay, a union must establish that "(1) [t]he hazard or physical hardship [is] not . . . considered in the classification of the employee's position pursuant to 5 U.S.C. § 5545(d)[;] (2) [t]he hazard or physical hardship [is] . . . listed in Appendix A to 5 C.F.R. Part 500[; and] (3) [the grievant is] . . . performing a hazardous duty within the definition of 5 C.F.R. 550.902." *U.S. Dep't of the Army, Alaska*, 54 FLRA 1117, 1122 (1998).

The Union argues that the award is based on a nonfact because the Arbitrator found, as a matter of fact, that the disputed hazardous duties were taken into account in the classification of the grievants' position. Exceptions at 13-14. As the Union itself concedes, this issue was disputed before the Arbitrator. *Id.* at 13 (acknowledging that at arbitration "the Agency argued that the Lock and Security Specialist's exposure to explosive munitions was considered when the position was classified"); *see also* Award at 16 (finding that the parties were "in disagreement about whether or not the hazards faced by the grievants working in the Armory [were] properly considered when the positions occupied by the grievants were classified and wage rates established"). Consequently, the Union's contention does not provide a basis for establishing that the award is based on a nonfact. *See U.S. Dep't of the Navy, Naval Surface Warfare Ctr., Dahlgren, Va.*, 44 FLRA 1118, 1122-23 (1992) (finding that the agency failed to establish that the award was based on a nonfact when it alleged that the arbitrator incorrectly determined that the performance of certain hazardous duties were not taken into account in the classification of the grievants' positions); *see also AFGE, Local 376*, 62 FLRA 138, 141 (2007) (Chairman Cabaniss concurring).

Accordingly, we deny the Union's exception.[4]

V. Decision

The Union's exceptions are dismissed in part and denied in part.

4. Based on this finding, we find it unnecessary to address the Union's contention that the award is contrary to law because it failed to award the grievants who were full-time Lock and Security Specialists a hazard pay differential.

APPENDIX

Article 6 -- Rights of the Employee

Section a. Each employee shall have the right to form, join, or assist a labor organization, or to refrain from any such activity, freely and without fear of penalty or reprisal, and each employee shall be protected in the exercise of such right . . . .

Section b. The parties agree that there will be no restraint, harassment, intimidation, reprisal, or any coercion against any employee in the exercise of any employee rights provided for in this Agreement and any other applicable laws, rules, and regulations, including the right: . . . to be treated fairly and equitably in all aspects of personnel management . . . .

Article 27 – Health and Safety

Section a. There are essentially two (2) distinct areas of concern regarding the safety and health of employees in the Federal Bureau of Prisons:

1. the first, which affects the safety and well-being of employees, involves the inherent hazards of a correctional environment; and

2. the second, which affects the safety and health of employees, involves the inherent hazards associated with the normal industrial operations found throughout the Federal Bureau of Prisons.

With respect to the first, the Employer agrees to lower those inherent hazards to the lowest possible level, without relinquishing its rights under 5 USC 7106. The Union recognizes that by the very nature of the duties associated with supervising and controlling inmates, these hazards can never be completely eliminated.

With respect to the second, the Employer agrees to furnish to employees places and conditions of employment that are free from recognized hazards that are causing or are likely to cause death or serious physical harm, in accordance with all applicable federal laws, standards, codes, regulations, and executive orders.

Exceptions, Jt. Ex. 2 at 10, 63.

65 FLRA No. 13

UNITED STATES
DEPARTMENT OF VETERANS AFFAIRS
SAN DIEGO HEALTHCARE SYSTEM
SAN DIEGO, CALIFORNIA
(Agency)

and

NATIONAL ASSOCIATION
OF GOVERNMENT EMPLOYEES/SEIU
(Union)

0-AR-4355

DECISION

August 31, 2010

Before the Authority: Carol Waller Pope, Chairman, and Thomas M. Beck and Ernest DuBester, Members

I. Statement of the Case

This matter is before the Authority on exceptions to an award of Arbitrator Charles A. Askin filed by the Agency under § 7122(a) of the Federal Service Labor-Management Relations Statute (the Statute) and part 2425 of the Authority's Regulations. The Union filed an opposition to the exceptions.

The Arbitrator determined that the Agency improperly denied hazard and/or environmental differential pay to five affected job classifications and ordered that the Agency pay the appropriate amounts of hazard pay to the affected General Schedule (GS) employee and environmental differential pay (EDP) to the affected Wage Grade (WG) employees. For the reasons that follow, we grant the Agency's exceptions in part and deny them in part.

II. Background and Arbitrator's Award

The grievants, who are responsible for handling medical waste products, filed a grievance alleging that the Agency improperly denied their entitlement to hazard pay and/or EDP. Award at 2. The issue framed by the Arbitrator was:

> Whether the [Agency] improperly denied hazard and/or environmental differential pay to five affected job classifications; and, if so, what is the appropriate remedy?

Award at 2.

The Arbitrator made the following findings regarding each of the job classifications at issue:

Wastes Manager Position (Environmental Protection Specialist) (GS position)

The Arbitrator found that the position description for Wastes Manager showed that the position's duties focus on administrative, management, and technical assistance. Award at 4, 16. Further, the description cites "occasional exposure to moderate risks" in certain hazardous areas and "regular and recurring exposure to moderate risks" that require safety precautions, including the use of personal protective equipment. *Id.* at 4, 17. He found that the job description "does *not* encompass regular direct handling or transport of hazardous materials, or indicate that there is a 'high potential' for exposure to medical wastes." *Id.* at 4. However, the incumbent in the position testified that she routinely handled hazardous waste and that this duty "did not involve mere speculative 'potential exposure." *Id.* at 5. The Arbitrator found that the incumbent in the Waste Manager position performed at least two hazardous duties: (1) the collection and transportation of "red bags" containing bio-hazardous waste and (2) the operation of equipment related to the disposal of medical and bio-hazardous waste material. Award at 15. Although the Arbitrator found that the latter duty occurred "only occasionally," he found that the collection and transportation of the containers of bio-hazardous waste materials occurred "daily – indeed, apparently for a significant period each work day." *Id.*; *see also id.* at 17 (noting the position's "direct, daily, hands-on contact with containers (red bags) of medical waste"). Further, the Arbitrator found that "protective devices [provided by the Agency] do not afford complete protection" from exposure to bio-hazardous waste. *Id.* at 16.

Hazardous Waste Disposer Position (WG position)

The Arbitrator noted that the position description for Hazardous Waste Disposer stated that ninety percent of the duties involve the processing of "bio-hazardous/infectious" medical waste and that the position "entails a high potential risk for exposure to regulated medical wastes." *Id.* at 6. He found that the testimony of the incumbent in the position was consistent with the position description. *Id.* In addition, the Arbitrator found that protective gear provided by the Agency did not provide complete protection from exposure to bio-hazardous waste. *Id.* at 6, 18.

Housekeeper Aid, Levels 1 and 2 (WG positions)

The Arbitrator found that the position descriptions for Housekeeper Aid, Levels 1 and 2 did not refer to: (1) any duties to handle hazardous waste or (2) any exposure or proximity to bio-hazardous or other hazardous waste materials. *Id.* at 7-8. However, the Arbitrator found that testimony and evidence showed that the incumbents in the positions were required to work with bio-hazardous waste on a daily basis and were exposed to a "high degree hazard of micro-organisms." *Id.* at 8, 18.

Housekeeper Aid, Level 3 (WG position)

The Arbitrator found that both the position description for Housekeeper Aid, Level 3 and testimony showed that incumbents in the position were required to work with bio-hazardous waste on a daily basis. In addition, the Arbitrator found that protective gear provided by the Agency was "insufficient to protect the body 'one hundred percent.'" *Id.* at 8, 18.

Based on the foregoing findings, the Arbitrator ruled, as to the Wastes Manager position, that, because the incumbent performed hazardous duties that were not part of her usual job responsibilities and not taken into account in the classification of her position, and because protective gear could not afford complete protection, she was entitled to a 25% hazard pay differential under 5 U.S.C. § 5545(d) and Appendix A to Subpart I of Part 550 of title 5 of the Code of Federal Regulations (Schedule of Pay Differentials).[1] *Id.* at 15-17. As for the Hazardous Waste Disposer and Housekeeper Aid, Levels 1, 2, and 3 positions, the Arbitrator could find no legal basis for the Agency's claim that, in order for these positions to be entitled to EDP, the job classifications "must not have taken into account the hazards of the particular position." *Id.* at 18. Based on the evidence and arguments, the Arbitrator found that, because the incumbents in each of these positions were exposed to "high degree hazard of micro-organisims," they were entitled to EDP of 8% pursuant to 5 U.S.C. § 5343(c)(4) and Appendix J to Subpart E of Part 532 of title 5 of the Code of Federal Regulations (Schedule of Environmental Differentials).[2] *Id.* at 18.

III. Positions of the Parties

A. Agency's Exceptions

The Agency alleges that the award is contrary to law because the employees' "exposure risk . . . [was]

1. 5 U.S.C. § 5545(d) provides, in pertinent part, that:

> The Office [of Personnel Management] shall establish a schedule or schedules of pay differentials for duty involving unusual physical hardship or hazard . . . . Under such regulations as the Office may prescribe . . . an employee to whom chapter 51 and subchapter III of chapter 53 of this title applies is entitled to be paid the appropriate differential for any period in which he is subjected to physical hardship or hazard not usually involved in carrying out the duties of his position. However, the pay differential –
>
> > (1) does not apply to an employee in a position the classification of which takes into account the degree of physical hardship or hazard involved in the performance of the duties thereof, except in such circumstances as the Office may by regulation prescribe; and
> > (2) may not exceed an amount equal to 25 percent of the rate of basic pay applicable to the employee.

Appendix A to Subpart I of Part 550 provides that a 25% differential is warranted for exposure to hazardous agents, work with or in close proximity to:

> (5) Virulent biologicals. Materials of micro-organic nature which when introduced into the body are likely to cause serious disease or fatality and for which protective devices do not afford complete protection.

2. 5 U.S.C. § 5343(c) provides, in pertinent part, that:

> The Office of Personnel Management, by regulation, shall prescribe practices and procedures for . . . establishing wage schedules and rates . . . . The regulations shall provide –
>
> . . . .
>
> (4) for proper differentials, as determined by the Office, for duty involving unusually severe working conditions or unusually severe hazards
>
> . . . .

Appendix J to Subpart E of Part 532 provides for EDP of 8% for

> Working with or in close proximity to micro-organisms which involves potential personal injury [for which] the use of safety devices and equipment . . . have not practically eliminated the potential for such personal injury.

practically eliminated through [the] use of the protective gear[.]" Exceptions at 3. According to the Agency, under both Agency guidance and Authority precedent, an employee is entitled to an environmental differential only "for exposure [to hazardous materials] . . . which cannot be practically eliminated." *Id.* at 3-6. Further, the Agency claims that the incumbent in the Wastes Manager position is not entitled to hazard pay because the employee "usually performed" the duties for which she was claiming hazard pay. *Id.* at 7. The Agency contends that employees are not entitled to hazard pay for duties that are usual, but rather, only for duties that are "not usually involved" or that are "unusually severe." *Id.* Finally, the Agency contends that the employees are not entitled to hazard pay and EDP because the employees' exposure to hazardous materials already was factored into their pay grades. *Id.* at 7-8.

B. Union's Opposition

The Union contends that the Agency's exceptions should be denied because they are mere disagreements with the Arbitrator's factual findings and, as such, do not provide a basis for finding the award deficient. Opposition at 3-4. Additionally, the Union contends that, to the extent the exceptions constitute a "contrary to law" argument, they should be denied because the Arbitrator correctly applied the applicable standards of law. *Id.* at 6-16.

IV. Preliminary Matters

A. Union's motion to strike.

The Union's opposition includes a Motion to Strike several portions of the Agency's exceptions. In its Motion to Strike, the Union argues that the Agency's counsel never mentioned, referred to, or submitted into evidence at the arbitration hearing or in the Agency's post-hearing brief "the statistical evidence of a ten year record of reported needle-stick and other potential blood-borne pathogen exposure[,]" referred to on pages 4 and 5 of the Agency's exceptions. Motion to Strike at 2. In its exceptions, the Agency states that it is "resubmit[ing] the statistical information that [it] referenced at the arbitration." Exceptions at 4. However, as the Union notes, the ten-year record includes an incident that occurred three days after the Arbitrator issued his decision and, thus, could not have been presented at the hearing. Motion to Strike at 3; *see also* Exceptions at 1 (stating date of award) and 5 (ten-year record listing event that occurred three days later).

Arbitration awards "are not subject to review on the basis of evidence that comes into existence after the arbitration hearing." *Office & Prof'l Employees Int'l Union, Local 268*, 54 FLRA 1154, 1156 n.1 (1998). Accordingly, because the statistical evidence came into existence after the arbitration hearing, we grant the Union's Motion to Strike.

B. The Agency's exceptions were timely filed.

The Union raises the question of whether the Agency's exceptions were timely filed. Opposition at 2-3. Section 7122(b) of the Statute requires that exceptions be filed thirty days from the date of service of the award. The Authority's Regulations, at 5 C.F.R. § 2429.22, provide that 5 days be added if the award is served by mail or commercial delivery. The award was sent via U.S. Mail on February 22, 2008. Opp'n at 2-3. Therefore, as the Union states, the Agency's exceptions should have been filed by March 27, 2008. *Id.* at 3. Because the Agency filed its exceptions via Federal Express, a commercial delivery service, the date of filing, at that time, would have been the date the Authority received the exceptions. 5 C.F.R. § 2429.21(b) (2008).[3] The record shows that the Authority received the exceptions on March 27, 2008. Accordingly, we find that the Agency's exceptions were timely filed.

V. Analysis and Conclusion

A. Whether the award is contrary to law.

When an exception involves an award's consistency with law, the Authority reviews any question of law raised by the exception and the award *de novo*. *See NTEU, Chapter 24*, 50 FLRA 330, 332 (1995) (citing *U.S. Customs Serv. v. FLRA*, 43 F.3d 682, 686-87 (D.C. Cir. 1994)). In applying the standard of *de novo* review, the Authority assesses whether an arbitrator's legal conclusions are consistent with the applicable standard of law. *See U.S. Dep't of Def., Dep'ts of the Army & the Air Force, Ala. Nat'l Guard, Northport, Ala.*, 55 FLRA 37, 40 (1998). In making that assessment, the Authority defers to the arbitrator's underlying factual findings. *See id.*

3. The Authority's Regulations, as amended effective November 8, 2009, now provide that a filing via a commercial delivery service that will provide a record showing the date the document was tendered to the delivery service is considered filed on the date the matter is deposited with the commercial delivery service. 5 C.F.R. § 2429.21(b) (2010).

As an initial matter, we find that the Agency's argument that the award is contrary to law because the employees' exposure risk . . . [was] practically eliminated through [the] use of protective gear" is not properly before the Authority. Exceptions at 3. Under § 2429.5 of the Authority's Regulations, the Authority will not consider issues that could have been, but were not, raised or presented to the Arbitrator. *See, e.g., U.S. Dep't of Homeland Sec., U.S. Customs & Border Prot., JFK Airport, Queens, N.Y.*, 62 FLRA 416, 417 (2008). There is no indication in the record that the Agency raised this argument before the Arbitrator.[4] Accordingly, the issue is not properly before the Authority. *See id.*[5]

1. Hazard Pay

The Agency contends that the incumbent in the Wastes Manager position is not entitled to hazard pay because the employee "usually performed" the duties for which she was claiming hazard pay. Exceptions at 7. According to the Agency, employees are not entitled to hazard pay for duties that are usual, but rather, only for duties that are "not usually involved." *Id.*

Pursuant to 5 U.S.C. § 5545(d), a GS employee is entitled to a hazardous duty differential for any period in which "he is subjected to physical hardship or hazard not usually involved in carrying out the duties of his position."[6] In *Adair v. United States*, the U.S. Court of Appeals for the Federal Circuit defined the term "usually involved in carrying out the duties of his position" as "inherent in a position, which regularly recurs, and which is performed for a substantial part of the working time." 497 F.3d 1244, 1253 (Fed. Cir. 2007).

Here, the Arbitrator found that the incumbent in the Waste Manager position performed at least two hazardous duties: (1) the collection and transportation of "red bags" containing bio-hazardous waste and (2) the operation of equipment related to the disposal of medical and bio-hazardous waste material. Award at 15. Although the Arbitrator found that the employee performs the latter duty "only occasionally," he found that she collects and transports containers of bio-hazardous waste materials "daily – indeed, apparently for a significant period each work day." *Id.*; *see also id.* at 17 (noting employee's "direct, daily, hands-on contact with containers (red bags) of medical waste"). These factual findings, which are undisputed, support a conclusion that this duty is inherent in the Waste Manager position, regularly recurs, and is performed for a substantial part of the working time. As such, it is usually involved in carrying out the duties of the Waster Manager position. Because a GS employee is entitled to a hazard duty pay only if the hazard duty is not usually involved in the employee's position, contrary to the Arbitrator's holding, the incumbent in the Waste Manager position is not entitled to such pay.[7]

Accordingly, we find that the Arbitrator's conclusion that the incumbent in the Waste Manager

4. Although the Union asserted before the Arbitrator that "[p]rotective measures, including the clothing provided, are incapable of practically eliminating the hazards" of the Hazardous Waste Disposer and the Housing Aids, Level 3, positions, *see* Award at 10, the Agency does not appear to have responded to this argument. Moreover, the Agency did not assert that the employees' exposure risk was practically eliminated through the use of protective gear in its Post-hearing brief.

5. Even if the issue were properly before the Authority, the Arbitrator made explicit factual findings that the risk of exposure to bio-hazards experienced by the Hazardous Waste Manager, Hazardous Waste Disposer, and Housekeeper Aid, Level 3 positions was not practically eliminated through the use of protective gear. *See* Award at 6 (Hazardous Waste Disposer position), 8 ((Housekeeper Aid, Level 3 position), and 16 (Hazardous Waste Manager position). As for the Housekeeper Aid, Levels 1 and 3 positions, the Arbitrator found that incumbents in those positions are required to carry "red bags" of bio-hazardous waste on a daily basis and, therefore, were entitled to EDP of 8 percent. *Id.* at 8, 17-18. In making these findings, the Arbitrator had before him the Union's evidence that spillage or leakage from the "red bags" could occur easily and that protective gear could not practically eliminate the risk of exposure to bio-hazardous waste. *See* Opp'n, Attach. Ex. A at 28. The Agency did not rebut that evidence. As stated above, in applying the *de novo* standard of review, the Authority must defer to the Arbitrator's factual findings.

6. In addition, hazard pay is not warranted where the classification of the position "takes into account" the fact of such exposure to hazards. 5 U.S.C. § 5545(d).

7. The Arbitrator also found that the employee's daily exposure to the bio-hazardous materials was not taken into account in classifying her position. Award at 17. In enacting 5 U.S.C. 5545(d), Congress noted that "unusual physical hardships or hazards which are inherent in a position, which regularly recurs, and which is performed for a substantial part of the working time, are best compensated for through the regular position classification process[,]" rather than enhanced compensation." *Adair*, 497 F.3d at 1253. We note that Article 13 of the parties' agreement describes the process that an employee may follow if she believes her position is improperly classified.

position was entitled to hazard pay is contrary to law and grant the Agency's exception.

2. EDP

Pursuant to 5 U.S.C. § 5343(c)(4), the Office of Personnel Management is required to provide for WG employees "proper differentials . . . . for duty involving unusually severe working conditions or unusually severe hazards." As the Arbitrator explained, those differential rates, 8% for high degree hazard and 4% for low degree hazard, are set out in Appendix J to Subpart E of Part 532.

Applying the legal standard in § 5543(c)(4) and the regulations, the Arbitrator found that the incumbents in the WG positions worked with, or in close proximity to, bio-hazardous waste and were exposed to a high degree of risk. Award at 17-18. The Agency claims, however, that the duties regularly performed by the WG positions are not "unusually severe" for purposes of § 5343(c)(4). Exceptions at 2, 7. Pursuant to § 5343(c)(4), OPM's regulations define "unusually severe" hazards warranting an EDP. The Arbitrator, based on the evidence and arguments, found that the WG positions fell within the "high degree hazard of micro-organisms" category within OPM's schedule of EDPs for "unusually severe" hazards, warranting an EDP of 8%. Award at 18. Except for its argument that the employees' exposure risk was practically eliminated -- an argument which, as discussed *supra*, is not properly before the Authority -- the Agency does not argue that the Arbitrator improperly placed the hazard within this EDP category. Moreover, contrary to the Agency's contention, unlike § 5545(d), § 5343(c)(4) does not provide that an employee is not entitled to EDP if the position's classification factored in exposure to hazards. *See supra* pages 2-3, nn.1-2.

Accordingly, we find that the Arbitrator's conclusion that the incumbents were entitled to EDP of 8% is consistent with the applicable standard of law. Therefore, we find that the award of EDP to the WG positions is not contrary to law and deny the Agency's exception.

VI. Decision

The Agency's exceptions are granted in part and denied in part.

65 FLRA No. 14

UNITED STATES
DEPARTMENT OF THE NAVY
NAVAL UNDERSEA WARFARE
CENTER DIVISION
NEWPORT, RHODE ISLAND
(Agency)

and

NATIONAL ASSOCIATION
OF GOVERNMENT EMPLOYEES
LOCAL R1-144
FEDERAL UNION
OF SCIENTISTS AND ENGINEERS
(Union)

0-AR-4289

ORDER DISMISSING EXCEPTIONS

August 31, 2010

Before the Authority: Carol Waller Pope, Chairman, and Thomas M. Beck and Ernest DuBester, Members[1]

I. Statement of the Case

This matter is before the Authority on exceptions to an award of Arbitrator Marilyn H. Zuckerman filed by the Agency under § 7122(a) of the Federal Service Labor-Management Relations Statute (the Statute) and part 2425 of the Authority's Regulations. The Union filed an opposition.

The Arbitrator directed the Agency to reimburse the grievant for fifty-three travel vouchers that were submitted to the Agency more than six years from the dates on which the expenses were incurred. The Arbitrator did not resolve the grievant's claim for "travel compensation/overtime associated with such travel" (overtime claim).

For the reasons that follow, we dismiss the exceptions, without prejudice, as interlocutory.

1. Member Beck's dissenting opinion is set forth at the end of this decision.

II. Background and Arbitrator's Award

When the grievant submitted travel vouchers to the Agency, the Agency refused to process fifty-three of those vouchers because the travel occurred more than six years prior to the date on which the grievant submitted the vouchers for payment. Award at 2. The grievant filed a grievance, which was unresolved and submitted to arbitration. *Id.*

At arbitration, the parties stipulated to the following issue: "Must the Agency compensate [the grievant] for the fifty[-]three travel vouchers that were submitted to the Agency in excess of six years from the date entitlement arose, *as well as . . . overtime associated with such travel*?" *Id.* at 6 (emphasis added). The parties also stipulated as follows:

> The [overtime claim] will be stayed pending resolution of the travel voucher claim. Should the Arbitrator find in favor of the Agency and deny the travel voucher grievance, the parties agree that the stayed issue will be considered resolved. However, if the Arbitrator rules in favor of the Union, the Arbitrator will retain jurisdiction over the [overtime claim] if the parties are unable to reach agreement.

Id.

In her award, the Arbitrator ruled in the Union's favor and found that the Agency must process the fifty-three vouchers and reimburse the grievant without interest, but did not rule on the overtime claim associated with such travel. *Id.* at 22. In this respect, the Arbitrator stated that, "[a]t the Union's request, [she] w[ould] retain jurisdiction over the [overtime claim] should the parties be unable to reach agreement on this issue." *Id.*

III. Positions of the Parties

A. Agency's Exceptions

The Agency argues that the award is contrary to law and regulation, and that the Arbitrator failed to correctly apply the doctrine of laches. Exceptions at 9-21.

B. Union's Opposition

The Union argues that the award is consistent with law and regulation and that the Arbitrator correctly held that the doctrine of laches does not apply. Opp'n at 2-6.

IV. Order to Show Cause and Agency's Response

The Authority issued an order, directing the Agency to show cause why its exceptions should not be dismissed as interlocutory.[2] *See* Order to Show Cause at 1-2. The Agency filed a response, in which it asserts that "the Arbitrator's act of ordering the Agency to compensate the grievant (without interest) for 53 travel vouchers is final as to that issue." Response at 1. The Agency argues that the Arbitrator's statement concerning her retention of jurisdiction for purposes of resolving the overtime claim is "in essence, . . . an offer to resolve possible problems related to the implementation of the [a]ward for travel voucher compensation." *Id.* at 2. According to the Agency, "[a]bsent the Arbitrator's award of compensation for travel vouchers, the parties would have had no authority to pursue or resolve the . . . overtime [claim] related to travel performed in conjunction with those vouchers." *Id.* Thus, the Agency asserts that the Arbitrator's award is final and the exceptions are not interlocutory. *Id.*

V. Analysis and Conclusions

Section 2429.11 of the Authority's Regulations pertinently provides that "the Authority . . . ordinarily will not consider interlocutory appeals." 5 C.F.R. § 2429.11. Thus, the Authority ordinarily will not resolve exceptions to an arbitration award unless the award constitutes a complete resolution of all the issues submitted to arbitration. *See, e.g., U.S. Dep't of Justice, Fed. Bureau of Prisons, Fed. Med. Ctr., Carswell, Tex.*, 64 FLRA 566, 567-68 (2010) (*Carswell*); *U.S. Dep't of the Army, Army Corps of Eng'rs, Norfolk Dist.*, 60 FLRA 247, 248 (2004) (*Army*); *U.S. Dep't of Health & Human Servs., Ctrs. for Medicare & Medicaid Servs.*, 57 FLRA 924, 926 (2002) (*HHS*). Consequently, an arbitration award that postpones the determination of an issue submitted does not constitute a final award subject to review. *See Carswell*, 64 FLRA at 567; *Army*, 60 FLRA at 248; *HHS*, 57 FLRA at 926. Similarly, the parties' agreement to conduct a separate hearing on a threshold issue does not operate to convert the arbitrator's threshold ruling into a final award subject to exceptions being filed under the Statute. *See, e.g., HHS*, 57 FLRA at 926. In this regard, "an award is not final merely because the parties agree to resolve the issues presented in separate proceedings." *AFGE, Local 12*, 61 FLRA 355, 357 (2005). However, where an arbitrator has ordered a remedy, the mere fact that the arbitrator retains jurisdiction to assist parties with the details of the remedy's implementation does not render exceptions to that award interlocutory.[3] *See, e.g., Office of Pers. Mgmt.*, 61 FLRA 358, 361 (2005) (then-Member Pope dissenting in part on unrelated grounds), *reconsideration denied*, 61 FLRA 657 (2006).

The Agency concedes that the Arbitrator has not resolved the overtime claim, but argues that the Arbitrator's retention of jurisdiction on this issue is to "resolve possible problems related to the implementation of the [a]ward for travel voucher compensation." Response at 2. However, in regard to the travel-voucher issue, the Arbitrator directed the Agency to "process the fifty[-]three claims and pay the [g]rievant what he is owed on them[,]" Award at 20, and the Agency does not explain how the Arbitrator's retention of jurisdiction over a claim for overtime "associated with" the grievant's travel would merely "implement[]" the Arbitrator's ruling on the vouchers. *Id.* at 6; Response at 2. In addition, it is undisputed that the parties stipulated that if the Arbitrator ruled in favor of the Union, then the Arbitrator would retain jurisdiction over the overtime claim "if the parties are unable to reach agreement." Award at 6. As the Arbitrator ruled in favor of the Union, and there is no assertion or record evidence that the parties have reached agreement regarding the overtime claim, that claim remains before the Arbitrator. Thus, although the Arbitrator's award may have resolved the Agency's liability as to the vouchers, it does not constitute a complete resolution of all the issues submitted to arbitration.[4] *See*

---

2. The Authority also gave the Union an opportunity to respond to the order to show cause, but the Union did not file a response.

3. The Authority has found interlocutory review to be appropriate where the exceptions present a plausible jurisdictional defect, the resolution of which will advance the ultimate disposition of the case. *U.S. Dep't of the Treasury, Customs Serv., Tucson, Ariz.*, 58 FLRA 358, 359 n.* (2002). Here, there is no claim that the exceptions raise a plausible jurisdictional defect.

4. The dissent asserts that "[t]he parties understood that, if the Agency was found to be obligated to pay [the] grievant for the old travel vouchers, it would also be obligated to compensate the grievant for overtime associated with that travel." Dissent at 5. The record does not support this assertion, as the parties stipulated that the overtime claim would be "considered resolved[]" only if the Arbitrator ruled that the Agency was *not* liable for the voucher claim, which she did not do. Award at 6. With regard to the dissent's reliance on the fact that the grievant prevailed in a

Carswell, 64 FLRA at 568; *AFGE, Local 12*, 61 FLRA at 356-57; *Army*, 60 FLRA at 248-49; *HHS*, 57 FLRA at 926.

For the foregoing reasons, we conclude that the Agency's exceptions are interlocutory. Accordingly, we dismiss the exceptions without prejudice. *See, e.g., AFGE, Local 12*, 61 FLRA at 357.

VI. Order

The exceptions are dismissed without prejudice.

prior grievance concerning overtime, that fact is immaterial because it involved "travel overtime in 1995[,]" while the grievance at issue in this case concerns travel occurring during 1997 through 2000. *Id.* at 2. Further, the fact that the Arbitrator retained jurisdiction "should the parties be unable to reach agreement" on the overtime claim, Award at 22, does not render the award final. *See, e.g., U.S. Dep't of HHS, Navajo Area Indian Health Serv.*, 58 FLRA 356, 357 (2003) (award was not final where arbitrator retained jurisdiction in the event the parties were unable to agree on a remedy); *U.S. Gov't Printing Office, Wash., D.C.*, 53 FLRA 17, 18 (1997) (same). Because the issue of the Agency's liability for the overtime claim remains before the Arbitrator, this case is distinguishable from the decisions cited by the dissent, in which only the determination of the specific amounts of monetary remedies, and/or the particular individuals entitled to those remedies, remained before the arbitrators. *See U.S. DOJ, Fed. Bureau of Prisons, USP Admin. Maximum (ADX), Florence, Colo.*, 64 FLRA 1168, 1170 (2010); *U.S. Dep't of Homeland Sec., Customs & Border Prot.*, 64 FLRA 989, 991 (2010); *U.S. Dep't of the Treasury, IRS*, 63 FLRA 157, 159 (2009).

Member Beck, Dissenting:

I do not agree with the Majority that the Agency's exceptions are interlocutory. That determination is not consistent with our recent decisions in *United States Department of Justice, Federal Bureau of Prisons, USP Admin. Maximum (ADX) Florence, Colorado*, 64 FLRA 1168 (2010), (*Bureau of Prisons*), *United States Department of Homeland Security, Customs and Border Protection*, 64 FLRA 989 (2010) (*DHS/CBP*) and *United States Department of the Treasury, Internal Revenue Service*, 63 FLRA 157 (2009) (*Treasury, IRS*).

Consistent with long-standing precedent, these cases conclude that the Authority will not resolve exceptions unless the arbitrator's award constitutes a complete resolution "of all the issues submitted to arbitration." *Bureau of Prisons*, 64 FLRA at 1169; *DHS/CBP*, 64 FLRA at 991; and *Treasury, IRS*, 63 FLRA at 158.

Here, the original grievance raised two related issues: (1) whether the Agency is required to compensate the grievant for the fifty-three travel vouchers that were submitted six years after entitlement "as well as" (2) whether the grievant is entitled to overtime compensation "associated with [that] travel." Award at 6. At arbitration, the parties jointly withdrew the second issue from the Arbitrator's jurisdiction, unless "the parties are unable to reach agreement." *Id.* The parties understood that, if the Agency was found to be obligated to pay grievant for the old travel vouchers, it would also be obligated to compensate the grievant for overtime associated with that travel.[1] Following the Arbitrator's determination regarding the vouchers, the only question left open was *how much* overtime compensation was owed to the grievant, not *whether* overtime compensation was owed.[2] As a result of the parties' stipulation, the Arbitrator had no jurisdiction to address the overtime issue. Award at 6. Consequently, the Arbitrator addressed (and resolved) all of the issues that were properly before him.

1. It is undisputed that the grievant prevailed in a prior grievance that established his entitlement to overtime while in a travel status. Award at 2.

2. The Union does not claim that the award is not final or that the exceptions are interlocutory. *See U.S. Dep't of Homeland Sec., Immigration & Customs Enforcement*, 64 FLRA 1003, 1006 (2010).

There is no substantive distinction between this case and those cited above that warrants a different outcome. In *Bureau of Prisons*, we found the arbitrator's award to be "final" even though the arbitrator retained jurisdiction "to assist the parties in the implementation of awarded remedies." 64 FLRA at 1170. We concluded that the arbitrator's retention of authority did not render the exceptions interlocutory. Two weeks earlier, we found another arbitrator's instructions (that directed the parties to "share information and determine individual employees' entitlement to backpay") and retention of jurisdiction did not render the agency's exceptions interlocutory. *DHS/CBP*, 64 FLRA at 991. Similarly, in *Treasury, IRS* we found exceptions were not interlocutory when "the only matter" over which the arbitrator retained jurisdiction "was the amount of back pay and expenses, if any" to be paid by the Agency. 63 FLRA at 159.

What the Majority has failed to explain is this: If the Agency is precluded from presenting its exceptions to the Authority now, at what point will the Agency be permitted to present its exceptions? The Arbitrator will weigh in on this matter again only "if the parties are unable to reach agreement" on the amount of overtime compensation owed. Award at 6. If (as seems likely) the parties reach agreement on the overtime question, there will be no further awards, remedies or rulings of any kind from the Arbitrator. In those circumstances, what triggering event will cue the Agency -- and the Authority -- that the Agency's exceptions are no longer interlocutory? What will have changed in terms of assessing whether the Arbitrator resolved all issues that were submitted to him? The answer to this question – "nothing" -- demonstrates that the extant Award resolved all issues that were actually placed before the Arbitrator for his resolution.

Accordingly, I would find that the Arbitrator's award is final and that the Agency's exceptions are not interlocutory.

65 FLRA No. 15

UNITED STATES
DEPARTMENT OF THE ARMY
UNITED STATES
ARMY DENTAL ACTIVITY
FORT BRAGG, NORTH CAROLINA
(Agency)

and

AMERICAN FEDERATION
OF GOVERNMENT EMPLOYEES
LOCAL 1770
(Union)

0-AR-4361

DECISION

August 31, 2010

Before the Authority: Carol Waller Pope, Chairman, and Thomas M. Beck and Ernest DuBester, Members

I. Statement of the Case

This matter is before the Authority on exceptions to an award (the fee award) of Arbitrator Robert G. Williams filed by the Agency under § 7122(a) of the Federal Service Labor-Management Relations Statute (the Statute) and part 2425 of the Authority's Regulations. The Union filed an opposition to the Agency's exceptions.

In the fee award, the Arbitrator awarded attorney fees. For the reasons that follow, we modify the fee award to provide that the amount of fees must be recalculated based on market rates prevailing at the time when the attorneys rendered their services, but otherwise deny the exceptions.

II. Background and Arbitrator's Awards

A. Merits Awards

In his original award, the Arbitrator sustained, in part, the grievances over the grievants' five-day suspensions. Specifically, although he sustained charges of absence without leave (AWOL) and failing to follow call-in procedures, he rejected charges of falsifying time cards. He mitigated the discipline to written reprimands for being AWOL and for failing to follow call-in procedures, and he awarded the grievants backpay. *U.S. Dep't of the Army, U.S. Army Dental Activity Headquarters, XVIII Airborne Corps & Fort Bragg, Fort Bragg, N.C.*, 62 FLRA 70, 70 (2007) (*Dep't of the Army*). In a supplemental award, the Arbitrator held that the reprimands must conform to the requirements set forth in 5 U.S.C. § 7503,[1] and he awarded attorney fees. *Id.*

The Agency filed exceptions, and the Authority concluded that the Arbitrator had misinterpreted § 7503 in directing the reprimands. Accordingly, the Authority vacated the award and remanded the matter to the parties for resubmission to the Arbitrator for a reassessment of whether the five-day suspensions were proper. *Id.* at 72. The vacating of the award was without prejudice to another petition for fees if the Arbitrator again awarded backpay. *Id.* at 73.

On remand (the remand award), the Arbitrator determined that the Agency failed to prove the falsification charge. Although he again sustained the charges of AWOL and failing to follow call-in procedures, he found that these charges were part of the same incident and were not separate offenses. He also found that the grievants were treated disparately with respect to the charge of failing to follow call-in procedures. On this basis, the Arbitrator again mitigated the five-day suspensions to written reprimands and awarded backpay. Fee Award at 2-3. The Agency did not file exceptions to the remand award, and the Union filed a petition for an award of attorney fees. *Id.* at 3.

1. Section 7503(a)-(b) provides, in pertinent part:

> (a) Under regulations prescribed by the Office of Personnel Management, an employee may be suspended for 14 days or less for such cause as will promote the efficiency of the service . . . .
>
> (b) An employee against whom a suspension for 14 days or less is proposed is entitled to--
>
> (1) an advance written notice stating the specific reasons for the proposed action;
>
> (2) a reasonable time to answer orally and in writing and to furnish affidavits and other documentary evidence in support of the answer;
>
> (3) be represented by an attorney or other representative; and
>
> (4) a written decision and the specific reasons therefore at the earliest practicable date.

B. Fee Award

As relevant to the Agency's exceptions, the Arbitrator addressed whether an award of fees was warranted in the interest of justice and whether the requested amount was reasonable within the meaning of 5 U.S.C. § 7701(g)(1) (§ 7701(g)(1)).[2] As to the interest of justice, the Arbitrator applied the criteria established by the Merit Systems Protection Board (MSPB) in *Allen v. United States Postal Service,* 2 M.S.P.R. 420 (1980) (*Allen*) and by the Authority for cases brought under the Statute.[3]

The Arbitrator considered whether criterion 5 of *Allen* was satisfied because the Agency "knew or should have known that it would not prevail on the merits" when it brought the disciplinary actions. *Allen*, 2 M.S.P.R. at 435. In this regard, the Arbitrator reiterated several findings that he had made in his original award with regard to the Agency's certification policy on time and attendance on which the falsification charges were based. Fee Award at 44. Specifically, he stated that: the Agency had a certification policy on time and attendance of only requiring employees to initial their time sheets; under this certification policy, employees were not responsible for time sheet omissions; and the Agency could not prove an intentional falsification charge on the basis of an omission. In addition, in the fee award, he found that the Agency should have known that it could not prove this charge when it brought the disciplinary actions. *Id.* at 44. Consequently, he concluded that fees were warranted in the interest of justice under criterion 5 of *Allen*. *Id.*

Although the Arbitrator recognized that fees are warranted in the interest of justice when any one of the criteria of *Allen* is satisfied, he also concluded that fees were warranted in the interest of justice under *Allen* criterion 2. *Id.* at 42. In addition, he further concluded that fees were warranted in the interest of justice under the Statute because of a service to the public in bringing the grievance. *Id.* at 46-47.

As to the reasonableness of the hourly rates charged by the Union's attorneys, the Union's attorneys provided the Arbitrator with the fee agreement, as well as affidavits and other evidence of prevailing market rates. In addressing the hourly rates, the Arbitrator focused on the fee agreement between the Union and the attorneys. The agreement provided that the attorneys may charge the Union "a reduced fee in the public interest[.]" *Dep't of the Army*, 62 FLRA at 73 (quoting the fee agreement). However, the agreement also provided that the attorneys would charge the Union hourly rates consistent with the "[a]djusted *Laffey* matrix" "upon receipt of a successful decision."[4] *Id.* The Arbitrator rejected the Agency's claim that the reduced rate was the attorneys' customary rate and the rate he was required to apply. Fee Award at 49. The Arbitrator found that his merit awards constituted a "successful decision" within the meaning of the fee agreement and that the agreement to pay rates consistent with the adjusted *Laffey* matrix applied. *Id.*

Next, the Arbitrator rejected the Agency's claim that the *Laffey* matrices could not apply because the attorneys' geographical area of practice is Baltimore,

2. Section 7701(g)(1) provides, in pertinent part, that the Merit Systems Protection Board (the Board or MSPB) "may require payment by the agency involved of reasonable attorney fees incurred by an employee . . . if the employee . . . is the prevailing party and the Board . . . determines that payment by the agency is warranted in the interest of justice[.]"

3. In *Allen*, the MSPB listed five broad categories of cases in which an award of attorney fees would be warranted in the interest of justice: (1) where the agency engaged in a prohibited personnel practices; (2) where the agency action was clearly without merit or wholly unfounded or the employee was substantially innocent of charges brought by the agency; (3) where the agency initiated the action in bad faith; (4) where the agency committed a gross procedural error; and (5) where the agency knew or should have known that the it would not prevail on the merits when it brought the proceeding. *Allen*, 2 M.S.P.R. at 434-35. An award of fees is also warranted in the interest of justice in cases brought under the Statute when there is a service to the federal workforce or a benefit to the public derived from maintaining the action. *U.S. Dep't of the Navy, Commander, Navy Region Haw., Fed. Fire Dep't, Naval Station Pearl Harbor, Honolulu, Haw.*, 64 FLRA 925, 928 (2010).

4. The *Laffey* matrix sets forth a method for determining the appropriate hourly rate for attorneys in the Washington, D.C. area. *AFGE, Local 2608*, 63 FLRA 486, 487 n.2 (2009). As recognized by the Arbitrator and as explained by the court in *Smith v. D.C.*, 466 F. Supp. 2d 151 (D.D.C. 2006), there are two versions of the matrix. One version is maintained by the Civil Division of the Office of the United States Attorney, which calculates the matrix rate for each year by adding the change in the overall cost of living as reflected in the United States consumer price index (CPI) for the Washington, D.C. area for the prior year and rounding that rate to the nearest multiple of $5. 466 F. Supp 2d at 156. That version is commonly referred to as the *Laffey* matrix. By contrast, the so-called "adjusted" *Laffey* matrix calculates the matrix rates for each year by using the legal services component of the CPI rather than the general CPI. *Id.*

Maryland, and the *Laffey* matrices apply only to attorneys practicing in Washington, D.C. *Id.* at 51-52. In this connection, the Arbitrator found that the attorneys' practice was not limited to Baltimore. *Id.* at 52. The Arbitrator also found that the adjusted *Laffey* matrix had the advantage in comparison with the *Laffey* matrix of being based specifically on the price of legal services. *Id.* at 50. In addition, the Arbitrator noted that, in the settlement of another case, the Agency had accepted, as reasonable, rates that were consistent with the adjusted *Laffey* matrix. *Id.* at 53.

For these reasons, the Arbitrator concluded that it was appropriate to apply rates consistent with the adjusted *Laffey* matrix. In calculating the amount of fees, the Arbitrator applied the adjusted *Laffey* rates existing at the time of the award, rather than the time of the performance of the legal services. He did so "because interest is not payable on attorney fees earned in prior periods." *Id.* at 54.

III. Positions of the Parties

A. Agency's Exceptions

The Agency contends that the Arbitrator erred by concluding that an award of fees was warranted in the interest of justice. As to *Allen* criterion 5, the Agency maintains that, when it brought the disciplinary actions, it relied on the uncontested facts that the grievants were absent from duty without approved leave. The Agency also maintains that it relied on the belief that the grievants were not credible and that the Arbitrator confirmed this belief by finding that they were not credible witnesses. Exceptions at 16. The Agency also notes that the Arbitrator found that it did not realize that its certification policy precluded proving the alleged charges. *Id.* In addition, although the Agency concedes that it did not file exceptions to the remand award, *id.* at 5, the Agency disputes the Arbitrator's finding in that award that the Agency could not prove an intentional falsification charge based on an omission, *id.* at 17. The Agency asserts that, contrary to the finding of the Arbitrator, it had a reasonable basis for charging the grievants with falsifying their time cards. *Id.* Further, the Agency argues that the Arbitrator erroneously determined that its actions were clearly without merit under *Allen* criterion 2, *id.* at 10-13, and that there was a benefit to the public in bringing the grievance, *id.* at 17.

Additionally, the Agency contends that, if an award of fees is warranted in the interest of justice, then the award is deficient because the hourly rates are not reasonable. The Agency argues that the fee agreement establishes the reduced fee amount as the maximum fee available under § 7701(g) because that fee constitutes the attorneys' customary billing rate. *Id.* at 19. Alternatively, the Agency argues that the Arbitrator erred by applying the adjusted *Laffey* matrix either because the attorneys practice in Baltimore or because he should have applied the *Laffey* matrix maintained by the Office of the U.S. Attorney, instead. *Id.* at 20-22. In addition, the Agency alleges that the Arbitrator inappropriately relied on the Agency's acceptance of the adjusted *Laffey* matrix in a settlement of another case because that case was a settlement rather than an arbitration award and the circumstances were not comparable. *Id.* at 21-22.

Finally, the Agency asserts that the Arbitrator erred by applying the adjusted *Laffey* matrix rates as they existed on the date of the award, rather than as they existed when the attorneys rendered their services. In this connection, the Agency maintains that the MSPB has held that fees may not be enhanced under § 7701(g) by applying current rates retroactively. *Id.* at 23.

B. Union's Opposition

As to the Agency's contention that an award of fees is not warranted in the interest of justice, the Union argues that *Allen* criterion 5 was satisfied because the evidence showed that the Agency knew or should have known that it would not prevail. Opp'n at 6. The Union also argues that *Allen* criterion 2 was satisfied and that an award of fees was warranted in the interest of justice under the Statute. *Id.* at 5, 7-8.

As to reasonableness of the amount, the Union asserts that the fee agreement did not establish the reduced fee amount as the maximum available under § 7701(g) and that the Arbitrator correctly awarded fees at the adjusted *Laffey* rates. *Id.* at 8, 10-17. In addition, the Union argues that the Arbitrator's determination of the appropriate billing rate is a factual finding to which the Authority must defer. *Id.* at 17. Finally, the Union alleges that awarding attorney fees at current prevailing rates is commonplace under other fee-shifting statutes. *Id.* at 18-19.

IV. Analysis and Conclusions

When an exception involves an award's consistency with law, the Authority reviews *de novo* any questions of law raised by the exception and the award.[5] *E.g., U.S. Dep't of the Navy, Commander, Navy Region Haw., Fed. Fire Dep't, Naval Station Pearl Harbor, Honolulu, Haw.*, 64 FLRA 925, 928 (2010) (*Dep't of the Navy*). In applying a standard of *de novo* review, the Authority assesses whether an arbitrator's legal conclusions are consistent with the applicable standard of law. In making that assessment, the Authority defers to the arbitrator's underlying factual findings. *Id.* In addition, the award in this case must be in accordance with the standards established under § 7701(g)(1). *Id.* The Agency contends that the award is not in accordance with these standards because, according to the Agency: (1) the award of fees is not in the interest of justice; and (2) the amount of fees is not reasonable. As such, we address only those requirements. *Id.*

A. Interest of Justice

The Authority resolves whether an award of fees is warranted in the interest of justice in accordance with § 7701(g)(1) by applying the criteria established by the MSPB in *Allen*. As recognized by the Arbitrator, an award of fees is warranted in the interest of justice if any one of the criteria is satisfied. *U.S. Dep't of the Air Force, Davis-Monthan Air Force Base, Tucson, Ariz.*, 64 FLRA 819, 821 (2010).

Under *Allen* criterion 5, an award of fees is warranted in the interest of justice when the agency "knew or should have known that it would not prevail on the merits" when it brought the proceeding. *Allen*, 2 M.S.P.R. at 435. This determination requires evaluation of the nature and weight of the evidence available to the agency at the time of the disputed action. *Soc. Sec. Admin., Balt., Md.*, 63 FLRA 550, 552 (2009). Accordingly, arbitrators must determine the reasonableness of the agency's actions and positions in light of the information available to it at the time of the disputed action. *Id.* The assessment of whether an agency knew or should have known that it would not prevail is primarily factual because it is based on the arbitrator's evaluation of the evidence and the agency's handling of that evidence. *Id.* Consequently, when the arbitrator's factual findings support the arbitrator's legal conclusion, the Authority denies an exception to the application of criterion 5. *Id.*

Here, the Arbitrator set forth specific factual findings in support of his legal conclusion that the Agency should have known that it would not prevail on the merits when it brought the disciplinary actions. Specifically, the Arbitrator found that, under the Agency's certification policy for time and attendance, it could not prove an intentional falsification charge on the basis of an omission from an employee's time sheet and that the Agency should have known this when it brought the disciplinary actions. These factual findings support the Arbitrator's legal conclusion that fees were warranted in the interest of justice because the Agency knew or should have known that it would not prevail when it brought the disciplinary actions. *See id.*

We reject the Agency's contention that these findings do not support the Arbitrator's legal conclusion because "the evidence presented did not show the agency *actually realized and understood* that its certification policy precluded proving the charges alleged." Fee Award at 45 (emphasis added). In this regard, *Allen* criterion 5, as quoted above, encompasses what the Agency "should have known" -- not only what it "knew" -- when it brought the disputed action. *Allen*, 2 M.S.P.R. at 435. Thus, the Agency's reliance on that statement does not demonstrate that the Arbitrator erred in concluding that *Allen* criterion 5 was satisfied. With regard to the Agency's assertion that the Arbitrator erroneously found in the remand award that it could not prove the falsification charges, the Agency concedes that it did not file exceptions to that award. As such, that award is final, and the Agency may not, at this stage, challenge these findings. *See U.S. Dep't of the Navy, Naval Undersea Warfare Ctr., Newport, R.I.*, 57 FLRA 32, 34 (2001). Accordingly, we defer to the Arbitrator's factual findings and deny the Agency's exception regarding whether an award of fees was warranted in the interest of justice.[6]

B. Reasonableness of Rate

The requirement of § 7701(g)(1) that the amount of fees be reasonable has two components: (1) reasonableness of the hourly rate; and (2) reasonableness of the number of hours expended. *See U.S. Dep't of Homeland Sec., Immigration & Customs Enforcement*, 64 FLRA 1003, 1007 (2010)

---

5. Contrary to the Union's claim, the Arbitrator's determination of hourly rate is a legal conclusion reviewed *de novo*. *See U.S. Dep't of Homeland Sec., Immigration & Customs Enforcement*, 64 FLRA 1003 (2010) (arbitrator's determination of hourly rate reviewed *de novo*).

6. As noted, an award of fees is warranted in the interest of justice if any one of the criteria is satisfied. Thus, we find it unnecessary to resolve the Agency's exceptions regarding the additional criteria on which the Arbitrator relied.

(*ICE*). Here, only the reasonableness of the hourly rate is disputed.

The fee agreement between the Union and the attorneys provides that the attorneys may charge the Union a reduced fee, but that the attorneys would charge hourly rates consistent with the adjusted *Laffey* matrix upon receipt of a successful decision. *Dep't of the Army*, 62 FLRA at 73. In *United States Department of Agriculture, Animal and Plant Health Inspection Service, Plant Protection and Quarantine*, 53 FLRA 1688, 1692 (1998) (*PPQ*), the Authority held that a similar fee agreement permitted the arbitrator to award fees at the law firm's non-retainer, billing rates as long as they were reasonable and consistent with prevailing market rates. Accordingly, on the basis of *PPQ*, we deny the Agency's exception contending that the reduced fee must apply.

In addition, the Authority has specifically identified the *Laffey* matrix as "the Washington, D.C./Baltimore rate" and applied it to an attorney whose "ordinary community of practice is the Washington, D.C./Baltimore area" while "home base[d]" in Baltimore. *AFGE, Local 2608*, 63 FLRA 486, 487-88 (2010). Moreover, the Authority's approach is consistent with the judicial approach to the matrix. *Cobell v. Norton*, 231 F. Supp. 2d 295, 302 (D.D.C. 2002) (describing the matrix as establishing a standard hourly rate for attorneys in "the Baltimore-Washington area"). Accordingly, the fact that the attorneys' office is located in Baltimore provides no basis for finding the application of adjusted *Laffey* matrix rates deficient.

The Arbitrator's application of the adjusted *Laffey* matrix, instead of the *Laffey* matrix, also provides no basis for finding the award deficient. Although the Authority has not addressed whether use of the adjusted *Laffey* matrix, rather than the *Laffey* matrix, is appropriate for an award of attorney fees in accordance with the standards of § 7701(g)(1), the court in *DL v. D.C.*, 256 F.R.D. 239 (D.D.C. 2009), noted that the U.S. Court of Appeals for the D.C. Circuit has not expressed a preference between the *Laffey* matrix and the adjusted *Laffey* matrix and has "suggested that the trial court should have discretion in determining the appropriate rates." 256 F.R.D. at 243 & n.4. In view of this approach by the court that established the matrices, we conclude that the Arbitrator was not precluded from applying the adjusted *Laffey* matrix as a matter of law.

The Agency further fails to demonstrate that the adjusted *Laffey* matrix does not establish reasonable hourly rates consistent with prevailing market rates for the Union's attorneys. In this regard, courts have affirmed the award of attorney fees at adjusted *Laffey* matrix rates as reasonable for attorneys practicing in the Washington, D.C./Baltimore, Maryland area. *Salazar v. D.C.*, 123 F. Supp. 2d 8, 15 (D.D.C. 2000). In addition, the Union's attorneys provided the Arbitrator with case citations demonstrating that they have been awarded attorney fees at adjusted *Laffey* matrix rates. Specifically, the Equal Employment Opportunity Commission awarded the Union's attorneys fees at adjusted *Laffey* matrix rates in *Doe v. SSA*, Case No. 120-2003-00498X (2007). The Union's attorneys also submitted arbitration awards in which arbitrators awarded them fees at adjusted *Laffey* matrix rates and settlement agreements in which other agency employers agreed to pay them fees at adjusted *Laffey* matrix rates. In view of this extensive precedent and evidence, the Agency's dispute with the Arbitrator's reliance on the settlement agreement in which the Agency agreed to pay adjusted *Laffey* matrix rates fails to establish that the award is deficient. *Cf. U.S. Dep't of Def., Educ. Activity, Arlington, Va.*, 57 FLRA 23, 26 (2001) (agency failed to establish that the hourly rate awarded by the arbitrator did not reflect the prevailing billing rate in the community for similar services by lawyers of reasonably comparable skill, experience, and reputation). Accordingly, we deny this exception.

In its final exception, the Agency contends that the Arbitrator's application of adjusted *Laffey* matrix rates as they existed on the date of the award, rather than as they existed when the attorneys rendered their services, is contrary to § 7701(g)(1), as interpreted and applied by the MSPB. When an exception contends that an award is contrary to § 7701(g)(1), the Authority looks to the decisions of the MSPB and follows its practices in resolving the exception. *AFGE, Local 2608*, 63 FLRA at 487. In interpreting and applying § 7701(g)(1), the MSPB has recognized that there is no explicit provision for interest on attorney fees. *Krape v. DOD*, 97 M.S.P.R. 430, 435 (2004). Consequently, the MSPB does not permit the retroactive application of current hourly rates to account for delay in payment of attorney fees. *Id.* The Arbitrator's application of adjusted *Laffey* matrix rates as they existed on the date of the award retroactively to account for no provision for interest is contrary to the MSPB's standards and practices established under § 7701(g)(1). *See id.* The Union does not dispute MSPB's practice, but claims, instead, that such enhancement is commonplace under other fee-shifting statutes. However, the standards of other fee-shifting statutes are not relevant because the Arbitrator's award must be in accordance with the standards established under § 7701(g)(1), which it is not. On this basis, we modify the award to provide that the amount of fees must be recalculated at the adjusted *Laffey* matrix rates as they existed at the time of performance of the legal services.

V. Decision

The fee award is modified to provide that the amount of fees must be recalculated at the adjusted *Laffey* matrix rates as they existed at the time of performance of the legal services. The remaining exceptions are denied.

65 FLRA No. 16

TIDEWATER VIRGINIA
FEDERAL EMPLOYEES
METAL TRADES COUNCIL
(Union)

and

UNITED STATES
DEPARTMENT OF THE NAVY
NAVAL FACILITIES
ENGINEERING COMMAND
MID-ATLANTIC (NAVFAC MIDLANT)
(Agency)

0-AR-4659

DECISION

September 9, 2010

Before the Authority: Carol Waller Pope, Chairman, and Thomas M. Beck and Ernest DuBester, Members

This matter is before the Authority on exceptions to an award of Arbitrator Edward C. Johnson filed by the Union under § 7122(a) of the Federal Service Labor-Management Relations Statute (the Statute) and part 2425 of the Authority's Regulations.*

Under § 7122(a) of the Statute, an award is deficient if it is contrary to any law, rule, or regulation, or if it is deficient on other grounds similar to those applied by federal courts in private sector labor-management relations. Upon careful consideration of the entire record in this case and Authority precedent, the Authority concludes that the award is not deficient on the grounds raised in the exceptions and set forth in § 7122(a). *See AFGE, Local 1668*, 50 FLRA 124, 126 (1995) (award not deficient on ground that arbitrator failed to provide a fair hearing where excepting party fails to demonstrate that the arbitrator refused to hear or consider pertinent and material evidence, or that other actions in conducting the proceeding so prejudiced a party so as to affect the fairness of the proceeding as a whole); *U.S. Dep't of Labor (OSHA)*, 34 FLRA 573, 575 (1990) (award not deficient as failing to draw its essence from the parties' collective bargaining agreement where excepting party fails to establish that the award cannot in any rational way be derived from the agreement; is so unfounded in reason and fact and so unconnected to the wording and purpose of the agreement as to manifest an infidelity to the obligation of the arbitrator; does not represent a plausible interpretation of the agreement; or evidences a manifest disregard of the agreement).

Accordingly, the Union's exceptions are denied.

* The Agency filed an opposition to the Union's exceptions. The Authority issued an Order to Show Cause (Order) requiring the Agency to show why its opposition should not be rejected as untimely. Order at 2. In its response, the Agency effectively concedes that it miscalculated the due date for filling its opposition. Agency's Response to Order at 1. As the Agency has failed to establish extraordinary circumstances warranting waiving the expired time limit, we will not consider the Agency's opposition. *See U.S. Dep't of Homeland Sec., U.S. Customs & Border Prot.*, 64 FLRA 916, 918-19 (2010) (union's opposition not considered where union conceded that its opposition was "technically untimely" and failed to establish extraordinary circumstances to excuse the lack of timeliness).

65 FLRA No. 17

UNITED STATES
DEPARTMENT OF THE AIR FORCE
RANDOLPH AIR FORCE BASE
SAN ANTONIO, TEXAS
(Respondent)

and

AMERICAN FEDERATION
OF GOVERNMENT EMPLOYEES
LOCAL 1840
(Charging Party/Union)

DA-CA-09-0109

DECISION AND ORDER

September 13, 2010

Before the Authority: Carol Waller Pope, Chairman, and Thomas M. Beck and Ernest DuBester, Members

I. Statement of the Case

This unfair labor practice case is before the Authority on exceptions to the attached decision of the Administrative Law Judge (Judge) filed by the General Counsel (GC). The Respondent filed an opposition to the GC's exceptions.

The complaint alleges that the Respondent violated § 7116(a)(1) and (5) of the Federal Service Labor-Management Relations Statute (the Statute) by refusing to bargain in good faith with the Union. The Judge found that the Respondent did not violate the Statute as alleged because the Union failed to submit substantive proposals to the Respondent, as required by the parties' collective bargaining agreement.*

Upon consideration of the decision and the entire record, we adopt the Judge's findings, conclusions, and recommended order and deny the GC's exceptions.

II. Order

The complaint is dismissed.

* In its exceptions, the GC challenges several of the Judge's factual findings and credibility determinations. In determining whether a judge's factual findings are supported, the Authority looks to the preponderance of the record evidence. *U.S. Dep't of Def., Def. Language Inst., Foreign Language Ctr., Monterey, Cal.*, 64 FLRA 735, 744 (2010) (*DOD*) (Member Beck dissenting in pertinent part). Additionally, the Authority will not overrule a judge's credibility determination unless a clear preponderance of all relevant evidence demonstrates that the determination was incorrect. *Id.* at 743. Here, the Judge's factual findings are supported by a preponderance of the record evidence, and the GC has failed to demonstrate, by a clear preponderance of all relevant evidence, that any of the Judge's credibility determinations were incorrect. Moreover, the plain wording of the parties' collective bargaining agreement (CBA) supports the Judge's interpretation of the CBA as requiring the submission of substantive proposals along with a request to renegotiate the CBA. *See* Judge's Decision at 3, 9. In this regard, the CBA distinguishes the "written proposals for negotiation[]" that a party must submit along with a request to renegotiate the CBA from "[g]round rules" proposals that the parties develop together. *See id.* at 3.

Member Beck notes that, for the reasons stated in his separate opinions in *U.S. Dep't of the Air Force, 12th Flying Training Wing, Randolph Air Force Base, San Antonio, Tex.*, 63 FLRA 256 (2009) and *U.S. Dep't of the Air Force, Air Force Materiel Command, Space & Missile Sys. Ctr., Detachment 12, Kirtland Air Force Base, N.M.*, 64 FLRA 166 (2009), he reviews the Judge's factual findings using a "substantial evidence in the record" standard rather than a "preponderance" standard.

Office of Administrative Law Judges

U.S. DEPARTMENT OF THE AIR FORCE
RANDOLPH AIR FORCE BASE
SAN ANTONIO, TEXAS
Respondent

and

AMERICAN FEDERATION
OF GOVERNMENT EMPLOYEES, LOCAL 1840
Charging Party

Case No. DA-CA-09-0109

Michael A. Quintanilla, Esq.
For the General Counsel

J. Todd Hedgepeth, Esq.
For the Respondent

Paul D. Palacio
For the Charging Party

Before: SUSAN E. JELEN
Administrative Law Judge

DECISION

This case arose under the Federal Service Labor-Management Relations Statute, Chapter 71 of Title 5 of the United States Code, 5 U.S.C. §7101, *et. seq.* (the Statute), and the Rules and Regulations of the Federal Labor Relations Authority (the Authority/FLRA), 5 C.F.R. Part 2423.

On February 4, 2009, the American Federation of Government Employees, Local 1840 (Charging Party or Union), filed an unfair labor practice charge with the Dallas Region of the Authority against the U.S. Department of the Air Force, Randolph Air Force Base, San Antonio, Texas (Respondent or Randolph AFB). (G.C. Ex. 1(a)) On October 30, 2009, the Regional Director of the Dallas Region of the Authority issued a Complaint and Notice of Hearing, which alleged that the Respondent violated section 7116(a)(1) and (5) of the Statute by refusing to bargain in good faith by refusing to negotiate a new collective bargaining agreement with the Union. (G.C. Ex. 1(d)) On November 24, 2009, the Respondent filed an Answer to the complaint, in which it admitted certain allegations while denying the substantive allegations of the complaint. (G.C. Ex. 1(h))

A hearing was held in San Antonio, Texas on January 19, 2010, at which time all parties were afforded a full opportunity to be represented, to be heard, to examine and cross-examine witnesses, to introduce evidence and to argue orally. The General Counsel and the Respondent filed timely post-hearing briefs, which have been fully considered.

Based upon the entire record, including my observation of the witnesses and their demeanor, I make the following findings of fact, conclusions and recommendations.

STATEMENT OF THE FACTS

The Respondent is an agency within the meaning of section 7103(a)(3) of the Statute. (G.C. Ex. 1(d), (h)) The Union is a labor organization within the meaning of section 7103(a)(4) of the Statute. (G.C. Ex. 1(d), (h)) Kim Bailey occupied the position of Labor Relations Officer at Randolph AFB from at least June 2008 through December 2008, and, at all times material to this matter, has been a supervisor and/or management official within the meaning of section 7103(a)(10) and (11) of the Statute. (G.C. Ex. 1(d), (h); Tr. 77)

Randolph AFB and the Union are parties to a collective bargaining agreement entitled *Memorandum of Agreement between Commander, 12th Support Group, Randolph Air Force Base, Texas and Local 1840, American Federation of Government Employees, AFL-CIO,* (Jt. Ex. 1)(CBA). The CBA was originally signed on August 6, 1993, and was rolled over at three year intervals in 1996, 1999, 2002, and 2005. Article 8, Duration of Agreement, states, in part:

> 8-2. This agreement will remain in effect for three years from the date of its approval by HQ AETC. On the third anniversary of its approval and each three years thereafter, it will automatically be renewed for an additional three year term unless, during the period between 105 and 60 days prior to the end of one of the three year terms, either Party gives written notice to the other Party of its desire to renegotiate the agreement. It is understood that this agreement will be terminated if it is officially determined that the Union is no longer entitled to exclusive recognition under Title VII.

> 8-3. Written notice of either Party's desire to renegotiate the agreement will be accompanied by the Party's written proposals for negotiation. Ground rules for the negotiations will be drawn up by mutual agreement and in compliance with applicable directives. The negotiations will be scheduled to begin within 60 days after the second Party receives the written notice, unless both Parties agree to a later date. The existing agreement will remain in effect until such time as the new agreement is signed by the Parties and approved by HQ AETC. (Jt. Ex. 1)

On June 9, 2008,[1] Vance Miller, President, AFGE, Local 1840, sent the following letter to Kim Bailey, Labor Relations Officer:

> Subject: Contract Negotiations
>
> 1. Pursuant to Memorandum of Agreement (Contract) between the American Federation of Government Employees, AFL-CIO (AFGE-Union) Local 1840 and 12th MSG, Article 8, Section 8-2, the Union is hereby providing notification of Intent to Re-Negotiate the Contract.
> 2. The Union desires to Re-Negotiate all Articles of the Contract.
> 3. The Union will provide its written proposal's (sic) and ground rules no later than ten (10) business days prior to the start of negotiations.
> 4. The Union request (sic) that negotiations of the Contract to start no later than October 1, 2008, and continue through completion.
> 5. Should there be any questions contact the undersigned.

(G.C. Ex. 2; Tr. 45, 57-58)

The Respondent did not furnish a written reply to the Union's demand to bargain; however, there were ongoing discussions between Bailey and Miller regarding the status of proposals from June through September 2008. Specifically, Miller testified that on several occasions he asked Bailey when he would be receiving the Respondent's ground rules proposals; while Bailey testified that on several occasions she asked Miller when the Respondent would be receiving the Union's ground rules and substantive proposals. (Tr. 59-60, 64, 81, 99)

Sometime in August, Miller contacted Paul Palacio, AFGE National Representative, regarding his frustrations with the Respondent's lack of action. Palacio contacted Bailey, who agreed to send him the Respondent's ground rules proposals.[2] (G.C. Ex. 3; Tr. 16-17, 19)

Miller, Palacio and Mark Gibson, AFGE, AFL-CIO Labor Relations Specialist, met in late September to discuss the status of the negotiations and the Union's ground rules proposals. The Union determined at that time that it wanted to poll its bargaining unit employees to determine what issues were the most important to them. The Union officials thought it would be helpful if they were allowed to have a meeting of employees at a facility at Randolph AFB. Miller agreed to contact Bailey for permission. According to Palacio, if Bailey would not agree to this group meeting, he intended to add this request to the Union's ground rules proposals, which he was still in the process of creating. (Tr. 20-21, 61-62)

On September 30, Miller approached Bailey to ask if the Union could meet with all the bargaining unit employees in an auditorium to present them with a survey that the Union created. (G.C. Ex. 6; Tr. 61-62, 80) While Bailey did not agree with the proposed group meeting, she did agree that the Union could present the survey to employees in their break rooms. (G.C. Ex. 4; Tr. 62) Bailey also informed Miller that she had not received the Union's ground rules proposals. (G.C. Ex. 4; Tr. 63)

In a series of emails in late September, Miller and Palacio discussed the survey and the status of the Union's ground rules proposals. (G.C. Ex. 4) Palacio reminded Miller of the decision to delay the ground rules proposals until Bailey responded to their request for the group meeting. Palacio asked Miller

1. All dates are in 2008, unless otherwise specified.

2. Bailey asserted that the document she sent to Palacio on August 30 was not the Respondent's ground rules proposal, but rather a sample of ground rules that she had used in a previous contract negotiation. (Tr. 79) She did change some of the information to reflect the correct parties and left certain date information blank to be filled in at a later time, following negotiations. Palacio appears to have assumed that the document was, in fact, the Respondent's ground rules proposal. However, I credit Bailey that this document was meant to serve as a sample for the Union's ground rules proposals. This is entirely consistent with the Respondent's position that the requesting party (in this case the Union) was required to submit the initial proposals.

if the break room drop was sufficient for his needs. (G.C. Ex. 4) On October 1, Miller responded that the break room drop was sufficient and that the Union was making 500 copies and would start distribution on the next Monday (which would be Monday, October 6, 2008). (G.C. Ex. 4, 6)

According to the Union, late on October 1, Palacio emailed the Union's ground rules proposal to Bailey. (G.C. Ex. 5) Bailey denies ever receiving this proposal from Palacio. (Tr. 79, 86)[3]

On October 2, Bailey sent the following Memorandum to Miller, titled *Contract Negotiations*:

1. On 9 June 2008, AFGE Local 1840 provided notice to this office of its intent to re-negotiate the contract (attachment 1). In accordance with Article 8, 8.3 "Written notice of either Party's desire to renegotiate the agreement will be accompanied by the Party's written proposals for negotiation." Since no proposals were received, your intent to request to begin contract negotiations is being returned without action. The timeframe to request full term negotiations has expired.

2. If you would like to request negotiations for mid-term bargaining, you may submit a written request identifying the articles you wish to negotiate along with the proposed changes. Such a request must be submitted no earlier than 16 months after the effective date of the contract and no later than 18 months after the effective date of the contract.

3. Should you have any questions please feel free to contact me at (210) 652-4658.

(G.C. Ex. 7)

The Union did make an attempt to get the negotiations back on track, but was unsuccessful. (Tr. 49-50, 95)

POSITIONS OF THE PARTIES

General Counsel

Counsel for the General Counsel (GC) asserts that the Union properly submitted a memo requesting to renegotiate the existing collective bargaining agreement on June 9, 2008. Respondent had a duty to bargain and by refusing to do so, by letter dated October 1, failed to bargain in good faith with the Union in violation of section 7116(a)(1) and (5) of the Statute. The GC argues that the parties' CBA does not provide the Respondent with a defense to do what would otherwise be a violation of section 7116(a)(1) and (5). *Internal Revenue Service, Wash., D.C.*, 47 FLRA 1091 (1993)(*IRS*); *Social Security Administration,* 64 FLRA 199, 202 (2009).

The GC argues that the parties were engaged in the bargaining of a new contract from June 9, 2008 through October 2, 2008. On June 9 the Union stated its desire to renegotiate the entire agreement and proposed negotiations begin no later than October 1. This was an obvious ground rules proposal, which did not foreclose the possibility that negotiations could begin earlier or later. The GC asserts that the Respondent's argument that the October 1 date was a "deadline" for negotiations which, if not met, foreclosed all negotiations, is ridiculous and should be disregarded. The GC also notes that another ground rules proposal contained in the June 9 memo concerned the submission of substantive proposals at least ten days before start of negotiations. Again, Respondent now argues that this "deadline" imposed an affirmative duty on the Union and, since it was not met, the Respondent was free to terminate negotiations. The GC argues that the Respondent's deadline theory is "exceptionally unreasonable". The GC argues that substantive negotiations were not set to begin on October 1, and to suggest that the parties agreed that the Union would submit written proposals ten days prior to October 1, whether or not negotiations were set to begin on that day or not is unsupported by the record.

3. I credit Bailey's testimony that she never received this document from the Union. I found her testimony straight forward throughout this proceeding. Although the General Counsel submitted emails regarding the service of this document, I find its late appearance in the record questionable. I note that the Union never referenced sending ground rules proposals to the Agency in its initial unfair labor practice charge in this matter, although it listed other correspondence. (G.C. Ex. 1(a)) Further, in its attempts to have the Agency renew the negotiations after the October 2 letter, it never mentioned that it had submitted ground rules proposals. (Tr. 54-55) The Union offered no explanation for these apparent inconsistencies.

The GC argues that the Respondent unilaterally terminated negotiations on October 2. The GC notes that, if the Respondent truly had an issue relating to the timing of the Union's substantive proposals, it could have refused to bargain in June. The Respondent did not do this, however, and continued to deal with the Union on a regular basis from June through September.

The GC specifically argues that the Respondent's interpretation of Article 8, Section 8-3 is unsupported by the record evidence. The Respondent claims that the Union was required to submit all proposals for the negotiation of a new contract when it submitted notice of its desire to renegotiate the parties' agreement. This interpretation ignores the realities of collective bargaining, in particular, term bargaining, which requires multiple exchanges of multiple proposals in a give and take exchange.

Finally, the GC argues that even if the judge concludes that the plain language of Article 8, Section 8-3 called for submission of any and all substantive proposals on the entire contract when it submitted its demand to bargain, there is substantial evidence in the record to demonstrate that the parties agreed to a different process for this particular negotiation.

Respondent

The Respondent argues that it did not violate the Statute in this matter, but that at all times it approached negotiations with a sincere resolve to reach agreement. It received the Union's request to negotiate and agreed to a requested extension for a "no later than" October 1, 2008 deadline. The Respondent also agreed to the Union's request that they provide its written proposals and ground rules no later than 10 business days prior to the start of the negotiations (thus, 10 days prior to October 1). The Respondent reminded the Union on numerous occasions that they needed to submit substantive proposals prior to the October 1 deadline. The Respondent provided sample ground rules to assist the Union in the drafting of their proposed ground rules. The Union, however, did nothing between June 9 and October 1.

The Respondent argues that it is important to look at the Union's behavior and not just the Respondent's. In order to protect their right to bargain, the Union must timely request to bargain, submit negotiable proposals, bargain in good faith, and timely request FSIP assistance if impasse is reached. *United States Dep't of Labor, Wash., D.C.*, 60 FLRA 68, 70 (2004). While the Union did timely request to bargain, they never submitted any negotiable proposals on any articles of the existing agreement. It was the Union that failed to bargain in good faith in this matter.

The Respondent argues that the negotiations on the CBA could not start until the Union provided written proposals on the articles of the agreement they desired to renegotiate. See Article 8, Section 8-3. Having received no written proposals in accordance with the Union's own request to negotiate, the Respondent properly returned their request to renegotiate without action.

ANALYSIS AND CONCLUSIONS

The GC asserts that after the Union submitted a timely notice of the reopening of the CBA, the Respondent was obligated to negotiate a new contract with the Union and its refusal to do so violated section 7116(a)(1) and (5) of the Statute. Since the Respondent justifies its conduct by an interpretation of the CBA, I am required by *IRS*, 47 FLRA at 1103, 1110 to determine the meaning of the disputed provisions.

In its *IRS* decision, the Authority held:

> [W]hen a respondent claims as a defense to an alleged unfair labor practice that a specific provision of the parties' collective bargaining agreement permitted its actions alleged to constitute an unfair labor practice, the Authority, including its administrative law judges, will determine the meaning of the parties' collective bargaining agreement and will resolve the unfair labor practice complaint accordingly.

Id. at 1103.

The Authority also stated:

> [O]nce the General Counsel makes a prima facie showing that a respondent's actions would constitute a violation of a statutory right, the respondent may rebut the General Counsel's showing . . . by establishing by a preponderance of the evidence that the parties' collective bargaining agreement allowed the respondent's actions.

Id. at 1110.

The basic facts in this matter are clear: on June 9, the Union timely requests to reopen the parties' collective bargaining, indicating its desire to negotiate all of the provisions of the agreement. No substantive proposals are included with the request, but the Union does request that the negotiations begin no later than October 1 and that its proposals be submitted ten days before the beginning of negotiations. There is no written response from the Respondent. Representatives of the Union (President and National Representative) and the Respondent (Labor Relations Officer) do have ongoing discussions about the negotiations, mainly regarding when either party will receive the other's proposals.[4]

In September, with the initial October date looming, the parties increase communications. At no time, however, does the Union ever submit substantive proposals. Finally, in the afternoon of October 1, the Union submits ground rules proposals, which the Respondent denies receiving. On October 2, the Respondent returns the Union's request to bargain over the parties' CBA, stating that it has no duty to bargain since the Union has not followed the contract and submitted substantive proposals.

The Respondent asserts that its actions were allowed by Section 8-3 of the parties' CBA. This section, as noted above, states in part:

> Written notice of either Party's desire to renegotiate the agreement will be accompanied by the Party's written proposals for negotiation. Ground rules for the negotiations will be drawn up by mutual agreement and in compliance with applicable directives.

Using the standards and principles for interpreting collective bargaining agreements applied by arbitrators and the Federal courts, in addition to Authority case law, I conclude that the CBA requires that written proposals accompany the written notice of the desire to renegotiate. The plain language of the article specifically states that "written notice . . . to renegotiate the agreement **will** be accompanied by the Party's written proposals for negotiation." (emphasis added) I find that this language requires the requesting Party to submit its substantive proposals on the new collective bargaining agreement with its request to renegotiate. It is undisputed that the Union did not submit substantive proposals with its request to renegotiate or at any time thereafter. *See U.S. Dep't of Justice, Immigration and Naturalization Service, Wash., D.C.,* 52 FLRA 256 (1996).

In support of its position, the GC cites to the D.C. Circuit's decision in *Nat'l Ass'n of Gov't Employees, Local R5-136 v. FLRA,* 363 F.3d 468 (D.C. Cir. 2004)(*NAGE Local R5-136*) , which reversed, in part, the Authority's decision in *Dep't of Veterans Affairs, Ralph H. Johnson Medical Center, Charleston, S.C.,* 58 FLRA 432 (2003)(*Johnson Med. Ctr.).* The Court stated that the Authority relied on "an entirely untenable interpretation of the parties' collective bargaining agreement" in finding that the Agency did not violate the Statute. The Court found that the Union, in a mid-term bargaining request, met the collective bargaining agreement's requirements by meeting the deadline for requesting negotiation in the matter and submitting a written proposal. The Court found that the provision of the collective bargaining agreement could not reasonably be interpreted to require the Union to put all plausible proposals on the table within that brief period or to foreclose negotiation of any proposal submitted thereafter.[5]

The GC argues that the contractual provision and demand to bargain in the *Johnson Med. Ctr.* case are analogous to Section 8-3 and the demand to bargain in this case. In *Johnson Med. Ctr.,* a unilateral change case, the Union made *a status quo* request and was required to submit its proposals after the review of the information provided in response to an information request. The GC argues that, in this case, the Union requested to negotiate all articles of the contract, requested a date to begin negotiations on or before October 1, 2008, and requested to submit its substantive proposals ten days prior to when negotiations would begin. While the facts differ, those differences do not alter the meaning that must be taken from that case. The Circuit Court's decision contains recognition that bargaining in the labor context necessarily involves multiple exchanges of

4. The GC asserts that, to the extent the Respondent suggests that Palacio was not a representative of the Union for the purpose of these negotiations, the record demonstrates that Palacio was acting on behalf of the Union. *See United States Dep't of the Air Force, 12th Flying Training Wing, Randolph AFB, San Antonio, TX.* 63 FLRA 256 (2009). The Respondent, however, has not raised this issue in its brief and a ruling in this matter is unnecessary.

5. In a footnote, the Respondent argued that the Authority's decision in *Johnson Med. Ctr.* is not relevant, particularly noting the dissent of then-Member Pope. The Respondent failed to discuss the Court's decision in this matter.

proposals. In both cases the Respondent interpreted those provisions to mean all substantive proposals had to be submitted with the request to negotiate.

I find no evidence that the Respondent was requiring that the Union submit all of its substantive proposals at the time it submitted its notice. The Respondent's primary argument was that the Union *never* submitted *any* substantive proposals, either at the time of its request to renegotiate the collective bargaining agreement or at any time thereafter. While there is language in the G.C. Exhibit 3 (the Respondent's sample ground rules proposals) regarding proposals – "Neither Management or the Union will be obligated to negotiate on any subject not included in said proposals." – I do not find this language sufficient to establish that the Respondent rejected the Union's request to renegotiate on the ground that it did not furnish all of its substantive proposals. This is not a position that the Respondent argued in its defense. Therefore, I do not find the GC's arguments regarding the applicability of *Johnson Med. Ctr.* persuasive.

The GC also argued that if it was concluded that the plain language of Section 8-3 of the CBA called for the submission of any and all substantive proposals on the entire contract when the Union submitted its demand to bargain, there is substantial evidence in the record to demonstrate that the parties agreed to a different process for this particular negotiation. Respondent admitted that it was free to reject the Union's proposal of providing proposals ten days prior to the beginning of negotiations, but did not do so; that it could have raised this issue in its proposed ground rules, but did not do so; and that it could have provided a definite date by which the Union would submit their proposals in writing, but did not do so. In essence the GC argued that the Respondent, by its actions between June 9 and October 2, negates the applicability of Section 8-3 of the CBA to allow its behavior in discontinuing negotiations and returning the Union's request to renegotiate.

The evidence clearly shows that the Respondent did not respond in writing to the Union's June 9 request and did engage in discussions with the Union regarding when its proposals, both ground rules and substantive, would be furnished. No actual negotiations took place during this time period. It is also clear that the Respondent accepted the Union's proposal of October 1 as the latest date for beginning negotiations on the new collective bargaining agreement. While the Respondent never communicated this agreement in writing to the Union, from the verbal communications, it appears that all of the parties were working with a target date of October 1.

The GC asserted that the Respondent's argument that the October 1 date was a "deadline" was ridiculous and should be disregarded. The Respondent argued that October 1 was a date that the Union itself proposed and the Respondent was willing to go along with. However, by October 1, when the Union had initially proposed bargaining should begin, the Union had done virtually nothing. There were no substantive proposals concerning the various articles of the collective bargaining agreement; and there were no formalized ground rules proposals to get the parties to the bargaining table. From June 9 to October 1, almost four full months, no proposals, other than those contained in the original request to renegotiate, were offered by the Union.

Article 8, Section 8-3 sets forth a specific procedure for the parties to follow if one of the parties desires to renegotiate the collective bargaining agreement. The issue then becomes whether the Respondent, when it did not specifically demand substantive proposals immediately after receipt of the Union's June 9 letter, can later rely on the language of Section 8-3. Even though both parties engaged in some communications regarding proposals for the new collective bargaining agreement, there is never any specific agreement that would change the actual language of the parties' CBA. I find that both parties are bound by the language of their own collective bargaining agreement and the obligations that it imposes on them with regard to renewing and/or renegotiating a new CBA.

The communications between the parties between June 9 and October 1 consist mainly of both parties trying to get the other side to submit proposals. Section 8-3 of the CBA requires the requesting party, in this case, the Union, to have the written notice of the desire to renegotiate the agreement accompanied by the Party's written proposals for negotiation. In this case, the Union failed to do so and I find that the Respondent's actions in refusing to negotiate because no substantive proposals had been submitted to be appropriate. The Respondent's intervening conduct between June 9 and October 1 does not negate its or the Union's obligations under the CBA.

I find that the Respondent's conduct in this matter did not violate section 7116(a)(1) and (5) of the Statute. Therefore, the GC has not established a violation of the Statute, and I recommend that the Authority adopt the following Order:

ORDER

It is hereby ordered that the complaint be, and hereby is, dismissed.

Issued, Washington, D.C. April 20, 2010

SUSAN E. JELEN
Administrative Law Judge

65 FLRA No. 18

NATIONAL AIR TRAFFIC
CONTROLLERS ASSOCIATION
(Union)

and

UNITED STATES
DEPARTMENT OF TRANSPORTATION
FEDERAL AVIATION ADMINISTRATION
(Agency)

0-AR-4444

DECISION

September 17, 2010

Before the Authority: Carol Waller Pope, Chairman, and Thomas M. Beck and Ernest DuBester, Members

I. Statement of the Case

This matter is before the Authority on exceptions to an award of Arbitrator James E. Conway filed by the Union under § 7122(a) of the Federal Service Labor-Management Relations Statute (the Statute) and part 2425 of the Authority's Regulations. The Agency filed an opposition to the Union's exceptions.

The Arbitrator denied the Union's grievance alleging that the Agency violated the parties' national agreement and the Statute when it discontinued a time-off program without bargaining over the change. For the reasons that follow, we deny the Union's exceptions in part and grant them in part, and remand the award to the parties for resubmission to the Arbitrator, absent settlement, to order an appropriate remedy.

II. Background and Arbitrator's Award

In 2001, the Agency and Union agreed to a program, which was memorialized in a local memorandum of understanding (MOU), pursuant to which local air traffic controllers who committed no operational errors or deviations were given nine hours of time off each year. Award at 1. Several years later, the Agency notified the Union that it planned to discontinue the program because it had failed to achieve its intended result of reducing the controllers' error rate. *Id.* at 4, 13. The Agency requested the Union's "impact and implementation proposal within 30 days." *Id.* at 2.

The Union, instead of responding directly to that request, proposed a new MOU, pursuant to which the previously agreed upon time off would be increased to sixteen hours. *Id.* The Agency replied, reiterating its intent to end the time-off program and proposing other incentive tools to take its place. *Id.* In response, the Union filed a grievance, which was submitted to arbitration. *Id.* The parties agreed to proceed without a hearing and submitted briefs. The parties stipulated to the following issue: "Did the Agency violate the [p]arties' collective bargaining agreement and [the Statute by refusing to bargain over the Union's proposed new MOU] and, if so, what should be the remedy. *Id.* at 2.

The Arbitrator found that the Statute generally requires the Agency to bargain over changes in conditions of employment and that the time-off program was a condition of employment. *Id.* at 10. However, the Arbitrator found that the Agency had no statutory duty to bargain over the substance of the Union's proposed MOU, explaining that the Agency's authority to reward performance was, in essence, authority to establish performance standards, which "touches upon the right to direct employees and assign work," and, as such, is nonnegotiable. *Id.* at 13-14. The Arbitrator also found that, although the Agency solicited impact proposals from the Union, "it [was] highly unlikely that anything the Union presented to the Agency . . . could reasonably be regarded as such 'procedures' or 'appropriate arrangements' under § 7106(b)(2) and (3) over which the Agency had any obligation to bargain." *Id.* at 16. Moreover, although the Arbitrator found that the sixteen-hour aspect of the Union's proposal was negotiable because it pertained only to the level of incentives instead of the substance of the time-off program, he also noted that negotiation of that aspect would be impossible because it was integrally intertwined with, and inseparable from, the program itself. *Id.* at 15-16. Accordingly, the Arbitrator concluded that the Agency did not violate the Statute. *Id.* at 19.

In addition, the Arbitrator found that neither the original MOU nor the Union's proposed MOU conformed to Article 21, Section 1[1] of the parties' national agreement, pursuant to which the Agency may consider granting awards for superior or exceptional performance. *Id.* at 14, 18. The Arbitrator found that the mere avoidance of errors and deviations "appears to have little in common with" any of the superior performance standards in Article 21, Section 1 with the possible exception of "significant contributions to the efficiency" of government operations. *Id.* at 14. As for that criterion, the Arbitrator found that uncontradicted facts demonstrated a decline in efficiency following the implementation of the time-off program. *Id.* In addition, the Arbitrator found that the original MOU was "offensive" to Article 102,[2] which bars provisions that conflict with the national agreement, and Article 7, Section 5,[3] which prohibits local or regional agreements from increasing or diminishing entitlements expressly contained in the national agreement. *Id.* at 18. As a result, the Arbitrator found that the Union's insistence on continuing the program was inconsistent with the national agreement and that no "compelling contractual arguments" had been presented "for requiring the Agency to persist in maintaining an MOU that failed to comply" with the agreement. *Id.* at 15.

The Arbitrator also addressed several other contentions of the Union. Specifically, he rejected the Union's argument that it was improper for the Agency to cancel the program based on performance of the facility rather than of individuals, finding that the purpose of the program was to improve operational efficiency instead of individual performance. *Id.* at 17. The Arbitrator also rejected the Union's contention that the Agency failed to establish that the operational necessity exception in Article 7, Section 4[4] of the national agreement excused the Agency from engaging in substantive bargaining before terminating the time-off program. *Id.* at 18. Instead, the Arbitrator found that the

1. Article 21, Section 1 provides, in pertinent part:

> The Parties agree that the use of awards is an excellent incentive tool for increasing productivity and creativity of bargaining unit employees by rewarding their contributions to the quality, efficiency, or economy of government operations. The Agency agrees to consider granting a cash, honorary, or informal recognition award, or grant time off without charge to leave or loss of pay to an employee individually or as a member of a group on the basis of:
> a. adoption or implementation of a suggestion or invention;
> b. significant contributions to the efficiency, economy, or improvement of government operations;
> c. exceptional service to the public, superior accomplishment, or special act or project on or off the job and contributions made despite unusual situations;
> d. recurring exemplary service . . . ;
> e. exceptional customer service or contributions . . .
> f. creative or innovative methods used to make work processes or results more effective and efficient;
> g. productivity gains;
> h. performance as reflected in the employee's most recent rating of record . . .
> i. unusual situations . . . in which an employee's efforts go beyond his/her normal duties.
>
> The Parties agree that this list is meant to be an example but is not all inclusive.

Exceptions, J. Ex. 1, Agreement at 53 54.

2. Article 102, Section 1 provides, in pertinent part:

> Any provision of this Agreement shall be determined a valid exception to, and shall supersede any existing or future Agency rules, regulations, directives, orders, policies and/or practices which conflict with the Agreement.

Id. at 172-73.

3. Article 7, Section 5 provides:

> The Parties at the local or regional levels may enter into written agreements or understandings on individual issues that do not conflict with this Agreement. However, unless specifically authorized by this Agreement, no such local or regional agreements may increase or diminish entitlements expressly contained in this Agreement.

Id. at 16.

4. Article 7, Section 4 provides, in pertinent part:

> The Agency will not implement the proposed change prior to completion of bargaining unless required by operational necessity. Operational necessity is defined as any change necessary to maintain the safety and efficiency of the air traffic system. Operational necessity is not to be invoked as a means to avoiding bargaining . . . . Operational necessity will only be invoked in those cases which meet the strict definition as set forth in this Article.

Id. at 16.

Agency's facts in support of operational necessity were not contradicted. *Id.* at 18-19.

III. Positions of the Parties

A. Union's Exceptions

The Union contends that the award is contrary to law because the Agency's unilateral termination of the time-off program violated § 7116(a)(5) of the Statute. Exceptions at 7, 10. In this regard, the Union contends that the Arbitrator should have viewed the proposal as "a mixture of both substantive and non-substantive proposals . . . [m]any [of which] were negotiable[.]" *Id.* at 12. The Arbitrator erred further, the Union claims, by finding that the Agency's unilateral action was not a breach of its bargaining obligation because it was "necessary to the functioning of the agency[.]" *Id.* at 14-16.

The Union also contends that the award is contrary to law because the Agency failed to abide by the terms of Article 7 of the national agreement, addressing midterm bargaining, and Article 21, Section 4, requiring the parties, at the local level, to develop jointly an operational error and deviation reduction program. *Id.* at 7-9, 13-14. In this regard, the Union contends that the Agency failed to raise the "operational necessity" exception in Article 7, Section 4 of the national agreement as a defense to the prohibition against implementing changes prior to the completion of bargaining. *Id.* at 14-16.

Finally, the Union contends that the award is contrary to public policy because it denies employees the right to bargain over the termination of an incentive awards program. Award at 5-6.

B. Agency's Opposition

The Agency contends that the Arbitrator properly determined that the Agency had not violated either the national agreement or the Statute when it terminated the time-off program and invited the Union to engage in impact and implementation bargaining. Opp'n at 3-13. Regarding the agreement, the Agency observes that the Union does not explicitly except to the award on the ground that it fails to draw its essence from the agreement or challenge the Arbitrator's determination that the terminated time-off program and the Union's proposal were inconsistent with Article 21, Section 1 and Article 102. *Id.* at 3 & 6. Instead, the Agency notes, the Union bases its argument that the award is contrary to the agreement on Article 21, Section 4,[5] a provision that was only a tangential basis for the Arbitrator's ruling. In addition, the Agency notes that the Union's argument that the Agency failed to comply with the mid-term bargaining requirements in Article 7 already had been considered and rejected by the Arbitrator. *Id.* at 6.

As for the Agency's compliance with the Statute, the Agency contends that Authority precedent supports the Arbitrator's finding that the Agency was not obligated to negotiate over the substance of the proposal because it interferes with management rights. *Id.* at 8-9.

Finally, the Agency argues that the award is not contrary to public policy as a denial of the right to bargain over incentive awards. *Id.* at 10. Instead, the Agency argues, the award finds only that the particular proposal at issue is not negotiable and is inconsistent with the national agreement. *Id.*

IV. Analysis and Conclusions

A. The award draws its essence from the national agreement.

We construe the Union's argument that the award is contrary to law because the Agency failed to abide by the terms of Article 7 and Article 21, Section 4 of the parties' national agreement as a claim that the award fails to draw its essence from the agreement. In reviewing an arbitrator's interpretation of a collective bargaining agreement, the Authority applies the deferential standard of review that federal courts use in reviewing arbitration awards in the private sector. *See* 5 U.S.C. § 7122(a)(2); *AFGE, Council 220*, 54 FLRA 156, 159 (1998). Under this standard, the Authority will find that an arbitration award is deficient as failing to draw its essence from the collective bargaining agreement when the appealing party establishes that the award: (1) cannot

---

5. Article 21, Section 4 provides:

> The Parties agree that a critical component of any effective quality assurance program is problem prevention. The Parties further agree it is desirable to identify and correct deficiencies and to recognize success in the area of Operational Error and Operational Deviation prevention. Therefore, the Parties at the local level shall meet to develop an operational error/deviation reduction program in accordance with FAA Order 7210.56.

Id. at 54-55.

in any rational way be derived from the agreement; (2) is so unfounded in reason and fact and so unconnected with the wording and purposes of the collective bargaining agreement as to manifest an infidelity to the obligation of the arbitrator; (3) does not represent a plausible interpretation of the agreement; or (4) evidences a manifest disregard of the agreement. *See U.S. Dep't of Labor (OSHA)*, 34 FLRA 573, 575 (1990). The Authority and the courts defer to arbitrators in this context "because it is the arbitrator's construction of the agreement for which the parties have bargained." *Id.* at 576.

Here, the Union contends that the award fails to draw its essence from the midterm bargaining requirements in Article 7 of the national agreement. In his consideration of the Union's argument that the Agency acted contrary to Article 7, the Arbitrator found that the Agency demonstrated "operation necessity" for its unilateral termination of the time-of program pursuant to Section 4 of Article 7 and that the Union did not rebut the facts on which the Agency based this demonstration. Nor does the Union rebut these facts in its exceptions. Additionally, the Arbitrator found that the Union's proposed MOU would require increased entitlements to air traffic controllers for performing their basic duties, which Article 7, Section 5 expressly prohibits. The Union contends further that the award fails to draw its essence from Article 21, Section 4 of the national agreement, which requires the parties jointly to develop an operational error and deviation reduction program. However, the award does not excuse the Agency from this requirement; it merely permits the Agency unilaterally to end one error reduction program and invite the Union to negotiate over an alternative program. As such, the Union fails to establish that the award is unfounded in reason or fact, unconnected with the wording or purpose of the national agreement or manifests a disregard of the agreement. Accordingly, we deny this exception.

B. The award is contrary to the Statute.

When an exception involves an award's consistency with law, the Authority reviews any question of law raised by the exception and the award *de novo*. *See NTEU, Chapter 24*, 50 FLRA 330, 332 (1995) (citing *U.S. Customs Serv. v. FLRA*, 43 F.3d 682, 686-87 (D.C. Cir. 1994)). In applying the standard of *de novo* review, the Authority assesses whether an arbitrator's legal conclusions are consistent with the applicable standard of law. *See U.S. Dep't of Def., Dep'ts of the Army & the Air Force, Ala. Nat'l Guard, Northport, Ala.*, 55 FLRA 37, 40 (1998). In making that assessment, the Authority defers to the arbitrator's underlying factual findings. *See id.*

The Union contends that the Agency violated § 7116(a)(5) of the Statute, which states that it is an unfair labor practice for an agency "to refuse to consult or negotiate in good faith with a labor organization . . . ." In this regard, the Union contends that the Agency terminated the MOU without giving the Union the opportunity to negotiate over the substance of the proposed change. Thus, the Union argues, the award is contrary to *NTEU v. FLRA*, 793 F.2d 371 (D.C. Cir. 1986) (*NTEU*), which, in vacating an Authority decision, held that a proposal determining the level of incentive pay for the performance of work was negotiable and was not an exercise of management's right to assign work. Exceptions at 11-12. While acknowledging this precedent, the Arbitrator found that the Agency had no statutory duty to bargain over the substance of the Union's proposed MOU, explaining that the Agency's authority to reward performance was, in essence, authority to establish performance standards, which "touches upon the right to direct employees and assign work[,]" and, as such, is nonnegotiable. Award at 13-14.

We agree with the Union that its proposed MOU involves the level of incentive pay for the performance of agency work, rather than the content of a performance standard. In this regard, the proposed MOU would provide a time-off incentive award based on the number of errors without regard to an employee's performance rating or appraisal. Exceptions at 12, Jt. Ex. 5 at 1 (stating that controllers "who have been both operation error-/deviation-free throughout the year will receive an award of 16 hours' time off"). Thus, like the proposal at issue in *NTEU*, the proposed MOU would reward the superior performance of assigned work, not establish a minimum standard of performance. *NTEU*, 793 F.2d at 374-75 (finding proposal that would provide additional compensation to employees who exceed certain requirements negotiable because it would reward superior performance of work, rather than establish "minimum levels of effort to avoid remedial action"). As a result, the proposal does not affect management's right to assign work and is negotiable.[6] Accordingly, we grant this exception.[7]

6. In finding the proposal to be within the duty to bargain, we make no judgment as to its merits.

7. In light of this determination, we find it unnecessary to resolve the Union's exception that the award is contrary to public policy.

V. Remedy

Consistent with our finding that the award is contrary to law, we set aside the award. The effect of our decision to set aside the award is to sustain the Union's grievance. *See NTEU, Chapter 207*, 60 FLRA 731, 735 (2005) (Chairman Cabaniss dissenting). The Arbitrator, however, did not make any determination with respect to remedy. As a result, we remand the award to the parties for resubmission to the Arbitrator, absent settlement, to order an appropriate remedy.

VI. Decision

The Union's exceptions are denied in part and granted in part. The award is deficient insofar as the Arbitrator found that the Agency's termination of the MOU without providing the Union an opportunity to negotiate over the substance of the proposed change did not violate the Statute. The award is remanded to the parties consistent with this decision.

65 FLRA No. 19

UNITED STATES
DEPARTMENT OF JUSTICE
FEDERAL BUREAU OF PRISONS
FEDERAL CORRECTIONAL COMPLEX
TUCSON, ARIZONA
(Agency)

and

AMERICAN FEDERATION
OF GOVERNMENT EMPLOYEES
LOCAL 3955
COUNCIL OF PRISONS
LOCAL 33
(Union)

0-AR-4670

DECISION

September 21, 2010

Before the Authority: Carol Waller Pope, Chairman, and Thomas M. Beck and Ernest DuBester, Members

This matter is before the Authority on an exception to an award of Arbitrator John F. Wormuth filed by the Agency under § 7122(a) of the Federal Service Labor-Management Relations Statute (the Statute) and part 2425 of the Authority's Regulations. The Union filed an opposition to the Agency's exception.

Under § 7122(a) of the Statute, an award is deficient if it is contrary to any law, rule, or regulation, or it is deficient on other grounds similar to those applied by federal courts in private sector labor-management relations. Upon careful consideration of the entire record in this case and Authority precedent, the Authority concludes that the award is not deficient on the grounds raised in the exceptions and set forth in § 7122(a). *See U.S. Dep't of Labor (OSHA),* 34 FLRA 573, 575 (1990) (award not deficient as failing to draw its essence from the parties' collective bargaining agreement where excepting party fails to establish that the award cannot in any rational way be derived from the agreement; is so unfounded in reason and fact and so unconnected to the wording and purpose of the agreement as to manifest an infidelity to the obligation of the arbitrator; does not represent a plausible interpretation of the agreement; or evidences a manifest disregard of the agreement).

Accordingly, the Agency's exception is denied.

65 FLRA No. 20

AMERICAN FEDERATION
OF GOVERNMENT EMPLOYEES
COUNCIL 236
(Union)

and

UNITED STATES
GENERAL SERVICES ADMINISTRATION
(Agency)

0-AR-4671

DECISION

September 21, 2010

Before the Authority: Carol Waller Pope, Chairman, and Thomas M. Beck and Ernest DuBester, Members

This matter is before the Authority on exceptions to an award of Arbitrator Joseph M. Pastore, Jr. filed by the Union under § 7122(a) of the Federal Service Labor-Management Relations Statute (the Statute) and part 2425 of the Authority's Regulations. The Agency filed an opposition to the Union's exceptions.

Under § 7122(a) of the Statute, an award is deficient if it is contrary to any law, rule, or regulation, or it is deficient on other grounds similar to those applied by federal courts in private sector labor-management relations. Upon careful consideration of the entire record in this case and Authority precedent, the Authority concludes that the award is not deficient on the grounds raised in the exceptions and set forth in § 7122(a).[*] *See U.S. Dep't of the Air Force, Lowry Air Force Base, Denver, Colo.*, 48 FLRA 589, 593-94 (1993) (award not deficient as based on a nonfact where excepting party either challenges a factual matter that the parties disputed at arbitration or fails to demonstrate that the central fact underlying the award is clearly erroneous, but for which a different result would have been reached by the arbitrator); *U.S. Dep't of Labor (OSHA)*, 34 FLRA 573, 575 (1990) (award not deficient as failing to draw its essence from the parties' collective bargaining agreement where excepting party fails to establish that the award cannot in any rational way be derived from the agreement; is so unfounded in reason and fact and so unconnected to the wording and purpose of the agreement as to manifest an infidelity to the obligation of the arbitrator; does not represent a plausible interpretation of the agreement; or evidences a manifest disregard of the agreement).

Accordingly, the Union's exceptions are denied.

[*] To the extent that the Union asserts that managers with "high salaries are able to assign . . . more money into their personal performance awards . . . provided they lower the number of employees receiving bonus money," such assertion was not raised before the Arbitrator, and therefore, is not properly before the Authority under 5 C.F.R. § 2429.5. Exceptions at 3. *See, e.g., AFGE, Local 1633*, 64 FLRA 732, 733 (2010). Accordingly, we dismiss this exception.

65 FLRA No. 21

UNITED STATES
DEPARTMENT OF JUSTICE
FEDERAL BUREAU OF PRISONS
USP ADMINISTRATIVE MAXIMUM (ADX)
FLORENCE, COLORADO
(Agency)

and

AMERICAN FEDERATION
OF GOVERNMENT EMPLOYEES
LOCAL 1302
COUNCIL OF PRISON LOCALS
(Union)

0-AR-4612
(64 FLRA 1168 (2010))

ORDER DENYING
MOTION FOR RECONSIDERATION

September 22, 2010

Before the Authority: Carol Waller Pope, Chairman, and Thomas M. Beck and Ernest DuBester, Members

I. Statement of the Case

This matter is before the Authority on the Agency's motion for reconsideration of an Authority order dismissing the Agency's exception in *United States Department of Justice, Federal Bureau of Prisons, USP Administrative Maximum (ADX), Florence, Colorado*, 64 FLRA 1168 (2010) (*DOJ*). The Union has not filed an opposition to the Agency's motion.

Section 2429.17 of the Authority's Regulations permits a party who can establish extraordinary circumstances to request reconsideration of an Authority final decision or order. For the reasons that follow, we deny the Agency's motion for reconsideration.

II. Decision in *DOJ*

In the underlying proceedings in *DOJ*, the Arbitrator concluded, as relevant here, that the Agency violated the Fair Labor Standards Act (FLSA) and the parties' agreement by failing to compensate Correctional Officers (Officers) for time spent performing certain pre- and post-shift activities. *DOJ*, 64 FLRA at 1168. The Arbitrator granted the Officers backpay in the amount of ten minutes per shift and liquidated damages. *Id.* The Arbitrator ordered the parties to meet and determine which Officers were entitled to compensation and the amount of compensation owed. *Id.*

The Agency filed an exception arguing that the Arbitrator's award of backpay was contrary to law, specifically, 5 C.F.R. § 551.412(a)(1).[1] *DOJ*, 64 FLRA at 1169. The Agency contended that, under § 551.412(a)(1), overtime compensation for prepatory activities is recoverable only if that time totals "*more than ten minutes*[.]" *Id.* (quoting Agency's Exception at 5) (emphasis in original). Because the Arbitrator awarded *only* ten minutes of overtime compensation, the Agency asserted that, even if the Officers' activities were recoverable, the award was inconsistent with § 551.412(a)(1). *Id.* at 1169. The Agency, accordingly, asked the Authority to set aside the award of backpay and liquidated damages. It presented no other arguments.

The Authority concluded that the Agency's exception was barred by § 2429.5 of the Authority's Regulations.[2] *Id.* at 1170. The Authority found that the Agency had ample notice throughout the arbitration process that the Union had requested, as a remedy, *only* ten minutes of overtime compensation in its grievance. *Id.* (citing Award at 15, 28; Exception at 1-2; Exception, Attach. B). Because the Agency had notice of the specific relief requested by the Union, the Authority stated that the Agency was required to present its argument concerning § 551.412(a)(1) to the Arbitrator. The Authority determined that the record did not establish that the Agency presented this argument to the Arbitrator; consequently, the Authority concluded that it could

1. 5 C.F.R. § 551.412, "Preparatory or concluding activities," provides, in pertinent part:

> If an agency reasonably determines that a preparatory or concluding activity is closely related to an employee's principal activities, and is indispensable to the performance of the principal activities, and that the total time spent in that activity is more than 10 minutes per workday, the agency shall credit all of the time spent in that activity, including the 10 minutes, as hours of work.

2. Section 2429.5 of the Authority's Regulations states, in relevant part, that "[t]he Authority will not consider evidence offered by a party, or any issue, which was not presented in the proceedings before the . . . arbitrator."

not consider this argument. *Id.* at 1170. The Authority, accordingly, dismissed the exception. *Id.*

III. Motion for Reconsideration

The Agency does not dispute that it neglected to present its argument concerning § 551.412(a)(1) to the Arbitrator. Instead, the Agency argues that extraordinary circumstances are established for reconsideration for two reasons.

First, the Agency contends that, by "allowing an award that is contrary to law to become binding[,]" the Authority erred in its conclusion of law. Motion for Reconsideration (Motion) at 5. The Agency contends that the Arbitrator's award is clearly prohibited by § 551.412(a)(1); as such, it asserts that, under principles of *de novo* review, the Authority cannot permit the award to become "final and binding." *Id.*

Second, according to the Agency, the Authority's decision to dismiss the Agency's exception allows "an improper monetary award against the United States Government to stand" even though principles of sovereign immunity require an express statutory waiver before the United States can be held liable for monetary damages. *Id.* (citations omitted). The Agency asserts that the Authority's dismissal of its exception contradicts Authority precedent that states issues of sovereign immunity may be raised at any time and that monetary awards "without proper statutory authority to waive sovereign immunity must be set aside." *Id.* at 6 (citations omitted). The Agency, accordingly, asks the Authority to grant its motion and set aside the Arbitrator's award of backpay and liquidated damages. *Id.* at 5, 5 n.2.

IV. Analysis and Conclusion

Section 2429.17 of the Authority's Regulations permits a party who can establish extraordinary circumstances to request reconsideration of an Authority order. The Authority has repeatedly recognized that a party seeking reconsideration under § 2429.17 bears the heavy burden of establishing that extraordinary circumstances exist to justify this unusual action. *See, e.g., U.S. Dep't of the Treasury, IRS, Wash., D.C.*, 56 FLRA 935, 936 (2000). The Authority has identified a limited number of situations in which extraordinary circumstances have been found to exist. These include situations: (1) where an intervening court decision or change in the law affected dispositive issues; (2) where evidence, information, or issues crucial to the decision had not been presented to the Authority; (3) where the Authority erred in its remedial order, process, conclusion of law, or factual finding; and (4) where the moving party has not been given an opportunity to address an issue raised *sua sponte* by the Authority in the decision. *See U.S. Dep't of the Air Force, 375th Combat Support Group, Scott Air Force Base, Ill.*, 50 FLRA 84, 86-87 (1995).

The Agency first argues that reconsideration of *DOJ* is warranted because a "basic tenet behind *de novo* review is that the Authority cannot allow an award that is contrary to law to become final and binding." Motion at 5; *see also id.* at 6. The Authority has rejected this argument as a basis for permitting reconsideration of an underlying decision. *See, e.g., U.S. Dep't of the Treasury, IRS*, 57 FLRA 592, 593-94 (2001) (rejecting argument that Authority was required to conduct *de novo* review of award and set it aside as inconsistent with Office of Personnel Management (OPM) regulation even though agency failed to raise regulation below). Accordingly, we reject this argument.

The Agency next argues that reconsideration is warranted because the remedy conflicts with § 551.412(a)(1) and is, therefore, not based on a valid waiver of sovereign immunity. The Agency further contends that Authority precedent states that: (1) agencies may raise issues of sovereign immunity at any time; and (2) monetary awards that are not based on proper waivers of sovereign immunity must be set aside. Motion at 6 (citing *U.S. Dep't of Transp., FAA, Detroit, Mich.*, 64 FLRA 325, 328-29 (2009) (*FAA*); *U.S. Dep't of the Treasury, IRS, Wash., D.C.*, 61 FLRA 146, 151 (2005) (*IRS I*) (then-Member Pope concurring) *aff'd sub nom. Dep't of the Treasury, IRS v. FLRA*, 521 F.3d 1148 (9th Cir. 2008) (*IRS II*)).

The question of sovereign immunity concerns whether Congress has validly waived the United States' immunity to monetary liability. *See, e.g., Dep't of the Army v. FLRA*, 56 F.3d 273, 277 (D.C. Cir. 1995) (citations omitted). The Agency does not dispute that the Arbitrator based his award, in part, on the FLSA. The Agency also does not dispute that, "[b]y authorizing suits against the United States, the [FLSA's amendment] waives the government's sovereign immunity[]" or that "[g]overnment employees were given the right to sue for violations of the FLSA[.]" *IRS II*, 521 F.3d at 1154 (citations omitted). Finally, the Agency does not dispute that the FLSA permits compensation for pre- and post-shift activities and that it does not prohibit payments for *de minimis* work.

Based on the foregoing, and contrary to the Agency's claim, the award *is* based on a valid Congressional waiver of sovereign immunity. Because the award is based on a valid waiver of sovereign immunity, i.e., the FLSA, any alleged conflict the remedy has with § 551.412(a)(1) provides no basis for concluding that the award is based on an invalid waiver of sovereign immunity. *See IRS I,* 61 FLRA at 151 (finding that remedy's alleged conflict with an OPM regulation provided no basis for concluding that sovereign immunity had not been validly waived where award was based on waiver under Portal-to-Portal Act); *see also IRS II,* 521 F.3d at 1156 (in affirming Authority's determination that award was based on valid waiver of sovereign immunity, court stated that alleged inconsistency with regulation did not address whether Portal-to-Portal Act was part of sovereign immunity found under FLSA).

The Agency's reliance on *IRS I* is misplaced. As explained above, in *IRS I,* the Authority rejected the agency's assertion that the waiver of sovereign immunity at issue was invalid because the arbitrator's remedy conflicted with an OPM regulation. *See IRS I,* 61 FLRA at 151; *see also IRS II,* 521 F.3d at 1156.

The Agency's reliance on *FAA* is likewise misplaced. *FAA* involves the Back Pay Act (BPA) -- not the FLSA -- which is a limited waiver of sovereign immunity. The BPA permits recovery of backpay if, among other things, it constitutes "pay, allowances, or differentials" within the meaning of the BPA. *FAA,* 64 FLRA at 329 (quoting *U.S. Dep't of HHS, Gallup Indian Med. Ctr., Navajo Area Indian Health Serv.,* 60 FLRA 202, 212 (2004) (Chairman Cabaniss dissenting in part; then-Member Pope dissenting in part)). Federal courts and the Authority have acknowledged that the foregoing requirement concerns whether sovereign immunity has been validly waived under the BPA. *See, e.g., SSA, Balt., Md.,* 201 F.3d 465, 471 (D.C. Cir. 2000) (stating that liquidated damages did not constitute "'pay, allowances, or differentials within the meaning of the statutory waiver of sovereign immunity" under the BPA); *U.S. DOL,* 61 FLRA 64, 66 (2005) (Chairman Cabaniss concurring) (citation omitted) (acknowledging that "pay, allowances, and differentials" under BPA concerned sovereign immunity); *U.S. Dep't of Transp., FAA,* 52 FLRA 46, 50 (1996) (citations omitted) (same); *cf. U.S. DOJ, Fed. Bureau of Prisons, Fed. Corr. Inst., Milan, Mich.,* 63 FLRA 188, 189-90 (2009) (finding that issue of whether remedy satisfied casual connection requirement of BPA was properly barred by § 2429.5 -- and would therefore not be considered on review -- even though it was part of agency's sovereign immunity argument). Thus, *FAA,* in accordance with related precedent, establishes only that sovereign immunity *under the BPA* has not been waived if certain requirements *under the BPA* have not been satisfied. *See FAA,* 64 FLRA at 329. Because this case does not involve the BPA, *FAA* is inapplicable.

Based on the foregoing, we deny the Agency's motion for reconsideration.

V. Order

The Agency's motion for reconsideration is denied.

65 FLRA No. 22

UNITED STATES
NUCLEAR REGULATORY COMMISSION
(Agency)

and

NATIONAL TREASURY
EMPLOYEES UNION
CHAPTER 208
(Union)

0-AR-4400

DECISION

September 23, 2010

Before the Authority: Carol Waller Pope, Chairman, and Thomas M. Beck and Ernest DuBester, Members

I. Statement of the Case

This matter is before the Authority on exceptions to an award of Arbitrator Stephen E. Alpern filed by the Agency under § 7122(a) of the Federal Service Labor-Management Relations Statute (the Statute) and part 2425 of the Authority's Regulations. The Union filed an opposition to the Agency's exceptions.

The Arbitrator found that the Agency violated the parties' agreement and § 7114(a)(2)(B) of the Statute by restricting a Union representative's participation in an investigatory interview. For the following reasons, we deny the exceptions.

II. Background and Arbitrator's Award

The Agency's employees are required to hold a security clearance in order to remain employed with the Agency. Award at 7. The Agency conducted an interview with an employee to determine whether the employee's security clearance should be withdrawn. *Id.* At the employee's request, a Union representative was present. *Id.* The Agency's representative "sought to restrict [the Union representative's] assistance of [the employee] during the interview." *Id.* Specifically, the Agency instructed the Union representative "not to communicate with [the employee] while [the employee] was responding to questions[,]" and instructed the employee that "he could only consult with [the Union representative] after a question was answered and that after he consulted with [the Union representative] he could not 'come back and redirect the question.'" *Id.* at 7-8. On a later date, the Agency sent further questions to the employee by email without notifying the Union representative.[1] *Id.*

The Union filed a grievance alleging that the Agency violated § 7114(a)(2)(B) of the Statute and Article 3.3 of the parties' agreement.[2] The grievance was unresolved and submitted to arbitration where, absent a stipulation of the issues by the parties, the Arbitrator framed the issues, in pertinent part, as follows:[3] "Are employees entitled to *Weingarten* rights[4] in examinations held to determine whether an employee's security clearance[s] should be revoked or suspended? . . . If so, were the employee's rights denied in this case? . . . If so, what shall the remedy be?" Award at 2.

The Arbitrator noted that the parties did not dispute that the Supreme Court's decision in *Department of the Navy v. Egan*, 484 U.S. 518 (1988)

1. The employee's security clearance was suspended and then revoked, and the employee "was apparently removed from the service and his removal was unsuccessfully challenged." Award at 8. Before the Arbitrator, the parties "stipulated that no remedy is available" to the employee. *Id.*

2. The pertinent wording of § 7114(a)(2)(B) is set forth below. Article 3.3 of the parties' agreement provides, in pertinent part, that "[t]he Union shall be given the opportunity to be represented at any examination of an employee in the unit by a representative of [the Agency] in connection with an investigation if: . . . [t]he employee reasonably believes that the examination may result in disciplinary action against the employee; and . . . [t]he employee requests representation." Award at 3.

3. The Arbitrator also framed issues regarding a "past practice" grievance, but those issues are not relevant here and will not be discussed further. Award at 6.

4. *Weingarten* rights are set forth in § 7114(a)(2)(B) of the Statute. In this regard, § 7114(a)(2)(B) "is intended to provide rights to Federal sector bargaining unit employees consistent with those provided in the private sector by the National Labor Relations Board (Board) in interpreting and applying the National Labor Relations Act and the Supreme Court's decision in *National Labor Relations Board v. J. Weingarten, Inc.*, 420 U.S. 251 (1975) (*Weingarten*)." *Headquarters, NASA., Wash., D.C.*, 50 FLRA 601, 606 (1995), *enforced* 120 F.3d 1208 (11th Cir. 1997), *aff'd* 527 U.S. 229 (1999).

(*Egan*) "precludes reviewing authorities from involving themselves in the substance of security clearance determinations." Award at 20. The Arbitrator also noted that "[i]f the purpose of the examination of [the employee] was solely to determine whether [his] clearance should be revoked, one could argue that" § 7114(a)(2)(B) of the Statute would not apply, "because revocation of a security clearance is not a disciplinary action." *Id.* However, the Arbitrator found that the record demonstrated that the interview "was an examination which could have resulted in disciplinary action, even if a determination had been made not to revoke [the employee's] clearance." *Id.* at 21. In this regard, the Arbitrator noted that, during the hearing, the Agency's counsel "acknowledged that information obtained in the course of a security clearance interview could be used in a disciplinary proceeding." *Id.* Thus, the Arbitrator concluded that "an employee has a reasonable fear that discipline, unrelated to security clearance matters, might result from the examination." *Id.*

The Arbitrator then stated:

> This is especially significant as, due to the potential broad scope of security clearance issues, all but the most minor of employee transgressions could become the subject of security clearance investigations. There is nothing in the Agreement to prevent the [Agency] from conducting all investigations into potential employee conduct under the umbrella of a security clearance investigation. Because of the fact that all [Agency] employees must have a security clearance, the [Agency] would have the ability to almost totally erode the rights, granted by both statute and the Agreement, to union representation in investigatory interviews.

Id. The Arbitrator concluded, in these circumstances, that the employee was entitled to Union representation during the interview. *Id.* at 22.

Next, the Arbitrator determined that the Agency "unduly restricted" the Union representative with regard to what he was permitted to do during the interview and that

> [t]hese undue restrictions included instructing [the Union representative] not to speak to [the employee] until [the employee] had completely answered a question; not allowing [the employee] to consult with [the Union representative] until after a question had been answered and then not permitting [the employee] to further answer the question; instructing [the Union representative] not to point to documents while [the employee] was answering questions; and, posing questions to [the employee] by e-mail without notifying [the Union representative].

Id.

In sum, the Arbitrator concluded that the Agency violated Article 3.3 of the parties' agreement and § 7114(a)(2)(B) of the Statute by restricting the Union representative's participation during the interview and by subsequently sending the employee the email. *Id.* at 23. To remedy the violations, the Arbitrator issued an order directing the Agency to: cease and desist from violating § 7114(a)(2)(B); and post a notice.

III. Positions of the Parties

A. Agency's Exceptions

The Agency asserts that the award is based on nonfacts because no evidence supports the Arbitrator's finding that most "employee transgressions" can be the subject of security-clearance investigations and that, as a result, the Agency could "totally erode" *Weingarten* rights by precluding union representation during security-clearance-related examinations. Exceptions at 31, 32. In this regard, the Agency asserts that the security-clearance process may not be used in connection with misconduct that lacks national-security implications. *Id.* at 33-34 (citing Executive Order (E.O.) 12,968, § 2.1(a); the Privacy Act, 5 U.S.C. § 552a(a)(7); and 10 C.F.R. § 10.2).[5] Also in this regard, the Agency contends that "the law presumes that Government

5. E.O. 12,968 Section 2.1(a) provides: "Determinations of eligibility for access to classified information shall be based on criteria established under this order. Such determinations are separate from suitability determinations with respect to the hiring or retention of persons for employment by the government or any other personnel actions." 10 C.F.R. § 10.2 provides, in pertinent part: "The criteria and procedures in this part shall be used in determining eligibility for [Agency] access authorization and/or employment clearance[.]" 5 U.S.C. § 552a(a)(7) provides, in pertinent part, that "the term 'routine use' means, with respect to the disclosure of a record, the use of such record for a purpose which is compatible with the purpose for which it was collected[.]"

officials will comply with the law and act in good faith in performing their duties." *Id.* (citing *Nat'l Archives & Records Admin. v. Favish*, 541 U.S. 157, *reh'g denied* 541 U.S. 1057 (2004) (*Favish*)). According to the Agency, but for the Arbitrator's alleged error, he would have reached a different conclusion. "For similar reasons[,]" the Agency asserts that the award is contrary to E.O. 12,968, the Privacy Act, 10 C.F.R. § 10.2, and *Favish*. *Id.* at 36 n.31.

In addition, the Agency argues that the award is contrary to law because, as a result of *Egan*, *Weingarten* rights do not apply to Agency determinations as to whether individuals are eligible for security clearances. In this connection, the Agency contends that § 7114(a)(2)(B) does not contain "any specific indication" that it applies in security-clearance-related examinations, and that *Egan* held that security-clearance examinations are not disciplinary in nature. *Id.* at 9. The Agency also contends that representation rights in security-clearance-investigatory interviews derive not from § 7114(a)(2)(B) but from E.O. 12,968 and 10 C.F.R. § 10.22(c), which do not incorporate *Weingarten* rights into the security-clearance process.[6] *Id.* at 13-14. Additionally, the Agency asserts that its security-clearance interview procedures "specifically prohibit cross-examination by the employee's representative, something that would be permissible in interviews where *Weingarten* rights apply." *Id.* at 14.

Further, the Agency claims that the award is contrary to law insofar as the Arbitrator found that the Agency unduly restricted the Union representative's conduct during the interview. *Id.* at 15. The Agency asserts that it is "not challenging the Arbitrator's factual determination[s]" regarding the interview. *Id.* at 20 n.21. However, the Agency contends that the Arbitrator's legal conclusion is erroneous because the Agency was entitled to insist on hearing the employee's own account of the matter under investigation, and it imposed reasonable restrictions to achieve this goal. *Id.* at 17-20 (citing *Dep't of the Treasury v. FLRA*, 707 F.2d 574, 580-81 (D.C. Cir. 1983) (*Treasury*); and *Headquarters, NASA, Wash., D.C.*, 50 FLRA 601 (1995) (*NASA*)). In this connection, the Agency asserts that it "did not impose any restriction before the interview . . ., but only did so after the Union representative's conduct substantially interfered with the Agency's right and interest in obtaining spontaneous answers" from the employee. *Id.* at 21-22. Specifically, the Agency states that its "witness testified that before the ground rules were imposed there were a 'handful of times' of [the Union representative] 'trying to stop [the employee] from answering questions, leaning over and cupping his hand, and whispering in [the employee's] ear and trying to actually answer questions for [the employee].'" *Id.* at 22 n.23. "On other occasions," the Agency claims, "the Union representative directed the employee's attention to text in documents by pointing." *Id.* at 4. According to the Agency, "[a]fter several instances of this behavior on the part of the Union representative, the Agency did insist that [the Union representative] refrain from speaking with or otherwise coaching the employee *while a question was pending*." *Id.* at 22 n.23. *Accord id.* at 21 ("after the Union representative repeatedly had been asked not to interject while a question was pending, the Agency made it clear on the record that once a question was asked, the employee was expected to answer the question unassisted."). However, the Agency contends that it did not prohibit the employee and the Union representative from consulting with each other after a question was answered or from taking breaks as needed. *Id.* at 22.

Moreover, the Agency argues that the award impermissibly expands the *Weingarten* right by applying it to questions sent to the employee by email. Exceptions at 22-27. Specifically, the Agency contends that most, "if not all[,]" of the requirements for finding a § 7114(a)(2)(B) violation are not met in connection with that incident. *Id.* at 25.

Finally, the Agency contends that the award is contrary to management's rights to determine internal-security practices and to discipline employees under § 7106 of the Statute. *Id.* at 27-31. To support its internal-security argument, the Agency cites *United States Nuclear Regulatory Commission v. FLRA*, 25 F.3d 229 (4th Cir. 1994) (*NRC*).

B. Union's Opposition

The Union argues that the award is not based on nonfacts. In this regard, the Union asserts that the Arbitrator determined that *Weingarten* rights applied because the employee reasonably feared discipline, and the Arbitrator's statements challenged by the Agency are "merely dicta[]" and were disputed before the Arbitrator. Opp'n at 57.

6. 10 C.F.R. § 10.22 provides, in pertinent part, that an "individual whose eligibility for an access authorization and/or an employment clearance is in question[]" must be presented with "[a] notification letter[]" that informs the individual "[t]hat the individual has the right to be represented by counsel or other representative at their own expense[.]" 10 C.F.R. § 10.22(c).

The Union also argues that the wording and legislative history of § 7114(a)(2)(B) of the Statute demonstrate that Congress did not exempt security-clearance interviews from the coverage of that statutory section. *Id.* at 17. In addition, the Union contends that *Egan* and its progeny do not apply because those decisions foreclose review of the merits of security-clearance determinations, not the procedural aspects of those determinations. *Id.* at 34.

Further, the Union contends that the Arbitrator correctly found that the Agency's restrictions on the Union representative's conduct during the interview violated § 7114(a)(2)(B). As an initial matter, the Union asserts that the Arbitrator found "a set of facts different than that portrayed in the Agency's exceptions," and that although "the Agency asserts it is not challenging the Arbitrator's factual determinations because the parties are largely in agreement as to what transpired during the interview, the Agency proceeds to do just that." *Id.* at 36, 35. With regard to the Agency's claim that it did not impose restrictions prior to the interview, the Union contends that there was conflicting testimony on that point, but that "[r]egardless of whether the restrictions were announced at the start of the interview or during the interview, the majority of the interview was clearly conducted under the ground rule." *Id.* at 40 n.9.

The Union acknowledges that, "[o]n several occasions, [its representative] did engage in efforts to confer, consult, or otherwise represent [the employee], but the Agency construed these attempts as interruptions and halted them." *Id.* at 5-6. "For example," the Union asserts, "at one point during the examination," the Union representative pointed to a document that had been written by the employee, in order to "tr[y] to remind [the employee] to discuss a particular fact so that [he] could provide a more complete answer." *Id.* at 6. According to the Union, when the Agency admonished the Union representative and told him that he could not give the employee answers, the employee stated, "He is not answering my questions. He is providing me representation." *Id.* The Union also acknowledges that the Union representative "whispered advice into [the employee's] ear[,]" but that, during the hearing, the Union representative explained that he was "just trying to ensure his answer's more complete; correct; accurate; and, more importantly, [that] favorable aspects that he was not completely answering" would be mentioned. *Id.* at 6-7. In addition, the Union contends that the Union representative was "even forbidden from communicating with the Agency before [the employee] completely answered the question[]" because when the Union representative "told the Agency that [the employee] wasn't finished answering a question, the Agency considered that to be an interruption." *Id.* at 41.

With regard to the Agency's claim that it did not prohibit the employee and the Union representative from consulting with each other after a question was answered or from taking breaks as needed, the Union asserts that "[o]mitted from the Agency's version of events is the Arbitrator's factual determination" that they could consult only "after questions were *completely* answered and the employee then *could not revise* his answer." *Id.* at 36. According to the Union, "[t]hese rules also applied to breaks[,]" and, consequently, the Union representative "was not able to clarify any questions to help the employee understand what he was being asked and assist the employee in answering." *Id.*

Moreover, the Union asserts that the award does not impermissibly expand the *Weingarten* right with regard to the email to the employee. *Id.* at 45. In this regard, the Union relies on the Authority's decision in *United States Immigration and Naturalization Service, United States Border Patrol, Del Rio, Texas*, 46 FLRA 363 (1992).

Finally, the Union contends that the award is not contrary to management's rights under § 7106 of the Statute because those rights "must be read in context with other parts of the Statute" and "cannot be read to trump *Weingarten* rights, as doing so would render § 7114(a)(2)(B) a nullity." *Id.* at 47-48 (citing *Fed. Bureau of Prisons, Wash., D.C.*, 55 FLRA 1250 (2000) (*Prisons*) (Member Cabaniss dissenting)).

IV. Analysis and Conclusions

A. The award is not based on nonfacts.

To establish that an award is based on a nonfact, the appealing party must show that a central fact underlying the award is clearly erroneous, but for which the arbitrator would have reached a different result. *See NFFE, Local 1984*, 56 FLRA 38, 41 (2000). However, the Authority will not find an award deficient on the basis of an arbitrator's determination of any factual matter that the parties disputed at arbitration. *See id.*

The alleged nonfacts cited by the Agency involve the Arbitrator's findings that most "employee transgressions" at the Agency can become the subject of security-clearance investigations and that, as a result, the Agency could "totally erode" *Weingarten* rights by precluding union representation during security-clearance-related examinations. Exceptions at 31, 32. The Arbitrator made the challenged findings only after he addressed the requirements of § 7114(a)(2)(B) – including the requirement that the employee reasonably feared discipline – and found those requirements met. *See* Award at 20-21. Thus, the challenged findings are dicta. *See Broad. Bd. of Governors, Office of Cuba Broad.*, 64 FLRA 888, 891-92 (2010) (citation omitted) (dicta are statements separate from the award and do not provide a basis for finding an award deficient). As such, the findings do not provide a basis for finding the award deficient. *See id.* Thus, we deny the nonfact exception and the related exception alleging that the challenged findings are contrary to law.

B. The award is not contrary to law.

When an exception involves an award's consistency with law, the Authority reviews any question of law raised by an exception and the award *de novo*. *See NTEU Chapter 24,* 50 FLRA 330, 332 (1995) (citing *U.S. Customs Serv. v. FLRA*, 43 F.3d 682, 686-87 (D.C. Cir. 1994)). In applying the standard of *de novo* review, the Authority assesses whether an arbitrator's legal conclusions are consistent with the applicable legal standard. *See U.S. DOD, Dep'ts of the Army & the Air Force, Ala. Nat'l Guard, Northport, Ala.*, 55 FLRA 37, 40 (1998). In making that assessment, the Authority defers to the arbitrator's underlying factual findings. *Id.*

1. The Finding that § 7114(a)(2)(B) Applies to Security-Clearance Examinations

Section 7114(a)(2)(B) of the Statute provides, in pertinent part, that "[a]n exclusive representative of an appropriate unit in an agency shall be given the opportunity to be represented at-- . . . any examination of an employee in the unit by a representative of the agency in connection with an investigation if . . . the employee reasonably believes that the examination may result in disciplinary action against the employee; and . . . the employee requests representation." The plain wording of § 7114(a)(2)(B) does not exclude security-clearance-related examinations from the definition of "examination[.]" In addition, the Agency does not cite any Authority or court decisions holding that § 7114(a)(2)(B) does not apply to security-clearance-related examinations. Although the Agency asserts that representation rights in security-clearance-investigatory interviews derive from E.O. 12,968 and 10 C.F.R. § 10.22(c), nothing in those authorities indicates that § 7114(a)(2)(B) is inapplicable to investigatory interviews that are conducted in connection with security-clearance investigations. *See supra*, notes 5 & 6. In addition, although the Agency asserts that its security-clearance interview procedures specifically prohibit "cross-examination" by the employee's representative, the Arbitrator did not find that the Union representative attempted to "cross-examin[e]" anyone. Exceptions at 14. As such, even assuming that the Agency's procedures could trump § 7114(a)(2)(B) in some circumstances, the Agency fails to demonstrate that § 7114(a)(2)(B) does not apply in this case.

In addition, the Agency's reliance on *Egan* is misplaced. In that decision, the Supreme Court held that the Merit Systems Protection Board lacks the authority to resolve the merits of an executive agency's security-clearance determination. 484 U.S. at 530-32. The Authority has held that, under *Egan*, neither arbitrators nor the Authority generally may review the merits of security-clearance determinations. *See IFPTE, Local 3*, 57 FLRA 699, 700 (2002); *P.R. Air Nat'l Guard, 156th Airlift Wing (AMC), Carolina, P.R.*, 56 FLRA 174, 181 n.10 (2000) (Chairman Wasserman dissenting in part). However, the Authority also has held that *Egan* does not preclude arbitrators from resolving issues that do not depend on a review of the merits of a security-clearance determination. *See AFGE, Local 1923*, 39 FLRA 1197, 1205 (1991); *U.S. Info. Agency*, 32 FLRA 739, 745-46 (1988) (*USIA*). For example, an arbitrator may review whether required procedural protections were satisfactorily provided to an employee in connection with the revocation of a security clearance. *See USIA*, 32 FLRA at 745.

The Arbitrator's assessment of whether the Agency violated § 7114(a)(2)(B) of the Statute did not involve a review of the merits of the Agency's security-clearance determination. In fact, as noted previously, the parties stipulated before the Arbitrator that no remedy was available to the employee in connection with the revocation of his security clearance. *See* Award at 8. Thus, nothing in *Egan* precluded the Arbitrator from assessing whether the investigatory interview violated § 7114(a)(2)(B).

For the foregoing reasons, we deny the exception.

2. The Finding that the Agency Denied the Employee the Right to Meaningful Union Representation

The Authority has held that "the purposes underlying [§] 7114(a)(2)(B) can be achieved only by allowing a union representative to take an active role in assisting a unit employee in presenting facts in his or her defense." *Bureau of Prisons, Office of Internal Affairs, Wash., D.C. & Phx., Ariz.*, 52 FLRA 421, 432 (1996) (Member Wasserman dissenting) (*Internal Affairs*) (quoting *NASA*, 50 FLRA at 607)). "A union representative's right to take an 'active role' includes not only the right to assist the employee in presenting facts but also the right to consult with the employee[.]" *Internal Affairs*, 52 FLRA at 432-33. In this connection, the Authority has held that "for the right to representation to be meaningful, the representative must have freedom to assist, and consult with, the affected employee." *Id.* at 433 (citation omitted). This is consistent with *Weingarten*,[7] where the Court stated that: "[a] single employee confronted by an employer investigating whether certain conduct deserves discipline may be too fearful or inarticulate to relate accurately the incident being investigated, or too ignorant to raise extenuating factors[;]" and "[a] knowledgeable union representative could assist the employer by eliciting favorable facts[.]" *Weingarten*, 420 U.S. at 262-63.

However, "a union's representational rights under [§] 7114(a)(2)(B) may not interfere with an employer's legitimate interest and prerogative in achieving the objective of the examination or compromise its integrity." *NASA*, 50 FLRA at 607 (citing *FAA, New Eng. Region, Burlington, Mass.*, 35 FLRA 645, 652 (1990)). In *Weingarten*, the Court, in summarizing the Board's litigative position, stated that an employer "is free to insist that he is only interested, at that time, in hearing the employee's own account of the matter under investigation." 420 U.S. at 260.

This wording from *Weingarten* has been interpreted as being "directed toward avoiding a bargaining session or a purely adversary confrontation with the union representative and to assure the employer the opportunity to hear the employee's own account of the incident under investigation." *NLRB v. Texaco*, 659 F.2d 124, 126 (9th Cir. 1981) (*Texaco*). Thus, where a union representative disrupts an interview by engaging in interruptions that are "verbally abusive" and "arrogantly insulting," an employer does not violate *Weingarten* rights by limiting the representative's participation. *Yellow Freight Sys., Inc.*, 317 NLRB 115, 124 (1995) (*Yellow Freight*) (representative "not entitled to disrupt the process by verbally abusive and arrogantly insulting interruptions, by conduct that grossly demeaned [an individual's] managerial status in front of an employee and fellow manager and that consisted of violent desk pounding and shouted obscenities, and finally by point-blank falsely calling [an individual] a liar and . . . refusing to immediately leave the office."). In addition, an employer does not violate *Weingarten* rights when it limits the union representative's participation after the representative has counseled an employee to answer a question only once and has prevented the employer from questioning the employee by engaging in persistent objections and interruptions. *Id.* (citing *N.J. Bell Tel. Co.*, 308 NLRB 277 (1992)).

However, the Authority has rejected the position that an employer is entitled to question an employee without *any* interruptions or intervention by the union representative. For example, in *United States Customs Service, Region VII, Los Angeles, California*, 5 FLRA 297 (1981), the Authority adopted a judge's decision in which the judge rejected an argument that an investigator "was entitled to obtain a statement from the employee without interruption from her representative." *Id.* at 307. Specifically, the judge held that "some interruption, by way of comments re[garding] the form of questions or statements as to possible infringement of employee rights, should properly be expected from the employee's representative." *Id.* In this connection, "[t]he employer always retains the option to refrain from conducting the examination in the event it decides that the interview, in the presence of a union representative, is not efficacious." *Id.* In addition, the judge found that even prohibiting the union representative from "pass[ing] notes" to the employee during the interview would impermissibly "circumscribe[] the effectiveness of the representative." *Id.*

The Authority reached a similar conclusion in *Norfolk Naval Shipyard*, 9 FLRA 458 (1982). In that decision, the Authority adopted the judge's finding of a *Weingarten* violation where, by intimidating the employees and attempting to silence their union

7. In interpreting § 7114(a)(2)(B), the Authority has found it appropriate to consider private-sector precedent involving *Weingarten* rights, but "has noted Congress' recognition that the right to representation might evolve differently in the private and Federal sectors, and that Board decisions would not necessarily be controlling in the Federal sector." *NASA*, 50 FLRA at 608 n.5.

representatives, the investigator interfered with protected rights. *Id.* at 473. The judge found a *Weingarten* violation despite the fact that the stewards continued to object, counsel and confer with the unit employees after being told to remain quiet. *Id.*

In addition, the Authority has held that meaningful representation includes the right to make statements that are part of the official record. In this connection, even where a representative has been permitted to confer with an employee and make statements "off the record," the Authority has found no "meaningful representation[]" where there was no indication that off-the-record statements would be considered in making a final determination regarding discipline. *Dep't of Veterans Affairs, Veterans Affairs Med. Ctr., Jackson, Miss.*, 48 FLRA 787, 798, 799 (1993), *on recon.* 49 FLRA 171, *recon. denied*, 49 FLRA 701 (1994) (*VAMC Jackson*).

The Board has reached similar conclusions regarding a representative's right to actively participate in an investigatory interview. Specifically, the Board has held that an employer's "right to regulate the role of the representative at the interview . . . cannot exceed that which is necessary to ensure the 'reasonable prevention of such a collective-bargaining or adversary confrontation with the statutory representative.'" *U.S. Postal Serv.*, 288 NLRB 864, 867 (1988) (citation omitted) (*USPS*). The principle that the employer may regulate the role of the union representative "does not state that the employer may bar the union representative from any participation[,]" which would be "wholly contrary to other language in the *Weingarten* opinion which explains that the representative should be able to take an active role in assisting the employee to present the facts." *Texaco*, 659 F.2d at 126. Accordingly, the Board has found a *Weingarten* violation when an interviewer silenced the union representative whenever the representative interrupted the interviewer's questioning of the employee. *USPS*, 288 NLRB at 868. *See also San Antonio Portland Cement Co.*, 277 NLRB 338, 339 (1985) (employer violated *Weingarten* rights by "cut[ting] off [union representative's] attempt to elicit information from employee and telling representative that he was "merely [present] as a witness and was not supposed to speak[]"); *Greyhound Lines, Inc.*, 273 NLRB 1443, 1448 (1985) (employer violated *Weingarten* rights by telling union representative that he must remain silent during interview); *U.S. Postal Serv.*, 254 NLRB 703, 707 (1981) (employer violated *Weingarten* rights where union representative was "not permitted to consult with nor counsel [the employee] in any way or to make any utterance *during the questioning*[]") (emphasis added).

Here, allowing the Union representative to counsel the employee while questions were pending was necessary to afford meaningful representation, particularly given the Arbitrator's finding that, once the employee had answered the question without assistance from the Union representative, he could not "further answer the question[.]" Award at 2. In this connection, as stated previously, § 7114(a)(2)(B) allows a union representative to "take an active role in *assisting a unit employee in presenting facts* in his or her defense.'" *Internal Affairs*, 52 FLRA at 432 (emphasis added). This is consistent with the policies underlying *Weingarten*, which, as stated above, include the considerations that an employee "may be too fearful or inarticulate to relate accurately the incident being investigated, or too ignorant to raise extenuating factors[,]" and that "[a] knowledgeable union representative could assist the employer by *eliciting favorable facts*[.]" *Weingarten*, 420 U.S. at 263 (emphasis added). *Accord Texaco*, 659 F.2d at 126 (representative entitled to "take an active role in *assisting the employee to present the facts[]*") (emphasis added). In addition, as stated previously, there is no "meaningful representation[]" when there is no indication that statements made by an employee with a union representative's assistance will be part of the official record that the employer considers in deciding whether discipline is warranted. *VAMC Jackson*, 48 FLRA at 799.

By not allowing the Union representative to counsel the employee before he answered questions, and then precluding the employee from adding to his answers after he had answered them without assistance, the Agency did not allow the Union representative to assist the employee in presenting facts in his own defense. Any counseling that the Agency permitted after the answers were completed did not preserve the Union representative's ability to provide meaningful representation to the employee, as required by § 7114(a)(2)(B).

The Agency asserts that it did not impose limitations on the Union representative until the representative "substantially interfered with" the Agency's "right and interest in obtaining spontaneous answers" from the employee. Exceptions at 21-22. However, the Union argues that the evidence was disputed with respect to whether the Agency imposed the limitations prior to, or during, the interview, and that, in either case, "the majority of the interview was clearly conducted under" the restrictions imposed by the Agency. Opp'n at 40 n.9. The Arbitrator did not make a factual finding that the Agency imposed its restrictions only after the start of the interview or after the Union representative interrupted the questioning. In addition, the Agency asserts that it is "not challenging the Arbitrator's factual determination[s]" regarding the interview. Exceptions at 20 n.21. Accordingly, there is no basis for the Authority to make a factual finding, not present in the award, that the Agency imposed the limitations only after the Union representative substantially interfered with the questioning.

Even assuming that the Agency imposed the limitations only after the Union representative intervened in some manner, the Agency's allegations regarding the nature of the alleged interventions do not support finding that the Union representative engaged in impermissible conduct during the interview. According to the Agency, the Union representative "directed the employee's attention to text in documents by pointing[,]" Exceptions at 4, and also engaged in "trying to stop [the employee] from answering questions, leaning over and cupping his hand, and whispering in [the employee's] ear and trying to actually answer questions for [the employee]." *Id.* at 22 n.23. However, the Agency does not corroborate this claim with any specific examples, and the Arbitrator did not make any findings that the representative acted as alleged. With regard to pointing to documents, the Union acknowledges that this occurred "at one point during the examination," but states that the document had been written by the employee himself and that the Union representative pointed to it only to "tr[y] to remind [the employee] to discuss a particular fact so that [he] could provide a more complete answer." Opp'n at 6. With regard to whispering in the employee's ear, the Union acknowledges that the Union representative whispered "advice" because he was "trying to ensure his answer's more complete; correct; accurate; and, more importantly, favorable aspects that he was not completely answering" would be mentioned. *Id.* at 6-7.

These circumstances provide no basis for finding that the Union representative: engaged in interruptions that were "verbally abusive" and "arrogantly insulting," *Yellow Freight*, 317 NLRB at 124; counseled the employee to answer questions only once, *id.*; prevented the Agency from questioning the employee by engaging in persistent objections and interruptions, *id.*; or attempted to convert the interview into "a bargaining session or a purely adversary confrontation[.]" *Texaco*, 659 F.2d at 126. In addition, although the Union representative attempted to assist the employee in answering questions, he did not preclude the Agency from "hear[ing] the employee's own account of the incident under investigation." *Id.* Further, as discussed previously, given the fact that the employee was not permitted to elaborate upon his initial answers to the Agency's questions, the only opportunity that the Union representative had to meaningfully elicit favorable facts from the employee was while questions were pending. Finally, *Treasury*, 707 F.2d 574, cited by the Agency, does not support setting aside the Arbitrator's finding of a violation, as that decision did not involve *Weingarten* rights under § 7114(a)(2)(B) of the Statute.

For the foregoing reasons, we conclude that the Arbitrator did not err by finding a violation of § 7114(a)(2)(B) in connection with the in-person interview.

With regard to the Arbitrator's finding that the Agency also violated § 7114(a)(2)(B) of the Statute by emailing the employee after the interview, the Authority has recognized that when an arbitrator bases an award on separate and independent grounds, an appealing party must establish that all of the grounds are deficient in order to demonstrate that the award is deficient. *See, e.g., U.S. Dep't of the Treasury, IRS, Oxon Hill, Md.*, 56 FLRA 292, 299 (2000). In such circumstances, if the excepting party does not demonstrate that the award is deficient on one of the grounds relied on by the arbitrator, then it is unnecessary to address exceptions to the other grounds. *See id.* As we have concluded that the Arbitrator did not err in finding a § 7114(a)(2)(B) violation with regard to the interview, and this finding provides a separate and independent basis for his finding of a § 7114(a)(2)(B) violation, we find it unnecessary to resolve the Agency's exceptions to the Arbitrator's finding regarding the email.

For the foregoing reasons, we deny the Agency's exceptions regarding § 7114(a)(2)(B).

3. Section 7106 of the Statute

The Agency asserts that the finding of a *Weingarten* violation is contrary to management's rights to determine internal security practices and discipline employees under § 7106 of the Statute. However, the Authority has stated that § 7106 "cannot be read as being so dominant that it negates congressionally-mandated, fundamental rights found in other parts of the Statute[,]" including "the *Weingarten* right to representation under [§] 7114(a)(2)(B)." *Prisons*, 55 FLRA at 1259 n.14.

As we have denied the exceptions to the Arbitrator's finding of a *Weingarten* violation, finding that the award is contrary to § 7106 would effectively "negate[]" the finding of that violation. *Id.* *NRC*, 25 F.3d 229, cited by the Agency, is inapposite because it involved an issue regarding whether proposals conflicted with the Inspector General Act, not § 7106 or § 7114(a)(2)(B) of the Statute. For these reasons, and consistent with *Prisons*, we deny the Agency's exceptions regarding § 7106 of the Statute.

V. Decision

The exceptions are denied.[8]

8. As there are no exceptions to the Arbitrator's cease-and-desist order and the direction to post a notice, we adopt those remedies.

65 FLRA No. 23

UNITED STATES
DEPARTMENT OF HOMELAND SECURITY
U.S. CUSTOMS AND BORDER PROTECTION
(Agency)

and

AMERICAN FEDERATION
OF GOVERNMENT EMPLOYEES
NATIONAL BORDER PATROL COUNCIL
(Union)

0-AR-4494

DECISION

September 24, 2010

Before the Authority: Carol Waller Pope, Chairman, and Thomas M. Beck and Ernest DuBester, Members

I. Statement of the Case

This matter is before the Authority on exceptions to an award of Arbitrator Joseph M. Sharnoff filed by the Agency under § 7122(a) of the Federal Service Labor-Management Relations Statute (the Statute) and part 2425 of the Authority's Regulations. The Union filed an opposition to the Agency's exceptions.

The Arbitrator found that the Agency violated the parties' agreement and the Statute by unilaterally making several changes to the Agency's body-armor policy (the policy), and he awarded a partial status quo ante (SQA) remedy.[1] For the following reasons, we deny the exceptions.

II. Background and Arbitrator's Award

The Agency made several changes to the policy without giving the Union notice and an opportunity to bargain. The Union filed a grievance, which was unresolved and submitted to arbitration. At arbitration, the parties stipulated to the following issue: "Did the Agency violate the Collective Bargaining Agreement and/or law when it unilaterally implemented [the policy] . . . without first notifying the Union and providing it was an opportunity to negotiate to the fullest extent of the law? If so, what is the remedy?" Award at 3.

The Arbitrator found that there was no dispute that the Agency had an obligation to bargain only the impact and implementation, not the substance, of the changes. *Id.* at 5, 7. The Arbitrator found that the reasonably foreseeable effects of several of the changes were greater than de minimis, *id.* at 7-14, but determined that the reasonably foreseeable effects of one of the changes were de minimis, *id.* at 15. As the Agency failed to engage in impact and implementation bargaining before making the changes that were greater than de minimis, the Arbitrator sustained the grievance "to the extent set forth in the Opinion." *Id.* at 18.

As to remedy, the Arbitrator applied the factors set forth in *Federal Correctional Institution*, 8 FLRA 604, 606 (1982) (*FCI*), for assessing whether SQA relief is appropriate.[2] The Arbitrator granted the request for SQA relief, "but only to the extent that the Union . . . claimed that the Agency's unilateral implementation of the . . . policy resulted in changes in working conditions which were not de minimis and which claims were upheld by the Arbitrator." Award at 18.

III. Positions of the Parties

A. Agency's Exceptions

The Agency argues that the SQA remedy is contrary to management's right to determine internal security practices under § 7106(a)(1) of the Statute.[3]

1. Although the Arbitrator did not expressly state that he found a violation of the Statute, there is no dispute that the violation of "law" asserted in the grievance, *see* Award at 2, and sustained in part by the Arbitrator, *see id.* at 18, is a violation of the Statute.

2. The *FCI* factors are: (1) whether, and when, notice was given to the union by the agency concerning the action or change decided upon; (2) whether, and when, the union requested bargaining on the procedures to be observed by the agency in implementing such action or change and/or concerning appropriate arrangements for employees adversely affected by such action or change; (3) the willfulness of the agency's conduct in failing to discharge its bargaining obligations under the Statute; (4) the nature and extent of the impact experienced by adversely affected employees; and (5) whether, and to what degree, an SQA remedy would disrupt or impair the efficiency and effectiveness of the agency's operations. 8 FLRA at 606.

3 We note that the Agency does not except to the Arbitrator's finding of an underlying statutory and

Exceptions at 5. In this connection, the Agency asserts that it had an internal security right to implement the policy. *Id.* at 8-9. In addition, the Agency asserts that, if it had complied with the law, then it would have given the Union the opportunity to engage in impact and implementation bargaining, but would not have maintained the status quo. *Id.* at 6-7. The Agency also asserts that it had "valid safety and operational impetuses" for making the changes, and it is "unreasonable" to direct the Agency to return to the status quo, as that "could result in scenarios that [would be] impractical, if not impossible[,]" including: requiring the Agency to issue body armor that is insufficient to protect employees; requiring the Agency to contract with vendors with whom the Agency no longer has contractual relationships; and allowing employees unfettered discretion as to whether to wear body armor on the range. *Id.* at 7-8. The Agency also asserts that the Authority, "in determining whether an ordered remedy is lawful, has examined cases concerning negotiability[]" and "utilized these negotiability determinations to decide whether an ordered remedy is permissible." *Id.* at 9 (citing *AFGE, Local 2006*, 58 FLRA 297 (2003) (*Local 2006*), and *U.S. INS, U.S. Border Patrol, San Diego Sector, San Diego, Cal.*, 43 FLRA 642 (1991) (*Border Patrol*)).

B. Union's Opposition

The Union argues that the award is not contrary to management rights. In this connection, the Union asserts that the Arbitrator did not require substantive, but only impact and implementation, bargaining. Opp'n at 7-8. In addition, the Union disputes the Agency's assertion that the remedy would force the Agency to issue less protective armor, and argues that the fact that the Agency may be required to contract with additional vendors does not demonstrate that the SQA remedy is inappropriate.[4] *Id.* at 11.

IV. Analysis and Conclusion

The Authority has held that "an arbitrator is empowered to fashion the same remedies in the arbitration of a grievance alleging the commission of an unfair labor practice as those authorized under [§] 7118 of the Statute." *NTEU*, 48 FLRA 566, 570 (1993). In addition, the Authority has held that § 7106(a) "limits the scope of bargaining rather than limiting the Authority's ability to issue remedial orders" under § 7118 of the Statute. *U.S. Dep't of the Air Force, 60th Air Mobility Wing, Travis Air Force Base, Cal.*, 59 FLRA 632, 639 (2004) (citing *Fed. Bureau of Prisons, Wash., D.C.*, 55 FLRA 1250, 1256-58 (2000)). Consistent with this principle, the Authority has held that the fact that management has a right to implement a change that adversely affects employees does not provide a basis for denying an SQA remedy. *U.S. Dep't of Energy, W. Area Power Admin., Golden, Colo.*, 56 FLRA 9, 13 (2000).

Consistent with this precedent, the Agency's argument that the award is contrary to management's right to determine internal security practices under § 7106(a)(1) does not provide a basis for finding that the Arbitrator erred in awarding SQA relief. In addition, the Agency does not assert, or provide any basis for finding, that the Arbitrator misapplied the *FCI* factors. To the extent that the Agency's claim regarding the SQA relief being "unreasonable" could be construed as raising the fifth *FCI* factor – whether, and to what degree, the remedy would disrupt or impair the efficiency and effectiveness of the Agency's operations – the Authority has held that a conclusion that an SQA remedy would be disruptive to the operations of an agency must be based on record evidence. *E.g., U.S. DHS, Customs & Border Prot.*, 64 FLRA 989, 996 (2010) (Member Beck dissenting in part). The Agency does not provide any record evidence to support its assertion and, thus, does not provide a basis for setting aside the SQA remedy on this ground.

Moreover, the decisions cited by the Agency do not support a contrary conclusion. *Local 2006* held that it is not improper for an arbitrator, in determining whether a proposed interpretation of an agreement would be inconsistent with law or

---

contractual violation; rather, the Agency excepts only to the SQA remedy.

4. The Union also asserts that it was contrary to law for the Arbitrator to direct the Agency to bargain only to the extent that the Arbitrator found individual aspects of the policy to be greater-than-de-minimis changes. *See* Opp'n at 12. The Union asserts that, "[i]f the Authority should find this argument is not within the scope of the exceptions raised by the Agency, then the Union requests that it be considered as a cross exception[]" or, alternatively, that the Authority "may address, sua sponte, matters that were not excepted to by the parties." *Id.* at 12 n.8 (citations omitted). To the extent that the Union is excepting to the award, the exception is untimely, as the award was served on the parties on January 25, 2009, and the Union filed its opposition on April 6, 2009. *See* 5 U.S.C. § 7122(b) (exception must be filed "during the 30-day period beginning on the date the award is served on the party"). In addition, this time limit cannot be extended or waived. 5 C.F.R. § 2429.23(d); *accord SSA, Balt., Md.*, 64 FLRA 306, 306 (2009). Accordingly, we do not consider the Union's assertion.

regulation, to rely on Authority negotiability precedent. 58 FLRA at 299. In *Border Patrol*, the Authority addressed the negotiability of a union's proposals in order to determine whether the agency violated the Statute by implementing a change after declaring the proposals nonnegotiable. 43 FLRA at 653-63. Neither decision held that an SQA remedy is limited by the negotiability of any union proposals, and, in any event, the Agency never gave the Union an opportunity to develop any proposals in this case. Thus, the decisions cited by the Agency are inapposite and do not provide a basis for setting aside the award.

For the foregoing reasons, the award is not contrary to management's right to determine internal security practices. Accordingly, we deny the exceptions.

V. Decision

The exceptions are denied.

65 FLRA No. 24

AMERICAN FEDERATION
OF GOVERNMENT EMPLOYEES
LOCAL 1547
(Union)

and

UNITED STATES
DEPARTMENT OF THE AIR FORCE
LUKE AIR FORCE BASE, ARIZONA
(Agency)

0-AR-4278

DECISION

September 28, 2010

Before the Authority: Carol Waller Pope, Chairman, and Thomas M. Beck and Ernest DuBester, Members

I. Statement of the Case

This matter is before the Authority on exceptions to an award of Arbitrator Donald Daughton filed by the Union under § 7122(a) of the Federal Service Labor-Management Relations Statute (the Statute) and part 2425 of the Authority's Regulations. The Agency filed an opposition to the Union's exceptions.

The Agency unilaterally changed the access requirements for its email system. Under the new requirements, bargaining unit employees could only access the system by using a "Common Access Card" (CAC) reader when they were at an off-base location. The Union grieved, arguing that this action constituted an unfair labor practice (ULP). The Arbitrator denied the grievance, finding that the Agency's action did not have an impact on the working conditions of bargaining unit employees.

For the reasons discussed below, we deny the Union's exception that the award is based on a nonfact. In addition, as discussed below, we deny in part and grant in part the Union's exceeded authority exception. Finally, with respect to the part of the exceeded authority exception that we grant, we remand the matter to the parties for resubmission to the Arbitrator, absent settlement, for further proceedings consistent with the Authority's decision.

II. Background and Arbitrator's Award

On November 22, 2006, for security reasons, Luke Air Force Base discontinued off-base access to its email system through the use of a password. Award at 2-3. Instead, off-base access to the Agency's email system was restricted to individuals with CAC readers. *Id.* Employees, including bargaining unit members, wishing to access the Agency's email system had to purchase their own CAC readers. When the Agency implemented the change without prior notice to the Union, the Union filed a grievance. The matter was not resolved and was submitted to arbitration.

The parties stipulated six issues for the Arbitrator to decide. The first issue, on which the Arbitrator ultimately resolved the grievance, concerned whether the Agency had changed bargaining unit employees' conditions of employment when it changed procedures for accessing the Agency's email system. Specifically, the first issue was:

> 1. Did [the Agency] violate the law by committing [ULPs], 5 USC § 7116, when it made the unilateral changes to the conditions of employment for the bargaining unit employees of Luke AFB?

Id. at 1.

The next four issues, which the Arbitrator did not reach, concerned whether the Agency had fulfilled various aspects of its bargaining obligation, assuming that it had changed bargaining unit employees' conditions of employment. Those issues were:

> 2. Did the [Agency] give proper notice of the change to the Union?
>
> 3. Did the [Agency] give the Union an opportunity to bargain?
>
> 4. Did the [Agency] negotiate the Impact and Implementation concerning the changes to the email systems?

> 5. Did [the Agency] violate Article III, Article IV and Article VI of the LMA [Labor Management Agreement] when it made unilateral changes to the email access for employees from off-base [Temporary Duty], etc.?[1]

Id. at 1-2.

The final issue, which the Arbitrator also did not reach, concerned the Agency's compliance with a Memorandum of Understanding (MOU) dated June 27, 2006. The sixth issue was:

> 6. Did [the Agency] violate the MOU dated June 27, 2006, concerning CAC and [Smart Card Login] access for [bargaining unit employees]?

Id. at 2.

The Arbitrator found that before the Agency changed its procedure for accessing the Agency's email system, employees could access the system from off-base with a password. Award at 3. This, he determined, enabled employees to utilize a "Federal Job Website" from off-base to apply for off-base job opportunities. *Id.*

The Arbitrator noted that when off-base access to its email system resulted in a number of security breaches, the Agency changed its access policy and restricted off-base access to individuals with CAC readers. *Id.* The new policy required an employee who wanted to access the Agency's email system from off-base to purchase his/her own CAC reader. *Id.* at 4. The Arbitrator determined that the Agency changed its access policy without prior notice to the Union. *Id.* at 3-4. He further found that the Union's "central complaint" about the change concerned the change's impact on the ability of employees to utilize a Federal Job Website via the Agency's email system to apply for off-base jobs. *Id.* at 4.

Focusing on the first stipulated issue, the Arbitrator identified the "core question" in the case as whether off-base email access through the use of a password was within the statutory definition of a "condition of employment." *Id.* The Arbitrator determined that it was not. He found that the elimination of password access to the Agency's email system "does not affect the ability of an employee to perform his or her duties and does not affect their day to day working conditions." *Id.* "Rather," the Arbitrator found, the elimination of off-base password access "simply limits a bargaining unit employee's ability to seek off-base employment through a Federal Job Website." *Id.* The Arbitrator concluded that "[n]o credible evidence was presented to show how this would affect a bargaining unit employee's working conditions . . . ." *Id.* at 4-5.

Because the Arbitrator found that "there is no factual basis . . . for finding conduct on the part of the [Agency] which impacts on the working conditions of the bargaining unit employees," he concluded that it was "unnecessary to resolve the remaining issues urged by the Union," apparently viewing them as moot. *Id.* at 5. The Arbitrator therefore denied the grievance.

III. Positions of the Parties

A. Union's Exceptions

The Union claims that the Arbitrator relied on a nonfact when he found that, as pertinent to the arbitration, bargaining unit employees needed off-base access to the email system to apply for "off-base job opportunities." Exceptions at 2-3. The Union asserts that the issues presented at arbitration did not concern the employees' ability to apply for off-base job opportunities, but rather focused on the employees' ability to apply for vacant Agency positions. *Id.*

The Union also argues that the Arbitrator exceeded his authority by not addressing all of the stipulated issues that were before him. *Id.* at 2. The Union does not make specific claims with regard to stipulated issues two through five. However, it does specifically address the sixth issue, asserting that the Arbitrator improperly failed to determine whether the Agency violated the 2006 MOU, in which the Agency agreed to "keep the Agency email systems available to employees . . . ." *Id.* at 4.

In addition, the Union claims that the Arbitrator exceeded his authority when he addressed an issue -- whether applying for vacant positions using the Agency's email system is a condition of employment -- that was not stipulated by the parties as part of the grievance. *Id.* at 3-4. According to the Union, under Article XXVII, § B of the parties' collective bargaining agreement, only issues presented during

1. Articles III, IV, and VI of the LMA concern bargaining obligations related to bargaining unit employees conditions of employment.

the grievance procedure and stipulated by the parties can be submitted to arbitration.[2] *Id.*

Finally, the Union argues that the award fails to draw its essence from the parties' agreement by failing to address all the stipulated issues and by not being limited to the issues stipulated by the parties, as required by Article XXVII of the parties' collective bargaining agreement.[3] *Id.* at 2-4.[4]

B. Agency's Opposition

The Agency does not address the Union's nonfact exception.

The Agency argues that the Arbitrator did not exceed his authority. It contends that the Arbitrator correctly decided the first issue when he found that the Agency's unilateral action modifying employee email access was not a ULP because it did not affect any conditions of employment. Opp'n at 1-4. The Agency further claims that the Arbitrator's conclusion concerning the first stipulated issue rendered the remaining issues moot. *Id.* at 4. Because the Agency had not changed unit employees' conditions of employment, there remained no issues concerning whether the Agency had fulfilled its obligation to bargain over changes to conditions of employment. *Id.* at 3-4.

The Agency also asserts that the Arbitrator did not exceed his authority when he addressed an issue that was not stipulated by the parties as part of the grievance. The Agency contends that, although it was not among the parties' stipulations, whether off-base email access is a condition of employment was directly related to the resolution of the first stipulated issue. The Agency notes that arbitrators do not exceed their authority by addressing issues that are necessary to decide a stipulated issue. *Id.* at 3-4.

Finally, the Agency claims that the Arbitrator's decision draws its essence from the parties' agreement. The Agency recognizes that the parties' agreement requires that the parties stipulate all issues to be arbitrated. However, the Agency argues that the condition of employment issue addressed by the Arbitrator, although not stipulated, had to be addressed in order to resolve the first stipulated issue. *Id.* at 4-5. The Agency asserts that the Union's essence exception is merely a disagreement with the Arbitrator's interpretation and application of the parties' agreement. *Id.* at 5.

IV. Analysis and Conclusions

A. The award is not based on a nonfact.

The Union disagrees with the Arbitrator's factual finding that, as pertinent to the arbitration, off-base email access was needed to apply for off-base job opportunities. It argues that off-base email access was needed to apply for Agency positions. Exceptions at 2-3.

In order to establish that an award is based on a nonfact, a party must show that a central fact underlying the award is clearly erroneous, but for which the arbitrator would have reached a different result. *U.S. Dep't of the Air Force, Lowry AFB, Denver, Colo.*, 48 FLRA 589, 593 (1993) (*Lowry AFB*).

The Union has not established that the Arbitrator's determination that bargaining unit employees needed off-base email access to apply for "off-base job opportunities" was clearly erroneous. Exceptions at 2-3. In support of its nonfact claim, the Union relies on two MOUs between the parties that reference employees' ability to access the Agency's computer system to self-nominate for positions (MOU dated 2001) and apply for jobs (MOU dated 2006).[5] However, the MOUs are ambiguous, as

2. Article XXVII, § B states in pertinent part:

> The parties agree that the issue(s) to be arbitrated will be consistent with those issue(s) presented during the grievance procedure. . . . The arbitrator shall confine his/her award to the issue(s) stipulated at the hearing and will not have the authority to make a decision on any issue(s) not so stipulated . . . .

Exceptions, Attach. 3 at 1.

3. The Union's claim that the award fails to draw its essence from the parties' LMA is substantively the same as its exceeded authority claims that the Arbitrator improperly failed to address all stipulated issues and addressed an issue that was not stipulated by the parties pursuant to the parties' LMA. *See* Exceptions at 2-4. Therefore, the Union's essence exception is not analyzed separately.

4. The Union is not challenging, on contrary to law grounds, the Arbitrator's conclusion that the disputed email access is not a condition of employment.

5. The 2001 MOU concerned the implementation of Air Force Manual 36-203-- Staffing Civilian Personnel Positions. The MOU provided that, upon request, email accounts would be provided to bargaining unit employees, and access to the computer system would be made

neither indicates whether employees need email access solely to apply for positions within the Agency. Moreover, neither MOU addresses which email access issues were raised before the Arbitrator. Ambiguous evidence is not sufficient to establish that an Arbitrator's factual determination is clearly erroneous. *See Lowry AFB,* 48 FLRA at 594. Consequently, we deny the Union's nonfact exception.

B. The Arbitrator exceeded his authority by failing to resolve a stipulated issue submitted to arbitration.

1. The Arbitrator did not exceed his authority by not addressing all of the stipulated issues.

The Union argues that the Arbitrator exceeded his authority by not resolving all of the stipulated issues. Exceptions at 2.

Arbitrators exceed their authority when they fail to resolve an issue submitted to arbitration. *See AFGE, Local 1617*, 51 FLRA 1645, 1647 (1996). Arbitrators, however, do not exceed their authority when they do not resolve issues that become moot as a consequence of the resolution of other issues. *Cf. AFGE, Local 987*, 58 FLRA 619, 621 (2003) (then-Member Pope dissenting) (finding that a grievance was barred by the Statute, the arbitrator did not exceed his authority by not resolving other claims raised before the arbitrator).

a. Stipulated issues numbers two through five.

The Arbitrator did not exceed his authority by not resolving stipulated issues two through five. The Arbitrator's determination not to reach those issues was based on his resolution of the first stipulated issue. That issue concerned whether the Agency committed a ULP when it unilaterally changed a condition of employment of bargaining unit employees. Award at 1. The condition of employment alleged to have been changed was the bargaining unit employees' ability to access their email accounts when off-base. *Id.* at 2. In this regard, the Arbitrator concluded that there was no duty to bargain because the Agency's decision to change its email policy did not have an impact on the working conditions of bargaining unit employees, and consequently that the Agency did not commit a ULP when it unilaterally changed the access to the email system.

When the Arbitrator found that the Agency's action did not have an impact on the working conditions of bargaining unit employees, it rendered stipulated issues two through five moot. These issues concerned whether the Agency had fulfilled various aspects of its bargaining obligation relating to Agency changes in conditions of employment. If the Agency had, in fact, changed a condition of employment, then it would have been pertinent to consider the issues raised by stipulated issues two through five. *See NTEU*, 64 FLRA 462, 464 (2010) (prior to changing conditions of employment, agencies must provide the exclusive representative notice of the change and an opportunity to bargain). However, here, the Arbitrator concluded that the change in the Agency's email policy did not affect employees' working conditions because off-base email access was not a condition of employment.

As the Arbitrator found that the Agency's action did not have an impact on the working conditions of bargaining unit employees, it became a moot point whether the Agency was required to give the Union notice of the change in policy (second issue); or to resolve whether the Agency was required to negotiate the impact and implementation of the changes to the email system (fourth issue). In addition, because the Arbitrator found that there was no duty to bargain, the issue of whether the Agency failed to give the Union an opportunity to bargain (third issue) became moot as well. Finally, as a result of the Arbitrator's conclusion with regard to the first issue, it also became moot for the Arbitrator to resolve whether there was a violation of Articles III, IV, and VI of the parties' LMA (fifth issue) because these articles also concern bargaining obligations over changes relating to conditions of employment.[6] Accordingly, as issues two through five became moot when the Arbitrator resolved the first issue, there was no need for the Arbitrator to address them. Consequently, the Arbitrator did not exceed his authority by not resolving issues two through five.

---

available in the employee's unit or squadron and/or Civilian Personnel Office. Exceptions, Attach. 2 at 1. The 2006 MOU provides, in pertinent part, that to access secure websites that require authentication from off-base locations or personal computers, a password may have to be established using the CAC at the work location. *Id.*, Attach. 1 at 1. The MOU also provides that systems, servers, and websites used by the employees to apply for jobs will remain accessible to employees through the "current" user identification password procedures on private computers. *Id.*

6. Articles III, IV, and VI of the parties' LMA are set forth in the Appendix.

b. Stipulated issue number six.

However, in contrast to issues two through five, the sixth stipulated issue did not become moot with the resolution of the first issue. The Arbitrator, therefore, exceeded his authority by not addressing issue number six. Unlike issues two through five, the sixth stipulated issue has nothing to do with whether the change in the Agency's email access policy had an impact on employees' working conditions. The sixth issue only required the Arbitrator to determine whether the Agency violated the 2006 MOU when it changed its policy regarding off-base email access. Award at 2. As indicated previously, supra note 4, the 2006 MOU provided, in part, that systems, servers, and websites used by employees to apply for jobs would remain accessible to employees through the then-current user id/password procedures on private computers. Exceptions, Attach. 1.

Accordingly, the Arbitrator exceeded his authority by failing to resolve a stipulated issue submitted to arbitration. *See U.S. Dep't of Def., Def. Contract Audit Agency, Cent. Region, Irving, Tex.*, 60 FLRA 28, 30 (2004) (arbitrator exceeded his authority when he failed to resolve an issue submitted to arbitration).

2. The Arbitrator did not exceed his authority when he resolved an issue that was not submitted to arbitration.

The Union also claims that the Arbitrator exceeded his authority because he resolved an issue -- whether off-base access to the Agency's email system is a condition of employment -- that was not submitted to arbitration. Exceptions at 2-3.

Arbitrators exceed their authority when they resolve an issue not submitted to arbitration. *AFGE, Local 1617*, 51 FLRA at 1647. However, arbitrators do not exceed their authority by addressing an issue that is necessary to decide a stipulated issue or by addressing an issue that necessarily arises from issues specifically included in a stipulation. *E.g., NTEU*, 64 FLRA 982, 986 (2010).

The Arbitrator did not exceed his authority by resolving whether off-base access to the Agency's email system was a condition of employment. As noted in Section B.1., above, in order to resolve whether the Agency committed a ULP when it unilaterally changed its email policy, it was necessary for the Arbitrator to address whether the change in email policy affected employees' working conditions. This in turn made it necessary for the Arbitrator to address whether off-base email access was a condition of employment.

As arbitrators do not exceed their authority by addressing an issue that is necessary to decide a stipulated issue, the Arbitrator here did not exceed his authority by addressing this issue.

V. Decision

We deny the Union's nonfact exception. We grant in part and deny in part the Union's exceeded authority and essence exceptions. We remand the award to the parties for resubmission to the Arbitrator, absent settlement, for further proceedings consistent with this decision.

APPENDIX

Article III, Section B

> *The Union has the right to negotiate with the Employer over changes to policies, programs, and procedures related to conditions of employment* which are within the authority of the Employer. The Union also has the right to submit mid-term proposals on subjects not covered by this agreement as well as all new laws, rules, and regulations.

Article IV, Section F

> The parties agree to work together in *promoting positive employee attitudes and esprit de corps with the objective of increased production,* reduced rates of errors, and more effective accomplishment of the mission of the base. To this end[,] Union representatives and Management officials will: Paragraph 3. *Promote friendly and harmonious working relationships* between supervisors and their subordinates and *between civilian and military personnel*[.] Paragraph 7. Strive to eliminate inequitable treatment of employees and any other practices which restrict and hamper efficiency and affect morale.

Article VI, Section A

> When a change will affect conditions of employment[,] *Management will notify the Union president.* Except in emergencies, *pending changes will not be implemented until required negotiations are completed.* The parties recognize that negotiations may be required even though the change, as a result of the emergency, has been implemented.

Exceptions, Attach. 5, Union's Post-Hearing Brief at 4.

65 FLRA No. 25

AMERICAN FEDERATION
OF GOVERNMENT EMPLOYEES
LOCAL 2924
(Union)

and

UNITED STATES
DEPARTMENT OF THE AIR FORCE
DAVIS-MONTHAN AIR FORCE BASE
TUCSON, ARIZONA
(Agency)

0-AR-4678

DECISION

September 28, 2010

Before the Authority: Carol Waller Pope, Chairman, and Thomas M. Beck and Ernest DuBester, Members

This matter is before the Authority on an exception to an award of Arbitrator Charles Cambridge filed by the Union under § 7122(a) of the Federal Service Labor-Management Relations Statute (the Statute) and part 2425 of the Authority's Regulations. The Agency filed an opposition to the Union's exception.*

Under § 7122(a) of the Statute, an award is deficient if it is contrary to any law, rule, or regulation, or it is deficient on other grounds similar to those applied by federal courts in private sector labor-management relations. Upon careful consideration of the entire record in this case and Authority precedent, the Authority concludes that the award is not deficient on the ground raised in the exception and set forth in § 7122(a). *See Prof'l Airways Sys. Specialists, Dist. No. 1, MEBA/NMU (AFL-CIO)*, 48 FLRA 764, 768-69 (1993) (award not deficient as contrary to law where excepting party fails to establish that the award is in any manner contrary to the law, rule, or regulation on which the party relies).

Accordingly, the Union's exception is denied.

* In its opposition, the Agency argues that the exception should be dismissed because the Union fails to state the basis of its exception and because the Union failed to comply with service requirements set forth in 5 C.F.R. § 2429.27. *See* Opp'n at 1. We reject the Agency's first argument because the Union's exception sufficiently states a claim that the award is contrary to an Agency regulation. *See* Exception at 1. As to the Agency's argument regarding service requirements, the Agency provides no support for this claim and, thus, we deny this claim as a bare assertion. *See, e.g., AFGE, Local 933*, 65 FLRA 9, 11 (2010). For these reasons, the Agency does not demonstrate that dismissal of the exception is warranted, and we consider the exception.

65 FLRA No. 26

UNITED STATES
DEPARTMENT OF HOMELAND SECURITY
UNITED STATES
CUSTOMS AND BORDER PROTECTION
WASHINGTON, D.C.
(Agency)

and

NATIONAL TREASURY
EMPLOYEES UNION
(Union)

0-AR-4367

DECISION

September 29, 2010

Before the Authority: Carol Waller Pope, Chairman, and Thomas M. Beck and Ernest DuBester, Members

I. Statement of the Case

This matter is before the Authority on exceptions to an award of Arbitrator Roger P. Kaplan filed by the Agency under § 7122(a) of the Federal Service Labor-Management Relations Statute (the Statute) and part 2425 of the Authority's Regulations. The Union filed an opposition to the exceptions.

The Arbitrator found that the Agency's use of Personal Appearance Standards (PAS) in selection and promotion decisions violated "merit system principles[,] . . . law, regulations and/or the [parties'] [a]greement[,]" Award at 29, and directed the Agency to cease implementation of the PAS. For the reasons that follow, we dismiss the exceptions in part, and deny them in part.

II. Background and Arbitrator's Award

The Agency implemented PAS that imposed restrictions on employees concerning such matters as hair style and length, facial hair, application of cosmetics, size and quantity of jewelry, and body piercings and tattoos. Award at 12. The Union filed a grievance alleging that the Agency's implementation of the PAS violated law, regulation, and the parties' agreement. *Id.* at 11. When the grievance was unresolved, it was submitted to arbitration, where, absent a stipulation by the parties, the Arbitrator framed the substantive issues[1] as follows: "[D]id the Agency violate the parties' . . . [a]greement, or applicable [f]ederal laws or regulations when it implemented the [PAS]? . . . If so, what is the appropriate remedy?" *Id.* at 2.

The Arbitrator found that the PAS constitute an "employment practice" within the meaning of 5 C.F.R. § 300.101 (§ 300.101).[2] *Id.* at 21. In this regard, the Arbitrator found that "the evidence showed that compliance with [the] PAS was necessary for initial and continued employment and for advancement." *Id.* at 20-21. He also found that "it was clear from the record that the PAS [were] used in making decisions regarding 'appointments' and 'promotions'." *Id.* at 28. Consequently, the Arbitrator found that the Agency violated 5 C.F.R. § 300.103 by promulgating the PAS without having conducted the job analysis required by that regulation.[3] *Id.* at 21-22. In this regard, the Arbitrator found that the Agency failed to demonstrate a rational relationship between the PAS and job performance, and that the record did not support a finding that the PAS were professionally developed. *Id.* at 24, 25. The Arbitrator found that because the Agency implemented an "unlawful 'employment practice[,]'" the Agency "violated merit system principles[,] . . . the law, regulations and/or

1. The Arbitrator also addressed an issue concerning whether the grievance was timely, and found that it was. Award at 15-19. As there are no exceptions to this finding, we do not address it further.

2. Section 300.101 states, in pertinent part, that the regulatory subpart in which it is contained establishes principles to govern "employment practices of [federal agencies] that affect the recruitment, measurement, ranking, and selection of individuals for initial appointment and competitive promotion in the competitive service[.]" Section 300.101 defines "employment practices" as including "the development and use of examinations, qualification standards, tests, and other measurement instruments."

3. 5 C.F.R. § 300.103 pertinently states that "[e]ach employment practice . . . shall be based on a job analysis to identify: (1) The basic duties and responsibilities; (2) The knowledges, skills, and abilities required to perform the duties and responsibilities; and (3) The factors that are important in evaluating candidates." It also states: "There shall be a rational relationship between performance in the position to be filled . . . and the employment practice used. The demonstration of rational relationship shall include a showing that the employment practice was professionally developed." *Id.*

the [parties'] [a]greement[,]" and, as a remedy, directed the Agency to "cease and desist" implementing the PAS. *Id.* at 28-29.

III. Positions of the Parties

A. Agency Exceptions

According to the Agency, "[t]he Arbitrator incorrectly ruled that compliance with the PAS was necessary for initial and continued employment and advancement and that an employee's failure to comply with the PAS would be considered . . . [in] evaluating the employee for advancement." Exceptions at 7. The Agency repeatedly asserts that "PAS are not used in selection decisions[,]" and that "[t]here is nothing in the record" to support the Arbitrator's contrary conclusion. *Id.* at 8, 7. In this regard, the Agency states that it "[c]learly . . . does not consider hair length, wearing of jewelry, and facial hair when selecting individuals for initial employment." *Id.* at 7.

The Agency asserts that the award is contrary to law "because it does not conform with applicable law with regard to the application of the terms 'employment practice' and 'qualification standard.'" *Id.* at 3. In this regard, the Agency argues that the PAS are a "condition of employment[,]" but not a "qualification standard[,]" *id.* at 6-7, and that the term "employment practice" in § 300.101 does not include the PAS because: (1) "'an individual agency action or decision that is not made pursuant to or as part of a rule or practice of some kind does not constitute an employment practice[,]'" *id.* at 5 (quoting *Wilcox v. MSPB*, Nos. 99-3314, 99-3315, 2000 WL 266481, at *2 (Fed. Cir. Mar. 9, 2000) (*Wilcox*)); and (2) "the term 'employment practice' is limited to actions that concern initial selection or promotion." *Id.* at 4-5 (citing *Meadows v. Palmer*, 775 F.2d 1193, 1198 (D.C. Cir. 1985) (*Meadows*)).

Additionally, the Agency argues that the Arbitrator's awarded remedy – directing the Agency to rescind the PAS – is contrary to law and exceeds the scope of the Arbitrator's authority. The Agency argues that the awarded remedy is contrary to law because the unit that filed the grievance no longer exists.[4] *Id.* at 11-13. In addition, the Agency argues that the Arbitrator exceeded his authority by instructing the Agency to rescind the PAS, which apply to *all* employees in the new unit, not only those who were formerly in the legacy unit that filed the grievance. *Id.* at 9-10.

B. Union Opposition

According to the Union, the Arbitrator properly found that the PAS are an employment practice within the meaning of § 300.101. Opp'n at 5-6. In addition, the Union argues that the Agency failed to raise its challenges to the remedy before the Arbitrator and that, in any event, the remedy is neither contrary to law nor outside the scope of the Arbitrator's authority. *Id.* at 9-16.

IV. Analysis and Conclusions

A. The award is not based on a nonfact.

We construe the Agency's argument that the Arbitrator incorrectly found that the Agency used the PAS in making selection and promotion decisions as a claim that the award is based on a nonfact. To establish that an award is based on a nonfact, the excepting party must establish that a central fact underlying the award is clearly erroneous, but for which the arbitrator would have reached a different result. *See U.S. Dep't of the Air Force, Lowry AFB, Denver, Colo.*, 48 FLRA 589, 593 (1993) (*Lowry*). However, the Authority will not find an award deficient on the basis of an arbitrator's determination of any factual matter that the parties disputed before the arbitrator. *Id.* at 593-94.

At arbitration, the Union argued, and the Agency disputed, that the Agency used the PAS as qualification criteria in making selection and promotion decisions. *See* Award at 19, 20. As the parties disputed this matter before the Arbitrator, the Agency's exception provides no basis for finding that the award is based on a nonfact. *See Lowry*,

4. We note, in this connection, that after the implementation of the PAS and the filing of the grievance, but prior to the arbitration hearing, the Authority certified a new bargaining unit (new unit) that includes, among other employees, all employees from the unit that filed the grievance (the legacy unit). *See* Award at 1, 14, 29-30; Exceptions, Attach., Hearing Transcript at 18; Exceptions at 3, 11. The Agency acknowledges that the Union was the elected exclusive representative for both the legacy unit and the new unit. Exceptions at 12-13.

48 FLRA at 593-94. Accordingly, we deny this exception.

B. The Arbitrator's finding that the PAS are an employment practice is not contrary to law.

When an exception involves an award's consistency with law, the Authority reviews any question of law raised by an exception and the award *de novo. See NTEU, Chapter 24,* 50 FLRA 330, 332 (1995) (citing *U.S. Customs Serv. v. FLRA,* 43 F.3d 682, 686-87 (D.C. Cir. 1994)). In applying a *de novo* standard of review, the Authority assesses whether the arbitrator's legal conclusions are consistent with the applicable standard of law. *See NFFE, Local 1437,* 53 FLRA 1703, 1710 (1998) (*Local 1437*). In making that assessment, the Authority defers to the arbitrator's underlying factual findings. *See id.*

Employment practices of the federal government that "affect the recruitment, measurement, ranking, and selection of individuals for initial appointment and competitive promotion in the competitive service" are subject to 5 C.F.R. part 300, subpart A. 5 C.F.R. § 300.101. Section 300.101 defines "employment practices" as including "the development and use of examinations, qualification standards, tests, and other measurement instruments." *See also NTEU*, 61 FLRA 554, 556 (2006). However, this term "should not be restricted to" these items, *Bush v. OPM*, 315 F.3d 1358, 1361 (Fed. Cir. 2003) (quoting *Prewitt v. MSPB*, 133 F.3d 885, 887 (Fed. Cir. 1998)), but should be given a "broad and inclusive meaning[.]" *NTEU*, 61 FLRA at 556 (quoting *Dowd v. United States*, 713 F.2d 720, 723 (Fed. Cir. 1983)). *See also Vesser v. OPM*, 29 F.3d 600, 603 (Fed. Cir. 1994) (refusing to interpret "employment practices" as only "the kinds of 'measurement instruments' that determine a candidate's ability to perform the duties and responsibilities of a job"); *Meadows*, 775 F.2d at 1198; *Saya v. Dep't of the Air Force*, 68 M.S.P.R. 493, 496 (1995) ("[p]ractices other than . . . merit-based tests also fall within the definition [of employment practice] if they affect selection.")

In finding that the PAS constitute an employment practice within the meaning of § 300.101, the Arbitrator stated, as discussed previously, that "compliance with [the] PAS was necessary for initial and continued employment and for advancement[,]" and that "the PAS [were] used in making decisions regarding 'appointments' and 'promotions.'" Award at 21, 28. As we have denied the Agency's nonfact exception above, we defer to these factual findings in reviewing the Agency's contrary-to-law exception. *See Local 1437*, 53 FLRA at 1710. Under the broad and inclusive meaning of employment practice, these findings support the Arbitrator's conclusion that the PAS are an employment practice. *See NTEU*, 61 FLRA at 556; *Bush*, 315 F.3d at 1360-61; *Prewitt*, 133 F.3d at 887; *Vesser*, 29 F.3d at 603; *Meadows*, 775 F.2d at 1198; *Dowd*, 713 F.2d at 723-24.

The decisions cited by the Agency do not support a contrary conclusion. *Wilcox*'s holding that "an individual agency action or decision that is not made pursuant to or as part of a rule or practice of some kind does not constitute an employment practice" is inapplicable because, here, the Arbitrator expressly found that the Agency engaged in the practice of using the PAS to make multiple appointment and promotion decisions. *See* Award at 28; *Wilcox*, 2000 WL 266481, at *2. Thus, whereas *Wilcox* concerned a single employee's allegation that one vacancy announcement was cancelled and another was not published in order to circumvent merit-system principles, here the Union alleged, and the Arbitrator found, that the Agency engaged in a pattern of making selection and advancement decisions using the PAS. *See* Award at 20-21, 28. In addition, the award is consistent with *Meadows*, which held that the term "employment practice" is "limited to actions which concern initial selection or promotion[,]" 775 F.2d at 1198, given the Arbitrator's finding that the Agency used the PAS "in making decisions regarding 'appointments' and 'promotions.'" Award at 28. Accordingly, the Agency has not established that the Arbitrator's conclusion that the PAS are an employment practice is contrary to law.

Further, because the term "employment practices" is to be broadly construed and is not limited to the terms specifically mentioned in § 300.101, including "qualification standards," the Agency's argument that the Arbitrator mischaracterized the PAS as a "qualification standard" does not provide a basis for finding deficient the Arbitrator's conclusion that the PAS are an employment practice. *See NTEU*, 61 FLRA at 556; *Bush*, 315 F.3d at 1360-61; *Prewitt*, 133 F.3d at 887; *Vesser*, 29 F.3d at 603; *Meadows*, 775 F.2d at 1198; *Dowd*, 713 F.2d at 723-24.

Based on the foregoing, we deny these exceptions.

C. Section 2429.5 of the Authority's Regulations bars the Agency's exceptions to the remedy directed by the Arbitrator.

Under § 2429.5 of the Authority's Regulations, the Authority will not consider issues that could have been, but were not, presented to the arbitrator. *See, e.g., U.S. Dep't of Homeland Sec., U.S. Customs & Border Prot., JFK Airport, Queens, N.Y.*, 62 FLRA 416, 417 (2008). Where a party makes an argument for the first time on exception that it could, and should, have made before the arbitrator, the Authority applies § 2429.5 to bar the argument. *See, e.g., U.S. Dep't of Justice, Fed. Bureau of Prisons, USP Admin. Maximum (ADX), Florence, Colo.*, 64 FLRA 1168, 1170 (2010) (*BOP*); *U.S. Dep't of Transp., FAA*, 64 FLRA 387, 389 (2010) (*FAA*).

Before the Arbitrator, the Union stated that the relief it was seeking included the rescission of the PAS. *See* Tr. at 18. The Agency could have, but did not, argue to the Arbitrator, as it does now, that the Authority's certification of the new unit would mean that awarding the Union's requested remedy would be contrary to law or exceed the Arbitrator's authority. Accordingly, we dismiss the Agency's exceptions to the remedy as barred by § 2429.5. *See BOP*, 64 FLRA at 1170 (§ 2429.5 barred argument that awarding remedy sought by union would violate law where the issue could have been, but was not, presented to the arbitrator); *FAA*, 64 FLRA at 390 (same).

V. Decision

The exceptions are dismissed in part and denied in part.

65 FLRA No. 27

FEDERAL DEPOSIT
INSURANCE CORPORATION
DIVISION OF SUPERVISION
AND CONSUMER PROTECTION
SAN FRANCISCO REGION
(Agency)

and

NATIONAL TREASURY
EMPLOYEES UNION
CHAPTER 273
(Union)

0-AR-4139

DECISION

September 29, 2010

Before the Authority: Carol Waller Pope, Chairman, and Thomas M. Beck and Ernest DuBester, Members[1]

I. Statement of the Case

This matter is before the Authority on exceptions to an award of Arbitrator Claude Dawson Ames filed by the Agency under § 7122(a) of the Federal Service Labor-Management Relations Statute (the Statute) and part 2425 of the Authority's Regulations. The Union filed an opposition to the Agency's exceptions.

The Arbitrator found that the Agency failed to fairly and equitably process the grievant's nomination for a Corporate Success Award (CSA). As a remedy, the Arbitrator ordered the Agency to award the grievant a CSA, with appropriate backpay.

The questions presented here are whether the award impermissibly affects management's rights to assign work and direct employees under 5 U.S.C. § 7106(a)(2)(A) and (B), and whether the award fails to draw its essence from the parties' agreement.

This case provides the Authority an opportunity to reexamine the restrictions that the Authority has placed on arbitrators' remedial powers in rendering awards that affect management rights under § 7106(a) of the Statute. The revised approach that we formulate for this and future cases, discussed in § IV.C. of this decision, gives arbitrators the same scope of remedial authority in such management rights cases as they routinely exercise in rendering awards that do not affect management rights.

For the reasons that follow, we deny the Agency's exceptions.

II. Background and Arbitrator's Award

The grievance claims that the Agency violated various Agency procedures and agreements with the Union when the Agency denied the grievant a CSA. A CSA is an annual award that provides Agency employees recognized as "top contributors" with a three percent increase in basic pay. Award at 3-4 (citing "Compensation Agreement Between FDIC and NTEU for the Years 2003-2005" (Compensation Agreement), § II.C). The percentage of employees to be recognized as "top contributors" in 2004 for their work in 2003 was to be set by the Agency's Chairman at "no less than 33 1/3 percent" of bargaining unit employees. Compensation Agreement, § II.C.

The Agency's CSA procedures for identifying top contributors are set forth in the Agency's "Procedures for Processing [CSAs]" Memorandum (the Memorandum) and "FDIC Directive System Circular 2420.1," Ch. 11, § 5 (Circular 2420.1). Award at 5-9. Circular 2420.1 is incorporated by reference in a Memorandum of Understanding between the parties (MOU).[2]

The CSA procedures have a number of steps. After supervisors numerically rank all nominated employees under their supervision, they submit the ranked nominations to the Assistant Regional Director (ARD) for their territory. *Id.* at 5-6. The ARD consolidates the nominations for evaluation by a first-level review panel consisting primarily of ARDs (the ARD Panel). *Id.* at 6. The ARD Panel evaluates each nomination, prioritizes the top one-third by assigning a numerical ranking, and submits those rankings to a second-level review panel consisting primarily of Deputy Regional Directors (DRDs) (the DRD Panel). *Id.* The DRD Panel evaluates and/or re-ranks each nominee and submits

1. Chairman Pope's separate opinion, concurring in part, is set forth at the end of the decision.

2. The relevant provisions of the Compensation Agreement, the Memorandum, Circular 2420.1, and the MOU are set forth in the attached Appendix.

the results to the Regional Director (RD) for approval. *Id.* The RD reviews the recommendations and submits the results to the Division Director. *Id.* The Compensation Agreement, the Memorandum, Circular 2420.1, and the MOU all require that CSAs be processed and distributed in a fair and equitable manner.

The grievant was nominated for a CSA for his work in 2003. His nomination was forwarded to the DRD Panel by the ARD Panel. *Id.* at 9. However, the DRD Panel did not forward his nomination to the RD for further review. Instead, the DRD Panel substituted another employee in place of the grievant. The substituted employee was not nominated before the nominations were submitted to the DRD Panel. By doing this, the Agency eliminated the grievant from consideration for a CSA. *Id.*

When the grievant learned how his nomination had been processed, he filed a grievance claiming that the Agency violated Circular 2420.1, the parties' collective bargaining agreement (CBA), and the Compensation Agreement by failing to award him a CSA. The grievance was not resolved, and was submitted to arbitration.

With no agreement on the issues, the Arbitrator determined that he would address both parties' submissions. The Union proposed: "Did management violate Circular 2420.1 when it failed to award [the grievant] a CSA? If so, what is the remedy?" *Id.* at 3. The Agency proposed: "Did the [Agency] abuse its discretion and violate Chapter 11 of Circular 2420.1 or Section 1 of the [MOU] when it did not give a [CSA] to [the g]rievant in 2004 based on his contributions for 2003? If so, what is the appropriate remedy?" *Id.*

The Arbitrator sustained the grievance. The Arbitrator held that the Agency violated the agreed-upon CSA selection process outlined in Circular 2420.1 and deprived the grievant of fair and equitable consideration for receipt of a CSA. *Id.* at 14-17. In the Arbitrator's view, the DRD Panel erred when it substituted another individual for the grievant. The Arbitrator found no evidence that the negotiated CSA selection process provided for the initiation of new nominations or for the removal of existing nominees at that stage of the process. *Id.* at 16.

Having found that the Agency "compromise[d] the selection [p]rocess[,]" the Arbitrator addressed the remedy. *Id.* at 19. Determining that re-running the CSA selection process would be "too problematic" to monitor and manage, the Arbitrator ordered the Agency to grant the grievant a CSA for 2003 with appropriate backpay. *Id.*

III. Positions of the Parties

A. Agency's Exceptions

The Agency presents two exceptions.[3] First, the Agency contends that the award is contrary to law because it impermissibly affects management's rights to assign work and to direct employees under 5 U.S.C. § 7106(a)(2)(A) and (B). Second, the Agency claims that the award fails to draw its essence from the Compensation Agreement.

The Agency argues in its first exception that the Arbitrator's award is deficient under the two-prong standard that has been used by the Authority to determine whether an award impermissibly affects management rights set forth in *United States Department of the Treasury, Bureau of Engraving and Printing, Washington, D.C.,* 53 FLRA 146 (1997) (*BEP*). The two *BEP* prongs are explained at § IV.A., below. The Agency only challenges the award under *BEP*'s second prong. The Agency contends that the award fails to satisfy *BEP* prong II because the award does not reflect a reconstruction of what the Agency would have done if it had not violated the agreed-upon CSA selection process. Exceptions at 11 n.9. According to the Agency, even assuming that the Arbitrator properly found that the Agency "violated the contract," he erroneously awarded the grievant a CSA pursuant to the Compensation Agreement without determining that the grievant actually deserved an award. *Id.* at 12-13. The Agency claims that, although there may have been a flaw in the application of the CSA selection process to the grievant, "management would still have had to determine whether the [g]rievant was in the top one-third of contributors" for the grievant to

3. The Agency argues that the Arbitrator exceeded his authority as a result of its exceptions claiming that: (1) the award impermissibly affects management's rights to assign work and to direct employees, and (2) the award fails to draw its essence from the agreement. An exception claiming that arbitrators have exceeded their authority requires a showing that they have failed to resolve an issue submitted to arbitration, resolved an issue not submitted to arbitration, disregarded specific limitations on their authority, or awarded relief to those not encompassed within the grievance. *See AFGE, Local 1617*, 51 FLRA 1645, 1647 (1996). As the Agency makes no specific argument to this effect, to the extent that this language was intended to constitute a separate exception, we find that the Agency has failed to establish that the Arbitrator exceeded his authority and deny the exception.

receive a CSA. *Id.* at 11. The Agency requests that the Authority modify the award to require the Agency only to reconsider the grievant for a CSA.

As its second exception, the Agency claims that the award fails to draw its essence from the Compensation Agreement. Noting that the grievant had not been determined to be a top contributor, the Agency claims that the award is inconsistent with the Compensation Agreement, which requires that CSAs be granted only to top contributors. *Id.* at 17. The Agency also claims that if it is required to award the grievant a CSA, more than one-third of bargaining unit employees would receive CSAs, in violation of the Compensation Agreement. *Id.* at 17-18. Because the award "does not represent a plausible interpretation of the agreement" and "evidences a manifest disregard of the agreement," *id.* at 17, the Agency argues it should be set aside.

B. Union's Opposition

The Union opposes the Agency's exceptions. First, regarding the Agency's *BEP* exception, the Union claims that the award correctly reconstructs what the Agency would have done if it had not violated CSA selection procedures by ordering the Agency to award the grievant a CSA. Among other things, the Union contends that evidence was presented at arbitration showing that the grievant was within the top twenty percent of employees nominated for a CSA before he was removed from consideration. Opp'n at 10-11.

Second, the Union contends that the award does not fail to draw its essence from the Compensation Agreement. In the Union's view, although the Compensation Agreement does not require the Agency to give CSAs to more than one-third of all bargaining unit employees, it also does not prohibit such action. *Id.* at 13. The Union argues that the Agency's exception should be denied because "[t]he question of the interpretation of the parties' agreement is a question solely for the arbitrator because it is the arbitrator's construction of the agreement for which the parties have bargained." *Id.* at 14 (citing *Panama Canal Comm'n,* 54 FLRA 1316 (1998)). Additionally, the Union alleges that the award does not fail to draw its essence from the Compensation Agreement because the agreement does not limit the Arbitrator's authority to award a remedy. *Id.* at 15. To the contrary, the Union argues that the remedy is consistent with the parties' CBA, which specifically grants the Arbitrator "the authority to make an aggrieved employee whole to the extent such remedy is not limited by law." *Id.* (citing CBA, Article 48, Section 4).[4] Thus, the Union claims that the Arbitrator's award does not "evidence a manifest disregard of the CBA[.]" *Id.* at 16. The Union requests that, if the Authority determines that the Arbitrator's remedy does not reconstruct what management would have done if it had not violated the contractual provision, then the Authority should remand the award to the Arbitrator for clarification.

IV. Analysis and Conclusions

In this case, the Authority has decided to revisit the issue of arbitrators' remedial authority when it entertains exceptions alleging that an award or arbitral remedy impermissibly affects management rights under § 7106 of the Statute. Our focus is on the analysis that applies after the Authority has determined that an award provides a remedy for a violation of a contract provision that was negotiated pursuant to § 7106(b) of the Statute.

A. Current Case Law

The legal framework that the Authority currently applies when analyzing arbitrators' awards claimed to impermissibly affect management rights set forth in 5 U.S.C § 7106(a) is stated in *BEP*, 53 FLRA at 151-54. The framework set forth in that decision has two prongs, both of which must be satisfied for an award to be upheld.

Under prong I, the Authority examines whether an award that affects management rights provides a remedy for a violation of either an applicable law, within the meaning of § 7106(a)(2) of the Statute, or a contract provision that was negotiated pursuant to § 7106(b) of the Statute. *See BEP*, 53 FLRA at 152-53 (reexamining the Authority's precedent in light of the Supreme Court's decision in *Dep't of the Treasury, IRS v. FLRA*, 494 U.S. 922 (1990) (*IRS*)); *see also Dep't of the Treasury, U.S. Customs Serv.*, 37 FLRA 309, 313-14 (1990) (*Customs Service*). If the award does not provide such a remedy, then the

---

4. Article 48, Section 4.B of the CBA provides, in pertinent part:

> The arbitrator shall have no power to add to, subtract from, or modify the terms of this Agreement. The award will be limited to the issues presented at arbitration. The arbitrator's decision will be final and binding and the arbitrator will have the authority to make an aggrieved employee whole to the extent such remedy is not limited by law.

Opp'n, Ex. 3 at 126.

award is contrary to law and cannot be upheld. *U.S. Dep't of Veterans Affairs, Med. Ctr., Northampton, Mass.*, 53 FLRA 1743, 1746 (1998).

Prong I's companion requirement, the reconstruction prong or "prong II," focuses on whether the arbitrator's remedy reflects a reconstruction of what management would have done if management had not violated the law or the contractual provision at issue. *See BEP*, 53 FLRA at 154. As with prong I, awards that fail to satisfy the reconstruction prong are not sustained. Thus, awards that fail to satisfy either prong of the Authority's current legal framework will be set aside, modified, or remanded. *Id.*

B. Origins and Development of Current Case Law

The Authority has modified both parts of its legal framework from time to time to reflect its own evolving understanding of the Statute's requirements and the nature of arbitration as Congress intended it to function in federal sector labor-management relations. This was the case when, for example, the Authority in *BEP* determined that the legal framework referred to as prong I should be applied generally to arbitration awards claimed to affect management rights under § 7106(a). *See BEP*, 53 FLRA at 153.

Drawing on prior precedent dealing with management's right to discipline, the Authority held in *BEP* that there was no basis in the Statute for not applying the same approach when reviewing awards claimed to affect other management rights in § 7106(a). *Id.* (citing *U.S. Dep't of Veterans Affairs, Med. Ctr., Birmingham, Ala.*, 51 FLRA 270, 274 (1995) (*VA Birmingham*)). As the Authority explained in *Customs Service*, on which *VA Birmingham* relied,

> [w]e are committed to the Statute's provision for final and binding arbitration and its purpose of facilitating the resolution of disputes. These are best served by ensuring that the decision of an arbitrator, selected by both parties to interpret and apply their collective bargaining agreement, will not be overridden on management rights grounds in order to relieve one party from the unwelcome result of that purposeful choice.

Customs Service, 37 FLRA at 316.

This same commitment to Congress' determination to use final and binding arbitration to facilitate and encourage the resolution of disputes under the Statute is evident in the evolution of the reconstruction requirement of the Authority's legal framework, prong II. The reconstruction requirement is traceable to the Authority's decision in *Social Security Administration*, 30 FLRA 1156 (1988) (*SSA*). In *SSA*, the Authority reexamined the remedial authority of arbitrators, based on its understanding of "the functions that arbitrators perform, and that Congress intended that arbitrators perform, under the Statute." *Id.* at 1161 (quoting *Newark Air Force Station*, 30 FLRA 616, 635-36 (1987)).

In *SSA*, the Authority rejected previously established restrictions on arbitrators' remedial authority; i.e., that arbitrators may not substitute their judgment for that of management when arbitrators resolve grievances over performance appraisal matters. Finding such a restriction "not warranted," the Authority held that arbitrators could exercise broader remedial power, substituting their judgment for that of management, when an arbitrator's remedy reflected a reconstruction of what management would have done had it acted properly. *SSA*, 30 FLRA at 1160. In the Authority's view, exercising this broader remedial discretion

> would not require an arbitrator to do anything other than what arbitrators do routinely in resolving other disputes, including those involving . . . other management rights .... This is precisely one of the functions that arbitrators perform, . . . under the Statute. In requiring parties to negotiate grievance procedures that result in binding arbitration, and in broadly defining what grievances could encompass, Congress fully expected arbitrators to review a wide variety of actions, including actions taken by management pursuant to § 7106.

Id. at 1161 (quoting *Newark Air Force Station*, 30 FLRA at 635-36). The Authority concluded: "To the extent that the resolution of grievances by arbitrators in this manner conflicts with § 7106(a)(2)(A) or (B), that conflict results from implementation of congressionally mandated grievance and arbitration procedures." *Id.* at 1162.

The Authority subsequently extended its *SSA* reconstruction precedent to arbitrators' awards claimed to impermissibly interfere with management rights other than those associated with performance appraisal matters. *VA Birmingham*, 51 FLRA at 274.

Continuing concerns about grievance arbitration's efficacy under the Statute have led to criticism of the Authority's reconstruction precedent. This criticism was expressed in *Social Security Administration, Boston Region (Region 1)*, 57 FLRA 264 (2001) (Member Wasserman, dissenting) (*SSA Boston*). In *SSA* Boston, the arbitrator found that a supervisor's search of the grievant's desk and related actions violated various contractual provisions.

In its decision, the Authority's majority acknowledged that the Authority's reconstruction requirement "ma[d]e it difficult [for the arbitrator] to construct meaningful remedies" in the case. *Id.* at 269. Nevertheless, finding the arbitrator's remedy "not a proper reconstruction," the majority set it aside, depriving the grievant of any make whole-type remedy for the contract violation the arbitrator found. *Id.*

Member Donald S. Wasserman, one of *BEP*'s two original authors, dissented.[5] The dissent found the majority's decision "bad law," and the reconstruction requirement "a framework that does not fit all cases and has no basis in the Statute." *SSA, Boston*, 57 FLRA at 270, 272 (Dissenting Opinion of Member Wasserman). Agreeing with the majority that reconstruction in the case was "not feasible," the dissent argued that "the requirement of reconstruction in all situations [i]s one that is not dictated by the Statute or the Supreme Court's decision in [*IRS*] . . . . [A]pplication of prong I of *BEP* properly and adequately protects management prerogatives under the Statute." *Id.* at 270. As for congressional intent, in the dissent's view, "when Congress authorized negotiations on matters covered in § 7106(b), that authorization included arbitration awards which give effect to those § 7106(b) matters the parties agree to negotiate. . . . In short, when Congress authorized bargaining on § 7106(b) matters, it also authorized arbitrators to issue awards to remedy violations of those provisions." *Id.* at 273.

The dissent in *SSA Boston* therefore disagreed with the majority's view "that the [reconstruction] standard is necessary to ensure that an agency's § 7106(a) rights are limited only to the extent bargained by the parties." *Id.* at 272. Rather, the dissent concluded, "it is by means of an essence challenge that impositions of contractual constraints never agreed to are addressed." *Id.*

Upon reexamination of the "reconstruction" standard reflected in *BEP*'s second prong, and as discussed in the following section, we determine that such a standard is not required by the Statute and, indeed, unduly limits the appropriate remedial authority of arbitrators. It is sufficient that an arbitrator's award that affects management rights under § 7106(a) of the Statute provides a remedy for a violation of either an applicable law, within the meaning of § 7106(a)(2) of the Statute, or a contract provision that was negotiated pursuant to § 7106(b) of the Statute.

C. Approach To Be Followed With Respect To The Remedial Authority of Arbitrators -- Elimination of the Reconstruction Requirement

The Authority concludes that the restriction on arbitrators' remedial authority imposed by *BEP*'s reconstruction requirement is not warranted. Rather, subject to any specific limitations set forth in the pertinent contract and to the requirement that an award provide a remedy for a properly negotiated contract provision, an arbitrator enjoys broad discretion to remedy a meritorious grievance even if the remedy affects management rights under § 7106(a). Exercise of this broad remedial discretion effectuates § 7106(a)'s explicit direction that management rights set forth in § 7106(a) are "subject to" provisions bargained under § 7106(b), and that "nothing in" § 7106 shall preclude the parties from negotiating such provisions. 5 U.S.C. § 7106(b). This broad remedial discretion exists even if, due to insufficient record evidence or other reasons, the arbitrator does not "reconstruct" what management would have done but for the legal or contract violation.

This approach is more consistent with the Statute and better serves the Statute's purpose of facilitating and encouraging the settlement of disputes than *BEP*'s reconstruction requirement. Neither the Statute's language nor its structure mandates particular arbitral remedies. To the contrary, Congress gave arbitrators extensive authority. "In requiring parties to negotiate grievance procedures that result in binding arbitration and in broadly defining what grievances could encompass, Congress fully expected arbitrators to review a wide variety of actions, including actions taken by management pursuant to § 7106." *SSA*, 30 FLRA at 1161. This wide-ranging authority includes authority to render

5. In deciding *BEP*, only two Members participated, Chair Phyllis N. Segal and Member Donald S. Wasserman. The Authority's third Member's office was vacant.

meaningful remedies tailored to the circumstances of particular cases. We find no indication that Congress intended to limit arbitrators' discretion in ordering such meaningful remedies by mandating remedies that "reconstruct" what agency management would have done if the agency had not violated law or its agreement with the exclusive representative. Accordingly, Authority decisions that impose a reconstruction requirement will no longer be followed. *See, e.g., FDIC,* 61 FLRA 738 (2006) (Chairman Cabaniss, writing separately); *SSA*, 61 FLRA 315 (2005) (then-Member Pope, dissenting in part).

It is thus our intent to reaffirm the Statute's policy of giving deference to arbitrators' wide-ranging remedial authority. However, such remedial authority is not unfettered. Rather, an arbitrator's award must still be reasonably related to the negotiated provisions at issue and the harm being remedied.

This limitation on arbitral remedy is not intended to establish a new two-pronged analytical framework that will be recited in every case involving an award alleged to violate management rights. We include the point simply to underscore for the parties and the arbitral community the legal requirements that apply to such awards. As in other types of arbitration cases, such awards must still withstand challenges raised in exceptions that the award does not satisfy the standards Congress established in the Statute for the Authority's review of arbitrators' awards. Where such a challenge establishes that an award imposes a constraint on management rights that was not agreed to by the parties, whether on essence grounds or otherwise, the award will be set aside.

On a practical level, parties to a collective bargaining agreement understand that (absent an express exclusion of a particular matter from arbitration) a violation of a negotiated contract provision is subject to being remedied by an arbitrator exercising his broad authority to remedy such violations. If an agency is concerned that the arbitral remedy for violating a particular contract proposal would impermissibly affect management rights, the agency need not agree to the proposal. However, if an agency agrees to include in its collective bargaining agreement a provision negotiated under § 7106(b), and that provision is applied by an arbitrator in a way reasonably related to the provision and the harm being remedied, a subsequent challenge to such an award is likely to be rejected by the Authority.[6]

D. Application of the Revised Analytical Framework

Applying the analytical framework described above, we conclude that the award in this case is not contrary to law. We also conclude that the award does not fail to draw its essence from the parties' agreement. We therefore deny the Agency's exceptions.

1. The award is not contrary to law.

We reject the Agency's exception arguing that the award's remedy is contrary to law.[7] This exception is based entirely on the assertion that the remedy does not reflect a reconstruction of what the Agency would have done if it had not violated the agreed-upon CSA selection process. As explained above, such "reconstruction" is not the standard to be applied to the remedy directed by an arbitrator. Moreover, the Agency concedes that the award enforces a properly negotiated contract provision. *See* Exceptions at 11 n.9. Consequently, we conclude that the award does not impermissibly affect management rights by failing to reconstruct what the Agency would have done if it had not violated the contract, and we deny the Agency's contrary to law exception.

6. Our concurring colleague claims that, under the new approach that we outline today, arbitrators' remedies "no longer may be found deficient based on management rights[.]" Concurring Opinion of Chairman Pope at 17. However, our colleague does not identify where in our decision we have said this – and indeed, we have not. The approach that we set forth today remains true to the Statute – and deviates not at all from the *BEP*/prong two approach that we are discarding – in this fundamental way: An arbitral remedy that affects management rights and is challenged on that basis will not be upheld if it enforces a contractual restraint on management rights for which the parties did not bargain pursuant to § 7106.

7. Although the Agency's contrary to law arguments are sometimes presented as an "exceeds authority" exception, we construe them to be a "contrary to law" exception. *U.S. DOD, Def. Contract Mgmt. Agency,* 59 FLRA 396, 398 n.6 (2003) (agency's argument that the arbitration award affected management rights set forth as an "exceeded authority" exception construed to be a "contrary to law" exception).

2. The Arbitrator's award does not fail to draw its essence from the parties' agreement.

We also reject the Agency's claim that the award fails to draw its essence from the parties' agreement. In reviewing an arbitrator's interpretation of a collective bargaining agreement, the Authority applies the deferential standard of review that federal courts use in reviewing arbitration awards in the private sector. *See* 5 U.S.C. § 7122(a)(2). Under this standard, the Authority will find that an arbitration award is deficient as failing to draw its essence from the collective bargaining agreement when the appealing party establishes that the award: (1) cannot in any rational way be derived from the agreement; (2) is so unfounded in reason and fact and so unconnected with the wording and purposes of the collective bargaining agreement as to manifest an infidelity to the obligation of the arbitrator; (3) does not represent a plausible interpretation of the agreement; or (4) evidences a manifest disregard of the agreement. *See U.S. Dep't of Labor (OSHA)*, 34 FLRA 573, 575 (1990) (*OSHA*). The Authority and the courts defer to arbitrators in this context because it is the arbitrator's construction of the agreement for which the parties have bargained. *Id.* at 576.

The Agency argues that the remedy portion of the award fails to draw its essence from the Compensation Agreement and should be set aside for two reasons. First, according to the Agency, the award is inconsistent with the Compensation Agreement, which requires that CSAs be granted only to top contributors. The Agency points out that the grievant has not been determined to be a top contributor. Second, the Agency claims that, if it were required to award the grievant a CSA, more than one-third of bargaining unit employees would receive CSAs, assertedly in violation of the Compensation Agreement.

With regard to the Agency's first argument, the record shows that the grievant's performance was at least sufficient for him to be nominated for a CSA by his first level supervisor, second and third level reviewers, Field Supervisors, and the ARDs under the negotiated CSA nomination procedures. *See* Award at 9. Based on the facts in the record, the Agency has not demonstrated that the Arbitrator's award: (1) cannot in any rational way be derived from the agreement; (2) is so unfounded in reason and fact and so unconnected with the wording and purposes of the collective bargaining agreement as to manifest an infidelity to the obligation of the arbitrator; (3) does not represent a plausible interpretation of the agreement; or (4) evidences a manifest disregard of the agreement. *See OSHA*, 34 FLRA at 575.

The Agency's second argument also lacks merit. The Compensation Agreement provides that "[t]he Chairman has sole discretion to set the percentage of bargaining unit employees who will be recognized as top contributors under the CSA program[,]" so long as that percentage is "no less than 33 1/3 percent." Award at 4. The Agreement's plain wording reflects that this is a minimum, and not a maximum, as argued by the Agency. *See FDIC,* 62 FLRA 356, 359 (2008) (*FDIC I*) (holding that the Compensation Agreement's 33 1/3 percent figure "is a minimum, not a maximum").

Thus, although the Compensation Agreement does not obligate the Agency to award CSAs to employees who are not in the top one-third of contributors, it also does not cap the number of bargaining unit employees eligible to receive CSAs at 33 1/3 percent. Consequently, awarding a CSA to the grievant does not necessarily preclude compliance with the requirements of the Compensation Agreement. *See id.*

Our conclusion on this point is not altered by the Compensation Agreement's language leaving it to the "sole discretion" of the Chairman to set the percentage of unit employees eligible to receive a CSA. Compensation Agreement at 2. The agreement includes other language mandating "fair and equitable treatment" for CSA candidates. *Id.* at 5. To the extent there is tension between these agreement provisions, we cannot say that the arbitrator's conclusion, that the grievant should receive a CSA, is not a plausible interpretation of the agreement as a whole.

For these reasons, the Agency has failed to demonstrate that the award fails to draw its essence from the Compensation Agreement. We therefore deny the Agency's exception.[8]

V. Decision

The Agency's exceptions are denied.

---

8. In reaching this conclusion, we are aware of our decision in *FDIC*, 64 FLRA 79 (2009) (Chairman Pope dissenting in part) (*FDIC II*), remanding on essence grounds an award arguably similar to the award in the instant case. To the extent that *FDIC II* is inconsistent with prior precedent represented by *FDIC I* and our reasoning in the instant case, *FDIC II* will no longer be followed.

APPENDIX

COMPENSATION AGREEMENT BETWEEN FDIC AND NTEU FOR THE YEARS 2003-2005

II. ANNUAL PAY

. . . .

C. Annual Pay Adjustment

Year 2003

Effective 2003, the Employer will provide an increase in basic pay of 3.2 percent for all employees who received a rating of "meets expectations" during the prior year's rating period. In addition, 2003 shall be a transition year for the Corporate Success Award, which is described below. . . .

Years 2004 and 2005

. . . .

A Corporate Success Award (CSA) will be established which provides that an additional 3.0 percent increase be made in basic pay for those employees recognized as top contributors. The Chairman has sole discretion to set the percentage of bargaining unit employees who will be recognized as top contributors under the CSA program. However, the percentage of bargaining unit employees to receive the CSA shall be no less than 33 1/3 percent. These awards shall be made on an annual basis.

. . . .

Opp'n, Attach. 4, Compensation Agreement Between FDIC and NTEU for the Years 2003-2005 at 1-2.

MEMORANDUM: PROCEDURES FOR PROCESSING CORPORATE SUCCESS AWARDS (November 17, 2003)

In order to ensure a fair and equitable distribution of the CSAs within the division, DSC will implement the following procedures for nominating employees.

Regional Office CSA Nomination Procedures

1. The supervisor prepares written CSA nominations for eligible employees.

2. The supervisor prioritizes and assigns a numerical ranking for all nominated employees within their span on control.

3. The supervisor submits the CSA nomination forms with numerical rankings to the Regional Office Assistant Regional Director, Administration (RO ARD-Admin).

. . . .

4. The RO ARD-Admin consolidates and prepares the CSA nomination forms for evaluation by first-level review panel consisting of the Assistant Regional Directors and the Deputy Regional Director – Compliance.

5. The first-level review panel evaluates each CSA recommendation and prioritizes the top-one third by assigning a numerical ranking.

6. The first-level review panel forwards their numerically ranked CSA recommendations to the second-level review panel consisting of the Deputy Regional Directors and Area Directors.

7. The second-level review panel evaluates and/or re-ranks each CSA recommendation and submits to the Regional Director for approval.

8. The Regional Director reviews the CSA recommendations, signs the appropriate justification forms, and submits the final Regional CSA recommendations to the Division Director.

. . . .

Opp'n, Attach. 7, Memorandum Regarding Procedures for Processing Corporate Success Awards (Zamorski Memorandum) at 1-2.

FDIC DIRECTIVE SYSTEM CIRCULAR 2420.1 (July 21, 2003)

CHAPTER 11
CORPORATE SUCCESS AWARDS

. . . .

11-2. Eligibility

All non-executive employees who have current performance ratings of record from the FDIC of "Meets Expectations" are eligible. . . .

. . . .

11-4. Criteria

The criteria below are intended to be achievable by any eligible employee in any position. Nominations for the award effecting in 2004 must be based on contributions made between January 1, 2003 and December 31, 2003. . . .

Nominations will be evaluated based on one or more of the following criteria. These are the only criteria permitted under the Corporate Success Award Program. Nominations will provide specific statements of the contributions by the employee that meet the identified criteria. Meeting one or more of these criteria does not entitle employees to be nominated to receive the Corporate Success Award.

A. Business Results: Consistently displays a high level of initiative, creativity, and innovation to produce results that reflect important contributions to the Corporation and/or its organizational components.

B. Competency: Demonstrates an exceptional degree of competency within his/her position, and is frequently relied upon by others for advice, assistance, and/or judgment that reflect important contributions to the Corporation and/or its organizational components.

C. Working Relationships: Builds extremely productive working relationships with co-workers, other Divisions/Offices, or other public or private sector agencies based on mutual respect that reflect important contributions to the Corporation and/or its organizational components.

D. Learning and Development: Takes an active part in developing personal skills and competencies and applies newly acquired skills and competencies that reflect important contributions to the Corporation and/or its organizational components.

11-5. Procedures

. . . .

B. Supervisors will nominate their top contributors by preparing form FDIC 2420/21, Corporate Success Award Nomination. Forms must be submitted to the designated reviewing official within 15 calendar days after the end of the consideration cycle. Employees may provide input to the appropriate supervisors for other employees to be considered for a [CSA].

C. Reviewing Officials, as designated in the Division/Office delegation of authority, will ensure the consistent application of Corporate Success Award criteria and the fair and equitable treatment of employees. The reviewing official shall sign the nomination form and forward it to the Division/Office Director within 30 calendar days after the end of the consideration cycle.

D. Each Division/Office Director or his/her designee will serve as the approving official for all Corporate Success Awards within their Division /Office. Directors are responsible for ensuring that the percentage of bargaining unit and non-bargaining unit employees recognized under the Corporate Success Award program equals the percentage identified by the Chairman. The Director, or his/her designee, will sign the nomination forms and forward them to their administrative officer for coordination with the Division of Administration, Human Resources Branch.

. . . .

F. The Chairman has sole discretion to set the percentage of bargaining unit and non-bargaining employees who will be recognized as top contributors under the Corporate Success Award (CSA) program . . . . However, the percentage of bargaining unit employees to receive the CSA will be no less than 33 1/3 percent.

Opp'n, Attach. 6, FDIC Circular 2420.1, Chapter 11 at 5-7.

MEMORANDUM OF UNDERSTANDING BETWEEN FDIC & NTEU
[March 13, 2003]

> 1. CSAs will be distributed to employees in a fair and equitable manner, and in accordance with the terms of the MOU and FDIC Circular 2420.1.

Opp'n, Attach. 5, Memorandum of Understanding Between FDIC & NTEU at 1.

Opinion of Chairman Pope, concurring in part:

The majority has decided that arbitral remedies may be challenged on private sector grounds only; remedies no longer may be found deficient based on management rights under § 7106 of the Statute. The majority's decision is flatly contrary to the Statute. Accordingly, although I agree with the ultimate conclusion to deny the Agency's exception in this case, I write separately.[1]

Section 7106(a) provides that "*Subject to subsection (b) . . . , nothing in this chapter shall affect*" the exercise of the management rights set forth therein. 5 U.S.C. § 7106(a) (emphasis added). An agency's authority to exercise the particular rights set forth in § 7106(a)(2) are constrained also by "applicable laws."[2] The Supreme Court has instructed that the words "nothing in this chapter", mean "nothing in the entire" Statute, including grievance arbitration under § 7121 of the Statute. *Dep't of the Treasury, IRS v. FLRA*, 494 U.S. 922, 928 (1990) (*IRS*). Accordingly, as relevant here, only those constraints on management rights properly negotiated under § 7106(b) are enforceable in arbitration. Put differently, "nothing" means "nothing outside § 7106(b)."

Consistent with the Statute and the Court's decision in *IRS*, the Authority established the two-pronged test set forth in *United States Department of the Treasury, Bureau of Engraving and Printing, Washington, D.C.*, 53 FLRA 146 (1997) (*BEP*).[3] The first prong of *BEP* asks, if raised in an exception, whether an arbitration award provides a remedy for a violation of "a contract provision that was negotiated pursuant to the exceptions to section 7106(a) that are set forth in section 7106(b)."[4] *Id.* at 153. The second prong of that test -- which the majority eliminates -- inquires, if raised in an exception, whether the awarded remedy constitutes a reconstruction of what management would have done had it complied with the relevant contract provision. *Id.* at 154.

It may well be that the term "reconstruction" was inartful in conveying the concept it embodies. However, whatever term is used, the Authority has made clear that the purpose of the second prong is to "ensure that an agency's section 7106(a) rights are limited only to the extent the parties bargained for." *SSA, Boston Region (Region 1), Lowell Dist. Office, Lowell, Mass.*, 57 FLRA 264, 270 (2001) (Member Wasserman dissenting in part) (*SSA, Boston*). Inquiring whether an award is based on an enforceable contractual provision is not enough; it is also necessary to inquire whether a remedy for violating that provision is properly based on that provision. Unless the term "nothing" in § 7106(a) means "nothing except arbitral remedies" -- an interpretation that the plain wording does not permit -- the latter inquiry is compelled by the Statute.[5]

In finding that an arbitrator's remedy may no longer be found deficient based on management rights, the majority draws a sharp line between a remedy and the remainder of an award. This line does not exist in the wording of the Statute or the

1. I agree that the award does not fail to draw its essence from the parties' agreement.

2. As the "applicable laws" provision is not relevant in this decision, I will not reference it further.

3. As set forth in *BEP*, the two-prong test was merely an extension of a similar limitation established years earlier with regard to awards resolving disputes over awards raising employees' performance ratings. 53 FLRA at 151 (citing *U.S. Dep't of HHS, SSA*, 34 FLRA 323 (1990)). Moreover, since at least 1984, the Authority has held that, consistent with management's right to select under § 7106(a)(2)(C), an arbitrator may not award a promotion absent a finding that "but for" the agency's contract violation, the grievant would have been selected for promotion. *AFGE, Local 12*, 15 FLRA 543 (1984). I note that, since *BEP*, twenty-four awards have been found deficient based on the second prong, including one award that was set aside over my dissent. *U.S. Dep't of Def., Tex. Nat'l Guard, Austin, Tex.*, 59 FLRA 437 (2003) (then-Member Pope dissenting).

4. By decision issued today in *United States Environmental Protection Agency*, 65 FLRA 113, 116-18 (2010) (Member Beck concurring), the Authority has modified its approach for resolving exceptions alleging that a contract provision is not enforceable under § 7106(b) and, as a result, an award is deficient under the first prong of *BEP*. In particular, the Authority has decided, consistent with the framework established 20 years ago in *Department of the Treasury, United States Customs Service*, 37 FLRA 309 (1990), that a provision is enforceable under § 7106(b) unless it abrogates a disputed management right. As the majority notes, the first prong of *BEP* is not in dispute in this case. Majority Op. at 4.

5. The majority's premise that an arbitrator's exercise of remedial authority effectuates the Statute's mandate that "nothing" shall preclude negotiation over subjects set forth in § 7106(b), Majority Op. at 8, does not hold water. *IRS* is crystal clear that "nothing" includes the entire Statute, including its grievance and arbitration provisions. 494 U.S. at 928.

extensive precedent interpreting it. Moreover, it is entirely artificial. In this regard, few parties (not to mention grievants) would find it meaningful. Indeed, management rights disputes in arbitration nearly always involve what the awards require agencies *to do (or stop doing)*: the remedy.[6] In addition, that the majority would (continue to) find remedies deficient on the other grounds set forth in § 7122 of the Statute is of no moment because, consistent with *IRS*, § 7106(a) provides an independent limitation on an arbitrator's remedial authority, and this limitation cannot be ignored.[7]

The majority states that an award must "be reasonably related to the negotiated provisions at issue and the harm being remedied." Majority Op. at 9. I agree that this is a legally permissible formulation of what I believe is a connection required by the Statute between a remedy disputed under § 7106(a) and the relevant contract provision. That is, I find that a "reasonable relation" standard, properly applied, is consistent with the Statute. Further, I would find that the remedy in this case is reasonably related to the contract provision and the harm remedied.

Applying the "reasonable relation" standard here, I agree with the majority that the award is not deficient. Regrettably, however, I part company with the majority on the reasoning used to reach this conclusion. Put simply, the majority is unwilling to adopt or apply "reasonable relation" as a standard for assessing whether a remedy is deficient based on management rights. Instead, only exceptions to remedies based on the "private sector grounds" set forth in § 7122(a)(2) of the Statute may be granted.[8] As the Statute requires *some* standard and the majority is unwilling to apply *any*, I am unable to bridge the gap.

For the foregoing reasons, I concur that the award is not deficient.[9]

---

6. To illustrate this point, I note but a few examples of the twenty four awards found deficient under the second prong of *BEP*. In *United States Department of Defense, Defense Contract Management Agency*, 59 FLRA 396 (2003) (then-Member Pope dissenting in part on other grounds) the arbitrator found that the agency failed to properly administer its incentive awards committee and, as a remedy, directed the agency to replace its performance appraisal system. In *United States Department of Defense, Departments of the Army and the Air Force, Alabama National Guard, Northport, Alabama*, 55 FLRA 37 (1998), the arbitrator found that two grievants had not been properly considered for one vacancy and, as a remedy, ordered both grievants promoted.

7. In this regard, the majority puts great stock in the policy that arbitrators have broad authority to fashion remedies. I do, too. However, there are other policies in play, including the policy decisions underlying the Congressional decision to enact § 7106(a). Despite my reluctance to overturn arbitral awards, I believe that scrutiny of remedies under § 7106(a) is required by the Statute and, if such scrutiny is to be eliminated, it must be done through legislative change. *See, e.g., United States v. Hopkins*, 427 U.S. 123, 125 (1976) (Court noted effect of application of statutory wording and stated that "'it is up to Congress to remedy this apparent harsh result[.]'" (quoting *Keetz v. United States*, 168 Ct. Cl. 205, 207 (1964)).

8. The majority's statement that its revised approach "deviates not at all . . . from the approach that [it is] discarding" undoubtedly creates confusion that will promote litigation to clarify the matter. Majority Op. at 10 n.6. In fact, it is quite clear that the revised approach discards the second prong of *BEP* and, as such, deviates completely from the prior approach. Moreover, although the majority disputes my claim that, under the revised approach, remedies will be found deficient based on private sector grounds only, *see id.*, the majority states repeatedly that a remedy will not be found deficient based on management rights alone. *See id.* at 2 (revised approach "gives arbitrators the same scope of remedial authority in . . . management rights cases as they . . . exercise in rendering awards that do not affect management rights"); 8 (under revised approach "[i]t is sufficient that an . . . award that affects management rights . . . provides a remedy for a violation of . . . an applicable law . . . or a contract provision . . . negotiated pursuant to § 7106(b) of the Statute"); 9 (awards alleged to violate management rights must withstand the same challenges "[a]s in other types of arbitration cases").

9. I note that the Authority has addressed awards of CSAs in several previous cases. In *FDIC*, 61 FLRA 735 (2006) (*FDIC I*) and *FDIC*, 61 FLRA 738 (2006) (*FDIC II*), the Authority sustained Agency exceptions based on the second prong of *BEP* to awards of CSAs and modified the awards to require the Agency to consider the grievants for CSAs. The Agency did not raise management rights in *FDIC*, 62 FLRA 356 (2008) (*FDIC III*), where the Authority denied the Agency's essence and exceeded-authority exceptions. In addition, the Union did not dispute the Agency's management rights claim in *FDIC I*, *FDIC II*, or here. In *FDIC*, 64 FLRA 79, 81 (2009) (Chairman Pope dissenting) (*FDIC IV*), where the Union did dispute the Agency's management rights exception, the Authority denied that exception. However, the majority (over my dissent) remanded the award in *FDIC IV* on essence grounds, *id.* at 82, a conclusion it now disavows. Majority Op. at 11 n.8. My understanding of the effect of today's decision is that *FDIC I* and *FDIC II* will no longer be followed with regard to management rights and the (majority) decision in *FDIC IV* will no longer be followed with regard to essence.

65 FLRA No. 28

UNITED STATES
ENVIRONMENTAL PROTECTION AGENCY
(Agency)

and

AMERICAN FEDERATION
OF GOVERNMENT EMPLOYEES
COUNCIL 238
(Union)

0-AR-4147

DECISION

September 29, 2010

Before the Authority: Carol Waller Pope, Chairman, and Thomas M. Beck and Ernest DuBester, Members[1]

I. Statement of the Case

This matter is before the Authority on exceptions to an award of Arbitrator Irwin Kaplan filed by the Agency under § 7122(a) of the Federal Service Labor-Management Relations Statute (the Statute) and part 2425 of the Authority's Regulations. The Union filed an opposition to the Agency's exceptions.

For the reasons that follow, we deny the exceptions. In so doing, we modify the Authority's existing test for determining whether a contract provision is enforceable in arbitration under § 7106(b)(3) of the Statute.[2] Specifically, in this and future cases we will make that determination by applying an abrogation (waiver) – rather than an excessive interference – standard.

II. Background and Arbitrator's Award

The parties negotiated National Reasonable Accommodation Procedures (the agreement), which provide for a National Reasonable Accommodation Coordinator (national coordinator) and local coordinators who process employees' reasonable accommodation requests. Under the agreement, the national coordinator may not delegate the duty of reviewing medical information to a local coordinator without the affected employee's approval.[3] The agreement was submitted for Agency-head review under § 7114 of the Statute. However, as the Agency did not complete the review within the thirty days allotted by § 7114(c)(3) of the Statute, the agreement went into effect.[4]

---

1. Member Beck's concurring opinion is set forth at the end of this decision.

2. The Authority has employed this test as "prong 1" of its analysis of arbitrators' awards claimed to impermissibly affect management rights set forth in 5 U.S.C. § 7106(a). *See U.S. Dep't of the Treasury, Bureau of Engraving & Printing, Wash., D.C.*, 53 FLRA 146, 154 (1997) (*BEP*). By decision issued today, the Authority is further modifying the analysis set forth in *BEP* by eliminating the requirement, referred to in *BEP* as "prong II," that a remedy "reconstruct" what agency management would have done if the agency had not violated law or its agreement with the exclusive representative. *See FDIC, Div. of Supervision & Consumer Prot., S.F. Region*, 65 FLRA 102, 106-07 (2010) (Chairman Pope concurring) (*FDIC*)). Although *BEP* and its "prongs" will no longer govern disposition of exceptions alleging that an award is contrary to management rights, it remains appropriate, for the reasons discussed below, to inquire whether an award enforces a provision negotiated under § 7106(b) or an applicable law.

3. The parties' agreement provides, in pertinent part:

> Official Access to Employee's Medical Information. There may be cases where the applicant or employee is uncomfortable with the [decision-maker] or supervisor having access to the employee's medical information. In this case the applicant or employee may ask that the [national coordinator] be the only EPA official to have access to any medical information that has been provided to the Agency. . . . ***The [national coordinator] will then be responsible for transmitting only pertinent information regarding functional limitations to the [decision-maker] if the information is needed to make a decision regarding [an] accommodation request. Alternatively, the [national coordinator] may advise the [decision-maker] without disclosing any medical information.***

Exceptions, Ex. 2 at 17.

4. Section 7114(c)(3) of the Statute provides:

> If the head of the agency does not approve or disapprove the agreement within the 30-day period, the agreement shall take effect and shall be binding on the agency and the exclusive representative subject to the provisions of this chapter and any other applicable law, rule, or regulation.

The Union filed a grievance alleging that the national coordinator transferred medical files to local coordinators in violation of the agreement. The parties did not resolve the grievance, and it was submitted to arbitration. The Arbitrator adopted the Union's formulation of the issue for resolution: "Whether the Agency violated the negotiated [agreement] by its [national coordinator] transferring confidential medical information of bargaining unit employees to a [local coordinator]? If so, what is the appropriate remedy?" Award at 2.

The Arbitrator concluded that, in negotiating the agreement, the parties had "voluntarily engaged in an appropriate arrangement . . . ." *Id.* at 12 (footnote omitted). The Arbitrator also stated that the parties had reached agreement on a permissive subject of bargaining. *Id.* at 13. In addition, the Arbitrator concluded that the Agency could not declare the agreement unlawful because the Agency head did not timely disapprove the agreement. *Id.* Further, the Arbitrator found that the Agency violated the agreement by transferring medical files from the national coordinator to a local coordinator. *Id.* at 14. Accordingly, the Arbitrator sustained the grievance and directed that the employees' files be returned to the national coordinator for processing. *Id.*

III. Positions of the Parties

A. Agency's Exceptions

The Agency argues that it may challenge the legality of the agreement even though the Agency-head review was untimely. *See* Exceptions at 4. The Agency also argues that the award is contrary to its right to assign work under § 7106(a)(2)(B) of the Statute. In this regard, the Agency contends that: (1) it determined that medical review should be performed by a local coordinator; (2) this determination is consistent with its right to assign work; and (3) any limitation on that right is unenforceable. *Id.* Moreover, the Agency contends that the matter of delegating duties to local coordinators does not involve the "method and means" of performing work under § 7106(b)(1) of the Statute. *Id.* at 9. Finally, the Agency contends that the Arbitrator's finding that the parties reached an agreement on an appropriate arrangement is based on a nonfact. *Id.* at 12.

B. Union's Opposition

The Union contends that, as the Agency-head review was untimely, the Agency may not challenge the agreement in this proceeding. *See* Opp'n at 6. The Union also contends that it is not unlawful to engage in collective bargaining on proposals that limit management's statutory rights, including the right to assign work, if an agency so chooses. *Id.* at 2. In this case, the Union contends that the Agency elected to negotiate with the Union on the roles of the coordinators involved in the processing of requests for reasonable accommodations. *Id.* at 2-3. The Union also argues that the agreement concerns the method and means of providing reasonable accommodations, within the meaning of § 7106(b)(1), and an appropriate arrangement, within the meaning of § 7106(b)(3) of the Statute. *Id.* at 4. Finally, with respect to the Agency's nonfact exception, the Union states that the agreement constitutes an arrangement. *Id.*

IV. Analysis and Conclusions

A. The Agency may challenge enforceability of the agreement.

As set forth above, § 7114(c)(3) of the Statute provides that, if an agency head does not approve or disapprove a collective bargaining agreement within thirty days after the date of its execution, then the agreement "shall take effect and shall be binding on the agency and the exclusive representative *subject to the provisions of [the Statute] and any other applicable law, rule, or regulation.*"[5] 5 U.S.C. § 7114(c)(3) (emphasis added). *Accord Point Mugu Joint Council of NAGE, Local R12-33 & NFFE, Local 1374*, 8 FLRA 389, 389 (1982). Because the Agency's disapproval was served on the Union more than thirty days after the agreement was executed, the agreement as negotiated and executed by the parties became effective and binding on the thirty-first day after execution -- but did so "subject . . . to" the Statute and any applicable law, rule, or regulation. *Id.*

Consistent with these principles, and with long-standing precedent, an agency may challenge the validity of a provision in an appropriate proceeding, such as this one. *Id.* at 390; *AFGE, AFL-CIO, Local 1858*, 4 FLRA 361, 362 (1980) (even after untimely disapproval, provisions found to violate "the Statute or any other applicable law, rule or regulation" are "deemed void and unenforceable[]"). In this regard, § 7122(a)(1) of the Statute charges the Authority with setting aside arbitration awards if they are "contrary to any law, rule, or regulation[.]" 5 U.S.C.

5. This statutory language is one indication that, as discussed in more detail below, management rights may not be waived as part of the bargaining process.

§ 7122(a)(1). There is no dispute that § 7106 of the Statute constitutes a "law[]" within the meaning of § 7122(a)(1). *Cf. U.S. Marshals Serv. v. FLRA*, 708 F.2d 1417, 1421 n.5 (9th Cir. 1983) ("The management rights section of the [Statute] is a law affecting conditions of employment[]"). Thus, an arbitration award that is contrary to § 7106 must be set aside. *See U.S. Dep't of Justice, Fed. Bureau of Prisons, Fed. Transfer Ctr., Okla. City, Okla.*, 57 FLRA 158, 162 (2001) (Chairman Cabaniss dissenting as to other matters) (*BOP, Oklahoma City I*) ("management rights cannot be waived[]"), *rev'd on other grounds, U.S. Dep't of Justice, Fed. Bureau of Prisons, Fed. Transfer Ctr., Okla. City, Okla.*, 58 FLRA 109, 110 (2002) (Chairman Cabaniss and Member Armendariz concurring; then-Member Pope concurring as to result) (*BOP, Oklahoma City II*) (citing *Wash. Plate Printers Union, Local No. 2, I.P.D.E.U.*, 31 FLRA 1250, 1255-57 (1988)).

For the foregoing reasons, the Agency may challenge the enforceability of the agreement -- as interpreted and applied by the Arbitrator in his award -- on the basis of § 7106 of the Statute.[6]

B. The award is not contrary to § 7106(a)(2)(B) of the Statute.

When an exception involves an award's consistency with law, the Authority reviews any question of law *de novo*. *See, e.g., NTEU, Chapter 24*, 50 FLRA 330, 332 (1995). In applying *de novo* review, the Authority assesses whether the arbitrator's legal conclusions are consistent with the applicable standard of law. *See, e.g., NFFE, Local 1437*, 53 FLRA 1703, 1710 (1998). In making that assessment, the Authority defers to the arbitrator's underlying factual findings. *See id.*

When a party contends that an award is contrary to a management right under § 7106(a) of the Statute, the Authority first assesses whether the award affects the exercise of the asserted right. *E.g., U.S. Dep't of the Navy, Puget Sound Naval Shipyard & Intermediate Maint. Facility, Bremerton, Wash.*, 62 FLRA 4, 5 (2007). If the award affects the right, then, under the applicable legal framework, the Authority examines, as relevant here, whether the award provides a remedy for a contract provision negotiated under § 7106(b) of the Statute.[7] *See FDIC*, 65 FLRA at 104-05; *Dep't of the Treasury, U.S. Customs Serv.*, 37 FLRA 309, 313-14 (1990). In this regard, § 7106(a) of the Statute provides that "*[s]ubject to subsection (b)* . . ., nothing in this chapter shall affect" the exercise of management rights. 5 U.S.C. § 7106(a) (emphasis added).[8] Accordingly, if an arbitrator's award affects a management right, then the award is contrary to law unless it enforces a contract provision negotiated under § 7106(b).

1. The award affects the Agency's right to assign work.

The right to assign work under § 7106(a)(2)(B) of the Statute includes the right to determine the particular duties to be assigned, when work assignments will occur, and to whom or what positions the duties will be assigned. *See U.S. Dep't of the Treasury, U.S. Customs Serv., El Paso, Tex.*, 55 FLRA 553, 558 (1999) (citation omitted). In addition, precluding the assignment of particular functions to particular individuals or positions affects the right to assign work. *E.g., NTEU, Chapter 243*, 49 FLRA 176, 181-82 (1994) (Member Armendariz dissenting as to other matters).

Under the parties' agreement, as interpreted and applied by the Arbitrator, the Agency may not assign to local coordinators certain of the processing functions for some employees' reasonable-accommodation requests, without the employees' prior consent. Thus, the award affects management's right to assign work. *See id.* The Union claims, and the Arbitrator concluded, that the parties agreed to an appropriate arrangement for employees seeking reasonable accommodations. Award at 12; Opp'n at 4. Applying *de novo* review to the Arbitrator's

---

6. We agree with our concurring colleague that the statutory scheme, which permits an agency to challenge an agreement provision, raises concerns regarding the efficient conduct of collective bargaining. Concurring Opinion at 12. However, as these concerns arise from the Statute itself, it is up to Congress to address them. *See Headquarters, NASA, Wash., D.C.*, 50 FLRA 601, 619 (1995) ("Should Congress disagree with our conclusion, it can amend the laws in accordance with its policy objectives."), *enforced*, 120 F.3d 1208 (11th Cir. 1997), *aff'd*, 527 U.S. 229 (1999).

7. If an award affects a management right under § 7106(a)(2) of the Statute, then the Authority may also consider whether the award enforces an "applicable law." *U.S. Dep't of Transp., FAA*, 63 FLRA 383, 385 (2009). As there is no claim that an applicable law is involved here, we do not discuss the matter further.

8. Further, Chairman Pope notes the Supreme Court's instruction that the words "nothing in this chapter" means "nothing in the entire" Statute, including grievance arbitration under § 7121 of the Statute. *Dep't of the Treasury, IRS v. FLRA*, 494 U.S. 922, 928 (1990).

legal conclusion, we assess whether, as interpreted and applied by the Arbitrator, the parties' agreement is enforceable under § 7106(b)(3).

2. The agreement is enforceable because it was negotiated under § 7106(b)(3) of the Statute.

In determining whether a provision was negotiated under § 7106(b)(3) of the Statute, the Authority assesses whether it ameliorates the adverse effects flowing from the exercise of a management right. *E.g.*, *U.S. DOJ, Fed. Bureau of Prisons, U.S. Penitentiary, Atlanta, Ga.*, 57 FLRA 406, 410 (2001) (Chairman Cabaniss dissenting) (*U.S. Pen.*). Here, the agreement, as interpreted and applied by the Arbitrator, limits the officials who may access the medical information of employees seeking reasonable accommodations, unless an employee consents to greater information sharing. *See* Award at 3-5; *see also supra* note 3. By requiring the Agency to seek an employee's permission before transferring medical files from the national coordinator to a local coordinator, the agreement ensures that an employee's medical information is kept confidential to the greatest extent practicable. In this regard, the Authority has previously recognized:

> [E]mployees have significant privacy interests in their medical records. Medical records, by their very nature, contain sensitive information about employees' medical history, and could reveal highly personal data about employees' physical, emotional, and mental conditions. . . . [T]he release of medical records . . . without the consent of the employees[] would result in a clear invasion of the employees' personal privacy[.]

AFGE, Local 1020, 47 FLRA 258, 268 (1993). Accordingly, the agreement, as interpreted and applied by the Arbitrator, ameliorates the adverse effects flowing from the exercise of management's right to assign the work of reviewing medical files.

The Agency asserts that the agreement is not an arrangement because the award does not enforce a provision that is tailored to benefit employees adversely affected by the exercise of a management right. However, because an arbitration award necessarily applies an agreement provision to actual, aggrieved parties, arbitration awards are inherently tailored to adversely affected employees, and the Authority does not conduct a tailoring analysis in resolving exceptions to arbitration awards. *E.g.*, *U.S. Pen.*, 57 FLRA at 410 n.5 (tailoring is part of the determination as to whether an arrangement is within the *duty to bargain*, not whether "an agreed-upon [provision,] incorporated into a collective bargaining agreement[,] is *enforceable* as negotiated pursuant to § 7106(b)(3)"). Therefore, the Agency's assertion provides no basis for finding that the award does not enforce an arrangement.[9]

Under the Authority's current standard for reviewing arbitral enforcement of provisions allegedly negotiated under § 7106(b)(3), the Authority determines whether an arrangement is "appropriate" by applying an excessive interference test. *See BOP, Oklahoma City II*, 58 FLRA at 110. A provision excessively interferes with the exercise of a management right if the benefits afforded employees under the provision are outweighed by the burdens on the exercise of management's rights. *Id.* at 111. This is consistent with the test that the Authority applies in the negotiability context. *Nat'l Ass'n of Indep. Labor, Local 7*, 64 FLRA 1194, 1197 (2010) (*NAIL*).

This case provides an opportunity for the Authority to reexamine whether "excessive interference" is the appropriate standard to use in proceedings reviewing arbitration awards. On reexamination, we find, for the following reasons, that it is more appropriate to assess whether a contract provision, as interpreted and applied by an arbitrator, "abrogates" – i.e., waives – management rights under § 7106(a) of the Statute. In so doing, we return to a standard adopted by the Authority twenty years ago. In particular, in *Department of the Treasury, United States Customs Service*, 37 FLRA 309 (1990) (*Customs Service*), the Authority established abrogation as the standard to be used in

---

9. We note that, in some arbitration decisions, the Authority has referenced tailoring in determining whether a provision is enforceable under § 7106(b)(3). *See, e.g., U.S. Dep't of Veterans Affairs, St. Cloud VA Med. Ctr., St. Cloud, Minn.*, 62 FLRA 508, 510-11 (2008); *U.S. Dep't of Commerce, Patent & Trademark Office*, 60 FLRA 839, 842 (2005); *NLRB*, 60 FLRA 576, 579 (2005) (Chairman Cabaniss concurring; then-Member Pope dissenting as to other matters). However, the dicta in these cases merely recognized that awards necessarily tailor relief to the harms suffered by adversely affected employees; none of the decisions set aside an award for failing to satisfy a tailoring analysis. *Cf. NTEU, Chapter 207*, 60 FLRA 731, 735 (2005) ("*As applied to the grievant*, [the provision] was a *properly tailored arrangement* that did not excessively interfere with management's rights." (Emphases added.)). Insofar as these decisions may be interpreted as requiring a tailoring analysis, they will no longer be followed.

the arbitration context. The Authority acknowledged that the abrogation standard differed from the excessive interference standard that the Authority applies in the negotiability context. In deciding that a different framework was warranted in reviewing arbitration awards, the Authority stated, in pertinent part:

> We expect that, as part of their negotiation process in reaching agreement on the provision, including it in their collective bargaining agreement, and subjecting the agreement to agency head review for legal sufficiency under [§] 7114(c) of the Statute, the parties will have assessed the effect of the provision on management's rights and the benefits to employees from the provision . . . .
>
> In our view, [the abrogation] approach to cases . . . more fully carries out the purposes of the Statute because it recognizes the fundamental differences under the Statute between the process for negotiation of a collective bargaining agreement and the process for enforcement of the collective bargaining agreement. The issue and determination of whether an arbitration award is deficient under [§] 7122(a)(1) is fundamentally different from the issue and determination of the extent of the duty to bargain under [§] 7117 of the Statute . . . .

Customs Service, 37 FLRA at 314-15.

The Authority acknowledged in *Customs Service* that there is an outer limit to what the parties may permissibly negotiate. In this regard, the Authority stated that "management rights are not waivable[.]" *Id.* at 316. However, the Authority found that "enforcement of an arrangement negotiated by the parties that does not abrogate management's rights does not involve a question of waiver." *Id.* Thus, the Authority found that if, as interpreted and applied by an arbitrator, an arrangement did not abrogate a management right, then the arrangement was appropriate – i.e., enforceable – and an arbitration award enforcing the provision would not be set aside by the Authority as contrary to § 7106. *Id.* at 317.

Subsequently, in *BOP, Oklahoma City II*, 58 FLRA at 110, the Authority reversed *Customs Service*. However, the majority in *BOP, Oklahoma City II* lacked a common rationale for doing so. In this regard, Chairman Cabaniss relied primarily on a finding that the Statute does not permit the use of one § 7106(b)(3) standard in the negotiability context and a different standard in the arbitration context. *Id.* at 113. Member Armendariz, by contrast, relied primarily on a finding that the Authority had not found an award to be deficient on abrogation grounds and, thus, application of the test had "effectively render[ed] the test meaningless and remove[ed] all of its utility." *Id.* at 115.

We find the rationale in *Customs Service* more persuasive than the separate rationales in *BOP, Oklahoma City II*. In so finding, we begin with the plain wording of the Statute. *See, e.g., U.S. Dep't of the Army, N. Cent. Civilian Pers. Operation Ctr., Rock Island, Ill.*, 59 FLRA 296, 301 (2003) (Chairman Cabaniss concurring). In this regard, neither § 7106(b)(3) nor any other provision of the Statute defines the standard to be used in determining whether an award is contrary to § 7106 and, as a result, contrary to law under § 7122(a)(1). Thus, the Statute does not expressly preclude the Authority from distinguishing between the standards used to determine whether a matter is within the duty to bargain under § 7106(b)(3) and the standard used to determine whether an award is contrary to law under § 7122(a)(1).

Further, as discussed in *Customs Service*, the negotiability and arbitration contexts are different in ways that warrant different analyses. In the negotiability context, where parties disagree over whether a proposal is within the duty to bargain under § 7106(b)(3), it is necessary that *the Authority balance* the competing burdens on management's rights against the benefits provided employees. *See NAIL*, 64 FLRA at 1197. By contrast, in the arbitration context, bargaining has concluded and it is reasonable to conclude that the *parties have balanced* the burdens and benefits themselves. As the Authority stated in *BOP, Oklahoma City I*, 57 FLRA at 162:

> parties should assess during bargaining the effect of the provision on management's rights and the benefits to employees from the provision. In other words, employers and unions should determine, through the collective bargaining process, what provisions best fit their working conditions and what arrangements are "appropriate." Thus, [the abrogation standard] reflects a justifiable reluctance on the part of the Authority to substitute its judgment on the wisdom of bargaining, or the merits of particular terms, for that of the parties who

have reached agreement on the contract provision.

Moreover, it is beyond dispute that many matters that are not within the duty to bargain are nevertheless not contrary to law. For example, an agency has no statutory duty to bargain over a matter encompassed by § 7106(b)(1) of the Statute. Nevertheless, once agreement has been reached over such a matter, it may not be disapproved by an agency head under § 7114(c)(3) and is fully enforceable in arbitration. *See U.S. Dep't of the Treasury, IRS, Wash., D.C.*, 56 FLRA 393, 395 (2000). Likewise, although there is no duty to bargain over matters that do not concern conditions of employment, agreements reached on those matters are fully enforceable. *See AFGE, Local 3302*, 52 FLRA 677, 680-83 (1996). Thus, the Statute recognizes that agency management is permitted to agree to a broader range of matters than those strictly within its duty to bargain. No basis is provided to conclude that the situation is any different when management rights under § 7106(a) are involved. Accordingly, short of waiver, agency management is permitted to agree to proposals affecting its management rights.

Finally, deference to parties' bargaining choices is consistent with the statutory "policies of: (1) promoting collective bargaining and the negotiation of collective bargaining agreements; and (2) enabling parties to rely on the agreements that they reach, once they have reached them." *NTEU*, 64 FLRA 156, 158 (2009) (Member Beck dissenting). Particularly after over thirty years' experience under the Statute, it is proper and reasonable to respect the choices and agreements made by the parties at the bargaining table.[10]

Based on the foregoing, we find that, in resolving exceptions to arbitration awards involving contract provisions alleged to be enforceable under § 7106(b)(3) of the Statute, we will assess whether the arrangement abrogates – i.e., waives – management rights. We will no longer apply an excessive-interference standard, and *BOP, Oklahoma City II* and other Authority decisions that have applied that standard in arbitration will no longer be followed.[11]

Applying the abrogation standard here, as interpreted and applied by the Arbitrator, the agreement limits the officials who may access the medical information of employees seeking reasonable accommodations, unless an employee consents to greater information sharing. *See* Award at 3-5; *see also supra* note 3. Specifically, the agreement ensures that, upon an employee's request, only the national coordinator will have access to the employee's full medical file, unless the employee thereafter consents to further dissemination. *See* Exceptions, Ex. 2 at 16-20. However, the Agency is incorrect in asserting that, under the agreement, local coordinators cannot assist in developing reasonable accommodations. *See* Exceptions at 7-8. In this regard, the Arbitrator found that, although there are "limit[s]" on the national coordinator's ability to share confidential medical information, the national coordinator is permitted to share with local coordinators or supervisors "the 'functional limitation' an employee faces, if the information is needed to make a decision" regarding a reasonable-accommodation request. Award at 12 n.4. Moreover, the agreement limits the national coordinator's ability to disclose certain employee medical information only where an employee requests such protection. Thus, the agreement will not necessarily preclude disclosure of employee medical records to local coordinators in all cases. The agreed-upon arrangement preserves the Agency's "right to request, obtain[,] and evaluate medical information in order to make a determination whether the employee qualifies for a [reasonable accommodation]." *Id.*

Consistent with the foregoing, we find that the agreement does not abrogate the Agency's right to

10. We therefore find the parties' agreement to a particular provision a relevant consideration in assessing whether the provision, as construed and applied by an arbitrator, constitutes an appropriate arrangement under § 7106(b)(3). However, because management rights may not be waived in collective bargaining, we are not able to join our concurring colleague in finding that the parties' agreement should be treated as a binding concession by the agency that the provision is a permissible limitation on management rights under § 7106(b). *See* Concurring Opinion at 12. Nevertheless, as stated previously, we agree with the concurrence that by permitting an agency to challenge a provision after agreement, the statutory scheme raises concerns regarding the efficient conduct of collective bargaining.

11. We note that our analysis calls into question whether abrogation also should be the standard applied in negotiability cases involving contract provisions (where agreement has been reached and subsequently disapproved), rather than proposals. *See BOP, Oklahoma City I*, 57 FLRA at 162 ("it appears appropriate to reexamine at the first opportunity the application of the excessive interference standard in cases where a provision has been disapproved under § 7114(c)"). However, as that issue is not raised here, we leave it for another day.

assign work. Thus, the agreement is enforceable under § 7106(b)(3) of the Statute and the award is not contrary to § 7106(a)(2)(B).[12]

C. The award is not based on a nonfact.

The Agency contends that the Arbitrator's finding that the parties reached an agreement on an appropriate arrangement is based on a nonfact. An arbitrator's conclusion that is based on an interpretation of the parties' collective bargaining agreement does not constitute a fact that can be challenged as a nonfact. *See NLRB*, 50 FLRA 88, 92 (1995). In finding that provisions of the parties' agreement constitute an appropriate arrangement, the Arbitrator interpreted and applied the language of the agreement. *See* Award at 14 ("The grievance is sustained . . . [because the] Agency[] . . . violated the [agreement] . . . ."). Thus, the Arbitrator's interpretation of the agreement as an appropriate arrangement cannot be challenged as a nonfact. Therefore, we deny the Agency's nonfact exception.

V. Decision

The Agency's exceptions are denied.

12. Because we have found that the award properly enforces an appropriate arrangement, it is unnecessary to address the award's alternative finding that the agreement resulted from negotiations on a permissive subject of bargaining under § 7106(b)(1) – namely, the methods or means of performing work.

Member Beck, Concurring:

I join Chairman Pope and Member DuBester in concluding that the Agency's exceptions should be denied. I also applaud my colleagues' move to abandon the "excessive interference" standard for assessing whether a contract provision that is being enforced by an arbitrator violates management's rights. Where I break ranks with my colleagues, however, is at their belief that we should engage in *any* assessment of whether a contract provision that is being enforced by an arbitrator violates management's rights.

The design of our Statute indicates that Congress intended for the evaluation of whether a given contract proposal impermissibly interferes with management rights to occur at the collective bargaining stage of the parties' labor relations -- not at the much later stage where the proposal has been adopted by the parties as a binding contract provision and arbitration about that provision has occurred. Once a proposal has been agreed to and has become a binding contract provision, the time for arguments about management's rights has passed.

Our Statute sets forth, at § 7106(a), certain critical management functions that are reserved to agency management (e.g., making determinations about budget, internal security, and the assignment of work). These are collectively known as "management rights." At the same time, at § 7106(b), the Statute unequivocally provides that an agency may agree to limitations on these management rights. The Statute expressly makes the management rights outlined in § 7106(a) "subject to" limitations that are negotiated pursuant to § 7106(b). Further, § 7106(b) tells us that "nothing" about § 7106(a) shall preclude the parties from negotiating limitations on management rights as described in § 7106(b). Reading § 7106 as a whole, one must conclude that Congress deemed the preservation of management rights to be important, and that it deemed the parties' freedom to negotiate limitations on these rights to be at least as important.

Our Statute also makes clear as crystal that management need not agree to impermissible limitations on its § 7106(a) management rights. When confronted with a collective bargaining proposal that, if implemented and enforced, would unduly infringe on management rights, agency negotiators may declare such a proposal to be non-negotiable. Whether the proposal is negotiable -- that is, whether it is or is not a permissible limitation on management rights -- then becomes a question to be resolved by the Authority. 5 U.S.C. §§ 7105(a)(2)(E), 7117(c). In addition, even if agency negotiators fail to raise negotiability objections during bargaining and tentatively agree to a union's proposal, the proposal may still be rejected as a result of agency head review. 5 U.S.C. § 7114(c).

Simply put, our Statute provides Federal agencies with ample opportunity to challenge a contract proposal based on its perceived interference with § 7106(a) management rights *before* such a proposal becomes a binding contract provision. Agencies are well aware that, if they do not reject a proposal at the bargaining table or through the mechanism of agency head review, the proposal "shall take effect and shall be binding." 5 U.S.C. § 7114(c)(3).

I presume that Federal agencies do not heedlessly agree to include in their collective bargaining agreements provisions that, if enforced in a reasonably foreseeable fashion, would impermissibly interfere with their management rights. As my colleagues correctly assert, once bargaining has taken place and a particular contract provision has been adopted, "it is reasonable to conclude that the *parties have balanced* the burdens and benefits themselves." Majority at 8 (emphasis in original). By agreeing to include in its collective bargaining agreement a provision that affects the management rights described in § 7106(a), the agency concedes that the provision is a permissible limitation on those rights under § 7106(b).

Consequently, once a contractual dispute has progressed to arbitration and the arbitrator has enforced a contract provision that was accepted by the agency as a permissible limitation on its management rights, the pertinent question is not whether the provision itself is an appropriate arrangement nor whether it excessively interferes with a § 7106(a) management right. Rather, at that point, the question is simply whether the remedy directed by the arbitrator enforces the provision in a reasonable and reasonably foreseeable fashion -- in other words, whether the remedy draws its essence from the agreement.

My colleagues note that, even after a proposal has been agreed to and has become a binding contractual provision, it remains "subject to the provisions of [the Statute]." 5 U.S.C. § 7114(c)(3). Therefore, they conclude, "an arbitration award that is contrary to § 7106 must be set aside." Majority at 4. I agree with this proposition. When an arbitral remedy affecting management rights is not properly derived from the contract provision that is being enforced, it "imposes a constraint on management rights that was not agreed to by the parties" and will be set aside. *FDIC, Div. of Supervision & Consumer Prot., S.F. Region*, 65 FLRA 102, 107 (2010); *see also id.* at 107 n.6. Thus, we ensure that a contract provision remains "subject to" the Statute by vacating an arbitral remedy that impermissibly interferes with management rights protected by § 7106(a) because it strays from the permissible limitation on management rights that the agency agreed to pursuant to § 7106(b).

I join in my colleagues' stated desire to show "deference to the parties bargaining choices" and I concur that "it is proper and reasonable to respect the choices and agreements made by the parties at the bargaining table." However, enabling parties, after the fact, to challenge as illegal contract provisions to which they voluntarily agreed does not reflect such deference and respect. And it profoundly undermines a principal goal of our Statute, which is "to provide the parties to [a collective bargaining] agreement with stability and repose with respect to matters reduced to writing in the agreement." *Dep't of the Navy, Marine Corps Logistics Base v. FLRA*, 962 F.2d 48, 59 (D.C. Cir. 1992).

To allow an agency to challenge the propriety of a given proposal under § 7106 *during* collective bargaining is consistent with Congress' mandate that our Statute "be interpreted in a manner consistent with the requirement of an effective and efficient Government." 5 U.S.C. § 7101(b). To allow an agency to mount a challenge under § 7106 *after* the agency has agreed to the provision and *after* an arbitrator has issued an award enforcing that provision can hardly be considered effective or efficient.

65 FLRA No. 29

AMERICAN FEDERATION
OF GOVERNMENT EMPLOYEES
LOCAL 3506
(Union)

and

SOCIAL SECURITY ADMINISTRATION
OFFICE OF DISABILITY
ADJUDICATION AND REVIEW
SAN ANTONIO, TEXAS
(Agency)

0-AR-4362

DECISION

September 29, 2010

Before the Authority: Carol Waller Pope, Chairman, and Thomas M. Beck and Ernest DuBester, Members

I. Statement of the Case

This matter is before the Authority on exceptions to an award of Arbitrator John B. Barnard filed by the Union under § 7122(a) of the Federal Service Labor-Management Relations Statute (the Statute) and part 2425 of the Authority's Regulations. The Agency filed an opposition to the Union's exceptions.

The Arbitrator found that the grievant's whistleblowing activities were a contributing factor in his nonselection for Hearing Office Director (HOD) and ordered the Agency to give the grievant priority consideration for the next HOD position in his region. For the reasons that follow, we deny the Union's exceptions.

II. Background and Arbitrator's Award

The Agency posted a vacancy announcement for a full-time permanent HOD. Award at 6. The grievant, who was President of the Union local, was one of eight applicants who qualified for the opening. *Id.* at 7. After the Agency decided not to select anyone for the position, the grievant filed a grievance concerning his non-selection. *Id.* Approximately three weeks later, the Agency posted a second vacancy announcement for the HOD position, this time for a full-time temporary position, not to exceed one year. *Id.* The grievant did not apply for this opening; rather, he filed a second grievance alleging that the temporary nature of the opening precluded his selection. *Id.* The Union made a discovery request for the promotion package related to the first vacancy announcement, but the Agency failed to produce it. *Id.* at 12-14. The grievant requested that an adverse inference be drawn from the Agency's non-production of the promotion package. *Id.* at 11-12

The Arbitrator addressed the following issues, which were proposed by one or both of the parties:

1. "As a threshold issue, is nonselection for a management position arbitrable under the parties' [collective bargaining agreement (CBA)] between the parties?"

2. "As a threshold issue, is management's decision to advertise a management position as temporary arbitrable under the CBA between the parties?"

3. "[Should] [a]n adverse inference be taken against the [A]gency for its failure/refusal to provide [the promotion package] related to [the first vacancy announcement]?"

4. "If the issue of non-selection for a management position is determined to be arbitrable, did the Agency violate the CBA by not selecting the grievant for the [permanent] HOD position . . . ? If so, what is the appropriate remedy?"

5. "If the issue of non-selection for a management position is determined to be arbitrable, did the Agency violate the CBA by advertising the . . . HOD position as temporary . . . ? If so, what is the appropriate remedy?"

6. "Was the grievant . . . not selected for [the permanent HOD position] because of his handicapping condition? If so, what shall the remedy be?"

7. "Were the grievant['s] . . . whistleblowing activities a contributing factor in the Agency's decision not to select him for [the permanent HOD

position]? If so, what shall the remedy be?"

8. "Was the grievant . . . not selected for [the permanent HOD position] because of his Union representational activities? If so, what shall the remedy be?"
9. "Was the grievant . . . not selected for [the permanent HOD position] because of his [Equal Employment Opportunity (EEO)] activities? If so, what shall the remedy be?"

10. "Was the grievant . . . not selected for [the permanent HOD position] because of the grievances that he filed? If so, what shall the remedy be?"

Id. at 2-3.

Regarding the first two issues, the Arbitrator found that the grievant's nonselection for a management position and the Agency's decision to post a temporary HOD position were arbitrable. *Id.* at 10-11. Regarding the third issue, the Arbitrator drew an adverse inference against the Agency for its failure to provide the Union with the promotion package related to the permanent HOD posting. *Id.* at 13-14. In this regard, the Arbitrator found that grievant's lack of access to the package denied him information central to his case and that the Agency offered no reasonable excuse for not having the package available. *Id.* at 14.

Regarding the fourth and fifth issues, the Arbitrator found that the Agency did not violate the CBA when it made no selection for the permanent HOD position and then posted a vacancy announcement for a temporary position. *Id.* at 11. As for the remaining issues, concerning whether certain factors contributed to the grievant's nonselection, the Arbitrator found that, with the exception of the whistleblowing activities, insufficient evidence had been presented to conclude that any of these were contributing factors. *Id.* at 18. As to the grievant's whistleblowing activities, the Arbitrator found that certain reports the grievant had made to both Congress and an Associate Commissioner of waste, fraud, and abuse in an awards program "could arguably be construed as having a chilling effect on the part of management when considerations are made in a promotional process." *Id.* at 19.

The Arbitrator considered and rejected the Agency's explanation that it did not make a selection from the first job announcement because it wanted to select the Hearing Officer Chief Administrative Law Judge (HOCALJ) before selecting the HOD. *Id.* at 15-16. The Arbitrator found that, because the Agency knew that the HOCALJ position was vacant when it posted for the permanent HOD, this explanation was both unsupported by sufficient evidence and unreasonable. *Id.* at 15, 17. In addition, the Arbitrator found that, because of the Agency's mishandling of the promotion package for the permanent HOD posting, he could not determine whether the grievant was on the well-qualified list or how he compared with the other applicants on the qualified list. *Id.* at 20. Under the circumstances, he found that a remedy short of placing the grievant in the position -- specifically, priority consideration for the next HOD position in the grievant's region -- was an appropriate and equitable remedy. *Id.*

III. Positions of the Parties

A. Union's Exceptions

The Union contends that the Arbitrator acted contrary to law and exceeded his authority when he ordered priority consideration as the remedy for the grievant's nonselection. Exceptions at 1. According to the Union, the appropriate remedy for a nonselection based on an applicant's whistleblowing activities is retroactive promotion to the denied position. *Id.* at 3. Further, the Union contends that the Arbitrator also exceeded his authority by failing to address, as possible motivating factors for the grievant's nonselection, the grievant's handicapping condition, representational activities, grievances, and EEO complaints. *Id.* at 5-8. The Union also contends that the Arbitrator improperly applied the adverse inference regarding the Agency's failure to produce the promotion package. In this regard, the Union contends that the adverse inference required the Arbitrator to find that the Union had met its evidentiary burden as to all contributing factors and to order a retroactive promotion.

B. Agency's Opposition

The Agency contends that the Arbitrator's award of priority reconsideration was consistent with law because the Arbitrator did not find that the Agency would have selected the grievant but for his whistleblowing activity. Opp'n at 6-7. Indeed, the Agency notes, the Arbitrator found that he could not make such a determination without the promotion package. *Id.* at 7. The Agency contends that there was clear and convincing evidence that the grievant would not have been selected, even if he had not engaged in whistleblower activities. *Id.* In support, the Agency notes that the grievant was a GS-13 applicant, that a selecting official testified that she always selected a GS-14 applicant for the HOD position, and that a GS-14 applicant was selected for the temporary HOD position. *Id.* at 8. Citing *Social Security Administration, Office of Hearings and Appeals, Paducah, Ky.*, 58 FLRA 124, 125-26 (2002), the Agency contends that an award of promotion and backpay is not appropriate when there is no causal connection between a prohibited personnel practice and a non-promotion.

The Agency contends that the Arbitrator did not exceed his authority because he addressed each of the factors that possibly could have contributed to the grievant's nonselection and found that there was sufficient evidence only as to the whistleblowing activities. *Id.* at 11. As for the adverse inference drawn by the Arbitrator, the Agency argues that it did not require the Arbitrator to find that all of the alleged factors were contributing factors to the grievant's nonselection. *Id.* at 14. Instead, the Agency contends, the adverse inference was tied only to the Arbitrator's finding that whistleblowing could have been a contributing factor. *Id.*

IV. Analysis and Conclusions

A. The award is not contrary to law.

When an exception involves an award's consistency with law, the Authority reviews any question of law raised by the exception and the award *de novo*. *See NTEU, Chapter 24*, 50 FLRA 330, 332 (1995) (citing *U.S. Customs Serv. v. FLRA*, 43 F.3d 682, 686-87 (D.C. Cir. 1994)). In applying the standard of *de novo* review, the Authority assesses whether an arbitrator's legal conclusions are consistent with the applicable standard of law. *See U.S. Dep't of Def., Dep'ts of the Army & the Air Force, Ala. Nat'l Guard, Northport, Ala.*, 55 FLRA 37, 40 (1998). In making that assessment, the Authority defers to the arbitrator's underlying factual findings. *See id.*

The Union contends that the Arbitrator's remedy of priority consideration is contrary to case law establishing that retroactive promotion is the appropriate remedy for a nonselection made in violation of the Whistleblower Protection Act.[1] However, none of the cases cited by the Union supports its contention. *Ruggieri v. Merit Systems Protection Board*, 454 F.3d 1323 (Fed. Cir. 2006), stands only for the proposition that an applicant's nonselection for a position for which the vacancy announcement is ultimately canceled is a "failure to take a personnel action" within the meaning of the Whistleblower Protection Act. *Id.* at 1326 (quoting 5 U.S.C. § 2302(a)(2)(A)(i)). The court made no finding as to the appropriate remedy for the nonselection. Likewise, in *Morgan v. Department of Energy,* 81 M.S.P.R. 48 (1999), the Merit Systems Protection Board (MSPB) did not hold that a retroactive promotion is always the appropriate remedy for a nonselection made in violation of the Whistleblower Protection Act. Instead, it held that, in an individual right of action proceeding brought under 5 U.S.C. § 1221 and concerning a nonselection, the MSPB, if it orders corrective action, *may* order a retroactive promotion with back pay. *Id.* at 55.[2] Finally, although in *Costin v. Department of Health and Human Services*, 72 M.S.P.R. 525 (1996), the MSPB found that the grievant had been retaliated against because of his whistleblowing and ordered the grievant be prospectively promoted, the MSPB did not find that the grievant was *entitled* to that or any other specific remedy. Moreover, under 5 U.S.C.

1. Under the Whistleblower Protection Act, an employer may not retaliate against an employee because of:

> (A) any disclosure of information by an employee or applicant which the employee or applicant reasonably believes evidences — (i) a violation of any law, rule, or regulation, or (ii) gross mismanagement, a gross waste of funds, an abuse of authority, or a substantial and specific danger to public health or safety, if such disclosure is not specifically prohibited by law and if such information is not specifically required by Executive order to be kept secret in the interest of national defense or the conduct of foreign affairs; or
> (B) any disclosure to the Special Counsel, or to the Inspector General of anagency or another employee designated by the head of the agency to receive such disclosures, of information which the employee or applicant reasonably believes evidences — (i) a violation of any law, rule, or regulation, or (ii) gross mismanagement, a gross waste of funds, an abuse of authority, or a substantial and specific danger to public health or safety[.]

5 U.S.C. § 2303(b)(8).

2. To the extent the Union suggests the Arbitrator exceeded his authority by not ordering the grievant be retroactively promoted, we reject this contention as well. Because the Arbitrator was not required to award this relief, he did not exceed his authority by failing to do so.

§ 1221(e)(1), the MSPB is authorized to order "such corrective action as the Board considers appropriate" when a whistleblowing violation has been established. This provision, thus, further supports a conclusion that there is no legal prohibition against the Arbitrator's chosen remedy of priority consideration.

The Union also contends that the Arbitrator improperly applied the adverse inference regarding the Agency's failure to produce the promotion package. In this regard, the Union contends that the adverse inference required the Arbitrator to find that the Union had met its evidentiary burden as to all contributing factors and to order a retroactive promotion. Exceptions at 8. The adverse inference principle, however, merely "permits an adverse inference to be drawn; it does not create a conclusive presumption against the party failing to" produce evidence. *Rockingham Machine-Lunex v. NLRB*, 665 F.2d 303, 305 (8th Cir. 1981). Moreover, the adverse inference that the Arbitrator drew from the Agency's failure to produce the promotion package is a finding of fact. *See* 31A C.J.S. *Evidence* § 255 (2010) ("The unfavorable . . . inference arising from the withholding of evidence is not conclusive against the party, but is merely a fact for the consideration of the" finder of fact.). As noted above, the Authority defers to an Arbitrator's factual findings, and the Union has not challenged the award on the basis of nonfact. Thus, contrary to the Union's contention, the Arbitrator was not required to find that the Union had met its evidentiary burden as to all contributing factors or order a retroactive promotion, and he did not err in failing to do so.

Accordingly, we find that the Arbitrator did not err in awarding the grievant priority consideration and properly applied the adverse inference regarding the Agency's failure to produce the promotion package and deny the exceptions.

B. The Arbitrator did not exceed his authority.

Arbitrators exceed their authority when they fail to resolve an issue submitted to arbitration, resolve an issue not submitted to arbitration, disregard specific limitations on their authority, or award relief to those not encompassed within the grievance. *See AFGE, Local 1617*, 51 FLRA 1645, 1647 (1996).

The Union contends that the Arbitrator exceeded his authority by failing to resolve certain issues that were before him. Specifically, the Union argues the Arbitrator failed to address whether the grievant's handicapping condition, representational activities, grievances, and EEO complaints were contributing factors in his nonselection. The Arbitrator, however, expressly considered each of these factors and concluded that "for the most part, while some arguments on each factor have possible merit, with the exception of the whistleblowing activities, there was not enough evidence presented to conclude a contributing factor." Award at 18. As a result, the Arbitrator resolved the issues before him.

Accordingly, we find that the Arbitrator did not exceed his authority and deny this exception.

V. Decision

The Union's exceptions are denied.

65 FLRA No. 30

UNITED STATES
DEPARTMENT OF VETERANS AFFAIRS
MEDICAL CENTER
HAMPTON, VIRGINIA
(Agency)

and

AMERICAN FEDERATION
OF GOVERNMENT EMPLOYEES
LOCAL 2328
(Union)

0-AR-4656

DECISION

September 29, 2010

Before the Authority: Carol Waller Pope, Chairman, and Thomas M. Beck and Ernest DuBester, Members

I. Statement of the Case

This matter is before the Authority on exceptions to an award of Arbitrator Louis J. D'Amico filed by the Agency under § 7122(a) of the Federal Service Labor-Management Relations Statute (the Statute) and part 2425 of the Authority's Regulations. The Union filed an opposition to the Agency's exceptions.

The Arbitrator found that the Agency violated the parties' agreement by changing the method for calculating employees' performance awards without providing the Union with advance notice or an opportunity to bargain over the impact and implementation of the change. For the reasons that follow, we deny, in part, and dismiss, in part, the Agency's exceptions.

II. Background and Arbitrator's Award

The Agency grants cash payments as "Superior Performance Awards" (performance awards) to deserving employees at one of the Agency's Medical Centers (the Center). Award at 5-6. When the Center's Director (the Director) reduced employees' performance awards based on patient surveys about the Center, the Union filed a grievance alleging that the reductions violated the parties' agreement. *See id.* at 7, 14. The grievance went unresolved, and the parties moved to arbitration. *See id.* at 16.

The Arbitrator stated that the grievance concerned only "Title 5 and [h]ybrid Title 38 employees" represented by the Union, and, consequently, it did not encompass employees belonging to a different union or "'[p]ure' Title 38 [e]mployees[,]" who were appealing their award reductions in a different forum.[1] *See id.* at 5, 10, 22. As to the covered group of employees, the Arbitrator framed the following issue for resolution:

> Did the Agency violate the collective bargaining agreement [(CBA)] by failing to notify the Union in advance of its decision to utilize the [Survey of Health Experiences of Patients (SHEP)] scores . . . [to] adjust[] the previously designated . . . Performance Award[s] . . . by 25% for employees encompassed by th[is] grievance?

Id. at 4.

The Agency argued that its regulations, rather than the CBA, controlled the administration of performance awards. *See id.* at 9. However, the Arbitrator found that both parties had previously acknowledged that the CBA concerned "the monetary awards under discussion[.]" *Id.* at 10, 12. Nevertheless, the Agency contended that the Director possessed unreviewable discretion to set the amount of performance awards, and, therefore, decisions on that particular issue could not be "appealed" at arbitration. *E.g.*, Agency's Closing Brief at 5 n.6. To the contrary, the Arbitrator determined that "[t]he Union was right to protest" reductions in performance awards through the CBA's negotiated grievance procedure because those reductions implicated employment conditions governed by the CBA; accordingly, "the Agency [h]andbook policy of

1. Title 38 refers to the portion of the United States Code that establishes an independent personnel system for many of the Agency's employees. *See generally* 38 U.S.C. Chapter 74. Title 5 is the portion of the United States Code that contains, among other provisions, the Statute. *See generally* 5 U.S.C. Chapter 71. "Hybrid Title 38" employees are those "who are subject to both title 38 and title 5 [of the United States Code]," and who, consequently, retain certain rights provided by title 5. *U.S. Dep't of Veterans Affairs v. FLRA*, 9 F.3d 123, 126 (D.C. Cir. 1993). By comparison, as relevant here, "pure Title 38 employees," i.e., *non*hybrid employees, are those who are subject solely to the title 38 personnel system. *Id.* at 125-26.

no right to appeal . . . performance awards does not bar the arbitration of th[e] grievance." Award at 13, 16.

The Agency also argued that the Union had previously acquiesced in the Director's award determinations, and, thus, the parties had not established a past practice regarding the awards. *See id.* at 8. However, the Arbitrator explained that past practices may include those that are "followed by one party and not challenged by the other[.]" *Id.* at 9 (internal quotation marks omitted). After setting forth the remaining criteria for a past practice, *see id.* at 11, the Arbitrator found that "for over 20 years," the Director determined award amounts and recipients on the basis of "(1) the employees' performance appraisal[s] . . . and (2) the availability of funds in the Agency's Budget[,]" and "nothing had been said before [the Director reduced the grievants' awards] . . . about . . . SHEP scores . . . affect[ing] . . . the awards[.]" *Id.* at 13.

Turning to the particular CBA provisions applicable to the dispute, the Arbitrator found that, because SHEP scores reflect the Center's *overall* performance and not that of *individual* employees, the Agency violated Article 26, Section 8(E) of the CBA when the Director reduced employees' performance awards based on a factor beyond their control.[2] *See* Award at 13, 22. Further, because the Arbitrator concluded that performance awards concerned conditions of employment, *id.* at 15, he found that the Agency violated Article 46, Section 4 of the CBA by using SHEP scores, in addition to performance ratings, as a factor in determining performance awards, without providing the Union with notice or an opportunity to bargain over the change in award criteria.[3] *See id.* at 14-15, 22.

Consequently, the Arbitrator granted the grievance. *See id.* at 24. Relying on Union Exhibit No. 6 to identify employees whose awards had been reduced, the Arbitrator directed the Agency to pay them compensation in the amount of their award reductions, with interest. *See id.* (citing Union Ex. 6).

III. Positions of the Parties

A. Agency's Exceptions

The Agency asserts that the Arbitrator erroneously interpreted CBA Articles 26 and 46 as provisions applicable to the parties' dispute. *See* Exceptions at 6 n.3, 11-12. According to the Agency, none of the CBA's provisions apply to the disputed performance awards, *see id.*, and, therefore, the regulations in the Agency's handbook govern the matter, *see id.* at 7-8. In this regard, the Agency argues that the handbook "does not allow an appeal of 'the amount of a superior performance award[,]'" and, because "an appeal" in this context is "synonymous" with "a grievance[,]" the award violates a governing Agency regulation. *Id.*

In addition, the Agency asserts that the Arbitrator erred in finding that the parties established a past practice regarding performance awards. *Id.* at 9-10. Alternatively, the Agency argues that, even if a past practice did exist regarding performance awards, the Arbitrator should have construed the past practice to allow the Director to determine performance awards in her "complete discretion." *Id.* at 10 & n.4, 11 n.5.

Consistent with its claim denying the existence of a past practice, the Agency further contends that it had no obligation to notify or bargain with the Union over a change to such a practice. *See id.* at 10-11. Thus, the Agency asserts that it could not have violated its notice or bargaining obligations regarding changes to conditions of employment, under CBA Article 46, Section 4, and that the Arbitrator's conclusion to the contrary fails to draw its essence from the CBA. *See id.* at 11-12 & n.6. The Agency similarly disputes the Arbitrator's findings regarding CBA Article 26, Section 8(E). In particular, the Agency contends that this section applies only to performance *appraisals*, and not performance *awards*. *See* Exceptions at 12. According to the Agency, the Arbitrator's flawed interpretation of this section resulted in his finding that employees' performance ratings were adjusted based on SHEP scores, which the Agency asserts is a nonfact. *See id.* at 12-13. Moreover, as the Agency contends that

---

2. Article 26, Section 8(E) of the agreement states, in pertinent part, "When evaluating performance, the [Agency] shall not hold employees accountable for factors which affect performance that are beyond the control of the employee . . . ." Award at 3.

3. Article 46, Section 4 provides in part:

> **Notification of Changes in Conditions of Employment**
> The [Agency] shall provide reasonable advance notice to the . . . Union . . . prior to changing conditions of employment. . . . All notifications shall be in writing . . ., with sufficient information to the Union for the purpose of exercising its full right to bargain.

Award at 3.

CBA Article 26, Section 8(E) does not concern performance awards, the Agency argues that the Director's use of SHEP scores in connection with performance awards did not violate that section, and that the Arbitrator's conclusion to the contrary fails to draw its essence from the CBA. *See id.* at 11-12.

Finally, the Agency argues that the Arbitrator exceeded his authority by granting relief to non-grievants. *Id.* at 13. The Agency asserts that Union Exhibit No. 6, which the Arbitrator used to identify the employees who were entitled to compensation for award reductions, lists all of the Agency's employees who received performance awards, and not merely the grievants. *Id.* at 14. Therefore, in the event that the Authority denies its other exceptions, the Agency requests that the Authority limit the awarded relief to the grievants. *See id.* at 15 & n.9.

B. Union's Opposition

The Union contends that the Agency is mistaken in its assertion that the CBA does not govern performance awards because, according to the Union, the CBA not only provides for performance-based monetary awards but also specifies that such awards will be based solely on an employee's performance rating. *See* Opp'n at 5-6. In addition, the Union contends that it is unnecessary for the Authority to limit the scope of relief awarded because the Arbitrator clearly stated that only those employee-grievants represented by the Union are covered by the grievance and award. *See id.* at 7.

IV. Analysis and Conclusions

A. The award is not contrary to Agency regulations.

The Agency argues that the award is contrary to governing regulations contained in the Agency's handbook, which does not allow performance-award appeals and which, as a result, renders the grievance substantively inarbitrable. An arbitration award that conflicts with a governing agency regulation is deficient under § 7122(a)(1) of the Statute. *See U.S. Dep't of Justice, Immigration & Naturalization Serv., Wash., D.C.*, 48 FLRA 1269, 1274-75 (1993). However, parties' agreements, rather than agency rules or regulations, govern the disposition of matters to which they both apply. *See U.S. Dep't of the Navy, Naval Training Ctr., Orlando, Fla.*, 53 FLRA 103, 108-109 (1997); *U.S. Dep't of the Treasury, U.S. Customs Serv., N.Y., N.Y.*, 51 FLRA 743, 746 (1996); *U.S. Dep't of the Army, Fort Campbell Dist., Third Region, Fort Campbell, Ky.*, 37 FLRA 186, 194 (1990). We note, in this regard, that when an arbitrator's substantive-arbitrability determination is based on law or governing regulations, the Authority reviews that determination *de novo*. *See, e.g., AFGE, Nat'l Border Patrol Council, Local 1929*, 63 FLRA 465, 466 (2009). However, in this case, the Arbitrator made his substantive-arbitrability determination on the basis of his findings that: (1) the parties previously acknowledged that the CBA governed "the monetary awards under discussion[,]" Award at 10, 12; (2) CBA Articles 26 and 46, in particular, applied to the parties' dispute; and (3) "the Agency [has not] asserted that the parties agreed to exclude this subject from their negotiated agreement[.]" *Id.* at 16. Because the Arbitrator's substantive-arbitrability determination was based on his interpretation of the parties' CBA, we review the Agency's challenge to this determination under the deferential essence standard, *infra* Part IV.C.[4] *See NATCA*, 56 FLRA 733, 735 n.3 (2000) (citing *AFGE, Local 1857*, 53 FLRA 1353 (1998)); *EEOC*, 53 FLRA 465, 481 n.20 (1997); *cf. NAGE, Local R4-45*, 55 FLRA 695, 699-700 (1999) (construing allegation that award violated law as claim that arbitrator erroneously interpreted parties' agreement to find that negotiated grievance procedure covered the subject matter of the dispute).

B. The award is not based on nonfacts.

The Agency contends that the award is based on nonfacts, namely, the Arbitrator's alleged determination that the parties established a past practice regarding performance awards,[5] and the

4. We note that, even if we were to review the Arbitrator's substantive-arbitrability determination *de novo* as a finding based on law, the Authority has held that regulations granting officials authority to make "final decisions" on certain matters do not exclude those matters from the parties' negotiated grievance procedure, unless the regulations provide "clear, specific indications that the . . . [regulatory] procedures were intended to be exclusive[.]" *AFGE, Local 3528*, 53 FLRA 1320, 1325-30 (1998) (quoting *NTEU, Chapter 15*, 33 FLRA 229, 235 (1988)). There are no clear, specific indications of exclusivity in the Agency's handbook regulations concerning performance awards.

5. In arbitration cases, the Authority addresses whether a past practice *exists* under the nonfact framework. *PASS*, 56 FLRA 124, 125 (2000). However, where a party alleges that an arbitrator improperly *interpreted* a past practice, the Authority considers the exception within the essence framework. *U.S. Dep't of Veterans Affairs, Med. & Reg'l Ctr., Togus, Me.*, 55 FLRA 1189, 1192-93 (1999). Thus, we review the Agency's argument that the parties had no past practice regarding performance awards as a nonfact

Arbitrator's alleged finding that employees' performance ratings were adjusted based on SHEP scores. To establish that an award is based on a nonfact, the appealing party must show that a central fact underlying the award is clearly erroneous, but for which the arbitrator would have reached a different result. *See NFFE, Local 1984*, 56 FLRA 38, 41 (2000). However, the Authority will not find an award deficient on the basis of an arbitrator's determination of any factual matter that the parties disputed at arbitration. *See U.S. Dep't of the Air Force, Lowry AFB, Denver, Colo.*, 48 FLRA 589, 594 (1993) (*Lowry AFB*) (citing *Nat'l Post Office Mailhandlers v. United States Postal Serv.*, 751 F.2d 834, 843 (6th Cir. 1985)).

The award does not contain an express finding as to the existence of a past practice regarding performance awards. However, even if the Agency is correct that the Arbitrator made such a factual finding, because the parties disputed this issue at arbitration, *see* Agency's Closing Brief at 8-9, Union's Closing Brief at 17-18, the award is not deficient on that basis. *See Lowry AFB*, 48 FLRA 589. Moreover, although the Agency alleges that the Arbitrator found that employees' performance ratings were adjusted based on SHEP scores, no such finding appears in the award. *Cf. SSA, Office of Hearings & Appeals*, 58 FLRA 405, 407 (2003) (nonfact exception denied because arbitrator did not make the finding alleged to constitute a nonfact). Accordingly, we deny the nonfact exceptions.

C. The award draws its essence from the parties' agreement.

The Agency contends that the Arbitrator's alleged conclusions regarding a past practice, as well as his interpretation and application of the CBA – including his determination of the substantive arbitrability of the grievance, *see supra* Part IV.A. – fail to draw their essence from the parties' agreement. In reviewing an arbitrator's interpretation of a collective bargaining agreement, the Authority applies the deferential standard of review that federal courts use in reviewing arbitration awards in the private sector. *See* 5 U.S.C. § 7122(a)(2); *AFGE, Council 220*, 54 FLRA 156, 159 (1998). Under this standard, the Authority will find that an arbitration award is deficient as failing to draw its essence from the collective bargaining agreement when the appealing party establishes that the award: (1) cannot in any rational way be derived from the agreement; (2) is so unfounded in reason and fact and so unconnected with the wording and purposes of the collective bargaining agreement as to manifest an infidelity to the obligation of the arbitrator; (3) does not represent a plausible interpretation of the agreement; or (4) evidences a manifest disregard of the agreement. *See U.S. Dep't of Labor (OSHA)*, 34 FLRA 573, 575 (1990). The Authority and the courts defer to arbitrators in this context "because it is the arbitrator's construction of the agreement for which the parties have bargained." *Id.* at 576.

As for the Agency's challenge to the Arbitrator's substantive-arbitrability determination, the award states that, in response to a specific query about whether the CBA governed the performance awards, both parties responded that the CBA governed "the monetary awards under discussion[.]" *See* Award at 10, 12. Because the Agency's exceptions do not deny the accuracy of that characterization, we find that the Arbitrator's substantive-arbitrability determination was not irrational, unfounded, implausible, or in manifest disregard of the CBA.

With regard to the Agency's contention that the award rests on a mistaken interpretation of a past practice concerning performance awards, as mentioned above in Part IV.B., it is not clear from the award that the Arbitrator found that a past practice existed or that he interpreted such a practice. However, even if the Arbitrator did interpret a past practice related to performance awards, that interpretation would not provide a basis for finding the award deficient because it would not affect the Arbitrator's determination that the Agency violated the CBA. *Cf. U.S. Dep't of Veterans Affairs, Veterans Affairs Med. Ctr., Louisville, Ky.*, 64 FLRA 70, 73 (2009) (finding that any alleged misinterpretation of past practice was "harmless error" because it did not affect the arbitrator's "pivotal finding" that Agency violated parties' agreement). Consequently, the Agency has not established that the Arbitrator's interpretation of a past practice renders the award deficient as failing to draw its essence from the parties' agreement.

With regard to CBA Article 26, Section 8(E), the Agency contends that the provision addresses only performance appraisals, not performance awards. However, the Arbitrator found that the parties agreed to base performance awards on performance ratings, which are the result of performance appraisals. In fact, the introductory paragraphs of Article 26 acknowledge that one purpose of performance

exception, and we analyze the Agency's argument that, even if a past practice did exist, the Arbitrator misinterpreted that practice, as an essence exception, *infra* Part IV.C.

appraisals is to determine performance awards. *See* Opp'n Attach., Agency Ex. 2 at 1-2 (quoting CBA Art. 26, § 1(B), (D), & (G)). Consequently, the Agency has not established that the Arbitrator's interpretation of Article 26, Section 8(E) is irrational, unfounded, implausible, or in manifest disregard of the CBA.

Because the Agency has failed to demonstrate a deficiency in the Arbitrator's finding of a violation of CBA Article 26, Section 8(E), we need not address the Agency's additional argument that it did not violate CBA Article 46, Section 4, because the finding of a violation of either contract provision is sufficient to support the award. *See, e.g., U.S. Dep't of Energy, Office of Scientific & Technical Info., Oak Ridge, Tenn.*, 63 FLRA 219, 220 (2009) (when an arbitrator has based an award on separate and independent grounds, an excepting party must establish that all of the grounds are deficient before the Authority can find that the award is deficient); *AFGE, Local 1546*, 59 FLRA 126, 128 (2003) (same).

For the foregoing reasons, we deny the essence exceptions.

D. The argument that the Arbitrator exceeded his authority is moot.

The Agency argues that the Arbitrator awarded relief to non-grievants. In this regard, arbitrators exceed their authority when they award relief to those not encompassed within the grievance. *See AFGE, Local 1617*, 51 FLRA 1645, 1647 (1996). Although the Arbitrator repeatedly stated that he was resolving a grievance that covered only those grievant-employees in the bargaining unit represented by the Union, the Agency is correct that the award directly refers to Union Exhibit No. 6 to indicate the employees who are owed compensation, and that exhibit includes non-grievant award recipients.

However, the Union contends that the awarded remedies extend only to those employees covered by the grievance. *See* Opp'n at 7. Where a party in opposition agrees with construing an award in the manner that an excepting party desires, the Authority has dismissed, as moot, exceptions that allege a deficiency based on a different construction of the award. *See, e.g., U.S. Dep't of Veterans Affairs, Veterans Affairs Long Beach Healthcare Sys., Long Beach, Cal.*, 63 FLRA 332, 334 (2009); *U.S. Food & Drug Admin., Detroit Dist.*, 59 FLRA 679, 683 (2004); *U.S. Dep't of Justice, INS, Jacksonville, Fla.*, 36 FLRA 928, 932 (1990). Construing the award consistently with the Union's contention that the Arbitrator provided relief only to grievant-employees in the bargaining unit represented by the Union, we dismiss the exceeded-authority exception as moot.

V. Decision

The Agency's exceptions are denied, in part, and dismissed, in part.

65 FLRA No. 31

AMERICAN FEDERATION
OF GOVERNMENT EMPLOYEES
LOCAL 1923
(Union)

and

UNITED STATES
DEPARTMENT OF THE NAVY
NAVAL FACILITIES
ENGINEERING COMMAND
(NAVFAC WASHINGTON)
(Agency)

0-AR-4662

DECISION

September 30, 2010

Before the Authority: Carol Waller Pope, Chairman, and Thomas M. Beck and Ernest DuBester, Members

This matter is before the Authority on exceptions to an award of Arbitrator Paul Greenberg filed by the Union[1] under § 7122(a) of the Federal Service Labor-Management Relations Statute (the Statute) and part 2425 of the Authority's Regulations. The Agency filed an opposition.[2]

Under § 7122(a) of the Statute, an award is deficient if it is contrary to any law, rule, or regulation, or if it is deficient on other grounds similar to those applied by federal courts in private sector labor-management relations. Upon careful consideration of the entire record in this case and Authority precedent, the Authority concludes that the award is not deficient on the grounds raised in the exceptions and set forth in § 7122(a). *U.S. Dep't of Veterans Affairs, Med. Ctr., N. Chi., Ill.*, 52 FLRA 387, 398 (1996) (award not deficient because of bias on the part of an arbitrator where excepting party fails to demonstrate that the award was procured by improper means, that there was partiality or corruption on the part of the arbitrator, or that the arbitrator engaged in misconduct that prejudiced the rights of the party); *U.S. Dep't of the Air Force, Lowry Air Force Base, Denver, Colo.*, 48 FLRA 589, 593-94 (1993) (award not deficient as based on a nonfact where excepting party either challenges a factual matter that the parties disputed at arbitration or fails to demonstrate that a central fact underlying the award is clearly erroneous, but for which a different result would have been reached by the arbitrator).

Accordingly, the exceptions are denied.

1. The exceptions in this case were prepared by the grievant and submitted with the Union's authorization.

2. The Agency filed an opposition to the Union's exceptions. The Authority issued an Order to Show Cause (Order), requiring the Agency to show why its opposition should not be rejected as untimely. Order at 1. In its response, the Agency claims that its opposition should be considered because the copy of the exceptions served on the Agency did not include a statement of service. Agency's Response to Order at 1-3. However, the Agency does not claim that it did not receive the exceptions. Under 5 C.F.R. § 2429.23(b), a waiver of an expired time limit must be based upon a showing of "extraordinary circumstances" justifying the waiver. 5 C.F.R. § 2429.23(b). As the Agency has failed to establish extraordinary circumstances warranting waiving the expired time limit, we will not consider the Agency's opposition. *See U.S. Dep't of Homeland Sec., U.S. Customs & Border Prot.*, 64 FLRA 916, 918-19 (2010) (union's opposition not considered where union failed to establish extraordinary circumstances to excuse the lack of timeliness).

In addition, both parties filed several unsolicited supplemental submissions. Section 2429.26 of the Authority's Regulations requires a party filing a supplemental submission to request permission to file such a submission. 5 C.F.R. § 2429.26. As neither party requested permission to file their respective supplemental submissions, we will not consider them. *See, e.g., AFGE, Local 933*, 65 FLRA 9, 10 (2010) (union's supplemental submission not considered where union did not request permission to file submission).

65 FLRA No. 32

UNITED STATES
DEPARTMENT OF THE ARMY
U.S. CORPS OF ENGINEERS
NORTHWESTERN DIVISION
(Agency)

and

UNITED POWER
TRADES ORGANIZATION
(Union)

0-AR-4651

DECISION

September 30, 2010

Before the Authority: Carol Waller Pope, Chairman, and Thomas M. Beck and Ernest DuBester, Members[1]

I. Statement of the Case

The matter is before the Authority on exceptions to an award of Arbitrator Jean A. Savage filed by the Agency under § 7122(a) of the Federal Service Labor-Management Relations Statute (the Statute) and part 2425 of the Authority's Regulations. The Union filed an opposition to the Agency's exceptions.

The Arbitrator sustained a grievance alleging that the Agency violated the parties' collective bargaining agreement (parties' CBA) when it denied the grievant's (the Union President) request for official time in May 2009. For the reasons that follow, we grant the Agency's exceptions in part and deny them in part.

II. Background and Arbitrator's Award

In November 2007, the Agency issued a memorandum (Agency Memo) informing managers about the procedures in the parties' CBA for requesting official time. Award at 4. The Union disagreed with the procedures set forth in the Agency Memo, contending that the CBA did not require the level of specificity outlined in the memo. The Union then filed a grievance, which the Agency denied. *Id.* The matter was submitted to arbitration. In October 2008, Arbitrator Kienast issued an award denying the grievance (Kienast Award).

Subsequently, Agency management and the grievant "agreed to an arrangement in which the [g]rievant could put asterisks [(Asterisk Procedure)] on days [that] he was requesting [official time] and attach a document listing purposes[.]"[2] *Id.* The Agency later informed the grievant that it "need[ed] more specificity to [his official time] request[s]." *Id.* The grievant did not comply. The Agency then denied his April 2009 requests for official time, stating that the requests were not in compliance with the CBA and the Kienast Award. *Id.* The Union then filed a grievance, which was also submitted to arbitration. In October 2009, Arbitrator Hauck issued an award sustaining the grievance (Hauck Award). *Id. at* 5.

In May 2009, the Agency again denied several of the grievant's official time requests, and the Union filed another grievance. The matter was not resolved and was submitted to arbitration on the following stipulated issue: "Whether the Agency violated the [CBA] and/or relevant law when it denied Union President's May, 2009 request for official time. If so, what is the remedy?" *Id.* at 2.

In the award now before the Authority, the Arbitrator sustained the grievance, concluding that the Agency violated Article 16.5 and 28.4 of the parties' CBA when it denied the grievant's official

---

1. Member Beck's separate opinion, dissenting in part, is set forth at the end of this decision.

2. The arrangement provided as follows:

> *
>
> The requested official time will be used for one or more of the following purposes:
>
> - Research and preparation for grievances or arbitrations.
> - Review and preparation of correspondence with management.
> - Administration of the CBA.
> - Phone calls in regards to the administration of the CBA.
>
> Past practice and the CBA [do] NOT require this level of specificity and it is given *under protest.* In addition, past practice has been established that "after the fact" changes have been allowed. These have been communicated to the Supervisor and approved by him. This practice will continue.

Award at 4 (emphasis in original).

time requests.[3] The Arbitrator found that the grievance, as it concerned the grievant's requests for May 11, 19, and 20, 2009, "is the same dispute that was resolved in the Hauck [A]ward." *Id.* at 7. Specifically, the Arbitrator found that, except for different dates, the parties, issue, contractual provisions, facts, arguments, and evidence were the same in both cases and that "there [were] no 'materially changed circumstances.'" *Id.* at 7 & 8. Moreover, after examining the transcript and Arbitrator Hauck's "reasoning and conclusions," the Arbitrator found that there had been a full and fair hearing and that the award was "not logically flawed or erroneous in its interpretation of the parties' [CBA]" *Id.* at 8. Accordingly, the Arbitrator held that it was appropriate to give the Hauck Award preclusive effect. *Id.* at 7.

The Arbitrator then noted that the Hauck Award held that the Asterisk Procedure "constituted practices that 'will be treated for all purposes as if they [were] incorporated into this [a]greement,' as provided in Article 28.4." *Id.* at 10. The Arbitrator, thus, found that the parties were contractually bound to implement the Asterisk Procedure, beginning on the date the Hauck Award was issued and until they are able to reach agreement on new procedures. *Id.*[4] Accordingly, as a remedy, the Arbitrator, among other things, directed the Agency to "implement the [A]sterisk [P]rocedure beginning on October 26, 2009, the date the Hauck [A]ward issued, until the parties are able to reach agreement on procedures for requesting official time." *Id.* at 14.

III. Preliminary Issue

The Union asserts that the Agency's exceptions are untimely. Opp'n at 4. The Union contends that the Arbitrator e-mailed the award to the parties on April 5, 2010,[5] and mailed signed copies of the award to the parties on April 6, the date of the postmark. *Id.* at 5. Citing Authority precedent, the Union argues that the award's date of service is the earlier of the two dates -- April 5 -- and, thus, to be timely, the exceptions must have been postmarked by May 4. *Id.* The Union contends that, as the Agency's exceptions were not filed until May 7, the exceptions are untimely. *Id.*

On June 18, the Authority's Office of Case Intake and Publication (CIP) issued to the Agency an order to show cause why its exceptions should not be dismissed as untimely (Order). In the Order, CIP stated that "when an award is served by two methods, timeliness is measured based on completion of the earliest method of service of the award." Order at 2 (citing *U.S. Dep't of Homeland Sec., U.S. Customs & Border Prot., U.S. Border Patrol*, 63 FLRA 345, 346 (2009), *recons. denied* 64 FLRA 807 (2010) (*Border Patrol*); *U.S. Dep't of the Treasury, IRS, Wash., D.C.*, 60 FLRA 966, 967 (2005) (*IRS*)). CIP stated that the award was "first e-mailed to the parties on April 5," and, as such, to be timely, any exceptions to the award had to be filed no later than May 4. *Id.* Because the Agency's exceptions were filed with the Authority by mail on May 7 (the date of the postmark), CIP stated that it appeared the exceptions were untimely. *Id.*

In response to the Order, the Agency asserts that Article 6.15 of the parties' CBA "limits the method of service to mail for arbitration awards." Agency Response to Order at 2. In particular, the Agency contends that Article 6.15 "clearly establishes the mailing of the award as the operative and proper method of service . . . ." *Id.* Moreover, the Agency asserts that the parties had an informal agreement that the award would be served "by mail" and that "mail would be the method of service for . . . the arbitration award." *Id.* at 2 & 3. The Agency contends that the award was served on the Agency by mail on April 6 and that because its exceptions were mailed to the Authority on May 7, the exceptions are timely.[6] *Id.* at 2.

In arbitration proceedings, the manner in which an arbitrator serves his or her award on the parties is a matter typically addressed informally by the arbitrator and the parties at, or after, the hearing; alternatively, it may be addressed in the arbitration

---

3. The relevant text of Articles 16 and 28 is set forth in the Appendix to this decision.

4. The Arbitrator also held that the Agency: (1) violated the parties' CBA when it denied the grievant's official time request for May 27 and (2) did not violate §§ 7102(1), 7131(d), or 7116(a)((1), (2), (5), or (8) of the Statute. Award at 12-13. As neither party excepts to these findings, we do not address them further.

5. All remaining dates are in 2010.

6. We note the Agency's claim that the Authority has allowed email service of arbitration awards in some cases without promulgating rules addressing that method of service. Agency Response to Show Cause Order at 3. We also note on July 21, 2010, the Authority issued its final rule clarifying the processing of arbitration cases, including email. *See* 75 FR 42283, 42290 (July 21, 2010) (§ 2425.2(c) of the Authority's Regulations concerns the methods of service of an arbitrator's award, including e-mail). The new regulations become effective on October 1, 2010.

provision of a collective bargaining agreement. *SSA Headquarters, Woodlawn, Md.*, 63 FLRA 302, 303 (2009) (*SSA*). Here, the Agency argues that Article 6.15 establishes mail as the method of service of arbitration awards. Article 6.15 provides, in relevant part, that an arbitrator's fee is reduced "for every day that the award is *mailed* later than the date required in this article." Award at 2. This wording supports the Agency's claim that mail is the method of service for the award. Accordingly, based on the parties' CBA and the Agency's undisputed assertions that the parties had an additional, informal agreement that the award would be served by mail, we find that the record demonstrates that the agreed-upon method of service for the award was mail.

The record shows that the award was served on the Agency by mail on April 6; as a result, to be timely, the Agency's exceptions had to be mailed by May 10. *Id.* at 2. Because the Agency's exceptions were mailed on May 7, they are timely.

IV. Positions of the Parties

A. Agency's Exceptions

The Agency asserts that the Arbitrator exceeded her authority by fashioning a remedy that was "beyond the scope of the stipulated issue." Exceptions at 11. Specifically, the Agency challenges the Arbitrator's order directing it to implement the "[A]sterisk [P]rocedure[.]" *Id.* at 7 & 8. The Agency asserts that requiring it implement this procedure "does not 'confine [itself] to those issues submitted to arbitration by the parties.'" *Id.* at 8.

In addition, the Agency contends that the Arbitrator failed to exercise "independent judgment" when she gave "preclusive effect" to the Hauck Award (citing *U.S. Dep't of Agric., Animal & Plant Health Inspection Serv., Plant Prot. & Quarantine*, 57 FLRA 4 (2001) (*Dep't of Agric.*)). *Id.* at 8, 9. The Agency asserts that the Arbitrator "did not independently analyze the merits of the case, nor did she . . . consider whether she agreed with Arbitrator Hauck's reasoning or result[s]." *Id.*

B. Union's Opposition

The Union asserts that the award directly addresses the stipulated issue, and that the Agency has not established that the award is deficient because the Arbitrator gave preclusive effect to the Hauck Award. Opp'n at 6, 7-8.

V. Analysis and Conclusions

A. The Arbitrator exceeded her authority to the extent the award applies to individuals other than the grievant.

Arbitrators exceed their authority when they fail to resolve an issue submitted to arbitration, resolve an issue not submitted to arbitration, disregard specific limitations on their authority, or award relief to those not encompassed within the grievance. *AFGE, Local 1617*, 51 FLRA 1645, 1647 (1996). In determining whether an arbitrator has exceeded his or her authority, the Authority accords an arbitrator's interpretation of a stipulated issue, or the arbitrator's formulation of an issue to be decided in the absence of a stipulation, the same substantial deference that it accords an arbitrator's interpretation and application of a collective bargaining agreement. *See NTEU*, 64 FLRA 982, 986 (2010) (citing *U.S. Info. Agency, Voice of Am.*, 55 FLRA 197 (1999). Nevertheless, if a grievance is limited to a particular grievant, then the remedy must be similarly limited. *See U.S. Dep't of Energy, Oak Ridge Office, Oak Ridge, Tenn.*, 64 FLRA 535, 538 (2010) (*Dep't of Energy*) (citing *U.S. Dep't of the Air Force, Air Force Logistics Ctr., Tinker Air Force Base, Okla.*, 45 FLRA 1234, 1240 (1992) (*Tinker AFB*).

In this case, the stipulated issue before the Arbitrator was: "Whether the Agency violated the [CBA] and/or relevant law when it denied [*the grievant's*] May, 2009 request for official time. If so, what is the remedy?" Award at 2 (emphasis added). The Arbitrator resolved this issue by determining that the parties were contractually bound to implement the "[A]sterisk [P]rocedure beginning on the date the Hauck [A]ward issued until they are able to reach agreement on [new] procedures." *Id.* at 10; *see also id.* at 14. Moreover, the Arbitrator's remedy requiring the Agency to implement the Asterisk Procedure until the parties are able to reach agreement on procedures is directly responsive to the issue. In this connection, it is well established that, where an arbitrator has found a contractual violation with regard to a particular agency action, the arbitrator may direct prospective relief, including directing the agency to comply with the violated contract provision in conducting future actions. *See, e.g., Air Force Space Div., L.A. Air Force Station, Cal.*, 24 FLRA 516, 517-20 (1986).

However, as set forth above, the grievance involved only the grievant's requests for official time. The Arbitrator, therefore, was authorized to award relief to the grievant only. *See Dep't of*

Energy, 64 FLRA at 538; *Tinker AFB*, 45 FLRA at 1240. The Arbitrator's remedy, however, directs the Agency to implement the Asterisk Procedure *generally* and does not limit its application to the grievant. *See* Award at 14 (directing the Agency to "implement the [A]sterisk [P]rocedure beginning on October 26, 2009, the date the Hauck [A]ward issued, until the parties are able to reach agreement on procedures for requesting official time."). Insofar as the award provides a remedy that applies to individuals other than the grievant, the award exceeds the Arbitrator's authority. Accordingly, we modify the award to clarify that this requirement applies only to the grievant.[7] *See, e.g., Dep't of Energy*, 64 FLRA at 538, and the cases cited therein.

B. The award is not contrary to law.

The Agency contends that the award is contrary to Authority precedent because the Arbitrator failed to exercise independent judgment in giving preclusive effect to the Hauck Award. Exceptions at 9. When an exception involves an award's consistency with law, the Authority reviews any question of law raised by the exception and the award *de novo*. *See NTEU, Chapter 24*, 50 FLRA 330, 332 (1995) (citing *U.S. Customs Serv. v. FLRA*, 43 F.3d 682, 686-87 (D.C. Cir. 1994)). In applying the standard of *de novo* review, the Authority assesses whether an arbitrator's legal conclusions are consistent with the applicable standard of law. *See U.S. Dep't of Def., Dep'ts of the Army & the Air Force, Ala. Nat'l Guard, Northport, Ala.*, 55 FLRA 37, 40 (1998). In so doing, the Authority defers to the arbitrator's underlying factual findings. *See id.*

The Authority generally has held that an arbitrator is not bound by another arbitrator's award. *See, e.g., Dep't of Agric.*, 57 FLRA at 6 (citing *AFGE, Local 2459*, 51 FLRA 1602, 1606 (1996)). In this regard, the Authority has found that arbitrators are required to exercise independent and impartial judgment on issues before them. *See id.* at 6 (citing *AFGE, Local 1273*, 44 FLRA 707, 712 (1992)). However, arbitrators may consider reasoning and conclusions in other arbitration awards. *See id.*

In this case, contrary to the Agency's contention, the record shows that the Arbitrator exercised independent judgment in deciding to give preclusive effect to the Hauck Award. In evaluating the disputed issue, the Arbitrator reviewed the hearing transcript in the Hauck Award and found that "there was a full and fair hearing before Arbitrator Hauck." Award at 8. Additionally, the Arbitrator stated that she had "carefully examined Arbitrator Hauck's reasoning and conclusions and [found] that his award [was] not 'logically flawed or erroneous in its interpretation of the parties' [CBA]". *Id.* Only after this examination did the Arbitrator decide to give preclusive effect to the Hauck Award.

These findings show that the Arbitrator exercised independent judgment concerning the issue before her. Consequently, we find that the award is not contrary to Authority precedent, and we deny this exception.

VI. Decision

The award is modified to apply to the grievant only. The remaining exceptions are denied.

---

7. We note the apparent inconsistency between the Arbitrator's finding that the Asterisk Procedure constituted a past practice that was incorporated into the parties' agreement and our determination that the remedy is limited to the grievant. This inconsistency, however, results from wording of the stipulated issue that the parties presented to the Arbitrator. Moreover, although the Arbitrator's remedy in this case should be limited to the grievant, the Arbitrator's underlying finding that the parties are contractually bound to implement the Asterisk Procedure is an integral part of the Arbitrator's resolution of the issue the parties placed before him.

APPENDIX

Article 6.15
ARBITRATION PROCEDURE

> Unless otherwise agreed by the parties, the Arbitrator shall furnish a complete report and award in writing to the [Agency] and the Union within thirty (30) calendar days following the close of the hearing or within thirty (30) calendar days of the *mailing* of the post hearing briefs, if the parties wish to file a brief. The Arbitrator's award shall be in writing and shall identify and discuss all issues raised by the parties . . . . The Arbitrator's fee shall be reduced by ten percent (10%) for every day that the *award is mailed* later than the date required in this article.

Agency's Response to Show Cause Order at 2 (emphasis in original). *See also* Award at 2.

Article 28
EFFECTIVE DATE, DURATION AND SCOPE OF THE AGREEMENT AND PAST PRACTICES

> 28.4 Laws, government[-]wide regulations and this Agreement take precedence over past practices. Existing and future working conditions, which are not inconsistent with this Agreement or law and are established through past practice, will be treated for all purposes as if they are incorporated into this Agreement and may only be modified or terminated through the exercise of the collective bargaining process.

Award at 3.

Member Beck, Dissenting In Part:

I agree with my colleagues' conclusion that the Arbitrator exceeded her authority by directing the Agency to apply the Asterisk Procedure to individuals other than the grievant. However, I disagree with my colleagues' determination that the Arbitrator was authorized to award prospective relief, as she did by directing the Agency to abide by the Asterisk Procedure in the future. Just as the stipulated issue before the Arbitrator was limited in terms of *whom* it covered (only the individual grievant), it was also limited in terms of the *time frame* that it covered -- only May of 2009.

To be sure, arbitrators have broad discretion in the fashioning of appropriate remedies. *See, e.g.*, *VA*, 24 FLRA 447, 450 (1986). However, despite this deference, the Authority has adhered to the fundamental principle that arbitrators must confine their awards and remedies to those issues submitted for resolution. *See id.*, and the cases cited therein. Arbitrators "must not dispense their own brand of industrial justice." *U.S. Dep't of the Treasury, U.S. Mint, Denver, Colo.*, 60 FLRA 777, 779 (2005) (then-Member Pope dissenting as to application) (quoting *VA*, 24 FLRA at 450).

The parties asked the Arbitrator to resolve the following stipulated issue:

> Whether the Agency violated the [parties'] collective bargaining agreement [CBA] and/or relevant law when it denied Union President's May, 2009 request for official time. If so, what is the remedy?

Award at 2. On its face, the issue was directed only at the Agency's processing of official time requests (1) submitted by the Union President for (2) May 2009. *Id.* at 10 (stating that the "parties limited the issue to be decided to the [Agency's] denial of several official time requests in May 2009"). Thus, the issue was specifically limited as to both the universe of employees affected *and* the time period involved. The Arbitrator's remedy should have been similarly limited. The Arbitrator here, however, ordered additional, prospective relief – that the Agency "implement the [A]sterisk [P]rocedure . . . *until the parties are able to reach agreement on procedures for requesting official time.*" *Id.* at 14 (emphasis added). This sweeping, prospective remedy is neither necessary nor appropriate given the specific and limited nature of the grievance.

Moreover, the Majority's approach – finding that the Arbitrator exceeded her authority to the extent that she awarded relief to individuals other than the grievant, but not with respect to the time period – leads to an anomalous result. In reaching her decision, the Arbitrator concluded that the Asterisk Procedure constituted a past practice and, accordingly, became part of the parties' agreement. The Arbitrator ordered the parties' to implement this procedure until they are able to reach a new agreement regarding requests for official time. In the Majority's view, this new requirement can be applied prospectively, but only with respect to the grievant. The Majority's conclusion, thus, creates two classes of employees – the Union President, who receives the benefit of this new requirement, and all other employees who request official time, who do not enjoy the benefit of the new requirement. Such inconsistency would not result, however, if the Majority recognized that the Arbitrator's authority was limited in two respects rather than in just one -- to the individual whose requests for official time had been denied and were in dispute and to the period of time covered by the requests.

Finally, I do not mean to suggest that an arbitrator can never order prospective relief. Indeed, one can imagine a stipulated issue that would have warranted the remedy directed by the arbitrator here. For example, the issue could have been stated as:

- "Does the agency violate Article 28.4 of the parties' CBA by demanding that requests for official time provide more detail than is contemplated by the Asterisk Procedure, and if so, what shall be the remedy?" Or,

- "Is the Asterisk Procedure a binding agreement or practice, and has the agency violated it by demanding that requests for official time provide more detail than is required by that Procedure, and if so, what shall be the remedy?" Or,

- "Has the Agency failed to comply with the Hauck Award, and if so, what shall be the remedy?"

Thus, the issue presented to the Arbitrator easily could have justified the imposition of the sort of generalized, prospective remedy that the Arbitrator directed. However, for their own reasons, the parties chose not to submit such an issue.

65 FLRA No. 33

UNITED STATES
DEPARTMENT OF THE AIR FORCE
82ND TRAINING WING
SHEPPARD AIR FORCE BASE, TEXAS
(Agency)

and

AMERICAN FEDERATION
OF GOVERNMENT EMPLOYEES
LOCAL 779
(Union)

0-AR-4455

DECISION

September 30, 2010

Before the Authority: Carol Waller Pope, Chairman and Thomas M. Beck and Ernest DuBester, Members

I. Statement of the Case

This matter is before the Authority on exceptions to an award of Arbitrator Harold E. Moore, filed by the Agency under § 7122(a) of the Federal Service Labor-Management Relations Statute (the Statute) and part 2425 of the Authority's Regulations. The Union filed an opposition to the Agency's exceptions.[1]

The Agency temporarily assigned the grievant to a higher-graded position for approximately nineteen months. Near the end of the grievant's assignment, the Agency retroactively detailed the grievant to the higher-graded position. The Arbitrator found that the Agency violated the parties' collective bargaining agreement (CBA) by failing to temporarily promote, rather than detail, the grievant to the position. For the reasons discussed below, we deny the Agency's exceptions.

II. Background and Arbitrator's Award

The Agency hired the grievant to fill a GS-7 position. Award at 2. The Agency then temporarily assigned the grievant to a higher-graded position for approximately nineteen months. *Id.* at 2-3. When the grievant was initially assigned to the higher-graded position, a position description classifying the position did not exist at the grievant's facility. *Id.* at 3. The Agency also did not initially document the grievant's temporary assignment as a detail. *Id.*

About fifteen months after the grievant was temporarily assigned to the higher-graded position, the Agency implemented a position description and classified the position at the GS-11 grade level. *Id.* Later, at approximately the eighteenth month of the grievant's temporary assignment, the Agency retroactively documented that it had detailed the grievant to the GS-11 position for the entire period. *Id.*

When the Agency decided to fill the position on a permanent basis, the grievant applied. Tr. at 43. However, the Agency hired another individual. *Id.*; Award at 3.

The employee grieved. The grievance alleged that the Agency violated the CBA. The grievance claimed that the Agency should have given the grievant a temporary promotion and paid him the differential between the GS-7 grade and the GS-11 grade. J. Ex. 2 at 2. When the grievance was not resolved, it was submitted to arbitration.

The Arbitrator adopted both parties' statements of the issues as follows:

> Whether [the Agency] violated Article Twenty-two of the [CBA[2]].

1. The Union's opposition also contained cross-exceptions. However the cross-exceptions were withdrawn and are not before the Authority.

2. The relevant portions of Article 22 state:

> Section 8. a. A detail is the temporary assignment of an employee to duties not within his job description. A detail does not change the employee's . . . grade, or pay rate.
> b. Details should be on a fair and equitable basis, consistent with employee qualification[s] and skills... [P]rolonged period[s] of details are discouraged.
> c. Details in excess of 30 continuous days will be recorded on Standard Form 50 . . . .
> d. Normally, a temporary promotion instead of a detail will be made when: (1) The employee is fully qualified for promotion; and, (2) The assignment [to] a higher graded position is expected to last for more than 90 days.

Award at 2.

> Whether the [g]rievant was entitled to have been temporarily promoted under the terms of the [CBA] due to his being temporarily assigned to a higher[-graded] position.

Award at 2.

The Agency argued that the grievant was only eligible for a detail. *Id.* at 4. The Agency took the position that the grievant was not entitled to a promotion because he had not met the regulatory time-in-grade requirement at the next lower grade below GS-11. *Id.* Conversely, the Union contended that the Agency can waive the time-in-grade requirement to avoid inequity to the grievant. *Id.* at 3-4. The Union also pointed out that the grievant was otherwise fully qualified for the job. *Id.* at 3.

The Arbitrator granted the grievance. *Id.* at 5. He ruled that the Agency violated a number of provisions of the CBA. *Id.* For instance, the Arbitrator held that the Agency violated Article 22, § (b), which specifies that details should be assigned on a "fair and equitable" basis. Applying this provision, he found that it was "inconsistent and inequitable" for the Agency to retroactively detail, rather than temporarily promote, the grievant solely because he did not meet the time-in-grade requirement. *Id.* The Arbitrator reasoned that the grievant filled the GS-11 position for more than nineteen months and possessed prior "academic and practical experience" otherwise qualifying him for the position's duties. *Id.* at 4-5.

The Arbitrator also found that the Agency violated Article 22, § 8(d) of the CBA. *Id.* at 5. Specifically, the Arbitrator found that the grievant satisfied the two provisions of Article 22, § 8(d) mandating a temporary promotion when: "(1) The employee is fully qualified for promotion; and, (2) The assignment to a higher graded position is expected to last for more than 90 days." *Id.* at 2. In applying the provisions, the Arbitrator found that the grievant, "by the Agency's stipulation, was qualified for the job, and supervision should have known during a nineteen months . . . period that the job was going to or had lasted more than ninety . . . days." *Id.* at 5.

As a remedy, the Arbitrator ordered the Agency to properly document the time the grievant spent performing the duties of the GS-11 position, and to pay the grievant the differential between the GS-11 and the grievant's GS-7 grade for the entire period of his temporary assignment. *Id.* at 6.

III. Positions of the Parties

A. Agency's Exceptions

The Agency contends that the award is deficient because: (1) the award is based on nonfacts; and (2) the award is contrary to law.

The Agency asserts that the award is based on nonfacts because the Arbitrator made two factual errors. The Arbitrator's first alleged error concerned how the Arbitrator understood the nature of the grievance. The Agency claims that the Arbitrator erroneously found that the "gist" of the grievance was that the grievant was not hired for the GS-11 position. Exceptions at 3. The Agency disagrees. Rather, the Agency argues, the grievance concerned the grievant's entitlement to additional pay and time in grade for the period of his alleged detail. *Id.*

The Arbitrator's second alleged error concerns the grievant's qualifications. The Agency argues that the award is based on a nonfact because the Arbitrator erroneously found as the award's central fact that the grievant was "qualified for the job" based on the Agency's stipulation. *Id.* at 3. The Agency claims that it never made such a stipulation. *Id.* at 3-4. Instead, the Agency argues, it presented evidence that the grievant was not fully qualified for the GS-11 promotion because he did not meet the requisite time-in-grade requirement. *Id.*

The Agency also makes a number of arguments in support of its contrary to law exception. First, the Agency asserts that the award is deficient because it is contrary to 5 C.F.R. § 300.604(b).[3] Specifically, the Agency argues that the grievant did not meet the time-in-grade requirement at the next lower grade below GS-11 so that he could be temporarily promoted to the GS-11 position. *Id.* at 4.

Further, the Agency argues that in any event, the grievant is not entitled to backpay under the Supreme Court's decision in *United States v. Testan*, 424 U.S. 392 (1976) (*Testan*) and other authority following *Testan*. *Id.* In particular, the Agency argues that an

---

3. The relevant portion of 5 C.F.R. § 300.604(b) states:

> (b) *Advancement to positions at GS-6 through GS-11.* Candidates for advancement to a position at GS-6 through GS-11 must have completed a minimum of 52 weeks in positions:
>
> (1) No more than two grades lower (or equivalent) when the position to be filled is in a line of work properly classified at 2-grade intervals[.]

employee is only allowed to receive the salary of his appointed position, even though the employee performed the duties of another position or claims he should have been classified at a higher grade. *Id.* (citing *Testan*, 424 U.S. at 955). Moreover, the Agency contends that if the grievant is entitled to a temporary promotion, he can seek a remedy under law other than the Back Pay Act. *Id.* at 5.

In addition, the Agency argues that the grievant may not be awarded backpay for misassignments to higher-level duties or improper classifications. *Id.* at 5. In support, the Agency cites authority holding that the Detail Statute, 5 U.S.C. § 3341 and the Federal Personnel Manual "do not require the granting of a temporary promotion for an overlong detail." [4]

B. Union's Opposition

The Union contends that the award is not based on nonfacts. Opp'n at 3. It argues that the Arbitrator found and the Agency admitted that the grievant was qualified for the GS-11 position in terms of education and experience. *Id.* Therefore, the issue of whether the grievant was qualified was not disputed at arbitration. *Id.* Instead, the Union contends that the central issue disputed at arbitration was whether the grievant met the requisite time-in-grade requirement to be entitled to a temporary promotion under the CBA. *Id.* at 3-4.

The Union further argues that the award is not contrary to law. *Id.* at 4. With regard to 5 C.F.R. § 300.604(b), the Union contends that a time-in-grade restriction may be waived to avoid undue hardship or inequity when a grievant would otherwise be entitled to a temporary promotion. *Id.* (citing *U.S. Dep't of Veterans Affairs Med. Ctr. Allen Park, Mich.*, 38 FLRA 688, 695-96 (1990) (*VAMC*)).

In addition, the Union asserts that *Testan* does not apply. Specifically, the Union points out that, unlike the plaintiffs in *Testan*, the grievant in this case is not seeking a retroactive reclassification of his position, but rather a temporary promotion for the time he performed higher-graded duties. *Id.* at 5. The Union asserts that grievances concerning whether a grievant is entitled under a collective bargaining agreement to compensation at a higher pay rate for performing the duties of a higher-graded position do not involve classification matters. *Id.* at 5-6.

IV. Analysis and Conclusions

A. The award is not based on nonfacts.

The Agency's first nonfact argument is that the Arbitrator erred when he found that the grievance concerned the Agency's hiring of another individual to fill the permanent GS-11 position. Exceptions at 3. To establish that an award is based on a nonfact, the appealing party must show that a central fact underlying the award is clearly erroneous, but for which the arbitrator would have reached a different result. *See NFFE, Local 1984*, 56 FLRA 38, 41 (2000) (*NFFE*). Moreover, the Authority will not find that an award relies on a nonfact based simply on the Arbitrator's allegedly erroneous determination of any factual matter that the parties disputed at arbitration. *Id.*

The Agency's argument does not establish that the award is based on a nonfact. Although the Arbitrator mentions that the grievant's nonselection for the GS-11 position generated the grievance, Exceptions at 3, the Agency does not explain how this finding is a central fact underlying the award. *See id.* Similarly, the Agency does not argue, *id.*, that the Arbitrator would have reached a different result but for this alleged error. *See AFGE, Local 1395*, 64 FLRA 622, 626 (2010) (award not based on nonfact where party failed to establish that arbitrator's reliance on erroneous fact, even if true, would have resulted in a different outcome). The Authority therefore rejects the Agency's nonfact assertions relating to how the Arbitrator characterized the grievance.

The Agency's second nonfact contention also lacks merit. The Agency contends in this connection

4. There is no evidence that the Agency raised this argument in the proceedings before the Arbitrator. Under § 2429.5 of the Authority's Regulations, the Authority will not consider issues that could have been, but were not, presented to the arbitrator. *See, e.g., U.S. Dep't of Homeland Sec., U.S. Customs & Border Prot., JFK Airport, Queens, N.Y.*, 62 FLRA 416, 417 (2008). Accordingly, the Authority will not consider the Agency's argument.

In addition, the Agency argues that the Award fails to draw its essence from the CBA because the CBA gives the Agency a "permissive right" to assign an employee higher graded duties without temporarily promoting the individual. Exceptions at 4. However, because the Agency fails to identify the basis for its argument in the CBA, the Authority rejects this argument as a bare assertion. *See, e.g., AFGE, Local 1858*, 59 FLRA 713, 715 (2004) (claim that award is inconsistent with collective bargaining agreement rejected as a bare assertion where party failed to explain or provide any support for statement).

that the Arbitrator's findings concerning the grievant's qualifications were erroneous. Exceptions at 3-4. In particular, the Agency argues that the Arbitrator erroneously found that the Agency stipulated that the grievant was qualified for the job. Exceptions at 3. However, even assuming that the Arbitrator erred concerning the Agency's stipulation, the Agency also points out that it argued that the grievant was not qualified for the temporary GS-11 position at arbitration. *Id.* at 4. As the Agency's nonfact argument relies on the Arbitrator's allegedly erroneous determination of a factual matter that was disputed at arbitration, the argument fails to demonstrate that the award is deficient on that basis. *See NFFE*, 56 FLRA at 41.

Accordingly, we deny the Agency's nonfact exceptions.

B. The award is not contrary to law.

The Agency claims that the award is contrary to a government-wide personnel regulation, 5 C.F.R. § 300.604(b), and to the Supreme Court's decision in *Testan,* 424 U.S. 392. When an exception involves an award's consistency with law, the Authority reviews any question of law raised by the exception and the award *de novo*. *See NTEU, Chapter 24*, 50 FLRA 330, 332 (1995) (citing *U.S. Customs Serv. v. FLRA,* 43 F.3d 682, 686-87 (D.C. Cir. 1994)). In applying this standard, the Authority assesses whether an arbitrator's legal conclusions are consistent with the applicable standard of law. *See U.S. Dep't of Def, Dep'ts of the Army & the Air Force, Ala. Nat'l Guard, Northport, Ala.*, 55 FLRA 37, 40 (1998). In making that assessment, the Authority defers to the arbitrator's underlying factual findings. *See id.*

1. The award is not contrary to 5 C.F.R. § 300.604(b).

The Agency argues that the award is contrary to 5 C.F.R. § 300.604(b) because the grievant did not meet the regulation's time-in-grade requirements to qualify for a temporary promotion. Exceptions at 4. As indicated previously, *see* note 3, *supra,* § 300.604(b) imposes a 52-week time-in-grade requirement at the GS-9 level for promotions to GS-11. However, a waiver of time-in-grade restrictions in temporary promotion cases is permissible under 5 C.F.R. § 300.603(b)(7) and Authority precedent. *See, e.g., U.S. Dep't of Veterans Affairs, W. L.A. Med. Ctr., L.A., Cal.*, 46 FLRA 853, 861 (1992) (*VA*). Under 5 C.F.R. § 300.603(b)(7), time-in-grade requirements may be waived "to avoid hardship to an agency or inequity to an employee[.]"

The Arbitrator explicitly found that the Agency had treated the grievant inequitably when it assigned him to the GS-11 position for more than nineteen months. Award at 4-5. The Agency does not argue, and it is not otherwise apparent, that applicable law or regulation would prevent the Agency from waiving § 300.604(b)'s time-in-grade requirements in reliance on § 300.603(b)(7) and complying with the award. The Authority therefore rejects the Agency's contrary to law exception pertaining to regulatory time-in-grade requirements.

2. The award is not contrary to the Supreme Court's decision in *Testan.*

The Agency contends that the award is deficient because the Supreme Court's decision in *Testan* bars a back pay remedy for the grievant. Exceptions at 4. However, the Agency's reliance on *Testan* and its progeny is misplaced.

Unlike this case, *Testan* dealt with employees' claims that their positions were wrongly classified. *See* 424 U.S. at 405-06. The Supreme Court ruled that federal employees are entitled to receive only the salary of the position to which they are appointed, even though they may have performed the duties of another position or claimed that they should have been placed in a higher grade. *See Testan*, 424 U.S. at 406. The Court concluded that "neither the Classification Act nor the Back Pay Act creates a substantive right in the respondents to backpay for the period of their claimed wrongful classifications." *Id.* at 407. Because this case does not involve any classification issues, *Testan* does not apply. *See U.S. Dep't of the Air Force, Warner Robins Air Force Logistics Ctr, Robins Air Force Base, Ga.*, 37 FLRA 155, 159 (1990) (*Testan* not applicable because grievant was not seeking reclassification of her position, but rather a temporary promotion for time in which she performed duties of a higher-graded position). The Authority therefore rejects the Agency's contrary to law exception based on *Testan.*

Accordingly, we deny the Agency's contrary to law exceptions.

V. Decision

The Agency's exceptions are denied.

65 FLRA No. 34

SOCIAL SECURITY ADMINISTRATION
HIGHLAND PARK, MICHIGAN
(Agency)

and

AMERICAN FEDERATION
OF GOVERNMENT EMPLOYEES
LOCAL 3239
(Union)

0-AR-4676

DECISION

September 30, 2010

Before the Authority: Carol Waller Pope, Chairman, and Thomas M. Beck and Ernest DuBester, Members

This matter is before the Authority on exceptions to an award of Arbitrator Joseph W. Gardner filed by the Agency under § 7122(a) of the Federal Service Labor-Management Relations Statute (the Statute) and part 2425 of the Authority's Regulations. The Union did not file an opposition to the Agency's exceptions.

Under § 7122(a) of the Statute, an award is deficient if it is contrary to any law, rule, or regulation, or it is deficient on other grounds similar to those applied by federal courts in private sector labor-management relations. Upon careful consideration of the entire record in this case and Authority precedent, the Authority concludes that the award is not deficient on the grounds raised in the exceptions and set forth in § 7122(a).[*] *See NFFE, Local 1827,* 52 FLRA 1378, 1385 (1997) (exception challenging an arbitrator's evaluation of the evidence and determination of the weight to be accorded such evidence provides no basis for finding an award deficient); *U.S. Dep't of Labor (OSHA)*, 34 FLRA 573, 575 (1990) (award not deficient as failing to draw its essence from the parties' collective bargaining agreement where excepting party fails to establish that the award cannot in any rational way be derived from the agreement; is so unfounded in reason and fact and so unconnected to the wording and purpose of the agreement as to manifest an infidelity to the obligation of the arbitrator; does not represent a plausible interpretation of the agreement; or evidences a manifest disregard of the agreement).

Accordingly, the Agency's exceptions are denied.

---

[*] To the extent that the Agency's statement concerning when an arbitrator exceeds his authority could be construed as an assertion that the Arbitrator exceeded his authority here, *see* Exceptions at 5, the Agency provides no argument in support of this statement. We thus reject this statement as a bare assertion. *See, e.g., AFGE, Local 446*, 64 FLRA 15, 16 (2009). To the extent that the Agency asserts that the award is contrary to management's right to determine the number of employees required to accomplish its mission under § 7106(a)(1) of the Statute, *see* Exceptions at 2-3, such assertion was not raised before the Arbitrator and, therefore, is not properly before the Authority under 5 C.F.R. § 2429.5. *See SSA, San Juan, P.R.*, 63 FLRA 589, 589 n.* (2009) (citing *AFGE, Local 1741*, 57 FLRA 696 (2002)). Accordingly, we dismiss this exception.

65 FLRA No. 35

AMERICAN FEDERATION
OF GOVERNMENT EMPLOYEES
COUNCIL OF PRISON LOCALS 33
(Union)

and

UNITED STATES
DEPARTMENT OF JUSTICE
FEDERAL BUREAU OF PRISONS
(Agency)

0-NG-3026

DECISION AND ORDER
ON A NEGOTIABILITY ISSUE

September 30, 2010

Before the Authority: Carol Waller Pope, Chairman, and Thomas M. Beck and Ernest DuBester, Members

I. Statement of the Case

This case is before the Authority on a negotiability appeal filed by the Union under § 7105(a)(2)(E) of the Federal Service Labor-Management Relations Statute (the Statute), and concerns the negotiability of one proposal. The Agency filed a statement of position (SOP), to which the Union filed a response. The Agency filed a reply to the Union's response.

For the reasons that follow, we find that the proposal is negotiable.

II. Background

The Agency proposed procedures for providing stab-resistant vests to correctional officers. *See* Record of Post-Petition Conference (Record) at 2. The Union sought, and the parties agreed to, post-implementation bargaining. *Id.* The Union filed a petition for review (petition) regarding the proposals on which the parties could not agree. The petition was placed in abeyance while the parties utilized the Authority's Collaboration and Alternative Dispute Resolution (CADR) Program. Agency's Reply at 1. Through the assistance of CADR, the parties entered into a memorandum of understanding (MOU), which provided, among other things, that: (1) the Agency will provide a stab-resistant vest to any correctional officer who requests one; (2) a correctional officer who requests a vest must wear it while on duty; and (3) after a six-month trial period, employees may be subject to discipline for failing to wear their vests while on duty. SOP at 10 n.1, Attach. A. The parties, however, failed to reach agreement on the proposal set forth below. Record at 2.

III. The Proposal

> It is understood by the parties that the fitted "Stab-Resistant Vest" is safety equipment. The Agency will maintain the employee's fitted vest in a secure area to be issued if the employee requests a vest. The fitted vest will be issued by the Agency to the employee in accordance with the Master Agreement, Article 28, Section (b). The cleaning of the vests will be negotiated locally.

Record at 2.[1]

IV. Meaning of the Proposal

The parties agree that the proposal seeks to require the Agency to: (1) consider the stab-resistant vests as safety equipment; (2) maintain the vests in a secure area for issuance to employees if they request them; (3) issue the vests in accordance with Article 28, Section (b) of the parties' Master Agreement; and (4) negotiate locally the cleaning of the vests. Record at 2.

In addition, the Agency asserts that the proposal is also intended to prevent management from

1. Article 28, Section (b) provides that:

> The Employer will ensure that adequate supplies of security and safety equipment are available for issue to and/or use by employees during the routine performance of their duties. This includes, but is not limited to, whistles, key chains, key clips, belts for equipment, disposable resuscitation masks and rubber gloves, handcuffs, two-way radios, body alarms, flashlights, hand-held metal detectors, weapons, ammunition, etc. Cases or holders, whichever is appropriate, to carry such equipment will also be available for these particular items of equipment normally using such cases or holders. Employees receiving such items will be accountable for them until they are returned to the Employer.

Union's Response, Attach. 1 at 1-2.

disciplining employees who do not wear their stab-resistant vests. SOP at 10-11 (citing Record at 3). The Agency's support for such an assertion arises solely from a statement that the Record attributes to the Union that the proposal is intended "to prevent employees from being disciplined for not wearing the vest or forgetting to bring it to work from home." Record at 3. However, the Union, in its Response, expressly notes that it does not concur with this statement in the Record. According to the Union, the proposal is not intended to preempt the disciplinary provisions in the parties' MOU, but instead is intended to reduce the risk of disciplinary action by ensuring that employees would be able to store their vests at the work site. Union's Response (Response) at 5.

When parties dispute the meaning of a proposal, the Authority will examine the wording of the proposal as well as the union's statement of intent to determine the meaning of the proposal. If the union's statement of intent comports with the plain words of the proposal, then the Authority will adopt the union's interpretation of the proposal for the purpose of construing what the proposal means and, based on its meaning, deciding whether it is consistent with law. *See AFGE, Local 1917,* 55 FLRA 228, 234 (1999) (citing *AFGE, Local 1900*, 51 FLRA 133, 138-39 (1995)).

The proposal's plain wording does not prevent the Agency from disciplining employees who fail to wear their vests. Because the Union's statement of intent comports with the plain wording of the proposal, we adopt the Union's interpretation. *See AFGE, Local 12*, 60 FLRA 533, 537 (2004).

V. Positions of the Parties

A. Agency's SOP

The Agency asserts that the proposal violates management's right to determine its internal security practices under § 7106(a)(1) of the Statute. *See* SOP at 4-5. The Agency contends that the proposal, by its plain meaning, would require the Agency to maintain an employee's stab-resistant vest -- which is specifically fitted and provided to each employee who requests one -- in a secure area of the prison when the employee is not on duty. *Id.* According to the Agency, "[d]etermining what items will be kept in a secure area and who will have access to the secure area" is inherently an internal security decision. *Id.* at 6. The Agency notes that the Authority has held that the need to control access to an agency's facilities or areas in its facilities is encompassed by management's right to determine its internal security practices. *Id.* at 6 (citing *Patent Office Prof'l Ass'n,* 41 FLRA 795, 837 (1991)). The Agency also notes that both the Supreme Court and the Authority have recognized that federal correctional institutions have more significant security concerns than other work environments and that, therefore, prison administrators are entitled to greater deference on the issue of internal security. SOP at 4-5.

The Agency argues that storing the stab-resistant vests in the secure area would impose the following burdens: (1) it would require more people to have access to the area to facilitate the collection, storage and distribution of the vests; (2) if every officer of the hundreds of officers at most correctional institutions requested a stab-resistant vest, then the institutions would not have the capacity to store those vests for each off-duty officer; and (3) because stab-resistant vests are worn under an employee's uniform, the Agency would be required to set up an area in the secure area where employees could remove their uniforms and don their vests and would have to account for this time in scheduling. *Id.* at 6-8.

The Agency disagrees with the Union's contention that stab-resistant vests should be treated in the same manner as bullet-proof vests in Article 28, Sections (b) and (d) of the parties' agreement. *Id.* at 7.[2] The Agency explains that, while bullet-proof vests are situational, given to relatively few employees, returned at the end of a shift and shared among officers, a stab-resistant vest is given to and fitted for each individual employee who requests one, and the employee is required to wear it at all times on any post to which he or she is assigned. Id. at 7-8. Therefore, according to the Agency, while it is necessary for the Agency to maintain bullet-proof vests, it is impractical to maintain each individual's stab-resistant vest. Id. Moreover, the Agency contends that the proposal's requirement that stab-

2. Article 28, Section (d) of the parties' agreement provides that:

> On armed posts, if the wearing of a bullet-proof vest is mandated or requested, there will be a sufficient supply of such vests provided by the Employer. The Employer will ensure that adequate numbers and sizes of such vests are available, including vests sized for female employees. The cleaning of these vests may be negotiated locally.

Union's Response, Attach. 1 at 2.

resistant vests be issued in accordance with Article 28, Section (b) means only that the Agency ensure that an adequate supply of equipment is available for issue and use, not that the Agency maintain all of the equipment. *Id.* at 9.

In addition, the Agency argues that the proposal is not an appropriate arrangement. *Id.* at 12. The Agency contends that, because the Union fails to address how the proposal is sufficiently tailored to specific, identified adverse effects on bargaining unit employees, the Union fails to assert that the proposal is an appropriate arrangement. *Id.* The Agency also argues that the Union fails to explain how the benefits of the proposal outweigh the broad, significant constraints the proposal places on the Agency's ability to determine its own internal security practices. *Id.* at 12 (citing *NTEU*, 53 FLRA 539, 541-42 (1997) (where a union offers no argument or authority to support a bare assertion that a provision is within the duty to bargain, the Authority will not consider such an assertion)).

The Agency also argues that the proposal violates management's right to discipline its employees because it is intended to prevent management from disciplining employees who do not wear their stab-resistant vests. *Id.* at 10-11 (citing Record at 3). According to the Agency, the Authority has held that provisions preventing management from disciplining employees for specified conduct are contrary to § 7106(a)(2)(A) of the Statute. *Id.* at 11 (citing *AFGE, Local 1345*, 48 FLRA 168, 202 (1993)). The Agency further alleges that this intended purpose also violates the MOU, in which the parties agreed that employees could be disciplined for failing to wear their vests. *Id.* at 11, Attach. A.

B. Union's Response

The Union contends that the proposal does not affect management's right to determine its internal security practices and that the cases cited by the Agency in support of its contention are inapposite. Union's Response (Response) at 1-4. The Union also argues that the Agency does not adequately explain how the storage of stab-resistant vests in a secure area differs from the storage of bullet-proof vests in accordance with Article 28, Section (d) of the parties' agreement. Id. at 4.

The Union next argues that the proposal is an appropriate arrangement that mitigates the adverse effects on employees flowing from management's practice of not only issuing stab-resistant vests to employees who request them, but also conditioning the issuance on mandatory daily use subject to discipline for noncompliance. Id. at 6-7. The Union identifies the adverse effects of the Agency's procedure as: (1) placing a great burden on employees to wear or carry the vest to work each day or face discipline such that employees could become discouraged from use and retention of the vest even though use of the vest would protect them from "clear and demonstrable dangers"; (2) creating a potential danger for a corrections officer who may be seen displaying the vest outside the corrections facility; (3) creating the risk of the vests being stolen; (4) creating an unnecessary possibility or likelihood of being disciplined for neglecting to bring the vest to work on a particular day; (5) creating the risk of exposing the employee to heat exhaustion or irritations associated with wearing the vest to and from work on hot and humid days; and (6) burdening the employee in a non-paid status with the cleaning and maintenance of the vest. *Id.* at 7-8.

The Union argues that the proposal at issue is similar to other proposals involving internal security that the Authority has determined to be negotiable. *Id.* at 9-12 (citations omitted). Moreover, the Union asserts that the storage of stab-resistant vests in secured areas when bullet-proof vests are already stored in those areas would be less of a burden and imposition on the Agency than the storage of weapons determined to be negotiable in other Authority cases. *Id.* at 8-12 (citing *NTEU*, 62 FLRA 321 (2007)).

In addition, the Union asserts that the Agency fails to argue that the portion of the proposal providing that "cleaning of the stab-resistant vests [will] be bargained locally" is not negotiable. *Id.* at 13. According to the Union, the Agency's assertion that bullet-proof vests are situational, whereas stab-resistant vests are not, is immaterial to the negotiability of the proposal regarding the storage and cleaning of the vests. *Id.* In addition, the Union alleges that the already existing procedure outlined in Article 28, Section (b) of the parties' agreement has not been shown to affect the authority of the Agency to determine its internal security practices. *Id.*

Regarding the right to discipline, as stated previously, the Union disagrees with the statement on page 3 of the Record that "[t]he Union explained that the proposal is intended to *prevent* employees from being disciplined . . . ." Response at 5 (quoting Record at 3) (emphasis added). The Union explains that the proposal is not intended to preempt the disciplinary provisions in the MOU. Instead, the

Union explains, the proposal is intended to "reduce the risk of disciplinary action." Id.

C. Agency's Reply

In reply to the Union's Response, the Agency contends that, even if the proposal constitutes an arrangement, it does not constitute an appropriate arrangement because it excessively interferes with management's rights. Agency's Reply (Reply) at 4. The Agency argues that the burdens on employees that the proposal is designed to address -- having to remember to wear the vest each day or having to wear it on hot days -- are minimal compared with the burden that the proposal would impose on the Agency. In this regard, the Agency asserts that its correctional institutions, each of which employs as many as 500-600 correctional officers, do not have the capability to store as many stab-resistant vests as the proposal would require. *Id.* at 6. The Agency alleges that the proposal, which would apply to every bargaining unit employee who requests such a vest, is not sufficiently tailored to mitigate the adverse effects that employees might experience. *Id.* at 7. According to the Agency, it has already addressed the potential adverse effects by not making use of the vests mandatory. *Id.* at 7-8.

VI. Preliminary Matter

The Union requests a hearing to resolve certain issues in this case. Record at 3, Petition at 5. Under 5 C.F.R. § 2424.31 of the Authority's Regulations, a hearing is appropriate "[w]hen necessary to resolve disputed issues of material fact . . . ." Here, the Union has not set forth any disputed issues of material fact for the Authority to consider at a hearing. Therefore, we deny the Union's request for a hearing. *See NFFE, Local 1998, IAMAW, Fed. Dist. 1,* 60 FLRA 141, 143 (2004); *Prof'l Airways Sys. Specialists,* 59 FLRA 25, 25 n.2 (2003).

VII. Analysis and Conclusions

A. The proposal does not affect management's right to discipline employees.

Management's right to discipline employees under § 7106(a)(2)(A) of the Statute extends to both performance-related and nonperformance-related conduct. *See AFGE, Local 1709,* 56 FLRA 549, 553 (2000). Proposals that preclude management from taking disciplinary action against employees for a particular offense affect management's right to discipline under § 7106(a)(2)(A) of the Statute. *See, e.g., AFGE, Local 1692,* 40 FLRA 868, 873 (1991); *Int'l Org. of Masters, Mates, & Pilots, Panama Canal Pilots Branch,* 32 FLRA 269, 275 (1988).

Although the Authority has held that provisions preventing management from disciplining employees for specified conduct are contrary to § 7106(a)(2)(A) of the Statute, the plain language of the proposal contains no restrictions on management's right to take disciplinary actions against employees. SOP at 11 (citing *AFGE, Local 1345,* 48 FLRA 168, 202 (1993)). As previously noted, the proposal is intended only to reduce the likelihood that an employee will fail to wear the vest at work, not to restrict management's right to take disciplinary action when such action occurs.[3] Accordingly, we find that the proposal does not affect management's right to discipline employees.

B. Assuming the proposal affects management's right to determine its internal security practices, the proposal is an appropriate arrangement.

The right to determine internal security practices includes the authority to determine the policies and practices that are part of an agency's plan to secure or safeguard its personnel, physical property or operations against internal and external risks. *AFGE, Fed. Prison Council 33,* 51 FLRA 1112, 1115 (1996) (*AFGE, FPC*). Furthermore, a federal correctional facility has special security concerns that may not be present at other work locations. *See AFGE, AFL-CIO, Local 683,* 30 FLRA 497, 500 (1987) (citing *AFGE, AFL-CIO, Council of Prison Locals, Local 1661,* 29 FLRA 990 (1987)).

For purposes of this decision, we assume without deciding that the proposal affects management's right to determine its internal security practices within the meaning of § 7106(a)(1) of the Statute, and, for the following reasons, we conclude that it is within the duty to bargain as an appropriate arrangement under § 7106(b)(3).

3. To the extent that the Agency asserts that the proposal violates the parties' MOU because the proposal is intended to prevent employees from being disciplined for failing to wear their vests, such argument is without merit. For the reasons stated above, the proposal is not intended to prevent management from disciplining employees for failing to wear their vests, but rather, to reduce the risk of disciplinary action against employees for such failure.

i. The proposal is an arrangement.

In determining whether a proposal or provision constitutes an appropriate arrangement within the meaning of § 7106(b)(3), the Authority applies the analytical framework articulated in *NAGE, Local R14-87,* 21 FLRA 24, (1986) (*KANG*). Under this framework, the Authority initially determines whether the proposal is intended to be an "arrangement" for employees adversely affected by the exercise of a management right. *See id.* at 33. In this regard, the Authority considers whether the proposal is "tailored" to compensate or benefit employees who are adversely affected by the exercise of a management right. *See, e.g., AFGE, Local* 1687, 52 FLRA 521, 523 (1996).

The Authority has held that proposals "intended to eliminate the possibility of an adverse effect, may constitute appropriate arrangements negotiable under [§] 7106(b)(3)[.]" *NTEU, Chapter 243,* 49 FLRA 176, 191 (1994). In particular, such "prophylactic" proposals will be found sufficiently tailored in situations where it is not possible to determine reliably which employees will be adversely affected by an agency action so as to draft a proposal to apply only to those employees. *Id.* An arrangement need not "target in advance the very individual employees who will be adversely affected." *U.S. Dep't of the Interior, Minerals Mgmt. Serv. v. FLRA*, 969 F.2d 1158, 1163 (D.C. Cir. 1992).

The Union identifies the adverse effects of the Agency's procedure as: (1) placing a great burden on employees to wear or carry the vest to work each day or face discipline such that employees could become discouraged from use and retention of the vest even though use of the vest would protect them from "clear and demonstrable dangers"; (2) creating a potential danger for a corrections officer who may be seen displaying the vest outside the corrections facility; (3) creating the risk of the vests being stolen; (4) creating and unnecessary possibility or likelihood of being disciplined for neglecting to bring the vest to work on a particular day; (5) creating the risk of exposing the employee to heat exhaustion or irritations associated with wearing the vest to and from work on hot and humid days; and (6) burdening the employee in a non-paid status with the cleaning and maintenance of the vest. Response at 7-8. The instant proposal is prophylactic in that it would eliminate the possibility that any of these adverse effects would occur. Moreover, the proposal is tailored to the extent possible. The proposal only applies to those bargaining unit employee who request a stab-resistant vest -- i.e., the very employees who would suffer the adverse effects of the Agency's practice. In this regard, the fact that employees are not required to wear stab-resistant vests does not, as the Agency argues, eliminate the adverse effects on those employees who request such vests; that fact merely precludes adverse effects on those employees who do not request a stab-resistant vest.

Therefore, we conclude that this proposal is sufficiently tailored and that the proposal is an arrangement. *See, e.g., AFGE, Local 171*, 64 FLRA 275, 277 (2009) (proposal applying only to those employees who are affected by the management right to determine internal security practice is an arrangement); *AFGE, Local 1770,* 64 FLRA 953, 959 (2010) (proposal applying to mitigate the adverse effects flowing from the exercise of management's right is an arrangement).

ii. The arrangement is appropriate.

If the proposal is an arrangement, then the Authority determines whether the arrangement is appropriate or whether it is inappropriate because it excessively interferes with management's rights. *See KANG,* 21 FLRA at 31. In making this determination, the Authority balances the proposal's benefits to employees against its burdens on management. *AFGE, Local 171,* 64 FLRA at 277.

The Union asserts that the proposal would benefit employees by relieving them of the burdens of wearing or carrying the vests to work each day and cleaning and maintaining the vests. According to the Union, the proposal also would benefit employees by reducing: (1) the potential dangers to correctional officers who may be seen wearing the vests outside the facility; (2) the possibility of employees being disciplined for failing to wear the vests; (3) the possibility of the vests being stolen; and (4) employees' exposure to heat exhaustion or other irritations from wearing the vests on hot or humid days. Response at 6-8.

The Agency contends that the proposal would affect its internal security because it would have to provide access to the secure area for each officer who requests a vest and for additional individuals to facilitate the collection, storage and distribution of the vests. SOP at 6. However, the proposal does not state that employees who receive the vests must be granted access to the secure area where the vests would be stored, or provide any indication as to how many (if any) additional employees would need access to such areas in order to collect, store and distribute the vests. Moreover, the Agency does not provide any basis for finding that the fact that stab-resistant vests are different from bullet-proof vests affects its internal security practice regarding access to storage areas.

The Agency also contends that no institution currently has the capability to store the number of vests that may be issued to correctional officers. Reply at 6-7. However, the Agency fails to provide sufficient information to support this assertion. Although the Agency has provided the number of employees at its facilities, it has failed to provide any evidence regarding the number of employees who have requested vests since the implementation of the plan -- i.e., the number of employees to whom the proposal would likely apply. The Agency also fails to support its assertion that the proposal would require the Agency to create a changing area in an area that is secure, as opposed to some other area.

In weighing the benefits to employees against the burdens placed upon the Agency's right to determine its internal security practices, the record establishes that the proposal would benefit employees. In contrast, the Agency has failed to support its claims that the proposal would significantly burden the Agency's right to determine its internal security practices. As such, we find that the proposal's benefits to employees outweigh its burdens on management's right to determine its internal security practices. *See, e.g., NTEU,* 62 FLRA 321 (benefits of proposal outweigh the burdens placed on management where Agency fails to establish that the proposal constitutes a significant burden on its right to determine internal security practices).

Accordingly, we find that the proposal is within the duty to bargain as an appropriate arrangement under § 7106(b)(3) of the Statute.

VIII. Order

The Agency shall, upon request, or as otherwise agreed to by the parties, negotiate over the proposal.[4]

4. In finding the proposal to be within the duty to bargain, we make no judgment as to its merits.

65 FLRA No. 36

AMERICAN FEDERATION
OF GOVERNMENT EMPLOYEES
LOCAL 1102
(Union)

and

UNITED STATES
DEPARTMENT OF JUSTICE
FEDERAL BUREAU OF PRISONS
FEDERAL DETENTION CENTER
SEATTLE, WASHINGTON
(Agency)

0-AR-4548

DECISION

October 1, 2010

Before the Authority: Carol Waller Pope, Chairman, and Thomas M. Beck and Ernest DuBester, Members

I. Statement of the Case

This matter is before the Authority on exceptions to an award of Arbitrator Joe H. Henderson filed by the Union under § 7122(a) of the Federal Service Labor-Management Relations Statute (the Statute) and part 2425 of the Authority's Regulations. The Agency filed an opposition to the Union's exceptions.

The Arbitrator concluded that the Agency's disclosure of medical information relating to the grievant's back injury was not unlawful because the Agency's disclosure was not willful or intentional. For the reasons set forth below, we deny the Union's exceptions, in part, and we remand the award to the parties for further action consistent with this decision.

II. Background and Arbitrator's Award

The grievant, who works at the Bureau of Prisons, Federal Detention Center in Seattle, Washington, sustained a back injury at work and took a leave of absence to recover. *See* Award at 3. After the grievant was injured, the Agency obtained medical information pertaining to the grievant's back injury and maintained this information in his medical file and his Office of Workers' Compensation Programs records. *See id.* at 5.

Shortly after his injury, management officials conversed about the grievant's injury and absence from work in the front lobby of the Agency's building. *Id.* at 3-4, 11. During their conversation, one of the officials stated that he had the paperwork relating to the grievant's workers' compensation claim on file. *Id.* at 12-13. At least one non-supervisory employee overheard their conversation.[1] *Id.* at 3-4, 11. In response to this incident, the Union filed a grievance. *Id.* at 4. The matter was unresolved and was submitted to arbitration. *Id.*

The parties did not stipulate to any issues, and the Arbitrator did not frame any issues. The Union's statement of the issue was whether "the Agency violate[d] [the grievant's] Rights to Confidentiality of Medical Information under the Americans with Disabilities Act [(ADA)] and the Rehabilitation Act? If [so], what is the appropriate remedy?" *Id.* at 3; *see also id.* at 11. As relevant here, the Agency's statement of the issue was whether it "violate[d] Article 6, Section B of the Labor Agreement when [it] discuss[ed] the [g]rievant's absence from work in the front lobby of the institution on May 6, 2008?"[2] *Id.* at 2.

The Arbitrator agreed with the Agency that management officials have the right to discuss work-related issues, including fellow employees' work-related injuries. *Id.* at 12. However, he determined that a public lobby was an inappropriate location "for management [officials] to engage in conversations about an employee." *Id.* The Arbitrator noted that, although the officials did not include anyone else in their conversation, a non-supervisory employee overheard a portion of their conversation, including the fact that the grievant was injured. *Id.* at 13. The Arbitrator determined that the information revealed was covered by the Privacy Act; that management officials disclosed this information to a third party; and the Agency's "disclosure had an adverse effect on the [g]rievant[.]" *Id.* However, the Arbitrator

1. At arbitration, the Agency and the Union disputed whether a second non-supervisory employee overheard the management officials' conversation; however, there is no dispute that at least one non-supervisory employee overheard the disclosure of the grievant's medical information. *See* Award at 9, 11.

2. The Agency also raised other issues before the Arbitrator. *Id.* at 2. Because no exceptions were filed to the Arbitrator's resolution of those issues, they are not before us.

found that the Agency's disclosure did not violate the Privacy Act because "[t]here was no showing that the 'disclosure was willful or intentional.'" *Id.* at 14. He noted that, even if the grievant's supervisor made a comment about the grievant's back injury in a sarcastic tone of voice, the Agency's disclosure of the grievant's medical information was not willful or intentional, but, rather, was careless and inadvertent. *Id.* According to the Arbitrator, "[a] 'willful act' is one done intentionally as distinguished from an act done carelessly or inadvertently." *Id.* (emphasis omitted). Finally, the Arbitrator suggested that the Agency should require the management officials to send a written apology to the grievant. *Id.*

III. Positions of the Parties

A. Union's Exceptions

The Union alleges that the award is contrary to law because it does not comply with the confidentiality provisions of the ADA and the Rehabilitation Act. Exceptions at 5-8. The Union claims that the Arbitrator added an additional, unnecessary requirement for proving a violation of the confidentiality provisions of the ADA and the Rehabilitation Act. *Id.* at 7. According to the Union, although the Privacy Act requires that an entity's disclosure of information be willful or intentional in order for that entity to be liable, the ADA and Rehabilitation Act contain no such requirement. *See id.* The Union alleges that, under the ADA and the Rehabilitation Act, "supervisors and managers may be informed regarding necessary restrictions on the work or duties of the employee and necessary accommodations[,]" but that, if the Agency discloses medical information in a manner that does not conform to the confidentiality provisions of the ADA, then its disclosure would violate the ADA and the Rehabilitation Act. *Id.* at 6-7 (citations omitted).

Moreover, the Union claims that, based on the "Agency's clear legal obligation to maintain the confidentiality of employee medical records," the Agency's disclosure clearly violates the confidentiality provisions of the ADA and the Rehabilitation Act. *Id.* at 8. According to the Union, it is undisputed that the grievant, before the disclosure occurred, provided the Agency with confidential medical information pertaining to his back injury and that Agency management officials "disclosed medical information, . . . that [the grievant] was out of work due to a back injury, to at least one bargaining unit employee . . . who had no prior knowledge of [the grievant's] injury." *Id.* at 7-8. Also, the Union claims that the Agency clearly "had no business[-]related reason for disclosing this information to" an individual who "was not a supervisor or manager responsible for determining the necessary restrictions on the work or duties of [the grievant]." *Id.* at 8. Furthermore, the Union alleges that, even if the disclosure occurred because the management officials were concerned about the grievant's health, the disclosure constitutes a violation of the confidentiality provisions of the ADA and the Rehabilitation Act. *Id.*

The Union also alleges that the award is contrary to law because it does not comply with the confidentiality provisions of the Privacy Act. *Id.* at 5, 9-10. The Union claims that the Arbitrator incorrectly found that the management officials did not disclose the grievant's medical information in an intentional or willful manner. *Id.* at 9-10. According to the Union, the Arbitrator misapplied the intent requirement by requiring the management officials to have intended to cause harm to the grievant, rather than merely intending to disclose the information. *Id.* at 10. The Union alleges that the Agency's disclosure was willful or intentional because the management officials admit that they were aware that a non-supervisory employee was standing mere steps away from them during their conversation. *Id.*

B. Agency's Opposition

The Agency argues that the award is not contrary to the confidentiality provisions of the ADA and the Rehabilitation Act. Opp'n at 4-6. The Agency contends that, although it is undisputed that management officials had a brief conversation in the lobby regarding the grievant's back injury that was overheard by at least one non-supervisory employee, their conversation did not reveal any confidential medical information pursuant to the regulations because it "did not contain any specific information regarding the grievant's diagnosis and/or symptoms." *Id.* at 5-6. Also, the Agency argues that "[i]t is undisputed that the brief conversation at issue contained no reference . . . to the relevant medical documentation . . . ." *Id.* at 6. Moreover, according to the Agency, the Equal Employment Opportunity Commission (EEOC) has held that statements made by an agency that an employee has used sick leave or that an employee is medically disabled for a position do not violate the Rehabilitation Act. *Id.* at 5-6 (citations omitted).

The Agency also contends that the award is not contrary to the confidentiality provisions of the Privacy Act. *Id.* at 6-9. The Agency argues that the Arbitrator did not misapply the intent requirement of the Privacy Act. *Id.* at 7-8. Also, the Agency contends that "[t]he Union simply disagrees with the Arbitrator's evaluation of the facts and is attempting through its exceptions to re-litigate the merits of the grievance before the Authority." *Id.* at 8 (citations omitted). Furthermore, the Agency argues that the Arbitrator rightfully used his discretion when he fashioned the award. *Id.*

IV. Analysis and Conclusions

When an exception involves an award's consistency with law, the Authority reviews any question of law raised by the exception and the award *de novo*. *See NTEU, Chapter 24*, 50 FLRA 330, 332 (1995) (citing *U.S. Customs Serv. v. FLRA*, 43 F.3d 682, 686-87 (D.C. Cir. 1994)). In applying the standard of *de novo* review, the Authority assesses whether an arbitrator's legal conclusions are consistent with the applicable standard of law. *See U.S. Dep't of Def., Dep'ts of the Army & the Air Force, Ala. Nat'l Guard, Northport, Ala.*, 55 FLRA 37, 40 (1998). In making that assessment, the Authority defers to the arbitrator's underlying factual findings. *See id.*

A. The Arbitrator's application of the confidentiality provisions of the Privacy Act is not contrary to law.

The Privacy Act limits the disclosure of information. *See U.S. Dep't of Veterans Affairs Med. Ctr., Charleston, S.C.*, 58 FLRA 706, 710 (2003) (*VAMC Charleston*). Section 552a(e)(2) of the Act permits federal agencies to disclose information only in accordance with the Act, and § 552a(g)(1)(D) and (g)(4) entitle an individual to relief if the agency intentionally or willfully fails to comply with the provisions of the Act. *Id.* (quoting 5 U.S.C. § 552(a)). To establish an unauthorized disclosure of information under 5 U.S.C. § 552(g)(1)(D), a claimant must prove the following four elements: (1) the information is covered by the Privacy Act as a "record" contained in a "system of records"; (2) the agency disclosed the information; (3) the disclosure had an "adverse effect" on the claimant; and (4) the disclosure was "willful or intentional." *See, e.g., AFGE, Local 1592*, 58 FLRA 584, 585 (2003) (quoting *Quinn v. Stone*, 978 F.2d 126, 131 (3d Cir. 1992)).

The Union alleges that the award is contrary to law because the Arbitrator incorrectly concluded that the Agency's disclosure was not willful or intentional. Exceptions at 9-10. The Union claims that the Arbitrator misapplied the intent requirement by requiring the management officials to have intended to cause harm to the grievant, rather than merely intending to disclose the information. *Id.* at 10.

The Union's argument is without merit. The Arbitrator's findings are consistent with case precedent. The Authority has found that the Privacy Act "does not make the [g]overnment strictly liable for every affirmative or negligent action that might be said technically to violate the Privacy Act's provisions" and that liability is imposed "only when the agency acts in violation of the Act in a willful or intentional manner, *either by committing the act without grounds for believing it to be lawful, or by flagrantly disregarding others' rights under the Act.*" *VAMC Charleston*, 58 FLRA at 710 (quoting *Albright v. United States*, 732 F.2d 181, 189 (D.C. Cir. 1984) (*Albright*)) (emphasis added).

Based on the Arbitrator's factual findings, the Agency did not disclose the grievant's medical information without grounds for believing its action to be lawful. The Arbitrator found that the management officials only intended to discuss the grievant's medical information among themselves. *See* Award at 13. The Arbitrator noted that, when the disclosure was made, the officials believed that they had the right to discuss work-related issues, including work-related injuries of employees. *Id.* at 12; *VAMC Charleston*, 58 FLRA at 710 (quoting *Albright*, 732 F.2d at 189) (citing *Wisdom v. Dep't of HUD*, 713 F.2d 422, 424 (8th Cir. 1983), *cert denied*, 465 U.S. 1021 (1984) & *Bruce v. United States*, 621 F.2d 914, 917 (8th Cir. 1980)) (finding that the Privacy Act is not violated when agencies have acted pursuant to regulations or other authority that they justifiably believed authorized their actions). Additionally, the Arbitrator determined that, although a public lobby was an inappropriate place to engage in a conversation about an employee's back injury, management officials were authorized to discuss the grievant's work-related injuries among themselves. Award at 12; 29 C.F.R. § 1630.14(c)(1) (authorizing "[s]upervisors and managers [to] be informed regarding necessary restrictions on the work or duties of the employee and necessary accommodations"); *VAMC Charleston*, 58 FLRA at 710 (citations omitted) (determining that, even when an agency does not follow proper procedures in order to fully comply with the authority that authorized its actions, no violation of the Privacy Act occurs). Consequently, the Arbitrator's findings demonstrate that the officials justifiably believed that they were authorized to discuss the grievant's medical condition among themselves.

Also, based on the Arbitrator's factual findings, the Agency did not flagrantly disregard the grievant's rights under the Act. Although the Union alleges that the Arbitrator misapplied the intent requirement by requiring the management officials to have intended to cause harm to the grievant, the Arbitrator simply determined that the Agency did not intentionally disclose the information. Exceptions at 10. The Arbitrator specifically found that the disclosure was not directed at any non-supervisory employees and that the disclosure was made carelessly or inadvertently, rather than willfully or intentionally. Award at 13, 14. Moreover, the Arbitrator determined that the Union's contention – that the grievant's supervisor commented on his medical condition in a sarcastic tone of voice – did not provide a basis for proving that the Agency's disclosure was willful or intentional. *Id.* at 14. Therefore, the Arbitrator's findings demonstrate that the Agency did not flagrantly disregard the grievant's rights under the Act.

Based on the foregoing, the Arbitrator's conclusion that the Agency's disclosure was not willful or intentional is not contrary to law. Accordingly, we deny the Union's exception.

B. The record is insufficient for a determination as to whether the award is contrary to law.

In this case, the Union alleges that the award is contrary to law because it does not comply with the confidentiality provisions of the ADA and the Rehabilitation Act. Exceptions at 5-8. The Union claims that the Arbitrator added an additional, unnecessary requirement for proving a violation of the confidentiality provisions of the ADA and the Rehabilitation Act. *Id.* at 7. According to the Union, although the Privacy Act requires that an entity's disclosure of confidential medical information be willful or intentional for that entity to be liable, the ADA and Rehabilitation Act contain no such requirement. *See id.*

Based on the record, the Arbitrator failed to address the merits of the Union's claim that the Agency's disclosure violated the confidentiality provisions of the ADA and the Rehabilitation Act. Although the Arbitrator noted the Union's statement of the issue and summarized the Union's arguments regarding the ADA and the Rehabilitation Act, he devoted his entire discussion to reiterating the parties' arguments and addressing the elements of the Privacy Act. Award at 11-14. Finally, the Arbitrator only set forth the legal standard for the Privacy Act, and his findings mirror the elements of that Act. *Id.* at 13-14.

Because the Arbitrator failed to address whether the Agency's disclosure violated the confidentiality provisions of the ADA and the Rehabilitation Act, we must determine whether the record permits us to ascertain whether the award is contrary to the ADA and the Rehabilitation Act or whether a remand is necessary. *See U.S. DOJ, Fed. BOP, U.S. Penitentiary, Terre Haute, Ind.*, 60 FLRA 298, 300 (2004) (finding that, in cases where an arbitrator fails to make requisite factual findings, the Authority may remand the award if the record does not permit it to make a determination on the merits) (*U.S. Penitentiary, Terre Haute*).

A party violates the confidentiality provisions of the ADA and the Rehabilitation Act by disclosing confidential medical information regarding the medical condition or history of any employee obtained during a medical examination or inquiry.[3] *See, e.g., Dominguez v. U.S. Postal Serv.*, EEOC Appeal No. 0120070258, 2009 WL 2205379, at *8 (July 15, 2009) (citing 29 C.F.R. § 1630.14(c)); *Goodman v. Dep't of the Navy*, EEOC Appeal No. 01A43290, 2004 WL 1719214, at *3 (July 22, 2004) (citations omitted). Not all medically-related information constitutes confidential medical information. *See, e.g., Coley v. Dep't of Transp.*, EEOC Appeal No. 0120101294, 2010 WL 3008274, at *2 (July 22, 2010) (noting that the agency did not disclose the complainant's confidential medical information when an agency attorney "stated that he had empathy for [c]omplainant 'because of her personal and mental health history'"); *see also Myrah v. Dep't of Agric.*, EEOC Appeal No. 01A52157, 2006 WL 1209770, at *4 (April 26, 2006) (determining that not all medically-related information "falls within the proscription of a confidential medical record" and that "a notation that an individual has taken sick leave or had a doctor's appointment [did] not [constitute] confidential medical information"). Moreover, 29 C.F.R. § 1630.14(c)(1) authorizes the release of confidential medical information in limited situations, including where "[s]upervisors and managers may be informed regarding necessary restrictions on the work or duties

3. The ADA confidentiality provisions apply to the Agency and unit employees through the Rehabilitation Act. *AFGE, Local 1045*, 64 FLRA 520, 522 (2010). Moreover, Congress has adopted the standards of the ADA for determining violations of the Rehabilitation Act. *Id.* (citing 29 U.S.C. § 791(g); *Office of Pers. Mgmt.*, 61 FLRA 358, 361 (2005)).

of the employee and necessary accommodations." Award at 4; *see also Tyson v. U.S. Postal Serv. (E. Area)*, EEOC Appeal No. 01992086, 2002 WL 1999045, at *2 (Aug. 23, 2002).

In this case, the record does not permit us to determine whether the confidentiality provisions of the ADA and the Rehabilitation Act were violated when management officials conversed about the grievant's back injury and leave status. As noted above, the Arbitrator failed to address the merits of the Union's claim that the Agency's disclosure violated the confidentiality provisions of the ADA and the Rehabilitation Act. Moreover, although there are sufficient factual findings for the Authority to establish whether a disclosure occurred under the ADA and the Rehabilitation Act, the record does not permit us to determine whether the information disclosed constituted confidential medical information. In this regard, it is impossible, based on the findings that the Arbitrator made, for the Authority to ascertain whether the information disclosed related to the grievant's medical condition or history or whether the information was obtained during a medical examination or inquiry. *See* Award at 3-4, 11-14 (containing no finding regarding whether "a back injury" is a medical condition, no discussion regarding how the information disclosed was obtained by the agency, and no determination regarding whether management officials conversed about grievant's confidential medical information). Consequently, the record does not permit us to determine whether the confidentiality provisions of the ADA and the Rehabilitation Act were violated. As a result, the award must be remanded to the parties for resubmission to the arbitrator, absent settlement, for further findings. *See AFGE, Local 1741*, 62 FLRA 113, 118 (2007) (citations omitted) (finding that, when the record does not contain sufficient findings for the Authority to resolve whether the award is contrary to law, the award should be remanded to the parties for resubmission to the arbitrator, absent settlement, for further findings); *U.S. Penitentiary, Terre Haute*, 60 FLRA at 300 (determining that, because the Arbitrator made no factual findings concerning whether the agency's violation was willful, and the record did not permit the Authority to make that determination, the case should be remanded); *see also Gibson v. U.S. Postal Serv.*, EEOC Appeal No. 0120082861, 2008 WL 4287707, at *1 (Sept. 10, 2008) (remanding the case to the agency because it failed to investigate whether it disclosed the complainant's confidential medical information in violation of the confidentiality provisions of the ADA and the Rehabilitation Act, and the "complainant . . . alleged a viable claim of unlawful medical disclosure").

Accordingly, we remand this case to the parties for resubmission to the Arbitrator, absent settlement. Upon remand, we ask the Arbitrator to determine whether the Agency violated the confidentiality provisions of the ADA and the Rehabilitation Act.

V. Decision

The Union's exception that the award is contrary to the Privacy Act is denied. The award is remanded to the parties for further action consistent with this decision.

65 FLRA No. 37

UNITED STATES
DEPARTMENT OF TRANSPORTATION
FEDERAL AVIATION ADMINISTRATION
(Agency)

and

NATIONAL AIR TRAFFIC
CONTROLLERS ASSOCIATION
(Union)

0-AR-4414

DECISION

October 20, 2010

Before the Authority: Carol Waller Pope, Chairman, and Thomas M. Beck and Ernest DuBester, Members

I. Statement of the Case

This matter is before the Authority on exceptions to an award of Arbitrator Joseph M. Sharnoff, filed by the Agency under § 7122(a) of the Federal Service Labor-Management Relations Statute (the Statute) and part 2425 of the Authority's Regulations. The Union did not file an opposition to the Agency's exceptions. The Agency also submitted a supplemental submission.[1]

The Union filed three grievances seeking the enforcement of a memorandum of understanding (MOU). The MOU set forth the Agency's procedures for reviewing the classification levels of air traffic control facilities. Exceptions at 5. The Arbitrator found the grievances arbitrable, sustained them, and ordered a *status quo ante* remedy. Award at 65.

For the following reasons, we deny one of the Agency's exceptions and dismiss the other two.

II. Background and Arbitrator's Award

The air traffic controller (controller) grievants work in Federal Aviation Administration (FAA) air traffic control facilities in Los Angeles, Houston, and Miami. FAA air traffic control facilities are classified from level 3 through level 12. Exceptions at 5. The classification level of a facility determines the controllers' pay at that facility. Award at 52. Controllers working at facilities with a classification of 12 receive the highest pay due to the facility's "high traffic count" and the complexity of the work performed. Exceptions at 5. Controllers working at facilities with lower classification levels receive lower pay because the work is not as complex as it is at the higher-rated facilities. *See id.*

The parties agreed to an MOU in 1999 that sets forth the procedures required when the Agency "validates" the classification level of facilities. *See* Award at 15-17. The Agency performs the validation process when a facility's traffic activity trend indicates the facility would be "eligible" for an upgrade or a downgrade. Award at 2-3. Under the MOU, the Agency must review and evaluate aircraft and traffic data collected pursuant to the procedures set forth in FAA Order 7210.57 (the Order). Exceptions at 5. The Agency must review this data within an appropriate time period. Award at 3, 17. The MOU requires that the Agency take prompt action to change a facility's classification level if, among other things, the data shows that the facility will be operating at the level required for the upgrade or downgrade for the subsequent 12 months. *Id.* at 3, 16-17.

The grievances allege that the Agency violated the parties' collective bargaining agreement (CBA), the MOU, and FAA rules, *inter alia*, when it failed to conduct the validation process required for the facilities' reclassification, and, if appropriate, their upgrade. *See* Award at 2-7, 53. The Agency denied the grievances and the matter was submitted to arbitration.

1. Under § 2429.26 of the Authority's Regulations, the Authority may, in its discretion, grant a party leave to file other documents as it deems appropriate. Here, the Agency requests leave because the Authority "might not have been aware of" a February 2009 case in which the United States District Court of Appeals for the District of Columbia found that the plaintiff air traffic controllers could not use the Administrative Procedure Act (APA) to "litigate their pay dispute" with the Agency. *See* Agency's Supplemental Submission at 3; *Filebark v. U.S. Dep't. of Transp.* 555 F.3d 1009, 1010 (D.C. Cir. 2009). We have considered the Agency's supplemental submission and find that it has no bearing on this case. *Filebark v. United States Department of Transportation* does not apply here, since the parties are not attempting to use the APA to litigate a pay dispute. Moreover, the two additional cases cited by the Agency in their supplemental submission are inapplicable to this case. Both cases pertain to individual position classifications which, as discussed below, are not at issue before the Authority in this proceeding.

The parties stipulated to the following issue to be resolved by the Arbitrator:

> Whether the Agency violated the terms of the November 3, 1999 MOU concerning facility grade levels, when it failed to conduct a validation study at Los Angeles center, Houston center and Miami center. If so, what shall the remedy be?

Id. at 8.

The parties each presented several arguments at arbitration. The Agency argued before the Arbitrator, *inter alia,* that the grievances were not arbitrable because they involved a classification matter under the CBA and § 7121(c)(5) of the Statute. *Id.* On the merits, the Union argued that the facilities at issue each complied with all of the steps required for the validation process to take place. In the Union's view, the Agency's failure to conduct the validation process violated the MOU and the Order. *Id.* at 53. The Agency claimed that the main reason why it did not conduct the validation process at the facilities involved was because the data that formed the basis for the validation process and "any resulting upgrade" was inaccurate. *Id.* According to the Agency, it properly delayed the validation process until the technical ability to obtain more accurate data became available. *Id.* at 54.

Addressing the threshold issue first, the Arbitrator determined that the grievances were arbitrable. *Id.* at 51-52. Specifically, the Arbitrator determined that the grievances were not excluded from the grievance process as matters concerning the classification of individual positions under § 7121(c)(5) of the Statute. The Arbitrator concluded that the MOU was negotiated by the parties to review the classification of air traffic control facilities, which the Arbitrator distinguished from the classification of individual controllers' positions. *Id.* In the Arbitrator's view, although controllers' pay would be affected by a reclassification of the facility at which they worked, the classification of controllers' positions would not be "directly" affected. *Id.* at 52. Accordingly, the Arbitrator found the grievances arbitrable.

The Arbitrator sustained the grievances on their merits. As relevant here, the Arbitrator found that the MOU requires facilities requesting an upgrade to have, among other things, "a complete and accurate set of data." *Id.* at 53. The Arbitrator found that the Order acknowledges that there are known problems with the data collection program used for the validation process. *Id.* at 56, 57. The Arbitrator further found that [the] Order nevertheless requires that the particular data collection system be used "'[u]ntil such time that appropriate automation capabilities are established[.]'" *Id.* at 57 (quoting the Order). Conversely, the Arbitrator also found that the Agency did not identify any language in the Order supporting its decision to not proceed with the validation process described in the Order at the time it was requested. *Id.* at 58.

For the reasons described above, the Arbitrator determined that the Agency's refusal to continue with the validation process based on the alleged inaccuracy of the data was "contrary to the commitments made by the Agency to conduct the validation process as a joint effort with [the Union]." *Id.* The Arbitrator concluded that "absent a revision of [the] Order and the MOU[,]" the Agency "was not free to ignore" these directives until it devised a better data source than the one that was being used. *Id.* at 62. In the Arbitrator's view, if, as the Agency claimed, there was a better data program to use, then the Agency could have revised the Order to take this into account. The Arbitrator also determined that the facilities at issue had each met the pre-conditions required for the validation process to be conducted. *Id.* at 58-62. Accordingly, the Arbitrator found that the validation process should have continued at each of the facilities at issue.

As a remedy, the Arbitrator ordered the parties to restart the validation process at the stage at which the Agency had interrupted its implementation. The Arbitrator directed the Agency to change the facilities' classification levels "[i]f the data is validated[.]" *Id.* at 65. The Arbitrator further ordered that the level change be made retroactive to a date "reasonably related" to the date by which the data could have been validated if the original validation process had been allowed to proceed. *Id.*

III. Agency's Exceptions

The Agency presents several arguments in its exceptions.

First, the Agency argues that the award is contrary to § 7121(c)(5) of the Statute and the CBA because the Arbitrator resolved a matter concerning classification. Exceptions at 2. The Agency asserts that just because it is exempt from the classification requirements under chapter 51 of Title 5 does not mean that § 7121(c)(5)'s exclusion of classification matters from the grievance process is inapplicable in this case. *Id.* at 5-6. According to the Agency, by ordering the Agency to review and potentially raise the facilities' classification levels, the Arbitrator effectively "ordered the reclassification of all positions at certain en route FAA facilities[.]" *Id.* at 8.

Second, on the merits, the Agency argues that the award affects management's right to determine its "methods and means of classifying and grading positions/facilities." *Id* at 11. According to the Agency, the Arbitrator "mandated a procedure for classification of positions" by ordering the Agency to review the facilities' classification levels according to the procedure previously agreed to by the parties in the MOU. *Id.* at 9-11.

Third, the Agency claims that "intervening events [have] render[ed] the arbitration award unenforceable." *Id.* at 12 (citing *U.S. Dep't of Labor, Wash. D.C.*, 61 FLRA 603 (2006) (*DOL*)). According to the Agency, a CBA that it implemented on June 5, 2006 (the 2006 CBA), "abolished" the MOU "which was the basis for the . . . award[.]" *Id.* at 12. Accordingly, the Agency claims, it is not required to comply with the terms of the award.

IV. Analysis and Conclusions

For the following reasons, we deny the Agency's exception based on § 7121(c)(5) of the Statute, and dismiss the other two exceptions.

The Agency claims that the award is contrary to law on three different bases, as described below. When an exception involves an award's consistency with law, the Authority reviews any question of law raised by the exception and the award *de novo*. *See NTEU, Chapter 24*, 50 FLRA 330, 332 (1995) (citing *U.S. Customs Serv. v. FLRA*, 43 F.3d 682, 686-87 (D.C. Cir. 1994)). In applying the standard of *de novo* review, the Authority assesses whether an arbitrator's legal conclusions are consistent with the applicable standard of law. *See U.S. Dep't of Def., Dep'ts of the Army & the Air Force, Ala. Nat'l Guard, Northport, Ala.*, 55 FLRA 37, 40 (1998) (*DOD*). In making that assessment, the Authority defers to the arbitrator's underlying factual findings. *See id.*

A. The award does not involve a classification matter under § 7121(c)(5) of the Statute and is therefore not contrary to law.

The Agency argues that the award is contrary to § 7121(c)(5) of the Statute because the Arbitrator resolved a classification matter within the meaning of that section. Section 7121(c)(5) of the Statute excludes from the coverage of negotiated grievance procedures any grievance concerning "the classification of any position which does not result in the reduction in grade or pay of an employee." 5 U.S.C. § 7121(c)(5).

The Authority has consistently described grievances concerning classification under § 7121(c)(5) as involving "the grade level of the duties assigned to, and performed by, the grievant[.]" *AFGE, Local 1858*, 59 FLRA 713, 715 (2004); *accord SSA*, 31 FLRA 933, 936 (1988). Consistent with this, the Authority has found that arbitration awards assessing whether a grievant's duties are improperly classified concern classification under § 7121(c)(5). *See, e.g., SSA*, 60 FLRA 62, 64-65 (2004) (arbitrator assessed duties permanently assigned to grievant's position and found that grievant should be compensated at higher grade); *U.S. Dep't of Veterans Affairs, Med. Ctr., Muskogee, Okla.*, 47 FLRA 1112, 1116-17 (1993) (arbitrator compared duties of positions with classification standards for higher-graded positions and found positions should be reclassified). However, the Authority has not found that an award involves classification under § 7121(c)(5) merely because the award involves the amount of employee's pay. *See, e.g., U.S. Dep't of Transp., FAA*, 61 FLRA 634, 636 (2006) (*FAA*) (citing *U.S. Dep't of Labor*, 12 FLRA 639, 640 (1983) (grievance concerning whether grievants were entitled to hazard differential pay did not involve classification under § 7121(c)(5)); *Int'l Org. of Masters, Mates & Pilots, Marine Div., Pan. Canal Pilots Branch*, 51 FLRA 333, 340 (1995) (proposals concerning the process of setting the amount of compensation to be assigned to a position classification that had already been established by the agency did not involve classification under § 7103(a)(14)(B)).

The record fails to substantiate the Agency's claim that the grievances are not arbitrable as matters concerning classification under § 7121(c)(5).[2] As the Arbitrator found, interpreting the parties' MOU, the classification actions involved in this case concern "the 'reclassification' of *air traffic control facilities,*" not the "distinct and different" matter of "the

2. The Agency correctly notes, Exceptions at 5-6, that its exemption from the requirements of chapter 51 of title 5 does not make § 7121(c)(5) inapplicable in this case. *See FAA*, 61 FLRA at 635. However, the Arbitrator did not resolve the grievances against the Agency on this basis. Therefore, this argument by the Agency does not provide any basis for finding the award deficient.

classification of individual positions or groups of similar positions[.]" Award at 51 (emphases in original). This process entails a "review and analysis of traffic data on record for each facility." *Id.* at 52 (quoting the MOU). Moreover, in a finding that the Agency does not specifically dispute, the Arbitrator concluded that "[n]o individual employee 'position' or the 'positions' of groups of similarly assigned employees will be affected directly by this review and analysis of traffic data and/or the resulting *reclassification of facilities.*" *Id.* (emphasis in original). The only effect that the Arbitrator found that the reclassification of facilities would have was an effect on controller pay. *Id.* We defer to the Arbitrator's undisputed factual findings. *See DOD,* 55 FLRA at 40. Additionally, as noted above, an effect on pay does not establish that a matter involves classification under § 7121(c)(5). *See FAA,* 61 FLRA at 636. Accordingly, we find that the award is not contrary to law because it involves a classification matter under § 7121(c)(5) of the Statute.

B. The Agency's exception that the award affects management's right to determine the methods and means of performing work under § 7106(b)(1) of the Statute is barred by § 2429.5 of the Authority's Regulations.

The Agency's argument that the award affects management's right to determine the methods and means of performing work, Exceptions at 11, is not properly before the Authority. Under § 2429.5 of the Authority's Regulations, the Authority will not consider issues that could have been, but were not, presented to an arbitrator. *See, e.g., U.S. Dep't of Homeland Sec., U.S. Customs & Border Prot., JFK Airport, Queens, N.Y.,* 62 FLRA 416, 417 (2008). Where a party makes an argument for the first time on exceptions that could, and should, have been made before the arbitrator, the Authority applies § 2429.5 to bar the argument. *See, e.g., U.S. Dep't of Justice, Fed. Bureau of Prisons, USP Admin. Maximum (ADX), Florence, Colo.,* 64 FLRA 1168, 1170 (2010); *U.S. Dep't of Transp., FAA,* 64 FLRA 387, 389 (2010).[3]

Although the Agency made several arguments before the Arbitrator, there is no indication in the record that the Agency argued, as it does in its exceptions, that the award affects management's right to determine the methods and means of performing work. The Agency could have, but did not, argue to the Arbitrator that awarding the Union's requested remedy would affect the Agency's right to determine the methods and means of performing work. Accordingly, we dismiss the Agency's exception based on that management right.

C. The Agency's exception that "intervening events" render the award unenforceable is barred by § 2429.5 of the Authority's Regulations.

Like the Agency's management rights argument discussed in the previous section, the Agency's argument that "intervening events" render the award unenforceable, Exceptions at 11-12, is not properly before the Authority.

There is no indication in the record that the Agency argued to the Arbitrator that its implementation of the 2006 CBA barred the Arbitrator's enforcement of the 1999 MOU. The Agency had ample opportunity, before the Arbitrator rendered his award in July 2008, to argue that the MOU had been rendered unenforceable by subsequent events; i.e., its implementation of the 2006 CBA in June 2006. However, the Agency did not. Accordingly, and apart from other considerations, we dismiss the Agency's exception based on its implementation of the 2006 CBA.

V. Decision

The Agency's exception based on § 7121(c)(5) of the Statute is denied. The remaining exceptions are dismissed.

---

3. Section 2429.5 was amended October 1, 2010. For purposes of this case, we apply the previous version of the regulation that was in effect at all times relevant to the processing of this case.

65 FLRA No. 38

UNITED STATES
DEPARTMENT OF JUSTICE
FEDERAL BUREAU OF PRISONS
FEDERAL CORRECTIONAL INSTITUTION
SHERIDAN, OREGON
(Agency)

and

AMERICAN FEDERATION
OF GOVERNMENT EMPLOYEES
LOCAL 3979
(Union)

0-AR-4630

DECISION

October 20, 2010

Before the Authority: Carol Waller Pope, Chairman, and Thomas M. Beck and Ernest DuBester, Members

I. Statement of the Case

This matter is before the Authority on exceptions to an award of Arbitrator Burton White filed by the Agency under § 7122(a) of the Federal Service Labor-Management Relations Statute (the Statute) and part 2425 of the Authority's Regulations. The Union filed an opposition to the Agency's exceptions.[1]

The Arbitrator directed the Agency to pay correctional officers (COs) for unpaid overtime. For the reasons that follow, we set aside the merits award in part, and remand it in part to the parties for resubmission to the Arbitrator, absent settlement.

II. Background and Arbitrator's Awards

The Union filed a grievance alleging that the Agency violated the Fair Labor Standards Act (FLSA), and the Federal Employees Pay Act, by failing to compensate COs for pre- and post-shift work activities. Merits Award at 7. When the grievance was unresolved, it was submitted to arbitration, where, absent a stipulation by the parties, the Arbitrator framed the substantive issues[2] as follows:

> [D]id [COs] work beyond their eight-hour day? . . . If so, did the Agency fail to compensate [COs] for work time over eight hours in a day? . . . If so, did the Agency act willfully by allowing the overtime to take place without appropriate compensation? . . . If [so], what is an appropriate remedy?

Id. at 3. The Arbitrator found that the Agency willfully failed to compensate COs for pre- and post-shift overtime. *Id.* at 18, 40, 44. In this regard, the Arbitrator found that some COs were required to stop at a control room to pick up equipment and/or a battery before their shift, and to drop it off after their shift, and that the Agency should have treated this activity as the beginning and end of the COs' compensable workdays. *Id.* at 4. The Arbitrator also found that those COs who did not need to stop at a control room to pick up equipment or a battery were required to stop at the office of the Operations Lieutenant before going to their post, and that this "was a pre-shift duty that was an integral part of the principal activity" of those COs, and, thus, began their compensable workdays. *Id.* at 39, 44.

The Arbitrator acknowledged that "federal courts consider overtime of ten minutes or less to be *de minimis*[,]" but stated that he would not apply this standard. *Id.* at 45. Rather, he computed overtime on the basis of the following language in Article 18(a) of the parties' agreement (Article 18): "Overtime work will be ordered or approved and paid in increments of one-quarter hour, with odd minutes rounded up or down to the nearest quarter hour." *Id.*

---

1. After issuing his first award in this matter (merits award), to which the Agency filed exceptions, the Arbitrator subsequently issued a remedy award. Upon the issuance of the remedy award, the Agency filed a second set of exceptions and asked the Authority to take official notice of its previously filed exceptions. As the Agency's second set of exceptions contains all of the arguments put forth in its prior exceptions, we find it unnecessary to separately consider the first set, and we refer to the second set as the Agency's exceptions. Similarly, in response to each set of the Agency's exceptions, the Union filed identical copies of its opposition, the second of which we refer to as the Union's opposition.

2. The Arbitrator also addressed an issue concerning whether the grievance was arbitrable, and found that it was. Merits Award at 14. As there are no exceptions to this finding, we do not address it further.

In an appendix to the merits award, the Arbitrator provided a table with estimations of the number of minutes spent on each compensable pre- and post-shift activity for ten groups of COs. Attachment to Merits Award (Appendix) at 1-2 (App.). In this appendix, the Arbitrator grouped the COs according to their assigned units, the types of compensable pre- and post-shift activities that they performed, and the relevant estimated walking times between compensable-activity locations. *See id.*

The Arbitrator explained that the "times [in the appendix] are minimum estimates. Post-shift activity is shown only if needed to meet the minimum for rounding under [Article 18]." Merits Award at 47. Consequently, for nine of the ten groups of COs identified in the appendix, the Arbitrator estimated only the number of minutes per day that the COs spent performing *pre*-shift activity. *See* App. at 1-2. The Arbitrator's estimates of time spent engaged in pre-shift activity for five of those nine groups (hereinafter "pre-shift COs") did not exceed ten minutes per day. *See id.* For the tenth group of COs – "Housing Unit CO starting at Lieutenant's office" (housing unit COs) – the Arbitrator estimated the number of minutes per day spent engaged in both pre- *and* post-shift activity, and the resulting total did not exceed ten minutes per day. *See id.*

As a remedy, the Arbitrator directed the Agency to compensate COs in all ten groups for fifteen minutes of overtime for each shift worked during the grievance period, including interest. Merits Award at 46. The Arbitrator solicited input from the parties on the matters of liquidated damages and attorney fees. *Id.* Subsequently, in the remedy award, the Arbitrator withdrew his previous order of interest, and awarded liquidated damages and attorney fees. Remedy Award at 1-3.

III. Positions of the Parties

A. Agency Exceptions

The Agency argues that the merits award is contrary to the FLSA and its implementing regulations because the Arbitrator awarded overtime pay to employees who performed less than ten minutes of pre- or post-shift work. Exceptions at 6-7 (citing 5 C.F.R. § 551.412(a)(1) (§ 551.412(a)(1));[3] *U.S. Dep't of Justice, Fed. Bureau of Prisons, U.S. Penitentiary, Leavenworth, Kan.*, 59 FLRA 593, 598 (2004) (*Leavenworth*), *recons. den.*, 59 FLRA 803 (2004)). In particular, the Agency argues that the Arbitrator erroneously directed the Agency to pay overtime compensation to housing unit COs despite the fact that he estimated that these employees spent less than ten minutes per day on pre- and post-shift activity. *Id.* at 7-8. In addition, the Agency states that the Arbitrator "appears" to have awarded overtime to pre-shift COs who worked ten minutes or less of overtime per day. *Id.* at 8. Regarding these COs, the Agency concedes that "[i]t is unclear from the [merits] [a]ward if the Arbitrator is including any post-shift activity [in] these totals." *Id.* at 8 n.4.

B. Union Opposition

The Union concedes that "time spent engaged in pre-shift and post-shift activities totaling fewer than 10 minutes per workday is considered *de minimis* under . . . § 551.412(a)(1) and not compensable." Opp'n at 3 (citing *Leavenworth*, 59 FLRA at 98). According to the Union, the Authority must remand the merits award for clarification because the Authority "cannot determine whether the total pre-shift and post-shift overtime compensation awarded actually exceeds 10 minutes[.]" *Id.* at 3-4. In this regard, the Union argues that the Arbitrator determined that COs' post-shift activities were compensable, but that the merits award is incomplete because the Arbitrator only estimated time spent engaged in post-shift activities "if it was necessary to exceed 7.5 minutes, which is the threshold required to 'round up [to fifteen minutes]' [under] Article 18[.]" Opp'n at 4, 5 n.2 (quoting Merits Award at 45). In addition, the Union argues that the Arbitrator listed a particular compensable post-shift activity – "'[p]erson needing to turn in equipment or paperwork to Lieutenant'" – in the section of the appendix concerning housing unit COs, but failed to include the estimated time that those COs spent engaged in this activity. *Id.* at 5-6 (quoting App. at 1).

IV. Analysis and Conclusions

When an exception involves an award's consistency with law, the Authority reviews any question of law raised by an exception and the award *de novo*. *See NTEU, Chapter 24,* 50 FLRA 330, 332 (1995) (citing *U.S. Customs Serv. v. FLRA,* 43 F.3d 682, 686-87 (D.C. Cir. 1994)). In applying a *de novo* standard of review, the Authority assesses whether the arbitrator's legal conclusions are consistent with the applicable standard of law. *See NFFE, Local 1437,* 53 FLRA 1703, 1710 (1998) (*Local 1437*). In making that assessment, the Authority defers to the arbitrator's underlying factual findings. *See id.*

3. The text of § 551.412(a)(1) is provided below.

The Agency contends that the merits award is contrary to the FLSA and § 551.412(a)(1) which provides, in pertinent part:

> If an agency reasonably determines that a preparatory or concluding activity is closely related to an employee's principal activities, and is indispensable to the performance of the principal activities, *and that the total time spent in that activity is more than 10 minutes per workday*, the agency shall credit all of the time spent in that activity, including the 10 minutes, as hours of work.

5 C.F.R. § 551.412(a)(1) (emphasis added). *See also Gen. Servs. Admin.*, 37 FLRA 481, 484 (1990) ("[p]reparatory and concluding activities *of more than 10 minutes per workday* are compensable as hours of work" when they are an integral and indispensable part of employees' principal activities) (emphasis added). Accordingly, as both parties concede, pre- and post-shift activities totaling ten minutes or less per workday are considered *de minimis* and not compensable under § 551.412(a)(1). *See Leavenworth*, 59 FLRA at 598.

In the appendix to the merits award, the Arbitrator estimated the time spent by housing unit COs engaged in several pre-shift activities. App. at 1. Under the phrase "Person needing to turn in equipment or paperwork to Lieutenant[,]" the Arbitrator estimated the time housing unit COs spent engaged in the post-shift activity "[w]alk from housing unit to Lieutenant's office[,]" and he provided "[t]otal" estimated time spent in pre- and post-shift activity for these COs. *Id.* The "[t]otal" pre- and post-shift activity estimates for these COs range from 7.6 minutes to 9.4 minutes. *See id.* The Union contends that these estimates are incomplete because the Arbitrator failed to estimate the time housing unit COs spent performing the post-shift activity "'[p]erson needing to turn in equipment or paperwork to Lieutenant[.]'" Opp'n at 5 (quoting App. at 1). However, when read in context, it is clear that the phrase "Person needing to turn in equipment or paperwork to Lieutenant" does not identify a type of compensable post-shift activity, but, rather, identifies the COs who perform the post-shift activity of "[w]alk[ing] from housing unit to Lieutenant's office[,]" for which the Arbitrator provided estimates. *See* App. at 1. Thus, the Arbitrator estimated the total time housing unit COs spent engaged in pre- *and* post-shift activity, and, as the estimates did not exceed ten minutes for any of those COs, the merits award is contrary to § 551.412(a)(1) insofar as it provides overtime compensation to those COs. *See Leavenworth*, 59 FLRA at 598. Accordingly, we set aside this portion of the merits award.

Regarding the pre-shift COs, the Arbitrator's estimates of the time these COs spent performing overtime work were each less than ten minutes per day. *See* App. at 1-2. Because the Arbitrator apparently reasoned that COs met the minimum threshold for compensable overtime under Article 18 if their pre- and post-shift activities exceeded 7.5 minutes per day, the Arbitrator did not determine how much, if any, time these COs spent engaged in *post*-shift activities. *See id.*; Merits Award at 47 ("[p]ost-shift activity is shown only if needed to meet the minimum for rounding under . . . Article 18"). In addition, the record does not provide sufficient information for the Authority to make that determination. Therefore, we are unable to determine whether the merits award directs the Agency to compensate these COs for activities that the parties concede to be noncompensable, *i.e.* pre- and post-shift activities totaling ten minutes or less per day. Accordingly, we remand the merits award to the parties for resubmission to the Arbitrator, absent settlement, to clarify how much time, if any, was spent by pre-shift COs engaged in post-shift activities. *See, e.g.*, *U.S. Dep't of Justice, Fed. Bureau of Prisons, Fed. Corr. Inst., Terminal Island, Cal.*, 63 FLRA 620, 625 (2009) (remanding award for clarification where record insufficient to determine which COs performed compensable activity and the amount of time they spent engaged in such activity).

V. Decision

The merits award is set aside insofar as it provides overtime compensation to housing unit COs, and the portions of the merits award concerning pre-shift COs are remanded to the parties for resubmission to the Arbitrator, absent settlement, for further findings.

65 FLRA No. 39

UNITED STATES
DEPARTMENT OF
HOMELAND SECURITY
U.S. CUSTOMS AND BORDER
PROTECTION
(Agency)

and

NATIONAL TREASURY
EMPLOYEES UNION
CHAPTER 164
(Union)

0-AR-4607

DECISION

October 26, 2010

Before the Authority: Carol Waller Pope, Chairman, and Thomas M. Beck and Ernest DuBester, Members[1]

I. Statement of the Case

This matter is before the Authority on exceptions to an award of Arbitrator Elvis C. Stephens filed by the Agency under § 7122(a) of the Federal Service Labor-Management Relations Statute (the Statute) and part 2425 of the Authority's Regulations. The Union filed an opposition to the Agency's exceptions.

The Arbitrator found that the Agency improperly suspended the grievant, and he awarded the grievant: (1) backpay and other related benefits for the time during which the grievant was affected by the suspension; (2) a make-whole remedy for the loss of pay and other benefits, including overtime and opportunities to earn overtime, that resulted from the Agency's withdrawal of the grievant's permit to carry a firearm; and (3) the opportunity to transfer to other parts of the Agency, if an opening exists.

For the reasons that follow, we set aside the make-whole remedy with respect to the removal of the grievant's firearm, and we deny the remaining exceptions.

II. Background and Arbitrator's Award

The grievant, a United States Customs and Border Protection Officer, worked at the Agency's port of entry in Danville, Washington. Award at 2. Sometime after moving to Danville in 2003, the grievant rented a house near a person (X). *Id.* Other agents at the Agency "gossiped" that X was "probably smuggling drugs[;]" however, "[t]here were no official briefings or official notices that [X] was a suspect[]" in connection with any drug-related crimes. *Id.* Moreover, X had never been arrested or indicted for dealing drugs. *Id.* However, the grievant had been to X's house for a party, had purchased a vehicle from X, and had X perform work on his car. *Id.* at 3. In addition, the grievant's wife had worked for X for approximately six months. *Id.* Around 2005, the grievant ceased contact with X. *Id.* at 2.

Beginning in July 2008, the Agency investigated the grievant regarding his possible inappropriate association with "individuals suspected of being drug smugglers[,]" including X. *Id.* at 3. Subsequently, the Agency issued to the grievant a proposed notice of removal, in which it charged the grievant with: (1) "improper association with individual(s) who are suspected or known to be connected to criminal activities[;]" and (2) "creating the appearance of improper association." *Id.* at 2-3. Upon review, the Director of Field Operations of the Agency's Seattle, Washington office upheld the first charge, but not the second. *Id.* Accordingly, she reduced the grievant's proposed removal to a five-day suspension. *Id.*

The Union filed a grievance, which was unresolved and submitted to expedited arbitration. *Id.* at 4. At arbitration, the parties stipulated to the following issues:

> 1. Whether [the grievant] committed the charge of [i]mproper [a]ssociation with [i]ndividual(s) who are [s]uspected or [k]nown to be [c]onnected to [c]riminal [a]ctivities; and
>
> 2. Whether the penalty of a five (5) day suspension for the conduct is reasonable.

Id. at 1.

Addressing the charge of improper association with X, the Arbitrator found that, although the

1. Member Beck's dissenting opinion is set forth at the end of this decision.

grievant may not have "exercised good judgment in his earlier behavior," X neither had been formally indicted or charged with any violation of drug laws, nor had been included, in the computer files reviewed by the Agency's officers, as a person "suspected" of such activity. *Id.* at 4-5. In the latter connection, the Arbitrator defined "suspected" as meaning "that the person has been identified as a suspect during a muster or other formal meeting, rather than as the subject of idle gossip." *Id.* at 5. The Arbitrator found that, at the time when the grievant associated with X, the grievant merely had heard gossip from other officers that "X is connected with drug smuggling[.]" *Id.* The Arbitrator determined that the Agency failed to prove that the grievant improperly associated with X.

In addition, the Arbitrator found that the grievant's association with X had ceased more than three years prior to the Agency's investigation. *Id.* at 4-5. In this connection, the Arbitrator noted that "[t]here was testimony of a personal[] conflict between" the grievant and his supervisor, "giving rise to the speculation of why [the supervisor] waited so long to" raise the issue of the grievant's association with X. *Id.* at 4. The Arbitrator determined that the extensive delay in investigating the grievant weighed against finding that the Agency timely disciplined the grievant. *Id.* The Arbitrator further determined that, in other disciplinary cases, arbitrators had found that the Agency violated Article 28 of the parties' agreement when it imposed discipline on grievants that was not timely or prompt.[2] *Id.* Moreover, the Arbitrator noted that the Director of the port of entry where the grievant worked had "no concern about [the grievant's] integrity and recommended him (twice) for a transfer to the Trusted Traveler Vetting Center [(the Center)]". *Id.* at 5.

The Arbitrator concluded that the Agency violated Article 28, Section 1.A of the agreement and that the grievant should be made whole for his loss of pay and benefits as a result of the suspension. *Id.* at 4-6. Accordingly, the Arbitrator awarded the grievant backpay and other related benefits for the time the grievant was affected by the unjustified and unwarranted personnel action. In addition, the Arbitrator awarded a make-whole remedy for the loss of pay and other benefits, including overtime and opportunities to earn overtime, due to the withdrawal of the grievant's permit to carry a firearm. Finally, the Arbitrator determined that, "given the situation" at the grievant's current work location, "he shall be given the opportunity to transfer" to other Agency ports of entry, or to the Center, "if an opening exists." *Id.* at 6.

III. Positions of the Parties

A. Agency's Exceptions

The Agency asserts that the Arbitrator based his award on a nonfact -- specifically, that the grievant ceased his associations with X in 2005 -- because the grievant admitted that he continued to associate with X until 2008. Exceptions at 9, 21.

The Agency also asserts that the Arbitrator failed to apply the appropriate legal standard when determining whether X was a "suspected law violator." *Id.* at 11-12. According to the Agency, the Arbitrator should have applied the standard set forth by the United States Court of Appeals for the Federal Circuit (the Federal Circuit) in *James v. Dale*, 355 F.3d 1375, 1378-79 (Fed. Cir. 2004) (*James*).

In addition, the Agency contends that the award is contrary to the Back Pay Act. According to the Agency, the Arbitrator summarily found that the Agency failed to prove the charge of improper association and that the Agency violated Article 28, Section 1 of the parties' agreement.[3] Exceptions at 13. The Agency contends that this summary conclusion does not satisfy the requirements of the Back Pay Act because there was no evidence that the grievant ever served his five-day suspension or that the suspension resulted in the reduction of the grievant's pay. *Id.* at 14.

The Agency also alleges that the Arbitrator exceeded his authority by addressing: (1) the removal of the grievant's firearm while the disciplinary action was pending; and (2) the grievant's non-selection for transfer. *Id.* at 8. The

2. Article 28, Section 1.A of the parties' agreement provides, in pertinent part, that: "In the interest of promoting a safe, efficient and effective work environment, and in order to minimize the cost of employee turnover and time off the job, the parties agree that misconduct should be remediated in a fair, impartial and timely manner." Award at 4. Article 28, Section 1.B provides that "instances of alleged misconduct should be raised and discussed in a timely manner . . . ." *Id.*

3. The Agency notes that this section of the parties' agreement states that "the parties agree that misconduct *should* be remediated in a fair, impartial and timely manner." Exceptions at 13 n.12 (emphasis in original). The Agency further notes that, contrary to the Arbitrator's conclusion, the parties' agreement does not "*require*" that discipline be timely. *Id.* at 14 n.12 (emphasis in original).

Agency contends that, because the propriety of the removal of the grievant's firearm and the non-selection of the grievant for transfer were not before the Arbitrator, the Arbitrator erred by providing remedies in connection with these issues. *Id.* The Agency also contends that it was "severely prejudiced" by the Arbitrator's consideration of the firearm issue, and that if it had known that the Arbitrator was going to resolve a transfer issue, it "would have offered evidence . . . and made arguments" regarding that issue. *Id.* at 19-20.

Finally, the Agency argues that the award is ambiguous. According to the Agency, it is unclear what the Arbitrator directed when he stated that the grievant should be given the opportunity to transfer to other ports of entry or the Center because all employees have such transfer opportunities, provided a vacancy is available. *Id.* at 8, 20. The Agency asserts that, if this portion of the award is not set aside, then the award should be remanded to the Arbitrator for clarification. *Id.* at 20.

B. Union's Opposition

The Union asserts that the Authority should deny the Agency's nonfact exception because it involves a fact that was disputed at arbitration and, even assuming that the Arbitrator erred, the Agency does not demonstrate that, but for the error, the Arbitrator would have reached a different result. Opp'n at 16-17. The Union also asserts that the award is not contrary to the decision in *James*, 355 F.3d 1375, because the instant case, unlike *James*, does not involve an adverse action under 5 U.S.C. §§ 4303 or 7512. Opp'n at 8. In addition, the Union contends that the award is not contrary to the Back Pay Act because the Arbitrator found that the Agency violated the parties' agreement and that, "because of this violation," the grievant "was affected by an unjustified and unwarranted personnel action, which resulted in his loss of pay and other benefits." *Id.* at 9 (quoting Award at 6).

Further, the Union argues that the Arbitrator did not exceed his authority by directing the Agency: (1) to compensate the grievant for losses suffered as a result of the withdrawal of his permit to carry a firearm; or (2) to provide the grievant an opportunity to transfer. *Id.* at 11, 13. According to the Union, these issues necessarily arose from the stipulated issues and were directly related to the Agency's disciplinary action. *Id.* at 10-11. With regard to the transfer issue, the Union argues that "[t]he record reveals, and the Arbitrator noted in his decision, that there was conflict between [the grievant] and his supervisor, . . . whose 2008 complaint resulted in the investigation and discipline at issue." *Id.* at 13. In addition, the Union contends that "the Arbitrator referred to 'the situation there' in [the grievant's] home port when awarding the opportunity to transfer[.]" *Id.* Finally, the Union contends that the award is not ambiguous because the intent of the award can be reasonably determined. *Id.* at 14.

IV. Analysis and Conclusions

A. The award is not based on nonfact.

To establish that an award is based on a nonfact, the appealing party must show that a central fact underlying the award is clearly erroneous, but for which the arbitrator would have reached a different result. *See NFFE, Local 1984*, 56 FLRA 38, 41 (2000). However, the Authority will not find an award deficient on the basis of an arbitrator's determination of any factual matter that the parties disputed at arbitration. *See id.*

The Agency asserts that the Arbitrator based his award on a nonfact, specifically, that the grievant ceased associating with X in 2005. Exceptions at 9, 21. This fact was disputed at arbitration. Exceptions, Attach., Jt. Ex. 3 (Agency contended grievant's statement proves that grievant continued to associate with X after 2005); *see also* Exceptions, Attach., Jt. Ex. 4(a) at 10 (Union contended grievant's alleged association with X occurred in November 2005); Award at 4 (Arbitrator found that grievant ceased associations with X in 2005). Consequently, the Agency's claim provides no basis for finding that the award is based on a nonfact, and we deny the exception. *See U.S. Dep't of the Air Force, Lowry Air Force Base, Denver, Colo.*, 48 FLRA 589, 593-94 (1993) (award not deficient based on a nonfact where excepting party challenges a factual matter that the parties disputed at arbitration).

B. The award of backpay for the removal of the grievant's firearm is contrary to law, but the remainder of the award is not contrary to law.

When an exception involves an award's consistency with law, the Authority reviews any question of law raised by the exception and the award *de novo*. *See NTEU, Chapter 24*, 50 FLRA 330, 332 (1995) (citing *U.S. Customs Serv. v. FLRA*, 43 F.3d 682, 686-87 (D.C. Cir. 1994)). In applying the standard of *de novo* review, the Authority assesses whether an arbitrator's legal conclusions are consistent with the applicable standard of law. *See*

U.S. Dep't of Def., Dep'ts of the Army & the Air Force, Ala. Nat'l Guard, Northport, Ala., 55 FLRA 37, 40 (1998). In making that assessment, the Authority defers to the arbitrator's underlying factual findings. *See id.*

i. Federal Circuit Precedent

Suspensions of fourteen days or less are not covered under 5 U.S.C. §§ 4303 or 7512. *See AFGE, Local 1770*, 51 FLRA 1302 (1996); *U.S. Dep't of the Air Force, Air Force Logistics Command, Hill Air Force Base, Utah*, 34 FLRA 986, 991 (1990). *See also U.S. Dep't of Justice, Immigration & Naturalization Serv., Jacksonville, Fla.*, 36 FLRA 928 (1990) (in a case involving a five-day suspension, the arbitrator was not bound to follow the same substantive standards of the Federal Circuit and the Merit Systems Protection Board). "[A]rbitrators considering suspensions of [fourteen] days or less may use and apply legal principles established by the Federal Circuit for review of adverse actions under § 7703; [however,] such use is not mandatory." *AFGE, Local 2172*, 57 FLRA 625, 629 (2001).

The Agency asserts that the award is contrary to law because the Arbitrator failed to apply the Federal Circuit's standard for determining whether an individual is a "suspected law violator." Exceptions at 11-12. As stated above, the use of principles established by the Federal Circuit for suspensions of less than fourteen days is not mandatory. Because the grievant's suspension here was for five days, the Arbitrator did not err in failing to apply the Federal Circuit's standard for determining whether X was a "suspected law violator." Accordingly, the award is not contrary to Federal Circuit precedent, and we deny this exception.

ii. The Back Pay Act

An award of backpay is authorized under the Back Pay Act only when an arbitrator finds that: (1) the aggrieved employee was affected by an unjustified or unwarranted personnel action; and (2) the personnel action resulted in the withdrawal or the reduction of an employee's pay, allowances, or differentials. *U.S. Dep't of the Air Force, Warner Robins Air Force Base, Ga.*, 56 FLRA 541, 543 (2000) (*Warner Robins*) (citing *U.S. Dep't of Health & Human Servs.*, 54 FLRA 1210, 1218-19 (1998) (*HHS*)).

a. The award of backpay for the grievant's five-day suspension is not contrary to the Back Pay Act.

A violation of a collective bargaining agreement constitutes an unjustified and unwarranted personnel action under the Back Pay Act. *See U.S. Dep't of Def., Dep't of Def. Dependents Schools*, 54 FLRA 773, 785 (1998)). The Arbitrator found that the Agency violated Article 28, Section 1 of the parties' agreement. Award at 4. The Agency has not demonstrated that this finding is deficient.[4] Accordingly, we find that the award satisfies the first requirement of the Back Pay Act.

The Arbitrator also found that the unwarranted and unjustified personnel action resulted in a reduction of the grievant's pay. Although the Arbitrator did not specify the amount of the loss incurred by the grievant, the Arbitrator did find that the action "resulted in [the grievant's] loss of pay and other benefits." Award at 6; *see also id.* at 5 (ordering that grievant be "made whole" for any loss of pay or benefits that were a direct result of the unjustified and unwarranted personnel action). This finding satisfies the second requirement of the Back Pay Act. *See, e.g., U.S. Dep't of the Air Force, Tinker Air Force Base, Okla. City, Okla.*, 63 FLRA 59, 61 (2008) (arbitrator's finding that the unwarranted and unjustified personnel action resulted in grievant's loss of pay was sufficient to satisfy the requirement under the Back Pay Act).

Moreover, an employee is only entitled to receive compensation "equal to all or any part of the pay, allowances, or differentials, as applicable which the employee normally would have earned or received during the period if the personnel action had not occurred[.]" 5 U.S.C. § 5596(b)(1)(A)(i). The award provides that the grievant should be "made whole" for the loss of any pay or benefits as a result of the suspension. Award at 6. Thus, the award does

4. The Agency asserts that Article 28, § 1 of the parties' agreement states that "the parties agree that misconduct *should* be remediated in a fair, impartial and timely matter" but does not "*require*" that the discipline be timely. Exceptions at 13 n.12. We construe this assertion as a claim that the award fails to draw its essence from the parties' agreement. As the Agency fails to provide any arguments to support this claim, we deny the claim as a bare assertion. *See U.S. Dep't of Homeland Sec., U.S. Customs & Border Prot., Port of Seattle, Seattle, Wash.*, 60 FLRA 490, 492 n.7 (2004) (when a party fails to provide any arguments or authority to support its exception, the Authority will deny the exception as a bare assertion).

not provide that the grievant be compensated for any losses not actually sustained as a result of that action.

For the foregoing reasons, we find that the award of backpay in connection with the suspension does not violate the Back Pay Act, and we deny the exception. *See HHS*, 54 FLRA at 1218-19 (award of backpay is warranted where the arbitrator found that the unjustified and unwarranted personnel action resulted in the loss of pay for the grievant).

b. The award of backpay for the removal of the grievant's firearm is contrary to the Back Pay Act.

As stated above, an award of backpay is authorized under the Back Pay Act only when an arbitrator finds that the unjustified or unwarranted personnel action resulted in the withdrawal or the reduction of an employee's pay, allowances, or differentials. *See Warner Robins*, 56 FLRA at 543. Here, the Arbitrator failed to find a nexus between the removal of the grievant's firearm and a loss in pay or benefits, as required by the Back Pay Act. Accordingly, the award of backpay for the removal of the grievant's firearm is contrary to the Back Pay Act, and we set it aside.[5] *See Portsmouth Naval Shipyard, Portsmouth, N.H.*, 49 FLRA 1522, 1533 (1994) (Authority declined to order an award of backpay where there was no nexus between the violation and a monetary loss).

C. The Arbitrator did not exceed his authority.

An arbitrator exceeds his or her authority when the arbitrator fails to resolve an issue submitted to arbitration, resolves an issue not submitted to arbitration, disregards specific limitations on his or her authority, or awards relief to persons who are not encompassed within the grievance. *See AFGE, Local 1617*, 51 FLRA 1645, 1647 (1996). In addition, an arbitrator is granted broad discretion to fashion a remedy that the arbitrator considers to be appropriate. *See U.S. DOD, Dependents Schools*, 49 FLRA 658, 663 (1994) (*DODDS*).

The Agency contends that the Arbitrator exceeded his authority by directing that the grievant be given an opportunity to transfer because that remedy addressed an issue -- i.e., the nonselection of the grievant for a position at the Center -- that was not before the Arbitrator. Exceptions at 8. For the following reasons, we find that the Agency's contention lacks merit.

The stipulated issues before the Arbitrator involved whether the grievant committed the charge of improper association and whether a five-day suspension for that conduct was reasonable. *See* Award at 1. Before the Arbitrator, the Union submitted evidence regarding both the grievant's prior applications for transfer and his relationship with his supervisor. *See* Exceptions, Attach., Jt. Ex. 5 at 5-6 (transcript of oral reply to notice of proposed removal discussing removal of firearm); *id.* at 32-37, 45-46 (transcript of oral reply to notice of proposed removal discussing the supervisor's conduct and alleging that the investigation was "driven entirely by" the supervisor's "false accusations"); Exceptions, Attach., Jt. Ex. 4(g) (letters regarding applications for transfer). In resolving the stipulated issues and finding that the suspension was improper, the Arbitrator considered the fact that the Agency's investigation into the grievant's conduct did not take place until years after the grievant ended his association with X. In this connection, the Arbitrator considered the fact that the grievant's supervisor raised the issue that led to the Agency investigation, and stated: "There was testimony of a personal[] conflict between" the grievant and his supervisor, "giving rise to the speculation of why [the supervisor] waited so long to" raise the issue of the grievant's association with X. Award at 4. Based on this evidence, the Arbitrator found that, "given the situation" at the grievant's work location, an appropriate remedy would be to award the grievant the opportunity to transfer to a different location. *Id.* at 6. In these circumstances, we find that this remedy directly relates to the stipulated issues.

We note the Agency's claim that, if it had known that the Arbitrator was going to resolve a transfer issue, then it "would have offered evidence . . . and made arguments" regarding that issue. Exceptions at 20. To the extent that the Agency's claim could be construed as arguing that the Agency was prejudiced by the Arbitrator's decision to award a transfer, we reject that argument. In this connection, as discussed above, the Union submitted evidence to the Arbitrator regarding both the grievant's prior applications for transfer and his relationship with his supervisor. There is no basis for finding that the Agency was denied an opportunity to address that evidence. Accordingly, there is no basis for finding that the Agency was unfairly prejudiced by the Arbitrator's resolution of this issue.

5. As we set aside the portion of the award concerning backpay for the removal of the grievant's firearm, we need not consider whether the Arbitrator exceeded his authority by ordering such a remedy.

For the foregoing reasons, we find that the Arbitrator did not exceed his authority by directing the transfer remedy, and we deny the exception.

D. The award is not incomplete, ambiguous, or contradictory.

The Authority will find an award deficient when it is incomplete, ambiguous, or so contradictory as to make implementation of the award impossible. *See U.S. Dep't of Labor, Mine Safety & Health Admin., Se. Dist.*, 40 FLRA 937, 943 (1991). For an award to be found deficient on this ground, the appealing party must show that implementation of the award is impossible because the meaning and effect of the award are too unclear or uncertain. *See U.S. Dep't of the Army, Corpus Christi Army Depot, Corpus Christi, Tex.*, 56 FLRA 1057, 1074 (2001).

Although the Agency alleges that the transfer remedy is ambiguous, the Agency does not argue, and there is no basis for finding, that the award is impossible to implement. Consequently, we find that the award is not deficient in this regard, and we deny the exception. *See U.S. Dep't of Homeland Sec., U.S. Customs & Border Prot.*, 64 FLRA 916 (2010) (finding award not deficient when agency, although alleging award was ambiguous, failed to allege that it was impossible to implement).

V. Decision

The award of backpay for the removal of the grievant's firearm is set aside, and the remaining exceptions are denied.

Member Beck, Dissenting in part:

I disagree with my colleagues' conclusion that the Arbitrator did not exceed his authority when he ordered that the grievant be given an opportunity to transfer within the Agency. Moreover, although I agree with my colleagues that the Arbitrator's award of backpay to the grievant due to the withdrawal of his permit to carry a weapon is contrary to law, I believe that the Arbitrator also exceeded his authority by awarding this remedy.

I recognize that arbitrators are granted broad discretion in the fashioning of appropriate remedies. *See, e.g., Veterans Admin.*, 24 FLRA 447, 450 (1986) (*VA*). However, despite the deference that we give to arbitrators in this regard, the Authority has adhered to the fundamental principle that arbitrators must confine their awards and remedies to those issues submitted for resolution. *See id.*, and cases cited therein. An arbitrator's discretion is not a license to address issues that are not presented by the parties. *U.S. Dep't of the Navy, Naval Sea Logistics Ctr., Detachment Atl., Indian Head, Md.*, 57 FLRA 687, 688 (2002). Although arbitrators may properly bring their judgment to bear in reaching a fair resolution of a dispute submitted to them, they may not decide matters that are not before them. *U.S. Dep't of the Treasury, U.S. Mint, Denver, Colo.*, 60 FLRA 777, 780 (2005) (then-Member Pope dissenting as to application).

Here, the parties specifically agreed that the Arbitrator would resolve the following two issues:

> 1. Whether [the grievant] committed the charge of [i]mproper [a]ssociation with [i]ndividual(s) who are [s]uspected or [k]nown to be [c]onnected to [c]riminal [a]ctivities; and
>
> 2. Whether the penalty of a five (5) day suspension for the conduct is reasonable.

Award at 1. The Arbitrator answered these questions when he found that the grievant had not committed the charge and implicitly found that the five-day penalty was unreasonable. Having so found, the Arbitrator possessed the authority to return the grievant to the position that he was in prior to the Agency's actions – i.e., to rescind the suspension and award to him the pay or benefits that he lost as a result of the suspension. The Arbitrator, however, went beyond this authority and awarded the grievant additional relief not warranted by the specific issues to which the parties stipulated – i.e., providing the grievant backpay due to the withdrawal of his permit to carry a firearm and the opportunity to transfer to other parts of the agency.[1]

This additional relief concerns issues that were not before the Arbitrator: First, whether the Agency had properly withdrawn the grievant's permit to carry a weapon, and second, the grievant's non-selection for transfer. As noted previously, the Arbitrator was neither asked to, nor authorized to, resolve these other issues, nor to direct remedies concerning them. *See VA,* 24 FLRA at 451 (holding that arbitrators may not decide matters that are not before them).

Accordingly, I would find that the Arbitrator exceeded his authority and would modify the award to vacate the portions of the award concerning these remedies.[2]

---

1. The Majority describes the Arbitrator's award of backpay due to the withdrawal of the grievant's permit to carry a firearm as "make-whole" relief. Majority at 1, 3. However, the Arbitrator failed to make any finding that the permit was withdrawn because of the charge against the grievant or that the grievant lost any pay or benefits due to the withdrawal. Accordingly, this award of backpay does not constitute make-whole relief.

2. Because I conclude that these additional remedies should be set aside, I would find it unnecessary to address the Agency's remaining exception that the award is ambiguous. Exceptions at 18. However, I concur with my colleagues' resolution of this issue.

65 FLRA No. 40

INTERNATIONAL FEDERATION
OF PROFESSIONAL AND
TECHNICAL ENGINEERS
LOCAL 4
(Union)

and

UNITED STATES
DEPARTMENT OF THE NAVY
PORTSMOUTH NAVAL SHIPYARD
PORTSMOUTH, NEW HAMPSHIRE
(Agency)

0-AR-4652

DECISION

October 26, 2010

Before the Authority: Carol Waller Pope, Chairman, and Thomas M. Beck and Ernest DuBester, Members

I. Statement of the Case

This matter is before the Authority on exceptions to an award of Arbitrator Tim Bornstein filed by the Union under § 7122 of the Federal Service Labor-Management Relations Statute (the Statute) and part 2425 of the Authority's Regulations. The Agency filed an opposition to the Union's exceptions.

As relevant here, the Arbitrator found that the grievance was not substantively arbitrable.[1] Award at 34. For the reasons discussed below, we deny the Union's exceptions.

II. Background and Arbitrator's Award

The Union filed a grievance alleging that the Agency's Equal Employment Opportunity (EEO) Program improperly "f[ell] under the Human Resources Office . . . in the [Agency's] organizational structure[,]" in violation of EEO regulations and Article 3, Section 5, and Article 5, Section 1, of the parties' agreement.[2] Award at 2-3. The Agency denied the grievance, and the Union invoked arbitration. *Id.* at 4-5.

The Arbitrator considered the Agency's claim that the grievance was not substantively arbitrable.[3] As relevant here, the Arbitrator noted the Agency's claim that the grievance "violates both statutory and contractual rights of management to determine its organization" under § 7106(a)(1) of the Statute and Article 2 of the parties' agreement.[4] *Id.* at 30. The Arbitrator also noted the Union's claim that an arbitrator may not rely on § 7106 of the Statute to determine that a grievance is not arbitrable. *Id.* at 32. The Arbitrator then stated:

> If the [S]tatute were the only relevant consideration here, the Union's position might be persuasive. But it is not[,] because the parties incorporated in Article 2 of their contract language respecting [§] 7106(a)(1) management rights. Accordingly, the question in this case is whether the parties intended that management's Article 2 rights could be challenged in Article 7's negotiated grievance procedure. Logically, it follows that, because the parties agreed to the incorporation of [§] 7106(a)(1) rights in Article 2 of their contract, those rights of

1. The Arbitrator also found that the grievance was procedurally arbitrable, and that the Union's request for information was "moot." Award at 33-34. As those finding are not at issue here, we do not discuss them further.

2. With regard to EEO regulations, the Union cited 29 C.F.R. part 1614, Equal Employment Opportunity Commission (EEOC) Management Directive 110, Ch. 6, IV(A), EEOC Management Directive 715, and Executive Order 13164. *See* Award at 2-4. With regard to the parties' agreement, Article 3, Section 5 states, in pertinent part, that "all employees in the unit will be treated fairly and equitably in the application and/or interpretation of the Statute, rules and regulations." *Id.* at 5-6. Article 5, Section 1 states, in pertinent part, that the parties agree that they are "governed by existing or future laws and regulations of appropriate authorities, such as Presidential Executive Orders[.]" *Id.* at 6.

3. The Arbitrator did not state what issues were before him, and the parties did not stipulate to what issues the Arbitrator would resolve.

4. Article 2 of the parties' agreement states, in pertinent part, that "nothing in this AGREEMENT shall affect the authority of the [Agency] . . . to determine the . . . organization . . . of the [Agency.]" Award at 5.

management are exempt from challenge in the grievance procedure.[[5]]

Id. at 33. Accordingly, the Arbitrator found that the grievance was not arbitrable, and he dismissed the grievance. *Id.* at 33-34.

III. Positions of the Parties

A. Union's Exceptions

The Union contends that the award fails to draw its essence from the parties' agreement because Articles 5 and 7 permit grievances alleging violations of law, and Article 7 permits grievances over matters "concerning . . . the effect or interpretation or a claim of breach" of the parties' agreement. Exceptions at 17-18. Additionally, the Union argues that Article 7, Section 2 "explicitly states that 'only' 11 discrete issues are excluded from coverage of this grievance procedure[,]" indicating that other matters, including the Union's grievance, are grievable.[6] *Id.* at 18. The Union further asserts that the grievance is arbitrable under Article 34, which the Union claims "contains . . . a directive to follow EEO laws[.]"[7] *Id.* at 17.

The Union also contends that the award is contrary to law for three reasons. First, the Union claims that the Authority has held that § 7106 does not bar arbitrability. *Id.* at 9-10 (citing *AFGE, Nat'l Border Patrol Council, Local 1929*, 63 FLRA 465, 466 (2009); *U.S. Dep't of Hous. & Urban Dev.*, 62 FLRA 52, 53 (2007); *U.S. Dep't of Homeland Sec., Customs & Border Prot. Agency, N.Y., N.Y.*, 61 FLRA 72, 75 (2005) (*DHS*)). Second, the Union asserts that the grievance "does not violate management's rights" because it seeks to "make the Agency follow the law." *Id.* at 15. Third, the Union alleges that the award is "contrary to law because it allows the Agency to use § 7106(a) to violate federal regulations." *Id.* at 14.

B. Agency's Opposition

The Agency contends that the award does not fail to draw its essence from the parties' agreement. Opp'n at 10. Additionally, the Agency asserts that the Union's contrary-to-law exceptions are misplaced because the Arbitrator based his award on "specific contract language found in Article 2 . . . and Article 7 . . . not upon statutory grounds." *Id.* at 6.

IV. Analysis and Conclusions

Where an arbitrator's determination regarding the substantive arbitrability of a grievance is based on his or her interpretation of a collective bargaining agreement, the Authority applies the deferential essence standard to review that determination. *See, e.g.*, *AFGE, Local 12*, 61 FLRA 456, 457-58 (2006) (citing *Nat'l Air Traffic Controllers Ass'n*, 56 FLRA 733, 735 n.3 (2000)). Here, the Arbitrator found that the grievance was not substantively arbitrable, and he based that finding on his interpretation of the parties' agreement. Award at 34.

---

5. Article 7, Section 1 of the parties' agreement states, in pertinent part, that a "grievance means any complaint . . . concerning . . . the effect or interpretation or a claim of breach of this AGREEMENT [or] any claimed violations, misinterpretation or misapplication of any law, rule or regulation affecting conditions of employment." Award at 6.

6. Article 7, Section 2 of the parties' agreement states:

> Only the following types of actions are specifically excluded from the provisions of Article[] 7 . . . . Matters thus excluded may be subject to administrative and/or statutory appeals and should be addressed to the appropriate authority . . . :
> a. Any claimed violation of Subchapter III of Chapter 73 of Title 5 of the United States Code (relating to political activities);
> b. Retirement, life insurance, or health insurance;
> c. A suspension or removal under Section 7532 of Title 5 of the United States Code;
> d. Any examination, certification, or appointment;
> e. The classification of any position which does not result in the reduction in grade or pay of an employee;
> f. Termination of a temporary employee;
> g. Oral admonishment or reprimand, letters of caution and letters of requirement;
> h. Substance of performance elements and standards;
> i. An allegation or complaint of discrimination reviewable under Part 713 of [Office of Personnel Management] regulations;
> j. Separation of probationers;
> k. Reduction-in-force.

Exceptions, Attach at 24-26; Opp'n, Attach. 4 at 24-26.

7. Article 34 states, in pertinent part: "All qualified employees are assured equal employment opportunities in employment matters . . . . The [Agency] will publish and disseminate an [EEO] affirmative action plan in accordance with existing law and directives." Exceptions, Attach. at 154.

Thus, the question is whether the award fails to draw its essence from the parties' agreement.

The Authority will find that an arbitration award is deficient as failing to draw its essence from the collective bargaining agreement when the appealing party establishes that the award: (1) cannot in any rational way be derived from the agreement; (2) is so unfounded in reason and fact and so unconnected with the wording and purposes of the collective bargaining agreement as to manifest an infidelity to the obligation of the arbitrator; (3) does not represent a plausible interpretation of the agreement; or (4) evidences a manifest disregard of the argument. *See U.S. Dep't of Labor (OSHA)*, 34 FLRA 573, 575 (1990). The Authority and the courts defer to the arbitrator in this context "because it is the arbitrator's construction of the agreement for which the parties have bargained." *Id.* at 576.

The Arbitrator interpreted Articles 7 and 2 of the parties' agreement, stating that the question before him was "whether the parties intended that management's Article 2 rights could be challenged in Article 7's negotiated grievance procedure." Award at 33. The Arbitrator found that the parties intended to exclude such challenges "because the parties agreed to the incorporation of [§] 7106(a)(1) rights in Article 2 of their contract[.]" *Id.* In response, the Union generically asserts that Articles 7 and 5 permit grievances alleging violations of law. However, the Union does not demonstrate that the Arbitrator's finding, that Articles 7 and 2 preclude grievances challenging management's right to determine its organization, is irrational, unfounded, implausible, or evidences a manifest disregard of the agreement. *See, e.g., AFGE, Local 3979, Council of Prisons Locals*, 61 FLRA 810, 815 (2006). Further, although Article 7, Section 2 of the parties' agreement states that certain matters are "specifically excluded" from the negotiated grievance procedure, that section does not foreclose the possibility that other provisions of the agreement, such as Article 2, might also provide a basis for excluding additional matters from the negotiated grievance procedure. Exceptions, Attach. at 25. Moreover, nothing in either Article 7 or Article 5 specifically states that matters regarding Article 2 rights of management to determine its organization are specifically *included* in the negotiated grievance process. Accordingly, we deny these essence exceptions.

As to Article 34 of the agreement, the Union does not explain how the award fails to draw its essence from that section, which "assure[s] equal employment opportunities" and states that the Agency "will publish . . . [an] affirmative action plan in accordance with existing law[.]" Exceptions, Attach. at 154. Where a party fails to support its claim that an award fails to draw its essence from a collective bargaining agreement, the Authority denies the exceptions as a bare assertion. *See, e.g., AFGE, Council of Prison Locals 33, Locals 1007 & 3957*, 64 FLRA 288, 291 (2009) (party failed to explain essence exception). Consistent with this precedent, we deny this essence exception as a bare assertion.

With regard to the Union's contrary-to-law exceptions, those exceptions are based on the erroneous premise that the Arbitrator relied on § 7106, and not on the parties' agreement, to determine that the grievance was not substantively arbitrable. *See* Exceptions at 10-11, 14. As the Arbitrator relied on the parties' agreement to determine that the grievance was not substantively arbitrable, the Union's statutory arguments are misplaced. *See AFGE, Local 779*, 64 FLRA 672, 674 (2010) (contrary-to-law exception to arbitrator's interpretation of contract misplaced). *Cf. NTEU, Chapter 260*, 52 FLRA 1533, 1538 (1997) (nothing required the arbitrator, as a matter of law, to interpret contract to find grievance arbitrable). Therefore, we deny the Union's contrary-to-law exceptions.

V. Decision

The Union's exceptions are denied.

65 FLRA No. 41

INTERNATIONAL ASSOCIATION
OF MACHINISTS AND
AEROSPACE WORKERS
NIPSIC LODGE 282
(Union)

and

UNITED STATES
DEPARTMENT OF THE NAVY
NAVAL FACILITIES ENGINEERING
COMMAND NORTHWEST
(Agency)

0-AR-4680

DECISION

October 28, 2010

Before the Authority: Carol Waller Pope, Chairman, and Thomas M. Beck and Ernest DuBester, Members

This matter is before the Authority on exceptions to an award of Arbitrator Kathryn T. Whalen filed by the Union under § 7122(a) of the Federal Service Labor-Management Relations Statute (the Statute) and part 2425 of the Authority's Regulations. The Agency filed an opposition to the Union's exceptions.*

Under § 7122(a) of the Statute, an award is deficient if it is contrary to any law, rule, or regulation, or it is deficient on other grounds similar to those applied by Federal courts in private sector labor-management relations. Upon careful consideration of the entire record in this case and Authority precedent, the Authority concludes that the award is not deficient on the grounds raised in the exceptions and set forth in § 7122(a). *See U.S. Dep't of the Navy, Naval Base, Norfolk, Va.*, 51 FLRA 305, 307-08 (1995) (award not deficient on ground that arbitrator exceeded his or her authority where excepting party does not establish that arbitrator failed to resolve an issue submitted to arbitration, disregarded specific limitations on his authority, or awarded relief to persons who were not encompassed within the grievance); *Prof'l Airways Sys. Specialists, Dist. No. 1, MEBA/NMU (AFL-CIO)*, 48 FLRA 764, 768-69 (1993) (award not deficient as contrary to law where excepting party fails to establish that the award is in any manner contrary to the law, rule, or regulation on which the party relies); *U.S. Dep't of the Air Force, Lowry Air Force Base, Denver, Colo.*, 48 FLRA 589, 593-94 (1993) (award not deficient as based on a nonfact where excepting party either challenges a factual matter that the parties disputed at arbitration or fails to demonstrate that a central fact underlying the award is clearly erroneous, but for which a different result would have been reached by the arbitrator); *U.S. Dep't of Labor (OSHA)*, 34 FLRA 573, 575 (1990) (award not deficient as failing to draw its essence from the parties' collective bargaining agreement where excepting party fails to establish that the award: cannot in any rational way be derived from the agreement; is so unfounded in reason and fact and so unconnected to the wording and purpose of the agreement as to manifest an infidelity to the obligation of the arbitrator; does not represent a plausible interpretation of the agreement; or evidences a manifest disregard of the agreement).

Accordingly, the Union's exceptions are denied.

* The Agency asserts in its opposition that the exceptions are not properly before the Authority because they were not dated or filed with a statement of service, as required by the Authority's Regulations. Opp'n at 1-2 (citing 5 C.F.R. § 2429.27). However, in response to an order from the Authority, the Union cured these deficiencies. *See* Deficiency Order (Sept. 13, 2010); Union's Cure of Deficiencies (Sept. 27, 2010). Thus, the exceptions are properly before the Authority, and we will consider them. *E.g., U.S. Dep't of Health & Human Servs., Appalachian Lab. for Occupational Safety & Health, Nat'l Inst. for Occupational Safety & Health, Ctrs. for Disease Control & Prevention*, 49 FLRA 1150, 1151 (1994).

65 FLRA No. 42

UNITED STATES
DEPARTMENT OF TRANSPORTATION
FEDERAL AVIATION ADMINISTRATION
(Agency)

and

NATIONAL AIR TRAFFIC
CONTROLLERS ASSOCIATION
(Union)

0-AR-4075

DECISION

October 29, 2010

Before the Authority: Carol Waller Pope, Chairman, and Thomas M. Beck and Ernest DuBester, Members

I. Statement of the Case

This matter is before the Authority on exceptions to an award of Arbitrator Kathryn Durham filed by the Agency under § 7122(a) of the Federal Service Labor-Management Relations Statute (Statute) and part 2425 of the Authority's Regulations. The Union filed an opposition to the Agency's exceptions.

The Arbitrator concluded that the Agency violated the parties' collective bargaining agreement by cancelling scheduled overtime assignments without proper notice. For the following reasons, we dismiss the Agency's exceptions pertaining to § 7106(a)(2)(A) and (D) and § 7101 of the Statute, and we deny the remaining exceptions.

II. Background and Arbitrator's Award

The parties submitted to arbitration several grievances alleging that the Agency had violated the parties' agreement by cancelling overtime assignments with less than seven days' notice. Award at 1. The Arbitrator found that Article 38, Section 8 (Section 8) of the agreement clearly specifies that the only situation in which the Agency can cancel overtime assignments with less than seven days' notice is when the overtime was assigned to an employee because of another employee's scheduled absence and the overtime was cancelled because that other employee returned to work.[1] *Id.* at 13. The Arbitrator determined that none of the grievances involved this situation and that, consequently, the Agency violated Section 8, as alleged. *Id.*

The Arbitrator addressed the Agency's claim that this interpretation of Section 8 is unenforceable as contrary to management's right to assign work under § 7106(a)(2)(B) of the Statute. *Id.* at 14. The Arbitrator noted that Section 8 provides that management is "normally" precluded from cancelling overtime without seven days' notice except in the specified circumstances. *Id.* at 13. She agreed with the Agency that including the standard "normally" into a provision does not necessarily render it negotiable, and she rejected the Union's argument that the inclusion of the term "normally" makes Section 8 negotiable and enforceable. *Id.* at 9, 13. Instead, she found that Section 8 constitutes an arrangement in which "the Agency bears the cost of 'doing business,' so to speak" in a limited number of "abnormal situations[.]" *Id.* at 14. In addition, she determined that Section 8's benefits to employees outweigh any effect on management's right. *Id.* Consequently, she concluded Section 8 is enforceable as an appropriate arrangement negotiated under § 7106(b)(3). Award Summary; Award at 14.

Accordingly, the Arbitrator sustained the grievances. She concluded that the grievants were entitled to the overtime pay that they would have earned if management had not violated the agreement, and she directed that the grievants be made whole. Award Summary.

III. Positions of the Parties

A. Agency's Exceptions

The Agency contends that the award is based on a nonfact because the Arbitrator "relies heavily" on an alleged, but unproven, past practice "of paying employees for overtime when scheduled overtime is cancelled with less than seven days notice." Exceptions at 28-29. The Agency further contends

---

1. Section 8 provides as follows:

> Overtime shall not normally be cancelled without seven (7) days notice. However, if an employee cancels or returns from annual or sick leave, any overtime scheduled to cover that absence may be canceled, provided that such overtime had been scheduled as a direct result of the returning employee's absence.

Award at 1.

that the award fails to draw its essence from Section 8 of the agreement. In this connection, the Agency asserts that the Arbitrator interpreted and applied the term "normally" to "declare" that Section 8 is "negotiable[.]" *Id.* at 33.

The Agency also contends that the award is contrary to management's rights to assign and direct employees under § 7106(a)(2)(A) of the Statute, and to take whatever actions are necessary to carry out the Agency mission during emergencies under § 7106(a)(2)(D). In addition, the Agency contends that the award is contrary to § 7101(a) of the Statute.

Finally, the Agency contends that the award is contrary to management's right to assign work under § 7106(a)(2)(B) of the Statute because the award affects the exercise of that right, and Section 8 is not enforceable pursuant to § 7106(b)(2) or (3). *Id.* at 12-21. With regard to § 7106(b)(3), the Agency asserts that the Arbitrator's interpretation of Section 8 requires the Agency to make "unacceptable choices" of either assigning an employee overtime work when there is no need for overtime work to be performed or paying the employee for the scheduled overtime. *Id.* at 20. The Agency argues that both options significantly burden management because they restrict management's ability to respond to the numerous situations that necessitate the cancellation of overtime on short notice. *Id.* at 20-21. Accordingly, the Agency contends that Section 8, as interpreted by the Arbitrator, excessively interferes with management's right to assign work and is not an enforceable appropriate arrangement under § 7106(b)(3).

B. Union's Opposition

The Union contends that the award is not based on a nonfact because the Arbitrator correctly found an established past practice of not cancelling overtime assignments with less than seven days' notice. Opp'n at 8-10. As to essence, the Union argues that the Agency's exception fails to meet the "high threshold" for showing that an award is deficient. *Id.* at 10-11. In addition, the Union asserts that the award is not contrary to § 7106(a)(2)(A) and (D) or § 7101 of the Statute. *Id.* at 6-7. Finally, the Union contends that the award is not contrary to management's right to assign work under § 7106(a)(2)(B) because Section 8 is an enforceable appropriate arrangement under § 7106(b)(3). *Id.* at 5-6.

IV. Preliminary Issue

The Authority's Regulations that were in effect when the Agency filed its exceptions provided that "[t]he Authority will not consider . . . any issue, which was not presented in the proceedings before the . . . arbitrator." 5 C.F.R. § 2429.5.[2] Before the Arbitrator, the Agency argued that to interpret Section 8 to allow cancellation of overtime with less than seven days' notice only when employees return from scheduled leave would excessively interfere with management's right to assign work under § 7106(a)(2)(B). Award at 6. There is no indication in the record that the Agency argued to the Arbitrator that such an interpretation of Section 8 would also conflict with § 7106(a)(2)(A) and (D) and § 7101. As these issues could have been, but were not, presented to the Arbitrator, § 2429.5 precludes the Agency from raising them for the first time in exceptions. Accordingly, we dismiss these exceptions.

V. Analysis and Conclusions

A. The award is not based on a nonfact.

To establish that an award is based on a nonfact, the appealing party must demonstrate that a central fact underlying the award is clearly erroneous, but for which the arbitrator would have reached a different result. *E.g., U.S. Dep't of the Treasury, IRS, Andover, Mass.*, 63 FLRA 202, 205 (2009) (*IRS*). The Authority will not find an award deficient on the basis of an arbitrator's determination on any factual matter that the parties disputed at arbitration. *Id.*

The Agency claims that the Arbitrator erroneously found a past practice of paying employees for overtime when scheduled overtime is cancelled with less than seven days' notice.[3]

2. The Authority's Regulations concerning the review of arbitration awards, as well as certain related procedural regulations, including § 2429.5, were revised effective October 1, 2010. *See* 75 Fed. Reg. 42,283 (2010). As the Agency's exceptions were filed before that date, we apply the earlier Regulations.

3. The Authority views an exception to an arbitrator's finding of whether a past practice exists as asserting a nonfact. The Authority views an exception to an arbitrator's interpretation of a past practice as asserting that the award fails to draw its essence from the agreement. *E.g., U.S. Dep't of the Army, Corps of Eng'rs, Nw. Div. & Seattle Dist.*, 64 FLRA 405, 408 n.5 (2010). As the Agency disputes the finding of a past practice, the Agency correctly challenges the award on nonfact grounds. *Id.*

However, the parties disputed this matter before the Arbitrator. Award at 8; Exceptions at 28-29 ("[T]he Agency produced witnesses to dispute past practice at the facilities involved in the grievances[.]"). Consequently, the Agency's exception provides no basis for finding that the award is based on a nonfact, and we deny the exception. *See IRS*, 63 FLRA at 205.

B. The award does not fail to draw its essence from the agreement.

For an award to be found deficient as failing to draw its essence from the collective bargaining agreement, it must be established that the award: (1) cannot in any rational way be derived from the agreement; (2) is so unfounded in reason and fact and so unconnected with the wording and purposes of the agreement as to manifest an infidelity to the obligation of the arbitrator; (3) does not represent a plausible interpretation of the agreement; or (4) evidences a manifest disregard of the agreement. *U.S. Dep't of Labor (OSHA)*, 34 FLRA 573, 575 (1990).

The Agency's essence exception misconstrues the award. In this connection, the Agency fails to show that the Arbitrator interpreted and applied the term "normally" to "declare" that Section 8 is "negotiable[.]" Exceptions at 33. To the contrary, the Arbitrator specifically concluded that the "inclusion of the standard 'normally' into an otherwise non-negotiable provision does not necessarily render it negotiable" and "does not insulate the provision from a challenge as to enforceability." Award at 9, 13. For this reason, the Arbitrator did not agree with the Union's argument that the term "normally" makes Section 8 negotiable and enforceable. *Id.* at 13. Instead, she concluded that Section 8's requirement to honor an overtime assignment, except in certain specified situations is enforceable as an appropriate arrangement negotiated under § 7106(b)(3). *Id.* at 9-13. Nothing in the Agency's exception establishes that the Arbitrator's interpretation and application of the term "normally" is irrational, unfounded, implausible, or manifestly disregards the agreement. Accordingly, we deny this exception.[4]

4. We note that the Arbitrator's interpretation of Section 8 is not necessarily the only plausible interpretation, and that the Agency's interpretation is also plausible. However, it is not the Authority's job to second-guess arbitrators by choosing the best among several interpretations of contract language and that, if an arbitrator's interpretation is plausible, then the Authority's inquiry ends.

C. The award is not contrary to law.

The Authority reviews questions of law raised by exceptions to an arbitrator's award *de novo*. *E.g.*, *NFFE Local 1437*, 53 FLRA 1703, 1709 (1998). In applying a standard of *de novo* review, we assess whether the arbitrator's legal conclusions are consistent with the applicable standard of law. *Id.* at 1710.

The Authority recently revised the analysis that it will apply when reviewing management-rights exceptions to arbitration awards. *See U.S. Envtl. Prot. Agency*, 65 FLRA 113, 115 (2010) (Member Beck concurring) (*EPA*); *Fed. Deposit Ins. Corp., Div. of Supervision & Consumer Prot., S.F. Region*, 65 FLRA 102 (2010) (Chairman Pope concurring) (*FDIC*). Under the revised analysis, the Authority will first assess whether the award affects the exercise of the asserted management right.[5] *EPA*, 65 FLRA at 115. If so, then, as relevant here, the Authority examines whether the award enforces a contract provision negotiated under § 7106(b).[6] *Id.* Also under the revised analysis, in determining whether the award enforces a contract provision negotiated under § 7106(b)(3), the Authority assesses: (1) whether the contract provision constitutes an arrangement for employees adversely affected by the exercise of a management right; and (2) if so, whether the arbitrator's enforcement of the arrangement abrogates the exercise of the management right. *See id.* at 116-18. In concluding

5. Member Beck agrees with the conclusion to deny the Agency's exceptions. He does not agree, however, with his colleagues' analysis of the contrary to law exception insofar as they address the question of whether the award affects the exercise of an asserted management right. For the reasons discussed in his Concurring Opinion in *EPA*, 65 FLRA 113, Member Beck concludes that, where, as here, the Arbitrator is enforcing a contract provision that has been accepted by the Agency as a permissible limitation on its management's rights, it is inappropriate to assess whether the provision itself is an appropriate arrangement or whether it abrogates a § 7106(a) right. *Id.* at 120. The appropriate question is simply whether the remedy directed by the Arbitrator enforces the provision in a reasonable and reasonably foreseeable fashion. *Id.*; *see also FDIC*, 65 FLRA at 107. Member Beck concludes that the Arbitrator's award is a plausible (even though not the only possible) interpretation of the parties' agreement. Accordingly, Member Beck agrees that the Agency's contrary to law exception should be denied.

6. When an award affects a management right under § 7106(a)(2) of the Statute, the Authority may also examine whether the award enforces an applicable law. *EPA*, 65 FLRA at 115 n.7.

that it would apply an abrogation standard, the Authority rejected continued application of an excessive-interference standard. *Id.* at 118.

It is not disputed that the award affects management's right to assign work. Consequently, we examine whether the Arbitrator enforced a contract provision negotiated under § 7106(b). The Arbitrator concluded that Section 8 was an enforceable appropriate arrangement under § 7106(b)(3). The Agency does not dispute that Section 8 is an arrangement, but argues that the Arbitrator's enforcement of Section 8 excessively interferes with the right to assign work. However, as stated above, we no longer apply an excessive-interference standard in determining whether an arbitrator has enforced a contract provision negotiated under § 7106(b)(3); rather, we apply an abrogation standard. *Id.*

The Authority has previously described an award that abrogates the exercise of a management right as an award that "precludes an agency from exercising" the right. *U.S. Dep't of the Army, Army Transp. Ctr., Fort Eustis, Va.,* 38 FLRA 186, 190 (1990) (*Ft. Eustis*) (quoting *Dep't of the Treasury, U.S. Customs Serv.,* 37 FLRA 309, 314 (1990)). In *Ft. Eustis*, the Authority concluded that the arbitrator's enforcement of the contract provision did not abrogate the exercise of a management right because, as interpreted by the arbitrator, the provision restricted management's right in only two situations and did not otherwise affect that right. *Id.* Here, the Arbitrator specifically found, and the Agency does not dispute, that Section 8 in no way precludes management from assigning an employee to work. Award at 14. Moreover, as interpreted by the Arbitrator, Section 8 restricts management's right to cancel overtime only in limited situations, specifically when management cancels with less than seven days' notice and for reasons other than those specified in Section 8. Consequently, the Agency fails to demonstrate that Section 8, as interpreted and applied by the Arbitrator, abrogates the exercise of the right to assign work. *See Ft. Eustis,* 38 FLRA at 190.

For the foregoing reasons, we conclude that the Arbitrator enforced a contract provision negotiated under § 7106(b)(3) of the Statute. Accordingly, the Agency fails to establish that the award is contrary to § 7106(a)(2)(B), and we deny this exception.

VI. Decision

The Agency's exceptions pertaining to § 7106(a)(2)(A) and (D) and § 7101 of the Statute are dismissed, and the remaining exceptions are denied.

65 FLRA No. 43

UNITED STATES
DEPARTMENT OF HEALTH
AND HUMAN SERVICES
OFFICE OF MEDICARE
HEARINGS AND APPEALS
(Agency)

and

NATIONAL TREASURY
EMPLOYEES UNION
CHAPTER 229
(Union)

0-AR-4137

DECISION

October 29, 2010

Before the Authority: Carol Waller Pope, Chairman, and Thomas M. Beck and Ernest DuBester, Members

I. Statement of the Case

This matter is before the Authority on exceptions to an award of Arbitrator Marvin E. Johnson filed by the Agency under § 7122 of the Federal Service Labor-Management Relations Statute (the Statute) and part 2425 of the Authority's Regulations. The Union filed an opposition to the Agency's exceptions.

The Arbitrator found that the Agency violated the parties' agreement when it denied the grievant's request to work from home two days per week under the Agency's flexiplace program. For the reasons discussed below, we dismiss the exceptions regarding the Privacy Act and the Health Insurance Portability and Accountability Act (HIPAA), and we deny the remaining exceptions.

II. Background and Arbitrator's Awards

The grievant, an attorney, applied to participate in the flexiplace program, which is set forth in Article 36 of the parties' agreement, two days per week.[1] Award at 2. The Agency approved only one day per week, citing the Agency's "newness" and "statutory case production mandates[]" as reasons for denying the second day. *Id.* When this ruling was upheld during the Agency's administrative-review process, the Union filed a grievance, which was submitted to arbitration. *Id.* The issue, as framed by the Arbitrator, was: "Did the Agency's denial of one of the two flexiplace days requested by the [g]rievant violate the parties' [a]greement? If so, what is the appropriate remedy?"[2] *Id.* at 3.

The Arbitrator noted that it was uncontested that the grievant met the eligibility requirements for flexiplace, and he found that the parties' agreement provides for a maximum of two flexiplace days per week "under most circumstances." *Id.* at 8. He determined that, under the parties' agreement, flexiplace applications are evaluated based on the requesting employee's program eligibility and ability to perform assigned duties at an alternative work station. The Arbitrator interpreted Article 36 both as containing a rebuttable presumption in favor of approving two days per week and as permitting the Agency to approve fewer than two days for "work-related reasons." *Id.* The Arbitrator found unpersuasive the Agency's argument that the Agency was too recently created to provide specific empirical "work-related reasons" in support of its denial of the grievant's second day of requested flexiplace. *Id.* at 8-9. The Arbitrator stated that the Agency's "lack of aggregate performance data . . . should not affect its decision" in relation to the grievant, who had a position description, work plan, and performance standards. *Id.* at 9.

The Arbitrator noted that the Agency had broad discretion under the parties' agreement to monitor and restrict participation in a flexiplace program if an employee's performance "impairs the Agency's mission or operations." *Id.* However, he found that, unless there is evidence that the grievant's "performance would suffer and/or impair the Agency's mission or office operations, her request should be granted." *Id.* The Arbitrator found that there was no evidence that the grievant's performance had been adversely affected in the four months since she began working one flexiplace day and no evidence that it would be adversely affected

---

1. The relevant portions of Article 36 are included in the appendix to this decision.

2. Although the Arbitrator did not state that he framed the issue, the issue presented in the Agency's post-hearing brief is different from the Arbitrator's. *See* Exceptions, Ex. 3 at 2. Accordingly, we assume that the issue was not stipulated.

by working two flexiplace days. *Id.* In view of the Agency's discretion and ability to monitor the grievant's performance, the Arbitrator also found that Article 36 did not conflict with management's rights under § 7106(a) of the Statute. *Id.* at 10. Accordingly, the Arbitrator concluded that the Agency violated Article 36 by failing to grant the grievant's request for two flexiplace days. *Id.*

III. Positions of the Parties

A. Agency's Exceptions

The Agency argues that the award is contrary to management's rights to assign work and determine internal security practices under § 7106 of the Statute. Both of the Agency's management-rights arguments are based on the assertion that Agency policy does not allow Medicare files, including paper and electronic copies of these files, to be transported to an employee's home. Exceptions at 5. With regard to the right to assign work, the Agency asserts that Authority precedent provides that the location at which work is performed is related to the right to assign work if the existence of a relationship between the job location and duties can be established. *Id.* at 6. According to the Agency, such a relationship exists in this case because employees do not have access to Medicare files while at home and, thus, cannot perform all of their assigned duties from home. *Id.* at 5-6. With regard to the right to determine internal security practices, the Agency argues that its policy of not allowing employees to take Medicare files home is part of its plan to safeguard its personnel, property, and operations, and the award – which would require the grievant to take such files home – would interfere with that policy. *Id.* at 6-8. In addition, the Agency argues that the award is based on an interpretation of Article 36 that would render Article 36 unenforceable.

The Agency also argues that the award is contrary to the Privacy Act because the Agency's published list of routine uses for Privacy-Act-protected information does not include transportation to and from employees' homes, and such use is contrary to the Privacy Act. *Id.* at 8-9. In addition, the Agency contends that the award is contrary to HIPAA because the notification that the Agency provides to its clients about how their Medicare files are used does not list transportation to employee homes. *Id.* at 10.

Further, the Agency alleges that the award is based on a nonfact because the Arbitrator based his award on evidence relating to matters that occurred after the Agency's decision to deny the grievant's flexiplace request. Specifically, the Agency argues that the grievant's performance on flexiplace is irrelevant to its decision to allow only one day of work from home. *Id.* at 11. The Agency also alleges that the Arbitrator exceeded his authority by considering this information. *Id.* According to the Agency, the Arbitrator avoided resolving the issue of whether the Agency's decision was improper by relying on information available only after the decision was made. *Id.* at 12.

B. Union's Opposition

In response to the Agency exception regarding the right to assign work, the Union argues that the Agency presented no evidence to support the claim that it has a policy against transporting Medicare files to employees' homes. Opp'n at 7. The Union also argues that the Agency's argument regarding the right to determine internal security practices should not be considered because it was not raised before the Arbitrator. *Id.* at 7-8. In the alternative, the Union argues that that the Agency presented no evidence to support its claim that the Agency's asserted internal security policy would restrict employees from working from home two days -- but not one day -- per week. *Id.* at 8. According to the Union, the award does not affect management rights but, if it does, then the award is not deficient because it enforces negotiable procedures. *Id.* at 10-11.

The Union argues that, under § 2429.5 of the Authority's Regulations, the Agency's exceptions related to the Privacy Act and HIPAA are barred because they were raised for the first time in exceptions. *Id.* at 4. Further, the Union maintains that the award is not based on nonfact because the Arbitrator properly considered evidence related to the grievant's performance on flexiplace. *Id.* at 11-12. The Union also maintains that the Agency has not established that the Arbitrator exceeded his authority because its exception does not fall into any of the categories recognized by the Authority. *Id.* at 12.

IV. Analysis and Conclusions

A. The award is not contrary to management's rights to assign work and to determine internal security procedures.

We review questions of law raised by exceptions to an arbitrator's award *de novo*. *See, e.g., NFFE, Local 1437,* 53 FLRA 1703, 1709 (1998). In applying a standard of *de novo* review, we determine whether the arbitrator's legal conclusions are consistent with the applicable standard of law. In making that determination, we defer to the arbitrator's underlying findings of fact. *See id.* at 1710.

The Authority has long held, and has recently reaffirmed, that in resolving whether an arbitrator's award is contrary to a management right under § 7106(a) of the Statute, we first examine whether the award affects the exercise of the right.[3] *See, e.g., U.S. Envtl. Prot. Agency,* 65 FLRA 113, 115 (2010) (Member Beck concurring) (*EPA*); *AFGE, Local 1441*, 61 FLRA 201, 205 (2005). If it does not, then we deny the exception. *See, e.g., Fed. Deposit Ins. Corp., Div. of Supervision & Consumer Prot., S.F. Region*, 64 FLRA 79, 81-82 (2009) (Chairman Pope dissenting in part on other grounds).

The Agency's management-rights exceptions are premised on the Agency's claim that it has a policy forbidding the removal of Medicare files from its offices. However, the Arbitrator made no finding about such a policy in his award, and the record contains no evidence regarding such a policy. As there is no evidence to establish the existence of this policy, and the Agency presented no other arguments related to management's rights on appeal, we find that the Agency has not established that the award affects the cited management rights as alleged. *See SSA, Chi. Region, Cleveland, Ohio Dist. Office, Univ. Circle Branch*, 56 FLRA 1084, 1088-89 (2001) (agency must support its claim that a given action constitutes the exercise of a right).

Accordingly, we deny the Agency's management-rights exceptions.

B. We dismiss the exceptions regarding the Privacy Act and HIPAA.

The Authority's Regulations that were in effect when the Agency filed its exceptions provided that "[t]he Authority will not consider . . . any issue, which was not presented in the proceedings before the . . . arbitrator." 5 C.F.R. § 2429.5.[4] The record indicates that arguments related to the Privacy Act and HIPAA were not raised before the Arbitrator. Further, there is no basis for finding that these arguments could not have been raised at that time. As the Agency could have, but did not, raise its Privacy Act and HIPAA arguments before the Arbitrator, the claims are not properly before the Authority. *See U.S. DOD, Def. Distrib. Depot, Anniston, Ala.*, 61 FLRA 108, 109 (2005) (Authority was barred from considering arguments raised for the first time on appeal). Accordingly, we dismiss the Agency's exceptions regarding the Privacy Act and HIPAA.

C. The award is not based on nonfact.

To establish that an award is based on a nonfact, the appealing party must show that a central fact underlying the award is clearly erroneous, but for which the arbitrator would have reached a different result. *See NFFE, Local 1984*, 56 FLRA 38, 41 (2000).

Although the Agency argues that the decision is based on a nonfact, it does not establish that evidence related to the grievant's performance on flexiplace was "clearly erroneous" or that the Arbitrator would have reached a different result if he had not considered the evidence. *See United Power Trades Org.*, 62 FLRA 493, 496 (2008) (nonfact exception denied where argument was "misplaced" and failed to establish elements of nonfact). Instead, the Agency challenges the Arbitrator's use of the evidence and, under Authority precedent, such challenges provide no basis for finding an award deficient. *NFFE, Local 1827,* 52 FLRA 1378, 1385 (1997). Accordingly, we deny this exception.

---

3. Member Beck agrees with the conclusion to deny the Agency's exceptions. He does not agree, however, with his colleagues' analysis that begins with the question whether the award affects the exercise of management's § 7106(a) rights. For the reasons discussed in his Concurring Opinion in *EPA*, 65 FLRA 113 (2010), Member Beck concludes that where, as here, the Arbitrator is enforcing a contract provision that has been accepted by the Agency as a permissible limitation on its management rights, it is inappropriate to assess whether the provision affects those rights. *Id.* at 120. The appropriate question is simply whether the remedy directed by the arbitrator enforces the provision in a reasonable and reasonably foreseeable fashion. *Id.* Member Beck concludes that the Arbitrator's award (directing the Agency to approve the grievant's request to work two telework days) is a reasonable implementation of the parties' agreement.

4. The Authority's Regulations concerning the review of arbitration awards, as well as certain related procedural Regulations, including 5 C.F.R. § 2429.5, were revised effective October 1, 2010. *See* 75 Fed. Reg. 42,283 (2010). As the Agency's exceptions in this case were filed before that date, we apply the prior Regulations.

D. The Arbitrator did not exceed his authority.

Arbitrators exceed their authority when they fail to resolve an issue submitted to arbitration, resolve an issue not submitted to arbitration, disregard specific limitations on their authority, or award relief to those not encompassed within the grievance. *See AFGE, Local 1617*, 51 FLRA 1645, 1647 (1996). In the absence of a stipulated issue, the arbitrator's formulation of the issue is accorded substantial deference. *AFGE, Local 933*, 58 FLRA 480, 482 (2003) (*AFGE*). In addition, in the absence of a stipulated issue, arbitrators do not exceed their authority when they resolve a matter relating to an issue they have formulated and their award is directly responsive to the formulated issue. *NFFE, Local Lodge 2276, IAMAW*, 61 FLRA 387, 389 (2005) (citing *AFGE, Local 1741*, 61 FLRA 118, 120 (2005)).

In this case, the parties did not stipulate to the issues before the Arbitrator, and, as such, we defer to the Arbitrator's formulation of the issue. *See AFGE*, 58 FLRA at 482. In resolving the issue that he framed, the Arbitrator found it necessary to determine whether the Agency relied on "work-related reasons" for denying the grievant's second requested flexiplace day, and, in resolving that issue, the Arbitrator found that the Agency had presented no evidence indicating that the grievant's performance would suffer or affect the Agency's mission or operations, or that it had done so. Award at 8-9. As the award is directly responsive to the formulated issue, the Agency has not demonstrated that the Arbitrator resolved an issue that was not properly submitted to arbitration. Accordingly, we find that the Agency has not demonstrated that the Arbitrator exceeded his authority, and we deny this exception.

V. Decision

The Agency's exceptions regarding the Privacy Act and HIPAA are dismissed, and the remaining exceptions are denied.

APPENDIX

Article 36: Flexiplace

. . . .

Section 2

A. All OS/AoA regional and Headquarters bargaining unit employees will have the option of applying for the flexiplace program, with the understanding that approval for participation requires meeting all program requirements . . . .

. . . .

Section 3

A. Employees who desire to work at an alternative duty station must complete a Statement of Interest to Participate in Flexible Workplace (Flexiplace) Program (Appendix 3). The employee must submit the form to his/her supervisor for consideration. The supervisor may recommend approval or disapproval, following which the form will be forwarded to the designated management official for final decision.

. . . .

Section 6

. . . .

B. For [regular and recurring] flexiplace, employees are approved to work a fixed number of days per week or per pay period.

1. Employees may be approved by supervisors for a maximum of two (2) days per week working at an alternate duty station under most circumstances.

2. If an employee requests to work at the alternate duty station two days per week, and s/he otherwise meets all eligibility requirements of the flexiplace program (including suitability and portability of her/his work to be performed at the alternate duty station), a rebuttable presumption in favor of approval of the two days will apply.

3. The [Agency] may approve less than an employee's requested two days per week of working at the alternate duty station for work-related reasons. If the supervisor reduces the number of days in this manner, the reason(s) for the reduction will be provided to the employee in writing.

Exceptions, Ex. 5.

65 FLRA No. 44

FEDERAL DEPOSIT
INSURANCE CORPORATION
(Agency)

and

NATIONAL TREASURY
EMPLOYEES UNION
CHAPTER 273
(Union)

0-AR-4184

DECISION

October 29, 2010

Before the Authority: Carol Waller Pope, Chairman, and Thomas M. Beck and Ernest DuBester, Members

I. Statement of the Case

This matter is before the Authority on exceptions to an award of Arbitrator Edna E. J. Francis filed by the Agency under § 7122(a) of the Federal Service Labor-Management Relations Statute (the Statute) and part 2425 of the Authority's Regulations. The Union filed an opposition to the Agency's exceptions.

The Arbitrator found that the Agency failed to fairly and equitably process the grievant's nomination for a Corporate Success Award (CSA). As a remedy, the Arbitrator ordered the Agency to award the grievant a CSA, with appropriate backpay and interest.

For the reasons that follow, we deny the Agency's exceptions.

II. Background and Arbitrator's Award

A CSA is an annual award that provides Agency employees recognized as "top contributors" with a three percent increase in basic pay. Award at 8; Opp'n, Attach. 3, "Compensation Agreement Between FDIC and NTEU for the Years 2003-2005" (Compensation Agreement)). The percentage of "top contributors" recognized in 2004 for their 2003 contributions, as set by the Chairman of the Agency under the Compensation Agreement, constitutes "33 1/3 percent of eligible bargaining unit employees." *Id.* at 15-16.

The Agency's CSA procedures for identifying top contributors as CSA recipients are set forth in the Agency's "Procedures for Processing [CSAs]" Memorandum (the Memorandum) and "FDIC Directive System Circular 2420.1," Chapter 11, § 5 (Circular 2420.1). *See id.* at 10-13; Opp'n, Attach. 5, Circular 2420.1; Opp'n, Attach. 6, the Memorandum. These procedures require supervisors to numerically rank all nominated employees under their command and to submit CSA ranked nominations to the Assistant Regional Director (ARD) for their territory. Award at 13. The ARD then consolidates and prepares those forms for evaluation by a first-level review panel, consisting of ARDs and the Deputy Regional Director (DRD) - Compliance. *Id.* The first-level review panel evaluates each CSA recommendation, prioritizes the top one-third by assigning a numerical ranking to the nominees, and submits those rankings to a second-level review panel consisting of DRDs and Area Directors (DRD Panel). *Id.* The DRD Panel evaluates and/or re-ranks each CSA nominee and submits the results to the Regional Director (RD) for approval. *Id.* The RD reviews the recommendations and submits the results to the Division Director. *Id.*

Circular 2420.1 is incorporated by reference in a Memorandum of Understanding between the parties (MOU). *Id.* at 9. The Compensation Agreement, the Memorandum, Circular 2420.1, and the MOU all require that CSAs be processed and distributed in a fair and equitable manner.[1]

When the grievant was nominated to receive a CSA, but was not selected, he filed a grievance. The grievance was not resolved and was submitted to arbitration. The Arbitrator framed the issues as follows: "Did the Agency violate Circular 2420.1 or the MOU when it failed to award [the grievant] a [CSA] in 2004? If so, what is the appropriate remedy?" *Id.* at 45.

The Arbitrator found that the process for considering the grievant's CSA nomination "was not fair and equitable" and thus violated the MOU and Circular 2420.1. *Id.* at 48. According to the Arbitrator, up to the point where the grievant's nomination was submitted to the DRD Panel, the

1. The relevant provisions of the Compensation Agreement, the Memorandum, Circular 2420.1, and the MOU are set forth in the appendix to this decision.

grievant ranked 64th on a list of 113 nominees who were in the top 33 1/3 percent of employees. *Id.* at 52. At the DRD phase of the process, the Arbitrator found irregularities which led him to conclude that "the DRD Panel did not, in any meaningful sense, re-rank the nominees." *Id.* Among the irregularities that she found, were the removal of the grievant's nomination from consideration, as well as that of eight other nominees. In this connection, the Arbitrator found that, although the DRD Panel was not required to keep the grievant on the list, it "should have been able to offer sound rationale for removing [the grievant] from consideration . . . ." *Id.* Having found that the "record lack[ed] such evidence[,]" the Arbitrator determined that this suggested that the DRD Panel "wanted to reach certain preconceived results." *Id.* Other irregularities found were the unexplained addition of one nominee, and, in the case of one CSA recipient, the consideration of contributions not corresponding to the 2003 work year for which the CSAs were being awarded. *Id.*

The Arbitrator thus concluded that the evidence established that, "except for the flawed and arbitrary process at the DRD Panel's level," the grievant's nomination would have remained among the top 33 1/3 percent of nominees and would have been forwarded to the RD for signature and ultimately submitted to the Director for approval. *Id.* at 56. Accordingly, the Arbitrator sustained the grievance and directed the Agency to award the grievant a CSA, effective 2004, for work performed in 2003, with backpay and interest.

III. Positions of the Parties

A. Agency's Exceptions

The Agency asserts that the Arbitrator's remedy is contrary to law because it affects management's rights to direct employees and to assign work under § 7106(a)(2)(A) and (B) of the Statute. Citing *United States Department of the Treasury, Bureau of Engraving and Printing, Washington, D.C.*, 53 FLRA 146 (1997) (*BEP*), the Agency first acknowledges that "Prong [I of the *BEP* framework] is not at issue" in this case because the "[a]ward provides a remedy for a purported violation of the parties' MOU and Circular [2420.1.]" Exceptions at 11 n.10. However, the Agency contends that the remedy does not "satisfy Prong [II]" of the *BEP* framework because it does not reflect a reconstruction of what the Agency would have done if it had not violated the contractual CSA nomination process. *Id.* at 11. The Agency asserts that the Arbitrator did not find that the grievant would have been recommended for a CSA by the RD. The Agency contends that the Arbitrator did not compare the grievant's contributions to those of other nominees and that, without making the requisite finding that the grievant should have received a CSA, the Arbitrator substituted her judgment for that of the Agency. The Agency requests that the Authority modify the remedy portion of the award to require the Agency to reconsider the grievant for a CSA. *Id.* at 16.

The Agency also argues that a remand is warranted because the Arbitrator exceeded her authority by substituting her judgment for that of the Agency when she granted the grievant a CSA without making the necessary findings under the CSA nomination process. *Id.* Additionally, the Agency asserts that the remedy fails to draw its essence from the "express language" of the Compensation Agreement and should be set aside because it requires the Agency to give the grievant a CSA "despite the absence of any findings as to how the [g]rievant's contribution compared with any of his co-workers or with any other CSA nominee." *Id.* at 19.

B. Union's Opposition

The Union argues that the Arbitrator did not exceed her authority and that she correctly reconstructed what the Agency would have done if the Agency had not violated the CSA nomination process. The Union also contends that the award does not fail to draw its essence from the Compensation Agreement because the Arbitrator found that, except for the flawed and arbitrary process at the DRD Panel's level, the grievant's nomination would have "remained among the top 33 1/3 percent of nominees[.]" Opp'n at 13 (quoting Award at 56). In addition, the Union asserts that the remedy is consistent with the parties' collective bargaining agreement (CBA), which specifically grants the Arbitrator "the authority to make an aggrieved employee whole to the extent such remedy is not limited by law." *Id.* (citing Article 48, Section 4).[2] The Union asserts that, if the Authority

---

2. Article 48, Section 4.B provides, in pertinent part:

> The arbitrator shall have no power to add to, subtract from, or modify the terms of this Agreement. The award will be limited to the issues presented at arbitration. The arbitrator's decision will be final and binding and the arbitrator will have the authority to make an

finds that the remedy is deficient, the award should be remanded to the Arbitrator for clarification.

IV. Analysis and Conclusions

A. The award is not contrary to law.

The Authority reviews questions of law raised by exceptions to an arbitrator's award *de novo*. *See NTEU, Chapter 24*, 50 FLRA 330, 332 (1995) (citing *U.S. Customs Serv. v. FLRA*, 43 F.3d 682, 686-87 (D.C. Cir. 1994)). In applying a standard of *de novo* review, the Authority determines whether the arbitrator's legal conclusions are consistent with the applicable standard of law. *See NFFE, Local 1437*, 53 FLRA 1703, 1710 (1998). In making that determination, the Authority defers to the arbitrator's underlying factual findings. *Id.*

The Authority recently revised the analysis that it will apply when reviewing management-rights exceptions to arbitration awards. *See EPA*, 65 FLRA 113, 115 (2010) (Member Beck concurring); *FDIC, Div. of Supervision & Consumer Prot., S.F. Region*, 65 FLRA 102, 106-07 (2010) (Chairman Pope concurring) (*FDIC, S.F. Region*). Under the revised analysis, the Authority will first assess whether the award affects the exercise of the asserted management right. *EPA*, 65 FLRA at 115. If so, then the Authority examines whether the award provides a remedy for a violation of either an applicable law, within the meaning of § 7106(a)(2) of the Statute, or a contract provision that was negotiated pursuant to § 7106(b) of the Statute. *Id.* In setting forth its revised analysis, the Authority specifically rejected the continued application of the reconstruction standard set forth in *BEP*. *FDIC, S.F. Region*, 65 FLRA at 106-107.

Applying this analysis, we reject the Agency's exception that the award's remedy is contrary to law. This exception is based entirely on the assertion that the remedy does not reflect a reconstruction of what the Agency would have done if it had not violated the agreed-upon CSA nomination process. As discussed above, such reconstruction is not the standard to be applied to the remedy directed by an arbitrator. Moreover, the Agency concedes that the award enforces a properly negotiated contract provision. *See* Exceptions at 11 n.10. Accordingly, we conclude that the award does not impermissibly affect management rights by failing to reconstruct what the Agency would have done if it had not violated the contract, and we deny the Agency's contrary to law exception.[3] *See, e.g., FDIC, S.F. Region*, 65 FLRA at 107.

B. The award does not fail to draw its essence from the parties' agreement.

In reviewing an arbitrator's interpretation of a collective bargaining agreement, the Authority applies the deferential standard of review that federal courts use in reviewing arbitration awards in the private sector. *See* 5 U.S.C. § 7122(a)(2); *AFGE, Council 220*, 54 FLRA 156, 159 (1998). Under this standard, the Authority will find that an arbitration award is deficient as failing to draw its essence from the collective bargaining agreement when the appealing party establishes that the award: (1) cannot in any rational way be derived from the agreement; (2) is so unfounded in reason and fact and so unconnected with the wording and purposes of the collective bargaining agreement as to manifest an infidelity to the obligation of the arbitrator; (3) does not represent a plausible interpretation of the agreement; or (4) evidences a manifest disregard of the agreement. *See U.S. Dep't of Labor (OSHA)*, 34 FLRA 573, 575 (1990). The Authority and the courts defer to arbitrators in this context "because it is the arbitrator's construction of the agreement for which the parties have bargained." *Id.* at 576.

The Agency asserts that the award fails to draw its essence from the Compensation Agreement because it requires the Agency to grant a CSA to the grievant without a finding that the grievant would have remained in the top one-third of contributors once he was compared with other nominees. Exceptions at 18.

Contrary to the Agency's assertion, the Arbitrator specifically found that, absent the Agency's violation of Circular 2420.1 and the MOU, the grievant's nomination "would have remained among the top 33-1/3 percent of nominees[.]" Award at 56. The Arbitrator further found that, "as a matter of course," the grievant's nomination, like those of others "listed among the top 33 1/3 percent," would have been submitted to the RD for signature and to the Director for approval and that the grievant would

---

aggrieved employee whole to the extent such remedy is not limited by law.

Opp'n, Attach. 2.

3. For the reasons set forth in her concurring opinion in *FDIC, S.F. Region*, 65 FLRA at 112, Chairman Pope agrees that the award is not deficient because the remedy is reasonably related to the negotiated provision and the harm being remedied.

have received a CSA. *Id.* As such, the Agency has not demonstrated that the award is irrational, implausible, unfounded, or evidences a manifest disregard of the Compensation Agreement. *See, e.g., FDIC, S.F. Region,* 65 FLRA at 108 (agency failed to show that award directing agency to award grievant a CSA was deficient on essence ground); *FDIC,* 62 FLRA 356, 359 (2008) (agency failed to show award finding agency failed to process grievant's CSA nomination form properly deficient on essence ground). Accordingly, we find that the Agency has failed to show that the award is deficient on essence grounds.

C. The award does not exceed the Arbitrator's authority.

Arbitrators exceed their authority when they fail to resolve an issue submitted to arbitration, resolve an issue not submitted to arbitration, disregard specific limitations on their authority, or award relief to persons who are not encompassed within the grievance. *See AFGE, Local 1617*, 51 FLRA 1645, 1647 (1996). When the parties fail to stipulate the issues, the arbitrator may formulate them on the basis of the subject matter of the grievance. *See U.S. Dep't of Def., Educ. Activity, Arlington, Va.*, 56 FLRA 887, 891 (2000) (citations omitted).

The Agency claims that the Arbitrator exceeded her authority by directing the Agency to award a CSA to the grievant. As stated above, the issue framed by the Arbitrator was whether the Agency violated Circular 2420.1 or the MOU when it failed to award the grievant a CSA in 2004, and if so, "what is the appropriate remedy?" Award at 45. The Arbitrator found a violation of Circular 2420.1 and the MOU and concluded that, had it not been for the violation, the grievant's nomination would have been submitted to the RD and the grievant would have received a CSA. As such, the Arbitrator's remedy directing the Agency to grant the grievant a CSA is responsive to the issue before her and is based on her evaluation of the evidence. Consequently, the Agency has not demonstrated that the Arbitrator exceeded her authority by ordering a CSA as a remedy.

Further, with respect to the Agency's claim that the Arbitrator exceeded her authority by ordering a remedy that fails to draw its essence from the Compensation Agreement, such claim does not provide a basis for finding the award deficient. When the Authority denies an exception claiming that an award fails to draw its essence from an agreement, and the appealing party essentially reiterates its essence arguments in contending that the arbitrator exceeded his or her authority, the Authority denies the exceeded-authority exception consistent with the denial of the essence exception. *See, e.g., NTEU*, 62 FLRA 45, 48 (2007) (citing *U.S. Dep't of Educ., Wash., D.C.*, 61 FLRA 307, 311 (2005) (Chairman Cabaniss concurring as to other matters); *U.S. Dep't of the Treasury, IRS., Austin, Tex.*, 60 FLRA 360, 362 (2004)). Consistent with the above conclusion that the award does not fail to draw its essence from Circular 2420.1 and the MOU, we find that the Agency has not demonstrated that the Arbitrator exceeded her authority and deny this exception.

V. Decision

The Agency's exceptions are denied.

APPENDIX

Compensation Agreement Between FDIC and NTEU for the Years 2003-2005

II. ANNUAL PAY

. . . .

C. Annual Pay Adjustment

Year 2003

Effective 2003, the Employer will provide an increase in basic pay of 3.2 percent for all employees who received a rating of "meets expectations" during the prior year's rating period. In addition, 2003 shall be a transition year for the Corporate Success Award, which is described below. . . .

Years 2004 and 2005

. . . .

A Corporate Success Award (CSA) will be established which provides that an additional 3.0 percent increase be made in basic pay for those employees recognized as top contributors. The Chairman has sole discretion to set the percentage of bargaining unit employees who will be recognized as top contributors under the CSA program. However, the percentage of bargaining unit employees to receive the CSA shall be no

> less than 33 1/3 percent. These awards shall be made on an annual basis.
>
> . . . .

Award at 8; Opp'n, Attach. 3 at 2.

Memorandum: Procedures for Processing Corporate Success Awards (November 17, 2003)

> The Regional Office CSA Nomination Procedure is set forth as follows:
>
> 1. The supervisor prepares written CSA nominations for eligible employees.
>
> 2. The supervisor prioritizes and assigns a numerical ranking for all nominated employees within their span on control.
>
> 3. The supervisor submits the CSA nomination forms with numerical rankings to the Regional Office Assistant Regional Director, Administration (RO ARD-Admin).
>
> . . . .
>
> 4. The RO ARD-Admin consolidates and prepares the CSA nomination forms for evaluation by a first-level review panel consisting of the Assistant Regional Directors and the Deputy Regional Director – Compliance.
>
> 5. The first-level review panel evaluates each CSA recommendation and prioritizes the top one-third by assigning a numerical ranking.
>
> 6. The first-level review panel forwards their numerically ranked CSA recommendations to the second-level review panel consisting of the Deputy Regional Directors and Area Directors.
>
> 7. The second-level review panel evaluates and/or re-ranks each CSA recommendations and submits to the Regional Director for approval.
>
> 8. The Regional Director reviews the CSA recommendations, signs the appropriate justification forms, and submits the final Regional CSA recommendations to the Division Director.
>
> . . . .

Award at 13.

FDIC DIRECTIVE SYSTEM Circular 2420.1 (July 21, 2003)

Chapter 11
Corporate Success Awards

> . . . .
>
> 11-2. Eligibility
>
> All non-executive employees who have current performance ratings of record from the FDIC of "Meets Expectations" are eligible.
>
> . . . .
>
> 11-4. Criteria
>
> The criteria below are intended to be achievable by any eligible employee in any position. Nominations for the award effective in 2004 must be based on contributions made between January 1, 2003 and December 31, 2003. . . .
>
> Nominations will be evaluated based on one or more of the following criteria. These are the only criteria permitted under the Corporate Success Award Program [(CSA)]. Nominations will provide specific statements of the contributions by the employee that meet the identified criteria. Meeting one or more of these criteria does not entitle employees to be nominated to receive the CSA.
>
> A. Business Results: Consistently displays a high level of initiative, creativity, and innovation to produce results that reflect important contributions to the Corporation and/or its organizational components.
>
> B. Competency: Demonstrates an exceptional degree of competency within his/her position, and is frequently relied upon by others for advice, assistance, and/or judgment that reflect important contributions to the Corporation and/or its organizational components.
>
> C. Working Relationships: Builds extremely productive working relationships with co-workers, other Divisions/Offices, or other public or private sector agencies based on mutual respect that reflect important contributions to the Corporation and/or its organizational components.

> D. Learning and Development: Takes an active part in developing personal skills and competencies and applies newly acquired skills and competencies that reflect important contributions to the Corporation and/or its organizational components.
>
> 11-5. Procedures
>
> . . . .
>
> B. Supervisors shall nominate their top contributors by preparing the form *FDIC Form 2420/21, Corporate Success Award Nomination.* Forms must be submitted to the designated reviewing official within 15 calendar days after the end of the consideration cycle. Employees may provide input to the appropriate supervisors for other employees to be considered for a CSA.
>
> C. Reviewing Officials, as designated in the Division/Office delegation of authority, will ensure the consistent application of CSA criteria and the fair and equitable treatment of employees. The reviewing official shall sign the nomination form and forward it to the Division/Office Director within 30 calendar days after the end of the consideration cycle.
>
> D. Each Division/Office Director, or his/her designee, will serve as the approving official for all CSA within their Division or Office. Directors are responsible for ensuring that the percentage of bargaining unit and non-bargaining unit employees recognized under the CSA program equals the percentage identified by the Chairman. The Director, or designee, will sign the nomination forms and forward them to the AO for coordination with the DoA, HRB.
>
> . . . .
>
> F. The Chairman has sole discretion to set the percentage of bargaining unit and non-bargaining employees who will be recognized as top contributors under the CSA program . . . . However, the percentage of bargaining unit employees to receive the CSA will be no less than 33 1/3 percent.

Opp'n, Attach. 5.

Memorandum of Understanding Between FDIC & NTEU (March 13, 2003)

> 1. CSAs will be distributed to employees in a fair and equitable manner, and in accordance with the terms of this MOU and FDIC Circular 2420.1.

Award at 9; Opp'n, Attach. 4.

65 FLRA No. 45

INTERNATIONAL FEDERATION
OF PROFESSIONAL AND
TECHNICAL ENGINEERS
LOCAL 77
PROFESSIONAL AND SCIENTISTS
ORGANIZATION
(Union)

and

UNITED STATES
DEPARTMENT OF THE NAVY
FLEET READINESS CENTER SOUTHWEST
(Agency)

0-AR-4613

DECISION

October 29, 2010

Before the Authority: Carol Waller Pope, Chairman, and Thomas M. Beck and Ernest DuBester, Members

I. Statement of the Case

This matter is before the Authority on exceptions to an award of Arbitrator Kenneth A. Perea filed by the Union under § 7122(a) of the Federal Service Labor-Management Relations Statute (the Statute) and part 2425 of the Authority's Regulations. The Agency filed an opposition to the Union's exceptions.[1]

The Arbitrator found that the Agency did not violate the parties' agreement when it required employees to use annual leave or leave without pay during a holiday shutdown. For the following reasons, we dismiss the Union's exceptions in part and deny them in part.

II. Background and Arbitrator's Award

The Agency proposed a temporary shutdown of its entire facility during the winter holidays, allegedly to reduce costs and production inefficiencies. Award at 2-3. The Agency assembled a team of various representatives to deliberate and make a recommendation regarding the proposal, but did not include the Union's president. *Id.* Shortly thereafter, the Agency ordered the shutdown, requiring employees to take annual leave or leave without pay during this period. *Id.* at 3-4.

The Union filed a grievance alleging that the Agency violated the parties' agreement by: (1) failing to demonstrate the necessity of the shutdown for productivity- improvement reasons; (2) denying the Union an opportunity to negotiate implementation of the shutdown; and (3) treating bargaining-unit members inequitably and unfairly by directing the shutdown. *Id.* at 4. The grievance was unresolved and submitted to arbitration. *Id.* at 5.

In his award, the Arbitrator framed the issues as:

> (1) Whether [the] Agency's action ordering [the facility] to cease operations and therefore require all members of the bargaining unit represented by the Union to utilize annual leave or take leave-without-pay . . . [was] in violation of Article 19 of the Agreement; and (2) If the answer to Issue No. 1 above is in the affirmative, what shall be the appropriate remedy?

Id. at 2.

As an initial matter, the Arbitrator found that the Union's parent organization participated in pre-shutdown discussions regarding the proposed shutdown. *Id.* at 3. In addition, he determined that Article 19, Section 5 of the parties' agreement provides that the Agency retains the right to shut down "the facility" for the "expressed and limited reasons[]" in that provision, including "productivity improvement," but does not permit the Agency to shut down only a *portion* of the facility.[2] *Id.* at 11.

1. In addition, the parties filed several supplemental submissions, which are discussed further below.

2. Article 19, Section 5 of the parties' agreement provides, in pertinent part:

> The [Agency] retains the right to order the facility to shut down for reasons such as emergencies, fiscal crises or productivity improvement, and to require employees to use annual leave during these shutdown periods . . . . Employees with inadequate annual leave to cover a shutdown period may elect to take leave-without-pay or to be detailed to a work assignment defined by the [Agency], if possible. The [Union] will be given the opportunity to negotiate the implementation of the shutdown.

Award at 6.

Therefore, he found that determining whether the shutdown was justified "must be examined on a facility-wide basis[.]" *Id.* at 11-12. Crediting testimony indicating that "61% percent of the Agency's workforce was absent during the . . . holidays before the Agency commenced implementing holiday shutdowns in 2005[,]" the Arbitrator found that "[i]t cannot be doubted that when such a large percentage of the workforce is absent from the facility during [the winter holidays], production is reduced significantly." *Id.* at 11. The Arbitrator acknowledged that individual bargaining-unit employees may not be less productive during that time, but determined that "total producti[vity] of the facility would be impacted were it to remain open during [the] holiday period." *Id.* Consequently, he found that "the facility shutdown . . . was necessary in the interest of 'productivity improvement'" because "[p]roductivity measured on an annual basis is . . . improved when the facility remains closed during the less productive holiday period[.]" *Id.* at 11-12. Thus, he found that the Agency did not violate the agreement by conducting the shutdown, and he denied the grievance. *Id.* at 12.

III. Positions of the Parties

A. Union's Exceptions

The Union claims that the Arbitrator should have found that the Agency committed an unfair labor practice (ULP) and violated Article 19, Section 5 of the agreement "[b]ased on the Agency's failure to bargain in good faith with the Union regarding the implementation of the 'shutdown[.]'" Exceptions at 4. The Union further claims that the Arbitrator's finding that the Agency could shut down the facility only for the "expressed and limited reasons" in the agreement would violate management's rights under § 7016(a) of the Statute to direct its mission and budget. *Id.* at 5.

In addition, the Union contends that the award is based on a nonfact because the Arbitrator erroneously found that the Union's parent organization participated in negotiations regarding the shutdown. *Id.* at 2-4. In this connection, the Union claims that the participating union was not its parent organization, and that the Arbitrator based his finding on "blatant and intentional misrepresentation[s]" made by the Agency in its post-hearing brief. *Id.* at 3-4.

The Union further maintains that the award is contrary to the Authority's decision in *United States Department of the Navy, Mare Island Naval Shipyard, Vallejo, California*, 49 FLRA 802, 810 (1994) (*Mare Island*). According to the Union, *Mare Island* established the principle that "a negotiated provision allowing an [a]gency to compel employees to use leave, or take leave without pay, cannot be abused and used wantonly." Exceptions at 3.

Next, the Union asserts that the award fails to draw its essence from the parties' agreement in several respects. The Union maintains that, in interpreting Article 19, Section 5, the Arbitrator erred by construing the term "the facility" as "the entire facility[.]" *Id.* at 6-7, 9. In this connection, the Union claims that this interpretation is inconsistent with testimony indicating that the parties intended the provision to protect only bargaining-unit members, rather than the entire facility, from arbitrary shutdowns. *Id.* at 5-6, 9. With respect the Arbitrator's findings under Article 19, Section 5 regarding "productivity improvement[,]" the Union argues that the Arbitrator erred by: (1) defining productivity only in terms of employee attendance; and (2) relying on testimony regarding decreased employee attendance during the winter holidays because that testimony concerned the attendance rate from a previous year, rather than the year at issue. *Id.* at 8, 10. In addition, according to the Union, there is "no evidence in the record that productivity is to be measured on an annual basis[,]" or "that total annual productivity of the facility would increase by shutting the facility down for a certain amount of time." *Id.* at 11. The Union asserts that because the agreement does not define "productivity" and "productivity improvement," those terms must be interpreted by considering their "common definition" or the parties' intent. *Id.* at 7, 10. In this regard, the Union cites testimony indicating that the parties intended the "productivity improvement" provision to apply only to "out of the ordinary and drastic" situations such as major overhauls. *Id.* at 5-8. Finally, the Union asserts that the award is "at odds" with Article 19, Section 2 of the agreement because it affords the Agency "unfettered control over Union members' leave."[3] *Id.* at 8-9, 11.

B. Agency's Opposition

The Agency asserts that the Union's exceptions should be dismissed because the Union failed to:

3. Article 19, Section 2 of the parties' agreement provides, in relevant part: "The primary purpose of annual leave is to provide an annual vacation period. The Employer will make an effort to approve an annual leave schedule that is consistent with the desires of employees and the dictates of workload and productivity." Exceptions, Attach. at 1.

(1) timely file its exceptions with the Authority; (2) serve the Agency until after the expiration of the filing period for exceptions; and (3) provide a certificate of service. Opp'n at 8-9. With respect to the Union's nonfact exception, the Agency contends that the Union has failed to demonstrate that a central fact underlying the award is clearly erroneous, but for which the Arbitrator would have reached a different result. *Id.* at 9. The Agency further argues that the Union has not shown that the award fails to draw its essence from the parties' agreement. *Id.* at 10-14.

IV. Preliminary Issues

A. We consider some, but not all, of the parties' supplemental submissions.

The Authority's Regulations do not provide for the filing of supplemental submissions. However, § 2429.26 of the Authority's Regulations provides that the Authority may, in its discretion, grant leave to file "other documents" as deemed appropriate. *See, e.g., Cong. Research Employees Ass'n, IFPTE, Local 75*, 59 FLRA 994, 999 (2004). The Authority generally will not consider submissions filed without requesting leave or permission. *See, e.g., Nat'l Ass'n of Indep. Labor, Local 6*, 63 FLRA 232, 232 n.1 (2009). However, the Authority may consider submissions filed without permission if those submissions address jurisdictional issues, such as the timeliness of exceptions. *See Bremerton Metal Trades Council*, 59 FLRA 583, 584 (2004) (*Bremerton Metal*) (timeliness of exceptions is jurisdictional); *AFGE, Council of Prison Locals, Local 171*, 52 FLRA 1484, 1489 n.7 (1997) (*Local 171*) (Authority considered jurisdictional arguments of supplemental submission filed without requesting permission).

On March 16, 2010, the Agency filed a supplemental submission including a declaration of Agency counsel in support of its opposition.[4] As this submission was filed within the time limit for filing the opposition, we consider this submission as part of the opposition.[5] *See Fed. Emps. Metal Trade Council*, 39 FLRA 3, 3 n.* (1991) (Authority considered addendum to opposition where it was filed within the time limit for filing the opposition).

On March 19, the Union filed a supplemental submission including: (1) a response to the Agency's claim in its opposition that the Union's exceptions were untimely; (2) a claim that the Union president personally delivered a copy of the Union's exceptions to an Agency representative on February 16 upon the Agency's request; and (3) an assertion that the Union had only two weeks to prepare its exceptions due to the shutdown, while the Agency had three months. *See* Union's Supplemental Submission (Mar. 19). Although the Union did not request leave to file the submission, the first issue addresses the timeliness of the exceptions, which, as stated above, is the type of issue that we consider even absent a party's request for permission to file a supplemental submission. *See Bremerton Metal*, 59 FLRA at 584; *Local 171*, 52 FLRA at 1489 n.7. Accordingly, we consider the March 19 submission to the extent that it addresses timeliness issues.[6] However, the Union's remaining assertions do not address that type of issue. As such, and as the Union did not request permission to file this submission, we do not consider these portions of the March 19 submission.

On April 30, the Authority's Office of Case Intake and Publication (CIP) issued an order directing the parties to cure procedural deficiencies in their respective filings. On May 14, the Union cured its deficiency, but also included documents in support of its exceptions that had not been filed with its original exceptions. As the time limit for filing exceptions had already expired, and the Union did not request leave to file these supplemental submissions, we do not consider them.

On May 27, the Agency filed a supplemental submission in response to the Union's May 14 submissions. However, the Agency did not request permission to file this submission, and the submission responds to arguments raised for the first time in submissions that we have not considered. Accordingly, we do not consider the May 27 submission. *See U.S. Dep't of the Army, Corps of Eng'rs, Portland Dist.*, 62 FLRA 97, 98 (2007) (*Corps of Eng'rs*) (submission was moot where it responded to arguments that were raised in a submission that was not considered by the Authority).

On June 17, CIP issued a Deficiency Order directing the Union to cure deficiencies in its filings. The Union timely cured the deficiencies. On July 1, the Agency requested leave to file a submission in response to the Deficiency Order. However, as the Order was not directed to the Agency, we do not

4. All dates in this section are from 2010.

5. The Agency's counsel's declaration is discussed *infra* Section IV.C.

6. The Union's argument regarding timeliness is considered *infra* Section IV.B.

consider the July 1 submission. *See U.S. Air Force, 82nd Training Wing, Sheppard Air Force Base, Wichita Falls, Tex.*, 61 FLRA 443, 443 n.1 (2006) (submission filed in response to order directed at opposing party was not considered by the Authority). Consequently, the Union's July 13 supplemental submission filed in response to the July 1 submission is rendered moot. *See Corps of Eng'rs*, 62 FLRA at 98. Further, as each of the parties' remaining supplemental submissions address arguments raised for the first time in supplemental submissions that are moot, we do not consider those submissions. *Id.*

B. The Union's exceptions were timely filed.

Section 7122(b) of the Statute provides, in pertinent part, that exceptions to an arbitrator's award must be filed "during the 30-day period beginning on the date the award is served on the party[.]" 5 U.S.C. § 7122(b). Under the Authority's Regulations that were in effect when the Union filed its exceptions, the first day of the thirty-day period is the date of service of the award. *See* 5 C.F.R. § 2425.1(b).[7] The Authority presumes, absent evidence to the contrary, that an award was served by mail on the date of the award. *See, e.g., Int'l Org. of Masters, Mates & Pilots*, 49 FLRA 1370, 1370-71 (1994) (*Masters, Mates & Pilots)*. If the last day of the thirty-day period falls on a weekend or federal holiday, then the due date for the exceptions is the next day that is not a weekend or federal holiday. 5 C.F.R. § 2429.21(a). In addition, if the award was served on the excepting party by mail, then the time period is extended an additional five days. 5 C.F.R. § 2429.22.

There is no evidence of the service date of the award other than the date of the award, which is December 11, 2009. Thus, the award is considered to have been served on December 11. *Masters, Mates & Pilots*, 49 FLRA at 1370. Counting thirty days beginning on December 11, the due date for filing exceptions was January 9, 2010. As January 9 was a Saturday, the due date for filing then became Monday, January 11. As the Authority presumes, absent evidence to the contrary, that an award was served by mail on the date of the award, the time period is extended for five days, until Saturday, January 16. *See id.* As January 16 was a Saturday, the due date for filing then became Monday, January 18, and as January 18 was a federal holiday, the due date was further extended until Tuesday, January 19. *See* 5 C.F.R. § 2429.21(a). The record shows, consistent with the Union's argument in its March 19 supplemental submission, that the Union's exceptions were postmarked on January 13. Accordingly, we find that the exceptions were timely filed.

C. The Union's exceptions are not procedurally deficient under § 2429.27(a) and (c) of the Authority's Regulations.

The Authority's Regulations provide that a party filing a document with the Authority must serve a copy on all counsel of record or other designated representatives of other parties, and must submit a statement of service to that effect. *See* 5 C.F.R. § 2429.27(a) and (c). Here, the Agency argues that the Union's exceptions should be dismissed because the Union did not serve the Agency with its exceptions until after the expiration of the filing period for exceptions and did not provide a certificate of service. Opp'n at 7-8. For support, the Agency cites the declaration of Agency counsel, in which he states that he received a copy of the Union's exceptions on February 16, 2010 without a certificate of service. *See id*; Agency Supplemental Submission (Mar. 16, 2010). However, the Union submitted a certificate of service showing service on the Agency on that date. *See* Union Cure of Deficiencies (July 1, 2010) at 2. Further, when timely filed exceptions have been served on the opposing party after the expiration of the filing period for exceptions, the Authority views such service to be procedurally sufficient unless the opposing party establishes that it was prejudiced by such service. *U.S. Dep't of Transp., FAA, Wash., D.C.*, 63 FLRA 492, 493 (2009) (citing *Office of Personnel Mgmt.*, 61 FLRA 358, 361 (2005) (then-Member Pope dissenting in part on unrelated grounds)). As the Agency does not claim that it was prejudiced by the Union's service, we deny the Agency's motion to dismiss the Union's exceptions.

D. Section § 2429.5 of the Authority's Regulations bars the Union's claims relating to Article 19, Section 2 of the parties' agreement and §§ 7106(a)(1) and 7116 of the Statute.

Under § 2429.5 of the Authority's Regulations, the Authority will not consider issues that could have been, but were not, presented in the proceedings before the arbitrator. *See, e.g., U.S. Dep't of the Air Force, Air Force Materiel Command, Robins Air Force Base, Ga.*, 59 FLRA 542, 544 (2003). There is no evidence that the Union argued below that:

7. The Authority's Regulations concerning the review of arbitration awards, as well as certain related procedural Regulations, were revised effective October 1, 2010. *See* 75 Fed. Reg. 42,283 (2010). As the exceptions in this case were filed before that date, we apply the prior Regulations.

(1) the Agency violated Article 19, Section 2 by directing the shutdown; (2) Article 19, Section 5's limits on the Agency's ability to direct a shutdown would violate management's rights under § 7106(a)(1) to direct its mission and budget; or (3) the Agency committed a ULP under § 7116 of the Statute. As the Union could have raised these issues before the Arbitrator, but did not, we dismiss these exceptions.

V. Analysis and Conclusions

A. The award is not based on a nonfact.

To establish that an award is based on a nonfact, the appealing party must show that a central fact underlying the award is clearly erroneous, but for which the arbitrator would have reached a different result. *See NFFE, Local 1984*, 56 FLRA 38, 41 (2000). However, the Authority will not find an award deficient on the basis of an arbitrator's determination of any factual matter that the parties disputed at arbitration. *See id.*

The Union's nonfact exception alleges that the Arbitrator erroneously found that the Union's parent organization participated in negotiations regarding the holiday shutdown. Exceptions at 2-4. Specifically, the Union claims that the participating union cited by the Arbitrator is not the Union's parent organization. *Id.* at 3-4. Although the Union asserts that the Arbitrator based his finding on alleged misrepresentations made in the Agency's post-hearing brief, the Union does not demonstrate that the Arbitrator clearly erred in making this finding. Accordingly, we deny the exception.

B. The award is not contrary to Authority precedent.

The Union contends that the award is contrary to the Authority's decision in *Mare Island*, 49 FLRA at 810. Exceptions contending that an award is contrary to Authority precedent are reviewed as contrary-to-law exceptions. *See, e.g., U.S. Dep't of the Treasury, IRS, Nat'l Distrib. Ctr., Bloomington, Ill.*, 64 FLRA 586, 592 (2010). As such, the Authority reviews the award *de novo*. In applying a *de novo* standard of review, the Authority assesses whether the arbitrator's legal conclusions are consistent with the applicable standard of law. *Id.*

The Union's reliance on *Mare Island* is misplaced. In *Mare Island*, the arbitrator found that the agency violated the agreement at issue in that case by failing to provide sufficient justification for its required use of annual leave during a temporary shutdown. The Authority denied the agency's essence exceptions to the arbitrator's interpretation of the agreement. *Mare Island*, 49 FLRA at 810. However, contrary to the Union's claim, the Authority did not hold, as a matter of law, that "a negotiated provision allowing an [a]gency to compel employees to use leave, or take leave without pay, cannot be abused and used wantonly." Exceptions at 3. As such, *Mare Island* does not provide a basis for setting aside, as contrary to law, the award at issue here, which involves a different arbitrator's interpretation of a different agreement. Accordingly, we deny the exception.

C. The award draws its essence from the parties' agreement.

In reviewing an arbitrator's interpretation of a collective bargaining agreement, the Authority applies the deferential standard that federal courts use in reviewing arbitration awards in the private sector. *See* 5 U.S.C. § 7122(a)(2); *AFGE, Council 220*, 54 FLRA 156, 159 (1998). Under this standard, the Authority will find that an arbitration award is deficient as failing to draw its essence from the collective bargaining agreement when the appealing party establishes that the award: (1) cannot in any rational way be derived from the agreement; (2) is so unfounded in reason and fact and so unconnected with the wording and purposes of the collective bargaining agreement as to manifest an infidelity to the obligation of the arbitrator; (3) does not represent a plausible interpretation of the agreement; or (4) evidences a manifest disregard of the agreement. *U.S. Dep't of Labor (OSHA)*, 34 FLRA 573, 575 (1990). The Authority and the courts defer to arbitrators in this context "because it is the arbitrator's construction of the agreement for which the parties have bargained." *Id.* at 576.

Article 19, Section 5 states, in pertinent part, that "[t]he [Agency] retains the right to order the facility to shut down for reasons such as . . . productivity improvement[.]" Award at 6. The Arbitrator found that "the facility" meant the *entire* facility, and that "the facility shutdown . . . was necessary in the interest of 'productivity improvement'" because "[p]roductivity measured on an annual basis is . . . improved when the facility remains closed during the less productive holiday period[.]" *Id.* at 11-12. The Union contends that these findings are inconsistent with testimony indicating that Article 19, Section 5 was intended to: (1) protect only bargaining-unit employees, rather than employees of the entire facility, from arbitrary shutdowns; and (2) apply only to "out of the ordinary and drastic" situations such as major overhauls. Exceptions at 6-9. However, the Union's reliance on this testimony does not provide a basis for finding that the Arbitrator's interpretation of Article 19, Section 5 is unfounded, implausible, and irrational or in manifest disregard of the parties' agreement. Accordingly, we deny this exception.

The Union also argues that the Arbitrator should have found that the Agency violated Article 19, Section 5 by "fail[ing] to bargain in good faith with the Union regarding the implementation of the 'shutdown[.]'" *Id.* at 4. This argument is premised on the Union's nonfact argument, specifically, the Union's claim that the union that participated in shutdown negotiations was not the Union's parent organization. As we have denied the nonfact exception, we also deny this exception. *See AFGE, Local 3937*, 64 FLRA 1113, 1115 (2010) (denying essence exception premised on party's previously rejected nonfact argument).

VI. Decision

The Union's exceptions are dismissed in part and denied in part.[8]

8. We note that the Union also asserts that the Arbitrator conducted an "improper hearing." Exceptions at 11. To the extent that the Union argues that it was denied a fair hearing, we deny the claim as a bare assertion. *See SSA, Balt., Md.*, 57 FLRA 690, 694 n.9 (2002) (denying unsupported fair hearing claim as a bare assertion).

65 FLRA No. 46

UNITED STATES
DEPARTMENT OF VETERANS AFFAIRS
VETERANS AFFAIRS MEDICAL CENTER
FAYETTEVILLE, NORTH CAROLINA
(Agency)

and

FAYETTVILLE VETERANS
ADMINISTRATION MEDICAL CENTER
BARGAINING UNIT EMPLOYEES
FAYETTVILLE, NORTH CAROLINA
(Petitioner)

and

AMERICAN FEDERATION
OF GOVERNMENT EMPLOYEES
LOCAL 1738, AFL-CIO
(Labor Organization)

WA-RP-10-0050

ORDER DENYING
APPLICATION FOR REVIEW

October 29, 2010

Before the Authority: Carol Waller Pope, Chairman, and Thomas M. Beck and Ernest DuBester, Members

I. Statement of the Case

This case is before the Authority on an application for review of the Regional Director's (RD's) Decision and Order (RD's Decision) filed by a group of bargaining unit employees at the United States Department of Veterans Affairs (VA), VA Medical Center, Fayetteville, North Carolina (Petitioner or employees) under § 2422.31 of the Authority's Regulations. The American Federation of Government Employees, Local 1738 (AFGE, Local 1738) filed an opposition to the application for review. The Petitioner filed a request for leave to file a supplemental submission responding to the opposition.

The RD dismissed the election petition as not properly before the Authority because it was not filed for any purpose set forth in the Authority's Regulations. To the contrary, the RD found that the petition concerned internal union matters over which the Authority does not have jurisdiction.

For the following reasons, we deny the application for review.

II. Background and RD's Decision

The group of employees who filed the petition work at the VA Medical Center, Fayetteville, North Carolina (Fayetteville VAMC). RD's Decision at 1. The employees are in a consolidated bargaining unit of nonprofessional employees at the VA. *Id.* The American Federation of Government Employees, AFL-CIO (AFGE) is the exclusive representative of the consolidated bargaining unit. *Id.* AFGE has designated AFGE, Local 1738, located in Salisbury, North Carolina, to represent bargaining unit employees located at the Fayetteville VAMC. *Id.*

The employees did not file their petition to change the bargaining unit's exclusive representative. Rather, the employees petitioned for an election to replace the local that the exclusive representative had designated to represent them with another local that the employees would like to establish. *Id.* at 2.

The RD dismissed the employees' petition, concluding that it was not properly before the Authority because it was not filed for any purpose set forth in §§ 2422.1 and 2422.2 of the Authority's Regulations.[1] *Id.* at 2-3. In addition, the RD concluded that the petition involves an internal union matter over which the Authority does not have jurisdiction. *Id.* at 3. According to the RD, the employees claim that they want to establish a new local because they are dissatisfied with the representation provided by AFGE, Local 1738. *Id.*

III. Positions of the Parties

A. Petitioner

The Petitioner does not challenge any of the RD's determinations. The Petitioner states that it "understand[s] the process and jurisdiction the Authority has in this case and [respects] the decision thus far." Application at 3. The Petitioner requests that the Authority "protect [employee] rights according to the Labor-Management Reporting and Disclosure Act (LMRDA) . . . and the [c]onstitution and [b]y-laws of [AFGE]." *Id.* Specifically, the

1. The text of §§ 2422.1 and 2422.2 is set forth in the attached appendix.

Petitioner claims that the exclusive representative, AFGE, established AFGE, Local 1738 to represent the employees at the Fayetteville VAMC without sufficiently considering the views of the affected employees. *Id.* at 2-3. Clarifying that they are not seeking to separate from AFGE, and noting their dissatisfaction with the services provided by AFGE, Local 1738, the employees state that they seek an election to establish a new local to represent them. *Id.* at 2.

B. AFGE, Local 1738

AFGE, Local 1738 opposes the application for review. AFGE, Local 1738 contends that the Petitioner has not asserted that review is warranted on any of the grounds set forth in § 2422.31(c) of the Authority's Regulations. Opp'n at 2. In addition, AFGE, Local 1738 argues that the RD correctly determined that the petition is not properly before the Authority under the Authority's Regulations. *Id.* Finally, AFGE, Local 1738 argues that the RD correctly determined that the petition concerns internal union matters over which the Authority does not have jurisdiction. *Id.* at 3-4.

IV. Preliminary Matters

This case involves two issues concerning supplemental submissions by the Petitioner. Section 2429.26 of the Authority's Regulations provides that the Authority may, in its discretion, grant leave to file supplemental submissions as deemed appropriate based on a showing of need. *See, e.g., AFGE, Local 2004*, 55 FLRA 6, 9 (1998).

First, along with its reply to an Authority order to cure certain deficiencies in its application, the Petitioner included additional information that was not originally included with its application. As the Petitioner failed to request permission to file this additional material as a supplemental submission under 5 C.F.R. § 2429.26, we do not consider the additional information. *See, e.g., U.S. Dep't of HHS, FDA*, 60 FLRA 250, 250 n.1 (2004).

Second, the Petitioner requests permission to respond to AFGE's opposition. The Petitioner's submission makes arguments that it raised or could have raised before the RD and in its application for review. As the Petitioner does not sufficiently explain why the Authority should consider arguments already raised in the application for review, or that could have been raised in the application, we do not consider this submission. *See, e.g., U.S. Dep't of the Air Force, Minot Air Force Base, N.D.*, 61 FLRA 366, 367 (2005) (citing *NTEU, Chapter 137*, 60 FLRA 483, 483 n.2 (2004)) (moving party needs to demonstrate why its supplemental submission should receive Authority review).

V. Analysis and Conclusions

Under § 2422.31(c) of the Authority's Regulations, the Authority may grant an application for review only when the application demonstrates that review is warranted on one or more of the following grounds: (1) the decision raises an issue for which there is an absence of precedent; (2) established law or policy warrants reconsideration; or (3) there is a genuine issue over whether the RD has: (i) failed to apply established law; (ii) committed a prejudicial procedural error; or (iii) committed a clear and prejudicial error concerning a substantial factual matter.

The Petitioner does not assert that review is warranted on any of the grounds set forth in § 2422.31(c) of the Authority's Regulations. Moreover, it is not otherwise apparent that the Petitioner intends to make any such claim. In its application, the Petitioner challenges neither the RD's decision to dismiss the petition as improperly before the Authority for failing to meet requirements under 5 C.F.R § 2422.1 and § 2422.2, nor her decision that the petition involves an internal union matter over which the Authority has no jurisdiction. *Id.* at 3. To the contrary, the Petitioner states that it "understand[s] the process and jurisdiction the Authority has in this case and [respects] the decision thus far." *Id.* As the Petitioner fails to assert any grounds for review set forth in § 2422.31(c), including any challenge to the RD's determinations, we conclude that review of the RD's decision is not warranted under the Authority's Regulations.[2]

VI. Order

The application for review is denied.

---

2. As noted above, the Petitioner requests that the Authority "protect [employee] rights according to the [LMRDA] . . . and the [c]onstitution and [b]y-laws of [AFGE]." Application at 3. A claim that a union's constitution was violated with respect to the LMRDA falls under the jurisdiction of the Assistant Secretary of Labor, Employment Standards Administration, Office of Labor-Management Standards (OLMS). *N.M. Army & Air Nat'l Guard*, 56 FLRA 145, 149 n.11 (2000).

APPENDIX

5 C.F.R. § 2422.1 provides:

§ 2422.1 Purposes of a petition.

A petition may be filed for the following purposes:

(a) *Elections or Eligibility for dues allotment.* To request:

(1)(i) An election to determine if employees in an appropriate unit wish to be represented for the purpose of collective bargaining by an exclusive representative, and/or

(ii) A determination of eligibility for dues allotment in an appropriate unit without an exclusive representative; or

(2) an election to determine if employees in a unit no longer wish to be represented for the purpose of collective bargaining by an exclusive representative.

(3) Petitions under this subsection must be accompanied by an appropriate showing of interest.

(b) *Clarification or Amendment.* To clarify, and/or amend:

(1) A recognition or certification then in effect; and/or

(2) Any other matter relating to representation.

(c) *Consolidation.* To consolidate two or more units, with or without an election, in an agency and for which a labor organization is the exclusive representative

5 C.F.R. § 2422.2 provides:

§ 2422.2 Standing to file a petition.

A representation petition may be filed by: an individual; a labor organization; two or more labor organizations acting as a joint-petitioner; an individual acting on behalf of any employee(s); an agency or activity; or a combination of the above: *Provided, however*, that

(a) Only a labor organization has standing to file a petition [seeking an election to determine if employees in an appropriate unit wish to be represented by an exclusive representative] pursuant to section 2422.1(a)(1);

(b) Only an individual has standing to file a petition [seeking an election to determine if employees in a unit no longer wish to be represented by an exclusive representative] pursuant to section 2422.1(a)(2); and

(c) Only an agency or a labor organization may file a petition [seeking to clarify and/or amend recognition of certification in effect and/or any other matter relating to representation] pursuant to section 2422.1(b) or (c).

65 FLRA No. 47

UNITED STATES
DEPARTMENT OF VETERANS AFFAIRS
VETERANS AFFAIRS REGIONAL COUNSEL
WINSTON-SALEM, NORTH CAROLINA
(Agency)

and

AMERICAN FEDERATION
OF GOVERNMENT EMPLOYEES
LOCAL 1738
(Union)

0-AR-4660

DECISION

October 29, 2010

Before the Authority: Carol Waller Pope, Chairman, and Thomas M. Beck and Ernest DuBester, Members[1]

I. Statement of the Case

This matter is before the Authority on exceptions to an award of Arbitrator Robert G. Williams filed by the Agency under § 7122(a) of the Federal Service Labor-Management Relations Statute (the Statute) and part 2425 of the Authority's Regulations. The Union filed an opposition to the Agency's exceptions.

The Arbitrator found that the Agency violated the parties' agreement when it improperly placed the grievant on a deficient performance improvement plan (PIP). He directed the Agency to expunge the PIP from the grievant's record, offer her an opportunity to attend a new training program, and provide her with a trainee position description (PD) and performance standards. For the following reasons, we deny the Agency's exceptions.

II. Background and Arbitrator's Award

The grievant was hired as a GS-9 Rating Veteran Service Representative (RVSR) and immediately began an eight-month training program. Award at 2-3. The Agency established "Training Benchmarks" to "provide clear markers for evaluation during a RVSR's formal training." *Id.* at 4. The grievant did not meet the "Training Benchmarks" at any point during the training program, but was nevertheless rated as "Fully Successful" at the end of that program. *Id.* at 11-13.

After starting work as a trained RVSR, the grievant failed to meet the performance standards for the position. *Id.* at 14-16. She received a warning of unacceptable performance and was placed on a PIP. *Id.* at 18. As a result, the Union filed a grievance that was unresolved and submitted to arbitration. *Id.* at 1-2. At arbitration, the Arbitrator framed the pertinent issue as: "was the [g]rievant properly placed on a valid [PIP] and, if not, what shall be the remedy?"[2] *Id.* at 2.

As an initial matter, the Arbitrator found that the grievant was hired as an "RVSR Trainee." *Id.* at 45. He also found that the grievant received a copy of the PD and performance standards applicable to trained RVSRs, but "apparently did not receive copies of [the] 'Training Benchmarks.'" *Id.* He determined that "[t]he Agency violated the [agreement] by failing to provide trainee [PDs] and standards that would lead to the development of trainees as qualified RVSRs." *Id.* at 49.

In addition, the Arbitrator found that the PIP was a "probationary period [that was] nothing more than a paid suspension" and a "disciplinary action as a prelude to an adverse action." *Id.* at 53. Further, he determined that the Agency's placement of the grievant on a PIP violated Article 26 of the parties' agreement in two respects.[3] First, he found that the PIP was deficient because it did not include "the causes of unacceptable performance and the remedial actions for correcting deficiencies." *Id.* at 54. Second, he determined that even if the PIP itself was not deficient, the Agency improperly placed the grievant on a PIP because "[t]he root of [her] inability to meet standards [was] found in the training, or lack of [a] training program." *Id.*

1. Member Beck's dissenting opinion is set forth at the end of this decision.

2. The Arbitrator also resolved an issue regarding whether the grievant was improperly denied promotion to the GS-10 level. Award at 2. As there are no exceptions regarding the Arbitrator's resolution of that issue, we do not address it further.

3. The pertinent provisions of Article 26 of the parties' agreement are set forth *infra*.

As remedies, the Arbitrator directed the Agency to expunge the PIP from the grievant's record and "provide the [g]rievant with an opportunity to attend an RVSR training program with a trainee [PD], performance standards and progress reviews that, if completed at the 'Fully Successful' level, will result in a trainee qualified to perform as a 'Fully Successful' RVSR." *Id.* at 57-58.

III. Positions of the Parties

A. Agency's Exceptions

The Agency argues that the award is based on nonfacts because the Arbitrator erred by finding that the Agency did not provide the grievant with a copy of the "Training Benchmarks" or rely on them during training. Exceptions at 1. In this connection, the Agency asserts that the grievant testified that she received the benchmarks, and that the record demonstrates that she initialed a copy of them. *Id.* at 26.

The Agency also argues that the Arbitrator's finding that the Agency violated the parties' agreement by failing to provide the grievant with a trainee PD and performance standards fails to draw its essence from Articles 9 and 26 of the parties' agreement and demonstrates that the Arbitrator exceeded his authority. *Id.* at 24-25, 27-28. In this regard, the Agency contends that Article 9 requires the Agency to provide RVSR PDs, but not trainee PDs.[4] Moreover, the Agency asserts that: (1) the grievant received a copy of the RVSR PD at the time of her assignment; and (2) even if Article 9 obligated the Agency to issue a trainee PD, the grievant never requested a copy of it as required by the provision. *Id.* at 28. With respect to Article 26, the Agency asserts that the grievant's appraisal period commenced when she entered the workforce as a fully trained RVSR, and that "[n]othing in the [parties' agreement] required the Agency to issue the [g]rievant her performance standards prior to the beginning of her appraisal period." *Id.* at 27.

The Agency further asserts that the award fails to draw its essence from Article 26 of the agreement insofar as the Arbitrator found that: (1) the PIP was deficient because it did not include "the causes of unacceptable performance and the remedial actions for correcting the deficiencies"; and (2) even if the PIP itself was not deficient, the Agency's placement of the grievant on a PIP was improper. *Id.* at 30-31, 34-36. In this connection, the Agency asserts that the grievant's PIP met the requirements set forth in Article 26 and that because the grievant failed to meet productivity performance standards from the beginning of her appraisal period, she was properly placed on a PIP. *Id.* at 31, 35-36.

Further, the Agency argues that the remedy -- directing the Agency to offer the grievant an opportunity to attend a new training program including a trainee PD and performance standards -- fails to draw its essence from the parties' agreement and demonstrates that the Arbitrator exceeded his authority. *Id.* at 25, 31-33. In this regard, the Agency contends that the remedy exceeds the relief specifically requested by the Union and is "not available under the [agreement] or any applicable regulations and/or policies." *Id.* at 31-33.

Finally, the Agency contends that the award is contrary to law. As an initial matter, the Agency asserts that arbitrators are bound by Merit Systems Protection Board (MSPB) precedent, that an agency "is entitled to use its managerial discretion in establishing the performance standards that measure an employee's performance[,]" and that the MSPB defers to an "agency's judgment concerning the use of performance deadlines and numerical measurements for a professional employee." Exceptions at 24. The Agency further contends that the award conflicts with MSPB precedent holding that agencies are not required to provide training during a PIP. *Id.* at 29. For support, the Agency cites *Daniel v. Department of Veterans Affairs*, 223 Fed. Appx. 986, 990 (Fed. Cir. 2007) (nonprecedential); *Thomas v. Department of Defense,* 95 M.S.P.R. 123 (2003), *aff'd* 117 Fed. Appx. 722 (Fed. Cir. 2004); *Goodwin v. Department of the Air Force*, 75 M.S.P.R. 204, 207 (1997); *Cornelius v. Nutt*, 472 U.S. 648 (1985); and *Siegelman v. Dep't of Hous. & Urban Dev.*, 14 M.S.P.R. 326 (1983). Finally, the Agency claims that the Arbitrator's finding that the PIP was "nothing more than a paid suspension" and a "disciplinary action as a prelude to an adverse action" is inconsistent with Title 5, Chapter 43 of the U.S. Code.[5] *Id.* at 30. In this regard, the Agency asserts that "performance actions taken under Chapter 43 are not adverse actions at all, but are considered performance based actions, as opposed to actions taken under Chapter 75." *Id.*[6]

4. The relevant wording of Article 9 of the parties' agreement is set forth *infra.*

5. Title 5, Chapter 43 of the U.S. Code is discussed further below.

6. The Agency also challenges the credibility of a portion of the grievant's testimony. Exceptions at 36. However, as

B. Union's Opposition

In response to the Agency's nonfact exception, the Union asserts that the Arbitrator's finding concerning whether the grievant received a copy of the "Training Benchmarks" is not a central fact underlying the award. Opp'n. at 10. Next, the Union argues that the Arbitrator did not exceed his authority because the award is "very narrow and limited" to the grievant and the Arbitrator has "broad latitude to determine how to implement a meaningful remedy." *Id.* at 10-11. Finally, the Union argues that the Agency's essence exceptions are "essentially a rehash of the arguments it made to the [A]rbitrator and that were properly rejected." *Id.* at 3-4.

IV. Analysis and Conclusions

A. The award is not based on nonfacts.

To establish that an award is based on a nonfact, the appealing party must show that a central fact underlying the award is clearly erroneous, but for which the arbitrator would have reached a different result. *See NFFE, Local 1984*, 56 FLRA 38, 41 (2000). However, the Authority will not find an award deficient on the basis of an arbitrator's determination of any factual matter that the parties disputed at arbitration. *See id.*

The Agency claims that the Arbitrator erred by finding that the Agency did not provide the grievant with a copy of the "Training Benchmarks" or use them during training. Exceptions at 1. However, the Arbitrator found that the Agency violated the parties' agreement in several respects, such as failing to provide trainee PDs and issuing a deficient PIP. Thus, even assuming that the Arbitrator made the two alleged factual errors, the Agency has failed to show that the Arbitrator would have reached a different result but for those errors. As such, the Agency has not demonstrated that the award is based on nonfacts, and we deny the exception.

B. The Arbitrator did not exceed his authority.

Arbitrators exceed their authority when they fail to resolve an issue submitted to arbitration, resolve an issue not submitted to arbitration, disregard specific limitations on their authority, or award relief to persons who are not encompassed within the grievance. *See U.S. Dep't of the Navy, Naval Base, Norfolk, Va.*, 51 FLRA 305, 307-08 (1995) (*Dep't of the Navy*). In the absence of a stipulated issue, an arbitrator's formulation of the issues is accorded substantial deference. *See AFGE, Local 933*, 58 FLRA 480, 482 (2003) (*AFGE*). An arbitrator does not exceed his or her authority where the award is directly responsive to the formulated issues. *See, e.g., AFGE, Local 4044, Council of Prisons Local 33*, 57 FLRA 98, 99 (2001). In addition, arbitrators have broad discretion to fashion remedies. *See, e.g., U.S. Dep't of the Air Force, Okla. City Air Logistics Ctr., Tinker Air Force Base, Okla.*, 47 FLRA 98, 101 (1993) (*Tinker AFB).*

The Agency argues that that the Arbitrator exceeded his authority by finding that the Agency's failure to provide trainee PDs and performance standards violated the parties' agreement. Exceptions at 24-25. However, the Agency does not argue that the Arbitrator resolved an issue not submitted to arbitration, disregarded specific limitations on his authority, or awarded relief to persons not encompassed in the grievance in making that finding. *See Dep't of the Navy*, 51 FLRA at 307-08. As the Agency fails to provide any support for its claim, we deny this exception as a bare assertion.[7] *See, e.g., U.S. Dep't of Homeland Sec., U.S. Customs & Border Prot., Port of Seattle, Seattle, Wash.*, 60 FLRA 490, 492 n.7 (2004).

The Agency also argues that the Arbitrator exceeded his authority by directing the Agency to provide the grievant with an opportunity to attend a training program, and to provide her with a trainee PD and performance standards. In this connection, the Arbitrator framed the relevant issue as: "Was the [g]rievant properly placed on a valid performance improvement plan, and if not, what shall be the remedy?" Award at 2. The ordered remedy is directly related to the framed issue of an appropriate remedy for the Agency's improper placement of the grievant on a PIP. With regard to the Agency's claim that the Union did not request these remedies, the Authority has held that "the fact that a [party] seeks a particular remedy does not, in and of itself, constrain the arbitrator's ability to fashion what he or she deems appropriate to any violation that is found." *See Dep't of the Air Force, Scott Air Force Base, Ill.*, 51 FLRA 675, 687 (1995). Thus, the Agency's argument is unpersuasive. Further, the Agency does not argue that the Arbitrator resolved an issue not submitted to arbitration, disregarded specific limitations on his authority, or awarded relief to

---

the Agency does not challenge any particular arbitral findings, we do not address the argument further.

7. We note that the Agency does argue that the Arbitrator's finding fails to draw its essence from the parties' agreement, as discussed below.

persons who are not encompassed within the grievance.

For the foregoing reasons, the Agency has not demonstrated that the Arbitrator exceeded his authority, and we deny the exception.

C. The award draws its essence from the parties' agreement.

In reviewing an arbitrator's interpretation of a collective bargaining agreement, the Authority applies the deferential standard that federal courts use in reviewing arbitration awards in the private sector. *See* 5 U.S.C. § 7122(a)(2); *AFGE, Council 220*, 54 FLRA 156, 159 (1998). Under this standard, the Authority will find that an arbitration award is deficient as failing to draw its essence from the collective bargaining agreement when the appealing party establishes that the award: (1) cannot in any rational way be derived from the agreement; (2) is so unfounded in reason and fact and so unconnected with the wording and purposes of the collective bargaining agreement as to manifest an infidelity to the obligation of the arbitrator; (3) does not represent a plausible interpretation of the agreement; or (4) evidences a manifest disregard of the agreement. *U.S. Dep't of Labor (OSHA)*, 34 FLRA 573, 575 (1990). The Authority and the courts defer to arbitrators in this context "because it is the arbitrator's construction of the agreement for which the parties have bargained." *Id.* at 576. Where an arbitrator interprets an agreement as imposing a particular requirement, the fact that the agreement is silent with respect to that requirement does not, by itself, demonstrate that the arbitrator's award fails to draw its essence from the agreement. *See, e.g., U.S. Dep't of Veterans Affairs, Ralph H. Johnson Med. Ctr, Charleston, S.C.*, 58 FLRA 413, 414 (2003) (*Johnson Med. Ctr.*); *U.S. Dep't of Def., Educ. Activity, Arlington, Va.*, 56 FLRA 901, 905-06 (2000) *(DOD)*; *U.S. Dep't of the Treasury, IRS, Wash., D.C.*, 56 FLRA 393, 394-95 (2000) (*IRS*); *U.S. Dep't of the Air Force, Ogden Air Logistics Ctr., Hill Air Force Base, Utah*, 35 FLRA 1267, 1271 (1990) (*Hill AFB*).

The Agency claims that the award fails to draw its essence from Articles 9 and 26 of the parties' agreement because these provisions do not require the Agency to provide: (1) trainee PDs; (2) trainee performance standards; and (3) "the causes of unacceptable performance and the remedial actions for correcting deficiencies" in a PIP.[8] Exceptions at 27-28, 30-31. However, even assuming that the agreement does not specifically impose these requirements, the fact that the agreement is silent with respect to these requirements does not demonstrate that the arbitrator's award fails to draw its essence from the agreement. *See Johnson Med. Ctr.*, 58 FLRA at 414; *DOD*, 56 FLRA at 905-06; *IRS*, 56 FLRA at 394-95; *Hill AFB*, 35 FLRA at 1271. The Agency also argues that the award conflicts with Article 9 because the grievant did not request a copy of a trainee PD. Exceptions at 28. However, the fact that Article 9 states that the Agency must provide a PD "at the time of assignment *and* upon request" does not show that the Arbitrator's finding that the Agency was required to provide the grievant with a trainee PD at the time of her assignment to that position, even absent a request, is irrational, unfounded, implausible, or in manifest disregard of the parties' agreement. Award at 28 (emphasis added). Accordingly, we deny the exception.

The Agency further contends that the award fails to draw its essence from Article 26 insofar as the Arbitrator found that the Agency improperly placed the grievant on a PIP.[9] Exceptions at 34-36. In this

---

8. Article 9 of the parties' agreement states, in pertinent part: "Employees will be furnished a current, accurate copy of the description of the position to which assigned at the time of assignment and upon request." Award at 28. Article 26, Section 5 provides, in pertinent part: "The rating official will establish and communicate in writing to employee(s) . . . performance standards, at the beginning of the appraisal period[.]" *Id.* at 32. Article 26, Section 10 of the parties' agreement states, in pertinent part:

> The PIP will identify the employee's specific performance deficiencies, the successful level of performance, the action(s) that must be taken by the employee to improve to the successful level of performance, the methods that will be employed to measure the improvement, and any provisions for counseling, training, or other appropriate assistance.

Id. at 36.

9. Article 26, Section 2 of the parties' agreement provides, in relevant part: "Appraisal period [is] [t]he established period of time for which performance will be reviewed and a rating of record will be prepared." *Id.* at 29. Article 26, Section 7 states, in pertinent part: "The performance appraisal process is used for making a basic determination that an employee is meeting their job requirements. It is also the basis for making certain personnel-related decisions." *Id.* at 34. Article 26, Section 8 provides, in

connection, the Agency asserts that because the grievant's supervisor determined that she was not meeting productivity standards from the beginning of her appraisal period, she was properly placed on the PIP. However, the Arbitrator determined that the grievant's performance problems were caused by circumstances outside of her control -- inadequate training -- and, therefore, the Agency's issuance of a PIP violated Article 26 of the agreement. Award at 54. The Agency provides no basis for finding that the Arbitrator's determination is irrational, unfounded, implausible, or in manifest disregard of the parties' agreement. Accordingly, we deny the exception.

The Agency also asserts that the Arbitrator's remedy requiring the Agency to offer the grievant an opportunity to attend a new training program and provide her with a trainee PD and performance standards fails to draw its essence from the parties' agreement because the agreement does not provide for such relief. As noted previously, arbitrators enjoy broad discretion in fashioning remedies. *See Tinker AFB*, 47 FLRA at 101. Moreover, the Agency does not cite any provision of the parties' agreement that addresses the remedies that are available in arbitration cases. *See U.S. Dep't of Veterans Affairs Med. Ctr., Detroit, Mich.*, 60 FLRA 306, 308 (2004). As such, the Agency provides no basis for finding that it was irrational, implausible, unfounded, or in manifest disregard of the agreement for the Arbitrator to order the challenged remedy, and we deny the exception.

D. The award is not contrary to law.

When an exception involves an award's consistency with law, the Authority reviews any question of law raised by the exception and the award *de novo*. *See NTEU, Chapter 24*, 50 FLRA 330, 332 (1995) (citing *U.S. Customs Serv. v. FLRA*, 43 F.3d 682, 686-87 (D.C. Cir. 1994)). In applying the standard of *de novo* review, the Authority assesses whether an arbitrator's legal conclusions are consistent with the applicable standard of law. *See U.S. Dep't of Def., Dep't of the Army & the Air Force, Ala. Nat'l Guard, Northport, Ala.*, 55 FLRA 37, 40 (1998). In making that assessment, the Authority defers to the arbitrator's underlying factual findings. *See id.*

The Agency contends that the award is deficient because the MSPB has held that agencies are not required to provide training during a PIP and that they enjoy managerial discretion and deference in establishing performance standards. Exceptions at 29. However, the Authority has held that MSPB decisions holding that agencies are not required to provide training during a PIP "do[] not prevent an agency from providing and . . . an arbitrator from requiring, training for an employee who has received an unacceptable performance rating as part of the assistance required under . . . the parties' collective bargaining agreement." *GSA*, 47 FLRA 1326, 1335 (1993). Moreover, the MSPB and court decisions cited by the Agency did not address whether an arbitrator who is enforcing a collective bargaining agreement properly may require an agency to provide performance standards in accordance with that agreement. Accordingly, these decisions are inapposite, and we deny this exception.

The Agency also contends that the Arbitrator's finding that the PIP was a "probationary period [that was] nothing more than a paid suspension" and a "disciplinary action as a prelude to an adverse action" is contrary to Title 5, Chapter 43 of the U.S. Code. Exceptions at 30. In this connection, the Agency noted that "[p]erformance actions taken under Chapter 43 are not adverse actions at all, but are considered performance based actions, as opposed to actions taken under Chapter 75." *Id.* Even assuming that the Arbitrator misinterpreted Article 43, he based his award on a finding that the Agency violated Chapter 43 *and* the parties' agreement. Award at 54-55. The Authority has held that where an arbitrator bases an award on separate and independent grounds, an excepting party must establish that all of the grounds are deficient in order to demonstrate that the award is deficient. *See, e.g., U.S. Dep't of the Treasury, IRS, Oxon Hill, Md.*, 56 FLRA 292, 299 (2000). We have denied the Agency's essence exceptions. Thus, as the Arbitrator's finding of a contractual violation

---

relevant part: "All bargaining unit employees will receive an annual performance appraisal for the period October 1 through September 30, or other dates agreed to by the national parties[.]" *Id.* at 34-35. Article 26, Section 10 states, in relevant part:

> If the supervisor determines that the employee is not meeting the standards of his/her critical elements(s), the supervisor shall identify the specific, performance-related problem(s). After this determination, the supervisor shall develop . . . a written PIP. . . . If the performance deficiency is caused by circumstances beyond the employee's control, the supervisor should consider means of addressing the deficiency using other than a PIP.

Id. at 36.

constitutes a separate and independent basis for his award, the Agency's contrary-to-law exception provides no basis for setting aside the award. Accordingly, we deny the exception.

V. Decision

The Agency's exceptions are denied.

Member Beck, Dissenting:

I do not agree with the Majority in several respects. I would vacate the award because the Arbitrator exceeded his authority and because the award fails to draw its essence from the parties' collective bargaining agreement.

The Arbitrator framed the issue in a way that can only be viewed as quite limited in scope: "Was the [g]rievant properly placed on a valid performance improvement plan [(PIP)] and, if not, what shall be the remedy?" Award at 2. Therefore, the Arbitrator exceeded his authority when he determined that the Agency violated Article 9 by failing to provide "trainee" position descriptions (PDs) and performance standards during the initial training period (*id.* at 45) and directed that the grievant be returned to a probationary training period under "trainee" performance standards and PD.[1] *Id.* at 55-56.

The grievant had successfully completed the training phase of her employment and had begun regular work as a Rating Veteran Service Representative (RSVR) before the PIP was initiated and, indeed, before she began the appraisal period that formed the basis of the PIP.[2] Consequently, matters of training were not encompassed within the issue framed by the Arbitrator.

I cannot conclude, as does the Majority, that the Arbitrator's award draws its essence from Articles 9 and 26 insofar as he requires the Agency to provide trainee PDs and trainee performance standards, and to specify the causes of unacceptable performance. None of these actions is required by the parties' CBA:

---

1. No evidence was presented that "trainee" performance standards or PDs exist. *See* Exceptions at 28 (citing *id.*, Attachs. B-3, B-5, and B-8). However, the grievant was provided "training benchmarks" during her initial training period. Exceptions, Attach. B-4. The Arbitrator found incorrectly that the grievant was not provided with these benchmarks during her training period. Award at 9-10.

2. I do not agree that the Agency's first exceeds authority exception (Arbitrator found that the Agency violated Article 9 by failing to provide trainee PDs and performance standards) is a "bare assertion." *See* Majority at 6. The arguments set forth by the Agency in its brief on pages 25-28 specifically support that exception. It is obvious that the arguments presented on pages 25-34 were intended to address both exceptions.

- Article 9 requires only that the employee receive a PD at the time of assignment. The grievant was provided the RVSR PD during both the training period (Award at 9) and upon actual assignment to the position (Exceptions, Attach. B-5).

- Article 26, Section 5 requires that standards be given "at the beginning of the appraisal period." The grievant was given (and signed for) performance standards when she was assigned to the RVSR position at the conclusion of her training period. Exceptions, Attach. B-8.

- Article 26, Section 10 requires that a PIP identify specific performance deficiencies, successful level of performance, corrective actions, measures of improvement, and training that will be provided. The PIP included all of these elements. Exceptions, Attach. B-12.

Without a doubt, arbitrators are afforded substantial latitude to interpret contract provisions and to fashion a remedy. *NFFE, Local 1442,* 64 FLRA 1132, 1134 (2010). However, that latitude is not without limits. Here, the Arbitrator took it upon himself to impose new and additional requirements that the parties chose not to include in their CBA. As such, the award is not a plausible interpretation of the agreement.[3]

Accordingly, I would vacate the Arbitrator's award.

---

3. As noted above, the Arbitrator here imposed new requirements that could not have been anticipated by the parties. *See supra* n.1. Accordingly, this case is distinguishable from those cited by the Majority. *See* Majority at 6. In those cases, the arbitrator merely applied a remedy in a manner that was rationally derived from (even if not specifically addressed by) the parties' agreement or was otherwise required by the circumstances of the violation. *U.S. Dep't of Veterans Affairs, Ralph H. Johnson Med. Ctr., Charleston, S.C.*, 58 FLRA 413, 414 (2003) (although agreement was silent regarding promotion, it was reasonable for arbitrator to require promotion to GS-8 after one year of "successful performance" where agency regulation required promotion after one year of satisfactory performance); *U.S. Dep't of Def., Educ. Activity, Arlington, Va.*, 56 FLRA 901, 902, 906 (2000) (reasonable for arbitrator to require payment of remedy within 30 days "because [the agreement] was silent as to a specific time frame" and the record demonstrated prior instances where the agency had delayed payment); *U.S. Dep't of the Treasury, IRS, Wash., D.C.*, 56 FLRA 393, 394-95 (2000) (reasonable for arbitrator to direct agency to submit bargaining impasse to Federal Service Impasses Panel where agency stipulated that the issue for the arbitrator included the question whether the agency's agreement to negotiate obligated the agency to submit to impasse procedures); and *U.S. Dep't of the Air Force, Ogden Air Logistics Ctr., Hill Air Force Base, Utah,* 35 FLRA 1267, 1271 (1990) (reasonable for arbitrator to interpret provision that required supervisor "to seek volunteers among qualified employees" to exclude employees on leave even though CBA did not define whether the term "qualified employee" excluded employees on leave).

65 FLRA No. 48

AMERICAN FEDERATION
OF GOVERNMENT EMPLOYEES
LOCAL 2441
COUNCIL OF PRISON LOCALS
(Union)

and

UNITED STATES
DEPARTMENT OF JUSTICE
FEDERAL BUREAU OF PRISONS
FEDERAL CORRECTIONAL INSTITUTION
MORGANTOWN, WEST VIRGINIA
(Agency)

0-AR-4399

DECISION

October 29, 2010

Before the Authority: Carol Waller Pope, Chairman, and Thomas M. Beck and Ernest DuBester, Members

I. Statement of the Case

The matter is before the Authority on exceptions to an award of Arbitrator Edward A. Grupp filed by the Union under § 7122(a) of the Federal Service Labor-Management Relations Statute (the Statute) and part 2425 of the Authority's Regulations. The Agency filed an opposition to the Union's exceptions.

The Arbitrator found that the Union failed to establish that the Agency, by its action in requiring the grievant to adhere to a certain dress code and restricting his use of the Agency's Groupwise system (Groupwise e-mail system), violated the parties' collective bargaining agreements or retaliated against the grievant because of his protected activities. For the reasons that follow, we deny the exceptions.

II. Background and Arbitrator's Award

The Agency (DOJ) operates a minimum security correctional institution under the Bureau of Prisons (BOP) in Morgantown, West, Virginia (facility). Award at 2. The grievant, the President of the Union at the facility, is a drug treatment specialist and a non-uniformed unit member. *Id.*

The grievant met with the Warden of the facility concerning a memorandum that notified unit employees on the day watch shift that they no longer had a 30-minute duty free lunch period. *Id.* at 3. At this meeting, the grievant was on "official time" and was "wearing jeans." *Id.* After the meeting, the grievant advised Union members, through the Agency's Groupwise e-mail system, that the "Union suggested employees who arrive early or stay late [request] overtime and require management to deny overtime in writing." *Id.*

The next day, the Warden met with the grievant and told him that jeans were not acceptable dress while on official time. *Id.* The following day, the grievant again wore jeans. *Id.* The Warden instructed him to change to appropriate trousers, which required the grievant to go home to change clothing. *Id.* at 3 & 6. The grievant complied with this instruction. Later, the Warden and the grievant discussed the matter further in the Warden's office. *Id.* at 3. At some point during this discussion, the grievant asked for a Union representative, which the Warden denied. *Id.* at 3 & 6. At this meeting, the Warden reminded the grievant that he should not be using the Groupwise e-mail system for matters that were not permitted under the parties' master agreement (MA). *Id.* at 3 & 6.

The Union considered the Warden's actions regarding the dress requirement and the Groupwise e-mail system to be retaliation against the grievant because of his protected union activities. *Id.* at 3. The grievant filed a grievance, which was not resolved and was submitted to arbitration. As relevant here, the Arbitrator framed the issues as: [1]

> Did the Warden coerce, intimidate and retaliate against [the] [g]rievant because of his protected activity by, denying him the right to wear "jeans" at the work place, threatening to deny him the opportunity to use a computer provide by the Agency, and requiring him to go home to secure other

1. A third issue concerning whether the Agency denied the grievant the right to a Union representative during the last meeting with the Warden was also before the Arbitrator. The Arbitrator found that the evidence did not establish that this meeting constituted an investigatory interview and, therefore, found that the Agency did not violate the agreements or law. Award at 12. Because the Union does not except to this finding, it will not be mentioned further in this decision.

> clothing in place of the "jeans" [the g]rievant was wearing?
>
> Did the Warden violate the Master Agreement [(MA)] when he told the grievant that he was using an Agency computer to circulate messages to employees throughout the [facility] which the Warden believed were matters pertaining to internal [U]nion matters and thus not permitted by the [MA] and informed [the] [g]rievant that the use of the internal Agency computer system would be denied him if he persisted in such use?

Id. at 1 & 2.

Before the Arbitrator, the Union argued that: (1) the grievant was on official time during the meetings with the Warden and thus was entitled to wear clothing of his choice without regard to Article 10 of the parties' supplemental agreement (SA); [2] and (2) the restriction of the grievant's use of the Groupwise e-mail system was retaliation for the e-mail that he sent concerning overtime use. *Id.* at 4. The Union argued that the Warden's actions constituted reprisal against the grievant because of his protected activities. *Id.* at 5. The Agency disputed the Union's assertions. *Id.* at 6-7.

The Arbitrator examined the parties' agreements and found that Article 10 of the SA contains a "prohibition against 'jeans[.]'" *Id.* at 9. After considering the wording of the parties' agreements, the Arbitrator concluded that the SA "does not make any exception which would cover the non-application of the dress code to persons on [o]fficial [t]ime[.]" *Id.* at 9; *see also id.* at 11. In this regard, the Arbitrator found that a Union officer on official time is not a "normally uniformed person, but rather a professional required to wear appropriate professional dress[.]" *Id.* at 9. The Arbitrator determined that, as a drug treatment specialist, the grievant comes into contact with inmates and his dress is considered to have some effect on his relationship with them. *Id.* Although recognizing that, while on official time, the grievant is not performing his regular work duties, the Arbitrator found that it was not "unreasonable to conclude that [the grievant] may not always be in the Union's office . . . , but may be [involved in situations in] the facility where he could be seen by inmates" under his professional care. *Id.* The Arbitrator also rejected the Union's argument that "past practice" supported the exemption of persons on Union business from the dress requirement, finding that the "evidence of past practice in this regard is scant." *Id.* Moreover, although recognizing "some inconsistency" with the "propriety of permitting 'jeans' to be worn on Dress Down Days" and the "strict requirement of adherence to the standard dress regulations on other occasions, including when [U]nion officials are on [o]fficial [t]ime," the Arbitrator stated that it was not "within [his] authority" to change the language of the agreement and that, if the Union "is dissatisfied with any . . . provision [in the SA,] it should be the subject of current negotiation[s]." *Id.* at 8.

The Arbitrator also found that the evidence was insufficient to conclude that the Warden's action concerning the grievant's wearing of jeans was reprisal or retaliation because of his protected activities. *Id.* at 9. The Arbitrator determined that, because the Warden had been assigned to the facility less than a month before his initial meeting with the grievant, "it was reasonable to conclude" that he was not aware of the jeans provision at that time. *Id.* Moreover, in reaching his conclusion, the Arbitrator noted that the Warden decided "to apply the rule on a consistent basis" and that, as a result, his decision also affected other employees, including supervisors. *Id.* Accordingly, the Arbitrator concluded that the evidence did not establish that the Warden enforced the dress requirement against the grievant as a reprisal or reprimand in an effort to retaliate against him because of his protected activities. *Id.* at 11.

The Arbitrator further found that the Warden's restriction on the grievant's use of the Groupwise e-mail system "was not taken as a reprisal because of [his] protected [U]nion activity." *Id.* The Arbitrator found that the parties' agreements "clearly restrict the use the Union may make of the system[.]" *Id.* The Arbitrator found that Article 12, Section (c) provides that, "[u]nder no circumstances will [Agency] manpower or supplies be used in support of internal Union business[,]" which is defined as "any activities performed by any employee relating to the internal business of a labor organization." *Id.* at 10. The Arbitrator examined e-mails submitted by the Agency and determined that the e-mails concerned internal Union business. *Id.* at 10 & 11. The Arbitrator also found that the Administrative Law Judge's (ALJ) decision in *SBA, Newark, N.J.*, FLRA ALJ Dec. Rep. No. 138, 1998 WL 964232 (*SBA*), cited by the Union, was not controlling because the parties' agreement in that case differed "markedly" "with respect to [the] restrictions on the use of

---

2. The relevant text of the parties' agreements is set forth in the appendix to this decision.

agency email by the union" from the parties' MA in the subject case. *Id.* at 11.

The Arbitrator denied the grievance, finding that the "evidence . . . [did] not establish that the Agency violated the [parties'] . . . agreements" or that it "took action against the [g]rievant as a reprisal or [retaliation] because of his Union activities." *Id.* at 11-12.

III. Positions of the Parties

A. Union's Exceptions

The Union asserts that the award fails to draw its essence from the parties' agreements. Exceptions at 1 & 7. The Union contends that the award "contradicts . . . the partie[s' MA] . . . to include but not limited to Articles 6, 12 and 32." *Id.* at 4. Specifically, the Union asserts that Article 12, Section (c) defines internal union business. The Union states that it "stipulated" that the Union could not "use the Groupwise [e-mail] system to conduct internal union business" as provided in the parties' MA and § 7131(b) of the Statute, but that testimony shows that it can use the system to conduct official business as provided by Article 12. *Id.* at 5. The Union asserts that the "[e-mail] advising bargaining unit staff of their right to overtime" concerning the lunch hour does not concern internal union business. *Id.* at 6.

In addition, the Union contends that the Arbitrator exceeded his authority. *Id.* at 1 & 5. According to the Union, by finding no violation of Article 12, the Arbitrator "change[d]" the meaning of this provision. *Id.* at 5.

The Union further asserts that the Arbitrator erred by finding that the evidence did not establish that the Agency retaliated against the grievant because of his protected activities and argues that such finding is contrary to §§ 7114, 7116(a)(1) and (2), and 7131(b) of the Statute. *Id.* at 4 & 7. The Union claims that the Agency's action in restricting the grievant's use of the Groupwise e-mail system and "enforc[ing the] dress requirement against [him]" while he was on official time was reprisal because of his protected activities. *Id.* at 6. The Union asserts that the "e-mail advising [unit employees] of their right to overtime" does not constitute internal union business within the meaning of § 7131(b) and that such activity is protected under § 7114. *Id.* The Union argues that *NTEU*, 6 FLRA 508 (1981), and *SBA* support its position that the e-mails did not concern internal union business under Article 12. *Id.* at 5-6.

B. Agency's Opposition

The Agency disputes the Union's claim that the award fails to draw its essence from the parties' MA. The Agency asserts that the Union cites Articles 6, 12, and 32, of the parties' MA, but only provides arguments concerning Article 12. Opp'n at 4. The Agency contends that the Arbitrator specifically found that the e-mails in dispute were not permitted pursuant to Article 12 because they dealt with internal union business. *Id.* at 5.

The Agency contends that the Union has not demonstrated that the Arbitrator exceeded his authority with respect to Article 12. *Id.* at 6-7. The Agency asserts that the award was directly responsive to the issues as determined by the Arbitrator. *Id.* at 7. The Agency also asserts that the Union has not demonstrated that the award is contrary to any law, rule, or regulation. *Id.* at 7-9.

IV. Analysis and Conclusions

A. The award does not fail to draw its essence from the parties' agreements.

In reviewing an arbitrator's interpretation of a collective bargaining agreement, the Authority applies the deferential standard of review that federal courts use in reviewing arbitration awards in the private sector. *U.S. Dep't of Homeland Sec., U.S. Customs & Border Prot., JFK Airport, Queens, N.Y.*, 62 FLRA 129, 132-33 (2007). Accordingly, the party appealing the award must establish that the award: (1) cannot in any rational way be derived from the agreement; (2) is so unfounded in reason and fact and so unconnected with the wording and purposes of the agreement as to manifest an infidelity to the obligation of the arbitrator; (3) does not represent a plausible interpretation of the agreement; or (4) evidences a manifest disregard of the agreement. *See U.S. Dep't of Labor (OSHA)*, 34 FLRA 573, 575 (1990). The Authority and the courts defer to arbitrators in this context "because it is the arbitrator's construction of the agreement for which the parties have bargained." *Id.* at 576.

The Union argues that the award "contradicts . . . the partie[s'] [MA] . . . to include but not limited to Articles 6, 12 and 32." Exceptions at 4. Specifically, the Union contends that, although it "stipulated" that the Union could not "use the Groupwise [e-mail] system to conduct *internal* union business" as provided in the parties' MA and § 7131(b) of the Statute, the Union can use the system to conduct *official* business as provided by Article 12. *Id.* at 5 (emphasis added). The Union asserts that the "[e- mail] advising bargaining unit staff of their right to overtime" concerning the lunch hour does not concern internal union business. *Id.* at 6.

The Arbitrator framed one of the issues before him as:

> Did the Warden violate the [MA] when he told [the g]rievant he was using an Agency computer to circulate messages to employees throughout the [facility] which the Warden believed were matters pertaining to internal union matters and thus not permitted by the [MA] and informed [the g]rievant that the use of the internal Agency computer system would be denied him if he persisted in such use?

Award at 2. In resolving this issue, the Arbitrator examined Article 12, Section (c) of the MA, which identifies Agency items available for the Union's use, including office equipment, and provides how the items may be used. *See id.* at 5. Article 12, Section (c) provides, in part, that "[i]t is understood that such use of these items is expected to promote efficient labor management relations. Under no circumstances will [Agency] manpower or supplies be used in support of internal Union business." *Id.* at 5.

Applying this provision, the Arbitrator found that, during a meeting with the grievant, the Warden instructed the grievant to "discontinue use of the Groupwise [e-mail] system for internal union business." *Id.* at 10. The Arbitrator found that the disputed Union e-mails demonstrated that the Union was using the Groupwise e-mail system in support of internal Union business, and that, therefore, the Agency's action in instructing the grievant to discontinue use of the Groupwise e-mail system for internal union business did not violate the parties' agreements. *See id.* at 10-11. The Arbitrator's finding was based on his evaluation of the evidence and his interpretation and application of Article 12. *See id.* As set forth above, the Authority defers to the Arbitrator's interpretation of the agreement "because it is the [A]rbitrator's construction of the agreement for which the parties have bargained." *OSHA*, 34 FLRA at 576. The Union has not demonstrated that the Arbitrator's interpretation of Article 12, Section (c) is irrational, implausible, or otherwise deficient.

Moreover, to the extent that the union claims that the award fails to draw its essence from other provisions of the parties' agreements, including Article 10, the Union fails to provide any explanation or arguments to support this claim. When a party fails to provide any arguments or authority to support its contention, the Authority will deny the exception as a bare assertion. *See, e.g., AFGE, Nat'l Joint Council of Food Inspection Locals*, 64 FLRA 1116, 1117 (2010). Therefore, we deny the claim as a bare assertion.

Accordingly, we find that the Union has not demonstrated that the award fails to draw its essence from the parties' agreements, and we deny this exception.

B. The Arbitrator did not exceed his authority.

The Union asserts that, by finding no violation of Article 12 of the parties' MA, the Arbitrator changed the meaning of this provision. Exceptions at 5. Arbitrators exceed their authority when they fail to resolve an issue submitted to arbitration, resolve an issue not submitted to arbitration, disregard specific limitations on their authority, or award relief to those not encompassed within the grievance. *AFGE, Local 1617*, 51 FLRA 1645, 1647 (1996). In the absence of a stipulated issue, the arbitrator's formulation of the issue is accorded substantial deference. *U.S. Dep't of the Air Force*, 61 FLRA 797, 801 (2006); *U.S. Dep't of the Army, Corps of Eng'rs, Memphis Dist., Memphis, Tenn.*, 52 FLRA 920, 924 (1997).

We find no merit to the Union's claim that the Arbitrator exceeded his authority. One of the issues framed by the Arbitrator was:

> Did the Warden violate the [MA] when he told [the g]rievant that he was using an Agency computer to circulate messages to employees throughout the [facility] which the Warden believed were matters pertaining to internal union matters and thus not permitted by the [MA] and informed [the g]rievant that the use of the internal Agency computer system would be denied him if he persisted in such use?

Award at 2. Interpreting and applying Article 12, Section (c) of the parties' MA, the Arbitrator found that, because the Union's e-mails concerned internal union business, the Agency did not violate the parties' MA by instructing the grievant not to use the Groupwise e-mail system for such matters. This finding is directly responsive to the framed issue. The Union has not provided any information that demonstrates that the Arbitrator's finding exceeds any limitations on his authority that are imposed by the parties' MA.

Accordingly, we deny this exception.

C. The award is not contrary to law.

When an exception involves an award's consistency with law, the Authority reviews any question of law raised by the exception and the award *de novo*. *See NTEU, Chapter 24*, 50 FLRA 330, 332 (1995) (citing *U.S. Customs Serv. v. FLRA*, 43 F.3d 682, 686-87 (D.C. Cir. 1994)). In applying the standard of *de novo* review, the Authority assesses whether an arbitrator's legal conclusions are consistent with the applicable standard of law. *See U.S. Dep't of Def., Dep'ts of the Army & the Air Force, Ala. Nat'l Guard, Northport, Ala.*, 55 FLRA 37, 40 (1998). In making that assessment, the Authority defers to the arbitrator's underlying factual findings. *See id.*

The Union asserts that the Arbitrator erred by finding that the evidence did not establish that the Agency retaliated against the grievant because of his protected activities and argues that such finding is contrary to §§ 7114, 7116(a)(1) and (2), and 7131(b) of the Statute. Although the record does not reveal whether the Union referenced a particular section of the Statute in the grievance, one of the issues framed by the Arbitrator was:

> Did the Warden coerce, intimidate and retaliate against [the] [g]rievant because of his protected activity by, denying him the right to wear "jeans" at the work place, threatening to deny him the opportunity to use a computer provided by the Agency, and requiring him to go home to secure other clothing in place of the "jeans" [g]rievant was wearing?

Award at 1. In addition, in alleging that the Agency retaliated against the grievant, the Union relied on *SBA,* which involved a § 7116(a)(1) and (2) allegation, and the Arbitrator distinguished that decision from the instant case. *See id.* at 11. These matters indicate that the Arbitrator resolved statutory issues.

Where statutory issues concerning union discrimination are raised, the Authority reviews the award under the statutory principles applicable to § 7116(a)(2). *See, e.g., NLRB*, 61 FLRA 197, 199 (2005); *AFGE,* 59 FLRA 767, 769-70 (2004). Section 7116(a)(2) of the Statute provides that it is an unfair labor practice (ULP) for an agency to encourage or discourage membership in a union by discrimination in connection with hiring, tenure, promotion, or other conditions of employment. When a grievance under § 7121 of the Statute involves an alleged ulp, the arbitrator must apply the same standards and burdens that would be applied by an administrative law judge in a ULP proceeding under § 7118. *See, e.g., AFGE, Local 3529*, 57 FLRA 464, 465 (2001). In a grievance alleging a ULP by an agency, the union bears the burden of proving the elements of the alleged ULP by a preponderance of the evidence. *See id.* As in other arbitration cases, the Authority defers to an arbitrator's findings of fact. *See id.*

Further, in cases alleging discrimination, the Authority applies the framework in *Letterkenny Army Depot*, 35 FLRA 113, 118 (1990) (*Letterkenny*). *See AFGE, Local 2145*, 64 FLRA 661, 664 (2010) (Member Beck dissenting, in part). Under that framework, the party making such an assertion establishes a *prima facie* case of discrimination by demonstrating that: (1) the employee against whom the alleged discriminatory action was taken was engaged in protected activity; and (2) such activity was a motivating factor in the agency's treatment of the employee. Once the *prima facie* showing is made, an agency may seek to establish the affirmative defense that: (1) there was a legitimate justification for the action; and (2) the same action would have been taken even in the absence of the protected activity.

Turning to the instant case, although the Arbitrator did not expressly apply the *Letterkenny* framework, the record is sufficient for the Authority to do so. In this regard, even assuming that the Union established a *prima facie* case of discrimination with respect to both the dress requirement and the Groupwise e-mail system, the Arbitrator's factual findings establish that provisions of the parties' agreements permitted the Agency's disputed actions – i.e., prohibiting the wearing of jeans and certain use of e-mail. *See IRS, Wash., D.C.*, 47 FLRA 1091, 1110 (1993) (an agency may rebut a *prima facie* showing that its actions would constitute a violation of a statutory right by establishing the parties' collective bargaining agreement permitted the agency's actions); *see also, SSA, Region VII, Kan. City, Mo.*, 55 FLRA 536, 538 (1999).

With respect to the dress requirement, Article 10 of the parties' SA concerns work attire for "[n]on-uniformed staff" and provides that "[u]nacceptable attire includes jeans[.]" Award at 4; Exceptions, Attach., SA at 6. The Arbitrator interpreted this provision and found that Article 10 applied to the grievant, a Union officer and non-uniformed member of the staff. *Id.* at 9. The Arbitrator further found that the parties' SA "does not make any exception which could cover the non-application of the dress code to persons on [o]fficial [t]ime" and that the Warden applied the rule on a "consistent basis which affected other employees as well as supervisors[.]" *Id.* As to the Groupwise e-mail system, the Arbitrator found that the parties' labor agreements "clearly restrict the use the Union may make of the system[.]" *Id.* at 11. In this regard, the Arbitrator found that Article 12, Section (c) of the parties' MA provides that, "[u]nder no circumstances will [Agency] manpower or supplies be used in support of internal Union business[,]" which is defined as "any activities performed by any employee relating to the internal business of a labor organization." *Id.* at 10. The Arbitrator examined e-mails submitted by the Agency as evidence and found that relevant e-mails fell within this contractual prohibition. *Id.* (e.g., grievant's e-mail to a unit employee questioning the employee's attendance at Union meetings and grievant's e-mail to unit employee regarding grievant's performance as a Union officer).

Moreover, the Union has not asserted that either of the relevant contract provisions is unenforceable, nor has it demonstrated that the award fails to draw its essence from the parties' agreements. As such, the Agency established its affirmative defense that provisions of the parties' agreements permitted the Agency to prohibit the grievant from wearing jeans and using the Groupwise e-mail system in support of internal Union business.

In addition, the cases cited by the Union provide no basis for finding the award deficient. In this regard, *NTEU* involved a proposal that concerned an announcement card that would be distributed to union members. *See NTEU,* 6 FLRA at 518. The proposal was found to be within the duty to bargain because the card simply advised employees of the union's status as exclusive representative and did not involve internal union business, as found here. *Id.* at 520. Further, *SBA* is non-precedential because it is an ALJ's decision to which no exceptions were filed. *See, e.g., PASS*, 56 FLRA at 125 n.*.

Accordingly, we find that the Union has not demonstrated that the award is contrary to law, and we deny this exception.

V. Decision

The Union's exceptions are denied.

APPENDIX

ARTICLE 10 of the parties' SA provides as follows:

ARTICLE 10 NON-UNIFORM WORK ATTIRE

> Non-uniformed staff may wear apparel that is deemed professional in nature. Unacceptable attire includes: jeans, skirts (including split skirts) and dresses above the knee, spandex, t-shirts, sweatshirts, sweatpants, shorts (except authorized uniforms), jogging suits, tank tops, leotards, high spiked heel shoes, sand[als], low cut, backless or sheer clothing, or any other item thought of as casual or recreational.

Exceptions, Attach., SA at 6.

ARTICLE 12 of the parties' MA provides as follows:

ARTICLE 12 USE OF OFFICIAL FACILITIES

> Section a. The [Agency] agrees to permit distribution of notices and circulars sponsored by the Union to all employees in the unit through regular internal distribution procedure provided that they:
>
> 1. are reasonable in size;
>
> 2. are signed by the local President or designee;
>
> 3. contain nothing that would seem to identify them as official [Agency] material or imply that they are sponsored or endorsed by the [Agency];
>
> 4. are limited to matters of direct concern to employees in relation to the Union or the [Agency], which will not endanger staff or the security of the institution; and
>
> 5. require no significant staff time.
>
> . . . .
>
> Section c. The use of [Agency] bulletin boards, office space, and office equipment is negotiable at the local level. It is understood that such use of these items is expected to promote efficient labor management relations. Under no circumstances will [Agency] manpower or supplies be used in support of internal Union business. Internal Union business is defined as: any activities performed by any employee relating to the internal business of a labor organization (including the solicitation of membership, elections of labor organization officials, and collection of dues).

Exceptions, Attach., MA at 35.

65 FLRA No. 49

UNITED STATES
DEPARTMENT OF TRANSPORTATION
FEDERAL AVIATION ADMINISTRATION
WASHINGTON, D.C.
(Respondent)

and

NATIONAL AIR TRAFFIC
CONTROLLERS ASSOCIATION
(Charging Party/Union)

WA-CA-06-0706

_____

DECISION AND ORDER

October 29, 2010

_____

Before the Authority: Carol Waller Pope, Chairman, and Thomas M. Beck and Ernest DuBester, Members

I. Statement of the Case

This unfair labor practice (ULP) case is before the Authority on exceptions to the decision of the Administrative Law Judge (Judge) filed by the Respondent. The General Counsel (GC) filed an opposition to the Respondent's exceptions.

The complaint alleges that the Respondent violated § 7116(a)(1) and (8) of the Federal Service Labor-Management Relations Statute (Statute) when it refused to participate in an arbitration proceeding with the Union in violation of § 7121 of the Statute. The complaint further alleges that the Respondent's participation was required by the parties' negotiated grievance procedure. The Judge concluded that the Respondent unlawfully refused to arbitrate in violation of § 7116(a)(1) and (8) of the Statute.

Upon consideration of the Judge's decision and the entire record, we adopt the Judge's findings, conclusions, and recommended Order.

II. Background and Judge's Decision

A. Background

The Union filed a grievance against the Respondent because the Respondent refused to upgrade the classification level of its Atlanta air traffic control facility. Judge's Decision at 4. The classification level of a facility determines controllers' pay at that facility. *See U.S. Dep't of Transp., FAA,* 61 FLRA 634, 634 n.1 (2006) (*FAA*).

When the parties were unable to resolve the grievance, it was submitted to arbitration before Arbitrator Jerome Ross, who was selected from the national panel of arbitrators the parties had established pursuant to their collective bargaining agreement (CBA). Judge's Decision at 4. The parties agreed that the Arbitrator would first rule on the grievance's arbitrability, and, if he found it arbitrable, would resolve the grievance's merits in a separate stage of the proceeding. *See id.* Arbitrator Ross subsequently ruled that the grievance was arbitrable and the Respondent filed exceptions. *Id.*

While the exceptions were pending, the Respondent notified Arbitrator Ross and the Union that it was invoking its contractual right to unilaterally remove Arbitrator Ross from the national panel of arbitrators. *Id.* However, the Respondent did not inform the Authority of its action. *Id.*

The Authority subsequently issued its decision on the Respondent's exceptions, remanding the case to the parties. *FAA,* 61 FLRA at 634. In its decision, the Authority identified Arbitrator Ross by name, *id.*, stating further: "The grievance is remanded to the parties for resubmission to the Arbitrator, absent settlement, for further findings consistent with this decision." *Id.* at 636; *see also* Judge's Decision at 5.

When the Respondent refused to resubmit the grievance to Arbitrator Ross, the Union filed a ULP charge against the Respondent. *Id.* at 1. The GC subsequently issued a complaint and a hearing was held before the Judge. *Id.* at 1-2.

B. Judge's Decision

The Judge found that the Respondent committed a ULP when it refused to allow the grievance to be resubmitted to Arbitrator Ross. The Judge based this conclusion on his resolution of three key issues. Those issues are whether the parties' CBA allows a party to unilaterally remove an arbitrator from consideration of a pending grievance, whether the parties established a past practice allowing for the unilateral removal of an arbitrator after his or her selection to hear a grievance, and whether Arbitrator Ross should not continue to arbitrate the grievance because of bias resulting from his removal by the Respondent from the parties' national panel.

The Judge found that the Respondent did not have the contractual right to unilaterally remove the Arbitrator from consideration of the grievance. In the Judge's view, the relevant language of the CBA is unambiguous. That language, set forth in Article 9, § 11, states:

> The Parties will create a national panel of three (3) mutually acceptable arbitrators. Each Party may unilaterally remove an arbitrator from the panel and another arbitrator shall be mutually selected to fill the vacancy. Within seven (7) calendar days after receipt of the request [to arbitrate], an arbitrator shall be selected from the panel by the Parties or by alternately striking names until one (1) remains or as otherwise mutually agreed.

Id. at 4 (quoting Respondent Ex. 1 at 26).

The Judge found that this language does not permit a party to remove an arbitrator from his or her assignment to a grievance during the pendency of the grievance. *Id.* at 7. Specifically, the Judge determined that the wording and order of the CBA's language reflect the parties' intent to distinguish the procedure for removing an arbitrator from the national panel, which is unilateral, from the procedure for selecting an arbitrator to hear a grievance, which is a joint process. *Id.* The Judge reasoned that, if the parties had wanted to allow for the unilateral removal of an arbitrator after joint selection to hear a grievance, then the CBA would have specifically stated this. *Id.* Furthermore, the Judge rejected the Respondent's contrary construction, that the CBA allows unilateral removal, because the Respondent's construction would lead to an incongruous result. In the Judge's opinion, "to accept the Respondent's construction . . . would be to allow for the removal of an arbitrator for any reason, including dissatisfaction with his preliminary rulings or a desire to redo the arbitration hearing." *Id.*

The Judge also rejected the Respondent's defense to the ULP complaint that the parties had a past practice of unilaterally removing an arbitrator after his or her joint selection. *Id.* The Judge found that the evidence did not substantiate the Respondent's claim. *Id.* Finally, the Judge rejected the Respondent's argument that Arbitrator Ross should not continue to arbitrate the grievance because of bias. *Id.* at 7. The Judge dismissed the Respondent's claim "out of hand," because "[t]o do otherwise would be to assume that Arbitrator Ross lacks the integrity to put aside any personal feelings he might have because of his removal from the [national] panel by the Respondent." *Id.*

Accordingly, the Judge found that the Respondent violated the Statute. He recommended as a remedy that the Respondent be ordered either to cease and desist from refusing to participate in proceedings before Arbitrator Ross, or to cooperate in choosing another arbitrator if Arbitrator Ross was unavailable. *Id.* at 8. Finally, the Judge recommended that the Respondent be ordered to post a nationwide notice at all of its facilities where workers are represented by the Union. The Notice would notify the employees that the Respondent would not refuse to arbitrate the grievance before Arbitrator Ross or in any manner interfere with its employees' exercise of their rights under the Statute. *Id.* at 9-10.

III. Positions of the Parties

A. Respondent's Exceptions

The Respondent argues that it did not commit a ULP because it is the Union and not the Respondent that is refusing to arbitrate the grievance. Exceptions at 4. The Respondent claims that it is willing to arbitrate the grievance in accordance with the Authority's decision in *FAA*, 61 FLRA at 634; however, its position is that the arbitrator who hears the grievance cannot be Arbitrator Ross. *Id.* The Respondent alleges that it is the Union that is delaying the process by refusing to select a different arbitrator. *Id.* at 4-5.

The Respondent further claims that the Authority should reject the Judge's determination that the Respondent had no right to remove Arbitrator Ross because the Judge misinterpreted the pertinent contract provision. *Id.* at 5-9. Citing contract language concerning the unilateral removal of an arbitrator from the national panel,[1] the Respondent

1. In its exceptions, the Respondent cites to Article 9, § 9 of the parties' CBA, which provides that "[t]he Parties shall create a panel of three (3) mutually acceptable arbitrators in each FAA Region. Either Party may unilaterally remove an arbitrator from the panel and another arbitrator shall be mutually selected to fill the vacancy. Arbitrators selected for panels must also agree to hear expedited arbitration cases as provided in Section 16." Exceptions, Respondent Ex. 1 at 23. The Judge relies on Article 9, § 11 of the CBA, which is set forth above in section II.B of this decision. Article 9, § 11 is comprised of all of the relevant portions of § 9 regarding arbitrators on the national panel, plus additional language regarding how the parties may choose an arbitrator from the panel to hear a grievance.

asserts that the clear language of the CBA allows it to unilaterally remove an arbitrator from consideration of a pending grievance at any time and for any reason. *Id.* at 6-7, 8.

The Respondent also urges the Authority to reject the Judge's recommended order that the Respondent participate in proceedings before Arbitrator Ross. The Respondent argues that Arbitrator Ross would be biased because of his awareness that the Respondent removed him from the national panel. *Id.* at 11. The Respondent posits that "any reinstatement of a terminated arbitrator would taint the impartiality of the procedures[,]" *id.* at 9, and "would have a negative [e]ffect" upon the outcome of the arbitration. *Id.* at 11.

Finally, the Respondent claims that, even if the Authority finds that the Respondent committed a ULP, the Authority should not order a nationwide posting because this case involves only an alleged contract violation rather than a violation of the Statute. *Id.* at 12. The Respondent argues that a nationwide posting is only appropriate when there is a statutory violation. The Respondent claims that if there is any violation at all here, it concerns only a question of contractual interpretation. *Id.*

B. GC's Opposition

The GC argues that the Judge properly rejected as irrelevant the Respondent's contention that it is willing to proceed with the pending grievance before a different arbitrator. Opp'n at 7. The GC notes that, while the Respondent cites cases regarding the need for an arbitrator to be removed where there is wrongdoing on the part of the arbitrator, here there is no such evidence of wrongdoing. *Id.* at 7-8.

The GC also contends that the contract language at issue does not specifically state that a party may unilaterally remove an arbitrator during the pendency of a grievance. *Id.* at 10. Furthermore, the GC alleges that there is no evidence that the parties had a past practice of unilaterally removing arbitrators after they had been selected to hear grievances. *Id.* at 10-11. In this connection, the GC asserts that there is only one documented attempt to do so – by the Union – and that this attempt was quickly rejected by both parties. *Id.* at 11.

The GC urges the Authority to reject the Respondent's argument that Arbitrator Ross should not continue as the arbitrator because he would be biased. *Id.* at 11-13. Specifically, the GC disagrees with the Respondent's position that the Arbitrator cannot be neutral and unbiased in light of the Respondent's conduct. *Id.* at 11-12. The GC argues that to accept this position means that any time a party asks for an arbitrator to be removed for any reason, the arbitrator should subsequently recuse himself or herself based on bias, a result the GC describes as "highly unusual" and "harsh and inequitable[.]" *Id.* at 12. In addition, the GC points out that there is no precedent supporting this contention. *Id.*

Finally, the GC contends that a nationwide posting is appropriate. *Id.* at 13. In the GC's view, the Judge correctly found that the Respondent violated the Statute and the remedy he recommended is consistent with the relief ordered by the Authority in such situations. *Id.* at 14. Furthermore, the GC contends that a nationwide posting is appropriate because the unit is nationwide, the grievance involved the parties at the national level, and the Respondent's improper conduct emanated from its national office.[2] *Id.*

IV. Analysis and Conclusions

For the following reasons, we deny the Respondent's first two exceptions and dismiss the third exception.

A. The Respondent committed a ULP by unlawfully refusing to participate in an arbitration proceeding pursuant to the parties' negotiated grievance procedure.

The Respondent argues that it is not refusing to arbitrate. Rather, the Respondent maintains that it wants to proceed to arbitration, but that the grievance cannot be resubmitted to Arbitrator Ross. The Respondent contends in this regard that the plain language of the contract concerning the right to unilaterally remove arbitrators from the national panel allows the Respondent to unilaterally remove Arbitrator Ross from consideration of the parties' pending grievance.[3]

---

2. The GC also argues that the Respondent attempts to bring new evidence before the Authority that was not presented to the Judge. Opp'n at 6. The evidence that the GC alleges that the Respondent presents to the Authority for the first time consists of facts such as that the parties have not used Arbitrator Ross since the Respondent removed him from the national panel and that the Union also once unilaterally removed an arbitrator from the panel. *Id.* at 6-7.

3. The Respondent also claims that the Authority's underlying decision upholding Arbitrator Ross's

1. Analytical framework.

Section 7121 of the Statute mandates binding arbitration for grievances that are not satisfactorily settled under the negotiated grievance procedure. *See* 5 U.S.C. § 7121(b)(1)(C)(iii). The Authority has found that an agency's refusal to participate in the arbitration process pursuant to a negotiated grievance procedure is in conflict with § 7121 of the Statute and is therefore a violation of § 7116(a)(1) and (8). *See Army Reserve Command,* 11 FLRA 55, 56 (1983). This is because a party's refusal to participate in the arbitration process results in the hindrance or obstruction of grievance resolution through binding arbitration, which is contrary to the mandate and intent of Congress in enacting § 7121. *Id.* In addition, choosing an arbitrator to hear a grievance, pursuant to the procedures the parties agree to for choosing arbitrators, is a fundamental component of the binding arbitration process. *Cf. AFGE, Local 1457*, 39 FLRA 519, 522, 528 (1991) (affirming Judge's finding that refusal to participate in selecting arbitrator is a ULP).

2. The Respondent's refusal to resubmit this grievance to arbitration before Arbitrator Ross constitutes a refusal to arbitrate.

The language in the CBA does not support the Respondent's claim that it is not refusing to arbitrate. In the matter before us, the process for selecting an arbitrator, set forth in Article 9, § 11 of the parties' CBA, addresses the selection of arbitrators in two different contexts: choosing an arbitrator to serve on the national panel and choosing an arbitrator who serves on the national panel to hear a grievance. As the Judge noted, when choosing an arbitrator to serve on the panel or filling a panel vacancy, Article 9, § 11 provides that the parties will act jointly. Judge's Decision at 4 (quoting Respondent Ex. 1 at 26). Section 11 also states that the parties may act unilaterally when removing an arbitrator from the panel. *Id.* (quoting Respondent Ex. 1 at 26).

However, when choosing an arbitrator to hear a grievance, the parties may only act jointly: they either mutually agree on an arbitrator who serves on the panel or they take turns striking names until they have one candidate left to hear the grievance. Nothing in the CBA indicates that the parties intended to allow unilateral action regarding the selection or removal of a specific arbitrator to hear a grievance. Specifically, the CBA is silent regarding the parties' right to act unilaterally regarding an arbitrator that has already been jointly selected. This, in conjunction with the fact that the parties are contractually authorized to act alone regarding only the removal of arbitrators from the national panel, supports the Judge's conclusion that taking action regarding an arbitrator already jointly selected requires further joint action. The Respondent was not contractually entitled to unilaterally remove the jointly selected arbitrator. Therefore, the Respondent's refusal to allow Arbitrator Ross to hear the grievance is inconsistent with the procedures the parties have established for choosing arbitrators to hear grievances. Accordingly, we deny the Respondent's exception and find that the Respondent committed a ULP when it refused to resubmit this grievance to arbitration before Arbitrator Ross.

B. A remedy requiring the Respondent to participate in proceedings before the arbitrator would not be inappropriate due to arbitrator bias.

The Respondent claims that the Judge's recommended order that the grievance be submitted to Arbitrator Ross is inappropriate. In support of this contention, the Respondent claims that Arbitrator Ross would be biased because the Respondent removed him from the national panel. Exceptions at 11.

The Respondent provides no evidence or legal support to establish that Arbitrator Ross should be excluded from hearing the grievance based on bias in the circumstances of this case. Specifically, the decisions that the Respondent cites are not binding on the Authority and are inapposite because they contain factual scenarios different from the circumstances presented in this case.[4] In addition, to accept the

---

determination that the grievance was arbitrable required the parties to resubmit the grievance to an arbitrator but not specifically to Arbitrator Ross. Exceptions at 2. However, in that decision, the Authority clearly indicated that the parties must resubmit the grievance to Arbitrator Ross. *FAA*, 61 FLRA at 636. Furthermore, upon receiving the Authority's decision in that case, the Respondent did not request reconsideration. *See* 5 C.F.R. § 2429.17.

4. For example, the Respondent relies on *Palmer Plastics, Inc. v. Rubin*, 108 N.Y.S.2d 514 (1951) (*Palmer Plastics*) to argue that Arbitrator Ross should be disqualified. However, this case concerns a very different factual situation. In *Palmer Plastics*, the arbitrator was chosen at a time when he was the personal attorney for both the president of Palmer Plastics and the respondent, who was a shareholder in Palmer Plastics. *Id.* at 516. However, by the time the arbitrator was called on to arbitrate a

Respondent's claim that Arbitrator Ross cannot now hear this grievance would only validate the Respondent's unlawful action. As the GC argues, it would be counterintuitive to find that Arbitrator Ross must now be removed due to bias against the Respondent that is the result of the Respondent's unlawful attempt to remove him. Opp'n at 11-12.

Finally, that the Respondent has vowed to file exceptions if Arbitrator Ross hears the grievance and finds against it has no bearing on the Authority's determination. As the Judge noted, either party may file exceptions to an arbitral award pursuant to § 7122 of the Statute. If the Respondent ultimately exercises its right to do so, its arguments will be considered by the Authority at that time. For these reasons, we deny the Respondent's exception that Arbitrator Ross cannot hear the grievance because he would be biased.

C. A nationwide posting is appropriate.

The Respondent argues that a nationwide posting is not appropriate. Exceptions at 12. Specifically, it claims that a nationwide posting is a remedy for a violation of the Statute, while the issue in this case concerns contractual interpretation. *Id.*

The Respondent's argument that a nationwide posting is not an appropriate remedy in this case is not properly before the Authority. Under § 2429.5 of the Authority's Regulations,[5] the Authority will not consider issues that could have been, but were not, presented to an administrative law judge. *See, e.g., U.S. Dep't of Transp., FAA, Wash. D.C.*, 64 FLRA 410, 412-13 (2010). Where a party makes an argument for the first time on exceptions that could have been, but were not, made before the judge, the Authority applies § 2429.5 to bar the argument. *See, e.g., id.* at 413-14; *U.S. Dep't of Transp., FAA, Houston, Tex.*, 63 FLRA 34, 36 (2008).

Although the Respondent made several arguments before the Judge, there is no indication in the record that the Respondent argued, as it does in its exceptions, that a nationwide posting is an inappropriate remedy in this case. In fact, the Respondent did not address remedies in either the ULP hearing or its post-hearing brief. The Respondent could have, but did not, argue to the Judge what it believed constitutes an appropriate remedy if the Judge were to find that it committed a ULP. Accordingly, we dismiss the Agency's exception that the Judge's recommended remedy is inappropriate.[6]

VI. Order

Pursuant to § 2423.41 of the Authority's Regulations and § 7118 of the Statute, the United States Department of Transportation, Federal Aviation Administration shall:

1. Cease and desist from:

(a) Refusing to participate in proceedings before Arbitrator Jerome Ross in the 2004 grievance concerning the Respondent's failure to upgrade the Air Traffic Control (ATC) level of its Atlanta facility (ATC grievance).

(b) In any like or related manner, interfering with, restraining, or coercing its employees in the exercise of their rights assured by the Statute.

2. Take the following affirmative action in order to effectuate the purposes and policies of the Statute:

(a) Participate fully in the proceedings before Arbitrator Ross concerning the ATC grievance.

(b) In the event that Arbitrator Ross is unavailable, cooperate in the selection of another arbitrator and participate fully in the proceedings before that arbitrator concerning the ATC grievance.

(c) Post at all of its facilities at which bargaining unit employees represented by the National Air Traffic Controllers Association are assigned copies of the attached Notice on forms to be

---

disagreement between the two, he no longer represented the president. *Id.* at 517. In addition, the arbitrator saw the shareholder socially and the arbitrator's wife had become involved in a business venture with the shareholder. *Id.* at 516-17. As a result of these circumstances and relationships, the court removed the arbitrator "in the interests of justice[.]" *Id.* at 520.

5. Section 2429.5 was amended October 1, 2010. *See* Fed. Reg. 42,283 (2010). For purposes of this case, we apply the previous version of the regulation that was in effect at all times relevant to the processing of this case.

6. Because we are denying or dismissing all of the Respondent's exceptions, we do not need to address the GC's preliminary argument that the Respondent relied on evidence in its exceptions to the Authority that it did not bring before the Judge. The Respondent's exceptions have no merit, even taking into account all of the allegedly new evidence it presents to the Authority.

furnished by the Authority. Upon receipt of such forms, they shall be signed by the Administrator of the Federal Aviation Administration and shall be posted and maintained for 60 consecutive days thereafter in conspicuous places, including all bulletin boards and other places where notices to employees are customarily posted. Reasonable steps shall be taken to insure that such Notices are not altered, defaced, or covered by other materials.

(d) Pursuant to § 2423.41(e) of the Authority's Regulations, notify the Regional Director of the Chicago Regional Office of the Authority, in writing, within 30 days of this Order, as to what steps have been taken to comply.

NOTICE TO ALL EMPLOYEES
POSTED BY ORDER OF THE
FEDERAL LABOR RELATIONS AUTHORITY

The Federal Labor Relations Authority has found that the United States Department of Transportation, Federal Aviation Administration (FAA) violated the Federal Service Labor-Management Relations Statute (the Statute) and has ordered us to post and abide by this notice.

WE HEREBY NOTIFY EMPLOYEES THAT:

WE WILL NOT refuse to participate in proceedings before Arbitrator Jerome Ross in the 2004 grievance concerning the FAA's failure to upgrade the Air Traffic Control (ATC) level of its Atlanta facility (ATC grievance).

WE WILL NOT, in any like or related manner, interfere with, restrain, or coerce our employees in the exercise of their rights assured by the Statute.

WE WILL participate fully in the proceedings before Arbitrator Ross concerning the ATC grievance.

WE WILL, in the event that Arbitrator Ross is unavailable, cooperate in the selection of another arbitrator and participate fully in the proceedings before that arbitrator concerning the ATC grievance.

____
(Respondent Representative)

Dated: _______ By:__________________________
(Signature) (Title)

This Notice must remain posted for 60 consecutive days from the date of posting, and must not be altered, defaced, or covered by any other material.

If employees have any questions concerning this Notice or compliance with its provisions, then they may communicate directly with the Regional Director, Chicago Regional Office, whose address is: Federal Labor Relations Authority, 55 West Monroe Street, Suite 1150, Chicago, IL 60603-9729, and whose telephone number is: (312) 886-3465.

Office of Administrative Law Judges

U.S. DEPARTMENT OF TRANSPORTATION
FEDERAL AVIATION ADMINISTRATION
WASHINGTON, D.C.
Respondent

and

NATIONAL AIR TRAFFIC CONTROLLERS
ASSOCIATION
Charging Party

Case No. WA-CA-06-0706

Thomas F. Bianco, Esq.
John F. Gallagher, Esq.
For the General Counsel

Patrick Daniel McGlone
Jessica Bartlett
For the Respondent

Sandra Riviears, Esq.
Marc S. Shapiro, Esq.
For the Charging Party

Before: PAUL B. LANG
Administrative Law Judge

DECISION

Statement of the Case

On September 20, 2006, The National Air Traffic Controllers Association, AFL-CIO (Union) filed an unfair labor practice charge (GC Ex. 1(a)) against the U.S. Department of Transportation, Federal Aviation Administration, Washington, DC (Respondent or FAA). On January 31, 2007, the Regional Director of the Chicago Region of the Federal Labor Relations Authority (Authority) issued a Complaint and Notice of Hearing (GC Ex. 1(b)) in which it was alleged that the Respondent committed an unfair labor practice in violation of §7116(a)(1) and (8) of the Federal Service Labor-Management Relations Statute (Statute) by refusing to participate in an arbitration proceeding in violation of §7121 of the Statute. The Respondent filed a timely Answer (GC Ex. 1(e)) in which it denied that it had committed the alleged unfair labor practice.[1/]

A hearing was held in Washington, DC on April 18, 2007. The parties were present with counsel and were afforded the opportunity to present evidence and to cross-examine witnesses. This Decision is based upon consideration of all of the evidence and of the post-hearing briefs submitted by the parties.

Preliminary Issue

The General Counsel moved to exclude all of the Respondent's evidence because the Respondent did not file its Pre-hearing Disclosure 14 days prior to the hearing as required by §2423.23 of the Rules and Regulations of the Authority. In fact, the Respondent did not file its Pre-hearing disclosure until I suggested to its counsel that he do so during the course of the pre-hearing conference which was held one week before the hearing.

Counsel for the Respondent presented two excuses for the late filing. One was that he had "inherited" the case from another attorney; the other was that the case had moved between two regional offices of the Authority. Neither of those excuses have the slightest merit. As to the first excuse, the Respondent's Answer was signed by its current counsel, thus indicating that he had responsibility for the case well before the Pre-hearing Disclosure was due. As to the second excuse, there is no logical connection between the transfer of the case between the Washington and Chicago regional offices and the Respondent's failure to comply with the pertinent regulation.

The above factors notwithstanding, neither the General Counsel nor the Union could identify any significant prejudice arising out of the late filing. Therefore, in order to allow the case to proceed on its merits rather than on a narrow, although important, procedural issue, I allowed the Respondent to submit testimony and evidence in accordance with its Pre-hearing Disclosure. It would be a serious mistake to interpret this ruling as establishing a precedent.

1. Shortly after the commencement of the hearing the Respondent amended paragraph 12 of the Answer so as to admit, with an explanation, that it had refused to submit the grievance to Arbitrator Ross (Tr. 13, 14).

Positions of the Parties

The General Counsel maintains that, by refusing to allow a pending arbitration to be resubmitted to Arbitrator Jerome Ross following a remand by the Authority, the Respondent breached its obligations under §7121 of the Statute. The General Counsel further maintains that the Respondent has failed to establish an affirmative defense under the collective bargaining agreement (CBA) between the parties. While, under the CBA, either party may unilaterally remove an arbitrator from the national panel, the CBA is silent as to the right of a party to unilaterally strike an arbitrator after selection. According to the General Counsel, the past practice of the parties is that an arbitrator may not be removed unilaterally after he or she has been selected to hear a specific grievance.

The Respondent maintains that the Authority's order of remand only requires that the pending grievance be resubmitted to arbitration, but not to any particular arbitrator. Therefore, the Respondent was entitled to exercise its contractual right to unilaterally remove Arbitrator Ross from the panel. The Respondent further maintains that the clear language of the CBA authorizes its action and that the parties have exercised their contractual right to unilaterally remove an arbitrator on numerous occasions.

The Respondent argues that, even if the Authority contemplated the remand of the grievance to Arbitrator Ross, the parties would not have been relieved of their obligation to proceed to arbitration if Arbitrator Ross was unavailable for any reason. The Respondent's exercise of its contractual right of unilateral removal rendered Arbitrator Ross unavailable, thereby obligating the parties to choose a different arbitrator. The Respondent emphasizes that it is not attempting to evade its obligation to resubmit the grievance to arbitration and has consistently expressed its willingness to cooperate with the Union in selecting another arbitrator. Furthermore, the Respondent was not motivated by a desire to influence the outcome of the pending grievance. Rather, it removed Arbitrator Ross because he engaged in unauthorized interest arbitration in another grievance.

The Respondent suggests that, since Arbitrator Ross is aware of his removal from the panel, his reinstatement would have a "negative affect [*sic*]" on the outcome of a future decision involving the Respondent and cites precedent in support of the proposition that an arbitrator may be removed because of the appearance of bias. The Respondent further states that, if the pending grievance is remanded to Arbitrator Ross and if he sustains the grievance, it will appeal on the grounds of prejudice arising out of this case. Such an appeal would further delay the resolution of the underlying dispute.

Findings of Fact

The Respondent is an agency within the meaning of §7103(a)(3) of the Statute. The Union is a labor organization as defined by §7103(a)(4) of the Statute. At all times pertinent to this case the Union and the Respondent were parties to a CBA (Resp. Ex. 1). Article 9 of the CBA, entitled "**GRIEVANCE PROCEDURE**", states, in Section 11, Step 2 (p. 26):

> The Parties will create a national panel of three (3) mutually acceptable arbitrators. Each Party may unilaterally remove an arbitrator from the panel and another arbitrator shall be mutually selected to fill the vacancy. Within seven (7) calendar days after receipt of the request [to arbitrate], an arbitrator shall be selected from the panel by the Parties or by alternately striking names until one (1) remains or as otherwise mutually agreed.

The Order of Remand

The facts surrounding the grievance at issue are undisputed. On March 9, 2004, the Union filed a grievance alleging that the Respondent wrongfully failed to upgrade the level of its Atlanta facility. The grievance was eventually referred to Arbitrator Ross and the parties agreed to bifurcate the grievance between the issues of arbitrability and merits. Arbitrator Ross ruled that the grievance was arbitrable and the Respondent thereupon filed exceptions. On July 27, 2006, the Authority directed the parties to resubmit the grievance to arbitration. (GC Ex. 1(b) and 1(e), ¶¶8-11).

Michael Herlihy, Respondent's Manager of Third Party Services for headquarters, testified that, at some point prior to the Authority's ruling on the Respondent's exceptions, the Respondent notified Arbitrator Ross and the Union that the Respondent was removing him from the panel (Tr. 32, 34).[2] The Respondent apparently did not inform the Authority of the removal (Tr. 18).

The order of remand by the Authority is to be found at 61 FLRA 634 dated July 27, 2006. The first sentence of the decision, under "Statement of the Case", refers to "Arbitrator Jerome H. Ross", but his name is not mentioned again. The decision contains a number of references to "the Arbitrator"; in the final sentence, under "Decision", the Authority states:

> The grievance is remanded to the parties for resubmission to the Arbitrator, absent settlement, for further findings consistent with this decision.

Past Practice

Although the evidence regarding past practice is also undisputed, the parties differ as to its significance. Marc S. Shapiro, an attorney for the Union, testified that, to the best of his understanding, the parties have in the past agreed to change an arbitrator after his selection but before he issued a decision. Shapiro further testified that he was unaware of any instance where such removal was effected unilaterally (Tr. 25).

Robert Taylor, the Director of Contract Administration and Training for the Union, described three incidents in which the parties agreed to remove an arbitrator after his selection (Tr. 39, 40).[3] Taylor also testified that, on August 21, 2002, as Director of Labor Relations for the Union, he sent a letter (GC Ex. 3) to Arbitrator Robert Harris notifying him that the Union was unilaterally removing him from the panel. Taylor was subsequently informed by William Osborne, outside counsel for the Union, that he could not unilaterally remove an arbitrator after his selection to hear a grievance. Taylor thereupon sent another letter to Arbitrator Harris on August 23 (GC Ex. 4) in which he rescinded the unilateral removal. Some time after Taylor sent the two letters to Arbitrator Harris he received a letter from Elizabeth J. Head, a Labor Relations Specialist for the Respondent, (GC Ex. 5) protesting the Union's attempt to unilaterally remove Arbitrator Harris and expressing the assumption that the Union would honor its contractual obligations by proceeding with the grievance that was before Arbitrator Harris. According to Taylor, this was the only prior instance in which either of the parties attempted to unilaterally remove an arbitrator after he had been selected to hear a grievance (Tr. 40-45).

Herlihy testified that the parties have unilaterally removed arbitrators on a number of occasions. However, he only cited the instance involving Arbitrator Harris as an example of either party even attempting to unilaterally removing an arbitrator after his selection to hear a grievance (Tr. 31).

Discussion and Analysis

The Authority has long held that the failure of a party to proceed to and participate in arbitration is inconsistent with the intent of §7121 of the Statute and is an unfair labor practice in violation of §7116(a)(1) and (8), *Department of Labor, Employment Standards Administration/Wage and Hour Division, Washington, D.C.*, 10 FLRA 316, 320 (1982). However, this case does not present a classic instance of a refusal to arbitrate since the General Counsel does not contest the fact that the Respondent has consistently indicated its willingness to proceed with the pending grievance before an arbitrator other than Arbitrator Ross. The disagreement between the parties centers on the meaning of the order of remand by the Authority and the intent of Article 9, Section 11 of the CBA.

The Respondent is correct in its assertion that the order of remand does not specifically address the issue of the effect of its unilateral removal of Arbitrator Ross. That is so because, whether by design or oversight, the Respondent did not raise the issue with the Authority. Simple logic indicates that the Authority assumed that the grievance would be remanded to Arbitrator Ross unless he became unavailable for reasons other than the unwillingness of one of the parties to use his services. If the Respondent was convinced that it was contractually entitled to unilaterally remove the Arbitrator during the pendency of the grievance, it could have informed the Authority of its action prior to the issuance of the decision, thus affording the Authority the opportunity to eliminate any purported ambiguity.

2. The General Counsel's Pre-hearing Disclosure (GC Ex. 2) cites a letter from the Respondent to Arbitrator Ross dated October 12, 2005, by which he was removed from the panel. The letter itself is not in evidence.

3. It is unclear whether Shapiro and Taylor were referring to the removal of an arbitrator from the panel or simply from the adjudication of an individual grievance.

The aforementioned factors notwithstanding, the threshold issue is whether the Respondent was contractually entitled to unilaterally remove Arbitrator Ross from the panel or, more precisely, whether his unilateral removal had any effect on his status with regard to the pending grievance. In *Dept. of Veterans Affairs, Ralph H. Johnson Medical Center, Charleston, South Carolina*, 57 FLRA 495, 498 (2001) the Authority held that, in ascertaining the meaning of contractual language, the Administrative Law Judge is to follow standards and principles applied by arbitrators and federal courts. It is axiomatic that contractual intent must, whenever possible, be determined from the language of the contract itself. Extrinsic evidence of past practice may only be considered to resolve ambiguous contract language, *Quick v. NLRB*, 245 F.3d. 231, 247 (3d Cir. 2001).

While the contractual language in question does not specifically state whether the parties may unilaterally remove an arbitrator during the pendency of a grievance, it can hardly be considered to be ambiguous. In the first place, the paragraph which establishes the right of unilateral removal from the panel then goes on to describe the procedure for the selection of an arbitrator from the panel to adjudicate an individual grievance. This language demonstrates the intent of the parties to distinguish the process of removing arbitrators from the panel, which allows for unilateral action, from that of selecting arbitrators for grievances, which requires joint action. It strains credibility to suppose that the parties intended to allow the unilateral removal of an arbitrator from consideration of a pending grievance, a highly unusual procedure, without specifically saying so. There is nothing in the record to rebut the Respondent's assertion that it sought to remove Arbitrator Ross for reasons having nothing to do with the pending grievance. Nevertheless, to accept the Respondent's construction of the CBA would be to allow for the removal of an arbitrator for any reason, including dissatisfaction with his preliminary rulings in a pending grievance or a desire to redo the arbitration hearing.

The Respondent's reliance on past practice is misplaced. The undisputed evidence shows that, although the Union attempted to unilaterally remove an arbitrator after his selection to hear a grievance, it was advised by Union counsel that it could not do so and a responsible representative of the Respondent espoused the same position. Even if I were to accept the far-fetched proposition, as put forward by the Respondent, that Head, as a Labor Relations Specialist, was not high enough on the management ladder to commit the Respondent to a contractual interpretation, the most that can be said is that past practice is neutral. The fact remains that the Union rescinded its unilateral removal of the arbitrator and that its decision to do so was not merely because it had a change of heart. The fact that the arbitrator later recused himself, almost certainly because of the Union's action, (Tr. 31) reinforces my conclusion that the parties did not intend to allow for unilateral removal of an arbitrator after his selection to hear a grievance.

I have dismissed out of hand any consideration of the Respondent's assertion that it will appeal an adverse decision by Arbitrator Ross because of the possibility of bias and that such an appeal would further delay the resolution of the underlying grievance. To do otherwise would be to assume that Arbitrator Ross lacks the integrity to put aside any personal feelings he might have because of his removal from the panel by the Respondent. The fact that the Respondent has made such an argument raises the question of whether it is attempting to induce the Union to abandon its position and to allow the grievance to go before another arbitrator.

Either party has the right to seek review of an arbitral award pursuant to §7122 of the Statute. However, it is unlikely that the Authority would set aside an award merely because of the possibility of bias arising out of a situation created by the Respondent.

The Remedy

It would be unrealistic not to anticipate the possibility that Arbitrator Ross might be unwilling or otherwise unavailable to hear the remainder of the grievance. I will therefore recommend an Order which requires the Respondent to cooperate in the submission of the grievance to another arbitrator if necessary.

For the foregoing reasons, I have concluded that the Respondent committed an unfair labor practice in violation of §7116(a)(1) and (8) of the Statute by refusing to allow the pending grievance to be resubmitted to Arbitrator Ross. Accordingly, I recommend that the Authority adopt the following Order:

ORDER

Pursuant to §2423.41(c) of the Rules and Regulations of the Authority and §7118 of the Federal Service Labor-Management Relations Statute (Statute), it is hereby ordered that U.S. Department of Transportation, Federal Aviation Administration, Washington, DC (Respondent), shall:

1. Cease and desist from:

(a) Refusing to participate in proceedings before Arbitrator Jerome Ross in the 2004 grievance concerning the Respondent's failure to upgrade the Air Traffic Control (ATC) level of its Atlanta facility (ATC grievance).

(b) In any like or related manner, interfering with, restraining or coercing its employees in the exercise of their rights assured by the Statute.

2. Take the following affirmative action in order to effectuate the purposes and policies of the Statute:

(a) Participate fully in the proceedings before Arbitrator Ross concerning the ATC grievance.

(b) In the event that Arbitrator Ross is unavailable, cooperate in the selection of another arbitrator and participate fully in the proceedings before that arbitrator concerning the ATC grievance.

(c) Post at all of its facilities at which bargaining unit employees represented by the National Air Traffic Controllers Association are assigned copies of the attached Notice on forms to by furnished by the Authority. Upon receipt of such forms, they shall be signed by the Administrator of the Federal Aviation Administration and shall be posted and maintained for 60 consecutive days thereafter in conspicuous places, including all bulletin boards and other places where notices to employees are customarily posted. Reasonable steps shall be taken to insure that such Notices are not altered, defaced or covered by other materials.

(d) Pursuant to §2423.41(e) of the Rules and Regulations of the Authority, notify the Regional Director of the Chicago Region of the Authority, in writing, within 30 days of this Order, as to what steps have been taken to comply.

Issued, Washington, DC, July 13, 2007.

PAUL B. LANG
Administrative Law Judge

65 FLRA No. 50

UNITED STATES
DEPARTMENT OF THE AIR FORCE
355 FIGHTER WING
DAVIS MONTHAN AIR FORCE BASE
TUCSON, ARIZONA
(Agency)

and

AMERICAN FEDERATION
OF GOVERNMENT EMPLOYEES
LOCAL 2924
(Union)

0-AR-4505
(63 FLRA 331 (2009))

DECISION

October 29, 2010

Before the Authority: Carol Waller Pope, Chairman, and Thomas M. Beck and Ernest DuBester, Members[1]

I. Statement of the Case

This matter is before the Authority on exceptions to an award (the fee award) of Arbitrator Frederick Day filed by the Union under§7122(a) of the Federal Service Labor-Management Relations Statute (the Statute) and part 2425 of the Authority's Regulations. The Agency filed an opposition to the Union's exceptions.

The Arbitrator denied the Union's application for an award of attorney fees. For the reasons that follow, we set aside the award and remand it to the parties for resubmission to the Arbitrator, absent settlement.

II. Background and Arbitrator's Awards

A. Merits Award

The Agency suspended the grievant on the basis of two charges: (1) failure to follow proper orders; and (2) inappropriate conduct.[2] The charge of failure to follow proper orders was based on the grievant's refusal of an order to disassemble an aircraft fuel cell. The charge of inappropriate conduct was based on the grievant's behavior towards his supervisor and his behavior in handing in his credentials, quitting his job, and leaving the worksite.[3] Merits Award at 2-6. The parties submitted to arbitration the stipulated issue of whether the Agency had just cause to suspend the grievant.

With regard to the charge of failure to follow proper orders, the Arbitrator acknowledged that, in refusing to disassemble the fuel cell, the grievant disputed whether the cell was "dry," as alleged by the Agency, and expressed safety concerns about exposure to contaminants and inadequate personal protective equipment. *Id.* at 5. As to the condition of the cell, the Arbitrator first noted the testimony of the Agency's occupational safety and health expert, who testified that, under the Agency's technical orders, a "wet" fuel cell is a cell containing jet fuel and a dry fuel cell is a cell in which the jet fuel has been drained and purged from the cell with oil. *Id.* The Arbitrator further noted that the Agency's expert conceded that dry fuel cells are not "literally dry" because they are wet with oil and residual jet fuel, but claimed that there should be only "minimal puddles" in a dry cell. *Id.*

Despite the testimony of the Agency's expert, the Arbitrator found that the grievant was also an expert in the matter of servicing fuel cells and was the only witness to the actual condition of the disputed fuel cell. *Id.* at 12. The Arbitrator credited the grievant's testimony that, although the Agency considers fuel cells purged with oil to be dry, they are often wet with jet fuel foam, puddles of jet fuel and oil, and leaking residual jet fuel from fuel lines. In addition, he found that the disputed fuel cell actually contained wet foam, puddles of jet fuel and oil, and leaky fuel valves that were different from the "ideal conditions" of dry fuel cells described by the Agency's safety expert and the Agency's technical

1. Member Beck's dissenting opinion is set forth at the end of this decision.

2. The Arbitrator noted that the Agency reduced the proposed suspension from fourteen days to five days and then to two days. Merits Award at 2 n.1. However, the Arbitrator acknowledged that the grievant had served a five-day suspension and further acknowledged the Union's claim that, as of the date of submission of its post-hearing brief, the grievant had not been reimbursed for the three days that he served over and above the two-day reduced penalty. *Id.*

3. The grievant, with the Agency's approval, subsequently rescinded his resignation. *Id.* at 5.

orders. *Id.* at 10. He also credited the grievant's testimony that, in working on such cells in the past, his coveralls became saturated with fuel and oil and partially deteriorated, soaking his clothes and body. *Id.* at 9-10. Accordingly, the Arbitrator determined that, when the grievant refused to enter the cell, his safety concerns about the fuel system were legitimate. Additionally, the Arbitrator found that, under the Agency's technical orders, the Agency should have provided the grievant with the proper protective equipment and that, under the parties' collective bargaining agreement, the grievant's supervisor should have requested an inspection of the disputed fuel cell by Agency safety or health officials instead of ordering the grievant to enter and disassemble the cell without examining the condition of the cell himself. *Id.* at 11-13.

For the foregoing reasons, the Arbitrator concluded that the grievant's refusal to follow the order was justified and that no discipline was warranted for the refusal. *Id.* at 13.

With regard to the charge of inappropriate conduct, the Arbitrator found that the grievant's conduct was abrupt, disrespectful, and inappropriate. He concluded that the Agency had just cause to reprimand, but not suspend, the grievant for this conduct. *Id.* at 14. The Arbitrator awarded the grievant backpay. *Id.*

The Agency filed exceptions to the merits award, and the Authority denied them. *U.S. Dep't of the Air Force, 355 Fighter Wing, Davis-Monthan Air Force Base, Tucson, Ariz.*, 63 FLRA 331 (2009). Thereafter, the Union filed an application for attorney fees.

B. Fee Award

In the fee award, as relevant here, the Arbitrator addressed whether an award of fees was warranted in the interest of justice under the criteria established by the Merit Systems Protection Board (MSPB) in *Allen v. USPS*, 2 M.S.P.R. 420 (1980) (*Allen*).[4] The Arbitrator considered whether criterion 5 of *Allen* was satisfied because the Agency knew or should have known that it would not prevail on the merits when it suspended the grievant. In this regard, the Arbitrator noted that the Agency's charge of failure to follow proper orders was based on the characteristics of a wet fuel cell, as set forth in the Agency's technical orders. He acknowledged that he had found, in the merits award, that the Agency was wrong about the actual condition of the disputed fuel cell. Fee Award at 10. Nevertheless, the Arbitrator found that the Agency's action was reasonable on the basis of its "by-the-book" view of the disputed fuel cell. *Id.*

In addition, he rejected the Union's contention that criterion 5 was satisfied because "the 'same evidence' presented at the arbitration hearing was available to the Agency" when the Agency decided to suspend the grievant. *Id.* Instead, he emphasized that, when the Agency made that decision, the Agency was under no obligation to credit the grievant's account of the incident because of its belief that he was attempting to avoid the assigned work. He also found that the Agency presented credible evidence at the arbitration hearing and that there was no evidence that the Agency was negligent. *Id.* at 10-11.

The Arbitrator also addressed the Union's claim that *Lambert v. Dep't of the Air Force,* 34 M.S.P.R. 501, 507 (1987), established a *per se* rule that fees are warranted in the interest of justice under criterion 5 whenever an agency's chosen penalty is mitigated. Fee Award at 11. The Arbitrator rejected this claim, noting that, in *Dunn v. Dep't of Veterans Affairs*, 98 F.3d 1308 (Fed. Cir. 1996) (*Dunn*), the court held that a "presumption of fees upon mitigation of a penalty runs counter to the statutory requirement that the employee show that the interests of justice warrant an award." Fee Award at 12 (quoting *Dunn*, 98 F.3d at 1313).

For the foregoing reasons, the Arbitrator concluded that fees were not warranted in the interest of justice under *Allen* criterion 5. In addition, he found that fees were not warranted under *Allen* criteria 1 and 2. Accordingly, he denied the Union's

4. In *Allen*, the MSPB listed five broad categories of cases in which an award of attorney fees would be warranted in the interest of justice: (1) where the agency engaged in a prohibited personnel practice; (2) where the agency action was clearly without merit or wholly unfounded or the employee was substantially innocent of charges brought by the agency; (3) where the agency initiated the action in bad faith; (4) where the agency committed a gross procedural error; and (5) where the agency knew or should have known that it would not prevail on the merits when it brought the proceeding. 2 M.S.P.R. at 434-35. An award of fees is also warranted in the interest of justice in cases brought under the Statute when there is a service to the federal workforce or a benefit to the public derived from maintaining the action. *E.g., U.S. Dep't of the Navy, Commander, Navy Region Haw., Fed. Fire Dep't, Naval Station Pearl Harbor, Honolulu, Haw.*, 64 FLRA 925, 928 (2010).

fee application without addressing the reasonableness of the amount of fees requested. *Id.*

III. Positions of the Parties

A. Union's Exceptions

The Union contends that the Arbitrator erred by concluding that *Allen* criterion 5 was not satisfied. Exceptions at 11. In this connection, the Union asserts that the Arbitrator failed to address and evaluate the evidence available to the Agency when it suspended the grievant, and notes that the Arbitrator found in the merits award that only the grievant actually knew the condition of the fuel tank. Accordingly, the Union claims that the merits award supports a conclusion that the Agency knew or should have known that it would not prevail when it suspended the grievant, and that the Arbitrator's conclusion otherwise is an inappropriate reexamination by the Arbitrator of his original findings. *Id.* at 12-13. The Union also argues that *Allen* criteria 1 and 2 were satisfied. *Id.* at 7-9. Finally, the Union contends that the award is deficient as based on a nonfact because the Arbitrator incorrectly stated that his merits award reduced a two-day suspension to a letter of reprimand. *Id.* at 14.

B. Agency's Opposition

The Agency contends that the Arbitrator did not err in concluding that an award of fees was not warranted in the interest of justice. Opp'n at 6-9. As to *Allen* criterion 5, the Agency notes that the Arbitrator specifically found in the fee award that there was no evidence that the Agency was negligent in its investigation or otherwise acted in a negligent manner. The Agency argues that the Authority should defer to these factual findings and deny the exception. *Id.* at 9. Further, the Agency contends that the Union fails to establish that the award is based on a nonfact. *Id.* at 10.

IV. Analysis and Conclusions

When an exception involves an award's consistency with law, the Authority reviews *de novo* any questions of law raised by the exception and the award. *E.g., U.S. Dep't of the Navy, Commander, Naval Region Haw., Fed. Fire Dep't, Naval Station Pearl Harbor, Honolulu, Haw.*, 64 FLRA 925, 928 (2010). In applying a standard of *de novo* review, the Authority assesses whether an arbitrator's legal conclusions are consistent with the applicable standard of law. The award in this case must be in accordance with the standards established under 5 U.S.C. § 7701(g)(1) § 7701(g)(1)).[5] *Id.* According to the Union, the award is not in accordance with the standard that an award of fees is warranted when in the interest of justice. As such, we only address this requirement. *Id.*

The Authority resolves whether an award of fees is warranted in the interest of justice in accordance with § 7701(g)(1) by applying the criteria established by the MSPB in *Allen*. In resolving whether an arbitrator properly applied the criteria, the Authority looks to the decisions of the MSPB and the United States Court of Appeals for the Federal Circuit. *NAGE, Local R5-188*, 54 FLRA 1401, 1406 (1998). In addition, an award of fees is warranted in the interest of justice if any one of the *Allen* criteria is satisfied. *E.g., U.S. Dep't of the Air Force, Davis-Monthan Air Force Base, Tucson, Ariz.*, 64 FLRA 819, 821 (2010).

Under *Allen* criterion 5, an award of fees is warranted in the interest of justice when the agency knew or should have known that it would not prevail on the merits when it disciplined the employee. *Allen*, 2 M.S.P.R. at 435. Making this determination requires the arbitrator to evaluate the reasonableness of the agency's actions and positions in light of the information available to it when it disciplined the employee. *U.S. Dep't of Homeland Sec., ICE*, 64 FLRA 1003, 1006-07 (2010) (*ICE*).

In disciplinary actions, the penalty imposed by the agency is an aspect of the merits of an agency's case, and fees are warranted in the interest of justice when the agency knew or should have known that its choice of penalty would not be sustained. *Id.* at 1006. The critical point is that agencies act unreasonably by imposing penalties that it knows or should know will not withstand scrutiny. *NATCA*, 64 FLRA 799, 801 (2010). In this regard, the MSPB has found that, when the penalty is mitigated based on evidence before, or readily available to, the agency at the time of the disciplinary action, and no new information was presented at the merits hearing that was not available to the agency at the time of the discipline, such mitigation establishes that the agency knew or should have known that its choice of penalty would not be sustained. *E.g., Miller v. Dep't of the*

5. Section 7701(g)(1) provides, in pertinent part, that the MSPB "may require payment by the agency involved of reasonable attorney fees incurred by an employee . . . if the employee . . . is the prevailing party and the [MSPB] . . . determines that payment by the agency is warranted in the interest of justice[.]"

Army, 106 M.S.P.R. 547, 551 (2007); *Del Prete v. USPS*, 104 M.S.P.R. 429, 434-35 (2007). In addition, the MSPB has held that "by imposing an unreasonably excessive penalty, an agency acts irresponsibly and . . . knows or should know that the penalty will not survive [MSPB] scrutiny." *Hutchcraft v. Dep't of Transp.*, 55 M.S.P.R. 138, 142 (1992).

An arbitrator's assessment of whether the agency knew or should have known that it would not prevail is *primarily* factual. *ICE*, 64 FLRA at 1007. When the arbitrator's factual findings support the arbitrator's *legal* conclusion, the Authority denies exceptions to the arbitrator's determination. *Id.* However, in resolving fee requests, arbitrators may not reexamine or reevaluate the findings on the merits of the grievance. *See Miller*, 106 M.S.P.R. at 552 (Chairman McPhie dissenting as to another matter) (administrative judge's decision on the merits of the disciplinary action is not subject to recharacterization in support of a fee decision). In other words, the arbitrator cannot disregard the findings in the merits award in determining whether the agency knew or should have known that it would not prevail. *See Brunning v. GSA*, 63 M.S.P.R. 490, 493 (1994) (*Brunning*). Consequently, when the arbitrator's findings in the merits award support a conclusion that the agency knew or should have known that it would not prevail, the Authority will find a legal conclusion to the contrary (in a fee award) deficient. *Dep't of Health & Human Servs., Public Health Serv., Region IV, Atlanta, Ga.*, 34 FLRA 823, 831 (1990) (*Public Health Service*).

In *Public Health Service*, the arbitrator concluded that an award of fees was not warranted in the interest of justice under *Allen* criterion 5. However, the Authority found that the arbitrator's factual findings established that the agency relied on incomplete facts and information. *Id.* at 832. As the complete facts and information were available to the agency at the time of its disputed actions, the Authority concluded that the agency should have known that it would not prevail in arbitration. *Id.* Accordingly, the Authority determined that the arbitrator's legal conclusion to the contrary was not consistent with his factual findings and was deficient. *Id.* at 831-32.

Applying these principles here, the Arbitrator found, in the merits award, that the parties' agreement provides, in pertinent part: "If the supervisor believes that the condition or corrected condition does not pose an imminent danger, but the employee still believes that an imminent danger situation exists, then the supervisor shall request an inspection by an agency safety or health official." Merits Award at 11. The Arbitrator then found that the grievant's supervisor, "instead of requesting 'an inspection by an agency safety or health official' as the [a]greement directs, ordered [the g]rievant to enter and disassemble the fuel cell." *Id.* Further, the Arbitrator determined that the supervisor, "who ordered [the g]rievant to enter the cell, had not himself inspected the cell[,]" and that, "by the condition of the cell and by the directives for entry into cells in such condition, the Agency should have had [appropriate protective equipment] available." *Id.* at 12. The Arbitrator then concluded that the Agency did not have just cause for the charge of failure to follow proper orders, and mitigated the suspension to a reprimand. *Id.* at 14. By finding that the Agency improperly failed to inspect the fuel cell, the Arbitrator implicitly – and necessarily – found that information regarding the actual condition of the fuel cell was before and available to the Agency at the time of the decision to suspend the grievant.[6]

The Arbitrator's own findings in the merits award, which he acknowledged in the fee award, support a conclusion that -- as a matter of law -- an award of fees was warranted in the interest of justice. In this connection, as in *Miller*, it is evident from the merits award that, in mitigating the suspension, the Arbitrator relied solely on evidence that was before, or reasonably available to, the Agency when it suspended the grievant. *See Miller*, 106 M.S.P.R. at 551. In addition, as discussed previously, these findings were not subject to reevaluation and could not be disregarded by the Arbitrator in concluding whether an award of fees was not warranted in the interest of justice. As in *Public Health Service*, the Arbitrator's findings establish that the Agency relied on incomplete facts and information in failing to determine the actual condition of the fuel cell and that the complete facts and information were available to the Agency when it suspended the grievant.

As the Agency knew or should have known that it would not prevail, the Arbitrator's general statements in the fee award with regard to the credibility of the Agency's evidence and the reasonableness of the Agency's investigation cannot establish otherwise. *See Brunning*, 63 M.S.P.R. at 493. The decision in *Dunn*, cited by the Arbitrator,

6. In addition, we note that the Agency does not argue that information regarding the actual condition of the fuel cell was not available to the Agency when it suspended the grievant.

also does not establish otherwise. The court in *Dunn* held that penalty mitigation alone does not create a presumption in favor of satisfaction of any of the *Allen* factors and that fees were not warranted in the interest of justice in that case because the record did not show that the agency chose the penalty negligently or in disregard of relevant facts. *Dunn*, 98 F.3d at 1313. We are not holding that fees are warranted merely because the imposed penalty was mitigated. Rather, we are holding that fees are warranted because the Arbitrator's findings from the merits award demonstrate that the Agency disregarded relevant facts in failing to determine the actual condition of the fuel cell and acted irresponsibly in its choice of penalty.

For the reasons set forth above, we conclude that fees are warranted in the interest of justice and that the Arbitrator's fee award is deficient in concluding otherwise.[7] As the Arbitrator did not make a determination as to a reasonable amount of fees, we remand the award to the parties for resubmission to the Arbitrator, absent settlement, to determine that matter.

V. Decision

The award is set aside and remanded to the parties for resubmission to the Arbitrator, absent settlement.

7. In view of this conclusion, it is unnecessary to address the Union's remaining exceptions.

Member Beck, Dissenting:

I do not agree with my colleagues that the Arbitrator's denial of attorney fees is contrary to law insofar as the Arbitrator concluded that fees are not warranted under the fifth criterion of *Allen v. USPS*, 2 M.S.P.R. 420 (1980) (*Allen*).

This case is a close call. The Authority has long held that we defer to an arbitrator's "underlying factual findings" when we review an interest of justice determination. *NTEU, Chapter 50*, 54 FLRA 250, 255 (1998). Therefore, when an arbitrator "fully articulates the reasons supporting one of the interest of justice criteria, the Authority will defer to the arbitrator's findings." *U.S. Dep't of Def., Def. Distrib. Region E., New Cumberland, Pa.*, 51 FLRA 155, 162 (1995).

Accordingly, I cannot conclude, as my colleagues, that the Arbitrator "disregarded" the findings that he made in the Merits Award and that the Agency acted irresponsibly in its choice of penalty.

In the Merits Award, the Arbitrator finds that the grievant's concerns were "reasonable" and that the supervisor could have requested "an inspection by an agency safety or health official." Merits Award at 11. Based on those findings, the Arbitrator concludes that the Agency did not have just cause for discipline. In the Fee Award, the Arbitrator concludes that, even though the Agency was "wrong based upon the actual, as opposed to the by-the-book, condition of the fuel [cell]," the Agency's case was "well reasoned" and that the Agency was under "no obligation to credit [g]rievant's accounts of the incident[.]" Fee Award at 10.

These conclusions are reasonable and consistent, unlike the inconsistent findings of the arbitrator in *Department of Health and Human Services, Public Health Service, Region IV, Atlanta, Georgia*, 34 FLRA 823, 831-32 (1990). The findings of the Arbitrator support his denial of fees and are entitled to our deference.

Accordingly, I would deny the Union's exception insofar as it relies on the "knew or should have known" criterion under *Allen*.

65 FLRA No. 51

UNITED STATES
DEPARTMENT OF VETERANS AFFAIRS
VETERANS CANTEEN SERVICE
MARTINSBURG, WEST VIRGINIA
(Respondent)

and

NATIONAL ASSOCIATION
OF GOVERNMENT EMPLOYEES
LOCAL R4-78
(Charging Party)

WA-CA-09-0247

DECISION AND ORDER

October 29, 2010

Before the Authority: Carol Waller Pope, Chairman, and Thomas M. Beck and Ernest DuBester, Members

I. Statement of the Case

This unfair labor practice (ULP) case is before the Authority on exceptions to the attached decision of the Administrative Law Judge (Judge) filed by the Respondent. The General Counsel (GC) and the Charging Party filed oppositions to the Respondent's exceptions.

The amended complaint alleges that the Respondent violated § 7116(a)(1) and (8) of the Federal Service Labor-Management Relations Statute (the Statute) by refusing to participate in the arbitration of a grievance. The Judge determined that the Respondent violated § 7116(a)(1) and (8) of the Statute and recommended that the Authority issue a cease and desist order, require the Agency to proceed to arbitration concerning the grievance at issue, and require the Agency to post a notice of the ULP finding within sixty days.

Upon consideration of the decision and the entire record, we deny the Respondent's exceptions and adopt the Judge's findings, conclusions, and recommended order.

II. Background and Judge's Decision

A. Background

The grievant, a supply clerk, was removed by the Respondent from her position. The Charging Party grieved her removal, and the Respondent denied the grievance. *Id.* at 3. The Charging Party then invoked arbitration. After the parties had selected an arbitrator, the Respondent informed the arbitrator that it would not participate in the arbitration. *Id.* The Charging Party then filed a ULP charge against the Respondent. *Id.* at 1. The Regional Director of the Washington Regional Office of the Authority issued a Complaint and Notice of hearing, alleging that the Respondent had violated § 7116(a)(1), (5), and (8) of the Statute by refusing to arbitrate the grievance. *Id.* at 1-2. The Respondent filed its Answer to the Complaint, admitting the factual allegations, but denying that it had committed a ULP. *Id.* at 2.

B. Judge's Decision

Before the Judge, the Respondent contended that the grievant, as a Veterans Canteen Service (VCS) employee, had no right to pursue arbitration under the negotiated grievance procedure of the parties' collective bargaining agreement. *Id.* at 5. According to the Respondent, VCS employees are appointed under 38 U.S.C. § 7802, which provides that such employees may be "removed by the Secretary without regard to the provisions of title 5 governing appointments in the competitive service and chapter 51 and subchapter III of chapter 53 of title 5."[1] *Id.*

1. 38 U.S.C. § 7802(e) provides:

> (e) Personnel.--The Secretary shall employ such persons as are necessary for the establishment, maintenance, and operation of the Service, and pay the salaries, wages, and expenses of all such employees from the funds of the Service. Personnel necessary for the transaction of the business of the Service at canteens, warehouses, and storage depots shall be appointed, compensated from funds of the Service, and removed by the Secretary without regard to the provisions of title 5 governing appointments in the competitive service and chapter 51 and subchapter III of chapter 53 of title 5. Those employees are subject to the provisions of title 5 relating to a preference eligible described in section 2108(3) of title 5, subchapter I of chapter 81 of title 5, and subchapter III of chapter 83 of title 5. An employee appointed under this section may be considered for appointment to a Department position in the competitive service in the same manner that a Department employee in

The Respondent asserted that, because, by its plain language, the statute provides that VCS employees may be removed "without regard to title 5," they do not have the right under 5 U.S.C. § 7512 to appeal their removals to the Merit Systems Protection Board (MSPB). *Id.* (citing *Chavez v. Dep't of Veterans Affairs,* 65 M.S.P.R. 590, 592-94 (1994) (*Chavez*)). The Respondent further contended that, because the grievant was also a nonpreference eligible excepted service (NEES) employee, she had no right to challenge adverse actions. *Id.* at 5-6.

The Respondent asked the Judge to resolve the question of arbitrability. *Id.* at 6. The Respondent acknowledged the general principle that parties must arbitrate all unresolved grievances, including questions of arbitrability, but contended that the Authority had carved out an exception from this general rule in *Director of Administration Headquarters, United States Air Force*, 17 FLRA 372 (1985) (*HQ, USAF*) for matters involving "clearly established" law. *Id.*

The Judge found that the language of 38 U.S.C. § 7802(e) was not as plain or as clear as the Respondent alleged and that an arbitrator would need to resolve significant issues of law and statutory construction in order to resolve the question of arbitrability. *Id.* In this regard, the Judge noted that, although the Respondent argued that the plain language of the statute provides that "VCS employees appointed under [§ 7802] may be removed . . . without regard to Title 5 provisions[,]" § 7802(e) actually provides that employees may be "removed by the Secretary without regard to the provisions of title 5 *governing appointments in the competitive service and chapter 51 and subchapter III of chapter 53 of title 5*." *Id.* (emphasis added). The Judge further noted that VCS employees are in the excepted service, not the competitive service, and under the plain language of the statute, would be excluded only from a narrow portion of title 5. *Id.* According to the Judge, the MSPB, in reaching a contrary conclusion in its *Chavez* decision, relied on legislative history from the 1982 amendments to 38 U.S.C. § 7802(e). The Judge stated that, even assuming the MSPB was correct, its interpretation of § 7802(e) was "far from obvious" and that its holding was not the "clearly established law" that the Authority had relied upon in *HQ, USAF*. *Id.*

Moreover, the Judge stated that, even if the MSPB's interpretation of § 7802(e) was correct with respect to the adverse action appeal rights of VCS employees under 5 U.S.C. § 7512, this "d[id] not automatically mean" that such employees "h[ad] no right to use the negotiated grievance procedure to challenge adverse actions." *Id.* The Judge noted that § 7121(e)(1) of the Statute requires employees whose cases are appealable under both 5 U.S.C. § 7512 and a negotiated grievance procedure to select one of these procedures. *Id.* at 9-10. The Judge characterized as "rather murky" the case law pertaining to the Respondent's contention that, if an employee is barred from a § 7512 appeal, she is also barred from using the negotiated grievance procedure. *Id.* at 10.

After outlining the case law "addressing the overlap between an employee's right to arbitration under a negotiated grievance procedure and her appeal rights under 5 U.S.C. § 7512 to the MSPB," the Judge concluded that a full hearing before an arbitrator was required. *Id.* at 10-11. He noted that, unlike the probationary employee's grievance in *HQ, USAF*, "it cannot be said that clearly established law bars [VCS] employees from grieving their removal."[2] *Id.* at 11 (citing *HQ, USAF*, 17 FLRA at 375).

The Judge then held that the Respondent committed a ULP in violation of § 7116(a)(1) and (8) of the Statute when it refused to proceed to an arbitration hearing regarding the grievance. *Id.* As a remedy, he recommended that the Authority issue a remedial order requiring that the Respondent:

---

the competitive service is considered for transfer to such position. An employee of the Service who is appointed to a Department position in the competitive service under the authority of the preceding sentence may count toward the time-in-service requirement for a career appointment in such position any previous period of employment in the Service.

2. In a footnote, the Judge also noted that the Respondent separately contended that, as an NEES employee, the grievant is precluded from grieving the merits of her removal under the Authority's decision in *National Labor Relations Board*, 35 FLRA 1116, 1117 (1990). According to the Judge, in that decision, the Authority held that NEES employees could not utilize the negotiated grievance procedure to appeal adverse actions because allowing such actions would subvert the integrated scheme Congress had created because it would provide adverse action appeal rights to some classes of employees, but not others. The Judge then noted that, after the Authority issued that decision, Congress granted MSPB appeal rights to most NEES employees. Accordingly, the Judge concluded that, if the Respondent were to prevail on its allegation of nonarbitrability of the grievant's removal, it would be based on her status as a § 7802 employee, not as an NEES employee. Judge's Decision at 10 n. 4.

(1) cease and desist from refusing to arbitrate the grievance and from restraining or coercing its employees in the exercise of their rights under the Statute; (2) proceed to arbitration over the grievant's grievance; (3) post a notice as required by the order; and (4) within thirty days, provide written notice to the Regional Director of the Washington Regional Office of the steps that the Respondent has taken to comply with the order. *Id.* at 12-13.

III. Positions of the Parties

A. Respondent's Exceptions

Reiterating the arguments that it made before the Judge, the Respondent contends that the plain language of 38 U.S.C. § 7802 establishes that removed § 7802 employees do not have grievance rights; that the MSPB has concluded that such language is "plain and clear" and has held that employees who are removed under § 7802 do not have appeal rights to the MSPB; and that the Authority should follow the MSPB's interpretation and find that such employees have no right to pursue arbitration under a negotiated grievance procedure. Exceptions at 4-6. Moreover, the Respondent contends that the Judge erred by finding: (1) that the MSPB's interpretation of the law "is far from obvious from the plain language of § 7802(e)" and (2) that the MSPB's "holding is not the 'clearly established law' that the Authority relied on" in *HQ, USAF*. *Id.* at 6 (quoting Judge's Decision at 9).

The Respondent also asserts that, under 5 C.F.R. § 752.401(d)(12), MSPB appeal rights are not available to employees who are excluded from title 5.[3] *Id.* at 6-7. The Respondent contends that it "would be nonsensical to allow for grievance rights when MSPB appeal rights, which are articulated in the same regulation [(5 C.F.R. § 752.405(b))] as grievance rights, are not available."[4] *Id.* at 7. The Respondent argues that 5 C.F.R. § 752.405(b), therefore, must be read to exclude § 7802 employees from a negotiated grievance procedure. *Id.* The Respondent contends that the Judge erred by finding that "case law on this issue is rather murky." *Id.* at 7. According to the Respondent, an arbitrator is subject to the same jurisdictional limitations as the MSPB and "may not issue awards which conflict with the applicable 'external law.'" *Id.* (quoting *Devine v. Levin*, 739 F.2d 1567, 1570 (Fed. Cir. 1984)).

The Respondent also contends that the Judge erred by concluding that, "[i]f the Respondent is to prevail on the nonarbitrability [of the grievant's] removal, it will be based on her status as a [§] 7802 employee, not as a NEES employee." *Id.* at 8 (citing Judge's Decision at 10 n.4). The Respondent asserts that the Judge improperly relied on the fact that, in *National Labor Relations Board*, the Authority "left open" the question whether NEES employees could use the grievance procedure to challenge adverse actions based on "alleged interference with protected union activity" because that issue is irrelevant to this case. *Id.* at 8-9 (citing *NLRB*, 35 FLRA 1116, 1125-26 (1990) (*NLRB*)). The Respondent also asserts that the Authority's decision in *Panama Canal Commission, Balboa, Republic of Panama*, 45 FLRA 1075 (1992), is likewise irrelevant because that decision failed to discuss an exception to the rule "that removed NEES employees do not have grievance rights as a matter of law." *Id.* at 9.

Finally, the Respondent asserts that the Authority should rule that, as a matter of law, § 7802 employees cannot grieve their removals. *Id.* at 9-11.

B. GC's Opposition

The GC contends that the Respondent's claims are without merit because the Respondent has not

3. 5 C.F.R. § 752.401(d)(12) provides, in pertinent part, that the following type of employee is excluded from coverage under this section:

> An employee whose agency or position has been excluded from the appointing provisions of title 5, United States Code, by separate statutory authority in the absence of any provision to place the employee within the coverage of chapter 75 of title 5, United States Code[.]

5 C.F.R. § 752.401(d)(12).

4. 5 C.F.R. § 752.405(b) provides:

> *Grievance rights.* As provided at 5 U.S.C. [§] 7121(e)(1), if a matter covered by this subpart falls within the coverage of an applicable negotiated grievance procedure, an[] employee may elect to file a grievance under that procedure or appeal to the [MSPB] under 5 U.S.C. [§] 7701, but not both. 5 U.S.C. [§] 7114(a)(5) and [§] 7121(b)(3), and the terms of an applicable collective bargaining agreement, govern representation for employees in an exclusive bargaining unit who grieve a matter under this subpart through the negotiated grievance procedure.

shown that the Judge failed to follow Authority precedent in concluding that the Respondent committed a ULP. GC's Opp'n at 2. The GC contends that it is well established that questions of arbitrability are solely for an arbitrator to decide and that an administrative law judge is precluded from making a determination of whether a grievance is arbitrable. *Id.* at 3. According to the GC, the Authority created a "one-time" exception to this rule in *HQ, USAF*, holding that "clearly established law" precluded a grievance regarding the termination of a probationary employee. *Id.* at 4 (citing *HQ, USAF*, 17 FLRA at 375). The GC argues that the Respondent's assertion that *HQ, USAF* provides a basis for the Authority to decide the arbitrability of the grievance at issue is incorrect. *Id.* at 4-5, 7. According to the GC, the authority cited by the Respondent in support of its position does not have the same "force and effect" as the precedent relied upon by the Authority in *HQ, USAF*. *Id.*

Further, the GC asserts that the Respondent's exception to "the Judge's characterization of the case law that addresses MSPB appeal rights in relation to grievance arbitrability as 'murky' misinterprets the Judge's point." *Id.* at 5. According to the GC, contrary to the Respondent's argument, the Judge did not state that an arbitrator is free to issue a decision that fails to comply with a governing statute. *Id.* Rather, the GC asserts, the Judge simply determined that the substantive arbitrability of a grievance concerning an NEES employee was not clear and, accordingly, determined that question should be resolved by an arbitrator. *Id.* at 5-6.

The GC contends that the Respondent's claim that arbitrators have no jurisdiction as a matter of law to determine the merits of a grievance filed by a NEES employee is incorrect and that its reliance on *NLRB* as support for this argument is misplaced. *Id.* at 6. According to the GC, due to the enactment of the Civil Service Due Process Amendments, Pub. L. No. 101-376, 104 Stat. 461 (1990), a NEES employee is permitted to use the negotiated grievance procedure to challenge an adverse employment action as long as the employee has completed two continuous years of service. *Id.* at 6-7 (citing *NTEU*, 52 FLRA 1265, 1269-71 (1997); *NTEU*, 39 FLRA 346 (1991)). The GC argues that the grievant had more than two years of continuous service at the time of her removal and, thus, is eligible to challenge her termination using the negotiated grievance procedure. *Id.* at 7.

Finally, the GC contends that, in the event that the Authority chooses to address arbitrability under § 7802(e), the language of that provision does not exclude arbitral review of termination actions. *Id.* at 7-9.

C. Charging Party's Opposition

The Charging Party asserts that the Judge did not err by finding that the Respondent committed a ULP when it refused to participate in the arbitration hearing regarding the grievant's removal. Charging Party's Opp'n at 3-4. The Charging Party alleges that it has negotiated and implemented a collective bargaining agreement with the Respondent that provides rights for employees of the VCS, including the grievant. *Id.* at 4. The Charging Party argues that Article 44 of the agreement establishes a clear negotiated grievance procedure, as well as a process for resolving questions of arbitrability, and that the Respondent has failed to show that the agreement does not govern the grievant's removal. *Id.*

Further, the Charging Party contends that the plain language of § 7802(e) does not establish that VCS employees who are removed do not have grievance rights and that the Authority should reject the Respondent's assertion that this issue has been clearly established. *Id.* at 5-6.

The Charging Party also contends that the Judge correctly determined that the grievant's status as a NEES employee would not affect the arbitrability of this matter. *Id.* at 8. The Charging Party contends that, in *Department of the Treasury, Office of Chief Counsel v. FLRA*, 873 F.2d 1467, 1472 (D.C. Cir. 1989), the D.C. Circuit recognized that, under § 7121(f) of the Statute, some employees in specialized personnel systems would negotiate for grievance procedures even though they have no statutory right of appeal. *Id.*

Finally, the Charging Party contends that the arbitrability issues raised by the Respondent are not properly resolved through this proceeding. *Id.* According to the Charging Party, the Authority has determined that negotiated grievance procedures may not confer jurisdiction regarding questions of arbitrability on the Authority and that, unless the parties agree otherwise, "negotiated grievance and arbitration procedures 'must be read as providing that all questions o[f] arbitrability not otherwise resolved shall be submitted to arbitration.'" *Id.* at 8-9 (quoting *DOL*, 10 FLRA 316 (1982)).

IV. Analysis and Conclusions

A. The Judge did not err by failing to find that the language of § 7802(e) was so clear that it was unnecessary for an arbitrator to interpret it.

Section 7121(a) of the Statute requires that collective bargaining agreements contain "procedures for the settlement of grievances, including questions of arbitrability." Additionally, § 7121(b)(1)(C)(iii) of the Statute requires that all such negotiated grievance procedures include procedures that "provide that any grievance not satisfactorily settled under the negotiated grievance procedure be subject to binding arbitration[.]" Such negotiated grievance and arbitration procedures "must be read as providing that all questions of arbitrability not otherwise resolved shall be submitted to arbitration." *DOL*, 10 FLRA at 318. The Authority has repeatedly held that a party refusing to arbitrate violates § 7116(a)(1) and (8) of the Statute. *See, e.g., Dep't of the Air Force, Langley AFB, Hampton, Va.*, 39 FLRA 966 (1991) (*Langley AFB*); *AFGE, Local 1457*, 39 FLRA 519 (1991).

Moreover, it is well established that questions of arbitrability are solely for an arbitrator to decide. *See* 5 U.S.C. § 7121(c); *Langley AFB*, 39 FLRA at 969. In *HQ, USAF*, the Authority created a limited exception to this rule, finding that "clearly established law" precluded a grievance regarding the termination of a probationary employee. *See HQ, USAF*, 17 FLRA at 374-75.

The Respondent does not dispute that, consistent with § 7122(a) of the Statute, the parties' agreement contains a negotiated grievance procedure, as well as a process for resolving questions of arbitrability. The Respondent also does not dispute that, consistent with § 7121(b)(1)(C)(iii) of the Statute, the parties' agreed-upon negotiated grievance procedure provides that any grievance not satisfactorily settled under the grievance procedure is subject to binding arbitration. Moreover, the Respondent does not dispute that the Authority has consistently held that questions of arbitrability are for an arbitrator to decide. Rather, the Respondent contends that the Judge erred in this case when he determined that the language of § 7802(e) and the MSPB's interpretation of that provision in *Chavez* are not the "clearly established law" that the Authority relied upon in *HQ, USAF*. Exceptions at 5-6.

We reject this contention. The "clearly established law" relied upon by the Authority in *HQ, USAF* involved an opinion of the United States Court of Appeals for the D.C. Circuit and several Authority decisions that directly interpreted an employee's rights under the Statute. Here, however, the Respondent relies upon an opinion of the MSPB that interprets an employee's right to appeal adverse actions to the MSPB.[5] Furthermore, in *HQ, USAF*, the Authority noted that "no threshold question or any other question of interpretation or statutory construction" was present that could "legitimately be resolved by an arbitrator." *HQ, USAF*, 17 FLRA at 375. In this case, however, several questions of interpretation and statutory construction must be answered in order to decide the arbitrability of the grievance that the Respondent refused to arbitrate. For instance, as an initial matter, the language of 38 U.S.C. § 7802(e) must be interpreted to determine what rights, if any, a VCS employee has under title 5. Moreover, as the Judge correctly explained, the answers to these questions are far from clear or straightforward. Judge's Decision at 9-11 (noting that the law "regarding the rights of [§] 7802 employees is far from clear" and that the case law regarding whether employees who do not have adverse action appeal rights also do not have grievance rights is "rather murky").

Accordingly, we find that the Judge did not err by finding that the language of § 7802(e) and the MSPB's interpretation of that provision is not the "clearly established law" that the Authority relied upon in *HQ, USAF* and denying this exception.

5. The Respondent also asserts, in this regard, that, because the MSPB has held that MSPB appeal rights are not available, it "would be nonsensical to allow for grievance rights" and contends that the Judge erred in concluding otherwise. Exceptions at 7. According to the Respondent, an arbitrator is subject to the same jurisdictional limitations as the MSPB and "may not issue awards which conflict with the applicable 'external law.'" *Id.* (quoting *Devine v. Levin*, 739 F.2d at 1570). To the extent that the Respondent is contending that the Judge found that an arbitrator is free to issue a decision that fails to comply with Federal laws, rules and regulations, we reject that contention. The Judge did not find that an arbitrator is free to issue a decision that fails to comply with applicable law. Rather, the Judge simply determined that the case law addressing the overlap between an employee's right to appeal adverse actions to the MSPB and his or her right to arbitration under a negotiated grievance procedure was not clear and, accordingly, determined that question should be resolved by an arbitrator.

B. The Judge did not err in finding that, "if the Respondent is to prevail on the nonarbitrability [of the grievant's] removal, it will be based on her status as a [§] 7802 employee, not as a [nonpreference-eligible excepted service employee]."

The Respondent also contends that the Judge erred in finding that, "[i]f the Respondent is to prevail on the nonarbitrability [of the grievant's] removal, it will be based on her status as a [§] 7802 employee, not as a [nonpreference-eligible excepted service employees]." Exceptions at 8 (citing Judge's Decision at 10 n.4). According to the Respondent, arbitrators have "no jurisdiction as a matter of law to determine the merits of [a] grievance" filed by a NEES employee. *Id.* at 8 (citation omitted).

We reject the Respondent's contention. Due to the enactment of the Civil Service Due Process Amendments, Pub. L. No. 101-376, 104 Stat. 461 (1990), an NEES employee is permitted to use the negotiated grievance procedure to challenge an adverse employment action as long as the employee has completed two continuous years of service. *See NTEU,* 52 FLRA at 1269-71. It is undisputed that the grievant had more than two years of continuous service at the time of her removal. GC's Opp'n at 7; Exceptions at 1. Thus, the grievant, as an NEES employee, is eligible to challenge her termination using the negotiated grievance procedure.

Accordingly, we find that the Judge did not err in finding that, if the Respondent were to prevail on the nonarbitrability of the grievant's removal, it would be based on her status as a § 7802 employee, not as an NEES employee, and deny the Respondent's exception.

V. Order

Pursuant to § 2423.41(c) of the Authority's Regulations and § 7118 of the Statute, it is hereby ordered that the Respondent shall:

1. Cease and desist from:

(a) Failing or refusing to arbitrate the grievance over the grievant's removal, after receiving notice from the Union of its desire to proceed to arbitration.

(b) In any like or related manner, interfering with, restraining, or coercing its employees in the exercise of their rights assured by the Statute.

2. Take the following affirmative action in order to effectuate the purposes and policies of the Statute:

(a) Proceed to arbitration concerning the grievance over the grievant's removal after receiving notice from the Union of its desire to proceed to arbitration.

(b) Post at its facilities where employees of the Veterans Canteen Service represented by the Union are located, copies of the attached Notice on forms to be furnished by the Authority. Upon receipt of such forms, they shall be signed by the Director of the Veterans Canteen Service and shall be posted and maintained for 60 consecutive days thereafter, in conspicuous places, including all bulletin boards and other places where notices to employees are customarily posted. Reasonable steps shall be taken to ensure that such Notices are not altered, defaced, or covered by any other material.

(c) Pursuant to § 2423.41(e) of the Authority's Regulations, notify the Regional Director of the Washington Regional Office, Federal Labor Relations Authority, in writing, within 30 days from the date of this Order, as to what steps have been taken to comply.

NOTICE TO ALL EMPLOYEES
POSTED BY ORDER OF THE
FEDERAL LABOR RELATIONS AUTHORITY

The Federal Labor Relations Authority has found that the United States Department of Veterans Affairs, Veterans Canteen Service, Martinsburg, West Virginia, violated the Federal Service Labor-Management Relations Statute (the Statute) and has ordered us to post and abide by this notice.

WE HEREBY NOTIFY EMPLOYEES THAT:

WE WILL NOT fail or refuse to arbitrate the grievant's grievance after receiving notice from the National Association of Government Employees, Local R4-78 of its desire to proceed to arbitration.

WE WILL NOT, in any like or related manner, interfere with, restrain, or coerce our employees in the exercise of their rights assured under the Statute.

WE WILL arbitrate the grievant's grievance.

____
(Respondent/Agency)

Dated: __________ By: ____________________
(Signature) (Title)

This Notice must remain posted for 60 consecutive days from the date of posting, and must not be altered, defaced, or covered by any other material.

If employees have any questions concerning this Notice or compliance with its provisions, they may communicate directly with the Regional Director, Washington Regional Office, whose address is: 1400 K Street, NW, 2nd Floor, Washington, DC 20424-0001, and whose telephone number is: (202) 357-6029.

Office of Administrative Law Judges

DEPARTMENT OF VETERANS AFFAIRS
VETERANS CANTEEN SERVICE
MARTINSBURG, WEST VIRGINIA
Respondent

AND

NATIONAL ASSOCIATION OF GOVERNMENT EMPLOYEES, LOCAL R4-78
Charging Party

Case No. WA-CA-09-0247

Neil P. Daly
For the General Counsel

Michael E. Anfang
For the Respondent

Sarah E. Suszczyk
For the Charging Party

Before: RICHARD A. PEARSON
Administrative Law Judge

DECISION

This is an unfair labor practice proceeding under the Federal Service Labor-Management Relations Statute, 5 U.S.C. §§ 7101-7135 (the Statute), and the Rules and Regulations of the Federal Labor Relations Authority (the Authority), 5 C.F.R. part 2423. The case was submitted to me in accordance with section 2423.26(a) of the Authority's Rules and Regulations, based on a waiver of a hearing and a stipulation of facts by the parties.

On March 12, 2009, National Association of Government Employees, Local R4-78 (the Union or Charging Party), filed an unfair labor practice charge against the Department of Veterans Affairs, Veterans Canteen Service (VCS), Martinsburg, West Virginia (the Agency or Respondent). After investigating the charge, the Regional Director of the Washington Region of the Authority issued a Complaint and Notice of Hearing on September 11, 2009, alleging that the Agency had violated section 7116(a)(1), (5) and (8) of the Statute by refusing to participate in the arbitration of a grievance. The Respondent filed its Answer to the Complaint on October 1, 2009, admitting the factual allegations of the Complaint but denying that it had a duty to arbitrate or that it committed an unfair labor practice.

A hearing was scheduled in the matter, but prior to the hearing the parties entered into a stipulation of facts and agreed that a hearing was not necessary. The parties filed a Joint Motion for Adjudication in Lieu of Hearing, which included a statement of facts not in dispute and documentary attachments. The hearing was therefore canceled. The General Counsel, the Respondent and the Charging Party have filed briefs, which I have fully considered.

Based on this record, I make the following findings of fact, conclusions of law, and recommendations.

FINDINGS OF FACT

Paragraphs 1 through 15 of the Joint Motion for Adjudication in Lieu of Hearing are hereby set forth verbatim, along with the references therein to Attachments 1 through 7, which I admit and will hereafter refer to as Joint Exhibits 1 through 7:

1. The charge in Case Number WA-CA-09-0247 was filed by the Charging Party with the Authority's Washington Regional Director on March 12, 2009. See Joint Exhibit 1 (Formal Papers for WA-CA-09-0247 including Charge, Complaint, and Answer to Complaint), paragraph 5 of Complaint and Answer.

2. The Respondent is an agency under 5 U.S.C. § 7103(a)(3). See Joint Exhibit 1, paragraph 2 of Complaint and Answer.

3. Ms. Angel Cottrell was employed as a Supply Clerk for the Respondent. See Joint Exhibit 2 (June 7, 2008, Standard Form 50 issued by Respondent removing Angel Cottrell from her position).

4. Ms. Cottrell was employed in her position under the authority of 38 U.S.C. § 7802. See Joint Exhibit 2.

5. Effective June 7, 2008, the Respondent removed Ms. Cottrell. See Joint Exhibit 2.

6. The National Association of Government Employees (NAGE) is the exclusive representative of a consolidated unit of employees appropriate for collective bargaining at the Department of Veterans Affairs.

7. The Charging Party is a labor organization under 5 U.S.C. § 7103(a)(4), and is NAGE's agent for employees in the bargaining unit at the Respondent, including Ms. Cottrell. See Joint Exhibit 1, paragraph 4 of Complaint and Answer.

8. During the time period covered by the Complaint, the Respondent and Charging Party were subject to a term collective bargaining agreement (CBA). See Joint Exhibit 3 (Department of Veterans Affairs – National Association of Government Employees Master Agreement effective November 28, 2003).

9. Articles 44 and 45 of the Agreement include a term that reads: "Grievance/Arbitrability will be resolved as threshold issues of arbitration, but must have been raised no later than the time the Step 3 decision is given." See Joint Exhibit 3, Articles 44 and 45.

10. In a memorandum dated June 13, 2008, and received June 19, 2008, the Charging Party, through its representative Ms. Dale Mills, grieved, at the third step, the Respondent's decision to remove Ms. Cottrell. See Joint Exhibit 4 (June 13, 2008, Step 3 Grievance filed by Dale Mills regarding Angel Cottrell's removal).

11. In a memorandum dated June 26, 2008, and received July 10, 2008, the Respondent, through its Associate Director of Field Operations Mr. Michael Wallace, denied the third-step grievance. See Joint Exhibit 5 (June 26, 2008, Step 3 Grievance Response signed by Michael Wallace).

12. On or about July 28, 2008, the Charging Party invoked arbitration of the third-step grievance. See Joint Exhibit 6 (July 28, 2008, electronic mail from Mills to Ray Tober invoking arbitration for the removal of Cottrell).

13. The Charging Party and Respondent agreed on or about December 18, 2008, that Arbitrator Richard Dissen would resolve the grievance described in paragraph 10.

14. On or about February 13, 2009, the Respondent, through its attorney, informed Arbitrator Dissen that the Respondent would not participate in arbitration of the grievance. See Joint Exhibit 7 (February 13, 2009, letter from Michael Anfang to Dissen informing Dissen that the Respondent would not participate in the arbitration of grievance regarding Cottrell's removal).

15. The Respondent has not participated in arbitration of the grievance described in paragraph 10.

DISCUSSION AND CONCLUSIONS

Positions of the Parties

General Counsel

The General Counsel argues that the Respondent violated section 7116(a)(1) and (8) of the Statute by refusing to proceed with an arbitration hearing to resolve Ms. Cottrell's grievance.[1] The GC insists that if the Agency believed the grievance was not arbitrable, based on Cottrell's status as an employee appointed pursuant to 38 U.S.C. § 7802 (a Section 7802 employee), the proper way of pursuing its position was to raise the arbitrability issue before the arbitrator. By refusing to conduct the hearing altogether, the GC says the Agency violated section 7121 of the Statute.

The General Counsel first quotes the language of section 7121(a), that "any collective bargaining agreement shall provide procedures for the settlement of grievances, including questions of arbitrability." Section 7121(b)(1)(C)(iii) further requires CBAs to "provide that any grievance not satisfactorily settled under the negotiated grievance procedure shall be subject to binding arbitration . . ." These are the statutory linchpins on which the Authority has repeatedly held that the refusal to participate in an arbitration is an unfair labor practice. *Dep't of the Air Force, Langley Air Force Base, Hampton, Va.*, 39 FLRA 966 (1991)(*Langley AFB*); *Dep't of Labor, Employment Standards Admin./Wage and Hour Division, Wash., D.C.*, 10 FLRA 316 (1982)(*DOL*). According to the GC, a party is not permitted to make its own unilateral determination of the nonarbitrability of a dispute, even when it appears clear on its face that a grievance is not arbitrable. *DOL*, 10 FLRA at 321-22. Similarly, the GC says that it is improper for an Administrative Law Judge to address or resolve arbitrability issues in such cases, citing *Dep't of the Navy, Portsmouth Naval Shipyard, Portsmouth, N.H.*, 11 FLRA 456, 457 (1983)(*Portsmouth*). It notes that arbitrators routinely deal with arbitrability questions and refuse to address the merits of the grievance if it is not arbitrable. *See, e.g., Bremerton Metal Trades Council*, 64 FLRA 103 (2009).

According to the GC, the only exception to the rule requiring arbitration involves adverse actions against professional employees appointed under title 38 of the U.S. Code. *See Veterans Admin. Central Office, Wash., D.C.*, 27 FLRA 835 (1987)(*VA Central Office*). There, an arbitrator conducted a hearing and ruled on the merits in favor of the employee, but the Authority upheld the agency's refusal to comply with the award, because the disciplinary procedures established by Congress for such cases under 38 U.S.C. §§ 4110-4119 were meant to be exclusive. *Id.* at 839-40. The GC argues that the instant case is completely different from *VA Central Office*: VCS employees are appointed under an entirely different chapter of title 38 than the professional employees involved in *VA Central Office*; the statutory provision relating to VCS employees contains none of the detailed procedures for disciplinary actions covering professional employees; and unlike section 4119 of title 38, section 7802 does not expressly reference the Statute or chapter 71 of title 5 in its exclusionary language.

Since the instant case does not fit within the one recognized exception to the general rule, the General Counsel submits that the Respondent was required to participate in the arbitration hearing scheduled in this case. By refusing to do so, the Respondent obstructed the procedure mandated by the Statute for resolving grievances and violated section 7116(a)(1) and (8).

Respondent

The Respondent begins its case by citing the statute that created the Veterans Canteen Service and authorizes the Secretary of the Department of Veterans Affairs to operate canteens, 38 U.S.C. § 7802. The law provides:

> (e) Personnel. – The Secretary shall employ such persons as are necessary for the establishment, maintenance, and operation of the Service, and pay the salaries, wages,

[1] The General Counsel has withdrawn, as cumulative, the allegation that the Respondent's actions violated section 7116(a)(5), and I will not consider that allegation further. G.C. Brief at 9 n.4.

> and expenses of all such employees from the funds of the Service. Personnel necessary for the transaction of the business of the Service at canteens, warehouses, and storage depots shall be appointed, compensated from funds of the Service, and *removed by the Secretary without regard to the provisions of title 5 governing appointments in the competitive service and chapter 51 and subchapter III of chapter 53 of title 5.*

38 U.S.C. § 7802(e)(emphasis added). The Respondent argues that since, by its "plain language," the statute provides that VCS employees may be removed without regard to title 5, they do not have the right under 5 U.S.C. § 7512 to appeal their removals to the Merit Systems Protection Board (MSPB). Resp. Brief at 5. The MSPB itself has held that it has no jurisdiction to hear adverse action appeals of VCS employees, citing 38 U.S.C. § 7802(e). *Chavez v. DVA,* 65 MSPR 590 (1994)(*Chavez).*

The Respondent then relies on section 7121(e)(1) of the Statute and 5 C.F.R. § 752.405(b) of the MSPB implementing regulations to argue that an employee who has no MSPB appeal rights also has no right to pursue arbitration under a CBA's negotiated grievance procedures (NGP). According to the Respondent, "[i]t would be nonsensical to allow for grievance rights when MSPB appeal rights, which are articulated in the same regulation as grievance rights, are not available." Resp. Brief at 6.

The Agency further notes that VCS employees are in the Federal excepted service, and that since Ms. Cottrell was a nonpreference eligible employee (NEES)(referring to the veteran's preference), such employees have no right to challenge adverse actions. Respondent cites several court opinions reversing the Authority's former rule that NEES employees could appeal their adverse actions through the NGP, and the Authority's ultimate reversal of that rule. *See, e.g., Dep't of the Treasury, Office of Chief Counsel v. FLRA,*873 F.2d 1467 (D.C. Cir. 1989), *cert. denied,* 110 S. Ct. 864 (1990)(*Treasury v. FLRA*); *National Labor Relations Board,* 35 FLRA 1116 (1990)(*NLRB*) .

Relying on the principle that an arbitrator is subject to the same jurisdictional limitations as the MSPB, the Respondent therefore submits that it has no obligation to participate in the NGP for the removal of VCS employees. It concedes that the Authority has never addressed this precise question, but it urges me and the Authority to do so, in order to enable the Respondent and the Union to resolve an issue that otherwise may continue to be the subject of continued litigation. It cites the Authority's decision in *Director of Administration, Headquarters, U.S. Air Force,* 17 FLRA 372 (1985)(*HQ, USAF*), as an appropriate analogy. There, the Authority upheld an agency's refusal to participate in the grievance and arbitration procedure regarding the removal of a probationary employee. While it noted and reaffirmed its basic principle, articulated in *DOL,* 10 FLRA at 320-21, that parties must arbitrate all unresolved grievances, including questions of arbitrability, the Authority carved out an exception for probationary employees. It reasoned that because probationary employees have been held, as a "matter of clearly established law", to have no right to appeal their removal, there is "no threshold question or any other question of interpretation or statutory construction which can legitimately be resolved by an arbitrator." *HQ, USAF*, 17 FLRA at 375.

Finally, the Agency cites an earlier arbitration case in which it successfully asserted the nonarbitrability of a removed VCS employee's grievance. *Veterans Canteen Service, Hot Springs, S.D. and AFGE Local 1539,* March 19, 2007, attached to Respondent's Brief. In that case, the arbitrator cited the MSPB decision in *Chavez, supra*, and ruled that he could not arbitrate the merits of a case in which the MSPB had no jurisdiction. Award at 3-4. While conceding that the arbitrator's ruling is not binding on me or the Authority, the Respondent asserts that the rationale of that case is persuasive, and urges the Authority to take a similar position, to prevent the Respondent from being forced to repeatedly litigate arbitrations around the country, when such hearings are a "pointless and hollow exercise". 17 FLRA at 375. It requests, therefore, that the complaint be dismissed.

Charging Party

The Union generally reiterates the arguments raised by the General Counsel, particularly the basic principle that the negotiated grievance procedure is the proper forum for raising all disputes among the parties to an CBA, even disputes as to arbitrability. Unlike the situation involving probationary employees in *HQ, USAF,* the rights of Section 7802 employees under the NGP is not a "matter of clearly established law" (17 FLRA at 375), as the Respondent itself concedes. Even within the Department of Veterans Affairs, arbitration decisions have produced conflicting results on the arbitrability of removal cases involving Section 7802 employees. Thus, in contrast to the arbitration award cited by the

Respondent, the Union cites and attaches three arbitrators' decisions involving the removal of VCS employees. In two of these, the arbitrators ruled on the merits of the grievances, while in the third the arbitrator ruled it was not arbitrable, but on different grounds than that asserted in the instant case. While none of these arbitrators addressed the issue of a Section 7802 employee's rights, the Union says that the Agency could have raised the issue but failed to do so.

The Union also relies on the language of the CBA (Joint Exhibit 3), particularly Article 44, Section 3, which lists a number of exclusions from the parties' grievance and arbitration procedure. Among those issues which are excluded are "[m]atters appealable to the Merit System [sic] Protection Board" and certain types of grievances relating to employees appointed under 38 U.S.C. §§ 7401, 7405 and 7422. Joint Exhibit 3 at 126-27. Grievances relating to Section 7802 employees are not excluded there or at any other place in the CBA, and this conveys, in the Union's view, the parties' intention to cover Section 7802 employees under the NGP.

Finally, the Union cites various classes of employees, working under "other personnel systems" as defined by the Authority under section 7121(e)(1), who have been found to have the right to use the NGP to appeal adverse actions over which the MSPB has no jurisdiction. *See U.S. Dep't of Transportation, Federal Aviation Administration,* 54 FRA 235 (1998)(employees in FAA personnel system); *U.S. Dep't of Defense, Army & Air Force Exchange Service, Dallas, Tex.,* 51 FLRA 1651, 1653 (1996)(employees of nonappropriated funds); *U.S. Dep't of Defense Dependent Schools, Germany Region,* 38 FLRA 1432, 1436 (1991)(DOD school system employees). These cases demonstrate, according to the Union, that employees are not necessarily prevented legally from utilizing the NGP simply because they are precluded from appealing adverse actions to the MSPB.

Analysis

On its most direct and straightforward level, this case is quite simple, and the case law is not really in dispute. Section 7121(a) of the Statute requires that collective bargaining agreements contain "procedures for the settlement of grievances, *including questions of arbitrability*."[2] (Emphasis added). Section 7121(b)(1)(C)(iii) requires all negotiated grievance procedures to include procedures that "provide that any grievance not satisfactorily settled under the negotiated grievance procedure shall be subject to binding arbitration which may be invoked by either the exclusive representative or the agency." The General Counsel, the Respondent and the Union further agree that the Authority has almost uniformly held, since its *DOL* decision in 1982, that a party refusing to arbitrate violates section 7116(a)(1) and (8). This is equally true for recalcitrant unions as it is for agencies. *See AFGE, Local 1457,* 39 FLRA 519 (1991); *Langley AFB,* 39 FLRA at 966.

For nearly as long as the Authority has been emphasizing the necessity of challenging arbitrability before the arbitrator, however, parties have been trying to carve out exceptions to this rule, usually by arguing that in their particular cases the nonarbitrability of the grievance is "clear" or the law is "settled." Thus in *Portsmouth,* the agency convinced the Judge that the CBA contained "clear and unmistakable" language excluding EEO disputes from the grievance procedure, and the ALJ ruled that the agency's refusal to arbitrate was justifiable. The Authority reversed, reiterating that "all questions of arbitrability" must be presented to arbitration, and that "the Judge erred by attempting to resolve the question of arbitrability himself." 11 FLRA at 457. In *Langley AFB,* the seemingly "clear" exclusion from the NGP involved separation actions, and the agency again argued that it would be a waste of everyone's time and money to arbitrate the grievance. Using language almost identical to that of Respondent's counsel in this case, the Air Force asserted, "there is no 'question' of arbitrability and therefore, no requirement (or purpose) for going to arbitration." 39 FLRA at 967; *see also* Resp. Brief at 9. The Authority rejected the argument again, stating: "Such a refusal may not be justified by a party's contention, however arguable or reasonable, that the parties intended the subject matter of the grievance to be excluded from the coverage of the

---

[2] It also allows parties to exclude any matter from the application of the grievance procedure, but nobody argues in this case that the Agreement contains such an exclusion for Section 7802 employees. On the contrary, while the Article 44 grievance procedure does contain an explicit exclusion of certain types of grievances involving employees appointed under chapter 74 of title 38, it contains no such reference to VCS employees, who are appointed under chapter 78 of title 38. Furthermore, Article 44, Section 6, Note 3 of the Agreement (Attachment 3 at 128) eliminates Step 2 of the grievance procedure at some VCS facilities and elevates those grievances directly to Step 3. It is thus indisputable that VCS employees have the right to present at least some grievances under the negotiated procedure.

negotiated grievance and arbitration procedures." 39 FLRA at 969. More recently, this point was articulated in a dissenting opinion: "Clearly, parties can dispute whether an issue is properly before an arbitrator and not commit an unfair labor practice, but that ability to dispute the arbitrability of an issue does not extend to asserting that the arbitrator has no authority to resolve the matter." *United States Dep't of Veterans Affairs, Veterans Affairs Med. Ctr., Phoenix, Ariz.*, 60 FLRA 405, 408 (2004)(Cabaniss, dissent).

The General Counsel and the Respondent each cite one exception to the above rule, but interestingly they each cite different cases: the General Counsel cites *VA Central Office*, while the Respondent cites *HQ, USAF*. The Air Force case is more directly applicable, as it involved an agency that refused to participate in a probationary employee's removal grievance, and it is the only Authority decision I have found since 1982 in which an agency's refusal to arbitrate was **not** held to be an unfair labor practice. The Authority reiterated its general rule from *DOL* that parties must arbitrate all unresolved grievances, but it created an exception for probationary employees, as the case law had "clearly established" that probationaries had no right to challenge their removal in any forum, including arbitration. 17 FLRA at 375.[3] While the *VA Central Office* decision did not involve an agency refusing to arbitrate, but rather one that refused to comply with an award, it is a useful reference nonetheless. Because the Authority and the courts had previously held that the VA's internal peer review process was intended to be the exclusive procedure for resolving professional competency actions against employees appointed under 38 U.S.C. § 4110, the arbitrator had no jurisdiction over the merits of the grievance, and thus the Authority would not enforce the award. I think it is safe to say that both of these cases represent exceptions to the Authority's general rule requiring arbitrability issues to be resolved by the arbitrator. The question then is whether Section 7802 employee removal actions warrant an additional exception.

The major problems with the Respondent's argument in favor of such an exception are that the "plain language" of 38 U.S.C. § 7802(e) is not so plain or clear, and while an arbitrator in this case may not have to make any factual determinations, he will need to resolve significant issues of law and statutory construction. The Respondent argues that "the plain language" of the law provides that "VCS employees appointed under 38 U.S.C. § 7802 may be removed from employment without regard to Title 5 provisions." Resp. Brief at 5. But section 7802(e) actually says that such employees may be "removed by the Secretary without regard to the provisions of title 5 governing appointments in the competitive service and chapter 51 and subchapter III of chapter 53 of title 5." As the Respondent notes elsewhere in its brief, VCS employees are in the excepted service, not the competitive service; thus the statutory language should "plainly" be interpreted to exclude VCS employees from only a narrow portion of title 5. The MSPB, in its *Chavez* decision holding that section 7802(e) should be read more broadly, so as to exempt VCS employees from all of title 5, including the right to appeal adverse actions to the Board, based its holding on the legislative history of the 1982 amendments to the 1946 VA statute. It noted that the original statutory language stated "without regard to civil-service laws" and that the 1982 amendments were labeled "technical amendments" that may not be construed as making a substantive change in the laws replaced. *Chavez*, 65 MSPR at 592-94. Assuming that the MSPB's reasoning is correct, its interpretation of the law is far from obvious from the plain language of section 7802(e), and its holding is not the "clearly established law" that the Authority relied on in *HQ, USAF*.

Further, while the MSPB may be correct in its interpretation of 38 U.S.C. § 7802(e) with respect to the adverse action appeal rights of VCS employees under 5 U.S.C. § 7512, that does not automatically mean that those employees have no right to use the negotiated grievance procedure to challenge adverse actions. Section 7121(e)(1) of the Statute requires employees whose cases are appealable under both 5 U.S.C. § 7512 and under the NGP to choose one of these procedures. The Respondent argues that if an employee is statutorily barred from a section 7512 appeal, she is also barred from using the NGP, but the case law on this issue is rather murky.

Initially, the Authority held in several decisions that NEES employees, who were barred by the Civil Service Reform Act (prior to 1990) from pursuing adverse action appeals under 5 U.S.C. § 7512, were nevertheless entitled to pursue such actions under their NGP. *See, e.g., National Treasury Employees Union*, 31 FLRA 993 (1988). Ultimately, however, the Authority overruled those decisions and adopted

[3] In fact, the Authority came to its decision in *HQ, USAF* only after the D.C. Circuit had reversed the Authority in another case involving the arbitration of a probationary's grievance. *Immigration and Naturalization Service v. FLRA*, 709 F.2d 724 (D.C. Cir. 1983).

the holdings of several courts that NEES employees could not utilize the NGP to appeal adverse actions. *NLRB,* 35 FLRA at 1117. The courts found that the CSRA established "an *integrated* scheme of administrative and judicial review" that granted adverse action appeal rights to some classes of employees and not to others, and it would therefore subvert that scheme to allow adverse action rights to unionized NEES employees that other NEES employees were denied. *Treasury v. FLRA*, 873 F.2d at 1469, quoting from *United States v. Fausto,* 484 U.S. 439, 445 (1988)(emphasis in original). However, based on the language of section 7121(e)(1) of the Statute, the D.C. Circuit also recognized that "Congress contemplated that some of these employees, who fall under specialized personnel systems apart from the main civil service system, would negotiate for grievance procedures although they have no statutory right of appeal." 873 F.2d at 1472. Moreover, when the Authority in *NLRB* acceded to the courts' position that NEES employees could not pursue adverse action appeals under their grievance procedure, it left open the question of whether NEES employees could use the grievance procedure to challenge adverse actions based on alleged interference with protected union activity. 35 FLRA at 1126.[4]

In *Panama Canal Commission, Balboa, Republic of Panama,* 45 FLRA 1075, 1083-85 (1992), the Authority compared the availability of adverse action appeal rights under negotiated grievance procedures for employees in several different personnel systems, all of whom were precluded from pursuing appeals to the MSPB. The Authority noted that when Congress amended the CSRA to give most NEES employees appeal rights to the MSPB, it expressly excluded NEES employees of the Panama Canal Commission; accordingly, the underlying premise of the Authority's *NLRB* holding continued to bar them from using the negotiated grievance procedures for adverse actions. 45 FLRA at 1083. By contrast, employees of the Department of Defense Dependent Schools are in a personnel system created by provisions in title 20 of the U.S. Code. *Id.* While the Authority did not directly address the question of whether title 20 employees are entitled to arbitration of adverse actions, it stated that such a right would not be inconsistent with the differing treatment of Panama Canal employees, "because, unlike the employees in the [*Panama Canal*] case, NEES employees in the title 20 system are not specifically excluded from the coverage of the Amendments [i.e., the 1990 amendments to the Civil Service Reform Act]." *Id.* Finally, the Authority looked at the grievance rights of nonappropriated fund (NAF) instrumentality employees, who (pursuant to 5 U.S.C. § 2105(c)) are not covered by most civil service laws but are covered by the Statute. Summarizing its previous decision in *NAGE, Local R5-82,* 43 FLRA 25 (1991), the Authority in *Panama Canal* stated: "Because of the unique nature of NAF employment, the fact that NAF employees are not covered by the Amendments does not mean that Congress specifically intended to deny those employees access to the negotiated grievance procedure." 45 FLRA at 1084.

In reviewing all of these decisions addressing the overlap between an employee's right to arbitration under a negotiated grievance procedure and her appeal rights under 5 U.S.C. § 7512 to the MSPB, I do not seek to answer the question of whether employees appointed under 38 U.S.C. § 7802 are barred from arbitrating their removals, although that is what the Respondent dearly wants me to do. Instead, the conclusion I reach from examining those decisions is that the interpretation of section 7802, and the balancing of section 7802 with the grievance rights of VCS employees under the Statute and the CBA, require a full hearing before an arbitrator. Unlike the probationary employee's grievance in *HQ, USAF,* it cannot be said that "clearly established law" bars Section 7802 employees from grieving their removal. 17 FLRA at 375. On the contrary, the law regarding the rights of Section 7802 employees under the Statute is far from clear. While the Respondent would have an arbitrator resolve only factual issues, the Authority noted in *HQ, USAF* that it is perfectly legitimate for arbitrators to resolve "question[s] of interpretation or statutory construction." *Id.* The Respondent has agreed in the CBA to resolve unsettled grievances by binding arbitration, and the Authority has repeatedly held that this includes "all" questions of arbitrability. *Langley AFB,* 39 FLRA at 969. It is far simpler for me to interpret the word "all" literally than it is to carve out a new exception to a thirty-year-old rule, and it would be far simpler

[4] In its brief (at 6-7), the Respondent separately argues that Ms. Cottrell, as an NEES employee, is precluded under the *NLRB* decision from grieving the merits of her removal. This was also a basis for the arbitrator's ruling in the *Hot Springs VA* case that the grievance was not arbitrable. *See* Attachment to Resp. Brief at 4. However, the CSRA was amended in 1990 to extend MSPB appeal rights to most NEES employees. *See* 5 U.S.C. §§ 4303, 7511, 7701 (Supp. II 1990); *see also Panama Canal Commission, Balboa, Republic of Panama,* 43 FLRA 1483, 1499 n.2, 1503 (1992). If the Respondent is to prevail on the nonarbitrability of Cottrell's removal, it will be based on her status as a Section 7802 employee, not as an NEES employee.

for the parties to a collective bargaining agreement to present their arbitrability disputes to the arbitrator than to undergo a lengthy unfair labor practice proceeding. While the Respondent might prefer that I resolve the question of arbitrability, the Authority has warned against just such a usurpation of the arbitrator's decision. *Portsmouth*, 11 FLRA at 457. Instead, I leave the parties to the bargain that they made: to air all aspects of their dispute before the arbitrator.

For all of the reasons stated above, I conclude that the Respondent committed an unfair labor practice, in violation of section 7116(a)(1) and (8) of the Statute, when it refused to proceed to an arbitration hearing in the Cottrell grievance.

Remedy

In order to remedy the unfair labor practice, a cease and desist order and the posting of a notice to employees are appropriate. The cease and desist order should require the Respondent to proceed to arbitrate the Cottrell grievance. While the grievance in question involved only the Respondent's Martinsburg, West Virginia, facility, the facts of the case make it clear that the Veterans Canteen Service's Central Office in St. Louis, Missouri, was involved in the refusal to arbitrate (Joint Exhibit 5); that the Respondent acted on a legal opinion given to it by the General Counsel of the Department of Veterans Affairs (Attachment to Joint Exhibit 7); and that the legal opinion applies throughout the Veterans Canteen Service. It is appropriate, therefore, that the notice be posted at all facilities where VCS employees represented by NAGE are located, and that it be signed by the Director of the Veterans Canteen Service. *See U.S. Dep't of Justice, Fed. Bureau of Prisons, Office of Internal Affairs, Wash., D.C.,* 55 FLRA 388, 394-95 (1999).

Accordingly, I recommend that the Authority issue the following remedial Order:

ORDER

Pursuant to section 2423.41(c) of the Authority's Rules and Regulations and section 7118 of the Federal Service Labor-Management Relations Statute (the Statute), it is hereby ordered that the Department of Veterans Affairs, Veterans Canteen Service, Martinsburg, West Virginia, shall:

1. Cease and desist from:

(a) Failing or refusing to arbitrate the grievance over Angel Cottrell's removal, after receiving notice from the National Association of Government Employees, Local R4-78 (the Union) of its desire to proceed to arbitration.

(b) In any like or related manner interfering with, restraining, or coercing its employees in the exercise of their rights assured by the Statute.

2. Take the following affirmative action in order to effectuate the purposes and policies of the Statute:

(a) Proceed to arbitration concerning the grievance over Angel Cottrell's removal after receiving notice from the Union of its desire to proceed to arbitration.

(b) Post at all of its facilities where employees of the Veterans Canteen Service represented by the Union are located, copies of the attached Notice on forms to be furnished by the Federal Labor Relations Authority. Upon receipt of such forms, they shall be signed by the Director of the Veterans Canteen Service and shall be posted and maintained for 60 consecutive days thereafter, in conspicuous places, including all bulletin boards and other places where notices to employees are customarily posted. Reasonable steps shall be taken to ensure that such Notices are not altered, defaced, or covered by any other material.

(c) Pursuant to section 2423.41(e) of the Authority's Rules and Regulations, notify the Regional Director of the Washington Region, Federal Labor Relations Authority, in writing, within 30 days from the date of this Order, as to what steps have been taken to comply herewith.

Issued, Washington, D.C., February 26, 2010.

RICAHARD A. PEARSON
Administrative Law Judge

NOTICE TO ALL EMPLOYEES
POSTED BY ORDER OF THE
FEDERAL LABOR RELATIONS AUTHORITY

The Federal Labor Relations Authority has found that the Department of Veterans Affairs, Veterans Canteen Service, Martinsburg, West Virginia, violated the Federal Service Labor-Management Relations Statute (the Statute), and has ordered us to post and abide by this Notice.

WE HEREBY NOTIFY OUR EMPLOYEES THAT:

WE WILL NOT fail or refuse to arbitrate the Angel Cottrell grievance after receiving notice from the National Association of Government Employees, Local R4-78 of its desire to proceed to arbitration.

WE WILL NOT in any like or related manner, interfere with, restrain, or coerce our employees in the exercise of their rights assured by the Statute.

WE WILL arbitrate the Angel Cottrell grievance.

____
(Agency/Activity)

Dated:_______By:____________________________
(Signature) (Title)

This Notice must remain posted for 60 consecutive days from the date of posting and must not be altered, defaced, or covered by any other material.

If employees have any questions concerning this Notice or compliance with any of its provisions, they may communicate directly with the Regional Director, Washington Region, Federal Labor Relations Authority, and whose address is: 1400 K Street, NW, 2nd Floor, Washington, DC 20424-0001 and whose telephone number is: (202) 357-6029.

65 FLRA No. 52

UNITED STATES
DEPARTMENT OF JUSTICE
FEDERAL BUREAU OF PRISONS
FEDERAL CORRECTIONAL INSTITUTION
SEAGOVILLE, TEXAS
(Activity)

and

AMERICAN FEDERATION
OF GOVERNMENT EMPLOYEES
COUNCIL OF PRISON LOCALS
LOCAL 1030
(Petitioner/Labor Organization)

DA-RP-10-0013

ORDER DENYING
APPLICATION FOR REVIEW

November 12, 2010

Before the Authority: Carol Waller Pope, Chairman, and Thomas M. Beck and Ernest DuBester, Members

I. Statement of the Case

This case is before the Authority on an application for review (application) filed by the United States Department of Justice (the Agency) under § 2422.31 of the Authority's Regulations.[1] The Petitioner/Labor Organization (the Union) did not file an opposition to the Agency's application.

As relevant here, the Regional Director (RD) determined that § 7112(b)(7) of the Federal Service Labor-Management Relations Statute (the Statute) does not bar the inclusion of a Special Investigative Support (SIS) Technician in the bargaining unit represented by the Union.[2] For the reasons that follow, we deny the Agency's application.

II. Background and RD's Decision

The Agency is a correctional institution. RD's Decision at 3. The Union filed a petition seeking to clarify the bargaining-unit status of the SIS Technician position. *Id.* at 1. In determining whether the disputed position should be excluded from the unit under § 7112(b)(7) of the Statute, the RD noted that the Authority equates "primarily engaged," within the meaning of that statutory section, with "preponderance." *Id.* at 5. He then found that the SIS Technician in dispute spends between thirty-five and forty percent of his time conducting staff investigations and, as a result, "the record evidence does not demonstrate that a preponderance of [the SIS Technician's] duties involved the investigation of staff." *Id.* The RD also noted the Agency's assertion that inmate investigations always have the potential to become staff investigations, but determined that "Authority precedent demonstrates that the 'potential for uncovering employee fraud, misuse of funds, or malfeasance' has been considered only in cases involving audits or investigations of agency programs or employees." *Id.* (citing *U.S. Dep't of Justice, Fed. Bureau of Prisons, U.S. Penitentiary, McCreary, Pine Knot, Ky.*, 63 FLRA 153, 155 (2009) (*McCreary*); *Small Bus. Admin.*, 34 FLRA 392, 401-02 (1990) (*SBA*); *U.S. Dep't of Labor, Office of Inspector Gen., Reg. I, Boston, Mass.*, 7 FLRA 834, 835-36 (1982) (*DOL*)). For these reasons, the RD concluded that the SIS Technician is not "primarily engaged in" staff investigations within the meaning of § 7112(b)(7), and he clarified the existing bargaining unit to include the disputed position. *Id.*

---

1. Section 2422.31 of the Authority's Regulations provides, in pertinent part:

> (c) *Review.* The Authority may grant an application for review only when the application demonstrates that review is warranted on one or more of the following grounds:
> . . . .
> (3) There is a genuine issue over whether the Regional Director has:
> (i) Failed to apply established law;
> . . . .
> (iii) Committed a clear and prejudicial error concerning a substantial factual matter.

5 C.F.R. § 2422.31(c)(3)(i), (iii).

2. Section 7112(b)(7) of the Statute provides that a bargaining unit is inappropriate if it includes "any employee primarily engaged in investigation or audit functions relating to the work of individuals employed by an agency whose duties directly affect the internal security of the agency, but only if the functions are undertaken to ensure that the duties are discharged honestly and with integrity." 5 U.S.C. § 7112(b)(7).

III. Agency's Application

The Agency requests review on the grounds that, in determining that the SIS Technician was not excluded under § 7112(b)(7) of the Statute, the RD: (1) committed a clear and prejudicial error concerning a substantial factual matter; and/or (2) failed to apply established Authority precedent. Application at 3.

With respect to the first ground, the Agency argues that the RD erred in finding that a preponderance of the SIS Technician's duties do not involve staff investigations because, according to the Agency, hearing testimony demonstrates that "approximately [fifty percent] of [the SIS's] current duties . . . pertain solely to conducting staff investigations[.]" *Id.* at 5. In this connection, the Agency asserts that the RD's reliance on *McCreary* is misplaced because the evidence in that decision indicated that only ten to twenty percent of the duties of the SIS Technicians at issue there involved staff investigations -- a much lower percentage than demonstrated in the instant case. *Id.* at 8-9.

With respect to the second ground, the Agency contends that, even assuming that the RD correctly found that up to forty-five percent of the SIS's duties consist of staff investigations, "the subject position should still be excluded . . . because it satisfies the 'preponderance' standard." *Id.* at 9. Further, the Agency maintains that the percentage of time spent by the SIS Technician investigating staff members is even greater than fifty percent because he also conducts inmate interviews, which "always have the potential to result in staff investigations." *Id.* at 8-9. In this connection, the Agency claims that the Authority has held that § 7112(b)(7) applies where employees perform internal investigations with "the potential for uncovering employee fraud, misuse of funds, or malfeasance[.]" *Id.* at 4 (citing *U.S. DOJ, Fed. Bureau of Prisons, U.S. Penitentiary, Marion, Ill.*, 55 FLRA 1243, 1248 (2000) (*USP Marion*); *SBA*, 34 FLRA at 402)). The Agency also claims that the RD misread *McCreary* "as establishing a *per se* rule that, henceforth, all [] SIS Technicians are automatically included in the bargaining unit unless they are engaged solely in staff investigations[,]" and that *McCreary* is distinguishable from the instant case because: (1) *McCreary* was based on "a limited and incomplete factual record" that "consisted solely of affidavits"; and (2) unlike here, "the SIS technician [in *McCreary*] did *not* assert that he received information about possible misconduct in the course of his inmate investigations." *Id.* at 7-8 (internal quotations omitted).

IV. Analysis and Conclusions

A. The RD did not commit a clear and prejudicial error concerning a substantial factual matter.

The Authority may grant an application for review if it is demonstrated that the RD committed a clear and prejudicial error concerning a substantial factual matter. 5 C.F.R. § 2422.31(c)(3)(iii). As set forth above, the Agency contends that the RD failed to properly consider hearing testimony indicating that approximately fifty percent of the SIS Technician's duties involve staff investigations. Application at 5.

The Agency relies on the testimony of the SIS Technician stating that approximately fifty percent of his duties pertain to staff investigations. *Id.* However, the SIS Technician's testimony was unclear. In this regard, the SIS Technician initially testified that seventy percent of his time involves investigatory work. Tr. at 144. He then reported spending half of his time conducting staff investigations, and the other half handling inmate investigations. *Id.* at 203, 205-06. It is unclear whether the SIS Technician meant that he evenly splits his *total* time, rather than the seventy percent pertaining to investigatory work, between staff and inmate investigations. The SIS Technician also later testified that approximately five percent of his time involves non-investigatory tasks, with the remainder of his time evenly split between staff and inmate investigations. *Id.* at 254-55. By contrast, both of the SIS Technician's former and current supervisors testified that one-third of the SIS Technician's duties involve staff investigations. *Id.* at 60, 115. In light of the SIS Technician's ambiguous statements, and the clear testimony of both his former and current supervisors, the Agency provides no basis for finding that the RD erred by declining to rely solely on one among the several unclear statements made by the SIS Technician, and, instead, reaching a conclusion consistent with the testimony of the supervisors. Accordingly, we find that the Agency has not established that the RD committed a clear and prejudicial error concerning a substantial factual matter.

B. The RD did not fail to apply established law.

The Authority may grant an application for review if it is demonstrated that the RD failed to apply established law. 5 C.F.R. § 2422.3l(c)(3)(i). In determining whether a specified investigative or audit position is properly excluded from a bargaining unit, the Authority considers whether: (1) the incumbents are "primarily engaged in investigation or audit functions"; (2) these functions "relat[e] to the work of individuals employed by an agency whose duties directly affect the internal security of the agency"; and (3) these functions are "undertaken to ensure that the duties are discharged honestly and with integrity." 5 U.S.C. § 7112(b)(7).

The Activity argues that, even assuming that the RD correctly found that up to forty-five percent of the SIS's duties consist of staff investigations, the "position should still be excluded . . . because it satisfies the 'preponderance' standard." Application at 9. In *McCreary*, the Authority held that where the RD found that "only ten to twenty percent of SIS Technicians' time involves investigations of staff members[,]" his conclusion that SIS Technicians' duties did not meet the "primarily engaged requirement" of § 7112(b)(7) "comport[ed] squarely with the 'preponderance' interpretation of 'primarily engaged' adopted in *AFGE, Local 3529*[, 57 FLRA 633, 637-38 (2001).]" 63 FLRA at 156. Although the Authority has not defined what percentage of an employee's duties constitutes a "preponderance" in this context, the Authority has interpreted "preponderance" to mean "a majority" in the context of interpreting the term as it appears in § 7103(a)(10) of the Statute.[3] *See U.S. Dep't of the Army, Parks Reserve Training Ctr., Dublin, Cal.*, 61 FLRA 537, 541 (2006) (citing *Veterans Admin. Med. Ctr., Fayetteville, N.C.*, 8 FLRA 651, 660 (1982)). There is no basis on which to define "preponderance" differently in the context of § 7112(b)(7) than it is defined in the context of § 7103(a)(10). The RD found that, at most, forty-five percent of the SIS Technician's duties involved staff investigations, and we have found no factual error. Consistent with the definition of "preponderance" as "a majority," *see id.*, we find that forty-five percent does not constitute a preponderance, and conclude that the RD did not fail to apply established law in this regard.

The Agency also argues that the preponderance standard is met in this case because the percentage of time spent by the SIS Technician investigating staff members is even greater than fifty percent, given that he conducts inmate interviews that "always have the potential to result in staff investigations." Application at 8. In this regard, the Agency argues that the Authority has held that § 7112(b)(7) "applies where individuals 'perform internal investigations of employee wrongdoing and fraud[]' with the potential for uncovering 'employee fraud, misuse of funds, or malfeasance[.]'" *Id.* at 4 (citing *SBA*, 34 FLRA at 399-402). However, in response to an identical argument, the Authority stated in *McCreary* that "Authority precedent demonstrates that the 'potential for uncovering employee fraud, misuse of funds, or malfeasance' has been considered only in cases involving audits or investigations of agency programs or employees." 63 FLRA at 155 (citing *SBA*, 34 FLRA at 401-02 ("potential" considered where auditors performed audits of agency "programs, contracts, operations and program participants"); *DOL*, 7 FLRA at 835 ("potential" considered where auditors conducted audits of agency "programs and the employees who run these programs")). The Authority also held in *McCreary* that "the potential for discovering staff misconduct ar[ose] in the context of inmate investigations, not employee investigations, as the precedent requires." *McCreary*, 63 FLRA at 155. Further, with respect to the Agency's arguments that *McCreary* is distinguishable from the instant case, neither the differences in record evidence between the cases nor the testimony in this case indicating that the potential for discovering staff misconduct always arises during inmate investigations provides a basis for finding that the RD erred as a matter of law. Accordingly, insofar as the RD failed to consider the potential for uncovering staff misconduct during the course of inmate investigations, we find that the Agency has not demonstrated that the RD failed to apply established law.

V. Order

The Agency's application for review is denied.

---

3. Section 7103(a)(10) of the Statute states, in pertinent part: "[T]he term 'supervisor' includes only those individuals who devote a preponderance of their employment time to exercising such authority[.]" 5 U.S.C. § 7103(a)(10).

65 FLRA No. 53

UNITED STATES
DEPARTMENT OF HOMELAND SECURITY
TRANSPORTATION SECURITY
ADMINISTRATION
(Agency)

and

AMERICAN FEDERATION
OF GOVERNMENT EMPLOYEES
AFL-CIO
(Labor Organization/Petitioner)

and

NATIONAL TREASURY
EMPLOYEES UNION
(Labor Organization/Petitioner)

WA-RP-10-0033
WA-RP-10-0036

DECISION AND ORDER ON REVIEW

November 12, 2010

Before the Authority: Carol Waller Pope, Chairman, and Thomas M. Beck and Ernest DuBester, Members[1]

I. Statement of the Case

This case is before the Authority on applications for review filed by the American Federation of Government Employees (AFGE) and the National Treasury Employees Union (NTEU) under § 2422.31 of the Authority's Regulations.[2] The Agency filed responses to AFGE's and NTEU's applications, and AFGE filed a response to NTEU's application. In addition, pursuant to § 2429.9 of the Authority's Regulations, the National Right to Work Legal Defense Foundation (the Foundation) requested, and received, permission to file an amicus curiae brief.[3]

AFGE and NTEU filed petitions under § 7111(b)(1)(A) of the Federal Service Labor-Management Relations Statute (the Statute).[4] AFGE's petition seeks "an election for exclusive recognition" of the Agency's transportation security officers (TSOs). AFGE Petition (Feb. 22, 2010). NTEU's petition "requests that a representation election be held[.]" NTEU Petition (March 17, 2010). The Regional Director (RD) found that the Authority's decision in *United States Department of Homeland Security, Border and Transportation Security Directorate, Transportation Security Administration*, 59 FLRA 423 (2003) (then-Member Pope dissenting) (*TSA*), precluded him from processing the petitions. Accordingly, he dismissed the petitions.

In two separate orders issued following the filing of the applications for review, the Authority granted the respective applications and deferred action on their merits. In the second order, the Authority also consolidated the cases.

For the reasons that follow, we reverse the RD's Decision and Order dismissing the petitions and order the RD to take appropriate action consistent with this decision.

II. Background

In November of 2001, Congress passed the Aviation and Transportation Security Act (ATSA), which created the Agency. As relevant here, in 49 U.S.C. § 44935 Note, Congress stated:

> Notwithstanding any other provision of law, the Under Secretary of Transportation for

1. Member Beck's dissenting opinion is set forth at the end of this decision.

2. Section 2422.31 of the Authority's Regulations provides, in pertinent part:

> (c) *Review.* The Authority may grant an application for review only when the application demonstrates that review is warranted on one or more of the following grounds:
> (1) The decision raises an issue for which there is an absence of precedent;.
> (2) Established law or policy warrants reconsideration; or,
> (3) There is a genuine issue over whether the Regional Director has:
> (i) Failed to apply established law[.]

3. Section 2429.9 of the Authority's Regulations provides, in pertinent part: "Upon petition of an interested person, . . . and as the Authority deems appropriate, the Authority may grant permission for the presentation of written . . . argument at any stage of the proceedings by an amicus curiae[.]"

4. The pertinent wording of § 7111 is set forth *infra*.

> Security [Under Secretary] may employ, appoint, discipline, terminate, and fix the compensation, terms, and conditions of employment of Federal service for such a number of individuals as the Under Secretary determines to be necessary to carry out the screening functions of the Under Secretary under section 44901 of title 49, United States Code. The Under Secretary shall establish levels of compensation and other benefits for individuals so employed.

Pursuant to this statutory authority, in 2003, the Under Secretary issued a memorandum (the Memo) that states, in pertinent part:

> I hereby determine that individuals carrying out the security screening function under section 44901 of Title 49, United States Code, in light of their critical national security responsibilities, shall not, as a term or condition of their employment, be entitled to engage in collective bargaining or be represented for the purpose of engaging in such bargaining by any representative or organization.

TSA, 59 FLRA at 424.

Subsequently, AFGE filed petitions seeking an election to determine whether the TSOs wished to be represented by AFGE for the purpose of collective bargaining. In *TSA*, 59 FLRA 423, the Authority found that § 7111 of the Statute permits employees to select an exclusive representative "for the purpose of collective bargaining[,]" and that "a union obtaining exclusive representative status under § 7111 obtains the full range of exclusive representative rights established by" the Statute. *Id.* at 428. Further, the Authority found that there was "no support for the argument that the Under Secretary meant to permit the creation or recognition of an exclusive representative having less than the full rights accorded to exclusive representatives under" the Statute, and that the Memo "precludes the recognition of an exclusive representative for any and all representational activity permitted by" the Statute. *Id.* at 429. Moreover, the Authority held that there was no evidence of Congressional intent to give the Authority power to determine an appropriate unit and conduct an election for any purpose other than to determine a representative for collective bargaining, or to create "some sort of hybrid exclusive representative[.]" *Id.* Finally, the Authority determined that, even if it agreed that a union could utilize the procedures encompassed by § 7111 to become recognized as a "hybrid exclusive representative having less than the full rights accorded by" the Statute, "the Under Secretary's exercise of his sole and exclusive discretion precludes such an outcome[.]" *Id.*

Later, AFGE and NTEU filed the petitions at issue here. As stated previously, AFGE seeks "an election for exclusive recognition" of the Agency's TSOs, while NTEU "requests that a representation election be held[.]" AFGE Petition (Feb. 22, 2010); NTEU Petition (March 17, 2010).

III. RD's Decision

The RD found that the decision in *TSA* required him to dismiss AFGE's and NTEU's petitions. RD's Decision at 4. In this connection, the RD determined that the ATSA, the Memo, and *TSA* "remain in full force and effect[,]" and that he was "bound to follow and apply" *TSA* because it is "the established precedent of the Authority." *Id.* In addition, the RD rejected an argument by AFGE that the Memo violates the United States Constitution. *Id.* at 4-5.

IV. Positions of the Parties

A. AFGE's Application

AFGE argues that established law or policy -- specifically, the Authority's decision in *TSA* -- warrants reconsideration. According to AFGE, the right to organize is a right that is "separate and distinct" from the right to engage in collective bargaining, and the ATSA does not deprive the Authority of jurisdiction to conduct an election and certify an exclusive representative for "any of several purposes under the Statute." AFGE's Application at 4. For support, AFGE cites *Firstline Transportation Security, Inc.*, 347 NLRB 447 (2006) (*Firstline*).[5]

AFGE also argues that, since the Authority issued its decision in *TSA*, the Agency has recognized AFGE for a variety of representational purposes. In this connection, AFGE alleges that: (1) the Agency

5. We note that AFGE also argues that the RD failed to apply established law when he "failed to examine" *Firstline*. AFGE's Application at 2 n.3. However, the RD did examine *Firstline* and found it not to apply because it involved private-sector screeners to whom the Memo does not apply. RD's Decision at 3 n.4. Thus, AFGE's argument is misplaced.

has established a "Partnership Office" that has met with, shared information with, and established an email address to solicit concerns from AFGE; (2) "AFGE has formed 37 Locals that represent employees at airports across the country[,]" and "[t]he leadership and membership from these Locals participate in meetings with the TSA Partnership Office, local airport management and Congressional representatives to discuss issues of importance to TSOs[;]" (3) the Agency provides for dues deduction to AFGE on behalf of TSOs; (4) the Agency has created its own grievance procedure in which AFGE represents employees, "and the [A]gency has recognized the right of employees to have representation in grievance proceedings, EEO cases, adverse action cases and peer review[;]" and (5) the Agency trains supervisors and managers to maintain neutrality in union-related matters and to refrain from discriminating against employees for their union activities, and "has issued guidance that makes it clear [that] employees can engage in union activities." AFGE's Application at 9-10. Thus, AFGE contends that it is "already functioning as the representative on behalf of TSOs" in these processes to the extent permitted by the Agency, and "it cannot be claimed that . . . there would be some barrier to TSOs exercising" statutory rights that do not involve collective bargaining. *Id.* at 10. AFGE also asserts that the Agency "has denied certain non-collective bargaining rights such as *Weingarten* rights," which underscores the importance of allowing employees to choose an exclusive representative.[6] *Id.*

Finally, AFGE contends that the RD failed to apply established law when he found that the Memo does not violate the Constitution. In this connection, AFGE asserts that the Memo's "prohibition of [TSOs] associating together for the purposes of collective discussion with their employer violates their right of free speech and association" under the First Amendment. *Id.* at 13. According to AFGE, the Memo improperly treats the Agency's TSOs differently from other Agency employees and airport screeners who work for private-sector companies. *Id.* at 15-17.

B. Agency's Response to AFGE's Application

The Agency argues that, given the Authority's decision in *TSA*, the RD correctly dismissed the petitions. However, the Agency asserts that if AFGE's petition seeks an election for purposes that do not include the right to bargain collectively, then *TSA* is not controlling, and the Agency does not object to an election for such limited purposes. Agency's Response to AFGE's Application at 3, 5. In this connection, the Agency concedes that it "provides, and has provided for some time, representation to TSOs -- separate and apart from collective bargaining[,]" and that this has "not been detrimental to the critical security responsibilities of TSOs or [the Agency's] mission imperatives to ensure transportation security." *Id.* at 4-5.

The Agency also argues that, if the Authority directs an election, then the Authority should also provide "a clear and full articulation of the legal authorization and implications of such a hybrid election[.]" *Id.* at 6 n.4. Further, the Agency states that it is "likely that [it] soon will conduct a thorough review of labor relations, including the issue of collective bargaining among TSOs" and that "the Authority should consider whether an election . . . should await the outcome of the Agency's review." *Id.* at 5-6. Finally, the Agency claims that, if the Authority grants review on the ground that it has authority to conduct an election for the purpose of collective bargaining or on grounds related to the constitutionality of the Memo, then the Authority should grant the Agency an opportunity to provide full briefing under § 2422.31(g) of the Authority's Regulations.[7] *Id.* at 4 n.2.

C. NTEU's Application

NTEU argues that there is "absolutely no precedent that squarely addresses basic statutory rights and obligations in a regime where there is exclusive representation without collective bargaining." NTEU's Application at 5. According to NTEU, if the Authority revisits *TSA*, then it "must address [several specific] basic questions about what exclusive representation without collective bargaining means" for the Agency's employees. *Id.* at 4.

D. Agency's Response to NTEU's Application

The Agency asserts that, if the Authority determines that it may conduct an election for a union

6. *Weingarten* rights are explained and discussed further below.

7. Section 2422.31(g) provides:

> *Briefs if review is granted.* If the Authority does not rule on the issue(s) in the application for review in its order granting review, the Authority may, in its discretion, afford the parties an opportunity to file briefs. The briefs will be limited to the issue(s) referenced in the Authority's order granting review.

that would lack collective-bargaining rights, then the Authority should address the issues raised by NTEU's application. Agency's Response to NTEU's Application at 3. In addition, the Agency reiterates that its Administrator is conducting a review of the issues, and that it would be "prudent to defer a decision on the novel approach that AFGE proposes" until the Administrator completes that review. *Id.*

E. AFGE's Response to NTEU's Application

AFGE asserts that addressing the issues raised by NTEU's application is unnecessary and "would only serve to delay" employees' opportunity to vote. AFGE's Response to NTEU's Application at 2. In addition, AFGE asserts that it is unnecessary for the Authority to wait for the Administrator to make a determination regarding collective bargaining before the Authority can direct an election. *Id.* at 4.

V. The Foundation's Amicus Curiae Brief

The Foundation argues that the Authority has no statutory authority to certify an exclusive representative because, under the ATSA, the Under Secretary continues to have unfettered discretion to decide whether TSOs can bargain collectively. Amicus Brief at 5-6. The Foundation also argues that TSOs are "the last line of defense against a terrorist boarding an airplane with a bomb or a weapon[,]" and that certifying TSOs would pose an "unacceptable threat to national security." *Id.* at 7, 6. In this regard, the Foundation asserts that ensuring national security requires flexibility and the ability to adapt quickly to threats, and that, if an exclusive representative is certified and a new security threat emerges, then "any changes to current . . . screening procedures would have to be negotiated[.]" *Id.* at 7-8. The Foundation also asserts that these same concerns prompted Congress not to allow unionization by members of the military and employees at the Federal Bureau of Investigation (FBI), the Central Intelligence Agency (CIA), and the Secret Service. *Id.* Further, the Foundation contends that, although the law prohibits TSOs from striking, the TSOs could ignore that prohibition and thereby "endanger vital public services[.]" *Id.* at 9. Moreover, the Foundation asserts that only twenty-five percent of TSOs voluntarily pay dues to AFGE or have joined AFGE Locals, and granting AFGE's petition would "force 75% of the proposed bargaining unit to be represented by an organization to which they clearly have no interest in belonging." *Id.* at 12. Finally, the Foundation contends that "[f]reedom of choice is the cornerstone of the United States Constitution[,]" and granting the petition would violate TSOs' "fundamental right . . . to speak for themselves in their workplace[]" and resolve workplace disputes on their own without relying on an exclusive representative. *Id.* at 12-13.

VI. Analysis and Conclusions

As discussed previously, in *TSA*, the Authority found, among other things, that there was "no support for the argument that the Under Secretary meant to permit the creation or recognition of an exclusive representative having less than the full rights accorded to exclusive representatives under" the Statute, and that the Memo "precludes the recognition of an exclusive representative for any and all representational activity permitted by" the Statute. 59 FLRA at 429.

It is undisputed that, since *TSA*, the Agency has recognized AFGE and NTEU as representatives of some employees for purposes of non-collective-bargaining activity. In fact, as noted previously, the Agency expressly states that it does not oppose an election for an exclusive representative, as long as the election is not for the purposes of certifying a union that could engage in collective bargaining. *See* Agency's Response to AFGE's Petition at 3-4. Thus, the premise of the decision in *TSA* -- that the Memo "precludes the recognition of an exclusive representative for any and all representational activity permitted by" the Statute, 59 FLRA at 429 -- is inconsistent with all parties' interpretations of the Memo as well as their current practice. Accordingly, we find it appropriate to reconsider *TSA* and reassess whether § 7111 of the Statute precludes processing election petitions with respect to TSOs.

Turning to that issue, § 7111 provides, in pertinent part:

> If a petition is filed with the Authority . . . by any person *alleging* . . . in the case of an appropriate unit for which there is no exclusive representative, *that 30 percent of the employees* in the appropriate unit *wish to be represented for the purpose of collective bargaining by an exclusive representative* . . . the Authority *shall* investigate the petition, and if it has reasonable cause to believe that a question of representation exists, it *shall* provide an opportunity for a hearing (for which a transcript shall be kept) after a reasonable notice. If the Authority finds on the record of the hearing that a question of representation exists, the Authority *shall* supervise or conduct an

election on the question by secret ballot and shall certify the results thereof.

5 U.S.C. § 7111 (emphasis added).

In other words, in order for the Authority to be obligated to process a representation petition seeking an election, the petition must include an allegation that thirty percent of employees in an appropriate unit "wish to be represented for the purpose of collective bargaining by an exclusive representative[.]" *Id.* The plain wording of § 7111 focuses on the wishes of *employees*, not the wishes or intentions of *employers*. Therefore, nothing in the plain wording of § 7111 indicates that the Authority may refuse to meet its statutory obligation to process representation petitions solely because an employer does not intend to accord its employees' exclusive representative the full range of collective-bargaining rights.[8]

In fact, such an interpretation of § 7111 would be inconsistent with the fact that the Authority consistently recognizes labor organizations as exclusive representatives even where those representatives have less than full collective bargaining rights under the Statute. *E.g., NAGE, Local R1-187, SEIU*, 64 FLRA 627, 628-29 (2010) (under 38 U.S.C. § 7422, Secretary of Veterans Affairs or designee has unreviewable discretion to determine that a matter concerns or arises out of professional conduct or competence and, thus, is not subject to collective bargaining); *NTEU*, 61 FLRA 871, 877 (2006) (then-Member Pope writing separately) (sole and exclusive discretion of Comptroller of the Currency barred negotiation over some, but not other, matters); *U.S. Dep't of the Interior, Bureau of Indian Affairs, S.W. Indian Polytechnic Inst., Albuquerque, N.M.*, 58 FLRA 246, 248-50 (2002) (agency had sole and exclusive discretion to determine whether to bargain over a demonstration project prior to its implementation); *Ass'n of Civilian Technicians, Tex. Lone Star Chapter 100*, 55 FLRA 1226, 1228 (2000), *aff'd* 250 F.3d 778, 784 (D.C. Cir. 2001) (National Guard technicians may not bargain concerning military aspects of civilian technician employment); *AFGE, Local 884*, 47 FLRA 884, 893-98 (1993) (Member Talkin dissenting in part), *aff'd sub nom. AFGE, Local 3295 v. FLRA*, 46 F.3d 73, 76 (D.C. Cir. 1995) (under 12 U.S.C. § 1462a(g), Director of Office of Thrift Supervision has sole and exclusive discretion to set pay and benefits, subject to a limited exception).[9]

Although the instant case is distinguishable from the above-cited decisions, in that the TSOs at issue here currently lack any right -- rather than a limited right -- to engage in collective bargaining, we find this to be a distinction without a meaningful difference in terms of whether the election petitions should be processed. In this regard, even if one of the labor organizations is certified but precluded from engaging in collective bargaining, the Statute provides exclusive representatives with several rights separate from negotiating collective bargaining agreements.[10] For example, § 7114(a)(1) provides exclusive representatives with not only the right to "negotiate collective bargaining agreements covering" unit employees, but also a separate right to "act for[]" those employees. Additionally, § 7117(d)(1) gives certain exclusive representatives the right to "consultation rights[,]" separate and apart from the right to engage in collective bargaining. Further, § 7114(a)(2)(A) entitles the exclusive representative to be represented at certain "formal discussion[s] . . . concerning any grievance or any personnel policy or practices or other general condition of employment[.]" In this connection, the Authority has held that the definition of "grievance" is not dependent on the scope of a negotiated grievance procedure. *See Luke Air Force Base, Ariz.*,

8. Nothing in the wording of AFGE's or NTEU's petitions precludes the Authority from processing those petitions. In this regard, as stated previously, AFGE's petition seeks "an election for exclusive recognition" of the TSOs, AFGE's Petition (Feb. 22, 2010), and NTEU's petition "requests that a representation election be held[.]" NTEU's Petition (March 17, 2010). We construe these broad statements as expressing an interest by TSOs to have the respective labor organizations represent them for purposes including, but not limited to, collective bargaining. In addition, although the parties argue that it would be appropriate to conduct an election for non-collective-bargaining purposes, they do not concede that they are seeking an election solely for such purposes. Thus, there is no basis for the dissent's assertion that, if an election is conducted, then employees will have selected an exclusive representative "for very limited purposes having nothing to do with collective bargaining[.]" Dissent at 14.

9 We acknowledge that the cited decisions are not representation decisions. Nevertheless, they demonstrate that labor organizations may be exclusive representatives under the Statute even if they have limited collective-bargaining rights.

10 We agree with the dissent that there is a difference between "*some* collective bargaining and *no* collective bargaining." Dissent at 13. However, in our view, there is an even more critical difference between being represented for all statutory purposes (including collective bargaining) and being unable to be represented for *any statutory purposes at all*.

54 FLRA 716, 730 (1998), *rev'd* 208 F.3d 221 (9th Cir. 1999). As such, the right of an exclusive representative to attend formal discussions under § 7114(a)(2)(A) does not require the existence of a collective bargaining agreement.

Moreover, § 7114(a)(2)(B) entitles the exclusive representative to be represented at any agency representative's examination of a unit employee (*Weingarten* discussion) if "the employee reasonably believes that the examination may result in disciplinary action" and "the employee requests representation." In this regard, the Authority has held that the rights regarding *Weingarten* discussions under § 7114(a)(2)(B) "are not tied to collective bargaining." *Dep't of Veterans Affairs, Veterans Affairs Med. Ctr., Jackson, Miss.*, 48 FLRA 787, 793 (1993), *recons. denied*, 49 FLRA 701 (1994). Thus, the fact that an exclusive representative lacks collective bargaining rights does not nullify *Weingarten* rights under § 7114(a)(2)(B).

In sum, a certified, exclusive representative has several rights under the Statute that are not dependent on the right to negotiate collective bargaining agreements.[11] *Cf. U.S. Dep't of Veterans Affairs, Wash., D.C. v. FLRA*, 1 F.3d 19, 21 (D.C. Cir. 1993) (although certain employees of the Veterans Administration "had no statutorily-protected right to negotiate collective bargaining agreements, or to administer such agreements through grievance arbitration procedures, they had and retain other rights protected by the [Statute], including 'the right to form, join, or assist a labor organization without fear of penalty or reprisal.'" (citation omitted)). The existence of these rights supports a conclusion that the Statute does not preclude the Authority from processing AFGE's and NTEU's election petitions merely because the Under Secretary exercised his statutory discretion to decline to accord exclusive representatives the right to engage in collective bargaining. Thus, we find no statutory basis for declining to process the petitions in this case.

Nothing in the Foundation's amicus brief supports a contrary conclusion. With regard to the Foundation's security-related concerns, even if AFGE or NTEU ultimately is certified as the TSOs' exclusive representative, that would not alter the Under Secretary's authority under the ATSA to set TSOs' conditions of employment and to decide whether and how to conduct collective bargaining. With regard to the Foundation's discussion of members of the military and employees of the FBI, CIA, and Secret Service, Congress specifically exempted "member[s] of the uniformed services" from the definition of "employee" under § 7103(a)(2)(B)(ii) of the Statute, and specifically exempted the FBI, CIA, and Secret Service from the definition of "agency" under § 7103(a)(3)(B), (C), and (H) of the Statute. The fact that Congress could have, but did not, specifically exempt TSOs or the Agency from the coverage of the Statute supports, rather than undercuts, a conclusion that Congress intended the Statute -- including § 7111 -- to apply to TSOs. *See AFGE, Local 3529*, 59 FLRA 619, 622 (2004) (noting that Congress expressly exempted one agency from coverage of a law and stating that, "had Congress intended to exclude [another agency], it would have done so"). With regard to the Foundation's argument that granting the petition would "force 75% of the proposed bargaining unit to be represented by" a labor organization, Amicus Brief at 12, that argument ignores the fact that, if that percentage of employees votes for no labor organization, then no labor organization will be certified. *See* 5 U.S.C. § 7111(a) (to be entitled to exclusive recognition, labor organization must be chosen by "a majority" of unit employees who vote). Finally, with regard to the Foundation's claim that processing the petition would violate TSOs' "fundamental right" to resolve workplace disputes without relying on an exclusive representative, the Foundation does not explain how the Statute's election procedures do not adequately protect the alleged right. Amicus Brief at 12. As such, the Foundation's arguments are misplaced.

For the foregoing reasons, we find that the decision in *TSA* warrants reconsideration, and, on reconsideration, we overrule *TSA* and reverse the RD's decision.[12]

11. The dissent claims that these statutory rights are merely "secondary" or "ancillary" to the right to engage in collective bargaining. Dissent at 13. We agree that the right to engage in collective bargaining, including the right to negotiate collective bargaining agreements, is significant. However, the other statutory rights discussed above also are significant, and neither the dissent nor the wording of the Statute provides any support for a conclusion that these rights are less significant than, or wholly dependent on, the right to engage in collective bargaining.

12. With regard to AFGE's additional argument -- that the RD failed to apply established law by failing to declare the Memo unconstitutional -- we note that the narrow issue before us in this case is whether the Memo precludes the Authority from conducting an election. We have found that it does not. As such, it is unnecessary to resolve whether the RD failed to apply established law by declining to

In so finding, we acknowledge NTEU's and the Agency's argument that, in directing an election, we should explain what exclusive representation means absent the right to engage in collective bargaining. To the extent that this argument suggests that we should articulate all of the details regarding how the Agency would be required to deal with AFGE or NTEU should either of those labor organizations be certified, it is neither necessary nor prudent to do so here. In this regard, although issues have been raised and questions posed, the record does not include the parties' arguments on these matters.[13] Moreover, although the parties' positions on these issues and questions could be obtained, doing so at this point would delay the election, and such delay is contrary to the purposes of the Statute. In this connection, the Authority has held that there is a "public interest[]" in "allowing employees to vote for the representative of their choice, without undue delay or the possible influence of extraneous factors caused by the passage of time[.]" *Dep't of the Army, U.S. Army Aviation Missile Command (AMCOM), Redstone Arsenal, Ala.*, 55 FLRA 640, 645 (1999) (Member Wasserman dissenting in part). *Accord Nat'l Ass'n of Agric. Emps.*, 61 FLRA 545, 548 (2006), *review dismissed*, 473 F.3d 983 (9th Cir. 2007) (denying request for stay of election). Thus, we reject NTEU's and the Agency's argument in this regard.

We also acknowledge the Agency's statement that we should await the outcome of the Agency's review of labor relations, including the issue of collective bargaining among TSOs and, potentially, the Memo. However, the Agency does not indicate how long this review will take.[14] Thus, granting the Agency's request could indefinitely preclude the TSOs from exercising the important statutory right discussed above, and we find it inappropriate to do so.

Finally, with regard to the Agency's request to provide further briefing, the Agency has had an opportunity to, and did, provide full briefing. In addition, granting the Agency's request also would unnecessarily delay the TSOs from exercising their statutory right to vote. Accordingly, we deny the Agency's request to provide additional briefing.

For the foregoing reasons, we reconsider and overrule *TSA*, reverse the RD's decision, and remand to the RD to process AFGE's and NTEU's petitions.

VII. Order

The RD is directed to take appropriate action consistent with this decision.

---

declare the Memo unconstitutional, and we do not resolve that issue.

13. We note that the dissent also poses several questions regarding what will occur if the petitions are processed, and asserts that the questions "demonstrate that our Statute does not countenance the election of an exclusive representative that has no collective bargaining rights." Dissent at 15. However, the dissent's questions do not have such far-reaching implications. They simply "demonstrate" that recognizing an exclusive representative with less than full collective bargaining rights has the potential to raise complex legal issues – the type of issues that the Authority frequently is faced with under the Statute. We may not abdicate our statutory responsibility to effect statutory rights merely because doing so may raise additional, complex questions.

14. Quoting the September 23, 2010 committee-hearing testimony of the Agency's Administrator, the dissent notes that the Agency has almost completed reviewing the issue of TSOs' collective-bargaining rights. *See* Dissent at 12 n.1. However, even assuming that a decision on this issue is imminent, we find no basis for further delaying the TSOs' exercise of their right to determine whether to select an exclusive representative, even if the contours of that exclusive representative's authority may change as a consequence of the Administrator's review.

Member Beck, Dissenting:

The question presented in this matter is not whether transportation security officers (TSOs) *should* enjoy collective bargaining rights, nor whether TSOs *should* be represented for certain purposes by one or more labor organizations. These are questions of policy that fall, in the first instance, to the Congress. When it created the Transportation Security Administration (TSA) in 2001, Congress left it to the Executive Branch, in the person of the TSA Administrator (formerly known as the "Under Secretary"), to answer these questions. *See* § 111(d) of the Aviation and Transportation Security Act, Pub. L. No. 107-71, *codified as* 49 U.S.C. § 44935 Note 2001.[1]

The crucial question presented by AFGE's and NTEU's petitions here is strictly a legal question: Does our Statute authorize the Authority to conduct an election through which employees may select an exclusive representative that is prohibited from engaging in any collective bargaining on their behalf? I conclude that it does not. Therefore, I disagree with my colleagues that the circumstances of this case require us to overrule *United States Department of Homeland Security, Border and Transportation Security Directorate, Transportation Security Administration*, 59 FLRA 423 (2003) (then-Member Pope dissenting) (*TSA*) and to reverse the Regional Director's decision.

Our Statute sets forth three propositions that are relevant to this question:

- The sole purpose of an election is to determine whether employees will be represented by an "exclusive representative." 5 U.S.C. § 7105(a)(2)(B). The Authority is not authorized to conduct an election for any other purpose.

- An election is held only to determine whether employees wish to select an exclusive representative "for the purpose of collective bargaining." 5 U.S.C. §§ 7111(b)(1)(A), 7111(f)(2). An election to select a representative that will engage in no collective bargaining is not contemplated by the Statute, and therefore is not authorized.

- The principal attribute of an "exclusive representative" is its ability to "negotiate collective bargaining agreements" for employees in the unit. 5 U.S.C. § 7114(a)(1). The Statute mandates that "any agency and any exclusive representative ... *shall meet and negotiate in good faith for the purposes of arriving at a collective bargaining agreement.*" 5 U.S.C. § 7114(a)(4) (emphasis added). Collective bargaining is the *sine qua non* of any exclusive representative. A labor organization that is unable to engage in any collective bargaining on behalf of the employees whom it purports to represent cannot be considered an "exclusive representative" within the meaning of our Statute.

In other words, the Authority may conduct an election only for the purpose of permitting employees to select an entity to act as their exclusive representative. An exclusive representative must be able to engage in collective bargaining. Consequently, the Authority may not conduct an election for the purpose of permitting employees to select an entity to represent them in some fashion that entirely excludes collective bargaining.

To this extent, I agree with the central holding of *TSA* -- that "[t]here is no evidence of Congressional intent to confer on the Authority the power to determine an appropriate unit and to conduct an election for any purpose other than to determine a representative for collective bargaining." 59 FLRA at 429.

The Majority correctly notes that exclusive representatives of employees in certain other agencies, such as the Comptroller of the Currency, Bureau of Indian Affairs, and Office of Thrift Supervision, have "less than full collective bargaining rights." Majority at 8. However, these exclusive representatives are able to engage in at least some collective bargaining on behalf of employees. There is not only a quantitative difference, but also a critical qualitative difference, between *some* collective bargaining and *no* collective

1. On September 23, 2010, in testimony before the Congress, TSA Administrator John Pistole stated that he is currently conducting a review on the question of whether TSOs should be given collective bargaining rights, that the review is "nearly complete," and that he expects to complete the review "in the near future" -- within "weeks rather than months." *Securing America's Transportation Systems: The Target of Terrorists and TSA's New Direction before the H. Subcomm. on Transp. Sec. & Infrastructure Prof.*, 111th Cong. (2010) (statement of John S. Pistole, Administrator, TSA).

bargaining. So long as a labor organization is able to engage in some collective bargaining on behalf of employees, it is carrying out the core function and responsibility of an "exclusive representative" within the meaning of our Statute. The same cannot be said of a labor organization that is able to engage in *zero* collective bargaining, which is the case for any labor organization seeking to represent TSOs as long as the Under Secretary's 2003 Memo is in effect.[2]

The Majority also correctly notes, as do the Unions in their respective Applications, that the Statute grants to exclusive representatives some rights and entitlements that are in addition to collective bargaining, such as the right to be present at formal discussions and, in certain circumstances, national consultation rights. However, the existence of such secondary rights enjoyed by an exclusive representative sheds no light on the question raised by the petitions. These rights are ancillary to – not instead of – collective bargaining, and they arise only if there is a collective bargaining relationship in place between the exclusive representative and the agency. A labor organization must first be an exclusive representative before it can enjoy these ancillary rights. As explained above, a labor organization cannot be an exclusive representative if it cannot engage in collective bargaining on behalf of the employees whom it purports to represent.[3]

Unprecedented and insuperable questions would flow from holding an election that results in the selection of a so-called "exclusive representative" that is completely prohibited from engaging in collective bargaining on behalf of employees. For example:

- Suppose an election were held and it resulted in one of the petitioning unions becoming the "exclusive representative" of TSOs. In the circumstances as they currently stand, the employees who voted in favor of that union would have done so understanding that they were voting for a union that lacks the status and legal authority to bargain collectively on their behalf. Thus, one could hardly conclude that employees either expected or wanted that union to represent them in collective bargaining.[4] If and when the new TSA Administrator reverses the extant Memo and grants collective bargaining rights to TSOs, what then is the status of this union? Should it be presumed that, because employees selected this union as their "exclusive representative" for very limited purposes having nothing to do with collective bargaining, these employees would also want the union to represent them in collective bargaining? What would be the basis for indulging in this assumption? Why would it be appropriate to assume that an entity selected by employees for certain very limited purposes would be selected by employees for different -- and much broader and consequential -- purposes?

2. This Memo may not remain in effect much longer. *See supra* n.1.

3. The Majority relies on *United States Department of Veterans Affairs, Washington, D.C v. FLRA*, 1 F.3d 19 (D.C. Cir. 1993) (*VA*) to support the proposition that "a certified, exclusive representative has several rights under the Statute that are not dependent on the right to negotiate collective bargaining agreements." Majority at 9. However, in that case, there was, nevertheless, an ongoing collective bargaining relationship between the union and the agency, and the historical circumstances underlying that relationship make it anomalous as a practical matter, and certainly inapposite to the question presented here. Long before the enactment of our Statute in 1978, the Veterans Administration voluntarily engaged in collective bargaining with, and entered into collective bargaining agreements with, various unions representing medical professionals. *See AFGE, Local 3884 v. FLRA*, 930 F.2d 1315, 1318 (8th Cir. 1991). This pre-1978 bargaining occurred, and these agreements were put in place, without the benefit of an election to select an "exclusive representative" within the meaning of our Statute. In stark contrast to the situation that evolved at the Department of Veterans Affairs, the instant petitions present the question of whether, *under our Statute*, we may hold an election to certify an exclusive representative that currently has no collective bargaining relationship with the agency, has no collective bargaining agreements in place, and is prohibited from engaging in any collective bargaining whatsoever.

4. There is no basis for the Majority's decision to "construe" the petitions as "expressing an interest by TSOs to have the respective labor organizations represent them for purposes of . . . collective bargaining." Majority at n. 8. Despite our Statute's explicit requirement that a petition must allege that employees in the affected unit "wish to be represented *for the purpose of collective bargaining*" (5 U.S.C. § 7111(b)(1)(A) (emphasis added)), these petitions pointedly omit such an allegation. More importantly, as all parties and my colleagues in the Majority agree, so long as the 2003 Memo is in effect, it is a legal impossibility for TSOs to be represented for purposes of collective bargaining. Therefore, the Majority's casual assumption that the petitions signify anything about TSOs' wishes with respect to collective bargaining can only be characterized as a profound misreading of both the petitions and the legal landscape in which the petitions are presented.

- Suppose that an election results in one of the petitioning unions becoming the "exclusive representative" with no authority, and therefore no apparent mandate from employees, to engage in collective bargaining. If and when the new TSA Administrator reverses the extant Memo and grants collective bargaining rights to TSOs, may a different union petition for a new election to determine which labor organization should represent employees for purposes of *collective bargaining*? What would be the Authority's response to such a petition? Would we treat the unit as one that is not currently represented for the purpose of collective bargaining (5 U.S.C. § 7111(b)(1)(a)), or would we treat the unit as one that is currently represented for purposes of collective bargaining (5 U.S.C. § 7111(b)(1)(b))? Would the election of an exclusive representative with no collective bargaining rights constitute a "valid election" for purposes of the 12-month election bar (5 U.S.C. § 7111(b)(2))?

To pose these questions is to demonstrate that our Statute does not countenance the election of an exclusive representative that has no collective bargaining rights.

Because, as a matter of law, there can be no exclusive representative that is entirely bereft of collective bargaining rights and responsibilities, the Authority is not permitted to conduct an election for such an entity. Accordingly, I disagree with the determination of my colleagues to overrule *TSA* and to reverse the Regional Director's decision.

65 FLRA No. 54

AMERICAN FEDERATION
OF GOVERNMENT EMPLOYEES
NATIONAL COUNCIL
OF EEOC LOCALS NO. 216
(Union)

and

EQUAL EMPLOYMENT
OPPORTUNITY COMMISSION
(Agency)

0-AR-4581

DECISION

November 15, 2010

Before the Authority: Carol Waller Pope, Chairman, and Thomas M. Beck and Ernest DuBester, Members

I. Statement of the Case

This matter is before the Authority on exceptions to an award of Arbitrator Steven M. Wolf filed by the Union under § 7122 of the Federal Service Labor-Management Relations Statute (the Statute) and part 2425 of the Authority's Regulations. The Agency filed an opposition to the Union's exceptions.[1]

In his original award (original award), the Arbitrator found that the Agency violated the Fair Labor Standards Act (FLSA) and further found, in a clarification award (clarification award), that affected employees were entitled to liquidated damages equal to the amount of overtime compensation owed minus compensatory time already used. For the reasons discussed below, we deny the Union's exceptions.

II. Background and Arbitrator's Award

The Union filed a grievance alleging, as relevant here, that the Agency violated 29 U.S.C. §§ 207 and 216(b) by effectively requiring employees to request compensatory time off in lieu of overtime compensation.[2] *See* Original Award at 1-2, 77. The Arbitrator framed the issue before him as: "[W]hether the Agency . . . violated the FLSA by . . . [creating] suffered or permitted overtime [by] . . . wrongly . . . granting . . . compensatory time instead of . . . overtime." *Id.* at 76-77. The Arbitrator sustained the grievance and, as relevant here, determined that the Agency owed any affected employees overtime compensation and liquidated damages. *See id.* at 77, 79. The Arbitrator directed the parties to attempt to determine which employees were owed overtime, and how much overtime each employee was owed.[3] *See id.* at 79.

After engaging in settlement discussions, the parties asked the Arbitrator to clarify how liquidated damages would be calculated. *See* Exceptions, Attach. 3 at 1-2 (Union Letter); Exceptions, Attach. 4 (Memo) at 1-4. In the clarification award -- the award at issue here -- the Arbitrator ruled, in pertinent part, that "liquidated damages shall be calculated after, not before, deduction of the monetary value of compensatory time granted and taken by eligible employees." Clarification Award at 1.

III. Positions of the Parties

A. Union's Exceptions

The Union asserts that the Arbitrator's "calculation of liquidated damages is contrary to the law" because the Arbitrator deducted compensatory time already paid from overtime compensation owed before determining the amount of liquidated damages. Exceptions at 4-5. (citing *U.S. Dep't of the Navy, Naval Sea Sys. Command*, 57 FLRA 543 (2001) (*Naval Sea Sys.*)). According to the Union, the Arbitrator thereby reduced liquidated damages which, the Union argues, "may only be reduced upon a showing of good faith by the employer[.]" *Id.* at 3

1. As discussed further below, the parties also submitted additional filings in connection with an Authority show-cause order.

2. 29 U.S.C. § 207(a) states, in pertinent part, that "no employer shall employ any of his employees . . . for a workweek longer than forty hours unless such employee receives compensation for his employment in excess of the hours above specified at a rate not less than one and one-half times the regular rate at which he is employed." As relevant here, 29 U.S.C. § 216(b) states that an employer who violates § 207 of the FLSA shall be liable to affected employees "in the amount of . . . their unpaid overtime compensation . . . and in an additional equal amount as liquidated damages."

3. Neither party filed exceptions to the original award. *See* Exceptions at 2; Opp'n at 1-2.

(citing 29 U.S.C. §§ 216(b) and 260;[4] *U.S. Dep't of the Navy, Naval Explosive Ordinance Disposal Tech. Div., Indian Head, Md.*, 56 FLRA 280, 286 (2000) (*Indian Head*)). *See also id.* at 4-5 (citing *U.S. Dep't of Commerce, NOAA, Office of Marine & Aviation Operations, Marine Operations Ctr., Norfolk, Va.*, 57 FLRA 559, 564 (2001) (*NOAA*)).

Additionally, the Union argues that the clarification award is contrary to law because the Arbitrator deducted unused compensatory time from the backpay award. *See* Exceptions at 5 (citing *SSA, Memphis, Tenn.*, 59 FLRA 564, 567 (2004) (*SSA*)).

B. Agency's Opposition

The Agency contends that the Union's exceptions are interlocutory because the Arbitrator did not "completely resolve all issues submitted for arbitration" including "the identification of the aggrieved individuals and the amounts of damages to which each is entitled[.]" Opp'n at 4 (citing *U.S. Dep't of Veterans Affairs, W. N.Y. Healthcare Sys., Buffalo, N.Y.*, 61 FLRA 173, 174-75 (2005) (*Veterans*); *Navy Pub. Works Ctr., San Diego, Cal.*, 27 FLRA 407, 408 (1987) (*Public Works*)). On the merits, the Agency alleges that the Arbitrator correctly calculated liquidated damages, as compensatory time already used does not constitute "unpaid" overtime under 29 U.S.C. § 216(b). Opp'n at 5. Further, the Agency asserts that the Arbitrator's calculation of liquidated damages is consistent with how Federal courts have calculated liquidated damages in similar contexts. *See id.* at 6-7 (citing *Coston v. Plitt Theatres, Inc.*, 831 F.2d 1321, 1330 (7th Cir. 1987) (*Coston*), *cert. denied*, 485 U.S. 1007 (1988), *vacated on other grounds*, 486 U.S. 1020 (1988), *on remand*, 860 F.2d 834 (7th Cir. 1988); *Lupien v. City of Marlborough*, 387 F.3d 83, 89-90 (1st Cir. 2004) (*Lupien*)). Finally, the Agency asserts that the award does not grant credit for unused compensatory time, as the Union claims. *See* Opp'n at 7.

IV. Analysis and Conclusions

A. Preliminary matter: The Union's exceptions are not interlocutory.

The Authority issued an order to show cause, directing the Union to show cause why the Authority should not dismiss the exceptions as interlocutory. *See* Order to Show Cause at 1-3. In its response, the Union asserts that the Arbitrator resolved all of the issues before him, as he "determined the remedy to be applied" in the original award, Response at 2, and his ruling in the clarification award as to how liquidated damages will be calculated constitutes a final award. *Id.* at 3. In the alternative, the Union claims that the Authority should consider the exceptions because "exceptional circumstances exist" that will materially advance the dispute in a way that would "assure the correct application of the law" and the "claims of individuals[.]" *Id.* at 3-4.

In a reply to the Union's response,[5] the Agency counters that "neither the [original award] nor the [clarification award] completely resolved all issues submitted for arbitration" because the Arbitrator had not resolved "the identification of aggrieved individuals or the amount of damages . . . to which they might be entitled." Reply at 4 (citing *U.S. Dep't of Health & Human Servs., Ctrs. for Medicare & Medicaid Servs.*, 57 FLRA 924, 925-26 (2002) (*HHS*)). Further, the Agency contends that the clarification award is "not a . . . clarification[]" because the Union did not adhere to the requirements for requesting a clarification under the parties' agreement. *See id.* Therefore, the Agency claims, "the [clarification award] cannot be treated as a clarification which can be the subject of an exception." *Id.* Finally, the Agency argues that the Union's exceptions do not present a plausible jurisdictional defect that would warrant review of an interlocutory appeal. *See id.* at 5.

Section 2429.11 of the Authority's Regulations provides, in pertinent part, that "the Authority . . . ordinarily will not consider interlocutory appeals." Accordingly, the Authority will not resolve exceptions to an arbitration award unless the award constitutes a complete resolution of all the issues submitted to arbitration. *See, e.g., U.S. Dep't of Transp., FAA, Wash., D.C.*, 60 FLRA 333, 334 (2004). Exceptions to an award are not interlocutory where an arbitrator has retained jurisdiction solely to assist the parties in the

4. As relevant here, 29 U.S.C. § 260 states that under the FLSA, if the employer "shows . . . that the act or omission giving rise to [the FLSA] action was in good faith and that he had reasonable grounds for believing that his act or omission was not a violation of t[he FLSA,]" then a court may "award no liquidated damages or award any amount thereof not to exceed the amount specified in" 29 U.S.C. § 216.

5. The order to show cause permitted the Agency to reply to any Union response. Order to Show Cause at 3.

implementation of awarded remedies, including the specific amount of monetary relief awarded. *See, e.g., U.S. Dep't of the Treasury, IRS*, 63 FLRA 157, 158 (2009) (*IRS*); *U.S. Dep't of the Air Force, Kirtland Air Force Base, Air Force Materiel Command, Albuquerque, N.M.*, 62 FLRA 121, 123 (2007). In addition, the Authority has held that an award holding an agency liable for unpaid overtime was final, and that exceptions to it were not interlocutory, even though the award did not identify, among other things, which employees were affected by the agency's actions. *See U.S. Dep't of Justice, Fed. Bureau of Prisons, USP Admin. Maximum (ADX), Florence, Colo.*, 64 FLRA 1168, 1170 (2010) (*ADX*).

Contrary to the Agency's claim, the original award completely resolved the issue submitted to arbitration -- whether the Agency violated the FLSA by failing to pay employees overtime compensation -- by finding that the Agency violated the FLSA and therefore owed affected employees overtime compensation and liquidated damages. *See* Original Award at 77, 79-80. Further, the fact that the Arbitrator did not identify the specific employees to whom overtime compensation was owed and did not determine the amount of overtime compensation owed, does not render the original award non-final for the purposes of determining whether the Union's exceptions are interlocutory. *See ADX*, 64 FLRA at 1170. Moreover, the clarification award, to which the exceptions here pertain, did not leave any submitted issues unresolved. Additionally, the decisions cited by the Agency do not demonstrate that either award is not final. In this regard, nothing in *Veterans*, 61 FLRA at 174-75, indicates that either the original award or the clarification award failed to completely resolve all of the issues submitted to arbitration. Moreover, unlike the situation here, the award in *Public Works*, 27 FLRA at 408, did not provide any type of remedy. Further, whereas the award in *HHS*, 57 FLRA at 926, entitled "Phase One Interim Award[,]" indicated, by its name, that the award was not final, neither the original award nor the clarification award in this case contains such indication. With regard to the Agency's claim that the Union did not adhere to the requirements of the parties' agreement in requesting a clarification of the award, the Agency does not provide any basis for finding the clarification award is not a final award to which the Union may file exceptions.

For the foregoing reasons, we find that the Union's exceptions are not interlocutory, and we consider them.[6]

B. The clarification award is not contrary to law.

When an exception involves an award's consistency with law, the Authority reviews any question of law raised by the exception and the award *de novo*. *See NTEU, Chapter 24*, 50 FLRA 330, 332 (1995) (citing *U.S. Customs Serv. v. FLRA*, 43 F.3d 682, 686-87 (D.C. Cir. 1994)). In applying the standard of *de novo* review, the Authority assesses whether an arbitrator's legal conclusions are consistent with the applicable standard of law. *See U.S. Dep't of Def., Dept's of the Army & the Air Force, Ala. Nat'l Guard, Northport, Ala.*, 55 FLRA 37, 40 (1998). In making this assessment, the Authority defers to the arbitrator's underlying factual findings. *See id.*

The FLSA provides that when an employer has not shown that it acted in good faith, the employer shall be liable for "*unpaid* overtime compensation . . . and . . . an additional equal amount [of] liquidated damages." 29 U.S.C. § 216(b) (emphasis added). Consistent with this wording, Federal courts have awarded or upheld awards of liquidated damages equal to *unpaid* overtime compensation, that is, overtime compensation minus compensatory time already paid. *See, e.g., D'Camera v. District of Columbia*, 722 F.Supp. 799, 803-04 (D.D.C. 1989) (*D'Camera*); *Roman v. Maietta Constr., Inc.*, 147 F.3d 71, 74, 76-77 (1st Cir. 1998) (*Roman*). *Cf. Coston*, 831 F.2d 1329-30 ("the amount of actual harm done the plaintiff must be determined prior to doubling the damage award as required to establish liquidated damages" such that "amounts earned in mitigation of the backpay compensatory award must be deducted prior to doubling" when determining damages under the Age Discrimination Employment Act, which incorporates the remedial scheme of the FLSA).

Consistent with the above precedent, the Arbitrator determined that liquidated damages should equal the actual harm to affected employees, i.e., the overtime compensation owed minus compensatory time already used. Moreover, the decisions cited by the Union are inapposite because they do not address

6. As we have found that the Union's exceptions are not interlocutory, it is not necessary to determine whether they present a plausible jurisdictional defect that would warrant review of an interlocutory appeal.

how liquidated damages should be calculated. *See Indian Head*, 56 FLRA at 286 (liquidated damages warranted where agency did not act in good faith under the FLSA); *NOAA*, 57 FLRA at 564 (agency acted in good faith under the FLSA); *Naval Sea Sys*, 57 FLRA at 545-48 (upholding award of backpay). As such, the Union has not demonstrated that the Arbitrator's calculation of liquidated damages is contrary to law. Therefore, we deny this exception.

Finally, the Union contends that the award improperly "provid[es] a credit for compensatory time granted" rather than compensatory time used. Exceptions at 5. Contrary to the Union's assertion, the award deducts "compensatory time *granted and taken* by eligible employees." Clarification Award at 1 (emphasis added). Thus, the award is not contrary to *SSA*, 59 FLRA at 567, where the Authority held that an award of overtime pay must be reduced to the extent that employees have already used compensatory time. *See* Exceptions at 5.

For the foregoing reasons, we deny the Union's exceptions.

V. Decision

The Union's exceptions are denied.

65 FLRA No. 55

UNITED STATES
DEPARTMENT OF JUSTICE
FEDERAL BUREAU OF PRISONS
UNITED STATES PENITENTIARY
ATWATER, CALIFORNIA
(Agency)

and

AMERICAN FEDERATION
OF GOVERNMENT EMPLOYEES
COUNCIL OF PRISON LOCALS
LOCAL 1242
(Union)

0-AR-4435
(64 FLRA 810 (2010))

_____

ORDER DENYING MOTION
FOR RECONSIDERATION

November 23, 2010

_____

Before the Authority: Carol Waller Pope, Chairman, and Thomas M. Beck and Ernest DuBester, Members

I. Statement of the Case

This matter is before the Authority on the Agency's motion for reconsideration of the Authority's decision to dismiss the Agency's exception in *United States Department of Justice, Federal Bureau of Prisons, United States Penitentiary, Atwater, California*, 64 FLRA 810 (2010) (*DOJ, Atwater*). The Union did not file an opposition to the Agency's motion for reconsideration.

Section 2429.17 of the Authority's Regulations permits a party who can establish extraordinary circumstances to request reconsideration of an Authority decision. For the reasons set forth below, we conclude that the Agency has failed to establish extraordinary circumstances warranting reconsideration. Accordingly, we deny the Agency's motion for reconsideration.

II. Decision in *DOJ, Atwater*

In the underlying proceedings in *DOJ, Atwater*, the Agency filed an exception challenging the Arbitrator's determination that its "willful" violation of the Fair Labor Standards Act (FLSA) warranted the application of a three-year, rather than a two-year, statute of limitations period to the scope of the remedy. Exception at 3-4. *See* 29 U.S.C. § 255(a) (providing for a two-year statute of limitations in which to bring a claim under the FLSA and a three-year statute of limitations where the violation of the law is willful). In resolving the exception, the Authority found that the Agency failed to address what it believed to be the appropriate statute of limitations period before the Arbitrator even though the Union requested that the Arbitrator apply the three-year statute of limitations. Therefore, the Authority dismissed the Agency's exception because "[t]he Authority will not consider . . . any issue, which was not presented in the proceedings before the . . . arbitrator." 5 C.F.R. § 2429.5.*

III. Motion for Reconsideration

The Agency claims that extraordinary circumstances exist warranting reconsideration of the Authority's decision in *DOJ, Atwater*. First, the Agency claims that the Authority erred in its findings of fact and its legal conclusions. Motion at 5. Specifically, the Agency claims that the Authority "misinterpreted" its arguments before the Arbitrator. *Id.* at 3. According to the Agency, it presented "substantial and persuasive evidence" at arbitration that was intended to show that it did not willfully violate the FLSA. *Id.* The Agency contends that the Authority should have understood that it presented this evidence to persuade the Arbitrator to apply the two-year statute of limitations without it having to use those "magic words." *Id.* at 5. Therefore, the Agency asks that the Authority reconsider its decision to dismiss the exception and render a decision on the merits of the case. *Id.* at 5-6.

Second, the Agency argues that the Authority legally erred by failing to ensure that the award is consistent with the law. *Id.* at 8. Specifically, the Agency argues that reconsideration is warranted because the remedy is not based on a valid waiver of sovereign immunity. The Agency explains that, although the FLSA provides a waiver of sovereign

* Section 2429.5 was amended October 1, 2010. *See* 75 Fed. Reg. 42, 283 (2010). For purposes of this case, we apply the previous version of the Regulation that was in effect at all times relevant to the processing of this case.

immunity, since the Arbitrator's factual findings do not support the application of the three-year statute of limitations under the FLSA, the waiver of sovereign immunity is invalid. Accordingly, the Agency claims, the Authority "is allowing an improper monetary award against the United States Government to stand," in violation of the doctrine of sovereign immunity. *Id.* at 6. As such, the Agency requests that the Authority grant its motion for reconsideration.

IV. Analysis and Conclusions

The Agency has failed to establish extraordinary circumstances warranting reconsideration.

Section 2429.17 of the Authority's Regulations permits a party that can establish extraordinary circumstances to request reconsideration of an Authority decision. The Authority has repeatedly recognized that a party seeking reconsideration under § 2429.17 bears the heavy burden of establishing that extraordinary circumstances exist to justify this unusual action. *See Int'l Ass'n of Firefighters, Local F-25*, 64 FLRA 943 (2010). The Authority has identified a limited number of situations in which extraordinary circumstances have been found to exist. These include situations where: (1) an intervening court decision or change in the law affected dispositive issues; (2) evidence, information, or issues crucial to the decision had not been presented to the Authority; (3) the Authority erred in its remedial order, process, conclusion of law, or factual finding; and (4) the moving party has not been given an opportunity to address an issue raised *sua sponte* by the Authority in its decision. *See id.*

First, we deny the Agency's claim that the Authority made erroneous findings of fact and legal conclusions that led to the improper dismissal of the Agency's exception under § 2429.5.

The record shows that, although the Agency provided the Arbitrator with factual assertions and background information relating to the parties' general dispute, the Agency failed to present any argument at arbitration relating to the applicable statute of limitations period. The case law interpreting 5 C.F.R. § 2429.5 makes clear that the Authority will not consider a contention that was not presented to the Arbitrator. *See U.S. Dep't of Justice, Fed. Bureau of Prisons, Fed. Corr. Complex, Oakdale, La.*, 63 FLRA 178, 179-80 (2009). In particular, the Authority will not consider arguments made by excepting parties who had notice of, and an opportunity to respond to, opposing parties' arguments prior to filing their exceptions with the Authority. *See U.S. Dep't of Justice, Fed. Bureau of Prisons, USP Admin. Maximum (ADX) Florence, Colo.*, 64 FLRA 1168, 1170 (2010) (*BOP, Florence*) (exception dismissed under § 2429.5 where agency had notice of specific remedy sought by union at arbitration and could have, but did not, present its argument to the arbitrator disputing that remedy); *U.S. Dep't of Homeland Security, U.S. Customs & Border Prot., JFK Airport, Queens, N.Y.*, 62 FLRA 416, 417 (2008) (same). Here, the record shows that the Agency had notice at the hearing that the Union was requesting that the Arbitrator apply the three-year statute of limitations period. However, the Agency failed to respond to the Union's argument or make a clear argument for a two-year statute of limitations prior to filing its exception. Accordingly, we reject the Agency's contention that reconsideration is warranted on the ground that extraordinary circumstances exist because the Authority erred in its findings of fact and its legal conclusions. *Cf. U.S. Dep't of Labor*, 60 FLRA 737, 738 (2005) (motion for reconsideration granted where agency challenged decision dismissing exception on § 2429.5 grounds where agency had no notification prior to union's post- hearing brief of argument under collective bargaining agreement).

Second, we deny the Agency's motion for reconsideration based on the doctrine of sovereign immunity. A claim of federal sovereign immunity can be raised at any time. *U.S. Dep't of the Treasury, IRS, Wash., D.C.*, 61 FLRA 146, 151 (2005) (citing *Dep't of the Army v. FLRA*, 56 F.3d 273, 275 (D.C. Cir. 1995); *accord Settles v. U.S. Parole Comm'n*, 429 F.3d 1098, 1105 (D.C. Cir. 2005) (sovereign immunity is a matter of "jurisdiction and may properly be raised at any time")). It is clear that a federal agency is subject to a monetary claim only if the statute on which the claim is based unambiguously establishes a waiver of sovereign immunity permitting such claim. *See Lane v. Pena*, 518 U.S. 187 (1996).

The Agency concedes that the FLSA constitutes a waiver of sovereign immunity, *see* Motion at 7, but argues that the requirements warranting a three-year statute of limitations under the FLSA were not met. Thus, the Agency's claim that the award contravenes the doctrine of sovereign immunity is merely a restatement of its claim that the Arbitrator erroneously applied the three-year statute of limitations under the FLSA — an issue that the Authority found untimely raised in *DOJ, Atwater*. The Agency has not provided any reason for us to reconsider the dismissal of the Agency's claim regarding the three-year statute of limitations issue. Moreover, the award is based on the FLSA and the FLSA provides a valid waiver of sovereign immunity. We therefore reject the Agency's contention that reconsideration is warranted because the award violates the doctrine of sovereign immunity.

Accordingly, because the Agency has failed to establish that extraordinary circumstances exist warranting reconsideration, we deny the Agency's motion for reconsideration.

V. Order

The Agency's motion for reconsideration is denied.

65 FLRA No. 56

UNITED STATES
DEPARTMENT OF VETERANS AFFAIRS
(Agency)

and

NATIONAL NURSES UNITED, AFL-CIO
(Petitioner/Labor Organization)

and

UNITED AMERICAN NURSES, AFL-CIO
(Exclusive Representative)

and

JUDIANN CHARTIER
(Interested Party)

WA-RP-10-0039

ORDER DENYING
APPLICATIONS FOR REVIEW

November 23, 2010

Before the Authority: Carol Waller Pope, Chairman, and Thomas M. Beck and Ernest DuBester, Members

I. Statement of the Case

This case is before the Authority on several applications for review filed by National Nurses United (NNU) bargaining unit members[1] under § 2422.31 of the Authority's Regulations.[2] The Petitioner, NNU, and the United States Department of Veterans Affairs (VA) each filed an opposition[3] to the applications for review.[4] Judiann Chartier, to whom the Regional Director (RD) granted interested party status on behalf of her clients, did not file any response to the applications for review.

An election was held in which VA nurses voted to change their affiliation with their exclusive representative from United American Nurses (UAN) to NNU. NNU and UAN subsequently filed a petition requesting that the certification held by UAN for the VA nurses be amended to reflect the bargaining unit's change in affiliation with its exclusive representative from UAN to NNU. The RD granted the petition, finding that NNU met the requisite conditions for the change in affiliation.

For the reasons that follow, we deny the applications for review.

II. Background and RD's Decision

NNU and UAN filed a petition requesting that the certification held by UAN for a unit of nurses working at the VA known as the National VA Council (NVAC) be amended to reflect NVAC's change in affiliation with its exclusive representative from UAN to NNU. RD's Decision at 1. The VA

---

1. The following individuals filed applications for review: (1) Alice Staggs; (2) Ruby Rose Hutchinson; (3) Donna King; (4) Linda Salvini; (5) Gina McLain; (6) Odell Anderson; (7) Rebecca Johnson; (8) Sandra McMeans; (9) Murrie Davis; and (10) Margaret Thompson.

2. Section 2422.31 of the Authority's Regulations provides, in pertinent part:

> (c) Review. The Authority may grant an application for review only when the application demonstrates that review is warranted on one or more of the following grounds:
>
> (1) The decision raises an issue for which there is an absence of precedent;
>
> (2) Established law or policy warrants reconsideration; or
>
> (3) There is a genuine issue over whether the Regional Director has:
>
> (i) Failed to apply established law;
>
> (ii) Committed a prejudicial procedural error;
>
> (iii) Committed a clear and prejudicial error concerning a substantial factual matter.

3. In addition to its original opposition addressing nine of the applications for review, NNU submitted an opposition specifically addressing Thompson's application for review and challenging her standing to file the application. As NNU's arguments in this opposition mirror those made in its original opposition submitted to the Authority, we do not address it further.

4. NNU also submitted two separate supplemental submissions replying to assertions made by the VA in its opposition. Section 2429.26 of the Authority's Regulations requires a party filing supplemental submissions to request permission to file such submissions. 5 C.F.R. § 2429.26. As NNU did not request permission to file either one of its supplemental submissions, we decline to consider them. *See, e.g., AFGE, Local 933*, 65 FLRA 9, 10 (2010) (union's supplemental submission not considered where union did not request permission to file submission).

stated that it agreed with the objective of the petition, "so long as there has been a proper following of the procedures for accomplishing a change in affiliation (i.e.[,] *Montrose* procedures)." *Id.* at 2; *see VA Hosp., Montrose, N.Y.,* 4 A/SLMR 858 (1974) (*Montrose*) (setting forth procedures to be followed during a change in affiliation), reaffirmed in *Florida Nat'l Guard, St. Augustine, Fla.,* 25 FLRA 728 (1987). The RD subsequently conducted an investigation.

The RD found that NVAC is a consolidated unit of nurses for twenty-two separate VA facilities in twelve states. *Id.* at 3. The NVAC bargaining unit includes approximately 8,725 bargaining unit employees, 2,403 of whom are dues-paying members. *Id.* at 3-4. The RD further found that UAN and the VA had a master agreement in effect for NVAC (UAN-VA master agreement). *Id.* at 3.

The RD determined that, in 2009, a number of nursing associations affiliated with UAN, including NVAC, began discussing plans to form a national nurses union. *Id.* A secret-ballot vote was conducted in November 2009 among the sixty-three delegates representing various UAN units, including those from NVAC. *Id.* The majority of the delegates who participated in the election supported the formation of NNU. *Id.* After the formation of NNU, a second election was held among NVAC members in early 2010. *Id.* at 7. In that election, the voters overwhelmingly supported the transfer of UAN's national bargaining rights to NNU. *Id.* at 8.

As required by Authority case law when determining whether to approve an affiliation change in these circumstances, the RD investigated whether appropriate due process procedures were followed in conducting the election. In order to amend a certificate of exclusive recognition to reflect a change in affiliation, the RD noted that the procedures set forth in *Montrose* must be followed. *Id.* (citing *Montrose,* 4 A/SLMR 858; *Fla. Nat'l Guard, St. Augustine, Fla.,* 25 FLRA 728). The RD found that, at a minimum, the Authority requires that: (1) a proposed change in affiliation should be the subject of a special meeting of the members of the incumbent labor organization, called for this purpose only, with adequate advance notice provided to the entire membership; (2) the meeting should be held at a time and place convenient to all members; (3) adequate time for discussion of the proposed change should be provided, with all members given an opportunity to raise questions within the bounds of normal parliamentary procedure; and (4) a vote by the members of the incumbent labor organization on the question should be taken by secret ballot, with the ballot clearly stating the change proposed and the choices inherent therein. RD's Decision at 8 (citing *Montrose,* 4 A/SLMR at 860).

The RD determined that the foregoing procedural *Montrose* requirements were satisfied. Specifically, the RD found that NVAC members all received several mailings that described the proposed change in affiliation and that special meetings were held to discuss the change at almost every VA facility. RD's Decision at 9. The RD also found that NVAC members received adequate notice of each of the meetings and that the meetings provided them with the opportunity to have their questions about the affiliation change answered in person. *Id.* In addition, the RD found that the ballot question was clearly written, and voters understood that the election was being held to decide whether the VA nurses should change their affiliation with their exclusive representative from UAN to NNU. *Id.* at 10.

As required under *Montrose,* the RD also investigated whether the proposed change in affiliation would "affect the continuity of unit employees' representation . . . [or] leave open any question concerning such representation." *Id.* at 9. The RD found that substantial information was provided to members over the course of several months which clearly stated that NNU would maintain existing NVAC officers, abide by all agreements entered into by UAN, and maintain the current dues amount. *Id.* at 10. The RD found that there had been no change to the NVAC officers, local officials, and business representatives. *Id.* The RD further found that, regardless of affiliation, the VA continued to work with the same representatives, including NVAC President Alice Staggs, and agreed that it could work with NNU. *Id.* Further, the RD found that NNU had stated that it was willing to adhere to the UAN-VA master agreement. Accordingly, because the procedures used to conduct the election for the change in affiliation met the required standards and there was the requisite continuity of representation, the RD granted the petition. *Id.*

III. Positions of the Parties

A. Applications for Review

The individuals filing applications for review (Applicants) make largely identical claims. The Applicants assert that NNU has not conducted itself as it said it would before the RD granted the petition changing the bargaining unit employees' exclusive representative affiliation from UAN to NNU. Specifically, the Applicants claim that, since the RD's decision to grant the petition, NNU has changed the structure of NVAC. *See, e.g.,* King Application at 1. In this regard, the Applicants point to NNU's removal of NVAC President Alice Staggs, NVAC Manhattan Local President Cathy Benjamin-Bovell[5], and business representative Hector Ramos, even though a document included in the ballot package stipulated that NVAC's leadership would remain the same until elections could be held. *See, e.g.,* Staggs Application at 2; Johnson Application at 2. The Applicants argue that they did not agree to these changes. *See, e.g.,* McMeans Application at 1-2. At least one Applicant claims that NNU has acted in "bad faith" and "violat[ed] . . . continuity of representation" by effecting these changes. McLain Application at 1. And another Applicant claims that NNU's conduct does not comply with an October 28, 2009 internal memorandum and a document distributed prior to the election, entitled, "Q & A Regarding Legal and Governance Issues Raised by UAN NVAC," which sets forth questions and answers about the transferring of bargaining rights from UAN to NNU. Hutchinson Application at 2.

The Applicants also explain that NNU has effected several other changes outside of the above-mentioned removals. For example, NNU has asked that NVAC presidents change their titles and that NVAC refer to its other officers as "'stewards.'" Salvini Application at 4, 6. NNU has also eliminated the office of Vice President, allegedly in violation of the UAN-VA master agreement to which it is bound. Johnson Application at 3. In addition, NNU informed NVAC that NVAC's by-laws would need to be replaced by "guidelines," even though, prior to the RD's decision, NNU had stated that NVAC's by-laws would remain in place. *See, e.g.,* Salvini Application at 4. Also, most of the Applicants mention that NNU has taken control of the local treasuries and is holding that money in escrow for the local organizations. *Id.*

Several of the Applicants note NNU's claim that at least some of these changes were made in response to an ongoing Department of Labor (DOL) investigation. *See, e.g.,* Salvini Application at 4; Johnson Application at 1-2. Several Applicants explain in this regard that NNU claims that DOL suspects that local NVAC units are in violation of reporting requirements, and that the changes NNU has undertaken are necessary to show DOL that the individual NVAC units are not "individual unions." Thompson Application at 1; Davis Application at 1. Several of the Applicants also note that, despite NVAC's request that NNU provide documentary evidence of DOL's investigation requiring these changes, NNU refused to provide any such documentation. Davis Application at 2. Accordingly, the Applicants ask that the Authority "reverse" the RD's decision to grant the petition to change NVAC's affiliation with its exclusive representative from UAN to NNU. *See, e.g.,* McLain Application at 1; Hutchinson Application at 1; Anderson Application at 1.

B. NNU's Opposition

NNU makes three claims in its opposition. First, NNU contends that none of the Applicants are parties to this case under the Authority's Regulations and that they therefore lack standing to file applications for review. NNU Opp'n at 2, 5-7. NNU argues that each Applicant filed the application for review on her own individual behalf. In NNU's view, the Applicants do not qualify as "parties" under the Authority's Regulations because none of them are petitioners, charged parties, respondents, or intervenors in the proceeding.[6] *Id.* at 7. According to NNU, as only a "party" may file an application for review with the Authority,[7] and as none of the Applicants meet the Authority's definition of a "party" under the Authority's Regulations, the Applicants do not have standing to file their applications for review. *Id.* at 7-8.

---

5. Some of the Applicants explain that Ms. Benjamin-Bovell was returned to her position shortly after being removed. *See, e.g.,* Salvini Application at 6.

6. *See* 5 C.F.R. § 2421.11, defining a "party," as relevant here, as:

> (a) Any labor organization, employing agency or activity or individual filing a charge, petition, or request;
>
> (b) Any labor organization or agency or activity
>
> (1) Named as
>
> (i) A charged party in a charge,
>
> (ii) A respondent in a complaint, or
>
> (iii) An employing agency or activity or an incumbent labor organization in a petition;
>
> (2) Whose intervention in a proceeding has been permitted or directed by the Authority[.]

7. *See* 5 C.F.R. § 2422.30(d), *Appeal of Regional Director Decision and Order,* which provides that "[a] party may file with the Authority an application for review of a Regional Director Decision and Order."

Second, NNU argues that the applications should be denied because the Applicants have failed to satisfy the criteria necessary for review set forth in 5 C.F.R. § 2422.31.[8] *Id.* at 2. Rather, NNU argues, the Applicants are "complain[ing] about an extraneous, internal union event that occurred subsequent to the [RD's] Decision." *Id.* According to NNU, "[t]he only argument advanced in support of the applications for review is based on the removal of Staggs as NVAC president following her extended and indefinite leave of absence from the VA." *Id.* at 9. NNU argues that "the Authority's practice in representation cases requires an assessment of the record based on the circumstances existing at the time of the hearing." *Id.* (emphasis omitted) (quoting *U.S. Dep't of the Army, U.S. Dep't of Def., Fort Detrick, Md.*, 62 FLRA 407, 409 (2008); and citing *N.M. Army & Air Nat'l Guard*, 56 FLRA 145, 149 (2000)). NNU further alleges that the Authority's inquiry must focus on whether a question concerning representation existed at the time of the RD's investigation into the matter. *Id.* Staggs was removed after the RD's investigation and decision to grant the petition. Therefore, NNU claims that the issues raised by the applications do not raise a question of representation. *Id.* at 9-10.

Third, NNU argues that, even if the Authority considers the applications for review, it must deny them because none of the applications sets forth a basis to grant review. According to NNU, the RD correctly found that the *Montrose* requirements were met and the change in affiliation has not affected bargaining unit members' continuity of representation. *Id.* at 10. NNU alleges that there is no Authority precedent providing that continuity of representation must last indefinitely. *Id.* at 10. Furthermore, NNU claims that it has maintained continuity of representation. *Id.* at 9. NNU explains that, with the exception of Alice Staggs, whose position was filled by NVAC's former vice-president, "all of the national positions representing [VA nurses] continue to be filled by the previous NVAC officers." *Id.* at 6. According to NNU, Staggs' removal has not undermined the continuity of representation for VA nurses. *Id.* at 10-11. NNU also notes that it continues to adhere to the UAN-VA master agreement and the VA continues to deal with NNU in all representational matters. Therefore, as substantial continuity of representation still exists, NNU requests that the Authority deny the applications for review. *Id.*

8. *See supra* at n.2.

C. VA's Opposition

The VA claims that the change in affiliation from UAN to NNU has had no effect on its relationship with the local bargaining units. VA Opp'n at 6. The VA further contends that the change in affiliation will not interfere with its mission, statutory labor obligations, or ability to adhere to the UAN-VA master agreement. *Id.* However, the VA is concerned that material facts may be in dispute regarding whether there is continuity of representation. Therefore, the VA asks that the Authority remand this matter to the Authority's San Francisco Regional Office for additional factual investigation and review. *Id.* at 7.

IV. Analysis and Conclusions

A. The Applicants have standing to seek review of the RD's decision.

For the following reasons, we find that the Applicants have standing to seek review of the RD's decision.

NNU argues that the Applicants lack standing to seek review of the RD's decision because they do not qualify as "parties" under § 2422.31(a) of the Authority's Regulations. However, the Authority rejected this argument in *United States Department of the Navy, Human Resources Service Center Northwest, Silverdale, Washington,* 61 FLRA 408 (2005) (*Navy*).

In *Navy*, an agency employee filed an application seeking review of an RD's decision that clarified several bargaining units following an agency reorganization. The union challenged the applicant's standing to file the petition, arguing that he was not a party under the Authority's Regulations. *See Navy,* 61 FLRA at 409. The Authority found that the applicant had standing to file the application for review under § 7105(f) of the Federal Service Labor-Management Relations Statute (the Statute) as an "interested person." *See Navy,* 61 FLRA at 410-11.

Section 7105(f) of the Statute provides that "the Authority may, upon application by any interested person filed within 60 days after the date of the action," review actions of the RD in representation matters. Since the applicant in *Navy* was an agency employee, and since that employee's exclusive representative was changed as a result of the decision, the Authority found that he was an interested person under the Statute and that he therefore had standing to file the application for review. *Id.* Similarly, here, as the Applicants are employees whose exclusive representative was changed as a result of the RD's decision, we find that the Applicants are interested persons under the Statute and that they therefore have standing to file applications for review.

B. The applications for review do not demonstrate that review is warranted on one of the required grounds set forth in § 2422.31.

Under § 2422.31(c) of the Authority's Regulations, the Authority may grant an application for review only when the application demonstrates that review is warranted on one or more of the following grounds: (1) the decision raises an issue for which there is an absence of precedent; (2) established law or policy warrants reconsideration; or (3) there is a genuine issue over whether the Regional Director has: (i) failed to apply established law; (ii) committed a prejudicial procedural error; or (iii) committed a clear and prejudicial error concerning a substantial factual matter.

The Applicants do not assert that review is warranted on any of the grounds set forth in § 2422.31(c) of the Authority's Regulations. Moreover, the record does not show that the Applicants intend to make any such claim. Instead, the Applicants ask the Authority to reverse the RD's decision based on events that took place after the RD completed the investigation and subsequently granted the petition. *See, e.g.,* Staggs Application at 1. The Applicants do not challenge the RD's decision to grant the petition and concede that they agreed to the change in affiliation based on the information that was presented to the RD and on which the RD made his decision to grant the petition. *See* Salvini Application at 7. Therefore, as the Applicants fail to challenge the RD's decision to grant the petition, and absent any other claim that comports with the requirements for review set forth in § 2422.31(c) of the Authority's Regulations, we find that review of the RD's decision is not warranted under the Authority's Regulations and deny the applications for review.[9] *See U.S. Dep't of Veterans Affairs, Veterans Affairs Med. Ctr., Fayetteville, N.C.*, 65 FLRA 191 (2010) (application denied for failing to assert any grounds for review set forth in § 2422.31(c), including any challenge to RD's determinations).

V. Order

The applications for review are denied.

9. As we deny the applications for review for failing to assert grounds for review pursuant to § 2422.31(c) of the Authority's Regulations, we find that it is unnecessary to address NNU's claim that it has maintained continuity of representation. For the same reason, we also find that it is unnecessary to address the VA's request that the Authority remand this matter to the Authority's San Francisco Regional Office for additional factual investigation and review.

65 FLRA No. 57

AMERICAN FEDERATION
OF GOVERNMENT EMPLOYEES
LOCAL 4044
(Union)

and

UNITED STATES
DEPARTMENT OF JUSTICE
FEDERAL BUREAU OF PRISONS
FEDERAL CORRECTIONAL INSTITUTION
THREE RIVERS, TEXAS
(Agency)

0-AR-4667

DECISION

November 24, 2010

Before the Authority: Carol Waller Pope, Chairman, and Thomas M. Beck and Ernest DuBester, Members

I. Statement of the Case

This matter is before the Authority on an exception to an award of Arbitrator Bruce Ponder filed by the Union under § 7122(a) of the Federal Service Labor-Management Relations Statute (the Statute) and part 2425 of the Authority's Regulations. The Agency filed an opposition to the Union's exception.

The Arbitrator concluded that the Union failed to establish a prima facie case that the Agency violated the Fair Labor Standards Act (FLSA). For the reasons set forth below, we deny the Union's exception.

II. Background and Arbitrator's Award

The grievants work the day shift as Correctional Officers (COs) at the Federal Correctional Institution (FCI) at Three Rivers, Texas. In resolution of an unrelated dispute, the Union and the Agency agreed to a settlement regarding portal-to-portal pay. Award at 2. As part of the settlement, the day shift became a straight eight-hour shift, without a duty-free lunch period. *Id.* at 2-3. However, despite the settlement agreement, the Union and the Warden orally agreed that the COs would continue to work 8 ½ hour shifts and take thirty-minute duty-free lunch periods. *Id.* at 3.

When a new Warden replaced the previous Warden, he noticed that the settlement agreement required the COs to work an eight-hour shift. The new Warden told the local Union President of the need to implement the eight-hour shift. *Id.* The Union President convinced him to delay implementation for one quarter, and requested another delay in implementation the next quarter. *Id.* The Warden implemented the eight-hour shift the following quarter.

The Union then filed a grievance alleging that the Agency violated the FLSA because, for a period of several years, day-shift COs worked 8 ½ hour shifts without being provided the opportunity for a thirty-minute duty-free lunch period. Opp'n at 3. The grievance was not resolved and was submitted to arbitration. *Id.* The issue before the Arbitrator was "[w]hether the [A]gency violated the collective bargaining agreement by requiring dayshift employees to work during thirty-minute lunch periods at FCI Three Rivers."[1] Award at 2.

The Arbitrator stated that the Union must prove by a preponderance of the evidence that the employees have performed work for which they were improperly compensated. *Id.* at 22-23 (citing *Anderson v. Mount Clemens Pottery*, 328 U.S. 680, 686-88 (1946)). The Arbitrator recognized that, under the FLSA, "to employ" includes "to suffer or permit to work," and that the Union must show that the Agency had actual or constructive knowledge of the grievants' overtime work. *Id.* at 23 (citing 29 U.S.C. § 203(g), 5 C.F.R. § 551.104[2]).

1. As a preliminary matter, the Arbitrator found that the FLSA's two-year statute of limitations applies rather than the collective bargaining agreement's forty-day statute of limitations. Award at 21. Because no exceptions were filed to the Arbitrator's resolution of this issue, it is not before us.

2. Although the Arbitrator actually cites to 29 C.F.R. § 551.104, the Agency points out that this seems to be a typographical error, and 5 C.F.R. § 551.104 contains the definition of "suffered or permitted work." Opp'n at 4 n.2. Suffered or permitted work means "any work performed by an employee for the benefit of an agency, whether requested or not, provided the employee's supervisor knows or has reason to believe that the work is being

After summarizing the testimony and evidence presented, the Arbitrator concluded that if, in fact, COs were working through lunch, then the Union had not provided sufficient evidence to show that the Agency was aware of the alleged problem, and, accordingly, had failed to establish a prima facie case. *Id.* at 28-29. In reaching this conclusion, the Arbitrator considered the following evidence:

1) Several COs testified that they often worked without receiving a lunch break, although they did not complain to their supervisors or file any overtime requests, *id.* at 4-9;

2) Some of the COs at issue attended labor management relations meetings at which lunch breaks were discussed and never raised the issue, *id.* at 27-28;

3) Several Agency officials testified that they were not aware of a problem with COs not getting lunch relief, they saw COs eating lunch in the break room, and, if a problem arose, it was resolved quickly, *id.* at 10-18; and

4) The Warden testified that he changed the shift hours to reduce potential Agency liability, *id.* at 29.

Therefore, the Arbitrator denied the Union's grievance. *Id.* at 30.

III. Positions of the Parties

A. Union's Exception

The Union argues that the Arbitrator's conclusion that the Agency had not violated the FLSA is contrary to 5 C.F.R. § 551.104. Exception at 1. According to the Union, the Arbitrator correctly cited the definition of "suffer and permit," but incorrectly applied the definition to the facts at hand. *Id.* at 2. The Union claims that, in denying the grievance, the Arbitrator incorrectly found it necessary for the employees to complain about not getting lunch breaks. *Id.* The Union argues that it is not the employees' responsibility to complain; rather, "it just must be proved the employee's supervisor knows or has reason to believe that the work is being performed and has an opportunity to prevent the work from being performed." *Id.* at 3.

The Union contends that the evidence shows that the COs did not receive thirty-minute lunch breaks, that the Agency was "well aware" of the problem, and that the Agency had the opportunity to prevent the work from being performed. *Id.* at 17-18. The Union asserts that the Agency's system for providing lunch breaks "rarely, if ever, produced the kind of duty-free 30 minute lunch break required under the FLSA[.]" *Id.* at 5. The Union argues that, because the Warden was aware that lunch breaks were a point of contention throughout the Agency, he must have had reason to believe that it was a problem specifically at FCI Three Rivers. *Id.* at 11-12. The Union also asserts that supervisors were aware of the problem because one supervisor testified that he could not guarantee that COs always received their lunch relief. *Id.* at 14. According to the Union, because the testimony shows that COs were working through lunch and the Agency was aware of it, the Arbitrator misapplied the "suffer or permit" standard and the award is contrary to law. *Id.* at 18.

B. Agency's Opposition

The Agency argues that the Arbitrator's findings are not contrary to 5 C.F.R. § 551.104. Opp'n at 3-4. The Agency asserts that the Union's arguments are actually just a disagreement with the Arbitrator's underlying factual finding, to which the Authority must defer. *Id.* at 5. The Agency asserts that the Arbitrator properly found that, if employees were working during their lunch periods, then their supervisors were not aware of it. Thus, the supervisors did not "suffer[ ] or permit[ ]" the COs to work overtime. *Id.* at 6. Moreover, according to the Agency, the Arbitrator did not improperly rely on the fact that the COs never complained or informed their supervisors because this evidence demonstrated that the supervisors did not have knowledge of any overtime work, if, in fact, such work occurred. *Id.* at 3.

IV. The award is not contrary to law.

The Union contends that the Arbitrator's award is contrary to 5 C.F.R. § 551.104. When an exception involves an award's consistency with law, the Authority reviews any question of law raised by the exception and the award *de novo*. *See NTEU, Chapter 24*, 50 FLRA 330, 332 (1995) (citing *U.S. Customs Serv. v. FLRA*, 43 F.3d 682, 686-87 (D.C.

---

performed and has an opportunity to prevent the work from being performed." 5 C.F.R. § 551.104.

Cir. 1994)). In applying the standard of *de novo* review, the Authority assesses whether an arbitrator's legal conclusions are consistent with the applicable standard of law. *See U.S. Dep't of Def., Dep'ts of the Army & the Air Force, Ala. Nat'l Guard, Northport, Ala.*, 55 FLRA 37, 40 (1998). In making that assessment, the Authority defers to the arbitrator's underlying factual findings. *See id.*

The FLSA defines "[e]mploy" as including "to suffer or permit to work." 29 U.S.C. § 203(g). As defined in 5 C.F.R. § 551.104, to suffer or permit to work means "any work performed by an employee for the benefit of an agency, whether requested or not, provided the employee's supervisor knows or has reason to believe that the work is being performed and has an opportunity to prevent the work from being performed."

The Arbitrator's assessment of whether the Agency supervisor knew or had reason to believe that COs were performing overtime work is a factual finding, to which the Authority must defer in this case as it is not alleged to constitute a nonfact. *AFGE, AFL-CIO, Local 3614*, 61 FLRA 719, 723 (2006) (*AFGE, Local 3614*); *see also Soc. Sec. Admin., Balt., Md.*, 63 FLRA 550, 552 (2009) (finding that a party's knowledge is a factual finding because "it is based on the arbitrator's evaluation of the evidence"). Thus, if the factual findings support the arbitrator's legal conclusion, the exceptions must be denied. *Id.* Additionally, "disagreement with an arbitrator's evaluation of the evidence and his determination of the weight to be accorded such evidence provides no basis for finding an award deficient." *AFGE, Local 3295*, 51 FLRA 27, 32 (1995).

The record shows that the Arbitrator evaluated whether the Agency supervisors knew or had reason to believe that COs may have worked during their lunch breaks. The Arbitrator weighed the conflicting testimony before him, acknowledged that it was a "mixed bag," but concluded that the Agency's testimony was "more credible." Award at 24, 29. Based on this evidence, the Arbitrator concluded that the Union did not meet its burden of establishing a prima facie case. *Id.* at 29.

Moreover, contrary to the Union's contention, the Arbitrator did not add a requirement that the grievants must complain in order to be eligible for overtime pay. Rather, the Arbitrator considered the absence of complaints to inform his decision of whether the Agency had actual or constructive knowledge of the alleged problem.

The Arbitrator's factual finding that supervisors were not aware of the alleged problem supports the legal conclusion that the supervisors did not suffer or permit the COs to work. *See AFGE, Local 3614*, 61 FLRA at 723. Therefore, we find that the award is not contrary to law, and we deny the exception. *See AFGE, Local 801, Council of Prison Locals 33*, 58 FLRA 455, 456-57 (2003) (citing *U.S. Dep't of the Air Force, Lowry Air Force Base, Denver, Colo.*, 48 FLRA 589, 594 (1993)) (finding the arbitrator's factual conclusion that the union had not presented evidence that employees worked overtime was not contrary to law).

V. Decision

The Union's exception is denied.

65 FLRA No. 58

UNITED STATES
DEPARTMENT OF JUSTICE
FEDERAL BUREAU OF PRISONS
FEDERAL CORRECTIONAL COMPLEX
TUCSON, ARIZONA
(Agency)

and

AMERICAN FEDERATION
OF GOVERNMENT EMPLOYEES
LOCAL 3955
(Union)

0-AR-4451

DECISION

November 24, 2010

Before the Authority: Carol Waller Pope, Chairman, and Thomas M. Beck and Ernest DuBester, Members

I. Statement of the Case

This matter is before the Authority on exceptions to an award of Arbitrator Richard L. Horn filed by both the Agency and the Union under § 7122(a) of the Federal Service Labor-Management Relations Statute (the Statute) and part 2425 of the Authority's Regulations. The Union filed an opposition to the Agency's exception, and the Agency filed an opposition to the Union's exceptions.

The Arbitrator concluded that the Agency violated: (1) the parties' collective bargaining agreement (parties' agreement) and federal laws when it failed to store properly explosive materials; and (2) the parties' agreement when it did not properly pay employees who stored, handled, and transported such materials. For the reasons set forth below, we grant the Union's exception regarding the Arbitrator's failure to require the payment of interest on the hazard pay differential award, modify the award to include interest consistent with the requirements of the Back Pay Act, and deny the parties' remaining exceptions.

II. Background and Arbitrator's Award

The grievants work as either Locksmiths or Assistant Locksmiths at the Federal Bureau of Prisons, Federal Correctional Complex located in Tucson, Arizona (Penitentiary). *See* Award at 17; Agency's Exception at 5-6. The positions involve a high level of risk for hazardous and stressful working conditions, and employees are required to know how to use "emergency entry equipment, riot control equipment, chemical munitions, and all Special Operations Response Team . . . equipment in order to maintain a high level of readiness at all times." Agency's Exception, Attach. D at 2 & Attach. E at 3.

During a conversation with management officials, the grievants expressed concern regarding their handling of explosive devices and the Agency's storage of such devices. *See* Award at 18. The grievants then sent a letter to the Agency regarding these concerns and inquiring about their potential entitlement to a hazard pay differential. *Id.* In its response to the grievants, the Agency noted that "a hazard pay differential was not in order because the hazardous work had already been taken into account in the pay rate for the Lock [and] Security Specialist job classification." *Id.* The grievants sent another letter to the Agency addressing, among other things, their entitlement to a hazard pay differential. *Id.* After the grievants failed to reach agreement with the Agency, the Union filed a formal grievance on their behalf. *See id.* at 19.

The matter was unresolved and was submitted to arbitration. The Arbitrator framed two issues regarding the merits of the case, one of which was whether the grievants were "entitled to be paid a hazard pay differential for working with or in close proximity to explosive material in accordance with applicable law? If so, what shall be the remedy?"[1] *Id.* at 2.

The Arbitrator found that the Agency violated the parties' agreement "when it did not properly pay [the grievants] who had the responsibility to store, handle, and transport . . . explosive devices." *Id.* at 31. The Arbitrator determined that, in his estimation, the job classifications did not contain language regarding the performance of the hazardous duties at issue. *Id.* at 30. Based on testimony, the Arbitrator inferred that the stun munitions, or flash

---

1. The Agency also raised other threshold issues before the Arbitrator. Award at 2. Because no exceptions were filed to the Arbitrator's resolution of those issues, they are not before us.

bangs, and tactical blast strips were explosive devices and that the Union had provided sufficient information regarding the hazardous nature of these explosive devices and the danger surrounding the improper storage of these munitions. *Id.* at 27-28. Also, the Arbitrator cited testimony indicating that the reference to equipment in the position descriptions "does not take in to consideration the stun munitions, because chemical munitions were listed separately, and explosive munitions were not listed, and are considered a serious hazard." *Id.* at 27. The Arbitrator found that the grievants were entitled to a hazard pay differential of 25 percent. *Id.* at 30. Furthermore, although the Arbitrator noted that a grievant testified that he became aware that he was responsible for handling and storing explosives in late 2006, he awarded the grievants backpay from the date that the grievance was filed, September 21, 2007. *Id.* at 19, 31.

III. Positions of the Parties

A. Agency's Exception

The Agency contends that the Arbitrator's conclusion that the grievants are entitled to a hazard pay differential is contrary to law. Agency's Exception at 4-7. According to the Agency, neither 5 U.S.C. § 5545(d) nor 5 C.F.R. § 550.904(a) authorizes the payment of a hazard pay differential to a grievant whose classification takes into consideration the hazardous duty that he has performed. *Id.* at 4-5. The Agency claims that "it is quite clear that the grievant's [sic] position descriptions take into account the hazards involved, specifically, working with and maintaining weapons, stun guns and other munitions." *Id.* at 5. Similarly, the Agency argues that "[b]oth position descriptions . . . clearly discuss the need for employees in these positions to be knowledgeable of weapons, weapons repair and to have technical and operational knowledge [of] riot control equipment and chemical munitions[,]" and that the position description for the GS-9 Assistant Locksmith position specifies that "employees in these positions must '[have the] ability to conduct technical inspections, test, and make repairs to maintain all weapons in good operational condition at all times.'" *Id.* at 6 (quoting Agency's Exception, Attach. D at 2 & Attach. E at 3).

Moreover, the Agency claims that the Arbitrator failed to refer to, evaluate, and make specific factual findings about the content of the position descriptions. *Id.* at 7 n.3. The Agency argues that the Arbitrator simply made a conclusory statement when he determined that, in his estimation, the classification of the positions did not contain language requiring the grievants to perform the relevant hazardous duties. *Id.* (citing Award at 30).

Finally, the Agency claims that testimony presented at arbitration demonstrates that the grievants' positions were classified to include the performance of hazardous duties. *Id.* at 6-7. According to the Agency, its own witness testified that "in no way can a position description contain each and every aspect of an employees [sic] duties . . ." and that the actual certifiers of the positions at issue told her that "the classification of these positions did specifically take into account the need to handle and work with hazardous materials." *Id.*

B. Union's Opposition

The Union argues that the Arbitrator's finding that the classifications did not take into account the hazardous duties in question is not contrary to law. Union's Opp'n at 8-9. The Union contends that the Arbitrator was hired to evaluate the relevant evidence and testimony and that the Agency simply disagrees with the Arbitrator's finding that the hazardous duties at issue were not taken into consideration in the classification of the positions. *Id.* at 5, 7-9.

Also, the Union argues that, contrary to the Agency's contention, the Arbitrator made specific findings regarding whether the relevant position descriptions mentioned explosive munitions. *Id.* at 5. Moreover, the Union contends that it put forth sufficient evidence for the Arbitrator to find that the relevant position descriptions did not include the hazardous duties performed by the grievants. *See id.* The Union argues that "[t]he position descriptions at issue do not at any point mention the requirement of the employee to handle, transport, store, or in any way work with explosive materials or devices." *Id.* The Union contends that, because chemical munitions are listed separately in the position descriptions, the clear absence of explosive munitions from the position descriptions demonstrates that the hazardous duties at issue were not included in the classification of the grievants' positions. *Id.* at 6.

The Union notes that, although the position descriptions do not mention explosive munitions, they do reference weapons, ammunition, and weapons repair. *Id.* at 5. However, the Union contends that, to the extent that the Agency is arguing that weapons include explosive devices in its exceptions, it is making this argument for the first time on appeal. *Id.* at 5-6.

Furthermore, the Union argues that, even if the position descriptions take into consideration working with explosive materials, "the fact that the Agency is violating federal regulations in the manner in which [it] require[s] the grievants to store these items would be relevant to whether or not these specific duties were considered in the classification of these positions." *Id.* at 7.

C. Union's Exceptions

The Union alleges that the Arbitrator's award of a hazard pay differential from the filing date of the grievance is contrary to law. Union's Exceptions at 5-10. The Union contends that, by calculating the hazard pay differential from the filing date of the grievance, the Arbitrator's award violates the Back Pay Act. *Id.* at 6-7, 10. According to the Union, the Back Pay Act authorizes an arbitrator to award backpay retroactively, up to six years before the filing date of the grievance, and requires that backpay must be awarded during "*the period for which the personnel action was in effect*[.]" *Id.* at 6 (citations omitted) (emphasis in original). Also, the Union contends that, where parties do not agree to a different contractual backpay recovery period, the statutory six-year recovery period applies and that "a clear distinction [exists] between contractual backpay recovery periods and contractual time periods for filing grievances." *Id.* at 9-10 (citation omitted). Furthermore, the Union alleges that, because the Arbitrator found that the grievance was timely filed, there is no reason to limit backpay from the date that the grievance was filed. *Id.* at 9.

The Union admits that, based on the testimony and evidence presented during the arbitration proceedings, the exact period of time that the grievants stored, handled, and transported explosives without being paid a hazard pay differential is unknown. *Id.* at 7. According to the Union, one witness testified that the grievants began performing these hazardous duties in late 2005 or early 2006. *Id.* Moreover, the Union asserts that, although a second witness testified that he discovered that he was storing explosive materials in late 2006, this witness meant to say that he began performing these hazardous duties in late 2005. *Id.* at 8. Ultimately, the Union claims that, because the Penitentiary "opened at some point in February 2006, at the very latest[,] the grievants should be entitled to back pay [sic] for the period beginning March 1, 2006 up to the date upon which the Agency makes the correction to their pay to include the hazard pay differential or ceases requiring the grievants to perform these hazardous duties." *Id.*

Also, the Union argues that the award is contrary to law because the Arbitrator failed to award interest in accordance with the Back Pay Act. *Id.* The Union claims that the Back Pay Act requires that interest be paid beginning on the date of the unjustified personnel action and "ending on a date not more than 30 days before the date on which payment is made." *Id.* (citations omitted). The Union asserts that, because the award does not explicitly award interest in addition to awarding backpay, it is contrary to law. *Id.*

D. Agency's Opposition

The Agency argues that the Arbitrator's award of a hazard pay differential from the filing date of the grievance is not contrary to law. Agency's Opp'n at 4-7. The Agency reiterates its contention that the grievants were not subjected to an unjustified or unwarranted personnel action because the grievants' positions were classified to include the storage, handling, and transportation of explosives. *Id.* at 4. The Agency argues that, even assuming the grievants were affected by an unjustified or unwarranted personnel action, the Back Pay Act does not specify an appropriate time period for an award of a hazard pay differential. *Id.* at 5. Additionally, the Agency contends that an arbitrator has great latitude in fashioning his remedy and that, because the Union failed to present clear evidence as to when the grievants were entitled to a hazard pay differential, the Arbitrator appropriately used his discretion in determining the time frame to award backpay.[2] *Id.* at 5-6.

IV. Analysis and Conclusions

When an exception involves an award's consistency with law, the Authority reviews any question of law raised by the exception and the award

2. Although the Agency argues in its opposition that "[h]azard pay is a type of [e]nvironmental [d]ifferential pay[,]" a hazard pay differential and environmental differential pay are distinct. Agency's Opp'n at 5 n.1. Whereas hazard pay differentials are governed by 5 U.S.C. § 5545(d) and apply to general schedule (GS) employees, the Office of Personnel Management is authorized under 5 U.S.C. § 5343(c)(4) to issue regulations providing for environmental differential pay to wage grade employees. *NAGE*, 43 FLRA 414, 422 & n.5, 424 (1991). Because the grievants, here, are GS employees, the Hazardous Duty Act, 5 U.S.C. § 5545, applies to them. Agency's Exception, Attach. D & Attach. E.

de novo. *See NTEU, Chapter 24*, 50 FLRA 330, 332 (1995) (citing *U.S. Customs Serv. v. FLRA*, 43 F.3d 682, 686-87 (D.C. Cir. 1994)). In applying the standard of *de novo* review, the Authority assesses whether an arbitrator's legal conclusions are consistent with the applicable standard of law. *See U.S. Dep't of Def., Dep'ts of the Army & the Air Force, Ala. Nat'l Guard, Northport, Ala.*, 55 FLRA 37, 40 (1998). In making that assessment, the Authority defers to the arbitrator's underlying factual findings. *See id.*

A. The Arbitrator's conclusion regarding the classification of the grievants' positions is not contrary to law.

The Agency claims that the Arbitrator's legal conclusion that the grievants are entitled to a hazard pay differential is contrary to law. Agency's Exception at 4-7. The Agency argues that, because "it is quite clear that the grievant's [sic] position descriptions take into account the hazards involved, specifically, working with and maintaining weapons, stun guns and other munitions[,]" the grievants are not entitled to a hazard pay differential. *Id.* at 4-5. Moreover, the Agency notes that the Arbitrator failed to refer to, evaluate, and make specific factual findings about the content of the position descriptions in his award. *Id.* at 7 n.3. Finally, the Agency claims that certain testimony demonstrates that the grievants' positions were classified to include a hazard pay differential. *Id.* at 6-7.

The threshold requirements for an employee's entitlement to a hazard pay differential originate from a statutory mandate, as well as government regulation. *U.S. Dep't of the Army, Alaska*, 54 FLRA 1117, 1122 (1998); *see also* 5 U.S.C. § 5545 & 5 C.F.R. Part 550, subpart I. As relevant here, a grievant must satisfy three requirements before he is entitled to a hazard pay differential: (1) the hazard or physical hardship must not have been considered in the classification of his position pursuant to 5 U.S.C. § 5545(d); (2) the hazard or physical hardship must be listed in Appendix A to 5 C.F.R. Part 500; and (3) he must be performing a hazardous duty within the definition of 5 C.F.R. § 550.902. *U.S. Dep't of the Army, Alaska*, 54 FLRA at 1122.

The Agency only contests the Arbitrator's conclusion with respect to the first requirement – i.e., whether the hazardous duty was considered in the classifications of the positions at issue. Agency's Exception at 5-7; Agency's Opp'n at 4. Therefore, the other requirements are not before us.

Based on the Arbitrator's factual findings, the award of a hazard pay differential is not contrary to law. In his award, the Arbitrator evaluated the credibility of evidence and testimony presented to him at arbitration before concluding that the classification of the grievants' positions did not take into account the performance of certain hazardous duties. Award at 26-28, 30-31. The Arbitrator cited specific testimony demonstrating that "the reference to equipment [in the position descriptions] does not take in to consideration the stun munitions, because chemical munitions were listed separately, and explosive munitions were not listed, and are considered a serious hazard." *Id.* at 27. Additionally, he noted that, based on certain testimony, it became clear to him that "the position description[s] did not include duties that were being performed by the grievants" and that, in his estimation, the job classifications did not contain language regarding the performance of the hazardous duties at issue. *Id.* at 30.

Further, to the extent that the Agency contends that the Arbitrator's award of a hazard pay differential is deficient because testimony demonstrates that the grievants' positions were classified to include a hazard pay differential, its contention is without merit. Agency's Exception at 6-7. The Agency's argument merely challenges the weight that the Arbitrator accorded to certain testimony; accordingly, the Agency has not established that the award is contrary to law. *See U.S. DOL*, 19 FLRA 300, 301-02 (1985) (finding that the arbitrator's award was not contrary to law when the arbitrator did not rely on certain classification standards and expert witness testimony indicating that the grievants' positions were classified to include a hazard pay differential when making his decision on the merits). Moreover, an arbitrator's failure to set forth specific findings, or to specify and discuss all allegations in a grievance, does not provide a basis for finding an award deficient. *U.S. Dep't of Commerce, Patent & Trademark Office,* 41 FLRA 1042, 1049 (1991) (citation omitted). In this regard, an arbitrator is not required to specify or discuss specific items of evidence on which an award is based or which otherwise were considered by the arbitrator. *See, e.g., U.S. Dep't of the Navy, Charleston Naval Shipyard, Charleston, S.C.*, 39 FLRA 987, 993 (1991) (citing *U.S. Dep't of Health & Human Servs., SSA, Balt., Md.*, 37 FLRA 766, 773-74 (1990)).

Consequently, given the Arbitrator's underlying factual findings, his conclusion that the classification of the grievants' positions did not take into account the performance of certain hazardous duties is not contrary to law. *See U.S. Dep't of the Army, Alaska*, 54 FLRA at 1123 (finding that, given the arbitrator's underlying factual findings, his legal conclusion that the grievants worked with, or in close proximity to, unstable and highly sensitive material, for which they were entitled to a hazard pay differential, was consistent with the applicable regulations).

Accordingly, we deny the Agency's exception.

B. The award of backpay from the filing date of the Union's grievance is not contrary to law.

The Union alleges that "the [a]ward [of backpay] is contrary to law because it was incorrectly calculated [as] beginning on the date the grievance was filed . . . ." Union Exceptions at 6. According to the Union, the grievants are entitled, under the Back Pay Act, to receive a hazardous pay differential during the period that they performed hazardous duties. *Id.*

Under Authority precedent, it is well established that arbitrators have broad authority and discretion to fashion remedies. *See, e.g., Nat'l Ass'n of Indep. Labor, Local 11*, 64 FLRA 709, 711 (2010) (citing *U.S. Dep't of the Air Force, Okla. City Air Logistics Ctr., Tinker Air Force Base, Okla.*, 47 FLRA 98, 101 (1993)). In particular, the Authority has found that the Back Pay Act's six year statute of limitations does not require an arbitrator to award backpay for a period of six years. *See id.* (citing *Nat'l Gallery of Art, Wash., D.C.*, 48 FLRA 841, 846 (1993) & *U.S. Dep't of HHS, SSA, Balt., Md.*, 47 FLRA 819, 829 (1993)). Moreover, the Authority has determined that Back Pay Act recovery periods are within the discretion of arbitrators, as long as awards do not exceed the maximum recovery authorized by law. *Id.* (citations omitted).

The Union's contention that the award of backpay from the date that the grievance was filed is contrary to the Back Pay Act is without merit. The Arbitrator has the discretion, under the Back Pay Act, to award the grievants a 25% hazard pay differential beginning on the date the grievance was filed. *See id.* The Arbitrator was not required, under the Back Pay Act, to award the grievants backpay for six years or however long the Union requested within that six-year period. *See id.* Moreover, the Union has not cited any other statute or regulation that obligates the Arbitrator to award backpay retroactive to the date that the grievants began performing the hazardous duties. *See U.S. Dep't of the Navy, Naval Surface Warfare Ctr., Crane Div., Crane, Ind.*, 49 FLRA 27, 31-32 (1994) (finding that the union failed to demonstrate that any other statute or regulation obligated the arbitrator to award backpay retroactive to the date the grievants were exempted from the FLSA). Consequently, the Union's exception provides no basis for finding the award deficient.

Accordingly, we deny the Union's exception.

C. The award is contrary to law for failing to include an award of interest.

The Union claims that the award is contrary to law because the Arbitrator failed to award interest in accordance with the Back Pay Act. Union Exceptions at 8. Under the provisions of the Back Pay Act, interest must be paid on backpay awards, beginning on the date of the unjustified and unwarranted personnel action, and the payment of interest must continue until a date selected by the Agency, which must not be more than 30 days before the date on which payment is made. *See, e.g., Nat'l Air Traffic Controllers Ass'n*, 64 FLRA 906, 907 (2010) (citing *U.S. Dep't of Def., Marine Corps Logistics Base, Barstow, Cal.*, 37 FLRA 796, 797 (1990)); *NTEU, Chap. 72*, 58 FLRA 447, 447 (2003); *U.S. Dep't of the Treasury, U.S. Customs Serv., El Paso, Tex.*, 57 FLRA 724, 728 (2002); 5 C.F.R. § 550.806(a)(2). Because the Arbitrator awarded a hazard pay differential to the grievants, the Union is entitled to an award of interest as a matter of law. *See U.S. Dep't of Agric., Animal & Plant Health Inspection Serv., Plant Prot. & Quarantine, Hyattsville, Md.*, 38 FLRA 1291, 1299 (1991) (awarding the union interest after denying the agency's exceptions to the backpay award).

Accordingly, we modify the award to include interest on the hazard pay differential award.

V. Decision

The Union's exception regarding the Arbitrator's failure to require the payment of interest on the hazard pay differential award is granted, the award is modified to include interest consistent with the requirements of the Back Pay Act, and the parties' remaining exceptions are denied.

65 FLRA No. 59

UNITED STATES
DEPARTMENT OF THE NAVY
NAVAL FACILITIES ENGINEERING
COMMAND MID-ATLANTIC
NORFOLK, VIRGINIA
(Activity/Petitioner)

and

INTERNATIONAL FEDERATION OF
PROFESSIONAL & TECHNICAL ENGINEERS
LOCAL 4
(Exclusive Representative/Petitioner)

and

INTERNATIONAL FEDERATION OF
PROFESSIONAL & TECHNICAL ENGINEERS
LOCAL 3
(Exclusive Representative)

and

METAL TRADES DEPARTMENT
AFL-CIO
(Exclusive Representative)

and

INTERNATIONAL ASSOCIATION OF
MACHINISTS & AEROSPACE WORKERS
DISTRICT LODGE 4
(Exclusive Representative)

and

AMERICAN FEDERATION
OF GOVERNMENT EMPLOYEES
LOCALS 23, 53, 2635, 2024, 1156, 1659 & 1698
AFL-CIO
(Exclusive Representatives)

and

NATIONAL ASSOCIATION
OF GOVERNMENT EMPLOYEES
LOCALS R1-178, R2-084, R1-100 & R1-134
(Exclusive Representatives)

and

LABORERS INTERNATIONAL UNION
OF NORTH AMERICA
LOCAL 1310
(Exclusive Representative)

BN-RP-09-0005
WA-RP-09-0039
WA-RP-09-0040
WA-RP-09-0041

ORDER DENYING
APPLICATION FOR REVIEW

November 24, 2010

Before the Authority: Carol Waller Pope, Chairman, and Thomas M. Beck and Ernest DuBester, Members

I. Statement of the Case

This case is before the Authority on an application for review filed by the National Association of Government Employees/SEIU (NAGE) under § 2422.31 of the Authority's Regulations.[1] The Agency (the United States Department of the Navy (DoN), Naval Facilities Engineering Command (NAVFAC) Mid-Atlantic, Norfolk, Virginia (NAVFAC Mid-Atlantic or Activity)) filed an opposition to NAGE's application for review.

As the result of a reorganization within the DoN, employees in 17 existing bargaining units at DoN facilities in Maine, New Hampshire, Rhode Island, Connecticut, Pennsylvania, New Jersey, and Virginia were transferred to the NAVFAC Mid-Atlantic. These bargaining units were represented by locals of

1. Section 2422.31 of the Authority's Regulations provides, in pertinent part:

> (c) *Review.* The Authority may grant an application for review only when the application demonstrates that review is warranted on one or more of the following grounds:
> (1) The decision raises an issue for which there is an absence of precedent;
> (2) Established law or policy warrants reconsideration; or,
> (3) There is a genuine issue over whether the Regional Director has:
> (i) Failed to apply established law;
> (ii) Committed a prejudicial procedural error;
> (iii) Committed a clear and prejudicial error concerning a substantial factual matter.

the International Federation of Professional and Technical Engineers (IFPTE), the Metal Trades Department, AFL-CIO (MTD), the International Association of Machinists (IAM), the American Federation of Government Employees (AFGE), NAGE, and the Laborers International Union of North America (LIUNA) (collectively, the Unions).

Following the transfer, IFPTE, Local 4 filed a petition to be certified under the successorship doctrine as the exclusive representative of the Activity's professional and nonprofessional employees at a DoN facility in Maine. The Activity filed cross-petitions, contending that, as a result of the reorganization, three separate Activity-wide units were appropriate: a professional unit, a general schedule (GS) nonprofessional unit, and a wage grade (WG) unit. The Unions disagreed, arguing that each continued as the exclusive representative of the respective unit of employees transferred to the Activity.

The Regional Director (RD) agreed with the Activity. Accordingly, the RD determined that GS nonprofessional employees are included in the existing unit of Activity employees represented by AFGE, Local 53; that WG employees are included in the existing unit of Activity employees represented by the Tidewater Virginia Metal Trades Council (Tidewater MTC); and that no question of representation existed concerning the Activity's unrepresented professional employees.

For the reasons that follow, we deny NAGE's application for review.

II. Background and RD's Decision

A. Background

The NAVFAC, headquartered in Washington, D.C., manages the planning, design, construction, contingency engineering, real estate, and public works support for the DoN shore facilities worldwide. RD's Decision at 3. NAVFAC consists of ten Facilities Engineering Commands (including the Activity), each of which reports to one of two NAVFAC Commands: NAVFAC Atlantic in Norfolk, Virginia (NAVFAC Atlantic) or NAVFAC Pacific in Pearl Harbor, Hawaii. *Id.*

The Activity, headquartered in Norfolk, Virginia, reports to NAVFAC Atlantic and supports U.S. Navy shore facilities from Maine to North Carolina. *Id.* In particular, it provides facilities engineering and acquisitions services through business lines and integrated product teams (IPT) organized into four areas, including public works (PW). The majority of employees in this case are involved in the PW function. *Id.* The Activity's workforce consists of 100 officers and enlisted personnel and over 3,300 civilian personnel. *Id.*

As relevant here, in January 2006, the Activity reorganized to include the PW operations at Naval Station Newport, Rhode Island (NAVSTA Newport); Naval Submarine Base, New London, Groton, Connecticut (Sub-Base Groton); and Portsmouth Naval Shipyard, Maine; as well as some operations in North Carolina. *Id.* at 4. Additionally, the Activity also established a new common PW Department (PWD) organizational structure at each of its approximately ten work sites, including the new Northeast sites. *Id.* The work of the PWD is closely aligned with the installation that it supports. *Id.* Each PWD is headed by a Public Works Officer (PWO), assisted by a deputy, who serves as the Activity's onsite manager. *Id.* Division heads and shop level supervisors are generally subordinate to the PWO and his deputy. *Id.* The PWO reports up the chain of command to the Commanding Officer through the Activity's Operation Officer. All of the PWO's superiors are located in Norfolk. *Id.*

At the time of the hearing, the Activity relied upon DoN human resources offices (HROs) to handle personnel and labor relations matters. *Id.* at 5. However, the Activity had requested that these functions be consolidated and administered by a single provider, HRO Norfolk, effective October 1, 2009. *Id.* At such time, HRO Norfolk "[began] provid[ing] the full range of services" to the Activity using "forward-deployed" human resources personnel, who reported directly to Norfolk. *Id.*

The reorganization affected employees in 17 bargaining units represented by IFPTE, MTD, IAM, NAGE, and LIUNA.[2] NAGE represented all professional, nonprofessional and WG employees at NAVSTA Newport, and all nonprofessional and WG employees at Sub-Base Groton. *Id.* at 11-12. As set forth above, various petitions were filed after the reorganization. *Id.* at 2.

In particular, as relevant here, NAGE argued on behalf of NAGE, Locals R1-100, R1-134, FUSE/RI-178 (R1-178), and R2-84, which represented the employees transferred to the Activity

2. LIUNA did not appear at the hearing and did not file a post-hearing brief. RD's Decision at 11 n.2.

from NAVSTA Newport and Sub-Base Groton.[3] *Id.* at 11-12. NAGE argued that the "post-transfer . . . units continue to remain appropriate . . . and that . . . its units retain an identifiable community of interest that is separate and distinct from that of other Activity employees[.]" *Id.* at 12. NAGE also asserted that the employees are geographically isolated from Norfolk and have limited interchange with other Activity employees. *Id.*

B. RD's Decision

In applying the Authority's framework set forth in *Naval Facilities Engineering Service Center, Port Hueneme, California*, 50 FLRA 363, 368 (1995) (*Port Hueneme*) for resolving successorship claims arising out of a reorganization, the RD first considered whether the "stand-alone successor units proposed by the [U]nions [(proposed separate units)]" were appropriate. *Id.* at 14. To make this determination, the RD considered whether the proposed separate units would: (1) ensure a clear and identifiable community of interest among the employees in the unit; (2) promote effective dealings with the Activity; and (3) promote the efficiency of the Activity's operations. *See* 5 U.S.C. § 7112(a). Applying these criteria, the RD concluded that the proposed separate units were not appropriate under § 7112(a) of the Federal Service Labor-Management Relations Statute (the Statute). *See* RD's Decision at 15 (citations omitted).

In this regard, the RD found that the record did not establish that the employees in the proposed separate units share a clear and identifiable community of interest that is separate and distinct from the other employees of the Activity. *See id.* at 14-15. In particular, the RD found that the record did not establish that the employees in these units have an employment relationship or work situation that is "materially different from the other employees of the Activity." *Id.* The RD found that employees in each of the proposed separate units and all of the other employees of the Activity: are part of the same organizational component; support the same mission; are subject to the same chain of command and to the same general working conditions; and have similar or related duties, job titles, and work assignments. *See id.*

The RD further found that these employees are governed by the same personnel and labor relations policies that are centrally established and administered at the Activity level. *Id.* In this regard, the RD found that, since the reorganization, work and safety processes of the PWDs have been "upgraded and streamlined" through the Activity-wide implementation of standard operating procedures (SOPs). *Id.* at 4. SOPs for "every type of job performed by the PW employees are stored in a computer database that can be assessed at the shop level at every PWD within NAVFAC Mid-Atlantic." *Id.* Moreover, the RD noted other items also have been standardized since the reorganization, including protective equipment, software programs used for tracking work, financial transactions, and attendance, and position descriptions. *Id.* at 5.

The RD considered the Unions' arguments that the affected employees are geographically separated, experience limited interchange and, as tenants, are subject to their local installation's security, safety and weather policies. *Id.* at 14. However, the RD found that, "such factors, taken as [a] whole, [did] not outweigh the numerous commonality of interests" described above. *Id.*

The RD also found that the proposed stand-alone successor units would not promote effective dealings. *Id.* at 15. According to the RD, such units "would require the Activity to negotiate and administer numerous separate [collective bargaining] agreements for . . . employees that share a community of interest" with the other Activity employees. *Id.* Moreover, the RD found that the evidence established that Activity supervisors at the local levels do not have the authority to establish policies, procedures or working conditions or to negotiate over such matters; rather, all personnel and labor relations matters, including the negotiation of collective bargaining agreements, are determined and managed centrally from the Activity level. *Id.*

The RD further determined that the proposed separate units would not promote efficiency of the Activity's operations. *Id.* In this regard, the RD found that the proposed separate units – which "are

3. NAGE, Local R1-100 represented, among others, a consolidated unit consisting of all wage grade (WG) and nonprofessional employees located at the Naval Submarine Base, New London, Groton, Connecticut; NAGE, Local Rl-134 represented all nonprofessional WG and GS employees of the Naval Station Newport, Newport, Rhode Island; NAGE, R1-178 represented all "appropriate-funded professional employees" employed at Naval Station Newport, Rhode Island; and NAGE, Local R2-84 represented WG and nonprofessional employees at the Naval Air Engineering Station, Lakehurst, New Jersey. RD's Decision at 6, 7, and 10. Because employees represented by NAGE, Local R2-84 are no longer employed by the Activity, their status is no longer involved in this case. *Id.* at 10.

based on the extent to which the affected employees were organized under their prior employer" – would result in an "artificial and unwarranted fragmentation of the Activity's centralized operations and structure[.]" *Id.* (citations omitted). Accordingly, the RD concluded that the units sought by the Unions, including NAGE, are not appropriate under § 7112(a).

The RD then examined the three alternative units proposed by the Activity. *Id.* at 16. According to the RD, the record shows that the employees in each of these units share a clear and identifiable community of interest. *Id.* In this regard, the RD found that employees in each unit: are part of the same organizational component; support the same mission; are subject to the same chain of command and to the same general working conditions; have similar or related duties, job titles and work assignments; and are governed by the same personnel and labor relations policies that are centrally established and administered at the Activity level. *Id.* The RD also found that these units would promote effective dealings and efficiency of agency operations. In this regard, the RD found that the units are "co-extensive with the Activity's operational and organizational structure and exist at the level where personnel and labor relations policies are established." *Id.* Accordingly, the RD concluded that separate Activity-wide units of professional, GS nonprofessional, and WG employees are appropriate. *Id.*

Finally, the RD addressed the representational status of the three Activity-wide units. The RD found that a "clear majority" of the professional employees were unrepresented and that none of the affected Unions had sought to represent an Activity-wide unit of professional employees. *Id.* The RD found that, because none of the affected Unions represented at least 30 percent of these employees, a genuine question concerning representation did not exist. *Id.* Accordingly, the RD found that there was no basis to direct an election among the professional employees. *Id.* (citations omitted).

With respect to the nonprofessional GS and WG employees, the RD noted that, under Authority precedent, new employees are automatically included in an existing bargaining unit where their positions fall within the express terms of the unit description and their inclusion would not render the bargaining unit inappropriate. *Id.* (citing *U.S. Dep't of the Air Force, Randolph Air Force Base, San Antonio, Tex.*, 64 FLRA 656, (2010) (*Randolph, AF Base*) (Member Beck dissenting) (citing *Dep't of the Army, Headquarters, Fort Dix, Fort Dix, N.J.*, 53 FLRA 287 (1997) (*Fort Dix*)). The RD found that AFGE, Local 53's certification defines the existing unit as including "[a]ll graded civil service employees assigned to the [NAVFAC Mid-Atlantic]" and that the TidewaterVirginia MTC's certification defines its existing unit as including "all employees of the [NAVFAC] Mid-Atlantic." *Id.* The RD further found that, because there was no dispute that the nonprofessional GS and WG employees who were transferred to the Activity are now working for and assigned to the NAVFAC Mid-Atlantic, these employees fall within the express terms of the certifications and, therefore, are automatically included in the respective units described above unless such inclusion would render the unit inappropriate. *Id.* at 17. Because there was "no contention or evidence" that such inclusion would render either unit inappropriate, the RD found that: (1) the Activity-wide unit of nonprofessional GS employees is represented by AFGE Local 53; and (2) the Activity-wide unit of nonprofessional WG employees is represented by the Tidewater MTC. *Id.*

III. Position of the Parties

A. NAGE's Application for Review

NAGE contends that the RD erred when he failed to apply established law and found that: (1) the proposed separate bargaining units sought by the Unions were not appropriate under § 7112(a) of the Statute; (2) separate Activity-wide units were appropriate; (3) GS employees are included in the existing unit of employees represented by AFGE, Local 53; (4) WG employees are included in the existing unit of employees represented by the Tidewater Virginia MTC; and (5) the professional employees are unrepresented. Application for Review (Application) at 17. Citing *Port Hueneme*, NAGE alleges that the RD failed to apply properly the appropriate unit criteria set forth in 5 U.S.C. § 7112(a). *See id.* at 13 & 17.

With respect to the community of interest criterion, NAGE argues that each of its proposed separate units "continues to share a clear and identifiable community of interest separate and distinct from NAVFAC Mid-Atlantic" employees at other locations. *Id.* at 17 & 18. In this regard, NAGE asserts that the record shows that there "have been no real changes in the day-to-day working conditions" of unit employees at Sub-Base Groton and NAVSTA Newport; that these employees continue to support the same mission and are subject to the same chain of command that they had before the reorganization; and that, "[w]hile the reorganization resulted in a change of command for the overall public works function[,]" the "direct supervision" of the employees remained the same. *Id.* at 18 & 19 (citing Tr. at 130 & 527-29). NAGE asserts that, before and after the reorganization, employees were under the direct command of the PWO — the highest level NAVFAC Mid-Atlantic manager. *Id.* at 19 & 20 (citing *U.S. Dep't of the Navy, Commander, Naval Base, Norfolk, Va.*, 56 FLRA 328 (2000) (*Naval Base, Norfolk*)). NAGE also contends that the RD "ignored evidence" that the NAVSTA local commander still has authority to impose discipline on employees. *Id.* at 21 (citing Tr. at 661-62). Further, NAGE asserts that the RD erred in finding that the affected employees and all other employees of the Activity: share the same skills; are involved in the same or similar jobs, functions, and responsibilities; and are subject to the same general conditions of employment. *Id.* at 22-24. NAGE asserts that employees in its proposed separate units would not be affected by a reduction-in-force (RIF) occurring at any other Activity location. *Id.* at 24 (citing Tr. at 190, 371-72).

NAGE further asserts that the RD erred by finding that the record did not establish that the NAGE-proposed separate units had "an employment relationship or work situation that [was] materially different from other employees of the Activity." *Id.* at 25. NAGE asserts that the record establishes that the units have specific local concerns unique from employees at other Activity locations. *Id.* at 26. NAGE contends that the local commander has "command and control" over day-to-day working conditions affecting NAVFAC employees located at his or her base, including decisions related to weather, access to the base, and security. *Id.* In this regard, NAGE asserts that its employees have different climate issues than employees in the Southern states, which, it contends, the local commander has the authority to address. *Id.* NAGE further contends that, because Sub-Base Groton is the only nuclear submarine base in the NAVFAC Mid-Atlantic region, employees assigned there are "subject to safety regulations that present unique safety and training issues." *Id.* at 27.

NAGE also contends that the RD erred when he "dismissed the fact" that NAGE employees are significantly distant from other Activity employees, especially those represented by the Unions in Norfolk, Virginia. *Id.* at 28. NAGE argues that, contrary to the RD's finding, record evidence does not establish "numerous commonality of interest[s]" among Activity employees that would warrant disturbing its bargaining units. *Id.* at 29 (citing *U.S. Dep't of the Navy, Commander, Navy Region Mid-Atlantic,* 63 FLRA 8 (2008) (*Navy Region Mid-Atlantic*)).

NAGE further contends that the RD erred by finding that the employees were administratively and organizationally integrated into the Activity. *Id.* at 32-33. According to NAGE, the record shows that employees in the three different locations do not regularly or frequently interact with each other. *Id.* NAGE contends that, if the RD's Decision "is affirmed[,] the Authority will have chosen to give weight to those factors that favor the Activity and ignore . . . factors . . . in the record that favor" employees. *Id.* at 29 & n.7 (citing *U.S. Dep't of the Navy, Fleet Readiness Ctr. Sw., San Diego, Calif.*, 63 FLRA 245 (2009) (*DoN, Fleet Readiness Center*), among five other cases, which it contends shows that Authority decisions "have been slanted towards . . . agencies").

NAGE asserts that the RD erred in finding that the proposed successor units would not promote effective dealings. *Id.* at 34. NAGE claims that the local units have enjoyed a long bargaining history at NAVSTA Newport and Sub-Base Groton, and that the record does not establish that the existence of separate bargaining units caused undue delay in addressing workplace issues. *Id.* at 34 & 37(citing Tr. at 421, 438, 440 & Activity Ex. 38, a spreadsheet tracking notices to Unions and bargaining status).

NAGE also contends that the local units would promote efficiency of agency operations. *Id.* at 38. NAGE asserts that, by "forward deploy[ing]" Human Resources (HR) and labor relations personnel, the Activity "acknowledges the cost savings and efficiency in [having] personnel and labor relations . . . located where employees are . . . ." *Id.* at 38 & 39. NAGE argues that, if such deployment promotes the efficiency of the Activity's operations, the RD should have found that allowing employees similar contact with their representative also promotes the efficiency of operations. *Id.* at 39.

For the reasons previously described, NAGE contends that Local R1-178, consisting of professional employees, continues to be an appropriate unit. *Id.* at 40. NAGE argues that the employees in this unit share a community of interest separate and distinct from Activity professional employees at other locations. *Id.* NAGE asserts that these employees have experienced no significant changes in their working conditions, job assignments, supervision, or work location as a result of the 2006 reorganization. *Id.* at 40-41 (citing Tr. at 577, 579, & 600). Moreover, NAGE contends that, because these employees are responsible for ensuring that the local commander at NAVSTA Newport complies with federal and state environmental laws and regulations, they "have certain local concerns" that are "unique to their location." *Id.* at 41-42 (citing Tr. at 142).

NAGE asserts that, "having erred in finding the NAGE units no longer appropriate, the RD failed to properly apply the rest of the successorship analysis." *Id.* at 42. According to NAGE, the record shows that its proposed successor units satisfy the remaining *Port Hueneme* criteria. *Id.* at 42-44.

NAGE asserts that "public policy . . . warrant[s] reconsideration of existing law." *Id.* at 44. According to NAGE, recent Authority decisions "analyzing the effective dealings criteria appear to focus exclusively on how the agency is impacted while completely disregarding the negative impact of these decisions on bargaining unit employees." *Id.* at 44 (citing decisions cited in Application for Review — *id.* at 29 n.7). NAGE states that, "[h]ad sufficient consideration been given to the negative impact . . . on the freedom of choice of bargaining unit employees in this case," the RD would have found that the proposed units that "dissolve certain units and — in the case of the professional employees [leave them] unrepresented — do nothing to promote effective dealings." *Id.* at 44. In this regard, NAGE asserts that one of its witnesses testified that unit employees had "voted out the very [U]nion that the [RD] seeks to force them to join." *Id.* at 45 (citing Tr. at 669).

B. Activity's Opposition

The Activity asserts that the RD properly considered all of the § 7112(a) criteria in determining whether the units sought by NAGE are appropriate. *See* Agency Opp'n to Application at 3. The Activity contends that NAGE's arguments are not supported by the totality of facts in this case. *Id.* at 7. The Activity asserts that NAGE "[has] not shown how the case law relied upon by the RD was [applied] erroneous[ly][.]" *Id.* at 8. The Activity also asserts that NAGE has "failed to identify a specific prejudicial error[]" or show that the RD neglected a substantial factual matter. *Id.*

The Activity contends that, in applying the *Port Hueneme* test, the RD "appropriately concluded that the record [did] not demonstrate that the employees in the stand-alone successor units proposed by the [U]nions share a clear and identifiable community of interest separate and distinct from the other employees of the Activity." *Id.* at 3. The Activity contends that NAGE's assertion that the RD "erred by concluding that the Activity's operations and personnel comprise a fully centralized and integrated enterprise" with all employees sharing the same mission, budget, chain of command, working conditions, and are subject to the same personnel and labor relations policies established and managed at the Activity level, "constitutes mere disagreement" with the RD's Decision. *Id.* at 4.

The Activity asserts that NAGE "points to 'unique' conditions . . . affecting . . . employees physically located at [Sub-Base Groton] due to the presence of the nuclear submarines." *Id.* However, according to the Activity, "the same condition[s] exist[] for [NAVFAC Mid-Atlantic] employees physically stationed at the Norfolk Naval Shipyard in Portsmouth, [Virginia]." *Id.* The Activity also contends that NAGE's contention concerning differences in weather/climate at the different locations does not "create a unique and distinct difference from one [PWD] to another." *Id.*

The Activity further contends that the RD properly concluded that the proposed separate units would not promote effective dealings or efficiency of the Activity's operations. *Id.* at 5. Moreover, the Activity argues that the RD properly concluded that there was no basis to direct an election among professional employees and that the GS and WG employees are represented by AFGE, Local 53 and the Tidewater MTC, respectively. *Id.* at 6-7.

IV. Analysis and Conclusions

A. The RD did not fail to apply established law.

The Authority will find that a gaining entity is a successor, and a union retains its status as the exclusive representative of employees who are transferred to the successor, when:

> (1) An entire recognized unit, or a portion thereof, is transferred and the transferred employees: (a) are in an appropriate bargaining unit . . . after the transfer; and (b) constitute a majority of the employees in such unit;
>
> (2) The gaining entity has substantially the same organizational mission as the losing entity, with the transferred employees performing substantially the

> same duties and functions under substantially similar working conditions . . .; and
>
> (3) It has not been determined that an election is necessary to determine representation.

Port Hueneme, 50 FLRA at 368.

Thus, under *Port Hueneme*, the first requirement for finding a new employing entity to be a successor employer is that the transferred employees continue to constitute a separate appropriate bargaining unit. *Id.* As set forth above, in determining whether a petitioned-for unit is appropriate, the Authority considers whether the unit would: (1) ensure a clear and identifiable community of interest among the employees in the unit; (2) promote effective dealings with the agency; and (3) promote efficiency of the operations of the agency. 5 U.S.C. § 7112(a); *see also U.S. Dep't of the Navy, Fleet & Indus. Supply Ctr., Norfolk, Va.*, 52 FLRA 950, 959 (1997) (*FISC*). A proposed unit must meet all three appropriate unit criteria in order to be found appropriate. *See id.* at 961 n.6. Determinations as to each of these criteria are made on a case-by-case basis. *U.S. Dep't of the Army, Military Traffic Mgmt. Command, Alexandria, Va.*, 60 FLRA 390, 394 (2004) (Chairman Cabaniss concurring in relevant part, dissenting as to other matters). The Authority has set out factors for assessing each criterion, but has not specified the weight of individual factors or a particular number of factors necessary to establish an appropriate unit. *See id.* However, for a petitioned-for separate bargaining unit to be appropriate, the employees at issue must have significant employment concerns or personnel issues that are different or unique from those of other employees. *See FISC*, 52 FLRA at 960; *see also U.S. Dep't of the Interior, Nat'l Park Serv., Wash., D.C.*, 55 FLRA 311, 315 (1999).

NAGE disputes the RD's finding that its former units would not constitute appropriate units. With regard to the first appropriate unit criterion — whether employees share a clear and identifiable community of interest — the Authority examines such factors as geographic proximity, unique conditions of employment, distinct local concerns, degree of interchange between other organizational components, and functional or operational separation. *See U.S. Dep't of the Navy, Naval Facilities Eng'r Command, Se. Jacksonville, Fla.*, 62 FLRA 480, 487 (2008) (*NFEC*). In addition, the Authority considers factors such as whether the employees in the proposed unit are part of the same organizational component of the agency; support the same mission; are subject to the same chain of command; have similar or related duties, job titles and work assignments; are subject to the same general working conditions; and are governed by the same personnel office. *See id.* at 487-88.

In this case, the RD found that employees in the proposed separate units are part of the same organizational component; support the same mission; and are subject to the same chain of command. *See* RD's Decision at 14. The RD further found that the employees have similar or related duties, job titles, and work assignments; are subject to the same general working conditions; and are governed by the same personnel and labor relations policies that are administered by the same personnel office that is centrally established and administered at the Activity level. *Id.* The RD, thus, found that the affected employees do not have significant employment concerns or personnel issues that are different or unique from other Activity employees. *Id.*

NAGE has not provided any basis for finding that the RD erred in his assessment of the community of interest factors. In this regard, while NAGE asserts that the day-to-day supervision of NAGE affected employees remained the same, a NAGE witness testified that, after the reorganization, the employees' fourth-level of supervision changed from the local commander to the commanding officer of NAVFAC Mid-Atlantic. *See* Tr. at 558. NAGE further contends that the RD ignored evidence that the local commander of NAVSTA Newport still has authority to impose discipline on employees. Application at 21 (citing Tr. at 661-62). However, the record shows that the third-step of the grievance process changed; rather than going to the local commander, the third-step appeal now goes to the NAVFAC Mid-Atlantic commander in Norfolk. *See* Tr. at 664. Moreover, the record supports the RD's finding that, since the reorganization, work and safety processes of the PWDs have been "upgraded and streamlined" through the Activity-wide implementation of SOPs. Furthermore, the RD noted other items also have been standardized since the reorganization, including protective equipment, software programs used for tracking work, financial transactions, and attendance, and position descriptions. RD's Decision at 4 & 5; *see also, e.g.*, Tr. at 284-85 (witness testified concerning standard operating procedures/safety, protective equipment); 331 (standard operating procedures for safety; business management system); 93-95 (standardized procedures for business/financial system).

NAGE further argues that the RD erred by finding that the employees in the proposed separate units share the same skills, are involved in the same or similar job, functions, and responsibilities, and are subject to the same general conditions of employment as other Activity employees. *See* Application at 22. NAGE has not demonstrated that the RD's findings in this regard are not supported by the record. *See* RD's Decision at 14; *see also, e.g.*, Tr. at 331-32 (after reorganization, employees' duties of providing carpentry, electrical work, and engineering design remained the same, but the manner in which performed changed according to either SOPs for safety or from business management system). NAGE's contention that employees in its proposed separate units have unique local concerns concerning climate also provides no basis for finding that the RD failed to apply the community of interest criterion properly. In this regard, the record does not establish that the affected employees' climate concerns required the RD to reach a different conclusion. *See* Tr. at 668 (witness testimony was not definite in that witness testified that "perhaps the environmental conditions" would make the employee conditions at NAVSTA Newport different than a Southern base). Moreover, its contention that employees located at Sub-Base Groton have unique working conditions due to the presence of nuclear submarines also is not supported by the record. Additionally, while the affected employees may be subject to separate competitive areas for purposes of a RIF, the existence of separate competitive areas for such purpose, like any other factor in evaluating community of interest, is not dispositive in resolving that issue. *See e.g.*, *U.S. Dep't of the Army, Army Materiel Command Headquarters, Joint Munitions Command, Rock Island, Ill.*, 62 FLRA 313, 318 (2007) (citing *AFGE, Local 2004*, 47 FLRA 969, 972 (1993) (factors that employees did not have in common, such as RIF competitive area, do not undermine the RD's determination that a community of interest exists)).

NAGE further claims that the affected employees' distance from Activity employees at other locations demonstrates that its units are unique. NAGE, however, has not established that the RD erred in applying this factor. Contrary to NAGE's contention, the RD did not "dismiss[] the fact" concerning the affected employees' locations. Application at 28. The RD specifically addressed the matter and found that, "[w]hile the affected employees are geographically separated, may experience limited interchange and, as tenants, are subject to their local installation's security, safety[,] and weather policies, such factors, taken as a whole, do not outweigh the numerous commonality of interests[.]" RD's Decision at 14.

NAGE's assertions concerning the professional employees, represented by Local R1-178 at NAVSTA Newport, also provide no basis for finding that the RD erred in applying the community of interest factors. The RD found, among other things, that the record did not demonstrate that the affected professional employees have duties that are different from those of other Activity employees, report to a different chain of command, or are subject to different or unique working conditions. *See* RD's Decision at 14. NAGE refers to certain testimony in the record that, it claims, shows that this unit has significant concerns that are unique to it. Specifically, NAGE contends that, because these employees are responsible for ensuring that the local commander complies with federal and state environmental laws and regulations, the employees have certain local concerns that are "unique to their location." Application at 42 (citing Tr. at 142). However, record testimony shows that, because regulations differ from state to state, employees at other Activity locations also must follow environmental regulations that are unique to their state. *See* Tr. at 142-43 & 582. Moreover, differences in environmental requirements are addressed through training via the Activity's environmental business line, which also is used by employees at NAVSTA Newport to obtain resources. *See id; see also id.* at 585-86. Accordingly, NAGE has not demonstrated that the RD erred in finding that the professional employees did not share a community of interest separate and distinct from other Activity employees.

Additionally, citing *Naval Base, Norfolk*, NAGE argues that the reorganization at issue here was merely a change in the chain of command that should not, by itself, render the existing units inappropriate. Contrary to NAGE's contention, the reorganization changed a variety of factors in addition to the chain of command. In this regard, as discussed above, since the reorganization, work and safety processes of the PWDs have been "upgraded and streamlined" through the Activity-wide implementation of SOPs, and personnel and labor relations policies are centrally established and administered at the Activity level. Additionally, other items have been standardized, including protective equipment, software programs used for tracking work, financial transactions, and attendance, and position descriptions. *See* RD's Decision at 4, 5 & 14-15. NAGE has thus failed to demonstrate that the reorganization at issue was merely a change in the chain of command. *See, e.g., U.S. Dep't of Health & Human Servs., Nat'l Insts. of Health, Nat'l Inst. of Envtl. Health Sciences Research, Triangle Park, N.C.*, 62 FLRA 84, 87 (2007).

Also, NAGE's reliance on *Navy Region Mid-Atlantic* provides no basis for finding the RD's Decision fails to comply with established law. Unlike the employees in *Navy Region Mid-Atlantic*, the employees here are not subject to different or unique working conditions. Rather, as previously described, the affected employees are part of the same organizational component, are subject to the same general working conditions, and are governed by the same personnel and labor relations policies. *See* RD's Decision at 14-15.

Further, NAGE's claim that, if the RD's Decision is affirmed, then the Authority "will have chosen to give weight to those factors that favor the Activity" provides no basis for finding the RD erred in finding that NAGE's proposed separate units are not appropriate. Application at 29. Under § 7112(a) of the Statute, the Authority is required to determine whether a proposed unit is an appropriate unit consistent with the three criteria listed therein. Moreover, as discussed above, the Authority makes determinations regarding whether these three criteria are satisfied on a case-by-case basis. *See Dep't of the Army*, 60 FLRA at 394. As found above, the RD's factual findings and the record evidence in this case fully support the RD's findings that the proposed separate units do not share a clear and identifiable community of interest, separate and distinct from other employees of the Activity. RD's Decision at 14. Because the record supports the RD's findings in this case, there is no basis to NAGE's claim that, should the Authority affirm the RD, the Authority will have chosen to favor the Activity.

As noted above, to be found appropriate, a proposed unit must meet all three appropriate unit criteria. Because NAGE has failed to demonstrate that the RD erred in finding that employees in NAGE's proposed separate units do not share a community of interest that is separate and distinct from other Activity employees, it is not necessary to address whether the RD correctly found that the proposed separate units would not promote effective dealings or the efficiency of the Activity's operations. *See U.S. Dep't of Commerce, Nat'l Weather Serv., Silver Spring, Md.*, 62 FLRA 472, 476 n.5 (2008).

Accordingly, as NAGE has not demonstrated that the RD erred in his conclusion that the separate units sought by the NAGE and the other Unions would not be appropriate, we find that NAGE has not established that the RD failed to apply established law.[4]

B. The application fails to demonstrate that review is warranted because established law or policy warrants reconsideration.

NAGE argues that "public policy . . . warrant[s] reconsideration of existing law." Application at 44. According to NAGE, recent Authority decisions "analyzing the *effective dealings* [factor] appear to focus exclusively on how the agency is impacted while completely disregarding the negative impact of these decisions on bargaining unit employees." *Id.* (citing decisions cited in Application — *id.* at 29 n.7) (emphasis added)). An assertion that "[e]stablished law or policy warrants reconsideration" is an established ground for challenging an RD's Decision. 5 C.F.R. § 2422.31(c)(2); *U.S. Dep't of Agric., Office of the Chief Info. Officer, Info. Tech. Servs.*, 61 FLRA 879, 883 (2006).

However, because NAGE has failed to demonstrate that the RD erred in finding that the employees in NAGE's proposed separate units do not share a community of interest that is separate and distinct from other Activity employees, we find that it is unnecessary to address NAGE's contention that recent Authority decisions warrant reconsideration of Authority precedent or established policy concerning effective dealings. Application at 44.

Accordingly, we find that NAGE has not demonstrated that established law or policy warrants reconsideration.

V. Order

NAGE's application for review is denied.

---

4. We note that NAGE contends that the RD committed a clear and prejudicial error concerning a substantial factual matter, and committed a prejudicial procedural error. *See* Application at 4. However, other than this bare assertion, NAGE provides no further arguments on these contentions. To the extent that its argument that the RD committed a clear and prejudicial error concerning a substantial factual matter could be construed as asserting the same arguments as made with respect to its contention that the RD failed to apply established law, such arguments have been addressed above. As to its contention that the RD committed a prejudicial procedural error, such contention is a bare assertion and provides no basis for finding the RD committed a prejudicial error. *See, e.g., NASA, Goddard Space Flight Ctr., Wallops Island Facility, Wallops Island, Va.*, 64 FLRA 580, 582 (2010).

65 FLRA No. 60

NATIONAL TREASURY
EMPLOYEES UNION
CHAPTER 193
(Union)

and

UNITED STATES
DEPARTMENT OF THE TREASURY
INTERNAL REVENUE SERVICE
SAN JUAN, PUERTO RICO
(Agency)

0-AR-4606

DECISION

November 30, 2010

Before the Authority: Carol Waller Pope, Chairman, and Thomas M. Beck and Ernest DuBester, Members

I. Statement of the Case

This matter is before the Authority on exceptions to an award of Arbitrator M. David Vaughn filed by the Union under § 7122(a) of the Federal Service Labor-Management Relations Statute (the Statute) and part 2425 of the Authority's Regulations. The Agency filed an opposition to the Union's exceptions.

The Arbitrator concluded that, although a probationary employee may bring a grievance challenging his removal from his position under certain circumstances, the provisions of the parties' collective bargaining agreement (parties' agreement) precluded the grievant from pursuing an unfair labor practice (ULP) complaint at arbitration. For the reasons set forth below, we deny the Union's exceptions.

II. Background and Arbitrator's Award

The grievant, a member of the bargaining unit, was terminated during his probationary period for excessive absences. Award at 7, 16. After his removal, the grievant filed a grievance alleging that he was removed from his position because he engaged in protected union activity. *Id.* at 17. The matter was unresolved and was submitted to arbitration. *See id.*

Prior to the hearing, the Arbitrator issued an initial decision and order, addressing an information request filed by the Union. Exceptions, Attach. 3 at 1, 2. The Agency then filed a motion for reconsideration, alleging that "the underlying grievance [was] not grievable or arbitrable because [the] [g]rievant [was] a probationary employee and the [a]greement, by its terms, makes the negotiated grievance procedure inapplicable to such employees." *Id.* at 1. In his second decision and order, the Arbitrator refused to address the arbitrability of the parties' dispute and ordered the hearing to proceed as scheduled. *Id.* at 3. The Arbitrator found that, although he was compelled to address the issue of arbitrability in advance of deciding the merits of the parties' dispute, he was not compelled to do so in advance of the hearing. *Id.* at 2-3.

At arbitration, the parties stipulated to the following issues:

> 1. [Does the Arbitrator] have jurisdiction to hear [the] [g]rievant's challenge to his termination during his probationary period?
>
> 2. If so, was [the] [g]rievant's termination motivated by his protected union activity and, if so, what shall be the remedy?

Award at 3.

The Arbitrator found that the Agency properly raised the issue of arbitrability. *Id.* at 35. The Arbitrator stated that he agreed with the Union's contention that, under Authority precedent, a probationary employee may challenge his removal if it was motivated by his engagement in protected activity.[1] *Id.* The Arbitrator also determined that a union is permitted "in lieu of filing a ULP with the

1. Although the Arbitrator was convinced by the Union's contention, he noted that the Agency cited to a series of cases where the Authority "rejected as non-negotiable a union's contractual proposal that would have allowed terminated probationary employees access to the negotiated grievance process in situations where the grievance would allege discrimination." Award at 36 (citing *NTEU*, 39 FLRA 848, 852-53 (1991) & *NTEU*, 25 FLRA 1067, 1078 (1987)). According to the Arbitrator, "[t]hose cases suggest that the Union's attempt to arbitrate might not survive a challenge, even if the . . . [a]greement were deemed to allow it." *Id.*

Authority, to allege in a grievance that an agency committed a ULP, unless the parties have excluded [ULP] grievances from the scope of their grievance procedure." *Id.* (citing *U.S. Dep't of Health & Human Servs., Region V*, 45 FLRA 737, 743 (1992) & *FDIC, Div. of Depositor & Asset Servs., Oklahoma City, Okla.*, 49 FLRA 894, 901 (1994) (*FDIC*)). The Arbitrator found that Article 41, Section 1 of the parties' agreement specifically excludes the issue of separation of probationary employees from the contractual grievance process. *Id.* at 36. The Arbitrator explained that

> while probationary employees are permitted to file ULP challenges with [the] FLRA (and [the] [g]rievant could have done so) and while non-probationary employees are in certain cases permitted to elect between the FLRA and their negotiated grievance procedure in contesting ULPs, the specific language [in Article 41, Section 1 of the parties' agreement] excluding the separation of probationary employees from the grievance procedure precludes [the] [g]rievant from pursuing his ULP complaint through the grievance arbitration process.[2]

Id. Further, the Arbitrator rejected the Union's contention that he ruled against the Agency's arbitrability claim in his second decision and order. *Id.* at 36-37. The Arbitrator noted that, in his second decision and order, he merely decided that he was not required to determine the arbitrability of the Union's grievance in advance of the hearing and that he specifically allowed the Agency to raise the issue of "arbitrability in its post-hearing brief." *Id.* at 37.

III. Positions of the Parties

A. Union's Exceptions

The Union argues that the award is contrary to law because the Arbitrator's arbitrability determination was based solely on the result of the alleged ULP, the grievant's separation. Exceptions at 8-9. The Union claims that, if the Agency had suspended the grievant or used any other sort of discipline, the case would have been arbitrable under the award. *Id.* at 9. Additionally, the Union contends that "[t]o allow arbitration in one case and not [in] another for the exact same action on the part of the Agency is inconsistent as the outcome of the ULP does not change whether or not a ULP occurred." *Id.*

Also, the Union claims that the award is contrary to law because the Arbitrator erroneously concluded that the parties' agreement "precludes challenges to the removal of probationary employees on the basis that the removal was motivated by protected activity." *Id.* (emphasis omitted). The Union asserts that, under the parties' agreement, the dispute is arbitrable. *Id.* at 9-11. The Union claims that, "while [the Arbitrator] recognized that the Union . . . could file ULP grievances[,] the Arbitrator brushed that aside and relied upon the statutory exclusion which is mirrored in the agreement prohibiting probationary employees from grieving their separation based on the merits of their performance or their misconduct." *Id.* at 10. The Union also argues that, in finding that the parties' agreement does not allow the grievant to arbitrate his removal, "the Arbitrator re-casts the dispute from a ULP challenge to one involving a garden variety contest over the grievant's performance or conduct." *Id.* Moreover, the Union claims that, based on Authority precedent, the grievance is arbitrable. *Id.* at 11. The Union notes that the Authority has found that "probationary employees are 'employees,' within the meaning of the [S]tatute and they have every right to pursue ULP charges before the Authority or through a negotiated grievance procedure unless the [parties' agreement] prohibits the grieving of ULP charges." *Id.* at 12.

B. Agency's Opposition

The Agency argues that the award is not contrary to law. Opp'n at 3. The Agency contends that "the Union oversteps when it argues that[,] because probationary employees may have their union file a grievance alleging a ULP, all such grievances must be arbitrable, as a matter of law." *Id.* Moreover, the Agency argues that the Arbitrator properly found that the grievance was not arbitrable because the agreement specifically prohibits probationary employees from utilizing the contractual grievance process in order to challenge their separations. *See id.*

2. Article 41 of the parties' agreement addresses the employee grievance procedure; Article 41, Section 1 provides that "[t]he grievance procedures of this Article shall not apply to the following: . . . 8. the separation of a probationary employee . . . ." Award at 5. Article 41, Section 2 defines a "grievance" as "any complaint . . . by an employee concerning any matter relating to the employment of the employee . . . [or] by an employee or the Union concerning . . . any claimed violation, misinterpretation, or misapplication of any law, rule, or regulation affecting conditions of employment." *Id.* at 5-6.

Also, the Agency contends that the award does not fail to draw its essence from the parties' agreement. *Id.* at 3-7. Although the Union only argues that the award is contrary to law in its exceptions, the Agency contends that "the Authority should construe the Union's argument that . . . [the] Arbitrator incorrectly read the contract language in this case as precluding the grievance as a contention that the Award fails to draw its essence from the parties' agreement." *Id.* at 5. According to the Agency, the instant action clearly differs from *FDIC* because the language in the parties' agreement plainly states that the grievance procedures do not apply to the separation of a probationary employee. *Id.* at 6-7 (citing *FDIC*, 49 FLRA at 901). Also, the Agency argues that, after considering the parties arguments, "the Arbitrator [correctly] determined that the lack of qualifying language meant that the parties had agreed to exclude *all* probationary separations from the contractual grievance procedure." *Id.* at 6 (emphasis in original). The Agency contends that "the parties got what they bargained for, the [A]rbitrator's construction of their agreement." *Id.* at 7. Furthermore, the Agency argues that the Arbitrator's award cannot be a manifest disregard of the parties' agreement because it gives the plainest meaning to the exclusion contained in Article 41, Section 1. *Id.*

IV. Preliminary Matter: Order to Show Cause

The Authority issued an Order to Show Cause (Order), directing the Union to demonstrate why it should not dismiss the Union's exceptions for lack of jurisdiction under § 7121(f) of the Statute. Order at 1-2.

The Union filed a response, asserting that, although the Authority "has no jurisdiction to review an arbitrator's award if it simply involves Chapter 75 misconduct or Chapter 43 performance based agency removals[,]" it "does have jurisdiction and has consistently exercised that jurisdiction to entertain challenges to an employee's removal if based on an underlying ULP claim." Union Response at 5, 4. In opposition to the Union's response, the Agency contends that, because the main issue is the grievant's separation, the Authority does not have jurisdiction to resolve the Union's exceptions. Agency Response at 3.

Based on applicable precedent, the Authority has jurisdiction to resolve the Union's exceptions to the award. *See Dep't of Def., Dependents Schs.*, 10 FLRA 312, 312 n.* (1982) (finding that the case was properly before the Authority to review because the removal of a probationary employee does not relate to any of the matters described in § 7121(f) of the Statute); *Dep't of HHS, SSA*, 32 FLRA 79, 83 (1988) (noting that, for purposes of § 7512, an employee is defined as "an individual in the competitive service who is not serving a probationary or trial period under an initial appointment . . .").[3] Accordingly, we address the exceptions.

V. Analysis and Conclusions

A. The award does not fail to draw its essence from the parties' agreement.

The Union alleges that the Arbitrator's interpretation of the parties' agreement is improper because he found that Article 41, Section 1 excluded all grievances involving the separation of a probationary employee regardless of the reasons for the employee's separation. Exceptions at 9. According to the Union, the language of Article 41, Section 1 simply mirrors "the statutory exclusion which . . . prohibit[s] probationary employees from grieving their separation based on the merits of their performance or their misconduct." *Id.* at 10. We construe this argument as a contention that the award fails to draw its essence from the parties' agreement.

In reviewing an arbitrator's interpretation of a collective bargaining agreement, the Authority applies the deferential standard of review that federal

3. We note that, to the extent that the Union is arguing in its exceptions, as it did before the Arbitrator, that the Arbitrator reversed his determination on the arbitrability of the dispute, such assertion is without merit. Exceptions at 7 (noting that, although the Arbitrator initially found that the matter was arbitrable in his second decision and order, he later determined, in his award, that the dispute was not arbitrable because the parties' agreement excludes a probationary employee from grieving and arbitrating his separation). Nothing in the record indicates that the Arbitrator ruled on arbitrability in his second decision and order. *See AFGE, Local 2172*, 57 FLRA 625, 628 (2001). Although the Arbitrator summarized the arguments made by the Union in his second decision and order, he ultimately determined that he was not compelled to address the issue of arbitrability in advance of the hearing. Exceptions, Attach. 3 at 2-3. Also, in his award issued to the parties, the Arbitrator made clear that, in his second decision and order, he "did not rule on the issue of arbitrability" and later "allowed the Agency to raise arbitrability in its post-hearing brief." Award at 37. Furthermore, the Union presented no evidence that the parties had agreed to a bifurcated procedure, with separate awards on arbitrability and the merits of the grievance. *See AFGE, Local 2171*, 57 FLRA at 628.

courts use in reviewing arbitration awards in the private sector. *See* 5 U.S.C. § 7122(a)(2); *AFGE, Council 220*, 54 FLRA 156, 159 (1998). Under this standard, the Authority will find that an arbitration award is deficient as failing to draw its essence from the collective bargaining agreement when the appealing party establishes that the award: (1) cannot in any rational way be derived from the agreement; (2) is so unfounded in reason and fact and so unconnected with the wording and purposes of the collective bargaining agreement as to manifest an infidelity to the obligation of the arbitrator; (3) does not represent a plausible interpretation of the agreement; or (4) evidences a manifest disregard of the agreement. *See U.S. Dep't of Labor (OSHA)*, 34 FLRA 573, 575 (1990). The Authority and the courts defer to arbitrators in this context because it is the arbitrator's construction of the agreement for which the parties have bargained. *Id.* at 576.

The Arbitrator determined that "the specific language [in Article 41, Section 1] excluding the separation of probationary employees from the grievance procedure precludes [the] [g]rievant from pursuing his ULP complaint through the grievance arbitration process." Award at 36. Contrary to the Union's argument, the Arbitrator's interpretation is not implausible or irrational. The Arbitrator's interpretation of the parties' agreement "gives the plainest meaning to the exclusionary phrase" contained in Article 41, Section 1. Opp'n at 7. The clear absence of qualifying language in Article 41, Section 1 also makes the Arbitrator's interpretation of the parties' agreement plausible. *See* Award at 5 (citing to the relevant provision in Article 41, Section 1, containing no qualifying language).

The Union claims that "[t]he phrase absent legal requirements [in the *FDIC* agreement] is synonymous with language in Article 2 of the parties' agreement essentially requiring that the instant agreement be administered according to law and legal requirements[.]" Union Response at 7 n.2. Its contention is without merit. In *FDIC*, the collective bargaining agreement excluded grievances over the separation of temporary employees "absent legal requirements to the contrary." 49 FLRA at 901. The Authority found that, because the exclusion contained the phrase "absent legal requirements to the contrary[,]" the Arbitrator's determination – that the quoted phrase meant that temporary employees could not be terminated as a result of engaging in protected activity and that a grievance alleging such a termination was grievable – did not fail to draw its essence from the collective bargaining agreement. *Id.* Because the exclusion in Article 41, Section 1 contains no qualifying language, the parties' agreement is distinguishable from the agreement in *FDIC*. Consequently, the Union has not demonstrated that the Arbitrator's interpretation of the parties' agreement is irrational, implausible, unfounded, or in manifest disregard of the agreement. *See U.S. Dep't of Transp., FAA*, 63 FLRA 15, 18 (2008).

Accordingly, we deny the Union's exception.

B. The award is not contrary to law.

When an exception involves an award's consistency with law, the Authority reviews any question of law raised by the exception and the award *de novo*. *See NTEU, Chapter 24*, 50 FLRA 330, 332 (1995) (citing *U.S. Customs Serv. v. FLRA*, 43 F.3d 682, 686-87 (D.C. Cir. 1994)). In applying the standard of *de novo* review, the Authority assesses whether an arbitrator's legal conclusions are consistent with the applicable standard of law. *See U.S. Dep't of Def., Dep'ts of the Army & the Air Force, Ala. Nat'l Guard, Northport, Ala.*, 55 FLRA 37, 40 (1998). In making that assessment, the Authority defers to the arbitrator's underlying factual findings. *See id.*

The Union claims that that the award is contrary to law because the Arbitrator's arbitrability determination was based solely on the result of the alleged ULP – i.e., the grievant's separation. Exceptions at 8-9. Also, the Union asserts that "[t]o allow arbitration in one case and not [in] another for the exact same action on the part of the Agency is inconsistent as the outcome of the ULP does not change whether or not a ULP occurred." *Id.* at 9. Finally, the Union alleges that the award is contrary to law because, based on Authority precedent, the grievance is arbitrable. *Id.* at 9-12. The Union claims that the Arbitrator wrongfully recasts the parties' dispute as "a garden variety contest over the grievant's performance or conduct" and that "probationary employees . . . have every right to pursue ULP charges before the Authority or through a negotiated grievance procedure unless the [parties' agreement] prohibits the grieving of ULP charges." *Id.* at 10, 11-12.

As a general matter, the termination of a probationary employee is not grievable or arbitrable as a matter of law. *See, e.g., GSA, Region 2, N.Y.C., N.Y.*, 58 FLRA 588, 589 (2008). The Authority has held that the termination of a probationary employee in violation of the Statute is a ULP. *See U.S. Dep't of Agric., Food & Nutrition Serv., Alexandria, Va.*,

61 FLRA 16, 22 (2005). The Authority has not addressed, however, whether the termination of a probationary employee is grievable and arbitrable when it is alleged to constitute a ULP. Even assuming that terminated, probationary employees are entitled to access the negotiated grievance procedure in such situations, the Arbitrator here found that the parties' agreement, as noted above, excludes complaints involving the separation of a probationary employee from the arbitration process, including those alleging a ULP. Award at 5, 36, 37; *see FDIC*, 49 FLRA at 900 (finding that a temporary employee may pursue a ULP complaint through the negotiated grievance procedure unless the parties agree to exclude his ability to do so in their agreement). The Authority has found that parties may agree to exclude any matter from the scope of their negotiated grievance procedure. *See, e.g., FDIC*, 49 FLRA at 900-01 (citing *U.S. Dep't of the Treasury, Customs Serv., Se. Region*, 43 FLRA 921, 925 (1992) (determining that, under the Statute, parties may choose to exclude any matter from the scope of negotiated grievance procedures)); *U.S. Naval Air Station, Kingsville, Tex.*, 35 FLRA 841, 842 (1990) (citation omitted) (finding that the parties may agree to exclude any matter, including disputes concerning contracting out, from the scope of their negotiated grievance procedure).

Although the Union claims that the award is unfair because it prevents only separated, probationary employees from using the negotiated grievance procedures, the parties themselves created this result when they limited the exclusion to complaints involving the separation of a probationary employee. Exceptions at 8-9. Moreover, the Union has not cited to a single case, in either its exceptions or at arbitration, "where a probationary employee, otherwise precluded from using the contractual grievance process, was nevertheless permitted to file a ULP utilizing that process." Award at 36. Consequently, the Union's contention – that the award is contrary to law because the Arbitrator failed to find that the grievant could pursue his ULP complaint through the negotiated grievance procedure – is without merit.[4]

Accordingly, we deny the Union's exceptions.

VI. Decision

The Union's exceptions are denied.

---

4. As the Arbitrator noted, the grievant here was not without recourse. Award at 36. As a probationary employee, he was entitled to pursue his ULP claim by filing a ULP charge with a regional office of the Authority. *Id.*

65 FLRA No. 61

SOCIAL SECURITY ADMINISTRATION
(Agency)

and

AMERICAN FEDERATION
OF GOVERNMENT EMPLOYEES
LOCAL 3239
(Union)

0-AR-4633

DECISION

November 30, 2010

Before the Authority: Carol Waller Pope, Chairman, and Thomas M. Beck and Ernest DuBester, Members

I. Statement of the Case

This matter is before the Authority on exceptions to an award of Arbitrator Margaret Nancy Johnson filed by the Agency under § 7122(a) of the Federal Service Labor-Management Relations Statute (the Statute) and part 2425 of the Authority's Regulations. The Union did not file an opposition to the Agency's exceptions.

The Arbitrator sustained a grievance alleging that the Agency did not have just cause to suspend the grievant for fourteen days for improperly accessing Agency records and disclosing the information contained in the records to a third party. Accordingly, she ordered that the grievant's fourteen-day suspension be mitigated to a two-day suspension and that the grievant be made whole for the excess time that she was suspended. For the reasons that follow, we deny the Agency's exceptions.

II. Background and Arbitrator's Award

The grievant, a Title II Claims Representative, works at the Agency servicing those individuals with retirement, disability, Medicare, or supplemental income benefits. Award at 1. The personal information of individuals receiving such benefits is stored in a computer system, and employees are issued an individualized PIN and password to track each time an employee enters the system. *Id.* Each time an employee accesses the system, he or she agrees not to access the data without proper authorization; assumes responsibility for safeguarding the information; and acknowledges potential consequences for misuse of the governmental program. *Id.*

The grievant was asked by her father to determine whether a social security number that he had found was that of a deceased relative. *Id.* at 3. The grievant accessed the Agency's computer system, determined that the social security number was her brother's, and reported her discovery to her father. *Id.* Subsequently, the Agency discovered that the grievant had accessed personal information for an individual with the grievant's maiden name. *Id.* The grievant acknowledged that she had accessed the information for her father. *Id.*

The Agency concluded that the actions of the grievant "could not be condoned regardless of [her] reasons for doing so" and recommended that the grievant be suspended for fourteen days. *Id.* at 3-4. The Assistant Regional Commissioner determined that the proposal notice was supported by a "preponderance of evidence" and suspended the grievant for fourteen calendar days, concluding that "no less severe penalty would effectively deter such conduct in the future." *Id.* at 4. In support of her decision, the Assistant Regional Commissioner noted that the discipline was the minimum prescribed in the Agency's Uniform Sanctions for Unauthorized Systems Access Violations (Sanctions Policy). *Id.*

The grievant filed a grievance seeking to have her suspension rescinded, which was unresolved and submitted to arbitration. The Arbitrator stated that the following issue was before her: "[W]as the fourteen (14) day suspension of [the grievant] for just cause, and, if not, to what remedy, if any, is the aggrieved entitled?" *Id.* at 2.

According to the Arbitrator, the dispute before her concerned the reasonable application of the Sanctions Policy, and "whether or not the use of a fourteen[-]day suspension in this instance comports with the just cause mandate negotiated into the [a]greement between the parties." *Id.* at 4. The Arbitrator held that the just cause requirement of

Article 23[1] of the parties' agreement required the Agency "to consider employee misconduct in the context in which it occurred, taking into account factors such as employment record, length of service, intent, and consequences, if any." *Id.* at 5.

The Arbitrator found that the Agency failed properly to analyze these factors when applying the Sanctions Policy to the grievant's infraction. *Id.* In this regard, the Arbitrator found that the grievant had more than twenty-five years of service to the Agency without any prior disciplinary record. *Id.* at 5, 8. The Arbitrator determined that the Agency, however, had improperly applied the grievant's length of service as an aggravating factor, rather than as a mitigating factor. *Id.* at 5. The Arbitrator further determined that there was no evidence that employees in other "cases involving improper access and disclosure [had] been issued a two[-]week disciplinary suspension or that the rule infraction carries with it a mandatory two[-]week suspension, regardless of mitigating factors." *Id.* at 6. The Arbitrator also found that the Agency had failed to show that the grievant's infraction had affected adversely the Agency's mission. *Id.* Moreover, the Arbitrator found unpersuasive the Agency's claim that such discipline was required to deter such conduct in the future, given the grievant's twenty-five years of service without prior discipline and given that, in this case, the disclosure was "to allay anxiety of an elderly parent." *Id.* at 7.

Noting that one of the issues before her was whether the decision to bypass progressive discipline was reasonable and proper, the Arbitrator concluded that, because the infraction was inadvertent and not calculated, "the purposes of the Agency could have readily been accomplished with a less onerous discipline." *Id.* at 7-8. Accordingly, the Arbitrator held that the two-week suspension "was excessively severe" and that a lesser penalty was proper. *Id.* at 8. As a result, she ordered that the grievant's two-week suspension be reduced to a two-day suspension and that the grievant be made whole for the excess suspension time. *Id.* at 8, 9.

III. Agency's Exceptions

The Agency contends that the Arbitrator misapplied the *Douglas* factors in determining that the penalty was not for just cause.[2] Exceptions at 6.

The Agency also contends that the Arbitrator's award fails to draw its essence from the parties' agreement because the Arbitrator ignored the Agency's contractual right to bypass progressive discipline where the grievant's conduct was a "serious violation[] of Agency policy." *Id.* at 1. According to the Agency, Article 23, Section 1 grants management the "discretion to bypass earlier steps of progressive discipline where it determines that misconduct is so serious that lesser penalties would not be appropriate." *Id.* at 4. The Agency asserts that the Arbitrator substituted her judgment for that of management and that her decision, accordingly, reflects a manifest disregard of the parties' agreement. *Id.* at 7.

The Agency further contends that the award is inconsistent with Authority precedent. According to the Agency, the Authority previously has found that Article 23, Section 1 provides management the discretion to bypass steps in progressive discipline for matters involving systems access. *Id.* at 4-5 (citing *Soc. Sec. Admin., St. Paul, Minn.*, 61 FLRA 92 (2005) (then-Member Pope dissenting) (*SSA*); *AFGE, Local 3342*, 58 FLRA 448 (2003)).

1. Article 2, Section 1 provides, in pertinent part:

> Section 1: Statement of Purpose and Policy
>
> The parties agree that the objective of discipline is to correct and improve employee behavior so as to promote the efficiency of the service. The parties agree to the concept of progressive discipline which is designed primarily to correct and improve employee behavior. A common pattern of progressive discipline is reprimand, short term suspension, long term suspension and removal. Any of these steps may be bypassed where management determines by the severe nature of the behavior that a lesser form of discipline would not be appropriate.
>
> The parties further agree that normally, discipline would be preceded by counseling and assistance including oral warnings which are informal in nature and not recorded. Counseling and warnings will be conducted privately and in such a manner so as to avoid embarrassment to the employee. Bargaining unit employees will be subject to disciplinary or adverse action only for just cause.

Award at 2.

2. In *Douglas v. Veterans Administration*, 5 M.S.P.R. 280 (1981), the Merit Systems Protection Board established thirteen factors to assist a deciding official in determining an appropriate penalty. These factors govern adverse actions under 5 U.S.C. §§ 4303 and 7512. *See, e.g., U.S. Gen. Servs. Admin., Ne. & Caribbean Region, N.Y., N.Y.*, 61 FLRA 68, 68 n.2 (2005).

Finally, the Agency asserts that, in the event that the award is found to be contrary to law, the record is sufficient to enable the Authority to assess the reasonableness of the Agency's decision to suspend the grievant for fourteen days, without remanding to the Arbitrator. *Id* at 8-9.

IV. Analysis and Conclusions

A. The award is not contrary to law.

The Authority has repeatedly held that arbitrators are bound by the same substantive standards as the Merit Systems Protection Board (MSPB) only when resolving grievances concerning actions covered by 5 U.S.C. §§ 4303 and 7512. *See IFPTE, Local 11*, 46 FLRA 893, 902 (1992). Suspensions of fourteen days or less are not covered under 5 U.S.C. §§ 4303 or 7512. *See AFGE, Local 1770,* 51 FLRA 1302 (1996); *U.S. Dep't of the Air Force, Air Force Logistics Command, Hill Air Force Base, Utah,* 34 FLRA 986, 991 (1990); *see also U.S. Dep't of Justice, Immigration & Naturalization Serv., Jacksonville, Fla.,* 36 FLRA 928 (1990) (in a case involving a five-day suspension, the arbitrator was not bound to follow the same substantive standards of the Federal Circuit and the MSPB).

The Agency argues that the Arbitrator misapplied the *Douglas* factors in determining that the penalty was not for just cause. Exceptions at 6-7. As noted, the use of principles established by the MSPB for suspensions of less than fourteen days is not mandatory. Although the Arbitrator considered the *Douglas* factors when he was not required to do so, the Agency's contention that he incorrectly applied them does not provide a basis for finding the award deficient. *See NATCA MEBA/MNU*, 52 FLRA 787, 792 (1996) (arbitrator's misapplication of factor when he was not required to apply that factor constituted, among other things, the arbitrator's reasoning and did not provide a basis for finding the award deficient); *see also AFGE, Local 3947,* 47 FLRA 1364, 1371 (1993) (award not deficient because arbitrator failed to apply *Douglas* factors where grievant received a fourteen-day suspension).

Accordingly, we reject the Agency's assertion that the award is contrary to law because the Arbitrator failed to apply correctly the *Douglas* factors and deny this exception.

B. The award does not fail to draw its essence from the parties' agreement.

In reviewing an arbitrator's interpretation of a collective bargaining agreement, the Authority applies the deferential standard of review that federal courts use in reviewing arbitration awards in the private sector. *See, e.g., AFGE, Council 220,* 54 FLRA 156, 159 (1998). Under this standard, the Authority will find that an arbitration award is deficient as failing to draw its essence from the parties' collective bargaining agreement when the appealing party establishes that the award: (1) cannot in any rational way be derived from the agreement; (2) is so unfounded in reason and fact and so unconnected with the wording and purposes of the collective bargaining agreement as to manifest an infidelity to the obligation of the arbitration; (3) does not represent a plausible interpretation of the agreement; or (4) evidences a manifest disregard of the agreement. *See, e.g., U.S. Dep't of Labor (OSHA)*, 34 FLRA 573, 575 (1990). The Authority and the courts defer to arbitrators in this context "because it is the arbitrator's construction of the agreement for which the parties have bargained." *Id.* at 576.

The Agency asserts that this case is similar to *SSA*, in which the Authority found an arbitrator's interpretation of the same provision of the parties' agreement failed to draw its essence from the agreement. Exceptions at 4 (citing *SSA*, 61 FLRA 92). The Agency contends that, in that case, like the case here, the agency bypassed the minimum sanction provided for in Article 23 and imposed a penalty that was consistent with the Sanctions Policy. *Id.*

In *SSA,* the Authority determined that the language of the parties' agreement provided the agency with the ultimate authority to determine the appropriate penalty for the grievant's infraction because the agreement provided the agency with the right to "bypass" lesser forms of discipline for "severe" infractions. *SSA,* 61 FLRA at 94 (then-Member Pope dissenting). The Authority found that, under Article 23, Section 1, the agency was "solely authorized" to determine the "degree of discipline" for "severe" behavior and held that, when serious conduct is involved, an arbitrator must uphold the agency's choice of discipline. *Id.* This interpretation, however, ignores that Article 23 also provides that all disciplinary action – including those assessed pursuant to management's right to bypass progressive discipline – must be for just cause. Moreover, this interpretation also ignores that "the Agency's exercise of authority under Article 23, like its exercise of authority under other contract provisions, is subject to arbitral scrutiny." *SSA*, 61 FLRA at 96 (dissenting opinion of then-Member Pope). Accordingly, we find that *SSA* was wrongly decided and overturn that decision.[3]

The Arbitrator here held that the just cause requirement of Article 23, Section 1 required the Agency to consider employee misconduct in the context in which it occurred, "taking into account factors such as employment record, length of service, intent, and consequences, if any." Award at 5. The Arbitrator further considered the Agency's ability to bypass progressive discipline, and concluded that, because the infraction was inadvertent and not calculated, the purposes of the Agency could have readily been accomplished with less severe discipline. *Id.* at 7-8. Such an interpretation is consistent with the express wording of the provision and gives full meaning to both parts of Article 23 at issue here – i.e., that "management may bypass progressive discipline when it determines, by the severe nature of the behavior, that a lesser form of discipline would not be appropriate" and that "bargaining unit employees will be subject to disciplinary or adverse action only for just cause." *Id.* at 2. Indeed, the Arbitrator herself ultimately determined that the violation was severe enough to bypass the initial step of progressive discipline provided for in Article 23, ordering that the grievant serve a two-day suspension, rather than simply receive a reprimand.

Accordingly, we find that the Arbitrator's interpretation is not implausible or unfounded and does not evidence a manifest disregard of the parties' agreement and deny this exception.

V. Decision

The Agency's exceptions are denied.

---

3. The Agency also argues that the Arbitrator's award is inconsistent with *AFGE, Local 3342*. We reject that contention. In *AFGE, Local 3342*, the Authority determined that the arbitrator's interpretation of the parties' agreement as permitting the agency to "skip counseling and warning" was not a manifest disregard of the agreement. *AFGE, Local 3342*, 58 FLRA at 450. Contrary to the Agency's assertion, however, the Authority did not hold that the provision of the parties' agreement — which is similar, but not identical to the provision at issue here — eliminates the arbitrator's authority to determine whether the penalty assessed was for just cause. *Id.* Accordingly, that case is inapposite.

65 FLRA No. 62

UNITED STATES
DEPARTMENT OF COMMERCE
PATENT AND TRADEMARK OFFICE
(Agency)

and

PATENT OFFICE PROFESSIONAL
ASSOCIATION
(Union)

0-AR-4128

DECISION

November 30, 2010

Before the Authority: Carol Waller Pope, Chairman, and Thomas M. Beck and Ernest DuBester, Members[1]

I. Statement of the Case

This matter is before the Authority on exceptions to an award of Arbitrator Salvatore J. Arrigo filed by the Agency under § 7122(a) of the Federal Service Labor-Management Relations Statute (the Statute) and part 2425 of the Authority's Regulations. The Union filed an opposition to the Agency's exceptions.

For the reasons that follow, we dismiss the exceptions in part and deny them in part.

II. Background and Arbitrator's Award

A. Background

In 2000, the Agency's patent examiners were paid under the General Schedule (GS). Award at 2. Because it was having difficulty recruiting and retaining employees, the Agency sought and received Office of Personnel Management (OPM) approval to pay employees special rates that were ten percent and fifteen percent higher than the GS rates. *Id.* at 2, 10. Under OPM regulations, employees paid a special rate receive the same general increases, but not the locality pay, that employees paid GS rates receive. *Id.* at 5. As a result, over time, special pay rates erode in value relative to the GS rates. Therefore, in conjunction with OPM's approval of the special rates, the Agency and the Union reached an agreement (the "Millennium Agreement," hereinafter "MA") that included Section A.2 (§ A.2), which provides as follows:

> The [Agency] shall request OPM approval for the next five years to increase the special pay schedule so as to maintain the 10% and 15% salary differentials relative to the updated GS rates, in a manner consistent with OPM regulations. If OPM refuses the request, the Agency shall enter into discussions with [the Union] in order to provide substantially equivalent alternatives.

Id. at 8.

B. 2002 Dispute

In 2002, federal employees in the Washington area received a 1.17 percent increase in locality pay in addition to the 3.6 percent general increase. *Id.* at 11. Consistent with the first sentence in § A.2, the Agency requested that OPM increase the Agency's special pay rate by 1.17 percent. *Id.* OPM denied the request, stating that the Agency no longer had recruitment and retention problems, and recommended that the Agency explore "the strategic use of other compensation flexibilities to address targeted recruitment and retention problems." *Id.*

Pursuant to the second sentence in § A.2, after OPM denied the Agency's request, the parties discussed ways in which a substantially equivalent alternative could be paid to employees. When the discussions failed to produce an agreement, the Union filed a grievance that was ultimately submitted to arbitration. *See id.* at 12. The arbitrator sustained the grievance and ordered the Agency to "engage in discussions with the Union 'in good faith with a sincere resolve to find a way to make-up for the lost locality pay,' without proposing or insisting on any other conditions." *U.S. Dep't of Commerce, Patent & Trademark Office*, 60 FLRA 839, 840 (2005), *pet. for review dismissed*, 180 F. App'x 176 (D.C. Cir. Mar. 21, 2006) (unpublished) (*PTO I*).

The Agency filed exceptions to the award. In resolving those exceptions, the Authority noted that the right to retain employees under § 7106(a)(2)(A) of the Statute "is the right to establish policies or practices that encourage or discourage employees from remaining employed by an agency." *Id.* at 841

---

1. Member Beck's separate opinion, dissenting in part, is set forth at the end of this decision.

(citation omitted). The Authority found that, as interpreted by the arbitrator, the second sentence of § A.2 effectively required the Agency to engage in good-faith discussions and to agree to an alternative to special pay increases, provided such alternative was lawful and within the Agency's funding ability. *Id.* The Authority further found that, as special rates "are a means to encourage retention of employees," the award affected management's right to retain employees. *Id.* at 841.

The Authority then addressed *the Union's claim that* § A.2 constituted an appropriate arrangement under § 7106(b)(3) of the Statute. The Authority stated that, in order for a provision to be enforceable as an appropriate arrangement, the provision must seek "to mitigate adverse effects flowing from the exercise of a management right." *Id.* at 842 (citation omitted). The Authority noted that, according to the arbitrator, § A.2 "was intended to address the adverse effect of special rate erosion that would occur over time as non-special rate employees received locality pay increases." *Id.* Because this "adverse effect [did] not result from the exercise of any management right, but by the operation of law," the Authority concluded that § A.2 was not an "arrangement" and, as a result, was not an appropriate arrangement under § 7106(b)(3). *Id.* at 842, 843.

The Authority rejected "as unsupported" the Union's argument that § A.2 was an arrangement for employees who were adversely affected by management's decision to eliminate paper files for patent searches and to include a customer-service element in employees' performance plans. *Id.* at 843. According to the Authority, "the [a]rbitrator made no findings that the second sentence of [§] A.2 was intended to ameliorate the alleged adverse effects cited by the Union." *Id.* at 842. Also according to the Authority, there was no basis in the wording of § A.2, and no other evidence, to support the Union's claims. *Id.* at 843. Accordingly, the Authority set aside the award.

C. Grievance and Award in this Case

In 2003, the locality pay rate for the Washington, D.C. area was again increased by 1.17 percent. However, the Agency concluded that it could not certify that it was "critical to the mission of the Agency" to amend the special pay rate, and it notified the Union that it would not request OPM to increase the special rate. Award at 13. The Union filed another grievance, and the matter was submitted to arbitration, where the Arbitrator adopted the issues as set forth by the Union:

1. Whether the [Agency] violated [§] A.2 of the [MA] when it refused to request OPM approval to increase the special pay schedule to maintain the 10% and 15% salary differentials following the increase in locality pay received by [GS] employees in the Washington, D.C. [area] in January 2003?

2. Whether the [Agency] violated [§] A.2 of the [MA] when it refused to engage in discussions to provide a substantially equivalent alternative following the increase in locality pay received by [GS] employees in the Washington, D.C. [area] in January 2003?

3. Assuming *arguendo* that either sentence of [§] A.2 interferes with management's right to retain employees, is [§] A.2 an appropriate arrangement for employees who were adversely affected by management's decision to eliminate the paper patent files and impose a customer service element in unit employees' performance plans?

4. Whether the [Agency's] refusal to request OPM approval to increase the special pay schedule or to engage in discussions to provide a substantially equivalent alternative constitute a clear and patent breach of a provision that goes to the heart of the [MA], thereby constituting a contract repudiation and unfair labor practice [(ULP)] in violation of 5 U.S.C. § 7116(a)(1) and (5)?

5. Whether the [Agency's] refusal to request OPM approval to increase the special pay schedule or to engage in discussions to provide a substantially equivalent alternative constitute a refusal to implement [§] A.2 of the [MA] in violation of the duty to negotiate in good faith as defined by § 7114(b)(5), thereby constituting [a ULP] in violation of 5 U.S.C. § 7116(a)(1) and (5)?

6. What shall the remedy be?

Award at 17-18.

The Arbitrator determined that the first sentence of § A.2 requires the Agency to make "yearly requests" to OPM for an increase in the special pay rate. *Id.* at 22. In this regard, he found that "the requirement to certify that the request . . . [is] necessary to ensure adequate staffing does not prevent the Agency from honestly certifying and explaining that the need is based upon the Agency's long-term needs . . . as the parties concluded in their discussions which led to the agreement." *Id.* The Arbitrator also found that the Agency did not petition OPM and, as a result, no refusal was made. *Id.* at 22-23. However, he concluded that the Agency was obligated to enter into discussions with the Union under the second sentence in § A.2 even though there was no refusal by OPM. *Id.* at 23. According to the Arbitrator,

> even if [§] A.2 does not specifically state so, the most reasonable and sensible interpretation of this section . . . is to require discussion, [as] set forth in the second sentence of [§] A.2, whenever application or consideration of the first sentence of [§] A.2 fails to achieve the agreed-upon and express objective of maintaining the 10% and 15% differential.

Id.

Because "the essential facts and circumstances" in the case before him were "substantially identical" to those found by the Authority in *PTO I*, the Arbitrator found, in accordance with that decision, that § A.2 of the MA affected management's right to retain employees. *Id.* at 24. The Arbitrator then addressed the Union's claim that § A.2 was intended to be an appropriate arrangement under § 7106(b)(3) of the Statute. Based on the record before him, the Arbitrator also found that "the entirety of [§] A," including § A.2, "was negotiated as a quid pro quo for the elimination of paper patents and the addition of customer service duties for employees[,]" two changes desired by the Agency and opposed by the Union. *Id.* (emphasis removed). According to the Arbitrator, the linkage between a special pay schedule and the paper file and customer service issues was established "in every document concerning the discussions between the parties[.]" *Id.* at 25. The Arbitrator determined that § A's provisions regarding the special pay schedule were a "balm" to "ameliorate the adverse effects upon employees for the Union's acceding to the Agency's desire to exercise its management rights regarding the elimination of paper files . . . and employees being assigned additional duties[,]" and were enforceable as appropriate arrangements under § 7106(b)(3). *Id.* at 25-26.

The Arbitrator also addressed the Union's claim that the Agency repudiated § A.2 of the MA. Assessing whether the Agency clearly and patently breached that provision, the Arbitrator found § A.2 to be "clear and unambiguous" in its requirements. *Id.* at 26. He noted the Agency's argument that the phrase "in a manner consistent with OPM regulations[,]" found in the first sentence of § A.2, should be interpreted as requiring the existence of supporting recruitment and retention data before the Agency would be obligated to submit a request to OPM. *Id.* at 21. The Arbitrator considered the parties' bargaining history and determined that the parties had "specifically rejected" such a prerequisite. *Id.* at 22. In this connection, the Arbitrator found that, during negotiations, the Agency had proposed such a prerequisite, but that the proposal had been "rejected based upon the parties' recognition that such data might not be present in a given year," despite the "long-term necessity for pay rates that would attract employees over the future years[.]" *Id.* at 21. In addition, the Arbitrator "credited testimony" that the Union proposed the "in a manner consistent with OPM regulations[]" wording, and that this wording merely expressed the Union's "concern . . . that it was essential that the Agency comply with all the aspects of the regulations in order to justify a special pay rate[,] stating that they wished assurance [that] the Agency presented to OPM a complete application containing all the required data." *Id.* at 22. The Arbitrator concluded that the Agency clearly and patently breached the agreement.

The Arbitrator also concluded that the breached provision "went to the heart of the parties' agreement." *Id.* at 27. In this regard, the Arbitrator found that § A.2 was a "critical part" of § A, which was, in turn, necessary to the Union's acceptance of the rest of the MA. *Id.* Therefore, according to the Arbitrator, the Agency repudiated the agreement in violation of § 7116(a)(1) and (5) of the Statute. *Id.*

In light of this violation, the Arbitrator concluded that the appropriate remedy was to "require the Agency to fulfill its obligations under the agreement and to 'enter discussions with [the Union] in order to provide substantially equivalent alternatives' to the erosion of the agreed-upon pay differentials set forth in the agreement." *Id.* at 29 (quoting § A.2). In this connection, the Arbitrator stated that the substantially equivalent alternatives should be "relative to updated GS rates from January 1, 2001, to January 2003, occasioned by raises in locality pay for Washington, D.C. GS employees during that period." *Id.* at 30. Citing the arbitrator's finding in the award set aside in *PTO I*, the Arbitrator stated that the object of the discussions should be to "find a lawful way to overcome the lost . . . locality pay and to compensate bargaining unit members[.]" *Id.* at 29 (citation omitted). The Arbitrator added that interest should be paid "on any money the employees might receive pursuant to the discussions envisioned in [§] A.2." *Id.* at 30.

III. Positions of the Parties

A. Agency's Exceptions

The Agency argues that the award is contrary to OPM regulations concerning special pay. In this regard, the Agency contends that the Arbitrator's interpretation of § A.2 violates: (1) the procedures for establishing and adjusting special pay rates set forth in 5 C.F.R. §§ 530.304-306; (2) the prohibition against receiving both special pay and locality pay set forth in 5 C.F.R. § 531.608; and (3) the requirement that the Agency certify to the necessity of adjusting special pay rates set forth in 5 C.F.R. § 530.[2] Exceptions at 19-23.

Relying on *PTO I*, the Agency also asserts that § A.2, as interpreted by the Arbitrator, is contrary to management's right to retain employees under § 7106(a)(2)(A) of the Statute. *Id.* at 2. The Agency argues that *PTO I* provides "binding Authority precedent" that § A.2 is not an arrangement because it ameliorates adverse effects resulting from "the operation of law, not the exercise of a management right." *Id.* at 14. The Agency maintains that the Arbitrator made no findings that the reduction in paper files or addition of a customer-service element to employees' performance plans either constituted the exercise of management rights or resulted in adverse effects. *Id.* at 15. In addition, according to the Agency, additional compensation is not a "balm" administered to mitigate adverse effects and is not "in any way narrowly tailored to compensate only those employees suffering adverse effects attributable to the Agency." *Id.* at 17.

The Agency also argues that the Arbitrator's finding of a repudiation of § A.2 is contrary to law. As an initial matter, the Agency asserts that, because the Arbitrator's interpretation and application of § A.2 is unlawful, the Agency's failure to comply with the provisions, as interpreted and applied by the Arbitrator, did not constitute repudiation. *Id.* at 24. In addition, the Agency contends that, even assuming that it breached § A.2 on one occasion, "this one-time breach is insufficient to establish" repudiation. *Id.* at 25. Further, the Agency asserts that it acted in accordance with a reasonable interpretation of § A.2. In this regard, the Agency contends that it was reasonable to interpret the first sentence of § A.2 as requiring it to submit a request to OPM "*only* in the event that it could lawfully and honestly make the required certification in good faith." *Id.* Moreover, the Agency asserts that the alleged breach does not go to the "heart" of the MA, as the heart of the MA "was to obtain the initial special pay rate from OPM." *Id.* at 26.

Additionally, the Agency argues that the award is contrary to the Back Pay Act, 5 U.S.C. § 5596, because the Arbitrator awarded interest without awarding backpay. *Id.* at 27-28. Finally, the Agency contends that the Arbitrator exceeded his authority. In this connection, the Agency asserts that the award "appears to effectively require the Agency to agree to substantially equivalent alternatives for 2002 and 2003[,]" but the grievance did not cover 2002. *Id.* at 29.

B. Union's Opposition

The Union asserts that the award is not contrary to OPM regulations because it neither requires the Agency to increase the special pay rate without approval nor grants employees special pay and locality pay. According to the Union, the award merely requires the Agency to enter discussions to make up for the lost locality pay. Opp'n at 32.

With respect to the Agency's management-rights argument, the Union contends that the award is not contrary to *PTO I* because the factual situation and legal arguments in the present case are different from that decision. *Id.* at 5-6. The Union also contends that, in *PTO I*, the Authority erroneously found that § A.2 affects management's rights. *Id.* at 8-9. The Union alternatively argues that, if the award affects management's rights, then the Arbitrator correctly found that the § A.2 is enforceable as an appropriate arrangement under § 7106(b)(3). *Id.* at 19. In this connection, the Union asserts that testimony at the arbitration hearing demonstrated that the elimination of paper files and the addition of a customer-service performance element negatively impacted employees. *Id.* at 23-24. The Union also claims that the Statute does not preclude negotiating additional compensation as an appropriate arrangement. *Id.*

In addition, the Union maintains that the Arbitrator did not err in finding a repudiation of the MA and that the award does not violate the Back Pay

2. The text of relevant provisions is in the appendix to this decision.

Act. Opp'n at 39-44. Finally, the Union argues that the Arbitrator did not exceed his authority because, contrary to the Agency's interpretation of the award, the Union "does not read [the] . . . award as to require any payment of a substantially equivalent alternative that the employees should have received during the year 2002." *Id.* at 44.

IV. Analysis and Conclusions

A. The award is not contrary to law.

The Agency alleges that the award is contrary to law in several respects. The Authority reviews questions of law *de novo*. *See NTEU, Chapter 24*, 50 FLRA 330, 332 (1995) (citing *U.S. Customs Serv. v. FLRA*, 43 F.3d 682, 686-87 (D.C. Cir. 1994)). In applying a standard of *de novo* review, the Authority determines whether the arbitrator's legal conclusions are consistent with the applicable standard of law. *NFFE, Local 1437*, 53 FLRA 1703, 1710 (1998). In making that determination, the Authority defers to the arbitrator's underlying factual findings. *See id.*

1. OPM Pay Regulations

The Agency argues that the award violates three provisions of OPM regulations by requiring the Agency to: (1) increase the special pay rate without OPM approval; (2) pay employees both special pay and locality pay; and (3) make false certifications to OPM regarding the need for special pay.

With regard to the arguments about special pay and locality pay, the Arbitrator did not find that the Agency was required to "increase the special pay rate" or to "provide employees with the locality pay increase[.]" Exceptions at 19, 21. Rather, he found that the MA required "discussion, [as] set forth in the second sentence of [§] A.2[,]" with the goal of achieving "the agreed-upon and express objective of maintaining the 10% and 15% differential." Award at 23. The Agency does not explain how these negotiations would constitute a violation of §§ 530.304, 530.305, or 530.306, which govern the formal creation of special pay rates. Likewise, the Agency does not explain how negotiations over methods of maintaining a pay differential would violate 5 C.F.R. § 531.608, which governs locality pay. The mere fact that the discussions would address some form of compensation does not mean that these OPM regulations would be violated. In this regard, we note that OPM recommended that the Agency explore "the strategic use of other compensation flexibilities" when it denied the Agency's request to increase the special pay rate for 2002. Award at 11.

In addition, contrary to the Agency's exception regarding 5 C.F.R § 530.305, the Arbitrator did not "require[] the Agency to submit a false certification" when finding that the Agency was required to make yearly requests to OPM for five years to increase the special pay rate. Exceptions at 22. In this regard, the Arbitrator found that the Agency could truthfully certify, in accordance with OPM regulations, that there was a long-term need for such increases. Award at 21-22. The Agency did not present any evidence to establish that the Arbitrator erred in this factual finding.

For the foregoing reasons, the Agency has not established that the award is in any manner contrary to the above cited provisions. *See Prof'l Airways Sys. Specialists, Dist. No. 1, MEBA/NMU (AFL-CIO)*, 48 FLRA 764, 769 (1993) (union failed to demonstrate that arbitrator conclusions were contrary to travel regulations); *Veterans Admin. Hosp., Newington, Conn.*, 5 FLRA 64, 66 (1981) (union failed to demonstrate that regulations mandated the remedy desired by the union and consequently failed to demonstrate that the award was in any manner contrary to those regulations). Accordingly, we deny these exceptions.

2. Section 7106(a)(2)(A) of the Statute

The Authority recently revised the analysis that it will apply when reviewing management-rights exceptions to arbitration awards. *See U.S. EPA*, 65 FLRA 113, 115 (2010) (Member Beck concurring) (*EPA*); *FDIC, Div. of Supervision & Consumer Prot., S.F. Region*, 65 FLRA 102 (2010) (Chairman Pope concurring) (*FDIC*). Under the revised analysis, the Authority assesses whether the award affects the exercise of the asserted management right. *EPA*, 65 FLRA at 115. If so, then, as relevant here, the Authority examines whether the award enforces a contract provision negotiated under § 7106(b).[3] *Id.* Also under the revised analysis, in determining whether the award enforces a contract provision negotiated under § 7106(b)(3), the Authority assesses: (1) whether the contract provision constitutes an arrangement for employees adversely affected by the exercise of a management right; and (2) if so, whether the

3. When an award affects a management right under § 7106(a)(2) of the Statute, the Authority may also examine whether the award enforces an applicable law. *EPA*, 65 FLRA at 115 n.7.

arbitrator's enforcement of the arrangement abrogates the exercise of the management right. *See id.* at 118. In concluding that it would apply an abrogation standard, the Authority rejected continued application of an excessive-interference standard. *Id.* at 113.

In his award, the Arbitrator found that, because "the essential facts and circumstances" in the case before him were "substantially identical" to *PTO I*, he was required to find that § A.2 of the MA affects management's right to retain employees. Award at 24. Neither the Agency nor the Union filed timely exceptions to this finding.[4] Accordingly, we find that the award affects management's right to retain employees.

Contrary to the arbitrator's determination in *PTO I*, the Arbitrator in this case expressly determined that § A, including § A.2, constitutes an arrangement under § 7106(b)(3) of the Statute. Award at 26. Although the Agency argues that the decision in *PTO I* precluded the Arbitrator from making this determination, the Authority has acknowledged that the enforceability of a contract provision depends on the particular circumstances of each case. In this connection, the Authority has held that if a particular arbitrator's interpretation of a contract provision is inconsistent with a management right, then the award will be set aside, but "the contractual provision, susceptible to a different and sustainable interpretation by a different arbitrator, will not be affected." *Dep't of the Treasury, U.S. Customs Serv.*, 37 FLRA 309, 314 (1990) (*Customs Serv.*). *Cf. NTEU*, 45 FLRA 1256, 1262 (1992) (in negotiability decision, Authority noted that union failed to demonstrate adverse effects and, "without addressing whether the Authority would conclude differently in another case," found that the provision was not an arrangement). As the Arbitrator was presented with different facts and arguments than were presented in *PTO I*, we find that *PTO I* did not preclude the Arbitrator from finding that § A is an appropriate arrangement.[5]

As for the Agency's claim that the Arbitrator erred on the merits in finding § A to be an appropriate arrangement, the Arbitrator found that the entire subject of special pay was negotiated "to provide a 'balm' to the Union which would ameliorate the adverse effects upon employees" of "the Agency's desire to exercise its management rights regarding the elimination of paper files[,]" among other things. Award at 25-26. Although the Arbitrator did not specify what management rights the Agency was exercising when it reduced the paper search files, the Authority previously has held, based on this Agency's undisputed assertions, that the Agency's determination to use a computerized patent-search system, rather than paper files, involved an exercise of the right to determine the methods and means of performing work under § 7106(b)(1) of the Statute. *See POPA*, 56 FLRA 69, 69, 87-91 (2000). Thus, Authority precedent supports the Arbitrator's conclusion that the Agency's reduction of paper search files constituted the exercise of a management right under § 7106 of the Statute. *Cf. AFGE, Council 215*, 60 FLRA 461, 464 (2004) (where arbitrator did not explain finding that agreement affected management rights, Authority relied on precedent to uphold finding). With regard to the Arbitrator's finding that the exercise of management's right adversely affected employees, before the Arbitrator, the Union submitted evidence regarding how the reduction of paper search files adversely affected employees. *See* Opp'n, Attach., Tr. at 52, 67, 71-73, 160, 163-69, 173-74 (testimony that electronic versions were more difficult to read than paper files, did not contain helpful notes that paper files contained, and slowed

4. To the extent that the Union's arguments related to whether management's rights are affected by § A.2 and the correctness of the Authority's findings in *PTO I* can be construed as exceptions, we do not consider them. In this connection, under the Authority Regulations that were in effect when the Arbitrator served his award and the parties had the opportunity to file exceptions, exceptions were required to be filed within 30 days of service of the award. *See former* 5 C.F.R. § 2425.1(b). As the Union did not file exceptions within that time period, its arguments are not timely raised. We note that the Authority's Regulations concerning the review of arbitration awards, as well as certain related procedural regulations, were revised effective October 1, 2010. *See* 75 Fed. Reg. 42,283 (2010). As the prior regulations were in effect during the time period when the Union had the opportunity to file exceptions, we apply the prior regulations.

5. To the extent that the Agency's exceptions can be construed as arguing that the Arbitrator was collaterally estopped from finding § A.2 to be an appropriate arrangement, we reject that argument. In this connection, before the doctrine of collateral estoppel can be applied, it must be demonstrated that, among other things, "the same issue was involved . . . [and] was litigated in" the previous decision. *U.S. Dep't of Energy, W. Area Power Admin., Golden, Colo.*, 56 FLRA 9, 11 (2000). For the reasons stated above, the "same issue" presented in this case – i.e., whether § A.2, as interpreted and enforced by *this* Arbitrator, is an appropriate arrangement – was not involved or litigated in *PTO I*. Accordingly, the Arbitrator was not collaterally estopped from finding § A.2 to be an appropriate arrangement.

down examiners' work in at least some instances). Accordingly, based on Authority precedent and the record in this case, we find that, by adopting the Union's position that the reduction in paper files adversely affected employees, the Arbitrator implicitly credited the Union's evidence of adverse effects.

Consistent with the foregoing, the management right affected by the award (the right to retain employees) is a right different from the management right that adversely affected employees (the right to determine the methods and means of performing work). However, the Authority has stated that, in determining whether a proposal or provision is an appropriate arrangement, "[t]he adverse effect . . . need not flow from the management right that a given proposal [or provision] affects." *Fraternal Order of Police, Lodge # 1F*, 57 FLRA 373, 381 (2001). In addition, the Authority previously held that various forms of monetary relief can constitute appropriate arrangements. *See, e.g., NATCA*, 61 FLRA 437, 440-41 (2006) (proposal requiring compensation to employees whose promotions are delayed by management assignment of training); *AFGE, Local 1827*, 58 FLRA 344, 346-47 (2003) (Chairman Cabaniss concurring in part and Member Armendariz dissenting in part) (voluntary separation incentive payments). Thus, the fact that the "balm" provided by § A is a potential increase in compensation does not demonstrate that the Arbitrator erred by finding § A to be an appropriate arrangement. Finally, with regard to the Agency's claim that § A is not sufficiently tailored to constitute an appropriate arrangement, the Authority does not apply a tailoring analysis in the arbitration context. *See EPA*, 65 FLRA at 116. Thus, the Agency's claim does not provide a basis for finding the award deficient.

For the foregoing reasons, we deny the exception to the Arbitrator's finding that § A2 was intended to be an arrangement.

With regard to whether the arrangement is appropriate, the Agency argues that the award excessively interferes with management's right to retain employees. However, as stated above, the Authority no longer applies an excessive-interference standard to determine whether an arrangement is appropriate. *See EPA*, 65 FLRA at 118. Rather, the Authority applies an abrogation standard, which the Authority has described as an assessment of whether the arbitration award "precludes [the] agency from exercising" the affected management right. *Customs Serv.*, 37 FLRA at 314. The Agency has provided no basis for finding that the award precludes the Agency from exercising its right to retain employees. Therefore, we find that the arrangement is appropriate within the meaning of § 7106(b)(3) of the Statute.

For the foregoing reasons, we find that the award is not contrary to management's right to retain employees under § 7106(a)(2)(A) of the Statute, and we deny the Agency's management-rights exception.

3. Section 7116(a)(1) and (5) of the Statute

When a grievance under § 7121 of the Statute involves an alleged ULP, the arbitrator must apply the same standards and burdens that would be applied by an administrative law judge in a ULP proceeding under § 7118. *E.g., NTEU*, 64 FLRA 462, 464 (2010). An allegation of repudiation in violation of § 7116(a)(1) and (5) of the Statute is analyzed using the standard set forth by the Authority in *Department of the Air Force, 375th Mission Support Squadron, Scott Air Force Base, Illinois*, 51 FLRA 858 (1996) (*Scott AFB*). Under that standard, the Authority examines two elements: (1) the nature and scope of the alleged breach of the agreement – i.e., was the breach clear and patent?; and (2) the nature of the agreement provision allegedly breached – i.e., did the provision go to the heart of the parties' agreement? *Id.* at 862. With regard to the first element, if the meaning of a particular agreement term is unclear and a party acts in accordance with a reasonable interpretation of that term, then that action will not constitute a clear and patent breach of the agreement. *E.g., SSA, N.Y., N.Y.*, 60 FLRA 301, 304 (2004). With regard to the second element, the Authority focuses on the importance of the provision that was breached, or allegedly breached, relative to the agreement in which it is contained. *E.g., U.S. Dep't of the Air Force, Aerospace Maint. & Regeneration Ctr., Davis Monthan Air Force Base, Tucson, Ariz.*, 64 FLRA 355, 357 (2009) (Member Beck concurring in part and dissenting in part on other grounds).

Applying that standard here, as for the first element, as stated previously, the first sentence of § A.2 states: "The [Agency] shall request OPM approval for the next five years to increase the special pay schedule so as to maintain the 10% and 15% salary differentials relative to the updated GS rates, in a manner consistent with OPM regulations." Award at 8. There is no dispute that the Agency refused to request OPM approval. The Agency argues that this refusal did not clearly and patently breach § A.2 because it would not have been "consistent with OPM regulations[]" to make the request. Exceptions at 25. However, as discussed previously, we have found that it would not have been inconsistent with OPM regulations to make the request. In addition, although the Agency asserts that a one-time breach cannot constitute a clear and patent breach of the agreement, the Authority has held that a one-time breach may constitute a repudiation, depending on the "nature and scope" of the breach. *Scott AFB*, 51 FLRA at 861 (quoting *DOD, Warner Robins Air Logistics Ctr., Robins Air Force Base, Ga.*, 40 FLRA 1211, 1219 (1991)). Further, § A.2 clearly requires the Agency to make a request "for the next five years[,]" Award at 8, and the Agency's refusal to do so one of those five years was in clear violation of the plain terms of that requirement. For these reasons, we find that the Agency clearly and patently breached the first sentence of § A.2.

As for the second element of the *Scott AFB* test, the Arbitrator found that "the entirety of [§] A," including § A.2, "was negotiated as a quid pro quo for the elimination of paper patents and the addition of customer service duties for employees[,]" and that, but for the inclusion of § A, "there would have been no agreement" to the MA. Award at 24, 27 (emphasis removed). The Agency does not assert that these factual findings are nonfacts; rather, its only argument in this connection is that, by making these findings, the Arbitrator was "attempt[ing] to evade th[e] binding precedent[]" of *PTO I*. Exceptions at 14. However, as discussed previously, we have found that *PTO I* did not bind the Arbitrator to reach a different conclusion in this case, given the differences in the record evidence before him. Thus, the Agency provides no basis for finding that the Arbitrator erred in his "quid pro quo" finding, and for the foregoing reasons, we find that the Arbitrator correctly determined that the Agency's breach of § A.2 went to the heart of the MA.

For the foregoing reasons, we conclude that the Arbitrator properly found that the Agency repudiated § A.2 of the agreement, and we deny the Agency's exception to that finding.

To the extent that the Arbitrator found a repudiation of the second sentence of § A.2, the Authority has held that, when an arbitrator bases an award on two or more separate and independent grounds, the appealing party must establish that all of the grounds relied on are deficient in order for the Authority to find the award deficient. *E.g., Broad. Bd. of Governors, Office of Cuba Broad.*, 64 FLRA 888, 892 (2010). Therefore, if the excepting party has not demonstrated that the award is deficient on one of the grounds relied on by the arbitrator, then it is unnecessary to address exceptions to the other ground. *Id.*

The Arbitrator's finding of repudiation of the first sentence of § A.2 provides a separate and independent basis for his finding of a violation of § 7116(a)(1) and (5) of the Statute. As such, it is unnecessary to determine whether the Arbitrator erroneously found a repudiation of the second sentence of § A.2, and to the extent that the Agency's exceptions challenge such a finding, we find it unnecessary to resolve the exceptions in that regard.[6]

4. The Back Pay Act

The Agency argues that the award is contrary to the Back Pay Act because it requires the award of interest without an underlying award of backpay. However, the Agency mischaracterizes the award. In this connection, the Arbitrator stated that interest should be paid "on any money the employees might receive pursuant to the discussions envisioned in [§] A.2." Award at 30. In other words, the Arbitrator did not award any backpay or interest, but merely determined that, if any backpay is found to be warranted, then the Agency must also pay interest on that backpay. This determination is consistent with the Back Pay Act, which provides that "interest must be paid" on backpay awards. *NATCA*, 64 FLRA 906, 907 (2010). Accordingly, we find that the Agency has not demonstrated that the award is contrary to the Back Pay Act, and we deny the exception.

B. The exceeded-authority exception is dismissed as moot.

Arbitrators exceed their authority when they fail to resolve an issue submitted to arbitration, resolve an issue not submitted to arbitration, disregard specific limitations on their authority, or award relief to those not encompassed within the grievance. *AFGE, Local 1617*, 51 FLRA 1645, 1647 (1996).

---

6. We note that the second sentence of § A.2 contains the requirement to engage in discussions with the Union, and that this sentence formed part of the basis of the Arbitrator's remedy. However, regardless of whether the Arbitrator correctly found a repudiation of this sentence, the Arbitrator found a breach of the second sentence, and the Agency did not file an exception alleging that the award fails to draw its essence from the agreement. Thus, the finding of a breach of the second sentence is undisturbed, and to the extent that the Arbitrator's remedy is based on that sentence, there is no basis for setting aside that remedy.

As stated previously, the Arbitrator addressed the issue of whether the Agency violated the MA by its actions "in January 2003[,]" but then directed the Agency to enter discussions with the Union to provide substantially equivalent alternatives to the loss in salary differentials "relative to updated GS rates from January 1, 2001, to January 2003[.]" Award at 18, 30. Also as stated previously, the Agency asserts that the award "appears to effectively require the Agency to agree to substantially equivalent alternatives for 2002 and 2003[,]" Exceptions at 29, while the Union "does not read [the] . . . award as to require any payment of a substantially equivalent alternative that the employees should have received during the year 2002." Opp'n at 44.

Where a party in opposition agrees with construing an award in a manner that an excepting party desires, the Authority has dismissed, as moot, exceptions that allege a deficiency based on a different construction of the award. *E.g., U.S. Dep't of Veterans Affairs, Med. Ctr., Hampton, Va.*, 65 FLRA 125, 129 (2010). Construing the award consistently with the Union's contention that the Arbitrator provided a remedy only as to 2003, not 2002, we dismiss the exceeded-authority exception as moot. *See id.*

V. Decision

The exceptions are dismissed in part and denied in part.

APPENDIX

The following provisions of 5 C.F.R. parts 530 and 531 were applicable at the time of the Arbitrator's award in 2006.

Sec. 530.304 Establishing or increasing special rates.

(a) OPM may increase the minimum rates of pay otherwise payable to a category of employees in one or more areas or locations, grades or levels, occupational groups, series, classes, or subdivisions thereof, when it is necessary to address existing or likely significant recruitment or retention difficulties. OPM will consider the circumstances listed in paragraph (b) of this section and the factors listed in Sec. 530.306 when evaluating the need for special rates. When OPM establishes a minimum special rate under this authority, corresponding increases also may be made in one or more of the remaining rates of the affected grade or level. For any given grade, a minimum special rate may not exceed the maximum rate of basic pay for the rate range (excluding any locality rate, other special rate, or similar payment under other legal authority) by more than 30 percent. A special rate is not payable if it exceeds the rate for level IV of the Executive Schedule.

(b) The circumstances considered by OPM in evaluating the need for special rates are the following:

(1) Rates of pay offered by non-Federal employers which are significantly higher than those payable by the Government within the area, location, occupational group, or other category of positions under GS pay system;

(2) The remoteness of the area or location involved;

(3) The undesirability of the working conditions or the nature of the work involved (including exposure to toxic substances or other occupational hazards); or

(4) Any other circumstances OPM considers appropriate.

(c) In setting the level of special rates within a rate range for a category of employees, OPM will compute the special rate supplement by adding a fixed dollar amount or a fixed percentage to all GS rates within that range, except that an alternate method may be used for grades GS-1 and GS-2, where within-grade increases vary throughout the range.

(d) If OPM establishes a special rate schedule that covers only law enforcement officers, OPM may compute the special rate supplement for grades GS-3 through 10 as a fixed percentage of LEO special base rates instead of GS rates. With respect to such a schedule, references to GS rates in Sec. 530.307 are deemed to be references to LEO special base rates.

Sec. 530.305 Agency requests for new or increased special rates.

(a) An agency may request that a special rate schedule be established or increased or that its employees be covered by an existing special rate schedule at any time. An authorized agency official in the agency headquarters office must submit to OPM any request to establish or increase special rates for a category of agency employees. The request must include a certification by the authorized agency official that the requested special rates are necessary to ensure adequate staffing levels to accomplish the agency's mission.

(b) The authorized agency official is responsible for submitting complete supporting data for any request for new or higher special rates. OPM may require that the supporting data include a survey of prevailing non-Federal pay rates in the relevant labor market.

(c) OPM may coordinate an agency special rate request with other agencies that have similar categories of employees. OPM may designate a lead agency to assist in coordinating the collection of relevant data. Each affected agency is responsible for submitting complete supporting data upon request to OPM or the lead agency, as appropriate, unless the agency determines that a category of its employees will not be covered by the proposed special rate schedule, as provided in Sec. 530.303(c).

Sec. 530.306 Evaluating agency requests for new or increased special rates.

(a) In evaluating agency requests for new or increased special rates, OPM may consider the following factors:

(1) The number of existing vacant positions and the length of time they have been vacant;

(2) The number of employees who have quit (i.e., voluntarily left Federal service), including, when available, a subcount of the number of employees who quit to take a comparable position offering higher pay;
(3) Evidence to support a conclusion that recruitment or retention problems likely will develop (if such problems do not already exist) or will worsen;
(4) The number of vacancies an agency tried to fill, compared to the number of hires and offers made;
(5) The nature of the existing labor market;
(6) The degree to which an agency has considered and used other available pay flexibilities to alleviate staffing problems, including the superior qualifications and special needs pay-setting authority in 5 C.F.R. § 531.212 and recruitment, relocation, and retention incentives under 5 C.F.R. part 575;
(7) The degree to which an agency has considered relevant non-pay solutions to staffing problems, such as conducting an aggressive recruiting program, using appropriate appointment authorities, redesigning jobs, establishing training programs, and improving working conditions;
(8) The effect of the staffing problem on the agency's mission; and
(9) The level of non-Federal rates paid for comparable positions. Data on non-Federal salary rates may be supplemented, if appropriate, by data on Federal salary rates for comparable positions established under a non-GS pay system.

(b) In determining the level at which to set special rates, OPM may consider the following factors:
(1) The pay levels that, in OPM's judgment, are necessary to recruit or retain an adequate number of qualified employees based on OPM's findings with respect to the factors set forth in paragraph (a) of this section;
(2) The dollar costs that will be incurred if special rates are not authorized;
(3) The level of pay for comparable positions; and
(4) The need to provide for a reasonable progression in pay from lower grade levels to higher grade levels to avoid pay alignment problems (e.g., such as might result from applying the two-step promotion rule in 5 U.S.C. 5334(b)).

(c) No one factor or combination of factors specified in paragraph (a) or (b) of this section requires OPM to establish or increase special rates or to set special rates at any given level.

Sec. 531.608 Relationship of locality rates to other pay rates.

(a) An employee must receive the greatest of the following rates of pay, as applicable--
(1) The scheduled annual rate of pay payable to the employee;
(2) A locality rate under this subpart;
(3) A special rate under 5 C.F.R. part 530, subpart C, or a similar
rate under other legal authority (e.g., 38 U.S.C. 7455); or
(4) A retained rate under 5 C.F.R. part 536 or a similar rate under other legal authority.

(b) A GS employee receiving a special rate is entitled to any applicable locality payment on the same basis as any other GS employee. The locality payment is computed based on the employee's scheduled annual rate of pay, which excludes any special rate. The employee is entitled to the higher of the locality rate or the corresponding special rate. As provided in 5 U.S.C. 5305(h) and 5 CFR 530.303(d), when an employee's locality rate exceeds a corresponding special rate, the employee's entitlement to the special rate is terminated.

Member Beck, Dissenting in Part:

I agree with my colleagues in all but one respect - I disagree that it is necessary to apply the Authority's revised framework (in *U.S. EPA*, 65 FLRA 113, 115 (2010) (Member Beck concurring)) to address the Agency's management's right exception.

The Arbitrator improperly purports to enforce contract language that the Authority has already found to be non-negotiable and an impermissible infringement on management rights. This contract language is therefore, unenforceable, and any arbitral remedy based on it must be vacated.

In *U.S. Dep't of Commerce, Patent & Trademark Office, petition for review dismissed,* 180 F. App'x 176 (D.C. Cir. Mar 21, 2006) (unpublished), 60 FLRA 839 (2005) (*PTO 1*), these same parties fully litigated precisely the same issue that is presented here: Whether the second sentence of Section A.2 was an appropriate arrangement under Section 7106(b)(3) of our Statute. The Authority concluded that this sentence is not an appropriate arrangement and set aside the arbitral award that was based on the sentence. *Id.* at 843. Thus, this Award, to the extent it relies on the second sentence of Section A.2, is precluded by our decision in *PTO 1*.

In *U.S. Dep't of the Air Force, Scott Air Force Base, Ill.*, 35 FLRA 978 (1990) (*Scott AFB*), the Authority determined that collateral estoppel applies when five requirements are satisfied:

(1) the same issue is involved in both cases;
(2) the same issue was litigated in the first case;
(3) the resolution of the issue was necessary to the decision in the first case;
(4) the prior decision is final; and
(5) the parties were fully represented at the prior hearing.

Scott AFB, 35 FLRA at 982-83. While the Agency does not use the specific term "collateral estoppel" in its arguments here, the arbitral proceedings and the Agency's exceptions are rife with collateral estoppel implications. Both parties and the Arbitrator recognized the implications of the Authority's prior decision (Award, at 19-20, 24, 25-26, 29), and the Agency addressed the impact of that decision throughout its exceptions. Agency Exceptions, at 5-7, 12, 29-30. Further, the Authority has applied the principle of collateral estoppel to such situations when, as here, an Arbitrator "expressly ignore[s]" a prior finding and makes "his own determinations on the same issues." *See Scott AFB,* 35 FLRA at 984.

It is plain to me that the Authority cannot permit an arbitrator to enforce contract language that the Authority has previously determined - after the question has been fully litigated by the same parties - to be unenforceable. Consequently, to the extent that the award is based on the second sentence of Section A.2, the award must be vacated.

65 FLRA No. 63

NATIONAL TREASURY
EMPLOYEES UNION
(Union)

and

FEDERAL DEPOSIT INSURANCE
CORPORATION
(Agency)

0-AR-4286

DECISION

December 6, 2010

Before the Authority: Carol Waller Pope, Chairman, and Thomas M. Beck and Ernest DuBester, Members

I. Statement of the Case

This matter is before the Authority on exceptions to an award of Arbitrator Jerome H. Ross filed by the Union under § 7122(a) of the Federal Service Labor-Management Relations Statute (the Statute) and part 2425 of the Authority's Regulations. The Agency filed an opposition to the Union's exceptions, and both parties filed supplemental submissions, which are discussed further below.

The Arbitrator found that the Agency's distribution of certain awards did not violate Title VII of the Civil Rights Act of 1964 (Title VII), the Age Discrimination in Employment Act (ADEA), or Agency Circular 2420.1 (Circular).

For the reasons that follow, we deny the Union's exceptions in part and remand the award in connection with the remaining exceptions.

II. Background and Arbitrator's Award

The Agency and Union negotiated the terms of an employee-reward program called the "Corporate Success Awards" (CSAs),[1] as well as the Circular and a memorandum of understanding (MOU) concerning the program.[2] The Union filed a grievance alleging that the Agency distributed CSAs in a manner that violated antidiscrimination statutes and provisions of the Circular and MOU, which require fair and equitable CSA distributions.[3] *See* Award at 2. When the grievance was unresolved, the parties proceeded to arbitration, where the Arbitrator framed the issue as follows: "Did the [Agency] violate Title VII . . ., the [ADEA,] or the 'fair and equitable' provision of [the] Circular . . . in its implementation of the [CSA] program for contribution year 2004?" *Id.* at 8.

The Union contended, on the basis of statistical analyses, that the "'subjective and undisciplined' procedures to select the employees to receive awards" resulted in an underrepresentation of certain employee groups among CSA recipients. *Id.* at 8-9. Specifically, the Union alleged that the award distributions resulted in statistically significant disparities in the awards received by eligible: (1) African-American and Hispanic employees, as compared to white employees; (2) employees forty years of age or older (forty-plus employees), as compared to those younger than forty; and (3) employees working at grade-level twelve and below, as compared to those working at grade-level thirteen and above. The Union argued that: (1) each of these group disparities violated the MOU and Circular; (2) the disparate impact on African-American and Hispanic employees violated Title VII; and (3) the disparate impact on forty-plus employees violated the ADEA. *Id.* at 8-10. The Agency disputed the Union's characterization of the awards process as subjective and undisciplined, as well as the significance and reliability of the Union's statistical analyses. *Id.* at 6-8.

Addressing the Union's Title VII and ADEA disparate-impact claims, the Arbitrator explained that, although he was "not prepared to resolve . . . th[e] dispute between the parties over the statistical

---

1. The Circular describes a CSA as "an annual award that provides for a 3.0 percent increase in basic pay . . . for those employees who are recognized as the top contributors within the [Agency]." Exceptions, Attach. C-6 (Joint Ex. 6-C: Circular 2420.1, § 11-1). In addition, the Circular states that CSAs "shall be distributed to employees in a fair and equitable manner." *Id.*

2. Although the Circular existed prior to the MOU, the parties negotiated revisions to the Circular in conjunction with the MOU. Acknowledging that both documents reflect the terms of the parties' agreement regarding CSAs, "[t]he MOU provides, in section 1, 'CSAs will be distributed to employees in a fair and equitable manner, and in accordance with the terms of this MOU and [the] Circular[.]'" Award at 2.

3. *See supra* notes 1 and 2 for the relevant Circular and MOU language.

tests applied[,] . . . it may not be unreasonable to conclude that [the Union's] analys[e]s disclose[] sufficient evidence of disparate impact ... with respect to selection of African-Americans, [forty-plus employees], and perhaps Hispanic employees" to establish *prima facie* cases for those claims. *Id.* at 14. On the basis of these "not ... unreasonable" conclusions, the Arbitrator "assum[ed], *arguendo*, that the record support[ed]" the Union's *prima facie* cases of disparate impact with regard to African-American, Hispanic, and forty-plus employees. *Id.* at 14-15, 17.

Proceeding to the next stage of the disparate-impact analysis under Title VII, the Arbitrator found that, in response to a *prima facie* showing, the Agency need only "produce evidence of a business necessity" to account for any disparities in the CSA distributions. *Id.* at 17. However, the Arbitrator did not determine whether the Agency had satisfied this burden. *Id.* Rather, he concluded that the "criteria to which the parties agreed [in the MOU, for the allocation of CSAs] . . . are general and less than specific. . . . [T]hey cry out for subjective evaluation. . . . Accordingly, little standardization could be expected[,] and a subjective process was logical and reasonable." *Id.* at 18.

Moving to the ADEA claim, the Arbitrator found that, in response to a *prima facie* showing, "the nature of [the Agency's] rebuttal is to present reasonable factors other than age [(RFOAs)] as possible bases for the disparate impact[,]" and he concluded that the Agency's "business objective[] . . . of identifying and rewarding top contributors was a legitimate goal, agreed to by the [Union in] . . . the MOU and . . . [the] Circular[.]" *Id.* at 18-19. As for the means that the Agency used to pursue that goal, the Arbitrator determined that "[o]nce the parties jointly agreed to the subjective course inherent in the [CSA] criteria, the argument that the process" produced unreasonably subjective outcomes "is not compelling." *Id.* at 19.

With respect to the Union's contention that CSA distributions underrepresented employees working at grade-level twelve and below, the Arbitrator determined that this complaint was "based on [an alleged violation of] the fair and equitable provision of [the] Circular[.]" *Id.* at 21. Although he found that "the data may well reflect a disparate impact" on employees working at grade-level twelve and below, the Arbitrator also concluded that the Union "offered no basis for defining the two groups for comparison purposes" at the "[grade-]level 12/13 breaking point[.]" *Id.* Because he found that the Union's chosen "breaking point" was "arbitrary," the Arbitrator determined that the resulting disparate-impact analysis "does not support a conclusion . . . that . . . the CSA selection process was . . . [un]fair [or in]equitable[,] in violation of [the] Circular[.]" *Id.*

Therefore, the Arbitrator denied the grievance as to all claims.

III. Positions of the Parties

A. Union's Exceptions

The Union argues that the Arbitrator erred by holding that, under Title VII, the Agency need only "produc[e] evidence" – but need not satisfy a burden of persuasion – to justify a racially disparate distribution of CSAs. Exceptions at 31, 36-38. In addition, the Union asserts that it was legal error for the Arbitrator to: (1) consider the MOU when determining the lawfulness of the CSA process, as employers cannot "rely on ... collective bargaining agreements to defend employment practices" against Title VII claims, *see id.* at 32, 43-45 (citing *Zipes v. Trans World Airlines, Inc.*, 455 U.S. 385 (1982); *Alexander v. Gardner-Denver Co.*, 415 U.S. 36 (1974) (*Alexander*)); and (2) conclude that the awards process was "job related" and consistent with "business necessity" merely because it seemed "logical" or "reasonable," *see id.* at 33, 46-48 (citing *Smith v. City of Jackson*, 544 U.S. 228 (2005) (*City of Jackson*); *N.Y.C. Transit Auth. v. Beazer*, 440 U.S. 568 (1979); *Albemarle Paper Co. v. Moody*, 422 U.S. 405 (1975) (*Albemarle*)). Consequently, the Union requests that the Authority find that the Arbitrator misallocated the parties' burdens under Title VII and that the Agency failed to establish that the CSA criteria and distribution processes were job related and consistent with business necessity. *Id.* at 33, 37-38, 48, 55-56 (citing 42 U.S.C. § 2000e-2(k)(1)(A)(i)[4]).

4. 42 U.S.C. § 2000e-2(k)(1)(A)(i) provides, in pertinent part:

> An unlawful employment practice based on disparate impact is established . . . if . . . a complaining party demonstrates that a[n employer] uses a particular employment practice that causes a disparate impact . . . and the [employer] fails to demonstrate that the challenged practice is job related for the position in question and consistent with business necessity[.]

Further, the Union asserts that the Arbitrator erred in determining whether the CSAs' disparate impact on forty-plus employees was justified by a "business necessity" or based on "reasonable factors other than age." *Id.* at 34, 56-59 (citing 29 U.S.C. §§ 623(a), 623(f)(1), 633a[5]). In this regard, the Union contends that, under the ADEA, it was legal error for the Arbitrator to: (1) rely upon the MOU to deny the claim; and (2) find that the subjective criteria and process for CSA distributions were "reasonable means" to serve a "legitimate goal" of the Agency, without conducting "an independent review of the reasonableness" of the Agency's methods. *Id.* at 57-59.

Moreover, the Union contends that the Arbitrator found that the Agency did not violate the "fair and equitable" provisions of the MOU and the Circular, and, according to the Union, this finding fails to draw its essence from those provisions because it disregards a provision of the MOU in which the Union reserved a right to challenge the implementation of CSA criteria.[6] *See id.* at 63-64. Finally, the Union contends that the Arbitrator's rejection of its claim that employees working at grade-level twelve and below "did not receive fair and equitable treatment" is based on the nonfact that the Union arbitrarily selected a breaking point for comparing lower and higher grade-level employees. *Id.* at 65-66.

B. Agency's Opposition

According to the Agency, because the Union "negotiated the terms of the CSA program . . . [and], in particular, the MOU and the Circular, the Union should be precluded from taking positions that are inconsistent with th[ose] agreements." Opp'n at 13 n.19. The Agency argues that the decisions cited by the Union fail to establish that a bargaining party may challenge the very agreement that it negotiated, where that agreement is not discriminatory on its face. *See id.* at 13-14.

The Agency contends that the Arbitrator properly applied Title VII standards. Specifically, the Agency contends that the Arbitrator found that: (1) the Agency "demonstrate[d] that the implementation of the CSA program was . . . consistent with a business necessity[;]" and (2) the CSA criteria were job related because they required that awards for "employee[s'] achievements reflect[] important contributions to the Agency." *Id.* at 5, 9-12.

With regard to the Union's claim that the award is contrary to the ADEA, the Agency contends that the claim ignores the Arbitrator's conclusion that the

---

5. 29 U.S.C. § 623 provides, in pertinent part:

§ 623. Prohibition of age discrimination

(a) Employer practices

It shall be unlawful for an employer –

(1) to . . . discriminate against any individual with respect to his compensation, terms, conditions, or privileges of employment, because of such individual's age; [or]

(2) to limit, segregate, or classify his employees in any way which would deprive or tend to deprive any individual of employment opportunities or otherwise adversely affect his status as an employee, because of such individual's age. . . .

. . . .

(f) Lawful practices; age an occupational qualification; other reasonable factors[.]

It shall not be unlawful for an employer . . . or labor organization –

(1) to take any action otherwise prohibited . . . where the differentiation is based on reasonable factors other than age . . . .

29 U.S.C. § 633a provides, in pertinent part:

§ 633a. Nondiscrimination on account of age in Federal Government employment

(a) Federal agencies affected

All personnel actions affecting employees . . . at least 40 years of age . . . in executive agencies . . . shall be made free from any discrimination based on age.

. . . .

(e) Duty of Government agency or official

Nothing contained in this section shall relieve any Government agency or official of the responsibility to assure nondiscrimination on account of age in employment as required under any provision of Federal law.

(f) Applicability of statutory provisions to personnel action of Federal departments, etc.

Any personnel action of any department [or] agency . . . referred to in subsection (a) of this section shall not be subject to, or affected by, any provision of [the ADEA], other than . . . the provisions of this section.

6. The MOU provides that, although the parties agree to a joint-review process for determining whether statistical disparities in CSA distributions "can be justified by a legitimate business reason or explained by the size(s) of the group(s) being compared[,] . . . this joint[-]review process does not waive the right of the Union or any employee to seek remedial relief in any appropriate legal forum." Exceptions, Attach. C-6 (Joint Ex. 6-B: MOU between FDIC & NTEU, cl. 3).

CSA process "for identifying and rewarding top contributors 'was a reasonable means to meet' the [Agency's] business objectives[.]" *Id.* at 16. The Agency further contends that it was the Union's "burden [to] show[] that the basis for the [Agency's] age neutral practices was unreasonable." *Id.* at 17-18 (citing *City of Jackson*, 544 U.S. at 242-43).

Responding to the Union's essence claim, the Agency argues that the Union is impermissibly attempting to relitigate contract-interpretation issues, despite the Arbitrator's finding that the CSA distributions were "fair and equitable." *Id.* at 18.

IV. Preliminary Matter: The Parties' Supplemental Submissions

The parties' supplemental submissions include: (1) the Union's reply (Union's reply) to the Agency's opposition to the exceptions; and (2) the Agency's opposition to the Union's reply (Agency's opposition to reply), in which the Agency contends that the Authority should not consider the Union's reply.

In addition, the parties' filed several submissions concerning a late-developing Supreme Court decision. In this regard, the Union's exceptions cited a decision of the United States Court of Appeals for the Second Circuit – *Meacham v. Knolls Atomic Power Laboratory*, 461 F.3d 134, 141-42 (2d Cir. 2006) (*Knolls*). Exceptions at 59-61. The Agency's opposition disputed the Union's characterization of *Knolls*. *See* Opp'n at 17 n.24. While the parties' dispute was pending before the Authority, the Supreme Court granted certiorari to review *Knolls*. *See* 552 U.S. 1162 (2008), *granting cert. to Knolls*, 461 F.3d 134. The Court ultimately vacated the Second Circuit's judgment. *See Meacham v. Knolls Atomic Power Lab.*, 554 U.S. 84 (2008) (*Meacham*), *vacating Knolls*, 461 F.3d 134. In connection with those legal developments, the parties filed the following supplemental submissions: (1) from the Union, a notice that the Supreme Court granted certiorari to review *Knolls*, *see* Notice of Recent Development (Jan. 25, 2008) (certiorari notice); (2) from the Union, a copy of the Supreme Court's decision in *Meacham* (decision text); (3) the Union's arguments as to how *Meacham* should affect the Authority's evaluation of the exceptions and opposition, *see* Notice of Relevant Development (June 23, 2008) at 1-2 (Union's *Meacham* arguments); and (4) the Agency's response to the Union's *Meacham* arguments, *see* Agency Response to Union's Notice of Relevant Development (July 1, 2008) (Agency's *Meacham* response). To summarize, the parties have filed six supplemental submissions: the Union's reply, the Agency's opposition to reply, and four submissions concerning *Meacham*.

Although the Authority's Regulations do not provide for the filing of supplemental submissions, § 2429.26 provides that the Authority may, in its discretion, grant leave to file "other documents" as deemed appropriate. *E.g.*, *Cong. Research Emps. Ass'n, IFPTE, Local 75*, 59 FLRA 994, 999 (2004) (*Cong. Research*). A filing party must demonstrate why its supplemental submission should be considered. *NTEU, Chapter 98*, 60 FLRA 448, 448 n.2 (2004). For example, the Authority has granted leave to file other documents where the supplemental submission responds to issues raised for the first time in an opposing party's filing. *See Cong. Research*, 59 FLRA at 999. Parties have also been granted leave to address the applicability of court decisions that issued while the parties' dispute was pending before the Authority. *E.g.*, *U.S. Dep't of Justice, Fed. Bureau of Prisons, Metro. Corr. Ctr., Chi., Ill.*, 63 FLRA 423, 423 n.1 (2009) (*Metro. Corr. Ctr.*) (citing *U.S. Customs Serv.*, 46 FLRA 1080, 1080 n.1 (1992)).[7]

However, where a party seeks to raise issues that it could have addressed in a previous submission, the Authority ordinarily denies requests to file a supplemental submission concerning those issues. *See, e.g.*, *U.S. Dep't of the Army, Corps of Eng'rs, Portland Dist.*, 61 FLRA 599, 601 (2006) (*Corps of Eng'rs*), *recons. denied*, 62 FLRA 97 (2007).[8] Finally, the Authority has denied requests for leave to file supplemental submissions on the basis of a party's contention that a party-opponent mischaracterized the party's position or misstated matters of law. *See Bremerton Metal Trades Council*, 64 FLRA 103, 104 (2009); *U.S. Dep't of the*

---

7. *But see U.S. Dep't of the Interior, Bureau of Reclamation, Mo. Basin Region*, 42 FLRA 820, 820 n.1 (1991) (finding "no circumstances warranting" consideration of supplemental submissions concerning decisions issued while parties' dispute was pending before Authority, but noting that Authority was "cognizant of the case law cited" in those submissions). As evidenced by *Metro. Corr. Ctr.*, the Authority's more recent practice has been to grant requests for leave to file arguments regarding relevant, intervening court decisions. 63 FLRA at 423 n.1.

8. However, the Authority has granted leave for a party to supplement its arguments in support of exceptions to an arbitration award, where the supplemental submission concerned a decision that issued one day before the party filed the exceptions. *See U.S. Dep't of HUD, Denver, Colo.*, 53 FLRA 1301, 1302 n.1, 1308-09 & n.6 (1998).

Navy, Naval Sea Sys. Command, 57 FLRA 543, 543 n.1 (2001) (*Naval Sea Sys. Command*).

A. Union Reply

The Union asserts that the Authority should consider its reply because: (1) the opposition "acknowledge[s], for the first time" that the Agency bore the burden of persuasion as to the business necessity of CSA processes resulting in disparate impact, Mot. for Leave to File Mem. in Reply at 2; (2) the opposition allegedly contains "a number of significant misstatements of the governing law[,]" *id.*; and (3) the matters in dispute "involve[] a number of complex legal issues . . . of first impression[,]" *id.* at 3.

The Union essentially requests leave to reiterate and elaborate its arguments regarding the burdens that parties bear in disparate-impact cases. However, the Union already had an opportunity to – and did in fact – address those issues in its exceptions. *See Corps of Eng'rs*, 61 FLRA at 601. Moreover, although the Union contends that the opposition contains "misstatements," Mot. for Leave to File Mem. in Reply at 2, such allegations do not merit granting leave to file a supplemental submission. *See Naval Sea Sys. Command*, 57 FLRA at 543 n.1. Finally, the Union has already been afforded an adequate opportunity to address the case's complexities. *See Corps of Eng'rs*, 61 FLRA at 601. Accordingly, we find that the Union has not demonstrated that its reply should be considered, and, therefore, we decline to consider it.[9] *See NTEU, Chapter 98*, 60 FLRA 448, 448 n.2 (2004).

B. Submissions Concerning *Meacham*

Although the Union filed both the *Meacham* decision text and its *Meacham* arguments, the Union did not request leave to file either submission. Similarly, the Agency did not request leave to file its *Meacham* response. Consistent with Authority precedent, the *Meacham* decision text and the holding reflected therein will be considered, to the extent appropriate, in resolving the exceptions. *See Metro. Corr. Ctr.*, 63 FLRA at 423 n.1. However, as leave was not requested to file the Union's *Meacham* arguments or the Agency's *Meacham* response, we decline to consider those submissions.[10] *See* 5 C.F.R. § 2429.26.

V. Analysis and Conclusions

A. The award is remanded with respect to the Arbitrator's findings regarding Title VII and the ADEA.

The Union argues that the award is contrary to Title VII and the ADEA. When an exception involves an award's consistency with law, the Authority reviews any question of law raised by the exception and the award de novo. *See NTEU, Chapter 24*, 50 FLRA 330, 332 (1995) (citing *U.S. Customs Serv. v. FLRA*, 43 F.3d 682, 686-87 (D.C. Cir. 1994)). In applying the standard of de novo review, the Authority assesses whether an arbitrator's legal conclusions are consistent with the applicable standard of law. *See U.S. Dep't of Def., Dep'ts of the Army & the Air Force, Ala. Nat'l Guard, Northport, Ala.*, 55 FLRA 37, 40 (1998) (*Ala. Nat'l Guard*). In making that assessment, the Authority defers to the arbitrator's underlying factual findings. *Id.*

As an initial matter, the Agency asserts that, because the Union agreed to the CSA criteria, the Union may not contest the award's determination that CSA distributions complied with Title VII and the ADEA. Opp'n at 13 & n.19. In effect, the Agency contends that the Union may not challenge the Agency's distribution of CSAs because the Union bargained for the MOU and Circular addressing CSAs.

"Title VII . . . concerns . . . an individual's right to equal employment opportunities. Title VII's strictures are *absolute* . . . . *Of necessity, the rights conferred can form no part of the collective-bargaining process* . . . ." *Alexander*, 415 U.S. at 51 (emphasis added). Thus, "[r]ights established under Title VII . . . are 'not rights which can be bargained away – either by a union, by an employer, or by both acting in concert[.]'" *Laffey v. Nw. Airlines, Inc.*, 567 F.2d 429, 447 (D.C. Cir. 1976) (quoting *Robinson v. Lorillard Corp.*, 444 F.2d 791, 799 (4th Cir. 1971) (*Robinson*)); *see also Grant v. Bethlehem Steel Corp.*, 635 F.2d 1007, 1014 (2d Cir. 1980) (*Bethlehem Steel*); *United States v. Allegheny-Ludlum Indus., Inc.*, 517 F.2d 826, 857 (5th Cir. 1975) ("Arbitration is a collective right; a Title VII cause of action is a personal right."); *United States v.*

9. Given this finding, the Agency's opposition to reply is moot, and we do not consider it. *See IBEW, Local 121*, 56 FLRA 1019, 1019 (2000) (declining to consider agency's response to union's unsolicited supplemental submission because supplemental submission itself would not be considered).

10. In light of the Supreme Court's decision in *Meacham*, as well as our consideration of that decision, the certiorari notice is moot, and we do not consider it.

N.L. Indus., Inc., 479 F.2d 354, 379 (8th Cir. 1973) (*N.L. Indus.*). In addition, as relevant here, decisions confirming the inalienability of Title VII rights also apply to similar ADEA rights. *See Trans World Airlines v. Thurston*, 469 U.S. 111, 121 (1985) (*Thurston*); *see also U.S. EEOC v. Calumet Cnty.*, 686 F.2d 1249, 1256 (7th Cir. 1982) ("[T]he decision in *Alexander* extends to the ADEA."). As employees' statutory EEO rights cannot be bargained away, and because employers may not rely on labor agreements to immunize their actions from Title VII or ADEA claims, we find that the Union is not prohibited from excepting to the award's legal determinations regarding CSA distributions. *See Alexander*, 415 U.S. at 51.

1. Parties' Burdens Under Title VII and the ADEA

Turning to the merits of the exceptions, as relevant here, Title VII and the ADEA require disparate-impact claimants to satisfy the same *prima facie* burden. "[T]o establish a *prima facie* case of [disparate-impact] discrimination, a [claimant] need only show that the facially neutral standards in question [result] in a significantly discriminatory pattern." *Dothard v. Rawlinson*, 433 U.S. 321, 329 (1977) (*Dothard*) (citing *Griggs v. Duke Power Co.*, 401 U.S. 424, 432 (1971) (*Griggs*)).

After the *prima facie* stage, Title VII and ADEA disparate-impact analyses differ. *See Gross v. FBL Fin. Servs., Inc.*, 129 S. Ct. 2343 (2009). Under Title VII, "[o]nce it is . . . shown that the [challenged] employment standards are discriminatory in effect, the employer [must defend those standards by] 'showing that any given requirement [has] . . . a manifest relationship to the employment in question.'" *Dothard*, 433 U.S. at 329 (quoting *Griggs*, 401 U.S. at 432). In particular, and as relevant here, in response to a Title VII *prima facie* showing, the employer must establish that the challenged standard or practice manifestly relates to the employment in question by "demonstrating" (i.e., proving) its job relatedness and consistency with business necessity. 42 U.S.C. § 2000e-2(k)(1)(A)(i), (B)(ii), *as extended to employees of the fed. gov't*, 42 U.S.C. § 2000e-16.[11] In this context, the "term 'demonstrates' means meets the burdens of production *and persuasion*." 42 U.S.C. § 2000e(m) (emphasis added), *as extended to employees of the fed. gov't*, 42 U.S.C. § 2000e-16.[12]

Although, as relevant here, an employer's only available defense to a Title VII disparate-impact claim is to prove that a challenged standard is job related and consistent with business necessity, potential defenses to an ADEA disparate-impact claim are not so limited.[13] Specifically, in response

11. *See supra* note 4 for the relevant language of 42 U.S.C. § 2000e-2(k)(1)(A)(i).

In pertinent part, 42 U.S.C. § 2000e-2(k)(1)(B)(ii) provides:

> If [an employer] demonstrates that a specific employment practice does not cause the disparate impact, the [employer] shall not be required to demonstrate that such practice is required by business necessity.

42 U.S.C. § 2000e-16 provides, in pertinent part:

> (a) Discriminatory practices prohibited; employees . . . subject to coverage
>
> All personnel actions affecting employees . . . in executive agencies . . . shall be made free from any discrimination based on race, color[,] . . . or national origin.
>
> . . . .
>
> (e) Government agency or official not relieved of responsibility to assure nondiscrimination in employment or equal employment opportunity
>
> Nothing contained in this Act shall relieve any Government agency or official of its or his primary responsibility to assure nondiscrimination in employment as required by the Constitution and statutes[,] or of its or his responsibilities under Executive Order 11478 relating to equal employment opportunity in the Federal Government.

12. To satisfy this burden, an employer must demonstrate more than a legitimate "business purpose" or "legitimate, nondiscriminatory reason" for the challenged practice or standard. *N.L. Indus.*, 479 F.2d at 365-66; *Bethlehem Steel*, 635 F.2d at 1015-17. Although each case must be evaluated on its particulars, demonstrations of business necessity may involve: (1) evidencing a strong correlation between a requirement and "highly effective [job] performance[,]" *Griggs*, 401 U.S. at 431-34; (2) establishing that a practice is essential for the safety and efficiency of business, *e.g.*, *Robinson*, 444 F.2d at 798; or (3) verifying, through an expert validation study, that evaluative criteria predict actual on-the-job performance or otherwise comply with the EEOC's Uniform Guidelines on Employee Selection Procedures, 29 C.F.R. pt. 1607. *See Albermarle*, 422 U.S. at 431 (finding validation study defective).

13. Just as in Title VII cases, an employer may defend against an ADEA disparate-impact claim by demonstrating job relatedness and business necessity. However, the Agency did not rely upon such a defense in this case; thus, we do not further address this defense in connection with the ADEA.

to an ADEA *prima facie* disparate-impact showing, an employer may defend "otherwise prohibited" employment actions by demonstrating that the "differentiation [of forty-plus employees and younger employees] is based on [RFOAs.]"[14] 29 U.S.C. § 623(f)(1).

2. Arbitrator's Application of Parties' Title VII and ADEA Burdens

With regard to Title VII, after noting that the Union had "argue[d] that the [Agency] is required to 'prove' a business necessity[,]" the Arbitrator stated that the Union "appears to overstate the [Agency]'s burden." Award at 17. The Arbitrator also stated that the Agency, as an employer, need only "produce evidence of business necessity." *Id.* As the Agency had a burden of persuasion – not merely a burden of production – concerning job relatedness and business necessity, *see* 42 U.S.C. §§ 2000e-2(k)(1)(A)(i), 2000e(m), *as extended to employees of the fed. gov't*, 42 U.S.C. § 2000e-16, the Arbitrator erred as a matter of law in this respect.

In addition, even if the Arbitrator had properly set forth the Title VII burdens, the Arbitrator also improperly considered the parties' collective bargaining agreements as evidence of job relatedness and business necessity. For the same reasons that the parties' agreement to the MOU and Circular cannot prohibit the Union from filing contrary-to-law exceptions, *see supra* Part V.A., the fact that the parties agreed to CSA criteria is irrelevant to determining whether they satisfied their respective burdens. Thus, the Arbitrator erred as a matter of law in treating the MOU and Circular as evidence that the Agency had satisfied its burden of proof.[15]

Similarly, with respect to the ADEA, the fact that the Union and Agency agreed to CSA criteria is not a legally permissible basis for: (1) rejecting employees' EEO claims; or (2) finding that the Agency satisfied its statutory burden. *See Thurston*, 469 U.S. at 121; *Alexander*, 415 U.S. at 51. Moreover, as discussed previously, after the award issued, the Supreme Court clarified that an employer bears a burden of persuasion regarding RFOAs. *See Meacham*, 554 U.S. at 91-95. The award is unclear as to whether the Arbitrator held the Agency to a burden of persuasion on the issue of RFOAs. *Compare* Award at 18 ("[T]he nature of [the Agency's] rebuttal is to *present* [RFOAs] as possible bases for the disparate impact." (emphasis added)), *with id.* at 19 ("[T]he [Union's] *argument* that the process reflects that [the Agency's] course was not reasonable . . . *is not compelling*." (emphases added)). However, this ambiguity need not be resolved in order to decide whether to grant the ADEA contrary-to-law exception because, regardless of whether the Arbitrator held the Agency to the proper statutory burden, the Arbitrator erred as a matter of law in relying on the MOU and Circular as the basis for denying the ADEA claims.

Further, with regard to both the Title VII and ADEA claims, the Arbitrator, at the first stage of disparate-impact analysis, *assumed* that the Union met its *prima facie* burdens, and, thus, he did not resolve the parties' factual disputes or weigh the evidence presented for and against the statutory claims. Similarly, because he assumed *prima facie* showings, the Arbitrator did not specify which of the parties' statistical analyses, if any, should be credited and why.[16] Therefore, the current record does not

14. We note that there is no dispute in this case that an RFOA affirmative defense is available to federal government employers.

15. As discussed above, the Union's agreement to CSA criteria cannot legitimize subjective employment standards that have a statistically significant disparate impact on protected groups. Consequently: (1) neither the Arbitrator's determination that the CSA criteria "are general[,] less than specific[, and] cry out for subjective evaluation[,]" Award at 14; (2) nor his finding that "little standardization could be expected and a subjective process was logical and reasonable[,]" *id.*, provides a legally cognizable basis for rejecting *statutory* EEO challenges to those standards. *See Alexander*, 415 U.S. at 51; *cf. Watson v. Fort Worth Bank & Trust*, 487 U.S. 977, 990-91 (1988) ("If an employer's undisciplined system of subjective decision[-]making has precisely the same effects as a system pervaded by impermissible intentional discrimination, it is difficult to see why Title VII's proscription against discriminatory actions should not apply.")

16. We note that a statistical report that incorporates data from similarly situated employees at different worksites should normally be considered probative of class-wide disparate impact if the employer uses substantially *similar* standards or practices at those sites, even when different individuals work at each site. *Cf., e.g., EEOC v. Am. Nat'l Bank*, 652 F.2d 1176, 1186 (4th Cir. 1981). *But see* Award at 13 ("[T]he premise of [the] report is questionable[]" because "employees in one division [were not] vying for selection against employees in another division.") Moreover, although the Arbitrator expressed doubts as to the probative value of statistics that aggregate award-distribution rates from different Agency divisions, *see* Award at 13-14, statistical aggregation is often the preferred method for establishing class-wide disparate impact among employees who are similarly situated with respect to the challenged employment standard or practice, but whose work locations or tenures differ. *See, e.g., EEOC v. Atlas Paper Box Co.*, 868 F.2d 1487, 1495

provide a sufficient basis for determining: (1) whether the Union satisfied its *prima facie* statutory burdens; or (2) whether the Agency satisfied its persuasive burdens as to its defenses.

Accordingly, we remand this matter to the parties for resubmission to the Arbitrator, absent settlement, for further findings and application of the proper statutory burdens. In doing so, we emphasize that the Arbitrator must first re-evaluate the evidence and determine whether the Union has satisfied its *prima facie* statutory burdens. *If* the Arbitrator finds that the Union has satisfied those burdens, *then* the Arbitrator must proceed to determine whether the Agency has satisfied its statutory burdens.

B. The award does not fail to draw its essence from the Circular.

The Union contends that the award fails to draw its essence from the "fair and equitable" provisions of the MOU and the Circular because, according to the Union, the Arbitrator erred in finding that the Union had arbitrarily chosen grade-level employee groups for CSA-distribution comparisons.[17] In this regard, the Union argues that the grade-level twelve/thirteen "breaking point" provided the appropriate basis for evaluating whether CSAs were fairly and equitably distributed to employees working at grade-level twelve and below. Exceptions at 66.

In reviewing an arbitrator's interpretation of a collective bargaining agreement, the Authority applies the deferential standard of review that federal courts use in reviewing arbitration awards in the private sector. *See* 5 U.S.C. § 7122(a)(2); *AFGE, Council 220*, 54 FLRA 156, 159 (1998). Under this standard, the Authority will find that an arbitration award is deficient as failing to draw its essence from the collective bargaining agreement when the appealing party establishes that the award: (1) cannot in any rational way be derived from the agreement; (2) is so unfounded in reason and fact and so unconnected with the wording and purposes of the collective bargaining agreement as to manifest an infidelity to the obligation of the arbitrator; (3) does not represent a plausible interpretation of the agreement; or (4) evidences a manifest disregard of the agreement. *See U.S. Dep't of Labor (OSHA)*, 34 FLRA 573, 575 (1990). The Authority and the courts defer to arbitrators in this context "because it is the arbitrator's construction of the agreement for which the parties have bargained." *Id.* at 576.

The Union has not identified a provision of the Circular that supports its contention that the Arbitrator erred in determining that the grade-level twelve-thirteen "breaking point" was an arbitrary basis for comparing CSA distributions among employees working at different grade levels. Exceptions at 66. In addition, the Union fails to identify language in the Circular to support a finding that the Arbitrator's interpretation of the phrase "fair and equitable" was irrational, unfounded, implausible, or in manifest disregard of the Circular. *OSHA*, 34 FLRA at 576. Consequently, we deny the essence exception.

C. The award is not based on a nonfact.

The Union contends that the award is based on a nonfact because the Arbitrator found that the Union's chosen "breaking point" for grade-level comparison groups of employees was arbitrary. Exceptions at 66. To establish that an award is based on a nonfact, the appealing party must show that a central fact underlying the award is clearly erroneous, but for which the arbitrator would have reached a different result. *See NFFE, Local 1984*, 56 FLRA 38, 41 (2000). However, an arbitrator's conclusion that is based on an interpretation of the parties' collective bargaining agreement does not constitute a fact that can be challenged as a nonfact. *See NLRB*, 50 FLRA 88, 92 (1995). As discussed previously, the Arbitrator's determination that the Union selected an arbitrary "breaking point" for comparison groups was based on his interpretation of the Circular – specifically, the Circular provision calling for "fair and equitable" CSA distributions. Award at 21. Such an interpretation does not constitute a fact that can be challenged as a nonfact. *See NLRB*, 50 FLRA at 92. Therefore, we deny the nonfact exception.

VI. Decision

The award is remanded to the parties for resubmission of the Title VII and ADEA claims to the Arbitrator, absent settlement. The remaining exceptions are denied.

(6th Cir. 1989); *Segar v. Smith*, 738 F.2d 1249, 1286 (D.C. Cir. 1984); *Capaci v. Katz & Besthoff, Inc.*, 711 F.2d 647, 654-56 (5th Cir. 1983).

17. As discussed previously, the Arbitrator determined that the Union's complaint regarding the distribution of CSAs to employees working at grade-level twelve and below was "based on [an alleged violation of] the fair and equitable provision of [the] Circular." Award at 21. Thus, the award does not resolve any alleged violations of the MOU, which also contains a "fair and equitable" CSA distribution provision, *supra* note 2. Therefore, we do not further address the Union's exception contending that the award fails to draw its essence from the MOU.

65 FLRA No. 64

UNITED STATES
DEPARTMENT OF DEFENSE
DEFENSE COMMISSARY AGENCY
RANDOLPH AIR FORCE BASE, TEXAS
(Agency)

and

AMERICAN FEDERATION
OF GOVERNMENT EMPLOYEES
LOCAL 1035
(Union)

0-AR-4190

DECISION

December 9, 2010

Before the Authority: Carol Waller Pope, Chairman, and Thomas M. Beck and Ernest DuBester, Members

I. Statement of the Case

This matter is before the Authority on exceptions to an award of Arbitrator Milden J. Fox Jr. filed by the Agency under § 7122(a) of the Federal Service Labor-Management Relations Statute (the Statute) and part 2425 of the Authority's Regulations.[1] The Union filed an opposition to the Agency's exceptions.

As relevant here, the Arbitrator found that the Agency admitted favoritism. For the reasons that follow, we set aside the award.

II. Background and Arbitrator's Award

The grievance alleges that the Agency violated Article 27, Section 2 of the parties' agreement by exhibiting favoritism toward a particular Computer Assisted Ordering Worker (CAO-1) in several respects.[2] The grievance was submitted to arbitration, where the Arbitrator framed the issue as follows: "Did the Agency violate any law, rule, regulation or [c]ontract in the way it treated CAO-1 in comparison to other members of the Randolph Commissary bargaining unit? If so, what, if any, is the remedy?" Award at 17.

The Arbitrator found that the Union "failed to prove that any employee was disadvantaged in a monetary or job performance manner." *Id.* at 26. However, the Arbitrator found that the Agency "admitted . . . that favoritism has taken place." *Id.* Accordingly, the Arbitrator sustained the grievance. *See id.* at 27.

1. The Arbitrator's award resolved three grievances, specifically, grievances pertaining to: (1) alleged Agency favoritism (the favoritism grievance); (2) light duty work for an employee who required safety shoes (the safety shoe grievance); and (3) an employee's termination (the termination grievance). We note that the Authority's Regulations concerning the review of arbitration awards, as well as certain related procedural regulations, were revised effective October 1, 2010. *See* 75 Fed. Reg. 42,283 (2010). As the prior Regulations were in effect during the time period when the parties had the opportunity to file exceptions, we apply the prior Regulations. Applying those Regulations, as the award was served on the parties on December 24, 2006, the thirty-day period for filing exceptions ended on January 22, 2007. *See former* 5 C.F.R. § 2425.1(b) (thirty-day period included date of service of award). As the award was served by regular U.S. mail, five days were added to the filing period, extending the due date until January 27, 2007. *See former* 5 C.F.R. § 2429.22. As that date was a Saturday, the due date was again extended until Monday, January 29, 2007. *See former* 5 C.F.R. § 2429.21. On January 25, 2007, the Agency filed timely exceptions. Although a cover sheet to the exceptions referred to both the favoritism grievance and the safety shoe grievance, the Agency's exceptions addressed only the favoritism grievance. On February 22, 2007, the Authority issued a deficiency order directing the Agency to submit four copies of its exceptions. On February 28, 2007, the Agency responded to the order by resubmitting its original exceptions regarding the favoritism grievance and, for the first time, submitting exceptions regarding the safety shoe grievance. As the latter exceptions were not filed by the January 29, 2007, due date for filing exceptions, those exceptions are untimely, and we do not consider them further. Additionally, as no exceptions were filed regarding the termination grievance, we do not consider that grievance further. Thus, our reference to the "award" herein concerns the award regarding the favoritism grievance.

2. Article 27, Section 2 of the parties' agreement provides that "[a]ll personnel shall be treated with fairness, equity, and dignity in all matters without favoritism or regard to political affiliation, race, color, religion, national origin, sex, marital status, age, or handicapping condition." Award at 5.

III. Positions of the Parties

A. Agency's Exceptions

The Agency contends that the Arbitrator's finding that the Agency admitted that favoritism had occurred is a nonfact. Exceptions at 2. The Agency states that, after the award issued, it contacted the Arbitrator to inquire about the basis for the finding of the admission and the Arbitrator responded that the admission was contained in the Agency's post-hearing brief. *See id.* at 4. In response, the Agency asserts that "[a]t no time did the Agency . . . admit that favoritism had occurred[,]" and contends that it was "not rational to draw an inference from the Agency's brief that it was admitting [to] . . . favoritism[.]" *Id.* The Agency also contends that the award is contrary to the Federal Rules of Evidence insofar as the Arbitrator relied on the Agency's post-hearing brief, as that brief does not constitute evidence. *See id.*

B. Union's Opposition

The Union contends that the Agency's nonfact exception provides no basis for finding the award deficient. In this regard, the Union asserts that the Authority will not find an award deficient on this ground if the alleged nonfact is based on an arbitrator's determination of a factual matter that the parties disputed at arbitration. *See* Opp'n at 2.

IV. Analysis and Conclusions

To establish that an award is based on a nonfact, the appealing party must show that a central fact underlying the award is clearly erroneous, but for which the arbitrator would have reached a different result. *See NFFE, Local 1984*, 56 FLRA 38, 41 (2000). The Authority will not find an award deficient on the basis of an arbitrator's determination of any factual matter that the parties disputed at arbitration. *See id.*

Here, the Arbitrator found that the Agency had admitted favoritism. *See* Award at 26. However, there is nothing in the award, or in the portion of the Agency's post-hearing brief relied on by the Arbitrator, supporting a conclusion that the Agency admitted favoritism. Thus, the finding is clearly erroneous. Moreover, the finding is central to the award. In this regard, the Arbitrator found that the Union did not establish that the Agency acted improperly, "[b]ut it has been admitted by the Agency that favoritism has taken place." *Id.* A review of the award as a whole leads to the conclusion that, but for the Arbitrator's erroneous finding, he would not have found favoritism. In addition, contrary to the Union's assertion, there is no basis to conclude that this particular factual finding — that the Agency conceded favoritism — was disputed below. Therefore, the central fact underlying the award is clearly erroneous, but for which the Arbitrator would have reached a different result. Accordingly, we find that the award is based on a nonfact, and set it aside.[3] *See, e.g., AFGE, Local 507*, 58 FLRA 378, 381 (2003) (Chairman Cabaniss dissenting).

V. Decision

The award is set aside.

3. As we find that the award is based on a nonfact, it is unnecessary to address the Agency's claim that the award is contrary to the Federal Rules of Evidence.

65 FLRA No. 65

NATIONAL LABOR RELATIONS BOARD
WASHINGTON, D.C.
(Respondent)

and

NATIONAL LABOR RELATIONS BOARD
PROFESSIONAL ASSOCIATION
(Charging Party)

WA-CA-09-0326

DECISION AND ORDER

December 14, 2010

Before the Authority: Carol Waller Pope, Chairman, and Thomas M. Beck and Ernest DuBester, Members

I. Statement of the Case

This unfair labor practice (ULP) case is before the Authority on exceptions to the attached decision of the Administrative Law Judge (Judge) filed by the Respondent. The General Counsel filed an opposition to the Respondent's exceptions.

The complaint alleges that the Respondent violated § 7116(a)(1), (5), and (8) of the Federal Service Labor-Management Relations Statute (the Statute) by refusing to bargain with the Union in a consolidated bargaining unit that had previously been certified by the Authority. For the reasons set forth below, we dismiss the complaint.

II. Background and Judge's Decision

A. Background

Prior to the events in this case, the Union was the bargaining representative of two units of employees of the Agency working at its Washington, D.C., headquarters: one unit comprised professional employees working for the National Labor Relations Board (NLRB) Chairman and Members (the Board), and the other comprised professional employees working in the NLRB's Office of the General Counsel (GC). Judge's Decision at 3. The Regional Director (RD) of the Authority's San Francisco Regional Office granted the Union's petition to consolidate the two units. *Id.* After the Respondent filed an Application for Review, the Authority affirmed the RD's decision and found that the proposed consolidated unit was appropriate. *NLRB, Wash., D.C.*, 63 FLRA 47 (2008) (*NLRB II*). Accordingly, the RD certified the Union as the exclusive representative for the consolidated unit. Judge's Decision at 3

Subsequently, the Union requested to bargain with the Agency concerning conditions of employment in the consolidated unit. In response, the Agency advised the Union that it had "elected to test the certification of the unit consolidated by the FLRA[,]" and therefore would "refuse to bargain in the consolidated unit." *Id.* The Agency offered instead to bargain "in separate Board[-]side and GC[-]side units." *Id.* at 3-4.

B. Judge's Decision

Before the Judge, the General Counsel filed a motion for summary judgment, arguing that there was no genuine issue of material fact, and that the undisputed facts warranted a finding that the Respondent had committed a ULP. *Id.* at 2. The Respondent opposed this motion, arguing that the Authority's decision in the underlying representation case improperly forced its Board and GC to act in concert for collective bargaining in violation of §§ 3(d) and 4(a) of the National Labor Relations Act (the Act).[1] *Id.* at 2, 4. The Respondent did not offer any additional evidence or factual allegations beyond those in the underlying representation case. *Id.* at 2.

The Judge stated that the Respondent's "request to reverse the Authority's decision in the [underlying] representation case is properly one that must be made to the Authority itself, or, failing there, to the Court

1. Section 3(d) of the Act pertinently provides: "The [GC] shall exercise general supervision over all attorneys employed by the Board (other than administrative law judges and legal assistants to Board members) and over the officers and employees in the regional offices." 29 U.S.C. § 153(d). Section 4(a) pertinently provides:

> The Board shall appoint . . . such attorneys, examiners, and regional directors, and such other employees as it may from time to time find necessary for the proper performance of its duties. The Board may not employ any attorneys for the purpose of reviewing transcripts of hearings or preparing drafts of opinions except that any attorney employed for assignment as a legal assistant to any Board member may for such Board member review such transcripts and prepare such drafts.

Id. § 154(a).

of Appeals." *Id.* at 5. The Judge found that he was bound to follow the Authority's holding that "a consolidated unit of Board-side and GC-side employees is appropriate." *Id.* (citing *NLRB II*, 63 FLRA at 51-52; *NLRB*, 62 FLRA 25, 31-34 (2007) (*NLRB I*)). Because the Judge found that "[t]he undisputed facts demonstrate that the Union made written requests to bargain with the Agency in the certified consolidated bargaining unit, and that the Agency refused to do so[,]" the Judge found that the Respondent violated § 7116(a)(1), (5), and (8) of the Statute "by refusing to negotiate and by otherwise refusing to accord the Union its statutory status as exclusive bargaining representative of the employees in the consolidated bargaining unit." *Id.* Accordingly, the Judge recommended that the Authority grant the General Counsel's motion for summary judgment. *Id.*

III. Positions of the Parties

A. Respondent's Exceptions

The Respondent asks the Authority to "dismiss the complaint because the unit consolidation decision upon which it relies is fatally flawed." Exceptions at 1.[2] In this regard, the Respondent asserts that the consolidated unit is barred by the explicit separation of supervisory authority over attorneys in the prosecutorial and adjudicatory components of the Agency mandated by §§ 3(d) and 4(a) of the Act. *Id.* at 5-10. Thus, the Respondent urges the Authority to correct its "erroneous decision" in *NLRB II*, 63 FLRA 47, in which the Authority found the consolidated unit to be appropriate. Exceptions at 1.

B. General Counsel's Opposition

The General Counsel asserts that the Judge properly rejected the Respondent's attempts to challenge the underlying certification of the consolidated unit by refusing to bargain. Opp'n at 2. Because the Respondent does not dispute that it refused to bargain with the Union concerning the certified unit, the General Counsel asks the Authority to uphold the Judge's finding that the Respondent violated § 7116(a)(1), (5), and (8) of the Statute. *Id.* at 2, 4.

IV. Analysis and Conclusions

In *NLRB I*, the Authority found that a consolidated unit different from the one in this case – composed of nonprofessional employees of the Board and GC, as well as nonprofessional and professional employees of the GC's regional offices – was appropriate. *See* 62 FLRA at 31-36. The Authority also found that the Respondent violated § 7116(a)(1), (5), and (8) of the Statute by refusing to negotiate with the Union as the exclusive representative of the employees in this consolidated unit in *NLRB, Wash., D.C.*, 63 FLRA 104, 107 (2009), *enforcement denied by NLRB v. FLRA*, 613 F.3d 275 (D.C. Cir. 2010) (*NLRB v. FLRA*).

On appeal, the United States Court of Appeals, District of Columbia Circuit (D.C. Circuit), denied enforcement of the ULP charges in *NLRB, Wash., D.C.*, because the court found that "subjecting the [GC]'s exercise of his supervisory authority to the consent of the Board," by requiring the GC and the Board to negotiate one contract with the consolidated unit, impermissibly interferes with the GC's independent authority. *NLRB v. FLRA*, 613 F.3d at 281. In this regard, the court held that, by providing that the GC "shall exercise general supervision" over all GC-side attorneys, § 3(d) of the Act "makes the [GC] independent of the Board with respect to the 'conditions of employment' that are subject to collective bargaining under § 7102(2) of the Statute." *Id.* at 280. Accordingly, the court held that "the Authority's unit determination conflicts with § 3(d) of the Act[,]" and that, consequently, the Authority "erred in holding the Board engaged in an unfair labor practice when it refused to bargain with the Union over the conditions of employment in that unit." *Id.* at 281, 282.

The consolidated unit at issue in this case comprises the GC and Board professional employees working at the NLRB's headquarters.[3] As relevant here, the Authority relied on *NLRB I* to find that the consolidated unit did not conflict with §§ 3(d) and 4(a) of the Act. *See NLRB II*, 63 FLRA at 51-52. The Authority has held that a respondent may not relitigate a certification in a ULP proceeding absent "new evidence or previously unavailable evidence or special circumstances[.]" *FDIC*, 40 FLRA 775, 782 (1991), *enf'd sub nom. FLRA v. FDIC*, No. 91-1207 (D.C. Cir. Sept. 1, 1992). We conclude that the decision in *NLRB v. FLRA* presents sufficient special

2. The Respondent filed exceptions and a "brief in support of its exceptions" with the Authority. Because the supporting brief contains the Respondent's arguments in detail, we refer to this document as the Respondent's "Exceptions."

3. We leave it to the RD to take appropriate action regarding the unit involved in *NLRB II* consistent with this decision.

circumstances for the Authority to consider the Respondent's admitted refusal to bargain in the context of the D.C. Circuit's holding that the Respondent lawfully refused to bargain with another consolidated unit composed of Board and GC employees because requiring such coordinated collective bargaining conflicted with § 3(d) of the Act. *See* 613 F.3d at 282.

In light of the decision in *NLRB v. FLRA*, and for the reasons discussed therein, we find that the Respondent did not violate the Statute when it refused to bargain with the Union over the conditions of employment in the consolidated bargaining unit. *See id.* Accordingly, the complaint must be dismissed.

V. Order

The complaint is dismissed.

Office of Administrative Law Judges

NATIONAL LABOR RELATIONS BOARD
WASHINGTON, D.C.
Respondent

and

NATIONAL LABOR RELATIONS BOARD
PROFESSIONAL ASSOCIATION
Charging Party

Case No. WA-CA-09-0326

Stephanie Arthur, Esq.
For the General Counsel

Barry F. Smith, Esq.
For the Respondent

Before: RICHARD A. PEARSON
Administrative Law Judge

DECISION ON MOTION FOR SUMMARY JUDGMENT

Statement of the Case

This is an unfair labor practice proceeding under the Federal Service Labor-Management Relations Statute, 5 U.S.C. §§ 7101-7135 (the Statute), and the Rules and Regulations of the Federal Labor Relations Authority (the Authority), 5 C.F.R. part 2423.

On September 3, 2009, the Regional Director of the San Francisco Region of the Authority issued a Complaint and Notice of Hearing, which alleged that the Respondent violated section 7116(a)(1), (5) and (8) of the Statute by refusing to bargain with the Charging Party in a consolidated bargaining unit that had previously been certified. On September 28, 2009, the Respondent filed its Answer, in which it admitted refusing to bargain in the consolidated unit, but denied that it had committed an unfair labor practice or otherwise violated the Statute. In its Answer, the Respondent also asserted as an affirmative defense that the Authority's decision certifying the consolidated unit was legally erroneous.

Subsequently, Counsel for the General Counsel filed a Motion for Summary Judgment, arguing that there was no genuine issue of material fact, and that the undisputed facts warranted a finding that Respondent had committed an unfair labor practice.

Respondent opposed the General Counsel's Motion for Summary Judgment and requested that the Authority set aside its earlier decision approving a consolidated unit. It further moved to incorporate by reference the full record of the underlying representation case, WA-RP-08-0002, into the instant case record, but it did not offer any additional evidence or factual allegations beyond that which was introduced in the representation case. Counsel for the General Counsel has not opposed the Respondent's Motion to Incorporate by Reference.

Based on these pleadings, the Chief Administrative Law Judge issued an Order on October 13, 2009, postponing the hearing indefinitely.

DISCUSSION OF MOTION FOR SUMMARY JUDGMENT

The Authority has held that motions for summary judgment, filed under section 2423.27 of its Regulations, 5 C.F.R. § 2423.27, serve the same purpose, and are governed by the same principles as motions filed in United States District Courts under Rule 56 of the Federal Rules of Civil Procedure. *Department of Veterans Affairs, Veterans Affairs Medical Center, Nashville, Tennessee*, 50 FLRA 220, 222 (1995); *Department of the Navy, U.S. Naval Ordnance Station, Louisville, Kentucky*, 33 FLRA 3, 4-5 (1988). If the pleadings, and additional evidence submitted in support thereof, demonstrate that there is no genuine issue of material fact and that the moving party is entitled to judgment as a matter of law, the motion for summary judgment should be granted. *Id.*

Along with its brief in support of its motion, the General Counsel has offered an affidavit and exhibits to corroborate the factual allegations of the Complaint. The Respondent's supporting brief does not dispute any of the General Counsel's factual allegations, nor does it offer any factual assertions of its own; rather, it disputes the legal arguments on which the Authority's decision in WA-RP-08-0002 was based, and it includes excerpts from the transcript of the representation hearing to support its own legal arguments. Further, as noted above, the Respondent moves to incorporate by reference the record in Case No. WA-RP-08-0002. Although (as I will discuss further below) the Respondent is not entitled to relitigate in this ULP proceeding issues that were or could have been raised in the underlying representation proceeding, the representation case record would be relevant if either party seeks review of the Authority's determination in this case in the United States Court of Appeals. Therefore, Respondent's motion to incorporate is granted.

After fully reviewing the pleadings and the documents in support of and in opposition to the motion for summary judgment, I agree with the General Counsel that there is no genuine issue of material fact in this case. Accordingly, it is appropriate to decide the case on the motion for summary judgment. Based on the entire record, I will summarize the material facts that are not in dispute, and based thereon, I make the following conclusions of law and recommendations.

Findings of Fact

The National Labor Relations Board, Washington, D.C. (Respondent or Agency) is an agency within the meaning of section 7103(a)(3) of the Statute. The National Labor Relations Board Professional Association (Charging Party or Union) is a labor organization within the meaning of section 7103(a)(4) of the Statute.

Prior to the events in this case, the Union was the bargaining representative of two units of employees of the Agency working at its Washington, D.C., headquarters: one unit was composed of professional employees working for the NLRB Chairman and Members, and the other was composed of professional employees working in the Office of the General Counsel. Affidavit of Leslie Rossen at 1, G.C. Exhibit 3 of Motion for Summary Judgment. On October 16, 2007, the Union filed a petition with the Authority seeking to consolidate these two units into one. The petition was docketed as Case No. WA-RP-08-0002. Rossen Affidavit at 1-2.

After holding a hearing, the Regional Director of the Authority's San Francisco Region issued a Decision and Order Granting the Petition for Consolidation. After the Respondent filed an Application for Review, the Authority issued a Decision and Order on Review, in which it affirmed the Regional Director's conclusion that the proposed consolidated unit was appropriate. *National Labor Relations Board, Washington, D.C.*, 63 FLRA 47 (2008). Accordingly, on December 18, 2008, the San Francisco Regional Director certified the Union as the exclusive representative for the consolidated unit, described as follows:

Included: All attorneys and other professionals performing comparable legal work, including permanent part-time employees, and law student employees (Student Assistants), in the Headquarters Office of the National Labor Relations Board and the Office of the General Counsel.

Excluded: Law students holding summer appointments and those on work-study programs; nonprofessional employees; management officials; supervisors; and employees described in 5 U.S.C. § 7112(b)(2), (3), (4), (6) and (7).

Exhibit A of Rossen Affidavit.

On March 5, 6, and 13, 2009, the Union requested to bargain with the Agency "in the certified bargaining unit" concerning quality step increases and a proposed revision to the Agency's information technology policy. Rossen Affidavit at 2-3; Exhibits B and C of Rossen Affidavit. On March 16, 2009, Lee Clark, the Agency's Chief of the Labor Relations Section, advised the Union that the Agency "has elected to test the certification of the unit consolidated by the FLRA", and that the Agency therefore would "refuse to bargain in the consolidated unit." Exhibit D of Rossen Affidavit. Clark offered instead to bargain "in separate Board side and GC side units." *Id.* Since that date, the Agency has not bargained with the Union regarding working conditions in the consolidated unit. Rossen Affidavit at 3.

DISCUSSION AND CONCLUSIONS

Positions of the Parties

The General Counsel notes first that the Respondent has admitted it is refusing to bargain with the Union in the consolidated unit that was recently certified by the Authority. The G.C. submits not only that the facts of this case are not in dispute, but that the unlawfulness of the Respondent's actions is also undisputed. The Respondent is knowingly defying the decision and order of the Authority in order to test the legal soundness of that decision in court; therefore, the G.C. argues that Respondent has clearly violated section 7116(a)(1), (5) and (8) of the Statute.

According to the General Counsel, the Respondent has defended its actions by attacking the Authority's decision in the representation case, reasserting the same arguments against a consolidated unit of Board-side and GC-side employees that it made in the representation case. The General Counsel cites *Federal Deposit Insurance Corporation,* 40 FLRA 775 (1991), *enf'd sub nom. FLRA v. Federal Deposit Insurance Corporation,* No. 91-1207 (D.C. Cir. Sept. 1, 1992)(*FDIC*), which applied similar principles from NLRB case law governing private sector labor relations. *See, e.g., Fred's Inc.,* 343 NLRB 138 (2004); *Texas Industries, Inc.,* 199 NLRB 671, 672 (1972). In both the private sector and in cases involving federal employees and agencies, a respondent in an unfair labor practice proceeding is not entitled to relitigate issues that were or could have been litigated in the underlying representation proceeding, absent newly discovered or previously unavailable evidence or special circumstances. *FDIC*, 40 FLRA at 782. Since the Respondent here has not offered any such evidence or demonstrated special circumstances, the General Counsel submits that it has violated section 7116(a)(1), (5) and (8) of the Statute, and urges that it be ordered to recognize and bargain with the Union on matters affecting the consolidated bargaining unit.

The Respondent argues that the Authority's decision in the underlying representation case improperly forces its Board and General Counsel to act in concert for collective bargaining, something that is contrary to sections 3(d) and 4(a) of the National Labor Relations Act, as amended, and that compromises the "complete separation" of the Agency's General Counsel and Board. The Authority has failed to give deference to the Respondent's longstanding interpretation of its own organic statute, and it has misinterpreted the Respondent's history of cooperative bargaining in the separate Board-side and GC-side units. While cooperative bargaining maintained the separation of the two entities within the Agency, Respondent insists that consolidation of the two units cannot similarly guarantee their independence. As a result, the Authority's representation decision creates a conflict between the National Labor Relations Act and the Statute, contrary to established rules of statutory construction. *Morton v. Mancari*, 417 U.S. 535, 549-51 (1974). Respondent urges that the

Authority reverse its previous decision and set aside the certification of the consolidated unit.

Analysis

Although the Respondent presents a lengthy and impassioned legal argument, it is asking me to do something that is not within my authority. Its request to reverse the Authority's decision in the representation case is properly one that must be made to the Authority itself, or, failing there, to the Court of Appeals. For my part, I must follow the Authority's decisions in this and similar cases, and the Authority has been quite consistent in holding that a consolidated unit of Board-side and GC-side employees is appropriate. *National Labor Relations Board, Washington, D.C.*, 63 FLRA 47, 51-52 (2008); *see also National Labor Relations Board,* 62 FLRA 25, 31-34 (2007)(representation case involving the consolidation of four other bargaining units of Respondent's employees, represented by a different union); *National Labor Relations Board, Washington, D.C.*, 63 FLRA 104, 107 (2009), *appeal docketed,* No. 09-1119 (D.C. Cir. 2009).

My discretion is even further constrained by the principles set forth in *FDIC, supra*, 40 FLRA at 782, which in turn follows the NLRB's own precedent regarding challenges to a union's certification in an unfair labor practice proceeding. *Texas Industries, Inc., supra,* 199 NLRB at 672. As the Authority stated most recently, "a respondent in a ULP proceeding is not entitled to relitigate issues that were or could have been litigated in a prior representation proceeding absent newly discovered or previously unavailable evidence or special circumstances." 63 FLRA at 107.

The Respondent has not offered any evidence other than that which was presented at the representation hearing, and it has not presented any special circumstances warranting a reconsideration of the Authority's earlier decision.

The undisputed facts demonstrate that the Union made written requests to bargain with the Agency in the certified consolidated bargaining unit, and that the Agency refused to do so. Paragraph 11 of Complaint, G.C. Exhibit 1 to Motion for Summary Judgment; Paragraph 11 of Answer, G.C. Exhibit 2; Exhibit D of Rossen Affidavit, G.C. Exhibit 3. Accordingly, the Respondent has violated section 7116(a)(1), (5) and (8) of the Statute by refusing to negotiate and by otherwise refusing to accord the Union its statutory status as exclusive bargaining representative of the employees in the consolidated bargaining unit.

I therefore recommend that the Authority grant the General Counsel's Motion for Summary Judgment and issue the following:

ORDER

Pursuant to section 2423.41(c) of the Authority's Rules and Regulations and section 7118 of the Federal Service Labor-Management Relations Statute (the Statute), it is hereby ordered that the National Labor Relations Board, Washington, D.C. (the Respondent):

1. Cease and desist from:

(a) Refusing to bargain with the National Labor Relations Board Professional Association (the Union), as the exclusive representative of the consolidated bargaining unit certified on December 18, 2008.

(b) Otherwise refusing to accord the Union its statutory status as the exclusive representative of the consolidated bargaining unit certified on December 18, 2008.

(c) In any like or related manner, interfering with, restraining, or coercing its employees in the exercise of their rights assured by the Statute.

2. Take the following affirmative action in order to effectuate the purposes and policies of the Statute:

(a) Recognize the Union as the exclusive representative for the following consolidated unit which was certified on December 18, 2008, and accord the Union its statutory status as the exclusive representative of the employees in the unit:

> Included: All attorneys and other professionals performing comparable legal work, including permanent part-time employees, and law student employees (Student Assistants), in the Headquarters Office of the National Labor Relations Board and the Office of the General Counsel.

Excluded: Law students holding summer appointments and those on work-study programs; nonprofessional employees; management officials; supervisors; and employees described in 5 U.S.C. § 7112(b)(2), (3), (4), (6) and (7).

(b) Upon request, negotiate in good faith with the Union over conditions of employment of its employees in the consolidated unit certified on December 18, 2008.

(c) Accord the Union and the employees in the consolidated bargaining unit certified on December 18, 2008, all rights and entitlements provided in the Statute.

(d) Post at its Headquarters offices where employees in the consolidated bargaining unit certified on December 18, 2008, are located, copies of the attached Notice on forms to be furnished by the Authority. Upon receipt of such forms, they shall be signed by the Respondent's General Counsel and shall be posted and maintained for 60 consecutive days thereafter, in conspicuous places, including all bulletin boards and other places where notices to employees are customarily posted. Reasonable steps shall be taken to ensure that such Notices are not altered, defaced, or covered by any other material.

(e) Pursuant to section 2423.41(e) of the Authority's Rules and Regulations, notify the Regional Director, San Francisco Region, Federal Labor Relations Authority, in writing, within 30 days from the date of this Order, as to what steps have been taken to comply.

Issued, Washington, DC, November 18, 2009.

____

RICHARD A. PEARSON
Administrative Law Judge

NOTICE TO ALL EMPLOYEES
POSTED BY ORDER OF THE
FEDERAL LABOR RELATIONS AUTHORITY

The Federal Labor Relations Authority has found that the National Labor Relations Board, Washington, D.C., violated the Federal Service Labor-Management Relations Statute (the Statute), and has ordered us to post and abide by this Notice.

WE HEREBY NOTIFY OUR EMPLOYEES THAT:

WE WILL NOT refuse to bargain with the National Labor Relations Board Professional Association (the Union) as the exclusive representative of the consolidated bargaining unit certified on December 18, 2008.

WE WILL NOT otherwise refuse to accord the Union its statutory status as the exclusive representative of the consolidated bargaining unit certified on December 18, 2008.

WE WILL NOT, in any like or related manner, interfere with, restrain, or coerce our employees in the exercise of their rights assured by the Statute.

WE WILL recognize the Union as the exclusive representative for the following consolidated bargaining unit which was certified on December 18, 2008, and accord the Union its statutory status as the exclusive bargaining representative of the employees in this unit:

Included: All attorneys and other professionals performing comparable legal work, including permanent part-time employees, and law student employees (Student Assistants) in the Headquarters Office of the National Labor Relations Board and the Office of the General Counsel.

Excluded: Law students holding summer appointments and those on work-study programs; nonprofessional employees; management officials; supervisors; and employees described in § 7112(b)(2), (3), (4), (6) and (7) of the Statute.

WE WILL, upon request, negotiate in good faith with the Union over conditions of employment of employees in the consolidated unit certified on December 18, 2008.

WE WILL accord the Union and the employees in the consolidated unit certified on December 18, 2008, all rights and entitlements provided in the Statute.

____
National Labor Relations Board

Dated:__________ By:______________________
(Title) (Signature)

This Notice must remain posted for 60 consecutive days from the date of posting and must not be altered, defaced, or covered by any other material.

If employees have any questions concerning this Notice or compliance with any of its provisions, they may communicate directly with the Regional Director of the Federal Labor Relations Authority, San Francisco Region, whose address is: 901 Market Street, Suite 220, San Francisco, CA 94103, and whose phone number is: (415) 356-5000.

65 FLRA No. 66

UNITED STATES
DEPARTMENT OF TRANSPORTATION
FEDERAL AVIATION ADMINISTRATION
(Agency)

and

NATIONAL AIR TRAFFIC
CONTROLLERS ASSOCIATION
(Union)

0-AR-4557

DECISION

December 14, 2010

Before the Authority: Carol Waller Pope, Chairman, and Thomas M. Beck and Ernest DuBester, Members

I. Statement of the Case

This matter is before the Authority on exceptions to an award of Arbitrator Ed W. Bankston filed by the Agency under § 7122(a) of the Federal Service Labor-Management Relations Statute (the Statute) and part 2425 of the Authority's Regulations. The Union filed an opposition to the Agency's exceptions.

After determining that the grievance was not moot and was arbitrable, the Arbitrator concluded that the Agency issued the disputed letter of reprimand without proper cause. The Arbitrator directed the Agency to rescind the letter of reprimand and make the grievant whole with backpay. The Arbitrator also awarded reasonable attorney fees. For the reasons that follow, we deny the Agency's exceptions.

II. Background and Arbitrator's Award

The Agency reprimanded the grievant for inattention to duty. Award at 5. He filed a grievance contending that the letter of reprimand was improper and contrary to the collective bargaining agreement. As a remedy, he requested that the Agency rescind the letter of reprimand and that he be awarded any other appropriate relief. *Id.* at 3, 7. The grievance was submitted to arbitration on the following stipulated issues:

> (1) Whether the grievance is moot, or in fact, arbitrable? If so,
> (2) Whether the Agency's issuance of the Letter of Reprimand to [the grievant] was for just cause and such as to promote the efficiency of the service? If not, what is the appropriate remedy?

Id. at 3.

Prior to the arbitration hearing, the Agency notified the grievant that it had removed the letter of reprimand from his official personnel folder. *Id.* at 8. The Agency then argued to the Arbitrator that the grievance was moot because "[t]his case was resolved with the canceling of the action prior to the . . . hearing and the [g]rievant suffered no loss of pay due to this reprimand." *Id.* The Arbitrator rejected the Agency's claim as follows:

> [T]he Agency is flat wrong with respect to arbitrability. We are here because it issued the Letter of Reprimand. We are here because the disciplinary action remained in effect for nearly a year . . . . We are here because the grievant wants the Letter of Reprimand "totally gone away." He wants his "name cleared," and the stigma gone. We are here because the Union grieved the efficacy of the Letter of Reprimand and whatever ill effects as may have befallen the grievant as a result.

Id. at 11 (citations omitted). In sum, the Arbitrator concluded that the grievance was arbitrable and was not moot. *Id.* at 11-12.

During the hearing, the Arbitrator denied the Agency's request to call as witnesses on the issue of arbitrability several Union representatives. He explained that the issue of arbitrability would be decided on the basis of the collective bargaining agreement and that, consequently, the testimony was not necessary to resolve the issue of arbitrability. Tr. at 35, 41. He also found that the testimony the Agency sought to elicit pertained to the merits of the case and had nothing to do with arbitrability. *Id.* at 39.

On the merits, the Arbitrator concluded that the Agency issued the letter of reprimand without proper cause and directed the Agency to rescind the letter of reprimand and expunge it and all associated documents from employee records. Award at 17. The Arbitrator also addressed the Union's claim that the grievant lost pay as a direct result of the letter of reprimand. In this regard, the Arbitrator noted that the grievant received a superior success increase (SCI) at level 2 that increased his annual salary by 0.6 percent. Citing testimony of the grievant's supervisor, the Arbitrator found that the supervisor admitted that "[b]ut for the Letter of Reprimand and the 'operational error,' wrongfully charged to the grievant, . . . the grievant would have received the 1.8 percent (Level 1) increase." *Id.* at 16. Accordingly, the Arbitrator additionally directed that the "grievant is to be made whole with respect to back pay plus interest to properly reflect the 1.2 percent loss of his SCI (Level 1) wage adjustment in accordance with the Back Pay Act." *Id.* at 17. The Arbitrator also awarded the grievant reasonable attorney fees. *Id.*

III. Positions of the Parties

A. Agency's Exceptions

The Agency contends that the award of backpay is contrary to law. The Agency first argues that the Arbitrator based the award of backpay on statements of the grievant's supervisor that the supervisor never made. Exceptions at 8. The Agency next argues that there is no causal connection between the letter of reprimand and the salary increase awarded by the Arbitrator because the grievant's lesser increase in pay was not the result of the reprimand and because there is "no obligation to pay an employee a performance award[.]" *Id.* at 9. The Agency further argues that, because there is no obligation to provide a performance award, the award is contrary to 5 U.S.C. § 4505 (§ 4505) and 5 C.F.R. § 451.104 (§ 451.104), which, according to the Agency, leave the granting of performance awards to the discretion of agencies. *Id.* at 10.

The Agency also contends that the Arbitrator exceeded his authority by addressing the issue pertaining to the letter of reprimand because the letter had been "rescinded[.]" *Id.* at 11. The Agency further contends that, by addressing the SCI salary increase issue, the award fails to draw its essence from the collective bargaining agreement and the Arbitrator exceeded his authority by disregarding the specific limitation set forth in Article 9.12 of the agreement.[1] *Id.* at 9. In this regard, the Agency asserts that the grievance made no mention of the SCI salary increase issue because it had not occurred at the time the grievance was filed. *Id.* at 6. The Agency also asserts that the SCI issue is precluded by Article 9.12 because the grievant filed a separate grievance disputing his salary increase that has not been submitted to arbitration. *Id.*

In addition, the Agency contends that, by refusing to allow the Agency to call Union witnesses, the Arbitrator denied the Agency a fair hearing and demonstrated bias against the Agency. *Id.* at 10. The Agency asserts that the testimony was crucial to the issues of the justification of the letter of reprimand and the preclusion of the SCI salary increase. *Id.*

Finally, the Agency contends that the award of attorney fees is contrary to law. The Agency asserts that the grievant is not a prevailing party because the Agency "rescinded" the letter of reprimand during the pendency of the grievance. *Id.* at 3. The Agency maintains that the award is in direct conflict with the Supreme Court's rejection of the "catalyst theory" in *Buckhannon Board and Care Home, Inc., v West Virginia Department of Health and Human Resources,* 532 U.S. 598 (2001) (*Buckhannon*).

B. Union's Opposition

The Union contends that the Arbitrator did not exceed his authority and disputes the Agency's assertion that it rescinded the letter of reprimand when it removed the letter of reprimand from the grievant's personnel file. The Union maintains that the Arbitrator properly concluded that the grievance was not moot because the merits of the grievance and the remedy were unresolved. Opp'n at 5. The Union further argues that nothing in Article 9.12 required the grievant to pursue a separate grievance to obtain relief. *Id.* at 7.

The Union also disputes the Agency's claim that the grievant is not a prevailing party for purposes of attorney fees. The Union asserts that the Arbitrator's award constitutes the required enforceable judgment and that the Agency did not voluntarily rescind the letter of reprimand, as it asserts. *Id.* at 8-9. Finally, the Union argues that the Agency does not establish that the Arbitrator's refusal to permit the Agency to call Union witnesses denied it a fair hearing or demonstrated bias against the Agency. *Id.* at 9-10.

---

1. According to the Agency, Article 9.12 provides that arbitrators are confined "to the precise issue(s) submitted for arbitration and shall have no authority to determine any other issue(s) not so submitted[.]" Exceptions at 9 (quoting Article 9.12).

IV. Analysis and Conclusions

A. The award of backpay is not contrary to law; the award does not fail to draw its essence from the collective bargaining agreement; and the Arbitrator did not exceed his authority.

When an exception involves an award's consistency with law, the Authority reviews de novo any questions of law raised by the exception and the award. *E.g., U.S. Dep't of Transp., Fed. Aviation Admin.,* 64 FLRA 922, 923 (2010) (*FAA*). In applying a standard of de novo review, the Authority assesses whether the arbitrator's legal conclusions are consistent with the applicable standard of law. In making that assessment, the Authority defers to the arbitrator's underlying factual findings. *Id.*

As relevant here, the Authority will find that arbitrators exceed their authority when they disregard a specific limitation on that authority or when they resolve an issue not submitted to arbitration. *E.g., U.S. DHS, U.S. Customs & Border Prot.,* 65 FLRA 160, 164 (2010). In assessing whether arbitrators have exceeded their authority, the Authority grants arbitrators broad discretion to fashion remedies that they consider appropriate. *Id.* In addition, as to asserted limitations set forth in a collective bargaining agreement, the Authority will find that the award fails to draw its essence from the agreement when the appealing party establishes that the award: (1) cannot in any rational way be derived from the agreement; (2) is so unfounded in reason and fact and so unconnected with the wording and purposes of the agreement as to manifest an infidelity to the obligation of the arbitrator; (3) does not represent a plausible interpretation of the agreement; or (4) evidences a manifest disregard of the agreement. *E.g., FAA,* 64 FLRA at 924.

In *FAA*, a grievant filed a grievance over his decertification that was submitted to arbitration on the stipulated issues of whether the decertification was in compliance with Agency regulations and, if not, what the remedy should be. The arbitrator found that the Agency improperly decertified the grievant and that, but for the unwarranted action, the Agency would have awarded the grievant an operational success increase (OSI) or an SCI. Accordingly, the arbitrator awarded the grievant backpay in the amount of the increase that the grievant would have received if he had not been decertified.

In its exceptions in *FAA,* the Agency claimed many of the same deficiencies that it has claimed in this case. In particular, the Agency claimed that the award of an OSI or SCI was contrary to the Back Pay Act because the grievant was not automatically entitled to an increase. Similarly, the Agency claimed that the award of an OSI or SCI was contrary to § 4505 and § 451.104 because such awards are discretionary. The Agency further claimed that the issue regarding an OSI and an SCI was not raised in the grievance and that, because the arbitrator addressed that issue, she exceeded her authority and the award failed to draw its essence from the same provision of the parties' agreement that is in dispute in this case. *Id.* at 922-23.

The Authority denied the Agency's exceptions. *Id.* at 924. As relevant here, the Authority noted that an award of backpay is authorized when an arbitrator finds that an unjustified or unwarranted personnel action directly resulted in a loss of pay, allowances, or differentials. The Authority stated that it does not look behind an award when the arbitrator finds a causal relationship and the finding is supported by other factual findings. The Authority concluded that the arbitrator found the requisite causal connection and that the finding was supported by other factual findings. *Id.* at 923-24. As to § 4505 and § 451.104, the Authority concluded that the arbitrator effectively found that, absent the unwarranted action, the Agency would have exercised its discretion and granted the grievant an OSI or SCI. *Id.* at 924. As to the claims that the arbitrator exceeded her authority and that the award failed to draw its essence from the agreement, the Authority noted that the parties expressly stipulated that the arbitrator could craft a remedy if the disputed decertification was improper, and the Authority stated that arbitrators enjoy particularly broad discretion in fashioning remedies when the parties specifically authorize them to determine the appropriate remedy for a violation. *Id.* In view of this stipulation and broad remedial discretion, the Authority rejected the Agency's claims. *Id.*

For the reasons set forth in *FAA*, we reject the similar claims raised by the Agency in this case. More specifically, the Agency provides no basis for finding the Arbitrator's award of backpay contrary to law. As in *FAA*, the Arbitrator in this case found the requisite causal connection, and the finding is supported by the Arbitrator's factual finding as to the testimony of the grievant's supervisor.[2] Also, as in

2. Although the Agency disputes the finding as to this testimony, as stated previously, the Authority defers to an arbitrator's underlying factual findings when assessing whether the award is contrary to law, *e.g., FAA*, 64 FLRA

FAA, the Arbitrator effectively found that, absent the unwarranted action, the Agency would have exercised its discretion and granted the grievant a SCI at level 1.

The Agency also provides no basis for finding that the Arbitrator exceeded his authority or that the award fails to draw its essence from the agreement. As in *FAA*, the parties expressly stipulated that the Arbitrator could craft a remedy. In this case, the parties expressly authorized the Arbitrator to craft a remedy if the issuance of the letter of reprimand was not for just cause. Award at 3. In view of this express authorization and the broad remedial authority it conveys, the Agency does not establish that the award of a SCI level 1 exceeded the Arbitrator's authority or disregarded the limitation of Article 9.12 of the agreement.

In this case, the Agency additionally argues that the Arbitrator exceeded his authority by addressing the issue pertaining to the letter of reprimand. However, the parties expressly stipulated that the Arbitrator would resolve whether the issuance of the letter of reprimand was for just cause if the Arbitrator found that the grievance was arbitrable. The Arbitrator specifically determined that the grievance was arbitrable and resolved the reprimand issue, as stipulated.[3] Consequently, the Agency provides no basis for finding that the Arbitrator exceeded his authority in this regard.

Accordingly, we deny these exceptions.

B. The Arbitrator did not deny a fair hearing and did not demonstrate bias against the Agency.

The Authority will find that an arbitrator denied a fair hearing when it is demonstrated that the arbitrator refused to hear or consider pertinent or material evidence or conducted the proceedings in a manner that so prejudiced a party as to affect the fairness of the proceedings as a whole. *E.g., U.S. Dep't of Commerce, PTO, Arlington, Va.*, 60 FLRA 869, 879 (2005) (*PTO*). However, the Authority has consistently held that arbitrators have considerable latitude in the conduct of hearings and that a party's objection to the manner in which the arbitrator conducted the hearing does not alone provide a basis for finding the award deficient. In particular, an arbitrator's exclusion of testimony alone does not establish that the arbitrator denied a fair hearing. *E.g., U.S. Dep't of HHS, SSA*, 24 FLRA 959, 961 (1986) (*SSA*). Arbitrators are required only to grant a fundamentally fair hearing, which provides adequate notice, a hearing on the evidence, and an impartial decision by the arbitrator. *PTO*, 60 FLRA at 879.

The Agency contends that the Arbitrator's refusal to allow it to call Union witnesses on the issue of arbitrability denied it a fair hearing and demonstrated bias against the Agency. In this regard, the Arbitrator stated to the Agency that he would decide the issue of arbitrability on the basis of the collective bargaining agreement and that the disputed testimony was not necessary to resolve the issue of arbitrability. Tr. at 35, 41. The Agency's assertions of the relevance of the testimony to the issues on the merits fail to demonstrate that the Arbitrator's refusal was not within his latitude to control the conduct of the hearing by ensuring that testimony was relevant and material to the resolution of the arbitrability issue. Consequently, the assertions provide no basis for finding that the Arbitrator failed to conduct a fair hearing. *See PTO*, 60 FLRA at 879; *SSA*, 24 FLRA at 961-62. Accordingly, we deny the exception contending that the Arbitrator denied a fair hearing.

When the Authority denies a party's fair hearing exception, and the party's bias exception is based on the asserted denial of a fair hearing, the Authority also denies the bias exception. *PTO*, 60 FLRA at 879. Consistent with this precedent, as the Agency's bias exception is based on its fair hearing exception, which we have denied, we also deny the bias exception.

C. The award of attorney fees is not contrary to law.

Awards of attorney fees under the Back Pay Act must be awarded in accordance with the standards established under 5 U.S.C. § 7701(g), which pertains to awards of attorney fees by the Merit Systems Protection Board (MSPB). *E.g., AFGE, Local 446*, 64 FLRA 15, 15-16 (2009). The standards established under § 7701(g) include the requirement

at 923, and the Agency does not contend that the finding is deficient as based on a nonfact.

3. To the extent that the Agency's argument is directed at the mootness determination, no basis is provided for finding the determination deficient. Under Authority precedent, the Arbitrator correctly determined that, as the grievance sought relief for the unjustified reprimand, the grievance was not moot. *See AFGE, Local 2145*, 62 FLRA 505, 506 (2008) (asserted claims for relief preclude an appeal from being moot); *AFGE, Local 1741*, 62 FLRA 113, 118 (2007) (party urging mootness must establish that interim relief or events completely or irrevocably eradicated the effects of the alleged violation).

that the employee must be the prevailing party. When exceptions concern the standards established under § 7701(g), the Authority looks to the decisions of the courts and the MSPB for guidance. *Id.* at 16. In regard to the requirement pertaining to prevailing party, the Authority applies the definition set forth in *Buckhannon* and adopted by the MSPB under § 7701(g). *Id.* Under this definition, a grievant is a prevailing party when the grievant obtains an enforceable judgment that benefited the grievant at the time of the judgment. *E.g., AFGE, Local 987,* 64 FLRA 884, 887 (2010).

Contrary to the claim of the Agency, the grievant is a prevailing party within the meaning of § 7701(g) and the Supreme Court's decision in *Buckhannon. See id.* at 887. The Arbitrator's award is an enforceable judgment that benefited the grievant at the time of the award. The Agency asserts that the grievant is not a prevailing party because it "rescinded" the letter of reprimand during the pendency of the grievance. Exceptions at 3. However, the Arbitrator rejected the Agency's claim that it had rescinded the reprimand and issued an award directing the Agency to rescind the reprimand and make the grievant whole, which, in accordance with our denial of the Agency's other exceptions, the Agency fails to establish is not enforceable.

Accordingly, we deny this exception.

V. Decision

The Agency's exceptions are denied.

65 FLRA No. 67

UNITED STATES
DEPARTMENT OF TRANSPORTATION
FEDERAL AVIATION ADMINISTRATION
(Agency)

and

NATIONAL AIR TRAFFIC
CONTROLLERS ASSOCIATION
(Union)

0-AR-4556

DECISION

December 15, 2010

Before the Authority: Carol Waller Pope, Chairman, and Thomas M. Beck and Ernest DuBester, Members

I. Statement of the Case

This matter is before the Authority on exceptions to an award of Arbitrator James A. McClimon filed by the Agency under § 7122(a) of the Federal Service Labor-Management Relations Statute (the Statute) and part 2425 of the Authority's Regulations. The Union filed an opposition to the Agency's exceptions.

The Arbitrator concluded that, because the parties had incorporated the Back Pay Act (BPA), 5 U.S.C. § 5596, into their agreement, the Agency was required to pay the grievant interest on backpay that it had paid to the grievant. For the reasons set forth below, we grant the Agency's contrary to law exception and set aside the Arbitrator's award.

II. Background and Arbitrator's Award

The grievant began employment with the Agency in 2003. Four years later, the grievant discovered that the Agency had set her pay incorrectly. Award at 6. The grievant asked the Agency to adjust her pay and give her backpay with interest. *Id.* Under the Agency's Personnel Management System (PMS), Agency employees are permitted to receive backpay for unjustified or unwarranted personnel actions; however, they cannot obtain interest. *Id.* at 4. The Agency, accordingly, adjusted the grievant's pay and gave her backpay, but it denied her request for interest. *Id.* at 6-7.

The Union filed a grievance arguing that the Agency violated the BPA and the parties' agreement by refusing to pay the grievant interest.[1] The parties stipulated to the following issue:

> Did the [Agency] violate the [BPA], 5 U.S.C. [§] 5596 and Article 37[2] of the contract when it refused to pay [the grievant] interest when the [Agency] corrected their mistake in setting her salary, if so what is the appropriate remedy?

Id. at 2.

The Arbitrator concluded that the Agency violated the parties' agreement. The Arbitrator found that Article 102, Section 1 establishes that the agreement serves as a "valid exception" to any Agency rule that conflicts with it.[3] *Id.* at 9 (quoting Article 102, Section 1). He further found that Article 102, Section 4 of the agreement incorporates the BPA into the agreement.[4] *Id.* Therefore, although the Agency's PMS prohibits interest on backpay, the Arbitrator concluded that the Agency nevertheless owed the grievant interest on her backpay because it had a contractual obligation to follow the BPA. *Id.*

---

1. Before the Arbitrator, the parties' disputed whether their 2003 or 2006 collective bargaining agreement controlled the resolution of this matter. The Arbitrator concluded that, because both agreements contained identical provisions, it was irrelevant which agreement controlled. Award at 6. Neither party challenges this finding; accordingly we will not address it further except to note that, for purposes of this decision, we will reference both agreements as if they were one document.

2. Article 37, Section 1 of the agreement provides: "In accordance with 5 USC Chapter 71, the Parties recognize the power of an appropriate authority to render a remedy in accordance with the provisions of 5 USC [§] 5596." Award at 3.

3. Article 102, Section 1 of the parties' agreement provides: "Any provision of this Agreement [Contract] shall be determined a valid exception to, and shall supersede any existing or future Agency rules, regulations, directives, order, policies and/or practices which conflict with the Agreement [Contract]." Award at 3.

4. Article 102, Section 4 of the parties' agreement provides: "Any provision of the United States Code (USC) or Code of the Federal Regulations (CFR) which is expressly incorporated by reference in this Agreement [Contract] is binding on the Parties." Award at 3.

at 9-10. The Arbitrator, accordingly, sustained the grievance and ordered the Agency to pay interest to the grievant. *Id.* at 11.

III. Positions of the Parties

A. Agency's Exceptions

The Agency contends that the award is contrary to law because the Arbitrator erroneously concluded that the BPA applies to the Agency through the parties' agreement. According to the Agency, Congress excluded the Agency from most of the provisions of Title 5 when it enacted the Department of Transportation Appropriations Act of 1996, Pub.L. No. 104-50, § 347, 109 Stat. 436, 460 (1995), codified at 49 U.S.C. § 40122 (DOT Act), including the BPA. Exceptions at 3. The Agency also states it has yet to incorporate the BPA into its PMS, even though Congress gave the Agency permission to adopt any portion of Title 5 when it authorized the Agency to develop its PMS. *Id.* Moreover, the Agency contends that legislation is currently pending before Congress that would make the BPA applicable to the Agency; according to the Agency, such legislation would be unnecessary if the BPA already applied to the Agency. *Id.* The Agency contends that the foregoing conclusively establishes that Congress excluded the Agency from the BPA, and that the incorporation of the BPA into the parties' agreement is insufficient to overcome this exclusion. *Id.* at 3-4.

Additionally, the Agency contends that, even if the BPA applies to the Agency, the award is nevertheless contrary to law because it does not satisfy several requirements of the BPA and PMS, Ch. II, § 9. *Id.* at 4-7.

B. Union's Opposition

The Union disputes on several grounds the Agency's contention that the BPA does not apply to the Agency. First, according to the Union, Congress amended the DOT Act to make the Statute applicable to the Agency; as such, the Agency is required to abide by agreements negotiated pursuant to its terms. Opp'n at 5. The Union contends that Article 37 of the parties' agreement passed Agency head review, and is, accordingly, a valid agreement negotiated under the Statute. Therefore, the Union alleges that the Agency is bound by Article 37. Opp'n at 4-5 (citing 5 U.S.C. § 7114(c)). Second, the Union argues that, under Authority precedent, parties may incorporate statutory language in an agreement so long as that language matches the language used by an agency under its own personnel system, i.e., agency rules. Opp'n at 5 (citing *NAGE, Local R1-203,* 55 FLRA 1081 (1999)). According to the Union, the Authority has further held that such contractual language trumps agency rules. Opp'n at 5 (citing *U.S. Dep't of Transp., FAA,* 61 FLRA 750 (2006)). The Union contends that the language of Article 37: (1) incorporates the BPA; and (2) mirrors the language contained in the Agency's PMS regarding backpay. Therefore, according to the Union, Article 37 controls over the Agency's PMS. *Id.* at 5, 10. Finally, the Union alleges that the Agency's arguments should be ignored because they are inconsistent with other arguments it has made in the past regarding whether the BPA applies to the Agency. *Id.* at 6-7 (citations omitted).

The Union contends that the Agency's remaining contrary to law arguments are barred by § 2429.5 of the Authority's Regulations because the Agency never presented them to the Arbitrator. *Id.* at 11, 16. Alternatively, the Union contends that these arguments are incorrect. *Id.* at 11-16, 16-21.

IV. The award is contrary to law.

When an exception involves an award's consistency with law, the Authority reviews any question of law raised by the exception and the award de novo. *See NTEU, Chapter 24*, 50 FLRA 330, 332 (1995) (citing *U.S. Customs Serv. v. FLRA*, 43 F.3d 682, 686-87 (D.C. Cir. 1994)). In applying the standard of de novo review, the Authority assesses whether an arbitrator's legal conclusions are consistent with the applicable standard of law. *See U.S. Dep't of Def., Dep'ts of the Army & the Air Force, Ala. Nat'l Guard, Northport, Ala.*, 55 FLRA 37, 40 (1998). In making that assessment, the Authority defers to the arbitrator's underlying factual findings. *See id.*

A. The BPA does not apply to the Agency.

The Agency argues that the Arbitrator's award of interest was improper because Congress has excluded the Agency from the coverage of the BPA. Exceptions at 3. The Agency further contends that the parties' agreement cannot serve as a basis to make the BPA applicable to the Agency. We construe the foregoing as a claim that the doctrine of sovereign immunity bars the award of interest.

1. The BPA does not apply to the Agency as a matter of law.

The United States, as sovereign, is immune from suit except as it consents to be sued. *U.S. Dep't of Transp., FAA*, 52 FLRA 46, 49 (1996) (*DOT*) (citing *U.S. v. Testan*, 424 U.S. 392, 399 (1976)). Thus, there is no right to money damages in a suit against the United States without a waiver of sovereign immunity. *DOT*, 52 FLRA at 49. In order to waive sovereign immunity, Congress must unequivocally express its intention to do so. *Id.* (citing *Lane v. Pena*, 518 U.S. 187, 192 (1996)). The Government's consent to a particular remedy also must be unambiguous. *DOT*, 52 FLRA at 49 (citing *Dep't of Army v. FLRA*, 56 F.3d 273, 277 (D.C. Cir. 1995). "As such, an award by an arbitrator that an agency provide monetary damages to a union or employee must be supported by statutory authority to impose such a remedy." *U.S. Dep't of the Air Force, Minot Air Force Base, N.D.*, 61 FLRA 366, 370 (2005) (*Minot*) (then-Member Pope dissenting in part on another matter) (citing *U.S. Dep't of HHS, FDA*, 60 FLRA 250, 252 (2004)). "In this regard, a collective bargaining agreement may require monetary payments to employees only where there is an underlying statutory authority for the payment." *Minot*, 61 FLRA at 370 (citation omitted). Absent a waiver of sovereign immunity, an arbitrator's monetary remedy is contrary to law. *See DOT*, 52 FLRA at 49.

Congress enacted the DOT Act, which authorized the Agency to develop its PMS. *See FAA*, 55 FLRA 1271, 1274-75 (2000) (Member Cabaniss concurring). The DOT Act also provided, in pertinent part, that Title 5 of the United States Code, with certain exceptions, did not apply to the PMS. 49 U.S.C. § 40122(g)(2); *see also FAA*, 55 FLRA at 1274. The BPA was not one of the exceptions specified.

When the Agency created its PMS, it established rules that allow Agency employees to obtain backpay in certain situations. *See* Award at 4 (citing PMS, Ch. II, § 9). However, the PMS does not permit interest for backpay paid by the Agency. *See id.* Additionally, the Agency chose not to incorporate the BPA into its PMS.

Congress subsequently amended § 347 of the DOT Act to extend additional portions of Title 5 to the PMS. *See* Pub. L. No. 104-122, 110 Stat. 876, codified at 49 U.S.C. § 40122(g)(2). Once again, Congress did not extend the BPA to the Agency; however, Congress did extend "chapter 71, relating to labor-management relations" to the Agency. 49 U.S.C. § 40122(g)(2)(C); *FAA*, 55 FLRA at 1274. Thus, the Agency is required to abide by the terms of the Statute.

Although Congress has extended the *Statute*, to the Agency, it has *not* extended the *BPA itself* to the Agency. *See* 49 U.S.C. § 40122(g)(2)(A)-(H) (listing only provisions of Title 5 that do apply to Agency). Therefore, apart from remedies of backpay awarded pursuant to the Statute, the Agency is exempt from the BPA. *See id.*; *cf. Brown v. Sec'y of the Army*, 918 F.2d 214, 216 (D.C. Cir. 1990) (concluding that BPA applied to matters arising under Title VII of the Civil Rights Act of 1964 because "text" of BPA provides "no hint of an exclusion of, or exemption for, federal sector Title VII adjudications[]"). As such, the BPA does not apply to the Agency when the Agency *itself* awards backpay to employees. The Agency awarded the grievant backpay under its PMS, not under the BPA.

Moreover, § 7122(b) of the Statute states that arbitrators may award grievants backpay "as provided in" the BPA. However, as stated above, the BPA does not apply to the Agency. Furthermore, the Arbitrator did not award any backpay under the BPA. Thus, there was no award of backpay "as provided in" the BPA in this case. As such, even assuming that § 7122(b) constitutes a requisite waiver of sovereign immunity for the payment of interest, it does not apply under the circumstances of this case because such a waiver could extend only as to an award of backpay made by an arbitrator and interest awarded by an arbitrator in conjunction with an award of backpay under the BPA.

2. The BPA does not apply to the Agency as a matter of contract.

The Union contends that, as a contractual matter, the grievant is entitled to interest on the backpay the Agency paid to her. "[A] collective bargaining agreement may require monetary payments to employees only where there is *underlying statutory authority* for the payment." *Minot*, 61 FLRA at 370 (emphasis added) (citation omitted). The "statutory authority" that the Union relies on is the BPA; however, as we have already held, Congress has not made the BPA applicable to payments of backpay made by the Agency. Nevertheless, the Union maintains that the BPA applies to the Agency because the parties negotiated Article 37 of their agreement pursuant to the terms of the Statute, which *is* applicable to the Agency.[5]

To the extent that the Union relies upon the Statute as a waiver of sovereign immunity, the Authority has rejected the assertion that the Statute itself constitutes a waiver as to monetary damages. *See, e.g., U.S. Dep't of Transp., FAA, Detroit, Mich.*, 64 FLRA 325, 329 (2009) (citing *Dep't of the Army*, 56 F.3d at 277).

The question, therefore, is whether the parties may rely on the Statute to negotiate a general waiver of the Agency's sovereign immunity to monetary relief under the BPA. The federal courts and the Authority have not directly addressed this issue. *Cf. Dep't of the Treasury, IRS v. FLRA*, 521 F.3d 1148, 1155 (9th Cir. 2008) (*IRS*) (in finding that Authority properly relied on Fair Labor Standards Act to find waiver of sovereign immunity, court noted, in *dicta*, that agency and union's contractual agreement was "plainly insufficient to show a waiver of sovereign immunity"); *see also id.* at 1156 (stating that "requisite statutory waiver" of sovereign immunity was "present, as opposed to an insufficient contractual waiver").

The United States may enter into contractual agreements, and be held liable for violations of the same, when Congress has enacted legislation permitting such agreements. *See, e.g., U.S. v. Navajo Nation*, 129 S.Ct. 1547, 1551-52 (2009) (*Navajo*) (discussing waiver of sovereign immunity for contracts for Indian Tucker Act); *U.S. v. Mitchell*, 463 U.S. 206, 215 (1983) (*Mitchell*) (discussing waiver of sovereign immunity for contracts under Tucker Act); *IRS*, 521 F.3d at 1153-54 (discussing waiver of sovereign immunity for contracts under Portal-to-Portal Act). Such legislation contains clauses that specifically permit the United States to be sued for violations of these agreements, and therefore, to be held liable for monetary remedies. *See, e.g., Navajo*, 129 S.Ct. at 1552; *Mitchell*, 463 U.S. at 215; *IRS*, 521 F.3d at 1154. The Authority has held that the Statute constitutes a waiver of the Agency's sovereign immunity as to the BPA within the context of an unfair labor practice (ULP). *FAA*, 55 FLRA at 1271. However, this case does not involve an ULP.

Moreover, "officers of the United States possess no power through their actions to waive [sovereign] immunity . . . in the absence of some express provision [of] Congress." *U.S. v. N.Y. Rayon Importing Co.*, 329 U.S. 654, 660 (1947). Parties "entering into an agreement with the Government take[] the risk of accurately ascertaining the authority of the agents who purport to act for the Government, and this risk remains with the contractor even when the Government agents themselves may have been unaware of the limitations on their authority." *Harbert/Lummus Agrifuels Projects v. U.S.*, 142 F.3d 1429, 1432 (Fed. Cir. 1998) *cert. denied* 525 U.S. 1177 (1999) (quoting *Trauma Serv. Group v. U.S.*, 104 F.3d 1321, 1325 (Fed. Cir. 1997)). The Union has failed to cite to any provision in the Statute that expressly authorizes an agency head, or other agency official, contractually to waive an agency's sovereign immunity as to monetary relief under the BPA. Consequently, even if the Agency head approved this provision of the parties' agreement, that would provide no basis for concluding that the Agency waived sovereign immunity. *See id.*

Furthermore, as to the specific matter at issue, the Statute is subject to multiple plausible interpretations. Specifically, although an interpretation of the Statute as permitting contractual waivers of sovereign immunity is a plausible one, an equally plausible interpretation of the Statute is that it does *not* permit contractual waivers. If a statute has multiple plausible interpretations, then that statute cannot be considered definitive enough to constitute a waiver of sovereign immunity. *See U.S. v. Nordic Village, Inc.*, 503 U.S. 30, 35 (1992).

Based on the foregoing, we conclude that the Statute does not permit parties contractually to waive sovereign immunity as to the BPA in situations not specifically addressed by the Statute. The Union's arguments as to why we should permit a contractual waiver of sovereign immunity are unpersuasive.

First, the Union argues that the Agency is bound by the BPA because, pursuant to the terms of the Statute, the Agency negotiated its inclusion into the parties' agreement. Opp'n at 5. However, as explained above, the Statute does not provide a basis for allowing parties contractually to waive sovereign immunity.

Second, the Union contends that the parties' agreement takes precedence over Agency rules; thus,

5. We note that Article 37 of the parties' agreement states only that an arbitrator can render remedies under the BPA "[i]n accordance with 5 USC Chapter 71[.]" Award at 3 (quoting Article 37, Section 1 of parties' agreement). This language suggests that the BPA is incorporated in the agreement *only* to the extent that it is consistent with the Statute. Nevertheless, both the parties and the Arbitrator agree that Article 37 fully incorporates the BPA; accordingly, we will limit our analysis to this interpretation.

the grievant is entitled to interest on her backpay even though the PMS prohibits it. *Id.* at 5, 10. To support this position, the Union relies on a decision in which the Authority held that language contained in a contract trumped a contrary Agency rule. *See* Opp'n at 5 (citing *U.S. Dep't of Transp., FAA,* 61 FLRA 750, 752 (2006)). However, this decision is inapplicable because there was no question that the contract provision in that case was valid. Moreover, that provision did not purport to waive sovereign immunity. By contrast, we have held that the provision in dispute here does not validly waive sovereign immunity. Thus, the Union's argument does not support its position.

Third, and finally, the Union asserts that the Agency's position should not be given deference because it is inconsistent with positions that it has taken in the past. Specifically, the Union contends that the Agency has previously relied on provisions of the BPA to overturn arbitration awards. Opp'n at 6-7 (citing *U.S. Dep't of Transp., FAA,* 63 FLRA 502 (2009); *U.S. Dep't of Transp., FAA, Wash., D.C.,* 63 FLRA 492 (2009) (*FAA, Wash., D.C.*); *U.S. Dep't of Transp., FAA, Airways Facility Serv., Nat'l Airway Sys., Eng'g Div., Okla. City, Okla.,* 60 FLRA 565 (2005) (*FAA, Okla.*)). Even if it were appropriate to examine whether the Agency's arguments are entitled to deference, the Union's argument lacks merit because, in each of the decisions cited by the Union, *the arbitrator* awarded backpay, not the Agency. *See U.S. Dep't of Transp., FAA,* 63 FLRA at 502; *FAA, Wash., D.C.,* 63 FLRA at 492; *FAA, Okla.,* 60 FLRA at 567. Thus, the Agency's current position is not inconsistent with these decisions.

V. Decision

The Agency's exception is granted and the award is set aside.[6]

6. Based on this decision, we find that it is unnecessary to address the Agency's remaining exceptions.

65 FLRA No. 68

AMERICAN FEDERATION
OF GOVERNMENT EMPLOYEES
LOCAL 1228
(Union)

and

UNITED STATES
DEPARTMENT OF VETERANS AFFAIRS
VA CENTRAL IOWA HEALTH CARE SYSTEM
DES MOINES, IOWA
(Agency)

0-AR-4409

DECISION

December 16, 2010

Before the Authority: Carol Waller Pope, Chairman, and Thomas M. Beck and Ernest DuBester, Members

I. Statement of the Case

This matter is before the Authority on exceptions to an award of Arbitrator David Gaba filed by the Union under § 7122(a) of the Federal Service Labor-Management Relations Statute (the Statute) and part 2425 of the Authority's Regulations. The Agency filed an opposition to the Union's exceptions.

The Union filed a grievance challenging the Agency's failure to temporarily promote the grievant during the period she was performing higher-graded duties prior to her noncompetitive promotion. The Arbitrator found that the parties' collective bargaining agreement (CBA) did not require the Agency to provide retroactive pay for the grievant for the time she spent performing higher-graded duties. He therefore denied the Union's grievance.

For the reasons set forth below, we deny the Union's exceptions.

II. Background and Arbitrator's Award

In 2001, the grievant was hired at the General Schedule (GS)-9 pay level as an addiction therapist for the Agency's Substance Abuse Program. Award at 4. During her years of employment, she took on many additional duties. In 2006, recognizing the grievant's accretion of duties, her supervisor requested that the Agency's Department of Human Resources review the grievant's position. *Id.* As a result of the review, the grievant was noncompetitively promoted to the GS-11 pay level and received a new position description. *Id.*

The Union subsequently filed a grievance claiming that the Agency failed to temporarily promote the grievant at the time she began accruing duties that were not part of her GS-9 position description, as required by Article 12 of the CBA.* *Id.* at 5. The Union claimed that the Agency should have provided the grievant GS-11 pay retroactive to the date she began to perform higher graded duties. *Id.* The matter was not resolved and was submitted to arbitration.

The parties agreed to the following statement of the issue: "Has the grievant . . . been performing the duties of a readjustment counseling therapist since shortly after she was hired in 2001? Should the grievant be compensated for the performance of these duties?" *Id.* at 2.

At the hearing, the Agency did not dispute that the grievant had accreted additional duties. *Id.* at 5. However, the Agency argued that the Arbitrator did not have jurisdiction to decide the grievance because it concerned the classification of the grievant's position, which was not arbitrable under the parties' CBA. *Id.* at 6.

The Arbitrator found, among other things, that the case law cited by the Union was not applicable because the cited cases covered prohibited personnel practices or situations where the individuals involved were not properly compensated while on detail or temporarily promoted under the governing CBA. *Id.* at 10. In this regard, the Arbitrator found that there was no evidence that the grievant had ever been detailed to a higher-graded position or that the Agency had committed any prohibited personnel practices. *Id.* The Arbitrator further found that the grievant voluntarily took on extra duties to assist her employer in providing better services to veterans. *Id.*

The Arbitrator noted that it would be equitable to make the grievant's promotion to GS 11 retroactive to the date she began to perform the higher graded duties. *Id.* at 11. However, he concluded that his duty was to interpret the CBA as negotiated by the

---

* The relevant provisions of the parties' CBA are set forth in the appendix to this decision.

parties, and that the CBA did not allow him to order retroactive pay for the grievant. *Id.* Therefore, the Arbitrator denied the grievance.

III. Positions of the Parties

A. Union's Exceptions

The Union argues that the award fails to draw its essence from the CBA. Exceptions at 9-11. Specifically, it asserts that the Arbitrator's award disregards Article 12, Section 2 of the parties' CBA, which requires that employees performing higher graded duties for more than ten consecutive days be temporarily promoted. *Id.* at 11. According to the Union, the Arbitrator found that the grievant began to perform higher-graded duties starting on the day she was hired. Therefore, the Union argues that under Article 12, Section 2 of the CBA, th e Arbitrator should have awarded the grievant a temporary promotion. *Id.*

In addition, the Union claims that the award is contrary to the Back Pay Act. *Id.* at 5-9. The Union contends that the Arbitrator's conclusion that he could not award backpay was based solely on his interpretation of the parties' CBA. *Id.* at 8. However, the Union asserts that arbitrators must consider all applicable laws when rendering their awards. Here, the Union claims that the Arbitrator failed to consider the applicability of the Back Pay Act, which authorizes arbitrators to award backpay. *Id.* The Union contends that the requirements of the Back Pay were met, including that there was an unwarranted personnel action. The Union argues that, had the Arbitrator made the appropriate finding under Article 12, Section 2 of the parties' CBA, he would have been required to apply the Back Pay Act. *Id.* at 8-9

B. Agency's Opposition

The Agency argues that the Arbitrator did not disregard the parties' CBA because the Arbitrator did not have before him the issue of whether the grievant received a temporary promotion. Opp'n at 4. In addition, the Agency claims that the facts do not establish that the grievant was ever detailed or temporarily promoted; rather, the facts show that she experienced an accretion of duties, which ultimately required a new position description. *Id.* Therefore, the Agency contends, the Arbitrator's finding that he could not award the grievant a temporary promotion showed a "manifest adherence" to the CBA. *Id.* at 5. The Agency also argues that the Arbitrator's award was consistent with Article 42, Section 2 (B)(5) of the parties' CBA, which does not permit grievances concerning the classification of any position that does not result in a reduction in grade or pay.

Finally, the Agency argues that the Arbitrator did not ignore the requirements of the Back Pay Act. The Agency claims that the Arbitrator correctly found that the Back Pay Act applied only if the grievant suffered a prohibited personnel practice or if she was not properly compensated while on a detail. *Id.* at 3. As neither of these situations was present here, the Agency asserts that the Arbitrator correctly found that he could not award backpay.

IV. Analysis and Conclusions

A. The award does not fail to draw its essence from the CBA.

The Authority will find that an arbitration award is deficient as failing to draw its essence from the collective bargaining agreement when the appealing party establishes that the award: (1) cannot in any rational way be derived from the agreement; (2) is so unfounded in reason and fact and so unconnected with the wording and purposes of the collective bargaining agreement as to manifest an infidelity to the obligation of the arbitrator; (3) does not represent a plausible interpretation of the agreement; or (4) evidences a manifest disregard of the agreement. *See U.S. Dep't of Labor* (*OSHA*), 34 FLRA 573, 575 (1990) (*Dep't of Labor*). The Authority and the courts defer to arbitrators in this context "because it is the arbitrator's construction of the agreement for which the parties have bargained." *Id.* at 576.

The Union argues that the award fails to draw its essence from the agreement because the award "disregards" Article 12, Section 2 of the parties' CBA, which provides that employees detailed to a higher-graded position for a period of more than ten consecutive work days must be temporarily promoted. Exceptions at 11. In the Union's view, the Agency had a contractual obligation to temporarily promote the grievant because she worked at a higher-graded position for more than ten consecutive work days. *Id.*

Contrary to the Union's claim, we find that the Arbitrator did not "disregard" Article 12, Section 2 of the parties' CBA. Although the Arbitrator found that the grievant performed higher-graded duties, he found that those duties were "voluntarily assumed[,]" and that there was a "lack of evidence" that the grievant was "ever detailed to a higher[-] graded position[.]" Award at 10 (internal quotations omitted). Because the Arbitrator found that the grievant was not actually detailed to a higher graded position, there was no basis for the Arbitrator to interpret Article 12, Section 2 of the parties' CBA as requiring the Agency to grant the grievant a temporary promotion. As such, the Union has failed to establish that the Arbitrator disregarded Article 12, Section 2 of the parties' CBA.

Consequently, the Union has not provided a basis for finding that the Arbitrator's interpretation of the parties' CBA is irrational, unfounded, implausible, or evidences a manifest disregard of the parties' CBA. *See AFGE, Local 217,* 60 FLRA 459, 461 (2004) (exception denied where union failed to show that arbitrator's award denying grievant's promotion was deficient on essence grounds). Accordingly, we deny the Union's essence exception.

B. The award is not contrary to law.

The Authority reviews questions of law raised by exceptions to an arbitrator's award de novo. *See NTEU, Chapter 24*, 50 FLRA 330, 332 (1995) (citing *U.S. Customs Serv. v. FLRA*, 43 F.3d 682, 686-87 (D.C. Cir. 1994)). In applying the standard of de novo review, the Authority assesses whether an arbitrator's legal conclusions are consistent with the applicable standard of law. *See U.S. Dep't of Def., Dep'ts of the Army & the Air Force, Ala. Nat'l Guard, Northport, Ala.*, 55 FLRA 37, 40 (1998). In making that assessment, the Authority defers to the arbitrator's underlying factual findings. *See id.*

An award of backpay is authorized under the Back Pay Act only when an arbitrator finds that: (1) the aggrieved employee was affected by an unjustified or unwarranted personnel action; and (2) the personnel action resulted in the withdrawal or the reduction of an employee's pay, allowances, or differentials. *U.S. Dep't of the Air Force, Warner Robins Air Force Base, Ga.*, 56 FLRA 541, 543 (2000) (citing *U.S. Dep't of Health & Human Servs.*, 54 FLRA 1210, 1218-19 (1998)).

The Union argues that the Arbitrator's conclusion that he could not award backpay was based solely on his interpretation of the parties' CBA and that the Arbitrator failed to consider the applicability of the Back Pay Act, which authorizes arbitrators to award backpay. Exceptions at 8. The Union further argues that, had the Arbitrator made the appropriate finding under Article 12, Section 2 of the parties' CBA, then he would have been required to apply the Back Pay Act. *Id.*

However, the Arbitrator did not find that the grievant was affected by an unjustified or unwarranted personnel action. Award at 10. Absent such a finding, there was no legal requirement for the Arbitrator to apply the Back Pay Act. Therefore, without a finding that the grievant was affected by an unjustified or unwarranted personnel action, we agree with the Arbitrator's conclusion that he did not have the authority to grant backpay under the Back Pay Act. *See AFGE, Nat'l Border Patrol Council, Local 2455*, 62 FLRA 37, 40 (2007) (award of back pay not authorized by Back Pay Act where arbitrator did not find that grievant was affected by an unjustified or unwarranted personnel action). Accordingly, the Arbitrator's conclusion that he was not authorized to award the grievant backpay is fully consistent with the requirements of the Back Pay Act. Consequently, we deny the Union's exception that the award is contrary to law.

V. Decision

The Union's exceptions are denied.

APPENDIX

Article 9 – Classification

Section 1 – General

> Employees dissatisfied with the classification of their positions should first discuss the problem with their supervisors. If a supervisor is unable to resolve the issue to the employee's satisfaction, the employee can discuss the matter with the Human Resources Manager or appropriate staff member who will explain the basis for the classification/job grading. An employee and/or the Local, upon request, will have access to the position description, evaluation report, if available, organizational and functional charts and other pertinent information directly related to the classification of the position. . . . When a desk audit is conducted, it will be completed within 90 days of the Union or employee request. . . . If the employee still believes there is an inequity, an appeal may be filed with the [Agency] or [the Office of Personnel Management] as appropriate. . . .

Award at 3.

Article 12 – Details, Reassignments and Temporary Promotions

Section 2 – Temporary promotions

> Employees detailed to a higher graded position for a period of more than ten (10) consecutive days must be temporarily promoted. The employee will be paid for the temporary promotion beginning the first day of the detail. The temporary promotion should be initiated at the earliest date it is known by management that the detail is expected to exceed ten (10) consecutive work days.

Id.

Article 42 – Grievance Procedure

Section 2 – Definitions

. . . .

> This Article shall not govern a grievance concerning: the classification of any position which does not result in the reduction in grade or pay of an employee.

Id. at 3-4.

65 FLRA No. 69

SOCIAL SECURITY ADMINISTRATION
OFFICE OF
DISABILITY ADJUDICATION AND REVIEW
REGION 1
(Agency)

and

AMERICAN FEDERATION
OF GOVERNMENT EMPLOYEES
LOCAL 1164
(Union)

0-AR-4370

DECISION

December 16, 2010

Before the Authority: Carol Waller Pope, Chairman, and Thomas M. Beck and Ernest DuBester, Members

I. Statement of the Case

This matter is before the Authority on exceptions to an award of Arbitrator Sharon Henderson Ellis filed by the Agency under § 7122(a) of the Federal Service Labor-Management Relations Statute (the Statute) and part 2425 of the Authority's Regulations. The Union filed an opposition to the Agency's exceptions.

The Union filed a grievance alleging that the Agency changed flexiplace benefits for senior case technicians (SCTs) without satisfying its bargaining obligations. The Arbitrator sustained the grievance, directed the Agency to bargain, and awarded monetary compensation to affected SCTs for commuting expenses.

For the reasons that follow, we grant the exceptions in part, set aside the award in part, and deny the exceptions in part.

II. Background and Arbitrator's Award

The Agency employs SCTs to organize and sequence information in its disability-claims case folders – a process referred to as "pulling cases." Award at 4. According to the parties' Flexiplace Agreement (Agreement), SCTs would be authorized to "pull cases" at an Alternate Duty Station (ADS) at least one day per week, unless supervisors determined that "insufficient work[,]" *id.* at 3, existed for such assignments. *Id.* at 3-4 (quoting Agreement, §§ 2, 4, 16).[1] As part of a flexiplace assignment, an SCT would take hard-copy, case-related documents to an ADS for "pulling." *Id.* at 4. Upon returning to a regular duty station, the SCT would bring back the cases that she or he had "pulled." *Id.* When the Agency began transitioning to electronic, paperless files (e-files), the parties adopted a memorandum of understanding (MOU) that explained the manner in which the Flexiplace Agreement could be changed, if necessary, to accommodate e-files.[2] *See id.* at 3-4, 10-11.

---

1. In relevant part, Section 2 of the Agreement provides:

> All employees who meet the . . . criteria [set forth in the Agreement] are eligible to participate in the Flexiplace Program. Eligible full-time employees will be authorized at least one day per week to work at an ADS. . . .

Award at 3 (quoting Agreement, § 2).

In pertinent part, Section 4 of the Agreement provides:

> If . . . [an] immediate supervisor determines that there is insufficient work for an employee to work at the ADS . . . , the employee will be informed in writing that his/her participation in Flexiplace is temporarily suspended until work is available.

Id. (quoting Agreement, § 4).

In addition, Section 16 of Agreement provides:

> The Agency reserves the right to temporarily suspend the Flexiplace Program . . . where operational exigencies require a return to the traditional 5-day workweek. . . . Prior to [the] extension of the suspension beyond one pay period, the Union will be notified, and the Agency agrees to fulfill its obligations in accordance with [the Statute].

Id. at 3-4 (quoting Agreement, § 16).

2. Section 1 of the MOU states, in pertinent part:

> Should management propose changes to existing Flexiplace Agreements, appropriate notice and opportunity to bargain will be provided to the Union in accordance with . . . [the] National Agreement and [the Statute].

See Award at 4-5, 13 (quoting MOU, § 1).

The Agency gradually converted more cases from paper files to e-files, which left increasingly fewer paper files available for pulling cases at an ADS. Because the Agency "deci[ded] that it could not take the security risk of providing SC[T]s [with] the [remote network] access" that the Agency believed was required to pull cases involving e-files at an ADS, "SCTs could not continue to perform work from home in any significant amounts[.]" *Id.* at 11. In light of the scarcity of portable, hard-copy files that required pulling, the Agency maintained that, even if SCTs no longer had any opportunities to work at an ADS, the Agency had done everything that the Agreement and MOU required of it. *See id.* at 6-7. Consequently, the Union filed a grievance alleging that the Agency violated the Agreement and MOU by curtailing SCTs' flexiplace benefits, without providing notice or an opportunity to bargain over the benefits change itself or the e-filing transition's impact on those benefits. *See id.* at 11; *see also* Exceptions, Attach., Letter from Union V.P. to Acting Chief A.L.J. (Mar. 9, 2007). When the grievance was unresolved, the parties proceeded to arbitration, where the Arbitrator framed the following issues for resolution: "Did the Agency violate the law and[/]or negotiated agreements or the parties' National Agreement when it altered or ended [f]lexiplace benefits for SCTs? If so, what shall be the remedy?" Award at 1.

The Arbitrator found that, in changing flexiplace for SCTs, the Agency had violated a "bargaining obligation . . . [that] is, itself, a product of negotiation." *Id.* at 13 (citing MOU, § 1; Agreement, § 16).[3] She determined that "minimally[,] Section 2 of the [Agreement] was changed" and, under Section 1 of the MOU, "that change in the [Agreement] required the Agency to give notice to, and bargain with, the Union." *Id.* at 19. Although she rejected the Union's request for restoration of the status quo ante because it "would prove too disruptive[,]" the Arbitrator directed the Agency to "meet . . . with the Union to negotiate about the change and/or impact of the electronic folder process on SCTs . . . ." *Id.* at 22, 23.

The Arbitrator emphasized that she was not "suggest[ing] that the Agency cannot continue to move forward in its quest to make the disability claims process a mostly electronic one." *Id.* at 21. Rather, she stated that she was directing the Agency to "attempt to do now what it did not do at the time [of its transition to e-filing,] when changes [to flexiplace] first appeared" – to "negotiate in good faith about the impact of the [e-filing transition on] the [f]lexiplace benefit for SCTs[,]" as required by the MOU. *Id.* at 21, 23. Therefore, the Arbitrator "require[d] the Agency to explore the wide range of work assignment[s] and technological options that the Agency has at its disposal and to bargain with the Union about that very issue." *Id.* at 23. The Arbitrator concluded her award by reiterating that "the Agency shall meet at reasonable times and places . . . to negotiate about the change and/or impact of the electronic folder process on SCTs[,]" and she directed that "SCTs shall also be reimbursed for reasonable parking and commuting expenses they incurred [due to missed flexiplace days.]" *Id.*

III. Positions of the Parties

A. Agency's Exceptions

The Agency contends that the award violates its right to assign work because, by directing the Agency to bargain over "that very issue[,]" the award would require it to "bargain substantively over [a] 5 U.S.C. [§] 7106(a)(2)(B)" matter, in violation of law. *Id.* at 6-7. The Agency also contends that the award violates its right under § 7106(b)(1) of the Statute to elect not to bargain over the technology of performing work. *Id.* at 9-10. In this regard, the Agency recognizes that it may elect to negotiate such matters but asserts that it has not elected to do so. *Id.* at 9. In addition, the Agency asserts that "substantive negotiations over the technology of performing the Agency's work could also improperly infringe on management's right to determine internal security practices[.]" *Id.* at 10 n.2 (citing 5 U.S.C. § 7106(a)(1)).

Finally, the Agency argues that, by ordering the Agency to reimburse SCTs for lost parking and commuting expenses, the award violates the doctrine of sovereign immunity because, according to the Agency, neither the Back Pay Act nor any other statute authorizes money reimbursements for "personal commuting expenses." *Id.* at 11-12 (citing *Immigration & Naturalization Serv., L.A. Dist., L.A., Cal.*, 52 FLRA 103, 105-06 (1996); *U.S. Customs Serv., Chicago-O'Hare*, 23 FLRA 366, 367 (1986) (*Chicago-O'Hare*)).

3. The Arbitrator reiterated this point later in the award: "Bargaining . . . in advance of known impending change . . . is, in this case, a negotiated agreement. . . . [T]he fact is inescapable that the Agency violated its own negotiated promise(s) to bargain when it changed the [f]lexiplace benefit . . . ." Award at 21.

B. Union's Opposition

The Union asserts that the award merely requires the Agency "to go to the bargaining table" and that, because the award does not mandate any particular outcome for the parties' negotiations, the Authority's consideration of the exceptions would constitute an impermissible advisory opinion on the legality of "[w]hat might eventually happen at the bargaining table[.]" Opp'n at 9-10 (citing 5 C.F.R. § 2429.10).[4] The Union also asserts that the Arbitrator directed the Agency to bargain to fulfill a contractual obligation, not a statutory one; thus, according to the Union, the Agency "cannot legitimately claim that the award [concerning contractual bargaining obligations] violates management rights." *Id.* at 1, 6 (citing *U.S. Dep't of Def., Nat'l Guard Bureau Adjutant Gen., Kan. Nat'l Guard*, 57 FLRA 934 (2002); *Soc. Sec. Admin., Balt., Md.*, 55 FLRA 1063 (1999); *AFGE, Local 3937*, 49 FLRA 785 (1994)). Finally, the Union contends that the Agency's arguments regarding sovereign immunity should be dismissed because, although the Agency was on notice that the Union was requesting remedies including commuting expenses, the Agency did not argue before the Arbitrator that sovereign immunity prevented her from awarding reimbursement for such expenses. *See id.* at 2, 10 (citing 5 C.F.R. § 2429.5).

IV. Preliminary Matter

The Authority has stated that an opinion as to matters that might occur in the future constitutes an advisory opinion. *See, e.g., AFGE, Local 1864*, 45 FLRA 691, 694-95 (1992). However, the Authority has considered exceptions to an arbitral direction to bargain where the agency challenged the legality of the direction itself and "not hypothetical events that might occur in the future[.]" *AFGE, Council 215*, 60 FLRA 461, 463-64 (2004). Here, the Agency does not assert that the results of bargaining would be contrary to law; the Agency objects to the direction to bargain itself. Specifically, the Agency contends that the award requires it to bargain over the substance of its rights under the Statute. As the Agency's exceptions concern a live legal dispute about its rights, and not hypothetical future events, the Authority would not be issuing an advisory opinion by evaluating the exceptions. *See AFGE, Council 215*, 60 FLRA at 463-64. As such, we consider the exceptions below.

4. Section 2429.10 of the Authority's Regulations states, in pertinent part, that "[t]he Authority . . . will not issue advisory opinions."

V. Analysis and Conclusions

A. The award does not violate management's rights under the Statute.

The Agency claims that the award is contrary to law because the Arbitrator directed it to bargain substantively over work assignments and the technology of performing work. The Authority reviews questions of law de novo. *See NTEU, Chapter 24*, 50 FLRA 330, 332 (1995) (citing *U.S. Customs Serv. v. FLRA*, 43 F.3d 682, 686-87 (D.C. Cir. 1994)). In applying the standard of de novo review, the Authority determines whether the arbitrator's legal conclusions are consistent with the applicable standard of law. *See NFFE, Local 1437*, 53 FLRA 1703, 1710 (1998). In making that determination, the Authority defers to the arbitrator's underlying factual findings. *See id.*

When evaluating exceptions to an arbitration award, the Authority considers the award and record as a whole. *See, e.g., AFGE, Local 2328*, 62 FLRA 63, 65 (2007) (consistency with law "clear from the record as a whole"); *AFGE, Local 3911*, 56 FLRA 480, 481 n.5 (2000) (determining relevant contract provision from "award as a whole"); *U.S. Dep't of Energy, Oak Ridge Operations Office, Oak Ridge, Tenn.*, 55 FLRA 1293, 1296 (2000) (reading "award as a whole" and finding agency "misconstrued the award"); *U.S. Dep't of Veterans Affairs, Med. Ctr., Fort Wayne, Ind.*, 39 FLRA 717, 721 (1991) (arbitrator's finding "apparent[] from a reading of the award as a whole"). In this regard, the Authority interprets the language of an award in context, without undue focus on isolated statements. *See, e.g., U.S. Dep't of Def., Def. Contract Audit Agency, Central Region, Irving, Tex.*, 60 FLRA 28, 29 (2004); *U.S. Dep't of the Navy, Naval Surface Warfare Ctr., Indian Head Div., Indian Head, Md.*, 56 FLRA 848, 850 (2000); *NTEU, Chapter 168*, 52 FLRA 1354, 1364 (1997); *U.S. Dep't of the Treasury, U.S. Customs Serv., El Paso, Tex.*, 52 FLRA 622, 628 n.5 (1996).

Based on the award and the record as a whole, we reject the Agency's claim that the award requires it to bargain over the substance of its rights to assign work and to determine the technology of performing work. In this regard, the Arbitrator found that the Agency's transition to e-filing did not "exonerate management from the obligation to bargain *the impact* of the change." Award at 12. To support that conclusion, the Arbitrator quoted from an Authority decision regarding impact-and-implementation bargaining. *Id.* at 13 (quoting *U.S. Dep't of HHS,*

SSA, Balt., Md., 41 FLRA 1309, 1317 (1991)). In addition, the Arbitrator stated that the Agency had violated the MOU by "mak[ing] significant changes in [f]lexiplace [benefits] . . . without first . . . negotiating *either* the change, *or* the impact of the change, on unit employees." *Id.* at 21 (emphases added). Consequently, the Arbitrator directed the Agency to "negotiate in good faith about the *impact of the change* to the [f]lexiplace benefit for SCTs." *Id.* at 23 (emphasis added). The Arbitrator concluded her award by reiterating that "the Agency shall meet at reasonable times and places . . . to negotiate about the change and/*or impact* of the electronic folder process on SCTs[.]" *Id.* (emphasis added).

The Agency correctly points out that, in addition to the foregoing, the award requires the Agency "to explore the wide range of work assignment[s] and technological options that the Agency has at its disposal and to bargain with the Union about that very issue." *Id.* at 23. In particular, the Agency focuses on the meaning of the phrase "that very issue." However, as used in the award, the meaning of "that very issue" is ambiguous. For example, the "issue" to which the phrase refers could be the "explor[ation]" of the parties' "options," or the "range" of options available for restoring flexiplace benefits. *Id.* In addition, the direction requires only that the Agency bargain "*about* that very issue"; it does not require the Agency to bargain *about the substance* of "that very issue." *Id.* (emphasis added). Accordingly, the Agency has not demonstrated that the aforementioned sections of the award require bargaining over more than the impact and implementation of the Agency's transition to e-filing, with particular attention to the impact on flexiplace benefits for SCTs.[5]

As the Agency does not allege that the Arbitrator's direction to engage in impact-and-implementation bargaining is contrary to law, we deny the Agency's exceptions regarding § 7106(a)(2)(B) and (b)(1) of the Statute.[6]

B. The award of commuting expenses violates the doctrine of sovereign immunity.

The Agency argues that the award of commuting expenses violates the doctrine of sovereign immunity. Exceptions at 11. The Union does not dispute that argument, but contends that the Agency's sovereign-immunity challenge should not be considered because it was not advanced before the Arbitrator. Opp'n at 2, 10-12 (citing 5 C.F.R. § 2429.5). Contrary to the Union's contention, however, "a claim of federal sovereign immunity can be raised by an agency at any time." *U.S. Dep't of the Treasury, IRS, Wash., D.C.*, 61 FLRA 146, 151 (2005) (citing *Dep't of the Army, U.S. Army Commissary, Fort Benjamin Harrison, Indianapolis v. FLRA*, 56 F.3d 273, 275 (D.C. Cir. 1995) (*Army*), *vacating in part* 48 FLRA 6 (1993)). Accordingly, we find that the Agency's sovereign-immunity exception has been properly raised for consideration, and, therefore, we consider it below.

The United States is immune from liability for money damages under the doctrine of sovereign immunity. *See Lane v. Pena*, 518 U.S. 187, 192 (1996). Because the award of "reimbursement" for "mileage and parking" expenses "to employees adversely affected by [f]lexiplace reduction[s,]" Award at 22-23, provides payment of a sum of money for the breach of the MOU, the remedy constitutes monetary damages. *See Army*, 56 F.3d at 276. A waiver of sovereign immunity will be found only if "unequivocally expressed in statutory text . . . and will not be implied[.]" *Lane v. Pena*, 518 U.S. at 192; *see also Army*, 56 F.3d at 277; *U.S. Dep't of Health & Human Serv., Food & Drug Admin.*, 60 FLRA 250, 252 (2004) (*Food & Drug Admin.*). Thus, the award of money damages for commuting expenses is only lawful if it is based upon an explicit waiver of sovereign immunity. *See Food & Drug Admin.*, 60 FLRA at 252.

The Agency claims that there is no statutory waiver of sovereign immunity to authorize payment for personal commuting expenses under the Back Pay Act, 5 U.S.C. § 5596, or any other statute. Under the Back Pay Act, an award of backpay is authorized only when an arbitrator finds, as relevant here, that an unjustified or unwarranted personnel action directly resulted in the withdrawal or reduction of a grievant's pay, allowances, or differentials. *See U.S. Dep't of Justice, Immigration & Naturalization Serv., San Diego, Cal.*, 51 FLRA 1094, 1097 (1996). The

5. When the Arbitrator describes the Agency's obligation to bargain over workplace changes or the impact of those changes, her use of the disjunctive word "or" indicates that the Agency may satisfy its obligation by negotiating over the impact of the changes alone. *See* Award at 21, 23.

6. To the extent that the Agency intended the reference in its exceptions to internal security practices to constitute an independent exception to the award, because we find that the award does not require substantive bargaining over the technology of performing work, we need not address whether an award requiring substantive bargaining over the technology of performing work would also violate the Agency's right to determine its internal security practices.

Authority has previously held that ordinary personal commuting expenses do not constitute pay, allowances, or differentials under the Back Pay Act. *See U.S. Dep't of Health & Human Servs.*, 54 FLRA 1210, 1222 (1998) (citing *Chicago-O'Hare*, 23 FLRA at 367-68). Moreover, the Authority has recognized that ordinary home-to-work mileage and parking costs constitute noncompensable personal commuting expenses. *See NTEU*, 30 FLRA 677, 678-79 (1987). Applying this precedent, we find that the Back Pay Act does not authorize reimbursement for SCTs' mileage and parking costs, and – as the Union does not cite another statutory waiver of sovereign immunity to support the monetary award – we set aside the portion of the award that directs payment to SCTs for personal commuting expenses.

VI. Decision

The Agency's sovereign-immunity exception is granted, and the award of personal commuting expenses is set aside. The Agency's remaining exceptions are denied.

65 FLRA No. 70

SOCIAL SECURITY ADMINISTRATION
(Agency)

and

AMERICAN FEDERATION
OF GOVERNMENT EMPLOYEES
COUNCIL 220
(Union)

0-AR-4485

DECISION

December 16, 2010

Before the Authority: Carol Waller Pope, Chairman, and Thomas M. Beck and Ernest DuBester, Members

I. Statement of the Case

This matter is before the Authority on exceptions to an award of Arbitrator Sean J. Rogers filed by the Agency under § 7122(a) of the Federal Service Labor-Management Relations Statute (the Statute) and part 2425 of the Authority's Regulations. The Union filed an opposition to the Agency's exceptions.

The Arbitrator found that the Agency violated the parties' agreement by implementing a policy that restricted when certain employees could use annual leave. For the reasons set forth below, we dismiss the Agency's exception that the award is contrary to § 7106(a)(2)(A) of the Statute and deny the Agency's remaining exceptions.

II. Background and Arbitrator's Award

The Agency employs Teleservice Representatives (Representatives). Representatives answer a nationwide toll-free number maintained by the Agency and are responsible for answering questions from individuals who call this number. Award at 7. The Agency enacted a nationwide annual leave guideline (guideline) to govern leave requests made by Representatives. At the Agency, the days of the week are designated with four different "Levels." *Id.* "Level 1" days are the days of the week with the highest volume of callers, whereas "Level 4" days are the days with lowest volume of callers. *Id.* Pursuant to the guideline, no more than 10 percent of Representatives nationwide would be permitted to use annual leave on "Level 1" and "Level 2" days, while no more than 15 percent of Representatives nationwide would be permitted to use leave on "Level 3" and "Level 4" days. *Id.* at 8.

The Union presented a grievance arguing that the Agency's implementation of the guideline violated Article 31, § 2B of the parties' agreement, which states, in relevant part, that the Agency will "make every reasonable effort to allow the maximum number of employees to use leave."[1] Award at 4 (citation omitted). The parties stipulated that the issue for resolution was "[w]hether the [Agency] violated the [parties' agreement] by implementing annual leave restriction guidelines for [the Representatives]? If so, what shall be the remedy?" Award at 3.

The Arbitrator concluded that the Agency violated Article 31, § 2B of the parties' agreement by enacting the guideline. The Arbitrator determined that § 2B is a "plain language, comprehensive and detailed provision covering the [p]arties' collectively bargained work rules and rights on the granting and denying of annual leave requests." *Id.* at 21. The Arbitrator concluded that the Agency "retains the right to deny annual leave for reasons described . . . by [§ 2B]." *Id.* at 20-21. However, he further determined that § 2B requires the Agency to "normally grant annual leave requests absent schedule conflicts and workload interference" and to make "every reasonable effort to allow the maximum number of employees to be on annual leave[.]" *Id.* at 20. Moreover, relying on his interpretation, the Arbitrator found that nothing in § 2B permitted the Agency to create or enact the guideline. *Id.* at 21, 24.

In reaching the above conclusion, the Arbitrator rejected the Agency's argument that Article 31, § 2B "limits" the Agency's management rights. *Id.* at 22; *see also id.* at 23 ("[Agency] had no management

1. Article 31, § 2B of the parties' agreement provides:

> Normally, leave requested in advance will be granted except when conflicts of scheduling or undue interference with the work of the [Agency] would preclude it. Leave may also be granted when it is not scheduled in advance and workload considerations permit . . . The [Agency] will make every reasonable effort to allow the maximum number of employees to use leave.

Award at 4 (citation omitted).

right to change the [parties' agreement].").
According to the Arbitrator, the Agency "never asserted" to the Union that § 2B violates any portion of the Statute. *Id.* at 22. Furthermore, the Arbitrator rejected the Agency's reliance on certain Authority decisions to support the proposition that the Agency had the right to create and implement the guidelines; according to the Arbitrator, those decisions were inapplicable to the resolution of the Union's grievance because they involved negotiability determinations. *Id.* at 23.

The Arbitrator sustained the Union's grievance. He ordered the Agency to rescind the guideline; "return to status quo ante" and grant and deny annual leave requests pursuant only to the criteria set forth in Article 31, § 2B; and cease and desist from imposing "unilateral changes" to § 2B. *Id.* at 24.

III. Positions of the Parties

A. Agency's Exceptions

The Agency asserts that the Arbitrator's award restricts the Agency's ability to deny leave and that, as such, it affects management's rights to direct employees and assign work under § 7106(a)(2)(A) and (B) of the Statute, respectively. Exceptions at 7. Accordingly, the Agency contends that the Authority should apply the two-prong test set forth in *United States Department of the Treasury, Bureau of Engraving and Printing, Washington, D.C.*, 53 FLRA 146 (1997) (*BEP*) and conclude that the award violates management's rights. *Id.* Specifically, the Agency contends that the award does not satisfy prong I of *BEP* because Article 31, § 2B, as interpreted by the Arbitrator, violates management's right to deny leave requests; as such, this provision is not an arrangement. *Id.* at 8-9. Further, the Agency argues -- without elaboration -- that, even if the provision is an arrangement, it is not appropriate because it "excessively interferes" with management rights. *Id.* at 9. Last, the Agency claims -- also without elaboration -- that the award does not satisfy prong II of *BEP* because the Arbitrator failed to reconstruct what action the Agency would have taken in the absence of the contractual violation found by the Arbitrator. *Id.*

The Agency also claims that the Arbitrator's award is contrary to law because the Arbitrator misapplied the Authority's "covered by" doctrine. *Id.* at 9-12. According to the Agency, the Arbitrator's determination that the Agency could not create the guideline because "the granting of annual leave is *covered by* Article 31, [§] 2B" inappropriately creates a "reverse covered by" doctrine that prohibits the Agency from exercising its management rights. *Id.* at 10-11 (quoting Award at 22) (emphasis in original). The Agency contends that the Arbitrator's decision inappropriately permits the parties' agreement to trump management's right to deny leave. *Id.* at 11.

Finally, the Agency contends that the Arbitrator's award fails to draw its essence from the parties' agreement. The Agency argues that Article 31, § 2B of the parties' agreement grants the Agency permission to deny leave requests to prevent "undue interference" with the Agency's workload, and that the guideline was enacted to prevent such interference. *Id.* at 12-13. According to the Agency, the Arbitrator's decision to rescind the guideline, therefore, creates doubt as to whether the Agency could *ever* deny leave requests. *Id.* at 13.

B. Union's Opposition

As a preliminary matter, the Union argues that the Agency's assertion concerning § 7106(a)(2)(A) of the Statute should be barred because it was not presented to the Arbitrator. Opp'n at 5.

Addressing the merits, the Union agrees that *BEP* applies to this case; however, it alleges that the award is nevertheless proper. The Union contends that the Arbitrator's interpretation of Article 31, § 2B satisfies prong I because this provision constitutes an arrangement for employees adversely affected by management's right to deny leave. *Id.* at 4 (citation omitted). Moreover, the Union contends that the provision is appropriate because it does not abrogate management's right to deny leave, it merely prevents the implementation of the guideline. *Id.* at 4-5 & n.2. The Union also asserts that the award satisfies prong II of *BEP* because: (1) there is a nexus between the Arbitrator's remedy -- rescinding the guideline -- and the Agency's violation of the parties' agreement; and (2) the Arbitrator properly reconstructed what action the Agency would have taken in the absence of its contractual violation. *Id.* at 5.

The Union also contends that the Arbitrator correctly found that the Agency was prohibited from implementing the guidelines because the use of leave is "covered by" Article 31, § 2B of the parties' agreement. *Id.* at 6. Based on this finding, the Union argues that the Arbitrator correctly found that the Union was not required to request to bargain over the matter. Further, the Union asserts that, regardless of whether the "covered by" doctrine applies, the

Agency was not permitted unilaterally to implement the guideline. *Id.* at 7.

The Union also rejects the Agency's claim that the Arbitrator's interpretation of Article 31, § 2B fails to draw its essence from the parties' agreement. Citing the Arbitrator's findings, the Union contends that the Arbitrator "clearly and methodically articulated his findings and rationale" in support of his conclusion that the guideline violated § 2B. *Id.* at 8. The Union asserts that it is not "reasonable to believe" that the Agency could still allow the "maximum number of employees to use leave[,]" as required by § 2B, *and* implement the guideline. *Id.* at 9.

IV. Preliminary Issue

The Authority's Regulations that were in effect when the Agency filed its exceptions provided that "[t]he Authority will not consider . . . any issue, which was not presented in the proceedings before the . . . arbitrator." 5 C.F.R. § 2429.5.[2] Before the Arbitrator, the Agency argued that interpreting Article 31, § 2B to prohibit the enactment of the guidelines would interfere with management's right to assign work under § 7106(a)(2)(B). Exceptions, Attach. 4 at 12 (Agency's post-hearing brief). There is no indication in the record that the Agency also argued to the Arbitrator that such an interpretation would conflict with § 7106(a)(2)(A). Because this issue could have been, but was not, presented to the Arbitrator, § 2429.5 precludes the Agency from raising it for the first time in exceptions. *See, e.g., U.S. Dep't of Transp., FAA*, 65 FLRA 171, 172 (2010) (Member Beck concurring as to other matters) (agency's exception concerning management rights was barred by § 2429.5 of the Authority's previous Regulations). Accordingly, we dismiss this exception.

V. Analysis and Conclusions

A. The award is not contrary to law.

The Authority reviews questions of law raised by exceptions to an arbitrator's award de novo. *See NTEU, Chapter 24*, 50 FLRA 330, 332 (1995) (citing *U.S. Customs Serv. v. FLRA*, 43 F.3d 682, 686-87 (D.C. Cir. 1994)). In applying a standard of de novo review, the Authority determines whether the arbitrator's legal conclusions are consistent with the applicable standard of law. *See NFFE, Local 1437*, 53 FLRA 1703, 1710 (1998). In making that determination, the Authority defers to the arbitrator's underlying factual findings. *Id.*

1. The award is not contrary to § 7106(a)(2)(B) of the Statute.

The Agency contends that the Arbitrator's award impermissibly affects management's right to assign work under § 7106(a)(2)(B) of the Statute. The Authority recently revised the analysis that it will apply when reviewing management rights exceptions to arbitration awards. *See U.S. Envtl. Prot. Agency*, 65 FLRA 113, 115 (2010) (Member Beck concurring) (*EPA*); *Fed. Deposit Ins. Corp., Div. of Supervision & Consumer Prot., S.F. Region*, 65 FLRA 102, 106-07 (2010) (Chairman Pope concurring) (*FDIC, S.F. Region*). Under the revised analysis, the Authority will first assess whether the award affects the exercise of the asserted management right. *EPA*, 65 FLRA at 115. If so, then, as relevant here, the Authority examines whether the award enforces a contract provision negotiated under § 7106(b). *Id.* Also, under the revised analysis, in determining whether the award enforces a contract provision negotiated under § 7106(b)(3), the Authority assesses: (1) whether the contract provision constitutes an arrangement for employees adversely affected by the exercise of a management right; and (2) if so, whether the arbitrator's enforcement of the arrangement abrogates the exercise of the management right. *See id.* at 116-18. In concluding that it would apply an abrogation standard, the Authority rejected continued application of an excessive interference standard. *Id.* at 118. Furthermore, in setting forth the revised analysis, the Authority rejected the continued application of the "reconstruction" requirement set forth in *BEP*. *FDIC, S.F. Region*, 65 FLRA at 106-07.

The parties do not dispute that the award affects management's right to assign work under § 7106(a)(2)(B) of the Statute. *See* Exceptions at 5-6; Opp'n at 3-4. Thus, we turn to whether the Arbitrator enforced a contract provision negotiated under § 7106(b). The Agency contends Article 31, § 2B does not constitute an appropriate arrangement under § 7106(b)(3) because it is neither an arrangement nor appropriate.

The Agency first asserts that § 2B, as interpreted and applied by the Arbitrator, is not an arrangement

2. The Authority's Regulations concerning the review of arbitration awards, as well as certain related procedural regulations, including § 2429.5, were revised effective October 1, 2010. *See* 75 Fed. Reg. 42,283 (2010). Because the Agency's exceptions were filed before that date, we apply the earlier Regulations.

because it conflicts with management's right to assign work. Exceptions at 8-9. However, this is not the standard that the Authority relies on when it decides whether a provision constitutes an arrangement; rather, the Authority examines whether a provision, as interpreted and applied by an arbitrator, ameliorates or mitigates adverse effects that flow from management's exercise of its management rights. *E.g., EPA*, 65 FLRA at 116 (citing *U.S. DOJ, Fed Bureau of Prisons, U.S. Penitentiary, Atlanta, Ga.*, 57 FLRA 406, 410 (2001) (Chairman Cabaniss dissenting)). Therefore, the Agency's claim that § 2B is not an arrangement because it conflicts with management's right to assign work is incorrect. Moreover, the Authority has held that provisions addressing the circumstances in which management can deny leave requests ameliorate the adverse affects flowing from management's right to deny leave requests. *See, e.g., NTEU*, 45 FLRA 696, 724 (1992) (citation omitted). Article 31, § 2B ameliorates or mitigates the adverse effects caused by management's exercise of its right to deny leave by addressing the circumstances when the Agency can deny leave requests. Accordingly, we find that Article 31, § 2B is an arrangement under § 7106(b)(3). *See id.*

The Agency next contends -- without elaboration -- that, even if Article 31, § 2B is an arrangement, it is not appropriate because it excessively interferes with management's right to assign work. However, as stated above, the Authority no longer applies an excessive interference standard in determining whether an arbitrator has enforced a contract provision negotiated under § 7106(b)(3); rather, it applies an abrogation standard. Moreover, the Agency offers no explanation as to why its right to assign work is burdened by § 2B. Accordingly, we find that the Agency has failed to establish that § 2B, as interpreted and applied by the Arbitrator, abrogates management's right to assign work. *See, e.g., U.S. Dep't of Homeland Sec., U.S. Customs & Border Prot.*, 61 FLRA 113, 116-17 (2005) (Member Armendariz dissenting) (citing *U.S. Dep't of the Treasury, U.S. Customs Serv., El Paso, Tex.*, 55 FLRA 553, 558 n.3 (1999)) (rejecting claim that provision was not appropriate, and that award was therefore contrary to management rights, where agency failed to explain how provision abrogated management's right to assign work)).[3]

Based on the foregoing, we find that Article 31, § 2B was negotiated under § 7106(b)(3) of the Statute.

The Agency also asserts -- with no explanation -- that, even if Article 31, § 2B is an appropriate arrangement, the award is deficient under *BEP* because the Arbitrator failed to reconstruct what management would have done had it complied with § 2B. However, as noted above, the Authority no longer requires that an arbitrator's remedy reconstruct what management would have done had it not violated the contract provision. *FDIC*, 65 FLRA 179, 181 (2010). Moreover, as we held above, Article 31, § 2B is a properly negotiated contract provision. The Arbitrator's award enforces this provision. Accordingly, we conclude that the award does not impermissibly affect management rights by failing to reconstruct what the Agency would have done had it not violated the contract, and we deny the Agency's contrary to law exception.[4] *See, e.g., id.* (citing *FDIC, S.F. Region*, 65 FLRA at 107).

2. Covered By Doctrine.

The Agency also argues that the award is contrary to law because the Arbitrator's interpretation of Article 31, § 2B created a "reverse covered by" doctrine that improperly prohibits the Agency from exercising its management right to assign work. Exceptions at 11. The Agency's argument is flawed. Although the Arbitrator used the phrase "covered by[,]" Award at 22, his award contains no indication that he relied on the covered by doctrine or any variation thereof. Moreover, the Agency's argument is based on the flawed assumption that § 2B is contrary to management's right to assign work;

3. Member Beck agrees with the conclusion to deny the Agency's exceptions. He does not agree, however, with his colleagues' analysis of the contrary to law exception insofar as they address the question of whether the award affects the exercise of an asserted management right. For the reasons discussed in his concurring opinion in *EPA*, 65 FLRA 113, Member Beck concludes that where, as here, the Arbitrator is enforcing a contract provision that has been accepted by the Agency as a permissible limitation on its management's rights, it is inappropriate to assess whether the provision itself is an appropriate arrangement or whether it abrogates a § 7106(a) right. *Id.* at 120. The appropriate question is simply whether the remedy directed by the Arbitrator enforces the provision in a reasonable and reasonably foreseeable fashion. *Id.*; *see also FDIC, S.F. Region,* 65 FLRA at 107. Member Beck concludes that the Arbitrator's award is a plausible interpretation of the parties' agreement. Accordingly, Member Beck agrees that the Agency's contrary to law exceptions should be denied.

4. For the reasons set forth in her concurring opinion in *FDIC, S.F. Region*, 65 FLRA at 112, Chairman Pope agrees that the award is not deficient because the Arbitrator's remedy is reasonably related to the negotiated provision and the harm being remedied.

however, as we held above, § 2B is *not* contrary to this right. Accordingly, we reject this argument.

B. The award does not fail to draw its essence from the parties' agreement.

In reviewing an arbitrator's interpretation of a collective bargaining agreement, the Authority applies the deferential standard of review that federal courts use in reviewing arbitration awards in the private sector. *See* 5 U.S.C. § 7122(a)(2); *AFGE, Council 220*, 54 FLRA 156, 159 (1998). Under this standard, the Authority will find that an arbitration award is deficient as failing to draw its essence from the collective bargaining agreement when the appealing party establishes that the award: (1) cannot in any rational way be derived from the agreement; (2) is so unfounded in reason and fact and so unconnected with the wording and purposes of the collective bargaining agreement as to manifest an infidelity to the obligation of the arbitrator; (3) does not represent a plausible interpretation of the agreement; or (4) evidences a manifest disregard of the agreement. *See U.S. Dep't of Labor (OSHA)*, 34 FLRA 573, 575 (1990) (*OSHA*). The Authority and the courts defer to arbitrators in this context "because it is the arbitrator's construction of the agreement for which the parties have bargained." *Id.* at 576.

The Agency claims that the Arbitrator's interpretation of Article 31, § 2B fails to draw its essence from the agreement because § 2B allows the Agency to deny leave when it would cause an "undue interference[,]" and the guideline was an attempt to prevent such interference. Exceptions at 13. After reviewing the language of § 2B, the Arbitrator concluded that it permits the Agency to deny leave requests when such requests would cause "undue interference" with the Agency's workload, Award at 20; however, he found that nothing in this language indicated that the Agency could create or enact any sort of leave guidelines. This conclusion was based on the Arbitrator's interpretation and application of § 2B. As set forth above, the Authority defers to the Arbitrator's interpretation of the agreement "because it is the [A]rbitrator's construction of the agreement for which the parties have bargained." *OSHA,* 34 FLRA at 576. The Agency's argument does not establish that the Arbitrator's interpretation of Article 31, § 2B is irrational, implausible, or otherwise deficient.

The Agency also argues that the Arbitrator's interpretation of Article 31, § 2B creates doubt as to whether the Agency could "ever deny requested annual leave." Exceptions at 13. However, as stated above, the Arbitrator determined that, under § 2B, the Agency unequivocally "retains the right to deny annual leave[.]" Award at 20-21; *see also id.* at 24 (Arbitrator reiterated his determination "that the granting *and denying* of annual leave" is governed by § 2B (emphasis added)). Consequently, this argument also fails to establish that the Arbitrator's interpretation is irrational, implausible, or otherwise deficient.

Accordingly, we find that the Agency has not demonstrated that the Arbitrator's interpretation of Article 31, § 2B fails to draw its essence from the parties' agreement.

VI. Decision

The Agency's exception regarding § 7106(a)(2)(A) is dismissed. The Agency's remaining exceptions are denied.

65 FLRA No. 71

UNITED STATES
DEPARTMENT OF THE NAVY
NAVY EXCHANGE
SAN DIEGO, CALIFORNIA
(Agency)

and

AMERICAN FEDERATION
OF GOVERNMENT EMPLOYEES
LOCAL 3723
(Union)

0-AR-4668

DECISION

December 16, 2010

Before the Authority: Carol Waller Pope, Chairman, and Thomas M. Beck and Ernest DuBester, Members

I. Statement of the Case

This matter is before the Authority on exceptions to an award of Arbitrator Jonathan S. Monat filed by the Agency under § 7122(a) of the Federal Service Labor-Management Relations Statute (the Statute) and part 2425 of the Authority's Regulations. The Union filed an opposition to the Agency's exceptions.

The Arbitrator concluded that the Agency violated the parties' Labor Management Agreement (Agreement) when it changed the hours of barber shop employees. As a remedy, he found that the grievant was entitled to backpay pursuant to the Back Pay Act and ordered the Agency to discuss the impact of the change with the Union. For the reasons set forth below, we dismiss the Agency's essence exception, grant the Agency's contrary to law exception, and set aside the award of backpay.

II. Background and Arbitrator's Award

The grievant works as a barber for the Navy Exchange (NEX) in San Diego, California, which is a nonappropriated fund instrumentality. The Agency, in response to customer complaints, changed the shift for barbers in the NEX barber shop to 12:00 p.m. to 8:30 p.m. Award at 3. The shift hours were previously 11:30 a.m. to 8:00 p.m. *Id.* After the shift change, the barber shop continued to close at 8:00 p.m. Exceptions at 2.

The Union presented a grievance alleging that the new schedule would have an adverse effect on the grievant's income because he works almost exclusively on commission. Award at 3. The Union also alleged that the Agency had violated the Agreement because it had failed to negotiate the schedule change with the Union. Exceptions at 2. The matter was not resolved, and was submitted to arbitration. *Id.* at 2-3. The parties stipulated to the following issue: "Did the Navy Exchange violate the . . . Agreement when it changed the starting and closing times of employees at the barber shop at Naval Base San Diego? If so, what is the appropriate remedy?" Award at 2.

The Arbitrator concluded that the grievant was adversely affected by the change in work schedule because he: (1) was no longer able to earn commissions between 11:30 a.m. and 12:00 p.m. and (2) was required to be at the shop without earning commissions 30 minutes after the shop closed. *Id.* at 6-7. Noting that Article 18, Section 6 of the Agreement provides that the Agency need not notify the Union of changes in hours of work unless the shift changes impact differential pay, the Arbitrator interpreted the phrase "differential pay" broadly to include commissions.[1] *Id.* at 8. According to the Arbitrator, because the grievant "los[t] the opportunity for commission" and, thus, "his pay [wa]s [a]ffected by the shift change, . . . the Union [wa]s entitled to be notified of the shift change." *Id.*

The Arbitrator then addressed the Union's argument that the Agency was required to negotiate the changes in work schedule pursuant to Article 6 of the Agreement. *Id.* The Arbitrator rejected the argument that the dispute was covered by Article 6 because that provision is silent on the specific subjects of hours and scheduling. *Id.* The Arbitrator instead concluded that the dispute was covered by Article 18, which specifically covers the subject of hours and scheduling. *Id.* at 8-9. The Arbitrator then found that Article 3, Section 2 of the Agreement states that nothing precludes the parties "from negotiating . . . arrangements for those who are adversely affected by the exercise of management's

1. The relevant statutory and contract provisions are set forth in the attached appendix.

rights" and that the grievant was adversely affected by the shift change. *Id.* at 9.

In conclusion, the Arbitrator found that the Agency "violated the . . . Agreement." *Id.* As a remedy, the Arbitrator awarded backpay consistent with the requirements of the Back Pay Act and directed the Agency to discuss the adverse impact of the schedule change with the Union. *Id.*

III. Positions of the Parties

A. Agency's Exceptions

The Agency asserts that the Arbitrator's conclusion that the term "differential pay" in Article 18, Section 6 includes commissions fails to draw its essence from the Agreement. Exceptions at 4-5. According to the Agency, the Arbitrator's interpretation disregards the plain language of Article 20, Section 1(a) of the Agreement, which defines differential pay. *Id.* at 5.

Additionally, the Agency argues that the award of backpay under the Back Pay Act is contrary to law. *Id.* at 6. The Agency claims that the grievant is not subject to the Back Pay Act because he is a nonappropriated fund instrumentality employee who is excluded from the definition of employee under 5 U.S.C. § 2105(c)(1), (2). *Id.* Alternatively, the Agency argues that, even if the grievant is subject to the Back Pay Act, he cannot show that he suffered any non-speculative damages as a result of the shift change. *Id.* Accordingly, because the grievant cannot prove that his pay was adversely affected by the change in his schedule, the Agency contends the award of backpay is deficient. *Id.* at 8.

B. Union's Opposition

The Union argues that the Arbitrator's award draws its essence from the plain language of the Agreement. Opp'n at 2. According to the Union, the Agency incorrectly excepted to the Arbitrator's interpretation of Article 18, Section 6 of the Agreement because the Arbitrator ultimately based his award on Article 3, Section 2. *Id.* at 2-3. The Union contends that, because Article 3, Section 2 of the Agreement states that the Agency and the Union may negotiate changes that adversely affect employees, the Arbitrator correctly concluded that the Agency violated the Agreement by failing to negotiate the shift change with the Union. *Id.* at 3.

Relying on *United Paperworkers International Union v. Misco, Inc.*, 484 U.S. 29, 34 (1987), the Union also contends that, even if the grievant is not subject to the Back Pay Act, the award of backpay is not contrary to law. *Id.* at 3-4. In this regard, the Union claims that the Arbitrator correctly determined that the grievant had suffered harm by not being allowed to earn commissions during the time when the barber shop was closed. *Id.* at 4.

IV. Analysis and Conclusions

A. The Agency's essence exception is barred by 5 C.F.R. § 2429.5.

The Authority's Regulations that were in effect when the Agency filed its exceptions provided that "[t]he Authority will not consider . . . any issue, which was not presented in the proceedings before the . . . arbitrator." 5 C.F.R. § 2429.5.[2] *See U.S. Dep't of Health & Humans Servs., Office of Medicare Hearings & Appeals*, 65 FLRA 175, 177 (2010). The Agency argues that the award fails to draw its essence from the Agreement because the Arbitrator disregarded the clear language of Article 20, Section 1(a). The Agency argued to the Arbitrator that the phrase "differential pay" in Article 18, Section 6 of the Agreement should be interpreted to mean "shift differential," but there is no evidence that the Agency cited to Article 20, Section 1(a) of the Agreement or presented that language to the Arbitrator. Exceptions, Attach., Tr. at 9. Because the Agency could have, and should have, argued to the Arbitrator that Article 20, Section 1(a) defines differential pay, § 2429.5 precludes the Agency from raising the issue for the first time in its exceptions. *See AFGE, Local 2382*, 64 FLRA 1163, 1165 (2010) (finding that an argument that the award manifestly disregards a provision of the agreement barred by § 2429.5 because that argument was not made before the arbitrator). Accordingly, we dismiss this exception. *See U.S. Dep't of Transp., Fed. Aviation Admin.*, 65 FLRA 171, 172 (2010).

B. The award is contrary to the Back Pay Act.

The Agency argues that the Arbitrator's award of backpay is contrary to law, specifically the Back Pay

---

2. The Authority's Regulations concerning the review of arbitration awards, as well as certain related procedural Regulations, including 5 C.F.R. § 2429.5, were revised effective October 1, 2010. *See* 75 Fed. Reg. 42,283 (2010). As the Agency's exceptions in this case were filed before that date, we apply the prior Regulations.

Act. When an exception involves an award's consistency with law, the Authority reviews any question of law raised by the exception and the award de novo. *See NTEU, Chapter 24*, 50 FLRA 330, 332 (1995) (citing *U.S. Customs Serv. v. FLRA*, 43 F.3d 682, 686-87 (D.C. Cir. 1994)). In applying the standard of de novo review, the Authority assesses whether an arbitrator's legal conclusions are consistent with the applicable standard of law. *See U.S. Dep't of Def., Dep'ts of the Army & the Air Force, Ala. Nat'l Guard, Northport, Ala.*, 55 FLRA 37, 40 (1998). In making that assessment, the Authority defers to the arbitrator's underlying factual findings. *See id.*

The Authority has long held that, under the Back Pay Act, an award of backpay is authorized only when an arbitrator finds that: (1) the aggrieved employee was affected by an unjustified or unwarranted personnel action; and (2) the personnel action has resulted in the withdrawal or reduction of the grievant's pay, allowances, or differentials. *See, e.g., U.S. Dep't of Health & Human Servs.*, 54 FLRA 1210, 1218-19 (1998).

The Arbitrator awarded backpay to the grievant pursuant to the Back Pay Act. Award at 9. The Agency argues that the award of backpay is contrary to law because the grievant is not an employee within the definition of 5 U.S.C. § 2105(c)(1) and is, therefore, not eligible for backpay. Employees of nonappropriated fund instrumentalities, such as NEX, are expressly excluded from the provisions of the Back Pay Act. *See Army & Air Force Exch. Serv. v. Sheehan*, 456 U.S. 728, 740 (1982) (concluding employee of a nonappropriated fund instrumentality is ineligible for backpay under the Back Pay Act); *U.S. Dep't of Agric., Farm Serv. Agency, N.Y. State Office, Malone, N.Y.*, 58 FLRA 508, 509 (2003) (finding employee excluded from the definition of employee to be excluded from coverage under the Back Pay Act).

Citing *Misco*, 484 U.S. at 41, the Union argues that, even if the grievant is not subject to the Back Pay Act, the award of backpay is still proper. Opp'n at 3. The Union's reliance on *Misco* is misplaced, however, as that case arises in the private sector and does not involve the Back Pay Act. The Union has not identified any statute other than the Back Pay Act that would entitle the grievant to backpay. Therefore, because the grievant may not recover backpay under the Back Pay Act, we find that the award of backpay is contrary to law and set it aside. *See Hamlet v. United States*, 63 F.3d 1097, 1106 (Fed. Cir. 1995) (finding that employees who are excluded from the Back Pay Act cannot recover backpay).

V. Decision

The Agency's essence exception is dismissed, the Agency's contrary to law exception is granted, and the award of backpay is set aside.

APPENDIX

Article 3, Section 2 provides:

> Nothing in this section shall preclude the Employer and the Union from negotiating:
>
> > a. procedures which management officials of the agency will observe in exercising any authority under this section;
> >
> > or;
> >
> > b. appropriate arrangements for associates adversely affected by the exercise of any authority under this section by such management officials.

Exceptions, Attach. E, Agreement at 3-4.

Article 18, Section 6 provides:

> There is no requirement on the Employer to notify the Union of changes in hours of work as long as the associate works the same total number of hours in a pay period and/or is on a rotational shift. The Union will be notified when shift changes are effected which impacts differential pay for associates on fixed schedules.

Id. at 24.

Article 20, Section 1(a) provides:

> A seven and one-half percent (7 ½%) shift differential will be paid for the entire shift when the majority of work performed is after 1500 hours. A ten percent (10%) shift differential will be paid when the majority of work performed is after 2300 hours.

Id. at 28-29.

5 U.S.C. § 2105(c)(1) provides:

> An employee paid from nonappropriated funds of the . . . Navy exchanges . . . and other instrumentalities of the United States under the jurisdiction of the armed forces conducted for the comfort, pleasure, contentment, and mental and physical improvement of personnel of the armed forces is deemed not an employee for the purpose of—
>
> > (1) laws administered by the Office of Personnel Management[.]

65 FLRA No. 72

FEDERAL DEPOSIT
INSURANCE CORPORATION
DIVISION OF SUPERVISION AND
CONSUMER PROTECTION
DALLAS REGIONAL OFFICE
(Agency)

and

NATIONAL TREASURY
EMPLOYEES UNION
CHAPTER 275
(Union)

0-AR-4106

DECISION

December 17, 2010

Before the Authority: Carol Waller Pope, Chairman, and Thomas M. Beck and Ernest DuBester, Members

I. Statement of the Case

This matter is before the Authority on exceptions to a supplemental award of Arbitrator Sandra Smith Gangle filed by the Agency under § 7122(a) of the Federal Service Labor-Management Relations Statute (the Statute) and part 2425 of the Authority's Regulations. The Union filed an opposition to the Agency's exceptions.

In her initial award, the Arbitrator found that the Agency violated the parties' agreements when it failed to fairly and equitably process the grievant's nomination for a Corporate Success Award (CSA), and she directed the Agency to reconsider the grievant's nomination. In the supplemental award, the Arbitrator reviewed the Agency's reconsideration of the nomination and again found that the Agency had failed to evaluate the grievant fairly and equitably. As a remedy, the Arbitrator directed the Agency to award the grievant a CSA with backpay, interest, and attorney fees. For the reasons that follow, we deny the Agency's exceptions.

II. Background and Arbitrator's Awards

The parties agreed through a Collective Bargaining Agreement (CBA), a Compensation Agreement, a Memorandum of Understanding (MOU), and an Agency Circular (Circular 2420.1), that the Agency would award a CSA to "top contributors" in the Agency and that such awards would be distributed in a "fair and equitable manner." *See* Initial Award at 4-8.[1] The parties agreed under the terms of the Compensation Agreement that the Agency's Chairman has "sole discretion to set the percentage of . . . employees who will be recognized as top contributors[,]" but that "the percentage of . . . employees to receive the CSA shall be no less than 33 1/3 percent." *Id.* at 6. Pursuant to that agreement, the Agency's Chairman determined that CSAs would be given to 33 1/3 percent of eligible employees. *Id.* at 12.

The grievant's supervisor nominated him to receive a CSA, and the grievant was ranked fifteenth on the list of nineteen nominees submitted to the Assistant Regional Director (ARD) of the Agency's Dallas Territory.[2] *Id.* at 13. The ARD Panel, which consists of ARDs and the Agency's Deputy Regional Director, evaluated the CSA candidates and made its recommendations to the Agency's Regional Director (RD), who subsequently made recommendations to the Agency's Division Director (Director). *See id.* at 11, 13-14. When the grievant was not selected to receive a CSA, he filed a grievance, which was unresolved and submitted to arbitration.

In her initial award, the Arbitrator found that the parties had agreed in the CBA, MOU, and Circular 2420.1 that the Agency would distribute CSAs in a "fair[,]" "objective[,]" and "equitable" manner. *Id.* at 17. According to the Arbitrator, the parties "intended that [the Agency] would maintain some objective evidence that the CSA criteria had been applied consistently and that employees had been treated fairly and equitably[,]" but the Agency had "used no organized rating system for comparing the

1. The relevant provisions of the CBA, Compensation Agreement, MOU, and Circular 2420.1 are set forth in the attached appendix.

2. The grievant is an employee of the Dallas Field Office. The Dallas Territory comprises the Dallas, Shreveport, and Austin Field Offices. The employees of the Dallas and Memphis Territories, along with the Regional Office Management Information Group (ROMIG), are considered together for purposes of calculating CSA distribution rates as required under the MOU. *See* Supplemental Award at 2; Initial Award at 9.

various contributions" of CSA nominees, and merely had compared nominees' contributions in a "verbal discussion" using "'personal knowledge.'" *Id.* at 18-19 (quoting an ARD's testimony).

Additionally, the Arbitrator found that the Agency did not comply with the "data-keeping requirement" of the MOU. *Id.* at 21. Specifically, the Arbitrator found that the MOU requires the Agency to maintain data about CSA distribution, including the division and office of each CSA recipient. *See id.* at 18. According to the Arbitrator, if the data indicated a rate of CSA distribution for a division or office that is less than 80% of the distribution rate for the division or office with the highest rate of CSAs awarded within the region, then the MOU requires that the Agency be prepared to show that the results can be justified by a legitimate business reason, or explained by the relative sizes of the groups. *See id.* In this regard, the Arbitrator observed that only about 13% of Dallas Field Office employees received CSAs, whereas 80% of ROMIG employees received CSAs. *See id.* at 20-21. The Arbitrator further found that the ARD Panel did not explain the "extraordinary divergence in the numbers" among the groups whose CSA nominations were submitted to the RD. *Id.* at 21.

Finally, the Arbitrator noted that the ARD Panel's decision to discount the grievant's service on additional assignments and on his two details was "not in keeping" with the CSA criteria identified in Circular 2420.1. *Id.*

For the foregoing reasons, the Arbitrator concluded that the Agency "failed to follow the contractual requirements," and sustained the grievance because the Agency "violated the contract." *Id.* at 21-22. As a remedy, the Arbitrator remanded the matter to the Agency in order for the ARD Panel to reconsider the grievant's nomination in comparison with the nominations of other employees, in a manner consistent with the CBA and the Arbitrator's decision. *Id.* at 23. The Arbitrator retained jurisdiction to resolve disputes regarding the implementation of the remedy. *Id.*

On reconsideration of the grievant's nomination, the Agency again denied the grievant a CSA. Supplemental Award at 3. The ARD Panel acknowledged that the variance in the distribution of CSAs among the groups of employees was greater than the percentage rate contemplated in the MOU, but asserted as a legitimate business reason that each of the previously selected CSA recipients "'demonstrated contributions that were *more deserving of the CSA* than the contributions of [the grievant.]'" *Id.* at 13 (quoting ARD affidavit) (emphasis added by Arbitrator). Thereafter, the Union requested that the Arbitrator review the Agency's decision on reconsideration to deny the grievant's CSA. In the supplemental award, the Arbitrator stated the issue as follows:

> Did the Agency violate the parties' [CBA] or [Circular 2420.1] or [the MOU], or any law, rule, or regulation or the [A]rbitrator's Award, when it failed to award the [g]rievant a [CSA], based on his contributions during [the performance year] following the Agency's recalculation and reconsideration process? If so, what is the appropriate remedy?

Id. at 3.

The Arbitrator found that the number of nominees recommended by the ARD panel was "significantly outside the [eighty] percent 'rule of thumb' that the parties had established as fair and equitable distribution[.]" *Id.* at 6. The Arbitrator also found that the reason provided by the Agency to justify the variance in CSA distribution rate in the grievant's Dallas Field Office, as compared with the other groups in the territory, was a "bald statement that begs the question" and did not constitute a legitimate business reason as required by the MOU. *See id.* at 13. In this regard, the Arbitrator found that permitting the Agency to explain a significant distribution variance by articulating such a "bald conclusion" as its "legitimate business reason" would "essentially eliminate[] the contractual requirement of . . . giving a compelling reason for the deviation" and would render the data-keeping requirements of the MOU and Circular 2420.1 "superfluous[.]" *See id.* at 13-15.

In addition, the Arbitrator found that the ARD Panel failed to meet its obligation to grant CSAs "'in a fair and objective manner'" because it did not appear to have developed any "measurable norms or standards" for assessing and comparing the various contributions of the nominees. *Id.* at 16 (quoting CBA). Because the ARD Panel reached its decision by using "verbal discussion" that was "by its very nature *subjective*," the Arbitrator concluded that the Agency did not apply "fair and objective" criteria as contractually required. *Id.* at 16-17. Similarly, the Arbitrator found that the RD and Director denied the grievant the CSA upon reconsideration using "a standard of subjectivity and discretion, rather than the standard of fair and equitable treatment, supported by objective evidence, that the parties' CBA required." *Id.* at 18. For the foregoing reasons, the Arbitrator concluded that the grievant was deprived, for a second time, of a reasonable opportunity to compete for a CSA. *See id.* at 17.

With regard to the appropriate remedy, the Arbitrator found that Article 48, Section 4.B. of the CBA authorized her to "make an aggrieved employee whole[.]" *Id.* at 18. Therefore, considering that the Agency twice failed to conduct a fair and equitable comparison of the grievant's contributions, that two years had passed since the issuance of the CSAs, and that it would be difficult to reconvene the ARD Panel, the Arbitrator fashioned a remedy. *Id.* at 18-19. In particular, the Arbitrator concluded that "[b]ut for the Agency's violation of the contractual requirements for fairly and equitably rating and comparing [CSA nominees], . . . the [g]rievant very likely would have received a CSA[.]" *Id.* at 19. In this regard, the Arbitrator stated that "[b]ut for the Agency's unjustified and unwarranted personnel action . . . in failing to follow the contractual requirements . . . the [g]rievant was deprived of . . . a CSA[.]" *Id.* at 20. Accordingly, the Arbitrator awarded the grievant a retroactive CSA, with interest and attorney fees. *Id.*

III. Positions of the Parties

A. Agency's Exceptions

The Agency argues both that the award fails to draw its essence from the parties' agreements and that the Arbitrator exceeded her authority because the Arbitrator: (1) improperly imposed her "own brand of objectivity" by finding that administration of the CSA process in the manner required by the CBA mandated the use of measurable "norms or standards[;]" Exceptions at 26; (2) erroneously required the Agency to demonstrate that the RD and Director had performed an objective review of the ARD panel's recommendations; *id.* at 28-29; and (3) awarded the grievant a CSA without rescinding one previously awarded and thereby exceeded the award limit imposed by the Agency's Chairman and agreed to by the parties. *See id.* at 30-32, 37.

In addition, the Agency contends that the award fails to draw its essence from the parties' agreements because the Arbitrator incorrectly found that the CSA selection process required the Agency to: (1) gather and share data about the CSA distribution rate among various employee groupings identified in the MOU during the CSA selection process rather than after it had awarded CSAs; *id.* at 21; (2) adjust the proposed CSA recipient list during the selection process if the rate of distribution did not meet an "'[eighty] percent standard[;]'" *id.* at 21-23 (quoting Supplemental Award at 15); and (3) demonstrate to the Union that any distribution variance was justified by a "legitimate business purpose" prior to the issuance of the awards. *Id.* at 25.

Further, the Agency asserts that the Arbitrator's remedy affects management's rights to direct employees and assign work under § 7106(a)(2)(A) and (B) of the Statute. *Id.* at 32. Citing *United States Department of the Treasury, Bureau of Engraving and Printing, Washington, D.C.*, 53 FLRA 146 (1997) (*BEP*), the Agency contends that the remedy "does not constitute a proper reconstruction of what the Agency would have done" if it had not violated the parties' agreements. Exceptions at 34. In this regard, the Agency argues that the Arbitrator "summarily concluded" only that, but for the Agency's violation of the contractual requirements, "'the [g]rievant *very likely* would have received a CSA[,]'" but did not find that the grievant's contributions placed him in the top one-third of bargaining unit employees. *Id.* at 36 (quoting Supplemental Award at 19) (emphasis added by Agency).

B. Union's Opposition

The Union argues that the Arbitrator did not exceed her authority and that the supplemental award is consistent with the CBA. In this regard, the Union argues that the Arbitrator's finding that the Agency failed to provide any objective evidence that it had used during the reconsideration process is consistent with her finding that the Agency failed to administer the CSA reconsideration process in the manner dictated by the parties' agreements. Opp'n at 3-4, 6-7. The Union further argues that the Arbitrator's remedy does not violate the parties' agreements because the agreements do not require the Arbitrator to rescind a CSA from one employee in order to award one to the grievant. *See id.* at 10. In addition, the Union contends that the award does not fail to draw its essence from the agreements because the Arbitrator required the Agency to provide distribution data and a "legitimate business reason" to explain the distribution variance after, not before, the Agency had completed its CSA reconsideration process. *See id.* at 3-6.

In addition, the Union asserts that the remedy reconstructs what management would have done absent the contractual violation. *See id.* at 11-12. According to the Union, the grievant is entitled to a

CSA because the top one-third of performers at the Agency are entitled to a CSA and the Arbitrator found that the grievant's nomination was "within the top one-third of the employees in [the Dallas/Shreveport] territory." Opp'n at 11-12 (quoting Supplemental Award at 19). In this regard, the Union further asserts that the Arbitrator found that "'[b]ut for the Agency's unjustified and unwarranted personnel action,'" the grievant would have received a CSA. *Id.* at 12 (quoting Supplemental Award at 20).

IV. Analysis and Conclusions

A. The award does not fail to draw its essence from the parties' agreements.

In reviewing an arbitrator's interpretation of a collective bargaining agreement, the Authority applies the deferential standard of review that federal courts use in reviewing arbitration awards in the private sector. *See* 5 U.S.C. § 7122(a)(2). Under this standard, the Authority will find that an arbitration award is deficient as failing to draw its essence from the collective bargaining agreement when the appealing party establishes that the award: (1) cannot in any rational way be derived from the agreement; (2) is so unfounded in reason and fact and so unconnected with the wording and purposes of the collective bargaining agreement as to manifest an infidelity to the obligation of the arbitrator; (3) does not represent a plausible interpretation of the agreement; or (4) evidences a manifest disregard of the agreement. *See U.S. Dep't of Labor (OSHA)*, 34 FLRA 573, 575 (1990) (*OSHA*). The Authority and the courts defer to arbitrators in this context because it is the arbitrator's construction of the agreement for which the parties have bargained. *Id.* at 576.

The Agency's essence exceptions challenge the Arbitrator's findings concerning both the CSA reconsideration process and the appropriate remedy for the alleged contractual violation. In regard to the reconsideration process, the parties' CBA provides that the Agency "will grant incentive awards in a fair and objective manner[.]" Initial Award at 4. Further, the parties' MOU requires that "CSAs will be distributed to employees in a fair and equitable manner and in accordance with the terms of this MOU and . . . Circular 2420.1." *Id.* at 6. Circular 2420.1 provides, in pertinent part, that CSAs "shall be distributed to employees in a fair and equitable manner[,]" and that "[r]eviewing [o]fficials . . . will ensure the consistent application of [CSA] criteria and the fair and equitable treatment of employees." *Id.* at 7-8.

Applying these provisions, in her initial award, the Arbitrator found that the Agency had obligated itself to grant awards in a "fair and objective manner," and should be able to demonstrate that it "had treated employees fairly and equitably when it identified the top contributors and issued [CSAs]." *See* Supplemental Award at 5. According to the Arbitrator, this obligation included the responsibility to evaluate employees using objective criteria rather than "subjective personal knowledge[.]" *Id.* at 6. Because the Agency reconsidered the grievant's nomination without making the modifications to its selection process that the Arbitrator found were contractually required, the Arbitrator determined that the Agency did not treat the grievant fairly and equitably as required by the parties' agreements. *See id.* at 13-18. Specifically, the Arbitrator found that the Agency had not produced any evidence to show that the contributions of the grievant and his fellow employees "had been reconsidered objectively, fairly and equitably[,]" *id.* at 17, and she also found that the ARD panel and the reviewing officials "used a standard of subjectivity and discretion, rather than the [contractually required] standard of fair and equitable treatment, supported by objective evidence[.]" *Id.* at 18. The Agency has not established that these findings are irrational, unfounded, implausible, or in manifest disregard of the parties' agreements. *See OSHA*, 34 FLRA at 575.

In regard to the significant distribution variance that occurred in the initial CSA selection process and was unchanged by the Agency's reconsideration, the Arbitrator found that the Agency's proffered "legitimate business reason" – that each of the CSA recipients "were more deserving of the CSA" than the grievant – did not meet the contractual requirement that such a divergence be explained in a manner that established that employees were compared "through an objective and fair rating process[.]" Supplemental Award at 13-15. In this connection, the Arbitrator reasoned that accepting such a "bald conclusion that a particular employee's contributions 'did not merit' an award" would "essentially eliminate[] the contractual requirement of . . . giving a compelling reason for the deviation[,]" and would render the data-keeping requirements of the MOU and Circular 2420.1 "superfluous[.]" *Id.* The Agency has also not established that these findings are irrational, unfounded, implausible, or in manifest disregard of the parties' agreements. *See OSHA*, 34 FLRA at 575.

In regard to the Agency's argument that the remedy fails to draw its essence from the parties' agreements, the Compensation Agreement provides that "[t]he Chairman has sole discretion to set the percentage of bargaining unit employees who will be recognized as top contributors under the CSA program[,]" so long as that percentage is "no less than 33 1/3 percent." Initial Award at 6. As the Authority has previously held, the 33 1/3 percent figure sets a minimum threshold, and not a maximum cap on the potential number of CSA recipients, as argued by the Agency. *See FDIC*, 62 FLRA 356, 359 (2008) (holding that the Compensation Agreement's 33 1/3 percent figure "is a minimum, not a maximum"). Thus, although the Compensation Agreement does not obligate the Agency to award CSAs to employees who are not in the top one-third of contributors, it also does not cap the number of bargaining-unit employees eligible to receive CSAs. *See FDIC, Div. of Supervision & Consumer Prot., S.F. Region*, 65 FLRA 102, 108 (2010) (*FDIC, SF Region*) (Chairman Pope concurring). Further, the Arbitrator specifically found that "[b]ut for" the Agency's violation of the parties' agreements, the grievant was deprived of a CSA. Supplemental Award at 20. Because the parties' agreements mandate "fair and equitable" treatment for CSA candidates, Initial Award at 7, the Agency has not established that the arbitrator's conclusion – that the grievant should receive a CSA as a remedy for repeated contractual violations – is not a plausible interpretation of the parties' agreements taken as a whole. *See FDIC, SF Region*, 65 FLRA at 108.

For the foregoing reasons, the Agency has not demonstrated that the supplemental award fails to draw its essence from the parties' agreements. Therefore, we deny the Agency's essence exceptions.[3]

B. The award is not contrary to law, rule, or regulation.

When an exception involves an award's consistency with law, the Authority reviews any question of law *de novo*. *See NTEU, Chapter 24*, 50 FLRA 330, 332 (1995) (citing *U.S. Customs Serv. v. FLRA*, 43 F.3d 682, 686-87 (D.C. Cir. 1994)). In applying *de novo* review, the Authority assesses whether the arbitrator's legal conclusions are consistent with the applicable standard of law. *See, e.g., NFFE, Local 1437*, 53 FLRA 1703, 1710 (1998). In making that assessment, the Authority defers to the arbitrator's underlying factual findings. *See id.*

The Authority recently revised the analysis that it will apply when reviewing management-rights exceptions to arbitration awards. *See U.S. EPA*, 65 FLRA 113, 115 (2010) (Member Beck concurring) (*EPA*); *FDIC, SF Region*, 65 FLRA at 106-07. Under the revised analysis, the Authority will first assess whether the award affects the exercise of the asserted management right. *EPA*, 65 FLRA at 115. If so, then the Authority examines whether the award provides a remedy for a violation of either an applicable law, within the meaning of § 7106(a)(2) of the Statute, or a contract provision that was negotiated pursuant to § 7106(b) of the Statute. *Id.* In setting forth its revised analysis, the Authority specifically rejected the continued application of the requirement, set forth in *BEP*, that an arbitrator's remedy "reconstruct" what management would have done but for the violation at issue. *FDIC, SF Region*, 65 FLRA at 106-07. The Authority further held in this regard that

> [a]s in other types of arbitration cases, such awards must still withstand challenges raised in exceptions that the award does not satisfy the standards Congress established in the Statute for the Authority's review of arbitrators' awards. Where such a challenge establishes that an award imposes a constraint on management rights that was not agreed to by the parties . . . the award will be set aside.

Id. at 107.

Applying this analysis, we reject the Agency's argument that the remedy is contrary to law. This exception is based entirely on the assertion that the remedy does not reflect a reconstruction of what the Agency would have done if it had not violated the

3. The Agency also argues that the Arbitrator "exceeded her authority" by: (1) imposing her "own brand of objectivity[;]" (2) requiring the Agency to demonstrate that the reviewing officials objectively reviewed the ARD panel's recommendations; and (3) awarding the grievant a CSA without rescinding one from another CSA recipient. *See* Exceptions at 26, 29, 37. As these contentions are restatements of some of the Agency's essence claims, we do not address them separately. *See SSA Balt., Md.*, 57 FLRA 690, 693 n.6 (2002) (as agency's claim that arbitrator exceeded his authority did nothing more than restate its essence claim, Authority did not address claims separately). *See also AFGE, Local 3627*, 64 FLRA 547, 550 n.3 (2010).

agreed-upon CSA selection process.[4] As discussed above, such "reconstruction" is no longer applicable. *See id.* Accordingly, we conclude that the award does not impermissibly affect management rights by failing to reconstruct what the Agency would have done if it had not violated the contract, and we deny the Agency's contrary-to-law exception.[5] *See, e.g., id.* at 107.

V. Decision

The Agency's exceptions are denied.

---

4. We note that the Agency concedes that the award enforces a properly negotiated contract provision. *See* Exceptions at 34 n.39. Accordingly, we do not address that issue further.

5. For the reasons set forth in her concurring opinion in *FDIC, SF Region*, 65 FLRA at 112, Chairman Pope agrees that the award is not deficient because the remedy is reasonably related to the negotiated provisions and the harm being remedied.

APPENDIX

Compensation Agreement Between FDIC and NTEU for the Years 2003-2005

II. ANNUAL PAY

. . . .

Year 2003

Effective 2003, the [Agency] will provide an increase in basic pay of 3.2 percent for all employees who received a rating of "meets expectations" during the prior year's rating period. In addition, 2004 shall be a transition year for the Corporate Success Award . . . .

Years 2004 and 2005

. . . .

A Corporate Success Award (CSA) will be established which provides that an additional 3.0 percent increase be made in basic pay for those employees recognized as top contributors. The Chairman has sole discretion to set the percentage of bargaining unit employees who will be recognized as top contributors under the CSA program. However, the percentage of bargaining unit employees to receive the CSA shall be no less than 33 1/3 percent. These awards shall be made on an annual basis.

. . . .

Initial Award at 5-6.

FDIC DIRECTIVE SYSTEM Circular 2420.1 (July 21, 2003) REWARDS AND RECOGNITION PROGRAM

Chapter 11
Corporate Success Awards

11-1. Definition

. . . .

[CSAs] shall be distributed to employees in a fair and equitable manner.

. . . .

11-4. Criteria: Nominations will be evaluated based on one or more of the following criteria. These are the only criteria permitted under the Corporate Success Award program. Nominations will provide specific statements of the contributions by the employee that meet the identified criteria. . . . .

A. Business Results: Consistently displays a high level of initiative, creativity, and innovation to produce results that reflect important contributions to the Corporation and/or its organizational components.

B. Competency: Demonstrates an exceptional degree of competency within his/her position, and is frequently relied upon by others for advice, assistance, and/or judgment that reflect important contributions to the Corporation and/or its organizational components.

C. Working Relationships: Builds extremely productive working relationships with co-workers, other Divisions/Offices, or other public or private sector agencies based on mutual respect that reflect important contributions to the Corporation and/or its organizational components.

D. Learning and Development: Takes an active part in developing personal skills and competencies and applies newly acquired skills and competencies that reflect important contributions to the Corporation and/or its organizational components.

11-5. Procedures

. . . .

B. Supervisors shall nominate their top contributors by preparing the [designated form]. Forms must be submitted to the designated reviewing official within 15 calendar days after the end of the consideration cycle. . . .

C. Reviewing Officials, as designated in the Division/Office delegations of authority, will ensure the consistent application of Corporate Success Award criteria and the fair and equitable treatment of employees. The Reviewing Official shall sign the nomination form and forward it to the Division/Office Director within 30 calendar days . . . .

. . . .

F. The Chairman has the sole discretion to set the percentage of bargaining unit and non-bargaining employees who will be recognized as top contributors under the Corporate Success Award program . . . . However, the percentage of bargaining unit employees . . . will be no less than 33 1/3 percent.

. . . .

Initial Award at 7-8.

Memorandum of Understanding Between FDIC and NTEU (March 13, 2003)

> 1. CSAs will be distributed to employees in a fair and equitable manner and in accordance with the terms of this MOU and FDIC Circular 2420.1.
>
> 2. The EMPLOYER agrees to provide data to NTEU in an electronic spreadsheet on bargaining unit Corporate Success Award (CSA) recipients in 2004 and 2005 (based on contributions made in 2003 and 2004, respectively) that will include the following fields: division/office, ...
>
> 3. If the data for one or more groups included in the fields identified in #2, above, indicates a rate of distribution that is less than 80% of the distribution rate for the group with the highest rate in that field, the FDIC and NTEU will conduct a joint review of the approved awards to determine if these results can be justified by a legitimate business reason or explained by the size(s) of the group(s) being compared. However, this joint review process does not waive the right of the Union or any employee to seek remedial relief in any appropriate legal forum.
>
> . . . .

Initial Award at 6-7.

FDIC AND NTEU COLLECTIVE BARGAINING AGREEMENT

Article 18, Section 1.B.

> The EMPLOYER will grant incentive awards in a fair and objective manner in accordance with this Agreement and applicable rules and regulations.

Initial Award at 4.

Article 48, Section 4.B.

> The arbitrator shall have no power to add to, subtract from, or modify the terms of this Agreement. The award will be limited to the issues presented at arbitration. The arbitrator's decision will be final and binding and the arbitrator will have the authority to make an aggrieved employee whole to the extent such remedy is not limited by law.

Initial Award at 5.

65 FLRA No. 73

UNITED STATES
DEPARTMENT OF HOMELAND SECURITY
U.S. CUSTOMS AND BORDER PROTECTION
(Agency)

and

NATIONAL TREASURY
EMPLOYEES UNION
(Union)

0-AR-4602

DECISION

December 17, 2010

Before the Authority: Carol Waller Pope, Chairman, and Thomas M. Beck and Ernest DuBester, Members

I. Statement of the Case

This matter is before the Authority on exceptions to an award of Arbitrator M. David Vaughn filed by the Agency under § 7122(a) of the Federal Service Labor-Management Relations Statute (the Statute) and part 2425 of the Authority's Regulations. The Union filed an opposition to the Agency's exceptions.

The Arbitrator concluded, among other things, that the Agency improperly designated the Auditors, encompassing positions at grades 9 through 13, (hereinafter Auditors) as exempt under the Fair Labor Standards Act (FLSA) and ordered the Agency to pay liquidated damages. Opinion and Interim Award at 45, 50; Opinion and Third Interim Award at 27. For the reasons set forth below, we deny the Agency's exceptions.

II. Background and Arbitrator's Award

The Agency employs roughly 300 Auditors nationwide who work in the Office of International Trade, Office of Regulatory Audit. Opinion and Interim Award at 5. The Union filed a grievance on behalf of these Auditors, asserting that the Agency had improperly classified them as FLSA exempt.[1] *Id.* at 1. After the Agency failed to respond to the Union's grievance, the Union invoked arbitration. *Id.* at 2. The parties stipulated to the following issue: "[w]hether the [Agency] improperly exempted employees covered by the grievance from the overtime provisions of the [FLSA?] . . . . If [so], what shall be the remedy?" *Id.* at 3.

In his opinion and interim award, the Arbitrator found that the Agency improperly designated the Auditors as FLSA exempt. *Id.* at 45, 50. The Arbitrator first examined whether the Auditors met the professional exemption.[2] *Id.* at 39-44. The Arbitrator determined that the Auditor position satisfied the primary duty test of this exemption. *See Id.* at 38, 40.

However, the Arbitrator found that the Agency failed to establish that the Auditor position satisfied the discretion and independent judgment test. *Id.* at 41-44. The Arbitrator determined that the Auditors do not exercise discretion and independent judgment because their work is constrained by the Focused Assessment Program (FA Program) policy and the Regulatory Audit Division Manual (RAD Manual), which "describe, in exacting, exhaustive detail the work to be performed by [the] Auditors." *Id.* at 41. According to the Arbitrator, testimony demonstrated that the Auditors consider the FA Program policy and the RAD Manual to be the "Bible" of their work and that "the purpose of the FA Program policy and the RAD Manual is to create uniform procedures for the conduct of the audits and to minimize the exercise of discretion by individual auditors." *Id.* Similarly, the Arbitrator noted that the Auditors must adhere to Government Accountability Office Generally Accepted Government Auditing Standards (GAGAS)

1. The Union also filed its grievance on behalf of Field Analysis Specialists, Chemists, Textile Analysts, and Information Technology Specialists. Opinion and Interim Award at 1. In addition to addressing the FLSA exemption status of the Auditors in his opinion and interim award, the Arbitrator addressed whether grade 14 Auditors and Field Analysis Specialists are FLSA exempt. *Id.* at 45-50. The Arbitrator also issued an opinion and second interim award which "resolved the [p]arties' dispute concerning the FLSA status of the bargaining unit employees in the Chemist (GS-1320), Textile Analyst (GS-1384) and Information Technology Specialist (GS-2210) [positions]." Opinion and Third Interim Award at 1-2. Because the Agency did not except to the Arbitrator's findings regarding the FLSA exemption status of these positions, they are not before us.

2. An employee is considered FLSA exempt under the professional exemption if the agency can establish that the primary duty, discretion and independent judgment, intellectual and varied work, and 80-percent tests are met. 5 C.F.R. § 551.207. The relevant provisions of 5 C.F.R. § 551.207 are set forth in the appendix to this decision.

and Agency policies when conducting audits. *Id.* Also, the Arbitrator determined that the Auditors' work is subject to extensive supervisory review and heavily edited by management officials. *Id.* at 41-42. The Arbitrator decided that the Auditors are not professional employees; rather, they are line or production employees because they follow policy instead of executing policy, and carry out the Agency's mission and day-to-day functions. *Id.* at 42, 43. Finally, relying upon 29 C.F.R. § 541.203(j), a Department of Labor (DOL) regulation involving the administrative exemption, the Arbitrator determined that, because the Auditors' work is similar to the duties performed by inspectors and investigators who are FLSA nonexempt, the Auditors' work fails to satisfy the professional exemption. *Id.* at 43-44.

Also, the Arbitrator found that the Agency failed to demonstrate that the Auditors were exempt from the FLSA under the administrative exemption.[3] *Id.* at 44-45. The Arbitrator noted that the administrative exemption contains the same discretion and independent judgment test as the professional exemption. *Id.* The Arbitrator determined that, because the Auditors rely heavily on the FA Program policy, the RAD Manual, and GAGAS requirements, they lack sufficient discretion and independent judgment. *Id.* at 45. Moreover, the Arbitrator noted that the Auditors do not satisfy the administrative exemption because, based on the record, "their work is essentially comparable to that of ordinary inspectors, as described in 5 CFR § 551.206(n)[,] who are FLSA [n]onexempt."[4] *Id.*

III. Positions of the Parties

A. Agency's Exceptions

The Agency asserts that the award is contrary to law because the Arbitrator improperly relied on non-controlling and obsolete DOL regulations. Exceptions at 6-8. The Agency claims that the Arbitrator's statement that "'[i]t is well-established that, in the event of [a] perceived conflict between DOL and [Office of Personnel Management (OPM)] guidance, DOL regulations govern'" is an incorrect statement of the law. *Id.* at 6 (quoting Opinion and Interim Award at 36); *see also id.* at 7. According to the Agency, the Arbitrator should have relied solely on OPM regulations to determine whether the Auditors are FLSA exempt because "OPM was given [the] responsibility . . . [of] administering the provisions of the FLSA with respect to the federal workforce." *Id.* at 7 (citations omitted). Moreover, the Agency claims that, even assuming the Arbitrator properly relied on DOL regulations in determining whether the Auditors are FLSA exempt, the DOL regulations that the Arbitrator cited in his award are obsolete. *Id.* (citing 69 Fed. Reg. 22,122-01 (Apr. 23, 2004)).

Also, the Agency claims that the award is contrary to law because the Arbitrator improperly relied on a "new" version of the OPM regulations. *Id.* at 8-9. The Agency asserts that the new OPM regulations are not applicable because "the Agency's decision to classify its Auditors as exempt from the FLSA . . . was made pursuant to an earlier version of the regulations (i.e., the 2006 version)." *Id.* at 8. According to the Agency, the Arbitrator should not have applied the new OPM regulations because OPM included a preamble "stating that these new regulations have 'no retroactive effects.'" *Id.* (citing 72 Fed. Reg. 52,753, 52,761 (Sept. 17, 2007)). Moreover, the Agency claims that, although the 2006 and the new OPM regulations are similar, the amendments modified the professional exemption's primary duty test by including additional requirements that did not exist in the 2006 regulations. *Id.* at 8-9.

The Agency asserts that the award is contrary to law because the Arbitrator applied the incorrect legal standard in assessing the professional exemption's primary duty test. *Id.* at 9-13. The Agency claims that the Arbitrator improperly "appli[ed] the primary duty test for the *administrative* exemption to conclude that the Agency's Auditors fail the primary duty test for the *professional* exemption." *Id.* at 10 (emphasis in original); *see also id.* at 12.

Finally, the Agency claims that the award is contrary to law because the Arbitrator failed to apply certain OPM and DOL regulations when analyzing the discretion and independent judgment test. *Id.* at 13-16. The Agency asserts that the Arbitrator

3. An employee is considered FLSA exempt under the administrative exemption if the agency can establish that the primary duty, nonmanual work, discretion and independent judgment, and 80-percent tests are met. 5 C.F.R. § 551.206. The relevant provisions of 5 C.F.R. § 551.206 are set forth in the appendix.

4. The Arbitrator also issued an opinion and third interim award in which the arbitrator ordered the agency to pay liquidated damages and determined that a three year statute of limitations period applied. Opinion and Third Interim Award at 26-27. Because the Agency does not except to the Arbitrator's findings in his opinion and third interim award, this opinion is not before us.

should have applied certain OPM regulations explaining that "employees can exercise discretion and independent judgment even if their decisions or recommendations are reviewed at a higher level." *Id.* at 15 (citing 5 C.F.R. § 551.104). Also, the Agency claims that the Arbitrator should have relied upon certain DOL regulations indicating that "'[t]he use of manuals, guidelines or other established procedures containing or relating to highly technical, scientific, legal, financial[,] or other similarly complex matters that can be understood or interpreted only by those with advanced or specialized knowledge or skills does not preclude exemption . . . .'" *Id.* at 15-16 (quoting 29 C.F.R. § 541.704). Finally, the Agency asserts that, instead of comparing the Auditors with inspectors, the Arbitrator should have taken into account the similarities between the Auditors and accountants, who are FLSA exempt.[5] *Id.* at 16.

B. Union's Opposition

The Union argues that the Arbitrator's conclusion that the Agency failed to demonstrate that the Auditors were FLSA exempt under either the professional exemption or the administration exemption was not contrary to law. Opp'n at 8-22.

The Union contends that the award is not contrary to law because the Arbitrator properly applied both the OPM and DOL regulations and did not rely on obsolete DOL regulations. *Id.* at 22-25. According to the Union, "the Authority has roundly rejected the argument that DOL regulations play no role in the analysis of the exemption status of federal employees." *Id.* at 22. Also, the Union argues that the Agency mischaracterizes the Arbitrator's reliance on the DOL regulations; the Union notes that the Arbitrator did not entirely disregard the OPM regulations as claimed by the Agency and never perceived a conflict between the OPM and DOL regulations. *Id.* at 24. Moreover, the Union contends that, "[w]hile the [a]ward does cite to pre-2004 DOL regulations, the provisions cited by the Arbitrator remain in effect." *Id.* at 25. According to the Union, because "[n]one of the propositions established in the 2004 regulations cited in the [a]ward were eliminated (or even substantially changed) in later revisions[,] . . . the Agency has not identified a single regulatory provision that is obsolete." *Id.* at 26.

Also, the Union argues that the award is not contrary to law even though the Arbitrator incorrectly applied the "new" version of the OPM regulations. *Id.* at 11 n.3, 26-28. The Union contends that, contrary to the Agency's interpretation of the award, "the Arbitrator did not [add] any additional requirements [to the primary duty test] and [found] *for the Agency* with respect to the primary duty test of the professional exemption." *Id.* at 27 (citing Opinion and Interim Award at 40) (emphasis in original). According to the Union, in stating that "there are more *tests* than just the positive education requirement[,]" the Arbitrator simply meant that, in addition to satisfying the primary duty test, the Agency must also demonstrate that an employee exercises discretion and independent judgment. *Id.* at 28 (citing Opinion and Interim Award at 40) (emphasis in original). Finally, the Union cites precedent indicating that, "even if an arbitrator uses the wrong legal analysis, the Authority [will] not disturb the conclusion if the correct result was reached." *Id.* at 27 n.7 (citing *U.S. Dep't of Commerce, Nat'l Oceanic & Atmospheric Admin., Office of Marine & Aviation Operations, Marine Operations Ctr., Va.*, 57 FLRA 430, 433 (2001)) (*Marine Operations Ctr.*).

The Union contends that the Arbitrator did not mistakenly apply the administrative exemption's primary duty test when determining whether the Auditors qualified for the professional exemption. *Id.* at 29-30. The Union argues that "the Arbitrator concluded both that the Auditors meet the primary duty test for the professional exemption because [employees must be educated in order to perform the work] and that the Auditors do not meet the primary duty test for the administrative exemption because they perform mission work." *See id.* at 30 (citing Opinion and Interim Award at 40, 42-43).

Finally, the Union argues that the Arbitrator properly found that the Auditors lack sufficient discretion and independent judgment to satisfy the professional and administrative exemptions. *Id.* at 30-32. The Union contends that "[t]he Arbitrator properly analyzed many factors, including the constraints placed on [the] Auditors by those documents, the routine nature of their work, and their lack of authority" before concluding that the Auditors lacked sufficient discretion and independent judgment. *Id.* at 31. Also, the Union argues that "[t]he Arbitrator did not conclude that *any* supervisory review would be sufficient to defeat a claim that [the] Auditors do not exercise discretion and independent judgment[;] [r]ather, . . . it was the extent of that review that defeated the claim." *Id.*

5. The Agency notes that the Arbitrator's comparison of the Auditors with ordinary inspectors was based solely on the new version of the OPM regulations. Exceptions at 14 (citing 5 C.F.R. § 551.206(n)). According to the Agency, the 2006 OPM regulations never mention the exemption status of the inspectors. *Id.*

(emphasis in original). According to the Union, it is irrelevant that some of the Auditors are Certified Public Accountants because a position's exemption status is dependent upon the actual duties performed. *Id.* at 32. Lastly, the Union argues that the Agency's claim that the Arbitrator should have compared the Auditors with accountants merely challenges the Arbitrator's factual findings and, ultimately, does not provide a sufficient basis for finding that the award is contrary to law. *Id.* at 31-32.

IV. Analysis and Conclusions

When an exception involves an award's consistency with law, the Authority reviews any question of law raised by the exception and the award de novo. *See NTEU, Chapter 24*, 50 FLRA 330, 332 (1995) (citing *U.S. Customs Serv. v. FLRA*, 43 F.3d 682, 686-87 (D.C. Cir. 1994)). In applying the standard of de novo review, the Authority assesses whether an arbitrator's legal conclusions are consistent with the applicable standard of law. *See U.S. Dep't of Def., Dep'ts of the Army & the Air Force, Ala. Nat'l Guard, Northport, Ala.*, 55 FLRA 37, 40 (1998). In making that assessment, the Authority defers to the arbitrator's underlying factual findings. *See id.*

A. The award is not contrary to law despite the fact that the Arbitrator relied on an outdated version of the DOL regulations.

The Agency asserts that the Arbitrator should have relied solely on OPM regulations in order to determine whether the Auditors are FLSA exempt and that the Arbitrator's statement – that the DOL regulations govern if a conflict exists between DOL and OPM regulations – is an incorrect statement of the law. Exceptions at 6-7. Moreover, the Agency claims that, even assuming the Arbitrator properly relied on DOL regulations in determining whether the Auditors were FLSA exempt, the DOL regulations that the Arbitrator cited in his award are obsolete. *Id.* at 7-8 (citations omitted).

The Agency's exception fails to establish that the award is deficient. Under Authority precedent, it is well established that an arbitrator may consider both OPM and DOL regulations when reviewing an employee's FLSA exemption status. *See NTEU*, 53 FLRA 1469, 1479-80 (1998) (applying both DOL and OPM regulations in order to determine whether the award exempting GG-11 level examiners from the FLSA was contrary to law). Moreover, the Authority has found that, although OPM regulations presumptively control, the DOL regulations are useful to arbitrators when interpreting the FLSA. *See U.S. Dep't of the Treasury, IRS, Wash., D.C.*, 46 FLRA 1063, 1072 (1992) (quoting *Adam v. United States*, 26 Cl. Ct. 782, 786 (1992) (*IRS, Wash. D.C.*) (finding that, "in construing [the OPM] regulations, the court is not barred, but[,] rather[,] encouraged to consider the DOL's regulations and other interpretations of the statute"). Here, although the Arbitrator improperly stated that DOL regulations control in the event of a conflict between the DOL regulations and the OPM regulations, the award is not deficient because the Arbitrator did not disregard the OPM regulations when making his determination that the Auditors are not FLSA exempt. Opinion and Interim Award at 36; *see IRS, Wash., D.C.*, 46 FLRA at 1072 (requiring arbitrators to consider OPM regulations when reviewing the FLSA exemption status of a federal employee). The Arbitrator discussed both the professional and administrative exemptions under the OPM and DOL regulations. Opinion and Interim Award at 33-36. Indeed, the Arbitrator cited almost exclusively to OPM regulations when he analyzed whether the professional and administrative exemption tests were met. *Id.* at 39-45. Thus, the Arbitrator's reliance on both DOL and OPM regulations does not render the award deficient.

Also, the Authority has found that an arbitrator's reliance on an outdated version of a statute does not render the award deficient unless the party excepting to the award can demonstrate that the award is inconsistent with the applicable version of the statute. *See U.S. Dep't of Def., Nat'l Guard Bureau Adjutant Gen., Kan. Nat'l Guard*, 57 FLRA 934, 936 (2002) (*Nat'l Guard*). Here, the Arbitrator cited to outdated DOL regulations involving the administrative and professional exemptions. Award at 34-35. However, although the Agency claims that significant updates were made to the DOL regulations, it does not cite to a single change in the 2004 version of the DOL regulations that would cause an inconsistency between the award and those regulations. Exceptions at 7 (citing 69 Fed. Reg. 22,122-01 (Apr. 23, 2004)) (failing to discuss how the DOL regulations changed and how the award is contrary to the 2004 version of the DOL regulations). Moreover, by failing to provide supporting arguments or authority, the Agency's contention constitutes nothing more than a bare assertion. *See, e.g., U.S. DHS, U.S. Customs & Border Prot., Port of Seattle, Seattle, Wash.*, 60 FLRA 490, 492 n.7 (2004) (determining that, if a party fails to provide any arguments or authority to support its exception, the Authority will deny the exception as a bare assertion). Consequently, the

Agency has failed to establish that the award is deficient. *See Nat'l Guard*, 57 FLRA at 936 (denying the agency's exception because, although the arbitrator relied on an outdated version of 32 U.S.C. § 709 in his award, the agency failed to prove that the award was inconsistent with 32 U.S.C. § 709 and that the arbitrator's reliance on an outdated version of that provision rendered the award deficient).

Accordingly, we deny the Agency's exception.

B. The Arbitrator's conclusion that the Auditors lack discretion and independent judgment is not contrary to law.

The Agency claims that the award is contrary to law because the Arbitrator wrongfully found that the Auditors lacked discretion and independent judgment. Exceptions at 13-16. The Agency asserts that the Arbitrator should have applied certain OPM regulations demonstrating that "employees can exercise discretion and independent judgment even if their decisions or recommendations are reviewed at a higher level." *Id.* at 15 (citing 5 C.F.R. § 551.104). Also, the Agency claims that the Arbitrator should have relied upon certain DOL regulations stating that "'[t]he use of manuals, guidelines or other established procedures containing or relating to highly technical, scientific, legal, financial, or other similarly complex matters that can be understood or interpreted only by those with advanced or specialized knowledge or skills does not preclude exemption . . . .'" *Id.* at 15-16 (quoting 29 C.F.R. § 541.704). Finally, the Agency asserts that, instead of only comparing the Auditors with inspectors, the Arbitrator should have taken into account the similarities between the Auditors and accountants who are FLSA exempt. *Id.* at 16.

Under OPM's implementing regulations, "[t]he designation of an employee as FLSA exempt or nonexempt ultimately rests on the duties actually performed by the employee." *U.S. Dep't of the Navy, Naval Explosive Ordnance Disposal Tech. Div., Indian Head, Md.*, 57 FLRA 280, 286 (2001) (quoting 5 C.F.R. § 551.202(h)(i)) (*U.S. Dep't of the Navy Indian Head II*). Moreover, it is the employer's burden to prove that employees are exempt. *Id.* (citing *Corning Glass Works v. Brennan*, 417 U.S. 188, 196-97 (1974)). Exemptions are construed narrowly against the employer who seeks to assert the exemptions. *Id.* (citing *Arnold v. Ben Kanowsky, Inc.*, 361 U.S. 388, 392 (1960)).

As an initial matter, the Agency asserts, and the Union concedes, that the Arbitrator improperly relied on the new version of the OPM regulations. Exceptions at 8-9; Opp'n at 11 n.3. We find that the Arbitrator erred by applying the new OPM regulations in his award because the grievance was presented and the Agency's decision to classify the Auditors as FLSA exempt occurred in 2006. The new OPM regulations became effective on October 17, 2007, and amendments to these regulations included changes to the administrative and professional exemptions. *See* 5 C.F.R. §§ 551.206, 551.208. For instance, new requirements were added to the professional exemption's primary duty test, and the 80-percent test was eliminated from both the administrative and professional exemptions. *See id.* However, there is no indication that the amendments were intended to be applied retroactively; in fact, OPM noted in its summary of the new OPM regulations that "[t]he regulations . . . [have] no retroactive effects[.]" 72 Fed. Reg. 52,753, 52,761 (Sept. 17, 2007); *see U.S. Dep't of the Interior, Bureau of Mines, Pittsburgh Research Ctr.*, 53 FLRA 34, 38 n.1 (1997) (*Bureau of Mines*) (determining that the Authority should apply the pre-amended version of the Training Act in existence at the time of the events giving rise to the grievance because there was no indication in the legislative history of the amendments that they were intended to be applied retroactively). Consequently, in reviewing the Agency's remaining exceptions, we apply the 2006 version of the OPM regulations. *See Bureau of Mines*, 53 FLRA at 38 n.1 (applying the pre-amended version of the statute in order to determine whether the award was contrary to law).

Under the 2006 version of the OPM regulations, an employee is considered FLSA exempt under the professional exemption if the agency can establish that the primary duty, intellectual and varied work, discretion and independent judgment, and 80-percent tests are met. 5 C.F.R. § 551.207. An employee is exempted from the FLSA under the administrative exemption if the agency can establish that the primary duty, nonmanual work, discretion and independent judgment, and 80-percent tests are met. 5 C.F.R. § 551.206; *see Marine Operations Ctr.*, 57 FLRA at 434 (determining that, under 5 C.F.R. § 551.206, an employee must meet all of the criteria to be exempted from FLSA overtime based on the administrative exemption). As noted by the parties, the discretion and independent judgment test is the same under both exemptions. Exceptions at 13; Opp'n at 21. In order to meet the test, an "employee [must] frequently [exercise] discretion and independent judgment, under only general supervision, in performing the normal day-to-day work." 5 C.F.R. §§ 551.206(c), 551.207(c).

Based on the Arbitrator's factual findings, his legal conclusion that the Auditors do not exercise discretion and independent judgment is not contrary to law. In his award, the Arbitrator evaluated the credibility of the evidence and testimony presented to him and considered the duties actually performed by the Auditors before concluding that the Auditors lack discretion and independent judgment. Opinion and Interim Award at 41-45; *see U.S. Dep't of the Navy Indian Head II*, 57 FLRA at 286 (indicating that an arbitrator must consider the duties actually performed by the grievant in determining whether that grievant is FLSA exempt). The Arbitrator found that, because the Auditors rely heavily on the FA Program policy, the RAD Manual, and GAGAS requirements, they lack sufficient discretion and independent judgment. Opinion and Interim Award at 41, 45; *see U.S. DHS, Bureau of Customs & Border Prot.*, 61 FLRA 485, 493 (2006) (*DHS*) (finding that it is not sufficient that employees exercise some discretion in the performance of their duties in order for them to qualify as professional employees). According to the Arbitrator, testimony demonstrated that the Auditors consider the FA Program policy and the RAD manual to be the "Bible" of their work and that "the purpose of the FA Program policy and the RAD Manual is to create uniform procedures for the conduct of the audits and to minimize the exercise of discretion by individual auditors." Opinion and Interim Award at 41; *see DHS*, 61 FLRA at 493 (determining that, although there were many decisions that Agricultural Specialists had to make in applying the manuals and performing their work, it was clear that the determinations that required judgment and extensive educational background, the hallmark of professional employees, were made by employees other than the Agriculture Specialist).

Although the Agency cites certain DOL regulations suggesting that employees may exercise discretion and independent judgment even if they rely upon manuals and guidelines in performing their duties, those regulations also state that "exemptions are not available . . . for employees who simply apply well-established techniques or procedures described in manuals or other sources within closely prescribed limits to determine the correct response to an inquiry or set of circumstances."[6] 29 C.F.R. § 541.704. Moreover, in concluding that the Auditors do not exercise sufficient discretion and independent judgment, the Arbitrator not only took into account the Auditors' reliance on the FA Program Policy, the RAD manual, and GAGAS requirements, but also considered other relevant factors. Opinion and Interim Award at 41-42.

For instance, the Arbitrator determined that the Auditors do not exercise discretion and independent judgment because their work is subject to extensive supervisory review and heavily edited by management officials. Opinion and Interim Award at 41-42. Although the Agency implies that, under the award, an employee cannot be subject to any supervisory review in order for the discretion and independent judgment to be met, the Arbitrator simply found that, in this case, the Auditors' work is subject to considerable supervisory review. Exceptions at 15; Opinion and Interim Award at 41-42. Finally, the Arbitrator compared the duties of the Auditors with those of ordinary investigators and determined that, like investigators, the Auditors lack discretion and independent judgment.[7] *See U.S. Dep't of the Navy, Naval Explosive Ordinance Disposal Tech. Div., Indian Head, Md.*, 56 FLRA

6. 29 C.F.R. § 541.704 provides as follows:

> The use of manuals, guidelines or other established procedures containing or relating to highly technical, scientific, legal, financial or other similarly complex matters that can be understood or interpreted only by those with advanced or specialized knowledge or skills does not preclude exemption under section 13(a)(1) of the Act or the regulations in this part. Such manuals and procedures provide guidance in addressing difficult or novel circumstances and thus use of such reference material would not affect an employee's exempt status. The section 13(a)(1) exemptions are not available, however, for employees who simply apply well-established techniques or procedures described in manuals or other sources within closely prescribed limits to determine the correct response to an inquiry or set of circumstances.

7. Although the Agency asserts that the Arbitrator relied solely on the inspector and investigator example contained in the new OPM regulations when he compared the duties of Auditors with those of inspectors, its assertion is without merit. Exceptions at 14 (citing 5 C.F.R. § 551.206(n)). In his award, the Arbitrator also cited an applicable DOL regulation, namely 29 C.F.R § 541.203(j), which notes that inspectors and investigators are not FLSA exempt because they do not exercise discretion and independent judgment. Opinion and Interim Award at 43-44. As noted previously, it is well established that an arbitrator may consider DOL regulations when reviewing an employee's FLSA exemption status. *See NTEU*, 53 FLRA at 1479-80.

280, 285 (2000) (citing *Piscione v. Ernst & Young, L.L.P.*, 171 F.3d 527 (7th Cir. 1999)) (finding that an arbitrator's determination regarding whether an employee's duties satisfy the requirements of an exemption may be based on a comparison of the employee's duties at issue with the duties of other employees whose exempt status has been determined) (*U.S. Dep't of the Navy, Indian Head I*).

To the extent that the Agency contends that the award is deficient because the Arbitrator failed to compare the Auditors' duties with those of accountants and failed to credit certain testimony, its contentions are without merit. Exceptions at 13-16. The Arbitrator's assessment of the weight to be accorded evidence and testimony is a factual finding, to which the Authority must defer in this case as it is not alleged to constitute a nonfact. *See AFGE, AFL-CIO, Local 3614*, 61 FLRA 719, 723 (2006). Moreover, because the Agency's arguments challenge the Arbitrator's evaluation of evidence and testimony and determination of the weight to be accorded such evidence and testimony, it has not established that the award is contrary to law. *See, e.g., AFGE, Local 4044*, 65 FLRA 264, 266 (2010) (finding that disagreement with an arbitrator's evaluation of the evidence and his determination of the weight to be accorded such evidence provides no basis for finding an award deficient); *SSA, Highland Park, Mich.*, 65 FLRA 141, 141 (2010). Consequently, based on the Arbitrator's factual findings, his conclusion – that the Agency failed to demonstrate that the Auditors are FLSA nonexempt because they lack sufficient discretion and independent judgment – is not contrary to law.[8]

Accordingly, we deny the Agency's exception.

8. As noted above, under both the professional and administrative exemptions, an employee must meet all of the criteria to be exempted from the FLSA. *See* 5 C.F.R. §§ 551.206, 551.207. Moreover, as also noted above, an employee must exercise discretion and independent judgment under both the professional and administrative exemptions. Exceptions at 13; Opp'n at 21. The Arbitrator's factual findings, to which we defer, demonstrate that the Agency has failed to prove that Auditors exercise discretion and independent judgment in accordance with 5 C.F.R. §§ 551.206 and 551.207. Opinion and Interim Award at 41-45. Consequently, it is not necessary to address the Agency's exception with respect to the primary duty test.

V. Decision

The Agency's exceptions are denied.

APPENDIX

5 C.F.R. § 551.206 Administrative exemption criteria.

An administrative employee is an advisor or assistant to management, a representative of management, or a specialist in a management or general business function or supporting service and meets all four of the following criteria:

(a) Primary duty test. The primary duty test is met if the employee's work –

(1) Significantly affects the formulation or execution of management programs or policies; or

(2) Involves management or general business functions or supporting services of substantial importance to the organization serviced; or

(3) Involves substantial participation in the executive or administrative functions of a management official.

(b) Nonmanual work test. The employee performs office or other predominantly nonmanual work which is –

(1) Intellectual and varied in nature; or

(2) Of a specialized or technical nature that requires considerable special training, experience, and knowledge.

(c) Discretion and independent judgment test. The employee frequently exercises discretion and independent judgment, under only general supervision, in performing the normal day-to-day work.

(d) 80-percent test. In addition to the primary duty test that applies to all employees, General Schedule employees in positions properly classified at GS-5 or GS-6 (or the equivalent level in other comparable white-collar pay systems) must spend 80 percent or more of the worktime in a representative workweek on administrative functions and work that is an essential part of those functions to meet the 80-percent test.

5 C.F.R. § 551.207 Professional exemption criteria.

A professional employee is an employee who meets all of the following criteria, or any teacher who is engaged in the imparting of knowledge or in the administration of an academic program in a school system or educational establishment.

(a) Primary duty test. The primary duty test is met if the employee's work consists of –

(1) Work that requires knowledge in a field of science or learning customarily and characteristically acquired through education or training that meets the requirements for a bachelor's or higher degree, with major study in or pertinent to the specialized field as distinguished from general education; or is performing work, comparable to that performed by professional employees, on the basis of specialized education or training and experience which has provided both theoretical and practical knowledge of the specialty, including knowledge of related disciplines and of new developments in the field . . . .

(b) Intellectual and varied work test. The employee's work is predominantly intellectual and varied in nature, requiring creative, analytical, evaluative, or interpretative thought processes for satisfactory performance.

(c) Discretion and independent judgment test. The employee frequently exercises discretion and independent judgment, under only general supervision, in performing the normal day-to-day work.

(d) 80-percent test. In addition to the primary duty test that applies to all employees, General Schedule employees in positions properly classified at GS-5 or GS-6 (or the equivalent level in other comparable white-collar pay systems), must spend 80 percent or more of the worktime in a representative workweek on professional functions and work that is an essential part of those functions to meet the 80-percent test.

65 FLRA No. 74

UNITED STATES
DEPARTMENT OF VETERANS AFFAIRS
MEDICAL CENTER
HAMPTON, VIRGINIA
(Activity)

and

AMERICAN FEDERATION
OF GOVERNMENT EMPLOYEES
AFL-CIO
(Petitioner/Union)

WA-RP-09-0062

DECISION AND ORDER ON REVIEW

December 17, 2010

Before the Authority: Carol Waller Pope, Chairman, and Thomas M. Beck and Ernest DuBester, Members

I Statement of the Case

This case is before the Authority on an application for review (application) filed by the Department of Veterans Affairs (Agency) under § 2422.31(c) of the Authority's Regulations.[1] The Union filed an opposition to the Agency's application.

The Regional Director (RD) determined that the Nurse Officer of the Day, Evening/Night Nurse III position (NOD) should not be excluded from the consolidated bargaining unit represented by the Union because the record did not indicate that NODs are supervisors within the meaning of § 7103(a)(10) of the Federal Service Labor-Management Relations Statute (the Statute).[2] For the reasons that follow, we deny the application.

II. Background and RD's Decision

This dispute involves four NODs who work at the Activity, a teaching hospital. RD's Decision at 1-2. The NODs work during "off-tours," a period of time that includes the evening shift, which starts at 3:30 p.m., and the night shift, which starts at midnight. *Id.* at 2. The NODs also work twelve hours every other weekend on a shift that also is considered an "off-tour." *Id.* at 2; Tr. at 11-12.

The RD found that NODs are responsible for ensuring that proper staffing is maintained. RD's Decision at 2. In this connection, NODs: assign tasks to employees; "float" employees from one unit to another; authorize overtime; temporarily change an employee's shift; grant unscheduled sick leave and up to two hours of emergency annual leave. *Id.* at 2, 4.

The RD also found that NODs are responsible for preparing a shift report. *Id.* at 3. The RD found that NODs prepare the shift report by reviewing information in earlier shift reports pertaining to inventory, patient care, and staff absences. *Id.* Then, the RD stated, NODs make "rounds" through the hospital, during which they gather information on patient needs, staffing, and supplies. *Id.* Next, NODs incorporate information from rounds, and from other nurses and previous shift reports, into the report. *Id.* at 4. Additionally, the RD determined that NODs respond to patient emergencies, disputes between employees, and requests for special

1. 5 C.F.R. § 2422.31 states, in pertinent part:

> (c) *Review.* The Authority may grant an application for review only when the application demonstrates that review is warranted on one or more of the following grounds:
>
> . . . .
>
> (2) Established law or policy warrants reconsideration; or,
>
> (3) There is a genuine issue over whether the Regional Director has:
>
> (i) Failed to apply established law;
>
> . . . .
>
> (iii) Committed a clear and prejudicial error concerning a substantial factual matter.

2 . 5 U.S.C. § 7103(a)(10) states:

> "[S]upervisor" means an individual employed by an agency having authority in the interest of the agency to hire, direct, assign, promote, reward, transfer, furlough, layoff, recall, suspend, discipline, or remove employees, to adjust their grievances, or to effectively recommend such action, if the exercise of the authority is not merely routine or clerical in nature but requires the consistent exercise of independent judgment, except that, with respect to any unit which includes firefighters or nurses, the term "supervisor" includes only those individuals who devote a preponderance of their employment time to exercising such authority[.]

equipment. *Id.* The RD found that NODs spend "very little time" on direct patient care. *Id.*

Analyzing these facts, the RD determined that NODs exercise supervisory authority only when they direct and assign employees. *Id.* at 6. In this regard, the RD found that NODs "assign and move employees among units, direct employees to perform specific job assignments, authorize overtime and adjust shift assignments[,]" and that NODs "approve sick and emergency annual leave." *Id.* at 6-7. Further, the RD found that NODs exercise independent judgment because they consider different factors about patient information and staffing levels, use independent and clinical judgment to "decide the appropriate staffing level[,]" and then "direct[] and assign[] employees as necessary to achieve the desired staffing level." *Id.* at 7. Because NODs make these considerations when directing and assigning employees, the RD determined that assigning and directing employees is "not a merely routine, clerical or perfunctory endeavor[.]" *Id.*

The RD then determined that "the record d[oes] not establish that the NODs spend a majority of their employment time on assigning and directing employees." *Id.* at 7. In this connection, the RD determined that two of the duties that NODs spend a significant amount of time performing -- conducting rounds and preparing shift reports -- do not involve directing and assigning employees, and thus do not involve the exercise of supervisory authority. *See id.* In this connection, the RD found that one NOD witness (NOD #1) spends "60 to 80 minutes conducting a single set of rounds" and "60 minutes reviewing and verifying the information in the [shift report][,]" and further found that NOD #1 spends "more time conducting rounds and . . . preparing and making copies of the [shift report] than she spends on any one of her other functions." *Id.* at 5. *See also id.* at 7. Moreover, the RD noted that the only duty that involved directing and assigning employees that NOD #1 specifically testified to was the "20 minutes" she spends each day "handling calls from employees and making calls to employees in connection with adjusting staffing[.]" *Id.* at 5. *Accord id.* at 7. With regard to the other NOD witness (NOD #2), the RD found that he spends only "two to three hours each shift" directing and assigning employees, specifically by "adjusting staffing levels by floating employees" and "calling employees to obtain replacements for absentees[.]" *Id.* at 5. *Accord id.* at 7.

In concluding that the record did not establish that NODs spend a majority of their time directing and assigning employees, the RD acknowledged that the Agency relied on testimony allegedly demonstrating that NOD #1 spends "90%" of her time performing supervisory duties, and that NOD #2 spends "100%" of his time performing supervisory duties. *Id.* at 5. However, the RD found this generalized testimony was outweighed by the more specific testimony discussed above. *See id.*

With the exception of directing and assigning employees, the RD found that NODs do not exercise supervisory authority. Specifically, the RD found that NODs do not adjust employee grievances or hire, promote, reward, transfer, furlough, layoff, recall, suspend, discipline, or remove employees, although the RD noted that NODs document employee misconduct and submit the documentation to supervisors, and may reassign employees who threaten patient care. *Id.* at 4. Further, the RD found that although NODs are generally the senior registered nurses on duty at the hospital during off-tours, charge nurses, rather than NODs, directly oversee the work performance of other nurses during off-tours. *Id.* at 2. In this regard, the RD found that NODs "generally are not assessing whether an employee is performing his or her job properly" when making rounds, *id.* at 3, and are not responsible for overseeing the performance of the hospital's staff. *Id.* at 4-5. Rather, the RD stated, "how an employee performs an assigned task is a matter for a [c]harge [n]urse[,]" *id.* at 3 who "directly oversee[s] the work performed by the [r]egistered [n]urses and other employees in the unit." *Id.* at 3, 2.

III. Positions of the Parties

A. Agency's Application

The Agency alleges that the RD committed clear and prejudicial errors concerning substantial factual matters. Application at 8. Specifically, the Agency asserts that the RD was "prejudicially selective" in considering testimony because he "did not appropriately consider the incumbents' testimony[,]" *id.* at 10, that NODs spend "'the majority,' or '90 percent,' or '100 percent,'" of their time engaged in "supervisory duties[.]" *Id.* at 11. Further, the Agency claims that because NODs spend little time performing hands-on patient care, the RD should have inferred that NODs spend "the vast majority" of their time "making rounds, ensuring staffing, and making other supervisory decisions that are eventually reflected in their report." *Id.* at 14.

The Agency also alleges that the RD failed to apply established law. In this regard, the Agency contends that, because NODs exercise supervisory authority during a preponderance of their employment time, they are supervisory employees under *Veterans Administration Medical Center, Fayetteville, North Carolina*, 8 FLRA 651, 660 (1982) (*Fayetteville*). *See* Application at 13-14. The Agency also claims the RD failed to apply *Fayetteville* by failing to find that NODs exercise supervisory authority when they conduct rounds and prepare shift reports. *Id.* at 14-15. Finally, the Agency asserts that NODs are supervisors because NODs "act as *the* one-and-only nurse supervisor at the facility" during off-tours, and argues that including NODs in the unit would result in an "extremely odd situation" that would be "prejudicial to the A[ctivity] due to the obvious conflict of interest[,]" because it would leave "up to 100 bargaining unit employees on duty without a single supervisor present."[3] *Id.* at 12.

B. Union's Opposition

The Union contends that the RD did not fail to apply established law and did not commit factual errors. Opp'n at 1. In this regard, the Union argues that there was "no evidence that the NODs exercised any supervisory authority when doing rounds[,]" during which time NODs "collect[] information" for the shift report. *Id.* at 2-3. Further, the Union contends, the Agency "does not explain how" preparing the shift report "involves the exercise of any of the supervisory indicia under § 7103(a)(10)." *Id.* at 2. With regard to the Agency's argument that the RD's Decision results in no supervisory nurses being present at the hospital during off-tours, Application at 12, the Union argues that the Authority previously has rejected a similar claim, Opp'n at 3 & n.3, and that unit employees are accountable to non-bargaining unit member nurse managers twenty-four hours per day, even when the nurse managers are not present at the hospital. *Id.* at 3.

IV. Analysis and Conclusions

A. The RD did not commit clear and prejudicial errors concerning substantial factual matters.

As noted previously, the Authority may grant review of an application if it is demonstrated that the RD committed a clear and prejudicial error concerning a substantial factual matter. 5 C.F.R. § 2422.31(c)(3)(iii). It is well settled that disagreement over the weight that an RD has accorded certain evidence is not sufficient to find that an RD committed a clear and prejudicial error concerning a substantial factual matter. *SSA, Office of Disability Adjudication & Review, Balt., Md.*, 64 FLRA 896, 902 (2010) (*SSA*).

The Agency contends that the RD did not sufficiently consider testimony that NODs spend "'the majority,' '90 percent,' or '100 percent,'" of their day allegedly exercising "supervisory duties[.]" Application at 11. In this connection, NOD #2 claimed, generally, that "100 percent" of his work was "in supervision[.]" Tr. at 150. However, the RD decided to credit NOD #2's more specific testimony that he spends only "two to three hours each shift" directing and assigning employees, and thus, only two to three hours each shift exercising supervisory authority. RD's Decision at 5. *Accord id.* at 7; Tr. at 153. In effect, the Agency challenges the weight that the RD accorded certain evidence, which, as stated above, is not sufficient to demonstrate that he committed a clear and prejudicial error concerning a substantial factual matter. *SSA*, 64 FLRA at 902.

With regard to NOD #1, the RD found that NOD #1 spends "more time conducting rounds and more time preparing and making copies of the [shift report] than she spends on any one of her other functions[,]" which necessarily include the duties that the RD found to be supervisory.[4] RD's Decision at 5. The RD based this finding on specific testimony that NOD #1 spends "60 to 80 minutes conducting a single set of rounds" and "60 minutes reviewing and verifying the information in the [shift report,]" and more time performing those non-supervisory activities than she spends performing activities in

3. The Agency also asserts that the Authority should review the RD's Decision because "established policy warrants reconsideration[.]" Application at 2. However, the Agency provides no support for this claim. Accordingly, we reject this claim as a bare assertion. *See U.S. Dep't of the Navy, Fleet Readiness Ctr. Sw., San Diego, Cal.*, 63 FLRA 245, 252 (2009).

4. As stated previously, the RD found that conducting rounds and preparing the shift report are not supervisory duties. As discussed further below, we find that the RD did not err as a matter of law in concluding that the NODs do not exercise supervisory duties when they conduct rounds and "think[] about" exercising supervisory authority while conducting rounds and preparing shift reports. Application at 15.

which she exercises supervisory authority. *Id. Accord id.* at 7; Tr. at 97, 113. Indeed, the RD noted that the one specific activity the witness testified to in which she directs and assigns employees is "handling calls from employees and making calls to employees in connection with adjusting staffing[,]" which takes her only "20 minutes each day[.]" RD's Decision at 5. *Accord* Tr. at 94.

The testimony that the Agency cites with regard to NOD #1 is a general, brief, unexplained response to a vague, multi-part question. Specifically, the Agency relies on the following exchange:

> [Agency Attorney]: .... I asked you about a number of categories of duties that you do. I asked you about granting leave, directing employees between units. We talked about resolving conflicts between employees, basically, all kinds of duties that relate to the nurses in your -- at the medical center. Do you have an estimate for what percentage of your time is spent on those duties?
>
> [NOD #1]: Probably 95 percent of the time. Let's say 90 percent because you spend time -- because we have reports that we do as well, that we have to do every day. So I'd say 90 percent.

Tr. at 85. Although NOD #1 testified that she spends "90 percent" of her time performing "a number of categories of duties" and "all kinds of duties that relate to the nurses[,]" *id.*, those general phrases do not necessarily equate to supervisory duties. Moreover, as with NOD #2, it was not a clear and prejudicial error for the RD to rely on NOD #1's more specific testimony discussed above rather than this more general testimony.

The Agency also relies on the testimony of the Activity's associate director of patient care services, an indirect supervisor of the NODs:

> [Agency Attorney]: .... Now, I talked with you about a number of duties that [NODs] do. We talked about directing employees, assigning employees, having some involvement in discipline, and granting leave. Those duties that we talked about, do you have an opinion on what percentage of their time is spent on those supervisory duties?
>
> [Indirect Supervisor Witness]: That's the majority of our duties. Outside of that small window where they provide -- they may be called upon to provide direct care, the majority of our responsibility is directing staff, ensuring the patient care delivery. You know, sometimes on the off[-]tour . . . they have to be responsible for calling in the nurses. So the majority of our role is spent making sure that patient care needs are met and coordinate the resources during the time where resources aren't readily available to make that happen.

Id. at 33-34.

Contrary to the Agency's claim, this testimony does not clearly demonstrate that NODs spend a majority of their time exercising supervisory authority. In this regard, the question generally refers back to "a number of duties" that the Agency attorney had asked the witness about, including one -- discipline -- that the RD found the NODs do not engage in. *Id.* at 33. In addition, the witness' response that the activities of "making sure that patient care needs are met" and coordinating resources "to make that happen[]" do not necessarily encompass supervisory duties and, in the case of patient care needs, could reasonably be interpreted as including making rounds and preparing the shift report, both of which the RD found were non-supervisory duties. *Id.* at 34. Finally, the Agency provides no support for its assertions that NODs exercise supervisory authority whenever they are not performing direct patient care. *See* Application at 14.

For the foregoing reasons, the Agency has not established that the RD committed clear and prejudicial errors concerning substantial factual matters.

B. The RD did not fail to apply established law.

As noted previously, under 5 C.F.R. § 2422.31(c)(3)(i), the Authority may grant an application for review when an application demonstrates that the RD failed to apply established law. When determining whether a nurse is a supervisor under § 7103(a)(10), the Authority determines, as relevant here, whether the employee spends a preponderance of his or her employment time exercising supervisory authority that requires the consistent exercise of independent judgment. *U.S. Dep't of the Army, Parks Reserve Training Ctr., Dublin, Cal.*, 61 FLRA 537, 543 (2006) (Chairman Cabaniss dissenting in part) (*Parks Reserve*)).

Here, the Agency asserts that the record indicates that NODs spend a majority of their time acting as supervisors and that under *Fayetteville*, an employee who is "primarily a supervisor . . . during a majority of their employment time" is a supervisor. Application at 13-14 & n.6. As we have previously rejected the argument that the NODs spend a majority of their time exercising supervisory authority, we find that the RD's decision is not inconsistent with *Fayetteville*, 8 FLRA at 660, in this regard.

The Agency further claims that the RD failed to apply *Fayetteville* because he failed to find that NODs exercise supervisory authority when they: (1) conduct rounds; and (2) "think[] about" exercising supervisory authority when conducting rounds and preparing shift reports. Application at 14-15. The nurses in *Fayetteville* exercised supervisory authority when they conducted rounds because they "evaluat[ed] the work of . . . subordinates in carrying out their assigned duties" and "act[ed] as . . . role model[s] in teaching or demonstrating proper procedures and techniques to . . . subordinates." *Fayetteville*, 8 FLRA at 662.

The record in this case does not show that NODs engage in similar activities, or any supervisory duties, when they conduct rounds. *See* RD's Decision at 3-4. Moreover, the RD specifically found, and the Agency does not dispute, that "NODs generally are not assessing whether an employee is performing his or her job properly" when making rounds. RD's Decision at 3. With regard to the Agency's assertion that *Fayetteville* indicates that "'thinking about' supervisory responsibilities" is the "same as exercising supervisory responsibilities[,]" the Agency does not cite any evidence indicating whether, or to what extent, NODs think about supervisory duties when conducting rounds or preparing shift reports. Application at 15. Thus, we find that the Agency has not demonstrated that the RD's decision is contrary to the Authority's decision in *Fayetteville*.

Finally, the Agency cites no law, rule, or regulation to support its claim that the RD's Decision is deficient because it would allegedly result in NODs being "*the* one-and-only nurse supervisor at the facility" during off-tours, *id.* at 12, and does not explain why the Activity is required to have supervisory staff on duty at all times, or why this necessitates a finding that the NODs are supervisors. Similarly, the Agency does not demonstrate that the alleged result of the RD's Decision -- that it would lead to an "obvious conflict of interest[,]" *id.* -- indicates that the RD failed to apply established law.

For the foregoing reasons, the Agency has not demonstrated that the RD failed to apply established law.

V. Order

The Agency's application is denied.

65 FLRA No. 75

UNITED STATES
DEPARTMENT OF THE TREASURY
INTERNAL REVENUE SERVICE
(Agency)

and

NATIONAL TREASURY
EMPLOYEES UNION
CHAPTER 238
(Union)

0-AR-4418

DECISION

December 21, 2010

Before the Authority: Carol Waller Pope, Chairman, and Thomas M. Beck and Ernest DuBester, Members

I. Statement of the Case

This matter is before the Authority on exceptions to an award of Arbitrator Frank Silver filed by the Agency under § 7122(a) of the Federal Service Labor-Management Relations Statute (the Statute) and part 2425 of the Authority's Regulations. The Union filed an opposition to the Agency's exceptions.

The Arbitrator concluded that the Agency violated agreements the parties had reached concerning employees affected by a reorganization. The Agency had refused to offer the grievant grade and pay retention after she accepted a position at a lower grade. The Agency had made the grievant's original, higher-graded position permanent before the grievant accepted the lower-graded position. The Arbitrator ordered the Agency to grant the grievant grade and pay retention.

For the reasons that follow, we grant the Agency's contrary to law exception and set aside the award.

II. Background and Arbitrator's Award

The grievant was a General Schedule (GS)-11 Management Analyst. Award at 4. A reorganization left the grievant without a permanent position within the new organization. *Id.* at 3. Consequently, as addressed in a provision of the Restructuring Agreement and Addendum (parties' agreement),[1] the Agency designated the grievant as a "transition employee" and assigned her to continue to perform work at her GS-11 grade and pay until placed in a permanent position. *Id.* at 4. Pursuant to another provision of the parties' agreement, [2] the grievant then applied for a GS-5 Revenue Officer position as a transition employee with grade and pay retention benefits. *Id.* at 4-5. The GS-5 position had been announced as eligible for transition benefits, including grade and pay retention. *Id.*

While the grievant's application was being processed, the Agency internally decided and advised the Union that all employees whose transition status had not been otherwise resolved would be made permanent in their current positions. *Id.* at 4. The Agency also determined that all transition benefits, including grade and pay retention, would cease. *Id.* at 6.

Shortly thereafter, the Agency notified the grievant that she would be made permanent in her GS-11 position at the same grade and pay level. *Id.* at 6, 11. Because the Agency decided to make the grievant's GS-11 position permanent, it processed the

---

1. The relevant portions of the parties' agreement provide:

> Section 2
> When a currently existing organization . . . no longer exists and there remains no organization, current or future, for employees not yet placed . . . [s]uch employees will remain at the same grade and post-of-duty, until placed . . . .
>
> . . . .
>
> V. Temporary Work Assignments While in Transition Status . . . Transition Employees will remain at their current grade and pay until permanently placed.

Award at 2.

2. The relevant portion of the parties' agreement provides:

> IV.E. Voluntary Change to Lower Grade . . . . In addition, Transition Employees who wish to be considered for voluntary placement in a position at a lower grade may apply for such position(s) as they are announced by the [Agency] . . . . If otherwise qualified, said Transition Employee will be placed in said position, with appropriate grade and pay retention . . . .

Award at 2.

grievant's application for the GS-5 position competitively. *Id.* at 5.

The Agency then offered the grievant the GS-5 position without grade and pay retention at the GS-11 level. *Id.* at 5-6. While the offer for the GS-5 position was pending, the Agency made the grievant's GS-11 position permanent. *Id.* at 11, 12. Two days after the Agency made the grievant's GS-11 position permanent, she accepted the offer of the GS-5 Revenue Officer position. *Id.* at 6, 11. As the Arbitrator found, the grievant accepted the lower-graded Revenue Officer position because, "[p]resumably, she was influenced by what she considered to be greater promotional opportunities in the [R]evenue [O]fficer job progression." *Id.* at 13.

The Union then filed a grievance claiming that the Agency violated the parties' agreement by failing to offer the GS-5 position with retained grade and pay at the GS-11 level. *Id.* at 7-8; Exceptions at 7-8. When the matter was not resolved, it was submitted to arbitration.

The issue, as framed by the Arbitrator, was: "Did the Agency fail to transition [the grievant] to a permanent . . . position, pursuant to the [parties' agreement]? If so, what is the appropriate remedy? Award at 2.

The Arbitrator held that the Agency's act of making the grievant permanent in her GS-11 position did not divest her of her contractual right under § IV.E of the parties' agreement to be placed in the GS-5 position while retaining GS-11 grade and pay. *Id.* at 14-15. The Arbitrator reasoned that at the time she applied for the GS-5 position, she met all pre-conditions to secure this contractual right. *Id.* at 12-13, 15. As a basis for this determination, he found that she secured this right by applying for and qualifying for the GS-5 position announced as eligible for transition benefits. *Id.* For these reasons, the Arbitrator found that her right to grade and pay retention at the GS-11 level as applied to the GS-5 position vested before she was made permanent in the GS-11 position. *Id.* at 14-15.

As a remedy, the Arbitrator ordered that the Agency provide the grievant with GS-11 grade and pay retention retroactive to the effective date of her placement in the GS-5 position. *Id.* at 15.

III. Positions of the Parties

A. Agency's Exceptions

The Agency asserts that the award is contrary to law and fails to draw its essence from the parties' agreement.

With regard to its contrary to law argument, the Agency asserts that the award violates 5 U.S.C. §§ 5361-5365 and 5 C.F.R. §§ 536.101-536.105, which govern grade and pay retention, and that the Agency had no independent contractual authority to provide this retention. Exceptions at 1, 16. Specifically, the Agency argues that it did not have discretion under these statutory and regulatory provisions to grant the grievant grade and pay retention in connection with the GS-5 position. *Id.*

The Agency maintains that the grievant was not entitled to grade retention under 5 C.F.R. § 536.103(b)[3] because the grievant's grade was no longer at risk of being reduced as a result of the reorganization after the Agency decided to make her GS-11 position permanent. *Id.* at 16. The Agency also claims that the grievant was not entitled to pay retention under § 536.104(b)[4] because the grievant's pay was not reduced as a result of a management action. *Id.* at 1, 16.

In addition, the Agency argues that 5 C.F.R. § 536.105(a)(3)[5] specifically excludes the grievant from grade or pay retention because her reduction in grade and pay was a matter of choice and thus "for personal cause." *Id.* at 1-2. The Agency contends that there is no legal basis that allows for grade and pay retention where the grievant voluntarily applies for and accepts a lower-grade position when she was already permanently assigned at the GS-11 grade and pay level. *Id.*

---

3. The relevant portion of 5 C.F.R. § 536.103(b) (2003) provides that an "agency may offer grade retention to eligible employees who are or might be reduced in grade as the result of a reorganization . . . announced by management in writing."

4. The relevant portion of 5 C.F.R. § 536.104(b) (2003) provides that an "agency may provide pay retention to eligible employees whose rates of basic pay would otherwise be reduced as the result of management action."

5. The relevant portion of 5 C.F.R. § 536.105(a)(3) (2003) provides that "(a) Grade and pay retention shall not apply to an employee who . . . (3) [i]s reduced in grade or pay for personal cause . . . . "

With regard to its essence exception, the Agency contends that the Arbitrator misinterpreted the parties' agreement to require the Agency to provide the grievant with grade and pay retention at the GS-11 level for accepting a GS-5 position. *Id.* at 2. The Agency asserts that the parties' agreement only entitles the grievant to grade and pay retention until the time she was permanently placed at the GS-11 grade and pay level. *Id.* at 15, 18. Therefore, the Agency argues that the Arbitrator wrongly applied the parties' agreement to entitle the grievant to grade and pay retention because the grievant accepted the GS-5 position after she was made permanent in her GS-11 position. *Id.*[6]

B. Union's Opposition

The Union asserts that the Agency's contrary to law claim is without merit. Opp'n at 6-12. Specifically, the Union argues that the issue raised by the contrary to law claim is solely one of contract interpretation because the parties' agreement incorporates regulations governing grade and pay retention. *Id.* at 6-7 (citing *AFGE, Local 2357*, 62 FLRA 375 (2008); *AFGE, Local 2703*, 59 FLRA 81 (2003); *see also*. In addition, the Union claims that the grievant did not accept the GS-5 position voluntarily. *Id.* at 9.

The Union also disagrees with the Agency's essence exception. *Id.* at 10-12.

IV. Analysis and Conclusions

For the reasons set forth below, the Authority grants the Agency's contrary to law exception.

The Agency contends that the Arbitrator's determination that the grievant is entitled to grade and pay retention at the GS-11 level after accepting the GS-5 position is contrary to 5 U.S.C. §§ 5361-5365 and 5 C.F.R. §§ 536.101- 536.105.[7] When an exception involves an award's consistency with law, the Authority reviews any question of law raised by the exception and the award de novo. *See NTEU, Chapter 24*, 50 FLRA 330, 332 (1995) (citing *U.S. Customs Serv. v. FLRA*, 43 F.3d 682, 686-87 (D.C. Cir. 1994)). In applying the standard of de novo review, the Authority assesses whether an arbitrator's legal conclusions are consistent with the applicable standard of law. *See U.S. Dep't of Def., Dep'ts of the Army & the Air Force, Ala. Nat'l Guard, Northport, Ala.*, 55 FLRA 37, 40 (1998). In making that assessment, the Authority defers to the arbitrator's underlying factual findings. *See id.*

Grade and pay retention have a specific statutory foundation. Title 5 U.S.C. §§ 5361-5365 govern the administration of grade and pay retention. In addition, Congress has, in 5 U.S.C. § 5365, authorized the Office of Personnel Management (OPM) to prescribe regulations governing the administration of grade and pay retention in circumstances beyond those specifically addressed in 5 U.S.C. §§ 5361-365.

As relevant here, OPM's regulations provided that an agency's authority to offer grade and pay retention was limited by the "conditions" and "criteria" prescribed in its government-wide regulations. 5 C.F.R. § 536.101. Specifically, § 536.103(b) provided that "the agency may offer grade retention to eligible employees who are or might be reduced in grade as the result of a reorganization . . . ." In addition, § 536.104(b) provided that an "agency may provide pay retention to eligible employees whose rates of basic pay would otherwise be reduced as the result of a management action."

Moreover, the Authority has held that government-wide regulations govern a matter in dispute to which they apply, even if the same matter is covered by a collective bargaining agreement under the Statute. *U.S. Dep't of the Army, Ft. Campbell Dist., Third Region, Fort Campbell, Ky.*, 37 FLRA 186, 193 (1990).

In its opposition, the Union raises a threshold argument that where the parties' agreement incorporates regulations governing a particular matter, the appropriate analysis is one of contract interpretation. Opp'n at 7. However, the Union's argument is unsupported. The Union relies on cases where the collective bargaining agreement incorporates agency, not Government-wide,

6. Because, for the reasons below, the Authority concludes that the award is contrary to law, it is unnecessary for the Authority to address the Union's additional exception that the award fails to draws its essence from the parties' agreement.

7. We apply the versions of 5 U.S.C. §§ 5361-5365 (2003) and 5 C.F.R. §§ 536.101- 536.105 (2003) in effect at the time of the actions giving rise to the grievance, rather than the revised versions of the code and regulations that subsequently went into effect.

regulations.[8] Here, the Agency argues that the award conflicts with Government-wide regulations. The cases on which the Union relies are therefore inapposite. Accordingly, we proceed to consider the Agency's contrary to law claim.

The award is inconsistent with § 536.103(b), as set forth above, by requiring the Agency to provide grade retention in conditions that do not meet the regulatory "conditions" and "criteria." The plain language of § 536.103(b) limits an agency's authority to offer grade retention "to employees who are or might be reduced in grade as the result of a reorganization . . . ." *See AFGE, Local 1709*, 57 FLRA 453, 455 (2001) (relying upon plain language to resolve a matter of statutory interpretation). Based on the Arbitrator's findings, shortly after the grievant applied for the GS-5 position, the Agency decided to make all remaining transition employees permanent in their current positions and so notified the Union, and later, the employee. It follows that when the Agency took these actions, the grievant, a transition employee, was no longer in a situation where she might be reduced in grade as a result of a reorganization. Award at 4. At that point, the "conditions" and "criteria" that govern grade retention ceased to exist. Therefore, when the Agency offered the grievant the GS-5 position after the Agency decided to make her GS-11 position permanent, and had so notified her, the Agency had no legal basis for providing grade retention. Accordingly, the Arbitrator's conclusion that the grievant is entitled to grade retention as applied to the GS-5 position is inconsistent with § 536.103(b).

Similarly, the award is inconsistent with § 536.104(b), also as set forth above, by requiring the Agency to provide pay retention. The plain language of § 536.104(b) limits an agency's authority to provide pay retention "to employees whose rates of basic pay would otherwise be reduced as the result of a management action." 5 C.F.R. § 536.104(b). As applied here, there is no indication that the grievant's pay would otherwise be reduced as the result of a management action. *Id.* Indeed, as indicated previously, shortly after the grievant applied for the GS-5 position, the Agency processed her application as ineligible for transition benefits because it intended to make transition employees permanent in their positions. Therefore, management never took any action to reduce her pay. To the contrary, as the result of "management['s] action," her rate of basic pay at the GS-11 level remained unchanged. *Id.* Therefore, the grievant's rate of basic pay was not at risk of being otherwise reduced when the Agency offered her the GS-5 position. Moreover, the grievant became permanent in her GS-11 position two days before she accepted the GS-5 position. Accordingly, the Arbitrator's conclusion that the Agency had the discretion to provide the grievant with pay retention at the GS-11 level for accepting the GS-5 position is inconsistent with § 536.104(b).[9]

Therefore, the award is contrary to 5 C.F.R. §§ 536.103(b) and 536.104(b)(2003). Accordingly, we grant the Agency's contrary to law exception and set aside the award.[10]

V. Decision

The Agency's contrary to law exception is granted and the award is set aside.

8. *See* cases Union relies on *supra* Part III.B.

9. The Authority's decision in *United States Department of the Treasury, Internal Revenue Service, Oklahoma City, Oklahoma*, 64 FLRA 615 (2010) (*IRS*) is distinguishable from this case. In *IRS*, the Authority upheld an award of grade and pay retention for an employee who accepted a lower-graded position based on the agency's assurances that she would retain grade and pay. In addition, the agency in *IRS* not only offered grade and pay retention, but permitted the grievant to receive retained pay for two years before it recognized an error and initiated actions to recoup the retained pay in a collection action. *IRS* is distinguishable because, *inter alia*, it involved a different version of the regulations regarding grade and pay retention; a much narrower agency argument (specifically, that a particular agency official was not an "authorized agency official" within the meaning of the regulations) than the broader arguments presented here; and an arbitration award that, unlike the award at issue here, was based in part on equitable estoppel.

10. The Agency asserts that the award is contrary to 5 C.F.R. § 536.105(a)(3), which sets forth certain exclusions for providing employees with grade and pay retention. Because the award is contrary to the regulations discussed above, it is unnecessary to address whether the award is also contrary to 5 C.F.R. § 536.105(a)(3).

65 FLRA No. 76

UNITED STATES
DEPARTMENT OF HOMELAND SECURITY
U.S. CUSTOMS AND BORDER PROTECTION
(Agency)

and

NATIONAL TREASURY
EMPLOYEES UNION
CHAPTER 164
(Union)

0-AR-4609

DECISION

December 21, 2010

Before the Authority: Carol Waller Pope, Chairman, and Thomas M. Beck and Ernest DuBester, Members[1]

I. Statement of the Case

This matter is before the Authority on exceptions to an award of Arbitrator Elvis C. Stephens filed by the Agency under § 7122(a) of the Federal Service Labor-Management Relations Statute (the Statute) and part 2425 of the Authority's Regulations. The Union filed an opposition to the Agency's exceptions.

The Arbitrator sustained a grievance alleging that the Agency had improperly suspended the grievant for five days and reassigned the grievant to another duty station (port). Accordingly, he directed the Agency to rescind the grievant's suspension; make him whole for any lost pay and benefits, including overtime; provide him with a "priority transfer to the Port of Bellingham when the next opening comes[;]" and reinstate his alternative work schedule (AWS) schedule at the new port. Award at 12.

For the reasons that follow, we deny the Agency's exceptions.

II. Background and Arbitrator's Award

The grievant, a U.S. Customs and Border Protection Officer who worked at the Port of Point Roberts, was charged with: (1) inattention to duty, for being asleep at his post; and (2) unprofessional conduct, for alleging that a supervisor was having an affair with a subordinate. *Id.* at 2-3. The Agency suspended the grievant for five days and reassigned him to the Blaine Port of Entry. *Id.* at 3. A grievance was filed and submitted to arbitration. *Id.*

The Arbitrator framed the issues before him as: "Whether a [five]-day suspension and [i]nvoluntary reassignment from the Point of Port Roberts for [i]nattention to [d]uty . . . and [u]nprofessional conduct . . . by [the grievant] would promote the efficiency of the [s]ervice? If not, what should be the appropriate penalty?" *Id.* at 1.

With regard to the inattention to duty charge, the Arbitrator found that the Agency had not penalized similar infractions in a similar manner, and concluded that "fact of disparate treatment is sufficient to resolve this charge in favor of [the grievant]." *Id.* at 10. With regard to the unprofessional conduct charge, the Arbitrator determined that the grievant's comments did "not rise to the level of flagrant misconduct[,]" and dismissed that charge. *Id.* at 11-12.

Based on the foregoing, the Arbitrator found that the grievant's five-day suspension was unjustified, and he directed the Agency to rescind it. *Id.* at 12. The Arbitrator also found that the disciplinary action "resulted in a loss of [the grievant's] pay" and that, "[b]ut for such action, [the grievant] would not have suffered such loss of pay." *Id.* Accordingly, the Arbitrator directed that the grievant "be made whole for any loss of pay and benefits, including any overtime assignments he would have worked." *Id.* In addition, the Arbitrator determined: "Given the situation[,] returning [the grievant] to Port Roberts would not be in the best interest of the service. Therefore, he shall be given a priority transfer to the Port of Bellingham when the next opening comes[.]" *Id.* Finally, the Arbitrator directed that the grievant's "AWS schedule shall be reinstated at the new port." *Id.*

III. Positions of the Parties

A. Agency's Exceptions

The Agency argues that the award is contrary to law because, in directing a rescission of the grievant's suspension because of disparate treatment, the

---

1. Member Beck's opinion, dissenting in part, is set forth at the end of this decision.

Arbitrator failed to find that a "similarly situated" employee received a different penalty for the same or similar offenses. Exceptions at 8-9. The Agency alleges that such a finding is required under the factors set forth in *Douglas v. Veterans Admin.*, 5 M.S.P.R. 280, 305 (1981) (*Douglas*).[2] Exceptions at 8.

Additionally, the Agency claims that the award is contrary to the Back Pay Act because, in ordering the Agency to "ma[k]e [the grievant] whole for any loss of pay and benefits, including any overtime [the grievant] *would have* worked[,]" the Arbitrator failed to find a "causal connection between the suspension and the loss of *overtime pay*." Exceptions at 9-10 (citing 5 U.S.C. § 5596(b); *U.S. Dep't of Justice, Fed. Bureau of Prisons, Fed. Corr. Complex, Beaumont, Tex.*, 59 FLRA 466, 468 (2003) (Chairman Cabaniss dissenting in part) (*Beaumont*); *U.S. Dep't of the Air Force, Okla. Air Logistics Ctr., Tinker Air Force Base, Okla.*, 58 FLRA 760, 762 (2003)(*Tinker AFB*)). Specifically, the Agency alleges that the Arbitrator did not make the requisite findings regarding "when, where, and the amount of overtime the grievant lost." *Id.* at 10 (citing *AFGE, Local 1857*, 35 FLRA 325, 328 (1990); *Navy Pub. Works Ctr., Norfolk, Va.*, 33 FLRA 592, 599 (1988) (*Navy*)).

Moreover, the Agency alleges that the Arbitrator exceeded his authority by awarding the grievant a "priority transfer" to the Port of Bellingham and reinstating the grievant's AWS schedule at that port. *Id.* at 13. In this connection, the Agency states that the issue before the Arbitrator was "[w]hether a [five]-day suspension and involuntary reassignment . . . would promote the efficiency of the Service? If not, what should be the appropriate *penalty*?" *Id.* (quoting Award at 1). According to the Agency, the Arbitrator answered both questions when he: (1) implicitly found that the five-day suspension and involuntary reassignment did not promote the efficiency of the service; and (2) determined that the five-day suspension should be rescinded. *Id.* By granting the grievant a priority transfer to a port other than his original duty station with "an otherwise unavailable" AWS, the Agency claims that the Arbitrator went "beyond the issue of an appropriate penalty[,]" providing "benefits" that were "completely unrelated to the matter being arbitrated." *Id.* at 14. The Agency also argues that, because the Union first sought this remedy in its closing brief, the "Arbitrator's willingness to award such a remedy" prejudiced the Agency because it was unable to timely raise any objection or offer additional evidence on this issue. *Id.* at 14-15.

In addition, the Agency asserts that the award fails to draw its essence from the parties' agreement because it conflicts with a memorandum of understanding (the Article) regarding AWS.[3] *Id.* at 11. Specifically, the Agency argues that the Article provides that employees covered by the Article may participate in AWS "only to the extent expressly provided under [a] locally negotiated agreement[]." *Id.* (quoting Exceptions, Attach. 7 at 1). The Agency interprets this clause to indicate that "[i]f AWS is not available at a particular port . . . then no employees at that port . . . will work an AWS." *Id.* According to the Agency, the Port of Bellingham "currently does not . . . have AWS available[,]" and, thus contends that the award conflicts with the Article. *See id.* at 12.

Finally, the Agency argues that the award is ambiguous. Specifically, the Agency contends that the Arbitrator's direction to provide a "priority transfer to the Port of Bellingham when the next opening comes" is unclear because such a personnel action does not exist at the Agency. *Id.* at 7, 15. The Agency asserts that, although existing personnel actions called "priority consideration" and "voluntary transfer" do "sound similar" to "priority transfer[,]" neither of those actions appears to be appropriate or intended here. *Id.* at 15-16.

B. Union's Opposition

The Union argues that the award is not contrary to law. Opp'n at 7-8. According to the Union, the Arbitrator was not required to apply the *Douglas* factors because this case involves a suspension for less than fourteen days. *Id.* at 8. In addition, the Union contends that the Arbitrator made the necessary findings to satisfy the requirements of the Back Pay Act. *Id.* at 9-10.

The Union also argues that the Arbitrator did not exceed his authority by ordering the Agency to give the grievant a "priority transfer" and to restore his AWS. *Id.* at 12-13 (citing *NATCA*, 62 FLRA 490 (2008)). The Union contends that, because the

2. The *Douglas* factors are rules developed by the Merit Systems Protection Board for evaluating whether a particular disciplinary action should be mitigated. *U.S. Dep't of the Air Force, Davis-Monthan Air Force Base, Tucson, Ariz.*, 64 FLRA 819, 820 n.3 (2010).

3. The Article states, in pertinent part: "[E]mployees covered by [the Article] may participate in a flexible or compressed work schedule only to the extent expressly provided under a locally negotiated agreement." Exceptions, Attach. 7 at 1.

Agency's imposed penalty included an involuntary reassignment that directly resulted in the loss of the grievant's AWS, the Arbitrator did not exceed his authority by providing a remedy for the Agency's unjustified action. *Id.* at 13-14. Moreover, according to the Union, if the grievant had returned to his original work station, then he would have been under the same management that took the unjustified personnel actions against him. *Id.*

In addition, the Union contends that the Arbitrator's award of an AWS does not fail to draw its essence from the Article because it is not excluded by the Article. Further, the Union asserts that an award of AWS is an appropriate "make whole" remedy for the grievant, who had an AWS prior to being disciplined in a manner that the Arbitrator found unjustified. *Id.* at 11-12.

Finally, the Union contends that the award is not ambiguous because the intent of the award can be reasonably determined. *Id.* at 15 (citing *U.S. EPA*, 63 FLRA 30, 33 (2008)). The Union argues that the award clearly intends for the grievant to receive a transfer to another port because of the Agency's unjustified involuntary reassignment. *Id.* at 15. The Union further argues that the Arbitrator used the term "priority" to indicate that the transfer was to be effective only "when and if an opening occurred at the specified port." *Id.*

IV. Analysis and Conclusions

A. The award is not contrary to law.

When an exception involves an award's consistency with law, the Authority reviews any question of law raised by the exception and the award de novo. *See NTEU, Chapter 24*, 50 FLRA 330, 332 (1995) (citing *U.S. Customs Serv. v. FLRA*, 43 F.3d 682, 686-87 (D.C. Cir. 1994)). In applying the standard of de novo review, the Authority assesses whether an arbitrator's legal conclusions are consistent with the applicable standard of law. *See U.S. Dep't of Def., Dep'ts of the Army & the Air Force, Ala. Nat'l Guard, Northport, Ala.*, 55 FLRA 37, 40 (1998). In making that assessment, the Authority defers to the arbitrator's underlying factual findings. *See id.*

1. The *Douglas* Factors

The Agency argues that the award is deficient because the Arbitrator failed to apply the *Douglas* factors when considering the penalty the Agency imposed. Exceptions at 8. As stated previously, the *Douglas* factors are factors applied by the Merit Systems Protection Board (MSPB) in evaluating whether a particular disciplinary action should be mitigated. Arbitrators are bound by the same substantive standards as the MSPB only when resolving grievances concerning actions covered by 5 U.S.C. §§ 4303 and 7512. *AFGE, Local 2128*, 47 FLRA 962, 967-68 (1993). As suspensions of fourteen days or less are not covered by §§ 4303 and 7512, an arbitrator's failure to apply the *Douglas* factors when considering such suspensions is not a ground for finding an award deficient. *See id.*

As the suspension at issue here is a five-day suspension, the Arbitrator was not required to apply the *Douglas* factors, and the Agency's exception does not provide a basis for finding the award deficient. *See id.* Accordingly, the award is not contrary to law in this regard, and we deny the exception.

2. The Back Pay Act

An award of backpay is authorized under the Back Pay Act when: (1) the aggrieved employee was affected by an unjustified or unwarranted personnel action; and (2) the personnel action resulted in a loss of pay, allowances, or differentials by the employee. *See, e.g., U.S. Dep't of Transp., FAA*, 63 FLRA 646, 648 (2009). As stated above, the Agency claims that the award is contrary to the Back Pay Act because the Arbitrator failed to find a "causal connection between the suspension and the loss of *overtime pay*." Exceptions at 10.

Contrary to the Agency's claim, the award ensures that any overtime backpay the grievant receives is causally connected to the unwarranted personnel action by limiting backpay to "any overtime assignments [the grievant] would have worked" had he not suffered the unwarranted personnel action. Award at 12. Because the Arbitrator conditioned an award of backpay on the existence of a causal connection as required by the Back Pay Act, the award is unlike awards in *Tinker AFB*, 58 FLRA at 762, *Beaumont*, 59 FLRA at 468, *AFGE, Local 1857*, 35 FLRA at 328, and *Navy*, 33 FLRA at 599, where the arbitrators awarded backpay without finding the causal connection required under the Back Pay Act.

Accordingly, the award is not contrary to the Back Pay Act, and we deny the exception.

B. The Arbitrator did not exceed his authority.

Arbitrators exceed their authority when, among other things, they resolve an issue not submitted to arbitration. *U.S. Dep't of the Treasury, IRS, Wash.*,

D.C., 64 FLRA 426, 434 (2010) (Member Beck dissenting in part as to other matters) (*IRS*). In cases in which the parties do not stipulate the issues for resolution, the Authority accords the arbitrator's formulation of the issue to be decided the same substantial deference that the Authority accords an arbitrator's interpretation and application of a collective bargaining agreement. *Id.* In this connection, when an arbitrator has formulated issues for resolution, the Authority will not find that the arbitrator exceeded his or her authority when the award is confined to the issues as the arbitrator framed them. *Id.*

Here, the Arbitrator framed the issues as follows: "Whether a [five]-day suspension and [i]nvoluntary reassignment from the Point of Port Roberts for [i]nattention to [d]uty . . . and [u]nprofessional conduct . . . by [the grievant] would promote the efficiency of the [s]ervice? If not, what should be the appropriate penalty?" Award at 1.

The Arbitrator resolved the issues by finding that the penalty imposed by the Agency -- the five-day suspension and the involuntary reassignment away from the Point of Port Roberts -- would not promote the efficiency of the service. Therefore, the Arbitrator rescinded the penalty of the suspension and effectively rescinded the penalty of the grievant's reassignment to the Blaine Port of Entry. *See* Award at 12. Having rescinded the penalty imposed by the Agency, the Arbitrator then determined what should be the appropriate "penalty[.]" *Id.* at 1. *See also id.* at 12. In this connection, the Arbitrator did not define "penalty" or give any indication that it was necessarily intended to mean "penalty against the grievant" as opposed to "penalty against the Agency," i.e., what remedial relief would be appropriate. Responding to the issue as he framed it, the Arbitrator determined that it would promote the efficiency of the service to provide the grievant a priority transfer to the Port of Bellingham, stating: "Given the situation[,] returning [the grievant] to Port Roberts would not be in the best interest of the service. Therefore, he shall be given a priority transfer to the Port of Bellingham when the next opening comes[.]" *Id.* As the Arbitrator's conclusion is responsive to the issues as the Arbitrator framed them, the Agency has not demonstrated that the Arbitrator exceeded his authority in this regard. *IRS*, 64 FLRA at 435 (2010).

With regard to the Agency's claim that it was prejudiced because the Union first sought priority consideration for transfer to the Port of Bellingham in its closing brief, the Agency, which improperly transferred the grievant, was aware that the issue of the grievant's work location was implicated by the grievance. *See* Award at 3 (grievance filed in response to Agency's decision to suspend and transfer grievant to a different work location). Thus, there is no basis for finding that the Agency was prejudiced by the Arbitrator's remedy. *Cf. U.S. Dep't of Justice, Fed. Bureau of Prisons, Fed. Corr. Inst., Marianna, Fla.*, 56 FLRA 467, 472 (2000) (rejecting exceeded-authority claim, noting that arbitrator's remedy was linked to harm alleged in grievance). We note, in this regard, that it is well established that arbitrators have broad discretion to fashion remedies, such as the remedy here. *See, e.g., U.S. Dep't of the Air Force, Okla. City Air Logistics Ctr., Tinker Air Force Base, Okla.*, 47 FLRA 98, 101 (1993) (*Air Logistics*).

Accordingly, we deny this exception.

C. The award does not fail to draw its essence from the parties' agreement.

The Authority will find that an arbitration award is deficient as failing to draw its essence from the collective bargaining agreement when the appealing party establishes that the award: (1) cannot in any rational way be derived from the agreement; (2) is so unfounded in reason and fact and so unconnected with the wording and purposes of the collective bargaining agreement as to manifest an infidelity to the obligation of the arbitrator; (3) does not represent a plausible interpretation of the agreement; or (4) evidences a manifest disregard of the agreement. *See U.S. Dep't of Labor (OSHA)*, 34 FLRA 573, 575 (1990). The Authority and the courts defer to the arbitrator in this context "because it is the arbitrator's construction of the agreement for which the parties have bargained." *Id.* at 576.

As stated above, the Agency asserts that the Article provides that employees may participate in AWS "only to the extent expressly provided under [a] locally negotiated agreement[]." Exceptions at 11. The Agency interprets this wording to require that "[i]f AWS is not available at a particular port . . . then no employees at that port . . . will work an AWS." *Id.* However, the Agency does not assert, and the Article does not indicate, that an arbitrator may not direct the continuation of an AWS as part of a remedy for the Agency's improper transfer of an employee. *See id.*; *id.* Attach. 7. In addition, it is well settled that arbitrators have broad discretion to fashion remedies. *See Air Logistics*, 47 FLRA at 101. Accordingly, we deny this exception.

D. The award is not incomplete, ambiguous, or contradictory.

The Authority will find an award deficient when it is incomplete, ambiguous, or so contradictory as to make implementation of the award impossible. *See U.S. Dep't of Labor, Mine Safety & Health Admin. Se. Dist.*, 40 FLRA 937, 943 (1991). For an award to be found deficient on this ground, the appealing party must show that implementation of the award is impossible because the meaning and effect of the award are too unclear or uncertain. *See U.S. Dep't of the Army, Corpus Christi Army Depot, Corpus Christi, Tex.*, 56 FLRA 1057, 1074 (2001).

Although the Agency argues that the award is ambiguous because it directs the Agency to provide a "priority transfer" to the Port of Bellingham, Exceptions at 15, a personnel action that the Agency claims does not exist at the Agency, the Agency does not argue, and there is no basis for finding, that the award is impossible to implement. Consequently, we find that the award is not deficient in this regard, and we deny the exception. *See U.S. Dep't of Homeland Sec., U.S. Customs & Border Prot.*, 64 FLRA 916, 919 (2010).

V. Decision

The Agency's exceptions are denied.

Member Beck, Dissenting in Part:

I disagree with my colleagues' conclusion that the Arbitrator did not exceed his authority by ordering that the grievant be given "priority transfer to the Port of Bellingham" and that "his AWS schedule shall be reinstated." Award at 12.

As I acknowledged in my dissent in *United States, Department of Homeland Security, U.S. Customs and Border Protection,* 65 FLRA 160, 165-66 (2010), arbitrators are granted broad discretion in the fashioning of appropriate remedies. *See, e.g., Veterans Admin.,* 24 FLRA 447, 450 (1986) (*VA*). Even so, the Authority has adhered to the fundamental principle that arbitrators must confine their awards and remedies to those issues submitted for resolution. *See id.*, and the cases cited therein. An arbitrator's authority to fashion a remedy does not extend to issues that are not submitted to arbitration. *U.S. Dep't of the Navy, Naval Sea Logistics Ctr., Detachment Atl., Indian Head, Md.,* 57 FLRA 687, 688 (2002). Although arbitrators may legitimately bring their judgment to bear in reaching a fair resolution of a dispute submitted to them, they may not decide matters that are not before them. *U.S. Dep't of the Treasury, U.S. Mint, Denver, Colo.*, 60 FLRA 777, 780 (2005) (then-Member Pope dissenting as to application).

Here, the Arbitrator framed the issue before him as:

> Whether a [five]-day suspension and [i]nvoluntary reassignment from the Point of Port Roberts for [i]nattention to [d]uty . . . and [u]nprofessional conduct . . . by [the grievant] would promote the efficiency of the [s]ervice? If not, what should be the appropriate penalty?

Award at 1. In other words, the Arbitrator was tasked with assessing whether the penalties that had been imposed on the grievant by the Agency were appropriate, and if not, whether some other penalty against the grievant would be more appropriate.[1]

The Arbitrator answered the first question when he implicitly found that the grievant's five-day suspension and involuntary reassignment did not promote the efficiency of the service. Award at 12. Having so found, the Arbitrator possessed the authority only to determine "the appropriate penalty." He was free to find -- and apparently did find -- that the appropriate penalty was no penalty at all. Thus, he could properly (1) rescind the suspension and award to the grievant the pay and benefits that he lost as a result of the suspension, and (2) return the grievant to his original work location. The Arbitrator, however, went beyond this authority and awarded to the grievant affirmative relief not contemplated by the specific issues that he framed – i.e., he ordered that the grievant be given a priority transfer to the Port of Bellingham and ordered the reinstatement of the grievant's AWS schedule at that port.

This additional relief concerns issues that were not before the Arbitrator. First, whether the grievant should be given a priority transfer to a specific port, and second, whether his AWS schedule should be reinstated there. The Arbitrator was neither asked to, nor authorized to, resolve these other issues, nor to direct remedies concerning them. By doing so, the Arbitrator exceeded his authority. *See Veterans Admin.,* 24 FLRA at 451 (finding arbitrator "exceed[ed] his authority by deciding, and awarding a remedy concerning an issue not submitted to arbitration"); *see also U.S. Dep't of Homeland Sec., U.S. Customs & Border Prot.,* 64 FLRA 916, 919-20 (2010); *U.S. Dep't of Homeland Sec., U.S. Customs & Border Prot.*, 62 FLRA 59, 62 (2007).

Accordingly, I would modify the award to vacate the portions of the award concerning these remedies.[2]

1. My colleagues' suggestion that the reference to a "penalty" refers to a "penalty against the Agency" is not plausible. The first sentence of the issue framed by the Arbitrator indisputably relates to the disciplinary penalty that was imposed on the grievant. If the Arbitrator's reference to a "penalty" in the second sentence were intended to indicate something entirely different -- a "penalty" that he might impose on the Agency -- he should have said so much more explicitly. Moreover, labor arbitrators are generally not asked to "penalize" employers who erroneously discipline employees.

2. Because I would find that these additional remedies should be set aside, I would find it unnecessary to address the Agency's remaining exceptions that the award fails to draw its essence from the parties' agreement or that the award is ambiguous. Exceptions at 11-12, 15-16.

65 FLRA No. 77

AMERICAN FEDERATION
OF GOVERNMENT EMPLOYEES
LOCAL 1770
(Union)

and

UNITED STATES
DEPARTMENT OF DEFENSE
DEFENSE COMMISSARY AGENCY
FORT BRAGG, NORTH CAROLINA
(Agency)

0-AR-4342

DECISION

December 21, 2010

Before the Authority: Carol Waller Pope, Chairman, and Thomas M. Beck and Ernest DuBester, Members

I. Statement of the Case

This matter is before the Authority on exceptions to an award of Robert W. Kilroy, filed by the Union under § 7122(a) of the Federal Service Labor-Management Relations Statute (the Statute) and part 2425 of the Authority's Regulations. The Agency filed an untimely opposition to the Union's exceptions.[1]

A grievance was filed disputing the grievant's performance review. Award at 2. The Arbitrator determined that the Agency did not violate the Master Labor Agreement (MLA) or the Agency's performance appraisal system in assessing the grievant's performance and denied the grievance. *Id.* at 6.

For the reasons set forth below, we both deny and dismiss the Union's exceptions.

II. Background and Arbitrator's Award

The Defense Commissary Agency operates commissaries at bases operated by the Department of Defense. The grievance arose when the grievant, working as a Sales Store Checker (Cashier), disputed her performance rating. *Id.* at 1.

The Agency implemented a performance appraisal system to use as the basis for making personnel decisions relating to pay increases, awards, grade reductions, reductions in force, and the like. *Id.* The performance appraisal system is comprised of performance elements for each position. Performance standards are applied to each of the elements to evaluate the employees' level of compliance with each element. The performance standards attempt to measure employees' performance by evaluating indicators such as quality of work, results achieved, manner of performance, and quantity and timeliness of work. *Id.* Once evaluations are complete, the performance appraisal system categorizes employees with one of the following five ratings: (1) unacceptable; (2) minimally acceptable; (3) fully successful; (4) excellent; or (5) outstanding. *Id.* at 2.

The grievant's duties as a Cashier are described as follows:

> Operates electronic cash register, scans grocery, meat and produce items. Accepts media from customers for payment, makes change and performs other duties as required, or assigned.

Id. The Arbitrator found that there are eight critical elements and one non-critical element that must be met to execute the duties of this position. *Id.*

1. The Agency concedes that its opposition was untimely filed. *See* Agency's Response to Order to Show Cause at 1. Under 5 C.F.R. § 2429.23(b), an expired time limit can be waived upon a showing of "extraordinary circumstances" justifying the waiver. The Agency requests that the Authority amend its Regulations so that submissions deposited with commercial delivery services for delivery to the Authority are considered filed on the day that they are deposited for delivery rather than when the submissions are received by the Authority. Effective November 9, 2009, 5 C.F.R. § 2429.21(b) was amended to provide that the filing date of submissions sent by commercial delivery is the date on which they are deposited with a commercial delivery service (rather than the date received by the Authority). However, as the Regulations that apply here are those that were in effect at the time the submission was filed, the opposition is still considered untimely. *See AFGE, Local 2145*, 61 FLRA 661 (2010). Further, as the Agency fails to make any claim that extraordinary circumstances warrant a waiver of the time limit, we will not consider the Agency's opposition.

In her grievance, the grievant argued that she incorrectly received a rating of "fully successful" from her supervisor rather than a rating of "excellent." *Id.* In order to achieve a rating of "excellent," employees must receive an "exceeded" grade on more than half of the critical performance elements assigned to their respective positions. The grievant received a rating of "exceeded" on four of the Cashier position's critical elements and a rating of "met" on the remaining four critical elements. *Id.* The grievant also received an "exceeded" rating on the one non-critical element of her position. *Id.* Accordingly, for the one-year rating period, the grievant's supervisor provided her with a rating of "fully successful." *Id.*

The grievant grieved her performance rating through the negotiated grievance procedure. The Agency denied the grievance and the matter was submitted to arbitration.

Each party presented arguments before the Arbitrator. The Union argued that the instances of "failures or errors" recorded in the grievant's evaluation should not be a bar to her receiving a rating of "excellent." *Id.* at 3. The Agency claimed that the grievant was aware that her "variances" under the critical elements and one customer complaint prevented her from achieving a rating of "excellent." *Id.* at 4.

The issue to be decided by the Arbitrator was whether the Agency violated Article 27 of the MLA and/or the performance appraisal system in its evaluation of the grievant.[2] *Id.*

First, the Arbitrator determined that the Union did not prove by a preponderance of the evidence that the Agency violated Article 27 of the MLA. The Arbitrator noted that the grievant's argument that she was not fairly evaluated was general and did not make any specific allegations under Article 27 of the MLA. *Id.* Accordingly, the Arbitrator found no violation.

Second, the Arbitrator found that the Union failed to prove by a preponderance of the evidence that the Agency violated its performance appraisal system. In the Arbitrator's view, the facts and circumstances did not demonstrate clear and convincing evidence of an abuse of discretion that would justify sustaining the grievance. In this respect, the Arbitrator noted that the grievant had two variances and one customer complaint. The Arbitrator determined that these were legitimate reasons why the grievant was not given a rating of "exceeds" on all of her critical elements. *Id.* at 6. Although the Union argued that the infractions were within the tolerances allowed, the Arbitrator noted that, if the grievant did not have any infractions at all, then she would have achieved a rating of "exceeds." *Id.* Accordingly, the Arbitrator found no violation of the performance appraisal system and denied the grievance. *Id.*

2. The text of Article 27, Employees Rights, is set forth in the attached appendix.

III. Union's Exceptions

In its exceptions, the Union lists several "issues presented" by the arbitration award, which appear to be the bases upon which it challenges the award. Exceptions at 2. As relevant here, the Union then argues that the Arbitrator erred as a matter of law in his assessment of the grievance and the performance standard.[3]

The Union claims that the Arbitrator erroneously imposed a heightened standard in evaluating the Union's challenge to the grievant's rating. According to the Union, the Arbitrator improperly required it to show that the rating was both incorrect and made in bad faith. *Id.* at 3. The Union contends that the grievant demonstrated that the performance standards were not properly applied to her. As there were no performance errors, the Union argues that the grievant should have received a higher rating. *Id.*

3. In addition to its contrary to law argument, the Union lists the following five issues: (1) Does the award fail to draw its essence from the MLA? (2) Did the Arbitrator exceed his authority by finding that the grievant was subject to an adverse action? (3) Did the Arbitrator exceed his authority when he decided the Agency violated the MLA under unspecified provisions other than those in the stipulated issues? (4) Did the Arbitrator exceed his authority when he ordered action taken that is properly under the purview of another organization? (5) Is the Arbitrator's award inconsistent with the Back Pay Act? The Union does not provide any arguments supporting these claims. Exceptions at 2. When a party fails to provide any arguments or authority to support its exceptions, the Authority will deny the exceptions as bare assertions. *See U.S. Dep't of Homeland Sec., U.S. Customs & Border Prot., Port of Seattle, Seattle, Wash.*, 60 FLRA 490, 492 n.7 (2004) (Chairman Cabaniss concurring). Therefore, to the extent that these "issues presented" were intended to operate as exceptions, we reject them as bare assertions.

The Union also argues that the award is contrary to law because the Arbitrator did not conclude that the performance standards were improper. *Id.* at 4. According to the Union, the performance standards merely describe the duties assigned rather than provide an objective standard by which performance can be measured. *Id.* at 5. The Union further claims that the standards are both "impermissibly vague" and "absolute."[4] *Id.* The Union maintains that a single customer complaint should not "lead[ ] to a failure of the standard." *Id.* In the Union's view, the performance standard is similar to other impermissible "absolute standards" invalidated by the Merit Systems Protection Board (MSPB). *Id.* (citing *Smith v. Dep't of Veterans Affairs,* 59 M.S.P.R. 340 (1993)). Accordingly, the Union argues that the award is contrary to law and asks that the Authority reverse the award on that basis.

IV. The award is not contrary to law.

The Union claims that the award is contrary to law because (1) the Arbitrator imposed a heightened standard in evaluating the Union's challenge to the grievant's performance rating, and (2) the performance standards upheld by the Arbitrator are inconsistent with the law. When an exception involves an award's consistency with law, the Authority reviews any question of law raised by the exception and the award de novo. *See NTEU, Chapter 24*, 50 FLRA 330, 332 (1995) (citing *U.S. Customs Serv. v. FLRA*, 43 F.3d 682, 686-87 (D.C. Cir. 1994)). In applying the standard of de novo review, the Authority assesses whether an arbitrator's legal conclusions are consistent with the applicable standard of law. *See U.S. Dep't of Def., Dep'ts of the Army & the Air Force, Ala. Nat'l Guard, Northport, Ala.*, 55 FLRA 37, 40 (1998) (*Dep't of Defense*). In making that assessment, the Authority defers to the arbitrator's underlying factual findings. *See id.*

The Union has failed to demonstrate that the award is contrary to law because the Arbitrator required it to meet a heightened standard of review. The Union does not cite any law to which the award is contrary. Additionally, the Union does not show how the Arbitrator required it to establish, as it claims, the Agency's "bad faith" when rating the grievant's performance. Instead, the Arbitrator determined whether the facts supported the grievant's rating. Specifically, the Arbitrator found that the grievant's supervisor identified events that prevented the grievant from receiving an overall rating of "excellent." In this respect, the Arbitrator found, and it is undisputed, that the grievant had two variances and was also the subject of a validated customer complaint. Award at 5. Accordingly, the Arbitrator concluded that the facts warranted the grievant's rating of "met" rather than "exceeds" on four of her critical elements and, therefore, an overall rating of "fully successful," rather than one of "excellent." *Id.* at 6. Thus, as the Arbitrator found that the facts supported the grievant's rating and that the Union failed to demonstrate that the Agency violated Article 27 of the MLA, he denied the grievance.

As indicated above, the Union does not cite any law to which the award is contrary. Moreover, deferring to the Arbitrator's undisputed factual findings in determining whether his legal conclusions are consistent with the law, *Dep't of Defense,* 55 FLRA at 40, the Union has not demonstrated that the Arbitrator rejected the Union's contentions because of a failure to show "bad faith" by the Agency. We therefore reject the Union's argument and deny the exception.

The Union's arguments that the performance standards are either impermissibly vague or absolute and that, therefore, the award is contrary to law, are not properly before the Authority. Section 2429.5 of the Authority's Regulations provides in pertinent part that "[t]he Authority will not consider . . . any issue, which was not presented in the proceedings before the . . . arbitrator."[5] 5 C.F.R. § 2429.5. Authority precedent makes clear that § 2429.5's provisions will be applied to bar consideration of a parties' exceptions where an issue could have been, but was not, presented to an arbitrator. *See, e.g., U.S. Dep't of Homeland Sec., U.S. Customs & Border Prot., JFK Airport, Queens, N.Y.,* 62 FLRA 416, 417 (2008).

4. Specifically, the Union claims that "performance standards 3 and 5 are absolute as written." Exceptions at 4.

5. The Authority's Regulations concerning the review of arbitration awards, as well as certain related procedural regulations, including § 2429.5, were revised effective October 1, 2010. *See* 75 Fed. Reg. 42,283 (2010). As the Agency's exceptions were filed before that date, we apply the earlier Regulations.

Application of § 2429.5's provisions in this case mandates dismissal of the Union's exception. There is no evidence in the record that the Union claimed before the Arbitrator that the performance standards were impermissibly vague or absolute. As the Union did not present, but could have presented those issues to the Arbitrator in the first instance, it may not do so now. We therefore dismiss the Union's exception.

V. Decision

The Union's exceptions are respectively denied and dismissed.

APPENDIX

ARTICLE 27
EMPLOYEE RIGHTS

Section 1. Pursuant to Title 5 Section 7102, United States Code, employees have the right, freely and without fear of penalty or reprisal, to form, join and assist the **UNION** or to refrain from such activity. The freedom of employees to assist the **UNION** shall extend to participation in the management of the **UNION** and acting for the **UNION** in the capacity of a **UNION** official.

Section 2. All personnel shall be treated with fairness, equity and dignity in all matters without favoritism or regard to political affiliation, race, color, religion, natural origin, sex, marital status, age or handicapping condition. Employees' constitutional rights will be protected and employees will be treated with proper regard and protection of their privacy. Employees have the right to fully pursue their private lives, personal welfare and personal beliefs without interference, coercion, or discrimination by management so long as such activities do not conflict with the government-wide ethics requirements as outlined in regulatory guidance or with job responsibilities; the standard of nexus shall apply.

Exceptions, Attach., MLA, at 70; *see also* Award at 3.

65 FLRA No. 78

NATIONAL ASSOCIATION
OF INDEPENDENT LABOR
LOCAL 7
(Union)

and

UNITED STATES
DEPARTMENT OF THE AIR FORCE
SEYMOUR JOHNSON AIR FORCE BASE
GOLDSBORO, NORTH CAROLINA
(Agency)

0-AR-4390

DECISION

December 22, 2010

Before the Authority: Carol Waller Pope, Chairman, and Thomas M. Beck and Ernest DuBester, Members

I. Statement of the Case

This matter is before the Authority on exceptions to an award of Arbitrator Glen M. Bendixsen filed by the Union under § 7122(a) of the Federal Service Labor-Management Relations Statute (the Statute) and part 2425 of the Authority's Regulations. The Agency filed an opposition to the Union's exceptions.

The Agency selected an employee (the selectee) to fill a vacant supervisory position. The Union subsequently filed grievances on behalf of two other candidates for the position, claiming that the Agency violated the parties' collective bargaining agreement (CBA) and an Agency regulation by improperly including the selectee on the referral certificate for the vacant position. The Arbitrator denied the grievances.

For the reasons that follow, we deny the Union's exceptions.

II. Background and Arbitrator's Award

The Agency posted a vacancy announcement for the Air Force Reserve Technician (ART) position of Sheet Metal Mechanic (Aircraft) Supervisor. Award at 8. As the vacancy was an ART position, it required both civilian and military (Air Force Reserve) qualifications.[1] *Id.* at 4.

In response to the vacancy announcement, the Agency received twenty applications, including those of the two grievants. Both grievants work in the Sheet Metal Shop as Aircraft Sheet Metal Technicians. *Id.* at 8.

The Agency evaluated the skills of the applicants to determine whether any met the civilian qualifications for the supervisory position. The Agency used a four-category rating system, rating applicants as unqualified, minimally qualified, best qualified, or the highest rating, highly qualified. *Id.* at 7-8. Applicants rated as minimally qualified, best qualified, or highly qualified were eligible to be placed on the referral list of qualified applicants for consideration by the selecting official. *See id.* at 9.

The evaluation panel ranked three applicants, including the two grievants, as "best qualified." *Id.* No applicants were rated "highly qualified," and one applicant was rated "minimally qualified." *Id.*

Due to the small number of best qualified applicants and the lack of any highly qualified applicants, the evaluation panel asked the selecting official whether he wished to include on the referral list applicants who were ranked as "minimally qualified." *Id.* at 9. The selecting official agreed that such applicants should be included. *Id.* Therefore, the evaluation panel included on the referral certificate the applicant who was ranked as "minimally qualified." *Id.* This applicant worked in the Maintenance Shop as a journeyman Machinist. *Id.* at 8-9. This addition increased the number of applicants on the referral certificate from three to four.

1. An ART is a reservist who works in a civilian position but is subject to performing reserve duty or being called for active duty in the Air Force. Award at 6. Reserve duty consists of two days duty per month and an additional period of two weeks duty per year. While on reserve duty, an ART occupies the same position and performs the same work, but does it in his or her military capacity and uniform. *Id.*

The evaluation panel sent the referral certificate to the selecting official. According to the Arbitrator:

> The evidence shows that the applicants on the certificate are listed alphabetically without any indication of their ranking; furthermore, that the selecting official routinely assumes that from among total applicants all on the certificate are 'best qualified' among all who applied.

Id. at 9. The four applicants subsequently appeared before an interview board, which provided its recommendations to the selecting official. *Id.*

The selecting official selected the applicant who was ranked minimally qualified to fill the vacant supervisory position. *Id.* at 9-10. Once the selecting official determined that the selectee had the necessary civilian qualifications, the Agency Chief of Personnel Employment, acting in her military capacity, then determined that the selectee met the qualifications of the military reserve equivalent of the supervisory position. *Id.*

The Union filed grievances on behalf of two applicants who had not been selected from the referral certificate. *Id.* at 10. The grievances alleged that the Agency violated the CBA and an Agency regulation by improperly placing on the referral list an applicant who was not qualified. *Id.* at 10-11. The grievances were not resolved and were submitted to arbitration.

The Arbitrator found that the issue before him was the "validity of the referral list from which the [selecting official] made his selection." *Id.* at 20. He determined that the Agency properly found that the selectee met the civilian and military qualifications to be included on the referral list. As relevant here, the Arbitrator concluded that Article 31, Section 6 of the CBA "was not violated by including a minimally qualified candidate on the referral list."[2] *Id.* at 22. The Arbitrator found that under Article 31, Section 6, an applicant who meets the minimal qualifications of a vacancy is "qualified." *Id.* Further, in the Arbitrator's view, Section 6's "mandate to select the 'best qualified' candidate" from the referral list did not rely upon the categories in which applicants were initially rated because the section did not make any reference to "highly qualified" applicants. *Id.* at 22-23. Rather, the Arbitrator interpreted Section 6's mandate to select the "best qualified" candidate as "clearly requir[ing] selection of the candidate deemed superior after a consideration of many factors[,]" including the recommendations of the interview board. *Id.* at 23. Finding that the interview board and the selecting official had made Section 6's "required 'evaluation' . . . to identify the 'best candidate'" from the referral list, the Arbitrator denied the grievances. *Id.*

III. Positions of the Parties

A. Union's Exceptions

The Union contends that the award fails to draw its essence from Article 31, Section 6 of the CBA. Exceptions at 2. The Union claims that the Arbitrator erred in interpreting Article 31, Section 6 of the CBA to permit the Agency to include on the referral certificate an applicant such as the selectee who is ranked as only minimally qualified. *Id.* at 2, 15-16. Rather, the Union argues, Article 31, Section 6 requires that of the qualified applicants, "only the Best Qualified . . . are referred over on the referral certificate" to the selecting official. *Id.* at 16. Because in the Union's view this did not happen, the Union asserts that the Arbitrator erroneously construed and applied the CBA when he denied the grievances.

In addition, the Union argues that the award is inconsistent with another arbitration award. *Id.* at 16-17 (citing *U.S. Dep't of the Army, Armament Research, Dev. & Eng'g Ctr., Picatinny Arsenal, N.J.*, 48 FLRA 873 (1993) (*U.S. Dep't of the Army, Picatinny*)). The Union claims that in that case, as in

---

2. Article 31, Section 6 of the CBA provides:

> All unit employee applications which meet minimum qualifications for a vacancy announcement are rated as qualified. Qualified candidates will be further evaluated in terms of the knowledge, skills, abilities (KSA's) required by the position to identify those best qualified candidates. Evaluation will be based on multiple assessment measures such as experience, education, and training to the extent that it is relevant to the position being filled. Rating criteria shall not be tailored to fit a certain employee or applicant. The Employer shall not use leave or medical records in rating candidates for promotion. Best [q]ualified candidates will be listed alphabetically. Promotion certificates will usually have the names of up to ten (10) persons.

Award at 5.

this case, an applicant did not possess the qualifications to be included on the referral list sent to the selecting official. In *U.S. Dep't of the Army, Picatinny*, the Authority denied exceptions to the arbitrator's award finding that the Agency violated, among other things, the parties' agreement by selecting an applicant who was not qualified for the position. *Id.* at 880.

B. Agency's Opposition

The Agency contends that the award is not deficient. It argues that the Arbitrator reasonably interpreted the CBA to include the selectee on the referral certificate and that the Union merely disagrees with the Arbitrator's interpretation of the CBA. Opp'n at 9. In addition, the Agency contends that the selectee was qualified to be placed on the referral certificate, according to the requirements of the Agency's regulations. *Id.* at 10.

IV. Analysis and Conclusions

A. The Union has not established that the award fails to draw its essence from the collective bargaining agreement.

The Union contends that the award fails to draw its essence from the CBA because the Arbitrator erroneously found that Article 31, Section 6 permits the Agency to include on the referral list an applicant such as the selectee who is ranked as minimally qualified.[3] In reviewing an arbitrator's interpretation of a collective bargaining agreement, the Authority applies the deferential standard of review that federal courts use in reviewing arbitration awards in the private sector. *See* 5 U.S.C. § 7122(a)(2); *AFGE, Council 220*, 54 FLRA 156, 159 (1998). Under this standard, the Authority will find that an arbitration award is deficient as failing to draw its essence from the collective bargaining agreement when the appealing party establishes that the award: (1) cannot in any rational way be derived from the agreement; (2) is so unfounded in reason and fact and so unconnected with the wording and purposes of the collective bargaining agreement as to manifest an infidelity to the obligation of the arbitrator; (3) does not represent a plausible interpretation of the agreement; or (4) evidences a manifest disregard of the agreement. *See U.S. Dep't of Labor (OSHA)*, 34 FLRA 573, 575 (1990). The Authority and the courts defer to arbitrators in this context "because it is the arbitrator's construction of the agreement for which the parties have bargained." *Id.* at 576.

The Union claims that the award fails to draw its essence from Article 31, Section 6 of the CBA because Section 6 requires that only the "best qualified" of the qualified candidates be referred to the selecting official on the referral list. Exceptions at 16. However, the only constraint that Section 6 imposes on referral lists is that such lists "will usually have the names of up to ten (10) persons." Moreover, although Section 6 requires that qualified applicants be further evaluated to determine which applicants are "best qualified," nothing in Section 6 bars the Agency from considering all qualified candidates "best qualified" for referral list purposes, where the total number of qualified candidates is under Section 6's presumptive limit of ten applicants on a referral list. In addition, the Union does not take issue with the Arbitrator's view that the overall goal of Section 6 is to assure that the "best candidate" is identified and selected. Award at 23. For these reasons, the Union does not provide any basis for finding that the Arbitrator's determination that the Agency did not violate Section 6 by including a minimally qualified candidate on the referral list is irrational, unfounded, implausible, or in manifest disregard of the CBA.

Accordingly, we deny this exception.

B. The Union has not established that the award is deficient because it conflicts with another arbitration award.

The Union contends that the award is deficient because it is inconsistent with an arbitration award upheld by the Authority in *U.S. Dep't of the Army, Picatinny*. Exceptions at 16-17. In that case, the arbitrator found that an agency violated the collective bargaining agreement by improperly placing a candidate on a referral certificate for a vacant position.

The Union's contention does not provide a basis for finding the award deficient. Arbitration awards are not precedential, and a contention that an

3. The Union also argues that the award is contrary Agency regulations, but does not demonstrate that the award is deficient in this regard. Specifically, the Union: (1) acknowledges that the Agency regulations state that additional candidates may be referred; and (2) argues that any discretion created by that wording "has been eliminated by contractual language." Exceptions at 15, 16. Thus, the Union's contrary to regulation argument essentially challenges the Arbitrator's contract interpretation.

arbitration award conflicts with other arbitration awards does not provide any basis for finding an award deficient under the Statute. *See IFPTE, Local 28, Lewis Eng'rs & Scientists Ass'n*, 50 FLRA 533, 536-37 (1995) (arbitrator not bound by awards resolving other disputes). Consequently, the Arbitrator was not required to conform the award in this case to a prior award resolving another dispute.

Accordingly, we deny this exception.

V. Decision

The Union's exceptions are denied.

65 FLRA No. 79

UNITED STATES
DEPARTMENT OF THE AIR FORCE
EDWARDS AIR FORCE BASE, CALIFORNIA
(Agency)

and

SPORT AIR TRAFFIC
CONTROLLERS ORGANIZATION
(Union)

0-AR-4625

DECISION

December 22, 2010

Before the Authority: Carol Waller Pope, Chairman, and Thomas M. Beck and Ernest DuBester, Members

I. Statement of the Case

This matter is before the Authority on exceptions to an award of Arbitrator Philip Tamoush, filed by the Agency under § 7122(a) of the Federal Service Labor-Management Relations Statute (the Statute) and part 2425 of the Authority's Regulations. The Union filed an opposition to the Agency's exceptions.

The Arbitrator determined that the Agency violated the parties' collective bargaining agreement (CBA) by unilaterally eliminating supervisory discretion to grant the grievants up to fifty-nine minutes of administrative leave during the last hour of the grievants' shifts when no duties are required.

For the reasons discussed below, we deny the Agency's exceptions in part and dismiss them in part.

II. Background and Arbitrator's Award

The grievants are air traffic controllers who support test and training missions in restricted airspace. Exceptions at 2. The grievants work four ten-hour shifts weekly. *Id.* at 3. During the final hour of a shift, the grievants may have no duties to perform, depending on varying mission needs and operational requirements. Award at 8; Exceptions at 2. In these situations, first-level supervisors have had the discretion to grant the grievants up to fifty-nine minutes of administrative leave. Award at 6.

The Agency unilaterally eliminated supervisory discretion to grant up to fifty-nine minutes of administrative leave at the end of the grievants' shifts. *Id.* at 3-7. The Union subsequently filed a grievance alleging that the Agency violated Article 24, Section 2 of the CBA[1] by eliminating supervisory authority to grant this leave in situations where no air traffic control operations are required. *Id.* at 6. When the grievance was not resolved, it was submitted to arbitration. *Id.* at 7.

At arbitration, the Union argued that Article 24, Section 2 of the CBA gives first-line supervisors the authority to grant the grievants up to fifty-nine minutes of administrative leave when they have no duties to perform at the end of their shifts. *Id.* at 8. Conversely, the Agency argued that Article 24, Section 2 gives first-line supervisors the authority to grant administrative leave for hazardous weather conditions only. *Id.* at 10.

In his award, the Arbitrator framed the issue, in relevant part, as follows:

> Did [the Agency] violate the [CBA] when it decided to abolish the "59-minute shove," as practiced previously? If so, what is the appropriate remedy?

Id. at 2.

The Arbitrator concluded that the Agency violated Article 24, Section 2 of the CBA by unilaterally eliminating the "59-minute shove." *Id.* at 14. The Arbitrator defined the "59-minute shove" as the first-line supervisors' authority to grant the grievants up to fifty-nine minutes of "time off with pay" during the final hour of the grievants' shifts. *Id.* at 11-12. The Arbitrator also construed Article 24, Section 2 as giving supervisors discretion to grant such leave only when "operations permit," which are times when the grievants have no duties to perform at the end of a shift because no air traffic control operations are required. *Id.* at 8, 12.

1. The relevant portion of Article 24, Section 2 of the CBA provides that "[t]he first[-]level supervisor has the authority to grant administrative leave up to 59 minutes." Exceptions, Attach., J. Ex. 1 at 10.

III. Positions of the Parties

A. Agency's Exceptions

The Agency argues that the award unlawfully requires the Agency to maintain a workweek amounting to less than the forty hours required by 5 U.S.C. § 6101(a)(2)(A).[2] Exceptions at 1. Specifically, the Agency argues that granting paid absences of fifty-nine minutes at the end of the grievants' shifts regularly occurs on about three out of every four shifts. *Id.* at 5. Therefore, the Agency maintains that granting such absences has become so routine as to reduce the workweek to thirty-seven hours on average, thereby contravening the forty-hour requirement of § 6101(a)(2)(A). *Id.* (citing *U.S. Dep't of Transp., FAA, Chi., Ill.*, 41 FLRA 1441, 1449-450 (1991) (*FAA*); *AFGE, AFL-CIO, Local 3231*, 25 FLRA 600, 603 (1987) (*AFGE*)). The Agency also argues that permitting supervisors to grant up to fifty-nine minutes of paid leave would establish a precedent in future CBAs eliminating any limits on the amount of administrative leave supervisors could grant. *Id.* at 7.

The Agency further contends that the Arbitrator's interpretation of the CBA renders the CBA "illegal" and "void in its entirety." *Id.* at 7-8. In support of this contention, the Agency claims that the Arbitrator interpreted the CBA to allow first-line supervisors "unfettered authority" to grant paid absences. *Id.* The Agency also argues that "as interpreted, the provision determines which manager performs a given task contrary to exclusive management rights." *Id.* at 8.

B. Union's Opposition

The Union asserts that the issue of whether Article 24, Section 2 contravenes 5 U.S.C. § 6101(a)(2)(A) was not raised during the arbitration. Opp'n at 2. The Union also contends that the CBA does not require employees to work less than a forty-hour workweek. *Id.* at 3.

In response to the Agency's argument that the Arbitrator's interpretation of the CBA renders it "illegal" and "void in its entirety," Exceptions at 7-8, the Union argues that the Agency has never sought to renegotiate Article 24, Section 2 during contract negotiations or any other period when the parties can reopen an existing agreement. Opp'n at 4.

IV. Analysis and Conclusions

The Agency argues that when the award upheld the routine granting of fifty-nine minutes of paid leave at the end of the grievants' shifts, it unlawfully reduced the workweek to thirty-seven hours on average, thereby contravening the forty-hour requirement of 5 U.S.C. § 6101(a)(2)(A). Exceptions at 5. As the Agency's exception challenges the award's consistency with law, the Authority reviews the question of law raised by the exception and the award de novo. *See NTEU, Chapter 24*, 50 FLRA 330, 332 (1995) (citing *U.S. Customs Serv. v. FLRA*, 43 F.3d 682, 686-87 (D.C. Cir. 1994)). In applying this standard, the Authority assesses whether an arbitrator's legal conclusions are consistent with the applicable standard of law. *See U.S. Dep't of Def., Dep'ts of the Army & the Air Force, Ala. Nat'l Guard, Northport, Ala.*, 55 FLRA 37, 40 (1998). In making that assessment, the Authority defers to the arbitrator's underlying factual findings. *See id.*

Under 5 U.S.C. § 6101(a)(2)(A), the head of each agency is directed to establish a "basic administrative workweek of 40 hours for each full-time employee in [the] organization[.]" The Agency does not demonstrate that the award is contrary to this obligation.[3] In this connection, although the Agency asserts that the award effectively allows employees to work a thirty-seven-hour workweek, the Union disputes this assertion, and the Arbitrator made no finding that the parties' current practice allows such a situation. There is no basis for the Authority to make a factual finding, not present in the award, that either the parties' current practice or the Arbitrator's award allows a thirty-seven-hour workweek on a regular basis. *See U.S. Nuclear Regulatory Comm'n*, 65 FLRA 79, 85 (2010) (Authority declined to make disputed factual finding not present in arbitrator's award). Thus, there is no basis for finding that the award requires the Agency to establish a thirty-seven-hour workweek.

The award simply enforces the Agency's agreement to permit supervisors broad discretion to approve administrative leave. In this regard, the

2. The relevant portion of 5 U.S.C. § 6101 provides that "(2) [t]he head of each Executive agency . . . shall— (A) establish a basic administrative workweek of 40 hours for each full-time employee in his organization . . . ."

3. The Union's assertion that the Agency did not raise the issue of whether Article 24, Section 2 contravenes § 6101 during the arbitration is without merit, as the record makes clear that the Agency did address this issue. *See* Exceptions, Attach., Agency's Post-Hearing Brief at 23.

Authority has recognized that agencies have broad discretion to grant administrative leave to employees for brief, occasional or sporadic periods of time when warranted by specific circumstances which are not a part of the daily routine of work. *See SSA, Balt., Md.*, 58 FLRA 630, 633 (2003) (administrative leave before Christmas holiday); *AFGE*, 25 FLRA at 603 ("essence of such leave is that it is only occasional or sporadic—when warranted by specific circumstances which are not a part of the daily routine of work"); *NLRB, Region 5*, 2 FLRA 327, 329-31 (1979) (*NLRB*) (administrative leave to cover tardiness in reporting to work); *see also U.S. Dep't of the Air Force, 439th Airlift Wing, Westover Air Reserve Base, Mass.*, 55 FLRA 945, 949 (1999) (administrative leave for time spent engaging in mandatory crew rest periods after long distance flights).

The award in this case is consistent with this Authority case law. As the Arbitrator noted, supervisory discretion to grant such leave is limited to fifty-nine minute increments. Award at 8, 11-12. Therefore, the leave is granted for brief periods only. As the Arbitrator also found, the supervisory discretion to grant this leave is limited to situations where "operations permit," which means where the grievants have no duties to perform because no air traffic operations are required. *Id.* Therefore, the leave is be granted on an occasional or a sporadic rather than a routine basis because whether employees have duties to perform varies depending on mission needs and operational requirements. *Id.* at 8; Exceptions at 2; *see also AFGE*, 25 FLRA at 603. Because the leave at issue here is brief and not granted on a routine basis, it does not unlawfully reduce the grievants' workweek to less than forty hours per week.

The circumstances in this case are distinguishable from the circumstances in cases the Agency relies on, *supra* Part III, where agencies were found to have no authority to grant administrative leave. In those cases, the Authority held that paid leave granted to cover employees' routine meal periods cannot count towards the forty-hour workweek. In both cases, the administrative leave was granted on a "regular, daily basis." *AFGE*, 25 FLRA at 603. Here, in contrast, the award does not require the Agency to regularly grant administrative leave at the end of the grievants' shifts. As discussed above, such leave is limited to brief, occasional periods when "operations permit." Therefore, the Agency has not demonstrated that its authority to grant administrative leave does not properly extend to the type of circumstance involved in this case. For these reasons, the award is consistent with § 6101(a)(2)(A) because it does not reduce employees' workweek to less than forty hours.

The Agency also argues that permitting supervisors to grant up to fifty-nine minutes of paid leave would establish a precedent in future CBAs eliminating any limits on the amount of administrative leave supervisors could grant. Exceptions at 7. However, this decision does not alter controlling Authority precedent that agency discretion is limited only to granting brief, occasional or sporadic periods of administrative leave.[4]

In sum, the Agency has not established that the Arbitrator's award unlawfully reduced the grievants' workweek to less than forty hours. Therefore, the Agency's exception provides no basis for finding that the award is contrary to 5 U.S.C. § 6101(a)(2)(A). Accordingly, we deny the Agency's exception.

V. Decision

The Agency's exceptions are denied in part and dismissed in part.

---

4. The Agency also excepts to the award on the basis that the Arbitrator's interpretation of the CBA renders the CBA "illegal" and "void in its entirety" because it allows first-line supervisors "unfettered authority" to grant paid absences. Exceptions at 7-8. We construe this as a contention that the award is contrary to law. However, this exception relies on the premise that the grievants' workweek has been unlawfully reduced to less than forty hours a week. As explained above, we reject this premise. Therefore, because the award does not unlawfully reduce the grievants' workweek, the Arbitrator's interpretation of the CBA is not "illegal" and the award cannot be found to be contrary to law on this basis. Accordingly, we deny this exception. In addition, the Agency asserts for the first time in its exceptions that the award is contrary to management rights because "as interpreted, the provision determines which manager performs a given task[.]" Exceptions at 8. There is no indication in the record that the Agency presented this argument to the Arbitrator. Because the issue was not presented to the Arbitrator, it is not properly before the Authority under § 2429.5 of the Authority's Regulations. *See, e.g. U.S. Dep't of the Army, The Adjutant General, Mo. Nat'l Guard, Bridgeton, Mo.*, 56 FLRA 1104, 1106 (2001). For these reasons, we dismiss this exception. We note, in this regard, that § 2429.5 was amended effective October 1, 2010. *See* 75 Fed. Reg. 42,283 (2010). For purposes of this case, we apply the prior Regulation that was in effect at all times relevant to the processing of this case.

65 FLRA No. 80

AMERICAN FEDERATION
OF GOVERNMENT EMPLOYEES
LOCAL 3380
(Union)

and

UNITED STATES
DEPARTMENT OF HOUSING
AND URBAN DEVELOPMENT
(Agency)

0-AR-4311

DECISION

December 22, 2010

Before the Authority: Carol Waller Pope, Chairman, and Thomas M. Beck and Ernest DuBester, Members

I. Statement of the Case

This matter is before the Authority on exceptions to an award of Arbitrator Irwin Kaplan filed by the Union under § 7122(a) of the Federal Service Labor-Management Relations Statute (the Statute) and part 2425 of the Authority's Regulations. The Agency filed an opposition to the exceptions.

As pertinent to the Union's exceptions, the Arbitrator denied the Union's grievance alleging that the Agency, by not selecting the grievant for a promotion, failed to follow merit staffing procedures in violation of the collective bargaining agreement (CBA) and applicable statutes and regulations. For the reasons that follow, the Authority denies the exceptions.

II. Background and Arbitrator's Award

The grievance arises from a vacancy announcement that the Agency posted for two permanent GS-13 Senior Project Manager positions to be filled at the Agency's Baltimore, Maryland; Washington, D.C.; and/or Richmond, Virginia locations. Award at 2. Applicants were instructed to submit one application for each location in which they were interested. *Id.* The grievant applied only for the Richmond location and was one of five applicants who made the best qualified list (BQL) for that location. *Id.* The grievant received the highest score possible under the crediting plan for the position. *Id.* at 4. The grievant then learned that two other applicants on the BQL were selected for the Richmond location. *Id.* at 2, 4. Both selectees received lower scores under the crediting plan than did the grievant. *Id.* at 4. A third applicant, who was on the BQL for the Baltimore location, was selected for that location under the same vacancy announcement. *Id.* at 2. Before the third applicant was selected, the Agency had not notified the grievant or the Union that a third permanent position would be filled. *Id.*

The selecting official, before making her selections, considered the applicants' recent experience in areas relevant to the position. She also consulted with the supervisors who would supervise the positions in Richmond and Baltimore to obtain their input on the applicants on the BQL. *Id.* at 5. The supervisor of the Richmond positions previously had worked with the grievant and gave negative feedback regarding that experience. *Id.* at 9.

The grievant filed a grievance alleging that the Agency failed to follow the merit staffing procedures set out in Article 13 of the CBA when it did not select the grievant for one of the Richmond positions and filled a third position without first notifying the grievant or the Union. *Id.* at 1. When the grievance was not resolved, it was submitted to arbitration, where the issues framed by the Arbitrator were:

1. Whether the Agency violated § 13.04 of the CBA, applicable law or regulation by failing to provide notice to the Union of management's intention to fill an additional vacancy that was not previously announced; and

2. Whether the application of the merit staffing principles/procedures for the position of Senior Project Manager . . . impacted the nonselection of the [g]rievant . . . for the position?

Id. at 3, 13, 15.

The Arbitrator determined that the Agency violated Section 13.04 of the CBA[1], finding its "plain

1. Section 13.04 of the CBA provides that: As a bargaining unit position "becomes available, [the Agency] agrees to notify promptly the Union of its intent to staff or cancel the vacant position." Exceptions, Ex. 2 at 52.

and unambiguous meaning" to be that when a bargaining unit position becomes available, the Agency must promptly notify the Union of its intent to staff or cancel the position. *Id.* at 14. Although the Arbitrator agreed with the Agency that the CBA permitted the Agency to reuse the selection roster for the vacancy announcement to fill the third position, the Arbitrator found that this did not excuse the Agency from the notification requirement. *Id.*

However, the Arbitrator also determined that the grievant's nonselection was not based on any misapplication by the Agency of the merit staffing procedures in Article 13 of the CBA. *Id.* at 16-18. Specifically, the Arbitrator found no violation of the CBA resulting from the selecting official's consideration of the recency of the applicants' relevant experience or her consultation with the supervisors of the Senior Project Manager positions. *Id.* at 16-17. In addition, the Arbitrator rejected the Union's contention that the selection for the Baltimore position impacted improperly on the grievant's nonselection, especially in light of the fact that the grievant had not applied for the Baltimore position. *Id.* at 17-18.

Finally, the Arbitrator rejected the Union's claim that the grievant was harmed because he would have filed an equal employment opportunity (EEO) complaint rather than the instant grievance had the Agency responded more promptly to the Union's request for the rating and ranking worksheet, the selection roster, and the crediting plan. *Id.* at 18. The Arbitrator based this determination on the Union's failure to take any actions to compel the Agency's production of these documents, the grievant's failure to let the Agency know that he was seeking them in contemplation of an EEO action, and the Union's failure to raise a discrimination claim in the arbitration. *Id.* 18-19.

As relief, the Arbitrator ordered the Agency to cease and desist from failing to comply with Section 13.04 of the CBA and to notify the Union in writing that it will comply with the notice requirement therein. *Id.* at 19.

III. Positions of the Parties

A. Union's Exceptions

The Union contends that the award fails to draw its essence from Article 13 of the CBA, which it interprets as prohibiting selecting officials from seeking feedback from other officials on an applicant's suitability for a position without the candidate's prior knowledge. Exceptions at 3-4. In support of its argument, the Union cites Section 13.10 of the CBA, which governs the evaluation phase of the selection process.[2] The Union notes that Section 13.10, which limits the information on which a candidate is to be rated and ranked to specific sources, does not include feedback from officials consulted without the candidate's knowledge. *Id.* at 3. The Union, while recognizing that the limitation on sources of information in Section 13.10 explicitly applies only to the evaluation phase, asserts that the selecting official is bound by it

2. Section 13.10 of the CBA provides, in pertinent part, that:

> Section 13.10 – Evaluation of Candidates.
>
> . . . . .
>
> (2) Criteria for Evaluation of Candidate Qualifications. The evaluation process shall be based on a comparison of the qualified candidates' qualifications against a set of job-related criteria that have been developed for the position to be filled.
>
> . . . . .
>
> (d) A candidate's rating shall be determined on the basis of relevant job-related information derived from a specified combination of the following sources:
> Appropriate application;
> Supplemental Qualifications Statements;
> Supervisory Appraisals;
> Structured interviews; and
> Written aptitude/ability tests (if required by the Office of Personnel Management).
>
> (3) Rating and Ranking of Candidates and Certificates.
>
> . . . . .
>
> (d) Merit Staffing Panel
>
> . . . . .
>
> 2. Members of the panel must evaluate candidates in accordance with the applicable crediting plan. They must take into consideration all job-related information derived from the application forms, supplemental qualifications statements, supervisory appraisals; and, if used, structured interviews and/or written tests.

Exceptions, Ex. 2 at 59-61.

because "the actual selection of an applicant is the end of the continuum of the evaluation process." *Id.*

The Union contends that the award also fails to draw its essence from the CBA to the extent that the Arbitrator found that it was appropriate for the selecting official to consider the recency of relevant experience of the applicants on the BQL for the Richmond location when recent experience was not listed as a selective placement factor in the vacancy announcement. *Id.* at 4-5.

Next, the Union contends that the Arbitrator exceeded his authority when he determined that it was not improper for the selecting official to have selected other candidates over the grievant for the Richmond positions based on the recency of relevant experience or to have consulted with the supervisors for the Senior Project Manager positions. *Id.* at 5-6. Further, the Union contends that the Arbitrator based his award on the "non-fact" that "the identity of the incumbent supervisor" for the position was a selective placement factor. *Id.* at 6. In this regard, the Union asserts that if the Arbitrator's finding that it was not improper for the Agency to unilaterally add or modify placement factors is allowed to stand, it would infringe upon the Union's rights under § 7106(b)(1) of the Statute to negotiate over the technology, methods, and means of performing work. *Id.*

Finally, the Union contends that the Agency's "illegal" delay in providing to the Union the rating and ranking worksheet, the selection roster, and the crediting plan harmed the grievant because it kept him from filing a timely discrimination complaint. *Id.* at 8. The Union claims it was only after the grievant received the documents that he realized that he had a basis for a discrimination complaint. *Id.*

B. Agency's Opposition

The Agency argues that the selecting official's consultations with the supervisors who actually would be supervising the successful applicants did not violate Section 13.10 of the CBA because that section governs only the rating and ranking stage of the selection process, and not the actions of the selecting official. Opp'n at 4. Nor, the Agency argues, did the consultations violate Section 13.11, the CBA provision governing the procedures to be followed by the selecting official. *Id.* at 5.[3] The Agency notes that all Section 13.11 contains is a provision that the selecting official may select, or not select, any candidate on the competitive placement certificate and a requirement that if one candidate on the certificate is interviewed, then all must be interviewed. *Id.* Therefore, the Agency contends, the Arbitrator's interpretation of the CBA as permitting the consultations was fair and rational. *Id.*

As for the Union's contention that the Arbitrator should have found it inappropriate for the selecting official to consider and compare the candidates' recency of relevant experience, the Agency argues that the selecting official acted appropriately even though recency of experience was not a selective placement factor per se. *Id.* at 9. If the Arbitrator were to find otherwise, the Agency argues, the selecting official would be precluded from drawing distinctions between candidates on the BQL if the distinctions were based on attributes, such as possession of an advanced degree, that were not listed as selective placement factors in the vacancy announcement. *Id.*[4]

The Agency contends that the Arbitrator did not exceed his authority when he determined that it was

---

3. Section 13.11 of the CBA provides, in pertinent part that:

> Section 13.11 Selection Consideration.
>
> . . . . .
>
> (1) Action by Selecting Official. The selecting official is entitled to select, or not select, any of the candidates on the Competitive Placement Certificate.
>
> (2) Interviewing Candidates.
>
> (a) The selecting official or a designee shall interview all or none of the BEST QUALIFIED candidates referred.
>
> (b) Telephone interviews are acceptable for candidates located outside of the local commuting area.

Exceptions, Ex.2 at 61-62.

4. The Agency also contends that the Union is raising, for the first time before the Authority, the issue of whether recency of relevant experience should have been a selective placement factor. Exceptions at 6-7. But, the Union is not raising that issue before the Authority. The Union's contention is not that recency of relevant experience should have been listed as a selective placement factor but that because it was not, a non-selection based on that factor resulted in a unilateral modification of the selective placement factors. *See id.* at 4-7. This contention, which the Union raised before the Arbitrator, Award at 16, is addressed below in Section IV.A.

appropriate for the selecting official to consult with the supervisors because this determination was in direct response to issues before him, specifically, whether the selection procedures used were permissible and whether they affected the grievant's nonselection. *Id.* at 12. As for the Union's argument that the Arbitrator's purported approval of the Agency's unilateral addition or modification of selective placement factors interfered with the Union's rights under § 7106(b)(1) of the Statute, the Agency notes that the Arbitrator made no factual finding that the Agency took such actions. Therefore, the Agency contends, this exception amounts to nothing more than a factual disagreement. Finally, the Agency contends that the Union fails to articulate how the Arbitrator's determination that the grievant was not harmed by the timing of the Agency's document production is contrary to any law, rule, or regulation. *Id.* at 15.

IV. Analysis and Conclusions

A. The award does not fail to draw its essence from the CBA.

In reviewing an arbitrator's interpretation of a collective bargaining agreement, the Authority applies the deferential standard of review that federal courts use in reviewing arbitration awards in the private sector. *See* 5 U.S.C. § 7122(a)(2); *AFGE, Council 220*, 54 FLRA 156, 159 (1998). Under this standard, the Authority will find that an arbitration award is deficient as failing to draw its essence from the collective bargaining agreement when the appealing party establishes that the award: (1) cannot in any rational way be derived from the agreement; (2) is so unfounded in reason and fact and so unconnected with the wording and purposes of the collective bargaining agreement as to manifest an infidelity to the obligation of the arbitrator; (3) does not represent a plausible interpretation of the agreement; or (4) evidences a manifest disregard of the agreement. *See U.S. Dep't of Labor (OSHA)*, 34 FLRA 573, 575 (1990). The Authority and the courts defer to arbitrators in this context "because it is the arbitrator's construction of the agreement for which the parties have bargained." *Id.* at 576.

The Arbitrator determined that the selecting official did not act contrary to Article 13 of the CBA when she considered the relative recency of the experience of the candidates for the Richmond positions and consulted with the supervisors. Award at 17. This determination is consistent with Section 13.11 of the CBA, which does not expressly prohibit a selecting official from considering candidates' relative experiences or consulting with their prospective supervisors. The Union has not explained how this determination is irrational, unfounded, implausible, or in manifest disregard of the CBA. Accordingly, the Authority denies this exception.

B. The Arbitrator did not exceed his authority.

Arbitrators exceed their authority when they resolve an issue not submitted to arbitration. *U.S. Dep't of the Interior, Nat'l Park Serv., Golden Gate Nat'l Recreation Area, S.F., Cal.*, 55 FLRA 193, 194 (1999). However, arbitrators do not exceed their authority by addressing an issue that is necessary to decide a stipulated issue, *NATCA, MEBA/NMU*, 51 FLRA 993, 996 (1996), or by addressing an issue that necessarily arises from issues specifically included in a stipulation. *See Air Force Space Div., L.A. Air Force Station, Cal.*, 24 FLRA 516, 519 (1986). In determining whether an arbitrator has exceeded his or her authority, the Authority accords an arbitrator's interpretation of a stipulated issue, or the arbitrator's formulation of an issue to be decided in the absence of a stipulation, the same substantial deference that it accords an arbitrator's interpretation and application of a collective bargaining agreement. *See U.S. Info. Agency, Voice of Am.*, 55 FLRA 197, 198 (1999).

The Union contends that the Arbitrator exceeded his authority when he determined that it was not improper for the selecting official to favor other candidates over the grievant or for her to consult the supervisors. Exceptions at 5. However, this determination was necessary to resolve what the Arbitrator identified as the principal stipulated issue, that is, whether the Agency's application of the merit staffing procedures impacted the grievant's nonselection. *See* Award at 3. Accordingly, the Authority denies this exception.

C. The award is not based on a nonfact.

To establish that an award is based on a nonfact, the appealing party must show that a central fact underlying the award is clearly erroneous, but for which the arbitrator would have reached a different result. *See NFFE, Local 1984*, 56 FLRA 38, 41 (2000). However, the Authority will not find an award deficient on the basis of an arbitrator's determination of any factual matter that the parties disputed at arbitration. *See id.*

The Union contends that the Arbitrator based his award on the "non-fact" that "the identity of the incumbent supervisor" for the position was a selective placement factor. Exceptions at 6. Stated otherwise, the Union contends that the Arbitrator erred when he determined that it was not improper for the selecting official to consider feedback from the incumbent supervisor even though she favored the selectees over the grievant. To the extent that the Arbitrator made a factual finding, the issue of whether the supervisor's feedback should have been requested and considered was disputed at the arbitration and, therefore, it cannot form a basis for finding the award deficient.

Similarly, whether the timing of the Agency's response to the Union's information request harmed the grievant was a factual matter disputed at the arbitration. Thus, this matter also cannot form a basis for finding the award deficient. Accordingly, the Authority denies this exception.

D. The award is not contrary to law.

When an exception involves an award's consistency with law, the Authority reviews any question of law raised by the exception and the award de novo. *See NTEU, Chapter 24*, 50 FLRA 330, 332 (1995) (citing *U.S. Customs Serv. v. FLRA*, 43 F.3d 682, 686-87 (D.C. Cir. 1994)). In applying the standard of de novo review, the Authority assesses whether an arbitrator's legal conclusions are consistent with the applicable standard of law. *See U.S. Dep't of Def., Dep'ts of the Army & the Air Force, Ala. Nat'l Guard, Northport, Ala.*, 55 FLRA 37, 40 (1998). In making that assessment, the Authority defers to the arbitrator's underlying factual findings. *See id.*

The Union contends that the Agency "illegally" denied the grievant a right to file an employment discrimination complaint because it took too long to respond to the Union's document request. Exceptions at 8. The Union also contends that the Arbitrator erred in finding that the grievant was not harmed by the timing of the Agency's document production. *Id.* However, the Union identifies no law with which the Arbitrator's finding is inconsistent. Accordingly, the Authority denies this exception.

V. Decision

The Union's exceptions are denied.

65 FLRA No. 81

UNITED STATES
DEPARTMENT OF THE AIR FORCE
AIR FORCE MATERIEL COMMAND
(Agency)

and

INTERNATIONAL ASSOCIATION
OF FIRE FIGHTERS
LOCALS F-78, F-88 & F-211
(Union)

0-AR-4433

DECISION

December 22, 2010

Before the Authority: Carol Waller Pope, Chairman, and Thomas M. Beck and Ernest DuBester, Members

I. Statement of the Case

This matter is before the Authority on exceptions to an award of Arbitrator Ann C. Wendt filed by the Agency under § 7122(a) of the Federal Service Labor-Management Relations Statute (the Statute) and part 2425 of the Authority's Regulations. The Union filed an opposition to the Agency's exceptions.

The Arbitrator found that, by not staffing each aircraft rescue fire fighting (ARFF) vehicle with at least three persons, the Agency violated an applicable Agency instruction, the parties' command labor agreement (CLA) and two local supplemental agreements (LSAs). For the following reasons, we dismiss the Agency's exceptions in part and deny them in part.

II. Background and Arbitrator's Award

The Agency dispatches pairs of ARFF vehicles to combat aircraft fires. Award at 10. As relevant here, the Agency previously staffed each ARFF vehicle with three persons. *Id.* The Agency then began dispatching pairs consisting of vehicles staffed with three persons and one person, respectively, at three of its bases (AFBs). *Id.* at 10, 14. The Union filed a grievance alleging that this action violated: Articles II, XXV, and XXX of the CLA; Department of Defense Instruction (DoDI) 6055.06; and the National Fire Protection Association (NFPA) 403 standard.[1] *Id.* at 9-14. The grievance was unresolved and submitted to arbitration, where the Arbitrator framed the issue as: "Did the [Agency] violate the [CLA], DoDI 6055.06, and/or (if applicable) NFPA 403, by reducing staffing on its [ARFF] vehicles, and if so[,] what is the remedy?" *Id.* at 1.

First, the Arbitrator found that the Agency violated Article II, Section 1 of the CLA by reducing the number of personnel per ARFF vehicle below the minimum standard set forth in DoDI 6055.06 without following proper deviation procedures. *Id.* at 16. In this regard, she determined that the Agency's rights under Article IV, Section 1 of the CLA "do[] not negate [its] obligation to comply with established procedures."[2] *Id.* at 17. Second, the Arbitrator determined that the Agency's actions violated Article XXV, Section 1 of the CLA because "redu[cing] manning of ARFF vehicles creates a safety hazard for the bargaining unit members." *Id.* at 17. In this connection, she found that "the 'two-in, two-out' rule [set forth in 29 C.F.R. § 1910.134] explicitly pertains to the firefighters[,]" and therefore, "[a] minimum of two ARFF vehicles manned with a driver/pumper and two fire fighters is essential to begin [an] initial fire fighting attack."[3] *Id.* She further found that, "contrary to the Agency's assertion that the safety of firefighters, flight crew [and] passengers [of] the aircraft [at the AFBs] is [its] first concern[,]" the

1. The relevant provisions of the CLA and DoDI 6055.06 are set forth in the appendix to this decision. As the Arbitrator did not rely on NFPA 403 in her award, we do not address it further.

2. Article VI, Section 1 of the CLA mirrors § 7106 of the Statute. Award at 5-6.

3. The parties do not dispute that Article XXV of the CLA requires the Agency to comply with DoDI 6055.06. DoDI 6055.06 Section 6.8 incorporates the "two-in/two-out" provisions of 29 C.F.R. § 1910.134, which states, in pertinent part:

> (4) Procedures for interior structural firefighting. . . . [T]he employer shall ensure that:
>
> > (i) At least two employees enter the [immediately dangerous to life or health (IDLH)] atmosphere and remain in visual or voice contact with one another at all times;
> > (ii) At least two employees are located outside the IDLH atmosphere[.]

Union Ex. 6 at 8; 29 C.F.R. § 1910.134.

staffing reduction posed a safety risk to each of these parties. *Id.* Third, the Arbitrator determined that the Agency violated Article XXX, Section 3 of the CLA by "ma[king] an arbitrary decision in the interest of budget reductions." *Id.* Finally, she found that LSAs negotiated at two of the three affected AFBs "stem[] from the CLA[,]" and that the Agency's reduction of staffing levels below the minimum requirements of DoDI 6055.06 violated provisions in each of those agreements.[4] *Id.* at 17-18.

As a remedy, the Arbitrator directed the Agency to either "[i]mmediately restore [the] minimum manning of ARFF vehicles to three (driver/pump operator and two fire fighters) per ARFF vehicle" or "[u]ndertake a risk analysis concerning the reduced manning, propose a time table [for] when the manning will be restored to meet the criteria of the DoDI 6055.06, request an appropriate waiver and notify the [U]nion of the waiver's status." *Id.* at 19. She also retained jurisdiction "until both parties notify the Arbitrator that one of the two remedy options is implemented." *Id.*

III. Positions of the Parties

A. Agency's Exceptions

The Agency asserts that the Arbitrator exceeded her authority "to the extent that her award focused in part on the safety [of] aircrews and passengers of Air Force aircraft." Exceptions at 5.

The Agency also asserts that the award is based on several nonfacts. *Id.* at 6-11. In this connection, the Agency maintains that the Arbitrator erred in finding that: (1) the Agency "made an arbitrary decision in the interest of budget reductions" by reducing the number of personnel per ARFF vehicle; (2) the LSAs were valid supplements to the CLA; (3) reducing the number of staff assigned to particular vehicles is inconsistent with the "two-in, two-out" rule incorporated into DoDI 6055.06; and (4) DoDI 6055.06 requires that a minimum of three persons be assigned to each ARFF vehicle. *Id.* Additionally, the Agency asserts that the Arbitrator erred by "ignor[ing] uncontroverted testimony that the Agency utilizes companies and cross staffing as well as mutual aid agreements to meet the requirements of DoDI 6055.06." *Id.* at 8.

Next, the Agency contends that the award fails to draw its essence from the parties' agreement. *Id.* at 5-6. In this connection, the Agency argues that the award is based on the Arbitrator's finding that the Agency violated LSAs that, according to the Agency, are not incorporated into the CLA. *Id.* at 6.

Finally, the Agency maintains that the award excessively interferes with management's rights under § 7106(a) of the Statute. *Id.* at 11-13. Specifically, the Agency asserts that the award interferes with management's rights to determine its organization, assign work, and determine its internal security practices by requiring the Agency to immediately restore minimum manning of ARFF vehicles to three persons per ARFF vehicle and, therefore, eliminating the Agency's discretion to determine how many firefighters to deploy and their optimal use at the scene of fire. *Id.* The Agency also asserts that the award interferes with management's right to determine the number of employees. *Id.* at 11.

B. Union's Opposition

The Union contends that the Arbitrator did not exceed her authority because she awarded relief only to persons encompassed within the grievance. Opp'n at 11. In this connection, the Union contends that the Arbitrator's comment regarding the impact of staffing changes on non-unit employees was a "fleeting discussion" that "was not in any way [the] basis for the award[.]" *Id.* at 12.

With respect to the Agency's nonfact exceptions, the Union argues that all of the findings challenged by the Agency were disputed at the hearing, and, moreover, are not clearly erroneous central facts, but for which the Arbitrator would have reached a different result. *Id.* at 15-22.

The Union also argues that the Agency has not demonstrated that the award fails to draw its essence from the parties' agreement. *Id.* at 13-14. In this regard, the Union asserts that, even if the LSAs are not valid supplements to the CLA, the award is not deficient because it is also based on the Arbitrator's finding that the Agency violated the CLA. *Id.* at 13.

Finally, as to management's rights, the Union disputes the Agency's claim that the award affects the rights cited by the Agency. *Id.* at 23-27. However, the Union maintains that, to the extent that the award does affect those rights, the award is not deficient because: (1) DoDI 6055.06 has the force and effect of law and, thus, constitutes an applicable law within the meaning of § 7106(a)(2) of the Statute; (2) the award provides a remedy for a

4. The relevant provisions of the LSAs are set forth in the appendix to this decision.

violation of Article II of the master agreement, a contractual provision negotiated pursuant to § 7106(b)(1); and (3) the award enforces a procedure and/or appropriate arrangement under §§ 7106(b)(2) and 7106(b)(3), respectively. *Id.* at 27-33.

IV. Preliminary Issue

Under § 2429.5 of the Authority's Regulations, the Authority will not consider issues that could have been, but were not, presented in the proceedings before the arbitrator.[5] *See, e.g., U.S. Dep't of the Air Force, Air Force Materiel Command, Robins Air Force Base, Ga.*, 59 FLRA 542, 544 (2003). In its exceptions, the Agency argues that the award, by requiring the Agency to "restore minimum manning of ARFF vehicles to three persons per ARFF vehicle[,]" violates management's rights to determine the organization and internal security practices of the Agency. Exceptions at 11-13. However, there is no indication in the record that the Agency raised arguments with respect to these rights before the Arbitrator.[6] The record establishes that the Agency could have done so, as the Union specifically requested as a remedy that the Arbitrator "hold that the [DoDI 6055.06] imposes minimum per-vehicle staffing of three personnel, and order the [Agency] to comply with DoDI 6055.06." Union's Post-Hearing Brief at 19. Moreover, the Agency did specifically raise arguments with respect to management's rights to assign work and determine the number of employees before the Arbitrator. *See* Award at 9. As the arguments concerning management's rights to determine organization and internal security practices could have been, but were not, raised below, we find that § 2429.5 bars the Agency from raising them in its exceptions. Accordingly, we dismiss these exceptions.

V. Analysis and Conclusions

A. The Arbitrator did not exceed her authority.

Arbitrators exceed their authority when they fail to resolve an issue submitted to arbitration, resolve an issue not submitted to arbitration, disregard specific limitations on their authority, or award relief to persons who are not encompassed within the grievance. *See U.S. Dep't of the Navy, Naval Base, Norfolk, Va.*, 51 FLRA 305, 307-08 (1995).

The Agency alleges that the Arbitrator exceeded her authority "to the extent that her award focused in part on the safety [of] aircrews and passengers of Air Force aircraft." Exceptions at 5. We construe this argument as a claim that the Arbitrator exceeded her authority by awarding relief to non-grievants. Although the Arbitrator found that the reduction in ARFF staffing "poses a serious safety issue in the context of the fire fighters, the crew and passengers of the aircraft and to the Agency[,]" Award at 17, there is no indication in the award that the Arbitrator extended relief to aircrews, passengers or any other persons not encompassed within the grievance. *Id.* at 19. Accordingly, the Agency has not demonstrated that the Arbitrator exceeded her authority, and we deny the exception.

B. The award is not based on nonfacts.

To establish that an award is based on a nonfact, the appealing party must show that a central fact underlying the award is clearly erroneous, but for which the arbitrator would have reached a different result. *See NFFE, Local 1984*, 56 FLRA 38, 41 (2000). However, the Authority will not find an

5. The Authority's Regulations concerning the review of arbitration awards, as well as certain related procedural Regulations, including 5 C.F.R. § 2429.5, were revised effective October 1, 2010. *See* 75 Fed. Reg. 42,283 (2010). As the Agency's exceptions in this case were filed before that date, we apply the prior Regulations.

6. Member Beck disagrees with his colleagues that these matters were not raised before the Arbitrator. As to the right to determine its organization, the Agency discusses "staffing" and "cross-staffing" throughout its post-hearing brief. Agency Post-Hearing Brief at 19, 31, 35, 39, 40, 43. The Arbitrator notes that the Agency argued that it has "the right to determine the personnel by which activity operations shall be conducted." Award at 9. The Authority has held that an agency's right to determine its organization encompasses staffing determinations and the distribution of responsibilities. *AFGE, Local 2004*, 56 FLRA 660, 661 (2000). As to the right to determine internal security practices, the Agency argued to the Arbitrator that any restriction on its ability to reduce staffing interfered with the management rights that are outlined in Article IV of the CLA. Award at 9, 17. Article IV, Section 1.a. of the CLA essentially repeats the same rights that are set forth in § 7106, including the right to determine internal security practices. *See* J.Ex. 1 at 7. In *United States Department of the Army, United States Army Signal Center, and Fort Gordon, Fort Gordon, Georgia*, we determined that "restricting [an] Agency's authority to staff a fire truck with fewer firefighters" affects an agency's "right to determine internal security practices under § 7106(a)(1)." 58 FLRA 511, 513 (2003). Accordingly, Member Beck would address (and deny) the Agency's right to determine organization and internal security exceptions for the same reasons that the right to assign work exception is denied.

award deficient on the basis of an arbitrator's determination of any factual matter that the parties disputed at arbitration. *See id.* Moreover, where the party in opposition contends that a matter alleged to be a nonfact was disputed before the arbitrator, and the excepting party does not argue to the contrary, the Authority has found no basis for finding the award deficient as based on a nonfact. *See U.S. Dep't of Energy, Nat'l Energy Tech. Lab.*, 64 FLRA 1174, 1175 (2010) (*Nat'l Energy*).

The Union contends that all of the matters raised in the Agency's nonfact exceptions were disputed at arbitration. *See* Opp'n at 15-22. The Agency does not argue to the contrary. Accordingly, consistent with *Nat'l Energy*, 64 FLRA at 1175, we deny the nonfact exceptions.

C. The award draws its essence from the parties' agreement.

In reviewing an arbitrator's interpretation of a collective bargaining agreement, the Authority applies the deferential standard that federal courts use in reviewing arbitration awards in the private sector. *See* 5 U.S.C. § 7122(a)(2); *AFGE, Council 220*, 54 FLRA 156, 159 (1998). Under this standard, the Authority will find that an arbitration award is deficient as failing to draw its essence from the collective bargaining agreement when the appealing party establishes that the award: (1) cannot in any rational way be derived from the agreement; (2) is so unfounded in reason and fact and so unconnected with the wording and purposes of the collective bargaining agreement as to manifest an infidelity to the obligation of the arbitrator; (3) does not represent a plausible interpretation of the agreement; or (4) evidences a manifest disregard of the agreement. *U.S. Dep't of Labor (OSHA)*, 34 FLRA 573, 575 (1990). The Authority and the courts defer to arbitrators in this context "because it is the arbitrator's construction of the agreement for which the parties have bargained." *Id.* at 576. Moreover, the Authority has held that where an arbitrator bases an award on separate and independent grounds, an excepting party must establish that all of the grounds are deficient in order to demonstrate that the award is deficient. *See, e.g., U.S. Dep't of the Treasury, IRS, Oxon Hill, Md.*, 56 FLRA 292, 299 (2000) (*Oxon Hill*).

The Agency contends that the award fails to draw its essence from the parties' agreement because it is based on a finding that the Agency violated LSAs that, according to the Agency, are not incorporated into the CLA. Exceptions at 6. However, in addition to her findings regarding the LSAs, the Arbitrator also found that the Agency violated the CLA. *See* Award at 18; *Oxon Hill*, 56 FLRA at 299. The Agency has not challenged the Arbitrator's interpretation of the CLA, which provides a sufficient basis for the award. Therefore, the finding of a CLA violation provides a separate and independent basis for the award, and, even assuming that the Arbitrator erroneously relied on the LSAs, the Agency's essence exception provides no basis for finding the award deficient. Accordingly, we deny the exception.

D. The award is not contrary to § 7106(a)(2)(B) of the Statute.

When an exception involves an award's consistency with law, the Authority reviews any question of law raised by the exception and the award de novo. *See NTEU, Chapter 24*, 50 FLRA 330, 332 (1995) (citing *U.S. Customs Serv. v. FLRA*, 43 F.3d 682, 686-87 (D.C. Cir. 1994)). In applying the standard of de novo review, the Authority assesses whether an arbitrator's legal conclusions are consistent with the applicable standard of law. *See U.S. Dep'ts of Def., Dep't of the Army & the Air Force, Ala. Nat'l Guard, Northport, Ala.*, 55 FLRA 37, 40 (1998). In making that assessment, the Authority defers to the arbitrator's underlying factual findings. *See id.*

The Authority recently revised the analysis that it will apply when reviewing management-rights exceptions to arbitration awards. *See U.S. EPA*, 65 FLRA 113, 115 (2010) (Member Beck concurring) (*EPA*); *FDIC, Div. of Supervision & Consumer Prot., S.F. Region*, 65 FLRA 102 (2010) (Chairman Pope concurring). Under the revised analysis, the Authority will first assess whether the award affects the exercise of the asserted management right.[7] *EPA*, 65 FLRA at 115. If so,

7. Member Beck agrees with the conclusion to deny the Agency's contrary to management's right to assign work exception. He does not agree, however, with his colleagues' analysis of the contrary to law exception insofar as they address the question of whether the award affects the exercise of an asserted management right. For the reasons discussed in his Concurring Opinion in *EPA*, 65 FLRA 113, Member Beck would conclude that, where, as here, the Arbitrator is enforcing a contract provision that has been accepted by the Agency as a permissible limitation on its management's rights, it is inappropriate to assess whether the provision itself is an appropriate arrangement or whether it abrogates a § 7106(a) right. *Id.* at 120; *see also U.S. Dep't of Health and Human Services, Off. of Medicare Hearings and Appeals*, 65 FLRA 175, 177

then, as relevant here, the Authority examines whether the award enforces a contract provision negotiated under § 7106(b). *Id.* When an award affects a management right under § 7106(a)(2) of the Statute, the Authority may also examine whether the award enforces an applicable law. *Id.* at 115 n.7.

1. The award affects management's right to assign work under § 7106(a)(2)(B) of the Statute.[8]

The right to assign work under § 7106(a)(2)(B) of the Statute includes the right to determine the particular duties to be assigned, when work assignments will occur, and to whom or what positions the duties will be assigned. *See U.S. Dep't of the Treasury, U.S. Customs Serv., El Paso, Tex.*, 55 FLRA 553, 558 (1999) (citation omitted). In addition, the Authority has found that requiring an agency to assign work to more employees than the number it would otherwise choose affects the right to assign work. *U.S. Dep't of Justice, Bureau of Prisons, Metro. Det. Ctr. Guayabo, P.R.*, 57 FLRA 331, 333 (2001) (Chairman Cabaniss dissenting) (*DOJ*) (citing *AFGE, Local 3807*, 54 FLRA 642, 646 (1998)).

Here, the award requires the Agency to assign firefighting duties to a minimum of three persons per ARFF vehicle, and therefore, at least six persons per pair of vehicles, despite the Agency's desire to staff them with a total of four persons per pair. Award at 10, 19. As the award requires the Agency to assign work to more employees than the number it would otherwise choose, we find that the award affects management's right to assign work. *See DOJ*, 57 FLRA at 333.

2. The award enforces an appropriate arrangement under § 7106(b)(3) of the Statute.

In determining whether the award enforces a contract provision negotiated under § 7106(b)(3), the Authority assesses: (1) whether the contract provision constitutes an arrangement for employees adversely affected by the exercise of a management right; and (2) if so, whether the arbitrator's enforcement of the arrangement abrogates the exercise of the management right. *EPA*, 65 FLRA at 118. In concluding that it would apply an abrogation standard, the Authority rejected continued application of an excessive interference standard. *Id.* at 113.

The Arbitrator found that reducing the number of staff per ARFF vehicle "poses a serious safety issue" and "multiplies the safety and health risks for all who are on the scene" by "immboliz[ing] some of the ARFF vehicles" at the scene of a fire. Award at 17. In so doing, she essentially found that the Agency's exercise of its right to assign work adversely affected the grievants. Here, the agreement provisions, as interpreted and applied by the Arbitrator, require the Agency to comply with all applicable regulations and instructions, including DoDI 6055.05. *Id.* at 16, 18-19. The Arbitrator found that "[t]o mitigate [safety] risks[,] it is essential that ARFF vehicles be manned in accordance with . . . DoDI 6055.06." *Id.* at 17. Thus, we find that the agreement provisions, as interpreted and applied the Arbitrator, ameliorate the adverse affects flowing from the exercise of management's right to assign work and, therefore, are arrangements.

With regard to whether the arrangements are appropriate, the Agency argues that the award excessively interferes with management's right to assign work.[9] Exceptions at 11-13. However, as stated above, the Authority no longer applies an excessive interference standard to determine whether an arrangement is appropriate. *See EPA*, 65 FLRA at 118. Rather, the Authority applies an abrogation standard, which assesses whether the arbitration award "precludes [the] agency from exercising" the affected management right. *Dep't of the Treasury, U.S. Customs Serv.*, 37 FLRA 309, 314 (1990). The Agency does not assert that the award precludes the Agency from exercising its right to assign work.

---

n.3 (2010), *and U.S. Dep't of Transp., Federal Aviation Adm.*, 65 FLRA 171, 173 n.5 (2010). The appropriate question is simply whether the remedy directed by the Arbitrator enforces the provision in a reasonable and reasonably foreseeable fashion. *EPA*, 65 FLRA at 120 (Concurring Opinion of Member Beck); *see also FDIC*, 65 FLRA at 107. Member Beck would conclude that the Arbitrator's award is a plausible interpretation of the parties' agreement and deny the exception.

8. We note that the Agency also contends that the award affects management's right to determine the number of employees under § 7106(a)(1). Exceptions at 11. However, as the Agency makes no argument in support of its claim, we deny this exception as a bare assertion. *See U.S. Dep't of Homeland Sec., U.S. Customs & Border Prot., Port of Seattle, Seattle, Wash.*, 60 FLRA 490, 492 n.7 (2004).

9. Although the Agency cites the abrogation standard set forth in *Department of the Treasury, United States Customs Service.*, 37 FLRA 309 (1990), it argues only that the award excessively interferes with management's rights. Exceptions at 11-12.

Moreover, the award specifically allows the Agency the option of continuing to staff ARFF vehicles with fewer than three persons, provided that it obtains a waiver via the procedures set forth in DoDI 6055.06. Therefore, we find that the arrangement is appropriate within the meaning of § 7106(b)(3) of the Statute.

For the foregoing reasons, we find that the award enforces an appropriate arrangement under § 7106(b)(3) of the Statute, we and deny the Agency's management rights exception.[10]

VI. Decision

The Agency's exceptions are dismissed in part and denied in part.

10. In light of this finding, it is not necessary to address the Union's arguments regarding § 7106(b)(1) and (b)(2) of the Statute, or its claim that DoDI 6055.06 is an applicable law within the meaning of § 7106(a)(2).

APPENDIX

Article II, Section 1 of the CLA states, in pertinent part:

> Within the context of [the Statute], it is agreed and understood that in the administration of all matters covered by the [CLA] and any [LSAs] thereto, the [Agency], the Union and unit employees are governed by applicable[,] existing and future laws and government-wide and Department of Defense (DOD) policies and regulations.

Award at 5.

Article XXV, Section 1 of the CLA provides, in relevant part:

> The Employer will assure that safe and healthful working and living conditions are provided for bargaining unit employees that are consistent with the provisions of applicable laws and regulations. The Parties agree that the AFMC Fire and Emergency Services Program shall comply with applicable DoD instructions, Air Force Instructions, NFPA Standards, OSHA Regulations and other applicable laws and regulations.

Id. at 6.

Article XXX, Section 3 of the CLA, provides, in pertinent part:

> The Employer agrees that the workplace will be free from arbitrary and capricious actions and decisions by supervisors. Decisions and/or actions taken by the Employer will be in accordance with applicable laws, rules[,] regulations and negotiated agreements.

Id.

Article X, Section 4 of the LSA between Wright-Patterson AFB and the International Association of Fire Fighters (AFL-CIO) Local F-88 states, in relevant part:

> The Employer agrees to staff and operate all required fire apparatus pursuant to the provisions of higher authority, law, rule, and regulations. The Employer agrees to negotiate with the Union of their desire to

> reduce the manning/staffing levels below the minimum requirements.
>
> *Id.*

Article XI, Section 6 of the LSA between the Oklahoma City Air Logistics Center Fire Department, [Tinker AFB] and the International Association of Fire Fighters (AFL-CIO) Local F-211 provides, in relevant part:

> The Employer agrees to staff and operate all required fire apparatus pursuant to the provisions of higher "authority" law, rule and regulation. The Employer agrees that any deviation to the minimum staffing requirements established by [the DOD] and the Department of the Air Force will only be accomplished after a waiver has been granted by the Secretary of the Air Force and/or his/her designee. The Employer further agrees to notify the Union in writing of their desire to reduce the manning/staffing levels below the minimum requirements.

Id. at 7.

DoDI 6055.06, provides, in pertinent part:

> 6.8. Immediately Dangerous to Life or Health (IDLH). Implement procedures to plan and respond to emergencies to IDLH atmospheres using established standards, local conditions' risk considerations, and the requirements of Part 1910.134 of 29 CFR . . . including the two-in/two-out provisions for interior structure and aircraft fires.
>
> . . . .
>
> 6.16. Deviation from Minimum Requirements. Deviation from minimum requirements increases risk. Conscious, informed decisions must be made to accept the risk posed by the deviation at an appropriate leadership level.
>
> 6.16.3. Long-Term Deviations. Long-term deviations are not expected to be remedied. Essentially long-term deviations waive the requirements of this Instruction. Document long-term deviations from minimum requirements in a document that contains:
>
> 6.16.3.1. An assessment of the risk caused by the deviation.
>
> 6.16.3.2. A description of measures to address the increased risk caused by the deviation.
>
> 6.16.3.3. A communication strategy for informing those affected . . . that a deviation has occurred and the measures being taken to minimize the risk of the deviation.
>
> 6.16.3.4. Approval by the applicable DoD component head. The approval shall contain clear statements that the approver has accepted the increased risk caused by the deviation and that the approval is not valid for more than 3 years. If the approval authority changes, deviation shall be briefed to the new approval authority. Expiring approval may be reviewed provided all steps in the approval process are reaccomplished or revalidated.

DoDI 6055.06, TABLE E3.T1 provides, in pertinent part:

MIMIMUM LEVEL OF SERVICE OBJECTIVES-OPERATIONS

PROGRAM ELEMENT	STAFF
ARFF	
Unannounced First Arriving Company	3
Announced First Arriving Company	3

Union Ex. 6 at 8, 10-11, 23.

65 FLRA No. 82

AMERICAN FEDERATION
OF GOVERNMENT EMPLOYEES
LOCAL 1148
(Union)

and

UNITED STATES
DEPARTMENT OF DEFENSE
DEFENSE SUPPLY CENTER
COLUMBUS, OHIO
(Agency)

0-AR-4685

DECISION

December 23, 2010

Before the Authority: Carol Waller Pope, Chairman, and Thomas M. Beck and Ernest DuBester, Members

I. Statement of the Case

This matter is before the Authority on exceptions to an award of Arbitrator Harry Graham filed by the Union under § 7122(a) of the Federal Service Labor-Management Relations Statute (the Statute) and part 2425 of the Authority's Regulations. The Agency filed an opposition to the Union's exceptions.

The Arbitrator determined that the Agency's five-day suspension of the grievant was without just cause. As a remedy, the Arbitrator ordered that the grievant be made whole for all monies lost as a result of the unjust suspension. In a subsequent award, the Arbitrator found that he was without authority to award attorney fees to the Union. For the reasons set forth below, we set aside the award and remand it to the parties for resubmission to the Arbitrator, absent settlement.

II. Background and Arbitrator's Award

The Agency suspended the grievant for five days for insubordination. *See* Exceptions, Ex. 6 at 3. The Union filed a grievance challenging the suspension. The matter was unresolved and was submitted to arbitration. In his initial award, the Arbitrator considered the following issue: "Did the [Agency] have just cause to discipline the [g]rievant? If not, what shall the remedy be?" *Id.* at 1. The Arbitrator sustained the grievance, finding that the suspension of the grievant was not for just cause. *Id.* at 10. Accordingly, the Arbitrator ordered that the grievant's suspension be rescinded and that he be compensated for any monies lost as a result of the suspension. *Id.* The Arbitrator retained jurisdiction for sixty calendar days from the date of his award. *Id.*

Approximately one month later, the Union submitted a request for attorney fees. Exceptions, Ex. 1. The Arbitrator found that he lacked authority to consider this request. According to the Arbitrator, Article 37, Section E of the parties' agreement provides that "[t]he arbitrator's award shall be limited solely to answering the question(s) put to him/her by the parties' submission." Award at 1. The Arbitrator concluded that, because the above issue was the sole issue presented to him, he did not have authority to award the fees requested by the Union. *Id.*

III. Positions of the Parties

A. Union's Exceptions

The Union contends that the award is contrary to law because the Arbitrator was authorized, by statute, to award attorney fees once the requirements of the Back Pay Act had been met. Exceptions at 5. The Union asserts that, while the parties' agreement limits an arbitrator's award to answering questions submitted by the parties, the issue presented to the Arbitrator included a possible remedy of attorney fees. *Id.* at 5-6. The Union contends that, because nothing in the parties' agreement "prohibits or circumscribes" the authority of an arbitrator to award attorney fees, the Arbitrator was authorized to consider the Union's fee request. *Id.* at 6 (citing *U.S. Dep't of the Army, Red River Army Depot, Texarkana, Tex.*, 39 FLRA 1215 (1991) (*Texarkana*)).

The Union also contends that the attorney fee award is contrary to law because it fails to provide a fully articulated and reasoned opinion, as required by Authority precedent. *Id.* at 8-9. The Union argues that remand is not necessary, however, as the record provides sufficient information for the Authority to analyze properly the statutory requirements. *Id.* at 9-15. In the alternative, the Union contends that the Authority should remand the award to the Arbitrator for specific findings. *Id.* at 15.

B. Agency's Opposition

The Agency's opposition addresses only "whether the [Authority] should render a decision on fees and expenses or whether the issue should be remanded to the parties for submission to the [A]rbitrator." Opp'n at 1. The Agency argues that the award fails to contain sufficient findings and analysis regarding whether an award of attorney fees is warranted under the Back Pay Act. *Id.* Accordingly, the Agency contends that, because there is "nothing in the record that could provide the basis" for the Authority to award attorney fees, the matter should be remanded to the Arbitrator. *Id.* at 2-3.

IV. The award is not contrary to law.

When an exception involves an award's consistency with law, the Authority reviews any question of law raised by the exception and the award de novo. *See NTEU, Chapter 24*, 50 FLRA 330, 332 (1995) (citing *U.S. Customs Serv. v. FLRA*, 43 F.3d 682, 686-87 (D.C. Cir. 1994)). In applying the standard of de novo review, the Authority assesses whether an arbitrator's legal conclusions are consistent with the applicable standard of law. *See U.S. Dep't of Def., Dep'ts of the Army & the Air Force, Ala. Nat'l Guard, Northport, Ala.*, 55 FLRA 37, 40 (1998). In making that assessment, the Authority defers to the arbitrator's underlying factual findings. *See id.*

A. The Arbitrator is authorized to consider the Union's request for attorney fees.

The Union contends that the award is contrary to law because the Arbitrator was authorized, by statute, to award attorney fees once the requirements of the Back Pay Act had been met. Exceptions at 5. The Back Pay Act confers jurisdiction on an arbitrator to consider a request for attorney fees at any time during the arbitration or within a reasonable period of time after the arbitrator's award of backpay becomes final and binding. *See, e.g., AFGE, Council of Prison Locals*, 55 FLRA 192 (1999) (citations omitted). In addition, parties can negotiate into their collective bargaining agreement time limits and other procedures to govern the filing of requests for attorney fees. *See id.* Moreover, a union may agree to language that clearly and unmistakably waives its statutory right to attorney fees. *See Texarkana*, 39 FLRA at 1221.

Here, the Arbitrator's underlying award rescinded the grievant's suspension and ordered that the grievant be awarded backpay for the loss that he suffered as a result of the unjust suspension. Exceptions, Ex. 6 at 10. Such an award conferred jurisdiction on the Arbitrator to consider the merits of a request for attorney fees. *See AFGE, Council of Prison Locals*, 55 FLRA at 192 (Back Pay Act conferred jurisdiction on an arbitrator to consider an attorney fee request where the remedy involved payment under the Back Pay Act). Thus, unless precluded by the parties' agreement, the Arbitrator was authorized to address the merits of the Union's request. *See id.* at 193.

The Arbitrator found that, because Article 37, Section E of the parties' agreement limited him to answering solely the questions put before him by the parties and those questions did not specifically include the Union's request for attorney fees, he lacked authority to consider the Union's request. As discussed above, however, the issues before the Arbitrator included resolution of the Union's request for attorney fees. Moreover, no provision of the parties' agreement prohibits or circumscribes the authority of an arbitrator to award attorney fees, nor does any provision of the agreement clearly and unmistakably waive the Union's statutory right to such fees.

Accordingly, we find that the Arbitrator had jurisdiction to consider the Union's request for attorney fees and grant the exception.

B. The record is insufficient for the Authority to resolve the Union's request for attorney fees.

Under the Back Pay Act, 5 U.S.C. § 5596, an award of attorney fees must be in accordance with the standards established under 5 U.S.C. § 7701(g). The threshold requirement for an award of attorney fees under the Back Pay Act is a finding that the grievant was affected by an unjustified or unwarranted personnel action, which resulted in a withdrawal or reduction of the grievant's pay, allowances or differential. *See U.S., Dep't of Def., Def. Distrib. Region E., New Cumberland, Pa.*, 51 FLRA 155, 158 (1995). The Back Pay Act further requires that an award of fees must be: (1) in conjunction with an award of backpay to the grievant on correction of the personnel action; (2) reasonable and related to the personnel action; and (3) in accordance with standards established under 5 U.S.C. § 7701(g). *See id.* The prerequisites for an award under § 7701(g) are that: (1) the employee must be the prevailing party; (2) the award of attorney fees must be warranted in the interest of justice;[*] (3) the amount of fees must be reasonable; and (4) the fees must have been incurred by the employee. *See id.* Furthermore, if an award fails to contain the findings necessary to enable the Authority to assess the arbitrator's legal conclusions, and those findings cannot be derived from the record, the case will be remanded to the parties for resubmission to the arbitrator so that requisite findings can be made. *See NFFE, Local 1437,* 53 FLRA 1703, 1712 (1998) (award remanded to parties for resubmission to the Arbitrator where award "under review is completely devoid of any discussion or analysis of the issue").

Here, the Arbitrator failed to address the Union's request for attorney fees. Moreover, the record is insufficient for the Authority to determine whether the Union's request met the statutory requirements set forth above. *See* Award at 1; Exceptions, Ex. 6 at 8-10 (e.g., containing no analysis or discussion regarding whether the assessment of fees is in the interest of justice or whether the fees charged by the Union were reasonable).

Accordingly, we find that the record is insufficient for the Authority to resolve the Union's request for attorney fees and remand the issue to the parties for resubmission to the Arbitrator, absent settlement, to consider this request.

V. Decision

The award is set aside and remanded to the parties for resubmission to the Arbitrator, absent settlement.

---

*. An award of attorney fees is warranted in the interest of justice if: (1) the agency engaged in a prohibited personnel practice; (2) the agency actions are clearly without merit or wholly unfounded, or the employee is substantially innocent of charges brought by the agency; (3) the agency actions are taken in bad faith to harass or exert improper pressure on an employee; (4) the agency committed gross procedural error which prolonged the proceeding or severely prejudiced the employee; or (5) the agency knew or should have known it would not prevail on the merits when it brought the proceeding. *See Allen v. U.S. Postal Serv.,* 2 M.S.P.R. 420 (1980). The Authority also has stated that an award of attorney fees is warranted in the interest of justice when there is either a service rendered to the Federal workforce or there is a benefit to the public derived from maintaining the action. *Texarkana,* 39 FLRA at 1223 (citing *Naval Air Dev. Ctr., Dep't of the Navy,* 21 FLRA 131, 139 (1986). An award of attorney fees is warranted if any of these criteria is satisfied. *See U.S. Dep't of Def., Def. Mapping Agency, Hydrographic/Topographic Ctr., Wash., D.C.,* 47 FLRA 1187, 1194 (1993).

65 FLRA No. 83

SOCIAL SECURITY ADMINISTRATION
DALLAS REGION
(Agency)

and

AMERICAN FEDERATION
OF GOVERNMENT EMPLOYEES, AFL-CIO
LOCAL 3506
(Union)

0-AR-3999

DECISION

December 23, 2010

Before the Authority: Carol Waller Pope, Chairman, and Thomas M. Beck and Ernest DuBester, Members

I. Statement of the Case

This case is before the Authority on exceptions to an award of Arbitrator Patrick E. Zembower filed by the Agency under § 7122(a) of the Federal Service Labor-Management Relations Statute (the Statute) and part 2425 of the Authority's Regulations. The Union filed an opposition to the Agency's exceptions.

The Arbitrator found that the Agency violated the parties' agreement by failing to give the grievant proper consideration and opportunity for promotion to a supervisory, paralegal specialist position. For the reasons that follow, we deny the Agency's exceptions.

II. Background and Arbitrator's Award

The grievant was one of nine candidates on the best-qualified list for promotion to a supervisory, paralegal specialist position, General Schedule (GS)-13. The recommending official, who was not the grievant's supervisor, interviewed all of the candidates except the grievant, who was on leave outside the country at the time the interview was scheduled and was to be conducted. The recommending official recommended a candidate other than the grievant, and the selecting official selected that candidate.

The grievant, an Asian-American female, filed a grievance alleging that the Agency violated the parties' agreement and Title VII of the Civil Rights Act of 1964 when it did not select her for the vacancy. Award at 14. Specifically, the grievant claimed that she was not selected because of her race. She additionally claimed that she was not afforded proper consideration because she was not interviewed and was not afforded the consideration required by the Agency's affirmative-action plan. *Id.* The parties did not resolve the grievance and submitted it to arbitration.

At arbitration, the parties were unable to agree on a stipulation of the issues, and the Arbitrator framed them as follows: "Was [the grievant] given proper consideration for promotion under [the vacancy announcement] and was she wrongly not selected? If so, what is the appropriate remedy?" *Id.* at 2. Specifically, the Arbitrator addressed whether the Agency: (1) afforded the grievant proper consideration for the vacancy; and (2) discriminated against the grievant because of her race. *Id.* at 15.

In regard to whether the grievant was given proper consideration, the Arbitrator addressed the selection process. He noted that the instructions on the best-qualified list "urge[d] the selecting official to do a couple of things: (1) interview; and (2) if there are two candidates that appear to be equally qualified, select[] the one who is of the underrepresented race." *Id.* at 15 n.2. He agreed with the Agency that it was not obligated to interview the candidates, but he determined that the Agency violated the agreement when it interviewed all of the candidates except the grievant. *Id.* at 15-16. As to the grievant being on leave, the Arbitrator stated: "If the [agreement] was followed[,] [then the grievant's] supervisor, the approving official[,] had [the leave] roster in her possession and should have known [the grievant's] situation when she [the recommending official] scheduled interviews." *Id.* at 7 n.1. The Arbitrator concluded that the Agency's failure to interview the grievant deprived her of the fair and equitable treatment required under Article 3, Section 2 of the parties' agreement.[1] *Id.* at 16. In so concluding, he stated that he did "not believe the reason of [the recommending official] as to why she could not

1. Article 3, Section 2 provides, in pertinent part: "All employees shall be treated fairly and equitably in all aspects of personnel management and without regard to political affiliation, race, color, national origin, sex, sexual orientation, marital status, age, or disabling condition, and with proper regard and protection of their privacy and constitutional rights." Award at 2.

accommodate [the grievant] for an interview" and that the asserted reason was a "pretext for discrimination." *Id.* at 16, 9. He also concluded that the failure to interview the grievant, as an Asian American, deprived her of equal opportunity and amounted to unlawful discrimination in violation of Article 18, Section 1 of the agreement.[2] *Id.* As a remedy, the Arbitrator directed the Agency to promote the grievant to the position of supervisory, paralegal specialist, GS-13, the next time a vacancy occurs in that position in the Agency's Fort Worth, Texas office. The Arbitrator further directed that, if a vacancy first occurs in that position elsewhere in the region, then the Agency will offer the position to the grievant without the grievant forfeiting her right to promotion in the Fort Worth office. *Id.* at 17.

III. Positions of the Parties

A. Agency's Exceptions

In support of its exceptions, the Agency submitted "sworn affidavits of key witnesses attesting to their testimony given during the arbitration hearing." Exceptions at 3. The Agency contends that this is necessary "[b]ecause the Arbitrator deliberately destroyed the record of the proceedings[.]" *Id.* In this regard, the Agency explains that it provided tapes and a tape recorder for the Arbitrator to record the hearing and requested the tapes so that it could transcribe the hearing. The Agency asserts that the Arbitrator denied the request, stated that the recording was for his exclusive use, and returned to the Agency blank tapes. *Id.*

With regard to the merits of the award, the Agency argues that the award is based on nonfacts. Specifically, the Agency contends that the Arbitrator "misstated the instructions listed on the [best-qualified] list" when he concluded that the instructions "required the selecting official to conduct interviews" and "mandate[d] that if there are two candidates that appear to be equally qualified, the selecting official must select the one who is of the underrepresented race." *Id.* at 15. The Agency also contends that the Arbitrator found that the recommending official should have known that the grievant was on leave when the official scheduled the interview because she was the "approving official" of the grievant's leave. *Id.* (citing Award at 7 n.1). The Agency argues that this finding is clearly erroneous because even the grievant stated that her supervisor had approved her leave. The Agency further argues that, but for this erroneous finding, the Arbitrator would have reached a different result. *Id.* at 15-17.

The Agency also argues that the award fails to draw its essence from Article 3, Section 2 of the parties' agreement. In this regard, the Agency argues that the Arbitrator's finding that Article 3, Section 2 requires "the Agency to interview all candidates for a vacancy, regardless of their availability" is inconsistent with the express wording of that article. *Id.* at 17. The Agency asserts that the Arbitrator acknowledged that the Agency was not obligated to interview any of the candidates, but failed to justify his finding of a violation of Article 3, Section 2. *Id.* at 18.

Finally, the Agency claims that the award is contrary to § 7106(a)(2)(C) of the Statute because the award "abrogate[s]" management's right to select employees for promotion. *Id.* at 9. In addition, the Agency contends that Article 3, Section 2 was not negotiated under § 7106(b)(3) of the Statute. *Id.* at 9-10. In this connection, the Agency maintains that the Arbitrator's interpretation of Article 3, Section 2 dictates that, if one candidate is interviewed, then all must be interviewed. The Agency claims that this interpretation of Article 3, Section 2 does not constitute an arrangement because it does not ameliorate the adverse effects of management's determination of whether to interview candidates. *Id.* at 11. Alternatively, the Agency argues that the award is deficient under prong II of the analytical approach set forth in *United States Department of the Treasury, Bureau of Engraving and Printing, Washington, D.C.*, 53 FLRA 146 (1997) (*BEP*), because the Arbitrator's remedy does not reconstruct what management would have done had it complied with Article 3, Section 2. *Id.* at 14.

---

2. Article 18, Section 1 provides, in pertinent part:

> The Administration and the Union affirm their commitment to the policy of providing equal opportunities to all employees and to prohibit discrimination because of race, color, religion, sex, national origin, disabling condition or age. . . . The parties agree that Equal Employment Opportunity shall be administered in accordance with Title 5 U.S.C., the Civil Rights Act of 1991, the Rehabilitation Act of 1973, as amended, the Age Discrimination in Employment Act (ADEA), Executive Order 11478, and other authorizing legislation, and applicable regulations.

Id. at 3.

B. Union's Opposition

As an initial matter, the Union contends that the Agency's affidavits should not be considered because they were not presented to the Arbitrator. Opp'n at 1. With regard to the Agency's nonfact exception, the Union argues that the Agency misstates the award and fails to establish that, but for the asserted nonfacts, the award would have been different. *Id.* at 8. As to essence, the Union claims that the Agency misstates the Arbitrator's interpretation of Article 3, Section 2. *Id.* at 9. As to management rights, the Union claims that the Arbitrator properly enforced Article 3, Section 2 and that the remedy reconstructs what management would have done had it not discriminated against the grievant. In this connection, the Union asserts that the Agency had no authority to make a selection based on illegal discrimination. *Id.* at 6-7.

IV. Preliminary Issue

The Union contends that the Agency should not consider the affidavits submitted by the Agency. The disputed affidavits attest to testimony that was provided at the hearing, and were prepared after the hearing because the Arbitrator denied the Agency's request for the tapes of the hearing so that the Agency could transcribe them.

The Authority previously has permitted a party to submit, in support of exceptions, a statement that sought to reflect what transpired in an arbitration proceeding that lacked a formal transcript. *See NTEU, Chapter 45,* 52 FLRA 1458, 1461 (1997). Specifically, the Authority has held that such a statement was not precluded by § 2429.5 of the Authority's Regulations, as in effect at that time,[3] which provided that the Authority would not consider any evidence that could have been, but was not, presented to the arbitrator. *Id.* Rather, the Authority has accepted such a statement insofar as it constituted arguments in support of exceptions. *Id.*

The disputed affidavits in this case are submitted in support of the Agency's exceptions and seek to reflect what transpired at the arbitration hearing, for which there is no formal transcript. Accordingly, consistent with *NTEU, Chapter 45,* we find that consideration of the affidavits is not precluded by § 2429.5 insofar as they constitute arguments in support of the Agency's exceptions.[4]

V. Analysis and Conclusions

A. The award is not based on nonfacts.

The Agency argues that the award is based on two nonfacts. To establish that an award is based on a nonfact, the appealing party must show that a central fact underlying the award is clearly erroneous, but for which the arbitrator would have reached a different result. *E.g., AFGE, Local 200,* 64 FLRA 769, 770 (2010); *AFGE, Local 1395,* 64 FLRA 622, 625 (2010).

The Agency's first nonfact argument claims that the Arbitrator misinterpreted the instructions on the best-qualified list when he concluded that the instructions "required the selecting official to conduct interviews" and "mandate[d] that if there are two candidates that appear to be equally qualified, the selecting official must select the one who is of the underrepresented race." Exceptions at 15. However, even assuming that the Arbitrator's interpretation of the instructions on the best-qualified list constitutes a factual determination subject to challenge as a nonfact, the Agency misstates the Arbitrator's interpretation. The Arbitrator noted that the instructions "urge[d] the selecting official to do a couple of things: (1) interview[;] and (2) if there are two candidates that appear to be equally qualified, selected [sic] the one who is of the underrepresented race." Award at 15 n.2. Consequently, the Arbitrator found that the instructions simply "urge[d]" the selecting official to conduct interviews and select the candidate of an underrepresented race when candidates are equally qualified; he did not interpret the instructions to require interviews or mandate a particular selection. Therefore, the Agency's argument provides no basis for finding that the award is based on a nonfact. *See AFGE, Local 1395,* 64 FLRA at 626.

3. The Authority's Regulations concerning the review of arbitration awards, as well as certain related procedural Regulations, including § 2429.5, were revised effective October 1, 2010. 75 Fed. Reg. 42,283 (2010). As the exceptions in this case were filed prior to October 1, 2010, we apply the prior version of the Regulations here. *See* 5 C.F.R. § 2425.1. However, we note that, like the prior version of § 2429.5, the revised version of § 2429.5 provides that the Authority will not consider any evidence that could have been, but was not, presented to the arbitrator.

4. In addition, we note that the Authority has accepted affidavits in support of exceptions alleging that the award was deficient on grounds that arose as a result of the award. *U.S. Dep't of Veterans Affairs Med. Ctr., N. Chi., Ill.,* 52 FLRA 387, 399 n.10 (1996).

The Agency's second nonfact argument contends that the Arbitrator erroneously found that the recommending official was the "approving official" of the grievant's leave. Exceptions at 15 (quoting Award at 7 n.1). However, even if the Arbitrator erred in this respect, the Agency does not establish that, but for such error, the Arbitrator would have reached a different result and found that the grievant was treated fairly and equitably. In this regard, the Arbitrator concluded that the grievant was not treated fairly and equitably because the Arbitrator did "not believe the reason of [the recommending official] as to why she could not accommodate [the grievant] for an interview" and found it to be a pretext for discrimination. Award at 16, 9. Consequently, the asserted error does not provide a basis for finding that the award is based on a nonfact. *See AFGE, Local 200,* 64 FLRA at 770.

Accordingly, we deny the nonfact exceptions.

B. The award does not fail to draw its essence from the agreement.

In reviewing an arbitrator's interpretation of a collective bargaining agreement, the Authority applies the deferential standard of review that federal courts use in reviewing arbitration awards in the private sector. *E.g., AFGE, Council 220,* 54 FLRA 156, 159 (1998). Under this standard, the Authority will find that an arbitration award is deficient as failing to draw its essence from the collective bargaining agreement when the appealing party establishes that the award: (1) cannot in any rational way be derived from the agreement; (2) is so unfounded in reason and fact and so unconnected with the wording and purposes of the collective bargaining agreement as to manifest an infidelity to the obligation of the arbitrator; (3) does not represent a plausible interpretation of the agreement; or (4) evidences a manifest disregard of the agreement. *E.g., U.S. Dep't of Labor (OSHA),* 34 FLRA 573, 575 (1990). The Authority and the courts defer to arbitrators in this context because it is the arbitrator's construction of the agreement for which the parties have bargained. *Id.* at 576.

As noted previously, Article 3, Section 2 of the parties' agreement provides, in pertinent part, that management shall treat all employees "fairly and equitably in all aspects of personnel management[.]" Award at 2. The Agency claims that the Arbitrator's interpretation of Article 3, Section 2 to require "the Agency to interview all candidates for a vacancy, regardless of their availability" is inconsistent with the express language of the agreement. Exceptions at 17. However, as the Agency acknowledges, the Arbitrator found that the Agency was not obligated to interview the candidates. Thus, the premise of the Agency's first essence assertion is misplaced and does not establish that the award is unfounded, irrational, implausible, or manifestly disregards the agreement.

The Agency also claims that the Arbitrator failed to justify his finding of a violation of Article 3, Section 2. However, the Arbitrator did justify the finding. Specifically, he determined that the Agency violated Article 3, Section 2 when it interviewed all of the candidates except the grievant in circumstances that the Arbitrator found to be a pretext for discrimination. The Agency provides no basis for finding that the Arbitrator's interpretation and application of Article 3, Section 2 is unfounded, irrational, implausible, or manifestly disregards the agreement.

Accordingly, we deny the essence exceptions.

C. The award is not contrary to § 7106(a)(2)(C) of the Statute.

The Authority reviews questions of law raised by exceptions to an arbitrator's award de novo. *E.g., NFFE, Local 1437,* 53 FLRA 1703, 1709 (1998). In applying a standard of de novo review, the Authority assesses whether the arbitrator's legal conclusions are consistent with the applicable standard of law. *Id.* at 1710.

The Authority recently revised the analysis that it will apply when reviewing exceptions alleging that awards are contrary to law because they are inconsistent with management rights. *See U.S. EPA,* 65 FLRA 113, 115 (2010) (Member Beck concurring) (*EPA*); *FDIC, Div. of Supervision & Consumer Prot., S.F. Region,* 65 FLRA 102 (2010) (Chairman Pope concurring) (*FDIC, S.F. Region*). Under the revised analysis, the Authority will first assess whether the award affects the exercise of the asserted management right. *EPA,* 65 FLRA at 115.[5]

---

5. For the reasons articulated in his recent concurring opinion and footnotes, Member Beck would conclude that it is unnecessary to assess whether the contract provision is an appropriate arrangement or whether it abrogates a § 7106(a) right. The appropriate question is simply whether the remedy directed by the Arbitrator enforces the provision in a reasonable and reasonably foreseeable fashion. *See EPA*, 65 FLRA at 120 (Concurring Opinion of Member Beck); *FDIC*, 65 FLRA at 107 (Concurring Opinion of Member Beck); *U.S. Dep't of the Air Force, Air Force Materiel Command,,* 65 FLRA No. 81, slip op. at 7

If so, then, as relevant here, the Authority examines whether the award enforces a contract provision negotiated under § 7106(b).[6] *Id.* Also under the revised analysis, in determining whether the award enforces a contract provision negotiated under § 7106(b)(3), the Authority assesses: (1) whether the contract provision constitutes an arrangement for employees adversely affected by the exercise of a management right; and (2) if so, then whether the arbitrator's enforcement of the arrangement abrogates the exercise of the management right. *See id.* at 118. In concluding that the Authority would apply an abrogation standard, the Authority rejected continued application of an excessive-interference standard. *Id.* at 113. In addition, in setting forth the revised analysis, the Authority rejected the continued application of the "reconstruction" requirement set forth in *BEP*. *FDIC, S.F. Region,* 65 FLRA at 106-07; *accord FDIC,* 65 FLRA 179, 181 (2010).

It is not disputed that the award affects management's right to select. The Agency contends that Article 3, Section 2 is not an appropriate arrangement within the meaning of § 7106(b)(3) because it does not constitute an arrangement.[7] As interpreted and applied by the Arbitrator, Article 3, Section 2 requires that management treat all employees fairly and equitably in exercising its right to make selections for promotion. To constitute an arrangement, Article 3, Section 2 must ameliorate or mitigate adverse effects that flow from management's exercise of its management rights. *E.g., U.S. Dep't of Veterans Affairs, Bd. of Veterans Appeals,* 61 FLRA 422, 425 (2005). The Authority has repeatedly found provisions requiring management to exercise its management rights fairly and equitably to constitute arrangements because they are intended to mitigate the adverse effects of the unfair or inequitable exercise of management's rights. *See, e.g., AFGE, Local 1367,* 64 FLRA 869, 876 (2010) (Member Beck dissenting as to other matters). Article 3, Section 2 ameliorates or mitigates the adverse effects on employees of all aspects of personnel management by ensuring that the Agency treats them fairly and equitably, without regard to various considerations, such as race, and with regard to their privacy and constitutional rights. For the foregoing reasons, we find that Article 3, Section 2 is an arrangement under § 7106(b)(3).

To the extent that the Agency's statement that the award "abrogate[s]" management's rights constitutes a claim that Article 3, Section 2 is not an appropriate arrangement, Exceptions at 9, the Authority has previously described an award that abrogates the exercise of a management right as an award that "precludes an agency from exercising" the right. *U.S. Dep't of the Army, Army Transp. Ctr., Fort Eustis, Va.,* 38 FLRA 186, 190 (1990) (*Ft. Eustis*) (quoting *Dep't of the Treasury, U.S. Customs Serv.,* 37 FLRA 309, 314 (1990)). The Arbitrator enforced Article 3, Section 2 to restrict management from interviewing all of the candidates except the grievant because, according to the Arbitrator, doing so deprived her of fair and equitable treatment. As interpreted and applied by the Arbitrator, Article 3, Section 2 does not preclude the Agency from exercising any of its rights; it merely requires the Agency to exercise them in a fair and equitable manner. Consequently, the Agency does not establish that the Arbitrator's enforcement of Article 3, Section 2 abrogates the exercise of a management right. *See Ft. Eustis,* 38 FLRA at 190. For the foregoing reasons, we find that Article 3, Section 2 was negotiated under § 7106(b)(3).

The Agency also argues that, if the Authority finds that Article 3, Section 2 constitutes a contract provision negotiated under § 7106(b)(3), then the award is deficient under *BEP* because the Arbitrator's remedy does reconstruct what management would have done had it complied with Article 3, Section 2. However, as noted above, the Authority no longer requires that an arbitrator's remedy reconstruct what management would have done had it not violated the contract provision. *FDIC,* 65 FLRA at 181. Thus, the Agency's argument does not provide a basis for setting aside the award. *See id.*

Additionally, as discussed above, the Arbitrator also concluded that the failure to interview the grievant constituted unlawful discrimination in violation of Article 18, Section 1. The Agency does not argue that the Arbitrator's enforcement of Article 18, Section 1 affects management rights or is otherwise deficient. The Arbitrator's relief is

---

n.7 (2010); *U.S. Dep't of Health and Human Services, Off. of Medicare Hearings and Appeals,* 65 FLRA 175, 177 n.3 (2010), and *U.S. Dep't of Transp., Federal Aviation Adm.,* 65 FLRA 171, 173 n.5 (2010). Member Beck would conclude that the Arbitrator's award is a plausible interpretation of the parties' agreement and deny the exception.

6. When an award affects a management right under § 7106(a)(2) of the Statute, the Authority may also examine whether the award enforces an applicable law. *EPA,* 65 FLRA at 115 n.7.

7. As discussed further below, in contending that the award is deficient, the Agency does not address the Arbitrator's enforcement of Article 18, Section 1.

intended to remedy the harm of the violation of Article 18, Section 1, as well as the harm of the violation of Article 3, Section 2. *See* Award at 16. As the Agency does not assert that Article 18, Section 1 is unenforceable, the Arbitrator's reliance on that contract provision further supports the remedy.[8]

For the foregoing reasons, we deny this exception.

VI. Decision

The Agency's exceptions are denied.

8. For the reasons set forth in her concurring opinion in *FDIC, S.F. Region,* 65 FLRA at 112, Chairman Pope agrees that the Agency provides no basis for finding the Arbitrator's remedy deficient as it pertains to the violation of Article 3, Section 2 because the remedy is reasonably related to Article 3, Section 2 and the harm being remedied. Chairman Pope agrees, in addition, that the uncontested violation of Article 18, Section 1, provides an additional basis for the remedy.

65 FLRA No. 84

AMERICAN FEDERATION
OF GOVERNMENT EMPLOYEES
LOCAL 987
(Union)

and

UNITED STATES
DEPARTMENT OF THE AIR FORCE
WARNER ROBINS AIR LOGISTICS CENTER
WARNER ROBINS AIR FORCE BASE, GEORGIA
(Agency)

0-AR-4653

DECISION

December 23, 2010

Before the Authority: Carol Waller Pope, Chairman, and Thomas M. Beck and Ernest DuBester, Members

I. Statement of the Case

This matter is before the Authority on exceptions to an award of Arbitrator William H. Holley, Jr. filed by the Union under § 7122(a) of the Federal Service Labor-Management Relations Statute (the Statute) and part 2425 of the Authority's Regulations. The Agency filed an opposition to the Union's exceptions.

The Arbitrator issued an award finding the grievance arbitrable and also finding that the Agency violated the parties' Master Labor Agreement (MLA). However, the Arbitrator did not discuss remedy issues and the award does not provide a remedy.

For the reasons discussed below, we grant the Union's exception that the Arbitrator exceeded his authority when he found a violation of the MLA. Consequently, we set aside the award with respect to that finding, and remand the award to the parties, absent settlement, for resubmission to the Arbitrator for further proceedings consistent with this decision.

II. Background and Arbitrator's Award

The Union's grievance concerns the Agency's failure to bargain with the Union over the implementation of a Multi-skill Training Program (MTP). The MTP was the subject of a 1997 Federal Service Impasses Panel (FSIP) decision, which was incorporated into a Memorandum of Agreement (MOA) between the parties. Award at 20-21 (citing *Dep't of the Air Force, Wright-Patterson Air Force Base, Headquarters, Air Force Materiel Command, Wright-Patterson Air Force Base, Ohio*, 97 FSIP 88 (1997)). In a subsequent proceeding, the Authority ruled that the MOA was binding on the parties and upheld an arbitrator's award finding that the Agency was compelled to implement the MOA pursuant to the FSIP-imposed agreement. *Id.* at 21, (citing *U.S. Dep't of the Air Force, Warner Robins Air Logistics Ctr., Robins Air Force Base, Ga.*, 56 FLRA 498, 499, 501 (2000)).

In February 2008, the Agency notified the Union that it intended to implement the MTP at the local level. The Union demanded to bargain with the Agency over the program's implementation. Award at 2. The Agency refused and responded that the demand to bargain was untimely. *Id.* at 6. The Union filed a grievance. When the parties could not resolve the grievance, the matter was submitted to arbitration.

Prior to the arbitration hearing, the Arbitrator and the parties agreed that the proceeding would be bifurcated: one hearing would be held on the grievance's arbitrability and another on its merits. Exceptions, Ex.6 at 7-8, 13-14. The Union's exceptions concern the Arbitrator's award following the arbitrability hearing. A separate hearing on the merits never occurred.

Based on the issues the parties proposed, the Arbitrator framed the issues as follows:

> Whether the [g]rievance is arbitrable.
>
> Whether the demand to bargain was timely.
>
> Whether the FSIP Imposed Agreement is still in effect. If so, does the FSIP Imposed Agreement allow for negotiations at the local level.

Award at 13.

The Arbitrator resolved the issues he framed. The Arbitrator found that the grievance was arbitrable, that the demand to bargain was timely, that the FSIP-imposed agreement was still in effect, and that the agreement allowed for negotiations at the local level. Award at 35, 38-39. However, the Arbitrator not only ruled on the issues he framed, he also ruled on a merits issue that was not among the framed issues. As to this additional merits issue, the Arbitrator found that the Agency's refusal to bargain with the Union over the implementation of the MTP was a violation of Article 33 of the MLA.[1] *Id.* at 38, 39. The Arbitrator also found that the Union's request to maintain the status quo until the completion of negotiations went beyond the requirements of Article 33. *Id.* at 38.

Although the Arbitrator concluded that the grievance was properly before him and that the Agency violated the MLA, the Arbitrator did not discuss remedy issues and the award does not provide a remedy.

III. Positions of the Parties

A. Union's Exceptions

The Union excepts to the award on three bases. The Union contends that the award fails to draw its essence from the parties' agreement, that the Arbitrator exceeded his authority, and that the Arbitrator failed to conduct a fair hearing. Exceptions at 5-8. However, the three exceptions raise a common complaint. With all three exceptions, the Union argues that when the Arbitrator reached the merits of the Union's contract violation claim, he went beyond the issues that he framed for the arbitration hearing. The Union asserts that, in doing so, the Arbitrator resolved a merits issue not before him. *E.g., id.* at 6-8. The Union requests that the award be remanded to the Arbitrator "to conduct a full hearing on the merits of the Union's grievance, including remedies."[2] *Id.* at 8.

B. Agency's Opposition

The Agency contends that the Union's exceptions are nothing more than disagreement with the Arbitrator's award. Opposition at 3. The Agency's position with regard to all three exceptions is that the proceeding involved only arbitrability issues, and that this is all the Arbitrator ruled on. *Id.* at 3-5. Therefore, the Agency asks the Authority to deny the Union's exceptions.

IV. Analysis and Conclusions

The Union claims that the Arbitrator exceeded his authority when he found a violation of Article 33 of the MLA. Arbitrators exceed their authority when they fail to resolve an issue submitted to arbitration, resolve an issue not submitted to arbitration, disregard specific limitations on their authority, or award relief to those not encompassed within the grievance. *See AFGE, Local 1617*, 51 FLRA 1645, 1647 (1996). In the absence of a stipulated issue, the arbitrator's formulation of the issue is accorded substantial deference. *See U.S. Dep't of the Army, Corps of Eng'rs, Memphis Dist., Memphis, Tenn.*, 52 FLRA 920, 924 (1997). However, although "[a]rbitrators may legitimately bring their judgment to bear in reaching a fair resolution of a dispute as submitted to or formulated by them, . . . they may not decide matters which are not before them." *Veterans Admin.*, 24 FLRA 447, 451 (1986).

It is undisputed that the issues before the Arbitrator did not include the merits of the Union's claim that the Agency violated Article 33 of the MLA.[3] Nevertheless, the Arbitrator resolved that claim. In these circumstances, we find that the Arbitrator exceeded his authority when he decided, prior to a hearing on the merits, that the Agency committed a contract violation.

Accordingly, the award is set aside with respect to the finding of a violation of Article 33 of the MLA and remanded to the parties, absent settlement, for resubmission to the Arbitrator to conduct a full hearing on the merits of the Union's grievance, including the remedies requested by the Union.[4] *U.S. Dep't of Def. Dependents Schools,* 49 FLRA

1. Article 33 sets forth the ground rules for negotiations during the term of the agreement. Article 33 is set forth in the appendix to this decision.

2. The remedies sought in the grievance are set forth in the Award at 9. They include a cease and desist order, a posting, and discipline of the Agency officials responsible for the failure to bargain.

3. There is nothing in the record that would explain why the Arbitrator went beyond the issues he framed. As we are constrained by the record before us, we must decide accordingly.

4. In light of this decision, it is unnecessary to address the Union's remaining exceptions.

120, 124 (1994) (where arbitrator exceeded authority award remanded to parties for resubmission to arbitrator in order to properly resolve grievance's remaining issues).

V. Decision

The Union's exception is granted. The award is set aside in part, and the matter is remanded to the parties, absent settlement, for resubmission to the Arbitrator for further proceedings consistent with this decision.

APPENDIX

Article 33-Ground Rules for Negotiations During the Term of the Agreement

Section 33.01: General

In an effort to continue to develop a productive labor-management relationship which benefits employees and their Union and the Employer, it is the intent of this article to encourage negotiations between the parties.

a. It is understood that neither party waives any rights under the Federal Service Labor-Management Relations Statute.

b. The parties do not intend to renegotiate the articles and provisions which already have been negotiated in this Agreement. The Parties agree to give notice and bargain over proposed changes in conditions of employment unless the matter is expressly contained in the contract.

c. The parties are committed to utilizing an interest-based, problem-solving approach to reach agreement during these negotiations. In this respect, during these negotiations neither party will file a grievance, institute any proceeding under the Stature, or declare a proposal nonnegotiable under the Statute concerning the matter. This process terminates when there is an agreement on the matter or either of the parties determines that it intends to rely on its statutory rights.

Section 33.02: Negotiations at Command Level

The Union will designate an official(s) to represent it in mid-term bargaining matters at Command level. The Union will provide an adequate staff to be located at HQ AFMC, WPAFB OH with authority to facilitate prompt response to the negotiations undertaken at Command level.

a. When a bargaining obligation is generated by a proposed directive at Command level or a directive issued above Command level, the following procedures will apply:

1. The Labor Relations Office will notify the designated Union official above of the intended changes in conditions of employment. A reasonable time period/date following the notification will be identified as the date management intends to implement. The union official designated above may request and be granted a meeting to discuss the change.

2. If the Union wishes to negotiate, in accordance with entitlements under CSRA, concerning proposed changes, the Union will submit written proposals to the Labor Relations Office not later than 15 workdays after receipt of Employer's notifications. The parties will determine a date on which negotiations will take place, the persons to be involved, the location, and the implementation procedures. Negotiations will normally begin within five workdays after receipt by the Labor Relations Office of the timely Union proposals. If necessary, the identified implementation date may be postponed by the Employer to complete negotiations.

b. When a bargaining obligation is generated by the union over a condition of employment which has not been covered by the contract and was not the subject of a matter previously submitted, but withdrawn, during negotiations, the following procedures will apply:

1. The union will notify, in writing, the Labor Relations Officer of the intended changes in conditions of employment. A reasonable time period/date following the notification will be identified as the implementation date. The Labor Relations Officer or designee may request and be granted a meeting to discuss the change.

2. If management wishes to negotiate, in accordance with entitlements under the CSRA, concerning the union's proposed changes, management will submit written counterproposals to the union not later than 15 workdays after receipt of the union's written notification. Negotiations will normally begin within five workdays after receipt by the union of the timely proposals. If necessary, the identified implementation date may be postponed to complete negotiations.

c. There shall be no implied consent or constructive implementation of any union proposal.

d. The parties may mutually agree to delegate responsibility for negotiations to subordinate activities and local Union officials.

e. Agreements reached under this Section will be promptly implemented by the Employer in the appropriate form such as regulation, letter, or operating instruction. Disputes over the application of the implementing directive will be subject to resolution under Article 6 (Grievance Procedure).

Section 33.03: Negotiations at Activity Level

a. Activity-wide changes in local conditions of employment, not covered by this MLA nor as a result of Command-wide negotiations under Section 33.02a above, which are within the discretion of the subordinate activity commander, will be brought to the attention of local Union officials prior to implementation in accordance with law and regulations. The Union will be given a specified reasonable implementation date as determined by mission requirements and the urgency for implementation.

1. If the Union wishes to negotiate, in accordance within Title VII, CSRA, the Union will submit written proposals to the activity labor relations office within ten calendar days of the date of notification if circumstances permit that much time. The local parties will determine a date on which negotiations will take place, the persons to be involved, the location, and the implementation procedures.

2. Upon notification that activities and local Unions have been delegated negotiation responsibilities in accordance with Section 33.02d, the activity will provide notice of the new or revised issuance or directive to the local president together with a specified reasonable implementation date. If the Union wishes to negotiate, it will respond in accordance with Section 33.03a(1) above and the provisions of that Section will be followed in discharging the bargaining obligations.

b. Changes in local conditions of employment at echelons below the activity commander will be brought to the attention of the Union representative designated to be contacted by the supervisor or manager making the changes. Arrangements will be made by such officials, if bargaining is requested, to discharge the bargaining obligation in a time frame consistent with the circumstances causing the needed change. Agreements reached may not violate any provisions of this MLA or Local Supplements.

c. When a bargaining obligation is generated by the union over a condition of employment which has not been covered by the contract and was not the subject of a matter previously submitted, but withdrawn, during negotiations, the following procedures will apply:

1. After review by the Council 214 President, the local Union President will notify, in writing, the Labor Relations Officer of the intended changes in conditions of employment. A reasonable time period/date following the notification will be identified as the proposed implementation date. The Labor Relations Officer or designee may request and be granted a meeting to discuss the change.

2. If management wishes to negotiate, in accordance with entitlements under the CSRA, concerning the union's proposed changes, management will submit written counterproposals to the union not later than 15 workdays after receipt of the union's written notification. Negotiations will normally begin within five workdays after receipt by the union of the timely proposals. If necessary, the identified implementation date may be postponed to complete registrations.

Award at 15-18.

65 FLRA No. 85

NATIONAL FEDERATION
OF FEDERAL EMPLOYEES
LOCAL 476
INTERNATIONAL ASSOCIATION OF
MACHINISTS AND AEROSPACE WORKERS
FEDERAL DISTRICT 1
(Union)

and

UNITED STATES
DEPARTMENT OF THE ARMY
U.S. ARMY COMMUNICATIONS-ELECTRONIC
RESEARCH, DEVELOPMENT AND
ENGINEERING CENTER
FORT MONMOUTH, NEW JERSEY
(Agency)

0-AR-4702

DECISION

January 6, 2011

Before the Authority: Carol Waller Pope, Chairman, and Thomas M. Beck and Ernest DuBester, Members

This matter is before the Authority on exceptions to an award of Arbitrator David M. Beckerman filed by the Union under § 7122(a) of the Federal Service Labor-Management Relations Statute (the Statute) and part 2425 of the Authority's Regulations. The Agency filed an opposition to the Union's exceptions.

Under § 7122(a) of the Statute, an award is deficient if it is contrary to any law, rule, or regulation, or it is deficient on other grounds similar to those applied by federal courts in private sector labor-management relations. Upon careful consideration of the entire record in this case and Authority precedent, the Authority concludes that the award is not deficient on the grounds raised in the exceptions and set forth in § 7122(a). *See U.S. Dep't of Labor (OSHA)*, 34 FLRA 573, 575 (1990) (award not deficient as failing to draw its essence from the parties' collective bargaining agreement where excepting party fails to establish that the award cannot in any rational way be derived from the agreement; is so unfounded in reason and fact and so unconnected to the wording and purpose of the agreement as to manifest an infidelity to the obligation of the arbitrator; does not represent a plausible interpretation of the agreement; or evidences a manifest disregard of the agreement); *AFGE, Local 1617*, 51 FLRA 1645, 1647 (1996) (award not deficient on grounds that arbitrator exceeded his authority where excepting party fails to establish that arbitrator did not resolve an issue submitted to arbitration, resolved an issue not submitted to arbitration, disregarded specific limitations on his authority, or awarded relief to those not encompassed within the grievance).[*]

Accordingly, the Union's exceptions are denied.

*. *See also U.S. Dep't of Justice, Fed. Bureau of Prisons, U.S. Penitentiary, Leavenworth, Kan.*, 53 FLRA 29, 32 (1997) (where collective bargaining agreement incorporates regulations with which award allegedly conflicts, issues concerning the arbitrator's interpretation of the regulations raise questions of contract interpretation that are reviewed under the essence standard).

65 FLRA No. 86

UNITED STATES
DEPARTMENT OF AGRICULTURE
FOOD SAFETY AND INSPECTION SERVICE
(Agency)

and

AMERICAN FEDERATION
OF GOVERNMENT EMPLOYEES
NATIONAL JOINT COUNCIL OF FOOD
INSPECTION LOCALS
(Union)

0-AR-4520

DECISION

January 7, 2011

Before the Authority: Carol Waller Pope, Chairman, and Thomas M. Beck and Ernest DuBester, Members

I. Statement of the Case

This matter is before the Authority on exceptions to an award of Arbitrator Gerard A. Fowler filed by the Agency under § 7122(a) of the Federal Service Labor-Management Relations Statute (the Statute) and part 2425 of the Authority's Regulations. The Union filed an opposition to the Agency's exceptions.

The Arbitrator found that the Agency violated the parties' agreement by failing to temporarily promote the grievant, and he awarded the grievant backpay with interest. For the following reasons, we deny the Agency's exceptions.

II. Background and Arbitrator's Award

The Union filed a grievance alleging that the grievant, a General Schedule (GS)-8, had performed the duties of a GS-9 twice a week, and that the Agency violated the parties' agreement by failing to compensate the grievant for performing those duties. Award at 2. The grievance was unresolved and submitted to arbitration. *Id.* at 3. At arbitration, the Arbitrator framed the relevant issues as: "Did the Agency violate . . . Article 19, [Sections] 2 and 3 [of the parties' agreement[1]] when it did not promote the [g]rievant . . . when he performed his assigned duties . . . . If so, what is the remedy?"[2] *Id.*

As an initial matter, the Arbitrator set forth several relevant agreement provisions, including Article 21, Section 8, which addresses temporary promotions.[3] *Id.* at 5-6. Next, the Arbitrator found that "[s]ince [the g]rievant was detailed to a GS-9 position consistently and met the minimum qualifications for the GS-9 position, the [parties' agreement] requires [that] he be granted a temporary promotion." *Id.* at 13. He then determined that "[t]he Agency violated [the parties' agreement] and committed an unjustified personnel action when it failed to pay [the g]rievant for work performed at the GS-9 level." *Id.* The Arbitrator also found that the "[g]rievant is eligible for backpay for the period [of] December 2006 . . . through June 2007[,]" but noted that 5 C.F.R. § 335.103(c) "is not applicable in this case" because "the number of days detailed amount[s] to less than 120 days[.]"[4] *Id.* at 12. The Arbitrator further determined that "[t]he Agency must . . . pay [the g]rievant for each day in which he was detailed to a GS-9 position in the relevant time period[,]" and he awarded the grievant backpay with interest. *Id.* at 12, 14.

III. Positions of the Parties

A. Agency's Exceptions

The Agency asserts that the Arbitrator exceeded his authority by awarding the grievant a retroactive temporary promotion because he framed the relevant issue as whether the Agency violated Article 19 of

1. Article 19, Section 2 of the parties' agreement states, in relevant part: "The Agency agrees that equal pay for substantially equal work shall be applied to all position classification actions." *Id.* at 4. Article 19, Section 3 of the parties' agreement provides, in pertinent part: "When significant changes in the duties and responsibilities of a position occur, the position description shall be amended or rewritten to accurately describe the assigned duties and responsibilities[.]" Agency's Post-Hearing Brief at 4.

2. The Arbitrator also resolved issues regarding whether the grievance was timely, non-arbitrable and/or non-grievable. Award at 1-2. As there are no exceptions regarding the Arbitrator's resolution of these issues, we do not address them further.

3. The pertinent wording of Article 21, Section 8 is set forth *infra*.

4. The pertinent wording of 5 C.F.R. § 335.103(c) is set forth *infra*.

the parties' agreement, which pertains to classification issues, rather than temporary promotions. Exceptions at 8.

The Agency further asserts that the award conflicts with Article 21, Section 8, which, according to the Agency, unambiguously provides that the Agency is not obligated to temporarily promote employees unless they have been detailed to a higher-graded position for more than sixty consecutive days. *Id.* at 5-6. In this connection, the Agency maintains that the Arbitrator failed to make a necessary finding that the grievant was detailed for more than sixty consecutive days. *Id.* at 6.

In addition, the Agency argues that the award is contrary to the Back Pay Act because "Article 21, Section 8 is the only relevant provision in [the parties' agreement] that addresses temporary promotions for higher graded duty[,]" and the Arbitrator failed to make the requisite findings to support an award of backpay based on that provision -- specifically, that the grievant was detailed for more than sixty consecutive days. *Id* at 7.

Finally, the Agency maintains that the award violates 5 C.F.R. § 335.103(c) and *United States Department of Veterans Affairs, Ralph H. Johnson Medical Center, Charleston, South Carolina*, 60 FLRA 46 (2004) (*Johnson Med. Ctr.*), because the Arbitrator directed a temporary promotion and backpay for a period exceeding 120 days. Exceptions at 8-9. In this connection, the Agency asserts that, by finding that the "[g]rievant [wa]s eligible for backpay for the period [of] December 2006 . . . through June 2007[,]" the Arbitrator awarded a temporary promotion without the use of competitive procedures for a period of seven months, and, therefore, in excess of 120 days. *Id.* at 9.

B. Union's Opposition

With regard to the Agency's exceeded authority exception, the Union argues that, at arbitration, the Agency had raised a classification argument, and the Union had argued at arbitration that the grievance "concerned a temporary promotion as opposed to a classification[.]" Opp'n at 10-11. Thus, the Union asserts that "resolution of the classification issue required the [A]rbitrator to consider the temporary promotion" issue, and he did not exceed his authority by addressing it. *Id.*

The Union also argues that the award is not contrary to the Back Pay Act because the Arbitrator "clearly found a causal connection between the Agency's unjustified action and the loss of pay for the grievant." *Id.* at 9. The Union further asserts that the Arbitrator was not required to cite a specific provision in his award because "both parties focused nearly entirely on Article 21 throughout the hearing and [their] briefs[.]" *Id.* at 8.

Finally, the Union contends that the award is not contrary to 5 C.F.R. § 335.103(c) because the Arbitrator "did not grant the grievant a promotion for the full seven months[,]" but rather, "limited the promotion to the specific days [that the grievant] was detailed, which amounted to less than 120 days." *Id.* at 12.

IV. Analysis and Conclusions

A. The Arbitrator did not exceed his authority.

Arbitrators exceed their authority when they fail to resolve an issue submitted to arbitration, resolve an issue not submitted to arbitration, disregard specific limitations on their authority, or award relief to persons who are not encompassed within the grievance. *See U.S. Dep't of the Navy, Naval Base, Norfolk, Va.*, 51 FLRA 305, 307-08 (1995). In the absence of a stipulated issue, an arbitrator's formulation of the issues is accorded substantial deference. *See AFGE, Local 933*, 58 FLRA 480, 482 (2003) (*AFGE*). In addition, an arbitrator does not exceed his or her authority where the award is directly responsive to the formulated issues. *See, e.g., AFGE, Local 4044, Council of Prisons Local 33*, 57 FLRA 98, 99 (2001).

Here, the Arbitrator framed the relevant issues as: "Did the Agency violate . . . Article 19, [Sections] 2 and 3 [of the parties' agreement] when it did not promote the [g]rievant . . . when he performed his assigned duties . . . . If so, what is the remedy?" Award at 2. Thus, the issue of the Agency's failure to "promote" the grievant was expressly included in the issues as the Arbitrator framed them. *Id.* Moreover, the Arbitrator identified Article 21, Section 8 of the parties' agreement as a relevant provision, *see id.* at 5-6, and there is no dispute that, before the Arbitrator, both parties provided arguments regarding that provision. In this regard, in summarizing the Agency's position, the Arbitrator stated that "with regard to the merits, the Agency asserts that [the g]rievant is not entitled to additional pay or to a promotion" and that "the Agency points to Article 21, [Section] 8 of [the parties' agreement]." *Id.* at 8; *accord* Union's Post-Hearing Brief at 16-20 (arguing that the grievant was entitled to a temporary promotion under Article 21, Section 8 because he met the applicable requirements and was not detailed for a brief period of fewer than sixty consecutive days). Thus, both the Arbitrator and the parties treated Article 21, Section 8 as relevant to the issues before the Arbitrator.[5] Accordingly, we find that the Arbitrator did not address an issue that was not submitted to arbitration, and we deny the exception.

B. The award draws its essence from the parties' agreement.

We construe the Agency's contention that the award conflicts with Article 21, Section 8 of the parties' agreement because the Arbitrator failed to find that the grievant was detailed for sixty consecutive days as a contention that the award fails to draw its essence from the parties' agreement.

In reviewing an arbitrator's interpretation of a collective bargaining agreement, the Authority applies the deferential standard that federal courts use in reviewing arbitration awards in the private sector. *See* 5 U.S.C. § 7122(a)(2); *AFGE, Council 220*, 54 FLRA 156, 159 (1998). Under this standard, the Authority will find that an arbitration award is deficient as failing to draw its essence from the collective bargaining agreement when the appealing party establishes that the award: (1) cannot in any rational way be derived from the agreement; (2) is so unfounded in reason and fact and so unconnected with the wording and purposes of the collective bargaining agreement as to manifest an infidelity to the obligation of the arbitrator; (3) does not represent a plausible interpretation of the agreement; or (4) evidences a manifest disregard of the agreement. *U.S. Dep't of Labor (OSHA)*, 34 FLRA 573, 575 (1990). The Authority and the courts defer to arbitrators in this context "because it is the arbitrator's construction of the agreement for which the parties have bargained." *Id.* at 576.

Article 21, Section 8 of the parties' agreement states, in relevant part: "Except for brief periods, not to exceed sixty (60) consecutive days, employees detailed to a higher grade position shall be given a temporary promotion if the employee meets applicable time in grade and Office of Personnel Management qualifications requirements." Award at 6. Thus, the provision provides that temporary promotions are not mandated when details do not "exceed sixty (60) consecutive days[.]" *Id.* However, the provision does not prohibit temporary promotions for details consisting of numerous nonconsecutive days over a period exceeding sixty days, which is the situation presented here. Thus, the Agency does not demonstrate that it was irrational, unfounded, implausible, or in manifest disregard of Article 21, Section 8 for the Arbitrator to award a temporary promotion in the circumstances of this case. Accordingly, we deny the essence exception.

C. The award is not contrary to law.

The Agency argues that the award is contrary to the Back Pay Act and 5 C.F.R. § 335.103(c). When a party's exceptions involve an award's consistency with law, the Authority reviews the questions of law raised by the arbitrator's award and the party's exceptions de novo. *NTEU, Chapter 24*, 50 FLRA 330, 332 (1995) (citing *U.S. Customs Serv. v. FLRA*, 43 F.3d 682, 686-87 (D.C. Cir. 1994)). In applying a de novo standard of review, the Authority assesses whether the arbitrator's legal conclusions are consistent with the applicable standard of law. *NFFE, Local 1437*, 53 FLRA 1703, 1710 (1998). In making that assessment, the Authority defers to the arbitrator's underlying factual findings. *See id.*

1. The Back Pay Act

As a general rule, an employee is entitled only to the salary of the position to which the employee is appointed. *U.S. Dep't of the Army, Fort Polk, La.*, 44 FLRA 1548, 1563 (1992) (*Fort Polk*) (citing *Cassandra G. McPeak and Wayne E. Dabney*, 69 Comp. Gen. 140 (1989) (*McPeak*)). An exception to this general rule exists, permitting compensation for the temporary performance of the duties of a higher-graded position, where, as relevant here, a collective bargaining agreement makes temporary promotions mandatory for details to higher graded positions, thereby establishing a nondiscretionary agency policy that would provide a basis for backpay. *U.S. Dep't of the Army, Army Armament Research, Dev. & Eng'g. Ctr.*, 49 FLRA 562, 565 (1994) (citing *Wilson v. United States*, 229 Ct. Cl. 510 (1981); *McPeak*, 69 Comp. Gen. at 140); *Fort Polk*, 44 FLRA at 1563. Where an arbitrator fails to identify such a non-discretionary agency policy, there is no unjustified or unwarranted personnel action that would entitle the grievant to an award of backpay under the Back Pay Act. *See U.S. Dep't of the Air Force, 81st Training Wing, Keesler Air Force Base, Miss.*, 60 FLRA 425, 429 (2004) (citing *U.S. Dep't of the Army, Headquarters, III Corps & Fort Hood, Fort Hood, Tex.*, 56 FLRA 544, 546 (2000)).

5. Although the Arbitrator did not specifically cite Article 21, Section 8 in finding a violation of the agreement, the parties do not dispute that he found a violation of that provision.

Here, the Agency argues that Article 21, Section 8 is the only relevant provision in the parties' agreement, and that the grievant is not entitled to backpay under that provision because the Arbitrator failed to find that the grievant was detailed for more than sixty consecutive days. Exceptions at 7. The Agency's argument effectively restates the Agency's essence exception, which we have denied. Accordingly, the Agency provides no basis for finding the award contrary to the Back Pay Act, and we deny this exception.

2. 5 C.F.R. § 335.103(c)

The Agency contends that the award is inconsistent with 5 C.F.R. § 335.103(c) because the Arbitrator directed the Agency to grant a temporary promotion without the use of competitive procedures for a period spanning seven months, and therefore, in excess of 120 days. Exceptions at 8-9. The Agency also contends that the award conflicts with the Authority's decision in *Johnson Med. Ctr*, 60 FLRA 46.

5 C.F.R. § 335.103(c)(1)(i) mandates the use of competitive procedures for promotions to higher-graded positions that last "more than 120 days[.]" Consistent with this regulation, the Authority held in *Johnson Med. Ctr.* that an award of a retroactive temporary promotion for a period of over two years violated 5 C.F.R. § 335.103(c)(1)(i). 60 FLRA at 49-50.

Here, the Arbitrator found that "the number of days detailed amount[ed] to less than 120 days" and that the Agency must "pay [the g]rievant for each day [that] he was detailed[.]" Award at 12. In this regard, there is no dispute that the grievant was detailed twice a week during the relevant period. Nothing in *Johnson Med. Ctr.* or 5 C.F.R. § 335.103(c)(1)(i) precludes an agency from noncompetitively, temporarily promoting a grievant for a series of time periods (here, twice a week), even if that series of periods -- when added to intermittent periods where the grievant was not temporarily promoted -- exceeds 120 days. Accordingly, the Agency does not demonstrate that the award is contrary to 5 C.F.R. § 335.103(c), and we deny the exception.

V. Decision

The Agency's exceptions are denied.

65 FLRA No. 87

AMERICAN FEDERATION
OF GOVERNMENT EMPLOYEES
COUNCIL 236
(Union)

and

UNITED STATES
GENERAL SERVICES ADMINISTRATION
(Agency)

0-AR-4707

DECISION

January 13, 2011

Before the Authority: Carol Waller Pope, Chairman, and Thomas M. Beck and Ernest DuBester, Members

This matter is before the Authority on exceptions to an award of Arbitrator Randall M. Kelly filed by the Union under § 7122(a) of the Federal Service Labor-Management Relations Statute (the Statute) and part 2425 of the Authority's Regulations. The Agency filed an opposition to the Union's exceptions.

Under § 7122(a) of the Statute, an award is deficient if it is contrary to any law, rule, or regulation, or it is deficient on other grounds similar to those applied by federal courts in private sector labor-management relations. Upon careful consideration of the entire record in this case and Authority precedent, the Authority concludes that the award is not deficient on the grounds raised in the exceptions and set forth in § 7122(a).* *See Prof'l Airways Sys. Specialists, Dist. No. 1, MEBA/NMU (AFL-CIO)*, 48 FLRA 764, 768-69 (1993) (award not deficient as contrary to law where excepting party fails to establish that the award is in any manner contrary to the law, rule, or regulation on which the party relies).

Accordingly, the Union's exceptions are denied.

* To the extent that the Union asserts that the Agency violated §§ 1(a) and 8(d) of the Agency's telework order, Exceptions at 1-2, such assertions were not raised before the Arbitrator, and therefore, are not properly before the Authority under 5 C.F.R. § 2429.5. We note that § 2429.5 was amended effective October 1, 2010. *See* 75 Fed. Reg. 42,283 (2010). Because these exceptions were filed after that date, we apply the revised Regulation.

65 FLRA No. 88

UNITED STATES
DEPARTMENT OF HOMELAND SECURITY
U.S. CUSTOMS AND BORDER PROTECTION
EL PASO, TEXAS
(Respondent)

and

AMERICAN FEDERATION
OF GOVERNMENT EMPLOYEES
NATIONAL BORDER PATROL COUNCIL
LOCAL 1929, AFL-CIO
(Charging Party)

DA-CA-09-0286

DECISION AND ORDER

January 20, 2011

Before the Authority: Carol Waller Pope, Chairman, and Thomas M. Beck and Ernest DuBester, Members

I. Statement of the Case

This unfair labor practice (ULP) case is before the Authority on exceptions to the attached decision of the Administrative Law Judge (the Judge) filed by the General Counsel (GC). The Respondent filed an opposition to the GC's exceptions.

The amended complaint alleges that the Respondent violated § 7116(a)(1) and (5) of the Federal Service Labor-Management Relations Statute (the Statute) by changing an established practice of granting certain employees administrative leave on their birthdays without bargaining, and by failing to respond to the Charging Party's (Union's) request to bargain over that matter. The Judge dismissed the amended complaint as untimely.

For the reasons that follow, we reverse the Judge's decision and remand the amended complaint for a resolution on the merits.

II. Background

The facts are set forth in detail in the Judge's decision and are only briefly summarized here. The Respondent had an established practice of first-line supervisors granting certain employees administrative leave on their birthdays (hereinafter "birthday leave"). Judge's Decision at 3. In July 2008, the Union's President (the President) "heard rumors" that the Respondent planned to eliminate that practice. *Id.* The President wrote a letter to the Respondent, in which the President "protested the termination of the practice and requested that the Respondent re-implement the practice immediately . . . ." *Id.* In response, the Respondent informed the Union that it was "rescinding the previous notice to the [employees]" regarding not granting birthday leave, and stated that "[i]f management determines to revisit this issue, the [U]nion will be given official notification." *Id.*

On July 29, 2008, the Respondent sent the President a letter stating, in pertinent part:

> This is to inform you that first line supervisors . . . do not have the authority or discretion to grant [employees birthday leave]. Therefore, effective December 28, 2008, management will terminate the practice of allowing first line supervisors the discretion of granting [birthday leave] . . . . Management will continue to approve or disapprove "excused absences" in accordance with regulations and policy.

Id. at 3-4.

On August 8, 2008, the President responded by letter stating, in pertinent part:

> While we are not entirely sure if the [Respondent's] proposal is intended to impact, in any way, the affected bargaining unit employees' entitlement to [birthday] leave,[1] we will, in an exercise of caution, nonetheless make known our demand to bargain over the proposed change(s), to the fullest extent allowed by law. Moreover, the Union hereby proposes and insists that the [Respondent] hold any change(s) pertaining to the [Respondent's] proposal in abeyance until the completion of all phases of bargaining . . . .

1. At the hearing, the President testified that he found it unclear whether the Respondent was proposing to change "what level of supervision[]" would be able to approve birthday leave, or whether the Respondent was proposing to change the entire practice of changing birthday leave. Tr. at 26. In this regard, the President testified that he believed that the Respondent would be obligated to bargain only in the latter situation, not the former. *Id.* at 27.

Id. at 4. The President then submitted five proposals and reserved the right to submit additional proposals. *Id.*

The Respondent did not respond to the President's letter or communicate further with the Union regarding this matter during 2008. *Id.* In 2009, an employee whose birthday was January 2 did not receive birthday leave. *Id.* Subsequently, other employees ceased receiving such leave. *Id.* at 4.

When the Union learned that employees had been denied birthday leave, the President contacted the Respondent's liaison with the Union (the liaison). *Id.* at 5. The liaison told the President that he would "look into the situation," but did not follow up with the President. *Id.* at 5. Later, the President again discussed the situation with the liaison, who suggested that the President should contact the Respondent's legal office. *Id.* The President did so, but on June 29, 2009, filed the ULP charge at issue in this case. *Id.*

III. Judge's Decision

The Judge noted that, in its prehearing disclosure, the Respondent argued that the ULP charge was not timely filed and, thus, that the complaint should be dismissed based on § 7118(a)(4)(A) of the Statute.[2] Judge's Decision at 5. Addressing this issue, the Judge found that "[t]he Union was not aware that the change had been implemented, specifically that . . . employees were no longer receiving [birthday leave] until employees began to complain in early 2009." *Id.* at 6. In this regard, the Judge found that "[t]he first known instance in which an employee was not given [birthday leave] was on January 2, 2009[,]" which the Judge found was a Friday "in the middle of a pay period." *Id.* The Judge then determined that "[a]pparently, the beginning of the pay period . . . was December 28, 2008, the date referenced in the Respondent's July 29, 2008, letter to the Union." *Id.*

The Judge stated that although the Respondent's July 29 letter "is framed in terms of first line supervisors no longer having certain authority, it is also apparent that the asserted change will impact on bargaining unit employees . . . ." *Id.* The Judge also stated that the July 29 letter "gave an implementation date of December 28, 2008, and, although the Respondent did not afford the Union the opportunity to bargain prior to implementation, it also never indicated to the Union that it had rescinded the implementation date." *Id.* The Judge then concluded: "The Union was aware of the impact of the change on bargaining unit employees in early January 2009 and, therefore, should have been aware that the implementation date for the change was December 28, 2008." *Id.* The Judge dismissed the amended complaint as based on an untimely charge. For support, the Judge cited *United States Department of Labor*, 20 FLRA 296 (1985), *rev'd on other grounds*, 834 F.2d 174 (D.C. Cir. 1987) (*DOL*), and *United States Department of the Treasury, IRS & United States Department of the Treasury, IRS, Houston District*, 20 FLRA 51 (1985), *petition for review denied*, 798 F.2d 113 (5th Cir. 1986) (*IRS*).

IV. Positions of the Parties

A. GC's Exceptions

The GC argues that the Judge erred in finding that the charge was untimely filed. Exceptions at 9. As an initial matter, the GC argues that the disputed change occurred on January 2, 2009, and that the Judge erred in finding that it occurred on December 28, 2008. In this connection, according to the GC, the Respondent "has consistently taken the position that the change announced on July 29, 2008, was an intra-management change" -- i.e., a change in which specific management officials could approve birthday leave -- "over which [the Respondent] had no duty to bargain with the Union." *Id.* at 5. Also according to the GC, the Respondent's July 29 notice did not indicate that the policy of allowing birthday leave would change, and that the Union's August 8 letter sought clarification regarding the scope of the change. In this regard, the GC contends that if the proposed change merely changed the identity of the management official that could approve birthday

---

2. Section 7118(a)(4) of the Statute provides, in pertinent part:

> (A) Except as provided in subparagraph (B) of this paragraph, no complaint shall be issued on any alleged [ULP] which occurred more than 6 months before the filing of the charge with the Authority.
> (B) If the [GC] determines that the person filing any charge was prevented from filing the charge during the 6-month period referred to in subparagraph (A) of this paragraph by reason of--
> (i) any failure of the agency . . . against which the charge is made to perform a duty owed to the person; or
> (ii) any concealment which prevented discovery of the alleged [ULP] during the 6-month period,
> the [GC] may issue a complaint based on the charge if the charge was filed during the 6-month period beginning on the day of the discovery by the person of the alleged [ULP].

leave, then the change would not be negotiable, but if it was intended to eliminate the entitlement to birthday leave entirely, then "this was a matter on which the Union wanted to bargain." *Id.* at 6. The GC asserts that, based on the Respondent's failure to respond to "the Union's request for clarification and bargaining[,]" the Union "interpreted the notice as meaning on its face [that] it was to be simply an internal management change." *Id.* Further, the GC asserts that the change actually implemented was different from the change announced, in that it discontinued the practice of granting birthday leave altogether, rather than merely change the first-line supervisors' authority to approve such leave. *Id.* at 7. The GC contends that, consequently, the Respondent's July 29 notice did not provide adequate notice of the change. *Id.* at 11.

The GC also argues that the Judge erred by relying on the Respondent's argument concerning § 7118(a)(4) because, even though the Respondent's pre-hearing disclosure raised the issue of timeliness, the Respondent did not raise timeliness as a defense in its answer or its post-hearing brief. *Id.* at 8. Further, the GC contends that the Judge erred by failing to draw an adverse inference from the Respondent's failure to call a particular witness during the hearing. *See id.* at 3-5. Finally, the GC requests that the Authority find that the Respondent violated § 7116(a)(1) and (5) of the Statute as alleged and order various remedies. *See id.* at 13.

B. Respondent's Opposition

The Respondent argues that the evidence supports the Judge's conclusion that the charge was untimely. Opp'n at 3. In this regard, the Respondent notes that the President was aware that several employees were denied birthday leave "during or before the summer of 2008[.]" *Id.* Further, the Respondent contends that the Judge appropriately exercised her discretion to decline to make an adverse inference. *Id.* at 5-7.

V. Analysis and Conclusions

Section 7118(a)(4)(A) of the Statute requires that a charge be filed within six months of the alleged ULP. *U.S. DHS, Border & Transp. Sec. Directorate, Bureau of Customs & Border Prot., Wash., D.C.*, 60 FLRA 943, 950 (2005) (then-Member Pope concurring in part and dissenting in part on other grounds), *rev'd on other grounds*, 446 F.3d 162 (D.C. Cir. 2006), *decision on remand*, 63 FLRA 406, *reconsid. denied*, 63 FLRA 600 (2009). The Authority has recognized that, at times, a charging party may not learn of an alleged ULP immediately, either due to a respondent's failure to perform a duty owed to the charging party or because of the respondent's concealment of the alleged ULP. 60 FLRA at 950. In such circumstances, § 7118(a)(4)(B) of the Statute permits the GC to issue a complaint when the charging party has filed a ULP charge within six months of discovery of the alleged ULP. *Id.*

In addition, the Authority has held that notice of a proposed change in conditions of employment must be sufficiently specific and definitive to adequately provide the exclusive representative with a reasonable opportunity to request bargaining. *U.S. DOD, Def. Commissary Agency, Peterson Air Force Base, Colo. Springs, Colo.*, 61 FLRA 688, 692 (2006). For example, the notice must apprise the exclusive representative of the scope and nature of the proposed change in conditions of employment, the certainty of the change, and the planned timing of the change. *Id.* In this regard, the Authority has stated that "[t]he notice must be sufficient to inform the exclusive representative of what will be lost if it does not request bargaining." *U.S. Army Corps of Eng'rs, Memphis Dist., Memphis, Tenn.*, 53 FLRA 79, 82 (1997). Further, the Authority has held that the obligation to bargain under the Statute includes, at a minimum, the requirement that a party respond to a bargaining request. *Pension Benefit Guar. Corp.*, 59 FLRA 48, 52 (2003) (then-Member Pope dissenting in part on other grounds).

Although the Judge stated that "the change was implemented, as announced, on December 28," Judge's Decision at 7, she did not find that the Respondent actually took any actions on that date. In addition, there is conflicting record evidence on this point. In this regard, while the employee whose birthday is January 2 testified that the Respondent announced the change "a week before my birthday," Tr. at 57, another employee testified that he "believe[d] it was the first of the year[]" when the Respondent announced the change. *Id.* at 66.

Even assuming that the Respondent actually implemented the change on December 28, the Union did not learn of the change immediately because the Respondent failed to perform duties owed to the Union. In this regard, the Respondent did not provide the Union with adequate notice of the scope and nature of the change -- specifically, whether it merely eliminated the authority of first-line supervisors to grant birthday leave, or whether it wholly eliminated employees' entitlement to such leave. Although the Union reasonably questioned the scope and nature of the proposed change and requested bargaining as "an exercise of caution," Judge's Decision at 4, the Respondent neither clarified the scope and nature of the change nor responded to the bargaining request. In these circumstances, even assuming that the Respondent wholly eliminated employees' entitlement to birthday leave on December 28, the Union's lack of awareness, prior to January 2, that management had done so was due to the Respondent's failure to perform duties that it owed to the Union -- in particular, its duties to provide adequate notice of the change and to respond to the Union's bargaining request. Thus, the above-cited Authority precedent supports a finding that the charge, which was filed within six months of January 2, was timely filed.

The decisions cited by the Judge do not support a contrary conclusion. In this regard, unlike the charging party in *DOL*, the President did not merely wait over eight months after discovering the ULP before filing the charge. *See* 20 FLRA at 297. Instead, the President repeatedly attempted to seek more information from the Respondent, and filed the charge only after those attempts were unfruitful. *See* Judge's Decision at 5. Thus, unlike the charging party in *DOL*, the President had a reasonable reason for not immediately filing the charge.

Further, in *IRS*, the Authority found that: the Respondent announced an immediate change at "open meetings of employees[,]" to which the Union was invited; "thereafter, with rare exception," the newly implemented rule was followed; and the incident that the union asserted was the first time that it learned of the new rule "was but a continuation of the open and undisguised enforcement of this rule." 20 FLRA at 52. Similar circumstances are not present here.

For the foregoing reasons, we find that the charge was timely filed, and we reverse the Judge's dismissal of the amended complaint.

With regard to the GC's request that the Authority find a violation of the Statute and order various remedies, where a judge erroneously dismisses a complaint without addressing the merits of the complaint, and the record does not provide a sufficient basis for resolving those merits, the Authority remands the case. *E.g., U.S. Dep't of the Army, Human Res. Command, St. Louis, Mo.*, 64 FLRA 140, 144 (2009) (Member Beck dissenting in part on other grounds) (remanding where judge erroneously found complaint barred by § 7116(d) of the Statute). Here, before the Judge, the Respondent raised various affirmative defenses that the Judge did not resolve. *See, e.g.,* GC Ex. 1(g) at 4 (Respondent's Answer to Complaint). As the Judge did not resolve those defenses, and there is an insufficient basis in the record for doing so, we remand the amended complaint to the Judge for a determination on the merits.[3]

VI. Order

The amended complaint is remanded to the Judge for a determination on the merits.

3. Accordingly, it is unnecessary to resolve the GC's remaining exceptions.

Office of Administrative Law Judges

DEPARTMENT OF HOMELAND SECURITY
U.S. CUSTOMS AND BORDER PROTECTION
EL PASO, TEXAS
RESPONDENT

AND

AMERICAN FEDERATION
OF GOVERNMENT EMPLOYEES
NATIONAL BORDER PATROL COUNCIL
LOCAL 1929, AFL-CIO
CHARGING PARTY

Case No. DA-CA-09-0286

Nora E. Hinojosa, Esq.
For the General Counsel

Mark W. Hannig, Esq.
For the Respondent

James Stack
For the Charging Party

Before: SUSAN E. JELEN
Administrative Law Judge

DECISION

This case arose under the Federal Service Labor-Management Relations Statute, Chapter 71 of Title 5 of the United States Code, 5 U.S.C. §7101, *et. seq.* (the Statute), and the Rules and Regulations of the Federal Labor Relations Authority (the Authority/FLRA), 5 C.F.R. Part 2423.

On June 29, 2009, the American Federation of Government Employees, National Border Patrol Council, Local 1929, AFL-CIO (Charging Party/Union) filed an unfair labor practice charge with the Dallas Region of the Authority against the Department of Homeland Security, U.S. Customs and Border Protection, El Paso, Texas (Respondent). (G.C. Ex. 1(a)) On March 31, 2010, the Regional Director of the Dallas Region of the Authority issued a Complaint and Notice of Hearing, which alleged that the Respondent violated section 7116(a)(1) and (5) of the Statute by failing to respond to the Union's request to negotiate over the termination of the practice of allowing first-line supervisors the discretion of granting excused absence/administrative leave to bargaining unit employees and by implementing said change without providing the Union with an opportunity to negotiate over this change to the extent required by the Statute. (G.C. Ex. 1(c)) On April 16, 2010, the Respondent filed an Answer to the complaint, in which it admitted certain allegations while denying the substantive allegations of the complaint. (G.C. Ex. 1(g)) On April 21, 2010, the Dallas Regional Director issued an Amended Complaint and Notice of Hearing, which alleged that the Respondent violated section 7116(a)(1) and (5) of the Statute by terminating the practice of allowing first-line supervisors the discretion of granting excused absence/administrative leave to bargaining unit employees, thereby discontinuing the practice of granting administrative leave on or near the birthdays of the Sector Enforcement Specialists at the El Paso Sector. (G.C. Ex. 1(h)) At the hearing, Counsel for the General Counsel amended the complaint to change the date of the alleged termination of the above practice to January 2, 2009. (Tr. 6).

A hearing was held in El Paso, Texas, on May 11, 2010, at which time all parties were afforded a full opportunity to be represented, to be heard, to examine and cross-examine witnesses, to introduce evidence and to argue orally. The General Counsel and the Respondent filed timely post-hearing briefs, which have been fully considered.[1]

Based upon the entire record, including my observation of the witnesses and their demeanor, I make the following findings of fact, conclusions and recommendations.

STATEMENT OF THE FACTS

The Respondent is an agency within the meaning of section 7103(a)(3) of the Statute. (G.C. Ex. 1(c), 1(g), 1(h)). Victor Manjarrez occupied the position of Chief Patrol Agent for the El Paso Sector from approximately 2008 through 2010. He has since transferred to the Tucson Sector of U.S. Customs and Border Protection; Randy Hill has been the interim Chief Patrol Agent since May 2010. (G.C. Exs. 1(c), 1(g), 1(h); Tr. 86-87) At all times material to this matter, Manjarrez has been a supervisor and/or management official within the meaning of section 7103(a)(10) and (11) of the Statute. (G.C. Ex. 1(c), 1(g), 1(h)).

1. The GC's unopposed Motion to Correct the Transcript is granted.

The Union is a labor organization within the meaning of section 7103(a)(4) of the Statute. James Stack is a border patrol agent within the El Paso Sector and has served as President of AFGE Local 1929 since January 1999. (Tr. 19) Included within the bargaining unit are Sector Enforcement Specialists (SES), who work in communications and serve as support for border patrol agents in the field. There are approximately fifty (50) SES, with forty-three (43) located in El Paso and seven (7) located in Deming. SES work 24 hours a day, seven days a week. There are three shifts: 8:00 a.m. to 4:00 p.m.; 4:00 p.m. to midnight; midnight to 8:00 a.m. (Tr. 19-21, 54, 63, 72, 110).

SES employees are considered essential personnel who must be present whenever border patrol agents are in the field. In general, this means when employees were granted administrative leave on Christmas Eve or New Year's Eve, SES employees remained at work, although they were apparently paid holiday pay for this time. (Tr. 32-33, 54-55) Prior to January 2009, a practice had developed that, in compensation for not being allowed to leave work on administrative leave like other employees, the SES employees were allowed administrative leave on or near their birthdays. The testimony indicated that this practice had been ongoing for several years, since around 1988. (Tr. 64) Employees were not required to request administrative leave for their birthdays and their birthdays were automatically included in the work schedules. If, somehow, a birthday was not on the schedule, the employee would ask about it and it would be placed on the schedule. Generally, employees took their specific birthday, but could also take the administrative leave at any time during that two week leave period. (Tr. 65-66, 76).[2]

In July 2008,[3] Stack heard rumors that the administrative leave for the SES was going to be eliminated and wrote to Alvon Williams, Supervisory Sector Enforcement Specialist, El Paso Sector. In his letter of July 3, Stack protested the termination of the practice and requested that the Respondent re-implement the practice immediately, while suggesting slight modifications to the manner in which the employees claim compensation for this date. (G.C. Ex. 2; Tr. 24).

2. This practice only existed in the El Paso office; the SES in Deming did not receive administrative leave on or around their birthdays. (Tr. 110).

3. All dates are in 2008 unless otherwise specified.

On July 22, Chief Patrol Agent Manjarrez sent a letter informing Stack that he was rescinding the previous notice to the SESs, regarding the granting of a paid day-off for their birthdays. The letter also stated that "If management determines to revisit this issue, the union will be given official notification." (G.C. Ex. 3; Tr. 25-26).

On July 29, Manjarrez sent a letter to Stack, pursuant to provisions of Article 3A of the Negotiated Agreement between U.S. Immigration and Naturalization Service and National Border Patrol Council, stating, in part:

> This is to inform you that first line supervisors for the El Paso Sector do not have the authority or discretion to grant the El Paso Border Patrol Sector, Sector Enforcement Specialists (SESs), nor any other employee, excused absence to offset for time off-duty provided to other employees on Christmas Eve and New Year's Eve. Therefore, effective December 28, 2008, management will terminate the practice of allowing first line supervisors the discretion of granting excused absence/administrative leave related to holidays or birthdays. Terminating this practice on this date should provide affected employees, that is, those currently employed within El Paso Border Patrol Sector as of the date of this notice, with an adequate adjustment period. Management will continue to approve or disapprove "excused absences" in accordance with regulations and policy.

(G.C. Ex. 4).

Stack responded on August 8, stating that the Union was in need of additional information and clarification. The Union referred to its July 3 letter to Alvon Williams (G.C. Ex. 2) and requested certain information.[4]

Stack then stated:

> While we are not entirely sure if the agency's proposal is intended to impact, in any way, the affected bargaining unit employees' entitlement to excused absences/administrative leave, we will, in an

4. The complaint in this matter does not include any allegations regarding section 7114 (b)(4) and this request for information.

> exercise of caution, nonetheless make known our demand to bargain over the proposed change(s), to the fullest extent allowed by law. Moreover, the Union hereby proposes and insists that the agency hold any change(s) pertaining to the agency's proposal in abeyance until the completion of all phases of bargaining, including any attendant third-party resolution procedures, such as, but not limited to, assistance from the Federal Mediation and Conciliation Service or the Federal Service(s) Impasses Panel.

The Union then submitted five proposals, while it reserved the right to submit additional proposals. (G.C. Ex. 5 at 2; Tr. 27-29).

The Union received no response from this letter and had no further communications with the Respondent on this issue until 2009.

Guillermo Acosta has been an SES since June 2006. He received administrative leave for his birthday, January 2, in 2007 and 2008. He did not receive administrative leave for his birthday in 2009. (Tr. 55) He expressed his concern to his supervisor (Tr. 59), as did other SESs. (Tr. 79) None of the other SESs have received administrative leave for their birthdays since January 2009. (Tr. 66, 76).

After learning that the SES were not receiving administrative leave for their birthdays, Stack contacted Bill Torres, a supervisory border patrol agent and the Respondent's liaison with the Union. Torres told him he would look into the situation, but Stack never heard from him. (Tr. 22, 42) Stack discussed this issue with Torres again, who suggested that Stack contact the Respondent's legal office. (Tr. 23) Stack spoke to attorneys in that office but eventually filed the unfair labor practice charge in this case on June 29, 2009. (G.C. Ex. 1(a); Tr. 23).

TIMELINESS

In its prehearing disclosure,[5] the Respondent raised the issue of timeliness, arguing that the unfair labor practice charge in this matter was not filed in a timely manner and thus, the complaint should be dismissed based on section 7118(a)(4)(A) of the Statute. The Respondent made no mention of this defense in its brief; however, the General Counsel (GC) did argue that the charge had been timely filed. Specifically, the GC asserted that the change in the established practice of granting eight hours of excused absence/administrative leave to the SES on or near their birthdays was implemented on January 2, 2009. The parties' collective bargaining agreement provides that the Union is to receive notifications from Respondent of intended changes and provide the appropriate level of bargaining when the Respondent proposes changes in the working conditions of bargaining unit employees. The GC asserts that the record evidence shows that adequate notice was not provided to the Union President of the change and that the Union was not provided an opportunity to bargain over the change prior to its implementation. Since the change was implemented on January 2, 2009, and the unfair labor practice charge in this matter was filed on June 29, 2009, the charge was timely filed and the Respondent's argument should be rejected.

Section 7118(a)(4) states:

> (A) Except as provided in subparagraph (B) of this paragraph, no complaint shall be issued on any alleged unfair labor practice which occurred more than 6 months before the filing of the chargewith the Authority.
>
> (B) If the General Counsel determines that the person filing any charge was prevented from filing the charge during the 6-month period referred to in subparagraph (A) of this paragraph by reason of –
>
> (i) Any failure of the agency or labor organization against which the charge is made to perform a duty owed to the person; or
>
> (ii) any concealment which prevented discovery of the alleged unfair labor practice during the 6-month period.

The General Counsel may issue a complaint based on the charge if the charge was filed during the 6-month period beginning on the day of the discovery by the person of the alleged unfair labor practice.

In *U.S. Army Armament Research, Development and Engineering Ctr., Picatinny Arsenal, N.J.,*

5. Section 2423.23 of the Authority's Rules and Regulations requires that the parties shall exchange information which includes "[a] brief statement of the theory of the case, including relief sought, and any and all defenses to the allegations in the complaint."

52 FLRA 527, 532 (1996), the Authority states that "[s]tatutes of limitation[s] are affirmative defenses and, as such, are waived unless raised in the pleadings or at trial." *Id.* at 532. The Authority further found that section 7118(a)(4) of the Statute "is an affirmative defense[.]" *Id.* at 534. Although the Respondent did not argue this defense in its brief, since the issue of timeliness was raised in the pleadings, I find this issue is properly before me.

The record evidence shows that the Respondent sent a letter to the Union on July 29, 2008, giving the Union notice that "... effective December 28, 2008, management will terminate the practice of allowing first line supervisors the discretion of granting excused absence/administrative leave related to holidays or birthdays. Terminating this practice on this date should provide affected employees, that is, those currently employed within El Paso Border Patrol Sector as of the date of this notice, with an adequate adjustment period...." (G.C. Ex. 4) The Union responded on August 8, requesting clarification and also requesting to bargain over the proposed change(s) to the fullest extent allowed by law. (G.C. Ex. 5) The Union received no further correspondence from the Respondent on this issue. The Union was not aware that the change had been implemented, specifically that SES employees were no longer receiving administrative leave/excused absence on or around their birthdays until employees began to complain in early 2009. The first known instance in which an employee was not given administrative leave for his birthday was on January 2, 2009. January 2 occurred on a Friday in 2009, which would be in the middle of a pay period. Apparently, the beginning of the pay period for the Respondent's employees was December 28, 2008, the date referenced in the Respondent's July 29, 2008, letter to the Union. (G.C. Ex. 4).

Although Respondent's July 29 notice to the Union is framed in terms of first line supervisors no longer having certain authority, it is also apparent that the asserted change will impact on bargaining unit employees, *i.e.* by essentially eliminating administrative leave on or around the SES birthdays. The evidence is clear that the Respondent's July 29 letter gave an implementation date of December 28, 2008, and, although the Respondent did not afford the Union the opportunity to bargain prior to implementation, it also never indicated to the Union that it had rescinded the implementation date. The Union was aware of the impact of the change on bargaining unit employees in early January 2009 and, therefore, should have been aware that the implementation date for the change was December 28, 2008. *See U.S. Dep't of the Treas., IRS and U.S. Dep't of the Treas., IRS, Houston District,* 20 FLRA 51 (1985) (Respondent's conduct did not prevent the Union from filing the charge within six months of the meetings where the dress code was announced.) *See also U.S. Dep't of Labor,* 20 FLRA 296 (1985).

Even though the GC amended the complaint to allege that the change was implemented on or about January 2, 2009, I find the record evidence establishes that the change was implemented, as announced, on December 28, 2008, rather than the date of the first affected employee's birthday. With the implementation date of December 28, 2008, the Union had six months from that date to file the charge in this matter. I find that the Respondent's conduct did not preclude the Union from filing the charge within six months. *Cf. Air Force Accounting and Finance Ctr., Lowry AFB, Denver, Colo.,* 42 FLRA 1226 (1991). Since the charge was filed on June 29, 2009, it was untimely filed under section 7118(4)(A) and thus no violation may be found.

Since I have found that the charge in this matter was untimely filed under section 7118(4)(A) of the Statute, no other discussion is necessary.

Accordingly, I recommend that the Authority adopt the following Order:

ORDER

It is ordered that the complaint be, and hereby is, dismissed.

Issued, Washington, D.C., September 16, 2010

SUSAN E. JELEN
ADMINISTRATIVE LAW JUDGE

65 FLRA No. 89

AMERICAN FEDERATION
OF GOVERNMENT EMPLOYEES
LOCAL 1815
(Union)

and

UNITED STATES
DEPARTMENT OF THE ARMY
U.S. ARMY AVIATION CENTER
OF EXCELLENCE
FORT RUCKER, ALABAMA
(Agency)

0-AR-4666

DECISION

January 20, 2011

Before the Authority: Carol Waller Pope, Chairman, and Thomas M. Beck and Ernest DuBester, Members

I. Statement of the Case

This matter is before the Authority on an exception to an award of Arbitrator William H. Mills filed by the Union under § 7122(a) of the Federal Service Labor-Management Relations Statute (the Statute) and part 2425 of the Authority's Regulations. The Agency filed an opposition to the Union's exception.[1]

The Arbitrator found that the grievance was substantively non-arbitrable. For the following reasons, we deny the Union's exception.

II. Background and Arbitrator's Award

The Agency requires employees to undergo periodic medical examinations. Award at 1-2. The Union filed a grievance on behalf of all bargaining unit employees requesting that the parties enter into a memorandum of agreement or memorandum of understanding to clarify whether the Agency or employees bore the responsibility for paying these medical examinations when performed by private physicians or medical facilities. *Id.* The grievance was unresolved and submitted to arbitration. *Id.* at 2.

Prior to the arbitration hearing, the Agency challenged the substantive arbitrability of the grievance, and the parties agreed that the Arbitrator should resolve the arbitrability issue before addressing the merits of the case. *Id.* Accordingly, the Arbitrator framed the threshold issue as: "Is the present dispute arbitrable?" *Id.* at 1.

As an initial matter, the Arbitrator noted that "[i]t seems inescapable that the Union's grievance is seeking to compel midterm bargaining." *Id.* at 14. Relying on the Supreme Court's decision in *National Federation of Federal Employees, Local 1309 v. Department of the Interior*, 526 U.S. 86 (1999) (*NFFE*), he further found that the Authority has "the sole power to determine 'whether, when, and where midterm bargaining is required[,]'" and, therefore, "an arbitrator obviously has no authority to compel it." Award at 16-17. Accordingly, the Arbitrator dismissed the grievance as non-arbitrable. *Id.* at 17.

III. Positions of the Parties

A. Union's Exception

The Union contends that the Arbitrator "appears to misunderstand that the matter grieved was simply a 'follow the prevailing law' [g]rievance issue . . . and [that] this matter was never a request to change or amend, add to, or delete from [the parties' agreement], . . . which is the predicate goal and intent of mid-term bargaining[.]" Exception at 1-2. The Union further argues that the "[i]nterpretation of pre-existing regulation[s] or issues between the two parties to the [parties' agreement] is not an attempt to initiate formal mid-term bargaining[.]" *Id.* at 2.

B. Agency's Opposition

The Agency asserts that the Union's exception does not "address with specificity . . . how the award violates [the] law or is otherwise deficient on other grounds[.]" Opp'n at 2. It also asserts that the Arbitrator made a procedural arbitrability determination, and that the Union's exception challenging that determination does not provide a basis for finding the award deficient. *Id.* at 3.

1. In addition, as discussed below, the Authority issued an Order to Show Cause why the exception should not be dismissed, and the parties filed supplemental submissions.

IV. Preliminary Issue

Although the Authority's Regulations do not provide for the filing of supplemental submissions, § 2429.26 of the Authority's Regulations provides that the Authority may, in its discretion, grant leave to file "other documents" as deemed appropriate. *See, e.g., Cong. Research Employees Ass'n, IFPTE, Local 75*, 59 FLRA 994, 999 (2004). The Authority generally will not consider submissions filed without requesting leave or permission. *See, e.g, NAIL, Local 6*, 63 FLRA 232, 232 n.1 (2009) (*NAIL*). In addition, where the Authority does not consider a submission, it also generally does not consider filings that respond to that submission. *See U.S. Dep't of the Army, Corps of Eng'rs, Portland Dist.*, 62 FLRA 97, 98 (2007) (*Corps of Eng'rs*).

The Union filed a motion to strike the Agency's opposition. *See* Union's Motion to Strike. As the Union failed to request permission to file its motion to strike, we do not consider it. *See NAIL*, 63 FLRA at 232 n.1.

The Agency requested leave to file a response to the Union's motion to strike. However, as the submission responds to arguments raised in a submission that we have not considered, we do not consider it. *See Corps of Eng'rs*, 62 FLRA at 98.

In addition, after the Authority issued an Order to Show Cause directing the Union to correct procedural deficiencies in the filing of its exception, the Union filed a response that includes arguments concerning the award. To the extent that these arguments constitute exceptions to the award, they are untimely, and we do not consider them.

The Agency filed a supplemental submission arguing that the Authority should not consider the additional merits arguments in the Union's response to the Order to Show Cause. As we have not considered those arguments, we need not consider the Agency's supplemental submission responding to those arguments. *Id.*

V. Analysis and Conclusions

As an initial matter, the Agency claims that the Union is challenging a procedural arbitrability determination. Procedural arbitrability involves "procedural questions, such as whether the preliminary steps of the grievance procedure have been exhausted or excused," and is distinguished from substantive arbitrability, which involves questions regarding whether "the *subject matter* of a dispute is arbitrable." *Fraternal Order of Police, New Jersey Lodge 173*, 58 FLRA 384, 385 (2003) (Chairman Cabaniss dissenting) (quoting Elkouri & Elkouri, *How Arbitration Works* 305) (Marlin M. Volz & Edward P. Goggin eds., 5th ed. 1997). As the Arbitrator's arbitrability determination was based on the subject matter of the grievance, not a procedural provision of the parties' agreement, he made a substantive -- not procedural -- arbitrability determination. Thus, we find that the Agency's argument does not provide a basis for declining to consider the merits of the Union's exception.

We construe the Union's contention that the Arbitrator "appears to misunderstand . . . the matter grieved" as an argument that the Arbitrator exceeded his authority by failing to resolve an issue submitted to arbitration and/or resolving an issue not submitted to arbitration. Arbitrators exceed their authority when they fail to resolve an issue submitted to arbitration, resolve an issue not submitted to arbitration, disregard specific limitations on their authority, or award relief to persons who are not encompassed within the grievance. *See U.S. Dep't of the Navy, Naval Base, Norfolk, Va.*, 51 FLRA 305, 307-08 (1995). In the absence of a stipulated issue, an arbitrator's formulation of the issues is accorded substantial deference. *See AFGE, Local 933*, 58 FLRA 480, 482 (2003) (*AFGE*). In addition, an arbitrator does not exceed his or her authority where the award is directly responsive to the formulated issues. *See, e.g., AFGE, Local 4044, Council of Prisons Local 33*, 57 FLRA 98, 99 (2001).

Here, the parties did not stipulate to the issues before the Arbitrator. The Arbitrator framed the issue as: "Is the present dispute arbitrable?" Award at 1. In resolving this issue, the Arbitrator determined that "the Union's grievance is seeking to compel midterm bargaining[,]" and that "an arbitrator . . . has no authority to compel it." *Id.* at 14, 17. In making the foregoing findings, the award was directly responsive to the issue as formulated by the Arbitrator. The Union provides no basis for finding that the Arbitrator either failed to resolve an issue that was properly before him or resolved an issue that was not properly before him. Thus, the Union has not demonstrated that the Arbitrator exceeded his authority, and we deny the exception.[2]

VI. Decision

The Union's exceptions are denied.

2. We note that the Arbitrator found that, based on the Supreme Court's decision in *NFFE*, he could not direct the parties to engage in mid-term bargaining. Award at 15-17. The issue before the Court in *NFFE* was whether the "duty to bargain extends to a clause proposed by a union that would bind the parties to bargain mid-term[.]" 526 U.S. at 88. In resolving that question, the Court concluded that "the Statute delegates to the FLRA the legal power to determine whether the parties must engage in mid-term bargaining[.]" *Id.* The Court did not address whether arbitrators may, or may not, direct parties to engage in mid-term bargaining. In any event, although the Union cites decisions involving the right to engage in mid-term bargaining, the Union's exception appears to be arguing that the issue of mid-term bargaining was not before the Arbitrator. Accordingly, we do not construe the exception as alleging that the award is contrary to law.

65 FLRA No. 90

UNITED STATES
DEPARTMENT OF HOUSING AND
URBAN DEVELOPMENT
(Agency)

and

AMERICAN FEDERATION
OF GOVERNMENT EMPLOYEES
NATIONAL COUNCIL OF HUD LOCALS 222
(Union)

0-AR-4586

DECISION

January 26, 2011

Before the Authority: Carol Waller Pope, Chairman, and Thomas M. Beck and Ernest DuBester, Members

I. Statement of the Case

This matter is before the Authority on exceptions to an award of Arbitrator Andrée Y. McKissick filed by the Agency under § 7122(a) of the Federal Service Labor-Management Relations Statute (the Statute) and part 2425 of the Authority's Regulations. The Union filed an opposition to the Agency's exceptions.

The Union filed a grievance alleging that the Agency violated the parties' agreement by failing to promote the grievants. *See U.S. Dep't of Hous. & Urban Dev.*, 59 FLRA 630, 630 (2004) (*HUD*). In her merits award (the MA), the Arbitrator sustained the grievance and awarded an "organizational upgrade" to the grievants. MA at 16. For the reasons that follow, we set aside the remedy and remand the MA to the parties for resubmission to the Arbitrator, absent settlement, to formulate an alternative remedy.

II. Background and Arbitrator's Award

The Union filed a grievance alleging that the Agency's advertising and filling of certain positions with promotion potential to General Schedule (GS)-13 deprived employees occupying similar positions with promotion potential to GS-12 of the opportunity to be promoted to GS-13. *HUD*, 59 FLRA at 630. In response, the Agency asserted, as relevant here, that the grievance was not arbitrable under § 7121(c)(5) of the Statute because it concerned the classification of positions.[1] *Id.* The parties proceeded to arbitration on the stipulated issue of arbitrability, and the Arbitrator issued an award (First Arbitrability Award, or First AA) finding that the grievance involved "the fairness of advertisements and vacancy announcements, not the proper classification of a position and one's concurrent duties." *Id.* (citing First AA at 6) (internal quotation marks omitted). Therefore, the Arbitrator found that the grievance was arbitrable.

The Agency filed exceptions to the First AA, and, in *HUD*, the Authority found that the Agency presented a plausible jurisdictional defect that warranted interlocutory consideration of the exceptions – namely, whether the grievance concerned classification, under § 7121(c)(5) of the Statute. 59 FLRA at 631. However, the Authority could not determine whether the Arbitrator had found that the grievance concerned "re*classifying* the grievants' permanent positions" or "re*assigning* the grievants to . . . newly-established, already-classified positions[.]" *Id.* at 632 (emphases added). The Authority stated that the "distinction between the two [findings] is critical because the Arbitrator: (1) would not have jurisdiction over a grievance concerning the promotion potential of employees' permanent positions; but (2) would have jurisdiction over a grievance alleging a right to be placed in previously-classified positions." *Id.* Accordingly, the Authority remanded the First AA for resubmission to the Arbitrator for clarification of the arbitrability issue. *Id.* On resubmission, the Arbitrator clarified that she found the "grievance [to be] alleging a right to be placed in previously-classified positions [with promotional potential to GS-13] and . . . thus arbitrable." Second Arbitrability Award (Second AA) (Opp'n, Attach., Ex. 2) at 1; *see also id.* at 6, 8.[2]

1. Under § 7121(c)(5) of the Statute, a grievance concerning "the classification of any position which does not result in the reduction in grade or pay of an employee" is excluded from the scope of the negotiated grievance procedure. 5 U.S.C. § 7121(c)(5).

2. The Agency filed exceptions to the Second AA, but the Authority's Office of Case Intake and Publication dismissed them as untimely filed. *See* MA at 2.

Thereafter, the Arbitrator issued the MA, which resolved the grievance's merits. In that award, the Arbitrator first recounted her earlier finding that the "grievance was arbitrable, as [it] was based upon the right to be placed in previously classified positions." MA at 2. She then stated that the issues for resolution in the MA were: "Whether the Agency violated the [c]ollective [b]argaining [a]greement [(CBA)], [l]aw[, r]ule, or other regulation [by] fail[ing] to treat bargaining unit employees fairly and equitably [at the time it] post[ed] vacancy announcement[s for newly-created positions] . . . until the present? If so, what are the appropriate remedies?" *Id.* at 3.

Because the Agency did not disclose information, including vacancy announcements, that the Arbitrator had previously directed it to provide to the Union, the Arbitrator drew an adverse inference against the Agency regarding the advertising and selection for newly-created positions with promotion potential to GS-13. *Id.* at 10-11. The Arbitrator also found that the Agency failed to rebut Union witnesses' testimony that "they were told by their supervisors that their applications to various [advertised, newly-created] positions would be destroyed, or not considered, and they should not apply." *Id.* at 12. Therefore, the Arbitrator concluded that the "evidence supports the Union's case that the [g]rievants were . . . not considered for selections [and were] dissuaded from applying" for positions with promotion potential to GS-13. *Id.* at 15.

The Arbitrator concluded that "but for these inequitable and unfair situations . . . , these affected positions [sic] should have been promoted to the journeyman level to GS-13 retroactively . . . ." *Id.* at 15. The Arbitrator found that the Agency's actions violated the following provisions of the CBA: (1) Article 4, Sections 4.01 and 4.06, "as these [g]rievants were unfairly treated and were unjustly discriminated against[;]" (2) Article 9, Section 9.01, "as classification standards were not fairly and equitably applied[;]" and (3) Article 13, Section 13.01, as the Agency "sought to hire external applicants, instead of promoting and facilitating the career development of internal employees." MA at 15. As for the appropriate remedy, the Arbitrator directed "an organizational upgrade of affected positions by upgrading the journeyman level for all the subject positions to [the] GS-13 level retroactively[.]" *Id.* at 16.

III. Positions of the Parties

A. Agency's Exceptions

The Agency contends that, by requiring an "organizational upgrade" of the grievants' positions, the award improperly: (1) classifies positions, in violation of law; (2) awards promotions, in violation of applicable regulations; (3) interferes with management's rights under the Statute; (4) exceeds the authority of the Arbitrator; and (5) violates the CBA. Exceptions at 2. According to the Agency, because the award directs "[t]he elevation of the grade of a position[,]" it "by definition[] requires [the position's] reclassification[,]" contrary to law. *Id.* at 2, 3 n.1. In addition, the Agency argues that the award provides the grievants with noncompetitive promotions, contrary to 5 C.F.R. § 335.103(c)(1)(v).[3] *Id.* at 3. Further, the Agency contends that the award "prohibits the Agency from removing duties from the positions encumbered by the grievants" and, consequently, violates its statutory rights to "determine its organization, assign work, and determine the grades of employees assigned to its organization." *Id.* at 4 (citing 5 U.S.C. § 7106(a), (b)(1)).[4] Moreover, the Agency contends that the award is deficient because the Arbitrator assumed classification authority that she did not possess under

---

3. 5 C.F.R. § 335.103 provides, in pertinent part:

> (c) Covered personnel actions--
>
> (1) Competitive actions. Except as provided in paragraphs (c)(2) and (3) of this section, competitive procedures in agency promotion plans apply . . . to the following actions:
>
> . . . .
>
> (v) Transfer to a position at a higher grade or with more promotion potential than a position previously held on a permanent basis in the competitive service . . . .

5 C.F.R. § 335.103(c)(1)(v).

4. The Agency notes that management's rights are incorporated into the CBA, and, therefore, the Agency argues that the award's alleged violations of management's rights contravene both the Statute and the CBA. *See* Exceptions at 4 (citing CBA Art. 3, § 3.06 (Exceptions, Attach. 3 at 7) (CBA provisions restating 5 U.S.C. § 7106(a)-(b)).

law or the CBA. *See id.* at 2-3 (citing CBA Art. 23, § 23.10(2) (Exceptions, Attach. 3 at 121)).[5] Finally, the Agency asserts that the award grants noncompetitive promotions in violation of the CBA. *Id.* at 3-4 (citing CBA Art. 13, § 13.09 (Exceptions, Attach. 3 at 58-59) (describing the application process "[t]o be considered for a vacancy")).

B. Union's Opposition

The Union asserts that the exceptions ignore the Arbitrator's clear statement that the MA determined "whether the bargaining unit employees were treated unfairly and inequitably with regard to *already* classified vacant positions[.]" Opp'n at 7 (citing MA). In this regard, the Union contends that the "remedy does not require [the] reclassification of employees presently at the GS-12 level, but rather [requires] that the Agency promote or reassign bargaining unit employees to the already classified positions."[6] *Id.* at 8. The Union argues that the remedy can be viewed as "direct[ing] the Agency to permanently[,] retroactively promote all affected [employees] into currently existing career ladder positions[.]" *Id.* at 16. In addition, the Union argues that an "organizational upgrade" will "remedy the Agency's failure to give the bargaining unit employees . . . proper consideration at the time of the competitive hiring/promotion actions." *Id.* at 11; *see also id.* at 9. In the alternative, the Union argues that the awarded "organizational upgrade can also be viewed as an accretion of duties, a valid and lawful remedy." *Id.* at 11. Finally, the Union contends that the award "is silent as to the prospective treatment of bargaining unit employees[,]" and, thus, does not violate management's rights by prohibiting the Agency from "removing duties from positions encumbered by bargaining unit employees[.]" *Id.* at 15.

IV. Analysis and Conclusions

The Agency argues that the award is contrary to law because it requires the reclassification of positions. When an exception involves an award's consistency with law, the Authority reviews any question of law raised by the exception and the award de novo. *See NTEU, Chapter 24*, 50 FLRA 330, 332 (1995) (citing *U.S. Customs Serv. v. FLRA*, 43 F.3d 682, 686-87 (D.C. Cir. 1994)). In applying the standard of de novo review, the Authority assesses whether an arbitrator's legal conclusions are consistent with the applicable standard of law. *See U.S. Dep't of Def., Dep'ts of the Army & the Air Force, Ala. Nat'l Guard, Northport, Ala.*, 55 FLRA 37, 40 (1998). In making that assessment, the Authority defers to the arbitrator's underlying factual findings. *See id.*

The Authority has repeatedly held that where the essential nature of a grievance concerns the grade level of the duties assigned to and performed by the grievant in his or her permanent position, the grievance concerns the classification of a position within the meaning of § 7121(c)(5) of the Statute. *E.g., U.S. Dep't of Labor, Wash., D.C.*, 64 FLRA 829, 830 (2010) (citing *U.S. EPA, Region 2*, 61 FLRA 671, 675 (2006) (*EPA*)); *SSA, Balt., Md.*, 20 FLRA 694, 694-95 (1985). In addition, a grievance concerns classification within the meaning of § 7121(c)(5) if it contends that the grievant's permanent position warrants a change in its journeyman level or promotion potential. *U.S. Dep't of Labor*, 63 FLRA 216, 218 (2009) (*DOL*) (citing *HUD*, 59 FLRA at 632). In contrast, "a disputed failure to promote a grievant under a competitive procedure . . . does not concern classification matters." *U.S. Dep't of the Air Force, Air Educ. & Training Command, Randolph Air Force Base, San Antonio, Tex.*, 49 FLRA 1387, 1389 (1994); *see also U.S. Dep't of the Army, Fort Campbell, Ky.*, 37 FLRA 1102, 1107, 1109 (1990).

Where an exception alleges that a grievance or award concerns classification in violation of § 7121(c)(5), the Authority may analyze *both* the nature of the grievance *and* the nature of the award including the awarded remedy – in order to determine whether the award is contrary to law. *E.g., U.S. Dep't of Veterans Affairs, Med. Ctr., Muskogee, Okla.*, 47 FLRA 1112, 1117 (1993); *U.S. Dep't of Agric., Agric. Research Serv., E. Reg'l Research Ctr.*, 20 FLRA 508, 509 (1985). In this regard, an award may be contrary to law because it concerns classification within the meaning of § 7121(c)(5) based on the remedy. *See U.S. Envtl. Prot. Agency, Region 2*, 59 FLRA 520, 524-25 (2003) (*EPA, Region 2*).

5. Article 23, Section 23.10(2) of the CBA provides, in relevant part, "The Arbitrator shall not have authority to add to, subtract from, or modify any of the terms of th[e CBA], or any supplement thereto." Exceptions, Attach. 3 at 121 (CBA Art. 23, § 23.10(2)).

6. According to the Union, "[t]his exact same remedy was addressed in the [parties' m]emorandum of [u]nderstanding, where the Agency agreed to the reassignment of employees to reclassified positions." Opp'n at 8.

In response to the Authority's decision in *HUD*, the Arbitrator found that the grievants "alleg[ed] a right to be placed in previously-classified positions[.]" Second AA at 1. The Arbitrator identified the previously-classified positions at issue as those newly-created positions – similar to the grievants' positions – with promotion potential to GS-13, and the Arbitrator credited the grievants' unrebutted testimony that they were "told by their supervisors that their applications to [these] various positions would be destroyed, or not considered, and they should not apply." MA at 12. The Arbitrator concluded that, "but for these inequitable and unfair situations[,]" the grievants would have been promoted to positions with GS-13 potential. *Id.* at 15. These findings support the Arbitrator's determination that the grievance was arbitrable because it did not concern classification within the meaning of § 7121(c)(5).

However, the remedy chosen by the Arbitrator – directing the Agency to perform an organizational *upgrade* of affected *positions* by *upgrading the journeyman level* for all the subject positions to GS-13 retroactively – involves classification. MA at 16 (emphases added); *see DOL*, 63 FLRA at 218; *cf. EPA, Region 2*, 59 FLRA at 525 (finding "substance of the grievance . . . [was not] barred by § 7121(c)(5)[,]" but setting aside award, in part, because remedial directions concerned classification, in part). In this regard, although the Arbitrator found that the grievance involved "previously-classified positions[,]" Second AA at 1, her remedy directs the Agency to *re*classify the grievants' *existing positions* by raising their journeyman level. As the Authority stated in *HUD*, the Statute does not authorize the Arbitrator to change the "promotion potential of employees' permanent positions[.]" *HUD*, 59 FLRA at 632. Moreover, although the Union asserts that a permanent-promotion remedy based on an accretion of duties to the grievants' positions would not involve classification within the meaning of § 7121(c)(5), the Authority has held to the contrary. *See, e.g.*, *EPA*, 61 FLRA at 675 (citing *AFGE, Local 2142*, 61 FLRA 194, 196 (2005)). For these reasons, the Arbitrator's remedy is contrary to law because it concerns classification matters, and we set it aside.

In cases where the Authority sets aside an entire remedy, but an arbitrator's finding of an underlying violation is left undisturbed, the Authority remands the award for determination of an alternative remedy. *See, e.g.*, *U.S. Dep't of Transp., FAA, Salt Lake City, Utah*, 63 FLRA 673, 676 (2009). As we have set aside the MA's entire remedy, we remand the MA to the parties for resubmission to the Arbitrator, absent settlement, to formulate an alternative remedy.[7]

V. Decision

For the foregoing reasons, we set aside the remedy and remand the MA to the parties for resubmission to the Arbitrator, absent settlement, to formulate an alternative remedy.

---

7. Because the Agency's remaining exceptions challenge the remedy that we set aside, they are moot, and we do not address them.

65 FLRA No. 91

AMERICAN FEDERATION
OF GOVERNMENT EMPLOYEES
LOCAL 3310
(Union)

and

UNITED STATES
DEPARTMENT OF THE ARMY
UNITED STATES
ARMY CORPS OF ENGINEERS
ENGINEER RESEARCH &
DEVELOPMENT CENTER
WATERWAYS EXPERIMENT STATION
VICKSBURG, MISSISSIPPI
(Agency)

0-AR-4259

DECISION

January 27, 2011

Before the Authority: Carol Waller Pope, Chairman, and Thomas M. Beck and Ernest DuBester, Members

I. Statement of the Case

This matter is before the Authority on exceptions to an award of Arbitrator William J. McGinnis filed by the Union under § 7122(a) of the Federal Service Labor-Management Relations Statute (the Statute) and part 2425 of the Authority's Regulations. The Agency did not file an opposition to the Union's exceptions.

The grievant was accused of stealing wire from the Agency and was suspended for fourteen days. The Union grieved the discipline. The Arbitrator denied the grievance, finding that the Agency had just cause to suspend the grievant.

For the reasons set forth below, the Union's exceptions are dismissed in part and denied in part.

II. Background and Arbitrator's Award

This case concerns the suspension of the grievant, an electrician, while a criminal charge was pending against him. An Agency surveillance camera recorded the grievant's truck exiting his place of employment with what the Agency alleged were two spools of wire that belonged to the Agency. The Agency contacted the police and the grievant was later arrested for criminal embezzlement. Award at 3.

The Agency conducted an investigation into the grievant's conduct. The Union requested that the Agency delay the administrative disciplinary proceeding until after final disposition of the criminal charge. The Agency refused. Two months after the alleged offense occurred, while the criminal charge was still pending, the grievant's supervisor issued a notice proposing that the grievant be suspended for fourteen days for the unauthorized possession of government property. The Agency subsequently imposed the suspension. *Id.* at 7-8.

The Union filed a grievance over the suspension. When the grievance was not resolved, it was submitted to arbitration. The Arbitrator framed the issues as: "Did the Agency have [j]ust [c]ause to suspend the [g]rievant for 14 days under the [c]ollective [b]argaining [a]greement [CBA]? If not, what shall the remedy be?" [1] *Id.* at 1. The Union requested that the Agency delay the arbitration hearing until after final disposition of the criminal charge. Once again, the Agency refused. The arbitration hearing was held while the criminal charge was still pending. *Id.* at 2-3.

Before the Arbitrator, the Union contended that the grievant's Fifth Amendment privilege against self-incrimination was violated because the Agency failed to delay the administrative disciplinary proceeding and the arbitration hearing until after final disposition of the criminal matter. *Id.* at 8.

Based on a preponderance of the record evidence, the Arbitrator concluded that the Agency established just cause for the grievant's suspension under the CBA.[2] *Id.* at 12-13, 15. The Arbitrator applied "Seven Tests" of just cause that, as the Arbitrator noted, "were developed by the renown[ed] Arbitrator Carroll R. Daugherty[.]" *Id.* at 10-11. The Arbitrator applied the "Seven Tests" because he found that "they have been acknowledged as the fair and equitable method to determine if the just cause

1. The relevant contract provisions are set forth in the attached appendix.

2. In his award, the Arbitrator determined that the burden was on the Agency to prove by a preponderance of the evidence that the grievant was suspended for just cause. Award at 10.

standard has been met by an employer." *Id.* at 11. As applied, the Seven Tests are: "Notice, Reasonableness of Rule or order, Investigation, Fair Investigation, Proof, Equal Treatment and Penalty." *Id.*

First, the Arbitrator found that the grievant had prior notice that the unauthorized possession of government property was an offense under Agency regulations. *Id.* Second, he found that the Agency regulation is reasonable. Third, the Arbitrator found that the Agency conducted a "thorough and extensive" investigation of the alleged offense prior to the imposition of the discipline. *Id.* He added that the administrative investigation was "relevant to the alleged offense" and produced sufficient evidence to make a determination as to whether the grievant committed an offense. *Id.* Fourth, the Arbitrator found that the Agency's investigation of the alleged offense was conducted objectively and without bias towards the grievant. *Id.* at 11-12. Fifth, the Arbitrator found that the evidence the Agency gathered during the investigation, including identification of the truck on the surveillance camera tape, constituted sufficient proof that the grievant should be disciplined. *Id.* at 12. Sixth, the Arbitrator found that there was no evidence that the Agency provided the grievant unequal treatment during the investigation. The Arbitrator stated that the Agency conducted the investigation fairly and without discrimination. *Id.* Seventh, the Arbitrator found the discipline reasonably related to the seriousness of the grievant's offense and the grievant's past record. *Id.*

Accordingly, applying the Seven Tests, the Arbitrator concluded that the Agency had established just cause under the CBA for the grievant's suspension. *Id.* at 12-13. In so concluding, the Arbitrator found that "[t]he grievant was given every opportunity to rebut the allegations against him[,]" but that he failed to do so. *Id.* at 13. In the Arbitrator's opinion, the grievant's "testimony on direct was significantly limited and failed to address the numerous issues raised during management's presentation of [its] case against him." *Id.* This was so despite "[a]ny alleged restraint on [the grievant's] ability to testify during the arbitration hearing was removed" based on "notice from his legal counsel . . . that he would not be indicted for embezzlement[.]" *Id.*

III. Union's Exceptions

The Union contends that the award violates the grievant's Fifth Amendment privilege against self-incrimination because the Agency failed to delay the administrative disciplinary proceeding and the arbitration hearing until after final disposition of the criminal matter. Exceptions at 7-8. The Union also argues that the Arbitrator erred in finding that any chilling effect on the grievant's ability to exercise his Fifth Amendment privilege was removed because, before the hearing, the grievant had been advised by his attorney that he would not be indicted. *Id.* at 7-8. The Union asserts that the grievant's concerns over his rights were not removed because the attorney's advice constituted merely "opinion." *Id.* at 7.

In addition, the Union contends that the award fails to draw its essence from Article 21 of the CBA on three grounds. *Id.* at 10-14. First, the Union argues that the award fails to comply with Article 21, Sections 2, 3, and 5, which require that disciplinary actions be timely imposed after the offense is committed. *Id.* at 10-11. The Union asserts that the award erroneously fails to find that the Agency did not timely impose the disciplinary action. *Id.* The Union states that the Agency imposed the proposed suspension approximately two months after the Agency completed the investigation. *Id.*

Second, the Union argues that the award fails to comply with Article 21, Section 2, which requires that discipline be for just cause. *Id.* at 11. The Union argues that the award is deficient because it fails to find that the Agency conducted the administrative investigation inconsistent with due process. *Id.* at 11, 12. The Union asserts, among other things, that the Agency did not provide the grievant an opportunity to confront his accusers. *Id.* at 11-12.

Third, the Union argues that the award fails to comply with Article 21, Sections 4 and 5, which require that the Agency attempt to ascertain all the pertinent facts both for and against the grievant before the imposition of disciplinary action. *Id.* at 13. The Union argues that the award erroneously finds that the Agency conducted a thorough and fair administrative investigation. The Union states that, in the course of the investigation, the Agency failed to gather evidence that supported the grievant's innocence such as statements from the grievant and employees who discovered the property missing. *Id.* at 12, 14.

Furthermore, the Union contends that the Arbitrator applied the incorrect burden of proof in this case. *Id.* at 14. The Union asserts that the correct burden is "beyond a reasonable doubt." *Id.* at 14-15.

Next, the Union contends that the award violates the Fourth and Fourteenth Amendments because the Agency conducted an unreasonable search and seizure by means of the surveillance camera tape. *Id.* at 4-7. Finally, the Union contends that the award is inconsistent with Agency rules and regulations concerning the administration of Agency property. *Id.* at 8-10.

IV. Preliminary Matters

The Authority's Regulations that were in effect when the Union filed its exceptions provided that "[t]he Authority will not consider . . . any issue, which was not presented in the proceedings before the . . . arbitrator." 5 C.F.R. § 2429.5.[3]

There is no indication in the record that the Union argued before the Arbitrator, as it does in its exceptions, that the Agency violated the Fourth and Fourteenth Amendments by conducting an unreasonable search and seizure by means of the surveillance camera tape. Exceptions at 4-7. In addition, there is no evidence in the record that the Union ever argued to the Arbitrator, as it does in its exceptions, that the Agency's investigation of the alleged offense was inconsistent with Agency rules and regulations concerning the administration of Agency property. *Id.* at 8-10. The Union could have presented these arguments to the Arbitrator but failed to do so. We therefore dismiss these exceptions as barred by § 2429.5 of the Authority's Regulations. *See U.S. DOD, Def. Distrib. Depot, Anniston, Ala.*, 61 FLRA 108, 109 (2005) (Authority will not consider arguments raised for the first time on appeal).

V. Analysis and Conclusions

A. The award is not contrary to the Fifth Amendment.

As noted above, the Union contends that the award violates the grievant's Fifth Amendment privilege against self-incrimination because the Agency failed to delay the administrative disciplinary proceeding and the arbitration hearing until after final disposition of the criminal matter. Exceptions at 7-8. When a party's exceptions challenge an award's consistency with law, the Authority reviews the exceptions de novo. *See NTEU, Chapter 24*, 50 FLRA 330, 332 (1995) (citing *U.S. Customs Serv. v. FLRA*, 43 F.3d 682, 686-87 (D.C. Cir. 1994)). In applying the standard of de novo review, the Authority assesses whether an arbitrator's legal conclusions are consistent with the applicable standard of law. *See NFFE, Local 1437*, 53 FLRA 1703, 1710 (1998). In making that assessment, the Authority defers to the arbitrator's underlying factual findings. *See id.*

The Fifth Amendment provides that no person "shall be compelled in any criminal case to be a witness against himself[.]" U.S. Const. amend. V. The privilege not only applies to a criminal prosecution but also applies to "any other proceeding, civil or criminal, formal or informal, where the answers might incriminate him in future criminal proceedings." *Lefkowitz v. Turley*, 414 U.S. 70, 77 (1973) (*Turley*). The Supreme Court extended this Fifth Amendment protection to public employment situations. *Garrity v. New Jersey*, 385 U.S. 493, 497-98 (1967) (*Garrity*) (Fifth Amendment extends to public employees). Based on the foregoing, the privilege could apply to an agency investigation and arbitration proceeding in the federal sector.

The Fifth Amendment privilege against self-incrimination is violated when an agency compels an employee to testify and the testimony could incriminate the employee. *Hoover v. Knight*, 678 F.2d 578, 581 (5th Cir. 1982) (*Hoover*) (citing *Turley*, 414 U.S. 70). Similarly, the Fifth Amendment is violated when an agency imposes a penalty upon an employee who elects to assert his or her Fifth Amendment privilege. *Id.* (citing *Garrity*, 358 U.S. 493).

Here, there is no evidence that, in the course of the administrative investigation, the Agency compelled the grievant to make statements on matters that could incriminate him. To the contrary, the record indicates that, during the investigation, the Agency contacted the grievant for a statement but that the grievant refused to provide one, on the advice of counsel. Tr. at 67.

Similarly, there is no evidence of any Fifth Amendment violation during the arbitration hearing. The grievant was not compelled to testify. Further, as found by the Arbitrator, the record reflects that the grievant was provided "every opportunity" to rebut the allegations against him, but failed to do so. Award at 13; *see also* Tr. at 214-16. Rather than assert a Fifth Amendment privilege, the grievant

3. The Authority's Regulations concerning the review of arbitration awards, as well as certain related procedural Regulations, including 5 C.F.R. § 2429.5, were revised effective October 1, 2010. *See* 75 Fed. Reg. 42,283 (2010). As the Union's exceptions in this case were filed before that date, we apply the prior Regulations.

chose to provide testimony that was "limited" and that "failed to address the numerous issues raised during management's presentation of [its] case against him." Award at 13. In these circumstances, the Union's claim that the award violates the Fifth Amendment lacks a foundation. *See Hoover*, 678 F.2d at 581 (as long as an employee is not required to surrender the constitutional privilege against self-incrimination, having to defend in two parallel proceedings does not raise constitutional questions).

Accordingly, we deny this exception.

B. The award does not fail to draw its essence from the CBA.

The Union contends that the award fails to draw its essence from Article 21 of the CBA on three grounds. Exceptions at 10-14. In reviewing an arbitrator's interpretation of a collective bargaining agreement, the Authority applies the deferential standard of review that federal courts use in reviewing arbitration awards in the private sector. *See* 5 U.S.C. § 7122(a)(2); *AFGE, Council 220*, 54 FLRA 156, 159 (1998). Under this standard, the Authority will find that an arbitration award is deficient as failing to draw its essence from the collective bargaining agreement when the appealing party establishes that the award: (1) cannot in any rational way be derived from the agreement; (2) is so unfounded in reason and fact and so unconnected with the wording and purposes of the collective bargaining agreement as to manifest an infidelity to the obligation of the arbitrator; (3) does not represent a plausible interpretation of the agreement; or (4) evidences a manifest disregard of the agreement. *See U.S. Dep't of Labor (OSHA)*, 34 FLRA 573, 575 (1990). The Authority and the courts defer to arbitrators in this context "because it is the arbitrator's construction of the agreement for which the parties have bargained." *Id.* at 576.

First, as noted, the Union argues that the award fails to comply with Article 21, Sections 2, 3, and 5, which require that disciplinary actions be timely imposed after the offense is committed. Exceptions at 10-11. The Union asserts that the award erroneously fails to find that the Agency did not timely impose the disciplinary action. *Id.* The Union states that the Agency imposed the proposed suspension approximately two months after the Agency completed the investigation. *Id.*

It is undisputed that the suspension of the grievant constitutes a formal disciplinary action and not an informal one. *See* Exceptions at 10. Article 21, Section 5 provides that an informal disciplinary action will be initiated within ten workdays. On the other hand, Article 21, Sections 2, 3, and 5 do not provide a time period for the initiation of a formal disciplinary action such as here. Thus, the Arbitrator's failure to find that the Agency did not timely impose the proposed suspension because the suspension was imposed approximately two months after the Agency completed the investigation provides no basis for finding that the Arbitrator's interpretation of Article 21, Sections 2, 3, and 5 is irrational, unfounded, implausible, or in manifest disregard of the agreement.

Second, the Union argues that the award fails to comply with Article 21, Section 2, which requires that discipline be for just cause. *Id.* at 11. However, the Arbitrator concluded, under the Seven Tests developed by arbitrator Carroll R. Daugherty, that the Agency had established just cause for the grievant's suspension under the CBA. Award at 11, 12-13. The Arbitrator found, among other things, that the Agency conducted a "thorough and extensive" investigation of the alleged offense prior to the imposition of the discipline. *Id.* at 11. He also found that the administrative investigation was "relevant to the alleged offense" and produced sufficient evidence to make a determination as to whether the grievant committed an offense. *Id.* In view of these findings by the Arbitrator, the Union provides no basis for finding that the Arbitrator's interpretation of Article 21, Section 2 is irrational, unfounded, implausible, or in manifest disregard of the agreement.

Third, the Union argues that the award fails to comply with Article 21, Sections 4 and 5, which require that the Agency attempt to ascertain all the pertinent facts both for and against the grievant before the imposition of disciplinary action. Exceptions. at 13. The Union argues that the award erroneously finds that the Agency conducted a thorough and fair administrative investigation. The Union states that, in the course of the investigation, the Agency failed to gather evidence that supported the grievant's innocence such as statements from the grievant and employees who discovered the property missing. *Id.* at 12, 14. However, as noted, the Arbitrator found that the Agency conducted a "thorough and extensive" investigation of the alleged offense prior to the imposition of the discipline. Award at 11. He also found that the Agency conducted a fair investigation. *Id.* at 12. In view of these determinations by the Arbitrator, the Union provides no basis for finding that the Arbitrator's interpretation of Article 21, Sections 4 and 5 is irrational, unfounded, implausible, or in manifest disregard of the agreement.[4]

Accordingly, we deny this exception.

C. The Arbitrator did not apply an incorrect burden of proof.

The Union contends that the Arbitrator applied the incorrect burden proof. Exceptions at 14. The Union asserts that the correct burden is "beyond a reasonable doubt." *Id.* at 14-15. If a burden of proof is set forth in applicable law, rule, or regulation, or in the parties' collective bargaining agreement, then an arbitrator must apply the prescribed burden. *AFGE, Local 2250*, 52 FLRA 320, 323-24 (1996). However, when no burden of proof is laid out, an arbitrator is empowered to prescribe whatever burden of proof he or she considers appropriate, and the award will not be found deficient on the basis that the arbitrator applied an incorrect burden of proof. *See id.* at 324. Moreover, unless otherwise provided, prescribing the burden of proof encompasses specifying which party has the burden of proof under the prescribed standard. *See id.*

In this case, the Union fails to establish that applicable law, rule, or regulation, or the CBA prescribed the burden of proof. Consequently, the Arbitrator was free to apply any appropriate burden, which he did when he found that the Agency had to prove by a preponderance of the evidence that the grievant was suspended for just cause. Therefore, as the Union fails to establish a prescribed burden of proof, the Union's claim that the Arbitrator applied an incorrect burden of proof provides no basis for finding the award deficient. *See id; see also* Elkouri & Elkouri, *How Arbitration Works*, 949 (Alan Miles Ruben, ed., BNA Books 6th ed. 2003) ("quantum of proof required to support a decision to discipline . . . is unsettled").

4. To the extent the Union's exceptions may be construed as challenging as a nonfact the Arbitrator' finding that the Agency conducted a thorough and fair investigation of the alleged offense prior to the imposition of discipline, the parties disputed this issue before the Arbitrator. Award at 4, 7. The Authority will not find an award deficient as based on a nonfact where the alleged nonfact was disputed by the parties at arbitration. *U.S. Dep't of the Air Force, Lowry Air Force Base, Denver, Colo.*, 48 FLRA 589, 594 (1993). Accordingly, the exceptions do not identify any basis for finding the award deficient as based on a nonfact.

Accordingly, we deny this exception.

VI. Decision

The Union's exceptions are dismissed in part and denied in part.

APPENDIX

ARTICLE 21
DISCIPLINE AND ADVERSE ACTIONS

SECTION 2. TIMELINESS OF DISCIPLINE.
If the Employer has just cause for disciplinary or adverse action, such action will be initiated timely after the offense was committed or made known to the Employer.

SECTION 3. INFORMAL DISCIPLINARY ACTIONS.
Oral admonitions and written warnings, if utilized, will be done in a timely manner, normally within ten (10) workdays in order to strengthen the relationship between the offending behavior and the discipline imposed. Informal disciplinary actions will be retained for a maximum period of twelve (12) months. The employee has the right to respond orally or in writing within 10 (ten) workdays. The Activity will consider the facts and the employee's response in determining the action to be taken. Normally, oral admonitions or written warnings shall not be given during the course of discussion between a supervisor and employee where the meeting is not specifically initiated for that purpose.

SECTION 4.
Before proposing and/or effecting disciplinary action against an employee of the bargaining unit, management officials shall attempt to ascertain all pertinent facts both for and against the employee.

SECTION 5.
When all the facts have been gathered and disciplinary action appears to be in order, discipline or a proposed notice thereof, as applicable, will be given promptly to the employee in accordance with the procedures set forth in the Code of Federal Regulation and this Contract. Subsequent to issuance, the employee will not be questioned further about the incident until he/she has been advised of their right to union representation. If representation is desired, no further discussion concerning this matter will take place with the employee until the representative is present.

Exceptions, Attach. 12.

65 FLRA No. 92

UNITED STATES
DEPARTMENT OF THE ARMY
FORT HUACHUCA, ARIZONA
(Agency)

and

AMERICAN FEDERATION
OF GOVERNMENT EMPLOYEES
LOCAL 1662
(Union)

0-AR-4343

DECISION

January 28, 2011

Before the Authority: Carol Waller Pope, Chairman, and Thomas M. Beck and Ernest DuBester, Members

I. Statement of the Case

This matter is before the Authority on exceptions to an award of Arbitrator John Phillip Linn filed by the Agency under § 7122(a) of the Federal Service Labor-Management Relations Statute (the Statute) and part 2425 of the Authority's Regulations. The Union filed an opposition to the Agency's exceptions.

The Arbitrator concluded that there was a preponderance of evidence establishing that the grievants failed to carry out the instructions of the Agency, but that the decision to suspend the grievants for one day did not promote the efficiency of the service. For the reasons set forth below, we deny the Agency's exceptions.

II. Background and Arbitrator's Award

The grievants are three firefighters at the Fort Huachuca Fire Department. The Fire Department implemented new Standard Operating Guidelines (SOGs) after failing an operational readiness inspection. Award at 3-4. The Union, including the grievants, helped develop the first twelve SOGs; the Agency subsequently created an additional seventy SOGs. *Id.* at 4.

The former fire chief sent a written communication to several management officials stating that all firefighters were required to review the SOGs, and that they would be given a month to initial that they had reviewed the SOGs. *Id.* In a subsequent communication, the former fire chief stressed the importance of having the employees read the SOGs and initial that they had done so. *Id.* at 5.

After a month had passed, eleven of the firefighters had not initialed stating that they had reviewed the SOGs. Five of the eleven had either forgotten to initial or needed a few more hours, but the other six, including the grievants, had refused to initial. *Id.*

The three grievants were each given a notice of proposed penalty, which stated that it was a critical safety issue that the firefighters read and understand the content of the SOGs. *Id.* at 6. Each grievant was then given a three-day suspension. *Id.* The Union presented a grievance challenging the suspensions. At the second step of the negotiated grievance procedure, the Director of Emergency Services mitigated the penalty to one-day suspensions. *Id.* at 6-7.

The matter was not resolved and was submitted to arbitration. The parties stipulated to the following issues:

1. Is the Agency's decision that [the grievants] failed to carry out the instructions of the Agency within the time required to review and initial the Fort Huachuca Fire Department [SOGs] supported by a preponderance of the evidence?

2. Is the Agency's decision to suspend [the grievants] for one (1) day a reasonable penalty, not excessive, for such cause as to promote the efficiency of the [f]ederal service, and consistent with the Douglas factors and the Army's table of penalties for various offenses?

Id. at 2-3.

According to the Arbitrator, the former fire chief believed that all of the firefighters were "[p]rofessional[s]" and, therefore, did not need training on the SOGs. *Id.* at 8. The Arbitrator found that the fire chief did not make any effort to test the firefighters' understanding of the new SOGs, and that two of the grievants "might be said to have acted for a higher cause" by not initialing because some of the firefighters who read and signed the SOGs actually might not have understood them. *Id.* The Arbitrator then determined that the Fire Department should have trained the firefighters. *Id.* at 9.

The Arbitrator concluded that a preponderance of the evidence supported the conclusion that the grievants failed to carry out the instructions of the Agency by failing to review and initial the SOGs. *Id.* at 10. However, he also found that the instructions of the Agency did not "promote the efficiency of the [f]ederal service." *Id.* Therefore, he rescinded the grievants' suspensions, ordered the Agency to pay each grievant for the amount of pay lost as a result of the suspension, and ordered the Agency to remove all reference of the grievants' suspensions from their official personnel files. *Id.*

III. Positions of the Parties

A. Agency's Exceptions

The Agency argues that the Arbitrator exceeded his authority by resolving an issue that was not before him. Exceptions at 6. The Agency contends that, after finding by a preponderance of the evidence that the grievants failed to carry out the Agency's instructions, the Arbitrator was charged with determining the reasonableness of the penalty. *Id.* at 5. Instead, the Agency asserts, the Arbitrator addressed the reasonableness of the Agency's *instructions*, an issue that was not before him. *Id.* at 4. In support of its argument, the Agency relies on *U.S. Department of Health and Human Services, Food & Drug Administration, New Orleans, Louisiana*, 54 FLRA 90, 95 (1998) (*FDA*), in which the Authority found that the Arbitrator exceeded his authority by "awarding a remedy concerning an issue not submitted to arbitration." Exceptions at 6. The Agency claims that the Arbitrator rescinded the grievants' discipline as a remedy for the Agency's faulty instructions, rather than because the suspension itself was unreasonable. *Id.* at 7.

The Agency also argues that the award fails to draw its essence from the parties' collective bargaining agreement (Agreement). *Id.* According to the Agency, the Arbitrator set aside the disciplinary action even though the Agency supported the charge by a preponderance of the evidence simply because he "did not like the directive issued to the grievants." *Id.* at 8. The Agency asserts that the award fails to draw its essence from Article 14, Section 7 of the Agreement and that the Arbitrator used the "just cause" standard in Article 14, Section 2 in a way unintended by the parties.[1] *Id.* at 8-9.

Finally, the Agency argues that the award is contrary to 5 U.S.C. § 7106 because it violates management's rights to assign work and to discipline. *Id.* at 9-10. The Agency contends that the Arbitrator's "prohibition on requiring the reading of the SOGs and initialing as having read them" interferes with the Agency's right to assign work. *Id.* at 10. Similarly, the Agency asserts that the Arbitrator's "refusal to allow discipline" violates management's right to discipline. *Id.*

B. Union's Opposition

The Union contends that the Arbitrator did not exceed his authority because, when taken as a whole, it is clear that he found that the Agency's decision to suspend the grievants was not a reasonable penalty. Opp'n at 7. According to the Union, the Arbitrator found the penalty to be unjust because "it was not possible for the grievants to fully understand the SOGs on their own" without training. *Id.* Further, the Union argues that the grievants' failure to follow the Agency's instructions was justified because the Arbitrator found the instructions were not safe. *Id.* at 8. However, the "Arbitrator's opinion that the order was unreasonable and potentially dangerous ha[d] no impact on anything or anyone other than the determination of the reasonableness of the penalties imposed on the grievants," which was one of the issues submitted to the Arbitrator. *Id.* at 11.

The Union also argues that the award draws its essence from the Agreement. The Union contends that the Arbitrator's finding that failing to follow instructions did not justify a suspension when all of the circumstances were considered is consistent with Article 14, Section 7 of the Agreement. *Id.* at 13. The Union asserts that the award draws its essence from Article 14, Section 2 of the Agreement because the Arbitrator failed to find "just cause" for the disciplinary action. *Id.* at 13-14.

---

1. The relevant Agreement provisions are set forth in the attached appendix.

Finally, the Union argues that the Arbitrator's award does not interfere with management's rights. *Id.* at 14-15. According to the Union, the award does not interfere with the Agency's right to assign work in the future or its right to discipline and, therefore, does not violate § 7106. *Id.*

IV. Analysis and Conclusions

A. The Arbitrator did not exceed his authority.

Arbitrators exceed their authority when they resolve an issue not submitted to arbitration. *See U.S. Dep't of the Interior, Nat'l Park Serv., Golden Gate Nat'l Recreation Area, S.F., Cal.*, 55 FLRA 193, 194 (1999). However, arbitrators do not exceed their authority by addressing a matter that is necessary to decide a stipulated issue, *NATCA, MEBA/NMU*, 51 FLRA 993, 996 (1996), or by addressing a matter that necessarily arises from issues specifically included in a stipulation. *See Air Force Space Div., L.A. Air Force Station, Cal.*, 24 FLRA 516, 519 (1986). In determining whether an arbitrator has exceeded his or her authority, the Authority accords an arbitrator's interpretation of a stipulated issue the same substantial deference that it accords an arbitrator's interpretation and application of a collective bargaining agreement. *See U.S. Info. Agency, Voice of Am.*, 55 FLRA 197, 198 (1999).

An arbitrator has broad discretion to "fashion a remedy that the arbitrator considers to be appropriate." *U.S. Dep't of the Air Force, 72nd Mission Support Group, Tinker Air Force Base, Okla.*, 60 FLRA 432, 434 (2004). Arbitrators routinely resolve whether disciplinary action was warranted, and, if so, whether the penalty imposed was appropriate. *See AFGE, Local 2382*, 58 FLRA 270, 271 (2002) (Chairman Cabaniss concurring) (finding that the arbitrator's reduction of a one-day suspension was within his authority even though he found the grievant did not conduct himself in an appropriate manner); *AFGE, Local 22*, 51 FLRA 1496, 1498-99 (1996) (denying an exception where the arbitrator found the grievant's behavior to be improper, but nonetheless reduced the grievant's suspension).

The issue submitted to the Arbitrator was whether the grievants' one-day suspensions promoted the efficiency of the federal service. Award at 2-3. In answering that question, the Arbitrator concluded that the Agency's "instructions" did not promote the efficiency of the federal service and, thus, rescinded the suspensions. *Id.* at 10. Accordingly, the issue of whether the instructions were proper necessarily arose from the stipulated issue of whether the suspensions for failing to follow those instructions promoted the efficiency of the service. *See U.S. Dep't of the Navy, Navy Inventory Control Point, Mechanicsburg, Pa.*, 59 FLRA 698, 698-99 (2004) (denying an exception that the arbitrator exceeded his authority where the remedy was directly responsive to the issue).

The Agency, relying on *FDA*, argues that the Arbitrator exceeded his authority by "awarding a remedy concerning an issue not submitted to arbitration." Exceptions at 7. However, in *FDA*, the arbitrator, after considering whether it was improper for the union to hold meetings off-site, also found a violation of a different provision of the parties' agreement, and ordered the agency to provide permanent office space to the union. *FDA*, 54 FLRA at 92. Because the issue of office space was not before the arbitrator, and was only "tangentially related" to the submitted issue, the Authority found that the remedy ordering the agency to provide office space exceeded his authority. *Id.* at 95. *FDA* is inapposite to the case at hand because the Arbitrator here decided a matter that necessarily arose from the stipulated issue, rather than one that was only tangentially related.

Therefore, we find that the Arbitrator did not exceed his authority in considering whether the Agency's instructions promoted the efficiency of the federal service and deny this exception.

B. The award draws its essence from the Agreement.

In reviewing an arbitrator's interpretation of a collective bargaining agreement, the Authority applies the deferential standard of review that federal courts use in reviewing arbitration awards in the private sector. *See* 5 U.S.C. § 7122(a)(2); *AFGE, Council 220*, 54 FLRA 156, 159 (1998). Under this standard, the Authority will find that an arbitration award is deficient as failing to draw its essence from the collective bargaining agreement when the appealing party establishes that the award: (1) cannot in any rational way be derived from the agreement; (2) is so unfounded in reason and fact and so unconnected with the wording and purposes of the collective bargaining agreement as to manifest an infidelity to the obligation of the arbitrator; (3) does not represent a plausible interpretation of the agreement; or (4) evidences a manifest disregard of the agreement. *See U.S. Dep't of Labor (OSHA)*,

34 FLRA 573, 575 (1990). The Authority and the courts defer to arbitrators in this context "because it is the arbitrator's construction of the agreement for which the parties have bargained." *Id.* at 576.

The Agency first argues that the award fails to draw its essence from Article 14, Section 7 of the Agreement because the Arbitrator rescinded "discipline stemming from the grievants' proven failure to follow a lawful order[.]" Exceptions at 8. However, while Section 7 provides that "employees are expected to obey lawful orders[,]" it also states that failure to do so "*may* result in disciplinary or adverse action." *Id.*, Attach. 3 at 13 (emphasis added). Discipline is not required for every failure to follow lawful instructions because, as listed in other sections of Article 14, the discipline must: "be based on just and sufficient cause[;]" "be in accordance with law, rule, regulation, and [the] Agreement[;]" "be processed in a timely manner[;]" and "promote the efficiency of the [f]ederal service." *Id.* at 12-13. Because discipline is not required for every failure to obey lawful orders, we find that the award draws its essence from Article 14, Section 7 of the Agreement. *See Soc. Sec. Admin.*, 65 FLRA 286, 288-89 (2010) (citation omitted) (finding that the agency's choice of discipline was subject to "arbitral scrutiny").

The Agency also argues that the Arbitrator used the "just cause" standard in a way unintended by Article 14, Section 2 of the Agreement because he "improperly applied the just cause standard to the directive itself and not [to] the discipline." Exceptions at 8-9. For the reasons stated above concerning whether the Arbitrator exceeded his authority, the Arbitrator found that the penalty was not imposed for just cause because the instructions failed to promote the efficiency of the service. The requirement that discipline be for the efficiency of the service is "functionally identical" to the requirement that discipline be for "just cause." *U.S. Dep't of Transp., Fed. Aviation Admin.*, 63 FLRA 383, 385 (2009) (*FAA*). Therefore, the requirement in Article 14, Section 2 of the Agreement that discipline be for "just and sufficient cause" is functionally identical to the requirement in Article 14, Section 4 of the Agreement that discipline will be "taken for such cause as will promote the efficiency of the [f]ederal service." Exceptions, Attach. 3 at 12-13. Therefore, we find that the award draws its essence from Article 14, Section 2 of the Agreement.

For the foregoing reasons, we deny this exception.

C. The award is not contrary to § 7106.

When an exception involves an award's consistency with law, the Authority reviews any question of law raised by the exception and the award de novo. *See NTEU, Chapter 24*, 50 FLRA 330, 332 (1995) (citing *U.S. Customs Serv. v. FLRA*, 43 F.3d 682, 686-87 (D.C. Cir. 1994)). In applying the standard of de novo review, the Authority assesses whether an arbitrator's legal conclusions are consistent with the applicable standard of law. *See U.S. Dep't of Def., Dep'ts of the Army & the Air Force, Ala. Nat'l Guard, Northport, Ala.*, 55 FLRA 37, 40 (1998). In making that assessment, the Authority defers to the arbitrator's underlying factual findings. *See id.*

The Authority recently revised the analysis that it will apply when reviewing management rights exceptions to arbitration awards, previously found in *U.S. Department of the Treasury, Bureau of Engraving and Printing, Washington, D.C.*, 53 FLRA 146, 154 (1997) (*BEP*). *See U.S. Envtl. Prot. Agency*, 65 FLRA 113, 115 (2010) (Member Beck concurring) (*EPA*); *Fed. Deposit Ins. Corp., Div. of Supervision & Consumer Prot., S.F. Region*, 65 FLRA 102 (2010) (Chairman Pope concurring) (*FDIC, S.F. Region*). Under the revised analysis, the Authority will first assess whether the award affects the exercise of the asserted management right. *EPA*, 65 FLRA at 115. If so, then, as relevant here, the Authority examines whether the award enforces a contract provision negotiated under § 7106(b). *Id.* Also, in determining whether the award enforces a contract provision negotiated under § 7106(b)(3), the Authority, under the revised analysis, assesses: (1) whether the contract provision constitutes an arrangement for employees adversely affected by the exercise of a management right; and (2) if so, whether the arbitrator's enforcement of the arrangement abrogates the exercise of the management right. *See id.* at 116-18. In concluding that it would apply an abrogation standard, the Authority rejected continued application of an excessive interference standard. *Id.* at 118.

It is not necessary to determine whether Section 14, as interpreted and applied by the Arbitrator, affects management's rights to assign work and to discipline because, even if it does, the Agency has not shown that the award is deficient. *See U.S. Dep't of Transp., Fed. Aviation Admin., Alaskan Region*, 62 FLRA 90, 92 (2007). In this regard, the Authority has found that provisions requiring that discipline be for just cause, or to promote the efficiency of the federal service, constitute appropriate arrangements within the meaning of § 7106(b)(3) of the Statute. *See FAA*, 63 FLRA at 385 (citing *Soc. Sec. Admin., Balt., Md.*, 53 FLRA 1751, 1754 (1998)). Because the Arbitrator was enforcing a provision that constituted an appropriate arrangement, the Agency has failed to show that the award is contrary to § 7106. Therefore, we deny this exception.[2]

V. Decision

The Agency's exceptions are denied.

2. Member Beck does not believe that it is necessary to evaluate whether the contract provision at issue constitutes an appropriate arrangement. For the reasons discussed in his concurring opinion in *EPA*, 65 FLRA 113, Member Beck concludes that where, as here, the Arbitrator is enforcing a contract provision that has been accepted by the Agency as a permissible limitation on its management's rights, it is inappropriate to assess whether the provision itself is an appropriate arrangement or whether it abrogates a § 7106(a) right. *Id.* at 120 (Concurring Opinion of Member Beck). The appropriate question is simply whether the remedy directed by the Arbitrator enforces the provision in a reasonable and reasonably foreseeable fashion. *Id.*; *see also FDIC, S.F. Region,* 65 FLRA at 107. Member Beck concludes that the Arbitrator's award is a plausible interpretation of the Agreement. Accordingly, Member Beck agrees that the Agency's contrary to law exceptions should be denied.

APPENDIX

Article 14, Section 2 provides:

> Disciplinary action is a responsibility of the Employer. Disciplinary actions must be based on just and sufficient cause, with emphasis on sound employee-management relations. The Employer recognizes that the prime objective of disciplinary action is generally rehabilitation. Discipline and adverse actions, when applied, will be in accordance with law, rule, regulation, and this Agreement.

Exceptions, Attach. 3 at 12-13.

Article 14, Section 4 provides:

> The Employer agrees that disciplinary actions will be processed in a timely manner and taken for such cause as will promote the efficiency of the Federal service.

Id. at 13.

Article 14, Section 6 provides, in pertinent part:

> The Employer agrees that supervisors will refer to the Table of Penalties for various offenses before deciding the appropriate penalty in a disciplinary action, and such actions will be administered in accordance with appropriate Douglas Factors . . . .

Id.

Article 14, Section 7 provides:

> All employees are expected to obey lawful orders. Failure to do so may result in disciplinary or adverse action.
>
> *Id.*

65 FLRA No. 93

UNITED STATES
DEPARTMENT OF TRANSPORTATION
FEDERAL AVIATION ADMINISTRATION
NASHUA, NEW HAMPSHIRE
(Agency)

and

NATIONAL AIR TRAFFIC
CONTROLLERS ASSOCIATION
NEW ENGLAND ENGINEERS
AND ARCHITECTS
(Union)

0-AR-4233

DECISION

January 28, 2011

Before the Authority: Carol Waller Pope, Chairman, and Thomas M. Beck and Ernest DuBester, Members

I. Statement of the Case

This matter is before the Authority on exceptions to an award of Arbitrator Harvey M. Shrage filed by the Agency under § 7122(a) of the Federal Service Labor-Management Relations Statute (the Statute) and part 2425 of the Authority's Regulations. The Union filed an opposition to the Agency's exceptions.

The Arbitrator concluded that the Agency was required to pay the grievant interest on pay that it gave the grievant in order to correct an error in his pay. The Arbitrator determined that the grievant was entitled to interest under the Agency's Personnel Management System (PMS) and the Back Pay Act (BPA), 5 U.S.C. § 5596. For the reasons set forth below, we grant the Agency's contrary to law exception and set aside the Arbitrator's award because it is inconsistent with the doctrine of sovereign immunity.

II. Background and Arbitrator's Award

In 1998, the Agency promoted the grievant to a General Schedule (GS)-11, Step 1; however, based on the Agency's 1998 Special Salary Rate Table, Number 0414 for Engineers (rate table), it should have promoted the grievant to a GS-11, Step 2. Award at 2. The grievant discovered this error several years later and contacted the Agency's human resources department (department). *Id.* He informed the department that, under the rate table, he was entitled to a promotion and a correction in pay. *Id.* To comply with the rate table, the Agency promoted the grievant and corrected his pay; however, it did not pay him any interest on his backpay. *Id.*

The Union filed a grievance arguing that the Agency violated the parties' agreement by refusing to pay interest to the grievant. *Id.* at 1. The parties did not stipulate to, and the Arbitrator did not specifically frame, an issue. However, the Arbitrator stated that the "essence of the issue [was] whether the [g]rievant was entitled to interest on the amount of monies he was paid as a result of not being placed at the proper step after his . . . promotion." *Id.* at 10 n.1. The Union argued that the grievant was entitled to interest under both Chapter II, § 9 of the Agency's PMS and the BPA, which allegedly applied to the Agency through Article 37 of the parties' agreement.[1] *See* Exceptions, Attach. 4, Union's Post-Hearing Brief at 12-13.

The Arbitrator first addressed whether an Agency employee could obtain interest under Chapter II, § 9 of the Agency's PMS.[2] The

---

1. Article 37, § 1 of the parties' agreement provides: "In accordance with 5 USC Chapter 71, the Parties recognize the power of an appropriate authority to render a remedy in accordance with the provisions of 5 USC [§] 5596." Award at 3.

2. Chapter II, § 9 of the Agency's PMS provides, in relevant part:

> (a) Agency funds may be used to pay back pay to an [Agency] employee or former employee who, as the result of a decision or settlement under the FAA Grievance Procedure, a collective bargaining agreement, the FAA Appeals Procedure, or the Executive System Appeals Procedure is found by an appropriate authority to have been affected by an unjustified or unwarranted personnel action that resulted in the withdrawal, reduction, or denial of all or part of the pay, allowances, and differentials otherwise due to the employee.
>
> . . . .
>
> (g) Agency funds may not be used to pay either interest or attorney fees as the result of a decision in the FAA Grievance Procedure, the FAA Appeals Procedure, or the Executive System Appeals Procedure.

Award at 7.

Arbitrator determined that, under § 9(a), an Agency employee could obtain backpay as a result of a "decision or settlement" arising under a collective bargaining agreement, the Federal Aviation Administration (FAA) Grievance Procedure, the FAA Appeals Procedure, or the Executive System Appeals Procedure. Award at 11. He also found that § 9(g) lists only three circumstance in which an employee could *not* receive interest on that backpay: the FAA Grievance Procedure, the FAA Appeals Procedure, or the Executive System Appeals Procedure. *Id.* at 12. Because a collective bargaining agreement is not excluded under § 9(g), the Arbitrator concluded that an employee could obtain interest under the PMS if he or she received backpay as a result of a decision or settlement under a collective bargaining agreement. *Id.*

Applying the foregoing analysis, the Arbitrator determined that the grievant was entitled to interest under the PMS. The Arbitrator found that the Agency corrected the grievant's pay in order "to comply with the [parties' agreement]"; thus, the grievant received a decision or settlement of backpay pursuant to the agreement. *Id.* at 11. Consequently, because the grievant received an award of backpay under the agreement, the PMS authorized the Agency to award interest. *Id.* at 11-12.

The Arbitrator also concluded that the grievant was entitled to interest under the BPA. *Id.* at 13-14. The Arbitrator rejected the Agency's arguments that the pay the grievant received did not satisfy several requirements of the BPA. *Id.* The Arbitrator did not explain how the BPA applies to the Agency.

III. Positions of the Parties

A. Agency's Exceptions

The Agency contends that the award is contrary to law. According to the Agency, Congress has excluded the Agency from the BPA; it also asserts that, although Congress gave the Agency permission to adopt any portion of Title 5 when Congress authorized the Agency to develop the PMS, the Agency has not incorporated the BPA into the PMS. Exceptions at 12-13. Therefore, the Agency contends that interest was not permitted under the BPA. *Id.* at 13. Alternatively, the Agency contends that, even if the BPA applies, the award does not satisfy several of its requirements. *Id.* at 13-16. Similarly, the Agency contends that the award of interest does not satisfy several requirements of the PMS. *Id.* at 8-12.

The Agency also contends that the Arbitrator's award of interest under the PMS was based on a nonfact. Specifically, the Agency contends that, contrary to the Arbitrator's finding, the Agency never acted pursuant to the parties' agreement when it decided to correct the grievant's pay. *Id.* at 3-4. The Agency further alleges that the award is deficient because the Arbitrator denied the Agency a fair hearing by relying on an article of the parties' agreement -- Article 39 -- that was first raised in the Union's post-hearing brief. *Id.* at 6-8.

B. Union's Opposition

The Union disputes the Agency's assertion that the award is contrary to law. First, according to the Union, the BPA applies to the Agency as a matter of law because of the Wendell H. Ford Aviation Investment and Reform Act for the 21st Century, Pub. L. No. 106-181, §§ 307(a), 308(b), 114 Stat. 61 (2000) (codified as amended 49 U.S.C. § 40122(g)(2)(H) & (g)(3). Opp'n at 16-17. Moreover, the Union asserts that the BPA applies to the Agency contractually because the parties negotiated its inclusion into Article 37 of their agreement. *Id.* at 17-18. Relying on the foregoing, the Union contends the grievant could receive interest under the BPA. The Union rejects the Agency's assertion that the award does not satisfy the requirements of the PMS and the BPA. *Id.* at 13-15, 17-18.

The Union also disagrees with the Agency's assertion that the Arbitrator based his award on a nonfact or deprived the Agency of a fair hearing. *Id.* at 6-9, 10-12.

IV. The award is contrary to law.

When an exception involves an award's consistency with law, the Authority reviews any question of law raised by the exception and the award de novo. *See NTEU, Chapter 24*, 50 FLRA 330, 332 (1995) (citing *U.S. Customs Serv. v. FLRA*, 43 F.3d 682, 686-87 (D.C. Cir. 1994)). In applying the standard of de novo review, the Authority assesses whether an arbitrator's legal conclusions are consistent with the applicable standard of law. *See U.S. Dep't of Def., Dep'ts of the Army & the Air Force, Ala. Nat'l Guard, Northport, Ala.*, 55 FLRA 37, 40 (1998). In making that assessment, the Authority defers to the arbitrator's underlying factual findings. *See id.*

The Arbitrator concluded that an award of interest was permissible under both the Agency's

PMS and the BPA. The Agency alleges that the award of interest is improper because the BPA does not apply through either the PMS or the BPA. *See* Exceptions at 12-13. We construe the Agency's assertion as a claim that the award of interest is contrary to the doctrine of sovereign immunity.

The United States, as a sovereign, is immune from suit except as it consents to be sued. *U.S. Dep't of Transp., FAA,* 52 FLRA 46, 49 (1996) (*DOT*) (citing *United States v. Testan*, 424 U.S. 392, 399 (1976)). Thus, there is no right to money damages in a suit against the United States without a waiver of sovereign immunity. *DOT,* 52 FLRA at 49. In order to waive sovereign immunity, Congress must unequivocally express its intention to do so. *Id.* (citing *Lane v. Pena*, 518 U.S. 187, 192 (1996)). The Government's consent to a particular remedy also must be unambiguous. *DOT*, 52 FLRA at 49 (citing *Dep't of the Army v. FLRA*, 56 F.3d 273, 277 (D.C. Cir. 1995)). "As such, an award by an arbitrator that an agency provide monetary damages to a union or employee must be supported by statutory authority to impose such a remedy." *U.S. Dep't of the Air Force, Minot Air Force Base, N.D.*, 61 FLRA 366, 370 (2005) (*Minot*) (then-Member Pope dissenting in part as to another matter) (citing *U.S. Dep't of HHS, FDA*, 60 FLRA 250, 252 (2004)). "In this regard, a collective bargaining agreement may require monetary payments to employees only where there is underlying statutory authority for the payment." *Minot*, 61 FLRA at 370 (citation omitted). Absent a waiver of sovereign immunity, an arbitrator's monetary remedy is contrary to law. *See DOT*, 52 FLRA at 49.

Based on the foregoing, we examine whether the PMS or the BPA contains a valid waiver of sovereign immunity for awards of interest.

A. The award of interest rendered pursuant to the PMS is contrary to sovereign immunity.

Congress enacted the Department of Transportation Appropriations Act of 1996, Pub.L. No. 104-50, § 347, 109 Stat. 436, 460 (1995), codified at 49 U.S.C. § 40122 (DOT Act). *See U.S. Dep't of Transp., FAA,* 65 FLRA 325, 327 (2010) (*FAA*). Congress, through the DOT Act, instructed the Agency to develop its own "personnel management system [i.e., the PMS] . . . [to] address the unique demands on the [A]gency's workforce." 49 U.S.C. § 40122(g)(1). The DOT Act states that the PMS should "provide for greater flexibility in the hiring, training, compensation, and location of personnel." *Id.* Additionally, the DOT Act states that Title 5 of the United States Code, with certain exceptions, "shall not apply" to the PMS. 49 U.S.C. § 40122(g)(2). "The BPA was not one of the exceptions specified." *FAA*, 65 FLRA at 327.

Relying on the above framework, the Agency created its PMS. The Agency decided not to make the BPA part of the PMS. *Id.* Nevertheless, the Agency drafted the PMS to state that backpay from different sources could be awarded in certain situations. *See* Award at 7 (quoting PMS, Ch. II, § 9). The PMS also states that interest on that backpay would not be permitted in several situations; backpay awarded for violations of the parties' collective bargaining agreement, however, was *not* one of those situations. *See id.* Based on the foregoing, the Arbitrator concluded the grievant could receive interest under the PMS because he received backpay for a violation of the parties' agreement.

Assuming without deciding that the Arbitrator's interpretation of the PMS was correct, nothing in the language of the DOT Act indicates that Congress waived the Agency's sovereign immunity to interest awarded as part of an award of backpay under the PMS. The DOT Act authorized the creation of the PMS. The DOT Act, however, contains no language that authorizes an employee to receive interest for an award of backpay awarded under the PMS. The only language in the DOT Act that could potentially provide for such an award under the PMS is the Act's statement that the PMS "should provide for greater flexibility in . . . *compensation*[.]" 49 U.S.C. § 40122(g)(1) (emphasis added). However, even assuming the term "compensation" encompasses backpay, this language contains no indication that it also allows *interest* for that backpay. *See id.* This provision, thus, does not unambiguously waive sovereign immunity as to interest for backpay awarded under the PMS. *See DOT,* 52 FLRA at 49 (stating that a waiver of sovereign immunity as to a particular remedy must be unambiguous). Additionally, as stated above, the BPA and its waiver of sovereign immunity as to awards of interest is not part of the PMS. *See FAA,* 65 FLRA at 327.

Based on the foregoing, the PMS does not constitute a valid waiver of sovereign immunity as to awards of interest as part of an award of backpay. Accordingly, the Arbitrator's award of interest under the PMS is deficient because it is contrary to the doctrine of sovereign immunity.

B. The award of interest rendered pursuant to the BPA is contrary to sovereign immunity.

The Agency contends that the Arbitrator's decision to award interest under the BPA is contrary to law because the BPA does not apply to the Agency. The Union asserts that the BPA applies to the Agency as a matter of law and contract. However, the Authority recently held that the BPA does not apply to the Agency as a matter of law or contract. *See FAA,* 65 FLRA at 327-28. Moreover, the Arbitrator did not award backpay under the BPA. Thus, as we explained in *FAA*, even if the BPA were applicable to the Agency, and the Agency's sovereign immunity to monetary damages under the BPA had been waived, the Arbitrator could not award interest under the BPA without first awarding backpay under the BPA. *See id.* at 327. Based on the foregoing, we find that the award of interest under the BPA is also contrary to sovereign immunity.

V. Decision

The Agency's contrary to law exception is granted and the award is set aside as inconsistent with sovereign immunity.[3]

3. Based on the foregoing conclusions, it is unnecessary to address the Agency's nonfact, fair hearing, and remaining contrary to law exceptions.

65 FLRA No. 94

AMERICAN FEDERATION
OF GOVERNMENT EMPLOYEES
LOCAL 3854
(Union)

and

UNITED STATES
DEPARTMENT OF THE AIR FORCE
AIR FORCE RESERVE COMMAND
MARCH AIR RESERVE BASE, CALIFORNIA
(Agency)

0-AR-4717

DECISION

January 31, 2011

Before the Authority: Carol Waller Pope, Chairman, and Thomas M. Beck and Ernest DuBester, Members

This matter is before the Authority on an exception to an award of Arbitrator Edna E. J. Francis filed by the Union under § 7122(a) of the Federal Service Labor-Management Relations Statute (the Statute) and part 2425 of the Authority's Regulations. The Agency filed an opposition to the Union's exception.[1]

Under § 7122(a) of the Statute, an award is deficient if it is contrary to any law, rule, or regulation, or it is deficient on other grounds similar to those applied by federal courts in private sector labor-management relations. Upon careful consideration of the entire record in this case and Authority precedent, the Authority concludes that the award is not deficient on the grounds raised in the exception and set forth in § 7122(a). *See, e.g., U.S. Dep't of the Treasury, IRS, Oxon Hill, Md.*, 56 FLRA 292, 299 (2000) (award not deficient where an arbitrator bases an award on separate and independent grounds, and the excepting party fails to establish that all of the grounds are deficient)[2]; *Prof'l Airways Sys. Specialists, Dist. No. 1, MEBA/NMU (AFL-CIO),* 48 FLRA 764, 768-69 (1993) (award not deficient as contrary to law where excepting party fails to establish that the award is in any manner contrary to the law, rule, or regulation on which the party relies).

Accordingly, the Union's exception is denied.

1. As the Union's arguments meet the requirements for granting review, we reject the Agency's request to dismiss the Union's exceptions. *See* 5 C.F.R. 2425.6(e)(1).

2. The award is based on the Arbitrator's findings that: (1) an Agency regulation did not authorize the grievant's supervisor to grant administrative leave; and (2) Comptroller General decisions regarding unauthorized administrative leave are controlling precedent. The Union's exception addresses only the Arbitrator's second finding.

65 FLRA No. 95

NATIONAL ASSOCIATION
OF GOVERNMENT EMPLOYEES
LOCAL R5-66
(Union)

and

UNITED STATES
DEPARTMENT OF VETERANS AFFAIRS
MEDICAL CENTER
MEMPHIS, TENNESSEE
(Agency)

0-AR-4658

DECISION

January 31, 2011

Before the Authority: Carol Waller Pope, Chairman, and Thomas M. Beck and Ernest DuBester, Members

I. Statement of the Case

This matter is before the Authority on an exception to an attorney fee award (fee award) of Arbitrator John E. Megley, III filed by the Union under § 7122(a) of the Federal Service Labor-Management Relations Statute (the Statute) and part 2425 of the Authority's Regulations. The Agency did not file an opposition to the Union's exception.

The Arbitrator found that the grievant was eligible for an award of attorney fees under the Back Pay Act, 5 U.S.C. § 5596, but reduced the amount of attorney fees requested by the Union by approximately half. For the reasons discussed below, we deny the Union's exception.

II. Background and Arbitrator's award

The grievant received a fourteen-day suspension for failure to follow his supervisor's instructions and for disorderly conduct. Original Award at 7. The Union filed a grievance claiming that the penalty imposed was inconsistent with the infraction. *Id.* at 10. The grievance was not resolved and proceeded to arbitration. As relevant here, the stipulated issue before the Arbitrator was: "Did the [Agency] violate the Collective Bargaining Agreement by suspending the [g]rievant, and if so, what shall the remedy be?" *Id.* at 4.

The Arbitrator mitigated the fourteen-day suspension to a written reprimand and ordered the grievant's personnel record purged of any reference to "rude and inappropriate conduct." *Id.* at 13. The Arbitrator also ordered backpay for lost wages and benefits, including night-time differential pay, for the time the grievant was suspended. *Id.* Subsequently, the Union requested attorney fees in the amount of $ 9,980.00. *See* Exception, Attach., Ex. C.

In his fee award, the Arbitrator found that the Union met the threshold requirement for attorney fees under the Back Pay Act because the grievant suffered an unwarranted personnel action, which resulted in the reduction of pay, allowances, or differentials. Fee Award at 4. The Arbitrator also addressed whether the Union's request for attorney fees met the criteria set forth in 5 U.S.C. § 7701(g). In this regard, he noted that § 7701(g) requires, as pertinent here, that the grievant be the prevailing party and that the fees be reasonable. *Id.* The Arbitrator found that because the Union did not prevail "in all aspects of the matter," the reasonable fees criterion warranted a proportional reduction of the attorney fees sought. *Id.* Specifically, the Arbitrator found that although the Union had prevailed in part by obtaining a reduction of the grievant's discipline and by obtaining backpay, the Agency also prevailed in part because the disciplinary charges were upheld, although the discipline was reduced. Accordingly, the Arbitrator awarded attorney fees in the amount of $ 4,490.00.[1] *Id.*

III. Union's Exception

The Union argues that the Arbitrator's fee award is contrary to the Back Pay Act, 5 U.S.C. § 5596, because it does not meet the standards set forth in 5 U.S.C. § 7701(g).[2] Specifically, the Union argues that the award does not meet the prevailing party and the reasonableness of the fee criteria. Exception at 3-4. The Union takes the position that it is entitled to the full amount of the attorney fees it requested. *Id.* at 7-8.

1. The record does not reflect why the Arbitrator reduced the requested attorney fees by slightly more than half. However, the precise amount of the award is not at issue in this case.

2. Section 7701(g)'s standards are discussed *infra* section V.

The Union bases its position on a number of principles. The Union acknowledges that to be eligible for an award of attorney fees under § 7701(g), a party must have been the prevailing party. *Id.* at 5. The Union further asserts that to be deemed a prevailing party under § 7701(g), a party must receive an enforceable judgment or settlement, which directly benefited the party at the time of the judgment or settlement. *Id.* Based on these principles, the Union argues that it was the prevailing party and that therefore, it was eligible to receive the full amount of the attorney fees requested. *Id.* at 7-8. The Union contends that although the Arbitrator initially found that the grievant was the prevailing party, he later improperly sought to avoid awarding full compensatory fees to the Union by "split[ting] the baby" and holding that neither party prevailed completely. *Id.* at 5.

With regard to the reasonableness of the fees, the Union claims that to determine whether the amount of attorney fees requested is reasonable within the meaning of § 7701(g), the extent to which the grievant was successful in the underlying action is the most critical factor. *Id.* at 6. The Union further asserts that because the grievant was the prevailing party, it was eligible to receive the full amount of attorney fees requested. *Id.* at 7-8. The Union also claims that the Arbitrator improperly applied the "[p]roportionality [p]rinciple" when he reduced the amount of fees requested by the Union. *Id.* at 6 (emphasis omitted). Citing *Hensley v. Eckerhart*, 461 U.S. 424, 440 (1983) (*Hensley*), the Union asserts that, in this case, there is no separate unsuccessful claim warranting the Arbitrator's reduction of the fees requested. *Id.* The Union claims that it should receive a fully compensatory fee because it achieved "truly excellent results." *Id.* at 7-8.

IV. The Arbitrator's reduction of the amount of the requested attorney fees is consistent with the requirements of 5 U.S.C. § 7701(g)(1), which the Back Pay Act incorporates.

The Union argues that the Arbitrator's fee award is contrary to the Back Pay Act, 5 U.S.C. § 5596, because it does not meet the standards set forth in 5 U.S.C. § 7701(g). Specifically, the Union argues that the award does not meet the prevailing party and reasonableness of the fees criteria. Exception at 3-4. We review the questions of law raised by the Union's exception to the Arbitrator's award de novo. *See NTEU, Chapter 24*, 50 FLRA 330, 332 (1995) (citing *U.S. Customs Serv v. FLRA*, 43 F.3d 682, 686-87 (D.C. Cir. 1994)). In applying a de novo standard of review, the Authority assesses whether the arbitrator's legal conclusions are consistent with the applicable standard of law. *See U.S. Dep't of Def., Dep'ts of the Army & the Air Force, Ala. Nat'l Guard, Northport, Ala.*, 55 FLRA 37, 40 (1998). In making that assessment, the Authority defers to the arbitrator's underlying factual findings. *See id.*

A. The statutory requirements for entitlement to attorney fees.

The threshold requirement for entitlement to attorney fees under the Back Pay Act, 5 U.S.C. § 5596, is a finding that the grievant was affected by an unjustified or unwarranted personnel action, which resulted in the withdrawal or reduction of the grievant's pay, allowances, or differentials. *Ala. Ass'n of Civilian Technicians*, 54 FLRA 229, 232 (1998) (*Ala. Nat'l Guard*). Once such a finding is made, the Act further requires that an award of fees be: (1) in conjunction with an award of backpay to the grievant on correction of the personnel action; (2) reasonable and related to the personnel action; and (3) in accordance with the standards established under 5 U.S.C. § 7701(g), which pertain to attorney fee awards by the Merit Systems Protection Board (MSPB). *Ala. Nat'l Guard*, 54 FLRA at 232.

Section 7701(g)'s standards for an award of attorney fees are as follows: (1) the employee must be the prevailing party; (2) the award of fees must be warranted in the interest of justice; (3) the amount of the fees must be reasonable; and (4) the fees must have been incurred by the employee. *See U.S. Dep't of the Treasury, IRS, Phila. Serv. Ctr., Phila., Pa.*, 53 FLRA 1697, 1699 (1998); *Allen v. U.S. Postal Serv.*, 2 M.S.P.R. 420, 427 (1980). When an exception concerns the standards established under § 7701(g), the Authority looks to precedent of the MSPB and the United States Court of Appeals for the Federal Circuit for guidance. *AFGE, Local 1061*, 63 FLRA 317, 319 (2009).

In this case, the Union challenges the Arbitrator's determination regarding the prevailing party and reasonableness of the fees criteria. Accordingly, we address only those requirements. *See, e.g., NFFE, Forest Serv. Council, Local 1771*, 56 FLRA 737, 741 (2000) (*Forest Serv. Council*) (addressing only the Back Pay Act issues raised by excepting party).

B. The Arbitrator's prevailing party determination is consistent with § 7701(g)(1).

The Union argues that to the extent that the Arbitrator found that the grievant was not the prevailing party, and on that basis awarded a reduced fee, the award is contrary to § 7701(g)(1).

The Authority applies the definition of "prevailing party" adopted by the MSPB. Under this definition, an employee is the prevailing party within the meaning of § 7701(g)(1) when the employee "received an enforceable judgment or settlement which directly benefited [the employee] at the time of the judgment or settlement." *AFGE, Local 987*, 64 FLRA 884, 886 (2010) (quoting *U.S. GSA, Ne. & Caribbean Region, N.Y., N.Y.,* 61 FLRA 68, 70 (2005) (citation omitted)). Under MSPB precedent, an employee who receives a mitigated penalty is considered to have received significant relief and is, therefore, a prevailing party. *E.g., Hutchcraft v. Dep't of Transp.*, 55 M.S.P.R. 138, 142 (1992), *aff'd,* 996 F.2d 1235 (Fed. Cir. 1993).

The Union's claim that the Arbitrator did not find that the grievant was the prevailing party appears to be based on a misinterpretation of the award. As the Arbitrator found, it was undisputed that the grievant was the prevailing party. Fee Award at 3.

However, the Arbitrator's finding that the grievant was the prevailing party does not totally resolve the fee issue. As the Arbitrator correctly recognized, the amount of the fees must also be reasonable. *Id.* at 4; *see Ala. Nat'l Guard*, 54 FLRA at 232. Accordingly, we find that the Arbitrator's determinations that the grievant was the prevailing party, but that the reasonableness of the fee must also be considered, are consistent with the applicable legal standard.

C. The Arbitrator's reasonable fee determination is consistent with § 7701(g)(1).

The Union argues that the award is contrary to law because the Arbitrator should not have considered the extent to which each party prevailed.

The Authority has held that it is reasonable to reduce requested attorney fees based on the degree of success achieved at arbitration. *See, e.g., Forest Serv. Council,* 56 FLRA at 742. In arriving at this conclusion, the Authority relied on Supreme Court cases holding that, when awarding attorney fees, the extent to which a plaintiff prevailed in the underlying litigation is the most critical factor to consider in determining the reasonableness of the fees. *Id.* (citing *Farrar v. Hobby*, 506 U.S. 103, 114 (1992)). In addition, the Authority has adopted the Supreme Court's ruling that "in cases involving a single successful claim, '[a] reduced fee award is appropriate if the relief, however significant, is limited in comparison to the scope of the litigation as a whole.'" *Id.* (quoting *Hensley,* 461 U.S. at 440). The Supreme Court has also held that "[t]here is no precise rule or formula" for reducing attorney fees, and that district courts "may simply reduce the award to account for . . . limited success[,]" so long as the reduction is otherwise consistent with the principles that the Court identified. *Hensley,* 461 U.S. at 436-37.

The Arbitrator's consideration of the Union's degree of success is consistent with the applicable legal standard. In this case, although the Arbitrator mitigated the penalty against the grievant from a fourteen-day suspension to a written reprimand, he also sustained both charges against the grievant that the parties pursued at arbitration. The Arbitrator concluded that a reasonable attorney fee award should reflect the grievant's degree of success. The Arbitrator's award in this regard, reducing the amount of fees requested, is consistent with the above-cited precedent. *See also NAGE, Local R4-6,* 54 FLRA 1594, 1599-1600 (1998) (upholding arbitrator's determination that it was reasonable to reduce requested attorney fees to an amount proportionate to degree of success achieved).

The Union acknowledges that an attorney fee award may be reduced by the number of hours devoted to unsuccessful claims. Exception at 6-7. However, the Union contends that a proportionate attorney fee award is not appropriate in this case because there is no separate claim in which the grievant was unsuccessful. *Id.* The Union's contention does not demonstrate that the award is deficient. As discussed above, under Authority precedent, arbitrators may reduce requested attorney fees based on the degree of success achieved even in situations involving a single successful claim. *Forest Serv. Council,* 56 FLRA at 742.

The Union also claims that it should receive a fully compensatory fee because it obtained "truly excellent results." Exception at 8. However, as stated above, arbitrators may reduce attorney fees based on the degree of success achieved. *Forest Serv. Council,* 56 FLRA at 742. Therefore, as the

Arbitrator here found that the Union did not prevail in all aspects of the matter, it was not impermissible for him to reduce the attorney fees sought. Accordingly, we find that the Arbitrator's determination regarding the reasonableness of the fee is consistent with § 7701(g)(1).

V. Decision

The Union's exception is denied.

65 FLRA No. 96

OFFICE AND PROFESSIONAL
EMPLOYEES INTERNATIONAL UNION
LOCAL 2001
(Union)

and

UNITED STATES
DEPARTMENT OF ENERGY
OAK RIDGE OFFICE
OAK RIDGE, TENNESSEE
(Agency)

0-AR-4689

DECISION

January 31, 2011

Before the Authority: Carol Waller Pope, Chairman, and Thomas M. Beck and Ernest DuBester, Members

I. Statement of the Case

This matter is before the Authority on exceptions to an award (supplemental award) of Arbitrator Robert G. Williams filed by the Union under § 7122(a) of the Federal Service Labor-Management Relations Statute (the Statute) and part 2425 of the Authority's Regulations. The Agency filed an opposition to the Union's exceptions.

The Arbitrator found that the Agency did not discriminate against the grievant when it failed to select him for a position. For the reasons that follow, we dismiss the Union's exceptions in part and deny them in part.

II. Background and Arbitrator's Award

When the grievant was not selected for a contract specialist position, General Schedule (GS)-1102-13, he filed a grievance that was submitted to arbitration. In an award resolving that grievance (initial award), as relevant here, the Arbitrator framed two issues before him as whether the Agency: (1) violated Office of Personnel Management (OPM) policies and regulations, and certain Agency policies, when it announced and filled the position;[1] and (2) engaged in unlawful discrimination against the grievant on the basis of his age, sex, or Union activity. *See* Initial Award at 2.

With regard to the first issue, the Arbitrator determined that the selection process violated the cited regulations and policies. *See id.* at 62-63, 65. As a remedy, the Arbitrator directed the Agency to redraft and repost the job announcement, and awarded backpay to the individual whom the Agency would ultimately select. *See id.* at 69-70.

With regard to the second issue, the Arbitrator stated that, "[g]iven the remedy ordered for the claims in issue number [one,] any consideration of discrimination claims would be premature until" the new selection process had been completed. *Id.* at 68-69. The Arbitrator determined that "[i]f the [g]rievant is not selected[]" in the new selection process, then the "Union may renew [its] discrimination claims based on evidence in the complying as well as the original erroneous selection process." *Id.* at 69. The Arbitrator "retain[ed] jurisdiction to hear any renewed discrimination claims." *Id.* at 70.

The Agency filed exceptions to the initial award with the Authority, and the Authority found that the Arbitrator's award of backpay was deficient, but otherwise denied the Agency's exceptions.[2] *See U.S. Dep't of Energy, Oak Ridge Office, Oak Ridge, Tenn.*, 64 FLRA 535, 537-39 (2010). After that decision, the Agency reposted the Contract Specialist, GS-1102-13 position and began a new selection process for the position. Supplemental Award at 1-2. The grievant, who is male, applied for the position, but the Agency selected a younger, female applicant (the selectee). *Id.* at 2. The Union then "renewed its discrimination claim first asserted

---

1. Specifically, the Arbitrator considered whether the Agency failed to comply with: (1) OPM policies when it announced the position, *see* Initial Award at 27, 41, 60; (2) 5 C.F.R. § 335.103(b)(3) by not considering candidates' performance evaluations and incentive awards, *see* Initial Award at 63; and (3) Agency policies, issued pursuant to 41 U.S.C. § 433, by selecting an applicant who did not meet certain experience-related requirements, *see* Initial Award at 43-46, 63-65.

2. Specifically, the Authority found that the Arbitrator exceeded his authority to the extent that his award granted backpay to an individual other than the grievant. *See U.S. Dep't of Energy, Oak Ridge Office, Oak Ridge, Tenn.*, 64 FLRA 535, 538 (2010).

in the original grievance[,]" *id.*, and the Arbitrator issued the supplemental award.

The parties did not stipulate, and the Arbitrator did not expressly set forth, issues to be decided in the supplemental award. *See id.* at 2, 5. The Arbitrator reiterated that he had stated, in the initial award, that he "retained jurisdiction 'to hear any renewed discrimination claims.'" *Id.* at 2 (quoting Initial Award at 70). The Arbitrator then stated that the Union "ha[d] the burden of showing that the Agency's selection of [the selectee] was a pretext to cover . . . discrimination in selecting her over the [g]rievant for the . . . announced position" in the new selection process. *Id.* at 5. Addressing that issue, the Arbitrator determined that the grievant was "unable to cite evidence that would constitute pretext[,]" i.e., evidence that the Agency was "pretending that the selectee's experience, education, or training was more than that of the [g]rievant." *Id.* at 6. As such, the Arbitrator concluded that the grievant was "unable to prove impermissible discrimination[,]" *id.* at 8, and denied the grievance, *see id.* at 5, 8-9.

III. Positions of the Parties

A. Union's Exceptions

The Union alleges that the Arbitrator exceeded his authority by not considering whether the Agency discriminated against the grievant during the *original* selection process. Exceptions at 3, 6, 12. The Union contends that the Arbitrator thereby failed to address the Union's claim that the Agency violated 5 U.S.C. § 2302(b)(6) during that process, *see* Exceptions at 5, 9, when it "rewr[ote]" the specialized experience requirements, *id.* at 4, and when the selecting official "prejudg[ed]" the grievant by determining prematurely not to select him,[3] *id.* at 9.

With regard to the new selection process, the Union asserts that although the selecting official from the original selection process was not the selecting official in the new selection process, her bias against the grievant nonetheless influenced the new selection process, in violation of § 2302(b)(6). *See id.* at 9-10. Additionally, the Union argues that the Arbitrator did not address the Union's argument that the new selection process violated 5 U.S.C. § 2301(b)(1) (§ 2301(b)(1)).[4] *Id.* at 7-8. In this connection, the Union asserts that the Agency was biased in favor of the selectee, given that choosing her allegedly would reduce the Agency's backpay liability with regard to grievances filed by the selectee and the grievant. *Id.* at 7. Further, the Union argues that the Agency violated 5 C.F.R. § 335.103(b)(3) (§ 335.103(b)(3)) by failing to consider applicants' performance evaluations and incentive awards.[5] *See* Exceptions at 11.

B. Agency's Opposition

The Agency contends that the Arbitrator did not exceed his authority because he resolved the issue before him of whether the grievant was discriminated against during the new selection process. *See* Opp'n at 5-7. As to the original selection process, the Agency argues that the Arbitrator's direction to "vacate the [original] selection decision and rerun the vacancy announcement . . . rendered it unnecessary for the Arbitrator to resolve the issue of discrimination as it related to the [original] selection action." *Id.* at 6. In addition, the Agency asserts that the Authority should not consider whether the Agency violated §§ 2301 and 2302 because the Union failed to argue those claims to the Arbitrator.

---

3. Section 2302(b)(6) states, in pertinent part, that any employee who has authority to take any personnel action shall not "grant any preference or advantage not authorized by law . . . to any . . . applicant for employment . . . for the purpose of improving or injuring the prospects of any particular person for employment[.]"

4. Section 2301(b) states, in pertinent part:

> Federal personnel management should be implemented consistent with the following merit system principles:
>
> (1) Recruitment should be from qualified individuals from appropriate sources in an endeavor to achieve a work force from all segments of society, and selection and advancement should be determined solely on the basis of relative ability, knowledge, and skills, after fair and open competition which assures that all receive equal opportunity.

5. Section 335.103(b) states, in pertinent part:

> Merit promotion requirements--
>
> . . . .
>
> . . . To be eligible for promotion or placement, candidates must meet the minimum qualification standards prescribed by the [OPM]. Methods of evaluation for . . . placement . . . must be consistent with . . . this chapter. Due weight shall be given to performance appraisals and incentive awards.

See Opp'n at 9-11 (citing 5 C.F.R. § 2429.5).[6] Alternatively, the Agency asserts that the Arbitrator was not obligated to consider those issues because the parties did not stipulate that the Arbitrator would consider them. *See* Opp'n at 9-12. Finally, the Agency disputes the Union's claim that the Agency violated § 335.103 by not considering the grievant's performance appraisals during the new selection process. *See id.* at 13.

IV. Analysis and Conclusions

A. Preliminary Matter: 5 C.F.R. § 2429.5 bars the Union's argument regarding 5 U.S.C. § 2301(b)(1), and bars one of the Union's arguments regarding 5 U.S.C. § 2302(b)(6).

The Authority's Regulations that were in effect when the Union filed its exceptions provided that "[t]he Authority will not consider . . . any issue[] which was not presented in the proceedings before the . . . arbitrator." 5 C.F.R. § 2429.5 (§ 2429.5).[7] Under § 2429.5, the Authority will not consider any issue that could have been, but was not, presented to the arbitrator. *See, e.g., U.S. Dep't of Homeland Sec., U.S. Customs & Border Prot., JFK Airport, Queens, N.Y.*, 62 FLRA 416, 417 (2008).

With regard to the Union's claim that the Agency violated § 2301(b)(1) during the new selection process, the Union did not argue to the Arbitrator that the Agency violated § 2301(b)(1). *See* Exceptions, Attach. 3, Letter from [Union] to Arbitrator (May 26, 2010) (May 26 Letter); Exceptions, Attach. 4, Letter from [Union] to Arbitrator (June 1, 2010) (June 1 Letter). As the Union could have, made that argument, we dismiss the Union's exception under § 2429.5.

The Union also claims that: (1) the selecting official was biased against the grievant during the original selection process; (2) the Agency violated § 2302(b)(6) during the original selection process; and (3) the Agency violated § 2302(b)(6) during the new selection process. *See* Exceptions at 5, 9-10; Opp'n at 11. Contrary to the Agency's assertion, the Union argued that the selecting official had "pre-nonselected" the grievant during the original selection process, May 26 Letter, and that the Agency violated § 2302(b)(6) during the original selection process, *see* June 1 Letter. However, the record indicates that the Union could have, but did not, argue to the Arbitrator that the Agency violated § 2302(b)(6) during the new selection process. *See* May 26 Letter; June 1 Letter. Accordingly, we will resolve the Union's exception alleging that the Agency violated § 2302(b)(6) in the original selection process, but, pursuant to § 2429.5, we dismiss the Union's exception alleging that the Agency violated § 2302(b)(6) during the new selection process.

B. The Arbitrator did not exceed his authority.

As relevant here, an arbitrator exceeds his or her authority when the arbitrator fails to resolve an issue submitted to arbitration. *U.S. Dep't of Transp., FAA*, 64 FLRA 680, 684 (2010). Where the parties have not stipulated, and the arbitrator has not expressly set forth, an issue to be decided, the Authority will look to the award to determine whether the issue is nevertheless apparent from the award. *See, e.g., U.S. Dep't of Veterans Affairs, Veterans Affairs Med. Ctr., Louisville, Ky.*, 64 FLRA 70, 72-73 (2009) (although arbitrator did not frame issues, purpose of arbitration hearing clear from record); *U.S. Dep't of the Navy, Navy Pub. Works Ctr., Norfolk, Va.*, 54 FLRA 338, 342 (1998) (Member Wasserman dissenting in part as to other matters) (issue "clear from the award as a whole") (*Navy*); *U.S. Dep't of Veterans Affairs, Med. Ctr. Providence, R.I.*, 49 FLRA 110, 116 (1994) (issue clear from award) (*Veterans*). Where parties have not stipulated to an issue to be decided, the Authority accords an arbitrator's formulation of the issues the same substantial deference accorded to an arbitrator's interpretation of the collective bargaining agreement. *Ass'n of Civilian Technicians, N.Y. State Council*, 61 FLRA 664, 665 (2006) (*ACT*). The Authority accords such deference even where the arbitrator has not expressly set forth the issue. *See Veterans*, 49 FLRA at 116 (deferring to arbitrator's apparent formulation of the issue before him). Further, when deferring to an arbitrator's formulation of the issues in the absence of a stipulation, the Authority grants an arbitrator "substantial discretion to . . . decline to consider issues[,]" *ACT*, 61 FLRA at 665, even if the Arbitrator's decision not to address certain issues is implicit in the award, *see Veterans*, 49 FLRA at 116 (arbitrator implicitly determined that an issue was not before him).

As discussed previously, the parties did not stipulate, and the Arbitrator did not expressly set forth, an issue for the Arbitrator to decide.

6. The pertinent wording of 5 C.F.R. § 2429.5 is set forth below.

7. The Authority's Regulations concerning the review of arbitration awards, as well as certain related procedural Regulations, including § 2429.5, were revised effective October 1, 2010. *See* 75 Fed. Reg. 42,283 (2010). As the Union's exceptions were filed before that date, we apply the earlier Regulations.

See Supplemental Award at 2, 5. The Arbitrator stated that the Union "ha[d] the burden of showing that the Agency's selection of [the selectee] was a pretext to cover . . . discrimination in selecting her over the [g]rievant for the . . . announced position" in the new selection process. *Id.* at 5. This statement, and the supplemental award as a whole, *see id.* at 8-9, support a conclusion that the Arbitrator viewed the issue before him as involving whether the Agency discriminated against the grievant during the new selection process. They also support a conclusion that the Arbitrator implicitly determined that the issues of whether the Agency discriminated against the grievant during the original selection process, and whether the Agency violated §§ 2302(b)(6) or 335.103(b) during that process, were issues that were not before him. *See* Supplemental Award at 5, 8-9. *Cf. Veterans*, 49 FLRA at 116. Because the Authority grants arbitrators substantial discretion to decline to consider issues when the parties have not stipulated to the issues to be decided, the Arbitrator's failure to consider issues regarding the original selection process is not a basis for finding that the award is deficient. *See ACT* 61 FLRA at 665-66. Therefore, we find that the Arbitrator did not exceed his authority by failing to resolve issues regarding the original selection process.

With regard to the claim that the Arbitrator did not address the Union's argument that the Agency was biased in favor of the selectee in the new selection process because choosing her allegedly would reduce the Agency's backpay liability, Exceptions at 7, the Authority has held that an arbitrator's failure to address every specific argument raised by a party does not render an award deficient. *See, e.g., AFGE, Local 3911*, 64 FLRA 686, 687 (2010). Thus, in resolving the issue of unlawful discrimination in the new selection process, the Arbitrator was not required to address the specific argument about backpay-motivated bias. Accordingly, we deny the exception.

For the foregoing reasons, we deny the Union's exceeded authority exceptions.

V. Decision

The Union's exceptions are dismissed in part and denied in part.

65 FLRA No. 97

UNITED STATES
DEPARTMENT OF JUSTICE
FEDERAL BUREAU OF PRISONS
FEDERAL CORRECTIONAL COMPLEX
TERRE HAUTE, INDIANA
(Agency)

and

AMERICAN FEDERATION
OF GOVERNMENT EMPLOYEES
LOCAL 720
COUNCIL OF PRISON LOCALS
COUNCIL 33
(Union)

0-AR-4502

DECISION

January 31, 2011

Before the Authority: Carol Waller Pope, Chairman, and Thomas M. Beck and Ernest DuBester, Members

I. Statement of the Case

This matter is before the Authority on exceptions to an award of Arbitrator Virginia Wallace-Curry filed by the Agency under § 7122(a) of the Federal Service Labor-Management Relations Statute (the Statute) and part 2425 of the Authority's Regulations. The Union filed an opposition to the Agency's exceptions.

The Arbitrator found that the Agency violated two settlement agreements when it stopped paying overtime compensation to certain employees. For the reasons that follow, we deny the Agency's exceptions.

II. Background and Arbitrator's Award

A. Background

This case is another in a series of cases involving disputes between Union locals and the Agency relating to overtime pay for pre-shift and post-shift activities. In a previous award, Arbitrator D'Eletto found that the Agency had violated the Fair Labor Standards Act (FLSA) by failing to compensate employees for certain pre-shift and post-shift activities. In *United States Department of Justice, Federal Bureau of Prisons, United States Penitentiary, Terre Haute, Indiana*, 58 FLRA 327, 330 (2003), the Authority found it "unclear whether [Arbitrator D'Eletto's] award include[d] compensation for picking up equipment at the control center and walking to the place of performance of principal activities, which the Agency concede[d was] legally permissible." Accordingly, the Authority remanded Arbitrator D'Eletto's award for clarification in this regard. *Id.*

Rather than resubmitting the award to Arbitrator D'Eletto for clarification, the parties executed a portal-to-portal settlement agreement (the portal-to-portal agreement), in which they agreed that "[s]hift starting and stopping times for all bargaining unit employees . . . shall begin and end at the [c]ontrol [c]enter[.]" Award at 1 (quoting the portal-to-portal agreement). The parties subsequently identified 120 posts where employees continued to perform compensable pre-shift and post-shift activities. *Id.* at 1-2.

When the Agency did not pay overtime to employees working the specified 120 posts, the Union requested a supplemental award from Arbitrator D'Eletto. Prior to a hearing before Arbitrator D'Eletto, the parties executed a settlement agreement (the settlement agreement), in which the Agency agreed to pay backpay and liquidated damages and to begin prospectively paying fifteen minutes of overtime per day to employees assigned to the specified 120 posts "until the Agency makes changes to the Correctional Services roster or takes other measures which eliminate pre-shift and post-shift work." *Id.* at 2 (quoting paragraph 4 of the settlement agreement). The settlement agreement also provided that "[s]hould the Agency exercise its rights under 5 U.S.C. § 7106, the Agency recognizes its obligation to negotiate appropriate arrangements for employees adversely affected by the exercise of authority and procedures with the Union in accordance with 5 U.S.C. § 7106 and the Master Agreement." *Id.* (quoting paragraph 4 of the settlement agreement).

Subsequently, the Agency notified the Union that the Agency had "eliminated or reorganized the assignment of pre-shift and post-shift tasks." *Id.* The Agency advised the Union that "the posts identified in the settlement agreement . . . will no longer be required to perform tasks associated with their principal activities while they are traveling to and from their assigned post." *Id.* Instead, shifts would begin and end at the post of duty rather than at the control center. Accordingly, the Agency ceased paying employees fifteen minutes of overtime per day for pre-shift and post-shift activities. *See id.* at 12-13.

The Union then filed the grievance in this case alleging that the Agency violated: (1) the settlement agreement when the Agency ceased paying the fifteen minutes of overtime; and (2) the portal-to-portal agreement when it ceased paying the overtime and when it changed the location at which shifts started and ended. *Id.* at 1. The parties were unable to resolve the grievance and submitted it to arbitration.

B. Arbitrator's Award

The Arbitrator framed the issue, as follows: "Did the Agency violate [the portal-to-portal agreement and the settlement agreement] when it made changes to the pre-shift and post-shift activities of the 120 posts in question, thus eliminating the payment of [fifteen] minutes of overtime?" *Id.* at 3. With regard to the Agency's unilateral change to the shift starting and ending point, the Arbitrator noted the Agency's argument that paragraph 4 of the settlement agreement allowed it to unilaterally take any measures to eliminate pre-shift and post-shift activities, including eliminating the control center as the shift starting and ending point. *Id.* at 14-15. The Arbitrator rejected the Agency's claim that it could act unilaterally and held that, if the Agency wanted to change the control center as the starting and ending point of each shift, then it was required to negotiate with the Union. *Id.* at 17. Accordingly, she concluded that the Agency violated the agreements "by unilaterally changing the shift starting and stopping point . . . from the [c]ontrol [c]enter to the assigned duty post and eliminating the compensable pre-shift and post-shift work." *Id.* at 14.

The Arbitrator further determined that, even if the Agency could unilaterally eliminate pre-shift and post-shift activities, "the proposal offered by the Agency to change the start/end point of the shift to the duty post d[id] not sufficiently eliminate the pre-shift and post-shift work." *Id.* at 16. In this regard, she found "that the Union raised undisputed allegations that some of the Agency's 'new' changes had been implemented prior to the [s]ettlement [a]greement without eliminating the pre and post-shift work." *Id.* In determining that the Agency had not sufficiently eliminated pre-shift and post-shift activities, she stated that "if it w[ere] so easy to eliminate the pre-shift and post-shift work by changing the starting and stopping point of the shift, the Agency would have done so long ago." *Id.* at 15-16.

For these reasons, the Arbitrator sustained the grievance and directed the Agency to comply with the portal-to-portal agreement requirement that shifts begin and end at the control center. As a remedy, she directed the Agency to pay such employees backpay and to begin prospectively paying employees assigned to the specified 120 posts fifteen minutes of overtime per day. *Id.* at 17.

III. Positions of the Parties

A. Agency's Exceptions

The Agency contends that the award fails to draw its essence from the portal-to-portal agreement and the settlement agreement. Exceptions at 8. Specifically, the Agency claims that the Arbitrator incorrectly found that paragraph 4 of the settlement agreement could not override the portal-to-portal agreement. In this connection, the Agency argues that paragraph 4 of the settlement agreement allowed it to make the disputed changes so that employees would no longer perform pre-shift and post-shift activities. *Id.* at 10.

The Agency additionally contends that the award is contrary to management's right to assign work under § 7106(a)(2)(B) of the Statute. The Agency argues that, by not allowing the disputed changes, the Arbitrator has applied the settlement agreement to prohibit the Agency from exercising its right to assign work. *Id.* at 11 n.6.

The Agency further contends that the award is contrary to the FLSA and 5 C.F.R. § 551.412(b) (§ 551.412(b)).[1] *Id.* at 4. In support, the Agency asserts that the Arbitrator found that the Agency had eliminated compensable pre-shift and post-shift activities when she found that the Agency had "chang[ed] the shift starting and stopping point . . . from the [c]ontrol [c]enter to the assigned duty post and eliminate[ed] the compensable pre-shift and post-shift work." *Id.* at 6 (quoting Award at 14). Consequently, the Agency maintains that, regardless

1. Section 551.412(b) defines "preliminary and postliminary activities" as "preparatory or concluding activity that is not closely related to the performance of the principal activities" and provides that time spent in such activities "is excluded from hours of work and is not compensable[.]"

of the Arbitrator's finding that the Agency was not authorized to make the changes, the Arbitrator has directed payment of overtime for work that was never performed. *Id.* at 6-7. The Agency also claims that the issue of whether the Agency bargained properly over the disputed changes was not at issue because the Union did not raise to the Arbitrator any issues of a failure to bargain over the changes or improper implementation of the changes. *Id.* at 6 n.4.

B. Union's Opposition

The Union contends that the award draws its essence from the portal-to-portal agreement and the settlement agreement. Opp'n at 7. The Union also contends that the award is not contrary to the FLSA and § 551.412. The Union claims that the Agency misstates the Arbitrator's factual findings on whether the Agency eliminated overtime work, and asserts that the Arbitrator "did not find that the Agency eliminated all compensable pre-shift and post-shift work." *Id.* at 5 (citing Award at 16). The Union additionally argues that, under the settlement agreement, the Agency was required to negotiate any such changes. *Id.* at 6.

IV. Analysis and Conclusions

A. The award does not fail to draw its essence from the parties' agreements.

In reviewing an arbitrator's interpretation of a collective bargaining agreement, the Authority applies the deferential standard of review that federal courts use in reviewing arbitration awards in the private sector. *E.g., AFGE, Council 220*, 54 FLRA 156, 159 (1998). Under this standard, the Authority will find that an arbitration award is deficient as failing to draw its essence from the agreement when the appealing party establishes that the award: (1) cannot in any rational way be derived from the agreement; (2) is so unfounded in reason and fact and so unconnected with the wording and purposes of the agreement as to manifest an infidelity to the obligation of the arbitrator; (3) does not represent a plausible interpretation of the agreement; or (4) evidences a manifest disregard of the agreement. *E.g., U.S. Dep't of Labor (OSHA)*, 34 FLRA 573, 575 (1990). The Authority and the courts defer to arbitrators in this context because it is the arbitrator's construction of the agreement for which the parties have bargained. *Id.* at 576.

The Agency argues that paragraph 4 of the settlement agreement permitted it to make the disputed changes. However, the Agency does not acknowledge that paragraph 4 also specifically obligated it to negotiate over procedures and appropriate arrangements pursuant to § 7106(b) if it exercised any management right under § 7106(a). In this regard, as stated previously, the Arbitrator held that "[i]f the Agency wants to change the [c]ontrol [c]enter as the starting/ending point of the shift, it must negotiate this with the Union." Award at 17. As the Agency asserts that the changes constituted an exercise of its right to assign work under § 7106(a)(2)(B) and makes no claim that it provided the Union with an opportunity to negotiate over procedures and appropriate arrangements under § 7106(b), the Agency provides no basis for finding that the award is irrational, unfounded, implausible, or manifestly disregards the settlement agreement. Accordingly, we deny this exception.

B. The award is not contrary to law.

When an exception involves an award's consistency with law, the Authority reviews de novo any questions of law raised by the exception and the award. *E.g., U.S. Dep't of the Air Force, Warner Robins Air Logistics Ctr., Warner Robins Air Force Base, Ga.*, 53 FLRA 1344, 1347 (1998) (*Warner Robins AFB*). In applying a standard of de novo review, the Authority assesses whether the arbitrator's legal conclusions are consistent with the applicable standard of law. *Id.*

1. Section 7106(a)(2)(B) of the Statute

The Agency first contends that the award is contrary to § 7106(a)(2)(B). The Authority recently revised the analysis that it will apply when reviewing exceptions alleging that awards are contrary to law because they are inconsistent with management rights. *See U.S. EPA*, 65 FLRA 113, 115 (2010) (Member Beck concurring) (*EPA*); *FDIC, Div. of Supervision & Consumer Prot., S.F. Region*, 65 FLRA 102 (2010) (Chairman Pope concurring). Under the revised analysis, the Authority will first assess whether the award affects the exercise of the asserted management right. *EPA*, 65 FLRA at 115.[2]

2. For the reasons articulated in his recent concurring opinion and footnotes, Member Beck would conclude that it is unnecessary to assess whether the award affects the exercise of the asserted management right. The appropriate question is simply whether the remedy directed by the Arbitrator enforces the provision in a reasonable and reasonably foreseeable fashion. *See EPA*, 65 FLRA at 120 (Concurring Opinion of Member Beck); *Soc. Sec. Admin., Dallas Region*, 65 FLRA 405, 408 n.5 (2010); *U.S. Dep't of the Air Force, Air Force Materiel Command*, 65 FLRA 395, 398 n.7; *U.S. Dep't of Health & Human Servs., Office*

If so, then, as relevant here, the Authority examines whether the award enforces a contract provision negotiated under § 7106(b).[3] *Id.*

It is not disputed that the award affects management's right to assign work. With regard to whether the award enforced a contract provision negotiated under § 7106(b), the Arbitrator enforced the settlement agreement to find that, if the Agency wants to change the starting and ending points of shifts, then the Agency must negotiate with the Union. The Authority has held that contract provisions that incorporate the bargaining obligations of the Statute constitute provisions negotiated under § 7106(b) of the Statute. *Warner Robins AFB*, 53 FLRA at 1349. Consequently, the Arbitrator was enforcing a provision negotiated under § 7106(b) of the Statute, and the Agency does not demonstrate that the award is contrary to management's right to under § 7106(a)(2)(B). *See id.* Accordingly, we deny this exception.

2. FLSA and § 551.412

The Agency contends that the award is contrary to the FLSA and § 551.412 because, regardless of the Arbitrator's finding that the changes were unauthorized, once the changes were made, no overtime work was performed. In this regard, the Agency alleges that the award confirms this and quotes the Arbitrator's statement that the Agency "eliminate[ed] the compensable pre-shift and post-shift work." Award at 14.

When evaluating exceptions to an arbitration award, the Authority considers the award and record as a whole. *See, e.g., U.S. Dep't of Energy, Oak Ridge Operations Office, Oak Ridge, Tenn.*, 55 FLRA 1293, 1296 (2000) (reading "award[] as a whole" and finding agency "misconstrued the award"). That is, the Authority interprets the language of an award in context. *See, e.g., U.S. Dep't of Def., Def. Contract Audit Agency, Central Region, Irving, Tex.*, 60 FLRA 28, 29 (2004).

The Agency relies on the Arbitrator's statement that the Agency "eliminate[ed] the compensable pre-shift and post-shift work." Award at 14. However, as stated previously, the Arbitrator found, more specifically, that: (1) even if the Agency could unilaterally eliminate pre-shift and post-shift activities, "the proposal offered by the Agency to change the start/end point of the shift to the duty post d[id] not sufficiently eliminate the pre-shift and post-shift work[,]" *id.* at 16; (2) "the Union raised undisputed allegations that some of the Agency's 'new' changes had been implemented prior to the [s]ettlement [a]greement without eliminating the pre and post-shift work[,]" *id.*; and (3) "if it was so easy to eliminate the pre-shift and post-shift work by changing the starting and stopping point of the shift, the Agency would have done so long ago[,]" *id.* at 15-16. Based on the award and the record as a whole, the Agency does not establish that the award confirms that employees no longer perform overtime work. Consequently, the Agency provides no basis on which to find that the award is contrary to the FLSA or § 551.412.[4]

Moreover, even assuming that the Agency eliminated pre-shift and post-shift activities, the Agency does not establish that the award is deficient. In this regard, the Authority has found that, even if employees did not actually work overtime, they may receive overtime pay under the Back Pay Act, 5 U.S.C. § 5596, if a contract violation resulted in their failure to work overtime. *E.g., U.S. Dep't of the Navy, Puget Sound Naval Shipyard*, 62 FLRA 4, 7-8 (2007) (quoting *U.S. Dep't of the Navy, Supervisor of Shipbuilding Conversion & Repair, Pascagoula, Miss.*, 57 FLRA 744, 746-47 (2002) (it is "well-settled that an employee may be awarded overtime compensation for overtime hours that were not worked because of a violation of a contract")); *see also Soc. Sec. Admin., Balt., Md.*, 57 FLRA 538, 542

of Medicare Hearings & Appeals, 65 FLRA 175, 177 n.3 (2010); *U.S. Dep't of Transp., Fed. Aviation Admin.*, 65 FLRA 171, 173 n.5 (2010). Member Beck would conclude that the Arbitrator's award is a plausible interpretation of the parties' agreement and deny the exception.

3. When an award affects a management right under § 7106(a)(2) of the Statute, the Authority may also examine whether the award enforces an applicable law. *EPA*, 65 FLRA at 115 n.7.

4. The Agency also claims that the issue of whether the Agency bargained properly over the disputed changes was not at issue because the Union did not raise to the Arbitrator any issues of a failure to bargain over the changes or improper implementation of the changes. However, the Union in its post-hearing brief alleged that the "Agency made a unilateral change to the shift starting and stopping point without negotiating with the Union as required by the [s]ettlement [a]greement." Opp'n, Attach. B, Union's Post-Hearing Brief at 8-9. Consequently, to the extent that the Agency is contending that the award is deficient because the Union did not raise an issue of a failure to bargain, the Agency's contention misstates the position of the Union, and, thus, provides no basis for finding the award deficient.

(2001) (citing approvingly 54 Comp. Gen. 1071 (1975), in which the Comptroller General confirmed that the "no work, no pay" rule no longer applies to preclude an award of backpay to remedy the violation of a collective bargaining agreement that causes an employee to lose pay).

As the Arbitrator found that the Agency violated the portal-to-portal agreement and the settlement agreement -- and as the Back Pay Act authorizes backpay to remedy the loss of overtime pay resulting from a violation of a collective bargaining agreement even when employees perform no overtime work -- the Agency's claim that the award is deficient because employees performed no overtime work provides no basis for finding the award deficient.

For the foregoing reasons, we deny this exception.

V. Decision

The Agency's exceptions are denied.

65 FLRA No. 98

AMERICAN FEDERATION
OF GOVERNMENT EMPLOYEES
LOCAL 2006
(Union)

and

SOCIAL SECURITY ADMINISTRATION
REGION III
(Agency)

0-AR-4675

DECISION

January 31, 2011

Before the Authority: Carol Waller Pope, Chairman, and Thomas M. Beck and Ernest DuBester, Members

I. Statement of the Case

This matter is before the Authority on exceptions to an award of Arbitrator Thomas Phelan filed by the Union under § 7122(a) of the Federal Service Labor-Management Relations Statute (the Statute) and part 2425 of the Authority's Regulations. The Agency filed an opposition to the Union's exceptions.

The Arbitrator concluded that the grievants were not eligible for overtime under Title 5, the Fair Labor Standards Act (FLSA), or the parties' National Agreement (Agreement) and that, as a result, the Union's information request was moot. For the reasons set forth below, we deny the Union's exceptions.

II. Background and Arbitrator's Award

The grievants are employees of the Mid-Atlantic Processing Center (the Center). Award at 6. All of the grievants work a flexible schedule. *Id.* All overtime at the Center is voluntary, and must be authorized and approved in advance. *Id.* at 7. To facilitate the requirement for authorization and approval, the Center uses a pre-approval process. Under this process, an employee informs a supervisor that he or she would like to work overtime and is listed on a pre-approved register. A second line supervisor then approves the listed employees in writing, except in emergencies. *Id.*

Employees are notified regarding available overtime opportunities by an electronic bulletin board. The board includes a reminder regarding the Agency's overtime policy, stating that "overtime is offered, authorized and approve[d] under the following parameters: Overtime must be worked in minimum 1-hour increments on weekdays and 3-hour increments on weekend days[;] Overtime worked in excess of the minimum must be in fifteen-minute increments up to the maximum scheduled[.]" *Id.* at 7-8. Employees who are authorized and approved to work overtime must record their time in, time out, and hours worked. *Id.* at 8.

The Union presented a grievance challenging, among other things, the Agency's policy requiring the grievants to work a minimum of one hour of overtime on weekdays and three hours of overtime on weekends (Minimum Overtime Policy). *Id.* at 3. The grievance also alleged that the Agency's policy of failing to pay the grievants for working "odd" minutes (i.e., less than 15 minute intervals) violated Title 5, the FLSA, and Article 10, Section 3 of the Agreement (Odd Minute Overtime Policy).[1] *Id.*

The matter was not resolved and was submitted to arbitration. As a preliminary matter, the Union filed a motion to compel information that it had requested as part of the grievance and the Agency had not provided. *Id.* at 6. The Arbitrator found that, because the information "was needed to identify the employees who had allegedly been damaged by the application of the Agency's overtime policy and the extent of the damages[,]" the information was not

1. Article 10, Section 3(B) provides that:

> When an employee, whether covered by the Fair Labor Standards Act or exempt, works regular overtime, such overtime will be scheduled and paid in increments of 15 minutes. When an employee, whether covered by the Fair Labor Standards Act or exempt, works irregular overtime, such overtime will be paid in increments of 15 minutes. Daily increments of less than 15 minutes, if such occur, will be accumulated during the workweek. At the end of the workweek, any increments of 7 minutes or fewer will be rounded down and any increments of 8 minutes or more will be rounded up to the next 15 minute interval.

Exceptions, Attach. 8, Union Statement of Issues at 6.

necessary unless the Union prevailed on the merits of its claims. *Id.* Accordingly, the Arbitrator bifurcated the case into two hearings – one on the merits and the other on damages, which was to be held at a later date if necessary. *Id.* The Arbitrator also denied the Union's motion to postpone the hearing. Exceptions at 6.

As relevant here, the issues before the Arbitrator were whether the Agency's Minimum Overtime Policy or Odd Minute Overtime Policy violated Title 5, the FLSA, or the Agreement.[2] *See* Award at 2; Exceptions at 3; Opp'n at 8.

The Arbitrator concluded that the Agency's Minimum Overtime Policy did not violate Title 5, the FLSA, or the Agreement. Award at 27. The Arbitrator noted that, while Title 5 and the FLSA require premium payment for overtime worked, the Agency has the right to establish policies for scheduling that overtime. *Id.* Accordingly, the Arbitrator found that the required one-hour and three-hour minimums did not violate Title 5, the FLSA, or the Agreement. *Id.* at 27-28.

The Arbitrator also concluded that the Agency's Odd Minute Overtime Policy did not violate Title 5 or the Agreement. The Arbitrator found that the requirement in Article 10, Section 3 of the Agreement – that odd minutes of overtime be accumulated at the end of each week – must be read in conjunction with the definitions of overtime provided in 5 U.S.C. § 6121(6) and Article 10, Section 2(D) of the Agreement, both of which require that overtime be officially ordered or approved.[3] *Id.* at 28-29. The Arbitrator noted that "it was uncontested" that employees who worked odd minutes of overtime did so without informing their supervisors and that the Agency's sign-in, sign-out system for recording overtime did not take those minutes into account. *Id.* Therefore, according to the Arbitrator, under both Title 5 and the Agreement, any odd minutes of overtime worked outside of a fifteen-minute interval were not overtime because they were not ordered or approved in advance by the Agency. *Id.*

Finally, the Arbitrator rejected the Union's argument that the odd minutes of overtime were required to be accounted for and compensated as "suffered or permitted" overtime under the FLSA.[4] *Id.* at 32. In this regard, the Arbitrator found that the Agency's Personnel Policy Manual (Manual) provides that flexible schedule employees are not able to earn "suffered or permitted" overtime. *Id.* at 30-31 (citing Section 3.1.1 of the Manual). The Arbitrator noted that the Manual is consistent with the Office of Personnel Management's (OPM's) Handbook on Alternative Work Schedules (AWS Handbook), which also excludes flexible schedule employees from earning "suffered or permitted" overtime. *Id.* at 31.

Therefore, the Arbitrator denied the Union's grievance. *Id.* at 33. Additionally, because he denied the grievance on the merits, the Arbitrator found that the information requested was unnecessary under § 7114(b)(4) of the Statute and denied the Union's information request. *Id.* at 33-34.

III. Positions of the Parties

A. Union's Exceptions

The Union argues that the Arbitrator's preliminary determinations are contrary to law, rule, or regulation. Exceptions at 4. The Union claims that the Arbitrator's bifurcation of the proceedings severely prejudiced the Union. *Id.* at 6. Citing *United States Department of Health & Human Services*, 33 FLRA 340, 341 (1988) (*DHHS*), the Union contends that an arbitrator may not unilaterally bifurcate an arbitration hearing without the agreement of both parties. *Id.* at 7. According to the Union, because it did not agree to bifurcation, the Arbitrator's decision was contrary to Authority precedent. *Id.* at 6. The Union also contends that the Arbitrator prejudiced the Union by refusing to postpone the hearing. The Union claims to have

2. The Arbitrator also addressed whether the grievance was timely and whether the Agency bypassed the Union in enforcing an unwritten overtime policy. Award at 24-26. Because no exceptions were filed to the Arbitrator's resolution of these issues, they are not before us.

3. 5 U.S.C. § 6121(6) defines overtime hours as "all hours in excess of 8 hours in a day or 40 hours in a week which are officially ordered in advance[.]" Article 10, Section 2(D) defines overtime as "work that is performed by an employee in excess of eight hours in a day or in excess of 40 hours in an administrative workweek and that is officially ordered or approved by the Agency." Exceptions, Attach. 8, Union Statement of Issues at 4.

4. As defined in the FLSA, "suffered or permitted" work is "work performed by an employee for the benefit of an agency, whether requested or not, provided the employee's supervisor knows or has reason to believe that the work is being performed and has an opportunity to prevent the work from being performed." 5 C.F.R. § 551.104.

received notice of the nature of the arbitration hearing only a few days before the hearing. *Id.* at 6-7.

The Union argues that the Arbitrator's award finding that the overtime was not ordered and approved is contrary to law because "the overtime work was officially ordered and approved[.]" *Id.* at 18-19. Relying on *Holzapfel v. Town of Newburgh, N.Y.*, 145 F.3d 516 (2d. Cir. 1998) (*Holzapfel*), the Union also asserts that the Agency's Minimum Overtime Policy violates the FLSA. *Id.* at 20-21. Moreover, the Union claims that the Arbitrator "misapplied the law" as it applies to flexible schedule employees and in denying the grievants' claim for "suffer or permit" overtime. *Id.* at 22. The Union also contends that the Agency's Odd Minute Overtime Policy conflicts with the Agreement. *Id.* at 21.

Finally, the Union claims that the Arbitrator's denial of its motion to compel was contrary to § 7114(b)(4) because its information request imposed a statutory requirement on the Agency "separate from the Agency's obligations in processing a [g]rievance." *Id.* at 5. The Union contends that the information is normally maintained by the Agency, is reasonably available, and is not unduly burdensome for the Agency to produce. *Id.* at 9-12. The Union further argues that it has shown the information is necessary and has stated a particularized need for the information. *Id.* at 12-17.

B. Agency's Opposition

The Agency argues that the Union's arguments do not show that the Arbitrator's award was contrary to law, but, rather, constitute a mere disagreement with the Arbitrator's conclusions. Opp'n at 7. Additionally, the Agency claims that the Union's arguments are unsupported assertions. *Id.*

With respect to the Union's exceptions relating to the motion to compel and motion to postpone, the Agency asserts that the exceptions are not properly before the Authority because they were not included in the framed issues. *Id.* at 8. Alternatively, the Agency argues that the motions are procedural matters, which the Arbitrator has "considerable latitude" to decide. *Id.* at 9-12 (citing *Commander, Carswell Air Force Base, Tex.*, 31 FLRA 620, 629-30 (1988)).

The Agency argues that the Arbitrator's decision that the Agency has the right to schedule overtime should be entitled to deference and that the Union's analogy to *Holzapfel* is inapposite. *Id.* at 21-22. Further, the Agency contends that the Arbitrator's conclusion that the Agency's Odd Minute Overtime Policy does not conflict with the Agreement is entitled to deference. *Id.* at 22-23.

The Agency claims that the Arbitrator's factual finding that the overtime allegedly worked by the grievants was not ordered or approved in advance is entitled to deference. *Id.* at 13-14. Additionally, the Agency contends that the Arbitrator was correct in holding that employees who work flexible schedules are ineligible for "suffer or permit" overtime as a matter of law because OPM regulations concerning overtime are entitled to deference under *Chevron, U.S.A., Inc. v. Natural Resources Defense Council, Inc.*, 467 U.S. 837, 842-43 (1984). *Id.* at 14-16.

Moreover, the Agency argues, even if, as a matter of law, Center employees are eligible for "suffer or permit" overtime, the Union cannot show that the grievants would meet the other requirements for such overtime. *Id.* at 17. The Agency claims that the Arbitrator found that the supervisors were not aware that employees were working unapproved overtime minutes. *Id.* at 19. Additionally, the Agency asserts that management acted reasonably to prevent employees from working unauthorized overtime. *Id.* at 20-21.

Finally, the Agency claims that the Arbitrator properly denied the Union's information request. *Id.* at 12. According to the Agency, because the Arbitrator determined that the grievants were not entitled to overtime, the information requested by the Union was no longer necessary. *Id.* at 13.

IV. Analysis and Conclusions

A. The Arbitrator did not fail to conduct a fair hearing.

The Union contends that the Arbitrator erred in: (1) denying the Union's motion to postpone the hearing and (2) bifurcating the proceeding. We construe these arguments as claims that the Arbitrator failed to conduct a fair hearing. *See AFGE, Local 171, Council of Prison Locals 33*, 61 FLRA 661, 663 (2006).

An award will be found deficient on the ground that an arbitrator failed to provide a fair hearing where a party demonstrates that the arbitrator refused to hear or consider pertinent and material evidence, or that other actions in conducting the proceeding so prejudiced a party as to affect the fairness of the proceeding as a whole. *See AFGE, Local 1668*, 50 FLRA 124, 126 (1995). It is well established that an arbitrator has considerable latitude in conducting a hearing and the fact that an arbitrator conducts a hearing in a manner that a party finds objectionable does not, by itself, provide a basis for finding an award deficient. *See AFGE, Local 22*, 51 FLRA 1496, 1497-98 (1996).

The Union argues that the Arbitrator failed to conduct a fair hearing by failing to grant its motion to postpone the hearing. The Union argues that it was prejudiced because it was under the impression that an informal mediation would be taking place, and only received notice that it would be an arbitration hearing twelve days beforehand. Exceptions at 4-7. However, the Union has not provided any evidence that it had a reasonable belief there would be an informal mediation or that twelve days' notice was inadequate. The Union further argues that the Arbitrator's denial was prejudicial because of the failure to receive the requested documents. *Id.* at 7. However, as discussed below, the Union was not entitled to the information pursuant to § 7114(b)(4). Therefore, as the Union has not shown how the alleged lack of notice prejudiced the Union and because the Arbitrator has considerable latitude in conducting a hearing, we deny this exception. *See AFGE, Local 1917*, 52 FLRA 658, 662 (1996) (finding that denial of a thirty-day postponement did not deny the union a fair hearing).

Additionally, the Union argues that the Arbitrator failed to conduct a fair hearing because he bifurcated the proceeding into separate hearings on liability and damages. The Union contends that bifurcation must be agreed to by both parties, relying solely on the Authority's decision in *DHHS*. Exceptions at 7. However, *DHHS* provides no support for this contention. In that decision, the Authority merely noted that the arbitrator had decided not to bifurcate the proceedings because the parties had not agreed to bifurcation, a decision which the Authority did not review or discuss further. *DHHS*, 33 FLRA at 341. The Arbitrator here exercised his considerable latitude in concluding that it was appropriate to bifurcate the proceedings, and the Union has not shown that the decision prejudiced the hearing as a whole. *See NAGE, Fed. Union of Scientists & Eng'rs, Local R12-198*, 63 FLRA 7, 7 n.* (2008) (denying an exception arguing that the arbitrator improperly bifurcated the proceedings). Therefore, we deny this exception.

B. The Agency's Minimum Overtime Policy and Odd Minute Overtime Policy are not contrary to Title 5 or the FLSA.

When an exception involves an award's consistency with law, the Authority reviews any question of law raised by the exception and the award de novo. *See NTEU, Chapter 24*, 50 FLRA 330, 332 (1995) (citing *U.S. Customs Serv. v. FLRA*, 43 F.3d 682, 686-87 (D.C. Cir. 1994)). In applying the standard of de novo review, the Authority assesses whether an arbitrator's legal conclusions are consistent with the applicable standard of law. *See U.S. Dep't of Def., Dep'ts of the Army & the Air Force, Ala. Nat'l Guard, Northport, Ala.*, 55 FLRA 37, 40 (1998). In making that assessment, the Authority defers to the arbitrator's underlying factual findings. *See id.*

1. Title 5

The Union argues that the Arbitrator erred in finding "that the overtour hours of work that failed to exceed the minimum hour and fifteen minute policies instituted by the Agency were not ordered and approved." Exceptions at 19. According to the Union, the grievants "are entitled to overtime pay under specific conditions," which, under Title 5, means work "in excess of 8 hours in a day or 40 hours in a week" if it is officially ordered in advance. *Id.* (citing 5 U.S.C. § 6121(6)). However, the Arbitrator's finding that the Agency did not officially order or approve the overtime is a factual finding that is not alleged to be a nonfact and to which the Authority must defer. *See AFGE, Local 607, Council of Prison Locals*, 61 FLRA 707, 710 (2006) (finding that the arbitrator's conclusions were not contrary to Title 5 where the arbitrator's factual findings were entitled to deference). Because the Arbitrator found that none of the work performed was ordered and approved, we find that neither the Minimum Overtime Policy nor the Odd Minute Overtime Policy is contrary to Title 5.

2. FLSA

Relying on *Holzapfel*, the Union argues that the Agency's Minimum Overtime Policy is contrary to the FLSA. However, in *Holzapfel*, the Second Circuit found that the employer's policy violated the FLSA because the employee was being forced to work unpaid overtime to care for his police dog. *Holzapfel*, 145 F.3d at 524-25. In contrast, the Agency's Minimum Overtime Policy does not force employees to work overtime or to work fewer hours than the required minimums. The Union has not identified any provision of the FLSA with which the Agency's Minimum Overtime Policy conflicts. Therefore, we find that the Agency's Minimum Overtime Policy is not contrary to the FLSA.

The Union also argues that the Arbitrator "misapplied the law" relating to "suffer or permit" overtime. Exceptions at 22. The Arbitrator rejected the Union's claim that the grievants were entitled to "suffer or permit" overtime because the Agency's Manual and the OPM AWS Handbook exclude flexible schedule employees from the ability to earn "suffered or permitted" overtime.[5] Award at 30-31. In reaching this conclusion, the Arbitrator deferred to the OPM AWS Handbook because he found it to be consistent with the FLSA. *Id.* at 31-32.

The Authority normally defers to OPM regulations on statutory matters OPM has been given authority to interpret as long as the regulations constitute a reasonable interpretation of the statutory language. *See NTEU, Chapter 41*, 57 FLRA 640, 644 (2001) (*NTEU*). However, the Authority only defers to other OPM guidance, such as opinion letters and manuals, to the extent that they have the power to persuade. *Id.* In a situation in which the OPM AWS Handbook was found to be consistent with the FLSA statutes and regulations, the Authority found it to carry persuasive weight. *See id.* at 644-45.

FLSA regulations provide that an employee is not entitled to overtime compensation under the FLSA for "hours of work that are not 'overtime hours,' as defined in 5 U.S.C. § 6121, for employees under flexible or compressed work schedules[.]" 5 C.F.R. § 551.501(a)(6). Section 6121 defines overtime hours as "all hours in excess of 8 hours in a day or 40 hours in a week which are officially ordered in advance." 5 U.S.C. § 6121. In other words, an employee covered by the FLSA who is on a flexible work schedule may not receive overtime unless ordered in advance. We find that the OPM AWS Handbook is consistent with these statutory and regulatory provisions and, therefore, carries persuasive weight. *See NTEU*, 57 FLRA at 644-45.

The Union also contends that the "legal reasoning and justification" behind denying "suffer or permit" overtime to flexible schedule employees diminishes as it applies to weekend work. Exceptions at 22. However, neither the FLSA nor the OPM AWS Handbook makes a distinction between weekday and weekend work in the context of being "suffered or permitted" to work.

The Union has not shown that the Arbitrator's decision relating to "suffer or permit" overtime is contrary to law. For the foregoing reasons, we deny the Union's exception.[6]

C. The award relating to the Odd Minute Overtime Policy draws its essence from the Agreement.

The Union argues that the Arbitrator's conclusion that the odd minutes of overtime were not compensable "is in conflict and superseded by the . . . Agreement[.]" Exceptions at 21. We construe this assertion as an argument that the award fails to draw its essence from the Agreement.

In reviewing an arbitrator's interpretation of a collective bargaining agreement, the Authority applies the deferential standard of review that federal courts use in reviewing arbitration awards in the private sector. *See* 5 U.S.C. § 7122(a)(2); *AFGE, Council 220*, 54 FLRA 156, 159 (1998). Under this standard, the Authority will find that an arbitration award is deficient as failing to draw its essence from the collective bargaining agreement when the appealing party establishes that the award: (1) cannot in any rational way be derived from the agreement; (2) is so unfounded in reason and fact and so unconnected with the wording and purposes of the collective bargaining agreement as to manifest an

5. Section (d)(1) of the OPM AWS Handbook provides, in relevant part: "Employees on flexible work schedules may not earn overtime pay as a result of including 'suffered or permitted' hours (under the FLSA) as hours of work." *See* Award at 31.

6. The Union asserts that the Arbitrator's award "ignored the advent of credit hours and compensatory time[.]" Exceptions at 22. However, because the issues before the Arbitrator solely related to overtime, the award has no bearing on the grievants' ability to earn credit hours or compensatory time. *See* 5 U.S.C. § 6121.

infidelity to the obligation of the arbitrator; (3) does not represent a plausible interpretation of the agreement; or (4) evidences a manifest disregard of the agreement. *See U.S. Dep't of Labor (OSHA)*, 34 FLRA 573, 575 (1990). The Authority and the courts defer to arbitrators in this context "because it is the arbitrator's construction of the agreement for which the parties have bargained." *Id.* at 576.

The Union argues that, because the Arbitrator determined that the odd minutes worked during the week were not compensable as overtime, his award conflicts with Article 10, Section 3(B) of the Agreement providing that odd minutes of overtime are to be accumulated at the end of each workweek. Exceptions at 21. The Arbitrator found that, because the additional minutes worked were not ordered or approved by the Agency, they did not meet the definition of overtime in Article 10, Section 2(D) and, therefore, were not compensable under Article 10, Section 3(B). Award at 29. The Arbitrator's conclusion is not unfounded, implausible, irrational, or in manifest disregard of the Agreement. *See U.S. Dep't of Veterans Affairs, Conn. Healthcare Sys., Newington, Conn.*, 57 FLRA 47, 49 (2001) (denying the agency's essence exception where the arbitrator interpreted the contractual definition of "facility"). Therefore, we find that the award draws its essence from the Agreement and deny this exception.

D. The award is not contrary to § 7114(b)(4).

Under § 7114(b)(4) of the Statute, an agency must furnish information to a union, upon request and "to the extent not prohibited by law," if that information is: (1) "normally maintained by the agency in the regular course of business;" (2) "reasonably available[;]" (3) "necessary for full and proper discussion, understanding, and negotiation of subjects within the scope of collective bargaining;" and (4) not "guidance, advice, counsel, or training[.]" 5 U.S.C. § 7114(b)(4).

In order to demonstrate that requested information is "necessary for full and proper discussion, understanding, and negotiation of subjects within the scope of collective bargaining" under § 7114(b)(4) of the Statute, a union "must establish a particularized need for the information by articulating, with specificity, why it needs the requested information, including the uses to which the union will put the information, and the connection between those uses and the union's representational responsibilities under the Statute." *IRS, Wash., D.C.*, 50 FLRA 661, 669 (1995).

The Union contends that the Arbitrator erred in denying its information request and motion to compel. According to the Arbitrator, because the odd minutes of overtime that the grievants may have worked were not compensable, the Union no longer required the requested information. Award at 33-34. The Union argues that the information is necessary, however, "to prove that bargaining unit employees worked outside their tour of duty hours on weekends and were not properly compensated for that time under the CBA, or federal law, rules and regulations." Exceptions at 13. The Union also argues that the information is necessary to prove that the Agency had knowledge that the Center employees were working overtime without being compensated for the time. *Id.* at 13-14.

As the Arbitrator correctly determined, because he denied the grievance on the merits, the Union's needs no longer exist. *See U.S. Dep't of Labor*, 63 FLRA 216, 218 (2009) (finding the fact that the grievance was barred mooted the information request where it was requested to help process a grievance). Because the Arbitrator found the minutes were not ordered or approved and could not be compensated as "suffer or permit" overtime, the information is not needed to prove whether the Center employees were working extra minutes, or whether the Agency had knowledge of it. Therefore, we find that the Arbitrator's decision denying the information request is not contrary to § 7114(b) and deny this exception.

V. Decision

The Union's exceptions are denied.

65 FLRA No. 99

AMERICAN FEDERATION
OF GOVERNMENT EMPLOYEES
LOCAL 3723
(Union)

and

UNITED STATES
DEPARTMENT OF THE NAVY
MARINE CORPS COMMUNITY SERVICES
MARINE CORPS AIR STATION MIRAMAR
SAN DIEGO, CALIFORNIA
(Agency)

0-AR-4706

DECISION

January 31, 2011

Before the Authority: Carol Waller Pope, Chairman, and Thomas M. Beck and Ernest DuBester, Members

This matter is before the Authority on an exception to an award of Arbitrator Myron L. Joseph filed by the Union under § 7122(a) of the Federal Service Labor-Management Relations Statute (the Statute) and part 2425 of the Authority's Regulations. The Agency did not file an opposition to the Union's exception.

Under § 7122(a) of the Statute, an award is deficient if it is contrary to any law, rule, or regulation, or it is deficient on other grounds similar to those applied by federal courts in private sector labor-management relations. Upon careful consideration of the entire record in this case and Authority precedent, the Authority concludes that the award is not deficient on the ground raised in the exception and set forth in § 7122(a). *See U.S. Dep't of Labor (OSHA)*, 34 FLRA 573, 575 (1990) (award not deficient as failing to draw its essence from the parties' collective bargaining agreement where excepting party fails to establish that the award cannot in any rational way be derived from the agreement; is so unfounded in reason and fact and so unconnected to the wording and purpose of the agreement as to manifest an infidelity to the obligation of the arbitrator; does not represent a plausible interpretation of the agreement; or evidences a manifest disregard of the agreement).

Accordingly, the Union's exception is denied.

65 FLRA No. 100

UNITED STATES
DEPARTMENT OF VETERANS AFFAIRS
MEDICAL CENTER
AUGUSTA, GEORGIA
(Agency)

and

NATIONAL NURSES UNITED
(Union)

0-AR-4719

DECISION

January 31, 2011

Before the Authority: Carol Waller Pope, Chairman, and Thomas M. Beck and Ernest DuBester, Members

This matter is before the Authority on an exception to an award of Arbitrator Allen D. Schwartz filed by the Agency under § 7122(a) of the Federal Service Labor-Management Relations Statute (the Statute) and part 2425 of the Authority's Regulations. The Union did not file an opposition to the Agency's exception.

Under § 7122(a) of the Statute, an award is deficient if it is contrary to any law, rule, or regulation, or it is deficient on other grounds similar to those applied by federal courts in private sector labor-management relations. Upon careful consideration of the entire record in this case and Authority precedent, the Authority concludes that the award is not deficient on the ground raised in the exception and set forth in § 7122(a). *See Prof'l Airways Sys. Specialists, Dist. No. 1, MEBA/NMU (AFL-CIO)*, 48 FLRA 764, 768-69 (1993) (award not deficient as contrary to law where excepting party fails to establish that the award is in any manner contrary to the law, rule, or regulation on which the party relies).

Accordingly, the Agency's exception is denied.

65 FLRA No. 101

AMERICAN FEDERATION
OF GOVERNMENT EMPLOYEES
LOCAL 12
(Union)

and

UNITED STATES
DEPARTMENT OF LABOR
WASHINGTON, D.C.
(Agency)

0-AR-4721

DECISION

January 31, 2011

Before the Authority: Carol Waller Pope, Chairman, and Thomas M. Beck and Ernest DuBester, Members

This matter is before the Authority on exceptions to an award of Arbitrator Ellen S. Saltzman filed by the Union under § 7122(a) of the Federal Service Labor-Management Relations Statute (the Statute) and part 2425 of the Authority's Regulations. The Agency filed an opposition to the Union's exceptions.

Under § 7122(a) of the Statute, an award is deficient if it is contrary to any law, rule, or regulation, or it is deficient on other grounds similar to those applied by federal courts in private sector labor-management relations. Upon careful consideration of the entire record in this case and Authority precedent, the Authority concludes that the award is not deficient on the grounds raised in the exceptions and set forth in § 7122(a). *See NFFE, Local 1827,* 52 FLRA 1378, 1385 (1997) (exception challenging an arbitrator's evaluation of the evidence and determination of the weight to be accorded such evidence provides no basis for finding an award deficient); *U.S. Dep't of Veterans Affairs, Med. Ctr., N. Chi., Ill.,* 52 FLRA 387, 398 (1996) (award not deficient because of bias on the part of an arbitrator where excepting party fails to demonstrate that the award was procured by improper means, that there was partiality or corruption on the part of the arbitrator, or that the arbitrator engaged in misconduct that prejudiced the rights of the party); *AFGE, Local 1668,* 50 FLRA 124, 126 (1995) (award not deficient on ground that arbitrator failed to provide a fair hearing where excepting party fails to demonstrate that the arbitrator refused to hear or consider pertinent and material evidence, or that other actions in conducting the proceeding so prejudiced a party so as to affect the fairness of the proceeding as a whole); *Prof'l Airways Sys. Specialists, Dist. No. 1, MEBA/NMU (AFL-CIO),* 48 FLRA 764, 768-69 (1993) (award not deficient as contrary to law where excepting party fails to establish that the award is in any manner contrary to the law, rule, or regulation on which the party relies).

Accordingly, the Union's exceptions are denied.

65 FLRA No. 102

UNITED STATES
DEPARTMENT OF THE TREASURY
INTERNAL REVENUE SERVICE
AUSTIN, TEXAS
(Agency)

and

NATIONAL TREASURY
EMPLOYEES UNION
CHAPTER 72
(Union)

0-AR-4178

DECISION

January 31, 2011

Before the Authority: Carol Waller Pope, Chairman, and Thomas M. Beck and Ernest DuBester, Members

I. Statement of the Case

This matter is before the Authority on an exception to an award of Arbitrator Marsha Kelliher filed by the Agency under § 7122(a) of the Federal Service Labor-Management Relations Statute (the Statute) and part 2425 of the Authority's Regulations. The Union filed an opposition to the Agency's exception.

The Arbitrator sustained the Union's grievance claiming that the Agency violated the parties' collective bargaining agreement (CBA) by limiting the assignment of overtime to Saturdays or Alternative Work Schedule (AWS) days-off.[1]

For the reasons set forth below, we deny the Agency's exception.

II. Background and Arbitrator's Award

Ordinarily, the Agency allowed employees to work overtime before or after the employees' regular work hours, on Saturdays, and on AWS days-off. The maximum amount of overtime the Agency would authorize for an employee was eight hours per week. In August 2005, for a two-week period, the Agency changed its policy concerning when overtime could be worked. For this particular two-week period, the Agency decided that overtime work could be performed only on Saturdays and AWS days-off. The Agency cited its interest in efficiency as the reason for the change.

The Union filed a grievance claiming that this limitation allowed employees on an AWS schedule more opportunities to work overtime than employees on a five-day a week schedule. The Union claimed that this violated Article 24, Section (2)(A)(1) of the parties' CBA, which requires that overtime be distributed "as equitably as possible."[2] Award at 1.

The Arbitrator framed the issue as: "Whether the assignment of overtime only on Saturdays or [AWS] days-off . . . was a violation of Article 24, Section (2)(A)(1) of the [CBA], and if so, what is the appropriate remedy?" *Id.* The Agency argued before the Arbitrator, among other things, that the right to assign work includes the determination of when overtime will be performed. *Id.*

The Arbitrator found that, if the Agency limited overtime to Saturdays or AWS days-off only, then employees on an AWS schedule would have twice the opportunity to work overtime as employees on other schedules. *Id.* at 2. The Arbitrator concluded that the distribution of overtime in this manner would therefore not be "as equitabl[e] as possible[,]" as required by the CBA. *Id.* Accordingly, the Arbitrator ordered that employees not on an AWS schedule be paid for sixteen hours of overtime with interest and attorney fees, less the amount of overtime actually worked, and not to exceed the average number of overtime hours worked per week by the affected employee from January 2005 through June 2005. *Id.*

III. Positions of the Parties

A. Agency's Exception

The Agency claims the award is contrary to law. The Agency contends that the award affects

1. The AWS is a work schedule that allows employees to be off from work one day of the regular five-day work week in return for working longer hours the other four days. Exception at 3.

2. Article 24, Section (2)(A)(1) provides in pertinent part: "Overtime will be distributed as equitably as possible among qualified employees." Opp'n, Attach., CBA at 75.

management's right to assign work under § 7106(a)(2)(B) of the Statute. Exceptions at 2. The Agency also asserts that Article 24, Section (2)(A)(1) of the CBA, as interpreted by the Arbitrator, is not enforceable pursuant to § 7106(b)(3). Specifically, the Agency claims that the CBA provison is not an arrangement because there is no adverse effect to ameliorate. In support, the Agency claims that all employees may work only a maximum of eight hours of overtime a week and the Arbitrator's interpretation of the provision does nothing more than provide employees on a five-day a week schedule more days on which to work overtime. *Id.* at 6. Therefore, the Agency alleges, the Arbitrator's interpretation of the provision at issue does not make the distribution of overtime more equitable. *Id.* at 6-7. Finally, the Agency asserts that Article 24, Section (2)(A)(1) of the CBA, as interpreted by the Arbitrator, is not enforceable pursuant to § 7106(b)(3) because it excessively interferes with management's rights by abrogating its right to assign work. *Id.* at 8-9.

B. Union's Opposition

The Union claims that allowing employees to work overtime during the week is a past practice that allows overtime to be distributed as equitably as possible, as required by the CBA. Opp'n at 3-4. The Union further argues that Article 24, Section (2)(A)(1) of the CBA and the past practice constitute a procedure for assigning overtime negotiated pursuant to § 7106(b)(2) of the Statute. *Id.* at 6-8.

IV. Analysis and Conclusions

The Agency argues that the award is contrary to management's right to assign work under § 7106(a)(2)(B) of the Statute. When an exception involves an award's consistency with law, the Authority reviews any question of law raised by the exception and the award de novo. *See NTEU, Chapter 24*, 50 FLRA 330, 332 (1995) (*NTEU*) (citing *U.S. Customs Serv. v. FLRA*, 43 F.3d 682, 686-87 (D.C. Cir. 1994)). In applying this standard, the Authority assesses whether an arbitrator's legal conclusions are consistent with the applicable standard of law. *See U.S. Dep't of Def., Dep'ts of the Army & the Air Force, Ala. Nat'l Guard, Northport, Ala.*, 55 FLRA 37, 40 (1998). In making that assessment, the Authority defers to the arbitrator's underlying factual findings. *See id.*

The Authority recently revised the analysis that it will apply when reviewing management rights exceptions to arbitration awards. *See U.S. Envtl. Prot. Agency*, 65 FLRA 113, 116-18 (2010) (*EPA*) (Member Beck concurring); *Fed. Deposit Ins. Corp., Div. of Supervision & Consumer Prot., S.F. Region*, 65 FLRA 102, 106-07 (2010) (*FDIC, SF Region*) (Chairman Pope concurring). Under the revised analysis, the Authority assesses whether the award affects the exercise of the asserted management right. *EPA*, 65 FLRA at 115. If so, then, as relevant here, the Authority examines whether the award enforces a contract provision negotiated under § 7106(b).[3] *Id.* Also, under the revised analysis, in determining whether the award enforces a contract provision negotiated under § 7106(b)(3), the Authority assesses: (1) whether the contract provision constitutes an arrangement for employees adversely affected by the exercise of a management right; and (2) if so, whether the arbitrator's enforcement of the arrangement abrogates the exercise of the management right.[4] *See id.* at 116-118. In concluding that it would apply an abrogation standard, the Authority rejected continued application of an excessive-interference standard. *Id.* at 118.

It is undisputed that the award affects management's right to assign work. *See AFGE, Council 215*, 60 FLRA 461, 464 (2004) (the right to assign work under the Statute includes the right to assign overtime and to determine when overtime will be performed). Consequently, we examine whether the Arbitrator enforced a contract provision negotiated under § 7106(b). Here, the Arbitrator enforced Article 24, Section (2)(A)(1) of the CBA. He determined that the Agency violated this provision by inequitably refusing to allow employees on a five-day a week schedule to work overtime during their regular work week before or after their regular work hours.

---

3. When an award affects a management right under § 7106(a)(2) of the Statute, the Authority may also examine whether the award enforces an applicable law. *EPA*, 65 FLRA at 115 n.7.

4. For the reasons articulated in his recent concurring opinion and footnotes, Member Beck would conclude that it is unnecessary to assess whether the contract provision is an appropriate arrangement or whether it abrogates a § 7106(a) right. The appropriate question is simply whether the remedy directed by the Arbitrator enforces the provision in a reasonable and reasonably foreseeable fashion. *See EPA*, 65 FLRA at 120 (Concurring Opinion of Member Beck); *FDIC, SF Region*, 65 FLRA at 107; *Soc. Sec. Admin., Dallas Region*, 65 FLRA 405, 408 n.5 (2010); *U.S. Dept of the Air Force, Air Force Materiel Command*, 65 FLRA 395, 398 n.7 (2010); *U.S. Dep't of Health & Human Servs., Office of Medicare Hearings & Appeals*, 65 FLRA 175, 177 n.3 (2010); *U.S Dep't of Transp., Fed. Aviation Admin.*, 65 FLRA 171, 173 n.5 (2010).

The Agency claims that Article 24, Section (2)(A)(1) of the CBA, as interpreted and applied by the Arbitrator, is not enforceable pursuant to § 7106(b)(3) because it is not an arrangement. In the Agency's view, limiting the days on which employees may work overtime does not have an adverse effect on those employees. Exception at 6-8. The standard set by the Authority to decide whether a provision constitutes an arrangement is whether the provision, as interpreted and applied by an arbitrator, ameliorates or mitigates adverse effects that flow from management's exercise of its management rights. *E.g., EPA*, 65 FLRA at 116 (citing *U.S. DOJ, Fed Bureau of Prisons, U.S. Penitentiary, Atlanta, Ga.*, 57 FLRA 406, 410 (2001) (Chairman Cabaniss dissenting)).

The Arbitrator's finding that employees on a five-day a week schedule were inequitably deprived of opportunities to work overtime during their regular work week supports the conclusion that the CBA provision enforced by the Arbitrator constitutes an arrangement. As the Arbitrator's award reflects, the Agency's decision to limit when overtime could be worked adversely affected these employees by significantly reducing their overtime work opportunities. Further, the Arbitrator's interpretation and application of the CBA provision has the effect of restoring those opportunities. Therefore, the Arbitrator's interpretation of Article 24, Section (2)(A)(1) ameliorates the adverse effects flowing from the exercise of management's right to assign the work. *EPA,* 65 FLRA at 116. Consequently, the Agency's assertion provides no basis for finding that the award does not enforce an arrangement.

The Agency also claims that Article 24, Section (2)(A)(1) of the CBA, as interpreted and applied by the Arbitrator, is not enforceable pursuant to § 7106(b)(3) because it excessively interferes with management's rights by abrogating management's right to assign work. Exception at 8-9. As stated above, the Authority no longer applies an excessive-interference standard in determining whether an arbitrator has enforced a contract provision negotiated under § 7106(b)(3); rather, it applies an abrogation standard. *EPA*, 65 FLRA at 116-18. The Authority has previously described an award that abrogates the exercise of a management right as an award that "precludes an agency from exercising" the right. *U.S. Dep't of the Army, Army Transp. Ctr., Fort Eustis, Va.,* 38 FLRA 186, 190 (1990) (quoting *Dep't of the Treasury, U.S. Customs Serv.*, 37 FLRA 309, 314 (1990)).

The Agency fails to demonstrate that Article 24, Section (2)(A)(1), as interpreted and applied by the Arbitrator, abrogates the exercise of the right to assign work. The Arbitrator did not interpret the provision to prevent management from assigning overtime. Article 24, Section (2)(A)(1), as applied by the Arbitrator, merely requires that overtime be distributed "as equitably as possible." Award at 2. Such a limitation, making equity a requirement in the assignment of overtime, does not preclude the Agency from exercising its right to assign work.

Based on the foregoing, the Agency has not shown that, as interpreted and applied by the Arbitrator, Article 24, Section (2)(A)(1) abrogates management's right to assign work. Accordingly, we find that the award is not contrary to management's right to assign work under § 7106(a)(2)(B) of the Statute.[5]

V. Decision

The Agency's exception is denied.

5. In view of this conclusion, we do not address whether the proposal constitutes a procedure under §7106(b)(2) of the Statute.

65 FLRA No. 103

SOCIAL SECURITY ADMINISTRATION
OFFICE OF DISABILITY
ADJUDICATION AND REVIEW
(Agency)

and

ASSOCIATION OF ADMINISTRATIVE
LAW JUDGES
JUDICIAL COUNCIL ONE
INTERNATIONAL FEDERATION
OF PROFESSIONAL AND
TECHNICAL ENGINEERS
(Union)

0-AR-4572

DECISION

January 31, 2011

Before the Authority: Carol Waller Pope, Chairman, and Thomas M. Beck and Ernest DuBester, Members

I. Statement of the Case

This matter is before the Authority on exceptions to an award of Arbitrator Andrée Y. McKissick filed by the Agency under § 7122(a) of the Federal Service Labor-Management Relations Statute (the Statute) and part 2425 of the Authority's Regulations. The Union filed an opposition to the Agency's exceptions.

The Arbitrator found that the Agency violated the parties' agreement by denying a Union representative's requests to receive travel authorizations identified as "no-cost travel orders" (NCTOs), and denying another Union representative's request for official time. For the reasons that follow, we set aside the award in part and deny the exceptions in part.

II. Background and Arbitrator's Award

This matter involves two grievances. In the first grievance, the Union alleged that the Agency violated the parties' agreement when it refused to issue a Union representative three NCTOs to travel on official time to represent Union members before the Merit Systems Protection Board. *See* Award at 2. In this connection, an NCTO is a type of travel authorization provided for by Article 9, Sidebar 2 of the parties' agreement.[1] Prior to its decision to end the practice, the Agency issued NCTOs to Union representatives for travel that was: (1) "on official time"; and (2) not paid for by the Agency. Award at 7. *See id.* at 9-10, 12, 16-17. *See also* Exceptions at 3 n.4, 8-9; Opp'n at 13-14; Opp'n, Attach. 2 at 19. Under Article 9, Sidebar 2, a Union representative who has received an NCTO is permitted to use his or her government "travel card," Award at 7, to book travel through the Agency's contracted travel agency and, thus, access discounted airfares that the U.S. General Services Administration (GSA) has negotiated with the airlines, also referred to as the GSA's "City Pair Program." Tr. at 225; Exceptions at 9, 12, 13 n.16, 14. *See* Award at 7, 17. *Cf.* Opp'n, Attach. 2, Union's Brief at 16 (Union's Brief).

In the second grievance, the Union alleged that the Agency violated the parties' agreement when it refused to: (1) grant another Union representative official time to attend a training seminar that was paid for by the Union and hosted by the Federal Mediation and Conciliation Service (FMCS); and (2) issue the representative an NCTO to attend the seminar. *See* Award at 2, 14-15. *See also* Exceptions, Attach. 5, Step Three Grievance at 7-9.

The grievances were unresolved and submitted to arbitration.[2] *See* Award at 2-3.

---

1. Article 9, Sidebar 2 of the parties' agreement states, in pertinent part:

> To the extent not precluded by law and regulation, for those situations in which [Union] representatives who are also unit employees and are on official time are not authorized the payment of transportation expenses by [the Agency, the Agency] agrees to issue [NCTOs]. This provision is limited to [Union] representatives who have a government travel card and who use that card for full payment of affected transportation expenses. [NCTOs] issued pursuant to this provision will not be used for personal travel.

Opp'n, Attach. 1, parties' agreement at 39. *Accord* Award at 7.

2. The Arbitrator did not frame the issues before her, but noted each party's statement of the issues. *See* Award at 3.

With regard to the first grievance, the Arbitrator found that, in Article 9, Sidebar 2 of the parties' agreement, "'the Agency agree[d] to issue [NCTOs].'" *Id.* at 15. The Arbitrator rejected the Agency's argument that *NTEU*, 30 FLRA 690 (1987) (*NTEU*), precludes the Agency from issuing NCTOs. Award at 13. Specifically, the Arbitrator stated that the "expansive language and inclusion of representational activities of Article 9, Section 1" of the parties' agreement "significantly widens the scope of 'official time' and its parameters."[3] *Id.* at 15. Thus, "the [parties' agreement] and its definitions in this regard has superseded the narrow limitations" of *NTEU*. *Id.* Accordingly, the Arbitrator determined the Agency was required to comply with Article 9, Sidebar 2, and directed the Agency to "cease and desist the denial of [NCTOs] and comply with Article 9, Sidebar [2] of the [parties' agreement]." *Id.* at 15-17. Additionally, the Arbitrator "disagree[d]" with the Agency's claim that Article 9, Sidebar 2 conflicts with the "Federal Travel Regulations (FTR), the Agency's Administrative Instructions Manual System (AIMS)[, and] Smartpay[,]"[4] *id.* at 16, and "disagree[d]" with the Agency's argument that employees are "protected under the Office of Workers Compensation Program (OWCP) of the Federal Employee[]s['] Compensation Act or the Federal Torts Claims Act (FTCA) without the concurrence of a[n] NCTO[.]" *Id.* at 17.

With regard to the second grievance, the Arbitrator determined that Article 9, Section 1 of the parties' agreement defines "official time" as including "'representational activities.'" *Id.* at 13 (quoting Article 9, Section 1). *See* Opp'n, Attach. 1, parties' agreement (Agreement) at 24. The Arbitrator also determined that Union-sponsored training is a "representational activity[.]" *See id.* at 13-14. In this connection, the Arbitrator found it persuasive that "the [s]tandard [f]orms located in Article 9, Section 11" of the parties' agreement "specif[y] 'Union-Sponsored training."[5] *Id.* at 14. The Arbitrator determined that the FMCS seminar was "not specifically excluded from coverage" in the parties' agreement, and concluded that the training seminar that the Union representative attended "falls within the ambit of 'Union-Sponsored training.'" *Id.* at 14-15. Additionally, the Arbitrator considered a contract between the Agency and the American Federation of Government Employees (AFGE) (AFGE contract), which states that "'Union-Sponsored training is an appropriate representational activity for which official time may be used[.']" *Id.* at 14 (quoting AFGE contract). The Arbitrator stated that "both the [parties' agreement] and the [AFGE contract] are supportive of training for representational purposes" and that both are "supportive of representational work and the development of those skills." *Id.* Accordingly, the Arbitrator found that the Agency violated the parties' agreement by failing to grant the Union representative official time, and she directed the Agency to "reinstate[] . . . three . . . days annual leave" that the representative was forced to use in lieu of official time to attend the training seminar.[6] *Id.* at 17. *See also id.* at 2.

III. Positions of the Parties

A. Agency's Exceptions

With regard to NCTOs, the Agency contends that the award is contrary to the Authority's decision in *NTEU*, 30 FLRA 690, because requiring the Agency to issue NCTOs results in Union representatives having access to government discount airfares through the City Pair Program even when their travel is not paid for by U.S. government. *See* Exceptions at 9, 12. Additionally, the Agency argues that the award is contrary to several of the FTR because they require that travel booked through the City Pair Program be for employees on "official business" traveling at "government expense." *Id.*

3. Article 9, Section 1 of the parties' agreement states, as relevant here, that "the term 'official time' shall include the purposes set forth in 5 U.S.C. § 7131, as well as other representational activities[.]" Award at 4.

4. The Arbitrator did not cite a specific section of the FTR or the AIMS. In addition, although the Arbitrator did not define "Smartpay[,]" there is no dispute what "Smartpay" is a government charge card program administered by the GSA. *See* Exceptions at 9, 14-15; *id.*, Attach. 11; Opp'n at 12, 20; Union's Brief at 16 & n.5.

5. Article 9, Section 11 of the parties' agreement states: "It is understood that nothing in this agreement is intended to limit the statutory rights to official time provided pursuant to 5 U.S.C. § 7131 or any other statute or regulation." Agreement at 32.

6. The Arbitrator further found that this Union representative "should have been granted a[n] [NCTO] to Washington DC for that representational training." Award at 15. However, the Arbitrator did not issue a remedy with regard to the NCTO, because the Union "waive[d] the issuance of any retroactive [NCTOs]." *Id.* at 12.

(citing 41 C.F.R. § 300-1.1, 301-1.3, 301-10.106, 301-10.110; *NTEU*, 30 FLRA at 691).[7] Because the award would result in Union representatives booking travel through the City Pair Program that was not "at government expense," the Agency further claims that the award would cause it to violate the GSA's City Pair contract with the airlines.[8] *See id.* at 13 (citing Exceptions, Attach. 13). The Agency further argues that the award is contrary to law because: (1) Union representatives traveling pursuant to Article 9, Sidebar 2, do not meet the "official travel" requirement allegedly set forth in *NTEU*, Exceptions at 12; (2) it is contrary to the "GSA's Smart[p]ay policy on the use of government credit cards[,]" *id.* at 14-15; (3) it is contrary to "the FTR governing the use of the government credit card[,]" *id.* at15 (citing 41 C.F.R. § 301-51.7).[9] Moreover, the Agency contends that the award fails to draw its essence from the parties' agreement, *id.* at 21, is based on nonfacts, *id.* at 25, 28, and is deficient because the Arbitrator exceeded her authority, *id.* at 26-27.

With regard to official time, the Agency asserts that the award is contrary to management's rights under § 7106 of the Statute. *See id.* at 16-20. In this connection, the Agency quotes § 7106(b)(1) and asserts that the award fails to satisfy both prongs of the two-pronged test set forth in *United States Department of the Treasury, Bureau of Engraving & Printing, Washington, District of Columbia*, 53 FLRA 146, 151-54 (1997) (*BEP*).[10] *See* Exceptions at 17, 20. The Agency also alleges that the award fails to draw its essence from the parties' agreement because Article 9, Section 1 is "silent regarding the question of whether the Union's representational activities include the use of official time to attend third-party seminars." *Id.* at 22. Finally, the Agency claims that the Arbitrator was not authorized under the parties' agreement to consider the AFGE contract. *Id.* at 23.

B. Union's Opposition

The Union contends that the award is "consistent with . . . governing laws and regulations." Opp'n at 11. First, in response to the Agency's claim that use of the City Pair Program is limited to those traveling "at government expense[,]" the Union asserts that "although not traveling at government expense, the [U]nion representatives were on 'official government business' satisfying the requirement for use of the City Pair[] Program." *Id.* at 14. Moreover, the Union contends that travel under Article 9, Sidebar 2 constitutes "official government travel" and that Article 9, Sidebar is enforceable. *Id.* at 13 (citing *NTEU*, 21 FLRA 6 (1986)). Additionally, the Union argues that *NTEU*, 30 FLRA 690, is "distinguishable" because it pertained to the negotiability of a bargaining proposal, not an agreed-upon contract. Opp'n at 12.

Next, the Union contends that the award is not contrary to § 7106. *Id.* at 14. In this regard, the Union asserts that the Agency "does not claim that the [a]ward interferes with any right delineated in [§] 7106(a)." *Id.* at 15. As to the Agency's argument regarding the AFGE contract, the Union argues that the award is "clearly based on the parties' . . . agreement and not on any collateral document." *Id.* at 17. As to the Agency's claim that the award is based on nonfacts, the Union asserts that "all of the alleged [nonfacts] are related to matters that were disputed below." *Id.*

7. 41 C.F.R. § 300-1.1 states, in pertinent part, that the FTR "implement[] statutory requirements . . . for travel by Federal civilian employees and others authorized to travel at [g]overnment expense."

41 C.F.R. § 301-1.3 states, in pertinent part, that "[e]mployees on official business" are "eligible for TDY allowances[.]" We note, in this regard, that "TDY" means temporary duty location, a "place, away from an employee's official station, where the employee is authorized to travel." 41 C.F.R. § 300-3.1.

41 C.F.R. § 301-10.106 states, in pertinent part, that "[i]f you are a civilian employee . . . you must always use a contract city-pair fare for scheduled air passenger transportation service unless one of the limited exceptions in § 301-10.107 exist."

41 C.F.R. § 301-10.110 states, in pertinent part, that an employee may not use "contract passenger transportation service for personal travel[.]" *See also* 41 C.F.R. § 300-2.22 (chapter 301, subchapter B addresses employees).

8. We note that the record indicates that an NCTO issued pursuant to Article 9, Sidebar 2, generally results in a Union representative using the City Pair Program. *See* Award at 7, 17; Exceptions at 9, 13. *Cf.* Union's Brief at 16. *Accord* 41 C.F.R. § 301-10.106.

9. 41 C.F.R. § 301-51.7 states, in pertinent part, that an employee "may not use the [g]overnment contractor-issued travel charge card for personal reasons while on official travel."

10. The *BEP* analysis, which the Authority no longer applies, is discussed below.

IV. Analysis and Conclusions

A. The portion of the award regarding NCTOs is contrary to law, but the portion of the award regarding official time is not contrary to law.

When an exception involves an award's consistency with law the Authority reviews any question of law raised by the exception and the award de novo. *E.g., AFGE, Local 3506*, 65 FLRA 30, 32 (2010). In applying the standard of de novo review, the Authority assesses whether an arbitrator's legal conclusions are consistent with the applicable standard of law. *Id.* In making that assessment, the Authority defers to the arbitrator's underlying factual findings. *Id.*

1. NCTOs

The Authority has previously found that the City Pair Program "applies only to individuals who are engaged in official travel conducted *at [g]overnment expense*[,]" based on the wording of a formerly-effective regulation, FPMR A-30. *NTEU*, 30 FLRA at 691 (emphasis added). FPMR A-30 prescribed policies and procedures "govern[ing] the use of carriers under contract to GSA to provide specified transportation services to 'Federal employees and other persons authorized to travel at *[g]overnment expense.*'"[11] *Id.* at 692 (emphasis added). The wording in FPMR A-30 is substantively identical to the wording in the current FTR. In this regard, 41 C.F.R. § 300-1.1 states that the FTR "implement[] statutory requirements and Executive branch policies for travel by Federal civilian employees and others authorized to travel *at [g]overnment expense.*" 41 C.F.R. § 300-1.1 (emphasis added). *Accord* 41 C.F.R. § 300-3.1 (defining "[c]ontract carriers" as U.S. air carriers which are "under contract with the government to furnish Federal employees and other persons authorized to travel *at [g]overnment expense* with passenger transportation service") (emphasis added). Thus, consistent with the Authority's interpretation of substantively identical language in *NTEU*, the FTR indicate that the City Pair Program does not apply to travel that is not at government expense. As it is undisputed that the award results in Union representatives having access to the City Pair Program for travel that is not at government expense, *see* Exceptions at 3 n.4, 8-9; Opp'n at 13-14; Agreement at 39; Union's Brief at 19, the award is contrary to the FTR.[12]

We note that, although the Union cites *NTEU*, 30 FLRA 690, for the proposition that travel on official time may constitute official travel, *see* Opp'n at 12, and *NTEU* 21 FLRA 6, for the proposition that what constitutes "official government travel" is left to the discretion of the Agency, Opp'n at 13, neither decision demonstrates that a Union representative may access the City Pair Program for travel that is not at government expense. *See NTEU*, 30 FLRA at 691; *NTEU*, 21 FLRA at 6-12. In this connection, although the Union claims that an employee "satisf[ies] the requirement for use of the City Pair[] Program" if he or she is on "'official government business[,]'" Opp'n at 14, the Union cites no law, regulation, or precedent to support its assertion that a Union representative who is not traveling at government expense may nevertheless access the City Pair Program. *See id.* at 12-14. Additionally, while the Arbitrator stated that *NTEU*, 30 FLRA 690, had been "superseded" by the parties' agreement, Award at 15, there is no basis for finding that the agreement can "supersede" the requirement of the FTR that the City Pair Program applies only to individuals who are engaged in official travel conducted at government expense. *See* 41 C.F.R. § 300-1.1; *NTEU*, 30 FLRA at 691-93.

For the foregoing reasons, we find that the Arbitrator's direction that the Agency cease and desist issuing NCTOs pursuant to Article 9, Sidebar 2 is inconsistent with the FTR. Thus, we set aside the award with regard to NCTOs.[13]

11. FPMR A-30 stated, in pertinent part: "This regulation prescribes policies and procedures governing the use of U.S. certified carriers in furnishing [g]overnment employees and other persons authorized to travel at [g]overnment expense with scheduled airline/rail passenger service between selected U.S. and international cities/airports at reduced fares." 51 Fed. Reg. 40805 (Nov. 10, 1986) (then to be codified at 41 C.F.R. Chapter 101, subchapter A, appendix). *Accord NTEU*, 30 FLRA at 691 & n.1.

12. The Authority has held that the FTR are government-wide regulations. *See, e.g., U.S. Dep't of Def. Dependents Sch., Arlington, Va.*, 52 FLRA 3, 7 (1996). Insofar as an arbitrator's award construes an agreement contrary to a government-wide regulation, the award is unenforceable. *See Soc. Sec. Admin., Office of Disability Adjudication & Review*, 64 FLRA 1000, 1002 n.5 (2010).

13. As we have found that the award is deficient on this ground, it is not necessary to address the Agency's remaining exceptions to the portion of the award that pertains to NCTOs.

2. Official Time

The Agency argues that the portion of the award regarding official time is contrary to management's rights. The Authority recently revised the analysis that it will apply when reviewing management-rights exceptions to arbitration awards. *See U.S. EPA*, 65 FLRA 113, 115 (2010) (Member Beck concurring) (*EPA*); *FDIC, Div. of Supervision & Consumer Prot., S.F. Region*, 65 FLRA 102, 106-07 (2010) (Chairman Pope concurring) (*FDIC*). Under the revised analysis, the Authority first assesses whether the award affects the exercise of the asserted management right. *EPA*, 65 FLRA at 115. If so, then the Authority examines whether the award provides a remedy for a violation of either an applicable law, within the meaning of § 7106(a)(2) of the Statute, or a contract provision that was negotiated pursuant to § 7106(b) of the Statute. *Id.* Also under the revised analysis, in determining whether the award enforces a contract provision negotiated under § 7106(b)(3), the Authority assesses: (1) whether the contract provision constitutes an arrangement for employees adversely affected by the exercise of a management right; and (2) if so, then whether the arbitrator's enforcement of the arrangement abrogates the exercise of the management right.[14] *See id.* at 118. In concluding that the Authority would apply an abrogation standard, the Authority rejected continued application of an excessive-interference standard. *Id.* at 113. In addition, in setting forth the revised analysis, the Authority rejected the continued application of the reconstruction requirement (i.e. the "second prong") set forth in *BEP*. *FDIC*, 65 FLRA at 106-07.

Here, although the Agency asserts that the award is contrary to management's rights, it does not cite a management right under § 7106(a). In addition, although the Agency quotes § 7106(b)(1) of the Statute, the Agency does not assert what right under § 7106(b)(1) is affected by the award. Accordingly, we deny the claim that the award affects management's rights as a bare assertion. *See U.S. Dep't of the Treasury, U.S. Customs Serv., El Paso, Tex.*, 55 FLRA 553, 558 n.3 (1999) (rejecting unsupported management right argument as a bare assertion). Additionally, with regard to the Agency's claim that the award fails to satisfy the second prong of *BEP*, as stated above, the Authority no longer applies a reconstruction standard. *See FDIC*, 65 FLRA at 106-07. Thus the Agency's claim does not demonstrate that the award is deficient.

For the foregoing reasons, we deny the Agency's management rights exception.

B. The award regarding official time does not fail to draw its essence from the parties' agreement.

The Authority will find that an arbitration award is deficient as failing to draw its essence from the collective bargaining agreement when the appealing party establishes that the award: (1) cannot in any rational way be derived from the agreement; (2) is so unfounded in reason and fact and so unconnected with the wording and purposes of the collective bargaining agreement as to manifest an infidelity to the obligation of the arbitrator; (3) does not represent a plausible interpretation of the agreement; or (4) evidences a manifest disregard of the agreement. *See U.S. Dep't of Labor (OSHA)*, 34 FLRA 573, 575 (1990). The Authority and the courts defer to the arbitrator in this context "because it is the arbitrator's construction of the agreement for which the parties have bargained[.]" *Id.* at 576. Additionally, when an arbitrator has based an award on separate and independent grounds, an appealing party must establish that all of the grounds are deficient in order to demonstrate that the award is deficient. *E.g.*, *Broad. Bd. of Governors, Office of Cuba Broad.*, 64 FLRA 888, 892 (2010) (*Cuba Broad.*).

Here, as stated previously, the Arbitrator found that the parties' agreement grants official time for "representational activities," including Union-sponsored training. Award at 13 (quoting Article 9, Section 1 of the parties' agreement). The Arbitrator determined that representational activities includes training, in part because "[s]tandard [f]orms located in Article 9, Section 11" of the parties' agreement "specif[y] 'Union-Sponsored training.'" *Id.* at 14. Additionally, the Arbitrator noted that official time for training is "not specifically excluded from coverage," and further found that the third-party held training was "Union-sponsored" because the Union

14. For the reasons articulated in his recent concurring opinion and footnotes, Member Beck would conclude that it is unnecessary to assess whether the contract provision is an appropriate arrangement or whether it abrogates a § 7106(a) right. The appropriate question is simply whether the remedy directed by the Arbitrator enforces the provision in a reasonable and reasonably foreseeable fashion. *See EPA*, 65 FLRA at 120 (Concurring Opinion of Member Beck); *FDIC*, 65 FLRA at 107; *U.S. Dep't of the Air Force, Air Force Materiel Command*, 65 FLRA 395, 398 n.7 (2010); *U.S. Dep't of Health & Human Servs., Office of Medicare Hearings & Appeals*, 65 FLRA 175, 177 n.3 (2010); *U.S. Dep't of Transp., Fed. Aviation Admin.*, 65 FLRA 171, 173 n.5 (2010).

paid for the seminar. *Id.* These findings support the Arbitrator's conclusion that the Agency violated the parties' agreement when it refused to grant official time to the Union representative who attended the Union-sponsored training, and there is no basis for finding the Arbitrator's interpretation of the parties' agreement to be irrational, unfounded, implausible, or in manifest disregard of the parties' agreement. With regard to the AFGE contract, the Arbitrator's interpretation of the parties' agreement is a separate and independent basis for the award. Thus, the Agency's claim that the Arbitrator's consideration of the AFGE contract is erroneous does not render the award deficient. *See Cuba Broad.*, 64 FLRA at 892-93.

Based on the foregoing, we deny this exception.

V. Decision

The portion of the award regarding NCTOs is set aside. The Agency's remaining exceptions are denied.

65 FLRA No. 104

UNITED STATES
DEPARTMENT OF AGRICULTURE
FARM SERVICE AGENCY
KANSAS CITY, MISSOURI
(Agency)

and

NATIONAL TREASURY
EMPLOYEES UNION
CHAPTER 264
(Union)

0-AR-4239

DECISION

February 3, 2011

Before the Authority: Carol Waller Pope, Chairman, and Thomas M. Beck and Ernest DuBester, Members

I. Statement of the Case

This matter is before the Authority on exceptions to an award of Arbitrator Marsha J. Murphy filed by the Agency under § 7122(a) of the Federal Service Labor-Management Relations Statute (the Statute) and part 2425 of the Authority's Regulations. The Union filed an opposition to the Agency's exceptions.

The Arbitrator concluded that the Agency's unilateral implementation of a five-tier performance appraisal system (PAS) violated the parties' collective bargaining agreement (CBA) and § 7116(a)(7) of the Statute. For the reasons that follow, we dismiss in part and deny in part the Agency's exceptions.

II. Background and Arbitrator's Award

The unit of employees involved here operated under a two-tier PAS specifically established by Article 27 of the parties' CBA. Award at 3. The Agency unilaterally decided to implement a five-tier PAS. The Agency notified the Union of its decision by providing the Union with copies of Notices PM-2482 and PM-2512. *Id.* at 3-4; Exceptions, Attach. C, Tr. at 17-22. Notices PM-2482 and PM-2512 are Agency notices announcing the implementation of a five-tier PAS. Exceptions, Attach. C, Tr. at 17-22. The Union challenged this proposed change on the ground that it conflicted with Article 27's two-tier PAS. Award at 4. However, the Agency subsequently implemented the five-tier PAS. *Id.*

The Union filed a grievance alleging that the Agency violated Article 27 of the CBA by implementing a five-tier PAS.[1] *Id.* at 2. The grievance was unresolved and was submitted to arbitration.

At arbitration, the parties stipulated to the following issues:

> Did the [Agency] violate Article 27, Article 45 (sections A and B), or Article 62 (Sections A, B and C) of the [CBA] [2] . . ; 5 USC Section 7114 (a); and/or 5 USC Section 7116 (a)(1)(5)(7) or (8) when it implemented a new performance appraisal system . . . ?

Id. at 3.

The Arbitrator granted the grievance in part. She ruled that the Agency violated a number of provisions of the CBA by implementing the five-tier PAS. *Id.* at 7. For instance, the Arbitrator held that the Agency violated Article 27, which established the two-tier PAS. *Id.* at 7-8. In addition, the Arbitrator held that the Agency violated Article 45, which provides that the CBA can be modified only if a statute, Executive Order, government-wide regulation, or judicial decision conflicts with a CBA provision. *Id.* at 6-7. The Arbitrator found that the Agency failed to prove that one of the outside authorities listed in Article 45 required implementation of a five-tier PAS. *Id.*

As relevant here, the Arbitrator also found that the Agency violated § 7116(a)(7) of the Statute when it implemented the five-tier PAS by "enforc[ing] any rule or regulation . . . which is in conflict with any applicable collective bargaining agreement . . . ." *Id.* at 8 (quoting 5 U.S.C. § 7116(a)(7)).

---

1. Article 27 sets forth the two-tier PAS in detail. *See* Exceptions, Attach. B.

2. The relevant text of Articles 45 and 62 of the CBA is set forth in the attached appendix.

As a remedy, the Arbitrator ordered the Agency to return to the two-tier PAS and make adversely affected employees whole. *Id.*

III. Positions of the Parties

A. Agency's Exceptions

The Agency contends that the award is deficient because: (1) the award is contrary to law; and (2) the award fails to draw its essence from the CBA.

The Agency makes three arguments in support of its contrary to law exception. First, the Agency contends that the award affects management's rights to direct employees and assign work under § 7106(a)(2)(A) and (B) of the Statute. Exceptions at 6-9. In addition, the Agency asserts that the provisions of the CBA, as interpreted by the Arbitrator, are not enforceable under § 7106(b)(3) because they excessively interfere with management's rights by dictating the performance levels of the PAS. *Id.* at 8-9. Last, the Agency argues that, even if the CBA provisions are enforceable under § 7106(b)(3), the award fails to reconstruct what action the Agency would have taken in the absence of the contract violation found by the Arbitrator. *Id.* at 9 n.20.

Second, the Agency argues that the award is contrary to § 7116(a)(7) of the Statute. *Id.* at 9-10. Specifically, the Agency asserts that the Arbitrator does not identify the "rule or regulation" within the meaning of § 7116(a)(7) that the Agency improperly enforced when it implemented the five-tier PAS. *Id.*[3]

Third, the Agency argues that the award is contrary to the Back Pay Act because the Arbitrator did not make the requisite findings to support a remedy of back pay. *Id.* at 11 n.23.[4]

B. Union's Opposition

The Union asserts that even if the award affects management's rights, it is still enforceable as an appropriate arrangement under § 7106(b)(3). Opp'n at 7.[5]

IV. Analysis and Conclusions

A. The award is not contrary to § 7106(a) of the Statute.

The Agency claims that the award is contrary to management's rights to direct employees and assign work under § 7106(a)(2)(A) and (B) of the Statute. When an exception involves an award's consistency with law, the Authority reviews any question of law raised by the exception and the award de novo. *See NTEU, Chapter 24*, 50 FLRA 330, 332 (1995) (*NTEU*) (citing *U.S. Customs Serv. v. FLRA*, 43 F.3d 682, 686-87 (D.C. Cir. 1994)). In applying this standard, the Authority assesses whether an arbitrator's legal conclusions are consistent with the applicable standard of law. *See U.S. Dep't of Def, Dep'ts of the Army & the Air Force, Ala. Nat'l Guard, Northport, Ala.*, 55 FLRA 37, 40 (1998). In making that assessment, the Authority defers to the arbitrator's underlying factual findings. *See id.*

The Authority recently revised the analysis that it will apply when reviewing management rights exceptions to arbitration awards. *See U.S. Envtl. Prot. Agency*, 65 FLRA 113, 115 (2010) (*EPA*) (Member Beck concurring); *Fed. Deposit Ins. Corp.*,

3. The Agency bases its essence exception on the claim that the Arbitrator failed to identify any rule or regulation enforced by the Agency that conflicted with the CBA when she found a § 7116(a)(7) violation. Exceptions at 10. This claim is substantively the same as its contrary to law claim that the Arbitrator erroneously found that the Agency violated § 7116(a)(7). Therefore, we do not separately analyze the Union's essence exception.

4. There is no evidence that the Agency raised this argument in the proceedings before the Arbitrator. Under § 2429.5 of the Authority's Regulations, the Authority will not consider issues that could have been, but were not, presented to the arbitrator. *See, e.g., U.S. Dep't of Homeland Sec., U.S. Customs & Border Prot., JFK Airport, Queens, N.Y.*, 62 FLRA 416, 417 (2008). In this regard, the Union, in its post-hearing brief, specifically requested make-whole relief. *See* Opp'n, Attach., Union's Post-Hearing Brief at 14. Although the Union's brief was filed after the Agency filed its post-hearing brief, nearly a month elapsed before the Arbitrator issued her award, and "the Agency does not argue that either the Arbitrator or the parties' CBA precluded the Agency from responding to the Union's post-hearing brief." *U.S. Dep't of Justice, Fed. Bureau of Prisons, Wash. D.C.*, 64 FLRA 1148, 1152 (2010) (where Agency failed to demonstrate that it had "no opportunity to respond" to union's attorney fee request, Authority dismissed exception under § 2429.5). For these reasons, there is no basis for finding that the Agency could not have raised its argument below, and we dismiss this exception.

5. The Union also argues that the issue of whether the award is contrary to management's rights was not raised before the Arbitrator within the meaning of § 2429.5 of the Authority's Regulations. The Authority finds that the Agency raised this issue before the Arbitrator. *See* Award at 5.

Div. of Supervision & Consumer Prot., S.F. Region, 65 FLRA 102, 106-07 (2010) (*FDIC, SF Region*) (Chairman Pope concurring). Under the revised analysis, the Authority assesses whether the award affects the exercise of the asserted management right. *EPA*, 65 FLRA at 115.[6] If so, then, as relevant here, the Authority examines whether the award enforces a contract provision negotiated under § 7106(b).[7] *Id.* Also, under the revised analysis, in determining whether the award enforces a contract provision negotiated under § 7106(b)(3), the Authority assesses: (1) whether the contract provision constitutes an arrangement for employees adversely affected by the exercise of a management right; and (2) if so, whether the arbitrator's enforcement of the arrangement abrogates the exercise of the management right. *See id.* at 116-18. In concluding that it would apply an abrogation standard, the Authority rejected continued application of an excessive-interference standard. *Id.* at 118. Furthermore, in setting forth its revised analysis, the Authority specifically rejected the continued application of the "reconstruction" requirement set forth in prior case law. *FDIC, SF Region,* 65 FLRA at 106-07.

It is not disputed that the award affects management's rights to direct employees and assign work. Consequently, we examine whether the Arbitrator enforced a contract provision negotiated under § 7106(b). Here, the Arbitrator enforced Articles 27, 45, and 62 of the CBA. He determined that the Agency violated these provisions by implementing a five-tier PAS because the parties already negotiated a two-tier PAS under Article 27. With regard to § 7106(b)(3), the Agency does not dispute that these provisions are arrangements, but argues that the Arbitrator's enforcement of these provisions excessively interferes with management's rights to direct employees and assign work by dictating the performance levels of the PAS. However, as stated above, the Authority no longer applies an excessive-interference standard in determining whether an arbitrator has enforced a contract provision negotiated under § 7106(b)(3); rather, it applies an abrogation standard. *EPA*, 65 FLRA at 116-18. The Authority has previously described an award that abrogates the exercise of a management right as an award that "precludes an agency from exercising" the right. *U.S. Dep't of the Army, Army Transp. Ctr., Fort Eustis, Va.*, 38 FLRA 186, 190 (1990) (quoting *Dep't of the Treasury, U.S. Customs Serv.*, 37 FLRA 309, 314 (1990)).

The Agency fails to demonstrate that Articles 27, 45, and 62, as interpreted and applied by the Arbitrator, abrogate the exercise of the rights to direct employees and assign work. The Arbitrator did not interpret the provisions to prevent management from establishing criteria to evaluate employees in their performance appraisals. The provisions agreed to by the Agency require it to limit its evaluation to two performance levels. Therefore, the provisions do not preclude the Agency from evaluating employees in their performance appraisals. Accordingly, the Agency has failed to establish that the provisions abrogate management's rights to direct employees and assign work. Based on the foregoing, the Authority finds that the contract provisions at issue were negotiated under § 7106(b) of the Statute.

The Agency also asserts, without elaboration, that even if the contract provisions are appropriate arrangements, the award is deficient because the award fails to "reconstruct" what the Agency would have done had it not violated those provisions. However, as discussed above, such "reconstruction" is no longer applicable. *See FDIC, SF Region,* 65 FLRA at 106-07. Accordingly, we find that the award does not impermissibly affect management's rights by failing to reconstruct what the Agency would have done if it had not violated the contract, and we deny this exception.

B. The award is not contrary to § 7116(a)(7) of the Statute.

The Agency argues that the award is contrary to § 7116(a)(7) of the Statute. As discussed above, when an exception involves an award's consistency with law, the Authority reviews any question of law

6. For the reasons articulated in his recent concurring opinion and footnotes, Member Beck would conclude that it is unnecessary to assess whether the contract provision is an appropriate arrangement or whether it abrogates a § 7106(a) right. The appropriate question is simply whether the remedy directed by the Arbitrator enforces the provision in a reasonable and reasonably foreseeable fashion. *See EPA*, 65 FLRA at 120 (Concurring Opinion of Member Beck); *FDIC*, 65 FLRA at 107; *SSA, Office of Disability Adjudication & Review*, 65 FLRA 477, 481 n.14 (2011); *U.S. Dep't of the Air Force, Air Force Materiel Command*, 65 FLRA 395, 398 n.7 (2010); *U.S. Dep't of Health & Human Servs., Office of Medicare Hearings & Appeals*, 65 FLRA 175, 177 n.3 (2010); *U.S. Dep't of Transp., Fed. Aviation Admin.*, 65 FLRA 171, 173 n.5 (2010).

7. When an award affects a management right under § 7106(a)(2) of the Statute, the Authority may also examine whether the award enforces an applicable law. *EPA*, 65 FLRA at 115 n.7.

raised by the exception and the award de novo. *See NTEU,* 50 FLRA at 332.

In deciding a grievance that alleges an unfair labor practice (ULP), "the arbitrator must apply the same standards and burdens that would be applied by an [Administrative Law Judge (ALJ)] in a ULP proceeding under § 7118." *NTEU, Chapter 168*, 55 FLRA 237, 241 (1990). That is, in resolving a grievance alleging a ULP under § 7116 of the Statute, an arbitrator functions as an ALJ. *NTEU*, 61 FLRA 729, 732 (2006).

Section 7116(a)(7) provides that "it shall be [a ULP] for an agency . . . to enforce any rule or regulation . . . which is in conflict with any applicable collective bargaining agreement . . . ." 5 U.S.C. § 7116(a)(7). The Authority has indicated that the terms "rule or regulation" as used in § 7116(a)(7) include internal agency policy issuances. *See Dep't of Health & Human Servs., Health Care Fin. Admin.*, 39 FLRA 120, 124, 132-33, 141 (1991) *enf'd sub. nom. U.S. DHHS, HCFA v. FLRA*, 952 F.2d 398 (4th Cir. 1991) (*HCFA*) (upholding ALJ decision finding § 7116(a)(7) violation based on agency's implementation of a policy issuance banning smoking, in conflict with parties' MOU).

The award is not contrary to § 7116(a)(7) of the Statute as the Agency claims. The Agency does not dispute the Arbitrator's factual findings that the Agency enforced Notices PM-2482 and PM-2512, which announced implementation of a five-tier PAS. Award at 3-4; Exceptions, Attach. C, Tr. at 17-22. *AFGE, Local 2054*, 63 FLRA 169, 173 (2009) (Authority may derive arbitrator's factual findings from record to assess arbitrator's legal conclusions). Notices PM-2482 and PM-2512 are policy issuances that constitute "rules or regulations" under § 7116(a)(7). *See HCFA,* 39 FLRA at 124, 132-33, 141. There is also no dispute that Notices PM-2482 and PM-2512 conflicted with the two-tier PAS specifically established by Article 27 of the CBA. Therefore, the Arbitrator's conclusion that the Agency violated § 7116(a)(7) of the Statute is consistent with the requirements of that provision.

Accordingly, as the Agency fails to establish that the award is contrary to § 7116(a)(7), we deny this exception.

V. Decision

The Agency's exceptions are dismissed in part and denied in part.

APPENDIX

The relevant portion of Article 45 of the CBA provides:

> Section B. Mandated Changes to This Agreement
>
> 1. If a future . . . government-wide regulation . . . requires the parties to change this Agreement, the Employer or the Union will notify the other, in writing, of proposed formal contract language to implement the change required. If either party desires to negotiate the impact and implementation of the change, to the extent permitted by law, it shall notify the other within five workdays. Such request to negotiate shall include a specific formal proposal for negotiations. Failure by either party to respond timely to the other's notice shall constitute a waiver of any right to negotiate on the proposed required change, and the proposed formal contract language will become part of this Agreement . . . . Neither party will be permitted to propose changes unrelated to the change specifically required by . . . government-wide regulation . . . .

Exceptions, Attach. B at 148.

The relevant portion of Article 62 of the CBA provides:

> Section A. Laws and Regulations
>
> In the administration of all matters covered by this Agreement, the Employer, the Union and employees are governed by existing and future laws and government-wide regulations.
>
> Section B. Agreement Duration
>
> For the duration of this Agreement, it will have the full force and effect of regulations within the bargaining unit. . . .

Id. at 187.

65 FLRA No. 105

UNITED STATES
DEPARTMENT OF VETERANS AFFAIRS
MONTGOMERY REGIONAL OFFICE
MONTGOMERY, ALABAMA
(Agency)

and

AMERICAN FEDERATION
OF GOVERNMENT EMPLOYEES
LOCAL 552
(Union)

0-AR-4566

DECISION

February 3, 2011

Before the Authority: Carol Waller Pope, Chairman, and Thomas M. Beck and Ernest DuBester, Members

I. Statement of the Case

This matter is before the Authority on exceptions to an award of Arbitrator William H. Holley, Jr. filed by the Agency under § 7122(a) of the Federal Service Labor-Management Relations Statute (the Statute) and part 2425 of the Authority's Regulations. The Union filed an opposition to the Agency's exceptions.

The Union filed a grievance alleging that the Agency raised production standards without first satisfying its bargaining obligations under the parties' Master Agreement (Agreement). The Arbitrator sustained the grievance and directed the Agency to return to the prior performance standards until it met its bargaining obligations. For the reasons that follow, we deny the Agency's exceptions.

II. Background and Arbitrator's Award

The Agency decided to raise the productivity element of the performance standards for its Rating Veterans Service Representatives (RVSRs) from 3.5 to 4.0 end products per day. Award at 45. When the Agency implemented the higher standard, the Union filed a grievance contending that the Agency did not meet its contractual bargaining obligations before effecting the change. *Id.* at 2-3. The grievance was unresolved and submitted to arbitration, where the Arbitrator framed the issues, in part, as follows: "Did the Agency violate the Agreement when it increased the production standard for the [RVSRs] from 3.5 to 4.0? If so, what is the remedy?"[1] *Id.* at 9.

The Arbitrator found that the parties engaged in pre-implementation discussions about the change in standards and that the Union proposed certain "stipulations . . . for agreement[,]" *id.* at 45, because the Union wanted the discussions to result in a Memorandum of Understanding (MOU) "to be agreed to and signed by" the Agency and Union, *id.* at 46. In this regard, the Arbitrator identified several ways in which the parties would benefit from a signed, written record of understandings reached in their discussions, but he found that the Agency representative participating in the discussions "refused to initial or sign any" such written statement. *Id.* at 47. The Arbitrator also determined that, although the Agency's participant in the discussions contended that she had reached an unwritten "[g]entlemen's [a]greement" with the Union concerning the change in performance standards, *id.*, the Union's letter proposing "stipulations . . . for agreement" stated, "[W]e've . . . not come to a clear understanding. . . . The Union's position is that we do not agree[,]" *id.* at 46.

The Arbitrator concluded:

> For these reasons, the Agency did not meet its bargaining obligations before the implementation of the 3.5 production standard. . . .[2] [B]ecause the Agency

1. The Arbitrator also resolved whether the Agency's response to the grievance was timely under the Agreement, and he found that the response complied with the Agreement in this regard. As there have been no timely filed exceptions to this finding, *see infra* note 3, we do not discuss it further.

2. The Arbitrator cited, among other provisions, the following sections of Article 26 of the Agreement as relevant to his determination that the Agency did not satisfy its bargaining obligations:

> Section 5 - Performance Standards
>
> A. . . . The [U]nion may provide input into any changes to performance standards and/or establishment of new performance standards.
>
> . . . .

> violated Article 26 [of the Agreement], . . . the Agency must return to the 3.5 production standard until it has met its bargaining obligations under the [Agreement].

Id. at 47; *see also id.* at 48.

III. Positions of the Parties

A. Agency's Exceptions

The Agency contends that the Arbitrator "failed to conform to law, rule, and regulation in finding the Agency did not meet its bargaining obligations under Article 26" because "committing an agreement to writing is not a requirement for meeting the Agency's obligation to bargain under the Agreement." Exceptions at 2-3.

In addition, the Agency argues that the award violates its right to assign work under § 7106(a)(2)(B) of the Statute because it directs changes to performance standards. *Id.* at 6. The Agency argues further that the remedy does not satisfy either the first or second prong of the test set forth in *United States Department of the Treasury, Bureau of Engraving & Printing, Washington, D.C.*, 53 FLRA 146 (1997) (*BEP*), for evaluating awards alleged to infringe on management rights. Exceptions at 6.

Moreover, the Agency asserts that the Arbitrator's direction "to change performance standards[,]" *id.* at 3, exceeds the Arbitrator's authority because: (1) the remedy does not "address" the Arbitrator's finding that the Agency failed to meet its bargaining obligations; and (2) a "more equitable remedy . . . would have been to order the parties to commit the agreement [that resulted from pre-implementation discussions] to writing." *Id.* at 4. Finally, the Agency contends that the Arbitrator exceeded his authority by directing a remedy that: (1) violates management's rights; and (2) fails to conform to the criteria that the Authority set forth in *Federal Correctional Institution*, 8 FLRA 604 (1982) (*FCI*), for assessing whether a status quo ante (SQA) remedy is appropriate. Exceptions at 4-5.

B. Union's Opposition

The Union argues that the Arbitrator correctly found that the Agency failed to meet its bargaining obligations before raising performance standards. Opp'n at 3. In addition, the Union contends that the Arbitrator did not exceed his authority by establishing new performance standards. *Id.* Instead, according to the Union, the Arbitrator directed the Agency to return to the previously agreed-upon performance standards until the Agency satisfied its bargaining obligations. *Id.* Further, although the Union recognizes that management has a right to assign work, the Union asserts that the Agency must exercise its right in compliance with the Agreement. *Id.*[3]

> E. The Union shall be given reasonable written advance notice . . . when [m]anagement changes, adds to, or establishes new elements and performance standards. Prior to implementation of the above changes to performance standards, management shall meet all bargaining obligations.
>
> Section 6 - Communications
>
> E. . . . [W]hen changes are made to performance standards[,] the [Agency] agrees that the supervisory personnel shall meet with their employees to discuss new or revised critical and non critical elements and standards . . . . The purpose of the meeting shall be to clarify any questions that the employees have concerning their performance standards . . . .

Award at 10-11; *see also* Award at 43.

3. The Union additionally requests that the Authority "review the decision on the grievance procedure[.]" Opp'n at 4; *see also supra* note 1. To the extent that the Union is excepting to the award, § 7122(b) of the Statute provides, in pertinent part, that exceptions to an arbitrator's award must be filed "during the 30-day period beginning on the date the award is served on the party[.]" 5 U.S.C. § 7122(b). Under the Authority Regulations in effect when this case was filed, the first day of the thirty-day period for filing exceptions was the date of service of the award. *See former* 5 C.F.R. § 2425.1(b) (2009). In this regard, the Authority presumes, absent evidence to the contrary, that an award was served by U.S. mail on the date of the award, and the Arbitrator's award is dated August 24. *See, e.g.*, *Int'l Org. of Masters, Mates & Pilots*, 49 FLRA 1370, 1370-71 (1994) (*Masters, Mates & Pilots*). Thus, the thirty-day deadline for filing exceptions was September 22. Under both the current and former Regulations, if an award is served on a party by U.S. mail, then five days are added to the thirty-day filing deadline. *See current* 5 C.F.R. § 2429.22 (2010); *former* 5 C.F.R. § 2429.22 (2009). As there is no evidence to the contrary, we assume that the award was served by U.S. mail, *see Masters, Mates & Pilots*, 49 FLRA at 1370-71, and add five days to the September 22 filing deadline, *see* 5 C.F.R. § 2429.22. Because the last day of that addition fell on Sunday, September 27, in accordance with 5 C.F.R. § 2429.21(a), the deadline for filing exceptions was Monday, September 28. Although the opposition bears a signature

IV. Analysis and Conclusions

A. The award is not contrary to law.

The Agency contends that the Arbitrator "failed to conform to law, rule, and regulation" in finding that the Agency violated Article 26 of the Agreement, and that the award violates management's right to assign work. Exceptions at 2, 6. When an exception involves an award's consistency with law, rule, or regulation, the Authority reviews any question of law raised by the exception and the award de novo. *See NTEU, Chapter 24*, 50 FLRA 330, 332 (1995) (citing *U.S. Customs Serv. v. FLRA*, 43 F.3d 682, 686-87 (D.C. Cir. 1994)). In applying the standard of de novo review, the Authority assesses whether an arbitrator's legal conclusions are consistent with the applicable standard of law. *See U.S. Dep't of Def., Dep'ts of the Army & the Air Force, Ala. Nat'l Guard, Northport, Ala.*, 55 FLRA 37, 40 (1998). In making that assessment, the Authority defers to the arbitrator's underlying factual findings. *See id.*

Although the Agency alleges that the Arbitrator "failed to conform to law, rule, and regulation" when he found that the Agency violated the Agreement, the Agency does not cite a law, rule, or regulation with which the Arbitrator allegedly failed to conform. "'A general assertion, absent more, is not sufficient to support a contention that an award is contrary' to law." *NFFE, Local 1442*, 61 FLRA 857, 859 (2006) (quoting *U.S. Dep't of Veterans Affairs, Ralph H. Johnson Med. Ctr., Charleston, S.C.*, 57 FLRA 489, 492 (2001)). Consequently, the Agency's allegation constitutes a bare assertion that does not establish that the award is deficient. *See AFGE, Local 217*, 60 FLRA 459, 460 (2004). Therefore, we deny this exception.[4]

With regard to the Agency's contentions that the award violates its right to assign work and that the remedy provided does not satisfy the *BEP* test, we note that the Authority recently revised the analysis that it will apply when reviewing management-rights exceptions to arbitration awards. *See U.S. EPA*, 65 FLRA 113, 115 (2010) (Member Beck concurring) (*EPA*); *FDIC, Div. of Supervision & Consumer Prot., S.F. Region*, 65 FLRA 102, 106-07 (2010) (Chairman Pope concurring) (*FDIC, S.F. Region*). Under the revised analysis, the Authority will first assess whether the award affects the exercise of the asserted management right. *EPA*, 65 FLRA at 115.[5] If so, then, as relevant here, the Authority examines whether the award enforces a contract provision negotiated pursuant to § 7106(b) of the Statute. *Id.* In setting forth its revised analysis, the Authority specifically rejected the continued application of the reconstruction standard (i.e., the "second prong") set forth in *BEP*. *FDIC, S.F. Region*, 65 FLRA at 106-07.

The Union does not challenge the Agency's contention that the award affects management's right to assign work. *See* Opp'n at 3. As for whether the award enforces a contract provision negotiated under § 7106(b), the Arbitrator found that the Agreement obligates the Agency to bargain over the impact and

---

date of September 28, *see* Opp'n at 4, the Union did not file the opposition with the Authority until November 4. *See* UPS Envelope from Union to FLRA (hand-dated Nov. 3, received Nov. 4) (on file with Authority's Office of Case Intake and Publication); *former* 5 C.F.R. § 2429.27(d) (2009) ("[D]ate of service . . . shall be the day when the matter served is . . . received from commercial delivery[.]"). Therefore, to the extent that the Union is excepting to the Arbitrator's procedural ruling, that exception is untimely, and we dismiss it.

4. We note that the Agency does not contend that the award fails to draw its essence from the Agreement. Nevertheless, even if the Agency's arguments were construed to raise an essence exception, the Agency does not provide any further explanation or identify any contractual language to substantiate its sole argument regarding the Arbitrator's interpretation of the Agreement: that "committing an agreement to writing is not a requirement for meeting the Agency's obligation to bargain under the Agreement." Exceptions at 3. Thus, even if construed as an essence exception, the Agency's claim is a bare assertion that does not provide any basis for finding the award deficient. *Cf. U.S. Dep't of Homeland Sec., U.S. Customs & Border Prot.*, 65 FLRA 160, 163 n.4 (2010) (argument that contractual provision permitted, but did not require, actions directed by arbitrator, without further explanation, found to be bare assertion).

5. For the reasons articulated in his recent concurring opinion and footnotes, Member Beck would conclude that it is unnecessary to assess whether the award affects the exercise of the asserted management right. The appropriate question is simply whether the remedy directed by the Arbitrator enforces the provision in a reasonable and reasonably foreseeable fashion. *See EPA*, 65 FLRA at 120 (Concurring Opinion of Member Beck); *U.S. Dep't of Justice, Fed. Bureau of Prisons, Fed. Corr. Complex, Terre Haute, Ind.*, 65 FLRA 460, 462-63 n.2 (2011); *Soc. Sec. Admin., Dallas Region*, 65 FLRA 405, 408 n.5 (2010); *U.S. Dep't of the Air Force, Air Force Materiel Command*, 65 FLRA 395, 398 n.7 (2010); *U.S. Dep't of Health & Human Servs., Office of Medicare Hearings & Appeals*, 65 FLRA 175, 177 n.3 (2010); *U.S. Dep't of Transp., Fed. Aviation Admin.*, 65 FLRA 171, 173 n.5 (2010). Member Beck would conclude that the Arbitrator's award is a plausible interpretation of the parties' agreement and deny the exception.

implementation (I & I) of changes to performance standards.[6] *See* Award at 47-48 (finding violation of Art. 26, § 5(E)); *see also id.* at 43 (quoting Art. 26, § 5(E)) ("Prior to implementation of . . . changes to performance standards, management shall meet all bargaining obligations[.]"). In this regard, the Authority has held that contractual requirements to bargain I & I before exercising management rights are enforceable § 7106(b) provisions. *See, e.g., U.S. Dep't of the Air Force, Warner Robins Air Force Base, Ga.*, 53 FLRA 1344, 1349 (1998) (*Warner Robins AFB*). Consequently, the Arbitrator's direction to the Agency to satisfy its I & I bargaining obligations under Article 26, Section 5(E) of the Agreement enforces a contract provision negotiated pursuant to § 7106(b) of the Statute. *See EPA*, 65 FLRA at 115; *Warner Robins AFB*, 53 FLRA at 1349. As to the Agency's contention that the award does not satisfy the reconstruction standard of *BEP*, as mentioned above, the Authority has rejected the continued application of that standard. *See FDIC, S.F. Region*, 65 FLRA at 106-07. Thus, the Agency's contention that the award is deficient under the second prong of *BEP* does not provide a basis for setting the award aside. For the foregoing reasons, we find that the Agency has not demonstrated that the award is contrary to management's right to assign work under § 7106(a)(2)(B), and we deny this exception.

B. The Arbitrator did not exceed his authority.

The Agency contends that Arbitrator exceeded his authority in several ways. Arbitrators exceed their authority when they fail to resolve an issue submitted to arbitration, resolve an issue not submitted to arbitration, disregard specific limitations on their authority, or award relief to those not encompassed within the grievance. *See AFGE, Local 1617*, 51 FLRA 1645, 1647 (1996).

As for the Agency's argument that the Arbitrator should have directed the "more equitable remedy" of reducing the parties' agreement to writing, Exceptions at 4, the argument proceeds from an incorrect premise: that the parties reached an I & I agreement on the changed performance standards, which, if written and signed, would fully satisfy the Agency's contractual I & I bargaining obligations. The Arbitrator did not find that such an agreement existed between the parties, and he noted that the Union expressly denied that any agreement had been reached. *See* Award at 46. Thus, the "more equitable remedy" that the Agency requests is inapplicable to circumstances of this case.

With regard to the Agency's contention that the Arbitrator failed to apply the *FCI* factors before granting an SQA remedy, the Authority has held that arbitrators have "great latitude in fashioning remedies[.]" *AFGE, Local 916*, 57 FLRA 715, 717 (2002) (*Local 916*) (quoting *NTEU, Chapter 68*, 57 FLRA 256, 257 (2001) (*Chapter 68*)); *Dep't of the Air Force, Warner Robins Air Logistics Ctr., Robins Air Force Base, Ga.*, 25 FLRA 969, 971 (1987). In particular, where an arbitrator finds that an agency's failure to bargain violates a collective bargaining agreement, the propriety of SQA relief is governed by the arbitrator's remedial authority under the violated agreement, not the *FCI* factors. *Chapter 68*, 57 FLRA at 257; *AFGE, Council 215, Nat'l Council of SSA OHA Locals*, 46 FLRA 1518, 1523-24 (1993) (*Council 215*). Although the Agency asserts that the Arbitrator contravened contractual limits on his remedial authority, the Agency does not identify a provision in the Agreement that limits the Arbitrator's authority in such a manner. *Cf., e.g., U.S. Dep't of the Air Force, Luke Air Force Base, Phoenix, Ariz.*, 62 FLRA 214, 215 (2007) (Chairman Cabaniss dissenting; Member Pope dissenting as to other matters) (excepting party failed to identify a specific contractual limitation on arbitrator's remedial authority); *Council 215*, 46 FLRA at 1524 (union did not establish that agreement required arbitrator to provide SQA relief for violations). In the absence of such a limitation, the Arbitrator's direction to the Agency is an appropriate exercise of his "great latitude" in fashioning remedies. *See Local 916*, 57 FLRA at 717 (quoting *Chapter 68*, 57 FLRA at 257).[7]

For these reasons, we find that the award is not deficient for disregarding specific limitations on the Arbitrator's remedial authority, and we deny this exception.

V. Decision

The Agency's exceptions are denied.

---

6. We note that the Agency does not dispute this obligation but contends that the obligation has been satisfied. *See* Exceptions at 2. The Arbitrator rejected that contention, *see* Award at 47-48, and the Agency provides no basis for finding that the Arbitrator erred in that regard.

7. Although the Agency also contends that the Arbitrator exceeded his authority because the award violates management's rights, as we have found that the award does not violate those rights, *supra* Part IV.A., we reject this contention as well.

65 FLRA No. 106

UNITED STATES
DEPARTMENT OF THE INTERIOR
BUREAU OF RECLAMATION
COLUMBIA-CASCADES AREA OFFICE
YAKIMA, WASHINGTON
(Activity)

and

INTERNATIONAL BROTHERHOOD
OF ELECTRICAL WORKERS
LOCAL 77, AFL-CIO
(Union/Petitioner)

SF-RP-10-0010

ORDER DENYING
APPLICATION FOR REVIEW

February 11, 2011

Before the Authority: Carol Waller Pope, Chairman, and Thomas M. Beck and Ernest DuBester, Members

I. Statement of the Case

This case is before the Authority on an application for review (application) filed by the Union under § 2422.31(c) of the Authority's Regulations.[1] The Activity filed an opposition to the Union's application.

In his decision, the Regional Director (RD) granted the Union's petition in part, and denied it in part. The RD found that the Activity was the successor employer of the Union's prevailing rate[2] employee bargaining unit, but denied the accretion of two wage grade[3] employees to the unit. The Union seeks review of the RD's decision denying accretion.[4]

For the reasons that follow, we deny the Union's application for review.

II. Background and RD's Decision and Order

A. Background

In 2009, the Pacific Northwest Region of the Bureau of Reclamation reorganized. RD's Decision at 6. The Upper and Lower Columbia area offices were combined to form the Columbia-Cascades Area Office (CCAO). *Id.* at 6-7. As a result of the reorganization, the Lower Columbia area office was closed. *Id.* at 7. The Green Springs Power Plant (GSPP) in Ashland, Oregon reported to the Lower Columbia area office. Only two employees are assigned to the GSPP; both are wage grade employees. *Id.* at 6-7, 9-10.

The Union represents a bargaining unit of prevailing rate employees assigned to the CCAO. *Id.* at 1. Wage grade employees are specifically excluded from the Union's unit description. *Id.* at 15. The prevailing rate employees of the Union's bargaining unit and the wage grade employees of the GSPP were reassigned to the newly created CCAO. *Id.* at 5.

The Union filed a petition seeking a determination that the GSPP wage grade employees

1 Section 2422.31(c) of the Authority's Regulations provides, in pertinent part:

> (c) *Review.* The Authority may grant an application for review only when the application demonstrates that review is warranted on one or more of the following grounds:
> (1) The decision raises an issue for which there is an absence of precedent;
> (2) Established law or policy warrants reconsideration; or
> (3) There is a genuine issue over whether the Regional Director has:
> (i) Failed to apply established law;
> (ii) Committed a prejudicial procedural error;
> (iii) Committed a clear and prejudicial error concerning a substantial factual matter.

2 Prevailing rate employees, also known as hourly employees, have the right to negotiate pay and pay practices in accordance with § 9(b) of the Prevailing Rate Systems Act and § 704 of the Civil Service Reform Act of 1978. These employees can also negotiate other conditions of employment that are otherwise not negotiable under the Federal Service Labor-Management Relations Statute (the Statute). RD's Decision at 4.

3 In contrast to prevailing rate employees, wage grade, also known as wage board employees, have their wages established by management based on special wage survey criteria established by the Office of Personnel Management and found in 5 C.F.R. § 532. RD's Decision at 5.

4 The RD's Decision is based on a stipulated record.

had accreted to the prevailing rate employee bargaining unit. The Activity disagreed. However, both parties agreed that the certification issued to the Union for its prevailing rate employee bargaining unit should be amended to show that CCAO is the successor employer for the bargaining unit. *Id.* at 2.

B. RD's Decision and Order

The RD found that the CCAO is the successor employer of the Union's prevailing rate employee bargaining unit.[5] The RD also found that the GSPP's two wage grade employees did not accrete to the Union's prevailing rate unit. Therefore, the RD dismissed the portion of the petition seeking accretion. *Id.* at 12-16.

Regarding the accretion issue, the RD found that the 2009 reorganization was a "triggering event" or change in agency operations and organization that satisfied a precondition for finding accretion. *Id.* at 14. However, the RD also found that other circumstances did not support the conclusion that the 2009 reorganization caused the accretion of the GSPP wage grade employees to the Union's prevailing rate unit. The RD found that accretion had not occurred because the reorganization did not bring about a "meaningful change" in the wage grade employees' duties, functions, or job circumstances. *Id.* at 15.

As to duties and functions, the RD found that the 2009 reorganization did not change the type of work performed by the wage grade employees. *Id.* As to job circumstances, the RD found that the reorganization also did not produce any meaningful changes. For example, the RD found that both before and after the reorganization there was no interaction or coordination between the two groups of employees. *Id.* at 16. Similarly, the RD found that the reorganization had not changed the limited interchange that the wage grade employees had with the prevailing rate employees. *Id.* Further, although after the reorganization the wage grade employees shared a first level supervisor with some prevailing rate employees, the RD did not view this change as meaningful, given that the employees have the same second level supervisor. *Id.* In addition, the RD found that the 2009 reorganization had not changed the way in which the wage grade employees received training or the frequency of their training. *Id.*

The RD also considered that after the reorganization both types of employees had the same area manager who had the authority to "set working conditions" for them. *Id.* However, as with the other job circumstances the RD considered, the RD concluded that the area manager's authority to set working conditions for both types of employees was also not a "meaningful change." *Id.* The RD noted in this regard that the prevailing rate unit continued to be distinguished by "unique features and special working conditions." *Id.* For example, as noted earlier, prevailing rate employees are unique in that they can negotiate their wages through collective bargaining. In contrast, wage grade employees have their wages established by management based on special wage survey criteria established by the Office of Personnel Management (OPM). Furthermore, the RD found that, historically, there had been limited interchange between these two groups of employees, and no interchange of jobs. *Id.* Consequently, the RD found that having the same area manager was not a "meaningful change" for the wage grade employees. *Id.* Accordingly, the RD found that the facts of the case do not support the conclusion that the 2009 reorganization caused the accretion of the wage grade employees to the Union's prevailing rate unit. *Id.*

In arriving at this conclusion, the RD rejected the Union's reliance on *International Communication Agency*, 5 FLRA 97 (1981) (*ICA*). *Id.* at 16-17. In *ICA,* the Authority found that wage grade radio broadcast technicians whose work location was New York City accreted to an existing prevailing rate unit of radio broadcast technicians in Washington, D.C. The Authority reached this conclusion without engaging in a "meaningful change" analysis.

The RD distinguished *ICA*. The RD noted specifically that it was only after *ICA* was decided that the Authority began applying the "triggering event" precondition, and the "meaningful change" requirement that framed the RD's analysis in the instant case. *Id.* at 17. The RD also cited a variety of factual differences between the cases. *Id.*

Finally, the RD rejected arguments that accretion accorded with public policy underlying federal collective bargaining, and that accretion should be found because the two groups were already thoroughly integrated, a proposition the RD rejected. *Id.*

---

5 The RD's determination regarding successorship is not at issue in this case.

III. Positions of the Parties

A. Union's Application for Review

The Union claims that the RD failed to apply established law by not finding that the GSPP employees accreted to its unit. Application at 2. In particular, the Union argues that the change in supervisory structure, given the area manager's authority over both groups of employees, was a "meaningful change." *Id.* at 4. According to the Union, after the 2009 reorganization, the area manager had the authority to set working conditions for both wage grade and prevailing rate employees, "impact[ing] everything that an employee does every day." *Id.* at 4-5.

The Union also claims that the RD misapplied the Authority's decision in *ICA*. *Id.* at 5. The Union argues that the instant case presents circumstances similar to those present in *ICA*, and therefore that the same result is warranted. The Union points out that considerations that led the Authority to find accretion in that case are also applicable here, such as the Authority's finding in *ICA* that accretion "will lead to more effective agency dealings." *Id.* at 6.

Finally, the Union claims that the accretion of the GSPP employees to its unit is in line with the public policy behind granting collective bargaining rights to federal employees. *Id.* at 7. The Union asserts that having two groups of employees doing the same work for the same employer, but subject to different conditions of employment and benefits can lead to lowered morale and dissatisfaction. According to the Union, "[t]he accretion of the GSPP employees into [its] unit is the only appropriate avenue for remedying the situation." *Id.* at 8.

B. Activity's Opposition

The Activity claims that the Union has not established grounds under 5 C.F.R. § 2422.31(c) for granting review of the RD's decision. Opp'n at 1.

First, interpreting the Union's "meaningful change" position as a challenge to a factual finding by the RD, the Activity claims the Union has not shown that the RD committed a clear prejudicial error concerning a substantial factual matter. *Id.* at 2. Second, the Activity contends that the RD did not misapply *ICA*. The Activity argues that the RD specifically considered the application of *ICA*, but found it distinguishable. *Id.* at 2-3. Finally, the Activity asserts that the Union's claim -- that accretion comports with public policy -- does not establish grounds for review under 5 C.F.R. § 2422.31(c). *Id.* at 3.

IV. The RD did not fail to apply established law.

The legal framework for resolving accretion issues is set forth in the Authority's case law. Accretion involves the addition of a group of employees to an existing bargaining unit without an election, based on a "triggering event" or change in agency operations or organization. *U.S. Dep't of the Interior, Bureau of Reclamation, Pacific Nw. Region, Grand Coulee Power Office, Wash.*, 62 FLRA 522, 524 (2008) (*Grand Coulee Power Office, Wash.*). Because accretion precludes employee self-determination, the accretion doctrine is narrowly applied. *See id.*

Where employees sought to be accreted have been "specifically excluded from the unit description in a bargaining certificate," these employees may "only be accreted into that unit" where there have been "meaningful changes" in the employees' duties, functions, or job circumstances that eliminate the original distinctions between employees and thus warrant their inclusion into the unit. *Def. Logistics Agency, Def. Supply Ctr., Columbus, Columbus, Ohio,* 53 FLRA 1114, 1123-1124 (1998) (*DLA Columbus*).

The Union claims that the RD failed to apply established law when he found that having the same area manager, who could establish working conditions for both groups of employees after the 2009 reorganization, was not a "meaningful change" in the GSPP employees' duties, functions, or job circumstances Application at 4-5. However, as discussed below, the Union fails to substantiate its claim.

The Union argues that having the same area manager is a "meaningful change" because the area manager "impacts everything that an employee does every day." *Id.* at 4-5. However, the Union fails to explain how a change in manager, or having the same manager as employees in the prevailing rate bargaining unit, changed GSPP employees' duties, functions, or job circumstances so as to constitute a "meaningful change." Therefore, the Union fails to demonstrate that the change in manager supports its claim that the RD failed to apply established law. *Accord DLA Columbus,* 53 FLRA at 1123-24 (finding no accretion where employees had new supervision after a reorganization, but continued to perform the same duties and functions, and where the reorganization did not result in any interchange of jobs with the other group of employees).

Furthermore, contrary to the Union's contentions, the RD did not fail to apply established law by not applying *ICA*. As the RD noted, *ICA* is distinguishable. After *ICA* issued, the Authority altered its accretion analysis and began applying the "meaningful change" rationale on which the instant case was decided. *See, e.g., DLA Columbus,* 53 FLRA at 1123-24. Thus, *ICA* was decided before the Authority established its current legal framework for use in accretion cases. Accordingly, the Union fails to demonstrate that the RD erred by reaching a result that differed from the result in *ICA*.

For the reasons stated above, we find that the RD did not fail to apply established law.[6]

V. Order

The application for review is denied.

6 The Union's contention that the public policy behind granting collective bargaining rights justifies accretion does not provide a basis for granting review of the RD's Decision. 5 C.F.R. § 2422.31(c). It is true that collective bargaining principles underlie many of the Authority's determinations under the Statute. However, there is no showing in this case that the Authority's accretion analysis, which the Union does not dispute, is inconsistent with those principles.

65 FLRA No. 107

NATIONAL ASSOCIATION
OF INDEPENDENT LABOR
LOCAL 5
(Union)

and

UNITED STATES
DEPARTMENT OF DEFENSE
DEFENSE LOGISTICS AGENCY
DEFENSE DISTRIBUTION DEPOT RED RIVER
(Agency)

0-AR-4592

DECISION

February 14, 2011

Before the Authority: Carol Waller Pope, Chairman, and Thomas M. Beck and Ernest DuBester, Members

I. Statement of the Case

This matter is before the Authority on exceptions to an award of Arbitrator George E. Larney filed by the Union under § 7122(a) of the Federal Service Labor-Management Relations Statute (the Statute) and part 2425 of the Authority's Regulations. The Agency filed an opposition to the Union's exceptions.

The Arbitrator concluded that, because the Agency failed to consult with the Union in accordance with Article VIII of the parties' collective bargaining agreement (parties' agreement) before transferring one of its bargaining unit General Schedule (GS)-5 Administrative Support Assistants (employee) to a position outside the bargaining unit, it should return that employee to the bargaining unit and place her in "a GS-05 . . . position comparable to her former position of record." Award at 13; *see also id.* at 11. For the reasons set forth below, we deny the Union's exceptions.

II. Background and Arbitrator's Award

The Agency transferred a bargaining unit employee to the newly created National Security Personnel System (NSPS), non-bargaining unit position of Secretary (Office Automation) without notifying the Union.[1] *Id.* at 6-7. As a result of the transfer, the employee's duties remained the same, but her total salary rose from $38,639.00 to $40,569.00. *Id.* at 6.

After the Union became aware that the employee had been transferred to the NSPS position, it filed a grievance. *Id.* at 6-7. In its grievance, the Union asserted that, in transferring the employee to the NSPS position, the Agency failed to comply with applicable provisions of the parties' agreement and Defense Logistics Agency Regulation (DLAR) 1404.4.[2] *See id.* at 7. The matter was unresolved and was submitted to arbitration. The parties stipulated to the following issue:

> Did the Agency violate DLAR 1404.4[,] Merit Promotion Program[,] and Article XXVI, the Staffing and Merit Promotion clause of the [parties' agreement] [,] . . . when [the Agency] permanently [moved] [reassigned] [the employee] from a GS-303-05 Administrative Support Assistant to a YB-318-01 NSPS pay band position of Secretary (Office Automation)[,] which is equivalent to a GS-06 rated position resulting in a higher rate of pay, without advertising the vacancy? If so, what shall be the proper remedy?[3]

Id. at 5.

The Arbitrator determined that, based on the contractual definition of the word "promotion," the employee received a promotion rather than a reassignment when she was transferred to the NSPS position. *Id.* at 11. According to the Arbitrator,

---

1. When the Agency moved the employee into the NSPS position, it eliminated her GS-5 Administrative Support Assistant position. Award at 13.

2. Pertinent sections of DLAR 1404.4 and the parties' agreement are set forth in the attached appendix.

3. The parties were able to agree on the statement of the issue regarding the merits of the dispute with the exception of one word; whereas the Union wanted to use the word "moved" to describe the employee's transfer from the GS-05 Administrative Support Assistant position to the NSPS position, the Agency requested that the transfer be described as a "reassignment." *Id.* at 5.

testimony demonstrated that "the GS Schedule and the NSPS System represent different pay plans/pay method categories and that . . . [the employee] received a higher rate of pay when she was moved from her GS-05 position of record to her new YB-1 rated position under the NSPS pay plan." *Id.* Also, the Arbitrator found that the only legitimate way that the Agency could have transferred the employee to the NSPS position was to honor the Union's national consultation rights by acting in accordance with Article VIII, Section 3 of the parties' agreement. *Id.* The Arbitrator determined that, if the Agency had complied with Article VIII of the parties' agreement, then the Union would have had notice of the proposed change in the employee's conditions of employment and would have had the opportunity to meet with the Agency to discuss the proposed change and to request negotiations and submit counterproposals. *Id.*

However, because the NSPS position was outside the bargaining unit, the Arbitrator noted that the Union was incorrect in arguing that, once the employee assumed the NSPS position, the provisions of the parties' agreement still applied to her. *Id.* Moreover, because the employee's "bargaining unit position was effectively abolished[,] coupled with the fact that negotiations never materialized pursuant to the provisions of" Article VIII, Section 3, the Arbitrator rejected the Union's assertion that the Agency violated Article XXVI and DLAR 1404.4 when it transferred the employee to the NSPS position. *Id.* at 11-12. As a result, the Arbitrator denied part of the Union's proposed remedy requesting that the vacancy be filled competitively pursuant to the provisions of Article XXVI and DLAR 1404. *See id.* 12, 13.

After finding a violation of the parties' agreement, the Arbitrator ordered two alternative remedies. *Id.* at 13. The Arbitrator ordered that the Agency vacate the NSPS position and place the employee in a GS-05 position comparable to her former position of record or, with the Union's consent, comply with Article VIII, Section 3 of the parties' agreement and "enter into negotiations with the Union to determine the disposition of [the employee's] position placement." *Id.*; *see also id.* at 11. Finally, "[g]iven the nature of the resolution of the subject grievance, the Arbitrator [found that he was] without a clear basis to designate a 'losing party' in th[e] proceeding" and that, in accordance with Article XXXI, Section 6 of the parties' agreement, the arbitration costs should be borne equally by the parties. *Id.* at 13.

III. Positions of the Parties

A. Union's Exceptions

The Union asserts that the award fails to draw its essence from the parties' agreement, that the award is based on a nonfact, and that the award is contrary to applicable law or regulation. Exceptions at 4.

The Union claims that, although the Arbitrator correctly set aside the employee's promotion, the Arbitrator incorrectly found that the Agency's personnel action did not violate Article XXVI, Section 4 of the parties' agreement and DLAR 1404.4. *Id.* at 5-6. According to the Union, "the [A]gency's action . . . permanently transferring [the employee] to a position with a higher rate of pay from the [GS] pay method category to the YB pay method category under NSPS" constitutes a promotion under Article XXVI of the parties' agreement. *Id.* at 7; *see also id.* at 8. Moreover, the Union claims that, because the employee received a promotion rather than a reassignment, the Agency was obligated to competitively fill the position, following the procedures set forth in Article XXVI of the agreement and DLAR 1404.4. *See id.* at 8-9. The Union notes that, because the Agency failed to follow the procedures set forth in Article XXVI and DLAR 1404.4, "bargaining unit members had no opportunity to apply for consideration for placement into the position based upon their qualifications." *Id.* at 9

Also, the Union asserts that the Arbitrator erred in requiring the Union and the Agency to split the arbitration costs. *Id.* According to the Union, because the Agency's improper personnel action was reversed, "the Union should be considered the winning party, and[,] as the losing party, the [A]gency should be ordered to pay the entire [A]rbitrator's fee and expenses pursuant to Article XXXI, Section 6 of the [parties' agreement]." *Id.*

Finally, the Union claims that the Arbitrator erred in finding that the vacant NSPS position should be filled in accordance with the prevailing NSPS rules. *Id.* at 9-10. The Union asserts that the vacant NSPS position "should be filled in accordance with Article XXVI of the [parties' agreement] and DLAR 1404.4, since these were the governing provisions at the time of the promotion[,] . . . rather than [the] Final NSPS rules which were not in effect at the time of the improper personnel action." *Id.* at 10.

B. Agency's Opposition

The Agency argues that, notwithstanding the Union's exceptions, the Authority should uphold the award. Opp'n at 8. The Agency contends that the Union's exceptions are not supported by the evidence. *Id.* According to the Agency, " it [is] quite clear that the Arbitrator's various determinations are detailed and definitively predicated upon record evidence of facts, law[,] and regulations, and that the Arbitrator's . . . [a]ward is not based on nonfact, [and] draws its essence from and cites to applicable provisions of the [parties' agreement]." *Id.* at 9. Moreover, the Agency contends that the Union's exceptions constitute mere disagreement with the award and that the Union has failed to provide evidence and arguments to support each basis for finding the award deficient. *Id.*

IV. Analysis and Conclusions

A. The award does not fail to draw its essence from the parties' agreement.

In reviewing an arbitrator's interpretation of a collective bargaining agreement, the Authority applies the deferential standard of review that federal courts use in reviewing arbitration awards in the private sector. *See* 5 U.S.C. § 7122(a)(2); *AFGE, Council 220*, 54 FLRA 156, 159 (1998). Under this standard, the Authority will find that an arbitration award is deficient as failing to draw its essence from the collective bargaining agreement when the appealing party establishes that the award: (1) cannot in any rational way be derived from the agreement; (2) is so unfounded in reason and fact and so unconnected with the wording and purposes of the collective bargaining agreement as to manifest an infidelity to the obligation of the arbitrator; (3) does not represent a plausible interpretation of the agreement; or (4) evidences a manifest disregard of the agreement. *See U.S. Dep't of Labor (OSHA)*, 34 FLRA 573, 575 (1990). The Authority and the courts defer to arbitrators in this context because it is the arbitrator's construction of the agreement for which the parties have bargained. *Id.* at 576.

The Union asserts that the Arbitrator incorrectly found that the Agency did not violate Article XXVI, Section 4 of the parties' agreement. Exceptions at 5-9. Moreover, the Union claims that, because the Agency's action constituted a promotion under Article XXVI of the parties' agreement, the Arbitrator should have found that the Agency was obligated to follow the procedures set forth in that provision to competitively fill that position. *Id.* at 7-9. We construe this argument as a claim that the award fails to draw its essence from the agreement. *See AFGE, Local 476*, 60 FLRA 41, 43 (2004) (construing the union's argument that the arbitrator erred in concluding that Article 13 of the parties' agreement excluded the remedies sought by the union as a claim that the award failed to draw its essence from the agreement).

The Union has failed to establish that the award fails to draw its essence from the agreement under any of the above tests. The Arbitrator reviewed the parties' agreement in its entirety and determined that, because Article XXVI was inapplicable, the Agency could not have violated that provision when it transferred the employee to the NSPS position. *See* Award at 11-12. The Union has not demonstrated why Article XXVI applies given that, in this case, the Agency transferred a bargaining unit employee to a non-bargaining unit position. Exceptions at 7-9 (arguing only that Article XXVI applies because the employee's transfer constitutes a promotion); *see Nat'l Fed'n of Fed. Emps., Local 1442*, 64 FLRA 1132, 1133, 1134-35 (2010) (*Local 1442*) (upholding the arbitrator's determination that Article 19, titled "Promotion," was inapplicable to the filling of two supervisory non-bargaining unit positions). Consequently, the Union has failed to prove that the Arbitrator's interpretation of the parties' agreement as applied to the facts of the case is irrational, implausible, unfounded, or in manifest disregard of the agreement. *See U.S. Dep't of Transp., FAA*, 63 FLRA 15, 18 (2008).

The Union also asserts that it should be designated as the winning party, and, as the losing party, the Agency should be ordered to pay all arbitration costs in accordance with Article XXXI, Section 6 of the parties' agreement. Exceptions at 9. We construe this argument as a claim that the award fails to draw its essence from the agreement. *See Nat'l Ass'n of Indep. Labor, Local 11*, 64 FLRA 709, 711-12 (2010) (construing the union's argument that the agency, as the losing party, should bear the costs of arbitration in accordance with the agreement as an allegation that the award failed to draw its essence from the agreement).

The Union's assertion is without merit. Article XXXI, Section 6 of the parties' agreement states that "[t]he Arbitrator's fees and expenses shall be borne by the losing party. The Arbitrator shall determine the losing party. If there is a split decision in which neither party can be designated as the losing party, the costs shall be borne equally." Exceptions, Attach. 5 at 48. In this case, the Arbitrator interpreted the provision and, pursuant to the discretion expressly granted to him by Article XXXI, Section 6 of the parties' agreement, determined that neither party was the clear losing party. Award at 13 (finding that, "[g]iven the nature of the resolution of the subject grievance, [he was] without a clear basis to designate a 'losing party' in this proceeding"). Although the Arbitrator sustained the grievance, he disagreed with the Union that the Agency violated Article XXVI and DLAR 1404.4 and denied part of the Union's proposed remedy. *Id.* at 11-12, 13. Consequently, given the discretion permitted under the provision, the Union has not established that the award cannot in any rational way be derived from the parties' agreement, evidences a manifest disregard of the agreement, or represents an implausible interpretation of the agreement. *See, e.g., NAGE, Local R4-27*, 60 FLRA 14, 16 (2004) (determining that, because the arbitrator had discretion under the agreement to split costs in the event that neither party could be designated as the losing party, the agency failed to establish that the award was irrational, implausible, or unconnected with the language of the agreement); *U.S. Dep't of the Air Force Headquarters, 92nd Air Refueling Wing, Fairchild Air Force Base, Wash.*, 59 FLRA 434, 435 (2003) (citing *NFFE, Local 2030*, 56 FLRA 667, 670 (2000)) (finding that, by splitting the fees, the arbitrator interpreted the agreement provision concerning the splitting of fees and, pursuant to the discretion expressly granted him by the agreement, determined that neither party was the clear losing party).

Accordingly, we deny the Union's exceptions.

B. The award is not contrary to law, rule, or regulation.

When an exception involves an award's consistency with law, the Authority reviews any question of law raised by the exception and the award de novo. *See NTEU, Chapter 24*, 50 FLRA 330, 332 (1995) (citing *U.S. Customs Serv. v. FLRA*, 43 F.3d 682, 686-87 (D.C. Cir. 1994)). In applying the standard of de novo review, the Authority assesses whether an arbitrator's legal conclusions are consistent with the applicable standard of law. *See U.S. Dep't of Def., Dep'ts of the Army & the Air Force, Ala. Nat'l Guard, Northport, Ala.*, 55 FLRA 37, 40 (1998). In making that assessment, the Authority defers to the arbitrator's underlying factual findings. *See id.*

The Union asserts that the Arbitrator should have found that the Agency violated DLAR 1404.4 when it transferred the employee from her GS-05 position of record to the NSPS non-bargaining unit position. Exceptions at 5-9. We construe the Union's argument as a claim that the award is contrary to law, rule, or regulation. *See AFGE, Local 476*, 60 FLRA at 43.

The Union's assertion that the award is contrary to DLAR 1404.4 is without merit. In this case, the Arbitrator found that, because DLAR 1404.4 was inapplicable, the Agency could not have violated that regulation when it transferred the employee to the NSPS position. *See* Award at 11-12. Moreover, an examination of DLAR 1404.4 does not establish that the Arbitrator erred. *See U.S. Dep't of the Air Force, San Antonio Air Logistics Ctr., Kelly Air Force Base, Tex.*, 51 FLRA 1624, 1628 (1996) (finding that an examination of the regulations that the union cited did not establish that the arbitrator was required to find that the grievant would have been selected for the improperly filled position). The purpose and scope of DLAR 1404.4 is to establish policy and procedures necessary "to ensure a systematic means of selection for promotion in the competitive service (GS/GM-15 and below)." Exceptions, Attach. 7 at 1. Because the vacant position at issue is an NSPS position rather than a GS/GM position, the policies and procedures contained in DLAR 1404.4 are not applicable to the vacant NSPS position. Consequently, the Union has not established that the award is inconsistent with DLAR 1404.4.

Also, the Union asserts that, rather than ordering the Agency to fill the newly vacant NSPS position in accordance with the prevailing NSPS Rules that were not in effect at the time the personnel action took place, the Arbitrator should have ordered that the position be filled in accordance with Article XXVI of the parties' agreement and DLAR 1404.4. Exceptions at 9-10. We construe the Union's argument as a claim that the award is contrary to law, rule, or regulation.

The Union's assertion is without merit. In his award, the Arbitrator did not require the Agency to fill the vacant NSPS position in accordance with prevailing NSPS rules; in fact, he did not address how the position should be filled. Instead, the Arbitrator simply ordered the Agency to comply with one of two alternative remedies. Award at 13. He determined that the Agency could either remove the employee from the NSPS position and place her into a GS-05 position comparable to her position of record or, after obtaining the Union's consent, comply with Article VIII of the parties' agreement and "enter into negotiations with the Union to determine the disposition of [the employee's] position placement." *Id.* at 13; *see also id.* at 11. Consequently, the Union has not established that the award is contrary to law.[4]

Accordingly, we deny the Union's exceptions.

V. Decision

The Union's exceptions are denied.

4. Because the Union provides no evidence to support its claim that the award is based on a nonfact and fails to identify any nonfact, we reject its claim as a bare assertion. *See AFGE, Local 405*, 63 FLRA 149, 152 n.9 (2009) (rejecting the union's nonfact exception as a bare assertion because it did not provide evidence to support its claim that the award was based on a nonfact); *AFGE, Local 446*, 64 FLRA 15, 16 (2009) (denying the union's nonfact exception as a bare assertion because it failed to make arguments to support its claim that the award was based on a nonfact).

APPENDIX

Article VIII – Matters Appropriate for Consultation or Negotiation

Section 1. Matters subject to consultation or negotiation are personnel policies and practices and matters affecting working conditions of unit employees which are within the discretion of the Employer so far as may be proper under applicable laws and regulations. These matters may include, but are not limited to, safety, training, labor-management relations, employee services, welfare and pay practices, methods of adjusting grievances, appeals, leave, promotion procedures, demotion practices, RIF practice, and hours of work.

Section 2. Upon request, the parties will negotiate:

(a) *at the election of the Employer*, on the numbers types and grades of employees or positions assigned to any organizational subdivision, work project, or tour of duty, or on the technology, methods, and means of performing work;

(b) procedures which management officials of the agency will observe in exercising any authority under the law; or

(c) appropriate arrangements for employees adversely affected by the exercise of any authority under the law by such management officials.

Section 3. The Employer will provide the Union with a copy of proposed new and revised regulations affecting unit employees and provide written notice of proposed changes in conditions of employment. *Upon request, the employer will schedule a meeting with the Union to discuss management's proposed regulations/ changes and intentions. After the meeting is held,* a reasonable amount of time, but not less than fifteen days, will be permitted to the Union to request negotiations and to submit written counter proposals. If written proposals are not received within the allocated time frame, it will be considered that the Union is in agreement with the proposal and the proposal will be implemented.

Exceptions, Attach. 5 at 12.

Article XXVI – Staffing and Merit Promotion

Section 1. The Employer recognizes the importance of, and benefits to be derived from, giving promotion opportunity to DDRT employees. *All vacant positions will be advertised except reassignments and those positions filled by re-promotion and/or reinstatement eligibles.* The initial area of consideration for a vacancy announcement will include the minimum area, DDRT.

Section 2. This agreement provides for concurrent consideration of DDRT employees, but does not restrict the right of the employer to fill positions by methods other than promotion.

. . . .

Section 4. Promotion is the change of an employee to a higher grade when both the old and the new positions are under the General Schedule, or under the same type graded wage schedule, or to a position with a higher rate of pay when both the old and new positions are under the same ungraded wage schedule or in different pay method categories.

Section 5. The Union and the Employer agree that the purpose of the local Merit Promotion Plan are [sic] to insure that employees are given full and fair consideration for advancement and to insure selection from among the best qualified candidates. It is further agreed that these procedures must be administered in such a way as to develop maximum employee confidence and to achieve the purpose of the plan as simply and as efficiently as possible.

. . . .

Id. at 38.

DLAR 1404.4 – Merit Promotion Program

I. *PURPOSE AND SCOPE.* This DLAR establishes the policy and procedures designed to ensure a systematic means of selection for promotion in the competitive service (GS/GM-15 and below). It implements Title 5, Code of Federal Regulations (CFRs), Part 335, and Federal Personnel Manual (FPM) chapter 335. It is applicable to HQ DLA, all DLA field activities, and Federal activities serviced by a DLA Office of Civilian Personnel (OCP). It does not apply to matters covered by Article 13 of the Master Agreement between DLA and the DLA Council of American Federation of Government Employees Locals.

A. Personnel Actions Covered. The competitive procedures of this DLAR must be applied to the following actions:

1. Temporary Promotions of More than 120 Calendar Days.

. . . .

3. Details of more than 120 calendar days to higher grade positions or to positions with known promotion potential.

. . . .

6. Transfer to a higher graded position.

. . . .

B. Personnel Actions Not Covered. The competitive requirements of this DLAR do not apply to the following actions:

. . . .

11. Transfer at the grade presently held on a permanent basis to a position at the same grade and with promotion potential that is no higher than that of the present position.

. . . .

II. POLICY

A. All positions which are required to be filled competitively under the provisions of this DLAR must be advertised by a JOA. JOAs may pertain to more than one position, may advertise open continuous announcements, and may be used to establish registers from which covered vacancies may be filled over a period of time.

. . . .

Exceptions, Attach. 7 at 1-2.

65 FLRA No. 108

NATIONAL ASSOCIATION
OF INDEPENDENT LABOR
LOCAL 5
(Union)

and

UNITED STATES
DEPARTMENT OF DEFENSE
DEFENSE LOGISTICS AGENCY
DEFENSE DISTRIBUTION DEPOT RED RIVER
TEXARKANA, TEXAS
(Agency)

0-AR-4577

DECISION

February 14, 2011

Before the Authority: Carol Waller Pope, Chairman, and Thomas M. Beck and Ernest DuBester, Members

I. Statement of the Case

This matter is before the Authority on exceptions to an award of Arbitrator George E. Larney filed by the Union under § 7122(a) of the Federal Service Labor-Management Relations Statute (the Statute) and part 2425 of the Authority's Regulations. The Agency filed an opposition to the Union's exceptions.

The Arbitrator concluded that, because the Agency failed to consult with the Union in accordance with Article VIII of the parties' collective bargaining agreement (parties' agreement) before transferring a bargaining unit General Schedule (GS)-9 Quality Assurance Specialists (employee) to a supervisory position outside the bargaining unit, it should return that employee to her GS-9 bargaining unit position of record. Award at 35, 47, 48, 49, 50. For the reasons set forth below, we deny the Union's exceptions.

II. Background and Arbitrator's Award

The Agency temporarily promoted the employee to a GS-11 Distribution Facilities Manager position. *Id.* at 28. Fourteen days after the employee was temporarily promoted, the Agency adopted the National Security Personnel System (NSPS), and, on that date, the GS-11 position was converted into an NSPS position. *Id.*; *see also id.* at 30. When the employee's temporary promotion ended, she was returned to her permanent bargaining unit position of record, the GS-9 Quality Assurance Specialist position. *Id.* at 30. Without notifying the Union, the Agency later transferred the employee to the NSPS supervisory non-bargaining unit position on a permanent basis.[1] *See id.*

After the Union became aware that the employee had been awarded the NSPS position on a permanent basis, it filed a grievance. *Id.* at 34. In its grievance, the Union asserted that the Agency violated its Merit Promotion Program, Defense Logistics Agency Regulation (DLAR) 1404.4, by not "allow[ing] all interested [e]mployees to apply for the position through the Merit Promotion competitive procedures . . . ." *Id.* (emphasis omitted). The matter was unresolved and was submitted to arbitration. *Id.* at 36, 37.

The parties could not agree on a stipulated issue regarding the merits of the case, and the Arbitrator did not frame an issue.[2] *See id.* at 6. The Union's statement of the issue was whether "the Agency violate[d] DLAR . . . 1404.4 . . . and Article XXVI [of the parties' agreement] . . . when [the Agency] permanently moved [the employee] from a GS-1910-09 Quality Assurance Specialist [position] to a GS-2030-11 Supervisory Distribution Facilities Specialist/YA-2030-02 Supervisory Distribution Facilities Specialist [position], resulting in a higher rate of pay without advertising the vacancy?"[3] *Id.* The Agency's statement of the issue was whether it "violate[d] 1404.4 of the [parties' agreement] when it temporarily promoted [the employee] to a GS-11 position, which was converted via NSPS, . . . and later reassigned [the employee] to the Supervisory Distribution Facilities Specialist [position] . . . ?" *Id.*

1. As a result of the employee's placement in the NSPS position, her adjusted basic pay rose from $49,546.00 to $52,023.00. Award at 28, 31.

2. The Agency also raised the issue of whether the grievance was timely filed before the Arbitrator. *Id.* at 5. Because no exceptions were filed regarding the Arbitrator's resolution of this issue, it is not before us.

3. Pertinent sections of DLAR 1404.4 and the parties' agreement are set forth in the attached appendix.

The Arbitrator found the Agency's contention that it merely reassigned the employee when it transferred her to the NSPS position on a permanent basis to be without merit. *Id.* at 46-47. The Arbitrator determined that the Agency disregarded the fact that, when it permanently transferred the employee to the NSPS position, she "continued to be in the status of a bargaining unit employee who had fully completed the initial [Agency] directed personnel action of a 120[-]day temporary promotion and therefore was not a[n] NSPS employee to be reassigned on a permanent basis to perform the duties of a[n] NSPS position." *Id.*

Also, the Arbitrator found that the Agency violated Article VIII of the parties' agreement by awarding the employee the NSPS position on a permanent basis. *Id.* at 47, 49. According to the Arbitrator, Article VIII recognizes that the Union possesses national consultation rights on matters such as promotion procedures, and Article VIII, Section 3 requires that the Agency provide the Union not only with a copy of proposed new and revised regulations impacting unit employees, but also with written notice of proposed modifications in conditions of employment. *Id.* at 47. The Arbitrator found that "once the Agency desired to move [the employee] on a permanent basis to the NSPS . . . position, it was contractually obligated to inform the Union of its desired intention and to furnish the Union with a copy of a proposal to accomplish this move, which represented a change in [the employee's] conditions of employment." *Id.* Moreover, the Arbitrator determined that, if the Agency had complied with Article VIII of the parties' agreement, then the Union would have had notice of the proposed change in the employee's conditions of employment and would have had the opportunity to meet with the Agency to discuss the proposed change and to request negotiations and submit counterproposals. *Id.*

However, contrary to the Union's contention, the Arbitrator found that that the Agency did not violate either Article XXVI of the parties' agreement or DLAR 1404.4. *Id.* at 47-48, 49. The Arbitrator determined that the Agency did not violate DLAR 1404.4 because, when the Agency adopted the NSPS system and "reassigned [the employee] while only a week into her initial 120[-]day temporary promotion[,] . . . [it] also converted the GS-11 bargaining unit position to the NSPS personnel system, placing it into the YA-2 pay band." *Id.* at 47. According to the Arbitrator, once the employee's 120-day temporary promotion ended, and she was returned to her GS-09 position of record, "there no longer existed the GS-11 bargaining unit position to which she was promoted and therefore, there no longer existed a vacancy in that GS-11 bargaining unit position to be filled . . . through competitive procedure by either [the employee] or any other bargaining unit employee." *Id.* at 47-48. Moreover, the Arbitrator noted that, although the Union claimed that the Agency's action violated Article XXVI of the parties' agreement and DLAR 1404.4, the facts demonstrated that the Agency violated Article VIII of the agreement. *Id.* at 49.

Also, the Arbitrator denied part of the Union's proposed remedy requesting that the vacancy be filled competitively pursuant to the provisions of Article XXVI and DLAR 1404.4. *See id.* at 47-48, 49. The Arbitrator determined that the only remedy available to the Union was to return the employee to her GS-9 position of record, and he, ultimately, ordered "the Agency to fill the subject vacant NSPS position in an appropriate manner consistent with the prevailing Final NSPS Rules." *Id.* at 49; *see also id.* at 48, 50.

Finally, "[g]iven the nature of the resolution of the subject grievance, the Arbitrator [found that he was] without a clear basis to designate a 'losing party' in this proceeding[,]" and that, in accordance with Article XXXI, Section 6 of the parties' agreement, the arbitration costs should be borne equally by the parties. *Id.* at 50; *see also id.* at 48.

III. Positions of the Parties

A. Union's Exceptions

The Union asserts that the award fails to draw its essence from the parties' agreement, that the award is based on a nonfact, and that the award is contrary to applicable law or regulation. Exceptions at 3.

The Union claims that, although the Arbitrator correctly set aside the employee's promotion, the Arbitrator incorrectly found that the Agency's personnel action did not violate Article XXVI, Section 4 of the parties' agreement and DLAR 1404.4. *Id.* at 4-5. According to the Union, testimony demonstrates that the NSPS pay band system and GS salary schedule are different pay method categories and that the employee received a higher rate of pay as an NSPS Supervisory Distribution Facilities Specialist than as a GS-9 Quality Assurance Specialist. *Id.* at 6-7. Moreover, the Union claims that, because the employee received a promotion rather than a reassignment, the Arbitrator should have found that the Agency was obligated to follow the procedures set forth in Article XXVI of the parties' agreement and DLAR 1404.4 in order to competitively fill the NSPS position. *See id.* at 7-8. The Union notes that, because the Agency failed to follow the procedures set forth in Article XXVI and DLAR 1404.4, "bargaining unit members had no opportunity to apply for consideration for placement into the position based upon their qualifications." *Id.* at 8.

Also, the Union asserts that the Arbitrator erred in requiring both the Union and the Agency to split the arbitration costs. *Id.* According to the Union, because the Agency's improper personnel action was reversed, "the Union should be considered the winning party, and as the losing party, the [A]gency should be ordered to pay the entire [A]rbitrator's fee and expenses pursuant to Article XXXI, Section 6 of the [parties' agreement]." *Id.*

Finally, the Union claims that the Arbitrator erred in finding that the vacant NSPS position should be filled in accordance with the prevailing NSPS rules. *Id.* at 8-9. The Union asserts that the vacant NSPS position "should be filled in accordance with Article XXVI of the [parties' agreement] and DLAR 1404.4, since these were the governing provisions at the time of the promotion[,] . . . rather than [the] Final NSPS rules[,] which were not in effect at the time of the improper personnel action." *Id.* at 9.

B. Agency's Opposition

The Agency argues that, notwithstanding the Union's exceptions, the Authority should uphold the award. Opp'n at 7. The Agency contends that the Union's exceptions are not supported by the evidence. *Id.* According to the Agency, "it [is] quite clear that the Arbitrator's various findings and conclusions are definitively predicated upon record evidence of facts, law[,] and regulations, and that the Arbitrator's . . . [a]ward draws it essence from and cites to applicable provisions of the [parties' agreement]." *Id.* Moreover, the Agency contends that the Union's exceptions constitute mere disagreement with the award and that the Union has failed to provide evidence and arguments to support each basis for finding the award deficient. *Id.*

IV. Analysis and Conclusions

A. The award does not fail to draw its essence from the parties' agreement.

The Union asserts that the Arbitrator incorrectly found that the Agency's personnel action did not violate Article XXVI, Section 4 of the parties' agreement. Exceptions at 4-8. Moreover, the Union claims that, because the Agency's action constituted a promotion under Article XXVI of the parties' agreement, the Arbitrator should have found that the Agency was obligated to follow the procedures set forth in Article XXVI of the parties' agreement in order to competitively fill the NSPS position. *Id.* at 6-8. We construe this argument as a claim that the award fails to draw its essence from the agreement. *AFGE, Local 476*, 60 FLRA 41, 43 (2004) (construing the union's argument that the arbitrator erred in concluding that Article 13 of the parties' agreement excluded the remedies sought by the union as a claim that the award failed to draw its essence from the agreement).

In reviewing an arbitrator's interpretation of a collective bargaining agreement, the Authority applies the deferential standard of review that federal courts use in reviewing arbitration awards in the private sector. *See* 5 U.S.C. § 7122(a)(2); *AFGE, Council 220*, 54 FLRA 156, 159 (1998). Under this standard, the Authority will find that an arbitration award is deficient as failing to draw its essence from the collective bargaining agreement when the appealing party establishes that the award: (1) cannot in any rational way be derived from the agreement; (2) is so unfounded in reason and fact and so unconnected with the wording and purposes of the collective bargaining agreement as to manifest an infidelity to the obligation of the arbitrator; (3) does not represent a plausible interpretation of the agreement; or (4) evidences a manifest disregard of the agreement. *See U.S. Dep't of Labor (OSHA)*, 34 FLRA 573, 575 (1990). The Authority and the courts defer to arbitrators in this context because it is the arbitrator's construction of the agreement for which the parties have bargained. *Id.* at 576.

The Union has failed to establish that the award fails to draw its essence from the agreement under any of the above tests. In this case, the Arbitrator reviewed the parties' agreement in its entirety and determined that, based on the facts of the case, Article VIII rather than Article XXVI was at issue. Award at 47, 49. The Union has not demonstrated why Article XXVI applies considering that, in this case, the Agency transferred a bargaining unit employee to a supervisory non-bargaining unit position. Exceptions at 6-8 (arguing only that Article XXVI is applicable because the employee's transfer constitutes a promotion); *see Nat'l Ass'n of Indep. Labor, Local 5*, 65 FLRA No. 107 (2011) (*NAIL*); *Nat'l Fed'n of Fed. Emps., Local 1442*, 64 FLRA 1132, 1133, 1134-35 (2010) (*Local 1442*) (upholding the arbitrator's determination that Article 19, titled "Promotion," was inapplicable to the filling of two supervisory non-bargaining unit positions). Moreover, an arbitrator's failure to set forth specific findings, or to specify and discuss all allegations in a grievance, does not provide a basis for finding an award deficient. *See, e.g., U.S. Dep't of Commerce, Patent & Trademark Office*, 41 FLRA 1042, 1049 (1991). Consequently, the Union has failed to prove that the Arbitrator's interpretation of the parties' agreement as applied to the facts of the case is irrational, implausible, unfounded, or in manifest disregard of the agreement. *See U.S. Dep't of Transp., FAA*, 63 FLRA 15, 18 (2008); *cf. Local 1442*, 64 FLRA at 1135 (finding that the award did not fail to draw its essence from the agreement because there was no evidence that the agency had elected to negotiate over the application of the parties' agreement to the filling of the two supervisory non-bargaining unit positions, and the arbitrator's conclusions were supported by controlling Authority case law).

Also, the Union asserts that it should be designated as the winning party, and, as the losing party, the Agency should be ordered to pay all arbitration costs in accordance with Article XXXI, Section 6 of the parties' agreement. Exceptions at 8. We construe this argument as a claim that the award fails to draw its essence from the agreement. *See Nat'l Ass'n of Indep. Labor, Local 11*, 64 FLRA 709, 711-12 (2010) (construing the union's argument that the agency, as the losing party, should bear the costs of arbitration in accordance with the agreement as an allegation that the award failed to draw its essence from the agreement).

The Union's assertion is without merit. Article XXXI, Section 6 of the parties' agreement states that "[t]he Arbitrator's fees and expenses shall be borne by the losing party. The Arbitrator shall determine the losing party. If there is a split decision in which neither party can be designated as the losing party, the costs shall be borne equally." Exceptions, Attach. 4 at 48. In this case, the Arbitrator interpreted the provision and, pursuant to the discretion expressly granted him by Article XXXI, Section 6 of the parties' agreement, determined that neither party was the losing party. Award at 50 (finding that, "[g]iven the nature of the resolution of the subject grievance, [he was] without a clear basis to designate a 'losing party' in this proceeding"). Although the Arbitrator sustained the grievance, he disagreed with the Union that the Agency violated Article XXVI and DLAR 1404.4 and denied part of the Union's proposed remedy. *Id.* at 47-48, 49. Consequently, given the discretion permitted under the provision, the Union has not established that the award cannot in any rational way be derived from the parties' agreement, evidences a manifest disregard of the agreement, or represents an implausible interpretation of the agreement. *See, e.g., NAGE, Local R4-27*, 60 FLRA 14, 16 (2004) (determining that, because the arbitrator had discretion under the agreement to split costs in the event that neither party could be designated as the losing party, the agency failed to establish that the award was irrational, implausible, or unconnected with the language of the agreement); *U.S. Dep't of the Air Force Headquarters, 92nd Air Refueling Wing, Fairchild Air Force Base, Wash.*, 59 FLRA 434, 435 (2003) (citing *NFFE, Local 2030*, 56 FLRA 667, 670 (2000)) (finding that, by splitting the fees, the arbitrator interpreted the agreement provision concerning the splitting of fees and, pursuant to the discretion expressly granted him by the agreement, determined that neither party was the clear losing party).

Accordingly, we deny the Union's exceptions.

B. The award is not contrary to law, rule, or regulation.

When an exception involves an award's consistency with law, the Authority reviews any question of law raised by the exception and the award de novo. *See NTEU, Chapter 24*, 50 FLRA 330, 332 (1995) (citing *U.S. Customs Serv. v. FLRA*, 43 F.3d 682, 686-87 (D.C. Cir. 1994)). In applying the standard of de novo review, the Authority assesses whether an arbitrator's legal conclusions are consistent with the applicable standard of law. *See U.S. Dep't of Def., Dep'ts of the Army & the Air Force, Ala. Nat'l Guard, Northport, Ala.*, 55 FLRA 37, 40 (1998). In making that assessment, the Authority defers to the arbitrator's underlying factual findings. *See id.*

The Union asserts that the Arbitrator should have found that the Agency violated DLAR 1404.4 when it transferred the employee from her GS-09 position of record to the NSPS supervisory non-bargaining unit position. Exceptions at 4-8. We construe the

Union's argument as a claim that the award is contrary to law, rule, or regulation. *See AFGE, Local 476*, 60 FLRA at 43.

The Union's assertion that the award is contrary to DLAR 1404.4 is without merit. In this case, the Arbitrator determined that DLAR 1404.4 did not apply because there was no vacant GS position to fill competitively. *See* Award at 47-48. An examination of DLAR 1404.4 does not establish that the Arbitrator erred in doing so. *See U.S. Dep't of the Air Force, San Antonio Air Logistics Ctr., Kelly Air Force Base, Tex.*, 51 FLRA 1624, 1628 (1996) (finding that an examination of the regulations that the union cited did not establish that the arbitrator was required to find that the grievant would have been selected for the improperly filled position). The purpose and scope of DLAR 1404.4 is to establish policy and procedures necessary "to ensure a systematic means of selection for promotion in the competitive service (GS/GM-15 and below)." Exceptions, Attach. 6 at 1. Because the vacant position at issue is an NSPS position rather than a GS/GM position, the Union has not established that the award is inconsistent with DLAR 1404.4.

Also, the Union claims that, rather than ordering that the newly vacant NSPS position be filled using the prevailing NSPS Rules that were not in effect at the time the personnel action took place, the Arbitrator should have ordered that the position be filled in accordance with Article XXVI of the parties' agreement and DLAR 1404.4. Exceptions at 8-9. We construe the Union's argument as a claim that the award is contrary to law.

This contention is without merit. The Union has not demonstrated that Article XXVI of the parties' agreement is applicable in filling the vacancy because the NSPS position is a supervisory position outside of the bargaining unit. *See NAIL*, 65 FLRA No. 107, slip op. at 5; *Local 1442*, 64 FLRA at 1133, 1134-35 (upholding the arbitrator's determination that article 19 titled promotion was inapplicable to the filling of two supervisory non-bargaining unit positions). Moreover, the Union has failed to demonstrate that DLAR 1404.4 is relevant in filling the vacant NSPS position because, as noted previously, the regulation's applicability is limited to GM/GS-15 positions and below.[4] Exceptions, Attach. 6 at 1.

Accordingly, we deny the Union's exceptions.

V. Decision

The Union's exceptions are denied.

---

4. Because the Union provides no evidence to support its claim that the award is based on a nonfact and fails to identify any nonfact, we reject its claim as a bare assertion. *See AFGE, Local 405*, 63 FLRA 149, 152 n.9 (2009) (rejecting the union's nonfact exception as a bare assertion because it did not provide evidence to support its claim that the award was based on a nonfact); *AFGE, Local 446*, 64 FLRA 15, 16 (2009) (denying the union's nonfact exception as a bare assertion because it failed to make arguments to support its claim that the award was based on a nonfact).

APPENDIX

Article VIII – Matters Appropriate for Consultation or Negotiation

Section 1. Matters subject to consultation or negotiation are personnel policies and practices and matters affecting working conditions of unit employees which are within the discretion of the Employer so far as may be proper under applicable laws and regulations. These matters may include, but are not limited to, safety, training, labor-management relations, employee services, welfare and pay practices, methods of adjusting grievances, appeals, leave, promotion procedures, demotion practices, RIF practice, and hours of work.

Section 2. Upon request, the parties will negotiate:

(a) *at the election of the Employer*, on the numbers types and grades of employees or positions assigned to any organizational subdivision, work project, or tour of duty, or on the technology, methods, and means of performing work;

(b) procedures which management officials of the agency will observe in exercising any authority under the law; or

(c) appropriate arrangements for employees adversely affected by the exercise of any authority under the law by such management officials.

Section 3. The Employer will provide the Union with a copy of proposed new and revised regulations affecting unit employees and provide written notice of proposed changes in conditions of employment. *Upon request, the employer will schedule a meeting with the Union to discuss management's proposed regulations/ changes and intentions. After the meeting is held,* a reasonable amount of time, but not less than fifteen days, will be permitted to the Union to request negotiations and to submit written counter proposals. If written proposals are not received within the allocated time frame, it will be considered that the Union is in agreement with the proposal and the proposal will be implemented.

Exceptions, Attach. 4 at 12.

Article XXVI – Staffing and Merit Promotion

Section 1. The Employer recognizes the importance of, and benefits to be derived from, giving promotion opportunity to DDRT employees. *All vacant positions will be advertised except reassignments and those positions filled by re-promotion and/or reinstatement eligibles.* The initial area of consideration for a vacancy announcement will include the minimum area, DDRT.

Section 2. This agreement provides for concurrent consideration of DDRT employees, but does not restrict the right of the employer to fill positions by methods other than promotion.

. . . .

Section 4. Promotion is the change of an employee to a higher grade when both the old and the new positions are under the General Schedule, or under the same type graded wage schedule, or to a position with a higher rate of pay when both the old and new positions are under the same ungraded wage schedule or in different pay method categories.

Section 5. The Union and the Employer agree that the purpose of the local Merit Promotion Plan are [sic] to insure that employees are given full and fair consideration for advancement and to insure selection from among the best qualified candidates. It is further agreed that these procedures must be administered in such a way as to develop maximum employee confidence and to achieve the purpose of the plan as simply and as efficiently as possible.

. . . .

Id. at 38.

DLAR 1404.4 – Merit Promotion Program

I. *PURPOSE AND SCOPE.* This DLAR establishes the policy and procedures designed to ensure a systematic means of selection for promotion in the competitive service (GS/GM-15 and below). It implements Title 5, Code of Federal Regulations (CFRs), Part 335, and Federal Personnel Manual (FPM) chapter 335. It is applicable to HQ DLA, all DLA field activities, and Federal activities serviced by a DLA Office of Civilian Personnel (OCP). It does not apply to matters covered by Article 13 of the Master Agreement between DLA and the DLA Council of American Federation of Government Employees Locals.

A. Personnel Actions Covered. The competitive procedures of this DLAR must be applied to the following actions:

1. Temporary Promotions of More than 120 Calendar Days.

. . . .

3. Details of more than 120 calendar days to higher grade positions or to positions with known promotion potential.

. . . .

6. Transfer to a higher graded position.

. . . .

B. Personnel Actions Not Covered. The competitive requirements of this DLAR do not apply to the following actions:

. . . .

11. Transfer at the grade presently held on a permanent basis to a position at the same grade and with promotion potential that is no higher than that of the present position.

. . . .

II. *POLICY*

A. All positions which are required to be filled competitively under the provisions of this DLAR must be advertised by a JOA. JOAs may pertain to more than one position, may advertise open continuous announcements, and may be used to establish registers from which covered vacancies may be filled over a period of time.

. . . .

Exceptions, Attach. 6 at 1-2.

65 FLRA No. 109

NATIONAL TREASURY
EMPLOYEES UNION
(Union)

and

UNITED STATES
DEPARTMENT OF THE TREASURY
BUREAU OF THE PUBLIC DEBT
WASHINGTON, D.C.
(Agency)

0-NG-3076

DECISION AND ORDER
ON NEGOTIABILITY ISSUES

February 14, 2011

Before the Authority: Carol Waller Pope, Chairman, and Thomas M. Beck and Ernest DuBester, Members[1]

I. Statement of the Case

This matter is before the Authority on a negotiability appeal filed by the Union under § 7105(a)(2)(E) of the Federal Service Labor-Management Relations Statute (the Statute), and concerns the negotiability of five provisions disapproved by the Agency head under § 7114(c) of the Statute.[2] The Agency filed a statement of position (SOP), the Union filed a response (response), and the Agency filed a reply (reply).

For the reasons that follow, we find that the provisions are not contrary to law, and we order the Agency to rescind its disapproval. In so doing, we modify the Authority's standard for determining, in the negotiability context, whether an agreed-upon contract provision constitutes an appropriate arrangement within the meaning of § 7106(b)(3) of the Statute. Specifically, in this and future cases we will make that determination by applying an abrogation (waiver) – not an excessive-interference – standard.

II. Article 11, Section 4B and Article 18, Section 14B

A. Wording

Article 11, Section 4B

> When a detail or temporary promotion is expected to be less than one hundred and twenty (120) days, the temporary supervisor shall discuss performance expectations with the employee at the beginning of the detail. Normally, this will occur within five (5) workdays from the beginning of the detail. Such performance expectations shall be confirmed in writing by the temporary supervisor before the employee can be held responsible for such performance expectations. When an employee on detail has performed under the performance expectations for at least ninety (90) days, but less than one hundred and twenty (120) days, an evaluation of the employee's performance while on such a detail shall be furnished in writing from the temporary supervisor of the detail to the employee's regular supervisor. When an employee on detail has performed under the performance expectation for less than ninety (90) days, an evaluation of the employee's performance while on detail may be furnished in the form of a memorandum from the temporary supervisor of the detail to the employee's regular supervisor. The employee's regular supervisor shall give appropriate consideration to such evaluations when evaluating the employee's overall performance.

Petition for Review (Petition) at 10.

Article 18, Section 14B

> When a detail or temporary promotion is expected to be less than one hundred and twenty (120) calendar days, the temporary supervisor shall discuss performance expectations with the employee at the beginning of the detail. Normally, this will occur within five (5) work days from the beginning of the detail. Such performance expectations shall be confirmed in writing

1. Member Beck's separate opinion, dissenting in part, is set forth at the end of this decision.

2. The petition for review (petition) originally involved fifty-five provisions. *See* Petition at 5. Five provisions remain at issue.

> by the temporary supervisor before the employee can be held responsible. If an employee is provided written expectations, a written evaluation is required when the employee has performed under the expectations for at least ninety (90) calendar days. The evaluation will be provided within thirty (30) calendar days of the end of the detail or temporary promotion.
>
> When an employee on detail has performed under the performance expectations for less than ninety (90) calendar days, an evaluation of the employee's performance while on detail may be furnished in the form of a memorandum from the temporary supervisor of the detail to the employee's regular supervisor. This memorandum will be provided within thirty (30) calendar days of the end of the detail or temporary promotion. The employee's regular supervisor shall give appropriate consideration to such an evaluation when evaluating the employee's overall performance.

Id. at 13.

B. Meaning

The parties agree that the provisions set forth a performance-appraisal process for employees detailed or temporarily promoted to a position for fewer than 120 days. Record of Post-Petition Conference (Record) at 1-2. Specifically, they provide processes for providing feedback to detailed or temporarily promoted employees at various periods of time during the details or temporary promotions. *Id.* at 2; Petition at 13. Under the provisions, performance expectations must be communicated to the detailed or temporarily promoted employee in writing before the employee may be held responsible for those expectations. Record at 2. The Union asserts, and the Agency does not dispute, that the written expectations may be submitted to an employee either by e-mail or hard copy. *See* Response at 11-12; Reply at 7-8. This undisputed assertion is consistent with the wording of the provisions, and we adopt it for the purposes of assessing the negotiability of the provisions. *See Int'l Ass'n of Machinists & Aerospace Workers, Local 726*, 31 FLRA 158, 170 (1988) (adopting undisputed contention as to the meaning of a provision that was consistent with the provision's wording) (*IAMAW*). In addition, the Agency asserts, and the Union does not dispute, that the provisions would prevent the Agency from holding an employee responsible for those expectations even if a supervisor has communicated the expectations to the employee orally. *See* SOP at 2; Response at 3, 7, 12; Reply at 2. As this undisputed assertion is consistent with the wording of the provisions, we adopt it for purposes of this decision. *See IAMAW*, 31 FLRA at 170.

C. Positions of the Parties

1. Agency

The Agency contends that the provisions affect management's rights to direct employees and assign work under § 7106(a)(2)(A) and (B) of the Statute because they prevent the Agency from "holding an employee accountable for performance expectations after the expectations have been communicated to the employee, but before they have been confirmed in writing." Reply at 2. The Agency also contends that the provisions are not appropriate arrangements under § 7106(b)(3) of the Statute because they excessively interfere with those management rights. *Id.* at 7-8. In this connection, the Agency asserts that the provisions "bar the exercise of . . . management['s] right to evaluate employees[,]" a burden that outweighs the "speculative" benefits the provisions would provide to employees. *Id.* at 8. For support, the Agency cites *Patent Office Professional Ass'n*, 48 FLRA 129 (1993) (Member Armendariz dissenting) (*POPA*), *petition for review denied sub nom. Patent Office Professional Ass'n v. FLRA*, 47 F.3d 1217 (D.C. Cir. 1995) (*POPA v. FLRA*). SOP at 3. Finally, the Agency contends that the provisions are not procedures under § 7106(b)(2) of the Statute because they place "significant limitations on a protected management right." Reply at 6.

2. Union

The Union contends that the provisions are appropriate arrangements under § 7106(b)(3) of the Statute. Response at 4, 9. In this regard, the Union argues that the provisions are arrangements for employees who "may be disciplined or suffer an adverse performance evaluation as a result of management not clearly stating performance expectations . . . ." *Id.* at 10. According to the Union, the provisions would benefit employees by: protecting them from "being disciplined or suffering an adverse performance evaluation[;]" ensuring that performance expectations are clearly defined and that employees are aware of those expectations; and providing employees with "written documentation" of those expectations to "serve as a reference" if an employee and a manager "disagree[] over the evaluation . . . of [an] employee's performance[.]" *Id.* at 11-12 (citing *Patent Office Prof'l Ass'n*, 47 FLRA 10 (1993)).

In addition, the Union contends that it is "hardly burdensome" to require a manager to send employees performance expectations via e-mail, which, the Union asserts, is "oftentimes . . . the predominant form of communication." *Id.* at 11. The Union also contends that, even if the performance expectations were submitted via hard copy, the provisions require the Agency to "perform a purely ministerial act by documenting performance expectations at the beginning of a detail[.]" *Id.* at 12. In this connection, the Union cites *AFGE, Local 32, AFL-CIO*, 28 FLRA 714, 718-20 (1987), as demonstrating that a provision is negotiable if it merely directs an agency to comply with the requirement of communicating performance standards to employees under 5 U.S.C. § 4302.[3] *See* Response at 12.

Finally, the Union argues that the provisions are procedures under § 7106(b)(2) of the Statute. Response at 8-9.

D. Analysis and Conclusions

1. The provisions affect management's rights to direct employees and assign work.

Management's rights to direct employees and assign work under § 7106(a)(2)(A) and (B) of the Statute include the rights to supervise employees and to determine the quantity, quality, and timeliness of employees' work. *AFGE, Local 3295*, 44 FLRA 63, 68 (1992) (*Local 3295*). The evaluation of employee performance is an exercise of management's rights to direct employees and assign work. *POPA*, 48 FLRA at 142. Thus, proposals or provisions that prohibit management from holding employees accountable for work performance affect the rights to direct employees and assign work. *See id.* Similarly, proposals or provisions that prohibit management from enforcing its established performance standards affect the rights to direct employees and assign work because they effectively alter the content of the standards. *See NTEU*, 47 FLRA at 710.

Here, the provisions would prohibit the Agency from holding an employee responsible for his or her performance expectations if those expectations have not been communicated to the employee in writing. Record at 2. As the provisions would prohibit management from holding employees accountable for work performance in these circumstances, we find that the provisions affect management's rights to direct employees and assign work under § 7106(a)(2)(A) and (B) of the Statute.

2. The provisions are appropriate arrangements.

i. Revised Analytical Framework

The Authority currently analyzes whether a proposal or provision is an appropriate arrangement under the framework set forth in *NAGE, Local R14-87*, 21 FLRA 24 (1986) (*KANG*). Under this framework, the Authority first determines whether a proposal or provision is intended to be an arrangement for employees adversely affected by the exercise of a management right. *AFGE, Nat'l Council of Field Labor Locals*, 58 FLRA 616, 617 (2003). To establish that a proposal or provision is an arrangement, a union must establish the effects or reasonably foreseeable effects that flow from the exercise of management's rights and demonstrate how those effects are adverse. *AFGE, Local 1770*, 64 FLRA 953, 959 (2010). Additionally, the claimed arrangement must be sufficiently tailored to compensate those employees suffering adverse effects attributable to the exercise of management rights. *Id.* However, "[p]rophylactic" proposals or provisions will be found sufficiently tailored in situations where it is not possible to determine reliably which employees will be adversely affected by an agency action so as to draft a proposal or provision to apply only to those employees. *Id.* at 959-60.

If the proposal or provision is an arrangement, then, under the Authority's current standard, the Authority determines whether the arrangement is appropriate or whether it is inappropriate because it "excessively interferes" with management's rights. *Id.* In making this determination, the Authority balances the proposal's or provision's benefits to employees against its burdens on management. *Id.*

For the following reasons, we reexamine and revise the standard that we apply in the negotiability

---

3. 5 U.S.C. § 4302 states, in pertinent part, that an agency's performance appraisal system shall provide for "communicating to each employee the performance standards and the critical elements of the employee's position[.]"

context for determining whether an agreed-upon contract provision constitutes an appropriate arrangement within the meaning of § 7106(b)(3) of the Statute. Specifically, we will no longer assess whether an arrangement is appropriate by applying an excessive interference standard. Rather, we will assess whether the provision "abrogates" – i.e., waives – the management right(s) that the provision affects.[4]

As an initial matter, it is well established that a bargaining proposal is outside the duty to bargain if it is contrary to law, rule, or regulation. *E.g., AFGE, Local 1226*, 62 FLRA 459, 462 (2008). However, as both the plain wording of the Statute and longstanding Authority precedent demonstrate, the mere fact that a proposal is outside the duty to bargain does not mean that it is contrary to law, rule, or regulation.

With regard to the plain wording of the Statute, § 7117(c) of the Statute provides that an exclusive representative may file a negotiability appeal "if an agency involved in collective bargaining with [the] exclusive representative alleges that the *duty to bargain* in good faith does not extend to any matter[.]" 5 U.S.C. § 7117(c) (emphasis added). By contrast, § 7114(c) of the Statute, which sets forth the process of agency-head review, does not speak in terms of whether an agreed-upon contract provision is within the duty to bargain. Rather, it provides, in pertinent part, that where an agency and an exclusive representative have reached an agreement, "[t]he head of the agency shall approve the agreement . . . if the agreement is *in accordance with the provisions of [the Statute] and any other applicable law, rule, or regulation* (unless the agency has granted an exception to the provision)." 5 U.S.C. § 7114(c)(2) (emphasis added).

It is well established that where Congress uses different terms in different parts of a statute, there is a presumption that Congress "did not view the two terms as being identical." *U.S. SEC, Wash. D.C.*, 61 FLRA 251, 255 (2005) (citing *Recording Indus. Ass'n of Am. v. Verizon Internet Serv.*, 351 F.3d 1229, 1235 (D.C. Cir. 2003)). That Congress did not state that an agency head may disapprove matters that are outside the "duty to bargain" is therefore significant. Put simply, Congress recognized that a matter may be outside the duty to bargain but, once agreed upon, may not be subject to agency-head disapproval unless it is contrary to the Statute or any other law, rule, or regulation. Further, the plain wording of § 7114(c)(2) states that an agency head "shall" – i.e., has no discretion not to – approve an agreed-upon contract provision unless that contract provision is contrary to the Statute or any other applicable law, rule, or regulation.

With regard to Authority precedent, consistent with the foregoing, the Authority has long held that the scope of what an agency head may disapprove is more limited than the scope of the duty to bargain. In this regard, in *National Ass'n of Government Employees, Local R4-75*, 24 FLRA 56 (1986) (*NAGE, Local R4-75*), the Authority stated that § 7114(c) of the Statute "strictly limits the occasions in which the head of the agency may invalidate an agreement[.]" *Id.* at 61 (quoting *AFGE v. FLRA*, 778 F.2d 850, 859 n.15 (D.C. Cir. 1985)). Specifically, the Authority found that, unless a contract provision negotiated under § 7106(b)(1) of the Statute is "otherwise inconsistent with applicable law, rule, or regulation," an agency head may not disapprove the provision because, in such circumstance, the provision is "not inconsistent with the Statute." *Id.* at 62. Consistent with *NAGE, Local R4-75*, and with the statutory wording discussed above, the Authority has held that although a matter may be a permissive subject of bargaining – and an agency may not be required to bargain over it – it may not be disapproved on agency-head review unless it is contrary to law, rule, or regulation. *See, e.g., NATCA, AFL-CIO*, 61 FLRA 336, 339 (2005) (provision regarding supervisory conditions of employment, a matter not within the duty to bargain, may not be disapproved on agency-head review); *id.* at 338 (same with regard to § 7106(b)(1) matter); *AFGE, Nat'l Mint Council*, 41 FLRA 1004, 1010 (1991) (agency-head review serves "limited purpose" of ensuring that contract provisions are not contrary to law, rule, or regulation).

In sum, although a particular proposal may be outside the duty to bargain because it is contrary to law, rule, or regulation, an agreed-upon contract provision is not contrary to law, rule, or regulation merely because, at the bargaining table, it was outside the duty to bargain.[5]

---

4. The excessive interference standard will continue to apply in negotiability cases involving contract proposals to which parties have not yet agreed.

5. Accordingly, the dissent's statement that the concept of a subject being contrary to the Statute "*includes*" the concept of being outside the duty to bargain is backwards; the former is narrower than the latter. Dissent at 20. Further, the dissent's references to "a proposal [that] proceeds to agency head review," *id.* at 19, and "a

The Authority has acknowledged this difference in the context of contract provisions that affect management rights under § 7106(a) of the Statute. In this connection, in *United States Environmental Protection Agency*, 65 FLRA 113 (2010) (Member Beck concurring) (*EPA*), the Authority addressed whether an arbitration award was contrary to management rights under § 7106(a) of the Statute. The Authority stated that "the Statute recognizes that agency management is permitted to agree to a broader range of matters than those strictly within its duty to bargain[,]" and "[n]o basis [was] provided to conclude that the situation is any different when management rights under § 7106(a) are involved." *Id.* at 118. Further, acknowledging that § 7122(a)(1) of the Statute charges the Authority with setting aside arbitration awards if they are "contrary to any law, rule, or regulation[,]" *id.* at 114, the Authority found it appropriate, in assessing whether an arbitrator is enforcing an appropriate arrangement under § 7106(b)(3) of the Statute, to apply a different standard than the Authority applies when determining whether a proposal is within the duty to bargain. Specifically, rather than applying the "excessive interference" standard that the Authority has applied in the negotiability context -- which involves assessing whether a proposal's burdens on management rights outweigh the proposal's benefits to employees -- the Authority found that a contractual arrangement that does not "abrogate" -- i.e., waive -- a management right is not contrary to law. *Id.* at 119.

Although *EPA* involved Authority review of exceptions to an arbitration award, rather than a negotiability appeal involving agency-head disapproval of contract provisions, the pertinent wording of § 7122(a) (governing Authority review of arbitration awards) is substantively identical to the wording in § 7114(c)(2) (governing agency-head review of agreements). Specifically, as stated previously, § 7122(a) provides that the Authority shall set aside an arbitration award if it is "contrary to any law, rule, or regulation[,]" and § 7114(c)(2) provides that an agency head shall approve an agreement if the agreement is "in accordance with the provisions of [the Statute] and any other applicable law, rule, or regulation . . . ." Thus, if a contract provision enforced by an arbitrator is not contrary to § 7106 of the Statute, then it cannot be disapproved by an agency head on the basis of § 7106. Consistent with this principle, as a contractual arrangement that does not abrogate a management right is not contrary to § 7106 in the arbitration context, *see EPA*, 65 FLRA at 118, it necessarily follows that an agency head may not rely on § 7106 to disapprove such an arrangement.[6]

provisionally-agreed-to proposal[,]" *id.* at 20, mischaracterize *provisions*, which are part of *contracts* that may be disapproved only on limited grounds.

6. We note that in *EPA*, the Authority did not identify as a relevant factor whether the agency head had timely disapproved the agreement. In fact, the Authority expressly stated that its analysis "call[ed] into question whether abrogation also should be the standard applied in negotiability cases involving contract provisions (where agreement has been reached and subsequently disapproved), rather than proposals." 65 FLRA at 118 n.11. The dissent concurred in *EPA* and "applaud[ed]" the majority's decision to abandon the excessive interference standard; unlike the majority, however, the dissent would not "engage in *any* assessment of whether a contract provision that is being enforced by an arbitrator violates management's rights." *Id.* at 119. In other words, in the arbitration context, the dissent would find that there is *no* level of interference with a management right -- whether excessive interference or abrogation -- that renders a provision unenforceable as long as parties have agreed to it.

In addition, the dissent's reliance on *AFGE, Local 2782 v. FLRA*, 702 F.2d 1183 (D.C. Cir. 1983) (*Local 2782*), and *AFGE v. FLRA*, 778 F.2d 850 (D.C. Cir. 1985) (*AFGE*), is misplaced. *Local 2782* involved an assessment of whether proposals were within the duty to bargain -- not whether agreed-upon provisions were enforceable -- and expressly left it "for the Authority to determine in the first instance[]" the meaning of the word "appropriate" in § 7106(b)(3). 702 F.2d at 1188. *AFGE* held only that the Authority reasonably had determined that an agency head may disapprove a contract that is contrary to law, rule, or regulation, even if that contract had been imposed by the Federal Service Impasses Panel (the Panel). Nothing in this decision is inconsistent with this principle, as we continue to find, consistent with *EPA*, that an arrangement that does not abrogate a management right is an appropriate arrangement and, thus, *not* contrary to law, rule, or regulation. In addition, although the court in *AFGE* stated that the purpose of agency head review is simply "to allow the head of the agency an extra [thirty] days to do that which his subordinates could have done earlier," 778 F.2d at 860 n.16, it did not hold that the scope of matters that an agency head may properly disapprove is coextensive with the scope of matters that may be declared outside the duty to bargain at the bargaining table. In fact, in dicta, the court stated that "an argument can be made that Congress'[] explicit policy to allow the head of an agency to invalidate an agreement may have even stronger justifications for terms imposed by the . . . Panel, than for those negotiated by the parties[,]" because "[i]n the latter case, the agency's own authorized representative has agreed to the terms." *Id.* at 858. In other words, the court acknowledged that the parties' agreement to a provision at the bargaining table may be a relevant consideration.

The decision to apply an "abrogation" standard in the arbitration context was based, in large part, on a policy of deferring to bargaining parties' choices. In this regard, in *EPA*, the Authority reiterated that, during bargaining, the parties' representatives are authorized to, and should, assess the burdens that a proposal would have on management rights and the benefits that the proposal would afford employees. *See* 65 FLRA at 117 (citing *U.S. DOJ, Fed. Bureau of Prisons, Fed. Transfer Ctr., Okla. City, Okla.*, 57 FLRA 158, 162 (2001) (Chairman Cabaniss dissenting) (*BOP, Okla. City*)). Specifically, the Authority stated that bargaining parties should assess "what provisions best fit their working conditions and what arrangements are 'appropriate.'" *Id.* (quoting *BOP, Okla. City*, 57 FLRA at 162). The Authority also stated that this policy reflected a "justifiable reluctance" on the part of the Authority to substitute its judgment for that of the parties who have negotiated an agreement. *Id.*

The Authority has deferred to bargaining parties' choices in the negotiability context as well. For example, in negotiability disputes involving agreed-upon contract provisions, the Authority defers to the parties who negotiated the provision -- not the agency head -- when assessing the provision's meaning. *See IBEW, Local 350*, 55 FLRA 243, 244 (1999) (deferring to the meaning provided by "the parties who agreed on the provision"). In addition, the Authority has held that a contract becomes effective even where an agency has not timely submitted the contract for agency-head review under § 7114(c) or where the agency head does not disapprove (or timely disapprove) a provision. *See U.S. Dep't of the Treasury, Bureau of Engraving & Printing*, 44 FLRA 926, 938-40 (1992). This recognizes that the bargaining parties' choices can have binding effects, without regard to the potential concerns of agency heads. Of course, a contract that becomes effective in these circumstances does so "subject to the provisions of [the Statute] and any other applicable law, rule, or regulation." 5 U.S.C. § 7114(c)(3). In that situation, as noted above, the provision is enforceable in arbitration unless it abrogates a management right.[7] *See EPA*, 65 FLRA at 118.

Deferring to the bargaining parties' choices and applying an "abrogation" standard in cases where the parties have agreed to contract provisions also is consistent with the Statute's requirement that agencies "be represented at . . . negotiations by duly authorized representatives prepared to discuss and negotiate on any condition of employment[.]" 5 U.S.C. § 7114(b)(2). In this connection, § 7114(b)(2) recognizes that agencies are required to provide bargaining representatives who adequately represent management's interests at the bargaining table *before* any agreement is reached. Thus, if a union proposal would impose burdens on an agency that the agency deems excessive, then those burdens should be assessed during negotiations – not after the parties have reached agreement.[8]

7. As noted above, such provision is enforceable, in the dissent's view, even if it abrogates a management right.

8. There is no basis for the dissent's speculation about what will occur under this revised approach; specifically, that agency heads will be more likely to get directly involved in collective bargaining, which, in turn, will impede the bargaining process. *See* Dissent at 21. As an initial matter, parties already have the ability to reach binding agreements with regard to a wide range of permissive subjects of bargaining -- including, but not limited to, "the numbers, types, and grades of employees or positions assigned to any organizational subdivision, work project, or tour of duty," and "the technology, methods, and means of performing work[,]" 5 U.S.C. § 7106(b)(1) -- and there is no evidence that this has resulted in the situation that the dissent predicts. In addition, there is no reasonable basis for finding that local agency representatives routinely fail to object to union proposals on management-rights grounds -- as evidenced by the plethora of Authority negotiability decisions in the past two years alone that have involved local agency negotiators declaring bargaining proposals outside the duty to bargain on those grounds. *See, e.g., AFGE, Local 221*, 64 FLRA 1153, 1155 (2010); *AFGE, Local 1345*, 64 FLRA 949, 950 (2010); *United Am. Nurses, D.C. Nurses Ass'n & United Am. Nurses Local 203*, 64 FLRA 879, 880 (2010); *AFGE, Local 1367*, 64 FLRA 869, 870 (2010) (Member Beck dissenting in part); *AFGE, Local 1547*, 64 FLRA 813, 813-14 (2010); *AFGE, Council of Prison Locals 33*, 64 FLRA 728, 728 (2010) (Member Beck concurring in the result); *NTEU, Chapter 83*, 64 FLRA 723, 724 (2010); *PASS*, 64 FLRA 474, 476 (2010) (Member Beck concurring in part and dissenting in part); *AFGE, Local 171, Council of Prison Locals 33*, 64 FLRA 275, 275 (2009); *AFGE, Local 2145*, 64 FLRA 231, 232 (2009); *NATCA*, 64 FLRA 161, 162 (2009); *NAGE, Local R1-109*, 64 FLRA 132, 133 (2009) (Member Beck dissenting); *AFGE, Local 801*, 64 FLRA 62, 63 (2009); *AFGE, Local 1156*, 63 FLRA 649, 649 (2009); *AFT, Indian Educators Fed'n, Local 4524*, 63 FLRA 585, 586 (2009); *AFGE, Local 1968*, 63 FLRA 481, 483 (2009); *AFGE, Local 1458*, 63 FLRA 469, 470 (2009); *NATCA*, 63 FLRA 387, 389 (2009); *AFGE, Local 1156*, 63 FLRA 340, 341 (2009); *AFGE, Local 1547*, 63 FLRA 174, 175 (2009). This is in stark contrast to the two negotiability decisions in the past two years that have involved agency-head disapproval of contracts on management-rights grounds. *See AFGE, Local 1770*, 64 FLRA 953, 955 (2010); *Nat'l Weather Serv. Emps. Org.*, 63 FLRA 450, 451 (2009). Further, although the dissent states that the Authority has not yet found that a contract provision abrogates a management right, *see*

For the foregoing reasons, in this and in future cases, we will find that a contractual arrangement is an "appropriate" arrangement within the meaning of § 7106(b)(3) of the Statute – and that an agency head may not disapprove such an arrangement on § 7106 grounds – unless the arrangement abrogates, or waives, a management right. Previous Authority decisions to the contrary will no longer be followed. In determining whether a contract provision abrogates a management right, we will assess whether the contract provision "precludes [the] agency from exercising" the affected management right. *U.S. Dep't of Transp., FAA*, 65 FLRA 171, 174 (2010).

ii. Application of Revised Analytical Framework

The Union contends that the provisions are arrangements for employees who are adversely affected by the Agency's exercise of its management right to evaluate employees' work performance. Response at 10. In this regard, the Union claims that the provisions will lessen the chance that an employee will receive an adverse performance evaluation, or will be disciplined, as a result of management "not clearly stating performance expectations[,]" thereby mitigating an adverse effect. *Id.* By contrast, the Agency does not explain how negative performance evaluations or discipline would not adversely affect employees, or how these harms are merely "speculative." Reply at 7. In addition, the Authority has found that a similar provision -- one that lessened the likelihood that an employee would be adversely affected by a negative performance evaluation because of matters beyond an employee's control -- constituted an arrangement. *See Patent Office Prof'l Ass'n*, 47 FLRA at 35-36. Moreover, as it is not possible to reliably determine in advance which employees are likely to be adversely affected, the provisions are prophylactic and are sufficiently tailored to benefit those employees who receive negative performance evaluations and suffer related adverse effects such as discipline. *See, e.g., AFGE, Council of Prison Locals 33*, 65 FLRA 142, 146 (2010). Consistent with the foregoing, we find that the provisions are arrangements.

With regard to whether the arrangements are appropriate, the provisions limit management's ability to hold employees accountable for work performance only in limited circumstances, specifically, where performance expectations have not been communicated to the employees in writing (including e-mail). As such, they do not preclude the Agency from exercising its rights to direct employees and assign work under § 7106(a)(2)(A) and (B) of the Statute. Therefore, the provisions do not abrogate those management rights and, thus, are appropriate arrangements.

For the foregoing reasons, the provisions are appropriate arrangements within the meaning of § 7106(b)(3) of the Statute and, thus, are not contrary to § 7106(a)(2)(A) and (B) of the Statute.[9]

III. Article 22, Section 3B

A. Wording

> In those cases where [the Agency] has sound reason to believe that an employee is abusing "emergency" annual leave, the employee shall be counseled concerning such abuse. If such counseling is unsuccessful, and the employee continues to abuse "emergency" annual leave, [the Agency] may issue a written notice to the employee that all subsequent "emergency" annual leave absences must be supported by credible evidence justifying such absences.

Petition at 57.

B. Meaning

The parties agree that the provision has the following meaning. If the Agency suspects an employee of abusing emergency annual leave, then the Agency must counsel the employee. Record at 2. If the employee continues to abuse emergency annual leave following the counseling, then the Agency could advise the employee in writing that he or she must provide supporting evidence to justify all subsequent uses of emergency annual leave. *Id.* Counseling must precede the written notice. *Id.* In addition, the Union asserts, and the Agency does not dispute, that, under the provision, the Agency could respond to a first offense of leave abuse with any form of discipline *other than* the issuance of a leave restriction notice. *See* Response at 2, 16. Because the provision is silent as to this matter, and the Union's clarifying explanation is consistent with the plain wording of the provision, the Authority adopts

Dissent at 19 n.1, if this proves anything at all, then it proves that parties are sufficiently sophisticated so as not to agree to contract provisions that abrogate management's rights.

9. As such, it is unnecessary to determine whether the provisions also are procedures under § 7106(b)(2).

this explanation for the purpose of construing what the provision means. *See, e.g., AFGE, Local 1770*, 64 FLRA 953, 958 (2010).

C. Positions of the Parties

1. Agency

The Agency contends that the provision affects management's right to discipline employees under § 7106(a)(2)(A) of the Statute "because it requires management to counsel an employee prior to being able to take disciplinary action." SOP at 6. In this regard, the Agency argues that the "issuance of a leave restriction letter is an inherently disciplinary act[,]" and that the Authority's precedent supports this position. Reply at 10 (citing *NFFE, Local 858*, 42 FLRA 1169, 1171-72 (1991) (*Local 858*)). *See also* SOP at 7 (citing *AFGE, Local 1156*, 42 FLRA 1157, 1161 (1991) (*Local 1156*)). In addition, although the parties' agreement provides that notices of *sick leave* restriction will not be considered disciplinary action, the Agency asserts that "there is no similar or parallel language . . . which would apply to notices of emergency annual leave restriction."[10] SOP at 6.

Additionally, the Agency argues that the provision is not an appropriate arrangement under § 7106(b)(3) of the Statute because the Authority has held that where, as here, a provision precludes management from issuing a leave-restriction letter until after counseling has taken place, the provision excessively interferes with management's right to discipline employees. Reply at 11 (citing *Local 858*, 42 FLRA at 1173). The Agency also argues that the provision is not a procedure within the meaning of § 7106(b)(2) of the Statute. *Id.* at 10-11.

2. Union

The Union argues that the provision is not contrary to management's right to discipline employees because "[a] requirement that the employee provide credible evidence in utilizing leave does not equate to discipline." Response at 13. In this regard, the Union contends that the provision in the parties' agreement stating that written notices of sick leave restrictions will not be considered disciplinary action also applies to written notices of emergency annual leave restrictions. *Id.* at 13 & n.1.

In addition, the Union argues that the provision is an appropriate arrangement under § 7106(b)(3) of the Statute because it "mitigates the adverse effects on employees when management exercises its right to discipline by requiring an employee to provide supporting documentation for emergency leave usage." *Id.* at 15. Further, the Union asserts that the provision does not delay or limit the Agency's ability to impose discipline for abuse of emergency annual leave, *id.* at 13, and that "nothing in [the provision] would limit the [Agency] from disciplining an employee while contemporaneously providing counseling[,]" *id.* at 16. According to the Union, the provision does not excessively interfere with management's right to discipline employees because it only limits the Agency's ability to notify an employee suspected of leave abuse that he or she must supply supporting evidence justifying future absences, while the Agency remains free to "discipline[e] employees for underlying offenses such as AWOL." *Id.* at 15-16.

Finally, the Union argues that the provision is a procedure within the meaning of § 7106(b)(2) of the Statute. *Id.* at 16-17.

D. Analysis and Conclusions

1. The provision affects management's right to discipline.

The Authority has held that "management's right to discipline includes placing an employee in a restricted leave use category." *NFFE, Local 405*, 42 FLRA 1112, 1131 (1991). Thus, the Authority has held that provisions or proposals that preclude management from imposing a leave restriction in response to a first offense of leave abuse affect management's right to discipline employees under § 7106(a)(2)(A). *See, e.g., NAGE, Local R5-82*, 43 FLRA 25, 28 (1991) (*NAGE*); *Local 858*, 42 FLRA at 1171-72; *Local 1156*, 42 FLRA at 1161.

Under the provision, the Agency would be precluded from requiring an employee to provide evidence justifying subsequent emergency annual leave absences until after the Agency has counseled the employee regarding the suspected leave abuse, given the employee an opportunity to improve, and seen no improvement. Thus, management would not be able to require an employee to provide evidence justifying future emergency annual leave absences based on the *initial* incident(s) giving rise to a "sound reason to believe" that the employee is "abusing 'emergency' annual leave[.]" Petition at 57. The Authority has held that similar provisions affect

10. Article 23, Section 4C of the parties' agreement provides, in pertinent part, that "written notices of sick leave restrictions . . . . will not be considered disciplinary action." Response, Attach., Article 23 at 4.

management's right to discipline under § 7106(a)(2)(A) of the Statute. *See NAGE*, 43 FLRA at 28; *Local 858*, 42 FLRA at 1172; *Local 1156*, 42 FLRA at 1162.

As stated previously, the Union cites a provision in the parties' agreement providing that written notices of sick leave restriction will not be considered disciplinary action in support of its argument that notices of emergency annual leave restriction are not discipline. Response at 13 & n.1. Contrary to the Union's claim, however, the plain wording of the cited provision applies specifically to notices of sick leave restrictions, not emergency annual leave restrictions, and the Union provides no basis for concluding that the provision has broader application. *See* Response, Attach., Article 23 at 4. Moreover, the Authority considered and rejected a virtually identical argument in *Local 1156*, 42 FLRA at 1162, and the Union provides no basis for reaching a different conclusion here.

For the foregoing reasons, we find that the provision affects management's right to discipline employees.

2. The provision is an appropriate arrangement under § 7106(b)(3) of the Statute.

As discussed previously, under the Authority's revised framework for determining whether a provision is an appropriate arrangement within the meaning of § 7106(b)(3) of the Statute, the Authority assesses: (1) whether the provision is intended to be an arrangement for, including being sufficiently tailored to compensate, employees adversely affected by the exercise of a management right; and (2) if so, then whether the contract provision abrogates the affected management right. *See supra*, § II.D.2.i. (citations omitted).

Applying that framework here, as the Union explains, the provision would "mitigate" the adverse effects of management's exercise of its right to discipline. Response at 15. In this regard, the provision would protect employees suspected of abusing emergency leave from being required to support future emergency annual leave requests with documentation without first receiving counseling and the opportunity to correct problematic emergency annual leave usage. Moreover, the proposal is tailored because it applies only to those employees whom management suspects of emergency annual leave abuse, but who have not yet received counseling that any future leave abuse may result in leave restriction. Accordingly, we conclude that the proposal is sufficiently tailored and that the proposal constitutes an arrangement for employees adversely affected by management's right to discipline.

As to whether the provision constitutes an appropriate arrangement, as stated above, the provision precludes management from requiring an employee to provide evidence justifying subsequent emergency annual leave absences until after the Agency has counseled the employee regarding the suspected leave abuse, given the employee an opportunity to improve, and seen no improvement. However, the provision does not preclude management from imposing other forms of discipline on the employee. Thus, the provision merely limits the circumstances in which management may exercise its right to discipline; it does not preclude the Agency from exercising that right. Accordingly, we find that the provision does not abrogate management's right to discipline employees under § 7106(a)(2)(A) of the Statute and, thus, is an appropriate arrangement.

For the foregoing reasons, we find that the provision is an appropriate arrangement within the meaning of § 7106(b)(3) of the Statute and, thus, is not contrary to § 7106(a)(2)(A) of the Statute.[11]

IV. Article 38, Section 2A, 2D

A. Wording

Article 38, Section 2

Unless contrary to law or regulation the Employer shall include, in its open market bid request, or request for proposals, the following requirements:

A. Employees who are identified as potentially adversely affected by the decision to contract shall receive right of first refusal by the Contractor, for employment openings for ninety (90) days after the beginning of contract performances.

. . . .

D. By the contract start date, the Contractor shall provide the Contracting Officer with the following:

11. As such, it is unnecessary to address whether the provision also is a procedure under § 7106(b)(2).

1. The names of potentially adversely affected Federal employees offered an employment opening.

2. The date the offer was made.

3. A brief description of the position.

4. The date of acceptance of the offer and the effective date of employment.

5. The date of rejection of the offer, if applicable.

6. The names of potentially adversely affected Federal employees who applied but were not offered employment and the reason(s) for withholding an offer.

Petition at 70, 72.

B. Meaning

The parties agree that, under Section A, employees who are identified as being potentially adversely affected by a decision to contract out work shall receive a right of first refusal for ninety days after the beginning of contract performance. Record at 2. This right of first refusal would be subject to the parties' negotiated grievance procedure unless making the right of first refusal subject to the negotiated grievance procedure is contrary to law or regulation, including Office of Management and Budget (OMB) Circular A-76 (A-76). *Id.* The parties agree that, under Section D, the Agency would be required to request that contractors provide the items listed in subsections 1-6. As with Section A, Section D would not operate if it is contrary to law or regulation. *Id.* at 2-3.

C. Positions of the Parties

1. Agency

The Agency contends that the provisions are inconsistent with A-76, a government-wide regulation, because they would subject matters that are provided for by A-76 to the negotiated grievance procedure. SOP at 12, 15 (citing *Dep't of the Treasury, IRS v. FLRA*, 494 U.S. 922 (1990) (*IRS*); *AFGE, Local 1345*, 48 FLRA 168 (1993)). The Agency maintains that these provisions are distinguishable from the proposal found negotiable in *AFGE, Local 1827*, 58 FLRA 344, 350 (2003). In this connection, the Agency asserts that the proposal at issue in *AFGE, Local 1827* did not apply in circumstances covered by A-76, while the provisions in this case would apply in such circumstances. *Id.* at 13, 15. Also in this connection, the Agency argues that the parties' collective bargaining agreement does not expressly preclude grievances over matters involving A-76. Reply at 13. Further, the Agency contends that the introductory language "[u]nless contrary to law or regulation" does not render the provisions negotiable. SOP at 13, 16-17.

2. Union

The Union contends that the provisions do not subject the rights afforded employees under A-76 to the negotiated grievance procedure. Response at 18. In this regard, the Union argues that the parties' agreement directly precludes alleged violations of A-76 from being grieved. *Id.* at 19. Finally, the Union contends that these provisions are distinguishable from the proposal in *IRS* because they do not provide for any sort of appeals procedure or access to the negotiated grievance procedure. *Id.* at 19-20.

D. Analysis and Conclusions

A-76 sets forth several requirements that federal agencies must follow when contracting out agency functions, and states, with certain exceptions not relevant here, that "*[n]oncompliance with [A-76]* shall not be interpreted to create a substantive or procedural basis to challenge agency action or inaction[.]" A-76 Revised, para. 5.g. (2003) (emphasis added). In *United States Department of the Treasury, IRS v. FLRA*, 996 F.2d 1246, 1248 (D.C. Cir. 1993) (*Dep't of the Treasury*), the court held that substantively identical wording in a previous version of A-76[12] precluded bargaining over a union proposal to subject alleged violations of A-76 to the negotiated grievance procedure. *Id.* at 1250. In this connection, the court stated that "collective bargaining over the method for resolving disputes concerning application of [A-76] and arbitration of claimed 'violations' of [A-76] would both be inconsistent with [A-76]." *Id.* Consistent with *Dep't of the Treasury*, the Authority has held that grievances over compliance with A-76 *itself* are

12. At the time of the court's decision, A-76 stated, in part, that except for an agency's internal appeal system, "This Circular and its Supplement shall not . . . establish and shall not be construed to create any substantive or procedural basis for anyone to challenge any agency action or inaction on the basis that such action or inaction was not in accordance with this Circular." *Dep't of the Treasury*, 996 F.2d at 1248. The court noted that a supplement to A-76 "add[ed] that a decision in the internal review process should not be subject to appeal outside the agency." *Id.*

barred, and that proposals subjecting disputes over compliance with A-76 *itself* are outside the duty to bargain. *See AFGE, Local 1513*, 52 FLRA 717, 719-22 (1993) (grievance not arbitrable); *AFGE, Local 1345*, 48 FLRA 168, 205-06 (1993) (Member Armendariz concurring and dissenting as to other matters) (proposal outside duty to bargain).

However, neither the plain wording of A-76 nor the above-cited court and Authority decisions support a conclusion that parties are precluded from agreeing to, and enforcing in arbitration, contract provisions that independently impose on agencies obligations that are the same as, or similar to, the requirements set forth in A-76. In this connection, the Authority has stated that a proposal was not contrary to A-76 where it would merely limit grievances "to the right guaranteed by the contract – not the right guaranteed by . . . A-76." *AFGE, Local 1827*, 58 FLRA at 350. As Article 38, Sections 2A and 2D do not subject enforcement of A-76 to the negotiated grievance procedure and the Agency does not argue that the provisions are otherwise contrary to law, we find that they are not contrary to law.

V. Order

The Agency shall rescind its disapproval of the provisions.

Member Beck, Dissenting:

My colleagues have chosen to jettison decades of precedent with respect to the standard by which we assess whether an agency head may, under § 7114(c)(2), reject a contract proposal that affects management's rights. They have decided to do so based on an exercise in statutory interpretation that is so strained as to be untenable. Further, they have created an inconsistency in approach that defies common sense; under their new regime, the same proposal that is legally invalid if it "excessively interferes" with management rights at the bargaining table magically becomes valid and binding when it lands on the agency head's desk.

Consequently, I must vigorously dissent.

In 1983, the D.C. Circuit examined the tension between management rights and the duty to bargain and concluded that a proposal affecting management rights should be deemed within the duty to bargain unless it interferes with statutory management rights "to an excessive degree." *AFGE, Local 2782 v. FLRA*, 702 F.2d 1183, 1188 (D.C. Cir. 1983). Notably, the Court did not say that a proposal must be considered negotiable unless it "abrogates" management rights. By taking care not to articulate what would have been an easy-to-apply, bright-line test -- abrogation, the Court indicated that the proper standard for assessing the negotiability of proposals that affect management rights is something short of total abrogation.

Since that time, the Authority has consistently applied the "excessive interference" standard to management assertions that bargaining proposals are outside the duty to bargain because they impermissibly interfere with management's rights under § 7106(a). *See, e.g., Nat'l Ass'n of Indep. Labor, Local 7*, 64 FLRA 1194, 1198 (2010) (proposal that would require bargaining unit employees to wear civilian uniforms provided by the agency when performing civilian duties excessively interferes with the right to determine methods and means of performing work); *Prof'l Airways Sys. Specialists*, 61 FLRA 97, 99 (2005) (proposal that requires agency to provide training in accordance with collective bargaining agreement excessively interferes with the right to assign work); *AFGE, Local 3529*, 57 FLRA 172, 179 (2001) (proposal that precludes agency from holding employees accountable for failing to accomplish task excessively interferes with right to direct employees and assign work); *AFGE, Local 1138, Council 214*, 51 FLRA 1725, 1735 (1996) (proposal that requires agency to place mechanics and operators on the same seniority list excessively interferes with the right to assign employees); *AFGE, Local 644*, 21 FLRA 658, 662 (1986) (proposal that requires agency to convert library space into office space excessively interferes with the right to determine internal security practices); *Ass'n of Civilian Technicians, Mont. Air Chapter*, 20 FLRA 717, 731 (1985) (proposal that would preclude management, regardless of circumstances, from obtaining additional personnel with skills unavailable in the bargaining unit excessively interferes with the right to provide numbers and types of employees to perform the agency's work).

This standard was applied whether the agency announced its position at the bargaining table or at the later stage of agency head review under § 7114(c). *Ass'n of Civilian Technicians, P.R. Army Chapter*, 60 FLRA 1000, 1008 (2005) (provision that requires the agency to reimburse employees for personal expenses related to cancelled leave excessively interferes with the right to assign work); *NFFE, Local 1214*, 49 FLRA 215, 221 (1994) (provision that would restrict agency's use of ethics and values in the evaluation of performance excessively interferes with the right to assign work and the right to discipline); *NTEU*, 31 FLRA 181, 185-86 (1988) (provision that would prevent the agency from detailing or temporarily promoting union officer or steward excessively interferes with the right to assign employees and to assign work); *AFGE, Local 1409*, 28 FLRA 109, 112 (1987) (provision that prevents agency from assigning duties that might conflict with any medical restrictions excessively interfere with the right to assign work).

The Majority now declares that it will apply a new standard of "abrogation" when a proposal that was provisionally accepted at the bargaining table is rejected as a result of agency head review. That is to say, *once a proposal proceeds to agency head review, it will be binding on the agency even if it "excessively interferes" with management's rights.* An agency head will now be permitted to reject a proposal only if it nullifies completely -- only if it eliminates entirely -- one or more statutory management rights. My research reveals *no case* in the past 20 years in which the Authority has found that a contract provision abrogates any management right; it just doesn't happen.[1] So, as a practical matter, post-bargaining table agency head review will no longer play any role in preserving the management prerogatives that Congress sought to protect through § 7106(a). This result is flatly inconsistent with Congressional intent. *See AFGE v. FLRA*, 778 F.2d 850, 863 (D.C. Cir. 1985) (Congress intended that the head of an agency may reject a contract term -- even a settlement imposed by the Federal Service Impasses Panel -- if "it is violative of management prerogatives under the Act").

The crux of my colleagues' reasoning is a bit of statutory interpretation that involves contrasting the language of § 7117(c)(1) (which relates to the statutory duty to bargain) with § 7114(c)(2) (which relates to agency head review). As identified by the Majority, the telling statutory language is as follows:

<u>§ 7117(c)(1)</u>	<u>§ 7114(c)(2)</u>
An exclusive representative may file a negotiability appeal "if an agency involved in collective bargaining with [the] exclusive representative alleges that the *duty to bargain* in good faith does not extend to any matter[.]" (Emphasis supplied by the Majority.)	Where an agency and an exclusive representative have reached an agreement, "[t]he head of the agency shall approve the agreement ... if the agreement is *in accordance with the provisions of [the Statute] . . . .*" (Emphasis supplied by the Majority.)

These two provisions reflect a couple of unremarkable propositions. First, § 7117(c)(1) tells us that a negotiability appeal involves questions about whether a proposal is outside the duty to bargain. Second, § 7114(c)(2) tells us that an agency head may reject a provisionally agreed-to proposal if

1. In 2002, the Authority abandoned the "abrogation" standard for the "excessive interference" standard when addressing management rights challenges to arbitral awards. At that time, Member Armendariz observed that, "in the 12 years that the abrogation standard [for arbitral awards] has been in existence, the Authority has never applied that standard in such a way to find that an award was deficient. Such a uniformly one-sided application effectively renders the test meaningless and removes all of its utility." *U.S. Dep't of Justice, Fed. Bureau of Prisons, Fed. Transfer Ctr., Okla. City, Okla.*, 58 FLRA 109, 115 (2002) (Concurring Opinion of Member Armendariz). My colleagues revived the abrogation standard in September 2010 (*see U.S. EPA*, 65 FLRA 113, 116 (2010) (*EPA*)) and have yet to conclude that the enforcement of any contract provision abrogates a management right.

he determines that it is not in accordance with the Statute.

For my colleagues in the Majority, it is a crucial point that "Congress did not state that an agency head may disapprove matters that are outside the 'duty to bargain.'" Majority at 6. For them, this apparent omission indicates that an agency head is prohibited from rejecting a proposal merely because it is outside the duty to bargain. To be sure, their observation about the statutory language is technically accurate (Congress did not expressly include "outside the duty to bargain" as a reason for agency head rejection of a proposal); however, the legal conclusion that they draw from it is wholly unjustified. What they have missed is that the two attributes -- (1) being outside the duty to bargain and (2) being not in accordance with the Statute -- are not mutually exclusive. The reference to the latter in § 7114(c)(2) does not *preclude* the former; rather, it *includes* the former.

Simply put, when a proposal impermissibly interferes with a management right, it is prohibited by § 7106(a). And a proposal that is prohibited by § 7106(a) can properly be characterized as being *both* outside the duty to bargain and not "in accordance with the provisions of [the Statute]." Such a proposal is subject to agency head rejection under § 7114(c)(2).[2] Rather than follow this axiomatic reading of the Statute, the Majority pursues a cramped interpretation that amounts to this: A proposal that violates § 7106(a) must nevertheless be treated by the agency head as being "in accordance with the provisions of [the Statute]."

Putting aside my colleagues' manifestly erroneous interpretation of the statutory language, the Majority's new regime just does not survive the test of common sense. What sense is there in applying a different test for negotiability at the stage of agency head review than is applied at bargaining table? As the D.C. Circuit has explained, the purpose of agency head review under § 7114(c) is simply "to allow the head of the agency an extra 30 days to do that which his subordinates could have done earlier." *AFGE v. FLRA*, 778 F.2d at 860 n.16.

Under the new approach announced by the Majority, a proposal runs afoul of the Statute if it "excessively interferes" with management rights when it is presented at the bargaining table; yet, when the same proposal reaches the agency head, it is somehow transmuted so that it now runs afoul of the Statute only if it "abrogates" management rights (which is virtually never found to occur).[3] The Statute does not possess the alchemic properties that the Majority ascribes to it. Nothing in the Statute's structure or purpose indicates that § 7106 means one thing at the bargaining table and something entirely different when agency head review takes place. Under § 7106, a proposal that affects management rights either is or is not a permissible limitation on those rights. Aside from its maladroit attempt to interpret § 7114(c)(2), the Majority offers no reason to apply a bifurcated standard of validity that is less rigorous at the stage of agency head review.

Of course, the practical effect of the Majority's new regime will be to impede normal labor relations and to slow the bargaining process. Knowing that they may no longer review new contract provisions

2. The Majority cites a few cases in which the Authority has held that a contract provision is not inconsistent with the Statute under § 7114(c)(2) merely because it was negotiated as a permissive subject of bargaining under § 7106(b)(1). Majority at 6-7. Based on this precedent, the Majority reaches the inappropriately broad conclusion that the concept of being not in accordance with the Statute excludes the concept of being outside the duty to bargain. *See* Majority at n.5. But these cases, in which an agency agreed to proposals on permissive subjects under § 7106(b)(1), tell us nothing about situations (like the one presented here) in which provisions negotiated under § 7106(b)(2) or (b)(3) are rejected because they impermissibly interfere with management rights. Provisions that are negotiated under § 7106(b)(1) are necessarily "in accordance with the provisions of [the Statute]" because such negotiation occurs entirely at the discretion of management and such proposals, by definition, cannot impermissibly interfere with management rights. In contrast, matters that an exclusive representative seeks to negotiate under § 7106(b)(2) or (b)(3) may impermissibly interfere with the management rights that Congress sought to protect under § 7106(a). If so, the proposal can hardly be characterized as being "in accordance with the provisions of [the Statute]" as contemplated by § 7114(c)(2).

3. The Majority mischaracterizes my view on provisions that have become binding contractual terms after agency head review and are then being enforced in arbitration. The Majority asserts that I view such a provision as "enforceable . . . even if it abrogates a management right." Majority at 9 n.7. As I explained in *EPA*, by agreeing to include a provision in its collective bargaining agreement (after agency head review) and to be bound by that provision in arbitration, an agency "concedes that the provision is a permissible limitation on [its management] rights under § 7106(b)." 65 FLRA at 120 (Dissenting Opinion of Member Beck). By definition, a contract provision that is being enforced in these circumstances can hardly be seen as an abrogation of management rights.

with an eye toward preserving their statutory management rights, agency heads are likely to delegate less authority to their labor relations officials in the field and reserve to themselves much more active and hands-on supervision of collective bargaining. My colleagues in the Majority are telling agency heads that the only meaningful review they now have is a review that occurs before -- not after -- preliminary agreement is reached at the bargaining table. As a consequence, each proposal that might affect management rights will languish in limbo until it is transmitted to, and reviewed by, the agency head -- an added step that is likely to increase substantially the time necessary to reach agreement on, or to resolve disagreements about, specific proposals.[4] This state of affairs can hardly be what Congress intended when it sought to promote "effective and efficient" federal-sector labor relations (§ 7101(b)) and "avoid unnecessary delays" in collective bargaining. § 7114(b)(3). As the D.C. Circuit has observed:

> Congress might have limited the head of the agency's review opportunity to the negotiation phase, but it apparently was unwilling to impose a continuous burden on the head of the agency to review each and every proposal as it arose in the course of day-to-day bargaining

AFGE v. FLRA, 778 F.2d at 858. My colleagues in the Majority have now decided to impose on agency heads precisely the burden that Congress sought to avoid.

As for the specific provisions at issue here, applying the "excessive interference" standard, I do not agree that the provisions in Articles 11, 18, and 22 constitute appropriate arrangements. I agree with my colleagues that the provisions in Article 38 are not contrary to law because they do not subject the Agency's decision to contract out specific functions to the parties' negotiated grievance procedure. *See AFGE, Local 1513*, 52 FLRA 717, 719-21 (1996); *see also U.S. Dep't of the Army, U.S. Army Corps of Eng'rs, Mobile Dist., Mobile, Ala.*, 64 FLRA 508, 512 (2010) (Dissenting Opinion of Member Beck).

---

4. Under § 7114(c)(3), there is a 30-day time limit on the post-bargaining table agency head review that the Majority has today eviscerated. There is no time limit placed on the earlier and more frequent agency head reviews that are likely to take place as a result of the Majority's new regime.

65 FLRA No. 110

SOCIAL SECURITY ADMINISTRATION
(Agency)

and

AMERICAN FEDERATION
OF GOVERNMENT EMPLOYEES
LOCAL 1760
(Union)

0-AR-4320

DECISION

February 16, 2011

Before the Authority: Carol Waller Pope, Chairman, and Thomas M. Beck and Ernest DuBester, Members

I. Statement of the Case

This matter is before the Authority on exceptions to an award of Arbitrator John B. Dorsey filed by the Agency under § 7122(a) of the Federal Service Labor-Management Relations Statute (the Statute) and part 2425 of the Authority's Regulations. The Union filed an opposition to the Agency's exceptions.

The Arbitrator found that the Agency violated the parties' national agreement (the agreement) by terminating the Local Union President's (the President's) access to certain aspects of the Agency's electronic communications system (the system) when he retired.

For the reasons that follow, we deny the Agency's exceptions.

II. Background and Arbitrator's Award

The President retired from the Agency, but continued to serve in his representational role as President. Award at 3. When he retired, the Agency terminated his access to the system, including the Agency's intranet and electronic mail (e-mail), as well as the Official Union Time Tracking System (OUTTS), which tracks Union officials' use of official time. *Id.*

A grievance was filed regarding this termination of access. *Id.* When the grievance was not resolved, it was submitted to arbitration, where the parties stipulated the issues, in pertinent part, as follows: "Did the [Agency] violate the . . . agreement when it terminated access of the . . . President to the . . . system, intranet, [e]-mail, and [the OUTTS]? If so, what shall be the remedy?" *Id.*

The Arbitrator noted that Article 4, Section 4 of the agreement provides that, when management proposes certain changes, the Agency must notify the Union electronically, and the Union must respond electronically.[1] *Id.* at 3-4. In addition, the Arbitrator found that Article 11, Section 9.A.8. of the agreement is "clear on its face[]" and provides the President the right to use the Agency's e-mail system to communicate with employees in the Local.[2] Award at 7.

The Arbitrator noted the Agency's claim that Article 11, Section 9.A.1. of the agreement requires the Union to comply both with Agency policies, including the Agency's Information Systems Security Handbook (the Handbook), and with a related Memorandum applying to the particular region where the President worked (the Memorandum), which

1. Article 4, Section 4 of the agreement provides, in pertinent part, that "[t]he designated Management representative will provide the designated Union representative with timely electronic notice of the Management initiated change(s) to a union-designated electronic mail box[,]" and "[t]he Union will request consultations and or negotiations . . . by submitting its request to a management designated electronic mailbox." Award at 3-4.

2. Article 11, Section 9.A. of the agreement provides, in pertinent part, that the Agency

> agrees to provide the Union with access to and use of the Agency's electronic mail subject to the following restrictions:
>
> 1. The Union agrees its access and use will comply with applicable government-wide and Agency policies and guidelines and the [agreement].
>
> . . . .
>
> 8. . . . [T]he [U]nion agrees that an e-mail message, with the exceptions noted below, will be transmitted to not more than 100 recipients at one time[.] . . . A Local president or a designee, however, is authorized to send one e-mail per week to each employee in his/her Local[,] in excess of the 100 recipient limit.

Exceptions, Attach., Ex. 5 at 11-5 - 11-6.

provide for terminating access to the system when employees depart the Agency.[3] Award at 7-8. Addressing that claim, the Arbitrator found that Section 9.A.1. "is hardly an example of clear contract language[,]" and that it "pledges the Union to comply with" the agreement, which "requires the Local President to use the [e]-mail system." *Id.* at 8. The Arbitrator also found that the Union is entitled to determine who will be its designee under the agreement, and that the President is entitled to serve in that role, despite his retirement. *Id.* Accordingly, the Arbitrator found that "the Agency must provide him with electronic notices of changes[,] and he must reply to management's electronic mail box." *Id.*

In addition, the Arbitrator noted that the parties had signed a Memorandum of Understanding regarding the OUTTS (the OUTTS MOU), and that Section 3 of the OUTTS MOU provides, in pertinent part, that "Local presidents and/or their designees shall have access to" the OUTTS. *Id.* at 5. The Arbitrator -- citing the parol evidence rule that prohibits, in certain circumstances, consideration of evidence extrinsic to a written agreement -- rejected the Agency's reliance on bargaining history to demonstrate that the OUTTS MOU was not intended to apply to retired individuals. *See id.* at 8-9.

Further, the Arbitrator addressed the Agency's claim that granting the President limited use of its system would compromise "the security of its entire electronic communications . . . ." *Id.* at 9. The Arbitrator determined that the Agency "presented no proof to back up that assertion." *Id.* In addition, the Arbitrator stated that it was undisputed that, "over his many years as a full time Union [o]fficial[,]" the President had limited access to the system, and "[t]here was not a single claim [that] it resulted in any security breach." *Id.* The Arbitrator also stated that "the Agency has not been consistent in applying what it maintains is an unbending policy[,]" because it has permitted another retired Union representative to continue using the system, and that the Agency "provided no explanation as to why [the President] should not be afforded equal treatment." *Id.*

3. The Handbook provides, in pertinent part: "Security officers should immediately deactivate the [personal identification numbers (PINs)] of employees who have departed the [A]gency . . . ." Exceptions, Attach., Ex. 6, Ch. 2.0 at 2 (emphasis omitted). The Memorandum directs Agency managers to complete a clearance form when employees leave the Agency, and lists "PIN deactivation[]" as a responsibility of the Agency's Center for Security and Integrity. Exceptions, Attach., Ex. 7 at 1.

Based on the foregoing, the Arbitrator concluded that the Agency violated the agreement when it terminated the President's intranet, e-mail, and OUTTS access. *Id.* As a remedy, he directed the Agency to restore that limited access. *Id.* at 10.

III. Positions of the Parties

A. Agency's Exceptions

The Agency argues that the award is contrary to management's right to determine its internal security practices under § 7106(a)(1) of the Statute because it interferes with the Agency's internal security policy-- set forth in the Handbook and the Memorandum -- of terminating employees' access to the system when they retire. Exceptions at 4, 6-7. According to the Agency, this policy is reasonably linked to its goal of safeguarding the system, which maintains personally identifiable information of every United States citizen. *Id.* at 8. Also according to the Agency, this policy is based on two principles: (1) "need to know[,]" i.e., the Agency grants system access only to employees; and (2) "least privilege[,]" i.e., even employees have access only to the information that they need in order to perform their jobs. *Id.* at 7. The Agency asserts that "proposals prescribing the actions management will take to ensure the security of its computer system directly interfere with" that management right. *Id.* at 5 (quoting *AFGE, Local 1712*, 62 FLRA 15, 17 (2007) (*Local 1712*)).[4] In addition, the Agency contends that the Arbitrator erred by finding that, merely because the President's prior access did not result in security breaches, there would be no security risk associated with his continued access. *Id.* at 8. With regard to the Arbitrator's finding that the policy has not been consistently applied, the Agency asserts that, although thousands of employees leave the Agency each year, the Union was able to cite only one example of a retiree who continued to have access -- and that situation was "pursuant to a specific negotiated agreement, and thus her access has been grandfathered in." *Id.* at 9. Further, the Agency also asserts that the Arbitrator was not enforcing an appropriate arrangement within the meaning of § 7106(b)(3) of the Statute. *Id.* at 10-11.

The Agency also argues that the award is contrary to the Handbook, which the Agency claims is a "rule" within the meaning of § 7122(a)(1) of the

4. Although the Agency cites "61 FLRA No. 6," Exceptions at 5, it appears that the Agency intended to cite *Local 1712*.

Statute because it was developed as a result of, and in order to bring the Agency into compliance with, various statutes and regulations.[5] *Id.* at 12.

Further, the Agency contends that the award fails to draw its essence from the agreement and the OUTTS MOU. With regard to the agreement, the Agency argues that the award "ignores" the wording in Article 11, Section 9.A.1. requiring that access to the system be consistent with, among other things, Agency policies. *Id.* at 14. With regard to the OUTTS MOU, the Agency contends that the Arbitrator's interpretation of that MOU is not plausible because the MOU does not provide an exhaustive list of who is excluded from computer access, and the Arbitrator ignored bargaining history evidence indicating that retired employees were intended to be excluded from access. *Id.* at 15.

B. Union's Opposition

The Union argues that the award is not contrary to management's right to determine internal security practices. Opp'n at 5. Specifically, the Union contends that the Agency failed to demonstrate a "link or reasonable connection" between its internal security objectives and its decision not to allow the grievant limited access to the system. *Id.* In this regard, the Union asserts that the Arbitrator directed reinstatement of the President's access to only e-mail, the intranet, and the OUTTS, and that the President would not have access to any secure data. *Id.* at 5-6. The Union also asserts that the Agency has applied its practice inconsistently. *Id.* at 6. Further, the Union contends that the Arbitrator was enforcing appropriate arrangements within the meaning of § 7106(b)(3) of the Statute, or, alternatively, contract provisions involving the technology, methods or means of performing work, within the meaning of § 7106(b)(1) of the Statute. *Id.* at 9-10.

With regard to the Agency's reliance on the Handbook, as an initial matter, the Union asserts that the Agency did not argue before the Arbitrator that the Handbook is a "rule" within the meaning of § 7122(a)(1) of the Statute and that, consequently, this argument must be dismissed under 5 C.F.R. § 2429.5.[6] *Id.* at 11. In addition, the Union claims that the award is not contrary to the plain wording of the Handbook. *Id.* at 10. In any event, the Union argues that the parties' agreement trumps any contrary Agency-wide regulations, and asserts that when an agreement incorporates the regulations with which an award allegedly conflicts, the matter becomes one of contract interpretation. *Id.* at 11.

Finally, the Union argues that the award draws its essence from the agreement and the OUTTS MOU. According to the Union, the Agency disputes the Arbitrator's "reasoned interpretation of the Agency regulations as incorporated into" the agreement. *Id.* In addition, the Union contends that the Agency has not demonstrated that the Arbitrator erred by relying on the parol evidence rule when he interpreted the OUTTS MOU. *Id.* at 13.

IV. Analysis and Conclusions

A. The award is not contrary to law.

The Agency alleges that the award is contrary to § 7106(a)(1) of the Statute and the Handbook. The Authority reviews questions of law de novo. *See NTEU, Chapter 24*, 50 FLRA 330, 332 (1995) (citing *U.S. Customs Serv. v. FLRA*, 43 F.3d 682, 686-87 (D.C. Cir. 1994)). In applying a standard of de novo review, the Authority determines whether the arbitrator's legal conclusions are consistent with the applicable standard of law. *NFFE, Local 1437*, 53 FLRA 1703, 1710 (1998) (*Local 1437*). In making that determination, the Authority defers to the arbitrator's underlying factual findings. *See id.*

1. Section 7106(a)(1) of the Statute

The Authority recently revised the analysis that it will apply when reviewing management rights exceptions to arbitration awards. *See U.S. EPA*, 65 FLRA 113, 115 (2010) (Member Beck concurring) (*EPA*); *FDIC, Div. of Supervision & Consumer Prot., S.F. Region*, 65 FLRA 102, 106-07 (2010) (Chairman Pope concurring). Under the revised analysis, the Authority assesses whether the award affects the exercise of the asserted

5. Specifically, the Handbook cites: (1) the "Federal Information Security Management Act of 2002 (FISMA)"; (2) the "Clinger Cohen Act of 1996"; (3) the "Freedom of Information Act of 1996"; (4) the "Federal Managers' Financial Integrity Act (FMFIA) of 1982"; (5) the "Privacy Act of 1974"; (6) "Records management by Federal Agencies (44 U.S.C. Ch. 31)"; (7) "Office of Management and Budget (OMB) Circulars A-123, A-127, and A-130"; and (8) "IRS Tax Information Security Guidelines for Federal, State and Local Agencies[.]" Exceptions, Attach., Ex. 6 at 1-2. The Agency does not contend that the award is contrary to these cited provisions.

6. The pertinent wording of 5 C.F.R. § 2429.5 is set forth below.

management right. *EPA*, 65 FLRA at 115.[7] If it does not, then the Authority denies the exception. *E.g., U.S. Dep't of Health & Human Servs., Office of Medicare Hearings & Appeals*, 65 FLRA 175, 177 (2010).

Management's right to determine its internal security practices under § 7106(a)(1) of the Statute includes the right to determine the policies and practices that are part of an agency's plan to secure and safeguard its personnel, property, and operations. *E.g., U.S. DHS, Customs & Border Prot. Agency, N.Y., N.Y.*, 61 FLRA 72, 76 (2005) (then-Member Pope concurring). Where an agency establishes a link or reasonable connection between the agency's goal of safeguarding personnel or property, or preventing disruption of agency operations, and the disputed practice, the Authority will find that the practice constitutes the agency's exercise of its right to determine its internal security practices. *Id.*

Here, the Arbitrator noted the Agency's claim that granting the President limited use of the system would compromise "the security of its entire electronic communications[,]" but he determined that the Agency "presented no proof to back up that assertion." Award at 9. The Agency does not argue that this factual finding is based on a nonfact, and, as stated previously, in assessing whether an arbitration award is contrary to law, the Authority defers to an arbitrator's factual findings. *E.g., Local 1437*, 53 FLRA at 1710. In addition, although the Agency emphasizes the sensitivity of the information contained in the system, the Agency does not assert that granting the President access to the system for very limited reasons -- specifically, intranet, e-mail, and the OUTTS -- would allow the President to access that sensitive information. In these circumstances, we find that the Agency has not established a link or reasonable connection between its goal of safeguarding this information and its practice of disallowing all retired employees, including the President, access to its intranet, e-mail, and the OUTTS. *Cf. Local 1712*, 62 FLRA 15, 17-18 (in negotiability case, agency established reasonable connection between security objective of safeguarding computer equipment and policy of keeping door to information technology office open). Accordingly, we find that the award does not affect management's right to determine its internal security practices and, therefore, we deny the Agency's management rights exception.[8]

2. The Handbook

As an initial matter, the Union argues that the Authority should not consider the Agency's claim that the award is contrary to "rule" because the Agency did not characterize the Handbook as a "rule" before the Arbitrator. Opp'n at 11. The Authority's Regulations that were in effect when the Agency filed its exceptions provided that "[t]he Authority will not consider . . . any issue, which was not presented in the proceedings before the . . . arbitrator." 5 C.F.R. § 2429.5.[9]

Before the Arbitrator, the Agency argued that the Handbook required termination of the President's access to the system. Exceptions, Attach., Ex. 2, Post-Hearing Brief at 1-2. Although the Agency did not specifically characterize the Handbook as a "rule or regulation," there is no dispute that the Handbook is an Agency regulation. Agency regulations are, as a matter of law, "rule[s] or regulation[s]" within the meaning of § 7122(a) of the Statute. *U.S. Dep't of the Army, Fort Campbell Dist., Third Region, Fort Campbell, Ky.*, 37 FLRA 186, 192 (1990). In addition, the Union points to no requirement that a party specifically characterize an Agency regulation as a "rule or regulation" before an arbitrator in order for the party to preserve its ability to later challenge the arbitrator's award as contrary to rule or

7. For the reasons articulated in his recent concurring opinion and footnotes, Member Beck would conclude that it is unnecessary to assess whether the award affects the exercise of the asserted management right. The appropriate question is simply whether the remedy directed by the Arbitrator enforces the provision in a reasonable and reasonably foreseeable fashion. *See EPA*, 65 FLRA at 120 (Concurring Opinion of Member Beck); *U.S. Dep't of Justice, Fed. Bureau of Prisons, Fed. Corr. Complex, Terre Haute, Ind.*, 65 FLRA 460, 462 n.2 (2011); *Soc. Sec. Admin., Dallas Region*, 65 FLRA 405, 408 n.5 (2010); *U.S. Dep't of the Air Force, Air Force Materiel Command*, 65 FLRA 395, 398 n.7 (2010); *U.S. Dep't of Health & Human Servs., Office of Medicare Hearings & Appeals*, 65 FLRA 175, 177 n.3 (2010); *U.S. Dep't of Transp., Fed. Aviation Admin.*, 65 FLRA 171, 173 n.5 (2010). Member Beck would conclude that the Arbitrator's award is a plausible interpretation of the parties' agreement and deny the exception.

8. Accordingly, it is unnecessary to resolve whether the Arbitrator was enforcing provisions negotiated under § 7106(b)(1) and (b)(3) of the Statute.

9. The Authority's Regulations concerning the review of arbitration awards, as well as certain related procedural Regulations, including § 2429.5, were revised effective October 1, 2010. 75 Fed. Reg. 42,283 (2010). As the Agency's exceptions in this case were filed before that date, we apply the prior Regulations.

regulation. *Cf. U.S. Dep't of Veterans Affairs, G.V. (Sonny) Montgomery VA Med. Ctr., Jackson, Miss.*, 65 FLRA 27, 29 (2010) (in dismissing exception on ground that agency did not challenge requested remedies as inconsistent with "[a]gency directives" before arbitrator, Authority did not address whether agency failed to properly characterize agency directives as laws, rules, or regulations). Consistent with the foregoing, we find that the Agency is not precluded from arguing that the Handbook is a rule or regulation within the meaning of § 7122(a) of the Statute.

Addressing the merits of the Agency's exception, when a collective bargaining agreement incorporates the agency regulation with which an award allegedly conflicts, the matter becomes one of contract interpretation because the agreement, not the regulation, governs the matter in dispute. *E.g., AFGE, Council of Prison Locals 33*, 59 FLRA 381, 382 (2003). The Authority has found that where, "as plainly worded and interpreted by the [a]rbitrator," a collective bargaining agreement provides that certain matters are required to be conducted in accordance with an agency regulation, "the agreement effectively incorporates" the regulation. *U.S. Dep't of Agric., Animal & Plant Health Inspection Serv., Plant Prot. & Quarantine*, 51 FLRA 1210, 1216-17 (1996) (*APHIS*).

Here, the Agency argues that the award is contrary to the Handbook. Specifically, the Agency claims, and there is no dispute, that the agreement requires that Union access to the system be consistent with Agency policies, including the Handbook. In these circumstances, consistent with *APHIS*, we consider the Handbook "effectively incorporate[d]" into the agreement, and we treat the matter as "one of contract interpretation[,]" *id.* Accordingly, below we apply an "essence" analysis to assess the Agency's argument.

B. The award does not fail to draw its essence from the parties' agreements.

The Agency challenges the Arbitrator's interpretation of the agreement and the OUTTS MOU. In reviewing an arbitrator's interpretation of a collective bargaining agreement, the Authority applies the deferential standard that federal courts use in reviewing arbitration awards in the private sector. *See* 5 U.S.C. § 7122(a)(2); *AFGE, Council 220*, 54 FLRA 156, 159 (1998). Under this standard, the Authority will find that an arbitration award is deficient as failing to draw its essence from the collective bargaining agreement when the appealing party establishes that the award: (1) cannot in any rational way be derived from the agreement; (2) is so unfounded in reason and fact and so unconnected with the wording and purposes of the collective bargaining agreement as to manifest an infidelity to the obligation of the arbitrator; (3) does not represent a plausible interpretation of the agreement; or (4) evidences a manifest disregard of the agreement. *U.S. Dep't of Labor (OSHA)*, 34 FLRA 573, 575 (1990). The Authority and the courts defer to arbitrators in this context "because it is the arbitrator's construction of the agreement for which the parties have bargained." *Id.* at 576.

With regard to the agreement, Article 11, Section 9.A. provides, in pertinent part, that the Agency "agrees to provide the Union with access to and use of the Agency's electronic mail subject to [certain] restrictions[.]" Exceptions, Attach., Ex. 5 at 11-5. One restriction, as the Arbitrator acknowledged, is Section 9.A.1., which provides that the Union's access to the system "will comply with applicable . . . Agency policies and guidelines in the [agreement]." *Id.* As discussed previously, the Arbitrator found Section 9.A.1. to be "hardly an example of clear contract language[,]" and noted that it required the Union to comply with not only Agency policies such as the Handbook, but also other provisions of the agreement -- including Article 4, Section 4, which "requires the Local President to use the [e]-mail system[]" to respond to management-proposed changes. Award at 8. Further, the Arbitrator found that, unlike Section 9.A.1., Section 9.A.8. -- which pertinently provides that "[a] Local president or a designee . . . is authorized to send one e-mail per week to each employee in his/her Local[,]" Exceptions, Attach., Ex. 5 at 11-6 -- is "clear on its face[]" and provides the President the right to use the Agency's e-mail system to communicate with unit employees. Award at 7. In these circumstances, the Agency has not demonstrated that the Arbitrator's finding that the parties' agreement entitles the President to continued, limited access to the system is irrational, unfounded, implausible, or a manifest disregard of the agreement.

With regard to the OUTTS MOU, the Agency asserts that the MOU does not exhaustively list every category of individual whose access is not permitted, and that the Arbitrator should have relied on evidence of bargaining history that indicates that retired employees were intended to be excluded. In effect, the Agency challenges the Arbitrator's decision, based on the Arbitrator's application of the parol evidence rule, not to rely on evidence of bargaining history. The Authority has held that exceptions contending that an arbitrator should, or should not, use parol evidence do not provide a basis for finding an award deficient. *NTEU*, 63 FLRA 299, 300 (2009). Consistent with this precedent, we conclude that the Agency's argument does not provide a basis for finding that the Arbitrator's interpretation of the OUTTS MOU fails to draw its essence from that MOU.

For the foregoing reasons, we deny the Agency's essence exceptions.

V. Decision

The Agency's exceptions are denied.

65 FLRA No. 111

UNITED STATES
DEPARTMENT OF HOMELAND SECURITY
U.S. IMMIGRATION AND
CUSTOMS ENFORCEMENT
(Agency)

and

AMERICAN FEDERATION
OF GOVERNMENT EMPLOYEES
LOCAL 1917
(Union)

0-AR-4649

DECISION

February 16, 2011

Before the Authority: Carol Waller Pope, Chairman, and Thomas M. Beck and Ernest DuBester, Members

I. Statement of the Case

This matter is before the Authority on exceptions to an award of Arbitrator Martin Ellenberg filed by the Agency under § 7122(a) of the Federal Service Labor-Management Relations Statute (the Statute) and part 2425 of the Authority's Regulations. The Union filed an opposition to the Agency's exceptions. The Agency and the Union also filed supplemental submissions.

The Arbitrator concluded that the letter of reprimand (reprimand) that the Agency issued to the grievant was not for just cause, as defined by the pertinent provisions of the parties' collective bargaining agreement (parties' agreement). Award at 15, 16. As a remedy, the Arbitrator ordered that the Agency void the reprimand and remove it, as well as any reference to it, from the grievant's personnel records. *Id.* at 16. For the reasons set forth below, we deny the Agency's exceptions.

II. Background and Arbitrator's Award

In a letter, the Agency informed the grievant, a Legal Assistant, that he was being placed on leave restriction. *Id.* at 2. The letter stated that the grievant must follow a set procedure for requesting sick and annual leave and warned him that, if he failed to follow these procedures, then "other disciplinary action for [absence without leave (AWOL)] and/or failure to follow instructions may be taken" against him. *Id.* After receiving this letter, the grievant was late to work on two separate occasions; in both instances, the grievant failed to follow the proper procedures for reporting his tardiness. *Id.* at 2-3. Subsequently, the grievant received a reprimand in which he was charged with failure to follow instructions and AWOL. *Id.*

The Union filed a grievance over the issuance of the reprimand.[1] *Id.* at 3. The matter was unresolved and was submitted to arbitration. *Id.* The parties stipulated to the following issue: "Was the . . . [r]eprimand . . . issued to [the grievant] for appropriate cause and to promote the efficiency of the [s]ervice? If not, what shall be the remedy?" *Id.*

The Arbitrator found that the Agency had not issued the reprimand for just cause.[2] *Id.* at 15-16. The Arbitrator determined that the Agency could not rely on Article 35, Section M of the parties' agreement to show that the reprimand was for just cause.[3] *Id.* at 14. The Arbitrator found that, because the language of Article 35, Section M of the parties' agreement states that "[h]abitual tardiness will not be excused and may be corrected through the implementation of disciplinary action[,]" the Agency may discipline an employee for tardiness only if it is habitual. *Id.* at 13; *see also id.* at 14. Although the Agency cited to a memorandum titled "Work Schedule Warning" that it had issued to the grievant four years prior to the reprimand, the Arbitrator found that the Agency never designated the

1. The Union also filed a grievance over the leave restriction; however, because that grievance was submitted to a different arbitrator, the validity of the leave restriction is not before us. Award at 3, 13.

2. The Arbitrator noted that, because the validity of the leave restriction was put before another arbitrator, the only issue before him was whether the issuance of the reprimand violated the parties' agreement. *See id.* at 13.

3. The relevant provisions of the parties' agreement are set forth in the attached appendix.

grievant's tardiness as habitual in the memorandum. *See id.* at 14. According to the Arbitrator, the Agency, in its memorandum, merely warned the grievant that, in the future, he could be disciplined for habitual tardiness if his attendance did not improve. *Id.* Moreover, the Arbitrator noted that "there [wa]s no evidence that habitual lateness was considered to be at least part of the basis for issuing the [r]eprimand . . . ." *Id.*

The Arbitrator also found that the Agency could not rely on Article 36, Section D of the parties' agreement to demonstrate that the reprimand was for just cause. *Id.* at 15. The Arbitrator noted that, under Article 36, Section D, the Agency is required to counsel an employee regarding his use of sick leave and may request that an employee provide a medical certificate for each subsequent absence if that employee continues to abuse sick leave. *See id.*; *see also id.* at 14. Moreover, according to the Arbitrator, Article 36, Section D makes clear that, to require a medical certificate for absences of three days or less, a pattern of abuse must exist or the Agency must reasonably doubt the validity of the claim for the use of sick leave. *Id.* at 15. Relying on testimony, the Arbitrator found that, at the time "the [r]eprimand was issued, the Agency . . . did not consider [the grievant's] lateness or absences to be abusive and warranting counseling or a warning of pending discipline" and "believed his explanations to be truthful." *Id.*

The Arbitrator further determined that, because Article 39, Subsection B references Article 36, the Agency could not rely on Article 39 in claiming that the reprimand was for just cause. *Id.* Finally, the Arbitrator noted that, although Article 40, Section A requires that "leave should be 'consistent with law and applicable regulations[,]'" it contains no language suggesting when disciplinary action is appropriate. *Id.*

III. Positions of the Parties

A. Agency's Exceptions

The Agency asserts that the Arbitrator exceeded his authority by adjudicating the validity of the leave restriction. Exceptions at 6-9. According to the Agency, the Arbitrator did not come simply "to conclusions regarding facts underlying the other grievance [that] . . . were integral to the matter before [him]." *Id.* at 8 (internal quotations omitted). Rather, the Agency claims that he ruled on the leave restriction when he determined that Article 36, Section D of the parties' agreement "precluded the Agency from restricting [the] [g]rievent's leave usage by requiring medical certificates – one of the instructions in the [l]eave [r]estriction." *Id.* at 7; *see also id.* at 8.

The Agency claims that the award is contrary to law because the "[A]rbitrator bases [his] award on an interpretation of [the parties' agreement] that excessively interferes with management's right to discipline under § 7106(a)(2)(A) of the Statute . . . ." *Id.* at 9 (citing *SSA*, 32 FLRA 712, 715-16 (1988)). The Agency asserts that, by limiting its ability to "discipline an employee for any absence or related failure to follow instructions . . . [unless] the employee has been habitually tardy, . . . formally notified . . . of the 'habitual' nature of the tardiness, and . . . continues to be tardy[,]" the award excessively interferes with management's right to discipline. *Id.* at 11. Moreover, the Agency claims that, by interpreting the parties' agreement to require that employees cannot be disciplined "for failure to follow procedures if [they] ha[ve] not been formally counseled prior to the issuance of such instructions" and by ignoring the Agency's ability to demand appropriate medical certifications from its employees, the award affects management's right to discipline. *Id.*; *see also id.* n.5.

Also, the Agency asserts that the award fails to draw its essence from the parties' agreement. *Id.* at 12. The Agency claims that the Arbitrator ignored the existence of Article 36, Section C of the parties' agreement, requiring an employee to notify the Agency of a sick leave-related absence, and that the Arbitrator wrongfully "conclud[ed] that the Agency was not able to instruct the [g]rievant to call in or provide evidence of incapacity." *Id.* at 13; *see also id.* at 12. The Agency further contends that the Arbitrator disregarded the plain language of Article 35, Section M in concluding "that only 'habitual tardiness' could form the basis for discipline." *Id.* at 13. According to the Agency, Article 35, Section M allows it to draw from an employee's annual leave, compensatory leave, or leave without pay or charge an employee with AWOL if that employee is tardy for sixty minutes or less. *Id.* Also, the Agency asserts that the Arbitrator's determination that Article 36, Section D "prevent[s] the Agency from disciplining the [g]rievant for failure to provide medical certification if managers ha[ve] not provided formal counseling prior to issuing limiting instructions" is contrary to the plain language of that provision. *Id.*; *see also id.* at 14. The Agency notes that, under that provision, counseling must occur when the supervisor requests that the employee provide a medical certificate. *Id.* at 14. Moreover, the Agency claims that the Arbitrator's finding that "Articles 39 and 40 [do] not allow discipline for leave abuse because they contain no language regarding discipline" disregards Article 31, which sets forth the only limitations on the Agency's ability to discipline as "just and sufficient cause" and "efficiency of the service." *Id.* at 14-15.

The Agency claims that the award is based on a nonfact because, although the Arbitrator noted both evidence and testimony demonstrating that the grievant was frequently absent from work and that the Agency engaged in various actions such as formal meetings, counseling, warnings, and removal of a desired assignment to address the grievant's tardiness, he improperly found that no discipline should be imposed. *Id* at 15-16. Additionally, the Agency asserts that the award is based on a nonfact because, in finding that the Agency failed to formally document "its displeasure with [the] [g]rievant's absences prior to the issuance of the [r]eprimand[,]" the Arbitrator "ignored the stipulated existence of the [l]eave [r]estriction, which specifically notes that the Agency finds [the] [g]rievant's pattern of unscheduled absences to be unacceptable." *Id.* at 16.

Finally, the Agency claims that the Arbitrator exceeded his authority by: (1) failing to adjudicate the stipulated issue and (2) addressing whether the grievant was habitually tardy, a charge not in dispute. *Id.* at 16-19.

B. Union's Opposition

The Union contends that the Agency has failed to prove that the award is deficient because arbitrators "have 'wide latitude to fashion remedies'" in disciplinary cases, and the Agency's exceptions essentially reflect its mere disagreement with the outcome. Opp'n at 5 (quoting *Dep't of the Air Force, Scott Air Force Base, Ill.*, 51 FLRA 675, 687 (1995)); *see also id.* at 6.

The Union also argues that the Agency's contention that the Arbitrator adjudicated the validity of the leave restriction is without merit. *Id.* at 6-10. The Union contends that the Arbitrator expressly acknowledged that he lacked jurisdiction over the leave restriction. *See id.* at 7. According to the Union, the Agency fails to offer any proof demonstrating that the Arbitrator found that the leave restriction was unenforceable. *Id.* at 7 & n.1. The Union contends that the Agency failed to demonstrate "that the other grievance somehow precluded the [A]rbitrator from considering the meaning and effect of Article 36[, Section D]" and that the Arbitrator's sole purpose in considering Article 36, Section D was to determine whether the Agency had cause to issue a reprimand. *Id.* at 7-8.

The Union contends that the Arbitrator's interpretation of the award does not affect management's right to discipline its employees. *Id.* at 10-13. The Union argues that an arbitrator has great latitude in interpreting and applying a collective bargaining agreement. *Id.* at 11 (citing *Dep't of the Treasury, U.S. Customs Serv.*, 37 FLRA 309, 316 (1990)). According to the Union, the Arbitrator's interpretation of Article 37, Section M does not "prevent the Agency [from] exercising its right to impose discipline." *Id.* at 13; *see also id.* at 12. Additionally, the Union contends that the Arbitrator's interpretation of Article 35, Section M is entitled to deference because the parties bargained for his interpretation of their agreement. *Id.* at 13.

Finally, the Union argues that the Agency's contention that the award is based on a nonfact is without merit because the Agency merely disagrees with the Arbitrator's interpretation of the evidence and testimony. *Id.* at 13-15. Moreover, the Union contends that the Agency's argument that the Arbitrator failed to adjudicate the stipulated issue is meritless because "[t]he [A]rbitrator engaged in extensive contract interpretation and determined that no 'cause' existed for the grievant's [r]eprimand." *Id.* at 15; *see also id.* at 16.

IV. Preliminary Matter

Although the Authority's Regulations do not provide for the filing of supplemental submissions, § 2429.26 of the Authority's Regulations provides that the Authority may, in its discretion, grant leave to file "other documents" as deemed appropriate. *See, e.g., U.S. Dep't of the Treasury, IRS, Nat'l Distribution Ctr., Bloomington, Ill.*, 64 FLRA 586, 589 (2010) (*IRS, Bloomington*); *Cong. Research Emps. Ass'n, IFPTE, Local 75*, 59 FLRA 994, 999 (2004)). The Authority has granted such leave where, for example, the supplemental submission responds to arguments raised for the first time in an opposing party's filing. *IRS, Bloomington*, 64 FLRA at 589. However, where a party's supplemental submission raises issues that the party could have raised in a previous submission, the Authority has denied a request to consider the supplemental submission. *Id.*

The Agency filed a motion requesting leave from the Authority, under 5 C.F.R. § 2429.26, to file a supplemental submission in order to respond to the Union's opposition. The Agency requests that the Authority review its supplemental submission because the Union raises a "new" argument in its opposition. Supplemental Submission at 1-3. The Agency claims that, for the first time in its opposition, the Union argues that the award cannot affect management's right to discipline because "the Arbitrator did not bar the Agency from imposing discipline . . . ." *Id.* at 1. Also, the Agency requests that the Authority review its supplemental submission because the Union makes two contradictory arguments in its opposition. *Id.* at 3-4. According to the Agency, the Union cannot argue both that the Arbitrator did not adjudicate the leave restriction and that the Arbitrator had the right to ignore the existence of the leave restriction. *Id.*

Although the Agency claims that the Union raised a "new" argument in its opposition, the Union merely responded to the Agency's exception challenging the award's impact on management's right to discipline. *See U.S. Dep't of the Army Corps of Eng'rs, Portland Dist.*, 61 FLRA 599, 601 (2006) (finding that, because the Union's opposition did not raise new matters that the agency did not have the opportunity to address in its exceptions, the agency should have raised its argument in its exceptions); *U.S. Dep't of the Treasury, U.S. Customs Serv., El Paso, Tex.*, 52 FLRA 622, 625 (1996); *cf. U.S. Dep't of the Army, Corps of Eng'rs, Walla Walla Dist., Pasco, Wash.*, 63 FLRA 161, 161-62 (2009) (considering the agency's supplemental submission because it challenged an issue first raised in the opposition, namely whether the agency was authorized to file the exceptions). Similarly, the Agency's argument that the Union made conflicting arguments in its opposition does not merit granting leave to file a supplemental submission. *See AFGE, Local 2823*, 64 FLRA 1144, 1146 (2010) (finding that the Union's allegation that the Agency's opposition contained conflicting statements did not merit granting leave to file a supplemental submission). Consequently, we deny the Agency's request and decline to consider the supplemental submission. *Id.* Because the Union's subsequent submission was intended to address the arguments raised for the first time in the Agency's supplemental submission, the Union's submission is moot and willnot be considered. *See U.S. Dep't of the Army, Corps of Eng'rs, Portland Dist.*, 62 FLRA 97, 98 (2007).

V. Analysis and Conclusions

A. The Arbitrator did not exceed his authority by adjudicating the validity of the leave restriction.

The Agency asserts that the Arbitrator exceeded his authority by adjudicating the validity of the leave restriction. Exceptions at 6-9. According to the Agency, the Arbitrator ruled on the leave restriction when he determined that Article 36, Section D of the parties' agreement "precluded the Agency from restricting [the] [g]rievant's leave usage by requiring medical certificates . . . ." *Id.* at 7; *see also id.* at 8.

Arbitrators exceed their authority when they fail to resolve an issue submitted to arbitration, resolve an issue not submitted to arbitration, disregard specific limitations on their authority, or award relief to those not encompassed within the grievance. *See AFGE, Local 1617*, 51 FLRA 1645, 1647 (1996). However, arbitrators do not exceed their authority by addressing an issue that is necessary to decide a stipulated issue or by addressing an issue that necessarily arises from issues specifically included in a stipulation. *See NATCA, MEBA/NMU*, 51 FLRA 993, 996 (1996); *Air Force Space Div., L.A. Air Force Station, Cal.*, 24 FLRA 516, 519 (1986). In determining whether an arbitrator has exceeded his or her authority, the Authority accords an arbitrator's interpretation of a stipulated issue the same substantial deference that it accords an arbitrator's interpretation and application of a collective bargaining agreement. *See U.S. Info. Agency, Voice of Am.*, 55 FLRA 197, 198 (1999).

The Agency's contention that the Arbitrator exceeded his authority by adjudicating the validity of the leave restriction is without merit. The Arbitrator did not resolve any issues not before him. The Arbitrator merely determined that, in this case, the Agency could not rely on Article 36, Section D to demonstrate that the *reprimand* was issued for just cause. Award at 15. Moreover, the Arbitrator expressly found that, because the validity of the leave restriction was put before another arbitrator, the only issue before him was whether the issuance of the *reprimand* violated the parties' agreement. *See id.* at 13. Consequently, the Agency has failed to establish that the Arbitrator exceeded the scope of his authority by resolving an issue not submitted to arbitration. *See U.S. Dep't of Labor*, 62 FLRA at 155; *U.S. Dep't of Educ.*, 59 FLRA 820, 823 (2004) (determining that, while the arbitrator considered events that had been adjudicated in prior grievances, the arbitrator did not resolve any issues not before him); *Gen. Serv. Admin.*, 47 FLRA 1326, 1331 (1993) (finding that the agency's contention that the arbitrator exceeded his authority by considering a performance evaluation that had been submitted to another arbitrator without merit because the arbitrator addressed an issue that was integrally related to the stipulated issue before him).

Accordingly, we deny the Agency's exception.

B. The award is not contrary to law.

The Authority reviews questions of law raised by exceptions to an arbitrator's award de novo. *See NTEU, Chapter 24*, 50 FLRA 330, 332 (1995) (citing *U.S. Customs Serv. v. FLRA*, 43 F.3d 682, 686-87 (D.C. Cir. 1994)). In applying a standard of de novo review, the Authority determines whether the arbitrator's legal conclusions are consistent with the applicable standard of law. *See NFFE, Local 1437*, 53 FLRA 1703, 1710 (1998). In making that determination, the Authority defers to the arbitrator's underlying factual findings. *Id.*

According to the Agency, the Arbitrator's determination that Article 35, Section M of the parties' agreement only allows the Agency to discipline an employee for being absent if his absence constitutes habitual tardiness excessively interferes with management's right to discipline. Exceptions at 11. Moreover, the Agency claims that, by interpreting Article 36, Section D of the parties' agreement to require that employees cannot be disciplined for failure to follow procedures unless they have been formally counseled and by ignoring the Agency's ability to demand appropriate medical certifications from its employees, the award improperly affects management's right to discipline. *Id.* & n.5.

The Authority recently revised the analysis that it will apply when reviewing management rights exceptions to arbitration awards. *See U.S. Envtl. Prot. Agency*, 65 FLRA 113, 115 (2010) (Member Beck concurring) (*EPA*); *Fed. Deposit Ins. Corp., Div. of Supervision & Consumer Prot., S.F. Region*, 65 FLRA 102, 106-07 (2010) (Chairman Pope concurring) (*FDIC, S.F. Region*). Under the revised analysis, the Authority will first assess whether the award affects the exercise of the asserted management right. *EPA*, 65 FLRA at 115. If so, then, as relevant here, the Authority examines whether the award enforces a contract provision negotiated under § 7106(b). *Id.* Also, in determining whether the award enforces a contract provision negotiated under § 7106(b)(3), the Authority, under the revised analysis, assesses: (1) whether the contract provision constitutes an arrangement for employees adversely affected by the exercise of a management right; and (2) if so, whether the arbitrator's enforcement of the arrangement abrogates the exercise of the management right. *See id.* at 116-18. In concluding that it would apply an abrogation standard, the Authority rejected continued application of an excessive interference standard. *Id.* at 118.

In this case, the Arbitrator set aside the reprimand, thereby affecting management's right to discipline. *See, e.g., U.S. DOT, FAA*, 63 FLRA 383, 385 (2009) (finding that, because the arbitrator set aside a five-day suspension, management's right to discipline was affected) (*DOT*); *U.S. Dep't of Energy, Sw. Power Admin., Tulsa, Okla.*, 56 FLRA 624, 625 (2000) (determining that, because the arbitrator mitigated a two-day suspension to a one-day suspension, management's right to discipline was impacted) (*Dep't of Energy*).

The Agency does not dispute that Article 35, Section M and Article 36, Section D constitute arrangements, but it asserts that the Arbitrator's interpretation of Article 35, Section M "excessively interferes with [its] right to discipline [because his interpretation] prevent[s] [it] from disciplining [employees in situations] where it has an undeniable rationale for doing so." Exceptions at 11; *see U.S. DOT, FAA*, 65 FLRA 171, 174 (2010) (noting that the agency did not dispute the arrangement requirement). The Agency's assertion is without merit. As interpreted and applied by the Arbitrator, Article 35, Section M of the parties' agreement precludes the Agency from disciplining an employee for tardiness only if tardiness is not habitual. Award at 13, 14. Although the Arbitrator's interpretation of the agreement limits the Agency's ability to discipline an employee for tardiness, the Agency is not precluded from disciplining an employee for tardiness in all cases. *See EPA*, 65 FLRA at 118 (finding that the agreement did not abrogate the agency's right to assign work because the agreement did not necessarily preclude disclosure of employee medical records to local coordinators in all cases). Instead, the parties' agreement, as interpreted by the Arbitrator, preserves the Agency's right to discipline an employee for habitual tardiness. *See id.* (finding that the agency's right to assign work was not abrogated because the agreed-upon arrangement preserved the agency's ability to request, obtain, and evaluate medical information).

Also, the Agency's contention that the Arbitrator's interpretation of Article 36, Section D excessively interferes with its right to discipline is meritless. The Agency misstates the Arbitrator's interpretation and application of Article 36, Section D. The Arbitrator did not find that the Agency may not discipline employees for failure to follow procedures unless they have been formally counseled. *See* Award at 13-14 (noting simply that Article 36, Section D states that an employee will be counseled). Moreover, the Arbitrator did not ignore the Agency's ability to demand medical certifications from its employees. *See id.* at 14, 15 (citing to Article 36, Section D which allows an employer to require an employee to provide a medical certificate under certain circumstances). Rather, the Arbitrator found that the Agency could not rely on Article 36, Section D in arguing that it issued the reprimand for just cause because the Agency failed to demonstrate that the prerequisites for requiring an employee to provide a medical certificate were met. *See id.* at 15. Based on testimony, the Arbitrator found that the Agency could not have properly disciplined the grievant for failing to provide a medical certificate because the Agency did not consider the grievant's absences to be abusive or doubt the validity of the grievant's claims. *Id.* Consequently, because Article 36, Section D preserves the Agency's right to discipline employees without formal counseling in some situations, the Agency has failed to demonstrate that the award abrogates its right to discipline its employees.[4]

Accordingly, we deny the Agency's exception.

4. Member Beck agrees with the conclusion to deny the Agency's exceptions. He does not agree, however, with his colleagues' analysis of the contrary to law exception insofar as they address the question of whether the award affects the exercise of an asserted management right. For the reasons discussed in his concurring opinion in *EPA*, 65 FLRA 113, Member Beck concludes that where, as here, the Arbitrator is enforcing a contract provision that has been accepted by the Agency as a permissible limitation on its management's rights, it is inappropriate to assess whether the provision itself is an appropriate arrangement or whether it abrogates a § 7106(a) right. *Id.* at 120 (Concurring Opinion of Member Beck). The appropriate question is simply whether the remedy directed by the Arbitrator enforces the provision in a reasonable and reasonably foreseeable fashion. *Id.*; *see also FDIC, S.F. Region*, 65 FLRA at 107. Member Beck concludes that the Arbitrator's award is a plausible interpretation of the parties' agreement. Accordingly, Member Beck agrees that the Agency's contrary to law exception should be denied.

C. The award does not fail to draw its essence from the parties' agreement.

The Agency asserts that the award fails to draw its essence from the parties' agreement. Exceptions at 12. The Agency claims that the Arbitrator ignored the existence of Article 36, Section C of the parties' agreement when he wrongfully "conclud[ed] that the Agency was not able to instruct the [g]rievant to call in or provide evidence of incapacity." *Id.* at 13; *see also id.* at 12. Also, the Agency asserts that the Arbitrator disregarded the plain language of Article 35, Section M when he concluded that "only 'habitual tardiness' could form the basis for discipline." *Id.* at 13. The Agency claims that the Arbitrator's determination that "Article 36[, Section D] prevent[s] the Agency from disciplining the [g]rievant for failure to provide medical certification" because managers did not formally counsel the grievant prior to issuing limiting instructions is contrary to the plain language of that provision. *Id.*; *see also id.* at 14. Finally, the Agency claims that the Arbitrator's finding that "Articles 39 and 40 [do] not allow discipline for leave abuse because they contain no language regarding discipline" disregards Article 31 which only limits the Agency's ability to discipline for just cause. *Id.* at 14; *see also id.* at 15.

In reviewing an arbitrator's interpretation of a collective bargaining agreement, the Authority applies the deferential standard of review that federal courts use in reviewing arbitration awards in the private sector. *See* 5 U.S.C. § 7122(a)(2); *AFGE, Council 220*, 54 FLRA 156, 159 (1998). Under this standard, the Authority will find that an arbitration award is deficient as failing to draw its essence from the collective bargaining agreement when the appealing party establishes that the award: (1) cannot in any rational way be derived from the agreement; (2) is so unfounded in reason and fact and so unconnected with the wording and purposes of the collective bargaining agreement as to manifest an infidelity to the obligation of the arbitrator; (3) does not represent a plausible interpretation of the agreement; or (4) evidences a manifest disregard of the agreement. *See U.S. Dep't of Labor (OSHA)*, 34 FLRA 573, 575 (1990). The Authority and the courts defer to arbitrators in this context because it is the arbitrator's construction of the agreement for which the parties have bargained. *Id.* at 576.

Contrary to the Agency's assertions, the Arbitrator's interpretation of the parties' agreement is not implausible or irrational. Although the Agency contends that the Arbitrator ignored the existence of Article 36, Section C in determining whether the reprimand was for just cause, the Arbitrator cited Article 36, Section C in his award. Award at 13. Moreover, the award does not fail to draw its essence from Article 36, Section C because the Arbitrator never found that the Agency could not require its employees to call in before taking anticipated sick leave. *See id.* (noting that Article 36, Section C requires an employee to notify the Agency about unanticipated sick leave).

Also, the Arbitrator's interpretation of Article 35, Section M is not implausible or irrational. The Arbitrator's interpretation of Article 35, Section M does not prevent the Agency from drawing on an employee's annual leave, compensatory leave, or leave without pay or charging an employee with AWOL if that employee is tardy for sixty minutes or less. *See id.* at 13, 14. Rather, as interpreted by the Arbitrator, Article 35, Section M simply prohibits the Agency from disciplining an employee for such tardiness unless it is habitual. *See id.* Consequently, the Arbitrator's interpretation of Article 35, Section M does not fail to draw its essence from the agreement.

Although the Agency asserts that the Arbitrator's interpretation of Article 36, Section D is contrary to the plain meaning of that provision, its assertion is without merit. As noted above, the Arbitrator never found that, because the Agency failed to provide counseling to the grievant before issuing limiting instructions, it was prohibited, under Article 36, Section D of the parties' agreement, from disciplining the grievant for failure to provide a medical certification. *See id.* at 15. Instead, the Arbitrator found that the Agency could not rely on Article 36, Section D to support its assertion that it issued the reprimand for just cause because the Agency failed to prove that it considered the grievant's absences to be abusive or doubted the validity of the grievant's claims. *Id.*

Finally, the Agency misinterprets the Arbitrator's findings regarding Articles 39 and 40. Contrary to the Agency's assertions, the Arbitrator did not determine that Articles 39 and 40 do not allow discipline for leave abuse. *See id.* Rather, the Arbitrator simply found that Articles 39 and 40 were inapposite. *See id.*

Accordingly, we deny the Agency's exception.

D. The award is not based on a nonfact.

To establish that an award is based on a nonfact, the appealing party must show that a central fact underlying the award is clearly erroneous, but for which the arbitrator would have reached a different result. *See NFFE, Local 1984,* 56 FLRA 38, 41 (2000). The Authority will not find an award deficient on the basis of an arbitrator's determination on any factual matter that the parties disputed at hearing. *AFGE, Local 376,* 62 FLRA 138, 141 (2007) (Chairman Cabaniss concurring). In addition, an arbitrator's conclusion that is based on an interpretation of the parties' collective bargaining agreement does not constitute a finding that can be challenged as a nonfact. *U.S. DHS, U.S. Customs & Border Prot., JFK Airport, Queens, N.Y.*, 62 FLRA 129, 131 (2007) (*DHS*). Further, a challenge to the weight accorded evidence and testimony does not provide a basis for finding that an award is based on nonfacts. *U.S. Dep't of Veterans Affairs Med. Ctr., Richmond, Va.*, 63 FLRA 553, 556 (2009).

The Agency asserts that the award is based on a nonfact because, although the evidence and testimony demonstrate that the grievant was frequently absent from work and that the Agency engaged in various actions to address the grievant's tardiness, the Arbitrator erroneously concluded that no discipline should be imposed. Exceptions at 15-16. Because the Agency's assertion effectively challenges the Arbitrator's interpretation of the term "habitual" in the parties' agreement, it provides no basis for finding the award deficient as based on a nonfact. *See DHS*, 62 FLRA at 131.

Also, the Agency claims that the award is based on a nonfact because, by finding that the Agency did not formally document its displeasure with the grievant's leave usage prior to issuing the reprimand, the Arbitrator disregarded the existence of the leave restriction. *Id.* at 16. Because the Agency does not point to, and the award does not contain, a factual finding on this point, its claim is without merit. *See SSA, Office of Hearings & Appeals*, 58 FLRA 405, 407 (2003) (denying the agency's nonfact exception because the arbitrator did not make the finding alleged to constitute a nonfact).

Accordingly, we deny the Agency's exception.

E. The Arbitrator did not exceed his authority by failing to adjudicate the stipulated issue and by addressing a matter not at issue.

As noted above, an arbitrator exceeds his or her authority when the arbitrator fails to resolve an issue submitted to arbitration, resolves an issue not submitted to arbitration, disregards specific limitations on his or her authority, or awards relief to persons who are not encompassed within the grievance. *See U.S. Dep't of Def., Army & Air Force Exch. Serv.*, 51 FLRA 1371, 1378 (1996).

The Agency's contentions that the Arbitrator exceeded his authority by failing to address the stipulated issue and by addressing whether the grievant was habitually tardy are without merit. The Arbitrator's award, which orders that the reprimand be voided and removed from the grievant's file because it was not issued for appropriate cause, is directly responsive and properly confined to the stipulated issue. *See AFGE, Local 3979, Council of Prisons Locals*, 61 FLRA 810, 815 (2006) (*AFGE, Local 3979*); *U.S. Dep't of Educ.*, 59 FLRA at 823 (finding that the arbitrator's award ordering a retroactive promotion with backpay for the grievant based on the requirements of Article 18 of the agreement was directly responsive and properly confined to the issue that he framed). Moreover, although the Agency did not charge the grievant with habitual tardiness, and the parties' stipulated issue does not include the phrase "habitual tardiness," the issue arose in the context of resolving whether the reprimand was issued for just and sufficient cause and is consistent with the arguments made before the Arbitrator. *See SSA, Balt., Md.*, 57 FLRA 181, 183 (2001) (finding that, although the parties' stipulated issue did not explicitly set forth the issue of bona fide consideration as the dispute, that issue arose in the context of resolving whether the grievant was improperly not selected and was consistent with the arguments made before the arbitrator). Consequently, because the Arbitrator's award is responsive and confined to the stipulated issue, the Agency has failed to demonstrate that the Arbitrator exceeded his authority.[5] *See AFGE, Local 3979*, 61 FLRA at 815. Accordingly, we deny the Agency's exception.

VI. Decision

The Agency's exceptions are denied.

5. To the extent that the Agency claims that the award is based on a nonfact because the Arbitrator failed to adjudicate the stipulated issue, its contention constitutes nothing more than a bare assertion. Exceptions at 16, 19; *see U.S. Dep't of Homeland Sec., U.S. Customs & Border Prot., Port of Seattle, Seattle, Wash.*, 60 FLRA 490, 492 n.7 (2004) (determining that, if a party fails to provide any arguments or authority to support its exception, the Authority will deny the exception as a bare assertion).

APPENDIX

Article 35, "Annual Leave," provides, in pertinent part:

> M. Habitual Tardiness. Habitual tardiness will not be excused and may be corrected through the initiation of disciplinary action. Tardiness of less than sixty (60) minutes, regardless of cause, at the discretion of the supervisor may be excused for adequate reasons. Depending on the circumstances the time may be charged to annual leave, compensatory leave, leave without pay or AWOL. If a charge against annual leave is made, it must be in multiples of fifteen (15) minutes, and the employee cannot be required to perform work for the period of leave charged against his or her account. . . .

Exceptions, Attach. 8 at 68.

Article 36, "Sick Leave," provides, in pertinent part:

> C. Sick Leave Request Procedures.
> (1) Anticipated Sick Leave. When an employee knows in advance that sick leave will be required, he or she shall request sick leave at the time the necessity for the leave is determined. Employees assigned to duty stations which have more than one 8-hour shift will provide notification at least one hour prior to beginning of the assigned shift.
> (2) Unanticipated Sick Leave. When the need for sick leave is unanticipated and sickness or injury prevents the employee from reporting to work, the employee shall notify the Employer as soon as possible. In no event shall the employee provide such notification to his or her supervisor later than one (1) hour after the normal time for reporting to work. When employees are assigned to a duty station which has an evening and/or midnight shift, the employee will provide notification at least one hour prior to the beginning of the assigned shift. If the degree of the employee's illness or injury prohibits compliance with the notification requirements provided above, the employee hall provide such notification as soon as possible. Acceptable evidence of such circumstances may be required.
>
> D. Evidence of Illness. Employees may be required to furnish acceptable evidence . . . to substantiate a request for sick leave if the sick leave exceeds three (3) consecutive workdays. . . . [S]upervisors may require medical certificates for absences of three (3) workdays or less when a pattern of abuse is reasonably suggested by an employee's chronic use of short periods of sick leave or when there is reasonable doubt as to the validity of the claim to such sick leave. When requiring medical certificates under such circumstances, the employee will be counseled by the supervisor that continued abuse of sick leave may result in a requirement to furnish a medical certificate for each subsequent absence or sick leave regardless of duration. . . .

Id. at 70.

Article 39, "Leave Without Pay," provides, in pertinent part:

> B. Matter of Right. The following employees are entitled, as a matter of right, to take leave without pay for the following purposes:
> . . . .
>
> (3) Family Necessity. An employee presenting acceptable documentation of need and who so requests in writing will be granted up to 12 weeks of leave without pay during any 12 month period as necessary to manage one or more of the following circumstances: . . . to care for a spouse, son, daughter, or parent of the employee when that person has a serious health condition. . . .

Id. at 74.

Article 40, "Leave for Family Responsibilities," provides, in pertinent part:

> G. Care for Family Members. Employees may take sick leave . . . to care for a family member who is incapacitated as the result of physical or mental illness, or injury. Annual Leave and Leave without Pay (including LWOP under the Family Medical Leave Act) may also be used for the purpose of caring for a family member. Employees may initially request leave for these purposes for a period of up to five (5) months. If circumstances require it, additional requests may be submitted. . . .

Id. at 77.

65 FLRA No. 112

UNITED STATES
DEPARTMENT OF JUSTICE
FEDERAL BUREAU OF PRISONS
FEDERAL CORRECTIONAL COMPLEX
VICTORVILLE, CALIFORNIA
(Agency)

and

AMERICAN FEDERATION
OF GOVERNMENT EMPLOYEES
LOCAL 3969
(Union)

0-AR-4596

DECISION

February 17, 2011

Before the Authority: Carol Waller Pope, Chairman, and Thomas M. Beck and Ernest DuBester, Members

I. Statement of the Case

This matter is before the Authority on exceptions to an award of Arbitrator Ruth Carpenter filed by the Agency under § 7122(a) of the Federal Service Labor-Management Relations Statute (the Statute) and part 2425 of the Authority's Regulations. The Union filed an opposition to the Agency's exceptions.

The Arbitrator found that the Agency improperly classified teachers in its correctional facility as exempt from the provisions of the Fair Labor Standards Act (FLSA), and that the Agency violated the parties' Memorandum of Agreement (MOA) by utilizing employees other than Vocational Training Instructors (VTIs) to cover for employees who were on sick and annual leave.

For the reasons that follow, we deny the Agency's exceptions.

II. Background and Arbitrator's Award

The Agency classified teachers at its correctional facility as exempt from the provisions of the FLSA, and assigned employees other than VTIs to cover employees' sick and annual leave. A grievance was filed, and, when the grievance was unresolved, it was submitted to arbitration, where the Arbitrator stated the issues, in pertinent part, as follows:

> Has . . . management properly classified "Teachers" at [the correctional facility] as [FLSA] exempt in accordance with federal law?
>
> If not, what shall be the remedy?
>
> . . . .
>
> Has . . . management violated the Master Agreement and/or the [MOA] . . . in regards to which employees in the Education Department are utilized as sick and annual leave coverage? If so[,] what shall be the remedy?

Award at 2.[1]

With regard to whether the teachers were properly classified as exempt from the FLSA, the Arbitrator found that the teacher position "requires greater qualifications to be hired" than the education specialist position, which the Agency classified as FLSA nonexempt. Award at 6. However, the Arbitrator also found that, like education specialists, the teachers' primary function is to perform "custody-officer type duties" rather than teaching. Award at 12. *Accord id.* at 6-7 (summarizing teachers' non-teaching duties). According to the Arbitrator, teachers "generally have [twelve to fifteen] hours per week where they are assigned teaching duties[.]" *Id.* at 6. In addition, the Arbitrator determined that teachers "may have to leave class to perform other duties to which they are assigned[,]" and that "[t]his can take up to [fifty percent] or longer of the class time." *Id.* at 12. For example, the Arbitrator found that teachers are "required to make sure all inmates are in the classroom, and if they are not, they must find them." *Id.* Accordingly, the Arbitrator found that teachers "only spend [fifty percent] of the class time actually in the class" and that, consequently, "some [teachers] only spend approximately six hours a week performing teaching duties." *Id.* at 6. The Arbitrator stated that "[a] few hours a week is not substantial and given the major focus and duties of the [t]eachers

---

1. The Arbitrator addressed additional issues, *see* Award at 2-3, but as those issues are not raised in the exceptions, we do not discuss them.

. . ., it cannot be said that limited teaching responsibilities are the predominant or defining facets of the position." *Id.* at 13. Thus, the Arbitrator concluded that the teachers' "primary duty" was not teaching, and that the Agency failed to establish that the teachers were properly classified as FLSA exempt. *Id.* Accordingly, she directed the Agency to pay teachers backpay until they are reclassified as FLSA nonexempt. *Id.* at 14.

With regard to whether the Agency inappropriately assigned employees other than VTIs to cover employees' sick and annual leave, the Arbitrator found that the MOA requires that only VTIs be utilized to cover absences caused by extended sick leave and scheduled annual leave, and that the Agency violated the MOA by utilizing non-VTI employees to cover such leave. *See id.* at 13. The Arbitrator noted that one employee who negotiated the MOA (the negotiator) testified that non-VTI employees would bid on their shifts on a six-month rotating basis, and that, "because the [VTIs] would not be required to rotate their shifts, it was agreed in . . . the MOA . . . that [VTIs] would be utilized for sick and annual leave coverage." *Id.* at 11. In addition, although the Arbitrator acknowledged the Agency's claim that "[m]anagement ha[s] the right to assign work[,]" she found that, by agreeing to the MOA, the Agency limited its ability to exercise that right. *Id.* at 13. As a remedy for the violation of the MOA, the Arbitrator directed that, in the future, VTIs will cover all extended sick leave and scheduled annual leave. *Id.* at 14.

III. Positions of the Parties

A. Agency's Exceptions

The Agency argues that the award is contrary to the FLSA and Office of Personnel Management (OPM) regulations implementing the FLSA. Specifically, the Agency contends that 5 C.F.R. § 551.208(h) exempts teachers from the FLSA, and that the Arbitrator "did not properly consider the unique necessities of being a teacher in a correctional institution."[2] Exceptions at 6. In this connection, the Agency asserts that: "[t]he time spent locating inmates who are absent from class is a part of a teacher's role in a correctional environment[;]" "[t]eaching inmates about punctuality and accountability should be considered teaching[;]" and "it is inappropriate for the Arbitrator to say teachers are not performing teachers' duties whey they are required to search inmates and provide for safety in the classroom." *Id.* at 7. In addition, the Agency claims that the Arbitrator "discounted the fact that teachers . . . are required to have an advanced degree in a specialized field of learning as contemplated by 5 C.F.R. § 551.208[,]" and asserts that "[t]he simple fact that education specialists are not required to have this degree and still do similar duties does not inherently mean that teachers should be [FLSA] non[]exempt as well." *Id.* at 8. Further, the Agency contends that "[i]t is reasonable to believe" that the teachers in *Wilks v. District of Columbia*, 721 F. Supp. 1383, 1386 (D.D.C. 1989) (*Wilks*), who were found to be exempt from the FLSA, "have the same or similar types of correctional duties as the teachers in the present case." Exceptions at 8 n.2.

The Agency also argues that the award is contrary to management's rights to assign work and assign employees under § 7106(a)(2)(B) and (a)(2)(A) of the Statute because it precludes management from assigning employees other than VTIs to cover sick and annual leave vacancies and may require management to use overtime assignments, cancel leave and/or training, or even assign management to vacant posts. *Id.* at 10, 12. The Agency also contends that the MOU, as interpreted by the Arbitrator, "does not constitute an arrangement for employees adversely affected by the exercise of a management right." *Id.* at 13. In this connection, the Agency asserts that: "[a]n arrangement must seek to mitigate adverse effects flowing from the exercise of a protected management right[;]" "[p]rovisions that are unrelated to management's exercise of its reserved rights do not constitute arrangements[;]" and "the purported arrangement must be sufficiently tailored to compensate or benefit employees suffering adverse effects resulting from the exercise of management's rights." *Id.* at 14. The Agency also asserts that the Arbitrator's remedy excessively interferes with management's rights, and that "the Arbitrator's remedy . . . is not a reconstruction of what the Agency would have done." *Id.* at 15, 17.

2. The pertinent wording of the OPM regulations at issue in this case is set forth below.

B. Union's Opposition

The Union argues that the award is not contrary to the FLSA. In this connection, the Union contends that the Agency had the burden of proving that the teachers are exempt from the FLSA, and that the record supports the Arbitrator's finding that the teachers' primary duty is to serve as correctional officers. Opp'n at 7-8. With respect to the Agency's claim that the teachers teach inmates about punctuality and accountability, the Union asserts that "there is no factual basis for this claim" because no witnesses testified that teachers perform that duty. *Id.* at 8.

With regard to the Agency's management rights exception, the Union argues that the award "certainly affects a management right[,] but that "[t]here is no doubt between the parties that the MOA constitutes an appropriate arrangement within the meaning of § 7106(b)(3) of the [S]tatute." *Id.* at 12. According to the Union, the question is whether the award would "abrogate the exercise of a management right[,]" and the award "does not limit the Agency's ability to assign work and assign employees any further than the Agency has chosen to limit itself." *Id.* Finally, the Union contends that the award reconstructs what management would have done if it had complied with the MOA. *Id.* at 12-13.

IV. Analysis and Conclusions

The Agency alleges that the award is contrary to the FLSA and § 7106 of the Statute. The Authority reviews questions of law de novo. *See NTEU, Chapter 24*, 50 FLRA 330, 332 (1995) (citing *U.S. Customs Serv. v. FLRA*, 43 F.3d 682, 686-87 (D.C. Cir. 1994)). In applying a standard of de novo review, the Authority determines whether the arbitrator's legal conclusions are consistent with the applicable standard of law. *NFFE, Local 1437*, 53 FLRA 1703, 1710 (1998). In making that determination, the Authority defers to the arbitrator's underlying factual findings. *See id.*

A. The FLSA

Under the OPM regulations implementing the FLSA, "[e]ach employee is presumed to be FLSA nonexempt unless the employing agency correctly determines that the employee clearly meets the requirements of one or more of the exemptions[.]" 5 C.F.R. § 551.202(a). In addition, "[e]xemption criteria must be narrowly construed to apply only to those employees who are clearly within the terms and spirit of the exemption." 5 C.F.R. § 551.202(b). Accordingly, "[t]he burden of proof rests with the agency that asserts the exemption[,]" and "[i]f there is a reasonable doubt as to whether an employee meets the criteria for exemption, the employee will be designated FLSA nonexempt." 5 C.F.R. § 551.202(c), (d).

With regard to the specific exemption alleged here, 5 C.F.R. § 551.208(h) provides, in pertinent part, that "[a] teacher is any employee with a primary duty of teaching, tutoring, instructing or lecturing in the activity of imparting knowledge[.]" In turn, 5 C.F.R. § 551.104 provides, in pertinent part, that "[p]rimary duty typically means the duty that constitutes the major part (over [fifty] percent) of an employee's work."[3] Thus, as relevant here, an employee is an FLSA-exempt teacher if he or she spends over fifty percent of his or her time teaching, tutoring, instructing or lecturing in the activity of imparting knowledge.

The Agency argues that the teachers' time spent locating inmates who are absent from class is a part of a teacher's role in a correctional environment, and that teaching inmates about punctuality and accountability should be considered teaching. The Agency also asserts that teachers are performing teaching duties when they are required to search inmates and provide for safety in the classroom. However, the Agency does not cite any authority to support its arguments, and the record provides no other basis for finding that these activities constitute teaching, tutoring, instructing or lecturing in the activity of imparting knowledge within the meaning of 5 C.F.R. § 551.208(h). Given that employees are presumed to be nonexempt, that exemption criteria must be construed narrowly, that the burden of proof

3. 5 C.F.R. § 551.104 also provides:

> A duty constituting less than [fifty] percent of an employee's work (alternative primary duty) may be credited as the primary duty for exemption purposes provided that duty:
>
> (1) Constitutes a substantial, regular part of the work assigned and performed;
>
> (2) Is the reason for the existence of the position; and
>
> (3) Is clearly exempt work in terms of the basic nature of the work, the frequency with which the employee must exercise discretion and independent judgment as discussed in § 551.206, and the significance of the decisions made.

The Agency neither asserts that the teaching is teachers' alternative primary duty nor addresses the requirements of the alternative primary duty test.

rests with the Agency, and that any reasonable doubt should result in finding employees nonexempt, *see* 5 C.F.R. § 551.202, the Agency's arguments do not provide a basis for setting aside the Arbitrator's finding that the teachers are nonexempt.

The Agency also argues that the nonexempt status of education specialists does not demonstrate that teachers also are nonexempt. Although the Arbitrator noted that education specialists are nonexempt, she based her determination regarding the teachers' FLSA status on the teachers' actual duties, not on the FLSA exemption status of education specialists. As such, the Agency's argument is misplaced and does not provide a basis for finding the award contrary to the FLSA.

With regard to the Agency's claim that the Arbitrator "discounted the fact that teachers . . . are required to have an advanced degree in a specialized field of learning[,]" Exceptions at 8, 5 C.F.R. § 551.208(a) states, in pertinent part: "To qualify for the learned professional exemption, an employee's primary duty must be the performance of work requiring advanced knowledge in a field of science or learning customarily acquired by a prolonged course of specialized intellectual instruction." As stated previously, the Arbitrator found that teachers' "primary duty" did not involve teaching. Award at 13. Thus, the Agency's claim is misplaced and does not provide a basis for finding the award contrary to 5 C.F.R. § 551.208(a).

Finally, the Agency provides no support for its assertion that "[i]t is reasonable to believe" that the teachers at issue here have the same or similar duties as those performed by the teachers in *Wilks*, 721 F. Supp. 1383. Exceptions at 8 n.2. As an initial matter, "[w]hile established position descriptions and titles may assist in making initial FLSA exemption determinations, the designation of an employee as FLSA exempt or nonexempt must ultimately rest on the duties actually performed by the employee." 5 C.F.R. § 551.202(e). Thus, it is not reasonable to assume that the teachers at issue here are exempt merely because the teachers at issue in *Wilks* also were exempt. Further, in *Wilks*, unlike here, there was no finding that the teachers spent a minority of their time performing teaching duties. Thus, *Wilks* does not provide a basis for finding that the award is contrary to the FLSA.

For the foregoing reasons, we deny the Agency's exceptions regarding the FLSA.

B. Section 7106 of the Statute

The Authority recently revised the analysis that it will apply when reviewing management rights exceptions to arbitration awards. *See U.S. EPA*, 65 FLRA 113, 115 (2010) (Member Beck concurring) (*EPA*); *FDIC, Div. of Supervision & Consumer Prot., S.F. Region*, 65 FLRA 102, 106-07 (2010) (Chairman Pope concurring) (*FDIC*). Under the revised analysis, the Authority assesses whether the award affects the exercise of the asserted management right. *EPA,* 65 FLRA at 115. If so, then, as relevant here, the Authority examines whether the award enforces a contract provision negotiated under § 7106(b).[4] *Id.* Also under the revised analysis, in determining whether the award enforces a contract provision negotiated under § 7106(b)(3),[5] the Authority assesses: (1) whether the contract provision constitutes an arrangement for employees adversely affected by the exercise of a management right; and (2) if so, whether the arbitrator's enforcement of the arrangement abrogates the exercise of the management right.[6] *See id.* at 118. In concluding that it would apply an abrogation standard, the Authority rejected continued application of an excessive-interference standard. *Id.* at 113. In addition, in setting forth the revised analysis, the Authority rejected the continued application of the "reconstruction" requirement set forth in *United States Department of the Treasury, Bureau of Engraving and Printing, Washington, D.C.*, 53 FLRA 146 (1997). *See FDIC*, 65 FLRA at 106-07.

The right to assign work under § 7106(a)(2)(B) of the Statute includes the right to determine the particular duties to be assigned, when work assignments will occur, and to whom, or what positions, the duties will be assigned. *E.g., U.S. Dep't of Commerce, PTO*, 65 FLRA 13, 15 (2010) (Member Beck dissenting on other grounds). The

4. When an award affects a management right under § 7106(a)(2) of the Statute, the Authority may also examine whether the award enforces an applicable law. *EPA,* 65 FLRA at 115 n.7.

5. The Union does not contend that the MOA was negotiated under § 7106(b)(1) or (2) of the Statute. Therefore, we do not consider that issue. *E.g., U.S. Dep't of Veterans Affairs, St. Cloud VA Med. Ctr., St. Cloud, Minn.*, 62 FLRA 508, 510 n.3 (2008).

6. Contrary to the Agency's claim that an arrangement must be "tailored[,]" Exceptions at 14, the Authority does not conduct a tailoring analysis in resolving exceptions to arbitration awards. *EPA*, 65 FLRA at 116.

right to assign employees under § 7106(a)(2)(A) of the Statute includes, among other things, the right to make temporary assignments. *E.g., NATCA*, 64 FLRA 161, 165 (2009). The award precludes management from assigning any employees other than VTIs to cover for employees who are on extended sick leave or scheduled annual leave. Thus, the award affects management's rights to determine to whom particular duties will be assigned and to make temporary assignments. Accordingly, the award affects management's rights to assign work and assign employees.

As for whether the Arbitrator was enforcing an appropriate arrangement within the meaning of § 7106(b)(3) of the Statute, the Arbitrator noted the negotiator's testimony that the MOA was negotiated to provide that VTIs would be utilized for extended sick and annual leave coverage because, unlike non-VTI employees, VTIs are not required to rotate their shifts every six months. *See* Award at 11. In this connection, the negotiator testified, without dispute, that the MOA "came about because the [VTIs] were given a set Monday through Friday day schedule, weekends, holidays off, without having to bid for any shift or post[]" and without having to "move out of their institution." Opp'n, Attach. 1 (Tr.) at 71. *Accord id.* at 54 (negotiator testified that VTIs "don't bid or rotate in their shifts or posts[,]" that "[t]heir schedule is set Monday through Friday days," and that "[t]hey don't ever have to change their shift or . . . place of work."). Put simply, in exchange for the instability that results from management's assignment of non-VTI employees to rotating shifts and posts, the parties agreed that those employees would be exempt from covering absences due to extended sick and annual leave -- and that, instead, the VTIs, whose schedules are stable, Monday-through-Friday day shifts, would cover that leave. Thus, the MOA was intended to ameliorate the adverse effects on non-VTI employees of management's right to assign those employees to shifts and posts that change every six months. Accordingly, we find that the MOA constitutes an arrangement within the meaning of § 7106(b)(3) of the Statute. *Cf. AFGE, Local 3157*, 44 FLRA 1570, 1580-81, 1591-92 (1992) (requirements that provided stability and predictability in employees' work schedules constituted arrangements).

With regard to whether the arrangement is appropriate, the Agency argues that the award "excessively interferes" with management's rights. Exceptions at 15. However, as stated above, the Authority no longer applies an excessive-interference standard to determine whether an arrangement is appropriate. *See EPA*, 65 FLRA at 118. Rather, the Authority applies an abrogation standard, which assesses whether the arbitration award "precludes [the] agency from exercising" the affected management right. *U.S. Dep't of the Air Force, Air Force Materiel Command*, 65 FLRA 395, 399 (2010) (citation omitted).[7] The Agency does not assert, and there is no basis for finding, that the award precludes the Agency from exercising its rights to assign work and assign employees. Therefore, we find that the arrangement is appropriate within the meaning of § 7106(b)(3) of the Statute.

Finally, the Agency claims that the Arbitrator's remedy "is not a reconstruction of what the Agency would have done[]" if it had complied with the MOA. Exceptions at 17. However, as stated above, the Authority no longer requires that an arbitrator's remedy reconstruct what management would have done if it had not violated the contract provision. *FDIC*, 65 FLRA at 118. Thus, the Agency's argument does not provide a basis for setting aside the award.

For the foregoing reasons, we deny the Agency's management rights exception.

V. Decision

The Agency's exceptions are denied.

---

7. For the reasons articulated in his recent concurring opinion and footnotes, Member Beck would conclude that it is unnecessary to assess whether the contract provision is an appropriate arrangement or whether it abrogates a § 7106(a) right. The appropriate question is simply whether the remedy directed by the Arbitrator enforces the provision in a reasonable and reasonably foreseeable fashion. *See EPA*, 65 FLRA at 120 (Concurring Opinion of Member Beck); *FDIC*, 65 FLRA at 107; *SSA, Office of Disability Adjudication & Review*, 65 FLRA 477, 481 n.14 (2011); *U.S. Dep't of the Air Force, Air Force Materiel Command*, 65 FLRA 395, 398 n.7 (2010); *U.S. Dep't of Health & Human Servs., Office of Medicare Hearings & Appeals*, 65 FLRA 175, 177 n.3 (2010); *U.S. Dep't of Transp., Fed. Aviation Admin.*, 65 FLRA 171, 173 n.5 (2010). Member Beck would conclude that the Arbitrator's award is a plausible interpretation of the parties' agreement and deny the exception.

65 FLRA No. 113

SOCIAL SECURITY ADMINISTRATION
(Agency)

and

AMERICAN FEDERATION
OF GOVERNMENT EMPLOYEES
LOCAL 3627
(Union)

0-AR-4584

DECISION

February 18, 2011

Before the Authority: Carol Waller Pope, Chairman, and Thomas M. Beck and Ernest DuBester, Members

I. Statement of the Case

This matter is before the Authority on exceptions to an award of Arbitrator Douglas F. Coleman filed by the Agency under § 7122(a) of the Federal Service Labor-Management Relations Statute (the Statute) and part 2425 of the Authority's Regulations. The Union filed an opposition to the Agency's exceptions.

The Arbitrator sustained the Union's grievance and found that the Agency violated the parties' agreement by relying on improper criteria to fill an Agency vacancy. For the reasons set forth below, we dismiss the Agency's exceptions.

II. Background and Arbitrator's Award

The Agency posted a vacancy announcement (the announcement) for three Senior Legal Assistant positions, General Schedule (GS)-6/GS-7/GS-8 (senior position(s)). *See* Award at 2; Exceptions, Attach. 5 at 2. The announcement required applicants to have familiarity with a certain set of duties, i.e., "specialized experience." Exceptions, Attach. 5 at 2. It also required applicants seeking a GS-6 senior position to have fifty-two weeks of "specialized experience at least *equivalent*" to a GS-5 level. *Id.* (emphasis added). However, it further stated that "specialized experience *must be gained at the next lower grade*" level. *Id.* (emphasis added).

Six employees applied; three applicants, including employee A, were placed on the best-qualified list. Award at 2. The Agency selected employee A to fill a GS-6 senior position. Employee A had held a GS-5 assistant position for only four months, Award at 5; however, she also had been a GS-10 supervisor at a different agency for over a year and that position involved many, but not all, of the same duties as a senior position, *id.* at 4-5.

The Union filed a grievance arguing that the Agency's selection of employee A violated Article 26 of the parties' agreement, which, in relevant part, requires the Agency to "ensure that applicants meet the minimum qualifications" for a position. Award at 2-3 (quoting Article 26, Section 10[A] of the parties' agreement). The Union contended that employee A should not have been selected because she did not meet the time and grade requirements for the position because she had held a GS-5 assistant position for four months rather than a full year. Award at 4; *see also* Exceptions, Attach. 4, Union's Grievance at 6-8. The Union requested that, if employee A did not meet the necessary requirements, the Agency vacate the selection and rerun the announcement. Award at 4; Exceptions, Attach. 4 at 4. The Arbitrator framed the issue as "[d]id the Agency violate the provisions of Article 26 Section[s] 1, 5A[,] 10A of the [parties' agreement] with respect to filing the Senior Legal Assistant vacancy[?]" Award at 2.

At the hearing, the Agency's Human Resources Specialist (specialist) responsible for creating the announcement and selecting employee A testified. She testified that she relied on Office of Personnel Management (OPM) classification standards (standards) and an OPM handbook (handbook) to select employee A. *See id.* at 7. The specialist acknowledged that the announcement stated that an applicant had to possess specialized experience at the next lower grade level for a period of a year and that employee A had been a GS-5 for only four months. *Id.* at 8. She also acknowledged that employee A did not have experience with all the duties necessary for the senior position. However, she testified that, under the standards and the handbook, employee A's time as a GS-10 supervisor satisfied the announcement's time and grade requirements and provided her with the experience necessary for the senior position. *Id.*

The Arbitrator concluded that the Agency violated the parties' agreement by selecting employee A. The Arbitrator determined that employee A did not satisfy the time and grade requirements of the announcement. According to the Arbitrator, the announcement unambiguously stated that an applicant "must" have relevant experience at the lower level for a full year. Award at 11 (quoting Exceptions, Attach. 5 at 2). Because employee A had been a GS-5 assistant for only four months, the Arbitrator held she did not satisfy this requirement. Award at 11-12. The Arbitrator determined that the requirements of the announcement could not be satisfied by employee A's year-long tenure as a GS-10 supervisor because that was contrary to the plain language requirements of the announcement. *See id.* at 10-11. Moreover, the Arbitrator found, contrary to the specialist's testimony, that employee A's GS-10 supervisor duties did not provide her with the skills necessary for the position. *See id.* at 11-12. The Arbitrator, accordingly, sustained the grievance.

III. Positions of the Parties

A. Agency's Exceptions

The Agency contends that the award is contrary to law because it impermissibly interferes with management's right to select under § 7106(a)(2)(C) of the Statute.[1] Exceptions at 6. Accordingly, the Agency asserts that the Authority should apply the two-prong test set forth in *United States Department of the Treasury, Bureau of Engraving & Printing, Washington, D.C.*, 53 FLRA 146 (1997) (*BEP*). *Id.* The Agency contends that the Arbitrator's award fails to satisfy prong I of *BEP* because the award excessively interferes with management's rights to fill positions and select appointments from properly ranked and certified candidates. *Id.* at 6-7. Specifically, the Agency alleges that the award creates this excessive interference, and is therefore contrary to § 7106(a)(2)(C), because: (1) the Arbitrator did not defer to the specialist's testimony regarding employee A's qualifications, *id.* at 8-9; (2) the award "affects the determination of whether applicants possess the requisite qualifications, skills and abilities[,] *id.* at 9; and (3) the Arbitrator improperly "second-guess[ed]" the specialist's interpretation of the announcement, *id.*

B. Union's Opposition

According to the Union, the Agency's assertion that the award excessively interferes with management's right to select is "incorrect[.]" Opp'n at 3. The Union contends that the specialist's testimony, in conjunction with the record, actually establishes that employee A did not have the necessary qualifications for the senior position. *See id.* The Union also asserts that, although the Agency may determine the necessary qualifications, skills, and abilities for a position, it must also determine that an applicant actually *has* the necessary qualifications, skills and abilities. *See id.* at 3-4.

IV. The Agency's exceptions are barred by § 2429.5 of the Authority's Regulations

The Authority's Regulations that were in effect when the Agency filed its exceptions provided that "[t]he Authority will not consider . . . any issue, which was not presented in the proceedings before the . . . arbitrator." 5. C.F.R. § 2429.5.[2]

As discussed above, the Arbitrator framed the issue as whether the Agency violated the parties' agreement by selecting employee A for the senior position. *See* Award at 2. The Union raised this allegation in its grievance. *See* Exceptions, Attach. 4 at 3-4. Moreover, in its grievance, the Union requested that the Agency vacate the selection if the selection was made in violation of the parties' agreement. *See id.* at 4. The Union requested similar relief at the hearing. *See* Award at 4. Thus, the Agency was aware that the Union was: (1) challenging the Agency's selection of employee A; and (2) seeking to vacate this selection. The Agency, therefore, had the opportunity to argue to the Arbitrator that the award could violate management's right to select by "affect[ing] the determination of whether applicants possess the requisite qualifications, skills and abilities[.]" Exceptions at 9. However, the record contains no indication that this argument was presented below.

---

1. Section 7106(a)(2)(C) of the Statute provides, in pertinent part:

> Subject to subsection (b) of this section, nothing in this chapter shall affect the authority of any management official of any agency . . . in accordance with applicable laws . . . with respect to filling positions, to make selections for appointments from (i) among properly ranked and certified candidates for promotion; or (ii) any other appropriate source[.]

5 U.S.C. § 7106(a)(2)(C)(i) & (ii).

2. The Authority's Regulations concerning the review of arbitration awards, as well as certain related procedural Regulations, including 5 C.F.R. § 2429.5, were revised effective October 1, 2010. *See* 75 Fed. Reg. 42,283 (2010). Because the Agency's exceptions in this case were filed before that date, we apply the prior Regulations.

Similarly, the Agency had an opportunity to argue to the Arbitrator that, under § 7106(a)(2)(C) of the Statute, the Arbitrator was required to defer to the specialist's examination of employee A's qualifications and her interpretation of the announcement. The specialist was the Agency's witness. *See* Award at 1. The record contains no indication, however, that the Agency argued at the hearing that the Arbitrator should defer to the specialist's testimony. Likewise, although the parties' filed post-hearing briefs, *see* Exceptions at 2, the record contains no indication that the Agency argued that a failure to defer to the specialist's testimony would excessively interfere with management's right to select.

Because the foregoing issues could have been, but were not, presented to the Arbitrator, we find that § 2429.5 of the Authority's Regulations precludes the Agency from raising them for the first time in its exceptions. *See, e.g., SSA, Newark, N.J.,* 64 FLRA 259, 260-61 (2009) (citations omitted) (Authority dismissed agency's argument that award violated management's right to select because agency failed to present argument below). Accordingly, we dismiss the Agency's exceptions.

V. Decision

The Agency's exceptions are dismissed.

65 FLRA No. 114

UNITED STATES
DEPARTMENT OF THE TREASURY
FINANCIAL MANAGEMENT SERVICE
EMERYVILLE, CALIFORNIA
(Agency)

and

NATIONAL TREASURY
EMPLOYEES UNION
CHAPTER 214
(Union)

0-AR-4677

DECISION

February 23, 2011

Before the Authority: Carol Waller Pope, Chairman, and Thomas M. Beck and Ernest DuBester, Members

I. Statement of the Case

This matter is before the Authority on exceptions to an award of Arbitrator Elinor S. Nelson filed by the Agency under § 7122(a) of the Federal Service Labor-Management Relations Statute (the Statute) and part 2425 of the Authority's Regulations. The Union filed an opposition to the Agency's exceptions.

The Arbitrator found that the Agency violated the parties' agreement by changing employees' work schedules, and directed the Agency to reinstate the employees' prior schedules. For the following reasons, we deny the Agency's exceptions.

II. Background and Arbitrator's Award

The grievants are production employees at the San Francisco Financial Center (SFFC), Payment Facilities Branch (PFB), which is responsible for printing and wrapping checks issued by the federal government. Award at 3. Because the grievants' previous supervisor arrived at the office by 6:45 a.m., the grievants were permitted to work from 6:45 a.m. until 3:15 p.m., although their official shift was 7 a.m. to 3:30 p.m. *Id.* at 5. The Agency later appointed two new supervisors, each of whom arrived at 7 a.m. *Id.* at 6. An experienced employee who arrived at 6:45 a.m. served as acting supervisor in the absence of the grievants' immediate supervisor. *Id.* In March 2008, the grievants' immediate supervisor issued a memorandum stating that employees were required to work during their official hours of duty. *Id.* at 7. He cited "a lack of cognizant supervision in the [PFB] prior to 7:00 a.m." and "production difficulties due to the different work schedules" as reasons for the change. *Id.*

The Union filed a grievance on behalf of all affected employees, alleging that the Agency violated the parties' agreement, past practice, and bargaining obligations by unilaterally changing the employees' work schedules. *Id.* at 9. The grievance was unresolved and submitted to arbitration. *Id.* at 10.

At arbitration, the parties stipulated to the following issues: "Was the Agency's . . . change in work schedules for employees . . . consistent with the [parties' agreement]? . . . If not, what shall be the remedy?" *Id.* at 2. As an initial matter, the Arbitrator found that Article 36, Section 8(B) of the parties' agreement allows for supervisor-initiated schedule changes in only two circumstances: (1) a change in workload; or (2) a lack of cognizant supervision.[1] *Id.* at 18.

With regard to workload, the Arbitrator acknowledged that "[i]n 2008, the SFFC was tasked with issuing congressionally-mandated federal stimulus payments . . . without increased staffing[,]" but found that "vague, unsupported testimony about federal stimulus mandates does not substitute for objective data showing affected employees' workloads changed and precipitated their schedule changes[.]" *Id.* at 3, 20-21. The Arbitrator then determined that "the Agency violated Article 36, Section 8[(B)] of the [parties' agreement] when it cited and used 'production difficulties due to the different work schedules' . . . as a reason for the [Agency's] change in employees' work schedules"

1. Article 36, Section 8(B) states, in pertinent part: "A supervisor may change an employee's established work schedule by providing the employee with written notice two (2) weeks before the effective date of the change if (1) the workload or (2) cognizant supervision no longer permits the employee to remain on the employee's then current schedule." Exceptions, Attach. 6, Master Labor Agreement at 128.

because the term "workload," as used in Article 36, Section 8(B), "does not equat[e] [to] 'production difficulties[.]'" *Id.* at 21, 20.

With respect to cognizant supervision, the Arbitrator found that, given the "long-standing, management-sanctioned practice of . . . consistently designating [an experienced employee] to act as a supervisor," the Agency failed to establish that a "lack of cognizant supervision[] precipitated [the] employees' work schedule changes[.]" *Id.* at 25, 24. In this regard, she determined that "the phrase 'cognizant supervision' [as] used in . . . Article 36 suggests that this phrase means 'adequate supervision.'" *Id.* at 25.

The Arbitrator concluded that the Agency violated Article 36, including the "spirit of Article 36, Section 1, when . . . it unilaterally changed the alternative employee work schedules[.]"[2] *Id.* at 19. As a remedy, she directed, among other things, that the Agency reinstate the status quo ante with respect to the affected employees' work schedules. *Id.* at 28.

III. Positions of the Parties

A. Agency's Exceptions

The Agency contends that the award fails to draw its essence from the parties' agreement on two grounds. Exceptions at 3-4, 6-7. First, the Agency asserts that the Arbitrator's finding that the term "workload" as used in Article 36 does not encompass "production difficulties" is an implausible interpretation of the agreement. *Id.* at 3-4. Second, the Agency maintains that the Arbitrator erred in finding that the Agency violated Article 36, Section 1 by failing to provide alternative work schedules (AWS) for employees. *Id.* at 6. In this connection, the Agency asserts that the award "completely ignores that Section 1 restricts AWS for shift workers, the very category of employees at issue." *Id.* at 6-7.

The Agency also contends that the remedy -- directing the Agency to reinstate the status quo ante with regard to employees' work schedules -- conflicts with the parties' agreement because it would permit some employees to work without supervision for up to thirty minutes. *Id.* at 8. In this regard, the Agency claims that "it is undisputed that Article 36 of the [p]arties' agreement contemplates the supervision of employees while they work." *Id.* The Agency also claims that "[a]rbitration awards that fail to reflect a reconstruction of the action management would have taken . . . are deficient and may be set aside." *Id.* (citing *U.S. Dep't of the Treasury, Bureau of Engraving & Printing*, 53 FLRA 146, 154 (1997) (*BEP*)).

The Agency further argues that the Arbitrator erred in finding that, despite the Agency's role in issuing the 2008 stimulus payments, the Agency failed to demonstrate that a change in workload precipitated the Agency's alteration of employees' work schedules. *Id.* at 4-5. In this connection, the Agency contends that the Arbitrator rejected "unchallenged testimony of an increased workload in 2008[.]" *Id.* at 5. Further, the Agency requests that the Authority take official notice of the "economic stimulus payments authorized by the U.S. Congress in 2008" because the payments were "widely discussed and reported by national news media[.]" *Id.* (citing *U.S. Dep't of Veterans Affairs, Ralph H. Johnson Med. Ctr., Charleston, S.C.*, 56 FLRA 381, 384 (2000)).

B. Union's Opposition

The Union argues that the Agency's essence exceptions constitute "nothing more than a disagreement with the Arbitrator's interpretation of the [a]greement." Opp'n at 4, 6-8. The Union also argues that, assuming that the Agency challenges the award on nonfact grounds, this exception is deficient because the "factual matter of workload was vigorously disputed at [the] hearing[.]" *Id.* at 6.

IV. Analysis and Conclusions

A. The award draws its essence from the parties' agreement.

In reviewing an arbitrator's interpretation of a collective bargaining agreement, the Authority applies the deferential standard that federal courts use in reviewing arbitration awards in the private sector. *See* 5 U.S.C. § 7122(a)(2); *AFGE, Council 220*, 54 FLRA 156, 159 (1998). Under this standard, the Authority will find that an arbitration award is deficient as failing to draw its essence from the collective bargaining agreement when the appealing party establishes that the award: (1) cannot in any rational way be derived from the agreement; (2) is so unfounded in reason and fact and so unconnected

2. The relevant wording of Article 36, Section 1 is set forth *infra*.

with the wording and purposes of the collective bargaining agreement as to manifest an infidelity to the obligation of the arbitrator; (3) does not represent a plausible interpretation of the agreement; or (4) evidences a manifest disregard of the agreement. *U.S. Dep't of Labor (OSHA)*, 34 FLRA 573, 575 (1990). The Authority and the courts defer to arbitrators in this context "because it is the arbitrator's construction of the agreement for which the parties have bargained." *Id.* at 576.

The Agency contends that the Arbitrator erred by finding that the term "workload," as used in Article 36, Section 8(B), does not encompass "production difficulties." Exceptions at 3-4. As noted previously, Section 8(B) provides, in pertinent part: "A supervisor may change an employee's established work schedule . . . if . . . the workload . . . no longer permits the employee to remain on the employee's then current schedule." Exceptions, Attach. 6, Master Labor Agreement (Master Labor Agreement) at 128. The Arbitrator found that "[p]roduction difficulties may indeed result in an increased, or decreased employee workload, but production difficulties and workload are not synonymous." Award at 20. The agreement does not define the term "workload," and the Agency provides no basis for concluding that the Arbitrator's interpretation was irrational, unfounded, implausible, or in manifest disregard of the parties' agreement. Accordingly, we deny the exception.

The Agency further argues that the Arbitrator erred in finding that the Agency violated Article 36, Section 1 by failing to provide AWS for affected employees in this case. *Id.* at 6. In this connection, the Agency asserts that the award "completely ignores that Section 1 restricts AWS for shift workers, the very category of employees at issue." *Id.* at 6-7. Article 36, Section 1(B) states, in pertinent part: "[The Agency] and [the Union] with the concurrence of affected employees is able to design a schedule that . . . would accommodate AWS where excluded by contractual provision (for example, shift workers), [and] the local parties will work in partnership to review the availability of AWS to these employees." Master Labor Agreement at 122. Contrary to the Agency's contention, this provision does not preclude the Agency from developing an enforceable practice whereby shift workers and other contractually excluded employees are permitted to participate in AWS. The Agency provides no basis for finding that the Arbitrator's interpretation of that provision was irrational, unfounded, implausible, or in manifest disregard of the parties' agreement, and, accordingly, we deny the exception.

The Agency also claims that the remedy -- directing the Agency to reinstate the status quo ante with regard to employees' work schedules -- conflicts with Article 36 of the parties' agreement because it would permit some employees to work without supervision for up to thirty minutes. Exceptions at 8-9. We construe this as a claim that the remedy fails to draw its essence from the agreement. The Arbitrator found that "the way in which the phrase 'cognizant supervision' is used in . . . Article 36 suggests that this phrase means 'adequate supervision[,]'" and "may encompass a 'knowledgeable [employee]' or a [l]ead who is directed to act for a supervisor during his/her absence[.]" Award at 25-26. However, the Arbitrator's interpretation of the agreement does not preclude the Agency from changing supervisors' schedules or designating a senior employee to serve as an acting supervisor, such that no work is performed without adequate supervision. Thus, the Agency's claim does not demonstrate that the remedy requires that employees perform work without "cognizant supervision" within the meaning of Article 36.

We note that, as an attachment to its exceptions, the Agency includes its post-hearing brief to the Arbitrator, along with two documents, drafted by external entities, that contain the word "cognizant" and allegedly demonstrate that the Arbitrator erroneously interpreted the term "cognizant supervision" as used in the parties' agreement. *See* Exceptions, Attach. 3. Although the Union moves to strike these documents, even assuming that the documents are properly before the Authority, they do not provide a basis for finding that the Arbitrator misinterpreted "cognizant" as the parties intended it to be used in the agreement. As such, the documents provide no basis for finding that it was irrational, implausible, unfounded, or in manifest disregard of the agreement for the Arbitrator to direct the remedy. Accordingly, we find it unnecessary to resolve the Union's motion to strike.

For the foregoing reasons, we deny the Agency's essence exceptions.

B. The award is not contrary to law.

We construe the Agency's claim that "arbitration awards that fail to reflect a reconstruction of the action management would have taken to resolve a [violation of] a . . . provision . . . are deficient and may be set aside[,]" and its citation to *BEP*, as a contention that the award's remedy is contrary to § 7106 of the Statute. When a party's exceptions involve an award's consistency with law, the Authority reviews the questions of law raised by the arbitrator's award and the party's exceptions de novo. *NTEU, Chapter 24*, 50 FLRA 330, 332 (1995) (citing *U.S. Customs Serv. v. FLRA*, 43 F.3d 682, 686-87 (D.C. Cir. 1994)). In applying a de novo standard of review, the Authority assesses whether the arbitrator's legal conclusions are consistent with the applicable standard of law. *NFFE, Local 1437*, 53 FLRA 1703, 1710 (1998). In making that assessment, the Authority defers to the arbitrator's underlying factual findings. *See id.*

The Authority recently revised the analysis that it will apply when reviewing management-rights exceptions to arbitration awards. *See U.S. EPA*, 65 FLRA 113, 115 (2010) (Member Beck concurring) (*EPA*); *FDIC, Div. of Supervision & Consumer Prot., S.F. Region*, 65 FLRA 102, 106-07 (2010) (Chairman Pope concurring) (*FDIC, S.F. Region*). Under the revised analysis, the Authority will first assess whether the award affects the exercise of the asserted management right. *EPA*, 65 FLRA at 115.[3] If so, then the Authority examines whether the award provides a remedy for a violation of either an applicable law, within the meaning of § 7106(a)(2) of the Statute,[4] or a contract provision that was negotiated pursuant to § 7106(b) of the Statute. *Id.* In setting forth its revised analysis, the Authority specifically rejected the continued application of the reconstruction standard set forth in *BEP*. *FDIC, S.F. Region*, 65 FLRA at 106-107. Accordingly, under the revised analysis, exceptions based on an alleged failure to reconstruct are denied. *See, e.g., FDIC, Div. of Supervision & Consumer Prot., Dallas Reg'l Office*, 65 FLRA 348, 352-353 (2010); *FDIC*, 65 FLRA 179, 181 (2010).

Here, the Agency's exception is based entirely on the Arbitrator's alleged failure to reconstruct what the Agency would have done if it had not violated the agreement. As discussed above, the Authority has rejected continued application of the former reconstruction standard. Accordingly, we deny the exception.[5]

C. The award is not based on a nonfact.

We construe the Agency's claim that the Arbitrator erred in finding that, despite the Agency's role in issuing the 2008 stimulus payments, the Agency failed to demonstrate that a change in workload precipitated the Agency's alteration of employees' work schedules as an argument that the award is based on a nonfact. To establish that an award is based on a nonfact, the appealing party must show that a central fact underlying the award is clearly erroneous, but for which the arbitrator would have reached a different result. *See NFFE, Local 1984*, 56 FLRA 38, 41 (2000). However, the Authority will not find an award deficient on the basis of an arbitrator's determination of any factual matter that the parties disputed at arbitration. *See id.*

Before the Arbitrator, the parties disputed whether a change in workload had occurred. *See* Award at 14 (Agency argued that SFFC "was tasked with issuing congressionally-mandated federal stimulus payments . . . which increased the workload without a staffing increase"); *id.* at 12 (Union argued that "[t]he workload in [PFB] did not justify a change to employees' work schedules"). With regard to the Agency's request that the Authority take official notice that Congress authorized stimulus payments in

3. For the reasons articulated in his recent concurring opinion and footnotes, Member Beck would conclude that it is unnecessary to assess whether the award affects the exercise of the asserted management right. The appropriate question is simply whether the remedy directed by the Arbitrator enforces the provision in a reasonable and reasonably foreseeable fashion. *See EPA*, 65 FLRA at 120 (Concurring Opinion of Member Beck); *U.S. Dep't of Justice, Fed. Bureau of Prisons, Fed. Corr. Complex, Terre Haute, Ind.*, 65 FLRA 460, 462 n.2 (2011); *Soc. Sec. Admin., Dallas Region*, 65 FLRA 405, 408 n.5 (2010); *U.S. Dep't of the Air Force, Air Force Materiel Command*, 65 FLRA 395, 398 n.7 (2010); *U.S. Dep't of Health & Human Servs., Office of Medicare Hearings & Appeals*, 65 FLRA 175, 177 n.3 (2010); *U.S. Dep't of Transp., Fed. Aviation Admin.*, 65 FLRA 171, 173 n.5 (2010). Member Beck would conclude that the Arbitrator's award is a plausible interpretation of the parties' agreement and deny the exception.

4. We note that the "applicable law" examination is applied only in cases involving management rights under §7106(a)(2). *See U.S. Dep't of Transp., Fed. Aviation Admin.*, 58 FLRA 175, 178 (2002).

5. For the reasons set forth in her concurring opinion in *FDIC, S.F. Region*, 65 FLRA at 112 (Concurring Opinion of Chairman Pope), Chairman Pope agrees that the award is not deficient because the remedy is reasonably related to the negotiated provisions and the harm being remedied.

2008, the Arbitrator acknowledged those payments, but found that "vague, unsupported testimony about federal stimulus mandates does not substitute for objective data showing affected employees' workloads changed and precipitated their schedule changes[.]" *Id.* at 20-21. Thus, the Agency's reliance on those payments does not demonstrate that the Arbitrator clearly erred in finding that no change in workloads occurred. In addition, in an attachment to its exceptions, the Agency includes its post-hearing brief, along with a graph that purports to show that the Agency's workload increased in 2008 due to the stimulus payments. *See* Exceptions, Attach. 3. Although the Union moves to strike this graph, even assuming that the graph is properly before the Authority, it does not demonstrate that the Arbitrator clearly erred in her factual findings. Accordingly, we find it unnecessary to resolve the Union's motion.

For the foregoing reasons, we find that the Agency has not demonstrated that the award is based on a nonfact, and we deny the exception.

IV. Decision

The Agency's exceptions are denied.

65 FLRA No. 115

NATIONAL ASSOCIATION
OF GOVERNMENT EMPLOYEES
LOCAL R1-144
FEDERAL UNION OF SCIENTISTS
AND ENGINEERS
(Union)

and

UNITED STATES
DEPARTMENT OF THE NAVY
NAVAL UNDERSEA WARFARE
CENTER DIVISION NEWPORT
NEWPORT, RHODE ISLAND
(Agency)

0-NG-3015

DECISION AND ORDER
ON A NEGOTIABILITY ISSUE

February 23, 2011

Before the Authority: Carol Waller Pope, Chairman, and Thomas M. Beck and Ernest DuBester, Members

I. Statement of the Case

This case is before the Authority on a negotiability appeal filed by the Union under § 7105(a)(2)(E) of the Federal Service Labor-Management Relations Statute (the Statute). The appeal involves the negotiability of one proposal. The proposal addresses the eligibility of Union officials to perform representational duties while teleworking on official time from their homes. Record of Post-Petition Conference at 2. The Agency filed a statement of position (SOP). The Union filed a response (Response) and a supplemental submission. The Agency did not file a reply.

For the reasons set forth below, we find that the proposal is negotiable.

II. Preliminary Issue

The Agency asks that the Authority dismiss the petition for review (petition) because the Union (1) mailed it to the wrong address and therefore failed to properly serve the petition on the Agency head and (2) failed to serve the Agency head's designee. SOP at 1-2. The Agency claims that the Union's service of the petition is thus in violation of 5 C.F.R. § 2424.2(g).[1] *Id.* at 2. The Agency claims that, as a result of the Union's defective service of the petition, it was not timely notified that the Union had filed a petition, consequently reducing the time that the Agency had to respond. *Id.* In the Agency's view, it was, therefore, "severely disadvantaged[.]" *Id.*

The Agency does not sufficiently support its request that the Authority dismiss the petition. First, even if the Union failed to properly serve the Agency head by mailing the petition to the wrong address, failure to serve an agency head where no prejudice is shown does not warrant the petition's dismissal. *See AFGE, Local 3342,* 36 FLRA 367, 374 (1990) (petition not dismissed based on union's failure to serve petition on agency head where agency timely filed SOP and did not show prejudice). Here, the Agency was able to timely file its SOP and has not otherwise shown that it was prejudiced by the defective service. Second, with regard to the Agency's argument that the Union "chose to flaunt the Authority's service regulation by ignoring its obligation to properly serve the Agency [h]ead's designee[,]" *see* SOP at 2, this regulation does not require that service be made on the Agency head's designee. *See* 5 C.F.R. § 2424.2(g). We therefore reject the Agency's request to dismiss the petition.[2]

III. Background

According to the Union, the proposal is intended to clarify the Agency's telework policy. The telework policy establishes policies and procedures for employees wishing to work from home.

---

1. 5 C.F.R. § 2424.2(g) provides that "*[s]ervice* means the delivery of copies of documents filed with the Authority to the other party's principal bargaining representative and, in the case of an exclusive representative, also to the head of the agency."

2. Although the Agency requests that the Authority take official notice that the petition was mailed to the incorrect address and that the Agency head's designee was not served, we decline to do so, as such action is not necessary to resolve the Agency's claims. In addition, the Union's supplemental submission addresses service issues regarding both the petition and the response. As the Agency was not prejudiced by the alleged service deficiencies with respect to the petition, and does not allege any service deficiencies with respect to the response, it is unnecessary to address the Union's supplemental submission or decide whether it is properly before us.

Response at 11. The Union contends that in 2004 and 2005, Agency policy permitted Union officials to telework. Petition at 5. However, now, the Union claims, Union officials are not allowed to perform representational duties while teleworking. Response at 11. Accordingly, the Union presented the Agency with the proposal set forth below, addressing Union officials' eligibility to perform representational duties while teleworking.

IV. Proposal

> Up to 5 full-time and/or part-time union officials are eligible for telework to perform union-related duties on official time at their home worksite, not to exceed 20 hours per week per person. This will not add to the overall amount of official time used by the union to perform representational duties.

Petition at 3.

V. Positions of the Parties

A. Agency

The Agency challenges the negotiability of the proposal on three bases. First, the Agency interprets the proposal as requiring it to allow Union officials to telework. On this basis, the Agency argues that the proposal is non-negotiable as affecting management's rights to assign and direct employees and determine its organization under § 7106(a) of the Statute. SOP at 8, 10, 13. The Agency also argues that the proposal violates 5 U.S.C. § 7131 because it would require management to permit Union officials to telework in contravention of the telework law. In the Agency's view, requiring the Agency to allow Union officials to telework while performing representational duties on official time essentially grants the Union officials additional "official time" beyond that which was intended by § 7131.[3] *Id.* at 14-15.

Second, the Agency interprets the proposal as requiring it to allow Union officials to work exclusively on representational duties while teleworking. On this basis, the Agency alleges, the proposal is non-negotiable as affecting management's rights to assign work, *see id.* at 6, and determine its budget under § 7106(a) the Statute. *Id.* at 13-14. For this same reason, the Agency also argues that the proposal is non-negotiable because it concerns representational duties and, therefore, does not concern "conditions of employment" as that term is defined in § 7103(a)(14) of the Statute. *Id.* at 11-12. In addition, the Agency claims that the proposal violates the Antideficiency Act by requiring it to allow Union officials to perform representational duties while teleworking. According to the Agency, this will require the Agency to expend appropriated funds for the Union's activities that have not been expressly provided for this purpose by legislative appropriations. *Id.* at 16.

Third, the Agency argues that by requiring it to allow Union officials to perform representational duties while teleworking, the proposal violates § 359 of Public Law 106-346 (the telework law). According to the Agency, in *American Federation of Government Employees, National Council of HUD Locals 222, AFL-CIO,* 60 FLRA 311 (2004) (*HUD*), the Authority held that, under the telework law, teleworking is only available to employees performing "official duties" and that representational duties do not qualify as "officially assigned duties" within the meaning of the law. *Id.* at 18 (citing *HUD,* 60 FLRA at 313). The Agency claims that subsequent Authority case law holding that the telework law does not prohibit parties from negotiating an agreement permitting union officials to perform representational duties on telework "has no precedential value" in this case. *Id.* at 19-20.

B. Union

The Union argues that a number of the Agency's contentions are based on its misinterpretation of the proposal. First, the Union argues that the Agency's contentions are based on the false premise that the proposal requires the Agency to allow Union officials to telework. Response at 13-14. According to the Union, this interpretation of the proposal is incorrect. Rather, the Union claims, under the proposal, all teleworkers, including Union officials, would need to be approved for telework by their supervisors. Therefore, the Union asks that the Authority reject the Agency's claims of non-negotiability based on this premise. Thus, the Union claims that the Authority should reject the Agency's arguments that the proposal affects management's rights to assign and direct employees and that it violates § 7131 of the Statute. *Id.* at 14, 17.

Second, the Union contends that a number of the Agency's arguments are based on the false premise

3. Section 7131(d) provides that the use of official time for representational activities other than negotiations or participation in Authority proceedings is subject to negotiation. 5 U.S.C. § 7131(d).

that the proposal would require the Agency to allow Union officials to work exclusively on representational duties while teleworking. According to the Union, this interpretation of the proposal is incorrect. Rather, the Union claims, Union officials' duties while on telework would not be limited to representational duties, but would also include duties assigned by the Agency. *Id.* at 15. Therefore, the Union asks that the Authority reject the Agency's claims of non-negotiability based on this premise - namely that the proposal affects management's rights to assign work, *see id.* at 14, determine its organization, and determine its budget under the Statute, *id.* at 17-20. Similarly, the Union argues that the Authority should reject the Agency's argument that the proposal is non-negotiable because it concerns only Union officials' representational duties, which do not constitute a condition of employment under the Statute. *Id.* at 18. In this same vein, the Union asks that the Authority reject the Agency's argument that the proposal violates the Antideficiency Act. *Id.* at 20.

Third, the Union contends that the proposal does not violate the telework law. The Union relies on Authority precedent holding that the telework law does not prohibit union officials from performing representational duties while teleworking on official time. *Id.* at 22.

VI. Meaning of the Proposal

The parties dispute what the proposal requires with regard to teleworking Union officials. First, the parties dispute whether the proposal requires management to allow Union officials to telework. Second, the parties dispute whether the proposal requires management to allow Union officials to work exclusively on representational duties while teleworking.

When parties dispute the meaning of a proposal, the Authority will examine the wording of the proposal as well as the union's statement of intent. If the union's explanation is consistent with the proposal's plain wording, then the Authority adopts that explanation for the purpose of construing what the proposal means. *Prof'l Airways Sys. Specialists,* 64 FLRA 474, 477 (2010) (citing *AFGE, Local 1900,* 51 FLRA 133, 138-39 (1995)). If the union's statement is not consistent with the wording of the proposal, however, the Authority will not adopt it for the purpose of determining whether the proposal is within the duty to bargain. *Id.* (citing *IFPTE, Local 3,* 51 FLRA 451, 459 (1995)).

First, the proposal's plain wording provides that Union officials are "eligible" for telework. Petition at 3. For an employee to be "eligible" for telework means that an employee is qualified to be chosen for telework.[4] It does not mean that there is a requirement that an employee be assigned to telework. Response at 13. Accordingly, under the proposal's plain wording, anywhere from 0 to 5 Union officials are eligible to be chosen for telework. Further, the Union expressly asserts that all teleworkers, including Union officials, would need to be approved for telework by their supervisors. *Id.* As the Union's statement of intent is consistent with the plain wording of the proposal, we adopt the Union's interpretation of this portion of the proposal. *See AFGE, Local 12*, 60 FLRA 533, 537 (2004).

Second, the proposal's plain wording provides that teleworking Union officials would perform representational duties "not to exceed 20 hours per week per person." Petition at 3. The "not to exceed" language provides a maximum number of hours that the Union officials must be allowed to perform representational duties while teleworking. The proposal does not provide a minimum amount of time that Union officials can spend performing representational duties while teleworking. Further, the Union expressly asserts that the proposal does not preclude the Agency from assigning the Agency's work to the teleworking Union officials, as needed. *See* Response at 15. As the Union's statement of intent with regard to this portion of the proposal is consistent with the proposal's plain wording, we adopt the Union's interpretation of this portion of the proposal.

VII. Analysis and Conclusions

For the reasons set forth below, we find that the proposal is negotiable.

A. The proposal does not affect management rights.

First, the Agency claims that the proposal would affect certain management rights because it would require management to allow Union officials to telework. SOP at 6-11. As discussed above, we find that the proposal does not require the Agency to allow Union officials to telework. Therefore, as the Agency premises its arguments that the proposal is

4. *See Webster's Third New International Dictionary* at 736 (3rd ed. 1986) (defining "eligible" as "fitted or qualified to be chosen").

non-negotiable as affecting its rights to assign and direct employees and its right to determine its organization on a misinterpretation of the proposal, we reject these management rights arguments.

Second, the Agency claims that the proposal would affect certain management rights because it would require management to allow Union officials to work exclusively on representational duties while teleworking. *Id.* at 6-11. As discussed above, we find that the proposal does not require the Agency to allow Union officials to work exclusively on representational duties while teleworking. Therefore, as the Agency premises its arguments that the proposal is non-negotiable as affecting its rights to assign work and determine its budget on a misinterpretation of the proposal, we reject these management rights arguments.

B. The proposal does not violate 5 U.S.C. § 7131.

The Agency claims that the proposal violates 5 U.S.C. § 7131 because it would require management to place Union officials on telework in contravention of the telework law. *See* 5 U.S.C. § 7131.[5] In this regard, the Agency argues that by mandating that the Agency allow Union officials to telework while performing representational duties on official time, the proposal essentially grants the Union officials additional "official time" beyond that which was intended by § 7131. SOP at 15. Consequently, the Agency claims the proposal is non-negotiable. As discussed above, we find that the proposal does not require the Agency to allow Union officials to telework. Therefore, as the Agency premises its argument regarding § 7131 on a misinterpretation of the proposal, we reject the Agency's claim.

C. The proposal concerns a condition of employment.

The Agency claims that the proposal is non-negotiable because it concerns representational duties and, therefore, does not concern "conditions of employment" as that term is defined in § 7103(a)(14) of the Statute. *Id.* at 11-12. Section 7103(a)(14) defines "conditions of employment" as "personnel policies, practices, and matters, whether established by rule, regulation, or otherwise, affecting working conditions . . . ." The proposal pertains to official time, which "shall be considered hours of work." *AFGE, Local 1770,* 64 FLRA 953, 958 (2010) (citing *ACT, Old Hickory Chapter*, 55 FLRA 811, 813 (1999) (quoting 5 C.F.R. § 551.424(b)) (rejecting claim that because a provision pertained to representational duties, the provision did not concern conditions of employment)). Therefore, we reject this argument.

D. The proposal does not violate the Antideficiency Act.

Citing 31 U.S.C. § 1341, the Agency claims that the proposal violates the Antideficiency Act because mandating that the Agency allow Union officials to perform representational duties while on telework will require it to spend appropriated funds on duties that are not the Agency's work. The Antideficiency Act precludes an agency from expending funds: (1) in excess of those appropriated for the fiscal year in which the expenditure is made; and (2) prior to their appropriation. *See* 31 U.S.C. § 1341(a)(1)(A) and (B); *see also AFGE, Local 1770,* 64 FLRA at 957; *Ass'n of Civilian Technicians, Evergreen & Rainier Chapters*, 57 FLRA 475, 483 (2001). The Agency, which did not claim that the proposal would require it to expend funds in excess of its appropriation for a given fiscal year or to expend funds prior to their appropriation, has failed to establish that the proposal is contrary to the Antideficiency Act. Therefore, we reject this argument.

E. The proposal does not violate the telework law.

The Agency argues that the proposal violates the telework law because the telework law does not authorize Union representatives to perform representational duties while teleworking on official time. SOP at 18 (citing *HUD,* 60 FLRA at 313). The Agency further claims that Authority precedent subsequent to *HUD,* holding that the telework law does not prohibit union officials from performing representational duties while teleworking on official time, is inapplicable in this case. *See U.S. Dep't of Agric., Food Safety & Inspection Serv.*, 62 FLRA 364, 367 (2008) (*DOA*); *see also U.S. Envtl. Prot. Agency*, 63 FLRA 30, 33 (2008) (*EPA*) ("§ 359 . . . does not prohibit union representatives from performing representational duties on official time from remote locations"). According to the Agency, those cases do not apply here because they involve instances in which there was a past practice of

5. Under § 7131(d), union representatives in the bargaining unit "shall be granted official time in any amount the agency and the exclusive representative involved agree to be reasonable, necessary, and in the public interest." 5 U.S.C. § 7131(d).

permitting Union officials to perform representational duties while teleworking on official time. SOP at 18-19.

The Agency's position that *DOA* and *EPA* do not apply to this case is incorrect. The Authority's holdings in *DOA* and *EPA* do not depend on the existence of a past practice allowing Union officials to telework on official time. Rather, in those cases, the Authority explained that even though *HUD* held that § 359 does not *require* union officials to be permitted to perform representational duties at home, that does not mean that § 359 *prohibits* parties from agreeing, pursuant to other authority, to contract terms or practices to that effect. *DOA,* 62 FLRA at 367; *EPA*, 63 at 33. Indeed, "the location at which official time is to be exercised" is a mandatory subject of bargaining. *U.S. Dep't of the Air Force, HQ Air Force Materiel Command*, 49 FLRA 1111, 1119 (1994). Thus, consistent with this precedent, we reject this argument.

VIII. Order

The Agency shall, upon request, or as otherwise agreed to by the parties, negotiate over the proposal.

65 FLRA No. 116

NATIONAL ASSOCIATION
OF INDEPENDENT LABOR
LOCAL 15
(Union)

and

UNITED STATES
DEPARTMENT OF THE NAVY
NAVAL SCHOOL EXPLOSIVE
ORDNANCE DISPOSAL
EGLIN AIR FORCE BASE, FLORIDA
(Agency)

0-AR-4687

DECISION

February 25, 2011

Before the Authority: Carol Waller Pope, Chairman, and Thomas M. Beck and Ernest DuBester, Members

I. Statement of the Case

This matter is before the Authority on an exception to an award of Arbitrator Andrew Dixon filed by the Union under § 7122(a) of the Federal Service Labor-Management Relations Statute (the Statute) and part 2425 of the Authority's Regulations. The Agency filed an opposition to the Union's exception.

The Arbitrator found that the grievant was not entitled to a hazard pay differential for performing underwater duties because the hazard that he faced was not listed in Appendix A to 5 C.F.R. part 550, subpart I. Award at 5-6. For the reasons set forth below, we deny the Union's exception.

II. Background and Arbitrator's Award

The grievant works for the Agency as an Explosive Ordnance Disposal Technician Instructor (EOD Instructor). *Id.* at 1-2. As an EOD Instructor, the grievant, among other things, "provides diving instructions in waters that may be murky, have rapid currents, [have] high waves, and may have restricted access to the surface." *Id.* at 2.

The Union presented a grievance on the grievant's behalf, asserting that "he had been denied [a hazard] . . . pay differential for his . . . underwater [duties], equipment and personnel transfers while at sea, and his handling of explosive devices." *See id.* The matter was unresolved and was submitted to arbitration. *Id.*

The principal issues were as follows: "[d]id the [Agency] violate Article 41[,] Section 1 of the Parties [sic] Collective Bargaining Agreement? If so, what should be the remedy?" *Id.* at 1.

The Arbitrator found that the grievant was not entitled to a hazard pay differential for performing underwater duties because the hazard that the grievant faced was not listed in Appendix A to 5 C.F.R. part 550, subpart I.[1] *Id.* at 5-6. The Arbitrator noted that Appendix A allows an employee to receive a hazard pay differential for underwater duty, such as "diving, required in scientific and engineering pursuits, or search and rescue operations, when: (a) at a depth of . . . [twenty feet] or more below the surface; or, (b) visibility is restricted; or, (c) in rapidly flowing or cold water; or, (d) vertical access to the surface is restricted[.]" Appendix A to 5 C.F.R. part 550, subpart I; *see also* Award at 5. The Arbitrator rejected the Union's interpretation of the relevant portion of Appendix A and found that, to be entitled to a hazard pay differential, an employee must not only qualify under (a) or (b) or (c) or (d), but must also be engaged in scientific and engineering pursuits or search and rescue operations while diving. *See* Award at 5. Moreover, the Arbitrator determined that, although the grievant, at times, "dive[d] at depths greater than [twenty] feet, in visibility restricted waters, or in cold or rapidly flowing waters[,]" and his vertical access to the surface was restricted during hull inspections, testimony demonstrated that "the [g]rievant's diving duties [were] not part of scientific and engineering pursuits or search and rescue operations."[2] *Id.* at 4, 5.

III. Positions of the Parties

A. Union's Exception

The Union asserts that the award is contrary to law, rule, or regulation because the Arbitrator failed

1. Pertinent statutory and regulatory provisions are set forth in the attached appendix.

2. The Arbitrator also addressed whether the grievant was entitled to a hazard pay differential for working with explosive devices and for boarding or leaving vessels in adverse conditions. Award at 4, 5-6. Because the Union did not except to the Arbitrator's findings regarding these issues, they are not before us.

correctly to interpret 5 U.S.C. § 5545. Exception at 5-9. The Union claims that the award is contrary to 5 U.S.C. § 5545(d) because the clear intent of the statute is "to pay an employee when exposed to hardship or hazard without concern over the nature of the mission." *Id.* at 5.

Also, the Union asserts that the award is contrary to law, rule, or regulation because the Arbitrator failed correctly to interpret the statute's implementing regulations. *Id.* at 7-8. The Union claims that, under the definition of hazardous duty in 5 C.F.R. § 550.902, the grievant's diving constitutes a hazardous duty because it could result in serious injury or death. *Id.* at 7. According to the Union, the Arbitrator conceded that the grievant dived at depths greater than twenty feet in visibility restricted or in cold or rapidly flowing waters and that, during training for hull inspections, his vertical access to the surface was restricted. *Id.* at 8. Also, the Union claims that the Arbitrator's interpretation of the relevant language in Appendix A is irrational because the hazard at issue here "is in the nature of the dive, not the mission the employee is on" and "[t]he purpose of the [hazard pay] differential is to provide an increase in pay for the exposure to the hazard." *See id.* 7-8. Moreover, the Union asserts that its interpretation of the regulation "is entirely consistent with the statute which makes no reference to the mission and only references the nature of the duties and if they involve physical hardship or hazard." *Id.* at 8. Finally, the Union claims that, in accordance with 5 C.F.R. part 550, subpart I, the grievant participated in the dives only occasionally and that the hazard that the grievant faced while diving was not considered in the classification of his position.[3] *Id.* at 8-9.

B. Agency's Opposition

The Agency argues that the award is not contrary to law, rule, or regulation. Opp'n at 1, 5. The Agency contends that, based on testimony presented, the Arbitrator properly concluded that the grievant was not entitled to a hazard pay differential because the grievant's duties were not listed in Appendix A of the implementing regulations. *See id.* at 2.

Also, the Agency argues that the language of the regulations is clear and unambiguous and that the Union, in its exception, asserts that the regulations' plain language should be ignored. *Id.* at 2, 3. Moreover, the Agency contends that the plain language of the regulations does not conflict with 5 U.S.C. § 5545(d). *Id.* at 3, 5. The Agency argues that "[n]othing in the [statute's] language limits [the Office of Personnel Management (OPM)] from considering the reason that duties are being performed when determining [whether the duty is] hazard[ous]." *Id.* at 5.

The Agency contends that the Union's assertion that "the grievant's diving duty *per se* meets the definition of hazardous duty set forth in 5 C.F.R. [§] 550.902, and that alone causes the grievant to be entitled to [a hazard pay differential]" is without merit. *Id.* at 3-4. According to the Agency, OPM, with the authority granted to it by 5 U.S.C. § 5545, "established the pay schedule set forth in Appendix A of 5 C.F.R. [p]art 550, [s]ubpart I, which provides for [a hazard] pay [differential] when diving is 'required in scientific and engineering pursuits, or search and rescue operations' and certain conditions are present." *Id.* at 4; *see also id.* at 2. Moreover, the Agency argues that the definition of hazardous duty contained in 5 C.F.R. § 550.902 does not confer a right or obligation on employees to receive a hazard pay differential. *Id.* at 4.

Finally, the Agency contends that, with regard to various hazardous duties listed in Appendix A, the mission is directly tied to the requirement for a hazard pay differential. *Id.* According to the Agency, "it make[s] sense that dives of [twenty] feet or more might be more hazardous in a search and rescue situation than they would be in a controlled training environment." *Id.* at 5.

IV. Analysis and Conclusion

When an exception involves an award's consistency with law, the Authority reviews any question of law raised by the exception and the award *de novo*. *See NTEU, Chapter 24*, 50 FLRA 330, 332 (1995) (citing *U.S. Customs Serv. v. FLRA*, 43 F.3d 682, 686-87 (D.C. Cir. 1994)). In applying the standard of *de novo* review, the Authority assesses whether an arbitrator's legal conclusions are consistent with the applicable standard of law. *See U.S. Dep't of Def., Dep'ts of the Army & the Air Force, Ala. Nat'l Guard, Northport, Ala.*, 55 FLRA 37, 40 (1998). In making that assessment, the Authority defers to the arbitrator's underlying factual findings. *See id.*

3. The Union notes that, at arbitration, the Agency argued that the hazards faced by the grievant were included in the classification of his position and that the Arbitrator did not reach this issue in his award. Exception at 8.

The threshold requirements for an employee's entitlement to a hazard pay differential originate from a statutory mandate, as well as government regulation. *U.S. DOJ, Fed. Bureau of Prisons, Fed. Corr. Complex, Tucson, Ariz.*, 65 FLRA 267, 270 (2010) (*Fed. Corr. Complex, Tucson*); *U.S. Dep't of the Army, Alaska*, 54 FLRA 1117, 1122 (1998); *see also* 5 U.S.C. § 5545 & 5 C.F.R. part 550, subpart I. As relevant here, a grievant must satisfy three requirements before he or she is entitled to a hazard pay differential: (1) the hazard or physical hardship must not have been considered in the classification of his position pursuant to 5 U.S.C. § 5545(d); (2) the hazard or physical hardship must be listed in Appendix A to 5 C.F.R. part 500; and (3) he or she must be performing a hazardous duty within the definition of 5 C.F.R. § 550.902. *Fed. Corr. Complex, Tucson*, 65 FLRA at 270; *U.S. Dep't of the Army, Alaska*, 54 FLRA at 1122; *U.S. Dep't of the Navy, Glenview Naval Air Station, Glenview, Ill.*, 48 FLRA 1420, 1429-30 (1994).

Hazard pay differentials are based on a schedule established by OPM and set forth in Appendix A to 5 C.F.R. part 550, subpart I. *NTEU, NTEU Chapter 51*, 40 FLRA 614, 621 (1991); 5 C.F.R. § 550.903(a) (noting that "[a] schedule of hazard pay differentials, the hazardous duties or duties involving physical hardship for which they are payable, and the period during which they are payable is set out as appendix A to this subpart and incorporated in and made a part of this section"). 5 C.F.R. § 550.904 states, in pertinent part, that "[a]n agency shall pay the hazard pay differential listed in appendix A of this subpart to an employee who is assigned to and performs any duty specified in appendix A of this subpart." *Id.* The Authority has found that, in order for an employee to receive a hazard pay differential, the hazardous duties that the employee performs must be included in Appendix A. *See VAMC, Leavenworth, Kan.*, 35 FLRA 14, 17 (1990).

The Union's claim that the award is contrary to 5 U.S.C. § 5545(d) is without merit. Although that provision provides for the establishment and payment of differentials for certain duties, it does not address or require the payment of a hazard differential for the underwater duty involved in this case. *See U.S. Dep't of the Interior, Bureau of Land Mgmt., Eugene Dist. Office*, 43 FLRA 761, 764 (1991) (*U.S. Dep't of the Interior*) (rejecting the union's contention that the award conflicted with 5 U.S.C. § 5545(d) because the statute did not address or require the payment of a hazard differential for the firefighting duties involved in the case). Consequently, the Union's claim provides no basis for finding the award deficient.

Similarly, the Union's assertion that the award conflicts with the implementing regulations is meritless. The Arbitrator determined that Appendix A only specifies diving as a hazardous duty when it is "required in scientific and engineering pursuits, or search and rescue operations[.]" Award at 5. The Arbitrator found that "the [g]rievant's diving duties [were] not part of scientific and engineering pursuits or search and rescue operations." *Id.* at 4, 5. Consequently, because the hazard that the grievant faced was not listed in Appendix A, the Arbitrator concluded that he was not entitled to a hazard pay differential. *Id.* at 5-6.

Although the Union's interpretation of these regulations differs from the Arbitrator's interpretation, the Union's assertions do not prove that the Arbitrator's interpretation conflicts with the plain wording of the regulations or is otherwise impermissible. *See U.S. Dep't of the Interior*, 43 FLRA at 764 (determining that, under § 7122(a) of the Statute, an award is deficient if the arbitrator's interpretation of a regulation conflicts with the plain wording of that regulation or is otherwise impermissible). Moreover, given the Arbitrator's underlying factual findings, which are undisputed and to which we defer, his legal conclusion that the grievant was precluded from obtaining a hazard pay differential because the underwater duty he performed was not listed in Appendix A to 5 C.F.R. part 550 is consistent with the applicable regulations. Finally, even assuming that the grievant participated in dives only occasionally and that the hazard that the grievant faced while diving was not considered in the classification of his position, the grievant would not be entitled to a hazard pay differential because the test, as noted above, mandates that the hazard faced by a grievant be included in Appendix A. *See Fed. Corr. Complex, Tucson*, 65 FLRA at 270; *U.S. Dep't of the Army, Alaska*, 54 FLRA at 1122; *VAMC, Leavenworth, Kan.*, 35 FLRA at 17 (upholding the arbitrator's determination that there was no entitlement to hazard pay because Appendix A did not list the item for which the hazard pay was sought). Consequently, the Union has failed to demonstrate that the award is deficient as contrary to 5 C.F.R. part 550, subpart I and Appendix A.

Accordingly, we deny the Union's exception.

V. Decision

The Union's exception is denied.

APPENDIX

5 U.S.C. § 5545(d), titled "Night, standby, irregular, and hazardous duty differential[,]" states, in pertinent part:

> The Office shall establish a schedule or schedules of pay differentials for duty involving unusual physical hardship or hazard . . . .

5 C.F.R. § 550.902, titled "Definitions[,]" states, in pertinent part:

> *Hazardous duty* means duty performed under circumstances in which an accident could result in serious injury or death . . . .

5 C.F.R. § 550.903, titled "Establishment of hazard pay differentials[,]" states, in pertinent part:

> (a) A schedule of hazard pay differentials, the hazardous duties or duties involving physical hardship for which they are payable, and the period during which they are payable is set out as appendix A to this subpart and incorporated in and made a part of this section.

5 C.F.R. § 550.904, titled "Authorization of hazard pay differential[,]" states, in pertinent part:

> (a) An agency shall pay the hazard pay differential listed in appendix A of this subpart to an employee who is assigned to and performs any duty specified in appendix A of this subpart. However, hazard pay differential may not be paid to an employee when the hazardous duty or physical hardship has been taken into account in the classification of his or her position, without regard to whether the hazardous duty or physical hardship is grade controlling . . . .

Appendix A to Part 550, Subpart I, titled "Schedule of Pay Differentials Authorized for Hazardous Duty Under Subpart I[,]" states, in pertinent part:

> Underwater Duty:
>
> (2) Diving. Diving, including SCUBA (self-contained underwater breathing apparatus) diving, required in scientific and engineering pursuits, or search and rescue operations, when:
>
> (a) at a depth of . . . [twenty feet] or more below the surface; or,
>
> (b) visibility is restricted; or,
>
> (c) in rapidly flowing or cold water; or,
>
> (d) vertical access to the surface is restricted by ice, rock, or other structure . . . .

65 FLRA No. 117

AMERICAN FEDERATION
OF GOVERNMENT EMPLOYEES
LOCAL 2923
(Union)

and

UNITED STATES
DEPARTMENT OF HEALTH AND
HUMAN SERVICES
NATIONAL INSTITUTE OF ENVIRONMENTAL
HEALTH SCIENCES
RESEARCH TRIANGLE PARK,
NORTH CAROLINA
(Agency)

0-AR-4443

DECISION

February 25, 2011

Before the Authority: Carol Waller Pope, Chairman, and Thomas M. Beck and Ernest DuBester, Members

I. Statement of the Case

This matter is before the Authority on exceptions to an award of Arbitrator Rochelle K. Kaplan filed by the Union under § 7122(a) of the Federal Service Labor-Management Relations Statute (the Statute) and part 2425 of the Authority's Regulations. The Agency filed an opposition to the Union's exceptions.

The Arbitrator found that the Agency had just cause to suspend the grievant based on an e-mail that he sent to several individuals, including individuals who were not Agency employees. For the reasons that follow, we dismiss in part, and deny in part, the Union's exceptions.

II. Background and Arbitrator's Award

When the Agency notified an employee (the employee) that it was terminating her, the employee notified the grievant, who is the Union Vice President. *See* Award at 2. Subsequently, the grievant e-mailed several individuals, including individuals who were not Agency employees. *See id.* The e-mail stated, in pertinent part, that "[t]here has seemingly been a long[,] continuous road of retaliation, discrimination, and injury against [the employee] by her current supervisor," *id.*, and described an exchange between the employee and her supervisor as a "blatantly and purposely humbling, racist, and unkind event[,]" *id.* at 3. The grievant signed the e-mail with his name and Union title. *See id.*

Based on this e-mail, the Agency suspended the grievant for fourteen days for "Making False and/or Malicious Statements Which Harm or Destroy the Reputation, Authority or Official Standing of an [Agency] Official." *Id.* A grievance was filed, and when the grievance was unresolved, it was submitted to arbitration. *See id.*

At arbitration, the Agency agreed to the Union's proposed issue statement, which the Arbitrator set forth as follows: "Whether the [fourteen]-day suspension of the [g]rievant was for just and sufficient cause? If not[,] what shall be the remedy?" *Id.* at 4. The Arbitrator noted that the grievance alleged that the suspension "violated various contractual and statutory provisions[,]" *id.* at 3, and then stated:

> Since the Union proffered and the Agency accepted the statement of the issue as simply just and sufficient cause for the suspension, the various statutory and contractual claims will not be addressed as they are deemed waived by the Union. To the extent that the Union has raised certain affirmative defenses to the discipline, among them being that the [g]rievant was acting as a [U]nion official when he sent out the e-mail, the Arbitrator will address the affirmative defenses.

Id. at 3 n.3.

The Arbitrator found that the e-mail "contain[ed] false or incorrect statements and/or statements made with reckless indifference to whether they were true or not." *Id.* at 28. The Arbitrator also found that "[t]he distribution of the e-mail to [several] individuals who had no need to know is evidence of his intention to harm the reputation of [the employee's supervisor] and the Agency[,]" and that the grievant "offered no other plausible explanation for broadcasting the e-mail to them." *Id.* The Arbitrator determined that the Agency proved its charges against the grievant. *See id.* at 29.

Next, the Arbitrator addressed the Union's affirmative defenses, including the Union's claim that the grievant was acting in his official Union capacity when he sent the e-mail. *See id.* at 32. The Arbitrator acknowledged that the grievant signed the e-mail by his name and Union title, but found that "merely signing it in that manner does not make it Union business or protected Union activity." *Id.* In this regard, the Arbitrator determined that "[t]he e-mail was not sent as a result of any ongoing labor/management dispute over the termination procedures[,]" and concluded that "the [g]rievant did not send the e-mail to [several outside] individuals for a valid Union purpose." *Id.* In addition, the Arbitrator stated that "Union [c]ounsel conceded at the hearing" that the Authority's "flagrant misconduct" test set forth in *Department of the Air Force, Grissom Air Force Base, Indiana*, 51 FLRA 7 (1995), "was not the standard to be used in assessing the [g]rievant's conduct, but then argued that it was the standard in her brief." Award at 32 & n.7. The Arbitrator then stated that "[e]ven using" that standard, "the [g]rievant's e-mail does not pass muster as proper Union conduct." *Id.* at 32. Thus, the Arbitrator rejected the Union's affirmative defenses, but concluded that, based on the nature of the offense, the grievant's years of service, and consistency with the Agency's Table of Penalties and other, similar offenses, the fourteen-day suspension was excessive and should be reduced to a seven-day suspension. *See id.* at 34.

III. Positions of the Parties

A. Union's Exceptions

The Union argues that the grievant's e-mail was protected speech under the First Amendment to the United States Constitution and that the Arbitrator erred by not applying the analysis set forth in *Pickering v. Board of Education*, 391 U.S. 563, 568 (1968) (*Pickering*), for assessing whether a government employer has violated an employee's free-speech rights. *See* Exceptions at 9-13. The Union also argues that the Arbitrator's finding that the grievant engaged in flagrant misconduct is contrary to law. *See id.* at 15-19.

Additionally, the Union contends that the Arbitrator's finding that the e-mail constituted flagrant misconduct is based on a nonfact. *See id.* at 14. In this connection, the Union asserts that it argued to the Arbitrator that "the flagrant misconduct standard was not applicable in this case, and that, even if it was, the [g]rievant's e-mail did not rise to the level of flagrant misconduct." *Id.* Further, the Union asserts that, at arbitration, "the Agency conceded" that the grievant did not engage in flagrant misconduct, and that the award is based on a nonfact because "the Arbitrator created a dispute of fact where there was none." *Id.*

B. Agency's Opposition

The Agency argues that, under 5 C.F.R. § 2429.5,[1] the Authority should dismiss the Union's exception regarding *Pickering* because the Union did not argue, before the Arbitrator, that the grievant's speech was protected under the First Amendment. *See* Opp'n at 5-6. Alternatively, the Agency argues that the exception should be denied on the merits. *See id.* at 7. In addition, the Agency contends that the Arbitrator's finding of flagrant misconduct is not contrary to law. *See id.* at 10-11. Further, the Agency asserts that the finding of flagrant misconduct is not based on a nonfact, and disputes the Union's claim that it conceded, before the Arbitrator, that the grievant had not engaged in flagrant misconduct. *See id.* at 8-9.

IV. Preliminary Issue

The Authority's Regulations that were in effect when the Union filed its exceptions provided that "[t]he Authority will not consider . . . any issue[] which was not presented in the proceedings before the . . . arbitrator." 5 C.F.R. § 2429.5 (§ 2429.5).[2] Under § 2429.5, the Authority will not consider any issue that could have been, but was not, presented to the arbitrator. *E.g., U.S. DHS, U.S. Customs & Border Prot., JFK Airport, Queens, N.Y.*, 62 FLRA 416, 417 (2008).

There is no evidence that the Union argued before the Arbitrator that the grievant's speech was protected under the First Amendment, or that the Arbitrator was required to apply a *Pickering* analysis. The Union could have done so. Therefore, consistent with § 2429.5, we dismiss the Union's exception regarding the *Pickering* analysis.

---

1. The pertinent wording of 5 C.F.R. § 2429.5 is set forth below.

2. The Authority's Regulations concerning the review of arbitration awards, as well as certain related procedural regulations, including § 2429.5, were revised effective October 1, 2010. *See* 75 Fed. Reg. 42,283 (2010). As the Union's exceptions were filed before that date, we apply the earlier Regulations.

V. Analysis and Conclusions

A. The award is not contrary to law.

The Union alleges that the Arbitrator's finding of flagrant misconduct is contrary to law. The Authority reviews questions of law de novo. *See NTEU, Chapter 24*, 50 FLRA 330, 332 (1995) (citing *U.S. Customs Serv. v. FLRA*, 43 F.3d 682, 686-87 (D.C. Cir. 1994)). In applying a standard of de novo review, the Authority determines whether the arbitrator's legal conclusions are consistent with the applicable standard of law. *NFFE, Local 1437*, 53 FLRA 1703, 1710 (1998) (*Local 1437*). In making that determination, the Authority defers to the arbitrator's underlying factual findings. *See id.*

The flagrant misconduct standard applies in cases where an agency is alleged to have violated § 7116 of the Statute by taking actions against an individual based on that individual's actions during the course of protected activity.[3] *See U.S. Dep't of Transp., FAA*, 64 FLRA 365, 369 (2009) (Member Beck concurring). Specifically, where an agency is alleged to have committed an unfair labor practice (ULP) on this basis, "a necessary part of the [agency's] defense" against the ULP allegation is that the individual's actions constituted flagrant misconduct or otherwise exceeded the bounds of protected activity. *Id.*

The Authority has held that arbitrators are required to apply statutory burdens of proof when resolving an alleged ULP. *E.g., U.S. GSA, Ne. & Caribbean Region, N.Y., N.Y.*, 60 FLRA 864, 866 (2005). By contrast, where an arbitrator resolves a claim under a collective bargaining agreement (CBA) rather than a statutory claim, "unless a specific burden of proof is required, an arbitrator may establish and apply whatever burden the arbitrator considers appropriate . . . ." *Id.* In this connection, the Authority distinguishes allegations that an agency lacked just cause for discipline under a CBA from allegations of unlawful interference with protected rights under the Statute. *See NAGE, Local R3-32*, 59 FLRA 458, 459 (2003) (Chairman Cabaniss concurring) (where parties stipulated a just-cause issue, Authority declined to consider claim of alleged violation of § 7102(a) of the Statute that was not raised before arbitrator). In addition, when an arbitrator is not required to apply a statutory standard, alleged misapplications of that standard do not provide a basis for finding the arbitrator's award deficient. *E.g., SSA*, 65 FLRA 286, 288 (2010).

Here, the Arbitrator found, and there is no dispute, that the Union "waived" any statutory claims, Award at 3 n.3, and that the issue before the Arbitrator was whether there was "just and sufficient cause" for the suspension, *id.* at 4 -- not whether the suspension violated § 7116 of the Statute. As such, the Arbitrator was not required to apply statutory standards, and the Arbitrator's alleged misapplication of the flagrant misconduct standard does not provide a basis for setting aside the award. *See SSA*, 65 FLRA at 288. Accordingly, we deny the exception.

B. The award is not based on a nonfact.

To establish that an award is based on a nonfact, the appealing party must show that a central fact underlying the award is clearly erroneous, but for which the arbitrator would have reached a different result. *E.g., U.S. Dep't of the Air Force, Lowry Air Force Base, Denver, Colo.*, 48 FLRA 589, 593 (1993). However, the Authority will not find an award deficient on the basis of an arbitrator's determination of any factual matter that the parties disputed at arbitration. *Id.* at 594. Further, where the premise of a nonfact exception is erroneous, the Authority denies the exception. *See U.S. DHS, Customs & Border Prot. Agency, N.Y., N.Y.*, 60 FLRA 813, 817 (2005) (*CBP NY*).

The Union's nonfact exception is premised on the Union's claim that the Agency conceded at arbitration that the grievant did not engage in flagrant misconduct. For support, the Union cites the transcript of the arbitration hearing, at which the Agency asserted that it was "not in agreement" that the flagrant misconduct standard was "applicable in this case." Exceptions, Attach., Tr. at 7. As the Agency argues in its opposition, and contrary to the Union's claim, the cited portions of the transcript do not demonstrate that the Agency conceded that the grievant's actions were not flagrant misconduct. As such, the premise of the Union's nonfact exception is erroneous, and we deny the exception. *See CBP NY*, 60 FLRA at 817.

VI. Decision

The Union's exceptions are dismissed in part and denied in part.

3. Section 7116(a)(2) of the Statute provides, in pertinent part, that it is an unfair labor practice for an agency "to encourage or discourage membership in any labor organization by discrimination in connection with hiring, tenure, promotion, or other conditions of employment[.]"

65 FLRA No. 118

AMERICAN FEDERATION
OF GOVERNMENT EMPLOYEES
LOCAL 0405
(Union)

and

UNITED STATES
DEPARTMENT OF JUSTICE
FEDERAL BUREAU OF PRISONS
FEDERAL CORRECTIONAL COMPLEX
BUTNER, NORTH CAROLINA
(Agency)

0-AR-4710

DECISION

February 25, 2011

Before the Authority: Carol Waller Pope, Chairman, and Thomas M. Beck and Ernest DuBester, Members

This matter is before the Authority on exceptions to an award of Arbitrator J. Douglas Hagewood filed by the Union under § 7122(a) of the Federal Service Labor-Management Relations Statute (the Statute) and part 2425 of the Authority's Regulations. The Agency filed an opposition to the Union's exceptions.

Under § 7122(a) of the Statute, an award is deficient if it is contrary to any law, rule, or regulation, or it is deficient on other grounds similar to those applied by federal courts in private sector labor-management relations. Upon careful consideration of the entire record in this case and Authority precedent, the Authority concludes that the award is not deficient on the grounds raised in the exceptions and set forth in § 7122(a). *See U.S. Dep't of Veterans Affairs, Med. Ctr., N. Chi., Ill.*, 52 FLRA 387, 398 (1996) (award not deficient because of bias on the part of an arbitrator where excepting party fails to demonstrate that the award was procured by improper means, that there was partiality or corruption on the part of the arbitrator, or that the arbitrator engaged in misconduct that prejudiced the rights of the party); *Prof'l Airways Sys. Specialists, Dist. No. 1, MEBA/NMU (AFL-CIO)*, 48 FLRA 764, 768-69 (1993) (award not deficient as contrary to law where excepting party fails to establish that the award is in any manner contrary to the law, rule, or regulation on which the party relies); *U.S. Dep't of the Navy, Long Beach Naval Shipyard, Long Beach, Cal.*, 48 FLRA 612, 618-19 (1993) (award not deficient as contrary to public policy where excepting party fails to establish that the award violates an explicit public policy based on well-defined and dominant laws and legal precedents); *U.S. Dep't of Labor (OSHA)*, 34 FLRA 573, 575 (1990) (award not deficient as failing to draw its essence from the parties' collective bargaining agreement where excepting party fails to establish that the award cannot in any rational way be derived from the agreement; is so unfounded in reason and fact and so unconnected to the wording and purpose of the agreement as to manifest an infidelity to the obligation of the arbitrator; does not represent a plausible interpretation of the agreement; or evidences a manifest disregard of the agreement).

Accordingly, the Union's exceptions are denied.

65 FLRA No. 119

UNITED STATES
DEPARTMENT OF THE ARMY
FORT CARSON, COLORADO
(Agency)

and

AMERICAN FEDERATION
OF GOVERNMENT EMPLOYEES
LOCAL 1345
(Union)

0-AR-4711

DECISION

February 25, 2011

Before the Authority: Carol Waller Pope, Chairman, and Thomas M. Beck and Ernest DuBester, Members

I. Statement of the Case

This matter is before the Authority on an exception to an award of Arbitrator Dorothy A. Fallon filed by the Agency under § 7122(a) of the Federal Service Labor- Management Relations Statute (the Statute) and part 2425 of the Authority's Regulations. The Union did not file an opposition to the Agency's exception.

The Arbitrator found that: (1) the Agency did not have just cause to issue the grievant a Letter of Reprimand and (2) the Agency had not issued the Letter of Reprimand within a reasonable period of time after the occurrence of the alleged offense. Award at 11-14. Accordingly, she ordered that: (1) the Letter of Reprimand be removed from the grievant's personnel file and (2) the Agency pay the grievant the "lost overtime and premium pay [that the grievant] would likely have earned for the period from [the date that the letter should have issued] up to the date he was returned to his normal assignments." *Id.* at 14. For the reasons set forth below, we deny the Agency's exception.

II. Background and Arbitrator's Award

The grievant, a civilian police officer, works in the Department of Emergency Services at Fort Carson, Colorado. *Id.* at 2. The grievant's assignments primarily involve escorting Absent Without Leave (AWOL) military personnel to their required locations. *Id.* During one such assignment, the person whom the grievant was escorting escaped. *Id.* at 5-6.

The Agency conducted an investigation into the incident. *Id.* at 6-7. While the incident was being investigated, the grievant "was assigned to administrative duties and restricted from his normal prisoner transport duties." *Id.* at 7. After completing its investigation, the Agency drafted a Letter of Reprimand in late November; however, the letter was not finalized and issued to the grievant until early January. *Id.* at 6-7. The grievant was then returned to his prisoner transport duties. *Id.* at 13.

The Union presented a grievance alleging that the Letter of Reprimand was not issued for just cause and that the Agency committed "an unjust and unwarranted action" by removing the grievant from his normal duties for three months before issuing the letter. *Id.* at 7. The grievance was unresolved and submitted to arbitration. *Id.* at 1-2. The issue before the Arbitrator was: "Did the Agency have just cause to issue a Letter of Reprimand when it did so [in January]? If not, what shall be the remedy?" *Id.* at 2.

The Arbitrator determined that the Agency failed to prove that the grievant had acted improperly during his transport of the prisoner. *Id.* at 11. The Arbitrator also found that the Agency violated Article 20, Section 2 of the parties' agreement, which requires that "'[]notices will be given to the employee within a reasonable period of time after the occurrence of the alleged offense[.]'" *Id.* at 11-12 (quoting parties' agreement). The Arbitrator found that the record showed that the investigation and draft Letter of Reprimand were completed by the last week in November; however, the grievant was not issued the letter until early January. *Id.* at 12. The Arbitrator found that the grievant's "discipline was delayed for no acceptable reason and caused [the grievant] harm beyond the" letter itself – "a more punitive financial result." *Id.* at 12-13.

In this regard, the Arbitrator found that, had the grievant been issued the letter in late November -- "a reasonable period from the date" of the incident -- "he would have been returned to his normal duties" and worked the "typical overtime required of all members of the unit." *Id.* at 13; *see also id.* at 7 (noting that grievant's assignment to administrative duties "resulted in his loss of all overtime opportunities while awaiting a decision on the level of discipline being imposed for the incident"). Although noting that overtime is not "guaranteed," the Arbitrator found that "officers of the AWOL unit are regularly required to transport prisoners over great distances, make regular determinations about how to go about their duties, and are regularly required to work beyond a normal forty-hour week." *Id.* at 13.

Accordingly, the Arbitrator sustained the grievance and ordered that: (1) the Letter of Reprimand be removed from the grievant's personnel file and (2) the Agency pay the grievant the "lost overtime and premium pay [that the grievant] would likely have earned for the period from [the date that the letter should have issued] up to the date he was returned to his normal assignments." *Id.* at 14.

III. Agency's Exception

The Agency contends that the award is contrary to the Back Pay Act, excepting only to "the [A]rbitrator's award of an undetermined quantum of back overtime and premium pay for lost opportunity, rather than for any overtime actually worked."* Exception at 3. The Agency notes that an award of backpay is authorized under the Back Pay Act only when an arbitrator finds that: (1) an employee was "affected by an unwarranted personnel action" and (2) the "unwarranted action directly resulted in the withdrawal or reduction of overtime pay that the employee[] would otherwise have received." *Id.* at 3 (quoting *Immigration & Naturalization Serv., U.S. Dep't of Justice,* 18 FLRA 412, 414 (1985)).

The Agency contends that, because the Arbitrator "did not find that the grievant would have been offered specific overtime assignments[,]" or that, even if he had been offered the work, he "would have been available to perform it or would have worked the amount of time necessary to receive overtime pay during the relevant time period[,]" the award of overtime pay fails to satisfy the second requirement of the Back Pay Act. *Id.* Citing *United States Department of Justice, Federal Bureau of Prisons, Federal Correctional Complex, Beaumont, Texas*, 59 FLRA 466, 467-68 (2003) (*Beaumont*); *United States Department of the Air Force, Warner Robins Air Force Base, Georgia,* 56 FLRA 541, 543 (2000) *(Warner Robins), American Federation of Government Employees, Local 1857*, 35 FLRA 325, 328 (1990) (*AFGE, Local,1857*)), *Navy Public Works Center, Norfolk, Virginia,* 33 FLRA 592, 599 (1988) (*Navy Public Works*), the Agency maintains that such findings "are precisely those that would be required for the Authority to sustain the [A]rbitrator's award of back overtime or premium pay." *Id.* at 3-4.

IV. The award is not contrary to the Back Pay Act.

When an exception involves an award's consistency with law, the Authority reviews any question of law raised by the exception and the award de novo. *See NTEU, Chapter 24*, 50 FLRA 330, 332 (1995) (citing *U.S. Customs Serv. v. FLRA*, 43 F.3d 682, 686-87 (D.C. Cir. 1994)). In applying the standard of de novo review, the Authority assesses whether an arbitrator's legal conclusions are consistent with the applicable standard of law. *See U.S. Dep't of Def., Dep'ts of the Army & the Air Force, Ala. Nat'l Guard, Northport, Ala.*, 55 FLRA 37, 40 (1998). In making that assessment, the Authority defers to the arbitrator's underlying factual findings. *See id.*

An award of backpay is authorized under the Back Pay Act only when an arbitrator finds that: (1) the aggrieved employee was affected by an unjustified and unwarranted personnel action and (2) the personnel action resulted in the withdrawal or the reduction of an employee's pay, allowances, or differentials. *See Warner Robins*, 56 FLRA at 543 (citing *U.S. Dep't of Health & Human Servs.,* 54 FLRA 1210, 1218-19 (1998)).

The Agency contends that the award fails to satisfy the second requirement of the Back Pay Act because the Arbitrator "did not find that the grievant would have been offered specific overtime assignments[,]" or that, even if he had been offered the work, he "would have been available to perform it or would have worked the amount of time necessary to receive overtime pay during the relevant time period." Exception at 3.

---

*. The Agency refers to the "back overtime and premium pay" awarded by the Arbitrator as "overtime pay." Exception at 3.

A violation of a collective bargaining agreement constitutes an unjustified or unwarranted personnel action under the Act. *See U.S. Dep't of Def., Dep't of Def. Dependents Sch.*, 54 FLRA 773, 785 (1998)). The Agency fails to challenge the Arbitrator's finding that it violated Article 20, Section 2 of the parties' agreement by delaying issuance of the Letter of Reprimand. *See* Award at 11-12. Accordingly, we find that the award satisfies the first requirement of the Back Pay Act.

The Arbitrator also found that the unwarranted and unjustified personnel action resulted in a reduction of the grievant's pay. *See id.* at 13. Although the Arbitrator did not enumerate the exact amount of the loss incurred by the grievant, the Arbitrator did find that the Agency's delay in issuing the letter "caused [the grievant] harm beyond" the letter itself -- "a more punitive financial result." *Id.* In this regard, the Arbitrator found that, had the grievant been issued the letter in late November, "he would have been returned to his normal duties" and worked the "typical overtime required of all members of the unit." *Id.*; *see also id.* at 7 (noting that grievant's assignment to administrative duties "resulted in his loss of all overtime opportunities while awaiting a decision on the level of discipline being imposed for the incident"). Moreover, although noting that overtime is not "guaranteed," the Arbitrator found that "officers of the AWOL unit are regularly required to transport prisoners over great distances, make regular determinations about how to go about their duties, and are regularly required to work beyond a normal forty-hour week." *Id.* at 13. These findings indicate that the Arbitrator found that the Agency's unjustified personnel action resulted in a loss of pay to the grievant. *See U.S. Dep't of the Air Force, Tinker Air Force Base, Okla. City, Okla.*, 63 FLRA 59 (2008) (arbitrator's finding that the unwarranted and unjustified personnel action resulted in grievant's loss of pay was sufficient to satisfy the requirement under the Back Pay Act).

Further, because the Arbitrator conditioned an award of backpay on the existence of a causal connection as required by the Back Pay Act, the award is unlike the awards in *Beaumont*, 59 FLRA at 468, *Warner Robins*, 56 FLRA at 543, *AFGE, Local 1857*, 35 FLRA at 328, and *Navy Public Works*, 33 FLRA at 599, where the arbitrators awarded backpay without finding the causal connection required under the Back Pay Act. Accordingly, we find that the Arbitrator's award satisfies the second requirement of the Back Pay Act.

Moreover, an employee is only entitled to receive compensation "equal to all or any part of the pay, allowances, or differentials, as applicable, which the employee normally would have earned or received during the period if the personnel action had not occurred[.]" 5 U.S.C. § 5596(b)(1)(A)(i). The Arbitrator's award provides that the grievant should be paid for the loss of any "overtime and premium pay he would likely have earned" due to the Agency's delay in the issuing the Letter of Reprimand. Award at 14. The award, thus, does not provide that the grievant be compensated for any losses not actually sustained as a result of the Agency's unjustified action.

Accordingly, we find that the Agency has failed to demonstrate that the Arbitrator's award violates the Back Pay Act and deny the Agency's exception.

V. Decision

The Agency's exception is denied.

65 FLRA No. 120

UNITED STATES
DEPARTMENT OF HEALTH
AND HUMAN SERVICES
SUBSTANCE ABUSE AND MENTAL
HEALTH SERVICES ADMINISTRATION
(Agency)

and

NATIONAL TREASURY
EMPLOYEES UNION
(Union)

0-AR-4626

DECISION

February 28, 2011

Before the Authority: Carol Waller Pope, Chairman, and Thomas M. Beck and Ernest DuBester, Members

I. Statement of the Case

This matter is before the Authority on exceptions to an award of Arbitrator Irwin Kaplan filed by the Agency under § 7122(a) of the Federal Service Labor-Management Relations Statute (the Statute) and part 2425 of the Authority's Regulations. The Union filed an opposition to the Agency's exceptions.

The Arbitrator determined that the Agency improperly rated the grievant's job performance. Award at 19, 20-22, 25-26. As a result, he canceled the Agency's ratings of two critical elements and ordered the Agency to raise those ratings to "exceptional."[1] *Id.* For the reasons set forth below, we deny the Agency's exceptions.

II. Background and Arbitrator's Award

The Agency utilizes a four-tier rating system to review its employees' annual performance. *Id.* at 2 n.4, 3. Under the four-tier system, employees are rated on various elements critical to their positions and then given an overall rating of exceptional, fully successful, minimally successful, or unacceptable. *See id.* at 2 n.4, 3-4.

The grievant works for the Agency as a General Schedule (GS)-14 statistician. *Id.* at 3. During the performance period in question, the grievant received only positive feedback from her first-line supervisor, was commended on the quality of the quarterly reports that she produced, and was awarded a Superior Internal Service Award. *Id.* at 5. At the end of the performance period, the grievant's first-line supervisor gave the grievant an exceptional rating on critical Element 2, a rating of fully successful on the remaining elements, and an overall performance rating of fully successful.[2] *Id.* According to the grievant's first-line supervisor, her "reports and work on certain projects did not show . . . sufficient innovation or creativity to warrant an exceptional rating for Elements 1 ("Transform the Healthcare System") and 4 (Collaborative Work Relationship)." *Id.* at 8. With regard to Element 3, the grievant's first-line supervisor rated her performance as fully successful because she did not thoroughly check errors on one of her reports and "did not 'do [anything] beyond her regular assignment of doing a regular statistical budget . . . and taking the lead on the quarterly reports' to warrant an exceptional rating[.]"[3] *Id.* (quoting Tr. at 207).

1. The critical elements used to evaluate the grievant's performance are as follows:

> (Element 1) Transform the Healthcare System; (Element 2) Lead and enhance [Center for Substance Abuse Treatment (CSAT)] projects and activities related to State performance management data systems development, [National Outcome Measures (NOMS)] reporting, and electronic health record (EHR); (Element 3) Services as CSAT statistical and data expert; (Element 4) Teamwork, Personal Growth, Collaboration; (Element 5) Program Management of Contracts[;] . . . and . . . (Element 6) Procurement Planning and Award Phase.

Award at 4 n.5.

2. During the previous rating period, the grievant received an exceptional rating on critical Element 4, a rating of fully successful on the remaining elements, and an overall fully successful rating. *Id.* at 3-4. After receiving the performance appraisal, the grievant met with her first-line supervisor and second-line supervisor to determine how she could receive a higher performance rating in the future. *Id.* at 4.

3. The grievant's second-line supervisor believed that the grievant deserved an exceptional rating on Element 3 because the work that she did on the quarterly reports went above and beyond what was expected of her. *Id.* at 8. At the second stage of the grievance procedure, the grievant's

The grievant was disappointed with her performance appraisal and met with her first-line supervisor to discuss what she could have done differently to have received a higher performance rating. *Id.* at 4, 5-6. According to the grievant, her first-line supervisor did not give her any constructive feedback during the meeting, and a follow-up meeting was canceled at the grievant's request because her first-line supervisor would not allow a Union representative to be present at the meeting. *Id.* at 6.

The Union presented a grievance over the grievant's performance appraisal. *Id.* at 4. The matter was unresolved and was submitted to arbitration. The principal issues were: (1) whether the Agency properly evaluated the grievant's performance in accordance with Article 30 of the parties' agreement . . . ?[4] (2) If so, what shall be the remedy?[5] *Id.* at 2-3.

The Arbitrator determined that the grievant was entitled to an exceptional rating for Element 4 and that the Agency's rating should be canceled. *Id.* at 21-22, 25. The Arbitrator found that, by not issuing the grievant an exceptional rating for Element 4, the Agency violated Article 30 of the parties' agreement. *Id.* at 21, 25. The Arbitrator noted that "Article 30, Section 6 of the [parties' agreement] mandates that 'when there is sufficient indication that performance is below the expected level, additional steps including meetings should be taken to provide feedback.'" *Id.* at 21. The Arbitrator determined that, "[g]iven the importance that [the grievant] conveyed to both [her first-line and second-line supervisors] in terms of getting an exceptional rating, the [A]gency was on notice of her expectation, particularly with regard to this element where the previous year the [g]rievant received an exceptional rating." *Id.* Moreover, the Arbitrator found that, because "the [g]rievant reasonably believed she was performing at the exceptional level, but was eyed as performing 'below' that level by her [first-line] supervisor, he was obligated to take measures, including meetings to provide negative feedback." *Id.* Finally, according to the Arbitrator, the record demonstrated that, if the Agency had acted in accordance with the standards set forth in Article 30, Section 6 of the parties' agreement, the grievant would have received an exceptional rating for Element 4.[6] *Id.* at 21, 22, 25.

III. Positions of the Parties

A. Agency's Exceptions

The Agency claims that the award is contrary to law. Exceptions at 1. According to the Agency, the award does not reflect a reconstruction of what it would have done had it not violated the parties' agreement. *See id.* at 4-5.

The Agency asserts that "the Arbitrator clearly overstepped his authority when he directed that the [g]rievant's appraisal for . . . Critical Element 4 be based on [her] reasonable belief and not the standards set out in the parties' agreement . . . ." *Id.* at 5. The Agency claims that, in making this finding, the Arbitrator not only misinterpreted, but also expanded, various provisions of the parties' agreement. *Id.*

The Agency asserts that, in accordance with Article 30, Section 2, the grievant was put on notice of the Agency's performance standards and that she never indicated that the performance standards were unclear in any way. *Id.* at 5-6.

Also, the Agency claims that the parties' agreement does not require that a rating be determined based on an employee's reasonable belief; rather, the agreement "stipulates that performance standards established by management . . . be used in regard to employee appraisals." *Id.* at 6 (emphasis omitted). According to the Agency, because "the award inserts the [g]rievant's reasonable belief as the major determining factor for the performance rating[,]" the award conflicts with the parties' agreement. *Id.*

The Agency asserts that, by obligating the grievant's first-line supervisor to take measures such

second-line supervisor changed her rating for Element 3 from fully successful to exceptional. *Id.* n.6.

4. Pertinent provisions of Article 30 are set forth in the attached appendix.

5. Another issue raised below was whether the Agency retaliated against the grievant for filing the instant grievance. Award at 3. Because the Agency did not except to the Arbitrator's findings regarding this issue, they are not before us.

6. The Arbitrator also determined that, while the grievant deserved an exceptional rating for Element 3, the record failed to demonstrate that the grievant was entitled to an exceptional rating for Element 1. *Id.* at 19-21, 25-26. Because the Agency has not excepted to the Arbitrator's findings regarding these elements, they are not before us.

as meetings to provide the grievant with negative feedback, the award contradicts the plain language of Article 30, Section 6 of the parties' agreement which "requires only one 'progress review during the rating period[.]'" *Id.* at 7; *see also id.* at 6. Finally, the Agency claims that the award conflicts with Article 30, Section 6 of the parties' agreement because a fully successful rating cannot reasonably be considered to be below the "expected level." *Id.* at 7.

B. Union's Opposition

The Union contends that, although the Agency correctly summarizes case law indicating that an arbitrator must reconstruct "how the [a]gency would have rated the grievant had it not acted improperly[,]" it does not point to anything "in the Arbitrator's [award] that reflects any misapplication of that law." Opp'n at 3. Moreover, the Union argues that, after considering the entire record, the Arbitrator properly reconstructed the grievant's rating for Element 4 and concluded that, but for the contract violations, the Agency would have given her an exceptional rating. *Id.* at 3-5.

Also, the Union contends that the Arbitrator did not overstep his authority by "simply impos[ing] the rating that [the grievant] expected to receive." *Id.* at 6. According to the Union, the Arbitrator simply found that, because the Agency violated Article 30, Section 6, the grievant was entitled to an exceptional rating for Element 4. *Id.*

The Union argues that the Agency's assertion that the grievant was on notice of the Agency's performance standards is a non sequitur because the grievant did not grieve the content of the performance standards. *Id.*

Furthermore, the Union contends that several of the Agency's claims constitute essence exceptions. *Id.* at 7. The Union argues that the award does not fail to draw its essence from the parties' agreement because it does not require the Agency to consider an employee's reasonable belief in addition to the standards set forth in the agreement when evaluating that employee's performance. *See id.* Also, the Union contends that the Arbitrator's finding that Agency management could not have issued the grievant a lower rating in Element 4 without providing her with negative feedback is not contrary to Article 30, Section 6 of the parties' agreement. *Id.* at 8. According to the Union, while Article 30, Section 6 only requires "that the supervisor 'conduct *at least* one (1) *documented* face-to-face progress review,'" the Article also "mandates that, 'when there is sufficient indication that performance is below the expected level, additional steps including meetings, should be taken to provide feedback.'" *Id.* (quoting Article 30, Section 6(A)(1), (3)) (emphasis in original). Finally, the Union contends that the Arbitrator's interpretation of the phrase "expected level" contained in Article 30, Section 6(A)(1) is reasonable considering that the grievant expected to receive the same rating as before, and her supervisors provided her with only positive feedback. *Id.* at 9.

IV. Analysis and Conclusions

A. The award is not contrary to law.

The Authority reviews questions of law raised by exceptions to an arbitrator's award de novo. *See NTEU, Chapter 24*, 50 FLRA 330, 332 (1995) (citing *U.S. Customs Serv. v. FLRA*, 43 F.3d 682, 686-87 (D.C. Cir. 1994)). In applying a standard of de novo review, the Authority determines whether the arbitrator's legal conclusions are consistent with the applicable standard of law. *See NFFE, Local 1437*, 53 FLRA 1703, 1710 (1998). In making that determination, the Authority defers to the arbitrator's underlying factual findings. *Id.*

The Authority recently revised the analysis that it will apply when reviewing management-rights exceptions to arbitration awards. *See U.S. EPA*, 65 FLRA 113, 115 (2010) (Member Beck concurring); *FDIC, Div. of Supervision & Consumer Prot., S.F. Region*, 65 FLRA 102, 106-07 (2010) (Chairman Pope concurring) (*FDIC, S.F. Region*). Under the revised analysis, the Authority will first assess whether the award affects the exercise of the asserted management right. *EPA*, 65 FLRA at 115. If so, the Authority examines whether the award provides a remedy for a violation of either an applicable law, within the meaning of § 7106(a)(2) of the Statute, or a contract provision that was negotiated pursuant to § 7106(b) of the Statute. *Id.* In setting forth its revised analysis, the Authority specifically rejected the continued application of the reconstruction standard set forth in *United States Department of the Treasury, Bureau of Engraving & Printing, Washington, D.C.*, 53 FLRA 146 (1997) (*BEP*). *FDIC, S.F. Region*, 65 FLRA at 106-107.

Applying this analysis, we reject the Agency's exception that the award's remedy is contrary to law. This exception is based entirely on the assertion that the remedy does not reflect a reconstruction of what the Agency would have done had it not violated the parties' agreement. Exceptions at 4-5. As discussed above, such reconstruction is not the standard to be applied to a remedy directed by an arbitrator. Moreover, the Agency concedes that the award enforces a properly negotiated contract provision. *See id.* (implying only that the remedy does not satisfy prong II of the *BEP* framework); *see also FDIC*, 65 FLRA 179, 181 (2010) (noting that the agency conceded that the award enforced a properly negotiated contract provision); *FDIC, S.F. Region*, 65 FLRA at 103, 107 (finding that the award enforced a properly negotiated contract provision when the agency only challenged the award under prong II of the *BEP* framework and it conceded that prong I was satisfied). Accordingly, we find that the award does not impermissibly affect management rights by failing to reconstruct what the Agency would have done if it had not violated the contract and deny the Agency's contrary to law exception.[7] *See, e.g., FDIC, S.F. Region*, 65 FLRA at 107.

B. The Arbitrator did not exceed his authority.

The Agency asserts that "the Arbitrator clearly overstepped his authority when he directed that the [g]rievant's appraisal for . . . Critical Element 4 be based on [her] reasonable belief and not the standards set [forth] in the parties' agreement . . . ." Exceptions at 5. We construe this argument as a contention that the Arbitrator exceeded his authority. *See AFGE, Local 933*, 58 FLRA 480, 482 (2003) (construing the union's assertion that the arbitrator "strayed far outside his authority" as a claim that the arbitrator exceeded his authority); *AFGE, Local 1668*, 51 FLRA 714, 718 (1995) (construing the union's claims that the award was deficient because the arbitrator failed to address specific provisions of the parties' agreement as contentions that the arbitrator exceeded his authority).

Arbitrators exceed their authority when they fail to resolve an issue submitted to arbitration, resolve an issue not submitted to arbitration, disregard specific limitations on their authority, or award relief to those not encompassed within the grievance. *See AFGE, Local 1617*, 51 FLRA 1645, 1647 (1996). In the absence of a stipulated issue, the arbitrator's formulation of the issue is accorded substantial deference. *See U.S. Dep't of the Army, Corps of Eng'rs, Memphis Dist., Memphis, Tenn.*, 52 FLRA 920, 924 (1997).

The Agency's assertion does not establish that any of the circumstances set forth above are present here; specifically, the Agency has not demonstrated that the Arbitrator failed to resolve an issue submitted, resolved an issue not submitted, disregarded any specific limitations on his authority, or awarded relief to anyone other than the grievant. *See U.S. Dep't of the Navy, Naval Base, Norfolk, Va.*, 51 FLRA 305, 307-08 (1995) (finding that the award was not deficient on the ground that the arbitrator exceeded his authority where the excepting party did not establish that the arbitrator failed to resolve an issue submitted to arbitration, disregarded specific limitations on his authority, or awarded relief to persons not encompassed by the grievance).

Accordingly, we deny the Agency's exception.

C. The award does not fail to draw its essence from the parties' agreement.

The Agency notes that, in accordance with Article 30, Section 2, it put the grievant on notice of the Agency's performance standards and that the grievant never indicated that the performance standards were unclear in any way. Exceptions at 5-6. Also, the Agency asserts that, because "the award inserts the [g]rievant's reasonable belief as the major determining factor for the performance rating[,]" the award contradicts the parties' agreement. *Id.* at 6. The Agency claims that the award is contrary to Article 30, Section 6(A)(1) because a fully successful rating cannot reasonably be considered as below the "expected level." *Id.* at 7. Finally, the Agency asserts that, by obligating the grievant's first-line supervisor to take measures such as additional meetings to provide the grievant with negative feedback, the award conflicts with Article 30, Section 6(A)(3) which "requires only one 'progress review during the rating period[.]'" *Id.*; *see also id.* at 6. We construe these assertions as claims that the award fails to draw its essence from the agreement. *See NTEU, Chapter 193*, 65 FLRA 281, 282, 283 (2010) (construing the union's argument as an essence exception despite the fact that the union only maintained that the award was contrary to law).

In reviewing an arbitrator's interpretation of a collective bargaining agreement, the Authority applies the deferential standard of review that federal courts use in reviewing arbitration awards in the private sector. *See* 5 U.S.C. § 7122(a)(2); *AFGE,*

7. For the reasons set forth in her concurring opinion in *FDIC, S.F. Region*, 65 FLRA at 112, Chairman Pope agrees that the Agency provides no basis for finding the Arbitrator's remedy deficient because the remedy is reasonably related to Article 30 and the harm being remedied.

Council 220, 54 FLRA 156, 159 (1998). Under this standard, the Authority will find that an arbitration award is deficient as failing to draw its essence from the collective bargaining agreement when the appealing party establishes that the award: (1) cannot in any rational way be derived from the agreement; (2) is so unfounded in reason and fact and so unconnected with the wording and purposes of the collective bargaining agreement as to manifest an infidelity to the obligation of the arbitrator; (3) does not represent a plausible interpretation of the agreement; or (4) evidences a manifest disregard of the agreement. *See U.S. Dep't of Labor (OSHA)*, 34 FLRA 573, 575 (1990) (*U.S. DOL (OSHA)*. The Authority and the courts defer to arbitrators in this context "because it is the arbitrator's construction of the agreement for which the parties have bargained." *Id.* at 576.

Although the Agency implies that the Arbitrator found that it violated Article 30, Section 2 of the parties' agreement, the Arbitrator did not find that the Agency violated the agreement because the grievant was unaware of the standards and elements used in her performance appraisal. *See* Exceptions at 5-6. Instead, the Arbitrator found that the grievant was unaware that her first-level supervisor viewed her performance as fully successful rather than excellent. *See* Award at 21. Moreover, the Arbitrator determined that, because the grievant's supervisor was aware that she expected to be rated at the exceptional level, the Agency violated Article 30, Section 6 of the parties' agreement by not taking necessary measures to provide the grievant with negative feedback. *Id.* Consequently, because its assertion is based upon a misunderstanding of the Arbitrator's award, it does not demonstrate that the award fails to draw its essence from the parties' agreement. *See NAGE, Local R4-45*, 55 FLRA 789, 794 (1999) (determining that, because the agency's exception was based on a misstatement of the arbitrator's award, the agency failed to demonstrate that the remedy failed to draw its essence from the agreement).

Similarly, the Agency's claim that the award conflicts with the parties' agreement because it "inserts the [g]rievant's reasonable belief as the major determining factor for the performance rating" is without merit. Exceptions at 6. As noted previously, the Arbitrator did not find that the Agency should have considered the grievant's evaluation of her own performance when issuing her a rating for Element 4. Award at 21. Rather, the Arbitrator simply took into account the grievant's reasonable expectation and the Agency's awareness of her expectation in determining that the Agency violated Article 30, Section 6 of the parties' agreement. *Id.* Therefore, because this assertion also is based upon a misunderstanding of the Arbitrator's award, it provides no basis for finding that the award fails to draw its essence from the parties' agreement. *See NAGE, Local R4-45*, 55 FLRA at 794.

Also, although the Agency asserts that the award conflicts with Article 30, Section 6 because a fully successful rating cannot reasonably be considered as below the "expected level," its assertion does not demonstrate that the award fails to draw its essence from the agreement under any of the pertinent tests. Exceptions at 7. Article 30, Section 6(A)(1) of the parties' agreement states that "when there is sufficient indication that performance is below the expected level, additional steps including meetings, should be taken to provide feedback." Opp'n, Attach. 2 at 100. Here, the Arbitrator considered the meaning of the term "expected level" from the grievant's perspective rather than from the Agency's perspective. *See* Award at 21. The Arbitrator determined that, in the grievant's case, the "expected level" of performance for Element 4 was the exceptional level because the grievant had received an exceptional rating during the prior performance rating period, and the grievant's first-line supervisor was on notice that she hoped to receive another exceptional rating for Element 4. *Id.* Although others likely would interpret the term "expected level" differently than the Arbitrator, his interpretation of "expected level" is not implausible. *See U.S. DOL (OSHA)*, 34 FLRA at 575-76 (determining that the Authority will not find that an award fails to draw its essence from the agreement even if a party believes that the arbitrator misinterpreted the agreement); *Dep't of Health & Human Servs., SSA*, 32 FLRA 79, 88 (1988) (finding that, although the agency or the Authority might have interpreted the agreement differently than the arbitrator, the agency's essence exception should be denied). Moreover, considering that the term "expected level" is not defined by the parties' agreement and that an arbitrator's interpretation of an agreement's provisions is accorded deference, the Agency has failed to demonstrate that the Arbitrator's interpretation of "expected level" is irrational. *See* Opp'n, Attach. 2 (containing no definition of the term "expected level"); *see also AFGE, Local 933*, 65 FLRA 9, 11 (2010) (finding that the union's reliance on a dictionary definition of the word "routine" did not demonstrate that the arbitrator's interpretation of "routine work assignments" was implausible, unfounded, irrational, or in manifest disregard of the agreement); *NTEU*, 63 FLRA 299,

300 (2009) (denying the union's essence exception because the term "Service-wide in nature" was not defined in the agreement and the union provided no basis to conclude that the arbitrator was constrained in his interpretation of the term).

Finally, the Agency's claim that the award expands the terms of Article 30, Section 6 by requiring it to take additional steps, including meetings, to provide feedback to the grievant, is without merit. Exceptions at 6-7. In this case, the Arbitrator found that, in accordance with Article 30, Section 6, the grievant's first-line supervisor was required to take necessary steps, such as meetings, to provide the grievant with negative feedback because he viewed her as performing below the "expected level." Award at 21. The Arbitrator's interpretation of Article 30, Section 6 of the parties' agreement is neither implausible nor irrational. Although Article 30, Section 6(A)(3) only requires that a hiring official conduct *at least* one face-to-face performance review with a subordinate, it does not preclude that hiring official from holding additional meetings. Opp'n, Attach. 2 at 100 (emphasis added). Also, as noted above, Article 30, Section 6(A)(1) of the parties' agreement requires that "when there is sufficient indication that [an employee's] performance is below the expected level, additional steps including meetings . . . be taken to provide [that employee with] feedback." *Id.* Consequently, the Agency has not demonstrated that the Arbitrator's interpretation of the parties' agreement is irrational, implausible, unfounded, or in manifest disregard of the agreement. *See U.S. Dep't of Transp., FAA*, 63 FLRA 15, 18 (2008).

Accordingly, we deny the Agency's exceptions.

V. Decision

The Agency's exceptions are denied.

APPENDIX

Article 30, titled "Performance Management Program," states, in pertinent part:

> Section 2: All employees will receive a performance appraisal based on a comparison of the employee's performance with the standards and elements established for the appraisal period.
>
> . . . .
>
> Section 6:
>
> A. Progress Reviews
>
> 1. The rating official shall communicate with the employee throughout the rating period concerning progress toward meeting standards in his/her Performance Plan. Formal face to face conversations are one way this communication can occur. Communication may also include such things as comments on written products the employee has submitted, e-mail comments regarding assignments, suggestions concerning better ways of conducting business, etc. Such feedback coupled with the regular mid year Progress Review will be sufficient for most employees to get feedback on expectations and measure progress toward meeting these expectations. However, when there is sufficient indication that performance is below the expected level, additional steps including meetings, should be taken to provide feedback.
>
> 2. The rating official may initiate discussions to provide feedback concerning performance. Each discussion should be candid and forthright and aimed at identifying performance strengths and weakness; barriers to success; methods for improving performance; training needed; etc.
>
> 3. The rating official shall conduct at least one (1) documented face-to-face progress review during the period between establishment of the Performance Plan and the end of the rating period, generally at mid-year. During any progress review, the rating official and employee may discuss:
>
>   a. the employee's accomplishments;
>
>   b. performance measures remaining to be accomplished and any barriers which may impede their accomplishment;
>
>   c. revisions to the plan which may reflect changes in work assignments or program initiatives;
>
>   d. deficiencies in performance and required improvements,and
>
>   e. training and developmental needs.
>
> . . . .

Opp'n, Attach. 2 at 97, 100-01.

65 FLRA No. 121

UNITED STATES
DEPARTMENT OF THE ARMY
MEDICAL ACTIVITY (MEDDAC)
FORT DRUM, NEW YORK
(Agency)

and

AMERICAN FEDERATION
OF GOVERNMENT EMPLOYEES
LOCAL 400
(Union)

0-AR-4690

DECISION

February 28, 2011

Before the Authority: Carol Waller Pope, Chairman, and Thomas M. Beck and Ernest DuBester, Members

I. Statement of the Case

This matter is before the Authority on exceptions to an award (fee award) of Arbitrator Mona N. Glanzer filed by the Agency under § 7122(a) of the Federal Service Labor-Management Relations Statute (the Statute) and part 2425 of the Authority's Regulations. The Union filed an opposition to the Agency's exceptions.

The Arbitrator granted the Union's application for attorney fees and gave the Agency thirty days to submit any objections to the amount of fees requested. None were filed and the amount requested was awarded.

For the reasons discussed below, we deny the Agency's exceptions.

II. Background and Arbitrator's Award

A. Merits Award

The Agency suspended the grievant, a physician's assistant, for his failure to control an incident in an examination room to the satisfaction of the patient's mother. Merits Award at 4-5; Fee Award at 2. The grievant was initially suspended for two weeks but prior to the arbitration the Agency reduced the suspension to seven days. Merits Award at 5.

The Arbitrator found that the grievant, who was hearing impaired, had past difficulties with the nursing staff, which was not accommodating to his disability. *Id.* at 3. The incident at issue involved a pediatric patient whom the grievant determined needed a catheterization procedure. The mother concurred but was apprehensive about the procedure. When the grievant left the room to attend to other patients, a nurse who had not followed the grievant's instructions before, decided unilaterally not to use the catheter and suggested another procedure to the mother. *Id.* at 4. When the grievant returned, he became visibly upset that his orders were not followed. He spoke to the mother, who agreed to go forward with the procedure, although she and the child were both upset. *Id.* The situation was described as chaotic and the procedure was eventually stopped. The next day a physician performed the catheterization on the first attempt. *Id.*

Finding that open frustration and anger does not promote patient care, and consequently, the Agency's reputation, the Arbitrator found that the Agency had reason to discipline the grievant. *Id.* at 7. She found, however, that the seven-day suspension was unreasonable. Balancing the Agency's interests with the "equity of the penalty imposed," the Arbitrator concluded that an anger management course was the proper penalty. *Id.* 7-8. The Arbitrator based her decision, in part, on the following facts: the grievant was an eight-year employee with excellent evaluations; his medical skills were never called into question; this was his first offense; a prior incident was written up and counseling recommended but never pursued; the nurse involved exacerbated the situation; and the penalty exceeded the guidelines. *Id.* Additionally, the Arbitrator found that the grievant's demeanor at the hearing indicated that his professional reputation was important to him and that any penalty would be taken seriously. *Id.* at 8. The Arbitrator therefore concluded that an anger management course would serve a purpose beyond being punitive in order to preserve a valued employee and enable him to better serve the Agency's mission. *Id.*

Accordingly, the Arbitrator found that the Agency did not have just cause to impose the seven-day suspension and ordered the grievant to take an anger management course as the remedy. *Id.* at 8. As neither party filed exceptions to the merits award, that award became final and binding.

B. Fee Award

Subsequent to the issuance of the merits award, the Agency imposed the seven-day suspension on the grievant, causing him to lose pay and benefits. The parties submitted a joint petition for clarification and the Arbitrator issued a supplemental award in which the Arbitrator repeated that the sole penalty imposed by the merits award was the anger management course. Fee Award at 2 (discussing supplemental award).

In the fee award at issue here, the Arbitrator granted the Union's request for attorney fees. *Id.* at 8. The Arbitrator addressed whether a fee award was warranted in the interest of justice under the criteria established by the Merit Systems Protection Board (MSPB) in *Allen v. USPS,* 2 M.S.P.R. 420 (1980).[1] *Id.* at 3. Recognizing that a fee award is warranted if any one of the *Allen* criteria is satisfied, the Arbitrator considered whether the Agency knew or should have known that it would not prevail on the merits when it suspended the grievant under *Allen* criterion 5. *Id.* at 4-7. The Arbitrator concluded that attorney fees were warranted because the Agency should have known that the seven-day suspension would be excessive under the circumstances. *Id.* at 7. In support of her conclusion, the Arbitrator noted that she had found the penalty unreasonable because "the penalty exceeded the guidelines, the behavior of a nurse exacerbated the problem, [the grievant's] medical judgment was correct, [the grievant] was an eight-year employee with excellent evaluations[,]" and this was "the first formal disciplinary action against him." *Id.* at 2.

Moreover, the Arbitrator found that the evidence at the hearing established that the Agency knew its decision would not stand because the Agency's reasons for exceeding the penalty guidelines were "suspect, particularly since there was no attempt throughout the process to look at relevant mitigating circumstances." *Id.* at 6.

Specifically, the Arbitrator found that the Agency had access to all witnesses and documents yet it failed to make any attempt to review the reasons for the grievant's failure to control the situation in the examination room. *Id.* at 6-7. The Arbitrator further found that "[w]ith minimal inquiry, [the Agency] would have to know that there were relevant mitigating circumstances." *Id.* at 7. In the Arbitrator's view, a minimal investigation would have revealed a single prior event in which the grievant had a previous conflict with the nurses but no disciplinary procedure was instituted and no one considered the nurses' failure to cooperate with the grievant as a contributing factor. The Arbitrator concluded that the same "limited vision" existed in this proceeding: although the grievant failed to maintain control, no one considered exonerating facts including the nurse's failure to follow the grievant's instructions, causing the patient's mother to question his medical judgment. *Id.* at 6-7. The Arbitrator further concluded that if the Agency had made any effort to investigate and evaluate mitigating circumstances, it would have discovered that even though the nurse took the mother to the patient advocate, no charges were filed against the grievant and no action was taken regarding his credentials. Because no attempt was made by the Agency to consider any mitigating factors, the Arbitrator determined that in the interest of justice, attorney fees were warranted under *Allen* criterion 5. *Id.* The Arbitrator found, however, that the fees were not warranted under *Allen* criterion 2 because the grievant was not "substantially innocent" of the charges against him and therefore the Agency's actions "were not wholly unfounded." *Id.* at 4.

In addition, the Arbitrator found that the Agency had no basis for continuing to impose the suspension in addition to the penalty imposed in the merits award. Consequently, the Arbitrator found that the matter had been unduly prolonged by the Agency. *Id.* at 7. Therefore, unlike the Agency's principal actions against the grievant, the Arbitrator found that this action was unfounded and without merit meeting both *Allen* criteria 2 and 5. In conclusion, the Arbitrator found that "[i]t is the magnitude of the injustice to the employee in light of all the facts and circumstances that justifies an award of attorney's fees." *Id.* (citation omitted).

1. Under *Allen,* an award of attorney fees is warranted in the interest of justice if: (1) the Agency engaged in a prohibited personnel practice; (2) the Agency's actions are clearly without merit or wholly unfounded, or the employee is substantially innocent of charges brought by the agency; (3) the Agency's actions are taken in bad faith to harass or exert improper pressure on an employee; (4) the Agency committed gross procedural error which prolonged the proceeding or severely prejudiced the employee; or (5) the Agency knew or should have known it would not prevail on the merits when it brought the proceeding. *See, e.g., AFGE, Local 3020,* 64 FLRA 596, 597 n.* (2010). An award of attorney fees is also warranted in the interest of justice when there is either a service rendered to the federal workforce or there is a benefit to the public derived from maintaining the action. *Id.*

III. Positions of the Parties

A. Agency's Exceptions

The Agency asserts that the Arbitrator's fee award is contrary to law because the requested attorney fees are not warranted in the interest of justice. Specifically, the Agency argues that neither the fee award nor the record establishes that the Agency knew or should have known that it would not prevail on the merits. *See* Exceptions at 11.[2] In this regard, the Agency argues that penalty mitigation, as here, where the suspension was reduced by an agency, does not create a presumption that fees are warranted. Instead, the fee award must be based on a specific factual finding that the Agency acted unreasonably. *Id.* The Agency further argues that the determination of what it "should have known" must be made in light of the information available to the Agency at the time the penalty was imposed and that the Arbitrator improperly considered the grievant's behavior after the initiation of the grievance in deciding that the penalty was unreasonable. *Id.* at 4, 12. Recognizing that what the Agency knew or should have known is primarily a factual determination in which the arbitrator evaluates the evidence, *id.* at 12, the Agency disagrees with the Arbitrator's interpretation of the record and argues that she either "ignored or gave no weight to" the Agency's witnesses, *id.* at 7. *See also id.* at 12-13, 17.

Finally, the Agency asserts that the Arbitrator did not base her fee award on the merits award. Rather, the Agency argues, the fee award is based solely on the delay brought about by the request for clarification and supplemental award. As such, the Agency asserts that the fee award is contrary to law because it is not based on a decision that the Agency acted unreasonably at the time it imposed the suspension. *Id.* at 8-9.

B. Union's Opposition

The Union contends that the Arbitrator used the proper legal standards when she determined that the Agency knew or should have known that the penalty was unreasonable because it failed to investigate the matter and consider mitigating factors. Opp'n at 21. The Union also argues that the Agency's exceptions do not demonstrate that the fee award is contrary to law because they only challenge the Arbitrator's factual conclusions and not the interpretation of the applicable law. *Id.* According to the Union, the Agency's claims that the Arbitrator misinterpreted the record are based on the Agency's disagreement with the Arbitrator's factual findings and credibility determinations. *Id.* at 13-16.

Additionally, the Union argues that the fee award is not based on the supplemental award, but rather is a correct decision in law and fact, based on the merits award in which the Arbitrator found the grievant at fault but the penalty to be unreasonable. *Id.* at 12. Therefore, the Union asks the Authority to deny the Agency's exceptions.

IV. Analysis and Conclusions

When an exception involves an award's consistency with law, the Authority reviews any question raised by the exception and the award de novo. *See NTEU, Chapter 24,* 50 FLRA 330, 332 (1995) (citing *U.S. Customs Serv. v. FLRA*, 43 F.3d 682-87 (D.C. Cir. 1994)). In applying the standard, the Authority assesses whether an arbitrator's legal conclusions are consistent with the applicable standard of law. *See U.S. Dep't of Def., Dep'ts of the Army & the Air Force, Ala. Nat'l Guard, Northport, Ala.* 55 FLRA 37, 40 (1998). In making that assessment, the Authority defers to the arbitrator's underlying factual findings. *See id.* In addition, the award in this case must be in accordance with the standards established under § 7701(g)(1).[3] *U.S. Dep't of the Navy, Commander, Navy Region Haw., Fed. Fire Dep't, Naval Station Pearl Harbor, Honolulu, Haw.,* 64 FLRA 925, 928 (2010). The Agency contends that the award is not in accordance with these standards because, according to the Agency, the award of fees is not in the interest of justice. As such, we address only this requirement. *Id.*

The Authority resolves whether an award of fees is warranted in the interest of justice in accordance

2. The Agency also argues that neither the fee award nor the record establishes that the Agency committed a prohibited personnel action or that the action was wholly unfounded and the employee was substantially innocent of the charges under *Allen* criteria 1 and 2. Exceptions at 9-11. In its opposition, the Union withdrew its contention that the fees are warranted under these criteria and relies exclusively on *Allen* criterion 5. Opp'n at 11.

3. Section 7701(g)(1) provides, in pertinent part, that the MSPB "may require payment by the agency involved of reasonable attorney fees incurred by an employee . . . if the employee . . . is the prevailing party and the [MSPB] . . . determines that payment by the agency is warranted in the interest of justice[.]" 5 U.S.C. § 7701(g).

with § 7701(g)(1) by applying the criteria established by the MSPB in *Allen*. As recognized by the Arbitrator, an award of fees is warranted in the interest of justice if any one of the criteria is satisfied. *U.S. Dep't of the Air Force, Davis-Monthan Air Force Base, Tucson, Ariz.*, 64 FLRA 819, 820-21 (2010).

Under *Allen* criterion 5, an award of fees is warranted in the interest of justice when the agency "knew or should have known that it would not prevail on the merits" when it brought the proceeding. *Allen*, 2 M.S.P.R. at 435. This determination requires an evaluation of the nature and weight of the evidence available to the agency at the time of the disputed action. *Soc. Sec. Admin., Balt., Md.*, 63 FLRA 550, 552 (2009) (*SSA*). Accordingly, arbitrators must determine the reasonableness of the agency's actions and positions in light of the information available at the time of the disputed action. *Id.* The assessment of whether an agency knew or should have known that it would not prevail is primarily factual because it is based on the arbitrator's evaluation of the evidence and the agency's handling of that evidence. *Id.* Consequently, when the arbitrator's factual findings support the arbitrator's legal conclusion, the Authority denies an exception to the application of criterion 5. *Id.*

Here, the Arbitrator held that "in light of all the facts and circumstances[,]" "[a]n award of attorney fees is warranted in the interests of justice." Fee Award at 7, 8. Specifically, the Arbitrator found that the Agency failed to consider any mitigating factors, which were readily available at the time of the disputed action, such as: the grievant's excellent eight-year employment record with no other formal discipline; the accuracy of the grievant's medical judgment; the nurse's conduct, which exacerbated the situation; and the penalty being in excess of the guidelines. *Id.* at 6-7. The Arbitrator determined that "[t]here was no evidence that [the Agency] considered these mitigating factors." *Id.* at 7. Finding that there was no investigation into these "exonerating" facts, the Arbitrator concluded that "[w]ith minimal inquiry [the Agency] would have to know that there were relevant mitigating circumstances." *Id.*

In view of the Arbitrator's factual findings, the legal conclusion that the Agency "should have known" that it would not prevail is not contrary to law. *See U.S. Gen. Servs. Admin., Ne. & Caribbean Region, N.Y., N.Y.*, 61 FLRA 68, 71 (2005) (agency's failure to consider mitigating circumstances such as grievant's superior employment record and misconduct of agency employee support arbitrator's legal conclusion that agency knew or should have known that it would not prevail); *U.S. Army Headquarters, XVIII Airborne Corps, Fort Bragg, N.C.*, 35 FLRA 390, 394 (1990) (citing *Yorkshire v. MSPB*, 746 F.2d 1454, 1457 (Fed. Cir. 1984)) (knew or should have known requirement satisfied when agency is negligent in conducting investigation). Therefore, although the Agency disagrees with the Arbitrator's factual findings and interpretation of the record, it has not established that the Arbitrator erred.[4] *See SSA*, 63 FLRA at 552 (agency's disagreement with arbitrator's factual findings does not establish that arbitrator erred in awarding attorney fees where agency failed to conduct thorough review of appropriate penalty for employee with excellent employment and flawless disciplinary records).

Further, the cases on which the Agency relies are inapposite. Although in each case the request for attorney fees was denied, there was no finding by the arbitrator, as there was here, that the agency should have known that the penalty it imposed would not prevail. In *Dunn v. Department of Veterans Affairs*, 98 F.3d 1308, 1313 (Fed. Cir. 1996), the court held that there was no presumption of a fee award based on a mitigation of the penalty. Similarly, *Sterner v. Department of the Army*, 711 F.2d 1563, 1570-71 (Fed. Cir. 1983), held that a finding of economic hardship does not create a presumption that a fee award is warranted.

Here, the Arbitrator did not base the fee award on a presumption that it was warranted because the penalty was mitigated. Rather, she concluded that with minimal investigation, the Agency should have known that the penalty imposed would not prevail. Moreover, the *Dunn* decision supports the Arbitrator's finding. There, the court noted that a negligently conducted investigation might give rise to an affirmative finding under *Allen* criterion 5. *Dunn* 98 F.3d at 1313; *cf. Nat'l Air Traffic Controller's Ass'n* 64 FLRA 799, 801 (2010) (Authority confirmed arbitrator's legal conclusion that fees were

4. The Agency also argues that the Arbitrator considered facts after the penalty was imposed; notably, that the conflict between the grievant and the nurses disappeared after the nurse involved in the incident left. Exceptions at 3-4. The Arbitrator recognized that the reasonableness of the penalty must be considered at the time it was imposed and stated that subsequent events were not the basis of the penalty but were mentioned as confirmation of the decision. Fee Award at 7. Thus, we conclude that the basis for the fee award was the Agency's actions at the time of the suspension. *Id.*

unwarranted where arbitrator made factual findings that agency conducted a thorough investigatory review before it imposed penalty). Finally, the Arbitrator distinguished *Department of the Air Force, Monthan Air Force Base, Tucson, Arizona,* 64 FLRA 819 (2010), and found that, unlike the arbitrator in *Monthan* who did not find that the agency knew or should have known the penalty it imposed would not prevail, the facts in this case "indicate that the [A]gency was aware that the penalty it imposed was problematic[.]" Fee Award at 5.

For the reasons set forth above, the Authority denies the exception because the award satisfies Allen criterion 5 and therefore is not contrary to the 5 U.S.C. § 7701 (g)(1).[5]

V. Decision

The Agency's exceptions are denied.

5. As noted, an award of fees is warranted in the interest of justice if any one of the criteria is satisfied. Thus, we find it unnecessary to resolve the Agency's exceptions regarding criterion 2 on which the Arbitrator also relied.

65 FLRA No. 122

UNITED STATES
DEPARTMENT OF DEFENSE
DEPARTMENT OF DEFENSE
DEPENDENTS SCHOOLS, EUROPE
(Agency)

and

FEDERAL EDUCATION ASSOCIATION
(Union)

0-AR-4401

DECISION

February 28, 2011

Before the Authority: Carol Waller Pope, Chairman, and Thomas M. Beck and Ernest DuBester, Members

I. Statement of the Case

This matter is before the Authority on exceptions to an award of Arbitrator Edward J. O'Connell filed by the Agency under § 7122(a) of the Federal Service Labor-Management Relations Statute (the Statute) and part 2425 of the Authority's Regulations. The Union filed an opposition to the Agency's exceptions.[1]

The Arbitrator sustained, in part, the grievance over the fourteen-day suspension of the grievant, and the Arbitrator directed that: the record of the suspension be expunged from the grievant's personnel file; and the arbitration award be placed in the grievant's permanent record. For the reasons that follow, we conclude that the Arbitrator's remedies are deficient, and we set them aside.

II. Background and Arbitrator's Award

The Agency suspended the grievant for fourteen days, and the Union filed a grievance on the grievant's behalf that was submitted to arbitration. Award at 7-8, 10. The Arbitrator denied the grievance, in part, and sustained the grievance, in part. The Arbitrator determined that, under all of the circumstances relating to the incident, the fourteen-day suspension was for just cause. *Id.* at 21. However, he explained that "a finding that[,] under the circumstances[,] the [g]rievant exercised poor judgment and must be punished does not end the inquiry." *Id.* He found that "the unique circumstances of this case require[d] modification of the full penalty imposed by the Agency." *Id.* at 24. Accordingly, he directed that: the record of the suspension be expunged from the grievant's personnel file; and the arbitration award be placed in the grievant's permanent record. *Id.* Because of the "unusual nature" of the ordered remedies, the Arbitrator retained jurisdiction to resolve any issues that might arise in their implementation. *Id.*

III. Positions of the Parties

A. Agency's Exceptions

The Agency contends that the Arbitrator's direction to expunge the record of the fourteen-day suspension from the grievant's personnel records is contrary to 5 C.F.R § 293.304 (§ 293.304).[2] The Agency maintains that § 293.304 prescribes that an employee's official personnel file (OPF) must contain all the long-term records affecting the employee's status and service that are required by Office of Personnel Management (OPM) instructions and that are designated in the OPM Guide to Personnel Recordkeeping (Recordkeeping Guide). Exceptions at 16. The Agency further maintains that the Recordkeeping Guide refers to the OPM Guide to Processing Personnel Actions (Personnel Actions Guide) for the identification of events that must be documented in an OPF, and that these events include suspensions, which are officially documented by a Standard Form 50 (SF-50). *Id.* The Agency also argues that the expungement is contrary to Department of Defense Educational Activity Regulation 5791.9, which the Agency claims requires it to maintain a file for all disciplinary actions taken.[3] *Id.* at 19.

The Agency further contends that the direction to place a copy of the award in the grievant's permanent personnel records is contrary to OPM regulatory requirements pertaining to the maintenance of

1. The parties also filed supplemental submissions, which are discussed below.

2. The pertinent wording of § 293.304 is set forth below.

3. The Agency does not provide the wording of Department of Defense Educational Activity Regulation 5791.9.

employee personnel records. In support, the Agency asserts that the Recordkeeping Guide specifically prohibits the placement of arbitration awards in permanent personnel records. *Id.* at 18.

The Agency also contends that the Arbitrator exceeded his authority by directing the expungement of the grievant's personnel file and the placement of the award in the grievant's permanent record. *Id.* at 4-13. In addition, the Agency contends that the award is deficient because the remedies are contradictory. *Id.* at 13-15. Finally, the Agency contends that the direction to expunge the grievant's records is deficient because it is contrary to management's right to take disciplinary action under § 7106(a)(2)(A) of the Statute. *Id.* at 20-22.

B. Union's Opposition

The Union contends that the Agency's exceptions are "premature" because of the Arbitrator's retention of jurisdiction and that the Authority should remand the award to the Arbitrator. Opp'n at 1.

IV. Preliminary Issues

As stated above, in its opposition, the Union contends that the Agency's exceptions are "premature" because of the Arbitrator's retention of jurisdiction, *id.*, which we construe as a claim that the Agency's exceptions are interlocutory. In response to the Union's opposition, the Agency filed a motion for leave to file a supplemental submission to address this issue and, in the submission, claims that its exceptions are not premature. Thereafter, the Union filed a response to the Agency's motion, claiming that the Authority should not consider the Agency's supplemental submission because the Agency did not request permission to file it.

With regard to the Agency's motion, as an initial matter, we note that, contrary to the Union's claim, the Agency did request permission to file its supplemental submission. As to whether we should grant that request, the Authority has granted leave to file supplemental submissions and has considered the submissions when the submissions respond to arguments raised for the first time in an opposing party's filing. *E.g., U.S. Dep't of Homeland Sec., Immigration & Customs Enforcement*, 64 FLRA 1003, 1005 (2010) (*ICE*). Here, as in *ICE*, the Union raised the issue of whether the Agency's exceptions are interlocutory for the first time in its opposition, and the Agency's supplemental submission addresses that issue. Accordingly, we grant the Agency's motion and consider its supplemental submission.

With regard to the Union's response, the Union did not request leave or permission to file the response. The Authority has declined to consider a response when the filing party did not request permission to file it. *E.g., AFGE, Local 1815*, 65 FLRA 430, 431 (2011) (*AFGE, Local 1815*). Accordingly, consistent with *AFGE, Local 1815*, we do not consider the Union's response.

With regard to the issue of whether the exceptions are interlocutory, the Authority has specifically held that "[e]xceptions to an award are not interlocutory where an arbitrator has retained jurisdiction solely to assist the parties in the implementation of awarded remedies[.]" *AFGE, Nat'l Council of EEOC Locals No. 216*, 65 FLRA 252, 253-54 (2010). As the Arbitrator viewed his remedies to be "unusual" and retained jurisdiction solely "to resolve any issues that may arise in [their] implementation[,]" Award at 24, we conclude that the exceptions are not interlocutory.

V. Analysis and Conclusions

Section 293.304 prescribes that an employee's OPF "shall contain long-term records affecting the employee's status and service as required by OPM's instructions and as designated in the [Recordkeeping Guide]." As discussed further below, the Recordkeeping Guide provides instructions not only for what documents must be contained in an employee's OPF, but also for what records may *not* be filed in the OPF. As § 293.304 specifically references the Recordkeeping Guide as governing the maintenance of records in the OPF, we interpret § 293.304 -- when read in conjunction with the Recordkeeping Guide -- as prescribing both the records that must be contained, and those that may not be contained, in OPFs.

With regard to the records that must be contained in OPFs -- i.e., "long-term records affecting the employee's status and service[,]" § 293.304 -- Section 3-F of the Recordkeeping Guide refers to the Personnel Actions Guide for a list of personnel actions that have long-term effects on an employee's status and service. The Personnel Actions Guide specifically identifies a "suspension that is effected under 5 U.S.C. chapter 75" and "[i]s for [fourteen] calendar days or less" as such a personnel action. Personnel Actions Guide, Ch. 15 at 15-12. The record that documents a fourteen-day suspension is an SF-50, and the Recordkeeping Guide provides that

SF-50s are filed in the OPF. Recordkeeping Guide, Section 3-F. Thus, we find that, when read in conjunction with the Recordkeeping Guide and the Personnel Actions Guide, § 293.304 requires that an OPF must contain an SF-50 documenting a fourteen-day suspension. As such, we find that the Arbitrator's direction to expunge the record of the grievant's fourteen-day suspension from his personnel file is contrary to § 293.304.[4]

With regard to the records that may not be contained in an OPF, Section 3-G of the Recordkeeping Guide provides, in pertinent part, "Do not file copies of decisions . . . in the personnel folder[,]" and specifically lists "[a]n arbitral award" as a decision that is not to be filed in the OPF. Recordkeeping Guide at 3-20. Accordingly, we find that the Arbitrator's direction to include his award in the grievant's permanent record is contrary to § 293.304.

For the foregoing reasons, we find that the Arbitrator's remedies are deficient, and we set them aside.

VI. Decision

The Arbitrator's remedies are contrary to § 293.304 and are set aside.[5]

4. OPM has advised the Authority that an agency may delete an SF-50 based on an administrative determination that the disciplinary action was unjustified or unwarranted. *Naval Plant Representative Office, Dallas, Tex.*, 2 FLRA 307, 311-12 (1979). As the Arbitrator specifically found that the fourteen-day suspension was for just cause, there is no administrative determination in this case that the suspension was unjustified or unwarranted.

5. In view of this decision, and as the remaining exceptions challenge the Arbitrator's remedies, we do not address those remaining exceptions.

65 FLRA No. 123

UNITED STATES
DEPARTMENT OF THE NAVY
MILITARY SEALIFT COMMAND
ATLANTIC REGION
HAMPTON, VIRGINIA
(Agency)

and

AMERICAN FEDERATION
OF GOVERNMENT EMPLOYEES
LOCAL 53
(Union)

0-AR-4227

DECISION

February 28, 2011

Before the Authority: Carol Waller Pope, Chairman, and Thomas M. Beck and Ernest DuBester, Members

I. Statement of the Case

This matter is before the Authority on exceptions to an award of Arbitrator M. David Vaughn filed by the Agency under § 7122(a) of the Federal Service Labor-Management Relations Statute (the Statute) and part 2425 of the Authority's Regulations. The Union filed an opposition to the Agency's exceptions.

The Arbitrator determined that the Agency improperly classified as exempt from the Fair Labor Standards Act (FLSA) certain positions held by bargaining unit employees. For the reasons that follow, we deny the Agency's exceptions.

II. Background and Arbitrator's Award

The Union submitted several grievances alleging that all of its bargaining unit members, General Schedule (GS)-12 and below, should be classified as non-exempt under the FLSA and should receive any backpay owed to them as a result of being classified as exempt. The Agency denied the grievances and the Union invoked arbitration. First Interim Opinion and Award (First Award) at 1, 6-7. Following an evidentiary hearing, the Arbitrator issued two separate interim awards.

In the first award, the Arbitrator identified the following issue:
"Is the grievance not arbitrable because of procedural defects?" *Id.* at 3. The Arbitrator found the dispute to be arbitrable. *Id.* at 2, 17-24.[1]

In a second interim opinion and award (Second Award), the Arbitrator framed the following issues:

> 1. Are the employees in the positions at issue in this proceeding properly exempt from coverage under the FLSA?
>
> 2. Did the Agency act in good faith and did it have reasonable grounds to believe that its acts and/or omissions were in compliance with the FLSA, so as to avoid the imposition of liquidated damages?
>
> 3. Did the Agency willfully violate the FLSA by failing to pay overtime, thereby requiring the application of a three-year statute of limitations?

Second Award at 3. The second award addressed only those positions for which evidence had been received. *Id.* at 93. The Arbitrator left the remaining positions and the second and third issues open for a subsequent hearing. *Id.* During the subsequent hearing, the parties reached a settlement agreement that resolved the remaining issues but the Agency retained its right to file exceptions regarding the Arbitrator's determination that electronics technicians (ET) and environmental protection specialists (EPS) were FLSA non-exempt. Third Opinion and Award (Third Award) at 1. The Arbitrator, upon reviewing the settlement agreement, issued a final award, the third award; deemed the first and second awards to be final awards; and retained jurisdiction to resolve any future issues arising from implementation of the settlement agreement. *Id.*

In the second award, the Arbitrator noted, as relevant here, that the FLSA contains a presumption that employees who work more than forty hours a week are entitled to overtime pay for the excess hours. Second Award at 41.[2] He also noted that an

1. As the Agency does not except to this finding, we do not address it further.

2. The remainder of this decision addresses only the ET and EPS positions.

employer claiming that an exemption to the FLSA applies to a particular position has the burden of proving that the position satisfies each requirement of the exemption being asserted. *Id.* at 41-42. During the arbitration, the Agency asserted that the administrative exemption under 5 C.F.R. § 551.206,[3] and/or the professional exemption under 5 C.F.R. § 551.207[4] applied to the positions in dispute. *Id.* at 9, 38.

The Arbitrator found that the duties of ETs include support of all Agency shipboard communications, navigation, radar, and electronic systems, and oversight of the repair of shipboard electronics by contractors. *Id.* at 65. He found that the case law, Department of Labor (DOL) Opinion Letters[5], and interpretations by the Office of Personnel Management (OPM) cited by the Union support a finding that ETs are FLSA non-exempt. *Id.* at 67-68. Further, he found that the Agency produced no evidence that its ETs have duties distinguishable from the ETs described in the cases and opinions cited by the Union. *Id.* at 68-69. Finally, the Arbitrator found that the record established that an ET is "plainly a technician" whose duties do not significantly affect the execution of management programs or policies, are line, rather than staff, in nature, and do not involve the frequent exercise of discretion and independent judgment. *Id.*

The Arbitrator found that duties of the sole EPS include coordinating the Agency's disposal of hazardous materials and conducting annual shipboard environmental assessments. *Id.* at 69. The Arbitrator found that the evidence established that the "overwhelming majority" of the EPS's work time is devoted to inspection work that does not involve any of the criteria of the administrative exemption that the Agency asserted. *Id.* at 73. In this regard, the Arbitrator found that EPS inspection work is governed by detailed guidelines and regulations. *Id.* For these reasons, the Arbitrator found that the Agency's determination that the EPS position is FLSA exempt was not supported by the evidence. *Id.* at 74.

The Arbitrator, having determined that the Agency erred in classifying the ET and EPS positions as FLSA-exempt, ordered that the Agency reclassify the positions as FLSA-non-exempt. *Id.* at 92.

III. Positions of the Parties

A. Agency's Exceptions

The Agency contends that the Arbitrator's determination that the ET and EPS positions are FLSA non-exempt is contrary to OPM and DOL government-wide regulations because it was based on position titles and "gross characterizations of duties" rather than on the duties that individuals holding these positions actually perform. Exceptions at 7. Among the "gross characterizations" that the Agency alleges the Arbitrator relied upon were statements in DOL regulations that ordinary inspection work is generally non-exempt and that work requiring reliance upon regulations is non-exempt. *Id.* The

---

3. Under 5 C.F.R. § 551.206, as it existed when the Arbitrator issued his awards, administrative employees had to meet all of the following criteria to be exempt:

> (a) *Primary duty test.* The primary duty test is met if the employee's work –
> (1) Significantly affects the formulation or execution of management programs or policies; or
> (2) Involves management or general business functions or supporting services of substantial importance to the organization serviced; or
> (3) Involves substantial participation in the executive or administrative functions of a management official.
> (b) *Nonmanual work test.* The employee performs office or other predominantly nonmanual work which is –
> (1) Intellectual and varied in nature; or
> (2) Of a specialized or technical nature that requires considerable special training, experience, and knowledge.
> (c) *Discretion and independent judgment test.* The employee frequently exercises discretion and independent judgment, under only general supervision, in performing the normal day-to-day work.

5 C.F.R. § 551.206 (2005). The current version of Subpart B of Part 551 of title 5 of the Code of Federal Regulations was amended on September 17, 2007.

4. Although the Agency contended before the Arbitrator that the professional exemption also applied, the Agency now claims that only the administrative exemption applies. *See* Exceptions at 8-9.

5. When the FLSA was enacted in 1938, the Secretary of Labor was given the authority to promulgate regulations to define the scope of FLSA exemptions. *See* 29 U.S.C. § 213(a)(1). When the FLSA was amended in 1974 to include specific groups of federal employees, it authorized the Civil Service Commission to promulgate such regulations applicable to those employees. OPM now performs that function. *See* 29 U.S.C. § 204(f).

Agency maintains that each position must be assessed on its particular facts, and that prior decisions by courts, OPM, or arbitrators about a named position carry little weight except to the extent that the actual duties performed were similar or identical. *Id.* at 8. Further, the Agency contends that the Arbitrator applied the independent judgment and discretion criteria of the administrative exemption in 5 C.F.R. § 551.206 to the ET and EPS positions so strictly as to effectively render the exemption meaningless. *Id.* at 9.

With regard to the ET position, the Agency contends that the Arbitrator's error is "obvious" because of evidence that the marine surveyor position, which the Arbitrator determined to be exempt, has duties similar to those of the ET position. *Id.* at 10. The Agency also contends that the Arbitrator failed to consider, or give appropriate weight to, evidence that the ET's duties are primarily administrative rather than technical, and that ETs represent management when performing their duties. *Id.* at 10-14.

With regard to the EPS position, the Agency contends that the evidence was undisputed that the sole EPS advises and acts as a representative of management and, therefore, is an administrative employee. *Id.* at 15. The Agency also contends that the record established that the EPS's work is varied and intellectual and the EPS must frequently exercise discretion and independent judgment in performing his work. *Id.* at 16-17. Finally, the Agency contends that the Arbitrator appeared to confuse the EPS position with the safety and occupational health specialist position even though the two positions involve substantially different duties. *Id.* at 18.

B. Union's Opposition

The Union contends that although the Agency's stated exception is that the Arbitrator's determinations are contrary to law, the Agency's actual disagreement is with the Arbitrator's findings of fact, the degree of consideration he gave to testimony, and his application of the regulations to the facts he found. Opp'n at 7, 13 & 15. Therefore, according to the Union, the Authority should reject the Agency's exceptions. *Id.*

Regarding the ET position, the Union asserts that it was appropriate for the Arbitrator to base his determination on prior decisions by courts, the OPM, and arbitrators concerning technicians with duties similar to those of the ETs,. and that the Agency failed to distinguish any of those decisions despite having had the opportunity to do so. *Id.* at 17-18. The Union also notes that the Arbitrator did not rely strictly on the precedents but also considered the ET position's actual duties as described in testimony. *Id.* at 19. As for the Agency's argument that the Arbitrator should have found the ET position to be exempt, as he did for the marine surveyor position, the Union contends that this runs counter to the Agency's argument that the Arbitrator should have based his determination on the actual duties of the ET position. *Id.* at 21. Moreover, the Union contends that the Arbitrator clearly distinguished the duties of the two positions. *Id.*

Regarding the EPS position, the Union contends that the Agency's exception is based on an allegation that the Arbitrator mischaracterized the position's duties and, as such, is not grounds for filing an exception. *Id.* at 23-24.

IV. Analysis and Conclusions

When an exception involves an award's consistency with law, the Authority reviews any question of law raised by the exception and the award de novo. *See NTEU, Chapter 24*, 50 FLRA 330, 332 (1995) (citing *U.S. Customs Serv. v. FLRA*, 43 F.3d 682, 686-87 (D.C. Cir. 1994)). In applying the standard of de novo review, the Authority assesses whether an arbitrator's legal conclusions are consistent with the applicable standard of law. *See U.S. Dep't of Def., Dep'ts of the Army & the Air Force, Ala. Nat'l Guard, Northport, Ala.*, 55 FLRA 37, 40 (1998). In making that assessment, the Authority defers to the arbitrator's underlying factual findings. *See id.*

OPM's regulations, at Subpart B of § 551 of title 5 of the Code of Federal Regulations, establish the criteria used to determine an employee's status under the FLSA. However, the designation of an employee as FLSA exempt or non-exempt rests on the duties actually performed by the employee. 5 C.F.R. § 551.202(e).[6] *See U.S. Dep't of the Navy, Naval Explosive Ordinance Disposal Tech. Div., Indian Head, Md.*, 56 FLRA 280, 284 (2000) (citing *Berg v. Newman*, 982 F.2d 500 (Fed. Cir. 1992) and other cases) (*U.S. Dep't of the Navy*). Section 551.202, sets out the following principles governing determinations as to whether an exemption applies to a position: (a) an employee is presumed to be FLSA non-exempt; (b) exemption criteria are to be narrowly

6. At the time the Arbitrator issued the awards, this provision was in 5 C.F.R. § 551.202(i).

construed; (c) the burden of proof rests with the agency that asserts the exemption; and (d) if there is reasonable doubt as to whether an employee meets the exemption criteria, the employee should be designated FLSA non-exempt. 5 C.F.R. § 551.202 (a) – (d) (2005).

The Agency argues that the Arbitrator failed to comply with OPM and DOL regulations because his determination was based on position titles and "gross characterizations of duties" instead of on the actual day-to-day duties. Exceptions at 7. However, the Arbitrator specifically recognized that his determination of the exemption status of the ET and EPS positions required consideration of the three criteria set out in the administrative exemption in 5 C.F.R. § 551.206. Thus, he applied the three criteria -- the "primary duty" test, the "nonmanual work" test, and the "discretion and independent judgment" test -- to the actual duties of the positions. Second Award at 65-74.[7] Further, the Arbitrator properly recognized that a position had to meet all criteria of the administrative exemption in order to be FLSA exempt. *Id.* at 73; *see also* 5 C.F.R. § 551.206 (an administrative employee must meet all exemption criteria).

Applying these criteria to the ET position, the Arbitrator considered testimony from both an ET incumbent and a supervisor regarding actual duties, and found their testimony to be consistent. Second Award at 24-26. In so doing, he found that the record establishes that the ET's duties do not meet the "primary duty" test in that the position's duties "do not significantly affect the execution of [m]anagement programs or policies and [the incumbent's] duties are fundamentally line, rather than staff, in nature." *Id.* at 68. Regarding the position's inspection duties, the Arbitrator found that these do not meet the "nonmanual work" test because the work "involves the use of skills and technical abilities in gathering factual information, applying known standards or prescribed procedures, determining what procedure to follow, or determining whether prescribed standards or criteria are met." *Id.* The Arbitrator based his finding on cases, DOL opinions, and OPM Letters describing the duties of electronics technicians as well as on the Agency's failure to produce any evidence that the ET position's duties are distinguishable. *Id.* at 68-69. As for the "discretion and independent judgment" test, the Arbitrator found that both the record and case precedents establish that the ET position's duties "do not involve the frequent exercise of discretion and independent judgment, but must be accomplished within [Agency] guidelines, regulations, and supervisory review and approval." *Id.* at 69.

Applying the administrative exemption criteria to the EPS position, the Arbitrator considered testimony from the EPS incumbent and a supervisor regarding actual duties, and found their testimony to be consistent. *Id.* at 27-28. In so doing, he found that the record establishes that inspection duties take up "the overwhelming majority of [the incumbent's] work time" and that this work does not meet any of the tests for the administrative exemption. *Id.* at 73. In addition, the Arbitrator found that the record establishes that the inspections are governed by detailed and comprehensive guidelines and regulations. *Id.*

As the Authority noted in *U.S. Dep't of the Navy*, in making FLSA exempt status determinations, "a trial court must have before it sufficient facts concerning the daily activities of the position to justify its legal conclusion." *U.S. Dep't of the Navy*, 56 FLRA at 284 (citation omitted). The Agency has not established that the Arbitrator failed to consider the positions' actual duties. Indeed, it is clear that the Arbitrator based his determinations on the testimony of position incumbents and supervisors regarding actual duties. Accordingly, the Authority finds that the award is in compliance with government-wide regulations because the determinations that the ET and EPS positions are exempt were based on evidence of actual duties.

With regard to the Agency's contentions that the Arbitrator failed to give appropriate weight to evidence that the ETs' duties are primarily administrative, that ETs represent management, that the work of the EPS is varied and intellectual, that the EPS frequently exercises discretion and independent judgment in performing his work, and that the duties of the EPS are similar to those of the exempt position of safety and occupational health specialist, the Authority will not find the award deficient on the basis of these contentions. The Authority has long held that disagreement with an arbitrator's evaluation of evidence and testimony, including the determination of the weight to be accorded such evidence, provides no basis for finding the award deficient. *See AFGE, Local 3295*, 51 FLRA 27,

7. These three tests are set out in greater detail at n. 3, *supra*. A fourth test contained in both exemptions, an "80-percent" test, was applicable only to GS-5 and GS-6 employees. Both the ET and EPS positions have higher grades.

32 (1995).[8] Finally, regarding the Agency's contention that the Arbitrator applied the criteria of the administrative exemption from the FLSA too strictly, the Authority finds that a strict application of the exemption is consistent with 5 C.F.R. § 551.202, in particular, with the principle in 5 C.F.R. § 551.202(b) that exemption criteria must be narrowly construed.

V. Decision

The Agency's exceptions are denied.

8. As the Agency does not provide any support for its claim that the Arbitrator's treatment of the EPS position as the same or similar to the Safety and Occupational Health Specialist position was "an obvious error of non-fact," Exceptions at 5 n.7, we deny the Agency's claim as a bare assertion. *See, e.g., U.S. Dep't of Homeland Sec., U.S. Customs & Border Prot., Port of Seattle, Seattle, Wash.*, 60 FLRA 490, 492 n.7 (2004) (citations omitted).

65 FLRA No. 124

UNITED STATES
DEPARTMENT OF JUSTICE
FEDERAL BUREAU OF PRISONS
FEDERAL PRISON CAMP
DULUTH, MINNESOTA
(Agency)

and

AMERICAN FEDERATION
OF GOVERNMENT EMPLOYEES
LOCAL 3935
COUNCIL OF PRISON LOCALS
COUNCIL 33
(Union)

0-AR-4500

DECISION

February 28, 2011

Before the Authority: Carol Waller Pope, Chairman, and Thomas M. Beck and Ernest DuBester, Members

I. Statement of the Case

This matter is before the Authority on an exception to an award of Arbitrator James A. Lundberg filed by the Agency under § 7122(a) of the Federal Service Labor-Management Relations Statute (the Statute) and part 2425 of the Authority's Regulations. The Union filed an untimely opposition to the Agency's exception.[1]

The Arbitrator concluded that the Agency: (1) violated Article 24 of the parties' agreement (Agreement) when a supervisory employee engaged in prohibited advocacy in seeking employment for his wife; and (2) violated Article 6 of the Agreement by conducting the grievant's reassignment in an inequitable manner. As a remedy the Arbitrator awarded, among other things: (1) bargaining to clarify the scope of the grievant's reassigned position; and (2) cross development training for the grievant. For the reasons set forth below, we deny the Agency's exception.

II. Background and Arbitrator's Award

The grievant is employed by the Agency as a medical secretary. The grievant was originally employed as a unit secretary prior to her current position as a medical secretary. Award at 2.

The Agency hired a new health services administrator (Mr. S) while there was an open medical secretary position. *Id.* at 3. His wife (Ms. S) requested and was granted a transfer to the open medical secretary position at the Agency after her husband took the health services administrator position. *Id.*

The warden submitted a U-2 Waiver for Supervision Request because Ms. S's employment in the medical secretary position violated Article 24 of the Agreement, which prohibits one relative from being in the supervisory chain of command over another.[2] *Id.* at 4. However, the Regional Director denied the waiver, believing that the Agency should avoid even the appearance of nepotism. *Id.* at 4-5. Ms. S then switched positions with the grievant, causing the grievant to be reassigned to the medical secretary position and Ms. S to be assigned to the unit secretary position. *Id.* at 5. The grievant was informed of the change by a reassignment letter, and then met with management at a reassignment meeting at which the Union was not present. *Id.* The grievant previously had told Mr. S that she was not interested in the medical secretary position. *Id.* at 4.

The Union requested to bargain with the Agency over "management's proposal to reassign a [u]nit secretary to the Health Services Department." *Id.* at 5. Subsequently, the Agency held a second reassignment meeting with the Union, at which the Agency asked the Union "what impact and implementation issues [it] wished to negotiate." *Id.* Rather than responding to the Agency's request, the Union presented a grievance, alleging that the

1. The Union concedes that its opposition was untimely filed. *See* Union Response to Show Cause Order at 2. Under 5 C.F.R. § 2429.23(b), an expired time limit can be waived upon a showing of "extraordinary circumstances" justifying the waiver. As the Union fails to make any claim that extraordinary circumstances warrant a waiver of the time limit, we will not consider the Union's opposition.

2. Article 24, Section (a)(2) provides: "There will be no prohibitions to the employment of a relative (including spouse) of an employee provided that: . . . there is no situation created in which one relative is in the supervisory chain of command over the other." Award at 6.

Agency improperly handled the consideration of Ms. S, failed to give the Union reasonable notice of the reassignment, failed to conduct impact and implementation bargaining, and failed to treat its employees fairly. *Id.* at 5-6. The Agency responded that it was exercising its right to assign work under 5 U.S.C. § 7106. *Id.* at 6. The matter was not resolved and was submitted to arbitration. *Id.*

The issue before the Arbitrator as framed by the Union was: "In the reassignment of [the grievant], did the [A]gency, in the exercise of its rights, violate the rights of the [U]nion as well as multiple articles of the [Agreement]? If this is found to be the case, what is the appropriate remedy?" *Id.* at 2. The issue as framed by the Agency was: "Did the [A]gency violate the Master Agreement, Article 3 section c, Article 6 section b, Article 7 section b and Article 24, with regards to the reassignment of [the grievant] from [u]nit [s]ecretary to [m]edical [s]ecretary at the [Agency]? If so, what is the appropriate remedy?" *Id.*

The Arbitrator concluded that conversations Mr. S had with the warden, as well as with secretaries in other units, constituted "prohibited advocacy," in violation of Article 24 of the Agreement.[3] *Id.* at 14-15.

The Arbitrator further concluded that the Agency violated Article 6, Section (b)(2) of the Agreement by conducting the reassignment in an inequitable manner.[4] *Id.* at 16. The Arbitrator found that the Agency provided the grievant less than a week's notice of the reassignment, reassigned her to a job she did not want, conducted the reassignment meeting without the Union present, and did not conduct impact and implementation bargaining prior to the reassignment. *Id.* Specifically, the Arbitrator found that the issues of work load, boundaries of work, cross-training, leave time, and work schedule should have been negotiated. *Id.* at 16-17.

As a remedy for the violations of Article 24 and Article 6 of the Agreement, the Arbitrator ordered that: (1) the parties negotiate over the issues listed in the ground rules agreed to by the parties; (2) the grievant maintain her current work station and not be moved without a legitimate work reason and notification to the Union; (3) the grievant be treated fairly and not be subject to retaliation; (4) the parties conduct "[n]egotiations over the scope of the [m]edical secretary position . . . for the purpose of clarifying the duties of the [m]edical secretary and establishing work expectations and boundaries[;]" (5) the grievant "be allowed to receive training in cross development courses without any limitation due to her work assignment as [m]edical secretary[;]" (6) the grievant receive priority consideration for future vacancies in her job series; and (7) the Agency not arbitrarily deny a request by any qualified secretary willing to exchange positions with the grievant. *Id.* at 18-19.

III. Agency's Exception

The Agency argues that the Arbitrator's award is contrary to law because it violates management's rights under § 7106 of the Statute. Exception at 4. The Agency asserts that two of the remedies ordered by the Arbitrator -- that the parties must negotiate to clarify "the scope of the [m]edical secretary position" and that the "grievant will be allowed to receive training in cross development courses without any limitation due to her work assignment as [m]edical secretary" -- affect management's right to assign work. *Id.* at 4-5. Accordingly, the Agency contends that the Authority should apply the two-prong test set forth in *United States Department of the Treasury, Bureau of Engraving & Printing, Washington, D.C.*, 53 FLRA 146 (1997) (*BEP*) and conclude that the award violates management's rights. *Id.*

The Agency claims that the award "clearly affects [its] right to assign work." *Id.* at 5. According to the Agency, the right to assign work includes the right to determine the particular duties to be assigned, when work assignments will occur, and to whom or what positions the duties will be assigned. *Id.* at 6. Additionally, the Agency argues that "the assignment of training constitutes the assignment of work." *Id.* at 7. Therefore, according to the Agency, the above remedies affect its right to assign work.

The Agency also argues that the Arbitrator's award does not satisfy prong I of *BEP* because Article 6 and Article 24 of the Agreement do not

3. Article 24, Section (a)(1) provides: "There will be no prohibitions to the employment of a relative (including spouse) of an employee provided that: (1) there is no evidence of advocacy of employment, either orally or in writing, by the relative (including spouse) already employed[.]" *Id.*

4. Article 6, Section (b)(2) grants to employees the right "to be treated fairly and equitably in all aspects of personnel management." *Id.* at 7.

constitute arrangements for employees adversely affected by the exercise of a management right. *Id.* at 8. According to the Agency, requiring it to bargain with the Union over the scope of the duties of the medical secretary position directly interferes with its right to assign work. *Id.* at 10. The Agency claims that these provisions, as interpreted by the Arbitrator, are not sufficiently tailored to be appropriate arrangements. *Id.* at 11. The Agency also argues that the portion of the award allowing the grievant to participate in cross development training "effectively abrogates" its right to assign work. *Id.*

Finally, the Agency argues that, even if the Arbitrator's interpretation of the Agreement is an appropriate arrangement, the award does not satisfy prong II of *BEP* because it is not a reconstruction of what the Agency would have done had it not violated the Agreement. *Id.* at 12-13. The Agency claims that, even if it had violated the Agreement, it would have only negotiated over the impact and implementation of the decision to reassign, and would not have bargained over the scope of the medical secretary duties. *Id.* at 13. Additionally, the Agency argues that it would not have granted the grievant an "unfettered right to training," but would have notified the Union and bargained over the impact and implementation of the reassignment. *Id.* at 13-14.

IV. The Arbitrator's award is not contrary to § 7106 of the Statute.

When an exception involves an award's consistency with law, the Authority reviews any question of law raised by the exception and the award de novo. *See NTEU, Chapter 24*, 50 FLRA 330, 332 (1995) (citing *U.S. Customs Serv. v. FLRA*, 43 F.3d 682, 686-87 (D.C. Cir. 1994)). In applying the standard of de novo review, the Authority assesses whether an arbitrator's legal conclusions are consistent with the applicable standard of law. *See U.S. Dep't of Def., Dep'ts of the Army & the Air Force, Ala. Nat'l Guard, Northport, Ala.*, 55 FLRA 37, 40 (1998). In making that assessment, the Authority defers to the arbitrator's underlying factual findings. *See id.*

The Agency contends that the Arbitrator's award enforcing Article 24 and Article 6 of the Agreement impermissibly affects management's right to assign work under § 7106 of the Statute. The Authority recently revised the analysis that it will apply when reviewing management rights exceptions to arbitration awards. *See U.S. Envtl. Prot. Agency*, 65 FLRA 113, 115 (2010) (Member Beck concurring) (*EPA*); *FDIC, Div. of Supervision & Consumer Prot., S.F. Region*, 65 FLRA 102, 106-07 (2010) (Chairman Pope concurring) (*FDIC, S.F. Region*). Under the revised analysis, the Authority will first assess whether the award affects the exercise of the asserted management right. *EPA*, 65 FLRA at 115. If so, then the Authority examines whether the award provides a remedy for a violation of either an applicable law, within the meaning of § 7106(a)(2) of the Statute, or a contract provision that was negotiated pursuant to § 7106(b) of the Statute. *Id.* Furthermore, in setting forth the revised analysis, the Authority rejected the continued application of the "reconstruction" requirement set forth in *BEP*. *FDIC, S.F. Region*, 65 FLRA at 106-07.

The Agency argues that the Arbitrator's award affects management's right to assign work. Exceptions at 5. The right to assign work under § 7106(a)(2)(B) of the Statute encompasses the right to determine the particular duties to be assigned, when work assignments will occur, and to whom or what positions the duties will be assigned. *See U.S. Dep't of Justice, Fed. Bureau of Prisons, Fed. Corr. Inst., Oakdale, La.*, 59 FLRA 277, 279 (2003) (citing *AFGE, Local 3529*, 56 FLRA 1049, 1050 (2001)). The right to assign work also encompasses "decisions as to the type of training to be assigned and the frequency and duration of [the] training." *U.S. Dep't of Homeland Sec., U.S. Customs & Border Prot.*, 61 FLRA 113, 116 (2005) (quoting *NTEU*, 45 FLRA 339, 358 (1992)). The Arbitrator's award requires the parties to negotiate to clarify the particular duties assigned to the grievant's position and allows the grievant to receive training without any limitation due to her current work assignment. Therefore, we find that the award affects management's right to assign work.

The Agency disputes that the Arbitrator's award enforces a contract provision that was properly negotiated pursuant to § 7106(b)(3) because the provision is not an appropriate arrangement. In determining whether the award enforces a contract provision negotiated under § 7106(b)(3), the Authority assesses: (1) whether the contract provision constitutes an arrangement for employees adversely affected by the exercise of a management right; and (2) if so, whether the arbitrator's enforcement of the arrangement abrogates the exercise of the management right. *EPA*, 65 FLRA at 116-18. In concluding that it would apply an abrogation standard, the Authority rejected continued application of an excessive interference standard. *Id.* at 118.

A contract provision constitutes an arrangement if the provision, as interpreted and applied by an arbitrator, ameliorates or mitigates adverse effects that flow from management's exercise of its management rights. *See Soc. Sec. Admin.*, 65 FLRA 339, 341-42 (2010) (citing *EPA*, 65 FLRA at 116). The Authority has held that provisions requiring an agency to exercise its management rights fairly and equitably, similar to Article 6, constitute arrangements within the meaning of § 7106(b)(3) of the Statute. *See U.S. Dep't of Justice, Fed. Bureau of Prisons, Fed. Corr. Complex, Beaumont, Tex.*, 62 FLRA 100, 102 (2007) (finding a "fair and equitable" provision to be an arrangement); *U.S. Dep't of the Navy, Supervisor of Shipbuilding, Conversion & Repair, Newport News, Va.*, 57 FLRA 36, 39 (2001) (same).[5] We find that Article 6, as interpreted and applied by the Arbitrator, constitutes an arrangement. An award abrogates the exercise of a management right if the award precludes the agency from exercising the right. *U.S. Dep't of Transp., Fed. Aviation Admin.*, 65 FLRA 171, 174 (2010). The Arbitrator's award does not, as the Agency alleges, preclude it from reassigning employees, but, rather, only precludes the Agency from conducting reassignments in an unfair manner. *See U.S. Dep't of the Army, Dugway Proving Ground, Dugway, Utah*, 57 FLRA 224, 226 (2001) (finding that, because the agreement provision preserved the agency's right to treat employees fairly, the award did not abrogate management's rights). We find that Article 6, as enforced by the Arbitrator, does not abrogate management's right to assign work. *See U.S. Dep't of the Air Force, Warner Robins Air Logistics Ctr., Warner Robins Air Force Base, Ga.*, 53 FLRA 1344, 1349 (1998) (finding that the arbitrator's award ordering the parties to negotiate over procedures and appropriate arrangements did not abrogate the agency's right to assign work). Accordingly, we find that Article 6, as interpreted by the Arbitrator, was properly negotiated pursuant to § 7106(b).[6]

The Agency further argues that even if the Arbitrator's award satisfies prong I of *BEP*, the remedy is not a reconstruction of what the Agency would have done had it not violated the Agreement. Exceptions at 12-13. However, as noted above, the Authority no longer requires that an arbitrator's remedy reconstruct what management would have done had it not violated the Agreement.[7] *FDIC*, 65 FLRA 179, 181 (2010).

For the foregoing reasons, we find that the Arbitrator's award is not contrary to § 7106 of the Statute and deny the Agency's exception.[8]

V. Decision

The Agency's exception is denied.

---

5. Moreover, although the Agency argues that the award is not sufficiently tailored to be an arrangement, "because an arbitration award necessarily applies an agreement provision to actual, aggrieved parties, arbitration awards are inherently tailored to adversely affected employees, and the Authority does not conduct a tailoring analysis in resolving exceptions to arbitration awards." *EPA*, 65 FLRA at 116.

6. Because we find that Article 6 was properly negotiated pursuant to § 7106(b), it is unnecessary to consider whether Article 24 was also negotiated pursuant to § 7106(b). *Cf. EPA*, 65 FLRA at 119 n.12 (finding it unnecessary to address an award's alternative finding after finding an appropriate arrangement).

7. For the reasons set forth in her concurring opinion in *FDIC, S.F. Region*, 65 FLRA at 112, Chairman Pope agrees that the Agency provides no basis for finding the Arbitrator's remedy deficient because the remedy is reasonably related to Article 6 and the harm being remedied.

8. Member Beck agrees with the conclusion to deny the Agency's exception. He does not agree, however, with his colleagues' analysis insofar as they address the question of whether the award affects the exercise of an asserted management right. For the reasons discussed in his concurring opinion in *EPA*, 65 FLRA 113, Member Beck concludes that where, as here, the Arbitrator is enforcing a contract provision that has been accepted by the Agency as a permissible limitation on its management's rights, it is inappropriate to assess whether the provision itself is an appropriate arrangement or whether it abrogates a § 7106(a) right. *Id.* at 120 (Concurring Opinion of Member Beck). The appropriate question is simply whether the remedy directed by the Arbitrator enforces the provision in a reasonable and reasonably foreseeable fashion. *Id.*; *see also FDIC, S.F. Region*, 65 FLRA at 107. Member Beck concludes that the Arbitrator's award is a plausible interpretation of the parties' agreement. Accordingly, Member Beck agrees that the Agency's exception should be denied.

65 FLRA No. 125

UNITED STATES
DEPARTMENT OF THE INTERIOR
BUREAU OF INDIAN AFFAIRS
NORTHERN PUEBLOS AGENCY
(Agency)

and

AMERICAN FEDERATION OF TEACHERS
INDIAN EDUCATORS FEDERATION
LOCAL 4524
(Union)

0-AR-4269

DECISION

February 28, 2011

Before the Authority: Carol Waller Pope, Chairman, and Thomas M. Beck and Ernest DuBester, Members

I. Statement of the Case

This matter is before the Authority on exceptions to an award of Arbitrator Bennett S. Aisenberg filed by the Agency under § 7122(a) of the Federal Service Labor-Management Relations Statute (the Statute) and part 2425 of the Authority's Regulations. The Union filed an opposition to the Agency's exceptions.

The Arbitrator sustained the Union's grievance finding that the Agency breached Article 31 of the parties' collective bargaining agreement (CBA) when it conducted a reduction-in-force (RIF) of the Northern Pueblo Agency (NPA) Hotshot Crew (NPA Crew). For the reasons set forth below, we dismiss the Agency's exceptions in part and deny them in part.

II. Background and Arbitrator's Award

At the beginning of 2005, the NPA Crew, a group of firefighters, "was designated as trainees." Award at 1. In a memorandum dated January 4,[1] the Director of Fire Management (the Director) for the Bureau of Indian Affairs (BIA) stated that all trainee crews within the BIA must become certified pursuant to the National Interagency Hotshot Crew process by September 30. *Id.* On June 21, the Agency sent a follow-up memorandum reiterating that, if any trainee crew did not have its certification by September 30, its funding would be terminated and the crew would be disbanded.
Id. at 2.

On August 1, the NPA Superintendent requested certification of the NPA Crew. On November 4, the NPA Crew was notified that it would not be recommended for certification because it lacked: (1) a Type 4 incident commander because the Assistant Superintendent failed to qualify for that position and (2) a squad boss because one resigned effective August 31. *Id.*

The Agency later notified the NPA Crew that it would be disbanded and that the employees would be terminated in a RIF. Exceptions at 2-3. The Union then filed a grievance. *Id.* at 3. The grievance was unresolved, and the matter was submitted to arbitration. The parties stipulated to the following issues:

> 1. Did [the Agency] breach Article 31[2] of the [CBA] when it conducted the [RIF] affecting the [NPA Crew] in 2006?
>
> 2. Was the 2006 [RIF] affecting the [NPA Crew] bona fide and conducted for a legitimate [m]anagement reason?

1. All dates refer to 2005 unless indicated otherwise.

2. Article 31, Section 1 of the CBA states:

> Through careful planning and use of other administrative techniques, to the extent it determines practicable and in the public interest, [Agency] officials at all organizational levels should seek to avoid the necessity of entering into a formal [RIF] action. Management will conduct a RIF only when the release is necessary for the reasons specified in [Office of Personnel Management] regulations, 5 CFR, which includes lack of work, shortage of funds, insufficient personnel ceilings, reorganizations, reclassify-cation due to a change in duties, or the exercise of reemployment rights or restoration rights.

Award at 3.

3. If the answer to issue 1 or issue 2 is favorable to the Union, what shall the remedy be?

Award at 3-4.

The Arbitrator found that Article 31, Section 1 of the CBA "places restrictions on the Agency's right to engage in a" RIF. *Id.* at 4. Specifically, the Arbitrator found that management must "seek to avoid the necessity of entering into formal [RIF] action through careful planning and use of other administrative techniques" and "will conduct a RIF only when the release is necessary for the reasons specified in OPM regulations," which includes, among other things, lack of work and shortage of funds. *Id.*

The Arbitrator observed that, even assuming that the Agency had the right to require the NPA Crew to obtain certification by September 30, "what followed . . . was totally under the control of [Agency] personnel, and the hotshot crew was solely at the [sic] their mercy." *Id.* He reasoned that certification could have occurred if the Agency had filed for certification earlier in May or June when there was a full complement of supervisory staff, and the question of whether the Assistant Superintendent was qualified for his position could have been resolved in favor of the NPA Crew. *Id.* at 4-5. The Arbitrator noted that either the Agency could have made a definitive determination that the Assistant Superintendent achieved Type 4 Incident Commander status, or it could have allowed him to achieve Type 4 Incident Commander status in the time allotted. *Id.* at 4-5. Instead, the Arbitrator pointed out, there was no testimony to indicate that the Agency ever made the NPA Superintendent or the NPA Crew aware that, as early as June, it considered the NPA Crew to have a supervisory deficiency. *Id.* at 5. The Arbitrator concluded that "it is clear" that the NPA Crew "had no control over the events that led to the denial of certification, and that [m]anagement did not satisfy the requirements of Article 31, [Section] 1." *Id.*

Finally, the Arbitrator found that, although the Agency had designated its employment action as a RIF, it had the characteristics of a disciplinary or adverse action, and the employees of the NPA Crew became the victims of the Agency's failure to follow the provision of Article 31, Section 1. *Id.* at 6. He stated that, although it is arguably proper under the CBA to conduct a RIF when there is a shortage of funds, he was "not convinced, based on the testimony, that there was an actual shortage of funds," noting that the Director testified that the half million dollars allotted to the NPA Crew was used elsewhere. *Id.* The Arbitrator concluded, however, that, even if there were a shortage of funds, "the Agency did not use careful planning and other administrative techniques to seek to avoid the necessity of entering into the [RIF]." *Id.*

Accordingly, the Arbitrator ordered the Agency to offer to all employees affected by the RIF reinstatement to their former positions, with back pay, including any proven lost premium pay. *Id.* The Arbitrator retained jurisdiction to resolve any disputes with regard to the remedy and to entertain any application for attorney fees. *Id.*

III. Positions of the Parties

A. Agency's Exceptions

The Agency contends that the award fails to draw its essence from the CBA. Specifically, the Agency argues that Article 31, Section 1 places no restrictions on management with regard to its ability to conduct a RIF, and that the Arbitrator's reliance on Article 31, Section 1 as a basis for overturning the RIF is contrary to the plain language of the provision. Exceptions at 7-8.

The Agency also argues that the Arbitrator exceeded his authority by reviewing management's actions with respect to its denial of the NPA Crew's certification. *Id.* at 9-11. According to the Agency, once an agency shows that its decision to conduct a RIF is in accordance 5 C.F.R. § 351.201(a)(2), an arbitrator, in reviewing the RIF, has no authority to review management considerations that underlie management's discretion. *Id.* at 10-11. The Agency argues that, because the RIF at issue here was conducted due to a shortage of funds and for a reorganization, the Arbitrator had no authority to review management's considerations underlying its discretion to effect the RIF. *Id.* at 11-12. Moreover, as part of this argument, the Agency challenges the Arbitrator's statements that the RIF had "'the characteristics of discipline or adverse action'" and that "'a RIF may not be a disguised adverse or performance[-]based action to remove an employee,'" asserting that such statements have no basis in fact. *Id.* at 11-12 (quoting Award at 6 & n.1).

Finally, the Agency contends that the award is contrary to law because it impermissibly interferes with management's rights as defined by § 7106(a)(2)(A) of the Statute.[3] Exceptions at 12-14. According to the Agency, "[b]y ruling that the employees are to be reinstated to their former positions with backpay, the Arbitrator effectively abrogate[d] management's rights – i.e.[,] the decisions that management made concerning" the NPA Crew. *Id.* at 14.

B. Union's Opposition

In its opposition, the Union moves to dismiss the Agency's exceptions. The Union contends that the Agency's exceptions should be dismissed because they contain arguments that could have been, but were not, presented to the Arbitrator. The Union contends that the Agency never argued before the Arbitrator or in its post-hearing brief that Article 31, Section 1 should be interpreted as placing no restriction on management's right to conduct a RIF. Opp'n at 20-21. Similarly, the Union contends that the Agency never raised below its argument that the Arbitrator had no authority to review whether the RIF was for bona fide reasons. *Id.* at 23. Finally, the Union argues that the Agency did not contend before the Arbitrator that the Union's grievance, its interpretation of Article 31, or the relief that it requested impermissibly interfered with management's rights under the Statute. *Id.* at 24-25.

As for the Award's merits, the Union argues that, even if the Agency argued below that the language of Article 31 did not place restrictions on management's right to conduct a RIF, the Agency's disagreement with the Arbitrator's interpretation of the language is not a basis for finding that the award failed to draw its essence from the CBA or for finding that the Award is otherwise deficient under the Statute. *Id.* at 22. The Union also contends that the Arbitrator did not exceed his authority when he reviewed whether the RIF was bona fide and accomplished for legitimate management reasons under OPM regulations, as well as whether the RIF independently violated the CBA. *Id.* at 23-24. Finally, the Union argues that the language of Article 31, Section 1 and the Arbitrator's interpretation of that provision does not impermissibly interfere with management's rights and notes that the Authority has upheld similar provisions previously. *Id.* at 25-26.

IV. Analysis and Conclusions

A. Preliminary Matter: 5 C.F.R. § 2429.5 bars certain of the Agency's arguments.

The Authority's Regulations that were in effect when the Agency filed its exceptions provided that "[t]he Authority will not consider . . . any issue, which was not presented in the proceedings before the . . . arbitrator." 5 C.F.R. § 2429.5.[4]

As set forth above, the parties asked the Arbitrator to resolve two issues: (1) whether the Agency breached Article 31 of the CBA when it conducted the RIF and (2) whether the RIF was bona fide and conducted for a legitimate management reason. Accordingly, the Agency had the opportunity to raise before the Arbitrator its arguments that Article 31, Section 1 places no restrictions on management's rights to conduct a RIF; that the Arbitrator had no authority to review either the "certification of th[e] crew as it relates to the reason for th[e] RIF" or whether the RIF was for bona fide reasons, *see* Exceptions at 12; and that Article 31, Section 1, if interpreted as argued by the Union at arbitration, as well as the remedy requested by the Union, improperly interfered with management's rights as defined by § 7106(a)(2)(A) of the Statute. However, there is no evidence in the record that the Agency did so.

The case law interpreting 5 C.F.R. § 2429.5 makes clear that the Authority will not consider a contention that could have been, but was not, presented to the Arbitrator. *See U.S. Dep't of the Air Force, Air Force Materiel Command, Robins Air Force Base, Ga.*, 59 FLRA 542, 544 (2003). Because there is no evidence in the record that the Agency raised any of these arguments before the Arbitrator, we conclude that these exceptions are not properly before the Authority.

3. Section 7106(a)(2)(A) of the Statute provides, in pertinent part:

> Subject to subsection (b) of this section, nothing in this chapter shall affect the authority of any management official of any agency . . . to hire, assign, direct, layoff, and retain employees in the agency . . . .

5 U.S.C. § 7106(a)(2)(A).

4. The Authority's Regulations concerning the review of arbitration awards, as well as certain related procedural Regulations, including 5 C.F.R. § 2429.5, were revised effective October 1, 2010. *See* 75 Fed. Reg. 42,283 (2010). Because the Agency's exceptions in this case were filed before that date, we apply the prior Regulations.

Based on the foregoing, we dismiss these exceptions.

B. The award is not based on a nonfact.

The Agency contends that Arbitrator's statements that the RIF had "the characteristics of discipline or adverse action" and that "a RIF may not be a disguised adverse or performance-based action to remove an employee" have no basis in fact. Exceptions at 11-12 (quoting Award at 6 & n.1). To the extent that these contentions could be construed as alleging that the Arbitrator's award is based on nonfacts, the Agency does not explain how these findings are central facts underlying the award. As a result, the Agency has failed to establish that the award is based on a nonfact. *See NFFE, Local 1984*, 56 FLRA 38, 41 (2000) ("To establish that an award is based on a nonfact, the appealing party must demonstrate that a central fact underlying the award is clearly erroneous, but for which a different result would have been reached by the arbitrator."). Accordingly, we deny this exception.

V. Decision

The Agency's exceptions are dismissed in part and denied in part.

65 FLRA No. 126

AMERICAN FEDERATION
OF GOVERNMENT EMPLOYEES
COUNCIL 220
(Union)

and

SOCIAL SECURITY ADMINISTRATION
REDDING DISTRICT OFFICE
REDDING, CALIFORNIA
(Agency)

0-AR-4617

DECISION

March 9, 2011

Before the Authority: Carol Waller Pope, Chairman, and Thomas M. Beck and Ernest DuBester, Members

I. Statement of the Case

This matter is before the Authority on exceptions to an award of Arbitrator Thomas Angelo filed by the Union under § 7122(a) of the Federal Service Labor-Management Relations Statute (the Statute) and part 2425 of the Authority's Regulations. The Agency filed an opposition to the Union's exceptions.

The Arbitrator determined that the Agency did not violate the law or the parties' National Agreement (Agreement) when it denied "suffer or permit" overtime to employees on alternative work schedules (AWSs).

For the reasons that follow, we deny the Union's exceptions.

II. Background and Arbitrator's Award

A. Background

The Union represents service and claims representatives at the Agency's Redding, California office. Award at 2-3. The Agreement provides for an AWS that allows employees to vary their arrival and departure times within the work day. *Id.* at 7.

The Redding office opens at 7:00 a.m. Work is not authorized to begin before that time. *Id.* at 5-6. The start time for AWS employees is either the time recorded on their time cards or 7:00 a.m., whichever is later. Overtime and credit hours are recorded on an Agency form. *Id.* at 4.

The Agreement recognizes two kinds of overtime, regular and irregular. *Id.* at 5. Regular overtime is planned and approved by management in advance. Irregular overtime is unplanned and is permitted at the Redding office only when a service call lasts beyond an employee's scheduled clock-out time. *Id.*

Some AWS employees became concerned that they were not being compensated for time they worked before 7:00 a.m., the authorized starting time. The employees became concerned because that time was not being recorded on the Agency overtime form as irregular overtime. The Union filed a grievance on their behalf seeking irregular overtime compensation. *Id.* at 2, 6. When the parties could not resolve the grievance, it was submitted to arbitration.

B. Arbitrator's Award

As relevant here, the parties stipulated to the following issue for resolution by the Arbitrator:

> Whether the [Agency] . . . denied compensation to employees for work performed beyond their tour of duty, and thereby violated the Agreement and/or the [Fair Labor Standards Act (FLSA)]. If so, what should the remedy be?

Id. at 3.

The Arbitrator first determined that all of the employees affected by the grievance were on AWSs. *Id.* at 7. In resolving the grievance, the Arbitrator considered the FLSA, its implementing regulation, 5 C.F.R. § 551.501(a)(6), and the Federal Employee Flexible and Compressed Work Schedules Act of 1982, 5 U.S.C. §§ 6120-6133 (the Act). *Id.* at 8-9.[1] Because the Union sought irregular overtime compensation for AWS employees for overtime work that was not ordered in advance by management, the Arbitrator construed the Union's argument to be based on the "suffer or permit" provisions of the

1. Pertinent provisions of these laws and regulations, as well as pertinent contract provisions, are set forth in the appendix to this decision.

FLSA, which provide for overtime compensation for such work.[2] *Id.* at 7, 9.

Applying the FLSA's "suffer or permit" overtime regulations, the Arbitrator determined that the FLSA allows AWS employees to earn overtime only if management orders the overtime in advance and the hours worked do not consist of credit hours. *Id.* at 7-8. The Arbitrator therefore concluded that AWS employees are not entitled to "suffer or permit" overtime because, by definition, it is not ordered in advance by management. Thus, the Arbitrator denied the grievance. *Id.* at 10. The Arbitrator found that the Office of Personnel Management's (OPM's) Handbook on Alternative Work Schedules (AWS Handbook) supported his decision. The AWS Handbook specifically states that "[e]mployees on flexible work schedules may not earn overtime pay as a result of including 'suffered or permitted' hours (under the FLSA) as hours of work." *Id.* at 8 (quoting AWS Handbook).

In the Arbitrator's view, the Union's position that AWS employees are entitled to "suffer or permit" overtime presumes that all employees are covered by the "suffer or permit" provisions of the FLSA regardless of whether they are on a flexible work schedule. *Id.* at 9. According to the Arbitrator, this position overlooks federal laws mandating that AWS employees are not entitled to any "suffer or permit" overtime. *Id.* Because AWS employees are not entitled to "suffer or permit" overtime, the Arbitrator concluded that it was unnecessary for him to determine whether management knew or should have known that AWS employees were starting work before 7:00 a.m. *Id.*

The Arbitrator did not determine whether the Agency denied AWS employees compensation under the Agreement for other "legitimate" overtime because he found that the Union failed to present sufficient evidence to prove this claim. *Id.* at 2.

2. The FLSA provides the federal minimum standards for wages and overtime. 29 U.S.C. §§ 201-219. 5 C.F.R. Part 551 sets forth the regulations implementing the FLSA in the federal sector. "Suffer or permit" overtime is overtime work performed for the benefit of an agency, whether requested or not, provided that management knows or has reason to know the work is being performed and does not prevent it. 5 C.F.R. §§ 551.104 & 401(a)(2).

III. Positions of the Parties

A. Union's Exceptions

The Union contends that the award is contrary to law and fails to draw its essence from the Agreement. Exceptions at 3. In support of its contrary to law claim, the Union argues that AWS employees are entitled to "suffer or permit" overtime because the regulations implementing the FLSA allow employees to be compensated for both regular and irregular overtime, including "suffer or permit" overtime. *Id.* at 4-6. Specifically, the Union argues that 5 C.F.R. § 551.401(a)(2) provides that all time spent by an employee performing work for the benefit of an agency under the direction and control of that agency constitutes hours of work. *Id.* at 4-5. According to the Union, such time includes "suffer or permit" overtime hours. *Id.* at 5. The Union reasons that, because "suffer or permit" hours constitute hours of work, AWS employees must be compensated for that time.

The Union claims that AWS employees are entitled to "suffer or permit" overtime under 5 C.F.R. § 551.501(c) because it is unscheduled overtime for which an employee must be paid.[3] The Union asserts that this regulation defines "irregular" overtime as overtime work that is not scheduled in advance of an employee's workweek. *Id.* Therefore, the Union argues, the Arbitrator erred in denying "suffer or permit" overtime to AWS employees. *Id.* at 5-6.

The Union further claims that the AWS Handbook does not support the Arbitrator's award. Specifically, the Union argues that the AWS Handbook, which states that "suffer or permit" overtime is not available to AWS employees, "is of little legal import" because it is only guidance and therefore not persuasive. *Id.* at 5. The Union further contends that, "contrary to [the Arbitrator's] assertions, the 'suffer or permit' or irregular overtime is authorized" by the regulations, not prohibited by the Act or the AWS Handbook, and is allowed by the Agency's Personnel Policy Manual. Therefore, the Union argues, the Arbitrator's decision that AWS employees are not permitted to work such irregular overtime is contrary to law. *Id.* at 6.

3. 5 CFR § 551.501 provides for overtime pay. Subpart (c) states: "In this subpart, 'irregular or occasional overtime work' is work that is not scheduled in advance of the employee's workweek."

Finally, the Union contends that the award fails to draw its essence from the Agreement because it is in conflict with the Agreement's general overtime provisions. *Id.* at 7-8. The Union cites the general overtime provisions of the Agreement, which provide compensation for both regular and irregular overtime.[4] *Id.* Therefore, the Union claims, the overtime provisions of the Agreement establish AWS employees' right to earn irregular overtime, including "suffer or permit" overtime. *Id.* at 7-9. In the Union's view, the award, which denies "suffer or permit" overtime, categorically denies all irregular overtime to AWS employees. Consequently, the Union argues, the award reflects a manifest disregard of the Agreement and is also unfounded, irrational, and not a plausible interpretation of the Agreement. *Id.* at 8-9.

B. Agency's Opposition

As a threshold matter, the Agency disputes the date the award was served on the Union and claims that the Union's exceptions were filed one day late. Opp'n at 2-3.

In regard to the merits, the Agency argues that the award is not contrary to law because it properly denies AWS employees both "suffer or permit" and irregular overtime. *Id.* at 3-4. The Agency contends that the Arbitrator correctly determined that "suffer or permit" overtime is not authorized for AWS employees because it is not overtime that is ordered in advance by management as required by 5 U.S.C. § 6121(6). *Id.* at 4-6. In the Agency's view, the Union's claim for overtime compensation is based on credit hours for which the law does not permit compensation.[5] *Id.* at 5. The Agency contends that the legislative history of the Act demonstrates Congress' intent to avoid the exact claim that is made here: a demand to be compensated for credit hours, which are accrued at the employee's election, by claiming entitlement to "suffer or permit" overtime even though it was not ordered in advance. *Id.* at 6-8.

Furthermore, the Agency contends that the Arbitrator was correct in giving the AWS Handbook persuasive weight when interpreting the Act's application to overtime because the Authority has done so in the past. *Id.* at 9 (citations omitted). Therefore, the Agency argues, the AWS Handbook, which states that AWS employees are not entitled to "suffer or permit" overtime, is persuasive authority that supports the award. *Id.* at 9-10. The Agency further notes that the Agency's Personnel Policy Manual also confirms the validity of the award because it states that employees on flexible work schedules cannot earn "suffer or permit" overtime. *Id.* at 6-7. Based on the foregoing, the Agency concludes that the Union has not shown that the Arbitrator's award is contrary to law.

The Agency also argues that the Union has not established that the award fails to draw its essence from the Agreement. *Id.* at 10-11. The Agency contends that the Union misinterprets the award. *Id.* at 10. Specifically, the Agency asserts that, while the Arbitrator determined that AWS employees are not entitled to "suffer or permit" overtime, he did not make a determination as to whether they are entitled to irregular overtime because the Union failed to provide evidence supporting this claim. *Id.* at 10-11. Therefore, the Agency argues, the Union fails to show that the award does not draw its essence from the Agreement.

IV. Preliminary Issue

The Agency disputes the date the award was served on the Union and claims that the Union's exceptions are untimely. *Id.* at 2-3.

Section 7122(b) of the Statute requires that exceptions be filed within thirty days from the date of service of the award. 5 U.S.C. § 7122(b). Section 2429.22 of the Authority's Regulations provides that five days be added if the award is served by mail or commercial delivery. 5 C.F.R. § 2429.22. The Regulations also provide that the date of filing exceptions by mail is the postmark date. 5 C.F.R. § 2429.21(b).

The Union submitted evidence establishing that it was served with the award by mail on December 29, 2009. Exceptions, Attach., Ex. 1.

4. Article 10, Section 3, General Overtime Provisions, provides in pertinent part:

> C. When an employee, whether covered by the Fair Labor Standards Act or exempt, works regular overtime, such overtime will be scheduled and paid in increments of 15 minutes. When an employee, whether covered by the Fair Labor Standards Act or exempt, works irregular overtime, such overtime will be paid in increments of 15 minutes . . . .

Exceptions, Attach., Ex. 2 at 56.

5. AWS employees are not compensated for credit hours unless they opt out of a flexible work program. *See* 5 U.S.C. §§ 6123(b) & 6126(b).

Therefore, adding five days as provided by 5 C.F.R. § 2429.22, the Union was required to file its exceptions by February 1, 2010.[6] The record indicates that the exceptions were postmarked January 29, 2010. Accordingly, the Union's exceptions were timely filed. *See U.S. Dep't of Veterans Affairs, San Diego Healthcare Sys., San Diego, Cal.*, 65 FLRA 45, 47 (2010).

V. Analysis and Conclusions

A. The award is not contrary to law.

The Union contends that the award is contrary to law because the Arbitrator misapplied the law concerning "suffer or permit" overtime under the FLSA. When an exception challenges an award's consistency with law, the Authority reviews the question of law raised by the exception and the award de novo. *See NTEU, Chapter 24*, 50 FLRA 330, 332 (1995) (citing *U.S. Customs Serv.*, 43 F.3d 682, 686-87 (D.C. Cir. 1994)). In applying this standard, the Authority assesses whether the arbitrator's legal conclusions are consistent with the applicable standard of law. *See NFFE, Local 1437,* 53 FLRA 1703, 1710 (1998). In making that assessment, the Authority defers to the arbitrator's underlying factual findings. *See id.*

The Arbitrator found that the Union's claim to irregular overtime was based on the "suffer or permit" provisions of the FLSA. "Suffer or permit" is overtime work performed for the benefit of an agency that management has not ordered in advance, but which management knows or has reason to know is being performed, and which management does not prevent. 5 C.F.R. §§ 551.104 & 401(a)(2). The regulations implementing the FLSA provide for overtime pay but exclude such pay "[f]or hours of work that are not 'overtime hours,' as defined in 5 U.S.C. § 6121, for employees under flexible . . . work schedules[.]" 5 C.F.R. § 551.501(a)(6). Overtime hours for employees on flexible work schedules, as defined in § 6121, are "all hours in excess of 8 hours in a day or 40 hours in a week which are officially ordered in advance, but [do] not include credit hours." 5 U.S.C. § 6121(6).[7] "In other words, an employee covered by the FLSA who is on a flexible work schedule may not receive overtime unless ordered in advance" by management. *AFGE, Local 2006*, 65 FLRA 465, 469 (2011). Furthermore, the AWS Handbook, which the Authority finds has persuasive weight on this issue, states that employees on flexible work schedules may not earn "suffer or permit" overtime. *Id.* (finding AWS Handbook persuasive and consistent with statutory and regulatory provisions precluding "suffer or permit" overtime for AWS employees).

The Arbitrator's legal conclusions are consistent with these principles. The Arbitrator found that all of the employees subject to the grievance are AWS employees. The Arbitrator then determined that AWS employees are only entitled to overtime if it is ordered in advance by management. The Arbitrator also found that "suffer or permit" overtime under the FLSA is overtime not ordered in advance. Therefore, the Arbitrator concluded that AWS employees are precluded from receiving "suffer or permit" overtime. Accordingly, the Union's contrary to law contentions do not provide a basis for finding the award deficient.

For the reasons set forth above, we deny the Union's exception that the award is contrary to law.

B. The award does not fail to draw its essence from the Agreement.

Relying on the general overtime provisions in the Agreement, the Union argues that the award fails to draw its essence from the Agreement. When reviewing an arbitrator's interpretation of a collective bargaining agreement, the Authority applies the deferential standard of review that federal courts use in reviewing arbitration awards in the private sector. *See* 5 U.S.C. § 7122(a)(2); *AFGE, Council 220*, 54 FLRA 156, 159 (1998). Under this standard, the Authority will find that an arbitration award is deficient as failing to draw its essence from the collective bargaining agreement when the appealing party establishes that the award: (1) cannot in any rational way be derived from the agreement; (2) is so unfounded in reason and fact and so unconnected with the wording and purposes of the collective bargaining agreement as to manifest an infidelity to the obligation of the arbitrator; (3) does not represent

6. The Authority's Regulations concerning the review of arbitration awards, as well as certain related procedural Regulations, including §§ 2429.21 and 2429.22, were revised effective October 1, 2010. 75 Fed. Reg. 42,283 (2010). As the exceptions in this case were filed prior to October 1, 2010, we apply the prior version of the Regulations here.

7. Credit hours are hours that are "in excess of an employee's basic work requirement and which the employee elects to work so as to vary the length of a workweek or a workday[.]" 5 U.S.C. § 6121(4).

a plausible interpretation of the agreement; or (4) evidences a manifest disregard of the agreement. *See, e.g., U.S. Dep't of Labor (OSHA)*, 34 FLRA 573, 575 (1990). This standard and the private sector cases from which it is derived make clear that an arbitrator's award will not be found to fail to draw its essence from the agreement merely because a party believes that the arbitrator misinterpreted the agreement. *See id.* at 575-76. The courts defer to the arbitrator's interpretation of the collective bargaining agreement "because it is the arbitrator's construction of the agreement for which the parties have bargained." *Id.* at 576.

The Union claims that the award fails to draw its essence from the Agreement by categorically denying all irregular overtime to AWS employees. However, the Arbitrator did not make such a categorical determination. To the contrary, the Arbitrator considered whether AWS employees are entitled to "legitimate" irregular overtime under the Agreement, and found that "the Union failed to present enough evidence that would allow for a conclusion to be drawn that the Agency denied legitimate overtime payments" to any employee, including AWS employees. Award at 2. Therefore, the Union fails to show that the award does not draw its essence from the Agreement on this basis.

The Union also claims that the award fails to draw its essence from the Agreement because the award is inconsistent with Article 10. The Union contends, in this regard, that Article 10 provides compensation for regular and irregular overtime, including "suffer or permit" overtime.

The Union's reliance on Article 10 is misplaced. Article 10 provides, in pertinent part: "When an employee . . . works irregular overtime, such overtime will be paid in increments of 15 minutes . . . ." Exceptions, Attach., Ex. 2 at 56. As this wording reflects, Article 10 does not establish any entitlement for AWS employees to earn "suffer or permit" overtime. The Arbitrator found that "the Agreement . . . contains some abstract provisions regarding the counting of incremental time with respect to irregular overtime[.]" Award at 2. As such, the Arbitrator's conclusion is not inconsistent with Article 10 because the article only addresses how employees will be paid for overtime they have earned. Consequently, the Union's claim does not provide any basis for finding that the Arbitrator's interpretation of the Agreement is unfounded, irrational, implausible, or in manifest disregard of the Agreement.

For the reasons set forth above, we deny the Union's exception that the award fails to draw its essence from the Agreement.

VI. Decision

The Union's exceptions are denied.

APPENDIX

Article 10 of the Agreement provides, in pertinent part:

> Section 3- General Overtime Provisions
>
> . . . .
>
> C. When an employee, whether covered by the Fair Labor Standards Act or exempt, works regular overtime, such overtime will be scheduled and paid in increments of 15 minutes. When an employee, whether covered by the Fair Labor Standards Act or exempt, works irregular overtime, such overtime will be paid in increments of 15 minutes. . . .

Exceptions, Attach., Ex. 2 at 56.

The Federal Employee Flexible and Compressed Work Schedules Act of 1982, 5 U.S.C. §§ 6120-6133 provides, in pertinent part:

5 U.S.C. § 6121 Definitions

> For purposes of this subchapter—
>
> . . . .
>
> (4) "credit hours" means any hours, within a flexible schedule established under section 6122 of this title, which are in excess of an employee's basic work requirement and which the employee elects to work so as to vary the length of a workweek or a workday;
>
> . . . .
>
> (6) "overtime hours", when used with respect to flexible schedule programs under sections 6122 through 6126 of the title, means all hours in excess of 8 hours in a day or 40 hours in a week which are officially ordered in advance, but does not include credit hours;

5 U.S.C. § 6123

> . . . .
>
> (b) Notwithstanding the provisions of law referred to in subsection (a)(1) of this section, an employee shall not be entitled to be compensated for credit hours worked except to the extent authorized under section 6126 of this title or to the extent such employee is allowed to have such hours taken into account with respect to the employee's basic work requirement.

5 U.S.C. § 6126

> . . . .
>
> (b) Any employee who is on a flexible schedule program under section 6122 of this title and who is no longer subject to such a program shall be paid at such employee's then current rate of basic pay . . . .

5 C.F.R. Part 551- Pay Administration Under the Fair Labor Standards Act provides, in pertinent part:

5 C.F.R. § 551.104 Definitions.

> . . . .
>
> Suffered or permitted work means any work performed by an employee for the benefit of an agency, whether requested or not, provided the employee's supervisor knows or has reason to believe that the work is being performed and has an opportunity to prevent the work from being performed.

5 C.F.R. § 551.401 Basic principles.

> (a) All time spent by an employee performing an activity for the benefit of an agency and under the control or direction of the agency is "hours of work." Such time includes:
>
> . . . .
>
> (2) Time during which an employee is suffered or permitted to work; . . . .

5 C.F.R. § 551.501 Overtime pay.

> (a) An agency shall compensate an employee who is not exempt under subpart B of this part for all hours of work in excess of 8 in a day or 40 in a workweek at a rate equal to one and one-half times the employee's hourly regular rate of pay, except that an employee shall not receive overtime compensation under this part --
>
> . . . .

> (6) For hours of work that are not "overtime hours," as defined in 5 U.S.C. § 6121, for employees under flexible or compressed work schedules[.]

. . . .

(c) In this subpart, "irregular or occasional overtime work" is work that is not scheduled in advance of the employee's workweek.

65 FLRA No. 127

UNITED STATES
DEPARTMENT OF HOMELAND SECURITY
U.S. CUSTOMS AND BORDER PROTECTION
(Agency)

and

AMERICAN FEDERATION
OF GOVERNMENT EMPLOYEES
LOCAL 2544
NATIONAL BORDER PATROL COUNCIL
(Union)

0-AR-4701

DECISION

March 14, 2011

Before the Authority: Carol Waller Pope, Chairman, and Thomas M. Beck and Ernest DuBester, Members

I. Statement of the Case

This matter is before the Authority on exceptions to an award of Arbitrator Jerome H. Ross filed by the Agency under § 7122(a) of the Federal Service Labor-Management Relations Statute (the Statute) and part 2425 of the Authority's Regulations. The Authority issued an Order to Show Cause (Order) directing the Agency to show cause why its exceptions should not be dismissed as interlocutory. The Agency filed a response to the Order. The Union filed a consolidated opposition to the exceptions and reply to the Agency's response to the Order.

The Arbitrator issued a supplemental award finding that the Union's request for attorney fees was warranted in the interest of justice. However, the Arbitrator found that issues remained regarding the reasonableness of the amount requested and remanded the case to the parties for resolution, retaining jurisdiction for the sole purpose of resolving the matter if the parties were unable to agree.

For the reasons discussed below, we dismiss the exceptions, without prejudice, as interlocutory.

II. Background and Arbitrator's Award

The grievant filed a grievance challenging his seven-day disciplinary suspension for failure to safeguard government property. Supplemental Award of Attorney Fees (Supplemental Award) at 1; Exceptions at 2. In the original award, the Arbitrator sustained the grievance and reduced the suspension to a written reprimand with backpay. Supplemental Award at 1. As neither party filed exceptions to the original award, it became final and binding.

Subsequent to the issuance of the original award, the Union filed a motion for attorney fees. The Union maintained that the attorney fees request was reasonable and warranted in the interest of justice. *Id.* at 1-2. The Agency filed an opposition asserting, as relevant here, that the Union was not entitled to an attorney fees award because the grievant failed to show that: (1) attorney fees were warranted in the interest of justice as required by the fifth *Allen* criterion[1]; and (2) the attorney fees request was reasonable. *Id.* at 2.

Although the Arbitrator did not frame the issues before him, it is reasonable, based on his summary of the parties' submissions, to construe the award as including issues regarding whether the fees were warranted in the interest of justice and whether the amount requested was reasonable. The Arbitrator determined that the Union's request for attorney fees satisfied *Allen*'s criterion 5, and as a result, a fee award was warranted in the interest of justice. The Arbitrator found that the Agency should have considered another case that was "virtually identical" to the grievant's in which an employee only received a written reprimand. *Id.* at 3. The Arbitrator

1. In *Allen v. U.S.P.S.*, 2 M.S.P.R. 420 (1980) (*Allen*), the Merit Systems Protection Board (MSPB) established criteria to determine whether a fee award was warranted in the "interest of justice." Under *Allen*, an award of attorney fees is warranted in the interest of justice if: (1) the Agency engaged in a prohibited personnel practice; (2) the Agency's actions are clearly without merit or wholly unfounded, or the employee is substantially innocent of charges brought by the agency; (3) the Agency's actions are taken in bad faith to harass or exert improper pressure on an employee; (4) the Agency committed gross procedural error which prolonged the proceeding or severely prejudiced the employee; or (5) the Agency knew or should have known it would not prevail on the merits when it brought the proceeding. *See, e.g., AFGE, Local 3020*, 64 FLRA 596, 597 n.* (2010). An award of attorney fees is also warranted in the interest of justice when there is either a service rendered to the federal workforce or there is a benefit to the public derived from maintaining the action. *Id.*

concluded that if the Agency had considered the consistency of the discipline, then the Agency would have known that it would not prevail on the merits. *Id.*

However, the Arbitrator postponed his determination as to the reasonableness of the attorney fees request because he found that issues remained unresolved regarding that requirement. *Id.* at 4. Although the Arbitrator determined that the rate "should be in line with the community rates of other attorneys," he did not determine what that rate should be. *Id.* The Arbitrator also found that there could be no resolution of the reasonableness issue without an itemized statement of hours worked in the record. Further, the Arbitrator expressed doubt concerning the reasonableness of the amount of time billed in preparation for the arbitration. *Id.* However, rather than deciding these issues, the Arbitrator remanded the reasonableness question to the parties "for resolution[,]" and retained jurisdiction for the "sole purpose of resolving this matter" if the parties were unable to agree. *Id.*

III. Positions of the Parties

A. Agency's Exceptions

The Agency excepts to the award as being contrary to law. The Agency asserts that the Arbitrator's factual findings do not support his legal conclusion that attorney fees are warranted "in the interest of justice" under the Back Pay Act, 5 U.S.C. § 596, 5 U.S.C. § 7701(g), and *Allen.* Exceptions at 7. The Agency also argues that the award is contrary to law because the fees awarded are unreasonable. *Id.* at 16-17.

With respect to whether the fees are warranted, the Agency claims that the Arbitrator misapplied the fifth *Allen* criterion. *Id.* at 11. According to the Agency, the award fails to describe how the Agency "knew or should have known" that it would not prevail when the Arbitrator based his decision on a previous case concerning a similar offense that occurred at least six years earlier involving different deciding officials. *Id.* at 12-14. The Agency also claims that to the extent the award is based on disparate penalties, the Arbitrator failed to conduct a proper analysis to determine whether the grievant was similarly situated to the employee in the previous case who received a lesser penalty. *Id.* at 15.

With regard to the reasonableness of the fees, the Agency takes exception to the Arbitrator's finding that the appropriate rate is the market rate in the community. *Id.* at 16-17. The Agency claims that the fees should be based on the fee agreement between the Union and its attorney as the Authority has ruled that there is a presumption that the rate agreed upon by the Union and its attorney is the maximum fee allowed absent evidence to the contrary. *Id.* According to the Agency, although the Union submitted an affidavit from an attorney in the community to establish the market rate, the Authority has held that such evidence does not demonstrate that an hourly rate higher than the fee agreement is reasonable. *Id.* at 17. Therefore, the Agency argues, the award is contrary to law because it establishes a fee rate without consideration of the fee agreement between the Union and its attorney. *Id.*

The Agency also challenges the number of hours billed by the Union's attorney. The Agency argues that it should not be responsible for the hours billed for preparation of the initial arbitration hearing because that hearing was cancelled by the Union. *Id.*, Agency's Brief in Opposition to Union's Motion, Ex. 8 at 10.

B. Union's Opposition

The Union contends that the Agency's exceptions are interlocutory and must be dismissed. Opp'n at 4. In the alternative, the Union argues that the Arbitrator properly found that attorney fees are warranted "in the interest of justice." *Id.* at 7. In the Union's view, the Agency "knew or should have know it would not prevail" when it elected to suspend the grievant because it had only issued a written reprimand in an earlier case with identical facts. *Id.* at 8.

With respect to the reasonableness of the fees requested, the Union argues that there are insufficient facts to determine this issue and consequently, the exceptions are interlocutory.[2] *Id.* at 13. Alternatively, the Union claims that although the Arbitrator did not determine a specific fee amount, a consideration of the available facts establishes that the amount requested is reasonable. *Id.*

2. The Union states that it inadvertently omitted its itemized statement of hours worked from the motion for attorney fees that it submitted to the Arbitrator, but that it sent a copy to both the Arbitrator and the Agency when it discovered the omission. Opp'n at 2. However, the Union states further that it was unaware when it submitted its itemized statement to the Arbitrator that the Arbitrator had already issued the supplemental award. *Id.*

IV. Order to Show Cause

As noted above, the Authority issued an order directing the Agency to show cause why its exceptions should not be dismissed as interlocutory. Order at 1. In response, the Agency asserts that two decisions made by the Arbitrator in his supplemental award are final: (1) the determination that the attorney fees are warranted "in the interest of justice"; and (2) the rate at which those fees should be paid. Response at 2. According to the Agency, Authority precedent provides that an award is final, and an exception is not interlocutory, when the Arbitrator retains jurisdiction for the sole purpose of determining the amount of the award. *Id.* In the Agency's view, the Arbitrator made a final decision that the fees are warranted and all that is left is for the Arbitrator to determine the amount owed. Therefore, the Agency argues, the award is ripe for review and the exceptions are not interlocutory. *Id.* at 2.

In addition, the Agency argues that the Arbitrator made a final determination as to the rate of pay at which the Union's attorney should be compensated. *Id.* The Agency admits that if it were disputing the actual amount of attorney fees awarded, then the matter would be interlocutory. However, the Agency claims that its exception is based on the Arbitrator's error in deciding the proper rate of pay. Therefore, the Agency argues, the Arbitrator's decision as to the rate of pay is final, not interlocutory, and contrary to law. *Id.* at 3.

The Union contends that the Arbitrator remanded more than just the computation issue. Opp'n at 3. According to the Union, on remand, the parties must: (1) determine the community rate; (2) resolve whether the Union's itemized hours are reasonable; and (3) resolve whether the hours spent by Union counsel are reasonable or repetitive because counsel prepared for the arbitration hearing twice. Once these issues are resolved, the Union argues, the Arbitrator must determine what fee amount should be awarded if the parties cannot agree on an amount. *Id.* The Union claims that if the parties cannot agree, additional litigation will require factual findings and legal determinations by the Arbitrator. The Union further contends that the Authority does not have sufficient facts in the record to make a decision regarding the amount of attorney fees that should be awarded. *Id.*

Finally, the Union argues that the cases cited by the Agency to support its contention that the award is not interlocutory are distinguishable. Specifically, the Union argues that those cases address appeals taken from a merits award in which the arbitrator retained jurisdiction to consider attorney fees "if a party sought them." *Id.* at 4. Here, in contrast, the Union asserts that the Agency filed exceptions to the fee award, not the merits award, and unlike the cases cited by the Agency, the sole issue being challenged by the Agency is the award of attorney fees. *Id.*

V. The exceptions are interlocutory.

Section 2429.11 of the Authority's Regulations pertinently provides that "the Authority . . . ordinarily will not consider interlocutory appeals." 5 C.F.R. § 2429.11. Thus, the Authority ordinarily will not resolve exceptions to an arbitration award unless the award constitutes a complete resolution of all the issues submitted to arbitration. *See, e.g., U.S. Dep't of Justice, Fed. Bureau of Prisons, Fed. Med. Ctr., Carswell, Tex.*, 64 FLRA 566, 567-68 (2010) (*Carswell*); *U.S. Dep't of the Army, Army Corps of Eng'rs, Norfolk Dist.*, 60 FLRA 247, 248 (2004) (*Army Corps of Eng'rs*); *U.S. Dep't of Health & Human Servs., Ctrs. for Medicare & Medicaid Servs.*, 57 FLRA 924, 926 (2002) (*HHS*). Consequently, an arbitration award that postpones the determination of an issue submitted does not constitute a final award subject to review. *See Carswell*, 64 FLRA at 567; *Army Corps of Eng'rs*, 60 FLRA at 248; *HHS*, 57 FLRA at 926. However, where an arbitrator has ordered a remedy but has not made a computation as to the amount of attorney fees, the mere fact that the arbitrator retains jurisdiction to assist parties with the details of the remedy's implementation does not render exceptions to that award interlocutory.[3] *See, e.g., Office of Pers. Mgmt.*, 61 FLRA 358, 361 (2005) (then-Member Pope dissenting in part on unrelated grounds), *reconsid. denied*, 61 FLRA 657 (2006).

The supplemental award does not constitute the Arbitrator's final award on attorney fees because it does not resolve all of the issues necessary to make that determination. With particular regard to the requirement that attorney fees awarded must be "reasonable," the Arbitrator postponed that determination by "remanding the question to the parties for resolution." Supplemental Award at 4. As the Arbitrator made clear, he would exercise his retained jurisdiction to render a final award resolving

3. The Authority has found interlocutory review to be appropriate where the exceptions present a plausible jurisdictional defect, the resolution of which will advance the ultimate disposition of the case. *E.g., U.S. Dep't of the Treasury, Customs Serv., Tucson, Ariz.*, 58 FLRA 358, 359 n.* (2002). There is no claim in this case that the exceptions raise a plausible jurisdictional defect.

the reasonableness of the attorney fees requested only "[i]n the event that [the parties] are unable to reach agreement" on this issue. *Id.*

The determination that the Arbitrator postponed concerning the reasonableness of the fees goes beyond a matter of computation. A reasonable attorney fee award "begins with an analysis of two objective variables: The attorney's customary billing rate; and the number of hours reasonably devoted to the case." *Stewart v. Dep't of the Army*, 102 M.S.P.R. 656, 662 (2006); *see also Dep't of the Air Force Headquarters, 832d Combat Support Group DPCE, Luke Air Force Base, Ariz.*, 32 FLRA 1084, 1100 (1988) (*Luke Air Force Base*). The Authority requires that fee requests "be closely examined to ensure that the number of hours expended was reasonable[,]" because "the number of hours expended are not necessarily those 'reasonably expended.'" *U.S. Dep't of Def., Def. Fin. & Accounting Serv.*, 60 FLRA 281, 286 (2004) (quoting *Luke Air Force Base*, 32 FLRA at 1101). Additionally, an arbitrator must support his or her determination as to the reasonableness of a fee request. *See U.S. Dep't of Def., Def. Distrib. Region E., New Cumberland, Pa.*, 51 FLRA 155, 158 (1995).

The standard of review as to the reasonableness of the number of hours awarded is deferential. In this connection, the MSPB has stated that the fact-finder is "in the best position to determine whether the number of hours expended is reasonable[.]" *McKenna v. Dep't of the Navy*, 108 M.S.P.R. 404, 411 (2008). "[A]bsent a specific showing that the [fact-finder's] evaluation was incorrect," the fact-finder's evaluation will not be second-guessed. *Id.* at 411. Consistent with this approach, the Authority has rejected an agency's "unsupported" exception to the number of hours that an arbitrator awarded a union attorney. *U.S. Dep't of Def., Educ. Activity, Arlington, Va.*, 57 FLRA 23, 26 (2001) (Chairman Cabaniss concurring in part and dissenting in part).

Based on the foregoing, it is evident that the Arbitrator left unresolved legal issues and factual determinations bearing on the reasonableness of the fees requested. Even though the Arbitrator determined that the rate "should be in line with the community rate of other attorneys," he did not determine what that rate should be. Supplemental Award at 4. Furthermore, the Arbitrator postponed a determination of the number of billable hours devoted to the case that would be considered "reasonably expended." *Luke Air Force Base*, 32 FLRA at 1101. Therefore, as the Arbitrator did not fully resolve the reasonableness issue, the supplemental award does not constitute a complete resolution of all the issues submitted to arbitration regarding the Union's entitlement to attorney fees, and the exceptions are interlocutory.

VI. Decision

The Agency's exceptions are dismissed, without prejudice, as interlocutory.

65 FLRA No. 128

UNITED STATES
DEPARTMENT OF JUSTICE
FEDERAL BUREAU OF PRISONS
FEDERAL CORRECTIONAL INSTITUTION
GREENVILLE, ILLINOIS
(Agency)

and

AMERICAN FEDERATION
OF GOVERNMENT EMPLOYEES
LOCAL 1304
COUNCIL OF PRISON LOCALS
(Union)

0-AR-4712

DECISION

March 14, 2011

Before the Authority: Carol Waller Pope, Chairman, and Thomas M. Beck and Ernest DuBester, Members

I. Statement of the Case

This matter is before the Authority on exceptions to an award of Arbitrator Steven Briggs filed by the Agency under § 7122(a) of the Federal Service Labor-Management Relations Statute (the Statute) and part 2425 of the Authority's Regulations. The Union did not file an opposition to the Agency's exceptions.

The Arbitrator awarded the Union attorney fees and costs. For the reasons that follow, we deny the Agency's exceptions.

II. Background and Arbitrator's Awards

The Union filed a grievance alleging that the Agency had failed to properly compensate employees for pre-shift and post-shift work. In his initial award, the Arbitrator found that the Agency had violated the Fair Labor Standards Act (FLSA), Agency regulations, and the parties' collective bargaining agreement, and he sustained the grievance. The Arbitrator directed the parties to negotiate over a remedy, including "reasonable attorney's fees." Supplemental Award on the Remedy at 7 (supplemental award). He retained jurisdiction to direct a remedy if the parties were unable to agree. *Id.* at 2.

When the parties were unable to agree to a remedy, the Arbitrator held a hearing, after which each party submitted a written position paper. In addition, the Union submitted a verified statement of attorney fees, the Agency submitted a response, and the Union submitted a brief for an award of attorney fees. *Id.* at 2-3. In his supplemental award, the Arbitrator awarded employees backpay with interest "consistent with the Back Pay Act." *Id.* at 6-7 (citation omitted). With regard to attorney fees, the Arbitrator noted that he had previously directed that "reasonable attorney's fees" should be included in any remedy. *Id.* at 7 (quoting Initial Award). Accordingly, he awarded as follows: "Since the Union is the prevailing party in this case[,] I hereby direct the Agency to pay the Union's reasonable attorney's fees and costs as part of the remedy in this case." *Id.* Specifically, the Arbitrator awarded attorney fees in the amount of $409,118.75, and costs in the amount of $24,372.66. *Id.* at 7-8.

III. Agency's Exceptions

The Agency contests only the Arbitrator's award of costs. Exceptions at 4. The Agency first contends that the Arbitrator's award of costs is contrary to the Back Pay Act, 5 U.S.C. § 5596. The Agency maintains that, under the Back Pay Act, an award of attorney fees including costs must be in accordance with the standards established under 5 U.S.C. § 7701(g) (§ 7701(g)), which standards require a fully articulated, reasoned decision setting forth the arbitrator's specific findings supporting the determination on each pertinent statutory requirement. *Id.* at 4-5. The Agency further maintains that § 7701(g) limits the award of costs to those that are "incidental and necessary expenses incurred in furnishing effective and competent representation." *Id.* at 7. The Agency asserts that the Arbitrator's award of costs is contrary to § 7701(g) because: (1) "the Arbitrator failed to provide a 'clear and reasoned explanation' of why the expenses claimed by the Union were recoverable[,]" *id.* at 5 (footnote omitted); and (2) the Union attorney's costs were not incidental and necessary expenses incurred in furnishing effective and competent representation, *id.* at 7.

The Agency also contends that the award of costs fails to draw its essence from the parties' collective bargaining agreement. *Id.* at 8. The Agency notes that, with exceptions not applicable in this case, Article 32, Section d (Section d) provides: "The arbitrator's fees and all expenses of the arbitration . . . shall be borne equally by the Employer and the Union." *Id.* at 9 (quoting agreement). According to the Agency, it is not disputed that the Arbitrator's award of costs includes the Union's share of the Arbitrator's fee and the Union's share of the hearing transcript fee. Thus, the Agency claims that the award "manifestly disregards" Section d. *Id.* In addition, the Agency asserts that the award, as it pertains to the transcript fee, also disregards Article 32, Section I of the parties' agreement.[1]

IV. Analysis and Conclusions

A. The award of costs is not contrary to the Back Pay Act.

The Authority held in *United States Department of the Navy, United States Naval Academy, Nonappropriated Fund Program Division*, 63 FLRA 100 (2009), that "awards of backpay should not be granted under the Back Pay Act where there is an independent statutory basis for such an award."[2] *Id.* at 103. In addition, the Authority found that the FLSA, 29 U.S.C. § 216(b) (§ 216(b)),[3] constitutes an independent statutory basis for awards of backpay and reasonable attorney fees. *Id.* at 102-03. Thus, the Authority held "the requirement under . . . § 7701(g)[(1)] that attorney fees are 'warranted in the interest of justice' is inapplicable" to award of fees made pursuant to the FLSA. *Id.* at 103.

In his supplemental award, the Arbitrator does not expressly identify the statutory authority for his award of fees and costs. However, for the reasons that follow, we conclude that it is implicit in the supplemental award that the Arbitrator awarded fees and costs under § 216(b).

As an initial matter, the award is specifically responsive to the Union's motion for an award of "attorney's fees" and costs of the case. Agency's Exceptions, Attach. E Union's Brief for Attorney's Fees Award (Union's Brief). The Union's motion is unequivocal as to the basis for the motion and the Arbitrator's statutory authority to award fees and costs: "29 U.S.C. § 216(b) of the FLSA mandates the payment of attorney's fees and costs of prevailing plaintiffs." Union's Brief at 3. Although the Union briefly discusses the requirements for an award of costs under the Back Pay Act, the Union is also unequivocal as to the Arbitrator's statutory authority to specifically award costs of the case: "The award of costs to the prevailing party is mandatory under the FLSA." *Id.* at 11. Further, the Arbitrator expressly quotes, without citation, § 216(b) in concluding that "reasonable attorney's fees" should be included in any remedy. Supplemental Award at 7 (quoting Initial Award). We note, in this regard, that § 216(b) (emphasis added) refers to "*attorney's* fee[,]" while the language of the Back Pay Act refers to "*attorney* fees." 5 U.S.C. § 5596(b)(1)(A)(ii) (emphasis added). In addition, the Arbitrator's award of fees and "costs" also tracks the language of § 216(b), while the Back Pay Act does not mention "costs." In this context, and with no reference in the supplemental award to the Back Pay Act with respect to fees and costs, we decline to construe the award of fees and costs as based on the Back Pay Act and, instead, find it implicit that the award is based on § 216(b).

For the foregoing reasons, we find that the Agency's reliance on the Back Pay Act is misplaced, and that its exception regarding the Back Pay Act provides no basis for finding the award deficient. Accordingly, we deny the exception.

B. The award of costs does not fail to draw its essence from the agreement.

For an award to be found deficient as failing to draw its essence from the collective bargaining agreement, it must be established that the award: (1) cannot in any rational way be derived from the agreement; (2) is so unfounded in reason and fact and so unconnected with the wording and purposes of the agreement as to manifest an infidelity to the obligation of the arbitrator; (3) does not represent a plausible interpretation of the agreement; and (4) evidences a manifest disregard of the agreement.

---

1. Article 32, Section I provides: "A verbatim transcript of the arbitration will be made when requested by either party, the expense of which shall be borne by the requesting party. If the arbitrator requests a copy, the cost of the arbitrator's copy will be borne equally by both parties. If both parties request a transcript, the cost shall be shared equally . . . ." Exceptions at 10 (quoting agreement); *id.*, Attach. F at 78 (same).

2. As noted above, the Arbitrator awarded employees backpay with interest consistent with the Back Pay Act. As the Agency does not contest this portion of the award, we do not address it further.

3. Section 216(b) provides that courts "shall, in addition to any judgment awarded to the plaintiff or plaintiffs, allow a reasonable attorney's fee to be paid by the defendant, and costs of the action."

U.S. Dep't of Labor (OSHA), 34 FLRA 573, 575 (1990).

Pursuant to § 216(b), as the prevailing party, the Union is entitled to have the Agency reimburse it for its "costs of the action[,]" i.e., the costs of bringing the FLSA case. In accordance with this statutory entitlement, the Arbitrator directed the Agency to pay the Union's costs, including the Union's share of the Arbitrator's fee and the Union's share of the hearing transcript fee. In its exception, the Agency does not dispute that the Union is statutorily entitled under § 216(b) to have the Agency reimburse the Union for the Union's costs of bringing the case and does not dispute that the Union's share of the Arbitrator's fee and the Union's share of the hearing transcript fee are "costs of the action" within the meaning of § 216(b). In addition, the Agency does not argue that the fee-sharing provisions of Article 32 were intended to supplant the cost provisions of § 216(b). As the costs were awarded under § 216(b), and there is no claim that Article 32 was intended to supplant § 216(b), the Agency does not demonstrate that the award manifestly disregards the agreement or is implausible, unfounded, or irrational.[4]

Accordingly, we deny the exception.

V. Decision

The Agency's exceptions are denied.

4. Member Beck notes that the parties' collective bargaining agreement explicitly provides that arbitrators' fees and expenses "shall be borne equally by the Employer and the Union." Exceptions, Attach. F at 76-77. Article 32, Section d. identifies several specific exceptions that apply to this shared-cost provision -- the cost for specific categories of witnesses to travel to arbitration hearings and for a limited number of witnesses (not to exceed five) to travel to hearings that arise from Council-level grievances -- for which the Agency bears the full cost. The parties could have negotiated an additional exception that would have required the Agency to pay for all costs associated with matters grieved under the FLSA but they did not do so. Therefore, in view of the agreement's clear language, Member Beck would conclude that the Arbitrator's interpretation is simply not a plausible interpretation of the parties' agreement.

65 FLRA No. 129

UNITED STATES
DEPARTMENT OF THE AIR FORCE
TYNDALL AIR FORCE BASE
TYNDALL AFB, FLORIDA
(Activity)

and

AMERICAN FEDERATION
OF GOVERNMENT EMPLOYEES
LOCAL 1113, AFL-CIO
(Union/Petitioner)

AT-RP-10-0016

ORDER DENYING
APPLICATION FOR REVIEW

March 16, 2011

Before the Authority: Carol Waller Pope, Chairman, and Thomas M. Beck and Ernest DuBester, Members

I. Statement of the Case

This case is before the Authority on an application for review (application) filed by the Activity under § 2422.31 of the Authority's Regulations.[1] The Union did not file an opposition to the Activity's application.

The Union filed a petition to determine whether the position of Air Force Police Officer (Officer) is properly within the bargaining unit. The Activity argued that Officers perform security work that directly affects national security within the meaning of § 7112(b)(6) of the Federal Service Labor-Management Relations Statute (the Statute) and thus are excluded from the bargaining unit. The Regional Director (RD) determined that Officers perform security work that involves national security; however, he concluded that the position's duties do not directly affect national security. The RD, accordingly, determined that Officers should not be excluded from the bargaining unit. For the reasons that follow, we deny the Activity's application.

II. Background and RD's Decision

A. Background

The Activity is a military base for the United States Department of the Air Force (Air Force). The Activity's mission is to support the combat functions of the Air Force by providing training, maintenance personnel, and managers that provide combat assistance. *See* RD's Decision at 8. The Activity houses over thirty tenants who assist with this mission. *Id.* at 3. These tenants perform various functions, including responding to air threats located in the Activity's region, *id.*; evaluating the Air Force's "air to air weapons system," *id.*; researching, discovering, and developing technologies to "further air base capabilities," *id.*; and providing "tools, practices, and professional support to maximize Air Force civil engineer capabilities[,]" *id.* (quoting Activity Ex. 1 at 17).

The Activity employs fifteen Officers, a civilian position that is responsible for several security functions on the base.[2] *Id.* at 4. The position is considered "non-critical, sensitive," and Officers have a "secret level of security clearance." *Id.* (citing Tr. at 34). All Officers receive training in "basic law enforcement techniques[.]" *Id.*

---

1. Section 2422.31 of the Authority's Regulations provides, in pertinent part:

> (c) Review. The Authority may grant an application for review only when the application demonstrates that review is warranted on one or more of the following grounds:
>
> (1) The decision raises an issue for which there is an absence of precedent;
>
> (2) Established law or policy warrants reconsideration; or
>
> (3) There is a genuine issue over whether the Regional Director has:
>
> (i) Failed to apply established law;
>
> (ii) Committed a prejudicial procedural error;
>
> (iii) Committed a clear and prejudicial error concerning a substantial factual matter.

2. At the hearing, the parties stipulated that the duties performed by two Officers who testified -- Officers K and T -- were representative of the duties performed by all fifteen Officers. RD's Decision at 2.

At the beginning of each shift, Officers receive verbal briefings about security issues. *Id.* at 4-5. The information they receive is not typically classified and is often "watered-down" information that is available to the public. *Id.* at 6 (citing Tr. at 165); *see also id.* at 5. Officers do not regularly "destroy[], reproduc[e], stor[e], or handl[e] classified information." *Id.* at 4 (citing Tr. at 66).

Officers are stationed at the Activity's front gates. *Id.* at 5. They are responsible for checking identification and passes for visitors who pass through the front gates. *Id.* However, Officers do not issue identification or passes, except on weekends when they may hand out visitors' passes. *Id.* On weekdays, commercial vehicles enter through a separate gate that is not staffed by Officers. *Id.* On weekends, however, commercial vehicles must come through the front gate. Officers visually inspect commercial vehicles that come through the front gate, but they do not use any equipment to do so. *Id.* Officers inspect other types of vehicles only when instructed to do so by the Activity as part of its "random anti-terrorist measure[.]" *Id.* at 5-6 (citing Tr. at 141).

Officers must respond to alarms that are activated at any of the Activity's facility buildings. *Id.* at 4. Facility buildings are critical buildings or buildings that contain classified information. *Id.* Responding to alarms at facility buildings comprises most of the Officers' duties and occurs, on average, twice a shift. *Id.* at 4, 6. When an alarm is activated, an Officer proceeds to the building and waits for a building custodian to arrive. *Id.* at 6. The Officer and the custodian walk through the facility to determine the cause of the alarm. *Id.* at 4. The facilities often contain classified information that the building owners must secure. *Id.* Officers potentially could view information that had been left unsecured, but none recalled actually seeing such information. *Id.* at 4, 6.

Officers also are responsible for responding to incidents involving suspicious packages or bomb threats. *Id.* at 5. If a suspicious package is reported, Officers and military police cordon off the area, evacuate unauthorized individuals inside the area, and prevent non-authorized individuals from entering it. *Id.* at 5, 6; Tr. at 168. Officers cordon-off the area until a fire chief (chief) with the Activity's fire department or other official determines no threat is present. RD's Decision at 6 (citing Tr. at 126-27, 137). Chiefs have the authority to send in bomb disposal units (disposal units) or military personnel with bomb-sniffing dogs. *Id.* at 5; Tr. at 137-38. The disposal units are part of the Activity's civil engineer unit and have no affiliation with the Officers. Officers cannot enter the cordoned-off area unless chiefs order them to do so. Tr. at 166. Officers also do not assist with the disposal of the package. *See id.*

B. RD's Decision

The RD noted that, under § 7112(b)(6) of the Statute, a bargaining unit is not considered appropriate if it includes "any employee engaged in intelligence, counterintelligence, investigative, or security work which directly affects national security[.]" RD's Decision at 7 (quoting 5 U.S.C. § 7112(b)(6)). The RD further stated that, in order to determine whether an employee fits within the foregoing standard, the Authority examines "whether employees are: (1) engaged in security work that (2) directly affects (3) national security." *Id.* (citing *U.S. Dep't of Def., Pentagon Force Prot. Agency, Wash., D.C.*, 62 FLRA 164, 171 (2007)).

The RD concluded that the Officers' duties involve security work within the meaning of § 7112(b)(6). *Id.* at 8. The RD reached this conclusion despite also finding that Officers "do not use classified information or have regular access to it." *Id.* at 7. The RD determined that, although Officers, when responding to alarms, search facilities containing classified information, there is little chance that Officers could view or use the classified information in these buildings. *See id.* He also found that Officers receive only "watered down" information during their security briefings. *Id.* at 8. Thus, the RD found that Officers do not use or have "regular" access to classified information. *Id.* at 7. He nevertheless concluded that the Officers' other duties -- including patrolling the base and its perimeter, monitoring the front gates, responding to suspicious packages and bomb threats, making routine traffic stops, monitoring gate cameras, responding to alarm facilities, and providing security for the Activity's tenants -- establish that they perform security work under § 7112(b)(6). *See id.* at 8.

The RD also determined that Officers' duties involve national security within the meaning of § 7112(b)(6) of the Statute.[3] *Id.* at 9.

Finally, the RD concluded that the Officers' duties do not directly affect national security. He

3. Neither party disputes this conclusion. Accordingly, we do not address it further.

stated that an employee's duties directly affect national security if they have "a straight bearing or unbroken connection that produces a material influence" on national security. RD's Decision at 8 (citing *SSA, Balt., Md.*, 59 FLRA 137, 144 (2003) (*SSA*) (Chairman Cabaniss concurring and then-Member Pope concurring in part and dissenting in part); *Dep't of Energy, Oak Ridge Operations, Oak Ridge, Tenn.*, 4 FLRA 644, 655 (1980) (*Oak Ridge*)). Relying on the foregoing standard, the RD examined several of the Officers' duties. As is relevant here, he analyzed their involvement with suspicious packages and the front gate.

The RD found that Officers must respond to incidents involving "bomb threats or suspicious packages[.]" *Id.* at 8. However, he found that Officers only secure and control the area containing these threats, whereas the fire chief or the bomb disposal unit deals with, and ultimately disposes of, the actual threat. *Id.* Thus, the RD concluded that the Officers' role in such situations is limited.

Examining the Officers' front gate duties, the RD found that Officers monitor gate cameras, check visitor identification and passes, perform random searches of non-commercial vehicles when ordered to do so during "random anti-terrorist measures[,]" and visually inspect commercial vehicles on weekends. *Id.* at 8-9. However, the RD also found that Officers do not actually determine who may access the base; indeed, the only time Officers issue visitors' passes is on the weekend, and visitors must be sponsored by someone else. *Id.* Further, the RD determined that Officers may not search non-commercial vehicles unless ordered to do so. *Id.* at 9. Additionally, the RD found that Officers are limited to searching commercial vehicles on the weekend and, even then, conduct only visual inspections. *Id.*

Based on the foregoing, the RD determined that the Officers' duties do not "have a clear, unbroken connection to national security." *Id.* The RD concluded that Officers should not be excluded from the bargaining unit because the duties they perform do not directly affect national security within the meaning of § 7112(b)(6) of the Statute. *See id.*

III. Activity's Application

The Activity requests that the Authority grant its application. The Activity argues that the RD's Decision is incorrect for three reasons.

First, the Activity contends that the RD "ignored facts" when he determined that the Officers' "relationship to national security is limited." Application at 1. Specifically, the Activity asserts that the RD did not properly evaluate how the Activity's "mission critically shortens the link between the [Officers'] duties and national security." *Id.* at 2. The Activity argues that its functions are "synonymous" with national security; as such, by protecting "a national security nerve center" like the Activity, a "link" is established between the Officers' duties and national security. *Id.* at 3. Therefore, according to the Activity, "[v]irtually every one of the criteria" in *Oak Ridge*, 4 FLRA at 655-56, is satisfied. *Id.*

Second, the Activity asserts that the RD "improperly" relied on his findings that Officers do not use, or have regular access to, classified information to support his conclusion that Officers do not directly affect national security. *Id.* at 4. The Activity contends that the RD should have limited the use of these findings to his analysis of whether Officers perform security work. *Id.* Based on this argument, the Activity also argues that the RD did not treat "access to" classified information and "use of" classified information equally. *Id.* According to the Activity, the RD improperly focused "on the use of classified information while" avoiding the Officers' "ease of regular access to classified materials." *Id.* at 5.

Third, the Activity contends that the RD "committed prejudicial error" by minimizing the Officers' duties concerning suspicious packages. *Id.* at 7. The Activity argues that the RD "gloss[ed] over" the Officers' duties by placing undue emphasis on the duties that the chief and the disposal units perform. *Id.* According to the Activity, in these situations, Officers respond to threats; "rapidly neutralize . . . the threat[,]" move people and assets away from the threat; apprehend suspicious persons; and "expose themselves to serious harm" by cordoning off the threat area. *Id.* Based on the foregoing, the Activity asserts that the chief and bomb technician's duties do not diminish the Officers' affect on national security. Furthermore, the Activity contends that the RD "inappropriately minimized" the Officers' duties with respect to the searching of commercial vehicles. *Id.* at 8. The Activity argues that the RD did not consider that, when Officers search commercial vehicles on the weekend, they search vehicles of various sizes. *Id.* at 8-9 (quoting Tr. at 134). Had the RD considered this fact, the Activity contends, he would have reached a different result. *See id.* at 8-9.

IV. Analysis and Conclusions

A. The RD did not commit clear and prejudicial error in connection with his examination of certain duties performed by Officers.

1. The RD did not commit clear and prejudicial error by disregarding facts linking the Activity's functions to the Officers' affect on national security.

The Activity first argues that the RD "disregarded facts" linking the functions performed by the Activity, the Officer's duties, and national security. Application at 1. According to the Agency, due to the importance of the Activity's work, the RD should have found that any security work performed on the base necessarily affects national security. *See id.* at 2-3. The Activity's argument is misplaced. In deciding whether a position directly affects national security within the meaning of § 7112(b)(6) of the Statute, the Authority has consistently looked *only* to the duties of the position at issue. *See, e.g., U.S. Dep't of the Air Force, Davis-Monthan Air Force Base, Ariz.*, 62 FLRA 332, 335 (2008) (Chairman Cabaniss concurring); *U.S. Dep't of Justice, Wash., D.C.,* 62 FLRA 286, 294 (2007) (Chairman Cabaniss concurring in part, dissenting in part); *Oak Ridge,* 4 FLRA at 655. The Authority has never stated that a position directly affects national security because of the duties performed by an activity. The Activity's argument is, therefore, incorrect.

Consistent with the foregoing, the Activity's reliance on *Oak Ridge* is misplaced. The Activity asserts that this matter satisfies "[v]irtually every one of the criteria" in *Oak Ridge*. Application at 3. The Activity does not explain what those "criteria" are, or how they apply in this matter. *Id.* Moreover, although the Authority in *Oak Ridge* examined the functions of the activity, it relied on the *duties of the position* at issue in order to determine whether that position directly affected national security. *See Oak Ridge*, 4 FLRA at 656. Consequently, *Oak Ridge* does not support the Activity's position.

Based on the foregoing, we deny the Activity's claim.

2. The RD did not commit clear and prejudicial error because he properly weighed the Officers' suspicious package duties.

The Activity contends that the RD committed prejudicial error because he failed to properly weigh: (1) the Officers' involvement with suspicious packages; and (2) the Officers' searching of commercial vehicles. As previously noted, under § 7112(b)(6) of the Statute, a bargaining unit is not appropriate if it includes any employee engaged in "security work which *directly affects* national security[.]" 5 U.S.C. § 7112(b)(6) (emphasis added). The Authority defines "direct effect" as "a straight bearing or unbroken connection that produces a material influence or [alteration]." *U.S. Dep't of Agric., Food Safety & Inspection Serv.,* 61 FLRA 397, 402 (2005) (*USDA*) (quoting *SSA,* 59 FLRA at 143); *Oak Ridge,* 4 FLRA at 655 (citing *Webster's Seventh New Collegiate Dictionary*). The Authority has found that a position does not directly affect national security if an intervening factor severs the position's affect on national security or otherwise limits it. *See, e.g., USDA*, 61 FLRA at 402.

The Activity first argues that the Officers' duties with respect to suspicious packages establish the Officers' direct effect on national security. The record reveals, however, that the Officers actual role in such situations is limited.

Officers are responsible for evacuating an area containing suspicious packages, cordoning-off the area, and preventing unauthorized individuals from entering the area. *See* RD's Decision at 8; Tr. at 126-27, 137. This is the extent of the Officers' functions; other positions are responsible for eliminating the threat posed by a suspicious package. A chief with the Activity's fire department is in charge of the situation and is the only individual who makes the decision as to how the situation should be resolved. RD's Decision at 6; Tr. at 137-38. To this end, only a chief can decide whether or not a disposal unit -- which contains no Officers -- or military personnel with bomb-sniffing dogs should be sent into the cordoned off area to dispose of the package. Tr. at 137-38. The disposal unit and military personnel are the only individuals who physically handle the package and ultimately decide how to dispose of it. *Id.* at 69-70. Moreover, although Officers cordon off the area, they do so in conjunction with military police. *Id.* at 168. Thus, even in the absence of Officers, other positions are available to cordon off the area. The Activity does not dispute any of the foregoing, nor has it averred that Officers have any involvement with the actual disposal of any suspicious packages. Accordingly, the record establishes that the Officers' ability to eliminate any threat posed by a suspicious package is quite "limited." *USDA*, 61 FLRA at 402 (position's limited duties in resolving threat to national security supported finding that position did not directly affect national security).

The Officers' discretion in resolving situations involving suspicious packages is similarly limited. Officers are required to follow a chief's orders. Officers cannot even enter the cordoned area unless a chief orders them to do so. Tr. at 169. Moreover, the Activity has not asserted, and the record does not reveal, that Officers have any control over the disposal unit or military personnel's actions or decisions. Thus, Officers have a "less than direct" impact on how suspicious package situations are resolved. *USDA,* 61 FLRA at 402 (position's limited discretion in deciding how to resolve threats supported finding that position did not directly affect national security).

The foregoing supports the RD's conclusion that Officers do not directly affect national security. Nevertheless, the Activity contends that Officers "are the actual threat response," Application at 8, because they "move people and assets out of harm's way,. . . apprehend suspicious persons, and . . . expose themselves to serious harm" by cordoning off the area, *id.* at 7. Although Officers do remove individuals from the area, as established above, Officers have little to no role in the disposal of suspicious packages, which is the "actual threat" at issue. *Id.* Additionally, the Activity cites to nothing in the record that establishes that Officers apprehend individuals associated with suspicious packages, nor do they explain how Officers being exposed to harm directly affects national security. The Agency's position, therefore, does not result in a different conclusion.

The Activity also contends that the RD committed prejudicial error because he failed to consider the fact that, when Officers search commercial vehicles on the weekend, they search vehicles of various sizes. Application at 8-9. Even if the RD failed to consider the distinction in commercial vehicle sizes, the Activity does not explain how such a distinction could directly affect national security. Thus, even if the RD committed the foregoing error, that error would not lead us to determine that his overall conclusion was erroneous.

Based on the foregoing, we reject the Activity's claim that the RD committed prejudicial error by failing to properly weigh certain duties.

B. The RD did not fail to apply established law.

The Activity argues that the RD impermissibly considered the Officers' involvement with classified information in his analysis of whether Officers directly affect national security. Application at 4. Based on this argument, the Activity also asserts that the RD did not treat the *use of* classified information and *access to* classified information equally. *Id.* at 4-5. We construe the foregoing arguments as assertions that the RD failed to apply established law.

The Activity's assertions are flawed. Contrary to the Activity's claim, the RD did not rely on the Officers' involvement with classified information to decide whether Officers directly affect national security. In his decision, the RD stated that, "[d]espite" the Officers' limited involvement with classified information, their other duties establish that they "are involved in *security work* under the meaning of [§ 7112(b)(6) of the Statute], thereby satisfying *the first prong* of the test." RD's Decision at 8 (emphasis added). The RD made no mention of the "directly affects" prong of § 7112(b)(6). 5 U.S.C. § 7112(b)(6). The foregoing language, therefore, demonstrates that the RD considered the Officers' involvement with classified information *solely* for the purposes of deciding whether Officers perform security work within the meaning of § 7112(b)(6). This is further reinforced by the fact that the RD's discussion of whether Officers directly affect national security contains *no* reference to the Officers' involvement with classified information. *See id.* at 8-9.

The Officers' non-use of, and limited access to, classified information was not part of the RD's consideration of whether Officers directly affect national security. Thus, the Activity's argument is incorrect, and we reject it. Because this argument is the basis of the Activity's assertion that the RD did not treat "access to" and "use of" classified information equally, we likewise reject that argument as well. Application at 4.

V. Order

The Activity's application for review is denied.

65 FLRA No. 130

UNITED STATES
DEPARTMENT OF VETERANS AFFAIRS
MEDICAL CENTER
RICHMOND, VIRGINIA
(Agency)

and

AMERICAN FEDERATION
OF GOVERNMENT EMPLOYEES
LOCAL 2145
(Union)

0-AR-4315

DECISION

March 17, 2011

Before the Authority: Carol Waller Pope, Chairman, and Thomas M. Beck and Ernest DuBester, Members

I. Statement of the Case

This matter is before the Authority on exceptions to an award of Arbitrator Frederick Day filed by the Agency under § 7122(a) of the Federal Service Labor-Management Relations Statute (the Statute) and part 2425 of the Authority's Regulations. The Union filed an opposition to the Agency's exceptions.

The Arbitrator found that the Agency violated the parties' agreement by terminating the Local Union President's (the President's) access to the Agency's computer system (system) following her discharge from employment. For the following reasons, we dismiss the Agency's exceptions in part and deny them in part.

II. Background and Arbitrator's Award

The President was discharged from her position at the Agency, but continued to serve in her representational role as President. Award at 3. When she was discharged, the Agency terminated her access to the system. *Id.*

A grievance was filed regarding this termination of access. *Id.* at 2. The grievance was unresolved and submitted to arbitration, where the parties stipulated the issues as follows: "Did the Agency violate the contract when it removed [the President's] computer access . . . ? If so, what shall be the remedy?" *Id.*

As an initial matter, the Arbitrator noted that the parties' agreement indicates that the "[Agency] and the Union have a mutual commitment to . . . a 'partnership[.]'" *Id.* at 7. The Arbitrator then found that Article 48, Section 1 of the agreement provides for Union "office space 'equipped with adequate telephone lines for [Federal Telecommunications System (FTS)], fax, and computer capabilities.'"[1] *Id.* The Arbitrator also noted that Article 48, Section 4 provides that the Agency shall also equip the Union office with various items, including "access to e-mail and administrative [Dynamic Host Configuration Protocol (DHCP)] functions . . . ."[2] *Id.*

The Arbitrator also found "no evidence that the [Union] is, in any way, non-compliant with all provisions of the Statute and the governing Union by[-]laws and governing mandates[,]" and that, therefore, "the [President] . . . has legal standing and status[.]" *Id.* at 8. In this connection, the Arbitrator found that "to deny her access to computer services is tantamount to the denial of the contractual service guaranteed the Union[,]" and would "isolate[e] the

---

1. Article 48, Section 1 states, in pertinent part:

> Section 1 – Local Union Office Space
> A. Management recognizes the importance and value of the Union's mission and purpose. Accordingly, management agrees to furnish office space to the Union appropriate for carrying out its representational and partnership duties[.]
> B. Each office will be equipped with adequate telephone lines for FTS, fax, and computer capabilities.

Award at 2.

2. Article 48, Section 4 provides, in pertinent part:

> Section 4 – Equipment
> A. The [Agency] will provide or make available to each Union office:
> 2. Personal computer with standard software, programs and capabilities compatible with the [Agency's] technology,
> 4. Access to e-mail and administrative DHCP functions in the Union office.

Id. at 2-3.

President [from] the most commonly used form of communications to carry out her mission[.]" *Id.* at 8-9. Accordingly, the Arbitrator sustained the grievance and directed the Agency to restore the President's system access. *Id.* at 10.

III. Positions of the Parties

A. Agency's Exceptions

The Agency argues that the award is contrary to management's right to determine its internal security practices under § 7106(a)(1) of the Statute because the award "excessively interferes with management['s] right to maintain security over its information [and] information systems." Exceptions at 4. In this connection, the Agency contends that the award "fails to address the lack of control that the [A]gency would be able to exercise over an individual who is not an employee but has access to its internal data and communications process[,]" and that the Arbitrator's remedy "fail[s] to reconstruct what management would have done." *Id.* at 4-5.

The Agency also argues that the award is based on nonfacts because the Arbitrator erroneously found that: (1) "the President and Union are one and the same under the contract"; and (2) "computer access is the most commonly used form of communications." *Id.* at 5, 6. In this regard, the Agency maintains that the President's "status with respect to . . . her right to computer access is no greater than that of a private citizen." *Id.* at 5. The Agency also maintains that the Arbitrator erred by citing the concept of "partnership" to "rationaliz[e] [the President's] status" because, according to the Agency, "partnership" was "voided by Executive Order [(EO)] 13203[.]" *Id.* at 6.

Further, the Agency contends that the award fails to draw its essence from the parties' agreement. *Id.* at 6-7. In this connection, the Agency asserts that the award "negates the contractual language defining the . . . Union" by finding it to be synonymous with the President. *Id.* at 7. The Agency also asserts that a Regional Director (RD) of the Authority has determined that the agreement "'does not address whether access must be provided to any [Union] representative.'" *Id.* at 7; *see also id.*, Attach., RD's Dismissal Letter, in Case No. WA-CA-04-0692 (January 31, 2005) at 1 (declining to issue an unfair labor practice (ULP) complaint concerning termination of a Union steward's computer access in conjunction with his notice of termination from employment and months after he stopped serving as a steward).

B. Union's Opposition

As an initial matter, the Union argues that the Authority should dismiss the Agency's exception regarding management's rights because the Agency raises the argument for the first time in its exceptions. Opp'n at 3. Further, the Union claims that "[t]here is no foundation for finding any impairment of the [A]gency's right to make security determinations." *Id.* at 4.

With respect to the nonfact exceptions, the Union contends that: (1) the Agency's arguments are "simply a disagreement with the Arbitrator as to the interpretation of the contract"; (2) there was "ample evidence" presented at the hearing demonstrating "the frequent use of e-mail communications"; and (3) "the [A]gency is confusing a particular partnership initiative" addressed by the EO with the general concept of "partnership" cited by the Arbitrator. *Id.* at 4-5.

Finally, the Union argues that the award draws its essence from the agreement because "[i]t is not implausible to interpret the language regarding computer access to include, at least, the president of the [Union]." *Id.* at 5. Further, the Union claims that the RD's decision cited by the Agency is "clearly inapplicable" because it "do[es] not constitute any sort of precedent" and involved different facts. *Id.* at 6.

IV. Preliminary Issues

A. The Authority has jurisdiction to resolve the Agency's exceptions.

Under § 7122(a) of the Statute, the Authority lacks jurisdiction to resolve exceptions to awards "relating to" a matter described in § 7121(f) of the Statute. Matters described in § 7121(f) include adverse actions, such as removals, that are covered under 5 U.S.C. § 7512 and are appealable to the Merit Systems Protection Board (MSPB) and reviewable by the United States Court of Appeals for the Federal Circuit (Federal Circuit). *See, e.g., U.S. Dep't of Commerce, Patent & Trademark Office, Arlington, Va.*, 61 FLRA 476, 477 (2006).

The Authority directed the Agency to show cause why its exceptions should not be dismissed for lack of jurisdiction pursuant to § 7122(a) of the Statute because the award "concerns a matter that could be considered 'inextricably intertwined' with a removal[.]" *See* Order to Show Cause at 1-2. In its response, the Agency asserts that "the loss of computer access is not an 'adverse action' appealable to the MSPB[,]" and that the Union "brought a separate grievance related to the [President's] proposed removal . . . ." Agency's Response at 4. Further, the Agency maintains that "the MSPB reviewed [the President's] termination, issued a decision, and did not address [the President's] computer access." *Id.* at 3. Finally, the Agency contends that the present matter of "whether the Agency may remove a [U]nion member's or officer's computer access . . . is not inextricably intertwined with [the President's] termination." *Id.*

The Authority will determine that an award relates to a matter described in § 7121(f) "when it resolves, or is inextricably intertwined with," a § 7512 matter. *See AFGE, Local 1013*, 60 FLRA 712, 713 (2005). In making that determination, the Authority looks not to the outcome of the award, but to whether the claim advanced in arbitration is one reviewable by the MSPB, and, on appeal, by the Federal Circuit. *See id.* The Authority has found that an award was inextricably intertwined with a removal where, for example, "the MSPB or an arbitrator w[ould] examine the propriety of an [absence without leave (AWOL)] charge in determining whether an employee was lawfully removed based on such a charge." *See U.S. Dep't of Veterans Affairs, Med. Ctr., Newington, Conn.*, 53 FLRA 440, 443 (1997) (*Newington*). The Authority has also found that a supplemental award that specifically granted remedies for an unlawful removal was inextricably intertwined with the removal. *See U.S. Dep't of Transp., Fed. Aviation Admin.*, 57 FLRA 580, 581 (2001) (*FAA*). The fact that a grievant has separately challenged his or her removal before the MSPB is not dispositive of whether the award is inextricably intertwined with the removal. *See Newington*, 53 FLRA at 441.

Here, the stipulated issue before the Arbitrator was whether "the Agency violate[d] the contract when it removed [the grievant's] computer access[?]" Award at 2. The Arbitrator expressly noted that "[a]t the time of the hearing in the instant matter, [the grievant's] discharge was [before the MSPB] and [as of] yet unresolved[,]" and his award did not address whether the President's removal was proper. *Id.* at 3. As such, we find that the award does not resolve a § 7512 matter.

With respect to whether the grievance is inextricably intertwined with the grievant's removal, in contrast to *Newington*, the action at issue here -- termination of system access -- is not a basis for the removal. In fact, there is no dispute that the termination of system access occurred *after* the grievant's removal. Moreover, the award specifically provides a remedy for the President's loss of system access -- not for her removal. *See FAA*, 57 FLRA at 581. As such, we find that the award is not inextricably intertwined with the President's removal and, therefore, the Authority has jurisdiction over the Agency's exceptions.

B. Section 2429.5 of the Authority's Regulations bars the Agency's claim relating to § 7106 of the Statute.

The Authority's Regulations that were in effect when the Agency filed its exceptions provided that "[t]he Authority will not consider . . . any issue, which was not presented in the proceedings before the . . . arbitrator." 5 C.F.R. § 2429.5.[3]

Before the Arbitrator, the Union requested that the Arbitrator "reinstate [the President] to 'full use and access to the computer system[.]" Award at 6. Thus, the Agency could have argued before the Arbitrator that restoring the grievant's access to the system would conflict with management's right to determine its internal security practices. There is no indication in the record that the Agency did so. As such, we dismiss this exception as barred by § 2429.5 of the Authority's Regulations. *See, e.g., U.S. DOD, Def. Distrib. Depot, Anniston, Ala.*, 61 FLRA 108, 109 (2005) (Authority will not consider arguments raised for the first time on exceptions).

V. Analysis and Conclusions

A. The award is not based on nonfacts.

To establish that an award is based on a nonfact, the appealing party must show that a central fact underlying the award is clearly erroneous, but for which the arbitrator would have reached a different result. *See NFFE, Local 1984*, 56 FLRA 38, 41 (2000). An arbitrator's conclusion that is based on an interpretation of the parties' collective bargaining agreement does not constitute a fact that can be challenged as a nonfact. *NLRB*, 50 FLRA 88, 92 (1995).

---

3. The Authority's Regulations concerning the review of arbitration awards, as well as certain related procedural Regulations, including § 2429.5, were revised effective October 1, 2010. *See* 75 Fed. Reg. 42,283 (2010). As the Agency's exceptions were filed before that date, we apply the prior Regulations.

The Agency argues that the award is based on a nonfact because the Arbitrator erred by finding that "the President and Union are one and the same under the contract." Exceptions at 5. In effect, the Agency's argument challenges the Arbitrator's interpretation of the parties' agreement. As stated above, an arbitrator's conclusion that is based on such an interpretation does not constitute a fact that can be challenged as a nonfact. *See NLRB*, 50 FLRA at 92. Accordingly, we deny this exception.

The Agency also argues that the Arbitrator erroneously found that "computer access is the most commonly used form of communications." Exceptions at 6. However, the Agency does not demonstrate that this finding is a clearly erroneous central fact, but for which the Arbitrator would have reached a different conclusion. Accordingly, we deny the exception.[4]

Finally, the Agency contends that the Arbitrator erred by citing the concept of "partnership" to "rationaliz[e] [the President's] status" because, according to the Agency, "partnership" was "voided by [EO] 13203." *Id.* However, the Agency does not explain how a central fact underlying the award is clearly erroneous, but for which the arbitrator would have reached a different conclusion. Accordingly, we deny the exception.

B. The award draws its essence from the parties' agreement.

In reviewing an arbitrator's interpretation of a collective bargaining agreement, the Authority applies the deferential standard that federal courts use in reviewing arbitration awards in the private sector. *See* 5 U.S.C. § 7122(a)(2); *AFGE, Council 220*, 54 FLRA 156, 159 (1998). Under this standard, the Authority will find that an arbitration award is deficient as failing to draw its essence from the collective bargaining agreement when the appealing party establishes that the award: (1) cannot in any rational way be derived from the agreement; (2) is so unfounded in reason and fact and so unconnected with the wording and purposes of the collective bargaining agreement as to manifest an infidelity to the obligation of the arbitrator; (3) does not represent a plausible interpretation of the agreement; or (4) evidences a manifest disregard of the agreement. *U.S. Dep't of Labor (OSHA)*, 34 FLRA 573, 575 (1990). The Authority and the courts defer to arbitrators in this context "because it is the arbitrator's construction of the agreement for which the parties have bargained." *Id.* at 576.

The Agency contends that the award fails to draw its essence from the parties' agreement because it "negates the contractual language defining the . . . Union" by finding it to be synonymous with the President. Exceptions at 7. Article 48, Section 4 of the parties' agreement states that the Agency "will provide . . . to each Union office . . . [a]ccess to e-mail and administrative DHCP functions in the Union office." Award at 2-3. The Arbitrator found that "to deny [the President] access to computer services is tantamount to the denial of the . . . computer services guaranteed [to] the Union . . . in the [parties'] [a]greement." *Id.* at 8. The Agency provides no basis for concluding that this interpretation is irrational, unfounded, implausible, or in manifest disregard of the agreement. Accordingly, we deny this exception.

With regard to the Agency's reliance on an RD's decision in an unrelated case not to issue a ULP complaint concerning termination of a Union steward's computer access, the Authority has held that "the decision not to issue a complaint is a nonreviewable, nonprecedential exercise of the General Counsel's prosecutorial responsibility" and, "[t]herefore, the dismissal of the charge is not binding on [an] [a]rbitrator or the Authority." *AFGE, Local 2823*, 64 FLRA 1144, 1147 (2010) (quoting *Dep't of Def., Dependents Schs.*, 30 FLRA 1092, 1096 (1988)). Thus, the RD's decision not to issue a complaint in an entirely different case provides no basis for finding that the award is deficient. Accordingly, we deny the exception.

VI. Decision

The Agency's exceptions are dismissed in part and denied in part.

4. We note that, although the Union claims that there "was ample evidence" presented at the hearing demonstrating that computers are the most commonly used form of communication, Opp'n at 4, the record does not indicate whether the parties disputed that factual issue below.

65 FLRA No. 131

UNITED STATES
DEPARTMENT OF VETERANS AFFAIRS
VA MARYLAND HEALTHCARE SYSTEM
(Agency)

and

AMERICAN FEDERATION
OF GOVERNMENT EMPLOYEES
LOCAL 331
(Union)

0-AR-4655

DECISION

March 17, 2011

Before the Authority: Carol Waller Pope, Chairman, and Thomas M. Beck and Ernest DuBester, Members

I. Statement of the Case

This matter is before the Authority on exceptions to an award of Arbitrator Janet M. Spencer filed by the Agency under § 7122(a) of the Federal Service Labor-Management Relations Statute (the Statute) and part 2425 of the Authority's Regulations. The Union filed an opposition to the Agency's exceptions.[1]

The Arbitrator sustained a grievance alleging that the Agency suspended the grievant without just cause. For the reasons that follow, we deny the Agency's exceptions.

II. Background and Arbitrator's Award

This dispute involves an altercation, discussed in further detail below, between the grievant, a Union president who is on 100 percent official time and works in the Union office, and another employee. As a result of the altercation, the Agency charged the grievant with "conduct unbecoming a federal employee based on physical intimidation and wrongful touching of another employee" and suspended the grievant for seven days. Award at 2 (emphasis omitted). The Union filed a grievance challenging the suspension, which was unresolved and submitted to arbitration. As stipulated by the parties, the issues at arbitration were: "Was the suspension of [the grievant] for just cause? If not, what should be the remedy?" *Id.*

The Arbitrator found that the altercation underlying the suspension arose after the Union prevailed in an arbitration case brought on behalf of two employees who later decided to withdraw from the Union. *Id.* at 3. When the employees went to the grievant's office to obtain his signature on dues deduction withdrawal forms, the grievant expressed his frustration that the employees were withdrawing despite the Union's efforts on their behalf, and accused the employees of being ungrateful. *Id.* The Arbitrator found that when one of the employees (the firefighter) said that the Union had not done anything for him, the grievant responded, "Well, if the Union didn't do anything for you, then don't call me," "or words to this effect[,]" to which the firefighter responded "If I call you anything, I'll call you an asshole." *Id.* at 4. The Arbitrator also found that, in response, the grievant became "irate and red-faced," approached the firefighter, and said, "Don't come down here acting all bad, I'm not afraid of you big boy" "or words to that effect[.]"[2] *Id.* at 12.

Before the Arbitrator, the firefighter testified that the grievant bumped him with his chest several times; the grievant denied that he physically touched the firefighter in any way. *Id.* at 10. The Agency submitted to the Arbitrator the statements of several individuals who had allegedly witnessed all or part of the altercation (witness statements), but those

1. The Authority ordered the Union to show cause why its opposition should not be considered untimely. The Union's response states that the opposition was timely filed based on the date of the Union's *receipt* of the exceptions. Response to Show Cause Order at 2. However, as the Authority's Regulations determine timeliness from the *date of service*, rather than receipt, and the Union does not allege "extraordinary circumstances" justifying a waiver of the expired time limit, *see* 5 C.F.R. § 2429.23(b), we do not consider the Union's opposition. *See U.S. Gen. Servs. Admin.*, 62 FLRA 341, 341 n.1 (2008).

2. With respect to the Arbitrator's finding that the grievant made the statement alleged by the Agency "or words to that effect," Award at 12, the only other version of the statement that appears in the award is the Arbitrator's quotation of the grievant's testimony that he said: "You're not going to come up here acting all big and bad because if you do, I will call the police[.]" *Id.* at 4.

individuals did not testify at the hearing, and the Arbitrator gave "no weight to their statements." *Id.* The Arbitrator also declined to "defer to the conclusions reached by the Agency's investigators based on their interviews with individuals who did not testify[.]" *Id.* In this regard, the Arbitrator stated that "[t]he right to cross-examine witnesses is fundamental to the fairness of the arbitration process" and that "[i]n a de novo proceeding such as this, the determination of credibility and weight must be made de novo by me." *Id.* The Arbitrator found that although the grievant may have been "closer to [the firefighter] than he says" and that the firefighter may have been "discomfited as a result[,]" the evidence was "inadequate . . . to establish that [the grievant] bumped against [the firefighter] with his chest or otherwise touched him[,]" and she credited the grievant's testimony that he did not do so. *Id.* at 11. In addition, the Arbitrator found that the firefighter could not "reasonably have *believed* that [the grievant] was contemplating a fight" or that the grievant "presented an ongoing danger to him." *Id.* at 11-12. The Arbitrator concluded that "the seriousness of the episode was exaggerated in the retelling, causing the escalation of an altercation into an unfounded charge of physical intimidation." *Id.* at 15.

The Arbitrator found that the Agency had not met its burden to prove that the misconduct underlying the suspension occurred. *Id.* at 9. In this regard, the Arbitrator found that, "[s]tanding alone," the grievant's statement, "Don't come down here acting all bad, I'm not afraid of you big boy" "or words to that effect[,]" was merely a defensive response to the firefighter's "hostile words[.]" *Id.*

The Arbitrator went on to state that "[b]ased on the Agency's analysis, it is possible the Agency would have found [the grievant] guilty of 'conduct unbecoming a federal employee based on physical intimidation' even in the absence of any finding of a physical touching." *Id.* at 12. However, the Arbitrator found that "the Agency's analysis . . . was flawed in several critical respects." *Id.* In this regard, the Arbitrator rejected the Agency's arguments that it could hold the grievant to a higher standard of conduct because he was a police officer and because, as Union President, he was in a leadership role akin to that of a supervisor. *Id.* at 12-13.

In addition, the Arbitrator found that "the altercation, properly evaluated, involved a matter of internal [U]nion affairs." *Id.* at 15. In this connection, she stated that the behavior of an employee acting in his or her capacity as a union official must be "significantly more egregious to justify discipline" "because representational interests of the employees are implicated." *Id.* at 13-14 (citing *Dep't of the Air Force, Grissom Air Force Base, Ind.*, 51 FLRA 7, 11 (1995)). The Arbitrator further found that: (1) there was no evidence that the altercation "disturbed employees performing their regular duties . . . or otherwise disrupted order in the workplace or interfered with the efficiency or mission of the Agency[;]" and (2) "[t]o the extent that the Agency's legitimate concern with violence in the work place was implicated, I have found there was no violence[.]" *Id.* at 14-15.

The Arbitrator concluded that the charge of "conduct unbecoming a federal employee based on physical intimidation" had not been "substantiated[,]" and that the suspension of the grievant was "not for just cause."[3] *Id.* at 12, 15, 16. Consequently, the Arbitrator awarded backpay and directed the Agency to remove all references to the suspension from the grievant's personnel records. *Id.* at 16.

III. Agency's Exceptions

The Agency contends that the Arbitrator erred by refusing to consider the witness statements. Exceptions at 10-11. In this regard, the Agency argues that because the statements were recorded at the time of the altercation, they were admissible despite the fact that the Union did not have an opportunity to cross-examine the witnesses. *Id.* at 10.

In addition, the Agency argues that the Arbitrator erred in two respects by improperly applying the protections of § 7102 of the Statute (§ 7102)[4] to the altercation between the grievant and the firefighter. First, the Agency argues that the grievant was "not representing his [U]nion or any employee" during the altercation. *Id.* at 4. Second, the Agency argues that the grievant's conduct exceeded the bounds of protected activity. *Id.* at 5-9 (citing *Dep't of the Air Force, 315th Airlift Wing v. FLRA*, 294 F.3d 192

3. The Arbitrator also found that there was no evidence that the Agency disciplined the grievant "in retaliation for his pursuing actions on behalf of the Union[.]" Award at 15. As there are no exceptions filed to this finding, we do not discuss it further.

4. In pertinent part, § 7102 protects an employee's "right to form, join, or assist any labor organization[] . . . freely and without fear of penalty or reprisal[.]" 5 U.S.C. § 7102.

(D.C. Cir. 2002); *AFGE, Local 987*, 63 FLRA 362 (2009) (*Local 987*)).[5]

IV. Analysis and Conclusions

A. The Arbitrator did not deny the Agency a fair hearing.

We construe the Agency's claim that the Arbitrator erred by refusing to consider the witness statements as a claim that the Arbitrator failed to provide a fair hearing. The Authority will find an award deficient on the ground that an arbitrator failed to conduct a fair hearing when it is demonstrated that the arbitrator refused to hear or consider pertinent and material evidence, or that other actions in conducting the proceeding prejudiced a party so as to affect the fairness of the proceeding as a whole. *AFGE, Local 1668*, 50 FLRA 124, 126 (1995). However, an arbitrator has considerable latitude in the conduct of a hearing and the fact that an arbitrator conducted a hearing in a manner that one party finds objectionable does not provide a basis for finding an award deficient. *AFGE, Local 22*, 51 FLRA 1496, 1497-98 (1996). In this regard, disputes over an arbitrator's evaluation of evidence, including the determination of the weight to be accorded such evidence, provide no basis for finding an award deficient. *U.S. Dep't of Veterans Affairs, Veterans Affairs Med. Ctr., Louisville, Ky.*, 64 FLRA 70, 72 (2009) (*Veterans Affairs*).

As an initial matter, although the Agency asserts that the Arbitrator "refused to consider" the witness statements, Exceptions at 11, the Arbitrator's award indicates that she considered the statements, but gave them "no weight[.]" Award at 10 (giving "no weight" to the written statements of witnesses who did not testify and declining to "defer to the conclusions reached by the Agency's investigators based on their interviews with individuals who did not testify[.]") To the extent that the Agency's arguments supporting the admissibility of the statements challenge the Arbitrator's discretion to evaluate evidence and determine the weight to be accorded such evidence, the arguments do not provide a basis for finding that the Arbitrator denied the Agency a fair hearing. *See Veterans Affairs*, 64 FLRA at 72. Consequently, we deny the exception.

B. The award is not contrary to law, rule, or regulation.

In reviewing arbitration awards for consistency with law, rule, or regulation, the Authority reviews questions of law raised by exceptions to an award de novo. *NTEU, Chapter 24*, 50 FLRA 330, 332 (1995) (citing *U.S. Customs Serv. v. FLRA*, 43 F.3d 682, 686-87 (D.C. Cir. 1994)). In applying the standard of de novo review, the Authority determines whether the arbitrator's legal conclusions are consistent with the applicable standard of law. *See NFFE, Local 1437*, 53 FLRA 1703, 1710 (1998). In making that determination, the Authority defers to the arbitrator's underlying factual findings. *See id.*

The Agency alleges that the Arbitrator improperly applied the protections of § 7102 to the conduct underlying the grievant's suspension. The scope of § 7102's protection and the Authority's standard for determining whether otherwise protected activity exceeds the boundaries of protected activity apply in cases where an agency is alleged to have violated § 7116 of the Statute (§ 7116),[6] thereby committing an unfair labor practice (ULP), by taking actions against an individual based on that individual's actions during the course of protected activity. *See, e.g.*, *Local 987*, 63 FLRA at 363.

The Authority has held that arbitrators are required to apply statutory burdens of proof when resolving an alleged ULP. *E.g.*, *U.S. GSA, Ne. & Caribbean Region, N.Y., N.Y.*, 60 FLRA 864, 866 (2005). By contrast, where an arbitrator resolves a claim under a collective bargaining agreement (CBA) rather than a statutory claim, "unless a specific burden of proof is required, an arbitrator may establish and apply whatever burden the arbitrator considers appropriate[.]" *Id.* In this regard, the Authority distinguishes allegations that an agency lacked just cause for discipline under a CBA from allegations of unlawful interference with protected

---

5. In addition, the Agency states that the award is "contrary to the parties' agreement" without providing any further explanation. Exceptions at 3. To the extent that the Agency is arguing that the award fails to draw its essence from the agreement, we deny the exception as a bare assertion. *See, e.g.*, *IFPTE, Local 4*, 65 FLRA 167, 169 (2010) ("Where a party fails to support its claim that an award fails to draw its essence from a collective bargaining agreement, the Authority denies the exceptions as a bare assertion.").

6. Section 7116 provides, in pertinent part, that it is an unfair labor practice for an agency "to encourage or discourage membership in any labor organization by discrimination in connection with hiring, tenure, promotion, or other conditions of employment[.]" 5 U.S.C. § 7116(a).

rights under the Statute. *See NAGE, Local R3-32*, 59 FLRA 458, 459 (2003) (Chairman Cabaniss concurring). In addition, where an arbitrator is not required to apply a statutory standard, alleged misapplications of that standard do not provide a basis for finding the arbitrator's award deficient. *E.g.*, *SSA*, 65 FLRA 286, 288 (2010).

Here, the record reflects, and there is no dispute, that the parties stipulated that the issue before the Arbitrator was whether there was "just cause" for the suspension of the grievant, Award at 2, not whether the suspension violated § 7116, and the Arbitrator found that "[t]he suspension of [the grievant] [was] not for just cause." *Id.* at 16. Because the issue before the Arbitrator was a contractual claim, the Arbitrator was not required to apply statutory standards, and the Arbitrator's alleged misapplication of the statutory standard concerning protected activity under § 7102 does not provide a basis for setting aside the award. *See SSA*, 65 FLRA at 288. Accordingly, we deny the exception.

V. Decision

The Agency's exceptions are denied.

65 FLRA No. 132

UNITED STATES
DEPARTMENT OF THE ARMY
UNITED STATES
ARMY CORPS OF ENGINEERS
NEW YORK DISTRICT
NEW YORK, NEW YORK
(Agency)

and

INTERNATIONAL FEDERATION
OF PROFESSIONAL AND
TECHNICAL ENGINEERS
LOCAL 98
(Union)

0-AR-4732

DECISION

March 21, 2011

Before the Authority: Carol Waller Pope, Chairman, and Thomas M. Beck and Ernest DuBester, Members

This matter is before the Authority on an exception to an award of Arbitrator Randi E. Lowitt filed by the Agency under § 7122(a) of the Federal Service Labor-Management Relations Statute (the Statute) and part 2425 of the Authority's Regulations.* The Union filed an opposition to the Agency's exception.

Under § 7122(a) of the Statute, an award is deficient if it is contrary to any law, rule, or regulation, or it is deficient on other grounds similar to those applied by federal courts in private sector labor-management relations. Upon careful consideration of the entire record in this case and Authority precedent, the Authority concludes that the award is not deficient on the ground raised in the exception and set forth in § 7122(a). *See U.S. Dep't of Labor (OSHA)*, 34 FLRA 573, 575 (1990) (award not deficient as failing to draw its essence from the parties' collective bargaining agreement where excepting party fails to establish that the award cannot in any rational way be derived from the agreement; is so unfounded in reason and fact and so unconnected to the wording and purpose of the agreement as to manifest an infidelity to the obligation of the arbitrator; does not represent a plausible interpretation of the agreement; or evidences a manifest disregard of the agreement).

Accordingly, the Agency's exception is denied.

---

* Pursuant to 5 C.F.R. § 2425.7, the Agency requested that the Authority issue an expedited decision in this dispute. The Union did not object to the Agency's request.

65 FLRA No. 133

AMERICAN FEDERATION
OF GOVERNMENT EMPLOYEES
LOCAL 1547
(Union)

and

UNITED STATES
DEPARTMENT OF THE AIR FORCE
LUKE AIR FORCE BASE, ARIZONA
(Agency)

0-AR-4354

DECISION

March 21, 2011

Before the Authority: Carol Waller Pope, Chairman, and Thomas M. Beck and Ernest DuBester, Members

I. Statement of the Case

This matter is before the Authority on exceptions to an award of Arbitrator Paul Eggert filed by the Union under § 7122(a) of the Federal Service Labor-Management Relations Statute (the Statute) and part 2425 of the Authority's Regulations. The Agency filed an opposition to the Union's exceptions.

The Arbitrator denied a grievance concerning a reduction in force (RIF) conducted by the Agency. For the reasons that follow, we deny the Union's exceptions.

II. Background and Arbitrator's Award

After the Agency conducted a RIF, the Union filed a grievance claiming that the Agency had failed to place four employees in positions to which they were entitled under law, regulations, and the parties' collective bargaining agreement (CBA). *See* Award at 2; Exceptions, Attach. 2, Grievance at 1. The grievance was unresolved and was submitted to arbitration.

Because the parties were unable to agree on a statement of the issue, the Arbitrator framed the issue as follows: "Did the Agency violate the terms of the [CBA] by its handling of the RIFs pertaining to [Employee 1], [Employee 2], [Employee 3] and [Employee 4]?" Award at 2. The Arbitrator found that, in addition to being bound by the CBA, the parties were bound by a related memorandum of understanding (MOU), which states that "RIFs will be run in accordance with applicable laws and regulations." *Id.* Thus, the Arbitrator determined that, "[i]n order to resolve the issue set forth in the [g]rievance, it is necessary to understand the rather complex RIF process set forth in federal statute and regulation and essentially incorporated by reference into the MOU." *Id.*

The Arbitrator explained that the computer-generated "retention register" that the Agency uses to make RIF decisions "ranks each employee in order of their relative job protection status[,]" and divides employees into "subgroups." *Id.* at 3. The Arbitrator stated that, within each subgroup, the retention register lists each employee in order of his or her "service computation date" (SCD), which is based upon an employee's combined government service as a military and/or civilian employee. *Id.*

The Arbitrator found that once an employee is "identified for release[,]" in certain circumstances, the employee may have a right to "bump" or "retreat" to a position for which he or she is qualified. *Id.* The Arbitrator proceeded to apply RIF regulations in order to determine the "retreat" and "bump" rights of each of the grievants. *See id.* at 3-8.

Regarding the right to "retreat[,]" the Arbitrator found that an individual (retreater) seeking to retreat to the position of another employee (retreatee) "must have held the job in question, or one 'essentially identical[,]' at some point in his *civil service* career[.]" *Id.* at 4. In addition, the retreater may retreat only to a position held by an employee in the "exact *same* subgroup[,]" and "[t]he retreater's SCD must trump that of the retreatee[.]" *Id.*

Turning to the specific circumstances of each grievant, the Arbitrator found that Employee 1 could not retreat to an explosives position because it was "undisputed" that he had "never held that grade and position previously in his civilian career." *Id.* Regarding Employee 2, the Arbitrator found that Employee 2's pre-RIF position was coded to signify that only a member of the United States Armed Forces Reserves could hold the position (reserve-membership position). *Id.* at 5. The Arbitrator also found that all of the comparable positions available after the RIF were coded to signify that they did not require reserve membership (non-reserve-membership positions). *Id.* In addition, the

Arbitrator found that "undisputed testimony showed that it [has] 'always' been an [Agency]-wide policy that [reserve-membership] positions not be treated as identical or substantially identical to parallel, [non-reserve-membership] positions in the event of RIFs, because of the reserve-membership difference." *Id.* As a result, the Arbitrator concluded that because Employee 2 "had never held a [non-reserve-membership] position before, and since his [reserve-membership] position was not 'substantially identical' to the [available non-reserve-membership] position[s], one of the conditions for retreat was not met." *Id.* at 6.

Regarding Employees 3 and 4, the Arbitrator found that, prior to the RIF, they both held the same position. *See id.* at 6, 8. Before the Arbitrator, the Union argued that the Agency should have assigned both employees to one of two related positions (proposed positions). *See id.* at 6, 8. The Arbitrator found that Employees 3 and 4 could not retreat to the proposed positions because those positions were not identical to any position that the employees had previously held. *Id.* at 6, 8. In this regard, the Arbitrator found that although the classification of one of the proposed positions appeared identical to that of the grievants' prior position, the duties were "substantially different," and, thus, the positions were not identical for purposes of retreat. *Id.* at 7-8. Regarding the second proposed position, the Arbitrator found that Employee 4 could not retreat because he had never held an identical position. *Id.* at 8. In addition, the Arbitrator rejected Employee 3's "unsupported suggestion" that his experience in a similar Grade 9 position qualified him to retreat to the proposed Grade 10 position. *Id.* at 6-7.

In explaining the right to "bump," the Arbitrator found that, first, the individual seeking to bump to a position (bumper) must belong to a higher subgroup than the individual who would be displaced (bumpee). *Id.* at 4. Second, the bumper need not have prior experience in the bumpee's position, but must be "qualified" for the position, which means "capable of performing the job fully at the time of [the] RIF, or within [ninety] days thereafter." *Id.* Finally, according to the Arbitrator, the relative SCDs of the employees are irrelevant for bumping purposes. *Id.*

The Arbitrator found that Employee 1 could not bump to the proposed explosives position because he was not "qualified" for the position within the meaning of the RIF regulations. *Id.* at 4-5. In this regard, the Arbitrator found that: (1) Employee 1's explosives experience was military, rather than civilian; (2) the available position called for "hands-on experience in dealing with explosives" and Employee 1's explosives experience "was more administrative in nature[;]" (3) Employee 1's explosives work was at Grade 8, which indicated "a substantially lesser skill level than that of the Grade 9 position he was seeking[;]" and (4) Employee 1 did not offer "additional, 'higher' experience from another source" or any "substantial detail to support his conclusory testimony that he was qualified." *Id.* at 5. The Arbitrator also found that Employees 2, 3, and 4 could not bump because none of the positions to which they were seeking to bump were held by someone in a subgroup lower than their own. *Id.* at 6, 8.

Based on the foregoing, the Arbitrator denied the grievance. *Id.* at 9.

III. Positions of the Parties

A. Union's Exceptions

The Union asserts that the Arbitrator "failed to properly apply . . . [g]overnment-[w]ide RIF [r]egulations as required by the parties['] MOU." Exceptions at 2. In this regard, the Union asserts that "[i]t was undisputed during the arbitration hearing that the [grievants] . . . were qualified for, previously held, and were coded for each of the respective positions sought[.]" *Id.* With regard to the Arbitrator's findings regarding the right to retreat, the Union contends that each of the employees had previously held the same, or "virtually the same" position as those to which they were seeking to retreat. *See id.* at 2-5. Regarding Employee 2, the Union argues that the "alleged" policy that reserve-membership positions could not be treated as identical to non-reserve-membership positions for purposes of RIF retreat rights "was not presented as evidence or in [any way] substantiated." *Id.* at 3. The Union also argues that the Arbitrator should have placed each of the grievants in the requested positions "instead of retaining less senior employees with lower RIF [SCDs]." *Id.* at 5. With regard to the Arbitrator's findings regarding the right to bump, the Union asserts that the grievants were "qualified for" the positions that they sought.* *Id.* at 2; *see also id.* at 3, 4.

---

*. In addition, the Union argues that the award fails to draw its essence from the parties' agreement because the Arbitrator failed to properly apply RIF regulations and that this failure was "contrary to the spirit of the parties['] agreement." Exceptions at 3; *see also id.* at 1, 3-4. As the

In addition, the Union argues that the Arbitrator "failed to resolve the issue that was before him in the Union's grievance." *Id.* at 5. In this regard, the Union asserts that the issue, as framed by the Arbitrator, concerned whether the Agency violated the CBA and MOU, but the grievance charged the Agency with violating RIF regulations, which are incorporated by reference into the MOU. *See id.* at 2. The Union also argues that the Arbitrator "exceeded his authority by failing to consider material facts and material evidence." *Id.* at 1. In a related argument, the Union asserts that the Arbitrator failed to conduct a fair hearing by failing to "consider material evidence presented in the arbitration hearing[,]" namely, the arbitration exhibits concerning each employee's relevant work experience and the "computer[-]generated RIF referral printouts from the Agency's . . . RIF computer program." *Id.* at 2.

B. Agency's Opposition

The Agency argues that the award is not deficient. Opp'n at 2-8. In this regard, the Agency contests the Union's claim that it was "undisputed" that each of the four employees was qualified for, previously held, and was coded for each of the positions that the Union sought for them in the grievance. *Id.* at 4. In addition, the Agency argues that the Arbitrator did not fail to resolve the issue before him because "the parties did not submit an agreed-upon statement of issue to the [A]rbitrator, thereby granting the Arbitrator the authority to define the issue." *Id.* at 8. The Agency also argues that the Arbitrator did not fail to consider material facts and evidence. *Id.* at 2.

IV. Analysis and Conclusions

A. The award is not contrary to law, rule, or regulation.

In reviewing arbitration awards for consistency with law, rule, or regulation, the Authority reviews questions of law raised by exceptions to an arbitrator's award de novo. *NTEU, Chapter 24*, 50 FLRA 330, 332 (1995) (citing *U.S. Customs Serv. v. FLRA*, 43 F.3d 682, 686-87 (D.C. Cir. 1994)). In applying the standard of de novo review, the Authority determines whether the arbitrator's legal conclusions are consistent with the applicable standard of law. *See NFFE, Local 1437*, 53 FLRA 1703, 1710 (1998) (*NFFE*). In making that determination, the Authority defers to the arbitrator's underlying factual findings. *See id.* Thus, exceptions that dispute an arbitrator's factual findings and evaluation of the evidence do not establish that an award is deficient. *See, e.g., U.S. Dep't of Veterans Affairs, Veterans Affairs Med. Ctr., Louisville, Ky.*, 64 FLRA 70, 72 (2009) (*Veterans Affairs*).

1. The right to retreat pursuant to RIF regulations.

RIF regulations provide that an employee may retreat only to a position that is "held by another employee with lower retention standing in the same tenure group and subgroup" and is "the same position, or an essentially identical position" as one "formerly held by the released employee on a permanent basis as a competing employee in a Federal agency[.]" 5 C.F.R. § 351.701(c).

The Union argues that the Arbitrator should have placed Employee 1 in the Grade 9 explosives position requested in the grievance because he had "previously held" the position. Exceptions at 5. However, the Arbitrator found that it was "undisputed" that Employee 1 had never held that grade and position in his civilian career, making him ineligible to retreat to the explosives position. Award at 4. The Union does not contend that the award is based on a nonfact in this regard and, as stated previously, the Authority defers to an arbitrator's factual findings when assessing whether the award is contrary to law. *See NFFE*, 53 FLRA at 1710. As the Arbitrator's factual findings support his legal conclusion that the Agency did not violate Employee 1's retreat rights under RIF regulations, we find that the award is not contrary to law in this regard.

Similarly, the Union argues that the Arbitrator should have placed Employees 3 and 4 in the proposed positions because it was "undisputed" that the positions sought were "virtually the same" as the positions the grievants previously held. *See* Exceptions at 4. However, the Arbitrator found that the duties of one of the proposed positions were "substantially different" from those of the positions held by the grievants, and, thus, the jobs were not identical for purposes of retreat. Award at 7-8. Regarding the second proposed position, the Arbitrator found that neither grievant had retreat rights because neither employee had held an identical position. *Id.* at 6-7, 8. The Union does not contend

Union's essence claim is based on its contrary-to-law claim that the Arbitrator erroneously applied RIF regulations, we do not separately analyze the Union's essence exception. *See, e.g., U.S. Dep't of Agric., Farm Serv. Agency, Kan. City, Mo.*, 65 FLRA 483, 484 n.3 (2011) (declining to separately analyze essence exception that was "substantively the same" as a contrary-to-law exception).

that the award is based on a nonfact in this regard and, as stated previously, the Authority defers to an arbitrator's factual findings when assessing whether the award is contrary to law. *See NFFE*, 53 FLRA at 1710. As the Arbitrator's factual findings support his legal conclusion that the Agency did not violate the retreat rights of Employees 3 and 4 under RIF regulations, we find that the award is not contrary to law in this regard.

In addition, the Union argues that the Arbitrator should have placed Employee 2 in one of the positions that he was seeking despite the fact that Employee 2 held a reserve-membership position prior to the RIF and the available, post-RIF positions were all non-reserve-membership positions. *See* Exceptions at 3-4. However, the Arbitrator found that Agency policy required treating reserve-membership positions as *not* "identical or substantially identical" to non-reserve-membership positions for the purposes of RIF rights. Award at 5. Although the Union argues that this policy was not "presented as evidence[,]" Exceptions at 3, the Arbitrator credited the "undisputed testimony" that the Agency could not treat these positions as identical for retreat right purpose, Award at 5. Further, the Union does not contend that the award is based on a nonfact in this regard and, as stated previously, the Authority defers to an arbitrator's factual findings when assessing whether the award is contrary to law. *See NFFE*, 53 FLRA at 1710. As the Arbitrator's factual findings support his legal conclusion that the Agency did not violate Employee 2's retreat rights under RIF regulations, we find that the award is not contrary to law in this regard.

The Union also argues that the Arbitrator erred by failing to place the grievants in positions held by employees with lower SCDs. Exceptions at 5. As discussed above, the RIF regulations provide that an employee may retreat only to a position held by an employee with "lower retention standing . . . *and* . . . [a position that is] the same position, or an essentially identical position, [as a position] formerly held by the released employee . . . ." 5 C.F.R. § 351.701(c) (emphasis added). As previously discussed, the Arbitrator found that none of the grievants had previously held positions that were identical, or essentially identical, to the positions to which they sought to retreat. Award at 4, 6, 8. The Union does not contend that the award is based on a nonfact in this regard and, as stated previously, the Authority defers to an arbitrator's factual findings when assessing whether the award is contrary to law. *See NFFE*, 53 FLRA at 1710. As the Arbitrator's factual findings support his legal conclusion that the grievants were not eligible to retreat to the positions that they sought, the allegedly lower SCDs of the employees that the Agency placed in those positions do not establish that the award is contrary to RIF regulations. *See* 5 C.F.R. § 351.701(c). Accordingly, we find that the award is not contrary to law in this regard.

Based on the foregoing, we find that the Union's arguments concerning retreat rights do not provide a basis for setting aside the award as contrary to law, and deny the contrary-to-law exceptions regarding retreat rights.

2. The right to bump pursuant to RIF regulations.

In order to bump to a position, an employee need not have previously held the position, but "[t]he employee must be qualified for the offered position." 5 C.F.R. § 351.701(a). In order to be "qualified" for a position, *id.*, the employee must have "the capacity, adaptability, and special skills needed to satisfactorily perform the duties of the position without undue interruption[,]" *id.* § 351.702(a)(4). RIF regulations define "[u]ndue interruption" to mean "a degree of interruption that would prevent the completion of required work by the employee [ninety] days after the employee has been placed in a different position" pursuant to RIF regulations. *Id.* § 351.203. In addition, RIF regulations provide that an employee may only bump to a position that is "held by another employee in a lower tenure group or in a lower subgroup within the same tenure group[.]" *Id.* § 351.701(b)(1).

The Arbitrator's finding that Employee 1 was ineligible to bump to the explosives position was based on the Arbitrator's findings that Employee 1's previous military, administrative, Grade 8 explosives experience did not "qualif[y]" him for the civilian, "hands-on[,]" Grade 9 explosives position that he was seeking. Award at 4-5. Although the Union disputes the Arbitrator's conclusion that Employee 1 was not qualified for the proposed position, Exceptions at 3, the Union does not dispute any of the Arbitrator's underlying factual findings or contend that the award is based on a nonfact in this regard, and, as stated previously, the Authority defers to an arbitrator's factual findings when assessing whether the award is contrary to law. *See NFFE*, 53 FLRA at 1710. As the Arbitrator's factual findings support his legal conclusion that the Agency did not violate Employee 1's bump rights under RIF regulations, we find that the award is not contrary to law in this regard.

To the extent that the Union's claim that no one with a lower SCD should have been placed in the positions sought by Employees 2, 3, and 4 could be construed as arguing that the Agency violated the bump rights of those grievants, the Arbitrator found that none of the positions to which these grievants proposed to bump were held by employees in a lower subgroup. Award at 6, 8. The Union does not argue that the award is based on a nonfact in this regard, and, as stated previously, the Authority defers to an arbitrator's factual findings when assessing whether the award is contrary to law. *See NFFE*, 53 FLRA at 1710. As discussed above, the absence of a potential bumpee in a lower tenure group or subgroup means that a mandatory precondition for bumping under RIF regulations was not met. *See* 5 C.F.R. § 351.701(b)(1). As the Arbitrator's factual findings support his legal conclusion that the Agency did not violate the bump rights of Employees 2, 3, and 4 under the RIF regulations, we find that the award is not contrary to law in this regard.

Based on the foregoing, we find that the Union's arguments concerning bump rights do not provide a basis for setting aside the award as contrary to law, and deny the contrary-to-law exceptions regarding bump rights.

B. The Arbitrator did not exceed his authority.

We construe the Union's assertion that the Arbitrator "failed to resolve the issue that was before him in the Union's grievance" as a claim that the Arbitrator exceeded his authority. Exceptions at 5; *see also id.* at 2. In addition, the Union argues that the Arbitrator "exceeded his authority by failing to consider material facts and material evidence." *Id.* at 1. Arbitrators exceed their authority when they fail to resolve an issue submitted to arbitration, resolve an issue not submitted to arbitration, disregard specific limitations on their authority, or award relief to persons who are not encompassed within the grievance. *See U.S. Dep't of the Navy, Naval Base, Norfolk, Va.*, 51 FLRA 305, 307-08 (1995). Where, as here, the parties fail to stipulate the issue for resolution, "the fact that the formulated issue[] differ[s] from the issue[] presented in the grievance provides no basis for finding that the award was in excess of the arbitrator's authority." *U.S. Dep't of the Treasury, IRS, Wash., D.C.*, 64 FLRA 426, 435 (2010). *See also AFGE, Local 933*, 58 FLRA 480, 482 (2003) (in the absence of a stipulated issue, an arbitrator's formulation of the issue is accorded substantial deference).

The Arbitrator stated, and the Union did not dispute, that the parties "were unable to agree on a statement of the issue in this matter[,]" which resulted in the Arbitrator framing the issue as whether the Agency had violated the CBA. Award at 2. The Arbitrator found that, in addition to being bound by the CBA, the parties were bound by the MOU's statement that "RIFs will be run in accordance with applicable laws and regulations." *See id.* As a result, the Arbitrator determined that, "[i]n order to resolve the issue set forth in the [g]rievance, it is necessary to understand the rather complex RIF process set forth in federal statute and regulation and essentially incorporated by reference into the MOU." *Id.* Thus, the Arbitrator expressly applied RIF regulations in order to determine the RIF rights of each of the four grievants, and, after analyzing the rights of each grievant to bump or retreat, the Arbitrator concluded that the Agency did not violate the RIF rights of any of the grievants. *See id.* at 5, 6, 8. Accordingly, the Union has not established that the Arbitrator failed to resolve the issue that was before him, and, thus, we deny the Union's exception claiming that the Arbitrator exceeded his authority in this regard.

The Union's argument that the Arbitrator "exceeded his authority by failing to consider material facts and material evidence" does not contend that the Arbitrator failed to resolve an issue submitted to arbitration, resolved an issue not submitted to arbitration, disregarded specific limitations on his authority, or awarded relief to persons who were not encompassed within the grievance. *See* Exceptions at 1. Rather, the Union's exceeded authority argument challenges the Arbitrator's evaluation of the evidence, and, as such, does not establish that the award is deficient. *See Veterans Affairs*, 64 FLRA at 72. Accordingly, we deny the exception.

C. The Arbitrator did not fail to conduct a fair hearing.

The Authority will find an award deficient on the ground that an arbitrator failed to conduct a fair hearing when it is demonstrated that the arbitrator refused to hear or consider pertinent and material evidence, or that other actions in conducting the proceeding prejudiced a party so as to affect the fairness of the proceeding as a whole. *AFGE, Local 1668*, 50 FLRA 124, 126 (1995). However, an arbitrator has considerable latitude in the conduct of a hearing and the fact that an arbitrator conducted a hearing in a manner that one party finds objectionable does not provide a basis for finding an award deficient. *AFGE, Local 22*, 51 FLRA 1496, 1497-98 (1996). In this regard, disputes over an arbitrator's evaluation of evidence, including the determination of the weight to be accorded such evidence, provide no basis for finding an award deficient. *Veterans Affairs*, 64 FLRA at 72. In addition, a party's unsubstantiated allegation that an arbitrator failed to consider evidence cannot establish that the arbitrator denied it a fair hearing. *See AFGE, Local 1547*, 59 FLRA 149, 151 (2003) (*Local 1547*). Further, an arbitrator is not required to specify or discuss specific items of evidence on which an award is based or that otherwise were considered by the arbitrator. *See id.*

As an initial matter, although the Union asserts that the Arbitrator "failed to consider material evidence presented in the arbitration hearing" concerning the grievants' work experience and the Agency's computer-generated RIF reports, Exceptions at 2, the Union has not cited any evidence in the record supporting these allegations. In addition, the Arbitrator expressly refers to the computer-generated retention register, and discusses each grievant's experience, in the award. *See* Award at 3, 4-8. Thus, the Union's unsubstantiated allegation that the Arbitrator failed to consider material evidence does not establish that the Arbitrator denied it a fair hearing. *See Local 1547*, 59 FLRA at 151. In any event, the Arbitrator was not required to specify or discuss specific items of evidence that he may have considered in formulating his award, *see id.*, and to the extent that the Union is challenging the Arbitrator's evaluation of evidence and determinations regarding the weight to be accorded such evidence, the Union does not provide a basis for finding that the Arbitrator denied the Union a fair hearing. *See Veterans Affairs*, 64 FLRA at 72. Consequently, we deny the exception.

V. Decision

The Union's exceptions are denied.

65 FLRA No. 134

NATIONAL TREASURY
EMPLOYEES UNION
CHAPTER 238
(Union)

and

UNITED STATES
DEPARTMENT OF THE TREASURY
INTERNAL REVENUE SERVICE
(Agency)

0-AR-4418
(65 FLRA 369 (2010))

ORDER DENYING MOTION
FOR RECONSIDERATION

March 21, 2011

Before the Authority: Carol Waller Pope, Chairman, and Thomas M. Beck and Ernest DuBester, Members

I. Statement of the Case

This matter is before the Authority on the Union's motion for reconsideration of the Authority's decision to grant the Agency's exception in *United States Department of the Treasury, Internal Revenue Service*, 65 FLRA 369 (2010) (*IRS*). The Agency filed an opposition to the Union's motion for reconsideration.

Section 2429.17 of the Authority's Regulations permits a party who can establish extraordinary circumstances to request reconsideration of an Authority decision. For the reasons set forth below, we conclude that the Union has failed to establish extraordinary circumstances warranting reconsideration. Accordingly, we deny the Union's motion for reconsideration.

II. Decision in *IRS*

In the underlying proceeding in *IRS*, the Arbitrator ordered the Agency to grant the grievant grade and pay retention after she accepted a lower-graded position subsequent to a reorganization. *IRS*, 65 FLRA at 369. The Authority granted the Agency's exception that the Arbitrator's award was inconsistent with government-wide regulations governing grade and pay retention. *Id.* at 371-72. In reaching this conclusion, the Authority deferred to the Arbitrator's factual findings that after the Agency underwent a reorganization that left the grievant without a permanent position, the grievant, who retained her higher-graded position as a "transition employee," applied for a lower-graded position. *Id.* at 372. The Authority also deferred to the Arbitrator's factual findings that the Agency decided to make her original, higher-graded position permanent before she was offered and she accepted the lower-graded position. *Id.* In these circumstances, the Authority concluded that the required regulatory conditions did not exist allowing the Agency to provide the grievant grade and pay retention in the lower-graded position. *Id.* at 371-72.

III. Positions of the Parties

A. Union's Motion for Reconsideration

The Union claims that extraordinary circumstances exist warranting reconsideration of the Authority's decision in *IRS* because the Authority erred in its factual findings. Motion for Reconsideration (Motion) at 1. The Union claims that the Authority erred by failing to consider and defer to "the Arbitrator's underlying factual finding that the Agency violated the contract when it failed to place the [grievant] into an appropriate position before it withdrew transition employee benefits from the grievant." *Id.* at 2.

B. Agency's Opposition

The Agency argues that the Authority should deny the Union's motion for reconsideration because: (1) the Union mischaracterizes legal conclusions made by the Arbitrator as factual findings to which the Authority must allegedly defer and, therefore, attempts to relitigate legal conclusions reached by the Authority, Opp'n at 3-5; (2) government-wide regulations govern the outcome of this case, rather than the Arbitrator's legal conclusions regarding the CBA, *id.* at 6; and (3) the Authority did not fail to consider the Arbitrator's factual findings, *id.* at 6-8.

IV. Analysis and Conclusions

Section 2429.17 of the Authority's Regulations permits a party that can establish extraordinary circumstances to request reconsideration of an Authority decision. The Authority has repeatedly recognized that a party seeking reconsideration under § 2429.17 bears the heavy burden of establishing that extraordinary circumstances exist to justify this unusual action. *See Int'l Ass'n of Firefighters, Local F-25*, 64 FLRA 943, 943 (2010). The Authority has identified a limited number of situations in which extraordinary circumstances have been found to exist. These include situations where: (1) an intervening court decision or change in the law affected dispositive issues; (2) evidence, information, or issues crucial to the decision had not been presented to the Authority; (3) the Authority erred in its remedial order, process, conclusion of law, or factual finding; and (4) the moving party has not been given an opportunity to address an issue raised sua sponte by the Authority in its decision. *See id.*

Although the Union claims that the Authority erred in its factual findings, the Union does not allege that any of the Authority's factual findings are erroneous. The only Authority factual finding that the Union discusses is that after the grievant applied for the lower-graded position, the Agency decided to make the grievant's original, higher-graded position permanent. Motion at 2. However, the Union does not allege that, or explain why this or any other factual finding made by the Authority is erroneous. Therefore, in this respect, the Union's motion for reconsideration does not establish that the Authority erred in its factual findings.

The Union only claims that the Authority erred by failing to consider and defer to "the Arbitrator's underlying factual finding that the Agency violated the contract when it failed to place the [grievant] into an appropriate position before it withdrew transition employee benefits from the grievant." *Id.* (emphasis omitted). However, the Arbitrator made no such finding. He found only that, at the time the grievant applied for the lower-graded position, she "met all pre-conditions" for grade and pay retention. *See IRS*, 65 FLRA at 370. In addition, to the extent that a contract violation is a factual finding, the Authority made no findings at all as to whether the Agency violated the contract. Therefore, in this respect as well, the Union's motion for reconsideration does not identify any erroneous factual finding that the Authority made or explain why such finding is erroneous.

Accordingly, because the Union has failed to establish that extraordinary circumstances exist warranting reconsideration, we deny the Union's motion for reconsideration.

V. Order

The Union's motion for reconsideration is denied.

65 FLRA No. 135

UNITED STATES
DEPARTMENT OF THE ARMY
WOMACK ARMY MEDICAL CENTER
FORT BRAGG, NORTH CAROLINA
(Agency)

and

AMERICAN FEDERATION
OF GOVERNMENT EMPLOYEES
COUNCIL 1770
(Union)

0-AR-4349

DECISION

March 24, 2011

Before the Authority: Carol Waller Pope, Chairman, and Thomas M. Beck and Ernest DuBester, Members

I. Statement of the Case

This matter is before the Authority on exceptions to an award of Arbitrator Clarence D. Rogers, Jr. filed by the Agency and the Union under § 7122(a) of the Federal Service Labor-Management Relations Statute (the Statute) and part 2425 of the Authority's Regulations. The Union and the Agency filed oppositions to each other's exceptions.

The Arbitrator determined that the Union satisfied the requirements for receiving attorney fees under the Back Pay Act, 5 U.S.C. § 5596, and awarded the Union a portion of the attorney fees it had requested. For the reasons discussed below, we dismiss the Agency's exceptions in part and grant them in part, and we find it unnecessary to resolve the Union's exceptions.

II. Background and Arbitrator's Awards[1]

The grievant asked for and received permission to use annual leave to take a day off. *See* Initial Award at 10. Later, the grievant realized that she could have taken that day off without using annual leave, because that day was treated as a holiday under the parties' agreement. *See id.* After the Agency failed to restore the grievant's annual leave, *see id.* at 2, the Union filed a grievance, which was unresolved and submitted to arbitration, *see id.* at 5.

In his initial award, the Arbitrator framed the issue as whether the Agency violated the parties' agreement by "requir[ing the grievant] to take annual leave" on her contractual holiday, and if so, what should be the remedy. *Id.* at 2. The Arbitrator found that the Agency violated the parties' agreement and that the grievant was "entitled to have the leave time . . . restored[.]" *Id.* at 11. Based on the testimony of two Agency witnesses, *see id.* at 8-9, the Arbitrator found that there was "evidence . . . that the Agency . . . already repaired any damage done by restoring the time . . . charged to [the grievant's] annual leave account" the day before the hearing, *id.* at 11-12. The Arbitrator concluded that there was "no reason" not to accept that evidence as being "anything less than true." *Id.* at 12. However, "out of an abundance of caution" the Arbitrator stated that the award would "include an order to do what has probably already been done." *Id.* The Arbitrator thus sustained the grievance and directed the Agency to "restore the annual leave that was charged to [the grievant's] account[.]" *Id.* The Arbitrator denied the Union's request for attorney fees, finding that there was "no evidence of bad faith or any other justification" that would warrant an award of attorney fees. *Id.*

Neither party filed exceptions to the initial award. *See* First Supplemental Award at 2. Approximately one month after the Arbitrator issued the initial award, the Union filed a motion with the Arbitrator, Exceptions, Attachment 2, Union's Motion for Clarification and Reconsideration (Union's Motion), alleging that the Agency had not restored the grievant's annual leave. *See* First Supplemental Award at 2. The Union also requested permission to file a brief in support of its request for attorney fees. *See id.* In response, Exceptions, Attachment 3, Agency's Response to Union Motion for Clarification and Reconsideration (Agency's Response), the Agency argued to the Arbitrator that it had restored the grievant's annual leave and that the Union was not entitled to attorney fees because it was not a prevailing party. *See* First Supplemental Award at 2.

In the first supplemental award, the Arbitrator granted the Union's request to file a brief in support of its request for attorney fees, and permitted the

1. The Arbitrator issued three awards in this matter: the initial award, the first supplemental award, and the second supplemental award.

Agency to file a response. *See id.* at 3. The Union then submitted a brief, Exceptions, Attachment 5, Union's Petition for Attorney Fees and Costs (Union's Brief), in support of its request for attorney fees, and the Agency filed a brief in opposition, Exceptions, Attachment 6, Agency's Response to the Union's Petition for Attorney Fees (Agency's Brief). *See* Second Supplemental Award at 2. In its brief, the Agency again argued that the Union was not a prevailing party, *see id.* at 4, and contended that the amount of fees requested by the Union was excessive, *see* Agency's Brief at 8-9.

In the second supplemental award, the Arbitrator stated that he was "clarifying" the initial award in certain respects. Second Supplemental Award at 5. First, the Arbitrator stated that the Agency "did not violate" the Arbitrator's direction in the initial award, *id.* at 4, because the Agency had in fact "restored" the grievant's annual leave "the day before the arbitration" hearing, *id.* at 5. Next, the Arbitrator stated that the grievant was a prevailing party and was therefore eligible for attorney fees, reasoning that the grievance caused the Agency to voluntarily restore the grievant's annual leave. *Id.* at 5-6. Further, the Arbitrator stated that the fact that he had sustained the grievance in the initial award was "indicative" that the grievant was a prevailing party. *Id.* at 5. The Arbitrator awarded the Union attorney fees, but at a lower hourly rate and for fewer hours than the Union had requested. *See id.* at 6-7.

III. Positions of the Parties

A. Agency's Exceptions

The Agency alleges that the Arbitrator exceeded his authority, arguing that under the doctrine of functus officio, the Arbitrator's authority to award attorney fees ceased once he denied the Union's request in the initial award. *See* Agency's Exceptions at 5. The Agency asserts, in this regard, that the Arbitrator did not retain jurisdiction after the initial award, and that the parties' agreement does not "permit an arbitrator to conduct further proceedings[.]" *Id.* Additionally, the Agency contends that the award is contrary to the Back Pay Act and 5 U.S.C. § 7701(g) (§ 7701(g)). Specifically, the Agency argues that the grievant is not a prevailing party under § 7701(g) because the Agency restored the grievant's annual leave prior to the hearing. *See id.* at 6-7.

B. Union's Opposition

The Union argues that the Arbitrator was authorized to clarify his initial award because that award was ambiguous. *See* Union's Opp'n at 2-3. Additionally, the Union argues that the grievant was a prevailing party because the Agency's "attempt to restore the leave before the [a]rbitration itself, and the [o]rder from the Arbitrator failed. . . . [L]eave was in fact not restored until afterwards." *Id.* at 4.

C. Union's Exceptions

The Union argues that the second supplemental award is contrary to Authority precedent because the Arbitrator failed to explain why he was awarding attorney fees for fewer hours and at a lower hourly rate than the Union had requested. *See* Union's Exceptions at 3, 7, 10.

D. Agency's Opposition

The Agency argues that the hourly rate on which the Arbitrator based his award is not contrary to law. *See* Agency's Opp'n at 3.

IV. Analysis and Conclusions

A. 5 C.F.R. § 2429.5 bars the Agency's exceeded authority exception.

The Authority's Regulations that were in effect when the Agency filed its exceptions provided that "[t]he Authority will not consider . . . any issue, which was not presented in the proceedings before the . . . arbitrator." 5 C.F.R. § 2429.5 (§ 2429.5).[2] Under § 2429.5, the Authority will not consider an issue that could have been, but was not, presented to the arbitrator. *See, e.g., U.S. Dep't of Homeland Sec., U.S. Customs & Border Prot., JFK Airport, Queens, N.Y.*, 62 FLRA 416, 417 (2008).

Here, the Agency was on specific notice that, subsequent to the initial award, the Union requested permission to address its request for attorney fees. *See* First Supplemental Award at 2. In response, the Agency could have raised its functus officio argument to the Arbitrator in either its Agency Response or Agency Brief. However, the Agency

2. The Authority's Regulations concerning the review of arbitration awards, as well as certain related Regulations, including § 2429.5, were revised effective October 1, 2010. *See* 75 Fed. Reg. 42,283 (2010). As the Union's exceptions were filed before that date, we apply the earlier Regulations.

did not raise the argument in either filing. *See* Agency's Response at 1-2; Agency Brief at 4-6. As the Agency could have, but did not raise this argument, we dismiss the Agency's exceeded authority exception.

B. The award is contrary to § 7701(g).

When an exception involves an award's consistency with law, the Authority reviews any question of law raised by the exception and award de novo. *See NTEU, Chapter 24*, 50 FLRA 330, 332 (1995) (citing *U.S. Customs Serv. v. FLRA*, 43 F.3d 682, 686-87 (D.C. Cir. 1994)). In applying the standard of de novo review, the Authority assesses whether an arbitrator's legal conclusions are consistent with the applicable standard of law. *See U.S. Dep't of Def., Dep'ts of the Army & the Air Force, Ala. Nat'l Guard, Northport, Ala.*, 55 FLRA 37, 40 (1998). In making that assessment, the Authority defers to the arbitrator's underlying factual findings. *See id.*

Awards of attorney fees under the Back Pay Act must be in accordance with the standards established under § 7701(g), which pertains to awards of attorney fees by the Merit Systems Protection Board (MSPB). *U.S. Dep't of Transp., FAA*, 65 FLRA 320, 323 (2010). The standards established under § 7701(g) include the requirement that the employee must be the prevailing party. *Id.* at 323-34. *See also U.S. Dep't of State*, 59 FLRA 129, 130 (2003) (grievant who is not a prevailing party is not entitled to attorney fees) (*State Department*).

The Authority has held that a grievant is not a prevailing party under § 7701(g) in instances where an agency has unilaterally rescinded a disputed action during the pendency of an appeal. *See AFGE, Local 446*, 64 FLRA 15, 16 (2009) (agency unilaterally rescinded suspension); *State Department*, 59 FLRA at 130 (same); *AFGE, Local 1547*, 58 FLRA 241 (2002) (agency voluntarily restored grievant's overtime). *Accord Sacco v. Dep't of Justice*, 90 M.S.P.R. 37, 41-42 (2001) (agency unilaterally rescinded constructive suspension).

In the initial award, the Arbitrator stated that there was "evidence . . . that the Agency . . . restor[ed]" the grievant's annual leave, Initial Award at 11, but "out of an abundance of caution[,]" the Arbitrator directed the Agency to restore the grievant's annual leave, *id.* at 12. In the second supplemental award -- the award at issue here -- the Arbitrator "clarif[ied]" the initial award to find expressly that the Agency had in fact "restored" the grievant's annual leave "the day before the arbitration" hearing. Second Supplemental Award at 5. Therefore, the Arbitrator's conclusion that the grievant was a prevailing party, and his award of attorney fees based on that conclusion, are contrary to § 7701(g). *See, e.g., State Department*, 59 FLRA at 130.

Based on the foregoing, we find that the award of attorney fees is contrary to § 7701(g), and we set it aside. As such, it is unnecessary to consider the Union's exceptions claiming that the Arbitrator's reduction in the amount of fees requested was contrary to Authority precedent.

V. Decision

The Agency's exceeded authority exception is dismissed, and the award of attorney fees is set aside.

65 FLRA No. 136

PENSION BENEFIT
GUARANTY CORPORATION
(Agency)

and

INDEPENDENT UNION
OF PENSION EMPLOYEES
FOR DEMOCRACY AND JUSTICE
(Petitioner/Labor Organization)

and

INTERNATIONAL FEDERATION
OF PROFESSIONAL AND
TECHNICAL ENGINEERS, AFL-CIO
UNION OF PENSION EMPLOYEES
(Incumbent Union)

WA-RP-10-0070

ORDER DENYING
APPLICATION FOR REVIEW

March 25, 2011

Before the Authority: Carol Waller Pope, Chairman, and Thomas M. Beck and Ernest DuBester, Members

I. Statement of the Case

This case is before the Authority on an application for review (application) filed by the Petitioner under § 2422.31(c) of the Authority's Regulations.[1] The Incumbent Union (UPE) filed an opposition to the application.[2]

The Regional Director (RD) determined that UPE is the incumbent exclusive representative of the bargaining unit at issue in the petition for an election and thus, under § 2422.8(d) of the Authority's Regulations, had a right to participate in the election.[3] For the reasons that follow, we deny the application.

II. Background and RD's Decision

On March 4, 2009, an RD of the Authority certified UPE as the exclusive representative of the bargaining unit at issue here. RD's Decision at 5 (citing Certification of Representative in Case No. WA-RP-09-0013). In the proceeding at issue here, the Petitioner filed a petition under § 7111(b) of the Federal Service Labor-Management Relations Statute (the Statute), requesting an election to determine whether employees of the Agency still wished to be represented by UPE or wished, instead, to be represented by the Petitioner. *Id.* at 1. Subsequently, the Petitioner filed a motion asserting that UPE is not automatically entitled to participate in this proceeding as the incumbent exclusive representative because it is not a "labor organization" within the meaning of § 7103(a)(4) of the Statute.[4] *Id.* at 2.

As relevant here, the RD found that, to meet the definition of "labor organization" under § 7103(a)(4), the organization must be composed of employees who participate and pay dues. *Id.* at 8. In this connection, the RD determined that it was not disputed that, in June 2010, UPE adopted a constitution that included a dues structure, and that dues withholding became effective August 15, 2010. *Id.* at 7. She also found it undisputed that, since that time, the Agency has been withholding dues payments of bargaining unit employees and transmitting the dues to UPE. *Id.* at 7-8. In addition,

1. 5 C.F.R. § 2422.31 states, in pertinent part:

> (c) *Review.* The Authority may grant an application for review only when the application demonstrates that review is warranted on one or more of the following grounds:
> (1) The decision raises an issue for which there is an absence of precedent;
> (2) Established law or policy warrants reconsideration; or,
> (3) There is a genuine issue over whether the Regional Director has:
> (i) Failed to apply established law;
> . . . .
> (iii) Committed a clear and prejudicial error concerning a substantial factual matter.

2. In its opposition, UPE states that, on February 3, 2011, it filed a petition to amend its certification to remove the reference to IFPTE. Opp'n at 2 n.2. As there is no allegation that this matter affects the application, we do not address it further. In addition, both the Petitioner and UPE filed supplemental submissions. As neither the Petitioner nor UPE requested permission to do so, we have not considered the submissions. *E.g., U.S. Dep't of Def., Dep't of Def. Dependents Sch., Europe*, 65 FLRA 580, 581 (2011).

3. The pertinent wording of § 2422.8(d) is set forth below.

4. Section 7103(a)(4) provides, in pertinent part, that "labor organization" means "an organization . . . in which employees participate and pay dues[.]"

the RD stated that the Authority has found that a newly formed organization may be a labor organization even before it has collected dues. *Id.* at 9 (citing *U.S. Dep't of Veterans Affairs, Wash., D.C. and U.S. Dep't of Veterans Affairs, Westside Med. Ctr., Chi., Ill.*, 35 FLRA 172, 178 (1990) (*Veterans Affairs*)). Accordingly, the RD concluded that employees participate in, and pay dues to, UPE and that, consequently, UPE is a labor organization within the meaning of § 7103(a)(4). *Id.* at 9-10.

Further, the RD stated that, under § 2422.8(d) of the Authority's Regulations, an incumbent exclusive representative is a party if any of the employees represented by the exclusive representative are affected by issues raised in a representation petition, and she found that employees represented by UPE are affected by the petition in this case. *Id.* at 10. As UPE is the incumbent exclusive representative, and in view of her conclusion that UPE is a labor organization under the Statute, the RD determined that UPE had a right under § 2422.8(d) to participate in the election. *Id.* at 10-11.

III. Positions of the Parties

A. Petitioner

The Petitioner contends that review is warranted because the RD failed to apply established law. Application at 2-3. Specifically, the Petitioner asserts that § 7103(a)(4) and the holding in *Veterans Affairs* require that UPE must actually have collected dues money no later than the date of its certification to qualify as a labor organization and that there is no exception for a "newly formed" organization. *Id.* at 21-22, 29. Consequently, the Petitioner asserts that the RD failed to properly apply § 7103(a)(4) in concluding that UPE qualified as a labor organization. *Id.* at 3.

The Petitioner also contends that review is warranted because the RD committed clear and prejudicial errors concerning substantial factual matters. Specifically, the Petitioner asserts that the RD erred in her application of *Veterans Affairs* because UPE did not have a dues structure and did not intend (or had only a speculative intent) to collect dues at relevant times, "including in November 2008 when it filed its representational petition with the [Authority], in February 2009 when the [Authority] conducted an election, and in March 2009 when UPE was certified." *Id.* at 35-38, 42-43. In addition, the Petitioner claims that the reference to a "newly-formed organization" in *Veterans Affairs*, 35 FLRA at 177, does not excuse the delay in actual dues collection. Application at 42. The Petitioner further alleges that the constitution adopted in June 2010 and its dues structure "are not valid or legitimate[,]" and that the Department of Labor is investigating issues related to this constitution. *Id.* at 37 & 38 n.22.

The Petitioner also contends that the RD committed clear and prejudicial errors as to substantial factual matters concerning the representation petition filed in November 2008 and UPE's affiliation with IFPTE. The Petitioner alleges that IFPTE, and not UPE, filed the petition and that the petition contained false information on UPE's affiliation with IFPTE. *Id.* at 30-34.

In addition, the Petitioner argues that review is warranted because there is an absence of precedent regarding whether a group can constitute a "labor organization" by simply having a dues structure and a speculative intent to collect dues, and regarding whether there is an exception for a newly formed organization. *Id.* at 21-22.

B. UPE

UPE contends that the application should be denied because the RD correctly applied established law to undisputed facts and correctly concluded that UPE is a "labor organization" within the meaning of § 7103(a)(4). Opp'n at 2. In this regard, UPE argues that the RD correctly found that, under § 7103(a)(4) and *Veterans Affairs*, UPE is a labor organization because it is undisputed that, in August 2010, the Agency began withholding dues and transmitting them to UPE. *Id.* at 6. For these reasons, UPE also contends that the RD's decision does not raise an issue for which there is an absence of precedent. *Id.* at 10-11. UPE further contends that the Petitioner fails to demonstrate that the RD committed any errors concerning any substantial factual matters because the RD identified and properly relied on undisputed facts in concluding that UPE is a labor organization. *Id.* at 15-18.

IV. Analysis and Conclusions[5]

As relevant here, § 2422.8(d) provides: "An incumbent exclusive representative . . . will be considered a party in any representation proceeding raising issues that affect employees the incumbent represents[.]" In turn, § 7103(a)(16)(A) of the

5. Although the Petitioner cites § 2422.31(c)(2) in its application, it does not allege that any established law or policy warrants reconsideration. Accordingly, we do not consider that issue further.

Statute pertinently defines "exclusive representative" as a "labor organization . . . which is certified as the exclusive representative[.]" There is no dispute that UPE is certified as the exclusive representative of the bargaining unit employees at issue in this proceeding, or that this proceeding affects these employees. There also is no dispute that, at the time of the RD's decision, UPE met the definition of labor organization. Consequently, there can be no dispute that, at the time of the RD's decision at issue here, UPE also met the definition of exclusive representative and constituted "[a]n incumbent exclusive representative" within the meaning of § 2422.8(d). Thus, under § 2422.8(d), UPE is entitled to be considered a party in this proceeding and to participate in any election.

The Petitioner argues that UPE did not meet the definition of labor organization by the time it was certified in 2009 and failed to meet the definition until it was "too late[.]" Application at 37. However, nothing in the wording of § 2422.8(d) or Authority precedent indicates that, in the context of an election petition where the unit employees are currently represented, the Petitioner may challenge the status of an incumbent exclusive representative on the basis that it did not constitute a labor organization as of the date on which it was certified by the Authority. *Cf. Def. Logistics Agency*, 5 FLRA 126, 127 (1981) (Authority adopted judge's conclusion that the certification of exclusive representative could not be collaterally attacked). In addition, § 7103(a)(4) and the Authority's decision in *Veterans Affairs* do not require that newly formed organizations must actually have collected dues money no later than the date of certification, or within any specific period of time thereafter, in order to qualify as a labor organization. Thus, the Petitioner's arguments provide no basis for finding that the RD erred in concluding that UPE is a labor organization and has a right under § 2422.8(d) to participate in any election. Accordingly, we deny the application.[6]

V. Order

The Petitioner's application for review is denied.

---

6. In connection with the Petitioner's claim that UPE is being investigated by the Department of Labor, the Authority has repeatedly acknowledged that the Assistant Secretary of Labor has exclusive jurisdiction over the type of claims raised by the Petitioner when they "do not fall under the purview of the [Statute]." *N.M. Army & Air Nat'l Guard*, 56 FLRA 145, 149 (2000) (then-Member Segal and then-Member Cabaniss concurring and Chairman Wasserman dissenting as to other matters). Here, the Petitioner makes no argument that the alleged matters are within the purview of the Statute. To the extent that the Petitioner is challenging UPE's certification on grounds other than UPE's failure to meet the definition of "labor organization[,]" the Petitioner may not raise any issue in its application that it did not raise to the RD. It is not clear that the Petitioner raised any challenge to the validity of the Authority's certification to the RD apart from whether UPE met the definition of labor organization.

65 FLRA No. 137

SOCIAL SECURITY ADMINISTRATION
(Agency)

and

AMERICAN FEDERATION
OF GOVERNMENT EMPLOYEES
COUNCIL 220
(Union)

0-AR-4327

DECISION

March 25, 2011

Before the Authority: Carol Waller Pope, Chairman, and Thomas M. Beck and Ernest DuBester, Members

I. Statement of the Case

This matter is before the Authority on exceptions to an award of Arbitrator Gail R. Smith filed by the Agency under § 7122(a) of the Federal Service Labor-Management Relations Statute (the Statute) and part 2425 of the Authority's Regulations. The Union filed an opposition to the Agency's exceptions.[1]

The Union filed a grievance alleging that the Agency violated the parties' collective bargaining agreement (CBA) when more than one management official (official) participated in mid-year performance discussions (mid-year discussions) with individual employees. The Arbitrator sustained the grievance and directed the Agency to conduct future mid-year discussions with only one management official participating. For the reasons that follow, we deny the Agency's exceptions.

II. Background and Arbitrator's Award

The Agency's bargaining-unit employees (employees) receive annual performance ratings. Award at 6-7. During each performance evaluation year (year), each individual employee has a mid-year discussion with management. *Id.* at 7. The Union filed a grievance alleging that the Agency violated the CBA when, in some instances, more than one official attended an employee's mid-year discussion. *Id.* at 8. When the grievance was unresolved, the parties proceeded to arbitration, where the Arbitrator defined the issue in dispute as follows: "Is Article 21[2] of the [CBA] [(Article 21)] violated when more than one individual participates on the Agency's behalf during a mid-year performance discussion with a[n employee]?" *Id.* at 9.

Before the Arbitrator, the Union asserted that, under the parties' previous agreement, "it was extremely rare" for more than one official to participate in a performance discussion with an employee and that, during negotiations for the new CBA, "the Agency never informed the Union that it wanted to have more than one management official involved in any of the performance discussions." *Id.* at 15-16. Thus, the Union argued that Article 21 should be read as an expression of the parties' continuing agreement that, except in rare circumstances, only one official would participate in mid-year discussions. *See id.* However, at the arbitration hearing, an Agency witness who had participated in negotiating the CBA "insisted that the Agency informed [the Union] that more than one . . . official [c]ould appear during the . . . mid-year . . . discussion[s]." *Id.* at 13. Moreover, the Agency contended that interpreting Article 21 in a manner that prohibited the attendance of multiple officials at such discussions would "violate[] management's right to assign work under [§] 7106(a)(2)(B) of . . . the Statute." *Id.* at 20 (internal quotation marks omitted).

1. A related matter involving these same parties is currently pending before the Authority on exceptions to an award of Arbitrator Charles Feigenbaum, and the exceptions to that award have been docketed as Case No. 0-AR-4509.

2. Article 21 of the CBA provides, in pertinent part:

> At least once during the appraisal period, management will have a documented performance discussion with each employee regarding the employee's performance. During the discussion, management should discuss the employee's contributions and results achieved . . .., reinforce expectations, and identify needs for performance management.
>
> . . . .
>
> Managers should document the content of performance discussions. . . .
> Employees and supervisors will sign the performance plan to acknowledge that the [mid-year] discussion was held.

Exceptions, Attach., Joint Ex. 1 at 131-32 (Art. 21, § 6.C.).

The Arbitrator found that Article 21 employed both singular and plural word forms – "including 'manager' or 'managers,' 'management,' 'the appraising official,' and 'supervisors'" – when referencing officials who would participate in performance discussions, and "there is no consistency as to when or how those terms are used." *Id.* at 17; *see also* *id.* at 17-19 (analysis of ambiguity in singular and plural contract terms). In light of the bargaining history and the parties' prior conduct, the Arbitrator concluded that "if the parties . . . had intended to allow for more than one [official] to attend [mid-year discussions]," then that intention would have been stated in "unambiguous language." *Id.* at 19. In the absence of such an unambiguous statement, she found that the parties "never jointly agreed . . . during the negotiations" that more than one official could participate in mid-year discussions. *Id.*

With regard to the Agency's contention that prohibiting more than one official from participating in mid-year discussions would violate management's rights, the Arbitrator found that, because management still "'retains discretion to choose who will evaluate an employee's performance'" and participate in the discussions, she was not interpreting Article 21 in a manner that would "adversely impact management's right to assign work[.]" *Id.* at 20-21 (quoting *NTEU*, 46 FLRA 696, 746 (1992)). Therefore, the Arbitrator concluded that the attendance of more than one official at mid-year discussions violated Article 21, and she directed the Agency "to cease from perpetuating this practice . . . in the future[.]" *Id.* at 21.

III. Positions of the Parties

A. Agency's Exceptions

The Agency argues that the award is contrary to management's rights to assign work and direct employees under § 7106(a) of the Statute and that management was "acting well within its right to assign work when it assigned more than one [official] to be present during" mid-year discussions. Exceptions at 3-7. In this regard, the Agency contends that the award precludes the assignment of particular duties to certain officials – including the assignment of "'additional supervisory duties to an employee who is already a supervisor[,]'" *id.* at 4 – which, according to the Agency, the Authority has found to be contrary to the right to assign work. *Id.* at 4-8 (citing *U.S. Dep't of VA, Alaska VA Healthcare Sys., Anchorage, Alaska*, 60 FLRA 968, 970 (2005) (*Alaska VA*); *U.S. Dep't of HHS, Health Care Fin. Admin.*, 57 FLRA 462, 463 (2001) (*HCFA*)). The Agency further contends that, although contract provisions negotiated pursuant to § 7106(b) of the Statute may not "completely prevent management from exercising its right to assign work[,]" the Arbitrator interpreted Article 21 so that it operates in such a manner. *Id.* at 9. Finally, the Agency asserts that the award fails to draw its essence from the plain wording of Article 21 of the CBA, which the Agency claims "does not prohibit or explicitly limit" the number of officials who may participate in mid-year discussions. *Id.*

B. Union's Opposition

The Union maintains that Article 21, as interpreted by the Arbitrator, is not contrary to management's rights. Opp'n at 1-2. According to the Union, Article 21, Section 6.C. of the CBA (Section 6.C.) is an enforceable procedure under § 7106(b)(2) of the Statute because: (1) it does not specify which official must participate in a mid-year discussion, *id.* at 4 n.1; and (2) although it provides "'the manner or guidelines'" for performance discussions between an official and an employee, it does not limit communications among officials, *id.* at 3. Finally, the Union argues that the Authority should reject the Agency's essence exception because it constitutes a request that the Authority reinterpret Article 21 of the CBA. *Id.* at 7.

IV. Analysis and Conclusions

A. The award is not contrary to management's right to assign work under § 7106(a)(2)(B) of the Statute.[3]

When an exception involves an award's consistency with law, the Authority reviews any question of law raised by the exception and the award de novo. *See NTEU, Chapter 24*, 50 FLRA 330, 332 (1995) (citing *U.S. Customs Serv. v. FLRA*, 43 F.3d 682, 686-87 (D.C. Cir. 1994)). In applying the standard of de novo review, the Authority assesses whether an arbitrator's legal conclusions are consistent with the applicable standard of law. *See U.S. Dep't of Def., Dep'ts of the Army & the Air Force, Ala. Nat'l Guard, Northport, Ala.*, 55 FLRA

3. Although the Agency also contends that the award is contrary to its right to direct employees, Exceptions at 3, 9, it provides no supporting arguments for this contention. Therefore, we deny the contention as a bare assertion. *See U.S. Dep't of Homeland Sec., U.S. Customs & Border Prot., Port of Seattle, Seattle, Wash.*, 60 FLRA 490, 492 n.7 (2004) (where a party does not provide any arguments or authority to support its exception, the Authority will deny it as a bare assertion).

37, 40 (1998). In making that assessment, the Authority defers to the arbitrator's underlying factual findings. *See id.*

The Authority recently revised the analysis that it will apply when reviewing management rights exceptions to arbitration awards. *See U.S. EPA*, 65 FLRA 113, 115 (2010) (Member Beck concurring) (*EPA*); *FDIC, Div. of Supervision & Consumer Prot., S.F. Region*, 65 FLRA 102, 106-07 (2010) (Chairman Pope concurring) (*FDIC*). Under the revised analysis, the Authority assesses whether the award affects the exercise of the asserted management right. *EPA*, 65 FLRA at 115.[4] If so, then, as relevant here, the Authority examines whether the award enforces a contract provision negotiated under § 7106(b).[5] *Id.*

The right to assign work under § 7106(a)(2)(B) of the Statute includes the right to determine the particular duties to be assigned, when work assignments will occur, and to whom or what positions the duties will be assigned. *See U.S. Dep't of the Treasury, U.S. Customs Serv., El Paso, Tex.*, 55 FLRA 553, 558 (1999) (citation omitted). For example, the Authority has held that a contract provision limiting the number of agency representatives at meetings with employees affects management's right to assign work. *See Alaska VA*, 60 FLRA at 970 (citing *HCFA*, 57 FLRA at 463 (award interpreting contract provision as restriction on agency's ability to assign more than one representative to Step 1 grievance meetings affected right to assign work)). The award limits the number of officials that the Agency may assign to conduct a mid-year discussion. Therefore, consistent with *Alaska VA* and *HCFA*, we find that the award affects the right to assign work.

The Union contends that Section 6.C. constitutes a procedure under § 7106(b)(2) of the Statute. The Authority has found that contract provisions affecting the number of employees, including officials, who perform a task may constitute procedures under § 7106(b)(2), so long as the provisions do not specify the particular persons or positions who will perform the task. *Compare Nat'l Ass'n of Indep. Labor*, 62 FLRA 1, 1-3 (2007) (Chairman Cabaniss concurring) (finding provision that required "supervisors," "peer panel," and "higher level management" to participate in review of performance plans constituted procedure, where management chose who would serve in those capacities), *and NFFE, Local 2099*, 35 FLRA 362, 363-68 (1990) (*Local 2099*) (finding provision that required use of rating and ranking panel, rather than single rating and ranking official, constituted procedure, where "[a]gency retain[ed] its ability to designate" members of the panel), *with AFGE, Local 2298*, 35 FLRA 1128, 1135-36 (1990) (finding proposal for rating and ranking panel did not constitute procedure, where proposal prohibited the assignment of selecting official to panel). The Arbitrator found, and the Union concedes, that the Agency retains the authority to choose any official to conduct any given mid-year discussion. *See* Award at 20-21; Opp'n at 4 n.1; *cf. Local 2099*, 35 FLRA at 363-68. Thus, consistent with the foregoing precedent, the fact that Section 6.C. affects the number of officials who may attend mid-year discussions does not preclude a finding that Section 6.C. constitutes a procedure under § 7106(b)(2).

In addition, when determining whether a contract provision involving performance discussions constitutes a procedure under § 7106(b)(2), the Authority has noted that agencies have a statutory duty, under 5 U.S.C. § 4302(a)(2) (§ 4302(a)(2)), to "encourage employee participation in establishing performance standards[.]" *E.g.*, *Patent Office Prof'l Ass'n*, 47 FLRA 10, 30-31 (1993); *Patent Office Prof'l Ass'n*, 29 FLRA 1389, 1389-92 (1987); *AFGE, AFL-CIO, Local 32*, 3 FLRA 783, 788-89 (1980) (*Local 32*). This duty includes an obligation "to bargain on procedures which management officials will observe in the development *and implementation* of performance standards[,]" *NTEU*, 35 FLRA 254, 256 (1990) (emphasis added), such as "the form of the employee participation" required by § 4302(a)(2), *Local 32*, 3 FLRA at 789. For example, in *NFFE*, 13 FLRA 426, 426-28 (1983), the Authority

4. For the reasons articulated in his recent concurring opinion and footnotes, Member Beck would conclude that it is unnecessary to assess whether the award affects the exercise of the asserted management right. The appropriate question is simply whether the remedy directed by the Arbitrator enforces the provision in a reasonable and reasonably foreseeable fashion. *See EPA*, 65 FLRA at 120 (Concurring Opinion of Member Beck); *U.S. Dep't of Justice, Fed. Bureau of Prisons, Fed. Corr. Complex, Terre Haute, Ind.*, 65 FLRA 460, 462 n.2 (2011); *Soc. Sec. Admin., Dallas Region*, 65 FLRA 405, 408 n.5 (2010); *U.S. Dep't of the Air Force, Air Force Materiel Command*, 65 FLRA 395, 398 n.7 (2010); *U.S. Dep't of Health & Human Servs., Office of Medicare Hearings & Appeals*, 65 FLRA 175, 177 n.3 (2010); *U.S. Dep't of Transp., Fed. Aviation Admin.*, 65 FLRA 171, 173 n.5 (2010). Member Beck would conclude that the Arbitrator's award is a plausible interpretation of the parties' agreement and deny the exception.

5. When an award affects a management right under § 7106(a)(2) of the Statute, the Authority may also examine whether the award enforces an applicable law. *EPA*, 65 FLRA at 115 n.7.

examined a proposal that required a supervisor to discuss a performance appraisal with an employee before discussing it with other higher officials. In finding that the proposal constituted a procedure under § 7106(b)(2), the Authority noted that the requirement to hold a discussion did not preclude the agency from taking whatever actions it deemed appropriate before or after that discussion occurred. *NFFE*, 13 FLRA at 426-28. Similarly, in *NTEU*, 42 FLRA 964, 972-79 (1991), the Authority found that a sentence of a provision requiring that the "establishment of performance standards and the documentation of accomplishments should be a joint planning and communication process between [the Union,] the employee, and his[or]her supervisor" was a procedure because it did not affect the content of performance standards, but merely established the "manner in which an agency meets the requirement of [§ 4302(a)(2)]."

As interpreted and applied by the Arbitrator, Section 6.C. does not preclude management from assigning the task of assessing an employee's performance, or developing feedback based on that assessment, to more than one official. Instead, it sets forth the parameters for a discussion with an employee of the conclusions *already reached* by whomever the Agency has previously assigned to assess the employee's performance and construct appropriate feedback based on that assessment. In that respect, Section 6.C. is similar to the proposal found to be a procedure in *NFFE*, 13 FLRA at 426-28. Moreover, Section 6.C. does not alter the content of performance standards. Rather, in keeping with the requirements of § 4302(a)(2), Section 6.C. regulates the manner in which the "joint planning and communication process" concerning performance standards will occur between management and an employee, and, in that respect, it is similar to the sentence of the provision in *NTEU*, 42 FLRA at 972-79, that the Authority found to be a procedure. Therefore, consistent with the precedents discussed above, we find that Section 6.C., as interpreted and applied by the Arbitrator, constitutes a procedure under § 7106(b)(2) and that, as a result, the award is not contrary to the right to assign work.

For the foregoing reasons, we deny the contrary-to-law exception.

B. The award draws its essence from the CBA.

The Agency contends that the award's restriction on the number of officials participating in mid-year discussions fails to draw its essence from the CBA. In reviewing an arbitrator's interpretation of a collective bargaining agreement, the Authority applies the deferential standard of review that federal courts use in reviewing arbitration awards in the private sector. *See* 5 U.S.C. § 7122(a)(2); *AFGE, Council 220*, 54 FLRA 156, 159 (1998). Under this standard, the Authority will find that an arbitration award is deficient as failing to draw its essence from the collective bargaining agreement when the appealing party establishes that the award: (1) cannot in any rational way be derived from the agreement; (2) is so unfounded in reason and fact and so unconnected with the wording and purposes of the collective bargaining agreement as to manifest an infidelity to the obligation of the arbitrator; (3) does not represent a plausible interpretation of the agreement; or (4) evidences a manifest disregard of the agreement. *See U.S. Dep't of Labor (OSHA)*, 34 FLRA 573, 575 (1990). The Authority and the courts defer to arbitrators in this context "because it is the arbitrator's construction of the agreement for which the parties have bargained." *Id.* at 576.

Although the Agency contends that the award ignores the CBA's plain wording, the Arbitrator found that the contractual wording is not plain because Article 21 employs both singular and plural word forms – "including 'manager' or 'managers,' 'management,' 'the appraising official,' and 'supervisors'" – when referencing officials who would participate in performance discussions, and "there is no consistency as to when or how those terms are used." Award at 17. Therefore, the Arbitrator determined that interpreting Article 21 required her to consider other contractual provisions and the parties' past conduct, including her findings that "it was extremely rare" for more than one official to participate in a performance discussion under the parties' previous agreement and that, "if the parties . . . had intended to allow for more than one [official] to attend [mid-year discussions]," then that intention would have been stated in "unambiguous language." *Id.* at 15-19. The Agency does not demonstrate that the Arbitrator's findings in this regard are irrational, unfounded, implausible, or in manifest disregard of the CBA. *See OSHA*, 34 FLRA at 575. Accordingly, we deny the essence exception.

V. Decision

The Agency's exceptions are denied.

65 FLRA No. 138

UNITED STATES
DEPARTMENT OF THE ARMY
U.S. ARMY CORPS OF ENGINEERS
SAINT LOUIS DISTRICT
ST. LOUIS, MISSOURI
(Agency)

and

NATIONAL FEDERATION
OF FEDERAL EMPLOYEES
LOCAL 405
(Union)

0-AR-4720

DECISION

March 30, 2011

Before the Authority: Carol Waller Pope, Chairman, and Thomas M. Beck and Ernest DuBester, Members

I. Statement of the Case

This matter is before the Authority on exceptions to an award of Arbitrator James L. Reynolds filed by the Agency under § 7122(a) of the Federal Service Labor-Management Relations Statute (the Statute) and part 2425 of the Authority's Regulations. The Union filed an opposition to the Agency's exceptions.

The Arbitrator found that the Agency did not have just cause to suspend the grievant for ten days. Award at 30. The Arbitrator ordered the Agency to set aside the grievant's suspension, expunge the suspension from his personnel records, and pay him backpay equal to what he would have earned had he not been suspended. *Id.* Additionally, the Arbitrator awarded interest and attorney fees as prescribed in 5 U.S.C. § 5596. *Id.* For the reasons set forth below, we remand the portion of the award granting attorney fees to the parties for resubmission to the Arbitrator, absent settlement. We deny the Agency's remaining exceptions.

II. Background and Arbitrator's Award

The grievant has worked for the Agency as a Park Ranger for approximately twenty-two years. *Id.* at 6. Approximately two years ago, the grievant was elected president of the Union. *Id.* The grievant uses official time to perform his Union duties. *Id.* at 7.

After the Agency received reports that employees were engaging in improper conduct while on duty, it scheduled employee interviews to investigate these reports. *See id.* at 11. The grievant met with a group of employees to discuss the upcoming interviews. *Id.* According to the grievant, bargaining unit members requested, at that time, to have Union representation at the interviews. *Id.* The grievant then requested and received official time from his first-line supervisor to represent bargaining unit members during the interviews. *Id.* As the interviews were about to begin, the grievant arrived with two Union stewards. *Id.* at 12. The Agency's labor counsel told the grievant that "he did not have a role in the interviews and that he should not be there because his presence had not been requested as a Union representative . . . by any employee." *Id.* Despite the grievant's protests, the interviews commenced without a Union representative present. *Id.*

Later that day, the grievant spoke with the labor counsel and a human relations representative in the hallway. *Id.* at 12-13. During their conversation, the grievant insisted that, because bargaining unit employees had requested his presence prior to the interviews, they "had a right to Union representation, and . . . he had an absolute right to talk to them." *Id.* at 13. Moreover, the grievant became animated, pointed his finger, and said "'what are you going to do about it' when asserting his right to represent the bargaining unit employees[.]" *Id.* at 28; *see also id.* at 13, 27. Following this incident, a threat management team met to discuss whether the grievant posed a threat to other employees. *Id.* at 14. The team determined that the grievant did not pose a threat. *Id.* at 14-15.

The Agency charged the grievant with committing an "overt [act] causing the apprehension of physical harm to at least two (2) [Agency] employees" and suspended him for ten days.[1] *Id.* at 24; *see also id.* at 5, 15. The Union timely grieved the suspension. *Id.* at 16. The matter was unresolved

---

1. The Agency also based the suspension on the grievant's conduct during an initial and follow-up meeting with his first-line and second-line supervisors regarding his use of official time. *See* Award at 5-6, 7, 8. Because the Agency does not except to the Arbitrator's findings regarding the grievant's conduct during these meetings, they are not before us.

and was submitted to arbitration. *See id.* At arbitration, the parties stipulated to the following issue: "[w]hether the [Agency] had just cause to suspend [the grievant] for two weeks ([e]ight [ten] hour work days)? If not, what shall the remedy be?" *Id.* at 3.

The Arbitrator determined that the grievant was acting in a representational capacity during the incident and that his conduct did not cross "the line of vigorous Union and management discussions." *Id.* at 27; *see also id.* at 25. Moreover, the Arbitrator found that, although the Agency conducted a thorough, fair investigation before imposing discipline, and the grievant was not disciplined for serving as president of the Union, the Agency did not have just cause to suspend the grievant. *See id.* at 23-24, 29, 30. According to the Arbitrator, "there [was] no evidence in the record that the [g]rievant 'threatened or attempted to inflict bodily harm without bodily contact.'" *Id.* at 28. The Arbitrator found that a reasonable person would not consider the grievant's words and actions to be threatening. *Id.* at 27. In this regard, the Arbitrator determined that the grievant's conduct was simply rude and boisterous and that the grievant's statement "what are you going to do about it" was merely rude and provocative. *Id.* at 28; *see also id.* at 27. Additionally, the Arbitrator found that the grievant's actions only could be considered "[d]iscourtesy," a lesser offense listed in the Agency's table of penalties. *Id.* at 28.

The Arbitrator ordered the Agency to set aside the grievant's suspension, expunge the suspension from his personnel records, and pay the grievant backpay equal to what he would have earned had he not been suspended. *Id.* at 30. Additionally, the Arbitrator awarded interest and attorney fees as prescribed in 5 U.S.C. § 5596. *Id.*

III. Positions of the Parties

A. Agency's Exceptions

The Agency argues that the award is based on a nonfact because "the [A]rbitrator was under the mistaken factual belief that he was without authority to mitigate the penalty imposed by management." Exceptions at 6. Moreover, the Agency claims that, absent the Arbitrator's misunderstanding, he likely would have ordered a different remedy. *See id.*

Also, the Agency contends that the Arbitrator exceeded his authority by not resolving "the second issue presented to him, i.e., 'what shall the remedy be?'" *Id.* at 7 (quoting Award at 3). According to the Agency, the Arbitrator had the authority "to fashion an appropriate remedy and not just uphold or overturn the grievant's suspension." *Id.*

Finally, the Agency claims that the award is contrary to law. *Id.* at 3-6, 7-9. The Agency argues that the award is contrary to § 7102 of the Statute because, as in *AFGE, Local 987*, 63 FLRA 362 (2009), the grievant's behavior exceeded the bounds of protected activity. *Id.* at 7-9.

Moreover, the Agency asserts that the Arbitrator's award of attorney fees is contrary to law because the Arbitrator failed to make "specific findings with regard to any of the pertinent statutory requirements associated with the award of attorney fees." *Id.* at 4; *see also id.* at 5. The Agency claims that the record is insufficient for the Authority to determine whether the Arbitrator properly awarded attorney fees. *Id.* at 5. As a result, the Agency asserts that the award "of attorney fees must be set side, or[,] in the alternative, be remanded to the parties for resubmission to the [A]rbitrator[,] absent settlement." *Id.* at 6.

B. Union's Opposition

The Union argues that the award is not based on a nonfact. Opp'n at 2. According to the Union, the Arbitrator properly rescinded, rather than mitigated, the suspension because he found that the Agency failed to prove that the grievant was guilty of the offense with which he was charged. *Id.*

Also, the Union argues that the Arbitrator's finding that the grievant's actions constituted protected activity is not contrary to law. *Id.* at 2-3. The Union notes that the Arbitrator found that the grievant's actions could not be considered threatening and "that the Agency, at most, proved that the [g]rievant acted in a discourteous manner." *Id.*

Finally, the Union contends that the award of attorney fees is not contrary to law because the

Arbitrator found that the grievant was disciplined improperly and rescinded the suspension.[2] *Id.* at 2.

IV. Analysis and Conclusions

A. The award is not based on a nonfact.

To establish that an award is based on a nonfact, the appealing party must show that a central fact underlying the award is clearly erroneous, but for which the arbitrator would have reached a different result. *See NFFE, Local 1984*, 56 FLRA 38, 41 (2000). The Authority has found that an exception challenging an arbitrator's legal conclusions will not demonstrate that an award is based on a nonfact. *See, e.g., U.S. Dep't of Health & Human Servs., Nat'l Insts. of Health*, 64 FLRA 266, 269 (2009); *NTEU*, 63 FLRA 198, 201 (2009); *AFGE, Local 3690*, 63 FLRA 118, 120 (2009).

The Agency contends that the award is based on a nonfact, but does not challenge any of the Arbitrator's factual findings. Instead, the Agency disputes the Arbitrator's opinion that, although arbitrators should not impose their own sense of appropriate discipline, they also should not hesitate to set aside discipline imposed by an agency when the record shows that it is excessive. Exceptions at 6; Award at 29. Consequently, the Agency's exception does not demonstrate that the award is based on a nonfact. *See AFGE*, 63 FLRA 627, 628 n.3 (2009) (denying the union's nonfact exception because it challenged the arbitrator's legal conclusion based on his interpretation of the evidence); *AFGE, Nat'l Border Patrol Council, Local 2455*, 62 FLRA 37, 40 (2007) (determining that the union failed to establish that the arbitrator's finding that an award of backpay was not authorized was based on a nonfact because his finding constituted a legal conclusion, rather than a factual determination).

Accordingly, we deny the Agency's exception.

B. The Arbitrator did not exceed his authority.

The Agency also contends that the Arbitrator exceeded his authority by not resolving "the second issue presented to him [at arbitration], i.e., 'what shall the remedy be?'" Exceptions at 7 (quoting Award at 3).

Arbitrators exceed their authority when they fail to resolve an issue submitted to arbitration, resolve an issue not submitted to arbitration, disregard specific limitations on their authority, or award relief to those not encompassed within the grievance. *See AFGE, Local 1617*, 51 FLRA 1645, 1647 (1996). In determining whether an arbitrator has exceeded his or her authority, the Authority accords an arbitrator's interpretation of a stipulated issue the same substantial deference that it accords an arbitrator's interpretation and application of a collective bargaining agreement. *See U.S. Info. Agency, Voice of Am.*, 55 FLRA 197, 198 (1999).

The Agency's contention that the Arbitrator exceeded his authority is without merit. The Arbitrator here clearly resolved the second issue presented to him by rescinding the grievant's suspension and awarding him backpay. Award at 30. Moreover, the Arbitrator's remedy is directly responsive and properly confined to the stipulated issues. *See U.S. Dep't of Homeland Sec., U.S. Immigration & Customs Enforcement*, 65 FLRA 529, 536 (2011) (determining that arbitrator's award, which ordered that reprimand be voided and removed from grievant's file because it was not issued for appropriate cause, was directly responsive and properly confined to the stipulated issues, namely whether the reprimand was for appropriate cause and, if not, what remedy was appropriate). Consequently, the Agency has failed to demonstrate that the Arbitrator exceeded his authority by failing to resolve an issue submitted to arbitration.

Accordingly, we deny the Agency's exception.

C. The award is not contrary to law, rule, or regulation.

When an exception involves an award's consistency with law, the Authority reviews any question of law raised by the exception and the award de novo. *See NTEU, Chapter 24*, 50 FLRA 330, 332 (1995) (citing *U.S. Customs Serv. v. FLRA*, 43 F.3d 682, 686-87 (D.C. Cir. 1994)). In applying the standard of de novo review, the Authority assesses whether an arbitrator's legal conclusions are

2. The Union concedes that precedent requires an arbitrator to provide detailed analysis when granting attorney fees and allows the Authority to remand an award to the parties for resubmission to the arbitrator, absent settlement, if the arbitrator fails to make detailed findings. Opp'n at 1 n.1. Also, the Union notes that, although it "offered to submit a fee petition to the Arbitrator[,] [t]he Agency decided to file exceptions instead." *Id.*

consistent with the applicable standard of law. *See U.S. Dep't of Def., Dep'ts of the Army & the Air Force, Ala. Nat'l Guard, Northport, Ala.*, 55 FLRA 37, 40 (1998) (*Ala. Nat'l Guard*). In making that assessment, the Authority defers to the arbitrator's underlying factual findings. *See id.*

1. The Arbitrator's finding that the Agency did not have just cause to suspend the grievant is not contrary to law.

The Agency asserts that that the award is contrary to § 7102 of the Statute because the grievant's behavior exceeded the bounds of protected activity. Exceptions at 7-9.

Under the Statute, a union official acting in a representative capacity may not be disciplined for actions taken in performing representative duties unless such actions constitute flagrant misconduct or otherwise exceed the bounds of protected activity. *See, e.g., U.S. Dep't of Veterans Affairs Med. Ctr., Richmond, Va.*, 63 FLRA 553, 555 (2009) (*VAMC Richmond*); *U.S. Dep't of the Air Force, Aerospace Maint. & Regeneration Ctr., Davis Monthan Air Force Base, Tucson, Ariz.*, 58 FLRA 636, 636 (2003).

The Authority has held that arbitrators are required to apply statutory burdens of proof when resolving an alleged unfair labor practice. *See, e.g., U.S. GSA, Ne. & Caribbean Region, N.Y., N.Y.*, 60 FLRA 864, 866 (2005). By contrast, where an arbitrator resolves a claim under a collective bargaining agreement rather than a statutory claim, an arbitrator may establish and apply whatever burden the arbitrator considers appropriate unless a specific burden of proof is required. *Id.* In this connection, the Authority distinguishes allegations that an agency lacked just cause for discipline under a collective bargaining agreement from allegations of unlawful interference with protected rights under the Statute. *AFGE, Local 2923*, 65 FLRA 561, 563 (2011). In addition, when an arbitrator is not required to apply a statutory standard, alleged misapplications of that standard do not provide a basis for finding the arbitrator's award deficient. *See Soc. Sec. Admin.*, 65 FLRA 286, 288 (2010).

Here, the issue before the Arbitrator was whether there was "just cause to suspend [the grievant] for two weeks[,]" not whether the suspension violated §7102 of the Statute. Award at 3. Moreover, although the Arbitrator found that the Agency did not have just cause to suspend the grievant, he made no determination regarding whether the Agency violated § 7102 of the Statute. *See id.* at 29, 30. Consequently, the Arbitrator was not required to apply statutory standards, and the Arbitrator's alleged misapplication of those standards does not provide a basis for finding the award contrary to law. *See AFGE, Local 2923*, 65 FLRA at 563 (finding that there was no need to address the union's claim that the arbitrator improperly applied the flagrant misconduct test when the issue before the arbitrator was whether there was "'just and sufficient cause' for the suspension" rather than whether the suspension violated the Statute).

Accordingly, we deny the Agency's exception.

2. The record is insufficient for the Authority to resolve the Agency's exception regarding the Arbitrator's award of attorney fees.

Under the Back Pay Act, 5 U.S.C. § 5596, an award of attorney fees must be in accordance with the standards established under 5 U.S.C. § 7701(g). The threshold requirement for an award of attorney fees under the Back Pay Act is a finding that the grievant was affected by an unjustified or unwarranted personnel action, which resulted in a withdrawal or reduction of the grievant's pay, allowances, or differentials. *See U.S. Dep't of Def., Def. Distrib. Region E., New Cumberland, Pa.*, 51 FLRA 155, 158 (1995). The Back Pay Act further requires that an award of fees must be: (1) in conjunction with an award of backpay to the grievant on correction of the personnel action; (2) reasonable and related to the personnel action; and (3) in accordance with standards established under 5 U.S.C. § 7701(g). *See id.* The prerequisites for an award under § 7701(g) are that: (1) the employee must be the prevailing party; (2) the award of attorney fees must be warranted in the interest of justice;[3] (3) the amount of

3. An award of attorney fees is warranted in the interest of justice if: (1) the agency engaged in a prohibited personnel practice; (2) the agency actions are clearly without merit or wholly unfounded, or the employee is substantially innocent of charges brought by the agency; (3) the agency actions are taken in bad faith to harass or exert improper pressure on an employee; (4) the agency committed gross procedural error which prolonged the proceeding or severely prejudiced the employee; or (5) the agency knew or should have known it would not prevail on the merits when it brought the proceeding. *See Allen v. U.S. Postal Serv.*, 2 M.S.P.R. 420 (1980). The Authority also has

fees must be reasonable; and (4) the fees must have been incurred by the employee. *See id.*

The Arbitrator did not articulate his reasons for granting attorney fees, and the record, as submitted to the Authority, does not assist the Authority in determining the Arbitrator's basis for granting attorney fees. *See* Award at 30 (awarding only reasonable attorney fees). In such situations, the Authority "take[s] the action necessary to assure that the award is consistent with applicable statutory standards." *U.S. Dep't of Agric., Animal & Plant Health Inspection Serv., Plant Prot. & Quarantine*, 53 FLRA 1688, 1695 (1998).

The record reveals that the grievant was the prevailing party. *See U.S. Dep't of Transp., Fed. Aviation Admin.*, 65 FLRA 320, 324 (2010) (finding that the grievant was the prevailing party when the arbitrator ordered the agency to rescind the reprimand and make the grievant whole); *AFGE, Local 933*, 64 FLRA at 718, 719 (determining that the grievant was clearly the prevailing party when the arbitrator rescinded the grievant's suspension). However, the record does not permit the Authority to resolve whether the fees requested were "warranted in the interest of justice," were reasonable, or were incurred by the employee. *See AFGE, Local 933*, 64 FLRA at 719. Accordingly, because the Arbitrator has not explained sufficiently the determination of pertinent statutory requirements, and the record does not permit the Authority to resolve the Agency's exception, we remand this portion of the award to the parties for resubmission to the Arbitrator, absent settlement, to clarify, consistent with the foregoing standards, his reasons for awarding reasonable attorney fees. *See U.S. Dep't of the Army, Womack Army Med. Ctr., Fort Bragg, N.C.*, 63 FLRA 524, 528 (2009) (finding that the award of attorney fees should be remanded to the parties for resubmission to the arbitrator, absent settlement, so that the arbitrator could clarify his reasons for awarding reasonable attorney fees).

stated that an award of attorney fees is warranted in the interest of justice when there is either a service rendered to the federal workforce or there is a benefit to the public derived from maintaining the action. *See, e.g., AFGE, Local 1148*, 65 FLRA 402, 404 n.* (2010). An award of attorney fees is warranted if any of these criteria is satisfied. *Id.*

V. Decision

The attorney fee award is remanded to the parties for resubmission to the Arbitrator, absent settlement. The Agency's remaining exceptions are denied.

65 FLRA No. 139

AMERICAN FEDERATION
OF GOVERNMENT EMPLOYEES
LOCAL 3615
(Union)

and

SOCIAL SECURITY ADMINISTRATION
OFFICE OF DISABILITY
ADJUDICATION AND REVIEW
(Agency)

0-AR-4695

DECISION

March 30, 2011

Before the Authority: Carol Waller Pope, Chairman, and Thomas M. Beck and Ernest DuBester, Members

I. Statement of the Case

This matter is before the Authority on exceptions to an award of Arbitrator Sean J. Rogers filed by the Union under § 7122(a) of the Federal Service Labor-Management Relations Statute (the Statute) and part 2425 of the Authority's Regulations. The Agency filed an untimely opposition to the Union's exceptions.

The Arbitrator concluded, as relevant here, that: (1) the Union's claim that the grievants were entitled to temporary promotions pursuant to Articles 26 and 27 of the parties' agreement (Agreement) was not arbitrable because the Union had failed to raise those provisions in its grievance, and (2) the Union's claim that the grievants were entitled to a higher rate of pay was not arbitrable because it involved a classification matter. For the reasons set forth below, we deny the Union's exceptions.

II. Background and Arbitrator's Award

The grievants are former General Schedule (GS)-334 Computer Specialists in the Agency's Division of Information and Integration, Office of Disability Adjudication and Review (ODAR). Award at 2. As a result of an Agency reorganization, approximately one-half of the GS-334 Computer Specialists in ODAR were reassigned to the Office of Systems (OOS); the other half remained in ODAR, but were moved to GS-343 Program Analyst positions. *Id.* at 13-14.

After the reorganization, the Office of Personnel Management (OPM) replaced the GS-334 Computer Specialist series with the GS-2210 Information Technology Management series. *Id.* at 14. Subsequently, OPM announced a new, special rate of pay for certain information technology positions, including the GS-334 position. *Id.* at 14-15. The OOS GS-334 Computer Specialists who had been converted to the GS-2210 Information Technology Management series received the new rate of pay, but the ODAR GS-334 Computer Specialists who had been moved to the GS-343 Program Analyst positions did not. *Id.* at 15.

The Union presented a grievance on behalf of the GS-343 Program Analysts, which alleged that the Agency violated Article 3, Section 2 and Article 28, Sections 2 and 4 of the Agreement by failing to find the grievants eligible for the GS-2210 special pay rate.[1] *Id.* The Union contended that the grievants were denied the proper pay because their current position descriptions did not accurately reflect their job responsibilities. *Id.* The Agency responded that the grievance was not arbitrable because it concerned classification of the grievants' positions. *Id.* at 2. The grievance was not resolved and was submitted to arbitration. *Id.* Subsequently, at the arbitration hearing, the Union also claimed that the grievants were entitled to temporary promotions pursuant to Articles 26 and 27 of the Agreement, raising these provisions for the first time. *Id.* at 38-39. The Arbitrator framed the relevant issues to be resolved as: (1) whether the Union's grievance is arbitrable, and (2) whether the Agency violated Article 3, Article 26, Section 16, Article 27, Section 4, or Article 28 of the Agreement, and if so, what shall be the remedy.[2] *Id.* at 5.

1. Article 3, Section 2 provides that "[a]ll employees shall be treated fairly and equitably in all aspects of personnel management . . . ." Award at 6. Article 28, Section 2 provides, in relevant part, that "position descriptions shall accurately state the principal duties and responsibilities of the position." *Id.* at 9.

2. The Agency also contended at the arbitration hearing that the grievance was untimely, a claim that the Arbitrator rejected. *Id.* at 34-35. Because no exceptions were filed to the Arbitrator's resolution of this issue, it is not before us.

The Arbitrator concluded that the Union's claim that the grievants were entitled to temporary promotions pursuant to Articles 26 and 27 of the Agreement was not arbitrable. *Id.* at 41. According to the Arbitrator, Article 24, Section 9 of the Agreement required the Union to plead in its grievance the specific provisions of the Agreement that had been violated.[3] Thus, the Union was not entitled to bring new claims at the arbitration hearing. *Id.* at 40-41. Because the Arbitrator found that the grievance only alleged that the Agency violated Articles 3 and 28 and did not mention Articles 26 and 27, he found that the Union's claim that the grievants were entitled to temporary promotions pursuant to Articles 26 and 27 was not arbitrable. *Id.* at 38-41.

The Arbitrator next considered the arbitrability of the grievants' entitlement to the GS-2210 special pay rate. *Id.* at 43-44. The Union asserted that the Agency's failure to pay the grievants at the GS-2210 special pay rate violated Article 3, Section 2 of the Agreement, which provides that employees are to be treated fairly and equitably. *Id.* at 44. The Arbitrator concluded that granting a special pay rate established by OPM to a different job series would involve a classification matter and, thus, he was without jurisdiction to decide the issue. *Id.* Therefore, he dismissed that portion of the grievance.[4] *Id.*

III. Preliminary Matter

The Agency submitted an opposition to the Union's exceptions by facsimile. The Authority issued an Order to Show Cause (Order) to the Agency because the Authority's Regulations do not permit an opposition to be filed by facsimile. Order at 1-2 (citing 5 C.F.R. §§ 2429.24(e) & 2429.27(b)). The Agency failed to respond to the Order in a timely manner.[5] Accordingly, we do not consider the Agency's opposition. *See AFGE, Local 933*, 64 FLRA 718, 718 n.* (2010) (refusing to consider the agency's opposition where it did not respond to the Authority's deficiency order in a timely manner).

IV. Union's Exceptions

The Union argues that the Arbitrator's determination that the Union was required to specifically plead a violation of Articles 26 and 27 of the Agreement in its grievance evidences a manifest disregard of Article 24, Section 9 of the Agreement. Exceptions at 6. According to the Union, Article 24, Section 9 does not require parties to specifically plead all alleged violations, just that they "normally" should do so. *Id.* at 7.

The Union also argues that the award is contrary to law because the Arbitrator improperly found that the Union's claim that the grievants were entitled to the GS-2210 special rate of pay was not grievable. *Id.* at 10. The Union claims that it is asking simply for a temporary promotion for the grievants by reason of their having performed higher-graded duties that have been previously classified. *Id.* at 11. According to the Union, the Arbitrator did not need to determine the proper grade level of the duties, but, rather, could have compared the grievants' duties to the GS-2210 position descriptions. *Id.* at 12.

Finally, the Union argues that the Authority should grant the grievants backpay for the entire period at issue rather than the 120-day period of backpay authorized by *United States Department of Veterans Affairs, Ralph H. Johnson Medical Center, Charleston, South Carolina*, 60 FLRA 46 (2004) (*Ralph H. Johnson*). Exceptions at 13-15. The Union asserts that "the years since the *Ralph H. Johnson* case have revealed that OPM's interpretation is plainly erroneous," and, as a result, the Authority should not limit the remedy to the time period set forth in the OPM opinion letter in that case. *Id.* at 15.

---

3. Article 24, Section 9 provides that "[t]he written grievance should normally contain a description of the matter(s) being grieved, include the article(s) of the agreement that is involved, and the requested relief, if known." *Id.* at 8.

4. In response to the Union's claim that the grievants' position descriptions were inaccurate, the Arbitrator awarded a desk audit intended to lead to the creation of accurate position descriptions. *Id.* at 41-48. Because no exceptions were filed to the Arbitrator's resolution of this issue, it is not before us.

5. Under 5 C.F.R. § 2429.23(b), an expired time limit can be waived upon a showing of "extraordinary circumstances" justifying the waiver. The Agency's arguments that it "misplaced" the Authority's Order and was not able to file a timely response "due to the holiday, emergency personal leave, and competing obligations," Agency's Motion for Leave to File Out of Time at 1, do not constitute extraordinary circumstances. *See AFGE, Local 2113*, 55 FLRA 414, 414 (1999) (finding no extraordinary circumstances where failure to comply with an Authority order was due to a party's own "inadvertence, accident, or mistake").

V. Analysis and Conclusions

A. The Arbitrator's finding with regard to the temporary promotion claim constitutes a procedural arbitrability determination.

The Union argues that the Arbitrator's determination that the Union did not plead Articles 26 and 27 with sufficient specificity does not draw its essence from Article 24, Section 9 of the Agreement. Exceptions at 6. This exception involves the Arbitrator's procedural arbitrability determination. *See AFGE, Local 1741*, 57 FLRA 696, 696 n.1 (2002). Procedural arbitrability involves questions of whether the procedural conditions to arbitrability have been met, while substantive arbitrability involves questions of whether the subject matter of a dispute is arbitrable. *See U.S. Dep't of Transp., Fed. Aviation Admin.*, 64 FLRA 680, 684 (2010). Here, the Arbitrator found the Union's temporary promotion claim was not arbitrable because it did not conform to the specificity requirements in Article 24, Section 9 of the Agreement and, thus, his conclusion is a procedural arbitrability determination. *See AFGE, Local 703*, 55 FLRA 507, 508 (1999) (finding an arbitrator's conclusion that a grievance did not meet the specificity requirements in the parties' agreement to be a procedural arbitrability determination).

The Authority generally will not find an arbitrator's ruling on the procedural arbitrability of a grievance deficient on grounds that directly challenge the procedural arbitrability ruling itself. *See, e.g., AFGE, Local 3882*, 59 FLRA 469, 470 (2003). However, the Authority has stated that a procedural arbitrability determination may be found deficient on the ground that it is contrary to law. *See id.* (citing *AFGE, Local 933*, 58 FLRA 480, 481 (2003)). In addition, the Authority has stated that a procedural arbitrability determination may be found deficient on grounds that do not directly challenge the determination itself, which include claims that an arbitrator was biased or that the arbitrator exceeded his or her authority. *See U.S. EEOC*, 60 FLRA 83, 86 (2004) (citing *AFGE, Local 2921*, 50 FLRA 184, 185-86 (1995)).

The Union's argument that the Arbitrator's award fails to draw its essence from the Agreement directly challenges the Arbitrator's procedural arbitrability finding and does not provide a basis for finding the award deficient. *See U.S. Dep't of Energy, Sw. Power Admin., Tulsa, Okla.*, 56 FLRA 624, 626 (2000) (finding that an agency's claim that the arbitrator erred in finding that the grievance met the specificity requirements in the parties' agreement directly challenged the procedural arbitrability determination). Therefore, we deny this exception.

B. The award is not contrary to § 7121(c)(5).

The Union argues that the Arbitrator's award is contrary to § 7121(c)(5) because the Arbitrator improperly found that the Union's claim for backpay at the GS-2210 special pay rate concerned a classification matter. When an exception involves an award's consistency with law, the Authority reviews any question of law raised by the exception and the award de novo. *See NTEU, Chapter 24*, 50 FLRA 330, 332 (1995) (citing *U.S. Customs Serv. v. FLRA*, 43 F.3d 682, 686-87 (D.C. Cir. 1994)). In applying the standard of de novo review, the Authority assesses whether an arbitrator's legal conclusions are consistent with the applicable standard of law. *See U.S. Dep't of Def., Dep'ts of the Army & the Air Force, Ala. Nat'l Guard, Northport, Ala.*, 55 FLRA 37, 40 (1998). In making that assessment, the Authority defers to the arbitrator's underlying factual findings. *See id.*

Under § 7121(c)(5) of the Statute, a grievance concerning "the classification of any position which does not result in the reduction in grade or pay of an employee" is removed from the scope of the negotiated grievance procedure. 5 U.S.C. § 7121(c)(5). The Authority has repeatedly held that, where the essential nature of a grievance concerns the grade level of the duties assigned to and performed by the grievant in his or her permanent position, the grievance concerns the classification of a position within the meaning of § 7121(c)(5) of the Statute. *See U.S. Dep't of Hous. & Urban Dev.*, 65 FLRA 433, 435 (2011). However, where the substance of a grievance is limited to the question of the accuracy of the grievant's position description, the grievance does not concern the classification of a position within the meaning of § 7121(c)(5). *See, e.g., U.S. Dep't of Def., Marine Corps Logistics Base, Albany, Ga.*, 57 FLRA 275, 277 (2001) (*Marine Corps*). Moreover, grievances concerning whether grievants are entitled to temporary promotions on the basis of having temporarily performed the established duties of a position other than their own are not barred by § 7121(c)(5). *U.S. Dep't of Labor, Wash., D.C.*, 64 FLRA 829, 830 (2010) (*DOL*).

Before the Arbitrator, the Union argued both that the grievants' position descriptions were inaccurate and that the Agency failed to compensate the grievants at the GS-2210 special pay rate. Award at 2. The Arbitrator found that the position description claim was arbitrable because it did not concern a classification matter, but that the claim requesting backpay at the GS-2210 special pay rate was not arbitrable because it did concern a classification matter. *Id.* at 41-43. The Union, in its exceptions, argues that the grievants were requesting only temporary promotions and that the Arbitrator erred in finding that claim concerned a classification matter. Exceptions at 12.

The Union has failed to establish that it requested only temporary promotions. The Union's grievance alleged "improper classification" of the grievants' permanent positions. Award at 15. Additionally, because the Arbitrator found the grievants' temporary promotion claim to have been improperly raised, the grievance, as advanced at arbitration, did not involve a temporary promotion claim. Therefore, we find that the Arbitrator did not err in concluding that the Union's request for backpay at the GS-2210 special pay rate concerned a classification matter, find that the award is not contrary to § 7121(c)(5), and deny this exception.[6] *See AFGE, Local 987*, 58 FLRA 453, 454-55 (2003) (finding a grievance to concern a classification matter where the grievance alleged that the grievant was improperly classified).

VI. Decision

The Union's exceptions are denied.

6. In light of this decision, it is unnecessary to address the Union's remaining exception.

65 FLRA No. 140

UNITED STATES
DEPARTMENT OF LABOR
BUREAU OF LABOR STATISTICS
(Agency)

and

AMERICAN FEDERATION
OF GOVERNMENT EMPLOYEES
LOCAL 12
(Union)

0-AR-4527

DECISION

March 30, 2011

Before the Authority: Carol Waller Pope, Chairman, and Thomas M. Beck and Ernest DuBester, Members

I. Statement of the Case

This matter is before the Authority on exceptions to an award of Arbitrator David P. Clark filed by the Agency under § 7122(a) of the Federal Service Labor-Management Relations Statute (the Statute) and part 2425 of the Authority's Regulations. The Union filed an opposition to the Agency's exceptions.

The Arbitrator concluded, among other things, that: (1) the Agency violated Articles 18 and 38 of the parties' agreement (Agreement); and (2) a desk audit was necessary to determine whether the Agency violated Article 20 of the Agreement, a matter over which he retained jurisdiction. For the reasons set forth below, we dismiss the Agency's exceptions, without prejudice, as interlocutory.

II. Background and Arbitrator's Award

The grievant works as a General Schedule (GS)-7 Support Services Assistant at the Agency's Bureau of Labor Statistics (BLS). Award at 15. When the grievant was transferred to his current location, he was told that he would be helping a GS-12 Program Analyst (the Program Analyst) with his duties. *Id.* at 16. In this capacity, the grievant worked on an almost daily basis with the Program Analyst. *Id.* For about two months, the grievant performed about 55% of the Program Analyst's duties while the Program Analyst worked on a "flexiplace" work schedule. *Id.* According to the Union, the grievant was told that he would be given an opportunity to compete for a Program Analyst position if one became available. Opp'n at 14.

Several months after the grievant began working with the Program Analyst, the Agency decided to hire two entry level Program Analysts through the Federal Career Intern Program (FCIP). Award at 17. The BLS posted information about the FCIP on its website, but did not post a vacancy announcement specifically for the Program Analyst positions, nor did it specifically notify the Union of the vacant positions. *Id.*

The Union presented a grievance arguing that the Agency violated the Agreement by: (1) failing to notify the Union of the vacant position and (2) failing to pay the grievant equal pay for substantially equal work.[1] *Id.* at 1. The grievance requested that the grievant "be placed in a career ladder Program Analyst position" and also requested backpay. *Id.* at 3. The matter was not resolved and was submitted to arbitration. The Arbitrator framed the relevant issues as follows:

> 1) Whether the Agency's decision to appoint a GS-9 Program Analyst pursuant to the Agency's component of the [FCIP], without announcing to the Union the existence of a vacancy for that position title, violated Article 18 of the . . . Agreement.
>
> 2) Whether the Agency failed to pay the [g]rievant for performing work that was substantially equal to that of a higher-paid Program Analyst, in violation of Article 20 of the . . . Agreement.

Id. at 2.[2]

1. Additionally, the Union argued to the Arbitrator that the failure to appoint the grievant was motivated by racial animus, in violation of Article 25 of the Agreement. Award at 1. The Arbitrator rejected the Union's argument on this issue. *Id.* at 25. Because no exceptions were filed to the Arbitrator's resolution of this issue, it is not before us.

2. The relevant provisions of the Agreement are set forth in the attached appendix.

During the hearing, the Agency objected to the Union's introduction of Article 18, Section 2, arguing that, because the Union did not allege a violation of that section in its step 2 grievance, it could not be considered by the Arbitrator. *Id.* at 20 n.4. The Arbitrator overruled the objection, finding that the Union did not allege a violation of Article 18, Section 2, but, rather, used that section to inform the "purpose and scope of the substantive articles articulated in the grievance." *Id.*

The Arbitrator first determined that the Agency must follow competitive merit staffing procedures in hiring through the FCIP because it "falls under the scope of Article 18" of the Agreement, as defined by Article 18, Section 2, because it "entails training and also qualifies appointees for eventual promotion." *Id.* at 19-20. The Arbitrator found that Article 18, Sections 4 and 7 of the Agreement required the Agency to notify the Union of the vacant Program Analyst positions. *Id.* at 20.

The Arbitrator then concluded that the Agency violated Article 18 by "failing to provide written notice to the Union of its intent to appoint Program Analysts pursuant to the BLS [FCIP]." *Id.* at 21. While the Arbitrator did not find any specific notification process to be required, he found that the Agency could have notified the Union through its "Spotlight" publication, in accordance with Article 18, Section 7 of the Agreement, and found untenable the Agency's position that there was no time to notify the Union because the hires were unanticipated. *Id.* As a remedy for the Agency's violation of Article 18, the Arbitrator ordered the Agency "henceforth to provide notice to the Union of its intention to hire Program Analyst positions through its Career Intern Program." *Id.* at 26.

The Arbitrator did not determine whether the Agency violated Article 20 of the Agreement; rather, he found a desk audit was necessary to decide whether the grievant was performing higher-graded duties. *Id.* at 23. While the Arbitrator recognized that he had no authority to determine the classification of the grievant pursuant to 5 U.S.C. § 7121(c)(5), he ordered the desk audit "so that the classification of the [g]rievant's work [could] be addressed" by the Agency. *Id.* The Arbitrator found that the desk audit would "not only affect the issue of back pay, but [could] also affect the issue of the appropriate remedy for the Agency's violation of Article 18" of the Agreement. *Id.* The Arbitrator retained jurisdiction over the desk audit matter, "in order to address, if necessary, the Union's requested remedy." *Id.*

III. Positions of the Parties

A. Agency's Exceptions

The Agency contends that the Arbitrator exceeded his authority by deciding whether Article 18, Section 2 of the Agreement applied because the Union did not raise that provision in its grievance. Exceptions at 6-7. According to the Agency, issues not raised in the Union's step 2 grievance are not arbitrable under Article 47, Section 7 of the Agreement. *Id.* The Agency asserts that the Arbitrator was incorrect that Article 18, Section 2 was simply background and, therefore, "relevant" to whether the Agency violated Article 18, Sections 1, 4, or 7 of the Agreement. *Id.* at 7-8.

The Agency also argues that the Arbitrator's remedy requiring the Agency to provide the Union with notice of open FCIP positions is contrary to law. *Id.* at 10. According to the Agency, the FCIP is in the excepted service and, thus, exempt from regular competitive service staffing requirements. *Id.* (citing Executive Order (E.O.) 13,162; 5 C.F.R. § 302). The Agency contends that, because there is no public notice requirement for positions in the excepted service, the Arbitrator's remedy that the Agency must notify the Union of positions in the FCIP is contrary to law. *Id.* at 10-11.

Finally, the Agency argues that the Arbitrator improperly engaged in classification when he ordered a desk audit. *Id.* at 12. According to the Agency, because the title of Article 20 is "Position Classification," the grievance challenges the grade level of the grievant's duties and whether he performed higher-graded work. *Id.* The Agency contends that the Arbitrator was making, analyzing, and identifying the grievant's position responsibilities. *Id.* at 14. Additionally, the Agency asserts that the Arbitrator's order that it conduct a desk audit is an attempt to force the Agency to do what the Arbitrator could not, i.e., make a classification determination. Therefore, the Agency claims that the Arbitrator's award of a desk audit is contrary to § 7121(c)(5) of the Statute. *Id.* at 15-16.

B. Union's Opposition

The Union responds that the Agency has not shown by a preponderance of the evidence that the

Arbitrator exceeded his authority by deciding an issue that was not before him. Opp'n at 8. The Union asserts that the Arbitrator properly interpreted Article 18 of the Agreement as requiring that the Union be given notice of advancement opportunities for unit employees. *Id.* at 9-10. The Union argues that, although it did not specifically mention Article 18, Section 2 in its grievance, the grievance indirectly raised that section. *Id.* at 11. Therefore, the Union argues, the Arbitrator did not exceed his authority in considering Article 18, Section 2 as relevant background.

The Union also argues that the Arbitrator's remedy that the Union must be provided notice of open Program Analyst positions is not contrary to law. *Id.* at 13-14. The Union contends that positions in the excepted service such as the FCIP are not exempt from all merit staffing requirements. *Id.* The Union asserts that various regulations and statutes and E.O. 13,162 require notice and that merit-based procedures be used for the recruitment and selection of candidates for the FCIP. *Id.* at 13-14 (citing E.O. 13,162; 5 C.F.R. § 213.3202(o); Department Personnel Regulation 213(2)(b)(1-2)).

Finally, the Union argues that the Arbitrator did not engage in classification in violation of § 7121(c)(5). *Id.* at 16. The Union claims that the Arbitrator should have awarded the grievant a temporary promotion because, for approximately one year, the grievant performed the same work as the Program Analyst. *Id.* The Union contends that the Arbitrator was measuring the accuracy of the grievant's position description. *Id.* at 16-17. Additionally, the Union argues that the act of ordering a desk audit does not, by itself, violate § 7121(c)(5) of the Statute. *Id.* at 17.

IV. Order to Show Cause

In an Order to Show Cause (Order), the Authority directed the Agency to show cause why its exceptions should not be dismissed as interlocutory. Order at 1. The Authority stated that, because the Arbitrator retained jurisdiction over the matter of the desk audit, his award did not "appear to constitute a final decision subject to review." *Id.* at 2-3.

In response, the Agency concedes that its exceptions are interlocutory because the Arbitrator "resolved one issue and retained jurisdiction of another issue." Response at 2. However, the Agency contends that it has presented a plausible jurisdictional defect, such that there are extraordinary circumstances warranting review. *Id.* The Agency claims that the Arbitrator lacked jurisdiction because "issues not identified by the Union in the grievance 'may not subsequently be considered by an arbitrator, should the grievance be invoked to arbitration'" pursuant to Article 47, Section 7 of the Agreement. *Id.* at 4. Therefore, the Agency argues that, because the Union did not allege a violation of Article 18, Section 2 in its grievance, the Arbitrator lacked jurisdiction to consider that section, and the entire award must be set aside. *Id.* at 3.

In the Order, the Union was granted leave to respond to the Agency's response. Order at 3. Instead, the Union filed a Motion to Correct and Amend Record before the Agency's response was filed. The Authority's Regulations do not provide for the filing of a supplemental submission. Therefore, it is incumbent upon the moving party to demonstrate a reason why the Authority should consider such supplemental submission. *See, e.g., U.S. Dep't of the Treasury, U.S. Customs Serv., El Paso, Tex.*, 52 FLRA 622, 625 (1996) (citing *Nat'l Union of Labor Investigators*, 46 FLRA 1311, 1311 n.1 (1993)). Section 2429.26 of the Authority's Regulations provides that the Authority may, in its discretion, grant leave to file "other documents" as deemed appropriate. Because the Union's Motion was not a response to the Agency's Response, and because the Union did not seek permission from the Authority to file supplemental briefing, nor demonstrate a reason why the Authority should consider such supplemental submission, we will not consider the Union's supplemental response.

V. Analysis and Conclusions

A. The exceptions are interlocutory.

The Authority will not generally grant interlocutory review of arbitration awards. 5 C.F.R. § 2924.11; *U.S. Dep't of Veterans Affairs, W. N.Y. Healthcare Sys., Buffalo, N.Y.*, 61 FLRA 173, 175 (2005) (*Veterans Affairs*). Therefore, the Authority will not consider exceptions to an arbitrator's award until the arbitrator has issued a final decision with respect to all issues submitted to arbitration. *U.S. Dep't of Justice, Fed. Bureau of Prisons, Fed. Med. Ctr., Carswell, Tex.*, 64 FLRA 566, 567 (2010); *U.S. Dep't of Health & Human Servs., Navajo Area Indian Health Serv.*, 58 FLRA 356, 357 (2003) (*DHHS*). If an arbitrator's award postpones the determination of a submitted issue or retains jurisdiction over at least one issue, then the decision does not constitute a final award. *AFGE, Local 12*, 38 FLRA 1240, 1246 (1990); *DHHS*, 58 FLRA at 357. In this case, the Agency conceded that its exceptions are interlocutory. Response at 2.

B. There is no plausible jurisdictional defect warranting interlocutory review.

Because the Agency's exceptions are interlocutory, the Authority will consider them only if there are extraordinary circumstances warranting review. *U.S. Dep't of the Interior, Bureau of Indian Affairs, Wapato Irrigation Project, Wapato, Wash.*, 55 FLRA 1230, 1232 (2000) (*BIA*). "[I]nterlocutory review should be reserved for those extraordinary situations where it is necessary," such as in the case of a plausible jurisdictional defect. *Id.* "[A] plausible jurisdictional defect is one that, on its face, is a credible claim, the resolution of which will advance the ultimate disposition of the case." *Library of Cong.*, 58 FLRA 486, 487 (2003) (then-Member Pope dissenting as to application).

1. Classification

The Agency argues that the Arbitrator's award is contrary to § 7121(c)(5) because the grievance concerned the classification of the grievant's position. Exceptions at 12-15. When an exception involves an award's consistency with law, the Authority reviews any question of law raised by the exception and the award de novo. *See NTEU, Chapter 24*, 50 FLRA 330, 332 (1995) (citing *U.S. Customs Serv. v. FLRA*, 43 F.3d 682, 686-87 (D.C. Cir. 1994)). In applying the standard of de novo review, the Authority assesses whether an arbitrator's legal conclusions are consistent with the applicable standard of law. *See U.S. Dep't of Def., Dep'ts of the Army and the Air Force, Ala. Nat'l Guard, Northport, Ala.*, 55 FLRA 37, 40 (1998). In making that assessment, the Authority defers to the arbitrator's underlying factual findings. *See id.*

An arbitrator does not have jurisdiction to determine "the classification of any position which does not result in the reduction in grade or pay of an employee." 5 U.S.C. § 7121(c)(5). The Authority has repeatedly held that where the essential nature of a grievance concerns the grade level of the duties assigned to and performed by the grievant in his or her permanent position, the grievance concerns the classification of a position within the meaning of § 7121(c)(5) of the Statute. *See U.S. Dep't of Hous. & Urban Dev.*, 65 FLRA 433, 435 (2011) (*HUD*). However, where the substance of a grievance concerns whether the grievant is entitled to a temporary promotion on the basis of having performed the established duties of a higher-graded position other than the grievant's own, the grievance would not be barred by § 7121(c)(5). *See U.S. Dep't of Labor, Wash., D.C.*, 64 FLRA 829, 830 (2010); *BIA*, 55 FLRA at 1232.

We find that the Agency has not established that the grievance concerns classification rather than a temporary promotion. *See U.S. Dep't of the Treasury, Internal Revenue Service, Agency-Wide Shared Servs., Florence, Ky.*, 63 FLRA 574, 578 (2009) (finding a grievance not to be barred by § 7121(c)(5) where the grievance concerned whether the grievant performed duties of a higher-graded position). The Arbitrator characterized the Union's argument at arbitration as "that the [g]rievant should be compensated for approximately a year of performing higher-graded work." Award at 14. Moreover, in its opposition, the Union contends that the Arbitrator should have awarded the grievant a temporary promotion. Opp'n at 16. Finally, it is undisputed that the duties allegedly performed by the grievant are of a position other than his own. *See U.S. Dep't of the Air Force, 81st Training Wing, Kesler Air Force Base, Miss.*, 60 FLRA 425, 428 (2004) (finding a grievance does not concern classification where the arbitrator compared the grievant's duties to another position).[3]

As a result, we find that there is no plausible jurisdictional defect warranting interlocutory review. *See U.S. Dep't of Transp., Fed. Aviation Admin.*, 62 FLRA 344, 347 (2008) (dismissing exceptions as interlocutory where the agency could not show that the arbitrator lacked jurisdiction); *BIA*, 55 FLRA at 1232 (finding no plausible jurisdictional defect where the union's classification claim was not sufficiently supported). Accordingly, we dismiss this exception, without prejudice, as interlocutory.[4]

3. We note that, although the Arbitrator at one point discussed the significance of the desk audit for the Agency's classification process, Award at 23, we interpret the Arbitrator to be using the desk audit to determine whether the grievant was entitled to backpay for the performance of higher-graded duties.

4. Member Beck notes that, should the Arbitrator make a classification determination following the results of the desk audit, such determination would violate § 7121(c)(5) of the Statute. *See HUD*, 65 FLRA at 436.

2. Exceeds Authority

The Agency also argues that the exceptions present a plausible jurisdictional defect because the Arbitrator decided an issue that was not before him and, thus, lacked jurisdiction to decide the entire award.[5] Response at 3-4.

The Agency argues that, pursuant to Article 47, Section 7 of the Agreement, issues not identified by the Union in the grievance may not later be considered by the Arbitrator. Exceptions at 6-7. The types of cases in which the Authority has reviewed interlocutory exceptions "have involved jurisdictional issues that arise pursuant to a statute." *Veterans Affairs*, 61 FLRA at 175. The Authority has consistently found that exceptions arising from the parties' agreement do not constitute extraordinary circumstances warranting review. *See U.S. Dep't of Homeland Sec., U.S. Immigration & Customs Enforcement*, 60 FLRA 129, 130 (2004) (concluding that the agency's exception claiming that the award failed to draw its essence from the agreement did not present a plausible jurisdictional defect); *AFGE, Local 446*, 59 FLRA 451, 454 (2003) (finding that an argument that the arbitrator exceeded his authority did not present a plausible jurisdictional defect).

Based on the foregoing, the Agency's argument that the grievance was not arbitrable under Article 47, Section 7 of the Agreement does not constitute a plausible jurisdictional defect warranting interlocutory review. *See U.S. Dep't of the Treasury, Bureau of Engraving & Printing, W. Currency Facility, Fort Worth, Tex.*, 58 FLRA 745, 746 (2003) (denying interlocutory review of the agency's exception where the agency argued that the matter was not grievable under the parties' agreement). Therefore, we dismiss these exceptions as interlocutory.

VI. Decision

The Agency's exceptions are dismissed, without prejudice, as interlocutory.[6]

5. The Agency's argument encompasses both the Agency's exceeds authority exception and its contrary to law exception.

6. Because we dismiss the exceptions as interlocutory, we make no determination on the merits of the Agency's claims.

APPENDIX

Article 18, Section 1 provides:

> The Department will adhere to all applicable Government-wide rules and regulations and the provisions in this Article in the administration of Merit Staffing. Moreover, the Department shall administer this Article in accordance with DPR 335, dated April 28, 2004, as specified or except as provided herein. Any future changes to this regulation will be handled in accordance with Article 38. The purpose and intent of this Article are to ensure that employees are given full and fair consideration and to ensure selection from among the best-qualified candidates. The Department and Local 12 also agree to fill positions in the bargaining unit on the basis of merit in accordance with systematic and equitable procedures adopted for this purpose.

Exceptions, Attach. 1, Agreement at 55.

Article 18, Section 2 provides, in relevant part:

> The following personnel actions are covered under competitive merit staffing procedures:
>
> . . . .
>
> d. Selection for training which is part of an authorized training agreement, part of a promotion program, or required by a formal training program before an employee may be considered for promotion;

Id.

Article 18, Section 4 provides:

> Vacancy announcements will be publicized in such a way as to ensure fair and open competition in accordance with Merit Systems Principles, 5 U.S.C. § 2301.

Id. at 57.

Article 18, Section 7 provides:

> The Department's Director of Human Resources will inform employees in the unit at least twice a year through a Spotlight or other issuance of the jobs, including qualification requirements that are likely to be filled at the entrance levels of career ladders during the year.

Id. at 58.

Article 20, Section 5 provides:

> The parties agree to the principle of equal pay for substantially equal work.

Id. at 60.

Article 38, Section 1 provides:

> In the administration of all matters covered by this Agreement and any supplements thereto, the parties are governed by existing or future laws and regulations of appropriate authorities; by published Department policies and regulations in existence at the time this Agreement became effective; and by subsequently published Department policies and regulations required by law or by the regulations of appropriate higher outside authorities.

Id. at 96.

Article 47, Section 7(a) provides, in relevant part:

> Issues and allegations that are not raised by the Union in the Step 2 process may not subsequently be considered by an arbitrator, should the grievance be invoked to arbitration.

Id. at 116.

65 FLRA No. 141

UNITED STATES
DEPARTMENT OF JUSTICE
EXECUTIVE OFFICE
FOR IMMIGRATION REVIEW
BOARD OF IMMIGRATION APPEALS
(Agency)

and

AMERICAN FEDERATION
OF GOVERNMENT EMPLOYEES
LOCAL 3525
(Union)

0-AR-4558

DECISION

March 30, 2011

Before the Authority: Carol Waller Pope, Chairman, and Thomas M. Beck and Ernest DuBester, Members[1]

I. Statement of the Case

This matter is before the Authority on exceptions to an award of Arbitrator Robert T. Moore filed by the Agency under § 7122 of the Federal Service Labor-Management Relations Statute (the Statute) and part 2425 of the Authority's Regulations. The Union filed an opposition to the Agency's exceptions.[2]

The Arbitrator found that the Agency violated its Performance Appraisal Program (PAP) in preparing the grievant's annual performance appraisal and denying her a within-grade increase (WIGI). The Arbitrator directed the Agency to rescind the erroneous appraisal, issue a new appraisal, provide the grievant a retroactive WIGI, provide supervisors training on performance appraisals, and post a notice. For the reasons discussed below, we deny the exceptions in part, and grant them in part.

II. Background and Arbitrator's Award

The Union filed a grievance on behalf of the grievant when she received an overall performance rating of "[u]nacceptable" on her annual performance appraisal and was denied a WIGI. Award at 10-11. The grievance was unresolved and was submitted to arbitration.

After the arbitration hearing, the grievant entered into a settlement agreement (SA) with the Agency to resolve a case pending before the Merit Systems Protection Board (MSPB). *Id.* at 6. Although the Agency provided the SA to the Arbitrator prior to the issuance of the arbitration award, the Arbitrator found that the SA had no "force or effect" in the pending arbitration. *Id.* at 7. He based this finding on: (1) the SA's statement that it "shall not be used, cited[,] or relied upon by any party in connection with any other judicial or administrative proceeding[;]" (2) the facts that the Union, rather than the grievant, was technically a party to the arbitration and that only the Union could withdraw the grievance; and (3) the fact that the SA was "so heavily redacted" that he could not determine whether it related to the arbitration or whether the grievant had received adequate consideration to make the SA binding. *Id.*

In his award, the Arbitrator stated the issues, in pertinent part, as: "Did the Agency comply with the requirements of the [parties' agreement] and Agency regulations in giving the grievant her annual performance appraisal . . . and if not what should the remedies be?" *Id.* at 1. Addressing the merits of the

1. Member Beck's concurring opinion is set forth at the end of this decision.

2. In its opposition, the Union argues that the Agency's exceptions should be dismissed for failure to comply with Article 7.7 of the parties' agreement, which states: "Prior to filing for an exception to the [Authority], written notification must be provided to the other party." Opp'n at 9. However, the Authority has held that a procedural requirement in a collective bargaining agreement does not provide a basis for dismissing exceptions that comply with the Authority's statutory and regulatory requirements. *See U.S. Army Aviation Sys. Command*, 22 FLRA 379, 379 n.* (1986) (*AASC*) (Authority did not dismiss exceptions for failure to comply with contract provision requiring ten-day notice prior to filing exceptions). The Union attempts to distinguish *AASC* on the basis that compliance with the ten-day notice requirement in that case would have deprived the excepting party of the entire thirty-day filing period, unlike the contractual provision here, which merely requires "prior" notice. Opp'n at 9 n.16. However, the Authority's decision to consider the exceptions in *AASC* was based upon the exceptions' compliance with Authority filing requirements, not the length of the contractual notice period at issue. *See AASC*, 22 FLRA at 379 n.*. Thus, *AASC* applies here, and, as the Agency's exceptions were timely filed in accordance with the requirements of § 7122(a) of the Statute and the Authority's Regulations, we consider the exceptions.

grievance, the Arbitrator found that the grievant was on detail outside the Agency to the Office of General Counsel (OGC) for the first six months of the relevant rating period and that she received an overall rating of "outstanding" from her supervisor there. *Id.* at 8-9. The Arbitrator also found that there was no "significant difference" between the grievant's duties on detail and her duties upon her return to the Agency. *Id.* at 11.

In addition, the Arbitrator found that when the grievant returned to the Agency, her supervisor directed her to undergo training to reacquaint her with the routines and procedures of the Agency. *Id.* at 9. The Arbitrator also found that after the grievant completed training, the grievant's trainer assessed her as being successful in all training elements and needing no further training before resuming her duties. *Id.* at 9-10, 13.

Further, the Arbitrator determined that when the grievant's supervisor prepared the grievant's annual appraisal at the end of the rating period, the appraisal covered only the period after the grievant's return to the Agency from her detail. *Id.* at 10. The Arbitrator found that, in preparing the appraisal, the supervisor "exclud[ed] from her consideration" the grievant's performance during both her training and her detail to the OGC. *Id.* at 13. The Arbitrator also found that the supervisor denied the grievant a WIGI "to which she was otherwise entitled by the length of time in her then current pay step, provided [that] her job performance was acceptable." *Id.* at 11.

As a result of these findings, the Arbitrator concluded that the grievant's supervisor violated the clear "mandate" of the PAP, which "unmistakably requires" that employees be reviewed on the basis of their performance over the entire performance year. *Id.* at 13. In this regard, the Arbitrator found that, under Section B of the PAP,[3] the Agency's appraisal period ran from April 1 to March 31 and was intended to create a record of an employee's performance for "*the entire rating period*[.]" *Id.* at 8 (quoting PAP) (emphasis added by Arbitrator). In addition, the Arbitrator found that the supervisor did not take into account that another manager had credited the grievant with "clearing out a substantial backlog of matters" upon her return to the Agency, and that this work entitled the grievant to a rating of at least "fully satisfactory" on individual rating elements and overall. *Id.* at 13-14. The Arbitrator concluded that the Agency had not overcome the "strong *prima facie* case" that the grievant would have received an overall rating of "outstanding" if she had been properly evaluated according to the PAP's requirements. *Id.* at 14.

To remedy the violations of the PAP, the Arbitrator directed the Agency to remove the performance appraisal from the grievant's file and replace it with an appraisal that rated her "fully successful" on all job elements and on her overall rating. *Id.* The Arbitrator also directed that an "assessor" "at the highest level of the personnel and labor relations structure of the Agency" should determine whether the grievant's appraisal rating for "any or all of her job elements and overall job performance" should be further elevated to "excellent" or "outstanding[.]" *Id.* In addition, the Arbitrator awarded the grievant the WIGI that she did not receive for the appraisal period, with interest. *Id.* at 14-15. The Arbitrator also directed the Agency to provide training on the PAP to the grievant's supervisor "and all other supervisors who serve as rating or reviewing officials under the PAP[.]" *Id.* at 15. Finally, the Arbitrator directed the Agency to post a notice regarding its adherence to the PAP requirements.[4] *Id.*

III. Positions of the Parties

A. Agency's Exceptions

The Agency argues that the Arbitrator erred in issuing an award after learning that, in the SA, the grievant had "agreed to dismiss any pending claim against the Agency[.]" Exceptions at 7. In this regard, the Agency contends that general waivers of claims, such as that included in the SA, apply to grievances unless grievances are "unambiguously excluded by the language of the agreement." *Id.* at 7-8 (citing *AFGE, Local 987*, 61 FLRA 245, 246

3. The pertinent wording of the PAP is set forth below.

4. The notice provides, in relevant part:

> The Agency will fairly and faithfully comply with all requirements of the . . . PAP and not allow the animus of any supervisor towards any employee to influence the job performance rating of that employee.
>
> The Agency has provided and, as necessary, will continue to provide training for all members of management and supervisors on their duties and obligations in their relations with subordinate employees including recognizing and respecting their rights to fair treatment under the . . . PAP and the [parties' agreement].

Award at 17.

(2005)). According to the Agency, because the Union has no claims independent from those that the grievant waived in the SA, the SA resolved all of the issues before the Arbitrator. *Id.* at 8.

The Agency also argues that the award violates an Agency regulation – the PAP – and that the PAP governs the matter in dispute because the Arbitrator was not enforcing any pertinent provisions in the parties' agreement. *Id.* at 11. In this regard, the Agency asserts that the Arbitrator's finding that there is a "mandatory" twelve-month appraisal period is contrary to the PAP, and that the Agency complied with the PAP's requirement that any appraisal be based on a minimum period of performance of ninety days. *Id.* at 12 (citing Section B.4 of the PAP). The Agency also asserts that the PAP does not require a reviewing official to consider an interim rating issued to an employee at the end of a detail to an office outside the Agency. *Id.* at 12-13 (citing Sections B.10 and B.12 of the PAP).

The Agency also challenges several of the Arbitrator's awarded remedies. Citing *United States Department of Treasury, Bureau of Engraving & Printing, Washington, D.C.*, 53 FLRA 146, 153 (1997) (*BEP*), the Agency asserts that the Arbitrator's cancellation of the grievant's performance rating is contrary to § 7106 of the Statute and that the PAP is not an "applicable law" for purposes of the Statute. Exceptions at 15. In addition, the Agency argues that the award of a WIGI is contrary to 5 C.F.R. § 531.404(a)[5] because the award requires the Agency to "prepare a rating of record that is inconsistent with the [Agency's] WIGI determination" and award the grievant a WIGI "even though her performance was not at an acceptable level of competence at the end of the waiting period for the WIGI." *Id.* at 9-11. Finally, the Agency argues that the Arbitrator exceeded his authority by awarding remedies that are too broad, specifically, his directions that the Agency: (1) post a notice to all employees regarding adherence to the PAP; (2) train its supervisors on the PAP, and (3) cancel the grievant's performance rating. *Id.* at 15-17.

B. Union's Opposition

The Union contends that the Arbitrator properly concluded that the SA had no bearing on the arbitration case. Opp'n at 10-11. In this connection, the Union argues that it was not a party to the SA and that the issue in the arbitration – whether the Agency must consider interim appraisals of employees on detail – is of continuing interest to the Union beyond the settlement of the grievant's individual MSPB claim. *Id.* at 12-13.

The Union also contends that the parties' agreement, rather than the PAP, governs the matter in dispute because Article 17 of the agreement[6] "clearly addresses performance evaluations, which is why the . . . PAP was developed in consultation with the Union." *Id.* at 17. In any event, the Union argues that the Arbitrator's decision is not contrary to the PAP, and that the Arbitrator correctly held "that the Agency simply cannot arbitrarily ignore the [grievant]'s performance on detail[.]" *Id.* at 20, 19.

In addition, the Union argues that the Arbitrator properly cancelled and replaced the grievant's performance appraisal, and that the award of a WIGI is not contrary to regulation because the Arbitrator found that the performance appraisal was not valid and, thus, that the denial of a WIGI was not valid. *Id.* at 14-16. The Union further argues that the Arbitrator had the authority to fashion remedies "specifically intended to benefit all members of the bargaining unit" because the issue before him had a "potential impact" on the entire bargaining unit. *Id.* at 21.

IV. Analysis and Conclusions

A. The Arbitrator did not err in failing to dismiss the grievance on the basis of the SA.

In finding that the SA had no "force or effect" in the arbitration, the Arbitrator interpreted the terms of the SA. Award at 7. Because settlement agreements are considered to be contracts, the Authority applies the deferential "essence" standard to review an arbitrator's interpretation of a settlement agreement. *AFGE, Local 12*, 61 FLRA 507, 508 (2006). *See, e.g., U.S. Dep't of the Army, Corps of Eng'rs, Nw. Div. & Seattle Dist.*, 64 FLRA 405, 409 (2010). Under the "essence" standard, the Authority will find that an arbitration award is deficient as failing to draw its essence from the settlement agreement when the appealing party establishes that the award: (1) cannot in any rational way be derived from the agreement; (2) is so unfounded in reason and fact and so unconnected with the wording and purposes of the agreement as to manifest an infidelity to the obligation of the arbitrator; (3) does not represent a plausible interpretation of the agreement; or

[5] The pertinent wording of 5 C.F.R. § 531.404 is set forth below.

[6] The wording of Article 17 is set forth below.

(4) evidences a manifest disregard of the agreement. *AFGE, Local 12*, 61 FLRA at 508. The Authority and the courts defer to arbitrators in this context "because it is the arbitrator's construction of the agreement for which the parties have bargained."[7] *U.S. Dep't of* Labor *(OSHA),* 34 FLRA 573, 576 (1990) (*OSHA*).

The SA provides, in pertinent part, that it "shall not be used, cited[,] or relied upon by any party in connection with any other judicial or administrative proceeding[.]" Award at 7. The Arbitrator interpreted this as meaning that it resolved only those issues currently or potentially before the MSPB and, therefore, found that it was not a sufficient basis for dismissing the grievance. *Id.* at 6-7. This interpretation is not inconsistent with the terms of the SA. *See AFGE, Local 12*, 61 FLRA at 509 (upholding arbitrator interpretation that "comports with the plain wording" of agreement). Although the Agency's contention that the agreement is a "general waiver[] of claims," Exceptions at 7, is one possible interpretation of the agreement, it does not establish that the Arbitrator's interpretation is irrational, unfounded, implausible, or manifestly in disregard of the agreement.

The precedent cited by the Agency is inapposite because it does not involve Authority review of an arbitrator's interpretation of a settlement agreement. *See AFGE, Local 987*, 61 FLRA at 246. As stated above, where an arbitrator has interpreted an agreement between the parties, the Authority will defer to that interpretation as long as it draws its essence from the agreement. *See OSHA*, 34 FLRA at 576.

Accordingly, we find that the Arbitrator's interpretation draws its essence from the SA. We note that the Agency also challenges the other bases for the Arbitrator's decision that the SA had no "force or effect" in the arbitration, specifically, his findings that: (1) only the Union could withdraw the grievance because the Union, not the grievant, was a party to the arbitration; and (2) the SA was so heavily redacted that the Arbitrator could not determine whether it related to the arbitration or whether the grievant had received adequate consideration to make it binding. *See* Award at 7; Exceptions at 7-9. The Authority has held that when an arbitrator has based an award on separate and independent grounds, an appealing party must establish that all of the grounds are deficient in order to have the award found deficient. *See, e.g.*, *AFGE, Council of Prison Locals 33, Locals 1007 & 3957*, 64 FLRA 288, 291 (2009). Because the Arbitrator's interpretation of the SA constitutes a separate and independent ground for his decision not to apply the SA, and the Agency has not shown that the award fails to draw its essence from the SA, we find that there is no need to consider the Agency's remaining arguments regarding the SA. *See id.*

B. The PAP governs the matter in dispute.

Under § 7122(a)(1) of the Statute, an arbitration award will be found deficient if it conflicts with any law, rule or regulation. *Overseas Educ. Ass'n*, 51 FLRA 1246, 1251 (1996). However, agency rules and regulations may govern the disposition of matters to which they apply only when the rules and regulations do not conflict with provisions of an applicable collective bargaining agreement. *U.S. Dep't of the Army, Fort Campbell Dist., Third Region, Fort Campbell, Ky.*, 37 FLRA 186, 195 (1990).

The parties dispute whether the PAP or their agreement governs the resolution of this exception. The Agency asserts that, because there is no contract provision addressing the issue submitted to arbitration, the PAP governs the dispute. Exceptions at 11. The Union counters that Article 17 of the parties' agreement "clearly addresses" the matter in dispute: performance evaluations.[8] Opp'n at 17.

---

7. The decisions cited in the concurrence are inapposite. In particular, none involves judicial review of an arbitrator's interpretation of a settlement agreement; all involve appellate court review of either a lower court's or an administrative agency's interpretation. It is well-established, in this regard, that judicial review of arbitral interpretations is deferential and not de novo. *See United Paperworkers Int'l Union v. Misco, Inc.*, 484 U.S. 29, 36-38 (1987).

8. Article 17, "Performance Evaluation[,]" provides as follows:

> 17.1 PRIMARY OBJECTIVE: The Parties agree that the primary objectives of the annual performance evaluation are to: recognize job requirements and standards and keep employees aware of them; improve individual performance; make and keep employees aware of their supervisor's judgment of their work performance; acknowledge employee accomplishments and good work; and strengthen supervisor-employee relationships.
>
> 17.2 SUPERVISOR/EMPLOYEE DISCUSSION: Unless mutually agreed otherwise by the relevant supervisor and employee, all supervisors are required to discuss

The Arbitrator found that the grievant's supervisor violated specific provisions of the PAP; he did not find that the supervisor violated the parties' agreement. *See* Award at 13-14. Further, Article 17 of the parties' agreement does not reference incorporation of the PAP,[9] and does not set forth the kind of procedural requirements that the Arbitrator found had been violated. *See* Exceptions, Attach. Q, Collective Bargaining Agreement (CBA) at 28. Thus, there is no basis for finding that the Arbitrator implicitly relied on Article 17. Accordingly, we find that the PAP, rather than the parties' agreement, governs the dispute.

C. The award is not contrary to law, rule, and/or regulation.

In reviewing arbitration awards for consistency with law, rule, or regulation, the Authority reviews questions of law raised by exceptions to an arbitrator's award de novo. *NTEU, Chapter 24*, 50 FLRA 330, 332 (1995) (citing *U.S. Customs Serv. v. FLRA*, 43 F.3d 682, 686-87 (D.C. Cir. 1994)). In applying the standard of de novo review, the Authority determines whether the arbitrator's legal conclusions are consistent with the applicable standard of law. *See NFFE, Local 1437*, 53 FLRA 1703, 1710 (1998). In making that determination, the Authority defers to the arbitrator's underlying factual findings. *See id.*

1. The PAP

Section B.4 of the PAP pertinently provides that the appraisal period "shall cover one year" and that "[t]he minimum appraisal period shall be no less than [ninety] days." Exceptions, Attach. R, PAP at 2 (PAP). Section B.9 provides that the purpose of performance appraisals is "to document the employee's performance over the entire rating period, and to assign an overall rating level." *Id.* at 3. In arguing that the award is contrary to the PAP, the Agency cites §§ B.10 and B.12, which concern, respectively, details and reassignments within the Agency. *Id.* at 4, 5.

The Arbitrator found that the Agency violated the clear "mandate" of the PAP, which "unmistakably requires" that employees be reviewed on the basis of their performance over the entire performance year. Award at 13. In this regard, the Arbitrator found that the grievant's supervisor erred by "excluding from her consideration" the grievant's performance during her detail and training. *Id.* Although the PAP does not directly address performance appraisals for employees who are on detail outside the Agency for part of the rating period, the PAP indicates that the appraisal should evaluate the employee's performance over the entire rating period, and none of the PAP provisions cited by the Agency states that a reviewing official may decline to consider an employee's performance on detail outside the Agency. In this regard, although Section B.4 states that the minimum appraisal period is ninety days, that does not establish that where, as here, an employee was working for the entire year-long rating period, the Agency may exclude a portion of the employee's performance so long as it considers the employee's performance over the ninety-day minimum appraisal period. *See* PAP at 2; Exceptions at 12.

The Agency also cites Section B.10, which provides that employees on details within the Agency to positions with "substantially different duties" shall receive an interim rating at the end of the detail. PAP at 4. However, there is no dispute that the grievant received an interim rating of "outstanding" from her supervisor while on detail. Award at 8. Thus, the issue here is not whether the grievant was entitled to an interim rating, but whether the grievant's supervisor violated the PAP by failing to *consider* the grievant's interim rating in preparing her annual performance appraisal.

The Agency also cites Section B.12, which provides that where an employee is reassigned within the Agency "to a position with substantially the same duties and responsibilities, the losing rating official will provide an interim rating to the gaining rating official . . . [and] [t]his rating will be considered in determining the annual appraisal." PAP at 5. Although Section B.12 requires consideration of interim ratings of performance during reassignments within the Agency, and the grievant returned from a detail outside the Agency, Section B.12 does not state that a reassignment within the Agency is the *only* circumstance in which a reviewing official should consider an interim rating. Thus, Section B.12 does not establish that the Arbitrator's finding that the Agency violated the PAP by failing to consider the

---

directly with the employee the annual performance rating.

Exceptions, Attach. Q, Collective Bargaining Agreement at 28.

9. In this regard, we note that although the Union contends that the PAP was "developed in consultation with the Union[,]" Opp'n at 17, the Union does not argue that the PAP itself is a negotiated agreement.

grievant's performance on detail in preparing her annual appraisal is deficient.

For the foregoing reasons, we find that the Agency has not demonstrated that the award is contrary to the PAP.

2. Section 7106(a)(2)(A) and (B) of the Statute

In resolving exceptions that contend that an award is contrary to a management right, the Authority first assesses whether the award affects the exercise of a right set forth in § 7106(a) of the Statute. *U.S. EPA*, 65 FLRA 113, 115 (2010) (Member Beck concurring). If the award affects the right, then the Authority examines whether the arbitrator was enforcing either an applicable law, within the meaning of § 7106(a)(2) of the Statute, or a contract provision negotiated pursuant to § 7106(b) of the Statute. *See FDIC, Div. of Supervision & Consumer Prot., S.F. Region*, 65 FLRA 102, 104 (2010) (Chairman Pope concurring).

The Agency cites *BEP*, 53 FLRA at 153, which involves the effect of an arbitrator's cancellation of performance ratings on an agency's rights to direct employees and assign work under § 7106(a)(2)(A) and (B) of the Statute. The Authority has held that an arbitrator's cancellation of a performance appraisal affects these management rights. *See, e.g., U.S. Dep't of the Navy, Naval Surface Warfare Ctr., Carderock Div., Acoustic Research Detachment, Bayview, Idaho*, 59 FLRA 763, 765 (2004) (Chairman Cabaniss concurring). As the Arbitrator directed the Agency to rescind the performance appraisal challenged by the grievant, we find that the award affects management's rights to direct employees and assign work.

As discussed above, the Arbitrator found that the Agency violated the PAP, but did not find any violations of the parties' agreement. *See* Award at 13-14. Because the Arbitrator's cancellation of the grievant's performance rating is based solely on the Agency's violations of the PAP, this remedy is valid only if the PAP constitutes an applicable law under § 7106(a)(2) of the Statute.[10]

An agency regulation constitutes an "applicable law" within the meaning of § 7106(a)(2) when it has "the force and effect of law." *NTEU*, 42 FLRA 377, 390-91 (1991), *enforcement denied on other grounds*, 996 F.2d 1246 (D.C. Cir. 1993); *see also U.S. Dep't of the Navy, Naval Undersea Warfare Ctr., Newport, R.I.*, 55 FLRA 687, 690 (1999) (*Navy*). Regulations have the force and effect of law when they: (1) affect individual rights and obligations; (2) were promulgated pursuant to an explicit or implicit delegation of legislative authority by Congress; and (3) were promulgated in conformance with any procedural requirements imposed by Congress. *Navy*, 55 FLRA at 690; *NTEU*, 42 FLRA at 391-93. Applying this standard, the Authority has held that agency performance appraisal regulations enacted under 5 U.S.C. § 4302 and corresponding Office of Personnel Management (OPM) regulations constitute "applicable law" under § 7106 of the Statute. *Navy*, 55 FLRA at 690-91.

The first requirement – that a regulation affect individual rights – is satisfied where the regulation is mandatory and establishes the obligations of agencies and the rights of employees. *Navy*, 55 FLRA at 690; *NTEU*, 42 FLRA at 391. As in *Navy*, the PAP regulations "oblige the agency to conduct the performance appraisal process in a particular manner and affect the rights of individual employees to obtain a particular summary performance rating." 55 FLRA at 690-91. Specifically, the section of the PAP violated by the Agency states that the "appraisal period *shall* cover one year[.]" PAP at 2 (emphasis added). This wording affects the obligation of the Agency and the right of the employees. Thus, the first requirement has been met.

The second requirement is that the regulation was promulgated pursuant to a Congressional delegation of legislative authority. *Navy*, 55 FLRA at 690; *NTEU*, 42 FLRA at 392. Under 5 U.S.C. § 4302, each agency is required to establish performance appraisal systems that are consistent with OPM regulatory requirements. *See Navy*, 55 FLRA at 691. The PAP lists both 5 U.S.C. chapter 43 and the OPM regulations as authority for its creation and references the OPM regulations throughout. PAP at 1, 2, 10-11. In addition, there is no claim that the PAP is inconsistent with either the requirements of 5 U.S.C. § 4302 or corresponding OPM regulations. Accordingly, the PAP meets the second requirement. *See Navy*, 55 FLRA at 691.

The final requirement is that the regulation was "promulgated in conformance with the procedural requirements imposed by Congress." *Id.* Section 553(a)(2) of Title 5 excepts agency rulemaking relating to agency management and personnel, such as the PAP, from the notice and comment requirement of the Administrative Procedure Act. *Id.*

10. As noted previously, there is no claim that the PAP is a negotiated agreement.

However, performance appraisal regulations must be promulgated under OPM regulations, which require agencies to submit their performance appraisal regulations to OPM for approval. *Id.*; 5 C.F.R. § 430.209. If OPM determines that an agency performance appraisal regulation does not meet statutory or regulatory requirements, then "it shall direct the agency to implement an appropriate system or program or to take other corrective action." 5 C.F.R. § 430.210. As a result, the Authority has held that where performance appraisal regulations have existed for an extended period of time and OPM has not directed an agency to take corrective action, the Authority may reasonably conclude that the regulations were promulgated in conformance with the appropriate procedural requirements. *See Navy*, 55 FLRA at 691. Here, neither party addresses this issue. However, the PAP had been in effect for over four and a half years at the time of the Arbitrator's award. *See* PAP at 2; Award at 16. Thus, we conclude that the PAP was promulgated in conformance with OPM requirements, and we find that the PAP was validly promulgated. *See Navy*, 55 FLRA at 691.

For the foregoing reasons, we find that PAP is an "applicable law" within the meaning of § 7106(a)(2), and that the award is not contrary to § 7106(a). Consequently, we deny this exception.

3. 5 C.F.R. § 531.404

The Agency argues that by requiring the Agency to "prepare a rating of record that is inconsistent with the [Agency's] WIGI determination" and award the grievant a WIGI "even though her performance was not at an acceptable level of competence at the end of the waiting period for the WIGI" the award is contrary to 5 C.F.R. § 531.404. Exceptions at 11. That regulation provides, in pertinent part, that: (1) an employee's performance must be rated as at least "[f]ully [s]uccessful" in order to receive a WIGI; and (2) when a WIGI decision is not consistent with the employee's most recent rating of record, "a more current rating of record must be prepared." 5 C.F.R. § 531.404(a).

As discussed previously, the Arbitrator determined that "had [the grievant] been properly judged in accordance with the requirements of the . . . PAP," she would have been rated "outstanding[.]" Award at 14. Moreover, as a remedy for the Agency's violations of the PAP, the Arbitrator directed the Agency to remove the grievant's most recent rating of record from her file and replace it with one rating her as "fully successful[.]" *Id.* Thus, as directed by the Arbitrator, the grievant's most recent rating of record will be at least "fully successful," and the corresponding award of a WIGI is not contrary to 5 C.F.R. § 531.404. Accordingly, we deny the exception.

D. The Arbitrator exceeded his authority in part.

Arbitrators exceed their authority when they fail to resolve an issue submitted to arbitration, resolve an issue not submitted to arbitration, disregard specific limitations on their authority, or award relief to persons who are not encompassed within the grievance. *U.S. Dep't of the Navy, Naval Base, Norfolk, Va.*, 51 FLRA 305, 307-08 (1995). The Authority has held that if a grievance is limited to a particular grievant, then the remedy must be similarly limited.[11] *See U.S. EPA*, 57 FLRA 648, 651-52 (2001) (*EPA*); *U.S. Dep't of the Air Force, Air Force Logistics Ctr., Tinker Air Force Base, Okla.*, 45 FLRA 1234, 1240-41 (1992) (*Tinker AFB*).

The issue before the Arbitrator was limited to whether the Agency acted improperly "in giving *the grievant* her annual performance appraisal[.]" Award at 1 (emphasis added). That is, the grievance was limited to the Agency's actions toward the grievant. Thus, as explained below, we find that the award is deficient to the extent that two of the Arbitrator's remedies extend to additional employees. *See Tinker AFB*, 45 FLRA at 1240-41.

Turning to the notice posting remedy, the Authority has held that where the parties submitted to an arbitrator the issue of whether the agency had violated the parties' agreement in its actions towards one employee, the arbitrator exceeded his authority by directing the agency to post a notice defining the rights of all bargaining unit employees. *EPA*, 57 FLRA at 651-52. Similarly, here, because the notice that the Arbitrator directed the Agency to post promises employees that the Agency will adhere to the PAP and that supervisor animus will not influence future performance appraisals for any employee, it defines rights for individuals who were not included in the grievance. *See* Award at 17.

---

11. However, where an agency's treatment of a grievant constitutes an unfair labor practice (ULP) in violation of the Statute, the Authority has upheld notice posting remedies. *See, e.g., U.S. Dep't of Housing & Urban Dev., L.A. Field Office, L.A., Cal.*, 64 FLRA 383, 386 (2010) (upholding notice posting where arbitrator found agency's discipline of union president was a ULP). Neither party has alleged that this case involves a ULP.

Accordingly, we find that this remedy is deficient because it exceeds the Arbitrator's authority. *See EPA*, 57 FLRA at 651-52.

The Agency also challenges the training remedy imposed by the Arbitrator. Exceptions at 17. The Authority has upheld a remedy requiring training for the supervisor(s) whose actions impermissibly affected a grievant's conditions of employment. *See, e.g., U.S. Dep't of the Air Force, Air Force Flight Test Ctr., Edwards Air Force Base, Cal.*, 48 FLRA 74, 87 (1993) (Member Talkin concurring) (arbitrator awarded sexual harassment training for the supervisor who sexually harassed grievant and the supervisor who failed to investigate the grievant's harassment complaints); *U.S. Dep't of Justice, U.S. Fed. Bureau of Prisons, U.S. Penitentiary, Lewisburg, Pa.*, 39 FLRA 1288, 1300-01, 1305 (1991) (arbitrator awarded "sensitivity training" for supervisor who violated parties' agreement by failing to give proper attention to grievant's medical concerns), *petition for review dismissed sub nom. U.S. Dep't of Justice v. FLRA*, 981 F.2d 1339 (D.C. Cir. 1993). Here, however, the awarded remedy of training for the grievant's supervisor *and* "all other supervisors who serve as rating or reviewing officials under the PAP" would affect the working conditions of employees beyond the grievant. *See* Award at 15. Accordingly, we find that the remedy of training is deficient to the extent that it applies to individuals other than the grievant's supervisor. *See Tinker AFB*, 45 FLRA at 1240-41.

In regard to the Arbitrator's cancellation of the grievant's performance rating, the Agency does not argue that the Arbitrator failed to resolve an issue submitted to arbitration, resolved an issue not submitted to arbitration, or awarded relief to persons who are not encompassed within the grievance. *See* Exceptions at 15. To the extent that the Agency argues that the Arbitrator disregarded a specific limitation on his authority, the authority cited by the Agency is § 7106 of the Statute, and we have found that the award is not contrary to § 7106. Accordingly, we find that the Arbitrator did not exceed his authority in directing the Agency to cancel the grievant's performance rating.

For the foregoing reasons, we grant the Agency's exceeded authority exceptions in part, and deny them in part.

V. Decision

The portions of the award directing the Agency to post a notice and train supervisors other than the grievant's supervisor are set aside, and the Agency's remaining exceptions are denied.

Member Beck, Concurring:

I agree with my colleagues that the Arbitrator exceeded his authority when he ordered a remedy – posting and training – directed at supervisors other than those to whom the grievant reported. I also agree that, under the circumstances of this case, the performance appraisal program (PAP) constitutes an applicable law, and that the Agency's remaining exceptions should be denied.

I disagree, however, with the Majority's assertion that we should accord "essence"-type deference to the Arbitrator's interpretation of the settlement agreement. Majority at 5. We grant extraordinary deference to an arbitrator's interpretation of a collective bargaining agreement because the agreement expressly makes the arbitrator the interpreter and enforcer of the agreement. *See U.S. Dep't of Labor (OSHA)*, 34 FLRA 573, 576 (1990) (it is the arbitrator's construction of the agreement for which the parties have bargained). However, this rationale does not apply to other contracts that other parties create outside of the labor relations context -- such as the settlement agreement here. It was an agreement between the Agency and an individual employee (not between the Agency and the Union) about an employment dispute outside of the traditional labor relations context. Under such circumstances, the parties have no particular expectation that the agreement will be subject to arbitration.

The Majority cites several cases where the Authority applied its highly deferential "essence" standard to an arbitrator's interpretation of a settlement agreement and then concludes that "courts defer to arbitrators in this context." Majority at 5 (citing *AFGE, Local 12*, 61 FLRA 507, 508 (2006); *U.S. Dep't of the Army, Corps of Eng'rs, Nw. Div. & Seattle Dist.*, 64 FLRA 405, 409 (2010)).[*] Contrary to this precedent, courts have held consistently and unequivocally that the interpretation of a settlement agreement is a question of law that is subject to de novo review. *Trustees of the 1199/SEIU Greater N.Y. Benefit Fund v. Kingsbridge Heights Rehab. Care Ctr.*, No. 09-4168-CV, 2010 WL 4140312, at *2 (C.A. 2 (N.Y.)) (interpretation of a settlement agreement is a question of law); *City of Emeryville v. Robinson,* 621 F.3d 1251, 1261 (9th Cir. 2010) (interpretation of a settlement agreement is a question of law subject to de novo review but we defer to any factual findings made by the trial court in interpreting the agreement unless they are clearly erroneous); *Greenhill v. United States*, 92 Fed. Cl. 385, 393 (2010) (citing *Mays v. U.S.P.S.*, 995 F.2d 1056, 1059 (Fed. Cir. 1993)) (the settlement agreement is a contract and its interpretation is a matter of law); *Lee v. U.S.P.S.*, 367 F. App'x 137, 139 (Fed. Cir. 2010) (interpretation of a settlement agreement is an issue of law; we review the MSPB's determination of law without deference); *Johnson v. U.S.P.S.*, 315 F. App'x 274, 277 (Fed. Cir. 2009) (interpretation of a settlement agreement is a question of law that we review de novo), (citing *King v. Dep't of the Navy*, 130 F.3d 1031, 1033 (Fed. Cir. 1997) (*King*)); *Kieffer v. M.S.P.B.*, 263 F. App'x 881, 883 (Fed. Cir. 2008) (interpretation of a settlement agreement is a matter of law which the court reviews without deference) (citing *King* ,130 F.3d at 1033). (My colleagues' citation, at footnote 7, to *United Paperworkers v. Misco, Inc.*, 484 U.S. 29, 36-38 (1987), does not support their contention that courts defer to arbitrators' interpretations of settlement agreements. The *Misco* Court was merely reaffirming the axiomatic proposition -- with which I agree -- that courts must defer to arbitrators' interpretations of *collective bargaining* agreements. *Misco* has nothing to say about how to review an arbitrator's interpretation of a different type of agreement that is entered into outside of the traditional labor relations context.)

To be sure, an arbitrator may interpret a settlement agreement when the circumstances of the dispute require him to do so. The Arbitrator here was called upon to determine whether the settlement agreement had any force or effect with respect to the grievance; however, his conclusion in that regard is not entitled to essence-type deference.

I would conclude that this settlement agreement, by which an individual employee released her individual claims against the Agency, did not waive the Union's institutional claims. Accordingly, I agree that the Arbitrator did not err by declining to dismiss the grievance because of the settlement agreement.

[*] The factual circumstances of these cases differ from the instant case in a key respect: The issue in each case directly presented to the arbitrator the question of whether the agency violated the parties' CBA by failing to comply with a prior settlement agreement.

65 FLRA No. 142

NATIONAL ASSOCIATION
OF INDEPENDENT LABOR
LOCAL 15
(Union)

and

UNITED STATES
DEPARTMENT OF THE NAVY
NAVAL SCHOOL EXPLOSIVE
ORDNANCE DISPOSAL
EGLIN AIR FORCE BASE, FLORIDA
(Agency)

0-AR-4687
(65 FLRA 557 (2011))

ORDER DENYING
MOTION FOR RECONSIDERATION

March 31, 2011

Before the Authority: Carol Waller Pope, Chairman, and Thomas M. Beck and Ernest DuBester, Members

I. Statement of the Case

This matter is before the Authority on the Union's motion for reconsideration of the Authority's decision to deny the Union's exception in *National Association of Independent Labor, Local 15*, 65 FLRA 557 (2011) (*NAIL*). The Agency filed an opposition to the Union's motion for reconsideration.

Section 2429.17 of the Authority's Regulations permits a party who can establish extraordinary circumstances to request reconsideration of an Authority final decision or order. For the reasons that follow, we conclude that the Union has failed to establish extraordinary circumstances warranting reconsideration. Accordingly, we deny the Union's motion for reconsideration.

II. Decision in *NAIL*

In the underlying proceedings in *NAIL*, the Arbitrator concluded, as relevant here, that the grievant was not entitled to a hazard pay differential for performing underwater duties because the hazard that he faced was not listed in Appendix A to 5 C.F.R. part 550, subpart I. *NAIL*, 65 FLRA at 557. In this regard, the Arbitrator noted that Appendix A allows an employee to receive a hazard pay differential for underwater duty, such as "diving, required in scientific and engineering pursuits, or search and rescue operations, when: (a) at a depth of . . . [twenty feet] or more below the surface; or, (b) visibility is restricted; or, (c) in rapidly flowing or cold water; or, (d) vertical access to the surface is restricted[.]" *Id.* (quoting Appendix A to 5 C.F.R. part 550, subpart I) (internal quotations omitted). The Arbitrator rejected the Union's interpretation of the relevant portion of Appendix A and found that, to be entitled to a hazard pay differential, an employee must not only qualify under (a) or (b) or (c) or (d), but must also be engaged in scientific and engineering pursuits or search and rescue operations while diving. *Id.* Moreover, the Arbitrator found that "the [g]rievant's diving duties [were] not part of scientific and engineering pursuits or search and rescue operations." *Id.* (quoting Award at 5) (internal quotations omitted).

The Union filed an exception to the award. *Id.* In its exception, the Union argued that the award was contrary to 5 U.S.C. § 5545(d) because the clear intent of the statute is "to pay an employee when exposed to hardship or hazard without concern over the nature of the mission." *Id.* at 558 (quoting Exception at 5) (internal quotations omitted). Also, the Union contended that the award was contrary to the statute's implementing regulations. *Id.* Specifically, the Union argued that, based on the definition of hazardous duty in 5 C.F.R. § 550.902, the grievant's diving constituted a hazardous duty because it could result in serious injury or death. *Id.* According to the Union, the Arbitrator conceded that the grievant dived at depths greater than twenty feet; that he dived in cold or rapidly flowing waters; that, while diving, his visibility was restricted; and that, during training for hull inspections, his vertical access to the surface was restricted. *Id.* The Union contended that the Arbitrator's interpretation of the relevant language in Appendix A was irrational because the hazard at issue "is in the nature of the dive, not the mission the employee is on[,]" and "[t]he purpose of the [hazard pay] differential is to provide an increase in pay for the exposure to the hazard." *Id.* (quoting Exception at 7-8) (internal quotations omitted). Moreover, the Union argued that its interpretation of the implementing regulations was consistent with the statute. *Id.* Finally, the Union contended that, in accordance with 5 C.F.R. part 550, subpart I, the grievant participated in the dives only occasionally and that the hazard that the grievant faced while diving was not considered in the classification of his position. *Id.*

The Authority concluded that the award was not contrary to 5 U.S.C. § 5545(d) because that provision did not address or require the payment of a hazard differential for the underwater duty performed by the grievant. *Id.* at 559. Also, the Authority found that the Union failed to prove that the Arbitrator's interpretation of the implementing regulations conflicted with the plain wording of those regulations or was otherwise impermissible. *Id.* The Authority determined that, given the Arbitrator's underlying factual findings, which were undisputed, his legal conclusion that the grievant was precluded from obtaining a hazard pay differential because the underwater duty he performed was not listed in Appendix A to 5 C.F.R. part 550 was consistent with the applicable regulations. *Id.*

Moreover, the Authority found that, even assuming that the grievant participated in dives only occasionally and that the hazard that the grievant faced while diving was not considered in the classification of his position, the grievant would not be entitled to a hazard pay differential because the hazard faced by the grievant was not included in Appendix A. *Id.* The Authority, accordingly, denied the Union's exception. *Id.* at 560.

III. Positions of the Parties

A. Motion for Reconsideration

In requesting that the Authority reconsider its decision in *NAIL*, the Union asserts that the decision is based on an erroneous conclusion of law. *See* Request at 1. In support of this assertion, the Union repeats the arguments it initially set forth in its exception to the award. *See id.* at 5-9; *NAIL*, 65 FLRA at 558.

The Union claims that the award is contrary to 5 U.S.C. § 5545(d) because legislative history indicates that the purpose of 5 U.S.C. 5545(d) is "to pay an employee when exposed to hardship or hazard without concern over the nature of the mission." Request at 6; *see also id.* at 1, 5, 8. Also, the Union asserts that the award is contrary to the statute's implementing regulations. *See id.* at 5-8. The Union claims that, under the definition of hazardous duty in 5 C.F.R. § 550.902, the grievant's diving constitutes a hazardous duty because it could result in serious injury or death. *Id.* at 7-8. The Union notes that, in the award, the Arbitrator conceded that the grievant dived at depths greater than twenty feet; that he dived in cold or rapidly flowing waters; that, while diving, his visibility was restricted; and that, during training for hull inspections, his vertical access to the surface was restricted. *Id.* at 8. The Union asserts that its interpretation of the implementing regulations is consistent with the statute and that the Arbitrator's interpretation of the relevant language in Appendix A is irrational because the hazard at issue "is in the nature of the dive, not the mission the employee is on" and "[t]he purpose of the [hazard pay] differential is to provide an increase in pay for the exposure to the hazard." *Id.* Finally, the Union claims that, in accordance with the regulations, the grievant dived only occasionally and that the hazard that he faced while diving was not considered in the classification of his position. *Id.* at 8-9.

B. Agency's Opposition

The Agency argues that the Union has failed to establish that extraordinary circumstances exist to warrant reconsideration of the Authority's decision in *NAIL*. Opp'n at 1-2. According to the Agency, the Union merely disagrees with the conclusion reached by the Authority. *Id.* at 2. Moreover, the Agency contends that the arguments that the Union makes in its motion for reconsideration are identical to those that it made in its exception. *Id.*

IV. Analysis and Conclusion

Section 2429.17 of the Authority's Regulations permits a party who can establish extraordinary circumstances to request reconsideration of an Authority decision. *See, e.g., U.S. Dep't of Justice, Fed. Bureau of Prisons, U.S. Penitentiary, Atwater, Cal.*, 65 FLRA 256, 257 (2010). The Authority has recognized repeatedly that a party seeking reconsideration under § 2429.17 bears the heavy burden of establishing that extraordinary circumstances exist to justify this unusual action. *Id.* The Authority has identified a limited number of situations in which extraordinary circumstances have been found to exist. *Id.* These include situations where: (1) an intervening court decision or change in the law affected dispositive issues; (2) evidence, information, or issues crucial to the decision had not been presented to the Authority; (3) the Authority erred in its remedial order, process, conclusion of law, or factual finding; and (4) the moving party has not been given an opportunity to address an issue raised sua sponte by the Authority in the decision. *See e.g., U.S. Dep't of the Air Force, 375th Combat Support Grp., Scott Air Force Base, Ill.*, 50 FLRA 84, 84 (1995).

In its motion for reconsideration, the Union presents the same arguments that it raised in its exception before the Authority. Request at 5-9; *NAIL*, 65 FLRA at 558. The Authority considered each of these arguments in *NAIL* and found that they must be denied for the reasons set forth in *NAIL*. *See NAIL*, 65 FLRA 559-60. The Union provides no additional argument to warrant a finding that the decision is based on an erroneous conclusion of law; rather, the Union is attempting merely to relitigate issues already presented and resolved. *See Bremerton Metal Trades Council*, 64 FLRA 543, 545 (2010). Consequently, the Union's arguments do not establish that reconsideration is warranted. *See e.g., U.S. Gen. Servs. Admin.*, 63 FLRA 254, 254-55 (2009); *U.S. Dep't of the Interior, Bureau of Indian Affairs, Navajo Area Office*, 54 FLRA 9, 13 (1998) (finding that the motion for reconsideration did not establish the extraordinary circumstances necessary to warrant reconsideration of the decision because the arguments that the union advanced in its motion were the same as those previously considered by the Authority in its decision); *U.S. Dep't of Health & Human Servs., Office of the Assistant Sec'y for Mgmt. & Budget, Office of Grant & Contract Fin. Mgmt., Div. of Audit Resolution*, 51 FLRA 982, 984-85 (1996) (denying the motion for reconsideration because, with one exception, the agency presented the same arguments raised in its exceptions before the Authority).

Accordingly, we deny the Union's motion for reconsideration.

V. Decision

The Union's motion for reconsideration is denied.

65 FLRA No. 143

UNITED STATES
DEPARTMENT OF THE ARMY
DEFENSE LANGUAGE INSTITUTE
MONTEREY, CALIFORNIA
(Agency)

and

AMERICAN FEDERATION
OF GOVERNMENT EMPLOYEES
LOCAL 1263
(Union)

0-AR-4531

DECISION

March 31, 2011

Before the Authority: Carol Waller Pope, Chairman, and Thomas M. Beck and Ernest DuBester, Members

I. Statement of the Case

The matter is before the Authority on exceptions to an award of Arbitrator Walter N. Kaufman filed by the Agency under § 7122(a) of the Federal Service Labor-Management Relations Statute (the Statute) and part 2425 of the Authority's Regulations. The Union filed an opposition to the Agency's exceptions.[1]

The Arbitrator concluded that the Agency violated the parties' agreement by failing to rate properly the grievant's job performance. He ordered the Agency to raise the grievant's rating. For the reasons set forth below, we deny the Agency's exceptions.

II. Background and Arbitrator's Award

The Agency utilizes a five-tier numerical rating system to determine its employees' annual performance rating (overall rating). *See* Award at 3-4. The highest possible number an employee can receive is a one and the lowest number is a five. *Id.* at 4 & n.1. The Agency determines an employee's overall rating by adding together the scores of eight performance standards (standards). *Id.* at 3. As with the overall rating, the Agency relies on a five-tier numerical scale to determine the score for each standard. Standards receiving a score of one are labeled with an "exceed"; twos and threes are labeled "successful"; fours are labeled as "fair" or "needs improvement"; and fives are labeled "unsuccessful" or "fails." *Id.* at 4 & n.1 (internal quotation marks omitted).

The grievant, a language teacher within the Agency, received a score of "exceed" for five standards for the 2006-07 rating period and a "successful" for the remaining three standards. *Id.* at 4. The standards rated as "successful" were "Teaching: Quality and Quantity," "Teaching: Use of Target Language" (Target Language), and "Technology[.]" *Id.* The Agency added the grievant's standard scores and determined that her overall rating was a two. *Id.* In her previous performance appraisal, the grievant received an "exceed" for all eight standards and a one for her overall rating. *Id.*

The Union filed a grievance arguing, as relevant here, that the grievant's three "successful" scores and her overall rating were a violation of Article 25, Sections 4[2] and 7(A)(2)[3] of the parties' agreement. *Id.* at 1 (citation

---

1. In its opposition, the Union asserts that it did not receive a complete copy of the Agency's exceptions. Opp'n at 1 n.1. The Agency filed a supplemental submission pursuant to § 2429.26 of the Authority's Regulations requesting leave solely to respond to the Union's assertion. *See* Agency Supplemental Submission at 1. The Union has not averred that it was prejudiced by the Agency's supposed error; thus, this error is not at issue. *See, e.g., IFPTE, Local 77, Prof'l & Scientists Org.*, 65 FLRA 185, 188 (2010) (where agency did not "claim that it was prejudiced" by alleged procedural deficiencies, Authority denied agency's motion to strike the exceptions). Because this error is not at issue, it is unnecessary to consider the Agency's supplemental submission addressing it. *See, e.g., U.S. Dep't of Homeland Sec., Border & Transp. Sec. Directorate, Bureau of Customs & Border Prot., Wash., D.C.*, 63 FLRA 406, 407 (2009) (citation omitted) (denying party's request to file supplemental submission because submission was deemed unnecessary), *reconsid. denied* 63 FLRA 600 (2009).

2. Article 25, Section 4 of the parties' agreement states:

> The employee's performance will be evaluated on a continuing basis. When there are indications that an employee is not meeting the established performance standards (i.e., the expressed measures of achievement[)] a meeting will be arranged with the employee to discuss the performance in question, and determine the efforts and/or training required to improve the employee's performance.

Exceptions, Attach. 3 at 38.

omitted). The Arbitrator framed the issue as "whether [the] [g]rievant's performance appraisal for the October 1, 2006-September 30, 2007 period was . . . in violation of applicable law or the [parties' agreement]; and if so, what the remedy should be."[4] Award at 2.

The Arbitrator concluded that the Agency violated the parties' agreement by scoring the grievant's Target Language standard as successful. *Id.* at 17. According to the Arbitrator, Article 25, Section 4 of the parties' agreement placed a duty on the Agency to inform the grievant if her performance was not "meeting the established performance standards[.]" *Id.* at 15 (quoting Article 25, Section 4). Similarly, the Arbitrator found that, under Article 25, Section 7(A)(2), the Agency was required to counsel the grievant if it discovered any shortcomings in her performance. *Id.* at 15 (quoting Article 25, Section 7(A)(2)). The Arbitrator found that the Agency had knowledge that the grievant's Target Language score could drop one level. *See id.* at 16. The Arbitrator, accordingly, determined that the Agency should have counseled the grievant about her performance. He further concluded that, had the Agency counseled the grievant, she would have taken steps to improve her score. *Id.* at 17.

In reaching the above conclusion, the Arbitrator rejected the Agency's claim that the parties' agreement does not mandate counseling when an employee's standard score drops one level. According to the Arbitrator, the agreement requires counseling when *any* "shortcomings" are identified; it is not limited to situations involving "imminent failure[.]" *Id.* at 15-16. The Arbitrator also found that Article 25, Sections 4 and 7(A)(2) are procedures and appropriate arrangements as defined in § 7106(b)(2) and (3) of the Statute, respectively. *Id.* at 16.

The Arbitrator sustained the Union's grievance in part and denied it in part.[5] "[B]y way of reconstructing" what action the Agency would have taken but for its contractual violation, the Arbitrator cancelled the grievant's "[succeed]" score for the Teaching Language standard and ordered the Agency to raise it to an "[exceed]." *Id.* at 17. Based on this change, the Arbitrator also ordered the Agency to raise the grievant's overall rating from a two to a one. *Id.*

III. Positions of the Parties

A. Agency's Exceptions

The Agency first argues that the award fails to draw its essence from the parties' agreement. According to the Agency, Article 25, Sections 4 and 7(A)(2) do not require the Agency to counsel an employee when one of her standard scores could drop from the previous year's score. *See* Exceptions at 4-5. The Agency avers that Section 4 defines the phrase "meeting the established performance standards" as the "expressed measure of achievement." *Id.* at 5 (emphasis omitted). Thus, according to the Agency, Section 4 mandates counseling only when an employee is not performing successfully; it does not address an employee's inability to maintain a higher score. *See id.* The Agency also argues that Section 7(A)(2) requires counseling only when a supervisor identifies "*shortcomings* in [an] employee's performance." *Id.* (emphasis in original). The Agency contends that dropping from an "exceed" score to a "succeed" score logically cannot be considered a "shortcoming"; as such, Section 7(A)(2) did not apply to the grievant. *Id.*

The Agency next asserts that the Arbitrator's award affects management's rights to direct employees and assign work under § 7106(a)(2)(A) and (B) of the Statute, respectively. *See id.* at 6 (citing *U.S. Dep't of the Army, U.S. Army Aviation & Missile Command, Redstone Arsenal, Ala.*, 58 FLRA 400, 403 (2003) (*Redstone*)). Accordingly, the Agency contends that the Authority should apply the two-prong test set forth in *United States Department of the Treasury, Bureau of Engraving & Printing, Washington, D.C.*, 53 FLRA 146, 153-54 (1997) (*BEP*) and conclude that the award violates management's rights. *See* Exceptions at 6 (citing *Redstone*, 58 FLRA at 403). The Agency contends that the award does not satisfy prong I of *BEP* because the Agency did not violate the parties' agreement. *See id.* at 7. The Agency further argues that

---

3. Article 25, Section 7(A)(2) of the parties' provides in relevant part:

> The evaluation given employees by their supervisors shall be objective and shall be prepared in accordance with the following . . . [i]f the immediate supervisor has identified shortcomings in the employee's performance, the employee will be notified as promptly as possible and at the six months discussion.

Exceptions, Attach. 3 at 39.

4. The Union also contended that the grievant's overall rating was reprisal for Union activities, Award at 6-8, a claim that the Arbitrator rejected, *id.* at 8. Neither party contests this determination. Accordingly, we do not address it further.

5. The Arbitrator found that the Agency scored the grievant's other two standards properly. Award at 13, 19. Neither party disputes these findings. Accordingly, we do not address them further.

the award does not satisfy prong II of *BEP* because the Arbitrator failed to reconstruct what action the Agency would have taken in the absence of its alleged contractual violation. *See id.* at 7-8.

B. Union's Opposition

The Union rejects the Agency's assertion that the award fails to draw its essence from the parties' agreement. The Union contends that Article 25, Section 7(2)(A) clearly requires the Agency to counsel an employee if that employee's standard score drops from the previous year's score, even if it only drops one level. *See* Opp'n at 3. The Union further argues that nothing in the parties' agreement states that the Agency will counsel an employee only when that employee is failing the Agency's performance standards altogether. *See id.* at 4 (citing Exceptions at 5).

The Union also disagrees that the award is contrary to law. The Union does not dispute the Agency's assertion that the award affects management's rights to direct employees and assign work; however, it contends the award was proper because the Arbitrator determined that the Agency violated the parties' agreement. *See id.* at 7. Further, the Union contends that the Arbitrator properly reconstructed what action the Agency would have taken in the absence of its contractual violation. *See id.* at 7-8.

IV. Analysis and Conclusions

A. The award does not fail to draw its essence from the parties' agreement.

In reviewing an arbitrator's interpretation of a collective bargaining agreement, the Authority applies the deferential standard of review that federal courts use in reviewing arbitration awards in the private sector. *See* 5 U.S.C. § 7122(a)(2); *AFGE, Council 220*, 54 FLRA 156, 159 (1998). Under this standard, the Authority will find that an arbitration award is deficient as failing to draw its essence from the collective bargaining agreement when the appealing party establishes that the award: (1) cannot in any rational way be derived from the agreement; (2) is so unfounded in reason and fact and so unconnected with the wording and purposes of the collective bargaining agreement as to manifest an infidelity to the obligation of the arbitrator; (3) does not represent a plausible interpretation of the agreement; or (4) evidences a manifest disregard of the agreement. *See U.S. Dep't of Labor (OSHA)*, 34 FLRA 573, 575 (1990) (*DOL*). The Authority and the courts defer to arbitrators in this context "because it is the arbitrator's construction of the agreement for which the parties have bargained." *Id.* at 576.

The Agency claims that the award fails to draw its essence from the parties' agreement because Article 25, Sections 4 and 7(A)(2) cannot be interpreted as mandating counseling when a standard score drops one level. Article 25, Section 4 of the parties' agreement states that "a meeting will be arranged with [an] employee to discuss [her] performance" when that "employee is not meeting the established performance standards (i.e., the expressed measures of achievement[)]." Exceptions, Attach. 3 at 38. Similarly, Article 25, Section 7(2)(A) states "[i]f the immediate supervisor has identified shortcomings in [an] employee's performance, the employee will be notified as promptly as possible[.]" *Id.*, Attach. 3 at 39. The Arbitrator interpreted the foregoing as meaning that the Agency must counsel an employee when his or her standard scores could drop from the previous year's scores. He also found that nothing in the foregoing language indicates that these contract provisions apply only when an employee is "failing to meet a standard altogether." Award at 15-16 (citation omitted). Although others may interpret the phrases "not meeting the established performance standards" and "shortcomings in an employee's performance" differently than the Arbitrator, his interpretations are not implausible. *See, e.g., U.S. Dep't of Health & Human Servs., Substance Abuse & Mental Health Servs. Admin.*, 65 FLRA 568, 572-73 (2011) (*DHHS*); *DOL*, 34 FLRA at 575-76.

The Agency's arguments do not lead us to a different conclusion. The Agency claims that Article 25, Section 4 defines the term "meeting the established performance standards" as the "expressed measure of achievement." Exceptions at 5. According to the Agency, this language mandates that Section 4 applies *only* when an employee is failing at their performance. *See id.* The Agency cites no language in Section 4 that states "meeting the established performance standards," or any other part of Section 4, applies solely to unsuccessful performances. *Id.* The Agency also asserts that "shortcomings," as used in Article 25, Section 7(A)(2), cannot logically be interpreted as referring to any situation where a standard score merely drops one level. *Id.* However, the Agency offers no language from the parties' agreement that defines "shortcomings," or otherwise states what, if any, limits are placed on the use of that word. *Id.* The foregoing, in conjunction with the deference afforded to the Arbitrator's interpretation of the agreement, does not lead to a conclusion that the Arbitrator's interpretation is irrational. *See DHHS*, 65 FLRA at 572-73.

Based on the foregoing, we find that the Agency has not demonstrated that the Arbitrator's interpretation of Article 25, Sections 4 and 7(A)(2) fails to draw its essence from the parties' agreement.

B. The award is not contrary to law.

The Authority reviews questions of law raised by exceptions to an arbitrator's award de novo. *See NTEU, Chapter 24*, 50 FLRA 330, 332 (1995) (citing *U.S. Customs Serv. v. FLRA*, 43 F.3d 682, 686-87 (D.C. Cir. 1994)). In applying a standard of de novo review, the Authority determines whether the arbitrator's legal conclusions are consistent with the applicable standard of law. *See NFFE, Local 1437*, 53 FLRA 1703, 1710 (1998). In making that determination, the Authority defers to the arbitrator's underlying factual findings. *Id.*

The Agency contends that the Arbitrator's award impermissibly affects management's rights to direct employees and assign work under §§ 7106(a)(2)(A) and (B) of the Statute, respectively. The Authority recently revised the analysis that it will apply when reviewing management-rights exceptions to arbitration awards. *See U.S. EPA*, 65 FLRA 113, 115 (2010) (Member Beck concurring) (*EPA*); *FDIC, Div. of Supervision & Consumer Prot., S.F. Region*, 65 FLRA 102, 106-07 (2010) (Chairman Pope concurring) (*FDIC, S.F. Region*). Under the revised analysis, the Authority will first assess whether the award affects the exercise of the asserted management right. *EPA*, 65 FLRA at 115. If so, then, as relevant here, the Authority examines whether the award enforces a contract provision negotiated under § 7106(b). *Id.* Furthermore, in setting forth the revised analysis, the Authority rejected the continued application of the "reconstruction" requirement set forth in *BEP*. *FDIC, S.F. Region*, 65 FLRA at 106-07.

The Union does not dispute the Agency's assertion that the award affects management's right to direct employees and assign work under the Statute. *See* Opp'n at 6-8. We, therefore, assume that the award affects the foregoing rights. *See, e.g., SSA*, 65 FLRA 339, 341 (2010). We next examine whether the award enforced properly negotiated provisions. *See id.*

The Agency asserts that the award is contrary to management's rights under the Statute because the Agency did not violate the parties' agreement. *See* Exceptions at 7. This is not the appropriate inquiry; rather, the Authority looks to whether the Arbitrator enforced properly negotiated contract provisions. *E.g., EPA*, 65 FLRA at 115. The Arbitrator found that Article 25, Sections 4 and 7(A)(2) are procedures and appropriate arrangements as defined in the Statute. *See* Award at 16. The Agency does not dispute this conclusion. Moreover, as stated above, the Arbitrator's determination that the Agency violated the parties' agreement is not deficient. Accordingly, we find that the award enforces properly negotiated contractual provisions.

The Agency next argues that the award is deficient under *BEP* because the Arbitrator failed to reconstruct what management would have done had it complied with the parties' agreement. However, as noted above, the Authority no longer requires that an arbitrator's remedy reconstruct what management would have done had it not violated the contract provision. *FDIC*, 65 FLRA 179, 181 (2010). Moreover, Article 25, Sections 4 and 7(A)(2) are properly negotiated contract provisions. The Arbitrator's award enforces these provisions. Accordingly, we find that the award does not impermissibly affect management's rights by failing to reconstruct what the Agency would have done had it not violated the contract.[6] *See, e.g., SSA*, 65 FLRA at 342 (citation omitted); *FDIC*, 65 FLRA at 181.

Accordingly, we find that the award is not contrary to management's rights to direct employees and assign work.[7]

V. Decision

The Agency's exceptions are denied.

---

6. For the reasons set forth in her concurring opinion in *FDIC, S.F. Region*, 65 FLRA at 112, Chairman Pope agrees that the Agency provides no basis for finding the Arbitrator's remedy deficient because the remedy is reasonably related to Article 25, Sections 4 and 7(A)(2) and the harm being remedied.

7. Member Beck agrees with the conclusion to deny the Agency's exception. He does not agree, however, with his colleagues' analysis insofar as they address the question of whether the award affects the exercise of an asserted management right. For the reasons discussed in his concurring opinion in *EPA*, 65 FLRA 113, Member Beck concludes that where, as here, the Arbitrator is enforcing a contract provision that has been accepted by the Agency as a permissible limitation on its management's rights, it is inappropriate to assess whether the provision itself is an appropriate arrangement or whether it abrogates a § 7106(a) right. *Id.* at 120 (Concurring Opinion of Member Beck). The appropriate question is simply whether the remedy directed by the Arbitrator enforces the provision in a reasonable and reasonably foreseeable fashion. *Id.*; *see also FDIC, S.F. Region*, 65 FLRA at 107. Member Beck concludes that the Arbitrator's award is a plausible interpretation of the parties' agreement. Accordingly, Member Beck agrees that the Agency's exception should be denied.

65 FLRA No. 144

UNITED STATES
DEPARTMENT OF THE NAVY
TRIDENT REFIT FACILITY
KINGS BAY, GEORGIA
(Agency)

and

INTERNATIONAL ASSOCIATION
OF MACHINISTS AND
AEROSPACE WORKERS
LOCAL LODGE 2783
(Union)

0-AR-4698

DECISION

March 31, 2011

Before the Authority: Carol Waller Pope, Chairman, and Thomas M. Beck and Ernest DuBester, Members

I. Statement of the Case

The matter is before the Authority on exceptions to an award of Arbitrator Samuel J. Nichols, Jr. filed by the Agency under § 7122(a) of the Federal Service Labor-Management Relations Statute (the Statute) and part 2425 of the Authority's Regulations. The Union filed an opposition to the Agency's exceptions.[1]

In his initial award (Merits Award), the Arbitrator concluded that the Agency violated a settlement agreement and past practice by failing to pay the grievants environmental differential pay (EDP). He ordered the parties to determine the amount of EDP the grievants should receive. After the parties were unable to reach agreement, the Arbitrator awarded the grievants $782,266.98 in EDP (Remedy Award). For the reasons set forth below, we dismiss the Agency's exceptions in part and deny the remaining exception.

II. Background and Arbitrator's Awards

The Agency and the Union entered into a settlement agreement, which, among other things, required the Agency to pay EDP to several groups of employees. Merits Award at 6-7. In October 2007, the Agency terminated this practice with respect to the grievants. *Id.* at 7. The Union presented a grievance challenging the Agency's action. The grievance was unresolved and proceeded to arbitration. The parties stipulated to the following issues: "(1) Whether [the Agency] terminated [EDP] in violation of the [parties' agreement], or other law, rule and regulation, by terminating compensation to the [g]rievants in shops 71A, 57A, 57B, and 38A"; and (2) "If so, what is the appropriate remedy?"[2] Opp'n at 7; Exceptions at 5-6; Exceptions, Attach. 4, Union's Closing Brief at 1.

On May 5, 2010, the Arbitrator issued his Merits Award. The Arbitrator concluded that the Agency violated the parties' agreement and past practice, and awarded the grievants EDP. Merits Award at 15. The Arbitrator did not award a specific amount of EDP; rather, he ordered the parties to consult "regarding the amount of EDP due." *Id.* The Arbitrator gave the parties sixty days to do so. *Id.* The Arbitrator stated that, before determining the final amount owed, he would "allow the parties to submit their respective computations" for his consideration. *Id.* The Arbitrator further stated that the Merits Award would "be made final upon the Arbitrator's certification of the EDP due on the grievance." *Id.* The Agency did not file exceptions to the Merits Award.

---

1. The Union filed a supplemental submission pursuant to § 2429.26 of the Authority's Regulations consisting of documents that it contends are "relevant and material" to the Agency's exceptions. Union Supplemental Submission at 2. The Union claims that these documents concern safety violations the Agency allegedly committed and that the documents did not come into existence until after the Agency filed its exceptions. *See id.* The Agency filed a response disputing the Union's claims that the documents are relevant. *See* Agency Supplemental Submission. The Union's proffered documents relate to the Agency's exceptions that challenge the Arbitrator's initial award; as discussed below, these exceptions are untimely. Because we do not consider the exceptions, it is unnecessary to address the Union's or the Agency's supplemental submissions addressing them. *See, e.g., U.S. Dep't of Homeland Sec., Border & Transp. Sec. Directorate, Bureau of Customs & Border Prot., Wash., D.C.*, 63 FLRA 406, 407 (2009) (citation omitted) (denying party's request to file supplemental submission because submission was deemed unnecessary), *reconsid. denied* 63 FLRA 600 (2009).

2. The Arbitrator did not set forth these issues in either of his awards. However, both parties agree that these were the stipulated issues. *See* Exceptions at 5-6; Opp'n at 7.

The parties were unable to agree on the amount of EDP that the grievants were owed; accordingly, they asked the Arbitrator to resolve their dispute. Remedy Award at 2. The Union requested $782,266.98 for the period covering 2007 to October 1, 2010; the Agency asserted that the grievants were not entitled to any EDP. *See id.* at 2-3. On September 9, 2010, the Arbitrator issued his Remedy Award and concluded that the Agency owed the grievants $782,266.98. *Id.* at 3. The Arbitrator stated that, if the Agency failed to implement this award by October 1, 2010, he would allow the Union to "submit additional calculations covering any and all hours recorded subsequent thereto." *Id.*

III. Positions of the Parties

A. Preliminary Issue

1. Agency's Threshold Issue

The Agency argues that the Authority should consider its exceptions because they are timely. *See* Exceptions at 3. The Agency avers that the Merits Award was not final because the Arbitrator ordered the parties to determine the amount of EDP the grievants should receive; thus, the award left an issue unresolved. *See id.* The Agency further notes that the Arbitrator stated that "[the Merits Award] will be made final upon the Arbitrator's certification of the EDP due on the grievance." *Id.* (quoting Merits Award at 14). Based on the foregoing, the Agency contends that it could not have filed exceptions to the Merits Award because they would have been interlocutory; thus, the Agency had to wait to file exceptions until the Arbitrator issued his Remedy Award. *See id.* at 3-4.

2. Union's Response

The Union does not dispute the Agency's assertion that its exceptions are timely. *See* Opp'n at 8.

B. Merits

1. Agency's Exceptions

The Agency claims that the Merits Award is deficient for three reasons. First, the Agency argues that the Arbitrator exceeded his authority because he was not asked to decide whether the Agency violated a past practice. *See* Exceptions at 5-8. Second, the Agency contends that the award of EDP is contrary to law because it conflicts with portions of the United States Code and the Code of Federal Regulations. *See id.* at 8-9. Third, the Agency argues that the Merits Award is incomplete and ambiguous because "it fails to provide any legal or factual basis for [the] conclusion that the grievants are entitled to EDP." *Id.* at 10-11.

The Agency argues that the Remedy Award is deficient because the Arbitrator exceeded his authority in two ways. First, the Agency avers that the Arbitrator exceeded his authority by failing to timely issue the Remedy Award. *Id.* at 7. The Agency contends that the parties' agreement requires an arbitrator to issue his or her award no more than thirty days after the conclusion of the hearing unless the parties agree otherwise. *Id.* (citing Article 33, Section 13 of the parties' agreement). The Agency claims that the Arbitrator took seven months to issue the Remedy Award without seeking an extension from either party. *Id.*

Second, the Agency contends the Arbitrator exceeded his authority by retaining jurisdiction after he issued the Remedy Award. *Id.* The Agency claims "[t]here is no authority" to support the Arbitrator's decision to retain jurisdiction to award additional EDP if the Agency failed to timely implement the award. *Id.* The Agency avers that the Arbitrator was asked "to review a finite issue, not to exercise continuing jurisdiction over all future EDP claims the grievants may choose to file." *Id.*

2. Union's Opposition

The Union argues that the Authority should deny the three Agency exceptions challenging the Merits Award. *See* Opp'n at 12-16, 21-33.

As to the exceptions contesting the Remedy Award, the Union disputes the Agency's assertion that the Arbitrator exceeded his authority by issuing an untimely award. *See id.* at 16. The Union contends that the Remedy Award was timely. *See id.* at 16-17.

The Union also rejects the Agency's argument that the Arbitrator exceeded his authority by retaining jurisdiction to assist with the implementation of the Remedy Award. The Union contends that it asked the Arbitrator to retain jurisdiction to award attorney fees and to assist with implementation in the event the Agency failed to pay EDP. *See id.* at 17-18. The Union argues that arbitrators are permitted to retain jurisdiction to "oversee[] the implementation of remedies[.]" *Id.* at 18 (quoting *U.S. Dep't of Veterans Admin., Med. Ctr., Leavenworth, Kan.*, 38 FLRA 232, 238-39 (1990)). The Union further contends that the Arbitrator did not retain jurisdiction to consider all future claims of EDP. *Id.* at 19.

IV. Preliminary Issues

A. The Agency's exceptions challenging the Merits Award are untimely.

The Agency argues that its exceptions to the Merits Award are timely. According to the Agency, the Merits Award was not final; as such, any exceptions filed as to the Merits Award would have been interlocutory.

Section 7122(b) of the Statute states that "[i]f no exception to an arbitrator's award is filed under [§ 7122(a) of the Statute] during the 30-day period beginning on the date the award is served on the party, the award shall be final and binding." 5 U.S.C. § 7122(b); *see also* 5 C.F.R. 2425.2(b).[3] The thirty day limit is jurisdictional; the Authority is unable to waive or extend it and must dismiss untimely filed exceptions. 5 U.S.C. § 7122(b); 5 C.F.R. § 2429.23(d);[4] *e.g., U.S. Dep't of Commerce, PTO, Arlington, Va.*, 60 FLRA 869, 877 (2005) (*PTO*). Parties must, therefore, file exceptions no later than thirty days after an award becomes final and is served on a party. *See* 5 U.S.C. § 7122(b).

An award is considered final for purposes of filing exceptions when it fully resolves all issues submitted to arbitration. *See, e.g., U.S. Dep't of Transp., FAA, Wash., D.C.*, 60 FLRA 333, 334 (2004). When an arbitrator orders a remedy but retains jurisdiction to assist the parties in the implementation of that remedy, all submitted issues are considered resolved. *See, e.g., U.S. Dep't of Justice, Fed. Bureau of Prisons, USP Admin. Maximum (ADX), Florence, Colo.*, 64 FLRA 1168, 1170 (2010) (award was final where arbitrator ordered backpay in initial award but retained jurisdiction to assist parties in determining the amount of backpay), *reconsid. denied* 65 FLRA 76; *U.S. Dep't of the Treasury, IRS*, 63 FLRA 157, 158-59 (2009) (same). However, where an arbitrator orders the parties to determine the remedy that should be awarded, the award is not considered final. *See, e.g., U.S. Dep't of HHS, Navajo Area Indian Health Serv.*, 58 FLRA 356, 357 (2003) (award was not final because arbitrator declined to issue remedy, and instead directed parties to determine the appropriate remedy); *U.S. Dep't of the Interior, Bureau of Indian Affairs, Wapato Irrigation Project, Wapato, Wash.*, 55 FLRA 1230, 1231-32 (2000) (same).

The foregoing precedent establishes that the Arbitrator's Merits Award was final for purposes of filing exceptions. The Arbitrator awarded a remedy of EDP and ordered the parties to determine the specific amount of EDP owed. Thus, the only issue left unresolved by the Merits Award was the amount that the grievants should recover. Because this was the only unresolved issue, the Merits Award constituted a final award for purposes of filing exceptions to it. *See, e.g., DOJ*, 64 FLRA at 1170 (award was final where it awarded a remedy of backpay, but left unresolved the amount of backpay that should be paid to the grievants).

The Arbitrator's statement that the Merits Award would not become final until he certified the amount of EDP owed does not alter our conclusion. An arbitrator's characterization of an award does not, by itself, demonstrate whether the award is final. *See, e.g., AFGE, Local 12*, 61 FLRA 355, 357 (2005) (finding that arbitrator's statements in award did not establish whether award was final).

The Merits Award was final for purposes of filing exceptions. The Agency, therefore, was required to file any exceptions to that award no later than thirty days after it received the award. *See* 5 U.S.C. § 7122(b). The Merits Award was issued and served upon the parties in May 2010. The Agency filed its exceptions with the Authority on October 8, 2010, well beyond the thirty days set forth in § 7122(b) of the Statute. Three of the five Agency's exceptions challenge the Arbitrator's conclusion, in his Merits Award, that the grievants were entitled to EDP.[5] *See* Exceptions at 5-9, 11.

3. 5 C.F.R. § 2425.2(b) states, in relevant part: "The time limit for filing an exception to an arbitration award is thirty (30) days after the date of service of the award. This thirty (30)-day time limit may not be extended or waived." We note that § 2425.2(b) was amended effective October 1, 2010. *See* 75 Fed. Reg. 42,283 (2010). Previously, § 2425.2(b) was located at 5 C.F.R. § 2425.1(b); however, the foregoing quoted language did not change. Accordingly, although we apply 5 C.F.R. § 2425.2(b), we rely on Authority precedent interpreting 5 C.F.R. § 2425.1(b).

4. 5 C.F.R. § 2429.23(d) states "[t]ime limits established in 5 U.S.C. [§§] 7105(f), 7117(c)(2) and 7122(b) may not be extended or waived under this section."

5. We note that, under Authority precedent, where an arbitrator issues a subsequent award that modifies the original award, the time limit for filing exceptions begins upon service of that subsequent award on the excepting party. *See, e.g., U.S. Dep't of Labor, Wash., D.C.*,

Because these three exceptions were filed more than thirty days after the Agency received the Merits Award, we find that they should be dismissed as untimely. *See, e.g., PTO,* 60 FLRA at 877.

The Agency's remaining two exceptions challenge the Remedy Award that was issued on September 9, 2010, and were filed by mail on October 8, 2010. *See* Exceptions, Certificate of Serv. These exceptions, therefore, were filed within the thirty day statutory timeline. Accordingly, we find that these two exceptions are timely.

B. The Agency's exception arguing that the Arbitrator failed to issue the Remedy Award within thirty days is barred by § 2429.5 of the Authority's Regulations.

Under § 2429.5 of the Authority's Regulations, the Authority will not consider issues that "could have been, but were not, presented" to the arbitrator.[6] 5 C.F.R. 2429.5; *see, e.g., AFGE, Council 236,* 65 FLRA 421, 421 n.* (2010) (*AFGE*); *see also U.S. Dep't of Transp., FAA,* 64 FLRA 387, 389 (2010). Exceptions raising such issues will be dismissed. *See AFGE,* 65 FLRA at 421 n.*. Where a party makes an argument before the Authority that is inconsistent with its position before the arbitrator, the Authority applies § 2429.5 to bar the argument. *See, e.g., U.S. Dep't of Transp., FAA, Detroit, Mich.,* 64 FLRA 325, 328 (2009) (*FAA*) (dismissing agency's argument that parties' agreement did not incorporate certain Office of Personnel Management regulations because agency conceded before arbitrator that agreement *did* incorporate those regulations).

In one of its exceptions to the Remedy Award, the Agency argues that the Arbitrator exceeded his authority because he did not issue the Remedy Award within thirty days of the Merits Award as required by the parties' agreement. The Arbitrator gave the parties sixty days to negotiate over the amount of EDP owed to the grievants; the Agency raised no objection. *See* Merits Award at 15; *see also* Remedy Award at 2. The Agency further expanded this timeframe by requesting an additional forty-five days to negotiate over the amount of EDP owed. *See* Opp'n at 16. This establishes that, while before the Arbitrator, the Agency tacitly agreed to extend the timeframe for the issuance of the Remedy Award well beyond thirty days. The Agency's position before the Arbitrator is inconsistent with the position the Agency has adopted before the Authority. Consequently, the Agency's exception is not properly before the Authority. *See, e.g., FAA,* 64 FLRA at 328.

Alternatively, even if the Agency did not agree to extend the timeframe for the issuance of the Remedy Award, the Agency failed to raise any objection to an extended timeframe. As established above, the Agency had clear and unambiguous notice that the Arbitrator, at a minimum, could take at least sixty days to issue his Remedy Award. *See* Merits Award at 15; *see also* Remedy Award at 2. Despite this notice, the Agency gave no indication such an action would be improper. Because the Agency failed to object below, even though it had a clear opportunity to do so, it may not object now. *See, e.g., AFGE,* 65 FLRA at 421 n.*.

Accordingly, we dismiss the Agency's exception.

V. The Arbitrator did not exceed his authority by retaining jurisdiction after he issued the Remedy Award.

The Agency contends that the Arbitrator had no authority to retain jurisdiction after he issued the Remedy Award; according to the Agency, the Arbitrator was not asked to decide all future claims for EDP that the grievants might file. *See* Exceptions at 7. Arbitrators exceed their authority when they fail to resolve an issue submitted to arbitration, resolve an issue not submitted to arbitration, disregard specific limitations on their authority, or award relief to those not encompassed within the grievance. *See AFGE, Local 1617,* 51 FLRA 1645, 1647 (1996). The Authority, like the federal courts, accords arbitrators substantial deference in the determination of the issues submitted to arbitration. *E.g., Veterans Admin.,* 24 FLRA 447, 450 (1986). In cases in which the parties have stipulated the issue for resolution, arbitrators do not exceed their authority by addressing any issue that is necessary to decide the stipulated issue or by addressing any issue that necessarily arises from issues specifically included in the stipulation. *Id.*

---

59 FLRA 131, 132 (2003) (Chairman Cabaniss concurring). The Agency does not assert that the Remedy Award modified the merits award. Our review of the Remedy Award likewise does not establish that the Arbitrator modified his Merits Award.

6. We note that § 2429.5 was amended effective October 1, 2010. *See* 75 Fed. Reg. 42,283 (2010). Because these exceptions were filed after that date, we apply the revised Regulation. *See, e.g., AFGE, Council 236,* 65 FLRA 421, 421 n.* (2010).

The Agency has not established that the Arbitrator exceeded his authority. The parties stipulated that the Arbitrator would decide: (1) whether the Agency violated law and the parties' agreement by failing to pay the grievants EDP; and (2), if so, what was the appropriate remedy. Opp'n at 7; Exceptions at 6. In response to these issues, the Arbitrator concluded that: (1) the Agency violated past practice by failing to pay the grievants EDP; and (2) as a result of this violation, the Agency owed the grievants a remedy of $782,266.98 in EDP by October 1, 2010. Merits Award at 15; Remedy Award at 3. The Arbitrator also determined that, if the Agency failed to pay the grievants this amount by October 1, he would allow the Union the opportunity to submit additional calculations "covering any and all hours recorded subsequent thereto." Remedy Award at 3. Thus, the Arbitrator did not state that he would consider additional EDP claims; rather, he merely held that he would consider additional calculations of EDP owed as result of the Agency's violation. The Agency has pointed to no language that suggests the Arbitrator retained jurisdiction to consider *all* possible future claims of EDP. The Remedy Award, therefore, is directly responsive to the stipulated issues. Accordingly, we find that the Arbitrator did not exceed his authority.

VI. Decision

The Agency's exceptions are dismissed in part and denied in part.

65 FLRA No. 145

UNITED STATES
DEPARTMENT OF LABOR
OFFICE OF THE ASSISTANT SECRETARY
FOR ADMINISTRATION AND MANAGEMENT
DALLAS, TEXAS
(Respondent)

and

AMERICAN FEDERATION
OF GOVERNMENT EMPLOYEES
NATIONAL COUNCIL
OF FIELD LABOR LOCALS
LOCAL 2139, AFL-CIO
(Charging Party/Union)

DA-CA-09-0273

DECISION AND ORDER

March 31, 2011

Before the Authority: Carol Waller Pope, Chairman, and Thomas M. Beck and Ernest DuBester, Members

I. Statement of the Case

This unfair labor practice (ULP) case is before the Authority on exceptions to the attached decision of the Administrative Law Judge (Judge) filed by the Respondent. The General Counsel (GC) filed an opposition to the Respondent's exceptions.

The complaint alleges that the Respondent violated § 7116(a)(1) and (5) of the Federal Service Labor-Management Relations Statute (the Statute) by refusing to engage in mid-term bargaining over parking at the Respondent's Dallas, Texas office. The Judge found that the Respondent violated § 7116(a)(1) and (5) the Statute and recommended that the Authority issue a cease and desist order, require the Respondent to bargain in good faith with the Union, and require the Respondent to post a notice of the ULP finding.

For the reasons discussed below, we deny the Respondent's exceptions and adopt the Judge's findings, conclusions, and recommended order.

II. Background and Judge's Decision

A. Background

The Respondent has employees at two locations in downtown Dallas. Judge's Decision at 2. The building located at 525 S. Griffin has a parking lot that is managed by the General Services Administration (GSA). *Id.* at 2-3. The parking lot contains 169 spaces, of which 48 are assigned to the Respondent.[1] *Id.* at 3. When the parking lot behind the 525 S. Griffin building closed, the Charging Party proposed that the parties conduct negotiations over the 48 parking spaces assigned to the Respondent. *Id.* In response, the Respondent stated that its spaces were assigned in accordance with the Department of Labor Manual Series (DLMS) and that it could not negotiate changes to the policy.[2] *Id.* The Respondent did not respond to subsequent emails on the issue and assumed the matter was concluded. *Id.* at 4.

The Charging Party then filed a ULP charge against the Respondent. *Id.* at 1-2. The Regional Director of the Authority's Dallas Regional Office issued a complaint, which alleged that the Respondent had violated § 7116(a)(1) and (5) of the Statute by refusing to engage in mid-term bargaining. *Id.* at 2. The Respondent filed an answer, admitting certain allegations, but denying the substantive allegations of the complaint. *Id.* A hearing was held and the parties filed post-hearing briefs. The Judge issued her decision based on the entire record. *Id.*

B. Judge's Decision

Before the Judge, the GC argued that the Respondent violated the Statute when it refused to engage in mid-term bargaining about parking. *Id.* at 5. The GC asserted that parking was not "covered

1. The remaining spaces are either: (1) assigned to other agencies located in the building or (2) unassigned and allocated to individuals through a process administered by the GSA. Judge's Decision at 3.

2. The DLMS contains the Respondent's internal regulations and policies regarding the administration and operation of the department, including parking at its facilities. DLMS Chapter 526 provides, in relevant part: "The following descending order of priority will govern allocation of [Department of Labor (DOL)] controlled parking spaces and will include the best interests of the DOL[.]" *Id.* at 4. The policy lists in order: "official needs, employees with disabilities, official necessity, van pools, and car pools." *Id.*

by" the parties' agreement, that the DLMS did not preclude bargaining over parking, and that the Respondent had not established a past practice regarding the DLMS. *Id.* In response, the Respondent argued that resolving parking issues using the DLMS constituted a past practice; as a result, under Authority precedent, the practice had been incorporated into the parties' agreement and was "covered by" the parties' agreement. *Id.* at 5-6. The Respondent further argued that, even if using the DLMS to resolve parking issues did not constitute a past practice, the DLMS had been incorporated into the parties' agreement through Article 2, Section 1 of the parties' agreement.[3] Respondent's Post-Hearing Brief at 8.

The Judge first rejected the Respondent's defense that using the DLMS to resolve parking issues constituted a past practice. Judge's Decision at 7. The Judge found that, although the Respondent had followed the practice of using the DLMS with regard to employee parking issues, there was "no evidence that the [Charging Party] ha[d] acquiesced to th[at] practice." *Id.* The Judge rejected the Respondent's argument that the Charging Party had agreed to be bound by the DLMS or had waived its right to bargain in *AFGE, Local 2139, National Council of Field Labor Locals*, 61 FLRA 654 (2006) (*AFGE, Local 2139*). Judge's Decision at 6-7.

The Judge also rejected the Respondent's second argument, finding that Article 2, Section 1 of the parties' agreement was insufficient to support the Respondent's "covered by" defense. *Id.* at 7. According to the Judge, the generalized reference to "policies and regulations" in that provision of the parties' agreement was not sufficient to incorporate the DLMS into the parties' agreement. *Id.*

Because the subject of parking was not "covered by" the parties' agreement, the Judge found that the Respondent violated § 7116(a)(1) and (5) of the Statute by refusing to bargain with the Charging Party. *Id.* Accordingly, the Judge recommended that the Authority adopt an order requiring the Respondent to cease and desist from refusing to bargain and post a notice at its facilities. *Id.* at 8.

---

3. Article 2, Section 1 provides, in relevant part: "In the administration of all matters covered by this Agreement, officials and employees are governed by existing or future laws and regulations of appropriate authorities; [and] by published Department and/or Agency policies and regulations in existence at the time this Agreement was approved[.]" *Id.* at 4.

III. Positions of the Parties

A. Respondent's Exceptions

The Respondent argues that the Judge erred in finding that using the DLMS to resolve parking issues did not constitute a past practice. Exceptions at 7. According to the Respondent, the parties have used the DLMS as guidance in resolving parking issues since 2004, and both parties have "recognized and consented to the supremacy" of the DLMS regarding parking issues. *Id.* The Respondent contends that the Charging Party has acquiesced in this practice by following the DLMS and by failing to file a grievance over the use of the DLMS. *Id.* at 8. The Respondent also asserts that the Charging Party has argued previously that the Respondent must abide by the terms of the DLMS as applied to parking arrangements within the Dallas Region. *Id.* at 8-9 (citing *AFGE, Local 2139*, 61 FLRA 654). Therefore, the Respondent argues, resolving parking issues by reference to the DLMS constitutes a past practice and, in effect, has been incorporated into the parties' agreement. *Id.* at 10.

The Respondent also argues that the Judge was collaterally estopped from finding that using the DLMS to resolve parking issues did not constitute a past practice. *Id.* at 11. According to the Respondent, in *United States Department of Labor, Mine Safety & Health Administration, Rocky Mountain District, Denver, Co.*, FLRA ALJ Dec. Rep. No. 111, 1993 WL 545336 (1993) (*DOL, MSHA*), a case involving the same parties, another judge found that "those regulations establish 'a past practice.'" Exceptions at 11 (quoting *DOL, MSHA*, 1993 WL 545336, at *3). The Respondent asserts that the five elements of collateral estoppel are met and that, as such, the Judge was precluded from finding that using the DLMS to resolve parking issues does not constitute a past practice. *Id.* at 11-12.

The Respondent also argues that, contrary to the Judge's opinion, it did not assert below that the DLMS was "covered by" the parties' agreement; rather, it contended that, "[b]ecause resolution of parking issues by reference to the DLMS has been established by past practice, that condition of employment [wa]s incorporated into and covered by the parties' . . . agreement." *Id.* at 13. Moreover, the Respondent asserts that Article 2, Section 1 expressly incorporates into the parties' agreement policies and regulations that were in existence at the time the parties' agreement was executed -- such as the

DLMS. *Id.* Therefore, the Respondent asserts that the Judge erred in finding that the DLMS had not been incorporated into the parties' agreement. *Id.* at 13-14.

B. GC's Opposition

The GC argues that the Judge reasonably found that using the DLMS to resolve parking issues did not constitute a past practice. Opp'n at 3. Specifically, the GC asserts that the Charging Party did not agree to be bound by the terms of the DLMS, did not participate in negotiations over the DLMS, and did not waive its right to object to the DLMS. *Id.* at 3-4. The GC argues that the way in which GSA deals with the remaining individual parking lot spaces is irrelevant to the 48 spaces that are controlled by the Respondent. *Id.* at 4-5. The GC also contends that, contrary to the Respondent's argument, the Charging Party's argument in *AFGE, Local 2139* that the proposal in that case was consistent with the DLMS does not mean that the Charging Party agreed that the DLMS controls all parking issues. *Id.* at 5.

The GC also argues that the elements of collateral estoppel are not met. *Id.* at 6-7. The GC asserts that, in *DOL, MSHA*, the judge did not find that the DLMS controlled all parking issues with the Respondent, but only that allowing inspectors to park their privately owned vehicles (POVs) at the Denver Federal Center constituted a past practice. *Id.*

Finally, the GC argues that the Judge was correct to find that, even if using the DLMS to resolve parking issues did constitute a past practice, Article 2, Section 1 was insufficient to establish that the issue of parking is "covered by" the parties' agreement. *Id.* at 7. According to the GC, the Respondent simply disagrees with the Judge's conclusion. *Id.*

IV. Analysis and Conclusions

A. The Judge did not err in concluding that the evidence did not demonstrate that the parties had a past practice that matters regarding parking at the Respondent's facilities were governed by the DLMS.

The standard for determining the existence of a past practice is whether a practice was consistently exercised for an extended period of time with the other party's knowledge and express or implied consent. *U.S. Dep't of the Treasury, Internal Revenue Serv., Louisville Dist., Louisville, Ky.*, 42 FLRA 137, 142 (1991). The practice must be "consistently exercised over a significant period of time and followed by both parties, or followed by one party and not challenged by the other." *Soc. Sec. Admin., Office of Hearing & Appeals, Montgomery, Ala.*, 60 FLRA 549, 554 (2005).

In determining whether a judge's factual findings are supported, the Authority looks to the preponderance of the record evidence. *U.S. Dep't of Transp., Fed. Aviation Admin.*, 64 FLRA 365, 368 (2009) (Member Beck concurring).[4] Applying these standards, we find that the Judge's conclusion that there was no established past practice of using the DLMS to resolve parking issues is supported by the record. The Judge found that, although the Respondent followed the practice of using the DLMS with regard to employee parking, there was no evidence that the Charging Party acquiesced in the practice. Judge's Decision at 7.

The Respondent argues that, because the Charging Party has been aware of the DLMS and has been applying to GSA for individual parking spaces as directed by the DLMS, the Judge erred in not finding that the Charging Party had acquiesced in the practice. Exceptions at 8. Further, relying on *AFGE, Local 2139* and *DOL, MSHA*, the Respondent argues that the Judge was precluded from finding that a past practice did not exist.

We reject the Respondent's arguments. The mere existence of the DLMS is not evidence of acquiescence by the Charging Party. Also, that a party has not objected to a practice does not, by itself, establish acquiescence. *See Marine Corps Logistic Base, Barstow, Cal.*, 46 FLRA 782, 799 (1992) (finding no acquiescence even though the union did not object to the practice because prior changes to the practice could have met with the union's approval) (*Marine Corps*). Moreover, the Respondent has not established that there were frequent disputes where consultation with the DLMS was necessary. *See U.S. Dep't of Homeland Sec., Border & Transp. Directorate, Bureau of Customs & Border Prot.*,

4. Member Beck notes that, for the reasons stated in his separate opinions in *U.S. Dep't of the Air Force, 12th Flying Training Wing, Randolph Air Force Base, San Antonio, Tex.*, 63 FLRA 256, 262-63 (2009) and *U.S. Dep't of the Air Force, Air Force Materiel Command, Space & Missile Sys. Ctr., Detachment 12, Kirtland Air Force Base, N.M.*, 64 FLRA 166, 179-80 (2009), he reviews the Judge's factual findings using a "substantial evidence in the record" standard rather than a "preponderance" standard.

59 FLRA 910, 914-15 (2004) (finding that, because the practice at issue was limited to isolated incidents, the evidence failed to demonstrate acquiescence).

AFGE, Local 2139 does not provide support for the Respondent's contention that the Judge erred in finding a past practice did not exist. In *AFGE, Local 2139*, a negotiability case, the Charging Party argued that its proposal concerning parking was "intended to require the Agency to comply with Agency regulations[,]" referring to the DLMS. *AFGE, Local 2139*, 61 FLRA at 654. However, the Charging Party did not assert that the DLMS always controlled or acquiesce in being bound by the DLMS simply because it argued in *AFGE, Local 2139* that its proposal was consistent with the DLMS.

The Respondent's reliance on *DOL, MSHA* to establish that the Judge was precluded by collateral estoppel is misplaced. As an initial matter, it is unclear whether the Respondent raised the precise issue of collateral estoppel before the Judge. However, even assuming the Respondent properly raised this issue, its claim is without merit. In *DOL, MSHA*, the judge found that permitting inspectors to park their POVs at a specific location while picking up their government owned vehicles was a past practice. *DOL, MSHA*, FLRA ALJ Dec. Rep. No. 111 at 3, 1993 WL 545336, at *3. Contrary to the Respondent's suggestion, the judge did not find that using the DLMS to resolve all parking issues constituted a past practice, nor was that issue litigated in that case. Because one element of collateral estoppel is that the issue must have been litigated in the previous case, the elements of collateral estoppel have not been met. *See U.S. Dep't of Energy, W. Area Power Admin., Golden, Colo.*, 56 FLRA 9, 11-12 (2000) (finding no collateral estoppel where the same issue was not litigated in both proceedings).

Accordingly, we find that the Judge did not err in finding that a past practice did not exist, reject the Respondent's argument that collateral estoppel applies, and deny this exception.[5]

B. The Judge did not err in concluding that, even assuming a past practice existed, parking was not "covered by" the parties' agreement.

The Authority has held that, absent a reopener clause, parties are not permitted to demand mid-term bargaining over matters that are covered by an agreement. *See, e.g., U.S. Dep't of Labor, Wash., D.C.*, 60 FLRA 68, 72 (2004) (citing *U.S. Dep't of Health & Human Servs., SSA, Balt., Md.*, 47 FLRA 1004, 1013 (1993) (*SSA I*).

A subject for negotiation is covered by a collective bargaining agreement if the matter is expressly contained in the agreement. *See SSA I*, 47 FLRA at 1018. If the agreement does not expressly contain the matter, then the Authority will determine whether the subject is inseparably bound up with, and thus plainly an aspect of, a subject covered by the agreement. *Id.* Consideration of the parties' bargaining history is an "integral component" of determining whether the matter is inseparably bound up with, and thus plainly an aspect of, the subject covered by the agreement. *U.S. Customs Serv., Customs Mgt. Ctr., Miami, Fla.*, 56 FLRA 809, 814 (2000). Moreover, in ULP cases that turn on the meaning of the parties' collective bargaining agreement, the Authority has held that, where a judge's interpretation of the meaning of the parties' agreement is challenged, it will determine whether the judge's interpretation is supported by the record and by the standards and principles applied by arbitrators and the federal courts. *IRS, Wash., D.C.*, 47 FLRA 1091, 1110-11 (1993).

Even assuming that the Respondent is correct that a past practice is incorporated into the parties' agreement, Exceptions at 13 (citing *AFGE, Local 2128*, 58 FLRA 519, 523 (2003)), because we find that the Judge correctly determined that using the DLMS to resolve parking issues does not constitute a past practice, the Respondent's argument does not support its "covered by" defense.

The Respondent also argues that the DLMS has been incorporated into the parties' agreement through Article 2, Section 1, which incorporates existing policies and regulations into the parties' agreement. Exceptions at 13. The Judge found that the generalized language of Article 2, Section 1 is insufficient to incorporate the DLMS into the parties' agreement. Judge's Decision at 7. We find that the Judge's decision is supported by the record. Article 2, Section 1 clearly refers to "the

5. The Respondent also argues that the Charging Party did not file a grievance protesting the application of the DLMS and for that reason should be said to have acquiesced in the practice. Exceptions at 8. The GC argues that the Respondent did not properly raise this issue before the Judge. Opp'n at 4 n.1. However, even assuming the Respondent did properly raise the issue, as noted above, failure to object does not establish acquiescence and, thus, would not be sufficient to overcome the Judge's finding. *See Marine Corps*, 46 FLRA at 799.

administration of *all matters covered by this Agreement* . . . ." GC's Post-Hearing Brief at 8-9. Because, as discussed above, we reject the Respondent's argument that use of the DLMS to resolve parking issues constituted a past practice and no other provision in the parties' agreement covers this issue, Article 2, Section 1 does not apply to the instant matter.

Accordingly, we reject the Respondent's argument that the DLMS has been incorporated into the parties' agreement such that the matter was "covered by" the parties' agreement and deny this exception.

V. Order

Pursuant to § 2423.41(c) of the Authority's Regulations and § 7118 of the Statute, it is hereby ordered that the Respondent shall:

1. Cease and desist from:

(a) Refusing to bargain mid-term with the Union, the exclusive representative of certain bargaining unit employees, regarding employee parking at 525 S. Griffin, Dallas, Texas.

(b) In any like or related manner, interfering with, restraining, or coercing its employees in the exercise of their rights assured by the Statute.

2. Take the following affirmative action in order to effectuate the purposes and policies of the Statute:

(a) Upon request, bargain in good faith with the Union, to the extent required by law, regarding employee parking at 525 S. Griffin Street, Dallas, Texas.

(b) Post at its facilities where bargaining unit employees represented by the Union are located, copies of the attached Notice on forms to be furnished by the Federal Labor Relations Authority. Upon receipt of such forms, they shall be signed by the Regional Administrator, and shall be posted and maintained for 60 consecutive days thereafter, in conspicuous places, including all bulletin boards and other places where notices to employees are customarily posted. Reasonable steps shall be taken to ensure that such Notices are not altered, defaced, or covered by any other material.

(c) Pursuant to § 2423.41(e) of the Authority's Regulations, notify the Regional Director, Dallas Regional Office, Federal Labor Relations Authority, in writing, within 30 days from the date of this Order, as to what steps have been taken to comply herewith.

NOTICE TO ALL EMPLOYEES
POSTED BY ORDER OF THE
FEDERAL LABOR RELATIONS AUTHORITY

The Federal Labor Relations Authority has found that the United States Department of Labor, Office of the Assistant Secretary for Administration and Management, Dallas, Texas, violated the Federal Service Labor-Management Relations Statute (the Statute) and has ordered us to post and abide by this notice.

WE HEREBY NOTIFY EMPLOYEES THAT:

WE WILL NOT refuse to bargain in good faith with the American Federation of Government Employees, National Council of Field Labor Locals, Local 2139, AFL-CIO (the Union), the exclusive representative of certain bargaining unit employees, regarding employee parking at 525 S. Griffin, Dallas, Texas.

WE WILL NOT, in any like or related manner, interfere with, restrain, or coerce our employees in the exercise of their rights assured by the Statute.

WE WILL, upon request, bargain in good faith with the Union to the extent required by law, regarding employee parking at 525 S. Griffin, Dallas, Texas.

____
(Respondent/Agency)

Dated: __________ By: ____________________
(Signature) (Title)

This Notice must remain posted for 60 consecutive days from the date of posting, and must not be altered, defaced, or covered by any other material.

If employees have any questions concerning this Notice or compliance with its provisions, they may communicate directly with the Regional Director, Dallas Regional Office, Federal Labor Relations Authority, and whose address is: 525 S. Griffin Street, Suite 926, LB-107, Dallas, Texas 75202-1906, and whose telephone number is: (214) 767-6266.

Office of Administrative Law Judges

U.S. DEPARTMENT OF LABOR
OFFICE OF THE ASSISTANT SECRETARY
FOR ADMINISTRATION AND MANAGEMENT
DALLAS, TEXAS
Respondent

AND

AMERICAN FEDERATION
OF GOVERNMENT EMPLOYEES
NATIONAL COUNCIL
OF FIELD LABOR LOCALS
LOCAL 2139, AFL-CIO
Charging Party

Case No. DA-CA-09-0273

Michael A. Quintanilla, Esq.
For the General Counsel

David L. Peña, Esq.
For the Respondent

Jeffrey P. Darby
For the Charging Party

Before: SUSAN E. JELEN
Administrative Law Judge

DECISION

This case arose under the Federal Service Labor-Management Relations Statute, Chapter 71 of Title 5 of the United States Code, 5 U.S.C. §7101, *et. seq.* (the Statute), and the Rules and Regulations of the Federal Labor Relations Authority (the Authority/FLRA), 5 C.F.R. Part 2423.

On June 18, 2009, the American Federation of Government Employees, National Council of Field Labor Locals, Local 2139, AFL-CIO (Charging Party/Union) filed an unfair labor practice charge with the Dallas Region of the Authority against the U.S. Department of Labor, Office of the Assistant Secretary for Administration and Management, Dallas, Texas (Respondent/OASAM). (G.C. Ex. 1(a)) On December 22, 2009, the Regional Director of the Dallas Region of the Authority issued a Complaint and Notice of Hearing, which alleged that the Respondent violated section 7116(a)(1) and (5) of the Statute by refusing to engage in mid-term bargaining over parking at the Respondent's Dallas, Texas offices. (G.C. Ex. 1(c)) On January 19, 2010, the Respondent filed an Answer to the complaint, in which it admitted certain allegations while denying the substantive allegations of the complaint. (G.C. Ex. 1(e)) At the hearing, the Respondent amended its answer to admit all but the final paragraph of the complaint. (Tr. 7).

A hearing was held in Dallas, Texas on March 10, 2010, at which time all parties were afforded a full opportunity to be represented, to be heard, to examine and cross-examine witnesses, to introduce evidence and to argue orally. The General Counsel and the Respondent filed timely Post-Hearing Briefs, which have been fully considered.

Based upon the entire record, including my observation of the witnesses and their demeanor, I make the following findings of fact, conclusions and recommendations.

STATEMENT OF THE FACTS

The Respondent is an agency within the meaning of section 7103(a)(3) of the Statute. (G.C. Ex. 1(d), (h)) At all times material to this matter, Kelley Pettit served as Regional Administrator and Earsie Johnson served as the Labor Relations Officer and both have been supervisors and/or management officials within the meaning of section 7103(a)(10) and (11) of the Statute. (G.C. Ex. 1(c), (e); Tr. 16, 49).

The Union is a labor organization within the meaning of section 7103(a)(4) of the Statute. (G.C. Ex. 1(c), (e)) Jeffrey Darby is the President of AFGE, Local 2139 and is Vice President of the National Council of Field Labor Locals. (Tr. 13).

OASAM is the consolidated agency for the Department of Labor (DOL), responsible for all administrative and management programs that serve all agencies within DOL, such as Human Resources, Financial Management, Administrative Services, Space, Telecommunications and Information Technology. (Tr. 50) The Dallas Region covers eleven states, including Texas. (Tr. 14, 50).

DOL has employees in at least two locations in downtown Dallas: 525 S. Griffin (also referred to as the A. Maceo Smith Building) and 1100 Commerce Street (also the Earle Cabell Building).[1]

1. Although Darby referenced the Earle Cabell Building during his testimony, the evidence reflects that the request

525 S. Griffin has a parking lot which is managed by the General Services Administration (GSA). (Tr. 51) There are 169 spaces in the parking lot; DOL has 48 agency-paid parking spaces as part of its lease agreement. (Tr. 52) There are nine different agencies, including DOL, which occupy space at 525 S. Griffin. (Tr. 52) DOL is the largest agency in the building. Not all parking spaces are assigned to a specific agency through its lease agreement, and the remaining spaces are available to individuals. The individuals pay GSA directly to park in a space and GSA administers the entire parking process. (Tr. 52-53) There is a waiting list for the next available parking spaces. (Tr. 50).

On March 17, 2009,[2] Darby sent an email to Pettit, stating the following:

> We understand the parking lot behind 525 S. Griffin will soon close. The NCFLL recognizes that the Department has absolutely no control over this situation.
>
> We propose negotiations on the parking lot located at 525 S. Griffin, specifically the spaces controlled by DOL. The NCFLL is interested in making a number of these available to BUEs in direct proportion with the size of the NCFLL BU vs. non-BUEs. It is patently unfair that non-BUEs have the lion's share of these spaces.
>
> Please let me know OASAM's position in this matter. Thank you.

(G.C. Ex. 2 at 3; Tr. 14-15).

Earsie Johnson responded on March 20, stating:

> We certainly empathize with the employees over the loss of the public parking across from the A. Maceo Smith building. As you indicated, we do not have any control over the parking availability in downtown Dallas, but have tried to be proactive in providing helpful information to our employees to assist them with locating alternative parking spots. (see attached).
>
> The parking lot behind the A. Maceo Smith building belongs to and is controlled by GSA. GSA maintains the access list and manages the process by which employees receive parking spots should one become available. Parking places that are allocated to a specific agency are determined between that agency and GSA, and are in strict accordance with DOL policy and we do not have the latitude to negotiate or break a Departmental policy.
>
> I hope this clarifies our position on this issue. Please let me know if you have any questions.

(G.C. Ex. 2 at 2; Tr. 16-17).

Darby reiterated the Union's request to bargain by emails dated March 23, April 13 and June 4. (G.C. Ex. 2; Tr. 17) The Respondent did not reply to these emails. (Tr. 17-18) Sometime in June, during a regularly scheduled labor-management meeting in Dallas, Pettit and Darby discussed the issue of parking and the Respondent assumed that the matter was concluded. (Tr. 61, 79) On June 18, however, the Union filed the unfair labor practice charge in this matter. (G.C. Ex. 1(a)).

The parties have a current National Agreement (NA)(G.C. Ex. 3) Article 2, Section 1 (Governing Laws and Regulations, Precedence of Laws and Regulations) states:

> In the administration of all matters covered by this Agreement, officials and employees are governed by existing or future laws and regulations of appropriate authorities; by published Department and/or Agency policies and regulations in existence at the time this Agreement was approved; and by subsequently published Department and/or Agency policies and regulations required by law or by the regulations of appropriate authorities.

Section 6 – Past Practices states:

> It is agreed and understood that any prior working conditions and practices and understandings which are not specifically covered by the Agreement or in conflict with it shall not be changed unless mutually agreed to by the parties.

(G.C. Ex. 3, p. 4-6).

The NA does not contain an article on employee parking, although Article 17 does deal with GSA Vehicles or Lease Vehicles. Section 2 contains a reference to employee POVs, and specifically states "...Where parking is provided for GOVs, employees

to bargain at issue in this matter only related to the building located at 525 S. Griffin.

[2] All dates are in 2009, unless specifically noted.

may park their POVs in vacant Agency spaces, provided that such use is not prohibited by law, regulation, or lease." (G.C. Ex. 3, p. 52).

The Department of Labor Manual Series (DLMS 2) contains the Respondent's internal regulations and policies regarding the administration and operation of the Department, including among other things, parking at DOL facilities. Chapter 520 contains the Parking Policy and was last updated on May 7, 2004. (Agency Ex. 1) Chapter 526 sets forth the parking priorities and states "The following descending order of priority will govern allocation of DOL controlled parking spaces and will include the best interests of the DOL as judged by the Director, BOC, or by delegation to the Regional Administrator, OASAM in regional offices, or other responsible administrative authorities in other facilities…." *Id.* at 4. The policy lists in order: official needs; employees with disabilities; official necessity; van pools, and carpools. *Id.*

POSITIONS OF THE PARTIES

General Counsel

The General Counsel (GC) asserts that the Respondent violated section 7116(a)(1) and (5) when it refused to engage in mid-bargaining over parking with the Union. The GC asserts that the Respondent offered no legitimate defense for this failure.

Specifically, the GC asserts that the Respondent's "covered by" defense should be rejected, citing *U.S. Dep't of HHS, Soc. Sec. Admin., Balt., Md.*, 47 FLRA 1004 (1993)(*SSA Baltimore*) and *Soc. Sec. Admin.*, 64 FLRA 199 (2009)(*SSA*). The GC notes that the parties' current NA (G.C. Ex. 3) does not contain an article concerning employee parking, and the matter therefore, is not expressly addressed in the parties' NA. The GC also argues that Article 2 of the parties' NA in conjunction with DLMS 2 must also be rejected as a defense to the refusal to bargain mid-term regarding employee parking.

The GC further argues that the DLMS 2, Chapter 520, et seq., does not preclude bargaining with the Union over employee parking. Under section 7117(b) of the Statute, an agency regulation does not bar negotiation over an otherwise negotiable proposal unless the agency has demonstrated a compelling need for the regulation under Subpart F, 2424.50 of the Authority's Regulations. *See AFGE, Local 2139, Nat'l Council of Field Labor Locals*, 61 FLRA 654, 656 (2006). The Respondent has made no such assertion nor has it presented evidence to demonstrate a compelling need to issue DLMS 2, Chapter 520. Thus, the existence of DLMS 2, Chapter 520 does not bar negotiation over employee parking.

Further, the GC argues that the policy does not preclude bargaining with the Union over parking. While the parking lot is controlled by GSA, there are forty-eight parking spaces allocated to various DOL agencies that were included within the normal leasing arrangements for space and are under the control of DOL agencies. The Respondent could bargain about these particular parking spaces, even under its own policy.

Finally, the GC argues that the Respondent has not established a practice where the Union has agreed to be bound by the terms of the DLMS 2 as part of the NA. The GC therefore asserts that the Respondent has failed to offer any legitimate defense to its refusal to bargain with the Union regarding parking and a violation of the Statute as alleged in the complaint, must be found.

Respondent

The Respondent denies that it violated the Statute as alleged in the complaint, asserting that it and the Union have a long-standing past practice that matters regarding parking at DOL facilities were governed by DLMS 2. Under Authority precedent, a past practice regarding working conditions constitutes an amendment to the parties' collective bargaining agreement (CBA), and, as such, the practice is "covered by" the CBA and not subject to mid-term bargaining. Under these circumstances, the Respondent's refusal to bargain was justified and the complaint should be dismissed.

ANALYSIS AND CONCLUSIONS

This case involves the Union's request to engage in mid-term bargaining over the parking spaces under the Respondent's control at the federal building located at 525 S. Griffin Street. The parties are in agreement that employee parking can be a proper subject of bargaining. The Respondent however, asserts that in this instance, it has no obligation to bargain mid-term over parking. Specifically, as noted above, the Respondent asserts that the subject of parking has been controlled by its regulations set forth in the DLMS 2 for a considerable period of time and such practice has become a part of the NA. Therefore, the Respondent is not obligated to bargain over the Union's mid-term bargaining request because the matter is "covered by" the parties' agreement.

The "covered by" doctrine is set forth in *SSA Baltimore* and applies only in cases alleging an unlawful refusal to bargain. *SSA,* 64 FLRA at 202. In particular, the doctrine is "available to a party claiming that it is not obligated to bargain because it has already bargained over the subject at issue." *U.S. Dep't of Energy, Western Area Power Admin., Golden, Colo.*, 56 FLRA 9, 12 (2000). The doctrine has two prongs. *U.S. Customs Serv., Customs Mgmt Ctr., Miami, Fla.*, 56 FLRA 809, 814 (2000). Under the first prong, a party properly may refuse to bargain over a matter that is expressly addressed in the parties' agreement. *Id.* Under the second prong, a party properly may refuse to bargain if a matter is inseparably bound up with, and thus, an aspect of a subject covered by the parties' agreement. *Id.* Although not expressly limited to situations like the instant case where an agency refuses to engage in union-initiated, mid-term bargaining, the covered by doctrine derives from, and is most naturally applied in, this type of scenario. *SSA, 64 FLRA* at 202.

The parties have engaged in little negotiation regarding parking. There is no evidence that there have been any previous requests by the Union for mid-term bargaining regarding parking. The one case cited by both parties, *AFGE, Local 2139,* 64 FLRA at 654, concerned the negotiability of a proposal to continue to pay for employee parking at the El Paso location. The Respondent relies on this case to assert that the Union was in agreement that the DLMS 2 was the proper source for dealing with parking issues, while the Union denies that its request that DOL follow the DLMS 2 was any sort of waiver of its right to bargain. In that case, the Union proposed that "The Agency will provide parking at the El Paso Field Office for bargaining unit employees who use their privately owned vehicles (POV) a majority of the time on Government business." The Union argued before the Authority that the proposal conformed to DLMS 2, Chapter 525.

As stated by both parties, in order to find the existence of a past practice, there must be a showing that the practice has been consistently exercised over a significant period of time and followed by both parties, or followed by one party and not challenged by the other. *U.S. Patent & Trademark Office,* 57 FLRA 185, 191 (2001). While the evidence indicates that the Respondent has followed the practice of using the DLMS 2 with regard to employee parking at its various locations, there is no evidence that the Union has acquiesced to this practice. A review of DLMS 2 does not reveal any prohibition against bargaining with the exclusive representative on the issue of parking. I do not find, that the single proposal noted above, although consistent with the DLMS 2, is sufficient to show that the Union has agreed to follow the DLMS 2 in all aspects of employee parking at various DOL facilities or that the Union has waived its right to bargain mid-term about parking.

Therefore, the Respondent's defense that resolution of parking issues by reference to the DLMS 2 has been established by past practice and has been incorporated into and covered by the parties' current NA, is rejected. *See AFGE, Local 2128 and U.S., Dept of Defense, Def. Cont. Mgmt. Agency, Dist. West, Hurst, Tex.*, 58 FLRA 519, 523 (2003). The issue of parking is not expressly addressed in the parties' agreement. The Respondent does not point to any specific article in the NA that deals with parking, rather it looks to Article 2, Section 1 as incorporating the DLMS 2 into the NA. I do not find, however, that Article 2, Section 1 of the agreement is sufficient to incorporate the DLMS 2, Chapter 525 into the agreement and therefore, it is not inseparably bound up with, and thus, an aspect of, a subject covered by the parties' agreement. *SSA,* 64 FLRA at 202.

Even assuming the evidence was sufficient to establish a past practice, I would reject the Respondent's covered by defense. In that regard, Article 2, Section 1 is inadequate to establish that the issue of parking is covered by the parties' agreement. The language has been carried over intact from contract to contract, except for elimination of the reference to Federal Personnel Manual. (*See* G.C. Ex. 4 at 4; G.C. Ex. 5 at 4; G.C. Ex. 6 at 4; G.C. Ex. 8 at 3) The language of the article itself, with its generalized references to policies and regulations, is not sufficient to incorporate the parking regulations into the NA. Therefore, the Respondent has failed to meet either prong of the covered by doctrine, since there is no specific article in the agreement related to parking, and the evidence fails to show that parking is inseparably bound up with and thus, a part of the agreement.

In this case, the Union has requested mid-term bargaining over the apportionment of parking spaces controlled by the Respondent. Since the subject of parking is not covered by the parties' agreement, the Respondent was obligated to bargain. The Respondent's refusal to bargain mid-term over parking arrangements at 525 S. Griffin was therefore in violation of section 7116(a)(1) and (5) of the Statute.

Accordingly, I recommend that the Authority adopt the following Order:

ORDER

Pursuant to section 2423.41(c) of the Authority's Rules and Regulations and section 7118 of the Federal Service Labor-Management Relations Statute (the Statute), it is hereby ordered that the U.S. Department of Labor, Office of the Assistant Secretary for Administration and Management, Dallas, Texas (Respondent), shall:

1. Cease and desist from:

(a) Refusing to bargain mid-term with the American Federation of Government Employees, National Council of Field Labor Locals, Local 2139, AFL-CIO (the Union), the exclusive representative of certain of our employees, regarding employee parking at 525 S. Griffin, Dallas, Texas.

(b) In any like or related manner, interfering with, restraining, or coercing its employees in the exercise of their rights assured by the Statute.

2. Take the following affirmative action in order to effectuate the purposes and policies of the Statute:

(a) Upon request, bargain in good faith with the Union, to the extent required by law, regarding employee parking at 525 S. Griffin Street, Dallas, Texas.

(b) Post at its facilities where bargaining unit employees represented by the Union are located, copies of the attached Notice on forms to be furnished by the Federal Labor Relations Authority. Upon receipt of such forms, they shall be signed by the Regional Administrator, and shall be posted and maintained for 60 consecutive days thereafter, in conspicuous places, including all bulletin boards and other places where notices to employees are customarily posted. Reasonable steps shall be taken to ensure that such Notices are not altered, defaced, or covered by any other material.

(c) Pursuant to section 2423.41(e) of the Authority's Rules and Regulations, notify the Regional Director, Dallas Region, Federal Labor Relations Authority, in writing, within 30 days from the date of this Order, as to what steps have been taken to comply herewith.

Issued, Washington, D.C. August 4, 2010

SUSAN E. JELEN
Administrative Law Judge

65 FLRA No. 146

UNITED STATES
DEPARTMENT OF THE TREASURY
INTERNAL REVENUE SERVICE
(Activity)

and

NATIONAL TREASURY
EMPLOYEES UNION
(Petitioner/Exclusive Representative)

WA-RP-09-0036

DECISION AND ORDER
ON REVIEW

March 31, 2011

Before the Authority: Carol Waller Pope, Chairman, and Thomas M. Beck and Ernest DuBester, Members[1]

I. Statement of the Case

This case is before the Authority on an application for review (application) filed by the Petitioner/Exclusive Representative (Union) under § 2422.31 of the Authority's Regulations.[2] The Activity filed an opposition. Pursuant to § 2429.9 of the Authority's Regulations, the American Federation of Government Employees (AFGE) requested, and received, permission to file an amicus curiae brief (amicus brief). The Activity filed a reply (reply) to AFGE's amicus brief.

The Union filed a petition to determine whether the position of Internal Revenue Police Officer (Officer) is properly within the bargaining unit represented by the Union. The Regional Director (RD) determined that the Officer position performs security work that directly affects national security and, therefore, should be excluded from the unit. In an order issued following the filing of the application for review, the Authority granted the Union's application and deferred action on the merits.

On review of the merits, and for the reasons that follow, we reverse the RD's Decision and Order, and we order the RD to take appropriate action consistent with this decision.

II. Background and RD's Decision

A. Background

The Activity utilizes three computer centers -- collectively known as the Enterprise Computing Center Division -- that oversee "the operations and maintenance requirements for all of the computers that run the [Activity's] tax processing system." RD's Decision at 2. The most critical of these computer centers is located in Martinsburg, West Virginia (the Center). The Center has a "Level 5" security rating -- the highest possible security rating under the Department of Justice rating system -- and is restricted to "authorized persons only." *Id.*

The Center contains the Master File, a computer system that contains the final processed tax return information for all individual and business tax returns in the country. *Id.* at 3. The Center also has a "mainframe computer" that is a "direct processing and handling engine" for five of the ten tax submission processing centers in the country. *Id.* Additionally, the Center has a "physical [l]edger" that essentially serves as "the nation's balance sheet," containing "a statement of receipts and disbursements." *Id.* at 3-4. The Center handles functions that cannot be performed at the other two computer centers; incapacitation of the Center would greatly impede the Activity's ability to process tax information. *Id.* at 3. The Center also is designated as a Continuity of Operations (COOP) site. *Id.* at 4. In the event of a "catastrophe," high ranking officials from the Department of the Treasury and the Activity who are "essential" to the continuity of the Activity's functions may congregate at the Center. *Id.*

The Center employs twelve Officers who are tasked with "protect[ing] the security" of the Center and its people. *Id.* It is the only Activity facility that has Officers. Officers have received extensive federal law enforcement training and carry firearms, batons, cell phones, and communication devices; they are also required to be present twenty-four hours a day, every day of the year.

1. Member Beck's separate opinion, dissenting in part, is set forth at the end of this decision.

2. As discussed further below, the Union argues that the Regional Director failed to apply established law. Section 2422.31 of the Authority's Regulations provides, in pertinent part, that the Authority may grant an application when "[t]here is a genuine issue over whether the Regional Director has[] . . . [f]ailed to apply established law[.]" 5 C.F.R. § 2422.31(c)(3)(i).

Officers have several duties. They are stationed at the Center's front gatehouse where they check incoming vehicles and passengers for proper identification and authorization to enter the building. *Id.* at 4. The Officers also perform vehicle patrols of the Center's grounds. *Id.* at 5. Additionally, Officers perform foot patrols of the Center's interior. As part of these patrols, Officers check card readers to ensure that they are functioning, and they also watch for suspicious individuals and may ask individuals to verify whether they have proper identification, or "challenge" their badges. *Id.* Contract security guards (Guards) also work the front gate and check card readers. *Id.* at 4, 5. Moreover, Guards are primarily responsible for determining which individuals may actually enter the building and providing visitors with identity badges. *Id.* at 5.

Officers have access to all areas within the Center and perform duties in areas to which access is "highly restricted." *Id.* Two of these highly restricted areas are the Treasury Secure Room (Secure Room) and the Treasury Cage (Cage). The Secure Room contains information that is more sensitive than the information contained in the Cage, and is used primarily by the Secretary of Treasury. *Id.* at 4. Officers do not have regular access to the Secure Room, but they can follow certain procedures to access the room in the event of an emergency. *Id.* at 5. Officers usually patrol the area adjacent to the Secure Room during a COOP event. *Id.* at 6. The Cage is a fenced-in room containing sensitive documents that are not maintained anywhere else in the country. *Id.* at 5; Tr. at 95, 111. Only authorized individuals, including Officers, may enter the Cage.

Officers also have duties during a COOP event. In particular, officers are extensively involved in the execution of COOP security plans and regularly participate in COOP preparation exercises. RD's Decision at 6. Moreover, during an actual COOP event, Officers must: patrol and monitor various areas in the Center; ensure that only authorized individuals enter the COOP area; and oversee the transfer of sensitive material from the Cage to the Secure Room.

B. RD's Decision

The RD stated that, under § 7112(b)(6) of the Statute, a bargaining unit is not appropriate if it includes "any employee engaged in . . . security work which directly affects the national security." RD's Decision at 6 (quoting 5 U.S.C. § 7112(b)(6)). Applying this section, the RD concluded that Officers' duties involve national security within the meaning of § 7112(b)(6) and that they perform security work.[3] *Id.* at 7-9. With regard to whether their duties directly affect national security, the RD stated that an employee's duties directly affect national security if they have "a straight bearing or unbroken connection that produces a material influence or alter[]ation" on national security. *Id.* at 9 (quoting *Dep't of Energy, Oak Ridge Operations, Oak Ridge, Tenn.*, 4 FLRA 644, 655 (1980) (*Oak Ridge*)).

As an initial matter, the RD found that the Officers' "routine foot patrols of the perimeter fence and the buildings" and "their work at the main gate" do not satisfy this standard. *Id.* at 10. However, the RD also found that the Officers' "access to and protection of" the Secure Room and the Cage directly affect national security. *Id.* With regard to the Secure Room, the RD acknowledged that Officers "do not routinely access" that Room, but found that " it is their duty to [e]nsure its protection in the event of an alarm or during a COOP event." *Id.* With regard to the Cage, the RD found that Officers "regularly patrol the . . . Cage and particularly at night, will walk through to [e]nsure that no documents are visible or computers left on." *Id.* In this connection, the RD stated that although the Officers "may not be required themselves to access or understand the documents or materials with which they may come into contact in the . . . Cage, it is their job to secure and protect this critical material." *Id.* Further, the RD stated that in a COOP event, the Officers "are responsible for guarding the sensitive materials that are moved from" the Cage to the Secure Room. *Id.* Moreover, the RD stated that although the Officers' performance of the foregoing duties is merely "occasional, . . . [it] is not incidental to their security work but is part and parcel of their mission to protect" the facility and its personnel. *Id.*

Based on the foregoing, the RD concluded that Officers are engaged in security work that directly affects national security within the meaning of § 7112(b)(6) of the Statute and, thus, should be excluded from the unit. *Id.*

III. Positions of the Parties

A. Union's Application for Review

The Union asserts that the RD failed to apply established law when he concluded that the Officers' work directly affects national security. *See* Brief by the Union in Support of Application for Review (Brief) at 12. According to the Union, any effect that the

3. The Union does not dispute either of these conclusions. *See* Brief by the Union in Support of Application for Review at 9 n.3.

Officers have on national security is limited by "low levels of discretion and by the existence of several intervening layers of personnel and processes[.]" *Id.* at 20-21. In this connection, the Union contends that the Officers' effect on national security is made indirect by: (1) the duties performed by the Guards; (2) the requirement that Officers must report serious matters to their supervisors; and (3) the fact that Officers do not write or implement security plans and are not the only personnel to respond to emergencies. *Id.* at 19-21. Based on the foregoing, the Union asserts that Officers' positions are similar to the position at issue in *United States Department of Agriculture, Food Safety and Inspection Service,* 61 FLRA 397 (2005) (*USDA*). Brief at 18-19.

In addition, the Union asserts that the Officers' duties with regard to the Secure Room do not directly affect national security. In this regard, the Union claims that: Officers do not access the Secure Room when they conduct their patrols; there are Officers who never have entered that Room; and "[o]nly one of the officers who testified at hearing had ever even entered the Room, and that was only once." *Id.* at 17 (footnote omitted). Also in this regard, the Union claims that "[i]f a special need to enter the [R]oom arises (i.e., to check an alarm that has been triggered)," then the Officer "must first sign out a special key and passcode from a safe in the command center[,]" and the individuals who staff the command center "would release the key and passcode to the [Officer] only after confirming the [Officer's] authority to enter the Secure Room[] and arranging for an escort to accompany the [Officer]." *Id.* (citing Tr. at 220-21, 419-20).

Finally, the Union contends that the Officers' duties with regard to the Cage do not directly affect national security. The Union relies on one Officer's testimony that, "once in the Cage, the [Officers] view and have access to very little -- nothing more than can be seen by the naked eye." *Id.* at 16 (citing Tr. at 356-57). Also according to the Union, "[i]n the event that an officer were to see something suspicious, or come across documents left unsecured, he would look for another person authorized to remedy the problem." *Id.* (citing Tr. at 358).

B. Activity's Opposition

As a preliminary matter, the Activity moves to strike the Union's brief in support of its application. According to the Activity, although the Authority's Regulations permit parties to file an "application for review," they do not permit parties to file briefs in support. Opp'n at 2 (quoting 5 C.F.R. § 2422.31(a)). Rather, the Agency contends that briefs are permitted only *after* the Authority grants an application for review. *Id.* (citing 5 C.F.R. § 2422.31(g)).[4]

With regard to the merits of the Union's application, the Activity contends that the RD properly concluded that the Center's work concerns national security, that Officers perform security work, and that the Officers' duties directly affect national security. *Id.* at 10, 14, 16. For support, the Agency cites: *Social Security Administration, Baltimore, Maryland,* 59 FLRA 137 (2003) (Chairman Cabaniss concurring and then-Member Pope concurring in part and dissenting in part on other grounds) (*SSA*); and *United States Department of the Treasury, Internal Revenue Service*, 62 FLRA 298 (2007) (Chairman Cabaniss and then-Member Pope concurring) (*IRS*).

C. AFGE's Amicus Brief

AFGE argues that, in concluding that Officers perform duties that directly affect national security, the RD failed to apply established law. In this connection, AFGE asserts that Officers rarely exercise independent judgment and, instead, generally follow "plans and procedures designed by others." Amicus Brief at 3. In addition, according to AFGE, the RD erroneously focused on what the Officers guard and patrol, rather than on the duties they perform while they guard and patrol. *Id.* at 2. Further, AFGE requests that the Authority "re-examine its current test for exclusion under § 7112(b)(6)[,]" *id.* at 8, which AFGE asserts often speculates as to a possible "chain of events" and "future duties" and how they could affect future circumstances.[5] *Id.* at 5-6.

---

4. 5 C.F.R. § 2422.31, "Application for review of a Regional Director Decision and Order[,]" states, in relevant part:

> (a) *Filing an application for review.* A party must file an application for review with the Authority within sixty (60) days of the Regional Director's Decision and Order.
>
> . . . .
>
> (g) *Briefs if review is granted.* If the Authority does not rule on the issue(s) in the application for review in its order granting review, the Authority may, in its discretion, afford the parties an opportunity to file briefs.

5. As neither party to this proceeding has requested reexamination of the Authority's current § 7112(b)(6) test, we do not address further AFGE's request. *See, e.g., UPS, Inc. v. Mitchell*, 451 U.S. 56, 61 n.2 (1981) (declining to resolve issue raised solely by amicus).

D. Activity's Reply to Amicus Brief

The Activity contends that "[c]onsideration of the national security implications of the thing being guarded is an *essential* part of any analysis of whether the security work is 'guarding, shielding or protecting' something that directly affects national security." Activity's Reply at 6-7. In addition, the Activity disagrees with AFGE's assertion that the Authority should modify its test for exclusion under § 7112(b)(6).

IV. Preliminary Issue

As stated previously, the Activity argues that the Authority should strike the Union's brief in support of the application. As the Activity correctly states, § 2422.31(a) of the Authority's Regulations authorizes parties to file an "application for review[.]" 5 C.F.R. § 2422.31(a). However, this section does not state that parties may *only* file an application, and nothing in § 2422.31 suggests that a party is prohibited from submitting a brief as part of its application for review. In addition, although § 2422.31(g) of the Authority's Regulations provides that the Authority has discretion to allow parties to file briefs after it grants an application for review, § 2422.31(g) does not state that briefs are permissible *only* in that situation. Accordingly, we deny the Activity's motion to strike the Union's brief.

V. Analysis and Conclusions

As the RD noted, under § 7112(b)(6) of the Statute, a bargaining unit is not appropriate if it includes any employee engaged in "security work which directly affects national security[.]" 5 U.S.C. § 7112(b)(6). It is undisputed that Officers are engaged in security work that involves national security. Consistent with the application for review, the issue is whether the RD erred by finding that the Officers' work *directly affects* national security, as required by § 7112(b)(6).

The Authority has interpreted and applied § 7112(b)(6) for more than thirty years -- since the Statute's enactment. In *Oak Ridge*, the Authority considered the "ordinary meaning" of the term "directly affects" and found that it means "a straight bearing or unbroken connection that produces a material influence or alter[]ation." 4 FLRA at 655. The plain terms of this definition -- that any bearing on national security must be "straight[,]" any connection must be "unbroken[,]" and any influence or alteration must be "material[,]" *id.* -- make it clear that § 7112(b)(6) does not permit the exclusion of positions merely because they have *some* relationship to national security.[6]

Applying § 7112(b)(6), the Authority, since *Oak Ridge*, has found that positions directly affect national security only in limited circumstances. For example, when there are "no intervening steps between the employees' failure" to satisfactorily perform their duties "and the potential effect [of that failure] on national security[,]" the Authority has found the requisite direct connection. *U.S. Dep't of the Air Force, Davis-Monthan Air Force Base, Ariz.*, 62 FLRA 332, 335 (2008) (Chairman Cabaniss concurring). By contrast, where an employee's role in protecting national security is "limited[,]" the Authority has not found the requisite direct connection. *U.S. Dep't of the Air Force, Tyndall Air Force Base, Tyndall AFB, Fla.*, 65 FLRA 610, 614 (2011) (*Tyndall AFB*); *USDA*, 61 FLRA at 402. Similarly, where employees must "go through another individual" before they may conduct a more extensive review of a situation that they believe may pose a security risk, the Authority has declined to find a direct effect. *USDA*, 61 FLRA at 403. *Cf. Tyndall AFB*, 65 FLRA at 613 (officers were responsible for evacuating and cordoning off areas containing suspicious packages, and preventing unauthorized individuals from entering the areas, but other positions were responsible for eliminating the threat posed by the packages). The Authority also has declined to find a direct effect where duties were "carried out in accordance with established procedures and provide[d] little opportunity for making choices[.]" *Oak Ridge*, 4 FLRA at 659. Further, the mere fact that employees' work may have a relationship to important national interests is not sufficient to find a direct effect on national security. *See, e.g., USDA*, 61 FLRA at 402-03 (declining to exclude inspectors who were involved in "guard[ing], shield[ing], and protect[ing] the food supply from the importation of unsafe, adulterated, damaged or ineligible food products[]").

The Authority's precedent applying § 7112(b)(6) is consistent with not only the plain wording of that statutory section, but also important statutory rights and policies discussed in *Oak Ridge*. In this connection, in *Oak Ridge*, the Authority emphasized that

> [e]xclusion from an appropriate unit deprives employees of the opportunity under the

---

6. We note that the dissent does not: squarely address the plain wording of "directly affects[;]" challenge how it has been interpreted since *Oak Ridge*; or explain how it permits any conclusion other than a conclusion that this language "should be interpreted narrowly[.]" Dissent at 12.

> Statute to determine whether or not they wish to be represented by a labor organization and of the opportunity to engage in collective bargaining with respect to conditions of employment through labor organizations. Labor organizations and collective bargaining in the civil service have been determined by the Congress to be "in the public interest." 5 U.S.C. § 7101(a). *Therefore*, the term "national security" must be interpreted to include only [certain activities].

Oak Ridge, 4 FLRA at 655 (emphasis added). This passage, which underscores the importance of the statutory rights and policies involved in this case, supports a narrow application of the "directly affects" requirement. Such an application is necessary to ensure that Congress' determination in § 7101(a) to "safeguard[] the public interest" through the institution of collective bargaining for federal employees is fully effectuated, rather than being unreasonably limited by constricted interpretations of the Statute that are not compelled by the Statute's plain language.

In addition, as particularly relevant in this case, the Authority's precedent applying § 7112(b)(6) is consistent with Congress' determination that federal employees who perform guard duties may be included in bargaining units with non-guard employees. In this connection, Executive Order (E.O.) 11,838, which preceded the Statute, amended E.O. 11,491, in pertinent part, "by eliminating the requirement that guards be represented in separate units and only by labor organizations which represented guards exclusively." *U.S. Dep't of the Treasury, Bureau of the Mint*, 2 FLRA 457, 460 (1980). In this connection, in a report that accompanied the issuance of E.O. 11,838, the Federal Labor Relations Council stated that "[g]uards have demonstrated no conflict of interest in performing their duties[]" and "[s]o long as the existing prohibition on strikes by federal employees is continued, such conflicts as might exist in the private sector need not be anticipated." *Labor-Mgmt. Relations in the Fed. Sector* (1975), at 30. This principle was continued when Congress enacted the Statute. *See Bureau of Indian Affairs, Wind River Agency, Fort Washakie, Wyo.*, 29 FLRA 935, 936, 938 (1987) (noting regional director's finding in this regard and declining to reconsider the policy created by E.O. 11,838). Thus, unlike certain other statutory exclusions -- such as management officials under § 7112(b)(1) -- there is no inherent conflict of interest arising when bargaining unit members perform guard duties. *Cf. Dep't of the Navy, Automatic Data Processing Selection Office*, 7 FLRA 172, 175 (1981) (noting "the intent reflected in the legislative history to exclude . . . officials who are identified with management and whose inclusion would result in an apparent conflict of interest[]").

Here, the RD found that the Officers' duties directly affect national security based on the Officers': (1) access to and protection of the Secure Room; (2) access to and protection of the Cage; and (3) guarding of sensitive materials when those materials are moved during a COOP. *See* RD's Decision at 10. For the following reasons, applying the terms of § 7112(b)(6) and the well-established Authority precedent cited above, we find that the record does not support the RD's conclusion that these duties (the disputed duties) demonstrate a direct effect on national security.[7]

As an initial matter, other individuals play an important role in securing the Center. In this connection, Guards also work the front gate and check card readers, and it is Guards, not Officers, who are primarily responsible for: (1) determining which individuals may actually enter the building; and (2) providing visitors with identity badges. *Id.* at 4-5. By controlling access to the facility, the Guards' duties have a substantial impact on the security of the facility. Further, the record indicates that Guards "man the command center," including the video monitors in that center, Tr. at 344, and dispatch Officers if Guards see something "that shouldn't be[,]" *id.* at 199. In this connection, one Officer testified that if he was not nearby when someone needed to be apprehended, the Guard could apprehend the individual and, in those situations, "would be the first line of defense[.]" *Id.* at 387. Another individual testified that Guards "can do . . . walk-throughs of the building, the card readers" and "help [Officers] in that respect[,]" and that although, "because of manpower, mainly, [the Guards are] . . . at the fixed post at the gate, . . . they can and they have helped do walk-throughs of th[e] buildings." *Id.* at 217. In addition to Guards, an information technology specialist testified that "[e]mployees are always told that security begins with us, so we're supposed to question if someone is not wearing their badge properly, if there is a suspicious package or if we get bomb threats," *id.* at 308, and that she "ha[s] actually challenged some people that didn't have their badges on," *id.* at 309. That employees other than Officers play such an important role in securing the

---

7. There is no basis for the dissent's statement that this decision "modif[ies] the Authority's approach to exclusion under § 7112(b)(6) of the Statute." Dissent at 12. We expressly apply the Authority's longstanding approach to § 7112(b)(6), as underscored by our conclusion that the RD "failed to apply *established law*" regarding § 7112(b)(6). *Infra* at 11 (emphasis added).

Center supports a conclusion that Officers do not directly affect national security.

In addition, the disputed duties occur within rooms that are accessible only by keys and/or card readers, and those rooms are within the Center, which, as stated previously, is accessible only by individuals who have been screened at the front gate. These additional layers of security render it less probable that the Officers' performance of the disputed duties within the secured Center would produce "a material influence or [alteration]" on national security. *SSA*, 59 FLRA at 143.

Further, in addition to the disputed duties, the Officers perform numerous other duties, including: checking incoming vehicles and passengers for proper identification and authorization to enter the building; performing vehicle patrols of the Center's grounds; and engaging in foot patrols of other areas of the Center's interior. RD's Decision at 5. That the Officers perform numerous, important duties unrelated to the disputed duties related to the Secure Room and the Cage is relevant to determining whether the Officers should be excluded from the unit.[8]

Moreover, the nature of the disputed duties does not demonstrate a straight or unbroken connection to national security. As an initial matter, we emphasize that the Officers are not stationed outside either the Secure Room or the Cage, checking badges of individuals who wish to enter the rooms. Rather, the Officers check on the rooms only as part of their foot patrols through the entire Center.

With regard to the Secure Room in particular, the record indicates that Officers generally do not access that Room. *See, e.g.*, Tr. at 420, 436 (Officer's testimony that he does not go into the Secure Room on a regular basis and had been informed that he was to "go into [it] only when [he] need[s] to[]" do so); *id.* at 356, 383 (other Officer's testimony that he "do[es] not have access to[]" the Secure Room). In particular, the record indicates that the circumstances under which Officers access that Room are limited. In this connection, one Officer testified only that he had "opened the door for the person that's supposed to be there[,]" that he had "checked a motion alarm before and c[o]me back out[,]" and that he sometimes checks "glass-break alarms" from the outside of the room. *Id.* at 418-19. In fact, that Officer testified that he does not know what is contained in, or what is done in, the Secure Room. *Id.* at 418 & 436. Further, in order to access the Room, Officers must obtain the assistance of other individuals. Specifically, one witness testified that the command center has an envelope with a sealed key, and the individuals in the command center must "make phone calls[] . . . to notify people that you're going in that room, and then you use that key and you can get in[.]" *Id.* at 220-21. As to the Officers' protection of the Secure Room, the record evidence is limited. For example, an Officer testified that "as long as the door [to the Room] is closed, that's usually enough[.]" *Id.* at 420.

Thus, Officers access the Secure Room only rarely and in limited circumstances, and they must obtain the assistance of other individuals in order to access it. In addition, the record evidence of their duties in protecting the Secure Room is limited. In these circumstances, we find that the record does not reflect that Officers' duties with respect to the Secure Room have "a straight bearing or unbroken connection that produces a material influence or [alteration]" on national security. *SSA*, 59 FLRA at 143.

With regard to the Officers' duties in and around the Cage, one Officer testified that when he enters the Cage, he's "checking for fire hazards, anything that would threaten the facility, any danger, and I don't do it on a daily basis." Tr. at 435. According to that Officer, employees work in the Cage during the weekday, *id.* at 421-22, and consequently, if he sees files laying out, he "wouldn't bother to look[]" because he would "assume somebody is working there." *Id.* at 454. In this connection, he stated that he has "never read [anything] on anybody's desk[.]" *Id.* at 453. Further, when asked whether he "look[s] for things like computers being on[,]" he testified: "I do not pay attention to the computers at all. I don't know who is in -- what people are doing in there. I don't know what

8. The RD's findings and the record do not establish how frequently the Officers perform the disputed duties. In this connection, the RD found both that Officers' "duties relative to" the Secure Room and the Cage are only "occasional[]" and that "[e]vidence demonstrates that [Officers] regularly patrol the . . . Cage and particularly at night, will walk through to insure that no documents are visible or computers left on." RD's Decision at 10. With regard to the record, one Officer testified that "when I'm doing a patrol of the annex, I would generally take a tour through" the Cage, Tr. at 357, while another Officer testified: "I don't go in there really unless I'm called, because if I'm doing my foot patrol through there, or a card reader, I go around the outside of it; and[] . . . if something is showing smoke or something, or I'm requested to go in there, I will go in, but it's not a regular thing for me to go in there." *Id.* at 421. Accordingly, it is not clear whether Officers "regularly patrol the Cage area" and "the interior of the Cage." Dissent at 15. In any event, that Officers perform numerous other duties indicates that the disputed duties are not the sole focus of their responsibilities, which informs our determination as to their unit status even if it is not a dispositive consideration.

they're doing and what they have on and what they need to have on." *Id.* at 435.

As for Officers on the night shift, another Officer testified that when he patrols the Cage, he looks for "computers that have been left on, any unsafe conditions that may exist." *Id.* at 358. For example, he said that "[t]here have probably been twice, in recent memory, where somebody has reported smoke, the smell of smoke[.]" *Id.* However, he also testified that he has "never found" a computer left on. *Id.* at 357. He further testified that, if he found a live computer on, then he would "attempt to get somebody to remedy the problem[,]" and "[i]f [he] can't find anybody in the area, [he] know[s] how to power down a computer and you just turn it off. That would be the extent of what [he] would do." *Id.* at 358. He also testified that he would also "look[] for a possibility that somebody left files or papers out[,]" *id.* at 373, but that he's "never seen any[]" documents and files lying out because "[g]enerally, everything is secured when [the employees who work in the Cage] leave." *Id.* at 357-58. As with the other Officer, he testified that he does not know what is performed in the Cage. *Id.* at 373.

Thus, the record indicates that other individuals work directly with the materials in the Cage. The record also indicates that at night, Officers who enter the Cage generally do not see documents left out or computers left on, and even if they did see a computer on, they would first contact someone else to address it and would turn it off only if someone was not available to address it. Given these circumstances, we find that the record does not reflect that Officers' duties with respect to the Cage have "a straight bearing or unbroken connection that produces a material influence or [alteration]" on national security. *SSA*, 59 FLRA at 143.

With respect to the guarding of sensitive materials when those materials are moved during a COOP, an Officer testified that he did not know what was in the "locked tubs[]" that are moved, and that the extent of the Officer's involvement is to "let the warehouse in and out[]" (sic), and provide for access and exit of the materials "[i]n and out of the dock areas[.]" Tr. at 430.[9] In other words, the Officers do not move any materials, and merely oversee the movement of the materials, which are in locked tubs. Given that other individuals are actually moving the materials, that the tubs are locked, and that the movement occurs only in COOP events and inside of an already secured facility, we find that any connection that this activity has to national security is not direct.

Taking all of the disputed duties together, we find that the Officers' duties do not directly affect national security. In so finding, we note that in the decisions cited by the Activity and the dissent, employees who were excluded from units under § 7112(b)(6) engaged in activities such as designing, analyzing, and /or installing security systems at the facilities involved. *See, e.g.*, *IRS*, 62 FLRA at 303;[10] *SSA*, 59 FLRA at 146. The Officers do not engage in similar activities. Thus, those decisions are distinguishable.

For the foregoing reasons, we find that the RD failed to apply established law when he found that the Officers' duties directly affect national security, and we direct the RD to clarify the unit to include the Officers.

VI. Order

The RD is directed to take appropriate action consistent with this decision.

---

9. We note the dissent's statement that the Officer "agreed that Officers provide '*secure* access and *secure* exit' of these materials." Dissent at 18 (citing Tr. at 430) (emphasis added in dissent). In fact, the Officer testified, "We let the warehouse in and out." When asked, "You provide for secure access and secure exit of these materials?", the Officer responded: "In and out of the dock areas, yes." Tr. at 430. Thus, the word "secure" was solely the questioner's, and the emphasis is solely the dissent's.

10. We note that, other than *IRS* -- which is distinguishable from this case for the reasons stated above -- the dissent cites no Authority precedent to support his position.

Member Beck, Dissenting in part:

I concur with my colleagues' conclusion to deny the Agency's motion to strike the Union's brief in support of its application for review (application). I also agree with my colleagues' decision not to consider AFGE's request to reexamine the Authority's approach under § 7112(b)(6) of the Statute. However, I disagree with the remainder of the Majority's decision.

Before addressing the merits of the Union's application, I address the Majority's decision to modify the Authority's approach to exclusion under § 7112(b)(6) of the Statute. Section 7112(b)(6) merely states that a bargaining unit is not appropriate if it contains "any employee engaged in . . . security work which *directly affects* national security." 5 U.S.C. § 7112(b)(6) (emphasis added). It contains no other qualifying language. Nevertheless, the Majority announces that the phrase "directly affects" should be construed "narrow[ly,]" because the Authority has interpreted it narrowly for the more than thirty years since the Authority issued its decision in *Dep't of Energy, Oak Ridge Operations, Oak Ridge, Tenn.*, 4 FLRA 644, 656 (1980) (*Oak Ridge*). Maj. Op. at 6-7. Despite this assertion, the Majority cites not a single case from those thirty-plus years that actually articulates this principle. Instead, the Majority offers three justifications as to why "directly affects" should be interpreted narrowly. These justifications do not withstand scrutiny.

First, the Majority argues that a narrow interpretation for this phrase is appropriate because the Authority supposedly has found that positions directly affect national security in limited circumstances. Maj. Op. at 6-7. In the Majority's cited decisions, the Authority did nothing more than decide whether a position's duties directly affected national security within the plain meaning of § 7112(b)(6). *See, e.g.*, *U.S. Dep't of the Air Force, Tyndall Air Force Base, Tyndall AFB, Fla.*, 65 FLRA 610, 613 (2011) (*Tyndall, AFB*) (Authority stated that it looked to whether intervening factors "limit[]" a position's direct effect on national security as that term is used in § 7112(b)(6) of the Statute) (citation omitted)[1];*U.S. Dep't of the Air Force, Davis-Monthan Air Force Base, Ariz.*, 62 FLRA 332, 335 (2008) (Chairman Cabaniss Concurring) (*Davis-Monthan*) (Authority found that "RD's conclusion that the disputed positions directly affect national security *within the meaning of § 7112(b)(6)* is supported by the record.") (emphasis added); *U.S. Dep't of Agric., Food Safety & Inspection Serv.*, 61 FLRA 397, 402-03 (2005) (*USDA*) (after noting Authority's definition of the phrase "direct effect," Authority concluded that RD properly found that position did not directly affect national security) (citation omitted)); *Oak Ridge*, 4 FLRA at 659 (after analyzing position's duties, administrative law judge concluded that position did not "engage[] in security work which *directly affects* the national security") (emphasis added)). The Majority does not explain how the Authority's decision to apply the plain language of § 7112(b)(6) leads to a conclusion that part of § 7112(b)(6) should be interpreted narrowly, particularly since none of the foregoing cases actually states this principle.

Second, the Majority contends that a narrow interpretation for "directly affects" is warranted because, in crafting the standard for exclusion under § 7112(b)(6), the Authority concluded that "[l]abor organizations and collective bargaining in the civil service have been determined by the Congress to be 'in the public interest.'" Maj. Op. at 7 (quoting *Oak Ridge* at 655). Although the Authority acknowledged that collective bargaining benefits the public interest, it also acknowledged that collective bargaining -- and hence the associated public interest -- is necessarily limited by § 7112(b)(6). *See Oak Ridge*, 4 FLRA at 656 (acknowledging that positions that were "directly related to the protection and preservation of the . . . United States" are excluded from bargaining units). Thus, from the outset, the Authority has recognized that the "important statutory rights and policies" that flow from the Statute have limits. Maj. Op. at 7. Not surprisingly, then, the Majority offers no language from *Oak Ridge* instructing that the phrase "directly affects" should be viewed narrowly. To the contrary, the only language the Majority cites refers solely to the phrase *national security* as it is used in § 7112(b)(6). Maj. Op. at 7 ("Labor organizations and collective bargaining in the civil service have been determined by the Congress to be 'in the public interest.' . . . *Therefore, the term 'national security'* must be interpreted to include only [certain activities].") (quoting *Oak Ridge*, 4 FLRA at 655 (emphasis added)).

Third, the Majority avers that Authority decisions interpreting the executive orders (E.O.) that preceded the Statute should inform the Authority's interpretation of § 7112(b)(6). Specifically, the Majority relies on

1. The Majority relies on the recently decided *Tyndall, AFB* to support its assertion that the Authority has applied the phrase "directly affects" narrowly. *See* Maj. Op. 7. *Tyndall, AFB* involved remarkably similar circumstances to this case in that there, as here, the Authority examined whether certain duties performed by police officers directly affected national security. *See Tyndall, AFB*, 65 FLRA at 613-14. Despite this striking similarity, *Tyndall, AFB* contains *absolutely no discussion* as to whether the phrase "directly affects" should be applied narrowly. *See id.*

decisions suggesting that, under the executive orders, the mixing of guards with other types of employees in a bargaining unit created no conflict. *See* Maj. Op. at 7-8 (citing *Bureau of Indian Affairs, Wind River Agency, Fort Washakie, Wyo.*, 29 FLRA 935, 938 (1987) (*Fort Washakie*); *U.S. Dep't of the Treasury, Bureau of the Mint,* 2 FLRA 457, 460 (1980)). However, the E.O. decisions cited by the Majority are inapplicable because they address a completely different provision of the Statute -- whether guards shared a "community of interest" with other employees, as that term is used in E.O. 11,491 and § 7112(a) of the Statute.[2] *See Fort Washakie*, 29 FLRA at 938 (activity's argument consisted of disagreement "with regard to the 'community of interest' criterion"). Decisions about the Authority's interpretation of *§ 7112(a)* tell us little about *§ 7112(b)(6)*. Indeed, the Majority offers no language from either of the executive orders, or decisions interpreting them, addressing the phrase "directly affects" as it appears in § 7112(b)(6). Thus, these decisions do not apply here. *See, e.g., Div. of Military & Naval Affairs (N.Y. Nat'l Guard), Latham, N.Y.*, 53 FLRA 111, 118 (1997) (*Latham*) (Authority chose not to rely on E.O. 11,491 to interpret § 7111(f)(1) of Statute because E.O. contained "no equivalent").

Moreover, even if the E.O. precedent were somehow helpful, a significant difference exists between the executive orders and § 7112(b)(6). The Statute, federal courts, and the Authority acknowledge that executive orders may inform interpretations of the Statute to the extent Congress intended their incorporation into the Statute. *See* 5 U.S.C. § 7135(b) ("[p]olicies, regulations, and procedures established under and decisions issued under [the executive orders] . . . shall remain in full force and effect . . . unless superseded by provisions of [the Statute.]"); *see also, e.g., Dep't of the Air Force, Sacramento Air Logistics Ctr., McClellan Air Force Base, Cal. v. FLRA*, 877 F.2d 1036, 1040-41 (D.C. Cir. 1989) (stating that executive order precedent could be used if Statute was unclear) (citation omitted); *U.S. Dep't of Homeland Sec., Bureau of Customs & Border Prot.*, 61 FLRA 485, 494 (2006) (applying executive order precedent that was consistent with language of Statute). However, these same authorities acknowledge that a difference between the executive orders and the Statute demonstrates the inapplicability of the former to the latter. *See* 5 U.S.C. § 7135(b); *see also, e.g., Air Force*, 877 F.2d at 1040-41 (noting that "Congress viewed the [S]tatute as a departure from the law that had developed under the [e]xecutive [o]rder structure," court found that Statute's failure to include language permitting certain travel expenses meant those expenses were no longer recoverable even though executive orders permitted such recovery); *Latham,* 53 FLRA at 118 (Authority chose not to rely on E.O. 11,491 to interpret § 7111(f)(1) of Statute because order contained "no equivalent").

E.O. 11,838 amended E.O. 11,491 to permit guards and other employees to be in the same bargaining unit; previously, guards were required to be in separate units. Thus, under E.O. 11,838, guards faced no obstacles to being in the same bargaining units as non-guards. Section 7112(b)(6) of the Statute altered this situation by mandating that guards could no longer be in *any* bargaining units if they perform duties that directly affect national security. *Compare Fort Washakie,* 29 FLRA at 938 (stating that E.O. 11,838 "eliminated the general exclusion of guards from units of other employees[]") *with U.S. Dep't of Justice,* 52 FLRA 1093, 1098 (1997) (Member Wasserman not participating) ("*Congress determined* in [§] 7112(b)(6) that a unit *may not include any* employee engaged in security work which directly affects national security[]" (emphasis added)). In other words, whereas, under E.O. 11,838, guards faced no impediments to being in a bargaining unit, under the Statute, guards may not be in *any* bargaining unit if their duties directly affect national security. The decisions upon which the Majority relies are inapplicable because they were superseded by § 7112(b)(6). *See* 5 U.S.C. § 7135(b).

Furthermore, the Majority's reliance on executive order precedent is misplaced for yet another reason. The Majority contends that the Authority's approach to guard duties under the executive orders supports a determination that "directly affects" under § 7112(b)(6) should be viewed narrowly. *See* Maj. Op. at 6-7. But the Majority's proffered decisions go solely to one position -- guards; by contrast, § 7112(b)(6) has been applied to a wide spectrum of positions. *See, e.g., Davis-Monthan,* 62 FLRA at 335 (secretary); *USDA*, 61 FLRA at 402-03 (food inspectors); *SSA, Balt., Md.*, 59 FLRA 137, 146 (2003) (Chairman Cabaniss concurring and then-Member Pope concurring in part and dissenting in part) (analyst). The Majority does not explain why viewing *one* position narrowly justifies viewing *all* positions narrowly.

---

2. E.O. 11,491 § 10(b) states, in relevant part, that "[a] unit may be established . . . which will ensure a clear and identifiable community of interest among the employees concerned[.]" E.O. 11,491 § 10(b). Section 7112(a) of the Statute states, in relevant part, that "[t]he Authority . . . shall determine any unit to be an appropriate unit only if the determination will ensure a clear and identifiable community of interest[.]" 5 U.S.C. § 7112(a).

The Majority's proffered justifications for a narrow interpretation of the phrase "directly affects" do not withstand scrutiny. Accordingly, I find no basis to conclude that the Authority's approach to exclusion under § 7112(b)(6) should be altered.[3]

Applying the proper standard for review under § 7112(b)(6), I conclude, in disagreement with my colleagues, that the duties of the Internal Revenue Police Officers (Officers) directly affect national security. As the Majority states, the RD found that Officers directly affect national security after he examined their: (1) access to and protection of the Treasury Cage (Cage); (2) access to and protection of the Secured Room; and (3) duties during a Continuity of Operations (COOP) event. *See* Maj. Op. at 8 (citing RD's Decision at 10). An analysis of the foregoing responsibilities establishes why the RD was correct.

Turning first to the Cage, as the Majority states, the Cage contains sensitive information that is not stored anywhere else in the country. RD's Decision at 5; Tr. at 95, 110. Moreover, it is a "restricted area" and access is limited *solely* to United States Department of Treasury officials, authorized individuals, and Officers. RD's Decision at 6; Tr. at 80; *see also id.* at 383 (Officer testified that "[t]he Cage . . . [has] very, very limited access."). Of the foregoing, only one group is charged with maintaining the security of this restricted area: Officers. Indeed, the Officers are the *only* security personnel with the authority to actually access the Cage. *See, e.g.,* Tr. at 219 (Officer testified that Contract Guards (Guards) "may not" enter the Cage).

Officers are charged with protecting the Cage and preventing unauthorized access to it. As the Director of Physical Security and Emergency Preparedness (Director) testified, Officers "make sure that the integrity of the Cage is maintained, and also . . . *ensure that no one is able to gain access to the Cage*, unless he or she is otherwise authorized to get in." Tr. at 80. (emphasis added). To this end, Officers regularly patrol the Cage area. *See* RD's Decision at 10. Additionally, Officers have the authority to question individuals approaching the Cage as to whether their identification badges are authorized. *See id.* at 5. Moreover, Officers check card readers to make sure they are functioning properly.

In addition to protecting the Cage itself, the Officers ensure the security of its contents. To that end, Officers regularly patrol the interior of the Cage. *See* RD's Decision at 10; *see also* Tr. at 357 (Officer testified that he "would generally take a tour" of the Cage while doing his patrol). When Officers tour through the Cage, they look for any documents that have been inadvertently left out or computers that have been left on by accident. Officers may not handle the documents; however, they are authorized to turn off the computers if no other authorized individual is available to do so. *See* Tr. at 358.

The Officers also perform security duties -- albeit limited ones -- in relation to the Secure Room. The Secure Room contains information that is more sensitive than the information stored in the Cage, and is primarily used by the Secretary of the Treasury. RD's Decision at 4. Managers at the Center do not even have access to this area. *See* Tr. at 81. As the Majority acknowledges, Officers check on the Secure Room during their foot patrols of the Center's interior. Maj. Op. at 9. Although the Majority is correct that Officers do not "generally" access the Secure Room, Officers nevertheless may access the room to check on emergencies such as fires, grant individuals access to the room, and check on matters that are out of the ordinary. *See, e.g.,* Tr. at 81, 418-19. Additionally, during a COOP event, Officers patrol the area that is adjacent to the Secure Room in order to maintain security. RD's Decision at 6. The record contains no indication that any other position has duties associated with the protection of the Secure Room.

Finally, the Officers perform several duties during a COOP event that also demonstrate how the Officers' duties affect national security. As stated by the Majority, Officers: are part of the execution of COOP security plans; are frequently a part of COOP preparation exercises; patrol and monitor areas of the Center during a COOP event; and prevent unauthorized individuals from accessing the Center during a COOP. Maj. Op. at 3. Moreover, as the record reveals, during a COOP event, Officers coordinate traffic, check the identification of individuals in the Center, check vehicles that pass through the Center, and search those vehicles. Tr. at 358-59. Additionally, Officers oversee the transfer of confidential documents during a COOP event. *See* Tr. at 429-30.

The foregoing establishes that all of the Officers' duties in question directly affect national security. The Majority disagrees, and claims the Officers' effect on national security is limited due to several reasons, all of which are erroneous.

The Majority first asserts that the Officers' effect on national security is limited because Guards perform

3. To be sure, I am not suggesting that the Authority should view the phrase "directly affects" broadly. Rather, the Authority should do no more and no less than continue to apply the plain language requirements of § 7112(b)(6), as it has done since *Oak Ridge*.

various security functions within and outside of the Center. Specifically, the Majority goes to great lengths to explain how the Guards' duties "play . . . an important role in securing *the Center*." Maj. Op. at 8 (emphasis added). Missing from the Majority's explanation is any citation to the record that explicitly or implicitly links the duties of the Guards to the safety of the restricted areas, *which are the only areas in dispute*. Unable to point to any portion of the record that actually states the Guards or other employees have any involvement with the restricted areas, the Majority merely assumes that the Guards' duties in relation to the Center as a whole make it "less probable" that the Officers' duties in the restricted areas directly affect national security. *Id.* at 9. However, the Majority does not dispute that Officers are the *only* employees that protect and secure the Center's restricted areas. Indeed, Guards have little effect if an unauthorized individual accesses the Center. Once such a situation occurs, Officers are almost always "[t]he first line of defense." Tr. at 83; *see also id.* at 228. *Only Officers* have the authority to arrest unauthorized individuals because "[t]hey are *the* law enforcement entity for [the Center]." *Id.* at 83 (emphasis added); *see also id.* at 86-87 (Director testified that she can "direct [Officers] to do things that [she could] not otherwise direct any of the [Guards]" to do). Indeed, Officers have the discretion to delegate certain duties to Guards in order to detain unauthorized individuals. *Id.* at 228. Furthermore, even though Guards assign badges to individuals, the Majority offers no testimony that Guards or other employees have ever checked badges at or near the restricted areas.

Second, the Majority argues that, because the Officers' disputed duties are not the "sole focus of their responsibilities," the Officers' effect on national security is limited. Maj. Op. at 9 n.9; *see also id.* at 9 ("That the Officers perform numerous, important duties unrelated to the disputed duties . . . is relevant to determining whether the Officers should be excluded from the unit."). The Majority does not produce a single Authority decision that states a position's effect on national security is lessened by the fact that the position performs other duties. This is because the relevant inquiry under § 7112(b)(6) is whether an employee performs "security work which directly affects national security[,]" not whether an employee performs "security work which directly affects national security" *all of the time*. 5 U.S.C. § 7112(b)(6). Indeed, in the recently decided *Tyndall, AFB*, although the police officers at issue performed several duties, *see Tyndall, AFB*, 65 FLRA at 611 (describing duties), the Authority analyzed *only* the two duties that were in dispute to determine whether the work of those officers directly affected national security. *See Tyndall, AFB*, 65 FLRA at 613-14 (analyzing solely suspicious package and commercial vehicle inspection duties). The Authority gave no indication that the effect on national security was reduced because the officers performed other duties. *See id.* at 613-14. The Majority does not explain why, in this nearly identical case, it has adopted a contrary approach.

Third, the Majority concludes "that the Officers' duties with respect to the Secure Room [do not] have 'a straight bearing or unbroken connection that produces a material influence or [alteration]' on national security." Maj. Op. at 10 (quoting *SSA, Balt., Md.*, 59 FLRA at 143 (2003)). The Majority is correct that the Officers' duties in relation to the Secure Room are limited. However, the Majority errs because it examines those duties in isolation, instead of in conjunction with the Officers' other disputed duties, to determine the Officers' effect on national security. When examining whether a position directly affects national security, the Authority examines *all* of the duties that are in dispute. *See, e.g., Tyndall, AFB,* 65 FLRA at 613-14 (examining disputed duties at issue in order to determine whether position directly affected national security); *U.S. Dep't of the Treasury, IRS*, 62 FLRA 298, 303-04 (2007) (Chairman Cabaniss concurring and then-Member Pope concurring) (*IRS*) (examining several duties at issue in order to determine whether position directly affected national security); *USDA*, 61 FLRA at 402-03 (same). Thus, the proper inquiry is not whether the Secure Room duties in and of themselves directly affect national security, but whether those duties *in addition* to the Officers' other disputed duties establish such an effect. The Majority's attempt to view those duties in isolation, therefore, is misplaced.

Fourth, the Majority asserts that the Officers' effect on national security is limited because Officers do not work with the materials in the Cage. *See* Maj. Op. at 10. This is unpersuasive. Although other individuals *work* with the materials in the Cage, Officers *protect* those materials. The Authority has found that positions directly affect national security where those positions' duties, in-part, include monitoring sensitive areas. *See, e.g., IRS,* 62 FLRA at 304; *cf. USDA*, 61 FLRA at 403 (finding that position did not directly affect national security, in part, because employees were not responsible for protecting physical premises).[4] Thus, the fact that Officers do not work with these materials is of no consequence.

4. The Majority claims that *IRS* is inapplicable because the employees in *IRS* "engaged in activities such as designing, analyzing, and/or installing security systems at the facilities involved." Maj. Op. at 11 (citations omitted). Although it is true that the employees in that case designed, analyzed,

Finally, the Majority contends that the Officers' COOP duties have a limited effect on national security because Officers "merely oversee the movement of . . . materials, which are in locked tubs[,]" through an already locked area, i.e., the warehouse. Maj. Op. at 11 (citation omitted). However, one of the Officers who regularly participates in COOP events agreed that Officers provide "*secure* access and *secure* exit" of these materials. Tr. at 430 (emphasis added).[5] Therefore, although the materials are moved in a secured area, the Officers are responsible for ensuring that the area is secured to begin with. Furthermore, regardless of whether the warehouse is locked, as stated above, employees directly affect national security where their duties include monitoring sensitive areas. *See, e.g., IRS,* 62 FLRA at 304; *cf. USDA,* 61 FLRA at 403.

Based on the foregoing, I would conclude that the Officers' duties at issue have a direct effect on national security.

---

and/or installed security systems, nothing in the decision suggests that the employees' duties directly affected national security *only* because they performed such duties. Thus, the Majority's attempt to distinguish this case is unpersuasive.

5. The Majority quizzically finds significance in the fact that the Officer did not himself state that Officers provide "secure access and secure exit" of materials during a COOP event, but only replied affirmatively when asked on cross-examination whether he performed such duties. Not only does this assertion ignore well-settled principles of evidence and trial technique, *see, e.g.,* 3 *Wigmore, Evidence* § 773 (Chadbourn rev. 1970) ("[I]t is well settled that on cross-examination of an opponent's witness, ordinarily no question can be improper as leading." (citations omitted)), but it also obfuscates the relevant issue -- that the Officer fully agreed to the question asked and, thus, unquestionably performs this duty. The Majority offers nothing that contradicts this point.

65 FLRA No. 147

UNITED STATES
DEPARTMENT OF THE ARMY
HEADQUARTERS, I CORPS
AND FORT LEWIS
FORT LEWIS, WASHINGTON
(Agency)

and

INTERNATIONAL ASSOCIATION
OF MACHINISTS AND
AEROSPACE WORKERS
DISTRICT LODGE 160/282
(Union)

0-AR-4198

DECISION

March 31, 2011

Before the Authority: Carol Waller Pope, Chairman, and Thomas M. Beck and Ernest DuBester, Members

I. Statement of the Case

This matter is before the Authority on exceptions to an award of Arbitrator Anthony D. Vivenzio filed by the Agency under § 7122(a) of the Federal Service Labor-Management Relations Statute (the Statute) and part 2425 of the Authority's Regulations. The Union did not file an opposition.

The Arbitrator found that the grievance was procedurally arbitrable. On the merits, the Arbitrator found that, although the Agency did not violate the parties' agreement when it transferred the grievant from the night shift to the day shift, it did violate the agreement by failing to return the grievant to the night shift after he had worked on the day shift for more than six months. For the reasons that follow, we deny the exceptions in part and modify the award in part.

II. Background and Arbitrator's Award

The grievant is a repair operator who worked on the night shift at a wastewater treatment facility. Award at 3. The Agency transferred the grievant to the day shift when it determined that the grievant failed to properly restart the facility after a power outage. *Id.* As a result of the transfer, the grievant no longer earned night differential pay. *See id.* at 21, 28-29. The Union filed a grievance, which was unresolved and submitted to arbitration. *Id.* at 1. The Arbitrator framed the issues before him as whether the grievance was procedurally arbitrable, whether the Agency violated the parties' agreement, and what the remedy should be. *Id.* at 2.

With regard to procedural arbitrability, the Arbitrator found that the Union had failed to request arbitration within the thirty-day limit required by Article 27 of the parties' agreement.[1] *Id.* at 16. The Arbitrator determined, however, that "behaviors of the parties" can indicate a "mutual waiver" of time limitations in a contract. *Id.* at 18. The Arbitrator found that the parties engaged in settlement negotiations and arbitrator selection long after the contractual time limit had expired. *See id.* In light of those actions, the Arbitrator concluded that the parties effectively waived the time limits in the agreement and that the grievance was "not barred for lack of literal compliance with Article 27[.]" *Id.*

With regard to the merits of the grievance, the Arbitrator found that it was "within the discretion of the [Agency]" to transfer the grievant, and that the transfer was a "proper exercise of its authority under Article 2[.]"[2] *Id.* at 26. However, the fact that the grievant had spent eight months on the day shift at the time of the hearing, *see id.* at 1, 26, led the Arbitrator to consider the "ramifications of maintaining the [g]rievant on the day shift" indefinitely. *Id.* at 26. In this connection, the Arbitrator stated that the grievant's "duties and activities underwent significant change as a result of the transfer[,]" as the grievant no longer engaged in activities "'affecting the plant's permit.'" *Id.* at 27 (quoting testimony). The Arbitrator found that the Agency "claimed that the transfer of the [g]rievant" was for the "purpose of improving his performance through closer supervision[,]" *id.*, which would give the grievant an "opportunity to demonstrate his ability to operate the plant for a return to the night shift[,]" *id.* at 28. The Arbitrator determined that "these things never materialized[.]" *Id.* The

1. Article 27 of the parties' agreement states, in pertinent part, that a written request for arbitration "must be submitted not later than thirty (30) calendar days after the fourth step decision letter is issued." Award at 16.

2. Article 2 states, in pertinent part, that "[i]t is the right of Management to . . . assign . . . employees" and "assign work[.]" *Id.* at 4.

Arbitrator stated that a "reassignment should be for a definite period of time if it is to be corrective," *id.* at 27, and concluded that the grievant's placement on the day shift "ripened into an adverse action over time." *Id.* at 28.

Noting the "history of the [g]rievant in this workplace" and "examining the range of previous reassignments," the Arbitrator determined that the "line" as to when the grievant's day-shift assignment became an adverse action "is to be drawn at six months." *Id.* The Arbitrator concluded that after the grievant had spent six months on the day shift, the "continuation of the reassignment of the [g]rievant to the day shift was . . . an adverse action, in violation of Article 18, Sections 1 and 2, of the [parties' agreement (Article 18)]."[3] *Id.*

To remedy the violation, the Arbitrator directed the Agency to reassign the grievant to the night shift and the duties that he previously had performed on that shift. *Id.* at 29. In addition, the Arbitrator found that the Agency's violation of Article 18 was an "unwarranted" personnel action that resulted in the withdrawal or reduction of the grievant's pay, allowances, and differentials. *Id.* at 28. The Arbitrator awarded the grievant backpay, without interest, for the time in excess of six months that the grievant had worked on the day shift. *Id.* at 29.

III. Agency's Exceptions

The Agency argues that the Arbitrator's procedural arbitrability determination is contrary to public policy. *See* Exceptions at 11. In this regard, the Agency argues that the award effectively punishes the Agency for having attempted to settle the grievance. *Id.* The Agency also argues that the award implies that the Agency should have refused to select an arbitrator, even though such a refusal "could have resulted in an unfair labor practice." *Id.*

With regard to the Arbitrator's resolution of the merits of the grievance, the Agency asserts that the award fails to draw its essence from the parties' agreement, arguing that the Arbitrator "mistakenly determined that the loss of night differential . . . constituted an adverse action under" Article 18. *Id.* at 7. In this connection, the Agency argues that Federal Personnel Manual (FPM) Chapter 752, referenced in Article 18, indicates that the grievant's transfer was not an adverse action because FPM Chapter 752 "excludes . . . from the definition of adverse action" a "'[r]eduction of an employee's rate of pay from a rate which is contrary to law or regulation to a rate which is required or permitted by law or regulation.'" *Id.* (quoting FPM Chapter 752).

The Agency also asserts that the award is contrary to 5 U.S.C. § 7512 (§ 7512) and 5 C.F.R. § 752.401 (§ 752.401). According to the Agency, the Authority should apply statutory standards to the Arbitrator's interpretation of Article 18 because the Authority has "applied statutory standards in assessing the application of contract provisions that mirror, or are intended to be interpreted in the same manner as, the Statute." *Id.* at 4 (quoting *AFGE*, 59 FLRA 767, 769 (2004) (Chairman Cabaniss concurring and then-Member Pope dissenting)). The Agency claims that the definition of "adverse action" under Article 18 "mirrors" the definitions of "adverse action" in § 7512 and § 752.401.[4] *Id.* at 4. The Agency argues that an adverse action did not occur under § 7512 because that section defines an adverse action as a reduction in pay, i.e., a reduction in basic pay, and not as a loss of night differential pay. *See* Exceptions at 5-6. For support, the Agency cites: *Spinks v. U.S. Postal Serv.*, 621 F.2d 987 (9th Cir. 1980) (*Spinks*), and *Allen v. Department of the Navy*, 13 M.S.P.R. 521 (1982) (*Allen*), *overruled in part by Robinson v. Department of the Army*, 21 M.S.P.R. 270, 272 & n.3 (1984). Alternatively, the Agency argues that the award is contrary to § 752.401 because the grievant's loss of night differential constituted a reduction in pay from a rate

---

[3] Article 18 states, in pertinent part:

> Section 1. Adverse actions are defined as suspensions for more than fourteen (14) days, removal, reduction in grade or pay, and furlough for thirty (30) days or less taken against career or career-conditional employees not serving a probationary . . . period. Excluded are those actions excluded under [Federal Personnel Manual (FPM)] Chapter 752.
>
> Section 2. Adverse actions will only be taken for just cause[.]

Award at 6.

4. As relevant here, § 7512 defines an adverse action as a removal, suspension for more than fourteen days, reduction in grade, reduction in pay, or furlough of 30 days or less. 5 U.S.C. § 7512. The version of § 752.401(a) in effect at the time of the actions giving rise to the grievance defined an adverse action similarly. *See* 5 C.F.R. § 752.401(a) (2006). Additionally, as relevant here, the version of § 752.401(b) in effect at the time of the actions giving rise to the grievance stated that actions excluded from the definition of adverse action include a "[r]eduction of an employee's rate of basic pay from a rate that is contrary to law or regulation." 5 C.F.R. § 752.401(b)(15) (2006).

that is contrary to law or regulation, and that such a reduction is not an adverse action under § 752.401(b)(15).[5] *See* Exceptions at 5.

Further, the Agency alleges that the remedy is contrary to § 7106 of the Statute because "moving the grievant to the night shift, and requiring the assignment of particular duties to the grievant, violates the exercise of management's rights to assign work and employees."[6] *Id.* at 10 (citing *Int'l Bhd. of Police Officers*, 47 FLRA 397, 404 (1993), and *AFGE, Local 1698, Local 1156*, 61 FLRA 615, 617 (2006)).

Finally, the Agency maintains that the award is contrary to the Back Pay Act because the Agency "did not violate" Article 18, Exceptions at 9, and, therefore, did not commit an unjustified or unwarranted personnel action, *id.* at 8. The Agency also asserts that the Arbitrator's award of backpay without interest is contrary to the Back Pay Act, but states that it will pay interest if the Authority upholds the award of backpay. *Id.* at 9 (citing *Nat'l Border Patrol Council, Local 2913*, 48 FLRA 657 (1993)).

IV. Analysis and Conclusions

A. The Arbitrator's procedural arbitrability determination is not deficient.

The Authority generally will not find an arbitrator's ruling on the procedural arbitrability of a grievance deficient on grounds that directly challenge the procedural-arbitrability ruling itself. *AFGE, Local 933*, 65 FLRA 9, 11 (2010) (*Local 933*). An arbitrator's determination regarding the timeliness of a grievance constitutes a determination regarding the procedural arbitrability of that grievance. *Id.* Additionally, questions of whether the "'preliminary steps of the grievance procedure have been exhausted or excused'" are questions regarding the procedural arbitrability of a grievance. *AFGE, Local 1815*, 65 FLRA 430, 431 (2011) (quoting *Fraternal Order of Police, N.J. Lodge 173*, 58 FLRA 384, 385 (2003) (Chairman Cabaniss dissenting)). The Authority has stated that a procedural arbitrability determination may be found deficient on grounds that do not challenge the determination itself, which include claims that an arbitrator was biased or that the arbitrator exceeded his or her authority. *Local 933*, 65 FLRA at 11.

By arguing that the Arbitrator's procedural arbitrability determination is contrary to public policy, the Agency directly challenges the procedural arbitrability ruling itself. *See id.* Accordingly, consistent with the foregoing, we deny the exception.

B. The award does not fail to draw its essence from the parties' agreement.

In reviewing an arbitrator's interpretation of a collective bargaining agreement, the Authority applies the deferential standard that federal courts use in reviewing arbitration awards in the private sector. *See* 5 U.S.C. § 7122(a)(2); *AFGE, Council 220, 54* FLRA 156, 159 (1998). Under this standard, the Authority will find that an arbitration award is deficient as failing to draw its essence from the collective bargaining agreement when the appealing party establishes that the award: (1) cannot in any rational way be derived from the agreement; (2) is so unfounded in reason and fact and so unconnected with the wording and purposes of the collective bargaining agreement as to manifest an infidelity to the obligation of the arbitrator; (3) does not represent a plausible interpretation of the agreement; or (4) evidences a manifest disregard of the agreement. *U.S. Dep't of Labor (OSHA)*, 34 FLRA 573, 575 (1990) (*OSHA*). The Authority and the courts defer to arbitrators in this context "because it is the arbitrator's construction of the agreement for which the parties have bargained." *Id.* at 576.

Article 18 of the parties' agreement states, in pertinent part, that "[a]dverse actions are defined as . . . [a] reduction in . . . pay[.]" Award at 6. The Agency claims that the Arbitrator erred in finding an adverse action under Article 18 because Article 18 excludes from the definition of adverse action any actions excluded in FPM Chapter 752, including a

5. In addition, the Agency claims that if the Authority were to find that an adverse action had occurred under § 7512, then the Authority would lack jurisdiction to resolve this dispute under 5 U.S.C. § 7121(f) (§ 7121(f)) and § 7122(a). *See* Exceptions at 6-7. Under § 7122(a), the Authority lacks jurisdiction to review an arbitration award "relating to a matter described in § 7121(f)[.]" The matters described in § 7121(f) include adverse actions, such as removals, which are covered under 5 U.S.C. § 4303 or § 7512 and are appealable to the Merit Systems Protection Board. *See U.S. Dep't of Justice, Fed. Bureau of Prisons, Fed. Det. Ctr., Miami, Fla.*, 57 FLRA 677, 678 (2002) (Member Armendariz concurring). Based on the fact, explained below, that the Arbitrator did not find an adverse action under § 7512, we find that §§ 7121(f) and 7122(a) do not prevent the Authority from considering the exceptions.

6. Section 7106 of the Statute states, in pertinent part that, "nothing . . . shall affect the authority of any management official . . . in accordance with applicable laws . . . to . . . assign . . . employees[,]" § 7106(a)(2)(A), or "assign work," § 7106(a)(2)(B).

reduction in an employee's "rate of pay." *See* Exceptions at 7-8. Article 18 does not define the terms "reduction in pay" or "rate of pay," and the Agency does not demonstrate that the Arbitrator erred by effectively finding that the grievant's loss of night differential pay was a reduction in pay -- and thus was an adverse action under Article 18 -- as opposed to a reduction in rate of pay within the meaning of FPM Chapter 752.[7] As the Agency has not shown that the Arbitrator's interpretation was irrational, unfounded, implausible, or in manifest disregard of the parties' agreement, we deny the exception.[8]

C. The award is contrary to law in part.

When a party's exceptions involve an award's consistency with law, the Authority reviews the questions of law raised by the arbitrator's award and the party's exceptions de novo. *NTEU, Chapter 24*, 50 FLRA 330, 332 (1995) (citing *U.S. Customs Serv. v. FLRA*, 43 F.3d 682, 686-87 (D.C. Cir. 1994)). In applying a de novo standard of review, the Authority assesses whether the arbitrator's legal conclusions are consistent with the applicable standard of law. *NFFE, Local 1437*, 53 FLRA 1703, 1710 (1998). In making that assessment, the Authority defers to the arbitrator's underlying factual findings. *See id.*

1. The award is not contrary to §§ 7512 or 752.401.

Previously, the Authority has denied exceptions to an arbitrator's contract interpretation where the exceptions alleged that the arbitrator misinterpreted a law or regulation. For example, when considering exceptions to an arbitrator's award interpreting the meaning of the term "detail" under a contract, the Authority found, in *AFGE, Local 779*, 64 FLRA 672 (2010) (*Local 779*), that an exception that claimed that the arbitrator failed to consider Office of Personnel Management regulations was misplaced. *See id.* at 674. Here, the Arbitrator interpreted Article 18, and not §§ 7512 or 752.401, to find that an adverse action occurred. *See* Award at 28. As such, *Local 779* supports a conclusion that the Agency's exceptions do not demonstrate that the award is contrary to §§ 7512 or 752.401. *See Local 779*, 64 FLRA at 674.

Although the Agency acknowledges that the Arbitrator resolved the matter based on his interpretation of Article 18, the Agency contends that the Authority should apply statutory standards because the "definition of adverse actions in [Article 18] mirrors the definition of adverse actions in both . . . § 7512 and . . . § 752.401." Exceptions at 4. As an initial matter, it is not clear that Article 18 mirrors, or was intended to be interpreted in the same manner as, §§ 7512 and 752.401, as Article 18 does not specifically reference or incorporate § 7512 or § 752.401. *See* Award at 6. Moreover, while the Authority has applied statutory standards to contract provisions that "mirror . . . *the Statute*[,]" *AFGE*, 59 FLRA at 769 (emphasis added), neither § 7512 nor § 752.401 is part of the Statute, i.e., part of chapter 71, title 5 of the United States Code. Moreover, the Arbitrator did not find that Article 18 mirrored, or was intended to be interpreted in the same manner as, §§ 7512 and 752.401. *See* Award at 26-28. In these circumstances, we do not apply statutory standards to resolve the Arbitrator's interpretation of Article 18. As such, the decisions cited by the Agency, which apply to § 7512 and/or Merit Systems Protection Board precedent, *see Spinks*, 621 F.2d at 988-89; *Allen*, 13 M.S.P.R. at 525 & n.4, do not apply here.

Based on the foregoing analysis, the Arbitrator's finding of an adverse action under Article 18 is not contrary to law.

---

7. We note that the FPM, referenced in Article 18, was abolished on December 31, 1994. *See, e.g.*, *Int'l Ass'n of Machinists & Aerospace Workers, Dist. Lodge 725, Local Lodge 726*, 60 FLRA 196, 197 n.2 (2004). However, there is no contention that the abolishment of FPM Chapter 752 is relevant to the issue before us.

8. Member Beck agrees that the "essence" exception, as framed by the Agency, should be denied. He notes that the Agency chose not to offer an "essence" argument that might have been more successful.

The Arbitrator explicitly found that the Agency's reassignment of the Grievant from the night shift to the day shift was not an adverse action and not subject to any arbitral remedy. Award at 26 ("The assignment of the Grievant to the day shift ... was within the discretion of the Employer and a proper exercise of the authority under Article 2 of the contract. The assignment was not ... arbitrary and capricious ... nor in violation of any other element of the contract.").

The "adverse action" the Arbitrator purported to remedy was the Agency's failure to transfer the Grievant from the day shift to the night shift at an arbitrary point in time that the Arbitrator conjured from thin air. But there is no plausible reading of Article 18 that makes this an "adverse action." An agency's decision not to transfer an employee from one shift to another cannot be considered a "suspension[] ... removal, reduction in pay or grade, [or] furlough." *Id.*, Article 18, Section 1 (explicitly defining what constitutes an "adverse action"). The Arbitrator treated as an "adverse action" something that the parties chose to exclude from the contractual definition of that term.

2. The award is not contrary to § 7106 of the Statute.

The Agency argues that the remedy is contrary to management's rights to assign work and employees under § 7106. The Authority recently revised the analysis that it will apply when reviewing management rights exceptions to arbitration awards. *See U.S. EPA*, 65 FLRA 113, 115 (2010) (Member Beck concurring) (*EPA*); *FDIC, Div. of Supervision & Consumer Prot., S.F. Region*, 65 FLRA 102 (2010) (Chairman Pope concurring) (*FDIC*). Under the revised analysis, the Authority will first assess whether the award affects the exercise of the asserted management right. *EPA*, 65 FLRA at 115. If an award affects the exercise of the asserted management right, then, as relevant here, the Authority examines whether the award enforces a contract provision negotiated under § 7106(b).[9] *See id.*

Where the Authority has found that an arbitrator was enforcing an appropriate arrangement within the meaning of § 7106(b)(3) of the Statute, the Authority has assumed, without deciding, that the award affected the management rights as claimed by the excepting party. *See U.S. Dep't of the Army, Fort Huachuca, Ariz.*, 65 FLRA 442, 443-46 (2011) (*Fort Huachuca*). In addition, the Authority has repeatedly found that contract provisions requiring agencies to take certain actions only for just cause are appropriate arrangements within the meaning of § 7106(b)(3). *See Fort Huachuca*, 65 FLRA at 445-46; *U.S. Dep't of Transp., FAA*, 63 FLRA 383, 385 (2009); *SSA, Balt., Md.*, 53 FLRA 1751, 1754 (1998). As Article 18 requires that actions covered therein will only be taken for just cause, and as the Authority has found that just cause provisions are appropriate arrangements under § 7106(b)(3), we find that the Arbitrator's interpretation and application of Article 18 was not contrary to § 7106.

3. The award is contrary to the Back Pay Act in part.

An award of backpay is authorized under the Back Pay Act when an arbitrator finds that: (1) the aggrieved employee was affected by an unjustified or unwarranted personnel action; and (2) the personnel action has resulted in the withdrawal or reduction of the grievant's pay, allowances, or differentials. *See, e.g., U.S. Dep't of Health & Human Servs.*, 54 FLRA 1210, 1218-19 (1998). The Authority has held that a violation of a collective bargaining agreement constitutes an unwarranted personnel action under the Act. *See id.* at 1218-19. In addition, under the provisions of the Back Pay Act, "interest must be paid" on backpay awards. *E.g., Nat'l Air Traffic Controllers Ass'n*, 64 FLRA 906, 907 (2010) (*NATCA*).

The Agency's first Back Pay Act exception asserts that the Agency did not violate Article 18 and, thus, that the Arbitrator awarded backpay without finding an unjustified or unwarranted personnel action. However, as the Arbitrator determined that the Agency violated Article 18, and as we have denied the Agency's essence exception challenging that determination, we find that the Agency has failed to demonstrate that the Arbitrator awarded backpay without finding an unjustified or unwarranted personnel action.

The Agency's second Back Pay Act exception asserts that the award is contrary to the Act because the Arbitrator awarded backpay without interest. *See* Exceptions at 9; Award at 28-29. As interest is required under the Act (and the Agency so concedes), *see NATCA*, 64 FLRA at 907, we modify the award to include an award of interest on the backpay.

V. Decision

For the foregoing reasons, we deny the Agency's exceptions in part and modify the award in part.

9. When an award affects a management right under § 7106(a)(2) of the Statute, the Authority may also examine whether the award enforces an applicable law. *EPA*, 65 FLRA at 115 n.7.

65 FLRA No. 148

AMERICAN FEDERATION
OF GOVERNMENT EMPLOYEES
LOCAL 648
NATIONAL COUNCIL
OF FIELD LABOR LOCALS
(Union)

and

UNITED STATES
DEPARTMENT OF LABOR
CHICAGO REGIONAL OFFICE
(Agency)

0-AR-4423

DECISION

April 8, 2011

Before the Authority: Carol Waller Pope, Chairman, and Thomas M. Beck and Ernest DuBester, Members

I. Statement of the Case

This matter is before the Authority on exceptions to an award of Arbitrator Anne L. Draznin filed by the Union under § 7122(a) of the Federal Service Labor-Management Relations Statute (the Statute) and part 2425 of the Authority's Regulations.[1] The Agency filed an opposition to the Union's exceptions.

The Arbitrator found that the Agency had just cause to suspend the grievant for fourteen days, but she directed the Agency to rescind any additional punishments that the Agency had imposed and to notify the Union and the grievant once it had done so.

For the reasons that follow, we dismiss the Union's exceptions in part and deny them in part.

II. Background and Arbitrator's Award

During a performance progress review meeting between the grievant and her first-line supervisor (the first-line supervisor), the grievant allegedly began "yelling and gesticulating in an 'unprofessional, disruptive and threatening' manner." Award at 5. The first-line supervisor and the grievant's second-line supervisor (the second-line supervisor) both asked the grievant to "calm down[,]" *id.* at 12, and when the grievant allegedly failed to do so, the first-line supervisor called the Federal Protective Service (FPS), which arrested the grievant, *id.* at 5. In addition, the Agency revoked the grievant's government credentials and building pass. *Id.* The second-line supervisor proposed to suspend the grievant for fourteen days for alleged violent and threatening behavior. *Id.* at 5-6.

Subsequently, the grievant hired outside counsel and filed an Equal Employment Opportunity (EEO) complaint alleging discrimination. *Id.* at 6. Then, after the Agency's Deputy Regional Director (Deputy RD) approved the proposed fourteen-day suspension, the grievant filed a grievance, which was unresolved and submitted to arbitration. *Id.*

Prior to the arbitration hearing, "the [g]rievant's attorney submitted a lengthy list of proposed witnesses." *Id.* The Arbitrator then had a pre-hearing conference call with the parties, in which she asked the parties to "limit their presentations to the

1. The Authority issued a deficiency Order on October 10, 2008 to the Union and required a response by October 24. (All dates in this footnote are from 2008.) Subsequently, on October 14, the Authority received a supplemental submission (dated October 2) designating Howard D. Weisman as the Union's representative. When the Union did not timely reply to the deficiency Order, the Authority issued an Order on November 7 directing the Union to show cause why the Authority should not dismiss the exceptions. On November 18, Mr. Weisman timely filed a response to the Order to show cause, asserting that the Authority should not dismiss the exceptions because: (1) he did not receive the Authority's October 10 Order; and (2) the Agency was not harmed by the Union's error. He also corrected the deficiency at issue in the October 10 Order. As (1) the Authority did not serve Mr. Weisman with the October 10 deficiency Order (because the Authority did not receive the designation of representative until October 14), (2) Mr. Weisman timely replied to the Order to show cause and corrected the deficiency, and (3) there is no basis for finding that the Agency would be prejudiced by considering the exceptions, we consider the exceptions. *See, e.g., U.S. DHS, U.S. Customs & Border Prot., U.S. Border Patrol, El Paso, Tex.*, 61 FLRA 4, 4 n.1, *recons. denied*, 61 FLRA 393 (2005) (where party did not timely receive deficiency order, Authority waived expired time limit and allowed filing); *U.S. Dep't of HHS, Appalachian Lab. for Occupational Safety & Health, Nat'l Inst. for Occupational Safety & Health, Ctrs. for Disease Control & Prevention*, 49 FLRA 1150, 1151 (1994) (Authority considered exceptions where party established that it did not receive Authority Order and other party was not prejudiced).

two days set aside for the hearing and modify their lists accordingly as much as possible." *Id.* Subsequently, "[c]ounsel notified the Arbitrator that they had discussed the matter and agreed upon how to handle the witness lists . . . ." *Id.*

At arbitration, the parties "agreed [that] the matter was appropriately before the Arbitrator." *Id.* In addition, they agreed to the following issues: "Whether or not the fourteen (14) day suspension which was given to [the grievant] was for just and sufficient cause and for reasons which will promote the efficiency of the [Agency] and[,] if not[,] what is the appropriate remedy?" *Id.* at 2.

The Arbitrator found that the decision to suspend was made based solely on information received from the first- and second-line supervisors. *Id.* at 8. As an initial matter, the Arbitrator rejected the Union's reliance on a letter from the second-line supervisor to the grievant (the second-line supervisor's letter) as evidence that the Agency promised the grievant a more thorough investigation. In this regard, the Arbitrator noted that the letter was a form letter that merely notified the grievant that her "credentials had been confiscated and would be returned when a determination had been made . . . as to what happened and what to do about it." *Id.* at 10. In addition, the Arbitrator found that the grievant and the Union had opportunities, but failed, to respond to the proposed suspension. *Id.* The Arbitrator determined that, without a response, the Deputy RD had no reason to investigate further. In addition, the Arbitrator rejected as "questionable[]" the Union's claim that the first- and second-line supervisors' accounts of the incident were unreliable because they were "parties to [the] incident . . . ." *Id.* at 12.

Further, the Arbitrator rejected the Union's attempts to challenge the credibility of the Agency's witnesses. The Arbitrator stated that

> [e]ven granting the Union's claims that [the first-line supervisor's] demeanor on cross examination indicated she was trying to hide something and there were inconsistencies in her story, it is easily conceivable that this was nothing more than witness over preparation and nervousness, a common problem with first time supervisors acting as witnesses about their actions.

Id. at 14. In addition, the Arbitrator noted that the grievant did not testify, and found that the Union's witnesses were not "fully present or knowledgeable" about relevant matters. *Id.* at 16. The Arbitrator determined that although calling the FPS may have been "an over reaction[,]" it provided "corroboration that the [g]rievant's conduct was outside the norms for professional office demeanor[.]" *Id.* at 13. The Arbitrator then determined that "the [g]rievant's actions were sufficiently problematic to provide basis for disciplinary action against her." *Id.* at 14. Accordingly, the Arbitrator concluded that the Agency had "just cause for discipline." *Id.* at 17.

In reaching this conclusion, the Arbitrator addressed the Union's claims that: (1) the Agency had failed to comply with a promise to have a Union steward present when the grievant was receiving performance reviews "in order to help keep the situation calm and to avoid outburst problems[,]" *id.* at 13; (2) the grievant had a "stellar" work record until she began working for the supervisors, *id.* at 15; and (3) the Agency began writing the grievant up for performance and disciplinary problems after the supervisors' arrival, which indicated supervisory "animosity" and a "conspiracy[,]" *id.* With regard to the first claim, the Arbitrator stated that, even assuming that the alleged promise existed, the Union steward (steward) "testified that she was lurking just outside" the first-line supervisor's door during part of the performance review, which the Arbitrator found indicated that the steward had been informed of the negative content of the evaluation beforehand and that both the steward and the first-line supervisor were concerned about how the grievant would respond to the review. *Id.* at 13.

With regard to the second and third claims, the Arbitrator noted that the grievant's work history was not introduced into the record, and she stated that it was "just as logical to assume that new supervisory personnel were brought in to instill a new work ethic in the office and that the spate of performance and disciplinary charges" that followed "were justified by what might be labeled as insubordinate conduct brought about by the animosity of the employee rather than the supervisor." *Id.* at 15. In this regard, the Arbitrator found that the steward's testimony and affidavit from another proceeding described the steward's belief that the new supervisors showed favoritism, but the Arbitrator found that the testimony and affidavit were not "dispositive[]" and that "no evidence was introduced that actually supported this perception." *Id.*

With regard to whether a fourteen-day suspension was the appropriate penalty, the Arbitrator found that the Agency's disciplinary notice cited a prior instance of discipline for similar offenses, and, citing Article 13, Section 1A of the parties' agreement,[2] she found that a fourteen-day suspension was "the next step in the progressive discipline." *Id.* at 17. Accordingly, the Arbitrator upheld the fourteen-day suspension. *Id.*

However, the Arbitrator found that additional punishment of the grievant was not warranted. *Id.* In this regard, she found that the Agency improperly denied reinstating the grievant's building pass and credentials, and she "order[ed] that [they] be returned to her immediately[,]" and that any issues resulting from the lack of credentials could "not be used as a basis for negative performance evaluation or discipline . . . ." *Id.* at 19. In addition, the Arbitrator noted that, in a letter (Congressional letter) responding to an inquiry from a member of Congress, the Agency implied that the grievant had engaged in misconduct, without acknowledging that a grievance had been filed and that arbitration proceedings were ongoing. *Id.* The Arbitrator "order[ed] that the Agency review all of the actions taken with respect to the [g]rievant," including the Congressional letter, with the goal to eliminate "inappropriate extra-contractual punishment." *Id.* at 21. Finally, the Arbitrator directed that once any extra-contractual punishment is "retracted, rescinded and/or stopped[,] . . . [c]onfirmation of such action shall be given to the Union and the [g]rievant . . . ." *Id.* at 22.

III. Positions of the Parties

A. Union's Exceptions

The Union argues that the Agency violated 5 U.S.C. § 2302(b)(9) (§ 2302(b)(9)),[3] and that "[o]nce the Arbitrator was informed of the civil rights investigation and the prohibited personnel practice of retaliation . . . the Arbitrator had the legal duty to address and resolve these issues . . . ." Exceptions at 7. In this connection, the Union asserts that the Arbitrator "would not allow the Union to introduce pertinent and material evidence" regarding this issue. *Id.*

In addition, the Union argues that the Arbitrator lacked jurisdiction over the grievance under both the parties' agreement and § 7121(d) of the Statute (§ 7121(d)).[4] *Id.* at 2-4. In this regard, the Union claims that the grievant's amended EEO complaint involved, among other things, the proposed suspension. *Id.* at 3. The Union contends that, when the suspension was made final, the proposed suspension "merged" with the final suspension. *Id.* In addition, the Union asserts that the parties' negotiated grievance procedure (NGP) excludes grievances over EEO matters. *Id.* at 4.

The Union also argues that the award is contrary to law in several respects. First, the Union contends that the Arbitrator's direction that the Agency review whether it imposed additional punishment and "submit additional material ex parte[,]" and her failure to grant a remedy for the failure to timely return the grievant's credentials, are contrary to law. *See id.* at 4-5 (citing *Totem Marine Tug & Barge, Inc. v. N. Am. Towing, Inc.*, 607 F.2d 649 (5th Cir. 1979); *Chevron Transp. Corp. v. Astro Vencedor Compania Naviera, S.A.*, 300 F.Supp. 179 (S.D.N.Y. 1969); *Katz v. Uvegi*, 187 N.Y.S.2d 511, 518 (N.Y.Sup. 1959), *aff'd*, 205 N.Y.S.2d 972 (N.Y.A.D. 2 Dep't 1960); *Giove v. Dep't of Transp.*, 230 F.3d 1333 (Fed. Cir. 2000) (*Giove*)). Second, the Union argues that, when the Agency imposed discipline, the Agency failed to consider the factors set forth by the Merit Systems Protection Board (MSPB) in *Douglas v. Veterans Administration*, 5 M.S.P.R. 280, 305 (1981) (*Douglas*), and that the Arbitrator "erroneously shifted the burden of applying the *Douglas* factors to the [g]rievant." Exceptions at 9-10 (citing *Devine v. Pastore*, 732 F.2d 213 (D.C. Cir. 1984); *Eichner v. U.S. Postal Serv.*, 83 M.S.P.R. 202 (1999)). Third, the Union claims that the Arbitrator improperly shifted the rebuttal burden to the grievant. *Id.* at 8 (citing *Kissner v. OPM*, 792 F.2d 133, 134-35 (11th Cir. 1986) (*Kissner*)). Fourth, the Union contends that, in

2. Pertinent wording from the parties' agreement is set forth below.

3. Section 2302(b)(9) provides, in pertinent part, that certain employees shall not "take or fail to take, or threaten to take or fail to take, any personnel action against any employee . . . because of-- (A) the exercise of any appeal, complaint, or grievance right granted by any law, rule, or regulation[] . . . ."

4. Section 7121(d) provides, in pertinent part:

> An aggrieved employee affected by a prohibited personnel practice under section 2302(b)(1) of this title which also falls under the coverage of the negotiated grievance procedure may raise the matter under a statutory procedure or the negotiated procedure, but not both. An employee shall be deemed to have exercised his option under this subsection to raise the matter under either a statutory procedure or the negotiated procedure at such time as the employee timely initiates an action under the applicable statutory procedure or timely files a grievance in writing, in accordance with the provisions of the parties' negotiated procedure, whichever event occurs first . . . .

making credibility determinations, the Arbitrator failed to consider numerous factors required by the MSPB. *Id.* at 11-13 (citing *Hillen v. Dep't of Army*, 35 M.S.P.R. 453, 458 (1987) (*Hillen*); *Barrett v. Dep't of Interior*, 65 M.S.P.R. 186, 194 (1994), *review reinstated*, 65 F.3d 187 (Fed. Cir. 1995) (*Barrett*)). Fifth, citing *NFFE, Local 615*, 17 FLRA 318 (1985), *petition for review denied*, 801 F.2d 477 (D.C. Cir. 1986) (*Local 615*), the Union claims that the Arbitrator failed to recognize "the difference between no investigation and a non-thorough investigation." Exceptions at 14.

Additionally, the Union contends that the Arbitrator exceeded her authority. In this regard, the Union argues that the Arbitrator failed to determine whether: (1) there was just cause for the suspension, *id.* at 9; (2) the delay in returning the grievant's credentials constituted "punishment, retaliation, or other misconduct", *id.* at 5; and (3) the Congressional letter harmed the grievant, *id.* at 5-6. In addition, the Union asserts that the Arbitrator exceeded her authority by "interpos[ing] her personal interpretations" of the second-line supervisor's letter, and by failing to note contradictions in the second-line supervisor's statements in the letter and in her testimony. *Id.* at 13.

Further, the Union challenges the Arbitrator's decision not to rely on certain testimony. *Id.* at 12. The Union also challenges the Arbitrator's decision not to discredit the supervisors' testimony, and asserts that the Arbitrator improperly found that inconsistencies in the testimony could be attributable to "witness overpreparation and nervousness" when "[a]n equally valid conclusion is that [the supervisor] was lying . . . ." *Id.*

Moreover, the Union asserts that although the Arbitrator acknowledged that Article 16, Section 5C of the parties' agreement requires that the record be kept open only in "unusual situations," the Arbitrator kept the record open without finding an unusual situation. *Id.* at 4. The Union also asserts that although Article 13, Section 1C of the parties' agreement requires that discipline be for just cause, the Arbitrator erroneously applied a "sufficiently problematic" standard, which does not equate to just cause. *Id.* at 9. In addition, the Union contends that the Arbitrator "wrongly applied" Article 13, Section 1A of the agreement when she found that the fourteen-day suspension was the next step in progressive discipline. *Id.* at 10.

The Union also asserts that the Arbitrator was biased. *Id.* at 14. In this regard, the Union asserts that the Arbitrator's statement that the steward was "lurking" outside the first-line supervisor's door casts doubt on the Arbitrator's objectivity. *Id.* at 15. In addition, the Union asserts that the Arbitrator routinely credited the Agency's witnesses over the Union's witnesses. *Id.* at 13. Further, the Union asserts that the Arbitrator exhibited bias when she "sided with" the Agency and found that the call to FPS "corroborat[ed]" the Agency's claim that the grievant acted improperly. *Id.* at 15.

Finally, the Union argues that the Arbitrator "ma[de] up evidence" and found that there was a non-thorough investigation, when there was "conflicting . . . evidence . . . as to whether an investigation was actually conducted." *Id.* at 14. The Union also argues that the Arbitrator "created . . . evidence" when she rejected the Union's claim regarding new management targeting the grievant. *Id.* at 12.

B. Agency's Opposition

The Agency argues that the Authority should not consider the Union's exception regarding § 2302(b)(9) because the Union did not raise its argument before the Arbitrator. Opp'n at 22-23. As for the Union's claim that the Arbitrator did not permit relevant witnesses in connection with the § 2302(b)(9) claim, the Agency asserts that the parties agreed on witness lists prior to the hearing and that the Union does not identify any witnesses that were not permitted to testify. *Id.* at 27.

The Agency also claims that the Arbitrator had jurisdiction to resolve the grievance. *Id.* at 14. As an initial matter, the Agency claims that § 7121(d) did not bar the grievance because that wording applies only when an NGP covers EEO matters, and the parties' NGP excludes such matters. *Id.* at 14-15. Even assuming that § 7121(d) applies, the Agency argues that it does not bar the grievance because the grievant never included the fourteen-day suspension as an issue in her EEO proceeding. *Id.* at 15.

In addition, the Agency contends that the award is not contrary to law. *Id.* at 27. In particular, the Agency argues that MSPB precedent does not apply because the Arbitrator was resolving a fourteen-day suspension. *Id.* at 30.

The Agency also argues that the Arbitrator did not exceed her authority because she resolved the issues submitted. *Id.* at 21-22. Further, the Agency argues that the Union's allegation of future "ex parte" receipt of evidence is "baseless[]" because the

Arbitrator expressly directed the Agency to advise the Union and the grievant of its determinations regarding any additional punishment that had been imposed. *Id.* at 18.

The Agency contends that the Union's challenges to the Arbitrator's credibility determinations do not demonstrate that the award is deficient. *Id.* at 30-31. The Agency also contends that the Arbitrator was not biased. *Id.* at 32-33. Finally, with regard to the Union's assertion that the Arbitrator "made[]up" facts, the Agency contends that disagreement with the Arbitrator's evaluation of evidence and the weight to accord that evidence is insufficient to demonstrate that the award is deficient. *Id.* at 31-32 (quoting Exceptions at 14).

IV. Preliminary Issues

The Authority's Regulations that were in effect when the Agency filed its exceptions provided that "[t]he Authority will not consider . . . any issue [] which was not presented in the proceedings before the . . . arbitrator." 5 C.F.R. § 2429.5 (§ 2429.5).[5] Under § 2429.5, the Authority will not consider any issue that could have been, but was not, presented to the arbitrator. *E.g.*, *U.S. DHS, U.S. Customs & Border Prot., JFK Airport, Queens, N.Y.*, 62 FLRA 416, 417 (2008). In addition, where a party makes an argument before the Authority that is inconsistent with its position before the arbitrator, the Authority applies § 2429.5 to bar the argument. *E.g.*, *U.S. Dep't of Transp., FAA, Detroit, Mich.*, 64 FLRA 325, 328 (2009).

There is no record evidence that the Union raised its argument regarding § 2302(b)(9) before the Arbitrator. Although the Union asserts that the Arbitrator precluded it from introducing evidence on this issue, the Union does not cite any record evidence that supports this assertion. In fact, the Arbitrator found the parties had "agreed upon how to handle the witness lists[,]" Award at 6, and there are no exceptions to that finding. As there is no evidence that the Union raised § 2302(b)(9) before the Arbitrator, and no basis for finding that it was improperly precluded from doing so, we dismiss the Union's exception regarding § 2302(b)(9).

With regard to the Union's claims that the Arbitrator lacked jurisdiction under both the parties' agreement and § 7121(d), the Authority has applied § 2429.5 to bar arguments challenging an arbitrator's contractual jurisdiction if those arguments were not raised before the Arbitrator. *See U.S. Dep't of the Air Force, Okla. Air Logistics Ctr., Tinker Air Force Base, Okla.*, 58 FLRA 760, 761 (2003). As the Union not only failed to argue before the Arbitrator that the parties' agreement precluded him from exercising jurisdiction but also expressly conceded that the grievance was properly before the Arbitrator, we find that § 2429.5 bars the Union from challenging the Arbitrator's contractual jurisdiction, and we dismiss the exception.

As for the Union's claim regarding § 7121(d), the Authority has declined to apply § 2429.5 to bar arguments challenging an arbitrator's *statutory* jurisdiction. *E.g.*, *U.S. Dep't of Agric., Food & Consumer Serv., Dallas, Tex.*, 60 FLRA 978, 980-81 (2005) (then-Member Pope dissenting in part on other grounds) (resolving merits of claim that arbitrator lacked jurisdiction under § 7121(c)(5) of the Statute, despite party's failure to raise claim to arbitrator). The Authority has applied this principle to the election of remedies provision in § 7121(d). *See U.S. DOJ, INS, El Paso, Tex.*, 40 FLRA 43, 49-52 (1991) (the Authority found claim regarding § 7121(d) was properly raised in exceptions despite excepting party's failure to raise it below). *Cf. U.S. Dep't of the Navy, Naval Air Eng'g Station, Lakehurst, N.J.*, 64 FLRA 1110, 1111 (2010) (considering argument regarding election-of-remedies provision in § 7116(d) of the Statute despite party's failure to raise it before arbitrator). There are significant factual distinctions between the cited precedent and this case.[6] However, even assuming

5. The Authority's Regulations concerning the review of arbitration awards, as well as certain related procedural Regulations, including § 2429.5, were revised effective October 1, 2010. *See* 75 Fed. Reg. 42,283 (2010). As the Union's exceptions were filed before that date, we apply the earlier Regulations.

6. In the above-cited Authority decisions, the excepting parties -- unlike the Union here -- did not expressly concede jurisdiction before the arbitrators and were not the parties that invoked arbitration. We note, in this regard, that had this case arisen in the private sector, the Union's actions at arbitration would have precluded it from challenging the Arbitrator's jurisdiction on appeal. *See, e.g.*, *United Indus. Workers v. Gov't of the Virgin Is.*, 987 F.2d 162, 168 (3rd Cir. 1993) ("[o]nce . . . parties have mutually agreed to refer a matter to an arbitrator, they are bound by his decision and may not later challenge his authority to resolve the claim"); *Howard Univ. v. Metro. Campus Police Officers Union*, 512 F.3d 716, 720 (D.C. Cir. 2008) (citations omitted) (absent "excusable ignorance of a predicate fact," a party that does not object to an arbitrator's jurisdiction during the arbitration may not later do so in court); *Int'l Paper Co. v. Schwabedissen Maschinen & Anlagen GMBH*, 206 F.3d 411, 418 (4th Cir. 2000) (party was estopped from claiming that his

that the Union's § 7121(d) claim is properly before us, we find, for the reasons discussed further below, that § 7121(d) does not apply in this case.

V. Analysis and Conclusions

A. The award is not contrary to law.

The Authority reviews questions of law *de novo*. *See NTEU, Chapter 24*, 50 FLRA 330, 332 (1995) (citing *U.S. Customs Serv. v. FLRA*, 43 F.3d 682, 686-87 (D.C. Cir. 1994)). In applying a standard of *de novo* review, the Authority determines whether the arbitrator's legal conclusions are consistent with the applicable standard of law. *NFFE, Local 1437*, 53 FLRA 1703, 1710 (1998). In making that determination, the Authority defers to the arbitrator's underlying factual findings. *See id.*

The Union claims that the award is contrary to § 7121(d), which provides that "[a]n aggrieved employee affected by a prohibited personnel practice under [§] 2302(b)(1) of this title *which also falls under the coverage of the negotiated grievance procedure* may raise the matter under a statutory procedure or the negotiated procedure, but not both." 5 U.S.C. § 7121(d) (emphasis added). Article 15, Section 2 of the parties' agreement excludes from the parties' NGP "a matter which is subject to a statutory appeal procedure . . . outside the [Agency] under law or the regulations of the . . . [Equal Employment Opportunity Commission] including . . . EEO [d]iscrimination[,]" for which the "[a]vailable [p]rocedure" is that set forth in "29 C[.]F[.]R[.] [part] 1614." Exceptions, Attach., Collective Bargaining Agreement at 35. Thus, the allegation of unlawful discrimination does not "fall[] under the coverage" of the NGP, within the meaning of § 7121(d). As a result, § 7121(d) does not apply and, consequently, cannot provide a basis for barring the grievance and finding that the award is contrary to law.[7]

In addition, the Union argues that the award is contrary to precedent prohibiting "ex parte" communications. Exceptions at 5. However, the Arbitrator directed that confirmation of the Agency's subsequent actions "be given to the Union and the [g]rievant[,]" Award at 22, and, thus, she did not direct any ex parte communications. With regard to the Union's reliance on *Giove*, 230 F.3d 1333, and its claim that the Arbitrator did not provide a remedy for the failure to timely return the grievant's credentials, the Arbitrator did provide a remedy by directing the Agency to restore the credentials. Accordingly, the premises of these legal arguments are inaccurate and do not provide a basis for finding the award contrary to law.

With regard to the Union's reliance on the *Douglas* factors, those factors are applied by the MSPB in evaluating whether a particular disciplinary action should be mitigated. *U.S. DHS, U.S. Customs & Border Prot.*, 65 FLRA 373, 375 (2010) (Member Beck dissenting in part on other grounds) (*CBP*). With regard to the Union's citation to *Kissner*, 792 F.2d 133, that Federal Circuit decision involved the burdens of proof that the MSPB applies when reviewing a removal action. Arbitrators are bound by the same substantive standards as the MSPB only when resolving grievances concerning actions covered by 5 U.S.C. §§ 4303 and 7512. *CBP*, 65 FLRA at 375. As suspensions of fourteen days or less are not covered by §§ 4303 and 7512, the Union's exception does not provide a basis for finding the award contrary to law. For the same reason, the Union's reliance on MSPB precedent regarding the factors that the MSPB applies in making credibility determinations and reviewing its administrative judges' credibility determinations is misplaced and provides no basis for finding the award deficient.

In addition, the Union, citing *Local 615*, 17 FLRA 318, asserts that the Arbitrator erred by failing to distinguish a non-thorough investigation from the failure to conduct any investigation. However, *Local 615* did not hold that agencies are required to take any particular actions in investigating proposed discipline and, thus, that decision does not provide any basis for finding that the award is contrary to law.

For the foregoing reasons, we deny the contrary-to-law exceptions.

---

lack of signature on written contract precluded enforcement of contract's arbitration clause when he had consistently maintained that other provisions of same contract should be enforced to benefit him). Nevertheless, in view of our determination that § 7121(d) does not apply in this case, it is unnecessary to decide whether the Union's § 7121(d) claim should be barred. *Cf. Pan. Area Mar./Metal Trades Council, AFL-CIO (M/MTC)*, 55 FLRA 1199, 1200 (1999) (Authority assumed, without deciding, that it had jurisdiction).

7. We note that the issue before the Arbitrator was whether the suspension was for just cause, not whether the suspension constituted unlawful discrimination.

B. The Arbitrator did not exceed her authority.

Arbitrators exceed their authority when they fail to resolve an issue submitted to arbitration, resolve an issue not submitted to arbitration, disregard specific limitations on their authority, or award relief to those not encompassed within the grievance. *AFGE, Local 1617*, 51 FLRA 1645, 1647 (1996). In addition, the Authority has held that arbitrators have great latitude in fashioning remedies. *E.g., U.S. Dep't of Veterans Affairs, Montgomery Reg'l Office, Montgomery, Ala.*, 65 FLRA 487, 490 (2011). Thus, an arbitrator is not required to provide a remedy for every violation of a collective bargaining agreement, *Nat'l Ass'n of Air Traffic Specialists, NAGE, SEIU*, 61 FLRA 558, 559 (2006), and the Authority has denied exceptions that constitute an attempt to substitute another remedy for that formulated by the arbitrator, *NAGE, Local R4-45*, 55 FLRA 789, 793 (1999).

The Union argues that the Arbitrator failed to decide whether there was just cause for the suspension. To the extent that the Union is claiming that the Arbitrator exceeded her authority in this regard, the Arbitrator directly addressed the just-cause issue and found that there was just cause for discipline. *See* Award at 17. Thus, the Union's claim does not demonstrate that the award is deficient. Similarly, we deny the Union's claim that the Arbitrator exceeded her authority by declining to find that the Agency acted improperly by failing to return the grievant's credentials and building pass and by failing to determine whether sending the Congressional letter harmed the grievant. In this connection, the Arbitrator did find that it was improper for the Agency to withhold the grievant's credentials, and she directed that the Agency take actions regarding the credentials and the Congressional letter. *Id.* at 19-22. Thus, the Union does not demonstrate that the Arbitrator failed to resolve issues before her.

Finally, the Union cites Article 16, Section 6A of the parties' agreement -- which states that arbitrators are confined to an interpretation of the agreement and Agency regulations -- and asserts that the Arbitrator credited testimony not in evidence. The Union's assertion does not provide a basis for finding that the Arbitrator failed to resolve an issue submitted, resolved an issue not submitted, disregarded specific limitations on her authority, or awarded relief to individuals not encompassed within the grievance. Accordingly, the assertion provides no basis for finding the award deficient.

For the foregoing reasons, we deny the exceeded-authority exceptions.

C. The Arbitrator did not deny the Union a fair hearing.

The Authority will find that an arbitrator denied a fair hearing when the excepting party demonstrates that the arbitrator refused to hear or consider pertinent or material evidence or conducted the proceedings in a manner that so prejudiced a party as to affect the fairness of the proceedings as a whole. *U.S. Dep't of Transp., FAA*, 65 FLRA 320, 323 (2010) (*FAA*). However, arbitrators have considerable latitude in the conduct of hearings, and a party's objection to the manner in which the arbitrator conducted the hearing does not alone provide a basis for finding the award deficient. *Id.* In addition, the Authority has held that disagreement with an arbitrator's evaluation of evidence, including the determination of the weight to be accorded such evidence, provides no basis for finding an award deficient. *U.S. Dep't of Veterans Affairs, Veterans Affairs Med. Ctr., Louisville, Ky.*, 64 FLRA 70, 72 (2009).

The Union argues that the Arbitrator erroneously declined to rely on certain testimony. We construe this as a claim that the Arbitrator failed to provide a fair hearing. *See, e.g., id.* (construing challenges to arbitrator's credibility determinations as fair-hearing claims). However, as stated above, the Authority has held that disagreement with an arbitrator's evaluation of evidence, including the determination of the weight to be accorded such evidence, provides no basis for finding an award deficient. *Id.* Accordingly, we deny the fair-hearing exception.

D. The award does not fail to draw its essence from the parties' agreement.

In reviewing an arbitrator's interpretation of a collective bargaining agreement, the Authority applies the deferential standard of review that federal courts use in reviewing arbitration awards in the private sector. *See* 5 U.S.C. § 7122(a); *AFGE, Council 220*, 54 FLRA 156, 159 (1998). Under this standard, the Authority will find that an arbitration award is deficient as failing to draw its essence from the collective bargaining agreement when the appealing party establishes that the award: (1) cannot in any rational way be derived from the agreement; (2) is so unfounded in reason and fact and so unconnected with the wording and purposes of the agreement as to manifest an infidelity to the obligation of the arbitrator; (3) does not represent a plausible interpretation of the agreement; or (4) evidences a manifest disregard of the agreement. *See U.S. Dep't of Labor (OSHA)*, 34 FLRA 573, 575 (1990). The Authority and the courts defer to arbitrators in this context because it is the arbitrator's construction of the agreement for which the parties have bargained. *Id.* at 576.

The Union asserts that, contrary to Article 16, Section 5C of the agreement, the Arbitrator kept the record open to receive additional, ex parte evidence from the Agency regarding whether the Agency imposed additional punishment on the grievant. Article 16, Section 5C of the agreement provides, in pertinent part, that "[e]xcept in unusual situations, the arbitrator will not have the authority to keep the record open in order to hear testimony of additional witnesses." Award at 4. However, the Arbitrator did not keep the record open in order to hear testimony of additional witnesses. Accordingly, the Union's assertion does not demonstrate that the award is deficient.

The Union also asserts that although the Arbitrator found that the grievant's conduct was "[s]ufficiently problematic" to support discipline, Article 13, Section 1C of the parties' agreement requires that discipline be for just cause. Exceptions at 9. Article 13, Section 1C provides: "No bargaining unit employee will be the subject of a disciplinary action except for just and sufficient cause and for reasons which will promote the efficiency of the [Agency]." Award at 2. As the Arbitrator expressly found that the discipline was for "just cause[,]" *id.* at 17, the Union does not provide a basis for finding that the Arbitrator's interpretation of Article 13, Section 1C was irrational, unfounded, implausible, or in manifest disregard of the agreement.

Further, the Union contends that the Arbitrator erroneously found that Article 13, Section 1A of the agreement is a table of penalties when, in fact, it merely defines what a disciplinary action is. Article 13, Section 1A provides, in pertinent part: "A disciplinary action, for the purposes of this Article, is defined as an oral admonishment confirmed in writing, a written reprimand or a suspension for [fourteen] calendar days or less." *Id.* at 2. The Arbitrator cited this provision and found that, after the grievant's previous discipline, a fourteen-day suspension was the next step in progressive discipline. The Union provides no basis for finding that it was irrational, unfounded, implausible, or in manifest disregard of the agreement for the Arbitrator to construe Article 13, Section 1A as providing a series of progressive steps of discipline.

For the foregoing reasons, we deny the essence exceptions.

E. The Arbitrator was not biased.

To establish that an arbitrator was biased, the moving party must demonstrate that the award was procured by improper means, that there was partiality or corruption on the part of the arbitrator, or that the arbitrator engaged in misconduct that prejudiced the rights of the party. *E.g., AFGE, Local 3438*, 65 FLRA 2, 3 (2010). The Authority has denied exceptions based on an arbitrator's remarks indicating concern with a party's conduct. *E.g., AFGE, Local 2382*, 64 FLRA 713, 717 (2010) (*Local 2382*). In addition, a party's assertion that all of an arbitrator's findings were adverse to that party, without more, does not demonstrate that an arbitrator was biased. *E.g., AFGE, Local 3354*, 64 FLRA 330, 332 (2009) (*Local 3354*). Further, where the Authority denies a party's fair-hearing exception, and the party's bias exception is based on its fair-hearing exception, the Authority also denies the bias exception. *E.g., FAA*, 65 FLRA at 323.

The Union argues that the Arbitrator's use of the term "lurking" to describe the steward's actions "brings into question the objectivity of the Arbitrator." Exceptions at 15. To the extent that this is a claim that the Arbitrator was biased because she made remarks that indicated concern with the steward's conduct, as stated previously, such claims do not establish that an arbitrator is biased. *See Local 2382*, 64 FLRA at 717.

Further, the Union argues that the Arbitrator improperly credited all of the Agency's witnesses' testimony while failing to credit the testimony of Union witnesses. To the extent that the Union is claiming that the Arbitrator was biased in this regard, as stated above, the fact that all of an arbitrator's findings are adverse to one party does not, without more, demonstrate that the arbitrator was biased. *See Local 3354*, 64 FLRA at 332. Accordingly, the Union's argument does not demonstrate that the Arbitrator was biased.

Finally, the Union argues that the Arbitrator was biased because she credited certain evidence. In effect, this argument repeats the Union's credibility challenge, which we previously have denied on fair-hearing grounds. As this argument merely repeats the fair-hearing argument, we also deny this exception. *See FAA*, 65 FLRA at 323.

For the foregoing reasons, we deny the bias exceptions.

F. The award is not based on nonfacts.

To establish that an award is based on a nonfact, the appealing party must show that a central fact underlying the award is clearly erroneous, but for which the arbitrator would have reached a different result. *E.g., AFGE, Local 3380*, 65 FLRA 390, 393 (2010) (*Local 3380*). However, the Authority will not find an award deficient on the basis of an arbitrator's determination of any factual matter that the parties disputed at arbitration. *Id.* In addition, the Authority has denied nonfact exceptions that challenge an arbitrator's credibility determinations, stating that exceptions disputing an arbitrator's evaluation of the credibility of witnesses and the weight to be given their testimony provide no basis for finding an award deficient. *U.S. Dep't of the Treasury, IRS, Kan. City, Field Compliance Serv.*, 60 FLRA 401, 403 (2004).

The Union argues that the Arbitrator "ma[de] up evidence" and found that there was a non-thorough investigation, when there was "conflicting . . . evidence . . . as to whether an investigation was actually conducted." Exceptions at 14. To the extent that the Union is claiming that the award is based on a nonfact, the Union's statement that there was "conflicting . . . evidence" on this factual issue concedes that the issue was disputed before the Arbitrator. *Id.* As such, the Union's argument provides no basis for finding the award based on a nonfact. *See Local 3380*, 65 FLRA at 393-94.

The Union also argues that the Arbitrator "created evidence" when she rejected the Union's claim that new management was targeting the grievant and, instead, found it "just as logical to assume" that management was brought in to instill a new work ethic and that the subsequent disciplinary and performance problems were justified by insubordinate conduct based on employee animosity. Exceptions at 12. To the extent that the Union is arguing that the award is based on a nonfact, the Union's claim does not explain how a central fact underlying the award is clearly erroneous, but for which the Arbitrator would have reached a different result. Thus, the claim does not provide a basis for finding that the award is based on a nonfact. *See Local 3380*, 65 FLRA at 393-94.

For the foregoing reasons, we deny the nonfact exceptions.

VI. Decision

The Union's exceptions are dismissed in part and denied in part.

65 FLRA No. 149

UNITED STATES
DEPARTMENT OF VETERANS AFFAIRS
NEBRASKA/WESTERN IOWA
VA HEALTH CARE SYSTEM
OMAHA, NEBRASKA
(Agency/Petitioner)

and

AMERICAN FEDERATION
OF GOVERNMENT EMPLOYEES
AFL-CIO
(Incumbent Labor Organization/Petitioner)

DE-RP-10-0017
DE-RP-10-0018
DE-RP-10-0028

ORDER GRANTING
APPLICATION FOR REVIEW

April 8, 2011

Before the Authority: Carol Waller Pope, Chairman, and Thomas M. Beck and Ernest DuBester, Members

I. Statement of the Case

This case is before the Authority on an application for review filed by the Nebraska/Western Iowa VA Healthcare System (Agency or NWI), under § 2422.31 of the Authority's Regulations. [1] The petitions filed in this case were filed as a result of a reorganization that led to the formation of NWI. RD's Decision at 2-3.

The Union filed two petitions: one seeking a unit of all professional employees at NWI, and one seeking a unit of all non-professional employees at NWI. In its petitions, the Union contends that each of the bargaining units should be formed through the doctrine of successorship. The Agency filed a cross-petition seeking four units within NWI.

The Regional Director (RD) granted the Union's two petitions, finding that NWI was the successor employer of VA Medical Center employees located in Omaha, Lincoln, and Grand Island, Nebraska and Community-Based Outpatient Clinic (CBOC) employees at various locations in Nebraska and Iowa. The RD also dismissed the Agency's cross-petition.

For the reasons that follow, we grant the application for review on the grounds that there is a genuine issue over whether the RD failed to apply established law and whether the RD committed a clear and prejudicial error concerning a substantial factual matter under § 2422.31(c)(3)(i) and (iii), respectively. On review, we conclude that the RD erred in both of these respects. We therefore remand the matter to the RD to issue appropriate certifications.

II. Background and RD's Decision

NWI was created by a reorganization in 1999. In 2010, three petitions were filed to resolve representation issues resulting from the reorganization. The petitions dealt with the realignment in 1999 of VA Medical Center employees located in Omaha, Lincoln, and Grand Island into NWI. The petitions also addressed the bargaining unit status of employees located at the Bellevue, Holdrege, Norfolk, and North Platte, Nebraska, and Shenandoah, Iowa CBOCs. RD's Decision at 1-2.

The RD found that, for years, the Union has been the exclusive representative of units of both professional and non-professional VA employees. *Id.* at 8. The RD determined that, at the time of the hearing, the American Federation of Government Employees (AFGE), Local 2219 represented the professional and nonprofessional employees located at Lincoln; AFGE, Local 2270 represented professional nurses and nonprofessional employees located at Omaha; and AFGE, Local 2601 represented the professional and nonprofessional employees located at Grand Island and the non-

1. Section 2422.31 of the Authority's Regulations provides, in pertinent part:

> (c) Review. The Authority may grant an application for review only when the application demonstrates that review is warranted on one or more of the following grounds:
>
> (1) The decision raises an issue for which there is an absence of precedent;
>
> (2) Established law or policy warrants reconsideration; or,
>
> (3) There is a genuine issue over whether the Regional Director has:
>
> (i) Failed to apply established law;
>
> (ii) Committed a prejudicial procedural error;
>
> (iii) Committed a clear and prejudicial error concerning a substantial factual matter.

professional employees located at the Holdrege CBOC. *Id.* at 9-10.

The Union filed two petitions: one seeking a unit of all professional employees at NWI, and one seeking a unit of all non-professional employees at NWI. In its petitions, the Union contends that each of the bargaining units should be formed through the doctrine of successorship.[2] *Id.* at 2. The Agency filed a cross-petition seeking four more limited units within NWI.[3] *Id.*

As pertinent here, the RD determined that the petitions raised the following issues:

1. Whether NWI is an appropriate unit for purposes of exclusive recognition; and

2. Whether NWI is a successor employer for any employees represented by AFGE.

Id. at 12.

The RD made the following findings in response to the issues identified above. First, applying the statutory criteria for determining whether a unit is an appropriate unit for exclusive recognition, the RD found that the Union's requested units of professional and non-professional employees at NWI are appropriate for exclusive recognition under § 7112(a) of the Federal Service Labor-Management Relations Statute (the Statute). *Id.* at 12-17. Second, the RD determined that NWI is a successor employer, as set forth below. With respect to the latter point, the RD applied the Authority's three-pronged framework described in *Naval Facilities Engineering Service Center (NFESC), Port Hueneme, Cal.*, 50 FLRA 363 (1995) (*Port Hueneme*), to determine whether NWI constituted a successor employer.

As set forth in *Port Hueneme*, an entity is considered to be a successor employer, and the labor organization involved retains its status as exclusive representative of the transferred employees, where:

(1) An entire recognized unit, or a portion thereof, is transferred and the transferred employees: (a) are in an appropriate bargaining unit . . . after the transfer; and (b) constitute a majority of the employees in such unit;

(2) The gaining entity has substantially the same organizational mission as the losing entity, with the transferred employees performing substantially the same duties and functions under substantially similar working conditions . . .; and

(3) It has not been demonstrated that an election is necessary to determine representation.

Id. at 368.

With regard to the first prong, the RD determined that the employees in each of the previously recognized units at Omaha, Lincoln, and Grand Island, and the professional employees at Holdrege, were "transferred" to NWI. RD's Decision at 19. Next, the RD reiterated his prior determinations that two units of all professional and non-professional NWI employees are appropriate. *Id.* Last, the RD determined that the transferred employees constitute a majority of the employees of each unit.[4] *Id.* Thus, the RD found, the first prong of the successorship framework is met.

The RD also made findings with respect to the second and third prongs of *Port Hueneme's* successorship framework. Regarding the second prong, the RD found that the creation of NWI did not change the overall mission of the entities involved to maintain the health and well-being of veterans. *Id.* at 19-20. The RD further found that the transferred employees perform substantially the same duties and functions under substantially similar working conditions at NWI as they did prior to their transfer. *Id.* at 20. The RD also found that, in any event, under the existing Master Labor Agreement the parties' Partnership Council would address any

2. The petition in Case No. DE-RP-10-0017 seeks to clarify the bargaining unit status of approximately 775 professional NWI employees working in the VA Medical Centers and five CBOCs. The petition in Case No. DE-RP-10-0018 seeks to clarify the bargaining unit status of approximately 1,034 non-professional NWI employees working in the VA Medical Centers and the five CBOCs. RD's Decision at 2.

3. The Agency's cross-petition is designated Case No. DE-RP-10-0028. In its application for review, the Agency does not maintain that the units sought in its petition should be established.

4. Specifically, the RD found that the Union represented a total of 641 professional employees, and 1,018 non-professional employees in the NWI units he found appropriate, while only 134 professional employees and 16 non-professional employees remain unrepresented. RD's Decision at 19.

changes to employees' job duties. Therefore, the RD concluded, the second prong of the framework is met. With regard to the third prong, the RD found that an election is unnecessary since the Union represents a clear majority of the employees. Therefore, the RD determined, the third prong of the framework is also met. *Id.*

Consequently, the RD concluded that NWI is a successor employer. The RD thus determined that the unit certifications should be amended to reflect the Union's status as exclusive representative of one professional unit and one non-professional unit of all employees assigned to NWI including all CBOC employees. *Id.*

III. Positions of the Parties

A. Agency's Application for Review

The Agency agrees with the RD's conclusions, with two exceptions. First, the Agency argues for the continued exclusion of the non-nurse professional Omaha employees from the NWI professional unit. The Agency points out that these employees had been specifically excluded from the Omaha professional employee unit transferred to NWI in 1999. Application for Review at 13. Second, the Agency contends that all CBOC employees, both professional and non-professional, who are located at CBOCs that were not in existence in 1999, should be excluded from each of the respective NWI units that the RD found appropriate. *Id.* at 11, 13-14.[5]

In support, the Agency makes a number of claims. First, the Agency argues that the RD failed to apply established law by erroneously applying *Port Hueneme* to include in the NWI professional unit the Omaha non-nurse professional employees who were specifically excluded from the Omaha unit transferred to NWI. *Id.* at 6. According to the Agency, to find successorship under *Port Hueneme's* framework, the employees transferred as a result of a reorganization must be part of an appropriate bargaining unit prior to the transfer. Here, the Agency argues, the Omaha professional employees were not part of an appropriate bargaining unit prior to the unit's transfer, but rather, were specifically excluded from the unit. Thus, the Agency claims, the doctrine of successorship cannot be used to include them in the unit following that transfer. *Id.* at 8

The Agency further argues that doing so would be inconsistent with the purpose behind the successorship doctrine, which is intended to preserve and maintain a pre-existing bargaining relationship that would otherwise be disrupted by a reorganization. As applied here, the Agency contends, the successorship doctrine would not preserve the existing bargaining relationship. Rather, the Agency claims, the application of the successorship doctrine would change the bargaining relationship by including employees in the unit who, previously, were specifically excluded from the bargaining unit. *Id.* Therefore, the Agency argues, the RD failed to apply established law.

In addition, the Agency argues that to include previously excluded employees in a post-transfer unit expansion, an additional test must be met. *Id.* at 9. Specifically, the Agency argues that there must be "'meaningful changes' in the employees' duties, functions, or job circumstances that eliminate the original distinctions between employees and thus warrant their inclusion into the unit." *Id.* (citing *Def. Logistics Agency Def. Supply Ctr. Columbus, Columbus, Ohio,* 53 FLRA 1114, 1124 (1998) (*DLA, Columbus*)).

Second, the Agency claims that, if *Port Hueneme* does not address the question raised by the Omaha professional employees who had been specifically excluded from the Union's bargaining unit, then the RD's decision raises an issue for which there is an absence of precedent. *Id.* at 10.

Third, the Agency contends that the RD failed to apply established law by determining that NWI is a successor employer for unrepresented CBOC employees who were not employed at NWI at the time of the reorganization. *Id.* at 10-12. According to the Agency, the successorship doctrine was meant to be applied at the time of the reorganization and resulting transfer of employees from the losing organization to the gaining organization. *Id.* at 11. Applying this principle, the Agency makes three main arguments. The Agency argues that, as the CBOC employees were hired directly into NWI

5. Thus, the Agency agrees to the formation of a single NWI professional unit and a single NWI non-professional unit, excluding only Omaha's non-nurse professional employees and employees of the CBOCs formed after 1999; that is, the Bellevue, Holdrege, and Norfolk, Nebraska, and Shenandoah, Iowa CBOCs. The record does not include the number of non-nurse professional employees who were specifically excluded from the Omaha professional unit. However, because their exclusion from the NWI professional unit, as the Agency seeks, would only reduce the number of unrepresented professionals in that unit, their exclusion would not alter the RD's conclusion that the represented employees are a "clear majority." RD's Decision at 20. *See also* n.4, *supra*.

several years after the 1999 reorganization that gave rise to this case, those employees could not have been transferred as part of that reorganization. *Id.* Further, the Agency asserts, as the CBOC employees were hired directly into NWI, they were not transferred at all. *Id.* Finally, the Agency argues, successorship principles allowing for the inclusion of formerly unrepresented employees in an appropriate successor unit do not apply because the disputed CBOC employees did not exist at the time of the transfer. *Id.*

Fourth, the Agency claims that, if Authority successorship precedent does not address the question raised by the unrepresented CBOC employees, then the RD's decision raises an issue for which there is an absence of precedent. *Id.* at 12.

Fifth, the Agency claims that the RD made a prejudicial factual error in finding that the Holdrege CBOC professional employees were transferred to NWI. *See* RD's Decision at 19; Application for Review at 12-13. The Agency claims that, contrary to the RD's factual findings, it was the North Platte employees, not the Holdrege professional employees, who were transferred to NWI as a result of the reorganization. According to the Agency, the North Platte CBOC was created in 1995, prior to the reorganization. Therefore, the Agency asserts, North Platte employees were capable of being "transferred" to NWI in the 1999 reorganization. *Id.* The Agency argues that the Holdrege CBOC only came into existence between 2007 and 2009 and therefore, could not have been transferred to NWI as part of the 1999 reorganization.[6]

Sixth, the Agency argues that the RD failed to apply established law by misapplying the third prong of the *Port Hueneme* test for successorship. *Id.* at 13. In this regard, the Agency claims that the RD erroneously determined that an election was not required because the unit employees who had been transferred to NWI constituted a majority of all transferred employees. *Id.* In the Agency's view, contrary to the RD's findings, an election is required as to the Omaha professional employees and the unrepresented CBOC employees. The Agency argues that the third prong of the test has not been met with regard to these employees because none of them were ever part of an appropriate bargaining unit, and because, aside from the CBOC employees located at the North Platte CBOC created in 1995, none of these employees were ever "transferred" to NWI. *Id.*

B. Union's Opposition

The Union contends that the RD correctly applied *Port Hueneme's* successorship framework. The Union agrees with the RD's appropriate unit findings. Specifically, the Union claims that the RD properly determined that excluding the Omaha non-nurse professional employees from the unit would promote unit fragmentation. Opp'n at 5. The Union argues that the RD properly applied Authority precedent in finding that one unit of NWI non-professional employees and one unit of NWI professional employees is appropriate. *Id.* at 1, 6.

Further, the Union agrees with the RD's finding that an election is not required in this case. The Union argues that the RD's determination in this regard was proper because a majority of the employees who were transferred to NWI were previously part of the Union's bargaining units. *Id.* at 1, 3, 5. The Union claims that, in finding this to be the case, the RD correctly treated the employees who are now employed by NWI, but who were not part of its bargaining unit at the time of the hearing, as "unrepresented." *Id.* at 4. The Union asserts that under Authority case law, an election is not necessary if the number of represented employees exceeds the number of unrepresented employees. *Id.* at 3. Thus, the Union argues, the previously excluded Omaha non-nurse professional employees transferred to NWI are properly included by the RD in the unit because the Union represents a majority of the transferred professional NWI employees. *Id.* at 4-5. The Union contends that to exclude these employees would promote unit fragmentation. *Id.* at 5.

Similarly, the Union argues that new hires, such as those employees located at the CBOCs formed by NWI after the reorganization in 1999, were also correctly determined by the RD to be included in the two appropriate NWI bargaining units. *Id.* at 5. The Union contends, in this connection, that Authority precedent requires that the RD consider the facts and circumstances at the time of the hearing, and at the time of the hearing, there were CBOC employees employed at NWI who shared a community of interest with the other NWI employees. *Id.* The Union further argues that the RD correctly included the CBOC employees in the unit because the reorganization took place over a period of time. *Id.*

6. The Agency notes that the non-professional employees at the Holdrege CBOC are now represented as the result of a recent election and does not oppose their inclusion in the non-professional unit. Application for Review at 3, 13. The Agency asks that the Authority take official notice of that certification, as set forth in Case No. DE-RP-09-0023.

The Union also claims that excluding the CBOC employees at issue would not effectuate the purposes of the Statute because the representational status of a portion of NWI employees would be left unresolved. *Id.* at 5-6. The Union asserts: "Given the integration and inter-reliance of NWI functions and employees it would promote fragmentation to separate *some* CBOC employees . . . from the remainder of NWI." *Id.* at 6.

In sum, the Union argues that the RD properly found that NWI is the successor employer to the Omaha, Lincoln, and Grand Island VA Medical Centers and the Bellevue, Holdrege, Norfolk, North Platte, and Shenandoah CBOCs. *Id.* at 1.

IV. Analysis and Conclusions

The Agency claims that the RD failed to apply established successorship law. The Authority's current successorship doctrine is based on the Authority's decision in *Port Hueneme*, 50 FLRA 363. In *Port Hueneme*, the Authority recognized that successorship promotes stability in labor-management relations, one of the Statute's fundamental purposes. *Id.* at 367. Accordingly, the Authority broadened the applicability of successorship to ensure that it was "flexible enough to apply . . . to the types of organizational changes being undertaken in Government at the present time." *Id.*

Previously, the Authority had restricted the doctrine's application to units of employees remaining "substantially intact" after transfer to a gaining entity. Furthermore, the appropriateness of "the unit" had to be "unimpaired in the gaining [entity]." *Dep't of Energy, W. Area Power Admin.*, 3 FLRA 77, 79 (1980). The Authority's decision in *Port Hueneme* modified these criteria by applying successorship not just to units remaining substantially intact after the transfer, but also to units in which only a portion of the unit has been transferred. *See Port Hueneme*, 50 FLRA at 370. Moreover, the Authority held that "successorship is possible . . . and a post-transfer unit may be found appropriate even if [the unit] has been expanded to include employees in addition to those transferred." *Id.*

In this case, the Agency agrees with the RD's application of the successorship doctrine in every respect save two: applying the doctrine to (1) include in the post-transfer professional unit Omaha non-nurse professional employees specifically excluded from the pre-transfer unit, and (2) include in the post-transfer units employees at CBOCs formed after 1999. Application for Review at 13-14. In other words, the Agency agrees to the formation, pursuant to the law of successorship, of a single NWI professional unit and a single NWI non-professional unit, with the exclusions noted. *Id.*

Resolving the Agency's application for review raises complex issues in the application of successorship law. These issues arise from the case's special circumstances, including the composition and number of predecessor units, as well as the extended period during which events pertinent to the Union's petitions occurred. With regard to the predecessor units, the professional unit certifications at Lincoln and Grand Island differ from Omaha's professional unit certification in one significant respect. Whereas the Lincoln and Grand Island professional units include all professionals at those locations; the Omaha professional unit specifically excludes most categories of professionals, essentially including only professional nurses. *See* RD's Decision at 9-10. In addition, with regard to the CBOCs, their establishment within NWI occurred for the most part at least eight, and as much as ten years after the reorganization that realigned the VA Medical Centers at Omaha, Lincoln, and Grand Island to create NWI. *Id.* at 5-6.

The RD's decision does not address these complex issues. The RD's application of the successorship doctrine is discussed below.

A. The RD failed to apply established law by determining that NWI is the successor employer of the Omaha non-nurse professional employees who were specifically excluded from the Omaha professional unit.

Successorship results in the continuation of a union's status as exclusive representative of an appropriate bargaining unit without a new, secret ballot election. *Port Hueneme* at 370-71. Thus, successorship depends on the union involved being the choice of the majority of employees in the claimed successor unit. *Id.* (citing *Def. Supply Agency, Def. Property Disposal Office, Aberdeen Proving Ground, Aberdeen, Md.*, 3 FLRC 789, 802 (1975)). Typically, the Authority has narrowly applied doctrines providing for the inclusion of employees in a bargaining unit without a self-determination election. *See, e.g., DLA, Columbus*, 53 FLRA at 1125 (the accretion doctrine is generally narrowly applied because it precludes employee self determination).

This case presents a situation to which both successorship principles and the principle of employees' right to self-determination apply. Under the successorship doctrine, where employees transferred from a recognized bargaining unit constitute a majority of the claimed successor's unit, employees other than the employees transferred from a recognized unit may become part of the successor unit as long as the unit remains appropriate with their inclusion. *See, e.g., Port Hueneme,* 50 FLRA at 370 n.7. In this regard, successorship situations will often involve previously unrepresented employees. Such unrepresented employees may include current employees of the successor employer when successorship conditions arise.

Here, not only were the unrepresented non-nurse professional Omaha employees not included in the recognized unit that was transferred, they had been specifically excluded from that unit's certification. RD's Decision at 9. The record is silent as to the reason why the non-nurse professional Omaha employees were specifically excluded from Omaha's professional unit. Nevertheless, reflecting the importance the Authority has placed on the right of self-determination, Authority case law addresses that special circumstance. In particular, specifically excluded employees may only be added to a unit without an election "where there have been 'meaningful changes' in the employees' duties, functions, or job circumstances that eliminate the original distinctions between employees[.]" *DLA, Columbus,* 53 FLRA 1123-24 (internal citation omitted); *see also U.S. Dep't of the Air Force, Langley Air Force Base, Va.*, 40 FLRA 111, 113, 117 (1991). This case law is pertinent in a successorship context because, under *Port Hueneme*, where successorship analysis must resolve the status of employees other than those transferred from a recognized bargaining unit, it must do so "consistent with established accretion principles." *Port Hueneme,* 50 FLRA at 370 n.7.

Consequently, although a straightforward application of successorship principles would resolve the status of a predecessor's unrepresented employees transferred to a successor, the same cannot be said as to the unrepresented non-nurse professional Omaha employees in this case.[7] Because Authority self-determination case law addresses their special situation, and because the RD did not resolve their situation consistent with that case law, we find that the RD failed to apply established law by determining that NWI is the successor employer of the non-nurse professional Omaha employees.[8] For the reasons discussed above, successorship law cannot be applied to include the unrepresented non-nurse professional Omaha employees in the NWI professional bargaining unit, and they must be excluded from the NWI professional unit in the certification issued by the RD.

B. The RD failed to apply established law by applying the successorship doctrine to include in the NWI bargaining units unrepresented CBOC employees hired by NWI several years after the reorganization creating NWI took place.

The Agency argues that the RD failed to apply established law when he resolved the bargaining unit status of unrepresented CBOC employees. The Agency points out that these employees are located at CBOCs that were formed years after the reorganization that created NWI. According to the Agency, as the CBOCs did not exist at the time of the reorganization, successorship principles should not be applied to their unrepresented employees. Application for Review at 11-12.

As discussed above, the successorship doctrine in *Port Hueneme* is applied to determine the representation rights of employees who are transferred as a result of a reorganization. In addition, successorship principles can operate to determine the representation rights of unrepresented employees employed by the gaining organization. *See, e.g., Port Hueneme,* 50 FLRA at 370 n.7, 374 n.11.[9] In this regard, such unrepresented employees

7. Thus, although we agree with the Union that avoiding unit fragmentation is a significant consideration in successorship law, *see* Opp'n at 5, 6, in the circumstances of this case such a consideration does not prevail over considerations relating to employee self-determination.

8. Given the conclusion that the RD failed to apply established law by including the non-nurse professional Omaha employees in the NWI professional bargaining unit, we find that there is no need to address the Agency's argument that there is an absence of precedent with regard to his decision concerning these employees.

9. We note that in *Fall River Dyeing & Finishing Corp. v. NLRB,* 482 U.S. 27 (1987) (*Fall River*), the Supreme Court found that a successorship existed despite a seven-month "hiatus" between the demise of a predecessor employer and the "start-up" of the successor. *Id.* at 45. Applying the National Labor Relations Board's "substantial and representative complement" rule, the Court recognized that a successor employer might have a "start-up period" postponing "the moment when the determination as to the

can become part of an appropriate successor unit when the employees transferred from a recognized bargaining unit constitute a majority of the employees in the post-transfer bargaining unit. *Id.* at 374-75.

Here, the RD erred by failing to find that the unrepresented CBOC employees were not part of the gaining organization at a time relevant for purposes of applying successorship law. Instead, the RD only considered whether it would be appropriate to include the unrepresented CBOC employees in the Union's proposed post-successorship unit under § 7112(a) of the Statute. As the unrepresented CBOC employees began their duties with NWI at a time too remote from events giving rise to the successorship issues in this case, successorship principles may not be applied to include them in the NWI bargaining units established pursuant to the reorganization in 1999.[10] Accordingly, we find that RD failed to apply established law by determining that the unrepresented CBOC employees should be included in the NWI bargaining units.[11] Consequently, these employees must be excluded from the NWI professional and non-professional units in the certifications issued by the RD.

V. Order

The application for review is granted and the case is remanded to the RD to issue appropriate certifications.

---

composition of the successor's work force is to be made." *Id.* at 47. The "start-up" period in *Fall River* was approximately four months. Therefore, almost one year elapsed before successorship determinations were made. The Authority referred approvingly to *Fall River's* holding regarding the "substantial and representative complement" rule in *Port Hueneme,* 50 FLRA at 371 n.9. However, no basis is argued to extend this principle to situations, as here, where eight to ten years elapsed before the establishment of the CBOCs and the hiring of their employees whose inclusion in the NWI units the parties dispute.

10. The record reflects that the same is true for the represented non-professional employees at the Holdrege CBOC, which was formed in 2008-09. RD's Decision at 6. Accordingly, to the extent that the RD found that any Holdrege employees were transferred to NWI for successorship purposes, *see* Application for Review at 12-13, we find that the RD committed a clear and prejudicial error concerning a substantial factual matter. Represented non-professional Holdrege employees voted in an election to be represented by the Union, and remain represented under the terms of the existing certification that applies to them, of which we take official notice.

11. Given the conclusion that the RD failed to apply established law in determining to include the unrepresented CBOC employees in the NWI bargaining units, we find that there is no need to address the Agency's argument that there is an absence of precedent with regard to the RD's decision concerning these employees. In addition, given the above determinations that the RD failed to apply established law with regard to the previously excluded non-nurse professional Omaha employees and the unrepresented CBOC employees, we find it unnecessary to separately address the Agency's argument that the RD failed to apply established law by misapplying the third prong of the *Port Hueneme* framework.

65 FLRA No. 150

AMERICAN FEDERATION
OF GOVERNMENT EMPLOYEES
LOCAL 4052
(Union)

and

UNITED STATES
DEPARTMENT OF JUSTICE
FEDERAL BUREAU OF PRISONS
METROPOLITAN DETENTION CENTER
GUAYNABO, PUERTO RICO
(Agency)

0-NG-3063

DECISION AND ORDER
ON A NEGOTIABILITY ISSUE

April 13, 2011

Before the Authority: Carol Waller Pope, Chairman, and Thomas M. Beck and Ernest DuBester, Members

I. Statement of the Case

This matter is before the Authority on a negotiability appeal filed by the Union under § 7105(a)(2)(E) of the Federal Service Labor-Management Relations Statute (the Statute). The appeal involves the negotiability of one proposal concerning the entrances that staff members may use to access a correctional institution.[1] The Agency filed a statement of position (SOP), to which the Union filed a response (response).[2] The Agency filed a reply to the response (reply).

For the reasons that follow, we find that the proposal is outside the duty to bargain. Accordingly, we dismiss the petition for review (petition).

1. The appeal originally concerned two proposals, Proposals 4 and 5. During the post-petition conference, the Agency withdrew its allegation of nonnegotiability with respect to Proposal 4. *See* Record of Post-Petition Conference at 2. Consequently, that proposal is no longer before the Authority.

2. As set forth below, the response was not timely filed.

II. Preliminary Issue

Section 2429.24(a) of the Authority's Regulations provides that documents must be filed with the Authority "between 9 a.m. and 5 p.m., Monday through Friday (except Federal holidays)." 5 C.F.R. § 2429.24(a). Therefore, consistent with this regulation, to be accepted for filing on a particular day, documents must be received by the Authority before 5 p.m. The Authority's Regulations also require that a response to an agency's statement of position be filed "in person, by commercial delivery, by first-class mail, or by certified mail." 5 C.F.R. § 2429.24(e).

The Union's response had to be filed with the Authority by January 18, 2011.[3] Order to Show Cause at 2. The Union transmitted its response by facsimile (fax) dated January 18. *Id.* The Authority issued an order stating that the response was not received until January 19. *Id.* The order also stated that fax transmission is not an authorized method of filing a response to an SOP. *Id.* Accordingly, the Authority directed the Union to show cause why it should consider the response. *Id.*

In its response to the order, the Union concedes that the response was required to be filed by January 18, but argues that extraordinary circumstances exist to warrant consideration of the response because: (1) the Union representative "did not have sufficient monetary funds" to submit the response by certified mail to the Authority and each Agency representative; and (2) the response was faxed to the Authority and was served by fax or certified mail on the Agency representatives on January 18. Response to Order to Show Cause at 2.

Requests for waivers of time limits may be granted only in "extraordinary circumstances." 5 C.F.R. § 2429.23. In addition, it is well established that parties filing documents with the Authority are "responsible for being knowledgeable" of the statutory and regulatory filing requirements. *AFGE, Local 2065*, 50 FLRA 538, 539-40 (1995).

With regard to the Union's claim that it filed the response on January 18, the transmission report that accompanied the response indicates that it was transmitted after 5 p.m. on that date. The Union does not address the regulatory requirement that documents be filed before 5 p.m., or claim extraordinary circumstances for failure to satisfy that requirement. Accordingly, the Union does not

3. All dates in this section are from 2011.

establish extraordinary circumstances for its failure to timely file the response.

With regard to the Union's claim concerning the cost of filing by certified mail, as stated above, § 2429.24(e) of the Authority's Regulations allows a union to file a response in several different ways; it does not *require* a union to file by certified mail. As such, the Union's argument concerning the costs of certified mail does not demonstrate extraordinary circumstances for its failure to comply with the Authority's filing requirements. Moreover, the Union's remaining claims do not provide a basis for excusing the Union's failure to comply with these filing requirements.

For the foregoing reasons, we do not consider the response.[4]

With regard to the reply, § 2424.26(a) of the Authority's Regulations provides that the "purpose of the agency's reply is to [respond to] any facts or arguments made for the first time in the [union's] response." As we do not consider the response, we also find that there is no reason for the Authority to consider the reply. *See IFPTE, Local 29, Goddard Eng'rs, Scientists & Technicians Ass'n*, 61 FLRA 382, 383 (2005).

III. Proposal

A. Wording

> Responsibilities: All staff assigned to Institution Entrances shall refer to the Institutional Post Orders for the proper equipment related to their duties in these assigned areas.
>
> A. Employees: There are primary three (3) entrances for staff to utilize, Front Entrance (Front Lobby)[,] Staff Entrance[,] and Rear Entrance (Rear Gate). All visitors will enter through the Front Lobby entrance to be processed into the institution. All unidentified staff, whether visiting or assigned, will present their Department of Justice, Federal Bureau of Prisons Identification Card upon request of staff at the designated entrance area, the Control Center Officer and/or any other institution staff requesting that the visitors identify themselves. (Staff are reminded that they are required to carry their BOP identification at all times while in the institution.)

Record of Post-Petition Conference (Record) at 2.

B. Meaning

The parties agree that the proposal would require the Agency to allow employees to enter the institution through any of the three entrances listed in the proposal. *Id.* at 2. In addition, the Agency asserts that the proposal would allow staff to use the Rear Entrance "regardless of whether or not they are on official assignment[.]" SOP at 5. As this assertion is both undisputed and consistent with the wording of the proposal, we adopt it for the purposes of assessing the negotiability of the proposal. *See Int'l Ass'n of Machinists & Aerospace Workers, Local 726*, 31 FLRA 158, 170 (1988) (adopting undisputed contention as to meaning that was consistent with the provision's wording).

IV. Positions of the Parties

A. Union

The Union argues that the proposal is intended to prevent staff from being visible to others when they walk between the "Front Lobby Visitors Entrance" and the gun locker. Petition at 7. In this regard, the Union claims that the proposal would alleviate the safety and security concerns associated with public exposure by permitting use of another entry. *Id.*

B. Agency

The Agency contends that the proposal violates management's rights to determine its internal security practices and assign work under § 7106(a)(1) and (a)(2)(B) of the Statute. SOP at 5-12. The Agency also contends that the Union has failed to specifically argue that the proposal is an appropriate arrangement or procedure within the meaning of § 7106(b)(2) or (3) and that, in any event, the proposal is neither an appropriate arrangement or a procedure. *Id.* at 12-19.

4. We note that, in responding to the order to show cause, the Union attached a copy of the response. However, as this copy was filed after January 18, it is untimely, and we do not consider it.

V. Analysis and Conclusions

Section 2424.32(c)(2) of the Authority's Regulations provides that "[f]ailure to respond to an argument or assertion raised by the other party will . . . be deemed a concession to such argument or assertion." Consistent with this regulation, when a union does not dispute an agency's claim that a proposal affects the exercise of management's rights, and does not argue that the proposal constitutes an exception to management's rights, the Authority will find that the proposal is outside the duty to bargain. *NATCA*, 62 FLRA 337, 340 (2008); *see also AFGE, Local 1712*, 62 FLRA 15, 16 (2007) (*AFGE*) (finding union's failure to address agency's management rights arguments a concession under 5 C.F.R. § 2424.32).

Here, the Union does not argue in the petition either that the proposal does not affect a management right or that the proposal is within the duty to bargain as an exception to management's rights.[5] Consequently, consistent with § 2424.32 and the above-cited precedent, we find that the Union has conceded that the proposal is contrary to the Agency's rights to determine internal security practices and assign work, and we find that the proposal is outside the duty to bargain. *See NATCA*, 62 FLRA at 340; *AFGE*, 62 FLRA at 16.

VI. Order

The petition for review is dismissed.

---

5. As discussed above, we do not consider the response.

65 FLRA No. 151

UNITED STATES
DEPARTMENT OF HOMELAND SECURITY
U.S. CITIZENSHIP AND IMMIGRATION SERVICES
(Agency)

and

AMERICAN FEDERATION
OF GOVERNMENT EMPLOYEES
LOCAL 3923
(Union)

0-AR-4727

ORDER DISMISSING EXCEPTIONS

April 22, 2011

Before the Authority: Carol Waller Pope, Chairman, and Thomas M. Beck and Ernest DuBester, Members

I. Statement of the Case

This matter is before the Authority on exceptions to an e-mail of Arbitrator Thomas Angelo filed by Immigration and Customs Enforcement (ICE)* under § 7122(a) of the Federal Service Labor-Management Relations Statute (the Statute) and part 2425 of the Authority's Regulations. The Union filed an opposition to ICE's exceptions.

In an initial award, the Arbitrator sustained the grievance and awarded the grievant priority consideration. In additional awards, the Arbitrator determined that the Agency had not complied with his awards and awarded remedial relief. Subsequently, in the e-mail to which ICE has filed exceptions, the Arbitrator denied ICE's motion to dismiss ICE from the arbitration proceedings.

For the reasons that follow, we dismiss the exceptions, without prejudice, as interlocutory.

* ICE states that ICE and U.S. Citizenship and Immigration Services (CIS) are separate components within the Department of Homeland Security (DHS). Exceptions, Attach. A at 2.

II. Background and Arbitrator's Awards

The grievant, an employee of CIS, filed a grievance when she was not selected for a position for which she had applied. The grievance was not resolved and was submitted to arbitration. In his initial award, the Arbitrator stated that the grievance arose out of a bargaining relationship between DHS, which he designated the "Agency[,]" and the Union. October 27, 2005 Award at 2. The Arbitrator sustained the grievance and awarded the grievant priority consideration for any published vacancy within the Agency's jurisdiction. *Id.* at 19.

In a subsequent award, the Arbitrator found that, in violation of the initial award, the Agency had failed to process the grievant's request for priority consideration and determined that the grievant was entitled to placement in the position of her choosing with backpay. January 30, 2007 Award at 29. The Agency filed exceptions to this award, but subsequently withdrew them. *See U.S. Dep't of Homeland Sec., U.S. Citizenship & Immigration Servs.*, 64 FLRA 335, 335-36 (2009).

In an additional award, the Arbitrator found that the Agency had failed to comply with the prior awards and directed it to comply. He awarded the grievant the next position, with backpay, within the Agency's facility at Glynco, Georgia, to which she applies and for which she is qualified. In addition, he directed the Secretary of DHS, or a responsible subordinate, to ensure that the Agency complies with the award. May 22, 2009 Award at 5.

In advance of a scheduled hearing on compliance with the awards, ICE submitted to the Arbitrator a motion to dismiss ICE from the arbitration on the basis that the Arbitrator lacked personal jurisdiction over ICE. ICE explained that the alleged lack of jurisdiction is based on the absence of any employee-employer relationship with the grievant in regard to the subject matter of the original grievance. ICE also contended that it had never been notified of the grievance, prior arbitration proceedings, or prior arbitration awards and that there was nothing substantive in any of the awards that concerns ICE. Exceptions, ICE's Motion to Dismiss for Lack of Jurisdiction, Attach. A at 1 n.2, 5.

The Arbitrator informed the ICE representative that the motion could be addressed at the outset of the compliance hearing scheduled for December 13, 2010. In conjunction with the hearing, the Union submitted a proposed order of "Final Compliance and

Clarification of Award" for the Arbitrator's approval and signature. In an e-mail, the Arbitrator denied ICE's motion to dismiss, stated that he was "adopting" the Union's proposed order, and cancelled the compliance hearing. December 3, 2010 e-mail.

III. Positions of the Parties

A. ICE's Exceptions

ICE maintains that the December 3, 2010 e-mail is an award and contends that it is contrary to law and that the Arbitrator was biased, exceeded his authority, and denied ICE a fair hearing. Exceptions at 3, 5, 7, 9. ICE also contends that the Arbitrator's exercise of jurisdiction over it is deficient. *Id.* at 11.

B. Union's Opposition

The Union contends that ICE's exceptions are interlocutory and should be dismissed. Opp'n at 1. The Union claims that the Arbitrator has not issued a final award. In this regard, the Union notes that the Arbitrator has yet to issue a final signed order. *Id.* at 3. In addition, the Union attaches an e-mail, dated January 3, 2011, from the Arbitrator to a representative of ICE in which the Arbitrator states: "As of this date I have not issued a final award." *Id.*, Union's Attach. A. Finally, the Union contends that there are no extraordinary circumstances warranting interlocutory review. *Id.* at 3.

IV. Order to Show Cause and Agency's Response

As it appeared that the December 3 e-mail did not constitute a complete determination of all issues submitted to arbitration, the Authority ordered ICE to show cause why its exceptions should not be dismissed as interlocutory. In its response to the show cause order, ICE makes two arguments.

First, ICE argues that the December 3 e-mail is not interlocutory as to ICE because the Arbitrator's denial of ICE's motion to dismiss is final as to the only issue involving ICE. Although ICE concedes that "it may be that the [A]rbitrator's award is in some manner less than final as between CIS and AFGE," ICE maintains that "[n]othing else that the [A]rbitrator may do in the future, short of reversing his decision and granting ICE's motion, will change his denial of ICE's motion." Response at 1, 3.

Second, and alternatively, ICE argues that interlocutory review is warranted because of a plausible jurisdictional defect, the resolution of which will advance the ultimate disposition of the case. In this connection, ICE claims that the Arbitrator lacks personal jurisdiction over ICE. *Id.* at 4. ICE acknowledges that the alleged lack of personal jurisdiction is not based on any statute and that, were interlocutory review to be granted, it would be the first time that the Authority did so when there is no statutory basis for a jurisdictional defect. *Id.* Nevertheless, ICE maintains that "[i]t is hard to imagine a stronger defect than the fact that an entity was not a party to the dispute which is before the [A]rbitrator." *Id.* Finally, ICE argues that interlocutory review would advance the ultimate disposition of the case because otherwise ICE must join CIS in expending funds on future proceedings. *Id.* at 4-5.

V. Analysis and Conclusions

The Authority's Regulations provide that the Authority "ordinarily will not consider interlocutory appeals." 5 C.F.R. § 2429.11 (§ 2429.11). An interlocutory appeal concerns a ruling that is preliminary to final disposition of a matter. In arbitration cases, this means that the Authority ordinarily will not resolve exceptions filed to an arbitration award unless the award constitutes a complete resolution of all issues submitted to arbitration. *See, e.g., U.S. Dep't of the Interior, Bureau of Indian Affairs, Wapato Irrigation Project, Wapato, Wash.*, 55 FLRA 1230, 1231 (2000) (*BIA*).

ICE contends that the December 3 e-mail is not interlocutory as to ICE because the Arbitrator's denial of ICE's motion to dismiss is final as to the only issue involving ICE. However, ICE does not argue that the e-mail constitutes a complete resolution of whether there has been compliance with the Arbitrator's prior awards, and, if not, what remedies are appropriate. To the contrary, ICE concedes that there may not be a complete resolution of these matters as to CIS. Consequently, ICE's exceptions are precisely the type of appeal that § 2429.11 is meant to preclude. *See U.S. Dep't of the Treasury, IRS, L.A. District*, 34 FLRA 1161, 1163 (1990) (*IRS*) (§ 2429.11 reflects the judicial policy of discouraging fragmentary appeals of the same case). Accordingly, we conclude that ICE's exceptions are interlocutory.

The Authority will review interlocutory exceptions when the exceptions raise a plausible jurisdictional defect, the resolution of which would advance the ultimate disposition of the case. *E.g., BIA*, 55 FLRA at 1232. However, the Authority reserves this review for "extraordinary situations[.]" *Id.*; *see U.S. Dep't of Homeland Sec.,*

U.S. Immigration & Customs Enforcement, 60 FLRA 129, 130 (2004) (exception dismissed as interlocutory because excepting party failed to demonstrate that "extraordinary circumstances" existed warranting interlocutory review). As ICE recognizes, these extraordinary situations have been found by the Authority only in situations in which it was alleged that the arbitrator lacked jurisdiction, as a matter of law, over subject matter of the grievance. *See, e.g., U.S. Dep't of Def., Nat'l Imagery & Mapping Agency, St. Louis, Mo.*, 57 FLRA 837, 837 n.2 (2002) (then-Member Pope dissenting as to other matters). Consequently, the Authority has repeatedly declined to extend interlocutory review to alleged jurisdictional defects that do not preclude arbitration of the grievance as a matter of law. *E.g., U.S. Dep't of Labor, Bureau of Labor Statistics*, 65 FLRA 651, 655 (2011) (alleged contractual exclusions from negotiated grievance procedure); *U.S. Dep't of Housing & Urban Dev.*, 62 FLRA 52, 53 (2007) (alleged exclusion based on § 7106 of the Statute); *U.S. Dep't of the Treasury, Bureau of Engraving & Printing, W. Currency Facility, Fort Worth, Tex.*, 58 FLRA 745, 746 (2003) (alleged contractual exclusions from negotiated grievance procedure).

In addition to establishing a plausible jurisdictional defect, the excepting party must also establish that interlocutory review will advance the ultimate disposition of the case. *BIA,* 55 FLRA at 1232. The Authority has described this situation as one in which resolving the exceptions would end the litigation. *See U.S. Dep't of the Interior, Bureau of Reclamation*, 59 FLRA 686, 688 (2004) (*Bureau of Reclamation*); *IRS,* 34 FLRA at 1163-64. For example, in *Bureau of Reclamation,* the Authority found that, to the extent the appealing party was contesting the arbitrator's jurisdiction over grievants who had failed to opt in to the grievance, it was uncontested that the arbitrator had jurisdiction over other grievants who had opted in. Consequently, the Authority determined that immediate resolution of the jurisdictional defect would not advance the ultimate disposition of the case because the case would still proceed to arbitration on the merits of the grievance as it pertained to the grievants who had opted in. *Bureau of Reclamation*, 59 FLRA at 687-88.

Here, ICE does not dispute that further arbitration proceedings may be necessary. Thus, even if we were to agree with ICE that it should be dismissed from further proceedings, ICE does not establish that interlocutory review of its exceptions will advance the ultimate disposition of this case. Moreover, no basis has been established to extend interlocutory review to alleged jurisdictional defects that do not preclude arbitration of the grievance as a matter of law. In this regard, the Authority has emphasized that the exceptional interlocutory review allowed by 28 U.S.C. § 1292 for federal courts of appeal specifically requires that the case must involve a controlling question of law. *IRS,* 34 FLRA at 1163-64.

Based on the foregoing, we conclude that interlocutory review is not warranted. Accordingly, we dismiss ICE's exceptions, without prejudice.

VI. Order

ICE's exceptions are dismissed, without prejudice, as interlocutory.

65 FLRA No. 152

AMERICAN FEDERATION
OF GOVERNMENT EMPLOYEES
COUNCIL 220
(Union)

and

SOCIAL SECURITY ADMINISTRATION
BALTIMORE, MARYLAND
(Agency)

0-AR-4509

DECISION

April 22, 2011

Before the Authority: Carol Waller Pope, Chairman, and Thomas M. Beck and Ernest DuBester, Members[1]

I. Statement of the Case

This matter is before the Authority on exceptions to an award of Arbitrator Charles Feigenbaum filed by the Union under § 7122(a) of the Federal Service Labor-Management Relations Statute (the Statute) and part 2425 of the Authority's Regulations. The Agency filed an opposition to the Union's exceptions.[2]

The Union filed a grievance alleging that the Agency violated the parties' collective bargaining agreement (CBA) when more than one management official (official) participated in initial performance discussions with individual employees (expectation discussions). The Arbitrator found that the Statute precluded him from adopting the Union's proposed interpretation of the CBA, and he denied the grievance.

For the reasons that follow, we grant the Union's contrary-to-law exception and remand the award to the parties for resubmission to the Arbitrator, absent settlement.

II. Background and Arbitrator's Award

At the beginning of the performance evaluation year (year), the Agency's bargaining-unit employees (employees) meet individually with management to conduct expectation discussions, in which the participants "attempt to arrive at a full and complete understanding" of employees' performance plans. Award at 3 (quoting CBA Art. 21, § 5 ("Expectation Discussions")). The Union filed a grievance alleging that the Agency violated the CBA when, in some instances, more than one official attended an employee's expectation discussion. *Id.* at 1-2, 4-5. When the grievance was unresolved, the parties proceeded to arbitration, where the Arbitrator defined the issues as follows:

> 1. *Threshold Issue* - Does the Agency have the management right under [§ 7106(a)(2)(B) of the Statute] to have two or more . . . officials present when conducting . . . expectation[] discussions . . .? If not,
>
> 2. *Substantive Issue* - Did the Agency violate the [CBA] by assigning two or more . . . officials to be present when conducting . . . expectation[] discussions . . .? If so, what shall be the remedy?

Id. at 2.

Addressing the threshold issue, the Arbitrator found that, although "the Union's interpretation of Article 21 [of the CBA] [(Article 21)] would not dictate . . . [whether] a specific individual or [position] could or could not attend an expectation discussion[,]" it would limit the number of officials who could attend an expectation discussion. *Id.* at 13. In this regard, the Arbitrator found that management's right to assign work under § 7106(a)(2)(B) of the Statute (§ 7106(a)(2)(B)) "includes the right to give a managerial task to more than one . . . official." *Id.* at 13-14 (citing *U.S. Dep't of VA, Alaska VA Healthcare Sys., Anchorage, Alaska*, 60 FLRA 968 (2005) (*Alaska VA*); *U.S. Dep't of HHS, Health Care Fin. Admin.*, 57 FLRA 462 (2001) (*HCFA*)). Thus, the Arbitrator concluded that the Union's interpretation of Article 21 "would impermissibly interfere with the management right to assign work" by limiting the number of officials at expectation discussions. *Id.* at 10-11; *see also id.* at 15.

---

1. Member Beck's separate opinion, concurring in the result, is set forth at the end of this decision.

2. This case relates to *Social Security Administration*, 65 FLRA 638 (2011) (*SSA*), which involved the same parties and a similar matter, but a different arbitrator.

The Arbitrator acknowledged that a prior arbitration award by a different arbitrator had enforced a similar provision of the CBA as a procedure under § 7106(b)(2) of the Statute (§ 7106(b)(2)) despite the limitation that the provision placed on the number of officials at performance discussions.[3] *Id.* at 11. However, the Arbitrator concluded that the Union's interpretation of Article 21 would constitute a "direct limitation" on the right to assign work and, thus, could not constitute a procedure under § 7106(b)(2). *Id.* at 15. Moreover, the Arbitrator determined that, because the threshold issue before him involved the correct "reading of a statute[,]" the rationales for giving deference to another arbitrator's "contract interpretation" did not apply. *Id.* at 11.

Based on his conclusion that he could not "issue an award that granted th[e] grievance . . . without violat[ing]" management's right to assign work under the Statute, the Arbitrator denied the grievance. *Id.* at 10-11; *see also id.* at 15.

III. Positions of the Parties

A. Union's Exceptions

The Union argues that the award is contrary to law because it "[i]nterprets [m]anagement's [r]ight to [a]ssign [w]ork under . . . § 7106(a)(2)(B) in an [o]verly [b]road and [e]xpansive [m]anner" that prevents the Union from "seek[ing] . . . enforcement . . . of contract provisions . . . negotiated pursuant to" § 7106(b). Exceptions at 5. The Union asserts that, because its interpretation of Article 21 would not prevent management from conducting expectation discussions or from determining which official participates in those discussions, *see id.* at 8, 11, the provisions of Article 21 concerning expectation discussions are enforceable as procedures under § 7106(b)(2), *id.* at 7, and the Arbitrator's failure to enforce them is contrary to law, *see id.* at 12. Although the Union recognizes that the Arbitrator "decided the case on a threshold question of law," the Union argues that the award fails to draw its essence from the CBA because the Arbitrator did not consider the Union's evidence in support of its interpretation of Article 21. *Id.* at 11-12.

3. We note that the prior arbitration award, to which the Arbitrator referred, was the award at issue in *SSA*, 65 FLRA 638. *See supra* note 2.

B. Agency's Opposition

The Agency argues that the right to assign work under § 7106(a)(2)(B) includes "the right to determine the particular duties to be assigned, when work assignments will occur, and to whom or what positions the duties will be assigned[,]" Opp'n at 3 (citing *Alaska VA*, 60 FLRA at 970; *HCFA*, 57 FLRA at 463; *AFGE, Local 1985*, 55 FLRA 1145, 1148 (1999) (*Local 1985*)), as well as "the right to 'assign additional supervisory duties to an employee who is already a supervisor[,]'" *id.* (citation omitted). The Agency argues further that the Union's interpretation of Article 21: (1) rests on a flawed assertion that management may effectively "bargain[] away" the right to assign work by agreeing to procedures under § 7106(b)(2), *id.*; and (2) conflicts with Authority decisions finding that procedures under § 7106(b)(2) may not "requir[e] an employee's supervisor to perform certain duties, or preclude that supervisor from performing certain duties," *id.* at 3, 5-7 (citing *AFGE, Local 3529*, 56 FLRA 1049, 1051-52 (2001) (*Local 3529*); *NAGE, Local R1-100*, 56 FLRA 268, 272 (2000) (*Local R1-100*); *U.S. Dep't of the Navy, Phila. Naval Shipyard, Phila., Pa.*, 49 FLRA 1363, 1368 (1994) (*Navy*); *AFGE, Local 1409*, 38 FLRA 747, 752-53 (1990) (*Local 1409*); *NFFE, Local 78*, 9 FLRA 819, 819-20 (1982) (*Local 78*)). Thus, the Agency contends that the Arbitrator correctly found that the Union's interpretation of Article 21 would be contrary to management's right to assign work. *Id.* at 8.

IV. Analysis and Conclusions

When an exception involves an award's consistency with law, the Authority reviews any question of law raised by the exception and the award de novo. *See NTEU, Chapter 24*, 50 FLRA 330, 332 (1995) (citing *U.S. Customs Serv. v. FLRA*, 43 F.3d 682, 686-87 (D.C. Cir. 1994)). In applying the standard of de novo review, the Authority assesses whether an arbitrator's legal conclusions are consistent with the applicable standard of law. *See U.S. Dep't of Def., Dep'ts of the Army & the Air Force, Ala. Nat'l Guard, Northport, Ala.*, 55 FLRA 37, 40 (1998). In making that assessment, the Authority defers to the arbitrator's underlying factual findings. *See id.*

The Authority recently revised the analysis that it will apply when reviewing management rights exceptions to arbitration awards. *See U.S. EPA*, 65 FLRA 113, 115 (2010) (Member Beck concurring) (*EPA*); *FDIC, Div. of Supervision & Consumer Prot., S.F. Region*, 65 FLRA 102, 106-

07 (2010) (Chairman Pope concurring). As relevant here, a contract provision interpreted so as to affect the exercise of a management right is contrary to law, as interpreted, unless it was negotiated under § 7106(b). *See EPA*, 65 FLRA at 115.

As discussed in *SSA*, 65 FLRA at 640, and as stated in the Agency's opposition, Opp'n at 3, the right to assign work under § 7106(a)(2)(B) includes the right to determine the particular duties to be assigned, when work assignments will occur, and to whom or what positions the duties will be assigned. *See Local 1985*, 55 FLRA at 1148 (citations omitted). For example, the Authority has held that a contract provision interpreted to limit the number of agency representatives at meetings with employees affects management's right to assign work. *See SSA*, 65 FLRA at 640 (contract provision interpreted to restrict agency's ability to assign more than one official to mid-year performance discussions affected right to assign work); *see also Alaska VA*, 60 FLRA at 970 (citing *HCFA*, 57 FLRA at 463 (contract provision interpreted to restrict agency's ability to assign more than one representative to Step 1 grievance meetings affected right to assign work)). The Union's proposed interpretation of Article 21 would limit the number of officials that the Agency may assign to conduct an expectation discussion. Therefore, consistent with the above-cited precedent, we find that, under the Union's proposed interpretation, Article 21 would affect the right to assign work.

However, as explained in *SSA*, so long as contract provisions do not specify the particular persons or positions who will perform a task, those provisions may constitute enforceable procedures under § 7106(b)(2) notwithstanding their effect on the number of employees, including officials, who will perform the task. *See* 65 FLRA at 640. Under the Union's proposed interpretation of Article 21, the Arbitrator found – and the Union concedes – that the Agency would retain the authority to designate the official who participates in any given expectation discussion. *See* Award at 13; Exceptions at 8, 11. Thus, consistent with *SSA* and the precedents discussed therein, the fact that the Union's proposed interpretation of Article 21 would affect the number of officials who may attend expectation discussions does not preclude a finding that the pertinent provisions of that article would operate as procedures under § 7106(b)(2).

Moreover, when determining whether contract provisions involving performance discussions constitute procedures under § 7106(b)(2), the Authority has noted that agencies have a statutory duty, under 5 U.S.C. § 4302(a)(2) (§ 4302(a)(2)), to "encourage employee participation in establishing performance standards[.]" *E.g., SSA*, 65 FLRA at 640 (citing *Patent Office Prof'l Ass'n*, 47 FLRA 10, 30-31 (1993); *Patent Office Prof'l Ass'n*, 29 FLRA 1389, 1389-92 (1987); *AFGE, AFL-CIO, Local 32*, 3 FLRA 783, 788-89 (1980) (*Local 32*)). This duty includes an obligation "to bargain on procedures which management officials will observe in the development *and implementation* of performance standards[,]" *NTEU*, 35 FLRA 254, 256 (1990) (emphasis added), such as "the form of the employee participation" required by § 4302(a)(2), *Local 32*, 3 FLRA at 789.

For example, in *SSA*, the Authority examined a contract provision that, as interpreted by the arbitrator, restricted the agency's ability to assign more than one management official to mid-year performance discussions. *See* 65 FLRA at 640. The Authority noted that, as interpreted, the provision at issue did not permit an employee to alter the content of performance standards or to select which management official would participate in the employee's mid-year discussion. *See id.* at 640-41 (citing *NFFE*, 13 FLRA 426, 426-28 (1983)). Rather, the Authority found that the arbitrator interpreted the provision in *SSA* so that it regulated the manner in which a "joint planning and communication process" concerning performance standards would occur between management and an employee. *See id.* (quoting *NTEU*, 42 FLRA 964, 972-79 (1991)) (internal quotation marks omitted). Consequently, the Authority found that the provision at issue operated as a procedure under § 7106(b)(2), which was consistent with the agency's obligation under § 4302(a)(2). *Id.*

As interpreted by the Union, the provisions of Article 21 concerning expectation discussions would operate in much the same way as the provision found to be a procedure in *SSA*. Thus, *SSA* and the other above-cited precedents support a conclusion that the pertinent provisions of Article 21, as interpreted by the Union, would operate as procedures under § 7106(b)(2).

The decisions cited by the Agency and Arbitrator do not support a contrary conclusion. In those decisions, the Authority found that contractual provisions, as interpreted, either: (1) did not constitute procedures under § 7106(b)(2) because they prescribed or precluded assignments to a particular individual *identified by name or title*; or (2) contravened management's rights *in the absence of any assertion* that the provisions were lawful under § 7106(b). *See Alaska VA*, 60 FLRA at 970 & n.2 (no assertion provision negotiated pursuant to § 7106(b)); *HCFA*, 57 FLRA at 463 (same); *Local 3529*, 56 FLRA at 1051 (provision requiring assignment of appraisal duties to every supervisor for whom a "Specialist performs 150 hours or more of work" not a procedure); *Local R1-100*, 56 FLRA at 272 (no assertion provision negotiated pursuant to § 7106(b)); *Navy*, 49 FLRA at 1368 (contract interpretation forbade additional assignments to supervisor "Simmons"); *Local 1409*, 38 FLRA at 752-53 (requiring "the Commander" to exercise discretion in a matter was "inconsistent with" right to assign work); *Local 78*, 9 FLRA at 819-20 (requiring "Assistant Director, Personnel Officer[,] and . . . Division Chief" to sit on selecting panel would "eliminat[e] . . . discretion inherent" in right to assign work). By contrast, as stated previously, the Union's proposed interpretation of Article 21 would *not identify* the official who would participate in any given expectation discussion, and the Union *does assert* that Article 21 operates pursuant to § 7106(b)(2). In addition, although the Authority in *Alaska VA* stated that it had not *previously* found a provision limiting the number of agency representatives at meetings with employees to constitute a procedure, the Authority made no finding as to whether such a provision *could* constitute a procedure, *see* 60 FLRA at 970. Thus, *Alaska VA* does not support finding that, as interpreted by the Union, the pertinent provisions of Article 21 would not constitute procedures.

For the foregoing reasons, we find that, under the Union's proposed interpretation of Article 21, the provisions of the article concerning expectation discussions would be enforceable as procedures under § 7106(b)(2), and the Arbitrator erred, as a matter of law, in concluding otherwise. Therefore, we grant the Union's contrary-to-law exception and remand the award to the parties for resubmission to the Arbitrator, absent settlement, so that he may determine the meaning of the CBA's provisions concerning expectation discussions and resolve the "substantive issue" set forth in the award.[4]

V. Decision

The Union's contrary-to-law exception is granted, and the award is remanded to the parties for resubmission to the Arbitrator, absent settlement.

Member Beck, Concurring in the result:

I agree with my colleagues that this matter should be remanded for resolution of the "substantive issue" presented by the Union's grievance. However, I arrive at this conclusion for different reasons than those employed by my colleagues.

My colleagues accept the Arbitrator's assertion that he was obliged to rule on the "threshold issue," Award at 2, which required him to engage in a legal analysis about management rights. They then address the same legal question that the Arbitrator purported to address and, applying a de novo standard of review, they arrive at a different conclusion than did the Arbitrator.

The problem with the Arbitrator's approach is that he need not have addressed – indeed, he should not have addressed – what he characterized as the "threshold issue." The Arbitrator was required only to interpret Article 21 and determine what contractual obligations or restrictions it imposed on the Agency in terms of conducting expectation discussions. It was beyond the Arbitrator's purview to determine whether Article 21 is or is not consistent with Section 7106(a)(2)(B) of the Statute; this question was answered when the Agency agreed to include Article 21 in the CBA and thereby conceded that, if it affects management's statutory rights at all, it is a permissible limitation on those rights.

4. The Union concedes that the award rests entirely on the Arbitrator's answer to a threshold question of law. Exceptions at 11. As the Arbitrator has not yet interpreted the CBA, the Union's essence exception is premature. Therefore, we decline to address the Union's essence exception.

65 FLRA No. 153

UNITED STATES
DEPARTMENT OF JUSTICE
FEDERAL BUREAU OF PRISONS
FEDERAL CORRECTIONAL COMPLEX
COLEMAN, FLORIDA
(Agency)

and

AMERICAN FEDERATION
OF GOVERNMENT EMPLOYEES
LOCAL 506
(Union)

0-AR-4371

DECISION

April 22, 2011

Before the Authority: Carol Waller Pope, Chairman, and Thomas M. Beck and Ernest DuBester, Members

I. Statement of the Case

This matter is before the Authority on exceptions to an award of Arbitrator Richard John Miller filed by the Agency under § 7122(a) of the Federal Service Labor-Management Relations Statute (the Statute) and part 2425 of the Authority's Regulations. The Union filed an opposition to the Agency's exceptions.

The Arbitrator directed the Agency to allow the placement of certain documents in the file that the Agency compiles when it investigates a guard alleged to have engaged in misconduct (guard's investigation file).

For the reasons discussed below, we dismiss the exceptions in part and deny them in part.

II. Background and Arbitrator's Award

The Union represents guards at a federal correctional complex. *See* Award at 8. At times, a special investigative agent (agent) will interview a guard alleged to have engaged in misconduct. *See id.* at 20. After the agent has interviewed the guard, the agent writes a statement that expresses the guard's answers in a narrative format (agent-authored affidavit). *See id.* at 21. The agent then presents the agent-authored affidavit to the guard for his or her signature. *See id.* at 21-22. Once the guard has had an opportunity to make changes or corrections, *see id.* at 21, the guard signs the agent-authored affidavit, *see id.* at 22. The agent-authored affidavit, along with other evidence, is placed in the guard's investigation file. *See id.* at 20.

The Union filed a grievance alleging that agent-authored affidavits should be written in a question-and-answer, rather than narrative, format. *See id.* at 11. The parties could not resolve the grievance and submitted it to arbitration. *See id.* As relevant here, the parties agreed to have the following issues resolved: (1) did the Agency violate the parties' agreement when it refused to have agent-authored affidavits written in a question-and-answer format; (2) does a guard have the right to have a copy of an agent's questions placed in the guard's investigation file; (3) does a guard have the right to submit a supplemental affidavit in his or her own words (guard-authored affidavit); and (4) if the answer to any of these questions is in the affirmative, then what should be the remedy. *See id.* at 7-8.

The Arbitrator rejected the Union's claim that agent-authored affidavits were required to be written in a question-and-answer format. *See id.* at 23, 31. As to the Union's claim that a guard has the right to have a copy of an agent's questions placed in the guard's investigation file, the Arbitrator stated that requiring this would "assist the [guards][,]" would "assist Agency reviewers . . . in ascertaining why [a guard] answered the question in [a] particular manner[,]" *id.* at 29-30, and would "assist everyone in the recalling of the information" at a hearing, *id.* at 30. Thus, the Arbitrator concluded that a guard has the right to have a copy of the questions placed in the guard's investigation file. *Id.* at 31. As to the Union's claim that a guard has the right to submit a guard-authored affidavit to the Agency, the Arbitrator stated that an Agency regulation, Internal Affairs Program Statement 1210.24, provides that the Agency will "prepare or accept in total the affidavit[s]."[1] *Id.* at 30. The Arbitrator determined that "accept in total" means that a guard "has the right to prepare an affidavit in his/her own words" and have the affidavit placed in the guard's

1. Internal Affairs Program Statement 1210.24 states, in pertinent part: "Affidavits addressing all salient issues will be obtained during an investigation. The Agency investigators will prepare or accept in total the affidavit." Award at 30.

investigation file. *Id.* Accordingly, the Arbitrator concluded that a guard has the right to provide a guard-authored affidavit to the Agency and have it placed in the guard's investigation file. *Id.*

III. Positions of the Parties

A. Agency's Exceptions

The Agency argues that the award is contrary to management's right to discipline under § 7106(a)(2)(A) of the Statute. *See* Exceptions at 4 (citing *AFSCME, Local 2830*, 60 FLRA 124, 127 (2004)) (*AFSCME*). Additionally, the Agency argues that the award is contrary to management's right to determine its internal security practices under § 7106(a)(1) of the Statute. *See id.* (citing *AFGE, Local 701, Council of Prison Locals 33*, 58 FLRA 128, 131 (2002) (Chairman Cabaniss concurring in part and dissenting in part; then-Member Pope dissenting in part)) (*Local 701*). The Agency asserts that the right to determine internal security practices includes the right to determine the "investigative techniques management will employ to attain its internal security objectives," and adds that "obtaining truthful and reliable information from interviewees constitute internal security practices[.]" *Id.* In addition, the Agency contends that the "limitations imposed by the Arbitrator on the information the Agency can include or exclude from its investigative files" affect the cited management rights because they "dictate[] to the Agency the manner in which it conducts investigations and gathers information." *Id.* Further, the Agency asserts that the award does not enforce a procedure under § 7106(b)(2) of the Statute or an appropriate arrangement under § 7106(b)(3) of the Statute. *Id.* at 4-5, 7.

B. Union's Opposition

The Union argues that the Agency's exceptions should be dismissed as untimely. *See* Opp'n at 1-2.

IV. Analysis and Conclusions

A. The Agency's exceptions were timely filed.

Where an arbitration award's date of service is not in the record, the date of an award is presumed to be the date of service. *E.g. FDIC*, 64 FLRA 1177, 1181 (2010) (*FDIC*). Exceptions to an arbitrator's award must be filed "during the [thirty]-day period beginning on the date the award is served on the party[.]" 5 U.S.C. § 7122(b). Under the Authority's Regulations that were in effect when the Agency filed its exceptions, the thirty-day period included date of service of award.[2] *See* 5 C.F.R. § 2425.1(b). When an award is served by mail, five days are added to the thirty-day filing period. *See* 5 C.F.R. § 2429.22.

The date of service of the award is not in the record. Thus, the date of the award, April 2, 2008, is presumed to be the date of service.[3] *See, e.g., FDIC*, 64 FLRA at 1181. Counting thirty days beginning on, and including, April 2, the due date for filing exceptions was May 1. *See* 5 C.F.R. § 2425.1(b). Because the award was served by mail, five days are added to that due date, resulting in a due date of May 6. *See* 5 C.F.R. § 2429.22. As the Agency filed its exceptions on May 6, the Agency's exceptions are timely. Accordingly, we consider the Agency's exceptions.

B. 5 C.F.R. § 2429.5 bars the Agency's exception regarding management's right to discipline under § 7106(a)(2)(A) of the Statute.

The Authority's Regulations that were in effect when the Agency filed its exceptions provided that "[t]he Authority will not consider . . . any issue, which was not presented in the proceedings before the . . . arbitrator." 5 C.F.R. § 2429.5 (§ 2429.5). Under § 2429.5, the Authority will not consider an issue that could have been, but was not, presented to the arbitrator. *See, e.g., U.S. Dep't of Homeland Sec., U.S. Customs & Border Prot., JFK Airport, Queens, N.Y.*, 62 FLRA 416, 417 (2008).

Here, the issues that the Agency agreed to permit the Arbitrator to determine included whether a guard has the right to have a copy of an agent's questions placed in the guard's investigation file, whether a guard has the right to submit a guard-authored affidavit, and if so, what should be the remedy. *See* Award at 7-8. As such, the Agency could have argued to the Arbitrator that requiring the Agency to place an agent's questions and a guard-authored affidavit in the guard's investigation file would affect management's right to discipline. *See, e.g.*,

2. The Authority's Regulations concerning the review of arbitration awards, including § 2425.1, as well as certain related procedural Regulations, including §§ 2429.5 and 2429.22, were revised effective October 1, 2010. *See* 75 Fed. Reg. 42,283 (2010). As the Union's exceptions were filed before that date, we apply the earlier Regulations.

3. All dates are in 2008 unless otherwise specified.

AFSCME, 60 FLRA at 127-28. The Agency did not do so. *See* Exceptions, Attach., Agency's Post-Hearing Brief at 16. Accordingly, we dismiss this exception under § 2429.5.

C. The award is not contrary to management's right to determine its internal security practices under § 7106(a)(1) of the Statute.

When an exception involves an award's consistency with law, the Authority reviews any question of law raised by the exception and award de novo. *See NTEU, Chapter 24*, 50 FLRA 330, 332 (1995) (citing *U.S. Customs Serv. v. FLRA*, 43 F.3d 682, 686-87 (D.C. Cir. 1994)). In applying the standard of de novo review, the Authority assesses whether an arbitrator's legal conclusions are consistent with the applicable standard of law. *See U.S. Dep't of Def., Dep'ts of the Army & the Air Force, Ala. Nat'l Guard, Northport, Ala.*, 55 FLRA 37, 40 (1998). In making that assessment, the Authority defers to the arbitrator's underlying factual findings. *See id.*

The Authority has recently revised the analysis that it will apply when reviewing management rights exceptions to arbitration awards. *See U.S. EPA*, 65 FLRA 113, 115 (2010) (Member Beck concurring) (*EPA*); *FDIC, Div. of Supervision & Consumer Prot., S.F. Region*, 65 FLRA 102, 106-07, (2010) (Chairman Pope concurring). Under the revised analysis, the Authority assesses whether the award affects the exercise of the asserted management right.[4] *EPA*, 65 FLRA at 115. If it does not, then the Authority denies the exception. *E.g.*, *Soc. Sec. Admin.*, 65 FLRA 523, 525-26 (2011) (*SSA*).

The right to determine internal security practices under § 7106(a)(1) of the Statute includes the authority to determine the policies and practices that are part of an agency's plan to secure or safeguard its personnel, physical property, or operations. *E.g.*, *U.S. DHS, Customs & Border Prot. Agency, N.Y.C., N.Y.*, 61 FLRA 72, 76 (2005) (then-Member Pope concurring) (*DHS*). Where an agency shows a link or reasonable connection between its objective of safeguarding its personnel, property, or operations and, as relevant here, an investigative technique designed to implement that objective, the Authority will find that an arbitration award that conflicts with the policy or practice affects management's right to determine internal security practices. *See Dep't of the Treasury, U.S. Customs Serv., El Paso, Tex.*, 56 FLRA 398, 403 (2000) (Member Wasserman concurring) (*Customs*). In this regard, although "techniques aimed at obtaining truthful and reliable information from interviewees [may] constitute internal security practices[,]" an agency must show a "link, or reasonable connection" between those techniques and the agency's internal security objectives in order to demonstrate that the award affects this management right. *Customs*, 56 FLRA at 403. *Cf. AFGE, Prison Council 33*, 51 FLRA 1112, 1116 (1996) (finding a connection between techniques designed to promote candid and truthful answers during investigations of employee wrongdoing and agency's internal security objectives).

If an agency fails to demonstrate a link or reasonable connection between its investigative techniques and its security objectives, then the Authority will find no effect on management's right to determine internal security. *See SSA*, 65 FLRA at 526 (agency failed to show link between safeguarding computer system and practice of disallowing retired employee to have access to agency e-mail and a limited number of other programs). *See also AFGE, Local 1547*, 63 FLRA 174, 176 (2009) (*Local 1547*) (agency failed to show link between collecting Social Security numbers and dates of birth for parking registration and agency's plan to secure its personnel, physical property, and operations); *DHS*, 61 FLRA at 76 (agency failed to demonstrate that the particular amount of ammunition available to employees to practice for firearms qualification had internal security ramifications); *NFFE, Local 2050*, 36 FLRA 618, 639-40 (1990) (agency failed to show link between notifying employees of criminal activity near agency office and agency's internal security practices).

4. For the reasons articulated in his recent concurring opinion and footnotes, Member Beck would conclude that it is unnecessary to assess whether the award affects the exercise of the asserted management right. The appropriate question is simply whether the remedy directed by the Arbitrator enforces the provision in a reasonable and reasonably foreseeable fashion. *See EPA*, 65 FLRA at 120 (Concurring Opinion of Member Beck); *U.S. Dep't of Justice, Fed. Bureau of Prisons, Fed. Corr. Complex, Terre Haute, Ind.*, 65 FLRA 460, 462 n.2 (2011); *Soc. Sec. Admin., Dallas Region*, 65 FLRA 405, 408 n.5 (2010); *U.S. Dep't of the Air Force, Air Force Materiel Command*, 65 FLRA 395, 398 n.7 (2010); *U.S. Dep't of Health & Human Servs., Office of Medicare Hearings & Appeals*, 65 FLRA 175, 177 n.3 (2010); *U.S. Dep't of Transp., Fed. Aviation Admin.*, 65 FLRA 171, 173 n.5 (2010). Member Beck would conclude that the Arbitrator's award is a plausible interpretation of the parties' agreement and deny the exception.

Here, the Agency asserts that the award imposes limitations that "dictate[] to the Agency the manner in which it conducts investigations and gathers information[,]" and asserts that "obtaining truthful and reliable information from interviewees" is an internal security practice. Exceptions at 4. However, the Agency does not cite a security objective to which the Agency's asserted investigative techniques -- specifically, declining to place a copy of an agent's questions and a guard-authored affidavit in a guard's investigation file -- are connected. *Cf. Local 1547*, 63 FLRA at 176 (agency "fail[ed] to explain even briefly how or why 'collection of information' is involved in its internal security procedures or policies"). In this connection, with regard to the third issue -- whether a guard has the right to submit a guard-authored affidavit -- the award does not affect the Agency's ability to conduct investigations and investigatory interviews as it always has, or to include agent-authored affidavits in a guard's investigation file as it always has, or to arrive at disciplinary decisions as it always has. In other words, the award does not alter the manner, scope, or results of any misconduct investigation.[5] As the Agency has not demonstrated a link or reasonable connection between its asserted investigative techniques and its security objectives, we find that the Agency has not demonstrated that the award affects management's right to determine its internal security practices. *See Local 1547*, 63 FLRA at 176. Further, *Local 701*, 58 FLRA at 131, cited by the Agency, does not support a contrary conclusion, because the union in *Local 701* conceded that the provision at issue affected the right to determine internal security practices, and, accordingly, the Authority did not address the issue. *See Local 701*, 58 FLRA at 132.

Based on the foregoing, we deny this exception. As the Agency's remaining exceptions are premised on the assumption that the award affects a management right, we find that it is unnecessary to consider the remaining exceptions. *See NFFE, Local 2050*, 35 FLRA 706, 715-16 (1990) (finding it unnecessary to determine whether proposal was an appropriate arrangement where proposal did not affect any management right).

V. Decision

The Agency's exceptions are dismissed in part and denied in part.

5. With regard to the second issue -- whether a guard has the right to have a copy of an agent's questions placed in the guard's investigation file -- we note that the Arbitrator resolved the issue by finding that placing a copy of an agent's questions in the guard's investigation file would "assist" the parties. Award at 30. The Arbitrator did not find that the Agency violated the parties' agreement or policy. *See id.* at 29-31. Nevertheless, the parties agreed that the second issue was whether a guard has a "right" to have a copy of an agent's questions placed in the guard's investigation file, *id.* at 4, and there is no contention that the Arbitrator exceeded his authority by resolving the issue.

65 FLRA No. 154

AMERICAN FEDERATION
OF GOVERNMENT EMPLOYEES
COUNCIL OF PRISON LOCALS
LOCAL 4052
(Union)

and

UNITED STATES
DEPARTMENT OF JUSTICE
FEDERAL BUREAU OF PRISONS
METROPOLITAN DETENTION CENTER
GUAYNABO, PUERTO RICO
(Agency)

0-AR-4650

DECISION

April 27, 2011

Before the Authority: Carol Waller Pope, Chairman, and Thomas M. Beck and Ernest DuBester, Members

I. Statement of the Case

This matter is before the Authority on exceptions to an award of Arbitrator Mark I. Lurie filed by the Union under § 7122(a) of the Federal Service Labor-Management Relations Statute (the Statute) and part 2425 of the Authority's Regulations. The Agency filed an opposition to the Union's exceptions.

The Arbitrator concluded that the Agency violated the parties' settlement agreement (Settlement Agreement) by unilaterally repudiating it, but that any remedy would excessively interfere with management's rights to determine its internal security practices and to assign work. For the reasons set forth below, we set aside the award and remand this matter to the parties for resubmission to the Arbitrator, absent settlement, to determine an appropriate remedy.

II. Background and Arbitrator's Award

Housing units at the Agency's Metropolitan Detention Center (MDC) in Guaynabo, Puerto Rico are designed to hold up to 140 inmates; the parties stipulated that a housing unit is overcrowded when 150 inmates are assigned to a single unit. Award at 4. To resolve a previous grievance regarding overcrowding, the parties entered into the Settlement Agreement, which, among other things, required the Agency to staff one additional officer, a "number two officer," to any housing unit at MDC that contained over 150 inmates.[1] Exceptions, Attach. 2 at 1; *see also* Award at 5 n.3.

Several years after entering into the Settlement Agreement, the Agency notified the Union that it would no longer assign a number two officer to housing units that had populations exceeding 150 inmates. Award at 2. The Union presented a grievance alleging that the Agency violated the Settlement Agreement by unilaterally repudiating it. Opp'n at 1. The grievance was not resolved and was submitted to arbitration. *Id.* at 2. The Arbitrator framed the relevant issue to be resolved as:

> Is the . . . Settlement [Agreement] a grievance settlement that is currently in effect, lawful in its purpose (contingent staffing) and enforceable according to its terms? And, if so, can its prescribed remedy be lawfully enforced by the Arbitrator and, if the remedy cannot be lawfully enforced, what should the remedy be?[2]

Award at 2 (emphasis omitted).

The Arbitrator found a general correlation between overcrowding in detention facilities and assaults on officers by inmates. *Id.* at 8. He also found that, "[w]here overcrowding has been a contributing factor to such assaults, paying staff to work overtime can reduce the assault rate." *Id.*

---

1. The Settlement Agreement acknowledges that the parties "agreed to the limit of 150 inmates per unit, before a number two officer was assigned." Exceptions, Attach. 2 at 1. The parties also agreed to pay overtime to any number two officer assigned as a result of overcrowding. *Id.*

2. The Agency argued to the Arbitrator that the Settlement Agreement was of finite duration implemented to address a specific situation at the time of the agreement. Award at 5. The Arbitrator found that the Settlement Agreement constituted a binding grievance settlement and found that the Agency violated the Settlement Agreement by unilaterally repudiating it. *Id.* at 19. Because no exceptions were filed to the Arbitrator's resolution of these issues, they are not before us.

However, the Arbitrator determined that most of the assaults at MDC were related, not to overcrowding, but to either an "officer's intercession in a crime in progress" or an "inmate with mental health problems." *Id.* at 10. Moreover, according to the Arbitrator, it was reasonable for the Agency to conclude that its enforcement of the Settlement Agreement could impose an unreasonable burden on its officers. *Id.* at 9. Therefore, the Arbitrator concluded that there was "no compelling need" to assign a number two officer at MDC when it is overcrowded. *Id.* at 11-12.

The Union argued before the Arbitrator that the Settlement Agreement did not excessively interfere with any management right because it did not "preclude the accomplishment of the Agency's internal security objectives" or "limit the Agency's capacity to relieve overcrowding." *Id.* at 13. The Agency responded that the Settlement Agreement excessively interfered with its rights to determine internal security and assign work because it "left no circumstance in which the Agency could not assign a [n]umber [two] [o]fficer" to an overcrowded facility, including emergency situations. *Id.* at 18.

The Arbitrator, in "[r]econstructing what [m]anagement would have done under these circumstances," found that the Agency would have assigned a number two officer only when overcrowding was accompanied by "additional, aggravating risk elements." *Id.* at 20. He, therefore, concluded that enforcement of the Settlement Agreement would excessively interfere with management's rights to determine its internal security practices and assign work. *Id.* at 20-21. The Arbitrator then decided that "no remedy can be or is awarded." *Id.* at 21.

III. Positions of the Parties

A. Union's Exceptions

The Union argues that the award is contrary to 5 U.S.C. § 7106(b)(3) of the Statute because the Arbitrator misapplied the test in *United States Department of the Treasury, Bureau of Engraving & Printing, Washington, D.C.*, 53 FLRA 146 (1997) (*BEP*). Exceptions at 5. The Union contends that the Arbitrator's reconstruction of what management would have done is improper because the "additional, aggravating risk" standard had no basis in law, regulation, or the Settlement Agreement. *Id.* at 8-9 (emphasis omitted).

The Union also asserts that the Authority should reinstate an "abrogation" standard and discontinue use of an "excessive interference" test when evaluating a remedy's effect on the exercise of a management right. *Id.* at 10-21. The Union argues that, applying an abrogation standard here, the Authority should remand the case to the Arbitrator to fashion an appropriate remedy, or, alternatively, should itself determine whether any remedy would abrogate the exercise of a management right. *Id.* at 21. According to the Union, the Arbitrator or the Authority could award a remedy that would allow the Agency to choose not to enforce the Settlement Agreement in emergency situations. *Id.* at 21-22 (citing *U.S. Dep't of Justice, Fed. Bureau of Prisons, Fed. Transfer Ctr., Okla. City, Okla.*, 58 FLRA 109 (2002) (*BOP, OKC*)). The Union also argues that such an exception may not be necessary because the Settlement Agreement does not abrogate management's rights. Exceptions at 22-23 (citing *U.S. Dep't of Justice, Fed. Bureau of Prisons, Fed. Transfer Ctr., Okla. City, Okla.*, 57 FLRA 158 (2001)).

Finally, the Union argues that several of the Arbitrator's findings are nonfacts, fail to draw their essence from the Settlement Agreement or the parties' agreement, or are contrary to the Statute. Exceptions at 6-10. According to the Union, the Arbitrator's conclusion that inmate assaults are unrelated to overcrowding fails to draw its essence from the Settlement Agreement or the parties' agreement and is a nonfact. *Id.* at 6-7. The Union also contends that the Arbitrator's finding that the officers "have not treated the threat as if it were real and immediate" by accepting overtime pay is a nonfact and fails to draw its essence from the parties' agreement. *Id.* at 8 (emphasis omitted). Further, the Union argues that the Arbitrator's use of a "compelling need" standard for determining whether a number two officer is necessary does not draw its essence from the Settlement Agreement or the parties' agreement and is contrary to the Statute. *Id.* at 9-10. The Union also claims that the Arbitrator did not consider all of the remedies it had requested and, therefore, his award does not draw its essence from the parties' agreement and he exceeded his authority. *Id.* at 10.

B. Agency's Opposition

The Agency argues that the Arbitrator correctly applied the "excessive interference" test set forth in *BOP, OKC*. Opp'n at 5-6. The Agency contends that the Arbitrator correctly determined that an award requiring it to comply with the Settlement Agreement would excessively interfere with its rights "because it leaves *no* circumstance under which the Agency could not assign a number two officer" when the population of a housing unit at MDC was overcrowded. *Id.* at 7. Also, the Agency claims that, even under an abrogation standard, enforcement of the Settlement Agreement would abrogate its rights because it would be forced to assign a number two officer "without any exception, limitation, or any room for the exercise of management discretion . . . ." *Id.* at 11.

The Agency also argues that the Union does not provide any support for its argument that the Arbitrator's findings fail to draw their essence from the Settlement Agreement or the parties' agreement. *Id.* at 12. According to the Agency, the Union's nonfact arguments simply constitute disagreement with the Arbitrator's conclusions. *Id.* at 15-16. The Agency also argues that the Arbitrator's decision not to grant certain remedies requested by the Union draws its essence from the parties' agreement because an arbitrator has great latitude in fashioning remedies. *Id.* at 13-14.

IV. Analysis and Conclusion: The award is contrary to § 7106 of the Statute.

When an exception involves an award's consistency with law, the Authority reviews any question of law raised by the exception and the award de novo. *See NTEU, Chapter 24*, 50 FLRA 330, 332 (1995) (citing *U.S. Customs Serv. v. FLRA*, 43 F.3d 682, 686-87 (D.C. Cir. 1994)). In applying the standard of de novo review, the Authority assesses whether an arbitrator's legal conclusions are consistent with the applicable standard of law. *See U.S. Dep't of Def., Dep'ts of the Army & the Air Force, Ala. Nat'l Guard, Northport, Ala.*, 55 FLRA 37, 40 (1998). In making that assessment, the Authority defers to the arbitrator's underlying factual findings. *See id.*

The Union contends that the Arbitrator erred in finding that the Settlement Agreement excessively interfered with management's rights to determine its internal security practices and to assign work. The Authority recently revised the analysis that it applies when reviewing management rights exceptions to arbitration awards. *See U.S. Envtl. Prot. Agency*, 65 FLRA 113, 115 (2010) (Member Beck concurring) (*EPA*); *FDIC, Div. of Supervision & Consumer Prot., S.F. Region*, 65 FLRA 102, 106-07 (2010) (Chairman Pope concurring) (*FDIC, S.F. Region*). Under the revised analysis, the Authority first assesses whether the award affects the exercise of the asserted management right. *EPA*, 65 FLRA at 115. If so, the Authority examines whether the award provides a remedy for a violation of either an applicable law, within the meaning of § 7106(a)(2) of the Statute, or a contract provision that was negotiated pursuant to § 7106(b) of the Statute. *Id.* In determining whether the award enforces a contract provision negotiated under § 7106(b)(3), the Authority assesses: (1) whether the contract provision constitutes an arrangement for employees adversely affected by the exercise of a management right; and (2) if so, whether the arbitrator's enforcement of the arrangement abrogates the exercise of the management right. *EPA*, 65 FLRA at 116-18. In concluding that it would apply an abrogation standard, the Authority rejected continued application of an excessive interference standard. *Id.* at 118. Furthermore, in setting forth the revised analysis, the Authority rejected the continued application of the "reconstruction" requirement set forth in *BEP*. *FDIC, S.F. Region*, 65 FLRA at 106-07.

The Arbitrator concluded that enforcement of the Settlement Agreement would "excessively interfere with the Agency's right to determine its internal security practices" and its right to assign work and, thus, that "no remedy can be or is awarded." Award at 20-21. However, the revised analysis requires us to determine whether the award abrogates the exercise of a management right.[3] An award abrogates the exercise of a management right if the award precludes the agency from exercising the right. *U.S. Dep't of Transp., Fed. Aviation Admin.*, 65 FLRA 171, 174 (2010). The Arbitrator's award does not preclude the Agency from exercising its rights to determine its internal security practices or to assign work because the Settlement Agreement does not require the Agency to assign a number two officer in all cases. Rather, the Settlement Agreement imposes this requirement only when the population at a housing unit at MDC reaches 150 inmates. *See U.S. Dep't of Justice, Fed. Bureau of Prisons, U.S. Penitentiary, Atlanta, Ga.*, 57 FLRA 406, 411 (2001) (finding that the arbitrator's award did not abrogate management's rights where the agency was not required to fill vacant posts in all situations). Therefore, the Settlement Agreement

3. The parties do not dispute that the Settlement Agreement affects management's rights to determine internal security practices and assign work. Opp'n at 8. Additionally, the parties do not dispute that the Settlement Agreement is an arrangement.

does not abrogate the cited management rights, and the Arbitrator erred by finding that he could not enforce it and provide a remedy. Accordingly, we set aside the award and remand this matter to the parties for resubmission to the Arbitrator, absent settlement, to determine an appropriate remedy.[4]

V. Decision

The award is set aside, and the matter is remanded to the parties for resubmission to the Arbitrator, absent settlement, to determine an appropriate remedy.[5]

---

4. Member Beck agrees with the conclusion to remand this matter for the determination of an appropriate remedy. For the reasons discussed in his concurring opinion in *EPA*, 65 FLRA 113, Member Beck concludes that, where, as here, the parties have agreed to a settlement provision, it is inappropriate for the Arbitrator to determine that the provision is not enforceable because it purportedly conflicts with statutory management rights. *Id.* at 120 (Concurring Opinion of Member Beck). Therefore, because the Arbitrator found that the Agency violated the Settlement Agreement by unilaterally repudiating it, Member Beck agrees that this matter should be remanded for the determination of an appropriate remedy.

5. Because the Union's remaining exceptions challenge the analysis that underlies the Arbitrator's conclusion that we set aside, it is unnecessary to address them. *See U.S. Dep't of Def., Def. Logistics Agency, Def. Contract Mgmt. Command, Def. Contract Mgmt. Area Operations Bos., Bos., Mass.*, 53 FLRA 210, 217 n.9 (1997).

65 FLRA No. 155

NATIONAL AIR TRAFFIC
CONTROLLERS ASSOCIATION
LOCAL ZHU
(Union)

and

UNITED STATES
DEPARTMENT OF TRANSPORTATION
FEDERAL AVIATION ADMINISTRATION
WASHINGTON, D.C.
(Agency)

0-NG-2982

DECISION AND ORDER
ON NEGOTIABILITY ISSUES

April 27, 2011

Before the Authority: Carol Waller Pope, Chairman, and Thomas M. Beck and Ernest DuBester, Members

I. Statement of the Case

This case is before the Authority on a negotiability appeal filed by the Union under § 7105(a)(2)(E) of the Federal Service Labor-Management Relations Statute (the Statute). The appeal concerns the negotiability of twelve proposals. The Agency filed a statement of position (SOP), to which the Union filed a response (response). The Agency did not file a reply to the Union's response.

For the reasons that follow, the Authority finds that Proposals 2, 6, 7, 9, 10, 11, and 12 are within the duty to bargain. In addition, the Authority dismisses the petition for review (petition) as to Proposals 3, 4, and 5 because the Agency has not raised a negotiability dispute with respect to those proposals, and dismisses the petition as to Proposals 1 and 8 because they are moot.

II. Background

The Agency component involved is an air route traffic control center. Record of Post-Petition Conference (Record) at 1. The Agency implemented the Lufkin Sector, which is a new sector within the airspace for which the center is responsible. *Id.* A sector is a section of airspace for which air traffic controllers (ATCs) perform separation duties. *Id.* The Lufkin Sector is part of the "Lufkin Specialty." *Id.* A specialty is a broader area of airspace composed of several sectors. *Id.* The Lufkin Sector was created after an existing sector, the Humble Sector, was split into two sectors. *Id.* at 1-2. Thus, the airspace that once composed the Humble Sector is now divided between the Humble Sector and the Lufkin Sector. *Id.*

ATCs are required to obtain certain certifications before working in a sector. *Id.* at 2. ATC pay is governed by the number of certifications obtained. Petition at 5. Once ATCs obtain certifications on all sectors within a specialty, they are classified as Certified Professional Controllers (CPCs). Record at 2. Establishment of the Lufkin Sector created two additional certifications within the specialty. *Id.* at 2-3.

III. Preliminary Matters

A. The proposals will be grouped as requested by the Union.

In its discussion regarding whether its proposals should be severed, the Union requests that Proposals 3, 4, and 5, and 11 and 12, be considered as two sets because the proposals in each proposed set concern the same subject matter.[1] Response at 16-17. This request does not involve "severance" as that term is defined in § 2424.2(h) of the Authority's Regulations because the Union is not requesting that the proposals be divided into separate parts.[2] 5 C.F.R. § 2424.2(h). However, because the Agency does not object to the Union's request, we will consider the proposals in

1. In its petition and response, the Union sometimes refers to the proposals as twelve sections of one proposal. However, the Union provides specific arguments to address each section separately in those documents. Additionally, during the post-petition conference, the Union claimed, without objection by the Agency, that the case involved twelve proposals. Record at 1. We therefore interpret the Union's position concerning severance as a request that the individual sections be treated as separate proposals. Accordingly, the Authority will consider them as separate proposals.

2. 5 C.F.R. § 2424.2(h) provides as follows:

> *Severance* means the division of a proposal or provision into separate parts having independent meaning, for the purpose of determining whether any of the separate parts is within the duty to bargain or is contrary to law. In effect, severance results in the creation of separate proposals or provisions. Severance applies when some parts of the proposal or provision are determined to be outside the duty to bargain or contrary to law.

each set together. *See NATCA, AFL-CIO*, 62 FLRA 174, 174-75 (2007) (Chairman Cabaniss concurring) (analyzing proposals together at union's request when agency did not object). As a result, if we find one of the proposals in a set nonnegotiable, then all of the proposals in that set will be found outside the duty to bargain. *Id.*

B. Proposals 1 and 8 are moot.

Where a proposal addresses an event that has already occurred, the Authority will find that the proposal is moot and will dismiss the petition.[3] *See, e.g., NTEU, Chapter 207*, 58 FLRA 409, 410 (2003) (Chairman Cabaniss dissenting) (*NTEU*); *IFPTE, Local 35*, 54 FLRA 1384, 1387-88 (1998) (Member Wasserman dissenting); *NFFE, Local 1482*, 45 FLRA 52, 65-66 (1992). In this connection, where a proposal has become moot, issuance of a ruling on the merits of the proposal would constitute an advisory opinion, which is prohibited under 5 C.F.R. § 2429.10. *AFSCME, Local 1418*, 53 FLRA 1191, 1195 (1998).

Proposals 1 and 8 address the implementation of the Lufkin Sector that has already occurred. In particular, Proposals 1 and 8 expressly require the Agency to take certain actions prior to that implementation. Accordingly, Proposals 1 and 8 are moot. *NTEU*, 58 FLRA at 410 (dismissing petition as moot where proposal referred to a specific event that had already occurred and required agency to take action by a date that had passed).

For the foregoing reasons, we dismiss the petition as to Proposals 1 and 8.

IV. Proposal 2

A. Wording

> Section 2: No employee currently holding certifications on the Humble Sector at [the Agency] will be required to certify on the Lufkin Sector. The implementation of this sector shall not affect an employee's [CPC] status.

Petition at 4.

B. Meaning

The parties agree that, under Proposal 2, ATCs who had already become certified on the Humble Sector before it was divided would not be required to obtain certifications on the Lufkin Sector. Record at 2. Conversely, ATCs who had not previously been certified on the Humble Sector would be required to obtain certifications on the Lufkin Sector. *Id.* In addition, CPCs' certification status and pay rate, which is governed by the number of certifications obtained, would be determined as if they had obtained the Lufkin Sector certifications. Petition at 5.

C. Positions of the Parties

1. Agency

The Agency asserts that the proposal is contrary to management's § 7106(a)(2)(B) right to assign work. SOP at 8. The Agency claims that the proposal would "restrict the Agency's ability to conduct recertification training." *Id.*

2. Union

The Union acknowledges that Proposal 2 would affect management's § 7106(a)(2)(B) right to assign work. Response at 4. However, the Union argues that the proposal is negotiable as an appropriate arrangement. *Id.* at 5. The Union contends that the proposal would prevent CPCs from losing pay by deeming them certified on the Lufkin Sector, thereby maintaining their fully-certified status for pay purposes. *Id.* at 5. The Union asserts that requiring CPCs to recertify on the Lufkin Sector would have the foreseeable effect of causing CPCs to lose their fully-certified status. *Id.* at 4-5. Because ATC pay is governed by the number of certifications obtained, this would reduce the pay of CPCs assigned to the Lufkin Specialty. *Id.* at 5. The Union further contends that the proposal is tailored to prevent CPCs from experiencing a pay loss. Finally, the Union explains that the proposal would not restrict the Agency from freely assigning certification training for the Lufkin Sector to all ATCs, including CPCs. *Id.*

D. Analysis and Conclusions

1. Proposal 2 affects management's § 7106(a)(2)(B) right to assign work.

The Union acknowledges that Proposal 2 would affect management's § 7106(a)(2)(B) right to assign work. *See id.* at 4. Where a union concedes that its proposal would affect management's rights under

3. The Agency does not argue that the negotiability dispute in this case is moot as to Proposals 1 and 8. However, mootness is a threshold jurisdictional issue and may be raised by the Authority sua sponte. *See, e.g., NTEU*, 52 FLRA 1265, 1278-79 (1997).

§ 7106(a) of the Statute, the Authority will find that the proposal would affect those rights. *See NATCA*, 61 FLRA 437, 439 (2006). Therefore, we find that this proposal would affect management's § 7106(a)(2)(B) right to assign work.

2. Proposal 2 is an appropriate arrangement.

The Union argues that Proposal 2 is negotiable as an appropriate arrangement under § 7106(b)(3). A proposal that would affect management's rights under § 7106(a) of the Statute is nevertheless negotiable if it constitutes an appropriate arrangement within the meaning of § 7106(b)(3) of the Statute. To establish whether a proposal constitutes an appropriate arrangement, the Authority first considers whether the proposal is intended to be an arrangement for employees adversely affected by the exercise of a management right. *See NAGE, Local R14-8*, 21 FLRA 24, 31 (1986) (*KANG*). The claimed arrangement must also be sufficiently tailored to compensate or benefit employees suffering adverse effects attributable to the exercise of management's rights. *See NTEU, Chapter 243,* 49 FLRA 176, 184 (1994). If the Authority finds the proposal to be an arrangement, then the Authority will determine whether it is appropriate or whether it is inappropriate because it excessively interferes with management's rights. *Id.* at 31-33. In doing so, the Authority weighs the benefits afforded to employees under the arrangement against the intrusion on the exercise of management's rights. *Id.*

As the Agency does not dispute that Proposal 2 is an arrangement, we find that the proposal constitutes an arrangement. *See* § 2424.32(c)(ii)(2) (agency's failure to respond to an assertion raised by union will, where appropriate, be deemed a concession to that assertion); *AFGE, Local 221*, 64 FLRA 1153, 1157 (2010) (where agency failed to address union's claim that proposals constitute arrangements, Authority determined that proposals constituted arrangements); *NTEU*, 61 FLRA 871, 874 (2006) (same).

With regard to whether the arrangement is appropriate, the Union asserts that Proposal 2 would benefit CPCs who are assigned to the Lufkin Specialty by maintaining their fully-certified status, therefore preventing a reduction in pay. By contrast, the Agency does not contest that Proposal 2 is "appropriate." Weighing the demonstrated benefits to ATCs against the absence of asserted or demonstrated burdens on the right to assign work, we find that Proposal 2 is an appropriate arrangement under § 7106(b)(3) of the Statute. *See AFGE, Local 1367*, 64 FLRA 869, 871-72 (2010) (Member Beck dissenting in part).

Based on the above, we find that Proposal 2 is within the duty to bargain.

V. Proposals 3, 4, and 5

A. Wording

Proposal 3

> Section 3: The implementation of the Lufkin Sector will not impact the pay progression of any employee currently undergoing initial qualification training in the Lufkin Specialty.

Petition at 5.

Proposal 4

> Section 4: Prior to the implementation of the Lufkin Sector, the Parties at the local level will develop a method for tracking any training delays, for employees undergoing initial qualification training, incurred as a consequence of any training and/or transition activities.[4]

Id. at 6.

Proposal 5

> Section 5: Any subsequent promotion(s) for employees will be backdated by the amount of time calculated as a training delay in Section 4.

Id. at 7.

4. Although Proposal 4 requires the Agency to have developed a method for tracking training delays prior to an event that has already occurred — implementation of the Lufkin Sector — the operation of the proposal is not limited by a particular event or timeframe. Rather, the proposal's operation will have a prospective impact on employees undergoing initial qualification training who incur training delays as the result of implementation of the Lufkin Sector. As such, the parties continue to have a legally cognizable interest in the outcome. *See NAGE, Local R1-109*, 64 FLRA 132, 133 (2009) (Member Beck dissenting as to another matter) (finding proposal not moot where proposal could benefit employees in future). Therefore, we find that Proposal 4 is not moot.

B. Meaning

The parties agree that under Proposal 3, any delay in ATCs obtaining certifications resulting from implementation of the Lufkin Sector will not affect such ATCs by reducing their pay, which is determined by the number of certifications obtained. Record at 2-3.

The parties agree that Proposal 4 would require the parties to jointly develop a mechanism for tracking any delays in certification training for ATCs attributable to other training associated with implementation of the Lufkin Sector. *Id.* at 3.

The parties agree that under Proposal 5, ATC pay increases based on the number of certifications obtained would be backdated by the amount of time certification training was delayed, as determined by the mechanism established in Proposal 4. *Id.*

C. Positions of the Parties

1. Agency

The Agency asserts that it has no duty to bargain over Proposals 3, 4, and 5 because ATC pay increases are "covered by" Article 108, Section 5 of the parties' collective bargaining agreement (CBA). SOP at 9-11.

2. Union

The Union contends that Proposals 3, 4, and 5 are not "covered by" the CBA. Response at 7-8.

The Union also argues that, although training generally falls within management's § 7106(a)(2)(B) right to assign work, Proposals 3, 4, and 5 are negotiable as appropriate arrangements. *Id.* at 6.

D. Analysis and Conclusions

The Agency's only claim with regard to Proposals 3, 4, and 5 is that they are "covered by" Article 108, Section 5 of the CBA. This claim raises a bargaining obligation dispute, which is defined in § 2424.2(a) of the Authority's Regulations as "a disagreement between an exclusive representative and an agency concerning whether, in the specific circumstances involved in a particular case, the parties are obligated to bargain over a proposal that otherwise may be negotiable." The Authority's Regulations specify that a bargaining obligation dispute includes a claim that a proposal "concerns a matter that is covered by a collective bargaining agreement[.]" 5 C.F.R. § 2424.2(a)(1). The Authority's Regulations further specify that a negotiability dispute "that concerns only a bargaining obligation dispute may not be resolved [in a negotiability proceeding]." 5 C.F.R. § 2424.2(d).

As the only issue raised by the Agency with regard to Proposals 3, 4, and 5 is a bargaining obligation dispute, we dismiss the petition as to Proposals 3, 4, and 5. *See NATCA*, 61 FLRA 341, 343-44 (2005); *Antilles Consol. Educ. Ass'n*, 61 FLRA 327, 331 (2005).

VI. Proposal 6

A. Wording

> Section 6: For a period of ninety days after the initial implementation of the Lufkin Sector, any and all operational errors or operational deviations occurring in any sector affected by this implementation will be attributed to the facility rather than an employee.[5]

Petition at 8.

B. Meaning

The parties agree that, under Proposal 6, for ninety days following implementation of the Lufkin Sector, bargaining unit members will be granted immunity from discipline or other adverse consequences resulting from any operational errors or deviations in sectors affected by the Lufkin Sector. Petition at 8; *see also* Record at 3.

C. Positions of the Parties

1. Agency

The Agency asserts that the proposal is contrary to management's § 7106(a)(2)(A) and (B) rights to discipline and to assign work. SOP at 12. Specifically, the Agency reasons that this proposal would excuse individual ATCs from responsibility for errors or deviations. *Id.* The Agency asserts that it

5. Although Proposal 6 refers to a timeframe that has already passed — ninety days following implementation of the Lufkin Sector — it will have a prospective impact on employees who are held accountable for any operational errors or deviations that occurred during those 90 days. As such, the parties continue to have a legally cognizable interest in the outcome. *See NAGE, Local R1-109*, 64 FLRA at 133 (finding proposal not moot where proposal could benefit employees in future). Therefore, we find that Proposal 6 is not moot.

would be restricted from requiring re-training for certification and from administering corrective discipline to individual ATCs who commit these errors or deviations. *Id.*

2. Union

The Union acknowledges that Proposal 6 would affect management's § 7106(a)(2)(A) and (B) rights to discipline and to assign work. Response at 9. However, the Union argues that the proposal is negotiable as an appropriate arrangement. *Id.* In support, the Union asserts that the proposal would allow ATCs assigned to the Lufkin Sector a "grace period" to familiarize themselves with the new changes before the Agency imposes performance or disciplinary-based measures on specific ATCs if an error occurs. *Id.* In addition, the Union contends that the proposal would not excessively interfere with management's rights because the proposal is limited to a brief ninety-day period. *Id.* The Union points out that, during the ninety-day period, the Agency could continue to investigate errors or conduct remedial training, but could not impose performance or disciplinary-based action on specific individuals. *Id.*

D. Analysis and Conclusions

1. Proposal 6 affects management's § 7106(a)(2)(A) and (B) rights to discipline and assign work.

The Union acknowledges that Proposal 6 would affect management's § 7106(a)(2)(A) and (B) rights to discipline and to assign work. *See id.* at 9. Therefore, consistent with Authority precedent dealing with a union's acknowledgement that a proposal would affect management's rights, *supra* Part IV.D, we find that this proposal would affect management's § 7106(a)(2)(A) and (B) rights to discipline and assign work.

2. Proposal 6 is an appropriate arrangement.

The Union argues that Proposal 6 is negotiable as an appropriate arrangement under § 7106(b)(3). Based on Authority precedent discussed *supra* Part IV.D, as the Agency does not dispute that Proposal 6 is an arrangement, we find that the proposal constitutes an arrangement.

With regard to whether the arrangement is appropriate, the Union asserts that Proposal 6 would benefit ATCs assigned to the Lufkin Sector by allowing for a "grace period" to familiarize themselves with the new changes before the Agency imposes performance or disciplinary-based measures on specific ATCs if an error occurs. By contrast, the Agency does not contest that Proposal 6 is "appropriate." Weighing the demonstrated benefits to ATCs against the absence of asserted or demonstrated burdens on the right to discipline and to assign work, we find that Proposal 6 is an appropriate arrangement under § 7106(b)(3) of the Statute. *See AFGE, Local 1367*, 64 FLRA at 871-72.

Based on the above, we find that Proposal 6 is within the duty to bargain.

VII. Proposal 7

A. Wording

> Section 7: The Lufkin Sector will be physically located in such a configuration so that the Radar position of the Lufkin Sector is immediately adjacent to the Radar position of the Houston Sector.

Petition at 8.

B. Meaning

The parties agree that Proposal 7 would require the radar scope position for the Lufkin Sector to be physically located next to the radar scope position for the Houston Sector. Record at 3. The radar scopes are in fixed positions, and the parties agree that the proposal is not intended to reposition the radar scopes. *Id.* at 3-4. Rather, the proposal would require that an existing radar scope position next to the pre-existing Houston radar scope position be assigned to the Lufkin Sector. *Id.* at 4. The radar scope position affects ATCs' spatial arrangement in the control center. Petition at 9.

C. Positions of the Parties

1. Agency

The Agency asserts that the proposal concerns a permissive subject of bargaining over which it has elected not to bargain. SOP at 13. In this regard, the Agency contends that the "configuration of an operational work area" concerns the methods and means of performing work under § 7106(b)(1) of the Statute. *Id.*

2. Union

The Union argues that the Agency has failed to explain how the proposal would interfere with the Agency's right to determine the methods and means of performing work. Response at 11. In this regard, the Union contends that the proposal would only require that the physical layout of the Lufkin Sector be adjacent to an existing sector in order to facilitate communication. The Union claims that this would not affect the ATCs' compliance with Agency directives and procedures. *Id.*

The Union also argues that the proposal is negotiable as an appropriate arrangement. *Id.* at 10. In support, the Union contends that the proposal would prevent errors due to poor communication between ATCs in the Lufkin Sector and ATCs in other sectors. *Id.* at 10-12. The Union further argues these errors would be minimized by physically aligning the Lufkin Sector with an existing sector in order to facilitate communication between ATCs. *Id.* at 11-12.

D. Analysis and Conclusions

The Agency argues that the proposal would infringe on management's right to determine the methods and means of performing work. SOP at 14. Even assuming that the proposal concerns the exercise of management's rights to determine the methods and means of performing work under § 7106(b)(1), the proposal is nevertheless negotiable because, for the reasons set forth below, it constitutes an appropriate arrangement. *See AFGE, Nat'l Council of Field Labor Locals*, 58 FLRA 616, 617 (2003) (*AFGE*) (assuming without deciding that proposal concerns exercise of management right to determine means of performing agency's work, but found proposal negotiable as appropriate arrangement).

The Union argues that Proposal 7 is negotiable as an appropriate arrangement under § 7106(b)(3). Based on Authority precedent discussed *supra* Part IV.D, as the Agency does not dispute that Proposal 7 is an arrangement, we find that the proposal constitutes an arrangement.

With regard to whether the arrangement is appropriate, the Union asserts that Proposal 7 would benefit ATCs by preventing errors due to poor communication between ATCs in the Lufkin Sector and ATCs in other sectors. Response at 10-12. By contrast, the Agency does not contest that Proposal 7 is "appropriate." Weighing the demonstrated benefits to ATCs against the absence of asserted or demonstrated burdens on the right to choose the methods and means of performing work, we find that Proposal 7 is an appropriate arrangement under § 7106(b)(3) of the Statute. *See AFGE, Local 1367*, 64 FLRA at 871-72.

Based on the above, we find that Proposal 7 is within the duty to bargain.

VIII. Proposal 9

A. Wording

> Section 9: Should the Agency determine to establish a training cadre, the Agency shall solicit volunteers for participation. The most senior qualified volunteer(s) shall be selected.

Petition at 10.

B. Meaning

The parties agree that, under Proposal 9, the Agency would have the option of establishing a training cadre, which would consist of a group of CPC training instructors. Record at 4. The parties also agree that the proposal would require the Agency to solicit volunteers and to select the most senior qualified volunteers to participate in the training cadre. *Id.* It is undisputed that the Agency would determine the qualifications for volunteers. Petition at 10.

C. Positions of the Parties

1. Agency

The Agency asserts that the proposal is contrary to management's § 7106(a)(2)(B) right to assign work. SOP at 15. Specifically, the Agency reasons that the proposal would restrict the Agency from determining which employees would be assigned to the training cadre. *Id.*

2. Union

The Union contends that the proposal is a procedure intended to minimize the impact of changes associated with the establishment of the Lufkin Sector by creating a training committee chosen by seniority. Response at 14.[6]

---

6. The Union also argues that, because the Agency did not submit a statement concerning Proposal 9, the Authority should deem the allegation of non-negotiability withdrawn. Response at 14. However, the Agency did submit a statement concerning Proposal 9. SOP at 15. Therefore, the Authority finds that the issue of Proposal 9's negotiability is properly before the Authority.

D. Analysis and Conclusions

1. Proposal 9 affects management's § 7106(a)(2)(B) right to assign work.

It is uncontested that the proposal affects management's § 7106(a)(2)(B) right to assign work. However, even if the proposal concerns the exercise of this management right, the proposal is nevertheless negotiable if it constitutes a procedure. *See NATCA, AFL-CIO*, 61 FLRA 336, 339 (2005) (*NATCA*) (proposal affecting management right under § 7106(a) nevertheless negotiable if it constitutes a procedure under § 7106(b)(2)).

2. The proposal constitutes a procedure under § 7106(b)(2).

It is also uncontested that the proposal is a procedure. The Union argues in its response that the proposal constitutes a procedure under § 7106(b)(2). Response at 14. The Agency did not address this claim in its SOP or file a reply. Therefore, the Authority finds that, consistent with the Agency's concession that the proposal is a negotiable procedure under § 7106(b)(2), this proposal is a negotiable procedure. *See* 5 C.F.R. § 2424.32(c)(ii)(2) (failure to respond to an assertion raised by other party will, where appropriate, be deemed a concession to that assertion); *NATCA*, 61 FLRA at 339 (where union did not dispute that provisions affected a management right, but agency failed to address union's claims that provisions constituted procedures, Authority determined that agency conceded that provisions constituted procedures and were therefore negotiable).

Based on the above, we find that Proposal 9 is within the duty to bargain.

IX. Proposal 10

A. Wording

Section 10: The Agency will provide space at all sectors for the posting of "strips" containing flight plan information for aircraft expected to be "non-radar."

Petition at 11.

B. Meaning

The parties agree that, under Proposal 10, the Agency would have to provide a small work area for ATCs to maintain printed flight plan information for aircraft expected to be outside the ATCs' radar coverage. Record at 4; Petition at 11. Employees are required to maintain this information. Record at 4; Petition at 11.

C. Positions of the Parties

1. Agency

The Agency asserts that the proposal concerns a permissive subject of bargaining over which it has elected not to bargain. SOP at 16. In this regard, the Agency contends that the "configuration of an operational work area" concerns the methods and means of performing work under § 7106(b)(1) of the Statute. *Id.*

2. Union

The Union argues that the configuration of work space to allow for the posting of certain flight plan information does not constitute a method and means of performing work. Response at 15. Rather, the Union claims that the proposal concerns the physical layout of ATCs' work space and ensures that sufficient space is allocated for maintaining the flight plan information. *Id.*

In addition, the Union contends that the proposal is negotiable as an appropriate arrangement. *Id.* In support, the Union argues that the proposal is designed to mitigate the impact of lack of sufficient space in the Lufkin Sector for the posting of such flight plan information. *Id.* In this regard, the Union argues that ATCs could be subject to disciplinary or performance-based action if they fail to post such information. *Id.*

D. Analysis and Conclusions

The Agency argues that the proposal would infringe on management's rights to choose the methods and means of performing work. SOP at 14. Even assuming that the proposal concerns the exercise of management's rights to determine the methods and means of performing work under § 7106(b)(1), the proposal is nevertheless negotiable because, for the reasons set forth below, it constitutes an appropriate arrangement. *See AFGE*, 58 FLRA at 617.

The Union argues that Proposal 10 is negotiable as an appropriate arrangement under § 7106(b)(3). Based on Authority precedent discussed *supra* Part IV.D, as the Agency does not dispute that Proposal 10 is an arrangement, we find that the proposal constitutes an arrangement.

With regard to whether the arrangement is appropriate, the Union asserts that Proposal 10 would benefit ATCs by preventing them from being subject to disciplinary or performance-based action for failing to post certain flight plan information. By contrast, the Agency does not contest that Proposal 10 is "appropriate." Weighing the demonstrated benefits to ATCs against the absence of asserted or demonstrated burdens on the right to choose the methods and means of performing work, we find that Proposal 10 is an appropriate arrangement under § 7106(b)(3) of the Statute. *See AFGE, Local 1367*, 64 FLRA at 871-72.

Based on the above, we find that Proposal 10 is within the duty to bargain.

X. Proposals 11 and 12

A. Wording

Proposal 11

Section 11: There shall be no local or regional supplements or modifications of this Agreement authorized.

Petition at 12; Record at 4.

Proposal 12

Section 12: Nothing in this Agreement shall be construed as a waiver of either Party's statutory or contractual rights.

Petition at 12.

B. Meaning

The parties agree that Proposal 11 would require that the agreement not be modified at the local level because it is national in scope. Record at 4.

The parties agree that under Proposal 12, the CBA would not constitute a waiver of either parties' statutory or contractual rights. *Id.*

C. Positions of the Parties

1. Agency

The Agency specifically states that it has no objection to the negotiability of Proposals 11 and 12. SOP at 17 & 18. However, the Agency does assert that the proposals are moot "in the absence of any negotiable proposals that would form the basis of [an agreement]." *Id.*

2. Union

The Union asserts that because Proposals 1 through 10 are negotiable, Proposals 11 and 12 are not moot. Response at 16.

D. Analysis and Conclusions

The Agency's only basis for asserting that Proposals 11 and 12 are non-negotiable is that they are "moot." The Agency's mootness claim is based on the premise that none of the Union's other proposals are negotiable. However, because we have determined that a number of the Union's other proposals are negotiable, we find that Proposals 11 and 12 are not moot, and that they are negotiable.

XI. Order

The Agency shall, upon request or as otherwise agreed to by the parties, negotiate with the Union over Proposals 2, 7, 9, 10, 11, and 12.[7] The petition for review as to Proposals 1, 3, 4, 5 and 8 is dismissed.

7. In finding these proposals to be within the duty to bargain, we make no judgment as to their merits.

65 FLRA No. 156

NATIONAL TREASURY
EMPLOYEES UNION
CHAPTER 302
(Union)

and

UNITED STATES
DEPARTMENT OF THE TREASURY
OFFICE OF THE COMPTROLLER
OF THE CURRENCY
(Agency)

0-AR-4681

DECISION

April 27, 2011

Before the Authority: Carol Waller Pope, Chairman, and Thomas M. Beck and Ernest DuBester, Members[1]

I. Statement of the Case

This matter is before the Authority on exceptions to an award of Arbitrator Charles Feigenbaum filed by the Union under § 7122(a) of the Federal Service Labor-Management Relations Statute (the Statute) and part 2425 of the Authority's Regulations. The Agency filed an opposition to the Union's exceptions.

The Arbitrator found that the Union's grievances were nonarbitrable based on the Authority's decision in *United States Department of Defense, National Imagery & Mapping Agency, St. Louis, Missouri*, 57 FLRA 837 (2002) (then-Member Pope dissenting) (*NIMA*).

For the reasons that follow, we reverse *NIMA*, and we set aside and remand the award to the parties for resubmission, absent settlement, to an arbitrator of their choice.

II. Background and Arbitrator's Award

An employee requested an Administratively Determined Pay Increase (ADPI) pursuant to the Agency's Policies and Procedures Manual (PPM) 3110-30.[2] When the Agency denied the request, the Union filed a grievance (the compensation grievance) alleging that the denial violated PPM 3110-30 and the parties' agreement. Award at 3. The grievance also requested certain information from the Agency pursuant to § 7114(b)(4) of the Statute.[3] In response, the Agency stated that ADPIs are "compensation tools[,]" and that "compensation issues are neither negotiable nor grievable as a matter of law" because, as the Authority held in *National Treasury Employees Union*, 59 FLRA 815, 816 (2004) (then-Member Pope dissenting), *pet. for review denied*, 435 F.3d 1049 (9th Cir. 2006) (*NTEU*), the Agency "has sole and exclusive discretion to determine such matters."[4] *Id.* As a result, the Agency stated that the Union's requested information was not "necessary for full and proper discussion, understanding and negotiation of matters falling within the scope of collective bargaining[,]" and it denied the information request. *Id.* The Union subsequently elaborated on its information request. *Id.* The Agency then denied the compensation grievance at step 1 of the parties' negotiated grievance procedure. *Id.* at 4.

Subsequently, the Union "raised the [compensation] grievance to step 2" of the parties' negotiated grievance procedure. *Id.* In so doing, the Union "disputed the Agency contention that the [compensation] grievance was a negotiation over compensation[,]" and stated that, instead, the grievance was about the Agency's "failure to

---

1. Member Beck's dissenting opinion is set forth at the end of this decision.

2. PPM 3110-30 sets forth the circumstances under which ADPIs will be granted. *See* Award at 2.

3. In pertinent part, § 7114(b)(4) of the Statute requires an agency to provide a union

> upon request, and to the extent not prohibited by law, data--
>
> (A) which is normally maintained by the agency in the regular course of business;
>
> (B) which is reasonably available and necessary for full and proper discussion, understanding, and negotiation of subjects within the scope of collective bargaining; and
>
> (C) which does not constitute guidance, advice, counsel, or training provided for management officials or supervisors, relating to collective bargaining[] . . . .

4. The "sole and exclusive discretion" doctrine is discussed further below.

implement its stated policy on pay disparities that is clearly delineated in PPM 3110-30." *Id.* The Agency denied the compensation grievance at both steps 2 and 3 of the negotiated grievance procedure. *Id.* at 5. The Union also filed a separate grievance over the Agency's refusal to provide the requested information (the information request grievance). *Id.*

When the grievances were unresolved, they were submitted to arbitration, where the Arbitrator stated the issues as follows: "The [Authority] has ruled that, under 5 U.S.C. §§ 481 and 482,[5] the Agency has no duty to bargain with the Union over pay issues. Does this bar the Union from using the negotiated grievance and arbitration procedures to challenge compensation determinations made by [the Agency]?" *Id.* at 1-2.

The Arbitrator noted that, in *NTEU*, 59 FLRA 815, the Authority held that the Agency has sole and exclusive discretion to establish employees' compensation. Award at 11. The Arbitrator noted that the Union "d[id] not dispute this finding of non-negotiability over compensation[,]" and that the issue was "what the finding means with respect to the grievance and arbitration procedures." *Id.* at 11-12. The Arbitrator found that the Authority's decision in *NIMA*, 57 FLRA 837, was "key" to resolving that issue, Award at 12, and that *NIMA* held that "neither the grievance nor arbitration procedure may be used to challenge a management compensation decision[,]" *id.* at 13. Accordingly, the Arbitrator concluded that the compensation grievance was neither grievable nor arbitrable. *Id.* The Arbitrator then stated: "That being the case, the same applies to the [information request] grievance . . . ." *Id.*

III. Positions of the Parties

A. Union's Exceptions

The Union argues that the award is contrary to law. The Union "concedes that *NIMA* precludes grievances over compensation" at the Agency, but asserts that *NIMA* was "wrongly decided" and that the Authority should "revisit" that decision. Exceptions at 7. In this regard, the Union asserts that: *NIMA* "confused the bargaining procedure with the grievance procedure," *id.* at 8; parties often reach agreements over matters that are not within the duty to bargain; and grievances that seek to require agencies to comply with those agreements and the agencies' "own regulations" are arbitrable, *id.* at 9. According to the Union, that the Agency has sole and exclusive discretion to establish compensation "does not mean that [the Agency] has unfettered discretion to unfairly implement the compensation policies that it adopted." *Id.* at 8. The Union requests that the Authority set aside and remand the award, while ordering the Agency to respond to the Union's information request. *See id.* at 10.

B. Agency's Opposition

The Agency argues that the award is not contrary to law. Specifically, the Agency asserts that, because it has sole and exclusive discretion to establish its employees' compensation, the Arbitrator correctly found that the grievance was not arbitrable. Opp'n at 6. In addition, the Agency contends that it has not negotiated compensation matters with the Union, and that the parties' agreement "stat[es] the Agency's position that matters related to compensation are not subject to the negotiated grievance and arbitration procedure." *Id.* at 9.

IV. Analysis and Conclusions

The Union alleges that the award is contrary to law. The Authority reviews questions of law de novo. *See NTEU, Chapter 24*, 50 FLRA 330, 332 (1995) (citing *U.S. Customs Serv. v. FLRA*, 43 F.3d 682, 686-87 (D.C. Cir. 1994)). In applying a standard of de novo review, the Authority determines whether the arbitrator's legal conclusions are consistent with the applicable standard of law. *NFFE, Local 1437*, 53 FLRA 1703, 1710 (1998). In making that determination, the Authority defers to the arbitrator's underlying factual findings. *See id.*

If a law indicates that an agency's discretion over a matter affecting employees' conditions of employment is intended to be "sole and exclusive," i.e., that it is intended to be exercised only by the agency, "then the agency is not obligated under the Statute to exercise that discretion through collective bargaining." *NTEU*, 59 FLRA at 816. In *NIMA*, the Authority held that an agency's sole and exclusive discretion to establish certain conditions of employment without bargaining also precludes grievances and arbitration over those conditions, once established. 57 FLRA at 842-43.

The Union argues that *NIMA* was wrongly decided and requests that the Authority reexamine that decision. For the reasons that follow, we agree. In so doing, we reject our dissenting colleague's view that reexamination of *NIMA* is not necessary because, even if *NIMA* was wrongly decided, the grievance is

5. The pertinent wording of §§ 481 and 482 is set forth below.

not arbitrable under the parties' agreement and PPM 3110-30. In this regard, the Arbitrator based his award solely on his interpretation of *NIMA;* he did not assess whether the grievance was nonarbitrable based on the parties' agreement, PPM 3110-30, or any other ground. It is well established that determining the meaning of an agreement is a matter for an arbitrator, rather than a de novo review by the Authority. *Cf. AFGE, Council 220*, 54 FLRA 156, 160 (1998) (remand to arbitrator appropriate where arbitrator failed to interpret potentially dispositive contract provision that appears to conflict with award). It also is well established that collective bargaining agreements, rather than agency regulations, govern the disposition of matters to which they both apply. *E.g., U.S. Dep't of the Treasury, IRS*, 64 FLRA 720, 722 (2010). Therefore, if the parties' agreement permits the grievance in this case, then any contrary terms in PPM 3110-30 are irrelevant. Further, if *NIMA* was correctly decided, then there would be no basis to remand for interpretation of the parties' agreement. As such, we reexamine *NIMA*.

In resolving this issue, two lines of Authority precedent are relevant. The first line of relevant Authority precedent involves the scope of negotiated grievance procedures. Section 7121 of the Statute provides, with certain exceptions not relevant here, that the negotiated grievance procedure "shall be the exclusive administrative procedures for resolving grievances which fall within its coverage." 5 U.S.C. § 7121(a)(1). The Authority has held that "Congress intended that '[a]ll matters that under the provisions of law could be submitted to the grievance procedures shall in fact be within the scope of any grievance procedures negotiated by the parties unless the parties agree as part of the collective bargaining process that certain matters shall not be covered by the grievance procedures.'" *NTEU, Chapter 15*, 33 FLRA 229, 236 (1988) (quoting Joint Explanatory Statement of the Committee on Conference, H.R. Rep. No. 1717, 95th Cong. 2d Sess., 157, *reprinted in* 1978 U.S. Code Cong. & Admin. News 2723, 2891)).

A law may expressly preclude grievances over a particular subject matter. *See, e.g.,* 5 U.S.C. § 7121(c) (excluding certain matters from the scope of the grievance procedure). In addition, a law may create an exclusive appeals procedure with regard to certain matters and thereby preclude the use of the negotiated grievance procedure to challenge those matters. "[W]here laws other than the Statute limit the scope of negotiated grievance procedures, there have been clear, specific indications that the statutory procedures were intended to be exclusive." *AFGE, Local 3258*, 53 FLRA 1320, 1325 (1998) (citations omitted) (*Local 3258*). In this connection, "where the exclusivity of an appeals procedure concerning certain challenges to an agency's conditions of employment decision is not established by the plain wording of a law, or its accompanying legislative history, the Authority has found that the negotiated grievance process is available." *Id.* at 1327. For example, "[w]here a statute states that an appeals procedure takes effect 'notwithstanding' any other law, such a statute constitutes a clear, specific indication that the statutory procedure is intended to be exclusive." *Id.* at 1326. In addition, "[e]ven where a law or regulation does not use such 'notwithstanding' language, the Authority will find matters excluded from the negotiated grievance process if the expressed intent to do so is unmistakable." *Id.*

Applying the first line of precedent here, 12 U.S.C. § 481 pertinently provides that the Comptroller shall employ certain individuals "without regard to the provisions of other laws applicable to officers or employees of the United States[,]" and 12 U.S.C. § 482 pertinently provides that, "[n]otwithstanding any of the provisions of [§] 481 . . . to the contrary, the Comptroller . . . shall fix the compensation . . . of, and appoint and direct, all employees of the Office of the Comptroller of the Currency."[6] Neither § 481 nor § 482 states that matters concerning compensation are excluded from negotiated grievance procedures. In addition, neither § 481 nor § 482 creates an exclusive procedure -- or *any* procedure, for that matter -- for appealing applications of the Agency's established compensation policy. Thus, the first line of Authority precedent lends support to a conclusion that individual applications of the Agency's established compensation system are subject to the parties' negotiated grievance procedure.

The second line of relevant Authority precedent involves the difference between the scope of bargaining and the enforceability of agreements -- including the use of the negotiated grievance

6. We note that §§ 481 and 482 have been amended to provide that the Agency's authority to fix compensation is "subject to chapter 71 of title 5, United States Code[.]" Dodd-Frank Wall Street Reform and Consumer Prot. Act, Pub. L. No. 111-203, § 318, 124 Stat. 1326 (2010). However, the amended wording is not yet effective. *See id.* at §§ 318(e) & 311(a) (effective date of § 318 is "the transfer date[,]" defined in § 311 as "1 year after the date of enactment of this Act[,]" which was July 21, 2010). In addition, there is no dispute that the pre-amendment wording applies here.

procedure to enforce those agreements. In this regard, it is well established that although a particular matter may be outside the duty to bargain as a permissive subject, if the parties reach an agreement over such a matter, then the agreement is enforceable in arbitration. *See, e.g., U.S. Dep't of the Treasury, IRS, Wash., D.C.*, 56 FLRA 393, 395 (2000), *reconsid. denied*, 56 FLRA 935 (2000) (contract provisions involving permissive subjects under § 7106(b)(1) of the Statute are enforceable in arbitration); *AFGE, Local 3302*, 52 FLRA 677, 680-83 (1996) (Member Armendariz concurring) (contract provisions involving matters that are not conditions of employment, and thus permissive subjects, are enforceable in arbitration). Further, federal employment is governed by a host of laws and government-wide regulations that establish various conditions of employment. For example, it is well established that most federal employees are not entitled to bargain over their wage rates because those rates are established by law. *E.g., Fraternal Order of Police, Lodge # 1F*, 57 FLRA 373, 383 (2001) (wage rates of General Schedule employees are outside the duty to bargain). Nevertheless, grievances regularly are filed regarding agencies' alleged misapplication of established wage rates. *E.g., U.S. Dep't of the Treasury, IRS, Small Bus./Self Employed Operating Div.*, 65 FLRA 23, 23 (2010) (grievance challenged agency's calculation of grievant's rate of pay upon her permanent promotion); *U.S. Dep't of the Treasury, IRS, Okla. City, Okla.*, 64 FLRA 615, 615 (2010) (grievance alleged improper termination of grievant's grade and pay retention). Therefore, there is a meaningful difference between what an agency is required to bargain over and what is grievable under a negotiated grievance procedure.

Applying that second line of precedent here, there is no dispute that the Agency had sole and exclusive discretion to establish employee compensation without bargaining. However, the mere fact that the Agency had no duty to *bargain* over compensation does not compel a conclusion that alleged misapplications of the Agency's established compensation system in PPM 3110-30 are not *grievable*. In this regard, there is no dispute that PPM 3110-30 is an Agency regulation. The Authority has held that "unless there is a specific exclusion in the agreement, a grievance concerning a violation of an agency regulation . . . is arbitrable under negotiated grievance procedures." *U.S. Dep't of the Treasury, IRS, Louisville Dist.*, 36 FLRA 375, 380 (1990). Thus, unless the parties' negotiated grievance procedure excludes alleged violations of PPM 3110-30 from its coverage -- a matter that the Arbitrator did not reach, because he relied solely on *NIMA* -- such alleged violations would be included within the scope of the negotiated grievance procedure. In addition, the compensation grievance alleged a violation of not only PPM 3110-30, but also the parties' agreement. Award at 3. For these reasons, the second line of Authority precedent also lends support to a conclusion that §§ 481 and 482 do not preclude the compensation grievance.

In *NIMA*, the Authority stated that it would be "incongruous" for Congress to give sole and exclusive discretion over a matter without also precluding grievances over that matter, and that "the more compelling and reasonable statutory construction" of the statutory wording at issue in *NIMA* was to preclude such grievances. 57 FLRA at 842. For support, the Authority cited: *Colorado Nurses Ass'n v. FLRA*, 851 F.2d 1486 (D.C. Cir. 1988) (*Colorado Nurses*); *NTEU v. FLRA*, 848 F.2d 1273 (D.C. Cir. 1988); *Local 3258*, 53 FLRA 1320; and *U.S. Dep't of Veterans Affairs, Med. Ctr., Danville, Ill.*, 34 FLRA 131, 134-35 (1990) (*VAMC Danville*).

However, the Authority did not address in *NIMA* the two lines of precedent discussed above or explain how its decision was consistent with that precedent. Moreover, the decisions on which the Authority relied do not support a conclusion that sole and exclusive discretion to establish a particular matter precludes grievances over that matter. In this regard, *Colorado Nurses* and *VAMC Danville* involved the application of title 38 of the United States Code, "an independent personnel system that . . . is exempt from all laws governing the terms and conditions of federal employment except as otherwise explicitly provided in" title 38. *Colorado Nurses*, 851 F.2d at 1489. By contrast, neither the laws at issue in *NIMA* nor the laws at issue here involve such an independent personnel system. In *Local 3258*, the Authority actually found that a particular matter was *not* barred from a negotiated grievance procedure, *see* 53 FLRA at 1327-30; thus, that decision did not support the Authority's conclusion in *NIMA*.[7]

7. We note that, in *Local 3258*, the Authority characterized *Illinois National Guard v. FLRA*, 854 F.2d 1396, 1402 (D.C. Cir. 1988) (*Ill. Nat'l Guard*), as holding that matters over which an agency head has sole and exclusive discretion may not be covered by a negotiated grievance procedure. However, *Ill. Nat'l Guard* addressed only the duty to bargain over union proposals regarding compressed work schedules, not whether a matter was grievable. Thus, *Ill. Nat'l Guard* also did not support the Authority's conclusion in *NIMA*.

Finally, in *NTEU v. FLRA*, the court found that allowing probationary employees to use the negotiated grievance procedure to challenge their discharges would be contrary to law because, according to the court, the Civil Service Reform Act "affirmatively intended agencies to retain the power to summarily terminate probationary employees[,]" and that Office of Personnel Management regulations allowed agencies to dismiss probationary employees "with only written notice and a brief statement of reasons, . . . and an exceedingly limited right to appeal[] . . . ." 848 F.2d at 1275. Here, by contrast, there are no statutory or regulatory provisions that either indicate that Agency applications of its established compensation system are not subject to review or specifically set out limited procedures for such review.

In sum, two lines of Authority precedent support conclusions that: (1) sole and exclusive discretion to establish certain conditions of employment does not preclude grievances over individual applications of those conditions of employment, once established; and (2) in reaching a contrary conclusion in *NIMA*, the Authority erred. Thus, we reverse *NIMA* and conclude that nothing in the Agency's sole and exclusive discretion to establish compensation precludes grievances over individual application of the Agency's established compensation system. Consequently, we set aside the award.

Where the Authority sets aside an arbitrator's determination that a grievance is not arbitrable, the Authority remands the matter to the parties for submission, absent settlement, to an arbitrator of their choice. *E.g.*, *AFGE, Local 2823*, 64 FLRA 1144, 1147 (2010). In those circumstances, the Authority also has declined to resolve additional arguments raised by parties. *See id.* (declining to order arbitrator to resolve merits of grievance because arbitrator could find grievance nonarbitrable on other grounds).

Here, the Union requests that the Authority order the Agency to provide the information that the Union requested -- in effect, requesting that the Authority resolve the merits of the information request grievance. The Arbitrator based his dismissal of that grievance solely on his finding that, as a result of *NIMA*, the compensation grievance was not arbitrable. As such, he did not address the merits of the information request grievance, including whether the information requests satisfied the requirements of § 7114(b)(4) of the Statute. Consistent with the foregoing precedent, we decline the Union's request to order the Agency to provide the information and, instead, remand the award to the parties for resubmission, absent settlement, to an arbitrator of their choice.[8]

V. Decision

The award is set aside and remanded to the parties for resubmission, absent settlement, to an arbitrator of their choice.

8. We note that nothing in this decision precludes an arbitrator from finding, on remand, that the grievance is nonarbitrable for reasons other than those set forth in *NIMA*.

Member Beck, Dissenting:

In light of the controlling statutory language, I cannot agree with my colleagues that the Comptroller's compensation decisions are subject to the grievance and arbitration procedure contemplated by our Statute.

The law provides, plainly and without qualification, that:

> the employment and compensation of . . . employees of the office of the Comptroller of the Currency . . . shall be *without regard to the provisions of other laws applicable to officers or employees of the United States.*

12 U.S.C. § 481 (emphasis added).

Unless one disagrees with the proposition that our Statute is a law applicable to employees of the United States, one must conclude that the Comptroller's compensation decisions are not subject to the coverage of our Statute. If the Comptroller's compensation decisions are not subject to the coverage of our Statute, then, *a fortiori*, they are not subject to the grievance and arbitration procedures that exist pursuant to our Statute.

The Comptroller might have agreed contractually to subject his compensation decisions to arbitral review, but he expressly declined to do so, stating in the CBA that:

> The Employer and Union disagree over whether matters related to compensation and benefits are subject to the grievance and arbitration procedure. It is the Employer's position that these matters are not subject to the negotiated grievance and arbitration procedure, as a matter of law . . . 12 USC 481, to set compensation "without regard to the provisions of other laws applicable to officers or employees of the United States."

Opp'n, Agency Ex.1, parties' agreement at 123 (Article 27, Section 1(A)(4) n.*).

Further, even the Agency policy upon which the Union relies explicitly provides that matters involving "[e]mployee compensation and decisions affecting permanent increases to employee base pay . . . *are not grievable* . . . [including], for example, the receipt of an *ADPI* . . ." Exceptions, Attach. 14, PPM 3110-30 at 3 (emphasis added).

The Union argues that we should reconsider *NIMA*, but fails to demonstrate that a different application of *NIMA* would result in a different outcome given the unambiguous language contained in the Agency's policy and the CBA. Exceptions at 6-10; *see NAGE, Local R1-109*, 61 FLRA 588, 591 (2006) (excepting party must establish that reconsideration of Authority precedent is "warranted"); *AFGE, Local 217*, 60 FLRA 459, 460 (2004) (union exception that does not demonstrate how award violates regulation is a bare assertion); *U.S. Dep't of the Army, Corps of Eng'rs Nw. Div., Portland Dist., Portland, Or.*, 59 FLRA 86, 88 (2003) (Member Armendariz dissenting) (excepting party bears burden to establish that award is inconsistent with regulatory language); *U.S. Dep't of the Navy, Naval Air Station, Jacksonville, Fla.*, 61 FLRA 139, 142 (2005) and *VA Med. Ctr., Long Beach, Cal.*, 41 FLRA 1370, 1380 (1991) ((excepting party must demonstrate that reconsideration of precedent is "require[d]").)

Therefore, it is unnecessary for us to re-examine our precedent in *NIMA* in order to resolve this case.

65 FLRA No. 157

UNITED STATES
DEPARTMENT OF HOMELAND SECURITY
U.S. CUSTOMS AND BORDER PROTECTION
U.S. BORDER PATROL
EL CENTRO SECTOR
(Agency)

and

AMERICAN FEDERATION
OF GOVERNMENT EMPLOYEES
NATIONAL BORDER PATROL COUNCIL
LOCAL 2554
(Union)

0-AR-4647

DECISION

April 27, 2011

Before the Authority: Carol Waller Pope, Chairman, and Thomas M. Beck and Ernest DuBester, Members

I. Statement of the Case

This matter is before the Authority on exceptions to an award of Arbitrator John P. McCrory filed by the Agency under § 7122(a) of the Federal Service Labor-Management Relations Statute (the Statute) and part 2425 of the Authority's Regulations. The Union filed an opposition to the Agency's exceptions.[1]

The Arbitrator found that the Agency violated the parties' agreement by suspending the grievant for fourteen days without just cause or reasons that would promote the efficiency of the service. For the reasons that follow, we deny the Agency's exceptions.

II. Background and Arbitrator's Award

A. Background

While on duty, the grievant attempted to free his Agency vehicle from the sand in which it was stuck, and, in the process, he dislodged its bumper. *See* Award at 3. Without the vehicle, he could not continue tracking a nearby group of suspected illegal aliens. *See id.* at 3, 12. The grievant's first-level supervisor directed him to write a memorandum concerning the incident (memo), which the grievant did. *See id.* at 3. In the memo's first three paragraphs, the grievant wrote that he was submitting the memo because he understood that it was required as a condition of employment but that he was reserving any protections afforded him by the United States Constitution or other laws, "especially under the [F]ifth and [F]ourteenth [A]mendments," as well as those protections recognized by certain Supreme Court decisions. *See id.* at 3-4 (citing *Garrity v. New Jersey*, 385 U.S. 493 (1967) (*Garrity*)). When the grievant's first-level supervisor instructed him to remove the first three paragraphs (the *Garrity* preamble, or preamble), he refused. *See id.* at 4.

After a discussion with his second-level supervisor, the grievant agreed to revise the memo. *Id.* Specifically, the grievant removed the *Garrity* preamble but replaced it with a new paragraph, in which he indicated that he was submitting the memo after receiving assurances from his second-level supervisor that the memo would neither leave the station nor result in discipline. *See id.* Upon reviewing the revised memo, the second-level supervisor directed him to remove the new paragraph because the second-level supervisor believed that it mischaracterized their earlier conversation. *See id.* The grievant responded by resubmitting the original version of his memo, including the *Garrity* preamble. *See id.*

After learning of the grievant's insistence that the *Garrity* preamble remain in the memo, the grievant's third-level supervisor met with him. *See id.* When asked whether he would remove the preamble, the grievant declined, in response to which his third-level supervisor stated that "if [the grievant] did not[,] he would be subjecting himself to insubordination." *Id.* After the grievant insisted that "he was relying on his constitutional rights in refusing to remove the preamble[,]" *id.* at 4-5 (footnote omitted), the third-level supervisor "gave him a direct order to remove the *Garrity* [p]reamble . . . , which the [g]rievant chose to disobey[,]" *id.* at 4. As a result, the Agency charged the grievant with insubordination and suspended him for fourteen days, the "sole basis for which . . . [was] his refusal to obey an order to remove the *Garrity* [p]reamble" from his memo. *Id.* at 6. The Union filed a grievance challenging the suspension, and when the matter was not resolved, the parties proceeded to arbitration.

B. Arbitrator's Award

The Arbitrator framed the following issue for resolution: "In accordance with . . . the parties' [a]greement, was the disciplinary action in this case taken for just cause and only for reasons that will promote the efficiency of the service?" *Id.* at 2 (citing Art. 32, § M of the parties' agreement).[2] The Arbitrator stated that the

1. The parties also filed several supplemental submissions, which are addressed *infra* Part III.

2. Article 32, Section M of the parties' agreement states, in pertinent part: "The parties agree that . . . suspension of less

"Agency ha[d] the burden . . . to establish, by a preponderance of the evidence," that the grievant's suspension complied with the parties' agreement. *Id.* at 10.

Addressing the propriety of punishing the grievant for his refusal to remove the preamble, the Arbitrator stated that the "government cannot penalize the assertion of the privilege" against self-incrimination by threatening to take serious disciplinary action against an employee because he or she invokes the privilege. *Id.* at 11-12 (citing *Lefkowitz v. Cunningham*, 431 U.S. 801, 806 (1977)). In this regard, the Arbitrator found that "the Agency, by the actions of its supervisor, had a direct role in causing" the grievant to "belie[ve] that termination could result from disobeying" the order to remove the *Garrity* preamble and that, consequently, the Agency had improperly penalized the grievant's assertion of his Fifth Amendment rights. *Id.* at 12. In response to the Agency's argument that the grievant should have obeyed the order to remove the preamble and grieved the issue later, the Arbitrator determined that "[o]rders that cause the surrender of constitutional rights" fall within a recognized exception to the "obey now[,] . . . grieve later rule[.]" *Id.* at 11 (citations omitted) (internal quotation marks omitted).

In addition, the Arbitrator found that other components of the Agency permitted employees to include a *Garrity* preamble in their memos and that permitting the grievant to do the same "would have been relatively costless to the Agency." *Id.* at 13. The Arbitrator also noted that the Agency had other alternatives, such as: agreeing to a memorandum of understanding recognizing the applicability of *Garrity* protections to all memos concerning on-duty performance; or providing routine *Garrity* rights notices to officers when they were required to write a memo, which would obviate the need for reservations of rights in the memos themselves. *Id.* The Arbitrator found that the availability of these "'relatively costless' alternative courses of action[, which] would address [the Agency's] stated concerns without infringing [on] the rights of agents[,]" belied the Agency's contention that permitting employees to include preambles in memos would "significantly undermine the efficiency of the Agency." *Id.* Accordingly, the Arbitrator found that the "Agency [did] not . . . establish just cause for the [g]rievant's suspension[,] or that the suspension was only for reasons as will promote the efficiency of the Agency." *Id.* at 14.

than fifteen days . . . will be taken only for appropriate cause as provided in applicable law. Such cause . . . shall be just and sufficient and only for reasons as will promote the efficiency of the [s]ervice." Award at 2; *see also* Exceptions, Attach., Joint Ex. 1 at 51.

III. Preliminary Matters

As noted previously, *supra* note 1, the parties filed several supplemental submissions. Specifically, the Agency filed a motion for leave to file a motion to strike certain attachments to the Union's opposition. *See* Mot. for Leave to File & Mot. to Strike (Motions) at 1 (citing 5 C.F.R. § 2429.26(a)).[3] In its concurrently filed motion to strike, the Agency contends that attachments to the Union's opposition either were not presented in the proceedings before the Arbitrator, although they could have been presented, or are irrelevant to the parties' dispute. *See* Motions at 2-3 (citing 5 C.F.R. § 2429.5).[4] In addition, the Agency requests that, if the Authority strikes attachments to the Union's opposition, then the Authority also strike any references to those attachments from the Union's arguments in opposition to the exceptions. *See id.* at 2. The Union filed a motion opposing the Agency's motion to strike. *See* Opp'n to Agency's Mot. to Strike at 1.

Section 2429.26 of the Authority's Regulations (the Regulations) requires a party filing a supplemental submission to request permission to do so. 5 C.F.R. § 2429.26; *see also AFGE, Local 1061*, 63 FLRA 317, 317 n.1 (2009). In addition, a filing party must demonstrate why its supplemental submission should be considered. *NTEU, Chapter 98*, 60 FLRA 448, 448 n.2 (2004) (Chairman Cabaniss dissenting as to other matters) (*Chapter 98*). The Authority has granted permission to file motions to strike where a moving party alleges that evidence or arguments presented for the Authority's consideration were not presented in the proceedings before the arbitrator. *E.g.*, *U.S. Dep't of the Interior, Nat'l Park Serv., Women's Rights Nat'l Historic Park, Ne. Region, Seneca Falls, N.Y.*, 62 FLRA 378, 379 (2008) (*Interior*). The Agency's motion to strike alleges that certain parts of the Union's opposition to the exceptions were not presented before the Arbitrator. Thus, consistent with *Interior*, we grant the Agency's motion for leave to file its motion to strike. *See Chapter 98*, 60 FLRA at 448 n.2. However, the Union did not request permission to file its opposition to the motion to strike. *See* 5 C.F.R. § 2429.26. Therefore, we decline to

3. 5 C.F.R. § 2429.26(a) states, in pertinent part: "The Authority . . . may in [its] discretion grant leave to file other documents as [it] deem[s] appropriate."

4. The Regulations concerning the review of arbitration awards, as well as certain related procedural Regulations – including § 2429.5 – were revised effective October 1, 2010. *See* 75 Fed. Reg. 42,283 (2010). As the exceptions and opposition in this case were filed before the effective date of the revised Regulations, we apply the prior version of the Regulations. Under the prior Regulations, 5 C.F.R. § 2429.5 stated, in pertinent part: "The Authority will not consider evidence offered by a party, or any issue, which was not presented in the proceedings before the . . . arbitrator."

consider the Union's opposing motion. *Cf. U.S. Dep't of Energy, Oak Ridge Office, Oak Ridge, Tenn.*, 64 FLRA 535, 535 n.1 (2010) (declining to consider motion to strike without request for leave to file).

Under § 2429.5 of the Regulations, the Authority generally will not consider evidence or arguments that could have been, but were not, presented to the arbitrator. *See supra* note 4 for text of § 2429.5; *see Soc. Sec. Admin.*, 57 FLRA 530, 534 (2001) (*SSA*) (citing *NAGE, Local R4-45*, 53 FLRA 517, 520 (1997); *U.S. Agency for Int'l Dev.*, 53 FLRA 187, 187 n.2 (1997)). In addition, the Authority has held that awards are not subject to review on the basis of evidence that comes into existence after arbitration. *See, e.g., U.S. Dep't of the Army, Corpus Christi Army Depot, Corpus Christi, Tex.*, 56 FLRA 1057, 1068 n.12 (2001) (*Corpus Christi*). However, § 2429.5 does not preclude consideration of arguments in support of exceptions where such arguments arise from the issuance of an award and could not have been presented at arbitration. *See NAGE, Local R3-77*, 59 FLRA 937, 940 (2004) (Chairman Cabaniss dissenting as to other matters) (*Local R3-77*) (citing *U.S. Dep't of the Navy, Supervisor of Shipbuilding Conversion & Repair, Pascagoula, Miss.*, 57 FLRA 744, 745 (2002)); *U.S. Dep't of Agric., Animal & Plant Health Inspection Serv., Plant Prot. & Quarantine*, 57 FLRA 4, 5 (2001) (Chairman Cabaniss concurring) (*USDA*) (citing *Prof'l Airways Sys. Specialists, Dist. No. 1, MEBA/NMU (AFL-CIO)*, 48 FLRA 764, 768 n.* (1993)).

The Union's attachment A provides the job title and describes the responsibilities of an Agency official who was promoted to a high-ranking position within the Agency after the award issued. *See* Opp'n, Attach. A; *see also* Opp'n at 1 (describing Union's purpose for submitting attachment A). The job title and responsibilities listed in the attachment are those of the official after his promotion. *See id.* The Union contends that, in his *former* position – which he held at the time that arbitration proceedings occurred in this case – this official was in charge of a component of the Agency that "entered into a Memorandum of Understanding [(MOU)] with the Union" permitting employees to reserve their *Garrity* rights in connection with any memo that the Agency compelled them to submit. *See* Opp'n at 1. According to the Union, the eventual promotion of this official reinforces the soundness of his decision, while occupying his former position, to enter into the aforementioned MOU. *See id.* As the promotion of this official occurred after the award issued, the information in the attachment came into existence after arbitration. *See Corpus Christi*, 56 FLRA at 1068 n.12. In addition, there is no indication that the promotion arose from (i.e., occurred because of) the issuance of the award. *Cf. Local R3-77*, 59 FLRA at 940 (§ 2429.5 does not preclude consideration of issues arising from award that could not have been presented at arbitration). Accordingly, we strike attachment A from the record.

Attachments B and C concern a grievance arbitration over an Agency employee's *Garrity* rights; that arbitration involved the same agency and union as this dispute but a different grievant. *See* Opp'n, Attachs. B & C. Both attachments are dated months before the Arbitrator issued the award at issue here. *See id.* However, there is no indication that the Union submitted these materials to the Arbitrator, although the Union presented other evidence at arbitration regarding the use of *Garrity* preambles by other Agency employees. *E.g.*, Award at 1, 6 ("The Union offered evidence regarding the use of the *Garrity* [p]reamble in the [Agency's other] Sectors."), 9, 13. Thus, the Union could have presented attachments B and C at arbitration. Because there is no indication that the Union did so, we strike attachments B and C from the record. *See* 5 C.F.R. § 2429.5; *SSA*, 57 FLRA at 534.

Attachments D and E are letters to another arbitrator addressing whether he should take official notice of the Arbitrator's award in the instant dispute, *see* Opp'n, Attachs. D & E, which establishes that the letters came into existence after the Arbitrator issued the award. However, the question of whether another arbitrator should take notice of the Arbitrator's award is a matter that arises from the issuance of the award and could not have been presented to the Arbitrator. *See Local R3-77*, 59 FLRA at 940; *USDA*, 57 FLRA at 5. Because § 2429.5 does not bar the consideration of matters that arise from the issuance of the award and could not have been presented to the Arbitrator, *see id.*, we deny the motion to strike attachments D and E from the record.[5]

Finally, the Union argues in its opposition to the exceptions that the Arbitrator's professional qualifications, as reflected in attachments F and G, counsel in favor of upholding his award. *See* Opp'n at 3. The Union would have had no reason to make this argument until after the award issued. *Cf. U.S. Dep't of Veterans Affairs Med. Ctr., N. Chi., Ill.*, 52 FLRA 387, 399 n.10 (1996) (submissions pertaining to whether award was deficient arose as result of award and, thus, were not barred by § 2429.5). Therefore, we deny the motion to strike attachments F and G. *See Local R3-77*, 59 FLRA at 940; *USDA*, 57 FLRA at 5.

5. Although the Agency objects to several of these attachments as irrelevant, a party need not demonstrate the relevance of the documents that it files with its exceptions or opposition in order for the Authority to accept those documents for consideration. *Cf. NFFE, Bureau of Indian Affairs Council*, 31 FLRA 3, 8 n.3 (1988) (although various documents were "of questionable relevance" to resolving the parties' dispute, they were not "of such nature to warrant granting a motion to strike"). In contrast, as discussed above, if a party requests permission to file a *supplemental* submission, then that party must demonstrate why its supplemental submission should be considered, *NTEU, Chapter 98*, 60 FLRA at 448 n.2, including that submission's relevance to the parties' dispute.

In accordance with the foregoing, we also grant the Agency's request to strike from the Union's opposition any references to attachments A, B, and C.

IV. Positions of the Parties

A. Agency's Exceptions

The Agency argues that the Arbitrator's finding that the grievant was compelled to submit the memo is based on the nonfact that the grievant reasonably believed that he was required to submit the memo or face termination. *See* Exceptions at 12, 23, 25. The Agency further argues that the award is contrary to *Garrity* and other judicial decisions concerning the employee protections first recognized in *Garrity*. *See, e.g.*, *id.* at 11, 12-13, 23, 31-32, 34. Finally, the Agency argues that the award is contrary to law because it does not require obedience to the "obey now, grieve later" rule. *See, e.g.*, *id.* at 36-38.

B. Union's Opposition

The Union disputes the Agency's assertion that the memo was not compelled. *See* Opp'n at 4-5. In addition, the Union contends that the award is consistent with *Garrity* and its progeny, as well as the "obey now, grieve later" rule. *See id.* at 9-10.

V. Analysis and Conclusions

A. The award is not based on a nonfact.

The Agency argues that the Arbitrator's finding that the grievant was compelled to submit the memo is based on the nonfact that the grievant reasonably believed that he was required to submit the memo or face termination. Exceptions at 12. To establish that an award is based on a nonfact, the appealing party must show that a central fact underlying the award is clearly erroneous, but for which the arbitrator would have reached a different result. *See NFFE, Local 1984*, 56 FLRA 38, 41 (2000). However, the Authority will not find an award deficient on the basis of an arbitrator's determination of any factual matter that the parties disputed at arbitration. *See id.* Even assuming that the Arbitrator's finding regarding compulsion constitutes a factual determination, the parties disputed this matter before the Arbitrator. *See* Award at 7 (Agency argued that grievant failed to establish compulsion to submit the memo), 9 (Union argued grievant included preamble in memo "to document that the statement was compelled and therefore protected"). Therefore, we deny the nonfact exception.

B. The award is not contrary to law.

The Agency alleges that the award is contrary to *Garrity* and the "obey now, grieve later" rule. When an exception involves an award's consistency with law, the Authority reviews any question of law raised by the exception and the award de novo. *See NTEU, Chapter 24*, 50 FLRA 330, 332 (1995) (citing *U.S. Customs Serv. v. FLRA*, 43 F.3d 682, 686-87 (D.C. Cir. 1994)). In applying the standard of de novo review, the Authority assesses whether an arbitrator's legal conclusions are consistent with the applicable standard of law. *See U.S. Dep't of Def., Dep'ts of the Army & the Air Force, Ala. Nat'l Guard, Northport, Ala.*, 55 FLRA 37, 40 (1998). In making that assessment, the Authority defers to the arbitrator's underlying factual findings. *See id.*

Although the Agency alleges flaws in the Arbitrator's legal analyses concerning *Garrity* rights and the "obey now, grieve later" rule, *e.g.*, Exceptions at 36-38, the issue framed by the Arbitrator involved whether "disciplinary action in this case [was] taken for just cause and only for reasons that will promote the efficiency of the service[.]" Award at 2 (citing Art. 32, § M of the parties' agreement). Where an arbitrator resolves a claim under a collective bargaining agreement (CBA) rather than a legal claim, "unless a specific burden of proof is required, an arbitrator may establish and apply whatever burden the arbitrator considers appropriate[.]" *U.S. Dep't of Veterans Affairs, VA Md. Healthcare Sys.*, 65 FLRA 619, 621 (2011) (*VA Md.*) (quoting *U.S. GSA, Ne. & Caribbean Region, N.Y.C., N.Y.*, 60 FLRA 864, 866 (2005)) (internal quotation marks omitted). In addition, where an arbitrator is not required to apply a particular legal standard, alleged misapplications of that standard do not provide a basis for finding the arbitrator's award deficient. *E.g.*, *SSA*, 65 FLRA 286, 288 (2010).

The Arbitrator found that the "Agency ha[d] the burden . . . to establish, by a preponderance of the evidence," that the grievant's suspension complied with the parties' agreement. Award at 10. For the reasons set forth *supra* Part II.B., the Arbitrator found that the "Agency [did] not . . . establish just cause for the [g]rievant's suspension[,] or that the suspension was only for reasons as will promote the efficiency of the Agency." *Id.* at 14. Because the issue before the Arbitrator was a contractual claim, the Arbitrator was not required to apply a particular legal standard, and the Arbitrator's alleged misapplication of *Garrity* rights doctrine or the "obey now, grieve later" rule does not provide a basis for setting aside the award as contrary to law. *See SSA*, 65 FLRA at 288. Accordingly, we deny the contrary-to-law exceptions. *Cf. VA Md.*, 65 FLRA at 621-22 (denying contrary-to-law exceptions challenging legal standard used by arbitrator, where arbitrator resolved grievance under parties' agreement on finding of no just cause for discipline).

VI. Decision

The Agency's exceptions are denied.

65 FLRA No. 158

UNITED STATES
DEPARTMENT OF THE AIR FORCE
U.S. AIR FORCE ACADEMY
COLORADO
(Respondent)

and

AMERICAN FEDERATION
OF GOVERNMENT EMPLOYEES
LOCAL 1867
(Charging Party/Union)

DE-CA-07-0305

DECISION AND ORDER

April 27, 2011

Before the Authority: Carol Waller Pope, Chairman, and Thomas M. Beck and Ernest DuBester, Members[1]

I. Statement of the Case

This unfair labor practice case is before the Authority on exceptions to the attached decision of the Administrative Law Judge (Judge) filed by the General Counsel (GC). The Respondent filed an opposition to the GC's exceptions.

The complaint alleges that the Respondent violated § 7116(a)(1) and (5) of the Federal Service Labor-Management Relations Statute (the Statute) by unilaterally eliminating the past practice of providing base taxi service to and from the office of the employees' exclusive representative (Union) without prior notice or opportunity to bargain.

The Judge found that the Respondent did not violate the Statute as alleged and recommended dismissal of the complaint.

Upon consideration of the Judge's decision and the entire record, we grant the GC's exceptions and issue the attached order.

1. Chairman Pope's separate opinion, dissenting in part, is set forth at the end of this decision.

II. Background and Judge's Decision

A. Background

The Respondent, located on an Air Force base, maintains a base taxi service. Judge's Decision at 25. Upon request to the dispatch office, the taxi service shuttles employees throughout base grounds. *Id.* The Union office is located on base about four or five miles from most employees' work stations. *Id.* at 26. Since at least the early 1990's, rather than drive, employees used the taxis for travel to and from the Union office. *Id.* at 28, 33-34. In early 2007, the Respondent discontinued this use of the taxis. *Id.* at 29. The Union then filed the unfair labor practice charge that resulted in the instant complaint.

B. Judge's Decision

The Judge found that the Respondent did not violate § 7116(a)(1) and (5) of the Statute. Although he recognized that employee use of the base taxis for travel to and from the Union office is a condition of employment, he found that the evidence did not establish that it was a past practice. *Id.* at 27, 35. In making this determination, the Judge applied the Authority's framework for establishing a past practice, which provides that the practice must have been (1) consistently exercised over a significant period of time and (2) either followed by both parties or followed by one party and not challenged by the other. *Id.* at 27 (citing *U.S. Patent & Trademark Office*, 57 FLRA 185, 191 (2001)).

Applying the first part of the Authority's framework, the Judge found that the practice of "employees [being] given taxi rides to and from the Union office whenever they wanted them" was consistently exercised "for several years at least," until it was unilaterally terminated by the Respondent in January of 2007. *Id.* at 28-29.

However, applying the second part of the test, the Judge determined that the GC did not present sufficient evidence to establish that the practice was followed by both parties, or followed by one party and not challenged by the other. Specifically, the Judge determined that the GC did not prove that the Respondent knew of the alleged past practice and that responsible management officials acquiesced to it. *Id.* at 33-34.

In finding that the Respondent had no direct knowledge of the practice, the Judge noted that the taxi logs documented only two instances of rides to the Union office from 2002 to 2007. *Id.* at 30. He reasoned that this number of rides did not suffice to establish the Respondent's direct knowledge of the practice, even though he also recognized that "dispatch logs are not a reliable record of the actual use of the base taxi service." *Id.* at 29.

The Judge also found that there was insufficient evidence to impute knowledge of the practice to the Respondent, even though the Judge cited unrefuted evidence showing that the Respondent's lead labor representative expressly agreed to employee use of the taxi service in the early 1990's. Specifically, the Judge cited the testimony of Michael R. Little, the former local Union President, that the Respondent's lead labor representative, Steve Furman, expressly agreed to this practice in a bargaining session. *Id.* at 33-34. Little testified that, in return, the Union withdrew its bargaining proposals that would have provided the Union with reserved parking spaces at every base building. *Id.* It was undisputed at the hearing that a need for employee use of the taxis existed because the Union office was a significant distance from the work stations of the bargaining unit members and parking spaces were limited. *See id.* at 28. However, the Judge found it unclear whether Furman's express agreement was made before or after the Union opened its office on base grounds. *Id.* at 34. The Judge also found it unclear whether the agreement could have applied to travel between locations where the bargaining unit members work rather than for travel to and from the Union office. *Id.*

The Judge therefore concluded that, while the cumulative testimony indicated that the Respondent may have known about this use of the taxis, to find so would be "conjecture," which is "no substitute for direct or circumstantial evidence . . . ." *Id.* at 34.

Moreover, the Judge found that there was no evidence that any responsible management official acquiesced to the practice. *Id.* at 30. The Judge noted that the Respondent has a duty to bargain only if it is established that responsible management officials knew of the alleged past practice and took no action to stop it. *Id.* However, the Judge determined that the GC did not present sufficient evidence establishing knowledge on the part of responsible management officials. *Id.*

In determining whether a responsible management official acquiesced to the practice, the Judge construed the term "responsible management official" to mean "a management representative with knowledge of and responsibility for the implementation of the Respondent's transportation policies." *Id.* at 33. Although the Judge acknowledged that Furman and his successor lead labor representatives had knowledge of the practice, he found that they did not qualify as responsible management officials because they "were not involved in matters related to the taxi service." *Id.*

III. Positions of the Parties

A. GC's Exceptions

The GC argues that the Judge erred in concluding that responsible management officials did not know of and acquiesce to the practice of providing taxi service for employee travel to and from the Union office. Exceptions at 1. Specifically, the GC alleges that the Judge erred in declining to impute knowledge of the practice to the Respondent. *Id.* at 9 (citing *Def. Distrib. Reg. W., Tracy, Cal.*, 43 FLRA 1539, 1560 (1992) (*Def. Distrib.*); *Lowry Air Force Base, Denver, Colo.*, 29 FLRA 566, 570 (1987) (*Lowry*)). In support, the GC relies on testimony of bargaining unit members that employees continuously used the taxis in this manner from the early 1990's to 2007. *Id.* at 11. The GC also asserts that the Judge should have relied on local Union President Little's unrefuted testimony regarding the express agreement made by the Respondent's lead labor representative, Furman, during bargaining. *Id.* at 7. Specifically, the Union contends that Furman and the Union agreed that it did not need reserved parking spaces because employees could use the taxis for travel to and from the Union office. *Id.* The GC argues that, as the Judge found, this testimony indicates that Furman was aware of the practice, as were his successors. *Id.* at 12.

The GC also contends that the Judge applied the wrong acquiescence standard. Specifically, the GC claims that the Judge required that actual knowledge on the part of management be proven to find acquiescence. *Id.* at 6. However, the GC asserts that either actual or imputed knowledge will suffice. *Id.*

Finally, the GC argues that the Judge erred in failing to find that responsible management officials acquiesced to the practice. *Id.* at 10-13. The GC claims that the Respondent acquiesced to the practice by never objecting to the employees' use of the taxis for travel to and from the Union office. *Id.* at 9. Furthermore, the GC asserts that Furman was a responsible management official because the express agreement he made with the Union, as addressed above, bound the Respondent to allow employees to use the taxi service for travel to and from the Union office. *Id.* at 10-12 In addition, the GC claims that, because Furman's successors had knowledge of this express agreement and the authority to bind the Respondent during bargaining, they also qualify as responsible management officials. *Id.* at 11. Therefore, the GC argues that the Judge should have found that responsible management officials acquiesced to the practice. *Id.* at 10-13.

B. Respondent's Opposition

The Respondent argues that there was no past practice of employees using the taxis for travel to and from the Union office. Opp'n at 14-15. Alternatively, the Respondent claims that, if there ever was such a practice, it was discontinued sometime prior to 2002, when the taxi dispatch logs were created. *Id.* In support, the Respondent notes that the logs reflect only two instances where management approved such taxi use. *Id.* at 7.

The Respondent further argues that it had no knowledge of any employee use of the taxis for travel to and from the Union office because such use was not "open and notorious." *Id.* at 5 (citing *Def. Distrib.*, 43 FLRA at 1560; *Lowry*, 29 FLRA at 566). In this regard, the Respondent asserts that the Union office was not in a location where management would notice taxi use for this purpose because the Respondent's transportation and labor relations offices are both located more than four miles away. *Id.* at 6-7. The Respondent also claims that the dispatchers hid the employees' use of the taxis for travel to and from the Union office, as evidenced by the lack of such requests in the dispatch logs. *Id.* at 7.

In addition, the Respondent claims that, contrary to the GC's assertion, the Judge applied the proper standard in finding that the Respondent did not acquiesce to the disputed practice. *Id.* at 3. The Respondent contends that the Judge properly refused to impute knowledge to the Respondent because the Judge never definitively found that the Respondent's labor representative and his successors knew of the disputed practice. *Id.* at 4.

Finally, the Respondent asserts that its labor representatives are not responsible management officials. Specifically, the Respondent claims that its labor representatives do not exercise any control over the taxi service, which is the responsibility of transportation department supervisors. *Id.* at 10-11. The Respondent further claims that its labor representatives cannot be considered responsible management officials merely because they are involved in collective bargaining negotiations. *Id.* at 11.

IV. Analysis and Conclusions

A. The employees' use of the taxi service for travel to and from the Union office constitutes a past practice.

The Authority recognizes that parties may establish conditions of employment through a past practice. *See Norfolk Naval Shipyard*, 25 FLRA 277, 286 (1987). In order for a condition of employment to be established through a past practice, there must be a showing that the practice "has been consistently exercised over a significant period of time and followed by both parties, or followed by one party and not challenged by the other." *Soc. Sec. Admin., Office of Hearings & Appeals, Montgomery, Ala.*, 60 FLRA 549, 554 (2005) (*OHA*); *see U.S. Dep't of Homeland Sec., Border & Transp. Directorate, Bureau of Customs & Border Prot.*, 59 FLRA 910, 914 (2004) (*DHS*). "Essential factors in finding that a past practice exists are that the practice must be known to management, responsible management must knowingly acquiesce in the practice, and the practice must continue for a significant period of time." *DHS*, 59 FLRA at 914. As with other established conditions of employment, a past practice may not be altered by either party absent agreement or impasse following good faith bargaining. *See id.*

As to the factor that the practice continued for a significant period of time, the Authority has found that a period of "several years" suffices for purposes of establishing a past practice. *See Soc. Sec. Admin.*, 64 FLRA 199, 203 (2009) (*SSA*). Applying this standard, the Judge found, and the record supports, that the practice of providing employees with taxi service for travel to and from the Union office was consistently exercised "for several years at least" until January of 2007. Judge's Decision at 28. We therefore find that this factor is established. We discuss the remaining factors below.

1. Responsible management officials knew about and acquiesced to the practice.

a. The Respondent's lead labor representatives are responsible management officials.

In addition to the factor discussed above, responsible management officials must know about and acquiesce to the practice in order to establish a past practice. *See DHS*, 59 FLRA at 914. Although the Judge found that the Respondent's lead labor representatives had knowledge of the practice, the Judge declined to impute their knowledge to the Respondent. In this connection, the Judge did not consider the Respondent's lead labor representatives to be responsible management officials. We reach a different conclusion.

Authority case law provides guidance on identifying responsible management officials. For example, in *SSA*, 64 FLRA at 203, the Authority held officials who occupied positions where they had special knowledge of the alleged practice to be responsible management officials. In other cases, the Authority has held that officials who had authority to act as agents for the agency with regard to the practice are responsible management officials. *See OHA*, 60 FLRA at 554; *U.S. Dep't of Health & Human Servs., Soc. Sec. Admin.,* 38 FLRA 193, 197 (1990).

These cases support the conclusion that the Respondent's lead labor representatives are responsible management officials. For example, Furman, the Respondent's lead labor representative in the early 1990's, and his successor lead labor representatives occupied positions in which they had special knowledge of the practice of employees using taxis to travel to and from the Union office. Indeed, the nature of these representatives' positions, as liaisons between the Union and Agency, put these representatives in a unique position to be aware of the customs and practices that existed between the Union and the Agency. Similarly, Furman and his successor lead labor representatives were in overall charge of the Respondent's labor relations with the Union, including being responsible for all matters relating to collective bargaining.

Furthermore, Furman and his successor lead labor representatives had authority to act as agents for the Respondent with regard to the practice. Therefore, as the Respondent's agents, they had the authority to enter into binding agreements on behalf of the Respondent. Furman exercised this authority by expressly agreeing to allow use of the taxi service "to bring employees" to and from the locations of Union representatives, which would include the Union office. Tr. at 159-60. In addition, Furman's successor lead labor representatives exercised their authority by not taking any actions to discontinue the practice.

On this basis, we conclude that Furman and his successors are responsible management officials for purposes of establishing that use of the taxis for travel to and from the Union office was a past practice.

b. Responsible management officials knew about the practice.

We now examine the extent to which responsible management officials knew about the practice. Under Authority precedent, management knowledge may be direct, or imputed in light of convincing circumstantial evidence. Direct knowledge exists where management exhibits actual knowledge of a practice. *See, e.g., Def. Distrib.*, 43 FLRA at 1559-1560 (finding direct management knowledge based on management's written acknowledgment of practice). Imputed knowledge exists where the facts are such that management has reason to know of the existence of a practice. *See, e.g., Lowry*, 29 FLRA at 570-71 (imputing management knowledge of union's practice of using a certain telephone service because management arranged for transfer of service during several office relocations and had access to routinely-maintained telephone records). Convincing circumstantial evidence "must establish that the conclusion sought is the only probable or at least the most reasonable explanation of what happened." *Mason & Hanger-Silas Mason Co.,* 167 NLRB 894, 907 (1967).

The Judge found that the Respondent's lead labor representatives knew about the practice. Judge's Decision at 33. That the Judge declined to "impute the knowledge of Berger, Furman and other of the Respondent's labor relations representatives to the Respondent" is immaterial, given our determination in Section IV.A.1.a. *supra* that the Respondent's lead labor representatives are themselves responsible management officials. *Id.*

The record supports the Judge's finding. For example, the record shows that labor representatives had direct knowledge that since the early 1990s employees were permitted to use the taxis to travel to the locations of the Union representatives. Tr. at 159-60; Judge's Decision at 15. This, by definition, included the Union office. The record also shows that, in return for this use of the taxis, the Union withdrew proposals for a Union office in every base building and reserved parking spaces at those buildings so that Union representatives could have access to unit members. Tr. at 159-60; Judge's Decision at 15.

Similarly, the record shows that Furman and his lead labor representative successor, "Terry Berger, . . . [and] everybody in . . . th[e] employee relations building, knew that [employees] were using the taxi service" to travel to and from the Union office. Tr. at 163; *see also* Tr. at 167. Little testified that this practice was subsequently authorized "by everybody else, Karen Christianson, Mike Cox, all these head of personnel people and all the personnel people that I dealt with, Terry Berger . . . . They recognized that we used the taxi service all the time." Tr. at 167.[2]

For these reasons, we find that responsible management officials had knowledge of the employees' use of the base taxis for travel to and from the Union office.

c. Responsible management officials acquiesced to the practice.

Finally, we examine whether responsible management officials acquiesced to the practice. Evidence of knowing acquiescence by responsible management officials may be express or implied. *See Def. Distrib.*, 43 FLRA at 1559-60 ("it is sufficient that employees consistently exercised a practice for an extended period of time, with the agency's knowledge and express or implied consent"). The Authority has described express acquiescence as occurring when management gives express consent to a practice. *See id.* Implied acquiescence is characterized as management's consent to a certain practice, given its knowledge of the practice, by failing to challenge it in a significant manner. *See id.* (finding implied acquiescence despite supervisors' occasional protests); *IRS & Brookhaven Serv. Ctr.*, 6 FLRA 713, 726-27 (1981) (finding implied acquiescence when, as a practice, management consistently met with more than one union representative without significant protest).

Here, the Respondent's lead labor representative, Furman, expressly acquiesced to the practice by agreeing to it in return for the Union's withdrawal of certain bargaining proposals. *See Def. Distrib.*, 43 FLRA at 1559-60. Moreover, the Respondent's continued acquiescence for almost twenty years may be implied because, as the Judge found, neither Furman nor his successors objected to the employees' use of the taxis for travel to and from the Union office. Judge's Decision at 29; *Def. Distrib.*, 43 FLRA at 1559-60. In addition, none of the Respondent's other management officials ever objected to this practice until 2007. Judge's Decision at 29.

For these reasons, we find that the Respondent's responsible management officials acquiesced to the employees' use of the base taxis for travel to and from the Union office. Based upon the foregoing, we conclude this use of the taxis constitutes a past practice.[3]

B. The Respondent violated § 7116(a)(1) and (5) of the Statute.

As discussed above, it is undisputed that the Respondent unilaterally discontinued use of the taxis for travel to and from the Union office without satisfying its bargaining obligations under the Statute. Therefore, we find that the Respondent violated § 7116(a)(1) and (5) of the Statute by unilaterally eliminating the past practice of providing base taxi service for travel to and from the Union office without giving the Union prior notice and an opportunity to bargain.

V. Order

Pursuant to § 2423.41(c) of the Authority's Regulations and § 7118 of the Statute, the Respondent shall:

1. Cease and desist from:

(a) Terminating the taxi service for employees to travel to and from the Union office, without first bargaining with the Union, to the extent required by the Statute.

(b) In any like or related manner, interfering with, restraining, or coercing unit employees in the exercise of their rights assured by the Statute.

---

2. Although the GC asserts that the Judge should have imputed knowledge of the practice to the Respondent, *see* Exceptions at 9, we find it unnecessary to resolve this exception because we find that responsible management officials had direct knowledge.

3. The dissent suggests that this case should be remanded. Dissent at 11 & 12. Specifically, the dissent claims that the Judge did not make sufficient factual findings regarding whether the Respondent knowingly acquiesced to the disputed practice and that the record does not permit the Authority to make such an assessment. *Id.* As discussed above, because we find the record is sufficient to make this assessment, a remand is unnecessary.

2. Take the following affirmative action in order to effectuate the purposes and policies of the Statute:

(a) Restore the base taxi service for employees requesting it to go to and from the Union office, a practice terminated on or about January 25, 2007.

(b) Upon the request of the Union, bargain concerning the taxi service for employees going to and from the Union office to the extent required by the Statute.

(c) Post at its facilities copies of the Notice to All Employees on forms to be furnished by the Authority. Upon receipt of such forms, they shall be signed by the Commander of the U.S. Air Force Academy, and shall be posted and maintained for 60 consecutive days thereafter, in conspicuous places, including all bulletin boards and other places where notices to employees are customarily placed. Reasonable steps shall be taken to ensure that such Notices are not altered, defaced, or covered by any other material.

(d) Pursuant to § 2423.41(e) of the Authority's Regulations, within 30 days from the date of this Order, notify the Regional Director, Denver Regional Office, Federal Labor Relations Authority, in writing, as to what steps have been taken to comply.

NOTICE TO ALL EMPLOYEES
POSTED BY ORDER OF THE
FEDERAL LABOR RELATIONS AUTHORITY

The Federal Labor Relations Authority has found that the United States Department of the Air Force, U.S. Air Force Academy, Colorado, violated the Federal Service Labor-Management Relations Statute and has ordered us to post and abide by this Notice.

WE HEREBY NOTIFY OUR EMPLOYEES THAT:

WE WILL NOT unilaterally terminate the practice of providing taxi service for employees to and from the Union office without first bargaining with the American Federation of Government Employees, Local 1867 (the Union), to the extent required by the Federal Service Labor-Management Relations Statute (the Statute).

WE WILL NOT in any like or related manner, interfere with, restrain, or coerce unit employees in the exercise of their rights assured by the Statute.

WE WILL, at the request of the Union, restore the practice of providing base taxi service for employees requesting it to go to and from the Union office.

WE WILL, at the request of the Union, bargain concerning the taxi service for employees going to and from the Union office to the extent required by the Statute.

____
Signature

Date: __________ By: ______________________
Commander

This Notice must remain posted for 60 consecutive days from the date of this posting, and must not be altered, defaced, or covered by any other material.

If employees have any questions concerning this Notice or compliance with its provisions, they may communicate directly with the Regional Director for the Denver Regional Office of the Federal Labor Relations Authority, whose address is: 1391 Speer Boulevard, Suite 300, Denver, Colorado, 80204-3581, and whose telephone number is: (303) 844-5224.

Chairman Pope, dissenting in part:

I agree with the majority that the Judge erred in refusing to find that the Respondent's lead labor representatives (the labor representatives) are responsible management officials for purposes of determining whether the Respondent knowingly acquiesced in a practice of unit employees using taxis to travel to and from the Union office. However, for the following reasons, I cannot join the majority in finding that the Respondent's labor (or any other) representatives knew about the disputed practice. Instead, I believe that it is appropriate to remand the complaint to the Office of Administrative Law Judges[1] for further action. Accordingly, I dissent in part.

The Judge found that a finding that the Respondent knew of the alleged past practice "could only be based on conjecture" and concluded that "the Respondent had no actual knowledge of" the disputed practice. Judge's Decision at 34. Elsewhere in his recommended decision, the Judge rejected the claim that management officials other than the labor representatives knew about the disputed practice. *Id.* at 32. Thus, the dispositive factual question is whether the labor representatives knew about the practice.

The Judge did not answer this question and, in my view, his findings do not permit the Authority to do so. For example, in finding (erroneously) that the labor representatives are not responsible management officials, the Judge stated that he did not "impute *the knowledge*" of those representatives to the Respondent. *Id.* at 33 (emphasis added). However, the Judge does not specify "the knowledge" to which he refers; the closest he comes is his statement that although Respondent's representatives "*might* have seen Union representatives and other bargaining unit members entering and leaving taxis, *such incidents would almost certainly have occurred other than at the Union office.*" *Id.* at 32 (emphasis added). Similarly, in addressing the alleged oral agreement between the parties permitting the disputed practice (in exchange for the Union withdrawing proposals for office space and reserved parking at various buildings), the Judge stated that "a logical quid pro quo" for the alleged Union concessions "could just as easily have been the use of the taxi service between locations where bargaining unit members were employed[,]" rather than between those locations and the Union office. *Id.* at 33-34.

1. The Judge who issued the recommended decision in this case is no longer with the Authority.

The majority states that "[t]he Judge found that the . . . [labor] representatives knew about the practice." Majority Op. at 7 (citing Judge's Decision at 33). However, as stated above, the Judge did not do so. Similarly, the majority states, as fact, that the Respondent's labor representative agreed "to allow use of the taxi service 'to bring employees' to and from the locations of Union representatives, *which would include the Union office.*"[2] *Id.* at 6 (emphasis added) (quoting Tr. at 159-60). However, the witness whose testimony the majority cites does not refer to the Union office. *See* Tr. at 165 ("[A labor representative] told me we could use the taxi service[]"); *id.* at 167 ("they authorized the use of the taxi service[]").

The majority acts at the Authority's peril in creating a complete record where only an incomplete record exists because it is well established that, for purposes of judicial review, the Judge's recommended decision is part of the record in this case. *See* 5 U.S.C. § 557(c) ("All decisions, including initial, recommended, and tentative decisions, are a part of the record."). More to the point, when assessing whether an agency's decision is based on substantial evidence, reviewing courts view such decisions in a less favorable light when the agency reaches a conclusion different from that of a judge. *See Universal Camera Corp. v. NLRB*, 340 U.S. 474, 496 (1951) ("[E]vidence supporting a conclusion may be less substantial when an impartial, experienced examiner who has observed the witnesses and lived with the case has drawn conclusions different from the [reviewing agency's] than when he has reached the same conclusion."). *See also NLRB v. Pinkston-Hollar Constr. Servs., Inc.*, 954 F.2d 306, 309-10 (5th Cir. 1992); *NLRB v. First Nat'l Bank of Pueblo*, 623 F.2d 686, 691-92 (10th Cir. 1980); *NLRB v. Fla. Med. Ctr., Inc.*, 576 F.2d 666, 674 (5th Cir. 1978); *Penasquitos Village, Inc.*, 565 F.2d 1074, 1077-78 (9th Cir. 1977); *NLRB v. Mid State Sportswear, Inc.*, 412 F.2d 537, 539 (5th Cir. 1969); *NLRB v. Ark. Grain Corp.*, 392 F.2d 161, 164-66 (8th Cir. 1968).

2. The majority also states that the labor representatives knew that, "since the early 1990s employees were permitted to use the taxis to travel to the locations of the Union representatives[]" and that "[t]his, by definition, included the Union office." Majority Op. at 7. However, that Union representatives are likely to be found at the Union office is not enough. The issue here is whether the Respondent had knowledge that taxis were used by employees to visit the Union office, not whether taxis were used to visit Union representatives at other locations. A "definitional" finding cannot resolve this issue, in my view.

In sum, the Judge did not make sufficient factual findings for an assessment of whether the Respondent knowingly acquiesced in the disputed practice and the record does not otherwise permit that assessment. In these circumstances, the Authority's general practice is to remand. *See SSA*, 64 FLRA 199, 204-05 (2009) (Member Beck dissenting in part); *SSA, Balt., Md. & SSA, Office of Hearings & Appeals, Kan. City, Mo. & SSA, Office of Hearings & Appeals, St. Louis, Mo.*, 60 FLRA 674, 680-81 (2005). Of course, "the Authority's normal function requires it to examine the entire record of a proceeding and make de novo findings of fact." *U.S. Dep't of the Air Force, Air Force Materiel Command, Space & Missile Sys. Ctr., Detachment 12, Kirtland Air Force Base, N.M.*, 64 FLRA 166, 171 (2009) (Member Beck concurring in part) (emphasis omitted). In my view, however, the sorry state of the record counsels against the Authority doing so in this case. Accordingly, I would remand.

Office of Administrative Law Judges

DEPARTMENT OF THE AIR FORCE
U.S. AIR FORCE ACADEMY, COLORADO
Respondent

AND

AMERICAN FEDERATION OF GOVERNMENT EMPLOYEES, LOCAL 1867
Charging Party

Hazel E. Hanley
For the General Counsel

Maj. Timothy J. Tuttle
For the Respondent

Before: PAUL B. LANG
Administrative Law Judge

DECISION

Statement of the Case

This case arises out of an unfair labor practice charge (GC Ex. 1(a)) which was filed on March 13, 2007, by the American Federation of Government Employees (AFGE), Local 1867 (Union) against the U.S. Air Force Academy. On January 24, 2008, the Regional Director of the Denver Region of the Federal Labor Relations Authority (Authority) issued a Complaint and Notice of Hearing (GC Ex. 1(b)) against the Department of the Air Force, U.S. Air Force Academy, Colorado (Respondent or Academy). In the Complaint it was alleged that the Respondent committed an unfair labor practice in violation of §7116(a)(1) and (5) of the Federal Service Labor-Management Relations Statute (Statute), by changing a past practice of providing base taxi service to and from the Union office for Union representatives and members of the bargaining unit represented by the Union. It was further alleged that the change was implemented without prior notice to the Union and without providing the Union with an opportunity to bargain over the change. On February 15, 2008, the Respondent filed a timely Answer (GC Ex. 1(e)) in which it denied that it had committed an unfair labor practice.

A hearing was held in Colorado Springs, Colorado on March 20, 2008. The parties were present with counsel and were afforded the opportunity to present evidence and to cross-examine witnesses. This Decision is based upon consideration of the evidence and of the post-hearing briefs submitted by the parties.

Positions of the Parties

The General Counsel maintains that, on or before January 25, 2007, there was a past practice whereby the Respondent's employees were allowed to use the base taxi service for trips to and from the Union office. The use of the taxi service was necessary because the Union office is approximately five miles from the work stations of bargaining unit members. It is not feasible for employees to use their own automobiles because employee parking is at a premium and the Respondent has encouraged the formation of car pools. Employees using their own automobiles to go to and from the Union office would lose their parking places. During the course of contract negotiations the Union dropped the subject of special parking spaces for Union representatives upon assurance by Respondent's representatives that they could use the taxi service.

According to the General Counsel the Respondent terminated the past practice on or about January 25, 2007, when a Union steward was refused taxi service from the Union office to his work station. Since that time, the Respondent has refused repeated requests for taxi service to and from the Union office. The Respondent did not provide the Union with advance notice of the change in conditions of employment and did not answer a request by the Union for bargaining over the termination of the past practice. By the Respondent's actions it has violated its statutory duty to negotiate in good faith.

The Respondent denies that the alleged past practice ever existed. The Respondent further maintains that the General Counsel has failed to support her burden of proof that taxi service to and from the Union office was provided other than in isolated incidents. Such incidents were neither authorized by nor known to responsible management representatives of the Respondent. Accordingly, the Respondent has no duty to bargain over the alleged change.

Summary of the Evidence

The nature of a past practice is such that the evidence of its existence is often anecdotal. The General Counsel submitted the following testimony on that issue:

Sterling Hiibschman. Hiibschman became an employee of the Respondent in 1994. He has been the President of the Union since March 3, 2005, and prior to that time, he was a steward and the First and Second Vice President. As President Hiibschman is on 100% official time (Tr. 12). Hiibschman identified a map of the Academy which is on its website (GC Ex. 4). According to Hiibschman the Union office[1] is located on the east side of the Academy grounds about a quarter of a mile from the intersection of Stadium Boulevard and Academy Drive and near the notation "Sand Barn" on the map. The Union office is four or five miles from the Cadet Area and approximately the same distance from the Civilian Personnel Office which is in the Community Center located in the central portion of the Academy grounds (Tr. 14).

Hiibschman testified that he used the taxi service extensively before he went on 100% official time and was working in Mitchell Hall.[2] He used the taxi service whenever he was on official time, which, between 1997 and 2005, was between two and three times a week (Tr. 15, 16). He knows that management officials were aware that he was using the taxi service since he often told them that he was late returning to work because he had to wait for a taxi. He has seen taxis dropping off employees at the Union office (Tr. 17). In preparation for the hearing, Hiibschman reviewed his appointment calendars (they were not offered in evidence) and found that he used the taxi service to travel to and from the Union office on January 10, 2005, and February 16, 2005. In both instances he requested official time from his supervisor (Tr. 18). Neither of those trips is shown in the records provided by the Respondent as part of its prehearing disclosure (Tr. 18, 19).[3]

In further preparation for the hearing, Hiibschman reviewed a memorandum from Major John C. Tobin, Acting Chief, Manpower, Organization and Quality for the Respondent, (Resp. Ex. 9) which was included with the Respondent's pre-hearing disclosure. In this memorandum, the Respondent sought the Union's agreement to the cancellation of a number of memoranda of understanding (MOUs) pursuant to the implementation of the Most Efficient Organization (MEO) program.[4] The Union agreed to the cancellation of the listed MOUs, none of which pertained to taxi service (Tr. 19, 20).

Hiibschman knows of no MOU between the Union and the Respondent concerning taxi service because it was never considered a problem. It was always assumed that a taxi would be available for "official business", which included Union business. Hiibschman cited Article 20, Section C of the collective bargaining agreement (CBA) (GC Ex. 2, p. 39) which states that, "Past practices remain in effect unless and until notice and bargaining obligations have been completed." (Tr. 20).

Hiibschman never received notice that the taxi service to the Union office was going to be terminated. He first learned of the change on January 25, 2007, when Roland Gallegos, a Union steward, got a taxi ride from Mitchell Hall to the Union office; when Gallegos called for a ride back he was told that he had the wrong number. Willy Rosaya, the Second Vice President, then called the dispatch office and was told that they "no longer" provided rides to and from the Union office (Tr. 20, 21).

After speaking with Gallegos and Rosaya, Hiibschman called Dwayne Clewell, the dispatchers' first line supervisor. Clewell informed him that Bobby Speights, the second line supervisor, had stated that activities carried out on official time were considered to be personal business for which the use of the taxi service was not permitted (Tr. 22).

On February 6, 2007, Hiibschman sent an e-mail to Clewell, Speights, Terence Berger, Eddie Queen, Charlie Dye and Larry Moore, as well as to Rosaya and Gallegos (GC Ex. 3)[5] in which he stated:

1/ The terms "Union office" and "Union hall" were used interchangeably throughout the hearing.

2/ Mitchell Hall is the cadet dining hall which is in the Cadet Area. Hiibschman is a food service worker.

3/ The records were eventually entered into evidence over the General Counsel's objection as Respondent's Exhibits 1 through 8.

4/ Moore testified that the MEO represented a joint, and ultimately successful, effort by the Union and the Respondent to preserve a number of civilian positions which, presumably, would otherwise have been assigned to contractors or eliminated entirely (Tr. 239). According to Tobin's memorandum the MEO was to go into effect on or around October of 2000.

5/ According to Rosaya's unchallenged testimony, the chain of command above the dispatchers is: Clewell, Vehicle Operations Supervisor; Speights, Vehicle Manager; Moore, Deputy Logistics Supervisor; and Dye, Chief of Logistics and Readiness (Tr. 65, 66). Berger is a labor relations representative for the Respondent (Tr. 90). Queen is a coach operator and the First Vice President of the Union (Tr. 87, 89).

> On January 25, 2007[,] Mr. Gallegos requested a taxi from the union hall back to his work area as he had been doing official business at the union. Mr. Gallegos was denied access to the taxi services by Dwayne Clewell who stated to me later in a telephone conversation that when stewards are on official time at the union that is different than official business but instead is personal business. I then asked Mr. Clewell who made this determination and definition of official time. I also articulated that official time is only given in the connection with official business. One must be on official time to do official business. Mr. Clewell said that Mr. Speights had made this determination and that is how it is. I indicated that this is a change in conditions of employment and that I personally took the taxi service to and from my workplace many times before becoming the President of the local. Please see that this matter is corrected immediately or we will pursue relief through FLRA. Thanks in advance!

Hiibschman received no response to his message (Tr. 22-24).

On cross-examination Hiibschman acknowledged that his statement about using the taxi service twice a week was a "guesstimate". He also admitted that there are no written records of his requests for taxi service. He explained this by stating that he did not have access to e-mail at Mitchell Hall, but acknowledged that he had such access at the Union office. However, he did not generate a paper trail because he did not anticipate that the use of taxi service would become an issue (Tr. 26-28).

Roseanne Pedrosa. Pedrosa has been employed by the Respondent since 1998. In 2000 she injured her hand and used the taxi service to take her to the hospital and to the Civilian Personnel Office where she filed a workers' compensation claim (Tr. 30, 31).

The next time Pedrosa needed a taxi was in midsummer of 2007. She had filed a grievance and had an appointment to discuss it at the Union office. When she called for the taxi she was told, "No, ma'am, we don't go down there anymore." Pedrosa described her experience to Les Clayter, a co-worker; Clayter called for a taxi and was told the same thing (Tr. 32-34).

On cross-examination Pedrosa testified that she had no documentation regarding her taxi ride in 2000 (Tr. 35).

Leslie Clayter. Clayter is a member of the bargaining unit but is not a Union member. He verified that he called for a taxi at Pedrosa's behest and that he was told that the policy had changed (Tr. 37, 38).

Clayter has never used a taxi to get to the Union office. He did use a taxi about two years ago to go to the base hospital for a hearing test. He did not find a notation of his taxi ride on the records provided by the Respondent, but acknowledged that the log entries do not include the names of passengers (Tr. 38-41).

Tammy Howard. Howard has been employed by the Respondent since 1995 as an accounting technician. She has on several occasions requested taxi service to the Union office and was told that the taxi service was for official business only. After arguing with the dispatcher, she would request an e-mail documenting the refusal so that she could claim reimbursement. At that point she would be provided with taxi service. Howard checked the dispatch logs for 2007 and could find no record of any taxis picking up passengers at Harmon Hall (where she worked) for trips to any destination (Tr. 47, 48).

On April 24, 2007, Howard called for a taxi to the Union office. It was sleeting and snowing at the time and she was told that she could only get a taxi if she walked across an area known as the Terrazo to the Cadet Clinic. According to Howard the Terrazo is slightly longer than a football field. When she arrived at the Cadet Clinic she could not find a taxi stand, but noticed a taxi. The driver asked her what she was doing there and when she said that she was told that this was the only place where she could get a taxi, he told her that they would have picked her up. Howard was under the impression that the taxi did not come in answer to her call, but just happened to be there (Tr. 49-51).

On July 6, 2007, Howard obtained a taxi to take her to an appointment at the Union office. After the meeting she called to get a taxi back to her work station and was told that they did not provide service to the Union office. Howard told Queen about the problem. Queen spoke with several different people on the telephone and eventually got a taxi for her. Howard checked the dispatch log and found nothing to show that she had taken a taxi on that date (Tr. 51, 52).

On March 5, 2007, Howard called for a taxi to take her to an appointment at the Civilian Personnel Office in order to discuss a grievance and an EEO complaint. She had to argue with the dispatcher over the definition of official business, but eventually got taxis to and from her destination. Again, she did not see any record of those trips in the dispatch log (Tr. 52).

On August 16, 2007, Howard's supervisor informed her that Berger indicated that she had an appointment at the Union office. When she called for a taxi the dispatcher told her that they no longer serviced the Union office. She then spoke to someone named Tyrone who told her that the policy had changed about a month before. When she asked for an e-mail to that effect she was given an address to send an e-mail. She did so, but never received a reply. Several days later she spoke to Speights who told her that they no longer serviced the Union office and that he was not going to send her an e-mail. He also told her that she would have to speak to Mr. Berger if she wanted taxi service to the Union office (Tr. 52-54). Howard did not say whether she ever spoke with Berger.

Howard identified an e-mail that she sent to Queen on August 22, 2007, in which she described her interaction with Speights (Tr. 54; GC Ex. 5). In the e-mail Howard wrote:

> . . . He [Speights] told me "We do not service the union office and never should have, and if I ever got a base taxi to the union office it was against his orders." . . . .

Howard's e-mail message directly contradicts her testimony that Speights implied a change in policy with regard to the use of taxi service by the Union. Consequently, I do not credit her testimony that Speights implicitly acknowledged the existence of the alleged past practice.

Howard further testified that she had a grievance in 2006 and took the base taxi to the Union office "all the time" (Tr. 55). In response to my question, Howard stated that she took a taxi between 15 and 20 times in 2007 and that 15 of those trips were to and from the Union office (Tr. 62). She gave no dates for those trips.

On cross-examination Howard acknowledged that none of her taxi rides were on the dispatching log and that, in the majority of cases, she was told that she could not use the taxi on Union business (Tr. 56). She also acknowledged that she usually spoke with someone named Walt. Her drivers were Mr. Gonzalez, Mr. Torrell and, on one or two occasions, someone with an English accent. Of the 15 trips that she remembered taking in 2007, Gonzalez drove on about 10, Torrell on three or more and the "British gentleman" on about 2 (Tr. 57-59).

Willy Rosaya, Jr. Rosaya is the Second Vice President of the Union and has worked for the Respondent since 1985 as a coach driver (Tr. 65). He is assigned as a taxi driver every day or every other day when he is not driving a bus or between bus runs. There are currently four regular taxi drivers, down from five. The numbers of taxis and drivers are not such as to keep the drivers and vehicles busy at all times (Tr. 67, 68).

According to Rosaya, he receives a trip ticket in the morning by which he is informed if he is to make taxi runs. After he makes each run he records the number of passengers on the trip ticket and, at the end of the day, deposits the trip ticket in a locked box in the break room. The next morning one of the dispatchers, usually Mr. Johnson, takes the tickets and enters the information into the computer. This procedure is only used for taxi runs that have been scheduled in advance. It does not apply to cases when the driver is assigned to a run that was not previously scheduled. He does not know if all of the information is sometimes not entered in the computer. That might occur when a taxi run which has not been previously scheduled is dispatched over the radio. He does not complete any paperwork for such runs (Tr. 68-71).

In January of 2006, Rosaya requested official time from his first line supervisor and had Timothy Stuehmeyer (presumably a driver) take him to and from the Union office. Rosaya verified his recollection with Stuehmeyer but did not see those rides recorded on the log for 2006 (Tr. 70, 71).

Rosaya also testified concerning an incident in January of 2007 involving Roland Gallegos, a Union steward. Rosaya was working in the Union office when Gallegos was present. He gave Gallegos the telephone number of the dispatch office; Gallegos dialed the number and was told that it was the wrong number. He then dialed again and was told by Russ Johnson that they no longer provided taxi service to the Union office. Rosaya got on the telephone and was told the same thing by Johnson. Rosaya then spoke to Clewell who also told him that they did not provide service to the Union office. Apparently Clewell did not imply that this was a change in past practice (Tr. 71, 72).

Later that month Clewell told Rosaya that he did not have a driver to take him to the Union office. Since that time Rosaya has used his personal vehicle so as to avoid a confrontation with Clewell; this amounts to one or two round trips each week (Tr. 72, 73).

When challenged on cross-examination as to why the purported lack of a driver for a previously requested run would provoke a confrontation if he requested a subsequent run, Rosaya would only say that, "you have to know Mr. Clewell" (Tr. 78). I do not credit this testimony since it makes no sense. Instead, I assume that Rosaya knew that Clewell would not authorize a taxi run to or from the Union office.

Rosaya stated that, in reviewing the dispatch logs, he did not find any notations of the identities of taxi passengers. He did, however, find a notation showing that a passenger had been delivered to the Union office (Tr. 74).

On cross-examination Rosaya admitted that he has never taken a passenger to the Union office. He has heard taxi drivers being dispatched over the two way radio but does not know whether the request for the taxi came in by telephone or by e-mail. When questioned as to whether Clewell or Speights ever authorized taxi service to the Union office, Rosaya answered that they would have because the dispatchers "represent management" and Clewell and Speights would know about such trips. Rosaya further stated that he knew that the dispatchers were in the bargaining unit, but that Speights and Clewell had stated that the drivers had to do what the dispatchers told them because they represent management (Tr. 75-78).

In response to my question Rosaya stated that he could not have driven himself to the Union office with a spare vehicle because his supervisor had said that they were not allowed to do so (Tr. 83).

On redirect examination Rosaya testified that Clewell and Speights had two way radios which they would keep on and that Moore and Dye also had radios. Consequently, Rosaya assumed that the supervisors would have heard taxis being dispatched to the Union office (Tr. 84).

Eddie Queen. Queen has been employed by the Respondent since 1974 and is currently a coach operator and the First Vice President of the Union (Tr. 87, 89). Since becoming a Union steward in 1975 Queen has used the taxi service to conduct Union business and has done so with the knowledge of management representatives. All of the waiter supervisors at Mitchell Hall were aware of this practice because he would use their telephones to call for taxis. Steve Furman, who preceded Berger as Labor Relations Officer, would see him getting out of a taxi at the Union office. Karen Christianson, the EEO manager, has seen him getting in and out of taxis.[6] Berger has seen him getting out of a taxi at Mitchell Hall. He would use the taxi service on an average of three times a week[7] (Tr. 90, 91).

Queen testified that he has been assigned as a taxi driver. The dispatcher would call him to the office and assign him to a run. He would receive his assignments from Phillip Patterson, Tyrone Smith and Russ Johnson. He does not give a passenger any type of paperwork, nor does he record the nature of the trip, the name of the passenger or the destination. The coach operators only log their bus runs on the trip tickets. Under a prior system the taxi drivers would record their runs on a form 868 (Tr. 91-93).

In May of 2007, a computer changeover was taking place at the Union office which involved government computers. Queen called the dispatch office and spoke to Johnson regarding a taxi ride to the computer center and back to the Union office so that he could pick up some equipment. Johnson told him that they did not support the Union anymore. Queen then called Dye who arranged for a taxi. That run does not appear in the dispatch log (Tr. 94-96). In early July of 2007 he became aware of Howard's problem obtaining a taxi. He spoke to Moore who arranged for a taxi; that run was not recorded in the dispatch log. Queen spoke with Moore after the incident with Howard, at which time Moore told him that it was illegal to provide taxi service to the Union and that he never would have authorized it (Tr. 96-98).

Queen testified that the transportation supervisors monitor the dispatch radio frequency virtually all of the time. He based that assertion on the fact that they could be reached on the radio (Tr. 98, 99).

Queen also testified that between 25 and 30 percent of his average of three weekly taxi runs on

[6]/ It is unclear whether this occurred at the EEO office or elsewhere.

[7]/ Queen's taxi trips were presumably on Union business, but it is unclear how many of them were to and from the Union office.

Union business were to the Union office. The dispatchers never questioned him as to the purpose of a trip when he called for a taxi to some place other than the Union office (Tr. 101, 103).

On cross-examination Queen acknowledged that he never took anyone to the Union office. He also maintained that Patterson, Smith and Johnson had dispatched drivers to the Union office and that, until the early part of 2007, such service had not been denied (Tr. 109). He also admitted that, other than on one occasion involving Howard, Moore had never approved taxi service to the Union office and that Berger had seen him getting out of a taxi in the late 1990's (Tr. 111).

Phillip Patterson. Patterson has been employed by the Respondent since 1994. He has been on a detail as a warehouseman since December of 2006, and before that he was the lead dispatcher, reporting to Clewell, Speights, Moore and Dye (Tr. 115-117). When he was lead dispatcher a person wanting a taxi would call the dispatch office. At one time, a representative of the dispatch office would complete a form 868 with the name of the person calling, that person's unit, the pickup location, time of pick up and destination. The form 868 was eventually replaced by OVIM, the Online Vehicle Management System. Patterson entered pertinent data in OVIM. Every taxi dispatch was recorded to the extent possible, but it depended on whether the drivers turned in their trip tickets. The purpose of the system is to keep track of the drivers' time and of the vehicles. The system is not designed to determine who was using the taxi service or where the taxis were going. Taxi runs might not be entered into the system if a driver was late in turning in a trip ticket or if dispatch office personnel were busy with other activities (Tr. 117-19).

Patterson testified that he would enter the data into the system and would run tallies of mileage at the end of each day and each week. The tallies were needed for the "war report" which enabled management to determine which vehicles needed maintenance. He acknowledged that he had been counseled by Clewell for not properly entering data, but denied that he was at fault because he was the only one entering data and would sometimes become overwhelmed. According to Patterson, OVIM entries could be changed and deleted (Tr. 119-21).

Patterson further testified that, as a Union steward, he used the taxi service on Union business; this included trips to various locations including the Union office. He dispatched taxis to the Union office "all the time". Management representatives could hear the dispatching to the Union office on their radios, but he was never told that trips to and from the Union office were unauthorized. Clewell usually carried his radio with him and could have heard the dispatches if it was turned on. Speights kept a radio on his desk which was usually turned on (Tr. 123-25).

According to Patterson, he first encountered a problem with taxi service in January of 2007. He was at the Union office with Gallegos, Queen and others when "Roland" (presumably Gallegos) stated that he needed a taxi to get back to his work station at Mitchell Hall. Patterson told him to call the dispatch office and, when he did so, he was advised that they no longer provided service to the Union office (Tr. 125).

Patterson also described an occasion when he was helping Howard with an EEO complaint. Howard had arrived at the Union office by taxi and they then took a taxi to the EEO office. After their business had been concluded, Patterson called for a taxi back to the Union office. After waiting for about 45 minutes he called the dispatch office to ask when the taxi was coming. Eventually, Patterson spoke to Clewell and, he thinks, to Speights after which he got a taxi to the Union office (Tr. 125-27). Patterson has not used the taxi service since that time, but has used the UDI service. This is a program by which a "you drive it" government vehicle is issued to an employee after his or her request has gone up the chain of command for approval and upon presentation of a civilian driver's license. The assignment of UDI vehicles is entered in the dispatch log, but not as a taxi run (Tr. 127-30). Patterson did not state whether he had been authorized to use a UDI vehicle for trips to and from the Union office.

On cross-examination[8] Patterson stated that he entered all taxi runs into the OVIM system and that he has no knowledge of any of the runs having been deleted from the system. He also testified that he dispatched all of the runs to the Union office over the radio. He never asked Speights for permission to do so and acknowledged that Speights never approved taxi runs to the Union office (Tr. 132-35).

8/ The transcript indicates that the cross-examination was conducted by Counsel for the General Counsel. This is an error; Patterson was a witness for the General Counsel and was cross-examined by Counsel for the Respondent.

On redirect examination Patterson testified that he did not have the discretion of denying anyone a taxi ride. He was once told this by Moore when he questioned whether he should dispatch a taxi to take someone to the base golf course (Tr. 135-37).

Barry Jencson. At the time of the hearing Jencson was a food service worker for the Respondent but, before that, was employed as a taxi driver. At various times Speights and Clewell were his first line supervisors, although Speights later became his second line supervisor. Moore and Dye were, respectively, his third and fourth line supervisors. Jencson stated that he would make from 5 to 15 taxi runs per day. He was sometimes dispatched to take employees to the Union office. His radio communications were mainly with the dispatchers; Clewell and Speights were "very seldom" on the radio (Tr. 141-43).[9]

In preparation for the hearing Jencson reviewed the taxi dispatch records provided by the Respondent for 2002 through 2006, the period during which he was a taxi driver. According to those records, he made about 100 runs in each of those years in spite of the fact that he did not work much in the last year. In reviewing the dispatch records, Jencson noted that the driver's name does not appear for all of the taxi runs and it is possible that some of those runs were made by him. Jencson was not concerned about accounting to his supervisor for his time and noted that on some days they did not use dispatch slips (Tr. 143-45).

On cross-examination Jencson acknowledged that, although some of his dispatches to the Union office came over the radio, for some "we had slips". He also admitted the possibility that Patterson sometimes merely told him to make a pickup at the Union office although his memory was hazy as to this point. He did state that, in general, "A lot of times I was just told to go make a run." Jencson dealt with his dispatcher and, to the best of Jencson's knowledge, Speights did not authorize any of his trips to the Union office (Tr. 146-48).

Richard DiBiasio. DiBiasio has been employed by the Respondent since 1988 as a food service worker in Mitchell Hall and has been a Union steward since around 1990. DiBiasio receives official time upon request. In counseling employees he tries to hold initial meetings in an informal dining room in Mitchell Hall, but about 55% of his meetings are in the Union office where he has access to a computer and records. DiBiasio travels to the Union office either in his own vehicle or by taxi. In the past three or four years he would use the taxi service if he were released to do Union business in the middle of the day and had to return to work. This is so because he did not want to lose his parking space and also wanted to save money (Tr. 151-53).

DiBiasio stated that he knew that his first line supervisor was aware that he was taking the base taxi because he had an arrangement with him whereby he (DiBiasio) would take his official time toward the end of his shift, thus avoiding the delay associated with the use of the taxi service.[10] DiBiasio's last use of a taxi on Union business was about a year prior to the hearing. The trip was to the Oracle Building rather than to the Union office. That trip does not appear in the dispatch log. He has used the taxi service for trips to the Union office about 20 times over the years (Tr. 153-56).

Michael Little. Little began work for the Respondent as a temporary employee in late 1976 or early 1977. He attained permanent status in or around March of 1977. He left the Respondent's employment in 1997 at which time he had the title of Master Gardener. He was the President of the Union from April 1, 1989, to December 8, 1997, when he became a national representative for AFGE. Prior to serving as President, Little was First Vice President and, before that, a steward (Tr. 158, 159).

Little testified that, although convenient parking was not available at all of the buildings where bargaining unit members worked, it was not a serious concern for him because Steve Furman, the head of Human Relations or Employee Relations for the Respondent, said that the Union could use the taxi service (Tr. 159, 160).

Little further testified that, when he became President of the Union, there was no Union office on the Academy grounds. After about three years Little and Furman negotiated the establishment of a Union office on base. At that time the Union office was on the flight line. Little often looked through his office window and saw employees arriving and leaving by

9/ I have construed Jencson's testimony to mean that Clewell and Speights seldom spoke over the radio since Jencson would have no way of knowing whether they were monitoring transmissions.

10/ It does not follow, and I do not conclude, that the supervisor's knowledge that DiBiasio was using the taxi could be inferred from his having allowed DiBiasio to take official time on occasions when he, according to his own testimony, might have used his personal vehicle.

taxi. He also saw Joseph Becker, the previous President, leave the area where they were both working and take a taxi to the Union office. According to Little, a number of management representatives in Employee Relations knew that Becker often took taxis. Little saw various Union stewards taking taxis to the Union office. In addition, a number of Union stewards would use the taxi service to take them from Jack's Valley[11] to and from the Union office (Tr. 161-64).

Little also testified that when he participated in negotiations with the Respondent over a collective bargaining agreement (CBA), the Union's proposals did not address the use of the taxi service. However, according to Little, all of the people he dealt with in the Respondent's personnel department knew that the taxi service was being used for trips to and from the Union office and for other Union business. Little did not press his proposals for reserved parking spaces because Furman assured him of the availability of the taxi service. Furthermore, R. Steven Boothee, a dispatch supervisor, was aware that the taxi service was frequently used for trips to and from the Union office. Boothee had formerly been a taxi driver and a Union steward (Tr. 166, 167).

On cross-examination Little acknowledged that his testimony was based upon events which occurred prior to 2002 (Tr. 168).

The Respondent presented the following witnesses:

Bobby Earl Speights. Speights became the Dispatch Supervisor around April of 2004 and Vehicle Operations Manager in June of 2005. As such, he is responsible for all ground transportation services. According to Speights, the Union is not allowed to use the base taxi service since the service is only for official government business. The policy was in effect when he became Vehicle Operations Manager. Speights further stated that he had been involved in vehicle operations for 34 years, including his military service, and that during that time Union use of official vehicles was not allowed (Tr. 173-75).

Speights testified that he was aware of an incident in 2007 in which someone wanted (and presumably obtained) taxi service for Union business and two incidents in 2006 in which the Union obtained taxi service; those incidents did not occur with his knowledge or authorization. He suspects that dispatchers sent taxi drivers to provide such service. Those taxi runs should have been logged into the OVIM system. Speights identified taxi dispatch logs (Resp. Ex. 1-8) which he personally printed out from the OVIM system. He found only two entries of trips to the Union office, both of which occurred in February of 2006 (Tr. 175-77).

Speights explained the meaning of each of the headings in the OVIM logs as follows:

CAT - the category of the run (01 denotes taxi runs, which are the only ones shown on the printouts in this case)

CON NUMBER - the confirmation number which is automatically assigned to each run

OFFICE SYMBOL - the office symbol of the requester's workplace

STAT CODE - a code showing that it is a vehicle run

PICKUP LOCATION - where the passenger is to be picked up

DEST - where the passenger is going

TIME REQ - when the passenger wants to be picked up

PAX - the number of passengers

TIME DSP - the time when the taxi was dispatched

TIME ARV - the time of arrival at the pickup point

TIME PU - the time of the actual pickup of the passenger(s)

TIME REL - the time of release, *i.e.*, arrival at the destination

RESP TIME - the time span between the call to the dispatch office and the pickup

TIME SRV - the total time of service from dispatch to the end of the run

REG NBR - the vehicle registration number

OPER - the name of the driver

[11] Jack's Valley is an area outside of the North Gate of the Academy where new cadets go through a boot camp.

OVIM is used throughout the Air Force for the management of all types of vehicles (Tr. 180-82).

Speights further testified that he created the computer run so that it would reflect only the taxi service for the relevant time periods and that he did not remove any data from the system. Most of the data as to the taxi runs is entered by dispatchers who are members of the bargaining unit. However, data is sometimes entered by Clewell, who is the supervisor (Tr. 183, 184). Customers have been asked to request taxi service by e-mail, but requests are also accepted by telephone. All requests should be entered into the OVIM system. The taxi drivers receive their instructions from the dispatchers, sometimes over the radio, but often in person when the drivers are sitting in the break area (Tr. 184, 185).

Speights stated that he knows that certain types of runs were not entered into OVIM. Those were trips in which a driver was taken by another driver in connection with the movement of a government vehicle to or from a repair shop outside of the base. When Speights was a Dispatch Supervisor he instructed the drivers to record the pertinent information on the form 868 if they were too busy to enter the data into OVIM. In this way the dispatchers could later log in the information on the runs. Speights also stated that he suspected that there had been trips to the Union office that had been dispatched in the break room and had not been logged in. The only way that he would know of such runs would be over the radio if a driver reported his location at the end of a run or if he overheard a radio conversation about a run to or from the Union office. He does not monitor every taxi run. He has a radio in his office which he neither carries with him nor keeps on all of the time.

Speights further stated that he is aware of only one trip to and from the Union office. That was an instance in which the hospital shuttle was diverted to transport Howard; it was not considered to be a taxi run. Speights has never authorized a taxi run to or from the Union office, although he has allowed vehicles to stop at the Union office while proceeding to or coming back from previously scheduled trips to other locations. There were no passengers involved in such occasions, and the drivers themselves wanted to stop at the Union office. Speights mentioned one occasion when he granted such a request by a bus driver. According to Speights, he allowed the stop because he was told that there was a controlling memorandum of understanding. Later, when no memorandum of understanding was produced, he stated that there would be no such permission in the future (Tr. 185-90).

In response to my question, Speights stated that the recorded runs of individual vehicles are not regularly checked against odometer readings to determine if the mileage is inconsistent with the recorded runs (Tr. 192-94).

On cross-examination Counsel for the General Counsel directed Speights' attention to various log entries in which the number of passengers was obviously excessive: for example, 48 passengers in one run (Resp. Ex. 3, p.17, second entry)[12], 26 in two others (Resp. Ex. 5, p.23 under October 15, 2004)[13] and 1500 in a third (Resp. Ex. 6, p. 21).[14] In one entry for September 28, 2004, there is no entry showing the number of passengers for a taxi run that apparently lasted for more than ten hours (Resp. Ex. 5, p.22, top entry)[15] (Tr. 198-204). Speights was also directed to numerous examples of incomplete entries.

Upon further cross-examination Speights stated that management officials in the transportation department do not monitor the radio throughout the day (Tr. 204, 205). He also acknowledged that a great deal of information was missing from the records, such as vehicle registration numbers and names of drivers, but that he depends on the dispatchers to log data into the system. According to Speights, he has counseled two dispatchers for failure to put all of the correct data into the OVIM system. When challenged as to the accuracy of the OVIM report that reflected only 102 taxi runs by Jencson in 2006, Speights opined that the figure could be accurate since Jencson and other drivers are assigned to clean vehicles, sometimes for an entire day, when they are not driving (Tr. 205, 206).

Counsel for the General Counsel confronted Speights with two entries showing that Richard

---

12/ This was a 4 hour run; the office symbol is shown as "VEHICLE OPERATIONS", the pickup location is "BMP", which stands for base motor pool (Tr. 207), and the destination is "LOCAL".

13/ One taxi run is recorded as being from "PREP SCHOOL" to "HOSPITAL/CADET CLINI", the other from "PREP SCHOOL" to "EEO".

14/ There are a number of other runs on the same page which show unrealistically high numbers of passengers.

15/ The entry shows "PREP SCHOOL" for the pickup location and "HOSPITAL/CADET CLINI" for the destination.

Gonzales, one of the taxi drivers, made two trips to the Union office on February 6 and 13, 2006 (Resp. Ex. 7, pp.4 and 5). Speights acknowledged that he took no action against Gonzales when he learned of the taxi runs (Tr. 207, 208).

On redirect examination Speights testified that the OVIM system is used primarily for manpower and budgetary purposes. He does not review the records every day because he does not have time and relies upon the dispatchers to "QC" (presumably, quality control) the data that goes into the system. In 2006 Patterson, as the dispatcher, was primarily responsible for logging data into OVIM. Speights stated that he had conversations with Patterson about Patterson's failure to properly log in data and also sent him a note on the subject. Speights denied having advance knowledge of Gonzalez' trips to the Union office. Any disciplinary action would have been directed to Patterson, since the drivers follow the dispatchers' instructions (Tr. 209, 210).

With regard to the obvious errors in numbers of passengers that were pointed out during cross-examination, Speights stated that they were the result of "fat fingering", or typing errors. Speights further stated that, when he noticed such errors, he mentioned them to the dispatchers. Speights explained one of the entries which showed 26 passengers (see *supra* note 13) as representing multiple trips to the Cadet Clinic (Tr. 210-12).

Dewayne Clewell. Clewell has been employed by the Respondent since 2002. He is now the Vehicle Dispatch Supervisor and has been involved with the taxi service since 2006. As Vehicle Dispatch Supervisor, Clewell oversees day-to-day operations, including the dispatching of drivers and the entry of data into OVIM. According to Clewell, the Union's use of the taxi service is unauthorized since activities on official time are considered personal business that does not support the mission of the Air Force. He bases this assertion on AFI.[16] This has been the policy since Clewell arrived at the Academy. He knows of no incidents involving taxi service to the Union office other than the runs which appear in the dispatch logs and the incident involving Howard. He has no knowledge of Patterson's purported use of the radio to dispatch runs to the Union office although he keeps his radio on most of the time (Tr. 215-17).

Clewell further testified that he has never authorized the Union to use the base taxi service and does not feel that there is a practice of allowing such use. However, he acknowledged that Patterson might not have been aware of the difference between official use and official time. Clewell was not at the Academy when Patterson was originally assigned to his position, although Patterson does have an understanding of AFI and the procedures for assigning and dispatching vehicles (Tr. 217).

On cross-examination Clewell was shown an entry for January 3, 2007 (Resp. Ex. 8, p.1), for which there is no vehicle registration number. When asked if he would request a dispatcher or vehicle scheduler to correct such omissions, Clewell stated that he does not review the logs on a daily basis. Counsel for the General Counsel then directed Clewell's attention to an entry for March 23, 2007 (Resp. Ex. 8, p.9), in which both the vehicle registration number and the name of the driver are missing. When Clewell sees such entries, he speaks to the dispatchers; however, an entry cannot be changed after it is closed (Tr. 218-20).

On redirect examination Clewell stated that the OVIM system does not allow a change in information after it has been entered. If such a change is attempted the system will generate an additional line indicating an amendment (Tr. 221).

Tyrone Smith. Smith has been a vehicle dispatcher for about three years. He described the procedure for dispatching taxis as follows:

1. Requests for taxis generally come in by e-mail. If a request is received by telephone, they usually tell the requester to also submit it by e-mail.

2. Information regarding the request is entered into OVIM, usually by Smith or by Russell Johnson. However, data is also entered by Walter Fedorczuk and Clewell. In addition, information is entered into a separate system that produces trip tickets. Occasionally a taxi run is not entered into the system because of the workload. However, Smith has never intentionally failed to enter such information.

3. Each morning the drivers go to the mailbox (presumably an electronic mailbox) and get trip tickets with the taxi runs for that day (Tr. 221-24).

According to Smith it is the Respondent's policy that the Union may not use the taxi service and he has never understood the policy to be otherwise. Smith acknowledged that the Union probably used the taxi

[16]/ Presumably AFI is an official Air Force publication. The Respondent did not offer it in evidence.

service on occasion, but he never knew about it. When Smith first assumed his duties he asked Patterson whether they were picking up Union personnel and Patterson responded that they were.

Smith further testified that he could not remember dispatching Queen to pick up Howard. When asked whether he had ever dispatched a taxi to the Union office, Smith responded that it was "hard to say" (Tr. 224, 225). I take that to mean that Smith has dispatched taxis to and from the Union office, but that he knew that he was not authorized to do so.

On cross-examination, Smith was shown a log entry for April 4, 2005 (Resp. Ex. 6, p.14). The run was from the base motor pool to Greeley, Colorado. The name of the driver was omitted and the run lasted for 70 hours and 60 minutes. Smith stated that the run had been incorrectly coded as a taxi run and that the category in the first column should have been 05, which is the code for a "u-drive". The entry for a u-drive run does not include the name of the driver.

Counsel for the General Counsel also directed Smith's attention to the second entry for May 25, 2005 (Resp. Ex. 6, p.20). That run was from "PREP SCHOOL" to "HOSPITAL/CADET CLINI" with 15 passengers over a period of two hours, and the driver's name does not appear. Smith stated that he thought that the entry was for the hospital shuttle and that he did not know why the driver was not identified. Smith acknowledged that missing information could be entered later after referring to the trip ticket. However, the omission would only be noticed when the weekly report was printed out. There would be no need to make a correction at that time since the information is already on the trip ticket (Tr. 225-28).

Counsel for the General Counsel then pointed out to Smith a number of entries for 2007 (Resp. Ex. 7) in which the names of drivers and/or vehicle registration numbers do not appear. Smith stated that those omissions were not crucial since the necessary information was available from other sources (Tr. 228-31).

Alfred Larry Moore. Moore has been Chief of Logistics Operations in charge of the Most Efficient Organization (MEO) for the past six years. According to Moore, the Respondent's position that the Union is not authorized to use the base taxi service is based upon Air Force and Department of Defense guidelines.[17] He further stated that the penalty for unauthorized use of government vehicles is severe and, in the case of civilians, includes suspension (Tr. 237).

Moore testified that the MEO is administered by the 10th Mission Support Group. Prior to the implementation of the MEO, the Union and the Respondent entered into an agreement to cancel a number of MOUs (Resp. Ex. 9).[18] Moore testified that, although the MEO does not address taxi service, that service has been substantially reduced due to a reduction in manning. Since the implementation of the MEO the Respondent no longer assigns taxi drivers to various locations on the Academy grounds in an attempt to reduce waiting time. Had there not been a reduction in manning, the Respondent would have lost the bid, thus necessitating a reduction in force. Moore could not state the number of available taxis prior to the implementation of the MEO, but estimated that there was a reduction of fifty percent (Tr. 237-39, 245-47).

Moore stated that he occasionally monitors the dispatch radio network, but has never heard about a run to the Union office. He further stated that the Union has not been permitted to use the taxi service since he has been in charge and, to the extent that it has occurred, it was without his knowledge or that of his managers (Tr. 247, 248).

On cross-examination Moore testified that the implementation of the MEO resulted in the elimination of taxi trips to the airport for temporary duty as well as intra-base trips for military personnel. They also stopped picking up certain commanders from their quarters and stopped transporting certain individuals to the airport (Tr. 248-51).

Walter Fedorczuk. Fedorczuk is currently a motor vehicle operator with additional duties involving scheduling and dispatching. According to Fedorczuk, although he is neither a manager nor a supervisor, he is not a member of the bargaining unit and is not represented by the Union. (The General Counsel did not challenge that assertion.) He was

---

17/ Moore did not elaborate on the alleged guidelines, nor did the Respondent cite them in its post-hearing brief.

18/ Counsel for the Respondent acknowledged that there was no MOU regarding the use of taxis by the Union and that there was no language in the MEO concerning past practices (Tr. 240, 243, 244).

originally hired by the Respondent in August of 2002, but was subsequently separated by a reduction-in-force and rehired in his present position on May 31, 2007 (Tr. 253, 254).

Fedorczuk enters UDI and bus requests into OVIM, but he does not recall having entered taxi requests and assumes that Johnson or Smith has done so. He dispatches taxis in response to telephone requests, but does not remember sending one to the Union office. Fedorczuk further stated that he might have denied such a request, but does not remember a specific instance. He denied any knowledge of the Union's use of the base taxi service other than having been told by his supervisors that they do not honor requests by the Union. The statements by his supervisors occurred some time between May 31, 2007 and January of 2008 (Tr. 254-56).

On cross-examination, Fedorczuk testified that it was possible to correct OVIM entries. On redirect examination, he stated that he did not know whether corrections could be made for taxi runs that had already occurred (Tr. 257-59).

Russell Johnson. Johnson has been a driver/scheduler for the Respondent for the past five years. He has been involved with the taxi service for something more than two years. Johnson described his duties as receiving requests for vehicles, entering the requests into the vehicle scheduling system and OVIM and assigning the runs to drivers. Entries into OVIM are made by him as well as by Smith and Fedorczuk. They receive vehicle requests from the secretary, Josephine Gallegos, who, in turn, receives them from the Logistics Department electronic mailbox. Drivers are normally informed of their runs by means of a daily trip sheet, but runs which are requested on short notice are dispatched by radio (Tr. 260, 261).

According to Johnson, data for every vehicle run is entered into the OVIM system except for unscheduled runs for purposes such as urgent vehicle maintenance or medical emergencies. Even in those cases, there is always "backup" so that the data can be entered after the run. Johnson stated that, other than because of short notice, he has never intentionally failed to enter information into the OVIM system. He knows that he is supposed to enter information into OVIM because he was trained that way "from day 1". (Tr. 261).

Johnson further stated that his understanding of the Respondent's policy is that the Union should not be using the base taxi service because such use does not support the mission of the Air Force. He has never dispatched a taxi to the Union office and, to the best of his knowledge, management has never authorized such a taxi run (Tr. 261, 262).

On cross-examination Johnson testified that the name of the driver who is assigned to a taxi run is normally not put into OVIM until the run has been completed. There is another system for vehicle scheduling which has the assignments of drivers to specific runs. OVIM can be corrected so as to reflect changes in the assignments of drivers (Tr. 264-66).

On redirect examination Johnson briefly scanned the dispatch sheets and indicated that pickup and destination data was shown for all of the runs. (The General Counsel has not alleged that this is not so.) Johnson testified that this information is necessary for the run to take place. If pickup and destination points are not entered, the system will not assign a number to the run (Tr. 267, 268).

Findings and Conclusions

Undisputed Facts

The Respondent is a unit of the United States Air Force which is an agency within the meaning of §7103(a)(3) of the Statute. The Union is a labor organization as defined by §7103(a)(4) of the Statute. At all times relevant to this case the Union was the exclusive representative of a unit of the Respondent's employees which is appropriate for collective bargaining (GC Exs. 1(b) and 1(e), ¶¶2-4).

The following facts are also undisputed, as shown by the aforementioned testimony:

1. The Respondent maintains a base taxi service which is available, upon request, to take military personnel and civilian employees to and from locations both on and off of the Academy grounds. (The scope of the taxi service will be discussed below.) The Respondent also maintains other vehicles, such as buses and ambulances.

2. Requests for taxi service are submitted to the dispatch office by telephone or e-mail. Requests which are received prior to the day when the taxis are required are, or should be, entered into the OVIM system.[19] Drivers access an electronic mailbox to

---

19/ The Respondent maintains another computer system which is used to assign drivers to taxi runs which have been requested prior to the day of service.

obtain daily trip tickets listing their assignments to pre-scheduled runs.

3. In the case of taxi runs which are requested on the date of service, dispatchers make assignments to drivers either by radio or personally by going to the drivers' break room. Same-day runs should also be entered into OVIM even in the case of urgent requests which are to be recorded and entered later.

4. The Union has an office on the Academy grounds which is beyond normal walking distance from the work stations of members of the bargaining unit. The Union maintains certain records in its office and uses the facility for meetings between Union representatives, bargaining unit employees and representatives of the Respondent.[20] The Union office is between four and five miles from the Cadet Area where most bargaining unit employees work.

5. Parking space for civilian employees is at a premium. Employees are encouraged by the Respondent to form carpools. Employees who move their vehicles during the day are at risk of losing their parking spaces.

The Legal Framework

The law pertinent to this case is well settled. In *U.S. Penitentiary, Leavenworth, Kansas*, 55 FLRA 704, 715 (1999) the Authority held that, prior to implementing a change in conditions of employment, an agency must provide the union with notice of the proposed change as well as an opportunity to negotiate over those aspects of the change that are within the duty to bargain. In determining whether a matter involves a condition of employment the Authority will consider (a) whether it pertains to bargaining unit employees, and (b) whether there is a direct connection between the matter and the work situation of bargaining unit employees, *Antilles Consolidated Education Association and Antilles Consolidated School System*, 22 FLRA 235, 237 (1986) (*Antilles*).

A condition of employment may arise out of a past practice. Consequently, a unilateral change in a past practice may trigger an obligation to bargain, *Dep't of the Treasury, Internal Revenue Service (Washington, DC), et al.*, 27 FLRA 322, 324 (1987). In order to establish the existence of a past practice, there must be a showing that the practice has been consistently exercised over a significant period of time and followed by both parties or that the practice has been followed by one party and not challenged by the other, *U.S. Patent and Trademark Office*, 57 FLRA 185, 191 (2001) (*Patent Office*).

The Significance of the Taxi Service

When measured according to the two-pronged test of *Antilles*, it is clear that the availability of the base taxi service is a condition of employment. As to the first prong, the use of taxis for transportation to and from the Union office is significant only to members of the bargaining unit. As to the second prong, the use of taxis affects the work situation of those employees since, in the absence of taxi service, an employee is faced with the choice of borrowing a vehicle, which may not be possible, rescheduling an appointment at the Union office, or using his or her own vehicle with the resulting inconvenience of a possible loss of a parking space or the disruption of a carpool schedule. Parenthetically, the denial of taxi service may delay an employee's return to work, thus adversely affecting the Respondent as well as the employee.

While the lack of taxi service to the Union office does not pose an insurmountable obstacle to the effective representation of bargaining unit employees by the Union, it undoubtedly makes such representation more difficult, both for Union officers and stewards and for the employees whom they serve. In *AFGE and Social Security Administration, et al.*, 25 FLRA 622, 625 (1987) the Authority held that, "Representation of employees in matters concerning their employment clearly affects the working conditions of those employees."

The Consistency and Duration of the Alleged Past Practice

The testimony as to the consistency and duration of the Union's use of the taxi service is far from definitive. I am skeptical of the assertions of certain of the General Counsel's witnesses as to the frequency of the trips. Hiibschman, for example, kept a diary of his appointments but had entries for only two rides to the Union office on January 10 and February 16 of 2005 (Tr. 18). Patterson's assertion that he dispatched taxis to the Union office "all the time" (Tr. 123) is not credible because he did not cite specific instances. The credibility of Patterson's testimony is further eroded by his assertion that he entered all of the taxi runs that he dispatched into OVIM, but did not explain the absence of entries of

[20]/ While there is no evidence on this point, it is logical to assume that the office is also used to conduct internal Union business.

all but two of the taxi runs to and from the Union office in the dispatch logs which are a product of OVIM.

Much of the testimony offered by the General Counsel's witnesses described the Union's use of taxis for trips between locations other than the Union office. Although the distinction between such trips and trips to and from the Union office may be arbitrary, the General Counsel has not alleged that the Union has been deprived of taxi service other than with regard to the Union office. I can only surmise that the Respondent was reluctant to order bargaining unit dispatchers to question other bargaining unit employees, much less Union representatives, as to whether they intended to use taxis on Union business. Such inquiries would be unnecessary for trips to and from the Union office which could only be for Union business.

In spite of the shortcomings of the testimony of the General Counsel's witnesses, it is sufficient to establish, by a preponderance of the evidence,[21] that, for several years at least, Union representatives and other bargaining unit employees were given taxi rides to and from the Union office whenever they wanted them. The Respondent has not challenged testimony as to the distance of the Union office from the work stations of bargaining unit employees, the scarcity of parking places and the encouragement of carpools by the Respondent. That testimony corroborates the proposition that employees would seek to use the taxi service to get to the Union office. Regardless of the frequency of such trips, there is no evidence or allegation of the refusal of taxi service prior to January of 2007. In *U.S. Customs Service, Customs Management Center, Miami, Florida*, 56 FLRA 809, 822 (2000), the Authority held that even an annual practice which has existed over a significant period of time can give rise to a bargaining obligation. While taxi trips to and from the Union office might not have been as frequent as suggested by the General Counsel's witnesses, taxi service was available when needed up until January of 2007.

The position of the Respondent as to this issue is not improved by the fact that the dispatch logs (Resp. Exs. 1-8) show only two trips to the Union office. There is ample testimony to the effect that all taxi runs were not entered into OVIM and that requests received on the day of the desired taxi service did not appear on the daily trip tickets. While all of the taxi runs that were entered into the OVIM system showed the pickup and destination points, the wide-spread omission of other data, such as the names of drivers and the number of passengers, shows that the dispatch logs are not a reliable record of the actual use of the base taxi service.

The Respondent's reliance on the MEO is similarly misplaced. The fact that the Union agreed to the cancellation of certain MOUs is of no consequence in view of the fact that none of the MOUs dealt with the availability of the taxi service. The argument that the intent of the MEO was to eliminate past practice is belied by the absence of any reference to past practice as well as by the language in the CBA (GC Ex. 2, p.39) to the effect that past practices remain in effect pending the completion of collective bargaining.

I have assigned no weight to the conclusory and unsupported testimony that the Union's use of the taxi service would be contrary to Air Force or Department of Defense regulations in view of the fact that the Respondent has neither cited such regulations nor offered them in evidence. It is safe to assume that there are regulatory as well as statutory prohibitions against the use of government property other than for official business.[22] However, the use of the taxi service by Union representatives on official time or by bargaining unit employees in connection with contractual grievances are not so obviously beyond the scope of official business as to justify my reaching such a conclusion in the absence of specific authority to that effect. There is, perhaps, an argument to be made as to a distinction between Union activities on behalf of bargaining unit members and activities related to internal Union business. However, the Respondent apparently has never drawn such a distinction and I will not do so now.

The Respondent's Knowledge or Acquiescence

There is no evidence that the Respondent specifically acquiesced to the Union's use of the base taxi service. To the contrary, Howard testified that she only received taxi service after initial refusals and was informed by Speights that such taxi runs were contrary to his orders (Tr. 48-52, 60; GC Ex. 5).

[21]/ This is the standard of proof required of the General Counsel pursuant to §2423.32 of the Rules and Regulations of the Authority.

[22]/ Several of the Respondent's witnesses testified that the Union's use of the taxi service did not "support the mission of the Air Force". This implies a somewhat broader definition of the circumstances under which such use would be permitted and supports my conclusion that the Union's use of the taxi service was not obviously improper.

Rosaya testified that he was told by Clewell that such service was not authorized (Tr. 72). Queen testified that he was told by Moore that the use of taxi service by the Union was illegal (Tr. 98).

In view of the fact that the Respondent did not acquiesce in the Union's use of the taxi service, it can only be charged with a duty to bargain under cases such as *Patent Office* if it knew of the alleged past practice and took no action to stop it. The Authority has made it clear that actual, rather than constructive, knowledge is required, *Dept. of Health and Human Services, Social Security Administration*, 17 FLRA 126, 139 (1985)(*HHS*). It is of no consequence that management representatives were lax in monitoring the use of the taxi service or that they could have learned of the Union's use of the service with only a slight effort.

As stated above, the absence of all but two taxi runs to the Union office from the OVIM dispatch logs does not prove that no such runs were made. However, the dispatch logs do support the proposition that responsible representatives of the Respondent were not aware of them. The overwhelming weight of the testimony of the General Counsel's and the Respondent's witnesses is that virtually all of the dispatching of taxis as well as the entry of the related data into the OVIM system was performed by dispatchers who are members of the bargaining unit. Consequently, the omission of such data from the dispatch logs means that the dispatching of taxis to and from the Union office was accomplished "off the books".

The absence of the records of all but two such taxi runs from June 11, 2001 to December 19, 2007, cannot rationally be considered as coincidental. Rather, it is the result of the efforts of certain dispatchers to accommodate the Union without the knowledge of the Respondent's responsible management representatives.[23] In any event, there is no written record of other than two taxi runs to and from the Union office. Therefore, if the Respondent is to be charged with knowledge of the practice, that knowledge must be found to have been attained by other means.

The position of the General Counsel is not enhanced by the fact that several employees were told that the Respondent would "no longer" provide taxi service to the Union. Those statements were made by dispatchers rather than by management officials and are not binding on the Respondent. In view of the fact that none of the dispatchers claimed to have been authorized to provide taxi service to the Union,[24] such statements by the dispatchers meant only that they no longer felt comfortable sending taxis to or from the Union office. The reluctance on the part of the dispatchers, as well as their selective lapses of memory, leads me to conclude that the dispatchers knew that the taxi runs to the Union office, as well as the other uses of the service by the Union, were unauthorized.

According to the evidence, management representatives only approved taxi rides to the Union office for Howard, after she argued about it (Tr. 48-52), and for Queen when he needed a ride between the Union office and the computer center in connection with a mandated change to government computers (Tr. 94, 95). Such *ad hoc* and atypical decisions by management representatives are insufficient to prove the existence of a binding past practice, *U.S. Dep't of Labor, Office of Workers' Compensation Programs, Boston, Massachusetts*, 56 FLRA 598, 603 (2000). In addition, Queen's reason for needing a taxi could logically have been considered to have fallen within even a narrow definition of official business.

The weight of the evidence is that some of the taxi runs to and from the Union office were dispatched by radio and it is undisputed that all of the supervisors in the dispatchers' chain of command had radios. However, it is also true that some taxi runs, to whatever destination, were dispatched on a face-to-face basis. I credit the testimony of the supervisors that they did not hear the dispatching of the taxi runs to and from the Union office because, to conclude otherwise, I would have to assume that the supervisors had nothing else to do but to monitor the dispatching of most, if not all, taxi and other vehicle runs. As previously stated, I have concluded that the taxi runs to and from the Union office were not as frequent as suggested by certain of the General

[23]/ The inability of Union representatives to find records of their taxi rides to other locations might have been due to sloppy record keeping or to the fact that the dispatch logs, even when completed properly, list only the number, but not the names, of passengers.

[24]/ Patterson testified that he was told by Moore that he (Patterson) did not have the authority to deny taxi service to anyone (Tr. 136). Patterson did not describe the context in which Moore made the statement. Furthermore, there is no evidence that Moore knew that the dispatch office was receiving requests for taxi service to and from the Union office.

Counsel's witnesses. Moreover, the failure of the dispatchers to log in the runs to and from the Union office suggests that, whenever possible, they would have avoided using the radio to dispatch the runs so as to avoid the attention of their supervisors.

While certain management representatives, including those involved in labor relations, might have seen Union representatives and other bargaining unit members entering and leaving taxis, such incidents would almost certainly have occurred other than at the Union office.[25] The Respondent apparently did not attempt to curtail trips to locations other than the Union office. Significantly, Hiibschman testified that he has not used the taxi service since he went on 100% official time and was acting only on behalf of the Union (Tr. 25).

In order for the General Counsel to meet her burden of proving the existence of a past practice, she must show that the practice occurred with the knowledge and acquiescence, direct or implied, of *responsible* management officials, *Norfolk Naval Shipyard*, 25 FLRA 277, 286 (1987). Although the term "responsible management official" is not specifically defined in Authority precedent, I feel confident in construing it in this case as denoting a management representative with knowledge of and responsibility for the implementation of the Respondent's transportation policies. Even though Queen's supervisor at Mitchell Hall allowed Queen to use his office telephone to request taxi rides to the Union office (Tr. 90), the knowledge of unidentified waiter supervisors is not binding on the Respondent since the nature of their positions does not, in the absence of additional evidence, suggest that they are responsible management officials in the context of this case.

DiBiasio, a food service worker, testified that his first line supervisor approved his use of official time and supposedly knew that he sometimes met with employees at the Union office. DiBiasio's supervisor, like Queen's, was not a responsible management official within the meaning of *Norfolk Naval Shipyard, supra*. Furthermore, the supervisor's knowledge of DiBiasio's use of official time does not translate into knowledge that he used the base taxi service, let alone that he was going to the Union office on a specific occasion. DiBiasio himself acknowledged that he sometimes used his own vehicle on Union business and that, at other times, he would meet with employees in Mitchell Hall (Tr. 152-54).

I do not impute the knowledge of Berger, Furman and other of the Respondent's labor relations representatives to the Respondent. It is undisputed that neither the CBA nor any MOU authorizes or prohibits the Union's use of the taxi service. Consequently, the Respondent's labor relations and personnel representatives were not involved in matters related to the taxi service.

The General Counsel maintains that the Respondent's knowledge of the alleged past practice is shown by Little's testimony to the effect that, some time around the early 1990's, Union representatives withdrew bargaining proposals For reserved parking spaces and office space in every building upon receipt of the Respondent's assurances that they could use the base taxi service (Tr. 160, 167). Curiously, that alleged understanding was never reduced to writing.[26] It is unclear whether the incidents described by Little occurred before or after the opening of the first Union office on Academy grounds. In any event, a logical *quid pro quo* for offices and parking spaces could just as easily have been the use of the taxi service between locations where bargaining unit members were employed. The Respondent apparently made good on its assurances to the Union since it has not been alleged that taxi service has been denied for trips other than to the Union office.

My review of the evidence leads me to conclude that, while it is possible that the Respondent knew of the alleged past practice, a finding to that effect could only be based on conjecture. Such conjecture is no substitute for direct or circumstantial evidence of the Respondent's actual, rather than constructive, knowledge of the Union's use of the base taxi service for trips to and from the Union office, *HHS*.

25/ Hiibschman testified that meetings with management representatives were sometimes held at the Union office and that bargaining unit employees could be seen through the window as they arrived in taxis (Tr. 17). I do not credit that testimony in the absence of further detail as to the identities of the management representatives or of verification of Hiibschman's suggestion that they were looking out of the window in the first place.

26/ According to Hiibschman, there is no MOU regarding taxi service because it had not been a problem (Tr. 20). Hiibschman's testimony does not adequately explain the failure of the Union to press for written language regarding what logically should have been considered as an important issue. The Union's inaction suggests that its representatives wanted to let sleeping dogs lie.

The evidence also leads me to the conclusion that the Respondent's oversight of the base taxi service was sporadic at best and that responsible management officials could have learned of the Union's use of the taxi service with a minimum of effort. However, the Authority has made it clear that it is of no consequence that the Respondent should have known of the alleged past practice, *HHS*. The fact remains that the Respondent had no actual knowledge of the alleged past practice and that the Respondent's ignorance was caused, in the first instance, by the failure of bargaining unit dispatchers to record the disputed taxi runs in the OVIMS system or in any other way so as to bring the runs to the attention of responsible management representatives.

It is unclear why the issue of taxi service to and from the Union office came to a head in January of 2007. If the curtailment of taxi service was caused by the implementation of the MEO, it would have occurred about six years earlier. Fortunately, I am not required to solve that mystery.

For the reasons stated above, I find that the General Counsel has not met her burden of proof as to the Respondent's knowledge of or acquiescence in the Union's use of the base taxi service for transportation to and from the Union office. Accordingly, I have concluded that no past practice existed such as to give rise to a bargaining obligation on the part of the Respondent. The Respondent did not commit an unfair labor practice by unilaterally denying such taxi service to the Union.[27]

In view of the above conclusion, I recommend that the Authority adopt the following Order:

ORDER

It is hereby ordered that the Complaint be, and hereby is, dismissed.

Issued, Washington, DC, June 11, 2008.

Paul B. Lang
Administrative Law Judge

[27]/ This Decision should not be construed as a determination as to whether the Respondent would be required to give the Union notice and an opportunity to bargain over the cessation of all taxi service to the Union.

65 FLRA No. 159

FRATERNAL ORDER OF POLICE
PENTAGON POLICE LABOR COMMITTEE
(Union)

and

UNITED STATES
DEPARTMENT OF DEFENSE
PENTAGON FORCE PROTECTION AGENCY
(Agency)

0-AR-4705

DECISION

April 27, 2011

Before the Authority: Carol Waller Pope, Chairman, and Thomas M. Beck and Ernest DuBester, Members

I. Statement of the Case

This matter is before the Authority on exceptions to an award of Arbitrator Stephen E. Alpern filed by the Union under § 7122 of the Federal Service Labor-Management Relations Statute (the Statute) and part 2425 of the Authority's Regulations.[1] The Agency filed an opposition to the Union's exceptions.

The Arbitrator sustained a grievance seeking payment for lost overtime opportunities resulting from the Agency's delay in returning the grievant to full duty status. Award at 2, 5. As a remedy, the Arbitrator awarded backpay; however, he denied the Union's request for attorney fees and for prospective relief. For the reasons that follow, we dismiss the Union's exceptions in part and deny them in part.

II. Background and Arbitrator's Award

The grievant is employed by the Agency as a police officer. *Id.* at 2. At the time of his hiring, the grievant had a high frequency hearing loss, a condition that he disclosed during an Agency medical examination. *Id.* The grievant was required to have annual medical examinations, each of which confirmed his hearing loss. *Id.* at 3. In 2007, the grievant was required to have a follow-up medical examination, which revealed the same hearing loss. *Id.* Based on this examination, on November 28, 2007, the Agency placed the grievant on light duty status pending an independent medical evaluation. *Id.* Because of this status, he was no longer eligible to work the same overtime as he did previously; as a result, his overtime work was "substantially reduced." *Id.*

On December 7, 2007, the grievant requested a medical waiver. *Id.* An Agency official determined that, because the grievant's case would be reviewed by a Medical Review Board (MRB) after the MRB received the results of the independent medical evaluation, a waiver was not appropriate at that time. *Id.* On December 14, 2007, the grievant was independently examined by an audiologist, who concluded that the grievant "could perform his police officer duties in a safe and effective manner." *Id.* at 3-4. The Agency's Medical Review Officer (MRO) concurred with this conclusion. *Id.* at 4. The grievant, however, remained on light duty. *Id.* In late January 2008, the grievant repeatedly inquired regarding the status of his waiver request. *Id.* at 4. An Agency official informed him that the MRB was "moving forward for a decision." *Id.* 4-5.

On March 14, 2008, the Union presented a grievance on the matter, which "sought, inter alia, a return to full duty status and payment for all lost overtime opportunities as a result of the [g]rievant's placement on light duty status." *Id.* at 5. On March 24, 2008, the Agency denied the grievance, noting that the grievant's reinstatement had been addressed by the MRB on March 19. *Id.* The Agency further stated that it had convened the MRB at the earliest opportunity and that the grievant's "reinstatement to full duty [had been] directed as a result of [that] deliberation . . . ." *Id.* The matter was unresolved and submitted to arbitration. The parties stipulated to the following issue: "Whether or not the Agency unreasonably delayed putting the [g]rievant back on full duty, and, if so, whether the [g]rievant was entitled to overtime." *Id.* at 2.

1. The Union also filed an unopposed motion for leave to supplement the record to add the Arbitrator's Supplemental Opinion and Award issued on December 13, 2010. *See* Union's Motion to Supplement Arbitral Record & Attach. We find that, even assuming that the document is properly before the Authority, it provides no basis for finding the award deficient. Accordingly, we find it unnecessary to resolve this motion. *See, e.g., U.S. Dep't of the Treasury, Fin. Mgmt. Serv., Emeryville, Cal.*, 65 FLRA 547, 549 (2011).

Before the Arbitrator, the Union asserted that the Agency's regulations require the MRB to conduct an "expeditious review" of the grievant's case; that the Agency had failed to conduct such a review; and that the Agency's unreasonable delay in convening the MRB caused the grievant to lose overtime. *Id.* at 6. The Union sought: (1) backpay for the overtime that he would have otherwise received; (2) an order "directing the Agency to conduct medical reviews in an expeditious manner"; (3) an order "directing the Agency to afford all qualified employees the right to overtime opportunities as set forth in the parties' agreement"; and (4) attorney fees. *Id.* The Agency asserted, among other things, that the grievant is "not entitled to attorney[] fees because it would not be in the interest of justice, as required by 5 U.S.C. § 7701(g)." *Id.* at 7.

The Arbitrator concluded that the Agency's delay in reviewing the grievant's case "was not reasonable." *Id.* at 8. In reaching this conclusion, the Arbitrator noted that the results of the grievant's December 2007 examination and the recommendations of the audiologist and the MRO "should have alerted" the MRB that "there was a substantial likelihood" that the MRB would find the grievant was able to "perform the full range of his law enforcement duties . . . ." *Id.* Further, because the grievant was being "substantially harmed" by remaining on light duty, the Arbitrator found the Agency should have "promptly" sought MRB review of the grievant's case. *Id.*

The Arbitrator rejected the Agency's claim that its standard practice was to delay consideration of a case until the MRB had other cases to review. *Id.* at 9. The Arbitrator found that, because the Agency's regulations entitle an employee to "expeditious" review, this practice "was not reasonable." *Id.* Noting that "expeditious" does not necessarily mean "immediate," the Arbitrator found that, under the circumstances, "it would have been reasonable for the MRB to take up to thirty days, or until January 18, 2008, to resolve" the [g]rievant's case. *Id.*

The Arbitrator rejected the Union's "request[]" for "an award of attorney fees." *Id.* at 12. As an initial matter, the Arbitrator noted that the grievant failed to "point to any specific criterion which he believes is satisfied and makes no argument as to why he should be awarded fees." *Id.* Applying the criteria set forth by the Merit Systems Protection Board in *Allen v. United States Postal Service*, 2 M.S.P.R. 420 (1980) (*Allen*) for an award of attorney fees, the Arbitrator found that the record before him "[did] not support a finding that any of the criteria were met." *Id.* In this regard, the Arbitrator found that: (1) the Agency did not engage in a prohibited personnel practice; (2) the Agency's action involving the delay of the grievant's case before the MRB and his return to full duty status was not clearly unfounded; (3) the Agency's action involving the delay of the grievant's case before the MRB and his return to full duty status was not taken in bad faith to harass or exert improper pressure on the grievant; (4) the Agency's action involving the delay of the grievant's case before the MRB and his return to full duty status did not involve a gross procedural error; and (5) the Agency did not know, nor should it have known, that it would not prevail on the merits when it sought review of the grievant's case before the MRB. *Id.*

The Arbitrator sustained the grievance and awarded the grievant backpay for the overtime that he lost as a result of the Agency's delay in returning him to full duty status. *Id.* at 13. The Arbitrator rejected the Union's request for remedial orders directing the Agency to "conduct medical reviews in an expeditious manner" and "afford all qualified employees the right to overtime opportunities" pursuant to the parties' agreement because the Union had failed to demonstrate that either order was warranted.[2] *Id.* at 11-12.

III. Positions of the Parties

A. Union's Exceptions

Initially, the Union asserts that its "exceptions involve the award['s] consistency with settled law. Exceptions at 1. Specifically, the Union argues that the Arbitrator's conclusion denying attorney fees is contrary to law. *Id.* at 7. The Union contends that, contrary to the "[A]rbitrator's implication," an award of attorney fees does not have to be made within the same proceeding that determines the merits of a grievance and that, had it "been afforded the opportunity" to file an application for fees, it "would have been able to demonstrate entitlement and reasonableness of the fees claim[ed]." *Id.* at 11.

The Union further argues that the requirements of the Back Pay Act were met. In this regard, the Union challenges the Arbitrator's finding that fees were not warranted in the interest of justice, contending that such fees are warranted under *Allen* criteria 2, 4, and 5. *Id.* at 11, 13-14. With respect to criterion 2, the Union asserts that the facts

2. The Arbitrator retained jurisdiction to resolve disputes concerning implementation of the award. Award at 13.

demonstrate that the Agency's actions were "clearly without merit or wholly unfounded." With respect to criterion 4, the Union asserts that the Agency was fully aware that it was not in compliance with its own procedural regulations; accordingly, the Union contends, the Agency's actions involved gross procedural error. *Id.* at 13-14. Finally, with respect to criterion 5, the Union asserts that, based on the "unreasonable and subjective interpretation" the Agency "placed on the meaning of the word expeditious" in its regulation, the Agency knew or should have known that it would not prevail on the merits when it brought the proceeding. *Id.* at 19.

Citing *United States Department of the Army, United States Corps of Engineers, Northwestern Division*, 65 FLRA 131 (2010) (Member Beck dissenting, in part) (*U.S. Dep't of the Army*), the Union contends that the Arbitrator erred in denying its request for prospective relief, specifically an order directing the Agency to "conduct medical reviews in an expeditious manner . . . ." *Id.* at 21. According to the Union, its requested remedy included "such further relief as is deemed necessary, appropriate, applicable and just." *Id.* As a result, the Union claims, the remedy "was not limited" to the grievant, but "included all police officers who might appear before the MRB." *Id.*

B. Agency's Opposition

The Agency asserts that the exceptions are barred by § 2429.5 of the Authority's Regulations because the arguments could have been, but were not, raised below. Opp'n at 6-8. The Agency contends that, as a remedy, the Union requested overtime payment, "attorney[] fees and costs now, and any other remedy the [A]rbitrator would deem appropriate or just under the circumstances." *Id.* at 4 (citing Tr. at 12). The Agency asserts that, although the Union requested such remedies before the Arbitrator, the Union did not "raise any arguments for them" at that time. *Id.* at 7.

Alternatively, the Agency contends that the award is consistent with law. *Id.* at 8-12. The Agency contends that its actions "were not clearly without merit or wholly unfounded," noting that the Arbitrator held the Agency's delay in placing [the] grievant back in full duty status was "'not clearly unfounded.'" *Id.* at 9 (quoting Award at 12). The Agency further asserts that the Arbitrator held that its "delay in placing the grievant back on full duty status 'did not involve gross procedural error.'" *Id.* at 10 (quoting Award at 12). Moreover, according to the Agency, "there is no evidence in the record, nor does the Union assert, that the Agency delayed the grievance process, or the arbitration . . . to harm [the] grievant." *Id.* at 11. Finally, the Agency contends that an award of attorney fees is not warranted because, as the Arbitrator found, it neither knew, nor should have known, that it would not prevail on the merits. *Id.* at 11-12.

The Agency contends that the denial of prospective relief is not contrary to law. *Id.* at 12-13. The Agency states that, at the arbitration hearing, "neither party offered testimony or documentary evidence concerning other individuals" because the issue before the Arbitrator "dealt only with the grievant." *Id.* at 13.

IV. Analysis and Conclusions

A. Preliminary Matter: The exceptions are barred, in part, by § 2429.5 of the Authority's Regulations.

Under 5 C.F.R. § 2429.5, the Authority will not consider "any evidence, factual assertions, arguments (including affirmative defenses), requested remedies, or challenges to an awarded remedy that could have been, but were not, presented in the proceedings before the . . . arbitrator."[3] 5 C.F.R. § 2429.5; *see also U.S. Dep't of Homeland Sec., U.S. Customs & Border Prot., JFK Airport, Queens, N.Y.*, 62 FLRA 416, 417 (2008) (exception dismissed under § 2429.5, where record established agency could have made argument before arbitrator but did not); 5 C.F.R. § 2425.4(c) (expressly prohibits exceptions from including "arguments (including affirmative defenses), requested remedies, or challenges to an awarded remedy that could have been, but were not, presented to the arbitrator").

There is no indication in the record that the Union argued to the Arbitrator, as it does in its exceptions, that fees were warranted in the interest of justice because *Allen* criteria 2, 4, and 5 were satisfied. *See* Award at 12. To the contrary, the Arbitrator found that, although the Union requested attorney fees, it failed to "point to any specific

3. The Authority's Regulations concerning the review of arbitration awards, as well as certain related procedural Regulations, including § 2429.5, were revised effective October 1, 2010. *See* 75 Fed Reg. 42,283 (2010). Because the Union's exceptions were filed after this date, we apply the revised Regulations here. *See* § 2429.1. We note that the revised version of § 2429.5 "merely incorporates into regulation" the Authority's practice under the prior version of § 2429.5. 75 Fed. Reg. 42,283 (2010).

criterion" that it believed was satisfied and "ma[de] no argument" regarding why fees should be awarded. *Id.* Because the Union could have, but did not, raise such arguments before the Arbitrator, it may not do so now. Accordingly, we dismiss this portion of the exceptions.

B. The Arbitrator's determination that the Union requested an award of attorney fees is not contrary to law.

The Union asserts that, "[c]ontrary to the [A]rbitrator's implication, an award of attorney fees does not have to be made within the same proceeding" and that, had it "been afforded the opportunity" to file its application for fees, it "would have been able to demonstrate entitlement and reasonableness of the fees claim[ed]." Exceptions at 11.

When an exception involves an award's consistency with law, the Authority reviews any question of law raised by the exception and the award de novo. *See NTEU, Chapter 24*, 50 FLRA 330, 332 (1995) (citing *U.S. Customs Serv. v. FLRA*, 43 F.3d 682, 686-87 (D.C. Cir. 1994)). In applying the standard of de novo review, the Authority assesses whether an arbitrator's legal conclusions are consistent with the applicable standard of law. *See U.S. Dep't of Def., Dep'ts of the Army & the Air Force, Ala. Nat'l Guard, Northport, Ala.*, 55 FLRA 37, 40 (1998). In making that assessment, the Authority defers to the arbitrator's underlying factual findings. *See id.*

The Back Pay Act expressly provides that an employee affected by an unjustified or unwarranted personnel action is entitled, on correction of the personnel action, to receive "reasonable attorney fees related to the personnel action." 5 U.S.C. § 5596(b)(1)(A)(ii). Regulations implementing this portion of the Act require that, to be awarded attorney fees by an arbitrator, the grievant or the grievant's representative must present a request for fees to the arbitrator, who must provide the employing agency with an opportunity to respond. *See* 5 C.F.R. § 550.807(a)-(b); *U.S. Dep't of the Army, Red River Army Depot, Texarkana, Tex.*, 54 FLRA 759, 762 (1998) (*Red River Army Depot*). Also, the Authority has held that it is not premature to request attorney fees as part of an arbitrator's award on the merits of a grievance. *See Health Care Fin. Admin., Dep't of HHS*, 35 FLRA 274, 289-90 (1990) (*HHS*) (quoting *Phila. Naval Shipyard*, 32 FLRA 417, 420 (1988) ("While such requests [for attorney fees] may be submitted during the course of an arbitration proceeding, nothing . . . requires that a request for attorney fees be made before an award is final and binding."). Further, the Authority has determined that "[a]rbitrators may rule on requests for attorney fees simultaneous to rendering a decision on the merits of a grievance." *See id.* at 290 (citations omitted).

In this case, we find that the Union has not demonstrated that the Arbitrator erred in deciding the issue of attorney fees. Before the Arbitrator, the Union stated that it was seeking, among other remedies, "attorney[] fees and costs now . . . ." *See* Exceptions, Attach. B, Tr. at 12; *see also* Award at 6 (noting that Union requested, among other things, "attorney[] fees under the Back Pay Act"). Moreover, the record reveals that, in response, the Agency asserted that the Union was "not entitled to attorney[] fees because it would not be in the interest of justice, as required by 5 U.S.C. § 7701(g)." Award at 7. In his award, the Arbitrator stated that the Union "request[ed] an award of attorney fees." *Id.* at 12. In these circumstances, the Union has not established that a request for attorney fees was not made before the Arbitrator. *See, e.g., HHS*, 35 FLRA at 289 (union's claim that no application for attorney fees request had been filed with arbitrator rejected because in its post-hearing brief union requested that "[c]ounsel for the [g]rievant . . . be awarded attorney[] fees in accordance with law" and arbitrator noted that grievant had requested attorney fees); *cf. Red River Army Depot*, 54 FLRA at 761 (union did not request fees as part of merits award because union "repeatedly stated in its post-hearing brief . . . that the [a]rbitrator retain jurisdiction in order to entertain a subsequent motion for an award of fees with supporting memorandum").

Accordingly, we deny this exception.

C. The Arbitrator's denial of the Union's request for prospective relief is not contrary to law.

The Union asserts that the "exceptions involve the award['s] consistency with settled law." Exceptions at 1. Citing *U.S. Dep't of the Army*, the Union contends that the Arbitrator erred in denying its request for prospective relief, specifically an order directing the Agency to "conduct medical reviews in an expeditious manner . . . ." *Id.* at 21.

Under 5 C.F.R. § 2425.6(b), a party arguing that an award is deficient on private-sector grounds -- including the ground that an arbitrator "[e]xceeded his or her authority[,]" *id.* § 2425.6(b)(1)(i) -- has an express duty to "explain how, under standards set forth in the decisional law of the Authority or Federal courts[,]" *id.* § 2425.6(b), the award is deficient. In addition, 5 C.F.R. § 2425.6(e)(1) provides that an exception "may be subject to dismissal or denial if[] . . . [t]he excepting party fails to raise and support a ground as required in" § 2425.6(b).

In support of its assertion that the award is contrary to law, the Union cites *U.S. Dep't of the Army*. However, the Union has not explained how, under *U.S. Dep't of the Army*, the award is deficient. Because the Union has not explained how the award is deficient under *U.S. Dep't of the Army* and has not cited any law that required the Arbitrator to grant the requested remedy, we find that the Union has failed to demonstrate that the award is contrary to law.

Accordingly, we deny this exception.

V. Decision

The Union's exceptions are dismissed in part and denied in part.

65 FLRA No. 160

NATIONAL ASSOCIATION
OF INDEPENDENT LABOR
LOCAL 5
(Union)

and

UNITED STATES
DEPARTMENT OF DEFENSE
DEFENSE LOGISTICS AGENCY
DISTRIBUTION RED RIVER, TEXAS
(Agency)

0-AR-4736

DECISION

April 28, 2011

Before the Authority: Carol Waller Pope, Chairman, and Thomas M. Beck and Ernest DuBester, Members

This matter is before the Authority on exceptions to an award of Arbitrator Carol Kyler filed by the Union under § 7122(a) of the Federal Service Labor-Management Relations Statute (the Statute) and part 2425 of the Authority's Regulations. The Agency filed an opposition to the Union's exceptions.

Under § 7122(a) of the Statute, an award is deficient if it is contrary to any law, rule, or regulation, or it is deficient on other grounds similar to those applied by federal courts in private sector labor-management relations. Upon careful consideration of the entire record in this case and Authority precedent, the Authority concludes that the award is not deficient on the grounds raised in the exceptions and set forth in § 7122(a). *See Fraternal Order of Police, Pentagon Police Labor Comm.*, 65 FLRA 781, 784-85 (2011) (denying a contrary-to-law exception where excepting party did not cite any law with which the arbitrator's award conflicted); *AFGE, Local 1802*, 50 FLRA 396, 398 (1995) (award not deficient as based on a nonfact where excepting party challenges a conclusion based on the arbitrator's interpretation of the parties' agreement); *U.S. Dep't of Labor (OSHA)*, 34 FLRA 573, 575 (1990) (award not deficient as failing to draw its essence from the parties' collective bargaining agreement where excepting party fails to establish that the award cannot in any rational way be derived from the agreement; is so unfounded in reason and fact and so unconnected to the wording and purpose of the agreement as to manifest an infidelity to the obligation of the arbitrator; does not represent a plausible interpretation of the agreement; or evidences a manifest disregard of the agreement).

Accordingly, the Union's exceptions are denied.

65 FLRA No. 161

SOCIAL SECURITY ADMINISTRATION
LOUISVILLE, KENTUCKY
(Agency)

and

AMERICAN FEDERATION
OF GOVERNMENT EMPLOYEES
LOCAL 3627
(Union)

0-AR-4350

DECISION

April 28, 2011

Before the Authority: Carol Waller Pope, Chairman, and Thomas M. Beck and Ernest DuBester, Members[1]

I. Statement of the Case

The matter is before the Authority on exceptions to an award of Arbitrator Michael L. Allen filed by the Agency under § 7122(a) of the Federal Service Labor-Management Relations Statute (the Statute) and part 2425 of the Authority's Regulations. The Union filed an opposition to the Agency's exceptions.

The Arbitrator found that the Agency violated the parties' agreements with regard to its distribution of Recognition of Contribution (ROC) awards. In addition, he directed the Agency to vacate the ROC awards that had been granted for the year at issue, stated that a particular management official (the Deciding Official) was required to personally evaluate and decide upon award nominations for that year, and retained jurisdiction over the implementation of remedies.

For the reasons that follow, we dismiss the Agency's exceptions in part and deny them in part.

II. Background and Arbitrator's Award

The parties have several agreements involving employee awards, including: (1) a 2000 nationwide agreement (the 2000 Agreement); (2) a 2005 nationwide agreement (the 2005 Agreement); (3) an additional agreement regarding ROC awards (the ROC Agreement); (4) a Memorandum of Understanding (MOU) setting forth the procedures that the Agency "must follow during the nomination process for ROC awards[;]" and (5) an Award Handbook (Handbook) containing the criteria that the Agency will consider in determining which employees would receive ROC awards. Award at 2-3.

When the Agency distributed ROC awards to certain employees but not others, the Union filed a grievance on behalf of nine employees who had not received such awards. *Id.* at 2-3. The grievance was unresolved and submitted to arbitration, where the Arbitrator framed the issues as follows:

> [W]hether the Agency complied with the [MOU[2]] . . . and/or Article 17 of the [2000 Agreement[3]], and/or Article 3, Section 2 of the [2005 Agreement[4]] in deciding whether to approve or deny "ROC" award nominations for nine (9) . . . personnel . . . ? If not, . . . whether the said . . . personnel were treated fairly and equitably by the Agency in its consideration of their ROC awards for said performance period? If either of the said questions is to be answered in the negative, then the final issue herein is the scope of the appropriate remedy.

Id. at 2.

The Arbitrator determined that the parties had agreed to several restrictions on "[m]anagement's otherwise virtually unfettered right to assess nominations[,]" including Article 3, Section 2A of the 2005 Agreement, which requires the Agency to

1. Member Beck's separate opinion, dissenting in part, is set forth at the end of this decision.

2. The pertinent wording of the MOU is set forth below.

3. Article 17, Section 2B of the 2000 Agreement provides, in pertinent part, that the Agency must consider the "relative significance and impact of [the employee's] contributions . . . in determining which type of awards would constitute appropriate recognition, and, for monetary awards, in determining the amount of money to be granted." Award at 10, 15-16.

4. The pertinent wording of the 2005 Agreement is set forth below.

"treat . . . its employees 'fairly and equitably.'" *Id.* at 16. The Arbitrator found that, under the review and approval process set forth in the agreements, "the Deciding Official -- and not the first-line supervisor -- must be the person who, 'decides to approve, deny or reject the ROC award nomination,' and who provides a written 'appropriate justification' for the said decision 'on the Action Form.'" *Id.* The Arbitrator found that "[p]recisely the opposite" occurred because first-line supervisors "not only nominated the ultimate recipients, but also made . . . the decision to approve the ROC awards, even providing the narrative justification and then 'rubber-stamping' the signature of the Deciding Official to the Action Form." *Id.* at 17. According to the Arbitrator, "[b]y relegating the decision-making autonomy to others, the appearance of 'fair and equitable treatment' was . . . seriously compromised[,]" in violation of the parties' agreements. *Id.* at 19.

With regard to remedy, although the Union proposed that each grievant receive a ROC award, *see id.* at 13, the Arbitrator declined to "adopt the proposal of the Union as to remedy[,]" *id.* at 19. Instead, he vacated the ROC awards that the Agency had granted and directed the Deciding Official to "personally review, evaluate and decide each of the nominations, explaining his reasons for approving or disapproving each nomination." *Id.* at 19-20. The Arbitrator also required that such actions be completed within sixty days of the date of his award and "expressly reserve[d] his jurisdiction to consider any complaint as to the decision of the Deciding Official." *Id.* at 20.

III. Positions of the Parties

A. Agency's Exceptions

The Agency claims that the award is contrary to management's right to assign work under § 7106(a)(2) of the Statute. *See* Exceptions at 6-11. In this connection, the Agency asserts that the award fails to satisfy both prongs of the two-pronged test set forth in *United States Department of the Treasury, Bureau of Engraving & Printing, Washington, D.C.*, 53 FLRA 146, 153-54 (1997) (*BEP*). With regard to prong I of *BEP*, the Agency contends that the MOU -- as interpreted by the Arbitrator to require the Deciding Official to review, evaluate, and decide upon each of the award nominations -- is not a contract provision that was negotiated under § 7106(b) of the Statute. *See* Exceptions at 6-9. With regard to prong II of *BEP*, the Agency argues that the remedy directed by the Arbitrator "does not reflect a reconstruction of what the Agency would have done" if it had not violated the MOU. *Id.* at 9.

The Agency also claims that the award fails to draw its essence from the MOU. *Id.* at 4. Specifically, the Agency asserts that, contrary to the Arbitrator's interpretation, the MOU does not require a "wet" signature or "preclude[] the Deciding Official from delegating completion of the award forms or the writing of the narrative to subordinate managers." *Id.* at 5 (citation omitted).

In addition, the Agency contends that the Arbitrator exceeded his authority by directing that all ROC awards for the year at issue be vacated. *Id.* at 10-11. In this connection, the Agency claims that the arbitration involved "whether or not [nine] employees were not given awards appropriately[,] not whether all awards were inappropriately granted." *Id.* at 10.

Finally, the Agency claims that "[t]he Arbitrator was functus officio" when he "reserve[d] . . . jurisdiction to consider any complaint as to the decision of the Deciding Official." *Id.* at 11 (quoting Award at 20). In this connection, the Agency asserts that the Arbitrator's retention of jurisdiction "bypasses the negotiated grievance procedures" set forth in the 2005 Agreement. *Id.*

B. Union's Opposition

The Union claims that the award is not contrary to management's right to assign work and that it draws its essence from the MOU. *See* Opp'n at 3, 2. The Union also claims that the Arbitrator was not functus officio because "it is not uncommon for an [a]rbitrator to retain jurisdiction for a period of time to resolve questions or problems that might arise concerning [an] award." *Id.* at 3.

IV. Preliminary Issues

The Authority's Regulations that were in effect when the Agency filed its exceptions provided that "[t]he Authority will not consider . . . any issue, which was not presented in the proceedings before the . . . arbitrator." 5 C.F.R. § 2429.5 (§ 2429.5).[5] Under § 2429.5, the Authority will not consider any

5. The Authority's Regulations concerning the review of arbitration awards, as well as certain related procedural regulations, including § 2429.5, were revised effective October 1, 2010. *See* 75 Fed. Reg. 42,283 (2010). Because the Agency's exceptions were filed before that date, we apply the earlier Regulations.

argument that could have been, but was not, presented to the arbitrator. *E.g., AFGE, Local 2923*, 65 FLRA 561, 562 (2011).

Before the Arbitrator, the Union argued that the Agency violated the MOU by allowing individuals other than the Deciding Official to take various actions, including approving awards. *See* Award at 13. Thus, the Agency could have argued to the Arbitrator that interpreting the MOU in this manner would be contrary to management's right to assign work. However, there is no evidence in the record that the Agency did so. Accordingly, under § 2429.5, we dismiss the Agency's exception alleging that the Arbitrator's interpretation of the MOU is contrary to management's right to assign work.

By contrast, it is unclear whether the Agency could have raised, before the Arbitrator, its management-rights challenge to the Arbitrator's chosen remedy. In this connection, the Arbitrator expressly declined to award the remedy requested by the Union and, instead, awarded a different remedy. *See id.* at 19. As there is no basis in the record for finding that the Agency could have raised to the Arbitrator its management-rights argument regarding the awarded remedy, we do not apply § 2429.5 to bar that argument. *Cf. U.S. Dep't of the Treasury, IRS, Andover, Mass.*, 63 FLRA 202, 205 (2009) (applying § 2429.5 where challenged remedies had been requested before arbitrator). Instead, we address that argument below.

For the foregoing reasons, we dismiss the Agency's management-rights exception regarding the Arbitrator's interpretation of the MOU, but we resolve the Agency's management-rights exception regarding the Arbitrator's chosen remedy.

V. Analysis and Conclusions

A. The Agency has not demonstrated that the remedy is contrary to § 7106 of the Statute.

The Agency alleges that the Arbitrator's remedy is contrary to § 7106 of the Statute. The Authority reviews questions of law de novo. *See NTEU, Chapter 24*, 50 FLRA 330, 332 (1995) (citing *U.S. Customs Serv. v. FLRA*, 43 F.3d 682, 686-87 (D.C. Cir. 1994)). In applying a standard of de novo review, the Authority determines whether the arbitrator's legal conclusions are consistent with the applicable standard of law. *NFFE, Local 1437*, 53 FLRA 1703, 1710 (1998) (*Local 1437*). In making that determination, the Authority defers to the arbitrator's underlying factual findings. *See id.*

The Authority recently revised the analysis that it will apply when reviewing management-rights exceptions to arbitration awards. *See U.S. EPA*, 65 FLRA 113, 115 (2010) (Member Beck concurring) (*EPA*); *FDIC, Div. of Supervision & Consumer Prot., S.F. Region*, 65 FLRA 102, 106-07 (2010) (Chairman Pope concurring) (*FDIC*). Under the revised analysis, the Authority assesses whether the award affects the exercise of the asserted management right. *EPA*, 65 FLRA at 115. If so, then the Authority examines whether the award provides a remedy for a violation of either an applicable law, within the meaning of § 7106(a)(2) of the Statute, or a contract provision that was negotiated under § 7106(b). *Id.* In setting forth the revised analysis, the Authority rejected the continued application of the "reconstruction" requirement set forth in *BEP*, 53 FLRA 146. *See FDIC*, 65 FLRA at 106-07.

Here, the Agency's exception is based entirely on the Arbitrator's alleged failure to reconstruct what the Agency would have done if it had not violated the MOU. As discussed above, the Authority has rejected continued application of the former reconstruction standard. Accordingly, we deny the exception.[6]

B. The award does not fail to draw its essence from the parties' agreements.

In reviewing an arbitrator's interpretation of a collective bargaining agreement, the Authority applies the deferential standard of review that federal courts use in reviewing arbitration awards in the private sector. *See* 5 U.S.C. § 7122(a)(2); *AFGE, Council 220*, 54 FLRA 156, 159 (1998). Under this standard, the Authority will find that an arbitration award is deficient as failing to draw its essence from the collective bargaining agreement when the appealing party establishes that the award: (1) cannot in any rational way be derived from the agreement;

---

6. For the reasons set forth in her concurring opinion in *FDIC*, 65 FLRA at 112 (Concurring Opinion of Chairman Pope), Chairman Pope would resolve this issue by determining whether the remedy is reasonably related to the negotiated provisions and the harm being remedied. *E.g., U.S. Dep't of HHS, Substance Abuse & Mental Health Servs. Admin.*, 65 FLRA 568, 571 n.7 (2011). Doing so, Chairman Pope would deny the exception. Here, however, in order to form a majority opinion on this issue and avoid an impasse in the resolution of this case, she agrees to deny the exception for the above-stated grounds. *See, e.g., AFGE, Local 727*, 62 FLRA 372, 374 (2008) (Separate Opinion of then-Member Pope) (joining majority opinion in order to avoid impasse in resolution of case).

(2) is so unfounded in reason and fact and so unconnected with the wording and purposes of the collective bargaining agreement as to manifest an infidelity to the obligation of the arbitrator; (3) does not represent a plausible interpretation of the agreement; or (4) evidences a manifest disregard of the agreement. *See U.S. Dep't of Labor (OSHA)*, 34 FLRA 573, 575 (1990). The Authority and the courts defer to arbitrators in this context "because it is the arbitrator's construction of the agreement for which the parties have bargained." *Id.* at 576.

The MOU states that "[o]nce the designated deciding official decides to approve, deny or reject the ROC award nomination, he/she will complete an [Action Form]." Exceptions, Attach. 3 at 5; Opp'n Ex. 1 at 5. The Action Form must include: (1) a written appropriate justification that "clearly articulate[s] the specific reason(s) that the employee's nomination(s) are approved, disapproved or rejected" and (2) the signature of the "designated deciding official[.]" Exceptions, Attach. 3 at 5; Opp'n Ex. 1 at 5, 10. Further, the MOU and Article 3, Section 2A of the 2005 Agreement expressly provide that employees shall be treated "fairly and equitably." Award at 16; Exceptions at 3.

Interpreting these provisions of the parties' agreements, the Arbitrator found that the "Deciding Official -- and not the first-line supervisor -- must be the person who, 'decides to approve, deny or reject the ROC award nomination,' and who provides a written 'appropriate justification' for the said decision 'on the Action Form.'" Award at 16. Requiring the "Deciding Official" to "personally review, evaluate[,] and decide each of the nominations" on the Action Form is consistent with the requirements set forth above, particularly where, as the Arbitrator found here, by "relegating" these actions to others, the Agency "seriously compromised" "the appearance of 'fair and equitable treatment[.]'" *Id.* at 19. The Agency does not establish that the Arbitrator's interpretation of the agreements is irrational, unfounded, implausible, or a manifest disregard of the agreements. Accordingly, the Agency does not demonstrate that the award fails to draw its essence from the agreements, and we deny the exception.

C. The Arbitrator did not exceed his authority by vacating all ROC awards for the year at issue.

An arbitrator exceeds his or her authority when the arbitrator fails to resolve an issue submitted to arbitration, resolves an issue not submitted to arbitration, disregards specific limitations on his or her authority, or awards relief to persons who are not encompassed within the grievance. *See AFGE, Local 1617*, 51 FLRA 1645, 1647 (1996). In addition, an arbitrator is granted broad discretion to fashion a remedy that the arbitrator considers to be appropriate. *See U.S. DOD Dependents Schs.*, 49 FLRA 658, 663 (1994). In this connection, although an arbitrator may not award relief to non-grievants, the mere fact that an arbitrator's remedy affects non-grievants does not demonstrate that the arbitrator exceeded his or her authority. *Compare SSA, Raleigh, N.C.*, 53 FLRA 43, 44-45 (1997) (arbitrator exceeded authority by awarding remedy to non-grievants), and *U.S. Dep't of the Air Force, Okla. City Air Logistics Ctr., Tinker Air Force Base, Okla.*, 42 FLRA 680, 685-86 (1991) (same), *with NLRB*, 50 FLRA 88, 94 (1995) (arbitrator did not exceed authority by directing rerunning of selection action).

Here, the Arbitrator framed the issues, in pertinent part, as whether the Agency complied with the parties' agreements "in deciding whether to approve or deny 'ROC' award nominations for nine (9) . . . personnel for the performance period[;]" "[i]f not . . . whether the said . . . personnel were treated fairly and equitably by the Agency in its consideration of their ROC awards for said performance period[;]" and "[i]f either of the said questions is to be answered in the negative, then the final issue herein is *the scope of the appropriate remedy*." Award at 2 (emphasis added). The Arbitrator found that the Agency violated the parties' agreements in its awards-selection process, and as an appropriate remedy, he directed that the awards be vacated and the awards process be rerun in accordance with the agreements. These findings were directly responsive to the issues framed by the Arbitrator. Although the Arbitrator's remedy has some effect on non-grievants, in that it sets aside their ROCs (at least until the process is rerun), that fact alone does not demonstrate that the Arbitrator exceeded his authority. *See NLRB*, 50 FLRA at 94. Accordingly, we deny the exceeded authority exception.

D. The Arbitrator was not *functus officio*.

Pursuant to the doctrine of *functus officio*, once an arbitrator has accomplished the resolution of the matter submitted, the arbitrator is without further authority. *See U.S. Dep't of the Army, Corpus Christi Army Depot, Corpus Christi, Tex.*, 58 FLRA 77, 80 (2002) (citation omitted) (then-Member Pope dissenting on other grounds); *AFGE, Local 2172*, 57 FLRA 625, 627 (2001). However, an arbitrator may retain jurisdiction for the purpose of overseeing the implementation of remedies, even absent a joint request of the parties. *E.g., U.S. Dep't of the Navy, Naval Surface Warfare Ctr., Indian Head Div., Indian Head, Md.*, 56 FLRA 848, 852 (2000).

The Arbitrator directed the Deciding Official to personally evaluate award nominations and explain his reasons for approving or disapproving each nomination. *See* Award at 19-20. The Arbitrator then "expressly reserve[d] . . . jurisdiction to consider any complaint as to the decision of the Deciding Official" in this regard. *Id.* at 20. Thus, the Arbitrator retained jurisdiction for the purpose of overseeing the implementation of his chosen remedies. Consistent with the foregoing principles, the Arbitrator was permitted to do so, and the Agency's exception does not demonstrate that the award is deficient in this regard. Accordingly, we deny the exception.

VI. Decision

The Agency's exceptions are dismissed in part and denied in part.

Member Beck, Dissenting In Part:

I agree with my colleagues' conclusions that the Agency's management-rights exception regarding the Arbitrator's interpretation of the MOU should be dismissed and that the award properly draws its essence from the agreements. I disagree, however, with their determination that the Arbitrator did not exceed his authority when he vacated all of the ROC awards for the year at issue.

To be sure, arbitrators are granted broad discretion in the fashioning of appropriate remedies. However, despite the deference that we accord to arbitrators in this regard, the Authority has adhered to the fundamental principle that arbitrators must confine their awards and remedies to those issues presented for resolution. *See, e.g., Veterans Admin.*, 24 FLRA 447, 450 (1986) and cases cited therein. An arbitrator's authority to fashion a remedy does not extend to issues that are not submitted to arbitration. *U.S. Dep't of the Navy, Naval Sea Logistics Ctr., Detachment Atl., Indian Head, Md.,* 57 FLRA 687, 688 (2002).

As the Majority acknowledges, the Arbitrator clearly specified that the issues before him were: (1) whether the Agency complied with the parties' agreements in approving or denying "award nominations for *nine (9)* Louisville office ODAR personnel" and (2) whether "*said ODAR personnel*" were treated "fairly and equitably . . . ." Award at 2 (emphasis added). On its face, the issue was directed only at the Agency's actions with respect to nine employees at the Louisville ODAR. Thus, the award nominations of *other* personnel at the Louisville ODAR were not before the Arbitrator. The Arbitrator's remedy, however, orders that *all* ROC awards for the Louisville ODAR for the year in question be vacated and reconsidered. *See id.* at 19-20. By vacating the awards for the entire Louisville ODAR, the Arbitrator exceeded his authority because he failed to confine his decision and any possible remedy to the issues as he unambiguously stated them. *See SSA, Raleigh, N.C.*, 53 FLRA 43, 44-45 (1997) (arbitrator exceeded his authority by awarding administrative leave to all bargaining unit employees rather than only to the twelve employees named in the grievance); *U.S. Dep't of the Air Force, Okla. City Air Logistics Ctr., Tinker Air Force Base, Okla.*, 42 FLRA 680, 685-86 (1991) (arbitrator exceeded his authority by ordering agency to conduct classification audits of all positions in certain wage grades where issue concerned only the grievant and did not refer to any other employee).

I do not mean to suggest that an arbitrator can never order relief that affects individuals who are not specifically identified in a grievance. Indeed, one can imagine an issue that might have warranted the remedy directed by the Arbitrator here. For example, the issue presented might have been: "Whether the Agency complied with the parties' agreements in approving or denying the award nominations for the Louisville ODAR personnel and, if so, what shall be the remedy?" However, the issue presented here was explicitly rather more limited.

Accordingly, I would find that the Arbitrator exceeded his authority by vacating ROC awards that were placed outside of his jurisdiction by the plain language of the issue presented.*

* Because I would vacate the portion of the award concerning this remedy, I would find it unnecessary to address whether the remedy is contrary to § 7106 of the Statute.

65 FLRA No. 162

UNITED STATES
DEPARTMENT OF HOMELAND SECURITY
U.S. IMMIGRATION AND CUSTOMS
ENFORCEMENT
(Agency)

and

AMERICAN FEDERATION
OF GOVERNMENT EMPLOYEES
LOCAL 1917
(Union)

0-AR-4290

DECISION

April 28, 2011

Before the Authority: Carol Waller Pope, Chairman, and Thomas M. Beck and Ernest DuBester, Members

I. Statement of the Case

This matter is before the Authority on exceptions to an award of Arbitrator Martin Ellenberg filed by the Agency under § 7122 of the Federal Service Labor-Management Relations Statute (the Statute) and part 2425 of the Authority's Regulations. The Union filed an opposition to the Agency's exceptions.

The Arbitrator sustained a grievance alleging that the Agency violated the parties' agreement when it issued a memorandum regarding fugitive cases worked by its Fugitive Operations (FUGOPS) teams (Memorandum). For the reasons that follow, we deny the Agency's exceptions.

II. Background and Arbitrator's Award

The Agency issued the Memorandum to all of its Field Office Directors. The Memorandum stated, in relevant part: "Effective immediately, fugitive cases worked by the [FUGOPS] teams will be prioritized by threats posed by the fugitive alien. This memorandum also establishes a new target goal of 1,000 fugitive apprehensions/cases closed per FUGOPS team." Award at 2.

Subsequently, the Union presented a grievance alleging that requiring FUGOPS teams "'to apprehend/close 1,000 targeted cases per year' is a 'significant change'" that affects deportation officers and support personnel and that, pursuant to Article 9(A) of the parties' agreement, the Agency "is contractually bound to notify the [U]nion of any significant changes that may affect the bargaining unit." *Id.* (quoting grievance). The grievance also stated that the Union had not been provided an opportunity to discuss with the Agency whether the "goals are realistic and attainable." *Id.* (internal quotation marks omitted).

The grievance was denied. The matter was unresolved and submitted to arbitration. The parties stipulated to the following issue: "Did the Agency violate Article 9(A) of [the parties' agreement] when it issued [the] Memorandum . . . ? If so, what shall be the remedy?"[*] *Id.* at 3.

The Arbitrator found that the Agency violated Article 9 of the parties' agreement when it issued the Memorandum "prior to engaging the Union in pre-decisional discussion." *Id.* at 11. In making this determination, the Arbitrator rejected the Agency's argument that, because the policy introduced in the Memorandum did not change the working conditions of unit employees, it was not required to provide notice to the Union pursuant to Article 9. *Id.* at 9 (noting that the Agency argued that, to determine whether a violation of Article 9(A) occurred, "there must first be a finding that the [Agency] changed unit employees' conditions of employment"). According to the Arbitrator, the issue to be decided was not "whether there ha[d] been a change in working conditions or whether an employee was, or may be in the future, inappropriately disciplined," but, rather, whether the Agency "violated Article 9 *when it issued* the Memorandum." *Id.* at 9-10 (emphasis in original).

The Arbitrator found that the "intent" of Article 9 is to avoid grievances and arbitration. *Id.* at 10. According to the Arbitrator, the language of the provision "does not suggest that the Union should be required to grieve or seek arbitration in order to have a new policy, which *may* impact on working conditions, explained or discussed prior to its publication." *Id.* (emphasis in original). The Arbitrator found that the Agency cannot "make a unilateral decision" that a "new policy does not impact" employees' working conditions "and then

[*] The relevant text of Article 9 is set forth in the appendix to this decision.

refuse to respond to the Union's questions concerning the policy." *Id.* The Arbitrator found that such conduct leaves the Union with "no course of action other than through the grievance procedure" – precisely "what Article 9 was intended to avoid." *Id.*

The Arbitrator further found that Article 9(B), "clearly defines the procedure to be followed" by the parties. *Id.* According to the Arbitrator, that provision provides that, "[w]ithin twenty-two (22) work days after being served with the notice of the proposed change, the [Union] . . . may request additional information necessary to clarify or determine the impact of the proposed change." *Id.* Finally, the Arbitrator noted that "Article 9 does not hamper the ability of the Agency to issue new policies" and that the Agency "is not required to secure the Union's agreement" to do so. *Id.*

The Arbitrator found that the Agency violated the "procedure clearly defined in Article 9 when it did not advise or permit the Union to 'engage in pre-decisional involvement prior to the [A]gency's formal presentation.'" *Id.* (quoting Article 9(A)); *see also id.* at 11 (finding that Agency violated Article 9(A) when it issued the Memorandum prior to engaging the Union in pre-decisional discussion). As a remedy, the Arbitrator directed the Agency to "promptly advise the Union in writing . . . of the explanation for the change in policy in accordance with the provisions of Article 9(A), thereby leaving the [U]nion to determine whether it wishes to pursue the procedures spelled out in Article 9(B)." *Id.* The Arbitrator retained jurisdiction to resolve any dispute concerning implementation of the award. *Id.*

III. Positions of the Parties

A. Agency's Exceptions

The Agency contends that the award does not draw its essence from the parties' agreement. Exceptions at 1-4. The Agency asserts that, contrary to the Arbitrator's interpretation, the parties' agreement does not require pre-decisional involvement, but, rather, "only encourages" such involvement "when there is a change in working conditions." *Id.* at 3 & 4; *see also id.* at 8 (noting that the parties' agreement "neither requires the Agency to notify the [U]nion, nor engage the Union in pre-decisional involvement, when there is no impact on working conditions"). The Agency contends that its interpretation is supported by the plain language of Article 9, which only "'encourage[s]' the parties to engage in pre-decisional involvement and further defines [the parties'] obligations when pre-decisional involvement is not used." *Id.* at 3 (quoting Article 9(A)).

The Agency also asserts that, because it is "not required to advise or permit the Union to engage in pre-decisional involvement[,]" the award is based on a nonfact. *Id.* at 4. According to the Agency, "[i]t is a fact that Article 9(A) defines the Agency's right to forego pre-decisional involvement;" accordingly the award "cannot state there is a violation of Article 9(A) when pre-decisional involvement is not used . . . ." *Id.*

Finally, the Agency contends that the award is contrary to law because it "allows the Union to bargain over the substance of a reserved management right when there is no change in working conditions." *Id.* at 9. The Agency asserts that Article 9 "is a procedures and appropriate arrangements (impact and implementation (I&I)) mid-term bargaining article that is intended to follow the rights identified in [§] 7106" of the Statute, and that, under its terms, the Agency is "to notify the [U]nion when there are changes in working conditions that create a duty to bargain over negotiable employment issues." *Id.* at 6-8. According to the Agency, because there was no change to the employees' working conditions, no bargaining obligation exists. *Id.* at 6.

B. Union's Opposition

The Union asserts that the Agency's essence contention is "mere disagreement" with the Arbitrator's interpretation of Article 9(A) and, accordingly, provides no basis for finding the award deficient. Opp'n at 2, 6 & 8. Moreover, according to the Union, the Authority previously has "recognized the Agency's duty to issue advance notice of proposed changes under Article 9(A)." *Id.* at 6 (citing *U.S. Dep't of Homeland Sec., U.S. Customs & Border Prot., JFK Airport Queens, N.Y.*, 62 FLRA 129 (2007)).

The Union also contends that, contrary to the Agency's contention, the plain language of the agreement supports the Arbitrator's interpretation. The Union notes that, although Article 9(A) refers to situations in which pre-decisional involvement is not used, Article 9(A) also provides that, in such situations, the Agency "shall present the changes and explanation of the changes, including the reasons for the changes, it wishes to make to existing rules, regulations, and existing practices to the Union in writing." *Id.* at 6 n.1 (internal quotation marks omitted). According to the Union, whether it is called "pre-decisional involvement," "notice . . . is clearly mandated under Article 9(A)." *Id.* (internal quotation marks omitted).

The Union also disputes the Agency's claim that pre-decisional involvement cannot be ordered pursuant to Article 9 absent a finding that the Agency's decision represents a change in conditions of employment. *Id.* at 7-8. According to the Union, the Arbitrator reasonably concluded "that Article 9(A) is a procedural provision intended to eliminate unnecessary grievances which would seek 'to have a new policy, which *may* impact on working conditions, explained or discussed prior to publication.'" *Id.* at 8 (quoting Award at 10) (emphasis in original).

With respect to the Agency's nonfact claim, the Union contends that the Agency has not identified any fact upon which the Arbitrator relied that is erroneous. *Id.* at 9. According to the Union, without such a fact, the Agency's claim has no merit. *Id.* at 9-10.

Finally, the Union contends that the Agency's assertion that the award is contrary to law is meritless. *Id.* at 10. The Union contends that the award – which merely requires the Agency to provide notice of proposed changes to policies and procedures and does not require the Agency to secure the Union's agreement regarding such changes – does not "infringe[] on any potential management rights to promulgate policies and procedures . . . ." *Id.* According to the Union, an award cannot be contrary to § 7106 "where it simply enforces an agreed[-]upon notice provision[,] but does not limit any management rights." *Id.*

IV. Analysis and Conclusions

A. The award draws its essence from the parties' agreement.

In reviewing an arbitrator's interpretation of a collective bargaining agreement, the Authority applies the deferential standard of review that federal courts use in reviewing arbitration awards in the private sector. *See* 5 U.S.C. § 7122(a)(2); *AFGE, Council 220*, 54 FLRA 156, 159 (1998). Under this standard, the Authority will find that an arbitration award is deficient as failing to draw its essence from the collective bargaining agreement when the appealing party establishes that the award: (1) cannot in any rational way be derived from the agreement; (2) is so unfounded in reason and fact and so unconnected with the wording and purposes of the collective bargaining agreement as to manifest an infidelity to the obligation of the arbitrator; (3) does not represent a plausible interpretation of the agreement; or (4) evidences a manifest disregard of the agreement. *See U.S. Dep't of Labor (OSHA)*, 34 FLRA 573, 575 (1990). The Authority and the courts defer to arbitrators in this context "because it is the arbitrator's construction of the agreement for which the parties have bargained." *Id.* at 576.

The Agency asserts that, contrary to the Arbitrator's interpretation, the parties' agreement does not require pre-decisional involvement, but, rather, "only encourages" such involvement "when there is a change in working conditions." Exceptions at 3.

Article 9 provides, in relevant part, that:

> The [p]arties are encouraged to engage in pre-decisional involvement prior to the agency's formal presentation of proposals for working conditions under this article. If the [p]arties are unable to reach an agreement through pre-decisional involvement or if pre-decisional involvement is not used, the [Agency] shall present the changes and explanation of the changes, including the reason for the change(s) it wishes to make to existing rules, regulations, and, existing practices to the Union in writing. . . . If the Union intends [to] exercise its bargaining rights regarding the proposed change, it must submit a timely bargaining demand including proposals, in accordance with the procedures and time frames specified below.

Award at 3. The Arbitrator found that the Agency violated this provision when it issued the Memorandum prior to engaging the Union in "pre-decisional discussion." *Id.* at 11. As a remedy, he directed the Agency to "promptly advise the Union in writing . . . of the explanation for the change in policy in accordance with the provisions of Article 9(A), thereby leaving the [U]nion to determine whether it wishes to pursue the procedures" provided in Article 9(B). *Id.*

The Agency has not identified any language in the parties' agreement that defines "change" in "working conditions." Further, Article 9(A) requires the Agency to provide the Union with notice of a proposed change even if pre-decisional involvement is not used and affords the Union the opportunity to determine whether to pursue the procedures provided under Article 9(B) with regard to the proposed change. Based on the wording of Article 9, the Agency has failed to demonstrate that the Arbitrator's interpretation and application of Article 9 manifests a disregard of the agreement or is implausible, irrational, or unfounded. Accordingly, we find that the Agency's exception provides no basis for finding that the award fails to draw its essence from the parties' agreement and deny this exception.

B. The award is not based on a nonfact.

To establish that an award is based on a nonfact, the appealing party must show that a central fact underlying the award is clearly erroneous, but for which the arbitrator would have reached a different result. *See U.S. Dep't of the Air Force, Lowry Air Force Base, Denver, Colo.*, 48 FLRA 589, 593 (1993). However, the Authority will not find an award deficient on the basis of an arbitrator's determination on any factual matter that the parties disputed at arbitration. *Id.* at 594 (citing *Nat'l Post Office Mailhandlers v. U.S. Postal Serv.*, 751 F.2d 834, 843 (6th Cir. 1985)). Additionally, an arbitrator's interpretation of a collective bargaining agreement does not constitute a matter that can be challenged as a nonfact. *See AFGE, Nat'l Council of EPA Locals, Council 238,* 59 FLRA 902, 904 (2004) (citing *U.S. Dep't of Veterans Affairs, Ralph H. Johnson Med. Ctr., Charleston, S.C.*, 57 FLRA 489, 493 (2001)).

The Agency's nonfact exception challenges the Arbitrator's interpretation of Article 9(A) of the parties' agreement, specifically his determination that the Agency violated the procedure defined in Article 9(A) when it did not advise or permit the Union to engage in pre-decisional involvement regarding the change to its FUGOPS teams. Because the Agency's exception challenges the Arbitrator's interpretation of the parties' agreement, it does not provide a basis for finding that the award is based on a nonfact. *See id.*

Accordingly, we deny this exception.

C. The award is not contrary to law.

The Agency contends that the award is contrary to law because it "allows the Union to bargain over the substance of a reserved management right when there is no change in working conditions." Exceptions at 9. The Agency asserts that Article 9 "is a procedures and appropriate arrangements [I&I] mid-term bargaining article that is intended to follow the rights identified in [§] 7106" of the Statute, and that, under its terms, the Agency is "to notify the Union when there are changes in working conditions that create a duty to bargain over negotiable employment issues." *Id.* at 6-8.

When an exception involves an award's consistency with law, the Authority reviews any question of law raised by the exception and the award de novo. *See NTEU, Chapter 24*, 50 FLRA 330, 332 (1995) (citing *U.S. Customs Serv. v. FLRA*, 43 F.3d 682, 686-87 (D.C. Cir. 1994)). In applying the standard of de novo review, the Authority assesses whether an arbitrator's legal conclusions are consistent with the applicable standard of law. *See U.S. Dep't of Def., Dep'ts of the Army & the Air Force, Ala. Nat'l Guard, Northport, Ala.*, 55 FLRA 37, 40 (1998). In making that assessment, the Authority defers to the arbitrator's underlying factual findings. *See id.* Also, where a grievance involves a dispute regarding a bargaining obligation as defined by the parties through an agreement, "the issue of whether the parties have complied with the agreement becomes a matter of contract interpretation for the Arbitrator." *Broad. Bd. of Governors, Office of Cuba Broad.*, 64 FLRA 888, 891 (2010) (*Broad. Bd.*) (citing *SSA, Balt., Md.*, 55 FLRA 1063, 1068 (1999) (*SSA*)). In those circumstances, the Authority applies the deferential standard to the arbitrator's contract interpretation. *See SSA*, 55 FLRA at 1069-70.

The instant dispute did not involve a claim that the Agency failed to satisfy its statutory bargaining obligation under the Statute; rather, the issue before the Arbitrator was whether the Agency met its contractual obligation under the notice provision of Article 9. The record shows that the Arbitrator noted the Agency's reference to § 7106 of the Statute and its argument that the "new policy introduced in the Memorandum did not change the working conditions of . . . unit employees . . . ." Award at 9. However, the Arbitrator expressly found that the stipulated issue before him was not "to determine whether there ha[d] been a change in working condition[s]," but, rather, "to determine whether the Agency violated Article 9 *when it issued* the [m]emorandum . . . ?" *Id.* at 9 &10 (emphasis in original). This finding is supported by the record evidence, which shows that the parties stipulated the issue as: "Did the Agency violate Article 9(A) . . . when it issued [the] Memorandum . . . ? If so, what shall be the remedy?" *Id.* at 3. Because the matter here involves a contractual violation, the Authority precedent cited by the Agency -- which involves the duty to bargain under the Statute -- is inapposite and provides no basis for finding the award contrary to law. *See, e.g., Broad. Bd.*, 64 FLRA at 891. *See also U.S. Dep't of Def., Nat'l Guard Bureau, Adjutant Gen., Kan. Nat'l*

Guard, 57 FLRA 934, 936-37 (2002). Moreover, as found above, the Agency failed to demonstrate that the Arbitrator's interpretation of this provision did not draw its essence from the parties' agreement.

Accordingly, we deny this exception.

V. Decision

The Agency's exceptions are denied.

APPENDIX

Article 9 - Impact Bargaining and Mid-Term Bargaining

A. *Notice of Proposed Change.* The Parties recognize that from time-to-time during the life of the Agreement, the need will arise for Management to change existing Service regulations covering personnel policies, practices, and/or working conditions not covered by this Agreement. The Parties are encouraged to engage in pre-decisional involvement prior to the agency's formal presentation of proposals for working conditions under this article. If the Parties are unable to reach an agreement through pre-decisional involvement or if pre-decisional involvement is not used, the Service shall present the changes and explanation of the changes, including the reason for the change(s) it wishes to make to existing rules, regulations, and, existing practices to the Union in writing. The Service recognizes that this obligation exists at the National, Regional and District level depending upon the level at which such changes originate. If the Service proposes a change in working conditions in locals in more than one region, such as for Telephone Centers or Service Centers, it shall serve the requisite notice on the Council at the National level. If the Union intends [to] exercise its bargaining rights regarding the proposed change, it must submit a timely bargaining demand including proposals, in accordance with the procedures and time frames specified below.

B. *Bargaining Procedures.* As applicable, mid-term bargaining shall be conducted in accordance with the following procedures and time frames:

(1) National Level Bargaining

(a) *Notice of Proposed Change.* When bargaining is appropriate at the National Level, Management shall serve its notice of the proposed change upon the President of the Council or his or her designee.

(b) *Demand to Bargain/Information.* Within twenty-two (22) workdays after being served with the notice of the proposed change, the President of the Council, or his or her designee, may request any additional information necessary to clarify or determine the impact of the proposed change. At the same time they shall serve any bargaining demand in writing upon the Chief, Labor and Employee Relations Policy Section, INS Headquarters, or such other person as may have been identified for this purpose in the Service's notice to the Union.

Award at 3; Exceptions, Attach. at 11-12.

65 FLRA No. 163

UNITED STATES
DEPARTMENT OF VETERANS AFFAIRS
CHARLES GEORGE VA MEDICAL CENTER
ASHEVILLE, NORTH CAROLINA
(Agency)

and

AMERICAN FEDERATION
OF GOVERNMENT EMPLOYEES
LOCAL 446
(Union)

0-AR-4550

DECISION

April 29, 2011

Before the Authority: Carol Waller Pope, Chairman, and Thomas M. Beck and Ernest DuBester, Members

I. Statement of the Case

This matter is before the Authority on an exception to an award of Arbitrator Richard H. Potter filed by the Agency under § 7122(a) of the Federal Service Labor-Management Relations Statute (the Statute) and part 2425 of the Authority's Regulations. The Union filed an opposition to the Agency's exception.

The Arbitrator issued an award ordering the Agency to reimburse the Union for dues that the Agency failed to deduct from a new employee's pay. The Arbitrator further ordered the Agency not to recover the amount paid to the Union from the employee.

For the reasons discussed below, we deny the Agency's exception.

II. Background and Arbitrator's Award

A newly-hired Agency employee signed an application to have union dues deducted from her pay. Award at 2. The Agency, however, failed to deduct the dues from the employee's pay and remit them to the Union for the employee's first two pay periods. *Id.* After the first two pay periods, the Agency began withholding the employee's dues, but did not reimburse the Union for the dues it had failed to withhold. The Agency admitted that it was at fault in failing to withhold the dues. *Id.* To resolve the matter, the Union requested that the Agency reimburse the Union for the dues it failed to remit, and not to deduct the dues from the employee's pay. *Id.*

The Agency refused to remit the dues. *Id.* The Agency believed that it did not have the authority to remit the dues without deducting them from the employee's pay. *Id.* at 2-3. The matter was ultimately submitted to arbitration. *Id.* at 2. The Arbitrator framed the issues as follows: "1. Should the Union be reimbursed for dues mistakenly not deducted and remitted? 2. If dues are remitted, should they be deducted from the employee?" *Id.* at 1.

The Arbitrator found that by signing the application for dues deduction, the employee expected the dues to be deducted from her pay, and that by law and the parties' agreement, "the Agency has a fundamental obligation to collect dues from Union members and remit them to the Union." *Id.* at 2-3. The Arbitrator further found that a year had passed and the Agency had still not fulfilled its obligation to remit the dues to the Union for the employee's first two pay periods. *Id.* at 3. The Arbitrator concluded that the Agency "is absolutely obligated to pay the dues the Union is owed" and that the issue concerning deduction from the employee's pay could have been resolved separately after the Agency fulfilled this obligation. *Id.* at 2-3. Therefore, the Arbitrator sustained the Union's grievance and ordered the Agency to reimburse the Union the dues it failed to withhold. The Arbitrator further ordered the Agency not to deduct that amount from the employee's pay. *Id.* at 3.

III. Positions of the Parties

A. Agency's Exception

The Agency claims that the award is contrary to law because it denies the Agency the right to recover the dues from the employee. Exception at 1. The Agency cites Comptroller General case law stating that after an agency reimburses a union for union dues an agency erroneously failed to collect, the agency "'must seek to recover the amount of the dues from the employees or exercise its power to waive collection from the employees under 5 U.S.C. § 5584[.]'" *Id.* at 3 (quoting *Hanley*, B-235386 (1989)).

B. Union's Opposition

The Union contends that the award is not contrary to law because the Agency has the authority to waive collection from the employee. Opp'n at 3-4 (citing *Dep't of Labor*, 60 Comp Gen. 93 (1980); *Hanley,* B-235386). The Union further argues that because the Agency has the authority to waive collection, such a waiver is properly required by the Arbitrator's award and past practice. *Id.* In the latter regard, the Union contends that the Agency has a past practice of waiving collection and reimbursing the Union when the Agency is at fault in failing to deduct and remit dues to the Union. *Id.* at 5. For these reasons, the Union argues, the Agency's exception should be denied. *Id.*

IV. Analysis and Conclusions

When an exception involves an award's consistency with law, the Authority reviews any question raised by the exception and the award de novo. *See NTEU, Chapter 24,* 50 FLRA 330, 332 (1995) (citing *U.S. Customs Serv. v. FLRA*, 43 F.3d 682, 686-87 (D.C. Cir. 1994)). In applying the standard, the Authority assesses whether an arbitrator's legal conclusions are consistent with the applicable standard of law. *See U.S. Dep't of Def., Dep'ts of the Army & the Air Force, Ala. Nat'l Guard, Northport, Ala.* 55 FLRA 37, 40 (1998). In making that assessment, the Authority defers to the arbitrator's underlying factual findings. *See id.*

The Arbitrator ordered the Agency to reimburse the Union for the dues it failed to withhold from the employee's pay. The Arbitrator further prohibited the Agency from recovering that amount from the employee. Award at 3. This amount represented an overpayment to the employee because the Agency failed to correctly deduct union dues from the employee's pay for the first two pay periods.

Claims by an agency against an employee for overpayment of pay and allowances are governed by 5 U.S.C. § 5584. *See U.S. Navy Public Works Ctr.*, 27 FLRA 156, 157-58 (1987) (*Navy Public Works).* Under § 5584(a), an agency may waive such a claim against an employee if: (1) collection "would be against equity and good conscience and not in the best interest of the United States"; (2) there is no indication of fraud, misrepresentation, fault, or lack of good faith on the part of the employee; and (3) the amount of the claim is not more than $1,500. 5 U.S.C. § 5584(a). Arbitrators' awards requiring an agency to waive such a claim against an employee are not contrary to law where the statutory criteria for such a waiver are met. *See Navy Public Works*, 27 FLRA at 157-58 (award not contrary to law where arbitrator ordered agency to waive collection of overpayment to employee due to agency error).

The Agency's exception does not provide a basis for finding the award deficient. The award effectively orders the Agency to waive its claim against the employee for its overpayment of her pay. Although the Agency argues that such an order is contrary to § 5584, the Agency does not address § 5584's waiver criteria. Regarding those criteria, the Agency's claim is well within the $1,500 statutory limit on the Agency's authority to waive the claim. Moreover, we defer to the Arbitrator's uncontested finding that the Agency, not the employee, was at fault. Therefore, because the Agency fails to show that it has no authority to waive its claim as required by the award, we find that the award is not contrary to law and deny the Agency's exception.

V. Decision

The Agency's exception is denied.

65 FLRA No. 164

AMERICAN FEDERATION
OF GOVERNMENT EMPLOYEES
LOCAL 1164
(Union)

and

SOCIAL SECURITY ADMINISTRATION
(Agency)

0-AR-4738

DECISION

April 29, 2011

Before the Authority: Carol Waller Pope, Chairman, and Thomas M. Beck and Ernest DuBester, Members

This matter is before the Authority on exceptions to an award of Arbitrator Elizabeth Bartholet filed by the Union under § 7122(a) of the Federal Service Labor-Management Relations Statute (the Statute) and part 2425 of the Authority's Regulations. The Agency filed an opposition to the Union's exceptions.

Under § 7122(a) of the Statute, an award is deficient if it is contrary to any law, rule, or regulation, or it is deficient on other grounds similar to those applied by federal courts in private sector labor-management relations. Upon careful consideration of the entire record in this case and Authority precedent, the Authority concludes that the award is not deficient on the grounds raised in the exceptions and set forth in § 7122(a). *See Fraternal Order of Police, Pentagon Police Labor Comm.*, 65 FLRA 781, 784-85 (2011) (denying a contrary-to-law exception where excepting party did not cite any law with which the arbitrator's award conflicted); *U.S. Dep't of the Treasury, IRS, Oxon Hill, Md.*, 56 FLRA 292, 299 (2000) (award not deficient where arbitrator bases award on separate and independent and excepting party fails to establish that all of the grounds are deficient);[*] *U.S. Dep't of the Navy, Naval Base, Norfolk, Va.*, 51 FLRA 305, 307-08 (1995) grounds, (award not deficient on ground that arbitrator exceeded his or her authority where excepting party does not establish that arbitrator failed to resolve an issue submitted to arbitration, disregarded specific limitations on his authority, or awarded relief to persons who were not encompassed within the grievance); *AFGE, Local 2921*, 50 FLRA 184, 185-86 (1995) (arbitrator's determination of the procedural arbitrability of a grievance is subject to challenge only on grounds other than those that directly challenge the procedural arbitrability determination).

Accordingly, the Union's exceptions are denied.

[*] Several of the exceptions challenge the Arbitrator's findings that the Agency did not violate the parties' agreement. However, with regard to certain of these challenged findings, the Arbitrator alternatively found that the grievant failed to timely raise her allegations, which provides a separate and independent basis for the award.

This page purposely left blank.

This page purposely left blank.

65 FLRA No. 165

NATIONAL TREASURY
EMPLOYEES UNION
LOCAL 233
(Union)

and

UNITED STATES
DEPARTMENT OF THE TREASURY
INTERNAL REVENUE SERVICE
SMALL BUSINESS/SELF EMPLOYED
OPERATING DIVISION
LAGUNA NIGUEL, CALIFORNIA
(Agency)

0-AR-4497

DECISION

April 29, 2011

Before the Authority: Carol Waller Pope, Chairman, and Thomas M. Beck and Ernest DuBester, Members

I. Statement of the Case

This matter is before the Authority on exceptions to an award of Arbitrator Frank Silver filed by the Union under § 7122(a) of the Federal Service Labor-Management Relations Statute (the Statute) and part 2425 of the Authority's Regulations. The Agency filed an opposition to the Union's exceptions.

In a merits award (the merits award), the Arbitrator found that the Agency's handling of the grievant's hardship reassignment request violated the parties' collective bargaining agreement (CBA). In a remedy award (the remedy award) – the award at issue here – the Arbitrator determined that the grievant was not entitled to backpay for a certain period of time. For the reasons that follow, we deny the Union's exceptions.

II. Background and Arbitrator's Award

In the merits award, the Arbitrator determined that the Agency violated the CBA when it did not consider placing employees who requested hardship transfers, including the grievant, in "not to exceed" (NTE) vacancies.[1] Award at 2. The Arbitrator remanded the matter to the parties to formulate an appropriate remedy, which would address "whether, in view of the [g]rievant's maternity leave, she would have been ready, willing, and able to accept [one of the NTE] positions [that were] announced" during the pendency of her hardship transfer request. *Id.* In this regard, the Arbitrator stated that "it was obviously the Union's burden to demonstrate [the grievant's] availability for work" as a prerequisite for any valid backpay claim. *Id.*

When the parties could not agree on a remedy, the Arbitrator issued the remedy award, in which he addressed the grievant's entitlement to backpay. *Id.* at 2-3. The Arbitrator found that, after the approval of the grievant's hardship transfer request but before her ultimate hardship reassignment in July 2005 (ultimate reassignment), the Agency posted two NTE announcements for positions at the grievant's desired reassignment location, and that the grievant was qualified for those positions. *Id.* at 4. The Arbitrator also found that the Agency cancelled the second of those announcements, so the second "announcement [was] disregarded[.]" *Id.* at 4-5. With regard to the remaining NTE announcement (the October 25 announcement), the Arbitrator determined that it "opened on October 25[, 2004,] and closed on November 8, 2004, [and] two individuals were selected on December 10, [2004,] with an *effective date of December 26*, 2004." *Id.* at 4 (emphasis added). The Arbitrator found that, in her sworn declaration, the grievant stated that she did not move to the location where she wished to be reassigned until December 27, 2004, and he found further that the grievant was scheduled to be on maternity leave until January 17, 2005. *Id.* at 3-4; *see also* Exceptions, Attach. 6 (Decl. of Grievant) at 11-12. Thus, the Arbitrator determined that the grievant was not ready, willing, and able to accept one of the two positions that had been filled under the October 25 announcement. Award at 4-5.

Although the Arbitrator "[p]resum[ed]" that the Agency had discretion to "hold open" a position with a December 26 effective date until the grievant was available for work, the Arbitrator noted that, in a sworn declaration, the Agency employee in charge of the hardship program (the Agency employee) stated

1. Although the award does not define the term "not to exceed vacancies," the *Code of Federal Regulations* states that agencies may fill "short-term position[s]" using "temporary appointment[s]" for a specified period "not to exceed" one year. 5 C.F.R. § 316.401(a)(1), (c)(1).

that he did not know whether management would have held open a position for the grievant. *Id.* at 5; *see also* Exceptions, Attach. 8 (Decl. of Human Resources Specialist). Consequently, the Arbitrator found that "whether [an NTE] position would have been held open [until the grievant was available for work] is entirely speculative on this record[.]" Award at 5. The Arbitrator found further that nothing in the CBA required the Agency to postpone the effective date of a position in order to offer it to the grievant. *Id.*

Because it could "not be concluded that the [g]rievant was ready, willing, and able to accept a position from the October 25 announcement," the Arbitrator found that she was not entitled to backpay for the period of time between the scheduled expiration of her maternity leave and her ultimate reassignment. *Id.* As an "additional reason" for denying backpay, the Arbitrator noted that the grievant chose to move to her desired reassignment location before she secured a job there, thus "mak[ing] herself unavailable to work [in] her old job" at her former location. *Id.* at 6 & n.4. Because he found that the grievant could have continued working in her former job until she secured her ultimate reassignment, the Arbitrator concluded that the grievant's "loss of pay would not have occurred but for the fact that she moved . . . in December and therefore made herself unavailable to return to her" former job. *Id.* at 5-6. For the foregoing reasons, the Arbitrator found that a backpay remedy "is not appropriate." *Id.* at 6.

III. Positions of the Parties

A. Union's Exceptions

The Union argues that the award is contrary to law – specifically, Title VII of the Civil Rights Act of 1964 (Title VII), as amended by the Pregnancy Discrimination Act,[2] 42 U.S.C. § 2000e(k) (§ 2000e(k)) – because the Arbitrator relied on the Agency employee's declaration stating that he did not know whether management would have held open a position for the grievant until her leave ended.[3] *See* Exceptions at 5. In this regard, the Union asserts that the Agency employee's declaration constitutes "direct evidence of discrimination against the [g]rievant." *Id.* at 10. The Union contends that "for all intent[s] and purposes, the Arbitrator[] relied on the Agency [employee's declaration] as justification for the Agency's failure to select the [g]rievant" for an NTE vacancy under the October 25 announcement, and, thus, the award permits the Agency's "direct discrimination against the [g]rievant due to her pregnancy-related condition." *Id.* at 11.

The Union argues further that the award fails to draw its essence from the CBA. The Union contends that the Arbitrator's decision to deny the grievant backpay because she moved from her former location misconstrues the CBA as imposing an "affirmative duty" on employees not to relocate due to hardship, where that relocation would "create a liability for the Agency if [the Agency] later violated" the CBA's provisions regarding hardship transfer requests. *Id.* at 12. The Union contends that imposing such an obligation on employees renders their contractual right to request hardship transfers "meaningless[,]" *id.*, and allows the Agency to "ignore" the CBA article regarding hardship transfers because "there will not be any substantive consequence for violating it[,]" *id.* at 14. *See also id.* at 15-18.

2. The Pregnancy Discrimination Act, Pub. L. No. 95-555, 92 Stat. 2076 (1978), amended Title VII by adding subsection (k) to the "Definitions" section. Subsection (k) provides, in pertinent part:

> [Unlawful employment practices] "because of sex" or "on the basis of sex" include, but are not limited to, because of or on the basis of pregnancy, childbirth, or related medical conditions; and women affected by pregnancy, childbirth, or related medical conditions shall be treated the same for all employment-related purposes, including receipt of benefits under fringe benefit programs, as other persons not so affected but similar in their ability or inability to work . . . .

42 U.S.C. § 2000e(k).

3. The Agency employee's declaration states, in pertinent part:

> I was . . . in charge of the [Agency's] hardship program [when the grievant's transfer request was pending]. . . . I understand that at the time of the effective date of the [NTE] position[s filled pursuant to the October 25 announcement, the grievant] was on extended leave[,] and [I] don't know if management would have held the position for her or chose to [bypass her] due to unavailability.

Exceptions, Attach. 8 (Decl. of Human Resources Specialist).

B. Agency's Opposition

The Agency contends that the Arbitrator correctly determined that the positions filled pursuant to the October 25 announcement had "an effective date prior to the [g]rievant's scheduled return to duty." Opp'n at 7 (citation omitted). With regard to the Union's pregnancy discrimination claim, the Agency asserts that Union failed to present such a claim to the Arbitrator and that the Agency employee's declaration, which the Union cites as evidence of discrimination, proves nothing more than the Agency employee's "lack of knowledge" as to whether a position would have been held open for the grievant until she was available to work. *Id.* at 11-12. In response to the Union's essence exception, the Agency argues that the law prohibited the Arbitrator from awarding backpay to the grievant for time when she was unavailable to work, and nothing in the CBA could authorize a backpay remedy "in violation of the law." *Id.* at 14-15.

IV. Preliminary Matter

The Agency contends that the Union did not raise its pregnancy discrimination argument before the Arbitrator. Under § 2429.5 of the Authority's Regulations (§ 2429.5), the Authority generally will not consider evidence or arguments that could have been, but were not, presented to the arbitrator.[4] *See Soc. Sec. Admin.*, 57 FLRA 530, 534 (2001) (*SSA*) (citing *NAGE, Local R4-45*, 53 FLRA 517, 520 (1997); *U.S. Agency for Int'l Dev.*, 53 FLRA 187, 187 n.2 (1997)). The parties each filed two briefs with the Arbitrator concerning the appropriate remedy for the Agency's violation of the CBA. *See* Exceptions, Attachs. 12 (First Agency Brief), 13 (First Union Brief), 14 (Second Agency Brief), & 15 (Second Union Brief).[5] In the First Union Brief, the Union cited § 2000e(k) to support its contention that the Arbitrator "should note that [the grievant's] pregnancy or subsequent maternity leave would not have barred her selection to [a] position" under the October 25 announcement. Exceptions, Attach. 13 at 6 (citation omitted). The Second Agency Brief – which followed the First Union Brief – included the Agency employee's declaration, *see id.*, Attach. 14 at 12, which the exceptions characterize as "direct evidence of discrimination[,]" Exceptions at 10. In the Second Union Brief – which followed the Second Agency Brief – the Union asserted that the Arbitrator should disregard the Agency employee's declaration because, in "the Union's view[,] . . . it would have been inappropriate for management not to select [the grievant] because she was on maternity leave." *Id.*, Attach. 15 at 2. To support this assertion, the Union cited its prior argument in the First Union Brief regarding § 2000e(k). *See id.* Therefore, we find that the Union presented to the Arbitrator its pregnancy discrimination argument concerning the Agency employee's declaration, and, consequently, we resolve the exception rather than dismissing it under § 2429.5.

V. Analysis and Conclusions

A. The remedy award is not contrary to law.

The Union contends that the award is contrary to § 2000e(k) because, "for all intent[s] and purposes, the Arbitrator[] relied on the Agency [employee's declaration] as justification for the Agency's failure to select the [g]rievant[.]" Exceptions at 11. When an exception involves an award's consistency with law, the Authority reviews any question of law raised by the exception and the award de novo. *See NTEU, Chapter 24*, 50 FLRA 330, 332 (1995) (citing *U.S. Customs Serv. v. FLRA*, 43 F.3d 682, 686-87 (D.C. Cir. 1994)). In applying the standard of de novo review, the Authority assesses whether an arbitrator's legal conclusions are consistent with the applicable standard of law. *See U.S. Dep't of Def., Dep'ts of the Army & the Air Force, Ala. Nat'l Guard, Northport, Ala.*, 55 FLRA 37, 40 (1998). In making that assessment, the Authority defers to the arbitrator's underlying factual findings. *See id.*

Section 2000e(k) requires that "women affected by pregnancy, childbirth, or related medical conditions . . . be treated the same for all employment-related purposes . . . as other persons not

4. The Authority's Regulations concerning the review of arbitration awards, as well as certain related procedural Regulations – including § 2429.5 – were revised effective October 1, 2010. *See* 75 Fed. Reg. 42,283 (2010). As the exceptions and opposition in this case were filed before the effective date of the revised Regulations, we apply the prior version of the Regulations.

5. The parties designated these briefs: (1) "Agency['s] Brief Regarding Remedies," Exceptions, Attach. 12; (2) "[Union's] Post Hearing Statement and Affidavits Regarding Remedies," *id.*, Attach. 13; (3) "Agency's Reply to Union's Statement Regarding Remedies. . .," *id.*, Attach. 14; and (4) "[Union's] Post Hearing Response to the Agency's Second Brief Regarding Remedies," *id.*, Attach. 15. To simplify the discussion, we refer to them, respectively, as "First Agency Brief," "First Union Brief," "Second Agency Brief," and "Second Union Brief."

so affected but *similar in their ability . . . to work*[.]" (Emphasis added.) Thus, as relevant here, § 2000e(k) requires employers to ensure the equal treatment of persons who are similarly *able to work*, regardless of pregnancy, childbirth, or related medical conditions. The Arbitrator made a factual finding that the grievant was *not* ready, willing, and *able to work* in time to accept one of the positions filled pursuant to the October 25 announcement, with an effective date of December 26, because: (1) the grievant did not move to the location where the positions were being filled until December 27; and (2) the grievant was scheduled to be on maternity leave until January 17, 2005. *See* Award at 3-4. Although the Union asserts that the Arbitrator was "simply wrong" to conclude that the grievant was unavailable to work until the end of her scheduled maternity leave, *see* Exceptions at 16 n.7, we note that: (1) the Union did not file a nonfact exception to this finding; and (2) the grievant's own declaration states that she did not move to her desired reassignment location until December 27, *see id.*, Attach. 6 (Decl. of Grievant) at 11-12. With regard to the latter, the grievant's declaration also specifically states that she was "ready, willing[,] and able to work" at her desired reassignment location as of December 27, *see id.* at 12, which was later than the effective date of the positions filled under the October 25 announcement.

The Arbitrator's factual finding regarding the grievant's inability to work supports his conclusion that the grievant was not entitled to backpay because she was not available to work on December 26, 2004, as required by the effective date of the positions filled under the October 25 announcement. *See* Award at 4-5. Although the Arbitrator referenced the statements in the Agency employee's declaration, he did so only in connection with his finding that "[w]hether a position would have been *held open* [until the grievant was available to work was] entirely speculative[,]" and that, consequently, he had no basis to conclude that the Agency was obligated to hold open such a position. *Id.* at 5 (emphasis added). As the Union has not established that the Agency would have accorded different treatment to another employee who, like the grievant, was unavailable to work, we deny the exception contending that the award is contrary to § 2000e(k).

B. It is unnecessary to resolve the Union's essence exception.

After concluding that the grievant was not entitled to backpay because she was unable to work in time to accept one of the positions filled under the October 25 announcement, the Arbitrator noted an "additional reason" for denying backpay to the grievant. *Id.* at 5-6. In this regard, the Arbitrator determined that the grievant could have continued working at her former location until her ultimate reassignment, and "[h]er loss of pay would not have occurred but for the fact that she moved . . . in December and therefore made herself unavailable to return to her" former job. *Id.* The Union argues that this determination fails to draw its essence from the CBA. *See* Exceptions at 14-18.

When an arbitrator has based an award on separate and independent grounds, an appealing party must establish that all of the grounds are deficient in order to have the award found deficient. *See, e.g.*, *U.S. Dep't of the Treasury, Internal Revenue Serv., Oxon Hill, Md.*, 56 FLRA 292, 299 (2000) (*Oxon Hill*). In such circumstances, if an excepting party does not demonstrate that the award is deficient on one of the grounds relied on by the arbitrator, then it is unnecessary for the Authority to resolve exceptions to the other ground. *See id.*

We have denied the Union's contrary-to-law exception to the Arbitrator's finding that the grievant was not ready, willing, and able to work in time to accept one of the positions filled under the October 25 announcement. *See supra* Part V.A. That finding regarding the grievant's ability to work constitutes a separate and independent basis for the Arbitrator's decision to deny the grievant's request for backpay. Accordingly, we find it unnecessary to resolve the essence exception to the Arbitrator's "additional" ground for denying backpay. *See Oxon Hill*, 56 FLRA at 299.

VI. Decision

The Union's exceptions are denied.

65 FLRA No. 166

UNITED STATES
DEPARTMENT OF TRANSPORTATION
FEDERAL AVIATION ADMINISTRATION
(Agency)

and

NATIONAL AIR TRAFFIC
CONTROLLERS ASSOCIATION
AIRCRAFT CERTIFICATION SERVICE
(Union)

0-AR-4608

DECISION

April 29, 2011

Before the Authority: Carol Waller Pope, Chairman, and Thomas M. Beck and Ernest DuBester, Members

I. Statement of the Case

This matter is before the Authority on exceptions to an award of Arbitrator Parker Denaco filed by the Agency under § 7122(a) of the Federal Service Labor-Management Relations Statute (the Statute) and part 2425 of the Authority's Regulations. The Union filed an opposition to the Agency's exceptions.

The Arbitrator issued an award finding that the grievant's one-day suspension was not for such cause as to promote the efficiency of the service. For the reasons discussed below, we deny the Agency's exceptions.

II. Background and Arbitrator's Award

The Agency suspended the grievant for one day for an alleged absence without leave in violation of her leave restriction letter. Award at 6, 8. The Union filed a grievance. When the parties were unable to resolve the grievance, they submitted it to arbitration.

The Union requested an expedited hearing pursuant to the parties' collective bargaining agreement (agreement). The agreement's expedited arbitration procedures require an arbitrator to issue a decision within twenty-one days after the arbitration hearing. *Id.* at 4. At the hearing, the parties stipulated the issue as: "Whether the [one]-day suspension imposed on the [g]rievant, . . . for unauthorized absence . . . was for such cause as to promote the efficiency of the service? If not, what shall the remedy be?" *Id.* at 10.

The arbitration hearing was held on November 10, 2009. *See id.* at 1-2. Upon completion of the hearing, the Arbitrator agreed to accept post-hearing briefs. *Id.* at 2; *see also* Exceptions at 5. The Union maintained that the parties' long-standing past practice in expedited arbitrations was to waive the twenty-one day deadline for the arbitrator's award and to mutually agree to a briefing schedule once the parties received the transcript. Opp'n at 3. The Agency, however, refused to deviate from the agreement's timeline and insisted that the award be issued within twenty-one days from the hearing. *Id.* at 4; *see also* Exceptions at 4-5; *id.*, Attach. 6. The Arbitrator agreed, and informed the parties that briefs would be due at least two weeks before the award's due date. Exceptions at 6.

The Union subsequently asked the Arbitrator for an extension of time until December 4 to file its brief, in order to obtain the transcript and attend to other pending matters. *Id.* at 7. The Arbitrator gave the parties a deadline of November 24 to submit their briefs. *Id.* at 7-8. On November 20, the Union submitted its brief to the Arbitrator by email and overnight mail. Exceptions, Ex. 6. On November 23, the Agency submitted its brief to the Arbitrator by overnight mail and to the Union by regular mail. Exceptions at 8.

The Arbitrator received the Union's brief on November 21 and the Agency's brief on November 24, but did not review either until November 24. Award at 2. On November 28, the Arbitrator issued his award. *Id.* at 26. He found that the grievant's one-day suspension did not promote the efficiency of the service and directed the Agency to rescind the suspension and expunge it from all of the Agency's systems of records. *Id.*

III. Positions of the Parties

A. Agency's Exceptions

The Agency contends that the award is contrary to law because the Arbitrator considered the Union's brief even though the brief was not served on the Agency Exceptions at 10-12. In support, the Agency claims that the Federal Mediation and Conciliation Service's (FMCS's) regulations, specifically 29 C.F.R. § 1404.4(b), mandate that the Arbitrator follow the Code of Professional Responsibility for Arbitrators of Labor-Management Disputes (Code of

Professional Responsibility).* The Agency argues that the Code of Professional Responsibility prohibited the Arbitrator from considering the Union's brief because the Agency was not served with a copy. *Id.* at 11-12.

The Agency also contends that the Arbitrator denied it a fair hearing by depriving the Agency of an opportunity to rebut any factual errors or new evidence that the Union's brief may have contained. *Id.* at 13-16.

B. Union's Opposition

The Union argues that the Arbitrator properly considered both briefs. Opp'n at 6. The Union also contends that the parties never agreed to an exchange of briefs and, "if the Agency did not receive a copy of the Union's brief, it was a mere oversight" on the Union's part. *Id.* at 7. In addition, the Union points out that the Agency could have contacted the Union to obtain a copy of the Union's brief, which the Agency has not done "to date." *Id.* at 5; *see also id.* at 7. The Union also asserts that the parties do not usually file rebuttal briefs and it is unlikely that the Agency would have requested leave to submit one here due to the twenty-one day timeline. *Id.* at 9. Finally, the Union argues, the Agency has failed to show that it was prejudiced by not receiving the Union's brief. Mere speculation that there may be prejudice, the Union argues, does not support a claim that the Arbitrator denied the Agency a fair hearing. *Id.* at 9-10.

IV. Analysis and Conclusions

A. The award is not contrary to law.

The Agency claims that the award is contrary to law because the Arbitrator considered the Union's brief in violation of 29 C.F.R. § 1404.4 and the Code of Professional Responsibility. When an exception challenges an award's consistency with law, the Authority reviews the question of law raised by the exception and the award de novo. *See NTEU, Chapter 24*, 50 FLRA 330, 332 (1995) (citing *U.S. Customs Serv. v. FLRA*, 43 F.3d 682, 686-87 (D.C. Cir. 1994)). In applying this standard, the Authority assesses whether the arbitrator's legal conclusions are consistent with the applicable standard of law. *See NFFE, Local 1437,* 53 FLRA 1703, 1710 (1998). In making that assessment, the Authority defers to the arbitrator's underlying factual findings. *See id.*

The FMCS has developed a set of standards for professional behavior of arbitrators. Arbitrators must meet the FMCS's standards to be listed on its roster of arbitrators. *See* 29 C.F.R. §1404.4. If an arbitrator on the roster fails to meet the standards, then a party may file a complaint with the FMCS and the FMCS may remove that arbitrator from the roster for violation of FMCS regulations or the Code of Professional Responsibility. *See* 29 C.F.R §§ 1404.4(f) and 1404.5(a) & (d).

The FMCS, however, has no authority to regulate arbitrators' actions. *See* 29 C.F.R. § 1404.4(d). Its regulations only set standards for arbitrators who want to be included on the roster. As relevant here, the only consequence for an arbitrator of not following the FMCS's regulations or the Code of Professional Responsibility is possible removal from the FMCS roster. Therefore, the cited FMCS regulations do not constitute a general restriction on arbitrators' authority and discretion with respect to arbitration proceedings. Consequently, that the Arbitrator may not have adhered to § 1404.4 and the Code of Professional Responsibility is not a basis for finding that the award is contrary to law. *Cf. Veterans Admin., Leavenworth, Kan.*, 34 FLRA 898, 902 (1990) (holding that Code of Professional Responsibility "is a privately developed set of standards for professional behavior and . . . is not a law, rule, or regulation . . . on which exceptions to an arbitration award can be predicated" (citations omitted)). Accordingly, we deny the Agency's contrary to law exception.

B. The Agency was not denied a fair hearing.

The Agency argues that the Arbitrator deprived the Agency of a fair hearing and prejudiced its rights by considering the Union's brief even though the Agency was not served with a copy. Exceptions at 13-16. The Authority will find an award deficient on the ground that the arbitrator failed to provide a fair hearing when it determines that an arbitrator's refusal to hear or consider pertinent and material evidence, or other actions in conducting the proceeding, prejudiced a party and affected the fairness of the proceeding as a whole. *See AFGE, Local 1668*, 50 FLRA 124, 126 (1995). An arbitrator, however, has considerable latitude in the conduct of the hearing. *See U.S. Dep't of Veterans Affairs Med. Ctr., Northport, NY,* 49 FLRA 630, 641-42 (1994) (arbitrator did not deny fair hearing by failing to afford agency an opportunity to respond to union's brief that was not served on agency); *U.S Dep't of Housing & Urban Dev.*, 42 FLRA 813, 819 (1991) (arbitrator's issuance of decision before union filed brief did not deny union fair hearing).

* 29 C.F.R.§ 1404.4 is set forth in the appendix to this decision.

The only ground on which the Agency claims that it was denied a fair hearing is that it was "improperly deprived of its right to review, respond, or . . . clarify any factual errors or new evidence that may have been contained" in the Union's brief. Exceptions at 16. The Agency, however, does not provide any evidence that it had such a right to file a rebuttal brief in this case. Moreover, it is undisputed that the Agency has not attempted to obtain a copy of the Union's brief to ascertain whether there would have been any need, in its view, to file such a rebuttal. *See id.*; Opp'n at 5, 7.

In these circumstances, the Agency has not shown that the Union's failure to serve a copy of its brief on the Agency prejudiced the Agency's ability to fully and completely present its position before the Arbitrator. The Agency's belief that it may have been prejudiced, without more, does not demonstrate that the Arbitrator denied the Agency a fair hearing by considering the Union's brief. Accordingly, we deny the Agency's fair hearing exception.

V. Decision

The Agency's exceptions are denied.

APPENDIX

29 C.F.R. § 1404.4

(a) The Roster. FMCS shall maintain a Roster of labor arbitrators consisting of persons who meet the criteria for listing contained in § 1404.5 and who remain in good standing.

(b) Adherence of Standards and Requirements. Persons listed on the Roster shall comply with FMCS rules and regulations pertaining to arbitration and with such guidelines and procedures as may be issued by the OAS pursuant to Subpart C of this Part. Arbitrators shall conform to the ethical standards and procedures set forth in the Code of Professional Responsibility for Arbitrators of Labor Management Disputes, as approved by the National Academy of Arbitrators, Federal Mediation and Conciliation Service, and the American Arbitration Association (Code).

(c) Status of arbitrators. Persons who are listed on the Roster and are selected or appointed to hear arbitration matters or to serve as factfinders do not become employees of the Federal Government by virtue of their selection or appointment. Following selection or appointment, the arbitrator's relationship is solely with the parties to the dispute, except that arbitrators are subject to certain reporting requirements and to standards of conduct as set forth in this part.

(d) Role of FMCS. FMCS has no power to:

(1) Compel parties to appear before an arbitrator;

(2) Enforce an agreement to arbitrate;

(3) Compel parties to arbitrate any issue;

(4) Influence, alter, or set aside decisions of arbitrators on the Roster;

(5) Compel, deny, or modify payment of compensation to an arbitrator.

(e) Nominations and Panels. On request of the parties to an agreement to arbitrate or engage in fact-finding, or where arbitration or fact-finding may be provided for by statute, OAS will provide names or panels of names for a fee. Procedures for obtaining these services are outlined in subpart C of this part. Neither the submission of a nomination or panel nor the appointment of an arbitrator constitutes a determination by FMCS that an agreement to arbitrate or enter fact-finding proceedings exists; nor does such action constitute a ruling that the matter in controversy is arbitrable under any agreement.

(f) Rights of persons listed on the Roster. No person shall have any right to be listed or to remain listed on the Roster. FMCS retains its authority and responsibility to assure that the needs of the parties using its services are served. To accomplish this purpose, FMCS may establish procedures for the preparation of panels or the appointment of arbitrators or factfinders which include consideration of such factors as background and experience, availability, acceptability, geographical location, and the expressed preferences of the parties. FMCS may also establish procedures for the removal from the Roster of those arbitrators who fail to adhere to provisions contained in this part.

65 FLRA No. 167

UNITED STATES
DEPARTMENT OF VETERANS AFFAIRS
MEDICAL CENTER
KANSAS CITY, MISSOURI
(Agency)

and

AMERICAN FEDERATION
OF GOVERNMENT EMPLOYEES
LOCAL 910
(Union)

0-AR-4171

DECISION

May 5, 2011

Before the Authority: Carol Waller Pope, Chairman, and Thomas M. Beck and Ernest DuBester, Members

I. Statement of the Case

This matter is before the Authority on exceptions to an award of Arbitrator Anthony Redwood filed by the Agency under § 7122(a) of the Federal Service Labor-Management Relations Statute (the Statute) and part 2425 of the Authority's Regulations. The Union filed an opposition to the Agency's exceptions. Both parties filed supplemental submissions.

The Union filed a grievance alleging that the Agency violated the parties' collective bargaining agreement (CBA) when it reassigned the grievant from his position as head of the Nephrology Section at the Kansas City Veterans Administration Medical Center (KC VAMC). The Arbitrator sustained the grievance. For the reasons set forth below, we set aside a portion of the award and deny the Agency's remaining exceptions.

II. Background and Arbitrator's Award

This case arises out of a grievance resulting from the grievant's reassignment from his position as head of the Nephrology Section at KC VAMC to that of a staff Nephrologist. According to the Chief of the Medical Subspecialties (Chief), the grievant's reassignment to a staff Nephrologist position was warranted due to the grievant's frequent public contradictions of the Chief, his public posting of notes about their discussions, his infrequent rounds on the dialysis unit, and the Chief's lack of confidence in the grievant's leadership abilities. Award at 5. Prior to reassigning the grievant, the Chief asked that a Board of Investigation (the Board) be convened to investigate what he believed to be research improprieties on the part of the grievant. Subsequent to the reassignment, the Board exonerated the grievant, finding that the Chief's allegations were unsubstantiated. *Id.*

The Arbitrator framed the issues to be decided at arbitration as follows:

> 1. As the grievant is a Title 38 employee, and as it is alleged that the grievance relates in part to professional conduct and to compensation, is the grievance arbitrable?
>
> 2. If yes, was the management right to reassign the grievant by removing him from the position of section head of [N]ephrology exercised in a manner consistent with the [CBA]? If not, what is the remedy?

Id. at 6.

The Arbitrator made two determinations on the arbitrability issue. First, the Arbitrator rejected the Agency's claim that, because the grievance dealt with professional conduct or competence, it was not arbitrable under 38 U.S.C. § 7422. The Arbitrator determined that the Agency's allegations concerning the grievant's professional conduct or competence did not involve the level of hands-on patient care or clinical competence required for its exclusion from arbitration under 38 U.S.C. § 7422(b).[1] *Id.* at 11; (citing 38 U.S.C. § 7422(b) & (c) and Article 42, Section 2(c), Note 1 of the parties' CBA).[2] The

1. 38 U.S.C. § 7422(b) precludes physicians and other selected medical professionals from filing grievances over matters concerning (1) professional conduct or competence, (2) peer review, or (3) the establishment, determination, or adjustment of employee compensation under this title. The relevant language of 38 U.S.C. § 7422(b) is set forth in the appendix to this decision.

2. The relevant language of Article 42, Section 2(c), Note 1 of the CBA as provided in the arbitration award and the relevant language of 38 U.S.C. § 7422 (c) are also set forth in the appendix.

Arbitrator further found that no evidence was presented at arbitration supporting any claim that the grievant failed to conduct himself professionally or lacked competence. The Arbitrator also noted that the Board of Investigation "totally exonerated" the grievant of allegations of professional incompetency. *Id.*

Second, the Arbitrator rejected the Agency's claim that, because the grievance dealt with employee compensation, it was not arbitrable under 38 U.S.C. § 7422. The Arbitrator determined that the grievance had more to do with the grievant's reputation than with compensation. *Id.* Accordingly, the Arbitrator found that the grievance should not be excluded from arbitration under 38 U.S.C. § 7422. As such, the Arbitrator concluded that the grievance was arbitrable. *Id.*

Turning to the grievance's merits, the Arbitrator first addressed the Agency's argument that the grievant's reassignment was within management's statutory right to assign work. *Id.* at 11. The Arbitrator noted that, although the Agency has the right to assign employees to duties and positions and "suspend, remove, reduce in grade or pay or take other disciplinary action against . . . employees[,]" that right is not absolute and must be exercised consistent with the negotiated provisions of the CBA. *Id.* at 11-12. As such, the Arbitrator considered whether the Agency's reassignment of the grievant from his position was in accordance with the CBA.

In determining whether the Agency was acting in accordance with the CBA when it reassigned the grievant from his position as head of the Nephrology Section to that of a staff Nephrologist, the Arbitrator considered the record. The Arbitrator found that the relationship between the Chief and the section heads, including the grievant, began deteriorating soon after the Chief joined KC VAMC's staff. *Id.* at 12. The Arbitrator noted that the Chief became "testy, confrontational, and ultimately retaliatory" when the grievant and other section heads presented him with input and suggestions. *Id.* Specifically, the Arbitrator determined that the Chief harassed the grievant and damaged his reputation by referring unfounded charges to the public Board of Investigation. *Id.* at 13. The Arbitrator further found that the Chief removed the grievant from his position before the Board of Investigation concluded its inquiry. *Id.* The Arbitrator also determined that the grievant was reassigned without any prior warning or counseling. *Id.* at 12.

The Arbitrator determined that the Agency's reassignment of the grievant violated several provisions of the CBA that were intended to limit the Agency's right to assign and reassign work, and its right to discipline employees. *Id.* at 11-12. First, the Arbitrator found that the Agency violated Article 12, Section 10, which provides that "reassignments shall not be used as punishment, harassment, or reprisal." *Id.* at 12-13, 15. Second, the Arbitrator concluded that the Agency's reassignment of the grievant violated Article 13, Section 4 of the CBA, providing that "administrative reassignments will not be used as discipline against any employees, unless appropriate procedures are followed." *Id.* at 13. Third, the Arbitrator determined that the Agency violated Article 13, Section 6 of the CBA, requiring that discipline be applied fairly and equitably and not be used to harass employees. *Id.* Lastly, the Arbitrator found that the Agency's reassignment of the grievant violated Article 16 of the CBA, which gives employees the right to (1) not be subjected to disciplinary or adverse action based on rumors or gossip; (2) receive instructions in such a manner that will avoid public embarrassment; and (3) be free from intimidation, coercion, harassment, or unreasonable working conditions, such as reprisal. *Id.* at 13-14. The Arbitrator concluded that the reassignment was neither fair nor reasonable, that it failed to meet due process standards and follow disciplinary process procedures, and that it was arbitrary and capricious. *Id.*

The Arbitrator sustained the grievance and granted the grievant both compensatory damages and equitable relief. Regarding compensatory damages, the Arbitrator found that working in a supervisory role was one factor considered in determining which physicians should be moved to a higher pay tier. *Id.* at 15. The Arbitrator further found that, had the grievant not been reassigned, he probably would have been placed in a higher pay tier, given the longevity of his service, his research and leadership record, and his status in the academic community. *Id.* Based on these facts, the Arbitrator concluded that the grievant's reassignment from his position as head of Nephrology foreclosed his consideration for higher compensation. *Id.* Consequently, the Arbitrator ordered the Agency to pay the grievant the difference between the actual compensation that the grievant received and the compensation that he would have received had he remained head of the Nephrology Section and, as a result, been placed in a higher pay tier. The Arbitrator also awarded the Union attorney fees. *Id.* at 16.

In addition, the Arbitrator awarded the grievant equitable relief. Noting that the parties agreed that the Arbitrator had full remedial authority, including the authority to reinstate the grievant, the Arbitrator ordered the reinstatement of the grievant to his former position as head of Nephrology or an equivalent leadership position. *Id.* at 15-16. The Arbitrator also determined that the grievant suffered harm to his reputation. As such, he ordered the Agency to publicly acknowledge, as agreed to by the Union, that the grievant had been "vindicated" by the arbitration and that his reassignment from head of Nephrology was unwarranted. *Id.* The Arbitrator also ordered that this public acknowledgement be made known to the appropriate officials at the University of Kansas Medical Center, where the grievant is a tenured professor.

III. Preliminary Matters

A. The Authority will not consider the parties' supplemental submissions.

Each party filed supplemental submissions concerning matters that arose after the Arbitrator issued the arbitration award. After submitting its exceptions to the Authority, the Agency requested the Secretary of Veterans Affairs (the Secretary) to make a determination as to whether the Arbitrator's award infringed on the Secretary's exclusive authority to make decisions on issues relating to (1) employee professional conduct or competence and (2) compensation, under 38 U.S.C. § 7422(d).[3] Title 38 Decision Paper (Decision Paper) at 1-3.[4] The Secretary's designee, the Under Secretary of Health (USH), addressed the Agency's request.[5] The parties each filed supplemental submissions with the Authority concerning the USH's decision on the issues raised by the Agency.

Although the Authority's Regulations do not provide for the filing of supplemental submissions, 5 C.F.R. § 2429.26 provides that the Authority may, in its discretion, grant a party leave to file "other documents" as deemed appropriate. *E.g., Cong. Research Emps. Ass'n, IFPTE, Local 75*, 59 FLRA 994, 999 (2004) (*Cong. Research*). A filing party must demonstrate why its supplemental submission should be considered. *NTEU, Chapter 98,* 60 FLRA 448, 448 n.2 (2004). For example, the Authority has granted leave to file other documents where the supplemental submission responds to issues raised for the first time in an opposing party's filing. *See Cong. Research*, 59 FLRA at 999. Parties have also been granted leave to address the applicability of court decisions that issued while the parties' dispute was pending before the Authority. *E.g., U.S. Dep't of Justice, Fed. Bureau of Prisons, Metro. Corr. Ctr., Chi., Ill.*, 63 FLRA 423, 423 n.1 (2009) (*Metro. Corr. Ctr.*) (citing *U.S. Customs Serv.,* 46 FLRA 1080, 1080 n.1 (1992)).

Here, neither party requested leave to file supplemental submissions addressing the merits of the Secretary's decision. Therefore, we decline to consider those submissions. *See* 5 C.F.R. § 2429.26.

B. A portion of the award is set aside based on the USH decision.

The USH addressed several issues raised in the Agency's exceptions to the arbitration award. The Secretary has the "exclusive authority" to make 38 U.S.C. § 7422 determinations. *See AFGE, Local 2145,* 61 FLRA 571, 575 (2006) (Secretary has authority to make § 7422 determination even after arbitration award resolves grievance pertaining to such matters) (*AFGE*) (citing *U.S. Dep't of Veterans Affairs, Veterans Affairs Med. Ctr., Asheville, N.C.*,57 FLRA 681, 683 (2002)). These determinations are not reviewable by the Authority. *See Veterans Admin., Long Beach, Cal.,* 48 FLRA 970, 975 (1993) (*VA, Long Beach*).

First, the USH determined that the grievant's reassignment was not a matter pertaining to professional conduct or competence within the meaning of § 7422(b). Decision Paper at 7.

3. 38 U.S.C. § 7422(d) provides:

> An issue of whether a matter or question concerns or arises out of (1) professional conduct or competence, (2) peer review, or (3) the establishment, determination, or adjustment of employee compensation under this title shall be decided by the Secretary and is not itself subject to collective bargaining and may not be reviewed by any other agency.

4. The Agency raised the same issues in its exceptions. Exceptions at 2.

5. Because the USH's decision bears upon the disposition of the § 7422(d) issue involved in this case, we take official notice of it. *See* 5 C.F.R § 2429.5 (Authority may take official notice of such matters as would be proper); *AFGE, Council 238,* 64 FLRA 223, 223 n.1 (2009) (official notice taken of documents submitted in arbitration appeal as relevant to resolution of negotiability case involving same parties where documents were relevant to disposition of negotiability determination).

Accordingly, the USH did not address the portion of the Arbitrator's award requiring the Agency to: (1) reinstate the grievant as head of Nephrology and (2) publicly acknowledge that the grievant had been vindicated by the arbitration. *Id.* As the USH found that the grievance did not address matters concerning professional conduct or competence, issues raised in the Agency's exceptions concerning the grievant's reassignment in this regard are not excluded from the Authority's review under § 7422(d). Accordingly, we will address the Agency's exceptions pertaining to those matters.

Second, the USH concluded that a portion of the award pertained to matters regarding compensation within the meaning of § 7422. *Id.* Accordingly, the USH invalidated the portion of the award regarding compensatory damages and attorney fees. Decision Paper at 6-7. As the Secretary has authority to make § 7422 determinations even after an arbitration award resolves a grievance pertaining to such matters, *see AFGE,* 61 FLRA at 575, we set aside that portion of the award. *See U.S. Dep't of Veterans Affairs, Veterans Affairs Med. Ctr., Amarillo, Tex.*, 49 FLRA 1511, 1516 (1994) (setting aside award where Chief Medical Director determined under § 7422(d) that the grievance concerned the peer review process and, therefore, was not arbitrable).

IV. Positions of the Parties

A. Agency's Exceptions

The Agency excepts to the arbitration award on several grounds. First, as relevant here, the Agency argues that reinstating the grievant to his former position as head of Nephrology affects management's right to assign work under the Statute. Exceptions at 6-7. According to the Agency, the CBA cannot be enforced so as to improperly deny the Agency the authority to exercise its management rights. *Id.* at 6. Thus, in the Agency's view, even if it violated the CBA by reassigning the grievant, an award reinstating the grievant to that position is unenforceable as violating management's right to assign work. *Id.* at 7, 20. As such, the Agency contends that the Authority should apply the two-prong test set forth in United States *Department of the Treasury, Bureau of Engraving & Printing, Washington, D.C.*, 53 FLRA 146, 153-54 (1997) (*BEP*) and conclude that the award violates management's rights. *See* Exceptions at 10.

The Agency contends that the award does not satisfy prong I of *BEP* because the Arbitrator failed to find that the CBA provisions addressing employee reassignments were negotiated under § 7106(b) of the Statute. *Id.* at 7-8. In addition, the Agency argues that the Arbitrator failed to establish that the reassignment of the grievant violated any applicable law. In this respect, the Agency argues that the Arbitrator erroneously found that the Agency violated provisions of Title 5, which are inapplicable in this case. Rather, the Agency claims, the Arbitrator should have looked at whether its actions were consistent with the provisions of Title 38, since the grievant was appointed under 38 U.S.C. § 7401(d). *Id.* at 8. The Agency further argues that the award does not satisfy prong II of BEP because the Arbitrator failed to reconstruct what action the Agency would have taken in the absence of its alleged contractual violation. *Id.* at 10.

Second, the Agency argues that the Arbitrator exceeded his authority. The Agency claims that the Arbitrator's order requiring it to publicly acknowledge, "*as agreed to by the Union,*" that the grievant has been vindicated by the arbitration impermissibly delegates the Arbitrator's authority to award appropriate remedies to the Union. *Id.* at 18-19. According to the Agency, the Union has no statutory, regulatory, or other right to exercise such authority. *Id.* at 19. In addition, the Agency contends that the Authority should not require it to provide notice to officials at the University of Kansas Medical Center that the grievant was vindicated at arbitration. According to the Agency, that institution is not involved in this case, and the Arbitrator does not have the authority to order the Agency to publicly acknowledge this result. *Id.*

Third, the Agency argues that the award is too ambiguous to implement because the Arbitrator did not provide any guidelines regarding what constitutes an appropriate "public acknowledgment." *Id.* The Agency contends that the Union could demand any number of things to be included in the public acknowledgement that the Arbitrator did not contemplate. Consequently, the Agency claims, the award is so ambiguous as to make implementation impossible and asks that that the Authority set it aside. *Id.*

Fourth, the Agency contends that all of its exceptions collectively demonstrate that the award fails to draw its essence from the CBA. *Id.* at 19-20.[6]

6. The Agency does not provide any specific arguments supporting its claim that the award fails to draw its essence from the agreement. When a party fails to provide any arguments or authority to support its exception, the Authority will deny the exception as a bare assertion. *See*

Therefore, the Agency asks that the Authority set aside the award.

B. Union's Opposition

The Union presents several arguments responding to the Agency's exceptions. First, the Union argues that the grievance does not involve the grievant's professional conduct or his competence as a physician under 38 U.S.C. § 7422. Opp'n at 5. Thus, the Union argues, the grievance is arbitrable. *Id.*

Second, the Union contends that the award does not violate management rights. *Id.* at 6-7. The Union argues that the right to assign work encompasses the right to determine particular duties to be assigned to employees and that the award does not preclude the Agency from determining the grievant's future duties. *Id.* at 9.

Third, the Union argues that the Arbitrator did not exceed his authority because, under the CBA, arbitrators have full authority to award appropriate remedies. *Id.* at 9 (citing CBA, Art. 40, Sect. 2(G)).

Fourth, the Union argues that the award draws its essence from the CBA because the Arbitrator did not exceed the broad remedial powers implicitly granted in the CBA. Opp'n at 15. The Union claims that arbitration awards are afforded a deferential standard of review. *Id.* at 16. As such, the Union argues, the award should be upheld.

V. Analysis and Conclusions

A. The award is not contrary to law.

The Agency claims that the award is contrary to its right to assign work under § 7106(a)(2)(B) of the Statute. When an exception involves an award's consistency with law, the Authority reviews any question of law raised by the exception and the award de novo. *See NTEU, Chapter 24*, 50 FLRA 330, 332 (1995) (citing *U.S. Customs Serv. v. FLRA*, 43 F.3d 682, 686-87 (D.C. Cir. 1994)). In applying the standard of de novo review, the Authority assesses whether an arbitrator's legal conclusions are consistent with the applicable standard of law. *See U.S. Dep't of Def., Dep'ts of the Army & the Air Force, Ala. Nat'l Guard, Northport, Ala.*, 55 FLRA 37, 40 (1998) (*Army*). In making that assessment, the Authority defers to the arbitrator's underlying factual findings. *See id.*

With regard to the Agency's contention that the award violates its right to assign work, we note that the Authority recently revised the analysis that it will apply when reviewing management-rights exceptions to arbitration awards. *See U.S. EPA*, 65 FLRA 113, 115 (2010) (Member Beck concurring) (*EPA*); *FDIC, Div. of Supervision & Consumer Prot., S.F. Region*, 65 FLRA 102, 106-07 (2010) (Chairman Pope concurring) (*FDIC, S.F. Region*). Under the revised analysis, the Authority will first assess whether the award affects the exercise of the asserted management right.[7] *EPA*, 65 FLRA at 115. If so, then the Authority examines whether the award provides a remedy for a violation of either an applicable law, within the meaning of § 7106(a)(2) of the Statute, or a contract provision that was negotiated pursuant to § 7106(b) of the Statute. *Id.* Also under the revised analysis, in determining whether the award enforces a contract provision negotiated under § 7106(b)(3), the Authority assesses: (1) whether the contract provision constitutes an arrangement for employees adversely affected by the exercise of a management right, and (2), if so, whether the arbitrator's enforcement of the arrangement abrogates the exercise of the management right. *Id.* at 116-18. In concluding that it would apply an abrogation standard, the Authority rejected continued application of an excessive-interference standard. *Id.* at 118. Furthermore, in setting forth its revised analysis, the Authority specifically rejected the continued application of the "reconstruction" requirement set forth in prior case law. *FDIC, SF Region,* 65 FLRA at 106-07.

U.S. Dep't of Homeland Sec., U.S. Customs & Border Prot., Port of Seattle, Seattle, Wash., 60 FLRA 490, 492 n.7 (2004). As such, we reject this claim as a bare assertion.

7. For the reasons articulated in his recent concurring opinion and footnotes, Member Beck would conclude that it is unnecessary to assess whether the award affects the exercise of the asserted management right. The appropriate question is simply whether the remedy directed by the Arbitrator enforces the provision in a reasonable and reasonably foreseeable fashion. *See EPA*, 65 FLRA at 120 (Concurring Opinion of Member Beck); *U.S. Dep't of Justice, Fed. Bureau of Prisons, Fed. Corr. Complex, Terre Haute, Ind.*, 65 FLRA 460, 462-63 n.2 (2011); *Soc. Sec. Admin., Dallas Region,* 65 FLRA 405, 408 n.5 (2010); *U.S. Dep't of the Air Force, Air Force Materiel Command,* 65 FLRA 395, 398 n.7 (2010); *U.S. Dep't of Health & Human Servs., Office of Medicare Hearings & Appeals,* 65 FLRA 175, 177 n.3 (2010); *U.S. Dep't of Transp., Fed. Aviation Admin.*, 65 FLRA 171, 173 n.5 (2010). Member Beck would conclude that the Arbitrator's award is a plausible interpretation of the parties' agreement and deny the exception.

The right to assign work under § 7106(a)(2)(B) of the Statute includes the right to determine the particular duties to be assigned, when work assignments will occur, and to whom, or what positions, the duties will be assigned. *E.g., U.S. Dep't of Commerce, PTO*, 65 FLRA 13, 15 (2010) (Member Beck dissenting on other grounds). As the award requires the Agency to assign the duties of the head of the Nephrology Section to the grievant, we find that the award affects management's right to assign work. *See U.S. Dep't of Veterans Affairs, Med. Ctr., Detroit, Mich.*, 61 FLRA 371, 373 (2005) (*VA Med. Ctr.*) (award returning grievant to previous position requires agency to assign certain duties to grievant and thus, affects management's right to assign work). We must therefore determine whether the Arbitrator enforced a contract provision negotiated pursuant to § 7106(b) of the Statute. *EPA*, 65 FLRA at 116.

The Arbitrator found that several provisions in the CBA are intended to limit the Agency's rights to assign and reassign work, and its right to discipline employees. Award at 11-12. The Arbitrator applied these provisions in finding that the Agency violated the CBA when it reassigned the grievant from his position as head of Nephrology to that of a staff Nephrologist. Specifically, the Arbitrator found that the Agency violated provisions of the CBA prohibiting reassignments from being used as punishment, harassment, or reprisal; provisions prohibiting reassignments from being used as discipline against employees without use of appropriate procedures; and provisions providing that discipline be applied "fairly and equitably" to employees. *Id.* at 12-15 (citing CBA Articles 12, 13 and 16).

The Authority has held that contractual provisions limiting the use of employee reassignments for disciplinary purposes are enforceable § 7106(b) provisions. *See, e.g., VA Med. Ctr.*, 61 FLRA at 372-74 (finding that contract provisions limiting the use of reassignments for disciplinary purposes were negotiated under § 7106(b)). In this connection, the Authority has held that such contract provisions constitute arrangements within the meaning of § 7106(b)(3) of the Statute. *U.S. Dep't of the Treasury, U.S. Customs Serv., N.Y., N.Y.*, 39 FLRA 278, 283 (1991) (*Treasury*) (contract provision setting forth limitations on reassignments found to be an arrangement); *IRS, Austin Dist.*, 9 FLRA 672, 674 (1982) (contract provision providing that reassignments would not be used in lieu of discipline constituted arrangement). Consequently, we find that the Arbitrator's direction to the Agency to reinstate the grievant to the position from which he was improperly reassigned enforces an arrangement negotiated pursuant to § 7106(b)(3) of the Statute. *See EPA*, 65 FLRA at 115.

Next, we must determine whether the Arbitrator's award reinstating the grievant abrogates the Agency's right to assign work to employees. *See EPA*, 65 FLRA at 116-18. The Authority has previously described an award that abrogates the exercise of a management right as an award that "precludes an agency from exercising" that right. *U.S. Dep't of the Air Force, Seymour Johnson Air Force Base, N.C.*, 55 FLRA 163, 167 (1999) (quoting *Dep't of the Treasury, U.S. Customs Serv.*, 37 FLRA 309, 314 (1990)). The CBA provisions, as interpreted and applied by the Arbitrator, do not prevent the Agency from assigning work to the grievant. By reinstating the grievant, the Arbitrator merely enforced the Agency's negotiated limitations on reassignments and discipline in the CBA as set forth above. Management still retains the right to assign work to employees within the limitations of the contractual provisions that it negotiated with the Union. Given these findings and that the Authority has concluded that similar CBA provisions constitute arrangements, *see, e.g., Treasury*, 39 FLRA at 283-84, we find that the provisions are enforceable under § 7106(b)(3) of the Statute and that Agency has not demonstrated that the award impermissibly affects management's right to assign work under § 7106(a)(2)(B). We therefore, deny the exception.[8]

B. The Arbitrator did not exceed his authority.

The Agency contends that the Arbitrator exceeded his authority for two reasons. First, it claims that the Arbitrator impermissibly delegated his authority to award appropriate remedies to the Union

---

8. Given this determination, we need not address the Agency's claim that the Arbitrator failed to establish that the reassignment of the grievant violated any applicable law. Further, we find it unnecessary to address the Agency's argument that the award is deficient under *BEP* because the Arbitrator failed to reconstruct what management would have done had it complied with the parties' agreement since the Authority no longer requires that an arbitrator's remedy reconstruct what management would have done had it not violated the contract provision. *FDIC*, 65 FLRA 179, 181 (2010). In addition, for the reasons set forth in her concurring opinion in *FDIC, S.F. Region*, 65 FLRA at 112, Chairman Pope agrees that the Agency provides no basis for finding the Arbitrator's remedy deficient because the remedy is reasonably related to the contract provisions at issue and the harm being remedied.

by allowing it to approve or disapprove the Agency's public acknowledgment of the arbitration's outcome. Second, the Agency argues that the Arbitrator does not have the authority to order the Agency to provide such public notification to the University of Kansas Medical Center.

An arbitrator exceeds his or her authority when the arbitrator fails to resolve an issue submitted to arbitration, resolves an issue not submitted to arbitration, disregards specific limitations on his or her authority, or awards relief to persons who are not encompassed within the grievance. *See U.S. Dep't of Def., Army & Air Force Exch. Serv.*, 51 FLRA 1371, 1378 (1996).

The Agency has not demonstrated that the Arbitrator exceeded his authority when he ordered the parties to agree on an appropriate public announcement acknowledging that the grievant had been vindicated at arbitration and to publicly inform the officials at the University of Kansas Medical Center of the grievant's vindication. *U.S. Dep't of Transp., Fed. Aviation Admin., Airways Facility Serv., Nat'l Airway Sys. Eng'g Div., Okla. City, Okla.*, 60 FLRA 565, 569 (2005) (exception claiming arbitrator exceeded authority denied where there was no violation of express limitation on authority). The Arbitrator found that the grievant's damages as a result of the Agency's breach of contract were largely to his reputation. *See* Award at 11. Thus, a public announcement of the arbitration's outcome at the grievant's longtime place of employment is directly responsive to any damage that may have occurred to the grievant's reputation as a result of the unsubstantiated accusations regarding the grievant's clinical research.

As the Agency has not demonstrated that the Arbitrator failed to resolve an issue submitted to arbitration, resolved an issue not submitted to arbitration, disregarded specific limitations on his authority, or awarded relief to persons who are not encompassed within the grievance, we deny the Agency's exception that the Arbitrator exceeded his authority.

C. The award is not too ambiguous to implement.

The Authority will find an award deficient when it is incomplete, ambiguous, or so contradictory as to make implementation of the award impossible. *See U.S. Dep't of Labor, Mine Safety & Health Admin. Se. Dist.*, 40 FLRA 937, 943 (1991). For an award to be found deficient on this ground, the appealing party must show that implementation of the award is impossible because the meaning and effect of the award are too unclear or uncertain. *See U.S. Dep't of the Army, Corpus Christi Army Depot, Corpus Christi, Tex.*, 56 FLRA 1057, 1074 (2001).

The Agency argues that the award is ambiguous because, in directing the Agency to publicly acknowledge the grievant's vindication at arbitration, the Arbitrator did not provide any guidelines regarding what constitutes an appropriate "public acknowledgment." Exceptions at 19. However, the Agency does not demonstrate that making such a public acknowledgment is impossible simply because it must issue the acknowledgment "in an appropriate public manner, as agreed to by the Union[.]" Award at 16. Accordingly, as there is no basis for finding that the award is impossible to implement, we find that the award is not deficient in this regard, and deny the exception. *See U.S. Dep't of Homeland Sec., U.S. Customs & Border Prot.*, 65 FLRA 373, 377 (2010).

VI. Decision

The portion of the award related to the grievant's compensation under 38 U.S.C. § 7422 is set aside and the Agency's remaining exceptions are denied.

APPENDIX

38 U.S.C. § 7422

§ 7422. Collective bargaining

. . . .

(b) Such collective bargaining (and any grievance procedures provided under a collective bargaining agreement) in the case of employees described in section 7421(b) of this title [38 USCS § 7421(b)] may not cover, or have any applicability to, any matter or question concerning or arising out of (1) professional conduct or competence, (2) peer review, or (3) the establishment, determination, or adjustment of employee compensation under this title.
(c) For purposes of this section, the term "professional conduct or competence" means any of the following:
(1) Direct patient care.
(2) Clinical competence.

. . . .

Article 42, Section 2, Grievance Procedure/Definition

C. Under Title 38 Section 7422, the following exclusions also apply:

1. Any matter or question concerning or arising out of professional conduct or competence such as direct patient care or clinical competence,
3. Any matter or question concerning or arising out of the establishment, determination, or adjustment of employee compensation under this Title.

Note 1: Any questions concerning . . . the exclusions in Paragraphs C1-C3 shall be resolved in accordance with the VA Partnership Council's Guide to Collective Bargaining . . . , which provides that these exclusions will be applied narrowly and only to those matters clearly and unequivocally involving direct hands-on patient care or clinical competence.

. . . .

Award at 4.

65 FLRA No. 168

UNITED STATES
DEPARTMENT OF COMMERCE
PATENT AND TRADEMARK OFFICE
(Agency)

and

NATIONAL TREASURY
EMPLOYEES UNION
CHAPTER 245
(Union)

0-AR-4697

DECISION

May 11, 2011

Before the Authority: Carol Waller Pope, Chairman, and Thomas M. Beck and Ernest DuBester, Members

I. Statement of the Case

This matter is before the Authority on exceptions to an award of Arbitrator George E. Marshall filed by the Agency under § 7122(a) of the Federal Service Labor-Management Relations Statute (the Statute) and part 2425 of the Authority's Regulations. The Union filed an opposition to the Agency's exceptions.

The Arbitrator determined that the Agency violated the parties' agreement, law, rule, and regulation when it changed its compensatory time policy to comply with 5 C.F.R. § 550.114 (§ 550.114). For the reasons discussed below, we grant the Agency's exceptions in part and deny them in part. In addition, we set aside the award to the extent that it applies to the period of time after the parties' agreement expired on January 19, 2008, and set aside the Arbitrator's direction to the Agency to reinstate its old compensatory time policy.

II. Background and Arbitrator's Award

The Agency had a policy (the old policy) that allowed employees to "carry over" up to eighty hours of compensatory time from "one year to the next" for an indefinite amount of time, Award at 2, in accordance with Article 18 of the parties' agreement,[1] *id.* at 1. In March 2007, the Office of Personnel Management revised § 550.114, which pertains to the use of compensatory time. *See* 72 Fed. Reg. 12032, 12035-36 (2007). The revised § 550.114 states, in pertinent part, that an employee "must use accrued compensatory time off . . . by the end of the 26th pay period after the pay period during which it was earned." 5 C.F.R. § 550.114(d). In November 2007, in order to comply with the revised § 550.114, the Agency replaced the old policy with a new compensatory time policy (the new policy). *See* Award at 2. Under the new policy, the Agency no longer allowed employees to carry over compensatory time indefinitely. *See id.* The Union filed a grievance challenging the new policy, and the grievance was unresolved and submitted to arbitration. *See id.* at 1.

The Arbitrator found that § 550.114 conflicted with the parties' agreement because § 550.114 would "prevent employees from carrying earned compensatory time forward for an indefinite period of time[.]" *Id.* at 2. The Arbitrator also found that the Agency was required to maintain the old policy, set forth in the parties' agreement, because the agreement existed before § 550.114 was implemented. *Id.* at 1-2. In this regard, the Arbitrator stated that the Agency could have terminated the agreement, but that the Agency did not notify the Union of its intent to do so, as required by the parties' agreement. *See id.* at 2 (citing *U.S. Dep't of the Army, Headquarters III Corps & Fort Hood, Tex.*, 40 FLRA 636 (1991) (*Fort Hood*)). According to the Arbitrator, the parties' agreement "expired and automatically renewed" on January 19, 2008. *Id.* at 2. Additionally, the Arbitrator found that under Article 3 of the agreement, "[a]ll past practices not in conflict with [the parties' agreement] shall continue, absent written notification by either party of their intent to discontinue or modify a particular practice."[2] *Id.* at 2-3. The Arbitrator determined that there was "no evidence in this record of such a notice being given." *Id.* at 3.

1. Article 18 of the parties' agreement states, in pertinent part, that an employee may not "carry forward more than . . . [eighty] hours of compensatory time . . . from one fiscal year to the next." Exceptions, Jt. Exs., Attach. 3 at 56.

2. Article 3 of the parties' agreement states, in pertinent part: "Past practices not in conflict with this Agreement shall continue, absent written notification by either party of their intent to discontinue or modify a particular practice." Exceptions, Jt. Exs., Attach. 3 at 6.

Based on the foregoing, the Arbitrator sustained the grievance and directed the Agency to rescind the new policy and to reinstate the old policy. *See id.* Additionally, the Arbitrator stated that employees who were adversely affected by the implementation should be made whole.[3] *Id.* The Arbitrator remanded the matter to the parties to determine which employees were adversely affected by the Agency's actions, and he retained jurisdiction to assist in the implementation of the remedies. *Id.*

III. Positions of the Parties

A. Agency's Exceptions

The Agency asserts that the Arbitrator erred as a matter of law when he determined that the Agency had not provided written notification of its intent to modify its compensatory time policy, pursuant to Article 3 of the parties' agreement. *See* Exceptions at 11 (citing *U.S. Dep't of Def., Def. Commissary Agency, Peterson Air Force Base, Colo. Springs, Colo.*, 61 FLRA 688, 692 (2006) (*Peterson AFB*)). Additionally, the Agency argues that the award is contrary to Authority precedent indicating that an agency may implement a government-wide regulation once the agreement with which the regulation conflicts has expired. *See* Exceptions at 9 (citing *GSA, Nat'l Capital Region*, 42 FLRA 121, 131 (1991) (*GSA*); *Fort Hood*, 40 FLRA at 641; *U.S. Dep't of Def., Def. Contract Audit Agency, Cent. Region*, 37 FLRA 1218, 1228 (1990) (*DCAA*)). The Agency claims in this regard that "[t]o the extent the Agency erred, it erred only in applying [§ 550.114] before" the agreement expired on January 19, 2008. *Id.* at 10. Further, the Agency contends that reinstating the old policy would conflict with § 550.114. *See id.* at 13-14.

B. Union's Opposition

The Union contends that the Agency's argument regarding notice should not be considered because the Agency "failed to raise the issue of timely notice" in its post-hearing brief. Opp'n at 12 (citing 5 C.F.R. § 2429.5 (§ 2429.5)).[4] Additionally, the Union argues that the Arbitrator's determination that the Agency was required to continue to follow the old policy is consistent with 5 U.S.C. § 7116(a)(7) (§ 7116(a)(7)).[5] *See id.* at 7-8. In response to the Agency's claim that the Agency did not violate § 7116(a)(7) once the parties' agreement expired, the Union argues that this is "very much in dispute" because the "plain language of the [parties' agreement] does not mention expir[ation]." *Id.* at 9.

IV. Analysis and Conclusions

When an exception involves an award's consistency with law, the Authority reviews any question of law raised by the exception and award de novo. *See NTEU, Chapter 24*, 50 FLRA 330, 332 (1995) (citing *U.S. Customs Serv. v. FLRA*, 43 F.3d 682, 686-87 (D.C. Cir. 1994)). In applying the standard of de novo review, the Authority assesses whether an arbitrator's legal conclusions are consistent with the applicable standard of law. *See U.S. Dep't of Def., Dep'ts of the Army & the Air Force, Ala. Nat'l Guard, Northport, Ala.*, 55 FLRA 37, 40 (1998). In making that assessment, the Authority defers to the arbitrator's underlying factual findings. *See id.*

Preliminarily, we address the Union's claim that the Agency's argument regarding notice should be dismissed under § 2429.5. Section 2429.5 provides, in pertinent part, that the Authority will not consider any "evidence, factual assertions, [or] arguments . . . that could have been, but were not, presented in the proceedings before the . . . arbitrator." 5 C.F.R. § 2429.5. *See also* 5 C.F.R. § 2425.4(c) (exceptions may not rely on any "evidence, factual assertions, [or] arguments . . . that could have been, but were not, presented to the arbitrator"). Here, the Agency asserted, in its post-hearing brief to the Arbitrator, that it notified the Union of its intent to implement the new policy. *See* Exceptions, Attach., Agency's Post-Hearing Brief at 6 ("[T]he Agency notified the unions . . . of its intended implementation of a comp time policy in compliance with the new regulation."). Further, the notice-related argument in the Agency's exceptions is based on evidence presented at arbitration. *See* Exceptions at 12. *Accord* Exceptions, Jt. Exs., Attach. 5 (Agency newsletter announcing new policy); Exceptions, Attach., Hr'g Tr. at 133, 137 (testimony regarding newsletter announcement). Thus, there is evidence that the Agency presented its argument regarding notice to the Arbitrator. Accordingly, we consider the Agency's argument.

---

3. Specifically, the Arbitrator stated that the remedy should include, but not be limited to, "[r]estoration and credit for any forfeited time" and "[p]ay for . . . employees who have separated from [the Agency] for unused compensatory time" that was forfeited. Award at 3. Additionally, the Arbitrator directed the Agency to post a cease and desist notice "concerning its violation." *Id.*

4. The pertinent wording of § 2429.5 is set forth below.

5. The pertinent wording of § 7116(a)(7) is set forth below.

With regard to the merits of that argument, the Authority has rejected as "misplaced" exceptions to an arbitrator's contract interpretation that challenge the arbitrator's interpretation of law. *Int'l Fed'n of Prof'l & Technical Engr's*, 65 FLRA 167, 169 (2010) (finding misplaced a contrary to law exception challenging arbitrator's interpretation of parties' agreement). *See also AFGE, Local 779*, 64 FLRA 672, 674 (2010) (same). *Cf. U.S. Dep't of the Treasury, IRS, Wash., D.C.*, 61 FLRA 352, 354 (2005) (Authority's unfair labor practice precedent irrelevant where arbitrator's award was limited to finding agency's notice of a reduction in force violated parties' agreement). Here, the Arbitrator interpreted and applied Article 3 of the parties' agreement to find that the Agency did not notify the Union that the Agency intended to change its compensatory time policy.[6] *See* Award at 2-3. Although the Agency claims that this finding is contrary to *Peterson AFB*, in which the Authority determined that an agency satisfied its *statutory* obligation to provide sufficient notice of a change, *see* 61 FLRA at 692-93, here the Arbitrator found only that the Agency did not satisfy its *contractual* obligations under the parties' agreement, *see* Award at 2-3. In this connection, the Authority has held that parties may negotiate contractual entitlements that are greater than statutory entitlements. *See United Am. Nurses, D.C. Nurses Ass'n & United Am. Nurses, Local 203*, 64 FLRA 879, 882 (2010) (entitlement to information under § 7114(b)(4) of the Statute is a "statutory floor and not a ceiling."). Also in this connection, the Authority has held that parties may agree to, and arbitrators may enforce, contract provisions requiring an agency to provide notification of various matters. *U.S. Dep't of Def., the Adjutant Gen., Nat'l Guard Bureau, Tenn. Air Nat'l Guard*, 56 FLRA 588, 591 (2000). Accordingly, the Agency's reliance on the statutory standard for adequate notice is misplaced and does not demonstrate that the Arbitrator erred as a matter of law by finding that the Agency failed to provide notice as required by the parties' agreement. Thus, we deny this exception.

With regard to the argument regarding the new policy's implementation, § 7116(a)(7) of the Statute states, in pertinent part, that it is an unfair labor practice for an agency to "enforce any . . . regulation . . . which is in conflict with any applicable collective bargaining agreement if the agreement was in effect before the date the . . . regulation was prescribed[.]" 5 U.S.C. § 7116(a)(7). The Authority interprets and applies § 7116(a)(7) "narrowly." *Fort Hood*, 40 FLRA at 641. Accordingly, provisions in a collective bargaining agreement "control over conflicting [g]overnment-wide regulations 'for the express term of the agreement during which the [g]overnment-wide regulation was first prescribed, *but no longer*.'" *Id.* (quoting *DCAA*, 37 FLRA at 1228) (emphasis added). Once a government-wide regulation that conflicts with a preexisting agreement is implemented, the government-wide regulation becomes enforceable by operation of law when the agreement expires. *See id.*

Here, the Arbitrator found that the parties' agreement expired on January 19, 2008.[7] *See* Award at 1-2. At that time, § 550.114 became enforceable by operation of law. *See Fort Hood*, 40 FLRA at 641. *See also GSA*, 42 FLRA at 131; *DCAA*, 37 FLRA at 1228. As such, the Arbitrator's conclusion that the Agency could not modify its compensatory time policy to comply with § 550.114, is contrary to Authority precedent insofar as it applies to the time after January 19, 2008. *See Fort Hood*, 40 FLRA at 642. Further, because the old policy conflicts with § 550.114, the Arbitrator's direction to reinstate that policy is contrary to § 550.114. *See SSA, Office of Disability Adjudication & Review*, 65 FLRA 477, 480 (2011) (setting aside award conflicting with government-wide regulations). Accordingly, we set aside the award to the extent that it applies to the period of time after the parties' agreement expired on January 19, 2008, and set aside the Arbitrator's direction to reinstate the old policy.

V. Decision

The Agency's exceptions are granted in part and denied in part. The award is set aside to the extent that it applies to the period of time after the parties' agreement expired on January 19, 2008, and the Arbitrator's direction to the Agency to reinstate the old policy is set aside.

---

6. We note that the Agency does not claim that the award fails to draw its essence from the parties' agreement, or that the Arbitrator's findings are based on nonfacts. *See* Exceptions at 11-13.

7. We note that the Union claims that this finding is "in dispute" because the agreement "does not mention expir[ation][.]" Opp'n at 9. To the extent that the Union's claim constitutes an exception to the award, the exception is untimely because the Union's opposition was not filed within thirty days of the service of the award. *See* 5 C.F.R. § 2425.2.

65 FLRA No. 169

UNITED STATES
DEPARTMENT OF THE AIR FORCE
LUKE AIR FORCE BASE, ARIZONA
(Agency)

and

AMERICAN FEDERATION
OF GOVERNMENT EMPLOYEES
LOCAL 1547
(Union)

0-AR-4410

DECISION

May 11, 2011

Before the Authority: Carol Waller Pope, Chairman, and Thomas M. Beck and Ernest DuBester, Members

I. Statement of the Case

This matter is before the Authority on exceptions to an award of Arbitrator Richard D. Sambuco filed by the Agency under § 7122(a) of the Federal Service Labor-Management Relations Statute (the Statute) and part 2425 of the Authority's Regulations. The Union filed an opposition to the Agency's exceptions.

As relevant here, the Arbitrator found that the Agency did not have just cause to remove one of two grievants from his position and ordered the Agency to return the grievant to his former position and to pay the grievant backpay. Award at 36. For the reasons set forth below, we grant the Agency's contrary to law exception and set aside the award.

II. Background and Arbitrator's Award

The grievants were employed by the Agency as temporary security guards. *Id.* at 7, 8. As a condition of their employment, the Agency required the grievants to sign a Statement of Understanding (Statement). *Id.* at 9. The Statement indicated that, as temporary limited employees hired for a period of one year or less, they were "not covered by the adverse action procedures under" 5 U.S.C. § 4303 and 5 U.S.C. § 7511, and could be "terminated at any time upon notice from the [A]gency." *Id.* at 11-12. After the grievants worked for the Agency for approximately two months, the Agency terminated their employment.[1] *See id.* at 9.

The Union filed a grievance on behalf of the grievants. *Id.* at 9-10. The matter was unresolved and was submitted to arbitration. *Id.* at 10. The Arbitrator framed the following issues: whether "the Agency violate[d] the language of the Labor Management Agreement [(parties' agreement)] when it terminated [the grievants]? If [so], what is the remedy?" *Id.*

The Arbitrator found that the Statement constituted an implied contract because it failed to contain an express disclaimer indicating that it was not "an express or implied contract of employment." *Id.* at 15 (internal quotation marks omitted); *see also id.* at 14, 33. The Arbitrator determined that, because the grievants were employed under an implied contract, they were not "at will" employees, and the Agency could terminate their employment only for just cause. *Id.* at 15, 22. The Arbitrator found that, although the first grievant's employment was terminated for just cause, the Agency did not have cause to remove the second grievant. *Id.* at 34-35, 36. The Arbitrator determined that the Agency did not have just cause to remove the second grievant because he did not have a prior disciplinary record, his absences were approved by his supervisor and "ostensibly granted due to [his] attempt to establish a work related injury[,]" and a bargaining unit employee rather than the direct supervisor signed his termination notice. *Id.* at 24; *see also id.* at 34, 36. Additionally, the Arbitrator found that the grievants were entitled to grieve their removals under the parties' agreement because the Union timely notified the Agency of its intent to negotiate a new agreement, and the provision prohibiting temporary employees from grieving their terminations was a

1. The Agency terminated the first grievant's employment because, on separate occasions, he failed to bring his ballistic vest to work, shave before work, and wear his ballistic vest properly, and because he was rude to the public. Award at 7. The Agency removed the second grievant from his position because he failed to bring his ballistic vest to work on two separate occasions and did not report for work on several occasions. *Id.* at 7-8.

permissive subject of bargaining that expired with the agreement.[2] *Id.* at 21-22, 34.

III. Positions of the Parties

A. Agency's Exceptions

The Agency claims that the award is contrary to law because, as temporary employees, the grievants are prohibited from grieving their terminations. Exceptions at 4-5. Moreover, the Agency asserts that the award is contrary to law because temporary employees "may be terminated without cause at any time." *Id.* at 5.

Also, the Agency claims that the Arbitrator exceeded his authority and that the award interferes with management's right to remove employees. *Id.* Specifically, the Agency asserts that the Arbitrator wrongfully concluded that the Statement was an implied contract and that the Agency could terminate the grievants' employment only for just cause. *Id.* According to the Agency, the "award excessively interferes with management's right . . . to terminate an employee not entitled to a hearing by law." *Id.* Moreover, the Agency claims that the Arbitrator exceeded his authority by asserting "jurisdiction over an issue specifically excluded from the grievance procedure" and by administering a remedy that he had no authority to grant under the law. *Id.*; *see also id.* at 6.

B. Union's Opposition

The Union argues that the grievance was properly before the Arbitrator and that the award does not fail to draw its essence from the parties' agreement because temporary employees are not excluded from the bargaining unit and the just cause provisions of the agreement apply to temporary employees. Opp'n at 3, 4-5. Also, the Union contends that the Arbitrator did not exceed his authority because he resolved the issue that was before him, and the issue that he framed corresponded to the statement of the issue in the grievance. *Id.* at 5. According to the Union, the Arbitrator properly found that the Agency did not have just cause to suspend the second grievant. *Id.* at 4-5, 6. Finally, the Union argues that the Agency, in its exceptions, ignores the fact that the provision prohibiting temporary employees from grieving their terminations was a permissive subject of bargaining and expired with the agreement. *Id.* at 3, 6.

IV. Analysis and Conclusion: The award is contrary to law.

When an exception involves an award's consistency with law, the Authority reviews any question of law raised by the exception and the award de novo. *See NTEU, Chapter 24*, 50 FLRA 330, 332 (1995) (citing *U.S. Customs Serv. v. FLRA*, 43 F.3d 682, 686-87 (D.C. Cir. 1994)). In applying the standard of de novo review, the Authority assesses whether an arbitrator's legal conclusions are consistent with the applicable standard of law. *See U.S. Dep't of Def., Dep'ts of the Army & the Air Force, Ala. Nat'l Guard, Northport, Ala.*, 55 FLRA 37, 40 (1998). In making that assessment, the Authority defers to the arbitrator's underlying factual findings. *See id.*

The Agency asserts that the award is contrary to law because the Arbitrator erroneously found that the grievants were not prohibited from grieving their terminations and could be terminated only for just cause. Exceptions at 4-5. As a general matter, the Authority has found that the termination of a temporary employee is not grievable or arbitrable as a matter of law. *See, e.g., Fed. Deposit Ins. Corp., Div. of Depositor & Asset Servs., Okla. City, Okla.*, 49 FLRA 894, 898 (1994) (finding that temporary employees are prohibited from contesting adverse and performance-based actions through the negotiated grievance procedure); *AFGE, AFL-CIO, Council of Marine Corps Locals, Council 240*, 39 FLRA 839, 846 (1991) (*AFGE, Council 240*); *Fed. Emps. Metal Trades Council*, 38 FLRA 1410, 1428-30 (1991) (*Mare Island*) (determining that an arbitrator is without authority to decide the appropriateness of the termination of a temporary employee based on an alleged failure to afford the employee the protections of 5 U.S.C. §§ 7511(a)(1) and 7513). Moreover, the Authority has determined that agencies retain the right to terminate temporary employees summarily with minimal due process protections. *See Mare Island*, 38 FLRA at 1428-30 (determining that, unlike competitive service employees, temporary employees are not afforded the protections of 5 U.S.C. § 7513 which requires an agency, among other things, to remove an employee "only for such cause as will promote the efficiency of

2. The Arbitrator also found that the Agency violated Article III, Section A of the parties' agreement "when it authorized Team Leaders (non-supervisory bargaining unit employees) to make entries into [their] Supervisor's Employee Work Folder (SEWF)." *Id.* at 35. Because the Agency does not except to this finding, it is not before us, and we do not address it further.

the service"). Consistent with that right, parties are prohibited from establishing any additional procedural protections that apply to the termination of temporary employees. *See AFGE, Council 240*, 39 FLRA at 843, 844-46 (implicitly rejecting the union's argument that temporary employees are not excluded from coverage of 5 U.S.C. §§ 7511 and 4303 in the same manner as probationary employees and finding that the union's proposal allowing temporary employees in the bargaining unit to grieve disciplinary and performance actions was nonnegotiable); *cf. U.S. Dep't of the Air Force, Nellis Air Force Base, Las Vegas, Nev.*, 46 FLRA 1323, 1326-27 (1993) (*Nellis AFB*) (determining that, because agencies retain the right to terminate probationary employees summarily with minimal due process protections, establishment through collective bargaining of any additional procedural protections applying to the termination of probationary employees is barred as inconsistent with law and regulation).

In this case, we find that the award is contrary to law. The Arbitrator's finding that the grievants were entitled to grieve their terminations under the parties' agreement is clearly erroneous because, as a matter of law, temporary employees are prohibited from contesting their terminations through the negotiated grievance procedure. *See, e.g., AFGE, Council 240*, 39 FLRA at 846; *Mare Island*, 38 FLRA at 1428-30. Also, the Arbitrator's determination that the grievants could be terminated only for just cause because they were employed under an implied contract is similarly without merit because agencies have the right to terminate temporary employees summarily, and parties are barred from establishing additional procedural protections that are not provided to terminated, temporary employees by statute.[3] *See AFGE, Council 240*, 39 FLRA at 844-46; *Mare Island*, 38 FLRA at 1428-30; *cf. Nellis AFB*, 46 FLRA at 1326-27.

Accordingly, we grant the Agency's contrary to law exception.

V. Decision

The award is set aside.

3. In view of our conclusion that the award is contrary to law, we find that it is unnecessary to consider the Agency's remaining exceptions. *See, e.g., U.S. Dep't of Transp., Fed. Aviation Admin., Nashua, N.H.*, 65 FLRA 447, 450 n.3 (2011) (finding that it was unnecessary to address the agency's remaining exceptions after setting aside the award as contrary to law); *Soc. Sec. Admin.*, 63 FLRA 313, 315 n.2 (2009) (same).

65 FLRA No. 170

NATIONAL INSTITUTES
OF HEALTH
(Agency)

and

AMERICAN FEDERATION
OF GOVERNMENT EMPLOYEES
LOCAL 2419
(Union)

0-AR-4692

DECISION

May 18, 2011

Before the Authority: Carol Waller Pope, Chairman, and Thomas M. Beck and Ernest DuBester, Members

I. Statement of the Case

This matter is before the Authority on exceptions to an award of Arbitrator Robert A. Creo filed by the Agency under § 7122(a) of the Federal Service Labor-Management Relations Statute (the Statute) and part 2425 of the Authority's Regulations. The Union did not file an opposition to the Agency's exceptions.

The Arbitrator concluded that the Agency violated the parties' agreement by denying the grievant's request for Union representation during a meeting (the meeting) where he was notified that his employment would be terminated. As a remedy, the Arbitrator ordered the Agency to conduct another meeting with the grievant and his Union representative, and to cease and desist from denying representation to similarly situated probationary employees. For the reasons set forth below, we grant the Agency's exception and set aside the award as contrary to law.

II. Background and Arbitrator's Award

The grievant's supervisor asked the grievant, a probationary employee, to attend a meeting. Award at 2. The grievant asked whether the meeting would be disciplinary and, if so, whether he needed to speak with a Union representative. *Id.* at 26. The supervisor informed him that a Union representative was not necessary as the sole purpose of the meeting was to "transmit documents." *Id.* At the meeting, the supervisor and a human resources specialist informed the grievant that the Agency had decided to terminate his employment; however, they also presented the grievant with a memorandum of understanding (MOU) that gave him the option of resigning. *Id.* at 2. The grievant was given seven days to consider the MOU. The grievant asked to speak to a Union representative. The supervisor and the specialist denied the grievant's request, but informed him that he could speak to one after the meeting. *Id.* Several days later, the grievant executed the MOU. *Id.* at 7.

The Union presented a grievance concerning the grievant's termination. The matter proceeded to arbitration, and the Arbitrator framed the following issues:

> 1) Is the [g]rievance arbitrable?[1]
>
> 2) Did the Agency violate the [parties'] [a]greement, applicable law[2] or regulations by its processing of the termination of [the grievant, a] probationary employee . . . ? If yes, what shall the remedy be?

Id. at 10.

As to the alleged contractual violation, the Union asserted that the Agency violated Article 28, Section 2 of the parties' agreement concerning probationary employees.[3] Exceptions, Attach. 4, Agency's Closing Brief at 3. The Union requested the grievant's reinstatement. Award at 23-24. The

---

1. The Agency argued that the grievance was not procedurally arbitrable because the Union did not file the grievance in accordance with filing procedures set forth in the parties' agreement. *See* Award at 24. The Arbitrator rejected this claim, *see id.* at 25, and the Agency does not challenge this conclusion. Accordingly, that issue is not before us.

2. Before the Arbitrator, the Union asserted that the Agency committed an unfair labor practice (ULP) by bypassing the Union when it offered MOUs and settlement agreements to other probationary employees facing termination. *See* Award at 23. Neither party addresses this issue; accordingly, it is not before us.

3. The relevant portions of the parties' agreement are set forth in the attached appendix.

Agency argued that reinstatement was not authorized because the Authority has consistently "held that a grievance concerning the separation of a probationary employee is excluded from the scope of negotiated grievance procedures based on the statutory and regulatory scheme for a probationary period of employment set forth in 5 U.S.C. [§] 3321 and 5 C.F.R. part 315, subpart H." Exceptions, Attach. 4, Agency's Closing Brief at 12 (citing *AFGE, Local 2006*, 58 FLRA 297, 298 (2003) (*AFGE*); *Dep't of Health & Human Servs., SSA*, 14 FLRA 164 (1984)).

The Arbitrator concluded that the Agency violated the parties' agreement by denying the grievant's request for representation during the meeting; however, he did not state which contract provision the Agency violated. Award at 25. The Arbitrator acknowledged that he could not review the merits of the grievant's termination; thus, he could not reinstate the grievant. *Id.* at 27. However, the Arbitrator ordered the Agency to hold a meeting with the grievant and a Union representative to discuss the grievant's termination. The Arbitrator stated that, although he could not mandate that the Agency reverse its decision to terminate the grievant, the Agency would not be permitted to convert the resignation into a termination. *Id.* The Arbitrator further ordered the Agency to cease and desist from "denying Union representation to probationary employees during meetings where they are issued discipline, including a notice of termination, which results in them being removed from the premises or otherwise suspended from reporting for their regular duty assignment." *Id.* at 28.

III. Agency's Exceptions

The Agency avers that the award is contrary to law for two reasons.

First, the Agency asserts that the award impermissibly expands the procedural protections afforded to probationary employees under Office of Personnel Management (OPM) Regulations. Exceptions at 8. The Agency avers that, under OPM Regulations, a probationary employee facing termination does not have the right to explain or defend himself/herself. *Id.* (citing *NTEU*, 39 FLRA 848 (1991) (*NTEU*)). The Agency further contends that collective bargaining agreements cannot be used to expand OPM's procedural protections. *Id.* Thus, according to the Agency, the award is contrary to "statutory and regulatory scheme for probationary periods of employment set forth in 5 C.F.R. part 315, subpart H." *Id.* (citing *AFGE*, 58 FLRA at 297).

Second, the Agency argues that the Arbitrator incorrectly concluded that the grievant was entitled to Union representation during the meeting. *Id.* at 5-6. The Agency claims that, under § 7114(a)(2)(B) of the Statute, the grievant did not have a right to representation because the meeting involved the notification of discipline, rather than the imposition of discipline. *Id.* at 6.

IV. Analysis and Conclusion: the award is contrary to law.

The Authority reviews questions of law de novo. *See NTEU, Chapter 24*, 50 FLRA 330, 332 (1995) (citing *U.S. Customs Serv. v. FLRA*, 43 F.3d 682, 686-87 (D.C. Cir. 1994)). In applying a standard of de novo review, the Authority determines whether the arbitrator's legal conclusions are consistent with the applicable standard of law. *NFFE, Local 1437*, 53 FLRA 1703, 1710 (1998). In making that determination, the Authority defers to the arbitrator's underlying factual findings. *See id.*

The Authority has held that a grievance concerning the termination of a probationary employee is excluded from the scope of negotiated grievance procedures based on the statutory and regulatory scheme for a probationary period of employment set forth in 5 U.S.C. § 3321 and 5 C.F.R. part 315, subpart H. *E.g., GSA, Region 2, N.Y.C., N.Y.*, 58 FLRA 588, 589 (2003) (*GSA*) (finding that grievance concerning agency's failure to abide by certain contractual provisions when it terminated grievant probationary employee was not substantively arbitrable) (citations omitted); *U.S. Dep't of the Air Force, Nellis Air Force Base, Las Vegas, Nev.*, 46 FLRA 1323, 1326-27 (1993) (*NAFB*) (same). In so holding, the Authority has consistently noted that parties may not use the collective bargaining process to provide procedural protections for probationary employees facing termination. *E.g., AFGE*, 58 FLRA at 298 (citation omitted); *NAFB*, 46 FLRA at 1326-27 (citations omitted). Of particular relevance, the Authority has found contrary to law a bargaining proposal requiring, among other things, that an agency provide a probationary employee with the option to request union representation during a meeting in which he or she faces termination. *See NTEU*, 39 FLRA at 852-53.

The award is contrary to law. The Union grieved whether the Agency processed the termination of a probationary employee in accordance with the parties' agreement when it denied the grievant's request for Union representation. *See* Award at 10. That portion of the grievance, therefore, concerned the termination of a probationary employee. *See, e.g., GSA*, 58 FLRA at 589 (grievance claiming that agency failed to follow contractual procedures when it terminated probationary employee concerned termination of probationary employee); *AFGE*, 58 FLRA at 298 (same). Such grievances are not substantively arbitrable. *See id.* Indeed, as noted above, contract provisions requiring that an agency provide a probationary employee with the option to request union representation during a meeting in which he or she faces termination are contrary to law.[4] *See NTEU*, 39 FLRA at 852-53. Accordingly, we find that the portion of the grievance concerning whether the Agency violated the parties' agreement was not substantively arbitrable; because the Arbitrator based his award on that portion, we set aside the award as contrary to law.[5] *See, e.g., GSA*, 58 FLRA at 589 (Authority set aside award after arbitrator erroneously concluded that a grievance concerning the termination of a probationary employee was substantively arbitrable).

V. Decision

The award is set aside.

APPENDIX

Article 28, Section 2 provides:

A. The purpose of this Section is to clarify certain rights of probationary employees where those rights may not be clear elsewhere in this Agreement.

B. The Agency agrees to provide probationary employees a reasonable and fair opportunity to improve job performance.

C. The Agency agrees to evaluate the performance of probationary employees during the probationary period and to counsel the employee concerning performance deficiencies. The Agency will give the employees the results of any interim review.

D. Probationary employees will usually be given a one-pay period's notice of their separation. This will not preclude the Agency [from] taking any action it deems appropriate for disciplinary and/or performance reasons in accordance with government-wide rules and regulations.

Award at 10-11.

---

4. We note that none of the contract provisions cited in the award mirrors rights set forth in the Statute.

5. As stated above, the issue concerning whether the Agency committed a ULP by bypassing the Union when it offered MOUs and settlement agreements to other probationary employees facing termination is not before us. We, therefore, do not address whether issue is substantively arbitrable. Furthermore, based on our decision, it is unnecessary to address the Agency's remaining exception.

65 FLRA No. 171

UNITED STATES
DEPARTMENT OF THE TREASURY
INTERNAL REVENUE SERVICE
(Agency)

and

NATIONAL TREASURY
EMPLOYEES UNION
(Union)

0-AR-4699

DECISION

May 23, 2011

Before the Authority: Carol Waller Pope, Chairman, and Thomas M. Beck and Ernest DuBester, Members

I. Statement of the Case

This matter is before the Authority on exceptions to an award of Arbitrator Stanley H. Sergent filed by the Agency under § 7122(a) of the Federal Service Labor-Management Relations Statute (the Statute) and part 2425 of the Authority's Regulations. The Union filed an opposition to the Agency's exceptions.

The Arbitrator sustained a grievance alleging that the Agency racially discriminated against the grievant when it failed to select her for a vacant position. For the reasons that follow, we deny the Agency's exceptions.

II. Background and Arbitrator's Award

While occupying a General Schedule, Grade 12 (GS-12) position with the Agency, the grievant applied for a vacant General Schedule, Grade 13 (GS-13) revenue agent position (the GS-13 position). Award at 2-3, 5-6. When the Agency selected another individual (the selectee) for the GS-13 position, the Union filed a grievance alleging, among other things, that the Agency racially discriminated against the grievant when it did not select her. *Id.* at 3. When the grievance was unresolved, the parties proceeded to arbitration. *Id.* at 4. As relevant here, the stipulated issue before the Arbitrator was whether the "Agency discriminate[d] against the grievant . . . based on race . . . when it did not select her for [the GS-13 position] . . . [, and,] [i]f so, what shall the remedy be?" *Id.*

The Arbitrator relied upon the *McDonnell Douglas* burden-shifting framework (the framework) – which complainants may use to "prov[e] a race discrimination case . . . in a Title VII[[1]] trial" – to assess the grievant's complaint of disparate treatment based on race. *Id.* at 17-19 (quoting and citing *McDonnell Douglas Corp. v. Green*, 411 U.S. 792, 802-03 (1973) (*McDonnell Douglas*)[2] (internal quotation marks omitted)). In this regard, the Arbitrator found that the Union satisfied the first-step burden under the framework by establishing a prima facie case of race discrimination. *Id.* at 19. He found further that the Agency satisfied the second-step burden under the framework by articulating "legitimate non-discriminatory reasons" for preferring the selectee over the grievant, including the Agency's contentions that the selectee: (1) "had the best interview . . ."; (2) was "ranked at the top of the best qualified list . . ."; and (3) had "recent relevant experience[.]" *Id.*

Moving to the third step of the framework, the Arbitrator determined that, in order to prevail on the disparate treatment claim, the Union had to "prove[] by a preponderance of the evidence that the Agency's [articulated reasons were] pretextual." *Id.* at 20. With regard to this third-step burden, the Arbitrator stated that he would not "second-guess[]" the Agency's proffered reasons for choosing the selectee unless the Union proved, as relevant here, that: (1) the reasons articulated were "unworthy of credence . . ."; or (2) the grievant's "qualifications were plainly[, demonstrably, or observably] superior to those of the selectee." *Id.* (citing *Burchfield v. Dep't of Treasury*, EEOC Appeal Nos. 01970152, 01941579 (Apr. 6, 2000)); *id.* at 27-28 (citing *Ash v. Tyson Foods, Inc.*, 546 U.S. 454 (2006)).

1. In this context, "Title VII" refers to the seventh title of the Civil Rights Act of 1964 (codified, as amended, at 42 U.S.C. §§ 2000e to 2000e-17).

2. Under the framework, an employee "must first establish a prima facie case of discrimination. If [the employee] does, [then] the employer must articulate a legitimate, nondiscriminatory reason for the challenged action. Finally, if the employer satisfies this burden, [then] the employee must show that the reason is pretextual[.]" *Dawson v. Entek Int'l*, 630 F.3d 928, 934-35 (9th Cir. 2011) (*Dawson*) (citation omitted).

As part of his assessment of whether the Agency's reasons were "worthy of credence," the Arbitrator examined the parties' compliance with their obligation under the master labor agreement (Agreement) to "mak[e] a complete record during the steps of the grievance procedure[.]" *Id.* at 25 (quoting Agreement Art. 41, § 8.A.1.).[3] The Arbitrator found that the Agency violated that contractual obligation because, although the Union "made a detailed presentation" at the second- and third-step grievance meetings to support the discrimination claim, the Agency never offered a "substantive reply" or "any definitive explanations for the grievant's non-selection [until arbitration]. Instead, it simply denied the grievance." *Id.* In addition, the Arbitrator found that the testimony of the selecting official for the GS-13 position was "not credible[,]" *id.* at 31, because the official articulated different reasons at arbitration than he had articulated to the grievant in a counseling session, which the Arbitrator found to be a violation of Article 13, Section 9.D. of the Agreement.[4] *See id.* at 21 (quoting Agreement Art. 13, § 9.D.), 24, 27-28, 31.

In light of the Agency's failure to satisfy its contractual obligation to fully articulate its reasons for the grievant's nonselection during counseling and at the second- and third-step grievance meetings, the Arbitrator found that the Agency's proffered reasons were "not credible . . . because they obviously ha[d] been devised for the arbitration" proceedings. *Id.* at 27. "Thus, the only conclusion that [the Arbitrator could] properly . . . draw[] from th[e] evidence [was] that the Agency's [reasons] . . . [were] pretext for discrimination based on race." *Id.*; *see also id.* at 25 (failure to provide "substantive response" prior to arbitration "suggest[ed] . . . pretext for . . . discrimination based on race"). As an additional ground for finding that the Agency's explanations at arbitration were pretextual, the Arbitrator found that the grievant's qualifications were "plainly superior" to those of the selectee. *Id.* at 28; *see also id.* at 27-31.

Because the Union had established its prima facie case and the Arbitrator found the Agency's articulated reasons for nonselection to be pretextual, the Arbitrator concluded that the Agency discriminated against the grievant on the basis of race and that, "in the absence of such discrimination[,] the Agency would have selected her for the . . . [GS-13 position]." *Id.* at 32. Therefore, the Arbitrator sustained the grievance, awarded the grievant a retroactive promotion to the GS-13 position, and directed the Agency to make her whole for any lost pay and benefits. *Id.* at 32-33.

III. Positions of the Parties

A. Agency's Exceptions

The Agency contends that the Arbitrator's conclusion that it discriminated against the grievant on the basis of race is contrary to Title VII. *See* Exceptions at 7, 11. In this regard, the Agency contends that the Arbitrator erred as a matter of law in determining that the Agency's articulated reasons for not selecting the grievant were pretextual. Specifically, the Agency argues that its "failure to provide [the] reason[s]" for the grievant's nonselection during earlier stages of the grievance process "is not sufficient to establish pretext." *Id.* at 11. Moreover, the Agency contends that the grievant's qualifications were not "plainly superior" to the selectee's, but rather, "the selectee['s] qualifications . . . [were] far more recent and relevant than the grievant's." *Id.* at 10. *See also id.* at 7 11 (arguments regarding the alleged superiority of the selectee's qualifications). Consequently, the Agency asserts that "the [A]rbitrator's finding of pretext [is] insufficient as a matter of law" to a support his conclusion that the Agency intentionally discriminated against the grievant on the basis of race. *Id.* at 13.

B. Union's Opposition

According to the Union, because the Arbitrator found that the "Agency's stated reason[s] [were] unworthy of credence" and that the grievant's

---

3. Article 41, Section 8 of the Agreement states, in pertinent part:

> A.
> 1. The parties will have the obligation of making a complete record during the steps of the grievance procedure. . . .
>
> D.
> With [exceptions not relevant here,] new issues may not be raised by either party unless they have been raised at [s]tep [two] of the grievance procedure. . . .

Opp'n, Attach. B at 131.

4. Article 13, Section 9.D. of the Agreement states, in pertinent part: "An applicant . . . who is not selected will, upon request, be entitled to counseling by the immediate supervisor or his or her designee . . . [and] additional counseling from the selecting official or his or her designee. The counseling will provide the reasons for [the applicant's] non-selection[.]" Opp'n, Attach. C at 53.

qualifications were "plainly superior" to those of the selectee, the Arbitrator correctly concluded that the Agency's articulated reasons were pretextual. Opp'n at 5; *see also id.* at 5-12, 15. Further, the Union asserts that the Authority has recognized that an arbitrator's findings of pretext constitute "factual findings[,]" to which the Authority defers. *Id.* at 15-16 (quoting *NTEU, Chapter 90*, 58 FLRA 390 (2000) (*NTEU*) (internal quotation marks omitted)). Finally, the Union argues that the Arbitrator applied the "correct legal standard" in his framework analysis, *id.* at 18, because his "disbelief of the reasons put forward" by the Agency, "together with the elements of the [Union's] prima facie case, suffice[d] to show intentional discrimination" by the Agency, *id.* at 10. *See id.* at 9-10, 18-19 (quoting and citing *St. Mary's Honor Ctr. v. Hicks*, 509 U.S. 502, 511, 519 (1993) (*St. Mary's*) (internal quotation marks omitted)).

IV. Analysis and Conclusions

The Agency asserts that the award is contrary to Title VII. When an exception involves an award's consistency with law, rule, or regulation, the Authority reviews any question of law raised by the exception and the award de novo. *See NTEU, Chapter 24*, 50 FLRA 330, 332 (1995) (citing *U.S. Customs Serv. v. FLRA*, 43 F.3d 682, 686-87 (D.C. Cir. 1994)). In applying the standard of de novo review, the Authority assesses whether an arbitrator's legal conclusions are consistent with the applicable standard of law. *See U.S. Dep't of Def., Dep'ts of the Army & the Air Force, Ala. Nat'l Guard, Northport, Ala.*, 55 FLRA 37, 40 (1998) (*Ala. Nat'l Guard*). In making that assessment, the Authority defers to the arbitrator's underlying factual findings. *See id.*

The Agency disputes the Arbitrator's findings that its articulated reasons for nonselection were pretextual. *See* Exceptions at 7-11. The question of whether an employer's stated reasons for an employment action are pretextual is a factual one. *See Raytheon Co. v. Hernandez*, 540 U.S. 44, 52 (2003) (quoting *McDonnell Douglas*, 411 U.S. at 804) (at third step of framework, claimant must establish that employer's "stated reason for [employment action] was *in fact* pretext" (emphasis added)); *Tex. Dep't of Cmty. Affairs v. Burdine*, 450 U.S. 248, 255 n.10 (1981) (pretext is a question for "trier of fact"); *Dawson*, 630 F.3d at 936 (circumstantial evidence undermining employer's stated reasons "raise[s] a material question of fact on pretext"); *Bonds v. Leavitt*, 629 F.3d 369, 386 (4th Cir. 2011) (claimant "failed to create a genuine issue of material fact regarding . . . pretext"); *see also Cones v. Shalala*, 199 F.3d 512, 520 (D.C. Cir. 2000) (where pretext determination "ultimately turns on witness credibility," agency's stated reason for employment action "presents a question of fact that is . . . 'quintessentially one for the finder of fact'"). As noted by the Union, Opp'n at 15-16, the Authority has held that it will defer to arbitral findings – in connection with an arbitrator's analysis at the third step of the framework – that the stated reasons for an adverse employment action were pretextual. *See NTEU*, 58 FLRA at 394. In this regard, the Authority defers to arbitral findings of pretext in the same manner that the Authority defers to other arbitral factual findings when applying the de novo standard of review. *See Ala. Nat'l Guard*, 55 FLRA at 40. Thus, we defer to the Arbitrator's factual finding that the Agency's stated reasons for not selecting the grievant for the GS-13 position were pretextual.

The Agency also contends that, as a matter of law, its failure to articulate legitimate, nondiscriminatory reasons earlier in the grievance process is insufficient to establish pretext. Exceptions at 11. The Agency does not cite any legal authority to support this contention, and it is not consistent with court decisions regarding this issue. *See, e.g., Hurlbert v. St. Mary's Health Care Sys., Inc.*, 439 F.3d 1286, 1298 (11th Cir. 2006) (holding that "employer's failure to articulate *clearly* and *consistently* the reason for an [adverse employment action] may serve as evidence of pretext" (emphasis added)); *Harvey v. Office of Banks & Real Estate*, 377 F.3d 698, 711 (7th Cir. 2004) (holding that fact finder "entitled to infer that [employer's] decision was in fact motivated by racial animus[,]" where employer did not offer "any legitimate reason" for demoting employee when it first notified him of the demotion); *Lamphere v. Brown Univ.*, 875 F.2d 916, 922 (1st Cir. 1989) (holding that "changing reasons, *failure to articulate reasons contemporaneously*, [or] conflicts among individuals' reasons" may suggest pretext for discrimination (emphasis added)). Thus, we find that the Agency has not established that the Arbitrator erred as a matter of law in this respect.

The Agency contends further that the Arbitrator erred, as a matter of law, in finding that the grievant's qualifications were "plainly superior" to those of the selectee. *See* Exceptions at 7-11. In this regard, the Authority has held that, when an arbitrator bases an award on two or more separate and independent grounds, the appealing party must establish that all of the grounds relied on are deficient in order for the Authority to find the award deficient. *E.g.*, *Broad.*

Bd. of Governors, Office of Cuba Broad., 64 FLRA 888, 892 (2010) (*Bd. of Governors*). If the excepting party has not demonstrated that the award is deficient on one of the grounds relied on by the arbitrator, then it is unnecessary to address exceptions to the other ground. *Id.* The Arbitrator identified two separate and independent grounds to support his finding that the Agency's articulated reasons were pretextual. Specifically, he found that: (1) the Agency's articulated reasons were "unworthy of credence"; and (2) the grievant's qualifications were "plainly superior[.]" Award at 20, 31; *see also id.* at 27-31. As discussed above, we have found that the Agency has not established that the Arbitrator erred in concluding that the Agency's reasons were "unworthy of credence[.]" As this conclusion provides a separate and independent ground for the award, we find it unnecessary to address the Agency's contention that the Arbitrator erred in finding that the grievant's qualifications were "plainly superior[.]" *See Bd. of Governors*, 64 FLRA at 892.

Finally, the Agency contends that the Arbitrator's findings of pretext do not support his ultimate conclusion that the Agency intentionally discriminated against the grievant. Exceptions at 13. However, the Supreme Court has expressly held that findings of pretext, together with the elements of a prima facie case, are sufficient to support a finding of intentional discrimination. *See St. Mary's*, 509 U.S. at 511, 519. Because we have found that the Arbitrator did not err in his findings of pretext, and as the Agency does not contest that the Union established a prima facie case, we find that the Arbitrator's framework analysis correctly applied the legal standard governing the disparate treatment claim.

For the foregoing reasons, we deny the Agency's exceptions contending that the award is contrary to law.

V. Decision

The Agency's exceptions are denied.

65 FLRA No. 172

BROADCASTING BOARD
OF GOVERNORS
(Agency)

and

AMERICAN FEDERATION
OF GOVERNMENT EMPLOYEES
LOCAL 1812
(Union)

0-AR-4571

ORDER DISMISSING EXCEPTIONS

May 23, 2011

Before the Authority: Carol Waller Pope, Chairman, and Thomas M. Beck and Ernest DuBester, Members

I. Statement of the Case

This matter is before the Authority on exceptions to an award of Arbitrator Suzanne R. Butler filed by the Agency under § 7122(a) of the Federal Service Labor-Management Relations Statute (the Statute) and part 2425 of the Authority's Regulations. The Union filed an opposition to the Agency's exceptions.

The Arbitrator found that the Agency suspended the grievant in violation of the parties' collective bargaining agreement (CBA), and she sustained the grievance. For the reasons that follow, we dismiss the Agency's exceptions.

II. Background and Arbitrator's Award

The Agency suspended the grievant for allegedly failing to follow instructions and Agency policy. Award at 6-7. The Union filed a grievance alleging that the Agency did not have sufficient cause under the CBA to suspend the grievant.[1] *Id.* at 2, 7. The grievance was unresolved and was submitted to arbitration, where, as relevant here, the parties stipulated to the following issues for resolution:

> 1. Did the Agency prove . . . that the [g]rievant failed to follow instructions . . ., as charged? If not, what shall be the remedy?
>
> 2. Did the Agency prove . . . that the [g]rievant failed to follow Agency policy . . ., as charged? If not, what shall be the remedy?

Id. at 2, 7.

Both the proposing and deciding officials (the officials) involved with the grievant's suspension testified at the arbitration hearing. *See id.* at 30. Based on their testimonies, the Arbitrator found that the Agency had suspended the grievant because the officials believed that he "intentionally act[ed] in insubordinate defiance of authority, disregard[ed] directive[s,] and refus[ed] to comply with a proper order," which were category fifteen offenses in the "Table of [Actions] incorporated into the [CBA.]" *Id.* (internal quotation marks omitted); *see also id.* at 4 (quoting category fifteen offenses from CBA's table of actions).

The Arbitrator found that the Agency failed to prove its charge of "intentional insubordination" in connection with the grievant's alleged failure to follow instructions. *See id.* at 30, 36, 39. With regard to whether the grievant failed to follow Agency policy, the Arbitrator found it uncontested that the grievant's actions were not consistent with the policy at issue. *Id.* at 37. Nevertheless, because the deciding official testified that she suspended the grievant based on her belief that he "knew or should have known" that the Agency policy applied to his circumstances, the Arbitrator found that the question before her involved whether "the [g]rievant *intentionally* failed" to follow a policy that "he knew or should have known" applied to his circumstances. *Id.* In that regard, the Arbitrator determined that the Agency did not prove that the grievant "intentionally failed to follow the [Agency] . . . policy as charged." *Id.* at 37-38; *see also id.* at 39.

Because she found that the Agency had not proven either charge "by a preponderance of the evidence," the Arbitrator sustained the grievance and

1. The CBA provides, in pertinent part: "An employee will be subject to disciplinary . . . actions only for such cause as will promote the efficiency of the Federal Service[.]" Award at 3 (quoting CBA Art. 20, § 1.B.); *see also id.* at 2 (identifying, among other provisions, CBA Art. 20, § 1.B. as "relevant contract language" in the parties' dispute).

directed the Agency to compensate the grievant for lost pay and to expunge the suspension from its records. *Id.* at 38-39.

III. Positions of the Parties

A. Agency's Exceptions

The Agency contends that the Arbitrator "relied on nonfacts" by finding that the charges against the grievant included "insubordination" and "an intentional failure to follow [Agency] policy[.]" Exceptions at 10 (internal quotation marks omitted). In addition, the Agency contends that the Arbitrator "re-formulat[ed]" the charges against the grievant in a manner contrary to law. *Id.* at 11. Specifically, the Agency asserts that the Arbitrator's "rewritt[en]" charges required the Agency to prove that the grievant intentionally violated instructions and Agency policy, whereas the Agency asserts that the grievant's intent was "irrelevant" to the charges for which the Agency disciplined him. *Id.* at 11-12 (citations omitted). Finally, the Agency alleges that the Arbitrator exceeded her authority by "re-defin[ing]" the charges to require a showing of intentionality. *Id.* at 8-9 (citations omitted).

B. Union's Opposition

The Union asserts that, before the Arbitrator, "the Agency's position" was that it suspended the grievant because he "intentional[ly]" failed to follow instructions and Agency policy. Opp'n at 14. For support, the Union quotes an exchange between the Arbitrator and the Agency's counsel at the hearing (Counsel), in which the Arbitrator asked Counsel to characterize the charges, and Counsel described them as "insubordinate defiance of authority, disregard of directive, [and] refusal to comply with [a] proper order[.]" *Id.* at 13 (quoting Tr. at 548). The Union asserts that Counsel's response included only "intentional misconduct charges[]" that qualified as category fifteen offenses under the CBA's table of actions, *id.*, and, when the Arbitrator inquired whether any of the Agency's charges qualified as category fourteen offenses under the table – i.e., a category of offenses that need not include intent – Counsel replied, "No[,]" *id.* (quoting Tr. at 547-48).

Further, the Union asserts that the Agency's post-hearing brief alleged that the grievant "*disregarded . . . instructions and decided to single-handedly call the shots . . . as he desired*" while on assignment. *Id.* (quoting Agency's Post-Hearing Br. at 12 (emphasis added by Union)). Moreover, the Union quotes the deciding official's testimony that she believed that the grievant "knew" that he was not following the Agency's policy, and that belief was her "basis for . . . upholding the two-day[]" suspension. *Id.* (internal quotation marks omitted) (quoting Tr. at 278-79). Based on the foregoing, the Union contends that the Authority should not "hear[] . . . argu[ments] on appeal [of the award that are] in opposition to the position [that the Agency] presented to the Arbitrator at [the] hearing." *Id.* at 20.

IV. Analysis and Conclusions

Under § 2429.5 of the Authority's Regulations (§ 2429.5), the Authority will not consider issues that could have been, but were not, presented to the arbitrator.[2] *See, e.g., U.S. Dep't of Homeland Sec., U.S. Customs & Border Prot., JFK Airport, Queens, N.Y.*, 62 FLRA 416, 417 (2008). Where a party makes an argument before the Authority that is inconsistent with its position before the arbitrator, the Authority applies § 2429.5 to bar the argument and to dismiss exceptions based on that argument. *See, e.g., U.S. Dep't of Transp., Fed. Aviation Admin., Detroit, Mich.*, 64 FLRA 325, 328 (2009) (*FAA*); *U.S. Dep't of the Treasury, Internal Revenue Serv.*, 57 FLRA 444, 448 (2001) (Chairman Cabaniss concurring).

The officials' testimonies, Counsel's assertions at the arbitration hearing, and the Agency's post-hearing brief all establish that, before the Arbitrator, the Agency argued that it had sufficient cause to suspend the grievant because he *intentionally* failed to follow instructions and Agency policy. *See* Exceptions, Attach. B(1) (hearing transcript, part 1) at 74-78, 84-85 (testimony of Proposing Official); *id.*, Attach. B(2) (hearing transcript, part 2) at 278-79 (testimony of Deciding Official); *id.* at 547-49 (exchange between Counsel and Arbitrator on category of offenses); Opp'n, Attach., CBA at 60 (listing offenses within categories fourteen and fifteen of table of actions); *id.*, Attach., Agency's Post-Hearing Br. at 10, 12 (alleging grievant "disregarded" instructions and "decided to

---

2. The Authority's Regulations concerning the review of arbitration awards, as well as certain related procedural Regulations – including § 2429.5 – were revised effective October 1, 2010. *See* 75 Fed. Reg. 42,283 (2010). As the exceptions in this case were filed before the effective date of the revised Regulations, we apply the prior version of the Regulations. Under the prior Regulations, § 2429.5 stated, in pertinent part: "The Authority will not consider evidence offered by a party, or any issue, which was not presented in the proceedings before the . . . arbitrator."

single-handedly call the shots . . . as he desired"). Moreover, in her award, the Arbitrator relied on those Agency allegations of intentionality when interpreting the issues and deciding the questions before her. *See* Award at 30, 37 (relying on officials' testimonies); *id.* at 2-4 (quoting CBA table of actions' wording of category fifteen offenses, but not category fourteen offenses, as "relevant contract language"); *id.* at 23-24 (summarizing Agency's position based on assertions in its post-hearing brief). In contrast, the premise of all of the Agency's exceptions is that the grievant was not charged with or suspended for intentionally failing to follow instructions and Agency policy. *E.g.*, Exceptions at 8-9, 10, 11-12. As such, the exceptions are inconsistent with the arguments that the Agency made before the Arbitrator, and we dismiss them as barred by § 2429.5. *See FAA*, 64 FLRA at 328.

V. Order

The Agency's exceptions are dismissed.

65 FLRA No. 173

AMERICAN FEDERATION
OF GOVERNMENT EMPLOYEES
LOCAL 1546
(Union)

and

UNITED STATES
DEPARTMENT OF DEFENSE
DEFENSE LOGISTICS AGENCY
(Agency)

0-AR-4745

ORDER DISMISSING EXCEPTION

May 23, 2011

Before the Authority: Carol Waller Pope, Chairman, and Thomas M. Beck and Ernest DuBester, Members

I. Statement of the Case

This matter is before the Authority on an exception to an award of Arbitrator Kathy Fragnoli filed by the Union under § 7122 of the Federal Service Labor-Management Relations Statute and part 2425 of the Authority's Regulations. The Agency filed an opposition.

The Arbitrator found that the Agency did not violate the parties' agreement when it reassigned the grievant. For the reasons that follow, we dismiss the Union's exception.

II. Background and Arbitrator's Award

The Agency reassigned the grievant to a new position. Award at 5-6. The Union filed a grievance challenging the reassignment as contrary to the parties' agreement. *Id.* at 6-7. The grievance was unresolved and submitted to arbitration, where the Arbitrator stated the issue, in pertinent part, as follows: "Did the Agency violate the terms of the [parties'] [a]greement when the [g]rievant was involuntarily reassigned . . . ?" *Id.* at 2. The Arbitrator found that the Agency did not violate the parties' agreement, and denied the grievance. *Id.* at 12.

III. Positions of the Parties

A. Union's Exception

The Union asserts that the award "conflicts with a Presidential Executive Order . . . ." Exception at 1.

B. Agency's Opposition

The Agency argues that § 2429.5 of the Authority's Regulations (§ 2429.5) bars the Union's exception because the Union failed to argue, before the Arbitrator, that the reassignment conflicts with an executive order. Opp'n at 4-5. The Agency also argues that the Union's exception lacks merit and fails to comply with §§ 2425.4 and 2425.6 of the Authority's Regulations. *See id.* at 3-4, 5-12. Finally, the Agency argues that the Authority lacks jurisdiction because the award relates to a reduction in pay covered under 5 U.S.C. § 7512. *Id.* at 5.

IV. Analysis and Conclusions

Under § 2429.5, "[t]he Authority will not consider any . . . arguments . . . that could have been, but were not, presented in the proceedings before the . . . arbitrator." 5 C.F.R. § 2429.5. *See also* 5 C.F.R. § 2425.4(c) (exceptions may not rely on any "evidence, factual assertions, [or] arguments . . . that could have been, but were not, presented to the arbitrator").

Here, the issues before the Arbitrator included whether the Agency's reassignment of the grievant violated the parties' agreement. Award at 2. In this regard, the Union argued to the Arbitrator that the reassignment violated the parties' agreement. *Id.* at 6-7. Although the Union could have also argued that the reassignment violated an executive order, there is no indication in the record that it did so. Accordingly, we dismiss this exception as barred by § 2429.5.* *See, e.g.*, *Fraternal Order of Police, Pentagon Police Labor Comm.*, 65 FLRA 781, 783-84 (2011).

V. Decision

The Union's exception is dismissed.

---

*Accordingly, we find it unnecessary to address the Agency's remaining arguments, including its claim that the Authority lacks jurisdiction. *See, e.g.*, *Pan. Area Maritime/Metal Trades Council, AFL-CIO (M/MTC)*, 55 FLRA 1199, 1200 (1999) (Authority assumed, without deciding, that it had jurisdiction, and dismissed exception pursuant to § 2429.5).

65 FLRA No. 174

NATIONAL ASSOCIATION
OF GOVERNMENT EMPLOYEES
LOCAL 888
(Union)

and

UNITED STATES
DEPARTMENT OF THE ARMY
ARMY GARRISON CAMP PARKS
CAMP PARKS, CALIFORNIA
(Agency)

0-AR-4735

DECISION

May 24, 2011

Before the Authority: Carol Waller Pope, Chairman, and Thomas M. Beck and Ernest DuBester, Members

This matter is before the Authority on an exception to an award of Arbitrator Jeffrey A. Belkin filed by the Union under § 7122(a) of the Federal Service Labor-Management Relations Statute (the Statute) and part 2425 of the Authority's Regulations. The Agency filed an opposition to the Union's exception.

Under § 7122(a) of the Statute, an award is deficient if it is contrary to any law, rule, or regulation, or it is deficient on other grounds similar to those applied by federal courts in private sector labor-management relations. Upon careful consideration of the entire record in this case and Authority precedent, the Authority concludes that the award is not deficient on the ground raised in the exception and set forth in § 7122(a). *See U.S. Dep't of the Air Force, Lowry Air Force Base, Denver, Colo.*, 48 FLRA 589, 593-94 (1993) (award not deficient as based on a nonfact where excepting party either challenges a factual matter that the parties disputed at arbitration or fails to demonstrate that the central fact underlying the award is clearly erroneous, but for which a different result would have been reached by the arbitrator).

Accordingly, the Union's exception is denied.

65 FLRA No. 175

AMERICAN FEDERATION
OF GOVERNMENT EMPLOYEES
LOCAL 3979
COUNCIL OF PRISON LOCALS
(Union)

and

UNITED STATES
DEPARTMENT OF JUSTICE
FEDERAL BUREAU OF PRISONS
FEDERAL CORRECTIONAL INSTITUTION
SHERIDAN, OREGON
(Agency)

0-AR-4741

DECISION

May 24, 2011

Before the Authority: Carol Waller Pope, Chairman, and Thomas M. Beck and Ernest DuBester, Members

This matter is before the Authority on exceptions to an award of Arbitrator Charles S. Loughran filed by the Union under § 7122(a) of the Federal Service Labor-Management Relations Statute (the Statute) and part 2425 of the Authority's Regulations. The Agency filed an opposition to the Union's exceptions.

Under § 7122(a) of the Statute, an award is deficient if it is contrary to any law, rule, or regulation, or it is deficient on other grounds similar to those applied by federal courts in private sector labor-management relations. Upon careful consideration of the entire record in this case and Authority precedent, the Authority concludes that the award is not deficient on the grounds raised in the exceptions and set forth in § 7122(a). *See U.S. Dep't of the Navy, Naval Base, Norfolk, Va.*, 51 FLRA 305, 307-08 (1995) (award not deficient on ground that arbitrator exceeded his or her authority where excepting party does not establish that arbitrator failed to resolve an issue submitted to arbitration, disregarded specific limitations on his authority, or awarded relief to persons who were not encompassed within the grievance); *U.S. Dep't of Labor (OSHA)*, 34 FLRA 573, 575 (1990) (award not deficient as failing to draw its essence from the parties' collective bargaining agreement where excepting party fails to establish that the award cannot in any rational way be derived from the agreement; is so unfounded in reason and fact and so unconnected to the wording and purpose of the agreement as to manifest an infidelity to the obligation of the arbitrator; does not represent a plausible interpretation of the agreement; or evidences a manifest disregard of the agreement).

Accordingly, the Union's exceptions are denied.

65 FLRA No. 176

AMERICAN FEDERATION
OF GOVERNMENT EMPLOYEES
LOCAL 1164
(Union)

and

SOCIAL SECURITY ADMINISTRATION
AUBURN DISTRICT OFFICE
AUBURN, MAINE
(Agency)

0-NG-3094

DECISION AND ORDER
ON NEGOTIABILITY ISSUES

May 25, 2011

Before the Authority: Carol Waller Pope, Chairman, and Thomas M. Beck and Ernest DuBester, Members

I. Statement of the Case

This matter is before the Authority on a negotiability appeal filed by the Union under § 7105(a)(2)(E) of the Federal Service Labor-Management Relations Statute (the Statute), and concerns the negotiability of two proposals. The Agency filed a statement of position (SOP), the Union filed a response, and the Agency filed a reply.

For the reasons that follow, we find that Proposal 1 is within the duty to bargain, and that Proposal 2 is outside the duty to bargain. Accordingly, we dismiss the petition with regard to Proposal 2, and direct the Agency to bargain over Proposal 1.

II. Proposal 1

A. Wording

> Additional adjudication time will be provided to all employees per the following procedure. All employees will be placed on a roster according to seniority by service computation date (SCD), with the most senior employee at the top of the roster. Each workday, the employee at the top of the roster will be given an adjudication day, and that employee's name goes to the bottom of the roster. If the top employee is not present that day, the next highest available employee will have an adjudication day and will then go to the bottom of the roster. The absent employee will remain at the top of the roster until present for the adjudication day. This rotation can be suspended for operational needs.
>
> Adjudication time provided under this procedure will be in addition to existing adjudication time procedures, such as the existing service representative rotation and the claims representatives' Wednesday duty rotation. Any changes to existing adjudication time procedures, arrangements, practices, and policies are subject to advance notice to the Union, consultation, and bargaining in accordance with 5 U.S.C. 71.

Petition at 1-2.

B. Meaning

In interpreting a disputed proposal, the Authority looks to its plain wording and any union statement of intent. If the union's explanation of the proposal is consistent with the proposal's plain wording, then the Authority adopts that explanation for the purpose of construing what the proposal means and, based on that meaning, deciding whether the proposal is within the duty to bargain. *See, e.g., NAGE, Local R1-144, Fed. Union of Scientists & Eng'rs*, 65 FLRA 552, 554 (2011) (*NAGE*). Where a proposal is silent as to a particular matter, the Authority will adopt a union's statement clarifying the matter if that statement is otherwise consistent with the wording of the proposal. *See, e.g., AFSCME, Local 2830*, 60 FLRA 671, 671 (2005) (*Local 2830*).

The parties agree that Proposal 1 would establish a rotational roster under which one employee per day would be selected to work an "adjudication day" during which the employee would work without interruption on adjudication "desk work" and not conduct interviews with members of the public. Record of Post-Petition Conference (Record) at 1-2. The parties also agree that employees would be listed on the roster in order of seniority, and that the "adjudication day" would be in addition to any "adjudication time" or "desk work" time that the employee is currently allotted. *Id.*

In addition, the Union explains, and the Agency does not dispute, that the statement in Proposal 1 that the "rotation can be suspended for operational needs[,]" Petition at 2, enables the Agency to "suspend the rotation for business reasons[,]" Record at 2. Although the Agency asserts that the wording of the proposal implies that such suspensions must be "in advance[,]" SOP at 10, nothing in the plain wording of "[t]his rotation can be suspended for operational needs[,]" Petition at 2, or the Union's statement of the proposal's meaning, prohibits the Agency from suspending the rotation for operational needs at any point during the work day. Accordingly, we interpret Proposal 1 as permitting the Agency to suspend the rotation for business reasons at any point during the work day.

Further, Proposal 1 requires the Agency to provide "all employees" with "[a]dditional adjudication time" by placing them on the roster. *Id.* at 1. In this regard, the Agency argues that "the only sensible way to interpret the [proposal] is by its clear statement that Proposal 1 applies to *all* employees." Reply at 2 (emphasis added). However, the Union explains that, for purposes of the roster described in Proposal 1, "all employees" means all of "those employees who have been assigned by the Agency to perform claims-related work, including adjudication of the claims." Response at 3. The Union's explanation is a reasonable interpretation of the proposal, as it is logical that the only employees who would be placed on a roster providing additional time for adjudication work would be those employees who perform that type of work. As the Union's explanation is consistent with the plain wording of the proposal, we adopt this interpretation. *See, e.g.*, *NAGE*, 65 FLRA at 554; *Local 2830*, 60 FLRA at 671.

Finally, the Agency argues that the last sentence of Proposal 1 – "Any changes to existing adjudication time procedures, arrangements, practices, and policies are subject to advance notice to the Union, consultation, and bargaining in accordance with 5 U.S.C. 71[,]" Petition at 2 – expands the Agency's future bargaining obligation "well beyond the requirements of the Statute[,]" SOP at 10-11. However, the Union explains that the sentence is intended to mean only that "where the Agency is otherwise required to notify the Union under the Statute of changes to conditions of employment, it would not be relieved of that requirement by operation of [the last sentence of Proposal 1]." Response at 3. As the Union's explanation is consistent with the plain wording of the proposal, we interpret the pertinent sentence as a restatement – not an expansion – of the Agency's bargaining obligations under the Statute. *See, e.g.*, *NAGE*, 65 FLRA at 554; *Local 2830*, 60 FLRA at 671.

C. Positions of the Parties

1. Agency

The Agency contends that Proposal 1 affects the Agency's right to assign work under § 7106(a)(2)(B) of the Statute.[1] SOP at 3. In this regard, the Agency asserts that all of the employees who would be included in the proposal's roster are responsible for both "interviewing the public and adjudicating the public's claims[.]" *Id.* Because "the idea of adjudication time is to provide uninterrupted desk time where the employee is not interrupted by having to take interviews or answer the telephone[,]" the Agency asserts that Proposal 1 prohibits the Agency from assigning interviewing duties to the employee selected to work an adjudication day pursuant to the roster without regard to the number of members of the public who are waiting to be interviewed. *Id.* at 4. For support, the Agency cites: *AFGE, Local 1164*, 54 FLRA 1327 (1998) (*Local 1164*); and *AFGE, Local 2879*, 49 FLRA 279 (1994) (*Local 2879*). *See* SOP at 4-7.

Additionally, the Agency argues that "Proposal 1 does not qualify as an arrangement" under § 7106(b)(3) of the Statute because "[t]he Union has not shown that Proposal 1 addresses adverse [e]ffects flowing from the exercise of a management right." *Id.* at 10. In this regard, the Agency contends that "employees . . . have sufficient time to perform adjudication duties[,]" *id.*, particularly if they take advantage of available flexible work schedules and adjudicate claims during hours when there is no interview work because the office is not open to the public, *id.* at 4. The Agency also contends that the "negligible" adverse effects of its assignment of work "impact different job positions and work assignments differently[,]" and, thus, the proposal's requirement that the Agency place all employees on the adjudication roster without consideration of the differences in "work units" and "job duties" demonstrates that Proposal 1 is not sufficiently tailored. *Id.* at 10.

1. Section 7106(a)(2)(B) of the Statute provides, in pertinent part, that "nothing . . . shall affect the authority of any management official of any agency . . . to assign work[.]"

In addition, the Agency asserts that Proposal 1 is not an "[a]ppropriate" arrangement under § 7106(b)(3), *id.* at 7 (emphasis omitted), because it "excessively interferes with the Agency's ability to get its job done[,]" *id.* at 10. In this regard, the Agency claims that "the unpredictable nature of day to day interviewing needs" and the fact that "removing employees from an office's interviewing schedule can lead to a serious break down in service to the public" demonstrate that Proposal 1's institution of mandatory non-interviewing time excessively interferes with management's rights. Reply at 2.

2. Union

The Union argues that Proposal 1 is an appropriate arrangement under § 7106(b)(3). Petition at 3; Response at 4-9. In support of its argument that Proposal 1 is an arrangement, the Union asserts that the Agency's exercise of its right to assign interview work during time that would otherwise be set aside for adjudication has resulted in employees having insufficient "uninterrupted" adjudication time. Response at 7. In this regard, the Union emphasizes that, currently, whenever the office is open to the public, employees are subject to being assigned interviews by management. *See id.* According to the Union, the Agency's work-assignment policies increase employees' "job stress," and adversely affect their "performance" and "performance appraisal[s]," and Proposal 1 would ameliorate these effects by assuring employees of "[at] least a day at a time to catch up on adjudication of claims, on a recurring basis[.]" Petition at 3. The Union also asserts that Proposal 1 is sufficiently tailored because it applies only to employees who both conduct interviews and adjudicate claims. Response at 6.

In determining whether Proposal 1 is an "[a]ppropriate" arrangement, *id.* at 6 (emphasis omitted), the Union argues that the Authority should apply the standard that it applied in *National Weather Service Employees Organization*, 64 FLRA 569, 571 (2010) (*NWS*) (Member Beck dissenting), and find that Proposal 1 would not "significantly hamper the ability of the agency to get its job done[,]" but, rather, would provide employees the "uninterrupted" time necessary to perform an "essential component" of the Agency's work, Response at 7. The Union further asserts that the proposal is an appropriate arrangement because it: (1) preserves the Agency's right to determine the duties of any position; (2) applies only to employees who have been assigned adjudication work by the Agency; and (3) does not limit the factors that the Agency may consider when determining whether an "operational need" to suspend the rotation exists. *Id.* at 8. Finally, the Union requests that the Authority sever the fourth, fifth, sixth, seventh, and/or eighth sentences of the proposal if the inclusion of any of those sentences renders Proposal 1 outside the duty to bargain. *Id.* at 2; Petition at 4; Record at 2.

D. Analysis and Conclusions

1. Proposal 1 affects management's right to assign work under § 7106(a)(2)(B) of the Statute.

Where a union does not respond to an agency argument that a proposal affects a management right under § 7106 of the Statute, the Authority finds that the union has conceded that the proposal affects the claimed management right. *See, e.g., AFGE, Local 1367*, 64 FLRA 869, 870 (2010) (*Local 1367*) (Member Beck dissenting in part). As the Union did not respond to the Agency's assertion that Proposal 1 affects management's right to assign work, the Union concedes that the proposal affects that right.

2. Proposal 1 is an appropriate arrangement under § 7106(b)(3) of the Statute.

In determining whether a proposal is an appropriate arrangement within the meaning of § 7106(b)(3) of the Statute, the Authority applies the analysis set forth in *NAGE, Local R14-87*, 21 FLRA 24 (1986) (*KANG*).[2] Under that analysis, the Authority first determines whether the proposal is intended to be an arrangement for employees adversely affected by the exercise of a management right. *Id.* at 31. To establish that a proposal is an arrangement, a union must identify the effects or reasonably foreseeable effects that flow from the exercise of management's rights and demonstrate how those effects are adverse. *Id.* Additionally, the claimed arrangement must be sufficiently tailored to compensate those employees suffering adverse effects attributable to the exercise of management's

---

2. In this regard, we note that the *NWS* standard cited by the Union was set forth by a reviewing court and applied by the Authority as the non-precedential "law of the case[,]" not adopted by the Authority as an alternative standard for determining whether a proposal constitutes an appropriate arrangement. *See NWS*, 64 FLRA at 571. We also note that, in decisions subsequent to *NWS*, the Authority has continued to apply the *KANG* standard, not the *NWS* standard. *See, e.g., AFGE, Council of Prison Locals 33*, 65 FLRA 142, 146 (2010).

rights. *AFGE, Local 1164*, 55 FLRA 999, 1001 (1999).

The Authority has recognized "employee stress" as an adverse effect, and has found that a proposal that sought to mitigate work-related stress resulting from management's exercise of its right to assign work was an arrangement. *See Local 1367*, 64 FLRA at 871. Although the Agency disputes employees' need for additional uninterrupted adjudication time, the Agency does not dispute that its current work-assignment policies have caused the adverse effects alleged by the Union with respect to employees' stress levels, performance, and performance appraisals. By providing one day of uninterrupted adjudication time on a rotating basis, Proposal 1 would reduce employees' stress and enable them to more efficiently perform the adjudication component of their job duties. In these circumstances, we find that the Union has demonstrated that Proposal 1 ameliorates the adverse effects of the Agency's exercise of its right to assign work. Accordingly, this case is distinguishable from the decisions cited by the Agency, in which the unions failed to either adequately identify the adverse effects flowing from the exercise of management's rights, or explain how the proposals would mitigate those effects. *See Local 1164*, 54 FLRA at 1333-34, 1342; *Local 2879*, 49 FLRA at 291, 295.

In addition, as discussed above, the employees who would be placed on Proposal 1's roster providing additional uninterrupted time for adjudication work are those whose job duties include both interviewing the public and adjudicating claims. *See* Response at 3, 6; SOP at 3. Accordingly, the proposal applies only to employees who potentially could suffer the adverse effects that result from insufficient uninterrupted adjudication time, and, thus, we find that Proposal 1 is sufficiently tailored. Consistent with the foregoing, we find that Proposal 1 is an arrangement.

If the Authority finds a proposal to be an arrangement, then the Authority will determine whether it is appropriate or whether it is inappropriate because it excessively interferes with management's rights. *KANG*, 21 FLRA at 31. In doing so, the Authority weighs the benefits afforded to employees under the arrangement against the intrusion on the exercise of management's rights. *Id.* at 31-33.

With respect to the benefits that Proposal 1 would afford employees, the Union argues that the proposal would mitigate the adverse effects of management's exercise of its right to assign interview work during time that would otherwise be spent adjudicating claims by affording employees "[at] least a day at a time to catch up on adjudication of claims, on a recurring basis[.]" Petition at 3. In this regard, the Union emphasizes that employees cannot effectively serve the mission of the Agency without sufficient uninterrupted adjudication time because "claims [are not] complete until [they are] adjudicated[.]" Response at 7. Thus, Proposal 1 would benefit employees by giving them additional uninterrupted adjudication time, which could reduce employee stress and result in better job performance and performance appraisals.

With respect to the burdens on management's right to assign work under § 7106(a)(2)(B) of the Statute, that right includes the right to determine the particular duties and work that will be assigned and the particular employees or positions to which the duties and work will be assigned. *See AFGE, Local 3509*, 46 FLRA 1590, 1598 (1993). That right also includes the right to determine the particular qualifications and skills needed to perform the work and to make a judgment as to whether a particular employee meets those qualifications. *Id.* The Agency asserts that the proposal "will expose the Agency to situations, with some frequency, where it will be unable to provide service to the public" because it "place[s] severe restrictions on the Agency's ability to deal with an interviewer shortage[,]" Reply at 3, 2, and that such shortages often arise unexpectedly due to heavy "walk-in traffic" and/or employees taking unanticipated sick or annual leave, SOP at 10. However, as discussed above, under Proposal 1, the Agency would retain the ability to suspend the rotation at any point in the work day for "operational needs[,]" Petition at 2, which are defined broadly as "business reasons[,]" Record at 2. In this regard, the flexibility retained by the Agency to deviate from the roster under Proposal 1 lessens the proposal's intrusion on the exercise of management's right to assign work. Further, although the Agency correctly argues that Proposal 1 would limit its ability to assign interviewing duties to the employee selected for an "adjudication day" according to the roster: (1) this limitation would be limited to one employee per day; (2) "the Agency would still decide . . . which employees are qualified to perform adjudication duty[,]" *id.* at 2; and (3) the employee selected by the roster would only be uninterrupted in performing work already assigned to him or her by the Agency, barring an "operational need[]" to suspend the roster, Petition at 2.

Weighing the benefits to employees against the burdens on the right to assign work, we find that the benefits to employees outweigh the relatively limited burdens on management's right to assign work. Therefore, we find that Proposal 1 is an appropriate arrangement within the meaning of § 7106(b)(3) of the Statute.[3]

With regard to the Agency's claim that the last sentence of Proposal 1 expands the Agency's future bargaining obligation "well beyond the requirements of the Statute[,]" SOP at 10-11, as stated previously, that sentence does not expand the Agency's bargaining obligations beyond those imposed by the Statute. Accordingly, to the extent that the Agency is claiming that Proposal 1 is outside the duty to bargain because it requires bargaining that the Statute does not require, this argument provides no basis for finding that Proposal 1 is outside the duty to bargain.

For the foregoing reasons, we find that Proposal 1 is within the duty to bargain.

III. Proposal 2

A. Wording

> In order to improve and maintain consistent service quality for both the Auburn and Rumford Service Areas and to mitigate the adverse impact (stress, backlogs, performance, etc.) on Auburn bargaining unit employees as a result of the increased workloads, Management will increase staff in the Auburn office by two bargaining unit positions. This increase will be in addition to any vacancies in Auburn existing prior to or during the negotiation of this Agreement.

Petition at 2.

B. Meaning

Proposal 2 refers to the Agency's decision to transfer work from one field office in Rumford, Maine (Rumford) to another field office in Auburn, Maine (Auburn). *See* SOP at 13-14. The parties agree that Proposal 2 would require the Agency to add two bargaining unit positions to Auburn by hiring or transferring two employees. Record at 2.

C. Positions of the Parties

1. Agency

The Agency contends that Proposal 2 affects the Agency's right to determine its organization under § 7106(a)(1) of the Statute,[4] its rights to hire, assign, and direct employees under § 7106(a)(2)(A),[5] and its right to determine the number of employees assigned to an organizational subdivision under § 7106(b)(1).[6] SOP at 14. In this regard, the Agency asserts that because the Agency is already "one person over its staffing allocation" for the region, *id.* at 13, Proposal 2 would require the Agency to reassign two employees from other offices in order to add two positions to Auburn, *id.* at 17, 18.

Additionally, the Agency argues that Proposal 2 is not an arrangement under § 7106(b)(3) of the Statute. *Id.* at 17-18. In this regard, the Agency contends that "[w]hatever . . . adverse [e]ffects there may [be], they [are] not related to an insufficiency of staff[.]" *Id.* at 17. The Agency also contends that the proposal's requirement that the Agency add two employees to "unspecified positions" is not sufficiently tailored. *Id.* at 18. Finally, the Agency asserts that Proposal 2 excessively interferes with management rights – and, thus, is not an "appropriate" arrangement – because it would require the Agency to reassign employees from other offices, thereby severely hampering the ability of the Agency to fulfill its mission in the offices being deprived of staff. *Id.*

2. Union

The Union argues that Proposal 2 is an appropriate arrangement under § 7106(b)(3). Petition at 3; Response at 9-12. In arguing that Proposal 2 is an "arrangement[,]" the Union contends that the Agency's exercise of its right to "consolidate

3. Because we find that Proposal 1 in its entirety constitutes an appropriate arrangement, it is unnecessary to address the Union's severance requests pertaining to this proposal.

4. Section 7106(a)(1) provides, in pertinent part, that "nothing . . . shall affect the authority of any management official of any agency . . . to determine the . . . organization . . . of the agency[.]"

5. Section 7106(a)(2)(A) provides, in pertinent part, that "nothing . . . shall affect the authority of any management official of any agency . . . to hire, assign, [and] direct . . . employees in the agency[.]"

6. Section 7106(b)(1) provides, in pertinent part, that "[n]othing . . . shall preclude any agency and any labor organization from negotiating . . . at the election of the agency, on the numbers, types, and grades of employees or positions assigned to any organizational subdivision[.]"

workloads and determine its organization" has resulted in "increased stress[,]" "increased difficulty in getting leave approved[,]" and "more difficulty in meeting performance expectations" for employees. Response at 10. The Union asserts that Proposal 2 would ameliorate these adverse effects "because there would be additional workers among whom to allocate the work, thereby easing the stress of performing more work, collectively; making the approval of leave requests more likely; and improving each employee's ability to achieve performance expectations." *Id.* at 10-11. The Union also asserts that Proposal 2 is sufficiently tailored because it applies specifically to "employees in the office to which the Agency has decided to transfer the Rumford workload[.]" *Id.* at 10. In determining whether Proposal 2 is an "appropriate" arrangement, the Union again argues that the Authority should apply the *NWS* standard, and asserts that Proposal 2 would not significantly hamper the ability of the Agency to process claims in Auburn because its provision of additional staff would "promote[] performance of the effective and efficient processing of claims by making more staff available to perform that work." *Id.* at 11 (citing *NWS*, 64 FLRA at 571). Finally, the Union requests that the Authority "sever sentence two from the first sentence of Proposal 2 – and thus address only sentence one – if the Authority determine[s] that the inclusion of sentence two would render Proposal 2 nonnegotiable." Record at 2.

D. Analysis and Conclusions

1. Proposal 2 affects management's right to determine its organization under § 7106(a)(1) of the Statute.

As discussed above, where a union does not respond to an agency argument that a proposal affects a management right under § 7106 of the Statute, the Authority finds that the union has conceded that the proposal affects the claimed management right. *See, e.g.*, *Local 1367*, 64 FLRA at 870. As the Union did not respond to the Agency's assertion that Proposal 2 affects management's right to determine its organization, the Union concedes that the proposal affects that right.

2. Proposal 2 is not an appropriate arrangement under § 7106(b)(3) of the Statute.

As set forth above, in determining whether a proposal is an appropriate arrangement within the meaning of § 7106(b)(3) of the Statute, the Authority applies the analysis set forth in *KANG*, 21 FLRA at 31-33.[7] As relevant here, if the Authority finds the proposal to be an arrangement, then the Authority will determine whether it is appropriate or whether it is inappropriate because it excessively interferes with management's rights. *Id.* at 31. In doing so, the Authority weighs the benefits afforded to employees under the arrangement against the intrusion on the exercise of management's rights. *Id.* at 31-33. Applying this standard, the Authority has found that a proposal that "absolutely require[s]" that a management right be exercised in a particular manner, without "any provision for exceptions or the weighing of individual circumstances[,]" and without "allow[ing] [the agency to] assess[] the effect of the proposal's requirements on the [a]gency's ability to conduct its operations effectively and efficiently[,]" places a "significant burden on the [a]gency." *Overseas Educ. Ass'n*, 39 FLRA 153, 161 (1991) (*OEA*). Even assuming that Proposal 2 constitutes an arrangement, for the following reasons, we find that it is not appropriate because it excessively interferes with management's right to determine its organization.

With respect to the benefits that Proposal 2 would afford employees, the Union argues that the addition of two employees would mitigate the adverse effects of the workload transfer on employees' stress levels, performance, performance appraisals, and leave requests by providing more employees to share the burden of the increased workload, thereby "making the approval of leave requests more likely . . . and improving each employee's ability to achieve performance expectations." Response at 10-11.

With respect to the degree of intrusion on the exercise of management's right to determine its organization under § 7106(a)(1) of the Statute, this right encompasses the right to determine the administrative and functional structure of the agency, including the distribution of responsibilities. *See AFGE, Local 3807*, 54 FLRA 642, 647 (1998) (*Local 3807*). In other words, this right includes the authority to determine how an agency will structure itself to accomplish its mission and functions. *Id.* Here, the first sentence of Proposal 2 "absolutely require[s]" that a management right be exercised in a particular manner without "any provision for exceptions or the weighing of individual circumstances[,]" *OEA*, 39 FLRA at 161, thereby

7. As noted previously, the Authority does not apply *NWS*, 64 FLRA 569, to determine whether a proposal is an appropriate arrangement within the meaning of § 7106(b)(3) of the Statute.

substantially restricting the Agency's ability to structure itself to accomplish its mission and functions, *see Local 3807*, 54 FLRA at 647. In addition, the Agency asserts, and the Union does not dispute, that because of a fixed regional staffing allocation, Proposal 2 would require the Agency to reassign two employees from other offices in order to add two positions to Auburn. SOP at 17, 18. According to the Agency, this would result in the overstaffing of Auburn while "severely hamper[ing] the ability of the [A]gency to get its job done in the locations having to give up staff." *Id.* at 18. Balancing the parties' respective interests, we find that the benefits to employees do not outweigh the significant burdens that Proposal 2 places on management. Accordingly, we find that Proposal 2 excessively interferes with the Agency's right to determine its organization under § 7106(a)(1) and, thus, is not an appropriate arrangement within the meaning of § 7106(b)(3) of the Statute.

The Union asks that the Authority "sever sentence two from the first sentence of Proposal 2 – and thus address only sentence one – if the Authority determine[s] that the inclusion of sentence two would render Proposal 2 nonnegotiable." Record at 2. In other words, in the event that the Authority finds Proposal 2 is outside the duty to bargain on the basis of the proposal's second sentence, the Union asks the Authority to consider the negotiability of the proposal's first sentence standing alone. However, as discussed above, the first sentence's requirement that the Agency "increase staff in the Auburn office by two bargaining unit positions[,]" Petition at 2, without "any provision for exceptions or the weighing of individual circumstances[,]" *OEA*, 39 FLRA at 161, excessively interferes with the Agency's right to determine organization. Thus, we find that Proposal 2's first sentence, standing alone, is outside the duty to bargain without regard to the second sentence. Accordingly, even assuming, without deciding, that the Union has sufficiently supported its severance request, severing the second sentence would not provide a basis for finding the proposal within the duty to bargain. Therefore, it is unnecessary to determine whether severance would be appropriate.

Accordingly, we find that Proposal 2 is outside the duty to bargain.[8]

IV. Order

The Agency shall, upon request, or as otherwise agreed to by the parties, negotiate over Proposal 1.[9] The petition for review as to Proposal 2 is dismissed.

---

8. In view of this finding, it is unnecessary to address the Agency's remaining assertions regarding Proposal 2. *See, e.g., NAGE, Local R1-109*, 61 FLRA 593, 597 & n.3 (2006) (where proposal violated right to assign work under § 7106(a)(2)(B) of the Statute, Authority found it unnecessary to address agency's claims that proposal also violated its right to determine its budget and concerned tours of duty under § 7106(a)(1) and § 7106(b)(1), respectively).

9. In finding this proposal within the duty to bargain, we make no judgment as to its merits.

65 FLRA No. 177

UNITED STATES
DEPARTMENT OF THE INTERIOR
BUREAU OF INDIAN AFFAIRS
FORT TOTTEN AGENCY
FORT TOTTEN, NORTH DAKOTA
(Agency)

and

INDIAN EDUCATORS FEDERATION
LOCAL 4524
AMERICAN FEDERATION OF TEACHERS
(Union)

0-AR-4281

DECISION

May 26, 2011

Before the Authority: Carol Waller Pope, Chairman, and Thomas M. Beck and Ernest DuBester, Members

I. Statement of the Case

This matter is before the Authority on exceptions to an award of Arbitrator Philip K. Kienast filed by the Agency under § 7122(a) of the Federal Service Labor-Management Relations Statute (the Statute) and part 2425 of the Authority's Regulations. The Union filed an opposition to the Agency's exceptions.

The Arbitrator concluded that the Agency violated the parties' collective bargaining agreement (CBA) when it separated the grievants from employment in a reduction-in-force (RIF) instead of reassigning them to new, lower-graded positions that the Agency had just created in the same line of work. As a remedy, the Arbitrator ordered the Agency to grant the grievants grade and pay retention in the lower-graded positions, for which the grievants had competed and been selected.

For the reasons set forth below, we dismiss in part and deny in part the Agency's exceptions.

II. Background and Arbitrator's Award[1]

The two grievants were full-time maintenance mechanics. *See* Award at 3. On July 13, 2006,[2] the Agency notified the Union that it would separate the grievants from employment in a RIF. *Id.* The Agency also advised the Union that there were no other positions available at the Agency for which offers could be made to the affected employees. *Id.* Although the Agency stated that there were no other positions available to offer to the affected employees, a proposed organization chart sent to the Union on December 8, 2006, indicated that the Agency planned to change the grievants' positions to lower-graded seasonal maintenance mechanic positions. *Id.*

Subsequently, the Agency notified the two grievants that they would be separated from employment pursuant to a RIF. *Id.* The grievants then applied for, were offered, and accepted lower-graded positions as seasonal maintenance employees. *Id.* The grievants were separated from employment on October 13 and reinstated two weeks later to the new, lower-graded positions. *Id.* at 3-4.

The Union filed a grievance alleging that the Agency violated the CBA. As a remedy, the Union argued that the grievants were entitled to grade and pay retention in their new, lower-graded positions. *Id.* at 2. The grievance was not resolved and was submitted to arbitration. *Id.*

As relevant here, the parties stipulated the issue as: "Are the grievants entitled to grade and pay retention in their new positions?" *Id.* The Arbitrator concluded that the Agency violated the CBA. The Arbitrator found that Article 31 of the CBA requires the Agency to seek "'to avoid the necessity of entering into RIF actions.'"[3] *Id.* at 3 (quoting Article 31). The Arbitrator noted that, at the same time the Agency was telling the Union that there were no other positions available to offer the grievants, the Agency was planning to change the grievants' positions to lower-graded seasonal positions. *Id.* The Arbitrator found that the Agency presented no evidence to explain "why it did not try to avoid the necessity of a RIF by simply reassigning

1. The parties agreed to "expedited arbitration" based on written submissions in lieu of a hearing. Award at 2. The parties stipulated to seventeen joint exhibits. *Id.*

2. Unless otherwise noted, all dates refer to 2006.

3. The pertinent text of Article 31 is set forth in the appendix to this decision.

the grievants to the [lower-graded] positions." *Id.* Determining that the Agency should have reassigned the grievants to the lower-graded positions, the Arbitrator concluded that the Agency violated Article 31 "by first separating the grievants and two weeks later appointing them to fill the new [lower-graded] positions." *Id.* at 3-4.

As a remedy, the Arbitrator ordered the Agency to grant the grievants grade and pay retention in their new, lower-graded positions. *Id.* at 4. The Arbitrator retained jurisdiction "for the ... purpose of ... deciding how to implement the grade and pay remedy absent agreement by the parties." *Id.* at 5.

III. Positions of the Parties

A. Agency's Exceptions

The Agency contends that the award is contrary to law and fails to draw its essence from the CBA.

Regarding its contrary to law contention, the Agency claims that the award is contrary to 5 U.S.C. §§ 5363(e)[4] and 2105.[5] Exceptions at 4. The Agency asserts that, under 5 U.S.C. § 5363(e), an employee who has a break in service of one workday or more is not eligible for grade and pay retention. The Agency argues that the award is inconsistent with 5 U.S.C. § 5363(e) because the employees had breaks in service of one or more days when they began their new positions following their terminations. Further, relying on 5 U.S.C. § 2105, the Agency asserts that, under 5 U.S.C. § 5363(e), grade and pay retention is limited to an individual who is a federal employee. The Agency argues that the award is inconsistent with 5 U.S.C. § 5363(e) because the grievants were not federal employees within the meaning of § 2105 when they began their new positions following their terminations. *Id.*

Next, the Agency contends that the award is inconsistent with an Office of Personnel Management (OPM) RIF regulation, 5 C.F.R. § 351.201(b),[6] that OPM issued pursuant to 5 U.S.C. § 1302.[7] *Id.* The Agency argues that the award is inconsistent with 5 C.F.R. § 351.201(b) because the Arbitrator found that the Agency erred when it conducted the RIF, even though the Agency complied with all RIF regulations. *Id.* at 6. Further, the Agency argues that the award is inconsistent with 5 C.F.R. § 351.201(b) because the Arbitrator found that the Agency should have reassigned the employees to the new, vacant positions, even though the RIF regulation does not require an agency to fill vacant positions. *Id.* at 6-7.

In addition, the Agency contends that the award is contrary to management's rights under § 7106(a)(1) and (2) of the Statute. *Id.* at 7. The Agency argues that the award "deprives management of its discretion to decide size, composition and location of the workforce." *Id.* at 7-9. The Agency also claims that the award violates purported management rights "to manage its available funds within current budget constraints[,]" *id.* at 9, and "to conduct the RIF according to OPM regulations[,]" *id.* at 10.

Regarding its essence contention, the Agency asserts that the CBA incorporates management's rights and OPM regulations that do not require the Agency to fill vacant positions in a RIF. *Id.* at 6-8. The Agency argues that, by finding that the Agency should have reassigned the riffed grievants to the new, vacant positions, the award not only violates management's rights and 5 C.F.R. § 351.201(b), but also fails to draw its essence from the comparable provisions of the CBA. *Id.* In addition, the Agency argues that Article 31 of the CBA cannot be interpreted to require the Agency to fill all vacant positions, because "[t]hat is not the language of Article 31." *Id.* at 7; *see also id.* at 8.

B. Union's Opposition

The Union contends that the award is not contrary to 5 U.S.C. § 5363(e). Opp'n at 9-10. The Union argues that the Agency intentionally did not reassign the grievants at the time of the RIF to the lower-graded positions to deprive the grievants of grade and pay retention to which they are entitled under RIF regulations. *Id.* at 9. The Union cites

---

4. The relevant text of 5 U.S.C. § 5363 is set forth in the appendix.

5. The text of 5 U.S.C. § 2105(a) is set forth in the appendix.

6. The relevant portion of 5 C.F.R. § 351.201 provides:

> (b) This part does not require an agency to fill a vacant position. However, when an agency, at its discretion, chooses to fill a vacancy by an employee who has been reached for release from a competitive level for one of the reasons in paragraph (a)(2) of this section, this part shall be followed.

7. Although the Agency cites 5 U.S.C. § 1302, Exceptions at 2, 4, 11, it does not explain how the award violates that provision.

case law in which the Merit Systems Protection Board (MSPB) has enforced a contractual provision requiring the filling of vacant positions in a RIF. *Id.*

Further, the Union contends that the award is not contrary to 5 C.F.R. § 351.201(b). *Id.* at 10-12. The Union argues that there is nothing in OPM regulations that precludes parties from agreeing to include in their collective bargaining agreements a requirement that an agency fill a vacant position during a RIF. *Id.* at 10-11. The Union repeats its assertion that the MSPB has enforced such contractual provisions. *Id.* at 11.

Next, the Union rejects the Agency's contention regarding the Arbitrator's interpretation of Article 31. *Id.* at 11-12, 16. The Union argues that the Arbitrator properly interpreted Article 31 to require the Agency to fill vacant positions in a RIF.

In addition, the Union contends that the Agency's arguments that the award is contrary to management's rights under § 7106(a) of the Statute are not properly before the Authority under § 2429.5 of the Authority's Regulations. *Id.* at 13. The Union claims that these arguments could have been, but were not, presented to the Arbitrator. *Id.*

IV. Preliminary Matter

The Agency contends that the award is contrary to management's rights under § 7106(a)(1) and (2) of the Statute. Exceptions at 7. The Agency argues that the award "deprives management of its discretion to decide size, composition and location of its workforce." *Id.* at 7-9. The Agency also claims that the award violates its purported management rights to "manage its available funds within current budget constraints[,]" *id.* at 9, and to "conduct the RIF according to OPM regulations[,]" *id.* at 10. The Union contends that the Agency's management's rights arguments are not properly before the Authority under § 2429.5 of the Authority's Regulations. Opp'n at 13.

The Authority's Regulations that were in effect when the Agency filed its exceptions provided that "[t]he Authority will not consider . . . any issue, which was not presented in the proceedings before the . . . arbitrator." 5 C.F.R. § 2429.5.[8] Under § 2429.5, the Authority will not consider any issue that could have been, but was not, presented to the arbitrator. *See, e.g., U.S. Dep't of Homeland Sec., U.S. Customs & Border Prot., JFK Airport, Queens, N.Y.*, 62 FLRA 416, 417 (2008) (*Customs & Border Prot., JFK Airport*).

There is no evidence in the record that the Agency raised its management rights arguments before the Arbitrator. Award at 3; Exceptions, Attach. 1, Agency's Opening Submission and Argument; Exceptions, Attach. 2, Agency's Response. Moreover, the record reflects that the Agency could have made these arguments below. The Union presented its claim to the Arbitrator that the Agency should have reassigned the grievants to the new, vacant positions. Award at 2. The Agency was therefore on notice of the reassignment issue to which the Agency now objects on management rights grounds. Consequently, the Agency could have presented its management rights arguments to the Arbitrator, but did not. Accordingly, the Authority dismisses this exception under § 2429.5. *See Customs & Border Prot., JFK Airport,* 62 FLRA at 417 (Authority will not consider arguments raised for the first time in exceptions).

V. Analysis and Conclusions

A. The award is not contrary to law.

The Agency contends that by ordering grade and pay retention, the award is contrary to law. Exceptions at 4. When an exception involves an award's consistency with law, the Authority reviews any question of law raised by the exception and the award de novo. *See NTEU, Chapter 24*, 50 FLRA 330, 332 (1995) (citing *U.S. Customs Serv. v. FLRA*, 43 F.3d 682, 686-87 (D.C. Cir. 1994)). In applying the standard of de novo review, the Authority assesses whether an arbitrator's legal conclusions are consistent with the applicable standard of law. *See U.S. Dep't of Def., Dep'ts of the Army & the Air Force, Ala. Nat'l Guard, Northport, Ala.*, 55 FLRA 37, 40 (1998). In making that assessment, the Authority defers to the arbitrator's underlying factual findings. *See id.*

Grade and pay retention have a specific statutory foundation. 5 U.S.C. §§ 5361-5365 govern the administration of grade and pay retention. In addition, Congress has, in 5 U.S.C. § 5365, authorized OPM to prescribe regulations governing

8. The Authority's Regulations concerning the review of arbitration awards, as well as certain related procedural Regulations, including 5 C.F.R. § 2429.5, were revised effective October 1, 2010. *See* 75 Fed. Reg. 42,283 (2010). As the Agency's exceptions in this case were filed before that date, we apply the prior Regulations.

the administration of grade and pay retention in circumstances beyond those specifically addressed in §§ 5361-5365.

As relevant here, an employee is entitled to grade and pay retention when "as a result of [RIF] procedures" an employee is placed in a position "which is in a lower grade than the previous position . . . ." 5 U.S.C. § 5362(a)(1); *see also* 5 U.S.C. § 5363; 5 C.F.R. §§ 536.201(a) & 301(a). "[RIF] procedures" are defined as "procedures applied in carrying out any [RIF] due to reorganization, due to lack of funds or curtailment of work, or due to any other factor . . . ." 5 U.S.C § 5361(7). An employee who has a break in service of one workday or more is not eligible for grade and pay retention. 5 U.S.C. § 5363(e). Under applicable regulations, an agency is not required to fill a vacant position in a RIF. 5 C.F.R. § 351.201(b). However, "an agency, at its discretion [may] choose[] to fill a vacancy by an employee who has been reached" in a RIF. *Id.*

1. The award is not contrary to 5 U.S.C. §§ 5363(e) and 2105.

The Agency contends that the remedy of grade and pay retention is inconsistent with 5 U.S.C. §§ 5363(e) and 2105. Exceptions at 4.

The Agency asserts that, under 5 U.S.C. § 5363(e), an employee who has a break in service of one workday or more is not eligible for grade and pay retention. The Agency argues that the award is inconsistent with 5 U.S.C. § 5363(e) because the grievants had a break in service of one or more days when they began their new positions as a consequence of their terminations. Further, relying on 5 U.S.C. § 2105, the Agency asserts that, under 5 U.S.C. § 5363(e), grade and pay retention is limited to an individual who is a federal employee. The Agency argues that the award is inconsistent with 5 U.S.C. § 5363(e) because the grievants were not federal employees within the meaning of § 2105 when they began their new positions following their terminations. *Id.*

With regard to saved grade and pay, the Arbitrator ordered the Agency to "pay the grievants at the grade of their old positions for two years from the date of their placement in the new [lower-graded] seasonal maintenance positions." Award at 4. However, the Arbitrator did not specify how the parties were to implement the remedy. Instead, the Arbitrator returned the matter to the parties to "meet and attempt to agree on how the [grade and pay retention] remedy . . . is to be implemented." *Id.* at 5. Moreover, the Agency does not claim that the award requires it to take particular personnel actions that are contrary to law or regulation, or that it is impossible to implement the remedy in a manner consistent with legal requirements. *See generally* OPM Guide to Processing Personnel Actions, ch. 3, subch. 2-2(a)(3) (discussing OPM's instructions on cancelling personnel actions and taking retroactive personnel actions "to implement," inter alia, "an arbitral award").

Accordingly, because the Agency's argument fails to take account of actions the Agency might take to lawfully implement the award, the argument fails to demonstrate that the award is contrary to 5 U.S.C. §§ 5363(e) and 2105.

For the foregoing reasons, we deny this exception.[9]

2. The award is not contrary to 5 C.F.R. § 351.201(b).

The Agency contends that the award is inconsistent with an OPM RIF regulation, 5 C.F.R. § 351.201(b), that OPM issued pursuant to 5 U.S.C. § 1302. Exceptions at 4-7. The Agency makes two arguments.

The Agency argues that the award is inconsistent with 5 C.F.R. § 351.201(b) because the Arbitrator

[9] Chairman Pope agrees with the decision to deny this exception but does not join in the majority's reasoning for doing so. In this regard, it is true enough that, as the majority states, "the Arbitrator did not specify how the parties were to implement the remedy." Majority Op. at 6. However, as the Arbitrator clearly awarded grade and pay retention, Chairman Pope would find that the lack of specificity as to "how" the award should be implemented is not relevant to the Agency's claim that the award is contrary to §§ 5363(e) and 2105. Addressing that issue, Chairman Pope would reject the Agency's claim -- that the grievants had a legitimate break in service -- on the grounds that: (1) the Arbitrator effectively found that the break in service was not legitimate because the Agency should have reassigned the grievants prior to that break; and (2) there is no dispute that, had the grievants been reassigned, they would have received grade and pay retention. In short, but for the Agency's contractual violation, the grievants would have received grade and pay retention. In these circumstances, the remedy is not contrary to law. *Cf. U.S. Dep't of the Navy, Puget Sound Naval Shipyard & Intermediate Maint. Facility, Bremerton, Wash.*, 62 FLRA 4, 7-8 (2007) (awards of overtime compensation warranted despite fact that employees did not actually work, where failure to work was due to agency's contract violation).

found that the Agency erred when it conducted the RIF, even though the Agency complied with all RIF regulations. *Id.* at 6. The Agency's contention is based on a misunderstanding of the award. The Arbitrator did not find that the Agency violated RIF regulations. Rather, the Arbitrator found that the Agency violated the CBA. Award at 3-4. Because this Agency argument neither addresses the Arbitrator's finding of a contract violation, nor asserts that the CBA is inconsistent with the cited regulation, the argument does not provide a basis for finding the award deficient as contrary to law.

Further, the Agency argues that the award is inconsistent with 5 C.F.R. § 351.201(b) because the Arbitrator found that the Agency should have reassigned the employees to the new, vacant positions, even though the RIF regulation does not require an agency to fill vacant positions. Exceptions at 5-7. The Agency's reliance on 5 C.F.R. § 351.201(b) is misplaced. Although 5 C.F.R. § 351.201(b) does not require an agency to fill a vacant position with an employee who has been reached for release in a RIF, the regulation also does not bar an agency from taking such an action. Indeed, the regulation specifically recognizes that "an agency, at its discretion [may] choose[] to fill a vacancy by an employee who has been reached for release" in a RIF. 5 C.F.R. § 351.201(b). Thus, the regulation does not preclude parties from entering into an agreement that obligates an agency to fill a vacant position in such circumstances. *See U.S. Dep't of Navy, U.S. Marine Corps*, 56 FLRA 265, 266 (2000) (where an agency has discretion under applicable law and regulation over a matter affecting conditions of employment, agency is obligated under Statute to exercise that discretion through bargaining unless governing law or regulation specifically requires that only agency may exercise that discretion). In this case, the award concludes that the Agency failed to exercise discretion that it possessed consistent with its valid contractual obligations. Therefore, the Agency's contention that the award is inconsistent with 5 C.F.R. § 351.201(b) because the Arbitrator found that the Agency should have reassigned the grievants does not provide a basis for finding the award deficient.

For the foregoing reasons, we deny this exception.

B. The award does not fail to draw its essence from the CBA.

The Agency argues that the award fails to draw its essence from the CBA. The Authority will find that an arbitration award is deficient as failing to draw its essence from the collective bargaining agreement when the appealing party establishes that the award: (1) cannot in any rational way be derived from the agreement; (2) is so unfounded in reason and fact and so unconnected with the wording and purposes of the collective bargaining agreement as to manifest an infidelity to the obligation of the arbitrator; (3) does not represent a plausible interpretation of the agreement; or (4) evidences a manifest disregard of the agreement. *See U.S. Dep't of Labor (OSHA)*, 34 FLRA 573, 575 (1990). The Authority and the courts defer to arbitrators in this context "because it is the arbitrator's construction of the agreement for which the parties have bargained." *Id.* at 576.

The Agency asserts that the CBA incorporates management's rights and OPM regulations that do not require the Agency to fill vacant positions in a RIF. Exceptions at 5, 6-7. The Agency argues that, as the award violates management's rights and the referenced RIF regulations, the award also fails to draw its essence from the CBA. *Id.* at 8. As discussed previously, the Agency's management's rights arguments are not properly before the Authority. In addition, as also discussed, the award is not contrary to 5 C.F.R. § 351.201(b). Consistent with those conclusions, the Agency has not established that the award fails to draw its essence from the CBA for these reasons.

In addition, the Agency argues that Article 31 of the CBA cannot be interpreted to require the Agency to fill all vacant positions because "[t]hat is not the language of Article 31." *Id.* at 7; *see also id.* at 8. As pertinent here, Article 31 states that "management officials . . . should seek 'to avoid the necessity of entering' into a RIF action." Award at 3 (quoting Article 31). The Arbitrator concluded that the Agency violated Article 31 when it separated the grievants from employment through a RIF instead of reassigning them to the new, lower-graded positions that the Agency had just created. *Id.* at 3-4.

The Agency does not demonstrate that the Arbitrator's finding that the Agency violated Article 31 when it riffed the grievants rather than reassign them fails to draw its essence from the CBA. In this connection, nothing in the language of Article 31 precludes such an interpretation. Further, the

Agency does not explain why the Arbitrator should be barred from interpreting the provision. *See, e.g.*, *AFGE, Council 220*, 65 FLRA 596, 599-600 (2011) ("The courts defer to the arbitrator's interpretation of the collective bargaining agreement 'because it is the arbitrator's construction of the agreement for which the parties have bargained.'" (quoting *U.S. Dep't of Labor (OSHA)*, 34 FLRA at 576)). Finally, the Agency does not explain why the Arbitrator's interpretation is irrational, unfounded, implausible, or evidences a manifest disregard of the CBA. Therefore, the Agency has not established that the award fails to draw its essence from the CBA for this reason.

For the foregoing reasons, we deny this exception.

VI. Decision

The Agency's exceptions are dismissed in part and denied in part.

APPENDIX

Article 31 provides, in pertinent part:

> Section 1. Policy
>
> Through careful planning and use of other administrative techniques, to the extent it determines practicable and in the public interest, management officials at all organizational levels should seek to avoid the necessity of entering into a formal reduction-in-force (RIF) action. Management will conduct a RIF only when the release is necessary for the reasons specified in OPM regulations, 5 CFR, which includes lack of work, shortage of funds, insufficient personnel ceilings, reorganizations, reclassification due to a change in duties, or the exercise of reemployment rights or restoration rights. Office of Personnel Management (OPM) regulations will be observed by Management and the Union in carry out their responsibilities throughout the RIF process. The provisions of this Article will apply to all RIF or transfer of function actions affecting unit employees under 5 CFR.

Award at 2.

The relevant portion of 5 U.S.C. § 5363 provides:

> (e) This section shall not apply, or shall cease to apply, to an employee who . . . (1) has a break in service of 1 workday or more . . . .

5 U.S.C. § 2105(a) provides, in pertinent part:

> (a) For the purpose of this title, "employee," except as otherwise provided by this section or when specifically modified, means an officer and an individual who is--
>
> (1) appointed in the civil service by one of the following acting in an official capacity--
>
> (A) the President;
>
> (B) a Member or Members of Congress, or the Congress;
>
> (C) a member of a uniformed service;
>
> (D) an individual who is an employee under this section;
>
> (E) the head of a Government controlled corporation; or
>
> (F) an adjutant general designated by the Secretary concerned under section 709(c) of title 32;
>
> (2) engaged in the performance of a Federal function under authority of law or an Executive act; and
>
> (3) subject to the supervision of an individual named by paragraph (1) of this subsection while engaged in the performance of the duties of his position.

65 FLRA No. 178

AMERICAN FEDERATION
OF GOVERNMENT EMPLOYEES
LOCAL 2018
(Union)

and

UNITED STATES MARINE CORPS
MARINE AIR GROUND TASK FORCE
TRAINING COMMAND
(Agency)

0-AR-4696

DECISION

May 27, 2011

Before the Authority: Carol Waller Pope, Chairman, and Thomas M. Beck and Ernest DuBester, Members

I. Statement of the Case

This matter is before the Authority on exceptions to an award of Arbitrator Jan Stiglitz filed by the Union under § 7122(a) of the Federal Service Labor-Management Relations Statute (the Statute) and part 2425 of the Authority's Regulations. The Agency filed an opposition to the Union's exceptions.

The Arbitrator concluded that the Agency properly suspended the grievant for making a false statement during the course of an investigation. For the reasons that follow, we deny the Union's exceptions.

II. Background and Arbitrator's Award

The grievant is a financial management analyst. Award at 2. He is also the Union's vice president. *Id.* The grievant met with an Agency attorney (meeting) to discuss a dispute concerning an employee's posting of a grievance on an Agency bulletin board. *Id.* During the meeting, the Agency attorney and the grievant engaged in a heated argument over whether the grievant had been authorized to conduct Union business. *Id.* at 2-3; Opp'n at 2.

Five days later, the grievant informed the Agency of his intent to file an unfair labor practice (ULP) charge alleging, among other things, a "battery upon a [U]nion official" based on an incident at the meeting. Award at 3. In response to the grievant's notice, the Agency conducted an investigation into what occurred at the meeting. *Id.* As part of the investigation, the Agency conducted an investigatory interview of the grievant concerning the meeting. *Id.* During the investigatory interview, an Agency representative asked the grievant whether the Agency attorney touched the grievant during the meeting. *Id.* at 3-4. In response, the grievant claimed that the Agency attorney "poked him in the chest with a finger." *Id.* at 3. Other witnesses who had been at the meeting provided statements to the Agency denying that the Agency attorney poked the grievant in the chest. *Id.*

After the investigation concluded, the Agency imposed a three-day suspension on the grievant for providing false information during the investigatory interview. *Id.* at 1-2. Specifically, the Agency determined that the grievant knowingly made the false statement at the interview that the Agency attorney poked him in the chest at the meeting. *Id.* at 3.

The Union grieved the suspension. Award at 1-2. The grievance was not resolved and was submitted to arbitration. As stipulated by the parties, the issues to be resolved by the Arbitrator were:

> 1. Did the Agency have just cause to suspend [the grievant] for three days based on the charge of providing false information during an investigation?
>
> 2. If not, what is the appropriate remedy?

Id. at 2.

The Arbitrator ruled that the Agency had just cause to impose the three-day suspension on the grievant for providing false information during an investigation. Specifically, the Arbitrator found that the grievant knowingly made the false statement during the investigatory interview that the Agency attorney poked him in the chest at the meeting. *Id.* at 15. The Arbitrator credited the testimony of witnesses at the meeting in finding that the Agency attorney did not poke the grievant in the chest. *Id.* Further, the Arbitrator concluded that the Union did not provide sufficient evidence to prove that the Agency attorney poked the grievant in the chest. *Id.* Therefore, the Arbitrator found, based on the evidence, that the grievant knowingly made a false statement during the investigatory interview. *Id.*

The Arbitrator also rejected the Union's argument that the grievant's false statement was protected activity under the Statute because of the grievant's status as a Union representative. *Id.* at 17. The Arbitrator determined that the grievant was not acting as a Union representative when he made the false statement at the investigatory interview. *Id.* The Arbitrator reasoned that although the questions at the investigatory interview may have related to events that took place while the grievant was acting as a Union representative, the Agency summoned him to the interview as an Agency employee. *Id.*

Moreover, the Arbitrator rejected the Union's argument that the suspension was based on the grievant's conduct at the meeting. Specifically, the Arbitrator found that the Agency did not consider the grievant's conduct at the meeting in deciding whether the grievant made the false statement at the investigatory interview. *Id.* However, the Arbitrator reasoned, the Agency properly considered what happened at the meeting in evaluating any mitigating circumstances bearing upon the range of discipline. *Id.* at 17-18.

III. Positions of the Parties

A. Union's Exceptions

The Union asserts that the award is contrary to law and is based on a nonfact.

The Union makes two contrary to law claims. First, the Union asserts that the Arbitrator's decision to uphold the grievant's three-day suspension is contrary to law because the grievant was engaged in protected activity at all times relevant to the suspension. Exceptions at 6-7. The Union argues that the grievant's conduct cannot be the basis for discipline because he was on 100 percent official time. Thus, the Union contends, the grievant was acting in a representational capacity at all times associated with the disciplinary action – at the meeting and at the investigatory interview. *Id.* at 6, 9. Because the grievant was acting in this capacity, the Union asserts, the grievant's false statement was protected activity and not subject to discipline because it did not exceed the bounds of protected activity. *Id.* at 9.

The Union also maintains that the award is contrary to 5 U.S.C. § 7503. The Union argues that § 7503 required the Agency to notify the grievant that the proposed suspension was based in part on his actions at the meeting, but that the Agency failed to do so.[1] The Union claims in this connection that one of the bases for the suspension was the grievant's actions at the meeting. *Id.* at 9-10.

Finally, the Union contends, the Arbitrator's conclusion that "the Agency's case stands unrefuted" and, "on the critical issue – did [the Agency attorney] poke [the grievant] with his finger – there were no inconsistencies," is based on a nonfact. *Id.* at 10. Specifically, the Union argues, the Arbitrator ignored conflicting evidence on this point presented at the arbitration hearing. *Id.* at 10-12.

B. Agency's Opposition

The Agency asserts that the Union's contrary to law claims are without merit. In response to the Union's first argument, the Agency contends that the grievant was not acting as a Union representative when he made the false statement that is the basis of the three-day suspension. Opp'n at 7-8. The Agency notes that it summoned the grievant to the investigatory interview as an Agency employee to provide information relevant to an alleged ULP that occurred at the meeting. *Id.* at 8. The Agency further asserts that the grievant was not summoned to the investigatory interview to discuss any labor-related issue on behalf of another member of the bargaining unit. *Id.* at 9. Moreover, the Agency also claims, even if the grievant was acting as a Union representative when he made the false statement, the statement exceeded the bounds of protected activity. *Id.* at 10-11.

In addition, the Agency argues that the award is not inconsistent with 5 U.S.C. § 7503. The Agency maintains that the Union misconstrues the Arbitrator's award to hold that the grievant was disciplined for his conduct at the meeting. *Id.* To the contrary, the Agency argues, the grievant's suspension was not based on his conduct at the meeting. *Id.* at 12.

Finally, the Agency argues, the Union's nonfact exception lacks merit. In the Agency's view, the Arbitrator weighed all relevant evidence presented at arbitration when he determined that the Agency

1. The relevant portion of 5 U.S.C. § 7503 provides: "(b) An employee against whom a suspension for 14 days or less is proposed is entitled to--(1) an advance written notice stating the specific reasons for the proposed action . . . ."

attorney did not poke the grievant in the chest. *Id.* at 4-6.

IV. Analysis and Conclusions

A. The award is not contrary to law.

The Union contends that the award is contrary to law because the grievant was engaged in protected activity at all times associated with the disciplinary action. When an exception involves an award's consistency with law, the Authority reviews any question of law raised by the exception and the award de novo. *See NTEU, Chapter 24*, 50 FLRA 330, 332 (1995) (citing *U.S. Customs Serv. v. FLRA*, 43 F.3d 682, 686-87 (D.C. Cir. 1994)). In applying the standard of de novo review, the Authority assesses whether an arbitrator's legal conclusions are consistent with the applicable standard of law. *See U.S. Dep't of Def., Dep'ts of the Army & the Air Force, Ala. Nat'l Guard, Northport, Ala.*, 55 FLRA 37, 40 (1998). In making that assessment, the Authority defers to the arbitrator's underlying factual findings. *See id.*

Whether an employer allegedly took actions against an individual during the course of protected activity applies in cases where an agency is alleged to have violated § 7116 of the Statute.[2] *See U.S. Dep't of Transp., FAA*, 64 FLRA 365, 369 (2009) (Member Beck concurring). Specifically, where an agency is alleged to have committed a ULP on this basis, "a necessary part of the [agency's] defense" against the ULP allegation is that the individual's actions constituted flagrant misconduct or otherwise exceeded the bounds of protected activity. *Id.*

The Authority has held that arbitrators are required to apply statutory burdens of proof when resolving an alleged ULP. *E.g., U.S. GSA, Ne. & Caribbean Region, N.Y., N.Y.*, 60 FLRA 864, 866 (2005). By contrast, where an arbitrator resolves a claim under a collective bargaining agreement (CBA) rather than a statutory claim, "unless a specific burden of proof is required, an arbitrator may establish and apply whatever burden the arbitrator considers appropriate . . . ." *Id.* In this connection, the Authority distinguishes allegations that an agency lacked just cause for discipline under a CBA from allegations of unlawful interference with protected rights under the Statute. *See U.S. Dep't of Veterans Affairs, VA Md. Healthcare Sys.*, 65 FLRA 619, 621 (2011) (where parties stipulated a just-cause issue, Authority declined to consider claim of alleged violation of § 7102(a) of Statute that was not raised before arbitrator); *AFGE, Local 2923*, 65 FLRA 561, 563 (2011) (finding that there was no need to address union's claim that arbitrator improperly analyzed whether grievant exceeded bounds of protected activity when issue before arbitrator was whether there was "'just and sufficient cause' for the suspension" rather than whether suspension violated the Statute). In addition, when an arbitrator is not required to apply a statutory standard, alleged misapplications of that standard do not provide a basis for finding the arbitrator's award deficient. *See Soc. Sec. Admin.*, 65 FLRA 286, 288 (*SSA*) (2010).

Here, the record reflects, and there is no dispute, that the parties stipulated that the issue before the Arbitrator was whether there was "just cause" for the grievant's suspension, not whether the suspension violated § 7116. Award at 2. Because the issue before the Arbitrator was a contractual claim, the Arbitrator was not required to apply statutory standards, and the Arbitrator's alleged misapplication of the statutory standard concerning protected activity under § 7116 does not provide a basis for setting aside the award. *See AFGE, Local 2923*, 65 FLRA at 563.

The Union also excepts to the award on the basis that it is contrary to 5 U.S.C. § 7503 because the Agency did not notify the grievant that his proposed suspension was based in part on his conduct at the meeting. Exceptions at 9-10. For the reasons explained above, the Arbitrator was not required to apply statutory standards, and the Arbitrator's alleged misapplication of the statutory standard concerning notice under 5 U.S.C. § 7503 does not provide a basis for setting aside the award. *See AFGE, Local 2923*, 65 FLRA at 563.

For these reasons, we deny the Union's contrary to law exceptions.

B. The award is not based on a nonfact.

The Union contends that the Arbitrator's finding, that "the Agency's case stands unrefuted" and, "on the critical issue—did [the grievant] poke [the Agency attorney] with his finger – there were no inconsistencies," are based on nonfacts. Exceptions at 10. To establish that an award is based on a nonfact, the appealing party must show that a central fact underlying the award is clearly erroneous, but for

2. Section 7116(a)(2) of the Statute provides, in pertinent part, that it is a ULP for an agency "to encourage or discourage membership in any labor organization by discrimination in connection with hiring, tenure, promotion, or other conditions of employment[.]"

which the arbitrator would have reached a different result. *See NFFE, Local 1984*, 56 FLRA 38, 41 (2000) (*NFFE*).

The Union's nonfact exception challenges the weight that the Arbitrator accorded testimony and other evidence. The Authority has long held that disagreement with an arbitrator's evaluation of evidence and the weight to be accorded such evidence does not provide any basis for finding an award deficient. *AFGE, Local 3295*, 51 FLRA 27, 32 (1995). Here, the Union simply disagrees with the Arbitrator's evaluation of the evidence that he found refuted the Union's case. Accordingly, we deny the Union's nonfact exception.

V. Decision

The Union's exceptions are denied.

65 FLRA No. 179

UNITED STATES
DEPARTMENT OF HOMELAND SECURITY
U.S. CUSTOMS AND BORDER PROTECTION
(Agency)

and

NATIONAL TREASURY
EMPLOYEES UNION
CHAPTER 164
(Union)

0-AR-4437

DECISION

May 27, 2011

Before the Authority: Carol Waller Pope, Chairman, and Thomas M. Beck and Ernest DuBester, Members[1]

I. Statement of the Case

This matter is before the Authority on exceptions to an award of Arbitrator Kenneth Cloke filed by the Agency under § 7122(a) of the Federal Service Labor-Management Relations Statute (the Statute) and part 2425 of the Authority's Regulations. The Union filed an opposition to the Agency's exceptions.

The Union filed a grievance alleging that the Agency improperly failed to bargain over a change in leave policy. The Arbitrator found that the Agency had a duty to bargain with the Union over the impact and implementation of the change,[2] and directed the Agency to bargain with the Union.

For the reasons that follow, we find that the award is deficient and set it aside.

II. Background and Arbitrator's Award

Prior to the events giving rise to the award in this case, the Agency implemented a Revised National Inspectional Assignment Policy (RNIAP), Award at 2, which states the Agency's election to: (1) cease negotiating with the Union over permissive subjects of bargaining under the Statute, *id.* at 7; (2) revoke any prior election to bargain at the local level, *id.* at 18; and (3) expressly override and replace any conflicting "'agreements, policies, documents or practices executed or applied by the parties previously, at either the national or local levels[,]'" *id.* at 24 (quoting RNIAP) (emphasis omitted). In regard to staffing levels, the RNIAP provides, in pertinent part, that "'[t]he number of personnel assigned to any inspectional activity, regardless of whether it is performed on a regular or overtime basis, on a regular workday or holiday, shall be determined by [A]gency managers to meet the operational needs and budgetary concerns.'" *Id.* at 8. The RNIAP also provides that "'[m]anagers will determine the number of employees that will be on leave during any scheduling period.'" *Id.* at 18.

The Agency reduced the number of employees who could qualify for short draw annual leave slots,[3] *id.* at 8, and the Union filed a grievance, which was unresolved and submitted to arbitration, *id.* at 2. Because the parties were unable to agree on a statement of the issues, the Arbitrator framed the issues as follows: "Did the [Agency] violate the [parties' agreement] or the . . . RNIAP . . . when it unilaterally reduced the number of short [draw] leave . . . slots available for bid by bargaining unit employees? . . . If so, what is the appropriate remedy?" *Id.* at 4.

Before the Arbitrator, the Union asserted that the Agency's reduction of short draw leave slots constituted a change in the parties' "established past practice" by which a one-to-one ratio of short draw to long draw leave slots was maintained. *Id.* at 16. The Union argued that it had sought to bargain over the "substance," as well as the "impact[] and implementation," of the Agency's reduction in the number of short draw leave slots. *Id.* at 9. The Union asserted that "[i]f the Agency had indicated

1. Member DuBester's dissenting opinion is set forth at the end of this decision.

2. As discussed *infra*, the Arbitrator denied the grievance as to the Agency's refusal to bargain over the substance of the change. *See* Award at 19, 25, 27-28. No exceptions were filed to this finding.

3. Annual leave includes "short draw" leave, which is for leave before, during, and after Thanksgiving, Christmas, and New Year's days, and "regular" or "long draw" leave, which is any other leave during the year. Award at 8. The Agency determines the number of people who can apply for "short draw" and "long draw" leave slots, and the Union administers the bid rotation that determines which employees receive the available slots. *Id.*

that this was a national issue, the [n]ational Union would have delegated bargaining to the local[,]" *id.* at 13, and that "even if [the] RNIAP preclude[d] local bargaining over local changes, it d[id] not eliminate the need of the Agency to bargain nationally[,]" *id.* at 24.

In response, the Agency argued that staffing levels – including the number of employees that may use leave on a given day – are "within management discretion based on the [RNIAP]." *Id.* at 16. According to the Agency, "[a]ll of the Union's attempts to negotiate were at a local level and there is no requirement to bargain locally on the determination of how many leave slots would be available." *Id.* at 16-17.

The Arbitrator found that the Agency's reduction in the number of short draw leave slots did not violate the parties' agreement or the RNIAP, regardless of the alleged past practice of maintaining a one-to-one ratio between the types of leave draw slots. *Id.* at 25, 27-28. In this regard, the Arbitrator stated that "setting aside the issue of impact and implementation," the short draw leave issues, including the issue of "whether short draw slots ought to be matched one-to-one with regular slots[,]" "are entirely local and were consistently treated that way by both sides." *See id.* at 25. Thus, the Arbitrator concluded that "the parties['] past practice regarding the ratio of regular to short draw leave slots represented a local practice that was overturned or bypassed by RNIAP." *Id.*

Although the Arbitrator found that the RNIAP relieved the Agency of its obligation to bargain over the substance of its decision to reduce the number of short draw leave slots, he also found that the RNIAP did not relieve the Agency of its obligation to bargain over the impact and implementation of its decision. *Id.* at 27. Accordingly, the Arbitrator directed the Agency to "meet and bargain with the Union over these issues at the Union's request." *Id.* at 28. In so doing, the Arbitrator did not address the Agency's argument that the Union's only attempts to bargain were below the level of recognition.

III. Positions of the Parties

A. Agency's Exceptions

The Agency argues that the portion of the award directing the Agency to bargain over the impact and implementation of its reduction in short draw leave slots is contrary to law because "there is no requirement to bargain, at the local level, inspectional assignment actions taken by the Agency under [the] RNIAP." Exceptions at 15. Citing the Arbitrator's statement that "'setting aside the issue of impact and implementation, the issues are entirely local and *were consistently treated that way by both sides*[,]'" *id.* at 16 (quoting Award at 25) (emphasis added by Agency), the Agency argues that where, as here, "there has been a factual finding that the only attempts to bargain impact and implementation of RNIAP-based actions were made, and refused, at the local level, the Authority has previously found that the Agency's obligation to bargain at the national level was not properly at issue[,]" *id.* (citing *NTEU, Chapter 137*, 61 FLRA 413, 416 (2005)). The Agency also argues that because the Arbitrator's direction to the parties to bargain "does not specifically exclude local bargaining, . . . it should be set aside as contrary to law." *Id.* at 15. Finally, the Agency argues that the Arbitrator exceeded his authority by reaching the issue of whether the Agency was obligated to bargain over the impact and implementation of its reduction in the number of short draw leave slots. *Id.* at 9-14.

B. Union's Opposition

The Union argues that the award is not contrary to law because both the Union and the Agency consistently treated the reduction in short draw leave slots as a local issue. *See* Opp'n at 11-12. In this regard, the Union argues that evidence at arbitration "clearly indicate[d] that had management asserted that the change in leave policy could only be bargained at the level of recognition, the Union was prepared to refer the matter to [the national Union] for further action." *Id.* at 11. However, according to the Union, the Agency's failure to respond to the Union's bargaining requests by referring to the RNIAP or asserting that the Union was attempting to bargain below the level of recognition makes the Arbitrator's award lawful and the precedent cited by the Agency distinguishable. *Id.* at 11-12. In addition, the Union argues that "[s]hould the Authority agree with the Agency[] . . . that an order of local bargaining is inappropriate in this case, the remedy can be clarified to require bargaining only at the level of recognition." *Id.* at 13. Finally, the Union argues that the Arbitrator did not exceed his authority. *Id.* at 6-10.

IV. Analysis and Conclusions

When an exception involves an award's consistency with law, the Authority reviews any question of law raised by an exception and the award de novo. *See NTEU Chapter 24,* 50 FLRA 330, 332

(1995) (citing *U.S. Customs Serv. v. FLRA*, 43 F.3d 682, 686-87 (D.C. Cir. 1994)). In applying a de novo standard of review, the Authority assesses whether the arbitrator's legal conclusions are consistent with the applicable standard of law. *See NFFE, Local 1437*, 53 FLRA 1703, 1710 (1998). In making that assessment, the Authority defers to the arbitrator's underlying factual findings. *See id.*

The Agency argues that because the Union's only attempts to bargain were at the local level, the Agency lawfully refused to bargain the impact and implementation of its reduction in short draw leave slots. *See* Exceptions at 16-17. In this regard, the Authority has repeatedly upheld the Agency's implementation of the RNIAP, which, as it relates to inspectional assignment matters, "terminated the Agency's obligation to bargain at the local level over such matters." *NTEU, Chapter 137*, 60 FLRA 483, 487 (2004) (*Chapter 137*) (Chairman Cabaniss concurring), *recons. denied,* 61 FLRA 60 (2005), *pet. for review dismissed sub nom. NTEU v. FLRA*, No. 05-1338, 2006 WL 2521320 (D.C. Cir. Aug. 14, 2006). *See also NTEU, Chapter 143*, 60 FLRA 922, 927-28 (2005) (*Chapter 143*) (Chairman Cabaniss concurring) (finding no obligation to bargain at the local level over the impact and implementation of assignment-policy changes) *pet. for review denied sub nom. NTEU v. FLRA*, 453 F.3d 506 (D.C. Cir. 2006); *U.S. Dep't of Homeland Sec., U.S. Customs & Border Prot.*, 60 FLRA 496, 499-500 (2004) (*DHS*) (Chairman Cabaniss dissenting) (same). Consistent with this precedent, the Agency did not violate the Statute if the Union attempted to bargain over the reduction in short draw leave slots only at the local level.

The Union does not dispute the Agency's argument that the Union attempted to bargain only at the local level. *See* Exceptions at 16-17. *See also* Award at 16-17. The Union claims only that it was *prepared* to bargain at the national level – not that it actually attempted to do so. In this regard, the Union asserts that the evidence at arbitration showed that "*had* management asserted that the change in leave policy could only be bargained at the level of recognition, the Union *was prepared* to refer the matter to National [Union] for further action." Opp'n at 11 (emphasis added). In support of this statement, the Union cites letters that the Union sent to local management notifying the Agency, as required by the parties' collective bargaining agreement, of the designated local Union stewards that the Agency should contact in the event of "intended changes in operational or administrative procedures impacting on employees[.]" Opp'n, Attach. 3 at 1 & 3 (emphasis omitted). These letters include the following statement:

> To the extent that [the Agency] believes that [its] bargaining obligation is only at the national level, please forward Article 37 notice to whomever you believe is the appropriate Agency representative at the national level and so advise [local Union] officers, so we can alert our national representative . . . and bargaining can occur at that level.[4]

Id. at 1, 3.

The foregoing letters do not refer to any particular subject of bargaining, including the Agency's reduction in short draw leave slots. Thus, the Union has not demonstrated that the letters constitute requests to bargain the reduction in short draw leave slots at the national level. Further, the Agency's implementation of the RNIAP informed the Union that the Agency was withdrawing any previously delegated authority to bargain assignment matters – including leave – at the local level. Award at 18. The Union cites no basis for concluding that the Agency was required to treat a request to bargain locally as a request to bargain at the national level.

The Arbitrator made no finding that the Union ever attempted to bargain at the national level, and the Union does not argue, or cite to any evidence, that it did so.[5] Because the Agency had no obligation to bargain at the local level, and the Union has not established that it attempted to bargain at anything other than the local level, Authority precedent supports a conclusion that the award is deficient. *See Chapter 143*, 60 FLRA at 927-28; *DHS*, 60 FLRA at 500; *Chapter 137*, 60 FLRA at 488.

---

4. The record does not include a copy of Article 37 of the parties' agreement.

5. In this regard, the dissent appears to find that, by informing the Agency of the Union's national-level contact, the Union was requesting to bargain at the national level. Dissent at 7. However, there is no basis for finding that, by providing contact information, the Union was requesting to bargain nationally over all subsequent changes in conditions of employment. Further, whether or not the Agency's "main argument before the Arbitrator" was that it had no obligation to bargain "at all," *id.*, the Agency also argued to the Arbitrator, as it does to the Authority, that the Union failed to request bargaining at any level other than the local level. Award at 16-17; Exceptions at 16-17. Thus, the Union's failure to request bargaining at the national level was before the Arbitrator, and is before the Authority.

The Union also cites no basis for concluding that the lawfulness of the Agency's refusal to bargain depends upon the reasoning that the Agency provided in its refusal. As discussed above, the Authority repeatedly has held that the RNIAP terminated any preexisting local bargaining agreements concerning assignment and, thus, the Agency did not violate the Statute by refusing to bargain at the local level over assignment matters. *See, e.g., Chapter 143,* 60 FLRA at 927-28; *DHS,* 60 FLRA at 500; *Chapter 137,* 60 FLRA at 488. These decisions do not require the Agency to refer to the RNIAP, or inform the Union of the need to request bargaining at the exclusive level of recognition, in order to lawfully refuse to negotiate with the Union at the local level. For example, although the agency in *NTEU, Chapter 137* explained its refusal to bargain by stating that management actions taken under the RNIAP could not be bargained locally, the Authority did not hold that the lawfulness of the agency's refusal to bargain at the local level depended upon the agency providing that explanation to the union. 61 FLRA at 414, 416-17.

In sum, because the Union did not establish that it attempted to bargain at the national level, the Arbitrator's finding that that the Agency improperly refused to bargain over the impact and implementation of its decision to reduce short draw leave slots is contrary to law.[6] *See Chapter 143,* 60 FLRA at 927-28; *DHS,* 60 FLRA at 500; *Chapter 137,* 60 FLRA at 488. Accordingly, we set aside the award.[7]

V. Decision

The award is set aside.

6. With regard to the dissent's reliance on "notification procedures[,]" Dissent at 7, the Union does not argue that the Agency failed to provide adequate notice; thus, we do not address that issue. Further, as there is no evidence that the Union argued to the Arbitrator – and the Arbitrator did not find – that the notice provided by the Agency was deficient, this case is distinguishable from *United States Department of Homeland Security, Customs & Border Protection,* 64 FLRA 989 (2010) (Member Beck dissenting), *pet. for review filed sub nom. United States Department of Homeland Security, Customs & Border Protection v. FLRA,* No. 10-1282 (D.C. Cir. Sept. 8, 2010), and the dissent's reliance on that decision is misplaced.

7. Because we find the award deficient as contrary to law, we do not address the Agency's other exceptions.

Member DuBester, Dissenting:

I do not agree with my colleagues that the Arbitrator's award should be set aside. Rather, I would find that the Agency was obligated to bargain over the impact and implementation (I&I) of its decision to reduce short draw leave slots, and deny the Agency's exceptions.

Among other things, as the decision acknowledges, the Union clearly and specifically advised the Agency of contact information at the national level for notices regarding changes in conditions of employment. Majority Op. at 4-5. The Union's communication, which pre-dated the events in this case, refers to this information as "official points of contact." Opp'n, Attach., Ex. 1B. In my view, therefore, the decision is not accurate when it concludes "the Union has not established that it attempted to bargain at anything other than the local level." Majority Op. at 5.

In addition, the Agency does not allege, and the award does not find, that the Agency followed those notification procedures for giving the Union effective notice at the national level concerning local changes in conditions of employment. Rather, the Agency's main argument before the Arbitrator was simply that it had no obligation at all, local or national, to bargain I&I. As indicated, the award, equally simply, finds that the Agency refused to bargain. The record supports that finding.

Finally, this case is very similar to *United States Department of Homeland Security, Customs & Border Protection,* 64 FLRA 989 (2010) (Member Beck dissenting) (*DHS, CBP*), *pet. for review filed sub nom. United States Department of Homeland Security, Customs & Border Protection v. FLRA,* No. 10-1282 (D.C. Cir. Sept. 8, 2010). That case was pending before the Authority when exceptions in the instant case were filed. Here, the Arbitrator cites, and the Agency discusses, *DHS, CBP* as possible precedent on the issue of the Agency's obligation to bargain at the national level over local changes in conditions of employment. In *DHS, CBP*, the Authority denied the Agency's exceptions to an award finding that the Agency committed unfair labor practices "by failing to provide notice and an opportunity to negotiate local assignment policy changes at the national level." *DHS, CBP,* 64 FLRA at 990. In my view, the instant case is comparable and the Authority should similarly uphold the Arbitrator's award.

65 FLRA No. 180

NATIONAL TREASURY
EMPLOYEES UNION
CHAPTER 299
(Union)

and

UNITED STATES
DEPARTMENT OF THE TREASURY
OFFICE OF THE COMPTROLLER
OF THE CURRENCY
(Agency)

0-AR-4731

DECISION

May 27, 2011

Before the Authority: Carol Waller Pope, Chairman, and Thomas M. Beck and Ernest DuBester, Members[1]

I. Statement of the Case

This matter is before the Authority on exceptions to an award of Arbitrator Jerome H. Ross filed by the Union under § 7122(a) of the Federal Service Labor-Management Relations Statute (the Statute) and part 2425 of the Authority's Regulations. The Agency filed an opposition to the Union's exceptions.

The Arbitrator found that the Union's grievance was neither grievable nor arbitrable based on the Authority's decision in *United States Department of Defense, National Imagery & Mapping Agency, St. Louis, Missouri*, 57 FLRA 837 (2002) (then-Member Pope dissenting) (*NIMA*). For the reasons that follow, we deny the Union's nonfact exception, set aside the award in part, and remand the award to the parties for resubmission, absent settlement, to an arbitrator of their choice.

II. Background and Arbitrator's Award

The Union filed a grievance alleging that certain employees did not receive the merit pay increases to which they were entitled under the Agency's national "Merit Pay & Bonus Guidelines" (National Guidance). Award at 2 & n.2. When the grievance was unresolved, it was submitted to arbitration, where the Arbitrator framed the following issue for resolution: "Is [the grievance] grievable/arbitrable under the parties' [collective bargaining agreement (CBA)]?"[2] *Id.* at 3.

As an initial matter, the Arbitrator rejected the Union's contention that the Agency's Policies and Procedures Manual (PPM) waived the Agency's right to contest the grievability of the parties' dispute. *See id.* at 4, 7 (citing PPM 3110-30).[3] In addition, the Arbitrator found that he was "constrained to follow" the Authority's decision in *NIMA*, *id.* at 6 (internal quotation marks omitted), and, as such, he determined that *NIMA* "require[d]" him to find that "merit pay determinations . . .[,] under [s]tatute[4] and case precedent, [are] within the sole and exclusive province of the Agency[,]" *id.* at 6, 7. Therefore, he concluded that the grievance was

1. Member Beck's dissenting opinion is set forth at the end of this decision.

2. In this regard, a footnote in the CBA's article on the negotiated grievance procedure (NGP) states, in pertinent part:

> The [Agency] and the Union disagree over whether matters related to compensation and benefits are subject to the grievance and arbitration procedures. It is the [Agency]'s position that these matters are not subject to the [NGP], as a matter of law, . . . pursuant to 12 [U.S.C. §]481. . . .

Award at 3 n.6 (quoting CBA Art. 27, n.*).

3. PPM 3110-30 states, in pertinent part:

> Employee compensation and decisions affecting permanent increases to employee base pay, lump-sum payments and salary differentials are not grievable. This includes, for example, . . . the amount of a merit pay increase . . . as long as the amounts awarded are consistent with [Agency] policies.

Award at 4.

4. The statutory provisions relevant to the Arbitrator's finding are 12 U.S.C. §§ 481 and 482. 12 U.S.C. § 481 pertinently provides that the Comptroller shall employ certain individuals "without regard to the provisions of other laws applicable to officers or employees of the United States[,]" and 12 U.S.C. § 482 pertinently provides that, "[n]otwithstanding any of the provisions of [§] 481 . . . to the contrary, the Comptroller . . . shall fix the compensation . . . of, and appoint and direct, all employees of the Office of the Comptroller of the Currency."

"neither grievable nor arbitrable under the . . . CBA[.]" *Id.* at 8.

III. Positions of the Parties

A. Union's Exceptions

The Union asserts that the Arbitrator's finding that PPM 3110-30 does not waive the Agency's right to contest the grievability of this dispute is based on a nonfact because "the PPM[,] as written[,] clearly establishes" that the Union may grieve inconsistent applications of the Agency's compensation policy. Exceptions at 4. In addition, the Union argues that the award is contrary to law because, according to the Union, it may grieve and arbitrate "decisions that [are] inconsistent with the Agency's unilaterally established pay policy." *Id.* at 3; *see also id.* at 6-7. In this regard, the Union contends that nothing in the CBA excludes matters involving the application of previously established compensation policies, such as the National Guidance, from the NGP. *See id.* at 6-7. Moreover, the Union contends that, for various reasons, the Arbitrator "erred in . . . applying the holding in *NIMA*" to the instant dispute. *Id.* at 8; *see also id.* at 5-7.

B. Agency's Opposition

The Agency argues that the Union's nonfact exception does not challenge a "fact" found by the Arbitrator. Opp'n at 7. In addition, the Agency asserts that the Arbitrator correctly found the grievance to be neither grievable nor arbitrable. *Id.* at 2-3. In this regard, according to the Agency, "[c]ompensation matters [involving the Agency's employees] are not grievable or arbitrable . . . because grievances over th[o]se matters would interfere with the Comptroller's authority . . . to set compensation 'without regard to the provisions of other laws applicable to officers or employees of the United States.'" *Id.* at 2 (quoting and citing 12 U.S.C. §§ 481, 482). Moreover, the Agency contends that "*NIMA* . . . is controlling in this case" and that the Arbitrator's grievability and arbitrability findings are consistent with *NIMA*. *Id.* at 8 (emphasis omitted); *see also id.* at 6, 8-9.

IV. Analysis and Conclusions

A. The award is not based on a nonfact.

The Union asserts that the Arbitrator's finding that PPM 3110-30 does not waive the Agency's right to contest the grievability of this dispute is based on a nonfact. Exceptions at 4-5. To establish that an award is based on a nonfact, the appealing party must show that a central fact underlying the award is clearly erroneous, but for which the arbitrator would have reached a different result. *See U.S. Dep't of the Air Force, Lowry Air Force Base, Denver, Colo.*, 48 FLRA 589, 593 (1993). However, an arbitrator's interpretation of applicable law and regulations is not a "fact" that can be challenged as a nonfact. *See U.S. Dep't of Transp., Fed. Aviation Admin., Wash., D.C.*, 58 FLRA 23, 26 (2002) (Chairman Cabaniss dissenting as to another matter) (*FAA*); *see also U.S. Dep't of the Air Force, San Antonio Air Logistics Ctr., Kelly Air Force Base, Tex.*, 51 FLRA 1624, 1630-31 (1996) (arbitrator's application of agency regulations is not a fact challengeable as a nonfact).

PPM 3110-30 is an Agency regulation. Therefore, the Arbitrator's interpretation of PPM 3110-30 is not a "fact" that can be challenged as a nonfact. *See FAA*, 58 FLRA at 26. Consequently, we deny the nonfact exception.

B. The Arbitrator's finding that the grievance is not grievable or arbitrable is contrary to law.

The Union argues that the award is contrary to law. The Authority reviews questions of law de novo. *See NTEU, Chapter 24*, 50 FLRA 330, 332 (1995) (citing *U.S. Customs Serv. v. FLRA*, 43 F.3d 682, 686-87 (D.C. Cir. 1994)). In applying a standard of de novo review, the Authority determines whether the arbitrator's legal conclusions are consistent with the applicable standard of law. *NFFE, Local 1437*, 53 FLRA 1703, 1710 (1998). In making that determination, the Authority defers to the arbitrator's underlying factual findings. *See id.*

If a law indicates that an agency's discretion over a matter affecting employees' conditions of employment is intended to be "sole and exclusive" – i.e., that it is intended to be exercised only by the agency – "then the agency is not obligated under the Statute to exercise that discretion through collective bargaining." *NTEU*, 59 FLRA 815, 816 (2004) (then-Member Pope dissenting), *pet. for review denied*, 435 F.3d 1049 (9th Cir. 2006). In *NIMA*, the Authority held that an agency's sole and exclusive discretion to establish certain conditions of employment without bargaining also precludes grievances and arbitration over those conditions, once established. 57 FLRA at 842-43.

The Arbitrator found that *NIMA* "require[d]" him to find the instant dispute neither grievable nor arbitrable. Award at 6. The Union argues that *NIMA* should not control the outcome of this dispute. *E.g.*, Exceptions at 8. For the reasons that follow, we agree.

In *National Treasury Employees Union, Chapter 302*, 65 FLRA 746 (2011) (Member Beck dissenting) (*Chapter 302*), the Authority reexamined and reversed *NIMA*, after concluding that: "(1) sole and exclusive discretion to establish certain conditions of employment does not preclude grievances over individual applications of those conditions of employment, once established; and (2) in reaching a contrary conclusion in *NIMA*, the Authority erred." *Id.* at 750; *see also id.* at 747-50 (analysis in support of reversing *NIMA*). Because *Chapter 302* held that "nothing in the Agency's sole and exclusive discretion to establish compensation precludes grievances over individual application of the Agency's established compensation system," *id.* at 750, the Arbitrator's finding that *NIMA* barred the grievance is contrary to law. Therefore, we grant the contrary-to-law exception and set aside the Arbitrator's finding that the grievance is neither grievable nor arbitrable.

Where the Authority sets aside an arbitrator's determination that a grievance is not arbitrable, the Authority remands the matter to the parties for submission, absent settlement, to an arbitrator of their choice. *E.g.*, *AFGE, Local 2823*, 64 FLRA 1144, 1147 (2010). Consistent with the foregoing precedent, we remand the award to the parties for resubmission, absent settlement, to an arbitrator of their choice.[5]

V. Decision

The nonfact exception is denied, the Arbitrator's finding that the grievance is neither grievable nor arbitrable based on *NIMA* is set aside, and the award is remanded to the parties for resubmission, absent settlement, to an arbitrator of their choice.

5. We note that nothing in this decision precludes an arbitrator from finding, on remand, that the grievance is nongrievable or nonarbitrable for reasons other than those set forth in *NIMA*.

Member Beck, Dissenting:

I disagree with my colleagues' determination to set aside the Arbitrator's finding that the grievance in this case is neither grievable nor arbitrable.

For the reasons that I articulated in my recent dissent in *National Treasury Employees Union, Chapter 302*, 65 FLRA 746, 751 (2011), compensation decisions of the Comptroller are not subject to the grievance and arbitration procedures that exist under our Statute.

65 FLRA No. 181

SOCIAL SECURITY ADMINISTRATION
REGION IX
(Agency)

and

AMERICAN FEDERATION
OF GOVERNMENT EMPLOYEES
COUNCIL 220
(Union)

0-AR-4334

DECISION

May 27, 2011

Before the Authority: Carol Waller Pope, Chairman, and Thomas M. Beck and Ernest DuBester, Members[1]

I. Statement of the Case

This matter is before the Authority on exceptions to an award of Arbitrator Thomas H. Hemer filed by the Agency under § 7122(a) of the Federal Service Labor-Management Relations Statute (the Statute) and part 2425 of the Authority's Regulations. The Union filed an opposition to the Agency's exceptions.

The Union filed a grievance alleging that the Agency suspended an employee without just cause, in violation of the parties' collective bargaining agreement (Agreement). The Arbitrator sustained the grievance and directed the Agency to compensate the grievant for lost pay and benefits and to remove the suspension from its records. For the reasons that follow, we deny the Agency's exceptions.

II. Background and Arbitrator's Award

The Agency suspended the grievant for misconduct related to her government credit card (Card). Award at 2. In this regard, the Agency alleged that the grievant: (1) used the Card while serving as a delegate to a Union caucus – an activity for which she had not scheduled official time or received Agency travel orders, *id.* at 5; (2) used the Card to purchase an airline ticket for another employee, *id.* at 2; and (3) failed to pay the Card bill in a timely manner, *id.* at 2. The Union filed a grievance contending, as relevant here, that the Agency punished the grievant for authorized uses of the Card. *See id.* at 3. The grievance was unresolved and submitted to arbitration on the stipulated issue of whether there was "just [c]ause for the . . . suspension of the [g]rievant[;]" and, "[i]f not, what shall the [r]emedy be?" *Id.* at 1.

A. Card Terms and Conditions

The Arbitrator examined the grievant's application for the Card (Application),[2] as well as the terms and conditions that appeared on the Application (Application Terms), which stated, in pertinent part, "By signing below, I . . . agree to use the [C]ard for *official travel* and *official travel related expenses* and to be bound by the . . . attached [a]greement governing the use of the [Card] . . . ." *Id.* at 3 (emphases added) (quoting "Government Card Application and Agreement"). In order to determine the meaning of the phrase "official travel[,]" the Arbitrator considered the "Title/Rank" assigned to the grievant on the Application. *Id.* In this regard, he found that the Application listed the grievant as "Claims Rep[resentative]/Union Rep[resentative]," which "establish[ed]" that the Card's authorized uses included travel and travel related expenses for "legitimate government business," including "both [o]fficial Agency and [o]fficial Union duties." *Id.* at 3-6. Consequently, the Arbitrator found that when the grievant traveled in connection with "official [U]nion duties," she engaged in "official travel," and the expenses she incurred because of that "official (Union) travel" constituted "official travel related expenses." *Id.* at 5-6. Although the Arbitrator also reviewed a "set of rules" that the Agency attached to the Application,[3] he concluded that those rules did "not

1. Member Beck's dissenting opinion is set forth at the end of this decision.

2. Although the Card Application and the "Citibank [Card] Program[,] Employee Information Packet" (hereinafter "Citi EIP"), *see* Exceptions, Attach., Agency Ex. 3, are part of "a commercial agreement . . . between the [g]rievant and a [c]redit [c]ard [c]ompany," the federal government "sponsored" that commercial agreement, and the Agency "enforce[s]" the provisions of the Card Application and Citi EIP as "condition[s] of employment." Award at 2.

3. The Arbitrator expressed some "doubt as to the admissibility of the [set of] rules" contained in the Citi EIP. *See* Award at 3-4. The Arbitrator noted that, although the Agency attached the Citi EIP to a copy of the grievant's Card Application and presented the Application and

alter the [Card's] original purpose[,]" as indicated by the Application itself. *Id.* at 3-4. The Arbitrator then proceeded to evaluate the Agency's allegations against the grievant, in accordance with his findings on the Card terms and conditions.

B. Agency's Allegations Against the Grievant

With regard to the grievant's use of the Card while serving as a delegate to a Union caucus, the Arbitrator concluded that the caucus involved internal Union business and occurred when the grievant would not otherwise have been in duty status. *Id.* at 5-6. The Arbitrator explained that, under the Agreement, the grievant could perform Union representational and labor-management functions on "official time" – when she "would otherwise be in duty status" – but the Statute required the grievant to conduct any internal Union business when she was in "non-duty status[.]" *Id.* at 4 (quoting 5 U.S.C. § 7131(b); Agreement, Art. 30, § 6(B)). As such, he found that the grievant could not have scheduled – and, thus, had no obligation to schedule – official time in order to make authorized use of the Card at the caucus. *Id.* at 5-6. Moreover, because the grievant, as a caucus delegate, performed "official [U]nion duties" while "on travel status, under the direction and control of the Union[,]" the Arbitrator found that the grievant had received the necessary "official (Union) travel" orders to "authorize[]" her use of the Card. *Id.* at 5-7. In this regard, the Arbitrator found that the grievant would receive travel orders from the Union in order to perform official duties under the Union's control, and she would receive travel orders from the Agency in order to perform official duties under the Agency's control. *Id.* at 5-6. The Arbitrator found further that, because the grievant did not seek reimbursement from the Agency for her expenses in connection with the Union caucus, charging those expenses to the Card did not "require specific authorization by anyone other than the [U]nion." *Id.* at 7. Thus, he concluded that the grievant used the Card for "official travel related expenses[,]" as she had a "right" to do under the "[c]redit [c]ard [a]greement[,]" including the Application Terms. *Id.* at 6-7.

Regarding the allegation that the grievant used the Card to purchase an airline ticket for another employee, *see id.* at 2, the Arbitrator determined that the grievant used the Card merely to reserve a ticket at a guaranteed favorable rate for another Union representative, and the airline "erroneously . . . conver[ted] . . . this guarantee into payment for the ticket[.]" *Id.* at 7. The Arbitrator found that the airline's "mistake . . . did not constitute 'misconduct'" by the grievant. *Id.*

As for the allegation that the grievant did not timely pay Card bills, the Arbitrator noted that the Agency had submitted its own reports of the grievant's account payment history, but not the credit card company's "official" account records. *Id.* at 7-8. Unlike "competent evidence" regarding the grievant's Card account, the Arbitrator found that the Agency reports constituted "hearsay" and lacked the details that the Arbitrator required to evaluate the alleged payment delinquencies, such as "[h]ow many late charges were imposed" and whether "punitive interest was applied[.]" *Id.* Therefore, he found that the Agency did not satisfy its burden of proving the allegation of payment delinquency. *Id.*

Based on the evidence and his "examination of . . . the Agreement and the Statute[,]" the Arbitrator concluded that "[j]ust [c]ause for the . . . suspension of the [g]rievant ha[d] not been established[,]" and he directed the Agency to compensate the grievant for lost pay and benefits and to remove the suspension from its records. *Id.* at 8.

III. Positions of the Parties

A. Agency's Exceptions

The Agency contends that the award is contrary to Agency rules, which the Agency states are based on the Federal Travel Regulation (FTR), Exceptions at 9, according to which employees "*must* have official travel orders to use the [C]ard *at all*[,]" *id.* at 7, and must "restrict the use of [the Card] to 'official travel related purposes[,]'" *id.* at 9. *See also id.* at 3-4 (citing Citi EIP, Agency Ex. 3 (Attach.) at 13-14), 8-9 (citing 41 C.F.R. § 301-51.6 (FTR); Admin. Instructions Manual Sys.

Citi EIP together as a single exhibit at arbitration, the "set of rules" contained in the Citi EIP governed accounts with Citibank, whereas the Application signed by the grievant indicated that her Card would be governed by rules for accounts with American Express. *See id.*

(AIMS), Agency Ex. 9 (Attach.) at 2).[4] According to the Agency, the grievant did not have travel orders for the Union caucus, and her attendance at the caucus did not constitute "official travel," within the meaning of Agency rules. *Id.* at 9. The Agency also contends that the award is contrary to management's right to discipline employees for "just cause" because the Arbitrator allegedly determined that "the Agency had no right to control [the grievant's] use of [the Card] when she was performing Union activities in an off-duty status." *Id.* at 7-8 (citing 5 U.S.C. § 7106(a)(2); Agreement, Art. 23, § 1). The Agency adds that the Arbitrator exceeded his authority because the award is contrary to management's right "to discipline its own employee[.]" *Id.* at 8.

In addition, the Agency asserts that the Arbitrator exceeded his authority by deciding an issue not before him – specifically, whether the Agency could "control" the grievant's Card use – rather than the stipulated issue of whether the grievant's actions warranted the discipline imposed. *Id.* at 7-10. As the result of deciding an issue not found in the grievance, the Agency asserts that the Arbitrator incorrectly determined that the Agency could not control the grievant's use of the Card. *Id.* at 7. The Agency further asserts that, although it did not allege that the grievant "should have [been on] official time" when she used the Card, the Arbitrator exceeded his authority by finding that the Agency failed to prove such an allegation. *Id.* at 9-10.

Moreover, the Agency argues that the award is based on nonfacts because the Arbitrator "completely ignored[,]" "inappropriately dismissed . . . as 'hearsay[,]'" or "apparently missed" the Agency's witness testimony and email exhibits allegedly establishing the grievant's delinquency in paying her Card bills. *Id.* at 10-11. The Agency argues that "a different result would have been reached" if the Arbitrator had considered all of the "pertinent, material evidence[.]" *Id.* at 11-12.

B. Union's Opposition

The Union contends that the exceptions mischaracterize the award as exempting Union officers from discipline. Opp'n at 9, 14, 21. Instead, the Union asserts that the award reflects the Arbitrator's findings that: (1) the grievant was authorized to use the Card at the Union caucus; (2) a mistake by an airline company did not constitute misconduct by the grievant; and (3) the Agency's hearsay evidence failed to establish bill payment delinquencies warranting a suspension. *See id.* at 8, 10, 14, 17-19. The Union further asserts that the exceptions inappropriately seek to re-evaluate the

---

4. Among others, the Agency cites the following provisions of the Citi EIP to support its contention that the award is contrary to Agency rules:

> *How is the Card to be Used?*
> The [Card] should be used to pay for major expenses connected with official [g]overnment travel (lodgings, meals, automobile rentals, etc.)
>
> . . . .
>
> *What Restrictions Apply to the Use of [the Card]?*
> [The Card] may be used to pay *only* for expenses authorized on your travel order for the purpose of conducting official [g]overnment business . . . .

Exceptions, Attach., Agency Ex. 3 at 13-14 ("Responses to Questions Most Commonly Asked").

As additional support for its contention that the award is contrary to Agency rules, the Agency cites the following provisions from its Administrative Instructions Manual System (AIMS):

> 07.32.02 *Policy*
>
> . . . .
>
> C. The [Card] shall be used only for authorized official travel expenses . . . as indicated on the travel order and approved by the travel authorizing official for employees under their line of authority. Employees are not authorized to use the [C]ard for family members, other persons, or personal expenses.
>
> . . . .
>
> 07.32.07 *Employee Rights and Obligations*
>
> . . . .
>
> C. The [Card] . . . [is] not to be used for . . . personal purposes and may only be used in connection with official [g]overnment travel. The [Card] may only be used for expenses authorized on a travel order . . . .

Exceptions, Attach., Agency Ex. 9 at 2, 4 (AIMS: "Government Contractor-Issued Charge Card Program").

Moreover, the Agency asserts that 41 C.F.R. § 301-51.6 supports its contention that the award is contrary to Agency rules. The pertinent wording of that provision is set forth *infra* Part IV.A.1.

Arbitrator's credibility determinations, factual findings, and determinations regarding the weight of evidence. *Id.* at 9, 11, 13, 15, 17-18, 19.

IV. Analysis and Conclusions

A. The award is not contrary to law, rule, or regulation.

The Agency asserts that the award is contrary to its rules, which are based on the FTR, and that the award is contrary to management's rights under the Statute. When an exception involves an award's consistency with law, rule, or regulation, the Authority reviews any question of law raised by the exception and the award de novo. *See NTEU, Chapter 24*, 50 FLRA 330, 332 (1995) (citing *U.S. Customs Serv. v. FLRA*, 43 F.3d 682, 686-87 (D.C. Cir. 1994)). In applying the standard of de novo review, the Authority assesses whether an arbitrator's legal conclusions are consistent with the applicable standard of law. *See U.S. Dep't of Def., Dep'ts of the Army & the Air Force, Ala. Nat'l Guard, Northport, Ala.*, 55 FLRA 37, 40 (1998) (*Ala. Nat'l Guard*). In making that assessment, the Authority defers to the arbitrator's underlying factual findings. *See id.*

1. The award is not contrary to Agency rules.

As to the Agency's assertions that the award is contrary to its rules, absent circumstances not relevant in this case, an arbitration award that conflicts with a governing agency rule or regulation will be found deficient under § 7122(a)(1) of the Statute. *See U.S. Dep't of the Army, Fort Campbell Dist., Third Region, Fort Campbell, Ky.*, 37 FLRA 186, 191-95 (1990). Because the Union does not dispute the Agency's contention that it may enforce the terms of the credit card agreement as Agency rules, we review the Arbitrator's interpretation of the credit card agreement as we would review an arbitral interpretation of Agency rules.

The Authority has held that arbitrators are empowered to interpret and apply agency rules in the resolution of grievances under the Statute. *See U.S. Dep't of Justice, Immigration & Naturalization Serv., Wash., D.C.*, 48 FLRA 1269, 1275 (1993) (*INS*). When evaluating exceptions asserting that an award is contrary to a governing agency rule or regulation, the Authority will determine whether the award is inconsistent with the plain wording of, or is otherwise impermissible under, the rule or regulation. *See U.S. Dep't of the Treasury, Internal Revenue Serv., Ogden Serv. Ctr., Ogden, Utah*, 42 FLRA 1034, 1056-57 (1991) (*IRS, Ogden*).

The Agency contends that the award is contrary to several of its rules restricting permissible uses of the Card to "'official [government] travel related purposes'" that have been authorized by "official travel orders" for the performance of "official [g]overnment business[.]" Exceptions at 3-4, 7-9; *see also supra* note 4 (text of rules in Citi EIP and AIMS). However, the Arbitrator found that the grievant complied with those Card use restrictions. *See* Award at 5-7. Significantly, the Agency rules do not define the terms "official travel," "official travel related expenses," or "government business," and, as a result, the Arbitrator had to determine the meaning to those terms in order to apply them to the particular circumstances at issue. *See INS*, 48 FLRA at 1275 (arbitrators may interpret agency rules). The Arbitrator first determined that the term "official travel" includes "official (Union) travel[.]" Award at 5-6. Employing that definition of "official travel," the Arbitrator found that the grievant attended the caucus "on travel status, under the direction and control of the Union." *Id.* at 7. The Arbitrator thus concluded that the grievant used the Card for "official travel related expenses" authorized by "official (Union) travel" orders, in the performance of "legitimate government business," *id.* at 4-6, and that the grievant's "official travel related expenses" did not require additional authorization from the Agency because the grievant did not request Agency reimbursement for those expenses, *id.* at 6-7. Because the Agency rules do not define the relevant terms – and, thus, do not provide an interpretation of those terms that differs from the Arbitrator's – the Agency does not demonstrate that the Arbitrator erred in concluding that the grievant complied with the Agency's Card use rules.

Although the Agency further asserts that 41 C.F.R. § 301-51.6 supports finding that the award is contrary to Agency rules, that provision limits Card use to "official travel related expenses" in the same manner as the Agency rules discussed above. In this regard, throughout 2002, 2003, and 2004 – i.e., the years during which events gave rise to the grievance – 41 C.F.R. § 301-51.6 stated: "*May I use the Government contractor-issued travel charge card for purposes other than those associated with official travel?* No, the Government contractor-issued travel charge card may be used only for official travel related expenses." 41 C.F.R. § 301-51.6 (2004) (year in which Agency initiated disciplinary actions related to grievant's Card activity); *id.* (2003) (year in which grievant used Card to reserve guaranteed favorable rate for another Union representative); *id.* (2002) (year of grievant's Card use at caucus, which was one ground Agency cited for initiating discipline). As discussed previously, the Arbitrator expressly found that the grievant used the Card for "official (Union) travel" in connection with the caucus and that the charges she incurred during that travel constituted "official travel related expenses[,]" for which she was "authorized" to use the Card. Award at 6. In addition, the Agency does not identify any wording in the FTR – as it existed at the time of the events that gave rise to the grievance – precluding a finding that "official (Union) travel" may constitute "official travel" or that "official travel related expenses" may include "official (Union) travel" related expenses. *Id.* Thus, the Agency does not demonstrate that the Arbitrator's finding that the grievant was authorized to charge "official (Union) travel" related expenses to the Card is contrary to 41 C.F.R. § 301-51.6, which limits Card use to "official travel related expenses."

We note that, while the exceptions in this case were pending before the Authority, the General Services Administration (GSA) amended the FTR. *See* 75 Fed. Reg. 24434 (May 5, 2010). In particular, the FTR amendments rephrased 41 C.F.R. § 301-51.6 and, *for the first time*, explicitly limited "official travel" to "[t]ravel under . . . the direction of a Federal agency." *See* 75 Fed. Reg. at 24,435. In amending the FTR, the GSA stated that the newly added definition of "official travel" applied only to "travel performed on and after June 4, 2010[,]" *id.* at 24,434, which would not include the grievant's travel at issue here. The Authority has previously held that, in the absence of any indication that amendments to governing legal provisions were intended to be applied retroactively, the Authority should apply the pre-amended versions of those provisions, as they existed when events gave rise to the grievance, in order to determine whether an award is consistent with the applicable legal standard. *See U.S. Dep't of the Interior, Bureau of Mines, Pittsburgh Research Ctr.*, 53 FLRA 34, 38 n.1 (1997) (*Bureau of Mines*) (applying pre-amended version of statute to evaluate whether award was contrary to law). As the final rule amending the FTR makes clear that retroactive application is not warranted, *see* 75 Fed. Reg. at 24434, and consistent with *Bureau of Mines*, 53 FLRA at 38 n.1, we do not rely upon the amended FTR in our evaluation of the Agency's exceptions. *See U.S. Dep't of Homeland Sec., U.S. Customs & Border Prot.*, 65 FLRA 356, 360 (2010) (in light of explanation of Office of Personnel Management that its regulatory amendments should not have retroactive effect, Authority declined to apply amendments retroactively when determining whether award was contrary to law). As discussed above, under the pre-amended version of the FTR, the Arbitrator's findings satisfy the FTR requirement – as it is incorporated by Agency rules – that the Card be used only for "official travel related expenses."[5]

Insofar as the Agency contends that the award is contrary to Agency rules prohibiting the grievant from using the Card to make purchases for another employee, the Arbitrator found that the grievant did not use the Card to make such a purchase, *see* Award at 7, and, as previously mentioned, the Authority defers to arbitral factual findings when conducting a de novo review. *See Ala. Nat'l Guard*, 55 FLRA at 40. Accordingly, such a contention does not provide a basis for finding the award contrary to Agency rules.

For the foregoing reasons, we deny the Agency's exceptions contending that the award is contrary to Agency rules.

2. The award is not contrary to management's right to discipline.

The Agency asserts that the award is contrary to its right to discipline employees. The Authority recently revised the analysis that it will apply when reviewing management rights exceptions to arbitration awards. *See U.S. EPA*, 65 FLRA 113, 115 (2010) (Member Beck concurring) (*EPA*); *FDIC, Div. of Supervision & Consumer Prot., S.F. Region*, 65 FLRA 102, 106-07 (2010) (Chairman Pope concurring). Under the revised analysis, the Authority will first assess whether the award affects the exercise of the asserted management right. *EPA*, 65 FLRA at 115. If so, then, as relevant here, the Authority examines whether the award enforces a

---

5. The dissent cites several decisions to support its conclusion that the award is contrary to Agency rules. *See* Dissenting Op. at 13-14 (citations omitted). Those decisions are inapposite. First, the decisions do not involve or interpret the Citi EIP. *Cf. U.S. Dep't of the Treasury, IRS, Small Bus./Self Employed Operating Div.*, 65 FLRA 23, 26 & n.4 (party's reliance on the interpretation of terms in other agencies' regulations failed to establish the definition of similar terms in the party's own regulation, where the party's own regulation did not contain definitions for the terms in dispute). Second, the decisions do not define "official government travel," which is the central disputed term in this case. Third, the decisions involve the agency authorization required to support employees' claims for *official time* when traveling or *reimbursement* for employees' travel expenses; the instant case does not involve either. *See* Award at 6-7.

contract provision negotiated pursuant to § 7106(b) of the Statute.[6] *Id.*

The Union does not dispute that the award affects management's right to discipline. *See* Opp'n at 14, 21. In addition, the Authority has previously held that an arbitrator's enforcement of a "just cause" contractual provision, which results in the rescission of an employee's suspension, affects management's right to discipline. *E.g., U.S. Dep't of Justice, Fed. Bureau of Prisons, Fed. Detention Ctr., Miami, Fla.*, 57 FLRA 677, 679 (2002) (Member Armendariz concurring) (citing *U.S. Dep't of Veterans Affairs, Med. Ctr., Coatesville, Pa.*, 53 FLRA 1426, 1429-30 (1998)). Thus, we find that the award affects management's right.

As for whether the award enforces a contract provision negotiated under § 7106(b), the Arbitrator concluded that "[j]ust [c]ause for the . . . suspension of the [g]rievant ha[d] not been established" based on his "examination of . . . *the Agreement* and the Statute[.]" Award at 8 (emphasis added). In addition, the Agency cites Article 23, Section 1 of the Agreement to support its claim that it has the right to discipline employees for "just cause."[7] *See* Exceptions at 7. Further, the Union does not dispute the contention that Article 23, Section 1 of the Agreement recognizes the Agency's right to discipline employees for "just cause." Consequently, as this point is uncontested by the parties, we find that the award enforces Article 23, Section 1 of the Agreement.

The Authority has held that contract provisions requiring just cause for discipline constitute appropriate arrangements within the meaning of § 7106(b)(3) of the Statute. *E.g., Soc. Sec. Admin., Balt., Md.*, 53 FLRA 1751, 1754 (1998). As Article 23, Section 1 of the Agreement requires just cause for discipline, we find that the award enforces a contract provision negotiated pursuant to § 7106(b)(3) of the Statute and, thus, is not contrary to management's right to discipline employees. Accordingly, we deny the Agency's exception that the award is contrary to law.

B. The Arbitrator did not exceed his authority.[8]

The Agency contends that the Arbitrator decided issues not before him and failed to decide a stipulated issue. As relevant here, arbitrators exceed their authority when they resolve an issue not submitted to arbitration or fail to resolve an issue submitted to arbitration. *See AFGE, Local 1617*, 51 FLRA 1645, 1647 (1996). However, arbitrators do not exceed their authority by addressing any issue that is necessary to decide a stipulated issue, *see Nat'l Air Traffic Controllers Ass'n, MEBA/NMU*, 51 FLRA 993, 996 (1996) (*NATCA*), or by addressing any issue that necessarily arises from issues specifically included in a stipulation, *see Air Force Space Div., L.A. Air Force Station, Cal.*, 24 FLRA 516, 519 (1986) (*Air Force*). Moreover, the Authority accords an arbitrator's interpretation of a stipulation of issues the same substantial deference accorded to an arbitrator's interpretation and application of a collective bargaining agreement. *See U.S. Info. Agency, Voice of Am.*, 55 FLRA 197, 198 (1999); *Air Force*, 24 FLRA at 518.

The Agency contends that the Arbitrator improperly resolved the issue of whether the Agency could "control" the grievant's use of the Card. Exceptions at 7. The Arbitrator made findings regarding the "control" that each party exercised over the grievant's official duties in order to determine whether the Agency or the Union would have been responsible for issuing any official travel orders for the grievant's trip to the Union caucus. *See* Award at 6. In this regard, the Arbitrator found that the grievant would receive travel orders from the Agency in order to perform official duties under the Agency's "control[,]" and she would receive travel orders from the Union in order to perform official duties under the Union's "control[.]" *Id.* at 5-6. The issue of which party could issue official travel orders for the grievant necessarily arose from the Agency's allegation that the grievant used the Card without official travel orders. Thus, it was necessary for the Arbitrator to assess the merits of that allegation in order to decide the stipulated issue of whether there

6. When an award affects a management right under § 7106(a)(2) of the Statute, the Authority may also examine whether the award enforces an applicable law. *EPA*, 65 FLRA at 115 n.7.

7. Article 23, Section 1 of the Agreement states, in pertinent part, "Bargaining unit employees will be subject to disciplinary or adverse action only for just cause." Exceptions, Attach., Joint Ex. 1 at 154.

8. The Agency contends that the Arbitrator exceeded his authority because the award is contrary to management's rights. As we deny the Agency's contention that the award is contrary to management's rights, *see supra* Part IV.A.2., we also deny this exceeded-authority exception. *See U.S. Dep't of Veterans Affairs, Montgomery Reg'l Office, Montgomery, Ala.*, 65 FLRA 487, 490 n.7 (2011) (as exceeded-authority exception merely restated management rights exception, exceptions were not addressed separately).

was "just [c]ause for the . . . suspension of the [g]rievant[.]" *Id.* at 1; *see NATCA*, 51 FLRA at 996; *Air Force*, 24 FLRA at 519. Consequently, we find that the Arbitrator did not exceed his authority by addressing the issue of which party controlled the grievant's official duties during her attendance at the Union caucus.

The Agency also contends that the Arbitrator found that it failed to prove an allegation that the grievant used the Card when she was not on official time, even though the Agency did not make that allegation. Exceptions at 9-10. This contention ignores that the Agency's rationale for imposing discipline addressed whether the grievant attended the caucus on official time; the decision to suspend the grievant quoted a provision regarding official time from Article 30 of Agreement. Exceptions, Attach., Joint Ex. 4 ("Decision to Suspend") at 3 (quoting Agreement, Article 30, App. F, pt. G ("Official Time and Labor Relations in Field Offices")). In these circumstances, we conclude that the issue of whether the grievant was obligated to schedule official time in order to use the Card necessarily arose from the stipulated "just cause" issue, and we find that the Arbitrator did not exceed his authority in this regard. *See NATCA*, 51 FLRA at 996.

Finally, the Agency asserts that the Arbitrator failed to resolve the issue of whether the grievant's actions merited discipline. Exceptions at 8. The Arbitrator expressly addressed that issue and found that the grievant's action did not warrant discipline because: (1) the grievant's use of the Card at the caucus was "authorized[;]" (2) the airline mistakenly charged another employee's ticket to the grievant's Card; and (3) the Agency failed to prove the grievant's delinquency in paying the Card bills. Award at 6-8. Therefore, we find that the Arbitrator did not fail to address a stipulated issue.

For the foregoing reasons, we deny the Agency's exceeded-authority exceptions.

C. The award is not based on nonfacts.

The Agency argues that the award is based on nonfacts because the Arbitrator "completely ignored[,]" "inappropriately dismissed . . . as 'hearsay[,]'" or "apparently missed" the Agency's witness testimony and email exhibits allegedly establishing the grievant's delinquency in paying her Card bills, and, but for those errors, the Arbitrator would have reached a different result. Exceptions at 10-12. To establish that an award is based on a nonfact, the appealing party must show that a central fact underlying the award is clearly erroneous, but for which the arbitrator would have reached a different result. *See NFFE, Local 1984*, 56 FLRA 38, 41 (2000). However, the Authority will not find an award deficient on the basis of an arbitrator's determination of any factual matter that the parties disputed at arbitration. *See id.* In addition, "disagreement with an arbitrator's evaluation of evidence and testimony, including the determination of the weight to be accorded such evidence, provides no basis for finding" that an award is based on a nonfact. *AFGE, Local 1102*, 65 FLRA 40, 43 (2010) (citing *U.S. Dep't of Veterans Affairs, Med. Ctr., Richmond, Va.*, 63 FLRA 553, 556 (2009); *AFGE, Local 3295*, 51 FLRA 27, 32 (1995)).

The Arbitrator directly addressed the evidence offered by the Agency to establish the grievant's payment delinquencies, and he found that the evidence was not "competent" to substantiate the charge against the grievant. Award at 7-8. The Agency's exceptions "disagree[] with [the A]rbitrator's evaluation of evidence and testimony, including the determination of the weight to be accorded such evidence, [which] provides no basis for finding the award deficient." *AFGE, Local 1102*, 65 FLRA at 43. Accordingly, we deny the Agency's nonfact exceptions.

V. Decision

The Agency's exceptions are denied.

Member Beck, Dissenting:

I disagree with my colleagues that the central premise of the Arbitrator's award – that travel to attend an internal Union caucus constitutes "official travel" – is consistent with Agency rules and government regulations. Maj. Op. at 6-8. The Arbitrator's finding on this point is contrary to both the Agency's travel credit card (travel card) policies and the General Service Administration's Federal Travel Regulation (GSA travel regulation). Concomitantly, his conclusion that rests on this finding – that is, that the Agency did not have just cause to suspend the grievant – is erroneous.

The Agency interpreted its rules and the GSA regulation as being limited to official government travel and business. Because the grievant attended an internal Union meeting while on non-duty status, the Agency concluded that she could not be on "official travel," and, therefore, impermissibly used her travel card. The Arbitrator reached a contrary conclusion. This conclusion, however, is inconsistent with the plain wording of the Agency's rule. As a result, under Authority precedent, the Arbitrator's conclusion is impermissible. *See, e.g., AFGE, Local 916*, 47 FLRA 735, 740 (1993) (*AFGE*) (analyzing whether award conflicted with "plain wording" of agency rule); *U.S. Dep't of the Interior, Bureau of Land Mgmt., Eugene Dist. Office*, 43 FLRA 761, 764 (1991) (same); *U.S. Dep't of the Treasury, IRS, Ogden Serv. Ctr., Ogden, Utah*, 42 FLRA 1034, 1056-57 (1991) (*Ogden*) (same).

The pertinent rules and regulations establish, in unmistakably clear language, that a travel card may be used only in connection with "official Government travel":

- The Agency's Citibank [Card] Program[,] Employee Information Packet (information packet) restricts the use of Government contractor-issued travel cards to "official Government travel." Exceptions, Attach., Agency Ex. 3 at 1.

- The information packet states that the travel card is "not to be used for personal purposes and may only be used in connection with official Government travel." *Id.* at 2, ¶ 5.

- The Agency's Administrative Instructions Manual System (instructions manual) states that the travel card "shall be used only for authorized official travel expenses and for making authorized ATM withdrawals as indicated on the travel order and approved by the travel authorizing official . . . ." Exceptions, Attach., Agency Ex. 9 at 2.

- The instructions manual also states that "[t]he [g]overnment contractor-issued charge card and ATM are not to be used for other persons or personal purposes and may only be used in connection with official Government travel." *Id.* at 4.

- The GSA travel regulation – upon which the instruction manual was based – explicitly notes that a government contractor-issued travel card "may be used only for travel related expenses." 41 C.F.R. § 301-51.6.*

The material facts also are not in dispute:

- The grievant was designated by the Union to attend a Union caucus as its delegate. Award at 6.

- The caucus was an internal "[U]nion affair" that did not qualify for "official time." *Id.* at 4; 5 U.S.C. § 7131(b). It took place on a Saturday and grievant attended in a non-duty status. Award at 5-6.

- The grievant used her travel card to charge expenses associated with her attendance at the caucus. *Id.* at 5, 7.

- The Agency concluded that the grievant had misused the travel card and

---

* Additionally, the Agency and Union entered into a memorandum of understanding (MOU) in which the Union acknowledged that travel cards "may only be used in connection with official Government travel" and that an employee (who is issued a travel card) must agree to use the card only "for official travel" and "in accordance with Agency/Organization policy." Exceptions, Attach., Union Ex. 10 at 1 (internal quotations omitted). Moreover, the MOU states that employees cannot use travel cards for "personal . . . purposes." *Id.* Although the MOU is not an agency rule, it nevertheless bolsters a conclusion that the Union had knowledge that the Agency limited the use of travel cards to "official Government travel."

imposed a five-day suspension. *Id.* at 2, 5.

Despite the clear restriction against using a travel card for other than "official Government travel," the Arbitrator concluded that the expenses incurred by the grievant while she was on "official (Union) travel" at the caucus became an "official Government expense . . . for which the use of the Government travel credit card is authorized." *Id.* at 5-6. This conclusion is inconsistent with governing legal principles.

Travel by a Union representative may be "regarded" as "official government business" under specific and limited circumstances – such as when a representative is engaged in collective bargaining or other representational activity that qualifies for "official time" pursuant to § 7131(a), (c), or (d). *Dep't of the Treasury, U.S. Customs Serv. v. FLRA*, 836 F.2d 1381, 1385 (D.C. Cir. 1988). Even then, travel is considered to be official government business only when the agency determines that the activity "serves the convenience of the agency or is otherwise in the primary interest of the government." *Id.*; *see also ACT, P.R. Army Chapter*, 62 FLRA 144, 145-46 (2007) (authorization for union representatives to travel are authorized only when the expenses are determined to be in the primary interest of the government). Such circumstances were not present here.

There is no dispute that the caucus was an internal "[U]nion affair," Award at 6; that the grievant attended at the "direction and control" of the Union, *id.* at 6; and that the grievant was required to attend in a non-duty status. 5 U.S.C. § 7131(b); *see also Dep't of Health & Human Servs., Soc. Sec. Admin.*, 46 FLRA 1118, 1123 (1993) (activities associated with internal union business are excluded from official time by § 7131(b)); *Dep't of Health & Human Servs., Soc. Sec. Admin.*, 27 FLRA 391, 396 (1987) (award of official time and travel related expenses is deficient when the predominant purpose of a meeting is for the benefit of a private organization and not the agency). Therefore, when the grievant attended the Union caucus she was not engaged in official business of the United States Government. She was engaged in Union business that served only Union interests.

The Arbitrator ignored this obvious conclusion and went on to assert that the Union possessed authority – comparable to that of the employing Agency – to authorize the grievant to use her travel card. According to the Arbitrator, the Agency may authorize travel in circumstances when the grievant performs her regular job duties, but the Union assumes the power to authorize travel – and consequently, use of the travel card – when the grievant performs duties at the direction and control of the Union. Award at 5-6.

Without a doubt, the Union had the prerogative to designate the grievant as its delegate to the Union caucus. However, the Arbitrator confuses that prerogative with the Agency's authority and responsibility to approve "official travel." It is well-established that only a Federal agency may authorize travel for its employees. *In re Anson*, 02-1 BCA ¶ 31,819, GSBCA No. 15708-TRAV, 2002 WL 243613 (G.S.B.C.A.) (department policy and Federal Travel Regulation establish authorization for government travel); *In re Raja*, 97-1 BCA ¶ 28,944, GSBCA No. 14029-TRAV, 1997 WL 166202 (G.S.B.C.A.) (reimbursement for official business travel requires agency approval); *Dep't of Navy, Supervisor of Shipbuilding Conversion & Repair, Boston, Mass.*, 33 FLRA 187, 189 (1988) (authority to direct when and how travel will occur is encompassed within management's right to assign work). Furthermore, the travel card agreement presupposes that the travel card will be used to make ATM cash withdrawals and for other travel expenses "in connection with official travel" once a valid "travel order and / or authorization" has been received from the Agency. Exceptions, Agency Ex. 3 at 2, Employees' Rights and Obligations, ¶¶ 1-5.

The fact remains that the grievant was not in a duty status when she attended the caucus and the Agency could not issue travel orders or authorization under these circumstances. As discussed above, she was required to attend the caucus in a non-duty status because it was an internal "[U]nion affair," Award at 6; 5 U.S.C. § 7131(b), and she did not qualify for "official time" because the caucus took place on a Saturday, a day when the grievant "otherwise would not be in a duty status." 5 U.S.C. § 7131(a), (c), and (d); *see U.S. Dep't of Transp., FAA, Sw. Region, Fort Worth, Tex.*, 59 FLRA 530, 532 (2003) (official time includes only representational duties that are performed during regularly scheduled duty hours). It is illogical to conclude that the Union could create an entitlement for the grievant to use the travel card when the Agency itself could not do so.

The Majority rejects the Agency's position because the rule and GSA travel regulation do not define certain terms, including "official travel." The Majority offers no other analysis or legal support for upholding the Arbitrator's enormously counterintuitive conclusion that the "official" use of a government credit card includes expenses associated with internal union business.

As stated previously, the Authority has held that an arbitrator's award must be consistent with the "plain wording" of the agency rule that is in dispute. *E.g., AFGE,* 47 FLRA at 740; *Ogden,* 42 FLRA at 1056-57. The definitions offered by the Arbitrator – and tacitly approved by the Majority – do not withstand scrutiny. As explained above, under established law, an employee on off-duty status attending an internal Union affair is not on "official travel." Equally apparent (I would think) is the notion that a non-government entity, i.e., the Union, does not enjoy the discretion to authorize expenditures on a travel card that was issued by the government. Simply stated, the Arbitrator's conclusion that an off-duty employee could use a government travel card solely for an internal union matter not only defies common sense, but is also inconsistent with the plain language of the relevant rules and regulation.

Moreover, the Arbitrator's analysis of the plain wording of the agency rule relies upon the addition of an entirely new word. Specifically, the Arbitrator found that the grievant's use of the travel card was permissible because the term "official travel" includes "official (Union) travel." Award at 5-6. It is difficult to square the Arbitrator's fabrication of a new word with the Authority's repeated admonition that an arbitrator should limit him or herself to the "plain wording" of an agency rule. *See, e.g., AFGE,* 47 FLRA at 740; *Ogden,* 42 FLRA at 1056-57. Not surprisingly then, the Majority offers not a single citation to any decisions where such a scenario occurred.

Accordingly, I would grant the Agency's contrary to law exception and find that the Agency had just cause to suspend the grievant. Based on this conclusion, I would find it unnecessary to address the Agency's remaining exceptions.

65 FLRA No. 182

UNITED STATES
DEPARTMENT OF HOMELAND SECURITY
U.S. CUSTOMS AND BORDER PROTECTION
(Agency)

and

AMERICAN FEDERATION
OF GOVERNMENT EMPLOYEES
NATIONAL BORDER PATROL COUNCIL
(Union)

0-AR-4404

DECISION

May 27, 2011

Before the Authority: Carol Waller Pope, Chairman, and Thomas M. Beck and Ernest DuBester, Members

I. Statement of the Case

This matter is before the Authority on exceptions to an award of Arbitrator M. David Vaughn filed by the Agency under § 7122(a) of the Federal Service Labor-Management Relations Statute (the Statute) and part 2425 of the Authority's Regulations. The Union filed an untimely opposition to the Agency's exceptions.

The Arbitrator sustained the Union's grievance alleging that the Agency's unilateral decision to reclassify a "rotational overseas duty location" and three "hardship stations" violated the Statute and the parties' agreement. Award at 3-4. For the reasons that follow, we grant the Agency's exceptions in part, deny the Agency's exceptions in part, and set aside a portion of the award.

II. Background and Arbitrator's Award

The Agency is organized into twenty geographic sectors, each of which consists of one or more stations. *Id.* at 3. The Agency classifies its sectors and stations pursuant to criteria set forth in its administrative manuals. *See id.* at 3, 4. The Agency has one sector in Puerto Rico, the Ramey sector; it classified the Ramey sector as a "'non-rotational overseas duty location.'" *Id.* at 3 (citation omitted). This classification included several benefits intended to encourage bargaining unit employees to accept assignments in that sector, including the ability to rotate out of the sector at government expense, home leave allowances, and access to nearby military exchanges and schools. *Id.* (citation omitted). The Ramey sector is currently the only sector located overseas. Tr. at 100. The Agency also classified three stations, in Presidio and Sanderson, Texas, and Ajo, Arizona, as "[h]ardship [s]tations." Award at 4. Employees who accept and stay in positions at hardship stations also receive certain benefits, including the ability to transfer out non-competitively at the end of a tour of duty. *Id.*

On October 21, 2004, the Agency notified the Union of its intent to reclassify the Presidio and Sanderson stations as non-hardship duty stations and the Ramey sector as a non-rotational overseas duty location. *Id.* at 5 (citation omitted). The Ajo station was not mentioned. In response, on November 18, 2004, the Union demanded bargaining, submitted fourteen bargaining proposals (2004 proposals), and made information requests concerning the Agency's notification.[1] *Id.* at 5-7. No other relevant action occurred until June 30, 2006, when the Agency notified the Union that the reclassification of the Ramey sector would go into effect on October 1, 2006; the Agency made no mention of the hardship stations.[2] *Id.* at 8; Union Ex. 9. In response, on July 31, 2006, the Union again demanded bargaining, submitted seventeen different proposals (2006 proposals) concerning solely overseas stations, and made information requests.[3] Award at 8-12. The Union also reminded the Agency of its 2004 proposals concerning the Agency's decision to reclassify the Ramey sector. Exceptions, Union Ex. 10 at 1. On August 28, 2006, the Agency responded to the Union, advising it that each of the 2006 proposals were non-negotiable and that its 2004 request to bargain was "moot" because of the passage of time. Award at 12. In addition, the Agency denied the Union's information requests. *Id.* In response, the Union sent a letter explaining in

1. The 2004 proposals are set forth in the appendix to this decision.

2. The Arbitrator stated that the Agency's June 30, 2006 communication informed the Union about the reclassification of the Presidio and Sanderson stations. *See* Award at 8. However, the Agency's communication contains no such information. *See* Exceptions, Union Ex. 9 at 1-2.

3. The 2006 proposals are set forth in the appendix to this decision.

greater detail the "particularized need" for the requested information and challenging the Agency's determination of non-negotiability. *Id.* Sometime after this letter was sent, the Agency changed the status of the Ramey sector to non-rotating and the statuses of the Presidio, Sanderson, and Ajo stations to non-hardship. *Id.* The Agency posted vacancy announcements for permanent positions in the Ramey sector and for positions in the former hardship stations reflecting the loss of hardship status. *Id.* at 13.

The Union presented a grievance, which the Agency denied. The Union then invoked arbitration. *Id.* The parties stipulated to the following issue:

> 1. Did the Agency fulfill its bargaining obligations before converting the Ramey sector to a non-rotational duty status and the Presidio, Sanderson, and Ajo stations to non- hardship duty stations?

Id. In addition, the Union proposed, and the Arbitrator accepted, the following issues:

> 2. Does the Agency have the legal authority to terminate the overseas status of the Ramey post?
>
> 3. If not, what is the remedy?

Id. at 13-14.

The Arbitrator determined that the Agency's proposed changes directly affected terms and conditions of employment, thereby triggering an obligation to notify the Union of the proposed changes and the Union's right to request information and bargaining. *Id.* at 25. The Arbitrator then assumed, for the sake of argument, that the Agency's reclassification of sectors and duty stations so as to affect the duration of assignments was the exercise of management's right to assign work. *Id.* at 26. Acknowledging that there is no right to bargain over the assignment of work, the Arbitrator nonetheless found that there was an obligation to bargain over the impact and implementation of the reclassifications. *Id.* As to the negotiability of the Union's 2004 proposals and its 2006 proposals, the Arbitrator found them all to be negotiable because they were "fashioned . . . to address and ameliorate the consequences of the Agency's actions." *Id.* at 27. Thus, he concluded that both sets of proposals were within the Agency's duty to bargain. The Arbitrator also found that the Union demonstrated a "particularized need" for the information it requested, and, as such, the Agency improperly denied the Union's information request.[4] *Id.* at 26-27.

The Arbitrator found that the Agency's refusal to provide the Union with the requested information, along with the Agency's failure to give notice in 2006 of its proposed changes to the hardship status of the three duty stations, its determination that all Union proposals were non-negotiable, and its refusal to bargain, established that the Agency violated its obligation under the Statute and the parties' agreement to bargain in good faith. *Id.* at 29. As a remedy, the Arbitrator ordered that the Agency provide to the Union the requested information, that the parties bargain over the Union's proposals, that the parties return to the status quo ante pending the results of bargaining, and that the Agency post a notice to all employees rescinding the reclassifications and agreeing to comply with the parties' agreement and the Statute prior to making any other changes to conditions of employment. *Id.* at 29-31.

III. Agency's Exceptions

The Agency contends that it complied with the Statute and the parties' agreement, and that the Arbitrator's conclusion to the contrary is contrary to law. Exceptions at 7-8. The Agency first argues that all seventeen 2006 proposals are "outside the duty to bargain" because they apply "to *all* employees in overseas locations," rather than just the Ramey sector employees. Exceptions at 15 (emphasis in original). The Agency also argues that the first twelve 2006 proposals are non-negotiable because they interfere with management's right to assign work under § 7106(a)(2)(B) of the Statute. *See id.* at 12-14.

The Agency also avers that the Arbitrator's conclusion that the Agency failed to provide the Union with notice and an opportunity to bargain over the reclassifications is contrary to law. The Agency contends that it provided the Union with notice of and opportunity to bargain over the proposed Presidio, Sanderson, and Ramey reclassifications in 2004 and 2006. *Id.* at 8-9. According to the Agency, the Union responded to both notices by submitting proposals, and the Agency responded by informing the Union that all of the proposals were non-negotiable. *See id.* According to the Agency, because the proposals submitted by the Union were

4. The Agency does not dispute this finding. Accordingly, we do not address it further.

non-negotiable, the Agency satisfied its bargaining obligation. *Id.* at 9.

IV. Preliminary Issue

Under the Authority's Regulations, a party may file an opposition to exceptions within thirty days after the date of service of the exceptions. 5 C.F.R. § 2425.1(c).[5] The Agency served its exceptions by mail on July 21, 2008, and, accordingly, the Union's opposition was required to be filed by August 25, 2008. Order to Show Cause at 1. The Union's opposition was postmarked August 26, 2008. *Id.* at 2. The Authority directed the Union to show cause why its opposition should be considered because it appeared to be untimely filed. *Id.* at 1.

The Authority finds, and the Union concedes, that the Union's opposition was filed one day after it was due. The Union explains that the cause of the untimely filing was "a simple mistake in computing when the opposition brief was actually due" and not extraordinary circumstances. Union Response to Show Cause Order at 2. The Authority previously has found that, where an opposition was filed one day late by commercial delivery, extraordinary circumstances did not exist warranting waiver of the expired deadline. *See NTEU*, 60 FLRA 226, 226 n.1 (2004); *see also U.S. Dep't of the Treasury, Customs Serv., San Diego Dist., San Diego, Cal.*, 58 FLRA 240, 241 n.1 (2002) (where a party did not dispute that its exceptions filed by commercial delivery were one day late under § 2429.21(b), the Authority refused to waive the expired time limit); *AFGE, Local 3369*, 55 FLRA 1074, 1074 n.1 (1999) (Authority refused to consider an opposition filed one day late); *AFSCME, Local 3870*, 50 FLRA 445, 448 (1995) ("a simple mistake in filing does not constitute a basis for a waiver of a[n expired] time limit"). Accordingly, we find that extraordinary circumstances do not exist here and that, as a result, we will not consider the Union's opposition.

V. Analysis and Conclusions

When an exception involves an award's consistency with law, the Authority reviews any question of law raised by the exception and the award de novo. *See NTEU, Chapter 24*, 50 FLRA 330, 332 (1995) (citing *U.S. Customs Serv. v. FLRA*, 43 F.3d 682, 686-87 (D.C. Cir. 1994)). In applying the standard of de novo review, the Authority assesses whether an arbitrator's legal conclusions are consistent with the applicable standard of law. *See U.S. Dep't of Def., Dep'ts of the Army & the Air Force, Ala. Nat'l Guard, Northport, Ala.*, 55 FLRA 37, 40 (1998). In making that assessment, the Authority defers to the arbitrator's underlying factual findings. *See id.*

Furthermore, when resolving a grievance that alleges an unfair labor practice (ULP) under § 7116 of the Statute, an arbitrator functions as a substitute for an Authority administrative law judge (ALJ). *U.S. Dep't of the Treasury, IRS, Wash., D.C.*, 64 FLRA 426, 431 (2010) (*IRS*). Consequently, in resolving the grievance, the arbitrator must apply the same standards and burdens that are applied by ALJs under § 7118 of the Statute. *Id.* In a grievance that alleges a ULP by an agency, the union bears the burden of proving the elements of the alleged ULP by a preponderance of the evidence. *Id.* As in other arbitration cases, in determining whether the award is contrary to the Statute, the Authority defers to the arbitrator's findings of fact. *Id.*

A. The Agency did not have an obligation to bargain over the 2006 proposals.

The Agency avers that all of the 2006 proposals are "outside the duty to bargain" because they apply to all overseas employees rather than only Ramey sector employees. Exceptions at 15. It is well established that, prior to implementing a change in conditions of employment, an agency is required to provide the exclusive representative with notice of the change and an opportunity to bargain over those aspects of the change that are within the duty to bargain if the change will have more than a de minimis effect on conditions of employment. *See, e.g., U.S. Dep't of the Air Force, Air Force Materiel Command, Space & Missile Sys. Ctr. Detachment 12, Kirtland Air Force Base, N.M.*, 64 FLRA 166, 173 (2009) (Member Beck concurring in part on other grounds); *U.S. Dep't of the Air Force, 355th MSG/CC, Davis-Monthan Air Force Base, Ariz.*, 64 FLRA 85, 89 (2009). Where such a change to conditions of employment falls within an agency's exercise of a management right under § 7106 of the Statute, the agency is nevertheless obligated to notify the exclusive representative and negotiate over the impact and implementation of the change. *See, e.g., U.S. Dep't of the Treasury, IRS*, 62 FLRA 411, 414

5. The Authority's Regulations concerning the review of arbitration awards, as well as certain related procedural Regulations, including the Regulations governing commercial filing, were modified effective November 9, 2009, *see* 74 Fed. Reg. 51,741 (2009), and again October 1, 2010, *see* 75 Fed. Reg. 42,283 (2010). As the exceptions in this case were filed prior to November 9, 2009, we apply the prior version of the Regulations here.

(2008). However, the Authority has held that, during such bargaining, an agency is obligated to bargain only over proposals that are reasonably related to the proposed change in conditions of employment. *See U.S. Dep't of Health & Human Servs., SSA, Balt., Md.*, 39 FLRA 258, 262 (1991) (*SSA*) (citing *Dep't of Health & Human Servs., SSA, Balt., Md.*, 31 FLRA 651, 656 (1988)); *U.S. Dep't of the Treasury, Customs Serv., Wash., D.C.*, 38 FLRA 770, 783 (1990). An agency, therefore, is not required to bargain over proposals that go beyond the scope of a proposed change. *See, e.g., FLRA v. U.S. Dep't of Justice*, 994 F.2d 868, 871-72 (D.C. Cir. 1993); *Dep't of the Air Force, Headquarters, Air Force Logistics Command, Wright-Patterson Air Force Base, Ohio*, 22 FLRA 502, 506 (1986) (*Wright-Patterson*).

The Union's 2006 proposals are not reasonably related to the change that they supposedly address. The Agency decided to reclassify the Ramey sector as a non-rotational overseas duty station. Award at 8, 12; Exceptions, Union Ex. 9 at 1. When it announced this decision, the Agency did not reference any other overseas stations/employees or mention any change to the Agency's guidelines concerning the classification of such stations. *See* Exceptions, Union Ex. 9 at 1-2. Consistent with its announcement, the Agency reclassified only the Ramey sector.[6] Despite this limited change, in 2006, the Union submitted proposals that address *all* overseas stations/employees. *See, e.g.,* Award at 9 (proposal one states that "[t]he initial tour of duty for all [Agency] employees assigned to *any overseas location* will be two years") (emphasis added); *id.* at 11 (proposal 14 states that "*[a]ll employees serving in overseas assignments* will accrue home leave in the amounts specified in government-wide regulations") (emphasis added); *id.* (proposal 15 states "*[a]ll employees serving in overseas assignments* will receive a cost-of-living allowance in the amount specified in applicable government regulations) (emphasis added).

The proposals contain no language that state they are limited to the Ramey sector. Indeed, when it submitted the 2006 proposals, the Union expressly stated that the proposals were not limited to the Ramey sector. *See* Exceptions, Union Ex. 10 at 3 n.4 (in setting forth 2006 proposals, Union stated it needed information from Agency "to determine the extent of the impact of the [Agency's] proposal on employees who are and will be assigned to the Ramey . . . Sector *and/or any other overseas location*, and to assist it in perfecting its bargaining proposals" (emphasis added)). Furthermore, although the Union president testified that the Ramey sector was the only overseas section, he did not testify that the 2006 proposals were limited to the Ramey sector. *See* Tr. at 100-01. Thus, if the proposals were adopted, they would apply to *any* overseas sector the Agency may create in the future.

The 2006 proposals concern *all* overseas stations and employees, including those that the Agency may create in the future. As a result, the 2006 proposals are not reasonably related to the relevant change in conditions of employment. *See Wright-Patterson*, 22 FLRA at 506 (where agency changed facial hair policy for employees that used respirators, Authority found that proposals concerning the general use of respirators were not reasonably related to that change in condition of employment).

The Arbitrator rejected this conclusion because he believed that the proposals went "directly to the changes proposed by the Agency." Award at 28. The Arbitrator's conclusion, however, is misplaced. As described above, the 2006 proposals were not limited to the relevant change in conditions of employment; as such, the proposals do not "go directly" to that change. *Id.*

Because the 2006 proposals are not reasonably related to the change in conditions of employment that they supposedly address, the Agency had no obligation to bargain over them. *See Wright-Patterson*, 22 FLRA at 506. Accordingly, we find that the Arbitrator's conclusion that the Agency was required to bargain over the 2006 proposals is contrary to law and should be set aside.[7] By extension, we also set aside the Arbitrator's determination that the Agency violated the Statute and the parties' agreement by failing to bargain over the 2006 proposals.

---

6. We note that, in 2006, the Agency also changed the hardship classifications of the Sanderson, Presido, and Ajo stations. *See* Award at 12. However, the 2006 proposals clearly were not related to that change because they addressed only the classification of overseas locations. *See id.* at 9-12 (setting forth 2006 proposals).

7. Based on this finding, it is unnecessary to address the Agency's assertion that proposals one through twelve of the 2006 proposals interfere with management's right to assign work under § 7106(a)(2)(B) of the Statute.

B. The Agency did not provide the Union with adequate notice and an opportunity to bargain.

The Agency contends that it provided the Union with adequate notice and an opportunity to bargain over the reclassifications because it informed the Union that its 2004 proposals were non-negotiable.[8] As discussed above, when an agency changes a condition of employment, it must provide a union with notice and an opportunity to bargain over the aspects of the change that are negotiable. This obligation to bargain is predicated on the union's submission of negotiable proposals. An agency may refuse to bargain where it contends that the proposals submitted by the union are nonnegotiable. *See PBGC,* 59 FLRA 48, 50 (2003) (then-Member Pope dissenting in part) (citing *U.S. Dep't of HUD,* 58 FLRA 33 (2002) (*HUD*)). However, the agency acts at its peril if it then implements the proposed change in conditions of employment. *See, e.g., SSA,* 39 FLRA at 262-63. If *all* pending union proposals are nonnegotiable, the agency will not be found to have violated the Statute by implementing the change without bargaining over them. However, if *any* pending union proposals are negotiable, the agency will be found to have violated the Statute by implementing the change without satisfying its obligation to bargain over the negotiable proposals and either reaching agreement or declaring impasse. *See, e.g., Fed. Bureau of Prisons, Fed. Corr. Inst., Bastrop, Tex.,* 55 FLRA 848, 852 (1999) (Chairman Segal concurring on other grounds) (citing *SSA,* 39 FLRA at 262-63).

The Arbitrator concluded that all of the 2004 proposals were negotiable. Award at 28, 30. The Agency does not challenge that conclusion. Consequently, as explained above, the Agency did not satisfy its bargaining obligation because it refused to bargain over negotiable proposals. *See HUD,* 58 FLRA at 35 (after determining that proposal at dispute was negotiable, Authority concluded that agency violated Statute by refusing to bargain over proposal on the basis that it considered proposal non-negotiable).

Accordingly, we find that the Arbitrator's conclusion that the Agency violated the Statute and the parties' agreement when it declined to bargain over the 2004 proposals is not contrary to law.

VI. Decision

The Agency's exceptions are granted in part and denied in part. The portion of the award concluding that the Agency violated the Statute and the parties' agreement by refusing to bargain over the 2006 proposals is set aside.

---

8. The Agency also argues that it provided the Union with adequate notice and an opportunity to bargain because it informed the Union that the 2006 proposals were non-negotiable. Because we find that the 2006 proposals are outside the Agency's duty to bargain, it is unnecessary to address this argument. We also note that the Agency has not asserted that the 2006 proposals replaced the 2004 proposals.

APPENDIX

The Union's 2004 proposals are as follows:

1. The Presidio and Sanderson, Texas Border Patrol stations shall remain designated as hardship duty locations.
2. Six months prior to fulfilling two years of service in the Presidio or Sanderson, Texas Border Patrol stations (or at any time of their choosing thereafter), employees shall be allowed to submit a list of at least five Border Patrol stations to which they desire to transfer, ranked in order of preference.
3. The Ramey, Puerto Rico Border Patrol Sector shall remain designated as rotational overseas location.
4. Six months prior to fulfilling three years of service in the Ramey, Puerto Rico Border Patrol Sector (or six months prior to fulfilling an overseas tour renewal agreement, or, if none has been executed, at any subsequent time of their choosing), employees shall be allowed to submit a list of at least five Border Patrol stations to which they desire to transfer.
5. If a vacancy exists in one of the stations on an employee's list of preferred stations, the employee's reassignment to the highest-ranked station on their list of preferences shall be approved unless the management official responsible for selections to that location articulates a *bona fide* reason for not doing so. Such explanation shall be set forth in writing and provided to the employee.
6. If no vacancies exist in any of the stations on an employee's list of preferred stations, management may, in its sole discretion, create one and reassign the employee to that station.
7. If the foregoing procedure does not result in an employee being approved for reassignment to one of his or her preferred locations, the employee shall be advised of this fact within thirty calendar days of submitting his or her initial preferences, and shall be requested to expand their list of preferences by at least five locations.
8. The aforementioned process shall continue until the employee is reassigned.
9. Employees assigned to the Presidio or Sanderson, Texas Border Patrol stations who are selected for reassignment under these procedures shall have their relocation approved and funded within thirty calendar days following their selection, unless their initial two-year tour of duty has not expired at that point, in which case their relocation shall be approved and funded within thirty calendar days following the expiration of their initial two-year tour of duty at that location.
10. Employees assigned to the Ramey, Puerto Rico Border Patrol Sector who are selected for reassignment under these procedures shall have their relocation approved and funded within thirty calendar days following the expiration of their initial or renewal overseas tour assignment.
11. Employees who are reassigned under these procedures are entitled to full reimbursement for all of their relocation expenses.
12. Employees do not waive their right to hardship or overseas rotation by inaction; they may invoke it at any time.
13. The Bureau shall take all reasonable steps to ensure that the eligible dependents of all employees assigned to the Ramey, Puerto Rico Border Patrol Sector, regardless of the duration of their assignment or their permanent place of residence, are able to participate in the Department of Defense Overseas Dependent School System.
14. The Bureau shall take all reasonable steps to ensure that all employees assigned to the Ramey, Puerto Rico Border Patrol Sector, regardless of the duration of their assignment or their permanent place of residence, have military base privileges.

Award at 6-7.

The Union's 2006 proposals are as follows:

1. The initial tour of duty for all Border Patrol employees assigned to any overseas location will be two years.
2. As an incentive for employees to remain overseas, the Bureau will offer relocation and/or retention bonuses of no less than 10% of the employees' annual rate of basic pay for each year that they extend their tour of duty.
3. Employees who are serving in an overseas assignment may request to renew their tour of duty in two-year increments. There will be no limit to the number of tour renewal requests. Such requests may be made at any time after an employee has completed 18 months of service overseas on a given tour

of duty, but must be made before the employee has completed 22 months of service for that tour of duty, at which point it will be assumed that the employee is desirous of rotating back to the continental United States.

4. An employee whose request for tour renewal is granted will receive tour renewal travel in accordance with the provisions of the Federal Travel Regulation.
5. Six months prior to fulfilling their tour of duty overseas, employees will be allowed to submit a list of at least five Border Patrol stations to which they desire to transfer.
6. If a vacancy exists in one of the stations on an employee's list of preferred stations, the employee's reassignment to the highest-ranked station on their list of preferences will be approved unless the management official responsible for selections to that location articulates a *bona fide* reason for not doing so. Such explanation will be set forth in writing and provided to the employee.
7. If no vacancies exist in any of the stations on an employee's list of preferred stations, management may, in its sole discretion, create one and reassign the employee to that station.
8. If the foregoing procedure does not result in an employee being approved for reassignment to one of his or her preferred locations, the employee will be advised of that fact within thirty calendar days of submitting his or her initial preferences, and will be requested to expand his or her list of preferences by at least five locations.
9. The aforementioned process will continue until the employee is reassigned.
10. Employees assigned to an overseas location who are selected for reassignment under these procedures will have their relocation approved and funded within thirty calendar days following the expiration of their initial or renewal overseas tour agreement.
11. Employees who are reassigned under these procedures are entitled to full payment for all of their relocation expenses.
12. Employees do not waive their right to overseas rotation by inaction; they may invoke it at any time.
13. Employees . . . are eligible for return travel and transportation . . . [from their] overseas duty station. . . .
14. All employees serving in overseas assignments will accrue home leave . . . .
15. All employees serving in overseas assignments will receive a cost-of-living allowance . . . .
16. All employees serving in overseas assignments who have dependent children will be entitled to utilize the Department of Defense Overseas Dependent School system . . . .
17. All employees serving in overseas assignments will be entitled to utilize military base privileges. . . .

Id. at 9-12.

65 FLRA No. 183

UNITED STATES
DEPARTMENT OF THE AIR FORCE
325th MISSION SUPPORT GROUP SQUADRON
TYNDALL AIR FORCE BASE, FLORIDA
(Respondent)

and

AMERICAN FEDERATION
OF GOVERNMENT EMPLOYEES
LOCAL 3240
(Charging Party/Union)

AT-CA-06-0163

DECISION AND ORDER

May 31, 2011

Before the Authority: Carol Waller Pope, Chairman, and Thomas M. Beck and Ernest DuBester, Members

I. Statement of the Case

This unfair labor practice (ULP) case is before the Authority on exceptions to the attached decision of the Administrative Law Judge (Judge) filed by the General Counsel (GC). The Respondent filed an opposition to the GC's exceptions.

The complaint alleges that the Respondent violated § 7116(a)(1) and (5) of the Federal Service Labor-Management Relations Statute (the Statute) when the Respondent reassigned two bargaining unit employees without giving the Union notice and an opportunity to negotiate to the extent required by the Statute. The Judge found that the Respondent did not violate the Statute and ordered that the complaint be dismissed.

For the reasons set forth below, we remand the case to the Judge for further proceedings consistent with this decision.

II. Background and Judge's Decision

A. Background

The bargaining unit represented by the Union includes laborers whose duties involve picking up garbage, performing ground maintenance, and distributing linens and supplies to housekeepers who maintain lodging areas, collectively known as the Sand Dollar Inn, at Tyndall Air Force Base (Tyndall AFB). Judge's Decision at 2. The lodging areas, which provide temporary accommodations for visitors, are located at various locations on the base. *Id.*

In May 2005, a lodging facility that had provided base housing was converted into an additional lodging area for visitors. This lodging area, which was designated Wood Manor, became part of the Sand Dollar Inn. *Id.* at 2-3. Two-, three-, and four-bedroom family units in Wood Manor replaced one-bedroom apartments in two other buildings that were closed. *Id.* at 3.

In January 2006, the Respondent reassigned two bargaining unit employees; one employee was assigned from another work site to Wood Manor (Employee A) and the other employee was assigned from Wood Manor to another work site (Employee B). After learning of these assignments, the Union filed a ULP charge. *Id.* at 1-2.

B. Judge's Decision

Before the Judge, the GC argued that the Respondent violated the Statute when it assigned the employees duties at different work sites without giving the Union notice and an opportunity to negotiate. *Id.* at 3. The GC asserted that the Respondent, by changing the location where the employees performed their assigned work, changed the employees' conditions of employment and that the impact of the change was more than de minimis. *Id.* at 3-4. In response, the Respondent "acknowledge[d] that the laborers primarily work some locations more often than others for purpose of continuity," but argued that, because the employees are required to work at all of the lodging areas as assigned, no change in the employees' conditions of employment occurred and that, even if such a change occurred, it was de minimis.[1] *Id.*

1. The Respondent also noted that the opening of Wood Manor was the subject of a separate ULP complaint. The Judge found that this complaint resulted in a finding that the Respondent had violated the Statute. Judge's Decision

The Judge concluded that the Respondent had not changed the employees' conditions of employment. *Id.* The Judge rejected the GC's assertion that "'a change in work location is itself a change in a condition of employment[,]'" noting that this principle does not apply in all circumstances. *Id.* at 4-5 (quoting *U.S. Dep't of Health & Human Servs. SSA, Balt., Md. and SSA, Fitchburg, Mass. Dist. Office, Fitchburg, Mass.*, 36 FLRA 655 (1990) (*SSA Fitchburg*)). The Judge found that the Authority has "made clear that determining a change in a condition of employment requires case-by-case analysis." *Id.* at 5 (citing *U.S. Immigration & Naturalization Serv., Houston Dist., Houston, Tex.*, 50 FLRA 140 (1995) (*INS, Houston*)). According to the Judge, even in *SSA Fitchburg*, the case primarily relied upon by the GC, the Authority noted that "'not all changes in office space will give rise to a bargaining obligation.'" *Id.* at 5-6 (quoting *SSA Fitchburg*, 36 FLRA at 668).

The Judge found that this case differed significantly from *SSA Fitchburg*. The Judge noted that, whereas the employees in *SSA Fitchburg* were expected to perform their duties in the same location on a daily basis, the laborers in this case had no such expectation. *Id.* at 6. The Judge found that "[t]here were no fixed assignments and no permanent duty stations at particular locations." *Id.* at 6-7. The Judge found, in this regard, that the Respondent's policy and practice "was to assign and alter which laborers would perform their duties at the various . . . locations . . . depending upon leave, availability, work load, and mission necessity." *Id.* at 6; *see also id.* at 3. Additionally, the Judge found that laborers were hired pursuant to a position description (PD) that clearly indicated that laborers were expected to perform the full range of custodial duties at all lodging locations. *Id.* at 6.

As further support for his conclusion, the Judge noted that the record showed that the work assignments at issue did not: (1) "result in a change to the substantive duties required of any laborer in the . . . unit"; (2) require a personnel action; (3) involve a formal detail; or (4) result in modification of pay.[2] *Id.* at 7. The Judge also noted that no evidence had been presented regarding "a past practice of notice and negotiation over the assignment of a primary work location at a particular lodging location . . . ." *Id.* at 7-8. Additionally, the Judge determined that, "[w]hile there was some evidence of health issues introduced on the part of [Employee A]," it was "far from clear or persuasive" that any health problem was caused by working at Wood Manor. *Id.* at 8.

The Judge found that, even if there had been a change in the employees' conditions of employment, the impact of the change was de minimis because the laborers were subject to performing substantially similar duties at the various lodging locations operated by the Respondent. *Id.* at 9. In this regard, the Judge found that: (1) the laborers were hired with the understanding that they would have to work at the various lodging locations in the Sand Dollar Inn System; (2) none of them had worked exclusively at the very same location for years; (3) their work assignments were made orally as needed; and (4) there was no evidence in the record that the assignment to different locations had any impact on the employees' pay. *Id.*

Accordingly, the Judge recommended that the complaint be dismissed.

III. Positions of the Parties

A. GC's Exceptions

The GC contends that the Judge erred by finding that the Respondent's action in reassigning Employees A and B did not constitute a change in the employees' conditions of employment. In particular, the GC contends that the Judge incorrectly interpreted the phrase in *SSA, Fitchburg* that "'not all changes in office space will give rise to a bargaining obligation'" to mean that "not all changes in office space constitute *changes in conditions of employment* . . . ." Exceptions at 2 (quoting Judge's Decision at 5) (emphasis in original). According to the GC, the Judge should have interpreted this language as meaning that "*some* changes in office space may not

at 3 n.1 (citing *U.S. Dep't of the Air Force, 325th Mission Support Group Squadron, Tyndall Air Force Base, Fla.*, Case No. AT-CA-05-0287, (Nov. 8, 2006), ALJ Rep. No. 202 (Dec. 27, 2006)). The decision did not include a status quo ante remedy. *Id.* The Judge found that, because no exceptions were filed to that decision, any assignment to the Wood Manor location made in January 2006 --"some eight months after operations started at that location" -- was not an assignment to a newly created location. *Id.*

2. The Judge noted that, in July 2006, the Respondent began treating Wood Manor differently from its other temporary lodging areas by using different time keeping methods and altering the supervisory structure. The Judge stated that, while these changes "give rise to legitimate questions regarding changes in conditions of employment, those issues were not raised by the [c]omplaint" in this case. Judge's Decision at 8 n.2.

give rise to a bargaining obligation because their effects were no more than *de minimis* – not because they were not changes in conditions of employment at all." *Id.* at 2-3 (emphasis in original).

The GC also argues that the Judge erred in finding that the reassignments at issue did not differ from past practice. *Id.* at 3. The GC asserts that, in concluding that "'assigning laborers to different lodging locations was an expected part of the job for laborers[,]'" the Judge "omits" that there is "no history of routinely changing the *permanent* duty stations of employees . . . ." *Id.* (emphasis in original) (quoting Judge's Decision at 6). The GC contends that the evidence instead shows that "past routine assignments to alternate work locations were *only* to cover for absences based on leave, illness, scheduled days off or some specific overriding project." *Id.* at 3-4 (emphasis in original). According to the GC, the only evidence of a permanent reassignment is the example cited by the Judge, in which the Agency accommodated a Union official by assigning him to a work area with access to a telephone. *Id.* at 4. The GC notes that, although the Union acquiesced regarding this change and did not request to bargain, its acquiescence cannot be "construed as a waiver of the Union's right to negotiate in this instance." *Id.*

The GC further contends that the Judge erred by relying on the PD. *Id.* at 5. The GC asserts that the PD does not "necessarily reflect everything that that the laborers do or don't do" and that the Respondent does not strictly adhere to the PD. *Id.* (citing Tr. at 208, 230-31).

The GC also contends that the Judge erred in suggesting that "no change [in conditions of employment] occurred until July 2006 . . . ." *Id.* at 8. The GC contends that the Respondent's July actions "simply confirmed what was already true -- that the Wood Manor assignment was separate and unique and not simply a routine assignment to an alternate work location . . . ." *Id.*

The GC further contends that the Judge erred in finding that any asserted change in conditions of employment was de minimis. *Id.* at 9. The GC asserts that the Judge omitted pertinent facts that prevented a full evaluation of the nature and extent of the change. *See id.* The GC argues that these facts would have shown that Wood Manor is substantially different from the other locations. *Id.* at 9-10. In this regard, the GC contends that the Judge omitted that: (1) Wood Manor consists of fifty-two separate buildings that can house families; (2) the size of the units increases the amount of trash and outside work; (3) outside work has virtually no shade; (4) there is only one break area and the availability of water is limited; (5) the site is in a remote location, a few miles from the other locations; (6) there are no restaurants or food services within walking distance; and (7) employees must use personal vehicles to get to the site or go to lunch. *Id.* at 10.

The GC also asserts that, in reaching the de minimis determination, the Judge improperly applied Authority precedent. *Id.* at 11-12. The GC contends that Employee A's work environment changed because "he was exposed to the outdoors more . . . ." *Id.* at 11. The GC asserts that this is a "significant factor considering the Florida location[,] even if [his] heart condition and medical emergencies are not taken into account . . . ." *Id.* (citing Judge's Decision at 8). According to the GC, Employee A's increased exposure to the Florida heat has as much impact as an employee's loss of a window in *SSA, Fitchburg* and an employee's loss of a window and office space in *Pension Benefit Guaranty Corp.*, 59 FLRA 48 (2003) (*PBGC*) (then-Member Pope dissenting in part as to another matter). *Id.* at 11-12.

B. Respondent's Opposition

The Respondent asserts that there was no change to the employees' conditions of employment. According to the Respondent, laborers do not have fixed duty stations, are routinely reassigned as needed, and were routinely assigned to Wood Manor, both before and after the facility was opened. Opp'n at 2-4 (citing Tr. at 33, 36, 42, 221, 224-225, among others).

The Respondent contends that the Judge appropriately considered the PD in determining whether there was a change in the employees' conditions of employment. *Id.* at 4-6 (citing *Office of Program Operations, Field Operations, SSA, S.F. Region*, 20 FLRA 97, 99-100 (1985)).

The Respondent further asserts that laborer duties and other terms or conditions of employment are essentially the same regardless of the location where the laborer performs those duties. *See id* at 6-7. Moreover, according to the Respondent, any change that occurred at Wood Manor took place in May 2005 or July 2006 and was not a part of the complaint. *See id.* at 8-9.

The Respondent contends that, because Employee B is "primarily used as a 'floater' to cover the various areas of lodging as needed or to perform other non-routine duties[,]" no change occurred with respect to his condition of employment. *Id.* at 9-10. According to the Respondent, although Employee B was "directed to work at Wood Manor" a couple of days a week from July 2005 until January 2006, he was never assigned to that location. *Id.* at 10.

The Respondent further asserts that, even if there was a change in the employees' conditions of employment, the effect, or reasonably foreseeable effect, of the change was no more than de minimis. *Id.* In this regard, the Respondent contends that: (1) the duties of the laborers are essentially the same regardless of the lodging area in which the employee works; (2) there was no change in employees' hours or compensation; (3) the employees routinely were asked to work at Wood Manor; (4) the location of the work area from the front gate is the same as other locations and is not remote; (5) employees at Wood Manor have access to water, break facilities, and food; and (6) there is no evidence to establish that the alleged change was permanent. *Id.* at 10-18. The Respondent also disputes the GC's contention that Employee's A assignment to Wood Manor exacerbated his medical condition. *Id.* at 14-16.

IV. Analysis and Conclusions

The GC contends that the Judge erred in concluding that: (1) the Respondent did not change the employees' conditions of employment; and (2) even if there was a change in the employees' conditions of employment, such change was de minimis.

The Authority has held that, in order to determine whether an agency's action violated the Statute, there must first be a finding that the agency changed unit employees' conditions of employment. *See, e.g., INS, Houston*, 50 FLRA at 143. The determination of whether a change in conditions of employment has occurred involves a case-by-case analysis and an inquiry into the facts and circumstances regarding the agency's conduct and employees' conditions of employment. *See id.* at 144; *92 Bomb Wing, Fairchild Air Force Base, Spokane, Wash.*, 50 FLRA 701, 704 (1995). Also, in determining whether a judge's factual findings are supported, the Authority looks to the preponderance of the record evidence.[3] *See, e.g., U.S. Dep't of Transp., Fed. Aviation Admin.*, 64 FLRA 365, 368 (2009) (Member Beck concurring).

Moreover, an agency is obligated to bargain over the impact and implementation of a change only where that change has more than a de minimis effect on conditions of employment. *See, e.g., PBGC*, 59 FLRA at 50. In assessing whether the effect of a change in conditions of employment is more than de minimis, the Authority looks to the nature and extent of either the effect or the reasonably foreseeable effect of the change. *Id.* at 51.

Applying the above legal standards to the facts in this case, we find that the Judge failed to make the necessary factual findings for us to determine whether the Respondent's reassignments of Employees A and B constituted a change in their conditions of employment, and, if so, whether such change was more than de minimis.

With respect to the change in conditions of employment, the Judge found that, within the Sand Dollar Inn, there were "no fixed assignments and no permanent duty stations at particular locations" and that the Respondent's policy and practice "was to assign and alter which laborers would perform their duties at the various . . . locations . . . depending upon leave, availability, work load[,] and mission necessity." Judge's Decision at 6-7. As further support for his conclusion, the Judge noted that the record showed that the work assignments at issue did not "result in a change to the substantive duties required of any laborer in the . . . unit." *Id.* at 7.

The GC disputes the Judge's findings, asserting that the Judge, in so holding, "omitted" pertinent facts, specifically that there was "no history of routinely changing the *permanent* duty stations of employees" and that "'past routine assignments to alternate work locations were *only* to cover for absences based on leave illness, scheduled days off or some specific overriding project." Exceptions at 3- 4 (citing Judge's Decision at 6) (emphasis in original). Moreover, the GC argues that the Judge omitted pertinent facts that would have shown that Wood Manor is substantially different from other locations, including that: (1) Wood Manor consists of fifty-two

3. Member Beck notes that, for the reasons stated in his separate opinions in *U.S. Dep't of the Air Force, 12th Flying Training Wing, Randolph Air Force Base, San Antonio, Tex.*, 63 FLRA 256, 262-63 (2009) (Concurring Opinion of Member Beck) and *U.S. Dep't of the Air Force, Air Force Materiel Command Space and Missile Sys. Ctr., Detachment 12, Kirtland Air Force Base, N.M.*, 64 FLRA 166, 179-80 (2009) (Concurring Opinion of Member Beck), he reviews the Judge's factual findings using a "substantial evidence in the record" standard rather than a "preponderance" standard.

separate buildings that can house families; (2) the size of the units increases the amount of trash and outside work; (3) outside work has virtually no shade; (4) there is only one break area and the availability of water is limited; (5) the site is in a remote location, a few miles from the other locations; (6) there are no restaurants or food services within walking distance; and (7) employees must use personal vehicles to get to the site or go to lunch. *Id.* at 9-10.

The Judge failed to discuss -- and thus failed expressly to credit or discredit -- much of the evidence presented regarding the employees' reassignments, including the duration and permanence of the employees' assignments,[4] as well as the substantive duties required of each employee at the relevant locations.[5] Because the Judge failed to make the necessary factual findings, we are unable to determine whether the Respondent's reassignment of Employees A and B constituted a change in their conditions of employment.

The Judge also found that, even if there had been a change in the employees' conditions of employment, the impact of the change was de minimis because the laborers were subject to performing substantially similar duties at the various lodging locations operated by the Respondent. Judge's Decision at 9. As noted above, the Judge failed to discuss much of the evidence regarding the substantive duties required of Employee A and Employee B at the relevant work locations. As a result, we are unable to determine whether the change in the employees' conditions of employment, if such change occurred, was more than de minimis.

Accordingly, because we are unable to determine whether the Respondent's reassignment of Employees A and B constituted a change in their conditions of employment, and, if so, whether, such change was more than de minimis, we remand the case to the Judge for further consideration. On remand, consistent with this decision, the Judge should, in determining whether a violation of the Statute occurred, evaluate the contrary evidence and make the necessary factual findings regarding the reassignments of Employees A and B.

V. Order

The case is remanded to the Judge for further consideration consistent with this decision.

4. We note that the record contains evidence that appears to contradict the Judge's finding that there were no fixed assignments or permanent duty stations at particular locations. Employee A testified that, before being assigned to Wood Manor, he was assigned to perform laborer duties in the same lodging area -- buildings 845, 1580, and 1582 -- for approximately "six years." Tr. at 95. Employee B testified that he performed work at Wood Manor for approximately six to eight months, until Employee A was reassigned there and he was reassigned to another location, and that he worked at Buildings 1615 and 1617 for a long period of time before he was assigned to Wood Manor. *See* Tr. at 139-140 &151. Additionally, there was testimony that laborers are assigned sometimes to a different location when circumstances require it -- e.g., to cover for an employee who may be on sick or annual leave, or to perform other tasks -- but that afterwards the laborer would return to his or her "regular" or "normal" assignment. Tr. at 36, 42, 77. The Judge, however, failed to discuss this testimony in his decision.

5. The Judge noted that, in July 2006, the Respondent began treating the temporary lodging area known as Wood Manor differently than its other temporary lodging areas by utilizing different time keeping methods and altering the supervisory structure for that location. Judge's Decision at 8 n.2. We note, as did the Judge, that the Respondent's action in this regard were not raised by the complaint and do not affect whether the violation alleged in the complaint actually occurred. *See id.*; GC Ex. 1(c); *see also, e.g., Air Force Flight Test Ctr., Edwards Air Force Base, Calif.*, 55 FLRA 116, 120-21 (1999) (Chair Segal concurring) (agency conduct after alleged change in working conditions not relevant with respect to whether change occurred on date alleged).

Office of Administrative Law Judges

U.S. DEPARTMENT OF THE AIR FORCE
325TH MISSION SUPPORT GROUP SQUADRON
TYNDALL AIR FORCE BASE, FLORIDA
Respondent

and

AMERICAN FEDERATION OF GOVERNMENT EMPLOYEES, LOCAL 3240, AFL-CIO
Charging Party

Richard S. Jones, Esquire
For the General Counsel

Major Robert M. Gerleman
For the Respondent

George White, President
For the Charging Party

Before: CHARLES R. CENTER
Chief Administrative Law Judge

DECISION

Statement of the Case

On February 6, 2006, the American Federation of Government Employees, Local 3240, AFL-CIO (Union) filed an unfair labor practice charge against the U.S. Department of the Air Force, 325th Mission Support Group Squadron, Tyndall Air Force Base (AFB), Florida (Respondent) alleging a "Change in Working Condition". GC-1(b). In the charge, the Union requested that the Federal Labor Relations Authority (Authority) issue a temporary restraining order, a legal remedy not provided by the Federal Service Labor-Management Relations Statute (Statute). On July 28, 2006, the Regional Director of the Atlanta Region of the Authority issued a Complaint and Notice of Hearing in which it was alleged that the Respondent committed an unfair labor practice in violation of §7116(a)(1) and (5) of the Statute on January 9, 2006, when it reassigned two bargaining unit employees without giving the Union notice and an opportunity to negotiate to the extent required by the Statute. GC-1(c). The Respondent filed a timely Answer on August 15, 2006 in which it denied the alleged violation of the Statute. GC-1(f). On August 16, 2006, the Respondent filed a motion for continuance of the hearing scheduled for October 11, 2006 and requested that the hearing be conducted on October 19, 2006. GC-1(g). Neither the General Counsel nor the Charging Party opposed the motion and it was granted. GC-1(i).

A hearing was held in Panama City, Florida on October 19, 2006, at which the parties were present with counsel and were afforded the opportunity to present evidence and cross-examine witnesses. This Decision is based upon consideration of all of the evidence, including the demeanor of witnesses, and of the post-hearing briefs submitted by the parties.

Findings of Fact

The Respondent is an "agency" within the meaning of §7103(a)(3) of the Statute. GC-1(f). The Union is a "labor organization" as defined by §7103(a)(4) of the Statute and is the exclusive representative of a unit of the Respondent's employees appropriate for collective bargaining. GC-1(b, c, f).

The bargaining unit includes laborers whose duties involve activities such as picking up garbage, performing ground maintenance, and distributing linens and supplies to the housekeepers who clean and maintain lodging areas collectively called the Sand Dollar Inn at Tyndall AFB, Florida. R-11, T-35, 138. These lodging areas exist at various locations on the base for the purpose of temporarily accommodating visitors to the base. T-33, 42, 77, 144, 221. Occupants of such lodging include students attending training, military and civilian personnel on temporary duty, and arriving or departing military families awaiting or clearing base housing. T-95 to 99.

In May 2005, the number of locations on Tyndall AFB at which the Sand Dollar Inn conducted temporary lodging operations was increased when 52 units of what was formerly base housing were converted into a temporary lodging facility designated as Wood Manor.[1/] T-41 to 43, 97 to 99, 178. These two, three and four bedroom family units replaced one-bedroom apartments in buildings 1615 and 1617 that were closed at another location on the

[1/] Although the opening of this location was the subject of a separate unfair labor practice complaint that resulted in an administrative law judge decision finding the Respondent violated the Statute, the decision did not include a *status quo ante* remedy and the Respondent was allowed to continue operations at this location. As no exceptions to that decision were filed, I find that any assignment to this location made in January 2006, some eight months after operations started at that location was not an assignment to a newly created location. *See Case No. AT-CA-05-0287.*

base. R-1, T-96, 97, 205, 206. The Agency's policy and practice for determining which laborers would perform the duties at each of the lodging locations were not changed when operations at the Wood Manor housing area were initiated and buildings 1615 and 1617 closed. T-178 to 185, 187 to 192, 203.

While laborers are routinely assigned to perform their laborer duties in the same lodging areas within the Sand Dollar Inn system each day for reasons of continuity and familiarity, responsibility for a particular lodging area is not fixed by any position description or personnel action, and the lodging area(s) to which a particular laborer is assigned on any given day is determined by leave, mission necessity or other factors. T-32 to 36, 49, 156, 157, 184 to 198, 202, 203, 224, 225. The laborer position description applicable to these bargaining unit employees states that the purpose of the laborer position is to "perform the full range of custodial duties in the Lodging areas", using a plural to describe the locations. R-11. The position description also indicates that laborers are to "Maintain ground maintenance of all Lodging areas in a timely and efficient manner." R-11.

Positions of the Parties

The General Counsel

The General Counsel contends that the Respondent violated §7116(a)(1) and (5) of the Statute on or about January 9, 2006, when it assigned bargaining unit laborers James Stephens and Chuck Hamilton to duties at different primary work locations without giving the Union notice and an opportunity to negotiate. GC-1(c); GC's Post-Hearing Brief, p. 10. The General Counsel maintains that in so doing, the Respondent changed the conditions of employment of Stephens and Hamilton and that the impact of that change was more than *de minimis*. The General Counsel essentially asserts that any change in the location where an employee performs his or her assigned work constitutes a change to his or her conditions of employment.

The Respondent

The Respondent contends that there was no change to a condition of employment because the duties of the laborers in question require them to work at all of the lodging areas at Tyndall AFB as assigned. Although the Respondent acknowledges that the laborers primarily work some locations more often than others for purpose of continuity, they have no fixed lodging location and are assigned duties at different lodging locations when required by mission necessity. Furthermore, the Respondent also asserts that even if a change in conditions of employment were to be found, that the foreseeable effect was no more than *de minimus*.

Discussion and Analysis

I. No Change to Conditions of Employment

The Complaint alleges the Respondent committed an unfair labor practice by changing the conditions of employment for a bargaining unit without giving notice and an opportunity to bargain. To conclude that the Respondent violated the Statute, it must be found that: (1) the Respondent's action in assigning two employees to work at differing locations within its temporary lodging system constituted a change in unit employees' conditions of employment; (2) such a change gave rise to duty to bargain; and (3) the Respondent failed to fulfill its duty to bargain. *See U.S. Immigration and Naturalization Service, Houston District, Houston, Texas*, 50 FLRA 140, 143-44 (1995) (*INS Houston*); *Dep't of Veterans Affairs, Veterans Administration Medical Center, Veterans Canteen Service, Lexington, Kentucky*, 44 FLRA 179, 187 (1992). For the reasons set forth below, I conclude that no change was made to the conditions of employment for bargaining unit employees in this case. Thus, there was no violation of the Statute and the Complaint should be dismissed.

The post hearing brief filed by the General Counsel cites a single case in support of the assertion that "a change in work location is itself a change in a condition of employment." *U.S. Dep't of Health and Human Services, Soc. Sec. Admin., Baltimore, Maryland and Soc. Sec. Admin., Fitchburg, Massachusetts District Office, Fitchburg, Massachusetts*, 36 FLRA 655, 668 (1990) (*SSA Fitchburg*). While that general axiom can be accurate under some circumstances, it is not true under all circumstances, as was pointed out in *INS Houston*, wherein the Authority made clear that determining a change in a condition of employment requires case-by-case analysis. *INS Houston* at 144. In fact, the Authority pointedly indicated in the *SSA Fitchburg* decision that ". . . not all changes in office space will give rise to a bargaining obligation. . .", *SSA Fitchburg* at 668. Thus, even the decision cited by the General Counsel stands for the proposition that not every change in the location at which an employee performs work will constitute a change in conditions of employment.

The portion of the *SSA Fitchburg* decision relevant to changing conditions of employment involved rearranging the seating location of four employees in a Social Security field office with sixteen bargaining unit employees. This change was prompted in part by the acquisition of new office furniture, a desire to gain efficiency from the centralization of Teleclaim work, and moving claims representatives who conducted in-person interviews closer to the clientele. While the Authority's decision did not directly address the question of whether such action constituted a change in conditions of employment because the unexplained determination of the judge was not challenged, the Authority did consider an exception alleging that the action was *de minimis*, and concluded that it was not. *SSA Fitchburg* at 668. However, it is important to note that the precedent relied upon by the Authority, *Library of Congress v. FLRA*, 699 F.2d 1280, 1286 (D.C. Çir. 1983) and *National Treasury Employees Union, Chapter 83 and Department of the Treasury, Internal Revenue Service*, 35 FLRA 398, 414 (1990), involved cases wherein entire bargaining units were moved to completely new physical locations, whereas *SSA Fitchburg* only involved moving four employees to different cubicles within existing physical workspace already assigned to the bargaining unit. Nonetheless, the precedent developed in cases involving the relocation of entire bargaining units to new physical locations, was, by virtue of the Authority's *SSA Fitchburg* decision, extended to cover the reseating of four employees at different cubicles in the same work space with little to no discussion for why such an extension was consistent with the Statute. While the Respondent's failure to file an exception to the judge's determination that such an action constituted a change in conditions of employment may explain why this extension was enacted with little explanation, the Authority was cognizant enough of the breadth of the expansion to cogently advise for future reference that ". . . not all changes in office space will give rise to a bargaining obligation. . .". *SSA Fitchburg* at 668.

While the Authority may have an opportunity to revisit and more fully explain the expansion it set forth in *SSA Fitchburg*, the precedent of that does not require a conclusion that assigning workers to perform laborer duties at differing temporary lodging locations on Tyndall AFB constituted a change to the conditions of employment for that bargaining unit. In fact, an essential difference between the Social Security employees in *SSA Fitchburg* and the laborers in this case leads to the opposite conclusion. The idea that altering the seating arrangements of employees within an established area of bargaining unit work space constitutes more than a *de minimis* change to conditions of employment when there is no change in the work being done is one upon which reasonable minds may differ; however, the issue ceases to be debatable when such alteration of work locations is a routine part of an agency's policy and practice. Because assigning laborers to different lodging locations was an expected part of the job for laborers working within the Sand Dollar Inn system, a case-by-case analysis of the facts distinguishes this case from the precedent of *SSA Fitchburg*.

In this case, the policy and practice of the Respondent was to assign and alter which laborers would perform their duties at the various lodging locations requiring their custodial services depending upon leave, availability, work load and mission necessity. Each of the laborers was hired pursuant to a position description that made clear the ability to perform the full range of custodial duties required at all of the locations was essential. The testimony from witnesses called by both sides indicated that laborers are typically assigned to work a particular area with which they are familiar, but that each employee was subject to being assigned to other areas when circumstances required it. Sometimes these differing assignments were made on a daily basis due to sick leave or other reasons, sometimes they would be on a weekly basis or longer to accommodate annual leave, and other times they took the form of altering the particular lodging area assigned to an employee. Whether the cause was employee unavailability, mission necessity, accommodating a union official by assigning him work in an area with access to a telephone, work loads or other reasons, the one constant that each of the laborers understood was that working at a particular location within the Sand Dollar Inn lodging system was never a certainty. There were no fixed assignments and no permanent duty stations at particular locations. It is the established fluidity in the assignment of laborer duties performed by the bargaining unit employees, as outlined in the position description and implemented in the policies and practices of the Respondent, which makes the precedent of *SSA Fitchburg* inapplicable in this case.

In *SSA Fitchburg*, there was no position description indicating that the ability to work at each cubicle was a requirement and that the employee would have to be able to perform the duties required at each cubicle. Further, there is nothing in the record demonstrating that Social Security Administration (SSA) field office managers assigned the employees duties at different cubicles on a routine basis. Thus, those SSA employees arguably had some reasonable expectation of performing their duties in the same cubicle on a daily basis and it can be argued that altering those static seating assignments impacted a condition of their employment in more than a *de minimis* manner. While I find such an argument dubious given the fact that bargaining unit employees continued to do the same type of work at the same physical location and within the very same floor space already assigned to that bargaining unit, I reject it outright when the facts of the case demonstrate that any expectation of working at the same lodging location within the Sand Dollar Inn system was not reasonable. One cannot accept a position for which he or she is told the job requires you to work at all lodging locations and then contend that the Respondent changed a condition of employment by assigning the employee to work at lodging location D instead of lodging location A.

In reaching this conclusion, it is important to note some of the factors that were not presented by the work assignments that are the subject matter of the General Counsel's Complaint. One, it did not result in a change to the substantive duties required of any laborer in the bargaining unit. All of the witnesses agreed that the general duties required of a laborer at any of the temporary lodging areas were basically the same. Two, the work assignment did not require a personnel action, did not involve a formal detail and did not result in modification of pay. Had such record keeping actions been necessary for personnel or pay reasons, it might indicate that the assignment of particular lodging location was something more than an assignment of work. However, no such evidence was presented. *See, U.S. Dep't of Veterans Affairs Medical Center, Leavenworth, Kansas*, 60 FLRA 315 (2004) (VA). Three, no evidence of a past practice of notice and negotiation over the assignment of a primary work location at a particular lodging location was presented. To the contrary, the witnesses agreed that previous changes in assignments were made without them being negotiated as changes in conditions of employment. In particular, the Union president testified that the location to which he was routinely assigned was changed without notice or bargaining in order to give him better telephone access. T-50, 88, 89. It appears that the driving force behind the Union's unfair labor practice charge was James Stephens' personal relationship with the Union president and Stephens' displeasure with working at the Wood Manor location. While there was some evidence of health issues introduced on the part of Stephens, it was far from clear or persuasive that any health problem was caused by working at this particular location. Furthermore, even if a causal relationship to the assignment were established, such health matters would not have been foreseeable given his full ability to perform at other temporary lodging locations involving substantially the same duties. *VA at 331.* Finally, another indication why the assignment of Stephens to Wood Manor was not a change in conditions of employment for the bargaining unit is the fact that if Stephens was not the laborer assigned to perform duties at Wood Manor, the responsibility of completing those tasks at that location would fall to another employee within the bargaining unit.[2] Thus, the only thing that would change is the individual performing the work and not the conditions under which they were performed by the bargaining unit.

II. Any Change was *De Minimis*

Although I find that there was no change to the conditions of employment for the bargaining unit in question, even if there were a change, its impact was *de minimus.* Therefore, the Respondent had no obligation to bargain the impact and implementation over the exercise of its management right to assign work at the various temporary lodging areas. The *VA* case discussed above was cited by neither the General Counsel nor the Respondent's briefs, however, it provides a clear indication that assigning laborers to various temporary lodging locations at Tyndall AFB had no more than a *de minimis* impact on the bargaining unit.

In the *VA* case, two nurses at the VA Medical Center in Leavenworth, Kansas were reassigned by formal detail from their positions in the Acute Medical/Surgical Ward, to other health care units located in different areas on the facility's campus. *VA* at 327. While these details involved performing substantially the same nursing duties, they required the two nurses to perform them at different physical locations separate and distinct from that at which they had previously worked for eight and nineteen years. Although the Authority concluded that the change was more than *de minimis*, it did so because the details resulted in one of the nurses losing the opportunity to earn more pay by virtue of a lost

---

[2] At some point in July 2006, the Respondent began treating the temporary lodging area known as Wood Manor differently than its other temporary lodging areas by utilizing different time keeping methods and altering the supervisory structure for that location. While those changes give rise to legitimate questions regarding changes in conditions of employment, those issues were not raised by the Complaint that was the subject of this hearing. T-116, 215 to 219.

opportunity for shift differential. In other words, despite being reassigned via formal detail to work at a new physical location after years of work at a prior work location, the Authority concluded that the reason the reassignment was more than *de minimis* was because it resulted in an assignment to a new unit where weekend work was not performed and shift differentials could not be earned; not because the nurses were physically relocated to new work locations. Thus, the act of moving the nurses to a new location on the medical campus was either *de minimis*, or not a change in conditions of employment at all.

The case at bar, involves laborers hired with the understanding that they would have to work at the various lodging locations in the Sand Dollar Inn system. None of the laborers had worked exclusively at the very same location for years on end, their work assignments were made orally as needed and there is no evidence in the record that the assignment to different lodging locations had any impact upon the pay they earned in the performance of their duties. For all of these reasons, the precedent of the *VA* case indicates that assignments made under the circumstances of this case have no more than a *de minimis* impact on the bargaining unit at Tyndall AFB because these laborers, like the nurses in *VA,* were subject to performing substantially similar duties at the various locations operated by the Respondent at all times. While each of the laborers experiences some change whenever he or she is assigned duties at a different lodging location, each change does not constitute a change to their conditions of employment that is more than *de minimis*.

For the reasons set forth above, I conclude that the Respondent did not violate the Statute and that the Complaint of the General Counsel should be dismissed.

ORDER

It is ordered that the Complaint be, and hereby, is dismissed.

Issued, Washington, DC, February 28, 2007.

CHARLES R. CENTER
Chief Administrative Law Judge

65 FLRA No. 184

AMERICAN FEDERATION
OF GOVERNMENT EMPLOYEES
LOCAL 3955
COUNCIL OF PRISON LOCALS 33
(Union)

and

UNITED STATES
DEPARTMENT OF JUSTICE
BUREAU OF PRISONS
FEDERAL CORRECTIONAL COMPLEX
TUCSON, ARIZONA
(Agency)

0-AR-4703

DECISION

May 31, 2011

Before the Authority: Carol Waller Pope, Chairman, and Thomas M. Beck and Ernest DuBester, Members[1]

I. Statement of the Case

This matter is before the Authority on exceptions to an award of Arbitrator Jay C. Fogelberg filed by the Union under § 7122(a) of the Federal Service Labor-Management Relations Statute (the Statute) and part 2425 of the Authority's Regulations. The Agency filed an opposition to the Union's exceptions.

The Arbitrator found that the Agency did not violate the parties' agreement by denying the grievant's request for sick leave. For the following reasons, we dismiss the Union's exceptions in part and deny them in part.

II. Background and Arbitrator's Award

The grievant, a physician's assistant in a correctional facility, requested sick leave because he was not feeling well after responding to an inmate's suicide attempt. Award at 3-4. The Agency denied his request due to a staffing shortage. *Id.* at 4. The grievant reported for his shift, but was later instructed to go home after a supervisor noticed that the grievant looked "tired and somewhat distressed." *Id.*

The Union filed a grievance on behalf of the grievant. *Id.* at 5. The grievance was unresolved and submitted to arbitration, where the Arbitrator framed the issue as: "Did the Agency violate Articles 20 and/or 27 of the [parties' agreement[2]], or the Code of Federal Regulations (if applicable) when it denied a request by the [g]rievant to take sick leave[?] If [so], what shall the appropriate remedy be?" *Id.* at 2.

---

1. Member Beck's separate opinion, dissenting in part, is set forth at the end of this decision.

2. Article 20 of the parties' agreement provides, in pertinent part:

> Section (a): Employees will accrue and be granted sick leave in accordance with applicable regulations, including:
> (1) sick leave may be used when an employee . . . is incapacitated for the performance of duties by sickness[;]
> . . . .
> (3) except in an emergency situation, any employee who will be or is absent due to illness or injury will notify the supervisor, prior to the start of the employee's shift or as soon as possible, of the inability to report for duty and the expected length of absence. . . . The actual granting of sick leave, however, will be pursuant to a personal request by the employee to the immediate supervisor, unless the employee is too ill or injured to do so, for each day the employee is absent, up to three (3) days, provided the supervisor has not approved other arrangements.

Article 27 of the parties' agreement states, in pertinent part:

> Section (a): There are essentially two (2) distinct areas of concern regarding the safety and health of employees in the [Agency]:
> (1) the first, which affects the safety and well-being of employees, involves the inherent hazards of the correctional environment; and
> (2) the second, which affects the safety and health of employees, involves the inherent hazards associated with the normal industrial operations found throughout the [Agency].

Exceptions, Attach. 4 at 52, 62.

As an initial matter, the Arbitrator stated that "it is widely held that, unless restricted by the language in a labor agreement, the granting or denial of a sick leave request is normally a right reserved to management." *Id.* at 10 (citation omitted). For support, he cited Elkouri & Elkouri, *How Arbitration Works*, 1083 (Alan Miles Ruben, ed., BNA Books 6th ed. 2003) (the arbitration manual). *Id.* The Arbitrator also stated that Article 20, Section (a)(1) of the parties' agreement provides that "sick leave may be used when an employee . . . is incapacitated for the performance of duties by sickness[.]" *Id.* at 11 (internal quotation marks omitted). The Arbitrator examined Article 20, Section (a)(3), and found that wording in that provision stating that "the actual granting of sick leave . . . will be pursuant to a personal request by the employee . . . *provided the supervisor has not approved other arrangements*" suggests that a sick leave request is subject to the approval of management. *Id.* at 11-12 (citations omitted). The Arbitrator determined that this interpretation of the provision is "consistent with the management rights language contained in Article 5[.]"[3] *Id.* at 12. In this connection, he noted that, in *AFGE, Federal Prison Council 33*, 51 FLRA 1112 (1996) (*Council 33*), the Authority held that judgment regarding the staffing necessary to maintain a secure facility is a management right. Award at 12. In addition, he stated that "there is nearly an equal amount of testimony and documentation in the record indicating that the facility was short[-]staffed[,] . . . and consequently had legitimate security and safety concerns that needed to be considered." *Id.* at 16-17.

The Arbitrator found that Article 32, Section (a) of the parties' agreement precluded him from considering the Union's argument that the Agency violated § 630.401(a).[4] *Id.* at 13-14. In this connection, the Arbitrator determined that the Union's grievance did not cite the regulation, and that there was no evidence that the parties agreed to modify the grievance pursuant to Article 32, Section (a). *Id.*

For the foregoing reasons, the Arbitrator found that the Union failed to demonstrate that the Agency violated the parties' agreement, and he denied the grievance. *Id.* at 17.

III. Positions of the Parties

A. Union's Exceptions

The Union argues that the award is deficient because the Arbitrator erred by: (1) relying on Article 32 of the parties' agreement as a basis for not considering the Union's argument concerning § 630.401(a); and (2) citing *Council 33*, 51 FLRA 1112, in support of his award. Exceptions at 7-9. The Union also argues that, by finding that the Agency's right to assign work justified its denial of the sick-leave request, the Arbitrator exceeded his authority. *Id.* at 7-8.

In addition, the Union asserts that the Arbitrator erred by failing to find that the Agency violated § 630.401(a). *Id.* at 5. The Union further claims that, by failing to find such a violation, the award fails to draw its essence from the parties' agreement because Article 20, Section (a) "clearly states [that] employees will accrue and be granted sick leave in accordance with applicable regulations." *Id.* In this regard, the Union also claims that the Arbitrator erred by: (1) relying on Article 20, Section (a)(3) because the grievance cited only the first clause of Article 20, Section (a); and (2) citing the arbitration manual, rather than the parties' agreement and applicable regulations, in rendering his decision. *Id.* at 4-5.

Finally, the Union argues that the Arbitrator's finding that "there is nearly an equal amount of testimony and documentation in the record indicating that the facility was short[-]staffed" is a "non-fact[]." *Id.* at 8 (emphasis omitted). Specifically, the Union maintains that, although there was "a small amount of testimony to the fact that the [facility] was short[-]staffed[,]" there is "no documentation in the record" to support the Arbitrator's finding. *Id.*

B. Agency's Opposition

The Agency argues that the award is not contrary to § 630.401. Opp'n at 6. With respect to the Union's essence exception, the Agency contends that

3. Article 5 of the parties' agreement mirrors § 7106 of the Statute. Exceptions, Attach. 4 at 8-9.

4. Article 32, Section (a) of the parties' agreement states, in relevant part: "[T]he party seeking to have an issue submitted to arbitration must notify the other party in writing of this intent prior to expiration of any applicable time limit. . . . However, the issues, the alleged violations, and the remedy requested in the written grievance may be modified only by mutual agreement." Exceptions, Attach. 4 at 76.

Section 630.401(a) provides, in pertinent part: "[A]n agency must grant sick leave to an employee when he or she . . . (2) [i]s incapacitated for the performance of his or her duties by physical or mental illness, injury, pregnancy, or childbirth[.]" 5 C.F.R. § 630.401(a); *see also* Award at 7.

the Arbitrator "properly read the relevant provision of the [parties' agreement] to give management the discretion to grant or deny sick leave requests." *Id.* at 4. Further, with regard to the Union's contention that the Arbitrator made "non-factual" findings, the Agency maintains that the Union's "assessment of the sufficiency of the evidence is not controlling." *Id.* at 6.

IV. Analysis and Conclusions

A. The Union's exceptions that fail to raise recognized grounds for review are dismissed under § 2425.6(e)(1) of the Authority's Regulations.

The Authority's Regulations concerning the review of arbitration awards, as well as certain related procedural Regulations, were revised effective October 1, 2010 and, thus, apply in this case. *See* 75 Fed. Reg. 42,283 (2010). The revised Regulations specifically enumerate the grounds that the Authority currently recognizes for reviewing awards. *See* 5 C.F.R. § 2425.6(a)-(b). In addition, the Regulations provide that if exceptions argue that an arbitration award is deficient based on private-sector grounds not currently recognized by the Authority, then the excepting party "must provide sufficient citation to legal authority that establishes the grounds upon which the party filed its exceptions." 5 C.F.R. § 2425.6(c).

Further, § 2425.6(e)(1) of the Regulations provides that an exception "may be subject to dismissal or denial if: . . . [t]he excepting party fails to raise and support" the grounds listed in § 2425.6(a)-(c), "or otherwise fails to demonstrate a legally recognized basis for setting aside the award[.]" 5 C.F.R. § 2425.6(e)(1). As originally proposed, § 2425.6(e)(1) provided for dismissal of exceptions that fail to raise or support an established ground. *See* 75 Fed. Reg. 22,540, 22,542 (2010). However, the final Regulation added the term "or denial," and explained that "a party's failure to *support* a properly raised ground for review may be subject to 'denial' rather than 'dismissal.'" *See* 75 Fed. Reg. 42,283, 42,285 (2010) (emphasis added). In other words, while an exception that does not *raise* a recognized ground is subject to dismissal under the Regulations, an exception that fails to *support* a properly raised ground is subject to denial.

The Union asserts that the award is deficient because the Arbitrator erred by: (1) relying on Article 32 of the parties' agreement as a basis for not considering the Union's arguments concerning § 630.401(a); and (2) citing *Council 33*, 51 FLRA 1112, in support of his award. Exceptions at 7-9. These exceptions fail to raise grounds currently recognized by the Authority, *see* 5 C.F.R. § 2425.6(a)-(b), and do not cite any legal authority to support a ground not currently recognized by the Authority, *see* 5 C.F.R. § 2425.6(c). For these reasons, we conclude that § 2425.6(e)(1) supports dismissing these two exceptions.

In reaching that conclusion, we emphasize that we decline to construe the exceptions as raising recognized grounds for review. In this connection, we acknowledge that, under the Authority's former arbitration regulations, the Authority frequently "construe[d]" parties' exceptions to raise recognized grounds when they could reasonably be construed as raising such grounds. *See, e.g., U.S. Dep't of the Navy, Supervisor of Shipbuilding, Conversion & Repair, Gulf Coast, Pascagoula, Miss.*, 62 FLRA 328, 330 (2007) (construing argument contesting arbitrator's interpretation of agreement provision as an essence exception). However, unlike the former regulations, as discussed above, the current Regulations both list each specific recognized ground for review and expressly provide that a failure to raise a recognized ground may result in dismissal of the exceptions. *Cf. former* 5 C.F.R. § 2425.1. One of the main purposes of the Authority's regulatory revisions was to clearly set forth the parties' burdens and explain the consequences of a failure to meet those burdens. We find that this purpose would be undercut by continuing to "construe" parties' exceptions as raising recognized grounds when parties have failed to state such grounds. Accordingly, for cases that are processed under the new Regulations, we will no longer construe parties' exceptions as raising grounds that the exceptions do not raise.

For the foregoing reasons, we dismiss these two exceptions.

B. The Arbitrator did not exceed his authority.

The Union contends that, by finding that the Agency's right to assign work justified its denial of the grievant's request for sick leave, the Arbitrator exceeded his authority. Exceptions at 7-8. Arbitrators exceed their authority when they fail to resolve an issue submitted to arbitration, resolve an issue not submitted to arbitration, disregard specific limitations on their authority, or award relief to persons who are not encompassed within the grievance. *See U.S. Dep't of the Navy, Naval Base, Norfolk, Va.*, 51 FLRA 305, 307-08 (1995).

The Union's contention does not assert that the Arbitrator failed to resolve an issue that was properly before him, resolved an issue that was not properly before him, disregarded specific limitations on his authority, or awarded relief to persons not encompassed within the grievance. Thus, the Union has not supported its exceeded-authority exception, and, consistent with 5 C.F.R. § 2425.6(e)(1) and the above-cited Authority precedent, we deny the exception.

C. The Union's exceptions that challenge the Arbitrator's determination regarding § 630.401(a) do not provide a basis for finding the award deficient.

The Union argues that the Arbitrator erred by failing to find that the Agency violated § 630.401(a). Exceptions at 5. The Union also argues that, by failing to find such a violation, the award fails to draw its essence from the parties' agreement because Article 20, Section (a) "clearly states [that] employees will accrue and be granted sick leave in accordance with applicable regulations." *Id.*

The Authority has held that questions of whether the "'preliminary steps of the grievance procedure have been exhausted or excused'" are questions regarding the procedural arbitrability of a grievance. *AFGE, Local 1815*, 65 FLRA 430, 431 (2011) (*Local 1815*) (quoting *Fraternal Order of Police, N.J. Lodge 173*, 58 FLRA 384, 385 (2003) (Chairman Cabaniss dissenting)). Here, the Arbitrator found that he could not consider the Union's argument with respect to § 630.401(a) because the Union's grievance did not cite the regulation, and there was no evidence that the parties agreed to modify the original grievance pursuant to Article 32, Section (a) of the parties' agreement. Award at 13-14. The Union's arguments essentially challenge the Arbitrator's determination that the Union failed to satisfy the procedural requirements set forth in the grievance procedure, which is a procedural arbitrability determination. *See Local 1815*, 65 FLRA at 431.

The Authority generally will not find an arbitrator's ruling on the procedural arbitrability of a grievance deficient on grounds that directly challenge the procedural arbitrability ruling itself. *AFGE, Local 933*, 65 FLRA 9, 11 (2010) (*Local 933*). However, a procedural arbitrability determination can be found deficient as contrary to law. *E.g., U.S. Dep't of Homeland Sec., U.S. Customs & Border Prot., U.S. Border Patrol, El Paso, Tex.*, 61 FLRA 122, 124 (2005) (*DHS*). In this connection, the Authority has recognized that "procedural requirements may be established [by statute] that apply to negotiated grievance procedures and . . . that a statute could be enacted establishing a filing period for grievances." *AFGE, Local 933*, 58 FLRA 480, 481 (2003) (citation omitted). Consequently, in order for a procedural arbitrability determination to be found deficient as contrary to law, the appealing party must establish that the determination is contrary to procedural requirements established by statute that apply to the parties' negotiated grievance procedure. *DHS*, 61 FLRA at 124.

With respect to the Union's contention that the Arbitrator erred by failing to find a violation of § 630.401(a), that regulation does not establish procedural requirements that apply to the parties' negotiated grievance procedure. Thus, the Union's contention does not provide a basis for finding the Arbitrator's procedural arbitrability determination contrary to law. *See id.* Similarly, the Union's essence argument regarding the failure to apply applicable regulations directly challenges the Arbitrator's procedural arbitrability finding and, thus, does not provide a basis for finding the award deficient. *See Local 933*, 65 FLRA at 11. Accordingly, we deny these exceptions.

D. The award draws its essence from the parties' agreement.

In reviewing an arbitrator's interpretation of a collective bargaining agreement, the Authority applies the deferential standard that federal courts use in reviewing arbitration awards in the private sector. *See* 5 U.S.C. § 7122(a)(2); *AFGE, Council 220*, 54 FLRA 156, 159 (1998). Under this standard, the Authority will find that an arbitration award is deficient as failing to draw its essence from the collective bargaining agreement when the appealing party establishes that the award: (1) cannot in any rational way be derived from the agreement; (2) is so unfounded in reason and fact and so unconnected with the wording and purposes of the collective bargaining agreement as to manifest an infidelity to the obligation of the arbitrator; (3) does not represent a plausible interpretation of the agreement; or (4) evidences a manifest disregard of the agreement. *U.S. Dep't of Labor (OSHA)*, 34 FLRA 573, 575 (1990). The Authority and the courts defer to arbitrators in this context "because it is the arbitrator's construction of the agreement for which the parties have bargained." *Id.* at 576.

The Union argues that the Arbitrator erred by: (1) relying on Article 20, Section (a)(3) because the grievance cited only the first clause of Article 20, Section (a)[5]; and (2) citing the arbitration manual in rendering his decision. Exceptions at 4-5. With respect to the first argument, the Union provides no basis for finding that the Arbitrator erred by relying on an agreement provision not specifically cited in the grievance. In fact, in similar circumstances, the Authority looks to the entire agreement in determining whether an award fails to draw its essence from the parties' agreement. *See Overseas Educ. Ass'n*, 4 FLRA 98, 102 (1980). As neither of the Union's arguments provides a basis for finding that the Arbitrator's interpretation of the agreement is implausible, irrational, or unconnected to the wording of the agreement, we deny the exceptions.

E. The award is not based on a nonfact.

The Union asserts that the Arbitrator's finding that "there is nearly an equal amount of testimony and documentation in the record indicating that the facility was short[-]staffed" is a nonfact. Exceptions at 8 (emphasis omitted). In this regard, the Union maintains that, although there was "a small amount of testimony to the fact that the [facility] was short[-] staffed[,]" there is "no documentation in the record" to support the Arbitrator's finding. *Id.*

To establish that an award is based on a nonfact, the appealing party must show that a central fact underlying the award is clearly erroneous, but for which the arbitrator would have reached a different result. *See NFFE, Local 1984*, 56 FLRA 38, 41 (2000). However, the Authority will not find an award deficient on the basis of an arbitrator's determination of any factual matter that the parties disputed at arbitration. *See id.*

The Union's assertion does not demonstrate that the Arbitrator's finding regarding documentation in the record is a clearly erroneous central fact, but for which the Arbitrator would have reached a different conclusion. Accordingly, the assertion does not demonstrate that the finding is a nonfact, and we deny the exception.

V. Decision

The Union's exceptions are dismissed in part and denied in part.

5. As noted previously, the first clause of Article 20, Section (a) of the parties' agreement states that "[e]mployees will accrue and be granted sick leave in accordance with applicable regulations[.]" Exceptions, Attach. 4 at 52.

Member Beck, Dissenting in Part:

I part ways with the Majority when they conclude that two of the Union's exceptions should be dismissed because the exceptions do not raise private-sector grounds that are recognized by the Authority.

Our recently revised regulations do not require parties to invoke any particular magical incantations when filing exceptions. A party is required only to "explain how" the award is deficient as contrary to law or on grounds similar to those applied by federal courts in private-sector arbitrations (5 C.F.R. § 2425.6(a)) or to "provide *sufficient citation* to legal authority" if the exception is based on a private-sector ground that is not listed in § 2425.6(b)(1)(i) through (b)(2)(iv). 5 C.F.R. § 2425.6(c) (emphasis added).

Here, the Union's arguments are sufficient to establish essence and contrary to law exceptions.* In one exception, the Union argues that the Arbitrator "erroneously interpret[ed] Article 32" when he failed to consider 5 C.F.R. § 630.401. Exceptions at 7. In the other exception, the Union argues that the Arbitrator erred by interpreting *AFGE, Fed. Prison Council 33*, 51 FLRA 1112 (1996) to support his conclusion that determinations regarding what manpower is required "to maintain a secure facility is a right reserved [to management] . . . with regard to denial [of] sick leave." Exceptions at 9 (emphasis omitted). Accordingly, I disagree with my colleagues that we would need to "construe" these arguments in order to find a recognized exception.

I would deny these additional exceptions using essence and contrary to law analyses but would not dismiss them under § 2425.6(e)(1).

* I contrast this case from our recent decision in *Fraternal Order of Police, Pentagon Police Labor Committee*, 65 FLRA 781, 784-85 (2011), where we dismissed the union's contrary to law exception because the union failed to explain how the award was deficient.

65 FLRA No. 185

UNITED STATES
DEPARTMENT OF JUSTICE
FEDERAL BUREAU OF PRISONS
FEDERAL CORRECTIONAL INSTITUTION
DUBLIN, CALIFORNIA
(Agency)

and

AMERICAN FEDERATION
OF GOVERNMENT EMPLOYEES
LOCAL 3584
(Union)

0-AR-4471

DECISION

May 31, 2011

Before the Authority: Carol Waller Pope, Chairman, and Thomas M. Beck and Ernest DuBester, Members

I. Statement of the Case

This matter is before the Authority on an exception to an award of Arbitrator Philip Tamoush filed by the Agency under § 7122(a) of the Federal Service Labor-Management Relations Statute (the Statute) and part 2425 of the Authority's Regulations.[1] The Union filed an opposition to the Agency's exception.

The Arbitrator found that the Agency violated the parties' collective bargaining agreement (CBA) by leaving certain work posts vacant and ordered the Agency to fill vacant posts.

For the reasons that follow, we deny the Agency's exception.

II. Background and Arbitrator's Award

The Agency schedules correctional officers to fill posts supervising prison inmates in its food services facilities. Award at 4. In certain locations, post orders call for more than one officer to be on duty at a time. *Id.* at 5. However, the Agency began leaving the additional officers' posts vacant. *Id.* This left one officer on duty to supervise twenty-five to thirty inmates. *Id.* at 4-5. The inmates were in both the kitchen and the dining areas, making the officer's supervision of all of the inmates "an almost impossible responsibility" and raising safety concerns. *Id.* at 5.

The Union filed a grievance alleging, as relevant here, that the Agency violated the CBA by leaving these posts vacant. *Id.* The grievance was unresolved and was submitted to arbitration. The Arbitrator adopted the Union's issue statement, which asked: "Did the Agency violate the [CBA] by vacating . . . posts at [the Agency]?" *Id.* at 2, 10.

The Arbitrator sustained the grievance. The Arbitrator found that the Agency violated the CBA by leaving posts vacant rather than filling them with regular staff officers or through overtime assignments. *Id.* at 11. The Arbitrator did not specify the provision of the CBA on which he relied. However, he referenced Article 27, entitled, "Health and Safety," in the "Relevant Contract Language" section of the award. *Id.* at 3. Article 27 of the CBA requires the Agency to reduce hazards to its employees "to the lowest possible level, without relinquishing its rights under 5 USC § 7106" of the Statute. Award at 3. The Arbitrator was also presented with the Union's argument that the CBA "mandates concern over health and safety issues inherent when [p]osts are not filled." *Id.* at 6-7. In addition, citing another arbitration award, the Union argued to the Arbitrator that "[m]anagement is permitted to vacate posts only for good reason[.]" *Id.* at 7. The Arbitrator concluded that "[m]anagement had a clear obligation[] . . . consistent with . . . prior arbitration cases cited by the Union, to cover and fill [p]ost positions." *Id.* at 12.

As a remedy, the Arbitrator ordered the Agency "to fill all vacant/abandoned posts by overtime or regular assignment forthwith." *Id.* at 13.

III. Positions of the Parties

A. Agency's Exception

The Agency claims that the award affects management's rights to determine its internal security practices and to assign work under § 7106(a)(1) and (a)(2)(B) of the Statute because the award precludes the Agency from leaving posts vacant. Exception

1. The Authority dismissed the Agency's exceptions to the initial award as interlocutory. Order at 1. The exceptions at issue here challenge both the initial award and the subsequent award. Exception at 1-2.

at 5, 6. The Agency further argues that, as interpreted and applied by the Arbitrator, Article 27 is not enforceable under § 7106(b)(3) because, by precluding the Agency from vacating posts, it excessively interferes with the exercise of management's rights. *Id.* at 7.

B. Union's Opposition

The Union argues that, although the award affects a management right, it is still enforceable as an appropriate arrangement under § 7106(b)(3) of the Statute. Opp'n at 7. According to the Union, the question is whether the award would abrogate the exercise of the Agency's management rights. *Id.* at 8. The Union contends that the award does not abrogate those rights because it does not prevent the Agency from determining "which and how many posts are necessary." *Id.* (citing *U.S. Dep't of Justice, Fed. Bureau of Prisons, U.S. Penitentiary, Atlanta, Ga.*, 57 FLRA 406 (2001) (*DOJ Atlanta*); *U.S. Dep't of Justice, Fed. Bureau of Prisons, Metro. Det. Ctr. Guaynabo, P.R.*, 57 FLRA 331, 333 (2001) (*DOJ Guaynabo*)).

IV. Analysis and Conclusions

The Agency claims that the award is contrary to management's rights to determine its internal security practices and to assign work under § 7106(a)(1) and (a)(2)(B) of the Statute. The Authority reviews questions of law raised by exceptions to an arbitrator's award de novo. *See NTEU, Chapter 24*, 50 FLRA 330, 332 (1995) (citing *U.S. Customs Serv. v. FLRA*, 43 F.3d 682, 686-87 (D.C. Cir. 1994)). In applying a standard of de novo review, the Authority determines whether the arbitrator's legal conclusions are consistent with the applicable standard of law. *See NFFE, Local 1437*, 53 FLRA 1703, 1710 (1998). In making that determination, the Authority defers to the arbitrator's underlying factual findings. *Id.*

The Authority recently revised the analysis that it will apply when reviewing management-rights exceptions to arbitration awards. *See U.S. EPA*, 65 FLRA 113, 115 (2010) (Member Beck concurring) (*EPA*); *FDIC, Div. of Supervision & Consumer Prot., S.F. Region*, 65 FLRA 102, 106-07 (2010) (Chairman Pope concurring) (*FDIC*). Under the revised analysis, the Authority will first assess whether the award affects the exercise of the asserted management right. *EPA*, 65 FLRA at 115.[2] If so, the Authority examines whether the award provides a remedy for a violation of either an applicable law, within the meaning of § 7106(a)(2) of the Statute, or a contract provision that was negotiated pursuant to § 7106(b) of the Statute. *Id.* Also, under the analysis, in determining whether the award enforces a contract provision negotiated under § 7106(b)(3), the Authority assesses: (1) whether the contract provision constitutes an arrangement for employees adversely affected by the exercise of a management right; and (2) if so, whether the arbitrator's enforcement of the arrangement abrogates the exercise of the management right. *Id.* at 116-18. In concluding that it would apply an abrogation standard, the Authority rejected continued application of an excessive interference standard. *Id.* at 118. Furthermore, in setting forth its revised analysis, the Authority specifically rejected the continued application of the reconstruction standard set forth in prior case law. *FDIC*, 65 FLRA at 106-07.

It is not disputed that the award affects management's rights to determine its internal security practices and to assign work under § 7106(a)(1) and (a)(2)(B) of the Statute. Consequently, we examine whether the Arbitrator enforced a contract provision negotiated pursuant to § 7106(b). Here, the Arbitrator enforced Article 27 of the CBA. He determined that the Agency violated the CBA "when it left post positions vacant, without filling them either by regular staff" or with "voluntary/mandatory overtime assignments." Award at 11.

With regard to § 7106(b)(3), the Agency does not dispute that this provision is an arrangement, but argues that the Arbitrator's enforcement of this provision excessively interferes with its management rights to determine its internal security practices and assign work by precluding the Agency from leaving posts vacant. Exception at 4, 6-7. However, as stated above, the Authority no longer applies an excessive interference standard in determining whether an arbitrator has enforced a contract

2. For the reasons articulated in his recent concurring opinion and footnotes, Member Beck would conclude that it is unnecessary to assess whether the contract provision is an appropriate arrangement or whether it abrogates a § 7106(a) right. The appropriate question is simply whether the remedy directed by the Arbitrator enforces the provision in a reasonable and reasonably foreseeable fashion. *See EPA*, 65 FLRA at 120 (Concurring Opinion of Member Beck); *FDIC*, 65 FLRA at 107; *SSA, Office of Disability Adjudication & Review*, 65 FLRA 477, 481 n.14 (2011); *U.S. Dep't of the Air Force, Air Force Materiel Command*, 65 FLRA 395, 398 n.7 (2010); *U.S. Dep't of Health & Human Servs., Office of Medicare Hearings & Appeals*, 65 FLRA 175, 177 n.3 (2010); *U.S. Dep't of Transp., Fed. Aviation Admin.*, 65 FLRA 171, 173 n.5 (2010).

provision negotiated under § 7106(b)(3); rather, it applies an abrogation standard. *EPA*, 65 FLRA at 116-18. The Authority has previously described an award that abrogates the exercise of a management right as an award that "precludes an agency from exercising" the affected management right. *U.S. Dep't of the Air Force, Air Force Materiel Command*, 65 FLRA 395, 399 (2010) (citation omitted).

The Agency fails to demonstrate that Article 27, as interpreted and applied by the Arbitrator, abrogates the exercise of its rights to determine its internal security practices and to assign work. The Arbitrator found that, consistent with cases cited by the Union permitting vacating posts for good reason, the Agency must cover and fill post positions. Award at 7, 12. Therefore, the award may reasonably be read as allowing the Agency to vacate posts for good reason, rather than precluding the Agency from vacating them in all circumstances. *See DOJ Atlanta*, 57 FLRA at 410-11 (award did not abrogate § 7106 right where award allowed Agency to leave posts vacant in certain circumstances); *DOJ Guaynabo*, 57 FLRA at 333-34 (same).

In addition, nothing in the award prevents the Agency from determining which and how many posts are necessary. The award does not preclude the Agency from determining the degree of staffing needed to maintain the security of its facility. *See DOJ Atlanta*, 57 FLRA at 410-11 (award did not abrogate § 7106 right where award did not prevent agency from determining which and how many posts are necessary); *DOJ Guaynabo*, 57 FLRA at 333-34 (same). Accordingly, the Agency fails to demonstrate that Article 27, as interpreted and applied by the Arbitrator, abrogates the exercise of its rights to determine its internal security practices and assign work. Based on the foregoing, we find that the contract provisions at issue were negotiated under § 7106(b) of the Statute and deny the exception.

V. Decision

The Agency's exception is denied.

65 FLRA No. 186

UNITED STATES
DEPARTMENT OF VETERANS AFFAIRS
CENTRAL TEXAS VETERANS
HEALTH CARE SYSTEM
TEMPLE, TEXAS
(Agency)

and

AMERICAN FEDERATION
OF GOVERNMENT EMPLOYEES
LOCAL 2109
(Union)

0-AR-4709

DECISION

May 31, 2011

Before the Authority: Carol Waller Pope, Chairman, and Thomas M. Beck and Ernest DuBester, Members

I. Statement of the Case

This matter is before the Authority on an exception to an award of Arbitrator Charles R. Greer filed by the Agency under § 7122(a) of the Federal Service Labor-Management Relations Statute (the Statute) and part 2425 of the Authority's Regulations. The Union filed an opposition to the Agency's exception.

The Arbitrator directed the Agency to pay the Union attorney fees. For the reasons that follow, we deny the Agency's exception.

II. Background and Arbitrator's Award

In his initial award dated September 17, 2010,[1] the Arbitrator, among other things, directed the Agency to pay the Union's attorney fees, "if allowed by federal regulations[.]" Initial Award at 9. On October 12, the Union submitted an "Application for Attorney's Fees" to the Arbitrator. Exception, Attach. at 21-40. As part of its application, the Union included the following items: (1) an affidavit from its attorney regarding his education, experience and current market rates; (2) an invoice of fees and costs; and (3) a statement of the prevailing market rate for similar work. *Id.* The invoice submitted by the Union reflected 44.5 total hours worked, including 36.5 hours spent on the case prior to the four-hour, three-witness hearing. *Id.* at 28-29. Just twelve days later, on October 24, the Arbitrator issued the following one sentence order (Attorney Fee Award): "After reviewing the Union's October 12, 2010 application for attorney's fees and attached documents, I find the application to be reasonable and supported by the facts, and hereby direct the Agency to pay the Union the sum of $15,048.46." Attorney Fee Award at 1.

On October 26, the Union notified the Arbitrator that the Agency was "not in compliance with [his] award" because, among other things, the Agency had failed to pay the attorney fees. Exception, Attach. at 46. In response, the Agency contended that the fees submitted by the Union were "excessive and violate[d] Title 5 statu[t]e 2430.4."[2] *Id.* at 44. According to the Agency, the requested fees were based on a $320 hourly rate, which exceeds the statutory hourly maximum of $125. *Id.* at 45. Moreover, the Agency argued that the amount of the attorney fees awarded was inconsistent with the arbitration award. *Id.* In this regard, the Agency asserted that: (1) it continues to make the same payments as before the award; (2) the Union's

1. All dates refer to 2010.

[2] Although the Agency, in its response, referred to "Title 5 statu[t]e 2430.4," it quoted 5 C.F.R. § 2430.4. Exceptions, Attach. at 4. Accordingly, we construe this argument as contending that the fees violated 5 C.F.R. § 2430.4. 5 C.F.R. § 2430.4 governs awards of attorney fees under the Equal Access to Justice Act (EAJA), 5 U.S.C. § 504, and provides, in relevant part:

> (a)(1)(i) No award for the fee of an attorney or agent under this part may exceed $125.00 per hour . . . .
>
> (b) In determining the reasonableness of the fee sought for an attorney, agent or expert witness, the following matters may be considered: (1) If the attorney, agent or witness is in practice, his or her customary fee for similar services, or, if an employee of the applicant, the fully allocated cost of the services; (2) The prevailing rate for similar services in the community in which the attorney, agent or witness ordinarily performs services; (3) The time actually spent in the representation of the applicant; (4) The time reasonably spent in light of the difficulty or complexity of the issues in the proceeding; and (5) Such other factors as may bear on the value of the services provided.

attorney is an appellant representative of the Union and is compensated by the Union "for services rendered;" and (3) "the fees submitted far exceed the arbitration expenses for both parties." *Id.* The Union replied that 5 C.F.R. § 2430.4 did not apply to this case. Rather, the Union argued, "attorney fees in arbitration are set in accordance with local market rates, which were fully documented" in the Union's application. *Id.* at 42.

The Arbitrator first found that 5 C.F.R. § 2430.4 was not relevant and that the parties' agreement "allows for reasonable attorney fees." Attorney Fee Award at 41. The Arbitrator then determined that the amount of fees requested by the Union was reasonable because the fees were based on average local fee data. *Id.*

III. Positions of the Parties

A. Agency's Exception

The Agency contends that the award of attorney fees is contrary to law, rule or regulation. Exception at 4. The Agency notes that it is "not disput[ing] the [A]rbitrator's authority to award attorney fees," but, rather, is contesting "the reasoning [the Arbitrator] used to justify the excessive amount awarded." *Id.* The Agency contends that, contrary to the Arbitrator's award, 5 C.F.R. § 2430.4 is relevant and provides "guidance on how to determine appropriate attorney fee amounts." *Id.* Referring to that regulation, the Agency argues that the amount of fees awarded is inconsistent with the complexity of the arbitration. *Id.* According to the Agency, the attorney invoice submitted by the Union is not justified by a "one day, 4 hour" arbitration, particularly when the Arbitrator denied part of the Union's requested relief and ordered the Union to pay its portion of the arbitrator's expenses. *Id.* As a result, the Agency requests that the Authority adjust the attorney fees awarded to an "appropriate amount." *Id.*

B. Union's Opposition

The Union agrees with the Agency that 5 C.F.R. § 2430 "provides guidance in the calculation of appropriate attorney fees." Opp'n at 3. However, it contends that the Agency's "analysis and application" of the regulation is "flawed." *Id.* As an initial matter, the Union contends it provided sufficient justification for the amount of fees that it requested and was awarded. *Id.* at 3-4. The Union further contends that the fees awarded are reasonable because: (1) the rate upon which the fees were based is within the prevailing market rate and (2) the hours expended working on the case are consistent with the facts and nature of the case. *Id.* at 4-7.

IV. Analysis and Conclusion: The award of attorney fees is not contrary to law.

The Agency contends that the award of attorney fees is contrary to law, rule or regulation. Exception at 4. The Agency bases its exception on 5 C.F.R. § 2430.4, which, it contends, provides "guidance on how to determine appropriate attorney fee amounts." *Id.* Referring to that regulation, the Agency argues that the amount of fees awarded is excessive because, among other things, the amount awarded is inconsistent with the complexity of the arbitration. *Id.*

The Agency's assertion is without merit. 5 C.F.R. § 2430 governs awards of attorney fees under the EAJA. *See U.S. Dep't of Def., Def. Distrib. Region E., New Cumberland, Pa.,* 51 FLRA 155, 163 n.7 (1995). However, the Authority has held that proceedings before arbitrators under the Statute are not adversary adjudications for purposes of the EAJA because they are not subject to the procedural requirements of the Administrative Procedure Act. *Id.* The attorney fees in this case, thus, were not awarded under the EAJA. Accordingly, 5 C.F.R. § 2430 is inapposite and does not demonstrate that the award is deficient.

Accordingly, we deny the Agency's exception.

V. Decision

The Agency's exception is denied.

65 FLRA No. 187

AMERICAN FEDERATION
OF GOVERNMENT EMPLOYEES
LOCAL 1547
(Union)

and

UNITED STATES
DEPARTMENT OF THE AIR FORCE
LUKE AIR FORCE BASE, ARIZONA
(Agency)

0-AR-4739

DECISION

May 31, 2011

Before the Authority: Carol Waller Pope, Chairman, and Thomas M. Beck and Ernest DuBester, Members

This matter is before the Authority on exceptions to an award of Arbitrator Kelly J. Hansen filed by the Union under § 7122(a) of the Federal Service Labor-Management Relations Statute (the Statute) and part 2425 of the Authority's Regulations. The Agency filed an opposition to the Union's exceptions.

Under § 7122(a) of the Statute, an award is deficient if it is contrary to any law, rule, or regulation, or it is deficient on other grounds similar to those applied by federal courts in private sector labor-management relations. Upon careful consideration of the entire record in this case and Authority precedent, the Authority concludes that the award is not deficient on the grounds raised in the exceptions and set forth in § 7122(a).[*] *See AFGE, Local 3615*, 65 FLRA 647, 649 (2011) (exceptions that directly challenge procedural arbitrability determinations on essence grounds provide no basis for finding the award deficient); *U.S. Dep't of the Navy, Naval Base, Norfolk, Va.*, 51 FLRA 305, 307-08 (1995) (award not deficient on ground that arbitrator exceeded his or her authority where excepting party does not establish that arbitrator failed to resolve an issue submitted to arbitration, resolved an issue not submitted to arbitration, disregarded specific limitations on his authority, or awarded relief to persons who were not encompassed within the grievance); *Prof'l Airways Sys. Specialists, Dist. No. 1, MEBA/NMU (AFL-CIO)*, 48 FLRA 764, 768-69 (1993) (award not deficient as contrary to law where excepting party fails to establish that the award is in any manner contrary to the law, rule, or regulation on which the party relies).

Accordingly, the Union's exceptions are denied.

[*] Although the Union asserts that the grievant was not notified of appeal rights to the Merit Systems Protection Board, the assertion was not raised before the Arbitrator and, therefore, is not properly before the Authority under 5 C.F.R. § 2429.5.

65 FLRA No. 188

NATIONAL TREASURY
EMPLOYEES UNION
CHAPTER 145
(Union)

and

UNITED STATES
DEPARTMENT OF HOMELAND SECURITY
U.S. CUSTOMS AND BORDER PROTECTION
LAREDO, TEXAS
(Agency)

0-AR-4492

DECISION

June 8, 2011

Before the Authority: Carol Waller Pope, Chairman, and Thomas M. Beck and Ernest DuBester, Members

I. Statement of the Case

This matter is before the Authority on exceptions to an award of Arbitrator Don B. Hays filed by the Union under § 7122(a) of the Federal Service Labor-Management Relations Statute (the Statute) and part 2425 of the Authority's Regulations. The Agency filed an opposition to the Union's exceptions.

The Arbitrator found that the issue of the propriety of the grievant's suspension was not arbitrable. For the reasons that follow, we set aside the award and remand this matter to the parties for submission, absent settlement, to an arbitrator of their choice.

II. Background and Arbitrator's Award

The grievant contacted an Agency Equal Employment Opportunity (EEO) counselor and alleged that the Agency was acting unlawfully in various ways, including the denial of opportunities to work overtime. Award at 4. The grievant elected to participate in an informal, precomplaint mediation process, but when that process was unsuccessful, the grievant filed a formal EEO complaint. *Id.* at 4 & 6. Although the official complaint form did not identify any specific unlawful actions, it was attached to a cover letter that mentioned, among other things, an Agency proposal to suspend the grievant for fourteen days. *Id.* at 6. The Agency dismissed the formal EEO complaint as untimely. *Id.*

Subsequently, the Agency mitigated the grievant's proposed suspension from fourteen to two days. *Id.* at 7. The Union appealed the two-day suspension by invoking expedited arbitration. *Id.* The Arbitrator framed the relevant issue as follows: "Does 5 U.S.C. § 7121 [(§ 7121)[1]] prohibit or otherwise limit the arbitration of the appeal of [the grievant's] two-day suspension [(the appeal)], because the subject matter[s] raised by [the appeal] were essentially the same 'matters' previously raised by the grievant in his original [EEO] complaint?"[2] *Id.* at 1.

The Arbitrator found that the formal EEO complaint and the appeal involved the same matters. *Id.* at 21. As such, and as the grievant filed his formal EEO complaint before the appeal, the Arbitrator determined that § 7121 barred the appeal. *Id.* The Arbitrator stated, in this regard, that the Agency had dismissed the formal EEO complaint "on the basis of *time limitations*[,]" *id.* at 6, and that "because of the previous (time) limitation forfeiture of [the grievant's] EEO claims, [the Arbitrator's] decision to summarily dismiss th[e] appeal will foreclose an independent 'due process' review[]" of "the alleged injustice" of the two-day suspension, *id.* at 20. Nevertheless, the Arbitrator found that "the mandates of § 7121[,] can neither be waived, forfeited nor ignored." *Id.* Accordingly, the Arbitrator dismissed the appeal. *Id.* at 20.

III. Positions of the Parties

A. Union's Exceptions

The Union argues that the award is contrary to § 7121(d), 29 C.F.R. § 1614.301,[3] and applicable case law. *See* Exceptions at 14. In this regard, the Union argues that § 7121(d) does not bar the appeal because the grievant "did not timely file an EEO complaint." *Id.* at 15. Also in this regard, the Union

1. The pertinent wording of § 7121 is set forth below.

2. The Arbitrator also framed an issue regarding the merits of the grievance but did not resolve that issue because, as discussed further below, he found the grievance nonarbitrable.

3. The pertinent wording of 29 C.F.R. § 1614.301 is set forth below.

contends that under 29 C.F.R. § 1614.301(a), only the filing of a formal EEO complaint constitutes an election under § 7121(d), and that pre-complaint counseling does not constitute an election. *Id.* at 16. In addition, the Union argues that § 7121(d) does not bar the appeal because: (1) the grievant could not have filed a valid EEO complaint over his suspension when it initially was proposed, *id.* at 17; (2) the negotiated grievance procedure expressly precludes proposed personnel actions, *id.* at 18; and (3) the subject of the EEO complaint and the subject of the appeal are not the "same matter[,]" *id.* at 21.

B. Agency's Opposition

The Agency argues that the Arbitrator did not err in finding that § 7121(d) bars the appeal. In response to the Union's claim that the grievant did not timely file his EEO complaint, the Agency states that § 7121(d) bars arbitration when the employee has "*timely initiate[d] an action*[,]" and that "*initiating an action* is not the same as *filing a complaint*." Opp'n at 10. The Agency claims that the grievant "timely *initiated* the EEO *action* as required by the statute and regulations, and then he filed his formal EEO complaint." *Id.* at 11. Finally, the Agency contends that the Union's remaining arguments do not demonstrate that the award is deficient. *See id.* at 11-26.

IV. Analysis and Conclusions

The Authority reviews questions of law de novo. *See NTEU, Chapter 24*, 50 FLRA 330, 332 (1995) (citing *U.S. Customs Serv. v. FLRA*, 43 F.3d 682, 686-87 (D.C. Cir. 1994)). In applying a standard of de novo review, the Authority determines whether the arbitrator's legal conclusions are consistent with the applicable standard of law. *NFFE, Local 1437*, 53 FLRA 1703, 1710 (1998). In making that determination, the Authority defers to the arbitrator's underlying factual findings. *See id.*

Section 7121(d) provides:

> An aggrieved employee affected by a prohibited personnel practice under [§] 2302(b)(1) of this title which also falls under the coverage of the negotiated grievance procedure may raise the matter under a statutory procedure or the negotiated procedure, but not both. An employee shall be deemed to have exercised his option under this subsection to raise the matter under either a statutory procedure or the negotiated procedure at such time as the employee *timely* initiates an action under the applicable statutory procedure or timely files a grievance in writing, in accordance with the provisions of the parties' negotiated procedure, whichever event occurs first.

5 U.S.C. § 7121(d) (emphasis added).

The Authority has held that, in order for § 7121(d) to bar a grievance, two requirements must be met: (1) the matter that is the subject of the grievance must be the same matter that was the subject of the action initiated under the statutory procedure; and (2) "such matter must have been earlier raised by the employee *timely* initiating an action under the statutory procedure." *AFGE, Local 2145*, 61 FLRA 571, 573 (2006). *Accord U.S. DoJ, U.S. Marshals Serv.*, 23 FLRA 414, 416 (1986) (*Marshals Serv.*). *Cf. Verkennes v. Cheney*, EEOC Appeal No. 01913941 at 3 n.1 (Dec. 10, 1991) (untimely filed grievance would not bar formal EEO complaint on the same matter); *Frankl v. Kemp*, EEOC Appeal No. 05910261 (May 13, 1991) (*Frankl*) (same).

In addition, the Authority has held that the "timely initiation of an action" under statutory EEO procedures occurs with the "filing of a formal written complaint." *AFGE, AFL-CIO, Nat'l INS Council*, 27 FLRA 467, 469-70 (1987) (*INS Council*). *Accord Marshals Serv.*, 23 FLRA at 417-18. This is consistent with Equal Employment Opportunity Commission regulations and precedent. *See* 29 C.F.R. § 1614.301(a) (stating, in pertinent part, that "[a]n election to proceed under this part is indicated only by the filing of a written complaint; use of the pre-complaint process . . . does not constitute an election for purposes of this section[]"); *Frankl*, EEOC Appeal No. 05910261.

There is no dispute that the grievant's formal EEO complaint was untimely. Although the Agency claims that § 7121(d) bars the appeal because the grievant "timely *initiated* the EEO *action*" before he filed his EEO complaint, Opp'n at 11, as stated above, it is the filing of the formal EEO complaint -- not any informal, precomplaint actions -- that is relevant for purposes of interpreting § 7121(d). *See INS Council*, 27 FLRA at 469-70; *Marshals Serv.*, 23 FLRA at 417-18. Thus, the Agency's claim is misplaced. As there is no dispute that the grievant's formal EEO complaint was untimely, the above-cited precedent supports a conclusion that the EEO complaint did not bar the appeal under § 7121(d). Accordingly, we find that the Arbitrator erred in relying on § 7121(d) to find the appeal nonarbitrable, and we set aside the award.

Where an arbitrator incorrectly dismisses a grievance as nonarbitrable, the Authority remands the matter to the parties for submission, absent settlement, to an arbitrator of their choice. *See AFGE, Local 2823*, 64 FLRA 1144, 1147 (2010). Consistent with this principle, we remand this matter to the parties for submission, absent settlement, to an arbitrator of the parties' choice.

V. Decision

The award is set aside, and this matter is remanded to the parties for submission, absent settlement, to an arbitrator of their choice.

65 FLRA No. 189

NATIONAL TREASURY
EMPLOYEES UNION
CHAPTER 164
(Union)

and

UNITED STATES
DEPARTMENT OF HOMELAND SECURITY
U.S. CUSTOMS AND BORDER PROTECTION
OROVILLE, WASHINGTON
(Agency)

0-AR-4693

DECISION

June 8, 2011

Before the Authority: Carol Waller Pope, Chairman, and Thomas M. Beck and Ernest DuBester, Members

I. Statement of the Case

This matter is before the Authority on exceptions to a supplemental award of Arbitrator Jerry B. Sellman filed by the Union under § 7122(a) of the Federal Service Labor-Management Relations Statute (the Statute) and part 2425 of the Authority's Regulations. The Agency filed an opposition to the Union's exceptions.

The Arbitrator issued an award (the initial award) sustaining the Union's grievance in part and denying it in part. Subsequently, the parties filed with the Arbitrator a joint petition for clarification. The Arbitrator issued a supplemental award finding that the Agency's proposal regarding the proper starting time for the day shift was in compliance with the initial award and did not violate the parties' collective bargaining agreement (the agreement) or 5 U.S.C. § 6101(a)(3).

For the reasons discussed below, we dismiss in part and deny in part the Union's exceptions.

II. Background and Arbitrator's Award

A. Background

This matter concerns work performed by bargaining unit Customs and Border Protection (CBP) officers who conduct inspections at land ports. The officers rotate between large ports and smaller ports. Initial Award at 6, 8. Each large port provides staffing for an outlying smaller port, and together the two ports constitute a single work unit. The smaller ports operate on a single fixed day shift from 9:00 a.m. to 5:00 p.m., while the large ports operate three shifts, including a day shift beginning at 8:00 a.m. and ending at 4:00 p.m. *Id.* at 8; Supplemental Award at 2.

The Union filed a grievance alleging that the Agency violated the agreement's bid, rotation, and placement (BRP) provisions when it refused to allow CBP officers to express both a shift and a port preference. When the parties could not resolve the grievance, the matter was submitted to arbitration. Initial Award at 2.

In the initial award, the Arbitrator sustained the portion of the Union's grievance claiming that the Agency violated the agreement's BRP provisions when the Agency refused to allow CBP officers to indicate a shift preference within their work units. *Id.* at 28; Supplemental Award at 3. The Arbitrator, however, denied the portion of the Union's grievance claiming that the Agency violated the BRP by not allowing officers to bid separately on the ports within each work unit. *Id.* In his award, the Arbitrator ordered the Agency to allow CBP officers to express a preference for a shift within their work units. Initial Award at 28-29. As neither party filed an exception to the initial award, that award became final and binding.

In attempting to implement the initial award, the parties disagreed regarding the proper starting time for the day shift. Supplemental Award at 1. The Agency proposed a collective day shift. The Agency's proposed collective day shift would encompass both the 8:00 a.m. to 4:00 p.m. shift at the large port and the 9:00 a.m. to 5:00 p.m. shift at the smaller port. *Id.* at 2. The Union claimed that such a collective day shift was in violation of the initial award and that CBP officers should be able to choose either the 8:00 a.m. to 4:00 p.m. or the 9:00 a.m. to 5:00 p.m. shift. *Id.* When the parties could not reach agreement on this issue, they filed a petition for clarification with the Arbitrator.

In the petition for clarification, the Union argued that the Agency's collective day shift proposal was in violation of the initial award. Exceptions, Attach., Clarification Petition. In addition, the Union, citing 5 U.S.C. § 6101(a)(3)(A) and (C), claimed that the CBP officers were entitled to state a preference for either the 8:00 a.m. or the 9:00 a.m. shift so that they could work the same hours each day.[1] *Id.* at 1-2. The Agency countered that adopting the Union's position would create separate de facto work units at the smaller ports in violation of the initial award. *Id.* at 2. The Arbitrator addressed the parties' petition for clarification by issuing the supplemental award.

B. Arbitrator's Supplemental Award

The Arbitrator did not frame the issue before him in the supplemental award. However, the Arbitrator addressed whether the Agency's collective day shift proposal complied with the initial award, the agreement, and the provisions of 5 U.S.C. § 6101(a)(3). *See* Supplemental Award at 1-2, 5. In resolving this issue, the Arbitrator credited the Agency's argument that it was prohibited from changing the hours at the smaller ports because those hours were established in the *Federal Register*. *Id.* at 2. Consequently, the Arbitrator found, the Agency could not change the day shift hours at the smaller ports to comport with the day shift hours at the large ports. *Id.* Therefore, the Arbitrator concluded, CBP officers would have to begin the day shift either at 8:00 a.m. or 9:00 a.m., depending on the port to which they were assigned. *Id.* at 3-4. The Arbitrator further determined that this did not violate the agreement's BRP provisions because those provisions contemplated a staggered shift to address the operational requirements of this specific region. *Id.* Accordingly, the Arbitrator concluded, the Agency's collective day shift proposal complied with the initial award and the agreement. *Id.* at 4.

The Arbitrator then addressed the Union's argument that the Agency's collective day shift proposal violated 5 U.S.C. § 6101(a)(3)(A) and (C). The Arbitrator rejected this argument. In rejecting the Union's argument, the Arbitrator relied upon the statute's exception, which allows an agency to avoid the statutory scheduling requirements if the agency head determines that the agency "would be seriously handicapped in carrying out its functions or that costs would be substantially increased . . . ." *Id.* at 4-5. The Arbitrator found that the statutory scheduling requirements would seriously handicap the Agency's ability to carry out its functions because the Agency demonstrated that it created the staggered day shifts to address the traffic flow in each port and to "carry out the operation and mission requirements of the . . . Agency[,] in this specific region[.]" *Id.* Therefore, the Arbitrator concluded, the statutory exception applied and consequently, the Agency's collective day proposal shift did not violate 5 U.S.C. § 6101(a)(3). *Id.*

III. Positions of the Parties

A. Union's Exceptions

The Union argues that the supplemental award is contrary to law because it permits the Agency to implement the collective day shift proposal in violation of 5 U.S.C. § 6101(a)(3). Exceptions at 4. First, the Union argues that a collective day shift is inconsistent with § 6101(a)(3)(A) and (C)'s statutory scheduling requirements that require the Agency to give CBP officers seven-days advance notice of any hours they are scheduled to work within a workweek. *Id.*

Next, the Union argues that the Arbitrator erred when he found that the statutory exception to § 6101(a)(3)'s scheduling requirements applied in this case. Specifically, the Union claims, the Agency was required to prove that the statutory scheduling requirements would have acted as a serious handicap to the Agency's operations or substantially increased the cost of its operations. *Id.* at 4, 15-16. However, according to the Union, the Agency argued only that the statutory scheduling requirements affected its "operational needs." *Id.* at 10, 13. The Union asserts that the statutory exception would be meaningless if all an agency had to do was declare operational needs to qualify for the exception. *Id.* at 18. Therefore, the Union claims, the Arbitrator misconstrued the law when he accepted the Agency's declaration of "operational needs" as being sufficient to establish that the Agency qualified for the statutory exception.

1. Section 6101(a)(3) provides in pertinent part:

> Except when the head of an Executive agency[] . . . determines that his organization would be seriously handicapped in carrying out its functions or that costs would be substantially increased, he shall provide, with respect to each employee in his organization, that—
>
> (A) assignments to tours of duty are scheduled in advance over periods of not less than 1 week;
>
> . . . .
>
> (C) the working hours in each day in the basic workweek are the same . . . .

Id. Consequently, the Union argues, the supplemental award is contrary to law.

B. Agency's Opposition

As an initial matter, the Agency contends that the Union's exceptions are untimely and should be dismissed. Opp'n at 7. In this regard, the Agency asserts that the award was served on the parties on September 2, 2010, and therefore the Regulations in effect on September 2, 2010 applied. Consequently, the Agency argues, the Union's exceptions were due thirty days from the date the award was served, which was October 1, 2010. As the Union filed its exceptions on October 4, 2010, the Agency contends they should be dismissed. *Id.*

With respect to the merits, the Agency contends that the Union's exceptions raise issues that the Union did not raise before the Arbitrator. *Id.* at 5, 9-10. Specifically, the Agency claims that the Union never argued to the Arbitrator that the collective day shift proposal was not in compliance with the seven-day advance notice requirement set forth in 5 U.S.C. § 6101(a)(3)(A). The Agency also claims that the Union never argued before the Arbitrator that the Agency failed to qualify for the statutory exception. *Id.* at 9-10. The Agency further contends that the Union has not produced any evidence that the Agency has failed to comply with the seven-day advance notice requirement. *Id.* at 5, 9-10. Rather, the Agency claims, the Union's exceptions are based on speculation that, at some unknown time in the future, the Agency may inconsistently schedule employees in violation of § 6101(a)(3)(A) and (C). *Id.* at 11. Such speculation, the Agency argues, cannot be construed as support for the Union's exceptions. *Id.*

Moreover, the Agency argues, the Arbitrator correctly found that the statutory exception to 5 U.S.C. § 6101(a)(3) applies here. Specifically, the Agency claims, it sufficiently demonstrated that staggered shift times are necessary to address the traffic flow of the Agency's operations in this region. *Id.* at 9. Therefore, the Agency argues, the collective day shift proposal is in compliance with both the agreement's BRP provisions and § 6101(a)(3).

IV. Preliminary Issue

The Authority ordered the Union to show cause why its exceptions should not be dismissed as untimely. Order to Show Cause at 1. Section 7122(b) of the Statute requires that exceptions be filed within thirty days from the date of service of the award. 5 U.S.C. § 7122(b). Under the Authority's revised Regulations, the thirty-day period for filing exceptions begins to run the day after the date of service of the award. *See* 5 C.F.R. § 2425.2(b).[2]

In response to the Order, the Union provided documentation showing that the award was served on the parties by e-mail on September 2, 2010. Because the exceptions were filed after the date that the new Regulations went into effect, pursuant to 5 C.F.R. § 2425.2(b), the first day of the filing period began on September 3, 2010, the day after the award was served on the parties. As the thirtieth day fell on Saturday, October 2, 2010, the Union was required to file its exceptions by the following Monday, which was October 4, 2010. *See* 5 C.F.R. § 2429.21(a). The Union filed its exceptions on Monday, October 4, 2010. Accordingly, we find that the exceptions are timely.

V. Analysis and Conclusions

Under § 2429.5 of the Authority's Regulations, the Authority will not consider arguments that could have been, but were not, presented to the arbitrator.[3] *See, e.g., U.S. Dep't of Transp., FAA*, 64 FLRA 387, 389-90 (2010) (*FAA*) (agency could not argue for first time in its exceptions that law limited arbitrator's authority). Where a party makes an argument for the first time on exception that it could, and should, have made before the arbitrator, the Authority applies § 2429.5 to bar the argument. *See, e.g., U.S. Dep't of Justice, Fed. Bureau of Prisons, USP Admin. Maximum (ADX), Florence, Colo.*, 64 FLRA 1168, 1170 (2010) (agency exception barred by § 2429.5 where agency failed to argue before arbitrator that union's requested relief was contrary to law); *U.S. Dep't of the Air Force, Warner Robins Air Logistics Ctr., Robins Air Force Base, Ga.*, 56 FLRA 498, 502 (2000) (agency exception barred by § 2429.5 where agency failed to argue

2. The Authority's Regulations concerning the review of arbitration awards, as well as certain related procedural Regulations, including §§ 2425.2 and 2429.21, were revised effective October 1, 2010. *See* 75 Fed. Reg. 42,283 (2010). Because the Union's exceptions were filed after this date, we apply the revised Regulations here. *See* 5 C.F.R. § 2425.1.

3. Section 2429.5 was also amended effective October 1, 2010. As discussed in note 2, because the Union's exceptions were filed after this date, we apply the revised Regulations here. In addition, we note that the revised version of § 2429.5 "merely incorporates into regulation" the Authority's practice under the prior version of § 2429.5. 75 Fed. Reg. 42,283, 42,289 (2010).

before the arbitrator that requested relief violated agency's management rights).

In the supplemental award, the Arbitrator determined that the Agency's collective day shift proposal was in compliance with the initial award, the agreement, and 5 U.S.C. § 6101(a)(3). Supplemental Award at 4-5. In reaching this conclusion, the Arbitrator found that the statutory exception to the scheduling requirements applied. *Id.*

The Union's primary exception to the supplemental award is that the Arbitrator misconstrued § 6101(a)(3)'s statutory exception when he applied it in this case. However, there is no indication in the record that the Union argued before the Arbitrator, as it does here, that the single statutory exception set forth in § 6101(a)(3) does not apply, even though the Union had the opportunity to do so. The Union cited § 6101(a)(3) in the clarification petition. Specifically, the Union cited subparts (A) and (C) of § 6101(a)(3) as support for its position that the Agency's collective day shift proposal violates both § 6101(a)(3) and the initial award.[4] Exceptions, Attach., Clarification Petition at 1-2. Therefore, the Union was sufficiently aware of § 6101(a)(3)'s provisions to have been able to make the corollary argument that § 6101(a)(3)'s single statutory exception is inapplicable to the facts of this case. Because the Union did not present an argument to the Arbitrator that the statutory exception does not apply, we find that § 2429.5 bars the Union from raising it before the Authority. Consequently, we dismiss the exception.[5]

VI. Decision

The Union's exceptions are dismissed in part and denied in part.

---

4. 5 U.S.C. § 6101(a)(3), including subparts (A) and (C), is set forth *supra* note 1.

5. As set forth above, we dismiss the Union's exception that the Arbitrator erred in finding that the statutory exception to § 6101(a)(3) applies. Therefore, the Union's arguments based on the remainder of § 6101(a)(3) cannot provide a basis for finding the award deficient. Accordingly, we deny that exception.

65 FLRA No. 190

SOCIAL SECURITY ADMINISTRATION
(Agency)

and

AMERICAN FEDERATION
OF GOVERNMENT EMPLOYEES
LOCAL 3239
(Union)

0-AR-4673

DECISION

June 13, 2011

Before the Authority: Carol Waller Pope, Chairman, and Thomas M. Beck and Ernest DuBester, Members

I. Statement of the Case

This matter is before the Authority on exceptions to an award of Arbitrator Richard D. Kimbel filed by the Agency under § 7122(a) of the Federal Service Labor-Management Relations Statute (the Statute) and part 2425 of the Authority's Regulations.

The Arbitrator determined that the Agency did not have just cause to suspend the grievant for three days, and mitigated the suspension to a written reprimand. For the reasons that follow, we dismiss the Agency's exceptions in part and deny them in part.

II. Background and Arbitrator's Award

The Agency suspended the grievant for three days for "inappropriate and discourteous behavior toward a manager, and disruption of the workplace[.]" Award at 2. The Union filed a grievance, which was unresolved and was submitted to arbitration. The Arbitrator stated the issues as follows:[1] "Was the three[-]day suspension of the [g]rievant for [j]ust [c]ause? If not[,] what shall be the remedy?" *Id.* at 3. The Arbitrator stated that the Agency had the burden of proving that the suspension was for just cause, which would require showing that: (1) the grievant "violate[d] an Agency rule or policy which warrants discipline[;]" and (2) the "discipline imposed is reasonable under the circumstances[.]" *Id.* The Arbitrator found that the first requirement was met because there was "no doubt . . . that the [g]rievant engaged in behavior in breach of the [parties' agreement]." *Id.* at 4.

In regard to the requirement that the discipline imposed be reasonable, the Arbitrator considered "mitigating circumstances." *Id.* In this regard, the Arbitrator credited "un-rebutted" testimony that the grievant's inappropriate behavior was "out of character[,]" *id.* at 5, and found that the grievant had a "long federal service record of over [twenty-two] years, a good overall work record, and . . . no prior discipline record[,]" *id.* at 6. Further, the Arbitrator cited Article 23, Section 1 of the parties' agreement (Article 23), which states that the "parties agree to the concept of progressive discipline[,]" *id.* at 5, but that the Agency may bypass steps of progressive discipline where it "determines by the *severe nature* of the behavior that a lesser form of discipline would not be appropriate[,]" *id.* at 6 (Arbitrator's emphasis). In this connection, the Arbitrator found that "there was a work disruption" resulting from the grievant's interaction with her supervisor, but that it was not "the degree of disruption that the Agency tried to portray." *Id.* at 5. The Arbitrator concluded that, under the circumstances, the Agency "*failed to meet its burden* of proving that the [g]rievant[']s behavior was *so severe* that it warranted the bypassing of a written reprimand." *Id.* at 6. Thus, the Arbitrator concluded that the three-day suspension was not reasonable under the circumstances and that, as a result, the second requirement for finding just cause was not met. *Id.* Accordingly, he directed the Agency to mitigate the suspension to a written reprimand, and awarded the grievant backpay. *Id.*

III. Agency's Exceptions[2]

The Agency argues that the mitigation of the suspension violates management's right to discipline employees under § 7106(a)(2)(A) of the Statute. Exceptions at 6-7. In addition, the Agency argues that the award fails to draw its essence from the parties' agreement because the mitigation reflects a "manifest disregard" of the Agency's right, under Article 23, to "bypass the earlier steps of progressive discipline where it determines that misconduct is so severe that lesser penalties would not be appropriate." *Id.* at 8. In this regard, the Agency asserts that the circumstances, including the

1. It is unclear from the record whether the parties stipulated the issues.

2. The Union did not file an opposition.

grievant's prior receipt of an oral warning, did not warrant the mitigation. *Id.* at 9-10. For support, the Agency cites: *SSA*, 64 FLRA 1119 (2010) (*SSA*) (Chairman Pope dissenting; Member DuBester concurring); *SSA, St. Paul, Minn.*, 61 FLRA 92, 93-94 (*St. Paul*) (then-Member Pope dissenting), *recons. denied*, 61 FLRA 256 (2005), *overruled by SSA*, 65 FLRA 286, 288-89 (2010) (*SSA II*); and *AFGE, Local 3342*, 58 FLRA 448, 449-50 (2003) (*Local 3342*). Exceptions at 8-9.[3]

IV. Analysis and Conclusions

A. Preliminary Issue: Whether § 2429.5 of the Authority's Regulations (§ 2429.5) bars the Agency's exception regarding management's right to discipline under § 7106(a)(2)(A) of the Statute.

The Authority's Regulations that were in effect when the Agency filed its exceptions provided that "[t]he Authority will not consider . . . any issue, which was not presented in the proceedings before the . . . arbitrator." 5 C.F.R. § 2429.5.[4] Under § 2429.5, the Authority will not consider an issue that could have been, but was not, presented to the arbitrator. *See, e.g., U.S. DOJ, Fed. Bureau of Prisons, Fed. Corr. Complex, Coleman, Fla.*, 65 FLRA 730, 731-32 (2011) (*DOJ*).

Here, the issues before the Arbitrator included whether the Agency's three-day suspension of the grievant was for just cause and the Arbitrator found, and the Agency concedes, that the just cause determination included the question of whether the penalty assessed was appropriate. *See* Award at 3; Exceptions at 3. Thus, the Agency could have argued to the Arbitrator that mitigating the Agency's chosen penalty would conflict with management's right to discipline. There is no indication in the record that the Agency did so. Accordingly, we dismiss this exception as barred by § 2429.5. *See, e.g., DOJ*, 65 FLRA at 731-32.

B. Whether the award fails to draw its essence from the parties' agreement.

In reviewing an arbitrator's interpretation of a collective bargaining agreement, the Authority applies the deferential standard of review that federal courts use in reviewing arbitration awards in the private sector. *See* 5 U.S.C. § 7122(a)(2); *AFGE, Council 220*, 54 FLRA 156, 159 (1998). Under this standard, the Authority will find that an arbitration award is deficient as failing to draw its essence from the collective bargaining agreement when the appealing party establishes that the award: (1) cannot in any rational way be derived from the agreement; (2) is so unfounded in reason and fact and so unconnected with the wording and purposes of the collective bargaining agreement as to manifest an infidelity to the obligation of the arbitrator; (3) does not represent a plausible interpretation of the agreement; or (4) evidences a manifest disregard of the agreement. *See U.S. Dep't of Labor (OSHA)*, 34 FLRA 573, 575 (1990). The Authority and the courts defer to arbitrators in this context because it is the arbitrator's construction of the agreement for which the parties have bargained. *Id.* at 576.

Article 23 provides, in pertinent part, that "[a] common pattern of progressive discipline is reprimand [followed by] short[-]term suspension," but that "[a]ny of the[] steps [of progressive discipline] may be bypassed where management determines by the severe nature of the behavior that a lesser form of discipline would not be appropriate." Exceptions, Attach. B (CBA) at 23-1. The Arbitrator found that the Agency had not demonstrated that the grievant's behavior was "*so severe* that it warranted the bypassing of a written reprimand[,]" Award at 6, and the Agency provides no basis for finding that the Arbitrator erred in this regard. In addition, although the Agency asserts that the grievant received an "oral warning" prior to the incident for which she was suspended, Exceptions at 10, Article 23 provides that "oral warnings . . . are informal in nature and not recorded[,]" CBA at 23-1. Thus, there is no basis for finding that an oral warning constitutes discipline or required the Arbitrator to find that the Agency was permitted to bypass the reprimand step of progressive discipline.

Further, the decisions relied upon by the Agency do not demonstrate that the award fails to draw its essence from the parties' agreement. In *SSA*, the Authority set aside an award where the arbitrator found just cause for discipline, but nonetheless mitigated a suspension. 64 FLRA at 1121-22. By contrast, here, the Arbitrator found that the Agency

---

3. We note that the Agency also cites an arbitration award. *See* Exceptions at 10 (citing *Dep't of Transp., FAA*, 98 F.L.R.R. 2-1112 (June 11, 1998)). However, as arbitration awards are not precedential, *see, e.g., U.S. Dep't of Homeland Sec., Customs & Border Prot.*, 63 FLRA 495, 499 (2009), we do not address this citation further.

4. The Authority's Regulations concerning the review of arbitration awards, as well as certain related procedural Regulations, including § 2429.5, were revised effective October 1, 2010. *See* 75 Fed. Reg. 42,283 (2010). As the Agency's exceptions were filed before that date, we apply the prior Regulations.

did *not* have just cause to suspend the grievant. Award at 6. In addition, the Agency's reliance on *St. Paul*, which also involved Article 23, is misplaced because the Authority overturned that decision in *SSA II*, 65 FLRA at 288-89. Finally, in *Local 3342*, the Authority denied an essence exception to an arbitrator's finding that the agency had established that an employee's misconduct warranted bypassing progressive discipline steps. 58 FLRA at 450. However, as discussed above, the Arbitrator here found that the Agency had *not* demonstrated that the grievant's misconduct warranted bypassing a written reprimand. Award at 6.

For the reasons stated above, the Agency provides no basis for finding that the Arbitrator's interpretation of Article 23 is irrational, unfounded, implausible, or in manifest disregard of the parties' agreement. Accordingly, we deny this exception.

V. Decision

The Agency's contrary-to-law exception is dismissed, and its essence exception is denied.

65 FLRA No. 191

UNITED STATES
DEPARTMENT OF THE AIR FORCE
AIR FORCE MATERIEL COMMAND
EGLIN AIR FORCE BASE, FLORIDA
(Agency)

and

AMERICAN FEDERATION
OF GOVERNMENT EMPLOYEES
LOCAL 1897
(Union)

0-AR-4716

DECISION

June 13, 2011

Before the Authority: Carol Waller Pope, Chairman, and Thomas M. Beck and Ernest DuBester, Members

I. Statement of the Case

This matter is before the Authority on exceptions to an award of Arbitrator Patricia S. Plant filed by the Agency under § 7122(a) of the Federal Service Labor-Management Relations Statute (the Statute) and part 2425 of the Authority's Regulations. The Union filed an opposition to the Agency's exceptions.

The Arbitrator found that the Agency failed to pay employees for time spent on standby duty (standby). For the reasons discussed below, we set aside the award.

II. Background and Arbitrator's Award

Prior to the onset of Hurricane Ida, *see* Award at 17-18, the Agency sent an e-mail to security personnel (Agency e-mail), notifying them that they were being placed on "[Six]-Ring Stand-By[,]" i.e., they were required to "answer [the] phone within [six] [r]ing[s] to receive instructions[.]" *Id.* at 17. The e-mail also stated that security personnel were to: (1) "be contactable at all time"; (2) have an "alternate number where your unit can reach you during a recall"; (3) refrain from going "hunting, camping or out of town"; (4) know that "even having a cell phone with you is no guarantee of contactability"; and (5) refrain from consuming alcohol. *Id.* The next day, the Agency issued a directive stating that certain employees would "[r]emain on [one]-hour standby after [the] hurricane passes, for possible [twenty-four] hour emergency recovery operations." *Id.* at 18. Approximately three weeks later, the Agency directed supervisors to "inform . . . personnel that we are no longer on six ring standby." *Id.*

The Union filed a grievance alleging that the Agency violated Article 36.03 of the parties' agreement (Article 36.03),[1] and 5 C.F.R. § 551.431 (§ 551.431),[2] by failing to pay security personnel for time spent on standby. *See id.* The matter was unresolved and was submitted to arbitration. *Id.*

An arbitration hearing was held. After the hearing, but before the issuance of the award, the Arbitrator e-mailed the Agency's attorney, asking her to "kindly check on the status of [the Arbitrator's] invoice[.]" Exceptions, Attach. 6 at 12-13. The Arbitrator and the Agency exchanged additional e-mails on this subject over the next two weeks. *See id.* at 4-13. Subsequently, the Arbitrator sent an e-mail to the Agency (Arbitrator's e-mail), where she stated: "[y]our finance office is at fault, less than thorough and totally responsible for the delay in my receiving my funds[;]" and "[y]our finance department has screwed me over for the last time." *Id.* at 4.

---

1. Article 36.03, entitled "STANDBY TIME[,]" states:

> Designated employees may be restricted to the official duty station or their living quarters, required to remain in a state of readiness to perform work, and have their activities substantially limited such that they cannot use the time effectively for their own purposes. In these situations, all time spent on standby is considered hours of work.

Award at 65.

2. As relevant here, § 551.431 pertains to time on standby that is considered hours of work for overtime pay purposes. *See U.S. Dep't of Transp., FAA*, 61 FLRA 750, 752 (2006). Section 551.431 states, in pertinent part:

> (a)(1) An employee is on duty, and time spent on standby duty is hours of work if, for work-related reasons, the employee is restricted by official order to a designated post of duty and is assigned to be in a state of readiness to perform work with limitations on the employee's activities so substantial that the employee cannot use the time effectively for his or her own purposes.

In her award, the Arbitrator did not define the issues before her, but noted how each party stated the issues to be resolved.[3] *See id.* at 18-19. According to the Union, the issues to be resolved were whether the Agency willfully violated the Fair Labor Standards Act (FLSA), related regulations, and the parties' agreement, when it "failed to pay [e]mployees [s]tandby [p]ay[.]"[4] *Id.* at 18. According to the Agency, the issues to be resolved were whether security personnel were "placed on standby as defined by [the parties' agreement]" and § 551.431, and, if so, whether a remedy of backpay was appropriate. *Id.* at 19.

The Arbitrator, citing Article 36.03, stated that the parties "mutually agreed as to the definition of [s]tandby time[,]" and emphasized that there was nothing "ambiguous . . . in what the [parties] set out as their agreed upon understand[ing] of the term 'standby.'" *Id.* at 65. The Arbitrator added that the Agency's head of security personnel used the "standby term" in the Agency e-mail. *Id.* at 69. The Arbitrator sustained the grievance and awarded backpay, liquidated damages, and attorney fees, pursuant to the FLSA and § 551.431(a)(1). *Id.* at 70. Additionally, as relevant here, the Arbitrator made comments that were critical of the Agency and some of its witnesses. *See id.* at 58, 61, 64, & 69.

III. Positions of the Parties

A. Agency's Exceptions

The Agency asserts that the award is contrary to § 551.431 because security personnel were not on standby during the period for which the Arbitrator ordered standby pay. *See* Exceptions at 9-10. In this regard, the Agency argues that security personnel were "not restricted to a designated post of duty, . . . assigned to be in a state of readiness to perform work, []or substantially limited in the use of their time." *Id.* at 10. Additionally, the Agency argues that the statements in the Arbitrator's e-mail, and the comments in the Arbitrator's award criticizing the Agency and some of its witnesses, indicate that the Arbitrator was biased. *See id.* at 15-16.

B. Union's Opposition

The Union maintains that the award is consistent with § 551.431. *See* Opp'n at 5 & n.6. In this connection, the Union argues that security personnel were on standby because they were: (1) "'restricted by official order;'" (2) directed to be in a state of readiness; and (3) substantially limited in their activities. *Id.* at 5 n.6 (quoting § 551.431). With regard to the "restricted" criterion, the Union asserts that the Agency e-mail was "viewed" by security personnel as an "official order to remain by the phone at home[,]" *id.* at 6, and that the Agency e-mail "effectively limited people to work and home[,]" *id.* at 11 n.10. The Union adds that "limit[ing] people to work and home" is "one of the elements related to standby pay - restricted by official order to a designated post of duty/living quarters[.]" *Id.* (citing § 551.431). Additionally, the Union argues that 5 C.F.R. § 2429.5 (§ 2429.5)[5] bars the Agency's bias claim, *see id.* at 13, and that, in any event, the Arbitrator was not biased, *see id.* at 14.

IV. Analysis and Conclusions

In reviewing arbitration awards for consistency with law, rule, or regulation, the Authority reviews questions of law raised by exceptions to an arbitrator's award de novo. *NTEU, Chapter 24*, 50 FLRA 330, 332 (1995) (citing *U.S. Customs Serv. v. FLRA*, 43 F.3d 682, 686-87 (D.C. Cir. 1994)). In applying the standard of de novo review, the Authority determines whether the arbitrator's legal conclusions are consistent with the applicable standard of law. *See NFFE, Local 1437*, 53 FLRA 1703, 1710 (1998). In making that determination, the Authority defers to the arbitrator's underlying factual findings. *See id.*

Section 551.431 states, in pertinent part, that "[a]n employee is on duty, and time spent on standby duty is hours of work if, for work-related reasons, the employee is restricted by official order to a designated post of duty[.]" 5 C.F.R. § 551.431. That is, an employee must be restricted to a "designated post of duty" in order to be on standby under § 551.431. *Id.* Unlike the former version of

3. In her award, the Arbitrator also resolved a procedural matter. *See* Award at 7, 12-17. As no exceptions were filed regarding that matter, we do not address it further.

4. The FLSA provides for the federal minimum standards for wages and overtime. 29 U.S.C. §§ 201-219. 5 C.F.R. Part 551 sets forth the regulations implementing the FLSA in the federal sector. *AFGE, Council 220*, 65 FLRA 596, 597 n.2 (2011).

5. Under 5 C.F.R. § 2429.5, the Authority will not consider "any evidence, factual assertions, arguments (including affirmative defenses), requested remedies, or challenges to an awarded remedy that could have been, but were not, presented in the proceedings before the . . . arbitrator." 5 C.F.R. § 2429.5.

§ 551.431[6] (which was not in effect at any times relevant here), *see* 5 C.F.R. § 551.431 (1999), and unlike Article 36.03, which uses wording similar to the wording in the former version of § 551.431, *see* Award at 65, the current version of § 551.431 does not provide that an employee may be on standby if restricted to his or her "living quarters." *See* 5 C.F.R. § 551.431. As such, the fact that security personnel were restricted to their homes, i.e., their living quarters, does not indicate that security personnel were on standby, as the Union argues. *See* Opp'n at 6, 11 n.10.

The Arbitrator found that security personnel were on standby without finding that security personnel were restricted to a designated post of duty, as required under § 551.431. *See* 5 C.F.R. § 551.431. *Cf. U.S. Dep't of Commerce, Nat'l Oceanic & Atmospheric Admin., Office of NOAA Corps Operations, Atl. Marine Ctr., Norfolk, Va.*, 55 FLRA 816, 820-21 (1999) (Chair Segal concurring; Member Wasserman dissenting) (arbitrator expressly found that grievants were restricted to a designated post of duty). Further, with regard to the Union's argument that the Agency restricted security personnel to their homes and were therefore on standby, the Arbitrator did not find, *see* Award at 65, 69, and there is no claim, *see* Opp'n at 5 & n.6, 6-7, 11 n.10, that security personnel's homes constitute a "designated post of duty" under § 551.431. Accordingly, we find that the Arbitrator's conclusion that security personnel were on standby is contrary to § 551.431.

With regard to the Arbitrator's reliance on Article 36.03, the Authority has held that parties may not negotiate over proposals that would entitle employees to standby pay unless such pay would be consistent with the requirements of § 551.431. *U.S. Dep't of Homeland Sec., U.S. Customs & Border Prot., Dall., Tex.*, 64 FLRA 603, 605 (2010) (*DHS*). As Article 36.03 permits standby pay to be granted to an employee who is restricted to his or her "living quarters" without regard to whether the employee is restricted to a "designated post of duty," *see* Award at 65, Article 36.03 is not consistent with the requirements of § 551.431 and, thus, cannot provide a basis for the Arbitrator's award of standby pay. *See DHS*, 64 FLRA at 605. *See also Soc. Sec. Admin., Office of Disability Adjudication & Review*, 64 FLRA 1000, 1002 n.5 (2010) (insofar as an arbitrator's award construes an agreement contrary to a government-wide regulation, the award is unenforceable).

For the forgoing reasons, we set aside the award as contrary to § 551.431. Consequently, we find that it is unnecessary to resolve the Agency's bias exception. *Cf. U.S. Dep't of Transp., FAA, Nashua, N.H.*, 65 FLRA 447, 450 n.3 (2011) (finding it unnecessary to address excepting party's remaining exceptions).

V. Decision

The award is set aside.

6. The Office of Personnel Management issued the revised version of § 551.431 in 1999, which became effective January 20, 2000. *See* 64 Fed. Reg. 69,165, 69,167, 69,180 (December 10, 1999). The former version of § 551.431 stated, in pertinent part:

> (a) An employee will be considered on duty and time spent on standby duty shall be considered hours of work if:
>
> . . . .
>
> (2) The employee, although not restricted to the agency's premises:
> (i) Is restricted to his or her *living quarters* or designated post of duty;
> (ii) Has his or her activities substantially limited; and
> (iii) Is required to remain in a state of readiness to perform work.

5 C.F.R. § 551.431 (1999) (emphasis added).

65 FLRA No. 192

AMERICAN FEDERATION
OF GOVERNMENT EMPLOYEES
LOCAL 1547
(Union)

and

UNITED STATES
DEPARTMENT OF THE AIR FORCE
LUKE AIR FORCE BASE, ARIZONA
(Agency)

0-NG-2924

DECISION AND ORDER
ON NEGOTIABILITY ISSUES

June 15, 2011

Before the Authority: Carol Waller Pope, Chairman, and Thomas M. Beck and Ernest DuBester, Members[1]

I. Statement of the Case

This case is before the Authority on a negotiability appeal filed by the Union under § 7105(a)(2)(E) of the Federal Service Labor-Management Relations Statute (the Statute). The appeal involves the negotiability of three proposals. The Agency filed a statement of position (SOP), to which the Union filed a response (response). The Agency did not file a reply to the Union's response.

For the reasons that follow, we find that Proposals 1 and 2 are within the duty to bargain, and that Proposal 9 is outside the duty to bargain.

II. Background

The Agency implemented several initiatives to reduce personnel. One of these initiatives was the Air Force Program Budget Decision 720 (PBD). The Union's proposals address aspects of the reduction-in-force (RIF) process contained in the PBD.

1. Member Beck's separate opinion, dissenting in part, is set forth at the end of this decision.

III. Proposal 1

A. Wording

> When the [e]mployer determines that a [c]ompetitive [s]ervice employee will be displaced by RIF, through Mock RIF[2] or otherwise, the [e]mployer will cross-reference all of the displaced [c]ompetitive [s]ervice employees['] experience brief job series with the job series held by the [e]mployer. If a position encumbered by a probationary [e]xcepted [s]ervice employee matches, in accordance with 5 CFR § 6.3, the [e]mployer will change the probationary employee's position to a "[t]erm" that will expire prior to the effective day of the applicable RIF, providing the [c]ompetitive [s]ervice employee has a higher Service Computation Date [(SCD)] than the probationary employee; the final RIF Retention Register [(RIF RR)] will include those vacated positions. These processes do not include temporary student positions identified in 5 CFR § 213.3202 and 5 CFR § 213.3102.

Petition at 3-4.

B. Meaning

As explained by the Union, Proposal 1 intends to lessen the adverse impact of a RIF on bargaining unit employees. Petition at 4. According to the Union, Proposal 1 would make more positions available for bump and retreat[3] for competitive service bargaining unit employees by converting appointments held by probationary excepted service Veterans Recruitment Appointments (VRAs)[4] to term appointments whose

2. A Mock RIF is a RIF retention register that is prepared before the actual RIF. Its function is to identify the names of potentially affected employees and provide those employees advance notice for early registration with the Agency's Priority Placement Plan and other available programs. Union's Petition (Petition) at 4.

3. "Bump and retreat" describes the process whereby employees released from their competitive levels displace employees with lower retention standings. This process is set forth in 5 C.F.R. § 351.701.

4. VRA appointments are excepted service appointments, made without competition, to positions otherwise in the competitive service. *See* 5 C.F.R. § 307.103. Upon completion of a two-year probationary period, these

terms would expire prior to the effective date of the RIF. Response at 2; *see also* Record of Post-Petition Conference (Record) at 2. As the proposal further explains, "those vacated positions" would then be included with other available positions under the RIF retention register. Petition at 3-4. As the Union's explanation of Proposal 1's meaning is not inconsistent with its plain wording, we adopt it for purposes of determining Proposal 1's negotiability. *E.g., NATCA*, 64 FLRA 161, 162 (2009).

C. Positions of the Parties

1. Agency

The Agency argues that Proposal 1 dictates procedures that are contrary to government-wide regulations governing RIFs. SOP at 2, 5. Specifically, the Agency argues that Proposal 1 is contrary to 5 C.F.R. § 351.201(a)(2) and (c), which concern RIFs generally; 5 C.F.R. §§ 351.403 and 404, which provide for the establishment of competitive levels and retention registers; and 5 C.F.R. §§ 351.501 and 502, which concern the order of retention in the competitive and excepted service, respectively.[5] *Id.* at 2, 9.

In addition, the Agency argues that Proposal 1 is contrary to 5 C.F.R. §§ 316.301 and 401, which are government-wide regulations governing term employment. *Id.* at 9. Furthermore, the Agency claims that VRA appointments are covered under 5 C.F.R. § 213[6] and that it cannot convert appointments occupied by excepted service VRA appointees to term appointments under 5 C.F.R. § 6.3. *Id.* at 8. The Agency also asserts that Proposal 1 interferes with management's right to assign employees under § 7106(a)(2)(A) because it requires that management reassign probationary excepted service employees to term positions that will expire prior to the effective date of the RIF. *Id.* at 2. In addition, the Agency argues that Proposal 1 would require the Agency to take specific personnel actions prior to conducting a RIF and that this would interfere with management's right to layoff employees under 5 U.S.C. § 7106(a). *Id.* The Agency further contends that Proposal 1 is not an appropriate arrangement under § 7106(b)(3) of the Statute. *Id.* at 2, 5.

2. Union

The Union asserts that Proposal 1 is not contrary to the RIF regulations because it does not dictate RIF procedures. Response at 1-2. The Union claims that the Agency has discretion to implement Proposal 1 because, under 5 C.F.R. § 6.3, it may change apppointments occupied by excepted service employees to term appointments. *Id.* at 2. The Union also argues that Proposal 1 does not interfere with management's rights to assign or layoff employees under 5 U.S.C. § 7106(a). Response at 1. The Union asserts that Proposal 1 would minimize the adverse impact of a RIF on bargaining unit employees. *Id.* at 2; Petition at 4.

D. Analysis and Conclusions

1. Proposal 1 is not inconsistent with the RIF regulations.

The Agency argues that Proposal 1 is contrary to 5 C.F.R. § 351.201(a)(2) and (c), which concern RIFs generally; 5 C.F.R. §§ 351.403 and 404, which provide for the establishment of competitive levels and retention registers; and 5 C.F.R. §§ 351.501 and 502, which concern the order of retention in the competitive and excepted service, respectively. SOP at 2, 9.

The Authority has found proposals requiring agencies to take certain personnel actions *prior* to conducting a RIF consistent with the RIF regulations in dispute here. *See, e.g., NAGE, Local R4-45*, 54 FLRA 218, 227 (1998) (proposal requiring that employees with lowest retention standing for their competitive level be reassigned thirty days prior to issuance of a RIF notice was not inconsistent with RIF regulations). Proposal 1 requires the conversion of appointments held by probationary VRA excepted service employees to term appointments, but only when the Agency determines -- through a mock RIF prior to conducting a RIF -- that a competitive service employee in the same job series as the probationary employee will be displaced in the actual RIF. As the actions required by Proposal 1 would occur *prior* to conducting a RIF, we find that Proposal 1 is not

positions automatically convert to competitive service positions. *See id.*

5. All relevant regulations are set forth, in pertinent part, in the appendix to this decision.

6. The Agency's references to 5 C.F.R. § 213 appear to be references to 5 C.F.R. Part 213, which generally regulates the excepted service. Excepted service positions include all positions in the executive branch of the federal government that are specifically excepted from the competitive service by or pursuant to statute, by the President, or by the Office of Personnel Management, and that are not in the Senior Executive Service.

inconsistent with the above referenced government-wide RIF regulations.

2. Proposal 1 is not inconsistent with 5 C.F.R. §§ 316.301 and 401, or with 5 C.F.R. § 6.3.

The Agency also claims that Proposal 1 is contrary to 5 C.F.R. §§ 316.301 and 401, which are government-wide regulations governing term employment. However, the Agency fails to explain the basis for its claim. Other than stating what the regulations provide, the Agency fails to make any claims based on the regulations. Under § 2424.32(b) of the Authority's Regulation, agencies have the burden of "raising and supporting arguments that the proposal . . . is outside the duty to bargain[.]" 5 C.F.R. § 2424.32(b). In the absence of any argument in support of its claim that the proposal is contrary to the cited regulations, the Agency's argument constitutes an unsupported assertion that is insufficient to establish that the proposal is outside the duty to bargain. *See* 5 C.F.R. § 2424.32(b); *AFGE, Local 3584, Council of Prison Locals C-33*, 64 FLRA 316, 317 (2009) (*Local 3584*). Consequently, we dismiss this claim as it is unsupported.

In addition, the Agency claims that it cannot convert appointments occupied by VRA excepted service appointees to term appointments under the discretion authorized by 5 C.F.R. § 6.3. SOP at 8. The Agency again fails to provide any arguments to support the basis for its claim. For the reasons stated above, the Agency's claim constitutes an unsupported assertion, and therefore it does not demonstrate that the proposal is outside the duty to bargain. 5 C.F.R. § 2424.32(b); *Local 3584*, 64 FLRA at 317. Consequently, we also dismiss this claim as it is unsupported.

3. Proposal 1 does not affect management's rights to assign and layoff employees under § 7106(a)(2)(A) of the Statute.[7]

The Agency argues that Proposal 1 interferes with management's right to assign employees under § 7106(a)(2)(A) because it requires that management reassign probationary excepted service employees to term positions. SOP at 2. The Agency also argues that Proposal 1's requirement that the Agency take specific personnel actions prior to conducting a RIF interferes with its management right to layoff employees under § 7106(a)(2)(A). *Id.*

Management's right to assign employees under § 7106(a)(2)(A) of the Statute includes the right to make initial assignments to positions, to reassign employees to different positions, and to make temporary assignments or details. *See NATCA*, 64 FLRA at 165. Proposal 1 does not affect management's right to assign employees because it does not require the assignment or reassignment of employees to any position. Proposal 1 only requires that when certain conditions are met, management will convert VRA appointments with a two-year probationary term to appointments with a term of less than two years. Proposal 1 does not affect what position the employee occupies. In this regard, under Proposal 1, a converted VRA employee would remain in the same position. Consequently, as Proposal 1 does not require the reassignment of employees, Proposal 1 does not affect management's right to assign employees under § 7106(a)(2)(A).

Management's right to layoff employees under § 7106(a)(2)(A) of the Statute includes the right to conduct a RIF and to exercise discretion in determining which positions will be abolished and which retained. *See, e.g., NTEU*, 60 FLRA 219, 222 (2004). Proposal 1 does not involve determining which positions will be abolished and which retained in a RIF. The proposal only operates "[w]hen the [e]mployer determines that a [c]ompetitive service

7. The Agency makes a general claim that, to the extent that any proposal in this case concerns a permissive subject of bargaining under § 7106(b)(1), it has elected not to bargain. SOP at 9-10. However, the Agency does not explain how any of the proposals constitute a permissive subject of bargaining under § 7106(b)(1). Accordingly, to the extent the Agency is claiming that any of the Union's proposals concerns a permissive subject of bargaining under § 7106(b)(1), we reject the Agency's claim as bare assertion. *See* 5 C.F.R. § 2424.32(b); *Local 3584*, 64 FLRA at 317.

employee will be displaced by RIF[.]" Petition at 3. Therefore, Proposal 1 does not affect management's right to layoff employees under § 7106(a)(2)(A) of the Statute.

For the foregoing reasons, Proposal 1 is within the duty to bargain.[8]

IV. Proposal 2

A. Wording

> When the [e]mployer determines to fill positions from an external source because of mission requirements, and after a notice of proposed RIF has been presented to the Union, unless the [e]mployer shows to the Union that the particular position being filled will be a job series not affected by the RIF, no positions will be filled with the discretionary VRA appointments until after all of the RIFs are completed. All "[t]emporary" and "[t]erm" positions will be included in the RIFs.

Petition at 5.

B. Meaning

The Union explains that the intent of Proposal 2 is that the Agency would suspend the filling of vacant positions with excepted service VRA employees until the RIF is completed. Petition at 6-7. According to the Union, Proposal 2 aims to protect employees by requiring that, when the Agency fills vacant positions, those positions be filled with competitive service employees whose positions will be available for bump and retreat purposes for bargaining unit employees affected by the RIF. *Id.* The Union clarifies that Proposal 2 is not intended to suspend or freeze the filling of positions from other appointment authorities, but rather to suspend the "discretional hiring" of excepted service employees that will take positions from the competitive service RIF. Response at 3.

With regard to the meaning of the last sentence of the proposal, the Union explains that Proposal 2 also intends that all positions filled with term or temporary appointments be included in the RIF in order to have those positions available for bump and retreat purposes for bargaining unit employees affected by the RIF. Record at 2. The Union further explains that it intends for Proposal 2 to encompass both competitive and excepted service temporary and term positions. *Id.*

As the Union's explanation of Proposal 2's meaning is not inconsistent with its plain wording, we adopt it for purposes of determining Proposal 2's negotiability. *E.g., NATCA*, 64 FLRA at 162.

C. Positions of the Parties

1. Agency

The Agency argues that Proposal 2 interferes with management's right to hire employees under § 7106(a). SOP at 3. The Agency contends that proposals that preclude an agency from exercising a management right unless or until other events occur are generally not within the duty to bargain. *Id.* The Agency also asserts that proposals that specify criteria pursuant to which management must exercise its rights interfere with management's rights. *Id.* Finally, the Agency argues that Proposal 2 is not an appropriate arrangement under § 7106(b)(3) of the Statute. *Id.* at 5.

2. Union

The Union asserts that Proposal 2 does not interfere with management's right to hire. Response at 2. According to the Union, Proposal 2 would not prevent management from hiring through other appointing authorities, but would only suspend the discretionary hiring of excepted service VRA employees that would make certain positions unavailable to competitive service employees for bump and retreat purposes. *Id.* at 2-3.

D. Analysis and Conclusions

The Agency argues that Proposal 2 affects management's right to hire employees under § 7106(a). SOP at 3. Even assuming that the proposal affects that management right, we find, for the following reasons, that it is within the duty to bargain as an appropriate arrangement under § 7106(b)(3) of the Statute.

---

8. The decisions on which the dissent relies do not support a different conclusion. One of the decisions, *NFFE, Local 2192*, 59 FLRA 868, 871 (2004), did not involve the management rights that are allegedly affected in this case. In the other decision, *AFGE, National Border Patrol Council*, 51 FLRA 1308, 1332-33 (1996), the Authority found that a provision requiring the agency to fill vacant positions that the agency elected to leave vacant affected the right to assign employees. Proposal 1 in the instant case does not impose a similar requirement.

To constitute an appropriate arrangement, a proposal must meet two requirements: it must be intended as an arrangement and it must be appropriate because it does not excessively interfere with the exercise of management's rights. *Id.; NAGE, Local R14-87*, 21 FLRA 24, 31 (1986) (*KANG*).

1. Proposal 2 is an arrangement.

In order to meet the first requirement, the Union must identify: (1) the adverse effects on employees that flow from the exercise of management's rights and (2) show that the arrangement is sufficiently tailored to compensate or benefit employees suffering those adverse effects. *Id.*

Proposal 2 satisfies the first *KANG* requirement. The impending RIF action and the possible consequence of termination from employment would have a severe, negative impact on any employee who undergoes them. *See U.S. Dep't of Def., Fort Bragg Dependents Sch., Fort Bragg, N.C.*, 49 FLRA 333, 352 (1994).

Proposal 2 is also sufficiently tailored because it benefits employees who could be affected by the RIF. The purpose of suspending the filling of positions with excepted service employees unless the positions are in a job series not affected by the RIF, or until after all of the RIFs are completed, is to prevent any decrease during the RIF in the number of positions available to competitive service employees for bump and retreat purposes. By doing this, the proposal mitigates the adverse effect of the RIF on affected employees. Therefore, Proposal 2 is an arrangement within the meaning of § 7106(b)(3) of the Statute.

2. The arrangement is appropriate.

In applying the second *KANG* requirement – that the proposal is appropriate because it does not excessively interfere with the exercise of management's rights – the Authority weighs the benefits the proposal affords to employees against the burden on the exercise of management's rights. *See KANG*, 21 FLRA at 31-33.

Although Proposal 2 limits the Agency's ability to use certain appointment authorities until the RIF is completed, it provides a substantial benefit to employees affected by the RIF. Proposal 2 protects against the reduction of employee bump and retreat opportunities during the RIF. In contrast, the burden on the Agency's ability to hire is not substantial. For example, under the proposal, the hiring limitation imposed on the Agency is not absolute. The proposal's hiring limitation only applies to RIF-affected positions. Further, although the Agency would be unable to hire VRA applicants into RIF-affected positions for the duration of the RIF, the Agency would still be able to fill vacancies during the RIF from other sources. Moreover, the hiring restriction is only effective until the termination of the RIF, which is ultimately a matter under the Agency's control. *See NTEU*, 24 FLRA 479, 481 (1986). Therefore, balancing the demonstrated benefit to employees against the burden on management's rights, we find that the proposal does not excessively interfere with management's rights and, therefore, constitutes an appropriate arrangement under § 7106(b)(3). *See AFGE, Local 1367*, 64 FLRA 869, 871-72 (2010).

For the foregoing reasons, Proposal 2 is within the duty to bargain.[9]

V. Proposal 9

A. Wording

> For the purposes to RIF, the [e]mployer will establish [c]ompetitive [l]evels based on the OPM identified [o]ccupational [s]eries (i.e. [j]ob [s]eries) and [p]ay [g]rade. Competitive [l]evels will not be broken down into any type of sub[]groups associated with locally created additional duties (i.e. multitasking, etc.) that may be identified in an employee's [c]ore

---

9. The decisions upon which the dissent relies are inapposite. In this regard, several of the decisions involved either no allegations, or bare assertions, regarding § 7106(b)(3). *See NAGE, Local R1-109*, 53 FLRA 403, 416-18 (1997); *AFGE, Local 1345*, 48 FLRA 168, 171-75 (1993) (Member Armendariz concurring in part and dissenting in part); *NAGE, Local R5-82*, 43 FLRA 25, 34-36 (1991) (*Local R5-82*); *Int'l Plate Printers, Die Stampers & Engravers Union of N. Am., AFL-CIO, Local 2*, 25 FLRA 113, 144-46 (1987). Finally, the proposals in the one remaining decision, *AFGE, Local 1923*, 44 FLRA 1405 (1992), placed a substantially greater burden on management's rights than does Proposal 2. Specifically, those proposals required the agency to fill certain vacancies, regardless of whether vacancies existed or whether management wanted to fill them. *See id.* at 1462-70. Proposal 2, which places temporary, partial restrictions on the Agency's ability to fill vacant positions, has no comparable effect.

> [d]ocument, or as applicable, [p]osition [d]escription.

Petition at 7-8.

B. Meaning

The Union states that the proposal is designed to lessen the impact of a RIF on the competitive service employees in the bargaining unit. Record at 3. The Union maintains that using employees' position descriptions to establish competitive levels would restrict or limit the ability of other employees in that series to bump and retreat into such designated positions. *Id.* The Union claims the proposal seeks to eliminate consideration of such subgroup designations during a RIF. *Id.* As the Union's explanation of Proposal 9's meaning is not inconsistent with its plain wording, we adopt it for purposes of determining Proposal 9's negotiability. *E.g., NATCA*, 64 FLRA at 162.

C. Positions of the Parties

1. Agency

The Agency first argues that Proposal 9 is contrary to the RIF regulations, specifically 5 C.F.R. Part 351, because it attempts to define RIF procedures. SOP at 3. The Agency also claims that Proposal 9 interferes with management's right to assign work, which includes the right to determine the particular duties that will be assigned. In addition, the Agency asserts that Proposal 9 interferes with management's rights because it defines competitive levels in a way that eliminates or interferes with management's discretion to determine qualifications for positions. *Id.* The Agency also argues that Proposal 9 is not an appropriate arrangement under § 7106(b)(3) of the Statute. *Id.* at 3, 5. Finally, the Agency claims that, as written, Proposal 9 would apply to non-bargaining unit employees and consequently is only negotiable at the election of the Agency. *Id.*

2. Union

The Union argues the Proposal 9 is not contrary to RIF regulations. Response at 3. The Union's position is that Proposal 9 is intended to establish competitive levels based on the Office of Personnel Management's (OPM's) established Occupational Job Series to allow each employee their bump and retreat rights within each of the occupational series in accordance with 5 C.F.R. Part 351. *Id.* The Union argues that Proposal 9 does not define qualifications, but rather uses OPM's definition for each of the occupational series instead of relying on descriptions of additional duties locally created by the Agency. *Id.* at 3. The Union further argues that Proposal 9 would not interfere with management's right to assign work. *Id.* The Union claims that the Agency has the discretion to establish competitive levels, and that the proposal would be an appropriate arrangement to minimize the adverse impact of a RIF on the bargaining unit. *Id.* Finally, contrary to the Agency's claim, the Union asserts that Proposal 9 does not concern any non-bargaining unit employees. *Id.*

D. Analysis and Conclusions

For the reasons that follow, we find that Proposal 9 is inconsistent with 5 C.F.R. § 351.403(a)(1) & (a)(2) and that it is therefore outside the duty to bargain under § 7117(a)(1) of the Statute.

Proposals that require that an agency act contrary to RIF regulations are inconsistent with government-wide regulations and are outside the duty to bargain. *AFGE, Local 1547*, 64 FLRA 813, 814-15 (2010); *see also NAGE, Local R4-6,* 52 FLRA 124, 127 (1996), and *Laborers' Int'l Union of N. Am., AFL-CIO-CLC, Local 1267,* 14 FLRA 686, 688 (1984).

By its terms, Proposal 9 affects the manner in which the Agency establishes the competitive levels of its employees. 5 C.F.R. § 351.403 dictates how competitive levels are established. Under § 351.403, competitive levels include:

> all positions in a competitive area which are in the same grade (or occupational level) and classification series, and which are similar enough in duties, qualification requirements, pay schedules, and working conditions so that an agency may reassign the incumbent of one position to any of the other positions in the level without undue interruption.

5 C.F.R. § 351.403(a)(1).

In addition, "[c]ompetitive level determinations are based on each employee's official position, not the employee's personal qualifications." 5 C.F.R. § 351.403(a)(2).[10]

[10] The current version of 5 C.F.R § 351.403(a)(2) was amended on August 11, 2008. 5 C.F.R § 351.403(a)(2)(i)

Proposal 9 is inconsistent with 5 C.F.R. § 351.403(a)(1) because it prevents the Agency from establishing competitive levels consistent with regulatory requirements. Specifically, Proposal 9 prevents the Agency from including in a competitive level positions which are "similar enough" to each other because they have similar position descriptions. *See id.* Proposal 9 is also inconsistent with 5 C.F.R. § 351.403(a)(2) because it contradicts the regulation's explicit direction that agencies base competitive level determinations on, among other things, official position descriptions. *See id.*

Consequently, as Proposal 9 is inconsistent with 5 C.F.R. §§ 351.403(a)(1) & (a)(2), it is outside the duty to bargain pursuant to § 7117(a)(1) of the Statute.[11]

VI. Order

The Agency shall, upon request, or as otherwise agreed to by the parties, negotiate over Proposals 1 and 2.[12] The petition for review is dismissed with regard to Proposal 9.

provides: "Except as provided in paragraph (a)(2)(ii) of this section for pay band positions, competitive level determinations are based on each employee's official position of record (including the official position description), not the employee's personal qualifications."

11. Given this conclusion, it is not necessary to address the Union's assertion that Proposal 9 is an appropriate arrangement. In this regard, a proposal that is contrary to law or government-wide regulation remains so regardless of whether it is a procedure or an appropriate arrangement. *See NTEU*, 55 FLRA 1174, 1181 (1999).

12. In finding the proposals to be within the duty to bargain, we make no judgment as to their merits.

APPENDIX

PART 351--REDUCTION IN FORCE

5 C.F.R. § 351.204 Responsibility of agency.

Each agency covered by this part is responsible for following and applying the regulations in this part when the agency determines that a reduction force is necessary.

5 C.F.R. § 351.403 Competitive level.

(a)(1) Each agency shall establish competitive levels consisting of all positions in a competitive area which are in the same grade (or occupational level) and classification series, and which are similar enough in duties, qualification requirements, pay schedules, and working conditions so that an agency may reassign the incumbent of one position to any of the other positions in the level without undue interruption.

(2) Competitive level determinations are based on each employee's official position, not the employee's personal qualifications.[13]

. . . .

(b) Each agency shall establish separate competitive levels according to the following categories:

(1) By Service. Separate levels shall be established for positions in the competitive service and in the excepted service.

. . . .

5 C.F.R. § 351.404 Retention register.

(a) When a competing employee is to be released from a competitive level under this part, the agency shall establish a separate retention register for that competitive level. The retention register is prepared from the current retention records of employees.

. . . .

5 C.F.R. § 351.501 Order of retention—competitive service.

(a) Competing employees shall be classified on a retention register on the basis

[13] *See supra* note 10.

of their tenure of employment, veteran preference, length of service, and performance in descending order as follows:

(1) By tenure group I, group II, group III; and

(2) Within each group by veteran preference subgroup AD, subgroup A, subgroup B; and

(3) Within each subgroup by years of service as augmented by credit for performance under § 351.504, beginning with the earliest service date.

5 C.F.R. § 351.502 Order of retention—excepted service.

(a) Competing employees shall be classified on a retention register in tenure groups on the basis of their tenure of employment, veteran preference, length of service, and performance in descending order as set forth under § 351.501(a) for competing employees in the competitive service.

PART 316 -- TEMPORARY AND TERM EMPLOYMENT

5 C.F.R. § 316.301 Purpose and duration.

(a) An agency may make a term appointment for a period of more than 1 year but not more than 4 years to positions where the need for an employee's services is not permanent. Reasons for making a term appointment include, but are not limited to: project work, extraordinary workload, scheduled abolishment, reorganization, contracting out of the function, uncertainty of future funding, or the need to maintain permanent positions for placement of employees who would otherwise be displaced from other parts of the organization. Agencies may extend appointments made for more than 1 year but less than 4 years up to the 4-year limit in increments determined by the agency. The vacancy announcement should state that the agency has the option of extending a term appointment up to the 4-year limit.

(b) OPM may authorize exceptions beyond the 4-year limit when the extension is clearly justified and is consistent with applicable statutory provisions. Requests to make and/or extend appointments beyond the 4-year limit must be initiated by the employing office and sent to the appropriate OPM service center.

5 C.F.R. § 316.401 Purpose and duration.

(a) *Appropriate use.* An agency may make a temporary limited appointment--

(1) To fill a short-term position (i.e., one that is not expected to last longer than 1 year);

(2) To meet an employment need that is scheduled to be terminated within the timeframe set out in paragraph (c) of this section for such reasons as abolishment, reorganization, or contracting of the function, anticipated reduction in funding, or completion of a specific project or peak workload; or

(3) To fill positions on a temporary basis when the positions are expected to be needed for placement of permanent employees who would otherwise be displaced from other parts of the organization.

(b) *Certification of appropriate use.* The supervisor of each position filled by temporary appointment must certify that the employment need is truly temporary and that the proposed appointment meets the regulatory time limits. This certification may constitute appropriate documentation of compliance with the limits set out in paragraph (c) of this section. The reason(s) for making a temporary limited appointment must be stated on the form documenting each such appointment.

(c) *Time limits--general.* (1) An agency may make a temporary appointment for a specified period not to exceed 1 year. The appointment may be extended up to a maximum of 1 additional year (24 months of total service). Appointment to a successor position (i.e., to a position that replaces and absorbs the position to which an individual was originally appointed) is considered to be an extension of the original appointment. Appointment to a position involving the same basic duties and in the same major subdivision of the agency and same local commuting area as the original appointment is also considered to be an extension of the original appointment.

(2) An agency may not fill a position by temporary appointment if that position has previously been filled by temporary appointment(s) for an aggregate of 2 years,

or 24 months, within the preceding 3-year period.

(d) *Exceptions to general time limits.*

(1) Agencies may make and extend temporary appointments to positions involving intermittent or seasonal work without regard to the requirements in paragraph (c) of this section, provided that:

(i) Appointments and extensions are made in increments of 1 year or less.

(ii) Employment in the same or a successor position under this and any other appointing authority totals less than 6 months (1,040 hours), excluding overtime, in a service year. The service year is the calendar year that begins on the date of the employee's initial appointment in the agency. Should employment in a position filled under this exception total 6 months or more in any service year, the provisions of paragraph (c) of this section will apply to subsequent extension or reappointment unless OPM approves continued exception under this section. An individual may be employed for training for up to 120 days following initial appointment and up to 2 weeks a year thereafter without regard to the service year limitation.

(2) OPM will authorize exceptions to the limits set out in paragraph (c) of this section only when necessitated by major reorganizations or base closings or other unusual circumstances. Requests based on major reorganization, base closing, restructuring, or other unusual circumstances that apply agencywide must be made by an official at the headquarters level of the Department or agency. Requests involving extension of appointments to a specific position or project based on other unusual circumstances may be submitted by the employing office to the appropriate OPM service center.

5 C.F.R. § 6.3 - Method of filling excepted positions and status of incumbents.

(a) The head of an agency may fill excepted positions by the appointment of persons without civil service eligibility or competitive status and such persons shall not acquire competitive status by reason of such appointment: Provided, that OPM, in its discretion, may by regulation prescribe conditions under which excepted positions may be filled in the same manner as competitive positions are filled and conditions under which persons so appointed may acquire a competitive status in accordance with the Civil Service Rules and Regulations.

(b) To the extent permitted by law and the provisions of this part, appointments and position changes in the excepted service shall be made in accordance with such regulations and practices as the head of the agency concerned finds necessary.

Member Beck, Dissenting:

I disagree with my colleagues' determinations that Proposal 1 does not affect management's rights to assign and layoff employees and that Proposal 2 constitutes an appropriate arrangement.

Proposal 1 requires the Agency to convert probationary excepted service employees to term appointments when specific circumstances -- defined solely by the Union -- occur. It then restricts how long the Agency may run the term appointment – until "the effective day of [the RIF]." Petition at 3-4. This Proposal unduly interferes with management's § 7106(a)(2)(A) rights to assign and layoff employees by imposing an absolute requirement on management to take a specific action and then requiring the Agency to terminate the action on a specific date.

We have found that similar provisions excessively interfere with management's rights. *See, e.g., NFFE, Local 2192*, 59 FLRA 868, 871 (2004) (proposal that imposes an absolute requirement on management to make certain work assignments not an appropriate arrangement); *AFGE, Nat'l Border Patrol Council*, 51 FLRA 1308, 1332-33 (1996) (provision that permits no exception to requirement that an employee be assigned to one of three positions identified by the employee is not an appropriate arrangement).

In similar fashion, Proposal 2 effectively restricts both *when* the Agency may fill a position -- not "until after all of the RIFs are completed," and *from what sources* -- it may make no "discretionary VRA appointments." Petition at 5.

We have held that "proposals that preclude an agency from exercising a management right *unless or until* other events occur are not within the duty to bargain." *NAGE, Local R1-109*, 53 FLRA 403, 418 (1997) (emphasis added) (proposal that prevents agency from detailing employees "until such time as" facilities are "formally and officially" consolidated is not within agency's duty to bargain), citing *AFGE, Local 1345*, 48 FLRA 168, 173-74 (1993).

Proposals that restrict the sources from which an agency can hire have similarly been found to fall outside an agency's duty to bargain:

- Requiring agency to fill positions with certain types of employees directly interferes with management's right to hire. *AFGE, Local 1923*, 44 FLRA 1405, 1465 (1992).

- Requiring agency to hire from a single source directly interferes with the right to select and is not an appropriate arrangement. *Id.* at 1468-70, citing *NAGE, Local R5-82*, 43 FLRA 25, 35-36 (1991).

- Requiring agency to hire from a particular source is non-negotiable because it violates the right to hire (§ 7106(a)(2)(A)) and the right to determine the personnel by which the agency's operations will be conducted (§ 7106(a)(2)(B)). *Int'l Plate Printers, Die Stampers & Engravers Union of N. Am., AFL-CIO, Local 2*, 25 FLRA 113, 145-46 (1987).

In this case, the Union's proposal would impermissibly prevent the Agency from using a particular source – VRA appointees.

Accordingly, I conclude that Proposals 1 and 2 excessively interfere with management's rights and do not constitute appropriate arrangements.

65 FLRA No. 193

AMERICAN FEDERATION
OF GOVERNMENT EMPLOYEES
LOCAL 1592
(Union)

and

UNITED STATES
DEPARTMENT OF THE AIR FORCE
HILL AIR FORCE BASE, UTAH
(Agency)

0-AR-4637
(64 FLRA 861 (2010))

DECISION

June 15, 2011

Before the Authority: Carol Waller Pope, Chairman, and Thomas M. Beck and Ernest DuBester, Members

I. Statement of the Case

This matter is before the Authority on an exception to an award of Arbitrator Barbara Bridgewater filed by the Agency under § 7122(a) of the Federal Service Labor-Management Relations Statute (the Statute) and part 2425 of the Authority's Regulations. The Union filed an opposition to the Agency's exceptions.

In an award on remand from the Authority (remand award), the Arbitrator found that the grievant is entitled to an award of attorney fees. For the reasons that follow, we deny the Agency's exception.

II. Background and Arbitrator's Awards

The Union filed a grievance challenging the Agency's denial of the grievant's request for compensatory time off. *See AFGE, Local 1592*, 64 FLRA 861, 861 (2010) (*Local 1592*). The grievance was not resolved and was submitted to arbitration. *See id.* In the award on the merits (merits award), the Arbitrator awarded the grievant three hours of compensatory time off (comp time), but denied the grievant's request for an award of attorney fees on the ground that comp time does not constitute "pay, allowance[s,] or differential[s]" within the meaning of the Back Pay Act (BPA), 5 U.S.C. § 5596. *See id.*

The Agency did not except to the award, but the Union excepted to the Arbitrator's denial of attorney fees. In *Local 1592*, the Authority found that the award of comp time constituted an award of pay, allowances, or differentials under the BPA. *See id.* at 862. Accordingly, the Authority concluded that the basis for the denial of fees was deficient and remanded the award to the parties for resubmission to the Arbitrator, absent settlement, for a resolution of the fee request. *See id.*

On remand, the Agency contended that, during the arbitration hearing on the merits of the grievance, it had granted the grievant the disputed comp time, and that the time had appeared in time and attendance records prior to the issuance of the merits award. Remand Award at 3. The Agency argued that, as a result, the grievant was not a prevailing party, as required for an award of attorney fees under 5 U.S.C. § 7701(g) (§ 7701(g)). *Id.* (citing *Buckhannon Bd. & Care Home, Inc. v. W. Va. Dep't of Health & Human Res.*, 532 U.S. 598 (2001) (*Buckhannon*)).

The Arbitrator acknowledged that the Agency had granted the grievant the disputed comp time prior to her merits award, but stated that she "did not have a factual basis for considering the instant matter to be moot." *Id.* In this connection, she stated that "because she awarded the [g]rievant [three] hours of . . . comp time in her [merits award], based on the merits of his grievance, the [g]rievant is a prevailing party." *Id.* at 4. Thus, she concluded that the grievant was entitled to an award of attorney fees. *Id.*

III. Positions of the Parties

A. Agency's Exception

The Agency contends that the remand award is contrary to the BPA and § 7701(g). *See* Exception at 2-4. In this regard, the Agency states that, under the definition of "prevailing party" set forth in *Buckhannon* and adopted by the Merit Systems Protection Board (MSPB) under § 7701(g), a grievant prevails only if he or she has received an enforceable judgment or settlement that directly benefited the grievant at the time of the judgment or settlement. *Id.* at 3-4. According to the Agency, the grievant is not a prevailing party because of the Agency's "voluntary and unilateral action" of granting the grievant the disputed comp time before the Arbitrator issued the merits award. *Id.* (citing *Buckhannon;*

Cole v. DoJ, 90 M.S.P.R. 627 (2001) (*Cole*); *Sacco v. DoJ,* 90 M.S.P.R. 37 (2001) (*Sacco*); *Nichols v. Dep't of Veterans Affairs,* 89 M.S.P.R. 554 (2001) (*Nichols*)).

B. Union's Opposition

The Union contends that the award is not contrary to law. In this connection, the Union asserts that, under *Buckhannon*, what is dispositive is that the grievant obtained a favorable and enforceable award on the merits of the grievance. Opp'n at 3. According to the Union, the Agency's reliance on the alleged unilateral grant of the disputed comp time is misplaced because that grant did not moot the grievance. *Id.* at 4. In this connection, the Union maintains that the Arbitrator issued an award sustaining the grievance and determined that it was not moot. *Id.* The Union also maintains that, if the Agency believed that the grievance was moot, then the Agency should have filed exceptions to the merits award. *Id.* Because the Agency did not do so, the Union claims that the grievant is the prevailing party as a result of the merits award. *Id.* at 4.

IV. Analysis and Conclusions

The Agency's exception challenges the consistency of the award with the BPA and § 7701(g). The Authority reviews de novo questions of law raised by the exception and the award. In applying a standard of de novo review, the Authority assesses whether the arbitrator's legal conclusions are consistent with the applicable standard of law. *E.g., U.S. Dep't of Transp., Fed. Aviation Admin.,* 65 FLRA 320, 322 (2010) (*FAA*).

In interpreting the term "prevailing party" in § 7701(g), the Authority has applied the definition of that term set forth in *Buckhannon* and adopted by the MSPB. Specifically, the Authority has held that a grievant is a prevailing party when he or she obtains an enforceable judgment that benefited him or her at the time of the judgment. *Id.* at 324.

Buckhannon, which set forth this definition, involved a lawsuit that challenged a particular requirement in a state law. *See* 532 U.S. at 601. While the lawsuit was pending, the challenged requirement was eliminated from the law, and, consequently, the district court dismissed the lawsuit as moot. *See* 532 U.S. at 601. In assessing whether attorney fees were appropriate, the Supreme Court rejected the petitioners' argument that fees were warranted under a "catalyst theory[,]" i.e., because their lawsuit brought about the change in the respondents' conduct. *Id.* at 605. Instead, the Court found that the term "prevailing party" requires the party to have been awarded some relief by a court, and, thus, only court judgments on the merits and settlement agreements enforced through consent decrees create the "alteration in the legal relationship of the parties[]" that is necessary for an award of fees. *Id.* at 603-05. In contrast, the Court found that a "voluntary change in conduct[] . . . lacks the necessary judicial *imprimatur* on the change." *Id.* at 605.

In reaching its conclusions in *Buckhannon*, the Court rejected the petitioners' claim that the catalyst theory was necessary to prevent defendants from unilaterally mooting an action before judgment in order to avoid an award of attorney fees. Specifically, the Court stated that "so long as the plaintiff has a cause of action for damages [rather than equitable relief], a defendant's change in conduct will not moot the case." *Id.* at 608-09. Moreover, the Court emphasized that "[i]f a case is not found to be moot, and the plaintiff later procures an enforceable judgment, the court may of course award attorney's fees." *Id.* at 609.

Consistent with *Buckhannon*, the MSPB has found that appellants were not prevailing parties in cases where agencies had unilaterally rescinded the appealed actions *and* the MSPB's administrative judges dismissed the employees' appeals. *See, e.g., Cole,* 90 M.S.P.R. at 628; *Sacco,* 90 M.S.P.R. at 39; *Nichols,* 89 M.S.P.R. at 555. In *Sacco* and *Nichols*, the administrative judges dismissed the appeals as moot, and in *Cole*, the administrative judge dismissed the appeal after the agency filed a motion to dismiss as moot and the employee withdrew his appeal. Consequently, in those decisions, there were no judgments on the merits on which the MSPB could base a finding that the employees were prevailing parties. Further, consistent with *Buckhannon* and this MSPB precedent, the Authority has found that a grievant was a prevailing party, despite an agency's claim that its voluntary action mooted the grievance, where the arbitrator rejected the mootness claim. *See FAA*, 65 FLRA at 324.

Unlike the above-cited precedent, here, in issuing the merits award, the Arbitrator did not find the grievance moot; instead, she sustained the grievance and awarded relief in the form of comp time. In the remand award, the Arbitrator specifically found that she "did not have a factual basis for considering the instant matter to be moot."[*] Remand Award at 3. The Agency did not except to the merits award and, thus, did not argue that the grievance was moot or challenge the Arbitrator's award of comp time, which the Authority subsequently found to be an award of pay, allowances, or differentials. In addition, the Agency's exceptions to the remand award do not expressly challenge the Arbitrator's statement that the matter was not moot. Thus, in the words of the Supreme Court, as this "case [wa]s not found to be moot" and the Arbitrator issued the merits award sustaining the grievance, "the [Arbitrator] may of course award attorney's fees." *Buckhannon*, 532 U.S. at 609.

Based on the foregoing, we conclude that the Agency has not demonstrated that the Arbitrator erred in finding that the grievant is a prevailing party. Accordingly, we deny the exception.

V. Decision

The Agency's exception is denied.

[*] The Arbitrator's conclusion that the Agency's actions did not moot the grievance distinguishes this case from *United States Department of the Army, Womack Army Medical Center, Fort Bragg, North Carolina,* 65 FLRA 632 (2011) (*Ft. Bragg*). In *Ft. Bragg*, the arbitrator stated that there was evidence that the agency had restored the disputed annual leave, but "out of an abundance of caution[,]" the arbitrator directed the agency to do what it had probably done, and, in a subsequent award, expressly found that the agency had in fact restored the disputed leave. *Ft. Bragg,* 65 FLRA at 634.

65 FLRA No. 194

AMERICAN FEDERATION
OF GOVERNMENT EMPLOYEES
LOCAL 1164
(Union)

and

SOCIAL SECURITY ADMINISTRATION
ROSLINDALE, MASSACHUSETTS
(Agency)

0-NG-3093

DECISION AND ORDER
ON NEGOTIABILITY ISSUES

June 16, 2011

Before the Authority: Carol Waller Pope, Chairman, and Thomas M. Beck and Ernest DuBester, Members

I. Statement of the Case

This matter is before the Authority on a negotiability appeal filed by the Union under § 7105(a)(2)(E) of the Federal Service Labor-Management Relations Statute (the Statute).[1] The appeal involves the negotiability of two proposals concerning the relocation of the Agency's Roslindale, Massachusetts Field Office (Field Office). The Agency filed a statement of position (SOP) to which the Union filed an untimely response (response).[2]

For the reasons that follow, we find that the proposals are outside the duty to bargain. Accordingly, we dismiss the petition for review (petition).

1. In response to the Authority's Order to Show Cause of March 9, 2011 (Order of March 9, 2011), the Union stated that two unfair labor practice charges filed in connection with this case, in Case Nos. BN-CA-11-0140 and BN-CA-11-0075, had been withdrawn and resolved, respectively. *See* Union's Response to Order of March 9, 2011 at 1-2.

2. For the reasons set forth in the Authority's Order dated April 8, 2011, the Union's response was untimely filed and will not be considered.

II. Background

On May 13, 2010, the Agency provided notice to the Union of its decision to relocate the Field Office. SOP at 1. The parties reached an agreement on all matters concerning the relocation except for two Union proposals that are the subject of the petition at issue here. *Id.*

III. Preliminary Issues

A. The Union's petition was timely filed.

The Agency claims that the Union's petition should be dismissed because it was untimely filed. SOP at 1-3. The record in this case indicates that the Agency provided the Union with an unsolicited written allegation of nonnegotiability (allegation). *See* Order to Show Cause of October 19, 2010 (Order of October 19, 2010) at 2. Subsequently, the Union requested an allegation from the Agency. *See* Union's Response to Order of October 19, 2010, Attach. 1, Union's e-mail of August 13, 2010. The Agency did not respond to the Union's request, claiming that it had already provided an allegation and that it was not required to support its allegation with specificity until it filed its statement of position. SOP at 2-3.

A union is not required to respond to an agency's unsolicited allegation. *See* 5 C.F.R. § 2424.11(c); *AFGE, Local 3369*, 49 FLRA 793, 794 (1994). Rather, the union may ignore the unsolicited allegation and instead elect to request a written allegation from the agency. *See id.* at 795. If an agency does not provide a written allegation in response to a union's written request, then a petition for review filed by the union is not subject to the time limits set forth in § 2424.21 of the Authority's Regulations, and the union may file its petition at any time. *See* 5 C.F.R. § 2424.21(b); *AFGE, AFL-CIO, Local 2052*, 30 FLRA 837, 839 (1987).

Here, the Union chose not to respond to the Agency's unsolicited allegation and instead requested an allegation. As the Agency did not provide an allegation in response to the Union's written request, the Union was not required to file its petition within any particular time frame. Consequently, the Union's petition was timely filed.

B. The Union's petition is not moot.

In its unsolicited allegation of nonnegotiability, the Agency indicated that it would implement the office relocation process. *See* Petition, Attach., Agency's July 29, 2010 Allegation. Noting that proposals that address events that have already occurred are moot, the Authority ordered the parties to show cause why the Union's petition should not be dismissed as moot. *See* Order of October 19, 2010 at 2. In its response to the Order, the Union asserts that its petition is not moot because the construction of the building has not been completed and the office relocation has not yet occurred. *See* Union's Response to Order of October 19, 2010 at 3-4. The Agency did not dispute the Union's assertion that the petition is not moot.

Section 2429.10 of the Authority's Regulations states that the Authority will not issue advisory opinions. *See* 5 C.F.R. § 2429.10. Thus, where the issues that led to the filing of a negotiability petition for review have been resolved, or where there is no longer a dispute between the parties, the Authority will dismiss the petition for review as moot. *See AFGE, Nat'l Veterans Admin. Council*, 41 FLRA 73, 74 (1991) (citing *AFGE, Local 85*, 32 FLRA 210, 211-12 (1988)). Mootness, therefore, is a threshold jurisdictional issue. *See AFGE, Council 238*, 64 FLRA 223, 225 (2009) (citing *Ass'n of Civilian Technicians, Show-Me Army Chapter*, 59 FLRA 378, 380 (2003)). The burden of demonstrating mootness is heavy and falls on the party urging mootness. *Id.*

In its Order of October 19, 2010, the Authority gave the parties an opportunity to show cause why the Union's petition should not be dismissed as moot. *See* Order of October 19, 2010 at 2. The record shows that the Union responded by asserting that its petition was not moot because the construction of the building has not been completed and the office relocation has not yet occurred. *See* Union's Response to Order of October 19, 2010 at 3-4. The record also shows that the Agency did not respond to the Authority's Order or dispute, in its SOP, the Union's claim that the petition was not moot. Accordingly, we find that the Agency has not met its burden of demonstrating that the petition is moot. *See NAGE, Local R1-109*, 61 FLRA 593, 596 (2006) (agency burden not met where agency failed to demonstrate that union's proposals were moot). Consequently, we find that the Union's petition is not moot.

IV. Proposal 3

A. Wording

> The final floor plan approved by the parties is attached to this [Memorandum of Understanding (MOU)]. A plotted floor plan identifying the employees['] seat/workstation locations will be provided to the Union when available. The floor plan will include a platform and ramp reception area similar to the current platform/ramp reception area. It will also have an FEI and backend workstation areas.

Petition at 3.

B. Meaning

The proposal describes the configuration of an office floor plan. Under the proposal, employees would have a separate Front End Interviewing (FEI) area where interviews with the public would take place. Petition at 4; Record of Post-Petition Conference (Record) at 1. The floor plan also describes a back-end area, away from the noise of the reception and interviewing areas, where the employees' work stations would be located in an atmosphere more conducive to concentration. Petition at 4.

The Union describes the FEI area as having windows built into a barrier wall with a raised reception counter and a platform with a ramp. This would allow employees who serve the public all day to remain seated in ergonomically correct workstations raised above ground level for added safety. *Id.* In the alternative, the Union suggests that the FEI area remain the same, but without the raised platform and ramp reception counter. *Id.* As the Union's explanation of Proposal 3's meaning is not inconsistent with its plain wording, we adopt it for purposes of determining Proposal 3's negotiability. *E.g., NATCA*, 64 FLRA 161, 162 (2009).

C. Positions of the Parties

1. Union

The Union argues that the proposed floor plan would provide a less stressful environment for employees, and would be more conducive to privacy, safety, efficiency, and productivity. Petition at 5.

The Union claims that the privacy of the barrier wall would safeguard the public's confidential information. *Id.* The Union also asserts that the barrier wall would provide a safer environment because it would prevent the general public from accessing the area where employees work on claims and where they may have files and other confidential case information displayed on their desks. *Id.* In addition, the Union argues that the backend area would provide a less stressful and noisy area that would be more conducive to efficiency and productivity. *Id.* at 5-6. The Union further asserts that the barrier wall would protect employees from direct contact with the public, safeguarding them from possible infectious diseases. *Id.* at 6.

The Union requests that Proposal 3 be severed into three parts, with the proposal's last two sentences each standing alone. *Id.* at 7.

2. Agency

The Agency argues that the proposal affects the Agency's rights to determine the methods and means of performing work under § 7106(b)(1) and to assign work under § 7106(a)(2)(B) of the Statute. SOP at 5-6. The Agency further claims that the proposal is not a procedure or an appropriate arrangement under § 7106(b)(2) and (3) of the Statute, respectively. *Id.* at 7-9. With regard to the Union's severance request, the Agency argues that there exist no grounds to sever the proposal. *Id.* at 10.

D. Analysis and Conclusions

A party's failure to respond to an argument or assertion raised by the other party will, where appropriate, be deemed a concession to such argument or assertion. *See* 5 C.F.R. § 2424.32(c)(2). Consistent with this regulation, when a union does not dispute an agency's claim that a proposal affects the exercise of management's rights, and does not argue that the proposal constitutes an exception to management's rights, the Authority will find that the proposal is outside the duty to bargain. *E.g., AFGE, Local 4052*, 65 FLRA 720, 722 (2011).

Here, the Union does not argue in the petition either that the proposal does not affect a management right or that the proposal is within the duty to bargain as an exception to management's rights.[3] Accordingly, consistent with § 2424.32 and the above-cited precedent, we find that the Union has conceded that the proposal is contrary to management's rights under § 7106(a) of the Statute.[4] *See AFGE, Local 4052*, 65 FLRA at 722. Consequently, we find that the proposal is outside the duty to bargain.[5]

V. Proposal 27

A. Wording

> This agreement will be effective upon Head of Agency approval per 5 U.S.C. [§] 7114. If any portion of this agreement is rejected[,] that portion will be reopened for bargaining within thirty (30) days of the Union's receipt of the notice of rejection. Such notice will be considered received when in the possession of the Union Chief Negotiator.

Record at 2.

B. Meaning

The term "agreement" in the proposal refers to the MOU that the parties are negotiating, which contains a floor plan to be used upon the relocation of the Field Office. Record at 2. The Union explains that the proposal would provide the Union with the right to reopen any portion of the MOU that is rejected on agency head review. *Id.* As the Union's explanation of Proposal 27's meaning is not inconsistent with its plain wording, we adopt it for purposes of determining Proposal 27's negotiability. *E.g., NATCA*, 64 FLRA at 162.

C. Positions of the Parties

1. Union

The Union asserts that the proposal seeks the right to bargain over issues that are rejected on agency head review. Petition at 8. The Union claims that it wants to preserve the right to bargain appropriate arrangements and procedures to mitigate the adverse impact that the Agency's proposed changes would have on the bargaining unit. *Id.*

3. Consistent with the Authority's Order of April 8, 2011, we do not consider the Union's response. *See* note 2, *supra*.

4. In view of this disposition, there is no need to address the Agency's management rights claim under § 7106(b)(1) of the Statute.

5. We deny the Union's request to sever Proposal 3. In this regard, the Union has not explained, pursuant to § 2424.22(c) of the Authority's Regulations, how Proposal 3 could be severed or demonstrated how potentially severed portions of the proposal could stand alone and be separately negotiable. *See Int'l Ass'n of Machinists & Aerospace Workers*, 59 FLRA 830, 831 n.3 (2004).

2. Agency

The Agency argues that Article 4, Appendix A, Section VI of the parties' collective bargaining agreement (CBA) covers situations and procedures available for re-opening bargaining after the Agency asserts that a Union proposal is nonnegotiable. SOP at 12. The Agency asserts that, as the subject of Proposal 27 is covered by the CBA, it is only negotiable at the election of the Agency. *Id.*

D. Analysis and Conclusions

Under § 7117 of the Statute and § 2424.2 of the Authority's Regulations, the Authority will consider a petition for review of a negotiability dispute only when it has been established that the parties are in dispute as to whether a proposal is inconsistent with law, rule, or regulation. 5 U.S.C. § 7117; 5 C.F.R. § 2424.2.

The Agency's only claim with regard to Proposal 27 is that it is "covered by" Article 4, Appendix A, Section VI of the CBA. SOP at 12. In the absence of an Agency contention that the Union's proposal is outside the duty to bargain because it is inconsistent with law, rule or regulation, it does not appear that there is an issue before the Authority that is appropriate for resolution in a negotiability appeal. *See, e.g., AFGE, Council 214*, 53 FLRA 131, 132 (1997).

Rather, the Agency's claim that the proposal is "covered by" Article 4, Appendix A, Section VI of the CBA raises a bargaining obligation dispute, which is defined in § 2424.2(a) of the Authority's Regulations as a disagreement between an exclusive representative and an agency concerning whether, in the specific circumstances involved in a particular case, the parties are obligated to bargain over a proposal that otherwise may be negotiable. *See* 5 C.F.R. § 2424.2(a). The Authority's Regulations specify that a bargaining obligation dispute includes a claim that a proposal "concerns a matter that is covered by a collective bargaining agreement[.]" 5 C.F.R. § 2424.2(a)(1). Under § 2424.30(b)(2), the Authority has discretion to resolve bargaining obligation issues when they are ancillary to the resolution of whether a proposal is inconsistent with law, rule, or regulation. *See* 5 C.F.R. § 2424.30(b)(2); *AFGE, Local 2143*, 48 FLRA 41, 43-44 (1993) (Member Talkin concurring as to another matter) (claimed existence of duty to bargain questions did not preclude determining negotiability of proposals that were otherwise properly before Authority). However, the Authority's Regulations further specify that a negotiability appeal "that concerns only a bargaining obligation dispute may not be resolved [in a negotiability proceeding]." 5 C.F.R. § 2424.2(d).

As the Agency does not claim that the Union's proposal is outside the duty to bargain because it is inconsistent with law, rule or regulation, there is no issue before the Authority as to Proposal 27 that is appropriate for resolution in a negotiability appeal. *See AFGE, Council 214*, 53 FLRA at 132. Consequently, as the only issue raised by the Agency with regard to Proposal 27 is a bargaining obligation dispute, we dismiss the petition as to Proposal 27. *See Nat'l Air Traffic Controllers Ass'n, Local ZHU*, 65 FLRA 738, 741 (2011).

VI. Order

The petition for review is dismissed.

65 FLRA No. 195

AMERICAN FEDERATION
OF GOVERNMENT EMPLOYEES
LOCAL 1547
(Union)

and

UNITED STATES
DEPARTMENT OF THE AIR FORCE
LUKE AIR FORCE BASE, ARIZONA
(Agency)

0-AR-4615

DECISION

June 20, 2011

Before the Authority: Carol Waller Pope, Chairman, and Thomas M. Beck and Ernest DuBester, Members

I. Statement of the Case

This matter is before the Authority on exceptions to an award of Arbitrator Douglas P. Hammond filed by the Union under § 7122(a) of the Federal Service Labor-Management Relations Statute (the Statute) and part 2425 of the Authority's Regulations. The Agency filed an opposition to the Union's exceptions.

As relevant here, the Arbitrator found that the due process and just cause standards incorporated in the parties' collective bargaining agreement (CBA) did not apply to the grievants' terminations from their positions as temporary employees.

For the reasons that follow, we deny the Union's exceptions.

II. Background and Arbitrator's Award

The grievants were employed by the Agency as temporary security guards. Award at 7. As a condition of their employment, the Agency required each grievant to sign a "Conditions of Temporary Limited Appointment Statement(s) of Understanding" (Statement). *Id.* at 10. The Statement indicated that, as temporary employees, they were "not covered by the adverse action procedures under 5 [U.S.C. §] 4303 and 5 [U.S.C. §] 7511" and could be "terminated at any time upon notice from the Agency." *Id.*

While on duty, the grievants had a fistfight. *Id.* at 7. An Agency supervisor gathered statements from other employees regarding the incident, but did not request statements from the grievants. *Id.* The Agency then notified each grievant that his employment was terminated based on "misconduct of fighting with another employee while on duty." *Id.* at 8.

The Union filed a grievance alleging that the Agency violated the CBA when it terminated the grievants' employment. *Id.* at 1. The matter was unresolved and was submitted to arbitration.

The Arbitrator framed the issues as whether "the grievance [is] properly before the Arbitrator in accordance with [the CBA]" and, if so, "was due process followed and was the termination of [the grievants] for just cause? If not, what is the appropriate remedy?" *Id.* at 3.

On the arbitrability issue, the Arbitrator found that the grievants were entitled to grieve their terminations under the CBA. *Id.* at 16. On the merits, the Arbitrator determined that the due process and just cause standards incorporated in the CBA did not apply to the grievants as temporary employees. *Id.* at 18-20. Finding that the Statement the grievants signed set forth the "conditions governing [their] temporary appointments," *id.* at 17, the Arbitrator further determined that "under [the] specific terms set forth in the signed statements[,]" the grievants' employment "could end for any legal reason[,]" *id.* at 18. In the Arbitrator's view, the grievants were not entitled to "commonly accepted due process requirement[s]" or "all the recognized steps . . . contained in the standard just cause provision." *Id.* at 18, 19. Therefore, the Arbitrator concluded, the grievants' "temporary appointments properly ended." *Id.* at 19.

III. Positions of the Parties

A. Union's Exceptions

The Union contends that the award is deficient because: (1) it fails to draw its essence from the CBA; and (2) it is contrary to law.

With respect to the essence exception, the Union argues that, contrary to the Arbitrator's interpretation, the CBA does not exclude the grievants from the due process and just cause standards incorporated in the CBA. Exceptions at 6. In this regard, the Union asserts that the grievants are part of the bargaining unit and no evidence was presented at arbitration that distinguishes temporary employees from the rest of the bargaining unit regarding disciplinary actions. *Id.* at 4. The Union also argues that the Arbitrator erred by finding that the grievants waived their contractual rights to due process and discipline for just cause by signing the Statement. *Id.* at 5-6. In addition, the Union contends that the Arbitrator failed to consider evidence presented at the arbitration hearing that other employees were given due process rights and an opportunity to respond to proposed disciplinary actions. *Id.* at 5, 7.

The Union also argues that the award is contrary to law "because it violate[s] the parties' [CBA]." *Id.* at 3.

B. Agency's Opposition

The Agency argues that it is irrelevant whether the Arbitrator erred in determining that the grievants waived certain of their rights under the CBA because the grievance was not arbitrable.[1] Opp'n at 2-3. Moreover, the Agency contends, even if the Arbitrator erroneously found that the grievants waived their rights, it was a "harmless error" because they had no rights to waive. *Id.* at 3-4. Finally, the Agency asserts, the Union's exceptions "merely disagree[]" with the award and mere disagreement with an award does not demonstrate that the award is deficient. *Id.* at 4.

IV. Analysis and Conclusions

The Union argues that the award fails to draw its essence from the CBA. Exceptions at 5-7. In reviewing an arbitrator's interpretation of a collective bargaining agreement, the Authority applies the deferential standard of review that federal courts use in reviewing arbitration awards in the private sector. *See* 5 U.S.C. § 7122(a)(2); *AFGE, Council 220*, 54 FLRA 156, 159 (1998). Under this standard, the Authority will find that an arbitration award is deficient as failing to draw its essence from the collective bargaining agreement when the appealing party establishes that the award: (1) cannot in any rational way be derived from the agreement; (2) is so unfounded in reason and fact and so unconnected with the wording and purposes of the collective bargaining agreement as to manifest an infidelity to the obligation of the arbitrator; (3) does not represent a plausible interpretation of the agreement; or (4) evidences a manifest disregard of the agreement. *See U.S. Dep't of Labor (OSHA)*, 34 FLRA 573, 575 (1990). The Authority and the courts defer to arbitrators in this context "because it is the arbitrator's construction of the agreement for which the parties have bargained." *Id.* at 576.

The Union bases its essence exception on three claims: (1) the CBA's due process and just cause standards apply to the grievants; (2) the grievants did not waive their contractual rights to due process and discipline for just cause by signing the Statement; and (3) the Arbitrator failed to consider evidence presented at the arbitration hearing concerning the rights other employees were afforded to respond to proposed disciplinary actions. Exceptions at 5-7.

With regard to the Union's argument that the CBA's due process and just cause standards apply to the grievants, as noted above, the Arbitrator rejected this claim based on the Statement each grievant signed when he was hired. The Statement provided that, as temporary employees, the grievants were "not covered by the adverse action procedures under 5 [U.S.C. §] 4303 and 5 [U.S.C. §] 7511" and that the grievants appointments "may be terminated at any time." Award at 10. Nothing in the language of the CBA's due process and just cause standards is inconsistent with the Arbitrator's interpretation. Moreover, the Arbitrator's finding that the CBA's due process and just cause standards do not apply to the terminations of temporary employees such as the grievants is consistent with Authority precedent. *See U.S. Dep't of the Air Force, Luke Air Force Base, Ariz.*, 65 FLRA 820, 822 (2011) ("[T]he Arbitrator's determination that the grievants could be terminated only for just cause . . . is . . . without merit because agencies have the right to terminate temporary employees summarily, and parties are barred from establishing additional procedural protections that are not provided to terminated, temporary employees by statute."). For the foregoing reasons, the Union fails to demonstrate that the award, finding that the due process and just cause standards incorporated in the CBA do not apply to the grievants, is irrational, unfounded, implausible, or in manifest disregard of the CBA.

With regard to the Union's argument concerning "waiver," for the reasons discussed above, the Union has not demonstrated that the Arbitrator erred in finding that the CBA's due process and just cause standards do not apply to the grievants. Therefore,

1. No exceptions were filed to the Arbitrator's finding that the grievance was arbitrable. Accordingly, that issue is not before us, and we do not address it further.

the grievants had no such contractual rights to "waive." Accordingly, the Union fails to demonstrate on this basis as well that the award is irrational, unfounded, implausible, or in manifest disregard of the CBA.

With regard to the Union's argument that the Arbitrator ignored certain evidence at the arbitration hearing concerning the rights afforded other employees, this argument does not demonstrate that the award is deficient for essence reasons under any of the tests set forth above. *See U.S. Dep't of the Navy, Naval Aviation Depot, Norfolk, Va.*, 36 FLRA 217, 222-23 (1990).

Accordingly, we deny the Union's essence exception.[2]

V. Decision

The Union's exceptions are denied.

2. In addition, the Union asserts that the award is contrary to law "because it violates the parties' [CBA]." Exceptions at 3. Because the Union has failed to identify any law with which the award allegedly conflicts, we reject the Union's exception as a bare assertion. *See, e.g., U.S. Dep't of Homeland Sec., U.S. Immigration & Customs Enforcement,* 61 FLRA 503, 505 n.4 (2006).

65 FLRA No. 196

AMERICAN FEDERATION
OF GOVERNMENT EMPLOYEES
LOCAL 738
(Union)

and

UNITED STATES
DEPARTMENT OF THE ARMY
COMBINED ARMS CENTER AND
FORT LEAVENWORTH
FORT LEAVENWORTH, KANSAS
(Agency)

0-AR-4726

DECISION

June 27, 2011

Before the Authority: Carol Waller Pope, Chairman, and Thomas M. Beck and Ernest DuBester, Members

I. Statement of the Case

This matter is before the Authority on exceptions to an award of Arbitrator Michael D. Gordon filed by the Union under § 7122(a) of the Federal Service Labor-Management Relations Statute (the Statute) and part 2425 of the Authority's Regulations. The Agency filed an opposition to the Union's exceptions.

The Arbitrator determined that the Agency did not violate applicable law or the parties' agreement in evaluating the grievant's performance, and denied the grievance. For the following reasons, we dismiss the Union's exceptions.

II. Background and Arbitrator's Award

The Union filed a grievance on behalf of the grievant after he received an "unsuccessful" overall rating on his performance evaluation. Award at 14. The grievance was unresolved and submitted to arbitration, where the Arbitrator framed the issue as: "Did [the] [g]rievant's . . . [p]erformance [e]valuation violate applicable law and/or the [parties' agreement][;] and, if so . . . [w]hat is the appropriate remedy?" *Id.* at 3.

As an initial matter, the Arbitrator identified Article XVIII, Sections 1 and 3 and Article XXIX, Section 2(c) as the relevant provisions of the parties' agreement.[1] *Id.* He found that "[a]n evaluation must be in good faith and supported by convincing, demonstrable facts that reflect Article XVIII['s] values and safeguards[,]" and that, "[i]n [the] instan[t] [case], the Agency satisfied these criteria[.]" *Id.* at 28. The Arbitrator further found that "[a]ny Article XXIX deficiencies either involve ministerial requirements with no direct impact on the evaluation itself or other collateral matters that [do] not diminish its legitimacy." *Id.* at 29. In addition, he determined that the Agency did not violate applicable law in evaluating the grievant. *Id.* at 23, 29. Accordingly, he denied the grievance. *Id.* at 29.

III. Positions of the Parties

A. Union's Exceptions

The Union argues that the Arbitrator "created harmful errors by asking management how he should rule[,]" "fighting with the Union rep[,]" and "not identifying or holding management accountable for [its] failure to comply with": (1) "due process in the evaluation and arbitration processes"; (2) "5 U.S.C. [C]hapter 43 and [§] 5307(d) and 5 C.F.R. [part] 430"; (3) "the Negotiated Agreement"; (4) its obligation to provide "truthful testimony," as well as data that is "legally required" under "5 U.S.C. § 7101"; and (5) the Union's "request for witnesses." Exceptions at 1-2. The Union also argues that the Agency failed to comply with "AR 690-400 Chapter 4302 Total Army Performance Evaluation System[,]" as well as "the Occupational Safety and Health Act [(OSHA)] of 1970, 29 [U.S.C.] [§] 660 & [§] 2112 of title 28, United States Code Pub. L. 98-620 &

---

1. Article XVIII, Section 1 provides, in pertinent part: "The performance appraisal system shall provide fair, accurate and objective evaluation of job performance. Each employee's evaluation shall be directly related to their official duties. Management shall provide assistance to employees in meeting performance standards." Award at 3.

Article XVIII, Section 3 provides, in pertinent part: "Standards used for the evaluation or performance shall be fair, valid, objective, attainable and communicated in writing to each employee at the beginning of the rating period." *Id.*

Article XXIX, Section 2(c), provides, in pertinent part: "A grievance is defined to be a dispute or complaint between the Employer and the Union or employee(s) covered by this agreement, pertaining to the following: . . . [m]atters involving . . . the interpretation and application of agency policies, regulation, and practices whether specifically covered by this agreement or not." *Id.* at 4.

SEC. 11, Executive Order 12196, OSHA 29 [C.F.R.] [part] 1960, DODI 6055.1, DODI 6055.5, AR 385-10 and AR 40-5[.]" *Id.* at 1. The Union's remaining exceptions quote testimony and summarize evidence presented at the hearing. *See id.* at 2-138.

B. Agency's Opposition

The Agency contends that "the creation of 'harmful errors' is not a specific ground for review of an arbitrator's award as provided for in 5 [C.F.R.] § 2425.6[,]" and, therefore, the exceptions "must be dismissed in [their] entirety." Opp'n at 4, 6. In this connection, the Agency asserts that the Union "does not provide any justification in support of its 'harmful errors' claim[] other than [its] reference to the arguments contained in its post-hearing brief." *Id.* at 6.

IV. Analysis and Conclusions

The Authority's Regulations specifically enumerate the grounds that the Authority currently recognizes for reviewing awards. *See* 5 C.F.R. § 2425.6(a)-(b). In addition, the Regulations provide that if exceptions argue that an arbitration award is deficient based on private-sector grounds not currently recognized by the Authority, then the excepting party "must provide sufficient citation to legal authority that establishes the grounds upon which the party filed its exceptions." 5 C.F.R. § 2425.6(c).

Further, § 2425.6(e)(1) of the Regulations provides that an exception "may be subject to dismissal or denial if: . . . [t]he excepting party fails to raise and support" the grounds listed in § 2425.6(a)-(c), "or otherwise fails to demonstrate a legally recognized basis for setting aside the award[.]" 5 C.F.R. § 2425.6(e)(1). Thus, an exception that does not raise a recognized ground is subject to dismissal under the Regulations. *AFGE, Local 3955, Council of Prison Locals 33*, 65 FLRA 887, 889 (2011) (Member Beck dissenting in part) (*Local 3955*).

The Union's contentions that the Arbitrator created "harmful errors" and that the *Agency* failed to comply with various laws do not constitute grounds currently recognized by the Authority for reviewing awards. *See* 5 C.F.R. § 2425.6(a)-(b). As the Union does not raise a recognized ground or cite legal authority to support a ground not currently recognized by the Authority, we dismiss the exceptions. *See Local 3955*, 65 FLRA at 889.[2]

V. Decision

The Union's exceptions are dismissed.

2. Member Beck notes that he would contrast this case from *AFGE, Local 3955, Council of Prison Locals 33*, 65 FLRA 887, 891 (2011) for the reasons articulated in his dissent in that case. He would instead compare this case with *Fraternal Order of Police, Pentagon Police Labor Committee*, 65 FLRA 781 (2011) where the Union failed to explain adequately how the award was deficient. In this case, the Union relies upon sheer volume (128 pages of testimony and evidence that was presented to the Arbitrator), rather than a clear and articulable ground, to support its exception.

65 FLRA No. 197

AMERICAN FEDERATION
OF GOVERNMENT EMPLOYEES
NATIONAL BORDER PATROL COUNCIL
LOCAL 2724
(Union)

and

UNITED STATES
DEPARTMENT OF HOMELAND SECURITY
UNITED STATES BUREAU OF CUSTOMS
AND BORDER PROTECTION
OFFICE OF BORDER PATROL
RAMEY SECTOR
RAMEY, PUERTO RICO
(Agency)

0-AR-4242

DECISION

June 27, 2011

Before the Authority: Carol Waller Pope, Chairman, and Thomas M. Beck and Ernest DuBester, Members

I. Statement of the Case

This matter is before the Authority on exceptions to an award of Arbitrator Thomas R. Skulina filed by the Union under § 7122 of the Federal Service Labor-Management Relations Statute (the Statute) and part 2425 of the Authority's Regulations.[1] The Agency filed an opposition to the Union's exceptions.

The Arbitrator denied a grievance alleging that the Agency violated Administrative Manual 2274 (AM 2274) with respect to the rotation of Border Patrol Agents (BPAs) from the Office of Border Patrol (OBP), Ramey Sector, Puerto Rico (Ramey Sector) duty location to the continental United States (CONUS). For the reasons that follow, we deny the Union's exceptions.

II. Background and Arbitrator's Award

The OBP was formerly part of the U.S. Immigration and Naturalization Service (INS). Award at 3. The INS was abolished under the Homeland Security Act of 2002, and, in March 2003, the OBP became a part of the U.S. Department of Homeland Security, U.S. Bureau of Customs and Border Protection. *Id.* The OBP is divided into twenty sectors nationwide, one of which is the Ramey Sector.

The grievants are BPAs assigned to the Ramey Sector. *Id.* at 2. BPAs can apply for a basic tour of duty at the Ramey Sector for a period of three years and can request up to two one-year extensions of their tours. *Id.* Upon completion of their tours and on request, BPAs are rotated back to CONUS. *Id.* "When an employee seeks rotation, the employee must list five (5) location preferences"; if "a position is not available at the preferred [location], the employee may be required to supplement their request of rotation locations." *Id.*; *see also id.* at 3 (stating that "procedure for rotation is for the eligible agent to make selections from a list of potentially available stations[,]" and, "[i]f the first five do [not] work, then the [BPA] may pick five more potential transfer points"); Exceptions, Attach., Jt. Ex. 2, Section 16.

In August 2005, the Union presented a grievance alleging that the Agency violated AM 2274 when it failed to rotate the grievants back to the CONUS in a timely manner.[2] Award at 2; Exceptions, Attach., Jt. Ex. 3(a). The parties were unable to resolve the grievance, and the matter was submitted to arbitration. Award at 1.

Because the parties could not agree on the issues, the Arbitrator framed the relevant issue as whether the Agency, with respect to the rotation of BPAs from the Ramey Sector to CONUS, violated AM 2274.[3] *Id.* The Arbitrator noted that the Union asserted, in this regard, that the Agency "failed to rotate employees to one of the preferred locations picked by the employee within sixty (60) days after the tour of duty ended, failed to submit requests to the appropriate sector[,] and failed to require the individual sector to acknowledge receipt of the employee's request to rotate [to] that sector." *Id.*

1. The Authority's Regulations concerning the review of arbitration awards, as well as certain related procedural Regulations, were revised effective October 1, 2010. *See* 75 Fed. Reg. 42, 283 (2010). Because the Union's exceptions were filed before that date, we apply the prior Regulations.

2. The relevant text of AM 2274 is set forth in the appendix to this decision.

3. The Agency also asserted that the grievance was untimely. No exceptions were filed regarding this issue. Accordingly, it is not before us.

The Arbitrator found that, "[w]hatever procedural difficulties took place," the Agency did not violate AM 2274 because the Agency had the authority "to rotate [employees] to [the] northern and southern border areas of CONUS as a priority instigated by Congress and management . . . ." *Id.* at 4.

Noting that Congress "makes appropriations," the Arbitrator found that "[f]iscal restraints could impact on rotations." *Id.* at 3; *see also* Exceptions, Jt. Ex. 2, Section 8a(2). The Arbitrator found that, for fiscal year 2005, Congress had earmarked funds to place more agents in the northern and southern borders and that the "evidence was clear that the [Agency] did not have the option to spend money other than how it was allocated." Award at 4. The Arbitrator further found that, in 2004, no BPAs applied for rotation to the northern and southern borders, which, he noted, was another prerequisite for rotation. *Id.; see also* Tr. at 20, 22 & 199.

The Arbitrator also found that AM 2274 provides management with "the authority to adjust tours of duty as needed to meet operational/administrative requirements" and that "there [was] no proof that there is any limitation" on such authority. Award at 3, 4. According to the Arbitrator, this authority is "well grounded" because the Agency deals with "awesome responsibilities generated by 911," as well as "many other potential border problems . . . ." *Id.* at 4.

Accordingly, the Arbitrator denied the grievance.

III. Positions of the Parties

A. Union's Exceptions

The Union argues that the award fails to draw its essence from AM 2274, Section 16. Exceptions at 13-25. According to the Union, although the Arbitrator acknowledged Section 8a(2) of the agreement, the Arbitrator did not address: (1) "whether the tours of duty were properly extended"; (2) whether the Agency improperly limited the stations available to Ramey Sector BPAs for rotation; or (3) the impact of Section 16a(3) of the agreement. *Id.* at 13-14. The Union asserts that Section 16a(3) of AM 2274 provides, in part, that "'[i]f an employee indicates locations where appropriate positions are not available or where turnover is limited, he/she will be requested to expand the area of availability.'" *Id.* at 16 (quoting Jt. Ex. 2 at 2274.10). The Union asserts that Section 16a(3) further provides, in part, that "'[w]henever an employee has not been rotated within 60 days after his/her tour of duty ends, the responsible Headquarters program manager will direct placement to a position at one of the preferred locations designated by the employee.'" *Id.* at 22-23 (quoting Jt. Ex. 2 at 2274.10). According to the Union, this provision requires that, once the Agency has decided to fill a BPA position, Ramey Sector BPAs who are eligible for rotation must be allowed to request that location and must be considered for that position. *Id.* at 23. The Union contends that this provision further requires that, "once [an employee's] tour of duty has ended, if the employee has not been rotated within sixty days, the [Agency] should direct placement of the employee to one of the locations designated by the employee, assuming that there is an appropriate position available . . . ." *Id.*

The Union further asserts that the award is contrary to law, rule or regulation. *Id.* at 26. In particular, the Union asserts that the Arbitrator's conclusion that "management's rights under [§] 7106 [of the Statute] take precedence over AM 2274, and therefore the Agency need not comply with the procedures set out in AM 2274" is contrary to law. *Id.* The Union asserts that § 7106(b)(2) and (3) is the "legal basis for the negotiation" of AM 2274 and, as such, AM 2274 is "an appropriate arrangement for employees adversely affected by the exercise of management's rights . . . ." *Id.*

The Union claims that the award is based on a nonfact because, according to the Union, the Arbitrator found that the Agency "did not have the option to spend money on the rotation of Ramey [Sector BPAs] back to CONUS." *Id.* at 29. The Union contends that testimony "does not support a finding that the Agency had no discretion in how its budget was spent[,]" but, rather, shows that the Agency did have discretion to spend money on the rotation of BPAs back to CONUS. *Id.*

The Union asserts that the award is "ambiguous, incomplete and contradictory." *Id.* at 30. According to the Union, the award is "replete with misstatements of fact" regarding the description of the parties' bargaining history, the rotation of BPAs during the relevant time period, and the procedure for BPAs to request rotation. *Id.* at 30-32 (citing Award at 3). The Union also contends that the Arbitrator "incorrectly summarized the issues raised by the Union when he failed to note that the Union also asserted that the [A]gency improperly limited the stations available to the Ramey [Sector BPAs] for rotation, and failed to timely rotate the employees after their tour of duty had ended." *Id.* at 30.

B. Agency's Opposition

The Agency asserts that the Union's contention that the award fails to draw its essence from AM 2274 constitutes "mere disagreement" with the Arbitrator's interpretation and application of the agreement. Opp'n at 5-6. The Agency also asserts that, because determination of the budget is a management right, the Union "cannot demand or force the [Agency] to reallocate or spend money on rotations that is not already designated for that . . . purpose." *Id.* at 7. Further, the Agency disputes the Union's claim that the Arbitrator did not address Section 16a(3) of AM 2274. *Id.* (citing Award at 3). The Agency contends that the Arbitrator "found that the [Agency] ha[s] the right under . . . § 7106 to adjust tours of duty and that this right is expressly preserved in AM 2274." *Id.* at 8.

The Agency asserts that the Union has not demonstrated that the award is contrary to law, rule, or regulation. *Id.* at 10. The Agency contends that the Union's assertion that the Arbitrator concluded that management's rights take precedence over AM 2274 "is an incorrect interpretation" of the award. *Id.* The Agency asserts that the Arbitrator "found, as a matter of contract interpretation, that AM 2274 did not waive management's right to assign employees." *Id.*

The Agency asserts that the Union has not shown that the Arbitrator's determination that the Agency could not spend money on rotating BPAs back to CONUS is a nonfact. *Id.* at 12. The Agency contends that this assertion is "merely a disagreement" with the Arbitrator's finding that Congress placed restrictions on the Agency's appropriations for the relevant years. *Id.* at 13. The Agency asserts that, in its closing brief to the Arbitrator, it provided an "in[-]depth explanation" of how it received its funding and how funding was earmarked for the relevant time period. *Id.* at 13 n.10 (citing Ex. B, Agency's Closing Brief at 8-11).

The Agency disputes the Union's assertion that the award is ambiguous, incomplete, and contradictory. *Id.* at 13. According to the Agency, because the Union has failed to show that implementation of the award is impossible, it has not shown that the award is deficient in this regard. *Id.*

IV. Analysis and Conclusions

A. The Arbitrator did not exceed his authority.

The Union contends that that the Arbitrator did not address whether the BPAs' tours of duty were properly extended and whether the Agency improperly limited the stations available to the Ramey Sector BPAs for rotation. We construe this claim as an assertion that the Arbitrator exceeded his authority by failing to resolve an issue submitted to arbitration.

Arbitrators exceed their authority when they fail to resolve an issue submitted to arbitration, resolve an issue not submitted to arbitration, disregard specific limitations on their authority, or award relief to those not encompassed within the grievance. *AFGE, Local 1617*, 51 FLRA 1645, 1647 (1996). In determining whether an arbitrator has exceeded his or her authority, the Authority accords an arbitrator's interpretation of a stipulated issue, or the arbitrator's formulation of an issue to be decided in the absence of a stipulation, the same substantial deference that it accords an arbitrator's interpretation and application of a collective bargaining agreement. *See U.S. Info. Agency, Voice of Am.*, 55 FLRA 197, 198 (1999).

Because the parties did not stipulate the issue, the Arbitrator framed the relevant issue as whether the Agency violated AM 2274 with respect to the rotation of BPAs from the Ramey Sector to CONUS. Award at 1. The Arbitrator also stated that, in this regard, the Union asserts that the Agency "failed to rotate employees to one of the preferred locations picked by the employee within sixty (60) days after the tour of duty ended, failed to submit requests to the appropriate sector[,] and failed to require the individual sector to acknowledge receipt of the employee's request to rotate [to] that sector." *Id.; see also* Exceptions, Attach., Nov. 9, 2006, Tr. at 98-100 (Arbitrator stated that, if the parties could not agree on the issue, he could formulate the issue after he "hear[d] the case").

Based on the issue before him and the record evidence, the Arbitrator denied the grievance, finding that the evidence did not support the Union's contention that the Agency violated AM 2274 with respect to the rotation of the Ramey Sector BPAs. The Arbitrator's finding is directly responsive to the issue before him. The Union has not demonstrated that the Arbitrator's determination exceeds his authority.

Accordingly, we deny this exception.

B. The award draws its essence from the parties' agreement.

The Union asserts that the award fails to draw its essence from AM 2274.[4] Exceptions at 13-25. In this regard, the Union contends that, although the Arbitrator "acknowledged" Section 8a(2) of the agreement, he failed to address the impact of Section 16a(3), which, the Union claims, sets out the Agency's obligations if an employee has not been rotated sixty days after his or her tour has ended. *Id.* at 13-14.

In reviewing an arbitrator's interpretation of a collective bargaining agreement, the Authority applies the deferential standard of review that federal courts use in reviewing arbitration awards in the private sector. *See* 5 U.S.C. § 7122(a)(2); *AFGE, Council 220*, 54 FLRA 156, 159 (1998). Under this standard, the Authority will find that an arbitration award is deficient as failing to draw its essence from the collective bargaining agreement when the appealing party establishes that the award: (1) cannot in any rational way be derived from the agreement; (2) is so unfounded in reason and fact and so unconnected with the wording and purposes of the collective bargaining agreement as to manifest an infidelity to the obligation of the arbitrator; (3) does not represent a plausible interpretation of the agreement; or (4) evidences a manifest disregard of the agreement. *See U.S. Dep't of Labor (OSHA)*, 34 FLRA 573, 575 (1990). The Authority and the courts defer to arbitrators in this context "because it is the arbitrator's construction of the agreement for which the parties have bargained." *Id.* at 576.

In finding that the Agency did not violate AM 2274, the Arbitrator examined and applied Section 8a(2), which concerns tours of duty, and Section 16, which concerns rotations, including Section 16a(3). *See* Award at 3. Under Section 8a(2), the Agency retains the authority to adjust tours of duty as needed to meet operational/administrative requirements. *See id.; see also* Exceptions, Jt. Ex. 2 at 2274.05. Section 16 provides for the rotation of an employee upon completion of a tour of duty, including the submission of the employee's list of preferred locations. *See* Exceptions, Attach., Jt. Ex. 2 at 2274.10. However, Section 16a(3) further provides that "[p]lacement at one of these offices [employee's preferred location] is not guaranteed" and that, "[i]f an employee indicates locations where appropriate positions are not available or where turnover is limited, he/she will be requested to expand the area of availability." *Id.*

Interpreting these provisions, the Arbitrator found that, for fiscal year 2005, funds were earmarked "to get more agents in the [n]orthern and [s]outhern borders" and that the "evidence was clear that the [Agency] did not have the option to spend money other than how it was allocated." Award at 3. In so finding, the Arbitrator determined that the Agency's authority was "well grounded" because the Agency deals with "awesome responsibilities generated by 911," as well as "many other potential border problems . . . ." *Id.* at 4. The Arbitrator considered the "procedural" requirements under Section 16, but found that the Agency did not violate AM 2274 because it had the authority to rotate employees to the northern and southern borders of CONUS as a "priority." *Id.*; *see also id.* at 3.

Based on the wording of Sections 8a(2) and 16a(3) of AM 2274, the Union has failed to demonstrate that the Arbitrator's interpretation and application of AM 2274 manifests a disregard of the agreement or is implausible, irrational, or unfounded. Moreover, an arbitrator's failure to set forth specific findings, or to specify and discuss all allegations in a grievance, does not provide a basis for finding an award deficient. *See, e.g., Nat'l Ass'n of Indep. Labor, Local 5*, 65 FLRA 502, 505 (2011); *see also U.S. Dep't of Justice, Fed. Bureau of Prisons, Corr. Inst., McKean, Pa.*, 49 FLRA 45, 49 (1994) (disagreement with an arbitrator's interpretation of the parties' agreement and his evaluation of the evidence provides no basis for finding an award deficient). The Union's exception, thus, provides no basis for finding the award deficient.

Accordingly, we deny this exception.

C. The Union's contrary to law exception does not provide a basis for finding the award deficient.

The Union asserts that the award is contrary to law, rule or regulation. Exceptions at 26. In particular, the Union asserts that the Arbitrator's conclusion that "management's rights under [§] 7106 [of the Statute] take precedence over AM 2274, and therefore the Agency need not comply with the procedures set out in AM 2274" is contrary to law. *Id.*

When an exception involves an award's consistency with law, the Authority reviews any question of law raised by the exception and the award

4. The parties concede that AM 2274 "is a negotiated agreement." *See* Exceptions at 3-4, 1; Opp'n at 1.

de novo. *See NTEU, Chapter 24*, 50 FLRA 330, 332 (1995) (citing *U.S. Customs Serv. v. FLRA*, 43 F.3d 682, 686-87 (D.C. Cir. 1994)). In applying the standard of de novo review, the Authority assesses whether an arbitrator's legal conclusions are consistent with the applicable standard of law. *See U.S. Dep't of Def., Dep'ts of the Army & the Air Force, Ala. Nat'l Guard, Northport, Ala.*, 55 FLRA 37, 40 (1998). In making that assessment, the Authority defers to the arbitrator's underlying factual findings. *See id.*

Here, the issue before the Arbitrator concerned whether the Agency violated AM 2274 with respect to the rotation of BPAs from the Ramey Sector. *See* Award at 1; Exceptions at 2; Opp'n at 1. The Arbitrator interpreted AM 2274 as permitting the Agency to adjust tours of duty as needed to meet operational/administrative requirements. *See* Award at 3-4; *see also* Exceptions, Jt. Ex. 2 at 2274.05. We have denied the Union's essence exception. Thus, even assuming that the Arbitrator also based his award on § 7106 of the Statute, the Union's assertion would not provide a basis for finding the award was contrary to law. *Cf. U.S. Dep't of the Treasury, IRS, Oxon Hill, Md.* 56 FLRA 292, 299 (2000) (finding that, when excepting party fails to demonstrate that award is deficient on one of the grounds relied on by the arbitrator, it is unnecessary to address exceptions to other grounds).

Accordingly, we deny this exception.

D. The award is not based on a nonfact.

To establish that an award is based on a nonfact, the appealing party must demonstrate that the central fact underlying the award is clearly erroneous, but for which a different result would have been reached by the arbitrator. *U.S. Dep't of the Air Force, Lowry Air Force Base, Denver, Colo.*, 48 FLRA 589, 593 (1993). However, the Authority will not find an award deficient on the basis of an arbitrator's determination on any factual matter that the parties disputed at arbitration. *Id.* at 594 (citing *Nat'l Post Office Mailhandlers v. U.S. Postal Serv.*, 751 F.2d 834, 843 (6th Cir. 1985)).

The Union's nonfact exception challenges the Arbitrator's finding that the Agency "did not have the option to spend money" on the rotation of Ramey Sector BPAs back to CONUS. Exceptions at 29; *see also* Award at 3. This issue was disputed before the Arbitrator. *See, e.g.*, Opp'n, Attach., Nov. 9, 2006, Tr. at 90, 105-06 & 108. As a result, the Union's exception provides no basis for finding the award deficient. *See, e.g., AFGE, Local 1658*, 57 FLRA 658, 661 (2001).

Accordingly, we deny this exception.

E. The award is not ambiguous, incomplete, or contradictory.

The Union asserts that the award is ambiguous, incomplete, and contradictory because the award is "replete with misstatements of fact" regarding the description of the parties' bargaining history, the rotation of BPAs during the relevant time period, and the procedure for BPAs to request rotation. Exceptions at 30-32 (citing Award at 3). The Union also contends that the Arbitrator "incorrectly summarized" certain issues that it raised. *Id.*

The Authority will find an award deficient when it is incomplete, ambiguous, or so contradictory as to make implementation of the award impossible. *See U.S. Dep't of Labor, Mine Safety & Health Admin., Se. Dist.*, 40 FLRA 937, 943 (1991). For an award to be found deficient on this ground, the appealing party must show that implementation of the award is impossible because the meaning and effect of the award are too unclear or uncertain. *See U.S. Dep't of the Army, Corpus Christi Army Depot, Corpus Christi, Tex.*, 56 FLRA 1057, 1074 (2001).

To the extent that the Union contends that the Arbitrator incorrectly summarized the issues that it raised, we construe this contention as a claim that the Arbitrator exceeded his authority by failing to address these issues, a claim that we rejected above.

As to the Union's claim that the award contains misstatements of fact, the Union has failed to show that, even if its claim is true, implementation of the award is impossible because the meaning and effect of the award are too unclear or uncertain. As a result, the Union has provided no basis for finding that the award is incomplete, ambiguous, or contradictory. *See, e.g., AFGE, Local 1395*, 64 FLRA 622, 624 (2010) (party's claim that arbitrator failed to address several issues and failed to define a certain term did not establish that award was incomplete, ambiguous, or contradictory).

Accordingly, we deny this exception.

V. Decision

The Union's exceptions are denied.

APPENDIX

The relevant Sections of AM 2274 are set forth below:

Section 8

8. TOURS OF DUTY

a. Tours of Duty:

. . . .

(2) Bargaining Unit: 2+1+1+1 Employees will serve a two-year initial tour of duty. When an employee requests an extension of tour, one year extensions may be granted at the discretion of appropriate management officials. (Exception: [BPA] positions in Puerto Rico – the tour of duty is 3 +1+1.)

. . . .

Management retains the authority to adjust tours of duty as needed to meet operational/administrative requirements.

. . . .

Exceptions, Attach., Jt. Ex. 2 at 2274.04-2274.05; *see also* Award at 3.

Section 16

16. ROTATION UPON COMPLETION OF TOUR OF DUTY

a. Employees who are completing their tours of duty outside the [CONUS], those not requesting extensions and those whose extensions are denied will, six months prior to completion of their tours:

(1) Submit a memorandum through official channels . . . designating at least five office locations in order of preference which are acceptable to them for return placement.

(2) If the request for rotation is to a location under the jurisdiction of another office, a copy of the request will be forwarded to the appropriate personnel officer. A further acknowledgement will be sent to the employee upon receipt by that office.

(3) Placement at one of these offices is not guaranteed. Whenever an employee has not been rotated within 60days after his/her tour of duty ends, the responsible Headquarters program manager will direct placement to a position at one of the preferred locations designated by the employee. . . . . If an employee indicates locations where appropriate positions are not available or where turnover is limited, he/she will be requested to expand the area of availability.

. . . .

Exceptions, Attach., Jt. Ex. 2 at 2274.10-2274.11; *see also* Award at 3.

65 FLRA No. 198

UNITED STATES
DEPARTMENT OF THE TREASURY
INTERNAL REVENUE SERVICE
WAGE AND INVESTMENT DIVISION
AUSTIN, TEXAS
(Agency)

and

NATIONAL TREASURY
EMPLOYEES UNION
CHAPTER 72
(Union)

0-AR-3977
(64 FLRA 39 (2009))

DECISION

June 27, 2011

Before the Authority: Carol Waller Pope, Chairman, and Thomas M. Beck and Ernest DuBester, Members

I. Statement of the Case

This matter is before the Authority on exceptions to an award of Arbitrator LeRoy R. Bartman filed by the Agency under § 7122 of the Federal Service Labor-Management Relations Statute (the Statute) and part 2425 of the Authority's Regulations. The Union filed an opposition to the Agency's exceptions.

In *United States Department of the Treasury, Internal Revenue Service, Wage & Investment Division, Austin, Texas*, 64 FLRA 39 (2009) (*IRS, Austin*), the Authority remanded an award to the Arbitrator for further findings. On remand, the Arbitrator awarded $200,000 in compensatory damages and restoration of the grievant's leave. For the reasons that follow, we deny the Agency's exceptions in part and grant them in part, and remand the award in part to the parties for further action consistent with this decision.

II. Background and Arbitrator's Award

A. Original Award

In his initial award (Original Award), the Arbitrator sustained a grievance claiming that the Agency violated the Rehabilitation Act (the Act) of 1973, as amended, 29 U.S.C. § 791, the parties' collective bargaining agreement (parties' agreement), and other laws, rules, or regulations by discriminating against the grievant based on his disability, creating a hostile work environment, and retaliating against the grievant for filing an Equal Employment Opportunity (EEO) complaint. The Arbitrator awarded the grievant $200,000 in compensatory damages and restoration of his leave.

B. Authority's Decision in *IRS, Austin*

In *IRS, Austin*, the Authority found that the record did not permit it to determine whether: (1) the amount of compensatory damages awarded was consistent with law or (2) the Arbitrator erred in restoring the grievant's leave. As a result, the Authority remanded these portions of the award to the parties for resubmission to the Arbitrator, absent settlement. 64 FLRA at 57.

With respect to the award of compensatory damages, the Authority found that the Arbitrator failed to cite any evidence as the basis for his award or make the necessary findings to substantiate his award. *Id.* at 55-56. Specifically, the Authority found that the Arbitrator "did not rely on any of the testimonial or documentary evidence in the record that establishes that the grievant is entitled to compensatory damages or to the amount of those damages." *Id.* at 55. The Authority noted that, although the Arbitrator did not set forth specific findings as required, his findings and the size of his award suggested that part of the sum may be punishment for the Agency's conduct toward the grievant and for his loss of future earnings. *Id.* The Authority further noted that punitive damages are not available in discriminatory conduct cases brought against federal agencies and that proof of entitlement to loss of future earnings involves evidence suggesting that an individual's injuries have narrowed the range of economic opportunities available to him. *Id.* (citations omitted). Stating that the record did not permit it to determine whether the amount of compensatory damages awarded was consistent with law, the Authority remanded this portion of the award to the parties for resubmission to the Arbitrator, absent settlement, for his clarification of the grievant's entitlement to compensatory damages based on the proper legal framework. *Id.* at 55-56 (citation omitted).

As to the restoration of the grievant's leave for the period 2002-2003, the Authority found that the Arbitrator made no findings linking the scope of the leave awarded and the scope of the Agency's illegal activity. *Id.* at 56. Because the record did not permit the Authority to make this determination, the Authority remanded this part of the award to the parties, instructing that, on remand, the Arbitrator should specify the amount of leave awarded and the manner in which the Agency's illegal actions are responsible for its use. *Id.*

C. Arbitrator's Award on Remand

On remand (remand award), the Arbitrator awarded the grievant a non-punitive compensatory award of $200,000 and restoration of lost benefits (sick leave and annual leave) for the years 2002-2003. Remand Award at 12-13, 15-16. The Arbitrator stated that, in so deciding, he had "reviewed all 831 pages of the . . . transcript, the joint exhibits, the Union's 130 exhibits and the Agency's 30 exhibits[,]" case law submitted by the parties, and testimony of witnesses. *Id.* at 10-11.

In awarding compensatory damages, the Arbitrator found that an award of $200,000 was supported by Equal Employment Opportunity Commission (EEOC) case law. *Id.* at 15-16 (citing *Franklin,* EEOC Appeal Nos. 07A00025 & 01A03882 (2001); *Rivers,* EEOC Appeal No. 01992843 (2002); *Ellis*, EEOC Appeal No. 01A13314 (2003); *Munno*, EEOC Appeal Nos. 01A01734 & 01A03001 (2001); *Mack*, EEOC Appeal No. 01983217 (2000), *recons. denied*, EEOC Appeal No. 01983217 (2000); and *Santiago*, EEOC Appeal No. 01955684 (1998)). For instance, the Arbitrator noted that, in *Franklin*, $150,000 in non-pecuniary damages was "based upon . . . evidence of emotional distress and the proven disability discrimination based upon a lack of reasonable accommodation." *Id.* at 15. The Arbitrator found that the record here "showed a lack of any good faith by the Agency to make any reasonable accommodation to prevent the stress which, according to testimony, was increased by" the grievant's supervisors. *Id.* Moreover, the Arbitrator stated that, in *Ellis*, the complainant's supervisor, like the grievant's supervisor here, "'picked apart her work[,]'" "'ostracized her in the work place'" and "'insinuated publicly that she was abusing sick leave.'" *Id.* (quoting *Ellis* at *2). The Arbitrator stated that this "treatment made the complainant's [medical condition] much worse, caused her intense physical and emotional pain and ultimately, compelled her to take disability retirement from the agency." *Id.* The Arbitrator found that record evidence shows that, like the grievant in *Ellis*, the grievant here "was forced into an approved medical retirement by the actions of the Agency." *Id.*

The Arbitrator further found that one physician's (Dr. 2's) examination of the grievant "provided the medical nexus between the increased severity of the [g]rievant's physical impairment to the increased stress he experienced at work." *Id.; see also id.* at 16 (finding that the medical assessment of Dr. 2, "in and of itself, substantiates . . . that the [g]rievant was entitled to the compensatory award of $200,000"). In this regard, the Arbitrator found that Dr. 2 determined, among other things, that:

- At the time of the examination, the grievant "'ha[d] not been able to work for several months. Each time he goes [back] to work, he develops increased wheezing and dyspnea which he attributes to the stress of his job'";

- "'[T]he pattern of deterioration'" that he observed in the grievant's condition from when he first saw him in September 2002 until May 2003 "'is consistent with his report of unrelieved stress, and he related that stress to what was happening to him at his job'"; and

- "'Had the amount and consistency of [the grievant's] stress been eliminated or greatly reduced, it is likely that the degree and rate of deterioration in [the grievant's] condition that precipitated Dr. [1's] referral of [the grievant] to [him] and that continued . . . would have been lessened or prevented altogether."

Id. at 13-15 (quoting Dr. 2's Letters dated May 18, 2003 (May 18 Letter) & April 6, 2004 (April 6 Letter)); *see also* Opp'n, Attach., Union Exs. 105 (May 18 Letter) & 128 (April 6 Letter).

In awarding restoration of the grievant's leave, the Arbitrator noted that the EEOC has held that a claim for restoration of sick leave hours allegedly taken because of discriminatory actions is recoverable under Title VII as a request for equitable damages and that, if an employee takes leave "'to avoid or recover from discriminating harassment, sick leave must be treated as excused leave in order to make the appellant whole and place [the employee] in a position [he/she] would have been absent the discrimination.'" Remand Award at 13 (quoting *Merriell*, EEOC Appeal No. 01890072 (1989)). After reviewing the evidence, including the medical findings of Dr. 2 described above and an audit of the grievant's leave forms, the Arbitrator found that the grievant took sick leave "to avoid or recover from discriminating harassment." *Id.* at 15. The Arbitrator noted that the record indicates that the grievant's leave usage increased from 37% in 2002 to over 70% in 2003. *Id.* at 13. As a result, the Arbitrator found that the grievant's "sick leave must be treated as excused leave in order to make the [grievant] whole or in the position [he] would have been absent the harassment." *Id.* at 15 (internal quotations omitted). Accordingly, the Arbitrator found that the grievant "was to receive an award of all lost benefits or other concurrent benefits of employment he would have earned." *Id.*

III. Positions of the Parties

A. Agency's Exceptions

The Agency asserts that the $200,000 award, which is "solely compensation for non-pecuniary damages" and is not for "loss of future earnings" or punitive damages, is contrary to law. Exceptions at 10 (citing Remand Award at 12 (emphasis omitted)).

The Agency asserts that the award of $200,000 in non-pecuniary damages is contrary to law because the harm suffered by the complainants in the cases relied upon by the Arbitrator differed significantly from the harm suffered by the grievant. *Id.* at 9-11. In this regard, the Agency contends that the Arbitrator does not explain why the harm suffered by the grievant was comparable to the harm suffered by the complainant in *Mack,* arguing that the Arbitrator identified no evidence that showed that the grievant suffered harm that "totally incapacitated" him for work or in his personal life. *Id.* at 15. The Agency also contends that the harm suffered by the grievant is dissimilar to the harm suffered by the complainants in *Franklin* and *Munno*. The Agency contends that the "remaining cases cited by the [A]rbitrator" -- i.e., *Ellis, Rivers*, and *Santiago* -- "have no relevance to the damages suffered by the [g]rievant . . . ." *Id.* at 14.

Further, the Agency asserts that, while it believes that the grievant "did not suffer catastrophic emotional damages and should not receive an award" greater than $100,000, the awards granted in *Ellis, Rivers,* and *Santiago*, which averaged about $122,000, "are more similar to the harm sustained by the [g]rievant . . . ." *Id.* at 15. The Agency contends that the case of *Carpenter*, EEOC Appeal No. 01945652 (1995), is even more similar. In that case, the Agency notes, the complainant, who suffered from asthma, was awarded $75,000 in compensatory damages for emotional distress. *Id.* at 15-16.

The Agency contends that the award does not address causation. The Agency asserts that the Arbitrator "did not cite any evidence to establish a connection between [its] discrimination and the harm" to the grievant. *Id.* at 17-18 (citing *Leperi,* EEOC Appeal No. 01964107 (1998)). The Agency further contends that the Arbitrator "disregarded the testimony" of a physician (Dr. 1), who testified that other factors beyond the grievant's working environment "contributed to the exacerbation of [his] asthma problems." *Id.* at 17 (citing Tr. at 465).

The Agency also contends that the grievant failed to prove that the delay between June 2002, when the grievant first requested a reasonable accommodation, and November 2002, when the Agency processed his request, was the "direct or proximate cause" of his "'fixed obstructive changes' consistent with [COPD]." *Id.* at 18 (quoting Opp'n, Attach., Union Exs. 105 & 128). The Agency further asserts that the Arbitrator based his finding that a "nexus existed between 'the increased severity of the [g]rievant's physical impairment' and the 'increased stress he experienced at work'" on evidence relating to Dr. 2 alone, but that Dr. 2 did not address the severity of his breathing impairment. *Id.* at 19 (quoting Remand Award at 14-16).

Concerning restoration of leave, the Agency asserts that, contrary to the Authority's decision in *IRS, Austin*, the Arbitrator did not make any findings linking the scope of the leave awarded to its actions, but, rather, "attribute[d]" the leave usage to its discriminatory conduct. *Id.* at 21. The Agency contends that, because the Arbitrator found that the Agency had subjected the grievant to discrimination from "May to November 2002[,]" the Arbitrator determined that the Agency ceased discriminating against the grievant in November 2002. *Id.* at 22 (citing Original Award at 23). As a result, the Agency contends, the Arbitrator had no basis to order the restoration of leave after November 2002. *Id.*

The Agency asks the Authority to reduce the award to an amount that is not "monstrously excessive" and is consistent with amounts awarded in similar cases, and that the Authority "not remand this case to the [A]rbitrator . . . ." *Id.*

B. Union's Opposition

The Union contends that the record "contains significant evidence of prolonged, serious and substantial harm to the [g]rievant stemming from the Agency's actions." Opp'n at 5. Relying on a number of cases, including *Franklin, Rivers, Ellis, Mack, Santiago,* and *Glockner*, EEOC Appeal No. 07A30105 (2004), the Union asserts that, contrary to the Agency's claim, the amount awarded by the Arbitrator is consistent with the amount awarded in similar cases. Opp'n at 7-12. Moreover, the Union contends, a pattern of discriminatory events, as occurred in this case, will generally lead to higher non-pecuniary compensatory damages than would be awarded in a case involving only one or two events. *Id.* at 5 (citing *Flythe*, EEOC Appeal No. 01972258 (2000)).

The Union further asserts that the EEOC has noted that "'the more inherently degrading or humiliating the agency action, the more reasonable it is to infer that [a] complainant[] would suffer humiliation or distress from the agency action.'" *Id.* at 12 (quoting *Heffley*, EEOC Appeal No. 07A40138 (2005) (citing *Glockner*)). The Union contends that the evidence shows that the grievant's supervisors sought to "increase rather than decrease [his] stress." *Id.* (citing Tr. at 181-82 (Union President testified concerning conversation where grievant informed her that his supervisor visited him in the hospital and discussed his performance)).

The Union contends that the Arbitrator addressed causation because the Arbitrator found a "direct nexus between the harm suffered by the [g]rievant and the Agency's unlawful conduct." *Id.* at 12. The Union further asserts that the Agency has not satisfied its burden of proof that the harm suffered by the grievant was caused by external factors. Opp'n at 14. The Union contends that "[a]t no point" during Dr. 1's testimony does he assert that "external factors" played "a role in exacerbating the [g]rievant's asthma" and that the Agency can "point to no . . . evidence" from Dr. 1 or any witness that supports this claim. *Id.* at 15 (citing Tr. at 465).

Finally, the Union contends that the evidence supports restoration of the grievant's leave for 2002-2003 and that the Agency has failed to present any "official leave records or other evidence" that rebuts the award. *Id.* at 21; *see also id.* at 16-21.

IV. Analysis and Conclusions

In remanding the original award, the Authority stated that the record did not permit the Authority to determine whether the amount of compensatory damages is consistent with law. *IRS, Austin*, 64 FLRA at 57. The Authority noted that the Arbitrator's "findings and the size of the award suggest that a part of this sum may be punishment for the Agency's conduct toward the grievant and for his loss of future earnings." *Id.* at 55. In the remand award, the Arbitrator indicated that the award of $200,000 is for "non-punitive compensatory" damages. Remand Award at 12; *see also id.* at 16. Based on the Arbitrator's award, we find that the award of $200,000 is limited to non-pecuniary compensatory damages. As set forth above, the Agency asserts that the award of $200,000 in non-pecuniary compensatory damages is contrary to law.

The Authority reviews questions of law raised by exceptions to an arbitrator's award de novo. *See NTEU, Chapter 24*, 50 FLRA 330, 332 (1995) (citing *U.S. Customs Serv. v. FLRA,* 43 F.3d 682, 686-87 (D.C. Cir. 1994)). In applying a standard of de novo review, the Authority determines whether the award is consistent with the applicable standard of law. *See NFFE, Local 1437*, 53 FLRA 1703, 1710 (1998). In making this determination, the Authority defers to the arbitrator's underlying factual findings. *See id.* When evaluating exceptions to an arbitration award, the Authority considers the award and record as a whole. *See, e.g., Soc. Sec. Admin., Office of Disability Adjudication & Review, Region 1*, 65 FLRA 334, 336 (2010) (citing, among other cases, *AFGE, Local 2328*, 62 FLRA 63, 65 (2007) (consistency with law "clear from the record as a whole")).

A. The portion of the award encompassing non-pecuniary damages is not contrary to law.

In a claim for compensatory damages, a grievant must demonstrate, through appropriate evidence, the harm suffered as a result of the agency's discriminatory action; the extent, nature, and severity of the harm suffered; and the duration or expected duration of the harm. *See IRS, Austin,* 64 FLRA at 54. The amount of compensatory damages awarded should reflect the extent to which the Agency's discriminatory action directly or proximately caused harm to the grievant and the extent to which other factors may have played a part. *See id.* and authorities cited therein. An award of compensatory damages should not be "monstrously excessive" standing alone, should not be the product of passion or prejudice, and should be consistent with the amount awarded in similar cases. *Id.* at 55. Awards of non-pecuniary damages in excess of $100,000 have resulted when the emotional damage has been catastrophic, leaving an employee unable to work for years to come, if ever. *See id.* at 54 (citing *Mack*).

Based on the evidence presented, the Agency has not demonstrated that the Arbitrator erred in awarding non-pecuniary damages. Medical and testimonial evidence show that the cumulative effect of the Agency's discriminatory actions resulted in the deterioration of the grievant's health and led to his developing COPD. Remand Award at 14 (quoting April 6 Letter) (noting that, in diagnosing the grievant's condition, Dr. 2 stated that "anxiety leads to flare-ups; flare-ups make controlling the asthma extremely difficult or impossible; poor control of severe asthma leads to COPD; COPD results in irreversible lung damage"); *see also* April 6 Letter (letter from Dr. 2 concerning the relationship between stress experienced at work by the grievant and the exacerbation of his medical condition). Further the record shows that, because of the increased deterioration of the grievant's health that resulted from the Agency's discriminatory actions, the grievant "was forced into . . . medical retirement" at approximately age forty-five, with irreversible lung damage. Remand Award at 15; *see also* Original Award at 22; *IRS, Austin*, 64 FLRA at 43.

In cases where victims of discrimination have suffered harm similar in degree to the grievant, the EEOC has awarded compensatory damages ranging from $100,000 to $200,000. *See, e.g., Mack* ($185,000 in non-pecuniary damages where, as a result of agency discrimination, complainant was left homeless for two years and suffered depression, emphysema, migraines and insomnia, and harm to family relationships); *Franklin* ($150,000 in non-pecuniary damages where, as a result of agency's discriminatory actions, complainant experienced extensive symptoms of emotional distress, resulting in changes in complainant's personality, the ending of his marriage, severe strains in his relationships with those close to him, including his children, and diminished enjoyment of life); *Glockner* ($200,000 in non-pecuniary damages where complainant suffered migraines, irritable bowel syndrome, depression, and stress that caused her to bite her cheeks so badly that surgery was required); and *Blount,* EEOC Appeal No. 0720070010 (2009), *recons. denied*, EEOC Appeal No. 0720070010 (2010) ($200,000 in non-pecuniary damages where agency failed to accommodate complainant resulting in his inability to work; complainant suffered from severe depression, for which he had taken medication).

The Agency contends that the Arbitrator does not explain why the harm suffered by the grievant is comparable to that suffered by the complainant in *Mack* and argues that the Arbitrator identified no evidence that showed that the grievant suffered harm that totally incapacitated him for work or in his personal life. Exceptions at 11-15. As stated above, awards of non-pecuniary damages in excess of $100,000 have resulted when the emotional damage has been catastrophic, leaving an employee unable to work for years to come, if ever. Here, the Arbitrator found that the Agency's discriminatory actions caused the grievant's health to deteriorate to the point where he was "forced into . . . medical retirement" at age forty-five. Remand Award at 15; *see also* Original Award at 22. Medical evidence also showed that the grievant's increased stress at work resulted in irreversible lung damage. Remand Award at 14 (citing April 6 Letter); *see also* May 18 Letter at 2 (stating that he believed that "much of [the grievant's] lung disease is fixed and not reversible" and that he did "not expect significant recovery in the future").

The Agency's contention that the harm suffered by the grievant is more similar to the harm suffered by the complainant in *Carpenter* also does not provide a basis for finding the Arbitrator erred. In that case, the EEOC, in awarding the complainant a lower amount of damages than he had sought, found that much of the damages about which he complained pre-dated the Civil Rights Act of 1991.

Accordingly, we find that the Agency has not demonstrated that the amount of damages awarded is contrary to law.

The Agency also contends that award is contrary to law because the Arbitrator "did not cite any evidence to establish a connection between the Agency's discrimination and the harm" to the grievant and, thus, the grievant did not meet his burden of proof. Exceptions at 18. Contrary to the Agency's contention, the Arbitrator examined the record regarding the nature, severity, and duration of the harm suffered by the grievant as a result of the Agency's discriminatory actions and found that the medical evidence provided a "nexus between the increased severity of the [g]rievant's physical impairment to the increased stress he experienced at work." Remand Award at 15; *see also id.* at 16 (finding that the medical assessment of Dr. 2, "in and of itself, substantiates . . . that the [g]rievant was entitled to the compensatory award of $200,000").

In addition to the medical evidence, the Arbitrator also found that the "record showed a lack of any good faith by the Agency to make any reasonable accommodation to prevent the stress, which according to testimony, was increased by [the grievant's] supervisors . . . ." *Id.* at 15. In this regard, the record shows, among other things, that: (1) the grievant requested a reassignment from supervisor 2 because of stress and was instructed by that supervisor to revise the letter, leaving out any references to his health, and resubmit it to supervisor 1; (2) the grievant's supervisors put pressure on him through "negative performance reviews despite his known medical problems"; (3) the grievant's appraisals were based upon a review of all the work he produced, instead of random samples; and (4) supervisor 1 shared the grievant's comments about on-the-job instructions he received from fellow workers with employees. *See* Original Award at 23; Remand Award at 6-7.

The Agency asserts that the Arbitrator "disregarded the testimony" of Dr. 1, who testified that "other factors beyond the [g]rievant's working environment contributed to the exacerbation of [his] asthma problems[,]" such as mold in his home and a seriously ill mother. Exceptions at 17 (citing Tr. at 465). However, there is nothing in the testimony referenced by the Agency that shows that Dr. 1 testified that the external factors mentioned increased the severity of the harm suffered by the grievant. The testimony shows that Dr. 1 responded to specific questions asked of him, but did not state that such external factors actually exacerbated the grievant's health problem.

Further, the Agency's contention that the grievant did not provide any proof that the delay between June 2002, when the grievant first requested a reasonable accommodation, and November 2002, when the Agency ultimately processed his request, was the direct or proximate cause of his health impairment also provides no basis for finding that the Arbitrator erred. During the period of June 2002 through November 2002, the Agency subjected the grievant to discrimination and harassment and created a hostile work environment. *See* Original Award at 23; *see also IRS, Austin*, 64 FLRA at 57. Moreover, evidence in the record shows that the cumulative effect of the Agency's actions resulted in the deterioration of the grievant's health. For example, Dr. 2 stated "'the pattern of deterioration'" that he observed in the grievant's condition "'from when [he] first saw him in September 2002 until . . . May 2003 is consistent with his report of unrelieved stress, and [that the grievant] related that stress to what was happening to him at his job.'" Remand Award at 14 (quoting April 6 Letter). Dr. 2 further stated that, "[h]ad the amount and consistency of [the grievant's] stress been eliminated or greatly reduced, it is likely that the degree and rate of deterioration in [the grievant's] condition ... would have been lessened or prevented altogether." *Id.* at 15 (quoting April 6 Letter).

In these circumstances, the Agency has not established that the Arbitrator failed to address causation. Accordingly, we find that the Agency has failed to establish that the Arbitrator erred in awarding the grievant $200,000 in non-pecuniary compensatory damages and deny this exception.

B. A remand of the portion of the award restoring leave to the grievant is necessary.

The Agency asserts that, contrary to *IRS, Austin*, the Arbitrator did not make any findings linking the scope of the leave awarded to its actions, but "attribute[d]" such usage to its discriminatory conduct. Exceptions at 20, 21.

In *IRS, Austin*, the Authority directed the Arbitrator to specify the amount of leave awarded the grievant and the manner in which the Agency's illegal actions are responsible for the use of that leave. 64 FLRA at 56; *see, e.g., Harrison*, EEOC Appeal No. 01A14848 (2002) (complainant provided sufficient documentation showing hours requested related to discrimination). "Whenever an agency is liable for unlawful employment discrimination, it must provide complainant with full, 'make-whole' relief to restore the complainant as nearly as possible to the position he or she would have been in absent the discrimination." *Ellis* at *2 (citation omitted). In the "federal sector, the agency's efforts in this regard should include (where appropriate) equitable relief . . . ." *Id.* (citation omitted). Restoration of leave taken because of discrimination suffered is a legitimate form of equitable relief. *Id.* (citation omitted).

As the Arbitrator found, the record establishes that the grievant took leave to "avoid or recover from discriminating harassment." Remand Award at 15. The Arbitrator directed the Agency to restore the grievant's leave for the "years 2002-2003." *Id.* at 13; *see also* Original Award at 23. However, while the evidence presented by the Union shows that the grievant used leave during the period that he was discriminated against by the Agency, the Arbitrator did not specify the amount of such leave or indicate when such leave was required because of the Agency's illegal activities. Moreover, the evidence submitted by the Union does not indicate clearly whether the grievant used leave for such purpose. *See, e.g.,* Opp'n, Attachs., Union Exs. 70(2) & 77 (notes from Dr. 1 requesting that the grievant be excused for certain days due to flu); Exs. 68, 69 (leave audit forms show grievant's leave usage, but do not explain reason for leave); Exs. 71-104 (medical certifications for grievant's use of sick leave include some pre-dating Agency's unlawful actions).

Accordingly, we remand this portion of the award to the parties for resubmission to the Arbitrator, absent settlement. On remand, the Arbitrator should specify the amount of leave awarded the grievant and the manner in which the Agency's illegal actions are responsible for the use of that leave.

The Agency requests that the award not be remanded to the Arbitrator. In *Alabama Association of Civilian Technicians*, 56 FLRA 231, 235 (2000) (Chairman Wasserman dissenting), the Authority noted "that a new arbitrator may be appointed to hear a matter where the original arbitrator resigns, dies, or is otherwise unable to act upon the issue." *Id.* at 235 (citing *Elkouri and Elkouri, How Arbitration Works,* 188 (5th Ed. 1997)); *see also How Arbitration Works,* 175-176 (6th Ed. 2003)). Here, the Agency has not explained why the award should not be remanded to the Arbitrator. Because the Agency has not provided any specific reasons why the award should not be remanded to the Arbitrator, there is no basis to conclude that this matter should be submitted to a new arbitrator.

Accordingly, we deny the Agency's request.

V. Decision

The Agency's exceptions are denied to the extent that the exceptions challenge the portion of the award granting $200,000 in non-pecuniary damages. With respect to the award of restoration of leave for the "years 2002-2003," this portion of the award is remanded to the parties for resubmission to the Arbitrator, absent settlement, for further findings consistent with this decision.

65 FLRA No. 199

SOCIAL SECURITY ADMINISTRATION
FREDERICKSBURG DISTRICT OFFICE
(Agency)

and

AMERICAN FEDERATION
OF GOVERNMENT EMPLOYEES
LOCAL 1923
(Union)

0-AR-4445

DECISION

June 29, 2011

Before the Authority: Carol Waller Pope, Chairman, and Thomas M. Beck and Ernest DuBester, Members

I. Statement of the Case

This matter is before the Authority on exceptions to an award of Arbitrator William W. Lowe filed by the Agency under § 7122(a) of the Federal Service Labor-Management Relations Statute (the Statute) and part 2425 of the Authority's Regulations. The Union filed an opposition to the Agency's exceptions.

The Union filed a grievance alleging that the Agency's performance rating of the grievant was contrary to law, rule, and/or the parties' collective bargaining agreement (CBA). The Arbitrator upheld the Agency's evaluation of the grievant as to one performance element, but determined that its evaluation as to a second element was contrary to the CBA. The Arbitrator thus sustained the grievance in part and denied it in part. For the reasons set forth below, we dismiss the Agency's exceptions in part and deny them in part.

II. Background and Arbitrator's Award

A. Background

The grievant worked as a Claims Representative. Award at 2. In the grievance, the Union alleged that the Agency improperly rated the grievant on three out of four of her performance elements. *Id.* at 4. The performance management and appraisal system that applies to the grievant has three tiers: Level 1 (Not Successful), Level 3 (Successful), and Level 5 (Outstanding). *Id.* at 3. The Agency rated the grievant at Level 3 (Successful) on all four of the performance elements: (1) Interpersonal Skills, (2) Participation, (3) Demonstrates Job Knowledge, and (4) Achieves Business Results. *Id.* at 2. This resulted in a summary performance rating of Successful Contribution. The Agency also gave her a performance award. *Id.* at 4, 23.

In the grievance, the Union claimed that the Agency should have rated the grievant at Level 5 on the Interpersonal Skills, Participation, and Achieves Business Results performance elements. The grievance also claimed that the Agency violated Article 3 of the CBA by not giving the grievant a rating that was fair and equitable when considering the quality and quantity of her work.[1] *See* Exceptions, Ex. 3 at 1; *see also* Opp'n, Exs. 1 & 2. Finally, the grievance argued that the grievant's performance award should be adjusted based on the change that the grievant sought in her performance rating. Exceptions, Ex. 3 at 1.

At the second step of the grievance process, the Agency raised the grievant's Achieves Business Results performance rating from Level 3 to Level 5. Opp'n, Ex. 1 at 3. However, the Agency did not raise the grievant's rating on the Interpersonal Skills and Participation performance elements. The parties then submitted the matter to arbitration to resolve the dispute concerning the two remaining performance elements.

The Arbitrator framed the issue as:

> Were the performance ratings given to [the grievant] in the elements Participation and Interpersonal Skills . . . a violation of the law, regulation and/or contract? If so, what is the appropriate remedy?

Award at 2.

1. Article 3, Section 2.A. provides, in pertinent part, that "[a]ll employees shall be treated fairly and equitably in all aspects of personnel management and without regard to political affiliation, race, color, religion, national origin, sex, sexual orientation, marital status, age, parental status or disabling condition, and with proper regard and protection of their privacy and constitutional rights." Exceptions, Ex. 5 at 3-1.

B. Arbitrator's Award

The Arbitrator sustained the grievance in part and denied it in part. As relevant here, the Arbitrator made several specific findings concerning the Union's claim that the Agency improperly rated the grievant on the Interpersonal Skills and Participation performance elements.

With regard to the Interpersonal Skills element, the Arbitrator determined that the evidence submitted by the grievant purporting to support a higher rating on that performance element did not address her interpersonal skills. *Id.* at 16. The Arbitrator further found that other evidence presented at arbitration demonstrated that the grievant's performance on the Interpersonal Skills element did not rise to Level 5. *Id.* at 17. The Arbitrator therefore concluded that the record did not support a change to the grievant's Interpersonal Skills performance rating from Level 3 to Level 5. *Id.*

With regard to the Participation element, the Arbitrator credited the testimony of several witnesses demonstrating that the grievant has a productive working relationship with others, that she is a team player, and that she regularly volunteers to help others when assistance is needed. *Id.* at 19-20. The Arbitrator found that this testimony showed that the grievant makes "significant and continuing contributions" above what is required by the Level 3 performance rating. *Id.* at 21-22. Accordingly, the Arbitrator determined, the Agency violated Article 3 of the CBA because it did not treat the grievant "fairly and equitably." *Id.* at 22.

The Arbitrator also cited Article 5 in his determination.[2] *Id.* Without any prior reference or further discussion, the Arbitrator similarly found that the Agency violated Article 5 by not treating the grievant fairly and equitably.[3]

For these reasons, the Arbitrator concluded that the record supported a change to the grievant's Participation performance rating from Level 3 to Level 5. *Id.* at 23. As this increased the grievant's overall element average from a three to a four, the Arbitrator directed the Agency to give the grievant a higher award, for which she was now eligible. Specifically, the Arbitrator ordered the Agency to give the grievant a Recognition of Contribution (ROC) award as a substitute for the performance award the grievant originally received. *Id.* The Arbitrator also ordered the Agency to pay the grievant the difference between the two awards. *Id.*

III. Positions of the Parties

A. Agency's Exceptions

The Agency excepts to the Arbitrator's award on the bases that it is contrary to law and fails to draw its essence from the CBA. Exceptions at 5, 10.

The Agency claims that the award is contrary to law because it affects management's rights to direct employees and assign work under § 7106(a)(2)(A) and (B) of the Statute. In this respect, the Agency argues that the arbitration award does not satisfy the two-prong test used by the Authority to determine whether an award resolving a performance appraisal grievance impermissibly affects management's rights to direct employees and assign work. Exceptions at 5-6 (citing *U.S. Dep't of the Treasury, Bureau of Engraving & Printing, Wash., D.C.,* 53 FLRA 146 (1997) (*BEP*)). Specifically, the Agency claims that the award fails to satisfy prong I of *BEP* because the Arbitrator erroneously failed to base his decision on a violation of the CBA. *Id.* at 7-8. The Agency also claims that the award fails to satisfy prong II of *BEP* because the Arbitrator did not reconstruct what management would have done had it not violated the CBA. *Id.* at 9-10.

Further, the Agency contends that the award fails to draw its essence from Article 3 of the CBA. *Id.* at 10. The Agency argues that the Arbitrator erred by finding that the grievant was not treated fairly and equitably under the CBA without comparing her performance rating to those of other similarly situated employees. Moreover, the Agency claims the Arbitrator did not base this finding on "any concrete evidence" that the grievant was discriminated against based on the protected classes set forth in the CBA. *Id.* at 11.

In addition, the Agency argues that the Arbitrator's finding that it violated Article 5 of the CBA fails to draw its essence from the CBA. *Id.* According to the Agency, Article 5 pertains to when the Union can request mid-term bargaining over certain negotiable subjects. The Agency claims that Article 5 has no relationship to this case and notes that the Union did not allege a violation of Article 5

2. Article 5 addresses Union-initiated mid-term bargaining, including the process and rules applicable to that activity. *See* Exceptions, Ex. 6.

3. As discussed below in Section V., we find it unnecessary to resolve the Agency's exception that the award fails to draw its essence from Article 5.

in its grievance. Therefore, the Agency claims, the award cannot in any rational way be derived from Article 5.

B. Union's Opposition

The Union argues that the award does not affect management's rights to assign work or direct employees under the Statute. Opp'n at 5. According to the Union, the award does not fail to meet the requirements of *BEP*. *Id.* at 8-10.

The Union further contends that the award does not fail to draw its essence from the CBA. *Id.* at 11. The Union claims that the Arbitrator's interpretation of Article 3 is entirely plausible. Accordingly, the Union argues, the Agency has not established that the award fails to draw its essence from the CBA. *Id.* at 14. Therefore, the Union requests that the Authority deny the Agency's exceptions.

IV. Preliminary Issue

The Agency claims for the first time in its exceptions that its rating of the grievant (1) was an exercise of its management rights to direct employees and assign work under § 7106(a)(2)(A) and (B), and (2) is consistent with Article 3's requirement that employees be treated fairly and equitably in personnel management matters.

Exceptions are barred by 5 C.F.R. § 2429.5 of the Authority's Regulations when they pertain to issues that could have been, but were not, presented to an arbitrator.[4] *See U.S. Dep't of Justice, Fed. Bureau of Prisons, USP Admin. Maximum (ADX), Florence, Colo.*, 64 FLRA 1168, 1170 (2010) (exception dismissed under § 2429.5 where agency had notice of specific remedy sought by union at arbitration and could have but did not present its argument to arbitrator disputing that remedy); *U.S. Dep't of Homeland Security, U.S. Customs & Border Prot., JFK Airport, Queens, N.Y.*, 62 FLRA 416, 417 (2008) (same); *cf. U.S. Dep't of Labor*, 60 FLRA 737, 738 (2005) (Chairman Cabaniss concurring as to another matter) (motion for reconsideration granted where agency challenged decision dismissing exception on § 2429.5 grounds where agency had no notification prior to union's post-hearing brief of argument under collective bargaining agreement).

The record indicates that the Agency did not raise either of its management rights arguments or its Article 3 argument before the Arbitrator even though it could have done so. At the arbitration hearing, the Union requested that the Arbitrator raise the grievant's performance rating and direct the Agency to consider the grievant for an ROC, an award higher than the award that she had originally received. *See* Award at 13. Although the Agency had notice of these requested remedies, it failed to present its management rights arguments to the Arbitrator and dispute the requested remedies on that basis. In addition, the record establishes that the Agency was on notice that the Union claimed, both in its grievance and before the Arbitrator, that the Agency violated Article 3 of the CBA because its ratings of the grievant on the Participation and Interpersonal Skills elements were unfair and inequitable. *Id.* at 12; *see also* Exceptions, Ex. 3 at 1; Opp'n, Exs. 1 & 2. However, the Agency failed to respond to the Union's argument, merely arguing to the Arbitrator that it "met all contractual and regulatory provisions" in evaluating the grievant. Award at 13.

The case law interpreting 5 C.F.R. § 2429.5 makes clear that the Authority will not consider a contention that could have been, but was not, presented to the Arbitrator. *See, e.g., U.S. Dep't of the Air Force, Air Force Materiel Command, Robins Air Force Base, Ga.*, 59 FLRA 542, 544 (2003). Here, the Agency's argument before the Arbitrator, that it followed all the rules, laws and regulations regarding the grievant's performance rating, Award at 13, is too general to sufficiently preserve its claims that its rating of the grievant was (1) an exercise of its management rights to direct employees and assign work under the Statute and (2) consistent with Article 3's requirement that employees be treated fairly and equitably in personnel management matters. *See, e.g., U.S. Dep't of the Air Force, Minot Air Force Base, N.D.*, 61 FLRA 366, 369 (2005) (then-Member Pope dissenting as to another matter) (internal quotations and citation omitted) (management rights exception dismissed under § 2429.5 because Agency assertion before the arbitrator that the action it took was to "ensure the safety of the crews and the protection of Air Force equipment" was insufficient to preserve ability to raise management rights claims before the Authority). As there is no evidence in the record that

4. The Authority's Regulations concerning the review of arbitration awards, as well as certain related procedural Regulations, including § 2429.5, were revised effective October 1, 2010. 75 Fed. Reg. 42,283 (2010). As the exceptions in this case were filed prior to October 1, 2010, we apply the prior version of the Regulations here. *See* 5 C.F.R. § 2425.1. However, we note that, like the revised version of § 2429.5, the prior version of § 2429.5 provides that the Authority will not consider any issue that could have been, but was not, presented to the arbitrator.

the Agency raised the arguments referenced above before the Arbitrator, we conclude that the Agency's exceptions on these bases are not properly before the Authority. Based on the foregoing, we dismiss the Agency's exceptions contending that the award is contrary to law and fails to draw its essence from Article 3 of the CBA.[5]

V. Analysis and Conclusions

One of the CBA's provisions that the Arbitrator found the Agency had violated was Article 5. Award at 22. The Agency claims that the award fails to draw its essence from Article 5 because that article, entitled "Union-Initiated Mid-Term Bargaining," has no relationship to this case. Exceptions at 11. Therefore, the Agency claims, the award cannot "in any rational way" be derived from Article 5. *Id.*

It is unnecessary to resolve this exception. When an arbitrator has based an award on separate and independent grounds, an appealing party must establish that all of the grounds are deficient in order to have the award found deficient. *See, e.g., U.S. Dep't of the Treasury, Internal Revenue Serv., Oxon Hill, Md.*, 56 FLRA 292, 299 (2000). In such circumstances, if an excepting party does not demonstrate that the award is deficient on one of the grounds relied on by the arbitrator, then it is unnecessary for the Authority to resolve exceptions to the other ground. *See id.*

Here, the Arbitrator found that the Agency violated both Articles 3 and 5 of the CBA because the Agency did not treat the grievant fairly and equitably. We have dismissed the Agency's essence exception to the Arbitrator's finding that the Agency violated Article 3 of the CBA. The Arbitrator's Article 3 determination constitutes a separate and independent basis for his decision finding that the Agency violated the CBA in its rating of the grievant. Accordingly, as we uphold the Arbitrator's Article 3 determination, we find it unnecessary to resolve the Agency's Article 5 essence exception and deny that exception. *See id.*

VI. Decision

The Agency's contrary to law exceptions and its Article 3 essence exception are dismissed. The Agency's Article 5 essence exception is denied.

5. Chairman Pope would deny on the merits the Agency's essence exception regarding Article 3. Although it is true enough that the Arbitrator *paraphrased* the Agency's position as arguing that it "met all contractual . . . provisions," Award at 13, the fact remains that the record does not disclose what the Agency *actually argued*. In the Chairman's view, it is reasonable to conclude that the Agency denied violating the same contract provision -- Article 3 -- the Union placed in dispute, especially since the Union makes no claim to the contrary. On the merits, Article 3 requires that employees "be treated fairly and equitably in all aspects of personnel management *and* without regard to" membership in certain protected categories. Exceptions, Attach., Ex. 5 (emphasis added). Contrary to the Agency's claim, nothing in this wording required the Arbitrator either to compare the grievant's performance rating to those of other similarly situated employees or to base his finding on evidence that the grievant was discriminated against based on membership in a protected category. *See* Exceptions at 11. Thus, Chairman Pope would find that the Agency does not demonstrate that the award fails to draw its essence from Article 3.

65 FLRA No. 200

UNITED STATES
DEPARTMENT OF TRANSPORTATION
FEDERAL AVIATION ADMINISTRATION
WASHINGTON, D.C.
(Agency)

and

PROFESSIONAL AIRWAYS
SYSTEMS SPECIALISTS
(Union)

0-AR-4267

DECISION

June 29, 2011

Before the Authority: Carol Waller Pope, Chairman, and Thomas M. Beck and Ernest DuBester, Members

I. Statement of the Case

This matter is before the Authority on exceptions to the final award of Arbitrator Suzanne R. Butler filed by the Agency under § 7122(a) of the Federal Service Labor-Management Relations Statute (the Statute) and part 2425 of the Authority's Regulations. The Union filed an opposition to the Agency's exceptions.[1]

In her final award, the Arbitrator ordered that the Agency immediately provide the Union with all of the information it had requested or "affirmatively show cause why specific parts of said information cannot be provided." Final Award at 20. For the reasons that follow, we deny the Agency's exceptions in part and dismiss them in part.

1. The Union also filed a motion to dismiss the Agency's exceptions because the Agency failed to serve the Union with a copy of the attachments to the Agency's exceptions. In response, the Agency timely re-served a copy of the attachments to its exceptions. Therefore, as the procedural issue underlying the Union's motion has been resolved, we deny the Union's motion.

II. Background and Arbitrator's Awards

A. Interim Award

In preparation for contract negotiations with the Union, the Agency commissioned a market survey from a private company (the contractor) comparing salaries of Agency employees to those of private sector employees doing comparable work. Interim Award at 5. The Union filed an information request seeking a copy of the actual survey, identification of the methodology used in conducting the survey, identification of the specific Agency positions and the private sector positions that were analyzed in the survey, and a copy of the contract between the Agency and the contractor. *Id.* at 9. When the Agency did not provide the requested information, the Union filed a grievance. *Id.* at 10-11. The parties were unable to resolve the grievance and an arbitration hearing was conducted.

The Arbitrator issued the interim award upholding the grievance and finding that the Agency improperly failed to provide the Union with the requested information. *Id.* at 34; Final Award at 4. The Arbitrator found the requested information relevant because, among other things, the Union had a particularized need for information regarding pay bands, as the CBA required the Agency to conduct annual pay band reviews. Interim Award at 28. The Arbitrator noted that the Agency had an interest in not disclosing this information due to the confidentiality restrictions contained in its agreement with the contractor. *Id.* at 28-29. However, the Arbitrator found that the Union's particularized need for the information prevailed because the Agency did not sufficiently explore the possibility of providing the Union with sanitized or redacted information. *Id.* at 29.

The Arbitrator directed that the parties "cooperate immediately in an effort to find alternative means for providing the requested information to the Union." *Id.* at 34. She also retained jurisdiction for ninety days over any disputes regarding implementation of the remedy. *Id.*; Final Award at 5.

B. Final Award

In response to the Arbitrator's interim award, the Agency sent the Union eighteen pages of information. Final Award at 5, 16. The Union e-mailed the Agency that it did not understand the information the Agency provided and requested a meeting. *Id.* at 5. When the Agency did not respond, the Union e-mailed the Agency again. *Id.* When the Agency still failed to respond, the Union contacted the Arbitrator and asked her to assert her retained jurisdiction. *Id.* at 6. The Arbitrator suggested a conference call and/or a face-to-face meeting. *Id.* This was within the ninety-day period during which the Arbitrator had retained jurisdiction. *Id.*

The Agency responded to the Arbitrator by stating that, because the Arbitrator had already sent the Agency her bill, her contract with the Agency was fulfilled and the interim award was final. *Id.* The Agency claimed that it had no authorization to expend additional funds on this matter and that there was no contract in place to cover the Arbitrator's fee for any additional services. Moreover, the Agency argued that the Arbitrator did not need to perform any additional services because the Agency was in compliance with the Arbitrator's award. *Id.* The Agency also claimed that it did not normally maintain the market information the Union had requested. Finally, the Agency claimed that, because the parties had entered into a new collective bargaining agreement covering employee compensation, the grievance regarding its failure to provide information relating to the market survey was moot. *Id.* at 6-7.

At this point, the Arbitrator again suggested a conference call with the parties. The Union responded by sending a letter to the Arbitrator stating that it did not "believe that an agency can override an arbitrator's express retention of jurisdiction by simply writing a check." *Id.* at 7. Therefore, it informed the Arbitrator, it had filed an unfair labor practice (ULP) charge. The ULP charge alleged that the Agency failed to recognize the Arbitrator's jurisdiction and refused to meet with the Arbitrator and the Union to resolve its lack of compliance with the award. *Id.*

After receiving the Union's letter, the Arbitrator informed the parties that she was holding the case in abeyance. *Id.*

A Regional Director of the Authority subsequently declined to issue a ULP complaint, stating that the award was not final and binding because the Arbitrator had directed the parties to develop an appropriate remedy on their own. *Id.* at 7-8. The Regional Director stated his view that the Agency's alleged refusal to participate in the arbitration proceeding was not a ULP because, when one party refuses to participate, an arbitrator has the authority to proceed ex parte on all matters properly before him or her. *Id.* at 8.

At this point, the Union requested that the Arbitrator take the case out of abeyance and assert her retained jurisdiction. *Id.* at 8-9. The Agency responded by claiming that it had closed out its contract with the Arbitrator, that her interim award had become final ninety days after it was issued, and that this post-award activity was not within the terms of her contract. *Id.* at 9. The Agency also reiterated that it was in compliance with the interim award and claimed that the Arbitrator was functus officio. *Id.*

The Arbitrator responded by informing the parties that she continued to retain jurisdiction over all disputes relating to remedy. *Id.* She stated that the Agency's functus officio argument was inapposite because an award does not become final if an arbitrator directs the parties to create a remedy. *Id.* at 9-10. The Arbitrator also informed the parties that, since the Agency was refusing to participate, she would exercise her authority to proceed ex parte and issue a final award. *Id.* at 10. Lastly, the Arbitrator indicated that invoices for her services would continue to be split equally between the parties. *Id.*

Absent a joint submission due to the Agency's refusal to participate, the Arbitrator framed the issue in the final award as follows: "Did the Agency fully comply with the [Interim] Award . . . ? If not, what shall be the remedy?" *Id.* at 2.

First, the Arbitrator examined the Agency's argument that she did not retain jurisdiction and that the interim award became final either on the date of the Arbitrator's invoice or ninety days after the award was issued. *Id.* at 14-15. The Arbitrator found these arguments unpersuasive. She determined that the interim award had not become final because she had not determined a remedy but rather remanded the matter to the parties so they could create a mutually acceptable remedy. *Id.* at 15. In addition, the Arbitrator noted the Union's request that she reassert her jurisdiction within the ninety-day period during which she specifically retained such jurisdiction. *Id.*

Next, the Arbitrator considered the Agency's claim that she was functus officio. She noted that the Authority will deem an award final if an arbitrator specifies a remedy but retains jurisdiction regarding any disputes that may arise over its implementation. *Id.* at 16. However, she also noted that the Authority will not find an award final if the arbitrator retains jurisdiction over the nature of the remedy. *Id.* The Arbitrator stated that, in this case, she had clearly done the latter.

The Arbitrator then considered the grievance's merits. As to whether the Agency satisfied the interim award's direction that the Agency supply the Union with the requested information, she noted that it was not unreasonable for the Agency to take two weeks to provide information to the Union. However, she found that the documents the Agency produced were not responsive and therefore did not establish its "reasonable, good faith 'cooperation'" with the Union, within the meaning of the interim award. *Id.* at 17 (quoting Interim Award at 34).

The Arbitrator recognized that the Agency provided eighteen pages of actual data to the Union. However, she found that this did not constitute compliance on the part of the Agency because the data was devoid of meaning without an explanation, which the Agency failed to provide. *Id.* at 18. Moreover, the Arbitrator recognized that the Union made several requests for explanatory meetings but the Agency never responded.

The Arbitrator similarly rejected the Agency's claim that there is no longer a need for the requested information because the parties have signed a new collective bargaining agreement. The Arbitrator found that market survey information relates to the bargaining unit members' pay bands, which the CBA requires the parties to review every year. *Id.*

Therefore, the Arbitrator ordered the Agency to provide the Union with the requested information immediately or "affirmatively show cause why specific parts of said information cannot be provided." *Id.* at 20. The Arbitrator also directed the Agency to meet with the Union to explain the information already provided and to post a notice "acknowledging that the Agency violated the Statute and the CBA by failing to provide the requested information and assuring employees of the Agency's intention to comply with the Statute and the CBA henceforth." *Id.*

III. Positions of the Parties

A. Agency's Exceptions

The Agency argues that the award fails to draw its essence from the CBA because the Union waited too long to file its grievance, thereby missing the deadline set forth in the CBA. The Agency claims that it informed the Union in 2000, 2002, and 2005 of its position regarding whether the information at issue could be provided. The Agency also cites Article 5, Section 9, Step 1 of the CBA, which states that a party has fifteen days from the date of the event giving rise to the incident to submit a grievance. Exceptions at 10.

In addition, the Agency claims that the Arbitrator did not have the authority to issue a second award because she was functus officio. *Id.* at 8. The Agency alleges that the Arbitrator only had jurisdiction for ninety days after the issuance of her interim award. *Id.* at 5. It also claims that it fully complied with the Arbitrator's interim award and subsequently paid her for its share of the cost of her services, as required by the CBA. *Id.* at 3, 7. Therefore, the Agency claims, the Arbitrator's final award exceeded the limits of her contractual authority. *Id.* at 2.

The Agency also argues that the Arbitrator exceeded her authority in the arbitration proceeding. In this connection, the Agency claims that the portion of the remedy directing it to post a nationwide notice was never previously raised before the Arbitrator or discussed by the parties. *Id.* at 13.

Repeating an argument it made before the Arbitrator, the Agency further excepts to the award's remedy that the Agency provide the Union with the information the Union requested because it claims the information is proprietary information held by the contractor. *Id.* at 14-15. The Agency argues that there are restrictions on the release of proprietary information that are similar to restrictions on the Federal Government's dissemination of copyrighted material. *Id.* at 17. The Agency also claims that requiring it to provide this information to the Union would cause the contractor and other companies that perform market-based surveys to exclude the Federal Government from participating. This, the Agency argues, would force the Federal Government to devise its own system for determining pay raises, which would cost a significant amount of money. Therefore, the Agency claims, requiring it to provide the Union with the requested information would interfere with management's right to contract out for services in the most cost-effective manner. *Id.* at 15. The Agency also contends that it does not have to provide the Union with the requested information because the Union has not proven that it has a particularized need for such information. *Id.* at 20. The Agency claims that there is no particularized need because the parties have already agreed to a new CBA that resolves the issues between the parties concerning pay. *Id.* at 20-21.

Finally, the Agency argues that it cannot provide the Union with the requested information because the information is held by the contractor. *Id.* at 20.

Therefore, the Agency alleges, the information is neither "readily" available to the Agency nor maintained by it. *Id.*

B. Union's Opposition

Regarding the Agency's arbitrability argument, the Union claims that its failure to file a grievance in 2000 or 2004 has no relevance to the grievance filed here because different information was involved. Opp'n at 16.

The Union also claims that the Arbitrator was not functus officio when she issued her final award. *Id.* at 11. In support, the Union points out that the interim award directed the parties to fashion a remedy and the Arbitrator retained jurisdiction for ninety days to resolve any remedy-related disputes. *Id.* at 11-14.

The Union interprets the Agency's argument that it cannot provide the requested information because it is proprietary information held by a private company as a contrary to law claim. However, the Union argues that the Agency never specifies which section of the Statute it claims the award violates. *Id.* at 14. Furthermore, the Union contends, if the Agency claims that certain information is restricted from disclosure, the Agency should at least specify which information cannot be divulged and provide its rationale. *Id.* at 15. This, the Union claims, would also satisfy the Agency's duty to consider alternative forms and means of disclosing the information.

The Union also argues that it has a particularized need for all of the information it requested. *Id.* at 24-25. In support of this argument, the Union notes that the parties are still following the 2000 CBA. Therefore, the Union claims, the information will help the Union with the present negotiations. *Id.* at 24. In addition, the Union argues, the information will assist it in preparing for future negotiations. *Id.* at 24-25. Also, the Union contends, this information may become the basis for future grievances concerning the propriety of the January 2005 pay adjustments, particularly in that some bargaining unit employees have been denied a pay increase. *Id.* at 25.

Finally, the Union asserts that the Agency's argument that the Agency does not maintain the information is meritless. *Id.* at 23-24. The Union claims that the Agency cannot argue that the information is not in its possession when the Agency relied on the information to create a summary of the market survey. *Id.* at 24.

IV. Analysis and Conclusions

A. The Arbitrator's procedural-arbitrability determination is not deficient.

The Agency argues that the final award does not draw its essence from the CBA. Exceptions at 9. The basis for the Agency's argument is that the Union's grievance is untimely because the Union had ample notice of the Agency's position that the requested information is proprietary. *Id.* at 9, 14. Specifically, the Agency claims that it advised the Union of this during negotiations in 2000, 2002, and 2007. *Id.* at 9-10. The Agency references Article 5, Section 9, Step 1 of the CBA as allowing either party to submit a grievance within fifteen days from the time of the event giving rise to the grievance. *Id.* at 10. Therefore, the Agency argues, since it previously informed the Union of its position regarding the proprietary nature of the information and the Union did not file a grievance at that time, the Union is contractually precluded from doing so now. *Id.* at 10-11. For this reason, the Agency claims that the award fails to draw its essence from the CBA. *Id.* at 11.

An arbitrator's determination regarding the timeliness of a grievance constitutes a determination regarding the procedural-arbitrability of that grievance. *United Power Trades Org.*, 63 FLRA 208, 209 (2009). The Authority generally will not find an arbitrator's ruling on the procedural-arbitrability of a grievance deficient on grounds that directly challenge the procedural-arbitrability ruling itself. *See, e.g., AFGE, Local 3882*, 59 FLRA 469, 470 (2003). However, the Authority has stated that a procedural-arbitrability determination may be found deficient on the ground that it is contrary to law. *See id.* (citing *AFGE, Local 933*, 58 FLRA 480, 481 (2003)). In addition, the Authority has stated that a procedural-arbitrability determination may be found deficient on grounds that do not directly challenge the determination itself, which include claims that an arbitrator was biased or that the arbitrator exceeded his or her authority. *See U.S. EEOC*, 60 FLRA 83, 86 (2004) (citing *AFGE, Local 2921*, 50 FLRA 184, 185-86 (1995)).

Here, the Arbitrator found that the Union's grievance was timely filed under the CBA. This finding constitutes a procedural-arbitrability determination. *See id.* As the Agency's exception directly challenges this procedural-arbitrability determination, we deny this exception.

B. The Arbitrator was not functus officio.

The Agency argues that the Arbitrator was precluded from issuing a final award because the Arbitrator was functus officio. Exceptions at 8. Under the principle of functus officio, once an arbitrator has resolved the matter submitted to arbitration, the arbitrator is without further authority. *See U.S. Dep't of Transp., Fed. Aviation Admin.*, 64 FLRA 574, 576 (2010) (*FAA*); *AFGE, Local 2172*, 57 FLRA 625, 627 (2001). Unless an arbitrator retains jurisdiction after issuance of the award, the arbitrator has no authority to take any further action without the joint request of the parties. *See FAA*, 64 FLRA at 576. However, where an arbitrator expressly retains jurisdiction to resolve disputes over interpretation or implementation of a remedy, the arbitrator may issue a supplemental award resolving such disputes. *See AFGE, Local 1156 & Laborers Int'l Union, Local 1170*, 57 FLRA 602, 603 (2001).

Here, the Arbitrator's interim award directed the parties to explore alternative means for providing the requested information to the Union and the Arbitrator specifically retained jurisdiction to resolve any disputes over the implementation of this remedy. Furthermore, the Agency provides no authority to support its allegation that the interim award became final because the Agency issued the Arbitrator a check.

As the Arbitrator expressly retained jurisdiction to resolve disputes over the implementation of her remedy, she was not functus officio. Therefore, we deny this exception.

C. The Arbitrator did not exceed her authority by addressing issues not contained in the grievance.

The Agency claims that the Arbitrator's remedy directing the Agency to post a notice acknowledging that it violated the Statute "was never mentioned or discussed by the parties[]." Exceptions at 13-14. We construe this as an allegation that the Arbitrator exceeded her authority by ordering a remedy that was not requested by the Union.

Arbitrators exceed their authority when they fail to resolve an issue submitted to arbitration, resolve an issue not submitted to arbitration, disregard specific limitations on their authority, or award relief to those not encompassed within the grievance. *See AFGE, Local 1617*, 51 FLRA 1645, 1647 (1996).

The Arbitrator did not err in requiring the Agency to post a notice. Even though the parties never addressed a notice posting as a potential remedy, Authority precedent gives arbitrators broad discretion to fashion remedies. *See, e.g., U.S. Dep't of the Air Force, Okla. City Air Logistics Ctr., Tinker Air Force Base, Okla.*, 47 FLRA 98, 101 (1993). Here, the Arbitrator framed the issue as encompassing fashioning of an appropriate remedy. Furthermore, the Authority has specifically upheld an arbitrator's order of a notice posting as a remedy. *See, e.g., Gen. Servs. Admin.*, 53 FLRA 925, 933 (1997) (upholding arbitrator's remedy of a notice posting for agency's failure to provide union with notice of and opportunity for representation at settlement negotiations).

Accordingly, we deny this exception.

D. The award is not contrary to law.

When an exception involves an award's consistency with law, the Authority reviews any question of law raised by the exception and the award de novo. *See NTEU, Chapter 24*, 50 FLRA 330, 332 (1995) (citing *U.S. Customs Serv. v. FLRA*, 43 F.3d 682, 686-87 (D.C. Cir. 1994)). In applying the standard of de novo review, the Authority assesses whether an arbitrator's legal conclusions are consistent with the applicable standard of law. *See U.S. Dep't of Def., Dep'ts of the Army & the Air Force, Ala. Nat'l Guard, Northport, Ala.*, 55 FLRA 37, 40 (1998). In making that assessment, the Authority defers to the arbitrator's underlying factual findings. *See id.*

1. The Agency has not met its burden to prove that the award should be set aside as contrary to law because it requires the Agency to provide the Union with proprietary information.

The Agency claims that it cannot furnish the requested information to the Union because the information is proprietary. We construe this as an exception that the award is contrary to law.

The Agency's understanding of the Arbitrator's awards is incorrect. Neither award specifies that the Agency's only recourse is to provide the Union with the requested information. The final award directed the Agency either to do so or to "affirmatively show cause why specific parts of said information cannot be provided." Final Award at 20. Similarly, the interim award directed that the parties "cooperate immediately in an effort to find alternative means for providing the requested information to the Union." Interim Award at 34. The interim award then specified that such means could include sanitization or redaction of protected information and/or attempting to obtain permission from the contractor to disclose the requested information. *Id.* Such a misconstruction of the award does not constitute a basis for finding the award contrary to law. *See, e.g., AFGE, Local 900*, 63 FLRA 536, 538-39 (2009) (because excepting party misinterpreted award, no basis was provided for finding that award was contrary to law).

Furthermore, the Agency has not provided a legal basis for its claim that it cannot be compelled to disclose proprietary information to the Union. Section 7114(b)(4) of the Statute states that an agency must furnish information to the exclusive representative involved "to the extent not prohibited by law." Although the Agency argues that it cannot be made to furnish the requested information to the Union, the Agency does not identify any statute, regulation, or appropriate judicial or administrative precedent that prohibits it from furnishing the requested information. *See U.S. Dep't of Health & Human Servs., SSA, Balt., Md.*, 50 FLRA 544, 547 (1995) (finding that nothing in statute cited by agency prohibited agency from disclosing proprietary information that Union requested).[2]

For these reasons, we deny this exception.

2. The Agency has not met its burden to prove that the award should be set aside as contrary to law because the Union has not shown a particularized need for the requested information.

The Agency argues that the Union did not prove it had particularized need for the information it requested because the parties have already agreed to a new CBA that resolves the issues between the parties concerning pay.

Where the parties are unable to agree on whether, or to what extent, requested information must be provided and the matter is presented for adjudication, each party must establish its reasons for requesting and denying a request for information. *E.g., U.S. Immigration & Naturalization Serv., U.S. Border Patrol, Del Rio, Tex.*, 51 FLRA 768, 774 (1996); *Dep't of the Air Force, Scott Air Force Base, Ill.*, 51 FLRA 675, 681 (1995). The Authority will find that an agency has unlawfully withheld information if the union has established a particularized need for the information and either: (1) the agency has not established a countervailing interest; or (2) the agency has established such an interest but it does not outweigh the union's demonstration of particularized need.

The Arbitrator found that the Union established it had particularized need for the requested information. Specifically, the Arbitrator found that, even though the parties had agreed to a new CBA, the requested market survey information relates to the bargaining unit members' pay bands, which the CBA requires the parties to review every year. In its exceptions, the Agency reiterates the argument it made to the Arbitrator, that the Union has not proven that it has a particularized need for the information because the parties have already agreed to a new CBA that resolves the issues between the parties concerning pay. However, the Agency does not dispute any of the Arbitrator's factual findings upon which she bases her determination that the Union has proven a particularized need for the information. Furthermore, although the Agency argues that its countervailing interest in the nondisclosure of the information is that the information is proprietary, the Authority has rejected that premise. *See supra* Section IV.D.1. Therefore, we find that the Agency's contrary to law argument concerning particularized need does not establish a basis upon which to find the Arbitrator's award deficient.

Accordingly, we deny this exception.

2. As noted above, the Agency argues that there are restrictions on the release of proprietary information that are similar to restrictions on the Federal Government's dissemination of copyrighted material. Exceptions at 17. However, the Agency's reliance on 17 U.S.C. § 105 and a decision regarding copyright law is misplaced because the Agency has not identified any legal restrictions on the dissemination of copyrighted material that is comparable to the legal restrictions on the dissemination of proprietary information. The Agency also claims that its asserted management right to contract out for services in a cost-effective manner would be violated if it is required to provide the Union with the requested information. However, this argument is based on the faulty premise that the Arbitrator's awards would necessarily result in the Agency being required to devise its own method for determining pay raises. Accordingly, we reject it.

E. 5 C.F.R. § 2429.5 bars the Agency's argument that the information the Union requested is not "readily" available to the Agency or maintained by the Agency.

The Agency claims that it cannot provide the information the Union requested because the information is held by the contractor and is therefore neither "readily" available to the Agency nor maintained by it. Exceptions at 20.

The Authority's Regulations that were in effect when the Agency filed its exceptions provided that "[t]he Authority will not consider . . . any issue, which was not presented in the proceedings before the . . . arbitrator." 5 C.F.R. § 2429.5 (§ 2429.5).[3] Under § 2429.5, the Authority will not consider an issue that could have been, but was not, presented to the arbitrator. *See, e.g., U.S. Dep't of Homeland Sec., U.S. Customs & Border Prot., JFK Airport, Queens, N.Y.*, 62 FLRA 416, 417 (2008).

A review of the record, including both the Arbitrator's interim and final awards, as well as the correspondence that the Agency sent to the Arbitrator and the Union, indicates that the Agency never presented these claims to the Arbitrator although it had the opportunity to do so. Because the Agency could have raised before the Arbitrator claims that the information sought is neither reasonably available to the Agency nor maintained by it and there is no evidence in the record establishing that the Agency did so, we dismiss this exception.

V. Decision

The Agency's exceptions are denied in part and dismissed in part.

3. The Authority's Regulations concerning the review of arbitration awards, as well as certain related procedural Regulations, including § 2429.5, were revised effective October 1, 2010. *See* 75 Fed. Reg. 42,283 (2010). As the Union's exceptions were filed before that date, we apply the earlier Regulations.

65 FLRA No. 201

AMERICAN FEDERATION
OF GOVERNMENT EMPLOYEES
LOCAL 1367
(Union)

and

UNITED STATES
DEPARTMENT OF THE AIR FORCE
LACKLAND AIR FORCE BASE, TEXAS
(Agency)

0-AR-4737

DECISION

June 29, 2011

Before the Authority: Carol Waller Pope, Chairman, and Thomas M. Beck and Ernest DuBester, Members[1]

I. Statement of the Case

This matter is before the Authority on an exception to an award of Arbitrator Louise B. Wolitz filed by the Union under § 7122(a) of the Federal Service Labor-Management Relations Statute (the Statute) and part 2425 of the Authority's Regulations. The Agency filed an opposition to the Union's exception.

The Arbitrator concluded that the grievant's five-day suspension was for just and sufficient cause. For the reasons set forth below, we deny the Union's exception.

II. Background and Arbitrator's Award

The Agency issued the grievant a notice of proposed suspension for five days, which alleged that the grievant was absent without leave (AWOL) on five days because he did not report to work and did not follow the established procedures for requesting leave. Award at 5. The resulting grievance was not resolved and was submitted to arbitration. *Id.* at 7. The parties stipulated to the following issue before the Arbitrator: "Did the Agency have just and sufficient cause to suspend the [g]rievant for five days based on the charges of unauthorized absence, failing to follow [a] supervisor's instructions and failure to request leave in accordance with established procedures? If not, what should the remedy be?" *Id.* at 5.

The Arbitrator found that prior to the absences at issue, the grievant's second-line supervisor (flight chief) instructed the grievant to request any unscheduled leave by calling the flight chief. *Id.* at 15. Over the next month and a half, the grievant was absent on five occasions, but the Arbitrator found that none of his leave requests for these days were approved. *Id.* at 16. On each of these occasions, the grievant either asked for leave from a supervisor other than the flight chief, or left answering machine messages at the office requesting leave without leaving a phone number where he could be reached (call-back number). *Id.* Whenever the grievant spoke to a supervisor to request unscheduled leave, the supervisor always instructed the grievant to contact the flight chief, but the grievant never did so. *Id.* After the first two absences, the flight chief again instructed the grievant to call him with any unscheduled leave requests, but the grievant continued not to do so. *Id.*

In her award, the Arbitrator cited several provisions of the parties' agreement including Article 13, Section 11 (Article 13),[2] which provides

1. Member Beck's separate opinion, concurring in the result, is set forth at the end of this decision.

2. Article 13, Section 11 of the parties' agreement pertinently provides:

> In case of illness or emergencies that cannot be foreseen, the following procedures apply in requesting sick or annual leave:
>
> > A. The employee will personally telephone his/her supervisor or the designated alternate if it is possible to do so. Otherwise, he/she will have an immediate family member or other responsible individual call for him/her as specified below.
> >
> > . . . .
> >
> > C. If the supervisor is not on duty, the employee will make his/her leave request to the person designated to act in the supervisor's place.
> >
> > . . . .
> >
> > F. If the first-line supervisor or alternate is temporarily unavailable, the employee will

procedures for requesting unscheduled leave, and Article 21 (Article 21),[3] which provides the parties' obligations in relation to disciplinary actions. *Id.* at 2. Before the Arbitrator, the Union argued that the grievant followed the procedures established in Article 13, and that the Agency's requirement that the grievant request unscheduled leave only from the flight chief conflicted with that provision. *Id.* at 14.

The Arbitrator found that it was "clear and uncontroverted" that the grievant was repeatedly instructed to call the flight chief to request unscheduled leave. *Id.* at 15. The Arbitrator determined that, even if the Agency's instructions were not proper or violated the parties' agreement, the grievant did not have the authority to determine that an instruction violated the parties' agreement and need not be followed. *Id.* at 15-16. Therefore, the Arbitrator concluded that, because the grievant "failed to follow instructions, failed to request leave according to the procedure clearly established by his . . . supervisor, and, therefore, was AWOL . . . as charged[,]" the Agency had just and sufficient cause to issue a five-day suspension. *Id.* at 16.

III. Positions of the Parties

A. Union's Exception

The Union argues that the award fails to draw its essence from the parties' agreement. Exception at 1. According to the Union, the Arbitrator "refused to address or resolve" the allegation that the Agency violated the parties' agreement by unilaterally creating new leave procedures that "directly conflict" with those in Article 13. *See id.* at 1, 6.

B. Agency's Opposition

The Agency argues that the award does not fail to draw its essence from the parties' agreement. *See* Opp'n at 1. In this regard, the Agency argues that the Union does not explain how the Arbitrator failed to apply Article 13, and that she could have determined that the grievant failed to comply with Article 13 by, for example, failing to leave a call-back number. *Id.* at 4-5.

IV. Analysis and Conclusion

In reviewing an arbitrator's interpretation of a collective bargaining agreement, the Authority applies the deferential standard of review that federal courts use in reviewing arbitration awards in the private sector. *See* 5 U.S.C. § 7122(a)(2); *AFGE, Council 220*, 54 FLRA 156, 159 (1998). Under this standard, the Authority will find that an arbitration award is deficient as failing to draw its essence from the collective bargaining agreement when the appealing party establishes that the award: (1) cannot in any rational way be derived from the agreement; (2) is so unfounded in reason and fact and so unconnected with the wording and purposes of the collective bargaining agreement as to manifest an infidelity to the obligation of the arbitrator; (3) does not represent a plausible interpretation of the agreement; or (4) evidences a manifest disregard of the agreement. *See U.S. Dep't of Labor (OSHA)*, 34 FLRA 573, 575 (1990). The Authority and the courts defer to arbitrators in this context "because it is the arbitrator's construction of the agreement for which the parties have bargained." *Id.* at 576.

The Arbitrator found that the Agency had just cause to suspend the grievant for his recurring failure to follow the repeated instruction that he should direct unscheduled leave requests to the flight chief. Award at 15-16. According to the Arbitrator, the Agency's alleged violation of Article 13 is irrelevant to this determination because the grievant did not have the authority to determine that an instruction violated the parties' agreement and need not be followed. *Id.* In this regard, the Union does not explain how the grievant's alleged compliance with Article 13 is inconsistent with the Arbitrator's finding that the Agency had just cause to suspend an employee who repeatedly refused to follow his supervisor's express instructions.[4] Furthermore, in

> leave a phone number where he/she can be contacted if circumstances permit. The supervisor will call the employee back in a short time and give a decision on the request. Otherwise, the employee should again contact the supervisor as soon as feasible.

Award at 2.

3. Article 21, Section 1 provides, in pertinent part, that "[e]mployees are expected to . . . respect the administrative authority of those directing their work . . . ." *Id.* Article 21, Section 2 provides: "It is the responsibility of the [e]mployer to take disciplinary action against an employee for just cause." *Id.*

4. Moreover, in light of the Arbitrator's finding that the grievant twice failed to leave a call-back number when leaving a message requesting unscheduled leave, *id.* at 16, it is not clear from the record that the grievant followed the

addition to Article 13, the Arbitrator cited Article 21 as a relevant provision of the parties' agreement, which requires that employees "respect the administrative authority of those directing their work[.]" *Id.* at 2. Accordingly, the Arbitrator interpreted the parties' agreement to find that the Agency had just cause to suspend an employee who repeatedly failed to follow his supervisor's instructions for requesting unscheduled leave, and, thus, was AWOL on five days. *Id.* at 16. As the Union has not established that this interpretation is irrational, unfounded, implausible, or in manifest disregard of the parties' agreement, the Union does not demonstrate that the award fails to draw its essence from the parties' agreement, and we deny this exception.[5]

V. Decision

The Union's exception is denied.

Member Beck, Concurring:

I join in my colleagues' decision to deny the Union's exception arguing that the Arbitrator's award fails to draw it essence from the parties' agreement. However, I believe my colleagues err when they fail to acknowledge and address the Union's additional contention that the Arbitrator exceeded her authority.

In its exceptions, the Union asserts that "the Arbitrator has refused to address or resolve the matter of the Agency's violation of the [parties' agreement]." Exceptions at 2. According to the Union, the Arbitrator "glosses over" the fact that the grievant was in compliance with the parties' agreement. *Id.* at 7, 9. Further, the Union argues that the Arbitrator found the propriety of the supervisor's instructions to be "completely irrelevant." *Id.* at 7; *see also id.* (noting that the Arbitrator stated that "it does not matter whether . . . [the] instructions were proper" or violated the parties' agreement or established procedure). In my view, these assertions constitute a separate and distinct argument that the Arbitrator exceeded her authority. *See AFGE, Local 1617*, 51 FLRA 1645, 1647 (1996) ("[a]rbitrators exceed their authority when they fail to resolve an issue submitted to arbitration").

Applying Authority precedent, I would find that the Arbitrator did not exceed her authority. The parties stipulated to the following issue: "[d]id the Agency have just and sufficient cause to suspend the [g]rievant . . . ." Award at 5. The Arbitrator resolved this issue when she determined that the grievant's failure to follow the Agency's clear instructions constituted just and sufficient cause to suspend the grievant for five days. *Id.* at 16. The issue of whether the Agency's instructions were in conflict with the parties' agreement and, thus, whether the Agency violated the agreement, was not included in the stipulated issue. As a result, the Arbitrator was not required to address this issue and did not fail to resolve an issue submitted to arbitration by not doing so. *See AFGE, Local 3911*, 64 FLRA 686, 688 (2010) (finding that the arbitrator did not exceed his authority when he failed to resolve a "predicate legal issue" that was not one of the stipulated issues); *U.S. Dep't of Veterans Affairs, Med. Ctr., Richmond, Va.*, 63 FLRA 553, 557 (2009) (finding that the arbitrator did not exceed his authority where the issue was whether there was just cause to suspend the grievant and did not include whether the agency violated the parties' agreement). Accordingly, I would deny this exception.

---

leave procedures prescribed by Article 13 in every instance. *See id.* at 2 (Article 13 requires an employee requesting leave to "leave a phone number where he/she can be contacted . . . .").

5. The Union does not argue that the Arbitrator exceeded her authority, and the Authority has held that "for cases that are processed under the [Authority's Regulations as revised effective October 1, 2010], we will no longer construe parties' exceptions as raising grounds that the exceptions do not raise." *AFGE, Local 3955, Council of Prison Locals 33*, 65 FLRA 887, 889 (2011) (Member Beck dissenting in part). Accordingly, we do not address whether the Arbitrator exceeded her authority.

65 FLRA No. 202

UNITED STATES
DEPARTMENT OF JUSTICE
FEDERAL BUREAU OF PRISONS
FEDERAL MEDICAL CENTER
CARSWELL, TEXAS
(Agency)

and

AMERICAN FEDERATION
OF GOVERNMENT EMPLOYEES
LOCAL 1006
COUNCIL OF PRISON LOCALS
COUNCIL 33
(Union)

0-AR-4641

DECISION

June 29, 2011

Before the Authority: Carol Waller Pope, Chairman, and Thomas M. Beck and Ernest DuBester, Members

I. Statement of the Case

This matter is before the Authority on exceptions to awards of Arbitrator Samuel J. Nicholas, Jr. filed by the Agency under § 7122(a) of the Federal Service Labor-Management Relations Statute (the Statute) and part 2425 of the Authority's Regulations. The Union filed an opposition to the Agency's exceptions.

In a series of awards, the Arbitrator found that the Agency violated the overtime compensation provisions of the Fair Labor Standards Act (FLSA), and he awarded backpay, liquidated damages, attorney fees, and costs.

For the reasons that follow, we dismiss the exceptions in part, deny the exceptions in part, set aside the awards in part, and remand the awards in part.

II. Background and Arbitrator's Awards

This case concerns an Agency medical center that is both a prison and a hospital. The Union filed a grievance alleging that the Agency was violating the FLSA by failing to compensate correctional officers and vocational nurses at the medical center for various pre-shift and post-shift activities. The grievance was not resolved and was submitted to arbitration.

The Arbitrator resolved the grievance in a series of six awards: two liability awards (Liability Awards Nos. 1 and 2); two damages awards (Damages Awards Nos. 1 and 2); and two attorney fees awards (Attorney Fees Awards Nos. 1 and 2).[1]

In an order prior to the hearing that resulted in Liability Award No. 1, the Arbitrator directed the Union to present evidence regarding nine of the posts and departments in dispute and directed the Agency to present its defenses. The Arbitrator stated that he would issue an award concerning any liability of the Agency with respect to those posts and departments. *See U.S. Dep't of Justice, Fed. Bureau of Prisons, Fed. Med. Ctr., Carswell, Tex.*, 64 FLRA 566, 566 (2010) (order dismissing earlier Agency exceptions) (*Fed. Med. Ctr.*).

In accordance with the Arbitrator's direction, the Union maintained that, prior to beginning their shifts, employees at the nine posts and departments report to the medical center's control center. The Union asserted that employees who are not assigned to the control center visit the control center to pick up batteries for their body alarms and radios, and then travel to their assigned posts or departments. The Union further asserted that, at the end of their shifts, they return the batteries to the control center. In this connection, the Union alleged that a charged battery is necessary for the employees to perform their job responsibility of maintaining the safety and security of the medical center. Liability Award No. 1 at 9. The Union also asserted that employees who are assigned to the control center are required to work prior to the beginning of their shifts and after the end of their shifts in order to accomplish their duties. *Id.* at 5. According to the Union, the Agency suffered or permitted employees to perform the asserted pre-shift and post-shift activities, and, therefore, the activities are compensable. *Id.* at 7-8.

1. For further identification, Liability Award No. 1 is dated November 26, 2008; Liability Award No. 2 is dated December 18, 2009; Damages Award No. 1 is dated March 3, 2009; Damages Award No. 2 is dated March 3, 2010; Attorney Fees Award No. 1 is dated May 14, 2009; and Attorney Fees Award No. 2 is dated March 4, 2010.

In Liability Award No. 1, the Arbitrator concluded that the Union had met its burden of proving that the employees assigned to the nine posts and departments perform compensable pre-shift and post-shift activities. *Id.* at 12-13. In particular, he agreed with the Union's assertion that the grievants pick up batteries at the control center prior to proceeding to their assigned posts or departments and return the batteries to the control center at the end of their shifts. In addition, he determined that these activities are compensable because they are indispensable to the performance of the employees' principal work activity. *Id.* at 11. More specifically, he found that batteries are essential to operative radios and body alarms and that, without operative radios and body alarms, the grievants cannot perform their principal work activity effectively and safely both for themselves and the inmates for whose safety they are responsible. *Id.* Consequently, he concluded that picking up batteries starts the work day and returning batteries ends the work day. *Id.*

In addition, he rejected the Agency's claim that picking up batteries is not necessary because charged batteries are already in place or can be delivered to employees at their posts. In this connection, he found that, because of safety concerns pertaining to operative radios and body alarms, employees cannot rely on the batteries in place or risk that the batteries might not be delivered to their posts. *Id.* With respect to the issue of whether the Agency "suffered or permitted" the disputed activities, the Arbitrator found that "management knew that correctional officers were picking up batteries at the control center and it never directed them to refrain from doing so." *Id.* at 12.

For these reasons, the Arbitrator sustained the grievance and directed the parties "to file a stipulation on the number of hours to be compensated and the monetary rate for quantifying the [a]ward relative to the total sum due." *Id.* He further directed that "[s]hould the parties fail to do so, the Arbitrator will make the calculations upon receiving advice of the parties." *Id.*

The parties were unable to stipulate the number of hours or the monetary rates at which the hours were to be compensated, and, accordingly, they filed statements of position with the Arbitrator. In its statement of position, the Union alleged that the employees assigned to the specified posts and departments worked, on average, twenty-two minutes of overtime each shift during the recovery period. Opp'n, Ex. Vol. II-6 at 5. For employees who are not assigned to the control center, the Union based this on the Arbitrator's finding that picking up and returning batteries started and ended the compensable work day. *Id.* at 3 (citing Liability Award No. 1 at 11). For employees assigned to the control center, the Union based this on the work they allegedly were required to perform before and after their shifts. *Id.* at 3-4. In addition, the Union proposed that the overtime be compensated on the basis of the average pay rates in the Agency of the correctional officer position (General Schedule (GS) grade 8, step 4) and vocational nurse position (GS-7, step 5) involved in the grievance (the disputed positions). *Id.* at 5.

In its statement of position, the Agency disagreed with the Union's allegation of twenty-two minutes of overtime each day. The Agency alleged that the testimony showed that the amount of time spent on pre-shift and post-shift activities was no more than ten minutes per shift and that, consequently, the amount of time was de minimis and not compensable.[2] Exceptions, Attach. B, Agency's Response at 2-3. The Agency also disagreed with the Union's proposed use of average rates of pay and claimed that backpay must be based on each employee's individual rate of pay at the time of the violation. *Id.* at 2.

In Damages Award No. 1, the Arbitrator adopted the Union's calculation of damages and awarded the grievants twenty-two minutes of overtime compensation for each shift at the Agency's average rates of pay of the disputed positions. Damages Award No. 1 at 13. He also awarded liquidated damages, found that the violation was willful, and calculated damages beginning three years before the grievance was filed.[3] *Id.*

Subsequently, the Union petitioned for an award of attorney fees under the FLSA, 29 U.S.C. § 216(b) (§ 216(b)).[4] In response, the Agency contended that the number of hours for which fees were requested was not reasonable. Exceptions, Attach. B, Agency's

2. As noted *infra* note 8, total time per workday must be more than ten minutes to be compensable.

3. The Agency filed exceptions to Liability Award No. 1 and Damages Award No. 1, and the Authority issued an order to show cause why the exceptions should not be dismissed as interlocutory. When the Agency did not respond, the Authority dismissed the exceptions without prejudice. *Fed. Med. Ctr.*, 64 FLRA at 566.

4. Section 216(b) provides that courts "shall, in addition to any judgment awarded to the plaintiff or plaintiffs, allow a reasonable attorney's fee to be paid by the defendant, and costs of the action."

Response to Union's Petition for Attorneys Fees at 3. In addition, the Agency attached a copy of the Union's statement of services provided and objected to specified entries. *Id.* at 4. The Agency also contended that costs could not be awarded because the parties' collective bargaining agreement requires such costs to be shared. *Id.* The Union filed a reply to the Agency's response.

In Attorney Fees Award No. 1, the Arbitrator found that the number of hours claimed was reasonable and that the requested hourly rates were based on the "updated" *Laffey* matrix (adjusted *Laffey* matrix)[5] and were, therefore, appropriate. Exceptions at 6 (citing Attorney Fees Award No. 1 at 4). He also found that the Union was entitled to recover costs.[6] *Id.*

In Liability Award No. 2, the Arbitrator addressed the same activities of picking up and returning batteries for employees assigned to disputed posts and departments that had not been addressed in Liability Award No. 1. For the reasons set forth in Liability Award No. 1, he determined that these activities are compensable. Liability Award No. 2 at 1, 3. Consequently, he directed the parties to file a stipulation on number of hours and hourly rates and stated that, if they were unable to do so, then he would make the necessary calculations after receiving their advice. *Id.*

The parties were unable to stipulate the number of hours and hourly rates, and they filed statements of position with the Arbitrator. The Union alleged that the employees assigned to the posts or departments in dispute worked from fifteen to twenty-five minutes of overtime per shift depending on the post or department.[7] The Union again proposed that the overtime be compensated on the basis of the average rates of pay of the disputed positions. Opp'n, Ex. Vol. III-22 at 9-10. The Agency again claimed that the compensable time of the grievants assigned to the disputed posts and departments was no more than de minimis and also incorporated its arguments from its first statement of position. Exceptions, Attach. B, Agency's Response to Remedy after Final Hearing at 2-3.

In Damages Award No. 2, the Arbitrator adopted the Union's calculation of damages and awarded the grievants the amount of backpay proposed by the Union. Damages Award No. 2 at 2. The Arbitrator stated that the amount was calculated on the basis of "twenty minutes overtime at the pay rate of GS[]8-4, this rate being the average pay rate for correctional officers[.]" *Id.* He also awarded liquidated damages and calculated damages beginning three years before the grievance was filed. *Id.*

The Union petitioned for an additional award of attorney fees, and the Agency did not file a response. In Attorney Fees Award No. 2, the Arbitrator awarded fees for the number of hours requested at the rates set forth in the adjusted *Laffey* matrix. Attorney Fees Award No. 2 at 2. He also awarded the Union its costs for this portion of the grievance. *Id.*

III. Positions of the Parties

A. Agency's Exceptions

The Agency contends that Damages Awards Nos. 1 and 2 are contrary to the FLSA. Exceptions at 7. The Agency argues that picking up and returning batteries at the control center are not indispensable to the primary activity of the grievants, as required by

---

5. The *Laffey* matrix sets forth a method for determining the appropriate hourly rates for attorneys in the Washington, D.C. area. *AFGE, Local 2608*, 63 FLRA 486, 487 n.2 (2009). As the Authority has recognized, there are two versions of the matrix. *U.S. Dep't of the Army, U.S. Army Dental Activity, Fort Bragg, N.C.*, 65 FLRA 54, 55 n.4 (2010) (*Army Dental Activity*). One version is maintained by the Civil Division of the Office of the United States Attorney, which calculates the matrix rate for each year by adding the change in the overall cost of living as reflected in the United States consumer price index (CPI) for the Washington, D.C. area for the prior year and rounding that rate to the nearest multiple of $ 5. That version is commonly referred to as the *Laffey* matrix. By contrast, the so-called "adjusted" *Laffey* matrix calculates the matrix rates for each year by using the legal services component of the CPI rather than the general CPI. *Id.* As the matrix used by the Arbitrator is commonly referred to as the adjusted *Laffey* matrix, rather than the updated *Laffey* matrix, we will use the common reference hereafter.

6. The Agency filed exceptions to Attorney Fees Award No. 1 and incorporated its previously noted exceptions to Liability Award No. 1 and Damages Award No. 1. The Authority dismissed the exceptions as interlocutory because the awards did not constitute a complete resolution of all issues submitted to arbitration. *Fed. Med. Ctr.*, 64 FLRA at 568.

7. Specifically, the Union contended that employees were entitled to the following amounts of overtime for each shift during the recovery period based on their assigned post or department: special housing unit #2 --twenty-two minutes; administrative unit #2 -- twenty-five minutes; compound #1 and #2 -- fifteen minutes; and the remaining posts or departments -- 17.5 minutes. Opp'n, Ex. Vol. III-22 at 9.

5 C.F.R. § 551.412 (§ 551.412).[8] *Id.* at 11. In this connection, the Agency maintains that "fully-charged batteries and phones are already available at every single post where they are needed when an officer arrives at the post[,]" and that "every correctional officer can call the compound officer and request an additional battery as needed [and] one will be delivered to them at their post." *Id.* at 10. Additionally, the Agency argues that officers were never "told or requested to pick up batteries at the control center[,]" that they "did so by their own choosing[,]" and that the Agency should not be found to have "constructive knowledge that this was constantly a practice." *Id.* at 10 & n.9. In regard to employees who worked "the Control Center # 1 post[,]" *id.* at 14, the Agency contends that the award of overtime is deficient because "they are not required to pick up any equipment prior to getting to their post and they are not required to return any equipment prior to completing their shift[,]" *id.* at 16.

In addition, the Agency asserts that in Damages Awards Nos. 1 and 2 the Arbitrator directed that overtime be paid "based on an average amount of minutes worked[.]" *Id.* at 17. The Agency argues that the posts at issue are located at different places throughout the medical center and are at varying distances from the control center. *Id.* at 18. The Agency alleges that, under Authority precedent, the awards are deficient because the Arbitrator fails to identify "the actual amount of time it takes for employees to get to individual posts[.]" *Id.* at 17 (citing *U.S. Dep't of Justice, Fed. Bureau of Prisons, Fed. Corr. Inst., Terminal Island, Cal.*, 63 FLRA 620 (2009) (*FCI, Terminal Island*)). In addition, the Agency contends that the Arbitrator's calculation of backpay on the basis of average rates of pay is also contrary to law because "[n]othing in the FLSA provides for employees to be paid an 'average' amount of a class of employees." *Id.* at 20.

The Agency further contends that Attorney Fees Award No. 1 is deficient because it "is impossible" that the number of hours claimed by the Union is reasonable. *Id.* at 22. The Agency also argues that the Arbitrator failed to "provide any independent analysis or discussion of the Union's fee request, despite the fact that the Agency specifically argued in its post-hearing brief that much of the Union's fee request was duplicative and redundant." *Id.* The Agency additionally contends that the Arbitrator's use of the adjusted *Laffey* matrix rather than the more commonly used *Laffey* matrix is deficient because the adjusted *Laffey* matrix is not reasonable. *Id.* at 23-24.

Finally, the Agency contends that the awards of costs in Attorney Fees Awards Nos. 1 and 2 fail to draw their essence from Article 32, Section d (Section d) of the agreement.[9] *Id.* at 25-27. In this regard, the Agency argues that the language of Section d "indicates that the parties have agreed that in all arbitrations between the parties, that all fees and expenses of the arbitration will be shared by the parties." *Id.* at 27. The Agency also argues that the award is deficient despite entitlement to costs under the FLSA because the Union "agreed to waive its right to seek" reimbursement of costs under the FLSA. *Id.* at 28.

B. Union's Opposition

The Union contends that the Arbitrator's findings that picking up batteries starts the compensable workday and that returning batteries ends the compensable workday are not contrary to the FLSA or § 551.412. Opp'n at 10. In addition, the Union claims that the Arbitrator's factual findings support a determination that the Agency suffered or permitted the disputed activities. *Id.* at 25. The Union also disagrees with the Agency's claims that batteries are available at the disputed posts or that they could be delivered. *Id.* at 15. The Union asserts that the testimony was to the contrary and that the Arbitrator factually determined that, for safety, it was necessary for the grievants to pick up the batteries at the control center. *Id.* at 14-15.

The Union agrees with the Agency that the control center officers do not pick up or return batteries, but contends that control center officers were properly awarded compensation because they are required to work before and after their scheduled shifts. *Id.* at 32, 35.

8. Section 551.412(a)(1) provides: "If an agency reasonably determines that a preparatory or concluding activity is closely related to an employee's principal activities, and is indispensable to the performance of the principal activities, and that the total time spent in that activity is more than [ten] minutes per workday, the agency shall credit all of the time spent in that activity . . . as hours of work." Section 551.412(b) defines "preliminary" and "postliminary" activities as "preparatory or concluding activity that is not closely related to the performance of the principal activities" and provides that time spent on such activities "is excluded from hours of work and is not compensable[.]"

9. Section d provides: "The arbitrator's fees and all expenses of the arbitration . . . shall be borne equally by the Employer and the Union." Exceptions at 26 (quoting Section d).

In regard to the Arbitrator's use of averages, the Union asserts that the Agency refused to stipulate to the number of hours and the pay rates and ignored the Union's request for documents that reflect when employees assume duty and are relieved of duty. *Id.* at 36-37. In addition, the Union maintains that it submitted a brief to the Arbitrator providing its advice on calculating damages, but that the Agency's brief to the Arbitrator offered no advice on calculating damages. The Union contends that the Agency challenges the calculation of damages for the first time in its exceptions. *Id.* at 48.

Alternatively, the Union contends that the Arbitrator's use of averages is consistent with court and Authority precedent. *Id.* at 38. In this connection, the Union argues that the Agency's failure to keep accurate and complete records authorized the Arbitrator to determine backpay by a "just and reasonable" inference. *Id.* at 38, 41 (quoting *Anderson v. Mt. Clemens Pottery Co.,* 328 U.S. 680, 687-88 (1946); citing *AFGE, Local 1741,* 62 FLRA 113, 119-20 (2007)). Further, the Union asserts that the Agency's reliance on *FCI, Terminal Island* is misplaced because this case is distinguishable from the "blanket award of [thirty] minutes for every shift, for every correctional officer regardless of testimony" in *FCI, Terminal Island. Id.* at 47. In particular, with respect to Damages Award No. 2, the Union maintains that the Arbitrator adopted the Union's calculation of damages, which was based on the posts or departments to which the grievants were assigned with the amounts of overtime requested varying from fifteen to twenty-five minutes. *Id.* at 44-45.

In regard to Attorney Fees Award No. 1, the Union contends that the Agency fails to establish that the number of hours awarded by the Arbitrator is deficient. The Union argues that the Arbitrator appropriately addressed the details of the Union's position and the Agency's objections in his award of fees. *Id.* at 52. Further, the Union contends that the Arbitrator's use of the adjusted *Laffey* matrix is not deficient. *Id.* at 54-56.

In regard to the Agency's essence exception, the Union contends that language of Section d does not address costs to which the Union is legally entitled. *Id.* at 58. The Union also argues that its entitlement to costs pursuant to the FLSA is a substantive right that overrides any conflicting agreement provision and that the Agency provides no support for its argument that the Union waived its right to seek reimbursement of costs under the FLSA. *Id.* at 60, 64.

IV. Preliminary Issue

The Authority's Regulations that were in effect when the Agency filed its exceptions provided that "[t]he Authority will not consider . . . any issue, which was not presented in the proceedings before the . . . arbitrator." 5 C.F.R. § 2429.5.[10] The Union contends that the Agency offered no advice to the Arbitrator on calculating damages and that the Agency challenges the calculation of damages for the first time in its exceptions. However, contrary to the Union's claim, in its statement of position to the Arbitrator in response to Liability Award No. 1, the Agency specifically disagreed with the Union's allegation of twenty-two minutes of overtime each day and alleged as to each post or department in dispute that the amount of time spent on pre-shift and post-shift activities was no more than de minimis. Exceptions, Attach. B, Agency's Response at 2. The Agency also specifically disagreed with the use of average rates of pay. *Id.* To the extent that the Union is also claiming that these issues are barred with respect to Damages Award No. 2, in its statement of position, the Agency alleged as to each post or department that the time spent on pre-shift and post-shift activities was no more than de minimis and incorporated by reference its earlier disagreement with the use of average rates of pay. *Id.,* Agency's Response to Remedy after Final Hearing at 2-3. Accordingly, we conclude that the Agency presented these issues to the Arbitrator and that the issues are not barred.

In regard to Attorney Fees Award No. 1, in its response to the Union's petition for fees, the Agency contended that costs could not be awarded because Section d requires that costs be shared. *Id.,* Agency's Response to Union's Petition for Attorney Fees at 4. However, the Agency did not acknowledge that the § 216(b) entitles the Union to reimbursement of its costs of bringing the case. The Agency also did not argue, as it does in its exception, that Section d supplants or waives the Union's entitlement to costs under that statutory provision. Accordingly, we conclude that the Agency may not argue, for the first time in exceptions, that Section d waives the Union's entitlement to costs under § 216(b).

10. The Authority's Regulations concerning the review of arbitration awards, as well as certain related procedural Regulations, including 5 C.F.R. § 2429.5, were revised effective October 1, 2010. 75 Fed. Reg. 42,283 (2010). Because the Agency's exceptions in this case were filed before that date, we apply the prior Regulations.

In regard to Attorney Fees Award No. 2, as the Agency did not file a response as it did in regard to Attorney Fees Award No. 1, the Agency did not argue that Section d precluded an award of costs. Accordingly, we conclude that the Agency's essence exception as to Attorney Fees Award No. 2 is barred.

V. Analysis and Conclusions

A. The Agency's contrary-to-law exceptions are granted in part and denied in part, and the awards are remanded in part.

When an exception involves an award's consistency with law, the Authority reviews de novo any questions of law raised by the exception and the award. *E.g., FCI, Terminal Island*, 63 FLRA at 623. In applying the standard of de novo review, the Authority determines whether an arbitrator's legal conclusions are consistent with the applicable standard of law. *Id.* In making that determination, the Authority defers to the arbitrator's underlying factual findings. *Id.*

1. The awards are remanded for clarification of the basis for the award of overtime to the grievants at the control center post who do not pick up and return batteries; the remaining exceptions regarding entitlement to overtime compensation are denied.

Section 551.412(a)(1) provides that preparatory and concluding activities that are closely related to, and indispensable to the performance of, an employee's principal activities constitute hours of work and are compensable when the time spent in the activities exceeds ten minutes per workday. Section 551.412(b) defines preliminary and postliminary activities as preparatory or concluding activities that are not closely related to the performance of the principal activities and provides that the time spent in such activities is not compensable.

Here, the Arbitrator found that picking up and returning batteries at the control center are activities indispensable to the performance of the employees' principal work activity because the batteries are essential to operative radios and body alarms and that, without operative radios and body alarms, the grievants cannot perform their principal work activities effectively and safely both for themselves and the inmates for whose safety they are responsible. The Agency does not dispute that fully charged batteries are indispensable to the performance of the grievants' principal activities. Instead, the Agency argues that picking up batteries at the control center is not necessary because charged batteries are already in place or can be delivered to employees at their posts or departments. However, the Arbitrator rejected this argument. He specifically found that picking up batteries was necessary because of safety concerns with relying on batteries being available at the post or by delivery. The Agency does not address in its exception the safety concerns on which the Arbitrator relied, or otherwise provide a basis for concluding that the Arbitrator erred in finding that picking up and returning batteries at the control center are compensable as activities that are indispensable to the performance of the grievants' principal work activity. Accordingly, we deny the Agency's argument that this finding is contrary to law.

In regard to the Agency's argument that the activities are not compensable because the Agency did not suffer or permit their performance, "suffered or permitted work" is defined as "any work performed by an employee for the benefit of an agency, whether requested or not, provided the employee's supervisor knows or has reason to believe that the work is being performed and has an opportunity to prevent the work from being performed." 5 C.F.R. § 551.104. Here, the Arbitrator specifically found that "management knew that correctional officers were picking up batteries at the control center and it never directed them to refrain from doing so[,]" Liability Award No. 1 at 12, and the Agency does not contend that the award is based on a nonfact. Accordingly, we defer to the Arbitrator's factual findings and deny the Agency's argument that this finding is contrary to law.

The Agency also contends that Damages Award No. 1 is deficient because it awards overtime to the grievants assigned to the control center post who do not pick up and return batteries. In Damages Award No. 1, the Arbitrator awarded the grievants assigned to the control center twenty-two minutes of overtime per shift. Damages Award No. 1 at 13. It is not disputed that the grievants assigned to the control center do not pick up and return batteries. Although the Union argued that the employees assigned to the control center were required to work prior to the beginning of their shift and after the end of their shift to accomplish their duties, in Liability Award No. 1, the Arbitrator specifically addressed only the activities of picking up and returning batteries and made no findings regarding the overtime allegedly performed by the grievants assigned to the control center. Consequently, it is not clear on this record what the Arbitrator's basis was for awarding these grievants twenty-two minutes of overtime for each shift in the control center. As a result, the record does not enable the Authority to determine whether the award is deficient as alleged by the Agency. Where the Authority is unable to determine whether an award is deficient, the Authority's practice is to remand the case to the parties for resubmission to the arbitrator, absent settlement, for a clarification of the basis for the award. *E.g., U.S. Dep't of the Army, Headquarters, III Corps & Fort Hood, Fort Hood, Tex.*, 56 FLRA 544, 547 (2000). Accordingly, we remand to have the Arbitrator clarify the basis for compensating the grievants assigned to the control center.

2. The awards are remanded for further findings regarding varying pay rates of individual grievants, and Damages Award No. 1 is remanded for further findings regarding the amount of time that the grievants spent in overtime; the exception regarding the amount of time that the grievants in Damages Award No. 2 spent in overtime is denied.

In Damages Award No. 1, the Arbitrator awarded the grievants twenty-two minutes of overtime compensation for each shift at the average rates of pay of the disputed positions. Damages Award No. 1 at 13. The Authority has specifically rejected an arbitrator's use of an "average amount of time expended per day per correctional officer" in calculating an award of backpay under the FLSA. *FCI, Terminal Island*, 63 FLRA at 624-25 (quoting arbitrator's award). As it was not disputed in *FCI, Terminal Island* that the time spent by correctional officers performing pre-shift and post-shift activities varied, in part on the basis of the length of time it takes correctional officers to travel between the control center and their assigned posts, the Authority held that the award did not correctly compensate the officers because the varying amounts of time must be taken into account under the FLSA. Accordingly, the Authority concluded that the award was contrary to the FLSA and set it aside. As the record did not provide sufficient information for the Authority to determine the amount of time that the correctional officers engaged in compensable activities, the Authority remanded the award to have the arbitrator account for the variations. *Id.* at 625.

As in *FCI, Terminal Island*, it is also not disputed in this case that the time spent by the grievants performing compensable activities varied. Thus, consistent with *FCI, Terminal Island,* we find that the Arbitrator's use of an average amount of overtime is contrary to the FLSA. As the record in this case does not provide sufficient information to determine the amount of time that the grievants engaged in compensable activities, based on the foregoing, we remand to have the Arbitrator take into account these varying amounts.

In Damages Award No. 1, the Arbitrator also used average pay rates within the Agency. The principle underlying the Authority's decision in *FCI, Terminal Island* applies equally to the use of average pay rates. There is no distinction apparent between an arbitrator's use of average amount of overtime and average pay rates. With the Authority having rejected in *FCI, Terminal Island* the use of average amount of overtime as contrary to the FLSA when the amount of time varied, there is no basis for permitting under the FLSA the use of average pay rates when the pay rates of the grievants concededly vary. Accordingly, we apply *FCI, Terminal Island* to the Arbitrator's use of average pay rates in Damages Award No. 1, and find that their use is contrary to the FLSA. As the record in this case does not provide sufficient information to determine the pay rates of the grievants, we remand to have the Arbitrator take into account the varying rates of pay of the grievants.

The Agency argues that Damages Award No. 2 is likewise deficient because it is based on an average amount of overtime of twenty minutes at average rates of pay. In Damages Award No. 2, the Arbitrator adopted precisely the total amount of backpay proposed by the Union and stated that the amount of backpay was calculated on the basis of twenty minutes of overtime at the average pay rate of correctional officers. Damages Award No. 2 at 2. In its opposition to the Agency's exceptions, the Union maintains that the Arbitrator adopted its exact calculation of damages and that the calculation was based on the individual posts or departments to which the grievants were assigned, with the amounts of overtime requested varying from fifteen to twenty-five minutes per shift. Opp'n at 44-45.

The Authority has repeatedly stated that when it resolves exceptions to an arbitration award, it considers the award and the record as a whole. In particular, the Authority interprets an award in context without undue focus on isolated statements. *E.g., Soc. Sec. Admin., Office of Disability Adjudication & Review, Region 1,* 65 FLRA 334, 336 (2010). Although the Arbitrator stated that the amount of backpay was calculated on the basis of twenty minutes of overtime at the average pay rate of correctional officers, he awarded the total precise amount proposed by the Union in its statement of position filed with the Arbitrator. Opp'n, Ex. Vol. III-22 at 9-10. As stated previously, the Union specifically contended in its statement that the grievants were entitled to the following amounts of overtime for each shift during the recovery period based on their assigned posts or departments: special housing unit #2 --twenty-two minutes; administrative unit #2 -- twenty-five minutes; compound #1 and #2 -- fifteen minutes; and the remaining posts or departments -- 17.5 minutes. *Id.* at 9. Thus, the Union's statement calculated backpay based on the varying amounts of time spent on pre-shift and post-shift activities, rather than on an average amount of overtime. Based on the record as a whole, we construe the backpay as calculated on the basis of varying amounts of overtime, and on the basis of the average rates of pay of the disputed positions and not solely the correctional officer position, as stated by the Arbitrator. As so construed, we deny the exception to Damages Award No. 2, as it pertains to the amount of overtime performed by the grievants per shift. However, for the reasons stated above in connection with Damages Award No. 1, the Arbitrator's use of average pay rates in Damages Award No. 2 is contrary to the FLSA. Accordingly, we set aside the Arbitrator's use of average pay rates in Damages Award No. 2. As with Damages Award No. 1, the record in this case does not provide sufficient information to determine the pay rates of the grievants. Accordingly, we remand to have the Arbitrator take into account the varying rates of pay of the grievants.

3. Attorney Fees Award No. 1 is remanded for further findings regarding the number of hours reasonably expended; the Agency's exception regarding the use of the adjusted *Laffey* matrix is denied.

With regard to the rates that the Arbitrator found appropriate, the Authority has held that arbitrators are not precluded, as a matter of law, from applying the adjusted *Laffey* matrix. *Army Dental Activity*, 65 FLRA at 58. Consistent with *Army Dental Activity*, we conclude that the Arbitrator's use of the adjusted *Laffey* matrix provides no basis for finding Attorney Fees Award No. 1 deficient.

In resolving whether an award of attorney fees is reasonable as required by the Back Pay Act, the Authority has taken into account court decisions applying other federal fee-shifting statutes with a similar requirement. *E.g., U.S. Dep't of Def., Def. Fin. & Accounting Serv.*, 60 FLRA 281, 286 (2004) (applying *Hensley v. Eckerhart,* 461 U.S. 424 (1983) (*Hensley*)). In particular, consistent with *Hensley,* the Authority reviews contested awards of attorney fees for the number of hours requested to ensure that the number of hours expended was reasonable. *Id.* When arbitrators have not made specific factual findings to support their conclusions that the number of hours expended is reasonable, the Authority has remanded to the parties for resubmission to the arbitrator for further findings. *E.g., U.S. Dep't of Veterans Affairs Med. Ctr., Detroit, Mich.*, 64 FLRA 794, 797 (2010) (*VAMC*). In this regard, remands are appropriate because the arbitrator, as the fact-finder, is in the best position to make determinations as to the reasonableness of the number of hours expended. *Id.*

As the foregoing precedent is expressly based on not only the Back Pay Act, but also other federal fee-shifting statutes, we apply this approach in this case involving an award of fees under the FLSA. Here, in view of the Agency's multiple challenges to specific expenditures of time of the Union's attorneys, the Arbitrator failed to set forth sufficient factual findings to support Attorney Fees Award No. 1. Accordingly, we remand the matter of the number of hours reasonably expended in relation to Attorney Fees Award No. 1 for specific findings by the Arbitrator.[11]

B. Attorney Fees Award No. 1 does not fail to draw its essence from the agreement.

For an award to be found deficient as failing to draw its essence from the agreement, it must be established that the award: (1) cannot in any rational way be derived from the agreement; (2) is so unfounded in reason and fact and so unconnected with the wording and purposes of the agreement as to manifest an infidelity to the obligation of the arbitrator; (3) does not represent a plausible interpretation of the agreement; or (4) evidences a manifest disregard of the agreement. *E.g., U.S. Dep't of Justice, Fed. Bureau of Prisons, Fed. Corr. Inst., Greenville, Ill.*, 65 FLRA 607, 608 (2011) (*FCI, Greenville*).

In accordance with our dismissal under § 2429.5, the Agency's argument under this exception is limited to the claim that Section d requires costs be shared by the parties. In *FCI, Greenville,* the arbitrator awarded costs under §216(b), and the Agency made the same argument as it does here. The

11. We note that we have dismissed pursuant to § 2429.5 of the Authority's Regulations this exception as it pertains to Attorney Fees Award No. 2.

Authority found that, in making this argument, the Agency did not dispute that, pursuant to § 216(b), a prevailing party in an FLSA action is entitled to reimbursement of the costs of bringing the FLSA case and did not allege that Section d was intended to supplant the cost provisions of § 216(b). *Id.* at 609. As a result, the Authority concluded that the Agency did not demonstrate that the award of costs under § 216(b) manifestly disregarded Section d or was implausible, irrational, or unfounded. *Id.*

Here, the Agency also does not dispute that, pursuant to § 216(b), a prevailing party in an FLSA action is entitled to reimbursement of the costs of bringing the FLSA case, and the Agency has not timely argued that Section d supplants or waives § 216(b). Consequently, consistent with *FCI, Greenville,* the Agency's essence argument does not provide a basis for finding the award of costs deficient. Accordingly, we deny this exception.

VI. Decision

The awards are remanded in part for clarification of the basis for the award of overtime to the grievants at the control center post who do not pick up and return batteries, and for further findings regarding varying pay rates of individual grievants. Damages Award No. 1 is remanded for further findings regarding the amount of time that grievants spent in overtime, and Attorney Fees Award No. 1 is remanded for further findings regarding the number of hours reasonably expended. The Agency's remaining exceptions are dismissed in part and denied in part.

65 FLRA No. 203

UNITED STATES
DEPARTMENT OF THE ARMY
WOMACK ARMY MEDICAL CENTER
FORT BRAGG, NORTH CAROLINA
(Agency)

and

AMERICAN FEDERATION
OF GOVERNMENT EMPLOYEES
LOCAL 1770
(Union)

0-AR-4305

DECISION

June 29, 2011

Before the Authority: Carol Waller Pope, Chairman, and Thomas M. Beck and Ernest DuBester, Members

I. Statement of the Case

This matter is before the Authority on exceptions to an award of Arbitrator Michele M. Hoyman filed by the Agency and the Union under § 7122(a) of the Federal Service Labor-Management Relations Statute (the Statute) and part 2425 of the Authority's Regulations. The Union filed an opposition to the Agency's exceptions and the Agency filed an opposition to the Union's exceptions.

The Arbitrator found that the grievant's promotion to General Schedule (GS)-12 was not lawful, but concluded that the Agency's failure to grant a waiver of the money the grievant had been paid improperly was an adverse event and ordered the Agency to grant the grievant a waiver. For the reasons set forth below, we dismiss the Agency's management rights exception, deny the Union's contrary to law exceptions, grant the Agency's exceeds authority exception, and set aside that portion of the award.

II. Background and Arbitrator's Award

The grievant has been employed by the Agency at Womack Medical Center (Womack) as a Registered Nurse (RN) for six years. Award at 3. Before becoming a Labor and Delivery Nurse for the Agency, the grievant gained "considerable experience" in labor and delivery, in the neonatal intensive care unit (NICU), and as a manager at other facilities. *Id.* While working at Womack, the grievant obtained a master's degree in midwifery, in part using the Agency's tuition assistance program. *Id.*

After completing her degree, the grievant responded to a Midwife vacancy announcement that was posted as a GS-11/training 12 position. *Id.* At the time the grievant applied for the position, she was serving at GS-10. The Agency's human resources department found that the grievant was not qualified at GS-12 because she did not have one year of specialized experience at GS-11. *Id.* at 4. The Agency informed the grievant that, because she was currently employed at GS-10 and there was a "ban on jumping one grade," she "might not be able to achieve the GS[-]12." *Id.* at 5. However, the Agency maintained a recruitment policy that allowed it to hire outside midwives at GS-12. *Id.* at 3-4.

After accepting the position at GS-11, the grievant received a Standard Form (SF)-50 Notice of Personnel Action indicating that she was classified at GS-12, Step 6. *Id.* at 6. She received pay at this level for approximately six months, until the Agency processed another SF-50 reclassifying the grievant at GS-11. *Id.* at 6-7. According to the Agency, the grievant had been mistakenly classified at GS-12. *Id.* at 7. After issuing the new SF-50, the Agency sent the grievant a bill for the difference between the GS-11 and GS-12 salary that she had been paid. *Id.* The grievant applied to the Defense Finance and Accounting Service (DFAS) for a waiver of the amount owed, but the waiver had not been granted by the time of the arbitration hearing. *Id.*

The Union presented a grievance alleging that the Agency violated Articles 27, 44, 38, and 2 of the parties' agreement by reclassifying the grievant at GS-11. *Id.* at 8. The matter was not resolved and was submitted to arbitration. The parties stipulated to the following issue: "[w]as the grievant's promotion to GS-12, Step 6 proper?" *Id.* at 2.

The Arbitrator concluded that "the promotion was not proper in the sense of lawful." *Id.* at 11. She also found that the promotion was "proper in the sense of being fair and meritorious on its face[.]" *Id.* The Arbitrator determined that she could not award the grievant a promotion or she would "fall afoul of the [Code of Federal Regulations (CFR)] and exceed her authority." *Id.* However, the Arbitrator encouraged the parties to achieve the fair result without being "paralyzed by legal technicalities." *Id.*

The Arbitrator found that the grievant accepted the position at GS-11 for three reasons: (1) it was "against regulations" to promote someone to GS-12 who was not at GS-11 for one year; (2) the GS-12 pay scale was only available to new hires according to the Agency's recruitment policy; and (3) the grievant did not qualify for any exceptions to the ban on advancing from GS-10 to GS-12. *Id.* at 5. However, the Arbitrator also found that the Agency could have credited the grievant as having one year of experience equivalent to GS-11 because she had experience as a labor and delivery nurse, experience in the NICU, prior management experience, and specialized skills. *Id.* at 13-14. Thus, the Arbitrator found that the grievant "had the qualifications of a GS-12." *Id.* at 14. Because the Arbitrator found herself limited to lawful remedies, she found that she could not "order the [A]gency to reinstate the [grievant's] GS-12 status . . . ." *Id.* at 16.

The Arbitrator then considered whether the Agency should have granted the grievant a waiver for the bill that DFAS sent her because she was "'mistakenly' given the GS-12." *Id.* at 14. The Arbitrator concluded that, by billing the grievant "for an [A]gency mistake," the grievant "experienced an adverse event which was a violation" of the parties' agreement. *Id.* Therefore, the Arbitrator ordered the Agency to grant a waiver and repay the grievant the money that she had already paid. *Id.* at 16.

III. Positions of the Parties

A. Agency's Exceptions

The Agency argues that award does not draw its essence from the parties' agreement, that the arbitrator exceeded her authority, and that the award is contrary to law. Agency's Exceptions at 3-4.

The Agency first argues that the award does not draw its essence from Article 39, Section 2 of the parties' agreement, which defines grievance as a complaint that, among other things, concerns a "claim of breach of" the parties' agreement and/or "any claimed violation . . . of any law, rule, or regulation . . . ." *Id.*, Attach. C, Contract Agreement at 60. According to the Agency, because Article 39 of the parties' agreement does not allow "the Arbitrator to make a decision on purely equitable grounds[,]" the award does not draw its essence from the agreement. *Id.* at 5.

The Agency also argues that the Arbitrator exceeded her authority. The Agency contends that the Arbitrator's authority ended when she determined that the promotion was not proper. *Id.* at 6. By then deciding whether the grievant was subject to an adverse action, she decided an issue not submitted to arbitration and exceeded her authority. *Id.* The Agency also argues that the Arbitrator exceeded her authority by finding a violation of the parties' agreement without specifying which provision the Agency had violated or how the Agency had done so. *Id.* at 7. According to the Agency, none of the provisions cited in the award was relevant to the stipulated issue before the Arbitrator. *Id.* at 7-8. Further, the Agency argues that the Arbitrator exceeded her authority by ordering the Agency to grant a waiver, which is in the "purview" of another organization, the DFAS, an entity that is not a party to the parties' agreement. *Id.* at 8-9.

The Agency argues that the award of backpay is contrary to the Back Pay Act. *Id.* at 9. According to the Agency, the Arbitrator did not make a finding that the grievant was subjected to an unjustified or unwarranted personnel action. *Id.* at 10. The Agency contends that, even if the unspecified violation of the parties' agreement is an unjustified personnel action, the Arbitrator has not shown how that action resulted in a loss of pay. *Id.* Further, the Agency argues that, because the Arbitrator "in essence" awarded the grievant a promotion, the award conflicts with 5 C.F.R. § 531.212(a) (§ 531.212(a)), which allows an agency to use its pay-setting authority for a reappointment only after a 90-day break in service or if the employee meets an exception to that requirement.[1] *Id.* at 11. The Agency contends that

---

[1] 5 C.F.R. § 531.212(a) provides:

> (1) An agency may use the superior qualifications and special needs pay-setting authority . . . for—
> (i) A first appointment . . . ; or
> (ii) A reappointment that is considered a new appointment . . . because it meets the conditions prescribed in paragraph (a)(2) and (3) of this section.
>
> (2) An agency may use the superior qualifications and special needs pay-setting authority for a reappointment only when the employee has had a break in service of at least 90 days . . . except as provided in paragraph (a)(3) of this section.

the grievant did not have a 90-day break in service or meet any of the exceptions. *Id.* Finally, the Agency argues that the award conflicts with § 7106 of the Statute because it violates management's rights to hire employees, determine a budget, and promulgate a recruitment and retention policy. *Id.* at 12.

B. Union's Opposition

The Union argues that the award draws its essence from the parties' agreement because the grievance procedure is properly used to address claims of unfairness. Union's Opp'n at 5.

The Union also argues that the Arbitrator did not exceed her authority. *Id.* at 5-6. The Union contends that the Arbitrator's use of the term "adverse action" is not a technical term, but, rather, a statement that the grievant experienced a loss of pay adverse to her interest. *Id.* at 6. According to the Union, it was reasonable for the grievant to believe that the Agency had properly granted her the promotion, and it would be unjust to require her to pay the money back to the Agency. *Id.* The Union also asserts that the Arbitrator did not exceed her authority by finding that the Agency violated the parties' agreement because it would be contrary to the parties' agreement to take money from the grievant improperly. *Id.* at 6-7. The Union also argues that the Arbitrator did not exceed her authority by ordering the Agency to reimburse the grievant and grant a waiver of the remaining money that she owed because the Agency can order DFAS to grant the waiver. *Id.* at 7.

The Union argues that the award is not contrary to the Back Pay Act because the grievant was subject to an improper personnel action – either the initial promotion or the Agency's rescission of the promotion – that was the result of an Agency error. *Id.* The Union also contends that the award is not contrary to law; according to the Union, the grievant met the time-in-grade requirement because the Arbitrator found that she had one year of equivalent experience at GS-11. *Id.* at 8. Additionally, the Union asserts that the grievant could have qualified for the exception in § 531.212(a)(3)(ii) for expert positions. *Id.* at 9.

C. Union's Exceptions

The Union argues that the Arbitrator's failure to grant the grievant a promotion to GS-12 is contrary to law. Union's Exceptions at 4. According to the Union, the grievant met the time in grade requirements because the grievant had one year of equivalent experience at GS-11. *Id.* at 4-5. The Union also contends that the grievant could have been hired at GS-12 even though the vacancy announcement listed the position at GS-11. *Id.* at 5.

The Union also argues that the grievant could have been hired at GS-12 because she met the exception in § 531.212(a)(3)(ii) for expert positions. *Id.* According to the Union, the grievant could have been qualified as an expert because she had "greater skill than a normal employee in that field" on the basis of her past private sector experience. *Id.* The Union contends that it does not need to show that the Agency would have been required to hire the grievant at the GS-12 level, but only that the Agency could have done so. *Id.* at 5-6.

D. Agency's Opposition

The Agency argues that the award is not contrary to law because the Union has failed to cite any provision of law with which the award conflicts. Agency's Opp'n at 2. Further, the Agency argues that the Arbitrator's refusal to grant a promotion is not contrary to any law or regulation. *Id.* at 2-3. According to the Agency, its recruitment policy forbids "any jump over a grade" without a 90-day break in service, which reflects the policy in § 531.212(a) that the Agency's pay-setting authority applies only to a reappointment after a break in service of 90 days. *Id.* at 3 (quoting Award at 12). The Agency contends that, because it is undisputed that the grievant was at GS-10 and had no break in service, the failure to grant her a promotion to GS-12 was not contrary to law. *Id.* at 3-4.

> (3) An agency may use the superior qualifications and special needs pay-setting authority for a reappointment without requiring a 90-day break in service if the candidate's civilian employment with the Federal Government during the 90-day period immediately preceding the appointment was limited to one or more of the following:
>
> . . . .
>
> (ii) Employment under an appointment as an expert or consultant under 5 U.S.C. [§] 3109 and 5 CFR part 304[.]

The Agency also argues that the grievant does not meet the definition of expert in § 531.212(a)(3)(ii). *Id.* at 4. According to the Agency, the regulation requires that, for the 90 days immediately preceding her appointment as a midwife, the grievant have served "under an appointment as an expert or consultant" pursuant to 5 U.S.C. § 3109 and 5 C.F.R. part 304. 5 C.F.R. § 531.212(a)(3)(ii). The Agency asserts that the grievant was serving as a GS-10 RN, not as an expert under § 3109. *Id.* at 4-5.

IV. Preliminary Issues

A. The Authority has jurisdiction to resolve the exceptions.

Under § 7122(a) of the Statute, the Authority lacks jurisdiction to resolve exceptions to awards "relating to" a matter described in § 7121(f) of the Statute. Matters described in § 7121(f) include adverse actions, such as removals, that are covered under 5 U.S.C. § 7512 and are appealable to the Merit Systems Protection Board (MSPB) and reviewable by the United States Court of Appeals for the Federal Circuit (Federal Circuit). *See, e.g., U.S. Dep't of Commerce, Patent & Trademark Office, Arlington, Va.*, 61 FLRA 476, 477 (2006).

The Authority directed the parties to show cause why their exceptions should not be dismissed for lack of jurisdiction pursuant to § 7122(a) of the Statute because the award "concerns a matter that related to a reduction in grade." *See* Order to Show Cause at 2. In its response, the Agency argues that the Authority has jurisdiction because 5 U.S.C. § 4303 and § 7512 cover only reductions in pay or grade that are based on "unacceptable performance" or qualify as an "adverse action." Agency's Response at 3. The Agency contends that, because the reduction in grade was the correction of an administrative error, it was not an adverse action and would not be covered under § 4303 or § 7512. *Id.* The Union, in its response, agrees that the Authority has jurisdiction because the issue before the Arbitrator was the propriety of the promotion, not the subsequent demotion. Union's Response at 2.

The Authority will determine that an award relates to a matter described in § 7121(f) "when it resolves, or is inextricably intertwined with," a § 7512 matter. *See AFGE, Local 1013*, 60 FLRA 712, 713 (2005). In making that determination, the Authority looks not to the outcome of the award, but to whether the claim advanced in arbitration is one reviewable by the MSPB, and, on appeal, by the Federal Circuit. *See id.* The Authority looks, therefore, to MSPB precedent for whether a matter is covered under § 7512. *See U.S. Dep't of Transp., Nat'l Highway Traffic Safety Admin.*, 58 FLRA 333, 336 (2003). The MSPB has found that, among other things, where an agency reduces an employee's grade or pay from a rate that would be "contrary to law or regulation[,]" the action is not an adverse personnel action under § 7512. *Gessert v. Dep't of the Treasury*, 113 M.S.P.R. 329, 332 (2010); *Deida v. Dep't of the Navy*, 110 M.S.P.R. 408, 412 (2009).

The Agency argues that the grievant could not have been promoted to GS-12 without spending one year at GS-11. Agency's Response at 5, 7. The Union argues that, to meet the time-in-grade requirements, the grievant only needed to have been in a GS-11 *equivalent* position for one year. Union's Exceptions at 4. A candidate for promotion must have spent fifty-two weeks "in a grade equivalent to or no more than one grade lower than the position for which the candidate is applying." *NATCA*, 51 FLRA 102, 107 (1995) (citing 5 C.F.R. § 300.604). 5 C.F.R. § 300.605, which explains what service is creditable for time-in-grade purposes, limits creditable service to the grade level of the "position[] to which [the employee is] appointed *in the Federal civilian service* . . . ." 5 C.F.R. § 300.605(a) (emphasis added). Once an employee accepts a GS position, that employee becomes "bound by the advancement restrictions contained in [§ 300.604]." *Ibrahim v. United States*, 26 Cl. Ct. 359, 363 (Cl. Ct. 1992).

It is undisputed that, at the time of her promotion, the grievant was at GS-10 and had never served at GS-11. As noted above, § 300.605(a) limits creditable experience for time-in-grade purposes to federal service and, thus, the grievant's previous private sector experience cannot be used to meet the time-in-grade requirements. *See* 5 C.F.R. § 300.605(a). Additionally, the grievant's federal experience must be credited at the grade level of position to which she was appointed; accordingly, the grievant could not have been credited with GS-11 experience while serving at GS-10. *Id.* Therefore, we find that, because the grievant did not meet the time-in-grade requirements of § 300.604, the grievant's promotion to GS 12 would have been contrary to law or regulation.[2]

---

2. In so finding, the Authority does not address the Arbitrator's factual finding that the grievant had one year of equivalent experience at GS-11. Award at 13-14. To be

Because the grievant's promotion would have been contrary to law or regulation, the Agency's correction of that mistake was not an adverse action covered under § 7512. *See White v. Dep't of the Air Force*, 32 M.S.P.R. 590, 592-93 (1987) (finding no jurisdiction over a reduction in pay action where the original promotion was unlawful). Accordingly, we find that the award does not relate to a matter described in § 7121(f) of the Statute and that the Authority has jurisdiction to resolve the exceptions. *See AFGE, Local 2986*, 51 FLRA 1549, 1154-55 (1996) (Member Armendariz dissenting).

B. The Agency's management rights exception is barred by § 2429.5.

Under § 2429.5 of the Authority's Regulations, the Authority will not consider issues that could have been, but were not, presented to the arbitrator.[3] *See, e.g., U.S. Dep't of the Air Force, Air Force Materiel Command, Robins Air Force Base, Ga.*, 59 FLRA 542, 544 (2003).

The Agency argues that the award conflicts with § 7106 of the Statute because it violates its management rights to hire employees, determine a budget, and promulgate a recruitment and retention policy. Agency's Exceptions at 12. There is no indication in the record that the Agency argued to the Arbitrator that a promotion would violate its management rights, even though the stipulated issue before the Arbitrator directly concerned the propriety of the promotion. Therefore, because the Agency could have raised, but did not raise, this issue before the Arbitrator, we find this exception is barred by § 2429.5 of the Statute and dismiss the Agency's exception. *See Soc. Sec. Admin., Newark, N.J.*, 64 FLRA 259, 260-61 (2009) (dismissing a management's rights exception where the agency did not make a management's rights argument to the arbitrator and where the agency was aware that the arbitrator might award a promotion).

V. Analysis and Conclusions

A. The Arbitrator exceeded her authority.

Arbitrators exceed their authority when they fail to resolve an issue submitted to arbitration, resolve an issue not submitted to arbitration, disregard specific limitations on their authority, or award relief to those not encompassed within the grievance. *See AFGE, Local 1617*, 51 FLRA 1645, 1647 (1996). In determining whether an arbitrator has exceeded his or her authority, the Authority accords an arbitrator's interpretation of a stipulated issue the same substantial deference that it accords an arbitrator's interpretation and application of a collective bargaining agreement. *See U.S. Info. Agency, Voice of Am.*, 55 FLRA 197, 198 (1999).

The Authority has held that, when an arbitrator decides the merits of a dispute and finds no violation of law or contract, the arbitrator has no authority to issue a remedy. *See Soc. Sec. Admin., Balt., Md.*, 64 FLRA 516, 518 (2010) (citing *NLRB, Tampa, Fla.*, 57 FLRA 880, 881 (2002)). As noted, the parties stipulated that the issue before the Arbitrator was whether "the grievant's promotion to GS-12, Step 6 [was] proper[.]" Award at 2. The Arbitrator resolved the stipulated issue by finding "that the promotion was not proper in the sense of lawful." *Id.* at 11. Even though the Arbitrator also found that the promotion was "proper" in the sense of "fair[,]" *id.*, she clearly found that "she cannot order the [A]gency to reinstate the GS-12 status for the grievant[,]" *id.* at 16. At that point, the Arbitrator had decided the merits of the dispute, found no violation of law or contract, and therefore possessed no authority to issue a remedy. *See U.S. Dep't of the Treasury, Internal Revenue Serv., Ogden Serv. Ctr., Ogden, Utah*, 63 FLRA 195, 197 (2009).

Additionally, the Authority has held that, where an arbitrator decides the merits of a stipulated issue, "the arbitrator has no authority to decide an issue not submitted to arbitration." *U.S. EPA, Region 2, N.Y.C., N.Y.*, 63 FLRA 476, 479 (2009) (citations omitted) (*EPA*). Notwithstanding the Arbitrator's conclusion regarding the grievant's promotion, the Arbitrator then determined that the Agency's billing

eligible for a promotion in the competitive service, an employee must meet both the Office of Personnel Management (OPM's) qualification standards and the time-in-grade requirements. *See U.S. Dep't of Veterans Affairs, Alaska Health Care Sys., Anchorage, Alaska*, 57 FLRA 590, 591 (2001). Equivalent experience may be used to satisfy OPM's qualification standards, but may not be used to meet time-in-grade requirements. *See* 5 C.F.R. § 300.604. Therefore, in finding that the grievant had one year of equivalent experience at GS-11, the Arbitrator could have found that the grievant met OPM's qualification standards, but not the time-in-grade requirements.

3. The Authority's Regulations concerning the review of arbitration awards, as well as certain related procedural Regulations, including 5 C.F.R. § 2429.5, were revised effective October 1, 2010. *See* 75 Fed. Reg. 42,283 (2010). As the Agency's exceptions in this case were filed before that date, we apply the prior Regulations.

the grievant for an Agency mistake was "an adverse event which was a violation of the [parties'] agreement . . . ." Award at 14. However, the issue of the waiver of the money the grievant owed was not before the Arbitrator. Rather, the only issue before her was whether the promotion was proper. Therefore, by deciding an issue not submitted to arbitration, the Arbitrator exceeded her authority. *See EPA*, 63 FLRA at 479 (finding that the arbitrator exceeded his authority by considering a different issue after resolving the stipulated issue).

Accordingly, we find that the Arbitrator exceeded her authority in finding that the Agency violated the parties' agreement, grant the Agency's exception, and set aside that portion of the award.[4]

B. The Union has failed to establish that the award is contrary to law.

The Union argues that the award is contrary to law because the grievant could have been properly promoted and because she was an expert under § 531.212(a)(3)(ii). Union's Exceptions at 4-5. When an exception involves an award's consistency with law, the Authority reviews any question of law raised by the exception and the award de novo. *See NTEU, Chapter 24*, 50 FLRA 330, 332 (1995) (citing *U.S. Customs Serv. v. FLRA*, 43 F.3d 682, 686-87 (D.C. Cir. 1994)). In applying the standard of de novo review, the Authority assesses whether an arbitrator's legal conclusions are consistent with the applicable standard of law. *See U.S. Dep't of Def., Dep'ts of the Army & the Air Force, Ala. Nat'l Guard, Northport, Ala.*, 55 FLRA 37, 40 (1998). In making that assessment, the Authority defers to the arbitrator's underlying factual findings. *See id.*

The Union argues that the award is contrary to law and that the Agency could have properly promoted the grievant to GS-12 because the grievant had one year of equivalent experience at GS-11. Union's Exceptions at 4-5. In making this argument, the Union fails to cite any law, rule, or regulation with which the Arbitrator's award conflicts. A general assertion is not sufficient to support a contention that an award is contrary to law. *See U.S. Dep't of Veterans Affairs, Montgomery Reg'l Office, Montgomery, Ala.*, 65 FLRA 487, 489 (2011). However, to the extent that the Union is asserting that the grievant satisfied the time-in-grade requirements, the Union's argument is without merit. As stated above, the grievant did not meet the time-in-grade requirements and, thus, was not entitled to a promotion to GS-12. Therefore, we find that the award is not contrary to law and deny this exception.

The Union also argues that the award is contrary to law because the grievant was an expert for purposes of the exception in § 531.212(a)(3)(ii). Union's Exceptions at 5. The Union asserts that the grievant was qualified as an expert because a "certified nurse midwife" is in the nursing series but is required to have additional education and expertise, and the grievant had additional expertise "based on her past private sector experience." *Id.* at 5, 6. However, the Union's argument is without merit. The exception in § 531.212(a)(3)(ii) requires an employee to have been actually appointed as an expert, and does not refer simply to those who have additional experience in their field. *See* 5 C.F.R. § 304.103. Additionally, the time served as an expert must have been "during the 90-day period immediately preceding the appointment" as a midwife; accordingly, the grievant's past private sector experience is irrelevant. 5 C.F.R. § 531.212(a)(3). Therefore, we find that the grievant did not qualify as an expert under the exception in § 531.212(a)(3)(ii) and deny this exception.

VI. Decision

The Agency's management rights exception is dismissed, the Union's contrary to law exceptions are denied, the Agency's exceeds authority exception is granted, and that portion of the award is set aside.

4. In light of our decision, we find that it is unnecessary to address the Agency's remaining exceptions. *See EPA*, 63 FLRA at 479 n.5.

65 FLRA No. 204

AMERICAN FEDERATION
OF GOVERNMENT EMPLOYEES
LOCAL 1738
(Union)

and

UNITED STATES
DEPARTMENT OF VETERANS AFFAIRS
MEDICAL CENTER
SALISBURY, NORTH CAROLINA
(Agency)

0-AR-4751

DECISION

June 30, 2011

Before the Authority: Carol Waller Pope, Chairman, and Thomas M. Beck and Ernest DuBester, Members[1]

I. Statement of the Case

This matter is before the Authority on an exception to an award of Arbitrator Bernard T. Holmes filed by the Union under § 7122(a) of the Federal Service Labor-Management Relations Statute (the Statute) and part 2425 of the Authority's Regulations. The Agency filed an opposition to the Union's exception.

The Arbitrator denied a grievance alleging that the Agency had violated the parties' agreement by failing to pay the grievants overtime for carrying pagers when they were off-duty. For the reasons that follow, we dismiss the Union's exception.

II. Background and Arbitrator's Award

The Union filed a grievance alleging that the Agency had violated the parties' agreement by failing to pay the grievants overtime for carrying pagers when they were off-duty. *See* Award at 5. The grievance was unresolved and submitted to arbitration where the parties were unable to stipulate to an issue. *Id.* at 2. The Arbitrator analyzed the issue set forth by the Union: "Did the Agency violate the [parties'] agreement by requiring the [grievants] to carry pagers when they were not in a pay status? And if so, what is the remedy. . . [?]" *Id.*; *see also id.* at 8. The Arbitrator found that the Agency had not violated Article 20 of the parties' agreement as alleged, and denied the grievance.[2]

III. Positions of the Parties

A. Union's Exception

The Union asserts that the award "should be reversed" because it is "contrary to the plain language of the negotiated agreement." Exception at 5; *see also id.* at 3. Specifically, the Union disputes the Arbitrator's interpretation of the "plain language" of Article 20, Section 5(e). *Id.* at 3-5.

B. Agency's Opposition

The Agency asserts that, based on the facts found by the Arbitrator, the grievants have not established that they are entitled to overtime pay under the parties' agreement. Opp'n at 23-27.

IV. Analysis and Conclusion

The Authority's Regulations specifically enumerate the grounds that the Authority currently recognizes for reviewing awards. *See* 5 C.F.R. § 2425.6(a)-(b). In addition, the Regulations provide that if exceptions argue that an arbitration award is deficient based on private-sector grounds not currently recognized by the Authority, then the excepting party "must provide sufficient citation to legal authority that establishes the grounds upon which the party filed its exceptions." 5 C.F.R. § 2425.6(c).

Further, § 2425.6(e)(1) of the Regulations provides that an exception "may be subject to dismissal or denial if: ". . . [t]he excepting party fails to raise and support" the grounds listed in § 2425.6(a)-(c), "or otherwise fails to demonstrate a legally recognized basis for setting aside the award[.]" 5 C.F.R. § 2425.6(e)(1). Thus, an exception that does not raise a recognized ground is subject to dismissal under the Regulations. *AFGE, Local 738*, 65 FLRA 931, 932 (2011) (*Local 738*); *AFGE, Local 3955, Council of Prison Locals 33*, 65 FLRA 887, 889 (2011) (Member Beck dissenting in part) (*Local 3955*).

1. Member Beck's separate opinion, concurring in the result, is set forth at the end of this decision.

2. The relevant portions of Article 20 are set forth in the appendix to this decision.

The Union's contention that the award is "contrary to the plain language of the negotiated agreement[,]" Exception at 5, does not constitute a ground currently recognized by the Authority for reviewing awards.[3] *See* 5 C.F.R. § 2425.6(a)-(b). As the Union does not raise a recognized ground or cite legal authority to support a ground not currently recognized by the Authority, we dismiss the exception. *See Local 738*, 65 FLRA at 932; *Local 3955*, 65 FLRA at 889.

V. Decision

The Union's exception is dismissed.

3. In accord with 5 C.F.R. § 2425.6, the Authority will "no longer construe parties' exceptions as raising grounds that the exceptions do not raise." *AFGE, Local 3955, Council of Prison Locals 33*, 65 FLRA 887, 889 (2011) (Member Beck dissenting in part). Thus, as the Union does not allege that the award fails to draw its essence from the parties' agreement, we do not address that issue. We note, in this regard, that three of the decisions cited by the concurrence were issued before 5 C.F.R. § 2425.6 went into effect, and are therefore inapposite. *See U.S. Dep't of Hous. & Urban Dev., Portland, Or.*, 64 FLRA 651 (2010) (Member Beck dissenting); *SSA, Office of Hearings & Appeals, Falls Church, Va.*, 59 FLRA 507 (2003); *U.S. Dep't of the Treasury, IRS*, 59 FLRA 507 (2003). In the remaining decision cited by the concurrence, the excepting party expressly raised an essence argument. *See U.S. Dep't of Homeland Sec., U.S. Immigration & Customs Enforcement*, 65 FLRA 529, 530, 534 (2011). Thus, that decision also is inapposite.

APPENDIX

Article 20 – Hours of Work and Overtime:

Section 4: General Overtime Provisions[:]

A. Overtime shall be distributed in a fair and equitable manner.

B. When an employee works overtime, whether covered by the Fair Labor Standards Act or exempt, such overtime will be paid in increments of fifteen (15) minutes.

C. Employees shall be paid differential and premium pay in addition to the overtime compensation in accordance with applicable regulations.

D. It is agreed that nonbargaining unit employees shall not be scheduled on overtime to perform the duties of bargaining unit employees for the sole purpose of eliminating the need to schedule bargaining unit employees for overtime.

. . . .

F. Employees who are called back to work for a period of overtime unconnected to their regularly scheduled tour or who work overtime on their day(s) off are entitled to a minimum of two (2) hours overtime pay. Employees called in for emergency work outside their basic workweek shall not normally be required to perform nonemergency functions. This does not preclude employees from being called in to provide coverage in nonemergency situations.

. . . .

J. Those employees eligible by Title 5 or Title 38 can accrue and use compensatory time when approved by Management.

Section 5: Paid On-Call/Standby:

A. Normally, volunteers will be used to perform on-call or standby duty before assigning such duty to nonvolunteers.

B. Scheduled on-call will be rotated among all qualified staff. Records of on-call shall be kept by management and made available to the Union upon request. If funding permits, employees scheduled for on-call duty shall be issued pagers or other mobile technology which will be used to notify them of a need for their return to duty.

. . . .

D. If on-call employees are called back to the station, they shall receive a minimum two (2) hours of pay.

E. Employees will not be required to stay at home or wear and respond to beepers/pagers unless they are in a pay status.

F. Employee participation in nonpaid, on-call status shall be voluntary.

G. Employees shall not be scheduled on-call while on annual leave.

. . . .

J. Those employee[s] currently in a standby pay retention status will continue to be paid under the provision of 38 USC 7457(c).

. . . .

Award at 2-4.

Member Beck, Concurring in the Result:

While I agree with my colleagues that the Union's exception should not be granted, I disagree with their conclusion that the Union's exception should be dismissed because it does not raise a private-sector ground that is recognized by the Authority.

As I stated in my dissent in *American Federation of Government Employees Local 3955, Council of Prison Locals* 33, 65 FLRA 887, 891 (2011) (Member Beck dissenting in part) (*Local 3955*), the Authority's revised regulations "do not require parties to invoke any particular magical incantations when filing exceptions." *Id.* The Union asserts both that the Arbitrator "ignored the plain language" of the parties' agreement and that his award is contrary to "[t]he plain language of Article 20, Section 5[.E.]" of that agreement. Exceptions at 3; *see also id.* at 5 (contending that "[t]he [a]ward is contrary to the plain language of the negotiated agreement"). Moreover, the Union claims, the Arbitrator based his determination "on a finding of ambiguity in a contract provision where none exists." *Id.* at 4. These assertions constitute an argument that the Arbitrator's award fails to draw its essence from the parties' agreement. *See, e.g., U.S. Dep't of the Treasury, IRS*, 59 FLRA 34, 37 (2003) (award fails to draw its essence from parties' agreement when it is implausible, irrational or in manifest disregard of the agreement). Indeed, in cases involving essence exceptions, the Authority has considered almost identical language to that used by the Union here. *See, e.g., U.S. Dep't of Homeland Sec., U.S. Immigration & Customs Enforcement*, 65 FLRA 529, 534 (2011) (agency claimed that arbitrator's finding was "contrary to the plain language of [contract] provision"); *U.S. Dep't of Housing & Urban Dev., Portland, Or.*, 64 FLRA 651, 653 (2010) (Member Beck dissenting) (agency argued that "[a]rbitrator ignored the 'plain language of the MOU'"); *SSA, Office of Hearings & Appeals, Falls Church, Va.*, 59 FLRA 507, 508-509, 510 (2003) (agency contended that award "ignor[ed] the plain language of [a]rticle 20").

I would find that the award does not fail to draw its essence from the agreement. Article 20, Section 5.E. provides that "[e]mployees will not be required to stay at home or wear and respond to beepers/pagers unless they are in a pay status." Award at 3 (quoting Article 20, Section 5.E.). The Arbitrator found that this provision requires the Agency to have placed "sufficiently restrictive limits on the movement and off duty activities" of the grievants to warrant placing them in a pay status, i.e. "'on-call.'" *Id.* at 16. The Arbitrator found "no such restrictive limits" had been placed on the grievants. *Id.* Thus, contrary to the Union's claim, the Arbitrator's factual findings show that he did not ignore Article 20, Section 5.E. Further, the Union has not provided any basis for finding that the Arbitrator erred in his interpretation and application of this provision. Accordingly, I would deny this exception.

65 FLRA No. 205

UNITED STATES
DEPARTMENT OF HOMELAND SECURITY
U.S. CUSTOMS AND BORDER PROTECTION
(Agency)

and

NATIONAL TREASURY EMPLOYEES UNION
(Union)

0-AR-4438

DECISION

June 30, 2011

Before the Authority: Carol Waller Pope, Chairman, and Thomas M. Beck and Ernest DuBester, Members

I. Statement of the Case

This matter is before the Authority on exceptions to an interim award and a remedial award of Arbitrator Margery F. Gootnick filed by the Agency under § 7122(a) of the Federal Service Labor-Management Relations Statute (the Statute) and part 2425 of the Authority's Regulations. The Union filed an opposition to the Agency's exceptions.

In her interim award, the Arbitrator determined that the Agency violated 5 U.S.C. § 6101(a)(3) and 5 C.F.R. § 610.121 when scheduling the work of Customs Officers. In her remedial award, the Arbitrator ordered remedial relief including backpay and attorney fees. For the reasons that follow, we dismiss the Agency's exceptions in part and deny them in part.

II. Background and Arbitrator's Award

The dispute involves the Agency's Revised National Inspectional Assignment Policy (RNIAP). Interim Award at 3. The RNIAP replaced an earlier National Inspectional Assignment Policy (NIAP) that had been negotiated by the Agency and the Union and that provided for local negotiation of matters set forth in § 7106(b)(1) of the Statute, including staffing levels and tours of duty at the local level.[1] The Union, after receiving complaints from Customs Officers that their work assignments were being changed without adequate notice because of flexibilities created by the RNIAP, requested bargaining over the RNIAP and a new "bid and rotation" system. *Id.* at 5. The Agency declined the request based, in part, on the existence of a question concerning representation (QCR), explaining that negotiating over the RNIAP would give the Union an unfair competitive advantage over competing labor organizations in the upcoming election. *Id.*[2] After the Agency refused the request, the Union presented a grievance alleging that the Agency violated 5 U.S.C. § 6101(a)(3), 5 C.F.R. § 610.121, § 7116(a)(1), (5), and (8) of the Statute, and the parties' collective bargaining agreement.[3] *Id.* at 6. When the Agency did not respond, the Union invoked arbitration.

A. Interim Award

Although the Agency and the Union proposed substantially similar issues, they were unable to stipulate the issues to be resolved. In her award, the Arbitrator addressed the following issues:

1. The Authority found, and the U.S. Court of Appeals for the District of Columbia Circuit affirmed, that the RNIAP was properly implemented and that it replaced the NIAP. Interim Award at 3-4 (citing *NTEU v. FLRA*, 414 F.3d 50 (D.C. Cir. 2005), *aff'g U.S. Dep't of the Treasury, Customs Serv., Wash., D.C.*, 59 FLRA 703 (2004) (Member Pope concurring)). However, the court was not presented with the issue now before the Authority – i.e., whether the provisions of the RNIAP are consistent with 5 U.S.C. § 6101(a)(3) and 5 C.F.R. § 610.121.

2. As the Arbitrator explained, the QCR arose from the creation of Customs and Border Protection as a component of the Department of Homeland Security and the consolidation of employees formerly in the Customs Service, Border Patrol, and the Plant Inspection Service – each exclusively represented by a different labor organization – into one agency. Interim Award at 27. In its letter to the Union declining the request to bargain, the Agency noted that the Authority was about to conduct an election in the Agency-wide bargaining unit and opined that it would be improper to begin negotiations just before an upcoming election. *Id.*

3. The text of the relevant statutory, regulatory, and contractual provisions is set forth in the appendix to this decision.

1. Whether the Agency violated 5 U.S.C. § 6101(a)(3), 5 C.F.R. § 610.121, and Article 21, Sections 3A and B of the parties' agreement when scheduling the work of Customs Officers? If so, what is the appropriate remedy?

2. Whether the Agency violated Article 37 of the parties' agreement and/or § 7116(a)(1) and (5) of the Statute when it failed to bargain over the RNIAP and/or a new bid and rotation policy as proposed by the Union? If so, what is the appropriate remedy?

3. Whether the Agency violated Articles 37 and 39 and/or § 7116(a)(1), (5), and (8) of the Statute when it declined to provide information in response to the information request attached to the Union's grievance? If so, what is the appropriate remedy?

Id. at 7-8, 17, 25, 30.

The Arbitrator found that the Customs Officers are protected by the work scheduling requirements in 5 U.S.C. § 6101(a)(3) and 5 C.F.R. § 610.121 (a) and (b) and that the RNIAP standards deviate from the requirements of the statute and regulation. *Id.* at 17-23. Moreover, the Arbitrator determined that, even if she "were to assume that the issuance of [RNIAP] . . . constituted an action attributable to 'the head of the Agency,'. . . there was no determination in [RNIAP] that carrying out the Agency's functions would be 'seriously handicapped' or that costs would be 'substantially increased'" if each Agency employee were provided the protections of 5 U.S.C. § 6101(a)(3). *Id.* at 20-21. Having made these findings, the Arbitrator found it unnecessary to address whether the Agency also violated Article 21, Sections 3A and B of the parties' agreement because those provisions were a verbatim recitation of the statute and regulation. *Id.* at 24-25.

Additionally, the Arbitrator found that the Agency had not violated § 7116(a)(1) and (5) of the Statute when it refused to bargain over the RNIAP or a new bid and rotation policy. The Arbitrator held that it was appropriate for the Agency to decline the Union's request to bargain during the pendency of a QCR. The Arbitrator noted that the Authority has held that an agency is not obligated to bargain during the pendency of a QCR but must, instead, maintain the status quo to the maximum extent possible. *Id.* at 28-29 (citing *U.S. Dep't of Justice, U.S. INS*, 9 FLRA 253, 283-86 (1982); *INS*, 16 FLRA 80, 87 (1984)).

Finally, the Arbitrator found that the Agency violated § 7116(a)(1), (5), and (8) of the Statute when it failed to respond to the Union's information request pertaining to the officers' work schedules. Award at 30-31. Moreover, because the Union had explained its need for the requested information with sufficient specificity, the Arbitrator ordered the Agency to provide the information. *Id.* at 33.

In addressing the appropriate remedy, the Arbitrator noted that the parties' agreement provides that the parties should discuss some aspects of the remedy, including compensation and attorney fees, for a period of 60 days following the issuance of the interim award. *Id.* at 34. As an interim remedy, the Arbitrator ordered the Agency to:

(1) Cease and desist from violating 5 U.S.C. § 6101(a)(3) and 5 C.F.R. § 610.121(a) and (b) and from failing to furnish necessary information requested by the Union; and

(2) Post appropriate notices wherever Customs Officers are assigned acknowledging the Agency's violations and promising not to commit such violations in the future.

Id. at 36-37. The Arbitrator retained jurisdiction for sixty days for the limited purpose of considering remedial issues and issuing an appropriate remedy. *Id.* at 37.

B. Remedial Award

After the interim award was issued, the Union advised the Arbitrator that the remedial issues remained unresolved and requested a decision both as to substantive relief and attorney fees. Remedial Award at 4.

The Arbitrator first addressed the appropriate recovery period under the Back Pay Act for those Customs Officers whose established work schedules were changed in violation of applicable law and regulation. *Id.* at 8. The Arbitrator found that, contrary to the Agency's assertion, retroactive adjustments in pay to which the affected officers were entitled should not be limited to the period starting with the date of the Union's grievance. *Id.* The Arbitrator found that the only limitation that the Back Pay Act imposes on the period of backpay recovery is that it cannot exceed six years from the filing of the Union's grievance and that, therefore, backpay was appropriate for the entire period since the RNIAP took effect. *Id.* at 9.

Next, the Arbitrator addressed the Agency's assertions regarding exclusions from 5 U.S.C. § 6101(a)(3) and 5 C.F.R. § 610.121. Referring to the reasons in her Interim Award, the Arbitrator again rejected the Agency's argument that Customs Officers are not covered by the statute or regulation. *Id.* at 10. In addition, the Arbitrator addressed several other exclusions asserted by the Agency. As to one of the asserted exclusions, the Arbitrator agreed that the Agency should not be liable for backpay whenever the Agency could demonstrate that a schedule change, otherwise inconsistent with applicable law, was implemented to accommodate an officer's request. *Id.* at 11. However, the Arbitrator rejected the Agency's assertion that an officer who volunteered for assignment to a special work team and, as a result, suffered a change in his established work schedule was not entitled to backpay. *Id.* at 11-12. Instead, she found that the Agency retained the discretion to accept or reject volunteers and to direct the assignment of Customs Officers to the teams. *Id.* Moreover, the Arbitrator agreed with the Agency that, where a change in an officer's work schedule is made to accommodate a court appearance, the Agency is not required to pay backpay. *Id.* at 13. Finally, the Arbitrator found that the Agency violated 5 U.S.C. § 6101(a)(3)(E) by changing work schedules, in at least some cases, in order to avoid overtime or holiday pay premiums. *Id.* at 13-14.

As for attorney fees, the Arbitrator found that the Union was the prevailing party, that the award of attorney fees was in the interest of justice, and that the fees sought by the Union were reasonable. *Id.* at 15-23. In her remedial award, the Arbitrator ordered the relief set out in her Interim Award, along with compensation under the Back Pay Act and attorney fees. *Id.* at 25-26.

III. Positions of the Parties

A. Agency's Exceptions

First, the Agency contends that the awards are contrary to law because the Arbitrator improperly subjected Customs Officers to the provisions of 5 U.S.C. § 6101 and its implementing regulations at 5 C.F.R. part 610, specifically, 5 C.F.R. § 610.121. Exceptions at 11-17. The Agency notes language in part 610 stating that the part applies only to "each employee to whom subpart A of part 550 applies." *Id.* at 12 (quoting 5 C.F.R. § 610.101). The Agency notes, in turn, that part 550, governing premium pay, excludes "overtime, night, Sunday, or holiday" services performed pursuant to "19 U.S.C. 261, 267, involving customs inspectors and canine enforcement officers." *Id.* (quoting 5 C.F.R. § 550.101(d)(1)). According to the Agency, this shows the Office of Personnel Management's (OPM's) recognition that Customs Officers have their own system for premium pay under the Customs Officer Pay Reform Act (COPRA), 19 U.S.C. §§ 261 and 267. *Id.*

The Agency argues, in the alternative, that the awards are contrary to law because the Commissioner's decision to except Customs Officers was made in accordance with congressional intent, 5 U.S.C. § 6101(a)(3), and 5 C.F.R. § 610.121. *Id.* at 18-34. In this regard, the Agency asserts that congressional intent supports the Commissioner's determination that Customs Officers are excepted from the scheduling requirements contained in 5 U.S.C. § 6101(a)(3) and 5 C.F.R. § 610.121. *Id.* at 18-23, 33. The Agency claims that language in several versions of a Department of Treasury, Bureau of Customs manual (Manual) supports its claim that the Commissioner properly excepted Customs Officers in accordance with 5 U.S.C. § 6101(a)(3). *Id.* at 23-26. Additionally, the Agency asserts that language contained in an Agency regulation, 19 C.F.R. § 24.16(d), and RNIAP supports its assertion that the Commissioner acted in accordance with 5 U.S.C. § 6101(a)(3) and 5 C.F.R. § 610.121. *Id.* at 27-33.

Next, the Agency contends that the Arbitrator's finding that employees who voluntarily participate on special work teams are entitled to backpay is based on a nonfact. *Id.* at 34-38. Specifically, the Agency contends that the Arbitrator erred in her conclusion that "it is clear that the Agency at all times has retained the discretion to accept or reject volunteers and to direct the assignment of Customs Officers to such teams." *Id.* at 34-35 (quoting Remedial Award at 11-12). In addition, the Agency contends that this conclusion fails to draw its essence from Article 20, Section 23 of the parties' agreement, which the Agency claims reinforces the voluntary nature of participation on the teams. *Id.* at 35.

Further, the Agency contends that the awards are based on a nonfact and are contrary to law because the Arbitrator failed to recognize that the Agency's scheduling practices were "holiday-blind." *Id.*

at 38-39. The Agency explains that it accommodated changes in workload during holidays so as to "avoid a serious handicapping to its mission or substantially increased costs . . . ." *Id.* at 40.

The Agency also asserts that the remedial award is contrary to law because relief under the Back Pay Act cannot be awarded for violations of 5 U.S.C. § 6101(a)(3). *Id.* at 42 (citing *Sanford v. Weinberger*, 752 F.2d 636 (Fed. Cir. 1985)).

Finally, the Agency contends that the awards violate equitable principles because they require the Agency to reimburse employees for the entire six-year period prior to the filing of the grievance. *Id.* at 43. Instead, the Agency contends, the retroactive award of backpay should not commence until the date that the Union filed the grievance because the Union "slept on its rights" by waiting for 5 ½ years after the RNIAP took effect before filing its grievance. *Id.* at 43-44.

B. Union's Opposition

The Union contends that the Arbitrator correctly ruled that Customs Officers are covered by 5 U.S.C. § 6101 and 5 C.F.R. § 610.121. Opp'n at 9-15. In this regard, the Union notes that the definition of "employee" in 5 U.S.C. § 6101(a)(1) contains an express exclusion for those individuals listed in 5 U.S.C. § 5541(2) and that Customs Officers are not included on that list. *Id.* at 10. Similarly, the Union notes, as does the Agency, that subpart A of part 610 applies to each employee to whom subpart A of part 550 applies. *Id.* at 11. The Union notes further that subpart A of part 550 provides that it applies to "each employee in or under an Executive agency, as defined in 5 U.S.C. 105, except those named in paragraphs (b) and (c) of this section." *Id.*[4] (quoting 5 C.F.R. § 550.101(a)). Observing that neither subsection (b) nor (c) of 5 C.F.R. § 550.101 excludes Customs Officers from the coverage of subpart A of part 550, the Union contends that Customs Officers are covered by 5 C.F.R. § 610.121. *Id.* at 11-12. The Union contends that the Agency's argument to the contrary contradicts the parties' agreement, which reflects the provisions set forth in 5 U.S.C. § 6101(a)(3) and 5 C.F.R. § 610.121(a) and requires the Agency to schedule Customs Officers in accordance with those provisions. *Id.* at 13.

Next, the Union contends that the Arbitrator correctly determined that the RNIAP work scheduling standards do not comply with 5 U.S.C. § 6101(a)(3) and 5 C.F.R. § 610.121(a). *Id.* at 15. In this regard, the Union contends that the Arbitrator correctly found that the RNIAP's scheduling regime did not incorporate the only available exception: that "the [A]gency would be seriously handicapped in carrying out its functions or that costs would be substantially increased." *Id.* In addition, the Union contends, there is no evidence that the Agency head made a determination that the Agency could not comply with 5 U.S.C. § 6101 and 5 C.F.R. § 610.121(a) because to do so would seriously handicap it in carrying out its functions or that its costs would be substantially increased. *Id.* at 17-23. Further, the Union contends that, as the Arbitrator found, the record contains numerous scheduling changes by the Agency that violated the statute and regulation. *Id.* at 23-24.

Additionally, the Union contends that the Arbitrator did not base her award on a nonfact when she determined that employees volunteering to participate in special work teams are entitled to the scheduling protections of 5 U.S.C. § 6101 and 5 C.F.R. § 610.121. *Id.* at 25. Instead, according to the Union, the record supports the Arbitrator's finding that the Agency maintained discretion over the assignment of employees to the teams. *Id.* at 8, 26. Nor, according to the Union, did the Arbitrator base her award on a nonfact when she determined that the Agency did not engage in holiday-blind scheduling. *Id.* at 26. The Union argues that the Agency's explanation that it changed employee schedules due to holiday workload is an admission that it violated the prohibition in 5 U.S.C. § 6101(a)(3)(E) and 5 C.F.R. § 610.121(a)(5) against "the occurrence of holidays . . . affect[ing] the designation of the basic workweek." *Id.* at 27.

Finally, the Union contends that the remedial award does not violate equitable principles by requiring the Agency to reimburse backpay for the entire six-year period prior to the filing of the grievance. *Id.* at 32.

IV. Preliminary Issues

The Authority's Regulations that were in effect when the Agency filed its exceptions provided that "[t]he Authority will not consider . . . any issue, which was not presented in the proceedings before

4. The parties do not dispute that the Agency, which is within an executive department, is an "Executive agency" as defined in 5 U.S.C. § 105.

the . . . arbitrator." 5 C.F.R. § 2429.5.[5] *See, e.g., U.S. Dep't of the Air Force, Air Force Materiel Command, Robins Air Force Base, Ga.*, 59 FLRA 542, 544 (2003) (the Authority will not consider issues that could have been, but were not, presented to the arbitrator).

The Agency asserts that the remedial award is contrary to law because relief under the Back Pay Act cannot be awarded for violations of 5 U.S.C. § 6101(a)(3). Exceptions at 42 (citing *Sanford v. Weinberger*, 752 F.2d 636 (Fed. Cir. 1985)). In addition, the Agency asserts that, under Article 20, Section 23 of the parties' agreement, employees volunteer to participate in the special work teams. *Id.* at 35.

The Agency could have made, but did not make, these arguments before the Arbitrator. Indeed, in its response to the Union's petition for attorney fees, the Agency acknowledged the applicability of the Back Pay Act, stating that: "[s]hould a remedial order for backpay be found appropriate, the Agency proposes that the remedial order be limited to the date of the grievance . . . and the specific relief be as simple as: The Agency is ordered to make impacted [Customs] Officers whole in accordance with the Back Pay Act." Opp'n, Ex.13 at 16. Likewise, there is no indication in the record that the Agency ever argued before the Arbitrator that, under Article 20, Section 23, participation in the special work teams is strictly voluntary. Because these arguments could have been presented below, but were not, we find that both of these arguments are barred by § 2429.5 and dismiss these exceptions.

V. Analysis and Conclusions

A. The award is not based on a nonfact.

To establish that an award is based on a nonfact, the appealing party must show that a central fact underlying the award is clearly erroneous, but for which the arbitrator would have reached a different result. *See NFFE, Local 1984*, 56 FLRA 38, 41 (2000). However, the Authority will not find an award deficient on the basis of an arbitrator's determination of any factual matter that the parties disputed at arbitration. *See id.*

The Agency contends that the award was based on two nonfacts: (1) that the Agency retained discretion over the assignment of employees to special work teams and that, therefore, employees participating in those teams were entitled to backpay; and (2) that the Agency's scheduling policies were not holiday-blind. However, both the Agency's degree of discretion over assignments to the special work teams and whether the Agency's adjustment of work schedules for holidays was for the purpose of avoiding holiday pay were factual matters that were disputed before the Arbitrator. *See* Remedial Award at 11-12 (special work teams), 13-14 (holidays affecting scheduling of basic workweeks). Accordingly, we deny this exception.

B. The award is not contrary to law.

When an exception involves an award's consistency with law, the Authority reviews any question of law raised by the exception and the award de novo. *See NTEU, Chapter 24*, 50 FLRA 330, 332 (1995) (citing *U.S. Customs Serv. v. FLRA*, 43 F.3d 682, 686-87 (D.C. Cir. 1994)). In applying the standard of de novo review, the Authority assesses whether an arbitrator's legal conclusions are consistent with the applicable standard of law. *See U.S. Dep't of Def., Dep'ts of the Army & the Air Force, Ala. Nat'l Guard, Northport, Ala.*, 55 FLRA 37, 40 (1998). In making that assessment, the Authority defers to the arbitrator's underlying factual findings. *See id.*

1. Customs Officers are covered by 5 U.S.C. § 6101 and 5 C.F.R. § 610.121.

The Agency contends that the awards are contrary to law because the Arbitrator improperly subjected Customs Officers to the provisions of 5 U.S.C. § 6101 and its implementing regulations at 5 C.F.R. part 610, specifically, 5 C.F.R. § 610.121. Exceptions at 11-17. According to the Agency, because 5 U.S.C. § 6101 provides OPM with the authority to promulgate implementing regulations, and because Congress has not indicated that OPM's regulations do not accurately reflect Congress's intent regarding 5 U.S.C. § 6101, "any exemption or exclusion from [p]art 610 necessarily reflects exclusion from the provisions of 5 U.S.C. § 6101." *Id.* at 12.

5. The Authority's Regulations concerning the review of arbitration awards, as well as certain related procedural Regulations, including 5 C.F.R. § 2429.5, were revised effective October 1, 2010. *See* 75 Fed. Reg. 42,283 (2010). Because the Agency's exceptions in this case were filed before that date, we apply the prior Regulations.

The Agency's argument is without merit. The definition of "employee" in 5 U.S.C. § 6101(a)(1) contains an express exclusion for those individuals listed in 5 U.S.C. § 5541(2). Customs Officers are not included on that list. In addition, the coverage provision of 5 C.F.R. part 610 states that it applies to "each employee to whom [s]ubpart A of [p]art 550 applies . . . ." 5 C.F.R. § 610.101. Subpart A of part 550 states that it applies "to each employee in or under an Executive agency . . . except those named in paragraphs (b) and (c) of this section." 5 C.F.R. § 550.101(a). Customs Officers do not fall within any of the exceptions set out in § 550.101(b). Moreover, as the Arbitrator explained, paragraph (c) merely recognizes that Customs Officers, among other groups of employees subject to the overtime pay provisions of Section 7 of the Fair Labor Standards Act and 5 C.F.R. part 551, are excluded from the overtime pay rules set out in subpart A of part 550. Interim Award at 18-19. It does not also mean that Customs Officers are excluded from the scheduling protections in 5 C.F.R. § 610.121.

The Agency argues that, because 5 C.F.R. § 550.101(d)(1) excludes overtime, night, Sunday, and holiday services conducted by Customs Officers and covered by the COPRA, these employees are not "employees" to which subpart A of part 550 applies and, therefore, they are excluded from the scheduling protections set out in 5 C.F.R. § 610.121. This interpretation ignores the plain language of 5 U.S.C. § 5541(2), in which Congress chose to exclude seventeen categories of individuals from the definition of "employee," but not Customs Officers. It also ignores the plain language of 5 C.F.R. § 550.101, paragraph (a), which covers Customs Officers, and paragraph (b), which explicitly excludes seventeen categories of individuals, but not Customs Officers. The Agency does not cite any legal precedent to support this strained interpretation of the foregoing statutes and regulations.[6] The Union, however, cites *Acuna v. U.S.*, 479 F.2d 1356, 1362 (Ct. Cl. 1973), *cert. denied*, 416 U.S. 905 (1974) (*Acuna*), which involved immigration inspectors, who have a special overtime pay system recognized by 5 C.F.R. § 550.101(d)(3). As is the case with the Customs Officers, subpart A of part 550 does not apply to the overtime, night, Sunday, and holiday services provided by immigration inspectors. Yet, the *Acuna* court analyzed the immigration inspectors' scheduling claims under 5 U.S.C. § 6101.

6. Nothing in the COPRA or its regulations at 19 C.F.R. § 24.16 excludes Customs Officers from the scheduling protections.

Accordingly, we find that the Customs Officers are covered by 5 U.S.C. § 6101 and 5 C.F.R. § 610.121, and deny this exception.

2. The Customs Officers are not excepted from the scheduling requirements in accordance with 5 U.S.C. § 6101(a)(3) and 5 C.F.R. § 610.121(a).

As noted by the Arbitrator, both 5 U.S.C. § 6101 and 5 C.F.R. § 610.121 contain an exception from compliance with the work scheduling requirements when the head of an executive agency "determines that his organization would be seriously handicapped in carrying out its functions or that costs would be substantially increased . . . ." 5 U.S.C. § 6101(a)(3); 5 C.F.R. § 610.121(a); *see also* Interim Award at 20. In order to qualify for this exception, an agency head must make a determination that "an exception from the normal scheduling was justified, in view of agency functions and the costs involved." *Acuna*, 479 F.2d at 1362. An agency head makes a determination that the agency would be "seriously handicapped" or that "costs would be substantially increased" when the agency head justifies the need for an exception with a "discussion of the nature of work performed" by the employees and "the inherent administrative difficulties in scheduling their hours of duty." *Id.* Although not requiring "exhaustive findings," such determination must be "reasoned." *Gahagan v. U.S.*, 19 Cl. Ct. 168, 179 (1989) (*Gahagan*). A serious handicap is one that "would jeopardize an agency's entire mission and demand priority attention throughout the organization." *Id.* Moreover, an agency head fails to make such a determination simply by instructing in a policy that schedulers will prepare workweek schedules to improve efficiency. *Id.* at 178-79.

The Agency's contention that the Commissioner's determination to except Customs Officers was made in accordance with 5 U.S.C. § 6101 and 5 C.F.R. § 610.121 is without merit. Although the Agency asserts that the Commissioner's determination to except Customs Officers is supported by congressional intent, this assertion fails to demonstrate that the Commissioner made a reasoned decision in accordance with 5 U.S.C. § 6101(a)(3) and 5 C.F.R. § 610.121(a). *See Gahagan*, 19 Cl. Ct. at 179 (determining that the agency must provide evidence which demonstrates that the agency head made a reasoned determination in accordance with § 6101(a)(3)).

Also, the Agency relies on language contained in the Manual to support its contention that the

Commissioner's determination to except Customs Officers was made in conformity with 5 U.S.C. § 6101 and 5 C.F.R. § 610.121. Exceptions at 23-26. However, because the Manual was superseded by the RNIAP, the Agency's reliance on it does not prove that the Commissioner excepted Customs Officers to avoid seriously handicapping the Agency in performing its functions or substantially increasing the cost of customs operations. *See id.* at 27, 29-34 (conceding that, after Congress passed the Consolidated Budget Reconciliation Act of 1993 (COBRA) containing the statutory provisions for COPRA, the Manual was no longer applied to customs inspectors and that the Agency implemented COPRA through RNIAP); Interim Award at 12 (noting that Section 3 of RNIAP states that "[t]he policies and procedures contained in this Handbook take precedence over any and all other agreements, policies, or other documents or practices executed or applied by the parties previously, at either the national or local levels, concerning the matters covered within this Handbook" and that "[t]he policies and procedures contained in this Handbook reflect the parties' full and complete agreement on the matters contained and addressed herein"); *see also NTEU, Chapter 137*, 60 FLRA 483, 487 (2004) (finding that, by its terms, Section 3 established RNIAP as the governing policies and procedures with respect to inspectional assignment matters over any and all other agreements and that, consistent with its clear terms, Section 3 terminated locally negotiated agreements concerning inspectional assignment matters).

Although the Agency asserts that language contained in an Agency regulation, namely 19 C.F.R. § 24.16(d), supports its assertion that the Commissioner excepted Customs Officers in accordance with 5 U.S.C. § 6101(a)(3) and 5 C.F.R. § 610.121, the language contained in § 24.16(d) does not state that the Agency's functions will be seriously handicapped, or that costs will be substantially increased, if work assignment priorities are not followed; rather, § 24.16(d) merely affirms that "[t]ours of duty should be aligned with the Customs workload" and that "[a]ll work assignments should be made in a manner which minimizes the cost to the government or party in interest." Because precedent indicates that changes to employees' hours of work are not justified under 5 U.S.C. § 6101 when made only to improve efficiency, the Agency has failed to demonstrate that the Commissioner properly excepted Customs Officers. *See Gahagan*, 19 Cl. Ct. at 179 (determining that the agency head did not make a determination that its costs would be substantially increased in the 1986 policy because improving efficiency might affect agency costs only marginally); *U.S. Dep't of Commerce, Nat'l Oceanic & Atmospheric Admin., Nat'l Weather Serv.*, 49 FLRA 1563, 1566 (1994) (quoting *Gahagan*, 19 Cl. Ct. at 179) (noting that "[i]mproving an agency's efficiency is different from seriously handicapping its functions" because a serious handicap, within the meaning of § 6101, would jeopardize an agency's mission).

Additionally, the Agency cites phrases such as "operational need" and "budgetary limitations" contained in RNIAP to support its contention that the Commissioner's determination to except Customs Officers was made in conformity with 5 U.S.C. § 6101 and 5 C.F.R. § 610.121. Exceptions at 29-33. However, because precedent demonstrates that changes made to employees' work schedules are not justified when made to further the agency's mission or to address budgetary limitations, the Agency's reliance on RNIAP does not prove that the Commissioner decided to except Customs Officers from the scheduling requirements contained in 5 U.S.C. § 6101 and 5 C.F.R. § 610.121 to avoid seriously handicapping the Agency in performing its functions or substantially increasing the cost of customs operations. *See Gahagan*, 19 Cl. Ct. at 179; *Veterans Admin. Med. Ctr., Palo Alto, Cal.*, 36 FLRA 98, 106 (1990) (*VAMC Palo Alto*) (finding that, although the agency argued that transporting patients on recreational outings furthered its mission and that budgetary limitations precluded regularly scheduled overtime, it failed to demonstrate that it changed the work schedules of motor vehicle operators to prevent serious handicapping of its functions or to prevent substantially increased costs).

Consequently, because the Commissioner did not make a reasoned "handicap" or "substantial cost" determination in order to justify his decision to except Customs Officers from the scheduling requirements of 5 U.S.C. § 6101 and 5 C.F.R. § 610.121, the Agency has failed to demonstrate that the award is deficient. *See Phila. Naval Shipyard*, 39 FLRA at 604-05 (upholding the arbitrator's determination that the agency did not meet the requirements of law (5 U.S.C. § 6101(a)(3)) and regulations when it modified the third shift production department employees' schedule). Accordingly, we deny this exception.

3. The Agency's scheduling practices for the holidays did not comply with 5 U.S.C. § 6101(a)(3)(E) and 5 C.F.R.§ 610.121(a)(5).

The Agency contends that its scheduling practices for the holidays were in compliance with 5 U.S.C. § 6101(a)(3)(E) and 5 C.F.R. § 610.121(a)(5) because: (1) the Agency's scheduling policies were holiday-blind and (2) it needed to adjust schedules to changed workloads during holidays in order to prevent serious handicapping and substantially increased costs in performing its mission. However, as discussed above, (1) the Arbitrator determined that the Agency's scheduling policies, in at least some cases, were not holiday-blind; and (2) based on the evidence, the Agency head failed to make a determination of "handicap" or "substantial cost" warranting an exception from the requirement that the occurrence of holidays not affect the designation of the basic workweek. Consequently, because the Agency's scheduling practices did not comply with the requirement that the occurrence of holidays not affect the designation of the basic workweek, the Agency has failed to demonstrate that the award is deficient. Accordingly, we deny this exception.

4. The Arbitrator did not err in determining that backpay was available under the Back Pay Act for the entire six-year period preceding the filing of the grievance.

The Agency contends that the awards violate equitable principles because they require the Agency to reimburse employees for the entire six-year period prior to the filing of the grievance even though, the Agency claims, the Union took too long to file it. Concerning the time period for which relief may be awarded, 5 U.S.C. § 5596(b)(4) provides, in relevant part, as follows: "[I]n no case may pay, allowances, or differentials be granted under this section for a period beginning more than [six] years before the date of the filing of a timely appeal[.]" The Authority has specifically held that this provision establishes the earliest date from which an award of backpay may commence. *AFGE, Local 1156*, 57 FLRA 602, 603 (2001); *accord AFGE, Local 933*, 58 FLRA 480, 482 (2003). In addition, the Authority has determined that Back Pay Act recovery periods are within the discretion of arbitrators, as long as awards do not exceed the maximum recovery authorized by law. *Id.* (citations omitted). Moreover, the Back Pay Act imposes no time restrictions on the filing of grievances. *See AFGE, Local 933*, 58 FLRA at 482 (finding that Back Pay Act does not, implicitly or explicitly, establish a filing period for negotiated grievance procedures). Accordingly, we find that the Arbitrator did not err in her interpretation of the Back Pay Act and deny this exception.

VI. Decision

The Agency's exceptions are dismissed in part and denied in part.

APPENDIX

5 U.S.C. § 6101 provides, in pertinent part:

> (a)(1) For the purpose of this subsection, "employee" . . . does not include an employee . . . excluded from the definition of employee in section 5541(2) of this title, except as specifically provided under this paragraph. . . .
>
> (a)(3) Except when the head of an Executive agency . . . determines that his organization would be seriously handicapped in carrying out its functions or that costs would be substantially increased, he shall provide, with respect to each employee in his organization, that –
>
> > (A) assignments to tours of duty are scheduled in advance over periods of not less than 1 week;
> >
> > . . . .
> >
> > (E) the occurrence of holidays may not affect the designation of the basic workweek . . . .

5 C.F.R. § 610.121 provides, in pertinent part:

> (a) Except when the head of an agency determines that the agency would be seriously handicapped in carrying out its functions or that costs would be substantially increased, he or she shall provide that --
>
> > (1) Assignments to tours of duty are scheduled in advance of the administrative workweek over periods of not less than 1 week;
> >
> > . . . .
> >
> > (5) The occurrence of holidays may not affect the designation of the basic workweek . . . .

Section 7116(a) of the Statute provides, in pertinent part:

> For the purpose of this chapter, it shall be an unfair labor practice for an agency –
>
> > (1) to interfere with, restrain, or coerce any employee in the exercise by the employee of any right under this chapter;
> >
> > . . . .
> >
> > (5) to refuse to consult or negotiate in good faith with a labor organization as required by this chapter;
> >
> > . . . .
> >
> > (8) to otherwise fail or refuse to comply with any provision of this chapter.

19 U.S.C. § 267 provides, in pertinent part:

> (b) Premium pay for customs officers
>
> > (1) Night work differential
> >
> > > (A) 3 p.m. to midnight shiftwork
> > >
> > > If the majority of the hours of regularly scheduled work of a customs officer occurs during the period beginning at 3 p.m. and ending at 12 a.m., the officer is entitled to pay for work during such period (except for work to which paragraph (2) or (3) applies) at the officer's hourly rate of basic pay plus premium pay amounting to 15 percent of that basic rate.
> > >
> > > (B) 11 p.m. to 8 a.m. shiftwork
> > >
> > > If the majority of the hours of regularly scheduled work of a customs officer occurs during the period beginning at 11 p.m. and ending at 8 a.m., the officer is entitled to pay for work during such period (except for work to which paragraph (2) or (3) applies) at the officer's hourly rate of basic pay plus premium pay amounting to 20 percent of that basic rate.

(C) 7:30 p.m. to 3:30 a.m. shiftwork

If the regularly scheduled work assignment of a customs officer is 7:30 p.m. to 3:30 a.m., the officer is entitled to pay for work during such period (except for work to which paragraph (2) or (3) applies) at the officer's hourly rate of basic pay plus premium pay amounting to 15 percent of that basic rate for the period from 7:30 p.m. to 11:30 p.m. and at the officer's hourly rate of basic pay plus premium pay amounting to 20 percent of that basic rate for the period from 11:30 p.m. to 3:30 a.m.

(2) Sunday differential

A customs officer who performs any regularly scheduled work on a Sunday that is not a holiday is entitled to pay for that work at the officer's hourly rate of basic pay plus premium pay amounting to 50 percent of that basic rate.

(3) Holiday differential

A customs officer who performs any regularly scheduled work on a holiday is entitled to pay for that work at the officer's hourly rate of basic pay plus premium pay amounting to 100 percent of that basic rate.

(4) Treatment of premium pay

Premium pay provided for under this subsection may not be treated as being overtime pay or compensation for any purpose.

Article 20, Section 23 provides, in pertinent part:

In the absence of local agreements, the following provisions apply:

A. The parties will solicit volunteers for participation in the assignment. . . .

B. Where workload requirements and/or staffing needs dictate and where there are no qualified volunteers on a waiting list (see F., below), the Employer may conduct additional solicitations during the course of the year; if additional solicitations are conducted, selections will be made pursuant to F., below.

. . . .

F. If there are too few volunteers, selections will be made by inverse order of seniority utilizing the procedures outlined in Section 5.B., above.

Exceptions, Ex. 20 at 136-37.

65 FLRA No. 206

UNITED STATES
DEPARTMENT OF VETERANS AFFAIRS
VA MEDICAL CENTER
DAYTON, OHIO
(Agency)

and

AMERICAN FEDERATION
OF GOVERNMENT EMPLOYEES
LOCAL 2209
(Union)

0-AR-4523

DECISION

June 30, 2011

Before the Authority: Carol Waller Pope, Chairman, and Thomas M. Beck and Ernest DuBester, Members

I. Statement of the Case

This matter is before the Authority on exceptions to an award of Arbitrator James Abernathy filed by the Agency under § 7122(a) of the Federal Service Labor-Management Relations Statute (the Statute) and part 2425 of the Authority's Regulations. The Union filed an opposition to the Agency's exceptions.[1]

The Arbitrator found that the Agency refused to promote the grievant to the General Schedule (GS)-7/11 prosthetics representative position as a result of her union activity and that, but for the Agency's failure to rate her properly and to interview her, she would have been selected for the position. *See, e.g.*, Award at 15, 19, 26, 35-36, 37. Moreover, the Arbitrator determined that the Agency's actions violated the parties' collective bargaining agreement (parties' agreement) and ordered the Agency to promote the grievant retroactively "to the position of [p]rosthetics [r]epresentative or a substantially equal position of GS-7/11." *Id.* at 37; *see also id.* at 18, 20, 21, 35-36. For the reasons set forth below, we dismiss the Agency's exceptions in part and deny them in part.

II. Background and Arbitrator's Award

When the grievant was hired by the Agency, she began working as a prosthetic clerk, but was promoted within a few months to the purchasing agent position in the prosthetics division. *Id.* at 5, 10. She worked as a purchasing agent for approximately four years. *Id.* During that time, the grievant was elected president of the Union.[2] *Id.* at 5. Subsequently, the grievant was assigned to the GS-6 health technician/purchasing agent position. *Id.* at 10. She has worked in that position for fourteen years. *Id.*

During her tenure as president, the grievant applied for a GS-7/11 prosthetics representative position. *Id.* Several weeks after the grievant applied for the position, she met with the head of prosthetics, who was also the selecting official, on Union business. *Id.* at 5-6. At their meeting, the selecting official asked the grievant whether she was on 100 percent official time as Union president. *Id.* She responded that she was on 100 percent official time. *Id.* at 6. A few weeks later, the grievant received a letter from an Agency human resources management specialist; the letter notified the grievant that, although she was qualified for the position at the GS-7 level, she had not been selected for the position. *Id.* Because the Agency rated the grievant as a GS-7, and the selecting official chose to interview only applicants rated at the GS-11 level, the grievant was neither interviewed nor selected for the position. *See, e.g., id.* After receiving the letter, the grievant discovered that the selecting official sent an email to a number of other employees indicating that the selectee accepted the position eight days after the grievant met with the selecting official and that the selectee planned to start working five days after accepting the position. *Id.* at 13.

The grievant presented a grievance requesting that the Agency promote her to the prosthetics

1. The Union also filed an addendum to its opposition. As its submission was filed within the time limit for filing the opposition, we consider this submission as part of the opposition. *See IFPTE, Local 77, Prof'l & Scientists Org.*, 65 FLRA 185, 187 (2010) (characterizing the agency's supplemental submission as an addendum to the opposition because it was filed within the time limit for filing the opposition); *Fed. Emps. Metal Trades Council*, 39 FLRA 3, 3 n.* (1991) (considering the union's addendum to its opposition because it was filed within the time limit for filing its opposition).

2. The grievant served as Union president for fourteen years and was on 100 percent official time during her tenure as president. Award at 5.

representative GS-7/11 position or an equivalent position. *Id.* at 6-7. The matter was unresolved and was submitted to arbitration. *See id.* at 7. The issue at arbitration was "[w]hether the Agency violated the [parties'] [a]greement or any law, statute, or regulation when it failed to promote [the] [grievant] to the position of [p]rosthetics [r]epresentative? If so, what shall be the remedy for the violation?" *Id.* at 4.

Among other things, the Arbitrator found that the Agency exhibited anti-union animus by improperly rating the grievant as a GS-7. *See, e.g., id.* at 17-18, 32, 36. The Arbitrator determined that, although the grievant's personnel file contained evidence indicating that she had a master's degree in legal and ethical studies, the Agency failed to consider the grievant's master's degree in rating her as a GS-7. *See, e.g., id.* at 17, 18, 28, 29. The Arbitrator noted that the Agency, as a matter of policy, did not consider the grievant's fourteen years of union experience when giving her a rating for the position and "may not have considered [the] [g]rievant's many years of prosthetics experience." *Id.* at 18; *see also id.* at 17, 21, 28, 32, 33. Also, the Arbitrator found that, because of the grievant's master's degree and her union experience, she was entitled to a GS-11 rating. *See, e.g., id.* at 26, 29. To support his finding, the Arbitrator relied on an Agency witness's testimony indicating that, if the Agency had considered the grievant's master's degree, it would have rated her at least at the GS-9 level. *See id.* at 19, 25, 26, 33. According to the Arbitrator, the witness testified that he would have graded the grievant "a GS-9 without taking into consideration [her] union experience[,]" that the grievant "should be a GS-9 or 'minimally' a GS-11[,]" and that he "got [the] [g]rievant to a GS-11 without considering her union experience." *Id.* at 19, 26; *see also id.* at 25, 33. Moreover, the Arbitrator determined that, by failing to rate the grievant properly, the Agency did not apply "the established standards pertaining to promotion in an equitable, fair, and non-discriminatory way" and, therefore, violated Article 22 of the parties' agreement.[3] *Id.* at 18.

Also, the Arbitrator found that the Agency exhibited anti-union animus by failing to interview the grievant. *See id.* at 24. According to the Arbitrator, the grievant was available to be interviewed, and the Agency "unfairly and unreasonably precluded [her] from participating in the interview process." *Id.* at 24; *see also id.* at 21, 35. Moreover, the Arbitrator determined that Article 22, Section 11 of the parties' agreement requires that, if the Agency uses interviews, it must interview all candidates who are reasonably available. *See, e.g., id.* at 21, 24, 31. The Arbitrator found that the Agency violated the parties' agreement when the selecting official arbitrarily chose to interview only applicants who were rated at the GS-11 level. *See, e.g., id.*

Ultimately, the Arbitrator ordered the Agency to promote the grievant retroactively "to the position of [p]rosthetics [r]epresentative or a substantially equal position of GS-7/11." *Id.* at 37; *see also id.* at 30. In so ordering the retroactive promotion, the Arbitrator found that the remedy did not violate management's right to select under § 7106(a)(2)(C) of the Statute. *Id.* at 34-36. In this regard, the Arbitrator noted that, as Union president, the grievant was engaged in protected activity. *Id.* at 34. The Arbitrator determined that the Agency violated the parties' agreement by rating the grievant improperly and by failing to interview her for the position. *Id.* at 35. Also, the Arbitrator found that the grievant was qualified to be promoted based on the Office of Personnel Management (OPM's) qualification standards and the Agency's Handbook (Handbook).[4] *See id.* at 21, 35. Finally, the Arbitrator determined that, but for the Agency's actions, the "[g]rievant would have been interviewed[,]" and, had "the [g]rievant been interviewed, [she] would have been found to be more qualified than the [s]electee and therefore promoted." *Id.* at 35.

III. Positions of the Parties

A. Agency's Exceptions

The Agency asserts that the Arbitrator's finding that the Agency should have rated the grievant as a GS-11 is contrary to the Handbook. Exceptions at 10-11. According to the Agency, the Handbook requires that, for an employee to be eligible for a promotion at the GS-11 level, the employee must have: (1) "[a]t least [one] year of experience equivalent to the next lower level, and must fully meet the [knowledge, skills, and abilities (KSAs)] at that level[;]" or (2) must have education "equivalent to [three] full years of progressively higher level graduate education or a Ph.D. or equivalent doctoral degree from an accredited university or college in the field of business; a medical field . . . ; public

3. The relevant provisions of Article 22 are set forth in the appendix to this decision.

4. The relevant portion of the Handbook is set forth in the appendix to this decision.

administration; health administration, or those in related courses of study." *Id.* at 10 (quoting Exceptions, Attach. 8 at 4) (internal quotation marks omitted) (emphasis removed). The Agency claims that the grievant is not entitled to a GS-11 rating because she does not have one year of experience at the lower level or three years of a higher level graduate education. *Id.* at 10-11.

Also, the Agency asserts that the award excessively interferes with management's right to select. *Id.* at 11-14. In this regard, the Agency claims that it did not act arbitrarily in violation of Article 22 when it opted only to interview applicants ranked and certified at the GS-11 level because, under 5 U.S.C. § 7106(a)(2)(C), it has "the statutory authority to interview, and select, from any group of 'ranked and certified candidates . . . .'" *Id.* at 13; *see also id.* at 12. The Agency asserts that the Arbitrator's interpretation of Article 22, Section 11 interferes with its right to select because, as interpreted by the Arbitrator, the provision provides that, if it "uses interviews, then all applicants must be interviewed, even if [the] position is posted at more than one grade level and [it] opts to fill the position at the highest grade level." *Id.* at 13. According to the Agency, "even with the 'hindsight review' conducted during the proceedings, [the] [grievant] was only qualified at the GS-9 level and therefore was not a candidate entitled to an interview or selection." *Id.* at 14; *see also id.* at 13. Moreover, the Agency claims that, because the grievant does not qualify as a GS-11 under the Handbook's qualification standards, the Arbitrator's remedy "is not a reconstruction of what would have been done 'but for' the alleged contractual violation." *Id.* at 14.

The Agency asserts that the award is based on a nonfact and that the Arbitrator committed "harmful due process error." *Id.* at 3-9. According to the Agency, the Arbitrator incorrectly recorded and reported an Agency witness's "hindsight evaluation" of the grievant's rating and then relied heavily on that testimony in determining that the grievant should have been rated as a GS-11. *Id.* In this regard, the Agency claims that the witness only testified that the grievant should have been qualified at the GS-9 level and that, based on the selectee's personnel folder, it was the selectee and not the grievant who qualified at the GS-11 level. *Id.* Moreover, the Agency asserts that the Arbitrator failed to consider evidence indicating that the selectee had prosthetics experience. *Id.* at 9.

Finally, the Agency claims that the Arbitrator exceeded his authority by finding that the grievant should have been rated as a GS-11. *Id.* at 14-15. The Agency notes that, based on the Handbook, the grievant does not qualify at the GS-11 level. *Id.* The Agency asserts that, by finding that the grievant would have been qualified at the GS-11 level if the Agency had considered her union experience, the Arbitrator, by default, determined "that [the] [g]rievant's 'union experience' qualified at the GS-9/GS-10 level." *Id.* at 15. According to the Agency, OPM, rather than the Arbitrator, has the authority to classify and/or grade positions. *Id.* Additionally, the Agency claims that the Arbitrator lacked authority to substitute his own standards for the qualification standards contained in the Handbook. *Id.*

B. Union's Opposition

The Union argues that the Agency's claims that the award is contrary to management's right to select and that the award is contrary to the Handbook should be dismissed because the Agency failed to raise these claims at arbitration. Opp'n at 9 & n.3, 10-11. Moreover, the Union contends that, even if the Authority decides to consider the Agency's claims, the Agency has failed to demonstrate that the award is contrary to law, rule, or regulation. *See id.* at 9-14.

Also, the Union argues that the award is not based on a nonfact. *Id.* at 15-20. According to the Union, all "of the supposed [nonfacts] raised by the Agency in its exceptions were in actuality disputed facts at arbitration . . . ." *Id.* at 15. The Union contends that, even if the Arbitrator misstated testimony, the award is not based on a nonfact because the Arbitrator independently found that the grievant was qualified at the GS-11 level by relying on the grievant's master's degree and union experience. *See id.* at 16-19. Moreover, the Union argues that, even if the Arbitrator improperly determined that the selectee had no prosthetics experience, the Arbitrator would not have reached a different result because he found that the grievant had more experience in prosthetics than the selectee. *Id.* at 19.

The Union contends that the Arbitrator did not deprive the Agency of a fair hearing. *Id.* at 20. According to the Union, the Agency has failed to demonstrate that it was prejudiced by the Arbitrator's "faulty memory" because the Arbitrator independently found that the Agency should have rated the grievant as a GS-11 and that the Agency should have interviewed the grievant. *Id.*

Finally, the Union argues that the Arbitrator did not exceed his authority in ordering a retroactive promotion because, in its grievance, the Union requested that the grievant "be promoted to the position of [p]rosthetics [r]epresentative, GS-7/11, or an equivalent position[,]" and the "Agency agreed to submit the issue to [a]rbitration." *Id.* at 15.

IV. Preliminary Issues

A. Section 2429.5 of the Authority's Regulations bars the Agency's exception regarding the Handbook.

The Agency asserts that the Arbitrator's determination that the Agency should have rated the grievant as a GS-11 is contrary to the Handbook. Exceptions at 10-11. According to the Agency, the grievant does not have one year of experience at the lower level or three years of a higher-level graduate education. *Id.*

Under § 2429.5 of the Authority's Regulations, the Authority will not consider issues that could have been, but were not, presented to the arbitrator. *See, e.g., U.S. Dep't of Homeland Sec., U.S. Customs & Border Prot., JFK Airport, Queens, N.Y.*, 64 FLRA 841, 843 (2010) (*JFK Airport*). However, where an issue arises from the issuance of the award and could not have been presented to the arbitrator, it is not precluded by § 2429.5. *See, e.g., U.S. Dep't of Justice, Fed. Bureau of Prisons, Fed. Corr. Complex, Oakdale, La.*, 65 FLRA 35, 38 (2010) (*Fed. Corr. Complex Oakdale*); *U.S. Dep't of Agric., Animal & Plant Health Inspection Serv., Plant Prot. & Quarantine*, 57 FLRA 4, 5 (2001) (citing *Prof'l Airways Sys. Specialists, Dist. No. 1, MEBA/NMU (AFL-CIO)*, 48 FLRA 764, 768 n.* (1993)).

The record establishes that the Agency was on notice that the Union argued that the grievant qualified at the GS-11 level. *See* Award at 19 (indicating that the Union argued below that the grievant was qualified at the GS-11 level); Exceptions at 5 (conceding that the issue of whether the grievant qualified as a GS-11 was crucial to the Union's case at arbitration). The Union clearly contended below that the grievant was rated improperly at the GS-7 level and that she should have been rated as a GS-11 and promoted based on OPM's qualification requirements and the Handbook. *See* Award at 8; Exceptions, Attach. 5 at 13-14; Exceptions, Attach. 6 at 5. Despite this notice, the record contains no indication that the Agency ever argued to the Arbitrator that, based on the qualification requirements in the Handbook, the grievant was not qualified at the GS-11 level. *See* Exceptions, Attach. 4 at 8 (arguing only that, even if an Agency witness testified that the grievant should have been rated as a GS-9, the Agency would not have interviewed the grievant and, thus, would not have selected her for the position). Because the Agency could have presented this argument to the Arbitrator but did not do so, it may not present this argument to the Authority on exceptions. *See Fed. Corr. Complex Oakdale*, 65 FLRA at 38 (concluding that, because agency did not present to the arbitrator its argument regarding the lack of a nondiscretionary agency policy requiring compensation for the temporary performance of higher-graded duties, its argument was barred by § 2429.5); *U.S. Dep't of Def., Def. Commissary Agency, Fort Lee, Va.*, 56 FLRA 855, 858 (2000) (*Def. Commissary Agency*) (finding that contentions made in an agency memorandum indicating that the grievant did not satisfy the minimum qualifications for the position were barred by § 2429.5 because the agency could have and should have presented these contentions to the arbitrator).

Accordingly, we dismiss the Agency's exception.

B. Section 2429.5 of the Authority's Regulations bars the Agency's exception regarding management's right to select under § 7106(a)(2)(C) of the Statute.

The Agency also claims that the award excessively interferes with management's right to select. Exceptions at 11-14.

As noted above, § 2429.5 bars the Agency from raising issues in its exceptions that could have been, but were not, presented to the arbitrator. *See, e.g., JFK Airport*, 64 FLRA at 843. Before the Arbitrator, the Union contended that, as a candidate, the grievant was entitled to be interviewed in accordance with Article 22 of the parties' agreement. *See* Award at 7, 21, 24 (noting that the Union argued that the grievant was readily available to be interviewed and should have been interviewed); Exceptions, Attach. 5 at 14 (arguing that the grievant was affected by the Agency's improper action when it failed to interview her for the position in accordance with Article 22 of the agreement). The Union argued that, under

OPM's requirements and the Handbook, the grievant qualified at the GS-11 level. *See* Exceptions, Attach. 5 at 13-14. Additionally, the Union contended that the Arbitrator should award the grievant a retroactive promotion and that the Arbitrator would not violate management's right to select by awarding the grievant a retroactive promotion. *See id.* at 11-12. However, there is no evidence in the record that the Agency argued below that interpreting Article 22, Section 11 as requiring it to interview all applicants would be contrary to management's right to select or that the grievant was not entitled to an interview because she was not a candidate for promotion. *See* Award at 9 (noting that the Agency stated that its selecting official had the right to interview arbitrarily from any grade level applicant); Exceptions, Attach. 4 at 7 (arguing only that it had "the option of interviewing applicants from just one certificate"). Similarly, the record does not indicate that the Agency argued below that, based on the qualification standards set forth in the Handbook, the proposed remedy would be contrary to management's right to select. *See* Exceptions, Attach. 4. at 1-10 (failing to counter the union's argument that ordering a retroactive promotion would not violate management's right to select). Consequently, because the Agency could have presented, but did not present, these arguments to the Arbitrator, it may not do so now. *See, e.g., U.S. Dep't of the Interior, Bureau of Indian Affairs, Fort Totten Agency, Fort Totten, N.D.*, 65 FLRA 843, 845 (2011); *Soc. Sec. Admin., Newark, N.J.*, 64 FLRA 259, 260 (2009) (finding that, in accordance with § 2429.5, agency's management rights exception was barred because the agency had notice that the arbitrator might award a retroactive promotion but failed to argue below that such a remedy would violate management's right to select); *U.S. Dep't of the Treasury, Internal Revenue Serv.*, 61 FLRA 304, 305 (2005) (barring agency's argument that the union's interpretation of a particular article would violate management's right to assign work because there was no indication in the record that the agency made that argument below, and the arbitrator ultimately accepted the union's interpretation of the article).

Accordingly, we dismiss the Agency's exception.

V. Analysis and Conclusions

A. The award is not based on a nonfact.

The Agency claims that the award is based on a nonfact because the Arbitrator incorrectly recorded and reported an Agency witness's "hindsight evaluation" of the grievant's rating and then relied heavily on that testimony in determining that the grievant was qualified as a GS-11. Exceptions at 3-9. In this regard, the Agency asserts that the witness only testified that the grievant should have been rated as a GS-9 and that, based on the selectee's personnel folder, it was the selectee rather than the grievant who qualified at the GS-11 level. *Id.* Moreover, the Agency claims that the award is based on a nonfact because the Arbitrator failed to consider evidence indicating that the selectee had prosthetics experience. *Id.* at 9.

To establish that an award is based on a nonfact, the appealing party must show that a central fact underlying the award is clearly erroneous, but for which the arbitrator would have reached a different result. *See, e.g., Soc. Sec. Admin., Se. Program Serv. Ctr., Birmingham, Ala.*, 64 FLRA 322, 323 (2009); *NFFE, Local 1984*, 56 FLRA 38, 41 (2000). However, the Authority will not find an award deficient on the basis of an arbitrator's determination of any factual matter that the parties disputed at arbitration. *See, e.g., NFFE, Local 1984*, 56 FLRA at 41.

The Agency's assertion that the award is based on a nonfact because the Arbitrator incorrectly reported and recorded testimony is without merit. Although the Agency discusses several instances where the Arbitrator allegedly misstated testimony, it has not established that the Arbitrator's findings were central facts underlying the award. *See* Exceptions at 3-9. In this regard, even if the Arbitrator incorrectly recorded and reported testimony, the Agency has not demonstrated that, but for the Arbitrator's mistake, he would have reached a different result; the witness only considered the grievant's master's degree in his hindsight evaluation, and the Arbitrator independently found that, because of the grievant's master's degree and union experience, she qualified at the GS-11 level. *See, e.g., AFGE, Local 2142*, 52 FLRA 739, 744 (1996) (finding that union failed to demonstrate that the arbitrator's determination that the grievant's ten-month detail was education and not training was a central fact underlying the award); *AFGE, Local 3947*, 47 FLRA 1364, 1372 (1993) (denying union's nonfact exception because, even if the arbitrator made an incorrect finding, the union did not demonstrate that, but for this finding, the arbitrator would have reached a different result).

Moreover, the issue of whether the selectee had prosthetics experience was disputed at arbitration. *See, e.g.,* Award at 20, 38 (addressing the issue of whether the grievant or the selectee had more prosthetics experience). The Authority will not find that an award relies on a nonfact based simply on the Arbitrator's allegedly erroneous determination of any factual matter that the parties disputed at arbitration. *See, e.g., Nat'l Ass'n of Gov't Emps., Serv. Emps. Int'l Union, Local R4-45*, 64 FLRA 245, 246 (2009); *U.S. Gov't Printing Office, Wash., D.C.*, 62 FLRA 419, 426 (2008); *NFFE, Local 1658*, 55 FLRA 668, 671 (1999) (finding that, because the parties contested below whether a particular candidate failed to apply for the position or did not apply in a timely fashion, the union's nonfact exception did not provide a basis for finding the award deficient); *NFFE, Local 186*, 55 FLRA 59, 60 (1999) (determining that union's contention that the arbitrator erroneously evaluated the evidence concerning the grievant's qualifications for other positions failed to demonstrate that the award was deficient as based on a nonfact because the issue was contested at arbitration). Consequently, the Agency's argument does not provide a basis for finding the award deficient.

Accordingly, we deny the Agency's exception.

B. The Arbitrator did not fail to provide a fair hearing.

The Agency asserts that the Arbitrator committed "harmful due process error" by incorrectly reporting and recording an Agency witness's "hindsight evaluation" of the grievant's rating and then relying heavily on that testimony in determining that the grievant was qualified as a GS-11. Exceptions at 3-9. Moreover, the Agency asserts that the Arbitrator committed "harmful due process error" when he failed to consider evidence demonstrating that the selectee had prosthetics experience. *Id.* at 9. The Authority has addressed similar arguments using a fair hearing analysis.[5] *See AFGE, Local 3627*, 64 FLRA 547, 550 (2010) (considering union's contention that award conflicted with the evidence and testimony as a fair hearing exception); *AFGE, Local 900*, 63 FLRA 536, 540 (2009) (considering union's claims that arbitrator misinterpreted testimony of a management official and failed to consider evidence and objections presented at the hearing as claims that the arbitrator failed to provide a fair hearing).

The Authority will find an award deficient on the ground that an arbitrator failed to conduct a fair hearing when it is demonstrated that the arbitrator refused to hear or consider pertinent and material evidence or that other actions in conducting the proceeding prejudiced a party so as to affect the fairness of the proceeding as a whole. *See, e.g., AFGE, Local 900*, 63 FLRA at 540; *AFGE, Local 1668,* 50 FLRA 124, 126 (1995). However, an arbitrator has considerable latitude in the conduct of a hearing; the fact that an arbitrator conducted a hearing in a manner that one party finds objectionable does not in and of itself provide a basis for finding an award deficient. *See, e.g., AFGE, Local 900*, 63 FLRA at 540; *AFGE, Local 22,* 51 FLRA 1496, 1497-98 (1996).

The Agency's assertions challenge the Arbitrator's evaluation of the evidence and testimony and the weight to accord them. The Authority has long held that disagreement with an arbitrator's findings of fact and evaluation of the evidence and testimony, including the credibility of witnesses and the weight given their testimony, provides no basis for finding an award deficient. *See, e.g., AFGE, Local 3627*, 64 FLRA at 551; *AFGE, Local 900*, 63 FLRA at 540. Consequently, the Agency's assertions do not establish that the Arbitrator denied it a fair hearing. *See AFGE, Local 900*, 63 FLRA at 540 (denying union's fair hearing exception, claiming, among other things, that the arbitrator misinterpreted testimony of a management official and failed to consider evidence presented at the hearing, because it merely challenged the arbitrator's evaluation of the evidence and testimony and the weight to accord them); *U.S. Dep't of Health & Human Servs., Ctrs. for Medicare & Medicaid Servs.*, 60 FLRA 437, 440, 443 (2004) (finding that agency's fair hearing exception, claiming that the arbitrator inappropriately relied on the rating panel's determination despite evidence that the panel process did not take place until after the priority consideration process was complete, did not demonstrate that the award was deficient).

Accordingly, we deny the Agency's exception.

5. We note that the exceptions were filed prior to the October 1, 2010 effective date of the Authority's revised arbitration Regulations.

C. The Arbitrator did not exceed his authority.

According to the Agency, the Arbitrator exceeded his authority by finding that the grievant should have been rated as a GS-11. Exceptions at 14-15. In this regard, the Agency asserts that, by default, the Arbitrator determined "that [the] [g]rievant's 'union experience' qualified at the GS-9/GS-10 level." *Id.* at 15. The Agency claims that OPM, rather than the Arbitrator, has the authority to classify and/or grade positions. *Id.* Moreover, the Agency asserts that the Arbitrator lacked authority to substitute his own standards for the qualification standards contained in the Handbook.[6] *Id.*

Arbitrators exceed their authority when they fail to resolve an issue submitted to arbitration, resolve an issue not submitted to arbitration, disregard specific limitations on their authority, or award relief to those not encompassed within the grievance. *See AFGE, Local 1617*, 51 FLRA 1645, 1647 (1996).

The Agency's contention that the Arbitrator exceeded his authority is without merit. The issue before the Arbitrator was "[w]hether the Agency violated the [parties'] [a]greement or any law, statute, or regulation when it failed to promote [the] [grievant] to the position of [p]rosthetics [r]epresentative? If so, what shall be the remedy for the violation?" Award at 4. The Arbitrator's finding that the grievant should have been rated at the GS-11 level was responsive to the issues before him. *See U.S. Dep't of Veterans Affairs, Ralph H. Johnson Med. Ctr., Charleston, S.C.*, 57 FLRA 72, 76 (2001) (*VAMC Charleston*) (determining that the arbitrator's finding that the grievant possessed the necessary specialized experience to qualify for a temporary promotion to the GS-12 level was responsive to the issue before him); *Laborers' Int'l Union of N. Am., Local 28*, 56 FLRA 324, 327 (2000) (noting that, in order for the arbitrator to decide the stipulated issue, it was necessary for her to consider the grade level of the traffic control duties performed by the grievant). Also, the Authority has found that a disputed failure to promote a grievant under a competitive procedure does not concern classification matters; thus, the Arbitrator did not disregard specific limitations on his authority by finding that the grievant should have been rated as a GS-11. *See U.S. Dep't of Hous. & Urban Dev.*, 65 FLRA 433, 435-36 (2011); *VAMC Charleston*, 57 FLRA at 76 (finding that, because the arbitrator was charged with determining whether the grievant possessed specialized experience equivalent to one year at the next lowest grade to a GS-12, the arbitrator did not exceed his authority by considering whether the grievant had performed the duties of that position); *U.S. Dep't of the Air Force, Air Educ. & Training Command, Randolph Air Force Base, San Antonio, Tex.*, 49 FLRA 1387, 1389 (1994) (noting that, where an arbitrator determines that a grievant is entitled to a competitive promotion, the award does not concern classification matters). Moreover, the Arbitrator did not substitute his own standards for the qualification standards contained in the Handbook. Rather, he determined that the grievant was qualified for the promotion under both OPM's and the Agency's qualification standards. *See* Award at 21, 35. Consequently, the Agency has failed to demonstrate that the Arbitrator exceeded his authority by disregarding specific limitations on his authority.

Accordingly, we deny the Agency's exception.

VI. Decision

The Agency's exceptions are dismissed in part and denied in part.

6. For the reasons stated above, the Agency's assertion that the Arbitrator exceeded his authority by finding that the grievant qualified as a GS-11 is barred by § 2429.5 of the Authority's Regulations. *See Fed. Corr. Complex Oakdale*, 65 FLRA at 38; *Def. Commissary Agency*, 56 FLRA at 858.

APPENDIX

Article 22 states, in pertinent part:

> *Section 1 – Purpose and Policy*
> The parties agree that the purpose and intent of the provisions contained herein are to ensure that promotions are made equitably and in a consistent manner. Promotions shall be based solely on job-related criteria, and without regard to political, religious, labor organization affiliation or nonaffiliation, marital status, race, color, sex, sexual orientation, national origin, nondisqualifying disabling condition, or age. . . .
>
> . . . .
>
> *Section 10 – Panel for Competitive Action*
>
> . . . .
>
> D. *Multiple Grade Levels or Locations*
> If an announcement pertains to more than one grade level or geographic location, a separate list of eligible persons will be developed for each grade level and location.
>
> . . . .
>
> *Section 11 – Sources of Information on Candidates*
>
> . . . .
>
> D. Interviews – If interviews are used, they must be job-related, reasonably consistent, and fair to all candidates. Also, if interviews are used, all candidates must be interviewed if reasonably available, in person or by telephone where circumstances warrant. If more than one management official is conducting the interview, a union representative may be present upon the employee's request.
>
> . . . .

Opp'n, Attach. 2 at 71, 80, 82, 83.

The Handbook states, in pertinent part:

> *3. GRADE REQUIREMENTS*
>
> . . . .
>
> b. *Grade Determination.* In addition to the basic requirements for employment, the following criteria must be met when determining the grade of candidates:
>
> . . . .
>
> (4) *GS-11*
>
> (a) *Experience.* At least 1 year of experience equivalent to the next lower level . . . .
>
> *OR,*
>
> (b) *Education.* Education equivalent to [three] full years of progressively higher level graduate education or a Ph.D. or equivalent doctoral degree from an accredited university or college in the field of business; a medical field, e.g., kinesiotherapy, occupational therapy, physical therapy, nursing, etc.; public administration; health administration; or those in related courses of study.

Exceptions, Attach. 8 at 2-4.

65 FLRA No. 207

UNITED STATES
DEPARTMENT OF JUSTICE
FEDERAL BUREAU OF PRISONS
FEDERAL CORRECTIONAL INSTITUTION
ALLENWOOD, PENNSYLVANIA
(Agency)

and

AMERICAN FEDERATION
OF GOVERNMENT EMPLOYEES
LOCAL 4047
COUNCIL OF PRISON LOCALS
COUNCIL 33
(Union)

0-AR-4691

DECISION

June 30, 2011

Before the Authority: Carol Waller Pope, Chairman, and Thomas M. Beck and Ernest DuBester, Members[1]

I. Statement of the Case

This matter is before the Authority on exceptions to an initial award (initial exceptions) and exceptions to a supplemental award (supplemental exceptions) of Arbitrator Gerard Scola filed by the Agency under § 7122(a) of the Federal Service Labor-Management Relations Statute (the Statute) and part 2425 of the Authority's Regulations. The Union filed an opposition to the initial exceptions (initial opposition) and an opposition to the supplemental exceptions (supplemental opposition).

In the initial award, the Arbitrator found that the Agency violated the Fair Labor Standards Act (FLSA), as amended by the Portal-to-Portal Act (the Act), 29 U.S.C. § 254, because it failed to compensate employees for pre-shift and post-shift work. In the supplemental award, he directed the Agency to pay backpay and liquidated damages, plus post-judgment interest, and to reimburse the Union for attorney fees and related expenses.

1. Member DuBester's separate opinion, dissenting in part, is set forth at the end of this decision.

For the following reasons, we deny the Agency's exceptions in part, set aside the initial award in part, modify the supplemental award to exclude the award of post-judgment interest, and remand the initial award to the parties for resubmission to the Arbitrator, absent settlement.

II. Background and Arbitrator's Awards

The Union filed a grievance alleging that the Agency violated the FLSA by failing to compensate correctional officers at a federal prison for various pre-shift and post-shift activities. The grievance was unresolved and submitted to arbitration, where the Arbitrator framed the issue as follows: "Did the [Agency] suffer or permit bargaining unit employees to perform compensable work before and[/]or after their scheduled shifts, without compensation, in violation of the [FLSA] and the parties' Master Agreement? If so, what is the remedy?" Initial Award at 7.

The Arbitrator found that, before their shifts, all correctional officers: visit the prison's Control Center to pick up equipment such as radios, keys, and handcuffs, as well as a charged battery for their radios; walk through the "Sally Port," which is the area between the Control Center and compound[2] entrance; flip a metal chit on the "accountability board" to indicate their presence in the compound; and travel through the compound to their assigned posts. *Id.* at 10-11. At the end of their shift, officers return to the Control Center. *Id.* at 12.

Each officer has a duty belt that holds his or her equipment. *Id.* at 9. At some point during the period of time covered by the grievance, the Agency instituted mandatory security screening for all employees. *Id.* at 38, 44. During the period after institution of the screening (post-screening period), officers were required to place their duty belts on an x-ray machine, and pass through a metal detector. *Id.* at 9. Officers would then once again don their duty belts before walking to the Control Center to begin the process discussed above. *Id.*

The Arbitrator determined that "hav[ing] a radio and body alarm that was working all the time" is "a 'principal activity' required by the Agency[.]" *Id.* at 40. In addition, the Arbitrator found that picking up a battery is "'integral and indispensable' to that principal activity, and therefore . . . should be

2. Although the Arbitrator did not define the term "compound," Initial Award at 10-11, there is no dispute that the compound is the area of the institution where prisoners are housed.

compensated." *Id.* The Arbitrator also found that "[o]nce the officer enters the Sally Port . . . and [he or she] turn[s] [his or her] chit on the 'Accountability Board' . . . the officer's day has begun." *Id.* at 42. In this regard, the Arbitrator determined that, prior to the institution of employee screening (the pre-screening period), "entrance into the Sally Port . . . [wa]s 'the first principal activity', and th[at] re[-]entry into the Sally Port, . . . carrying equipment back to the Control Center . . . [wa]s 'the last principal activity', that describe[ed] the outer limits of the officer's work day[.]" *Id.* at 43. According to the Arbitrator, "[o]nce the Agency made [going through] the metal detector in the screening room a requirement, it became the officer's 'first principal activity' of the day[,]" and "the donning of the duty belt [and] the stop at the Control Center . . . be[came] part of [his or her] workday." *Id.* at 44, 45 (emphasis omitted).

Based on the foregoing, the Arbitrator sustained the grievance. *Id.* at 51. With respect to the pre-screening period, he awarded compensation ranging from fifteen to thirty minutes of overtime per day[3], depending on the assigned post. *Id.* at 49-50. With respect to the post-screening period, the Arbitrator awarded the same amount of compensation, plus an additional five minutes for each post, with one exception not relevant here.[4] *Id.* at 50.

In the supplemental award, the Arbitrator directed the Agency to pay backpay and liquidated damages, and to reimburse the Union for attorney fees and related expenses. Supplemental Award at 2. He also directed the Agency to pay post-judgment interest on the total amount of the award for a period beginning on November 16, 2010, if it failed to pay the Union in full prior to that date. *Id.* at 3.

III. Positions of the Parties

A. Agency's Initial Exceptions

The Agency contends that the initial award is contrary to law in several respects. First, the Agency argues that the award is contrary to the FLSA and the Act "because it explicitly grants overtime compensation for the simple act of flipping a chit on an accountability board[.]" Exceptions at 6-9 (internal quotations omitted) (citing *IBP, Inc. v. Alvarez*, 546 U.S. 21, 40 (2005) (*Alvarez*); *U.S. Dep't of Justice, Fed. Bureau of Prisons, USP Terre Haute, Ind.*, 58 FLRA 327, 329 (2003) (*Terre Haute*)). Second, the Agency asserts that the Arbitrator erred by awarding compensation to all officers for time spent traveling between the Sally Port and their duty posts, regardless of whether or not they engage in principal activities prior to traveling. *Id.* at 16-20 (citing *Alvarez*, 546 U.S. at 37; *Terre Haute*, 58 FLRA at 330). Third, the Agency argues that the "screening procedures are not integral and indispensable such that they should be compensable" under the FLSA and the Act. *Id.* at 11-13 (citing *Bonilla v. Baker Concrete Constr., Inc.*, 487 F.3d 1340, 1344 (11th Cir. 2007) (*Bonilla*); and *Gorman v. Consol. Edison Corp.*, 488 F.3d 586, 593 (2d Cir. 2007) (*Gorman*)). Fourth, the Agency alleges that the Arbitrator failed to consider whether time spent in pre-shift and post-shift activities was de minimis under 5 C.F.R. § 511.412(a)(1), and, therefore, non-compensable.[5] *Id.* at 13-16 (citing *U.S. Dep't of Justice, Fed. Bureau of Prisons, USP Leavenworth, Kan.*, 59 FLRA 593, 598 (2004) (*Leavenworth*)).

B. Union's Initial Opposition

As an initial matter, the Union contends that the Agency's initial exceptions, which were filed on September 21, 2010,[6] should be dismissed as untimely. Initial Opp'n at 4-7. In this regard, the Union asserts that the Arbitrator served the award via e-mail on August 19, and, as such, any exceptions had to be filed by September 17. *Id.* at 4.

With respect to the merits of the Agency's exceptions, the Union contends that the Arbitrator did not err by awarding compensation for time spent by officers flipping an accountability chit and traveling between the Sally Port and their posts because those activities occurred during their continuous workday. Initial Opp'n at 9-17 (citing *U.S. Dep't of Justice, Fed. Bureau of Prisons, Fed. Corr. Inst., Jesup, Ga.*, 63 FLRA 323, 327 (2009); *Alvarez*, 546 U.S. at 37). With regard to the employee security screening, the Union asserts that it is integral and indispensable to officers' principal activities because it is: (1) conducted at a location separate from the location where visitors are screened; (2) necessary to officers' principal work "due to the dangerous nature of the

3. Although the Arbitrator did not specify the unit of time over which he awarded minutes of compensation, there is no dispute that the award grants compensation in terms of minutes per day.

4. Employees assigned to the Perimeter Patrol Post were not awarded an additional five minutes of compensation. Initial Award at 50.

5. The relevant wording of 5 C.F.R. § 551.412(a)(1) is set forth *infra*.

6. All dates in this paragraph, and in the discussion of the timeliness issue below, are from 2010.

correctional environment"; and (3) performed for the benefit of the employer because officers must "maintain a high level of professionalism" and "be prepared to respond in the event of an emergency" when at the screening site. *Id.* at 17-19.

With respect to compensation for time spent donning duty belts, the Union claims that "courts have consistently found that donning and doffing specialized equipment -- for example, a police officer's duty belt -- is an integral and indispensable activity that would begin the compensable continuous workday." *Id.* at 21 (citing *Nolan v. City of L.A.*, 2009 U.S. Dist. LEXIS 70764, at *40 (C.D. Cal., May 5, 2009); *Maciel v. City of L.A.*, 569 F. Supp. 2d 1038, 1049 (C.D. Cal. 2008)). The Union also argues that the donning of the duty belt in this case is indispensable and integral because the belt is required by the Agency, necessary for officers to perform their duties, used primarily for the benefit of the Agency, and required to be donned on the Agency's premises. *Id.* at 24-29. In this connection, the Union contends that "the requirement that donning occur at the place of employment weighs heavily in favor of finding that the donning act is integral [and] indispensable[.]" *Id.* at 28-29 (internal quotation marks omitted) (citing *Jordan v. IBP, Inc.*, 542 F. Supp. 2d 790, 806 (M.D. Tenn. 2008) (*Jordan*); *Ballaris v. Wacker Siltronic Corp.*, 370 F.3d 901, 911 (9th Cir. 2004) (*Ballaris*); *Alvarez v. IBP, Inc.*, 339 F.3d 894, 903 (9th Cir. 2003) (*IBP*); and *Dep't of Labor Wage and Hour Advisory Memorandum No. 2006-2* at 2 (May 31, 2006)).

Finally, the Union contends that the award does not grant compensation for de minimis time. *Id.* at 29-31.

C. Agency's Supplemental Exceptions

The Agency argues that the supplemental award is contrary to the FLSA because it awards both liquidated damages and post-judgment interest. Supplemental Exceptions at 20-23.

D. Union's Supplemental Opposition

The Union argues that "the Arbitrator properly awarded liquidated damages because the Agency failed to prove that it acted in good faith or on reasonable grounds." Supplemental Opp'n at 30.

IV. Preliminary Issue

The Authority ordered the Agency to show cause why the initial exceptions should not be dismissed as untimely (Order). Section 7122(b) of the Statute requires that exceptions be filed within thirty days from the date of service of the award. 5 U.S.C. § 7122(b). Under the Authority's Regulations that were in effect when the Agency filed its initial exceptions, the first day of the thirty-day period for filing exceptions was the date of service of the award. *See former* 5 C.F.R. § 2425.1(b).[7] The Authority has held that when an award is served by two methods, timeliness is measured based on completion of the earliest method of service of the award. *U.S. Dep't of Homeland Sec., U.S. Customs & Border Prot., U.S. Border Patrol*, 63 FLRA 345, 346 (2009), *recons. denied*, 64 FLRA 807 (2010); *U.S. Dep't of the Treasury, IRS, Wash., D.C.*, 60 FLRA 966, 967 (2005). Section 2429.22 of the Authority's Regulations provides that five days will be added if the award is served by mail or commercial delivery. 5 C.F.R. § 2429.22.

In response to the Order, the Agency asserts that the Arbitrator served his initial award by mail on August 18 -- one day prior to his service by e-mail on August 19. Agency's Response to the Order at 4. The record substantiates the Agency's assertion by showing that the initial award was postmarked on August 18. *Id.*, Attach. A at 1. Thus, the thirty-day deadline for filing the initial exceptions was September 16. As the initial award was first served by mail, five days were added to the filing period, extending the due date until September 21. The Agency's initial exceptions were filed by personal delivery on September 21. Accordingly, we find that the initial exceptions are timely.

V. Analysis and Conclusions

When a party's exceptions involve an award's consistency with law, the Authority reviews the questions of law raised by the arbitrator's award and the party's exceptions de novo. *NTEU, Chapter 24*, 50 FLRA 330, 332 (1995) (citing *U.S. Customs Serv. v. FLRA*, 43 F.3d 682, 686-87 (D.C. Cir. 1994)). In applying a de novo standard of review, the Authority assesses whether the arbitrator's legal conclusions are consistent with the applicable standard of law. *NFFE, Local 1437*, 53 FLRA 1703, 1710 (1998). In making that assessment, the Authority defers to the arbitrator's underlying factual findings. *See id.*

7. The Authority's Regulations concerning the review of arbitration awards, as well as certain related procedural Regulations, including 5 C.F.R. § 2429.5, were revised effective October 1, 2010. *See* 75 Fed. Reg. 42,283 (2010). Because the Agency's exceptions in this case were filed before that date, we apply the prior Regulations.

A. The initial award is contrary to the FLSA and the Act in part.

In passing the Act, Congress distinguished between "the principal activity or activities that an employee is hired to perform," which are compensable, and "activities which are preliminary to or postliminary to said principal activity or activities," which are not compensable. 29 U.S.C. § 254(a)(1) & (2). *See AFGE, Local 1482*, 49 FLRA 644, 646-47 (1994); *Gen. Servs. Admin.*, 37 FLRA 481, 484 (1990). *See also Reich v. N.Y.C. Transit Auth.*, 45 F.3d 646, 649 (2d Cir. 1995) (*N.Y.C. Transit*). Any activities that are integral and indispensable to an employee's principal activity or activities are themselves principal activities under the Act. *Alvarez*, 546 U.S. at 33 (citing *Steiner v. Mitchell*, 350 U.S. 247, 253 (1956)).

In determining whether given activities are an integral and indispensable part of employees' principal activities, "what is important is that such work is necessary to the business and is performed by the employees, primarily for the benefit of the employer, in the ordinary course of that business." *Dunlop v. City Electric Inc.*, 527 F.2d 394, 401 (5th Cir. 1976) (*Dunlop*). In addition, activities that take place between the first and last principal activities of the day, including those which would otherwise be excluded from compensation under the Act, are covered by the FLSA because they occur during the continuous workday. *Alvarez*, 546 U.S. at 29-30, 37, 40; *see also* 29 C.F.R. § 790.6(a)-(b).

The Arbitrator awarded compensation for two separate periods: the pre-screening period and the post-screening period. We address these periods separately below.

1. Pre-Screening Period

The Arbitrator found that picking up a battery at the Control Center is integral and indispensable to the officers' principal activities. Initial Award at 40. The Agency does not dispute this finding, which, as a matter of law, supports a conclusion that the picking up of the battery is a principal activity. *See Alvarez*, 546 U.S. at 33. The Arbitrator also found, and the Agency does not dispute, that re-entry into the Sally Port is the last principal activity of the day. Initial Award at 43. It is undisputed that the flipping of the accountability chit and travel between the Sally Port and duty posts occur after the pick-up of batteries at the Control Center and before re-entry into the Sally Port from the compound at the end of the day. *Id.* at 40. As these activities occur between the first and last principal activities of the day, they are part of the continuous workday.[8] *Alvarez*, 546 U.S. at 29-30.

The Agency's reliance on *Terre Haute* is misplaced because the flipping of the accountability chit and the travel in that case, unlike here, occurred before the start of the continuous workday. Further, with regard to the Agency's claim that the Arbitrator compensated travel time to all officers, regardless of whether they engage in principal activities prior to traveling, the Arbitrator found that "all of the workers pick up a charged battery" -- the first principal activity of the day. Initial Award at 10. Therefore, the Arbitrator's factual finding, which the Agency does not challenge as a nonfact, supports his determination that all officers who travel between the Sally Port and their duty posts are entitled to compensation for the flipping of the accountability chit and travel time as part of the continuous workday. *Alvarez*, 546 U.S. at 29-30, 37.

For the foregoing reasons, we deny the exceptions regarding the pre-screening period.

2. Post-Screening Period

The Agency contends that the award is deficient because the time spent passing through the security screening is not compensable under the FLSA and the Act. Courts that have addressed this issue consistently have held that time spent participating in security screening is not compensable under the FLSA. *See Bonilla*, 487 F.3d at 1345 (concluding that time spent going through airport security to report to work was not compensable under the FLSA); *Gorman*, 488 F.3d at 592-93 (holding that while security procedures including "waiting in line and passing through a radiation detector, x-ray machine, and explosive material detector" were necessary "in the sense that they were required and serve the essential purpose of security," they were not "integral" to the nuclear power station's employees' principal activities and therefore noncompensable).

8. We note that the Arbitrator identifies several activities, including the flipping of the accountability chit, as the beginning of the workday or "first principal activity." *See* Initial Award at 42-44. However, as discussed previously, the Arbitrator found that picking up a battery at the Control Center occurs prior to these other activities and is integral and indispensable to officers' principal activities. *Id.* at 10, 40. Therefore, for the purposes of the FLSA, the picking up of the battery at the Control Center is actually the officers' first principal activity and, thus, the beginning of the continuous workday.

The Union argues that the security screening in the instant case is integral and indispensable to officers' principal activities because it is: (1) conducted at a location separate from where visitor screening is conducted; (2) necessary to officers' principal work "due to the dangerous nature of the correctional environment"; and (3) performed for the benefit of the Agency because officers must "maintain a high level of professionalism" and "be prepared to respond in the event of an emergency" when at the screening site. Initial Opp'n at 17-19. However, there is no basis in the above-cited precedent for finding that these factors have any bearing on whether the screening is "integral and indispensable" to officers' principal activities. Accordingly, we find that, consistent with *Gorman* and *Bonilla*, passing through the security screening is not compensable as a principal activity, and set aside that portion of the initial award.[9]

The Arbitrator also compensated officers for time spent donning their duty belts and traveling to the Control Center after passing through the security screening because he found those activities to be part of the continuous workday. However, as we have set aside the Arbitrator's finding that the security screening is a principal activity, such time is compensable only if the donning of the duty belt is a principal activity sufficient to commence the continuous workday, or if officers engage in principal activities during their travel from the security screening area to the Control Center. *See Terre Haute*, 58 FLRA at 330.

As stated previously, activities that are integral and indispensable to an employee's principal activity or activities are themselves principal activities under the Act. *Alvarez,* 546 U.S. 21. Also as stated previously, in determining whether given activities are an integral and indispensable part of employees' principal activities, "what is important is that such work is necessary to the business and is performed by the employees, primarily for the benefit of the employer, in the ordinary course of that business." *Dunlop*, 527 F.2d at 401. Further, some courts have held that an employer-imposed requirement that donning occur at the employer's premises weighs heavily in favor of finding that the donning is a compensable activity. *See Jordan*, 542 F. Supp. 2d at 806 (citing *Ballaris*, 370 F.3d at 911). In addition, the donning of protective gear is generally compensable only if it is specialized or unique, rather than generic. *See, e.g.*, *Gorman*, 488 F.3d at 594; *N.Y.C. Transit*, 45 F.3d at 649; *Reich v. IBP, Inc.*, 38 F.3d 1123, 1126 (10th Cir. 1994).

As an initial matter, the Arbitrator neither found that the donning of the duty belt is an integral and indispensable activity, nor assessed the factors relevant to determining whether that activity is integral and indispensable. The Arbitrator found that each officer *has* a duty belt, and that because officers cannot wear these belts when passing though the security screening, they need to don their belts on the Agency's premises after passing through the security screening. Initial Award at 9. However, the Arbitrator made no findings regarding whether officers are actually required by the employer to wear the duty belt. Thus, in contrast to the precedent cited by the Union, it is unclear whether the donning of the duty belt on the premises is an activity that is required by the employer. *Cf. Jordan,* 542 F. Supp. 2d at 806 (finding that requirement that employees don required frocks on the employer's premises weighed heavily in favor of compensability); *Ballaris*, 370 F.3d at 903, 911-12 (holding that donning of uniforms at employer's premises was compensable work where employees were required to wear the uniforms); *IBP*, 339 F.3d at 898 n.2, 904 (finding that donning of required protective gear at employer's premises was a compensable activity).

Further, the Arbitrator did not address whether the duty belt, if required, must be donned immediately after passing through screening, such that travel from the screening area to the Control Center is compensable as part of the continuous workday. Moreover, if the duty belt is required, but can be donned at any point after passing through the screening, travel to the Control Center is compensable only if officers engage in principal activities during their travel. It is unclear from the

9. The dissent contends that: (1) the Arbitrator determined that officers are essentially on duty while passing through screening; and (2) it is undisputed that officers can be required to respond to emergencies while at the screening site. *See* Dissent at 11. However, the Arbitrator found only that after officers pass through screening *and* begin to collect equipment, "their focus shifts" from civilian to correctional officer. Award at 44 (emphasis added). In addition, the dissent does not explain why it would be relevant to consider whether screening is conducted at separate locations for employees and visitors (as in the instant case) or at one location for everyone (as in *Gorman*); in both cases, everyone is screened. Moreover, the fact that the employer in *Bonilla* was required to conduct employee screening is immaterial because, as *Gorman* demonstrates, even when an employer is not required to conduct screening, the act of passing through screening before engaging in principal activities is not compensable. Finally, the dissent is based solely on attempts to distinguish precedent; the dissent cites no precedent actually supporting its position.

record whether officers engage in such activities while traveling from the screening area to the Control Center. In addition, the Arbitrator did not address whether the duty belt is a type of protective gear (i.e., helmet, safety glasses, or steel-toed boots), and, if so, whether it is unique or generic. *See Gorman*, 488 F.3d at 594.

Where an arbitrator has not made sufficient factual findings for the Authority to determine whether the award is contrary to law, and those findings cannot be derived from the record, the Authority will remand the award to the parties for further action. *See, e.g., AFGE, Local 2054*, 63 FLRA 169, 172 (2009); *U.S. Dep't of Transp., Maritime Admin.*, 61 FLRA 816, 822 (2006); *NFFE, Local 1437*, 53 FLRA 1703, 1710-11 (1998). Accordingly, we remand the award to the parties for resubmission to the Arbitrator, absent settlement, to determine: (1) whether the donning of the duty belt is an activity that is integral and indispensable to officers' principal activities, including, among other things, whether the duty belt is a type of unique protective gear; (2) if so, whether officers are required to don the belt immediately after passing through screening; and (3) whether officers engage in principal activities during their travel from the security screening area to the Control Center.

B. It is premature to determine whether the initial award is contrary to 5 C.F.R. § 511.412(a)(1) in part.

The Agency alleges that the initial award is contrary to 5 C.F.R. § 511.412(a)(1) because the Arbitrator failed to consider whether the time spent in the compensated activities was de minimis. 5 C.F.R. § 511.412(a)(1) provides, in pertinent part:

> If an agency reasonably determines that a preparatory or concluding activity is closely related to an employee's principal activities, and is indispensable to the performance of the principal activities, and that the total time spent in that activity is more than [ten] minutes per workday, the agency shall credit all of the time spent in that activity, including the [ten] minutes, as hours of work.

5 C.F.R. § 551.412(a)(1).

The Authority has held that "[an] award is contrary to 5 C.F.R. § 511.412(a)(1)" where "the total time awarded by the Arbitrator . . . does not exceed [ten] minutes per workday[.]" *See Leavenworth*, 59 FLRA at 598. Here, the Arbitrator awarded no less than fifteen minutes of compensation for eligible officers.[10] *See* Initial Award at 49-50. As the total time awarded by the Arbitrator for these employees exceeds ten minutes per workday, and we have upheld the Arbitrator's remedy for the pre-screening period, we deny the exception with respect to that time period.

In addition, as stated previously, we are remanding the award with respect to the Arbitrator's remedy concerning the post-screening period. Thus, it is unclear whether, following remand, the award of compensation for this period will exceed a total of ten minutes per workday. As such, we find it premature to address the exception with regard to that time period. *See Terre Haute*, 58 FLRA at 330 (finding it premature to address cross-exceptions regarding damages under the FLSA where remand was ordered to determine whether award granted compensation for certain activities).

C. The supplemental award of post-judgment interest is contrary to law.

The Arbitrator directed the Agency to pay liquidated damages plus interest on the total amount of the award in accordance with the Back Pay Act if it failed to pay the Union in full by November 15, 2010. In *Social Security Administration, Baltimore, Maryland v. FLRA*, 201 F.3d 465, 473 (D.C. Cir. 2000), a decision concerning post-judgment interest, the court held that "liquidated damages are not pay, allowances, or differentials[,]" and that because of this, "the Back Pay Act does not authorize the [Authority] to require an agency to pay interest on liquidated damages awarded under the FLSA." Moreover, the Authority has held that "an employee may not recover the full amount of both liquidated damages and interest" under the FLSA. *U.S. Dep't of Commerce, Nat'l Oceanic & Atmospheric Admin., Office of Marine & Aviation Operations, Marine Operations Ctr., Va.*, 57 FLRA 430, 436 (2001). Accordingly, we find that the supplemental award is contrary to law.

Where the Authority is able to modify an award to bring it into compliance with applicable law, it will do so. *See, e.g., U.S. Dep't of Energy, Oak Ridge Office, Oak Ridge, Tenn.*, 64 FLRA 535, 538 (2010). As the award is deficient to the extent that it grants both post-judgment interest and liquidated damages,

10. As noted previously, there is no dispute that the award grants compensation in terms of minutes per day.

we modify it to exclude the award of post-judgment interest.[11]

VI. Decision

The Agency's exceptions are denied in part, the initial award is set aside in part, the supplemental award is modified to exclude the award of post-judgment interest, and the initial award is remanded to the parties for resubmission to the Arbitrator, absent settlement.

11. However, we note that the actual amount of backpay and liquidated damages may change as a result of the remanded issues.

Member DuBester, Dissenting in Part:

Contrary to my colleagues, and in agreement with the Arbitrator, I would find that the time spent by the correctional officers passing through security screening is compensable.

It appears from the facts as found by the Arbitrator that the time spent passing through security screening is an integral part of the officers' principal activities. As the Arbitrator determined, officers are essentially on duty while going through screening. Initial Award at 44. It is undisputed that officers can be called on to respond to an emergency while at the screening site. As the Arbitrator found, *id.*, as officers pass through the metal detector, their focus shifts from being civilians to being correctional officers.

In making this judgment, I find the cases on which the majority relies distinguishable. *Gorman v. Consol. Edison Corp.*, 488 F.3d 586 (2nd Cir. 2007) (*Gorman*); *Bonilla v. Baker Concrete Constr., Inc.* 487 F.3d 1340 (11th Cir. 2007) (*Bonilla*). In both *Gorman* and *Bonilla*, employees were not engaged in doing their jobs until after they passed through security screening. Also in contrast to *Gorman* and *Bonilla*, the security screening here meets the test of *Dunlop v. City Electric Inc.*, 527 F.2d 394 (5th Cir. 1976) (*Dunlop*), cited by the majority. *Dunlop* sets forth the test for determining whether a given activity is an integral and indispensable part of employees' principal activities, namely: "that such work is necessary to the business and is performed by the employees, *primarily for the benefit of the employer, in the ordinary course of that business.*" *Id.* at 401 (emphasis added). In *Bonilla*, the screening was required by the FAA, not the employer, and was not based on the employer's discretion for its benefit. In *Gorman*, unlike here, the security measures were required for everyone entering the plant, including visitors. Here, the screening is only for officers, with the public being subject to different security procedures.

In light of my view on this issue, I would also uphold the Arbitrator's finding that officers should be compensated for time spent donning their duty belts and traveling to the control center, and would not find a remand necessary to determine whether those activities are part of the continuous workday.

65 FLRA No. 208

AMERICAN FEDERATION
OF GOVERNMENT EMPLOYEES
LOCAL 2022
(Union)

and

UNITED STATES
DEPARTMENT OF THE ARMY
BLANCHFIELD ARMY
COMMUNITY HOSPITAL
(Agency)

0-AR-4756

DECISION

June 30, 2011

Before the Authority: Carol Waller Pope, Chairman, and Thomas M. Beck and Ernest DuBester, Members

This matter is before the Authority on exceptions to an award of Arbitrator James T. Ellis filed by the Union under § 7122(a) of the Federal Service Labor-Management Relations Statute (the Statute) and part 2425 of the Authority's Regulations. The Agency filed an opposition to the Union's exceptions.

Under § 7122(a) of the Statute, an award is deficient if it is contrary to any law, rule, or regulation, or it is deficient on other grounds similar to those applied by federal courts in private sector labor-management relations. Upon careful consideration of the entire record in this case and Authority precedent, the Authority concludes that the award is not deficient on the grounds raised in the exceptions and set forth in § 7122(a). *See AFGE, Local 3955, Council of Prison Locals 33,* 65 FLRA 887, 890 (2011) (Member Beck dissenting as to other matters) (denying exceeded-authority exception where excepting party failed to support its exception); *Fraternal Order of Police, Pentagon Police Labor Comm.,* 65 FLRA 781, 784-85 (2011) (denying contrary-to-law exception where excepting party did not cite any law with which the arbitrator's award conflicted);[*] *U.S. Dep't of the Air Force, Lowry Air Force Base, Denver, Colo.,* 48 FLRA 589, 593-94 (1993) (award not deficient as based on a nonfact where excepting party challenges a factual matter that the parties disputed at arbitration).

Accordingly, the Union's exceptions are denied.

[*] We note that, as with the Union's contrary-to-law exception, the Union's public policy exception does not cite to a public policy with which the award conflicts.

65 FLRA No. 209

UNITED STATES
DEPARTMENT OF THE NAVY
NAVAL AIR STATION
PENSACOLA, FLORIDA
(Agency)

and

AMERICAN FEDERATION
OF GOVERNMENT EMPLOYEES
LOCAL 1960
(Union)

0-AR-4688

DECISION

June 30, 2011

Before the Authority: Carol Waller Pope, Chairman, and Thomas M. Beck and Ernest DuBester, Members

I. Statement of the Case

This matter is before the Authority on exceptions to an award of Arbitrator Frederick P. Ahrens filed by the Agency under § 7122(a) of the Federal Service Labor-Management Relations Statute (the Statute) and part 2425 of the Authority's Regulations. The Union filed an opposition to the Agency's exceptions.

The Arbitrator concluded that the Agency violated the parties' collective bargaining agreement (the agreement) by failing to authorize uniform allowances for certain of its employees in accordance with applicable government-wide and Agency regulations.

For the reasons that follow, we dismiss in part and deny in part the Agency's exceptions.

II. Background and Arbitrator's Award

The Agency requires its police officers and its firefighters to wear uniforms. Award at 4. Article 36, Section 36.02 of the agreement requires the Agency to authorize a uniform allowance for employees required to wear uniforms. [1] The uniform allowance is to be "in accordance with applicable regulations." *Id.* at 5 (quoting Article 36, Section 36.02).

The uniform allowance that the Agency authorized has two components: an initial uniform allowance and an annual uniform allowance. *See* Award at 6. Employees receive an initial uniform allowance when they are first hired. *See* Exceptions at 2-3; *id.*, Attach., Encl. 14 at 2. Employees also receive an annual uniform allowance to defray the cost of replacement uniforms. Exceptions at 3; *id.*, Attach., Encl. 14 at 3.

The Arbitrator found that the Agency increased the initial and the annual uniform allowances in 2007. Award at 4. However, the Agency did not begin implementing the increases until 2010. *See id.* at 4, 10. As part of the implementation process, the Agency required employees to fill out a "self-certification form[,]" certifying the amount of the initial and annual uniform allowances they had received in prior years, and the amount of personal funds they had spent for required uniform articles. *Id.* at 4. Employees were then paid a make-up annual uniform allowance based in part on what they had actually paid for required uniform articles. *Id.* at 4-5.

The Union, which had not agreed to the self-certification procedure, filed a grievance. *Id.* at 1. The grievance raised the issue whether the Agency violated Article 36, Section 36.02 of the agreement by failing to pay employees the proper uniform allowance in accordance with the applicable regulations. *Id.* at 1-3. When the grievance was not resolved, it was submitted to arbitration.

The Arbitrator framed a threshold arbitrability issue and a merits issue, respectively, as follows:

> Does the Arbitrator have the authority to issue[] an award in this matter?
>
> . . . .
>
> Did the [Agency] violate the [a]greement, Article 36, Section 36.02[,] by not authorizing a revised uniform allowance in accordance with applicable regulations? If not, what is the proper remedy?

Award at 2 & 3.

1. Article 36, Section 36.02 states that "[i]f the Employers require UNIT employees to wear uniforms[,] the Employers will authorize uniform allowances in accordance with applicable regulations." Exceptions, Attach., Encl. 3 at 1; *see also* Award at 5.

As to the threshold matter, the Agency contended that the grievance was not arbitrable because the Agency was not the proper party to the grievance. Instead, the Agency claimed that the Commander Navy Region Southeast (the Region) was the proper party to the grievance.[2] *Id.* at 1-2. The Arbitrator rejected this contention and determined that the Agency was the proper party. *Id.* at 3. The Arbitrator found that the agreement specifically designates the Agency and the Union as parties to the agreement. *Id.* He further found that the parties had not agreed to substitute the Region for the Agency as a party to the agreement pursuant to Article 40, Section 40.03,[3] which addresses the procedures for modifying the agreement. *Id.* For these reasons, the Arbitrator determined that the grievance was arbitrable. *Id.*

Addressing the merits, the Arbitrator determined that the Agency violated Article 36, Section 36.02 of the agreement by failing to authorize uniform allowances for its employees in accordance with applicable government-wide and Agency regulations. *Id.* at 10. Specifically, he found that the regulations did not allow the Agency to determine the amount of the annual uniform allowance based on the employees' uniform replacement costs. *Id.* at 9. Rather, the Arbitrator found, this amount must be based on the cost of all required uniform articles "pro-rated for the estimated life" of those articles. *Id.* at 8-9 (citing Agency Notice CNIC 12594).[4]

The Arbitrator also found that the applicable regulations do not require employees to self-certify out-of-pocket expenses for the Agency's use in determining the initial or annual uniform allowances. *Id.* However, he found that employees may be required to provide evidence, acceptable to the Agency, such as receipts, of their initial purchase of uniforms, for the Agency's use in determining an employee's initial uniform allowance. *Id.* at 9. The Arbitrator specifically noted that this requirement did not extend to determination of the annual uniform allowance because the annual uniform allowance is based on the proration of uniform costs over estimated uniform life. *Id.* at 9-10.

Finally, the Arbitrator limited his award to determinations of uniform allowances for previous time periods, under the parties' agreement that expired on April 22, 2010. *Id.* at 10. The Arbitrator stated that subsequent uniform allowances are governed by the parties' new collective bargaining agreement. *Id.*

III. Positions of the Parties

A. Agency's Exceptions

The Agency asserts that the award is contrary to law and fails to draw its essence from the agreement.

According to the Agency, the Arbitrator's arbitrability determination is contrary to law because the Arbitrator erroneously failed to recognize that the Agency and the Union are not the proper parties to the grievance. Exceptions at 5-6. Specifically, the Agency claims, after the consolidation petition was granted, the parties were no longer bound to the agreement's grievance procedure. *Id.* Moreover, the Agency asserts, after consolidation, statutory rights such as filing grievances could be exercised only by certain representatives of the parties. Here, the Agency asserts, those representatives are the Region and the national Union. *Id.* Therefore, the Agency argues, it is not a proper party to the grievance. *Id.* Furthermore, the Agency claims, the Union did not have standing to file the grievance because the national Union did not authorize it to act on the issue of employees' uniform allowances. *Id.* at 6.

The Agency also argues that the Arbitrator's arbitrability determination fails to draw its essence from the agreement. Specifically, the Agency argues

2. During the term of the agreement, the Region filed a representation petition in Case No. AT-RP-08-0003 to consolidate several local bargaining units into one national unit. Exceptions at 2. One of these local units included the Agency's employees. *Id.* The consolidation petition was granted and a new certification of representative issued. As a result, a new consolidated unit, referred to as Commander, Navy Installations Command (CNIC), was created. *Id.*, Attach., Encl. 4. The agreement involved in this case remained in effect until a new collective bargaining agreement covering CNIC was negotiated. *Id.* at 2-3, 5.

3. Article 40, Section 40.03 provides:

> No agreement, alteration, understanding, variation, waiver, or modification of any terms or conditions contained herein shall be made unless such agreement is made and executed in writing between both PARTIES and has been ratified by the UNION and approved by the Department of Defense.

Exceptions, Attach., Encl. 3 at 78-79; *see also* Award at 3.

4. The relevant portion of CNIC 12594 states that the Region "shall determine and document the appropriate amount of annual uniform allowance paid to employees based on the cost pro-rated for the estimated life of the minimum required uniform articles . . . as well as any additional uniform items the Region deems necessary." Exceptions, Attach., Encl. 14 at 3.

that the Arbitrator failed to consider Article 40.01[5] of the agreement, which addresses circumstances that terminate the agreement. *Id.* at 11.

On the merits, the Agency asserts that the award is contrary to 5 C.F.R. § 591.103(c), under which the Agency "establish[es] policies to administer the uniform allowance program, including uniform standards acceptable to the agency." *Id.* at 6 (quoting 5 C.F.R. § 591.103(c)). Citing the preamble to this regulation,[6] as published in the Federal Register, the Agency argues that § 591.103(c) requires that employees provide the Agency evidence of their uniform purchases. *Id.* at 6 (citing 72 Fed. Reg. 20,701 (April 26, 2007)). However, the Agency claims, the Arbitrator erroneously determined that employees are not required to provide evidence of their uniform purchases for the Agency's use in determining the amount of the annual uniform allowance. *Id.* at 7-8.

The Agency also contends that the award is contrary to § 591.103(c) because it conflicts with the regulation's preamble, as published in the Federal Register, which grants the Agency sole discretion to decide what evidence is acceptable to verify employees' purchase of uniforms. *Id.* at 9 (citing 72 Fed. Reg. at 20,701). Based on the Agency's discretion to determine "uniform purchase documentation requirements," the Agency argues that the Arbitrator erred when he determined that employees' self-certifications of out-of-pocket uniform expenses may not be utilized to determine the uniform allowance. *Id.* at 8-9.

The Agency further argues that the award is contrary to CNIC 12594(5)(d).[7] *Id.* at 8-10. Specifically, the Agency argues that it may require employees to complete self-certification forms because this process satisfies the regulation's requirement that the Agency establish and maintain records of employee uniform purchases. *Id.* at 9-10. Therefore, the Agency contends, the Arbitrator erred when he determined that the Agency cannot require employees to provide self-certification forms as evidence of their uniform purchases.

B. Union's Opposition

The Union asserts that the Agency cannot argue that the parties are not the proper parties to the grievance because the validity of the agreement was never challenged at arbitration. Opp'n at 1. In the alternative, the Union claims that the agreement remained in effect until a collective bargaining agreement covering the consolidated units, including the Agency, was negotiated. *Id.* Therefore, the Union asserts, the Arbitrator correctly found that the agreement was enforceable by the parties at the time the grievance was filed. *Id.* at 2.

In addition, the Union opposes the Agency's essence exception, claiming that the Agency never argued before the Arbitrator that the agreement had terminated pursuant to Article 40.01. *Id.* at 3.

On the merits, the Union contends that the Agency's argument that the award is contrary to § 591.103(c) fails because this regulation does not require employees to provide the Agency with self-certifications of their out-of-pocket uniform expenses. *Id.* at 2-3. This regulation, the Union argues, only requires the Agency to establish a policy verifying that employees spent their allowances on uniforms. *Id.* at 3. The Union also asserts that the Agency cannot use the self-certification forms to determine the initial or annual uniform allowances. *Id.* at 2-3.

IV. Preliminary Issue

The Agency claims that the award is contrary to law because the award fails to recognize that the Agency and the Union are not the proper parties to the grievance. Exceptions at 5.

The Authority generally will not find an arbitrator's ruling on the procedural arbitrability of a grievance deficient on grounds that directly challenge the procedural arbitrability ruling itself. *See AFGE, Local 3882*, 59 FLRA 469, 470 (2003). However, a procedural arbitrability determination may be directly challenged and found deficient on the ground that it is contrary to law. *See id.* (citing *AFGE, Local 933*, 58 FLRA 480, 481 (2003)). In order for a procedural arbitrability determination to be found deficient as contrary to law, the appealing party must establish that the determination is contrary to procedural

5. Article 40.01 of the agreement provides that "this agreement shall terminate at any time it is determined that the UNION is no longer entitled to exclusive recognition under the [Statute]." Exceptions, Attach., Encl. 3 at 77.

6. The relevant portion of the preamble provides:

> At a minimum, OPM expects such policies will . . . require employees to provide evidence acceptable to the agency of the employee's purchase of one or more uniforms . . . .

7. The relevant portion of CNIC 12594(5)(d) provides that the Agency is "responsible for developing and maintaining records that verify all required uniform articles are purchased and/or issued to each employee [and] the cost breakdown of each item purchased." Exceptions, Attach., Encl. 14 at 3.

requirements established by statute that apply to the parties' negotiated grievance procedure. *See U.S. Dep't of Homeland Sec., U.S. Customs & Border Prot., U.S. Border Patrol, El Paso, Tex.*, 61 FLRA 122, 124 (2005).

The Arbitrator's determination that the Agency and the Union are the proper parties to the grievance concerns the grievance's procedural arbitrability. *See U.S. Dep't of Veterans Affairs, Louis Stokes Med. Ctr., Cleveland, Ohio*, 64 FLRA 911, 912-13 (2010) (Authority determined that exception concerning whether employee was proper grievant involved arbitrator's procedural arbitrability determination); *AFGE, Local 1931*, 50 FLRA 279, 281 (1995) (arbitrator's finding that grievance was not arbitrable because grievant did not fall within contractual definition of employee under parties' negotiated grievance procedure was procedural arbitrability determination). However, the Agency has failed to identify any procedural requirements established by statute that apply to the parties' negotiated grievance procedure, with which the Arbitrator's award conflicts. Therefore, the Agency's contention provides no basis for finding the Arbitrator's determination deficient.[8]

Accordingly, we deny the Agency's contrary to law exception that alleges that the grievance is not arbitrable.

8. In addition, the Agency asserts for the first time, as an essence exception, that the Arbitrator failed to consider Article 40.01 of the agreement, which addresses circumstances that terminate the parties' agreement. Exceptions at 10-11. Under § 2429.5 of the Authority's Regulations, the Authority generally will not consider evidence or arguments that could have been, but were not, presented to the arbitrator. *See Soc. Sec. Admin.*, 57 FLRA 530, 534 (2001) (citing *NAGE, Local R4-45*, 53 FLRA 517, 520 (1997); *U.S. Agency for Int'l Dev.*, 53 FLRA 187, 187 n.2 (1997)). There is no indication in the record that the Agency raised this argument in the proceedings before the Arbitrator. Moreover, the Agency could have raised the argument because the issue of whether the agreement was in effect was in dispute before the Arbitrator. Because the issue raised by Article 40.01 was not presented to the Arbitrator, but could have been, it is not properly before the Authority under § 2429.5 of the Authority's Regulations. *See, e.g. U.S. Dep't of the Army, The Adjutant General, Mo. Nat'l Guard, Bridgeton, Mo.*, 56 FLRA 1104, 1106 (2001). For this reason, we dismiss the Agency's essence exception challenging the grievance's arbitrability. We note that § 2429.5 was amended effective October 1, 2010. *See* 75 Fed. Reg. 42,283 (2010). For purposes of this case, we apply the prior Regulation that was in effect at all times relevant to the processing of this case.

V. Analysis and Conclusions

A. The award is not contrary to 5 C.F.R. § 591.103(c).

The Agency argues that contrary to 5 C.F.R. § 591.103(c), the Arbitrator erroneously determined that employees are not required to provide evidence of their uniform purchases for the Agency's use in determining the amount of the annual uniform allowance. When an exception involves an award's consistency with law, the Authority reviews any question of law raised by the exception and the award de novo. *See NTEU, Chapter 24*, 50 FLRA 330, 332 (1995) (citing *U.S. Customs Serv. v. FLRA*, 43 F.3d 682, 686-87 (D.C. Cir. 1994)). In applying the standard of de novo review, the Authority assesses whether an arbitrator's legal conclusions are consistent with the applicable standard of law. *See U.S. Dep't of Def., Dep'ts of the Army & the Air Force, Ala. Nat'l Guard, Northport, Ala.*, 55 FLRA 37, 40 (1998). In making that assessment, the Authority defers to the arbitrator's underlying factual findings. *See id.*

As noted above, Section 591.103(c)'s plain language requires an agency to "establish policies to administer the [agency's] uniform allowance program[.]" *See AFGE, Local 1709*, 57 FLRA 453, 455 (2001) (relying on plain language to resolve a matter of statutory interpretation). However, contrary to the Agency's argument, § 591.103(c)'s plain language does not require employees to provide evidence of their uniform purchases for the Agency's use in determining their annual uniform allowance.

Similarly, the Agency contends that contrary to 5 C.F.R. § 591.103(c), the Arbitrator erroneously determined that employees' self-certifications of their uniform purchases may not be utilized to determine the uniform allowance. Exceptions at 8. However, the plain language of § 591.103(c), set forth above, also does not include such a requirement.

In addition, to the extent the Agency relies on the preamble to § 591.103(c), as published in the Federal Register, to argue that the award is contrary to the regulation, the Agency's reliance is misplaced. The Agency relies on the preamble to argue that, under § 591.103(c), employees are required to provide the Agency with evidence of their uniform purchases, and that the Agency has sole discretion to decide what evidence is acceptable. However, as with § 591.103(c)'s plain language, the language of the preamble does not address the particular evidence of their uniform purchases that employees may be required to provide or the utilization of such evidence to determine the annual uniform allowance. In sum, § 591.103(c) neither sets forth any evidentiary requirements employees must meet in connection with the determination of their annual uniform allowances, nor requires employees to submit self-certifications of their uniform purchases.

Accordingly, we deny the Agency's exception that the award is contrary to 5 C.F.R. § 591.103(c).

B. The award does not fail to draw its essence from the agreement.

The Agency argues that the award is contrary to Agency regulation CNIC 12594(5)(d). Specifically, the Agency asserts that employees must complete self-certification forms because that process satisfies CNIC 12594(5)(d)'s requirement that the Agency develop and maintain records of uniform purchases.

The Agency claims, and there is no dispute, that Article 36, Section 36.02 of the agreement requires the Agency to authorize uniform allowances consistent with Agency regulations, including CNIC 12594(5)(d). When a collective bargaining agreement incorporates the agency regulation with which an award allegedly conflicts, the matter becomes one of contract interpretation because the agreement, not the regulation, governs the matter in dispute. *E.g., AFGE, Council of Prison Locals 33*, 59 FLRA 381, 382 (2003). The Authority has found that where, "as plainly worded and interpreted by the [a]rbitrator," a collective bargaining agreement provides that certain matters are required to be conducted in accordance with an agency regulation, "the agreement effectively incorporates" the regulation. *U.S. Dep't of Agric., Animal & Plant Health Inspection Serv., Plant Prot. & Quarantine*, 51 FLRA 1210, 1216-17 (1996) (*APHIS*).

In these circumstances, consistent with *APHIS*, we find that CNIC 12594(5)(d) is effectively incorporated into the agreement, and we treat the matter as one of contract interpretation. *Id.* Accordingly, we apply an essence analysis to assess the Agency's argument.

In reviewing an arbitrator's interpretation of a collective bargaining agreement, the Authority applies the deferential standard that federal courts use in reviewing arbitration awards in the private sector. *See* 5 U.S.C. § 7122(a)(2); *AFGE, Council 220*, 54 FLRA 156, 159 (1998). Under this standard, the Authority will find that an arbitration award is deficient as failing to draw its essence from the collective bargaining agreement when the appealing party establishes that the award: (1) cannot in any rational way be derived from the agreement; (2) is so unfounded in reason and fact and so unconnected with the wording and purposes of the collective bargaining agreement as to manifest an infidelity to the obligation of the arbitrator; (3) does not represent a plausible interpretation of the agreement; or (4) evidences a manifest disregard of the agreement. *U.S. Dep't of Labor (OSHA)*, 34 FLRA 573, 575 (1990). The Authority and the courts defer to arbitrators in this context "because it is the arbitrator's construction of the agreement for which the parties have bargained." *Id.* at 576.

The Agency claims that employees must complete self-certification forms because this process satisfies CNIC 12594(5)(d)'s requirement that the Agency develop and maintain records. Exceptions at 9. Therefore, the Agency asserts, the award is contrary to CNIC 12594(5)(d) because the award precludes the Agency from requiring employees to provide self-certification forms as evidence of their uniform purchases.

CNIC 12594(5)(d) states that the Agency is "responsible for developing and maintaining records that verify all required uniform articles are purchased and/or issued to each employee [and] the cost breakdown of each item purchased . . . ." Exceptions, Attach., Encl. 14 at 3. As the Arbitrator found, the plain language of CNIC 12594(5)(d) does not mandate the use of self-certification forms. Award at 9. Therefore, the Arbitrator's conclusion that the Agency is precluded from using self-certification forms to determine the initial and annual uniform allowances is consistent with CNIC 12594(5)(d). Accordingly, the award is a plausible interpretation of the agreement and there is no basis for concluding that the award is irrational, unfounded, implausible, or in manifest disregard of the agreement.

Accordingly, we deny the Agency's exception.

VI. Decision

The Agency's exceptions are dismissed in part and denied in part.

65 FLRA No. 210

AMERICAN FEDERATION
OF GOVERNMENT EMPLOYEES
LOCAL 12
(Union)

and

UNITED STATES
DEPARTMENT OF LABOR
(Agency)

0-AR-4541

ORDER DISMISSING EXCEPTIONS

July 11, 2011

Before the Authority: Carol Waller Pope, Chairman, and Thomas M. Beck and Ernest DuBester, Members

I. Statement of the Case

This matter is before the Authority on exceptions to an award of Arbitrator Merry C. Hudson filed by the Union under § 7122(a) of the Federal Service Labor-Management Relations Statute and part 2425 of the Authority's Regulations. The Agency filed an opposition to the Union's exceptions.[1]

The Arbitrator found that the Agency did not violate the parties' agreement or law when it removed the grievant from federal service. For the reasons that follow, we dismiss the Union's exceptions.

II. Background and Arbitrator's Award

The Agency gave the grievant a "minimally satisfactory" performance rating and placed him on a performance improvement plan (PIP). Award at 6. After the PIP period ended, the supervisor informed the grievant that his performance had not been successful, and that the grievant could request a downgrade as an alternative to removal. *See id.* at 7. After a Union representative informed the supervisor that the grievant would consider requesting a downgrade, the grievant e-mailed the supervisor a settlement proposal that provided for a downgrade if certain additional conditions were met. *See id.* at 7-8. The supervisor rejected the settlement proposal, and the grievant decided not to request a downgrade. *Id.* at 8. Subsequently, the Agency removed the grievant from federal service for failing to meet the requirements of his PIP. *Id.*

The Union filed a grievance challenging the grievant's removal, and when the grievance was unresolved, it was submitted to arbitration. *See id.* at 2, 10. At arbitration, the Union argued, as relevant here, that the "performance-based removal of the [g]rievant" violated the parties' agreement and 5 U.S.C. chapter 43. *Id.* at 4. The Union also argued that the Agency removed the grievant to retaliate against him for involving the Union in the dispute, and thereby committed an unfair labor practice (ULP). *See id.* at 4, 12-13.

The Arbitrator framed the issue before her as whether the Agency "removed [the] [g]rievant from his position . . . in violation of the [parties' agreement] or federal law and, if so, what shall be the remedy." *Id.* at 3. The Arbitrator found that the grievant's removal was justified, and determined that the Agency complied with the parties' agreement and 5 U.S.C. chapter 43. *See id.* at 10. In addition, the Arbitrator found that the Agency "considered both [the] [g]rievant's past performance[] and his performance during the PIP period." *Id.* at 17. With regard to the Union's ULP claim, the Arbitrator found that the Union "failed to show that the Agency's decision" to remove the grievant was "in any way influenced by [the] [g]rievant's exercise of his right to obtain union representation." *Id.* at 14. Based on the foregoing, the Arbitrator denied the grievance. *Id.* at 17.

III. Positions of the Parties

A. Union's Exceptions

The Union asserts that the Arbitrator "erred in finding that [the] Agency had not engaged in" a ULP, Exceptions at 10, and maintains that the Arbitrator "erred in finding that [the] Agency had lawful reasons to explain its" decision to remove the grievant, *id.* at 11. Additionally, the Union argues

1. As discussed further below, the parties also filed supplemental submissions in response to an Authority Order to Show Cause, and we consider those submissions. Further, the Union and the Agency filed additional supplemental submissions. However, the parties did not request permission to file those submissions. Thus, consistent with the Authority's Regulations and precedent, we decline to consider those submissions. *See* 5 C.F.R. § 2429.26; *AFGE, Local 1061*, 63 FLRA 317, 317 n.1 (2009).

that the award is contrary to 5 C.F.R. § 432.105(a),[2] and that the Arbitrator "erroneously concluded that the Agency could remove employees based on pre-PIP performance." *Id.* at 17.

B. Agency's Opposition

The Agency contends that the Authority lacks jurisdiction to consider the Union's exceptions because the grievant's removal was a performance-based action arising under 5 U.S.C. § 4303 (§ 4303). *See* Opp'n at 2-3. The Agency also contends that the Arbitrator correctly rejected the Union's remaining arguments, including its ULP allegation. *See id.* at 11-15.

IV. Order to Show Cause and Parties' Responses

The Authority directed the Union to show cause why its exceptions should not be dismissed for lack of jurisdiction pursuant to § 7122(a) of the Statute because the award "concerns the Agency's removal of an employee[.]" Order to Show Cause at 1.

In its response to the show-cause order (Union's response), the Union asserts that it "appealed to the Authority" because the removal "flowed from the Agency's commission of" a ULP, and "only the [Authority] can determine whether the Union's charge is correct." Union's Response at 1.

In a reply to the Union's response (Agency's reply), the Agency contends that the Authority does not have jurisdiction because the award is "inextricably intertwined" with a matter covered by § 4303. Agency's Reply at 2; *accord id.* at 3 (citing, inter alia, *U.S. Dep't of Veterans Affairs, Carl T. Hayden Med. Ctr., Phoenix, Ariz.*, 59 FLRA 569, 570 (2004) (Chairman Cabaniss concurring) (*VA*)).

V. Analysis and Conclusions

Under § 7122(a) of the Statute, the Authority lacks jurisdiction to resolve exceptions to awards "relating to" matters described in § 7121(f) of the Statute.[3] *See, e.g., AFGE, Local 491*, 63 FLRA 307, 308 (2009) (*Local 491*). Matters described in § 7121(f) include adverse actions, such as removals for unacceptable performance, that are covered under 5 U.S.C. § 4303 and are appealable to the Merit Systems Protection Board (MSPB) and reviewable by the United States Court of Appeals for the Federal Circuit (Federal Circuit).[4] *See, e.g., U.S. Dep't of Commerce, Patent & Trademark Office, Arlington, Va.*, 61 FLRA 476, 477 (2006) (*PTO*).

The Authority will determine that an award relates to a matter described in § 7121(f) "when it resolves, or is inextricably intertwined with," a § 4303 matter. *See Local 491*, 63 FLRA at 308. In making that determination, the Authority looks not to the outcome of the award, but to whether the claim advanced in arbitration is one reviewable by the MSPB, and, on appeal, by the Federal Circuit. *Id.*

It is undisputed that the grievant was removed from employment for unacceptable performance, pursuant to 5 U.S.C. chapter 43, and that the claim advanced at arbitration challenged the Agency's decision to remove the grievant for his unacceptable performance. *See* Award at 1, 4-5, 8, 10; Union's Response at 1-3; Exceptions at 1, 3, 6; Agency's Reply at 1-2, 4; Opp'n at 4. As the award at issue relates to the grievant's removal for unacceptable performance under 5 U.S.C. chapter 43, the award relates to a matter described in § 7121(f). *See PTO*, 61 FLRA at 477-78 (grievant's removal for unacceptable performance "inextricably intertwined" with § 4303). Thus, the above-cited precedent supports a conclusion that the Authority lacks jurisdiction to consider the Union's exceptions to the award.

The Union asserts that the removal "flowed from the Agency's commission of" a ULP, and asserts that "only the [Authority] can determine whether" this assertion is correct. Union's Response at 1. However, the Authority previously has dismissed exceptions under § 7121(f) even where the conduct at issue in the arbitration proceeding was alleged to constitute a ULP. *See VA*, 59 FLRA at 570 (Authority lacked jurisdiction to consider exceptions

2. 5 C.F.R. § 432.105(a) states, in pertinent part, that "[o]nce an employee has been afforded a reasonable opportunity to demonstrate acceptable performance . . . an agency may propose a reduction-in-grade or removal action if the employee's performance . . . is unacceptable[.]"

3. Section 7122(a) provides, in pertinent part: "Either party to arbitration . . . may file with the Authority an exception to any arbitrator's award pursuant to the arbitration (other than an award relating to a matter described in section 7121(f) of this title)." Section 7121(f) provides, in pertinent part: "In matters covered under sections 4303 and 7512 of this title which have been raised under the negotiated grievance procedure . . . section 7703 of this title pertaining to judicial review shall apply to the award of an arbitrator . . . ."

4. Section 4303, states, in pertinent part: "[A]n agency may reduce in grade or remove an employee for unacceptable performance."

to award that found, among other things, that agency committed a ULP when it suspended grievant for thirty days). In addition, although the MSPB may not adjudicate whether a ULP occurred, it "not only can but *must* address issues that could properly underlie [ULP] charges where such issues are raised as affirmative defenses alleging 'prohibited personnel practices.'" *Wildberger v. FLRA*, 132 F.3d 784, 791 (D.C. Cir. 1998) (citing 5 U.S.C. § 2302(b)(9); *Ireland v. Dep't of HHS, SSA*, 34 M.S.P.R. 614 (1987); *Bodinus v. Dep't of the Treasury*, 7 M.S.P.R. 536, 540-42 (1981)). *See also Dep't of Commerce, Bureau of the Census v. FLRA*, 976 F.2d 882, 890 (4th Cir. 1992). Accordingly, the MSPB addresses claims that employee removals violate 5 U.S.C. § 2302(b)(9) because they were taken in retaliation based on union activities. *See, e.g., Gustave-Schmidt v. DoL*, 87 M.S.P.R. 667, 675 (2001). For these reasons, the claim advanced at arbitration in this case is one that could have been reviewed by the MSPB, and, on appeal, by the Federal Circuit. Even if that were not the case, the possibility that there may be no forum in which a party may challenge an arbitration award does not provide a basis for finding that the Authority has jurisdiction. *E.g., PTO*, 61 FLRA at 478 (citing *U.S. Dep't of Veterans Affairs, Med. Ctr., Newington, Conn.*, 53 FLRA 440, 443 (1997)).

For the foregoing reasons, the Authority lacks jurisdiction to consider the Union's exceptions to the award. Accordingly, we dismiss the exceptions.

VI. Order

The Union's exceptions are dismissed.

65 FLRA No. 211

AMERICAN FEDERATION
OF GOVERNMENT EMPLOYEES
LOCAL 3627
(Union)

and

SOCIAL SECURITY ADMINISTRATION
OFFICE OF DISABILITY ADJUDICATION
AND REVIEW
TAMPA, FLORIDA
(Agency)

0-AR-4752

DECISION

July 11, 2011

Before the Authority: Carol Waller Pope, Chairman, and Thomas M. Beck and Ernest DuBester, Members

This matter is before the Authority on exceptions to an award of Arbitrator Cecile Steele filed by the Union under § 7122(a) of the Federal Service Labor-Management Relations Statute (the Statute) and part 2425 of the Authority's Regulations. The Agency filed an opposition to the Union's exceptions.

Under § 7122(a) of the Statute, an award is deficient if it is contrary to any law, rule, or regulation, or it is deficient on other grounds similar to those applied by Federal courts in private sector labor-management relations. Upon careful consideration of the entire record in this case and Authority precedent, the Authority concludes that the award is not deficient on the grounds raised in the exceptions and set forth in § 7122(a). *See AFGE, Local 3615*, 65 FLRA 647, 649 (2011) (exceptions that directly challenge procedural arbitrability determinations on essence grounds provide no basis for finding the award deficient); *U.S. Dep't of Veterans Affairs, Med. Ctr., N. Chi., Ill.*, 52 FLRA 387, 398 (1996) (award not deficient because of bias on the part of an arbitrator where excepting party fails to demonstrate that the award was procured by improper means, that there was partiality or corruption on the part of the arbitrator, or that the arbitrator engaged in misconduct that prejudiced the rights of the party); *AFGE, Local 1869*, 50 FLRA 172, 174 (1995) (award not deficient as being incomplete, ambiguous, or contradictory where excepting party fails to establish that implementation of the award is impossible); *AFGE, Local 1668*, 50 FLRA 124, 126 (1995) (award not deficient on ground that arbitrator failed to provide a fair hearing where excepting party fails to demonstrate that the arbitrator refused to hear or consider pertinent and material evidence, or that other actions in conducting the proceeding so prejudiced a party so as to affect the fairness of the proceeding as a whole).

Accordingly, the Union's exceptions are denied.

65 FLRA No. 212

UNITED STATES
DEPARTMENT OF THE AIR FORCE
AIR FORCE FLIGHT TEST CENTER
EDWARDS AIR FORCE BASE, CALIFORNIA
(Agency)

and

SPORT AIR TRAFFIC CONTROLLERS
ORGANIZATION
(Union)

0-AR-4620

ORDER DISMISSING EXCEPTIONS

July 11, 2011

Before the Authority: Carol Waller Pope, Chairman, and Thomas M. Beck and Ernest DuBester, Members

I. Statement of the Case

This matter is before the Authority on exceptions to an award of Arbitrator Edna E.J. Francis filed by the Agency under § 7122(a) of the Federal Service Labor-Management Relations Statute (the Statute) and part 2425 of the Authority's Regulations. The Union filed an opposition to the Agency's exceptions.

The Arbitrator found that the Agency violated the parties' agreement and the Statute by failing to fulfill its bargaining obligations before changing a past practice. The Arbitrator directed the Agency to return to the status quo until it satisfied its bargaining obligations, and directed the parties to agree on a remedy for affected employees. For the reasons that follow, we dismiss the exceptions, without prejudice, as interlocutory.

II. Background and Arbitrator's Award

The Union filed a grievance alleging, in pertinent part, that the Agency violated the parties' agreement and the Statute when it refused to follow the past practice of granting administrative leave in the amount necessary for employees to receive a minimum of twelve hours of rest after working an overtime shift (rest policy). Award at 2. The grievance was unresolved and submitted to arbitration.

Before the Arbitrator, the Agency conceded that it ceased following the rest policy, but argued that it had fulfilled its bargaining obligation by offering the Union the opportunity to submit impact and implementation proposals concerning its new policy under which the Agency would ensure an eight-hour minimum interval between shifts. *Id.* at 10-11.

The Arbitrator found that the Agency's notice to the Union was insufficient, *id.* at 22-23, and that the Agency violated the parties' agreement and the Statute by changing the rest policy past practice before fulfilling its statutory bargaining obligations, *id.* at 24. As one element of the remedy, the Arbitrator directed the Agency to "return to the status quo ante" and "cease and desist from enforcing the change in past practice until it has satisfied its statutory bargaining obligations." *Id.*

In addition, the Arbitrator found that the Agency's failure to continue following the rest policy affected employees. *See id.* at 18. In this regard, the Arbitrator found that there was "no dispute" that, on several occasions, employees were "offered irregular and unscheduled overtime on their regular day off . . . and were not granted administrative leave" consistent with the rest policy. *Id.* The Arbitrator also found that, on a particular date, the Union president "was forced to work overtime and was not granted administrative leave in the amount necessary" under the rest policy. *Id.* Because the Arbitrator found that the Agency changed the rest policy past practice before it had satisfied its bargaining obligations, the Arbitrator stated:

> [T]he Agency and the Union shall attempt to fashion a remedy regarding the case of any bargaining unit employee who, [during the relevant time period], declined overtime as a result of the change in past practice or worked overtime or an irregular shift but was . . . denied administrative leave [consistent with the rest policy].

Id. at 24. The Arbitrator retained jurisdiction "in the event the parties are unable to resolve issues regarding implementation of the remedy[,]" but noted that her jurisdiction would expire if extension of her jurisdiction was not requested by a specified date. *Id.*

III. Positions of the Parties

A. Agency's Exceptions

The Agency argues that the award is contrary to law because the Arbitrator imposed additional requirements not required by law when evaluating the adequacy of the Agency's notice and invitation to bargain. Exceptions at 1-2.

B. Union's Opposition

The Union argues that the award is not contrary to law. Opp'n at 1-5.

IV. Order to Show Cause

In an Order to Show Cause (Order), the Authority directed the Agency to show cause why its exceptions should not be dismissed as interlocutory. Order at 1. The Authority stated that, because the Arbitrator directed the parties "'to attempt to fashion a remedy'" for any employee who declined overtime as a result of the change in past practice, or worked overtime or an irregular shift but was denied administrative leave consistent with the rest policy, *id.* at 2 (quoting Award at 24), "it is unclear whether the award 'completely and unambiguously' resolves the remedy," *id.* (quoting *AFGE, Local 1923*, 48 FLRA 1117, 1121 (1993)).

In response, the Agency argues that the award is final because the Authority has previously upheld the finality of awards in which arbitrators directed the parties to reach agreement regarding remedies. Response at 1 (citing *U.S. Dep't of Justice, Fed. Bureau of Prisons*, 63 FLRA 132 (2009) (*Prisons*); *SSA, Balt., Md.*, 60 FLRA 32 (2004) (Chairman Cabaniss concurring) (*SSA*)). In addition, the Agency asserts that it is "not aware of any . . . employees entitled to a remedy under the award[,]" and that the Union has not provided the Agency with a list of employees allegedly entitled to a remedy.[*] *Id.* at 2.

In reply, the Union argues that: (1) the Agency's exceptions are interlocutory, Reply at 1; (2) the Arbitrator has extended her jurisdiction until after the Authority issues a decision, *id.* at 2; and (3) "[i]t is undisputed that the parties have not yet fashioned a remedy as required by the [a]ward[,]" *id.* at 3. Further, the Union disputes the Agency's claim that it is unaware of any employees entitled to a remedy. *Id.* at 2.

V. Analysis and Conclusions

Under § 2429.11 of the Authority's Regulations, the Authority "ordinarily will not consider interlocutory appeals." 5 C.F.R. § 2429.11. Thus, the Authority ordinarily will not resolve exceptions to an arbitration award unless the award constitutes a complete resolution of all the issues submitted to arbitration. *See, e.g., U.S. Dep't of Homeland Sec., U.S. Customs & Border Prot.*, 65 FLRA 603, 605 (2011). Consistent with this principle, the Authority has held that where an arbitrator declines to issue a remedy, directing instead that the parties attempt to develop an appropriate remedy on their own, the award does not constitute a final decision to which exceptions can be filed. *See U.S. Dep't of Health & Human Servs., Navajo Area Indian Health Serv.*, 58 FLRA 356, 357 (2003) (*Navajo*); *U.S. Dep't of the Interior, Bureau of Indian Affairs, Wapato Irrigation Project, Wapato, Wash.*, 55 FLRA 1230, 1231-32 (2000) (*Interior*).

In this case, the Arbitrator found that it was undisputed that employees were adversely affected by the Agency's failure to follow the rest policy, Award at 18, directed the parties to "attempt to fashion a remedy" for affected employees, and retained jurisdiction in the event the parties were unable to resolve the remedy issue, *id.* at 24. Consequently, consistent with the decisions cited above, the award is not a final decision. *See Navajo*, 58 FLRA at 357; *Interior*, 55 FLRA at 1231-32.

The decisions cited by the Agency are inapposite. In *SSA* and *Prisons*, the arbitrators specified the nature of the awarded remedies, but directed the parties to confer concerning the details of those remedies, such as the exact amount of costs to be recovered, *SSA*, 60 FLRA at 32, and the number of backpay claims of affected employees, *Prisons*, 63 FLRA at 133. Here, by contrast, the Arbitrator did not specify the type of remedy to which the affected employees were entitled and merely direct the parties to agree on the details of the awarded remedy; rather, the Arbitrator left the entire nature of the remedy up to the parties to decide. Accordingly, the Arbitrator's award is not a final decision and, thus, the Agency's exceptions are interlocutory.

VI. Order

The Agency's exceptions are dismissed, without prejudice, as interlocutory.

[*] In addition, although the Agency originally argued that the Arbitrator's jurisdiction had expired because the Union failed to request an extension of her jurisdiction, Response at 1, the Agency filed a supplemental submission (Addendum) clarifying that, at the request of the Union, the Arbitrator extended the period during which the parties may request that she reassert jurisdiction until sixty days after the Authority issues a decision on the Agency's exceptions. Addendum at 1. *See also* Reply at 2.

65 FLRA No. 213

NATIONAL TREASURY
EMPLOYEES UNION
CHAPTER 145
(Union)

and

UNITED STATES
DEPARTMENT OF HOMELAND SECURITY
U.S. CUSTOMS AND BORDER PROTECTION
LAREDO, TEXAS
(Agency)

0-AR-4492
(65 FLRA 898 (2011))

ORDER DENYING
MOTION FOR RECONSIDERATION

July 14, 2011

Before the Authority: Carol Waller Pope, Chairman, and Thomas M. Beck and Ernest DuBester, Members

I. Statement of the Case

This matter is before the Authority on the Agency's motion for reconsideration (motion) of the Authority's decision in *National Treasury Employees Union, Chapter 145*, 65 FLRA 898 (2011) (*NTEU*). The Union did not file an opposition to the Agency's motion.

Section 2429.17 of the Authority's Regulations permits a party that can establish extraordinary circumstances to request reconsideration of an Authority final decision or order. For the reasons that follow, we conclude that the Agency has failed to establish extraordinary circumstances warranting reconsideration. Accordingly, we deny the Agency's motion.

II. Decision in *NTEU*

In the arbitration award at issue in *NTEU*, the Arbitrator held that § 7121(d) of the Federal Service Labor-Management Relations Statute (§ 7121(d)) barred a grievance concerning the propriety of the grievant's suspension because the grievant previously had filed a formal Equal Employment Opportunity (EEO) complaint regarding the suspension.[1] *See* 65 FLRA 898, 898. On the Union's exceptions to the award, the Authority found that there was no dispute that the grievant's formal EEO complaint had been untimely, and held that the award was contrary to law because § 7121(d) does not bar a grievance where the previously filed, formal EEO complaint is untimely. *See id.* at 899-900. In so holding, the Authority: (1) considered the plain wording of § 7121(d) and Authority and Equal Employment Opportunity Commission (EEOC) precedent interpreting that wording; (2) considered the plain wording of 29 C.F.R. § 1614.301 (§ 1614.301) and EEOC precedent interpreting that wording;[2] and (3) expressly rejected the Agency's claim that § 7121(d) requires only that a grievant timely initiate an EEO "*action*[,]" rather than timely initiating a formal EEO complaint, in order for the grievance to be barred. *Id.* The Authority set aside the award and remanded the matter to the parties for submission, absent settlement, to an arbitrator of their choice. *Id.* at 900.

III. Agency's Motion

The Agency asserts that the Authority erred in its conclusion of law in *NTEU* and that, consequently, extraordinary circumstances warrant reconsideration of that decision. Motion at 1. According to the Agency, § 7121(d) and pertinent precedent "only require timely initiation of an action[,]" *id.* at 1, not "a timely formal EEO complaint[,]" *id.* at 4, and the grievant "timely initiated an EEO action" before he filed his untimely, formal EEO complaint, *id.* The

---

1. Section 7121(d) provides:

> An aggrieved employee affected by a prohibited personnel practice under [§] 2302(b)(1) of this title which also falls under the coverage of the negotiated grievance procedure may raise the matter under a statutory procedure or the negotiated procedure, but not both. An employee shall be deemed to have exercised his option under this subsection to raise the matter under either a statutory procedure or the negotiated procedure at such time as the employee timely initiates an action under the applicable statutory procedure or timely files a grievance in writing, in accordance with the provisions of the parties' negotiated procedure, whichever event occurs first.

2. Section 1614.301(a) provides, in pertinent part, that "[a]n election to proceed under this part is indicated only by the filing of a written complaint; use of the pre-complaint process . . . does not constitute an election for purposes of this section."

Agency asserts that § 1614.301 does not include the word "timely[,]" which indicates that the formal EEO complaint need not be filed timely in order to bar a grievance. *Id.* at 5. The Agency also asserts that allowing *NTEU* to "stand[] . . . would be contrary to the legislative purpose [behind § 7121(d), as] cited in" Authority precedent discussed in *NTEU*. *Id.*

IV. Analysis and Conclusions

Section 2429.17 of the Authority's Regulations permits a party that can establish extraordinary circumstances to request reconsideration of an Authority decision. *E.g., Nat'l Ass'n of Indep. Labor, Local 15*, 65 FLRA 666, 667 (2011). The Authority repeatedly has recognized that a party seeking reconsideration under § 2429.17 bears the heavy burden of establishing that extraordinary circumstances exist to justify this unusual action. *Id.* The Authority has identified a limited number of situations in which extraordinary circumstances have been found to exist, including, as relevant here, a situation where the Authority erred in its conclusion of law. *Id.* However, where a party's motion for reconsideration presents the same arguments that were rejected by the Authority in its decision, the Authority has denied the motion. *See id.* In this connection, the Authority repeatedly has held that attempts to relitigate conclusions reached by the Authority are insufficient to establish extraordinary circumstances. *E.g., Sport Air Traffic Controllers Org.*, 64 FLRA 1142, 1143 (2010).

In its motion, the Agency relies on arguments that the Authority rejected in *NTEU* and, thus, attempts to relitigate conclusions that the Authority reached in *NTEU*. Consistent with the foregoing, those arguments do not demonstrate extraordinary circumstances warranting reconsideration of *NTEU*. Accordingly, we deny the motion.

V. Order

The Agency's motion is denied.

65 FLRA No. 214

UNITED STATES
DEPARTMENT OF THE ARMY
WOMACK ARMY MEDICAL CENTER
FORT BRAGG, NORTH CAROLINA
(Agency)

and

AMERICAN FEDERATION
OF GOVERNMENT EMPLOYEES
LOCAL 1770
(Union)

0-AR-4595

DECISION

July 20, 2011

Before the Authority: Carol Waller Pope, Chairman, and Thomas M. Beck and Ernest DuBester, Members

I. Statement of the Case

This matter is before the Authority on exceptions to an award of Arbitrator Edward E. Hales filed by the Agency under § 7122(a) of the Federal Service Labor-Management Relations Statute (the Statute) and part 2425 of the Authority's Regulations. The Union filed an opposition to the Agency's exceptions.

The Arbitrator found that the Agency violated the parties' agreement by paying several employees at the General Schedule (GS)-6, rather than GS-7, grade level. For the reasons that follow, we deny the Agency's exceptions and the Union's request for a remand.

II. Background and Arbitrator's Award

The Agency posted vacancies for certain "GS 6/7" positions. Award at 3. The Agency's Human Resources Consultant (the Consultant) offered the positions to five applicants (the grievants) at the GS-7 level, and they accepted the positions at that level. *See id.* at 12-13. However, when the grievants began work, the Agency processed their paperwork and began paying them at the GS-6 level. *See id.* at 13.

Subsequently, the Union filed a grievance on behalf of the five grievants, alleging that they were "improperly downgraded" from the GS-7 level to the GS-6 level "upon commencing their jobs." *Id.* at 1. When the grievance was unresolved, it was submitted to arbitration, where the Arbitrator framed the issues as follows:

> 1. Did the Agency improperly downgrade the [grievants] to the GS-6 grade level, after they applied for and were offered and accepted the . . . position[s] at the [GS]-7 level, as asserted by the Union?
>
> 2. Were the [g]rievants properly hired at the GS-6 grade level, as asserted by the Agency[,] for the . . . position[s] based on their qualifications and after it was determined that they were erroneously offered the position[s] at the GS-7 grade level?

Id. at 11.

As an initial matter, the Arbitrator rejected the Agency's claim that the grievance was not arbitrable because it concerned a classification matter within the meaning of § 7121(c)(5) of the Statute (§ 7121(c)(5)). Specifically, the Arbitrator found that the grievance "d[id] not involve an attempt to reclassify a position[]" and that there was no dispute regarding "whether the wrong job classification was involved for the type of work that the [g]rievants were performing . . . ." *Id.* at 17. Instead, the Arbitrator stated that the grievants "were seeking employment to a position for which they had been qualified . . . by the . . . Consultant[,]" *id.* at 17-18, and that the grievance "concern[ed] whether the [g]rievants were improperly downgraded to the GS-6 grade level[,]" *id.* at 17.

Addressing the merits of the grievance, the Arbitrator found that the evidence supported a conclusion that the grievants were qualified for the GS-7 level. In this regard, the Arbitrator stated that the Agency's argument that they were not qualified at that level was "not persuasive when considering the evidence [that] appears to be to the contrary." *Id.* Specifically, the Arbitrator found that, before offering the grievants the positions, the Consultant had "qualified" them, *id.* at 17, and that the Agency "ha[d] not presented any evidence[] [that] credibly demonstrates that [they] were not qualified for the GS-7 grade level[,]" *id.* at 18. Instead, the Arbitrator found that the Agency "made a tacit decision to process the [g]rievants for employment at the GS-6 grade regardless of their qualifications." *Id.*

The Arbitrator determined that Article 3, Section 1(e)(1) of the parties' agreement (Article 3) requires the promotion of an employee "properly ranked and certified for promotion." *Id.* As the Consultant had determined that the grievants were qualified for the GS-7 level, the Arbitrator found that the Agency violated the agreement by "improperly downgrad[ing] the [g]rievants from the . . . GS-7 grade level to the GS-6 grade level."[1] *Id.* Accordingly, the Arbitrator sustained the grievance and directed the Agency to pay the grievants backpay at the GS-7 level. *Id.*

III. Positions of the Parties

A. Agency's Exceptions

The Agency claims that the award is based on two nonfacts. First, the Agency asserts that the Arbitrator erred by finding that "a 'downgrade' had occurred[,]" because, according to the Agency, the grievants were never employed at the GS-7 level. Exceptions at 4. Second, the Agency argues that the award is based on a nonfact because the Arbitrator erred in finding a violation of Article 3. *See id.* at 7-8. In this regard, the Agency contends that Article 3 does not require the Agency to "advance every individual solely because they meet the qualifications[,]" and that the Arbitrator's interpretation of Article 3 "would lead to the untenable situation where the Agency would be forced to hire all qualified candidates regardless of how many vacancies exist." *Id.* at 8.

The Agency also claims that the award is contrary to § 7121(c)(5) because the grievance concerned classification and, thus, was not arbitrable. *See id.* at 2-4. In particular, the Agency contends that, "[i]n order for the [A]rbitrator to claim jurisdiction in this matter[,] he had to rely on the nonfact that a 'downgrade' had occurred." *Id.* at 4.

Additionally, the Agency asserts that the award is contrary to 5 C.F.R. § 300.604(b) because the record evidence does not support a conclusion that the grievants met the requirements for a promotion to the GS-7 level at the time they were hired.[2] *See id.* at 5-6.

Finally, the Agency contends that the award is contrary to the Back Pay Act, 5 U.S.C. § 5596 (the BPA). *See id.* at 6. In this regard, the Agency asserts that classifying the positions at the GS-6 level was not unjustified or unwarranted because the Agency was acting in accordance with 5 C.F.R. § 335.103(b)(3),[3] which requires the Agency to comply with 5 C.F.R. § 300.604(b). *See id.* at 6-7. In addition, the Agency asserts that there was no withdrawal or reduction of the grievants' pay, allowances, or differentials because they were never employed or paid at a level higher than GS-6. *See id.* at 7.

B. Union's Opposition

The Union argues that the award is not based on nonfacts. *See* Opp'n at 8. In this connection, the Union contends that, contrary to the Agency's assertion, the Arbitrator did not find that the Agency must promote and select every individual that is properly ranked and certified. *See id.* at 9.

The Union also argues that the award is not contrary to § 7121(c)(5) because, as the Arbitrator found, the grievance did not attempt to reclassify the positions. *See id.* at 4-5. In addition, the Union contends that the award is not contrary to 5 C.F.R. § 330.604. *See id.* at 5. In this regard, the Union asserts that the Agency's arguments do not take into account 5 C.F.R. § 300.603(b)(1), which provides an exclusion for appointments based on selection from a competitive examination register of eligibles or under

1. We note that the Arbitrator did not find that the grievants were ever actually employed at the GS-7 level, and there is no dispute that they were not employed at that level. In this regard, the Arbitrator appears to have used the term "downgrade" to refer to the grievants being initially processed and paid at the GS-6 level after accepting positions at the GS-7 level. *Cf.* Award at 1 (Arbitrator characterized grievance as alleging that grievants had been "improperly downgraded . . . *upon commencing their jobs.*") (emphasis added). Thus, this case does not involve a "reduction in grade[]" within the meaning of 5 U.S.C. § 7512(3), and § 7122(a) of the Statute does not preclude the Authority from exercising jurisdiction.

2. 5 C.F.R. § 300.604 provides, in pertinent part:

> The following time-in-grade restrictions must be met unless advancement is permitted by § 300.603(b) of this part:
>
> . . . .
>
> (b) Advancement to positions at GS-6 through GS-11. Candidates for advancement to a position at GS-6 through GS-11 must have completed a minimum of [fifty-two] weeks in positions:
>
> . . . .
>
> (2) No more than one grade lower (or equivalent) when the position to be filled is in a line of work properly classified at [one]-grade intervals . . . .

3. 5 C.F.R. § 335.103(b)(3) provides, in pertinent part, that "[m]ethods of evaluation for promotion and placement[] . . . must be consistent with instructions in part 300, subpart A, of this chapter."

a direct-hire authority.[4] *See id.* at 6. The Union also asserts that 5 C.F.R. § 300.601 states that the regulations are intended to prevent excessively rapid promotions and, because the grievants were initial hires, the regulatory requirements regarding eligibility for promotions are inapposite.[5] *See id.* Even assuming that the regulations apply, the Union contends that the Arbitrator made factual findings that support his legal conclusion that the grievants were qualified at the GS-7 level. *See id.* at 6-7.

Further, the Union argues that the award is consistent with the BPA because the grievants were hired at the GS-7 level and then improperly "downgraded" to the GS-6 level. *Id.* at 7. In addition, the Union asserts that it has not yet requested attorney fees from the Arbitrator, and requests that the Authority remand this case for a decision regarding such fees. *See id.* at 9.

IV. Analysis and Conclusions

A. The award is not based on nonfacts.

To establish that an award is based on a nonfact, the appealing party must show that a central fact underlying the award is clearly erroneous, but for which the arbitrator would have reached a different conclusion. *See U.S. Dep't of the Air Force, Lowry Air Force Base, Denver, Colo.*, 48 FLRA 589, 593 (1993). However, the Authority will not find an award deficient on the basis of an arbitrator's determination on any factual matter that the parties disputed at arbitration. *Id.* at 594 (citing *Nat'l Post Office Mailhandlers v. U.S. Postal Serv.*, 751 F.2d 834, 843 (6th Cir. 1985)). Additionally, an arbitrator's interpretation of a collective bargaining agreement does not constitute a matter that can be challenged as a nonfact. *E.g.*, *U.S. DHS, U.S. Immigration & Customs Enforcement*, 65 FLRA 792, 795 (2011) (*ICE*).

The Agency's first nonfact claim is that the Arbitrator erred by finding that "a 'downgrade' had occurred[,]" because the grievants were never employed at the GS-7 level. Exceptions at 4. As noted previously, the Arbitrator did not find that the grievants were ever actually employed at the GS-7 level; rather, the Arbitrator appears to have used the term "downgrade" to refer to the grievants being initially processed and paid at the GS-6 level after accepting positions at the GS-7 level. *See supra*, note 1. There is no basis for finding that the Arbitrator's statement that this action constituted a "downgrade" is a clearly erroneous factual finding, but for which the Arbitrator would have reached a different conclusion. Accordingly, we deny the exception.

The Agency's second nonfact claim is that the Arbitrator erred in finding a violation of Article 3. Exceptions at 7-8. As stated above, an arbitrator's interpretation of a collective bargaining agreement does not constitute a matter that can be challenged as a nonfact. *See ICE*, 65 FLRA at 795. Accordingly, we deny the exception.[6]

B. The award does not fail to draw its essence from the parties' agreement.

The Authority will find that an arbitration award is deficient as failing to draw its essence from a collective bargaining agreement when the appealing party establishes that the award: (1) cannot in any rational way be derived from the agreement; (2) is so unfounded in reason and fact and so unconnected with the wording and purposes of the collective bargaining agreement as to manifest an infidelity to the obligation of the arbitrator; (3) does not represent a plausible interpretation of the agreement; or (4) evidences a manifest disregard of the agreement. *See U.S. DoL (OSHA)*, 34 FLRA 573, 575 (1990). The Authority and the courts defer to arbitrators in this context "because it is the arbitrator's construction

4. 5 C.F.R. § 300.603 provides, in pertinent part:

> (a) Coverage. This subpart applies to advancement to a [GS] position in the competitive service by any individual who within the previous [fifty-two] weeks held a [GS] position under nontemporary appointment in the competitive or excepted service in the executive branch, unless excluded by paragraph (b) of this section.
>
> (b) Exclusions. The following actions may be taken without regard to this subpart but must be consistent with all other applicable requirements, such as qualification standards:
>
> (1) Appointment based on selection from a competitive examination register of eligibles or under a direct hire authority. . . .

5. 5 C.F.R. § 300.601 provides, in pertinent part, that "[t]he restrictions in this subpart are intended to prevent excessively rapid promotions in competitive service [GS] positions and to protect competitive principles. . . ."

6. Alternatively, we construe the Agency's claim as arguing that the award fails to draw its essence from the parties' agreement, and we address that issue below. In doing so, we note that the Agency's exceptions were filed prior to the October 1, 2010 effective date of the Authority's revised arbitration Regulations.

of the agreement for which the parties have bargained." *Id.* at 576.

The Agency argues that the Arbitrator erred in finding a violation of Article 3 because that provision does not require the Agency to "advance every individual solely because they meet the qualifications[,]" and that the Arbitrator's interpretation of the provision "would lead to the untenable situation where the Agency would be forced to hire all qualified candidates regardless of how many vacancies exist." Exceptions at 8. However, the Arbitrator did not find that Article 3 requires the Agency to either advance or hire all qualified individuals. Thus, the premise of the Agency's argument is incorrect, and we deny the exception.

C. The award is not contrary to law.

The Agency asserts that the award is contrary to law in several respects. The Authority reviews questions of law de novo. *See NTEU, Chapter 24*, 50 FLRA 330, 332 (1995) (citing *U.S. Customs Serv. v. FLRA*, 43 F.3d 682, 686-87 (D.C. Cir. 1994)). In applying a standard of de novo review, the Authority determines whether the arbitrator's legal conclusions are consistent with the applicable standard of law. *NFFE, Local 1437*, 53 FLRA 1703, 1710 (1998). In making that determination, the Authority defers to the arbitrator's underlying factual findings. *See id.*

1. Section 7121(c)(5)

Under § 7121(c)(5), a grievance concerning "the classification of any position which does not result in the reduction in grade or pay of an employee" is removed from the scope of the negotiated grievance procedures. *U.S. Dep't of the Army, U.S. Army Corps of Eng'rs, Nw. Div., Portland, Or.*, 59 FLRA 443, 445 (2003) (*Army*). The Authority has viewed the meaning of "classification" under § 7121(c)(5) in the context of 5 C.F.R. chapter 511. *Id.* 5 C.F.R. § 511.101(c) defines classification of a position as "the analysis and identification of a position and placing it in a class under the position-classification plan established by OPM under chapter 51 of title 5, United States Code." Under the system established by OPM, classification entails the identification of the appropriate title, series, grade, and pay system of a position. *See Army*, 59 FLRA at 445 (citing 5 C.F.R. § 511.701(a)).

Where the essential nature of a grievance concerns the grade level of the duties assigned to and performed by the grievant in his or her permanent position, the grievance concerns the classification of a position within the meaning of § 7121(c)(5). *E.g., U.S. Dep't of HUD*, 65 FLRA 433, 435 (2011) (*HUD*). In addition, a grievance concerns classification within the meaning of § 7121(c)(5) if it contends that the grievant's permanent position warrants a change in its journeyman level or promotion potential. *Id. See also U.S. DoL*, 63 FLRA 216, 218 (2009).

In contrast, a grievance that alleges a right to be placed in previously classified positions does not concern classification. *See HUD*, 65 FLRA at 436. Similarly, a grievance alleging that an agency failed to promote a grievant under a competitive procedure does not concern classification matters. *Id.* In this regard, the Authority has held that where an arbitrator determines that a grievant is entitled to a career-ladder, temporary, or other noncompetitive promotion based on previously classified duties, the award does not concern a classification matter. *See U.S. Dep't of HUD, Wash., D.C.*, 59 FLRA 630, 631 (2004); *see also U.S. Dep't of HHS, Nat'l Inst. for Occupational Safety & Health, Cincinnati Operations, Cincinnati, Ohio*, 52 FLRA 217, 221 (1996). Further, a grievance concerning a delay in receiving a career-ladder promotion does not concern classification. *See U.S. Dep't of HUD*, 47 FLRA 1053, 1061 (1993).

Here, there is no dispute that the journeyman level of the grievants' positions is GS-7. In addition, the grievance did not challenge the journeyman level of the positions or require the Arbitrator to assess the grade level of the duties assigned to and performed by the grievants in those positions. Instead, it argued that the Agency erred by processing the grievants' paperwork, and paying them, at the GS-6 level, rather than the full journeyman level of GS-7. As such, the grievance is more analogous to a grievance alleging a right to be placed in a previously classified GS-7 position, or a grievance challenging a delay in a career-ladder promotion, than it is to a grievance alleging that a position is improperly classified. Accordingly, we find that the grievance did not involve classification within the meaning of § 7121(c)(5), and we deny the exception.

2. 5 C.F.R. § 300.604(b)

5 C.F.R. § 300.604(b) provides, in pertinent part, that "[c]andidates for advancement to a position at GS-6 through GS-11 must have completed a minimum of [fifty-two] weeks in positions . . . [n]o more than one grade lower (or equivalent) when the position to be filled is in a line of work properly classified at [one]-grade intervals[.]" 5 C.F.R. § 300.604(b)(2). The Agency asserts that the award

is contrary to this regulation because the record evidence does not support a conclusion that the grievants were qualified for promotions to the GS-7 level at the time they were hired. *See* Exceptions at 5-6.

Even assuming that 5 C.F.R. § 300.604(b) applies to the hiring of the grievants,[7] the Arbitrator found that the evidence supported a conclusion that the grievants were qualified at the GS-7 level when they were hired, and that the Consultant had made such a determination. The Agency provides no basis for concluding that the Arbitrator erred in making these findings. Thus, the premise of the Agency's exception regarding 5 C.F.R. § 300.604(b) is incorrect, and we deny the exception.

3. The BPA

An award of backpay is authorized under the BPA when an arbitrator finds that: (1) the aggrieved employee was affected by an unjustified or unwarranted personnel action; and (2) the personnel action has resulted in the withdrawal or reduction of the grievant's pay, allowances, or differentials. *E.g., U.S. Dep't of the Army, Headquarters, I Corps & Fort Lewis, Fort Lewis, Wash.*, 65 FLRA 699, 703 (2011). A violation of a collective bargaining agreement constitutes an unjustified or unwarranted personnel action under the BPA. *Id.*

The Arbitrator found that the Agency violated the parties' agreement, which supports a conclusion that the Agency committed an unjustified and unwarranted personnel action. *See id.* Although the Agency argues that its action was not unjustified or unwarranted because it was complying with 5 C.F.R. § 335.103(b)(3), which requires the Agency to comply with 5 C.F.R. § 300.604(b), we have rejected the Agency's claim that the award is contrary to 300.604(b). As such, the premise of the Agency's claim -- that 5 C.F.R. § 300.604(b) compelled the Agency's action -- is unfounded.

With regard to whether the violation resulted in the withdrawal or reduction of the grievants' pay, allowances, or differentials, the Agency argues that the grievants did not suffer such a loss because they were never paid at the GS-7 level. However, the Arbitrator found that the Agency improperly "downgraded" the grievants from GS-7 to GS-6. Award at 18. Thus, he implicitly found that, but for the Agency's improper action, the grievants would have been paid at the GS-7 level. This finding supports a conclusion that the violation resulted in the withdrawal or reduction of the grievants' pay, allowances, or differentials.

For the foregoing reasons, the Arbitrator's findings support a conclusion that the award is consistent with the BPA, and we deny the BPA exception.

D. We deny the Union's request for a remand.

The Union acknowledges that it has not yet requested attorney fees from the Arbitrator, but requests that the Authority remand the award for a determination regarding such fees. Under 5 C.F.R. § 550.807(a), an award of attorney fees is premised on the request of a grievant or a grievant's representative. *U.S. Dep't of the Army, Corps of Eng'rs, Huntington Dist., Huntington, W. Va.*, 59 FLRA 793, 799 (2004). Such a request must be made to the arbitrator, who is the "appropriate authority" under 5 C.F.R. § 550.807(a) to render such an award in the case of an arbitration proceeding. *Id.* Further, there is no legal requirement that arbitrators issue a fee award at the time that they issue an award on the merits of the grievance. *Id.* Rather, the BPA confers statutory jurisdiction on an arbitrator to consider an attorney-fee request filed after the arbitrator's decision awarding backpay. *Phila. Naval Shipyard*, 32 FLRA 417, 421 (1988).

As the BPA confers statutory jurisdiction on the Arbitrator to resolve any Union request for attorney fees, there is no need for the Authority to remand the matter for a determination of fees. Accordingly, we deny the Union's request for a remand.

V. Decision

The Agency's exceptions and the Union's request for a remand are denied.

---

7. As noted previously, 5 C.F.R. § 300.604(b) applies to "*[a]dvancement*" of employees, and 5 C.F.R. § 300.601 pertinently provides that the restrictions in 5 C.F.R. § 300.604(b) "are intended to prevent excessively rapid *promotions* . . . ." (emphases added). The plain wording of these regulations suggests that 5 C.F.R. § 300.604(b) does not apply to the grievants, who were initial hires.

65 FLRA No. 215

UNITED STATES
DEPARTMENT OF VETERANS AFFAIRS
BLACK HILLS HEALTH CARE SYSTEM
HOT SPRINGS, SOUTH DAKOTA
(Agency)

and

AMERICAN FEDERATION
OF GOVERNMENT EMPLOYEES
LOCAL 1539
(Union)

0-AR-4744

DECISION

July 27, 2011

Before the Authority: Carol Waller Pope, Chairman, and Thomas M. Beck and Ernest DuBester, Members

This matter is before the Authority on exceptions to an award of Arbitrator David A. Singer, Jr. filed by the Agency under § 7122(a) of the Federal Service Labor-Management Relations Statute (the Statute) and part 2425 of the Authority's Regulations. The Union filed an opposition to the Agency's exceptions.

Under § 7122(a) of the Statute, an award is deficient if it is contrary to any law, rule, or regulation, or it is deficient on other grounds similar to those applied by federal courts in private sector labor-management relations. Upon careful consideration of the entire record in this case and Authority precedent, the Authority concludes that the award is not deficient on the grounds raised in the exceptions and set forth in § 7122(a).* *U.S. Dep't of the Air Force, Lowry Air Force Base, Denver, Colo.*, 48 FLRA 589, 593-94 (1993) (award not deficient as based on a nonfact where excepting party either challenges a factual matter that the parties disputed at arbitration or fails to demonstrate that the central fact underlying the award is clearly erroneous, but for which a different result would have been reached by the arbitrator); *U.S. Dep't of Labor (OSHA)*, 34 FLRA 573, 575 (1990) (award not deficient as failing to draw its essence from the parties' collective bargaining agreement where excepting party fails to establish that the award: cannot in any rational way be derived from the agreement; is so unfounded in reason and fact and so unconnected to the wording and purpose of the agreement as to manifest an infidelity to the obligation of the arbitrator; does not represent a plausible interpretation of the agreement; or evidences a manifest disregard of the agreement).

Accordingly, the Agency's exceptions are denied.

---

* Because the Agency could have presented to the Arbitrator, but did not, its exceeded-authority and contrary-to-law arguments, these arguments are not properly before the Authority under 5 C.F.R. §§ 2425.4(c) and 2429.5 (2011), and these exceptions are dismissed. *See AFGE, Local 1546*, 65 FLRA 833, 833 (2011).

65 FLRA No. 216

UNITED STATES
DEPARTMENT OF HOMELAND SECURITY
U.S. CUSTOMS AND BORDER PROTECTION
SWANTON, VERMONT
(Respondent)

and

AMERICAN FEDERATION
OF GOVERNMENT EMPLOYEES
AFL-CIO, LOCAL 2774
NATIONAL BORDER PATROL COUNCIL
(Charging Party/Union)

BN-CA-09-0171

DECISION AND ORDER

July 27, 2011

Before the Authority: Carol Waller Pope, Chairman, and Thomas M. Beck and Ernest DuBester, Members

I. Statement of the Case

This unfair labor practice (ULP) case is before the Authority on exceptions to the attached decision of the Administrative Law Judge (the Judge) filed by the General Counsel (GC). The Respondent filed an opposition to the GC's exceptions.

The complaint alleges that the Respondent violated § 7116(a)(1) and (8) of the Federal Service Labor-Management Relations Statute (the Statute) by refusing to fully comply with a final and binding arbitration award. The Judge found that the Respondent did not violate the Statute as alleged, and he recommended dismissing the complaint.

For the reasons that follow, we: deny the GC's exceptions that challenge the Judge's factual findings and allege that the Judge committed prejudicial procedural errors; find that the Respondent violated the Statute as alleged; deny the GC's request for a reinstatement remedy; and grant the GC's remaining requested remedies.

II. Background

The facts are set forth in detail in the Judge's decision and are only briefly summarized here. A Border Patrol agent (the affected employee) was removed from federal service for making false statements in the course of his duties. Judge's Decision at 3. The Charging Party (Union) filed a grievance on the affected employee's behalf, challenging the removal. *Id.* The grievance was unresolved and submitted to arbitration. *Id.* On December 5, 2008, an arbitrator (the arbitrator) issued an award (the award) in which he found that the Respondent had violated the parties' collective bargaining agreement and, as relevant here, directed the Respondent to vacate the removal and reinstate the affected employee. *Id.* In addition, the arbitrator retained jurisdiction "as to any requests for clarification, interpretation[,] and/or implementation" of the award. Jt. Ex. 1 (Arbitration Award) at 30.

The Office of Personnel Management (OPM) did not appeal the award on the Respondent's behalf,[1] and the Respondent proceeded with reinstating the affected employee. Judge's Decision at 3. Shortly before the affected employee's return date of January 5, 2009,[2] officials at the Respondent's national headquarters (HQ) contacted the Respondent's Office of Internal Affairs (Internal Affairs), which informed the HQ officials that the affected employee was due for a periodic background reinvestigation (PRI). *Id.* at 4. The HQ officials determined that a PRI was necessary in order for the affected employee to have access to the Respondent's computer systems, which they asserted was necessary for the affected employee to perform duties as a Border Patrol agent (agent). *Id.* Accordingly, the HQ officials directed the Respondent not to assign the affected employee agent duties. *Id.* Instead, the Respondent assigned him to perform duties as a mission support specialist, but after a day or two in that position, the Respondent determined that those duties required computer access. *Id.* Accordingly,

1. As discussed further below, only the Director of the OPM could appeal the award on the Respondent's behalf, and only after seeking reconsideration from the arbitrator. At the ULP hearing, the Respondent conceded that OPM did not request reconsideration from the arbitrator. *See* Tr. at 9. However, the Judge did not address, and the record does not indicate, whether the Respondent requested OPM to do so.

2. In this regard, a Respondent witness testified, without dispute, that he contacted Internal Affairs "a few days" before the affected employee's return and was informed of the need to conduct a PRI. Tr. at 128.

the Respondent placed the affected employee on paid administrative leave. *Id.* Subsequently, Internal Affairs conducted the PRI and, in approximately September 2009, informed the Respondent that the PRI was completed and that the affected employee did not pass it. *Id.*

The Union filed a charge, and the GC issued a complaint, alleging that the Respondent violated § 7116(a)(1) and (8) of the Statute by failing to fully comply with the award. *Id.* at 1-2.

III. Judge's Decision

The Judge found that the award had clearly directed the Respondent to return the affected employee to his duties as an agent. Judge's Decision at 7-8. In addition, the Judge determined that the Respondent failed to fully comply with the award because it reinstated the affected employee for only two days before placing him in a non-duty status. *Id.* at 7. The Judge found that, while the affected employee was in a non-duty status, he did not have "the opportunity to earn administratively uncontrollable overtime and other types of premium pay or to be considered for training, details or promotion." *Id.* at 4.

In addressing whether the Respondent had a valid justification for failing to fully comply, the Judge stated that there is "little or no Authority precedent on this point, particularly in employee removal cases," but that there is a "substantial body" of Merit Systems Protection Board (MSPB) precedent. *Id.* at 8. In this regard, the Judge found that the MSPB has held that agencies may decline to return reinstated employees to their former positions when the agencies have a "strong, overriding interest" for doing so. *Id.* (citations omitted). The Judge also found that the MSPB has held that agencies are entitled to "special deference" when compliance issues are "entwined with security concerns[,]" and that the MSPB has upheld employee removals when the employees' security clearances have been revoked. *Id.* at 9.

In addition, the Judge found that 5 C.F.R. § 732.201(a) requires agencies to designate as sensitive any position that could have a "material adverse effect on the national security[,]" and that "Critical-Sensitive[]" is one designation for a sensitive position. *Id.* at 10. He also found that the agent position is a "Critical-Sensitive" position and that, under the Respondent's Personnel Security Handbook (the Handbook), "[a]ll employees are subject to a [PRI] to ensure continued suitability for employment." *Id.* The Judge noted that the Handbook addresses PRIs separately from security clearances, and stated that the record does not indicate whether agents are required to have security clearances. *Id.* He also noted that MSPB precedent on which he relied involved security clearances, and he stated that it was "not entirely clear . . . whether the same principles of 'special deference' to executive decisions on security clearances are applicable to cases involving [PRIs]." *Id.* at 11. While acknowledging that PRIs "are not, in and of themselves, security clearance determinations," the Judge determined that, because both security clearances and PRIs raise national security concerns, there was no "meaningful distinction" between them in the context of this case. *Id.*

Further, the Judge determined that agents who have been "off rolls" and return to active duty must pass a PRI before they may access the Respondent's computer systems, "unless they have a current PRI in their files." *Id.* at 12. In this connection, the Judge stated that until the affected employee passed a PRI, "he would not have access to the [Respondent's] computer systems or email, precluding him from performing his duties as a[n] [agent]." *Id.* at 4. In addition, the Judge determined that the affected employee had been in a non-duty status from 2005 until January 2009, and that his previous PRI had been performed in 1997. *Id.* at 12. Thus, the Judge found that the Respondent's "normal security procedures" required a new PRI for the affected employee. *Id.* In addition, the Judge found that the Respondent had not raised the issue of the affected employee's PRI during the arbitration proceedings that resulted in the award "because the need to perform a PRI did not arise" until after the arbitrator directed the Respondent to reinstate the affected employee. *Id.*

Moreover, the Judge found that, in order for the Respondent to fully comply with the award and fully reinstate the affected employee as an agent, the Respondent would have been required to "override or violate the procedures requiring PRIs[]" because "[i]t would have had to give access to the [Respondent's] automated systems (and all the sensitive information that might be contained therein) to a person whose 'continued employment' has been determined not to be 'consistent with the interests of the national security.'" *Id.* (quoting 5 C.F.R. § 732.203). In addition, the Judge determined that directing the Respondent to do so would "not merely review the substance of the PRI determination, but override the PRI entirely." *Id.* Accordingly, the Judge concluded that the Respondent had "compelling and overriding reasons" for placing the affected employee on administrative leave until he passed his PRI, and in keeping him off active duty when he later failed his PRI. *Id.* at 13. In this connection, the Judge found that after the affected employee failed his PRI, he could not have computer access and, thus, was "unable to perform a significant component of his duties as a[n] . . . [a]gent." *Id.* at 12.

The Judge also found that the Respondent's actions did not constitute a "collateral attack" on the award because the Respondent was not disputing the arbitrator's factual or legal conclusions but, instead, "based its actions on additional facts that did not exist at the time of the arbitration hearing: [the affected employee's] failure to pass his PRI and his consequent inability to perform the duties of a[n] [agent]." *Id.* at 13.

Based on the foregoing, the Judge found that the Respondent did not violate the Statute as alleged, and he recommended dismissing the complaint. *Id.* at 14.

IV. Positions of the Parties

A. GC's Exceptions

The GC asserts that the Judge's factual findings omit relevant evidence in two respects. First, the GC contends that the record supports a "reasonable inference" that, during the arbitration proceedings, the Respondent could have anticipated, and notified the arbitrator of the possibility, that the affected employee would need a PRI in the event that he was ultimately reinstated. GC's Exceptions at 6. Second, the GC argues that the Judge's finding that lack of computer access precluded the affected employee from performing agent duties is "not entirely accurate," because the Respondent could have assigned him administrative duties as an agent, and hearing testimony indicated only that the affected employee could not perform agent duties "efficiently" without computer access -- not that he could not have performed them at all. *Id.*

The GC also asserts that the Judge's findings are "internally inconsistent and arbitrary" because the Judge "effectively equat[ed]" PRIs and security clearances after finding no evidence that agents are required to have security clearances and stating that it was unclear whether agency determinations regarding PRIs are entitled to the same deference as determinations regarding security clearances. *Id.* at 12-13. In addition, the GC argues that the Judge erred by finding that, in order for the Respondent to comply with the award, it would have had to grant computer access to an individual whose continued employment "'*has been determined*'" not to be consistent with the interests of national security. *Id.* at 15 (quoting Judge's Decision at 12 (emphasis added by GC)). In this connection, the GC asserts that, when the Respondent failed to reinstate the affected employee to agent duties in January 2009, no such determination had been made because the affected employee had not yet failed his PRI. *Id.*

The GC also argues that the Judge erred by admitting the Handbook into evidence. *Id.* at 9. In this regard, the GC asserts that the Respondent did not list the Handbook in its prehearing disclosure, as required by § 2423.23 of the Authority's Regulations,[3] but that the Handbook was admitted at the Judge's prompting and over the GC's objection. *Id.* at 9-10. According to the GC, without the Handbook, there is no record evidence to support the Judge's findings regarding the purported "national security" implications of a PRI. *Id.* at 11. Thus, the GC claims that the Judge denied the GC due process because he then "used the Handbook to invent" a national security defense that the Respondent had not presented. *Id.*

Moreover, the GC argues that the Judge erred by relying on MSPB precedent to conclude that the Respondent had a valid justification for failing to comply with the award. *Id.* at 6-7. In this regard, the GC contends that, in the ULP forum, a respondent may not collaterally attack an arbitration award, *see id.* at 14-16, and a party cannot defend its noncompliance with a final and binding arbitrator's award on grounds that could have been raised on review under 5 U.S.C. § 7122, *see id.* at 7. The GC asserts that because "OPM did not appeal . . . [the a]ward, the Respondent has no options left but to comply" with it. *Id.* at 9. Further, the GC contends that the Authority's decision in *United States Department of Transportation, Federal Aviation Administration*, 54 FLRA 480 (1998) (*FAA*), is "directly on point" and precludes the Respondent's defense here. GC's Exceptions at 8. Moreover, the GC argues that, contrary to the Judge's finding, an order directing the Respondent to comply with the award would not require the Authority to review the PRI determination, because the unlawful conduct was placing the affected employee on administrative leave in January 2009, before the PRI was conducted. *Id.* at 13. Nevertheless, the GC requests that the Authority issue an order that includes a direction to reinstate the affected employee. *See id.* at 19. The

3. The pertinent wording of § 2423.23 of the Authority's Regulations is set forth below.

GC also requests a make-whole remedy for the affected employee, as well as a nationwide posting of a notice signed by the highest official of the Respondent. *See id.* at 17-19.

B. Respondent's Opposition

The Respondent asserts that the record supports the Judge's factual findings. Respondent's Opp'n at 2. With regard to whether the Respondent could have informed the arbitrator about the potential need for a PRI, the Respondent contends that the record evidence indicates that, although there was speculation that the affected employee was due for a PRI, the PRI was initiated by Internal Affairs' Personnel Security Division, and the Respondent neither had control over the PRI process nor knew what the outcome of that process would be. *Id.* at 4.

The Respondent also asserts that the Judge properly exercised his discretion in admitting the Handbook into evidence. *Id.* at 8. In addition, the Respondent argues that the Judge did not "invent" a defense for the Respondent, but found persuasive a defense that the Respondent had "repeatedly raised[.]" *Id.* at 9.

Further, the Respondent argues that the Judge correctly determined that there was a compelling reason for the Respondent not to fully implement the award. *Id.* at 4. The Respondent also argues that the Judge correctly determined that the Respondent did not collaterally attack the award because the factors that limited the affected employee's ability to return to duty did not exist at the time of the arbitration hearing. *Id.* at 12. Finally, the Respondent claims that the Judge correctly determined that, in order for the Respondent to comply with the award and fully reinstate the affected employee, the Respondent would be required to "override or violate the procedures requiring PRIs." *Id.* at 11.[4]

4. In addition, the Respondent claims that it acted in accordance with its "reasonable" construction of the award. Respondent's Opp'n at 6-7. However, the Judge rejected the Respondent's claim that it "acted reasonably[,]" Judge's Decision at 7, and the Respondent did not except or cross-except to that finding. Accordingly, we do not address the Respondent's claim further.

V. Analysis and Conclusions

A. The Judge's factual findings are not deficient.

Several of the GC's arguments effectively challenge the Judge's factual findings and his failure to make other factual findings. In determining whether a judge's factual findings are supported, the Authority looks to the preponderance of the record evidence.[5] *U.S. Dep't of Transp., FAA*, 64 FLRA 365, 368 (2009) (Member Beck concurring).

The GC claims that the evidence supports a "reasonable inference" that, during the arbitration proceedings, the Respondent could have anticipated that the affected employee would need to undergo a PRI if he were ultimately reinstated. However, the Judge found that the Respondent's HQ officials did not become aware of the need for the affected employee to undergo a PRI until *after* the award issued, when they contacted Internal Affairs and were informed that the affected employee was due for a PRI. *See* Judge's Decision at 12. A preponderance of the record evidence supports this factual finding. *See, e.g.*, Tr. at 129 (Respondent witness testified that he did not ask Internal Affairs whether the affected employee was due for next PRI "until after the arbitration award came out"); *id.* at 161 (testimony that, in January 2009, human resources contacted Internal Affairs and asked whether a PRI was needed); *id.* at 162 (testimony that the affected employee "was officially off rolls, so he would not have come up" in the system that notifies the Respondent when an employee's PRI is due); *id.* at 114 & 125 (Respondent witness testified that, although he believed the affected employee "probably" needed a PRI, he "didn't know"); *id.* at 128 (testimony that management contacted Internal Affairs "a day or two" before the affected employee's reinstatement); *id.* at 131 (Respondent witness testified that he was not "privy" to "most of the

5. Member Beck notes that, for the reasons stated in his separate opinions in *Social Security Administration*, 64 FLRA 199, 207 (2009) (Dissenting Opinion of Member Beck), *United States Department of the Air Force, Air Force Materiel Command, Space and Missile Systems Center, Detachment 12, Kirtland Air Force Base, New Mexico*, 64 FLRA 166, 179-80 (2009) (Concurring Opinion of Member Beck), and *United States Department of the Air Force, 12th Flying Training Wing, Randolph Air Force Base, San Antonio, Texas*, 63 FLRA 256, 262-63 (2009) (Concurring Opinion of Member Beck), he reviews the Judge's factual findings using a "substantial evidence in the record" standard rather than a "preponderance" standard.

particulars" of the case). In addition, the Judge found that agents who have been "off rolls" and are returning to active duty must pass a PRI in order to gain access to the Respondent's computer systems, "*unless* they have a current PRI in their files." Judge's Decision at 12 (emphasis added). In other words, if an agent has a current PRI in his or her files, then the agent is not required to have a PRI conducted. Thus, it was reasonable for the Respondent to have been unaware, at the time of the arbitration proceedings, that the affected employee needed a PRI before he could be fully reinstated. For these reasons, there is no basis for concluding that the Judge erred in failing to find that, at the time of the arbitration proceedings, the Respondent should have anticipated and raised the possibility that the affected employee might need to undergo a PRI in the ultimate event of his reinstatement.

The GC also challenges the Judge's finding that lack of computer access precluded the affected employee from performing agent duties. *See* GC's Exceptions at 6. In this connection, the Judge stated that until the affected employee passed his PRI, "he would not have access to the [Respondent's] computer systems or email, precluding him from performing his duties as a[n] [agent]." Judge's Decision at 4. However, the Judge also stated that a lack of access to the Respondent's "computer and security systems" after the affected employee failed to pass his PRI resulted in him being "unable to perform a *significant component* of his duties as a[n] . . . [agent]." *Id.* at 12 (emphasis added). Reading the two statements together, it is apparent that the Judge found only that the lack of computer access precluded the affected employee from performing a "significant component" of agent duties, *id.* -- not that it precluded him from performing *any agent duties at all*. Thus, the premise of the GC's argument is misplaced and does not provide a basis for finding that the Judge erred in this regard.

In addition, the GC alleges that the Judge's findings are "internally inconsistent and arbitrary" because the Judge "effectively equat[ed]" PRIs and security clearances after finding no evidence that agents are required to have security clearances and stating that it was unclear whether agency determinations regarding PRIs are entitled to the same deference as determinations regarding security clearances. GC's Exceptions at 12-13. In this connection, the Judge acknowledged that security clearances and PRIs are not the same thing, but found that, in the context of this case, there is no "meaningful" distinction between them. Judge's Decision at 11. The GC does not explain, or provide any basis for finding, that these findings are "internally inconsistent" or "arbitrary." GC's Exceptions at 12. Thus, the GC does not demonstrate that the Judge erred in this regard.

Finally, the GC asserts that the Judge erred in stating that, in order to comply with the award, the Respondent would have had to give computer access to a person whose continued employment "*has been determined*" not to be consistent with the interests of national security. GC's Exceptions at 15 (quoting Judge's Decision at 12 (emphasis added by GC)). According to the GC, at the time when the affected employee was reinstated, such a national security determination had not yet been made. Even assuming that the Judge's use of the phrase "has been determined" is a misstatement, there is no basis for finding that this alleged misstatement is material. In this regard, the Judge also found that the Respondent could not fully comply because the affected employee could not be reinstated to all of his former duties until he passed his PRI, and the GC does not demonstrate that this finding is deficient. Thus, the GC's assertion does not provide a basis for reversing the Judge.

For the foregoing reasons, we find that the Judge's factual findings are not deficient.

B. The Judge did not commit prejudicial procedural errors.

The GC claims that the Judge deprived the GC of due process, and acted contrary to § 2423.23 of the Authority's Regulations, by allowing the Handbook into evidence and then relying on it to "invent" a national security defense that the Respondent had not presented. GC's Exceptions at 11. With regard to the GC's due-process argument, the Respondent -- not the Judge -- raised a national security defense in the first instance. In this connection, the Respondent's prehearing disclosure stated, in pertinent part: "Pursuant to 5 C.F.R. § 732.203, [the affected employee] was required to undergo his [PRI] after being reinstated[,]" and "[b]ecause of [this and other] concerns, the Respondent had a compelling reason to place [the affected employee] on administrative leave after reinstating him as a[n] [agent]." Disclosure at 2. As the Judge stated, 5 C.F.R. § 732.203 addresses "national security." Judge's Decision at 10. Further, in its post-hearing brief, the Respondent again raised concerns regarding the PRI process, and made arguments and cited MSPB precedent regarding the loss of security clearances. *See* Respondent's Post-Hearing Brief at 8, 14-15. Thus, the Respondent raised a national security defense, separate and apart from the Handbook, and the Judge did not "invent" such a defense for the Respondent. GC's Exceptions at 11.

With regard to whether admission of the Handbook denied the GC due process, during the hearing, after extensive witness testimony regarding the PRI process, the Judge asked the Respondent's attorney whether he intended to admit into evidence "whatever regulation . . . governs these [PRIs]." Tr. at 145. In this connection, the Judge stated that "to the degree that [the Respondent was] essentially raising a defense that the decision to keep [the affected employee] off of active duty was based on the concern that he was not going to pass the [PRI], I think it is relevant to have the regulation itself for me to consider. And so rather than asking a lot of questions of either this or the next witness about all that, having the regulation itself might be more straightforward." *Id.* at 146. During the questioning of the next witness, the Respondent then moved to introduce the Handbook. *Id.* at 151. Although the GC objected to its admission, the Judge did not deprive the GC of the opportunity to ask questions or present evidence or arguments regarding it, and the GC could have made arguments regarding it in its post-hearing brief. Further, as discussed above, the Respondent's pre-hearing disclosure and witness testimony expressly raised and discussed the PRI process. Thus, there is no basis for finding that the GC was prejudiced by the Judge's admission of the Handbook.

With regard to the GC's reliance on § 2423.23 of the Authority's Regulations, that Regulation, entitled "Prehearing disclosure[,]" provides, in pertinent part: "*Unless otherwise directed or approved by the Judge*, the parties shall exchange[] . . . the following items at least [fourteen] days prior to the hearing: . . . (b) *Documents.* Copies of documents, with an index, proposed to be offered into evidence[.] . . ." (emphasis added). Under the plain terms of the Regulation, the Judge had discretion to allow the Respondent to introduce the Handbook, even though it had not been included in the Respondent's prehearing disclosure. Further, it is well established that, under § 2423.31(b) of the Authority's Regulations, the determination of matters to be admitted into evidence is within the discretion of the administrative law judge. *E.g., U.S. Dep't of Veterans Affairs, Golden Gate Nat'l Cemetery, San Bruno, Cal.*, 59 FLRA 956, 959 n.7 (2004) (Chairman Cabaniss dissenting in part). Thus, the Judge did not act contrary to § 2423.23 by admitting the Handbook into evidence.

For the foregoing reasons, we find that the Judge did not commit prejudicial procedural errors.

C. The Judge erred by finding that the Respondent did not violate § 7116(a)(1) and (8) of the Statute as alleged.

Under § 7121(e) of the Statute, a party may challenge an adverse action within the meaning of 5 U.S.C. § 7512 (§ 7512), such as a removal, under either the appellate procedures of the MSPB or the parties' negotiated grievance procedure (NGP) if such matters have not been excluded from the NGP. *U.S. Army, Adjutant Gen. Publ'ns Ctr., St. Louis, Mo.*, 22 FLRA 200, 203-04 (1986) (*Army*). If the action is challenged under the NGP and the matter is submitted to arbitration, then the arbitrator is governed by 5 U.S.C. § 7701(c)(1), pertaining to the appellate procedures of the MSPB. *See id.* at 204.

In addition, § 7121(f) of the Statute (§ 7121(f)) states that 5 U.S.C. § 7703 (§ 7703), which deals with judicial review of final MSPB decisions, also applies to arbitration awards pertaining to matters covered under §§ 7303 and 7512. *See id.* at 204-05. Thus, a party that wishes to appeal such an award may not file exceptions with the Authority. *See id.* at 203. Further, pursuant to the framework for judicial review set forth in §§ 7121(f) and 7703, agencies may not directly obtain judicial review of such awards. *See id.* at 205. Rather, § 7703(d) provides, in pertinent part:

> The Director of . . . [OPM (the Director)] may obtain review of any final order or decision of the [arbitrator] by filing, within [sixty] days after the date the Director received notice of the final order or decision of the [arbitrator], a petition for judicial review in the United States Court of Appeals for the Federal Circuit [(the Federal Circuit)] if the Director determines, in his discretion, that the [arbitrator] erred in interpreting a civil service law, rule, or regulation affecting personnel management and that the [arbitrator's] decision will have a substantial impact on a civil service law, rule, regulation, or policy directive. If the Director did not intervene in a matter before the [arbitrator], the Director may not petition for review of [an arbitrator's] decision under this section unless the Director first petitions the [arbitrator] for a reconsideration of [his or her] decision, and such a petition is denied. . . . The granting of the petition for

judicial review shall be at the discretion of the Court of Appeals.

5 U.S.C. § 7703(d).

If the Director does not file a timely petition for review of the arbitration award, then the award is considered final and binding. *See Army*, 22 FLRA at 207-08. At that point, a party that fails to comply with the award's unambiguous terms constitutes a ULP. *Id.* at 208. Thus, although the Authority lacks jurisdiction to resolve exceptions to an award regarding a § 7121(f) matter, the Authority may review in a ULP proceeding the alleged noncompliance with such awards. *Id.* at 207. In doing so, as with other awards, the Authority will not allow the respondent to collaterally attack the award. *See id.* at 206. *Cf. FAA*, 54 FLRA 480, 484 (review of arbitration award finding ULP for failure to comply with previous arbitration award); *U.S. Dep't of the Air Force, Carswell Air Force Base, Tex.*, 38 FLRA 99, 107 (1990) (in non-§ 7121(f) cases, claim that award is inconsistent with law, rule or regulation should be raised as an exception to award, and if party fails to do so, then it "must comply" with final award). In this connection, the Authority has held that to allow for such a collateral attack would circumvent congressional intent with respect to statutory review procedures and the finality of arbitration awards. *See Army,* 22 FLRA at 206.

In assessing whether an agency has failed to comply with a final and binding arbitration award regarding a removal, the Authority previously has relied on the fact that the agency failed to request OPM to seek Federal Circuit review of the award. Specifically, in *FAA*, the Authority stated that, following the issuance of an award directing an agency to reinstate a grievant, "[i]f the [a]gency had any concerns about reinstating [the grievant] to [the] duties [of her position] . . . , the [a]gency could have either raised them before [the] [a]rbitrator . . . or asked the Director of OPM to seek review of the award in the Federal Circuit in accordance with [§] 7703(d)." 54 FLRA at 485. As "[t]he [a]gency did neither[,]" the Authority found that the "award became final and binding, and [§] 7122(b) of the Statute mandated that the [a]gency comply with the . . . award." *Id.*

Here, as stated previously, the Respondent became aware of the need to conduct a PRI for the affected employee shortly before his return date of January 5, 2009. In his December 5, 2008 award, the arbitrator had retained jurisdiction "as to any requests for clarification, interpretation[,] and/or implementation of th[e] [a]ward[,]" and did not limit the period of time of his retention of jurisdiction. Arbitration Award at 30. Thus, there is no basis for finding that the Respondent could not have raised its concerns about the PRI to the arbitrator when it became aware of the need to conduct a PRI. There also is no dispute that the Respondent could have requested OPM to petition the arbitrator for reconsideration and, if that was unsuccessful, to petition the Federal Circuit for review. However, there is no claim or record evidence that the Respondent took any of these actions. As such, *FAA* supports a conclusion that the "award became final and binding, and [§] 7122(b) of the Statute mandated that the [Respondent] comply" with it by reinstating the affected employee to agent duties. 54 FLRA at 485. As the Respondent did not comply with the award by reinstating the affected employee to agent duties, we find that the Respondent failed to fully comply with the arbitration award and thereby violated § 7116(a)(1) and (8) of the Statute.

D. We grant the GC's requested remedies in part and deny them in part.

The GC requests an order to reinstate the affected employee. The Authority has found it appropriate to consider "intervening events" in assessing the propriety of requested remedies. *U.S. DoL, Wash., D.C.*, 61 FLRA 603, 605 (2006) (then-Member Pope dissenting in part on other grounds). *See also U.S. Dep't of the Air Force, Aerospace Maint. & Regeneration Ctr., Davis-Monthan Air Force Base, Tucson, Ariz.*, 64 FLRA 355, 361 (2009) (Member Beck concurring in part and dissenting in part) (*Davis-Monthan*) ("in considering the remedy for [a] ULP, it is appropriate to take into account the remedies awarded in other appeals processes" such as MSPB proceedings); *U.S. Dep't of Transp. & FAA*, 48 FLRA 1211, 1214 n.2 (1993), *pet. for review denied sub nom., PASS v. FLRA*, 52 F.3d 1123 (D.C. Cir. 1995) (unpublished) (assessment of whether status quo ante relief is appropriate "necessarily may result in consideration of events that have transpired subsequent to, and as a consequence of, a unilateral implementation of a change in conditions of employment").

Here, after the affected employee returned to work and was placed on administrative leave, Internal Affairs conducted, and the affected employee failed, a PRI. There is no claim or record evidence that the failure to pass the PRI resulted from any unlawful conduct by the Respondent. Thus, an intervening event -- the affected employee's failure to pass a PRI -- resulted in the employee being unable to perform the duties of his position. In these circumstances, we find that a reinstatement remedy is not warranted, and deny the GC's request for such a remedy. Although the GC claims that directing the Respondent to fully comply with the award would not require the Authority to review the PRI determination, directing the Respondent to fully comply with the award and reinstate the affected employee to agent duties would "override the PRI entirely[,]" as the Judge found. Judge's Decision at 12. Accordingly, we reject the GC's argument.

With regard to the GC's request for make-whole relief, the Authority regularly grants such a remedy in ULP cases. *See, e.g., Davis-Monthan*, 64 FLRA at 361; *SSA*, 64 FLRA 199, 205 (2009) (Member Beck dissenting in part on other grounds). The Judge found that while the affected employee was on administrative leave, he did not have "the opportunity to earn administratively uncontrollable overtime and other types of premium pay or to be considered for training, details or promotion." Judge's Decision at 4. The Respondent does not address, and thus does not oppose, the GC's request for these forms of make-whole relief. Accordingly, we grant an appropriate make-whole remedy for the period of time between the affected employee's placement on administrative leave and the time that he failed his PRI in September 2009.[6]

Finally, the GC requests a nationwide posting signed by the highest official of the Respondent. In determining the scope of a posting requirement, the Authority considers the two purposes served by the posting of a notice. *E.g., SSA, Balt., Md. & SSA, Office of Hearings & Appeals, Kan. City, Mo. & SSA, Office of Hearings & Appeals, St. Louis, Mo.*, 60 FLRA 674, 681 (2005) (*SSA*). First, the notice provides evidence to unit employees that the rights guaranteed under the Statute will be vigorously enforced. *Id.* Second, in many cases the posting is the only visible indication to those employees that a respondent recognizes and intends to fulfill its obligations under the Statute. *Id.* In applying this test, a relevant factor is whether the national office of a respondent was involved in the statutory violations. *Id.* at 682. *See also U.S. Dep't of the Treasury, IRS*, 56 FLRA 906, 913 (2000) (*IRS*). Where that has been the case, and the Authority has directed a nationwide posting, the Authority also has directed the highest official of the national office to sign the posting. *See, e.g., SSA*, 60 FLRA at 682; *IRS*, 56 FLRA at 914.

The Judge found, and there is no dispute, that the Respondent's national HQ directed the Respondent not to assign agent duties to the affected employee upon his reinstatement. *See* Judge's Decision at 4. In addition, the Respondent does not address, and thus does not oppose, the GC's request for a nationwide posting signed by the highest official of the Respondent's national office. In these circumstances, we grant the GC's request for a nationwide posting signed by the Chief of the Border Patrol.

VI. Order

Pursuant to § 2423.41 of the Authority's Regulations and § 7118 of the Statute, the Respondent shall:

1. Cease and desist from:

(a) Failing and refusing to fully comply with the award issued by Arbitrator Parker Denaco on December 5, 2008 (the Denaco award).

(b) In any like or related manner, interfering with, restraining, or coercing its employees in the exercise of their rights assured them by the Statute.

2. Take the following affirmative action in order to effectuate the purposes and policies of the Statute:

(a) Make whole the employee whose removal was at issue in the Denaco award by paying him backpay, with interest, for all pay that he lost as a result of the Respondent's failure to comply with the Denaco award, through the time of his failure to pass his periodic reinvestigation in September of 2009.

(b) Post at its facilities, where bargaining unit employees represented by the Union are located, copies of the attached Notice on forms to be furnished by the Authority. Upon receipt of such forms, they shall be signed by the Chief of the Border Patrol, and shall be posted and maintained for 60 consecutive days thereafter in conspicuous places, including all bulletin boards and other places where notices to employees are customarily posted.

6. We note that undisputed record evidence indicates that "if an agent is performing his or her responsibilities in the course of th[e] five years [between PRIs], ordinarily that agent just continues his responsibilities while the [PRI] is being done[.]" Tr. at 127. By contrast, if an agent has been "inactive" in the Respondent's computer systems for more than forty-five days, then the agent is "locked out" of the system and must have access restored. *Id.* at 136. Thus, if the affected employee had been continuously performing agent duties, then he would have continued to have access to the computer systems while his PRI was conducted.

Reasonable steps shall be taken to ensure that such Notices are not altered, defaced, or covered by any other material.

(c) Pursuant to § 2423.41(e) of the Authority's Regulations, notify the Regional Director, Boston Regional Office, Federal Labor Relations Authority, in writing, within 30 days from the date of this Order, as to what steps have been taken to comply.

NOTICE TO ALL EMPLOYEES
POSTED BY ORDER OF THE
FEDERAL LABOR RELATIONS AUTHORITY

The Federal Labor Relations Authority has found that the United States Department of Homeland Security, U.S. Customs and Border Protection, Swanton, Vermont, violated the Federal Service Labor-Management Relations Statute and has ordered us to post and abide by this notice.

WE HEREBY NOTIFY OUR EMPLOYEES THAT:

WE RECOGNIZE that the Federal Service Labor-Management Relations Statute (the Statute) requires an agency to take the actions required by an arbitrator's final award.

WE WILL NOT fail and refuse to fully comply with the award issued by Arbitrator Parker Denaco on December 5, 2008 (the Denaco award).

WE WILL NOT in any like or related manner interfere with, restrain, or coerce bargaining unit employees in the exercise of their rights assured them by the Statute.

WE WILL make whole the employee whose removal was at issue in the Denaco award by paying him backpay, with interest, for all pay that he lost as a result of the Respondent's failure to comply with the Denaco award, through the time of his failure to pass his periodic reinvestigation in September of 2009.

____
(Respondent)

Dated: ________ By: ____________________
(Signature) (Title)

This Notice must remain posted for 60 consecutive days from the date of the posting, and must not be altered, defaced, or covered by any other material.

If employees have any questions concerning this Notice or compliance with its provisions, they may communicate directly with the Regional Director, Boston Regional Office, Federal Labor Relations Authority, whose address is: Thomas P. O'Neill, Jr. Federal Building, 10 Causeway Street, Suite 472, Boston, MA 02222, and whose telephone number is: (617) 565-5100.

Office of Administrative Law Judges

DEPARTMENT OF HOMELAND SECURITY
U.S. CUSTOMS AND BORDER PROTECTION
SWANTON, VERMONT
Respondent

and

NATIONAL BORDER PATROL COUNCIL,
AMERICAN FEDERATION OF GOVERNMENT
EMPLOYEES, AFL-CIO, LOCAL 2774
Charging Party

Gerard M. Greene
For the General Counsel

David A. Markowitz
For the Respondent

Patricia T. Nighswander
For the Charging Party

Before: RICHARD A. PEARSON
Administrative Law Judge

DECISION

STATEMENT OF THE CASE

This is an unfair labor practice proceeding under the Federal Service Labor-Management Relations Statute, 5 U.S.C. §§ 7101-7135 (the Statute), and the Rules and Regulations of the Federal Labor Relations Authority (the Authority), 5 C.F.R. part 2423.

On March 3, 2009, the National Border Patrol Council, American Federation of Government Employees, AFL-CIO, Local 2774 (the Union or the Charging Party) filed an unfair labor practice charge against the Department of Homeland Security, U.S. Customs and Border Protection, Swanton, Vermont (the Agency or the Respondent). After investigating the charges, the Acting Regional Director of the Boston Region of the Authority issued a Complaint and Notice of Hearing on December 18, 2009, alleging that the Agency had refused to fully comply with a final arbitration award as required by Sections 7121 and 7122 of the Statute, and that such refusal constituted an unfair labor practice in violation of section 7116(a)(1) and (8) of the Statute. The Respondent filed its Answer to the Complaint on January 12, 2010, denying that it refused to comply with the award or committed any unfair labor practice.

A hearing was held in this matter on February 3, 2010, in Burlington, Vermont. All parties were represented and afforded the opportunity to be heard, to introduce evidence, and to examine witnesses. The General Counsel and Respondent filed post-hearing briefs, which I have fully considered.

Based on the entire record[1] including my observation of the witnesses and their demeanor, I make the following findings of fact, conclusions of law, and recommendations.

FINDINGS OF FACT

Ross D. Schofield was hired by the Immigration and Naturalization Service (which later merged into the Respondent) in 1997 as a Border Patrol Agent. In February of 2005, he was working as a GS-1896-11 Border Patrol Agent assigned to the Newport, Vermont, Border Patrol Station, which is one of eight stations in the Swanton Sector that covers the U.S.-Canada border in New York and Vermont. At that time, Agent Schofield and two other agents were involved in the apprehension and release of a drug smuggling suspect and the seizure of 60 pounds of marijuana. Jt. Ex. 1 at 8-9. In the weeks after the incident, officials of the Agency, as well as officials of Immigration and Customs Enforcement, the Drug Enforcement Administration and the Newport police, came to believe that the three agents had falsified information on the documents relating to the drug seizure: although the documents prepared by the agents indicated that they had found the marijuana "abandoned" on a roadside and concealed the fact that a suspect in possession of the drugs had initially been arrested, contradictory details began to surface. *Id.* at 10-11. Upon further questioning, Schofield and the other two agents admitted that they had falsified details of their reports in order to utilize the drug suspect as an informant and to provide the suspect with a plausible alibi for losing his drugs. *Id.* at 9-10, 12, 18-20. They believed that such falsification was justifiable based on a prior case at the Newport Station. *Id.* at 10, 13.

---

[1] The General Counsel noted some corrections to the transcript in its post-hearing brief. While these corrections were untimely under 5 C.F.R. § 2423.21(b)(4), I have independently determined that they, as well as other corrections are appropriate, as follows: 1) Wherever the name "Aguila" occurs, it should be replaced with "Aguilar"; 2) On page 9, line 6, "McCole" should be replaced with "make whole"; 3) On page 75, line 25, "his" should be replaced with "your"; and 4) On page 125, line 17, "OPF" should be replaced with "OPM."

After an investigation, the agents were indicted in November 2005 by a Federal grand jury on a series of charges including conspiracy and the making of materially false statements to Federal officials. Shortly thereafter, Schofield was placed on indefinite suspension by the Agency, based on his indictment. *Id.* at 13. However, the criminal charges against Schofield were dropped by the U.S. Attorney in July 2006, causing the Agency to rescind his suspension, place him on paid duty status and on administrative leave pending further disciplinary investigation. *Id.* The case was presented to the Agency's National Disciplinary Review Board, and in November 2007 the Agency issued a notice of intent to remove Agent Schofield from the Federal service. The Agency characterized his series of false statements as "wrong and deceptive," alleging that he had "jeopardized the mission and significantly damaged the credibility of the CBP/Border Patrol as a law enforcement agency," and that he had "demonstrated complete disregard for the drug interdiction process and the interagency coordination that exists." *Id.* at 14.

The Union filed a grievance on Agent Schofield's behalf, challenging the removal; after conducting a hearing on the grievance, Arbitrator Parker Denaco issued a decision and award on December 5, 2008. Jt. Ex. 1 (the Award). The Union challenged the Agency's removal of Agent Schofield both on the merits of the case and on the ground that the Agency had violated Article 32(G) of the collective bargaining agreement, which requires the Agency to furnish employees with notices of proposed adverse actions "at the earliest practicable date[.]" The arbitrator analyzed prior arbitration precedent between these parties concerning Article 32(G), concluding that the provision is not merely procedural but substantive, thus obviating the need for the grievant to show harmful error from a delay. *Id.* at 23-24. Noting that the Agency proposed Schofield's removal 33 months after the alleged misconduct, or 16 months after the Federal indictment against Schofield was dismissed, the arbitrator determined that the latter period was unjustifiable; thus he concluded that the Agency had violated Article 32(G). *Id.* at 24-25.

Arbitrator Denaco stated that his finding of an Article 32(G) violation was "dispositive of this case", but he went on nonetheless to express reservations concerning the substantive charges against Schofield. *Id.* at 27-28. He found that the Agency did not prove that Schofield knew the actions of his fellow agents were improper or that they had received training on the use of informants. *Id.* at 27. He also cited mitigating factors that might have weighed in favor of a lesser penalty than removal. *Id.* at 28. Based on his conclusion that the Agency had violated Schofield's Article 32(G) rights under the CBA, the arbitrator ordered the Agency to vacate the adverse action against the grievant, to expunge all records referring to the adverse action, and to reinstate the grievant with back pay and benefits from the date of his removal; he further gave Schofield the right to request reassignment out of his current chain of command. *Id.* at 29-30.

Upon receiving the arbitrator's decision and award, the Agency did not appeal, but rather began to implement it. Schofield was put back on active duty on January 5, 2009 and told to report to the Newport Station headquarters. Tr. 17. The parties stipulated that he was paid back pay and benefits from the date of his removal to his reinstatement. Jt. Ex. 3. However, Schofield's service on active duty was short-lived. Officials at the Agency's national headquarters initially directed Swanton Sector's Chief Patrol Agent not to put Schofield in uniform and instead to assign him to administrative duties. Tr. 75, 79, 118. Schofield had been either suspended, removed or on administrative leave since early 2005, and until he passed a periodic background reinvestigation (PRI) he would not have access to the Agency's computer systems or email, precluding him from performing his duties as a Border Patrol Agent.[2] Tr. 115, 162. They were also concerned that Federal prosecutors would refuse to pursue future criminal cases involving Schofield, because Schofield's prior actions in the drug seizure had compromised his credibility and might trigger a "*Giglio*" obligation.[3] Headquarters officials checked with the Agency's Office of Internal Affairs and ascertained that Schofield was due to have a PRI performed. Tr. 118. They considered a variety of positions for Schofield and decided to assign him to the Swanton Sector headquarters as a mission support specialist, but after a day or two in that position, Agency officials determined that there was little or no work that Schofield could do, in light of his inability to access the computer systems; instead, Schofield was placed on (paid) administrative leave, and he has remained in that status since approximately January 7, 2009.

[2] An official of the division within the Office of Internal Affairs that performs employee security clearance investigations and periodic reinvestigations testified that the position of Border Patrol Agent is classified as "critical sensitive" and that all such employees must have a "single scope background investigation" performed every five years. Tr. 150, 154-55; *see also* Resp. Ex. 1.

[3] *Giglio v. United States,* 405 U.S. 150 (1972)(*Giglio*), requires Federal prosecutors to disclose to defense counsel information that bears on the credibility of a government witness.

Schofield was notified by the Agency's Office of Internal Affairs on January 22, 2009, that it was beginning Schofield's PRI. Tr. 161. The result of this process was that Schofield did not "clear" his reinvestigation; that is, he did not pass. Tr. 163. These results were turned over to Agency management in approximately September 2009 to determine what further action would be taken. Tr. 145, 147, 168. At the time of the hearing, Schofield remained on administrative leave, receiving pay and benefits but not working or having the opportunity to earn administratively uncontrollable overtime and other types of premium pay or to be considered for training, details or promotion. Tr. 19-20, 39-40, 45, 46, 51.

DISCUSSION AND CONCLUSIONS

Positions of the Parties

General Counsel

The General Counsel (GC) argues that the Respondent has intentionally refused to comply with the Award, by allowing Agent Schofield to work only for two days before placing him back on administrative leave, a status in which he is unable to earn a variety of premiums or to be considered for promotion, training or details. Although the GC agrees that the Agency paid Schofield full back pay, expunged any references to the adverse action from Schofield's personnel file, and briefly reinstated him to duty status, it argues that this does not constitute full compliance with the Award, citing *Kerr v. National Endowment for the Arts,* 726 F.2d 730, 733 (Fed. Cir. 1984). Because Schofield is not being allowed to perform the duties he performed before his adverse action, and because he is not enjoying many of the benefits of active employment, the clear intent and purpose of the Award is being thwarted.

The General Counsel further submits that the Authority has long held that an agency's failure to comply with a final arbitration award, even in termination cases on which the agency cannot file exceptions under section 7122(a) of the Statute, constitutes an unfair labor practice under section 7116(a)(1) and (8). *U.S. Army Adjutant General Publications Center, St. Louis, Mo.,* 22 FLRA 200 (1986)(*Army Adjutant General*). Once an award has become final and binding, either through the denial of exceptions, the failure to file exceptions, or the Federal Circuit's denial of a petition for judicial review, the Authority will not review the merits of the award in an unfair labor practice proceeding. *Id.* at 206. Accordingly, the GC argues that the Respondent's justifications for putting Schofield on administrative leave are nothing more than collateral attacks on the Award and must be rejected.

The GC recognizes that the Merit Systems Protection Board (MSPB), which directly reviews appeals of agency adverse actions and enforces compliance with its own decisions, will excuse an agency's refusal to reinstate an employee to his former position, notwithstanding a Board decision in favor of the employee and a *status quo ante* remedial order, when the agency shows "that an outside event or determination rendered the appellant incapable of performing the duties of his prior position." *Marcotrigiano v. Dep't of Justice*, 95 MSPR 198, 204 (2003). In *Marcotrigiano,* the Board held that the agency did not have to reinstate an INS investigator to his former position after he was acquitted on charges of pornography and his removal was overturned, because two U.S. Attorneys had advised the employee's supervisors that they would not use him as a witness, based on *Giglio*-type concerns related to his criminal trial. While the Board recognized that the credibility concerns about the employee were related to matters that had been raised in his removal appeal, the Board noted that these concerns had been raised not by the agency itself but by Federal prosecutors. *Id.* at 203-05. The General Counsel argues, however, that *Marcotrigiano* is distinguishable from the instant case, because here the *Giglio* concern was raised by Agency officials, not outside prosecutors, and that it was mere speculation at the time Schofield was removed from duty. Similarly, the GC argues that in January 2009, Agency management could only speculate as to whether Schofield would pass his PRI. Even if Schofield did not pass the reinvestigation, the decision of what action to take against Schofield rests with the Respondent, not the division investigating him. Finally, the GC notes that the Agency's concerns – both those relating to possible *Giglio* problems and those relating to Schofield's inability to pass a reinvestigation – were based on the same conduct as that which was litigated in his arbitration hearing. Thus, the GC argues that the Respondent is improperly attempting to collaterally attack the Award itself, which considered all of the same facts and found that Schofield should be reinstated.

Respondent

The Respondent defends its actions on several grounds. First, it asserts that it fully complied with the Award, arguing that its reinstatement of Schofield on January 5, 2009, fulfilled the requirements of the Award, and that its decision to place him on administrative leave two days later was a distinct and separate action that was justified by the facts of the case. Citing the case of *Noble v. Dep't of Justice*, 68 MSPR 524 (1995), Respondent asserts that an agency is not prohibited from instituting a subsequent personnel action against an employee after rescinding his prior removal. Citing *U.S. Dep't of the Treasury, IRS, Austin Serv. Ctr., Austin, Tex.*, 25 FLRA 71 (1987), Respondent further argues that its compliance with the Award must be evaluated in terms of whether its construction of the Award was reasonable, and that in the circumstances of this case, it acted reasonably in placing Schofield on administrative leave until his PRI was completed. It noted testimony that Border Patrol Agents cannot perform most of their work without access to the Agency's computer systems, and that employees who have been in a non-duty status for as long as Agent Schofield must pass a PRI before being allowed access to those systems. In this context, the Respondent's removal of Schofield from duty status on January 7, 2009, was a reasonable precaution, based not on the conduct for which Schofield had been removed, but on Schofield's inability to perform the duties of his job until he passed a PRI.

Additionally, the Respondent submits that it had a "strong overriding interest" justifying its refusal to keep Schofield on duty status. *LaBatte v. Dep't of the Air Force,* 58 MSPR 586, 594 (1993). In *LaBatte,* the MSPB upheld an agency's refusal to return an employee to his former position because his security clearance had been revoked; in *Marren v. Dep't of Justice,* 32 MSPR 285, 287 (1987), the Board upheld the agency's revocation of a Border Patrol Agent's government driver's license, despite the fact that the agent's removal for causing a serious car accident in his government vehicle and for related conduct had been overturned. The Respondent also cites the *Marcotrigiano* decision for this same principle. In all of these cases, the Board held that despite prior decisions ordering an employee's reinstatement, the lack of some required job qualification (a government driver's license, a security clearance) justified the agencies' refusal to return the employees to their former jobs. Similarly, Respondent argues here that all its Border Patrol Agents must have passed a PRI in order to access the Agency's computer systems and to perform their duties, and they must also be able to testify in criminal cases against people they investigate. The Respondent submits that Schofield lacked the former qualification when he was reinstated in January 2009, and that they reasonably feared he would not be able to meet the latter qualification.

The Respondent agrees that once an arbitration award is final and binding, as the Award was in this case, it cannot be collaterally attacked. *U.S. Dep't of Transportation, Fed. Aviation Admin., Northwest Mountain Region, Renton, Wash.*, 55 FLRA 293, 296-97 (1999). It insists that it is not attacking the Award here, but rather that an "outside event or determination" rendered Schofield incapable of performing his duties. Resp. Brief at 19, paraphrasing the *Marcotrigiano* decision, 95 MSPR at 204.

Analysis

If this case simply involved the question whether Respondent complied with the Award, it would be fairly straightforward, and it would be resolved in favor of the General Counsel. It is not that simple, however, and requires a consideration of precedent from the MSPB as well as the Authority, ultimately tipping the scales in favor of the Respondent.

As noted by the General Counsel, the Authority has long held that once an arbitration award is final, the parties must comply with it and may not collaterally attack it. *Army Adjutant General, supra,* 22 FLRA at 202. The Respondent recognizes that the Award in this case was final and binding. Resp. Brief at 19. A party's refusal to comply with a final award is an unfair labor practice enforceable by the Authority, even when the Authority lacks jurisdiction (pursuant to section 7121(f) of the Statute) to hear exceptions to the award. *Dep't of HHS, SSA*, 41 FLRA 755 (1991). Where the award is unambiguous, a strict compliance test is employed. *See United States Dep't of the Treasury, IRS, Austin Compliance Ctr., Austin, Tex.*, 44 FLRA 1306, 1315 (1992). Where the award is ambiguous, the test for compliance is whether the agency's action is consistent with a reasonable construction of the award; *United States Dep't of Justice, Fed. Bureau of Prisons, Fed. Corr. Inst., Marianna, Fla.*, 59 FLRA 3, 4 (2003).

In accordance with these precedents, the Respondent argues that it acted reasonably in reinstating Schofield and then putting him on administrative leave, in light of the logistics involved in putting an agent back on the rolls within a short time frame. This argument is premised, however, on the notion that the Award was ambiguous, and I cannot accept that premise. There was nothing ambiguous about the arbitrator's order to reinstate Agent Schofield. Reinstating Schofield for two days and then placing him in a non-duty status was considerably less than full compliance with the Award, and it cannot be rationalized in terms of administrative difficulties in fulfilling the arbitrator's demands. The Agency was not simply looking for a few additional weeks to put Schofield back into a full duty status;[4] rather, it was citing a new basis for keeping him off duty. Respondent's argument conflates the issue of whether it complied with the Award and the separate issue of whether it had legitimate reasons for refusing to do so. Although, as I explain later, I agree that it was justified in putting Schofield on extended administrative leave, I will not indulge in the illusion that this constituted compliance with the Award.

The Award directs the Respondent, *inter alia,* to reinstate Agent Schofield, to make him whole in regard to pay and benefits, to expunge all records of the adverse action, and not to use those records in the future to detract from Schofield's promotional opportunities or other administrative actions. Jt. Ex. 1 at 29. The Respondent was further directed to grant any request Schofield might make in the subsequent year for reassignment out of his current chain of command. *Id.* The Award is clear in its intent to return Schofield to his original duty status and to enable him to resume his career as a Border Patrol Agent. While he is currently being paid his base salary while on administrative leave, he is not earning administratively uncontrollable overtime (which can routinely amount to a quarter of an agent's base pay) or premiums such as night differential and Sunday pay, and he is not being considered for promotions or career-enhancing details or training. Tr. 19-20, 39-40, 45, 46, 51. The Award clearly intended that Schofield be allowed to work as a Border Patrol Agent and to have the advancement opportunities of other agents, and both these purposes are being frustrated by the Respondent's actions.[5]

The true issue in this case is not whether the Respondent complied with the Award, but whether it had a valid justification for refusing to comply. There is little or no Authority precedent on this point, particularly in employee removal cases, but there is a substantial body of precedent at the MSPB, whose jurisdiction covers most Federal employee removals, and whose case law also applies to arbitration proceedings challenging such removals. Section 7121(e)(2) of the Statute; *see also Cornelius v. Nutt,* 472 U.S. 648, 652 (1985). The Board has long held that while an agency is generally required to return a reinstated employee to his former position, it may refuse to do so when there is "a strong, overriding interest" against doing so. *Payne v. U.S. Postal Service,* 55 MSPR 317, 319-20 (1992). In *Payne,* an employee's removal for mishandling of the mails was overturned, but subsequently he was convicted on criminal charges arising out of the same actions for which he had been removed. The Board noted that the criminal conviction was directly related to the employee's official duties and held that it was "a compelling reason for not returning appellant to active duty status[.]" *Id.* at 320, 321. The Board cited *Burrell v. Dep't of the Navy,* 43 MSPR 174 (1990), where the agency successfully argued that despite an order to reinstate a motor vehicle operator, the employee's convictions for reckless driving and driving under the influence rendered him unfit to transport explosives.[6] Moreover, in *Yokley v. U.S. Postal Service,* 57 MSPR 482, 285-86 (1993) and *Connor v. U.S. Postal Service,* 50 MSPR 389, 392-93 (1991), the Board held that the agency was justified in requiring the employees to undergo fitness for duty examinations as a prerequisite for reinstatement, based on the nature of their prior actions and the length of time the employees had been off duty. The case law in this area was summarized by the Board in *Sink v. U.S. Postal Service,*
65 MSPR 628, 632-34 (1994).[7]

In the *Sink* decision, the Board also noted that agencies are entitled to "special deference" when "the issue of compliance [is] entwined with security concerns." *Id.* at 634, citing *LaBatte,* 58 MSPR at 594. In *LaBatte,* a firefighter holding a sensitive position requiring a security clearance was removed for using cocaine, and while his removal action was pending, the agency suspended his security clearance. The MSPB overturned the removal and ordered him

[4] *See, e.g., Dep't of HHS, SSA,* 22 FLRA 270, 282-84 (1986).

[5] In analogous situations, the MSPB has held that placing an employee on administrative leave following his reinstatement is not full compliance with a reinstatement order. *Special Counsel v. Dep't of Transportation,* 72 MSPR 104, 107 (1996); *Rauccio v. U.S. Postal Service,* 44 MSPR 243, 245 (1990).

[6] In *Burrell,* the agency agreed to place the appellant in a lower position, but in *Payne,* the agency's insistence that it had no other position for the appellant was upheld by the Board.

[7] The Board has also held that an agency's concern (pursuant to the Supreme Court's 1972 *Giglio* decision) that prosecutors would not allow an employee to testify in court may justify its refusal to place an employee into a job that requires him to appear in court. *Marcotrigiano, supra.* In our case, Respondent cites this as an additional justification for its refusal to put Schofield back onto active duty. But in *Marcotrigiano,* the agency's concern was based on letters from two U.S. Attorneys' offices that they would not call the appellant as a witness. 95 MSPR at 202. In the instant case, no prosecutors have raised *Giglio* concerns about Schofield to the Agency, and the Agency's fears are thus speculative to this point. Accordingly, I do not consider this to be a sufficient reason to keep Schofield off active duty, and I do not discuss it further.

reinstated, but in a subsequent compliance proceeding it held that the agency was justified in placing him in another job until his security clearance was reinstated. "The lack of a security clearance constitutes a compelling reason not to return the appellant to his Firefighter position." 58 MSPR at 595. *See also King v. Dep't of the Navy*, 98 MSPR 547, 555 (2005).

In *LaBatte,* the appellant's return to his old job was merely delayed, but the Board has also upheld the outright removal of employees due to the revocation of their security clearance. *See, e.g., Payne, supra,* and *Egan v. Dep't of the Navy,* 28 MSPR 509, 522 (1985), which was ultimately affirmed by the Supreme Court in *Dep't of the Navy v. Egan,* 484 U.S. 518 (1988)(*Egan*). Similarly, in *Blagaich v. Dep't of Transportation,* 90 MSPR 619 (2001), the agency removed an air traffic control specialist (a position requiring a security clearance) after he was criminally convicted on several unspecified charges. An arbitrator reduced his removal to a suspension and ordered him reinstated, but after receiving the arbitration decision the agency revoked his security clearance based on the same underlying misconduct and removed him once again. Despite the prior arbitration decision, the Board refused to apply the doctrine of *res judicata* or to overturn the employee's removal. *Id.* at 623-24. It held that the initial removal had been based on the misconduct leading to his criminal conviction, while the subsequent removal was based on separate and distinguishable grounds: his loss of the security clearance that was required for his job. *Id.* Pursuant to the Supreme Court's decision in *Egan, supra,* 484 U.S. at 530, the Board stated that it could not review the merits of a decision to revoke a security clearance. In light of the employee's loss of his security clearance, the Board held that his removal was valid. *Blagaich*, 90 MSPR at 626. Finally, the Board held in *Blagaich* that the agency was not required to place the employee in a nonsensitive position. Citing *LaChance v. Jowanowitch,* 144 F.3d 792, 793 (Fed. Cir. 1998), the Board found no statute, agency regulation or other evidence that the employee had a right to reassignment to a nonsensitive position. As in *LaChance,* Blagaich had been hired for a position requiring a security clearance, and once he lost that clearance he could not perform his job. 90 MSPR at 626. *See also Lyles v. Dep't of the Army,* 864 F.2d 1581, 1583 (Fed. Cir. 1989).

In the case at bar, Schofield was employed as a Border Patrol Agent, which is designated by the Agency as a "Critical-Sensitive" position, which requires employees to undergo periodic reinvestigation every five years. Tr. 155. *See also* Resp. Ex. 1 at 9, 16 (Personnel Security Handbook, HB 1400-07, December 2006) and 5 C.F.R. §§ 732.201(a) and 732.203. 5 C.F.R. § 732.201(a) provides:

> For purposes of this part, the head of each agency shall designate, or cause to be designated, any position within the department or agency the occupant of which could bring about, by virtue of the nature of the position, a material adverse effect on the national security as a sensitive position at one of three sensitivity levels: Special-Sensitive, Critical-Sensitive, or Noncritical-Sensitive.

5 C.F.R. § 732.203 requires periodic reinvestigations of all Critical-Sensitive employees every five years and further states: "The employing agency will use the results of such periodic reinvestigation to determine whether the continued employment of the individual in a sensitive position is clearly consistent with the interests of the national security."

Pursuant to the above regulation, Chapter 1, Section 4 of the Agency's Personnel Security Handbook provides, in regard to Position Sensitivity Designation, "CBP [Customs and Border Protection] positions are designated High Risk Public Trust or Critical-Sensitive National Security." Resp. Ex. 1 at 9. It defines Critical-Sensitive positions as "hav[ing] the potential for causing exceptionally grave damage to national security." *Id.* Later, it states: "All employees are subject to a periodic reinvestigation (PRI) to ensure continued suitability for employment." *Id.* at 16.

It should also be noted that the definition section of the Personnel Security Handbook contains a separate definition for "Security Clearance" than for "Position Sensitivity Designation," (*Id.* at 10) and it devotes separate chapters for periodic reinvestigations and for security clearances. It appears that while all CBP employees are designated as either High Risk Public Trust or Critical-Sensitive National Security positions, and that Border Patrol Agents are designated as Critical-Sensitive National Security, not all CBP employees are required to have security clearances. *See* Resp. Ex. 1 at 19. The record does not indicate whether Border Patrol Agents are required to have a security clearance.

The *Egan, LaBatte, Blagaich* and *LaChance* decisions cited above all, involve the removal of employees from, or reinstatement to, positions requiring a security clearance. Pursuant to *Egan,* reviewing agencies and courts are prohibited from examining the substance of an agency decision to revoke a security clearance. 484 U.S. at 530. It is not entirely clear, based on the evidence of record and the case law, whether the same principles of "special deference" to executive decisions on security clearances are applicable to cases involving periodic reinvestigation. *Sink, supra,* 65 MSPR at 634.

The Authority has applied the holding and underlying principles of *Egan* in a variety of contexts, although not in circumstances analogous to the instant case. Pursuant to *Egan,* it stated in *United States Information Agency,* 32 FLRA 739, 745 (1988), that an arbitrator may not review the merits of an agency's security clearance determination. In *IFPTE, Local 3,* 57 FLRA 699, 700 (2002), the Authority stated that it "has consistently indicated that proposals which would permit arbitrators to review the merits of security clearance determinations would not be negotiable under *Egan.*" Yet it has also held that *Egan* "does not foreclose examination of other issues not related to the merits of an agency's clearance determination[.]" *AFGE, Local 1923,* 39 FLRA 1197, 1205 (1991). Accordingly, in *Puerto Rico Air National Guard, 156th Airlift Wing (AMC), Carolina, P.R.,* 56 FLRA 174 (2000), the Authority held that an agency committed an unfair labor practice when it suspended several employees' security clearances in retaliation for lawful picketing. The Authority reasoned that it was not barred under *Egan* from making such a determination, as the agency had stated unequivocally that it suspended the employees' security clearances because of their picketing. Thus, the Authority said it did not need to examine the substance of the agency's security clearance decision in order to find an unfair labor practice.

Although the PRIs performed by the Respondent's Office of Internal Affairs are not, in and of themselves, security clearance determinations, it is clear from the quoted language of the regulation and the Agency's handbook that a PRI directly involves questions of national security. 5 C.F.R. part 732, on which the classification of the position of Border Patrol Agent as Critical-Sensitive is based, is entitled "National Security Positions," and by definition an employee holding a Critical-Sensitive position may have "a material adverse effect on the national security[.]" 5 C.F.R. § 732.201(a). The record in our case does not contain any substantive information about the PRI performed on Agent Schofield in the months prior to the hearing, but a determination that he failed the PRI inherently indicates that his "continued employment . . . in a sensitive position is [not] clearly consistent with the interests of the national security." 5 C.F.R. § 732.203. In these respects, and in the limited context of this case, it is difficult to discern any meaningful distinction between the failure to pass a PRI and the revocation of a security clearance. Both Deputy Division Chief Viens and Respondent's Internal Affairs official testified that agents returning to a duty status cannot have access to the Agency's computer and security systems until they have passed a PRI, and as a result they would not be able to perform the duties of their job. Tr. 115, 162. This is not a mere technicality or personnel rule, but an issue that directly involves national security. The classification system that has been established within the Executive Branch to protect national security, as described by the Supreme Court in *Egan,* 484 U.S. at 527-30, is indistinguishable from the Respondent's system that has been outlined in the present case requiring Border Patrol Agents to pass Periodic Reinvestigations in order to demonstrate the continued ability to perform the duties of their jobs. Accordingly, if the Authority is asked to compel an agency to reinstate an employee to a Critical-Sensitive position, it should not do so if this would require the Authority to evaluate the substance of a PRI determination.

Arbitrator Denaco ordered the Respondent to reinstate Schofield as a Border Patrol Agent. The issue of Schofield's PRI was not raised in that proceeding, because the need to perform a PRI did not arise until Schofield was ordered to be reinstated. Schofield had been in a non-duty status from 2005 to January 2009. The record establishes that Border Patrol Agents who have been "off rolls" and are returning to active duty must pass a PRI before having access to the Agency's computer systems, unless they have a current PRI in their files. Tr. 115, 162. Schofield's last PRI had been performed in 1997, and a lesser form of investigation was performed in 2003. Tr. 162-3. Thus the Agency's normal security procedures required a new PRI to be performed for Schofield, and the Agency followed these procedures in initiating such a PRI in January 2009. Several months later, in approximately September 2009, the PRI was completed, and Schofield did not pass. Tr. 147, 168. As a result, Schofield has not had access to the Agency's computer and security systems, and is unable to perform a significant component of his duties as a Border Patrol Agent. Tr. 115, 168.

In order for the Respondent to reinstate Schofield fully as a Border Patrol Agent in January 2009, and to comply with the Award, it would have had to override or violate the procedures requiring PRIs. It would have had to give access to the Agency's automated systems (and all the sensitive information that might be contained therein) to a person whose "continued employment" has been determined not to be "consistent with the interests of the national security." 5 C.F.R. § 732.203. As the *Egan* court stated with regard to security clearances, the process is "an attempt to predict his possible future behavior and to assess whether . . . he might compromise sensitive information. . . . Predictive judgment of this kind must be made by those with the necessary expertise in protecting classified information." 484 U.S. at 528-29. Needless to say, neither I, nor the Authority, possess the expertise necessary to decide whether Schofield should be allowed access to the Agency's sensitive information. Placing Schofield in his former position as a Border Patrol Agent, and affording him all the career opportunities to which an agent is entitled, would require the Agency to assume a national security risk that its Office of Internal Affairs determined was unacceptable. Such an order would not merely review the substance of the PRI determination, but override the PRI entirely.

On the basis of *Egan* and related Authority and MSPB precedent, I conclude that the Respondent was justified in placing Schofield on administrative leave until he passed a PRI. Although Internal Affairs had not yet begun its PRI on Schofield when he was reinstated on January 5, 2009, Agency officials checked and learned that Schofield was due to have a PRI in order to return to full duty status, and the PRI was initiated later that month. Tr. 114, 118, 134, 147, 161. In these circumstances, I find that the Respondent had compelling and overriding reasons to keep Schofield off active duty until he passed his PRI. Since he subsequently failed the PRI, the Respondent was justified in keeping him off active duty.

Contrary to the assertion of the General Counsel, Respondent's actions in this case do not represent a collateral attack on the Award. Respondent has not disputed here either the factual or legal conclusions of the arbitrator, but rather it has based its actions on additional facts that did not exist at the time of the arbitration hearing: Schofield's failure to pass his PRI and his consequent inability to perform the duties of a Border Patrol Agent. The MSPB made a similar analysis in *Blagaich, supra,* 90 MSPR at 623-24, and in a somewhat different context in *Marcotrigiano, supra,* 95 MSPR at 203-05. I believe the reasoning is applicable here as well. The arbitration addressed the proposed removal of Schofield based on his conduct in 2005; Respondent's action placing him on administrative leave in 2009 was based on Schofield's inability to perform the duties of his job until he passed a PRI. This is a separate and independent basis for taking action against Schofield, and this distinguishes it from cases such as *U.S. Dep't of Transportation, Fed. Aviation Admin.,* 54 FLRA 480 (1998). Respondent is not claiming that Arbitrator Denaco's Award is contrary to law or regulation. Rather, it is arguing that once Schofield became eligible for reinstatement in January 2009, a basic requirement of his position was passing a PRI. Until he passed the PRI, he could not perform the duties of his job because he did not have access to basic information necessary for his work; after he failed the PRI, his inability to work as a Border Patrol Agent was further established. As in *Blagaich* and *Marcotrigiano,* Respondent's actions concerning Schofield in 2009 were based on facts and events separate from those decided by Arbitrator Denaco.

This does not mean that Agent Schofield is without recourse in seeking to regain his job. There may be internal Agency procedures for him to appeal the outcome of his PRI; moreover, the Agency will have to institute an adverse action against him if it wishes to change his status as an employee on administrative leave and to remove him permanently from his position, thereby entitling him to statutory appeal procedures. This case also does not address whether there are other jobs that Schofield can perform or whether the Agency is required to find such a position for him. The current decision simply means that the FLRA is not the appropriate forum for overturning the determination of an employee's national security-based periodic reinvestigation.

For all of these reasons, I conclude that the Respondent did not commit an unfair labor practice when it removed Schofield from active duty in January 2009. Accordingly, I recommend that the Authority issue the following Order:

ORDER

It is ordered that the complaint be, and hereby is, dismissed.

Issued, Washington, DC, September 29, 2010.

RICHARD A. PEARSON
Administrative Law Judge

65 FLRA No. 217

UNITED STATES
DEPARTMENT OF JUSTICE
FEDERAL BUREAU OF PRISONS
FEDERAL CORRECTIONAL COMPLEX
COLEMAN, FLORIDA
(Agency)

and

AMERICAN FEDERATION
OF GOVERNMENT EMPLOYEES
COUNCIL OF PRISON LOCALS
LOCAL 506
(Union)

0-AR-4560

DECISION

July 29, 2011

Before the Authority: Carol Waller Pope, Chairman, and Thomas M. Beck and Ernest DuBester, Members

I. Statement of the Case

This matter is before the Authority on exceptions to an award of Arbitrator J. J. Pierson filed by the Agency under § 7122(a) of the Federal Service Labor-Management Relations Statute (the Statute) and part 2425 of the Authority's Regulations. The Union filed an opposition to the Agency's exceptions.

The Arbitrator found that the Agency violated the parties' agreement by the manner in which it reassigned a correctional officer (the grievant), and denied him the opportunity to work overtime, while his conduct was under investigation. As a remedy, the Arbitrator directed the Agency to pay the grievant for lost overtime. For the reasons that follow, we deny the exceptions, but modify the award to correct a typographical error.

II. Background and Arbitrator's Award

When the grievant entered a correctional institution to begin his shift with prohibited items in his possession, the Agency opened an investigation into the matter (the investigation). Award at 2. During the investigation, the Agency reassigned the grievant to a phone-monitoring post in the central administrative building – outside the correctional institution – and did not permit him to work overtime. *Id.* The Union filed a grievance alleging that the Agency had not taken these actions against similarly situated employees and thereby violated the parties' agreement, particularly Article 6 (Article 6),[1] "by failing to treat [the grievant] fairly and equitabl[y]." *Id.* at 3. The Arbitrator framed the issue as follows: "Did the Agency . . . violate the [parties'] [a]greement by reassigning [the grievant] to work outside the institution during the period he was being investigated for his conduct . . . and by denying him the opportunity to work overtime [during that period]? If so, what shall be the remedy?" *Id.* at 1.

The Arbitrator found that, although the suspicion that prompted the investigation was "neither unreasonable nor unjustified[,]" *id.* at 21, the Agency's treatment of the grievant was "less than fair and equitable," *id.* at 24. In this regard, the Arbitrator found that, unlike in situations involving other employees under investigation, the Agency reassigned the grievant from the correctional institution to a post "where he was in view of other officers and administrators[,]" which caused him "embarrassment and humiliation[.]" *Id.* at 22. In addition, the Arbitrator found it "unwarranted" for the Agency to deny the grievant the opportunity to work overtime, *id.*, because "others were not denied overtime opportunities when reassigned from regular duties or under investigation." *Id.* at 23. Thus, the Arbitrator concluded that the reassignment of the grievant and the denial of overtime violated the parties' agreement, was "unjustified and unwarranted[,]" *id.* at 27, and "caused the [g]rievant to lose substantial overtime opportunities and income[,]" *id.* at 24.

The Arbitrator determined that an appropriate remedy would be "an award for lost overtime opportunities, calculated by past records of performance and in response to the actual monetary loss of income by [the grievant]." *Id.* at 25. The Arbitrator noted the Agency's arguments that "the Union could not prove that [the grievant] would have been offered specific overtime assignments on specific dates[,]" and that "the overtime opportunities had been markedly decreased" at the institution during the period of the investigation. *Id.* at 25 n.35. However, the Arbitrator found that: (1) the grievant was prohibited from working overtime for seventeen

1. The pertinent text of Article 6 is provided below.

weeks, *id.* at 26; (2) "overtime opportunities were a regular and routine assignment in the institution[,]" *id.* at 25; and (3) the grievant "previously worked an extensive amount of regular and voluntary overtime shifts[,]" *id.* The Arbitrator also stated that "[t]here was no contention that the [g]rievant ever refused overtime." *Id.* The Arbitrator "acknowledge[d] that the [g]rievant would not have worked every available overtime hour . . . each week[,]" but concluded that "based on his prior personnel and pay records, it is not unreasonable to conclude that [the grievant] would have worked forty . . . hours of overtime each week[.]" *Id.* at 26. As a result, the Arbitrator directed the Agency to pay the grievant $16,388 as compensation for lost overtime income. *Id.* Later in the award, the Arbitrator directed the Agency to pay the grievant $17,388 "as calculated in the above [o]pinion." *Id.* at 28.

III. Positions of the Parties

A. Agency's Exceptions

The Agency argues that the award fails to draw its essence from the parties' agreement. Specifically, the Agency claims that the award is inconsistent with Article 30, Section g (Article 30)[2] of the agreement. Exceptions at 22.

In addition, the Agency argues that the award is contrary to law because the parties' agreement, as interpreted by the Arbitrator, affects management's rights to assign work, assign employees, and determine internal security practices under § 7106(a) of the Statute[3] and does not constitute an appropriate arrangement under § 7106(b)(3).[4] *Id.* at 7-18. In this regard, the Agency argues that the Arbitrator's interpretation of the agreement "would never allow management to temporarily reassign a correctional officer . . . while [he or she is] under investigation for potential security breaches[,]" *id.* at 15-16, and "completely prevents the Agency from choosing where to reassign an employee[,]" *id.* at 17. The Agency also argues that "the agreement as interpreted by the Arbitrator [is] not sufficiently tailored to constitute [an] appropriate arrangement[]." *Id.* at 16. In support of its management rights arguments, the Agency cites: *United States Department of Justice, Federal Bureau of Prisons, Federal Correctional Institution, Lompoc, California*, 58 FLRA 301 (2003) (*BOP Lompoc*) (Chairman Cabaniss concurring and then-Member Pope dissenting); *United States Department of Justice, Federal Bureau of Prisons, Federal Correctional Institution, Sheridan, Oregon*, 58 FLRA 279 (2003) (*BOP Sheridan*) (Chairman Cabaniss concurring and then-Member Pope dissenting); *IFPTE, Local 1*, 49 FLRA 225 (1994) (*IFPTE*) (Member Talkin dissenting in part); and *NTEU, Chapter 26*, 22 FLRA 314 (1986) (*Chapter 26*). Exceptions at 16-18. Further, the Agency contends that the award is deficient under prong II of the test set forth in *United States Department of the Treasury, Bureau of Engraving & Printing, Washington, D.C.*, 53 FLRA 146 (1997) (*BEP*), because the remedy does not reconstruct what management would have done if it had complied with the agreement. Exceptions at 18-20.

Additionally, the Agency argues that the Arbitrator's award of allegedly lost overtime pay is contrary to the Back Pay Act, 5 U.S.C. § 5596 (BPA). Exceptions at 22-31. In this regard, although the Agency concedes that a contract violation can constitute an unjustified or unwarranted personnel action under the BPA, the Agency contends that, for the reasons set forth in its essence and management rights exceptions, it did not commit an unjustified or unwarranted personnel action. *Id.* at 23. In addition, the Agency argues that the Union did not establish "that overtime was available to the grievant on specific days and that the grievant was specifically available on those days to work it." *Id.* at 24-25. In this connection, the Agency asserts that: (1) "[t]he overtime available for staff to work after the investigation commenced markedly decreased[,]" *id.* at 28-29; (2) "the Union provided no evidence as to specific dates that [the grievant] would have been available" to work overtime, *id.* at 28; and (3) "each and every overtime assignment would not have been available" to the grievant because overtime is assigned using a seniority-based rotation, *id.* at 26-27. As a result, the Agency argues that the Arbitrator's calculation of lost overtime opportunities based on the amount of overtime that the grievant worked prior to the investigation was "speculative[.]" *Id.* at 28. For support, the Agency cites: *United States Department of Justice, Federal Bureau*

---

2. The pertinent text of Article 30 is provided below.

3. Section 7106(a) of the Statute provides, in pertinent part, that "nothing . . . shall affect the authority of any management official of any agency . . . to determine . . . internal security practices[,] . . . assign . . . employees . . . , or . . . to assign work[.]"

4. Section 7106(b)(3) provides, in pertinent part, that "[n]othing in this section shall preclude any agency and any labor organization from negotiating . . . appropriate arrangements for employees adversely affected by the exercise of any authority under this section by such management officials."

of Prisons, Federal Correctional Complex, Beaumont, Texas, 59 FLRA 466 (2003) (*BOP Beaumont*) (Chairman Cabaniss dissenting in part); *United States Department of the Air Force, Warner Robins Air Force Base, Georgia*, 56 FLRA 541 (2000) (*Warner Robins*); *AFGE, Local 1857*, 35 FLRA 325 (1990) (*Local 1857*); and *Naval Air Rework Facility, Norfolk, Virginia*, 21 FLRA 410 (1986) (*Naval Air*). Exceptions at 24, 28-29, 31.

B. Union's Opposition

As a preliminary matter, the Union argues that, because the Agency "failed to raise any argument based on management's rights under § 7106" to the Arbitrator, § 2429.5 of the Authority's Regulations bars the Agency from making such an argument to the Authority. Opp'n at 8.

In regard to the merits of the Agency's exceptions, the Union argues that the award does not fail to draw its essence from the agreement because the Arbitrator enforced "the mandates of the [parties'] [a]greement requiring the Agency to treat all employees in a fair [and] equitable manner." *Id.* at 14. In addition, the Union argues that the award is not contrary to § 7106 because Article 6 constitutes an appropriate arrangement under § 7106(b)(3). *See id.* at 12. In this connection, the Union claims that the award merely requires that, in exercising its management rights, "the Agency do so in a manner [that] is fair and equitable to all employees, as is required by Article 6[.]" *Id.*

Additionally, the Union argues that the award does not violate the BPA. In this connection, the Union contends that the Arbitrator made the necessary specific factual findings to support the amount of overtime awarded, and that "a finding of causal connection under the [BPA] may be implicit from the award." Opp'n at 16 (citing *U.S. Dep't of the Treasury, U.S. Customs Serv., Portland, Or.*, 54 FLRA 764 (1998) (*Customs*); *U.S. Dep't of the Army, Anniston Army Depot, Anniston, Ala.*, 46 FLRA 974 (1992) (*Army Depot*)). Further, the Union asserts that the Arbitrator "implicitly rejected the Agency's argument as to the amount of overtime [the grievant] would have worked." Opp'n at 17.

IV. Analysis and Conclusions

A. Preliminary Issue: § 2429.5 does not bar the Agency's management rights exceptions.

The Union claims that the Agency's management rights arguments should be dismissed under § 2429.5. The Authority's Regulations that were in effect when the Agency filed its exceptions provided that "[t]he Authority will not consider . . . any issue, which was not presented in the proceedings before the . . . arbitrator." 5 C.F.R. § 2429.5.[5] Under § 2429.5, the Authority will not consider an issue that could have been, but was not, presented to the arbitrator. *See, e.g., U.S. Dep't of Agric., Forest Serv.*, 64 FLRA 931, 933 (2010). In its post-hearing brief to the Arbitrator, the Agency cited 5 U.S.C. § 7106(a)(1)-(a)(2), and argued that "the parties' . . . [a]greement, *consistent with the . . . Statute*, gives the Warden the right to assign . . . . [and] the right to determine the internal security practices of the institution." Exceptions, Attach. B at 11 (emphasis added). Thus, the record demonstrates that the Agency presented its management rights arguments to the Arbitrator. Accordingly, we reject the Union's claim, and address the Agency's management rights arguments.

B. The award does not fail to draw its essence from the parties' agreement.

In reviewing an arbitrator's interpretation of a collective bargaining agreement, the Authority applies the deferential standard of review that federal courts use in reviewing arbitration awards in the private sector. *See* 5 U.S.C. § 7122(a)(2); *AFGE, Council 220*, 54 FLRA 156, 159 (1998). Under this standard, the Authority will find that an arbitration award is deficient as failing to draw its essence from the collective bargaining agreement when the appealing party establishes that the award: (1) cannot in any rational way be derived from the agreement; (2) is so unfounded in reason and fact and so unconnected with the wording and purposes of the collective bargaining agreement as to manifest an infidelity to the obligation of the arbitrator; (3) does not represent a plausible interpretation of the agreement; or (4) evidences a manifest disregard of the agreement. *See U.S. Dep't of Labor (OSHA)*,

5. The Authority's Regulations concerning the review of arbitration awards, as well as certain related procedural Regulations, including § 2429.5, were revised effective October 1, 2010. *See* 75 Fed. Reg. 42,283 (2010). As the Agency's exceptions were filed before that date, we apply the prior Regulations.

34 FLRA 573, 575 (1990). The Authority and the courts defer to arbitrators in this context because it is the arbitrator's construction of the agreement for which the parties have bargained. *Id.* at 576.

Article 30 provides, in pertinent part, that the Agency has "the right to respond to an alleged offense by an employee" that raises security concerns by "reassign[ing] the employee to another job within the institution or remov[ing] the employee from the institution pending investigation and resolution of the matter[.]" Award at 5. The Agency argues that the award is inconsistent with this wording because it "limit[s] where an employee can be reassigned during an investigation . . . ." Exceptions at 22. However, the Union alleged before the Arbitrator that the Agency violated Article 6, which requires that employees "be treated fairly and equitably in all aspects of personnel management[.]" Exceptions, Attach. C (Collective Bargaining Agreement (CBA)) at 10. *See also* Award at 3; Opp'n, Attach. (Union's Post-Hearing Brief) at 14-15, 18. The Arbitrator found that the grievant was "entitled to be treated fairly and equitably[,]" Award at 21, but "received treatment different from other employees[,]" *id.* at 23, and that the Agency treated the grievant "in a manner less than fair and equitable," *id.* at 24. In so finding, the Union argues, and there is no dispute, that the Arbitrator was enforcing Article 6. *See* Opp'n at 12, 14. Thus, although Article 30 provides management with certain rights, the Arbitrator effectively found that Article 6 limited those rights by requiring the Agency to treat employees fairly and equitably. *See* Award at 21-24, 27. The Agency provides no basis for concluding that this finding is unfounded, irrational, implausible, or manifestly disregards the agreement. Accordingly, we deny the Agency's essence exception.

C. The award is not contrary to law, rule, or regulation.

When an exception involves an award's consistency with law, the Authority reviews any question of law raised by an exception and the award de novo. *See NTEU, Chapter 24,* 50 FLRA 330, 332 (1995) (citing *U.S. Customs Serv. v. FLRA,* 43 F.3d 682, 686-87 (D.C. Cir. 1994)). In applying a de novo standard of review, the Authority assesses whether the arbitrator's legal conclusions are consistent with the applicable standard of law. *See NFFE, Local 1437,* 53 FLRA 1703, 1710 (1998) (*Local 1437*). In making that assessment, the Authority defers to the arbitrator's underlying factual findings. *See id.*

1. The award is not contrary to § 7106 of the Statute.

The Authority recently revised the analysis that it will apply when reviewing exceptions alleging that awards are contrary to law because they are inconsistent with management rights under § 7106 of the Statute. *See U.S. EPA*, 65 FLRA 113, 115 (2010) (Member Beck concurring) (*EPA*); *FDIC, Div. of Supervision & Consumer Prot., S.F. Region*, 65 FLRA 102 (2010) (Chairman Pope concurring) (*FDIC, S.F. Region*). Under the revised analysis, the Authority will first assess whether the award affects the exercise of the asserted management right under § 7106(a). *EPA*, 65 FLRA at 115.[6] If so, then, as relevant here, the Authority examines whether the award enforces a contract provision negotiated under § 7106(b).[7] *Id.* Also under the revised analysis, in determining whether the award enforces a contract provision negotiated under § 7106(b)(3), the Authority assesses: (1) whether the contract provision constitutes an arrangement for employees adversely affected by the exercise of a management right; and (2) if so, then whether the arbitrator's enforcement of the arrangement abrogates the exercise of the management right. *See id.* at 118. In concluding that the Authority would apply an abrogation standard, the Authority rejected continued application of an excessive-interference standard. *Id.* at 113. In addition, in setting forth the revised analysis, the Authority rejected the continued application of the "reconstruction" requirement set forth in *BEP*. *FDIC, S.F. Region*, 65 FLRA at 106-07.

---

6. For the reasons articulated in his recent concurring opinion and footnotes, Member Beck would conclude that it is unnecessary to assess whether the contract provision is an appropriate arrangement or whether it abrogates a § 7106(a) right. The appropriate question is simply whether the remedy directed by the Arbitrator enforces the provision in a reasonable and reasonably foreseeable fashion. *See EPA*, 65 FLRA at 120 (Concurring Opinion of Member Beck); *FDIC, S.F. Region*, 65 FLRA at 107; *SSA, Office of Disability Adjudication & Review*, 65 FLRA 477, 481 n.14 (2011); *U.S. Dep't of the Air Force, Air Force Materiel Command*, 65 FLRA 395, 398 n.7 (2010); *U.S. Dep't of Health & Human Servs., Office of Medicare Hearings & Appeals*, 65 FLRA 175, 177 n.3 (2010); *U.S. Dep't of Transp., Fed. Aviation Admin.*, 65 FLRA 171, 173 n.5 (2010).

7. When an award affects a management right under § 7106(a)(2) of the Statute, the Authority may also examine whether the award enforces an applicable law. *EPA*, 65 FLRA at 115 n.7.

The Agency argues that the Arbitrator's award affects management's rights to assign work, assign employees, and determine internal security practices under § 7106(a) of the Statute. Exceptions at 9. Where the Authority has found that an arbitrator was enforcing an appropriate arrangement within the meaning of § 7106(b)(3) of the Statute, the Authority has assumed, without deciding, that the award affected the management rights as claimed by the excepting party. *See, e.g., U.S. Dep't of the Army Headquarters, I Corps & Ft. Lewis, Ft. Lewis, Wash.*, 65 FLRA 699, 703 (2011). As discussed below, we find that the Arbitrator was enforcing an appropriate arrangement. Accordingly, we assume without deciding that the award affects the Agency's rights to assign work, assign employees, and determine internal security practices.

As discussed above, the Arbitrator's finding that the Agency violated the parties' agreement was based in part on his application of Article 6, which requires the Agency to treat employees "fairly and equitably in all aspects of personnel management[.]" CBA at 10. "The Authority has repeatedly found provisions requiring management to exercise its management rights fairly and equitably to constitute arrangements because they are intended to mitigate the adverse effects of the unfair or inequitable exercise of management's rights." *SSA, Dallas Region*, 65 FLRA 405, 409 (2010) (*SSA*). *See also U.S. Dep't of Justice, Fed. Bureau of Prisons, Fed. Prison Camp, Duluth, Minn.*, 65 FLRA 588, 591 (2011) (*BOP Duluth*); *U.S. Dep't of the Army, Dugway Proving Ground, Dugway, Utah*, 57 FLRA 224, 226 (2001) (*Dugway*) (Chairman Cabaniss dissenting). Further, although the Agency argues that the award is not sufficiently tailored to be an arrangement, "the Authority does not conduct a tailoring analysis in resolving exceptions to arbitration awards." *EPA*, 65 FLRA at 116. Accordingly, we find that Article 6, as interpreted and applied by the Arbitrator, constitutes an arrangement.

In arguing that, as interpreted by the Arbitrator, the agreement is not an "appropriate" arrangement, Exceptions at 15, the Agency cites several decisions in which the Authority determined that arbitrators' enforcement of contracts excessively interfered with management rights, *id.* at 17-18 (citing *BOP Lompoc*, 58 FLRA at 302-03; *BOP Sheridan*, 58 FLRA at 284; *IFPTE*, 49 FLRA at 249). However, as stated above, the Authority no longer applies the excessive-interference standard in determining whether an arbitrator has enforced a contract provision negotiated under § 7106(b)(3); rather it applies the abrogation standard. *EPA*, 65 FLRA at 116-18. Thus, the Agency's reliance on these decisions is misplaced.

With regard to whether the award abrogates management rights, an award abrogates the exercise of a management right if the award precludes the agency from exercising the right. *See U.S. Dep't of Transp., Fed. Aviation Admin.*, 65 FLRA 171, 174 (2010). However, the Authority previously has found Article 6, as interpreted by another arbitrator, to be an appropriate arrangement under § 7106(b)(3) because the provision did not "preclude [an agency] from reassigning employees, but, rather, only preclude[d] the [a]gency from conducting reassignments in an unfair manner." *BOP Duluth*, 65 FLRA at 591. *Cf. SSA*, 65 FLRA at 409 (provision requiring management to exercise its rights fairly and equitably does not abrogate management's rights); *Dugway*, 57 FLRA at 226 (same). Similarly, the award in this case does not, as the Agency alleges, preclude the Agency from temporarily reassigning an employee under investigation, Exceptions at 15-16, or "completely prevent[] the Agency from choosing where to reassign an employee[,]" *id.* at 17. Instead, the award requires the Agency to manage the reassignment and overtime opportunities of an employee under investigation in a "fair and equitable" manner. Award at 24. Thus, this case is distinguishable from the decisions cited by the Agency because they each involved awards or proposals that effectively precluded an agency's exercise of its management rights. *See BOP Lompoc*, 58 FLRA at 303 (award "effectively remove[d] . . . [a]gency's authority to determine the staffing necessary to maintain the security of its facility"); *BOP Sheridan*, 58 FLRA at 284 (award "totally over[o]de any [a]gency internal security staffing determinations"); *IFPTE*, 49 FLRA at 249 (award imposed "absolute" restriction on agency's ability to assign work); *Chapter 26*, 22 FLRA at 317 (proposal "could totally preclude [an] [a]gency from exercising its right to assign work").[8] Because the award in this case does not impose similar restrictions on the Agency's exercise of its management rights, the Agency does not establish that the Arbitrator's enforcement of Article 6 abrogates management's rights to assign work, assign employees, or determine internal security practices. Accordingly, we find that Article 6, as interpreted by the Arbitrator, is an appropriate arrangement under § 7106(b)(3).

---

8. Further, as noted above, in *BOP Lompoc*, 58 FLRA at 303, *BOP Sheridan*, 58 FLRA at 284, and *IFPTE*, 49 FLRA at 249, the Authority was applying the excessive-interference standard, rather than the abrogation standard.

The Agency also argues that the award is deficient under *BEP* because the remedy does not reconstruct what management would have done if it had not violated the parties' agreement. Exceptions at 18-20. However, as noted above, the Authority no longer requires that an arbitrator's remedy reconstruct what management would have done if it had not violated the parties' agreement. *FDIC, S.F. Region*, 65 FLRA at 106-07. Thus, the Agency's argument does not provide a basis for setting aside the award.[9] *See id.*

For the foregoing reasons, we find that the award is not contrary to § 7106 of the Statute, and deny the Agency's management rights exceptions.

2. The award is not contrary to the BPA.

Under the BPA, an award of backpay is authorized only when an arbitrator finds that: (1) the aggrieved employee was affected by an unjustified or unwarranted personnel action; and (2) the personnel action has resulted in the withdrawal or reduction of the grievant's pay, allowances, or differentials. *See, e.g., U.S. Dep't of Health & Human Servs.*, 54 FLRA 1210, 1218-19 (1998). A violation of a collective bargaining agreement constitutes an unjustified or unwarranted personnel action under the BPA. *See id.* Thus, the Arbitrator's finding that the Agency violated the parties' agreement supports a conclusion that the award satisfies the first requirement of the BPA. Although the Agency argues that this requirement is not met, its argument is premised on its essence and management rights exceptions. As we have denied these exceptions, we also reject the Agency's argument in this connection.

With respect to the second BPA requirement, the Authority has held that a direct causal connection may be implicit from the record and the award. *See Customs*, 54 FLRA at 770-71; *Army Depot*, 46 FLRA at 976; *AFGE, Local 31*, 41 FLRA 514, 518-19 (1991) (*Local 31*). In this regard, the Authority has found that where an agency disputed before an arbitrator a grievant's availability to work overtime, but the arbitrator nevertheless awarded backpay for overtime, the arbitrator "implicitly rejected" the agency's argument and found that, but for the agency's unjustified or unwarranted personnel action, the grievant would have worked overtime and received the backpay awarded. *Customs*, 54 FLRA at 771; *Army Depot*, 46 FLRA at 976.

In this case, the Arbitrator found that the Agency's denial of overtime opportunities to the grievant violated the parties' agreement, Award at 28, and determined that an appropriate remedy would be "an award for lost overtime opportunities, calculated by past records of performance and in response to the actual monetary loss of income by [the grievant][,]" *id.* at 25. Both parties offered evidence concerning the number of overtime opportunities denied the grievant and the grievant's history of working overtime. *Id.* at 8, 15-16, 18, 25-26. Based on that evidence, the Arbitrator found that: (1) the grievant was prohibited from working overtime for seventeen weeks, *id.* at 26; (2) "overtime opportunities were a regular and routine assignment in the institution[,]" *id.* at 25; and (3) the grievant "previously worked an extensive amount of regular and voluntary overtime shifts[,]" *id.* The Arbitrator concluded that, "based on his prior personnel and pay records, it is not unreasonable to conclude that [the grievant] would have worked forty . . . hours of overtime each week[.]" *Id.* at 26. In this regard, the Arbitrator noted that "[t]here was no contention that the [g]rievant ever refused overtime[,]" Award at 25, and implicitly rejected the Agency's argument that the Union failed to establish the grievant's availability to work overtime on specific dates. *See, e.g., Customs*, 54 FLRA at 771; *Army Depot*, 46 FLRA at 976. Similarly, the Arbitrator acknowledged, but implicitly rejected, the Agency's arguments about the amount of overtime assignments that would have been offered the grievant. *See* Award at 25 n.35. Further, the Arbitrator "acknowledge[d] that the [g]rievant would not have worked every available overtime hour . . . each week[,]" when he determined that the grievant would have worked forty hours of overtime per week, rather than the seventy-two hours per week suggested by the Union. *Id.* at 26. As a result of these findings, the Arbitrator "calculate[d] and determine[d] that [the grievant] lost $964 of overtime opportunity each week . . . during the seventeen[-]week period of reassignment[.]"[10] *Id.*

9. For the reasons set forth in her concurring opinion in *FDIC, S.F. Region*, 65 FLRA at 112, Chairman Pope agrees that the Agency provides no basis for finding the Arbitrator's remedy deficient because the remedy is reasonably related to Article 6 and the harm being remedied.

10. We note that the rate of pay used by the Arbitrator in his calculation of backpay for the grievant's "lost overtime opportunities" does not appear to be consistent with the Back Pay Act or Fair Labor Standards Act. Award at 25. Backpay for loss of overtime opportunity is paid at an appropriate overtime rate. *See Dep't of the Navy, Phila. Naval Shipyard, Phila., Pa.*, 28 FLRA 574, 575-76 (1987). Here, the Arbitrator bases his calculation of damages on a "straight-time hourly rate" but offers no justification for

By arguing that this calculation is too "speculative" to satisfy the BPA, Exceptions at 29, the Agency effectively challenges the Arbitrator's factual findings discussed above. However, where, as here, a party has not demonstrated that an award is based on a nonfact,[11] the Authority defers to an arbitrator's factual findings. *See Local 1437*, 53 FLRA at 1710. Further, the Arbitrator's factual findings distinguish this case from those cited by the Agency in which the Authority found backpay awards deficient because the arbitrators' factual findings did not support a backpay award. *See BOP Beaumont*, 59 FLRA at 467-68 (arbitrator awarded grievant the "average" overtime amount paid to coworkers during the relevant time period without finding the grievant would have been offered, or available to work, overtime); *Warner Robins*, 56 FLRA at 543 (arbitrator expressly found "potential" as opposed to "actual" monetary loss); *Local 1857*, 35 FLRA at 326-27 (arbitrator awarded sixteen hours of overtime pay "[b]ased on what is, admittedly, pure conjecture"); *Naval Air*, 21 FLRA at 412 (arbitrator awarded backpay despite finding that there was "no evidence that any of the [grievants] were actually available and willing to work" during the missed overtime opportunities).

Although the Agency characterizes the Arbitrator's award of $17,388.00 as a "mysterious amount," Exceptions at 19, that violates the BPA, *id.* at 22, this figure appears to be the result of a typographical error. In this regard, earlier in the award, the Arbitrator found that the grievant lost $964 of overtime per week, for a total of "$16,388.00" in lost overtime pay for the seventeen-week investigation period. Award at 26. Later in the award, the Arbitrator directed the Agency to compensate the grievant for "his loss of overtime income in the amount of $17,388.00, as calculated in the above [o]pinion." *Id.* at 28. Because the former amount is consistent with the Arbitrator's calculations, and the latter amount appears to be merely a typographical error, we modify the award to correct that error.

For the reasons stated above, we find that the award, as modified above, is not contrary to the Back Pay Act.

---

this aberration other than his "view" that the "straight-time" rate is "more reasonable." Award at 26. However, as there are no exceptions to this aspect of the award, we do not discuss it further.

11. The Agency has not asserted that the award is deficient because it is based on a nonfact.

V. Decision

The award is modified to correct a typographical error in the amount of backpay, and the Agency's exceptions are denied.

65 FLRA No. 218

UNITED STATES
DEPARTMENT OF THE AIR FORCE
AIR FORCE MATERIEL COMMAND
EGLIN AIR FORCE BASE, FLORIDA
(Agency)

and

AMERICAN FEDERATION
OF GOVERNMENT EMPLOYEES
LOCAL 1897
(Union)

0-AR-4716
(65 FLRA 908 (2011))

ORDER DENYING
MOTION FOR RECONSIDERATION

July 29, 2011

Before the Authority: Carol Waller Pope, Chairman, and Thomas M. Beck and Ernest DuBester, Members

I. Statement of the Case

This matter is before the Authority on the Union's motion for reconsideration (motion) of the Authority's decision in *United States Department of the Air Force, Air Force Materiel Command, Eglin Air Force Base, Florida*, 65 FLRA 908 (2011) (*Eglin AFB*). The Agency did not file an opposition to the Union's motion.

Section 2429.17 of the Authority's Regulations permits a party that can establish extraordinary circumstances to request reconsideration of an Authority final decision or order. For the reasons that follow, we conclude that the Union has failed to establish extraordinary circumstances warranting reconsideration. Accordingly, we deny the Union's motion.

II. Decision in *Eglin AFB*

In the underlying proceedings in *Eglin AFB*, the Union filed a grievance alleging that the Agency violated Article 36.03 of the parties' agreement (Article 36.03),[1] and 5 C.F.R. § 551.431 (§ 551.431),[2] by failing to pay security personnel for time spent on standby. *See Eglin AFB*, 65 FLRA at 908. Citing Article 36.03, the Arbitrator sustained the grievance and awarded backpay, liquidated damages, and attorney fees, pursuant to the Fair Labor Standards Act and § 551.431. *See id.* at 909. The Agency filed exceptions to the award. *Id.* at 908.

The Authority determined that the Arbitrator's award was contrary to § 551.431 because she found that security personnel were on standby without finding that they were restricted to a designated post of duty. *See id.* at 910. The Authority found that because Article 36.03, as interpreted by the Arbitrator, was inconsistent with § 551.431, Article 36.03 could not provide a basis for the Arbitrator's award of standby pay. *See id.*

III. Union's Motion

The Union asserts that, in *Eglin AFB*, the Authority erred in its factual findings because it did not "defer[] to the Arbitrator's findings of fact[.]" Motion at 5. In addition, the Union argues that the Authority erred in its conclusions of law, asserting that the Arbitrator "met the requirements to prove a standby claim under [§] 551.431[,]" *id.* at 6, because she found that security personnel were "'restricted by official order[,]'" *id.* at 5 n.1 (quoting § 551.431). In this regard, the Union asserts that "to the extent the Arbitrator applied the incorrect standard[,] the Authority should have remanded this case for the Arbitrator to apply the correct standard." *Id.* at 6

1. Article 36.03, entitled "STANDBY TIME[,]" states:

> Designated employees may be restricted to the official duty station or their living quarters, required to remain in a state of readiness to perform work, and have their activities substantially limited such that they cannot use the time effectively for their own purposes. In these situations, all time spent on standby is considered hours of work.

Eglin AFB, 65 FLRA at 908 n.1 (quoting Award at 65).

2. Section 551.431 states, in pertinent part:

> (a)(1) An employee is on duty, and time spent on standby duty is hours of work if, for work-related reasons, the employee is restricted by official order to a designated post of duty and is assigned to be in a state of readiness to perform work with limitations on the employee's activities so substantial that the employee cannot use the time effectively for his or her own purposes.

(citing *NTEU*, 64 FLRA 395 (2010); *U.S. Dep't of Health & Human Servs., SSA, Kan. City, Mo. Dist.*, 39 FLRA 22 (1991) (*SSA*)). Finally, the Union contends that the Authority "raised [an issue] sua sponte" because the Authority determined that the Arbitrator "relied on . . . Article 36.03 to support her finding of standby." *Id.* In this connection, the Union argues that the Agency "never mentioned in its exception that the reliance on Article 36.03 was improper[,]" and did not "state in its exception that Article 36.03 was in contradiction with the regulation." *Id.* As such, the Union asserts that the Authority "should have remanded the case to the Arbitrator to clarify her award based on the Authority's determination that Article 36.03 was inconsistent with [§] 551.431[.]" *Id.* (citing *IRS, Indianapolis Dist.*, 30 FLRA 850 (1987) (*IRS*)).

IV. Analysis and Conclusions

Section 2429.17 of the Authority's Regulations permits a party that can establish extraordinary circumstances to request reconsideration of an Authority decision. *E.g., Nat'l Ass'n of Indep. Labor, Local 15*, 65 FLRA 666, 667 (2011) (*NAIL*). A party seeking reconsideration under § 2429.17 bears the heavy burden of establishing that extraordinary circumstances exist to justify this unusual action. *Id.* The Authority has identified a limited number of situations in which extraordinary circumstances have been found to exist. *See, e.g., U.S. Dep't of Justice, Fed. Bureau of Prisons, U.S. Penitentiary, Atwater, Cal.*, 65 FLRA 256, 257 (2010) (*BOP*). These include situations where: (1) an intervening court decision or change in the law affected dispositive issues; (2) evidence, information, or issues crucial to the decision had not been presented to the Authority; (3) the Authority erred in its remedial order, process, conclusion of law, or factual finding; and (4) the moving party has not been given an opportunity to address an issue raised sua sponte by the Authority in its decision. *Id.* A party does not establish such extraordinary circumstances by repeating the arguments that the Authority rejected in the underlying dispute. *See NAIL*, 65 FLRA at 667. In this connection, the Authority has repeatedly held that attempts to relitigate conclusions reached by the Authority are insufficient to establish extraordinary circumstances. *E.g., Sport Air Traffic Controllers Org.*, 64 FLRA 1142, 1143 (2010).

The Union asserts that the Authority erred in its factual findings without citing a factual finding, erroneous or otherwise, that the Authority made. *See* Motion at 5-6. In addition, although the Union claims that the Authority failed to "defer[] to the Arbitrator's findings of fact," *id.* at 5, the Union does not cite a finding of fact to which the Authority did not defer, *see id.* at 5-6. Accordingly, this argument does not establish a basis for reconsideration.

Next, the Union asserts that the Authority erred in its conclusions of law because the Arbitrator's award was consistent with § 551.431. *See id.* at 6. This is the same argument that the Authority rejected in *Eglin AFB*. *See* 65 FLRA at 909-10. Thus, this argument does not establish a basis for reconsideration. *See NAIL*, 65 FLRA at 667. Additionally, neither *NTEU*, 64 FLRA at 397, nor *SSA*, 39 FLRA at 25-26, holds that the Authority must remand a matter to an arbitrator if he or she applied an incorrect standard of law. Therefore, the Union does not demonstrate that the Authority erred in *Eglin AFB* by not remanding the matter to the Arbitrator in this regard.

Finally, the Union asserts that the Authority "raised [an issue] sua sponte" when it found that the Arbitrator "relied on . . . Article 36.03 to support her finding of standby." Motion at 6. However, as stated in *Eglin AFB*, the Union's grievance alleged that the Agency violated Article 36.03, and the Arbitrator relied on Article 36.03 in rendering her award. *See* 65 FLRA at 908-09. Thus, the Authority did not raise Article 36.03 sua sponte. In addition, we note that the Union could have addressed the enforceability of Article 36.03 in its opposition to the Agency's exceptions. *See id.* at 909. Accordingly, the Union was not deprived of an opportunity to address this issue. *See BOP*, 65 FLRA at 257. Therefore, the Union does not establish a basis for reconsideration. As to the Union's argument in this connection regarding remand, the Union's premise, that the Authority considered Article 36.03 sua sponte, *see* Motion at 6, is incorrect. Further, nothing in *IRS*, 30 FLRA 850, indicates that the Authority should have remanded this matter to the Arbitrator. Accordingly, the Union provides no basis for finding that the Authority erred in *Eglin AFB* by not remanding the matter to the Arbitrator in this regard.

For the foregoing reasons, the Union has not demonstrated extraordinary circumstances warranting reconsideration of *Eglin AFB*. Accordingly, we deny the Union's motion.

V. Order

The Union's motion is denied.

65 FLRA No. 219

AMERICAN FEDERATION
OF GOVERNMENT EMPLOYEES
LOCAL 3627
(Union)

and

SOCIAL SECURITY ADMINISTRATION
OFFICE OF DISABILITY
ADJUDICATION AND REVIEW
JACKSONVILLE, FLORIDA
(Agency)

0-AR-4749

DECISION

July 29, 2011

Before the Authority: Carol Waller Pope, Chairman, and Thomas M. Beck and Ernest DuBester, Members

I. Statement of the Case

This matter is before the Authority on an exception to an award of Arbitrator Douglas F. Coleman filed by the Union under § 7122(a) of the Federal Service Labor-Management Relations Statute (the Statute) and part 2425 of the Authority's Regulations. The Agency filed an opposition to the Union's exception.

The Arbitrator denied the Union's grievance, finding that the Agency had the right to suspend temporarily the flexiplace program due to a lack of available work. For the reasons set forth below, we deny the Union's exception.

II. Background and Arbitrator's Award

The grievant is employed as a Decision Writer in the Agency's Office of Disability Adjudication and Review (ODAR). Award at 4. In addition to a national collective bargaining agreement, the Agency and the Union negotiated a flexiplace agreement for the purpose of establishing a flexible workplace program. *Id.* at 1.

The flexiplace agreement provides that employees have the ability to work at an Alternative Duty Station (ADS) at least one, but up to three, days a week. *Id.* at 10. Employees must request leave to participate in the flexiplace program every six months. *Id.* The grievant's supervisor approved the grievant's timely request for three ADS days. *Id.* However, shortly thereafter, the hearing office director (Director) sent an email approving only one ADS day a week for all employees because there was insufficient work available to support employees working three ADS days. *Id.* at 10-11.

The Union presented a grievance, alleging that the Agency violated the flexiplace agreement by unilaterally changing the ADS assignments. *Id.* at 1. The matter was not resolved and was submitted to arbitration. The Arbitrator framed the issue as follows: "Did the [Director] unilaterally change the Flexiplace Program [Flex Plan] from 3 days to 1 day after the immediate Supervisor had approved a 3-day plan for [the grievant]?" *Id.* at 2 (second alteration in original).

The Arbitrator found that, under the flexiplace agreement, supervisors had the right to change an employee's ADS days or temporarily to suspend the employee's participation in the flexiplace program based on workload availability. *Id.* at 10. Further, the Arbitrator determined that a Director may review ADS requests before they are approved by the immediate supervisor to determine if enough work is available. *Id.* at 12. Accordingly, because the Arbitrator found that the Agency had the authority to change or suspend the flexiplace program, he denied the grievance. *Id.* at 12-13.

III. Positions of the Parties

A. Union's Exception

The Union notes that the issue it submitted to the Arbitrator was: "Did the Agency violate the [flexiplace agreement] when it unilaterally changed the terms of the flexiplace agreements properly and timely entered by bargaining unit employees and the appropriate management official in the Jacksonville, Florida [ODAR]?" Exception at 1. According to the Union, the Agency's submitted issues were: (1) "Whether the [A]gency violated the Agreement by limiting Decision-Writers to working at home one day per week . . . ?"; (2) "Whether the Agency violated the Agreement by retracting work plans signed in error by a Group Supervisor . . . ?"; and (3) "Whether the relief requested by the [U]nion is available under law, rule, regulation or collective bargaining agreement?" *Id.*

The Union argues that the Arbitrator "did not resolve the issue submitted to him by the Union, . . . the issues submitted to him by the Agency, . . . [or] the issue as he framed it himself." *Id.* Additionally, the Union claims that the Arbitrator "limited the scope of the case" to the individual grievant, even though the Union filed the grievance on behalf of all the Agency's Decision Writers in Jacksonville. *Id.* at 2.

B. Agency's Opposition

The Agency argues that the Union did not "provide sufficient citation" to establish the grounds upon which it relied in filing its exception. Opp'n at 7 (quoting 5 C.F.R. § 2425.6(c)).

Further, the Agency asserts that the Arbitrator did not exceed his authority because he is "free to formulate the issues based on the subject matter of the grievance" and that the Authority must give "substantial deference" to the Arbitrator's formulation. *Id.* at 8. In this regard, the Agency contends that the Arbitrator did not err in "limiting the applicability of his decision" to the grievant because he "may choose to frame the issue narrowly." *Id.* at 9. The Agency claims that the Arbitrator is not required to resolve issues that he did not frame for resolution. *Id.* at 8.

The Agency also argues that the Arbitrator did not fail to resolve his formulated issue. *Id.* at 10. The Agency claims that the Arbitrator reviewed the flexiplace agreement and the hearing testimony before concluding that the Directors may approve or reject employee requests for ADS days "based on projected workloads and employee availability." *Id.* (citing Award at 11-12). The Agency contends that the Union does not contest the Arbitrator's findings. *Id.* According to the Agency, the Arbitrator resolved the issue that was before him and the Union's exception should be denied. *Id.* at 10-11.

IV. Analysis and Conclusion: The Arbitrator did not exceed his authority.

The Union argues that the Arbitrator failed to resolve the issues submitted to arbitration. Exception at 1-2. Arbitrators exceed their authority when they fail to resolve an issue submitted to arbitration, resolve an issue not submitted to arbitration, disregard specific limitations on their authority, or award relief to those not encompassed within the grievance. *See AFGE, Local 1617*, 51 FLRA 1645, 1647 (1996). In the absence of a stipulated issue, the arbitrator's formulation of the issue is accorded substantial deference. *See U.S. Dep't of the Army, Corps of Eng'rs, Memphis Dist., Memphis, Tenn.*, 52 FLRA 920, 924 (1997).

The Authority's Regulations specifically enumerate the grounds that the Authority currently recognizes for reviewing awards. *AFGE, Local 3955, Council of Prison Locals 33*, 65 FLRA 887, 889 (2011) (Member Beck dissenting in part) (citing 5 C.F.R. § 2425.6(a)-(b)) (*AFGE, Local 3955*). Further, "an exception 'may be subject to dismissal or denial if[] . . . [t]he excepting party fails to raise and support a ground as required in' § 2425.6(b)." *Fraternal Order of Police, Pentagon Police Labor Comm.*, 65 FLRA 781, 785 (2011) (quoting 5 C.F.R. § 2425.6(e)) (*Pentagon Police*). In other words, as the Authority has explained, "an exception that fails to support a properly raised ground is subject to denial." *AFGE, Local 3955*, 65 FLRA at 889.

In arguing that the Arbitrator failed to resolve the issues submitted to him in arbitration, the Union has raised a ground recognized by the Authority – that the Arbitrator exceeded his authority. *See* 5 C.F.R. § 2425.6(b)(1)(i). However, the Union has failed to offer any support for its contention. The Union has provided no record citations to demonstrate how it or the Agency articulated the issues presented to the Arbitrator. However, even accepting as true the Union's assertion that its grievance was filed on behalf of all of the Decision Writers and that the Arbitrator formulated the issue as only relating to the grievant, the Union has failed to establish whether the Arbitrator's formulation was outside his authority. The Union does not provide any legal standard by which to analyze its argument, nor does it cite to any case law, from the Authority or otherwise, in support of its position. Additionally, the Union has not demonstrated how the Arbitrator's decision does not resolve the issue as he framed it. The Union offers no explanation for its assertion beyond its statement that review of the various issues "will clearly show" that none of the issues were resolved by the Arbitrator in his award. Exception at 2. In other words, the Union has failed to "explain how" the

Arbitrator exceeded his authority as required by § 2425.6(b).[1]

Accordingly, the Union has failed to support the ground upon which it relied in filing its exceptions and, thus, we deny the Union's exception.[2] *See Pentagon Police*, 65 FLRA at 785.

V. Decision

The Union's exception is denied.

---

1. Chairman Pope finds that the Union has not raised a "ground[]" for finding the award deficient under § 7122(a)(2) of the Statute and § 2425.6 of the Authority's Regulations. In this connection, failure to "resolve the issues submitted[,]" Exceptions at 2, is not one of the recognized grounds for review. Rather, it is a *standard* that the Authority applies in determining whether one of the enumerated grounds -- that the arbitrator exceeded his or her authority -- has been established. *See U.S. Dep't of the Navy, Naval Base, Norfolk, Va.*, 51 FLRA 305, 307-08 (1995). As the Union has not cited one of the grounds for review that the Authority recognizes -- which grounds are easily found in § 2425.6(a)-(b) of our Regulations -- or provided citation to legal authority that establishes the purported ground on which the Union relies under § 2425.6(c), Chairman Pope would dismiss the exception under § 2425.6(e). *See, e.g., AFGE, Local 738*, 65 FLRA 931, 932 (2011); *AFGE, Local 3955, Council of Prison Locals 33*, 65 FLRA 887, 889 (2011) (Member Beck dissenting in part).

2. We disagree with our colleague that failing to "resolve the issues submitted" is not a valid articulation of the exceeds-authority ground, Exception at 2, and that this articulation is substantively different from the ground itself. Authority precedent recognizes this articulation as a component of the exceeds-authority ground. *See, e.g., U.S. EPA, N.Y.C., N.Y.*, 64 FLRA 227, 230 (2009) (resolving a claim that the arbitrator "resolved an issue not submitted to arbitration and thus disregarded a specific limitation of his authority" as an exceeds-authority exception); *U.S. Dep't of the Navy, Puget Sound Naval Shipyard, Bremerton, Wash.*, 53 FLRA 1445, 1447 (1998) (Member Wasserman dissenting) (resolving an argument that the arbitrator "erred when he reframed the stipulated issue" as an exceeds-authority exception).

Further, Member Beck notes that a requirement that parties submitting exceptions must use only certain preferred words placed in a certain preferred order can be found in neither our Statute nor § 2425.6 of our Regulations. Member Beck also notes that insisting on such precision exalts form over substance and creates pitfalls of hypertechnicality to the unnecessary detriment of the parties who come before us.

65 FLRA No. 220

UNITED STATES
DEPARTMENT OF THE NAVY
SUPERVISOR OF SHIPBUILDING,
CONVERSION AND REPAIR
NEWPORT NEWS, VIRGINIA
(Respondent)

and

NATIONAL ASSOCIATION
OF INDEPENDENT LABOR
LOCAL 2
(Charging Party)

and

INTERNATIONAL FEDERATION
OF PROFESSIONAL AND
TECHNICAL ENGINEERS
LOCAL 1
(Charging Party)

WA-CA-08-0207
WA-CA-08-0208

DECISION AND ORDER

July 29, 2011

Before the Authority: Carol Waller Pope, Chairman, and Thomas M. Beck and Ernest DuBester, Members

I. Statement of the Case

This consolidated unfair labor practice (ULP) case is before the Authority on exceptions to the attached decision of the Administrative Law Judge (the Judge) filed by the General Counsel (GC) and the National Association of Independent Labor, Local 2 (NAIL). The Respondent filed an opposition to the exceptions of the GC and NAIL.

The consolidated complaint alleges that the Respondent violated § 7116(a)(1) and (5) of the Federal Service Labor-Management Relations Statute (the Statute) by repudiating an agreement that it reached with the Charging Parties[1] concerning parking at the Respondent's facility. The Judge found that the Respondent did not violate the Statute as alleged, and he recommended dismissing the consolidated complaint.

For the reasons that follow, we deny the GC's and NAIL's exceptions, and we dismiss the consolidated complaint.

II. Background

The Respondent's employees work at a facility that the Respondent operates (Respondent's facility). Judge's Decision at 2-3. The employees of several other components of the Department of the Navy (Agency) also work at the Respondent's facility, and the employees of those other Agency components are referred to as "tenant command" personnel. *See id.* at 3. The Charging Parties – NAIL and the International Federation of Professional and Technical Engineers, Local 1 (IFPTE) – are the exclusive representatives of some of the Respondent's employees. *See id.* The American Federation of Government Employees, Local 53 (AFGE) is the exclusive representative of some of the tenant command personnel who work at the Respondent's facility (AFGE-represented personnel). *See id.*

The Respondent assigns parking privileges to its employees, as well as tenant command personnel, in accordance with procedures in a written instruction. *See id.* The Respondent invited the Charging Parties to negotiate a revision to the instruction, and the Charging Parties proposed revisions that would, among other things, change the parking privileges of AFGE-represented personnel. *Id.* After receiving those proposals, the Respondent contacted the Agency component that employs the AFGE-represented personnel – the Fleet Industrial Supply Center, Norfolk (FISC) – to suggest that FISC inform AFGE of the proposed revisions. *Id.* The Respondent then continued bargaining without further involvement by either FISC or AFGE, and, eventually, the Respondent and the Charging Parties negotiated and signed a revised instruction (Revision J).[2] *Id.* at 3-4. Under Revision J, the

1. Although there are two Charging Parties to this case, only NAIL filed exceptions.

2. Revision J states, in pertinent part:

> Eligible [parking space] applicants will be assigned to specific parking assignment groups. Parking lot and space assignment will occur in assignment group order as follows:
>
> (1) Group I – Special designated parking . . . [.]
> (2) Group II – Handicapped personnel.

Respondent would first designate eligible parking applicants as members of one of five prioritized "assignment groups," and applicants would then receive parking assignments in the order dictated by their assignment group's priority status. *Id.* at 3-4 & n.3. In keeping with the Charging Parties' proposals, Revision J's lowest priority assignment group consisted entirely of tenant command personnel, including AFGE-represented personnel. *Id.*

When the Respondent began reallocating spaces under Revision J, it realized that some FISC employees would lose their parking spaces as the result of an unanticipated parking shortage. *Id.* at 4. The Respondent was unsuccessful in obtaining additional spaces, and it informed FISC of the effect that the shortage would have on FISC employees. *See id.* Thereafter, AFGE sent the Respondent a demand to cease changes to parking at the Respondent's facility in order to afford AFGE an opportunity to bargain with FISC on the matter. *Id.* The Respondent then notified the Charging Parties that it was not implementing Revision J. *See id.* The Charging Parties filed ULP charges, and the GC issued a complaint, alleging that the Respondent unlawfully repudiated Revision J. *Id.*

III. Judge's Decision

Before the Judge, the GC argued that the Respondent repudiated a lawful agreement in violation of § 7116(a)(1) and (5) of the Statute,[3] whereas the Respondent contended that it did not violate the Statute because implementing Revision J would have unlawfully permitted the Charging Parties to negotiate substantive changes to the working conditions of AFGE-represented personnel. *See id.* at 5. The Judge explained that, although it was undisputed that the Respondent refused to implement Revision J, the "Authority . . . will not find an unlawful repudiation where the agreement allegedly repudiated is contrary to law." *Id.* at 6 (citing *U.S. Dep't of Transp., Fed. Aviation Admin., Atlanta, Ga.*, 60 FLRA 985, 986 (2005) (*FAA*)). In this regard, the Judge determined that Revision J is contrary to § 7114(a)(1) of the Statute (§ 7114(a)(1)) because it would allow the Charging Parties "to directly determine, or regulate, the conditions of employment of employees in the AFGE . . . bargaining unit[, which] runs afoul of the principle of exclusive recognition[.]"[4] *Id.* at 7; *see also id.* (citing *NAGE, Local R1-109*, 61 FLRA 593, 597 (2006) (*Local R1-109*)). Therefore, the Judge concluded that the Respondent's refusal to implement the agreement did not constitute unlawful repudiation, and he recommended that the Authority dismiss the consolidated complaint.[5] *Id.* at 8.

IV. Positions of the Parties

A. GC's Exceptions

The GC argues that the Judge erred in finding that Revision J is contrary to law and that, consequently, he erred in finding that the Respondent did not unlawfully repudiate the agreement. GC's Exceptions at 3, 6. The GC contends that both the Authority and the U.S. Court of Appeals for the District of Columbia Circuit (D.C. Circuit) have recognized that agreements providing bargaining unit members with preferential access to limited resources are lawful, even where their effects are "inconvenient" or "unseemly[.]" *Id.* at 7 (quoting *U.S. Dep't of the Navy, Naval Aviation Depot, Cherry Point, N.C. v. FLRA*, 952 F.2d 1434, 1441 & n.8 (D.C. Cir. 1992) (*Cherry Point*)) (internal quotation marks omitted); *see also id.* at 6-8. In particular, the GC asserts that the agreement to afford employees represented by the Charging Parties priority access to a finite benefit – i.e., parking spaces

---

(3) Group III – [Respondent Employee] and Tenant Command Carpools.
(4) Group IV – [Respondent Employee] individuals.
(5) Group V – Tenant Command individuals.

Judge's Decision at 4 n.3 (quoting GC Ex. 4 at 4).

3. Section 7116(a) of the Statute states, in pertinent part:

> [I]t shall be an unfair labor practice for an agency . . . (1) to interfere with, restrain, or coerce any employee in the exercise by the employee of any right under this chapter; [and] . . . (5) to refuse to consult or negotiate in good faith with a labor organization as required by this chapter[.]

4. Section 7114(a)(1) of the Statute provides, in pertinent part: "A labor organization . . . accorded exclusive recognition is the exclusive representative of the employees in the unit it represents and is entitled to act for, and negotiate collective bargaining agreements covering, all employees in the unit."

5. The Judge also found that the Respondent justifiably refused to implement Revision J because honoring it would have unlawfully interfered with the bargaining relationship between FISC and AFGE. *See* Judge's Decision at 7. However, because the consolidated complaint is fully resolvable on the basis of the Judge's § 7114(a)(1) finding alone, *see infra* Parts V.-VI., we find it unnecessary to address the Judge's additional finding concerning unlawful interference, or the exceptions to that finding.

– is lawful and enforceable even though it effectively reduces the number of parking spaces available to other individuals, including AFGE-represented personnel. *Id.* at 6-8 (citing *AFGE, Local 2139*, 61 FLRA 654, 656 (2006) (*Local 2139*); *Soc. Sec. Admin., Office of Hearings & Appeals, Region II, Buffalo Office of Hearings & Appeals, Buffalo, N.Y.*, 58 FLRA 722, 727 (2003) (*SSA*); *AFSCME, Local 2910*, 53 FLRA 1334, 1338 (1998) (*AFSCME*)).

B. NAIL's Exceptions

Like the GC, NAIL argues that the Judge erred in finding that the agreement is contrary to § 7114(a)(1) and in concluding that the Respondent did not unlawfully repudiate Revision J. *See* NAIL's Exceptions at 1. According to NAIL, the Judge's decision – rather than Revision J – is contrary to § 7114(a)(1) because it deprives NAIL of its rights "to represent employees of [the] Respondent[,] . . . to negotiate and reach agreement with [the] Respondent, and to have those agreements implemented." *Id.* at 2. In that regard, NAIL asserts that the Judge's reasoning would make "practically every agreement" between the Charging Parties and the Respondent meaningless because the Respondent could always refuse to implement those agreements based on their effects on employees represented by another union. *Id.* at 3.

C. Respondent's Opposition

The Respondent contends that, contrary to the GC's arguments in its exceptions, *Cherry Point* actually supports the Judge's decision in this case. *See* Opp'n 3-4. According to the Respondent, "[w]hile *Cherry Point* acknowledges that union proposals within the scope of mandatory bargaining . . . may have '*some impact*' on personnel outside the bargaining unit[,]" *Cherry Point* does not sanction agreements by one exclusive representative that "actually regulate[]" the conditions of employment of a bargaining unit with a different exclusive representative. *Id.* at 4-5 (quoting *Cherry Point*, 952 F.2d at 1440) (internal quotation marks omitted).

With regard to NAIL's exceptions, the Respondent contends that, although reaching lawful agreements over facility-wide matters may require coordinated bargaining with other unions as well as the Charging Parties, negotiations regarding "employer-specific matters[,] such as flexible schedules, telework, training, travel, [and] merit staffing procedures" for the Respondent's employees, need not include exclusive representatives other than the Charging Parties. *Id.* at 10 n.4.

V. Analysis and Conclusions

As the Judge stated, although unlawfully repudiating a negotiated agreement is contrary to § 7116(a)(1) and (5) of the Statute, the "Authority will not find an unlawful repudiation where the agreement allegedly repudiated is contrary to law." *FAA*, 60 FLRA at 986 (citing *Gen. Servs. Admin., Wash., D.C.*, 50 FLRA 136, 139 n.7 (1995)) (agency did not unlawfully repudiate agreement if it was contrary to Back Pay Act). Under § 7114(a)(1), once a union is certified as the exclusive representative of an appropriate unit of employees, that union has the exclusive right to bargain with respect to the conditions of employment of employees in that certified unit. *See AFGE, Local 2879, AFL-CIO*, 49 FLRA 1074, 1087-89 (1994) (*Local 2879*). An agency may not negotiate with one exclusive representative to regulate the conditions of employment for a unit represented by another union because such negotiations would run afoul of the principle of exclusive representation. *See AFGE, Local 32 v. FLRA*, 110 F.3d 810, 815 (D.C. Cir. 1997) (*Local 32*) (unions may not negotiate agreements that "*govern*" the working conditions of employees in other bargaining units or that "b[i]nd" an agency with respect to the rights of those employees). *Cf. Local R1-109*, 61 FLRA at 597 (applying *Cherry Point* to find proposals that "directly determine" conditions of employment for employees in another bargaining unit outside duty to bargain); *AFGE, Local 32*, 51 FLRA 491, 507-08 (1995) (applying *Cherry Point* to find proposals "directly implicating" employees in other bargaining units outside duty to bargain); *Local 2879*, 49 FLRA at 1088-89 (applying *Cherry Point* to find proposals that "seek to regulate" conditions of employment of employees in another bargaining unit outside duty to bargain).[6]

6. We note that private-sector precedent under the National Labor Relations Act (NLRA) holds that it is a ULP for parties to apply the terms of a collective bargaining agreement negotiated by one union to employees represented by a different union. *See, e.g.*, *Sperry Sys. Mgmt. Div., Sperry Rand Corp. v. NLRB*, 492 F.2d 63, 67 n.4 (2d Cir. 1974) ("Demands by a union to represent employees outside the certified uni[t] are unfair labor practices[.]"); *id.* at 69 ("[A]n employer commits [an] unfair labor practice . . . when it imposes on employees of one unit the contract and bargaining agent of another unit."); *Local 7-210, Oil, Chemical, & Atomic Workers, Int'l Union, AFL-CIO v. Union Tank Car Co.*, 475 F.2d 194, 197 (7th Cir. 1973) (under NLRA, employer properly

According to the GC and NAIL, Revision J merely "affects" the conditions of employment of AFGE-represented personnel but does not run afoul of the principle of exclusive recognition. *See* GC's Exceptions at 6-8; NAIL's Exceptions at 3. However, the wording of Revision J establishes that it does more than merely affect the conditions of employment of AFGE-represented personnel. In particular, Revision J expressly determines the access of "tenant command" personnel to parking, *see supra* note 2, even though AFGE – the exclusive representative of some of the tenant command personnel – had no part in negotiating the revised instruction. Thus, the above-cited precedent supports a conclusion that Revision J is contrary to § 7114(a)(1).

Moreover, Revision J is unlike the proposals discussed in *Cherry Point*, *Local 2139*, *SSA*, and *AFSCME*, which the GC cites in support of its exceptions. The GC contends that Revision J is comparable to a hypothetical proposal discussed in *Cherry Point*, which would have called for "all parking at [the agency's facility] [to] be reserved for employees" represented by the union making the proposal. *See Local 32*, 110 F.3d at 815 (internal quotation marks omitted) (discussing the hypothetical proposal in *Cherry Point*). As the D.C. Circuit explained in *Local 32*, although the hypothetical proposal in *Cherry Point* would have "severely limited" the parking options available to employees not represented by the proposing union, the proposal would have been lawful because it did not "define[the] parking privileges . . . for members of other bargaining units[.]" *Id.* In a similar manner, the lawful proposal in *Local 2139* was limited to address only the parking privileges of "bargaining unit employees" represented by that union. 61 FLRA at 654. Revision J, on the other hand, is *not limited* to bargaining unit employees represented by the Charging Parties, and it directly *defines* the parking privileges of AFGE bargaining unit members by expressly identifying "tenant command individuals" as a particular parking "assignment group." *See supra* note 2. As a result, Revision J is not comparable to the hypothetical proposal discussed in *Cherry Point* or the proposal found negotiable in *Local 2139*.

As for the other decisions cited by the GC, in *SSA*, a proposed ULP remedy required an agency to restore the status quo ante (SQA) with regard to the parking privileges of one group of employees at its facility. *See* 58 FLRA at 727. The Authority held that "the fact that the [r]espondent had bargaining obligations with more than one labor organization regarding parking privileges d[id] not justify not imposing an SQA order." *Id.* However, the Authority did not authorize the charging party in *SSA* to negotiate an agreement that would directly determine the conditions of employment of other bargaining units, and, thus, *SSA* does not support the GC's exceptions. In *AFSCME*, the Authority applied *Cherry Point* to find that "nothing on the face of th[e] proposal [under consideration] indicates a direct effect on non-unit employees."[7] 53 FLRA at 1338. By contrast, Revision J on its face directly affects employees in a unit other than those represented by the Charging Parties because it expressly identifies them as "tenant command individuals" and then precisely regulates their parking privileges by placing them in a certain parking "assignment group." *See supra* note 2.

With regard to NAIL's argument that the Judge's decision violates NAIL's § 7114(a)(1) rights "to represent employees of [the] Respondent[,] . . . to negotiate and reach agreement with [the] Respondent, and to have those agreements implemented[,]" NAIL's Exceptions at 2, the Judge's decision does not prevent NAIL from reaching lawful agreements with the Respondent regarding the working conditions of employees represented by NAIL. Rather, the decision prevents NAIL from attempting to negotiate or enforce agreements that govern the conditions of employment of a bargaining unit represented by a different exclusive representative. As NAIL does not have § 7114(a)(1) rights to negotiate or enforce agreements on behalf of AFGE-represented personnel, *see Local R1-109*, 61 FLRA at 597, the Judge's decision on that point is not inconsistent with § 7114(a)(1).

NAIL argues further that the Judge's decision will render meaningless its ability to negotiate

---

refused to apply union's contract to workers certified as members of another unit with a different bargaining representative).

[7] Proposal 1 in *AFSCME* stated, in relevant part:

> *Unit employees represented by the [union]* shall be given access to parking spaces in the same proportion as the number of unit members to the [agency] population as a whole. . . . The [agency] will assign *bargaining unit employee parking spaces* in the following order of priority: . . . 1. permanently handicapped employees; 2. employees who work unusual hours; 3. car pools and van pools; 4. all other vehicles.

53 FLRA at 1334 (emphases added).

agreements on behalf of its members because the Respondent could always refuse to implement them based on the effects they have on other bargaining units. NAIL's Exceptions at 3. However, the Judge did not find that the Respondent could refuse to implement agreements simply because they "affect" other bargaining units. He found that the Respondent could not lawfully implement agreements negotiated with the Charging Parties that "directly determine, or regulate, the conditions of employment of employees" in other bargaining units. Judge's Decision at 7. Thus, NAIL's argument is based on a misinterpretation of the Judge's decision and does not provide a basis for finding the decision deficient.

For the foregoing reasons, we find that Revision J directly determines the parking privileges of AFGE-represented personnel, and, consequently, it is inconsistent with the principle of exclusive recognition. *See Local 32*, 110 F.3d at 815; *Local R1-109*, 61 FLRA at 597. Therefore, we deny the exceptions to the Judge's findings that Revision J is contrary to § 7114(a)(1) and that, as a result, the Respondent did not unlawfully repudiate Revision J by refusing to implement it.

VI. Order

The consolidated complaint is dismissed.

Office of Administrative Law Judges

DEPARTMENT OF THE NAVY
SUPERVISOR OF SHIPBUILDING, CONVERSION AND REPAIR, NEWPORT NEWS, VIRGINIA
Respondent

and

NATIONAL ASSOCIATION OF INDEPENDENT LABOR, LOCAL 2
Charging Party

and

INTERNATIONAL FEDERATION OF PROFESSIONAL AND TECHNICAL ENGINEERS, LOCAL 1
Charging Party

June M. Marshall, Esq.
For the General Counsel

Joseph R. Barco, Labor Relations Specialist
For the Respondent

Before: CHARLES R. CENTER
Chief Administrative Law Judge

DECISION ON MOTIONS FOR SUMMARY JUDGMENT

STATEMENT OF THE CASE

This case arose under the Federal Service Labor-Management Relations Statute (Statute), 5 U.S.C. §§ 7101-7135 and the revised Rules and Regulations of the Federal Labor Relations Authority (Authority), Part 2423.

A Consolidated Complaint and Notice of Hearing was issued on December 28, 2009, based on two separate unfair labor practice charges filed on February 7, 2008, against the Department of the Navy, Supervisor of Shipbuilding, Conversion, and Repair, Newport News, Virginia (Respondent). Case No. WA-CA-08-0207 was filed by the National Association of Independent Labor, Local 2 (NAIL), and Case No. WA-CA-08-0208 was filed by the International Federation of Professional and Technical Engineers, Local 1 (IFPTE). The Consolidated Complaint alleges that the Respondent repudiated an agreement it entered into with NAIL and IFPTE concerning vehicle parking and violated §7116(a)(1) and (5) of the Statute.

On February 16, 2010, the General Counsel filed a Motion for Summary Judgment in the consolidated complaint asserting that there were no material facts in dispute, and it was entitled to judgment as a matter of law. On February 17, 2010, the Respondent filed a response to the motion for summary judgment in which it agreed that there were no material facts in dispute, but contended that summary judgment should be made in favor of the Respondent.[1]

Based upon the assertions of the Respondent and General Counsel, there were no genuine issue of material facts in dispute, and an Order Indefinitely Postponing the hearing was issued on February 18, 2010.

MOTIONS FOR SUMMARY JUDGMENT

The Authority has held that motions for summary judgment filed under §2423.27 of its Regulations serve the same purpose and are governed by the same principles, as motions filed in the United States District Courts under Rule 56 of the Federal Rules of Civil Procedure. *Dep't of Veterans Affairs, Veterans Affairs Med. Ctr, Nashville, Tenn.*, 50 FLRA 220, 222 (1995); *Dep't of the Navy, U.S. Naval Ordnance Station, Louisville, Ky.*, 33 FLRA 3, 4-5 (1988) (*NOS, Louisville*), *rev'd on other grounds*, No. 88-1861 (D.C. Cir. Aug. 9, 1990). The motion is to be granted if the "'pleadings, depositions, answers to interrogatories, and admissions on file, together with affidavits, if any, show that there is no genuine issue as to any material fact and that the moving party is entitled to a judgment as a matter of law.'" *NOS, Louisville* at 4, quoting Rule 56(c). After reviewing the pleadings, affidavits, and exhibits submitted by the parties, I agree that there is no genuine issue of material facts with respect to the consolidated complaint before me.

Accordingly, it is unnecessary to hold a hearing in this case, and it is appropriate to decide the case on the motions for summary judgment. The summary of the undisputed material facts and my conclusions of law and recommendations are set forth below.

---

[1] The "response" to the General Counsel's motion submitted by Respondent is for all intents and purposes a cross-motion for summary judgment and it is treated as such.

FINDINGS OF FACT

The Respondent is an agency under §7103(a)(3) of the Statute. (GC Ex. 2, 3) The Respondent's facility is not located on a military installation or other federal property, but rather is situated at the Northrop Grumman Shipyard in Newport News, Virginia. (Resp. App. A) In addition to its own employees, there are other federal personnel located at the Respondent's facility who provide support to the Respondent's mission and are considered "Tenant Command Personnel". (*Id.*) The largest tenant command having employees at Respondent's facility is the Integrated Logistics Support Department, which is organizationally aligned under the Fleet Industrial Supply Center, Norfolk (FISC, Norfolk). (*Id.*)

The Charging Parties in this case, NAIL and IFPTE are labor organizations within the meaning of §7103(a)(4) of the Statute. (GC Ex. 2, 3) NAIL is the exclusive representative of a unit of Respondent's employees appropriate for collective bargaining at the Newport News facility; IFPTE is also the exclusive representative of a unit of Respondent's employees at the same facility. (*Id.*). The American Federation of Government Employees, Local 53 (Local 53), is the exclusive representative of a bargaining unit that includes employees employed by FISC, Norfolk. (Resp. Apps. A, B at 2) Some of the employees in Local 53 bargaining unit are assigned to one of the tenant commands at the Respondent's Newport News facility and are located there.[2] (Resp. Apps. A, B)

In addition to office space, Northrop Grumman Shipbuilding, Newport News, provides 378 parking spaces for the Respondent and its tenant commands at the Newport News facility. (Resp. App. A) In the summer of 2007, the Respondent began the process of revising its instruction for the distribution and use of parking spaces. (*Id.*) During the course of the negotiations associated with this revision IFPTE and NAIL proposed, among other things, that the former practice of assigning individuals to a parking lot, but leaving the choice of specific parking spaces to a daily first-come, first-served basis, be replaced with one that assigned all parking spaces by numbers, to individuals and carpools. (*Id.*) Another proposal put forward by IFPTE and NAIL was that individuals employed by tenant commands be assigned parking spaces only after individuals in four other categories that included employees of the Respondent, received parking space assignments. (*Id.*) Respondent notified FISC, Norfolk of the IFPTE/NAIL proposals which would change a working condition of FISC employees located at the Newport News facility, and suggested that FISC, Norfolk inform Local 53 of the proposals. (*Id.*) During the ensuing negotiations between Respondent and IFPTE and NAIL, there was no discussion between the Respondent and either FISC, Norfolk or Local 53. (*Id.*)

On or about August 8, 2007, negotiations with IFPTE and NAIL were completed and an agreement was reached and signed. The agreement took the form of SUPSHIPNN Instruction 5560.1J (Revision J), which set forth policies concerning the allocation of vehicle parking at the Respondent's Newport News facility. (GC Ex. 2, 3, 4; Resp. App. A at 2) Revision J included the proposals described above that were made by IFPTE and NAIL.[3] (GC Ex. 4; Resp. App. A)

In October 2007, the Respondent made an initial allocation of parking spaces using the process set forth in Revision J and discovered there were approximately 25 fewer spaces than what was needed to meet demand. (Resp. App. A) Under the prior first-come, first-served process for allocating parking spaces, daily absences based on such reasons as leave, official travel, and alternative work schedules

---

2 The FISC, Norfolk employees located at the Respondent's facility had previously been employees of the Respondent. (Resp. Response at 2; Resp. App. B) As a consequence of a reorganization that was effective in 2005, they were "organizationally reassigned in place" to FISC, Norfolk which was another component within the Department of the Navy. (Resp. App. B) In a decision issued in 2006, the Regional Director of the Authority's Denver Regional Office found that the employees who previously were included in the bargaining unit represented by NAIL had accreted to the bargaining unit represented by AFGE, Local 53. (Resp. App. B)

3 Revision J provides in relevant part:

> 7. Space Assignment
>
> > b. Eligible applicants will be assigned to specific parking assignment groups. Parking lot and space assignment will occur in assignment group order as follows:
> >
> > (1) Group I – Special designated parking as listed in enclosure (1)
> > (2) Group II – Handicapped personnel.
> > (3) Group III – SUPSHIPNN and Tenant Command Carpools.
> > (4) Group IV – SUPSHIPNN individuals.
> > (5) Group V – Tenant Command individuals.
>
> (GC Ex. 4 at 4)

had masked this shortfall. (*Id.*) Under the new approach set forth in Revision J tenant command personnel were relegated to the last group in line to receive assigned parking spaces. Thus, they would absorb the entire shortage and would lose their parking spaces. (*Id.*) After unsuccessfully attempting to obtain additional parking spaces, Respondent notified FISC, Norfolk of the parking shortage and its effect on FISC personnel. (*Id.*)

On January 7, 2008, Respondent received a demand from Local 53 for an opportunity to bargain prior to the implementation of the changes in parking. (Resp. App. A at 3) In February 2008, the Respondent agreed to delay implementation of the Revision J process for several weeks to afford FISC, Norfolk and Local 53 an opportunity to conduct discussions on the matter. (*Id.*) At that point, Respondent informed IFPTE and NAIL that Revision J had not been implemented. On February 7, 2008, IFPTE and NAIL both filed unfair labor practice charges alleging that the Respondent repudiated the agreement reached in August 2007. (GC Ex. 1(a), (b))

By memoranda dated April 7, 2008, Respondent informed IFPTE and NAIL that it would not implement Revision J because of the effect it would have on the working conditions of employees in the AFGE, Local 53 bargaining unit. (GC Ex. 5, 6; Resp. Apps. C, D) The memoranda included "Draft SUPSHIPNNINST.5560.1K" (Draft Revision K), which the Respondent characterized as an effort to solve the parking problem that resulted from Revision J for the review of IFPTE and NAIL. (GC Ex. 5, 6; Resp. Apps. C, D, E)[4] In the April 7, 2008, memoranda, the Respondent invited IFPTE and NAIL to request consultation/negotiation. (Resp. Apps. C, D; GC Ex. 5, 6) No negotiations occurred. (Resp. App. A)

DISCUSSION AND ANALYSIS

Position of the Parties

A. General Counsel

The General Counsel (GC) contends that the Respondent, IFPTE and NAIL reached an agreement on parking at Respondent's facility and that the Respondent repudiated in violation of §7116(a)(1) and (5) of the Statute. The General Counsel acknowledges that repudiation is not a violation in circumstances where the agreement term at issue is contrary to law. (GC Brief at 3). The GC asserts that in this case there is no showing that any provision of the agreement is contrary to law and the impact of the agreement on employees in a bargaining unit represented by a labor organization other than the two who are parties to the agreement, does not render it illegal. (*Id.*) Rather than failing to implement the agreement reached with IFPTE and NAIL, the GC argues that the Respondent has the obligation to bargain with the representative of the other bargaining unit affected. (*Id.*)

As a remedy, the General Counsel seeks an order requiring the Respondent to cease and desist, implement Revision J, and post a notice to employees.

B. Respondent

The Respondent asserts that its actions in refusing to implement Revision J did not violate the Statute as alleged. (Resp. Response at 3) Respondent contends its actions were driven by its realization that implementation of Revision J would change the conditions of employment of employees in a third unit of recognition whose exclusive representative was not afforded an opportunity to bargain over the change. (*Id.*) Respondent avers that implementation of Revision J without the third union being afforded an opportunity to bargain would have subjected it to an allegation that it violated the Statute. (*Id.* at 4.) Additionally, the Respondent maintains that the remedy sought by the General Counsel would allow IFPTE and NAIL to negotiate a substantive change in a working condition of members of AFGE, Local 53 bargaining unit. (*Id.*)

Discussion and Analysis

A. The Respondent Refused to Implement the Agreement

It is undisputed that the Respondent entered into an agreement with IFPTE and NAIL that established a process for assigning the parking spaces under its control at its Newport News facility. That agreement was embodied in Revision J. It is also undisputed that Respondent refused to implement Revision J.

---

[4] Resp. App. E includes, in addition to Draft Revision K, pages 1 and 8 from Revision J. As it appears that those pages were inadvertently included in Resp. App. E, I will disregard those two pages.

B. The Respondent's Refusal to Implement the Agreement Did Not Constitute Unlawful Repudiation

A failure or refusal to honor an agreement constitutes a violation of the Statute when the breach of contract amounts to a wholesale repudiation of the collective bargaining agreement. *See, e.g., Dep't of Defense, Warner Robins Air Logistics Ctr, Robins Air Force Base, Ga.*, 40 FLRA 1211, 1217-19 (1991). The Authority, however, will not find an unlawful repudiation where the agreement allegedly repudiated is contrary to law. *E.g., U.S. Dep't of Transportation, Fed. Avia. Admin., Atlanta, Ga.*, 60 FLRA 985, 986 (2005). In this case, the Respondent essentially asserts that it could not lawfully implement Revision J because of the effect it would have on the working conditions of employees included in a bargaining unit represented by an exclusive representative that was not a party to the negotiations.

As discussed above, Revision J represented an agreement the Respondent reached with IFPTE and NAIL. In addition to determining conditions of employment of the employees in the bargaining units represented by those two labor organizations, Revision J directly determined conditions of employment of employees of the tenant organizations located at the Respondent's Newport News facility, some of whom are represented by the AFGE, Local 53. In particular, Revision J prescribed the order in which parking spaces would be assigned to employees located at the Respondent's Newport News facility including those employees represented by Local 53, *supra* note 3 above. Thus, Revision J is not an agreement reached with IFPTE and NAIL that merely has "some impact" on employees in the AFGE bargaining unit, instead, it is an agreement reached with those two unions that actually "regulates" and eliminates a condition of employment previously enjoyed by employees in the AFGE, Local 53 bargaining unit. *See, e.g., Am. Fed'n of Gov't Employees, Local 2879, AFL-CIO*, 49 FLRA 1074, 1086-90 (1994).

Under §7114(a)(1) of the Statute, when a labor organization has been accorded exclusive recognition, it is the exclusive representative of the employees in the unit it represents and is entitled to act for and negotiate collective bargaining agreements covering all employees in the unit. Correlatively, once a union is certified as the exclusive representative of an appropriate unit of employees, an agency must "deal only with" that representative concerning matters affecting the conditions of employment of the employees in that unit. *See, e.g., Am. Fed'n of Gov't Employees, Nat'l Council of HUD Locals 222*, 54 FLRA 1267, 1276 (1998) (*HUD*). Allowing a union to directly determine the conditions of employment of employees in a bargaining unit for which another union holds exclusive recognition "would run afoul of the principle of exclusive recognition." *Nat'l Ass'n of Gov't Employees, Local R1-109*, 61 FLRA 593, 597 (2006), quoting *HUD*. If follows that allowing IFPTE and NAIL to directly determine, or regulate, the conditions of employment of employees in the AFGE Local 53 collective bargaining unit runs afoul of the principle of exclusive recognition as set forth in §7114 of the Statute.

Despite the absence of a collective bargaining relationship between the Respondent and the AFGE, Local 53, the Respondent nevertheless, had an obligation to honor AFGE's status as the exclusive representative of the employees of FISC, Norfolk located at its facility. In this regard and as noted earlier, AFGE, Local 53's bargaining relationship was with FISC, Norfolk which was a tenant of the Respondent insofar as those FISC employees located at the Respondent's Newport News facility. The record shows that prior to Revision J, the FISC, Norfolk employees located at the Respondent's Newport News facility were provided parking in the spaces controlled by the Respondent at the facility. Parking arrangements for employees generally concern employees' conditions of employment and a change in parking arrangements generally constitutes a change in conditions of employment. *E.g., Soc. Sec. Admin., Office of Hearings and Appeals, Charleston, S.C.*, 59 FLRA 646, 649 (2004), *aff'd as to other matters*, 397 F.3d 957 (D.C. Cir. 2005). In view of the fact that FISC, Norfolk had the bargaining relationship with AFGE, Local 53that entity had the responsibility for fulfilling the bargaining obligation owed to that union in conjunction with any change in the parking arrangements for the employees in its unit of recognition. *See, e.g., Headquarters, Def. Logistics Agency, Washington, D.C.*, 22 FLRA 875, 879-80 (1986) (*DLA*). Despite the fact that it was the responsibility of FISC, Norfolk rather than the Respondent, to fulfill the bargaining obligation owed to AFGE, Local 53 prior to changing the parking arrangements that applied to the employees in Local 53, Respondent would be in violation of the Statute if it took action that interfered with the bargaining relationship between the parties to that exclusive recognition. *See, e.g., DLA*. Although the theory of the violation would differ based on the relationship between the two organizational entities, such interference can occur regardless of whether the entities involved are in a superior/subordinate relationship in the same chain of command or are simply different organizational entities in the same agency. *See, e.g., id.; see also Air Force Logistics Command, Wright-Patterson Air Force Base, Ohio,* 46 FLRA 1184, 1186-87 (1993). Respondent was not free to disregard the exclusive recognition that AFGE held for the FISC, Norfolk employees and could not enter into an agreement with IFPTE and NAIL that directly affected conditions of employment for employees in the AFGE, Local 53 bargaining unit without violating the Statute.

I find that the Revision J agreement the Respondent reached with IFPTE and NAIL was contrary to §7114(a)(1) of the Statute because the detailed guidance regarding precedence in the assignment of assigned parking spots directly affected the conditions of employment for bargaining unit employees represented by AFGE, Local 53 as they were placed last in priority for the assignment of parking spaces when an insufficient number of spaces were available. Thus, parking that was previously provided to the Local 53 bargaining unit would be unilaterally taken away without bargaining. In view of this, the Respondent's action in refusing to implement the Revision J agreement bargained with two other unions, did not constitute unlawful repudiation.

For the reasons outlined above, I recommend that the Authority grant the Respondent's cross-motion for summary judgment and dismiss the consolidated complaint. Accordingly, it is recommended that the Authority adopt the following Order:

ORDER

It is ordered that the consolidated complaint be, and hereby is, dismissed.

Issued, Washington, D.C., March 29, 2010.

CHARLES R. CENTER
Chief Administrative Law Judge